W9-COL-267

Famous First Facts

By the Same Author

FACTS ABOUT THE PRESIDENTS

Famous First Facts

A Record of First Happenings,
Discoveries and Inventions
in the United States

By

Joseph Nathan Kane

Third Edition

THE H. W. WILSON COMPANY
NEW YORK   1964

PREFACE

Thirty years have passed since the first edition of FAMOUS FIRST FACTS was published. Numerous printings of the several editions have been made. They have brought in thousands of letters and thousands more have resulted from a year's broadcast of "Famous Firsts" on a coast-to-coast network and a syndicated newspaper feature "Who Was First?" The various claims made for "firsts" were carefully considered and only two vital changes have been made.

Despite this record, the author has continued on the elusive chase for facts. Much supplementary material has been added to the text as well as many new entries. Most statements have been compiled from original source material, much of which has not been published. Inventors and participants have been interviewed and a large correspondence has increased the number of items. To aid those interested in further information, suggested sources for further consultation are often listed. These are books which are generally accessible to the average reader and not necessarily the sources from which the printed statements are obtained.

The author still has a large collection of facts which have not been included as it has not been possible to obtain the necessary substantiation and verification. Perhaps these may take another thirty years before they will be ready for the next edition.

For their assistance and friendly cooperation, I want to thank John Jamieson, editor of general publications of The H. W. Wilson Company, and Ruth Ulman, assistant editor, who helped to make a tedious task less burdensome.

JOSEPH NATHAN KANE

December 1963

CONTENTS

FAMOUS FIRST FACTS

THE FIRST

ABDOMINAL OPERATION. *See* Surgical operation: Abdominal operation

ABERDEEN-ANGUS CATTLE IMPORTATION. *See* Animals: Cattle (Aberdeen-Angus) importation

ABOLITION NEWSPAPER. *See* Newspaper: Abolition newspaper

ABOLITION SOCIETY was "The Society for the Relief of Free Negroes Unlawfully Held in Bondage," formed April 14, 1775, in Philadelphia, Pa. The first president was John Baldwin. It was reorganized in 1784 and a new constitution adopted in 1787. It was incorporated in 1789 as the "Pennsylvania Society for Promoting the Abolition of Slavery and for the Relief of Free Negroes Unlawfully Held in Bondage and for Improving the Condition of the African Race." *(Pennsylvania Magazine of History and Biography.* Vol. 36, No. 1. January 1912.)

ABRASIVE for commercial use, to perform work that previously was possible only with diamond dust, was boron carbide (B_4C). It is lighter than aluminum and its density is 2.52 grams per c.c. It was produced by the Research Laboratories of the Norton Company, Worcester, Mass., and introduced to the world through a technical paper read before the Electrochemical Society in New York on September 27, 1934.

ABRIDGMENT OF LAWS. *See* Law digest

ABSENTEE VOTING LAW. *See* Election law: Absentee voting law (state)

ABSOLUTE MONARCH TO VISIT THE UNITED STATES. *See* Visiting celebrities: Absolute monarch

ACADEMY was "The Academy and College of Philadelphia" founded by Benjamin Franklin in 1749 in Philadelphia, Pa. Franklin drew up the constitution for the academy and on November 13, 1749, was appointed its president. The academy opened August 13, 1751. Seven men graduated May 17, 1757, at the first commencement, six as Bachelors of Arts and one as Master of Arts. State legislation enacted September 13, 1791, united the University of the State of Pennsylvania with the College Academy and Charitable School of Philadelphia

THE FIRST

under the name of the Trustees of the University of Pennsylvania. The first meeting was held November 8, 1791, at Independence Hall, Philadelphia, Pa. Inasmuch as many of the academies were elementary schools and the title "academy" was used indiscriminately, there is considerable conflict as to which was the first academy. *(Ellwood Patterson Cubberley—The History of Education)*

ACADEMY OF ART. *See* Art organization: Art organization

ACADEMY OF ARTS AND LETTERS. *See* Arts and letters society: Arts and letters society (national)

ACADEMY OF ARTS AND SCIENCE. *See* Arts and science society: Arts and science society (national)

ACADEMY OF DESIGN. *See* Art organization: Artists' society of importance

ACADEMY OF POLITICAL AND SOCIAL SCIENCE. *See* Political science society: Political and social science society (national)

ACADEMY OF SCIENCE. *See* Arts and science society; Science association: National Academy of Sciences

ACCIDENT (automobile). *See* Automobile accident

ACCIDENT (railroad). *See* Railroad accident

ACCIDENT INSURANCE. *See* Insurance: Accident insurance company

ACCIDENT REPORT
  Industrial accident reports required from employers were demanded by Massachusetts, under the Employers' Liability Act, Chapter 270 of the Acts of 1887 passed May 14, 1887, effective September 1, 1887, entitled "An act to extend and regulate the liability of employers to make compensation for personal injuries suffered by employees in their service." Section 3 of the act relates to the filing of notice.

THE FIRST

THE FIRST

ACCORDION PATENT was issued January 13, 1854, to Anthony Faas of Philadelphia, Pa., and bore patent No. 11,062.

ACCOUNTANCY DEGREE. *See* Degrees (academic and honorary): Doctor of philosophy in accounting degree

ACCOUNTANCY LAW (state) was Chapter 312, "an act to regulate the profession of public accountants" signed April 17, 1896, by Governor Levi Parsons Morton of New York. Charles Waldo Haskins was appointed the first chairman of the New York Board of Certified Public Accountant Examiners.

ACCOUNTANT to be made a certified public accountant was Frank Broaker of New York City who received certificate No. 1 on December 1, 1896 from the New York State Board of Certified Public Accountant Examiners. His name was first on the alphabetical list of thirty accountants certified on that date.

ACCOUNTANTS' SOCIETY
Accountants' society was the Institute of Accountants and Bookkeepers, organized July 28, 1882, in New York City. The name was changed on June 23, 1886, to the Institute of Accounts.

Accountants' society formed by a state group was the New York State Society of Certified Public Accountants, which was organized in New York City, March 30, 1897, following the passage of the New York State Certified Public Account Law of April 17, 1896 (Chapter 312). Charles Waldo Haskins was the first president. It was incorporated January 25, 1897.

Accountants' society to become a national organization was the American Association of Public Accountants formed in New York City on December 22, 1886, although it was not incorporated until August 20, 1887. The first president was James Yalden.

"ACE." *See* Aviation—Aviator: American ace; Aviation—Aviator: Naval ace

ACETYLENE or carbide gas was made May 4, 1892, by Thomas Leopold Willson of the Willson Aluminum Company in Spray, N.C. He was experimenting to produce metallic calcium by fusing lime and coal tar in an electric furnace. The experiment was unsuccessful and when the molten slag-like mass was dumped into a nearby stream, it was seen that a gas was liberated. The gas which the carbide liberated on contact with water was recognized as acetylene. Shortly afterwards acetylene was manufactured on a commercial scale. Acetylene had been made previously, however, on a laboratory scale. (*The Story of Carbide—National Carbide Sales Corporation*)

ACHROMATIC LENS. *See* Lens: Achromatic lens

ACIDOPHILUS MILK. *See* Milk: Acidophilus milk

ACQUISITION OF LAND BY THE U.S. GOVERNMENT. *See* Territorial expansion: Acquisition of land by the federal government

ACTOR
Actor of American birth was John Martin, who appeared at the Old Southwark Theatre, Philadelphia, Pa., March 13, 1790, as Young Norval in a play entitled *Douglas.* (*Charles Durang—History of the Philadelphia Stage*)

Actor to have an exclusive contract. *See* Moving picture actor: Actor to have an exclusive contract

Actor to receive curtain applause was Edmund Keene, who appeared in a group of special performances in Boston, Mass., in 1821. (*Eugene Tompkins—History of the Boston Theatre*)

American actor to appear abroad was James Henry Hackett, who made his English debut on April 5, 1827, at Covent Garden, London, England. His first appearance on the stage was in a small role in Newark, N.J., in 1816 when he was sixteen years of age, but his professional debut was made March 1, 1826, when he appeared as Judge Woodcock in *Love in a Village* at the Park Theatre, New York City. (*Montrose Jonas Moses—Famous Actor Families in America*)

English actor of note to perform in the United States was George Frederick Cooke of Covent Garden, London, England, who left Liverpool, England, October 4, 1810. He arrived in New York City, November 16, 1810, and made his debut November 21, 1810, as Richard the Third in the play of the same name at the Park Theatre, New York City, before two thousand people. His manager, Thomas Apthorpe Cooper, paid him $125 a week for ten months, a traveling fee of 25c per mile, and expenses. Cooke died in New York City, September 26, 1812. (*William Dunlap—Memoirs of George Frederick Cooke*)

Matinee idol was John Henry, an Irish actor, who made his debut at Covent Garden, London, England, in 1762. His American debut was made in Philadelphia, Pa., October 6, 1766, as Publius Horatius in *The Roman Father.* (*Arthur Hornblow—History of American Theatre*)

ACTORS' EQUITY ASSOCIATION. *See* Actors' union

THE FIRST

ACTORS' NATIONAL PROTECTIVE UNION. *See* Actors' union

ACTORS' UNION was the Actors' National Protective Union, New York City, chartered by the American Federation of Labor, January 4, 1896. It combined with the White Rats (established June 1900) and the Actors' Equity Association (organized May 26, 1913) to form the Associated Actors and Artists of America (chartered August 28, 1919). A strike which was called August 7, 1919, in thirteen theaters in New York City and which spread to other cities was settled in the union's favor September 6, 1919. *(George Fuller Golden—My Lady Vaudeville and Her White Rats)*

ADAPTO CAR. *See* Railroad car: Freight car (Adapto Car)

ADDING MACHINE
Adding machine absolutely accurate at all times was the "Comptometer," which was invented by Dorr Eugene Felt of Chicago, Ill. The model was constructed in November 1884, in Chicago. A patent was applied for in March 1887 and issued on October 11, 1887 (No. 371,496). Felt entered into partnership with Robert Tarrant on November 28, 1887. This firm was later incorporated on January 25, 1889, as the Felt & Tarrant Company. Up to 1902 this machine was the only multiple order key-driven calculator on the market. *(J. A. V. Turck—Origin of Modern Calculating Machines)*

Adding machine successfully marketed was invented by William Seward Burroughs of St. Louis, Mo., who on August 21, 1888, obtained a patent (No. 388,118), for which he had applied January 10, 1885. In January 1886 he incorporated the business as the American Arithmometer Corporation of St. Louis, Mo., with an authorized capitalization of $100,000. This company was acquired on January 16, 1905, by the Burroughs Adding Machine Company, organized under the laws of Michigan with a capital stock of $5 million. *(Burroughs Bulletin. March 9, 1929)*

Adding machine to employ depressible keys was made by Du Bois D. Parmelee of New Paltz, N.Y., who received patent No. 7,074 on February 5, 1850. He called his machine a "calculator." It was neither practical nor generally used. *(J. A. V. Turck—Origin of Modern Calculating Machines)*

Adding machine to print totals and subtotals was made in 1872 by Edmund D. Barbour of Boston, Mass., who obtained patent No. 133,188 on November 19, 1872. His machine, which was called a "calculating machine," was not practical.

THE FIRST

ADDRESSOGRAPH was invented in 1892 by Joseph Smith Duncan of Sioux City, Iowa. The first model consisted of a hexagonal wood block upon which was glued rubber type torn from rubber stamps. The block revolved, advancing a new name and address to the printing point and inking the type simultaneously at each operation. This model was never marketed. The model "Baby 'O'" was put into production on July 26, 1893, in one small back room in the old Caxton Building on Dearborn Street, Chicago, Ill. Duncan obtained patent No. 558,936, April 28, 1896, on an "addressing machine."

ADHESIVE AND MEDICATED PLASTER
Adhesive and medicated plaster used in the treatment of fractures was reported in *Anatomy, Physiology and Diseases of the Bones and Joints,* by Samuel David Gross, published in 1830 in Philadelphia, Pa. *(American Journal of Medical Science. June 1897)*

Adhesive and medicated plaster patent was No. 3965, issued March 26, 1845, to Dr. Horace Harrel Day of Jersey City, N.J., and Dr. William H. Shecut. They dissolved rubber in a solvent, such as benzine, turpentine and bisulphide of carbon which they spread with a brush on fabric. They sold the process to Dr. Thomas Allcock, who introduced Allcock's Porous Plaster. *(American Journal of Pharmacy. Vol. 82. 1910)*

Adhesive and medicated plaster with a rubber base to be successfully manufactured was produced by Robert Wood Johnson and George J. Seabury in 1874 at East Orange, N.J. In 1886 Johnson separated from Seabury and formed Johnson & Johnson, New Brunswick, N.J., which introduced a full line of pharmaceutical plasters with an India rubber base.

ADHESIVE STAMP. *See* Postage stamp: Adhesive stamp

ADJUTANT GENERAL. *See* Army officer: Adjutant General

ADMIRAL. *See* Naval officer: Admiral

ADMIRAL IN THE COAST GUARD. *See* Coast Guard (U.S.): Vice Admiral in the Coast Guard

ADMIRAL IN THE MERCHANT MARINE. *See* Merchant Marine: Merchant Marine officer to hold the rank of rear admiral

ADMIRAL KILLED IN ACTION. *See* Naval officer: Admiral killed in action in World War II

THE FIRST

ADMIRAL WHO WAS A GENERAL.
See Army officer: General to become a rear
admiral

ADVENTIST. *See* Seventh Day Adventist
church

ADVERTISEMENT
Advertisement appeared May 1-8, 1704, in
the Boston *News-Letter.* Three ads occupied
four inches in a single column. The only
display was a two-line initial letter in the
text and the word "Advertisement" above
them. One offered "At Oysterbay on Long
Island in the Province of New York . . . a
very good Fulling Mill to be Let or Sold, as
also a Plantation, having on it a large new
Brick house, and other good house by it for a
Kitchin and workhouse, etc." Another offered
a reward for the capture of a thief and the return of certain wearing apparel, and the third
was a notice of the loss of two anvils. In the
first issue, April 17-24, 1704, an announcement
was made that advertisements would be published. (*James Melvin Lee—History of American Journalism*)

Advertisement to occupy a half-page appeared on July 18, 1743, in the New York
Weekly Journal, the first newspaper in America
established by a political faction. It advertised
a "curious musical machine" imported from
England which was exhibited for a fee at Mr.
Pacheco's at Petticoat Lane.

Advertising or commercial radio broadcast.
See Radio broadcast: Advertising or commercial radio broadcast

Automobile advertisement in a national
magazine of general circulation appeared in
the March 31, 1900, *Saturday Evening Post,*
Philadelphia, Pa. The W. E. Roach Company,
Philadelphia, featured its slogan, "Automobiles
That Give Satisfaction." The *Scientific American,* however, on July 30, 1898, had published
a one-column advertisement of the Winton
Motor Car Co., Cleveland, Ohio, under the
caption "Dispense with a Horse."

Magician's advertisement appeared March
18, 1734, in the New York *Weekly Journal*
and announced that on March 18, Joseph
Broome would "perform Wonders of the
World by Dexterity of Hand" at the home of
Charles Sleigh, on Duke Street, New York,
and invited "all to be Spectators of his Ingenuity." The admission fees were 1s, 9d, and
6d (25c, 18c and 12c). (*John Mulholland—
Quicker Than the Eye*)

Newspaper advertisement printed on aluminum foil. *See* Newspaper: Newspaper advertisement printed on aluminum foil

THE FIRST

Newspaper with perfumed advertising
page. *See* Newspaper: Newspaper with perfumed advertising page

Radio broadcasting contract for FM broadcasting. *See* Radio advertising: Radio advertising contract for frequency modulation
broadcasts

Three-dimensional newspaper advertisement was published June 12, 1953, in the
Daily Freeman, Waukesha, Wis. The Hale-
Frame Associates, decorators, used a full page
to advertise carpets. A cardboard cut-out with
a red and blue lens to see the third-dimensional
effect was supplied with the newspaper. On
consecutive days, starting July 13, 1953, Bullock's Downtown used six full-page three-
dimensional advertisements in the Los Angeles
Times.

ADVERTISING AGENCY was opened by
Volney B. Palmer in Philadelphia, Pa., in 1841,
for the reception of advertisements. He thus
became the first commercial advertising agent.
(*V. B. Palmer's Business Men's Almanac—
1849*)

ADVERTISING COURSE. *See* Radio
instruction: Radio-advertising course

ADVERTISING LAW
Advertising legislation (state) was "an act
to regulate the sale of merchandise and to prevent misleading and dishonest representations
in connection therewith," chapter 657 of the
Laws of New York passed April 30, 1898.
Those whose advertisements are "intended to
have the appearance of an advantageous offer,
which is untrue or calculated to mislead, shall
be guilty of a misdemeanor."

Outdoor advertising legislation (state)
was passed by New York March 28, 1865,
which amended Chapter 573 Laws of 1853
entitled "an act for the more effectual prevention of wanton and malicious mischief
and to prevent the defacement of natural
scenery." Painting and printing upon stones,
rocks, trees and the defacement of natural
scenery in certain localities constituted a misdemeanor punishable by a fine not exceeding
$250, or six months imprisonment, or both.
(*Chapter 222 Laws of 1865.*)

ADVERTISING MAGAZINE was the
Advertising Agency Circular, a monthly
founded by George Presbury Rowell and published by George P. Rowell & Co., New York
City. It was issued from 1865 until December 1866, when the name was changed to the
Advertiser's Gazette. On Thursday, April 1,
1875, it was first issued as a weekly. (*Advertiser's Gazette. April 1, 1875. Vol. 9, No. 1*)

THE FIRST

ADVERTISING ORGANIZATION to combat business abuses by advancing truth and fair practice in business was the Vigilance Committee of the Advertising Club of New York, New York City, organized at a meeting called December 1911 by Lewellyn E. Pratt, program committee chairman. Investigation work commenced March 1912. On May 19, 1912, the Associated Advertising Clubs of America in convention at Dallas, Tex., formed a national committee with Harry D. Robbins as chairman. (*Hurnard Jay Kenner—The Fight for Truth in Advertising*)

ADVERTISING STANDARDIZATION. *See* Billboard standardization

ADVISORY COMMITTEE FOR AERO-NAUTICS (national). *See* Aviation: Advisory committee for aeronautics (national)

AERIAL CAMERA. *See* Camera: Aerial camera (nine-lens) for large-scale mapping

AERIAL FERRY BRIDGE. *See* Bridge: Aerial ferry

AERIAL FOREST PATROL. *See* Forest service: Forest service aerial patrol

AERIAL LIFT BRIDGE. *See* Bridge: Aerial ferry

AERIAL MOTION PICTURES. *See* Aviation: Airplane moving picture show

AERIAL PHOTOGRAPH. *See* Photograph: Aerial photograph

AERIAL POLICEWOMAN. *See* Police: Policewoman on the aerial force

AERO CLUB OF AMERICA LICENSE. *See* Aviation—License: Pilot's license issued by the Aero Club of America

AEROCYCLE. *See* Helicopter: Aerocycle

AERONAUTIC INTERNATIONAL EX-POSITION. *See* Aviation—Expositions and meets: Aeronautic international exposition

AERONAUTICAL BOARD. *See* Aviation: Air control municipal board

AERONAUTICAL ENGINEERING COURSE. *See* Aviation—School: Aeronautical engineering course

AERONAUTICAL STOWAWAY. *See* Aviation: Aeronautical stowaway

THE FIRST

AERONAUTICAL TROPHY. *See* Aviation: Aeronautical trophy

AERONAUTICS. *See* Aviation

AERONAUTICS (CIVIL) AUTHORITY (U.S.). *See* Civil aeronautics authority (U.S.)

AFRICAN CHURCH was the Bethel African Methodist Episcopal Church, founded in 1793 by Richard Allen, a Negro, at Sixth and Lombard Street, Philadelphia, Pa. It was opened for public worship July 17, 1794 and dedicated July 29, 1794, by Bishop Francis Asbury. On October 12, 1794, the Reverend Robert Blackwell announced from the pulpit that the congregation was received in full fellowship in the Methodist Episcopal Church. It was incorporated March 28, 1796, as the "Minister, Church, Wardens and Vestrymen of the African Episcopal Church of St. Thomas in the City of Philadelphia. (*Carter Godwin Woodson—History of the Negro Church*)

AFRICAN METHODIST EPISCOPAL CHURCH. *See* Methodist Episcopal Church: African Methodist Episcopal Church

AFRICANDER CATTLE. *See* Animals: Cattle (Africander cattle)

AGENCY (advertising.) *See* Advertising agency

AGRICULTURAL ADJUSTMENT AD-MINISTRATION was authorized by act of Congress (H.R. 3835, 73d Congress) "to relieve the existing national economic emergency by increasing purchasing power." The act, approved May 12, 1933 (48 Stat.L.31) was known as the Agricultural Adjustment Act. The first administrator was Henry Agard Wallace, Secretary of Agriculture.

AGRICULTURAL APPROPRIATION by a state for carrying out extension training work along agricultural lines was made by New York, May 12, 1894, when Governor Roswell Pettibone Flower signed the act "to amend the agricultural law in relation to agricultural experiment stations within this state, and to make an appropriation therefor," chapter 675. The appropriation was $16,000.

AGRICULTURAL "BOARD" (state) was provided for in New York State by a law passed April 7, 1819, but was not actually organized until January 20, 1820. It was made up wholly of agricultural society delegates, and was a quasi-public organization. (*Edward Wiest—Agricultural Organization in the U.S.*)

THE FIRST

THE FIRST

AGRICULTURAL BOOK

Agricultural book was *The Husbandman's Guide: In Four Parts. Part First. Containing many Excellent Rules for Setting and Planting of Orchards, Gardens and Woods, the times to Sow Corn, and all sorts of Seeds. Part Second. Choice Physical Receipts for divers dangerous Distempers in Men, Women and Children. Part Third. The Experienc'd Farrier. . . . Part Fourth. Certain rare Receipts to make Cordial Waters, Conserves, Preserves. . . .*" It was a 107-page reprint of an English book and was published in 1710 for Eleazar Phillips by John Allen, Boston, Mass.

Agricultural book distinctly American was *Essays upon Field Husbandry in New England* by Jared Eliot. It consisted of six essays, originally printed separately, which were printed and sold by Edes and Gill in Boston, Mass., in 1760. The first essay appeared in 1748, the second in 1749, the third in 1751, the fourth in 1753, the fifth in 1754, and the sixth in 1759. (*Franklin Bowditch Dexter—Biographical Notices of the Graduates of Yale College 1701-1745*)

AGRICULTURAL DICTIONARY. *See* Dictionary: Agricultural dictionary

AGRICULTURAL ENCYCLOPEDIA was

Anthony Florian Madinger Willich's *The Domestic Encyclopedia, or A Dictionary of Facts, and useful knowledge, comprehending a concise view of the latest discoveries, inventions and improvements, chiefly applicable to rural and domestic economy . . . ,* a five-volume set, published in Philadelphia, Pa., in 1804 by William Young Birch and Abraham Small. It had originally appeared in England. (*Percy Wells Bidwell and John Ironside Falconer—History of Agriculture in Northern United States*)

AGRICULTURAL EXPERIMENT STATION

Agricultural experiment farm was ten acres set aside by Savannah, Georgia in 1735. A skillful botanist was appointed "to collect the seeds of drugs and dying-stuffs in other countries in the same climate, in order to cultivate such of them as shall be found to thrive well in Georgia." (*Collections of Georgia Historical Society—1840—Vol. 1*)

State agricultural experiment station was the Connecticut Agricultural Experiment Station, established in Connecticut by Act approved July 20, 1875. Orange Judd, editor and proprietor of the *American Agriculturist,* offered $1,000, and the trustees of Wesleyan University at Middletown, Conn., offered the free use of the chemical laboratory of Orange Judd Hall on condition that the legislature appropriate

$2,800 per annum for two years. The appropriation was made October 1, 1875, and work begun January 1, 1876. Professor Wilbur Olin Atwater was made the first director of this first regularly organized state experiment station and served until April 9, 1877. (*Bulletin 80. Office of Experimental Stations—U.S. Department of Agriculture.*)

AGRICULTURAL FAIR. *See* Fair: Agricultural fair

AGRICULTURAL IMPLEMENTS. *See* Plow; Reaper

AGRICULTURAL JOURNAL

Agricultural journal was the *Agricultural Museum,* a sixteen-page octavo issued July 4, 1810, under the sponsorship of the Columbian Agricultural Society. It was edited by the Reverend David Wiley and printed by W. A. Rind at Georgetown, D.C. The first volume was semi-monthly, but beginning with volume two it was issued monthly. Subscription was $2.50 for 24 numbers. Publication ceased May 1812. (*Agricultural History. April 1928. Vol. 2 No. 2*)

Agricultural journal to attain prominence was the *American Farmer,* an eight-page quarto size weekly, which was founded in Baltimore, Md., April 2, 1819, by John Stuart Skinner. It flourished under various names until 1897. (*William Edward Ogilvie—Pioneer Agricultural Journalists*)

AGRICULTURAL LAND GRANT pro-

posal was made by Justin Smith Morrill. He advocated giving each state an allotment of land, the income from which should be used to support at least one agricultural college in each state. The bill was vetoed by President James Buchanan in 1857, but was signed by President Abraham Lincoln on July 2, 1862 (12 Stat.L. 503), after certain modifications had been made. It was known as the Morrill Act, and its full title was an "Act donating public lands to the several states and territories which may provide colleges for the benefit of agriculture and the mechanic arts." (*George Washington Atherton—The Legislative Career of Justin S. Morrill*)

AGRICULTURAL SCHOOL

Agricultural college (state) to be chartered was the Farmers High School of Pennsylvania, incorporated April 13, 1854. The charter was repealed and it was reincorporated February 22, 1855. The school opened February 16, 1859. In the first session, 119 students were admitted. The Bachelor of Scientific and Practical Agriculture degree (B.S.A.) was awarded to those who completed a four-year course and submitted a dissertation. The name was changed on May 6, 1862, to the Agricultural College of Pennsylvania.

THE FIRST

Agricultural college (state) to open was the Agricutural College of Michigan, Lansing, Michigan, which was chartered on February 12, 1855, and opened on May 13, 1857. On May 14, 1857, the faculty of six conducted classes for the 63 students. The first president was Joseph Ricketson Williams. The school was later renamed the Michigan State College of Agriculture and Applied Science.

Vocational agricultural school with dormitory facilities which was a department of a state university was the School of Agriculture of the University of Minnesota, established October 18, 1888 at St. Anthony Park, St. Paul, Minn. The first principal was William Wirt Pendergast.

AGRICULTURAL SEED DISTRIBUTION (national) was undertaken in 1836-37 by the Commissioner of Patents, Henry Leavitt Ellsworth at his own expense and without Congressional authorization. In 1838, the cost of agricultural statistics and seeds was $126.40. In 1839, about 30,000 packets were distributed, the expense being about $1,000. Seed distribution was discontinued June 30, 1923.

AGRICULTURAL SOCIETY
Agricultural society on the American continent was the Philadelphia Society for the Promotion of Agriculture, which was organized on March 1, 1785. Meetings were scheduled every two months. The promotion of agriculture was undertaken as one of the functions of the New Jersey Society for Promoting Agriculture, Commerce and Arts, established in 1781. A meeting was held September 7, 1781, in Trenton, N.J. Samuel Witham Stockton was secretary. *(Early Development of Agricultural Societies in the U.S.—Agricultural Historical Society Papers)*

Agricultural society for dairymen was the Vermont Dairymen's Association, organized October 27, 1869, at Montpelier Vt., "to improve the dairy interests of Vermont, and all subsidiary interests." *(Annual Report 1875—Vermont Department of Agriculture)*

Agricultural society of national importance was the National Grange of the Patrons of Husbandry, which was organized in Washington, D.C., December 4, 1867, with William Saunders of the Department of Agriculture as master, and Oliver Hudson Kelley, a native of Boston, Mass., as secretary. This was the first important cooperation undertaken by farmers. The movements and meetings of the society were carried on in secret. *(Solon Justus Buck—The Granger Movement)*

AGRICULTURAL SOIL CONFERENCE of importance was the International Congress of Soil Science which met in Washington,

THE FIRST

D.C., from June 13 to 22, 1917. Delegates were present from over twenty countries. *(International Congress of Soil Science—Proceedings and Papers of the First International Congress)*

AGRICULTURAL STATE COLLEGE. *See* Agricultural school: Agricultural college (state) to be chartered

AGRICULTURAL STATION. *See* Agricultural experiment station: State agricultural experiment station

AGRICULTURE
Crop limitation law was passed October 16, 1629, by the Virginia General Assembly. Act five limited the planting of tobacco. *(William Wallace Hening—Statutes at Large. Vol. 1)*

Crop surplus destruction was ordered January 6, 1639, by the Virginia General Assembly: "Tobacco by reason of excessive quantities made, being so low that the planters could not subsist by it or be enabled to raise more staple commodities or pay their debts, enacted that the tobacco of that year be viewed by sworn viewers and the rotten and unmerchantable, and half the good to be burned, so the whole quantity made would come to 1,500,000 pounds without stripping and smoothing." *(William Wallace Hening—Statutes at Large. Vol. 1)*

Federal Crop Insurance Corporation. *See* Federal Crop Insurance Corporation

Grain Stabilization Corporation. *See* Grain Stabilization Corporation

AGRICULTURE BUREAU
Agriculture bureau (hitherto a section of the Patent Office) was made a separate entity on May 15, 1862, by an act "to establish a Department of Agriculture" (12 Stat.L.387) and was administered by a Commissioner of Agriculture until February 9, 1889 (25 Stat.L. 659), when it was made the eighth executive department in the federal government. The first Superintendent of Agriculture under the Department of the Interior was Thomas Green Clemson who served from February 3, 1860 to March 4, 1861. Isaac Newton was appointed Commissioner of Agriculture by President Abraham Lincoln on July 1, 1862, and served until June 19, 1867. *(Records in Bureau of Plant Industry—Department of Agriculture, Washington, D.C.)*

Agriculture bureau scientific publication was *A Report on the Chemical Analysis of Grapes*, a four-page leaflet, by Charles Mayer

AGRICULTURE BUREAU—*Continued*
Wetherill, Ph.D., M.D., dated October 15, 1862,
printed by the Government Printing Office,
Washington, D.C. *(Edgar Fahs Smith—
Charles Mayer Wetherill)*

AGRICULTURE   DEPARTMENT
(state)
State department of agriculture was cre-
ated by Georgia by act of February 28, 1874.
The first commissioner was Dr. Thomas P.
Janes, who served for six years.

AGRICULTURE DEPARTMENT (U.S.)
Agriculture Departemnt distinguished service gold medal. *See* Medal: Agriculture Department distinguished service gold medal

Office of Markets was created May 16,
1913, by the Secretary of Agriculture under
authority of March 4, 1913 (37 Stat.L.854),
which appropriated $50,000 for its operation.
The first chief was Charles John Brand, who
served from May 16, 1913, to June 30, 1919.
In the appropriation act of June 30, 1914 (38
Stat.L.440), a similar paragraph was headed
"Office of Markets" and the amount increased
to $200,000. The Office of Markets and the
Office of Rural Organization were combined
on July 1, 1914, and the resulting unit was
called the Office of Markets and Rural Organization. It was changed to the Bureau of Markets by the act of March 4, 1917 (39 Stat.L.
1162).

**Secretary of the Department of Agricul-
ture** was Norman Jay Colman of Missouri,
who was appointed February 13, 1889, by
President Grover Cleveland and who served
until March 5, 1889. Previously he had served
as Commissioner of Agriculture from April
4, 1885, to February 12, 1889. *(William Lawrence Wanlas—U.S. Department of Agriculture, Washington, D.C.)*

AGRICULTURE PROFESSOR in a college was Samuel Latham Mitchill, who was
appointed by Columbia College, New York City,
on July 9, 1792, as Professor of Natural History, Chemistry, Agriculture, and the other
related sciences. Part of his course included
the "theory of vegetation and application of its
principles to practical agriculture, nutrition and
food of plants, with the history of manures,
multiplication, dissemination and habitations of
plants. Chemical history of various vegetable
products, Sap, Gum, Resin, Farina, etc., with
their preparation and application to the uses
of man. Vegetable colors, vegetable poisons,
baking,   brewing,   tanning,   etc." *(Alfred
Charles True—History of Agricultural Education in the U.S.)*

AIR (compressed) for tunnel construction
was employed in 1879. This method was
introduced by Dewitt Clinton Haskin and was

used in the construction of the famous Hudson
River tunnel between Hoboken, N.J., and Morton Street, New York City. The tunnel plans
called for two tubes, each sixteen feet wide
and eighteen feet high. During the construction, on July 21, 1880, the compressed air blew
a hole through the soft silt of the roof about
360 feet from the Hoboken shaft, flooding the
tubes and drowning twenty workmen. Work
was discontinued and the tunnel was not completed and opened until February 25, 1908.
(Archibald Black—The Story of Tunnels)

AIR (liquid) was economically produced in
1895 by Charles Eastman Tripler of the Tripler
Liquid Air Company, New York City. His
invention reduced the cost of production from
$500 a pint to $4 a gallon. *(New Hampshire
Medical Society. Transactions. May 25, 1899—
"Liquid air"—J. Milnor Coit)*

**AIR BOAT COMMERCIAL LINE SERV-
ICE.** *See* Aviation: Hydroplane commercial
line service

AIR BRAKE was invented by George Westinghouse, Jr., of Schenectady, N.Y., who received patent No. 88,929 on April 13, 1869, on a
"steam power brake." It was used on an
experimental train carrying officials of the
Panhandle Railroad. It immediately demonstrated its value. But inasmuch as it took longer
for the air to reach the last cars of a train,
each car stopped at a different time. A "triple
air brake" which corrected this fault was patented by Westinghouse (No. 124,405) on March
5, 1872. He invented an automatic brake fifteen
years   later. *(Bulletins—Westinghouse   Air
Brake Co.)*

AIR BRUSH PATENT was No. 248,579,
which was granted to Leslie L. Curtis of Cape
Elizabeth, Me., on October 25, 1881, for his
"atomizer for coloring pictures."

AIR-CONDITIONED   AUTOMOBILE.
See Automobile: Air-conditioned automobile

AIR-CONDITIONED   FACTORY.   *See*
Factory: Air-conditioned factory

**AIR-CONDITIONED   OFFICE   BUILD-
ING.** See Building: Air-conditioned office
building

AIR-CONDITIONED RAILROAD CAR.
See Railroad car: Air-conditioned car

AIR-CONDITIONED   THEATER.   *See*
Theater: Theater provided with scientific air
distribution

AIR-CONDITIONED TRAIN. *See* Railroad: Air-conditioned train

THE FIRST

THE FIRST

AIR CONFERENCE (international). *See* Aviation—Expositions and Meets: Air conference (international)

AIR CONTROL MUNICIPAL BOARD. *See* Aviation: Air control municipal board

AIR DEFENSE COMMAND (U.S.) was created February 26, 1940, with headquarters at Mitchel Field, Long Island, N.Y., pursuant to War Department Orders, dated February 26, 1940, for defense against air attack through the practical application of the coordinated effort of aviation, anti-aircraft artillery, and aircraft warning agencies, including fixed military and civilian installations. It was charged with the development of a system for unified air defense of an area and the determination of tasks within the capabilities of the various combinations of tactical units which might be assembled for the air defense of cities, continental bases, manufacturing and industrial areas, or of armies in the field. The first Commander was Brigadier General James Eugene Chaney.

AIR FORCE
Air Force Secretary was William Stuart Symington of Missouri, who was sworn in by Chief Justice Frederick Moore Vinson in Washington, D.C., on September 18, 1947. He served until April 24, 1950, when his successor, Thomas Knight Finletter, was sworn in.

AIR FORCE ACADEMY (U.S.)
Air Force Academy was authorized April 1, 1954 (68 Stat.L.47). Temporary headquarters were established July 11, 1955, at the Lowry Air Force Base, Denver, Colo. The first commandant was Lieutenant General Hubert Reilly Harmon. The first advisory board consisted of Dr. Arthur Holly Compton, Dr. Virgil Melvin Hancher, Dr. John Alfred Hannah, Kaufman Thuma Keller, Charles Augustus Lindbergh, and General Carl Spaatz. The $135,000,000 academy at Colorado Springs, Colo., received its first cadets on August 29, 1958. The first graduating class (207 cadets) was commissioned June 3, 1959, the commencement address being delivered by James Henderson Douglas, Secretary of the Air Force. First in the graduating class was Bradley C. Hosmer of Dunseith, N.D. The four-year course consisted of 1,548 hours of the humanities, 1,629 hours of science, and 2,178 hours of airmanship.

Air Force Academy woman officer was Captain Naomi M. McCracken of Redding, Calif., who took over her duties as assistant director of cadet records at the Air Force Academy temporary headquarters, Denver, Colo., on April 26, 1957.

AIR FORCE FLAG. *See* Flag: Air Force flag

AIR FORCE OFFICER
Air Force chairman of the Joint Chiefs of Staff was General Nathan Farragut Twining, who was sworn in August 15, 1957, in Washington, D.C., by President Dwight David Eisenhower. On September 29, 1960, the day before Twining retired as Chief of Staff, President Eisenhower decorated him with the Distinguished Service Medal.

Air Force Surgeon General was Major General Malcolm Cummings Grow, who served from July 1, 1949, to November 30, 1949. Air Force General Order No. 35 of June 8, 1949, authorized the U.S. Air Force Medical Service and the Office of Surgeon General. Grow had previously served as Air Surgeon from January 1946 to July 1, 1949.

Brigadier General (Negro) in the Air Force was Benjamin Oliver Davis, Jr., of Washington, D.C., director of Operations and Training of the Far East Air Force, who was named October 27, 1954. He was the son of Brigadier General Benjamin Oliver Davis of the U.S. Army.

Judge Advocate General of the U.S. Air Force was Colonel Reginald Carl Harmon, who was nominated by President Harry S. Truman on September 8, 1948, for a four-year term as the first Judge Advocate General of the Air Force with the rank of major general.

AIR FORCE SURVIVAL SCHOOL. *See* Aviation—School: Air Force survival school

AIR MAIL SERVICE
Air mail contractor (domestic) was the Varney Air Line, which operated a single-engine Swallow biplane on April 6, 1926, between Pasco, Wash., and Elko, Nev., where connections were made with the Post Office Department's transcontinental line. Chief pilot Leon Cuddeback took off from Pasco. Franklin Rose, who took off from Elko, Nev., crashed in the desert.

Air mail experimental route was flown May 15, 1918, between Washington, D.C., Philadelphia, Pa., and New York City by planes and pilots supplied by the War Department. Lieutenant Torrey H. Webb in a Curtiss JN-4 left Belmont Field, Long Island, with two sacks containing 2,457 pieces of mail and flew to Philadelphia. Lieutenant James Clark Edgerton continued the trip to Potomac Field, Washington, D.C. in a relief plane. The 218 miles were covered in 3 hours and 20 minutes. A similar service started from Washington, with Lieutenant George L. Boyle flying east. A broken

AIR MAIL SERVICE—*Continued*
propeller forced his descent at Waldorf, Md.
The mail was carried by motor truck to Philadelphia, then flown to New York City by
Lieutenant H. Paul Culver.

Air mail flyer's medal of honor. *See* Medal:
Air Mail Flyer's Medal of Honor

Air mail long-distance night service was
established on July 1, 1925, from New York
City to Chicago, Ill., over a 774-mile course.
The first plane, from Hadley Field, New
Brunswick, N.J. (the New York area) was
piloted by D. C. Smith. It was followed by a
second plane piloted by J. D. Hill. The first
plane eastward was simultaneously dispatched
from Chicago, and was piloted by Shirley
Short, and was likewise followed by a second plane carrying the surplus mail.

Air mail pilot was Earl Lewis Ovington,
who was sworn in on September 23, 1911, at
Garden City, Long Island, N.Y., as "air mail
pilot number one." In his Blériot monoplane,
"Dragonfly," he delivered air mail from Postmaster General Frank Harris Hitchcock at
Garden City, to postmaster William McCarthy
at Mineola, L.I., a distance of six miles, inaugurating the first official air mail service
authorized by the Post Office Department. The
first mail consisted of 640 letters and 1,280 postcards. This was not a regular scheduled flight
as the service was performed without expense
to the Post Office Department. *(Records in
Division of Main Service. Post Office Department, Washington, D.C.)*

Air mail regular service was established
August 12, 1918, by the Post Office Department
between New York City and Washington, D.C.
Ben B. Lipsner was the first superintendent of
air mail. The pilots were Ed. V. Gardner,
Maurice Newton, Max Miller, and Robert F.
Shank.

**Air mail service between North and South
America** was inaugurated May 14, 1929, from
Miami, Fla.

Air mail service from ship to shore was
inaugurated August 13, 1928, by the Trans-
Atlantic Aerial Company when an amphibian
was launched from the "Ile de France," 400
miles at sea. Three sacks of mail, including
two packages of films, were delivered at New
York City fifteen hours before the ship docked.
Service was discontinued September 28, 1928.

Air mail service to a steamer at sea was
made August 14, 1919, when an Aeromarine flying boat piloted by Cyrus Johnston Zimmermann dropped a bag of mail on the forward

deck of the White Star liner "Adriatic," an
hour and a half after she had left her pier in
New York City.

Air mail stamp. *See* Postage stamp: Air
mail stamps

Air mail transatlantic service was inaugurated on May 20, 1939, with a flight from New
York City to Marseilles, France, via Bermuda
and Portugal.

Air mail transcontinental flight was from
San Francisco, Calif., to New York City. The
plane left San Francisco at 4:30 A.M., February 22, 1921, and arrived at Hazelhurst Field,
Long Island, N.Y., at 4.50 P.M. on February
23, 1921, 33 hours and 20 minutes later. The
actual flying time was 25 hours and 16 minutes;
the average speed for the 2,629 miles was 104
miles an hour.

Air mail transcontinental service (combination airplane-railroad) began on September 8, 1920, when 16,000 letters reached the
west coast in 22 hours less than the best train
time. The mail was carried by planes during
the day and by trains at night, a service of 63
hours for the flight west and 78½ hours for
the eastward flight. The various sections and
the dates of first service were: New York City
to Cleveland, July 1, 1919; Cleveland to Chicago, May 15, 1919; Chicago to Omaha, May
15, 1920, and from Omaha to San Francisco,
September 8, 1920.

**Air mail transcontinental through regular
service** was established between New York
City and San Francisco, Calif., July 1, 1924,
when the air mail-railroad service was discontinued. The first westward flight of this
service was made by Wesley L. Smith, who flew
from New York City to Cleveland, Ohio, and
the first eastward flight by Claire K. Vance,
who flew from San Francisco, Calif., to Reno,
Nev. The service was daily including Sunday,
with fourteen stops en route.

Airplane mail pick-up by which planes
snatch mail from the ground without landing
was demonstrated on October 1, 1929, by Pennsylvania-Central Airlines at Washington, D.C.
Despite rain, 253 successful pick-ups were made
in 255 attempts. The pick-up device was authorized by the Post Office Department for use
on PCA, now known as the Capital Airlines,
and was used on regular schedules at Beaver
Falls and Newcastle, Pa., and Youngstown,
Ohio, on the Pittsburgh-Cleveland route.

**Autogiro mail delivery direct to a post
office** took place May 25, 1935, in Philadelphia, Pa. Pilot Louis Levy landed an autogiro
on the roof of the Market Street Post Office

THE FIRST

and handed a sack of mail from the Central Airport, Camden, N.J., to Postmaster General James Aloysius Farley. A few minutes later, pilot James Garrett Ray swooped down in another autogiro, took a sack of mail, and followed Levy back to the airport.

Autogiro mail delivery regular service began July 6, 1939, when Captain John MacDonald Miller flew an Eastern Air Line autogiro from the roof of the Philadelphia Post Office to the Central Airport, Camden, N.J., six miles away, in six minutes. The autogiro made the round trip to its starting place in fourteen minutes.

Balloon flight carrying mail. *See* Balloon: Balloon flight carrying mail

Helicopter air mail and express service was inaugurated October 1, 1947, by Los Angeles Airways, Inc., Los Angeles, Calif., to serve the San Fernando Valley area. On May 20, 1947, the company received the first Civil Aeronautics Board certificate, which covered a three-year period. Service was extended October 15, 1947, and January 8, 1948, to serve forty-two communities. During the first three-year period, 200,000 flights were made and 13 million pounds of mail carried. Pilots on the first flight were Boyd Kesselering and John De Blauw.

Helicopter air mail and express service to carry passengers was the Los Angeles Airways, Inc., which instituted the combined service on November 22, 1955, between Los Angeles and Long Beach, Calif.

Helicopter air mail delivery by commercial helicopter was made July 5, 1946, between the Bridgeport, Conn., post office and the airport. The pilot was D. D. ("Jimmy") Viner, chief pilot of Sikorsky Aircraft, Bridgeport, Conn.

Helicopter air mail experimental tests were made July 8, 1946, from the Lockheed Airport, Burbank, Calif., by the Post Office Department and the Army Air Force. For three weeks, two weekly trips were made to Long Beach, Calif., to the north, and to Santa Ana to the south, serving twenty-four post offices en route.

International air mail was inaugurated March 3, 1919, between Seattle, Wash., and Victoria, British Columbia (74 miles) by Edward Hubbard of the Hubbard Air Service, who piloted a Boeing Type C open cockpit biplane with pontoons. William Edward Boeing was a passenger on the flight. Regular service under contract commenced October 14, 1920, and continued under successive contracts until June 30, 1937.

THE FIRST

Jet propelled airplane to transport mail was a P-80 Shooting Star which on June 22, 1946, carried a letter addressed to President Harry S. Truman. It was piloted by Captain Robert Atkinson Baird III of Clarksdale, Miss., who left the Schenectady County Airport, Schenectady, N.Y., and arrived at the National Airport, Washington, D.C. (370 miles) in 49 minutes. Another jet propelled P-80, piloted by Major Kenneth Oscar Chilstrom of Elmhurst, Ill., left for Dayton, Ohio, with a letter for Orville Wright and, after a stopover at Wright Field, arrived at Chicago, Ill., in 2 hours and 2 minutes.

Letter to encircle the world by commercial air mail flight. *See* Postal service: Letter to encircle the world by commercial air mail

Missile mail (official) was dispatched from the submarine U.S.S. "Barbero" (SSC-317), about 100 miles at sea off the Atlantic coast to the Mayport Naval Auxiliary Station, near Jacksonville, Fla., on June 8, 1959. Bearing four-cent postage rather than seven-cent air mail stamps, 3,000 letters were shot in a 36-foot Regulus 1 winged missile at about 600 miles an hour. The missile landed 22 minutes after being launched. The letters, signed by Postmaster General Arthur Ellsworth Summerfield, were addressed to President Dwight David Eisenhower and to other government officials and important personages. The project was under the supervision of Captain Arnold Schade.

Pacific air mail flight and the first air crossing from California to the Philippines was made by the "China Clipper" of Pan American Airways, Inc., commanded by Edwin Charles Musick. The plane left San Francisco, Calif., November 22, 1935, at 3:46 A.M. Pacific Standard Time and made stops at Honolulu, Midway, Wake, and Guam, landing at Manila, P.I., November 28, 1935 at 11:31 P.M., having covered 8,210 miles in 59 hours and 48 minutes. It carried 58 sacks of mail containing 110,865 letters. The return trip started December 1, 1935, from Manila and was completed December 6, 1935 at 10:37 A.M. at San Francisco, Calif. The eastbound flight was made in 63 hours and 24 minutes, the total flying time being 123 hours and 12 minutes. *(William Stephen Grooch—From Crate to Clipper)*

Parcel post domestic air service was authorized June 29, 1948, (62 Stat.L.1097) and began September 1, 1948. The country was divided into eight postal zones, the maximum rate being 80 cents for the first pound and 65 cents for each additional pound or fraction thereof.

Parcel post international air service was inaugurated March 15, 1948, between the United

THE FIRST

AIR MAIL SERVICE—*Continued*
States and twenty-one countries in Europe.
Service to South America was instituted on
September 4, 1948, and to the Pacific area on
September 11, 1948.

Rocket air mail flight was made February
23, 1936, at Greenwood Lake, N.Y., in the
"Gloria," an eleven-foot rocket with a fifteen-
foot wing spread. The fuel was liquid oxygen
and alcohol. The inventors of the rocket were
Willy Ley, Louis Goodman, and Hugh Franklin Pierce. The flight was sponsored by Frido
W. Kessler. The rocket carried 4,323 letters
and 1,826 postcards. Each cover was franked
with special rocket stamps in addition to the
regular postage stamps.

Woman aviator to pilot an air-mail transport. *See* Aviation—Aviator: Woman aviator to pilot an air mail transport

AIR MAIL STAMP. *See* Postage stamp:
Airmail stamps

AIR MEDAL. *See* Medal: Air medal (U.S.)
awarded to a woman

AIR MEET. *See* Aviation—Expositions and
meets: Aviation meet

**AIR PASSENGER INTERNATIONAL
STATION.** *See* Aviation—Airport: Air passenger international station

AIR PATROL (U.S.) (Civil). *See* Civil
air patrol (U.S.)

AIR RACE, INTER-CITY. *See* Aviation
—Races: Inter-city airplane race

AIR RAID SHELTER
Air raid community shelter was the Highlands Community Shelter, Inc., Boise, Idaho,
which was completed on July 1, 1961. It was
designed to accommodate 1,000 people. Family
membership cost $100. The shelter cost $142,000
of which $122,000 was government research
funds obtained from the Office of Civil Defense.

Air raid shelter was built by Howard
Moyer Gounder at Fleetwood, Pa., R.F.D.
#1, and completed November 1, 1940. Stone
walls eighteen inches thick set in concrete with
eighteen-inch retaining walls built alongside a
mountain boulder supported an eight-inch reinforced concrete roof, weather-conditioned
with asphalt tar. Movable bunks on one wall
accommodated six people. The floors were made
of cement. Heavy double doors, one opening
inward, the other outward, contained small
windows. Electric wiring encased in iron pipes

THE FIRST

supplied illumination. A stove provided heating
and cooking facilities, while ventilation was
afforded by a protected chimney in the rear.

See also Building: House with a built-in
nuclear bomb shelter

AIR-RAIL PASSENGER SERVICE. *See*
Aviation: Air-rail passenger transcontinental
service

AIR RIGHTS LEASE was made by the
New York Central Railroad Company in February 1910 to the Grand Central Palace, New
York City for $30,000 a year. The Palace was
permitted to build its structure over the New
York Central Railroad tracks. The air rights
idea was originated by Ira A. Place.

AIR SERVICE (U.S.). *See* Aviation: Air
service of the United States Army

AIR SPRAY (paint). *See* Paint spraying
device

AIR SQUADRON. *See* Aviation: Air
squadron (complete)

AIR STATION (COAST GUARD). *See*
Aviation: Coast guard air station

AIR STEWARDESS. *See* Aviation: Air
stewardess

AIR TERMINAL. *See* Aviation—Airport:
Air terminal

AIR-TO-AIR ROCKET. *See* Rocket: Air-
to-air rocket

AIR TRAFFIC REGULATION COURSE.
See Traffic regulation course: Air traffic
regulation course

AIR TRAINING SCHOOL (Naval). *See*
Aviation—School: Naval air training school

**AIRBOAT COMMERCIAL LINE SERV-
ICE.** *See* Aviation: Hydroplane commercial
line service

**AIRCRAFT BATTLE FORCE COM-
MANDER.** *See* Naval officer: Naval officer
designated Commander, Aircraft Battle
Force

AIRCRAFT CANNON. *See* Ordnance:
Automatic aircraft cannon

AIRCRAFT CARRIER. *See* Ship: Aircraft
carrier

THE FIRST

AIRCRAFT LIABILITY INSURANCE. *See* Insurance: Aircraft liability and property damage insurance

AIRCRAFT OWNED BY U.S. FOREST SERVICE. *See* Forest service: Aircraft owned by the Forest Service

AIRMAIL. *See* Air mail service

AIRPLANE. *See* Aviation—Airplane

AIRPLANE-AUTOMOBILE COMBINATION. *See* Automobile: Automobile-airplane combination

AIRPLANE FLYING SCHOOL. *See* Aviation—School: Airplane flying school

AIRPLANE HIGH-SPEED TANK. *See* Aviation—airplane high-speed tank to test airplanes

AIRPLANE INSTRUCTOR'S LICENSE. *See* Aviation—License: Airplane instructor's license

AIRPLANE LEGISLATION. *See* Aviation—Legislation: Aviation legislation

AIRPLANE MAIL PICK-UP. *See* Air mail service: Airplane mail pick-up

AIRPLANE PASSENGER (official). *See* Aviation—Passenger: Airplane passenger (official)

AIRPLANE PASSENGER (woman). *See* Aviation—Passenger: Woman airplane passenger

AIRPLANE POST OFFICE. *See* Post office: Airplane post office

AIRPLANE POSTAGE STAMPS. *See* Postage stamps: Air mail stamps

AIRPLANE RACE. *See* Aviation—Races: Airplane race

AIRPLANE SALE. *See* Aviation—Airplane: Airplane sold commercially

AIRPLANE TELECAST. *See* Television—Telecast: Airplane telecast (network)

AIRPLANE TO RACE A TRAIN. *See* Aviation—Races: Airplane to race a train

THE FIRST

AIRPLANE TORPEDO. *See* Torpedo: Airplane torpedo

AIRPLANE TRANSCONTINENTAL PASSENGER (woman). *See* Aviation—Passenger: Woman airplane passenger (transcontinental)

AIRPLANE WEDDING. *See* Wedding: Airplane wedding

AIRPORT (federally owned). *See* Aviation—Airport: Airport (federally owned and operated)

AIRPORT HOTEL. *See* Aviation—Airport: Airport hotel

AIRPORT MANAGER (woman). *See* Aviation—Airport: Airport manager (woman)

AIRSHIP. *See* Aviation—Airship

AIRSHIP BOMBING. *See* Aviation—Airship: Airship bombing

AIRSHIP CARRIER. *See* Ship: Aircraft carrier

AIRSHIP DISASTER. *See* Aviation—Airship: Airship disaster

AIRSHIP (U.S. Navy). *See* Aviation—Airship: Airship of the U.S. Navy

AIRWAYS ILLUMINATION. *See* Aviation: Airways illumination

ALARM. *See* Burglar alarm: Burglar alarm

ALARM CLOCK. *See* Clock: Alarm clock

ALBANY REGENCY. *See* Political machine

ALBERT MEDAL. *See* Medal: Albert medal presented to a native-born American

ALCOHOL
Power alcohol plant was established by the Bailor Manufacturing Company, Atchison, Kan., which sold power alcohol October 2, 1936. Five per cent of the total output was butyl alcohol and acetone which were blended with ethyl alcohol, which in turn was blended with gasoline. Raw materials used were rye, oats, sweet potatoes, barley, milo, kafir corn, molasses and rice.

ALCOHOL CONTROL ADMINISTRATION. See Federal alcohol control administration

ALFALFA is supposed to have been introduced into California in 1854 from Chile, but John Spurrier, in his book *The Practical Farmer,* dedicated to Thomas Jefferson and published at Wilmington, Del., in 1793, described alfalfa, which he called "lucerne." *(Joseph Elwyn Wing —Alfalfa Farming in America)*

ALGEBRA BOOK
See also Arithmetic

Algebra book was *Arithmetic, or the art of ciphering, according to the coins, measures and weights of New York, together with a short treatise on algebra (Arithmetica of Cyffer-Konst, Volgens de Munten Maten en Gewigten, te New York, gebruykelyk als mede een kort ontwerp van de Algebra),* a Dutch text book by Pieter Venima printed by Peter Zenger in 1730 in New York City. *(Lao Genevra Simons—Bibliography of Early American Textbooks on Algebra)*

Algebra book by a native American was Nicholas Pike's *A New and Complete System of Arithmetic, composed for the use of the citizens of the United States,* published in 1788 by John Mycall, Newburyport, Mass. It contained 512 pages, of which 39 were devoted to algebra. *(Lao Genevra Simons—Bibliography of Early American Textbooks on Algebra)*

ALIEN CITIZENSHIP. *See* Immigration:

Alien registration

ALIEN DISCRIMINATORY LAW was the "act respecting aliens" passed July 6, 1798 (1 Stat.L.577) which required that aliens "not actually naturalized shall be liable to be apprehended, restrained, rescued and removed as alien enemies."
See also Immigration

ALIEN REGISTRATION. *See* Immigration: Alien registration

"ALL-BLIND" AIRPLANE FLIGHT. *See* Aviation—Flights: All-blind flight

ALL-GLASS WINDOWLESS STRUCTURE. *See* Building: All-glass windowless structure

ALL-STEEL PASSENGER CAR. *See* Car: Steel passenger railroad coach

ALL-STEEL RAILWAY BRIDGE. *See* Bridge: Railway all-steel bridge

ALLERGY MAGAZINE. *See* Medical periodical: Allergy magazine

ALLIGATOR FARM was established in 1892 at Anastasia Island, St. Johns County, Fla., by George Reddington.

ALMANAC
Almanac was *An Almanak for the Year of Our Lord, 1639, Calculated for New England* by William Peirce, printed in 1638 at Cambridge, Mass., by Stephen Day's Cambridge Press. The months began with March. *(Clarence Saunders Brigham—An Account of American Almanacks)*

Almanac bibliography was *A Preliminary Check List of American Almanacs 1639-1800,* 160 pages, by Hugh Alexander Morrison of the Library of Congress which was published in 1907 by the Government Printing Office, Washington, D.C. The entries were arranged geographically by states.

Nautical almanac was Samuel Stearns' *The Universal Kalendar, Comprehending the Landsman's and Seaman's Almanack for the Year 1783,* published December 29, 1782, in Boston, Mass., by Benjamin Edes and Son.

Patent medicine almanac was *Bristol's Free Almanac for 1844 being bissextile or leap year and of American Independence, the 68th containing astronomical calculations and other useful and entertaining matter,* calculated by Lucas Seaver and published at Batavia, N.Y., in 1843. It contained 24 pages, including 10 of testimonials, and was issued by C. C. Bristol, manufacturer of Bristol's Sarsaparilla, Buffalo, N.Y.

ALTERNATING CURRENT POWER PLANT. *See* Electric power plant: Alternating current power plant

ALTERNATING CURRENT POWER TRANSMISSION. *See* Electric power plant: Alternating current power plant

ALTERNATOR (electric). *See* Electric alternator

ALUMINUM
Aluminum was produced in commercial quantities in November 1888 by the Pittsburgh Reduction Company (which later developed into the Aluminum Company of America). It was based upon the invention of Charles Martin Hall, completed on February 23, 1886. On July 9, 1886, Hall applied for a patent, which he obtained on April 2, 1889 (No. 400.766), on reducing aluminum by electrolysis. Hall produced aluminum electrically instead of chemically, greatly reducing its cost. He dissolved alumina in a bath of cryolite (the double fluoride of aluminum and sodium) and passed an electric current through the solution. *(Joseph William Richards—Aluminum)*

THE FIRST

Aluminum girder-type highway bridge. *See* Bridge: Welded aluminum girder-type highway bridge

Aluminum used commercially in a transmission conductor was employed November 30, 1899, by the Hartford Electric Light Company of Hartford, Conn., on a transmission from its water power plant at Tariffville, Conn., to Hartford, Conn.

Newspaper advertisement printed on aluminum foil. *See* Newspaper: Newspaper advertisement printed on aluminum foil

ALUMINUM-FACED BUILDING. *See* Building: Aluminum-faced building

ALUMINUM STREET CAR. *See* Street Car: Aluminum street car

ALUMNI ASSOCIATION (COLLEGE). *See* College alumni association

AMALGAM FOR FILLING TEETH. *See* Dentistry: Amalgam for filling teeth

AMATEUR FENCERS LEAGUE OF AMERICA. *See* Fencing: Fencing league (national)

AMBASSADOR. *See* Diplomatic service: Ambassador

AMBASSADOR (Japanese). *See* Japanese ambassador

AMBASSADOR TO ENGLAND. *See* Diplomatic service: Ambassador to England

AMBULANCE
Hospital ambulance service was introduced by the Commercial Hospital (now the General Hospital) Cincinnati, Ohio, prior to 1865. The list of employees for the year ending February 28, 1866, names James A. Jackson, employee No. 27, as "driver of ambulance" at an annual salary of $360. A similar service was started in June 1869 by Bellevue Hospital, New York City, under the direction of Dr. Edward Barry Dalton.

Incubator ambulance service maintained for transportation of premature infants was instituted by the city of Chicago, Ill. The ambulance was ordered February 26, 1935, and made its first run March 21, 1935.

AMBULANCE AIR SERVICE. *See* Aviation: Ambulance air service

THE FIRST

AMBULANCE CORPS (Army). *See* Army ambulance corps

AMBULANCE SHIP. *See* Ship: Ambulance ship

AMENDMENT TO THE CONSTITUTION. *See* Constitutional amendment (U.S.): Constitutional amendment

"AMERICA" (as a geographical designation) was first used by Martin H. Waldseemüller, also called Ilacomilus or Hylacomylus, in his *Cosmographiae Introductio,* published in April 1507, at St. Dié in the Vosges mountains of Alsace. The first delineation of the New World was made in 1506 by Giovanni Matteo Contarini, an Italian, and the map was engraved by Francesco Roselli of Florence, Italy. (*Geographical Review. October 1930*)
See also Map: Globular map published showing the western hemisphere

"AMERICA" (the song) was first publicly sung July 4, 1832, in the Park Street Church, Boston, Mass., by the school children of Boston. The song was written on a scrap of paper in half an hour by Dr. Samuel Francis Smith, a Baptist minister. The original manuscript is in the Harvard University Library.

"AMERICAN" (as an adjective) to be used instead of "United States," was officially recommended by Secretary of State John Hay, who instructed American diplomatic and consular officers under date of August 3, 1904, to use "American" instead of "United States" as an adjective. In strictly formal documents and in notarial acts performed by consular officers, the adjective form of designation is not used but the full name of the country is given as, for example, "Government of the United States of America," "Embassy of the United States of America," etc.

AMERICAN ACADEMY OF ARTS AND LETTERS. *See* Arts and letters society: Arts and letters society (national)

AMERICAN ACADEMY OF ARTS AND SCIENCES. *See* Arts and science society: Arts and science society (national)

AMERICAN ACADEMY OF POLITICAL AND SOCIAL SCIENCE. *See* Political science society: Political and social science society (national)

AMERICAN "ACE." *See* Aviation—Aviator

AMERICAN ANTIQUARIAN SOCIETY. *See* Historical society: Historical society (national)

AMERICAN ANTI-VIVISECTION SO-CIETY. *See* Anti-vivisection society

AMERICAN ASSOCIATION FOR THE ADVANCEMENT OF ATHEISM. *See* Atheism society

AMERICAN ASSOCIATION FOR THE ADVANCEMENT OF SCIENCE. *See* Science association: Scientific society (national organization)

AMERICAN ASSOCIATION FOR THE HARD OF HEARING. *See* Deaf—Association: National social organization for the hard of hearing

AMERICAN ASSOCIATION OF PUBLIC ACCOUNTANTS. *See* Accountants' society: Accountants' society to become a national organization

AMERICAN BANKERS ASSOCIATION. *See* Bankers Association: National bankers association

AMERICAN BIBLE SOCIETY. *See* Bible society: Bible society (national organization)

AMERICAN BIRD BANDING ASSOCIATION. *See* Bird banding society

AMERICAN BOWLING CONGRESS. *See* Bowling tournament: Bowling convention

AMERICAN BRASS ASSOCIATION. *See* Trade association

AMERICAN CHEMICAL SOCIETY. *See* Chemical society: Chemical society (national)

AMERICAN COLLEGE OF SURGEONS. *See* Medical society: American College of Surgeons

AMERICAN ECONOMIC ASSOCIATION. *See* Economics asociation

AMERICAN EXPEDITIONARY FORCE
American Expeditionary Force to leave the United States (since the Mexican war) and the first to leave for a destination beyond the western hemisphere sailed May 25, 1898, from San Francisco, Calif., on the "Australia," "City of Pekin," and "City of Sydney," bound for Manila, Philippines, a distance of 6,220 miles. The expeditionary force consisted of 115 officers and 2,386 enlisted men, commanded

by General Wesley Merritt. They arrived off Manila, June 30, 1898, and landed July 1, 1898. Admiral George Dewey and General Merritt demanded the surrender of Manila, August 7, 1898, but the city did not comply until August 13, 1898.

American Expeditionary Force Air Service chief was Colonel Mason Mathews Patrick, appointed May 29, 1918. On July 6, 1918, the Senate approved his nomination as major general. On June 26, 1923, at the age of 60, he qualified as a pilot at Bolling Field, Washington, D.C. *(Mason Mathews Patrick—United States in the Air)*

American expeditionary force to land in Africa. *See* World War II: American expeditionary force to land in Africa

American expeditionary force to land on the European continent in World War II. *See* World War II: American expeditionary force to land on the European continent

AMERICAN FEDERATION OF LABOR. *See* Labor union: Labor union of importance

AMERICAN FLAG. *See* Flag: American flag

AMERICAN FORESTRY ASSOCIATION. *See* Forestry society: National forestry association

AMERICAN GEOLOGICAL SOCIETY. *See* Geological society (national)

AMERICAN GUERNSEY CATTLE CLUB. *See* Cattle Club: Cattle club (Guernsey cattle)

AMERICAN HISTORICAL ASSOCIATION. *See* Historical society: Historical society (general)

AMERICAN HISTORY CHAIR. *See* History instruction: American history chair

AMERICAN HUMANE ASSOCIATION. *See* Humane Society: Humane association national organization

AMERICAN JERSEY CATTLE CLUB. *See* Cattle club: Cattle club (Jersey cattle)

AMERICAN LANGUAGE
Book on Americanisms was John Pickering's *A vocabulary, or collection of words and phrases which have been supposed to be*

THE FIRST

peculiar to the United States of America; to which is prefixed an essay on the present state of the English language in the United States, a 206-page book published in 1816 by Cummings and Hilliard, Boston, Mass.

AMERICAN LEAGUE. *See* Baseball league: American league

AMERICAN LEGION. *See* War veterans society: American legion

AMERICAN LIBRARY ASSOCIATION. *See* Library society: Library association (national

AMERICAN LUTHERAN CHURCH. *See* Lutheran church: American Lutheran church

AMERICAN MEDICAL ASSOCIATION. *See* Medical society: Medical society (national)

AMERICAN METROLOGICAL SOCIETY. *See* Weights and Measures Standardization: National organization to improve systems of weights, measures and moneys

AMERICAN NEWSPAPER PUBLISHERS ASSOCIATION. *See* Newspaper: Newspaper association

AMERICAN PARTY or "Know-Nothing Party" was organized about 1854. The first national convention was held June 5, 1855, in Philadelphia, Pa. The party was really a secret organization rather than a political party. Membership was divided into three degrees. The first included members who were American-born and were wholly unconnected with the Roman Catholic Church. They were obliged to vote as the society determined. The second degree included members who were permitted to hold office inside the organization. The third degree was composed of members who were eligible for office outside the organization. On February 18, 1856, a convention held in Philadelphia, Pa., abolished the secret character of the organization and made presidential nominations—former President Millard Fillmore of New York for President and Andrew Jackson Donelson of Tennessee for Vice President. Fillmore received only eight electoral votes. The name American Party was used by organizations in 1874 and 1887, but each was a distinct and separate party.

AMERICAN PHARMACEUTICAL ASSOCIATION. *See* Pharmacy society (national)

AMERICAN PHILOLOGICAL ASSOCIATION. *See* Philological society: Philological society (national)

AMERICAN PHILOSOPHICAL SOCIETY. *See* Science association: Scientific society

AMERICAN PHYSICAL SOCIETY. *See* Physics: National physics association

AMERICAN PHYSIOLOGICAL SOCIETY. *See* Physiological society: Physiological society

AMERICAN POLITICAL SCIENCE ASSOCIATION. *See* Political science society: Political science association

AMERICAN PSYCHOLOGICAL ASSOCIATION. *See* Psychological society: Psychological society (national organization)

AMERICAN RED CROSS was organized in Washington, D.C., on May 21, 1881, by Clara Barton, who became its first president. The constitution was adopted May 21, 1881, and the society was incorporated July 1, 1881, under the laws of the District of Columbia and reincorporated April 17, 1893. The society was again incorporated, by act of Congress, June 6, 1900, as the American National Red Cross (31 Stat.L.277), and again January 5, 1905 (33 Stat.L.599). Jean Henri Dunant had proposed an international Red Cross organization agreed to by sixteen nations at a preliminary conference October 26-29, 1863, and also at a convention August 22, 1864, at Geneva, Switzerland. The treaty was ratified March 16, 1882, (22 Stat.L.940) by the U.S. Senate, making the United States the thirty-second nation to join. (*Mabel Thorp Boardman—Under the Red Cross Flag*)

AMERICAN REPUBLICS CONFERENCE. *See* Conference: Conference of American republics

AMERICAN SOCIAL SCIENCE ASSOCIATION. *See* Social science society (national)

AMERICAN SOCIETY FOR THE PREVENTION OF CRUELTY TO ANIMALS. *See* Humane society: Humane society

AMERICAN SOCIETY OF CIVIL ENGINEERS. *See* Engineering society: Civil engineering national society

AMERICAN SOCIETY OF COMPOSERS, AUTHORS AND PUBLISHERS. *See* Music society: Music society for the literary protection of composers and authors

THE FIRST

AMERICAN SOCIETY OF DENTAL SURGEONS. *See* Dental society: Dental society of importance

AMERICAN SOCIETY OF MECHANICAL ENGINEERS. *See* Engineering society: Mechanical engineering national society

AMERICAN SOCIOLOGICAL SOCIETY. *See* Sociological society: Sociological society (national)

AMERICAN STATISTICAL ASSOCIATION. *See* Statistical society

AMERICAN THEOSOPHICAL SOCIETY. *See* Theosophical society

AMERICAN UNITARIAN ASSOCIATION. *See* Unitarian society: National organization of the Unitarian churches of the United States and Canada

AMERICIUM. *See* Element: Element 95

AMMUNITION. *See* Ordnance

AMNESTY proclamation to citizens was issued by President Abraham Lincoln on December 8, 1863. He also issued another similar proclamation, March 26, 1864. President Andrew Johnson issued supplementary proclamations May 29, 1865, September 7, 1867, July 4, 1868 and December 25, 1868. (*Henry Jarvis Raymond—Lincoln, His Life and Times*)

AMPHIBIOUS SEAPLANE GLIDER. *See* Glider: Amphibious seaplane glider

AMPHIBIOUS VEHICLE. *See* Steam-operated amphibious vehicle

AMUSEMENT DEVICES. *See* Carrousel; Ferris wheel; Loop the loop centrifugal railway; Railroad: Switchback railway

ANAESTHESIA. *See* Anesthesia

ANARCHIST was Josiah Warren, who was known as the "father of anarchy." He was of the intellectual type and was not an advocate of violence. In 1827 he opened a "time store" in Cincinnati, Ohio, to vindicate his theory of "labor for labor." He sold merchandise at cost, plus 7 per cent for handling and a labor charge for the clerk's hire. He advocated the transference of government activities to private persons. (*William Bailie—Josiah Warren, The First American Anarchist*)

ANATOMY BOOK. *See* Medical book: Anatomy book

THE FIRST

ANATOMY LECTURES (Scientific). *See* Medical instruction: Anatomy lectures (scientific)

ANATOMY RESEARCH INSTITUTE. *See* Research institute: Anatomy research institute

ANCIENT AND MODERN HISTORY CHAIR. *See* History instruction: Ancient and modern history chair

ANCIENT ARABIC ORDER OF NOBLES OF THE MYSTIC SHRINE. *See* Freemasons: Ancient Arabic order of nobles of the mystic shrine

ANCIENT MYSTICAL ORDER ROSAE CRUCIS, the Rosicrucian order, often abbreviated AMORC, a non-sectarian fraternity devoted to the investigation and study of the higher principles of life as found expressed in man and nature, was first established in America in 1694 by Magister Kelpius, appointed in England to become the first master of the order in America. The first lodge, temple, and laboratories of the order were erected in 1694 in what is now Fairmount Park, Philadelphia, Pa. The national headquarters of the Grand Lodge of the Rosicrucian Order of the North and South Jurisdiction is located at Rosicrucian Park, San Jose, Calif. Each jurisdiction is under the direction of an Imperator who has a Supreme Council as an advisory board which charters lodges and chapters.

ANESTHESIA
   Anesthetic (general) was sul-ether used by Dr. Crawford Williamson Long of Jefferson, Ga., in December 1841 and January 1842. He removed a cystic tumor about half an inch in diameter from the back of the neck of James M. Venable on March 30, 1842, applying ether under a towel. His bill for the operation amounted to $2.25: for sulphuric ether 25 cents and for excising the tumor $2. This discovery antedates that of Morton by four years and that of Wells by two years. It was not reported, however, until 1852, when the Georgia State Medical Society was notified. (*Francis Randolph Packard—History of Medicine in the U.S.*)

   Anesthetic in dentistry was used by Dr. Horace Wells, a dentist of Hartford, Conn., who discovered the anesthetic property of nitrous oxide (laughing) gas. On December 11, 1844, while under the influence of gas, he had one of his teeth extracted by Dr. John M. Riggs. The use of the gas was not successful, as he did not know it had to be combined with oxygen, a discovery which was not made until twenty-four years later. (*Yale Journal of Biology and Medicine. May 1933*)

THE FIRST

Ether administered in childbirth was employed December 27, 1845, by Dr. Crawford Williamson Long during the delivery of his second child, Fanny (Long) Taylor, at Jefferson, Ga.

Painless surgery demonstration was given on October 16, 1846, at the Massachusetts General Hospital, Boston, Mass. Dr. John Collins Warren operated on Gilbert Abbott, who had a swelling on the right side of his jaw, and removed a tumor, using the drug of William Thomas Green Morton of Charleston, Mass. Morton was refused admission to hospitals until he divulged the name of the secret drug. Although he is credited with the discovery of anesthetics, eight or ten others have also claimed the honor.

Spinal anesthesia report was "The Growing Importance and Value of Local and Regional Anesthesia in Minor and Major Surgery" by Dr. Rudolph Matas of New Orleans, La., which was published in 1900 in the *Journal of the Louisiana State Medical Society.* On November 10, 1899, he anesthetized a patient by "spinal subarachnoid method." *(New Orleans Medical and Surgical Journal. February 1928)*

Trifluoroethyl vinyl ether given to a human was administered on April 10, 1953, to Dr. Max Samuel Sadove, Professor of Anesthesiology at the University of Illinois, by Dr. John Christian Krantz, Jr., Professor of Pharmacology of the University of Maryland, at the Research and Educational Hospitals of the University of Illinois, Chicago, Ill. This anesthetic takes effect in less time than standard ether.

ANGINA OPERATION. *See* Surgical operation: Heart operation for the relief of angina pectoris

ANGLE IRON. *See* Iron: Angle iron

ANGLING BOOK. *See* Fishing treatise

ANIMAL BREEDING SOCIETY
Artificial animal breeding cooperative society was the artificial Breeding Unit No. 1 of the New Jersey Holstein-Friesian Cooperative Association, organized May 16, 1938, in Hunterdon, Somerset, and Warren Counties, N.J. Dr. James Arnold Henderson was in charge. The original membership consisted of 102 dairymen, who entered 1,050 Holstein cows.
See also Horse breeding society

ANIMAL GLUE FACTORY. *See* Glue factory

THE FIRST

ANIMAL HOSPITAL. *See* Veterinary hospital

ANIMAL HUSBANDRY
Animal husbandry federal appropriation. *See* Animal industry bureau (U.S.): Animal husbandry federal appropriation

Animal husbandry professor was John Alexander Craig of the Wisconsin Agricultural Experiment Station, University of Wisconsin, Madison, Wis., who served from 1890 to 1897. His specialty was sheep husbandry.

ANIMAL INDUSTRY BUREAU (U.S.)
Animal husbandry federal appropriation was approved April 23, 1904 (33 Stat.L.281), an "act making appropriations for the Department of Agriculture for the calendar year ending June 30, 1905." For experiments in animal breeding and feeding in cooperation with state agricultural stations, $25,000 was appropriated, part of an appropriation of $1,362,880 to the Bureau of Animal Industry. The first expenditure was July 1, 1904.

Bureau of Animal Industry of the United States Department of Agriculture was established by act of Congress, May 29, 1884 (23 Stat.L.31). The first chief of the Bureau of Animal Industry was Dr. Daniel Elmer Salmon, who served from May 31, 1884, to October 31, 1905.

Dairy division of the Bureau of Animal Industry was organized July 1, 1895. Major Henry Elijah Alvord was appointed first chief. His original staff consisted of one assistant and two clerks. *(Ulysses Grant Houck—Bureau of Animal Industry)*

Pathological division of the Bureau of Animal Industry was established April 1, 1891. Dr. Theobald Smith was appointed the first chief. *(Ulysses Grant Houck—Bureau of Animal Industry)*

ANIMAL-INFECTING VIRUS TO BE CRYSTALLIZED. *See* Virus: Virus (human- or animal-infecting virus) to be crystallized

ANIMAL POUND. *See* Pound (enclosure for animals)

ANIMAL TRAPS. *See* Traps: Steel animal traps

ANIMAL VIVISECTION. *See* Anti-vivisection society; Vivisection

ANIMALS

Animal awarded a Distinguished Service Cross. *See* Medal: Distinguished service cross awarded an animal

Animals fired into space and rescued from a rocket. *See* Rocket: Animals fired into space and rescued from a rocket

Aquatic mammals. *See* Aquatic mammals

Bear (white) brought to the United States was Ursa Major, a nine-month-old cub, caught in Davis Strait, on the western coast of Greenland, which was exhibited January 18, 1733, at Clark's Wharf, North End of Boston. It was brought by Captain Atkins from Greenland and kept in a large cage. It was shipped to London on February 27, 1734. *(Boston Weekly News Letter. January 18, 1733)*

Birds. *See* Birds

Camel imported was an "African camel . . . 7 feet high and 12 feet long," exhibited in Boston, Mass., and advertised in the Boston *Gazette* of October 2, 1721.

Camels imported for commercial purposes were landed May 14, 1856, at Indianola, Tex. Lieutenant David D. Porter of Chester, Pa., left Smyrna February 15, 1856, on the "Supply," a Navy store-ship, and arrived at Powder Horn, three miles below Indianola, on May 1, 1856, but the camels were not landed until later. The shipment consisted of thirty-four camels. *(Bibliographical Society of America—Transactions. Vol. 46, 4th quarter.)*

Cattle (Aberdeen-Angus) importation was made in 1873 by George Grant, Victoria, Kan., who imported four bulls, two of which were exhibited the same year at Kansas City, Mo. The bulls, imported from Scotland, were crossed with native longhorn Texas cattle.

Cattle (Africander cattle) arrived December 11, 1931, in New York City. Sixteen bulls and thirteen cows and heifers left Capetown, South Africa, November 14, 1931, and were held in quarantine from December 12, 1931, to March 9, 1932, at the United States Department of Agriculture, Animal Quarantine Station, Clifton, N.J. William Henry Black, in charge of Beef Cattle Investigations, Bureau of Animal Industry, selected the cattle and had complete supervision until arrival at final destination, March 14, 1932, at King Ranch, Kingsville, Tex.

Cattle club. *See* Cattle club

Cattle exportation was made from Savannah, Ga. A shipment of 16 steers was exported

in 1755, and in 1770, 28 steers and cows. In 1772, 136 steers and cows were shipped from that port, probably to the West Indies. It is possible that prior shipments were made, but there is no known record of them.

Cattle exportation to Great Britain is believed to have been made in 1868 by Nelson Morris who shipped a few live cattle from Chicago, Ill., to London and Glasgow. The first large shipment was made in October 1876 by William Colwell, a cattle dealer of Boston, Mass., who shipped a cargo of 450 live cattle to Liverpool on the steamship "Istrian" of the Leyland Line. *(Rudolf Alexander Clemen— The American Livestock and Meat Industry)*

Cattle (Guernsey cattle) imported were one bull and two heifers which arrived at Boston, Mass., in 1831. They were taken to the farm of General Moody Adams Pillsbury at Guernsey Island, Lake Winnepesaukee, N.H.

Cattle importation law (U.S.) prohibiting the importation of diseased cattle from foreign countries was the "act to prevent the spread of foreign diseases among the cattle of the United States" passed December 18, 1865 (14 Stat.L.1). The first application of the law took place on July 31, 1875, when meat, cattle, and hides from Spain were excluded on account of the presence of the foot-and-mouth disease in that country.

Cattle importation of purebred shorthorns was effected by the Ohio Company for Importing English Cattle, which was organized at Chillicothe, Ohio, on November 2, 1833. The company issued 92 shares at $100 each, which were held by 48 persons, 28 of whom held one share each. To further purebred strains, the society sent Felix Renick to England to buy purebreds. On May 20, 1834, he purchased 7 bulls and 12 cows, which were shipped to Philadelphia, Pa., and driven overland to Chillicothe, Ohio, where they arrived in June 1834. Although cattle had been imported since 1624, this was the first society organized for importing purebred stock. *(Ohio Archaeological and Historical Quarterly. Vol. 33. January 1924)*

Cattle (shorthorn) public auction sale was held October 29, 1836 at Felix Renick's Indian Creek Farm, Chillicothe, Ohio when forty-three head sold for $34,540, an average of $803.25 apiece.

Cattle tuberculosis test was made March 3, 1892, on a herd of cattle belonging to Dr. J. E. Gillingham, Claremont Farms, Villa Nova, Pa. The herd was tested with tuberculin brought from Europe by Dr. Leonard Pearson, Dean of the Veterinary Department of the University of Pennsylvania, Philadelphia.

THE FIRST

Chinchilla farm that was successful was established February 22, 1923, at Los Angeles, Calif., by Mathias Farrell Chapman with eleven chinchillas imported from Peru and Chile. The farm, later moved to Inglewood, Calif., contained about 1,300 animals.

Cow flown in an airplane was Elm Farm Ollie, a Guernsey, which went aloft on February 18, 1930, with a corps of reporters. She was milked during the flight and the milk was sealed in paper containers and parachuted over St. Louis, Mo.

Cows were imported from Devon, England, in March 1624, by Edward Winslow, who on January 1, 1633, became governor of the Plymouth Colony (Mass.). In 1632 "no farmer was satisfied to do without a cow; and there was in New England, not only a domestic, but an export, demand from the West Indies, which led to breeding for sale. But the market was soon overstocked, and the price of cattle went down from fifteen pounds and twenty pounds to five pounds; and milk was a penny a quart." Cows were raised principally for their hides; secondly, for meat; and only very incidentally for their milk. (*Albert Sidney Bolles—Industrial History of the United States*)

Dog race. *See* Dog race

Dog show. *See* Dog show

Dogs trained to guide the blind were taught at "The Seeing Eye," Nashville, Tenn., in 1928. "The Seeing Eye" was incorporated January 9, 1929, under the laws of Tennessee as an association not for pecuniary profit. Mrs. Harrison Eustis was the first president. The organization moved to Morristown, N.J., in May 1929 and was incorporated on April 30, 1932, under the laws of New Jersey. "Buddy," the first Seeing Eye dog to guide a blind man, was a shepherd dog brought over from Vevey, Switzerland, in June 1928 by Morris S. Frank, to whom it had been presented on April 25, 1928.

Dugong. *See* Aquatic mammals: Dugong

Elephant arrived on the "America" April 13, 1796, at New York City from Bengal, India. She was two years old, six and a half feet high, and was exhibited by Jacob Crowninshield at the corner of Beaver Street and Broadway. The elephant's habits were described as follows: "It eats thirty pounds of rice besides hay and straw—drinks all kinds of wine and spirituous liquors, and eats every sort of vegetable; it will also draw a cork from a bottle with its trunk." (*New York Argus. April 23, 1796*)

Fishes. *See* Fishes

THE FIRST

Fur-bearing animals raised commercially were minks reared in Oneida County, N.Y., in 1866 by H. Ressegue. Prices of skins were high, and live animals for breeding stock brought $30 a pair.

Giant panda was Su-Lin, imported from China by Mrs. William H. Harkness, Jr., on the "President McKinley." It weighed about 5 pounds when it arrived at San Francisco, Calif., December 18, 1936. Su-Lin died April 1, 1938, in the Brookfield Zoo, Chicago, Ill., which had purchased it for $8,750.44. The giant panda was discovered on November 9, 1936. Bearlike in appearance but related to the raccoon, it ranges in bamboo jungles on mountainous land between China and Tibet. Its head and neck are white. Splotchy black fur encircles its eyes, and its tiny ears are grayish black. Forelegs, chest, shoulders, and hind legs are black. Grayish white fur covers its back and sides. It eats shoots and roots of bamboo and grows to a weight of 300 pounds, a length of 5 feet, and a height of 3 feet. (*Ruth Harkness—The Lady and the Panda*)

Goat show. *See* Goat show

Gorilla born in captivity was Colo, born December 22, 1956, at the Columbus, Ohio, zoo. She weighed 3¼ pounds and was the offspring of Baron (11 years old, 380 pounds), and Christiana (9 years old, 260 pounds).

Horse. *See* Horse

Leopard was exhibited February 2, 1802, by Othello Pollard, near the Columbian Museum, Boston, Mass. An admission fee of twenty-five cents was charged to see the "import from Bengal." (*Boston Independent Chronicle—February 8, 1802. No. 2177*)

Lion was exhibited November 26, 1716, in Boston, Mass., by "Captain Arthur Savage, at his house in Brattle Street, where is to be shewn by William Nichols, a Lyon of Barbary, with many other rarities, the like never before in America." (*Boston News Letter No. 659. November 26-December 3, 1716*)

Monkey trained to perform was "a creature called a Japanese, of about two feet high, his body resembling a human body in all parts except the feet and tail" exhibited February 25, 1751, at the house of Mr. Edward Willet, New York City. Admission of a shilling was charged for the performance in which the monkey walked a tightrope, exercised a firelock (gun), and danced.

Mule was bred from a jack sent to President George Washington. The exportation of full-blooded jacks from Spain was prohibited,

THE FIRST

ANIMALS—*Continued*
but Charles III of Spain, learning of Washington's interest, sent him two jacks which arrived in Boston, Mass., on October 26, 1785. These were the first jacks to arrive in the United States. *(Paul Leland Haworth—George Washington, Country Gentleman)*

Okapi was imported August 4, 1937, at New York City. It was 21 months old, weighed 235 pounds, and was 49 inches tall at the shoulder. It resembled a cross between a zebra and a giraffe, and had a mahogany red body with white stripes on its buttocks and upper legs. It consumed 8 bananas, 4 heads of cabbage, 3 bunches of carrots, and 6 liters of condensed milk and water daily. It was captured in the Belgian Congo and shipped July 22, 1937 on the Red Star liner "Pennland" under the personal care of Dr. William Reid Blair, director of the Bronx Zoo, New York City, to which it was delivered.

Platypus. *See* Aquatic mammals: Platypus (duck-billed)

Porpoise. *See* Aquatic mammals: Porpoise

Pronghorn antelope bred and reared in captivity was born in the City Park Zoo, Denver, Colo., in 1903. The event was noted by Theodore Roosevelt, who congratulated the zoo director, Alfred Hill.

Reindeer born in the United States was a jet black calf born on May 31, 1929, at Lodgepole Ranch, the estate of Otis Emerson Dunham at North Beverly, Mass.

Rhinoceros was exhibited September 13, 1826 at Peale's Museum and Gallery of the Fine Arts, New York City. Advertisements stated "its body and limbs are covered with a skin so hard and impervious that he fears neither the claws of the tiger nor the proboscis of the elephant; it will turn the edge of a scimitar and even resist the force of a musket ball." The exhibit, scheduled to close October 13, was extended to November 25.

Sheep were imported into America in 1609, when the London Company brought over a shipment to Jamestown, Va.

Sheep (Karakul fur sheep) imported were 5 rams and 10 ewes which arrived at New York City in 1908 from Russia on the S.S. "Esthonia." They were placed in quarantine at Athenia, N.J., preparatory to shipment to the ranch of Dr. C. C. Young at Holliday, Texas. *(U.S. Department of Agriculture Yearbook 1915)*

THE FIRST

Sheep (Merino sheep) were imported in 1802 by Colonel David Humphreys, United States Minister to Spain, who shipped 100 of them from Lisbon to Derby, Conn. In 1809 they were valued at $1,500 each. It is also recorded that in 1793 three merino sheep were smuggled in by William Foster, but were eaten, their value being unknown at the time. *(Francis Little—Early American Textiles)*

Sheep (Merino sheep) exhibition was in 1807 at Pittsfield, Mass. by Elkanah Watson, a native of Plymouth, Mass. Two sheep were on display "under the great elm tree in the public square of Pittsfield." *(Louis George Connor—A Brief History of the Sheep Industry in the United States)*

Snakes (cobra). *See* Cobra: King cobra snakes

ANIMATED BOOK. *See* Flicker

ANIMATED CARTOON. *See* Moving picture: Animated cartoon

ANIMATED CARTOON ELECTRIC SIGN. *See* Electric sign: Animated cartoon electric sign

ANIMATED CARTOONING SCHOOL. *See* Cartoon school

ANIMATED PHOTOGRAPHIC PICTURE PROJECTION. *See* Moving picture: Animated photographic picture projection before a theater audience

ANNEXATION OF TERRITORY. *See* Territorial expansion: Annexation of territory

ANNUAL was *Le Souvenir, or Picturesque Pocket Diary, Containing an Almanack, Ruled Pages for Memoranda, Literary Selections and a Variety of Useful Information for 1825* published at Philadelphia, Pa., by A. R. Poole in 1825. It was 24-mo. and contained 108 pages, including a calendar for 1826. It was issued in a cardboard slip case. It preceded the *Atlantic Souvenir—Christmas and New Year's Offering 1826*, copyrighted October 3, 1825, edited by Henry D. Gilpin, published by [H. C.] Carey and [I.] Lea, Philadelphia, Pa. *(Ralph Thompson—American Literary Annuals and Gift Books)*

ANNUNCIATOR was invented by Seth Fuller of Boston, Mass., who obtained a patent on December 26, 1833. It was installed at the Tremont House, Boston, Mass., and was known as "hanging bells." There were 140 bells which occupied a space 57 feet long, 6 feet high, and

1 foot deep. A small hammer hitting a gong caused the sound and vibrated a card showing a number corresponding with the room number. Each bell was in a glass-enclosed box. They were placed in operation when the hotel opened, October 16, 1829.

ANSWERING SERVICE (telephone). See Telephone: Telephone company answering service

ANTARCTIC EXPEDITION. *See* Discovery: Discovery of Antarctica

ANTARCTICA DISCOVERY. *See* Discovery: Discovery of Antarctica

ANTELOPE (Pronghorn). *See* Animals: Pronghorn antelope

ANTHEM (National). *See* National anthem

ANTHOLOGY (American) was *American Poems, Selected and Original,* 304 pages, compiled by Elihu Hubbard Smith, published in 1793 in Litchfield, Conn., by [Thomas] Collier and [David] Buel. (The two-volume work *Select Poems on Various Occasions, Chiefly American,* printed by S. Hall, Boston, Mass., in 1787, contained English as well as American poems.)

ANTHRACITE COAL. *See* Coal: Anthracite coal

ANTHRAX VACCINE. *See* Vaccine: Anthrax vaccine for humans

ANTHROPOLOGY LABORATORY was the Laboratory of Anthropology which was formally opened to the public on September 1, 1931, at Santa Fe, N.M. Jesse Logan Nusbaum was in charge. Dr. Alfred Vincent Kidder was chairman of the board of trustees. (*American Civic Annual. Vol. 3. 1931*)

ANTI-DISCRIMINATION COMMISSION. *See* Labor: Labor anti-discrimination commission (state)

ANTI-LYNCHING STATUTE. *See* Lynch law (state)

ANTI-MASONIC PARTY was formed in 1827 in western New York. The first national convention was held in Philadelphia, Pa. in September 1830 and was attended by 96 delegates from 10 states. On September 26, 1831, 113 delegates from 13 states attended a convention at Baltimore, Md. at which they voted for their first presidential candidates. William Wirt of Maryland was nominated for

President and Amos Ellmaker of Pennsylvania for Vice President. In the 1832 elections Wirt received 7 electoral votes as compared with 219 cast for the Democratic nominee, Andrew Jackson.

ANTI-MONOPOLY PARTY was formed May 14, 1884, at a convention held in Chicago, Ill. The existence of "The Anti-Monopoly Organization of the United States," as it was named, was of short duration, as its members joined the People's Party. General Benjamin Franklin Butler of Massachusetts was nominated for the presidency by the Anti-Monopoly Party, and General Absolom Madden West of Mississippi for the vice presidency; both were also nominated by the Greenback Labor Party at its national convention. They received 175,370 votes as compared with 4,874,986 cast for Grover Cleveland of New York, the Democratic candidate, in the election of November 4, 1884.

ANTI-PRICE DISCRIMINATION LAW. *See* Price regulation law: Price regulation law (state)

ANTIQUARIAN BOOK STORE. *See* Book store (antiquarian)

ANTIQUARIAN SOCIETY. *See* Historical society: Historical society (national)

ANTIQUITIES COLLECTION (Egyptian). *See* Egyptian antiquities collection

ANTI-SALOON LEAGUE. *See* Temperance society: Anti-saloon league

ANTI-SIT-DOWN STRIKE LEGISLATION. *See* Strike: Anti-sit-down strike legislation (state)

ANTI-SLAVERY PARTY was the Liberty Party, which held its first convention in Warsaw, New York, November 13, 1839. James Gillespie Birney of Kentucky was nominated for the presidency and Francis Julius LeMoyne for the vice presidency. The nominations were confirmed on April 1, 1840, despite the unwillingness of the candidates to accept, and in the Harrison-Van Buren election they polled 7,069 votes. The first national convention of the Liberty Party was held in New York City on May 12, 1841. (*Theodore Clarke Smith—The Liberty and Free Soil Parties in the Northwest*)

ANTI-SLAVERY SOCIETY. *See* Abolition society

ANTITOXIN LABORATORY was established in September 1894, by the New York City Department of Health. Dr. William Hal-

THE FIRST

ANTITOXIN LABORATORY—*Continued*
lock Park was in charge. This was also the first
antitoxin laboratory in the world established
by a public health organization and the first to
provide for the free distribution of antitoxin
to the poor. (*Wade Wright Oliver—The Man
Who Lived for Tomorrow*)

ANTI-TRUST LAW. *See* Trust: Anti-
trust law

ANTI-TUBERCULOSIS VACCINE. *See*
Vaccine: Tuberculosis vaccine

ANTI-VIVISECTION PLAY. *See* Play
(drama): Anti-vivisection play

ANTI-VIVISECTION SOCIETY was the
American Anti-Vivisection Society organized
February 23, 1883, at Philadelphia, Pa. Its object according to its charter was "the restriction of the practice of vivisection within proper
limits, and the prevention of the injudicious and
needless infliction of suffering upon animals
under the pretense of medical and scientific research." The founder of the society was Mrs.
Caroline Earle White. The first president was
Dr. Thomas George Morton. The first annual
meeting was held January 30, 1884, in Philadelphia, Pa. (*Anti-Vivisection Society—Annual
Report 1884*)
See also Vivisection

APARTMENT HOUSE. *See* Building:
Apartment house with a modern lay-out

**APARTMENTS SOLD BY A DEPART-
MENT STORE.** *See* Business: Department
store to sell apartments

APOSTOLIC DELEGATE (Catholic). *See*
Catholic apostolic delegate

APOTHECARY. *See* Druggist

APPENDECTOMY. *See* Surgical operation: Appendicitis operation

APPENDICITIS OPERATION. *See* Surgical operation: Appendicitis operation

APPLE PARER was invented on February
14, 1803, by Moses Coats, a mechanic of Downington, Pa.

APPLES were imported from England in
1629 by John Winthrop, colonial governor of
Massachusetts. The first apples grown in this
country were probably obtained from trees
planted in Boston, Mass., from which "ten fair
pippins" were plucked on October 10, 1639.
Governor John Endicott planted the first nurs-

THE FIRST

ery of young fruit trees at Danvers, Mass.
(*George Kirby Holmes—Progress of Agricul-
ture in the United States—1899 Yearbook—
Department of Agriculture*)

**APPLIED CHEMISTRY PROFESSOR-
SHIP.** *See* Chemistry professor: Professorship of applied chemistry

APPORTIONMENT (Congressional). *See*
Congressional apportionment

**APPRENTICE   CONTINUATION
SCHOOL.** *See* Continuation school: Apprentice continuation school

AQUARIUM
Aquarium for monsters of the deep was
Marineland, eighteen miles south of St. Augustine, Fla., built at an approximate cost of
$500,000. Ground was broken May 15, 1937,
and the dedication and formal opening took
place June 23, 1938. The marine studios consisted of two adjacent open-air steel and concrete tanks (one rectangular, 100 feet by 40 feet,
and 18 feet deep; the other circular, 75 feet in
diameter, and 11 feet deep) with 200 portholes.

Aquarium (inland salt water) was installed in Chicago, Ill., for the 1893 Columbian
Exposition by Marshall McDonald. Medals
were conferred upon him by Belgium, England,
France, Germany, and Russia for his efforts in
increasing and bettering the hatching and propagation of fish.

AQUATIC MAMMALS
Dugong arrived at the Steinhart Aquarium, San Francisco, Calif., on November 16,
1955, and was on display until December 27,
1955, when it died. It belongs to the order
Sirenia and is a sea mammal. The mammary
glands are located under the fore limbs and not
near or towards the hind quarters as in most
other mammals.

Platypus (duck-billed) (ornithorhynchus
anatinus) was publicly exhibited July 15, 1922,
by the New York Zoological Society at Bronx
Park, New York City. It arrived at San
Francisco, Calif., from Australia. The platypus
is a small fur-bearing aquatic animal with
webbed feet and a bill like that of a duck.
Though a mammal, it is oviparous (egg-
laying).

Porpoise born in captivity was born February 14, 1940, at Marineland, Fla. The porpoise was born dead.

Whale. *See* Whale; Whaling

AQUATIC PLAY. *See* Play: Aquatic play

THE FIRST

AQUEDUCT BRIDGE. *See* Bridge: Wire cable suspension aqueduct bridge

ARABIC DAILY NEWSPAPER. *See* Newspaper: Arabic daily newspaper

ARABIC MAGAZINE was *The Star of America (Kowkab America),* a weekly, edited by Abraham Mitrie Rihbany, which was published in New York City in 1892. *(Abraham Mitrie Rihbany—A Far Journey)*

ARBITRATION
Arbitration proceeding in the Hague Permanent Court of Arbitration was the Pious Fund Case of the Californias, a dispute between the United States and Mexico. The protocol of agreement was signed May 22, 1902, and the award of the court was made October 14, 1902. Mexico was forced to pay $1,420,682.67 in Mexican currency and $43,059.99 annually, beginning February 2, 1903. The issue was whether the claim of the United States for indemnity in behalf of the Roman Catholic Archbishop of San Francisco and the Bishop of Monterey was governed by the principle of *res judicata,* by virtue of the arbitral sentence of Sir Edward Thornton of November 11, 1875. The contention of the United States that the claim should be so governed was sustained by a unanimous court. The Pious Fund was money collected by Jesuits in Mexico for missions in California. After 1848, when Upper California was ceded to the United States, Mexico refused payment of income to churches in California. *(Charles Cheney Hyde —International Law)*

Arbitration tribunal was established by the Chamber of Commerce, New York City, New York, on May 3, 1768, and consisted of seven members to adjust "any differences between parties agreeing to leave such disputes to this Chamber." A different committee was appointed for each meeting. *(Joseph Bucklin Bishop—A Chronicle of One Hundred and Fifty Years— The Chamber of Commerce of the State of New York, 1768-1918)*

Colonial arbitration law was "an act for the more easy and effectually finishing of controversies by arbitration," passed at the legislative session held from October 11, 1753, to November 2, 1753, in New Haven, Conn. Each side appointed an arbitrator and the court appointed one. The court was granted power to levy and collect the awards. *(Charles Jeremy Hoadly—The Public Records of the Colony of Connecticut from May 1751 to February 1757.)*

Federal arbitration law was "an act to make valid and enforceable written provisions or agreements for arbitration of disputes arising out of contracts, maritime transactions or com-

THE FIRST

merce among the States or Territories or with foreign nations" (43 Stat.L.883), approved February 12, 1925, to take effect January 1, 1926.

Federal Board of Mediation and Conciliation (labor relations only) was the United States Board of Mediation and Conciliation, authorized by the act of March 4, 1913 (37 Stat. L.739), and giving the secretary of labor "power to act as mediator and to appoint commissioners of conciliation in labor disputes whenever in his judgment the interests of industrial peace may require it."

Interstate carrier arbitration law was the act of October 1, 1888 (25 Stat.L.501), "an act to create boards of arbitration or commission for settling controversies and differences between railroad corporations and other common carriers engaged in interstate and territorial transportation of property or passengers and their employees." It provided for two methods of settling disputes, namely, voluntary arbitration (not used in ten years) and investigation (applied only once, ineffectively, in the Pullman strike of 1894).

National Mediation Board. *See* Labor: National mediation board

State arbitration law was Chapter 21, "An act for amending and declaring the law in the cases therein mentioned," passed December 15, 1778, by the General Assembly of Maryland, at Annapolis, which ruled "it shall be lawful to and for such court to give judgment upon the award of the person or persons to whom such submission and reference shall be made." *(Clement Dorsey—The General Public Statutory Laws and Public Local Law of the State of Maryland from the year 1692 to 1939 inclusive with annotations thereto and a copious index)*

State arbitration law (modern), under which an agreement to arbitrate controversies which may arise from a contract is recognized as valid and enforceable, was the "Arbitration Law" of New York, an "act in relation to arbitration constituting chapter seventy-two of the consolidated laws," Chapter 275 of the Laws of 1920, New York, which became effective April 19, 1920, the date when it was signed by Governor Alfred Emanuel Smith. Many laws were passed between 1886 and 1920 by several states, but they were not effective.

State Board of Mediation and Arbitration was the New York Board of Mediation and Arbitration, organized June 1, 1886, under authority of an act of May 18, 1886. The commissioners were William Purcell, Gilbert Robertson, Jr., and Florence F. Donovan. On

ARBITRATION—*Continued*
June 2, 1886, Massachusetts authorized a state
arbitration board "for the settlement of differences between employers and their employees."

Strike settlement. *See* Strike: Strike settlement

ARBITRATION ASSOCIATION
Arbitration association devoted exclusively
to advancing principle and practice in this field
was the Arbitration Society of America, Inc.,
formed at New York City on May 15, 1922. On
January 29, 1926, the American Arbitration
Association was formed by a merger of the
Arbitration Society of America, Inc., the Ar-
bitration Foundation, Inc., and the Arbitration
Conference. The first officers of the American
Arbitration Association were Anson W. Bur-
chard, president; Lucius Root Eastman and
Frances Keller, vice presidents; and J. Noble
Braden, executive secretary.

ARBOR DAY. *See* Holiday: Arbor day

ARC LIGHT. *See* Electric lighting: Electric arc lights

ARCADE was the Philadelphia Arcade,
which extended from Chestnut Street through to
Carpenter Street between Sixth and Seventh
Streets, Philadelphia, Pa. It was erected by the
Arcade Company of which John Haviland was
architect. The cornerstone was laid on May 3,
1826, and the building finished in September
1827. The cost of construction was $112,000;
$42,500 was paid for the land.

ARCH BRIDGE (steel). *See* Bridge: Steel
arch bridge

ARCH RAILROAD BRIDGE (stone). *See*
Bridge: Stone arch railroad bridge

ARCHAEOLOGICAL SOCIETY
Archaeological society (national) was the
Archaeological Institute of America which was
founded May 10, 1879, at Boston, Mass. The
constitution was adopted May 17, 1879. The
first annual meeting was held May 15, 1880, at
Boston, Mass. It was incorporated by act of
Congress, May 26, 1906. Its purpose was to
promote and direct archaeological research. The
first president was Charles Eliot Norton. *(First
Annual Report of the Executive Committee of
the Archaeological Institute of America)*

ARCHERY CLUB
Archery association (national) was the
National Archery Association, formed January
23, 1879, in Crawfordsville, Ind., by representatives of eight archery clubs. The first president
was Maurice Thompson. The first grand annual
meeting and the first tournament were held

August 12-14 in Chicago, Ill., at which twenty
women and sixty-nine men competed. High
score was made by Will H. Thompson, who won
with 172 hits and a score of 624. *(Robert Potter
Elmer—American Archery)*

Archery club was the United Bowmen
of Philadelphia, founded in 1825 by Franklin
Peale, Titian Ramsey Peale, Robert E. Griffith,
M.D., Samuel P. Griffith, Jr., Jacob M. Morris,
and Thomas Sully. The club was not formally
organized until 1828, when membership, was limited to twenty-five. Members dressed in frock
coats of Lincoln green, ornamented with gold
braid, and wore broad straw hats with three
black ostrich plumes.

ARCHITECT
Landscape architect was John Reid, gar-
dener to Sir George Mackenzie of Rosebaugh,
Lord Advocate under Charles II, who left
Aberdeen, Scotland, August 28, 1683, on the
"Exchange," accompanied by his wife and three
daughters. He landed at Staten Island, N.Y.,
December 19, 1683. *(New Jersey Historical
Society Proceedings—January 1937)*

Woman architect to enter the architectural
profession was Louise Blanchard Bethune, who
opened an independent office in 1881 in Buffalo,
N.Y. She was the first woman member of the
American Institute of Architects, elected to
full membership on September 15, 1890.

ARCHITECTURAL BOOK
Architectural book distinctly American was
*The Country Builders' Assistant; containing a
collection of new designs of carpentry and
architecture*, by Asher Benjamin. It contained
30 plates and was printed in 1797 by Thomas
Dickman, Greenfield, Mass.

Architectural book printed in America was
Abraham Swan's *British Architect; or the
Builders Treasury of Staircases*, published in
1775 by R[obert] Bell in Philadelphia, Pa., for
J. Norman. It was a reprint of the edition
published in London, England, in 1745.

ARCHITECTURAL SCHOOL
Architectural school of collegiate rank was
established February 20, 1865, by the Massachusetts Institute of Technology, Boston,
Mass., which opened a Department of Architecture. William Robert Ware was the first
head of the department and received the title
of professor.

Landscape architecture course for women
was offered September 15, 1901, by the Lowthorpe School of Architecture, Groton, Mass.
The director of the school was Mrs. Edward
Gilchrist Low. Degrees were not conferred, but
certificates were given. First certificates were
awarded June 10, 1903 to three students.

THE FIRST

ARCHIVAL ADMINISTRATION comprehensive program for training of archivists was offered September 25, 1940, by the School of Public Affairs, American University, Washington, D.C. John Clarke Patterson was Director of the Graduate School and the School of Public Affairs.

ARCHIVAL COURSE was "Archives and Historical Manuscripts," offered September 29, 1938, by Columbia University, New York City, under Dr. Solon Justus Buck, director of publications, National Archives, Washington, D.C.

ARCHIVIST OF THE UNITED STATES was Robert Digges Wimberley Connor appointed October 10, 1934. The position was created by act of Congress (48 Stat.L.1122) an "act to establish a National Archives of the United States Government," approved June 19, 1934, by President Franklin Delano Roosevelt, which established the Archives Bureau. The archivist has an official seal and is chairman of a National Publications Committee.

ARCTIC EXPEDITION. *See* Expedition: Arctic expedition

ARCTICS. *See* "Artics"

ARITHMETIC
See also Algebra book

American Arithmetic by a native American was Isaac Greenwood's *Arithmetick—Vulgar and Decimal with the Application Thereof to a Variety of Cases in Trade and Commerce*, which was published in 1729 in Boston, Mass., by S. Kneeland and T. Green for T. Hancock at the Sign of the Bible and Three Crowns in Ann Street. It contained 158 pages, 4 pages of index and 4 pages of advertisements. *(David Eugene Smith and Jekuthiel Ginsburg—History of Mathematics in America Before 1900)*

Arithmetic to be printed in the colonies was James Hodder's *Arithmetick; or that necessary art made most easy. Being explained in a way familiar to the capacity of any that desire to learn it in a little time*, printed by J. Franklin, Boston, Mass., in 1719 for S. Phillips. *(Louis Charles Karpinski—Bibliography of Mathematical Works Printed in America Through 1850)*

ARMISTICE DAY. *See* Holiday: Armistice day

ARMOR PLATE CONTRACT (U.S. NAVY) was awarded to the Bethlehem Iron Company, South Bethlehem, Pa., on June 1, 1887. Six thousand seven hundred tons were ordered at $536 a ton for the battleships

THE FIRST

"Maine" and "Texas" and the monitors "Puritan," "Amphitrite," "Monadnock" and "Terror." *(American Iron and Steel Association—History of the Manufacture of Armor Plate for the United States Navy)*

ARMOR-PLATED VESSELS. *See* Ship: Iron-clad naval vessel

ARMORED CAR. *See under* Automobile

ARMORED COMMERCIAL CAR HOLD-UP. *See* Automobile robbery: Armored commercial car hold-up

ARMORED TANK. *See* Army armored tank

ARMORY. *See* Arsenal

ARMY
American Army division to cross the Rhine river. See World War I: American army division to cross the Rhine river

Army aviator. *See* Aviation—Aviator

Army Engineering Department of the Continental Army was authorized by the Continental Congress, June 16, 1775. It established a separate engineering department in the army composed of one chief engineer, who received $60 a month, and two assistant engineers at $20 a month. The first chief engineer was Colonel Richard Gridley who was appointed in June 1775 under the resolve of the Continental Congress of June 16, 1775. A formal "Corps of Engineers" was established March 11, 1779, but was disbanded November 3, 1783, upon the dissolution of the Revolutionary Army.

Army expeditionary force. *See* American expeditionary force

Army flag (official). *See* Flag: Army flag (official)

Army Veterinary Corps was established as part of the Medical Department of the Army by the National Defense Act of 1916 (39 Stat.L.166) enacted June 3, 1916. The legislation authorized two officers for each regiment of cavalry, one for every three batteries of field artillery, and one for each mounted battalion of engineers. The Army, however, had previously used civilians as meat inspectors for the Army Veterinary Corps.

Automobiles ordered for the U.S. War Department. *See* Automobile: Automobiles ordered for the U.S. War Department

THE FIRST

ARMY—*Continued*

Ballistic missile operational unit was the 259th Field Artillery Missile Battalion, which completed training November 1954 at Fort Bliss, Tex. The unit was deployed to Europe in February 1955 to provide guided missile supports for units in the U.S. Seventh Army.

Battle fought by U.S. troops. *See* War: Battle fought by U.S. troops

Brevet was authorized by the Continental Congress on July 20, 1776, for Jacques Antoine de Franchessin, a Knight of the Order of St. Louis, an experienced officer in the service of France, who received a brevet commission of lieutenant colonel.

Brevet conferred upon an American was authorized November 19, 1777, by the Continental Congress, which granted the rank of lieutenant colonel, and a sword valued at $100, to Major Walter Stewart. *(James Barnet Fry—The History and Legal Effect of Brevets in the Armies of Great Britain and the United States)*

Cavalry unit was the Regiment of Dragoons, later known as the 1st Regiment of Dragoons, organized at Jefferson Barracks, Mo., in August 1833. Colonel Henry Dodge assumed command August 29, 1833. The designation of this organization was changed to the 1st Cavalry by act of Congress of August 3, 1861 (12 Stat.L.287). On March 5, 1792, Congress gave the President power to raise a squadron of cavalry at his direction to serve for three years. *(Records in Adjutant General's Office, War Department, Washington, D.C.)*

Confederate general killed in the Civil War. *See* Civil war: Confederate general killed in the Civil War

Dental Corps of the U.S. Army. *See* Dental Corps (U.S. Army): Dental Corps of the U.S. Army

Doctor (woman) commissioned in the regular Army. *See* Army officer: Woman doctor commissioned in the regular Army

Engineer Corps of the United States Army was established by Act of March 16, 1802 (2 Stat.L.132), "fixing the military peace establishments of the United States." The corps consisted of one engineer (major), two assistant engineers (captains), two other assistants (second lieutenants), and ten cadets. The first engineer in charge was Major Jonathan Williams, appointed April 13, 1802. *(Jonathan Williams—Plan of Jonathan Williams for Fortifying the Narrows)*

THE FIRST

Gas regiment of the United States Army, authorized August 15, 1917 by General Order 108, was organized by Colonel Earl James Atkisson. The first year it was known as the Thirtieth Engineers, and later it was named the First Gas Regiment. The first battalion was organized October 16, 1917. Its first independent action took place June 18, 1918, against Germans in the Toul sector, France.

Helicopter battalion activated was the Eighth Transportation Battalion (helicopter), consisting of three helicopter companies and one maintenance company, formed April 1, 1954, at Fort Bragg, N.C., under command of Major Robert Kolb.

Law (federal) authorizing military service for Negroes was introduced July 16, 1862, by Senator Henry Wilson of Massachusetts and signed July 17, 1862, by President Abraham Lincoln. It empowered the President to accept "persons of African descent, for the purpose of constructing intrenchments or performing camp competent." *(George Washington Williams—A History of the Negro Troops in the War of the Rebellion)*

Law (state) conferring military privileges and duties on the Negro was chapter 24 of the Public Acts of Tennessee, passed June 28, 1861. The governor was authorized to receive "all male free persons of color between the ages of 15 and 50 . . . to do all such menial service for the relief of the volunteers."

Medical corps of the U.S. Army is generally claimed to have been organized by the Reorganization Act of April 14, 1818 (end section—3 Stat.L.426), under which Joseph Lovell was appointed surgeon general. Medical officers previously were generaly appointed for special regiments. Richard Allison of Pennsylvania was appointed surgeon of a corps of 700 rank and file, which the first Congress had authorized on September 29, 1789. From this date to 1798, medical officers were appointed for regiments as they were authorized by Congress. The Act of May 28, 1798 (1 Stat.L.558) provided for the appointment of a physician general, for which post James Craik of Virginia was selected. The Act of March 3, 1813 (2 Stat.L.819) authorized the appointment of a physician and surgeon general. Dr. James Tilton of Delaware was appointed physician and surgeon general, and Francis Le Baron of Massachusetts was appointed apothecary general.

Military airplane. *See* Aviation: Airplane in actual military operation

Military leader of the Puritan settlers. *See* Military leader

THE FIRST

Moving picture for training soldiers. *See* Moving picture: Moving picture for training soldiers

Newspaper published by soldiers in the field. *See* Newspaper: Newspaper published by soldiers in the field

Railroad to carry troops. *See* Railroad: Railroad to carry troops

Reserve Officers Training Corps was authorized by the National Defense Act of June 3, 1916 (39 Stat.L.191), an "act for making further and more effectual provision for the national defense and for other purposes." Men were accepted for military training in times of peace to take the place of officers in time of war.

Reserve Officers Training Corps course in mountain and winter warfare was announced October 3, 1947, by President Homer Levi Dodge of Norwich University, Northfield, Vt. The course began in December 1947. The equipment included 150 pairs of skis, 130 pairs of snowshoes, 6 toboggans, sleds, etc.

Reserve Officers Training Corps Units were infantry units established, under authority of War Department Bulletin No. 44, October 21, 1916, at the University of Arkansas, Fayetteville, Ark.; University of Maine, Orono, Me.; St. John's College, Annapolis, Md.; Agricultural and Mechanical College of Texas, College Station, Tex.; College of St. Thomas, St. Paul, Minn., and the Citadel, Charleston, S.C. *(John Dickinson—The Building of an Army)*

Signal Corps was authorized as a separate branch of the U.S. Army by act of Congress March 3, 1863 (12 Stat.L.753). The corps was established under act of June 1, 1860 (12 Stat.L.66), which appropriated $2,000 "for the manufacture or purchase of apparatus and equipment for field signals" and the appointment of one signal officer. On June 27, 1860, Assistant Surgeon Albert James Myer was appointed signal officer with the rank of major.

Soldier to receive seven decorations at one time. *See* Medal: Soldier to receive seven decorations at one time

Soldier to win the three highest ranking decorations. *See* Medal: Soldier to win the three highest ranking decorations

Strike in which federal troops were called in peacetime. *See* Strike: Strike in which federal troops were called in peacetime

THE FIRST

Woman to become a member of the Women's Army Corps. *See* Army auxiliary corps: Woman to become a member of the women's army corps

Women's Army Medical Specialist Corps was authorized under the Army-Navy Nurses Act of 1947, April 16, 1947 (61 Stat.L.41), which established a dietitians' section, a physical therapists' section, and an occupational therapists' section to consist of 24 majors and 385 captains and first and second lieutenants.

ARMY AMBULANCE CORPS

Army ambulance corps was established August 2, 1862, by Major General George Brinton McClellan, who issued General Order No. 147 authorizing one captain to each army corps as the commandant of the Ambulance Corps, a first lieutenant for a division, a second lieutenant for a brigade, and a sergeant for each regiment. The members of the corps wore a green band on the cap, a green half chevron two inches broad on each arm above the elbow. *(Medical and Surgical History of the War of the Rebellion—Vol. 2, Surgical History Part 3)*

Army Ambulance Corps established by congressional action was authorized by the "Act to Establish a Uniform System of Ambulances in the Armies of the United States," approved March 11, 1864 (13 Stat.L.20), which provided each army corps with two-horse ambulances in accord with their strength. Infantry regiments of from 200 to 500 men were entitled to two ambulances, while those of over 500 men were entitled to three. Cavalry regiments with fewer than 500 men were entitled to one ambulance, while those of over 500 were entitled to two.

ARMY ARMORED CAR UNIT

in the United States Army was Troop A, 1st Armored Car Squadron, which was organized at Fort George G. Meade, Md., in 1928. It was commanded by Captain Harold G. Holt.

ARMY ARMORED TANK

manned by United States troops in the U.S. Army was the French Renault tank used in the Battle of St. Mihiel on September 12, 1918. The first chief of the Tank Corps was Brigadier General Samuel Dickerson Rockenbach, appointed June 1919. No American-built tanks were used in World War I. *(Records in Office of the Chief of Infantry—War Department.)*

See also Ordnance: Tank

ARMY AUXILIARY CORPS

Legion of Merit medal awarded a Women's Army Corps member. *See* Medal: Legion of Merit medal awarded a Women's Army Corps member

ARMY AUXILIARY CORPS—*Continued*
Woman to become a member of the Women's Army Corps, Regular Army, was Technician Third Grade Vietta M. Bates of Camden, N.J., who was sworn in July 8, 1948, in Washington, D.C., by General Omar Nelson Bradley, Army Chief of Staff. The ceremony was televised.

Women's Army Auxiliary Corps (WAAC) was authorized May 14, 1942 (56 Stat.L.278), an "act to establish a Women's Army Auxiliary Corps for service with the Army of the United States," under the command of a director who was to receive $3,000 annually plus allowances. The director was Oveta Culp Hobby (Mrs. William Pettus Hobby), appointed May 15, 1942, who assumed command the following day, when she was sworn in by Secretary of War Henry Lewis Stimson. On September 30, 1943, the Women's Army Auxiliary Corps became the Women's Army Corps (WAC).

Women's Army Auxiliary Corps (WAAC) training course commenced July 20, 1942 at Fort Des Moines, Des Moines, Iowa, and concluded August 29, 1942 when 346 women were commissioned third officers.

ARMY AVIATOR. *See* Aviation—Aviator

ARMY BALLOON CORPS of the U.S. Army was the Balloon (Aeronautic) Corps of five balloons and fifty men under the command of Thaddeus Sobieski Coulincourt Lowe, chief aeronaut of the Army of the Potomac, formed October 1, 1861. Four balloons were ready for service November 10, 1861, and were used for reconnaissance and for directing artillery fire via telegraph in Virginia. (*Official Records of the Union and Confederate Armies, Series 1*)

ARMY BALLOON SCHOOL was established on April 6, 1917, by Major Albert Bond Lambert on ground leased at Grand and Meramec Streets, St. Louis, Mo. When the first class of twelve graduated, May 15, 1917, all the equipment was offered without compensation to the War Department, which operated it until November 1917, when winter quarters were opened at San Antonio, Tex. In May 1918, the school was transferred to Camp John Wise at San Antonio.

ARMY CAMP
Army camp for "limited service" selectees was opened at Camp McCoy, Wis. Company No. 1, consisting of eighty-five enlisted men, was activated July 19, 1942. The commanding officer was Major William Lutz Krigbaum.

Army Camp for training Negro officers was established June 15, 1917, at Fort Des Moines, Des Moines, Iowa, and was known as

the 17th Provisional Training Regiment. On October 15, 1917, the first commissions were granted, 106 Negroes being commissioned as second lieutenants.

Army Citizens' Military Training Camp was established in 1921 with an enrollment of 10,299. The camps were authorized by the amendment to the National Defense Act of June 4, 1920 (41 Stat.L.759)

ARMY DENTAL CORPS. *See* Dental Corps (U.S. Army)

ARMY DENTIST. *See* Dental Corps (U.S. Army): Dentist officially employed in the U.S. Army

ARMY "E" AWARD. *See* Navy "E" award: Army-Navy "E" award

ARMY EXCLUSION LAW imposing a penalty for excluding soldiers in uniform from public places was Chapter 1562 passed May 5, 1908, by Rhode Island. The bill was sponsored by Theodore Francis Green. This act was amended from Section 32 of Chapter 283 of the General Laws of 1896.

ARMY EXECUTION in the American Army occurred on June 27, 1776. A treacherous guard, Thomas Hickey, plotted with others to capture George Washington and deliver him to Sir William Howe. Hickey was tried, convicted, and formally executed in New York City. All the officers and men off duty belonging to the brigades of Spencer, Heath, Sterling, and Scott assembled under arms at their respective barracks and at ten o'clock marched to the grounds, a field near the Bowery Lane. Hickey was hanged in the presence of twenty thousand persons.

ARMY FIELD HOSPITAL. *See* Hospital: Army field hospital

ARMY FIELD RANGE, or "Moving Kitchen," drawn by horses, was introduced by Captain Daniel Frank Craig, 4th Field Artillery, on a 21-day march in May 1908, while he was serving on the staff of Colonel Alexander Brydie Dyer at Vancouver, Wash. It was mounted on a two-wheeled truck or trailer and was drawn behind a rations wagon. It was never officially adopted by the War Department, although extensively used.

ARMY HELIPORT. *See* Heliport: Military heliport

ARMY HOSPITAL. *See* Hospital: Army field hospital

ARMY INSIGNIA

Chevrons for non-commissioned army uniforms were authorized by General Regulations for the Army of the United States, 1847, which provided three bars and an arc for sergeant-major, three bars and a tie for quartermaster sergeant, three bars and a lozenge for first sergeant, three bars for a sergeant, and two bars for a corporal. *(Henry Loomis Nelson— The Army of the United States)*

Shoulder sleeve insignia, known as a "shoulder patch," depicted a wildcat in a circle and was authorized October 19, 1918, for the Eighty-first Division, nicknamed the "Stonewall Jackson Division," the "Bobcat Division," and the "Wildcat Division."

Shoulder sleeve insignia issued to an independent air unit was authorized July 20, 1937, for the General Headquarters Air Force. It consisted of an ultramarine blue three-bladed propeller outlined against an orange disk. (An independent air unit was one directly under the command of the War Department, not under a commander who in turn was under the War Department.)

Special insignia or marking to designate regiments was instituted by the Massachusetts Provincial Congress on July 5, 1775, which "resolved that thirteen thousand coats be provided . . . and one thereof given to each non-commissioned officer and soldier in the Massachusetts Forces . . . and that the Committee of Supplies . . . are to cause all the coats to be buttoned with pewter buttons, and that the coats for each regiment, respectively, have buttons of the same number stamped on the face of them."

Wound chevron was authorized, pursuant to General Orders No. 6, War Department, on January 2, 1918. It was a gold chevron, identical with that of war service, worn on the left sleeve.

ARMY LANGUAGE SCHOOL

began courses in Japanese November 1, 1941, at Crissey Field, Presidio of San Francisco, Calif. It was deactivated, and activated as the Military Service Language School, Camp Savage, Minn., on June 1, 1942. It was moved to Fort Snelling, Minn., on August 15, 1944, and to the Presidio of Monterey, Calif., on June 11, 1946. The school was redesignated the Army Language School on September 1, 1947. In 1953 the school offered courses in twenty-four languages.

ARMY LODGE (Masonic).

See Freemasons: Military masonic loge

ARMY MEDICAL BOOK.

See Medical book: Medical book for army medical use

ARMY-NAVY FOOTBALL GAME. *See* Football game: Army-Navy football game

ARMY NURSE CORPS (female)

was established as a permanent organization of the Army by section 19, Act of February 2, 1901 (31 Stat.L.753), to consist of one superintendent ($1,800 annual compensation) and nurses and reserve nurses who received $40 a month within the continental limits of the United States and $50 a month when on foreign service and transportation and necessary traveling expenses when traveling under orders. Quarters, subsistence, and medical attendance were also provided. The first superintendent was Mrs. Dita H. Kinney, who was appointed March 15, 1901, and who resigned July 31, 1909. Anita Newcomb McGee, Acting Assistant Surgeon, United States Army, appointed August 29, 1898, had organized the nurses who remained with the Army after the Spanish American War into a corps under the Surgeon General. She served until December 31, 1900. *(Julia Catherine Stimson—History and Manual of the Army Nurse Corps)*
See also Army Officer—Woman

ARMY OFFICER

Adjutant General in the Continental Army was Horatio Gates, whose commission was signed June 19, 1775, by John Hancock. He received $125 a month and the rank of brigadier general. The resolution to establish this office was passed June 16, 1775. Gates was chosen June 17, 1775, and on May 16, 1776, became a major general. He had a hectic military career, resigned from service, reentered it, was suspended, and was later reinstated. *(Samuel White Patterson—Horatio Gates)*

Air Surgeon of the War Department was Colonel David Norvell Walker Grant, Chief of the Medical Division of the Office of the Air Corps, who was named to the post on October 24, 1941. He was rated a flight and air surgeon on July 3, 1942, and was assigned as Chief Surgeon under the Commanding General of the Army Air Forces.

American general missing in action in World War II. *See* World War II: American general missing in action in World War II

Army aviator (Negro) to down an Axis airplane. *See* Aviation—Aviator: Negro Army aviator to down an Axis airplane

Army Dental Corps Major General. *See* Dental Corps (U.S. Army): Army Dental Corps Major General

Army Medical Specialist Corps male officer commissioned was Second Lieutenant Sheldon Saffren of Philadelphia, Pa., who was

ARMY OFFICER—*Continued*
commissioned December 30, 1955, at the University of Pennsylvania Physical Therapy School, Philadelphia. The Army-Navy Nurses Act of April 16, 1947 (61 Stat.L.4) was amended on August 9, 1955, by the Bolton Amendment (69 Stat.L.579), which extended nurses' commissions to male personnel.

Brigadier General (Negro) was Benjamin Oliver Davis, commanding officer of Harlem's 369th Coast Artillery (National Guard), appointed October 25, 1940, to command a brigade in the 2nd Cavalry Division at Fort Riley, Kan.

Chaplain (Catholic) appointed by the President was the Reverend Francis Edward Boyle of the District of Columbia. He was appointed June 13, 1862, accepted June 16, 1862, and was assigned to Stone Hospital, Washington, D.C.

Chaplain (Catholic) of the Continental Army was the Reverend Louis Eustace Lotbiniere, appointed January 26, 1776, by General Benedict Arnold, to act as chaplain to the regiment of Colonel James Livingston. *(Peter Force—American Archives. Vol. 1)*

Chaplain (Catholic) of the U.S. Army was the Reverend Samuel H. Milley who served as post chaplain at Monterey, Calif., from September 28, 1849, to February 1850. *(Aidan Henry Germain—Catholic Military and Naval Chaplains)*

Chaplain (Chief) of the U.S. Army was John Thomas Axton, a clergyman of the Congregational Church appointed July 15, 1920, with the rank, pay, and allowance of colonel. He retired April 6, 1928. The office of Chief of Chaplains was established pursuant to Section 15 of an Act of Congress approved June 4, 1920 (41 Stat.L.769).

Chaplain (Jewish) of the U.S. Army was the Reverend Jacob Frankel of Philadelphia, Pa., who was appointed September 10, 1862, and who accepted September 18, 1862. This appointment expired by constitutional limitation, March 4, 1863. He was reappointed April 22, 1863, to the United States Hospital, Philadelphia, Pa., and was honorably mustered out of service July 1, 1865. Michael Mitchell Allen was regimental chaplain of the 65th regiment of the Fifth Pennsylvania Cavalry, resigning September 26, 1861, but he was not a "regularly ordained clergyman." *(War Department—Records of Chaplains Commissioned in 1862)*

Chaplain killed in action was Chaplain John Rosbrugh of Allen Township, Pa., who served as chaplain of Northampton County. He

was commissioned December 26, 1776, and was killed at the battle of Assunpink, or the second battle of Trenton, on January 2, 1777. *(John Cunningham Clyde—Rosbrugh, a Tale of the Revolution)*

Chaplain (Negro) of the U.S. Army was Henry McNeal Turner, pastor of the Israel African Methodist Episcopal Church, Washington, D.C. He was commissioned chaplain of the United States Colored Troops by President Abraham Lincoln in 1863. Turner enlisted in the First United States Colored Infantry, otherwise known as the First District Regiment of Columbia, and was present and active in all its military engagements. He was mustered out of service in September 1865, and was appointed a chaplain in the regular army by President Andrew Johnson. *(Richard Robert Wright—Centennial Encyclopedia of the African Methodist Episcopal Church)*

Chaplain of the U.S. Army was the Reverend John Hurt, who was appointed March 4, 1791, and who resigned April 30, 1794. He served during the Revolution as chaplain of the Sixth Virginia Infantry beginning October 1, 1776. He became brigade chaplain on August 18, 1778, and served as such to the close of the war. *(Francis Bernard Heitman—Officers of the Continental Army, 1775-1783)*

Chemical Warfare Chief was Brigadier General Amos Alfred Fries, who served from July 16, 1920, to March 4, 1921, and from March 28, 1921, to March 27, 1929. On February 24, 1925, he was advanced to Major General.

Chief engineer of the Continental Army was Colonel Richard Gridley, who served from June 17, 1775, to August 5, 1776. On June 16, 1775, the Continental Congress authorized one chief engineer at $60 a month, and two assistants at $20. *(Andrew Atkinson Humphreys—Historical Sketch of the Corps of Engineers)*

Flight surgeon of the U.S. Army was Dr. John Patrick Kelly, who reported for duty at the Signal Corps School of Aviation, College Park, Md., on June 30, 1911, and who moved with the school to Augusta, Ga., on November 29, 1911.

General appointed from civilian rank was William Signius Knudsen, director general of Office of Priority Management, appointed a lieutenant general on January 16, 1942, by President Franklin Delano Roosevelt.

General (Continental Army) was George Washington, appointed June 15, 1775, by the Second Continental Congress assembled at the State House, Philadelphia, Pa. Congress resolved "that five hundred dollars per month be

THE FIRST

allowed for the pay and expenses of the general." Washington was made general and commander-in-chief of the army of the United Colonies and served without pay.

General killed in World War II. *See* World War II: American general killed in World War II

General of the Armies of the United States was General John Joseph Pershing, whose appointment was unanimously confirmed by the U.S. Senate on September 4, 1919. The position was created by "act relating to the creation of the office of General of the Armies of the United States" (41 Stat.L.283), approved September 3, 1919. Pershing's was the only appointment under the act.

General of the U.S. Army was Ulysses Simpson Grant, appointed July 25, 1866. He served until March 4, 1869, when he was inaugurated President of the United States.

General to be consecrated a bishop was Major General William Richard Arnold, former chief of chaplains of the United States Army, in active service as a major general in the Inspector General's office when consecrated Titular Bishop of Phocaea on October 11, 1945, in St. Patrick's Cathedral, New York City, by Archbishop Francis Joseph Spellman.

General to become a rear admiral was Samuel Powhatan Carter, who organized the Tennessee Brigade and became a brigadier general of volunteers May 1, 1862. He was breveted major general March 13, 1865, for gallantry and meritorious service and was mustered out of volunteer service January 15, 1866. On June 23, 1865, he was a lieutenant commander in charge of the gunboat "Monocacy" on the Asiatic station. He was appointed rear admiral May 16, 1882, and retired August 6, 1882.

General wounded in action in World War II. *See* World War II: American general wounded in action in World War II

Generals to wear the five-star insignia as Generals of the Army were Henry Harley Arnold, Dwight David Eisenhower, Douglas MacArthur, and George Catlett Marshall, whose appointments were ratified December 15, 1944, by the Senate. The grade of General of the Army was established by Public Law No. 482, approved by Act of Congress, December 14, 1944 (58 Stat.L.802).

Judge Advocate of the Continental Army was Lieutenant Colonel William Tudor, who served from July 29, 1775, to April 9, 1777. On August 10, 1776, he was made lieutenant colonel.

THE FIRST

Judge Advocate of the U.S. Army was Captain Campbell Smith of the 4th Infantry, who served from March 3, 1797, to March 16, 1802.

Major General of the Continental Army, next in rank to George Washington, was Artemas Ward, who was appointed on June 17, 1775, by an Act of the Continental Congress, and who served until April 23, 1776, when he resigned with the rank of major general. *(Charles Martyn—The Life of Artemas Ward)*

Major (Negro) was Martin Robinson Delany, who received his commission on February 8, 1865. On April 5, 1865, he was ordered to report to Charleston, S.C. *(Alrutheus Ambush Taylor—The Negro in South Carolina During the Reconstruction)*

Male nurse commissioned was Second Lieutenant Edward L. T. Lyon of Kings Park, N.Y., who was sworn in October 6, 1955, by First Army Surgeon Brigadier General Harold Willard Glattly in the chapel of St. Cornelius the Centurion on Governors Island, N.Y. The Army-Navy Nurses Act (61 Stat.L.41) of April 16, 1947, was amended on August 9, 1955, by the Bolton Amendment (69 Stat.L.579), which extended nurses' commissions to male personnel.

Paymaster of the U.S. Army was Caleb Swan, appointed May 9, 1792. His office was authorized by act of May 8, 1792 (1 Stat.L. 271). He resigned June 30, 1808. He received $60 a month and was required "to reside near the headquarters of the troops of the United States." The first Pay Department, by that name, was organized under the Act of April 24, 1816 (3 Stat.L.297).

Paymaster General of the Continental Army was James Warren of Massachusetts, appointed June 27, 1775. On June 16, 1775, the Continental Congress established a separate department in the army to take care of payments to troops. The department consisted of the paymaster general, who received $100 a month, and a deputy at $50 a month. Warren resigned April 19, 1776. *(Massachusetts Historical Society—Warren-Adams Letters)*

Quartermaster of the Continental Army was Major Thomas Mifflin, who served from August 14, 1775, to November 7, 1777. *(Lancaster County Historical Society Papers, 1889)*

Regimental Jewish chaplain was Rabbi Elkan Cohen Voorsanger, commissioned as chaplain first lieutenant November 15, 1917, in Paris, France. He served with the American Expeditionary Forces and was promoted to the grade of captain on February 22, 1919. The act of June 3, 1916 (39 Stat.L.176) authorized

ARMY OFFICER—*Continued.*
the appointment of one chaplain for each regiment of cavalry, infantry, field artillery, and engineers, and 1200 of coast artillery. The act of October 6, 1917 (40 Stat.L.394) authorized the appointment of twenty chaplains-at-large.

Surgeon General of the Continental Army was Benjamin Church, who served from July 27, 1775, to October 16, 1775. He held the position of Director General and Chief Physician and received $4 a day compensation. On November 1, 1775, he was jailed for treason. (*Allen French—General Gage's Informers*)

Surgeon General of the U.S. Army to whom the title was officially applied was James Tilton of Delaware, who was Physician and Surgeon General of the U.S. Army from June 11, 1813, until June 15, 1815, when he was honorably discharged. His office was established by act of March 3, 1813 (2 Stat.L.819). Tilton, in 1813, wrote "Economical Observations on Military Hospitals," which was published at Wilmington, Del., by J. Wilson. The first medical officer to fill the position now known as Surgeon General of the Army was Joseph Lovell, who served from April 18, 1818, until his death, October 17, 1836. His salary was $2,500 per annum. The position was authorized by act of April 14, 1818 (3 Stat.L.426), an "act regulating the staff of the Army." (*Francis Bernard Heitman—Historical Register and Dictionary of the U.S. Army*)

Woman army officer (other than those in the medical department) to be sworn in in the regular U.S. Army was Colonel Mary Agnes Hallaren, who took the oath of office December 3, 1948. After the oath, Secretary of the Army Kenneth Claiborne Royall announced her selection as director of the Women's Army Corps, Regular Army. The ceremony took place in the office of General Omar Nelson Bradley, Army Chief of Staff, the oath being administered by Major General Edward Fuller Witsell, Adjutant General.

See also Army Nurse Corps (Female)

Woman assistant army surgeon was Dr. Mary Edwards Walker, who served as a contract surgeon from March 11 to August 23, 1864, and from September 22, 1864, to June 15, 1865. She wore male attire. The Congressional Medal of Honor awarded her, January 24, 1866, was, by adverse action of the Board of Medal Awards, stricken from the list February 15, 1917, nothing having been found in the records to show the specific act or acts for which the decoration was originally awarded.

Woman doctor commissioned in the regular Army was First Lieutenant Fae Margaret Adams of San Jose, Calif., sworn in March 11, 1953, in Washington, D.C. Pre-

viously, she had been a WAC reserve medical officer. She obtained her degree under the GI bill of rights.

Woman officer in the Judge Advocate General's Department was Captain Phyllis Ladora Propp, who was detailed May 3, 1944. She was a WAC officer and served on active duty from October 3, 1942, to September 21, 1949.

Woman to be appointed a Regular Army officer (Colonel) was Florence Aby Blanchfield, who on July 9, 1947, was appointed lieutenant colonel in the U.S. Army with permanent rank under authority of Army Nurses Law of April 16, 1947. The ceremony was held at the Pentagon, Washington, D.C. General Dwight David Eisenhower, Chief of Staff, presented her with her commission. On June 1, 1943, she had been appointed Superintendent of Army Nurses.

Woman with rank corresponding to colonel in the United States Army was Julia Otteson Flikke, Army Nurse Corps, who received the relative rank of Colonel, Army of the United States, on March 13, 1942. She was appointed to the Army Nurse Corps, March 8, 1918.

Woman with rank corresponding to major in the United States Army was Julia Catherine Stimson, superintendent of the Army Nurse Corps. Relative rank was conferred by Act of Congress, June 4, 1920 (41 Stat.L.767).

ARMY PARACHUTE TROOPS consisted of a test platoon of two officers and forty-eight men from the 29th Infantry who started training July 1, 1940. The first United States Army Parachute Battalion was the 501st, organized October 1, 1940, at Fort Benning, Ga., under the command of Major William Maynadier Miley.

ARMY RADIO CAR. *See* Radio car (military)

ARMY SCHOOL
Army school was the Military Academy of the United States, established at West Point, N.Y., by Act of Congress (2 Stat.L.132) of March 16, 1802, for the purpose of educating and training young men in the theory and practice of military science. The first superintendent was Jonathan Williams, who served from April 15, 1802, to June 20, 1803, with the rank of major. He resigned, but at the request of President Thomas Jefferson returned to the same position on April 19, 1805, and served as lieutenant colonel until July 31, 1812, when he resigned. During the interim following his first resignation, the senior officers assumed command of the Academy.

THE FIRST

THE FIRST

Army school graduate (Jewish) was Simon Magruder Levy of Maryland, a cadet from March 2, 1801, to October 12, 1802, when he graduated and was commissioned a second lieutenant in the Corps of Engineers. He was appointed a cadet for his good conduct as orderly sergeant at the Battle of Maumee Rapids, August 20, 1794. He resigned from the Army September 30, 1805, and died in 1807 in Georgia.

Army school graduate killed in military action was George Ronan. In the War of 1812 with Great Britain, he was engaged in Captain Nathan Heald's desperate battle near Ft. Chicago, Ill., August 15, 1812, against a vastly superior force of Indians, when he was struck down—not, however, before killing two Indians in a hand-to-hand fight and continuing the struggle, on his knees and weak from loss of blood, until the last moment. *(George Washington Cullum—Biographical Register of the Officers and Graduates of the U.S. Military Academy)*

Army school graduate (Negro) was Henry Ossian Flipper. He was appointed a second lieutenant in the 10th Cavalry on June 15, 1877, and remained in service until June 30, 1882, when he was dismissed for conduct unbecoming an officer and a gentleman. He was a cadet from May 20, 1873, to June 14, 1877. The first Negro admitted to the Army School was James Webster Smith, who was appointed by Congressman Solomon Lafayette Hoge, and who reported on May 31, 1870. *(Henry Ossian Flipper—The Colored Cadet at West Point).*

Army school graduates were Joseph Gardner Swift of Massachusetts and Simon Magruder Levy of Maryland. Both graduated from the Military Academy at West Point, N.Y., October 11, 1802, and were appointed second lieutenants the following day. Levy resigned September 30, 1805. Swift was made a brigadier general on February 19, 1814, for meritorious service in the defense of New York. They were the only graduates of the original class of ten: five from Massachusetts, and one each from Connecticut, Maryland, Missouri, New York, and Virginia. *(George Washington Cullum—Biographical Register of the Officers and Graduates of the U.S. Military Academy)*

Army training school to teach security troops, federal and state, was the First Corps Area Tactical School opened June 13, 1942, at Concord, Mass., under General Sherman Miles, commander of the First Corps Area. The instructors included army officers, scouting experts and Bert "Yank" Levy, author of *Guerilla Warfare.*

ARMY SCHOOL FOR CHAPLAINS. *See* Chaplains' school: Army school for chaplains

ARMY SCHOOL OF NURSING. *See* Nursing school: Army school of nursing

ARMY SECRET SERVICE BUREAU was inaugurated in 1861 by President Abraham Lincoln, who appointed Allan Pinkerton to be in charge. The identity of Pinkerton, who was the first chief of this bureau, was not revealed, and he served as "Major Allan." He was attached to the staff of General George Brinton McClellan.

ARMY SURGEON. *See* Army officer: Surgeon general

ARMY UNIFORM was standardized by order of the Continental Army in October 1779 when Washington, as the commander-in-chief, prescribed a uniform through a general order. The coat was blue. The facings for the infantry were varied—white, buff, red, and blue; the artillery and artificers' coats were faced with scarlet and had scarlet linings; and the light dragoons' coats were faced with white and had white buttons and linings.

ARMY VOTE was tabulated in 1864. The soldiers in the field were allowed to vote in the election of November 8, 1864. Of a total of 150,635 votes cast by the soldiers, 116,887 were for Abraham Lincoln, Republican, and 33,748 for George Brinton McClellan, Democrat.

ARMY WAR COLLEGE was authorized by War Department general orders No. 155 on November 27, 1901, to furnish advanced military instruction to regularly commissioned army officers; $20,000 was authorized by Congress, May 26, 1900 (31 Stat.L.209). The first class of sixteen officers was convened November 1, 1904, and terminated May 31, 1905. The first president was Major General Samuel Baldwin Marks Young. The cornerstone of the War College, Washington, D.C., was laid February 21, 1903, and the building opened June 20, 1907. Quarters were rented until the building was completed.

ARSENAL of the U.S. Government was the Springfield Armory, Springfield, Mass. (originally established in April 1778 as a laboratory for the preparation of all kinds of ammunition), established April 2, 1794 (1 Stat.L.352), as a National Armory for the manufacture of small arms. The manufacture of small arms began in 1795. The first superintendent was David Ames and the master armorer was Robert Orr. The first gunlock was filed by hand by Alexander Crawford after a struggle of three days. It took a month to complete twenty muskets. Only 245 were completed the first year. *(Moses King—Handbook of Springfield)*

THE FIRST

THE FIRST

ART AUCTION IN A DEPARTMENT STORE.

See Business: Department store to hold a public art auction

ART COMMISSION (public)

and the first important commission for a painting with more than one figure was "The Last Supper," an oil on canvas, 117½ inches wide and 35 inches high, by Gustavus Hesselius, ordered painted September 5, 1721, by the Vestry of St. Barnabas' Church, Queen Anne's Parish, Prince Georges County, Md. It was put in place as an altar piece on November 26, 1722. Hesselius was paid "£17 currt. money" for the painting and installation. *(Philadelphia Museum of Art —Gustavus Hesselius. 1682-1755)*

ART COURSE

Art course in true fresco painting was offered September 14, 1936, by the Department of Fine Art, Louisiana State University, University, La. Two courses, Mural Painting and Advanced Mural Painting were offered by Conrad Albrizio. Students were required to mix and put up their own plaster.

Industrial camouflage course met October 15, 1940, at Kansas City Art Institute, Kansas City, Mo. The instructor was Keith Martin. No points or credits were given for the twelve-week course.

ART DEPARTMENT IN A COLLEGE.

See Fine arts department: Fine arts department in a college

ART GALLERY (WPA).

See Works progress administration: Works progress administration federal art project gallery

ART ORGANIZATION

Art organization of importance was the Pennsylvania Academy of Fine Arts, which was established in Philadelphia, Pa., on December 26, 1805, "to promote the cultivation of the Fine Arts in the United States of America, by introducing correct and elegant copies from works of the first masters in sculpture and painting." It was incorporated March 28, 1806. The first president of the Academy was George Clymer.

Artists' society of importance was the New York Drawing Association, organized November 8, 1825, in New York City. On January 18, 1826, fifteen of the membership were empowered to select fifteen other artists to form the National Academy of Design, which was incorporated April 5, 1828. Samuel Finley Breese Morse was elected president and Thomas Seir Cummings treasurer, both of whom served from January 18, 1826, to May 14, 1845. On April 7, 1906, the Society of American Artists merged with the academy, their members auto-matically becoming members of the academy. *(Thomas Seir Cummings—Historic Annals of the National Academy of Design)*

ARTICLES OF CONFEDERATION

were adopted November 15, 1777, and were formally engrossed, July 9, 1778, in Philadelphia, Pa. South Carolina was the first state to ratify them, February 5, 1778, and Maryland was the last of the thirteen states to accept them, January 30, 1781. The articles as ratified by the thirteen states were formally announced to the public on March 1, 1781. *(Merrill Jensen—The Articles of Confederation)*

"ARTICS" were patented on February 2, 1858 by Thomas Crane Wales of Dorchester, Mass., who obtained patent No. 19,269 on waterproofing boots and gaiters. They were originally known as "Wales Patent Artic Gaiter." They were made then, as now, of rubber and cloth and were both waterproof and coldproof.

ARTIFICIAL BREEDING.

See Animal breeding society: Artificial animal breeding cooperative society

ARTIFICIAL EYE.

See Eye: Artificial eye

ARTIFICIAL FERTILIZER.

See Fertilizer (artificial)

ARTIFICIAL HEART

was a spirally coiled glass tube and pump invented in 1935 by Dr. Alexis Carrel, assisted by Colonel Charles Augustus Lindbergh. The apparatus consisted of a culture chamber and the electrically operated glass pump. An extirpated organ was suspended in the culture chamber and the main artery and vein connected with the glass tubes of the pump, which circulated a nutritive fluid through the organ and kept it alive. The experiments were carried on in Rockefeller Institute in New York City. *(Science Magazine Vol. 81. June 21, 1935)*

ARTIFICIAL INSEMINATION.

See Impregnation (human) by means of artificial insemination

ARTIFICIAL LEG.

See Leg (artificial) patent

ARTIFICIAL LIGHTING.

See Acetylene; Electric lighting; Gas

ARTIFICIAL LIGHTNING.

See Lightning (artificial)

ARTIFICIAL SNOW.

See Snow: Artificial snow

THE FIRST

ARTIFICIAL TEETH. *See* Dentistry: Patent for artificial teeth

ARTIST
See also
Engraver   Pastellist
Etcher   Sculptor
Lithographer

American artist of importance was John Singleton Copley, who sailed from Boston, Mass., in 1774 for England, where he painted the portraits of the king and queen. The "Death of Chatham" is one of his most widely known works. He is credited with more than 269 oil paintings, 35 crayons, and 14 miniatures. *(Augustus Thorndike Perkins—A Sketch of the Life and Some of the Works of John Singleton Copley, R. A.)*

American artist to win distinction was Benjamin West, who on March 24, 1792, became president of the Royal Academy of London, succeeding Sir Joshua Reynolds. His first discourse to the students of the Royal Academy was delivered December 10, 1792. Born October 10, 1738, near Swarthmore, Pa., he went to Italy in 1760, arriving in Rome on July 10. He studied there for three years and afterwards remained abroad. *(Henry Ezekiel Jackson—Benjamin West, His Life and Work)*

Artist to arrive in America was Jacques Le Moyne de Morgues, who accompanied the French expedition to Florida in 1564 under Laudonnière. They sailed from Havre de Grace, France, April 20, 1564, and reached Florida (New France) June 22, 1564, remaining until September 25, 1565. Le Moyne's work consisted principally of scenic and historical views. *(Narrative of Le Moyne. Translated by Fred B. Perkins from the Latin of De Bry and printed for William Appleton—Boston. 1874)*

Artist successful in commercial art was Matthew Pratt, who painted signboards in Philadelphia, Pa., in 1768. He sailed from Philadelphia, Pa., for London on June 24, 1764, and studied under Benjamin West. On March 20, 1768, he sailed from Bristol, England, and returned to Philadelphia. *(William Sawitzky—Matthew Pratt. 1734-1805, A Study of His Work)*

English artist in territory now a part of the United States was John White, Governor of Sir Walter Raleigh's Virginia Colony, and grandfather of Virginia Dare, the first white child born in America. His drawings were made in Virginia and Florida from 1585 to 1590 *(Theodore de Bry—America)*

Woman painter (and the first pastellist in America) was Henrietta Johnston. She worked

THE FIRST

with colored chalk, producing most of her paintings between 1707 and 1720. Her subjects were mostly women of South Carolina, but her best work is a likeness of "His Excellency Robert Johnson, Captain General, Governor and Commander-in-Chief in and over His Majesty's Province of Carolina," which was made in 1718. *(The Antiquarian. September 1928)*

ARTS AND LETTERS SOCIETY

Arts and letters society (national) was the American Academy of Arts and Letters, founded April 23, 1904 (incorporated April 17, 1916, 39 Stat.L.51), as a section of the National Institute of Arts and Letters. The latter organization was founded in September 1898 (incorporated February 4, 1913 (37 Stat.L.600). The first membership of the American Academy of Arts and Letters consisted of William Dean Howells, Augustus Saint-Gaudens, Edmund Clarence Stedman, John La Farge, Samuel Langhorne Clemens, John Hay, and Edward MacDowell. The first member added to the original group was Henry James, January 7, 1905. *((American Academy of Arts and Letters—Proceedings in Commemoration of the Twenty-Fifth Anniversary)*

National Institute of Arts and Letters gold medal. *See* Medal: National Institute of Arts and Letters gold medal

Negro member of the National Institute of Arts and Letters was Dr. William Edward Burghardt Du Bois, head of the Department of Sociology of Atlanta University, Atlanta, Ga., who was elected to membership on December 22, 1943.

Woman elected to the American Academy of Arts and Letters was Julia Ward Howe, author of "The Battle Hymn of the Republic," who was elected January 28, 1908. *(Laura Elizabeth Richards and Maud Howe Elliott—Julia Ward Howe, 1819-1910)*

Woman elected to the National Institute of Arts and Letters was Julia Ward Howe, who was elected January 25, 1907

ARTS AND SCIENCE SOCIETY

Arts and science society (national) was the American Academy of Arts and Sciences, founded in Boston, Mass., and chartered on May 4, 1780, "to cultivate every art and science which may tend to advance the interest, dignity, honor and happiness of a free, independent and virtuous people." The first president was James Bowdoin, who served from 1780 to 1790. *(Centennial Volume. Memoirs VII)*

Woman elected to the American Academy of Arts and Sciences was Maria Mitchell, elected unanimously May 30, 1848. At Nantucket, Mass., she had discovered a telescopic

THE FIRST

THE FIRST

ARTS AND SCIENCE SOCIETY—*Cont.*
comet on October 1, 1847, for which King
Frederic VI of Denmark had also presented
her with a gold medal. *(Proceedings. American
Academy of Arts and Sciences. May 1890)*

**ASHKENAZIC JEWISH CONGREGA-
TION.** *See* Jewish congregation: Jewish
congregation (Ashkenazic)

ASPHALT PAVEMENT. *See* Road: Sheet
asphalt pavement

ASSAY OFFICE BUILDING (federal)
was authorized March 3, 1853 (10 Stat.
L.212), and erected on Wall Street, New York
City, in 1854. The first assayer in charge was
John Torrey. An assay office was opened in
Philadelphia, Pa., in 1828 as a department of
the Mint and not as a separate institution (4
Stat.L.278). The assay offices of the govern-
ment were placed under the Bureau of the
Mint when the Bureau was authorized (12
Stat.L.424), on February 12, 1873, to control
all the mints and assay offices. The first direc-
tor of the Mint was Henry Linderman. *(Jesse
Paul Watson—The Bureau of the Mint)*

ASSEMBLY, LEGISLATIVE. *See* Legislative assembly

ASSOCIATE JUSTICE (woman). *See*
Judge: Woman associate justice

**ASSOCIATION FOR THE ADVANCE-
MENT OF SCIENCE.** *See* Science association: Scientific society (national organization)

ASTRONAUTS
American astronaut to orbit the earth was
Lieutenant Colonel John Herschel Glenn, Jr.,
of New Concord, Ohio, who was blasted off at
9:48 A.M. E.S.T. on February 20, 1962, from
Cape Canaveral, Fla., in an Atlas D, 93 feet
high with a 16-foot maximum base diameter.
The bell-shaped capsule, which weighed 4,265
pounds at launch, 2,987 pounds at orbit insertion, and 2,422 pounds on recovery, traveled
around the earth three times, covering 83,450
miles at an average speed of 17,400 miles an
hour. The capsule came down at 2:43 P.M. in
the Atlantic Missile Range and Glenn was
taken aboard the U.S.S. "Noa" at 3:04 P.M.

Astronauts chosen by the National Aero-
nautics and Space Administration for Project
Mercury were trained at the Langley Research
Center, Hampton, Va. The selection of the
seven men was announced April 7, 1959. They
were Air Force Captains Leroy Gordon
Cooper, Jr., of Carbondale, Colo., Virgil Ivan
Grissom of Mitchell, Ind., and Donald Kent
Slayton of Sparta, Wis.; Navy Lieutenants
Malcolm Scott Carpenter, of Boulder, Colo.,

and Walter Marty Schirra, Jr., of Hackensack, N.J.; Navy Lieutenant Commander Alan
Bartlett Shepard, Jr., of East Derry, N.H.;
and Lieutenant Colonel of Marines John
Herschel Glenn, Jr., of New Concord, Ohio.

Space flight by an American astronaut
was made by Commander Alan Bartlett Shepard, Jr., whose 15-minute suborbital flight in
a capsule rocketed by a Redstone missile with
about 75,000 pounds of thrust took place on
May 5, 1961. The capsule, weighing slightly
more than 2,000 pounds, made a 302-mile trip
down-range from Cape Canaveral, Fla., at a
ground speed of 4,500 miles an hour; it
reached an altitude of 115 miles before re-
entering the earth's atmosphere. Shepard experienced a 5-minute period of weightlessness.
See also Medal: National Aeronautics and
Space Administration distinguished service
medal

ASTRONOMER
Astronomer of note in the American
colonies was John Winthrop of Cambridge,
Mass., who made sunspot observations on
April 19, 20, and 22, 1739. No observations
were made on April 21 as it was cloudy. The
observations consist of one-page reports in the
University Archives, Harvard University Library, and have never been published.

Astronomer to acquire fame after the
Revolution was Nathaniel Bowditch, who in
1802 wrote *The New American Practical Navigator, being an epitome of navigation, containing all the tables necessary to be used with the
nautical almanac in determining the latitude
and the longitude by lunar observations, and
keeping a complete reckoning at sea,* published
in Newburyport, Mass. This book corrected
over 8,000 errors in other works and was
adopted by the U.S. Navy Department as the
standard authority on navigation. *(Henry
Ingersoll Bowditch—Sketch of the Life and
Character of Nathaniel Bowditch)*

Astronomer to measure the size of a fixed
star was Dr. Francis Gladheim Pease, who
on December 13, 1920, at Mount Wilson Observatory, Mount Wilson, Calif., measured Betel-
geuse, the bright red star in the right shoulder
of Orion, by means of an inferometer designed
by Professor Albert Abraham Michelson. He
found the star to be 260 million miles in
diameter. *(Astrophysical Journal—Vol. 53.
1921)*

Woman astronomer employed in the U.S.
Naval Observatory was Eleanor Annie Lamson, a graduate of George Washington University, Washington, D.C., who was employed on
July 20, 1900, and who served until her sudden
death, July 27, 1932. She computed all the
results for gravity determination made by Dr.

THE FIRST

Felix Andries Vening-Meinesz's observations on his submarine cruise to the West Indies and was working on the reports of his second expedition, the East Indian cruise, at the time of her death.

ASTRONOMICAL EXPEDITION to record an eclipse of the sun consisted of Professors Samuel Williams, Stephen Sewall, James Winthrop, Fortesque Vernon, and six students, who were sent, October 9, 1780, from Harvard College, Cambridge, Mass., to Penobscot Bay. The Commonwealth of Massachusetts supplied a boat. Although the country was at war with England, the British officer in command at Penobscot Bay permitted the expedition to land and observe the eclipse of October 27, 1780, which lasted from 11:11 A.M. to 1:50 P.M. *(Memoirs—American Academy of Arts and Sciences. 1785)*

ASTRONOMICAL OBSERVATIONS BOOK was James Melville Gillis' *Astronomical Observations made at the Naval Observatory, Washington, under Orders of the Honorable Secretary of the Navy, Dated August 13, 1838.* It consisted of 671 pages and was a catalog of 1,248 stars. It was printed in Washington, D.C. *(Biographical Memoirs—National Academy of Science. Vol. 1)*

ASTRONOMICAL OBSERVATORY. *See* Observatory; Planetarium

ASTRONOMY
  Meteoric display ("shooting stars") on record was observed by Andrew Ellicott on November 12, 1799, off the Florida Keys. The "whole heaven appeared as if illuminated with sky rockets, flying in an infinity of directions, and I was in constant expectation of some of them falling on the vessel. They continued until put out by the light of the sun after day break." *(Andrew Ellicott—The Journal of Andrew Ellicott)*

  Moving picture of an eclipse of the sun taken from a dirigible. *See* Moving picture: Moving picture of an eclipse of the sun taken from a dirigible

  Planet found beyond Neptune was Pluto, discovered at the Lowell Observatory, Flagstaff, Ariz., February 18, 1930, by Clyde William Tombaugh, on plates made in a systematic long-continued search begun under the direction of the late Dr. Percival Lowell, who had mathematically predicted and located the planet many years before, almost exactly in the position where found. The announcement was withheld even after it had been observed many times and completely checked, until March 13, 1930, the anniversary of Lowell's birth (and of Herschel's discovery of Uranus). *(Scientific Monthly. Vol. 34. January 1932)*

THE FIRST

  Planet (asteroid) named for an American President was Hooveria. It was discovered in March 1920 by Professor Johann Palisan of the University of Vienna, Austria, and named for Herbert Hoover, who at that time was engaged in feeding the distressed European peoples.

ASTRONOMY MAGAZINE presenting a popular exposition of astronomy was *The Sidereal Messenger,* published by Ormsby Mac-Knight Mitchel, editor and director of the Cincinnati Observatory. It cost $3 a year. The first issue was published July 1846 by Derby Bradley & Company, Cincinnati, Ohio, and consisted of eight pages. Publication ceased October 1848.

ATHEISM SOCIETY of importance was the American Association for the Advancement of Atheism, the first society in the United States to use the word "Atheism" or any of its forms as a title. The society was organized in New York City in October 1925, and was incorporated November 16, 1925, in New York State. The charter was at first denied by the Supreme Court. The first president of the Association was Charles Smith. *(American Association for the Advancement of Atheism—Annual Report. Vol. 1)*

ATHLETE TO WIN FOUR PRIZES AT THE OLYMPIC GAMES. *See* Olympic games: American athlete to win four prizes in one year at the Olympic games

ATHLETIC ASSOCIATION. *See* Intercollegiate athletic association; Sports: Athletic club

ATHLETIC CLUB. *See* Sports: Athletic club

ATHLETIC COMPETITIONS. *See* Sports; *see also under specific headings*

ATHLETIC GAMES. *See* Sports; *see also under specific headings*

ATHLETICS DEPARTMENT. *See* Physical culture department

ATLANTIC CABLE. *See* Cable: Cable across the Atlantic ocean

ATLANTIC OCEAN BROADCAST. *See* Radio broadcast: Transatlantic broadcast

ATLANTIC OCEAN FLIGHT. *See* Aviation—Aviator: Aviator to fly one hundred times across the Atlantic ocean; Aviation—Flights (transatlantic)

THE FIRST

THE FIRST

ATLANTIC OCEAN SCHEDULED AIR SERVICE. *See* Aviation—Flights (transatlantic): Atlantic ocean scheduled air service

ATLAS issued by a state was *The Atlas of the State of South Carolina, made under the authority of the Legislature; prefaced with a geographical statistical and historical map of the state.* It was prepared under the direction of Robert Mills and printed for the state in 1825 by John D. Toy, Baltimore, Md. It contained a map of the state of South Carolina and twenty-eight district maps scaled 21 miles to the inch which were engraved by H. S. Tanner and assistants. The atlas was 18 inches by 24 inches and included the location of the roads, rivers, bridges, ferries, factories, taverns, many of the plantations, etc.

ATOMIC BOMB
Atomic bomb dropped from an airplane over water was released from "Dave's Dream," an Air Force B-29 Superfortress, on June 30, 1946 (21:01 Greenwich Civil Time) over the Bikini Lagoon in the Pacific Ocean. The shot, designated "Able," was part of Operation Crossroads. It had a 520-foot height of burst and caused the sinking of two transports (the "Gilliam" and the "Carlisle") and damage to 18 other ships which were among a group of 73 vessels used as a target.

Atomic bomb explosion occurred July 16, 1945 (12:29:15 G.C.T.) in a desert area at Alamogordo Air Base, 120 miles southeast of Albuquerque, N.M. The shot, designated "Trinity," was part of Operation Trinity. It was a tower shot with 100-foot height of burst.

Atomic bomb explosion over enemy territory took place on August 6, 1945, over Hiroshima, Japan, from the "Enola Gay," a B-29 airplane. The pilot was Colonel Paul W. Tibbets, Jr., of Miami, Fla., and the bombardier was Major Thomas W. Ferebee of Mocksville, N.C. *(William Leonard Laurence—Dawn Over Zero, the Story of the Atomic Bomb)*

Atomic bomb underground explosion was detonated November 29, 1951 (19:59:59.7 G.C.T). at Frenchman Flat, Nev., and witnessed by a group of congressmen and military officers headed by Chief of Staff General Joseph Lawton Collins. The explosion, which caused a hole about 800 feet in diameter and 100 feet deep, was designated as "Uncle," a part of Operation Buster-Jangle.

Atomic bomb underwater explosion took place July 24, 1946 (20:35 G.C.T.) in the Pacific Ocean, three miles off Bikini. The bomb was dropped from an airplane at a height of 7,000 feet and exploded 90 feet under water. The shot, designated "Baker,"

was part of Operation Crossroads. It resulted in the sinking of 10 vessels (including the battleship "Arkansas") which were set up as a target.

Atomic explosion witnessed by troops as part of a war maneuver was designated "Dog." It was part of Operation Buster-Jangle, which took place November 1, 1951 (15:30:01.6 G.C.T.), in New Mexico. The 11th Airborne Division of Camp Campbell, Ky., witnessed the air-drop explosion.

Atomic fusion (thermonuclear) bomb was detonated October 31, 1952 (19:14:59.4 G.C.T.) and designated as "Mike" of Operation Ivy. It was a tower shot with a burst of 20 feet at the Elugelab Atoll at the Eniwetok Proving Ground, Marshall Islands.

Atomic fusion (thermonuclear) bomb dropped from an airplane exploded May 20, 1956 (17:50:38.7 G.C.T.) over Namu Atoll at the northwest edge of the Bikini Atoll. It was designated as "Cherokee," a part of Operation Redwing. It created a fireball four miles in diameter.

Rocket with an atomic warhead. *See* Rocket: Rocket with an atomic warhead

ATOMIC BOMB-RESISTANT FEDERAL BUILDING. *See* Building: Atomic bomb-resistant federal building

ATOMIC CANNON. *See* Ordnance: Atomic cannon

ATOMIC ELECTRIC GENERATING STATION (full scale). *See* Electric power plant: Atomic electric generating station (full scale)

ATOMIC ENERGY
Atomic-powered cruiser. *See* Ship: Atomic-powered cruiser

Atomic-powered merchant ship. *See* Ship: Atomic-powered merchant ship

Atomic-powered submarine. *See* Submarine: Atomic-powered submarine

Electric power from nuclear energy was obtained through the use of Experimental Breeder Reactor I (EBR-I), placed in operation during the summer of 1951 at the National Reactor Testing Station operated by the United States Atomic Energy Commission near Idaho Falls, Idaho. EBR-I is a fast breeder reactor designed and operated by the Argonne National Laboratory, Argonne, Ill. The core in use at the time of the first production of electricity enabled the reactor to pro-

THE FIRST

duce 1,400 thermal kilowatts and 150 electrical kilowatts. On December 20, 1951, the reactor supplied steam to a turbo-generator which produced electrical energy of more than 100,000 watts to operate the pumps and other reactor equipment and to provide light and electrical facilities for the building in which the reactor was housed.

Electric power generated from atomic energy to be sold commercially. *See* Electric power plant: Electric power generated from atomic energy to be sold commercially

Electric power generated from atomic energy to illuminate an entire town. *See* Electric power plant: Electric power generated from atomic energy to illuminate an entire town

Self-sustaining nuclear chain reaction demonstration was made December 2, 1942, by Enrico Fermi and his staff at the Metallurgical Laboratory of the University of Chicago, Chicago, Ill., before approximately forty persons, when energy of the atom was released and controlled. Atomic particles known as neutrons, spontaneously released by atoms of metallic uranium or uranium oxide, embedded in a suitable pattern throughout a block of graphite, were permitted to collide with neighboring atoms of uranium or uranium oxide, causing these neighboring uranium atoms to split. The uranium atoms thus split released additional neutrons, which caused further similar reactions with still other uranium atoms, and so on at a rapidly increasing rate.

ATOMIC ENERGY COMMISSION

Atomic Energy Commission was established by the Atomic Energy Act, approved August 1, 1946 (60 Stat.L.755), which created a five-man commission of civilians to develop and utilize atomic energy toward improving the public welfare, increasing the standard of living, strengthening free competition in private enterprise, and promoting world peace. The commission, appointed October 28, 1946, by President Harry S. Truman and confirmed April 9, 1947, by the Senate, consisted of chairman David Eli Lilienthal, Robert Fox Bacher, Sumner Tucker Pike, Lewis Lichtenstein Strauss, and William Wesley Waymack. The first meeting was held November 13, 1946.

Atomic Energy Commission Patent Compensation Board award was made November 21, 1951, to Cyril Elwin McClellan of Glen Burnie, Md., who was awarded $7,500 for a method of separating isotopes used at the Brookhaven National Laboratory, Upton, Long Island, N.Y. The invention was assigned to the Atomic Energy Commission. McClellan applied for a patent December 22, 1942. It was placed under security order but was removed February 18 1949.

THE FIRST

Hospital completely devoted to the study of the atom in the treatment of cancer. *See* Hospital: Hospital completely devoted to the study of the atom in the treatment of cancer

ATOMIC ENERGY MUSEUM. *See* Museum: Museum devoted exclusively to atomic energy

ATOMIC POWER CLOCK. *See* Clock: Clock to operate by atomic power

ATOMIC REACTOR

Atomic reactor for research and development designed to determine the feasibility of plutonium-containing fuels for power reactors reached criticality on November 25, 1960. This reactor was part of the Plutonium Recycle Program (PRP) conducted by the General Electric Company for the Atomic Energy Commission at the Hanford Atomic Products Operation, Richland, Wash. The use of plutonium-239 as an enrichment material instead of uranium-235 would permit the operation of enriched fuel reactors without dependence on expensive uranium isotope separation facilities. It would increase the amount of energy recovered from a given amount of raw uranium and provide a way of utilizing for peaceful purposes plutonium not needed for weapons use.

Atomic reactor (privately operated) was the Raleigh Research Reactor, Raleigh, N.C., placed in operation September 5, 1953, by the North Carolina State College of Agriculture and Engineering and the University of North Carolina. Completely independent of the Atomic Energy Commission or other federal government financial support, the reactor is free of secret or classified data and is available without restriction to the general public for observation and to students and staff for study and research.

Atomic reactor system to be patented by a private company was a water boiler type invented by John William Flora of Canoga Park, Calif., who on May 17, 1960, received U.S. patent No. 2,937,127, which was assigned to North American Aviation, Inc. The reactor, 8 feet high and 8 feet in diameter, was built by Atomics International, a division of North American Aviation, Inc. It was fueled by enriched uranium in solution.

Atomic reactor to produce plutonium was placed in operation in September 1944 at the Manhattan district, U.S. Army Corps of Engineer's Hanford Engineering Works, Richland, Wash. The Hanford plant was originally constructed and operated by the E. I. duPont de Nemours Company and was valued at $347,000,000. Since 1946, the plant has been operated by the General Electric Company and has been expanded to represent an investment of $1,136,500,000.

ATOMIC REACTOR—*Continued*

Military nuclear power plant designed for air shipment of major components was dedicated at the U.S. Army Engineer Research and Development Laboratories, Fort Belvoir, Va., on April 29, 1957, by Secretary of the Army Wilber Marion Brucker. The Army Package Power Reactor, designated the SM-1, was the result of studies initiated in 1952 to determine the feasibility of applying nuclear power to military uses. The first plant, serving as a prototype, was a pressurized water type producing 1,855 kilowatts of electricity. A single core loading operates the plant from 1½ to 2 years at a power factor of .8. The plant was designed and constructed by Stone and Webster Engineering Corporation and Alco Products, Inc.

Nuclear reactor built for private industrial research was a 50,000 watt research reactor (L-47) designed and built by Atomics International, a division of North American Aviation, Inc., which began operating June 28, 1956. The reactor is located on the campus of the Illinois Institute of Technology, Chicago, Ill., and is operated by the Armour Research Foundation. It is of the "solution" type, fueled by enriched uranium, with a reactor core surrounded by graphite bars arranged in a stack (8 feet by 5 feet by 5 feet) which acts as a reflector. The rate of fission in the reactor is controlled by four boron bars. The reactor produces neutrons and gamma rays and is not used to generate electrical power. The reactor cost about $700,000. Twenty-four industrial companies contributed about $20,000 each toward the total cost. The first director of the project was Dr. Richard Franklin Humphreys.

Sodium reactor (experimental) (SRE) was built by Atomics International, a division of North American Aviation, Inc., for the Atomic Energy Commission in the Santa Susana Mountains, about 30 miles northwest of Los Angeles, Calif. The atomic power reactor went critical on April 25, 1957. It generates about 6,000 kilowatts of electricity.

Thorium-uranium reactor (privately owned) to supply light and power was designed and fabricated by the Babcock and Wilcox Company for the Consolidated Edison Company's Indian Point nuclear electric generating station at Buchanan, N.Y., a 275,000 kilowatt plant built at a cost of $100,000,000. This was the first reactor designed to supplement fissionable uranium-235 with fertile thorium-232. Construction began January 28, 1958.

ATOMIC VESSELS. *See* Navy: Atomic submarine division, *and also under* Ship; Submarine

ATTACHÉ (naval). *See* Naval officer: Naval attaché

ATTORNEY GENERAL

Assistant attorney general (state) who was a woman was Ella Louise Knowles (later Mrs. Haskell), who was admitted to the Montana bar on December 28, 1889. In 1892 she was a candidate for Attorney General on the Populist ticket. She ran 5,000 votes ahead of her ticket in a state casting only 50,000 votes. Her Republican opponent, Henry Joseph Haskell, who won the election and whom she later married, appointed her assistant attorney general.

Attorney General of the United States was Edmund Jennings Randolph, who was appointed by President Washington on September 26, 1789, and who entered on his duties on February 2, 1790, and served till January 1, 1794. The office was created by act of Congress September 24, 1789 (1 Stat.L.73), an "act to establish the Judicial Courts of the United States." His salary was $1,500 a year. (*Albert George Langeluttig—Department of Justice*)

Opinion by a U.S. Attorney General was rendered by Edmund Randolph to the Secretary of the Treasury on August 21, 1791, the government at that time being in Philadelphia, Pa. The opinion held that interest on certificates issued pursuant to the Act of Congress passed August 4, 1790, was not allowable and the courts would embarrass a system of finance by a determination in favor of interest for the year 1791. (*U.S. Justice Department—Digest of the Official Opinions of the Attorneys General of the U.S. 1885*)

ATTORNEY OF THE UNITED STATES

was Samuel Sherburne, Jr., of New Hampshire who was appointed United States Attorney in and for the New Hampshire District on September 26, 1789. Twelve other attorneys, one for each state district, were appointed on the same date.

AUCTION (book). *See* Book auction

AUCTION BRIDGE CHAMPIONSHIP

(duplicate) was held July 9, 1914, at the Lake Placid Club, Lake Placid, N.Y. The four-man team of the New York Bridge Whist Club defeated the team of the Knickerbocker Whist Club of New York City by seven tricks on forty-eight boards to win the American Whist League's Hamilton Trophy, symbolic of the whist championship of the United States and Canada.

See also Bridge whist organization

AUCTION OF ART OBJECTS BY A DEPARTMENT STORE. *See* Business: Department store to hold a public art auction

AUDIENCE PARTICIPATION TELECAST. *See* Television—Telecast: Audience participation telecast

AUDION TUBE. *See* Radio Tube: Radio tube

AUGER (screw auger) was manufactured in 1810 by Walter French in Seymour, Conn. He was also the first to put a screw point on augers. Previously, only pod augers without screws had been used and a gouge was required to start the hole before an auger could be made to work. *(Connecticut Magazine—July 1900)*

AUREOMYCIN
Aureomycin chlortetracycline, the first broad-spectrum antibiotic, was released to the American physician in November 1948. It was developed and produced by Lederle Laboratories, a division of American Cyanamid Company, Pearl River, N.Y. Discovered by Dr. Benjamin Minge Duggar, the antibiotic is a yellow crystalline substance obtained from a mold named *Streptomyces aureofaciens. (Annals of New York Academy of Sciences. November 1948. Vol. 51. p. 175)*

AURORA BOREALIS display recorded in America took place in New England on December 11, 1719. "This evening, about eight o'clock, there arose a bright and red light in the E.N.E. like the light which arises from an house when on fire (as I am told by several credible persons who saw it, when it first arose) which soon spread itself through the heavens from east to west, reaching about 43 or 44 degrees in height, and was equally broad." *(Massachusetts Historical Society Collections.* **Vol. II)**

AUSTRALIAN BALLOT SYSTEM. *See* Election law: Australian ballot system

AUTHOR
Author whose livelihood was obtained exclusively by writing was Charles Brockden Brown of New York and Philadelphia. His first book was *Alcuin, a Dialogue,* one of the earliest known works by an American championing the rights of women. It was published anonymously and was first announced April 28, 1798, by T. & J. Swords, New York City. His first novel was *Wieland, or the Transformation,* which was published in New York City in 1798. The scenes were set on the banks of the Schuylkill, and the complications were mainly created by ventriloquism. The book was the first American example of the "Gothic" horror novel. *(David Lee Clark—Charles Brockden Brown— Pioneer Voice of America)*

Sports writer was Henry William Herbert, who used the nom de plume "Frank Forester,"

and who acquired fame in 1834 as an authority on outdoor sports. *(David Wright Judd—Life and Writings of Frank Forester)*

Successful woman serial writer was Anna Sophia Winterbotham Stephens, whose poems "The Tradesman's Boast" and "The Polish Boy," published in 1834, brought her fame. She edited *Peterson's Magazine* and *Godey's Lady's Book,* and was the author of thirty books, many of which appeared as serials.

Woman author in America is claimed to be Anne (Dudley) Bradstreet, whose poems were printed in 1640 in a volume entitled *Several Poems, compiled with great variety of Wit and Learning, full of delight; wherein especially is contained a compleat Discourse and Description of the Four Elements, Constitutions, Ages of Man, and Seasons of the Year, together with an exact Epitome of the Three first Monarchies, viz; The Assyrian, Persian, and Grecian; and the beginning of the Roman Commonwealth to the end of their last King, with divers other pleasant and serious Poems; by a Gentlewoman of New England.* She was the daughter of Governor Thomas Dudley and wife of Governor Simon Bradstreet, both of Massachusetts. *(Samuel Eliot Morison—Builders of the Bay Colony)*

Woman author to make writing a profession was Hannah Adams. Her income from this source was very limited. In 1784 her first book appeared, *Alphabetical Compendium of the Various Sects which Have Appeared from the Beginning of the Christian Era to the Present Day. (Dedham Historical Register. July 1896)*

"AUTOBANK." *See* Bank: "Autobank" complete service

AUTOGIRO
Autogiro flown was at Pitcairn Field, Willow Grove, Philadelphia, on December 19, 1928. It was brought to this country by Harold Frederick Pitcairn, who formed the Pitcairn-Cierva Autogiro Company of America for licensing the manufacture of the autogiro in this country. On January 19, 1931, the name of the company became the "Autogiro Company of America." *(The Autogiro—Pitcairn-Cierva Autogiro Company of America)*

Autogiro mail delivery. *See* Air mail service: Autogiro mail delivery direct to a post office

Autogiro manufactured with a closed cabin was the Kellett Convertible K2 model, powered with a 165 h.p. Continental engine, which was flown October 21, 1931 at the Philadelphia Municipal Airport, Philadelphia, Pa. It had a

AUTOGIRO—*Continued*
door which opened part of the roof, and a window on the pilot's side. It seated two passengers and could be transformed into an open model at will.

Autogiro rotary wing aircraft fellowship was the Juan de la Cierva Fellowship established at the College of Engineering, New York University. The first recipient of the fellowship was Samuel B. Sherwin of New York City, who enrolled September 8, 1939.

Autogiro to land on the White House lawn was a Pitcairn-Cierva piloted by James Garrett Ray of Philadelphia, Pa., who landed April 22, 1931. He was presented with the 1930 Collier Trophy by President Hoover.

Autogiro to land packages on a moving ship was piloted by James Garrett Ray of the Pitcairn Company, Philadelphia, Pa. He lowered several rolls of film to the "Ile de France" on April 30, 1931, as the departing steamer left New York City for Europe.

Autogiro to loop the loop publicly was demonstrated by John MacDonald Miller at the National Air Races, Cleveland, Ohio, August 27, 1932.

Autogiro to tow a glider was piloted by John MacDonald Miller at Valley Stream, Long Island, N.Y., on May 23, 1933. The glider was piloted by Jack O'Meara.

Autogiro (wingless direct control) for military purposes was the KD-1, a two-place open cockpit tandem type with dual controls, manufactured by the Kellett Autogiro Corporation, Philadelphia, Pa., in 1934. Control is accomplished by means of the rotor system, which is inclined by moving the control stick in conventional manner. The autogiro has a gross weight of 2,050 pounds and has a cruising range of 3½ hours—361 miles. It was first flown December 9, 1934, at the Philadelphia Airport, Philadelphia, Pa.

Autogiro with side-by-side seating arrangement was a Kellett Autogiro K2 model with a 165 h.p. Continental engine. The design was planned January 13, 1931, and the ship was completed and tested April 17, 1931, at the Philadelphia Municipal Airport, Philadelphia, Pa.

Parachute jump from an autogiro. *See* Aviation—Parachute: Parachute jump from an autogiro

Transcontinental autogiro flight was made by John MacDonald Miller, who left Pitcairn Field, Willow Grove, Philadelphia, Pa., May

14, 1931. Many stops were made en route to California to exhibit the machine. The autogiro landed May 28, 1931 at the North Island Naval Air Station, San Diego, Calif.

AUTOGRAPH TIME RECORDER. *See* Time recorder: Autograph time recorder

AUTOMAT (restaurant). *See* Restaurant: Restaurant with an automatic arrangement for vending food

AUTOMATED SUBWAY TRAIN. *See* Subway: Train to run automatically without conductors or motormen

AUTOMATIC AIRCRAFT CANNON. *See* Ordnance: Automatic aircraft cannon

AUTOMATIC COMPUTING SCALE. *See* Scale: Automatic computing pendulum-type scales

AUTOMATIC HEADLIGHT CONTROL. *See* Headlight: Automatic headlight control

AUTOMATIC PARKING METER. *See* Parking meter (automatic)

AUTOMATIC PILOT. *See* Aviation: Automatic pilot

AUTOMATIC RECORD CHANGER. *See* Phonograph: Phonograph with an automatic record changer

AUTOMATIC RIFLE. *See* Ordnance: Semi-automatic rifle

AUTOMATIC TELEPHONE. *See* Telephone: Automatic telephone system (successful)

AUTOMATIC TOLL COLLECTOR. *See* Toll collector (automatic)

AUTOMATON
Automaton was imported from England on May 3, 1743, and was exhibited by Mr. Pacheco of New York City, who charged one shilling admission. It performed "several strange and diverting motions to the admiration of the spectators" and was advertised in the *New York Weekly Journal* of July 18, 1743.

Automaton to operate by long-distance control, electronically geared to duplicate simultaneously the exact motions of a master machine at long distances, was the machine nicknamed "Yes Man." The automaton was made by the General Electric Company's General Engineering Laboratory, Schenectady, N.Y., for the Aircraft Nuclear Propulsion Department under contract with the U.S. Air Force, and its manufacture was announced on May 23, 1956. It was designed to perform remote-control mechanical jobs in dangerously radioactive areas from any required distance.

AUTOMOBILE

Air-conditioned automobile was manufactured by the Packard Motor Car Company, Detroit, Mich., and publicly exhibited November 4-12, 1939, at the 40th Automobile Show, Chicago, Ill. Air in the car was cooled to the temperature desired, dehumidified, filtered, and circulated. Heat was provided in the winter. The refrigerating coils were located behind the rear seat in an air duct, with heating coils in another compartment of the same duct. The capacity of the unit was equivalent to 1.5 tons of ice in twenty-four hours when the car was driven at 60 m.p.h., or 2 tons at 80 m.p.h.

Armored car was designed by Colonel Royal Page Davidson in May 1898. A Colt automatic machine gun was mounted on the car, which was intended for military use. The automobile was manufactured by the Duryea Automobile Company of Peoria, Ill., and was used by the Northwestern Military and Naval Academy of Lake Geneva, Wis.

Armored commercial car was employed by Brink's Incorporated, Chicago, Ill., in 1918. It had one thickness of armor-plate steel, but was not of all-steel construction throughout.

Armored commercial car completely protected was put in service February 1, 1920, by Michael Francis Sweeney of the Sweeney Detective Bureau, Inc., St. Paul, Minn. Construction was started in March 1919 by the Boyd Auto Shops, Minneapolis, Minn. The side walls and roof were steel, welded-steel construction; no wooden walls or roof supports were used. The glass was "polished plate wired glass." Hinged steel plates were placed over the windshield and window glass. They were so arranged that the tripping of a catch caused the steel plates to cover the glass windows and windshield.

Army armored car. *See* Army armored car unit; Army armored tank

Automobile-airplane combination was the Arrowbile, built by the Waterman Arrowplane Corporation, Santa Monica, Calif., completed for testing February 20, 1937. Delivery of five Arrowbiles was made August 15, 1937, to the Studebaker Corporation, South Bend, Ind. In the air, its top speed was 120 miles an hour

and its cruising speed was 105 miles an hour. It had a six-cylinder Studebaker engine which developed 100 h.p.

Automobile exhibited at a circus. *See* Circus: Circus to feature an automobile as an attraction

Automobile (gasoline-electric combination) was placed in service about 1910. It was equipped with the Owen magnetic drive and a generator in a combined unit.

Automobile (new type gasoline-electric combination) was delivered on August 30, 1929, to Colonel Edward Howland Robinson Green by the General Electric Company of Schenectady, N.Y. It was capable of developing 60 h.p. and had no clutch or gear-shifting device. There were only two foot pedals, one at the left for the brake and the other at the right for acceleration. To start the car the driver stepped on the starting button and then fed the engine gas.

Automobile regularly made for sale was manufactured by the Duryea Motor Wagon Company, which was organized in Springfield, Mass., in 1895. Charles Edgar Duryea, America's pioneer automobile manufacturer, began building his automobile in August 1891. It was completed at his shop, 47 Taylor Street, Springfield, Mass., and successfully operated April 19, 1892.

Automobile slung beneath airplane fuselage in flight. *See* Aviation—Flights: Airplane flight with an auto slung beneath the fuselage

Automobile snow cruiser. *See* Snow cruiser (automobile)

Automobile to exceed the speed of a mile a minute was driven on November 16, 1901, by A. C. Bostwick on a straightaway course at Ocean Parkway, Brooklyn, N.Y., in a race sponsored by the Long Island Automobile Club. He covered the distance in 56⅗ seconds. This record was held only a few minutes as Henry Fournier lowered it to 51⅘ seconds in a 40 h.p. gasoline automobile, and Foxhall Keene lowered it to 54⅗ seconds. Both Fournier and Keene raced in French automobiles. Bostwick used a 40 h.p. Winton. *(Smithsonian Institution—Smithsonian Report for 1901)*

Automobile to exceed the speed of 200 miles an hour was a 1,000 h.p. "Mystery Sunbeam" driven by Major Henry O'Neil de Hane Segrave on March 29, 1927, at Daytona Beach, Fla., at an average speed of 203.79 miles both ways. *(Henry O'Neil de Hane Segrave—The Lure of Speed)*

THE FIRST

THE FIRST

AUTOMOBILE—*Continued*

Automobile to exceed the speed of 300 miles an hour was a Bluebird Special driven by Sir Malcolm Campbell, who on September 3, 1935, at Bonneville Salt Flats, Utah, drove a mile at the rate of 304.331 miles an hour, and made a return run at 298.013 miles an hour, an average speed of 301.1292 miles an hour.

Automobile to exceed the speed of 400 miles an hour was a Railton Mobil Special, driven by John Cobb on September 16, 1947, at Bonneville Salt Flats, Utah, on a fourteen-mile straightaway. His speed was 385.645 miles per hour in the first test and 403.135 miles in the second.

Automobile with a circulating lubrication system was the Autocar model of 1904, manufactured at Ardmore, Pa.

Automobile with left-hand steering was the Northern four-cylinder car of 1907, manufactured by the Northern Motor Car Company of Detroit, Mich. The automobile was also equipped with air brakes. The designer of these improvements was Charles Brady King, one of America's pioneer automobile inventors.

Automobiles ordered for the U.S. War Department were purchased in 1899 from the Woods Motor Vehicle Company of Chicago, Ill. "The automobiles were provided for ordinary horse transportation when they serve to furnish electrical power in the field for use of telegraphy, telephony, signal lights, etc., while, when circumstances permit, the same power is available for transportation itself."

Collection and delivery of mail in automobiles. *See* Postal service: Collection and delivery of mail in automobiles

Diesel engine automobile. *See* Diesel engine: Diesel engine automobile trip

Electric storage battery automobile was designed by William Morrison and built by Morrison & Schmidt, Des Moines, Iowa, in the summer of 1891. It was powered by twenty-four storage-battery cells, placed under the seats, which took ten hours to charge, and could run continuously for thirteen hours. It carried twelve people, had a 4 h.p. motor, and was capable of a speed of fourteen miles an hour. It was sold to J. B. McDonald, president of the American Battery Company of Chicago, in 1892. (*Scientific American. January 9, 1892*)

Electric taxicabs were introduced in New York City in the spring of 1897 by the Electric

Vehicle Company, whose office and garage were located at 1684 Broadway, New York City. (*Horseless Age. Vol. 3. No. 7. October 1898*)

Field hospital automobile with X-ray equipment was designed at Lake Geneva, Wis., by Colonel Royal Page Davidson and was first used in May 1915 at the Northwestern Military Academy, Lake Geneva, Wis. The necessary electric current was generated by the automobile motor.

Foreign automobile exhibited was displayed at the World's Fair in Chicago in 1893 by Karl Benz of Germany. It was built by Gottlieb Daimler of Germany and was named after his daughter, Mercedes.

Free piston automobile was the XP-500, an advanced-design experimental model built by the research staff of the General Motors Corporation, Detroit, Mich. The first public announcement was made April 15, 1956; the first public display took place May 16, 1956, at the dedication of the GM Technical Center. The engine had two horizontal cylinders, each containing two opposed pistons. These cylinders and pistons served to produce hot gases which turned a turbine wheel geared to the rear wheels of the car. The engine generated 250 horsepower.

Gas turbine automobile was the XP-21 Firebird, built by the General Motors Corporation, and tested by Mauri Rose in October 1953 at the GM Proving Ground, near Milford, Mich. Its first public appearance was January 21-26, 1954, at the GM Motorama, Waldorf Astoria Hotel, New York City. A 370 h.p. Whirlfire turbo-power jet was installed in the rear of the car. The total weight of the engine unit, including the gasifier and power sections, was 775 pounds, the over-all weight of the entire car being 2,500 pounds. It had a plastic body and accommodated only the driver. Its speed was 150 miles per hour, but it was believed capable of 235 miles per hour. At it consumed fuel faster than conventional cars, it was not commercially produced.

Gas turbine automobile operated on city streets was a 1955 Plymouth sedan which was first operated in Detroit, Mich., on April 19, 1955.

Miniature automobile manufactured in the U.S. was offered for sale by Powell Crosley, Jr., on April 28, 1939. It had an 80-inch wheelbase and was 10 feet long from bumper to bumper. It had two cylinders, three forward speeds and a reverse, four-wheel mechanical brakes, a four-gallon capacity tank, and safety glass. The two-passenger convertible coupe and the four-passenger con-

THE FIRST

THE FIRST

vertible sedan sold for $325 and $350, F.O.B. Richmond, Ind. On June 19, 1939. the Crosley cars were put on sale in R. H. Macy's basement in New York City.

Mobile telephone commercial service. *See* Telephone: Mobile telephone commercial service

Plastic automobile was manufactured by the Ford Motor Company, Dearborn, Mich., in August 1941. Fourteen plastic panels were mounted on a tubular welded frame; windows and windshield were of acrylic sheets, which resulted in approximately a 30 per cent decrease in weight. On January 13, 1942, patent No. 2,269,451 was obtained by Henry Ford, Dearborn, Mich., on the automobile body construction, an auto body chassis frame made from steel tubes or pipes designed for use with automobiles made from plastics. *(Modern Plastics. September, 1941)*

Plastic laminated fiberglas body sports car was the Chevrolet Corvette, produced June 30, 1953, by the Chevrolet Motor Division of the General Motors Corporation plant at Flint, Mich. Two experimental models had been made in January 1953. The list price was $3,250, including a 1953 powerglide automatic transmission as standard equipment. The car was only 33 inches at the door (body height), 70 inches wide, and 167 inches long on a 102-inch wheelbase. Its curb weight was approximately 2,900 pounds.

President to ride in an automobile. *See* President (United States): President to ride in an automobile

Production of more than 100,000 passenger cars in one year was achieved in 1909, when 123,990 cars were manufactured. More than 1 million cars (1,525,578) were manufactured in 1916; more than 5 million cars (5,119,466) in 1949; more than 7 million cars (7,920,186) in 1955. *(Automobile Manufacturers Association—Automobile Facts and Figures)*

Production of more than one million passenger cars of one make in one year was achieved in 1949, when 1,109,958 Chevrolets were manufactured by the Chevrolet Motor Division of General Motors Corporation, Detroit, Mich.

Radio car (military). See Radio car (military)

Right-hand-drive automobile for the delivery of mail was a Crosley, placed in service in Cincinnati, Ohio, from December 27, 1951, to January 6, 1952, for special delivery service.

On January 7, 1952, it was placed in service for letterbox delivery on a mounted route. It is possible that some of the early makes of automobile, which had right-hand drives, may have been used earlier.

Sedan type automobile was the 1913 Hudson Sedan, manufactured by the Hudson Motor Car Company, Detroit, Mich. It was officially shown January 11, 1913, at the Thirteenth National Automobile Show, New York City. It carried all accessories as standard equipment.

Shaft-driven automobile was constructed in 1901 by the Autocar Company of Ardmore, Pa. It was driven in 6 hours and 15 minutes from Ardmore to Madison Square Garden, New York City, where it was exhibited in the New York Automobile Show of December 1901. The first eight hundred cars were equipped with steering levers, but the later ones were equipped with steering wheels. *(Autocar Messenger. Vol. 13. No. 10)*

Steam automobile was invented in 1866 by Henry Alonzo House. It was driven through the streets of Bridgeport, Conn., and surrounding towns for several months. On October 6, 1866, House and his brother, James A. House, co-inventor, drove the car to Stratford, Conn., taking a party of men to a vessel-launching.

Steam-operated amphibious vehicle. *See* Steam-operated amphibious vehicle

Sun-powered automobile was a fifteen-inch sunmobile built by William G. Cobb of General Motors Corporation and publicly demonstrated August 31, 1955, at the General Motors Powerama, Chicago, Ill. It had twelve photoelectric cells made of selenium which converted light into electric current. The current powered a tiny electric motor with a driveshaft connected to the rear axle by a pulley.

Transparent-top automobile in regular production was the Mercury "Sun Valley," a sports coupe with transparent green tinted plexiglas replacing the steel over the front section of the roof, announced December 7, 1953, by the Ford Motor Company, Detroit, Mich.

Two-way radio in an automobile. *See* Radio telephone: Two-way radio in an automobile

AUTOMOBILE ACCIDENT occurred in New York City, May 30, 1896, when Henry Wells of Springfield, Mass., in a Duryea Motor Wagon, collided with Evylyn Thomas, a bicycle rider, who was taken to the Manhattan Hospital. Her leg was fractured and Wells

THE FIRST

AUTOMOBILE ACCIDENT—*Continued*
spent the night in jail awaiting the report as
to the extent of the injuries. *(New York Daily
Tribune. May 31, 1896)*
See also Automobile Fatality

AUTOMOBILE ADVERTISEMENT. *See*
Advertisement: Automobile advertisement

**AUTOMOBILE-AIRPLANE COMBINA-
TION.** *See* Automobile: Automobile-airplane combination

AUTOMOBILE BRAKE (four wheels)
was invented by Otto Zachow and William Bes-
serdich of Clintonville, Wis., who obtained
patent No. 907,940, December 29, 1908 on
"power applying mechanism."

AUTOMOBILE BUS
Automobile sightseeing bus was the Motor
Tally-Ho owned and operated by Isaac Harris
in Brooklyn's Prospect Park. It was operated
by gasoline and had a 60 h.p. engine and 4
cylinders with a three-bearing crank-shaft. It
carried nineteen passengers and the driver. It
was built by the Mack Motor Truck Corporation, Brooklyn, N.Y., in 1900 and sold for
approximately $3,000.

Bus night coach was built by the Pickwick
Corporation in Los Angeles, Calif., and placed
in service in July 1929 between Los Angeles
and San Francisco, Calif. The car was of
metal construction, chiefly of duralumin, and
provided sleeping and seating accommodation
for twenty-six people. The bus had two lavatories, a kitchen and pantry and carried a crew
of three: pilot, steward and porter.

Bus operated by a railroad for the transportation of passengers was used by the Spokane, Portland and Seattle Railway Company.
The railroad organized the Spokane, Portland
and Seattle Transportation Company, which
was incorporated on July 23, 1924, and began its highway operations on August 25,
1924. *(Automotive Transportation and Railroads—Commission on Commerce and Marine.
American Bankers Association.)*

Bus with a double deck was imported from
France and introduced on Fifth Avenue, New
York City, by the Fifth Avenue Coach Company in 1906. The Di Dion Bouton type bus
was used. An experimental model propelled by
electricity supplied by a battery was tested in
1904. *(Motor Coach. June-July 1924)*

Bus with a double-deck body and chassis
made in the United States was constructed
in 1915 by the Fifth Avenue Coach Company
of New York City.

THE FIRST

Bus with cross seats was introduced by
the Fifth Avenue Coach Company, New York
City. The double-deck buses were fitted with
cross seats on March 17, 1914, and the single-
deck buses on August 27, 1915. All seats had
been longitudinal before that. The single-deck
buses seated 16 people, the double-deck 44.
(Motor Coach. July 1928)

Coast to coast through bus line was the
"Yelloway Bus Line," which began service
on September 11, 1928, from Los Angeles,
Calif., to New York City. Three 26-passenger
buses departed daily from each terminal, covering 3,433 miles in 5 days and 14 hours.

Gas turbine bus was the GM Turbocruiser,
a modified GMC coach built by the research
staff of the General Motors Corporation, Detroit, Mich., which was publicly announced
June 10, 1954, after it had already logged more
than 2,000 miles. The engine used a single
burner and two turbine wheels, one to drive
the centrifugal compressor, the other to drive
a transmission which was connected to the rear
wheels of the bus.

Transcontinental no-change bus service
was instituted September 8, 1953, by Continental Trailways, which started its through
service at 9 P.M. from the Port Authority Bus
Terminal, New York City, to San Francisco,
Calif. The fare for the 3,154-mile trip was
$56.70. The time was 88 hours 50 minutes, of
which 77 hours 19 minutes was the actual
riding time.

Two-way radio equipped bus. *See* Radio
telephone: Two-way radio equipped bus

AUTOMOBILE CATALOG was a one-
sheet four-page circular, issued in 1895 by the
Duryea Motor Wagon Company of 285 Main
Street, Springfield, Mass. The retail price for
a "two-seater" automobile was $1,000, for a
"four-seater," $2,000. The automobile was de-
scribed as follows: "It has two actual 3 horsepower motors. . . . It uses ordinary stove gasoline and costs less than ½ cent per mile. . . . It
has 34 inch front and 38 inch rear wheels. . . .
It weighs 700 pounds or about 300 pounds more
than a similar common wagon. . . . It is steered
by a sidewise motion of the lever and speeded
by a vertical motion. . . ."

AUTOMOBILE CLUB was the American
Motor League, which held its preliminary meet-
ing November 1, 1895, in Chicago, Ill., with
sixty members. On November 29, 1895, a
constitution was adopted and officers elected.
No president was selected, but four vice presi-
dents, Charles Edgar Duryea of Illinois, Hiram
Percy Maxim of Connecticut, Henry Gurney
Morris of Philadelphia, and H. D. Emerson
of Cincinnati, Ohio, were elected. Dr. Joseph
Allan Hornsby was elected secretary and
Charles Brady King, treasurer.

THE FIRST

AUTOMOBILE COMPANY incorporated was the Duryea Motor Wagon Company of Springfield, Mass., incorporated September 21, 1895, under the laws of Maine.

AUTOMOBILE DRIVER (woman) was Genevra Delphine Mudge (Mrs. Eva Mudge Nelson), who drove a Waverly Electric in 1898 in New York City. On December 31, 1899, she participated in an automobile race in New York City, driving a Locomobile which skidded on the snow and knocked five spectators down.

AUTOMOBILE DRIVING COURSE in a high school, including both classroom work and behind-the-wheel training, was offered at State College High School, State College, Pa., from February 17, 1934, to June 11, 1934. The first instructor was Amos Earl Neyhart. Students who completed the course received Pennsylvania automobile operators' licenses.

See also Automobile school

AUTOMOBILE ELECTRIC SELF-STARTER

Automobile electric self-starter, applied commercially to an automobile, was offered to the public in May 1911 by the Cadillac Motor Car Company of Detroit, Mich. The self-starter was patented by Charles Franklin Kettering, who obtained patent No. 1,150,523 on August 17, 1915, on an "engine starting device."

Automobile electric self-starter patent was No. 745,157, which was granted on November 24, 1903, to Clyde Jay Coleman of New York City. He invented the self-starter in 1899, but the invention was impractical. The license was purchased by the Delco Company, which was taken over by the General Motors Corporation.

AUTOMOBILE FATALITY was Henry H. Bliss, a real estate broker, 68 years old, who was knocked down and run over as he was alighting from a southbound street car at Central Park West and 74th Street, New York City, on September 13, 1899. He was taken to Roosevelt Hospital, where he died. Arthur Smith, the driver, was arrested and held in $1,000 bail.

See also Automobile accident

AUTOMOBILE FINANCE COMPANY was the Bankers Commercial Corporation, New York City, organized February 1915, an affiliate of the Commercial Security Company, Inc. (formerly the Fidelity Contract Company), Chicago, Ill.

AUTOMOBILE GARAGE. *See* Garage (public)

THE FIRST

AUTOMOBILE HILL CLIMBING CONTEST was sponsored by the Automobile Club of America and held September 9, 1901, at Nelson Hill, just outside of Peekskill, N.Y., as one of the feature events in the 500-mile test run from New York City to Buffalo, N.Y. The Class A race was won by the Grout Brothers, automobile manufacturers of Orange, Mass., who entered a steam-propelled open Stanhope automobile of their own manufacture. The car weighed 920 pounds and seated two people, including the driver. The climb took 2 minutes, 45 seconds. The hill was 226 feet high and 2,372 feet long with a slant varying from 12 to 17 degrees. *(Automobile Club of America—Five Hundred Mile Endurance Contest)*

AUTOMOBILE INSURANCE. *See* Insurance: Automobile compulsory insurance act (state)

AUTOMOBILE LEGISLATION

Automobile seat belt safety legislation requiring automobiles to be equipped with attachments (frame holes) to which seat belts could be fastened was enacted by Illinois on June 27, 1955, and signed by Governor William Grant Stratton on July 6, 1955. The law provided that on or after July 1, 1956, no new motor vehicle could be registered unless equipped with seat belt attachment conforming to the specifications of the Society of Automotive Engineers.

Federal motor carrier legislation was the act of August 9, 1935 (49 Stat.L.543), "to amend the Interstate Commerce Act, as amended, by providing for the regulation of the transportation of passengers and property by motor carriers operating in interstate or foreign commerce." *(Parker McCollester—Federal Motor Carrier Legislation)*

State motor car legislation was passed by the General Assembly of Connecticut, "An act regulating the speed of motor vehicles," approved May 21, 1901. Robert Woodruff of the town of Orange, a representative in the Connecticut Assembly, presented the bill which provided that the speed of all motor vehicles should not exceed twelve miles an hour on country highways and eight miles an hour upon highways within the limits of the city. A substitute bill was presented, however, which provided that "no motor vehicle shall run on any highway or public place outside the limits of the city at a speed to exceed fifteen miles an hour . . . or within the limits of the city to exceed twelve miles an hour. A person having charge of a powerful vehicle shall have such vehicle under their control and shall reduce the speed of such vehicle until said crossing of such street or road shall have been passed. Upon meeting or passing any vehicle drawn by a horse, the person having charge of the power of the vehicle shall reduce the speed and if the

AUTOMOBILE LEGISLATION—*Cont.*

horse drawing such vehicle appears to be frightened the person in charge of said motor vehicle shall stop."

AUTOMOBILE LICENSE BOARD was

the Board of Examiners of Operators of Automobiles authorized July 6, 1899, by Chicago, Ill. It consisted of Edward Beach Ellicott, City Electrician, chairman; Dr. Arthur Rowley Reynolds, Commissioner of Health; John Ericson, City Engineer; and James Furlong, secretary, appointed to ascertain the qualifications of persons seeking licenses.

AUTOMOBILE LICENSE (federal)

Common carrier license issued by the Interstate Commerce Commission was MC-60785, granted December 22, 1936, to Rodger's Motor Lines, Inc., Scranton, Pa., to become effective January 21, 1937.

Contract carrier license issued by the Interstate Commerce Commission was MC-81,751, issued December 29, 1936, to Howard W. Juett, Cartersville, Ga., effective as of December 29, 1936. This permit authorized his operations as a contract carrier of certain specified commodities to and from Cincinnati, Ohio, to points in the state of Florida, as specified therein.

AUTOMOBILE LICENSE PLATES

Automobile license plates were required by New York State in 1901 under "an act to amend the highway law, in relation to the use of highways by automobiles or motor vehicles and requiring the owners of such vehicles to register with the Secretary of State." The act became a law April 25, 1901, and took effect immediately. Registration was required within thirty days. Owners of automobiles were obliged to register their names and addresses and a description of their machines. The registration fee was $1. In 1901, fees totaling $954 were received and in 1902, $1,082. The licenses bore the owners' initials and were required to be over three inches in height.

Permanent license plates were issued by Connecticut and became effective March 1, 1937. The plates were made of aluminum with black letters against a natural background. The annual number was located directly in the middle and at the bottom of the plate. The colored insert is designed so that it may be easily removed and changed each year.

Plastic license plate tabs were issued December 15, 1942, by the Massachusetts Department of Public Utilities for 1943 truck registrations. They were made of a laminated phenolic compound by the General Electric Company, Schenectady, N.Y. Printed resin-impregnated sheets of paper, backed by a suit-

able filler, covered by a translucent sheet, were bonded together under approximately 250° Fahrenheit temperature and 1500 pounds pressure.

AUTOMOBILE MAGAZINE was *The Horseless Age,* published November 1895 in New York City by Edward P. Ingersoll.

AUTOMOBILE MAIL DELIVERY. *See* Postal service: Collection and delivery of mail in automobiles

AUTOMOBILE MAIL WAGON built especially for mail collection service was constructed by the Winton Motor Vehicle Company of Cleveland, Ohio, in 1899. A test was made in Cleveland over a 22-mile route, when mail was collected from 120 boxes. Although the test was made in a severe snow storm under adverse conditions, the trip took 2 hours and 27 minutes, whereas the horse and wagon trip required 6 hours. The test was authorized by Mr. Dewston, Cleveland's postmaster. (*Automobile Magazine. Vol. 1. February 1900*)

AUTOMOBILE PARADE was held at Newport, R.I., September 7, 1899. Society leaders of Boston, New York, and Philadelphia participated. The vehicles were all profusely decorated with flowers and flags. A prize was awarded to Mrs. Hermann Oelrichs, whose automobile was overhung with wisteria. Upon the radiator was a flock of pure white doves that appeared to be drawing the carriage. Nineteen cars were in the line. (*Automobile Magazine. October 1899*)

AUTOMOBILE PARKING REGISTER. *See* Parking meter (automatic)

AUTOMOBILE PATENT was No. 549,160, filed on May 8, 1879, by George Baldwin Selden, an attorney of Rochester, N.Y. It was granted to him on November 5, 1895, and embodied his claims to the original application of the internal combustion hydrocarbon motor to a road vehicle.

AUTOMOBILE   POLICE   PATROL WAGON was designed by Frank Fowler Loomis of Akron, Ohio, and was placed in service by the Akron Police Department in June 1899. It had three speeds and made sixteen miles an hour. It was operated by electric power and weighed 5,500 pounds, including the batteries. (*Automobile Magazine. May 1900*)

AUTOMOBILE RACE

Automobile race was held on November 28 (Thanksgiving Day), 1895, over snowy roads from Chicago to Waukegan, Ill., a distance of approximately 52 miles. Of the eighty-odd entries, only six could start: three foreign cars, two American-made cars, and one American gasoline car. The race and the $2,000 prize offered by the Chicago *Times-Herald* were won by James Franklin Duryea, who drove an automobile invented by his brother, Charles Edgar Duryea. Arthur M. White, umpire, rode with him. Only one other entry finished, an American rebuilt Benz electric, which was pushed many miles. The Duryea entry had a water-cooled gasoline engine with a water pump, a bevel-gear transmission with three speeds forward and reverse, and electric ignition. It was equipped with a rigid front axle with steering knuckles at the ends. It was steered by a tiller handle, the up-and-down motion of which changed the speed. The average speed in the race was 7½ miles an hour.

Automobile race from New York to Paris via Seattle and Yokohama started February 12, 1908, from Times Square, New York City. Six automobiles were entered: three French cars, one Italian, one German, and one American. The race was won by George Shuster, driver, George J. Miller, mechanic, and Montague Roberts, assistant mechanic, in a car made by the E. R. Thomas Motor Company, Buffalo, N.Y. The elapsed time was 170 days, of which 88 were spent in actual driving. The average daily run was 152 miles; the longest daily run 420 miles. It was not necessary for the same mechanic or helpers to accompany the cars throughout the trip. The Thomas car returned to New York City on August 1, 1908. The race was sponsored by the New York *Times* and the Paris newspaper *Le Matin*.

Automobile race (long distance) was held September 9-14, 1901, under the auspices of the Automobile Club of America, which sponsored a 500-mile race from its club house, Fifth Avenue and 58th Street, New York City, to Buffalo, N.Y. The race was won by David Wolfe Bishop, who drove a Panhard automobile manufactured by Panhard-Levassor of Paris, France. The car carried one passenger and driver and was operated with gasoline. It weighed 2,800 pounds when fully equipped. The average speed was 15 miles an hour. There were 87 entries in the race with 80 starters. The race was not a speed or endurance test but a reliability test. The exact mileage was 464.2 miles, divided into day trips with stops at Poughkeepsie, Albany, Herkimer, Syracuse, Rochester, and Buffalo. (*Automobile Club of America—Five Hundred Mile Endurance Contest*)

Automobile race on a track was held September 7, 1896, at Narragansett Park, Cranston, R.I., as a feature of the Rhode Island State Fair and was witnessed by 40,000 spectators. Six gasoline and two electric automobiles raced, the winner being an electric Riker made by the Riker Electric Motor Car Co., Brook-

lyn, N.Y., with a speed of approximately 24 miles per hour. The driver was A. H. Whiting and the passenger was A. L. Riker, the owner. The time for the winner was 15 minutes 1¾ seconds. The race was for five heats of five miles each on a one-mile dirt track, one heat to be raced each afternoon of the Fair week. The prize offered was $1,000 each day.

Automobile race on a track (long distance) took place May 30, 1911, at the Indianapolis Speedway, Indianapolis, Ind., and was won by Ray Harroun, 29 years old, who drove a 16-cylinder Marmon "Wasp" over the 2½ mile oval course for a distance of 500 miles in 6 hours 41 minutes and 8 seconds, an average of 74.7 miles per hour. Only 38 of the 44 cars entered completed the race. One contestant was killed in an accident. The race was witnessed by 85,000 spectators.

Transcontinental automobile race started June 1, 1909, from New York City and ended June 22, 1909, at Seattle, Wash., scene of the Alaska-Yukon Pacific Exposition. Mayor George Brinton McClellan fired the starting gun. There were six entrants: an Acme, an Itala, a Shawmut, a Stearns, and two model T Fords. The Stearns failed to start. The race was won by Bert W. Scott and C. James Smith, who drove one of the Ford cars. They received a silver prize and a $2,000 award from H. Robert Guggenheim.

Transcontinental automobile race (for a time record) was won by Dwight B. Huss of Detroit, Mich., who left New York City May 8, 1905, in "Old Scout," an Oldsmobile runabout, and arrived at Portland, Ore., on June 21, 1905. He was accompanied by Milford Wigle of Detroit. (*Olds Motor Works—From Hell Gate to Portland*)

Vanderbilt Cup Race started at Hicksville, Long Island, N.Y., October 8, 1904, on a 10-lap course over a 30-mile circuit. Five Mercedes cars, three Panhards, two Fiats, two Pope-Toledos, and one each of Renault, De Dietrich, Clement-Bayard, Simplex, Packard, and Royal Tourist were entered. The race was concluded when two cars finished. The winner was George Heath in a Panhard, with average speed of 52.2 miles per hour. The first American winner of the Vanderbilt Cup Race was George H. Robertson in a 90 h.p. Locomobile on October 24, 1908, over a 23.46-mile circuit (distance 11 rounds, 258.06 miles) at the Motor Parkway, Long Island, N.Y. His average speed was 64.3 miles per hour; his time 4 hours, 48⅕ seconds.

AUTOMOBILE RACE TRACK
Automobile race track (asphalt covered) was opened on September 18, 1915, at the Narragansett Speedway, Cranston, R.I., where two world records were broken.

AUTOMOBILE RACE TRACK—*Cont.*

Automobile speedway (board track) was the Los Angeles Motordrome, near Playa del Rey, Calif., started January 30, 1910. It was made of wood, "pie pan" in shape, with a circumference of 5,281 feet and was under the direction of Fred Evans Moskovics. The motordrome was opened April 7, 1910, although trial races were held March 23, 1910.

AUTOMOBILE RIM. *See* Automobile tire: Demountable tire-carrying rim

AUTOMOBILE ROAD MAP. *See* Map: Automobile road map

AUTOMOBILE ROBBERY

Armored commercial car hold-up was staged March 11, 1927, by the "Flatheads" gang, about seven miles from Pittsburgh, Pa., on the Bethel Road on the way to Coverdale. An armored truck carrying a $104,250 payroll of the Pittsburgh Terminal Coal Company was dynamited while passing over a mine placed under the roadbed by the bandits. Five guards were badly injured.

AUTOMOBILE SCHOOL

See also Automobile driving course

Automobile school was established in 1903 by the Department of Education of the Young Men's Christian Association, Boston, Mass., to train chauffeurs, mechanics, and prospective owners of cars. The course consisted of lectures on the construction and operation of cars together with laboratory, machine shop, and repair work. Enrollment the first year was approximately 250 students.

Truck-driving training school was opened in June 1954 by the Bedford Motor-Transport Drivers Training Program, Inc., Bedford, Pa., and the first class graduated July 31, 1954.

AUTOMOBILE SERVICE STATION

Drive-in service station was opened by the Gulf Refining Company on December 1, 1913, at the intersection of Baum Boulevard and St. Clair Street, Pittsburgh, Pa. The station remained open all night and provided free crankcase service. Only thirty gallons of gasoline were sold the first day. Frank McLaughlin was the first manager.

AUTOMOBILE SHOW was held at Madison Square Garden, New York City, November 3 through November 10, 1900, under the auspices of the Automobile Club of America. There were 51 exhibitors, 31 of whom showed cars, and the others, accessories. A ramp was built to show the hill-climbing ability of the cars, and barrels were placed on the floor to show their steerability. Braking (stopping)

contests and starting contests were held. Admission to the "horseless horse show" was 50 cents.

AUTOMOBILE SPEEDING ARREST

Driver arrested for speeding was Jacob German, operator of Cab No. 1,565 for the Electric Vehicle Company, who was arrested May 20, 1899, by Bicycle Roundsman Schuessler for driving at a "breakneck speed" of twelve miles an hour on Lexington Avenue, New York City. German was booked and jailed in the East 22nd Street stationhouse.

AUTOMOBILE TIRE

Balloon tire production on a regular basis was introduced April 5, 1923, by the Firestone Tire and Rubber Company of Akron, Ohio. Earlier, on several occasions, thin-walled tires with small bead diameters were used experimentally or for special purposes. No prior commercial use, however, was made. (*India Rubber Review. February 1924*)

Clincher tire was manufactured in 1899 by B. F. Goodrich Company of Akron, Ohio, in sizes ranging from 28 x 2½ inches to 36 x 3 inches. The tire was of 19-ply construction.

Cord tire for commercial use was manufactured in 1910 by the B. F. Goodrich Company of Akron, Ohio.

Demountable tire-carrying rim was invented by Louis Henry Perlman of New York City, who applied for a patent May 21, 1906. Patent No. 1,052,270 was granted February 4, 1913. (*James Rood Doolittle—The Romance of the Automobile Industry*)

Non-skid tire of the modern type was patented by Stacy G. Carkhuff of the Firestone Tire and Rubber Company, Akron, Ohio. The patent was applied for on September 4, 1908, and granted on April 14, 1914, as No. 1,093,310. The angle formation of the edges of the raised portions molded on the tire provided against skidding in all directions. The tires were manufactured in Akron, Ohio. (*Cycle and Trade Journal. November 1, 1908*)

Pneumatic tire was made in 1895 by the Hartford Rubber Works, Hartford, Conn., owned by the Pope Manufacturing Company, now a subsidiary of the United States Rubber Company. It was used in March 1895 on the Duryea automobile that won the *Times-Herald* race November 28, 1895. (*Henry Clemens Pearson—Pneumatic Tires*)

Pneumatic tire patent was No. 488,494 awarded December 20, 1892, to Alexander T. Brown and George F. Stillman of Syracuse, N.Y.

THE FIRST

Rubber tire patent. *See* Rubber: Rubber tire patent

Synthetic rubber tire was commercially marketed by the B. F. Goodrich Company, Akron, Ohio, which exhibited on June 5, 1940, passenger car tires made of butadiene, synthesized from soap, gas, petroleum and air. These tires were trademarked "Ameripol."

Tubeless automobile tires were manufactured by the B. F. Goodrich Company, Akron, Ohio, which announced the manufacture on May 11, 1947. The tires automatically sealed themselves when punctured. They were marketed in Indiana, Kentucky, Ohio, and West Virginia before being offered for national distribution.

AUTOMOBILE TIRE CHAIN was invented by Harry D. Weed of Canastota, N.Y., who obtained patent No. 768,495 on August 23, 1904, on a "grip-tread for pneumatic tires." Weed licensed manufacture to the Weed Chain Tire Grip Company, which later was acquired by the American Chain and Cable Company.

AUTOMOBILE TRACK. *See* Automobile race track

AUTOMOBILE TRACTOR

Diesel engine tractor with an American-built engine was assembled May 1930 by the Cummins Engine Company, Columbus, Ind. A Cummins model U4-cylinder, 4½-by-6-inch bore and stroke diesel engine, which developed 50 h.p. at 1,000 revolutions per minute and weighed 1,400 pounds, was placed in an Allis-Chalmers Track Type Tractor.

Diesel-powered tractor offered on the market was the "Caterpillar" Diesel Tractor, manufactured by the Caterpillar Tractor Company, Peoria, Ill. It was a track-type, weighed 24,390 pounds, and developed 68 maximum drawbar horsepower. It was powered with a four-cylinder four-cycle diesel engine, the first of which was delivered in October 1931. (*Caterpillar Tractor Company, Peoria, Ill.*)

Endless chain tractor was invented by Charles Dinsmoor of Warren, Pa., who obtained patent No. 351,749 November 2, 1886, on a "vehicle." The endless chain tractor, or track-type tractor, did not become a commercial and practical reality until Benjamin Holt of the Holt Manufacturing Company of Stockton, Calif., produced such a tractor in 1906 and proceeded to build and sell them in quantities. (*Scientific American. December 18, 1886*)

Gasoline tractor was manufactured in 1892, by John Froelich of Froelich, Iowa, who shipped one of his tractors on September 6, 1892, to Langford, S.D., where it was employed from

THE FIRST

September 24, 1892, to November 16, 1892, in threshing. It had a Van Duzen vertical single-cylinder gasoline engine mounted on wooden beams to operate a J. I. Case threshing machine. Froelich formed the Waterloo Gasoline Traction Engine Company, Waterloo, Iowa, January 10, 1893, incorporated for $50,000, and later acquired by the John Deere Plow Company.

Steam tractor was made by Daniel Best of San Leandro, Calif., in 1886. One of his "Best" tractors was loaded on a car at San Leandro, February 8, 1889.

AUTOMOBILE TRANSCONTINENTAL TRIP

Gas turbine automobile to make a transcontinental trip was the "Turbine Special," a 1956 stock four-door Plymouth sedan, which left New York City on March 26, 1956, at 9:45 A.M. E.S.T. and arrived at Los Angeles, Calif., on March 30, 1956, at 11:55 A.M. E.S.T. covering 3,020 miles in 95 hours and 15 minutes elapsed time (74 hours and 19 minutes driving time). It was driven by two-man teams of turbine research engineers under the direction of George John Huebner, Jr., executive engineer in charge of research for the Chrysler Corporation.

Transcontinental automobile group tour was begun June 26, 1911, when ten Premier automobiles with forty occupants, a pilot car, and a truck, left Atlantic City, N.J., on an "ocean to ocean" tour. They arrived at Los Angeles, Calif., on August 10, 1911, and concluded the trip August 13, 1911, at Venice, Calif., covering 4,617.6 miles.

Transcontinental automobile trip by a nonprofessional driver in his own car was made by Dr. Horatio Nelson Jackson of Burlington, Vt., a physician, with Sewell K. Crocker of Seattle, Wash., as his mechanic. The car was a 20 h.p. $2,500 Winton, manufactured by the Winton Motor Carriage Company of Cleveland, Ohio. Jackson and Crocker left San Francisco, Calif., on May 23, 1903, and arrived in New York City on July 26, 1903. The average daily run was 125 miles. The trip consumed 63 days, of which 44 were spent traveling and 19 awaiting supplies. (*Motor World. July 23 and July 30, 1903*)

Transcontinental automobile trip by a woman was made by Alice Huyler Ramsey (Mrs. John R. Ramsey) of Hackensack, N.J., and Nettie R. Powell, Margaret Atwood, and Hermine Jahns, who left New York City on June 9, 1909, in a 30 h.p. Maxwell-Briscoe open car and arrived at San Francisco, Calif., on August 6, 1909. Mrs. Ramsey was president of the Women's Motoring Club of New York. (*Alice Huyler Ramsey—Veil, Duster and Tire Iron*)

THE FIRST

THE FIRST

AUTOMOBILE TRANSCONTINENTAL TRIP—*Continued*

Transcontinental family automobile trip requiring only a month was made by Mr. and Mrs. Jacob M. Murdock of Johnstown, Pa., and their children (Lillian, 18; Alice, 14; and Milton, 10), who left Los Angeles, Calif., on April 24, 1908, in a four-cylinder 30 h.p. Packard. They arrived in New York City on May 26, 1908, having covered 3,693.8 miles in 32 days, 5 hours, and 25 minutes. No distance was covered at night, on the five Sundays, on one rainy day, or on one day of visiting at Johnstown. Only one tire blowout occurred. The family was accompanied by a mechanic, Philip De May. (A similar trip made by a family in 1906 had required 175 days.)

AUTOMOBILE TRUCK

Automobile truck was designed and built in Pittsburgh in 1898 and 1899 by Louis Semple Clarke and his associates. They were organized as the Pittsburgh Motor Vehicle Company and later incorporated as the Autocar Company. The first truck was pictured and described in the Autocar's 1899 catalog as "a delivery wagon which can be made of any size or design, that will be fitted with five to eight horsepower motors. Complete with motors it will weigh from 900 to 1400 pounds—so simple in construction that any driver of ordinary intelligence can operate it with more safety than he could drive a horse." (*Twenty-Fifth Anniversary—Autocar Co.*)

Automobile truck completely streamlined from the ground up was introduced by the White Motor Company, Cleveland, Ohio, on September 4, 1935.

AUTOMOBILE TRUCKING SERVICE

Automobile inter-city trucking service began October 29, 1904, when William B. Chenoweth placed a six-cylinder motor truck in service between Colorado City, Colo., and Snyder, Tex.

Automobile trucking service by railroad motor coaches was inaugurated on January 8, 1923, by the Baltimore, Chesapeake and Atlantic Railway between Cambridge, Salisbury, and Tyaskin, Md., and served six stations.

AUTOMOBILE TWO-WAY RADIO. *See* Radio telephone: Two-way radio in an automobile

AUTOMOBILE WRECKING CRANE. *See* Crane: Automobile wrecking crane

AUTOMOTIVE ENGINEER (woman). *See* Woman: Woman automotive engineer

AUTOPSY

Autopsy is recorded to have taken place at Salem, Mass., in September 1639. "This boy was ill-disposed, and his master gave him unreasonable correction and used him ill in his diet. After the boy gate a bruise on his head, so as there appeared a fracture in his skull, being dissected after his death." Marmaduke Perry of Salem, Mass., was arraigned for the death of his apprentice. (*John Winthrop—History of New England*)

Autopsy and verdict of a coroner's jury was recorded in Maryland on September 24, 1657. The surgeon received his fee of "one hogshead of tobacco" for "dissecting and viewing the corpse" of a Negro slave supposed to have been murdered by his master.

AVIATION

See also

Air mail service	Aviation—Flights
Autogiro	(Transpacific)
Aviation—Airplane	Aviation—Flights
Aviation—Airplane	(World)
bombing	Aviation—Legislation
Aviation—Airport	Aviation—License
Aviation—Airship	Aviation—Magazine
Aviation—Aviator	Aviation—Parachute
Aviation—Exposi-	Aviation—Passenger
tions and Meets	Aviation—Races
Aviation—Flights	Aviation—School
Aviation—Flights	Balloon
(Transatlantic)	Glider
Aviation—Flights	Helicopter
(Transcontinental)	

"Ace." *See* Aviation—Aviator: American ace; Aviation—Aviator: Naval ace

Admiral in uniform to ride in an airplane. *See* Aviation—Passenger: Admiral in uniform to ride in an airplane

Advisory Committee for Aeronautics (National) was established by act of Congress (U.S.C. title 50, sec. 151), approved March 3, 1915. The membership, appointed by the President, consisted of two representatives each from the aviation sections of the War and Navy Departments, and one each from the Smithsonian Institution, Weather Bureau, Bureau of Standards, and eight others "acquainted with the needs of aeronautical science, either civil or military, or skilled in aeronautical engineering or its allied sciences." The first chairman was Brigadier General George Percival Scriven. Naval Constructor Holden Chester Richardson was secretary. The committee was appointed April 2, 1915, and the organization meeting held April 23, 1915. (*National Advisory Committee for U.S.—Aeronautics—Annual Report 1915*)

Aerial photography. *See* Photography: Demonstration of rapid aerial photography

THE FIRST

Aerial policewoman. *See* Police: Policewoman on the aerial force

Aeronautic international exposition. *See* Aviation—Expositions and meets: Aeronautic international exposition

Aeronautical Division of the United States War Department was authorized August 1, 1907, by Brigadier General James Allen, Chief Signal Officer of the Army. Captain Charles De Forest Chandler headed the division.

Aeronautical patent was granted October 28, 1799, to Moses McFarland of Massachusetts on a "federal balloon."

Aeronautical stowaway was William Ballantyne, a rigger, a member of the original crew of the British dirigible R-34. Ballantyne and two other men had been laid off in order to lighten the load for a transatlantic crossing to America, but Ballantyne stowed away on the flight. The R-34 left East Fortune, Scotland, 2 A.M., July 2, 1919, and arrived 9:54 A.M. at Roosevelt Field, Long Island, N.Y., July 6, 1919.

Aeronautical trophy was awarded by the *Scientific American* in New York City in 1908. It was valued at $2,500. It was to become the property of the flyer taking it three years in succession, the conditions for winning to be changed each year according to the progress of aviation. Flights were to be made before official witnesses at a pre-announced time and place. Glenn Hammond Curtiss was the first trophy winner. His first flight was made for the trophy on July 4, 1908, at Hammondsport, N.Y., at 7:30 P.M. in his "June Bug" at a speed of forty miles an hour. The "June Bug" was equipped with an eight-cylinder air-cooled Curtiss engine with a six-foot propeller on the rear of its crankshaft. (*Scientific American. July 18, 1908*)

Air combat of an American organization in World War I. *See* World War I: Air combat of an American organization in World War I

Air control municipal board was the San Diego, Calif., Board of Air Control which was created by Municipal Ordinance No. 11,485 on December 19, 1927. Prior to its formation aircraft operations were controlled by Municipal Ordinance No. 10,035, adopted June 25, 1925.

Air defense command. *See* Air defense command (U.S.)

Air mail stamps. *See* Postage stamp: Airmail stamps

THE FIRST

Air passenger-mile traffic volume to exceed first-class rail traffic volume was recorded in 1951, when scheduled United States domestic, territorial, and local service (feeder) carriers flew 10,556,139,000 revenue passenger-miles, compared with parlor and sleeping car traffic on class one railroads of 10,225,525,000 miles.

Air-rail passenger transcontinental service was inaugurated on June 14, 1929, by the New York Central Lines in cooperation with the Universal Air Lines and the Santa Fe Railroad. Planes were used only across the level Midwest, from Cleveland, Ohio, to Garden City, Kan., a distance of 1,181 miles.

Air service of the United States Army originally came into being on July 18, 1914, when the aviation section was created within the Signal Corps with an allotted strength of 60 officers and 260 men. The entire equipment consisted of six planes. War Department General Order 75 of December 14, 1913, prescribed a provisional aero squadron with 20 officers and 90 enlisted men.

Air squadron (complete) of American D.H.4 planes with Liberty motors crossed the German lines on an independent mission on August 7, 1918. All the planes returned safely. The first American-built De Havilland airplane with a Liberty motor took to the air in France on May 17, 1918.

Air squadron of the United States Army in World War I was Squadron No. 1, assigned to the front on April 8, 1918, for observation duty. The first combat action took place on April 12, 1918, when the First Aero Squadron was attacked while on a reconnaissance mission.

Air stewardess was Ellen Church, who made her first flight May 15, 1930, between San Francisco, Calif., and Cheyenne, Wyo., on United Air Lines.

Air stewardess (Negro) was Ruth Carol Taylor, a graduate nurse of Ithaca, N.Y., who made her first flight on February 11, 1958, from Ithaca to New York City on Mohawk Airlines.

Aircraft carrier. *See* Ship: Aircraft carrier

Aircraft owned by the Forest Service. *See* Forest service: Aircraft owned by the forest service

Airline to install rear-facing passenger seats aboard its planes was North American Airlines, Burbank, Calif. The first flight of a

THE FIRST

THE FIRST

AVIATION—*Continued*
plane equipped with these seats was made from Burbank, Calif., to La Guardia Field, New York City, on June 1, 1953.

Airplane commutation tickets were placed on sale May 1, 1929, by the Colonial Division of American Airways, which inaugurated commutation tickets on the Newark-Boston line. These commutation tickets were for ten and fifty trips.

Airplane diesel engine was manufactured by the Packard Motor Car Company of Detroit, Mich., in 1928. The engine was 225 h.p. and weighed 510 pounds. It was used in a Stinson Detroiter airplane and made its first flight September 19, 1928.

Airplane fatality occurred on September 17, 1908, at Fort Myer, Arlington Heights, Va., when a propeller blade struck an overhead wire because of the wearing through of a fitting to which the guy wire was attached. Thomas Etholen Selfridge, U.S. Army, was killed as a result of a skull fracture and Orville Wright received multiple hip and leg fractures.

Airplane fatality (woman) was Julie Clark of Denver, Colo., who was killed June 17, 1912, at the Illinois State Fair Grounds, Springfield, Ill., when her Curtiss biplane struck the limb of a tree and turned turtle while circling the field at 40 m.p.h. Her death was the 151st in a heavier-than-air craft.

Airplane "fly-it-yourself" system was started by the Saunders Drive It Yourself Company on September 15, 1929, at the Fairfax Airport, Kansas City, Kan. The idea was not profitable and operations ceased on May 15, 1930.

Airplane high-speed tank to test airplanes was designed in 1929 and completed May 1931 by the National Advisory Committee for Aeronautics, Washington, D.C. It was the first towing tank in which the towing carriage ran with pneumatic wheels on steel rails, and in which very large models could be tested at relatively high speeds. The dimensions were 2,020 feet (length) by 24 feet (width) by 12 feet (depth). Towing speeds up to 50 miles an hour could be obtained.

Airplane human pick-up was accomplished September 5, 1943, when the pilot, Captain Norman Rintoul, picked up Paratrooper First Lieutenant Alexis Doster of Washington, D.C., with an airplane from which a hook was suspended from a 185-foot, half-inch-thick nylon rope, at the Clinton County Army Air Base at Wilmington, Ohio. An electric reeling motor weighing 200 pounds was used to hoist the pick-up.

Airplane in actual military operation by the United States Army was used in March 1916 when the 1st Aero Squadron, composed of 11 officers, 82 enlisted men, 1 civilian mechanic, and 8 JN airplanes, was ordered to proceed to Casa Grandes, Mexico, for active duty with the punitive expedition under General John Joseph Pershing. Airplanes had been previously used, however, in February 1913, when the Army Aviation School, then at Augusta, Ga., was transferred to Texas City, Tex., for the purpose of providing aviation for ground troops stationed on the Mexican border to prevent disorders. (*Records in Office of the Chief of the Air Corps, War Department, Washington, D.C.*)

Airplane loop the loop. *See* Aviation—Flights: Airplane loop the loop

Airplane merchandise shipment was delivered to the Morehouse-Martens Company of Columbus, Ohio, by pilot Philip Parmelee. Five bolts of "Rajah" silk manufactured by Rogers and Thompson of New York City, valued at $600, were shipped from New York City to Dayton and taken from there to Columbus by the plane, which landed at the old Columbus Driving Park. The silk was cut up and stamped, "This silk is a piece of the first merchandise ever carried in an airplane—Dayton to Columbus, November 7, 1910." The distance of 60 miles was made in 56 minutes. The delivery was a publicity stunt for which $5,000 was paid. The shipping rate was $71.42 a pound.

Airplane moving picture show was given on October 8, 1929, by Transcontinental Air Transport, Inc., in a Ford transport plane 5,000 feet in the air. A current newsreel and two cartoon comedies were shown with the cooperation of the Universal Newsreel Company and the Duograph Company. The machine was installed by J. Frankenberg, its originator. The projector weighed about eight pounds, the entire apparatus together with batteries less than thirty-four pounds. A delicate filament lamp specially designed to operate on low voltage was unaffected by the vibration of the motors.

Airplane rescue at sea was effected January 30, 1911, by the destroyer "Terry," which picked up James A. D. McCurdy within four minutes after his 50 m.p.h. biplane en route from Key West, Fla., to Camp Columbia, Havana, Cuba, landed on the sea 10 miles from Havana as a result of a faulty oil connection. The plane's pontoons kept it afloat. The pilot had been in the air 2 hours and 8 minutes and had made the first sea flight out of sight of land.

Airplane rescue at sea effected by another airplane was made by Hugh Robinson on August 14, 1911, over Lake Michigan. Pilot

THE FIRST

Rene Simon dived down in his monoplane to wave to some motorboats. Unable to rise, he crashed into Lake Michigan. Robinson, in a Curtiss hydroplane, flew over to Simon and found him in his floating plane smoking a cigar. Robinson hailed several people in motorboats, and they towed Simon and his monoplane to the shore.

Airplane sleeping berths were introduced by American Airways of Chicago, Ill., in March 1933. The berths were made by folding two of the plane's chairs to form a cot. The first airplane with nonconvertible sleeping berths was placed in service October 5, 1933, by Eastern Air Transport between Atlanta, Ga., and New York City. The plane was a Curtiss-Wright Condor and was designed to contain eight berths and five seats, but on the initial trip only two berths were installed, an upper and a lower. The berths were 6 feet 5 inches long and 2 feet 4 inches wide. The first passengers to occupy the berths were Captain Edward Vernon Rickenbacker and Alexander Strong. The plane was equipped in the company's shops at the Atlanta Municipal Airport, where the first trip started.

Airplane take-off from a hotel roof was made by a Curtiss biplane at 2:35 P.M., June 11, 1912. In a light rain Silas Christoferson took off from the Multnomah Hotel, Portland, Ore., on a 170-foot board runway built over obstructions. Christoferson, who had not yet won his pilot's license, crossed the Willamette and Columbia rivers on the flight.

Airplane tank discharger was patented by John Hays Hammond, Jr., Gloucester, Mass., who received patent No. 2,038,998, April 28, 1936, on a "gas tank discharger for airplanes." A cylinder of compressed carbon dioxide cut off the supply of gasoline to the carburetor and dumped it into space.

Airplane to land on the White House lawn was the "Moth," piloted by Harry N. Atwood, who landed on July 14, 1911, about 3 P.M., and was presented by President William Howard Taft with the gold medal of the Aero Club of Washington. Atwood circled the Capitol and the Library of Congress and flew down Pennsylvania Avenue and over the Washington Monument and the Executive Mansion.

"Airplane train." *See* Aviation—Flights: "Airplane train"

Airways illumination was attempted August 21, 1923, when forty-two landing fields on the Chicago-Iowa City-Omaha-North Platte-Cheyenne route were lit by thirty six-inch electric arc beacons which made complete revolutions three times a minute. The lights were of 5,300,000 candle power and were visible for fifty miles.

THE FIRST

Ambulance air service to transport sick people by airplane to hospitals was organized on October 21, 1929, by the Colonial Flying Service and the Scully Walton Ambulance Company of New York.

Automatic pilot, an instrument which can be set to take over and relieve the pilot in flying modern aircraft, was developed by William Green and used on a Gates-Day Standard J5 airplane on October 8, 1929, at Cleveland, Ohio in a Pennsylvania-Central Airlines (now Capital Airlines) plane flown by Captain Trow Sebree from Cleveland to Pittsburgh, Pa.

Aviation gasoline. *See* Gasoline: Aviation gasoline

Aviation trainer was the Link Trainer, an aircraft-like mechanical-electrical device complete with hooded cockpit, controls, and a full complement of flight instruments. The trainer behaves like an airplane but does not leave the ground. It was invented by Edwin Albert Link. The first sale was made in 1929 to the Link Flying School, Binghamton, N.Y. It was adopted by the U.S. Navy in 1931, and by the U.S. Army Air Corps in 1934.

Aviation trainer (jet) was the C-11, completed March 1949 by Link Aviation, Inc., Binghamton, N.Y., and shipped to Air Materiel Command Headquarters, Wright-Patterson Air Field Base, Dayton, Ohio, on March 16, 1949. Final inspection was accomplished and the trainer approved and accepted by the U.S. Air Force on October 3, 1949. Flight evaluation tests were held November 15-18, 1949. The trainer was put into service at Tyndall Air Force Base, Panama City, Fla., in September 1950. Production models of this trainer weighed 6,840 pounds and were 17 feet 9 inches long.

Battleship sunk by an airplane was the "Ostfriesland," a former German battleship, which was sunk July 21, 1921, near Hampton Roads, Va., in a bombing demonstration conducted by General William Mitchell. Three direct hits were made out of five attempts, each of the five bombs weighing 1,000 pounds. Later, the Martin bombers dropped seven 2,000-pound bombs, and sank the battleship within twenty-one minutes after the attack. Near misses were preferred to direct hits since the former would shake open the seams and cause the battleship to topple. These seven bombs caused the dreadnaught to turn on her port side and sink stern first.

Caterpillar Club. *See* Caterpillar club: Caterpillar club member

Civil air patrol (U.S.). *See* Civil air patrol (U.S.)

AVIATION—*Continued*

Coast Guard air station was established March 24, 1920, at Morehead City, N.C. It operated until July 1, 1921, when it was decommissioned because of lack of funds.

Coast Guard aviation unit was formed under Act of Congress August 29, 1916 (39 Stat.L.601) which authorized the Secretary of the Treasury "to establish, equip, and maintain aviation stations, not exceeding ten in number, for the purpose of saving life and property along the coasts of the United States and at sea contiguous thereto."

Floating seaplane ramp (municipally owned) was launched August 15, 1934, at the Brooklyn Navy Yard, N.Y. It was formally dedicated September 5, 1934, by Bernard Seymour Deutsch, president of the Board of Aldermen of the City of New York. The New York and Suburban Airlines, Inc., a subsidiary of the National Aviation Corporation, operated the Bellanca Airbus on floats furnishing a commuting service between the downtown area and Oyster Bay and adjacent points on Long Island, and week-end service to Martha's Vineyard and Nantucket, Mass. The first passenger flight was made July 16, 1934, from Oyster Bay to the foot of Wall Street in 19½ minutes. The landing was made at an improvised float.

Flying medical clinic. *See* Medical clinic: Flying medical clinic

Forest service aerial patrol. *See* Forest service: Forest service aerial patrol

Gyroscope automatic stabilization for aircraft that was successful was demonstrated by Lawrence B. Sperry and Lieutenant Patrick Nelson Lynch Bellinger in August 1913 at Lake Keuka, Hammondsport, N.Y., in a Curtiss-F boat. Stabilization was longitudinal and lateral.

Hydroplane commercial line service started January 1, 1914, between St. Petersburg, Fla., and Tampa, Fla. The planes were built by the Benoist Aircraft Company and were operated by the St. Petersburg-Tampa Airboat Line. The first plane was piloted by Antony (Tony) Jannus. Mayor Abram Cump Pheil of St. Petersburg, Fla., paid $400 for the first round trip. Noel Mitchell paid $175 for the second trip. Two round-trip flights were made daily. The regular round-trip fare was $10. The planes flew 80 feet above the water across Tampa Bay, an air distance of 18 miles in 23 minutes.

Hydroplane commercial line service (international) was established by Aeromarine Airways, Inc., on November 1, 1920, from Key West, Fla., to Havana, Cuba. The service employed two three-plane flying boats. The fare was $50. Mail was also carried.

Jet drone target missile was a Ryan Firebee pilotless jet plane made by the Ryan Aeronautical Company, San Diego, Calif., and first flown April 23, 1954, at Holloman Air Development Center, Alamogordo, N.M. It was powered by a 1,000-pound thrust jet engine (Continental Turbojet J69-T19) and was able to fly at a speed of more than 600 miles per hour at altitudes up to 42,500 feet. It was air- or ground-launched, pilotless, and flown by electronic remote control from a ground station. It was 17 feet 3 inches long, and 5 feet 10 inches high, had a wing span of 11 feet 2 inches, and weighed 1,848 pounds gross.

Moving picture from an airplane. *See* Moving picture: Moving picture from an airplane

Physiological research laboratory of the U.S. Army Air Corps was completed January 1, 1937, at the Air Corps Materiel Division, Wright Field, Dayton, Ohio. Its purpose was to investigate and devise means to alleviate the distressing symptoms occurring during air travel and to furnish information to the engineer which would enable him to provide conditions aloft most favorable for the efficient functioning of the pilot and observer. (*Aviation Medicine. June 1937*)

Propeller blade of hollow steel made from a single piece of steel tubing was placed in mass production by the American Propeller Corporation, Toledo, Ohio, in June 1942. The process was developed at the Lycoming Division of the Aviation Corporation, Williamsport, Pa. Over 80,000 hollow steel propeller blades were made from tubing in three years.

Radio broadcast from an airplane. *See* Radio broadcast: Radio broadcast sent from an airplane

Radio telephone communication between the ground and an airplane. *See* Radio telephone: Radio telephone communication between the ground and an airplane

Refueling attempt in mid-air was made at Rockwell Field, Coronado, Calif., on June 27, 1923, at 4:43 A.M. in a De Havilland plane piloted by Captain Lowell Herbert Smith, Air Corps, with Lieutenant John Paul Richter, Air Corps, as receiver of fuel. A 40-foot steel-wire-encased hose was lowered to the fuel-receiving plane. They refueled in flight and remained aloft 37 hours, 15 minutes, and 14⅘ seconds. (*Records in Headquarters Rockwell Field, Office of the Commanding Officer. Coronado, Calif.*)

THE FIRST

Secretary of the Air (U.S.) *See* Defense department (U.S.)

Sermon from an airplane was delivered Sunday, April 16, 1922, by Belvin W. Maynard, "the Flying Parson," an ordained Baptist minister, who preached a sermon broadcast from his Fokker airplane. Listeners were asked to donate to the Veterans Mountain Camp, Tupper Lake, N.Y.

Telegram dispatched from an aerial station. *See* Telegram: Telegram dispatched from an aerial station

War night-flying scout group was the 185th Pursuit Squadron, which went to the front on October 5, 1918, assigned to the Meuse-Argonne sector in France.

Wedding in an airplane. *See* Wedding: Airplane wedding

Women's Auxiliary Ferrying Squadron (WAFS, later WASPS) to ferry training and liaison aircraft from factory to domestic airfields was under the supervision of Mrs. Nancy Harkness Love of Newcastle, Del., whose appointment was announced September 10, 1942, by Lieutenant General Henry Harley Arnold. The pilots received Civil Service status and $3,000 a year.

AVIATION—AIRPLANE

See also

Autogiro	Glider
Aviation—Airship	Helicopter
Balloon	

Airplane (commercial) stabilized was the Curtiss Condor No. 5, built in 1931 by the Curtiss Aeroplane and Motor Company in its factory at Garden City, Long Island, N.Y. The plane was powered by two liquid-cooled twelve-cylinder engines, 650 h.p., and was equipped with both a Sperry stabilizer and an automatic pilot which were placed in a box under the pilot's seat. The airplane carried eighteen passengers, two pilots, and a hostess, and was operated by the Eastern Air Transport airlines between New York City and Miami, Fla.

Airplane equipped with radio to cross the Atlantic ocean was the tri-motored Fokker monoplane "The America," which took off from Roosevelt Field, N.Y., at 5:24 A.M. on June 29, 1927, with a four-man crew, Commander Richard Evelyn Byrd, pilots Bert Acosta and Lieutenant Bernt Balchen, and radioman Lieutenant George O. Noville. The plane landed July 1, 1927, near the shore at Ver-sur-Mer, France, after a 4,200-mile flight, in 43 hours and 21 minutes.

THE FIRST

Airplane fatality. *See* Aviation: Airplane fatality

Airplane (heavier-than-air) to make any long sustained flight under its own power was Samuel Pierpont Langley's model No. 5, which was tested May 6, 1896, on the shores of the Potomac River. This unmanned model "aerodrome" weighed 26 pounds, was 16 feet in length, and had four cambered single-tier wings, each about 14 feet from tip to tip. It was driven by a one-horsepower steam engine. It was catapulted from a platform 20 feet above the water and flew a distance of about ¾ mile, remaining aloft 1½ minutes during one of its flights. As the fuel was exhausted, the plane descended gently to the water. It was picked up, dried off, refueled, and relaunched the same afternoon. Langley predicted that airplanes would be used to carry men, but his friends and the press scoffed. (*Nature—May 28, 1896*)

Airplane outfitted with a machine gun was a Wright biplane flown at College Park, Md., May 7, 1912, by pilot Lieutenant Thomas de Witt Milling. Charles de Forest Chandler of the Army Signal Corps was in charge of a Lewis machine gun. (*Scientific American. July 6, 1912*)

Airplane post office. *See* Post office: Airplane post office

Airplane purchased by the United States Government was a Wright biplane which was given its first official flight on July 30, 1909, and accepted from Orville and Wilbur Wright of Dayton, Ohio, on August 2, 1909. The purchase price was $25,000, but a bonus of $5,000 was given because the specified speed, 40 miles an hour in still air, was exceeded. The plane, built at Dayton, Ohio, was powered by a 25 h.p. motor and averaged a fraction over 42 miles an hour. It was known as "Miss Columbia." Lieutenant Frank Purdy Lahm and Wilbur Wright made the first flight under government ownership at College Park, Md., on October 8, 1909.

See also Aviation—Aviator: Army aviator to solo

Airplane smoke screen. *See* Smoke screen

Airplane sold commercially was the "Gold Bug," delivered by Glenn Hammond Curtiss June 16, 1909, to the New York Aeronautical Society at Hammondsport, N.Y., for $5,000. Flying instructions were given to two members. (*Chelsea Curtis Fraser—Famous American Flyers*)

Airplane telecast. *See* Television—Telecast: Airplane telecast (network)

AVIATION—AIRPLANE—Continued

Airplane to receive national acclaim was constructed by the Wright brothers. On December 17, 1903, at Kitty Hawk, N.C., with Orville Wright at the controls, this machine "raised itself into the air in full flight, sailed forward without reduction in speed, and finally landed at a point as high as that from which it started." The plane, with the 179-pound four-cylinder engine, weighed 745 pounds. The engine made 1200 r.p.m. and developed 12 h.p. The plane was launched from a monorail after a 35- to 40-foot run. Four flights were made against a 21-mile wind. The average speed developed was 31 miles. The longest flight was 852 feet in 59 seconds. (*Century Magazine.* *1908*)

Airplane "train." *See* Aviation—Flights: "Airplane train"

Airplane used by a newspaper was a Canadian Curtiss 75-mile-an-hour biplane, piloted by Lieutenant William D. Tipton, which was placed in service by the *Evening Sun* of Baltimore, Md., on September 1, 1920, when it reported a railroad wreck at Back River. Two days later it flew out to sea and located the submarine S-5 in trouble off the Delaware Capes.

Airplane with eight engines was the Hercules, a Hughes Flying Boat, built by Howard Hughes at Culver City, Calif., and first test-flown by him at Long Beach harbor, Calif., on November 2, 1947, when it flew a mile at an altitude of about 70 feet. It was designed to carry 700 troops, or 350 stretcher cases, with doctors, nurses, and medical supplies, or a 60-ton tank, assembled and ready for action upon landing.

Bomber (all-wing jet) was the Northrop Flying Wing XB-49, which had its taxi trial, October 21, 1947, at Northrop Field, Hawthorne, Calif. It had a span of 172 feet and weighed in excess of 88,000 pounds. The eight-jet XB developed thrust equivalent to 32,000 h.p. "Clean" design obtained by eliminating the drag-producing tail surfaces and fuselage boosted the XB-49's speed and range over that of a comparable conventional model.

Bomber with the Flying Wing design was the Northrop XB35, built by Northrop Aircraft, Inc. which took off from Northrop Field, Hawthorne, Calif., on June 25, 1946, and made a successful flight of 85 miles to the U.S. Army Air Force Base at Muroc, Calif. It weighed 209,000 pounds in gross overload condition and had a 172-foot wing span with a 53-foot overall length. It had an operational range of about 10,000 miles and could carry 56,000 pounds of bombs.

Catapulted airplane. *See* Aviation—Flights: Airplane catapulted

Child born in an airplane. *See* Births: Child born in an airplane

Cow flown in an airplane. *See* Animals: Cow flown in an airplane

Dirigible. *See* Aviation—Airship: Dirigible

Fighter airplane was the Kirkham Fighter, designed by Charles Kirkham, manufactured by the Curtiss Aeroplane and Motor Company, Garden City, Long Island, N.Y., and tested at Garden City, August 19, 1918, when it attained a speed of 162 miles an hour. It established a world's record on October 11, 1918, when it made a ceiling climb of 26,300 feet.

Fighter airplane carrying a cannon was the P-39 (Airacobra), tested by pilot Jimmy Taylor at Wright Field, Dayton, Ohio, on April 6, 1938. It was built by the Bell Aircraft Corporation at the Niagara Falls Airport, Niagara Falls, N.Y. The armament consisted of a 37mm. cannon located on the fuselage centerline, the gun barrel projecting through the reduction gear box and propeller hub; two .50 caliber machine guns in the forward fuselage; and four .30 caliber free-firing machine guns installed in pairs in each outer wing panel. (*Aviation. May 1943*)

Gas turbine propeller-driven airplane was the XP-81, a fighter, designed and produced by the Vultee Field, Downey, Calif., division of Consolidated Vultee Aircraft Corporation and first flight tested February 11, 1945, at an Army Air Force base in Muroc, Calif. Its wing span was 50 feet 6 inches and its fuselage 44 feet 8 inches long. It weighed 19,500 pounds and traveled at a speed greater than 500 miles an hour. In the nose was a propeller drive gas turbine type TG-100, built by the General Electric Company. Between the cockpit and the tail was a I-40 jet engine, also built by the General Electric Company.

Hydroplane that was successful was the "Flying Fish," which was flown by its inventor, Glenn Hammond Curtiss, at San Diego, Calif., on January 26, 1911. On September 29, 1909, Wilbur Wright had flown from Governors Island, N.Y., to and around the Statue of Liberty, and back, a distance of 19½ miles, in an airplane that carried a canoe.

Hydroplane flight to and from a ship. *See* Aviation—Flights: Hydroplane flight to and from a ship

Hydroplane of stainless steel built for commercial purposes was the Sea Bird, de-

THE FIRST

THE FIRST

signed and constructed by Fleetwings, Inc., Bristol, Pa., with welding apparatus especially designed by the company. It was first flown experimentally by Daniel Johnson Brimm, test pilot, off the Delaware River at Bristol, Pa., on September 4, 1936. It weighed 2,320 pounds empty (gross load 3,425 pounds) and had a cruising speed of 135 m.p.h. (The Edward G. Budd Manufacturing Company of Philadelphia, Pa., had built an experimental stainless steel plane in 1931 duplicating a Savois Marchetti design already existent in wood.)

Hydroplane with a multi-engine was the "America" financed by Rodman Wanamaker and christened June 22, 1914, at Hammondsport, N.Y. It had two Curtiss 1,250 r.p.m., 90 h.p. engines and attained a speed of 65 m.p.h. The "America" weighed 3,000 pounds empty (5,200 pounds fully loaded) and had five watertight compartments. Length over-all was 34 feet. The upper wing span was 74 feet, lower wing span 46 feet. A third motor was added in July 1914 but was rejected.

Jet airplane to land on a ship was the FD-1 Phantom piloted by Lieutenant Commander James J. Davison, which landed July 21, 1946, on the deck of the carrier "Franklin D. Roosevelt," 60 miles east of Cape Henry, Va. The plane was airborne after a 360-foot run. It was designed and built by the McDonnell Aircraft Corporation of St. Louis, Mo., and had a service ceiling over 7 miles and a top speed in excess of 500 m.p.h. It was a single-seat, low-wing monoplane of conventional monocoque design, with twin axial-flow Westinghouse turbo-jet engines built into the wing roots. Total weight with full combat load was less than 10,000 pounds. The wings folded electrically and when rigged for stowage the plane was 16 feet wide.

Jet magnesium airplane was an F-80C Shooting Star, flown June 11, 1955, at Mitchel Air Force Base, Long Island, N.Y., by Captain Richard Otto Ransbottom. It was designed and manufactured for the Air Research and Development Command of the U.S. Air Force by East Coast Aeronautics, Inc., Pelham Manor, N.Y., a subsidiary of the Barnum Steel Corporation.

Jet propelled airplane designed and built in the United States was the XP-59, an Airacomet, built by the Bell Aircraft Corporation, Buffalo, N.Y., and flown for the first time October 1, 1942, at a secret testing base in Muroc, Calif., by Robert Morris Stanley. It was rated over 400 m.p.h. and in excess of 40,000 feet. The higher the altitude (up to a certain maximum altitude) the faster it flew. It employed two turbo-jet engines built by General Electric Company, Lynn, Mass., from designs of the British inventor Group Captain Frank Whittle. The fuel was generally kerosene, although anything that burns could be used. There was no propeller.

Jet propelled fighter plane to be accepted by the U.S. Army Air Forces for combat purposes was the P-80 Shooting Star, designed by Clarence L. Johnson, and constructed in 143 days by the Lockheed Aircraft Corporation, Burbank, Calif. It had a wing span of 38 feet 10½ inches, an over-all length of 34 feet 6 inches, and a height of 11 feet 4 inches. The first flight was made January 1944, and in February 1945, it was announced by the Army as perfected for actual combat.

Jet propelled fighter plane (four-engine) for the U.S. Army was the Curtiss XP-87, built by the Curtiss-Wright Corporation, Columbus, Ohio, and tested September 15, 1947. It had a 60-foot wing span and an approximate over-all length of 65 feet. The engines, built by the Westinghouse Electric Corporation, were placed in pairs in housings built into the wings. The plane was tested in flight at Muroc, Calif., on March 1, 1948.

Jet propelled landing on an aircraft carrier was made November 6, 1945 by Ensign Jake C. West in an FR-1 Fireball on the escort carrier "Wake Island," off San Diego, Calif. The Fireball, a Ryan-built Navy fighter plane, was powered by both a turbo-jet and a conventional reciprocating engine, which normally uses its reciprocating power plant for take-off and landing, switching over to the jet as either an exclusive or supplementary propulsive force once it is in the air. As West was landing, the reciprocating engine power failed and he landed using jet power.

Jet propulsion four-engine bomber was the XB-45, built by North American Aviation, Inc., Los Angeles, Calif., which made its test flight March 6, 1947, at Muroc, Calif. It was flown by George Krebs. It had a wing span of 89½ feet and was 74 feet long and 25 feet high from ground to tail top. The engines were arranged in pairs in single nacelles in each wing.

Jet transport commercial airplane built in the United States was the Boeing jet Stratoliner Model 707, first tested July 15, 1954, by Alvin M. ("Tex") Johnston at Renton, Wash., where it was built by the Boeing Airplane Company. It had four Pratt & Whitney J-57 engines with more than 10,000 pounds thrust. It weighed 190,000 pounds and cost about $20 million. It was designed to carry about 150 passengers across the Atlantic Ocean at a speed of 550 m.p.h. The first transport was delivered August 16, 1958, to Pan American Airways.

Letter to encircle the world by commercial air mail. *See* Postal service; Letter to encircle the world by commercial air mail

AVIATION—AIRPLANE—*Continued*

Molded plywood airplane was the "Whistling Bill," a two-place fighter, built in 1918 by the Curtiss Aeroplane and Motor Company, Garden City, Long Island, N.Y. The fuselage was made of four 3/32-inch longitudinal sheets of Haskelite, three-ply birch plywood, steamed and formed to contour in a concrete die. The wings were not of plywood. The cooling radiators were of the tubular type, located on the sides of the fuselage. The plane was of 400 h.p. carried two .30 caliber machine guns, and had a sea-level speed of 170 m.p.h. It was designed by Charles Kirkham.

Monoplane (American) was the Walden III, invented by Dr. Henry W. Walden and test-flown at Mineola, Long Island, N.Y., on December 9, 1909. It was equipped with a 1909 Anzani three-cylinder motor which developed 22 h.p. and flew at a speed of 52 m.p.h. *(U.S. Naval Institute Proceedings. March 1934)*

Naval airplane was the Curtiss Amphibian Triad, delivered July 1911. It was equipped with dual controls permitting two pilots to operate them in flight. It was tested at Lake Keuka, Hammondsport, N.Y. The first naval pilots were Lieutenants Theodore Gordon Ellyson and John Henry Towers. Funds were obtained from a $25,000 congressional appropriation passed March 4, 1911 (36 Stat.L.1268), "for experimental work in the development of aviation for naval purposes."

Naval patrol bomber launched like a ship was the 140,000-pound Glenn L. Martin Company's XPB2M-1, christened "Mars," November 8, 1941, in Baltimore, Md., by Mrs. Artemus Land Gates, wife of the Assistant Secretary for the Navy for Air. The keel was laid August 22, 1940. The bomber had a 200-foot wing span and four engines each of 2,000 h.p. It was the first flying boat accorded Navy keel-laying and launching ceremonies.

Photograph from an airplane. *See* Photograph: Photograph from an airplane

Plastic bonded airplane to be awarded a Type certificate by the Civil Aeronautics Administration was an open two-place tandem low-wing full-cantilever type monoplane built by the Timm Aircraft Corporation, Van Nuys, Calif., in July 1940. It was approved April 5, 1941. It was a training plane, the fuselage, wings, and all control surfaces of which were fabricated from a special material formed by binding several laminations of plywood with liquid plastic and pressing in a precision mold to the exact contour and size desired. The entire airplane structure contained less than 7 per cent aluminum.

Postage stamp to picture an airplane. *See* Postage stamp: Postage stamps to picture an airplane

Radio message sent from an airplane. *See* Radio broadcast: Radio broadcast sent from an airplane

Rocket airplane (military) was the MX-324, built by the Northrop Aircraft, Inc., Hawthorne, Calif., and flown July 5, 1944, by Harry Crosby, pilot. It had a prone cockpit in which the pilot lay flat to withstand the pull. An Aerojet XCAL-200 rocket motor was used with monoethylaniline as fuel. The craft was known as the Rocket Ram. It was originally tested as a glider on October 2, 1943, by John Myers.

See also Aviation—Flights: Airplane to exceed the speed of sound

Rocket plane built in the United States designed for supersonic flight to carry a human was the Army XS-1, manufactured by the Bell Aircraft Corporation, Buffalo, N.Y. The craft, which was an orange-colored needle-nose plane 31 feet long with a 28-foot wingspan and a 210-pound engine, carried fuel that incorporated oxygen. After a series of glide tests, the XS-1 made its first powered flight on December 8, 1946, when it was released from a B-29 bomber at 25,000 feet. It remained aloft 19 minutes, seven of which were under power. The test pilot, Chalmers ("Slick") Goodlin of New Alexandria, Pa., landed the plane at Muroc Army Air Field, Calif.

Skywriting. *See* Skywriting

Symphony to call for an airplane propeller. *See* Symphony: Symphonic work to call for an airplane propeller

Telecast from an airplane. *See* Television —Telecast: Airplane telecast (network)

Telephone communication between the ground and an airplane. *See* Radio telephone: Radio telephone communication between the ground and an airplane

Three-motor airplane was an eight-passenger Curtiss Eagle which made its first public flight on July 24, 1919, at Garden City, Long Island, N.Y., developing a top speed of 99 m.p.h. It had three 150 h.p. K-6 engines, a wing span of 61 feet 4 inches, and a wing area of 770 square feet. Its gross weight was 7,450 pounds. On October 29, 1919, at Washington, D.C., this machine made 82 flights and carried 496 people, mostly prominent government officials.

Transatlantic hydroplane flight. *See* Aviation—Flights (transatlantic): Transatlantic hydroplane flight

THE FIRST

Transatlantic robot pilotless airplane was the Skymaster, a U.S. Army C-54, four-engine military transport which took off from Stephensville, Newfoundland, on September 22, 1947, and arrived 10 hours and 15 minutes later at Brise Norton, four miles from London, England (2,400 miles). The robot piloting device was not touched after the throttles were opened to start the airplane. The plane carried fourteen persons, including Colonel James Milligan Gillespie, the pilot and commander.

Transport airplane designed especially for trans-oceanic service was the Pan American Clipper, a 19-ton flying boat powered by four Hornet air-cooled, geared, and super-charged engines, each developing 750 h.p. It was an all-metal monoplane, 68 feet long, with a wing-spread of 118 feet 2 inches. It carried within its hull and in the wings and pontoons a fuel load of more than 8½ tons, adequate for a flight range of 3,500 miles. Under the command of Captain Edwin C. Musick, the first Clipper took off April 16, 1935, at 6:50 P.M. from San Francisco, Calif., and arrived 12:59 P.M. on April 17, 1935, at Pearl Harbor, Honolulu, covering 2,301 air miles in 18 hours, 39 minutes. The return trip was begun April 22, 1935, at 8:59 P.M. from Pearl Harbor, and the transport landed at Alameda Airport, Calif., April 23, 1935, at 5:59 P.M.

Turbine propeller light-airplane was flown November 5, 1952, at Wichita, Kan., by Hank Waring, who piloted the XL-19B Bird Dog, built by the Cessna Aircraft Company, Wichita. It was powered by a 250-pound Boeing turbine engine with a rating of 210 h.p on take-off and a cruise rating of 175 h.p. It utilized the exhaust gases from the jet power-producing section to drive a propeller shaft through a second-stage turbine wheel and a reduction gear system.

Twin-engine pressurized airplane was the Convair Liner, a 300-mile-an-hour, 40-passenger airliner, equipped with two 2,400 h.p. Pratt and Whitney engines. Its wing span was 91 feet 9 inches; its length 74 feet 8 inches; its height 26 feet 11 inches. The Convair's jet exhaust propulsion principle was used for added speed. The plane was produced at the Consolidated Vultee Aircraft Corporation's San Diego, Calif., plant. It was first test-flown on March 16, 1947.

Two-way conversation between a glider and the land. *See* Radio telephone: Two-way conversation between a glider and the land

AVIATION—AIRPLANE BOMBING
See also World war II (American bombing mission)

Airplane bombing experiment was made June 30, 1910, by Glenn Hammond Curtiss at

THE FIRST

Hammondsport, N.Y. Curtiss released lead missiles attached to colored streamers from a height of 50 feet upon a target 500 feet by 90 feet. He scored ten hits and four misses. (*Aeronautics. August 1910*)

Airplane bombing experiment with explosives was carried out by Philip O. Parmelee and Lieutenant Myron Sidney Crissy upon a test range at San Francisco, Calif., January 7-25, 1911.

Airplane bombing in the United States occurred on November 12, 1926, during a Prohibition feud between rival illicit beer and rum factions, the Sheltons and the Birgers in Williamson County, Ill. A plane swooped low and dropped three bombs over the farmhouse of Charles Birger, but as they were crudely made, they failed to explode, a failure which probably saved the lives of Birger and his companions, for the marksmanship of the flyer was unusually good.

Airplane bombing raid by an American air unit was made by the 96th Bombardment Squadron. The unit left the airdrome at Amanty, in Breguet airplanes on June 12, 1918, and bombed the railroad yards at Dommary Baroncourt, 24 miles northwest of Metz. (*Records in Office of the Chief of the Air Corps, War Dept. Washington, D.C.*)

Hydrogen bomb dropped from an airplane. *See* Atomic bomb: Atomic fusion (thermonuclear) bomb dropped from an airplane

AVIATION—AIRPORT
Air passenger international station was established at Meacham Field, Key West, Fla., the first flight being made by the Pan American World Airways on October 28, 1927, to Havana, Cuba. The airport facilities consisted of a small frame building that served as the station. Maintenance facilities were housed in an old fort nearby and in a small frame structure that served as a radio shack. Federal Health, Customs, and Immigration officials came to the station when notified of the arrival or departure of a plane.

Air terminal (not located at an airport) was opened January 27, 1941, in New York City, for American Airlines, Eastern Airlines, Pan American Airways System, Transcontinental & Western Air, Inc., and United Airlines.

Airport (federally owned and operated) (not Army) was the Washington National Airport, Washington, D.C., opened for regular traffic June 16, 1941. The cornerstone of the Terminal Building was laid by President Frank-

AVIATION—AIRPORT—Continued

lin Delano Roosevelt, September 28, 1940. The Civil Aeronautics Administration was in charge, and John Groves was the manager.

Airport hotel was the Oakland Airport Inn, in Oakland, Calif., built by the Board of Port Commissioners. It was opened July 15, 1929, and operated by the Interstate Company.

Airport manager (woman) was Laurette Schimmoler, appointed May 28, 1932, at Port Bucyrus, Ohio, at a salary of $510 a year. (*Charles E. Planck—Women With Wings*)

Airport municipal legislation was enacted at Modesto, Calif., July 8, 1910 (Article 3 Section 6) and ratified September 14, 1910, at a special election which authorized the city to acquire "aviation landings." An airfield was not erected within the city limits until 1918. (*California Laws. 39 Session. 1911*)

Airport municipally owned was the Tucson Municipal Airport, east of Tucson, Ariz. The first plane landed on November 20, 1919, and was piloted by "Swede" Myerhofer. (*Arizona Yearbook. 1930*)

Airport to receive an A1-A rating from the Department of Commerce was the Pontiac, Mich., Municipal Airport, which obtained the rating on February 11, 1930. The field covers 240 acres.

AVIATION—AIRSHIP

Airplane catapulted. *See* Aviation—Flights: Airplane catapulted

Airship bombing was suggested by John Wise, an aeronaut, who petitioned Congress in 1851 for funds with which to carry out his plan. He wrote *A System of Aeronautics* published in Philadelphia, Pa., in 1850.

Airship disaster occurred on May 23, 1908, at Berkeley, Calif., when the 450-foot cigar-shaped balloon invented by John A. Morrell collapsed and exploded, injuring the inventor and fifteen passengers. It was 46 feet in diameter at the center, and contained six gasoline engines which generated 200 h.p. each.

Airship (lighter-than-air) was the British dirigible R-34. It was under the command of Major George Herbert Scott, who left East Fortune, Scotland, on July 2, 1919, and arrived at Roosevelt Field, New York, on July 6, having flown 3,130 nautical miles in 108 hours, 12 minutes. The airship returned to Pulham, England, a few days later flying 3,200 miles in 74 hours and 56 minutes. (*Edward Maitland Maitland—The Log of H.M.A. R-34 Journey to America and Back*)

Airship of the U.S. Navy was the DNI, a twin-engine non-rigid 115,000-cubic-foot dirigible. The envelope was built at New Haven, Conn., and the car at Boston, Mass. It was acquired under contract of June 1, 1915, at a cost of $45,636.25. It was too overweight to leave the ground and the twin-engine was replaced with a single engine. The first flight was made at Pensacola, Fla., April 1917. Only three flights were made as the airship was damaged in handling and did not justify repairing.

Airship of the U.S. Navy that was successful was the F1, built to U.S. Navy specifications under contract dated March 14, 1917, by the Goodyear Tire and Rubber Company, Akron, Ohio. The ship was assembled at a Chicago, Ill., amusement park and the first flight made from Chicago to Wingfoot Lake, near Akron, May 30, 1917.

Airship to land on a roof was the A4, a 160-foot dirigible with a 95,000-cubic-foot gas capacity, which took off from the Wingfoot Lake Naval Air Station, near Akron, Ohio, and landed on a 30-by-30-foot platform on the roof of the Statler Hotel, Cleveland, Ohio, on May 23, 1919. Two of the five passengers alighted, one of them Ralph Hazlett Upson, designer of the dirigible. The pilot was James Shade.

Airship with an enclosed cabin was the non-rigid dirigible "Pilgrim," a 51,000-cubic-foot airship built by the Goodyear Tire and Rubber Company, Akron, Ohio. The first flight was made June 3, 1925, with John Maloney Yolton as pilot.

Atlantic Ocean regular commercial airship service. *See* Aviation—Flights (transatlantic): Atlantic Ocean regular commercial airship service

Balloon. *See* Balloon

Catholic mass in an airship over the ocean. *See* Catholic holy mass: Catholic mass in an airship over the ocean

Dirigible was designed and built by Caesar Spiegler. The flight was scheduled for July 3, 1878, with John Wise of Lancaster, Pa., as the pilot. The dirigible was of the cigar shape and supported a wicker-cage partition with a door and window.

Dirigible (American-built rigid) and the first of the Zeppelin type to use helium gas, the ZR1, was christened "Shenandoah"— "daughter of the stars"—by Mrs. Edwin Denby, on October 10, 1923. Commanded by Lieutenant Commander Zachary Lansdowne, it was destroyed in a storm on September 3, 1925, over

THE FIRST

Caldwell, Ohio. Lansdowne and fourteen members of the crew were killed. It was launched August 20, 1923, and tested in flight September 4, 1923, at Lakehurst, N.J. *(Charles Emery Rosendahl—Up Ship)*

Dirigible balloon contracted for by the United States Government was built by Captain Thomas Scott Baldwin. Designed by Glenn Curtiss, it was 96 feet long, and equipped with an engine of 20 h.p. It was demonstrated to the government representatives at Fort Myer, Va., in August 1908, Baldwin acting as pilot and Curtiss as engineer. It was subsequently purchased from Captain Baldwin and used by the Signal Corps at Omaha, Neb., for several years. Its engine, the first water-cooled engine which Curtiss made, is now in the National Museum. It averaged 19.61 m.p.h. and stayed aloft 2 hours. It was sold for $5,737.50.

Dirigible for private commercial operation was delivered on May 22, 1930, by the Goodyear Zeppelin Corporation of Akron, Ohio, to the New England Airship Company of Bedford, Mass. It was chartered by Bird & Son, Inc., of East Walpole Mass., and as a good-will messenger made 1,380 flights, carrying more than 6,000 passengers in less than five months.

Dirigible landing and taking off from an ocean-going steamship was the non-rigid dirigible "Mayflower," a blimp of the Goodyear Fleet. On July 31, 1930, as the S.S. "Bremen" reached New York City, the "Mayflower" lowered itself to the deck (which was 85 feet long by 36 feet wide) and picked up a passenger, Paul Weeks Litchfield, president of the Goodyear Tire and Rubber Company. The railings of the ship were covered with mattresses to prevent the puncturing of the sides of the dirigible. The "Mayflower" was 128 feet long and 37 feet wide and contained 86,000 cubic feet of gas.

Dirigible made completely of metal was the ZMC-2, which was constructed by the Detroit Aircraft Corporation, Detroit, Mich. It was tested at Grosse Ile Airport, Mich., August 19, 1929, and was manned by Captain William E. Kepner and a crew of four who stayed aloft 49 minutes and 55 seconds. The ship was 149 feet 5 inches long and 52 feet 8 inches in diameter and had a displacement of 202,200 cubic feet of helium gas. Its weight, empty, was 9,115 lbs. It carried a total load of 12,242 pounds. On June 24, 1926, President Calvin Coolidge had signed House Resolution 9690 appropriating $300,000 towards its construction. The contract with the Navy had been signed on August 18, 1926, under the administration of the first Assistant Secretary of Navy for Aeronautics, Edward Pearson Warner. *(The Metalclad Airship—Detroit Aircraft Corporation.)*

THE FIRST

Dirigible merchandise shipment sent to the United States by air was a shipment of toys brought over in 1924 by the German dirigible ZR3 (later the "Los Angeles"), which flew from Friedrichshafen, Germany, on October 12, to Lakehurst, N.J., where it arrived on October 15, 1924. It was manned by a crew of 33 men and made the 50,000-mile trip in 81 hours and 17 minutes.

Dirigible passenger transfer to an airplane. *See* Aviation—Passenger: Dirigible passenger transfer to an airplane

Dirigible transfer of mail to a train was effected on June 15, 1928, by an Air Corps blimp piloted by Lieutenant Karl S. Axtater and Lieutenant Edward H. White, who flew directly over an Illinois Central train near Scott Field, Belleville, Ill., and dipped low enough to permit the railway mail clerk to reach the sack of mail which was suspended by means of a rope. The blimp was a "C" type dirigible, 210 feet long, with a crew of six.

Flights. *See* Aviation—Flights (transatlantic); Aviation—Flights (transcontinental); Aviation—Flights (transpacific); Aviation—Flights (world)

Stock order from a Zeppelin. *See* Brokerage: Stock order from a Zeppelin

Transatlantic dirigible flight. *See* Aviation—Flights (transatlantic): Transatlantic dirigible flight

Transcontinental airship voyage. *See* Aviation—Flights (transcontinental): Transcontinental airship voyage

Woman airship passenger was Mary P. Miller, who ascended at 8 P.M. on August 11, 1906, from Franklin, Pa., in the 40-h.p. 22,500 cubic-foot airship owned by her husband, Major Charles J. S. Miller, and piloted by Leo Stevens, the inventor and builder of the airship. It rose about 600 feet and flew one eighth of a mile before the engine stopped. The airship landed and Mrs. Miller alighted. Stevens then adjusted the engine, ascended again and crossed the city in total darkness. He landed a mile from town.

Woman Zeppelin passenger. *See* Aviation—Passenger: Woman Zeppelin passenger (paying)

AVIATION—AVIATOR

American ace under American colors was Lieutenant Douglas Campbell, who shot down a German aviator on April 14, 1918. His fifth victory, which qualified him as an "ace," occurred May 31, 1918.

AVIATION—AVIATOR—Continued
American ace in World War II was First Lieutenant Boyd D. ("Buzz") Wagner of Johnstown, Pa. While serving in the Army Air Corps in the Philippines, Wagner was attacked on December 12, 1941, by five Japanese pursuit planes. He shot two planes out of the air and machine-gunned twelve on the ground, leaving five burning. He was awarded the Distinguished Service Cross and mentioned by Lieutenant General Douglas MacArthur in one of his communiqués.

American ace (jet) was Captain James Jabara, of Wichita, Kan., a member of the Fourth Fighter Interceptor Wing, who in an F-86 Sabre Jet airplane shot down his fifth and sixth Communist MIG jet airplanes on May 20, 1951, in battle over Sinuiju, northwest Korea. Later, he defeated his fifteenth Communist MIG over Korea, becoming the second triple jet ace, the first being Captain Joseph McConnell, Jr., who scored sixteen MIG victories.

American Ace of Aces was Captain Edward Vernon Rickenbacker, of Columbus, Ohio, who was credited wth 26 victories (22 airplanes and 4 balloons). His first victory took place in the Baussant region, in the Toul sector, France, April 29, 1918, and his last in the St. Juvin region, October 30, 1918. (Sender Garlin—The Real Rickenbacker)

American ace (triple jet) in Korea was Captain Joseph Christopher McConnell, Jr., who shot down sixteen MIG-15's in his F-86 Sabre Jet. On May 18, 1953, he downed three in one day. He completed 106 missions in Korea, and on August 10, 1953, a residence known as "Appreciation House" was presented to him by his neighbors in Apple Valley, Calif., who built it in forty-five hours. He was killed August 25, 1954, at Edwards Air Base, north of Rogers Dry Lake, Calif., while testing a new plane, an F-86 H.

American aviator killed while a pilot in the Lafayette Escadrille, an American flying squadron in the service of France, was Victor Emmanuel Chapman, who was shot down June 23, 1916, northeast of Douamont in the Verdun sector. From August 1914 to August 1915 he was in the Foreign Legion. (Bert Hall—One Man's War, The Story of the Lafayette Escadrille)

American aviator shot down in World War I was H. Clyde Balsley of the Lafayette Escadrille, who was attacked by a German squadron at a height of 10,000 feet above Verdun, France, on June 18, 1916. Although wounded, he managed to land his airplane within the Allies' lines. He received the Military Medal and the War Cross for his bravery. (Edwin C. Parsons—The Great Adventure; the Story of the Lafayette Escadrille)

American bombardier over German occupied territory. See World War II: American bombardier over German occupied territory

American pilot to shoot down a German fighter plane. See World War II: American pilot to shoot down a German fighter plane

Army aviator to win a victory over an enemy airplane was First Lieutenant Stephen W. Thompson, First Aero Squadron, whose victory is recorded as of February 5, 1918, at Saarbrucken, Germany, where he downed an Albatross pursuit plane.

Army aviator to solo was Second Lieutenant Frederic E. Humphreys, who on October 26, 1909, at College Park, Md., made two circuits of the field in three minutes. He was followed by Lieutenant Frank Purdy Lahm, who went six times around and made some small circles as well, remaining aloft thirteen minutes. Lieutenant Humphreys then resumed his solo flying for eight minutes. (Scientific American. November 13, 1909)

See also Aviation: Airplane purchased by the United States Government

Aviator (American) to establish an altitude record was Louis Paulhan, who flew a Farman biplane on January 12, 1910, to a height of 3,967 feet at an aviation meet at Aviation Camp, Los Angeles, Calif. About 50,000 spectators witnessed his flight, which lasted 50 minutes and 46 1/5th seconds. His descent was made in 7 minutes and 30 seconds.

Aviator to down two enemy fighter airplanes in one day in Korea was Air Force First Lieutenant Robert Earl Wayne of Garden City, Long Island, N.Y., who in an F-80 jet airplane shot down two enemy airplanes over Korea on June 27, 1950. He was one of the flight leaders with the Thirty-fifth Fighter Squadron of the Eighth Fighter Group. He was also the first jet pilot to down an enemy aircraft.

Aviator to fire a gun from an airplane was Lieutenant Jacob Earl Fickel of the 29th Infantry, who fired rifle shots at a target on August 20, 1910, at the Sheepshead Bay Race Track, New York City, from a single-seater Curtiss plane piloted by Glenn Hammond Curtiss.

Aviator to fly a million miles in a jet airplane was Melvin C. Garlow of Alexandria, Va., who flew his millionth mile on March 7, 1959. His first jet flight was made January 1955 in a Capital Viscount.

Aviator to fly one hundred times across the Atlantic Ocean was Captain Robert Oliver Daniel Sullivan, who completed his hundredth trip on December 28, 1942, from New York to Lisbon, Portugal. His first flight across the Atlantic was made January 28-29, 1938, from New York to Marseilles, France.

Jet plane combat victor in the Korean War was First Lieutenant Russell John Brown of Pasadena, Calif., who on November 8, 1950, while flying a U.S. Air Force F-80, destroyed a MIG-15 over North Korea in a jet-versus-jet combat.

Marine aviator. *See* Marines: Marine aviator

Naval ace in Korea was Lieutenant Guy Bordelon, who in a World War II vintage propeller-driven F-4U Corsair achieved his fifth victory on July 17, 1953. He was awarded a Navy Cross.

Naval ace in World War I was David Sinton Ingalls of the U.S. Naval Aviation Forces, who while attached to the 213th Squadron of the British Royal Air Force "alone and in conjunction with other pilots shot down at least four enemy aeroplanes and one or more enemy balloons." He was awarded the Distinguished Flying Cross by the British government on October 25, 1918, and the Distinguished Service Medal by the United States on November 11, 1920. He served as Assistant Secretary of the Navy for Aeronautics from March 16, 1929, to March 15, 1932.

Naval ace in World War II was Lieutenant Edward Henry O'Hare who, alone and single-handed, attacked nine twin-engine Japanese heavy bombers, shot down five, and damaged a sixth on February 20, 1942, in the southwest Pacific in an action of about five minutes' duration.

Negro airplane pilot on a scheduled passenger line was Perry H. Young of Orangeburg, S.C., who was hired as a flight crewman on December 17, 1956, by New York Airways. He started regular passenger flights on February 1, 1957, as a copilot in a helicopter.

Negro Army aviator to down an Axis airplane was First Lieutenant Charles Hall of Brazil, Ind., who in a Warhawk in a fighter squadron escorting bombers shot down a German Focke-Wulf 190 over Sicily on July 2, 1943. Lieutenant Colonel Benjamin Oliver Davis, Jr., of Washington D.C., was squadron commander.

Negro flier of the U.S. Naval Reserve was Jesse Leroy Brown of Hattiesburg, Miss., who was commissioned ensign on April 15, 1949. He

crashed December 4, 1950, near the Changjin Reservoir in Korea, the first Negro flier killed in action in Korea.

Pilot to receive the Congressional Medal of Honor, granted by the President with the approval of Congress, was awarded to 2nd Lieutenant Frank Luke for extraordinary heroism in action at Murvaux, France, September 12-15, 1918. The award was made April 14, 1919, for the destruction of eight enemy balloons in four days and was posthumously presented at Phoenix, Ariz., on May 29, 1919, to his father, Frank Luke, Sr. Luke was a member of the 27th Aero Squadron when he was killed in action. He is officially credited with 18 victories, a record that was surpassed in World War I only by Captain Edward Vernon Rickenbacker who was credited with 26 victories and who later also received the Medal of Honor. *(Norman Shannon Hall—The Balloon Buster, Frank Luke of Arizona)*

Woman aviator to fly across the Atlantic Ocean east to west was Amy Johnson Mollison, who, accompanied by her husband, James Allan Mollison, left Pendine, Wales, July 22, 1933, at 7 A.M. in the "Seafarer" on a non-stop flight. They crashed July 23, 1933, at 9:30 P.M. at Stratford, Conn., about 55 miles from their ultimate goal. They flew 3,190 miles in 38½ hours.

Woman aviator to fly solo across the Pacific Ocean was Amelia Earhart Putnam. She left Wheeler Field, Honolulu, at 10:15 P.M. Friday, January 11, 1935, and arrived at the Oakland Airport, Oakland, Calif., at 4:31 P.M. Saturday, covering 2,408 miles in 18 hours 16 minutes at an average speed of 133 m.p.h. *(George Palmer Putnam—Soaring Wings, a Biography of Amelia Earhart)*

Woman aviator to make a public flight was Blanche Stuart Scott, a pupil of Glenn Hammond Curtiss, who made a solo flight October 23, 1910, at the Driving Park, Fort Wayne, Ind. She used an Ely machine and rose to a height of 12 feet and sailed across the field. After the flight, she stated, "I believe I could have turned and circled the track, but Mr. Curtiss has absolutely forbidden me attempting the turns until I have mastered the straightway flights." *(Fort Wayne Journal—Gazette. Oct. 24, 1910)*

Woman aviator to pilot an air-mail transport on a regular schedule was Helen Richey, who flew from Washington, D.C., to Detroit, Mich., via Pittsburgh and Cleveland, on December 31, 1934. She was appointed a copilot by Central Airlines and flew a Tri-Motored Ford 12-passenger transport.

AVIATION—AVIATOR—*Continued*
Woman test pilot to test standard production aircraft was Alma Heflin, who made her first production test flight November 12, 1941, for the Piper Aircraft Corporation, Lock Haven, Pa.

Woman to pilot an airplane faster than the speed of sound was Jacqueline Cochran (Mrs. Floyd Bostwick Odlum), who on May 18, 1953, flew a North American F-86 Canadair over Rogers Dry Lake, Calif., at the speed of 652.337 m.p.h.

AVIATION — EXPOSITIONS AND MEETS
Aeronautic international exposition was held in New York City May 9-18, 1912, at the Grand Central Palace under the auspices of the Aero Club of America. An invitation to attend was extended to Rear Admiral Hugo Osterhaus on the opening day by Robert Joseph Collier, president of the Aero Club of America, who flew from Keyport, N.J., to the U.S.S. "Washington" moored in the Hudson River. (*Aero Club of America—First Annual International Aeronautical Exhibition*)

Air conference (international) was held August 1-4, 1893, in Chicago, Ill. The opening address was delivered by Octave Chanute. Other speakers were Charles Edgar Duryea, Samuel Pierpont Langley, and Professor Albert Francis Zahn of Notre Dame University. (*Proceedings of the International Conference on Aerial Navigation. 1893*)

Aviation meet was held in Los Angeles, Calif., January 10-20, 1910. American planes had an opportunity of proving their power in competition with foreign planes. Two Farman biplanes and two Blériot monoplanes were foreign exhibits. Three Curtiss biplanes of American manufacture were shown, piloted by Glenn Hammond Curtiss, Charles Keeney Hamilton, and Charles Foster Willard. At the meet Louis Paulhan broke the altitude record of the world with a flight to 4,165 feet.

Intercollegiate air meet was held May 7, 1920, at Mitchel Field, Long Island, N.Y., under the auspices of the Intercollegiate Flying Association, the U.S. Air Service, and the American Flying Club. The Air Service loaned the fliers Curtiss JN-4 planes. Yale University won with nine points, Williams was second with six points, and Princeton and Columbia tied for third place with five points each. The other college entries were Cornell, Harvard, Lehigh, Pennsylvania, Pittsburgh, Rutgers, and Wesleyan.

AVIATION—FLIGHTS
Airplane altitude flight to exceed 28,000 feet was made September 18, 1918, by Captain Rudolph William Schroeder, who reached

an altitude of 28,900 feet at Wilbur Field, Fairfield, Ohio, while flying a 300-h.p. Hispano-Suiza motor-powered Bristol fighter.

Airplane catapulted successfully was a Curtiss hydro-airplane, catapulted from the Washington Navy Yard, Washington, D.C., on November 12, 1912. The catapult was built under the direction of Captain Washington Irving Chambers, assisted by Naval Constructor Holden Chester Richardson and Admiral Nathan Crook Twining of the Bureau of Ordnance. The airplane was piloted by Lieutenant Theodore Gordon Ellyson. Similar attempts had been made previously at Annapolis, Md., but were not successful. (*Aviation Magazine. February 28, 1921*)

Airplane catapulted from a dirigible was a Vought two-seater observation plane which was released on May 20, 1930, from the airship "Los Angeles." It was piloted by Lieutenant Commander Charles Ambrose Nicholson, who flew it to the carrier "Saratoga."

Airplane endurance flight exceeding one hour was made September 9, 1908, by Orville Wright, who flew a Wright airplane with a Wright motor at Fort Myer, Va., for 1 hour 2 minutes and 15 seconds.

Airplane endurance flight exceeding 400 hours was made by Dale Jackson and Forest O'Brine, who took off at 7:17 A.M. on July 13, 1929, in the "St. Louis Robin" from the Lambert-St. Louis Field, St. Louis, Mo., and landed there at 7:38:30 P.M. on July 30 after a flight of 420 hours, 21 minutes, and 30 seconds. Each flier earned $15,672.50 for the flight, which was sponsored by the Curtiss-Robertson Airplane Manufacturing Company.

Airplane endurance flight exceeding 1,200 hours (50 days) was made by Jim Heth and Bill Burkhart, who took off from Garland-Dallas Airport, Dallas, Tex., at 7:01 P.M. on August 2, 1958, in a single-engine Cessna 172 with a Continental engine. The plane remained in the air 1,200 hours, 18 minutes, and 30 seconds before landing at 7:18:30 P.M. on September 21, 1958.

Airplane flight was made August 14, 1901, near Bridgeport, Conn., by Gustave Whitehead, who made four flights, one of which covered a distance of a mile and a half, in his airplane "No. 21." (*Stella Randolph—Lost Flights of Gustave Whitehead*)
See also Aviation—Airplane: Airplane (heavier-than-air) to make any long-sustained flight

Airplane flight (commercially scheduled) over a single route linking four continents was made by the 42½-ton "Dixie Clipper," with ten passengers and eleven in the crew. Commanded by Captain Harold Edwin Gray, the plane left La Guardia Field, New York City, February 1, 1941, on an 11,348-mile trip. Stops were made at Bermuda; Lisbon, Portugal; Bolama, Portuguese Guinea; Port of Spain, Trinidad; and San Juan, Puerto Rico. The plane returned to the starting field February 9, 1941. This was also the first airplane of commercial United States registry to land at an African airport.

Airplane flight from a ship was made on November 14, 1910, when Eugene Ely, a civilian pilot of the Curtiss Company, took off from the deck of the scout cruiser "Birmingham" at Hampton Roads and flew two miles through fog and rain to Norfolk, Va. The runway was 83 feet long with a 5 degree slope, allowing only a 26-foot take-off, as the length of the plane was 57 feet. On January 18, 1911, Ely flew 13 miles from Camp Selfridge, Calif., and alighted safely upon the platform built on the deck of the U.S. cruiser "Pennsylvania" in San Francisco harbor.

Airplane flight with an auto slung beneath the fuselage was made February 11, 1935, from Floyd Bennett Field, N.Y., with Lou Reichers at the controls. An Uppercu-Burnelli transport with a cabin twelve feet wide supported a Ford roadster fastened and braced with struts between the wheels of the landing gear. The test was made to demonstrate the quick starting ability of a branded gasoline but was valuable because it demonstrated the possibility of transporting tanks behind enemy lines in battle.

Airplane loop the loop was made by Lincoln Beachey at North Island, San Diego, Calif., on November 18, 1913. At a 1,000-foot level, he brought his machine up with a swoop and a moment later was flying head downward. The loop was completed at a 300-foot level. On November 28, 1913, he made a triple loop.

Airplane night scheduled passenger flight was made April 1, 1927, when a three-engine Fokker of the Colonial Air Transport Company took off for Boston, Mass., from Hadley Field, N.J., then the only lighted airport with a lighted runway.

Airplane round trip, made in one day between two large cities, was made on June 13, 1910, when Charles Keeney Hamilton, flying in a Curtiss biplane equipped with a Curtiss motor, made the round trip between Governors Island, N.Y., and Philadelphia, Pa. He left Governors Island at 7:36 A.M. and arrived at Front Street and Erie Avenue, Philadelphia, at 9:26 A.M. The average speed for his flight of 1 hour and 50 minutes was 46.92 m.p.h. He left Philadelphia 11:33 A.M. and, after a detour, landed at South Amboy,

N.J., at 12:54 P.M., in a swamp instead of on a green. He repaired a broken spark plug and reascended at 6:17 P.M. and landed at Governors Island at 6:40 P.M. The flying time for the round trip was 3 hours and 34 minutes. For this accomplishment, he won a $10,000 prize offered by the New York *Times* and the Philadelphia *Ledger*. *(Lyman J. Seely—Flying Pioneers of Hammondsport)*

Airplane to exceed a mile in altitude was a Wright biplane flown by Walter Richard Brookins to an altitude of 6,234 feet on July 9, 1910 over Atlantic City, N.J. The gasoline gave out when he descended to 5,800 feet, and the engine stopped, but Brookins glided the airplane to safety. He was in the air 1 hour, 2 minutes, and 35 seconds. For his feat he won a $5,000 prize offered by the Atlantic City Aero Club.

Airplane to exceed the speed of 200 miles an hour was piloted by Lieutenant Lester James Maitland on October 14, 1922, at the national airplane meet at Selfridge Field, Mount Clemens, Mich. Maitland flew a Curtiss pursuit plane with a 375 h.p. engine, at a speed of 216.1 m.p.h. for 50 kilometers.

Airplane to exceed the speed of 300 miles per hour was flown September 4, 1933, over Glenview, Ill., by James R. Wedell of Patterson, La., who won the Phillips Trophy Race. He made four consecutive runs over a three-kilometer course at an average speed of 304.980 m.p.h., in a monoplane of his own design (Wedell-Williams No. 44) fitted with 300 h.p. Wasp supercharged engine.

Airplane to exceed the speed of 600 miles per hour was piloted by Army Air Force Colonel Albert Boyd of Asheville, N.C., on June 19, 1947, at Muroc Air Field, Calif. He flew a jet propelled Lockheed P-80R at 623.738 m.p.h. over a 1.86-mile course, flying four times, twice in each direction, and at one time attaining a speed of 632 m.p.h.

Airplane to exceed the speed of 800 miles an hour was a North American F-100C Super Sabre Jet, which reached 822.135 m.p.h. on August 20, 1955, over the Mojave Desert at Palmdale, Calif. It was piloted by Colonel Horace Albert Hanes at a 40,000-foot altitude.

Airplane to exceed the speed of 1,300 miles an hour was the D-558-2 Skyrocket, a jet built for the U.S. Navy by the El Segundo, Calif., division of the Douglas Aircraft Company. Piloted by Scott Crossfield of the National Advisory Committee for Aeronautics, it attained a speed of 1,327 m.p.h. in a three-minute flight on November 20, 1953, over Edwards Air Force Base, Muroc, Calif. It was designed under the direction of chief engineer Edward H. Heinemann and first flew in 1947 at Muroc, Calif.

AVIATION—FLIGHTS—*Continued*

Airplane to exceed the speed of 4,000 miles an hour was the X-15 flown November 9, 1961, by Major Robert White at the Edwards Air Force Base, Calif. A speed of 4,070 miles an hour was sustained for 86 seconds.

Airplane to exceed the speed of sound and break the sound barrier was the Bell X-1, a U.S. Army rocket airplane, flown October 14, 1947, at Edwards Air Force Base, Muroc, Calif., by Air Force Major Charles E. (Chuck) Yeager. The rocket engine was built by Reaction Motors, Inc., Rockaway, N.J. The plane attained the speed of 967 m.p.h. and an altitude of 70,140 feet. The official announcement did not come, however, until released June 10, 1948, by Air Secretary William Stuart Symington. Alcohol and liquid oxygen were used as fuel, forced into the burners by gaseous nitrogen. The plane was equipped with rockets which could keep it in the air only 10 minutes. It had to be dropped from a bomber while at a high altitude. (At sea level, the speed of sound is 760 m.p.h.)

Airplane to exceed the speed of sound which was piloted by a civilian was piloted by Herbert Henry Hoover of Knoxville, Tenn., chief test pilot in charge of the National Advisory Committee for Aeronautics, who on March 10, 1948, from Edwards Air Force Base, Calif., made a supersonic flight in a Bell X-1 rocket-propelled research airplane.

See also Aviation—Airplane: Rocket plane; Aviation—Aviator: Woman to pilot an airplane faster than the speed of sound

Airplane to fly a distance exceeding 500 miles was a two-year-old obsolete Curtiss biplane which was flown a distance of 590 miles from Chicago, Ill., to Hornell, N.Y., on November 19, 1916, by Ruth Law. She left at 8:25 A.M. and arrived at 2:10 P.M., in 5 hours and 45 minutes flying time. She landed and refueled and continued on to Binghamton.

Airplane to land on the White House lawn. *See* Aviation: Airplane to land on the White House lawn

"Airplane train" soared from Floyd Bennett Field, N.Y., August 2, 1934, at 10:44 A.M. It consisted of a Wright-Eaglerock airplane piloted by Elwood Keim which towed three gliders, piloted by Jack O'Meara, Dr. Roswell Earl Franklin, and Stanley Smith. The gliders were to be released from the train at Philadelphia, Baltimore, and Washington. The flight was arranged by the Lustig Sky Train Corporation, and each glider carried about 75 pounds of mail. Because of heavy winds, the air train was forced down at Philadelphia at 1:20 P.M.

All blind cross-country test of instrument or "blind" flying and landing was made on March 21, 1933, from College Park, Md., to Newark, N.J., by James Kinney, pilot, accompanied by Harry Diamond, U.S. Bureau of Standards scientist, who helped develop the instrument landing system, and William La Violette, radio technician.

All blind distance flight by the U.S. Army was made April 6, 1940, by Major Carl B. McDaniel, assisted by Captain William A. Matheny, Lieutenant William P. Ragsdale, and four enlisted men, in a four-motored 22½-ton craft from Mitchel Field, Long Island, N.Y., to Langley Field, Va. Two civilian passengers were carried in the 2 hour and 2 minute flight.

All blind flight was made September 24, 1929, at Mitchel Field, Long Island, N.Y., by Lieutenant James Harold Doolittle in a Consolidated-Wright biplane. He made a complete flight in an enclosed cockpit without seeing the ground or any part of the airplane except an illuminated instrument board. He was guided by a radio beacon. Lieutenant Benjamin Kelsey accompanied him in the event of an emergency.

All blind solo flight by the U.S. Army was made May 7, 1932, by Captain Albert Francis Hegenberger at Patterson Field, Dayton, Ohio, in an Army Douglas BT-2 plane equipped with standard Air Corps instruments. He took off and landed the plane completely enclosed in the hooded cockpit, with no external vision from start to finish. (*U.S. Air Forces. July 1932*)

Balloon flight. *See* Balloon: Balloon flight

California-Hawaii flight. *See* Aviation—Flights (transpacific): California-Hawaii flight

Glider flight. *See* Glider

Helicopter flight. *See* Helicopter

Honolulu squadron flight. *See* Aviation—Flights (transpacific): Honolulu squadron flight

Hydroplane flight to and from a ship was made by Glenn Curtiss to the U.S.S. "Pennsylvania" in the Pacific Ocean on February 17, 1911, from North Island, San Diego, Calif. He landed alongside the ship and was hoisted aboard. Then the procedure was reversed. He received the Robert F. Collier Trophy in 1912 for outstanding contributions to American aviation.

THE FIRST

Inter-city airplane flight by a U.S. officer was made July 30, 1909, by Lieutenant Benjamin Delahauf Foulois, who flew with Orville Wright as the pilot from Fort Myer, Va., to Alexandria, Va. They traveled 10 miles at an altitude of 600 feet averaging 42 miles an hour, thereby establishing three world's records for distance, speed, and altitude.

Jet passenger commercial service. *See* Aviation—Flights (transatlantic): Jet passenger commercial service

Jet passenger international trip was made April 18, 1950, in an Avro Canada Jetliner from Malton Airport, Toronto, Canada, to the International Airport, New York City, a distance of 359 miles in one hour. Chief pilot was Donald Howard Rogers. Four Rolls-Royce Derwent jet engines were mounted in pairs in the two underslung nacelles, which also housed the main landing wheels. The plane carried three passengers, a crew of three, and 15,000 airmail letters marked with an official Canadian government cachet, the first mail carried in a jet transport.

Jet passenger trip was made January 10, 1951, when an Avro Jetliner, four-engine turbo-jet piloted by Donald Howard Rogers took off from Chicago, Ill., at 11:07 A.M., and arrived at New York City in 1 hour and 42 minutes, setting a new speed record of 442 m.p.h.

New York-Alaska flight, 4,345 miles each way, was made by four United States planes of the Alaskan Flying Expedition which left Mitchel Field, Long Island, N.Y., July 15, 1920, and arrived at Nome, Alaska, August 25, 1920. The expedition left Nome, August 29, 1920, and returned to Mitchel Field, October 20, 1920, making sixteen stops en route. The average flying speed of the trip was 80 m.p.h. The crew consisted of Captain St. Clair Streett, in command; First Lieutenant Clifford Cameron Nutt; Second Lieutenants Ross C. Kirkpatrick, Erik Henning Nelson, and Clarence E. Crumrine; Sergeants James Long and Joseph E. English; and Captain Howard Douglas, advance officer.

New York-Bermuda flight was made on April 1, 1930, by Captain Lewis Alonzo Yancey, navigator, William Alexander, pilot, and Zeh Bouck, radio operator, in the Stinson monoplane "Pilot," equipped with a Wright Whirlwind motor. They landed 60 miles from their goal on the ocean and floated overnight. They resumed flight and arrived at Hamilton, Bermuda, on April 2, 1930. Each member of the crew received $1,000 from the Bermuda Board of Trade.

THE FIRST

New York-Chicago non-stop flight was made by Captain E. F. White, April 19, 1919, piloting a De Havilland-4 army biplane. He covered the 727 miles in 6 hours, 50 minutes flying time, an average speed of 106 miles an hour.

New York-Panama non-stop flight was made by Captain Roy W. Ammel of Chicago in his Lockheed-Sirius monoplane, the "Blue-flash." He made the 3,189-mile trip from Floyd Bennett Field, Brooklyn, N.Y., to France Field, Panama, on November 9, 1930, in 24 hours and 34 minutes.

Night flight was made by Walter Richard Brookins on April 18, 1910, at Montgomery, Ala.

North Pole flight was made by Lieutenant Commander Richard Evelyn Byrd, U.S.N. retired, and Floyd Bennett on May 9, 1926. In the "Josephine Ford," a triple-engine Fokker monoplane, they flew from King's Bay, Spitzbergen, to the Pole and back, without stopping, covering 1,545 miles in 15 hours and 30 minutes. *(Richard Evelyn Byrd—Skyward)*

North Pole flight in a single-engine airplane was made by Captain Charles Francis Blair, Jr., of Port Washington, Long Island, N.Y., from Bardu Foss, Norway, to Fairbanks, Alaska, in 10 hours and 29 minutes (non-stop), on May 29, 1951, in the "Excalibur III," a converted flame-red Mustang fighter plane with a 12-cylinder V-type engine. The take-off was at 4:02 P.M. (11:02 A.M., New York time) and the landing was at 3:29 P.M. (9:29 P.M., New York time) at the Ladd Air Force Base. About 3,000 letters were carried on this air mail polar flight.

North Pole jet crossing was made September 20, 1951, in a six-jet medium Boeing B-47 Stratojet which took off and returned to Eielson Air Force Base, near Fairbanks, Alaska. The plane was piloted by Colonel Richard Cox Neeley of Salt Lake City, Utah, and copilot Colonel John Gibbons Foster of New York City. The third member of the crew was radar operator-navigator Captain David Jacob Haney of Copperhill, Tenn.

North Pole landing by an airplane at the geographic pole was made by a U.S. Air Force ski-wheeled C-47 which landed May 3, 1952. It took off from Fletcher's Ice Island, about 115 miles from the Pole, and carried ten Air Force officials and scientists. It was piloted by Lieutenant Colonel William Pershing Benedict of San Rafael, Calif., and copilot Lieutenant Colonel Joseph Otis Fletcher of Shawnee, Okla.

AVIATION—FLIGHTS—*Continued*
Over-water flight was made by Glenn Hammond Curtiss, who on August 31, 1910, flew in his biplane from Euclid Beach Park, Cleveland, Ohio, to Cedar Point, Sandusky, Ohio, a distance of 70 miles over Lake Erie in 78 minutes nonstop. He flew at an altitude between 400 and 500 feet.

Over-water round-trip flight was made by Glenn Luther Martin in a biplane pusher type, on May 10, 1912. The trip was made in 37 minutes at an altitude in excess of 2,000 feet for an approximate distance of 31 miles over the Pacific Ocean from Newport Bay to Avalon, Catalina Island, Calif. The return flight was from Catalina Island via San Pedro and down the coast to Newport Bay, covering 45 miles in 51 minutes. An inflated tire tube on the fuselage served as a life preserver.

President to fly in a twin-engined airplane. *See* President (United States): President to fly in a twin-engined airplane

President to fly in an airplane while in office *See* President (United States): President to fly in an airplane while in office

Sky-train international round-trip flight was made from Key West, Fla., May 14, 1935, at 1:40 P.M. to Havana, Cuba. The flight lasted 1 hour and 45 minutes, the average speed being 64 m.p.h. The sky-train consisted of an airplane and two gliders towed by the plane. The plane was piloted by Elwood Keim of New York City, and the gliders by E. Paul du Pont, Jr., of Wilmington, Del., and Jack O'Meara of New York City. The return flight was made from Havana, May 19, 1935.

South Pole flight was made on November 28, 1929, by Lieutenant Commander Richard Evelyn Byrd, U.S.N. retired, from his base, Little America, in the Antarctic. The crew consisted of Bernt Balchen, pilot; Harold I. June, radio operator; and Captain Ashley C. McKinley, photographer. They reported that they reached the Pole about 8:55 A.M. (New York time) on November 29, 1929, and dropped a United States flag there. *(Richard Evelyn Byrd—Little America)*

Stratoliner commercial flight was made July 8, 1940, by Transcontinental & Western Air, with a Boeing 307-B four-engine plane. It flew normally 4 miles above the earth. This was the first commercial flight to use supercharged cabins. It was a 33-passenger plane by day and a 25-passenger plane at night. The cabin was designed with 9 individual seats and 4 compartments, each of 6-passenger capacity. At night, these compartments were converted into sleepers of 4 berths each. The first eastbound transcontinental commercial flight was

made in 12 hours and 22 minutes (11 hours and 55 minutes flying time), and the westbound trip in 14 hours and 17 minutes (14 hours flying time). Stops were made at Kansas City. The terminals were La Guardia Airport, New York City, and the Lockheed Air Terminal, Burbank, Calif.

AVIATION—FLIGHTS (transatlantic)
Air mail transatlantic service. *See* Air mail service: Air mail transatlantic service

Airplane flight (commercially scheduled) over a single route linking four continents. *See* Aviation—Flights: Airplane flight commercially scheduled over a single route linking four continents

Atlantic Ocean regular commercial airship service was inaugurated by the "Hindenburg," of the German Zeppelin Transport Company, which departed from Friedrichshafen, Germany, at 9:30 P.M. (Central European Time) on May 6, 1936, and landed May 9, 1936, at the United States Naval Air Station, Lakehurst, N.J., at 6:08 A.M. (Eastern Standard Time), completing the voyage of approximately 4,000 miles in 61 hours and 38 minutes, an average speed of 65 m.p.h. Fifty-one passengers and fifty-six officers and crew made the flight. The ship was in the command of Captain Ernst August Lehmann, under the general direction of Dr. Hugo Eckener. *(Ernst August Lehmann—Zeppelin, The Story of Lighter-than-Air Craft.)*

Atlantic Ocean scheduled air service was inaugurated by Pan American Airways on May 20, 1939, when the "Yankee Clipper," a 4-engine, 4½-ton flying boat took off from Manhasset Bay, Port Washington, Long Island, N.Y., and arrived at Lisbon, Portugal in 26½ hours (20 hours and 16 minutes actual flying time). It was commanded by Captain Arthur Earl La Porte and carried a crew of 14, 3 PAA employees, and 1,680 pounds of mail.

Aviator to fly one hundred times across the Atlantic Ocean. *See* Aviation—Aviator: Aviator to fly one hundred times across the Atlantic Ocean

Ballon Atlantic crossing attempt. *See* Balloon: Balloon Atlantic crossing attempt

Jet passenger commercial service was inaugurated October 4, 1958, by the British Overseas Airways Corporation, whose jets crossed the Atlantic Ocean in both directions. The flight from New York City to London, piloted by Captain Thomas B. Stoney, was made in 6 hours and 12 minutes with a stop at Gander, Newfoundland. The flight from London to New York was made in 10 hours and 26 minutes with a 1 hour and 10 minute stop at Gander, Newfoundland. The planes, Comet IV's, averaged 580 m.p.h. and flew at an altitude of 34,000 to 40,000 feet. First class passage was $435.

Jet transatlantic flight west to east was made July 20, 1948, by sixteen Lockheed P-80 Shooting Stars from Mount Clemens, Mich., to Odiham, England (4,283 miles) in 10 hours and 40 minutes under the command of Colonel David Carl Schilling, of Raleigh, N.C., commander of the Fifty-sixth Fighter Group. Stops were made at Goose Bay, Labrador; Bluie West Two, Greenland; Keflavik, Iceland; and Stornoway, in the Outer Hebrides, off Scotland.

Jet transatlantic non-stop flight east to west was made on September 22, 1950, by Colonel David Carl Schilling of Raleigh, N.C., commanding officer of the Thirty-first Escort Wing, from Manston, England, to the Air Force Base, Limestone, Me. (3,300 miles) in a single-engine F-84E Republic Thunderjet. The flight took 10 hours and 1 minute. Schilling made three aerial refueling contacts with Air Force tanker planes. Lieutenant Colonel William D. Ritchie, who also took off in an F-84, was forced to bail out over Labrador.

Jet transatlantic non-stop flight west to east was made by two Boeing B-47 Stratojets of the Strategic Air Command's 306th Medium Bombardment Wing, based at MacDill Air Force Base, Tampa, Fla., on April 7, 1953. The flight was made from Limestone, Me., to Fairford, England, in 5 hours and 38 minutes—a distance of 3,120 miles at an average speed of 555 m.p.h. The lead plane was piloted by Colonel Michael Norman Wright McCoy; Lieutenant Colonel Michael Irwin Berkowitz, observer; and Lieutenant Colonel George Purnell Birdsong, Jr., copilot. In the second plane were Colonel Lloyd Dean Griffin, copilot, and Lieutenant Colonel Lawrence Harry Grant, observer.

Transatlantic dirigible flight was attempted by Walter Wellman on October 15, 1910, when he and his companions left Atlantic City, N.J., in a non-rigid dirigible, "The America," en route to Ireland. The dirigible was 228 feet long with a 52-foot diameter. They were forced down after 71½ hours by storms and fogs after flying 1,008 miles. The entire crew was rescued about 375 miles east of Cape Hatteras, N.C.

Transatlantic foreign squadron flight to the United States was led by General Italo Balbo, Italian Air Minister, who was in command of a squadron of 24 Italian seaplanes manned by 98 men. The flight cost was approximately $3 million, including an estimated value of $56,000 for each plane. The planes covered 6,100 miles in 47 hours and 52 minutes.

The squadron left Orbetello, Italy, Sunday, July 2, 1933, at 12:40 A.M. and flew to Amsterdam, Holland; Londonderry, North Ireland; Reykjavik, Iceland; Cartwright, Labrador; Shediac, New Brunswick; and Montreal, Canada before landing in Chicago, Ill., at 7 P.M. on July 15. *(Italo Balbo—My Air Armada)*

Transatlantic hydroplane flight was made by Americans, but it was not a single non-stop flight. The NC 4, commanded by Lieutenant Commander Albert Cushing Read, left Rockaway, Long Island, N.Y., on May 8, 1919, in company with the NC 1 and NC 3, but was the only plane to finish the trip. Stops were made at Trepassey, Newfoundland; Horta and Ponta Delgada, in the Azores; and Lisbon, Portugal. The final destination, Plymouth, England, was reached on May 31—a total distance of 4,500 miles. Read's crew was composed of Lieutenants Elmer Fowler Stone, Walter Hinton, and James Lawrence Breese; Ensign Herbert Charles Rodd; and Chief Machinist's Mate Eugene Saylor Rhoads. *(George Conrad Westervelt—The Triumph of the N.C.'s)*

Transatlantic non-stop flight from America was made in a Vickers "Vimy" Bomber, a bimotored Rolls Royce airplane with four-bladed propellers which was piloted by Captain John Alcock of the Royal Air Force and navigated by Lieutenant Arthur Whitten Brown of the Royal Flying Corps. They left St. John's, Newfoundland, Saturday, June 14, 1919, and arrived in Clifton, Ireland, 16 hours and 12 minutes later, covering a distance of 1,960 miles at the average speed of 120 m.p.h. *(Arthur Whitten Brown—Flying the Atlantic in Sixteen Hours)*

Transatlantic non-stop flight from Europe to the United States and the first flight from Europe to the mainland of North America was made by Captain Dieudonné Coste and his mechanic, Maurice Bellonte, in a red sesquiplane, "The Question Mark." They arrived at Valley Stream, N.Y., at 7:12 P.M. on September 2, 1930, completing the first non-stop flight from France to the United States, a trip which consumed 37 hours and 18½ minutes. This trip was the fourteenth conquest of the North Atlantic by airplane and the fifth westward flight. *(Dieudonné Coste—Paris-New York)*

Transatlantic regular commercial airplane service, flying the "southern route" was undertaken by the 41½ ton "Dixie Clipper" of the Pan American Airways, commanded by Captain Robert Oliver Daniel Sullivan, which left Port Washington, Long Island, N.Y., June 28, 1939, at 1:59 P.M., with 12 crew members and 22 passengers. It was powered by four 1,550 h.p. Wright Cyclone engines. Stops were made at Horta, in the Azores, and Lisbon, Portugal. The plane landed at Marseilles, France, June 30, 1939, at 8:21 A.M. The fare was $375.

AVIATION—FLIGHTS (transatlantic)—
Continued

Transatlantic round-trip flight from the United States was made in the "Lady Peace" by Richard Merrill and Harry Richman who left Floyd Bennett Field, New York, September 2, 1936, at 4:37 A.M., and arrived September 3, 1936 about 10:30 A.M., in a forced landing at Llwyncelyn, Carmarthenshire, Wales, 175 miles from the Croyden Airdrome. The return trip was made from Southport, England, September 13, 1936 and they crash-landed at Musgrave Harbor, Newfoundland, about 100 miles from Harbor Grace, Newfoundland, returning to New York City a week later.

Transatlantic solo flight was made by Charles Augustus Lindbergh on May 20, 1927, from New York to Paris. He flew about 3,610 miles in 33 hours and 32 minutes in the "Spirit of St. Louis," a Ryan monoplane equipped with a single 225 h.p. Wright Whirlwind motor. He left Roosevelt Field at 7:52 A.M. on May 20, 1927, and arrived at 5:24 P.M. (New York time) the following day at Le Bourget field, Paris. *(Charles Augustus Lindbergh—We)*

Transatlantic solo flight by a woman was made by Amelia Earhart Putnam, who left Harbor Grace, Newfoundland at 5:50 P.M. Friday, May 20, 1932, and arrived at London-derry, Ireland, at 8:46 A.M. Saturday, May 21, 1932. Her flight was made exactly five years after Lindbergh's flight. Lindbergh flew 3,610 miles in 33 hours and 32 minutes, while Amelia Earhart flew 2,026 miles in 14 hours and 56 minutes. *(Amelia Earhart—Fun of It)*

Transatlantic solo westward flight was made by James Allan Mollison. He left Port-marnock, Ireland, August 18, 1932, 6:33 A.M., and landed at 12:45 A.M., August 19, 1932, at Pennfield Ridge, New Brunswick. He made the trip in "The Heart's Content," a De Havil-land Puss Moth with a Gipsy III inverted en-gine. Accompanied by his wife, Amy Mollison, he made another east-west flight across the Atlantic Ocean, thus becoming the first man to have twice crossed the Atlantic in a west-ward flight. He took off from Wales, July 22, 1933, in the "Seafarer," a De Havilland Drag-on plane, and landed July 23, 1933, at Stratford, Conn., where the plane crashed. *(James Allan Mollison—Death Cometh Soon or Late)*

Woman airplane passenger to cross the Atlantic Ocean. *See* Aviation—Passenger: Woman airplane passenger to cross the Atlantic Ocean

Woman aviator to fly across the Atlantic Ocean. *See* Aviation—Aviator: Woman avi-ator to fly across the Atlantic Ocean east to west

AVIATION—FLIGHTS (transcontinental)

Air mail transcontinental flight. *See* Air mail service: Air mail transcontinental flight

Air mail transcontinental service. *See* Air mail service: Air mail transcontinental serv-ice

Air mail transcontinental through regular service. *See* Air mail service: Air mail trans-continental through regular service

Jet passenger commercial transcontinental service began January 25, 1959, when a four-engine American Airlines Boeing 707 made the trip between Los Angeles, Calif., and New York City with 112 passengers and 8 in the crew in 4 hours, 3 minutes, and 3 seconds. The plane was piloted by Captain Charles Macatee of Huntington, Long Island, N.Y. Another flight from New York to Los Angeles was made in 6 hours and 33 minutes. The fare was $158.85 one way plus tax and $301.90 round trip plus tax.

Stratoliner commercial flight. *See* Aviation —Flights: Stratoliner commercial flight

Transcontinental airplane flight was made by Calbraith Perry Rodgers, who left Sheeps-head Bay, N.Y., September 17, 1911, in his Burgess-Wright biplane and was 49 days en route to California, arriving in Pasadena on November 5, 1911. He was followed by a special train carrying spare parts. The distance was 3,417 miles (2,567 air-line miles), which he covered in 70 hops. His actual flying time was 3 days, 10 hours, and 14 minutes. His best day's coverage was 231 miles and his best single flight was 133 miles from Stovall to Imperial Junction. Weather was responsible for the loss of 11 days, and 13½ days were consumed in making repairs. On November 12, at Compton, Calif., he crashed and was badly injured, but on December 10 he continued his journey to the Pacific and landed at Long Beach, Calif.

Transcontinental airplane flight by a woman was made by Laura Ingalls, who left Roosevelt Field, N.Y., on October 5, 1930, in a Moth biplane. She made nine stops before reaching Glendale, Calif., on October 9, 1930, in 30 hours and 27 minutes flying time. On October 18 she made a return flight in 25 hours and 35 minutes.

Transcontinental airplane flight (east-bound) was made by Robert Grant Fowler, who left Los Angeles, Calif., on October 19, 1911, in a model B Wright biplane equipped with a 30 h.p. four-cylinder Wright engine. He made 65 landings en route in California, Arizona, New Mexico, Texas, Louisiana, Ala-bama, Georgia, and Florida, and landed at Jacksonville, Fla., on February 8, 1912.

THE FIRST

Transcontinental airship voyage was made by the "Shenandoah," a dirigible of the Zeppelin type, which left Lakehurst, N.J., October 7, 1924, under the command of Lieutenant Commander Zachary Lansdowne, and arrived at San Diego, Calif., October 11, 1924. The "Shenandoah" made the return flight and arrived at Lakehurst, October 25, 1924. The airship was originally the ZR1. It made its maiden trip September 4, 1923, and was christened the "Shenandoah" October 10, 1923, at Lakehurst, N.J. It crashed at Caldwell, Ohio, September 3, 1925.

Transcontinental autogiro flight. *See* Autogiro: Transcontinental autogiro flight

Transcontinental commercial overnight transport service was inaugurated August 1, 1934, by the Transcontinental and Western Air. A twin-motored Douglas monoplane, the "Sky Chief," piloted by Otis Frank Bryan, took off from the Newark Airport, Newark, N.J., August 1, 1934, at 5:24 P.M. and arrived at Kansas City, Mo. Here the passengers transferred to a plane piloted by M. O. Brown and flew to the Glendale Airport, Los Angeles, Calif., where they arrived at 7:13 A.M., August 2, 1934.

Transcontinental dirigible flight (non-rigid dirigible) was made by the C2, which left Langley Field, Newport News, Va., on September 14, 1922, and arrived at Ross Field, Arcadia, Calif., on September 23, 1922. The dirigible was 192 feet long, 64 feet wide, and 67 feet high, and contained 172,000 cubic feet of hydrogen gas. It was powered by two 150 h.p. Wright motors and commanded by Major Harold A. Strauss and Captain George W. McEntire. On its return trip on October 17, 1922, the bag ripped while being towed out of the hangar at San Antonio, Tex., causing an explosion which injured seven of the eight-man crew.

Transcontinental flight in 24 hours flying time was made by Lieutenant William Devoe Coney of the 91st Aero Squadron, who took off from Rockwell Field, San Diego, Calif., at 7:00 P.M., February 21, 1921. He was forced down at Bronte, Tex., by a snowstorm. He completed his flight at Pablo Beach, Jacksonville, Fla., on February 24, 1921, at 7:27 A.M. He covered 2,079 miles in 36 hours and 27 minutes elapsed time and 22 hours and 27 minutes flying time.

Transcontinental flight made by Negroes in their own plane was made by Charles Alfred Anderson of Bryn Mawr, Pa., holder of a transport license, and Dr. Albert Ernest Forsythe of Atlantic City, privately licensed pilot. They took off from Bader Airport, At-

THE FIRST

lantic City, N.J., July 17, 1933, at 2:49 A.M. and arrived at Los Angeles, Calif., July 19, 1933, at 5:30 P.M.

Transcontinental flight within 24 hours was made June 23, 1924, by Lieutenant Russell Lowell Maugham of the Army Air Service in a twelve-cylinder Curtiss PW8 pursuit plane equipped with a 430 h.p. engine. The airplane weighed 2,230 pounds (gross weight 3,599 pounds). The flight started at 3:00 A.M. (New York time), from Mitchel Field, Long Island, N.Y., and concluded at Crissy Field, San Francisco, Calif., 2,670 miles, at 9:48 P.M. (Pacific time). Stops were made to refuel at Dayton, Ohio; St. Joseph, Mo.; North Platte, Neb.; Cheyenne, Wyo.; and Salduro, Utah. The elapsed time was 21 hours and 48 minutes, and the total flying time was 18 hours and 52 minutes.

Transcontinental glider flight. *See* Glider: Glider towed across the continent

Transcontinental non-stop east-west flight by a woman was made by Laura Ingalls in a Wasp-powered Lockheed Orion monoplane, the "Auto da Fé," which left Floyd Bennett field, Brooklyn, N.Y., July 10, 1935, and arrived at Burbank, Calif., 18 hours and 19½ minutes later.

Transcontinental non-stop eastward scheduled service was inaugurated October 19, 1953, when a Trans World Airlines Lockheed Super-Constellation took off from International Airport, Los Angeles, Calif., at 7:09 P.M. (10:09 P.M. New York time) and arrived at Idlewild, New York International Airport, New York City, at 6:26 A.M. (New York time), on October 20, 1953. On westward flights, a stop-over at Chicago, Ill., was made.

Transcontinental non-stop flight was made by Lieutenants Oakley G. Kelly and John A. Macready, of the Air Service, U.S.N. On May 2, 1923, the aviators, piloting a Fokker T2 monoplane equipped with a Liberty Engine, took off from Roosevelt Field, New York, at 11:36 P.M., and arrived at Rockwell Field, Coronado Beach, Calif., at 12:26 P.M., the next day, covering a distance of 2,700 miles in 26 hours and 50 minutes.

Transcontinental non-stop flight by a woman was accomplished by Amelia Earhart Putnam. She took off from Los Angeles, Calif., August 24, 1932, at 4:26 P.M. (New York time), in her red Wasp-powered Lockheed airplane, and arrived at the Newark, N.J., Metropolitan Airport, 11:32 A.M. (New York time). She flew approximately 2,600 miles in 19 hours and 5 minutes.

AVIATION—FLIGHTS (transcontinental)
—Continued

Transcontinental regularly scheduled through air service was opened October 25, 1930, simultaneously from New York City and Los Angeles, Calif., by Transcontinental & Western Air, Inc., a merger of TAT-Maddux Airlines and Western Air Express. The westward flight required 39 hours, of which 25 hours and 35 minutes were in actual flight. Ground time was consumed in stops at Philadelphia, Harrisburg, Pittsburgh, Columbus, Indianapolis, St. Louis, Kansas City (overnight), Wichita, Amarillo, Albuquerque, Winslow, and Los Angeles. The eastbound flight, operating on the same schedule of stations, including the overnight stop at Kansas City, required a total of 34 hours and 18 minutes. Actual time aloft was 23 hours and 43 minutes. The one-way fare was $200.

Transcontinental regularly scheduled two-way non-stop service was instituted November 29, 1953, by American Airlines, using Douglas DC-7's, between International Airport, Los Angeles, Calif., and Idlewild, New York International Airport, New York City. The eastbound flight was scheduled for 7 hours and 15 minutes and the westbound flight for 7 hours and 55 minutes. Preliminary test runs over the 2,540 mile course were made November 20, 1953.

Transcontinental round-trip airplane flight within one day was made June 12, 1946, when a jet-propelled P-80 Shooting Star fighter plane, piloted by Colonel Leon Gray of Casa Grande, Ariz., Major Robin Olds of Beverly Hills, Calif., and Lieutenant Jack Richardson of Oklahoma City, Okla., left March Field, Calif., and arrived at Andrews Field, Md., in 5 hours and 31 minutes with a 34-minute stop at Oklahoma City to refuel. They returned in 6 hours and 45 minutes with stops to refuel at Scott Field, Ill., and Midland, Tex. The trip of approximately 4,540 miles was made in 12 hours and 15 minutes. Total elapsed time, including a drive to Washington, D.C., for luncheon and return to the field, was 14 hours and 51 minutes.

Transcontinental round-trip solo flight between sunrise and sunset was made May 21, 1955, by First Lieutenant John M. Conroy of Van Nuys, Calif., who took off from Los Angeles, Calif., in the "California Boomerang," an F-86 Sabre Jet airplane, at 5:59:45 A.M. (Pacific time), and covered 5,085 miles in 11 hours, 18 minutes, and 27 seconds elapsed time. On the eastbound flight he made stops at Columbus, Ohio; Tulsa, Oklahoma; and Albuquerque, N.M. On the return flight, after a 32-minute stop at Mitchel Field, N.Y., he landed at Denver, Colo., and Springfield, Ill.

AVIATION—FLIGHTS (transpacific)
California-Hawaii flight was made on June 28-29, 1927, by Lieutenants Lester J. Maitland

and Albert Francis Hegenberger, who flew in a triple-engine Fokker monoplane from Oakland, Calif., to Wheeler Field, Oahu Island, Hawaii, 2,400 miles, in 25 hours and 50 minutes. (Lester J. Maitland—Knights of the Air)

Honolulu squadron flight was made by six U.S. Navy seaplanes under the command of Lieutenant Commander Knefler McGinnis. The planes, with 30 aviators, left San Francisco, Calif., January 10, 1934, 2:22 P.M. and arrived at Pearl Harbor, Hawaii, 2,408 miles distant, 24 hours and 56 minutes later, crossing the ocean at an average speed of 100 miles an hour.

Jet transpacific non-stop flight was made July 29, 1952, by a four-jet RB-45 Tornado bomber from Elmendorf Air Force Base at Anchorage, Alaska, to Yokota Air Base, Japan, a distance of 3,460 miles in 9 hours and 50 minutes at an average speed of 350 m.p.h. The plane was refueled twice in flight by B-29 tanker aircraft. The flight was under the command of Major Louis H. Carrington of Austin, Tex., Captain Wallace D. Yancey of Fort Worth, Tex., was copilot, and Major Frederic W. Shook of Fort Worth, Tex., was navigator.

Pacific air mail. See Air mail service; Pacific air mail flight

Transpacific non-stop flight was made by Clyde Pangborn and Hugh Herndon, Jr. who landed at Wenatchee, Wash., October 5, 1931, having covered the 4,458-statute-mile hop from Sabishiro, Japan, in 41 hours and 13 minutes in a single-motored 425 h.p. Bellanca monoplane. This was the last lap of their round-the-world trip.

Woman aviator to fly solo across the Pacific Ocean. See Aviation—Aviator: Woman aviator to fly solo across the Pacific Ocean

AVIATION—FLIGHTS (world)
Jet round-the-world non-stop flight was made by three B-52 Air Force Stratofortress bombers which flew 24,325 miles in 45 hours and 19 minutes at an average speed of 525 m.p.h. under the command of Major General Archie J. Old, Jr., of the 15th Air Force. The take-off was from Castle Air Force Base, Merced, Calif., on January 16, 1957, and the landing was made at March Air Base, Riverside, Calif., on January 18, 1957. The planes were refueled in flight by KC aerial tankers. Each eight-engine jet carried a crew of nine. The route was via Newfoundland, French Morocco, Saudi Arabia, the coasts of India and Ceylon, the Philippines, and Guam.

Round-the-world civil air service began June 17, 1947, when a Pan American airplane, commanded by Hugh Gordon, left La Guardia

Field, New York City, with 21 passengers and a crew of 10. The route, 22,297 miles, was via Gander, London, Istanbul, Karachi, Manila, Bangkok, Calcutta, Shanghai, Tokyo, Guam, Wake, Honolulu, and San Francisco. The first trip took 309 hours and 21 minutes, with 101 hours and 32 minutes actual flying time. Round-trip fare for the world flight was $1,700.

Round-the-world flight over the North Pole on a regularly scheduled commercial air route began November 15, 1954, when the Scandinavian Airlines System, using DC-6B's, inaugurated simultaneous service in both directions between Copenhagen, Denmark, and Los Angeles, Calif. The eastbound flight with 40 passengers left International Airport, Los Angeles, Calif., at 8:23 P.M. (Greenwich Mean Time) and arrived at Copenhagen on November 16, 1954, at 8:18 A.M. (Greenwich time), an elapsed time of 23 hours and 55 minutes (20 hours and 38 minutes flying time) for the 5,800 miles. The westbound flight was made in 24 hours and 11 minutes flying time (27 hours elapsed time).

Round-the-world non-stop airplane flight was made in 94 hours and 1 minute by a B-50 Superfortress, "Lucky Lady II," under the command of Captain James Gallagher. The plane left Carswell Air Force base, Fort Worth, Tex., on February 26, 1949, at 11:21 A.M. It carried a crew of 14 and averaged 249 m.p.h. on its 23,452-mile trip. It was refueled four times in the air by B-29 tanker planes and landed March 2, 1949, at 9:22 A.M.

World flight was made by three of the planes that took part in the round-the-world flight of the U.S. Army Service: the "Chicago," piloted by Lieutenant Lowell Herbert Smith; the "Boston," piloted by Lieutenant Leigh Wade; and the "New Orleans," piloted by Lieutenant Erik Henning Nelson. The "Chicago" and the "New Orleans" crossed the Atlantic from Kirkwall, Scotland, to Indian Harbor, Labrador, stopping at Iceland and Greenland, completing the first round of the world flight. The flight began at Seattle, Wash., April 6, 1924, and ended there on September 28, 1924. The "Boston" was forced down near Faroe Islands in the north Atlantic. This trip also marked the first crossing of the China Sea and the first crossing of the Atlantic via Iceland and Greenland. The flight was made in 57 hops, averaging 483 miles each; and in circumnavigating the globe the aviators touched or traversed 21 countries, 25 states, and 1 territory of the United States. The distance flown was 26,103 miles, the total time 175 days, flying time 351 hours and 11 minutes. *(Lowell Jackson Thomas—The First World Flight)*

World flight by a commercial airplane was made by the "Pacific Clipper," of Pan

American Airways, which left San Francisco, Calif., December 2, 1941, under Captain Robert Ford, and a 10-man crew, and returned to New York City, January 6, 1942, covering 31,500 miles in 209½ hours flying time. The return trip from New Zealand, because of war conditions, was over the Coral Sea, Netherlands East Indies, Indian Ocean, Java Sea, Bay of Bengal, Arabian Sea, Persian Gulf, Red Sea, the Nile and Congo rivers, overland to West Africa, thence to Brazil, and finally to New York.

World solo airplane flight was made by Wiley Hardeman Post in a Lockheed Vega monoplane, the "Winnie Mae." He took off from Floyd Bennett Field, New York City, Saturday, July 15, 1933, at 5:10 A.M. and landed in Berlin, Germany, at 6:55 A.M. the following day (25 hours and 45 minutes). Other stops were at Koenigsberg, Moscow, Novosibirsk, Irkutsk, Rukhlovo, Khabarovsk, Flat, Fairbanks and Edmonton. Post returned to Floyd Bennett Field, Saturday, July 22, 1933, at 11:59:30 P.M., making the round-the-world circuit of 15,596 miles in 7 days, 18 hours, and 49 minutes, of which 115 hours, 36 minutes, and 30 seconds was flying time. His airplane was equipped with a Sperry automatic pilot and a directional radio. Accompanied by Harold Gatty, Post had previously made a round-the-world flight in the "Winnie Mae." Starting from Roosevelt Field, N.Y., on June 23, 1931, they covered a total of 15,474 miles at an average speed of 145.8 m.p.h. They returned July 1, 1931, after an elapsed time of 8 days, 15 hours, and 51 minutes. This trip was 21 hours and 2 minutes longer than the later solo flight by Post, the first man to fly around the world twice. *(Wiley Post—Around the World in Eighty Days)*

AVIATION INSTRUCTION. *See* Aviation—School

AVIATION—LEGISLATION
Airport municipal legislation. *See* Aviation—Airport: Airport municipal legislation

Aviation legislation (national) dealing with the operation of civil aircraft was the Air Commerce Act of 1926 (44 Stat.L.568), approved May 20, 1926, "to encourage and regulate the use of aircraft in commerce, and for other purposes." It was the basis for the formation of the Aeronautics Branch of the Department of Commerce. Legislation dealing with the Army Air Corps and Naval Aeronautics was passed prior to 1926.

Aviation legislation (state) was passed by Connecticut, June 8, 1911 (page 1348, Chapter 86, Public Acts of 1911). The act "concerning the registration, numbering, and use of air ships and the licensing of operators thereof" was recommended by Governor Simeon Eben Baldwin. It required all airships to be regis-

AVIATION—LEGISLATION—Continued

tered ($5 fee) and all applicants for a pilot's license to be tested (fee not over $25). A license to operate and direct airships was required by each pilot ($2 fee). The law also provided as penalty for nonobservance a $100 fine and six months' imprisonment. (Earlier, in 1905, Tennessee passed an act in statutory form which authorized a tax on aircraft, but it did not attempt to regulate or control aircraft.) On May 10, 1927, the legislature of Connecticut authorized the organization of the Connecticut Department of Aviation, the first independent state department for the control and regulation of aeronautics in the United States (Chapter 324). Offices were opened July 1, 1927, at Brainard Field, Hartford, Conn. The first commissioner of aeronautics was Clarence Moore Knox, who served until March 1931.

AVIATION—LICENSE

Airplane instructor's license issued under the Civil Aeronautics Authority created by the Civil Aeronautics Act approved June 23, 1938 (52 Stat.L.973) was a rerated license issued to Arthur J. Banks, Atlanta, Ga., September 27, 1939. The first woman licensed was Evelyn Pinckert Kilgore, San Bernardino, Calif., October 13, 1939. In the early days, "instructor" could be written on a private pilot's license after 200 hours of flight.

Cargo airlines licensed by the Civil Aeronautics Board were the Flying Tiger Line, Inc., Slick Airways, Inc., United States Airlines, and Airnews, Inc., which were issued licenses on April 29, 1949, effective June 24, 1949.

Civil Aeronautics Administration honorary license was awarded to Orville Wright on August 19, 1940, under authority of act of Congress passed June 13, 1940 (54 Stat.L.1283). It authorized the issuance to Orville Wright of "honorary aircraft pilot's certificate numbered one in recognition of the outstanding service rendered by him in advancing the science of aeronautics."

Glider license awarded a woman by the National Aeronautic Association was No. 10 Class "A" issued to Maxine Dunlap (Mrs. Bennett) on February 5, 1931. Requirements were a flight of one-minute duration with two "S" curves and a normal landing.

Glider license Class "C" issued by the National Aeronautic Association (for a flight above the starting point of at least five minutes or a flight of at least five minutes without loss of altitude recorded by a barograph) was license No. 1 issued February 5, 1931, to Commander Ralph Stanton Barnaby, U.S.N. The

first woman to receive the license was Mrs. Hattie Meyer Barnaby, Washington, D.C., who was awarded license No. 37, August 12, 1931.

Glider pilot's license issued by the National Aeronautic Association was awarded to Leonard A. Wiggins, Akron, Ohio, on October 7, 1930. He was the first to receive both the "A" license (for a flight of one-minute duration with two "S" curves and normal landing) and the "B" license (for a starting, 360-degree turn both to the left and the right).

Glider pilot's license (honorary) was No. 1, which was issued to Clarence Marshall Young, assistant Secretary of Commerce for Aeronautics, on November 7, 1929. Licenses were issued for student, commercial, and non-commercial classes. (Records in Aeronautics Branch, Department of Commerce. Washington, D.C.)

Pilot's license granted to a woman by the U.S. Department of Commerce was issued to Mrs. Phoebe Fairgrave Omlie, who, on June 30, 1927, obtained Transport License No. 199. (Records in Aeronautics Branch, Department of Commerce. Washington, D.C.)

Pilot's license issued by the Aero Club of America, the first society officially recognized by the Fédération Aéronautique Internationale, was license No. 1, which was awarded to Glenn Hammond Curtiss on June 8, 1911.

Pilot's license issued by the U.S. Department of Commerce was Private Pilot's License No. 1, awarded on April 6, 1927, to William Patterson MacCracken, Jr., former Assistant Secretary of Commerce for Aeronautics. (Records in Aeronautics Branch, Department of Commerce. Washington, D.C.)

President to hold an airplane pilot's license. See President (United States): President to hold an airplane pilot's license

Woman aviator to pass the test of the Aero Club of America was Harriet Quimby of New York, who on August 1, 1911, successfully passed her license test. (F.A.I. License #37). She was also the first woman to cross the English channel in a plane.

AVIATION—MAGAZINE

Aviation magazine was Aeronautics, published from October 1893 to September 1894 by the American Engineer and Railroad Journal, New York City. It was edited by Matthias Nace Forney, and featured reports and articles about airplanes, gliders, and balloons. It contained 16 pages and sold for 10 cents a copy or $1 a year.

THE FIRST

Aviation magazine devoted primarily to airplanes was *Fly,* published November 1908 in Philadelphia, Pa., by (Alfred William) Lawson and (John F.) Kelley. It contained 20 pages and sold for 10 cents a copy or $1 a year. The cover showed a girl seated on the back of an American eagle beckoning to the aviators piloting the only two airplanes that could fly. (*The American Magazine of Aeronautics,* published in July 1907, was devoted to balloons, kites, etc., as well as to airplanes.)

AVIATION—MEDICINE (book). *See* Medical book: Aviation medicine book

AVIATION—PARACHUTE

Aviator to bail out of a disabled airplane was Lieutenant Harold R. Harris, chief of the flying section of McCook Field, Dayton, Ohio, who jumped from a 'Loening monoplane on October 20, 1922, 2,000 feet over North Dayton, Ohio, before his plane crashed.

Aviator to bail out of an airplane flying at supersonic speed was George Franklin Smith of Manhattan Beach, Calif., who was propelled into the air when his seat automatically detached itself from an F-100A Super Sabre Jet fighter on February 26, 1955, above the Los Angeles International Airport, Los Angeles, Calif. He was at an altitude of 6,500 feet at the supersonic speed of 777 m.p.h. His clothes were cut to ribbons, and his socks, helmet, and oxygen mask were stripped off. He felt deceleration of 40 G's so that his organs weighed forty times normal. He landed in the ocean and was rescued by a passing boat off Laguna Beach, Calif. He was hospitalized about six months.

Moving picture actor to stage a parachute jump. *See* Moving picture actor: Stunt actor

Nylon parachute jump was made June 6, 1942, from an airplane at Brainard Field, Hartford, Conn., by Adeline Gray, parachute rigger of the Pioneer Parachute Company, Manchester, Conn.

Parachute known as the "free parachute" —the type with which the operator jumps before pulling the rip cord—was developed by the Army Air Corps under the direction of Major Edward L. Hoffman. The first person to jump with the Army chute was Leslie Le Roy Irving at McCook Field, Dayton, Ohio, on April 28, 1919. (*Records in Air Corps Materiel Division. Wright Field, Dayton, Ohio*)

Parachute jump from a balloon was made by Charles Guille, who ascended August 2, 1819, from Vauxhall Gardens, New York City, in a wicker basket decorated with flowers suspended from a 25,000-cubic-foot prepared-silk

THE FIRST

balloon which cost $3,000. Avoiding a squall, he jumped from a height of two miles with an umbrella-shaped parachute and fell 300 feet before it expanded. He drifted across the East River and in 15 minutes was out of sight, landing at New Bushwick, Long Island, four miles from the city. He carried two phials of hartshorn and cologne water to counteract dizziness.

Parachute jump from an airplane was made March 1, 1912 by Captain Albert Berry from a Benoist Pusher plane, piloted by Antony Jannus, at Jefferson Barracks, St. Louis, Mo. Berry jumped from an altitude of 1,500 feet while the plane was traveling 50 miles an hour.

Parachute jump from an airplane by a woman was made by Georgia ("Tiny") Broadwick, 18 years old, on June 21, 1913, over Griffith Field, Los Angeles, Calif., from an airplane piloted by Glenn Martin and flying at a 1,000-foot altitude and a speed of 30 m.p.h. After a 100-foot drop, her "life boat," an 11-pound silken parachute, opened and she landed in a barley field.

Parachute jump from an autogiro was made November 15, 1931, by Frankie Hammond, a parachute jumper of West Paterson, N.J., from a Pitcairn Autogiro at an air circus at Caldwell, N.J. The air show was for the benefit of the family of Victor Brooks, Keyport aviator, who was killed November 1, 1931, when his plane crashed during a race at Stanhope, N.J.

Parachute tower for training parachute jumpers was a free-drop tower built April 1935, at Hightstown, N.J., by the Safe Parachute Jump Company, Hightstown, N.J. The tower was 125 feet high, with a horizontal arm at the top capable of being rotated 360 degrees.

Parachute wedding. *See* Wedding: Parachute wedding

AVIATION—PASSENGER

Admiral in uniform to ride in an airplane was Rear Admiral Bradley Allen Fiske, U.S.N., who flew over the Hudson River and New York City on May 10, 1912, in a plane piloted by Walter Brookins and Robert Joseph Collier. (*Bradley Allen Fiske—From Midshipman to Rear Admiral*)

Airplane passenger (official) was Lieutenant Frank Purdy Lahm, who flew 6 minutes and 26 seconds at Fort Myer, Va., on September 9, 1908, in a Wright plane piloted by Orville Wright. The first passenger to fly was Charles W. Furnas, who went aloft May 14, 1908, with Wilbur Wright at the controls.

THE FIRST

AVIATION—PASSENGER—*Continued*
Dirigible passenger transfer to an airplane
was effected on August 29, 1929, at the Cleveland, Ohio, Air Show. Lieutenant Adolphus W. Gorton of the U.S. Navy attached a hawser, stretched between two uprights on the top wing of his plane, to a hook attached to a ladder of metal girders lowered from the keel of the dirigible "Los Angeles." Lieutenant Calvin Bolster then descended to the plane.

Woman airplane passenger was the wife of Captain Ralph Henry Van Deman of the General Staff of the U.S. Army, who made a 4-minute flight October 27, 1909, at College Park, Md., with Wilbur Wright at the tiller.

Woman airplane passenger to cross the Atlantic Ocean was Amelia Earhart, who rode as the passenger of Wilmer Stultz, the pilot, and Louis Gordon, the mechanic, in the "Friendship," a tri-motored Fokker airplane. They left Trespassey, Newfoundland, on June 17, 1928, and in 20 hours and 40 minutes arrived at Burry Port, Wales. Miss Earhart (later Mrs. George Palmer Putnam) was the first American aviatrix to whom the International Aeronautic Federation awarded a pilot's license. The award was made in 1923. (*Amelia Earhart —Twenty Hours Forty Minutes*)

Woman airplane passenger (transcontinental) was Lillian Gatlin of Santa Ana, Calif., who in a U.S. Post Office De Havilland mail plane equipped with a 400 h.p. Liberty motor, left San Francisco, Calif., October 5, 1922. Stops were made at Reno, Salt Lake City, Rock Springs, Cheyenne, North Platte, Omaha, Iowa City, Chicago, and Cleveland. The flight covered 2,680 miles in 27 hours and 11 minutes flying time. The final lap from Cleveland, Ohio, to Mineola, N.Y., was made by pilot Elmer C. Leonhardt, who landed at Curtiss Field, October 8, 1922.

Woman flown in a U.S. Army plane from one country to another was Senora Herminia Davila, wife of Carlos Davila, former President of Chile. She was ill and was taken on board on a stretcher December 7, 1939, at Mitchel Field, Long Island, N.Y., and arrived at Santiago, Chile, on December 9, 1939.

Woman to fly entirely around the world by commercial heavier-than-air plane was Marjorie Shuler (Mrs. Felix Charles), who left Southampton, England, on June 4, 1938, and flew across Europe, down into Africa, across Asia, to Australia, back to Bangkok, to Hongkong, and across the Pacific, and from San Francisco, Calif., to New York City. She took off from Port Washington, Long Island, N.Y., June 17, 1939, and completed her trip at Marseilles, France, June 19, 1939, covering the last leg of her flight from New York to

THE FIRST

Marseilles, 4,650 miles, in 42 hours and 28 minutes. (*Marjorie Shuler—A Passenger to Adventure*)

Woman Zeppelin passenger (paying) was Clara Adams of Tannersville, Pa., who left Lakehurst, N.J., on Monday, October 29, 1928, in the Graf Zeppelin on its eastward return flight to Germany.

AVIATION—RACES
Airplane passenger race around the world to test commercial flying routes started September 30, 1936, from Lakehurst, N.J. Three reporters, Dorothy Kilgallen, Herbert Roslyn Ekins, and Leo Kiernan, made the trip by different routes. The race was won by Ekins of the New York *World Telegram*, who returned to Lakehurst, October 19, 1936, covering 25,654 miles in 18 days, 11 hours, 14 minutes, and 33 seconds. The average speed was 127 m.p.h. The total flying time was 8 days, 10 hours, and 6 minutes. (*Dorothy Kilgallen—Girl Around the World*)

Airplane race (of importance) in which both men and women were contestants was the National Air Race, August 30-31, 1931, from Los Angeles, Calif., to Cleveland, Ohio, in which 36 men and 16 women competed. It was a handicap derby scored on the basis of comparative power of motor and speed of plane. It was won by Phoebe Fairgrave Omlie of Memphis, Tenn., to whom an award was given on August 31, 1931. She also won the grand prize and the prize for the women's division.

Airplane race won by an American in Europe was the First International Air Race held at Rheims, France, during the week of August 22, 1909. The fastest time on the 20-kilometer course was 15 minutes, 50 6/10 seconds. The race was won by Glenn Hammond Curtiss, who was also the first to win the James Gordon Bennett trophy in aeronautics.

Airplane to race a train was piloted by Glenn Hammond Curtiss, who took off May 29, 1910, from Van Rensselaer Island, Albany, N.Y., at 7:02 A.M. At 8:30 A.M. he landed at Poughkeepsie, N.Y., where he refueled the plane with 8 gallons of gasoline and 1½ gallons of oil. Another stop was made at 214th Street, New York City, before the landing at Governors Island, N.Y. The distance of 150 miles was covered in 4 hours and 57 minutes, of which 2 hours and 46 minutes was flying time. The plane weighed 1,000 pounds and had a 30-foot length and a 30-foot wing spread. It was powered by an 8-cylinder, 40 h.p. V engine built by the Elbridge Engine Company, Rochester, N.Y. Curtiss won a $10,000 prize offered by the New York *World*. Although this event had been scheduled as a race, the train really served as an observation train. (*Clara Studer —Sky Storming Yankee*)

THE FIRST

Inter-city airplane race was held August 5, 1911, between New York City and Philadelphia, Pa. Three Curtiss machines with Curtiss engines left Governors Island, N.Y. The race was won by Lincoln Beachey, who covered the 83 miles in 1 hour and 50 minutes time. Hugh Robinson completed the trip in 2 hours, 8 minutes, and 47 seconds, while Eugene Ely was forced to land at Princeton, N.J.

Transcontinental air race was held October 8, 1919. Fifteen planes left San Francisco, Calif., and forty-eight left Roosevelt Field, Mineola, N.Y., in a 5,400-mile race across the continent and back in the aerial derby sponsored by the American Flying Club of New York. Lieutenant Belvin W. Maynard, in a De Havilland-4 with a Liberty motor, crossed the continent in 24 hours, 59 minutes, and 48½ seconds actual flying time. He left Mineola, October 8, 1919, 9:24 A.M. and landed at the Presidio, San Francisco, October 11, in the elapsed time of 3 days, 6 hours, and 4 minutes. He left the Presidio, October 14, 1:19 P.M. and arrived at Roosevelt Field, October 19, in the elapsed time of 3 days, 21 hours, and 31 minutes. Maynard won by elapsed time, but his actual flying time he was eclipsed by three others.

AVIATION—SCHOOL

Aeronautical engineering course (complete college course) was given in 1913-1914 under the Department of Naval Architecture and Marine Engineering, Massachusetts Institute of Technology, Cambridge, Mass. Lectures in aeronautics were given in 1912 and 1913. The first regular instructor in aeronautical engineering was appointed in 1913. The aerodynamic laboratory was placed in operation and a graduate course was established leading to the degree of Master of Science in Aeronautical Engineering in 1914.

Air Force Academy (U.S.) *See* Air Force Academy (U.S.): Air Force Academy

Air Force survival school was conducted by the 3904th Composite Wing, Strategic Air Command, in December 1949. It was moved to Stead Air Force Base, Reno, Nev., in 1952. Training began in July 1952. The Stead Air Force Base and the survival school became a part of the Air Training Command's Crew Training Air Force on September 1, 1954, at which time the 3635th Combat Crew Training Wing was activated. Colonel Burton E. McKenzie assumed command of the Training Wing in July 1955. The course lasted 17 days and was devoted to instruction in survival under adverse conditions with limited food supplies.

Airplane flying school was opened by the Curtiss Exhibition Company in September 1910. It gave military officers free instruction in fly-

THE FIRST

ing at the field at Lake Keuka, Hammondsport, N.Y. Glenn Hammond Curtiss was the instructor. The first officer of the U.S. Army assigned to these courses was Captain Paul N. Beck, who became the first "military aviator." The Navy Department also sent officers for instruction in flying.

Airplane flying school operated by a woman was the Stinson School of Flying, San Antonio, Tex., owned and opened in 1914 by Emma B. Stinson (mother of Jack, Eddie, and Katherine Stinson). On January 20, 1916, a field of about 200 acres was leased from the city of San Antonio for $5 a year.

High school aviation course was instituted by Haaren High School, New York City, in September 1929 with eleven students under the direction of William Arnheim. In September 1931 an aviation annex was organized and the 833 boys enrolled in the aviation course were transferred to this building. In 1944, 3,500 students were enrolled.

Naval air training school was the U.S. Navy Aeronautic Station, Pensacola, Fla., opened December 1, 1914, under the command of Captain Henry Croskey Mustin. The first staff consisted of three instructors and a dozen mechanics. The name was later changed to the U.S. Naval Air Station. From 1911 to 1914, flight training was given at a camp at Greensbury Point, near Annapolis, Md.

AVOCADO was imported by Henry Perrine in 1833 and planted at Santa Barbara, Calif. *(Wilson Poppenoe—Manual of Tropical and Subtropical Fruits)*

AXE manufacturing plant was erected in 1800 at Johnstown, N.Y., by William Mann. The business was continued by his family at various locations and was sold in 1890 to the American Axe and Tool Co.

AXMINSTER CARPETS. *See* Carpet loom: Carpet power loom to weave Axminster carpets

BABIES' HOSPITAL. *See* Hospital: Babies' hospital designed exclusively for infants

BABY CARRIAGE was made by Charles Burton in 1848 in New York City. Protests were heard because the people wheeling them showed a tendency to hit pedestrians. Burton moved to England where he opened a factory and obtained orders for his "perambulator" from Queen Victoria, Queen Isabella II of Spain, and the Pasha of Egypt. *(Chronicles of a Baby Carriage—F. A. Whitney Carriage Co.)*

THE FIRST

BABY CARRIAGE FACTORY successfully operated was started in 1858 in Leominster, Mass., under the firm name of F. W. & F. A. Whitney. This later became the F. A. Whitney Carriage Company. The carriages had two wheels, with a long tongue and supporting standard in front, and were made of wood. The first year only 75 carriages were built.

BABY SHOW was held at Springfield, Ohio, October 5, 1854, more in a spirit of jest than with a serious object. It met with instant favor and 127 babies were entered, the prize baby being the 10-month old daughter of William Ronemus of Vienna, Ohio, who was awarded a silver plate service including a large salver worth $300. Three other prizes were awarded.

BABY SITTERS' INSURANCE POLICY. See Insurance: Baby sitters' insurance policy

BACHELOR TAXES. See Tax: Bachelor tax

BACHELOR'S DEGREES. See under Degrees (academic and honorary)

BACK-PEDAL BICYCLE BRAKE. See Bicycle: Bicycle with a back pedal brake

BACTERIOLOGY INSTRUCTION. See Medical instruction: Bacteriology courses in a college

BACTERIOLOGY LABORATORY
Bacteriology diagnostic laboratory, as an integral part of the work of a health department, was the Division of Pathology, Bacteriology and Disinfection, established by the Department of Health of New York City in 1892. The first director of the laboratory was Dr. Hermann Michael Biggs, who served from September 14, 1892, to February 3, 1902. (Wade Wright Oliver—The Man Who Lived for Tomorrow)

Bacteriology laboratory was the Hoagland Laboratory, 335 Henry Street, Brooklyn, N.Y., incorporated February 21, 1887, and opened for experimentation in February 1889. The first "Director of Laboratory and Department of Bacteriology" was Dr. George Miller Sternberg, who demonstrated the microbe of pneumonia in saliva. The laboratory is a privately endowed institution and retains its corporate identity although affiliated with the Long Island College of Medicine, Brooklyn, N.Y. (Private bacteriology laboratories had been established earlier by individual physicians.)

BACTERIOLOGY LECTURES. See Medical instruction: Bacteriology lectures

THE FIRST

BACTERIOLOGY TEXTBOOK. See Medical book: Bacteriology textbook

BAGS (PAPER). See Paper bag manufacturing machine

BAHA'I HOUSE OF WORSHIP was opened at Wilmette, Ill., for public lectures and guided tours on May 1, 1931. The site was blessed by Abdu'l-Baha, son of Baha'u'llah on May 1, 1912. The temple was dedicated for public worship on May 2, 1953.

BAKING POWDER MANUFACTURER was Benjamin Talbert Babbitt, whose Star Yeast Powder was introduced to the public in 1870.

BAKING SODA (bicarbonate of soda) commercial production was undertaken by John Dwight and Dr. Austin Church in 1846, in New York City. In 1847 they organized John Dwight & Company.

BALL BEARING commercial installation was made October 30, 1794, on the weathervane topping the steeple of the Evangelical Lutheran Church of the Holy Trinity, Lancaster, Pa. The brick portion of the tower rises 86 feet and includes the bell chamber, above which rises a spire from an octagonal base to a height of 195 feet, on top of which is the weather vane. The bearings were of the anti-friction roller type with a pin through them.

BALL-BEARING SKATE PATENT. See Roller skate: Ball-bearing skate patent

BALL-POINT PEN. See Pen: Ball-point pen patent

BALLET was presented February 7, 1827, in "The Deserter," at the Bowery Theatre, New York City. The danseuse, Madame Francisquy Hutin, who introduced the modern ballet, wore a dress of gauze, and "a sort of subdued expression of fear and terror simultaneously rose from the ladies present, and at the next instant, as if inspired by one idea, they fled from the house." (New York Clipper, November 23, 1872)

BALLISTIC MISSILE. See Rocket: Ballistic missile

BALLISTIC MISSILE OPERATIONAL UNIT. See Army: Ballistic missile operational unit

BALLISTIC MISSILE SUBMARINE. See Submarine: Ballistic missile submarine

THE FIRST

BALLOON
See also Aviation—Airship

Balloon Atlantic crossing attempt was made by the 300,000-cubic foot "Daily Graphic," which was launched on October 6, 1873, in Capitoline Gardens, Brooklyn, N.Y. Instead of a basket, a life boat supported by two slings was used. The crew consisted of Captain Washington Harrison Donaldson, George Ashton Lunt, and a newspaperman, Alfred Ford. The balloon left the earth at 9:19 A.M. Later the crew ran into a storm and jumped, near New Canaan, Conn., at 1:15 P.M. (*Washington Harrison Donaldson—History of Donaldson's Balloon Ascensions*)

Balloon carrier. *See* Ship: Balloon carrier

Balloon circular flight was made by the "California Arrow," constructed by Captain Thomas Scott Baldwin and equipped with a Curtiss motor. It made its first circular flight on August 3, 1904, at Oakland, Calif.

Balloon corps (army). *See* Army balloon corps

Balloon destroyed by enemy gun fire was shot down by the Spaniards July 1, 1898, at Santiago, Cuba. It was piloted by Colonel George Derby of the Army Engineer Department who advised the Army as to the enemy's movements. The balloon was above the American troops, and the soldiers were glad that it was brought down as it drew fire in their direction.

Balloon filled with helium gas as a substitute for hydrogen was the C-7, a non-rigid United States Navy dirigible. On December 1, 1921, it sailed from the naval air station at Hampton Roads, Va., to Washington, D.C., and returned. It contained 181,000 cubic feet of gas.

Balloon flight was made by Edward Warren, 13 years old, on June 23, 1784, at Baltimore, Md., in Peter Carnes' balloon, 35 feet in diameter and 30 feet high, made of silk of various colors. The air was rarefied by a cylindrical stove of iron suspended under the balloon. Carnes attempted a flight on July 17, 1784, at Philadelphia, Pa., but the balloon burst into flames. (*Maryland Journal and Baltimore Advertiser. June 24, 1784*)

Balloon flight by a native-born American in the United States was made by Charles Ferson Durant, the first to make aeronautics a profession. On September 9, 1830, at Castle Garden, New York City, he gave an exhibition in a balloon which he constructed at his own home and flew to Perth Amboy, N.J. Durant

THE FIRST

was the first person to land on board a ship, a feat which he performed in Chesapeake Bay on the "Independence." For his accomplishment he was awarded a gold medal in 1836 by the American Institute. (*Eric Adolphus Dime—Charles Ferson Durant—America's First Aeronaut*)

Balloon flight carrying mail was made by John Wise in the "Jupiter" on August 17, 1859, from Lafayette, Ind. He carried 123 letters and 23 circulars in a pouch. His destination was New York City, but instead he landed at Crawfordsville, Ind., about 27 miles south of the take-off. On July 1, 1859, he endeavored to fly mail from St. Louis, Mo., to New York City, but he jettisoned it in a storm.

Balloon flight in which a presidential order was carried was a 40-minute flight made by Jean Pierre Blanchard of France, who left Philadelphia, Pa., at 10:16 A.M., January 9, 1793, in the presence of President George Washington and other officials. He was permitted the use of the courtyard of the prison at Germantown, Philadelphia, and the roar of artillery announced the moment of his departure. President Washington presented him with an order "To all to whom these presents shall come" directing that he be allowed "to pass in such direction and to descend in such places as circumstances may render most convenient." The balloon reached about one mile in altitude. He landed in Deptford Township, Gloucester County, N.J., about 15 miles away. (*Jean Pierre Blanchard—Journal of My 45th Ascension, Being the First Performed in America*)

Balloon flight to exceed an altitude of 40,000 feet was made by Captain Hawthorne C. Gray of the U.S. Army Air Service, who ascended on May 4, 1927, from Scott Field, Ill., in a free balloon 80,000 cubic feet in capacity with 3,800 pounds of sand ballast. He reached an altitude of 42,470 feet in a flight of 1 hour and 57 minutes. Trouble developed over Grayville, Ill., and the balloon descended too rapidly. Abandoning the balloon at an altitude of 8,900 feet, he parachuted and landed at Golden Gate, Ill.

Balloon flight to exceed an altitude of 70,000 feet was made November 11, 1935, by Captains Orvil A. Anderson and Albert William Stevens, U.S. Army Air Forces, from Rapid City, S.D., in the Explorer II which ascended to 72,394 feet. It landed 12 miles from White Lake, S.D., about 240 miles east of the starting point. The 3,700,000 cubic foot capacity free balloon was aloft 8 hours and 13 minutes.

Balloon flight to exceed an altitude of 100,000 feet was made by the Winzen Research Balloon flown as part of project "Man-

BALLOON—*Continued*
high" from Crosby, Minn., on August 19,
1957. It descended at Elm Lake, S.D., August
20, 1957, having reached an altitude of 101,516
feet during its 32 hours in the stratosphere.
For approximately 26 hours, its altitude was
over 90,000 feet. Major David Goodman
Simons, medical officer of the U.S. Air Force,
was awarded the Distinguished Flying Cross
for this flight on August 24, 1957.

Balloon marriage ceremony. *See* Wedding:
Balloon wedding

Balloon parachute descent. *See* Aviation—
Parachute: Parachute jump from a balloon

Balloon wedding. *See* Wedding: Balloon
wedding

Dirigible. *See* Aviation—Airship: Dirigible

BALLOON CORPS (army). *See* Army
balloon corps

BALLOON RACE
Balloon cup race for the James Gordon
Bennett Aeronautic Cup was won by Lieutentant
Frank Purdy Lahm, pilot of the balloon "United
States," who on September 30, 1906, with Major
Henry Blanchard Hersey, flew from Paris,
France, to Whitby, England, covering 410 miles
in 22 hours and 17 minutes. Sixteen balloons
from seven countries were entered. The first
race in the United States was held October 21,
1907, at St. Louis, Mo., and won by the German
balloon "Pommern," which, with Oscar Erbslon
and Henry Holm Clayton as pilots, flew 880
miles to Asbury Park, N.J. in 39 hours, 59
minutes, and 25 seconds. There were nine
balloon entrants in the 1907 race.

Dirigible balloon race was held at St.
Louis, Mo., October 4-9, 1909, at which time
four dirigibles, all the existing dirigibles in the
United States, flew from Forest Park and
Clayton Road to Kingshighway and Lindell
Avenues and back. The first prize of $1,000
was won by Lincoln Beachey. Roy Knabenshue
and Captain Thomas Baldwin were close run-
ners-up. Cornwall Dixon, using foot power, was
carried over the city and landed in East St.
Louis. The four dirigibles were housed in improvised tents and were filled with hydrogen
produced by a slow process with sulphuric acid
and iron filings.

BALLOON SCHOOL (army). *See* Army
balloon school

BALLOON TIRE. *See* Automobile tire:
Balloon tire production

BALLOT. *See* Election: Printed ballot

BALLOT SYSTEM (Australian). *See* Election law: Australian ballot system

BANANA IMPORTATION was recorded
in 1804, when the schooner "Reynard" brought
thirty bundles of bananas from Cuba. (*Philip
Keep Reynolds—The Banana*)

BAND SAWMILL. *See* Sawmill: Band
sawmill

BAND WAGON utilized for the distribution
of samples and advertising matter was employed in 1871 by Benjamin Talbert Babbitt,
who used eight imported white Arabian stallions to pull the wagon. The band was seated
on top of the wagon. His slogan, "For All
Nations," appearing on advertising cards over
the doors of the Broadway street cars, was
prominently featured. (Babbitt had the distinction of being one of the first to advertise
in cars and buses.) (*John William Leonard—
History of the City of New York*)

BANDING (bird). *See* Bird banding: Bird
banding

BANJO CLOCK PATENT. *See* Clock:
Banjo clock patent

BANK
"Autobank" complete service was instituted November 12, 1946, by the Exchange National Bank of Chicago. Ten tellers' windows
protected by heavy bullet-proof glass and im-
pregnable corrugated steel were equipped with
automatic slide-out drawers to enable motorists
to transact business without leaving their automobiles.

Bank chartered by Congress was the
Bank of North America in Philadelphia, Pa.,
which was organized on November 1, 1781. It
commenced business on January 7, 1782, with a
total capital of $400,000, of which amount the
government subscribed $250,000. Thomas Will-
ing was elected president and Tench Francis,
cashier. Later the bank entered the National
Banking System. (*Laurence Lewis—A History
of the Bank of North America, the First Bank
Chartered in the United States.*)

Bank established in a foreign country by
a United States bank was opened November 10,
1914, by the National City Bank of New York
in Buenos Aires, Argentina. The Federal Reserve Act (38 Stat.L.251) approved December
23, 1913, permitted American banks to establish
branches abroad.

THE FIRST

Bank for Negroes operated by Negroes was the savings bank of the Grand Fountain of the United Order of True Reformers, a special order founded by William W. Browne, which was incorporated in 1881 in Richmond, Va. The bank, chartered in March 2, 1888, began operations April 3, 1889, with a paid-up capital of $4,000. The first day's deposits were $1,268.69. The board of directors was elected by the society. (The Freedman's Savings and Trust Company, established in 1865, was not a Negro bank, but a bank operated by whites for Negroes.) *(New England Magazine. Vol. 32. 1905.)*

Bank for Negroes privately operated by Negroes and independent of fraternal connections was the Capitol Savings Bank of Washington, D.C., organized October 17, 1888, with a capital of $6,000.00. *(Association for the Study of Negro Life and History, Inc. Arnett Grant Lindsay, John Henry Harmon, and Carter Godwin Woodson—The Negro as a Business Man)*

Bank of the United States was sponsored by the Federalist Party and was chartered February 25, 1791, by "an act to incorporate the subscribers to the Bank of the United States" (1 Stat.L.191), in Philadelphia, Pa. Although the charter made no specific provision for the deposit of government funds, the Secretary of the Treasury, Alexander Hamilton, used the bank as a fiscal agent. The charter expired in 1811 and was not renewed by Congress because of the opposition of the Democratic-Republicans. The closing of the bank was partly responsible for the panic of 1814. The second Bank of the United States was authorized on April 10, 1816 (3 Stat.L.266) and was opened on January 7, 1817. It ceased functioning as a national institution in March 1836. *(Louis Carroll Root—The First United States Bank)*

Bank open day and night was the Night and Day Bank, New York City, opened May 1, 1906, with a capital of $200,000, a surplus of $200,000, and a reserve of $100,000. Oakleigh Thorne was the first president. The idea was originated by Thomas Benedict Clarke. The bank closed at midnight June 5, 1910. It later became the Harriman National Bank.

Bank payments to depositors of a closed insured bank were made by the Federal Deposit Insurance Company on July 3, 1934, to the depositors in the Fond du Lac State Bank, East Peoria, Ill., which suspended business May 28, 1934, and went into receivership June 25, 1934. The insured deposits were approximately $104,000.

Bank president (Negro woman) was Maggie Lena Walker, who founded the Saint Luke Penny Savings Bank, Richmond, Va., incor-

THE FIRST

porated July 28, 1903. It had a paid-in capital of $25,000. The first day's deposits exceeded $8,000. *(Sadie Iola Daniel—Woman Builders)*

Bank to operate a window in a subway station for the convenience of subway riders was the Bowery Savings Bank, New York City, which opened two tellers' windows in a glass-enclosed cubicle in the Grand Central Station of the Interborough Rapid Transit subway on September 26, 1955. The windows have bullet-resistant glass. A special receptacle for passing money and bankbooks permits only one side to be open at a time.

Checkmaster plan (checking account service with no minimum balance requirements) was introduced June 27, 1935, by the National Safety Bank and Trust Company, New York City. A charge of five cents was made for each check drawn and each item deposited.

Christmas savings club was originated by Merkel Landis, treasurer of the Carlisle Trust Company, Carlisle, Pa., in 1909, and placed in operation by that bank the same year. The first payment was received December 1, 1909.

Clearing house was the New York Clearing House, organized August 23, 1853, by 16 presidents, 1 vice president, and 21 cashiers representing 38 banks, at the Merchants Bank, New York City. The plan was presented August 31, 1853, and was adopted September 13, 1853. The exchange was opened October 11, 1853, at 14 Wall Street. Total clearings the first day were $22,648,109.87 and the balances $1,290,-572.38. The New York Clearing House Association charter, drawn by George Curtis, was adopted June 6, 1854. *(James Sloan Gibbons—The Banks of New York)*

Drive-in bank. *See* Bank: "Autobank" complete service

Export-Import Bank of Washington, D.C., was organized February 8, 1934, pursuant to Executive Order No.6581 dated February 2, 1934, "to aid in financing and to facilitate exports and imports and the exchange of commodities" between the United States, its territories, insular possessions, and any foreign country or its agencies or nations. The bank is a District of Columbia corporation, the certificate of which was filed February 12, 1934. Officers were elected February 13, 1934. The first president was George Nelson Peek, the first secretary Warren Lee Pierson. The capital stock of the corporation was $1 million par value of common stock and $10 million par value of preferred stock.

Federal Home Loan Bank Board. *See* Federal Home Loan Bank Board

BANK—*Continued*

Federal reserve system was placed in operation on November 16, 1914, when the twelve Federal Reserve Banks were formally opened. The Federal Reserve Act, approved December 23, 1913 (38 Stat.L.251), was an "act to provide for the establishment of Federal Reserve Banks, to furnish an elastic currency . . . to establish a more effective supervision of banking in the United States."

Freedmen's bank was the Freedman's Savings and Trust Company, for the Negro, chartered by Congress (13 Stat.L.510) March 3, 1865. A central bank was established in Washington, D.C., with branches in 34 cities. The bank was in operation about eight years, during which time it received deposits amounting to $57 million. The depreciation in security values due to the panic of 1873 caused the trustees to vote to close the bank, the affairs of which were placed in the hands of three commissioners.

Joint stock land bank chartered was the Iowa Joint Stock Land Bank of Sioux City, Iowa. It was chartered April 24, 1917, and authorized to do business in the states of Iowa and South Dakota. The charter was granted under the Federal Farm Loan Act of July 17, 1916 (39 Stat.L.360).

National bank under the national banking law of February 25, 1863 (12 Stat.L.665), an "act to provide a national currency," was the first National Bank of Davenport, Iowa, now the Union Savings Bank and Trust Company. The application for the charter was mailed from Davenport, Iowa, on February 24, 1863, one day prior to President Abraham Lincoln's signing the bill. Charters were numbered in the order in which they were received in Washington, D.C. Davenport, being located some distance from Washington received charter No. 15, dated June 22, 1863. Subscription books were opened on May 25 and in three days the capital stock of $100,000 had been subscribed. The first stockholders' meeting was held Saturday, May 30, and the first directors were elected June 6, 1863, to serve until January 12, 1864. The first president was Austin Corbin. The bank was opened on June 29, 1863. For two days the bank was the only national bank in operation under the new act.

National bank branch legally operated was the Pascagoula National Bank of Moss Point, Miss., Charter No. 8,593. This bank was a conversion of the Bank of Moss Point, a state association, with a branch at Scranton, Miss. (now known as Pascagoula). This branch was retained and operated by the Pascagoula National Bank of Moss Point under authority conferred by the Act of March 3, 1865 (13 Stat.L.484), which provided that "any bank or banking association organized under state laws, and having branches, the capital

being joint and assigned to and used by the mother bank and branches in definite proportions, may, if it becomes a national banking association in conformity with existing laws, retain and keep in operation its branches, or such one or more of them as it may elect to retain." The Pascagoula National Bank of Moss Point was chartered on March 14, 1907, and is still in operation, together with the branch at Pascagoula, Miss. The branch at Pascagoula has operated continually since the opening of the parent bank at Moss Point.

National bank chartered was the First National Bank of Philadelphia, Pa., Charter No. 1. This bank, chartered on June 20, 1863, was no conversion of a state bank into the national system, but a primary organization. It opened for business July 11, 1863.

National bank failure was the First National Bank of Attica, N.Y., placed in receivership April 14, 1865. The failure was due to injudicious banking and failure of large debtors. The receivership was terminated January 2, 1867.

National bank woman president was Frances Estelle (Mason) Moulton, who was elected January 11, 1938, as president of the Limerick National Bank, Limerick, Me., to fill the vacancy caused by the death of her father, Jeremiah Miller Mason.

Postal savings bank was authorized by President William Howard Taft on June 25, 1910 (36 Stat.L.814), when he signed the "act to establish postal savings depositories for depositing savings at interest," introduced by Senator Thomas Henry Carter of Montana on January 26, 1910, an act which created a board of trustees consisting of the Postmaster General, the Secretary of the Treasury, and the Attorney General, severally, acting ex officio, for the control, supervision, and administration of the postal savings system. Postal savings service was established initially at 48 second-class post offices on January 3, 1911. The service was gradually extended to other post offices. Attention was drawn to postal savings by Postmaster General John Angel James Creswell in 1871, but no action was taken despite the fact that 80 such bills were introduced into Congress between 1873 and 1910. Deposits in 11 months reached a total of $11,000,000 which was distributed among 2,710 national and state banks.

Savings bank was the Bank for Savings in the City of New York, which was conceived on November 29, 1816, but for which the charter was not granted until March 26, 1819. The bank opened for business on July 3, 1819. The deposits on the first day, received from eighty depositors, amounted to $2,807. The statement

THE FIRST

for the first six months showed a loss of $27 suffered as a result of the bank's accepting counterfeit money and a short change loss of $23.92. (*Emerson Willard Keyes—History of Savings Banks*)

Savings bank actually to receive money on deposit was the Philadelphia Saving Fund Society, Seventh and Walnut Streets, Philadelphia, Pa., which opened for business on December 2, 1816, in the office of George Billington, the secretary-treasurer, on the west side of Sixth Street. Billington received a salary of $250 a year. The affairs of the bank were conducted by twelve managers. Andrew Bayard was the first president. The bank was chartered February 25, 1819. Condy Raguet, on November 25, 1816, suggested the idea of the bank to four others.

Savings bank to become a corporation was the Provident Institution for Savings in Boston, Mass., which was chartered December 13, 1816, and opened for business on February 19, 1817. It paid interest at the rate of 5 per cent per annum and was under the management of 1 president, 12 vice presidents, and 24 other trustees who had the power to elect a treasurer and other officers. (*Edward Levi Robinson— One Hundred Years of Savings Banking*)

Savings bank with a half-billion dollar deposit was the Bowery Savings Bank of New York, which, according to its statement of March 31, 1932, had more than $502 million, owned by 378,000 depositors.

Savings group to teach children to save their money in a methodical manner was started March 16, 1885, by Professor John Henry Thiry of Long Island City, N.Y., who established a system of fund collections in schools and a school savings bank. (*Edward Levi Robinson —One Hundred Years of Savings Banking*)

Trailer bank was the Meadow Brook National Bank, West Hempstead, Long Island, N.Y., which opened a branch trailer bank at Locust Grove, Long Island, N.Y., on May 26, 1956, in a 46-foot air-conditioned trailer. It had four tellers' windows opening out on one side of the trailer. The first day, over $100,000 was received in deposits. The trailer was used pending the erection of a permanent structure adjacent to the trailer.

Travelers' check. *See* Check: Travelers' checks

Trust company permitted to do a trust business was the Farmer's Fire Insurance and Loan Company of New York City, which was incorporated February 28, 1822. It became the

THE FIRST

City Bank Farmer's Trust Company and later the First National City Trust Company. The first company to use "Trust Company" as part of its title was the New York Life Insurance and Trust Company of New York City. The company was chartered on March 9, 1830, with an authorized capital of $1 million. The organization meeting was held on April 12, 1830, and William Bard was chosen the first president. In 1922 it merged with the Bank of New York and National Banking Association, forming the Bank of New York and Trust Company. The first company organized to do a trust business exclusively was the United States Trust Company of New York, which was incorporated on April 12, 1853. The first president was Joseph Lawrence. (*Study Course— American Institute of Banking*)

World bank was the International Bank for Reconstruction and Development, which entered into force on December 27, 1945, when it was subscribed to by 21 countries, whose subscription amounted to $7,173,000,000. The United States subscription was $3,175,000,000. The first loan was made on May 9, 1947 to France—a 30-year loan of $250,000,000 at 3¼ per cent and $150,000,000 at 3 per cent.

BANK LEGISLATION

Bank guaranty legislation was the Glass-Steagall Act, the "Banking Act of 1933," which was passed by Congress, June 16, 1933 (48 Stat.L.162) to provide for the safer and more effective use of the assets of banks, to regulate interbank control, to prevent the undue diversion of funds into speculative operation, effective January 1, 1934. It insured deposits up to $2,500 each in all Federal Reserve banks and, on July 1, 1934, deposits in approved banks— 100 per cent up to $10,000; 75 per cent from $10,000 to $50,000; 50 per cent over $50,000. "An act to provide for the sound, effective and uninterrupted operation of the banking system, and for other purposes" (49 Stat.L.684) approved August 23, 1935, limited the insurance to $5,000 for any one depositor.

Bank legislation (state) to insure depositors was the Safety Fund Banking Law of New York, chapter 94, "an act to create a fund for the benefit of the creditors of certain monied corporations," enacted April 2, 1829. Banking organizations were assessed one-half of one per cent of the capital stock, until three per cent was set aside for a bank fund. Three commissioners, known as Bank Commissioners of the State of New York, were appointed for two-year terms at an annual salary of $1,500. Banks, their officers, and servants were required to be examined under oath, at least once every four months.

National banking system was created by statute on February 25, 1863. This act provided for a Comptroller of Currency under the Treas-

THE FIRST

THE FIRST

BANK LEGISLATION—*Continued*
ury Department. The first incumbent was Hugh
McCulloch, who served from May 9, 1863, to
March 8, 1865. (*Amos Kidder Fiske—The
Modern Bank*)

BANK ROBBERY
Bank robbery occurred Saturday, March
19, 1831, when two doors of the City Bank,
Wall Street, New York City were opened by
duplicate keys and the bank was robbed of
$245,000. Edward Smith, an Englishman (alias
Jones, alias James Smith, alias James Honey-
man), was indicted by the Grand Jury and
arraigned May 2, 1831, at the Court of General Sessions. On May 11, 1831, he was sentenced to five years at hard labor at Sing Sing.
Over $185,000 of the loot was recovered. (*New
York Gazette. March 12, 1831*)

BANKERS' ASSOCIATION
Bankers' association formed by a state
group was the Texas Bankers' Association
which was organized July 23, 1885, at Lampasas,
Tex., with an initial membership of 31. The
first president was James Francis Miller and
the first secretary Frank R. Malone.

National bankers' association was the
American Bankers Association, which was organized on May 24, 1875. The first national
convention was held at Saratoga, N.Y., July 20-
22, 1875, at which time Charles Bingley Hall
was elected president. The objects of the association were self-protection against frauds,
standardization of rules, and bettering of conditions between the banks and their clients.
(*Banker's Magazine. August 1875*)

BANKRUPTCY ACT was the act of April
4, 1800 (2 Stat.L.20) "to establish a uniform
system of bankruptcy in the United States."
It contained 64 sections and applied to "any
merchant or other person residing within the
United States, actually using the trade of merchandise, by buying and selling in gross, or by
retail, or dealing in exchange as a banker,
broker, factor, underwriter or marine insurer."
It was repealed in December 1803. It did not
permit voluntary bankruptcy and applied to
traders only. (*Charles Warren—Bankruptcy in
United States History*)

BAPTISM occurred in March 1540. Two
Indian guides called Peter and Mark were baptized in the Ocmulgee River near Macon, Ga.
(*John C. Butler—Historical Record of Macon
and Central Georgia*)

BAPTIST CHURCH
Baptist Church in America was probably
established by Roger Williams, "the Apostle of
Religious Liberty," in Providence, R.I., in 1639.
The First Baptist Church of Newport, R.I.,
founded by Dr. John Clarke, its first pastor

(now the First Baptist John Clarke Memorial
Church), was definitely called a Baptist Church
in 1644. A church and a meeting house, however, are believed to have been erected as early
as 1638. (*Edward Francis Rines—Old Historic
Churches of America*)

Baptist Church (Negro) was established
in 1773 by a Mr. Palmer at Silver Bluff, S.C.,
a small settlement opposite Augusta on the
Savannah River. George Galphin became a
patron and permitted David George to be
ordained for this special work after having
previously allowed George Liele to preach there.
(*Carter Godwin Woodson—History of the
Negro Church*)

German Baptists (also known as Dunk-
ards, Dunkers, and Tunkers) held their first
immersion December 25, 1723, at Wissahickon
Creek, Germantown, Philadelphia, Pa. The first
chosen elder was Peter Becker and the first
congregation was the Coventry Congregation,
which met September 7, 1724. (*Martin Grove
Brumbaugh—History of the German Baptist
Brethren in Europe and America*)

Seventh Day Baptist Church was organ-
ized at Newport, R.I., in 1671, by Stephen
Mumford, an English Sabbatarian Baptist. The
first deacon was William Weeden. (*Albert
Henry Newman—History of the Baptist
Churches in the United States*)

BAR ASSOCIATION. *See* Lawyers' association

BARBED WIRE. *See* Wire: Barbed wire

BARGE (concrete). *See* Ship: Concrete
barge

BARLESS ZOO. *See* Zoological garden:
Barless zoological garden of naturalistic rock
construction

BARRAGE (mine). *See* Mine barrage

BASEBALL
Baseball (yellow) was used April 27, 1938,
in the Columbia-Fordham game, New York
City. It was a regulation National League ball
dyed yellow, with red stitches, and was developed by Frederic Rahr.

Cork center baseball was invented by Benjamin F. Shibe of Bala, Pa., who obtained
patent No. 924,696 on June 15, 1909. It was
manufactured by A. G. Spalding & Bros., Chicago, Ill., and used in occasional league games in
1909 and in regular play in 1910. The ball was
first used in World Series games on October 20,

THE FIRST

22, and 23, 1910, in Chicago, Ill., between the Philadelphia (American League) and the Chicago (National League) teams.

BASEBALL BATTING AND FIELD-ING CAGE was built at Yale University, New Haven, Conn., in the fall of 1885 by Captain Philip Battell Stewart. The candidates for the team worked there during the winter of 1886. The building was about 70 feet long and 20 feet wide and had skylights protected by wire. It was the forerunner of the expensive cages and field houses so common in American colleges and universities.

BASEBALL BOOK was Robin Carver's *The Book of Sports,* published in 1834 in Boston, Mass., by Lilly, Wait, Colman and Holden. It was based on an English edition of the *Boy's Own Book.* Similar rules applied to the game of rounders were published in 1829.

BASEBALL CATCHER'S MASK was invented by Frederick Winthrop Thayer of Waverly, Mass., captain of the Harvard University Baseball Club, who obtained Patent No. 200,358 on February 12, 1878, on a "face guard or safety mask." It was made by a Cambridge, Mass., tinsmith, tried out in the gymnasium in the winter of 1876-1877, and used by James Alexander Tyng in a game with the Live Oaks at Lynn, Mass., April 12, 1877. Louis Trauschke, catcher of the Foster Baseball Club, Lawrence, Mass., who had been hurt by a pitched ball, adopted the mask. It was manufactured by Peck & Snyder, New York City. (*H Book of Harvard Athletics*)

BASEBALL "DICTATOR" was Judge Kenesaw Mountain Landis, elected November 12, 1920, for a seven-year term from 1921 to 1928. He received $42,500 a year and $10,000 expenses to rule the sixteen American and National League Baseball Clubs. He served from January 12, 1921, to November 24, 1944. (He was reelected in 1925, 1935, and 1942.) He died November 24, 1944, and was succeeded by Senator Albert Benjamin ("Happy") Chandler of Kentucky, elected April 24, 1945, for a seven-year period at $50,000 a year.

BASEBALL GAME
Baseball is attributed to Colonel Abner Doubleday, who later became a general in the U.S. Army. In 1839 he laid out the first regular baseball diamond at Cooperstown, N.Y., and formulated the rules of play.

Baseball game at night was played June 2, 1883, at League Park, Fort Wayne, Ind., between a club of boys known as the M.E. College and the Quincey professionals. The score was Quincey 19, College 11. The field was illuminated by 17 lights of 4,000 candlepower each. Only 7 innings were played. The game

THE FIRST

was witnessed by 2,000 people. A preliminary test was made May 29, 1883, using 11 of the 16 lights then set up. (*Fort Wayne Journal-Gazette. June 3, 1883*)

Baseball game at night by a regular league team took place in Grand Rapids, Mich., on July 8, 1909. It was played between the Grand Rapids and Zanesville teams in the Central League. Grand Rapids won 11 to 10.

Baseball game at night by major league teams was played at Crosley Field, Cincinnati, Ohio, May 24, 1935, when the Cincinnati Reds defeated the Philadelphia Phillies 2 to 1 before a paid attendance of 20,422. President Franklin Delano Roosevelt in Washington, D.C., pressed a button which turned on 363 lights (1,000 kilowatts each) on 8 giant towers for this National League game.

Baseball game broadcast with a play-by-play description. *See* Radio broadcast: Baseball game broadcast with a play-by-play description

Baseball game for which admission was charged. *See* Baseball game: Baseball series

Baseball game telecast. *See* Television—Telecast: Baseball game (collegiate) televised

Baseball game (World Series) broadcast. *See* Radio broadcast: Baseball (World Series) broadcast

Baseball playoff series for a National League pennant took place October 1, 1946, in St. Louis, Mo., and October 3, 1946, in Brooklyn, N.Y., after the Brooklyn Dodgers and the St. Louis Cardinals had tied on September 29, 1946, both teams having won 96 and lost 58 games for a .623 average in the National League. The Cardinals won the first two of the two-out-of-three series by the score of 4-2 and 8-4, thus winning the National League pennant and the right to play the Boston Red Sox of the American League in the World Series. The series opened October 6, 1946, in St. Louis, Mo. The Cardinals won four games of the seven-game series.

Baseball series was played July 20, August 17, and September 10, 1858, at the Fashion Race Course, Long Island, N.Y., between teams representing Brooklyn and New York. New York won two of the three games with the Brooklyn Atlantics. The first time spectators were charged admission to see a baseball game was July 20, 1859, on which date 1,500 people paid a fifty-cent admission fee. The players did not receive remuneration until 1858, when they received a share of the gate receipts. (*Seymour Roberts Church—Baseball. The His-*

BASEBALL GAME—*Continued*
tory, Statistics and Romance of the American National Game from Its Inception to the Present)

Baseball series world championship was won by the National League Providence team in 1884, which won three out of a series of five games. The opposing team was the Metropolitans of the American Association. Providence won 6-0, 3-1, 12-2. *(Francis C. Richter —History and Records of Baseball)*

Double no-hit nine-inning baseball game in the major leagues was played May 2, 1917, at Weeghman Park, Chicago, Ill., by the Chicago Cubs (Jim Vaughn, pitcher) and the Cincinnati Reds (Fred Toney, pitcher). Both players pitched a full nine-inning game without allowing a hit. In the tenth inning, the Cincinnati team brought in a run. The score was Cincinnati 1, Chicago 0.

Intercollegiate baseball game was played on July 1, 1859, between Amherst and Williams Colleges, in Pittsfield, Mass. Amherst won by a score of 73 to 32. The game began at 11 A.M., and continued four hours without interruption. Each team had 13 players and the game lasted 26 innings. The captain of Amherst was James Fitzgerald Claffin, and Williams' captain was Humphrey S. Anderson. *(Statistics of Intercollegiate Contests—Athletic Council, Williams College)*

Major league game in which the majority of the players on one team were Negroes was played July 17, 1954 between the National League Brooklyn Dodgers and Milwaukee Braves at Milwaukee, Wis. The Braves won 6 to 1. The Negro players on the Brooklyn team were Don Newcombe, pitcher; Roy Campanella, catcher; Jim Gilliam, second base; Jackie Robinson, third base; and Edmundo Isasi ("Sandy") Amoros, left field.

No-hit nine-inning baseball game was pitched by Joseph E. Borden of the Philadelphia team of the National Association on July 28, 1875, in Philadelphia, Pa., against Chicago. The score was Philadelphia 4, Chicago 0.

No-run nine-inning baseball game was played May 11, 1875, at Red Stocking Park, St. Louis, Mo., between the Chicago White Stockings and the St. Louis Reds of the National Association. The score of the 1 hour and 35-minute game was Chicago 1, St. Louis 0. Chicago made six base hits and scored one run; St. Louis made three base hits and did not score. George ("Charmer") Zettlein was the Chicago pitcher and Joseph Myles Blong the St. Louis pitcher.

President to pitch a ball to open the baseball season. *See* President: President to pitch a ball to open the baseball season

Triple play unassisted by a player in organized baseball was made May 8, 1878 by Paul Hines playing in center field on the Providence team. The game was played at Providence, R.I., between Providence and Boston, the former winning 3 to 2.

Triple play unassisted in a modern major league game was made by shortstop Neal Ball of the Cleveland American League team on July 19, 1909, at Cleveland, Ohio, in the second inning of the first game of a doubleheader against the Boston American League team. Ball caught Amby McConnells' liner; touched second, retiring Honus Wagner, who was on his way to third; and tagged Jake Stahl as he came up to second. When Ball came to bat in the same inning, he hit a home run. Cleveland defeated Boston 6 to 1 in the first game. Boston defeated Cleveland 8 to 2 in the second game.

Triple play unassisted in a World Series was made October 10, 1920, in the fifth game of the series, at Cleveland, Ohio by Bill Wambsganss, second baseman of the Cleveland American League team, in a game with the Brooklyn National League team. In the fifth inning, Wambsganss caught Otto Miller's drive, tagged Kilduff for a double play, ran to first, and tagged Clarence Mitchell. The Cleveland Indians defeated the Brooklyn Robins 8 to 1.

World Series baseball game broadcast. *See* Radio broadcast: Baseball (World Series) broadcast

World Series baseball games to gross a million dollars were played October 10-15, 1923, in New York City between the New York Yankees of the American League (Miller J. Huggins, manager) and the New York Giants of the National League (John Joseph McGraw, manager). Receipts were $1,063,815, of which the players' share was $368,783.04 The Yankees won 4-2. *(Frank Graham—The New York Yankees)*

BASEBALL GLOVE was worn by Charles C. Waite, first baseman of Boston, in 1875. It was flesh color so as not to be conspicuous and had a large round opening at the back for ventilation. *(Albert Goodwill Spalding—America's National Game)*

BASEBALL HALL OF FAME. *See* Hall of fame: Hall of fame (baseball)

THE FIRST

BASEBALL LEAGUE

American League was organized on January 29, 1900, in Philadelphia, and originally consisted of eight teams, Buffalo, Chicago, Cleveland, Detroit, Indianapolis, Kansas City, Milwaukee, and Minneapolis. The first president of the league was Byron Bancroft ("Ban") Johnson, who served from 1900 to 1927.

Baseball league association was the National Association of Professional Baseball Leagues, which was organized at the Leland Hotel, Chicago, Ill., on September 5-6, 1901, by seven presidents of the minor leagues: the Western League, the Western Association, the Pacific Northwest League, the Eastern League, the New York State League, the New England League, and the Three-I-League. The first president was Patrick Thomas Powers, and the first secretary was John H. Farrell of New York. The first annual meeting was held at the Fifth Avenue, Hotel, New York City on October 23-25, 1902.

Baseball league of importance was the National Association of Base-Ball Players, organized March 17, 1871, in New York City. James N. Kerns of Troy, N.Y., was elected president. The member clubs were the Athletics of Philadelphia; the Mutuals of New York; the Kekiongas of Fort Wayne; the Olympics of Washington; the Haymakers of Troy; the Bostons of Boston; the White Stockings of Chicago; Cleveland; and Rockford. Each club paid an entry fee of ten dollars. The first game was played May 4, 1871, at Fort Wayne, Ind. (The score was Fort Wayne 2, Cleveland 0.) The series consisted of three out of five games with the other teams. The champion team was the Athletics of Philadelphia (manager Elias Hicks Hayhurst), winning 22 games and losing 7 (.759). Chicago was second, winning 20 games and losing 9 (.690). Boston was third, winning 22 games and losing 10 (.688).

Juvenile baseball league was the Waynesburg, Pa., Juvenile Baseball League, formed in 1908 by 3 teams—the Colts, the North Side Cubs, and the Times Pirates (the last composed of carrier boys for the Waynesburg *Times*). An admission fee of 10 cents was charged for each game, the seasonal proceeds of $60 being donated to a library fund.

National League was formed on February 2, 1876, and consisted of eight baseball teams, Boston, Chicago, Cincinnati, Hartford, Louisville, New York, Philadelphia, and St. Louis. The first president was Morgan Gardner Bulkeley, who served from February 2, 1876, to December 7, 1876.

BASEBALL MANAGER

Baseball manager to guide the same club on three different occasions was Stanley Raymond ("Bucky") Harris, who managed the American League Washington Senators from 1924 to 1928 (winning first place twice, third place once, and fourth place twice); from 1935 to 1942 (winning fourth place once, fifth place once, sixth place four times, and seventh place twice); and from 1950 to 1954 (winning fifth place three times, sixth place once, and seventh place once).

Baseball manager to win pennants in both leagues was Joseph Vincent ("Marse") McCarthy, non-playing manager of the Chicago National League team, whose team on October 6, 1929, earned the pennant by winning 98 games and losing 54 games. As manager of the New York American League team he won the pennant on September 23, 1932, winning 106 games and losing 46 games. On October 2, 1932, the New York American League team also won the world championship, defeating the Chicago National League team in four straight games.

BASEBALL PLAYER

Baseball "Home Run King" to achieve 25 home runs in one season was John ("Bucky") Freeman, outfielder of the Washington club of the National League, who hit 25 home runs and 27 triples in 1899.

Baseball "pinch hitter" was John Joseph Doyle, a substitute catcher, ordered to bat in the ninth inning by Pat Tebeau of the Cleveland Spiders in a game played June 7, 1892, in Brooklyn, N.Y., against the Brooklyn Ward's Wonders. Doyle made a single, advancing Jack O'Connor from first to third base. The 1891 rules allowed substitutions anywhere at any time during a game.

Baseball pitcher to curve a ball is reported to be William Arthur ("Candy") Cummings, who introduced this innovation in 1866. He played with the Excelsior Junior Nine and the Stars of Brooklyn. Others for whom the claim is made are Fred Goldsmith of the Chicago White Stockings and George McConnell.

Baseball pitcher to pitch a perfect no-hit, no-run, no-walk World Series game was Don Larsen of the American League New York Yankees. On October 8, 1956, in the fifth game of the World Series played with the National League Brooklyn Dodgers, at the Yankee Stadium, New York City, Larsen pitched a perfect game. The score was New York 2, Brooklyn 0.

Baseball pitcher to pitch three no-hit games was Larry Corcoran of the Chicago Nationals, who pitched a no-hitter against Boston on August 19, 1880, against Worcester on September 20, 1882, and against Providence on June 27, 1884.

BASEBALL PLAYER—*Continued*

Baseball player to catch a ball dropped from the Washington Monument, Washington, D.C.(500-foot level) was Billy ("Pop") Schriver of the Chicago National League club, who accomplished this feat on August 29, 1892, and again on August 25, 1895. Charles ("Gabby") Street, catcher of the Washington club of the American League, caught a baseball dropped from the top of the monument on August 21, 1908.

Baseball player to hit a home run in an All-Star game was George Herman ("Babe") Ruth of the American League New York Yankees, who on July 6, 1933, at Comiskey Park, Chicago, Ill., hit a home run in the third inning of the first game of the annual series. The run brought in Charles Leonard Gehringer of Detroit. The American League won 4 to 2. William Anthony ("Wild Bill") Hallahan was the National League pitcher and Jimmy Wilson was the catcher, both of the St. Louis Cardinals.

Baseball player to hit four consecutive home runs in one game was Lou Gehrig of the American League New York Yankees, who hit home runs in the first, fourth, fifth, and seventh innings on June 3, 1932, in a game in Philadelphia, Pa., against the American League Philadelphia Athletics. The score was Yankees 20, Athletics 13. (Minor league players had performed the same feat earlier.)

Baseball player to hit four home runs in one game was Bobby Lowe, second baseman of the Boston National League team, who achieved this distinction in Boston, Mass., on May 30, 1894, in the third (two runs), fifth, and sixth innings in a game against Cincinnati. The score was Boston 20, Cincinnati 11.

Baseball player to hit over .400 was Ross Barnes of the National League Chicago White Stockings, who in 1876 batted .404 in 66 games.

Baseball player to score more than 4,000 hits was Tyrus Raymond ("Ty") Cobb who played in 3,033 games in 24 years (Detroit, American League, 1905-1926) ; Philadelphia, American League, 1927-1928) scoring 4,191 hits in his 11,429 times at bat.

Baseball player to win the Most Valuable Player Award three times was Stan Musial of the National League St. Louis Cardinals, who won the award for 1943, 1946, and 1948.

Major league baseball player to pitch two successive no-hit no-run games in a season was Johnny Vander Meer of the National League Cincinnati Reds, who on June 11, 1938, shut out Boston by 3 to 0 in Cincinnati, Ohio.

Only three men reached first base, all on walks. On June 15, 1938, he defeated the Brooklyn Dodgers in New York City, 6-0.

Negro baseball player was Moses Fleetwood ("Fleet") Walker, catcher on the Toledo team of the American Association. He played in 41 games in 1884 and hit .251.

Negro major league baseball player was Jackie Robinson of the National League Brooklyn Dodgers, who played in an exhibition game on April 11, 1947, against the New York Yankees. He played at first base in the exhibition game and during the season. *(Carl T. Rowan and Jackie Robinson—Wait Till Next Year)*

Professional baseball player was Alfred James Reach, outfielder of the Philadelphia Athletics of the National Association from 1871 to 1875. In 1874, he received $1,000 for playing fourteen games.

Woman baseball pitcher engaged by an organized male baseball team was Virne Beatrice ("Jackie") Mitchell, nineteen, who on April 1, 1931, was engaged by the Chattanooga Baseball Club of the Southern Association.

BASEBALL RULES

Baseball rule code was adopted September 23, 1845, by the Knickerbocker Club of New York. *(J. Austin Fynes—Athletic Sports in America)*

Baseball rules standardizing the game were adopted May 1858, in New York City by the National Baseball Association. The rules provided that the bat was not to exceed 2½ inches in diameter and the ball 10½ inches in circumference, the latter to weigh 6½ ounces. The game was to last 9 innings or until one team won 21 runs. Previously each team had played under its own set of rules. Three delegates from each of the following clubs attended the meeting: Atlantic, Baltic, Bedford, Continental, Eagle, Empire, Excelsior, Eckford, Gotham, Harmony, Knickerbocker, Nassau, Olympic, Putnam, and Union.

BASEBALL TEAM

Baseball team was the Knickerbocker Club of New York, organized September 23, 1845, by Alexander Joy Cartwright, which played the New York Baseball Club at the Elysian Field in Hoboken, N.J., on June 19, 1846. Duncan F. Curry was the first president. The game lasted four innings and was won by the New York Baseball Club with the score of 23 to 1. At this date, there was no standard baseball, and as each home club supplied the ball it often varied in size, elasticity, and content. Three seasons later the Knickerbockers adopted a blue and white uniform and were the first team uniformly outfitted. *(By-Laws, Regulations and Rules of the Knickerbocker Base Ball Club of New York)*

Baseball team (Negro professional) was the Cuban Giants, organized in New York City in 1885. S. K. Govern was manager. The players received expenses and weekly salaries according to positions: pitchers and catchers, $18, infielders $15, and outfielders $12. *(Sol White—History of Colored Baseball)*

Baseball team to receive a regular salary for its services was the Red Stockings of Cincinnati, led by Harry and George Wright, which traveled in 1869 to various cities, engaging local teams. Through 1869 and up to June 1870, they played without losing a game. A salary of $1,400 was paid to George Wright, shortstop; $1,200 to Harry Wright, captain and center field; $1,100 to Asa Brainard, pitcher; $1,000 to Fred Waterman, third base; and $800 each to the first and second basemen, the catcher, the left and right fielder, and the substitute.

Baseball team to tour was the Brooklyn Excelsiors, under the management of Captain Joseph B. Leggett, which left June 30, 1860, for Albany, N.Y. They played at Troy, Buffalo, and cities in the west and south.

Baseball team to win three World Series in succession was the American League New York Yankees, which won the world championship October 6, 1936, October 9, 1937, and October 9, 1938.

Baseball team to win five World Series in succession was the American League New York Yankees, managed by Casey Stengel, which won the world championship on October 9, 1949, from the Brooklyn Dodgers (4 games to 1); on October 7, 1950, from the Philadelphia Phillies (4 games to 0); on October 10, 1951, from the New York Giants (4 games to 2); on October 7, 1952, from the Brooklyn Dodgers (4 games to 3); on October 5, 1953, from the Brooklyn Dodgers (4 games to 2).

Baseball teams to go on a world tour were the Chicago and All America teams. They started their world tour October 20, 1888, and returned April 20, 1889. They played 53 games of 4 innings and over, in Australia, Ceylon, Egypt, Italy, France, England and the United States. Twenty-eight games were won by the All America team, 22 by the Chicago team, and 3 were tied. Their first game abroad was played December 10, 1888, in Auckland, New Zealand. *(Henry Clay Palmer—Athletic Sports in America)*

Baseball teams to travel beyond the confines of the U.S. were the Boston Red Stockings and the Philadelphia Athletic Blue Stocking teams of the National Association which played a series of fifteen exhibition games from July 30, 1874, to August 27, 1874, in England and Ireland. *(Henry Chadwick—De Witt's Base-Ball Guide for 1875)*

Professional league baseball team to win three pennants in succession was the Chicago Cubs of the National League, who won pennants in 1880, 1881, and 1882. In 1880 the team won 67 games, lost 17; in 1881 it won 56 games, lost 28; in 1882 it won 55 games, lost 29. Adrian Constantine Anson was the manager. *(Adrian Constantine Anson—A Ball Player's Career)*

Women's baseball team was the Young Ladies Base Ball Club No. 1, which toured the country in 1890 playing men's teams. W. S. Franklin was the manager. The players were May Howard, pitcher and captain; Nellie Williams, catcher; Kittie Grant, first base; Angie Parker, second base; Edith Mayres, third base; Effie Earl, shortstop; Alice Lee, left field; Rose Mitchell, right field; Annie Grant, center field. *(National Police Gazette. September 20, 1890)*

BASEBALL UMPIRE

Baseball umpire (major league) to wear eyeglasses was Eddie Rommel, who wore them in the game between the New York Yankees and the Washington Senators on April 18, 1956, in Washington, D.C. He became an umpire in the American League in 1938.

Negro umpire in organized baseball was Emmett Littleton Ashford of the Class C Southwestern International League, who was authorized as a substitute umpire on February 20, 1952, by president Les Powers.

BASILICA. *See* Catholic church: Catholic church raised to the dignity of a basilica

BASKETBALL

Basketball was invented in 1892 by James Naismith, who introduced the game in the International Young Men's Christian Association Training School in Springfield, Mass. As the game was originally played it was necessary for the players to use a ladder to get up and remove the ball from the basket. *(James Naismith and Luther Gulick—Basket Ball)*

Basketball collegiate team to win the National Invitation Tournament and the National Collegiate Athletic Association trophy was the Beavers of the City College of New York, coached by Nat Holman, who defeated

THE FIRST

THE FIRST

BASKETBALL—*Continued*
Bradley University, Peoria, Ill., 69 to 61, on
March 18, 1950, and 71 to 68 on March 28,
1950.

Basketball game telecast. *See* Television—
Telecast: Basketball game to be televised

Basketball intercollegiate five-man team
game was played in New Haven, Conn., on
March 20, 1897, when Yale University, New
Haven, defeated the University of Pennsylvania, Philadelphia, 32-10.

Basketball intercollegiate game was played
December 10, 1896, in New Haven, Conn., between Wesleyan University, Middletown, Conn.,
and Yale University, New Haven. Wesleyan
won 4-3. Seven men were on each team.

Basketball played at a women's college
was introduced in 1892 by Senda Berenson,
director of physical education at Smith College,
Northampton, Mass.

Basketball player (professional) to score
more than 15,000 points was Dolph Schayes
of the Syracuse Nationals of the National
Basketball Association. On January 12, 1960,
in Philadelphia, Pa., Schayes tallied 34 points
in a 127-120 triumph over the Boston Celtics,
raising his score to 15,013 points. Schayes
played professional basketball for 12 years.

Basketball team (college) was formed at
Mount Union College, Alliance, Ohio. H. S.
Jones introduced basketball as a collegiate
game at the Morgan Gymnasium at Mount
Union College in December 1892 and it was
accepted as an intercollegiate sport.

National Basketball Association Negro
player was Charles Henry Cooper, all-star
player, who was drafted April 24, 1950, by the
Boston Celtics and who played his first game
for that team on November 1, 1950, in Fort
Wayne, Ind.

Olympic games basketball championship.
See Olympic games: Olympic games basketball championship

BASKETBALL RULES
Basketball rule book was *Rules for Basketball* by James Naismith, instructor in the International Young Men's Christian Association
Training School, Springfield, Mass., published
in 1892 by the Springfield Printing and Binding Company, Springfield, Mass. *(James Naismith—Basketball, Its Origin and Development)*

Basketball rules were published in the
Triangle Magazine, Springfield, Mass., January 15, 1892.

BATHHOUSE
Bathhouses owned and operated by a municipality were the L Street baths of Boston,
Mass., built in 1865. They were first opened
to the general public in 1866 and were under
the supervision of the Board of Bath Commissioners, which had charge of all baths and
gymnasiums up to 1913. *(John Koren—Boston
1822 to 1922. The Story of Its Government
and Principal Activities During One Hundred
Years)*

Legislation concerning public baths which
provided for the establishment of free public baths in cities, villages, and towns of
50,000 or over, in such number as determined
necessary by local health boards, was Chapter
351, "An act to promote the public health and
to amend chapter 473 of the laws of 1892 entitled 'An act to establish free public baths in
cities, villages and towns,'" passed by New
York State, April 18, 1895. The law required
the baths to be kept open not less than fourteen
hours a day and to be provided with hot and
cold water. This law was mandatory, whereas
Chapter 473 of the laws of 1892 had permitted
cities to erect free public baths if they desired
to do so. *(William Paul Gerhard—On Bathing
and Different Forms of Baths)*

Public bath and washhouse was opened
January 1, 1852, by the New York Association
for Improving the Condition of the Poor in
Mott Street, near Grand Street, New York
City, now the Community Service Society. The
first year 80,375 bathers and 10,038 washers
availed themselves of the advantages.

Public baths with showers were provided
by the People's Bath, New York City, formally opened August 17, 1891. The bath cost
$25,922 and was operated by the Association
for Improving the Condition of the Poor, now
the Community Service Society. There was a
charge of five cents for the use of a shower,
including soap and towel. During the first
thirteen and a half months there were 69,944
bathers.

Steam baths for curing disease were
advocated by Samuel Thomson, who in 1796
experimented with steam in the treatment of
his daughter, whom physicians were unable to
cure. He traveled on horseback through New
Hampshire, Maine, Vermont, and Massachusetts, advocating treatment by steam as well
as by the use of herbs. *(Samuel Thomson—A
Narrative of the Life and Medical Discoveries
of Samuel Thomson)*

Turkish bath was opened October 6, 1863,
by Dr. Charles H. Shepard at 81 Columbia

Heights, Brooklyn, N.Y. It was known as "The Hammam," the name used in the East. Admission was a dollar. Only one bather came the first day and only fifty the first month. (*Journal American Medical Association. March 10, 1900*)

BATHROOMS (hotel). *See* Hotels: Hotel to install bathrooms

BATTERY
Battery to convert radioactive energy into electrical energy was a radioelectric cell invented by Philip Edwin Ohmart of Cincinnati, Ohio, which was announced on December 31, 1951. It consisted of two electrochemically dissimilar electrodes separated by a filling gas which was ionized by exposure to nuclear energy to produce an electrical current.

Solar battery to convert useful amounts of the sun's energy into electricity was invented by Gerald Leondus Pearson, Calvin Souther Fuller, and Daryl M. Chapin at the Bell Telephone Laboratories, New York City, and announced April 25, 1954. Made of specially treated strips of silicon, the battery needed no fuel other than the light of the sun. It had no moving parts, nothing in it was consumed or destroyed, and theoretically it was possible for it to last indefinitely.

Solar energy battery manufactured commercially was made by the National Fabricated Products, Inc., Chicago, Ill., in 1955. It consisted of a disc, the size of a half-dollar, which was hermetically sealed. It generated a half-volt from its two terminals. The battery was first advertised May 20, 1955, in *Electronic Design,* and the first shipment was made June 1, 1955.

BATTING AND FIELDING CAGE (baseball). *See* Baseball batting and fielding cage

BATTLE. *See* under names of various wars, e.g. Civil war; also War

BATTLESHIP. *See* Ship: Battleship of importance

BATTLESHIP SUNK BY AN AIRPLANE. *See* Aviation: Battleship sunk by an airplane

BAUXITE was discovered in 1887 at a point a few miles northeast of Rome, Floyd County, Ga. A few fragments of the unknown mineral were picked up on the Holland lot, two miles north of the Ridge Valley Iron Company's furnace at Hermitage, Ga. Bauxite mining began in April 1888, when the deposits on the Holland

property, lot 61, 23rd district of Floyd County, were first opened and worked. The first shipments of the ore were made in May 1888 to the Pennsylvania Salt Company, Natrona, Pa., and to Greenwich Point, Pa. This ore is said to have been used for the manufacture of both alum and metallic aluminum. (*Geological Survey of Georgia. Bulletin No. 11*)

BAZOOKA ROCKET GUN. *See* Ordnance: Bazooka rocket gun

BEACON. *See* Lighthouse

BEACONS (radio). *See* Radio beacons

BEADS (glass). *See* Glass bead

BEAR. *See* Animals: Bear (white)

BEATIFICATION (Catholic). *See* Catholic beatification

BED
Box spring was imported from France in 1857 by James Boyle, Chatham Square, New York City, a manufacturer of bedding. Made reversible, it was about 12 inches deep. The frame was made in 8 sections, 1¼-inch lumber boards joined together with strips of ticking. The center of the spiral was attached to the center of the frame, and then came the usual ties of twine.

"Concealed bed" was manufactured by the Murphy Door Bed Company in San Francisco, Calif., in 1909. The beds, known as "In-a-door" beds, operated on a pivot and could be swung out of sight behind doors or in closets.

Folding bed manufacture was successfully accomplished in 1875-1876 at Sixth and Filbert Streets, Philadelphia, Pa., by the Hale and Kilburn Manufacturing Company, now known as Hale and Kilburn Company. The folding bed was invented by a man in the company's employ named Everett and was improved upon by H. S. Hale. The bed was designed because of the then beginning apartment house idea and the necessity of economy in space. The beds were equipped with a "flexible spring" which afterwards developed into what was called a "sectional spring bed," or the ordinary bedspring divided into three sections, lengthwise, each being filled with springs and enclosed in a canvas covering. This spring developed into the box spring now in use.

BEEF EXPORTS. *See* Meat: Beef export

BEER
Beer was brewed at the Roanoke Colony (Virginia) of Sir Walter Raleigh in 1587.

THE FIRST

THE FIRST

BEER—*Continued*
According to Thomas Hariot's account, "Wee made of the same [pagatowr, or maize] . . . some mault, whereof was brued as good ale as was to bee desired. So likewise by the help of hops thereof may bee made as good beere." *(Thomas Hariot—A Briefe and True Report of the New Found Land of Virginia)*

Beer in cans. See Cans: Beer in cans

Lager beer was manufactured in Philadelphia, Pa., in 1840 by John Wagner, who had an eight-barrel kettle in his home. It was stored in a cellar under the brewhouse.

BEER (root). *See* Root beer

BEET SUGAR. *See* Sugar: Sugar beets

BELL. *See* Electric bell

BELLS. *See* Carillon; Chimes

BELT (cartridge belts). *See* Cartridge belt patent

BELT CONVEYOR SYSTEM
  Belt conveyor more than four miles long was manufactured by the Goodyear Tire and Rubber Company, Akron, Ohio for the Weirton mine of the National Mines Corporation to convey coal 10,900 feet from a West Virginia mine to the Monongahela River. The conveyor was installed in 1949 in a single loop of belting more than four miles in total circumference. It traveled at a speed of 300 feet a minute to deliver 300 tons of coal an hour.

  Belt conveyor system was described by Oliver Evans in his book *The Young Millwright and Millers Guide* published in Philadelphia, Pa., in 1795. Evans illustrated a flat belt receiving material on its upper run and discharging it over the end, on a broad endless strap of thin pliant leather or canvas revolving over two pulleys in a case or trough. *(Greville Bathe and Dorothy Bathe—Oliver Evans, a Chronicle of Early American Engineering)*

BELTING sold to manufacturers is recorded in the account books of Pliny Jewell, a leather dealer of Hartford, Conn. There is an entry in 1826 of the sale of a leather belt three inches wide. Manufacturers who required belting usually bought skins, cut them to the desired thickness, and by nailing the ends of the pieces to the floor when wet, and driving wedges between the leather and floor, half-way between the ends, stretched them taut.

BELTS OF LEATHER for transmitting power from shaft to shaft were devised by Paul Moody, who used them in the Appleton cotton mill in Lowell, Mass., in 1828. Up to this time all transmissions had been by means of iron gears. Belting, however, had previously been used in some mills to carry power from shafts which in turn were driven by gears from a water wheel. *(Louis W. Arny—National Association of Leather Belting Manufacturers. Report. November 20, 1918)*

BENEFIT PERFORMANCE. *See* Play (drama): Benefit performance

BENEVOLENT AND PROTECTIVE ORDER OF ELKS was organized February 16, 1868, in New York City from an older social and benevolent organization, "The Jolly Corks." The presiding officer of the Jolly Corks at the time of adopting the B.P.O.E. title was Charles A. S. Vivian. The first exalted B.P.O.E. ruler was George W. Thompson. The Grand Lodge was incorporated on March 10, 1871, in New York and the first Grand Exalted Ruler was George J. Green. *(Charles Edward Ellis—An Authentic History of the Benevolent and Protective Order of Elks)*

BERKELIUM. *See* Element: Element 97

BESSEMER STEEL CONVERTER. *See* Steel: Bessemer steel converter

"BEST SELLER." *See* Book: Best seller novel

BETATRON
  See also Bevatron

  Betatron was built at the University of Illinois, Urbana, Ill., by Professor Donald William Kerst and placed in operation July 15, 1940. It had an output energy of 2.3 million electron volts. The betatron is a machine to accelerate electrons by the use of a magnetic field and can produce either a sharp beam of high-energy X-rays or a free beam of high-energy electrons.

  Mobile betatron was placed in operation on November 12, 1948, at the United States Naval Ordnance Laboratory, White Oak, Md. It was built by the General Engineering and Consulting Laboratory of the General Electric Company, Schenectady, N.Y., and was a 10 million-volt X-ray generator capable of penetrating 16 inches of steel.

  Photograph of high-volt X-rays. *See* Photograph: Photograph of a beam of 1 billion-volt X-rays

BEVATRON was built for the Radiation Laboratory of the University of California at Berkeley, and placed in operation on February 15, 1954. It has a maximum beam energy of 6.25 billion volts. It is housed in a circular building 220 feet in diameter and 69 feet high.

See also Betatron

BIBLE
Bible for the blind in embossed form, the old line letter system, was issued in 1835 by the American Bible Society, New York City. This society was also the first to supply the blind with the Bible in New York Point, and in the more recent Braille.

Bible in an Indian language translation was finished in 1661 by John Eliot, "the Apostle to the North American Indians." It was entitled *"The New Testament of Our Lord and Saviour Jesus Christ,"* and was dedicated in English to Charles II. It contained 130 printed leaves without pagination and two title pages, one in English and the other in the Algonquin Indian dialect. The text was in double columns with marginal references. In 1663, *"The Holy Bible, Containing the Old Testament and the New, Translated into the Indian Language"* was printed in quarto size. From Genesis to the end of the Old Testament, it contained 414 leaves, and from St. Matthew to the end of the New Testament, 126 leaves. Both Bibles were "ordered to be printed by the Commissioners of the United Colonies in New England, at the charge and with the consent of the corporation in England for the propagation of the gospel amongst the Indians in New England" and were printed in Cambridge, Mass., by Samuel Green and Marmaduke Johnson. *(Samuel Eliot Morison—Builders of the Bay Colony)*

Bible in folio size to be illustrated was *The Holy Bible, containing the Old and New Testaments: With the Apocrypha. Translated out of the original tongues and with the former translations diligently compared and revised by the special command of King James I of England,* published in 1791 by I[saiah] Thomas, Worcester, Mass. It contained 1,012 pages and about 50 plates. *(Edwin A. R. Rumball-Petre —Rare Bibles)*

Bible printed in English was printed by Robert Aitken of Philadelphia, Pa., in 1782. The frontispiece read, *"The Holy Bible, containing the Old and New Testaments—newly translated out of the original tongues; and with the former translations diligently compared and revised.* Printed and sold by R. Aitken, at Pope's Head, Three doors above the Coffee House, in Market Street, Philadelphia, Pa., 1782." It was a duodecimo of 353 pages without pagination. The venture, though authorized by Congress, September 21, 1782, was unsuccessful financially. The New Testament was

printed in 1781 by Aitken. *(Robert Rowland Dearden and Douglas Sloane Watson—The Bible of the American Revolution)*

Bible printed in German was printed by Christoph Sauer (also spelled Saur or Sower), Germantown, Pa., in 1743 from the text of the 32nd Halle edition with type obtained from Frankfurt, Germany. Its title was *Biblia Das ist; Die Heilige Schrift Altes und Neues Testaments, Nach der Deutschen Uebersetzung D. Martin Luthers, mit jedes Capitels Kurtzen Summarien, auch Beygefügten vielen und richtigen parallelen; nebst einem gewöhnlichen anhang des dritten und vierten buchs Esra und des dritten Buchs der Maccabäer.*

Bible translated into English in America was *The Holy Bible, containing the old and new covenant, commonly called the Old and New Testament; translated from the Greek,* issued in four volumes with unnumbered pages. It was printed in Philadelphia, Pa., by Jane Aitken in 1808. It was copyrighted September 12, 1808, in the District of Pennsylvania by the translator, Charles Thomson, who had been Secretary to the Continental Congress.

Bible translation by a woman was made by Julia Evelina Smith of Glastonbury, Conn., and published in Hartford, Conn., in 1876 by the American Publishing Company. Her knowledge of Latin, Greek, and Hebrew enabled her to make the translation. In the historical narratives, the verbs were translated in the future tense. The Old Testament consisted of 892 pages and the New Testament 276 pages. The full title was *The Holy Bible, containing the Old and New Testaments: translated literally from the original tongues.*

Bibles in hotel rooms were placed there in October 1908, in the Superior Hotel, Iron Mountain (now Superior), Mont., by the Gideons, the Christian Commercial Traveling Men's Association. The organization was founded in 1899 at Boscobel, Wis. The first president was Samuel Eugene Hill. This work has grown until at the present time more than 2 million Bibles have been distributed to hotels, hospitals, penal institutions, and public schools.

Catholic Bible in English was a 990-page quarto printed by Carey, Stewart & Co., Philadelphia, Pa., in 1790. It was printed from new type cast in the foundry of John Baine, Philadelphia, and was intended to be issued in 48-page sections every Saturday. The first section was issued December 12, 1789. The title was *The Holy Bible, translated from the Latin Vulgate: diligently compared with the Hebrew, Greek and other editions, in divers languages; and first published by the English College at Douai, anno 1609. Newly revised and corrected, according to the Clementine edition of*

THE FIRST

THE FIRST

BIBLE—*Continued*
the Scriptures, with annotations for elucidating the principal difficulties of Holy Writ. It was based on the New Testament published in 1582 in Rheims, France, and the Old Testament published in Douai, Flanders, in 1609.

Greek Testament was *The New Testament in Greek*, 478 pages, 16 mo., printed in 1800 by Isaias [Isaiah] Thomas, Worcester, Mass.

Hebrew Bible published in America was *Biblia Hebraica*, printed in 1814 by Thomas Dobson, Philadelphia, Pa., from type imported from Amsterdam, Holland. *(Publications Jewish Historical Society—1926)*

Phonetic Bible was *The New Testament of Our Lord and Saviour Jesus Christ, translated out of the original Greek, and with the former translations diligently compared and revised*, 397 pages, by Andrew Comstock, M.D., published in 1848 in Philadelphia, Pa. Comstock used a character for each of the 38 elementary sounds and 6 for compound letters. The text was set in double columns.

BIBLE CONCORDANCE was a reprint of an edition published in London in 1643. It was published in Cambridge, Mass., in 1683. In 1720 it was published as the *Cambridge Concordance* by Samuel Newman of Cambridge, Mass.

BIBLE SCHOOL to train missionaries was the Missionary Training College for Home and Foreign Missionaries and Evangelists, New York City, founded 1882 and formally opened October 1, 1883, with an enrollment of four students. The course consisted of one year of study, including courses in English, Christian Evidences, Bible Study and Interpretation, Church History, and Christian Life and Work. The first commencement was May 1884. The school was founded by Dr. Albert Benjamin Simpson, who was the first president. The name was changed to the Missionary Training Institute in April 1894. On October 24, 1897, opening exercises were held at South Nyack, N.Y., present location of the school.

BIBLE SOCIETY
Bible society was the Bible Society of Philadelphia, organized December 12, 1808, at Philadelphia, Pa. The name was changed to the Pennsylvania Bible Society in 1840. The Reverend William White, D.D., was the first president and B. B. Hopkins, the first secretary. The society was governed by 24 managers from whom were selected a president, 4 vice presidents, 2 secretaries, and a treasurer. The initiation fee was $5 and the dues $2 a year. Life membership was $50. *(An Address of the Bible Society Established at Philadelphia to which is subjoined the constitution of said society and the names of the managers)*

Bible society (national organization) was the American Bible Society, formed by delegates from 35 Bible societies for the sole purpose of increasing the circulation of the Holy Scriptures. The delegates met May 8, 1816, in New York City, and organized the society on May 11, 1816. The first president was Elias Boudinot, who served from 1816 to 1821. In the first year, 6,140 Bibles were distributed. *(American Bible Society—Bible Society Manual)*

BIBLICAL LITERATURE BIBLIOGRAPHY. *See* Bibliography: Bibliography of theological and biblical literature

BIBLICAL STUDENTS SUMMER CONFERENCE was organized by Dwight Lyman Moody, July 7, 1886, at the Mount Hermon School, Northfield, Mass. The conference, at which 250 students from 85 colleges in 22 states were present, marked the beginning of the Student Volunteer movement which has sent thousands of missionaries into all parts of the world. The students devoted their time to a study of the Bible and to methods of evangelical work. *(William Revell Moody—The Life of D. L. Moody)*

BIBLIOGRAPHY
Bibliography of Americana in English was *Bibliotheca Americana; or a Chronological Catalogue of the most curious and interesting books, pamphlets, state papers, etc. upon the subject of North and South America, from the earliest period to the present in print . . .*, published in 1789 in London, England, for J. Debrett. It contained 271 pages and included an introductory study on the state of literature in North and South America.

Bibliography of theological and biblical literature was Cotton Mather's *Manuductio Ad Ministerium; directions for a candidate of the ministry, wherein first, a right foundation is laid for his future improvement, and, then, rules are offered for such a management of his academical and preparatory studies, and thereupon, for such a conduct after his appearance in the world, as may render him a skilful and useful minister of the gospel.* The work was printed in 1726 for Thomas Hancock and sold at his shop in Ann Street, Boston, Mass. It contained 151 pages, and a catalog for a young student's library.

BIBLIOGRAPHY COURSE was offered in 1878 by the University of Michigan, at Ann Arbor. Raymond Cazallis Davis, the librarian, gave a lecture once a week during November and December. *(University of Michigan—Catalogue 1878-79)*

BIBLIOGRAPHY SOCIETY (national) was the Bibliographical Society of America, organized October 18, 1904, in St. Louis, Mo., "to promote bibliographical research and to issue bibliographical publications." The first officers were William Coolidge Lane, president; Herbert Putnam, first vice president; Reuben Gold Thwaites, second vice president; and Wilberforce Eames, librarian.

BICAMERAL LEGISLATURE. *See* Legislature: Legislature with two chambers

BICARBONATE OF SODA. *See* Baking soda

BICYCLE
Bicycle velocipedes or "swift walkers," as they were then called, were imported in 1819. The first one in New York City made its appearance on May 21, 1819. The Common Council met on August 19, 1819, and in solemn session passed a law "to prevent the use of velocipedes in the public places and on the sidewalks of the city of New York."

Bicycle with a **back pedal brake** was patented on December 24, 1889, by Daniel C. Stover and William A. Hance of Freeport, Ill., who received patent No. 418,142.

Bicycle with a **rotary crank** was patented (No. 59,915) on November 20, 1866, by Pierre Lallemont of Paris, France. It was known as a "bone shaker." He rode on it from Ansonia, Conn., to New Haven, Conn. The fore wheel was axled to the jaws of a depending bar, which was pivoted in the frame, and turned by a horizontal lever bar, which was revolved by a treadle crank.

BICYCLE CLUB. *See* Bicycle society

BICYCLE CORPS (military) was organized in 1894 by Colonel Royal Page Davidson and was made up of cadets in the Northwestern Military Academy, Lake Geneva, Wis. It was composed of 16 bicycles, each equipped with special clips for carrying rifles, etc. One of the feats of the corps was a maneuver in which the riders put themselves and their bicycles, which with their military equipment weighed 54 pounds each, over a 16-foot wall in 2 minutes and 48 seconds. Numerous long cross-country trips were made. On June 7, 1897, eleven cadets left Chicago, Ill., carrying a message from Major General John R. Brooks of Fort Sheridan, Ill., over the mountains and the National Pike to Washington, D.C., where it was delivered to Russell Alexander Alger, Secretary of War, on June 26, 1897. (*Bicycle World—July 2, 1897*)

BICYCLE FACTORY was established in 1877 by Colonel Albert Augustus Pope, who organized the Pope Manufacturing Company. His first machines were manufactured by the

Weed Sewing Machine Company of Hartford, Conn. The first order was in 1878 for fifty "Columbia" bicycles. (*Herbert Alfred Garratt—The Modern Safety Bicycle*)

BICYCLE MAGAZINE was *The American Bicycling Journal*, published December 22, 1877 in Boston, Mass. It contained 16 pages and cost 10 cents a copy. It appeared every other Saturday. Frank William Weston was the editor.

BICYCLE PATENT
Bicycle patent was granted to William K. Clarkson, Jr., of New York City on June 26, 1819, for an "improved curricle." Bicycles were then known as "curricles," "velocipedes," or "swift walkers."

Water velocipede patent was No. 95,531, granted on October 5, 1869, to F. A. Spofford and Matthew G. Raffington of Columbus, Ohio.

BICYCLE RACE
Intercollegiate bicycle race was held May 27, 1896, at the Manhattan Beach Track, New York City, under the auspices of the Intercollegiate Association of Amateur Athletes of America. Five races were held—¼ mile, ½ mile, 1 mile, 1 mile tandem, and 5 miles. Contestants scored 5 points for each first place, 2 points for each second place, and 1 point for each third place. The score was Columbia 20, Yale 8, Pennsylvania 5, Columbian University of Washington 5, and Harvard 2.

International six-day bicycle race was held in Madison Square Garden, New York City, from midnight Sunday, October 18, 1891, to midnight Saturday, October 24, 1891, and was won by William Martin, who rode a "high wheeler" bicycle. There were 40 contestants but only 6 finished. Martin covered 1,466 miles and 4 laps and won a $2,000 prize. Ten laps constituted a mile. The first two-man team event was held from February 12, 1899, to February 17, 1899, and was won by Miller and Waller, who rode a combined total of 2,733.4 miles.

Motorcycle-paced bicycle race was a 100-mile race for a $1,000 prize held July 29, 1899, at the Manhattan Beach Track, Manhattan Beach, New York. There were four entries: Harry Elkes, Frank Waller, Charles Miller, and Burns Pierce. Pierce covered the course in 3 hours, 27 minutes, and 5⅖ seconds, beating the nearest competitor by 7⅓ miles. The contestants were on bicycles. The motorcycle was used to pace them.

Paired six-day bicycle race was held at Madison Square Garden, New York City, December 9-14, 1901. The winners of the $1,500

BICYCLE RACE—*Continued*
team prize were Robert Walthour of Atlanta, Ga., and Archie McEachern of Toronto, Canada, who pedaled 2,555 miles. Sixteen professional riders from nine nations competed. Paired races were instituted as the law prohibited one man from being on the track more than twelve hours a day.

Women's six-day bicycle race was held at Madison Square Garden, New York City, January 6-11, 1896. It was promoted by William Madden and David Holland. Frankie Nelson, closely followed by Helen Baldwin, covered 418 miles. About 4,000 spectators attended the final session.

BICYCLE RACE TRACK OF WOOD was built by the Bay City Club, San Francisco, Calif., and placed in use July 1, 1893. The outer edges of the track were built on an incline.

BICYCLE RACER
Bicycle racer to attain the speed of a mile a minute was Charles Minthorn Murphy, known as Mile-A-Minute-Murphy, who on June 30, 1899, rode a mile in 57 4/5 seconds, riding behind a Long Island Railroad train from Farmingdale, Long Island, to Maywood, Long Island, N.Y., on a 3-mile measured track. He followed the train, which was equipped with an extension top and sides so that he raced in a comparative vacuum.

Woman bicycle champion of the National Amateur Bicycle Association was Doris Kopsky of Belleville, N.J., who on September 4, 1937, in Buffalo, N.Y., covered a mile in 4 minutes and 22.4 seconds.

Woman bicycle champion of the National Amateur Bicycle Association to win twice was Mildred Marie Dietz of St. Louis, Mo., who won at Humboldt Park, Chicago, Ill., on August 18-19, 1945, and at Columbus, Ohio on August 17, 1946.

BICYCLE SCHOOL for velocipede riding was opened in New York City on December 5, 1868, at 932 Broadway, by Pearsall Brothers.

BICYCLE SOCIETY
Bicycle club was the Boston Bicycle Club formed February 11, 1878, in Boston, Mass., by fourteen members. George B. Woodward was president, Thatcher Goddard was captain, and Harry S. Mann was secretary and treasurer. The uniform was a gray jacket, shirt, breeches, and stockings and a blue Glengarry Scotch cap with a small visor in front. The first meet was held March 9, 1878. (*The Wheelman. March 1883*)

Bicycle society (national organization) was the League of American Wheelmen formed

May 31, 1880, at Newport, R.I., by 128 members representing 28 cycling clubs. The first officers were president Charles Ed Pratt of Boston, Mass.; vice president Thomas K. Longstreth of Philadelphia, Pa.; and Commander C. K. Munroe of New York City. (*Bicycling World. June 12, 1880*)

BICYCLE TIRE
Bicycle tire (cord) was invented by John F. Palmer of Chicago, Ill., who obtained patent No. 476,680 on June 7, 1892. The patent covered a self-healing tire in which the tread portion of the rubber was placed under compression, so that a puncture would tend to close rather than gape open. The tire was manufactured in 1892 by the B. F. Goodrich Company of Akron, Ohio, and was first exhibited at the Philadelphia Cycle Show in February 1893.

Bicycle tire (pneumatic) was made in the tire factory of the George R. Bidwell Cycle Company of New York City in April 1891 for use on its bicycles. (*William Chauncey Geer—Reign of Rubber*)

Rubber tire patent. *See* Rubber: Rubber tire patent

BICYCLE TRAFFIC COURT was held at Racine, Wis., June 18, 1936, under authority of Grover Cleveland Lutter, chief of police. The judges of the court were Sergeant Wilbur Hansen and Officer Alphonse Costabile of the Racine Police Department. Sessions were held Saturday mornings. Section 12.71 of Code of the General Ordinance of the City of Racine passed by Common Council May 4, 1937, approved May 8, 1937, required all bicycles to be registered with the police department.

BICYCLE TRIP
Bicycle rider to cross the continent in less than three weeks was Eugene McPherson, 22 years old, of Ohio State University who left Santa Monica, Calif., on September 1, 1949, and arrived at New York City on September 21, 1949, covering 3,054 miles in 20 days, 4 hours and 29 minutes.

Bicycle trip around the world was made by Thomas Stevens, who started from San Francisco, Calif., on April 22, 1884, on a 50-inch bicycle (diameter of the large front wheel). He pedaled across the United States, arriving at Boston, Mass., on August 24, 1884. He left for Europe by ship. He visited England, France, Germany, Austria-Hungary, Serbia, Bulgaria, Turkey, Persia, India, China, and Japan. On December 17, 1886, he landed at Yokohama, Japan, having actually wheeled about 13,500 miles. He left Yokohama on the "City of Peking" and arrived at San Francisco January 4, 1887. (*Thomas Stevens—Around the World on a Bicycle*)

THE FIRST

Bicycle trip of 100 miles sponsored by a club took place September 6, 1882, when the Boston Bicycle Club, Boston, Mass., sponsored a trip from Worcester, Mass., to Boston. The trip started at 4:38 A.M. and ended at 9:30 P.M. with frequent stop-offs for food, refreshments, and repairs. The elapsed time was 16 hours and 52 minutes, of which 12 hours and 6 minutes was the actual riding time. Seven men covered the complete 102½ miles, but many others rode along for varying distances. The route was via South Framingham, Natick, Wellesley, Dedham, Stoughton, Brockton, Randolph, Braintree, Quincy, Mattapan, Waltham, and Newton.

BIFOCALS. *See* Lens: Bifocal contact lens; Lens: Eyeglass bifocals

BILL. *See* Money: Bill

BILL OF RIGHTS. *See* Constitutional amendment (U.S.)

BILLBOARD LEGISLATION. *See* Advertising law: Outdoor advertising legislation (state)

BILLBOARD STANDARDIZATION was attempted by the owners of outdoor advertising services who reorganized and formed the Associated Bill Posters and Distributors of the United States and Canada on July 15, 1891, in Chicago, Ill. At a meeting held in Kansas City, Mo., October 16-20, 1925, the name was changed to the Outdoor Advertising Association of America, Inc., by virtue of the absorption of the Painted Display Advertising Association. Billboards were usually from 50 to 100 feet in length. In 1912 the boards were divided into sections 25 feet long. The posters were all of the same height, 8 feet 10 inches, but their length varied. The 8-, 12-, 16-, and 24-sheet posters were in general use. The 24-sheet poster was 19 feet 8 inches long. The difference between the size of the poster and the billboard allowed for the use of a white border which tended to intensify the pictorial poster. At later dates the height of the billboard was changed until it was as high as 15 feet from the ground line, with 3 feet of lattice apron border at the base.

BILLIARD BALL of composition material resembling ivory was invented by John Wesley Hyatt, the winner of a $10,000 prize offered by Phelan and Collender of New York City for the best substitute for an ivory ball. Hyatt obtained patent No. 50,359, October 10, 1865, on a billiard ball; patent No. 76,765, April 14, 1868, on a compound for billiard balls; patent No. 88,634, April 6, 1869, on a method of coating and painting; and patent No. 105,338, July 12, 1870, on celluloid. *(Journal of Industrial and Engineering Chemistry. Vol. 6. No. 2)*

THE FIRST

BILLIARD BOOK was *Billiards Without A Master; a full and complete set of rules for the government of the game of billiards and the various games of pool, etc; hints to players, advice to amateurs, keepers of saloons, etc.,* by Michael Phelan, containing 127 pages and 50 copperplate diagrams. It was published in 1850 in New York City by D. D. Winant.

BILLIARD MATCH
Billiard match of importance was played May 13, 1854, for a $200 stake at Malcolm Hall, Syracuse, N.Y., by Joseph N. White of New York City and George Smith of Watertown, N.Y. It was a four-ball carom game, 500 points up, on a six-by-twelve four-pocket table. White won by a score of 500 to 484. The score of runs and averages was not kept. *(Michael Phelan—American Billiard Record)*

Billiard match to attain international prominence was played in Detroit, Mich., on April 12, 1859, between Michael Phelan of New York City and John Seereiter of Detroit for the championship of the world and a $15,000 purse. Phelan, known as the "father of billiards," won the championship by a score of 2,000 against his competitor's 1,904. The best run made by Phelan was 129 points. The game was played on a six-by-twelve four-pocket table with four balls. Pushing and crotching were allowed.

Billiard three-ball match on a six-by-twelve carom table was played for a $500 stake April 30, 1855, at San Francisco, Calif., between Michael Phelan, then of San Francisco, and M. Damon of Paris, France. Phelan conceded his opponent 20 points in 100, and won two out of three games. *(Brooklyn Daily Eagle Almanac—1887)*

Intercollegiate billiard match was played July 25, 1860, in Worcester, Mass., when freshmen of Harvard and Yale engaged in a "grand trial of skill." A six-pocket, six-by-twelve table was used. Four balls, white, spotted, light red and dark red, each 2⅜ inches, were used. Pushing and crotching were allowed. Benjamin Thompson Frothingham and William Stackpole of Harvard won with 800 points against 720 for George St. John Sheffield and Theodore C. Bacon of Yale. The best run was 45, made by Bacon. *(Michael Phelan—American Billiard Record)*

BILLIARDS were brought to America by the Spaniards who settled in St. Augustine, Fla., in 1565.

BINDER (book). *See* Book binder

BINET-SIMON SCALE. *See* Intelligence test

BIOGRAPHY COURSE
Biography department in a college was established at Carleton College, Northfield, Minn., in the college year 1919-20. It was organized by Dr. Ambrose White Vernon as a separate department of the college.

BIOLOGY
Biology course (general) offered in a college was conducted by Professor Edmund Beecher Wilson, professor of biology, at Bryn Mawr College, Bryn Mawr, Pa., beginning September 23, 1885. Five lectures were given weekly with eight hours of laboratory practice. The students examined the structure of typical animals and plants, first of familiar species, then of unicellular organisms, working thence progressively upwards and taking the higher animals and plants, and ending with the embryological development of the chick. An advanced class was engaged in the study of animal morphology. Lectures on specific phases of biology had, however, been given earlier.

Biology instruction. *See* Physiological laboratory

BIRD BANDING
Bird banding was done at Mill Grove Farm, Montgomery County, 24 miles northwest of Philadelphia, Pa., in 1803 by John James Audubon, who used silver wire to band a brood of phoebes (Sayornis phoebe) and was fortunate in obtaining two returns.

Bird banding by federal authorities was done by the United States Biological Survey. Bands were attached to different species of ducks and other water birds during the summer of 1914 by Dr. Alexander Wetmore who was making investigations of the duck sickness at the Bear River marshes, Utah. (*U.S. Agricultural Bulletin No. 1145. May 1923*)

BIRD BANDING SOCIETY
was the American Bird Banding Association, formed in New York City by thirty charter members on December 8, 1909. The society was dissolved in 1920, when records and effects were turned over to the Bureau of Biological Survey of the United States Department of Agriculture, Washington, D.C. (*The Auk. Vol. 38, 1921*)

BIRD LEGISLATION (international)
was the Migratory Bird Treaty for the protection of migratory birds in the United States and Canada, signed August 16, 1916, by the United States and Great Britain at Washington, D.C. (39 Stat.L.1702). It was signed by President Woodrow Wilson, September 1, 1916, and ratified by Great Britain October 20, 1916. Ratifications were exchanged in Washington, D.C., December 7, 1916, and the treaty proclaimed December 8, 1916.

BIRD MONUMENT. *See* Monument: Monument to a bird

BIRD PROTECTION AGENCY (federal)
was begun on July 1, 1885, as a section of Economic Ornithology, Division of Entomology, Department of Agriculture. It became the Bureau of Biological Survey on July 1, 1905, was transferred to the Department of Interior on July 1, 1939, and consolidated with the Bureau of Fisheries on June 30, 1940, to form the present Fish and Wildlife Service.

BIRD REFUGE authorized by a state
was established at Lake Merritt, Oakland, Calif., by authority of Chapter 109, Act of February 14, 1872.

BIRD RESERVATION (national)
was established by Executive Order of President Theodore Roosevelt on March 14, 1903, at Pelican Island, situated in the Indian River near Sebastian, Fla. The refuge was enlarged by Executive Order of January 26, 1909, to include adjacent mangrove and other islands. (*Records in Bureau of Biological Survey, Department of Agriculture. Washington, D.C.*)

BIRD SANCTUARY for wild birds
was the Hawk Mountain Sanctuary, Drehersville, Pa., which received options on the area, August 29, 1934.

BIRDS
Bird for which a definite crossing of the Atlantic has been recorded is that of a common tern (Sterna hirundo) that was banded at Eastern Egg Rock, Me., on July 3, 1913, and found dead in August 1917 at the mouth of the Niger River, West Africa. (*Frederick Charles Lincoln—Migration of American Birds*)

Eagle depicted on a postage stamp. *See* Postage stamp: Postage stamps depicting the American eagle

Ostrich farm was established at South Pasadena, Calif., by Edwin Cawston in 1886. He imported fifty ostriches from Africa, eighteen of which survived the trip and were landed at Galveston, Tex., in 1886. In order to discourage the exportation of ostriches from Africa, an export tax of $500 was placed on each ostrich and $25 on each egg, but this shipment escaped the tax as the boat sailed from Africa a few hours before the tax became effective.

Partridge propagation was encouraged in 1790 when Richard Bache, son-in-law of Benjamin Franklin, stocked his plantation at Beverly, N.J. Four years previously, General Lafayette had sent a few partridges to George Washington (*Technical Bulletin No. 61—United States Department of Agriculture*)

THE FIRST

Ptarmigan (Eskimo chicken) hatched and reared in captivity was hatched July 24, 1934, at Ithaca, N.Y., from one of ten eggs obtained from Churchill, Manitoba, Canada, by Arthur Augustus Allen, Professor of Ornithology, Cornell University, Ithaca, N.Y. The ptarmigan was 110 days old when it died of enterohepatitis (commonly called blackhead).

Quetzal bird (adult) (pharomacrus costaricensis) was imported October 4, 1940, by Dr. Victor Wolfgang Von Hagen, New York City, who had captured it. It was acquired by the St. Louis Zoo, St. Louis, Mo., but was exhibited until October 7, 1940, at the Bronx Zoo, New York City. It was a male, three years old, pigeon size, with a crimson breast. The back and head were emerald green with a gold trim. The wings were jet black and the tail black and white; over the tail was a green train about a yard long, and four additional feathers. On October 29, 1937, Dr. Von Hagen had brought back nine young quetzals, which were shown at the Bronx Zoo until April 1939, when the last one died. (*Victor Wolfgang Von Hagen—Jungle in the Clouds*)

Snow goose bred in captivity was hatched in 1934 in the City Park Zoo, Denver, Colo. This gosling was the first seen anywhere. Three eggs were laid; one hatched, one was destroyed, and one was given to the Colorado Museum of Natural History, in the City Park Zoo, Denver, Colo. Clyde E. Hill was the director of the zoo.

Sparrows were imported under the auspices of Nicholas Pike and other directors of the Brooklyn Institute in 1850 for the purpose of protecting shade trees from foliage-eating caterpillars. Eight pairs of English sparrows were imported. The birds were kept in cages until liberated in the spring of 1851. They did not thrive and in 1852 a larger number were imported. (*Frederick William Evans—English Sparrows*)

BIRLING. *See* Log rolling (birling) national championship

BIRTH CONTROL CLINIC. *See* Medical clinic: Birth control clinic

BIRTH REGISTRATION
Birth Registration Law (state) was passed by the state of Georgia, December 19, 1823. It required the "clerks of the court of ordinary, in each county respectively to enter and register in a book" the dates of births of all persons upon due proof made by affidavit or oath. The clerk was entitled to charge 25 cents for each registration. (*Georgia Law, Extract General Appropriation Bill, Page 192, Approved December 19, 1823*)

THE FIRST

Birth registration uniform system for the numbering of birth certificates was adopted March 18, 1948, by the American Association of Registration Executives. The Council on Vital Records and Vital Statistics approved this resolution of the regislation executives at a meeting on August 30, 1948. The system was inaugurated January 1, 1949. Each state was assigned a number: 101 for Alabama, 102 for Arizona, 103 for Arkansas, etc. A second number refers to the year, and a third number to the order of the birth in the state's record. The lowest number in the classification was awarded to Leonard Blake Gunnells of Prattville, Ala., whose name was the first on the roll of the first county in Alabama's alphabetical county list. His number was 101-49-000001.

BIRTHS
Birth (human) to be televised. *See* Television—Telecast: Birth (human) to be televised

Child born in an airplane was the daughter of Mr. and Mrs. T. W. Evans, born on October 28, 1929, in a transport plane over the city of Miami, Fla.

Child born in the White House, Washington, D.C., was James Madison Randolph, the son of Thomas Mann Randolph and Martha (Jefferson) Randolph, the daughter of President Thomas Jefferson, born January 17, 1806. He died January 23, 1834. The Randolphs were married February 23, 1790. (*Robert Isham Randolph—The Randolphs of Virginia*)

Child born in the White House, Washington, D.C., the offspring of a President, was Esther Cleveland, born September 9, 1893. She was the second child of President Grover Cleveland and Frances Folsom Cleveland, who were married June 2, 1886, in the Blue Room of the White House, Washington, D.C. (*Gibson Willets—Inside History of the White House*)

Child born of English parents in America was Virginia Dare. She was born at Roanoke Island, North Carolina, on August 18, 1587, and was the daughter of Ananias Dare and Eleanor (White) Dare, and granddaughter of John White, governor of the colony sent out from England by Sir Walter Raleigh on May 8, 1587. Only the first nine days of her life are known to history. On May 8, 1587, three vessels left England with 150 colonists, including 25 women and children. They landed at Cape Hatteras on July 22, cruised up what is now Pamlico Sound to the "iland called Roanoac." Two vessels returned immediately and the third with John White sailed on August 27 for more supplies. When he returned four years later, the colonists were all gone and the fort was in ruins. (*North Carolina Booklet Vol. 1. #1 May 10, 1901—Major Graham Daves—Virginia Dare*)

THE FIRST

THE FIRST

BIRTHS—*Continued*
Child born of European parents on American soil was Snorro, the son of Thorfinn Karlsefni and Gudrid, the widow of Thorstein Ericsson (Leif Ericsson's brother). About 160 Norse volunteers arrived in America in 1007 to form a settlement in Vinland, which may have been Nova Scotia or the coast of Maine. Snorro returned to Iceland and took an important part in its government.

Child born on a vessel passing through the Panama Canal was the child of Mr. and Mrs. M. Niezes of Panama. The baby was born on June 2, 1930, on the Dutch steamship "Baralt," passing through Gatun locks.

Quadruplets delivered by Caesarean operation were Maureen, Kathleen, Eileen and Michael Cirminello, born to Mr. and Mrs. Joseph Cirminello on November 1, 1944, in Philadelphia, Pa. The Caesarean section was performed under spinal anesthesia. The obstetrician in charge was Dr. John Calvin Ullery of Upper Darby, Pa.

Quintuplets were five boys born February 13, 1875, in Watertown, Wis., to Mrs. Edna Beecham Kanouse, wife of Edward Cole Kanouse. All five died within two weeks. (The birth of quintuplets in 1776 is claimed for Mars Bluff, S.C., and in 1800 for Monticello, Ill.)

Sextuplets were three boys and three girls born September 8, 1866, in Chicago, Ill., to James and Jennie A. Lewis Bushnell. The attending physician was Dr. James Edwards and the midwife was Priscilla Bancroft. One of the sextuplets—Lucy—died at the age of two months, and one—Laberto—died at eight months. Of the surviving four, one—Norberto—died at 68, and three—Alberto, Alice Elizabeth (Mrs. Hughes), and Alincia L. (Mrs. Parker)—were over 70 when they died. (According to the *Boston Medical and Surgical Journal* of 1847 [Vol. 35, p. 27], sextuplets were born on June 27, 1846, to a Mrs. Marr of Phipsburg, Maine, but the report may have been a hoax.)

Telecast (public) of a human birth. *See* Television—Telecast: Birth (human) to be televised for the public

White child of French Protestant parentage was born in 1565 in the French settlement of Fort Caroline, Fla., established in 1564 by René Goulaine de Laudonnière, a Huguenot. In August 1565 the original settlement was reinforced with the arrival of Captain Jean Ribaut's expedition, bringing women, children, agricultural implements, etc. (*Thomas Frederick Davis—Historic St. Johns Bluff, near Jacksonville, Fla.*)

World War baby was born on June 7, 1918, to ·Mrs. Kate Lewis, who married William Lewis of the American Expeditionary Force in London, England, on July 14, 1917.

BISHOP (Catholic). *See* Catholic bishop

BISHOP (general). *See* Army officer: General to be consecrated a bishop

BISHOP'S HERESY TRIAL. *See* Heresy trial of a bishop

BLACKOUT
Blackout lighting demonstration was made May 14, 1941, when twelve specially designed blackout luminaries spaced 100 feet apart along Parkland Avenue, Lynn, Mass., were illuminated. Each lighting fixture used a 2½ watt Argon (gaseous) lamp and gave off light in the form of ultraviolet rays invisible to observers in planes at a height of 20,000 feet.

Blackout outdoor light control was instituted by Seattle, Wash., May 11, 1942, which required all outside types of lighting to be controlled by manual control, master control wire, photoelectric cell, or radio switch, and subject to permit.

BLANKET
Blanket factory was the Burleigh Blanket Mills, established by Captain John H. Burleigh in 1854, on the Piscataqua River, Me. The factory was located on the site originally selected by Ferdinando Gorges in 1620 for a grist mill, at what is now South Berwick, Me.

Blanket robe and carriage lap robe business was successfully undertaken at Sanford, Me., in 1867 by Thomas Goodall. (*William Morrell Emery—History of Sanford, Me.*)

Electronic blanket was manufactured by Simmons Company on October 9, 1946, in Petersburg, Va. Temperature was regulated by an "electronic" thermostatic control. It sold for $39.50.

Horseblankets were manufactured by Thomas Goodall at Troy, N.H., in 1852. The only horseblankets then in use were imported and were square in shape. Goodall cut them to fit and put on buckles. He sold out his interest in 1865 to a group of financiers from Keene, N.H. (*M. T. Stone—Historical Sketch of the Town of Troy, N.H.*)

BLAST FURNACE. *See* Iron: Iron blast furnace

BLASTING (sand). *See* Sand blasting

THE FIRST

BLIND

Bible for the blind. *See* Bible: Bible for the blind in embossed form

Book for the blind. *See* Book: Book for the blind

Correspondence school for the blind to offer instruction in the Braille system of embossed print was the Hadley Correspondence School for the Blind, Winnetka, Ill., which offered courses, in August 1921, in English grammar, business correspondence, and the study of Scriptures, as well as instruction in the Braille system. The school, founded by William Aaron Hadley, was incorporated in Illinois, January 2, 1922.

Dogs trained to guide the blind. *See* Animals: Dogs trained to guide the blind

Kindergarten for the blind. *See* Kindergarten: Kindergarten for the blind

Magazine for the blind. *See* Periodical: Magazine for the blind

Music magazine published in Braille. *See* Music magazine: Music magazine published in Braille

School for the blind was the New England Asylum for the Blind, Boston, Mass., incorporated March 2, 1829. The school was founded by Dr. John Dix Fisher and opened under Dr. Samuel Gridley Howe in August 1832 with six pupils. On April 1, 1839, the name was changed to the Perkins Institution and the Massachusetts Asylum for the Blind in honor of Thomas Handasyd Perkins, who in 1833 offered his Boston home with open grounds around it for a school building. On October 3, 1877, the word "asylum" was dropped and the name changed to the Perkins Institution and Massachusetts School for the Blind. The present name of the school, now at Watertown, Mass., is the New England Institution for the Education of the Blind. (*Paul Monroe—Cyclopedia of Education*)

School for the blind to adopt the Braille system was the Missouri School for the Blind, St. Louis, Mo. In 1859, Dr. Simon Pollak, a trustee of the school, introduced it direct from Paris, France. Three letters were changed and it was used in music, spelling, etymology, and other subjects.

School for the Negro blind was the State School for the Blind and the Deaf opened in Raleigh, N.C., on January 4, 1869, with 26 pupils. (*Seventieth Anniversary of the State School for the Blind and the Deaf. Raleigh, N.C.*)

THE FIRST

State school for the blind was the Ohio Institution for the Blind, authorized April 3, 1837, and opened July 4, 1837, with five pupils, in the Presbyterian Church, Columbus, Ohio, in the presence of 900 people. Anson W. Penniman was the first teacher. The first superintendent was William Chapin, who served from May 1, 1840, to October 1, 1846. On April 25, 1902, a law was enacted to change the name to the Ohio State School for the Blind.

Talking book. *See* Talking book

Telephone switchboard with Braille markings. *See* Telephone: Telephone switchboard with Braille markings

"BLIND" AIRPLANE FLIGHT. *See* Aviation—Flights: All blind flight

BLOCK SIGNAL SYSTEM (railroad). *See* Railroad signal system

BLOCK TIN BUTTON. *See* Button: Pewter or block tin buttons

BLOCKADE was effected on April 30, 1778, from West Point, N.Y., to Constitution Island, N.Y. A huge chain was forged at the Sterling Iron Works, Orange County, N.Y., from ore mined in the same county and was carried in sections to West Point, where it was joined and stretched across the Hudson to prevent British ships from passing. The chain weighed 180 tons and was 1,700 feet long; each link was 2½ inches wide and 30 inches long. It was placed in position April 16 and on April 30, 1778, was secured at both ends. In the summer of 1776, a chain of chevaux-de-frise and sunken ships had been extended between Fort Washington, N.Y., and Fort Lee, N.J., but the British passed it October 9, 1776, without firing a gun. (*Macgrane Coxe—The Sterling Furnace and the West Point Chain*)

BLOOD BANK

Blood bank to preserve by refrigeration blood for transfusions was established March 15, 1937, by the Cook County Hospital, Chicago, Ill. (*Journal of the American Medical Association. July 10, 1937*)

Blood serum (human) (dried) was prepared by Dr. Earl William Flosdorf and Dr. Stuart Mudd of the School of Medicine, University of Pennsylvania, Philadelphia, Pa., on December 21, 1933, with glass apparatus made by them. The powdered dried blood serum was used successfully for transfusions for the prevention and treatment of children's diseases at a hospital at Philadelphia, Pa. The method was first described at a meeting of the American Chemical Society at St.

BLOOD BANK—*Continued*
Petersburg, Fla., in April 1934. More recently, the applications and uses of the dried blood serum have been greatly extended.

BLOOD GROUPING TEST. *See* Medical legislation: Blood grouping test laws

BLOOD SERUM (dried). *See* Blood bank: Blood serum (human) (dried)

BLOODSHED IN THE CIVIL WAR. *See* Civil war: Bloodshed in the Civil War

BLOOMERS were introduced at the First Woman's Rights Convention at Seneca Falls, N.Y., which met at Lyceum Hall on July 19, 1848, the name being derived from their sponsor, Mrs. Amelia Jenks Bloomer. The costume is supposed to have been devised by Mrs. Elizabeth Smith Miller. *(Dexter Chamberlain Bloomer—Life and Writings of Amelia Bloomer)*

BLOTTING PAPER was made in New Haven, Conn., by Joseph Parker & Son Company in 1856 at the West Rock Paper Mill on a Fourdrinier machine. Until this time only small quantities had been imported from England as sand-boxes were in general use. *(Paper World—August 1881)*

BLOWPIPE was invented in 1801 by Professor Robert Hare of Philadelphia, Pa., who called it a "hydrostatic blowpipe." He reported his discovery to the Chemical Society of Philadelphia in *A Memoir of the Supply and Application of the Blow-Pipe, Containing an Account of the new method of supplying the Blow-Pipe either with common air or oxygen gas; and also of the effects of the intense heat produced by the combustion of the hydrogen and oxygen gases. (Edgar Fahs Smith—Life of Robert Hare)*

BLUE LAW
　Blue law was enacted by the first legislative body assembled in America, the Virginia House of Burgesses, at its first session in 1619. The law provided that "all persons whatsoever upon the Sabbath days shall frequent divine service and sermons, both forenoon and afternoon." The Anglican church was established by law and the creed of the church was the rule of the colony. *(Gustavus Myers—Ye Olden Blue Laws)*

　Blue law regulating gambling was passed in 1624 by the Virginia Assembly. It specified that "Mynisters shall not give themselves to excesse in drinking or yette spend their tyme idelie by day or by night, playing at dice, cards or any unlawful game."*(Catherine Perry Hargrave—History of Playing Cards)*

　Gambling legislation (colonial). *See* Gambling legislation

BLUE SKY LAW. *See* Trust: Blue sky laws

BOARD OF EDUCATION (state). *See* Education: State board of education

BOARDING SCHOOL FOR INDIANS. *See* Indian school: Indian school (boarding) on a reservation

BOARDWALK was erected in 1870 at Atlantic City, N.J. To finance it, $5,000 was obtained by the sale, at a 10 per cent discount, of scrip which could be used to pay taxes. The boardwalk rested on the sand and was 8 feet wide. It was completed on June 26, 1870. It was conceived by a hotel man, Jacob Keim of the Chester County House, and Alexander Boardman, a railroad conductor on the Camden and Atlantic Railroad.

BOAT CLUB
　Boat club was the Knickerbocker Boat Club of New York, organized in 1811. The club had a white boat, with green gunwales and gilt stripes, named the "Knickerbocker," built by John Baptist. John Palmerton was coxswain, and William Cracker, John Burt, Thomas Dixon, and Thomas Palmerton were the oarsmen. The "Knickerbocker" raced the "Invincible," built by John and William Chambers, from Harsimus, N.J., to the Battery, New York City. On the crew of the "Invincible" were William Chambers, coxswain, and John Chambers, James Rush, Peter Snider, and John Swinburn, oarsmen. The club disbanded in 1812. *(New York Mirror, July 15, 1837)*

　Boat club association of amateur clubs was the Castle Garden Amateur Boat Club Association, which operated a boathouse at Castle Garden, N.Y., from 1834 to 1842. Annual regattas around Bedloe Island and back were held, the last one on July 4, 1842. Some of the boats entered were the "Wave," "Gull," "Gazelle," "Pearl," "Cleopatra," "Halcyon," "Ariel," "Minerva," and "Gondola." *(Robert F. Kelley—Amateur Rowing)*

BOAT RACE
　See also Rowing; Yacht race

　Fisherman's boat race was held May 1, 1886, over a triangular course. The start was off the Boston Light, Little Brewster Island, Boston, to and around Davis Ledge buoy off Minot's Ledge, thence to and around Half Way Rock off the Marblehead shore, and back to Boston Light. The "John H. McManus" won the first prize of $1,500, finishing two miles ahead of the "Sarah H. Prior," which was a few minutes ahead of the "Gertie S. Windsor." The pilot schooner "Hesper" won the race and the cup, but not the prize money, as it was not truly a fisherman's boat. *(Wesley George Pierce—Goin' Fishin')*

Intercollegiate boat race, in eight-oared boats, took place August 3, 1852, between Yale and Harvard on a two-mile course on Lake Winnepesaukee, Centre Harbor, N.H. Harvard's lone entry, the "Oneida," a 38-foot boat captained by Joseph Mansfield Brown, won by two lengths over Yale's "Shawmut," followed by Yale's "Undine" and "Atlanta." *(James Wellman—Story of the Harvard-Yale Race 1852-1912)*

Intercollegiate regatta was held July 26, 1859, at Lake Quinsigamond, Worcester, Mass. Harvard defeated both Yale and Brown over a 3-mile course. A regatta was scheduled July 23, 1858, at Springfield, Mass., but was postponed as a member of the Yale crew had drowned the day before.

International boat race was held August 17, 1869, on the Putney-Mortlake course on the Thames, London, England. An Oxford crew of four beat the Harvard crew by three clear lengths.

International lifeboat race was held September 7, 1927, from the Statue of Liberty to Pier A, New York City, under the auspices of the Neptune Association. Eleven boats of different sizes, shapes, and weights from seven different nations competed. A prize cup was presented to Captain John F. Milliken of the M.S. "Segundo" of Norway whose team of eight men covered the course in 15 minutes, 27 seconds. Second honors went to the crew of the M.S. "Titania" of Norway (16 minutes, 27 seconds) and third place to the crew of the "De Grasse" of France (17 minutes, 7 seconds). Later races developed uniform conditions.

Motor boat race under organized rules was held June 23-24, 1904, under the jurisdiction of the Columbia Yacht Club, 86th Street and Hudson River, New York City. A 32-mile race was held for the Gold Cup of the Challenge Cup Series, from the clubhouse to a point 16 miles north and back. The trophy was won by C. C. Riotte in the "Standard," 100 h.p., 59 feet long, average speed 22.57 statute miles (19.67 nautical miles) per hour. The contest was decided by a point system and the rules were formulated on April 22, 1903, by the American Power Boat Association, which was organized by seven yacht clubs on

January 20, 1903. *(American Power Boat Association—Story of Its Origin and Its Development)*

Regatta. *See* Yacht race: Regatta

Yacht race (international). *See* Yacht race: Yacht race (international)

BOATS. *See* Catamaran; Ferryboat; Life boat; Motor boat; Ship

BOBSLED COMPETITION

Four-man bob-team competition was held February 14-15, 1932, at the Third Olympic Winter Games at Lake Placid, N.Y., with thirteen teams from six nations competing. First place was won by the United States team of William L. Fiske, driver, and Edward F. Eagan, Clifford B. Gray, and Jay O'Brien, brakemen, in a contest which covered the four heats in a total time of 7 minutes, 53.68 seconds.

Two-man bob-team competition was held February 9-10, 1932 at the Third Olympic Winter Games at Lake Placid, N.Y., with fifteen teams from eight nations entered in the competition. First place was won by the United States (J. Hubert Stevens, driver, and Curtis Stevens, brakeman) in 8 minutes, 14.74 seconds for the four heats.

BOBSLED RUN of international specifications was the Mt. Van Hoevenberg bobsled run at North Elba, N.Y., on the highway between Lake Placid and Elizabethtown, N.Y., designed by Stanislaus Zentzytzki. Work was begun August 4, 1930, and the run was open to the public December 25, 1930.

BOHEMIAN AMERICAN CHURCH was St. John Nepomuk Church, St. Louis, Mo., opened April 20, 1855, by the first pastor, Reverend Henry Lipowsky, a former lieutenant in the Austrian Army. The first solemn High Mass was sung by Father de Smet, the famous Jesuit missionary among the Indians, on May 16, 1855, the patronal feast.

BOHEMIAN - AMERICAN DICTIONARY. *See* Dictionary: Bohemian-American dictionary

BOHEMIAN NEWSPAPER (Czech). *See* Newspaper: Czech language newspaper

BOILER

Carbon monoxide boiler to achieve complete conversion of waste gases into useful power was designed and developed by the Sinclair Oil Corporation and placed in operation November 1953 at its Houston, Tex., refinery.

THE FIRST

BOILER—*Continued*
Carbon monoxide (CO) was converted into carbon dioxide (CO_2) by injecting a stream of air into the waste gases from the generator. The catalyst was regenerated in the catalytic oil cracking process.

BOILER INSURANCE COMPANY. *See* Insurance: Boiler insurance company

BOILER LEGISLATION was the state boiler inspection law, approved July 9, 1864, by Connecticut. Chapter 67 authorized the governor to appoint an "Inspector of Boilers" to check every steam boiler used for manufacturing or mechanical purposes.

BOILER PLATES were made between 1816 and 1825 by Dr. Charles Lukens' mill, the "Brandywine Mill" at Coatesville, Pa. The mill was originally started at Rokeby, Pa., by Isaac Pennock in 1790 as the Federal Slitting Mill. Iron slabs were heated in an open charcoal fire, rolled out into plates, and then slit up into rods for general blacksmiths' use. In 1810 Pennock purchased a sawmill at Brandywine, which he converted into the Brandywine Iron Mill. The organization has remained in the hands of Lukens' descendants, and is now known as the Lukens Steel Company, one of the world's largest plate mills.

BOLL WEEVIL. *See* Cotton-boll weevil

BOLT FACTORY. *See* Nut and bolt factory

BOLT MACHINE. *See* Nut and bolt machine

BOMB EXPLOSION (atomic). *See* Atomic bomb: Atomic bomb explosion

BOMB SHELTER. *See* Air raid shelter; Building: House with a built-in nuclear bomb shelter

BOMBER. *See* Aviation—Airplane

BOMBING MISSION (AMERICAN) OVER ENEMY-OCCUPIED TERRITORY. *See* World War II: American bombing mission over enemy-occupied territory in Europe

BOMBING ON CONTINENTAL AMERICAN SOIL. *See* World War II: Bombing on continental American soil

BOND
Bonds of the United States Government were the interest-bearing obligations which were authorized by the Act of August 4, 1790

THE FIRST

(1 Stat.L.138), for the refunding of the domestic debt and that part of the state debt which was assumed by the Federal Government. The total issue amounted to $64,456,963.90; $30,088,-397.75 drew interest at 6 per cent; $19,719,-237.39 at 3 per cent; and $14,649,328.76 drew interest at 6 per cent after 1800. Practically the entire issue was retired by 1836. *(Liquidating the Revolutionary War—Commissioner of the Public Debt. Treasury Dept.)*

Bonds payable specifically in United States gold coins were issued under authority of a financial bill, an "act to define and fix the standard of value, to maintain the parity of all forms of money issued or coined by the United States, to refund the public debt," March 14, 1900 (31 Stat.L.45).

Liberty bond. *See* Loan: Liberty bond subscriptions

Treasury notes (interest-bearing) were authorized by the act of June 30, 1812 (2. Stat.L.766). The President was authorized to issue treasury notes to an amount not exceeding $5 million. The act provided "that the said treasury notes shall be reimbursed by the United States, at such places, respectively, as may be expressed on the face of the said notes, one year, respectively after the day on which the same shall have been issued; from which day of issue they shall bear interest at the rate of five and two-fifths per centum a year, payable to the owner or owners of such notes, at the treasury, or by the proper commissioner of loans, at the places and times respectively designated on the face of said notes for the payment of principal." *(John Jay Knox—United States Notes, A History of the Various Issues of Paper Money by the Government of the United States)*

War bond. *See* War bond

BONDED WAREHOUSE. *See* Warehouse legislation

BONDING COMPANY. *See* Insurance: Bonding company (exclusive)

BONDING LAW (state). *See* Insurance: Bonding law (state)

BONE BANK. *See* Medicine: Bone bank

BONE BANK CENTER. *See* Deaf—Bone Bank: National temporal bone bank center for ear research

BOOBY TRAP. *See* Land mines

THE FIRST

BOOK

See also under specific type of book or subject, e.g.,

Agricultural book   Novel
Almanac   Pharmacopoeia
Bible   Social Register

Best seller novel was *Charlotte, a Tale of Truth,* by Mrs. Rowson (Susanna Haswell Rowson), an actress of the New Theatre, Philadelphia, Pa., and author of *Victoria* (1786), *The Inquisitor* (1788), *Rebecca, or the Fille de Chambre* (1792), etc. *Charlotte* was printed by D. Humphreys for M. Carey, Philadelphia, Pa., in two volumes in 1794. An English edition of *Charlotte* was printed in London in 1790. Later it was entitled *Charlotte Temple.* About 200 editions have been printed. *(American Antiquarian Society—Proceedings, Vol. 42, April 1932)*

Best seller other than a text or purely theological work was *In His Steps, or What Would Jesus Do?* by the Reverend Charles Monroe Sheldon. It was written in the winter of 1896 and was a Utopian fantasy of what the world might be like if people lived literally according to Christ's teachings. It was read by the author a chapter at a time to his Sunday evening congregation in the Central Congregational Church, Topeka, Kan. He sold the story for $75 to the Chicago *Advance* and it was printed as a serial in 1897. As only parts of the serial were sent to the copyright office, the copyright was declared defective. Over 8 million copies in various editions were published by different publishers. *(Charles Monroe Sheldon—Charles M. Sheldon—His Life Story)*

Book bound with a pre-printed offset cloth was Gertrude Stein's *Portraits and Prayers,* a 264-page book published November 7, 1934, by Random House, New York City. The cover showed a portrait of Gertrude Stein made at her home in Belignin, France by Carl Van Vechten. The cloth was supplied by Columbia Mills, Inc., Syracuse, N.Y.

Book entered for copyright was *The Philadelphia Spelling Book arranged upon a plan entirely new, adapted to the capacities of children and designed as an immediate improvement in spelling and reading the English language,* which was registered in the clerk's office of the first district of Pennsylvania, June 9, 1790, by John Barry, the author. It was printed in Philadelphia, Pa., in 1790 by Carey, Stewart and Co. It was also issued as *The American Spelling Book.*

Book for the blind was the *Gospel of St. Mark,* published in 1833 in Philadelphia, Pa., by the Pennsylvania Institution for the Instruction of the Blind. It was printed in

THE FIRST

embossed roman letters, upper and lower case. Jacob Snider, Jr., recording secretary of the Pennsylvania Institute proposed the publication and the funds were donated by Nathan Dunn and Edward Coleman. *(Pennsylvania Institution for the Instruction of the Blind— Second Annual Report—March 2 1835)*

Book (full size) published in the colonies was Stephen Day's (Steeven Daye's) *The Whole Booke of Psalmes, Faithfully Translated into English Metre whereunto is prefixed a Discourse declaring not only the lawfulness, but also the necessity of the heavenly ordinance of singing scripture psalmes in the Churches of God.* The book contained 296 pages and was published in July 1640 by the Cambridge Press, Cambridge, Mass. It was a new metrical version of the psalms, a revision of those of Sternhold and Hopkins. Seventeen hundred copies were printed and sold for 20 pence each, netting a profit of almost £80. *(George Emery Littlefield—The Early Massachusetts Press)*

Book intended for circulation in the English colonies was Martin Luther's *Little Catechism,* translated into the Algonquin Indian language in 1656 by Johannes Campanius, a clergyman, who dedicated it to King Karl X Gustav of Sweden. About 600 copies of this 160-page book were printed in 1696, forty years later, in Stockholm, Sweden, by Thomas Campanius Holm, Campanius' grandson. The title was *Lutheri Catechismus oswersatt på American-Virginiste Sprätet.* It was intended for missionary work among the Indians in the colony of New Sweden and also contained a small vocabulary in the Algonquin Indian language.

Book list. *See* Book index

Book of Common Prayer in use in what is now the United States was the one used by the Reverend Francis Fletcher, chaplain and chronicler of Drake's ship, the "Golden Hind," June 24, 1579. A great stone cross in Golden Gate Park, San Francisco, Calif., commemorates the event.

Book of Common Prayer (in the Mohawk Indian language) was *The morning and evening prayer, the litany, church catechism, family prayers, and several chapters of the Old and New Testament,* translated into the *Mahaque Indian language by Lawrence Claesse, interpreter to William Andrews, Missionary to the Indians from the Honourable and Reverend the Society for the Propagation of the Gospel in Foreign Parts.* The book contained 115 pages and was published in 1715 by William Bradford in New York City.

Book of folio size, other than laws, was Samuel Willard's *A Compleat Body of Divinity in Two Hundred and Fifty Expository Lec-*

BOOK—*Continued*

tures on the Assembly's Shorter Catechism wherein the doctrines of the Christian religion are unfolded, their truth confirm'd . . . etc., published in 1726 in Boston, Mass., by [Bartholomew] Green and [Samuel] Kneeland. It was published posthumously, and contained 1,000 pages printed in two columns. There is an error in pagination as the work was printed by two presses.

Book (of size) completed entirely by one man was *Old Papermaking,* by Dr. Dard Hunter, published in 1923 by the author at Chillicothe, Ohio. It consisted of 140 pages, size 9 x 11½ inches, printed on handmade paper from linen and cotton cloth. Dr. Hunter not only was the author, but he manufactured the paper, designed the book, cut and cast the type, printed the book, etc.

Book on cornstalk paper was *Farm Products in Industry,* by George McCullough Rommel, which was printed in June 1928 by Rae D. Henkle Co. Inc., New York City.

Book on microcards. *See* Microcard: Book on microcards

Book on vellum was George Allen's *The Life of Philidor, Musician and Chess Player,* published in 1863 by E. H. Butler & Co., Philadelphia, Pa. Only two copies of the regular edition were printed on vellum.

Book (pamphlet) on vellum was *The First Plymouth Patent, Granted June 1, 1621,* a small quarto, of sixteen pages. It was edited by Charles Deane and published in 1854 in Cambridge, Mass. Only four copies were printed. It was bound in full brown levant morocco with a gilt border and fillets enclosing an ornamental inside border on the sides.

Book printed in the Indiana Territory was *Laws for the Government of the District of Louisiana, passed by the Governor and Judges of the Indiana Territory at their first session begun and held at Vincennes on Monday the first day of October 1804.* The book was published by territorial authority and printed by E. Stout in 1804 in Vincennes, Indiana Territory.

Book printed on American paper with American-made plates and bound in America was Charlotte (Turner) Smith's *Elegiac Sonnets and Other Poems,* printed in October 1795 by Isaiah Thomas, Worcester, Mass. The five oval plates were by Joseph H. Seymour, Jr. The 126-page book was a reprint of an English edition.

Book privately printed was John Eliot's *Communion of Churches; or, The Divine Management of Gospel-Churches by the Ordinance of Councils, Constituted in Order According to the Scriptures,* printed in 1665 by Marmaduke Johnson, Cambridge, Mass. It contained 40 pages. It was not for general sale. *(Charles Evans—American Bibliography)*

Book review telecast. *See* Television—Telecast: Book review to be televised

Book series microfilmed. *See* Microfilm: Book series microfilmed

Book set by linotype was *The Tribune Book of Open Air Sports,* edited by Henry Hall and published in 1887 by the Tribune Association, New York City. The foreword states, "This book is printed without type—being the first product in book form of the Mergenthaler machine which wholly supersedes the use of movable type."

Book set by the Photon process. *See* Typesetting machine: Photographic type-composing machine

Book with color plates was *The City of Philadelphia in the State of Pennsylvania North America as it appeared in the year 1800 consisting of twenty-eight plates drawn and engraved by W. Birch and Son,* published December 31, 1800, in Philadelphia, Pa. It was a large oblong folio containing 26 separate views drawn and engraved and two preliminaries. It was originally issued in fourteen numbers (two parts) in wrappers. It sold for $28.00 uncolored, $41.50 hand tinted in unbound boards, and $44.50 bound. *(Pennsylvania Magazine of History and Biography—July 1949. Vol. 73, No. 3)*

Comic books. *See* Periodical: Comic books

Hymn book. *See* Music book: Hymn book

Map made in the United States published in a book. *See* Map: Map made in the United States published in a book

Miniature book was William Secker's *A Wedding Ring, Fit for the Finger, or the Salve of Divinity on the Sore of Humanity. With directions to those men that want wives, how to choose them; and to those women that have husbands, how to use them.* The book contained 92 pages and was published in 1705 in Boston, Mass., by T. Green for Nicholas Buttolph. The size was approximately 2 by 3½ inches. It was a reprint of a work published in 1658 in London, England.

THE FIRST

Novel. *See* Novel

Profane poetry translation prepared in the colonies to be published was George Sandys' translation of Ovid's *Metamorphoses,* which was published in 1626 in London, England as *Ovid's Metamorphoses Englished, Mytholized and Represented in Figures.* A second edition was published in 1632 to which was added a translation of Virgil's *Æneid.* Sandys was treasurer of the Virginia Company. *(Richard Hooper—The Poetical Works of George Sandys)*

Stereotyped book was *The Larger Catechism,* which bore on the title page "The first book ever stereotyped in America. Stereotyped and printed by J. Watts and Co., New York, June 1813." The process was introduced by John Watts and was a combination of the systems of Firmin Didot and Charles Mahon, Earl of Stanhope. *(George Adolf Kubler—A New History of Stereotyping)*

Translated classic published was Cato's *Moral Distichs Englished in Couplets,* which was translated by James Logan, President of the Council and Chief Justice of the Province of Philadelphia. It was printed and sold in 1735 by Benjamin Franklin, Philadelphia, Pa. It consisted of 24 pages of precepts of morality and moral apothegms. It sold for one shilling and was announced in the December 18, 1735, *Pennsylvania Gazette.*

Typewritten book manuscript. *See* Typewritten book manuscript

BOOK AUCTION was authorized April 18, 1662, by the Court of Burgomasters and Schepens of New Amsterdam: "Anna Claas Croezens, widow of Daniel Litschoe, deceased, requests by petition to be allowed to sell by the Baliff some books which she has belonging to Sir Henry Moedy, as according to obligation she has a claim on him for a considerable sum." *(Records of New Amsterdam from 1653 to 1674. Vol. 4. p. 64)*

BOOK AUCTION CATALOG
Book auction catalog was announced in the *Boston News Letter,* Monday, May 18, 1713, No. 475: "On Thursday next, the 28th current being the day after the election, there will be exposed to sale by public vendue or outcry at the house of Mr. Ambrose Vincent, silk dyer in Wings Lane, Boston, a good collection of books, to be seen at the said house two days before the sale, etc. Catalogues will be posted at public places." *(Clarence Saunders Brigham —History of Book Auctions in America.)*

Book auction printed catalog was *A Catalog of Curious and Valuable Books Belonging to the Late Reverend and Learned Mr. Ebene-*

THE FIRST

zer Pemberton, Consisting of Divinity, Philosophy, History, Poetry and Generally Well Bound, which described the books "to be sold by auction at the Brown Coffee House in Boston, Mass." on July 2, 1717, at 3 P.M. The catalog was printed by B. Green in 1717 and was obtainable gratis at the shop of Samuel Gerrish, bookseller. *(George Leslie McKay— American Book Auction Catalogues 1713-1934)*

BOOK BINDER in America was John Ratliffe, who in 1663 was commissioned to bind Eliot's "Indian Bible" and "take care of the binding of 200 of them strongly and as speedily as may bee with leather, or as may bee most serviceable for the Indians." On August 30, 1664 he sent a letter to the Commissioners of New England stating that he was not well satisfied with the prices paid him for binding, and that 3 shillings, 4 pence, or 3 shillings, 6 pence was the lowest price at which he could bind books.

BOOK CATALOG of publishers was *The Uniform Trade List Annual, Embracing the Full Trade Lists of American Publishers, Together with Advertisements and Business Cards of Prominent Firms Connected with the Book and Stationery Trades,* published in October 1873 by *Publishers' Weekly,* 37 Park Row, New York City.

BOOK CLUB
Book-of-the-Month Club was established in New York City, April 1926, by Harry Scherman, with Robert Haas as president. The original book judges were Dorothy Canfield, Heywood Broun, Henry Seidel Canby, William Allen White, and Christopher Morley. On April 16, 1926, the first book selection, *Lolly Willowes, or the Loving Huntsman,* by Sylvia Townsend Warner, published by Viking Press, was distributed to 4,750 members.

BOOK COLLECTORS' MAGAZINE. *See* Book Trade Magazine: Book collectors' magazine

BOOK COURSE was given in a college by Dr. Edwin Osgood Grover, Professor of Books, appointed in the fall of 1926 by President Hamilton Holt of Rollins College, Winter Park, Fla. The first instruction was given September 22, 1926. The idea of a "professorship of books" was suggested by Ralph Waldo Emerson in his essay "Books" (January 1858—Vol. 1, No. 3, *Atlantic Monthly*) and was advocated by the U.S. Bureau of Education in 1876 but no college accepted the idea until 1926.

BOOK FAIR was held in the Coffee House on Beaver Street, New York City, on June 1, 1802, to display offerings of publishers and booksellers. Hugh Gaines was chairman and Mathew Carey of Philadelphia was secretary.

BOOK FAIR—*Continued*
This literary fair was attended by 46 booksellers, and proved so successful that the following year a similar one was held in Philadelphia, Pa., after which the fairs alternated between those cities.

BOOK INDEX
Book index was the *American Book Circular*, published in 1843 by Wiley and Putnam, New York City. It contained 64 pages, of which 55 were devoted to a list of 1,172 original works in 2,474 volumes. It classified "some of the most important and recent American publications."

General catalog of books was *The Catalogue of All the Books Printed in the United States, with the prices and places where published.* . . . It was printed January 1804 for the booksellers of Boston, Mass., and contained 80 pages. It sold for 10 cents. The books were classified according to subjects: law, physic, divinity, Bibles, and miscellanies, school books, and singing books.

Government Publications Index. *See* Index of government publications

Monthly cumulative index of books was the *Cumulative Book Index*, published February 1898 by Morris & Wilson, Minneapolis, Minn. It listed 9 pages of books published during January 1898. The cumulative feature was begun a few months later, when all the books listed in previous issues were cumulated in one alphabet.

BOOK LIST. *See* Book index: Monthly cumulative index of books

BOOK MATCHES. *See* Match: "Book matches"

BOOK PLATE by an American engraver of which there is any record was made by Nathaniel Hurd of Boston, Mass., in 1740 for Thomas Dering. *(David McNeely Stauffer—American Engravers upon Copper and Steel)*

BOOK PUBLISHER of denominational books was the Methodist Book Concern, organized at a conference in the John Street Methodist Episcopal Church, New York City, May 1789. The Reverend John Dickins advanced the capital, $600, from his private savings and started publishing in Philadelphia, Pa. The first book issued was *The Christian's Pattern*, Wesley's version of Thomas À Kempis' *Imitation of Christ*. *(Henry C. Jennings—The Methodist Book Concern, a Romance of History)*

BOOK REVIEW
Book review editor was Sarah Margaret Fuller (later the Marchioness Ossoli), who was hired in December 1844 by Horace Greeley for his New York *Tribune*. In addition to her salary, the contract provided that she be given a home with Greeley's family and allowed her the privilege of writing when she desired. She wrote under the name of Margaret Fuller and served until August 1846, when she made a trip to Europe. *(Sarah Margaret Fuller Ossoli—Memoirs of Margaret Fuller Ossoli)*

Book review newspaper supplement was the Book Review Supplement of the New York *Times*, issued Saturday, October 10, 1896. It contained 8 pages of 4 columns each, the last page devoted to a full-page advertisement of the Sunday magazine supplement. The first editor was Francis Whiting Halsey. On January 29, 1911, it was issued on Sunday as a 16-page supplement.

BOOK STORE (antiquarian) was established July 10, 1830, in Boston, Mass., by Samuel Gardner Drake, who specialized in writing about American Indians. *(Potter's American Monthly, October 1875)*

BOOK TRADE MAGAZINE
Book collectors' magazine was *The Philobiblion, a Monthly Biographical and Literary Journal Containing Critical Notices of and Extracts from Rare, Curious and Valuable Old Books,* published on India paper by J. W. Bouton, New York City. The first issue was dated December 1861. George Philip Philes was the editor.

Book trade magazine was the *Bookseller's Advertiser & Monthly Chronicle of Literary Enterprises,* also known as the *Bookseller's Advertiser & Monthly Register of New Publications,* which appeared January 1, 1834 (published by West & Trow, New York City), and contained 8 printed quarto pages. Subscription was $1 yearly. It listed 275 "Original American Works published in 1833" and American reprints of foreign works.

Successful book trade magazine was the *American Publishers' Circular and Literary Gazette,* a weekly for booksellers and libraries, issued September 1, 1855, by the New York Book Publishers' Association, of which William Henry Appleton was president; Alfred Smith Barnes, vice president; and George Palmer Putnam, secretary. It was absorbed by *Publishers' Weekly.*

BOOK WAGON. *See* Library: Book-wagon

BOOKKEEPER. *See* Accountant

THE FIRST

BOOKS OF POSTAGE STAMPS. *See* Postage stamp: Books of postage stamps

BOOKSELLER of importance in the colonies was Hezekiah Usher, who started in business in Cambridge, Mass., in 1639. He later had a monopoly on printing the laws of the General Court of Massachusetts and superintended the publications of the London Society for the Propagation of the Gospel Among the Indians. *(Isaiah Thomas—History of Printing)*

BOOKSELLERS' ASSOCIATION was the American Company of Booksellers organized June 7, 1801, in New York City "to improve quality, to avoid interference, to discontinue importations, to favor a literary fair, to recommend correspondence and to promote the general interest." The first president was Mathew Carey of Philadelphia, Pa. *(Adolph Growall— Book Trade Bibliography in the United States in the Nineteenth Century)*

BOOKSELLER'S CATALOG of first American editions of American authors was the *Catalogue of First Editions of American Authors, Poets, Philosophers, Historians, Statesmen, Essayists, Dramatists, Novelists, Travelers, Humorists, etc.,* published in 1885 by Leon and Brother, booksellers, of New York City. It consisted of 58 pages and listed the various American authors in alphabetical order and the current prices for first editions of their works. In addition to the regularly issued catalog, there were also interleaved copies on hand-made paper.

BOOSTER (locomotive). *See* Locomotive booster

BORAX was discovered by Dr. John A. Veatch, January 8, 1856, in mineral water from Tuscan Springs, Tehama County, Calif. Commercial production began at Borax Lake, Lake County, Calif., in 1864, when pure crystals were refined by immersion in solution and permitted to crystallize out again, thus disposing of an apparently very minute amount of impurities. This deposit supplied the United States until 1868, when larger deposits were found in Nevada. *(John Randolph Spears—Illustrated Sketches of Death Valley and Other Borax Deserts of the Pacific Coast)*

BORDER PATROL
Border patrol organization under the Immigration and Naturalization Service was established June 1, 1924, under authority of an act of May 28, 1924 (43 Stat.L.240). It originally consisted of 427 men. William Walter Husband was Commissioner General of Immigration, but there was no officer directly in charge of all the border patrol units as they operated under the supervision of the various district heads.

THE FIRST

Border patrolman was Jefferson Davis Milton, United States Immigration and Naturalization Service, who served from April 13, 1904, to June 30, 1932. He was appointed under authority of annual appropriation acts before the border patrol was formally established by act of Congress on May 28, 1924, and patrolled the border to prevent the smuggling of Orientals across the Mexican border.

BOREALIS. *See* Aurora borealis

BORON CARBIDE. *See* Abrasive

BOTANIC GARDEN was planned and made by John Bartram, who laid out about five or six acres with his own hands in 1728. The garden is located at 43d and Eastwick Streets, Philadelphia, Pa., on the banks of the Schuylkill River. Bartram at one time acted as botanist to George III. He corresponded with Linnaeus, who considered him the "greatest natural botanist in the world." *(William Jay Youmans—Pioneers of Science in America)*

BOTANIC SCIENTIFIC EXPEDITION to study and classify botanical species was made in the New England area by Manasseh Cutler, who set out from Ipswich, Mass., on July 19, 1784, for Mt. Washington, N.H. He examined 350 species and classified them according to the Linnaean method. *(William Parker Cutler and Julia Perkins Cutler—Life, Journals and Correspondence of Rev. Manasseh Cutler)*

BOTANIST
Botanist to become a prominent landscape gardener was Andrew Jackson Downing of Newburgh, N.Y. In 1841 he wrote *A Treatise on the Theory and Practice of Landscape Gardening Adapted to North America,* the first serious discussion on the subject. *(Knickerbocker Magazine. October 1852)*

Woman botanist to distinguish herself in America was Jane Colden, daughter of Cadwallader Colden. She manifested her interest in botany in 1728, at the age of 4; and by the age of 34, in 1758, had described 400 plants according to the Linnaean method, using English terms. *(William Darlington—Memorials of John Bartram and Humphry Marshall)*

BOTANY BOOK
Botany book (elementary work) was *The Elements of Botany, or Outlines of the Natural History of Vegetables,* by Benjamin Smith Barton. It was illustrated with 30 plates. It was originally printed in Philadelphia, Pa., in 1803 and was reprinted in 1804 in London, England. Barton was appointed Professor of Natural History and Botany in the College of Philadelphia in 1789.

THE FIRST

BOTANY BOOK—*Continued*
Botany book strictly American and the first treatise on American plants written by a native American and printed in this country was *Arbustrum Americanum; the American Grove, or an alphabetical catalogue of forest trees and shrubs, natives of the American United States . . . also some hints of their uses in medicines, dyes and domestic economy,* 174 pages, by Humphry Marshall of Chester County, Pa., published in 1785 by Joseph Crukshank, Philadelphia, Pa. *(William Darlington—Memorials of John Bartram and Humphry Marshall)*

BOTANY PROFESSOR was Adam Kuhn, who was appointed in January 1768 by the Philadelphia College, Philadelphia, Pa. He occupied his post for 21 years. His schooling was obtained in Sweden under Linnaeus. *(Eclectic Repertory. April 1818)*

BOTTLE
Bottle blown in America was made in a factory set up in the woods one mile from Jamestown, Va., in 1608, twelve years before the landing of the Pilgrims. The common glass bottle bears the distinction of being the first manufactured product exported from this country. This factory, the first glass factory in America, was destroyed in 1622 by the Indians who massacred the inhabitants of Jamestown. *(Fifty Years of Achievement—Illinois Glass Co.)*

Milk bottles were made by Louis Porter Whiteman, owner of the Warren Glass Works, Cumberland, Md., who manufactured the "Warren Glass Works Glass Air Tight Milk Jars" in 1879. They were used by the Echo Farms Dairy Company, New York City. To commemorate the event, the Pennsylvania State Agricultural Society presented a plaque to Whiteman.

Screw cap bottle with a pour lip was patented May 5, 1936, by Edward A. Ravenscroft, Glencoe, Ill., who received patent No. 2,039,345. The bottles were manufactured by the Abbott Laboratories, North Chicago, Ill.

BOTTLE CAP with the crown cork was invented in 1892, by William Painter, founder of the Crown Cork and Seal Co., Baltimore, Md., who obtained U.S. Patent No. 468,226 on February 2, 1892. The crown cork is a simple bit of tin with a corrugated rim or skirt into which is inserted a disc of natural or composition cork.

BOTTLER OF MINERAL WATER was Elie Magloire Durand, who also invented a machine for bottling it under pressure. Durand opened a drug store in 1825 at the corner of

THE FIRST

Sixth and Chestnut Streets, Philadelphia, Pa., *(Thomas Meehan—Proceedings Academy of Natural Sciences of Philadelphia. 1873)*

BOUNTY was granted under authority of Act 5 of the General Assembly held at James City, Va., October 5, 1646. It was signed by Sir William Berkeley, Knight Governor, and provided that "what person soever shall after publication hereof kill a wolfe and bring in the head to any commissioner, upon certificate of said communication to the county court, he or they shall receive one hundred pounds of tobacco for so doing to be raised out of the county where the wolfe is killed." *William Waller Hening—Virginia Statutes at Large)*

BOWIE KNIFE, which is shorter than the regular sword, was invented by Colonel James Bowie in Texas about 1835. It is variously claimed that he made the first knife out of a file; that the weapon was originally used by the Mexicans; and that in an encounter with Mexicans his original sword broke to within twenty inches of the hilt, leaving the balance of the sword, which was the first Bowie knife, easier to handle. The knife had but one edge and a curved point which necessitated its being carried in a sheath. *(Evelyn Brogan—James Bowie; a Hero of the Alamo)*

BOWLER
Bowler to make a perfect score of 300 in an American Bowling Congress tournament was William Knox of Philadelphia, Pa., who rolled a perfect game on March 10, 1913, in Toledo, Ohio in the thirteenth international bowling tournament. It was the fourteenth perfect game recognized with a gold medal.

Bowler to roll two perfect games in a sanctioned league competition was Frank Caruana of Buffalo, N.Y., who rolled two perfect games in succession on March 5, 1924, in Buffalo, N.Y. He had five strikes on a third game, rolling 29 strikes in succession.

Woman bowler to obtain a perfect score in a sanctioned competition under conditions of the Woman's International Bowling Congress was Emma Fahning (Mrs. Charles Fahning) of the Germain Cleaning Team, who bowled a perfect game on March 4, 1930, in Buffalo, N.Y.

BOWLING MAGAZINE was *Gut Holz* issued August 9, 1893, in New York City. It was originally printed in German. On May 19, 1894, it became the *Bowlers' Journal.*

BOWLING RULE STANDARDIZATION was undertaken November 13, 1875, when 27 delegates met at Germania Hall, New York City, and organized a National Bowling Association. The association soon went out of existence, however, as did the American Amateur Bowling Union, which was organized in 1890.

THE FIRST

The first important bowling convention to standardize rules was held by the American Bowling Congress, when it organized September 9, 1895, in New York City. *(American Bowling Congress 1895-1945—Just Fifty Years)*

BOWLING TOURNAMENT

Bowling convention of importance was the American Bowling Congress held in New York City September 9, 1895.

Bowling match recorded is that of January 1, 1840, played at the Knickerbocker Alleys, New York City.

Bowling tournament for women under the auspices of the Women's International Bowling Congress (organized November 29, 1916; incorporated October 20, 1919) was held March 17, 1917, in St. Louis, Mo. Eight five-woman teams, sixteen two-woman teams and twenty-four individuals participated. The individual high score was won by Mrs. M. Koester with an average of 162.

Bowling tournament sponsored by the American Bowling Congress convened in Chicago, Ill., January 8-11, 1901. Forty-one five-man teams, 79 two-man teams and 115 individuals participated in the contest. The prize money was $2,500. The individual winner was Frank ("Pop") Breill (or Brill) of Chicago, Ill., with a score of 648. A two-man team, J. Voorhies and C. K. Starr, of the Metropolitan Bowling Club of New York, rolled 1,203 points and won $80. The Standard Bowling Club of Chicago rolled 2,720 points, defeating the Crescents of Chicago, who had 2,692 points, and winning $200.

Gold medal award to a perfect-score bowler by the American Bowling Congress was made in 1909. Three perfect scores were entered: Al Rothwell of St. Louis on February 26, 1908, whose claim was rejected as his league was not sanctioned; Homer Sanders of St. Louis on April 4, 1908; and A. C. Jellison on December 15, 1908. A roll-off for the medal was held March 11, 1909, in Pittsburgh, Pa., and was won by Jellison, who received a gold medal, while Sanders received a silver medal. The awards were not for perfect scores, but for high scores.

BOX SPRING. *See* Bed: Box spring

BOXING. *See* Prize fight

BOY SCOUTS OF AMERICA

Boy Scout to become an eagle scout was Arthur Rose Eldred of the Oceanside, Long Island, N.Y., troop, who received this distinction

THE FIRST

on August 21, 1912. Others may have qualified at about the same time, but his name is the first recorded.

Boy Scout uniformed troop was Troop No. 1, organized at the Central Y.M.C.A., Troy, N.Y., in the fall of 1911. The uniform was designed by Charles M. Connally of Troy and has since become standard equipment. *(Rutherford Hayner—History of Troy and Rensselaer County)*

Boy Scouts of America, an organization for boys from nine years upwards, was incorporated in the District of Columbia, on February 8, 1910, and was granted a federal charter by an act of Congress of June 15, 1916. The motto of the organization is "Be Prepared."

BOYCOTT LAW was passed September 26, 1903, by Alabama (Chapter 176). The law declared it a misdemeanor for two or more persons to conspire to prevent persons from carrying on a lawful business, to print or circulate stickers, cards, etc., and to use threats. The fine was not less than $50 nor more than $500, or imprisonment of not more than 60 days at hard labor. *(Code of Alabama—1903)*

BOYS' CAMP. *See* Camp for boys

BRAILLE

Braille Bible. *See* Bible: Bible for the blind in embossed form

Braille magazine. *See* Periodical: Magazine for the blind

Braille music magazine. *See* Music magazine: Music magazine published in Braille

Braille schools. *See* Blind: School for the blind

BRAKE. *See* Air brake; Automobile brake

BRAKE PATENT

Brake patent was granted August 29, 1828, to Robert Turner of Ward (now Auburn), Mass., on a "self-regulating wagon brake."

Railroad brake patent was issued September 19, 1838, to Ephraim Morris of Bloomfield, N.J., on "eccentric brakes for cars."

BRANDING LEGISLATION was enacted February 5, 1644, by Connecticut. It provided that all cattle and swine (but not horses) older than six months be earmarked or branded before May 1, 1644, and that the marks be regis-

THE FIRST

BRANDING LEGISLATION—*Continued* tered. The penalty for violation was five shillings a head, two of which were paid to informers.

BRASS was rolled in 1802 by Abel Porter & Company of Waterbury, Conn. The factory was owned by Abel Porter and Levi Porter, who were also the first to make brass by the direct fusion of copper and zinc. *(Joseph Anderson—Town and City of Waterbury. Vol. II)*

BRASS AND COPPER SEAMLESS TUBES were manufactured in 1851 by the American Tube Works at Somerville, Mass. The process was introduced by Joseph Fox. Previously strips of rounded metal with brazed edges had been used. *Brass Pipe—80th Anniversary—American Tube Works)*

BRASS AND IRON FOUNDRY in America was opened at Lynn, Mass., in 1645, by Joseph Jencks (or Jenks), who manufactured the first kitchen utensils, tools and machines in the new world.

BRASS CLOCK WORKS. *See* Clock: Brass clock works

BRASS KETTLES were made in 1834 in Wolcottville, now Torrington, Conn., by Israel Coe, who organized the Coe Brass Company. They used the so-called battery process.

BRASS ROD was drawn in 1873 by the Coe Brass Company of Torrington, Conn.

BRASS SPINNING was invented by Hiram Washington Hayden of Waterbury, Conn., who obtained patent No. 8589 on December 16, 1851, on machinery for making kettles and articles of like character from discs of metal. A disc was mounted in a chuck which was rotated at a uniform speed. A tool was then pressed against the metal which was thus shaped to the die. The process was first attempted at Wolcottville, now Torrington, Conn., and was later sold to the Waterbury Brass Company. *(William Gilbert Lathrop—The Brass Industry in the United States.)*

BRASS WIRE. *See* Wire: Brass wire

BRASS WIRE DRAWING AND TUBE MAKING MACHINERY was imported in 1831 from England by Israel Holmes for his firm, Holmes and Hotchkiss, established in 1830 in Waterbury, Conn.

BRAWL IN CONGRESS. *See* Congress (U.S.)—House of Representatives: Brawl

BREACH OF PROMISE SUIT was instituted June 14, 1623, in the Virginia Council of State, Charles City County, Va. The Reverend Greville Pooley brought suit against Cicely (Sysley) Jordan, the widow of Captain Samuel Jordan, who had jilted him in favor of William Ferrar (or Farrar). The penalty for a third offense was either corporal punishment, or fine, or otherwise. *(Alexander Brown—The First Republic in America)*

BREAD
Bread made from unbolted flour, which later became known as graham bread, was invented and introduced by Sylvester Graham in 1847. Bakers disliked the product and started riots, threatening Graham's life if he persisted in its manufacture. *(Franklin Bowditch Dexter —Biographical Sketches of the Graduates of Yale College)*

Completely automatic bread plant was installed and opened July 1, 1910, by the Ward Baking Company, Chicago, Ill. The dough was not touched nor the bread handled except when it was placed on the wrapping machine.

Frozen bread was offered to stores November 3, 1952, by Arnold Bakers, Inc., Port Chester, N.Y.

BREAKFAST FOOD
Breakfast foods (ready to eat) were introduced principally by Charles William Post, who produced "Grape Nuts" in 1897. He manufactured "Post Toasties" in 1915, and "Post's Bran" in 1922. *(Products of General Foods— General Foods Corporation.)*

Shredded wheat biscuits were made by Henry D. Perky, and William H. Ford of Watertown, N.Y., who obtained patent No. 502,-278 on August 1, 1893, on a machine for making the shreds or filaments of wheat. The Cereal Machine Company, Denver, Colo., was formed in 1893 to manufacture them.

BREECH-LOADING CANNON. *See* Ordnance: Cannon (breech loading)

BREEDING SOCIETY (animal). *See* Animal breeding society

BREVET. *See* Army: Brevet conferred upon an American

BREWERY to remain in business for 200 years was that of the Francis Perot's Sons Malting Company of Philadelphia. The original concern was established in 1687 by Anthony Morris, 2d, in Philadelphia, Pa., on the east side of Front Street, below Walnut, facing the Delaware River, and was incorporated in 1887.

THE FIRST

THE FIRST

The concern is still in business, having descended from father to son for eight generations. It is the oldest brewery firm with a continuous existence. (*Historical Sketch of the Oldest Business House in America*)

BRICK

Brick building. *See* Building: Brick building

Brick insulating was supplied to the trade by the Armstrong Cork Company of Lancaster, Pa., in June 1913 under the trade name Nonpareil Insulating Brick. This brick is used in high temperature equipment such as industrial furnaces, ovens, oil stills, blast furnaces, stoves, and similar apparatus. Diatomaceous earth is pulverized, mixed with finely ground cork and a small quantity of clay added for a binder. It is molded into brick form and then fired. The cork is consumed, leaving the finished brick terra cotta in color and extremely cellular in structure. Because of the many small voids left when the particles of cork are burned out, and because of a large amount of non-circulating air, the ability of the brick to hold heat is exceptionally high.

Brick pavement. *See* Road: Brick pavement

Brick roofing tile. *See* Tile: Brick roofing tile

Fire brick was made by the Salamander Works of Woodbridge, N.J., in 1825. Although definite records are not obtainable, it is believed an attempt was made to manufacture fire bricks in 1812. (*Heinrick Ries and Henry Leighton—History of Clay Working Industry in the United States.*)

Fire brick to withstand high heat was manufactured in 1841 by the "Mount Savage" Fire Brick Works of Mount Savage, Md., now the Union Mining Company of Allegany County, Md.

Light-weight brick was developed in 1927 by Charles Frederick Burgess of the C. F. Burgess Laboratories, Inc., Madison, Wis. It is porous, one fifth the weight of ordinary brick, and yet resistant to the entrance of water. It floats in water and has adequate compressive strength for use in all types of buildings for load-bearing walls.

Terra cotta was manufactured by James Renwick in 1853 in New York City. He conceived the idea of introducing terra cotta as a building material and substitute for cut stone work. (*Walter Geer—Story of Terra Cotta*)

Terra cotta factory to be successful was established by J. N. Glover in Louisville, Ky.,

in 1867. After a series of successive changes of locale and management it gradually developed into the Northwestern Terra Cotta Co., Chicago, Ill.

BRICK KILN in America was established in Salem, Mass., in 1629.

BRICK MACHINE for the production of soft mud bricks was designed and built by Henry Martin in 1857 and installed in Hartford, Conn. The clay was pushed from the press box through a die or jack mold into sanded wooden molds by a process similar to the method of pressing the clay by hand into wood or steel molds.

BRIDGE

Aerial ferry was put in operation April 9, 1905, over the ship canal from Lake Avenue, Duluth, to Minnesota Point, Minn. The car was suspended in the air from a superstructure which had a clear height over Lake Superior of 135 feet. The truss in the center was 51 feet, making a total height at the highest part of the superstructure of 186 feet above water level. The width, center to center of trusses, was 34 feet, and the clear span was 393.75 feet in length. The car platform was 34 by 50 feet, with room enough to accommodate six automobiles and two glassed-in cabins, each 7 by 30 feet, for passengers, and with a carrying capacity of 125,000 pounds. The platform was 12 feet above the water line. The round trip could be made in ten minutes. (*Henry Grattan Tyrrell—Transporter Bridges*)

Bridge was erected in 1634 over the Neponset river from Milton to Dorchester, Mass., by Israel Stoughton. Authority to build a bridge and mill was extended April 1, 1634, by the Massachusetts General Court. (*Albert Kendall Teele—History of Milton*)

Bridge of flowers was instituted at the suggestion of Mrs. Walter Burnham in 1929, when a 400-foot five-arch concrete span bridge over the Deerfield River between Shelburne and Buckland, Mass., was abandoned with the passing of the trolley line. The bridge at Shelburne Falls, Mass., was converted into a walk, both sides being lined with innumerable species of flowering plants and shrubs.

Bridge to a foreign country. *See* Bridge: Railway suspension bridge

Bridge with open mesh steel flooring was the University Bridge, Seattle, Wash., opened for traffic April 7, 1933. The flooring, 80 per cent open, self-cleaning and self-draining, was originated by Walter Edward Irving of the Irving Subway Grating Company, Inc., Long Island City, N.Y., who obtained patent No. 1,991,154 on February 12, 1935.

BRIDGE—*Continued*

Bridge with piers sunk in the open sea was the Golden Gate suspension span, San Francisco, Calif. Actual construction was officially started January 5, 1933. Joseph Baermann Strauss was appointed chief engineer. The length of the main structure of the bridge is 8,940 feet, with towers 746 feet above water and a minimum clearance of 220 feet. The Golden Gate bridge was the first built across the outer mouth of a major ocean harbor.

Cantilever bridge was designed by Charles Shaler Smith for the Cincinnati Southern Railroad to cross the Kentucky River. It was built in 1876-1877, near Harrodsburg (Mercer County), Ky. A contract for an iron truss bridge was let to the Baltimore Bridge Company on July 9, 1875, for $377,500. Construction started October 12, 1876, and was completed February 20, 1877. The bridge was tested April 20, 1877. It had three spans, each 375 feet long.

Cast iron bridge was built in 1835 over Dunlap's Creek at Brownsville, Pa., by John Snowdon from the design of and under the direction of his foreman, John Herbertson. It has five tubular arch ribs of 85-foot span and is 25 feet wide. (*Engineering Record. June 6, 1908*)

Cast iron girder bridge was built by Earl Trumbull over the Erie Canal in 1840 at Frankfort, N.Y. It had a span of 77 feet. (*Wrought Iron Record. Vol 1. No. 3— Wrought Iron Research Association.*)

Concrete arch highway bridge was designed by Carl A. Trik, Superintendent of Bridges, Bureau of Highways, Philadelphia, Pa., and erected in 1893 to carry Pine Road over Pennypack Creek, Philadelphia. It consisted of two arched spans, each 25 feet, 4¾ inches wide, with a rise of 6 feet, 6 inches, supported by concrete abutments and a concrete pier, built on a light skew. It is 34 feet wide and carries a 26-foot wide macadam roadway with two granite-paved gutters on concrete foundations. The entire bridge, including the appurtenances and the thorough renovation of the retaining walls on both approaches cost $9,288.12 (*Report of 1893—Philadelphia Superintendent of Bridges*)

Concrete cantilever bridge was erected over Indian Creek at Marion, Iowa, in 1905 for the Marion Street Railway Company. It had three 50-foot spans with two longitudinal ribs 12 inches wide supported on concrete columns and floor slabs on transverse beams.

Double-deck bridge of importance was the Queensboro Bridge, over the East River, New York City, which was opened to traffic on

March 30, 1909. The Manhattan Suspension Bridge, also a double-deck bridge over the East River, was opened to traffic on December 31, 1909. The total cost of the land and construction of the Queensboro Bridge was approximately $17 million and of the Manhattan Suspension Bridge about $31 million. (*Records in the Department of Plants and Structures. New York City*)

Hanging railroad bridge was built in 1879 at a location several miles east of Canon City, Colo., where the Royal Gorge of the Arkansas River is only thirty feet wide and entirely filled by the river. Sheer rock cliffs rise for more than 1,000 feet on each side. The bridge was built above and parallel to the river, one side imbedded in the rock cliff and the other suspended over the stream by means of overhead V-type beams. It was designed by Charles Shaler Smith.

Iron truss bridge with parallel chords and open web was designed by Richard Osborne, chief engineer of the Reading Company. Construction of trusses began January 1845 at Pottstown, Pa., and was completed in March. The bridge had a 34.2-foot span, with a 4-foot space between tracks, and was erected a half mile east of Flat Rock Tunnel, north of West Manayunk station. Erection was begun Saturday night, May 3, 1845, and the bridge was finished Sunday, May 4, 1845. It remained until 1901 on the main line of the Philadelphia and Reading Railroad Company, now the Reading Company. (*Henry Gratton Tyrrell—History of Bridge Engineering*)

Iron wire suspension bridge was the Schuylkill River bridge at Philadelphia, Pa., designed and constructed by Erskine Hazard and Captain Josiah White. It was 408 feet long with a board floor 18 inches wide. It had a 33-foot sag and could not support more than six or eight persons at a time. It weighed 4,702 pounds, cost $125, and was opened to traffic June 1816. A toll of a cent a person was charged until the tolls defrayed the cost. (*Engineering News—March 16, 1905*)

Pile bridge was designed and constructed by Major Samuel Sewall and built across the York River at York, Me., in 1761. Thirteen bands of piles were hammered upright, the ends protruding above the water, upon which a 270-foot wooden bridge was erected. (*George Alex Emery—Ancient City of Gorgeana*)

Pontoon bridge was floated into place at Collins' Pond, Lynn, Mass., in 1804. The Board of Directors authorized Captain Moses Brown to bridge the pond, which was of great depth. The pond had a soft, peaty bottom which did not permit the use of any feasible means of constructing bridge piers. The pontoon bridge was 511 feet in length and 28 feet wide. It consisted of five layers of pine timber, each at right angles to the one below it. The lowest course was of logs hewn on one side and the next three courses were about a foot square. The whole mass was secured together by three-inch dowels. Including the top planking it was about 5 feet thick. *(Historical Collection of the Essex Institute. Vol. 36. "The Floating Bridge at Lynn"—Charles Jeptha Hill Woodbury)*

Pontoon bridge of reenforced concrete was the Lake Washington Floating Bridge, Seattle, Wash., begun December 29, 1938, and dedicated July 2, 1940. It was composed of 25 pontoons bolted together, each having two or more 65-ton anchors. Its total length was 34,021 feet. It was financed by a PWA grant of $3,794,000 and a bond issue of $5,500,000 to be repaid by toll charges.

Railway all-steel bridge was the Glasgow Bridge, a 2,700-foot structure built by the Chicago and Alton Railroad Company over the Missouri River at Glasgow, Mo. The contract for steel was dated October 12, 1878, and the bridge was placed in service about November 1, 1879. *(Archibald Black—The Story of Bridges)*

Railway bridge across the Mississippi River was the Rock Island Railroad Bridge, between Rock Island, Ill., and Davenport, Iowa, built of wood resting on stone piers. The piers were completed June 1854. The bridge was fully completed and a locomotive sent across it on April 21, 1856. On April 22, 1856, a train consisting of three locomotives and eight passenger cars crossed as a test.

Railway suspension bridge was the Niagara Falls Suspension bridge over the gorge at Niagara, which was completed in 1854. It had a span of 825 feet and two decks, the lower one carrying a highway 15 feet wide, partially enclosed at the side by timber stiffening trusses. The upper deck, 24 feet wide and 245 feet above high water, had a single railway track in the center and was floored over to separate it from the highway below. The bridge was started in 1853 by Charles Ellet, who withdrew from the work. It was completed by John Augustus Roebling. The first train crossed the bridge March 8, 1855. *(John Augustus Roebling—Memoir of the Niagara Falls and International Suspension Bridge)*

Rolling lift bridge was the Van Buren Street bridge, located over the Chicago River, Chicago, Ill., which was opened to traffic February 4, 1895. It consists of two arms meeting at the center of the river which when open provide a clear channel 82 feet in width, measured along the line of the stream. Each arm consists of three trusses which carry two road-

ways, each 18 feet wide, and two sidewalks, each 8 feet wide. The bridge is operated by two 50 h.p. electric motors on each side of the river. The total construction cost was $169,700. The bridge's construction was patented by William Scherzer of Chicago, Ill.

Steel arch bridge was built across the Mississippi River at St. Louis, Mo., by James Buchanan Eads. It was started in 1869 and opened July 4, 1874. It had a center span of 520 feet and two side spans of 502 feet each. *(Henry Grattan Tyrrell—History of Bridge Engineering)*

Stone arch railroad bridge in the world was the Carrollton Viaduct of the Baltimore and Ohio Railroad, spanning Gwynn's Falls at Baltimore, Md. It was named after Charles Carroll, who laid the last stone in the bridge several weeks prior to its official opening and inspection by the president and board of directors on December 21, 1829. It is 300 feet long and 70 feet high and has two arches—a large 80-foot span over the stream and a small arch through which, originally, a wagon road passed. The bridge was built by James Lloyd and is still in use, supporting a double-track line. The heaviest freight trains of the Baltimore and Ohio Railroad pass over it at undiminished speed. *(Joseph Gurn—Carroll of Carrollton)*

Stone bridge in America was built in 1697-1698 at Pennepecka, near Germantown, Pa. William Penn wrote from Pennsburg on June 22, 1700, to "urge the justices about the bridge at Pennepecka and Poquessin forthwith for a carriage or I cannot come down" to attend a local meeting. *(Site and Relic of Germantown —Reports)*

Suspension bridge was erected in 1796 by James Finley across Jacob's Creek, Westmoreland County, Pa. It had a 70-foot span and cost $6,000. He patented his design in 1801. The bridge was on the turnpike between Uniontown, Pa., and Greensburg, Pa.

Suspension bridge of importance having steel towers insead of the customary masonry towers was the Williamsburg Bridge, connecting Brooklyn and Manhattan, New York City, which was opened on December 19, 1903. The cost was $24,100,000 for land and construction. *(Records in Department of Plants and Structures. New York City)*

Timber trestle pier of lattice construction was started in June 1840 at the Long Hollow Crossing, Shuman's Station, Pa., and was originally on the Little Schuylkill and Susquehanna Railroad, later the Catawissa Branch of the Reading Company. The pier was designed by James F. Smith and was 740 feet long and 122 feet high. The timber piers were later replaced

THE FIRST

BRIDGE—*Continued*
with stone masonry; then the trusses with
wooden trestles; then the wooden trestles with
iron and steel viaducts. Finally all were replaced with concrete bridges and fill. *(Catawissa Railroad Company—Annual Report)*

Toll bridge was erected by Richard Thur-
low (variously spelled Thorla, Thorlo, and
Thurley) in 1654 over the Newbury River at
Rowley, Mass. He built the bridge at his own
cost and on May 3, 1654, the General Court of
Massachusetts fixed a rate of toll for animals.
Passengers were permitted free passage. The
bridge remained a toll bridge until 1680.
(Joshua Coffin—History of Newbury)

Tubular plate girder bridge was built in
1841 by James Millholland for the Baltimore
and Ohio Railroad Company near Bolton Depot, Md. The bridge had a 50-foot span. The
sides and bottom were wholly of wrought iron,
but the flange was reinforced with 12 by 12
inch timbers. The plates were 38 inches wide
and 6 feet long. The whole bridge weighed
14 tons and cost approximately $2,200. *(Henry
Grattan Tyrrell—History of Bridge Engineering)*

**Welded aluminum girder-type highway
bridge** was a four-span structure, 36 feet
wide and 222 feet long, on Clive Road, about
one mile north and one mile west of Urban-
dale, Iowa, erected for the Iowa State Highway Commission by the Jensen Construction
Co., and United Contractors of Des Moines,
Iowa. It was completed September 24, 1958,
at a cost of approximately $125,000.

Wire cable suspension aqueduct bridge
was built in Pittsburgh, Pa., across the Alleghany River by John Augustus Roebling.
There were seven spans of 162 feet each, consisting of a wooden trunk to hold water, and
supported by a continuous wire cable on each
side, 7 inches in diameter. The length of the
aqueduct without extensions was 1,140 feet,
the cables 1,175 feet. The total weight of the
water in the aqueduct was 2,100 tons. The cost
of construction and removal of the old wooden
bridge was $62,000. The bridge was completed
in May 1845. *(Charles Beebe Stuart—Lives
and Works of Civil and Military Engineers)*

Wire suspension bridge for general traffic
was erected over the Schuylkill River at Fairmount, Pa., by Charles Ellet. The bridge was
opened on January 2, 1842. It had a 358-foot
span, was supported by wire cables, five at
each side, and had a width of 25 feet. It cost
$35,000.

**Wooden railroad bridge of a purely truss
type** was built in 1838 by Benjamin Henry
Latrobe for the Baltimore and Ohio Railroad

THE FIRST

Company across the Patapsco River at Elys-
ville (now Alberton), Md. It consisted of two
spans, each about 150 feet in length. The
bridge was completed in 1839 and was replaced
in 1852 by iron Bollman trusses. *(William
Hubert Burr and Myron Samuel Falk—Design
and Construction of Metallic Bridges)*

Wrought iron lattice girder railroad bridge
was built by the New York Central across the
Mohawk River at Schenectady, N.Y., in 1859.
Howard Carroll was the engineer in charge.
(Wrought Iron Record. Vol. 1. No. 3)

"Y" bridge was authorized by the General
Assembly of Zanesville, Ohio, on January 21,
1812. The bridge, in the form of the letter "Y,"
spanned the Licking and Muskingum Rivers
and was opened for traffic in 1814. The present
concrete bridge is the fourth structure to have
occupied the site. *(The Sohioan. August 1929)*

**BRIDGE CHAMPIONSHIP TOURNA-
MENT.** *See* Auction bridge championship
(duplicate)

BRIDGE TABLE. *See* Electric bridge table

BRIDGE WHIST ORGANIZATION of
importance was the American Whist League,
which convened at the Athenaeum, Milwaukee,
Wis., April 14-17, 1891, in response to a call
made by Cassius M. Paine, president of the
Milwaukee Whist Club. Thirty-six clubs represented by 83 delegates standardized the rules
and adopted a 61-section code. The first president was Eugene S. Elliott of the Milwaukee
Whist Club, and Robert Frederick Foster of
the Manhattan Club of New York City was
secretary. *(John T. Mitchell—Duplicate Whist,
Its Rules and Methods of Play)*
   See also Auction bridge championship

BRIDGE WHIST RULE BOOK was *The
Whist Player's Hand Book, containing most
of the maxims of the old school and several
new ones exemplified by apposite cases; with
a method of acquiring a knowledge of the principles on which they are grounded to which
are added observations on short whist, also the
games of Boston and euchre.* The book was
written by Thomas Matthews and published in
1844 in Philadelphia, Pa., by Isaac M. Moss.
It contained 96 pages, 75 of which were devoted to whist.

BRIDGE WHIST TOURNAMENT

Duplicate whist tournament was held April
15, 1891, in Milwaukee, Wis., by the American Whist League. Forty-eight delegates participated. Twelve tables were arranged in
pairs, each with two teams of two players each.
The eight players of each pair of tables
changed positions after every deal. The medal

winner was E. Price Townsend of the Hamilton Club, Philadelphia, Pa. The rules were substantially Cavendish with a few slight modifications to suit the American game.

BRIGADIER GENERAL (Negro). *See* Army officer: Brigadier general (Negro)

BRITANNIA WARE was manufactured in 1824 in Taunton, Mass., by Isaac Babbitt and William Crossman. On July 17, 1839, Isaac Babbitt of Boston, Mass., obtained patent No. 1,252 on a "wheel box with anti-friction rollers." An act of Congress of August 29, 1842 (5 Stat.L.547) authorized the Secretary of the Navy to pay $20,000 for the "right to use Babbitt's anti-attrition metal." *(George Sweet Gibb—The Whitesmiths of Taunton)*

BRITISH PARLIAMENT MEMBER (American woman). *See* Woman: American woman to become a member of Parliament

BRITISH SETTLEMENT. *See* Colonist: English settlement

BROADCASTING. *See* Radio broadcast

BROADCLOTH was produced in Pittsfield, Mass., in 1793 from fleeces of the merino sheep of Arthur and John Scholfield. Soon after 1793 they manufactured 24½ yards of broadcloth. *(Joseph Edward Adams Smith—History of Pittsfield)*

BROADSIDE. *See* Newspaper

BROADWAY PLAY TO BE TELEVISED. *See* Television—Telecast: Play to be televised with its original Broadway cast

BROKERAGE
Clearing house for stocks and bonds was the Philadelphia Clearing House, which was organized in Philadelphia, Pa., in August 1870 as an adjunct of the Board of Brokers, Philadelphia stock exchange.

Curb exchange in history to transact more business in a day than the New York Stock Exchange was the New York Curb, on June 15, 1929, when the volume for the Curb was 1,287,900 shares, as compared with 1,260,400 for the Stock Exchange.

Exchange to specialize in mining securities was the San Francisco Stock and Exchange Board, September 11, 1862. It has been in continuous operation since its inception, but its name has twice been changed—to San Francisco Stock Exchange and then to San Francisco Mining Exchange. It was organized by

a group of 37 independent brokers determined to establish fixed positive prices for shares of the Comstock mining companies. The Comstock Lode in Nevada in 1859 produced $680 million, enough to pay the entire cost of the Civil War. The companies issued shares which were widely traded at prices ranging from $1,000 to $2,000 each.

Financial "corner" took place in New Amsterdam (New York) in 1666. Frederick Phillipse cornered the market in wampum by creating a shortage. He buried several hogsheads of it in order to force those who had to use this medium of exchange to purchase wampum from him at a higher price.

Investment trust is claimed to have been the New York Stock Trust, a general portfolio statutory trust, which was organized in New York City in 1889. *(John Francis Fowler, Jr. —American Investment Trusts)*

Ocean-going brokerage office was opened on the French liner "Ile de France" on August 15, 1929, orders being taken as the boat left Le Havre. A special wireless station, independent of the ship's wireless equipment, was installed in a space adjoining the board room. Three radio channels, one to receive continuous quotations, the second to transmit orders to New York, and the third to receive executions were available for use.

Stock exchange was the New York Stock Exchange, the outgrowth of an agreement signed on May 17, 1792, by 24 brokers to fix the rates of commission on stocks and bonds. The first meeting was held at the Merchants Coffee House, 2d and Gold Streets, New York City. The first president was Matthew McConnell. This protective league existed until 1817 when the New York Stock Exchange, organized on its present lines. *(Edmund Clarence Stedman—History of the Stock Exchange)*

Stock exchange at which more than a million shares were traded in one day was the New York Stock Exchange, New York City, whose transactions on December 15, 1886, totaled 1,096,509 shares.

Stock order from a Zeppelin was radioed on August 8, 1930, from the Graf Zeppelin. The radio message was picked up at Tuckerton, N.J., and the order sent to Portland, Me., by telegraph. The order was sent by Alexander Godfrey of Boston, Mass.

Telegraph ticker used by a brokerage concern. *See* Telegraph: Telegraph ticker used by a brokerage concern

BROKERAGE—*Continued*
Visitor to open the New York Stock Exchange was Leonard Ross, a ten-year-old boy from California, who was introduced on April 24, 1956, by Keith Funston, president of the exchange, and who pressed the button which activated the opening gong. Young Ross had won $100,000 on the television show "The Big Surprise."

Woman brokerage office owner was Victoria Claflin Woodhull, who, with her sister Tennessee Celeste Claflin, opened offices in 1869 in the Hoffman House, New York City. Their company, Woodhull, Claflin & Co., showed a net profit of $750,000 for the first six weeks. A newspaper cartoon depicted them driving a chariot drawn by two bullocks and two bears, with the heads of the largest financiers of the time. Tennessee was holding the reins while Victoria was whipping from right to left. The wheels of the chariot were crushing financiers while others embodied as ducks, with crutches under their wings, were trying to fly away. (*Theodore Tilton—Biographical Sketch of Victoria C. Woodhull*)

Woman director of a stock exchange was Mary Gindhart Roebling of the Trenton Trust Company, Trenton, N.J., who on October 28, 1958, became one of the 32 governors of the American Stock Exchange, New York City. As a governor she was entitled to go on the floor of the exchange. She was one of the three so-called public members not connected with the Wall Street community.

Woman president of a major stock brokerage concern was Josephine Perfect Bay (Mrs. Charles Ulrick Bay), who on December 1, 1956, became chairman and president of A. M. Kidder & Co., Inc., New York City.

Woman stock exchange member (commodity exchange) was Gretchen B. Schoenleber of the Ambrosia Chocolate Company, Milwaukee, Wis., who was admitted September 3, 1935, to membership in the New York Cocoa Exchange, Inc., New York City.

Woman to sell securities on the floor of the New York Curb Exchange, New York City, was motion picture actress Linda Darnell, who occupied Post 29 on November 19, 1941, to sell U.S. Defense Bonds and stamps.

BRONCHITIS TREATISE. *See* Medical book: Bronchitis treatise

BRONZE EQUESTRIAN STATUE. *See* Monument: Bronze equestrian statue

BRONZE SKYSCRAPER. *See* Building: Bronze and glass skyscraper

BRONZE STAR. *See* Medal: Bronze star

BRONZE STATUE (full length) was executed by Ball Hughes in 1847 and placed in the cemetery at Mount Auburn, Cambridge, Mass. It represented the astronomer Dr. Nathaniel Bowditch, seated and holding a copy of his translated work, La Place's *Mécanique Céleste*, with a globe and a quadrant beside him. The statue was imperfect and was recast by Gruet Jne. Fondeur of Paris, France, in 1886. (*Boston Courier—June 16, 1847*)

BRUSHES were manufactured at Medfield, Mass., in 1808 by Artemas Woodward in a shop that stood near the present site of the Orthodox parsonage. (*William Smith Tilden—History of the Town of Medfield*)

BUDDHIST TEMPLE was established July 15, 1904, in Los Angeles, Calif., in a meeting room. The chief priest was Rinban Izumeda. Most of the congregation belonged to the Shinshu Sect of Buddhism, a branch of the home Hompa Hongwanji Buddhist Temple.

BUDGET BUREAU (United States) was created by Act of Congress (42 Stat.L.22) approved June 10, 1921. The Bureau was then part of the Treasury Department, but under the immediate direction of the President. The first director of the budget was Brigadier General Charles Gates Dawes, who served until July 1, 1922. (*William Franklin Willoughby—National Budget System*)

BUDGET COMMISSIONER OF A STATE (Woman). *See* Woman: Woman state budget commissioner

BUILDING
Air-conditioned factory. *See* Factory: Air-conditioned factory

Air-conditioned office building was the Milam Building, San Antonio, Tex., which opened January 1, 1928. The building is 21 stories high, contains nearly 3 million cubic feet of space, and has 247,779 square feet of gross floor area. It was the first air-conditioned office building in the world with the air conditioning a part of the original construction.

Air raid shelter. *See below* House with a built-in nuclear bomb shelter; *see also* Air raid shelter

All-glass windowless structure was the Owens-Illinois Glass Company's packaging laboratory, Toledo, Ohio, completed January 15, 1936. Eighty thousand translucent water-clear hollow glass blocks weighing about 150 tons were used in the two-story building, which had

THE FIRST

39 rooms and an aggregate floor area of 20,000 square feet. The blocks were manufactured at the company's Muncie, Ind., plant and were a part of the structural strength of the building.

Aluminum-faced building was the Alcoa Building, Pittsburgh, Pa., a 30-story, 410-foot skyscraper, completed August 1, 1953, for the Aluminum Company of America. The exterior walls were thin stamped aluminum panels, 6 by 12 feet, bolted to angles on the spandrel beams and backed up with four inches of perlite-concrete sprayed on slotted aluminum lath and reinforcing bars.

Apartment house with a modern lay-out was erected in New York City in 1869. It was known as the "Stuyvesant Apartments" and was located at 142 East 18th Street. It contained "four distinct suites of apartments" on each of the four floors. The fifth and top floor was arranged for artists' studios. The annual rental for the apartments varied from $1,200 to $1,800 each, while $200 was charged for the studios. The architect was Richard Morris Hunt and the owner Rutherford Stuyvesant. *(Annual Report of the Superintendent of Buildings, New York 1862-1869)*

Atom bomb-resistant federal building was the laboratory for the Armed Forces Institute of Pathology, Walter Reed Army Medical Center, Washington, D.C., which was occupied March 13, 1955, and dedicated by President Dwight David Eisenhower on May 23, 1955. The 8-story reinforced concrete bomb-resistant building contains 8 floors, 5 above ground and 3 underground. It has a gross area of approximately 215,000 square feet and a net usable area of 130,000 square feet. It was constructed by the Cramer-Vollmerhousen Co., Inc., of Washington, D.C.

Brick building was erected in 1633 in New Amsterdam (New York City) as a residence for Wouter Van Twiller, the fifth Dutch governor. Several other brick structures were likewise erected within the fort. The bricks were imported from Holland. *(Charles Thomas Davis—Practical Treatise on the Manufacture of Bricks, Tiles and Terra Cotta)*

Bronze and glass skyscraper was a 519-foot structure, 38 stories high, at 375 Park Avenue, New York City. It contained 3,650,000 square feet of glass divided into 3,800 windows. The steel framework was put together by use of high-tensile steel bolts instead of steel rivets. Mies van der Rohe and Philip Johnson were the architects and Kahn & Jacobs the associated architects with the George A. Fuller Company, the general contractors. The highest point of steel construction was reached on December 17, 1956. The building was completed in November 1957.

THE FIRST

Building built inside a factory completely ready for occupancy, and the first building floated across a river, was a 41-ton 5-room house and garage (32 by 42 feet), fully equipped with furnace, cooling system, laundry, and plumbing, and partly furnished. It was built by R[obert] G[ilmour] Le Tourneau, Inc., Peoria, Ill. It was towed across the Illinois River on its own bottom from Peoria to the Le Tourneau test farm in East Peoria, Ill., on September 17, 1938.

Building constructed wholly of cast iron was a factory five stories high which was built by James Bogardus at the corner of Centre and Duane Streets in New York City in May 1848. *(John W. Thomson—Cast Iron Buildings; Their Construction and Advantages)*

Building devoted entirely to highway traffic was erected by the Eno Foundation for Highway Traffic Control, Inc., at Saugatuck, Conn. Ground was broken July 18, 1938, the cornerstone laid August 29, 1938, and the building completed July 1, 1939. The organization was incorporated April 22, 1921, and affiliated with Yale University, New Haven, Conn., February 15, 1933.

Building erected by the Government in Washington, D.C., was the Executive Mansion. It was modeled after the palace of the Duke of Leinster in Ireland and was designed by James Hoban. The cornerstone was laid October 13, 1792. The Executive Mansion was first occupied by President John Adams in 1800, and the first New Year's reception was held there on January 1, 1801. The Executive Mansion was burned by the British in 1814 and only the four walls were left standing. It was restored in 1818 and in order to obliterate the marks of fire, the stones were painted white. Since that time the Executive Mansion has been known as the White House. When Adams first took occupancy, there was only a path through an elder swamp leading from the President's house to the Capitol. *(Charles Hurd—The White House, a Biography)*

Building erected in the United States for public use, under the authority of the Federal Government, was a structure for the U.S. Mint. This was a plain brick edifice, on the east side of Seventh Street, near Arch, in Philadelphia, Pa. The mint was established by the Act of April 2, 1792 (1 Stat.L.246), an "act establishing a mint and regulating the coins of the United States." The cornerstone was laid by David Rittenhouse, Director of the Mint, on July 31, 1792.

Building for telephone directory compilation and printing was built for the General Telephone Directory Company, a subsidiary of the General Telephone Corp., in Des Plaines,

BUILDING—*Continued*
Ill., and dedicated April 30, 1953. It has a total of 30,000 square feet of working area. The company produces directories for 2,500 communities and 2 million telephones in 34 states.

Building heated by steam was the Eastern Hotel of Boston, Mass., erected in 1845. Small wrought iron pipes conveyed the steam and the heat was diffused by coils of pipe.

Building in all-Gothic architecture was Trinity Episcopal Church, New Haven, Conn., designed by Ithiel Town of New Haven in 1814. It had seam-faced traprock with brownstone trim. *(Roger Hale Newton—Town and Davis, Architects)*

Building in which wrought iron beams were used was erected for Harper & Brothers in New York City in 1854. Wrought iron beams were rolled for the first time in the United States in 1854 at the Trenton, N.J., Iron Works, of which Peter Cooper was the principal owner. These beams were intended for the Cooper Union building, but they were not ready in time as it took two years to prepare them. They were 7 inches deep, weighed 81 pounds per yard, and were of the type known as deck beams. Previously cast iron beams had been used in construction work. *(More Than One Hundred Years of Publishing—Harper & Bros.)*

Building known as a Quonset hut was built in September 1941 at Quonset Point air station, Greenwich, R.I., for the U.S. Navy by the Great Lakes Steel Corporation, Stran-Steel Division, Detroit, Mich. The structures were built around a framework of Stran-Steel members, a light steel building material distinguished by a patented groove into which nails can be driven. They are officially designated by the U.S. Navy as U.S. Navy Arch-Rib Huts.

Building known as a skyscraper was a ten-story steel-skeleton building erected by the Home Insurance Company of New York at La Salle and Adams Street, Chicago, Ill. Designed by Major William Le Baron Jenney, it was started on May 1, 1884, and completed in the fall of 1885. It was constructed of marble and flanked by four columns of polished granite supporting a marble balcony. Two additional stories were added to it later. A steel frame supported the entire weight of the walls instead of the walls themselves carrying the weight of the building. *(William Aiken Starrett—Skyscrapers and the Men Who Build Them)*

Building of fireproof construction was the Fireproof Building, which was designed and built by Robert Mills in 1822-1823 on Meeting Street, between Queen and Broad Streets, Charleston, S.C. It was built for the preservation of the county records and was a stone and iron structure. Even the window sashes were made of iron. The building is still in use. *(Charleston Courier. March 30, 1822)*

Building of pressed structural steel was a 2-story 14-room building designed and built in June 1907 by the Taft-Howell Co., of Cornwall Landing, N.Y., for the Tuxedo Park Association, Tuxedo Park, N.Y. The pressed steel, known by its trade name, Metal Lumber, was developed by Harry Merrill Naugle, chief engineer of the Berger Manufacturing Company, Canton, Ohio. The building had structural members substituting in every detail for what normally would be wood studs and joists in balloon frame construction for dwellings.

Building with a high steeple was Trinity Church, New York City, which was begun October 17, 1839, and dedicated May 21, 1846, Ascension Day. A small admission fee was charged visitors, who climbed the 308 steps to the Trinity steeple, "with suitable resting places provided" to a point 34 feet below the peak. The steeple was 284 feet above Broadway, and was the highest point until 1893, when the Manhattan Life Insurance Company erected its 17-story building and tower, which thrust its pinnacle 60 feet above the Trinity spire.

Building with prefabricated walls of mosaic concrete was completed in February 1935. It is located on the Colesville Pike, north of Washington, D.C., and was built by the Earley Process Corporation, Washington, D.C. The walls of the house consisted of 32 panels, 2 inches thick, approximately 9 feet high, and from 4 to 10 feet wide, heavily reinforced with electrically welded steel mesh, fireproof, weatherproof, and waterproof. Color and texture were determined by the color of the crushed quartz and quartz sand used in the concrete.

Capitol building. *See* Capitol

Circular office building was the Capitol Tower, Hollywood and Vine Streets, Los Angeles, Calif., dedicated April 6, 1956. It was 150 feet high (13 stories), and had a diameter of 92 feet. Above the roof was a 90-foot spire from which a beacon light flashed the word "Hollywood" in Morse code. Welton Becket was the architect.

Commercial building heated by the sun was the Solar Building, Albuquerque, N.M., a single-story building. The heating system, designed by Frank Hillman Bridgers and Donald Paxton, was completed August 1, 1957. One wall of the building, sheathed in glass tilted to

THE FIRST

face the sun, collects heat from the sun's rays and heats panels containing water which flows through a conventional heating system.

Elevator in an office building. *See* Elevator: Elevator in an office building

Fire escapes for tenements. *See* Fire escapes for tenements

Fraternity house. *See* Fraternity (Greek letter): Fraternity house

House completely sunheated was built in Dover, Mass., and occupied on December 24, 1948. The house traps the sun's energy through a unit consisting of a black sheetmetal collector behind two panes of glass. The solar heat is stored in a "heat bin" containing an inexpensive sodium compound. Electric fans blow the stored heat through vents as desired. The experiments were sponsored by Amelia Peabody. The house was designed by Eleanor Raymond and the heating system was developed by Dr. Maria Telkes.

House with a built-in nuclear bomb shelter was exhibited May 24, 1959, at Hi-Tor Woods, Pleasant Hills, Pa. It was built by the Obie Construction Co., Pittsburgh, Pa., and contained a fully equipped underground integral shelter with bunks to sleep four persons, sanitary facilities, a food storage area and refrigerator, a transoceanic radio, a first aid kit, a weather-warning device, a Geiger counter, a fire extinguisher, and other equipment. The main part of the shelter was 22 feet long and 8 feet wide. Another section contained an auxiliary power plant, heating equipment, an air filtering system, and an oxygen tank. The walls were made of concrete blocks 10 inches thick; lead was used for insulation against radiation. The shelter had a concrete escape tunnel.

Library building. *See* Library: Library building

Marble building. *See* Marble building

Monolithic concrete building was the Milton House, Milton, Wis., a hotel built in 1845 by Joseph Goodrich on the corduroy road between Chicago, Ill., and Madison, Wis. It replaced a log house built in 1837 and a frame building of 1839. The walls were 18 inches thick. A hexagonal tower three stories high served as a lookout for Indians; the remaining portion was two stories high. *(Concrete Age. August 1924)*

Penitentiary building. *See* Prison: Penitentiary building (national)

THE FIRST

Post office building (U.S.). *See* Post office: Post office building (U.S.)

"Presidential mansion." *See* "Presidential mansion"

Solar-heated and radiation-cooled house was built by Raymond Whitcomb Bliss in Tucson, Arizona. The system, built at a cost of nearly $4,000 for labor and materials, was placed in operation January 15, 1955. A large slanting slab of steel and glass converted the sunlight into heat, which was brought into the house by ducts. The same fans, controls, ducts, etc., were used for summer cooling.

Steam-heated factory. *See* Factory: Steam-heated factory

Steel-frame building was the Tacoma Building in Chicago, Ill., completed in 1887. It was designed by Holabird & Roche and built by George Allon Fuller. This building embodied the principles upon which all modern skyscrapers are designed and erected.

Steel-frame residence was the Copper House, built in 1890, at Shore Road and 88th Street in the Bay Ridge section of Brooklyn, N.Y. The house was constructed with copper sheets riveted to the exterior. It was built by Niels Poulson, who resided in it from 1890 until his death in 1911. *(American Scandinavian Review. February 1931)*

Tenement house was built in New York City in 1833 on Water Street, on a site now within the limits of Corlears Park. It was four stories high, with arrangements for one family on each floor. This was the beginning of the system of grouping many homes under one roof.

Theater. *See* Theater: Theater

"White House." *See* Building: Building erected by the Government in Washington, D.C.

"White House of the Confederacy" was used as a residence by Jefferson Davis from February 18, 1861, to May 22, 1861. It is located at 626 Washington Street, Montgomery, Ala. Davis arrived at Montgomery on February 16, 1861, and remained at a local hotel for a few days.

Windowless factory. *See* Factory: Windowless factory

Woman to have her name placed on the cornerstone of a United States Government

THE FIRST

BUILDING—*Continued*
building. *See* Woman: Woman to have her name placed on the cornerstone of a United States Government building

BUILDING AND LOAN ASSOCIATION was the Oxford Provident Building Association, which was organized on January 3, 1831, in Thomas Sidebotham's Tavern, 4219 Frankford Avenue, Frankford, Pa. The organizers were Jesse Castor, secretary, Samuel Pilling, treasurer, and Jeremiah Horrocks. The company was succeeded by the Decatur Building Association. The first loan was $500, made on April 11, 1831, to Mr. Comly Rich. *(Robert Riegel—The Building and Loan Association)*
See also Federal savings and loan association

BULL MOOSE PARTY. *See* Progressive party

BULLFIGHT
Bullfight was held July 4, 1884, in Dodge City, Kan. The first bull put up a good fight but was not killed. The next four bulls showed little inclination to fight and likewise were spared. To appease the crowd, the first bull was returned to the ring and was killed by Captain Gregorio Gallardo. Among the bulls were Ringtailed Snorter, Iron Gall, Sheriff, Rustler, Loco Jim, Ku Klux, and Eat-em-up Richard. Another bullfight was held the following day. (On Saturday, July 31, 1880, at 5 P.M., a steer-baiting contest had been held in New York City before 4,000 spectators, but rubber caps had been placed on the bulls' horns and the matadors were not permitted to kill the bulls. The rosettes were not stuck into the bulls, but glued on.) *(Kansas Historical Quarterly. Vol 2, no.3. August 1933)*

Woman bull fighter (professional) was Patricia McCormick, of Big Spring, Tex., whose professional debut was made January 20, 1952, in Ciudad Juarez, Mexico. On that occasion she killed two bulls. In her first two years, she killed eighty bulls. *(Patricia McCormick—Lady Bullfighter)*

BUNTING manufacture was undertaken in 1838 by Michael Hodge Simpson at the New England Worsted Company, Saxonville, Mass.

BUREAU OF FOREIGN AND DOMESTIC COMMERCE. *See* Commerce Department (U.S.): Foreign and domestic commerce bureau

BUREAU OF IDENTIFICATION. *See* Police: Police bureau of identification

BUREAU OF MEDICINE AND SURGERY (Naval). *See* Navy: Bureau of Medicine and Surgery

BUREAU OF NAVIGATION. *See* Navigation Bureau (U.S.)

BUREAU OF STANDARDS. *See* Standards Bureau (U.S.)

BURGLAR ALARM
Burglar alarm was installed by Edwin Thomas Holmes on February 21, 1858, in Boston, Mass. The releasing of a spring by the opening of a door or window made a contact which caused a short circuit of the wires. *(Edwin Thomas Holmes—A Wonderful Fifty Years)*

Burglar alarm operated by ultrasonic or radio waves using the Doppler effect was the "Alertronic," invented by Samuel Bagno of New York City, who obtained patent No. 2,655,645 on October 13, 1953, on a movement detection system for intruders or fire. It was manufactured by the Alertronic Corporation, Long Island City, N.Y., and first sold in June 1950. Reflected waves of 19,000 cycles a second, pitched too high for normal human ears, are recorded through a microphone into an alarm, generally stationed at a convenient location. The noise made by an intruder, having a slightly different frequency, causes the alarm gong to sound.

Burglar alarm system in which the protected premises were connected by wire to a central office system which was immediately apprised of entry was installed by the Holmes Burglar Alarm Company, New York City, in 1872. The alarms served safe cabinets and bank vaults specifically instead providing general protection for stores and houses.

BURIAL PLOT (Jewish). *See* Cemetery: Jewish burial plot

BURLESQUE SHOW. *See* Play (drama): Burlesque show

BUS. *See* Automobile bus

BUSINESS
Chain store organization is ascribed to many, but the first of the existing chain stores was the Great Atlantic and Pacific Tea Company. George Huntington Hartford was in the hide and leather business in New York City in 1857 and in 1859 added tea to his merchandise. In 1864 he originated the Great American Tea Company, which in 1869 developed into the Great Atlantic and Pacific Tea Company, the presidency of which he kept until his death, August 29, 1917. Despite the name, the first store on the Pacific coast was not opened until January 1930.

THE FIRST

Commercial rating agency was established in New York City on August 1, 1841, as the Mercantile Agency, by Lewis Tappan, who founded the *Journal of Commerce* in 1828. The first place of business of the agency was at the corner of Hanover Street and Exchange Place, New York City. Branch houses were later opened, the first in Boston, Mass., in February 1843. On May 1, 1859, the firm was taken over by R. G. Dun & Company.

Department store was the Zion's Co-Operative Mercantile Institution created by Brigham Young in 1868 in Salt Lake City, Utah. In the beginning, each department was housed in its own store. One handled dry goods and carpets, another men's clothing. Groceries were carried in a different store, while another was a drug store. The following year, they were all housed under the same roof.

Department store television sales demonstrations (large-scale). *See* Television—Telecast: Department store sales demonstrations (large-scale)

Department store to hold a public art auction was Gimbel Brothers, New York, City, on November 14 and 15, 1941, when 303 items were auctioned by the Kende Galleries, Inc. The sales totaled $12,066.

Department store to sell apartments was Gimbel Brothers, Philadelphia, Pa., which on January 13, 1953, invited the public to the furniture floor to see full-size furnished duplicates of Philadelphia's first cooperative apartments. Over a million dollars' worth of apartments were contracted for the first day.

Department store to sell insurance of various types was Carson Pirie Scott & Co., Chicago, Ill. The first sale was made September 29, 1953, on a wedding present and personal effects floater for $2,500. The premium was $20.

Five-cent store was opened in Utica, N.Y., on February 22, 1879, by Frank Winfield Woolworth. The store was a great disappointment as its sales after a few weeks were as low as $2.50 a day. Woolworth moved his store in June 1879 to Lancaster, Pa., where it proved a success. His idea was developed on September 24, 1878, in Watertown, N.Y., when during the week of the country fair he originated a "five-cent table" in the store of Moore and Smith. The first joint venture of the Woolworth brothers in Harrisburg, Pa., was called "Great 5 Cent Store." (*Fifty Years of Woolworth*— *F. W. Woolworth Co.*)

"Food-O-Mat" was installed in the Grand Union Company store, Carlstadt, N.J., on May

THE FIRST

24, 1945. It was invented by Lansing Peter Shield. The patented merchandise display fixture operates on a gravity-feed, rear-load principle. Stockmen working behind the unit place cans, jars, and packages, label upright, on inclined runways. The items reach the shopper brand name uppermost. As the customer picks out an item, another slides in place by gravity.

Installment finance company to purchase installment contracts from retail dealers was the Fidelity Contract Company, Rochester, N.Y., which held its first directors' meeting April 7, 1904. The company, organized by Lee Richmond, Frederick Zoller, and George Gale Foster, became the Bankers Commercial Corporation of New York City.

Keedoozle store was opened in Memphis, Tenn., on May 15, 1937, by the Keedoozle Corporation of Memphis, Tenn., of which Clarence Saunders was president. Sample merchandise was displayed behind rows of tiny glass windows. The customer made purchases by inserting a notched rod into a keyhole beside the items desired. The mechanism automatically recorded the selections. The merchandise was automatically collected and wrapped when the insertion of the key in a final slot released the contents to a conveyor for wrapping. "Keedoozle" is a coined word for "key-does-all."

Mail-order house was established by Aaron Montgomery Ward in 1872 in a 12 by 14 foot room at 825 North Clark Street, Chicago, Ill., with $2,400 capital, one third of which was advanced by George R. Thorne. The first catalog consisted of a single-sheet price list, 8 by 12 inches, without illustrations. Afterwards, catalogs with descriptive pictures were issued and a 15-cent charge made for them. The first free catalogs, more than 3 million weighing four pounds each, were mailed in 1904. (*History and Progress of Montgomery Ward and Co.*—*Montgomery Ward and Co.*)

Nurse employed by an industrial organization. *See* Nurse: Nurse employed by an industrial organization

Sales meeting televised. *See* Television—Telecast: Sales meeting televised

BUSINESS ECONOMICS COURSE, under the title "Commerce, Political Economy and Statistics," was established by the University of Louisiana (now Tulane University), New Orleans, La., in 1849; and was conducted by Professor James Dunwoody Brownson De Bow.

BUSINESS EXPOSITION. *See* Fair: Industrial exposition

THE FIRST

THE FIRST

BUSINESS HISTORY CHAIR was the Isidor Straus Professorship of Business History, established in 1923 by the Graduate School of Business Administration, Harvard University, Cambridge, Mass. The first incumbent was Norman Scott Brien Gras, appointed in 1927.

BUSINESS LIBRARY. *See* Library: Business library supported by taxes

BUSINESS MACHINES. *See* under specific kinds of machine, e.g., Adding machine; Cash register; Postage meter; Telautograph

BUSINESS MANUAL was John Hill's *The Young Secretary's Guide; or a Speedy help to learning* . . . printed by B[artholomew] Green and J[ohn] Allen for S. Phillips in 1703 in Boston, Mass. It was based on an English work, contained 192 pages of instructions on writing business and social letters, punctuation rules, a dictionary of "hard words," and examples of bonds, bills, letters of attorney, deeds of sale, mortgage forms, warrants of attorney, deeds of gift, bills of sale, bills of exchange, assignments, etc. *(Louis Charles Karpinski—Bibliography of Mathematical Works printed in America Through 1850)*

BUSINESS PUBLICATION was the *New York Prices Current,* a weekly started in New York City in 1795 by James Oram. The date of the earliest known existing copy of this publication is January 2, 1797.

BUSINESS SCHOOL
  Business collegiate school was the Wharton School of Commerce and Finance in Philadelphia, Pa., established in 1881 by the University of Pennsylvania through a $100,000 gift of Joseph Wharton. *(Thomas Harrison Montgomery—A History of the University of Pennsylvania)*

  Business high school was the Washington Business High School, Washington, D.C., authorized June 11, 1889, by the Board of Education. It opened September 22, 1890, in an unused grade school building of seven rooms. Allan Davis was the first principal. *(Reports of the Board of Trustees of the Public Schools in Washington, D.C., 1885-1900)*

  Business school was opened in Rochester, N.Y., in 1842 by George Washington Eastman, and was known as the Eastman Commercial College.

  Commercial high school. *See* Commercial high school

BUSTLE was patented by Alexander Douglas of New York City, who obtained patent No. 17,082 on April 21, 1857, on an "improvement in bustles."

BUTTON
  Buttons of fresh water pearl were manufactured in Muscatine, Iowa, in 1890 by John F. Boepple, assisted by William Molis and R. Kerr. The pearl was obtained from domestic fresh water clam shells. *(U.S. Bureau of Fisheries. Vol. 36. 1917-18)*

  Cloth-covered buttons were made by hand in Easthampton, Mass., in 1826 by Mrs. Samuel Williston, who was the first to introduce their use commercially in the United States. Her husband formed a partnership with Joel Hayden, who invented the first machine for making covered buttons. The partnership lasted until 1848, when Williston bought out his partner and conducted the business alone.

  Gilt buttons to be commercially manufactured were produced in 1802 by Abel Porter & Company of Waterbury, Conn. The faces were all gilded, and gold was used extensively in the manufacture. This concern later developed into the Scovill Manufacturing Company of Waterbury, Conn. *(Henry Bronson—History of Waterbury)*

  Pewter or block tin buttons were manufactured in 1790 in Waterbury, Conn., by Henry, Silas, and Samuel Grilley, three brothers who established a small factory on Bunker Hill, an elevated section of the city. The buttons were cast in molds. The eyes were originally cast of the same material. Later, wire eyes were used. *(Homer Franklin Bassett—Waterbury and Her Industries)*

BUTTONHOLE SEWING MACHINE. *See* Sewing machine: Sewing machine to stitch buttonholes

CAB LOCOMOTIVE. *See* Locomotive: Locomotive with a cab

CABIN AIRSHIP. *See* Aviation—Airship: Airship with an enclosed cabin

CABINET OF THE UNITED STATES
  Cabinet was appointed by President George Washington during his first term, April 30, 1789, to March 3, 1793. Members of the cabinet were Thomas Jefferson of Virginia, Secretary of State; Alexander Hamilton of New York, Secretary of the Treasury; Henry Knox of Massachusetts, Secretary of War; Samuel Osgood of Massachusetts, Postmaster General; and Edmund Jennings Randolph of Virginia, Attorney General. The seat of the Federal

Government at that time was New York City. (*Henry Barrett Learned—The President's Cabinet*)

Cabinet appointee rejected by the Senate was Roger Brooke Taney of Maryland, nominated by President Andrew Jackson June 24, 1834 as Secretary of the Treasury. (*William Henry Smith—History of the Cabinet of the United States of America*)

Cabinet conference telecast was presented on June 3, 1953, from the White House, Washington, D.C. President Dwight David Eisenhower conferred for half an hour with Mrs. Oveta Culp Hobby, Secretary of Health, Education and Welfare; George Magoffin Humphrey, Secretary of the Treasury; Ezra Taft Benson, Secretary of Agriculture; and Herbert Brownell, Attorney General. The telecast was carried by four networks.

Cabinet member convicted of a crime committed while a member of a President's cabinet was Albert Bacon Fall, who was tried in the District of Columbia Supreme Court. He was found guilty by Justice William Hitz on October 25, 1929, of receiving and accepting a bribe of $100,000 from Edward Laurence Doheny in connection with the Elk Hills Naval Oil Reserve in California, a bribe given with a view to influencing Fall, as Secretary of the Interior in President Warren G. Harding's cabinet, to grant valuable oil leases to Doheny's Pan-American Petroleum and Transport Company. On November 1, 1929, Fall was sentenced to one year in prison and was fined $100,000.

Cabinet member who was a brother of a President was Robert Francis Kennedy, who took office as Attorney General in the cabinet of President John Fitzgerald Kennedy on January 21, 1961.

Cabinet member who was a Catholic was Roger Brooke Taney of Maryland, Attorney General in Andrew Jackson's cabinet from July 20, 1831, until September 23, 1833, and Secretary of the Treasury from September 23, 1833, until June 25, 1834.

Cabinet member who was Jewish was Oscar Solomon Straus of New York, who was Secretary of Commerce and Labor during President Theodore Roosevelt's second administration. He was appointed on December 12, 1906, and served from December 17, 1906, to March 3, 1909. (*Oscar Solomon Straus—Under Four Administrations from Cleveland to Taft*)

Cabinet officer to address a joint session of Congress was Secretary of State Cordell Hull, who reported on November 18, 1943,

that the tripartite conference at Moscow pointed towards the maintenance of peace and security in the postwar world. The two houses, being in recess, assembled to hear him, but technically it was not a "joint session."

Cabinet session held at a place other than the seat of the United States Government was held November 22, 1955, at President Dwight David Eisenhower's farm at Gettysburg, Pa. It was attended by the President, the Vice President, the ten cabinet officers, and four other government officials.

Cabinet session telecast. *See* Television—Telecast: Cabinet session to be televised

Confederate to serve in the cabinet was David McKendree Key, a senator from Tennessee, who served from March 12, 1877, to August 24, 1880, as Postmaster General in the cabinet of President Rutherford Birchard Hayes. He had been a lieutenant colonel in the 43rd Regiment of Tennessee and had been wounded and captured at Vicksburg.

Father and son to occupy the same cabinet posts were Henry Cantwell Wallace, Secretary of Agriculture under Presidents Warren Gamaliel Harding and Calvin Coolidge, March 5, 1921, to October 25, 1924, and Henry Agard Wallace, Secretary of Agriculture under President Franklin Delano Roosevelt, March 4, 1933, to August 26, 1940.

Full cabinet sworn in at the same time and place by the same official took office on March 4, 1933, when Justice Benjamin Nathan Cardozo of the Supreme Court of the United States swore nine men and one woman as President Franklin Delano Roosevelt's cabinet in the library on the second floor of the White House.

Negro sub-cabinet member was James Ernest Wilkins of Chicago, Ill., who was appointed Assistant Secretary of Labor for International Affairs by President Dwight David Eisenhower on March 4, 1954, and sworn in March 18, 1954, in Washington, D.C. On August 18, 1954, with Secretary of Labor James Mitchell and Under Secretary Arthur Larson out of town, he was the first Negro representative of a department to attend a cabinet meeting. (William Henry Lewis, a Boston Negro attorney, was Special Assistant Attorney General from March 26, 1911, to April 1, 1913, but the "special" in his title deprived him of sub-cabinet rank.)

Postmaster general of the United States to become a member of the President's cabinet. *See* Postmaster: Postmaster general of the United States to become a member of the President's cabinet

CABINET OF THE UNITED STATES
—*Continued*
Secretary of Health, Education and Welfare was Oveta Culp Hobby (Mrs. William Pettus Hobby) of Houston, Tex., who was sworn in April 11, 1953, by Frank Kesler Sanderson, White House administrative officer, in President Dwight David Eisenhower's office, the White House, Washington, D.C., as the tenth officer in the President's cabinet. She was in charge of 37,500 workers in 550 offices in the country. Previously, she had been Administrator of the Federal Security Agency.

Vice President to preside over a cabinet meeting. *See* Vice President of the United States: Vice President to preside over a cabinet meeting

Woman cabinet member was Frances Perkins (Mrs. Paul Caldwell Wilson), appointed Secretary of Labor by President Franklin Delano Roosevelt. She served from March 4, 1933, to June 30, 1945. She had been Industrial Commissioner for New York prior to this appointment. *(U.S. Department of Labor —Frances Perkins, a Bibliographical List)*

Woman sub-cabinet member was Annette Abbott Adams, who was appointed Assistant Attorney General on June 26, 1920, by President Woodrow Wilson. She resigned August 15, 1921. *(Arthur J. Dodge—Origin and Development of the Office of the Attorney General)*

CABLE (telegraph)
Cable was an insulated copper wire laid October 18, 1842, by Samuel Finley Breese Morse in New York Harbor between the Battery and Governors Island. On the following day, while transmitting signals, the cable ceased to work because a vessel in raising its anchor had caught and wrecked 200 feet of the cable. Another cable was laid in New York Harbor for commercial use in 1843 by Samuel Colt. It was insulated with cotton yarn, beeswax, and asphaltum encased in a lead pipe, and connected New York City with both Fire and Coney Islands. *(Edward Wright Byrn—Progress of Invention in the Nineteenth Century) (Samuel Irenaeus Prime—Life of S. F. B. Morse)*

Cable across the Atlantic Ocean was completed on August 5, 1858, through the efforts of Cyrus West Field. Two unsuccessful attempts had been made previously. On July 28, 1858, a splice was made in mid-ocean, and on the following day four ships, belonging to England and the United States, paid out the cable as they sailed for home—the "Agamemnon" and "Valorous" bound for Valentia, Ireland, and the "Niagara" and the "Gorgon" for Trinity Bay, Newfoundland, which were

to be the terminals. The cable was 1,950 statute miles long and over two thirds of it was laid more than two miles deep. Introductory and complimentary messages were exchanged by President James Buchanan and Queen Victoria on August 16, 1858. The cable was weak and the current insufficient, and service was suspended September 1, 1858. *(Isabella Field Judson—Cyrus W. Field, His Life and Work)*

Cable across the Atlantic Ocean was paid out on August 6, 1857. The American frigate "Niagara" and the British warship "Agamemnon" attempted the task, but the cable broke and it was impossible to mend the break or complete the cable. *(Henry Martyn Field— History of the Atlantic Telegraph)*

Cable across the Pacific Ocean was paid out on December 14, 1902, between San Francisco, Calif., and Honolulu, Hawaii, a distance of 2,277 nautical miles (2,620 miles) by the cableship "Silverton" and was landed on the beach near Honolulu, January 1, 1903. The first message was sent at 11:03 P.M. (San Francisco time) on that day. This cable was opened for public use on January 5, 1903.

Cable across the Pacific Ocean between Honolulu, Midway, Guam, and Manila was completed and spliced at Manila on July 3, 1903. After testing, the first official message was sent by President Theodore Roosevelt from his home at Oyster Bay, N.Y., at 10:50 A.M., July 4, 1903, to Governor William Howard Taft at Manila, who immediately answered it. Another message was sent westward across the Pacific and around the world to Clarence Hungerford Mackay, president of the Commercial Pacific Cable Company, who was with President Roosevelt at his home. The transmission time of the message was eleven minutes. The message was answered by Mr. Mackay, his message going eastward to London and over the system of the Eastern Telegraph Company to Manila, thence over the new Pacific cable and back to Oyster Bay, transmission time of the message being nine minutes. The cable from San Francisco, Calif., to Manila via Honolulu was 7,876 nautical miles (9,060 miles).

Coaxial cable was invented by Lloyd Espenschied of Kew Gardens, N.Y., and Herman A. Affel of Ridgewood, N.J., whose application for a patent was filed May 23, 1929. They were awarded patent No. 1,835,031 on December 8, 1931, on a "concentric conducting system" which was assigned to the American Telegraph and Telephone Company, New York City.

News dispatch by cable was received August 26, 1858, and was published in the New York *Sun*, August 27, 1858. It stated that a treaty of peace had been concluded by China in which England and France obtained all their

THE FIRST

demands including the establishment of embassies at Peking and indemnification for military expenses.

Submarine cable plow. *See* Plow: Submarine cable plow

Submarine telegraph cable that was practical was laid by Ezra Cornell, an associate of Samuel Finley Breese Morse. In 1845 he laid twelve miles of cable enclosed in lead pipes across the Hudson River connecting Fort Lee, N.J., with New York City. This cable was carried away by ice in 1846. (Later a steel wire was suspended from high masts erected on opposite shores, but sleet and snow caused the wire to snap.) Before the cable was installed, messages for Philadelphia, Pa., and Washington, D.C., were carried across the Hudson by messengers in boats. *(Alonzo B. Cornell—True and Firm, Biography of Ezra Cornell)*

Submarine telegraph cable to be insulated with gutta percha, was made by Samuel T. Armstrong and Lorenzo Higgins at a factory on Water Street, Brooklyn, N.Y., in May 1848. It was laid across the North (Hudson) River for the Magnetic Telegraph Co. *(Transactions American Institute, 1847)*

CABLE CAR. *See* Street car: Cable car

CAESAREAN OPERATION (successful). *See* Surgical operation: Caesarean operation (successful)

CAFETERIA was opened in 1895 in Chicago, Ill., on Adams Street between Clark and La Salle Streets by Ernest Kimball. In 1899 he moved it to the basement of the New York Life Building, where it was located until 1925.
See also Restaurants

CALCULATING MACHINE. *See* Adding machine

CALICO printery was established in Boston, Mass., by George Leason and Thomas Webber, who advertised in the Boston *News Letter,* April 21-28, 1712, that they had "set up a Callender-Mill and Dye House in Cambridge Street, Boston, near the Bowling Green where all gentlemen, Merchants, and others may have all sorts of Linnens, callicoes, stuffs or Silks Callendered: Prints all sorts of Linnens."

CALIFORNIA CONSUL. *See* Diplomatic Service: Consul to California

CALIFORNIA-HAWAII FLIGHT. *See* Aviation—Flights (transpacific): California-Hawaii flight

THE FIRST

CALIFORNIA MISSION was dedicated and blessed by Father Junipero Serra on July 16, 1769. After High Mass, the royal standard of Spain was unfurled over the Mission which was named in honor of San Diego de Alcala. The mission was the first of a chain of 21 which were erected. It is located in what is now San Diego, Calif. *(Trowbridge Hall— California Trails)*

CALIFORNIUM. *See* Element: Element 98

CALIPER (screw) was constructed by John Edson Sweet in 1874 in the shops of Sibley College (Cornell University), Ithaca, N.Y. The screw of the machine had 16 threads per inch and its divided circle had 625 readings, the calibration reading to $1/_{10,000}$ inch. The machine stood on three legs. *(Frederick Arthur Halsey—Methods of Machine Shop Work)*

CALL BOX (TELEGRAPH). *See* Telegraph: Telegraph call boxes

CALLIOPE was invented by Joshua C. Stoddard of Worcester, Mass., who on October 9, 1855, received patent No. 13,368. He formed the American Steam Music Company in Worcester, Mass., in 1855. The first marine exhibition was held August 6, 1856, on the large side-wheel tugboat "Union." *(John Harrison Morrison—History of American Steam Navigation)*

CALL BOX (telegraph). *See* Telegraph: Telegraph call boxes

CAMEL race took place April 7, 1864, at Agricultural Park, Sacramento, Calif. The proceeds obtained from the sale of tickets were used to aid the poor. *(May Humphreys Stacey —Uncle Sam's Camels)*

CAMELS. *See under* Animals

CAMERA
Aerial camera (nine-lens) for large-scale mapping was designed by personnel of the U.S. Coast and Geodetic Survey in 1934 under the direction of Lieutenant Oliver Scott Reading and built under contract by the Fairchild Aerial Camera and Instrument Company, Jamaica, N.Y., in 1935. It was placed in operation in 1936. It was 29 inches wide, 27 inches fore and aft, 31 inches high, and weighed 306 pounds net. Gross weight with all equipment for photography was 750 pounds. The nine lenses photographed the terrain simultaneously on one piece of film. The camera was loaded with a strip of film 23 inches wide and 200 feet long, and could take 100 exposures without reloading. When flown at a height of

CAMERA—*Continued*
13,750 feet, the camera photographed 121 square miles at one exposure at a scale of 1 inch to 1,667 feet.

Camera to take, develop, and print pictures on photographic paper was the Polaroid camera, invented by Edwin Herbert Land and demonstrated on February 21, 1947, at a meeting of the Optical Society of America meeting at the Hotel Pennsylvania, New York City. The camera contained a specially prepared photographic paper with a "pod" of developer and hypo sandwiched with the film. The turning of a knob squeezed open one of the pods, which developed the negative and made the print. The picture was produced in about one minute.

Fluoro-record reflector camera. *See* X-ray: Fluoro-record reflector camera

Moving picture camera (portable) was the Victor Cine Camera, manufactured by the Victor Animatograph Company, Inc., Davenport, Iowa, in 1923. It was 3 by 6 by 8 inches, weighed 5 pounds, and cost $55. It was advertised August 12, 1923.

Non-electronic device for observing in total darkness was the Evaporograph, built by Baird Associates, Inc., Cambridge, Mass., an affiliate of the American Research and Development Corporation, and announced to the public on February 15, 1956. It cost $9,500 and was housed in a cabinet 18 by 14 by 11 inches. It was designed to observe radiation differences corresponding to temperature variations of one to several thousand degrees of Fahrenheit.

Photo-finish camera (electric eye) installed at a race track was placed in operation January 16, 1936, at the Hialeah Race Course, Hialeah, Fla.

Roll film camera, which did not require a table or tripod for support, was Kodak No.1, a fixed-focus box camera, announced in June 1888 by George Eastman of Rochester, N.Y. It weighed 22 ounces and had a lens fast enough to make instantaneous exposures. It used a roll of film of 100 exposures and took a round picture 2½ inches in diameter. It was covered by patent No. 388,850 dated September 4, 1888, and the name "Kodak" was registered on the same date.

Tintype camera was patented by Professor Hamilton Lamphere Smith, professor of natural sciences, Kenyon College, Gambier, Ohio, who obtained patent No. 14,300, on February 19, 1856, on "photographic pictures on japanned surfaces." The photographs were collodion positives on black or chocolate-colored iron plates. (*Robert Taft—Photography and the American Scene*)

CAMERA EXPOSURE METER. *See* Photography: Camera exposure meter

CAMOUFLAGE was undertaken as a scientific study by Abbott Henderson Thayer who presented a valuable treatise on protective coloration entitled "The Law Which Underlies Protective Coloration," which appeared in the April 1896 issue of *The Auk*, an ornithological journal, published in New York City.

CAMOUFLAGE COURSE. *See* Art course: Industrial camouflage course

CAMP (army). *See* Army camp

CAMP FIRE GIRLS organization was developed by Mrs. Luther Halsey Gulick at her camp at Lake Sebago, Maine. The name and ranks were suggested by W. C. Langdon. The society, an organization for young girls, was made public March 17, 1912. The watchword is "Wohelo," made from the first two letters of each of the words, Work, Health and Love. (*Luther Halsey Gulick—Campfire Girls of America*)

CAMP FOR BOYS' outdoor recreation was Camp Comfort, Welch's Point, Milford, Conn., established in August 1861, when Frederick William Gunn, founder of the Gunnery School, took fifty boys on a two-week camping trip. The camp was organized again in August 1863 and in August 1865. In 1867, Gunn started another camp at Point Beautiful on Lake Waramaug, Washington, Conn., which was opened for a two-week period in August for twelve successive years.

CAMP FOR CONSCIENTIOUS OBJECTORS. *See* Conscientious objectors camp

CAMP MEETING was held in 1803 by James M'Geary, William McGee (Presbyterian), and John McGee (Methodist) in a little log church on the Gaspar River in Logan County, Ky. (*G. W. Gorham—Camp Meeting Manual*)

CAMPAIGN MEDAL. *See* Medal: "Campaign medal"

CAMPAIGN (POLITICAL) TELECAST. *See* Television—Telecast: Political campaign telecast

CAMPAIGN (PRESIDENTIAL) CO-MANAGER (WOMAN). *See* Woman: Woman presidential campaign co-manager

CANAL
Canal was built around the falls of the Connecticut River at South Hadley Falls,

Mass., in 1793. It was chartered by "the Proprietors of the Upper Locks and Canals on the Connecticut River in the County of Hampshire." The canal was two miles long and was opened to traffic in 1794. Benjamin Prescott was the engineer. Boats were run into movable caissons filled with water and were hauled by cables operated by water power. The canal had two levels connected by an incline, up and down which boats were raised or lowered in a tank of water and propelled by cables operated by water wheels. (*Alonzo Barton Hepburn—Artificial Waterways and Commercial Development*)

Canal for creating water power was dug by English settlers in 1639-1640 at Dedham, Mass., at Mill Creek, or Mother Brook as it is commonly called, and was used to run a mill. It conveyed water from the Charles River into the Neponset River. The order for the construction of the canal follows: "The 25th of ye 1 month, Commonly Called March. 1639. Assembled whose names are vnderwritten vizt. . . . . . Ordered y^t a Ditch shalbe made at a Common Charge through purchased Medowe vnto ye East Brooke. y^t may both be a pticon fence in ye same; as also may serve for a Course vnto a water mill." (*Early Records of the Town of Dedham, Mass. Dedham Historical Register. Vol. 6. No. 4*)

Canal of importance was the Erie Canal, which connected the waters of Lake Erie at Buffalo with the waters of the Hudson at Albany, N.Y. Lake Erie lies 550 feet above the level of tide water in the Hudson. The canal was 360 miles in length, 40 feet wide at the top and 28 feet wide at the bottom, and 4 feet deep. The canal was authorized on April 15, 1817, and construction started July 4, 1817. The first boat plied between Rome and Utica on October 22, 1819. The canal was opened for traffic on October 26, 1825. The original cost was approximately $9,000,000. (*Historical Catechism. 8th ed. Utica. 1835*)

Great Lakes to the Gulf waterway became an accomplished fact on June 21, 1933, upon arrival at Chicago, Ill., of the first tow from New Orleans, La. On June 1, 1933, the Federal Barge Line steamer "Vicksburg" with barges laden with coffee, sisal, and general merchandise left New Orleans, La. The tow was transferred to the "Hoover" at Memphis, Tenn.; to the "Sawyer" plying the Illinois River; and to the "Warner" at Ottawa, Ill., which brought it to Chicago. The completion of the Lakes to the Gulf Waterway was officially celebrated in Chicago, June 22, 1933.

Saint Lawrence Seaway, 2,342 miles from the Atlantic Ocean to Duluth, Minn., was opened April 25, 1959. The first ship to enter the 400-mile system between Montreal and Lake Erie was the Canadian government ship "d'Iberville" a 6,000-ton ice-breaker; the first

commercial ship was the "Simcoe" of the Canada Steamship Lines; the first ocean-going ship was the "Prins Willem George Frederik"; the first United States ship was the "Santa Regina" of the Grace Lines. The seaway was formally opened June 26, 1959, by Queen Elizabeth II and President Dwight David Eisenhower.

CANAL LOCKS made of concrete were built by the United States Government for the Illinois and Mississippi Canal (the Hennepin canal), which connected Lake Michigan at Chicago, Ill., with the Mississippi River, south of Rock Island, Ill. Excavation work commenced July 1892 and the first section, the Milan section, was opened to traffic on April 17, 1895. (*Illinois and Mississippi Canal—Annual Report of the Chief Engineer—1908*)

CANCER CLINIC. *See* Medical clinic: Cancer clinic

CANCER HOSPITAL. *See* Hospital: Cancer hospital

CANCER LABORATORY, exclusively for the study of cancer, was the New York State Pathological Laboratory for the Study of Cancer established in May 1898 under a $10,000 appropriation made by the New York State legislature on April 29, 1898, Chapter 606, "for the faculty of the medical department of the University of Buffalo for the equipment and maintenance of a laboratory to be devoted to an investigation into the causes, nature, mortality rate and the treatment of cancer." Dr. Roswell Park was the first director and Dr. Harvey Russell Gaylord, associate. (*First Annual Report of the Director of the New York State Pathological Laboratory—1899*)

CANCER RESEARCH FUND was the Collis P. Huntington Fund for cancer research established in 1902 by Mrs. Collis Potter Huntington. The fund, amounting to $100,000, was used by the New York Cancer Hospital, New York City. It enabled the hospital to administer X-ray treatments and install new equipment. (*Reports of the Collis P. Huntington Fund for Cancer Research of the General Memorial Hospital*)

CANDLE FACTORY for making spermaceti candles was established by Benjamin Crabb in Newport, R.I., in 1748. It was destroyed by fire in 1750.

CANE SUGAR. *See* Sugar: Sugar cane

CANNING
See also Cans

Canning was introduced in 1819 by Ezra Daggett, and his nephew, Thomas Kensett, who canned salmon, oysters, and lobsters in

CANNING—*Continued*
New York City. On January 19, 1825, they obtained a patent to "preserve animal substances in tin." Cans were in use in 1825, but the real development of the canning industry did not start until after the Civil War. (*Henry Meech Loomis—The Canning of Foods*)

Salmon cannery was erected in 1864 at Washington, Yolo County, Calif., on the banks of the Sacramento River by Hapgood, Hume and Company. The firm consisted of Andrew S. Hapgood, George W. Hume, and William Hume. About 2,000 cases of salmon were canned the first year. Approximately 50 per cent of the first production spoiled because the cans were not hermetically sealed. (*R. D. Hume—The Salmon of the Pacific Coast*)

Sardine cannery that was successful was established in 1876 in Eastport, Me., by Julius Wolff of Wolff and Reesing, New York City. The cans, as originally used, were made of three pieces, top, bottom, and side, which were soldered together. (*Frederick Clarence Weber —The Maine Sardine Industry. U.S. Department of Agriculture, Bulletin No. 908*)

CANNING BOOK was a translation of François Appert's *L'Art de Conserver, pendant plusieurs années, toutes les substances animales et végétales,* published in 1812 by [David] Longworth, New York City.

CANNON. *See* Ordnance: Cannon (breech loading)

CANNON IN A FIGHTER AIRPLANE. *See* Aviation—Airplane: Fighter airplane carrying a cannon

CANOE ASSOCIATION was the American Canoe Association, formed August 3, 1880, by 25 canoeists at Crosbyside Park, Lake George, N.Y. The first commodore was William Livingston Alden and the first secretary Nathaniel Holmes Bishop. (*American Canoe Association Yearbook—1895*)

CANOE CLUB was the New York Canoe Club founded in New York City in 1870. A clubhouse was built in 1879 during which year a regatta was held. The club was dissolved August 3, 1880. (*C. Bowyer Vaux—Canoe Handling*)

CANONIZATION OF NORTH AMERICANS. *See* Catholic canonization of North Americans

CANS
Beer in cans for retail sale was packed by the Krueger Brewing Company at Newark, N.J., and placed on sale in Richmond, Va., on January 24, 1935.

Can (tin) with a key opener was invented by J. Osterhoudt of New York City who obtained patent No. 58,554 on October 2, 1866, for an "improved method of opening tin cans." The can had a projecting lip and key.

CANTALOUPE. *See* Melons

CANTILEVER BRIDGE. *See* Bridge: Cantilever bridge

CANTOR
Jewish woman cantor was Betty Robbins (Mrs. Sheldon Robbins) of Massapequa, Long Island, N.Y., whose first service was sung on September 15, 1955, the eve of Rosh Hashanah or the Jewish New Year, at Temple Avodah, Oceanside, Long Island, N.Y.

School for cantors was the Hebrew Union School of Education and Sacred Music, New York City, which opened October 16, 1948. Cantor-educator diplomas were awarded June 17, 1951, to the graduating class of ten men.

CAPITAL PUNISHMENT
See also Execution

Capital punishment authorized by federal law made the killing of a federal officer a mandatory capital offense. The law was enacted May 18, 1934 (48 Stat.L.780), and the first case to be tried was that of *United States vs. John Paul Chase.* On March 25, 1935, Chase was convicted of first-degree murder for the killing of Samuel Cowley, Department of Justice agent, on November 27, 1934, in Barrington, Ill. Judge Philip Sullivan sentenced Chase to life imprisonment on March 28, 1935, as the jury did not recommend the death penalty since he was not the principal in the matter. The first execution was that of George W. Barrett, for the murder of federal agent Nelson Bernard Klein in College Corner, Ind., on August 16, 1935. He was tried before U.S. District Judge Robert C. Baltzell, convicted December 14, 1935, and hanged March 24, 1936, at the Marion County Jail, Indianapolis, Ind.

Death penalty was first abolished by Michigan law, enacted May 4, 1846, effective March 1, 1847. The gallows were still retained, however, for treason against the state. On April 22, 1794, Pennsylvania had abolished the death penalty except for murder in the first degree. *(Michigan History Magazine. Vol. 29, No.1)*

Woman judge to sentence a man to death. *See* Judge: Woman judge to sentence a man to death

CAPITOL was a statehouse on Duke of Gloucester Street, Williamsburg, Va., in which the General Assembly met. The building was erected in 1698 by Governor Francis Nicholson, who was the first person to apply the term "capitol" to a government building.

CAPITOL (of the United States) was designed by Dr. William Thornton, whose plan was accepted as the most suitable one submitted in a national contest. On July 16, 1790, the site for the Capitol was chosen, and on January 24, 1791, George Washington directed a survey for the Capitol. The cornerstone of the Capitol was laid in Washington, D.C. on September 18, 1793. George Washington delivered an oration and the Grand Master of the Maryland Masons an appropriate address. After the laying of the cornerstone, the assembly retired to an extensive booth to enjoy a barbecue feast. George Washington laid the cornerstone on the southeast corner of the central (oldest) section. The central section is of Virginia sandstone painted white to make it harmonize with the Massachusetts marble of the two wings. *(Rufus Rockwell Wilson—Washington, the Capitol City)*

CAPTAIN. *See* Naval officer: Captain

CAR. *See* Automobile; Railroad car; Street car

CARBIDE BORON. *See* Abrasive

CARBIDE FACTORY to manufacture commercial quantities of carbide was established in 1894 by Thomas Leopold Willson in Spray, N.C. He obtained United States patents No. 541,137 and No. 541,138 on June 18, 1895, on carbide (calcium carbide), a compound of calcium and carbide. He produced it by fusing calcium or lime with coke at a very high temperature. *(The Story of Carbide—National Carbide Sales Corp.)*

CARBIDE GAS. *See* Acetylene

CARBON MICROPHONE. *See* Radio microphone (carbon)

CARBON MONOXIDE BOILER. *See* Boiler: Carbon monoxide boiler

CARBON TETRACHLORIDE (CCl_4) was manufactured by Charles Ernest Acker who introduced his process in 1908. He also invented the Acker process of manufacturing caustic soda by the electrolysis of molten salt in 1896 for which he received the Elliott Cresson Gold Medal of the Franklin Institute in 1902. He was also the first to produce carbon and tin tetrachloride on a commercial scale.

"CARBORUNDUM," a trade-marked abrasive, to be used in place of emery, corundum, and other similar materials, was invented by Edward Goodrich Acheson in 1891 in Monongahela City, Pa. By running a current of electricity through a mixture of silica and carbon, he obtained a material hard enough for rough-polishing diamonds, rubies, sapphires and other precious and semi-precious stones. He obtained patent No. 492,767 February 28, 1893, on the production of artificial crystalline carbonaceous materials. The first sale of this material was 10 carats at the rate of 40 cents a carat or $880 a pound. *(The Story of Carborundum—The Carborundum Co.)*

CARD TIME RECORDER. *See* Time recorder: Card time recorder

CARDINAL (Catholic). *See* Catholic priest —Catholic priest to be elevated to the cardinalate

CARDING MACHINE. *See* Spinning, carding, and roping machines

CARDS (Christmas). *See* Christmas cards

CARDS (postal). *See* Postal card

CARGO SUBMARINE. *See* Submarine: Cargo submarine to cross the Atlantic ocean

CARGO VESSEL. *See* Ship

CARICATURE was Nathaniel Hurd's "The True Profile of the Notorious Doctor Seth Hudson," published in 1762 in Boston, Mass. It depicted Dr. Hudson in pillory and Howe, his assistant, at the whipping post, in punishment for forging the provinces' paper money. *(William Murrell—A History of American Graphic Humor)*
See also Cartoon

CARILLON
Carillon was installed in the belfry of the Old North Church (now Christ Church), Boston, Mass., in 1745. Eight bells were ordered in 1744 from Abell Rudhall's foundry, Gloucester, England, by Thomas Gunther, who put

CARILLON—*Continued*
up a bond to guarantee payment. They were shipped on the "Two Friends" on March 9, 1745, the total cost being £560, 4 shillings, 10 pence. (*New England Historical and Genealogical Register—1904—Vol. 58*)

Carillon (**modern**) was installed in the Church of Our Lady of Good Voyage, Gloucester, Mass., and blessed by His Eminence Cardinal O'Connell on July 2, 1922. The bells and apparatus, weighing 28,000 pounds, were made and installed by John Taylor & Co., Loughborough, England, and consisted of 31 bells, the largest weighing 2,826 pounds. They were played for the first time by carillonneur George B. Stevens. (*William Gorham Rice—Carillon Music and Singing Towers of the Old World and the New*)

CARNEGIE HERO FUND COMMISSION was established on March 12, 1904, by Andrew Carnegie, who transferred to the Commission $5 million of first collateral 5 per cent bonds of the United States Steel Corporation. The by-laws were adopted May 20, 1904, in Pittsburgh, Pa. The first award was a bronze medal which was presented to Louis A. Baumann, Jr., 17, a laborer, who saved Charles Stevick, 16, also a laborer, from drowning, near Wilkinsburg, Pa., July 17, 1904. Baumann dived into Sulphur Pond in water 10 feet deep, and after three attempts, rescued Stevick, who was panic-stricken. In the first year, 248 cases were considered, and 3 silver and 6 bronze medals awarded.

CARPET FACTORY
Carpet mill was founded in 1791 by William Peter Sprague in North Second Street, Philadelphia, Pa. He manufactured Axminster carpets on handlooms, and one of his earliest designs represented the arms and achievements of the new republic of the United States.

Carpet mill to make ingrain carpets was established in 1810 by George M. Conradt in Frederick, Md. The carpets were produced on handlooms on a drum having rows of pegs, and were of two- or three-ply, the warp being worsted or cotton with a wool filling.

CARPET LOOM
Carpet power loom was invented by Erastus Brigham Bigelow of West Boylston, Mass., who obtained patent No. 169 on April 20, 1837. It was employed by the Lowell Manufacturing Company of Lowell, Mass., in the weaving of carpets.

Carpet power loom to weave Axminster carpets was invented in 1876 by Halcyon Skinner, employed by the Alexander Smith & Sons Carpet Company of Yonkers, N.Y. Axminster carpets have a fluffy thick pile with a

linen or hemp warp and chenille filling. Skinner obtained patent No. 186,374 on January 16, 1877, jointly with Alexander Smith.

Carpet power loom to weave ingrain carpets was used by the Lowell Manufacturing Company of Lowell, Mass. In 1841 the company adopted the power machinery invented by Erastus Brigham Bigelow, and within two years hundreds of the machines were in operation.

CARPET SWEEPER that was practical was invented in 1876 by Melville Reuben Bissell of Grand Rapids, Mich., who obtained patent No. 182,346 September 19, 1876. Although the idea had been introduced earlier, no practical sweeper was invented until he devised the "broom-action" principle by which, through variable pressure on the handle, a sweeper could be made responsive to the different grades of floor coverings. Bissell organized the Bissell Carpet Sweeper Company in Grand Rapids, Mich.

CARPETING
Carpeting of tufted plastic was manufactured at La Fayette, Ga., by the E. T. Barwick Mills and offered for sale January 4, 1953, for April 1, 1953, delivery. The carpeting, made of Saran fibers, is immune to moths, mildew, and fungi and is almost completely resistant to ink and other stains. It will soften, char, and decompose in flame, but will not support combustion.

Carpeting (velvet) and tapestry were manufactured in Newark, N.J., in 1855 by John Johnson.

CARRIAGE (baby). *See* Baby carriage

CARRIAGE LAP ROBE. *See* Blanket: Blanket robe and carriage lap robe business

CARRIER (aircraft). *See* Ship: Aircraft carrier

CARRIER (commercial electric power line). *See* Electric transmission: Electric power line commercial carrier

CARRIER SYSTEM. *See* Cash carrier system

CARROUSEL
Carrousel patent was No.117,336, granted on July 25, 1871, to Willhelm Schneider of Davenport, Iowa. It was a two-story carrousel and not very successful or practical.

Carrousel with the jumping horse mechanism was invented by Charles Wallace Parker of the C. W. Parker Amusement Company, Leavenworth, Kan. He started manufacturing it in 1896 and completed it in April 1898 in Abilene, Kans. The first one was sold to his brother, William T. Parker.

Portable carrousel was a "Carry-Us-All" manufactured in 1896 in Abilene, Kan., by the C. W. Parker Amusement Company. It weighed 20 tons and consisted of 16 sections.

CARTEL. *See* Trust: Cartel

CARTOON
See also Caricature; Newspaper: Newspaper Sunday comic section

Cartoon awarded a Pulitzer prize was "On the Road to Moscow," by Rollin Kirby, which appeared August 5, 1921, in the New York *World.* The award of the $500 prize was announced on May 21, 1922.

Democratic cartoon, in which the emblem of the party was represented as a donkey appeared in *Harper's Weekly,* New York City, January 15, 1870. The drawing, by Thomas Nast, was entitled "A Live Jackass Kicking a Dead Lion." The jackass was tagged "Copperhead papers" and the dead lion represented Edwin McMasters Stanton, Lincoln's Secretary of War. The background showed an eagle perched on a rock and in the far background the United States Capitol. *(Albert Bigelow Paine—"Th. Nast")*

Newspaper cartoon was "Join or Die" designed by Benjamin Franklin and published in Philadelphia, Pa., in his newspaper, the *Pennsylvania Gazette,* on May 9, 1754. It was printed in the first column of the second page and was 2⅞ by 2 inches. It depicted a snake cut up into segments, each representing a colony. *(James Melvin Lee—History of American Journalism)*

Newspaper cartoon strip was published September 11, 1875, in the New York *Daily Graphic* and showed seventeen successive pictures on one full page. It was entitled "Professor Tigwissel's Burglar Alarm."

Republican cartoon, in which the emblem of the party was represented as an elephant, appeared in *Harper's Weekly,* New York City, November 7, 1874. The drawing by Thomas Nast was entitled "The Third-Term Panic" and referred to the possibility that Grant might seek a third term. It depicted an ass, labeled "N.Y. Herald" in a lion's skin labeled "Caesarism," frightening numerous timid animals labeled "N.Y. Times," "N.Y. Trib.," etc., while a berserk elephant, labeled "Republican vote," about to fall into "Chaos," tossed platform planks to right and left. The quotation, "An

Ass having put on the Lion's skin, roamed about the Forest, and amused himself by frightening all the foolish Animals he met with in his wanderings," accompanied the title.

Uncle Sam cartoon appeared in the New York *Lantern,* a comic weekly, on March 13, 1852. It was called "Raising the Wind" and depicted the struggle between a United States shipowner and the Cunard Company, with John Bull actively helping his line while Uncle Sam was an onlooker. The cartoonist was Frank Henry Temple Bellew. The original "Uncle Sam" was Samuel Wilson of New Hampshire, who was the official inspector in Troy, N.Y., of provisions purchased for the United States troops in the War of 1812. All shipments as inspected were branded "U.S." by Wilson, whose nickname was "Uncle Sam." The coincidence of initials suggested the application of the nickname to the government.

CARTOON ELECTRIC SIGN. *See* Electric sign: Animated cartoon electric sign

CARTOON SCHOOL giving courses in the production of animated cartoons was the Hastings School of Animation, New York City, organized February 1938. Instruction began April 1938.

CARTRIDGE. *See* Ordnance: Cartridge loading machinery

CARTRIDGE BELT patent was No. 67,898 granted on August 20, 1867, to Anson Mills, Brevet Lieutenant Colonel, U.S. Army, Fort Bridger, Utah. Moisture had previously affected the cartridge belts. Mills invented a woven cartridge belt, and the machinery for making it, which was adopted by both the Army and Navy. *(Anson Mills—My Story)*

CARTRIDGE LOADING MACHINE. *See* Ordnance: Cartridge loading machinery

CASEIN FIBER was produced December 1935 by Earle Ovando Whittier and Stephen Philip Gould of Washington, D.C., who obtained patent No. 2,140,274 on December 13, 1938, and dedicated it "to the free use of the people of the United States of America."

CASH CARRIER SYSTEM was invented by David Brown of Lebanon, N.J., who obtained patent No. 165,473 on July 13, 1875, on "an apparatus for transmission of goods, packages, etc." It had a wire rail with endless rope pulleys. William Stickney Lamson installed it in his ladies' furnishing store in Lowell, Mass., in February 1879. By means of two overhead wires, a small basket was conveyed from the salesman to the cashier. In the spring of 1881, he organized the Lamson Consolidated Store

THE FIRST

CASH CARRIER SYSTEM—_Continued_
Service Company to manufacture these carriers for others and in January 1882 incorporated the Lamson Cash Railway Company. _(Frank Pierce Hill—Lowell Illustrated)_

CASH REGISTER was invented in 1879 by James J. (Jake) Ritty, a businessman of Dayton, Ohio, who while on a trip to Europe observed the workings of a recording device on the steamship which marked the revolutions of the ship's propeller and gave to its officers each day a complete and accurate record of the speed of the boat. He returned to the United States and invented a machine for registering receipts of cash and totaling them. He manufactured the machine in Dayton, but it was not accurate, and in the following year, 1880, he produced a machine that gave some evidence of being practical. James Ritty and John Ritty of Dayton obtained patent No. 221,360 on a "cash register and indicator" on November 4, 1879. In 1884 the National Cash Register Company took over the business, which in 5 years' time had gone through three changes, and developed from a plant with 20 workmen to an organization with a staff of more than 15,000 persons. _(Brief History of the Cash Register —National Cash Register Co.)_

CAST IRON BRIDGE. _See_ Bridge: Cast iron bridge

CAST IRON BUILDING. _See_ Building: Building constructed wholly of cast iron

CAST IRON PIPES (city waterworks). _See_ Iron: Cast iron pipes used in a city waterworks system

CAST STEEL. _See_ Steel: Cast steel for plows

CASTER for furniture was patented by Philos Blake, Eli Whitney Blake, and John A. Blake, of New Haven, Conn. They were awarded patent No. 821 on June 30, 1838, on a "mode of constructing casters and applying them to bedsteads."

CATALOG (automobile). _See_ Automobile catalog

CATALOG (fraternity). _See_ Fraternity catalog

CATALOG (stamp). _See_ Postage stamp catalog

CATALOG OF THE LIBRARY OF CONGRESS. _See_ Library catalog: Catalog of the Library of Congress

THE FIRST

CATALYTIC CRACKING PROCESS. _See_ Gasoline: Aviation gasoline

CATAMARAN, a jointed boat, used principally by life guards at public beaches, was patented by Nathanael Greene Herreshoff of Providence, R.I., who received patent No. 189,459 on April 10, 1877, on two parallel hulls.

CATAPULTED AIRPLANE. _See_ Aviation —Flights: Airplane catapulted

CATCHER'S MASK. _See_ Baseball catcher's mask

CATERPILLAR CLUB
Caterpillar Club member was John Boettner, pilot of the "Wing Foot" balloon of the Goodyear Tire and Rubber Company, Akron, Ohio, who parachuted 1,200 feet to safety on July 21, 1919, while his balloon crashed into a building at La Salle Street and Jackson Boulevard, Chicago, Ill. The crash resulted in the death of 3 persons and injuries to 28. "Caterpillar Club" is a name used to designate those persons whose lives have been saved by parachute jumps from aircraft in distress. _(Office of the Chief of the Air Corps—Roster of the Caterpillar Club)_

Father and son Caterpillar Club members were Paul Fisk Collins, who jumped November 19, 1928, north of Brookville, Pa.; and Lieutenant Paul Liske Collins, who jumped on February 11, 1944, 50 miles south of Fairbanks, Alaska.

Woman Caterpillar Club member was Mrs. Irene McFarland, who jumped from her plane June 28, 1925, over Grissard Field, Cincinnati, Ohio. She tested a parachute which was packed in a container fastened to the plane, so that when she jumped her weight would cause the container to break and permit the parachute to slip and blow out. Officials also required her to use an army parachute. She jumped and her parachute jammed, suspending her under the fuselage, from which she swung like a pendulum. She could not release herself and Lieutenant Watson, her pilot, could not land. He motioned to her to release the army parachute, which she did, the force breaking the cords which held her tied to the airplane. Had the original parachute worked Mrs. McFarland would not have been eligible for membership in the Caterpillar Club.

CATHEDRAL
Cathedral was the Cathedral of the Assumption of the Blessed Virgin Mary, in Baltimore, Md., a primatial see of the Catholic Church. The cornerstone was laid July 7, 1806, and the building was dedicated May 31, 1821, by Archbishop Ambrose Marechal. It

was completed in 1851. In 1936, the Baltimore Cathedral was raised to the rank of a minor basilica by Pope Pius XI. The first diocese (of Baltimore) was created by Pope Pius VI on November 6, 1789.

Episcopal cathedral was the Cathedral of Our Merciful Saviour, Faribault, Minn., built by the Right Reverend Henry Benjamin Whipple, First Bishop of Minnesota, as his own church. The cathedral was begun in 1862 and completed in 1869 at a cost of $100,000. A tower was added in 1902.

Serbian Orthodox cathedral. *See* Serbian Orthodox cathedral

CATHOLIC APOSTOLIC DELEGATE

(permanent) was Monsignor Francesco Satolli, representative of Pope Leo XIII, who arrived January 24, 1893, in Washington, D.C. He was created Cardinal November 29, 1895, with the title of Santa Maria in Ara Coeli. (*Catholic University Bulletin. Vol. 16, No. 2. Feb. 1910*)

CATHOLIC BEATIFICATION

Catholic beatification of an American citizen took place at St. Peter's Basilica, Rome, Italy, November 13, 1938, when Mother Frances Xavier Cabrini, founder of the Institute of the Missionary Sisters of the Sacred Heart, was beatified.

Catholic beatification of an American Indian took place on May 9, 1939, when the Cardinals of the Congregation of Rites in Rome, Italy, recommended the beatification of Kateri Tekakwitha, "the lily of the Mohawks," who was born in 1656 at Ossernenon, near Auriesville, N.Y. Their decision was sanctioned by Pope Pius XII on May 19, 1939.

CATHOLIC BIBLE. *See* Bible: Catholic bible

CATHOLIC BISHOP

See also Catholic priest

Catholic bishop to exercise episcopal functions was Frai Juan Cabezas de Altamirano, son of Juan Cabezas and Doña Ana Calzado, appointed Bishop of Santiago de Cuba in 1603. He visited the Provinces of Florida in 1607 and at St. Augustine administered the sacrament of confirmation to many Spaniards and converted Indians.

Catholic bishop appointed to serve in the United States was the Right Reverend John Carroll, "Superior of the Missions in the thirteen United States of North America." A

petition for appointment of a bishop was sent to Pope Pius VI on March 12, 1788, and was acted upon favorably June 23, 1788. Bishop Carroll received 24 of the 25 votes, and the result was confirmed by the Pope on November 6, 1789. The Right Reverend Charles Walmesley (Bishop of Rama and Vicar Apostolic of the Western District, England), consecrated John Carroll bishop August 15, 1790, in the chapel of Lulworth Castle, Dorset, England. On April 8, 1808, he became an archbishop. (*An Account of the Consecration by One Bishop of the First Romish Bishop in the United States*)

Catholic bishop (Negro) was Bishop James Augustine Healy, consecrated June 21, 1875 as Bishop of Portland, Me., with jurisdiction over Maine and New Hampshire. He was ordained a priest in 1854 in Paris, and was assigned to St. James' Church (white), Boston, Mass., in 1866.

Catholic bishop (Negro) consecrated in the United States was Bishop Joseph Oliver Bowers, consecrated on April 22, 1953, by Francis Cardinal Spellman at the Church of Our Lady of the Gulf, Bay St. Louis, Miss.

Native bishops of the South were the Right Reverend Domenic Manucy, Bishop of Mobile, and his cousin Anthony Dominic Ambrose Pellicier, Bishop of San Antonio, who were ordained August 15, 1850, in Mobile, Ala. They were born in St. Augustine and educated at Spring Hill College, Ala. (*Francis Xavier Reuss—Biographical Cyclopedia of the Catholic Hierarchy*)

CATHOLIC CANONIZATION of North

Americans took place in a three-day celebration commencing June 30, 1930. Each of those canonized was credited with having performed two miracles and having met a heroic death. The laymen were René Goupil and John Lalande. The Jesuit priests were Isaac Jogues, John De Brébeuf, Noel Chabanel, Anthony Daniel, Gabriel Lalemant, and Charles Garnier. The Pontifical Mass was celebrated at the Vatican by Archbishop Forbes of Ottawa, Canada.

CATHOLIC CHAPLAIN (U. S. Army).

See Army officer: Chaplain (Catholic)

CATHOLIC CHURCH

Catholic church raised to the dignity of a basilica was the Sanctuary of Our Lady of Victory, Lackawanna, in the Diocese of Buffalo, N.Y. It was dedicated and consecrated on May 25, 1926, as Our Lady of Victory Shrine, and on July 28 by Apostolic Decree of Pope Pius XI it was dignified with the title of "Basilica of Our Blessed Lady of Victory."

THE FIRST

CATHOLIC CHURCH—*Continued*
Catholic parish church for Negroes was St. Francis Xavier's, Baltimore, Md., purchased October 10, 1863, and dedicated February 21, 1864.

CATHOLIC COLLEGE. *See* College: Catholic college

CATHOLIC CONVENT. *See* Convent

CATHOLIC DIOCESE was the Diocese of Baltimore, Md., established April 6, 1789, and raised to the dignity of the first Archdiocese in the United States, April 8, 1808. By a decree of the Sacred Congregation of the Propaganda, July 19, approved by Pius IX, July 5, 1858, prerogative of place was conferred on the Archdiocese of Baltimore, so that it is known as "The Premier See" of the country.

CATHOLIC FUNERAL
Catholic funeral attended by the U.S. Continental Congress was that of Philippe Charles Jean Baptiste Tronson du Coudray, French officer. On September 15, 1777, while crossing the Schuykill River at Middle Ferry on a ferry to join Washington's army, his horse became frightened and plunged overboard. Tronson du Coudray, who had assumed the post of inspector-general of the American Army, was drowned. Congress resolved that he should be buried with military honors and that the members of Congress should attend his funeral, which was held in Philadelphia, Pa., September 17, 1777. (*John Thomas Scharf and Thompson Wescott—History of Philadelphia*)

CATHOLIC HOLY ORDERS were conferred by Don Gabriel Díaz Vara Calderón, Bishop of Santiago de Cuba, on a visit to St. Augustine, Fla., August 24, 1675. Minor orders were conferred on seven candidates.

CATHOLIC MAGAZINE
Catholic magazine was the weekly journal *Courier de Boston*, which appeared on April 23, 1789, and continued publication weekly for six months. It was published in French in Boston, Mass., and was edited by Paul Joseph Guérard de Nancrède, instructor in French at Harvard University. (*Apollinaris William Baumgartner—Catholic Journalism*)

Catholic magazine in English was the *Michigan Essay or Impartial Observer*, a weekly, which was issued August 31, 1809. It was printed and published in Detroit, Mich., by James M. Miller and was only semi-Catholic in scope. The idea was advocated by the Reverend Gabriel Richard of Detroit. The weekly consisted of 4 pages, 9¼ by 16 inches, of which a small part was printed in French. The rates

THE FIRST

were: $5 a year for subscribers living in the city; $4.50 in upper Canada; and $4 elsewhere. (*Paul J. Folk—Pioneer Catholic Journalism*)

CATHOLIC MASS
Catholic Mass was celebrated June 1526 in the present territory of the United States by the Dominican Fathers Antonio Montesino and Antonio de Cervantes, for the several hundred colonists under the leadership of Lucas Vásquez de Ayllón on the Atlantic coast. Masses may also have been said for the earlier Norse explorers.

Catholic Mass for nightworkers was held May 5, 1901, at the Church of St. Andrew, New York City. Father Luke J. Evers obtained special permission from the Pope to institute this service as church law did not permit mass before sunrise.

Catholic Mass in an airship over the ocean was conducted in the Zeppelin "Hindenburg" May 7, 1936, the Feast of the Apparition of St. Michael the Archangel, by Father Paul Schulte of the Oblates of Mary Immaculate.

Catholic Mass in an airship over the ocean by an American priest was conducted in the Zeppelin "Hindenburg" on August 6, 1936, by Father James Renshaw Cox of St. Patrick's Church, Pittsburgh, Pa.

Catholic Mass (midnight) telecast. *See* Television—Telecast: Catholic Mass (midnight) to be televised

CATHOLIC NEGRO UNIVERSITY. *See* College: Negro university (Catholic)

CATHOLIC NUNS
See also Convent

Catholic nuns (cloistered community) were the Magdalen Sisters at the Convent of the Good Shepherd, Baltimore, Md., founded April 24, 1922.

Catholic nuns (colored community) were the Oblate Sisters of Providence, founded by Jacques Hector Nicholas Joubert de la Muraille on July 2, 1829, in Baltimore, Md. Pope Gregory XVI approved the order October 2, 1831.

Nun who professed her vows in the United States was Sister St. Stanislas Hachard of the Ursuline Convent, New Orleans, La., who took her holy vows March 15, 1729. (*The Ursulines in New Orleans and Our Lady of Prompt Succor*)

THE FIRST

Nun who was born in the United States was Mary Turpin of Illinois, born in 1731, who entered the Ursuline Convent, New Orleans, La., in 1748. She began her novitiate July 2, 1749, and made her profession of faith January 31, 1752. She died November 20, 1761, at the age of 30.

CATHOLIC PARISH was the parish of St. Augustine, Fla., founded September 8, 1565, on the day of the Feast of the Nativity of the Blessed Virgin, by Don Pedro Menéndez de Avilés. The first parish register is also owned by this church and consists of fifteen volumes beginning January 1, 1594, and continuing down to the time of the British occupation of Florida in 1763. The first parish priest was Don Martín Francisco López de Mendozo Grajales.

CATHOLIC PRESIDENT. *See* President (United States) : President who was a Catholic

CATHOLIC PRESIDENTIAL NOMINEE. *See* Presidential candidate: Presidential candidate who was a Catholic

CATHOLIC PRIEST
See also Catholic bishop

Catholic cardinal whose see was west of the Rockies was James Francis Cardinal McIntyre, Archbishop of Los Angeles, who was elevated to the Sacred College of Cardinals on January 12, 1953, by Pope Pius XII.

Catholic priest ordained in the United States was Father Stephen Theodore Badin, ordained May 25, 1793, by Bishop John Carroll at the Cathedral of St. Peter, Baltimore, Md. He was appointed to the Mission of Kentucky and held his first mass in Kentucky on the first Sunday of Advent, 1793, in the house of Dennis McCarthy in Lexington, Ky. *(Benedict Joseph Webb—Centenary of Catholicity in Kentucky)*

Catholic priest to be elevated to the cardinalate was John McCloskey who was preconized cardinal in the Consistory of March 15, 1875. The investiture was made in the cathedral on Mott Street, New York City, on April 27, 1875. He was made a cardinal under the title of "Santa Maria supra Minervam."

Catholic priest to receive his full theological training in the United States was Demetrius Augustine Gallitzin (Dimitri Augustin Golitzyn) who was ordained a Catholic bishop by Bishop John Carroll on March 18, 1795, in Baltimore, Md. *(Sarah M. Brownson—Life of Demetrius Augustine Gallitzin)*

THE FIRST

Native Catholic priest was Father Francisco de Florencia, who joined the Jesuit order in 1643. He was born in St. Augustine, Fla., in 1620. *(Francisco de Florencia—Origen de los Dos Célebres Santuarios de la Nueva-Galicia Obispado de Guadalaxara en la América Septentrional)*

Negro Catholic priest ordained to work in the United States was the Reverend Augustus Tolton. He was ordained at the College of Propaganda, Rome, Italy, on April 24, 1886, and opened a mission in Quincy, Ill., in the Diocese of Springfield (Ill.) *(John Thomas Gillard—The Catholic Church and the American Negro)*

Negro Catholic priest ordained in the United States was Charles Randolph Uncles, who was ordained in the Baltimore Cathedral, Baltimore, Md., December 19, 1891, by Cardinal Gibbons.

Roman Catholic priest to serve in Congress. *See* Congressman (U.S.): Roman Catholic priest to serve in Congress

CATHOLIC PROVINCIAL COUNCIL of the Roman Catholic Church convened in Baltimore, Md., October 4, 1829, and consisted of 5 prelates. Four bishops were unable to attend. The council enacted 28 decrees. The first plenary session of the National Council assembled in Baltimore, Md., May 10, 1852, and consisted of 6 archbishops, 23 bishops, 40 theologians, and 18 other ecclesiastics. *(Henry Stanislaus Spalding—Catholic Colonial Maryland)*

CATHOLIC SAINT. *See* Saint (Catholic)

CATHOLIC SEMINARIANS (Negro) to be ordained to the priesthood by a Negro bishop were ordained on June 29, 1953, by Bishop Joseph Oliver Bowers, S.V.D., at St. Augustine's Seminary, Bay St. Louis, Miss.

CATHOLIC SEMINARY for the education of Negro priests was opened by the Missionaries of the Society of the Divine Word, at Bay St. Louis, Miss., and was dedicated September 16, 1923.

CATHOLIC SETTLEMENT (permanent) was made in 1565 in St. Augustine, Fla., where a Catholic congregation was founded.
See also Catholic Mass: Catholic Mass

CATHOLIC STUDENT to seek admission to the American College of the Roman Catholic Church of the United States, a pontifical college

THE FIRST

THE FIRST

CATHOLIC STUDENT—*Continued*
founded in Rome, Italy, on December 8, 1859, was Michael Augustine Corrigan. He was consecrated May 4, 1873, in St. Patrick's Cathedral, Newark, N.J., as Bishop of Newark. He was later made an archbishop, the palladium being conferred on him on March 4, 1881.

CATHOLIC WORK written by an American Catholic was published in Annapolis, Md., in 1784. The author was John Carroll, whose article was entitled "An Address from the Roman Catholics of the United States of North America," and answered an attack made by an ex-Jesuit. (*Daniel Brant—Biographical Sketch of . . . John Carroll, First Archbishop of Baltimore*)

CATTLE. *See under* Animals

CATTLE BRANDING LEGISLATION (state). See Branding legislation

CATTLE CLUB
See also Dairy Breed Organization

Cattle club (Guernsey cattle) was the American Guernsey Cattle Club, formed March 1, 1876, at the home of Augustus Ward, Farmington, Conn. A permanent organization was effected February 7, 1877, when eleven men from five states met in New York City. The first annual meeting was held December 19, 1877.

Cattle club (Jersey cattle) was the American Jersey Cattle Club, formed July 1868, at Newport, R.I., by forty-three dairymen who signed a tentative constitution. The first annual meeting was held April 5, 1869, at the Astor House, New York City. It was incorporated May 25, 1880. Its object was to record and perpetuate the breed of Jersey cattle. The first president was Samuel J. Sharpless of Philadelphia, Pa. Colonel George E. Waring was secretary, and Thomas J. Hand, treasurer. (*Robert M. Gow—The Jersey*)

CAUCUS (Congressional). *See* Congressional caucus

CAVALRY UNIT. *See* Army: Cavalry unit

CELESTIAL PHOTOGRAPH. *See* Photograph: Celestial photograph

CELLOPHANE was made in the early part of 1924 by the Du Pont Cellophane Company at its plant in Buffalo, N.Y., with machinery manufactured in its own shops. Cellophane originally sold for $2.65 a pound. (*Du Pont Magazine. Fall 1925*)

CELLULOID was invented by John Wesley Hyatt of Albany, N.Y., and Isaiah Smith Hyatt of Rockford, Ill., who obtained patent No. 91,341 on June 15, 1869. This invention won a $10,000 prize offered by Phelan & Collender of New York City for a substitute for ivory in billiard balls. The inventors dissolved pyroxyline and camphor in alcohol, then subjected the mixture to heat and pressure in molds. They began manufacturing it in 1872, organized the Newark Celluloid Manufacturing Company, and obtained United States trademark registration No. 1102 on January 14, 1873, on the word "celluloid," which they derived from the combination of *cellulose* and *-oid*, meaning "like." (*Edward Chauncey Worden—Nitro-Cellulose Industry*)

CELLULOID PHOTOGRAPHIC FILM. *See* Photographic film: Celluloid photographic film

CELLULOSE NITRATE PATENT was No. 4,874, issued to Christian Frederick Schoenbein of Basle, Switzerland, on December 5, 1846. It covered the use of cotton wool in an explosive compound. He obtained an English patent on October 8, 1846.

CELLULOSE SPONGE. *See* Sponge: Oxidized cellulose (sponge)

CEMENT
Cement was introduced into the United States from England about 1870. Because of its weight it was brought over as ballast. American portland cement was invented by David Oliver Saylor of Allentown, Pa., who perfected a process for making hydraulic cement from argillo-magnesium and argillo calcareous limestone and received patent No. 119,413 on September 26, 1871. European cement was regarded as superior and it was not until 1897 that the use of American cement exceeded importations from Europe. (*Cement and Concrete—Portland Cement Association*)

Natural cement rock was discovered in 1818 by Canvas White near Fayetteville, Onondaga County, N.Y. He obtained a patent on a cement manufacturing process which he sold to New York State for $10,000. (*Robert Whitman Lesley—History of the Portland Cement Industry in the United States*)

CEMENT STADIUM. *See* Stadium: Cement stadium

CEMETERY
Congressional cemetery was established in Washington, D.C., in a section of Christ Church known as the Washington Parish Burial Ground. Records show that burials were made early in 1804 but the date of the deed which is

THE FIRST

recorded is March 31, 1812. The cemetery at 18th and E Streets, S.E., is more familiarly known as the Congressional Cemetery and occupies thirty acres alongside the Anacostia River.

Federal cemetery in the United States to contain graves of both Union and Confederate soldiers was opened in Springfield, Mo., by act of Congress dated March 3, 1911 (36 Stat.L.1077). The Confederate cemetery, which was maintained by the state of Missouri prior to 1911, was deeded to the Federal Government on June 21, 1911. A stone wall separates the graves of the Confederate troops from those of the Union soldiers. The cemetery contains over 3,100 graves. (*Jonathan Fairbanks and Clyde Edwin Tuck—Past and Present of Greene County, Mo.*)

Foreign service women interred in the Arlington National Cemetery, Arlington, Va., were Section Officer Monica M. Daventry of Worcester, England, and Section Officer Ruth P. Watson of Hampstead, England, members of the British Women's Auxiliary Air Force, interred November 19, 1942. Returning from duty, they were killed in an automobile accident. American soldiers served as pallbearers and twelve Waves as honorary pallbearers.

Jewish burial plot was established by Congregation Shearith Israel in 1656. The plot occupied a piece of ground in the section now known as Chatham Square, New York City. (*American Jewish Historical Society Publications. Vol. 18*)

National cemeteries as they exist today were authorized by the Act of July 17, 1862 (12 Stat.L.596). Prior to this act a number of cemeteries had been established for the burial of military dead, although it was not until later that they were designated "national cemeteries." Among these are the following: Mexico City (Mexico) National Cemetery, 1851; Ft. Leavenworth (Kan.) National Cemetery, 1861; Loudon Park (Baltimore, Md.) National Cemetery, 1861; Lexington (Ky.) National Cemetery, 1861; Soldiers' Home (Washington, D.C.) National Cemetery, 1861; and Cypress Hills (Brooklyn, N.Y.) National Cemetery, 1862. The national cemetery in Mexico City was established in 1851 although it was not designated as a national cemetery until the Act of July 17, 1862. (*Records in Office of the Quartermaster General, War Dept. Washington, D.C.*)

President buried in the National Cemetery at Arlington. *See* President: President buried in the National Cemetery at Arlington, Va.

THE FIRST

CENSORSHIP
State board of censorship on literature was appointed by Georgia in March 1953 under authority of an act approved February 19, 1953, "an act to provide for the creation, membership and compensation of a State Literature Commission; to provide for certain definitions; to provide for recommendations of prosecution by the commission; to provide for identification of 'literature'; to repeal conflicting laws; and for other purposes." The committee consisted of James Wesberry, chairman, Hubert Dyan, and William Boswell. Newspapers were not subject to review or censorship.

CENSORSHIP BOARD (moving pictures). *See* Moving picture censorship: Moving picture censorship board

CENSUS
Census in which the population of the United States exceeded 10,000,000 was fifth census, the census of 1830, which showed a population of 12,866,620. The tenth census, the census of 1880, listed the population as 50,155,783, the first over the 50,000,000 mark.

Census of the United States was authorized by act of March 1, 1790 (1 Stat.L.101), "providing for the enumeration of the inhabitants of the United States." The census compilation cost $44,377 and utilized the services of 17 marshals and 650 assistants. The enumeration, as of August 1, 1790, showed a population of 3,939,326 located in 16 states and the Ohio territory. Virginia with 747,610 was the most populous state. New York City had a population of 33,131, Philadelphia had a population of 28,522, and Boston had a population of 18,320. (*Bureau of Census—Story of the Census*)

Census which included the deaf, dumb and blind was taken in 1830. Previously, those so afflicted were not enumerated at all.

City to exceed 1,000,000 in population was New York City whose population according to the census of 1880 was 1,206,299, not including Brooklyn, which was then an independent city. New York City was also the first with a population exceeding 5,000,000. The population of the five boroughs of New York City was 5,620,048 in 1920.

State to exceed 5,000,000 in population was New York State, with a population, according to the census of 1880, of 5,082,871. According to the 1920 census, New York State with 10,385,227 was the first to exceed the 10,000,000 mark.

CENSUS—*Continued*
States to exceed 1,000,000 in population were New York State, 1,372,812; Virginia, 1,065,366; and Pennsylvania, 1,049,456, according to the 1820 census.

CENTER AISLE RAILROAD CAR. *See* Railroad car: Car with a center aisle

CENTRAL HEATING. *See* Heating system

CENTRAL STATISTICAL BOARD (U.S.) was created by Executive Order No. 6225, dated July 27, 1933, under authority vested in the President by the National Industrial Recovery Act "to formulate standards for and to effect coordination of the statistical services of the Federal Government incident to the purposes . . . of the National Industrial Recovery Act." It was organized August 9, 1933, and was originally composed of eight members. The first chairman was Winfield William Riefler. (*U.S. Budget Bureau—Statistical Standards Division—Report for the Period July 27, 1933-February 12, 1934*)

CENTRIFUGAL LOOP THE LOOP RAILWAY. *See* Loop the loop centrifugal railway

CENTRIFUGAL MILK SEPARATOR. *See* Cream separator: Centrifugal cream separator

CERAMICS SCHOOL was started by Ohio State University, Columbus, Ohio, in 1894 under the guidance and direction of Professor Edward Orton, Jr. (*Heinrich Ries and Henry Leighton —History of the Clay Working Industries in the United States*)

CERTIFICATES (gold). *See* Money: Gold certificates

CERTIFIED PUBLIC ACCOUNTANT. *See* Accountant

CERTIFIED SCHOOL PLAN FOR COLLEGE ENTRANCE. *See* College: College entrance "certified school plan"

CHAIN-STITCH SEWING MACHINE. *See* Sewing machine: Chain-stitch single-thread sewing machine

CHAIN STORE ORGANIZATION. *See* Business: Chain store organization

CHAIN STORES TAX. *See* Tax: Chain stores tax (state)

CHAIR
Dental chair. *See* Dental chair

Folding theater chair was invented by Aaron H. Allen of Boston, Mass., who obtained patent No. 12,017 December 5, 1854, on an "improvement in seats for public buildings."

Recumbent chair patent was No. 2,100, issued May 22, 1841, to Henry Peres Kennedy, a cabinet-maker and upholsterer of Philadelphia, Pa. A spiral spring was placed horizontally between the back rail of the seat and the front rail of the chair.

Rocking chair is believed to have been invented by Benjamin Franklin about 1760. This date is not verified and no authentic instance of a prior rocker has come to light. (*Walter Alden Dyer and Esther Stevens Fraser—The Rocking Chair, an American Institution*)

Steamer chair or deck chair was introduced in 1891 by Heinrich Conried, impresario of the Metropolitan Opera House, New York City. He built 500 chairs and formed the Ocean Comfort Company to distribute and rent them. At one time 5,000 chairs were on rental to steamship companies which did not provide their own chairs for the decks. The first rental contract was signed with Albert Ballin, general director of the Hamburg-American lines. (*Montrose Jonas Moses—Life of Heinrich Conried*)

CHAIR FACTORY was established by Lambert Hitchcock in Hitchcockville (now Riverton) Conn., in 1818. The chairs were generally hand-painted on the back. They were shipped "knocked-down" and sold extensively in the South.

CHAMBER MUSIC ORGANIZATION. *See* Music: Chamber music organization

CHAMBER OF COMMERCE
Chamber of Commerce of the United States of America was founded in 1912 by approximately five hundred representatives of commercial organizations, trade associations, and individual establishments, who were invited to participate in a series of discussions by President William Howard Taft and Secretary of Commerce and Labor Charles Nagel. The headquarters of the Chamber of Commerce of the United States, one of the finest buildings in Washington, D.C., was dedicated May 20, 1925.

Chamber of Commerce (state) was the New York Chamber of Commerce, formed April 5, 1768, by twenty merchants at a meeting at Fraunces Tavern, New York City. John Cruger was the first president, and Anthony Van Dam the first secretary. The preamble

THE FIRST

to a resolution adopted at that time reads: "Whereas Mercantile Societies have been found very useful in trading cities for promoting and encouraging commerce, supporting industry, adjusting disputes relative to trade and navigation, and procuring such laws and regulations as may be found necessary for the benefit of trade in general, etc. . . ." The Chamber of Commerce was incorporated March 13, 1770, under a royal charter from King George III. Its motto was "Non Nobis Nate Solum" (Not born for ourselves alone). *(Joseph Bucklin Bishop—A Chronicle of One Hundred and Fifty Years)*

Junior Chamber of Commerce was organized October 13, 1915, as the Young Men's Progressive Civic Association in St. Louis, Mo. The name was changed to the Junior Chamber of Commerce in 1918. On January 21, 1921, delegates from twenty-four cities assembled in St. Louis to establish the United States Junior Chamber of Commerce. The first national convention was held in St. Louis June 17-18-19, 1920. Henry Giessenbier, Jr., was elected president.

CHANDELIER. *See* Glass crystal chandelier

CHANNEL SWIMMER (American-born). *See* Woman: American woman to swim the English Channel

CHAPEL CAR. *See* Railroad car: Chapel car.

CHAPLAIN. *See under* Army officer; Naval officer

CHAPLAINS' SCHOOL

Army school for chaplains was the Army Chaplain School, Fort Monroe, Va., organized February 9, 1918. It was moved to Camp Taylor, Ky., on April 9, 1918.

Naval chaplains' school conducted by the U.S. Navy was the Chaplains' School, Naval Operating Base, Norfolk, Va., which held its first session February 23, 1942.

CHARITY BOARD (state) was the Massachusetts State Board of Charities established April 29, 1863 (Chapter 240—Acts of 1863). Five members and a general agent were sworn in October 7, 1863. Otis Norcross was the first chairman. The only compensation received by board members was traveling expenses.

CHAUTAUQUA ORGANIZATION was formed August 4, 1874, by the first Sunday School Teachers Assembly at a meeting held in Fair Point, N.Y., at the suggestion of John

THE FIRST

Heyl Vincent and Lewis Miller. On August 10, 1878, home study courses were offered and the name Chautauqua Literary and Scientific Circle adopted. *(Rebecca Richmond—Chautauqua, an American Place)*
See also Home study course

CHECK

Check sent by radio across the Atlantic Ocean. See Radio facsimile transmission: Check sent by radio across the Atlantic Ocean

Travelers' checks were devised in 1891 by Marcellus Fleming Berry, who was then General Agent of the American Express Company. In the first year only 248 checks amounting to $9,120 were sold. *(Alden Hatch—American Express)*

CHECK PHOTOGRAPHING DEVICE

was the Checkograph invented by George Lewis McCarthy, who received patent No. 1,748,489, February 25, 1930. Commercial manufacture was undertaken May 1, 1927, by the Eastman Kodak Company, Rochester, N.Y., which marketed the device as the "Recordak" and made the first installation May 1, 1928, at the Empire Trust Company, New York City. The machine photographs checks on 16mm motion picture film. The first application of the machine, other than by banking institutions, was made in 1929 by the United States Treasury. The first application in libraries was made in 1935 when the New York *Times* and the New York Public Library cooperated in photographing copies of the New York *Times* of World War I period on microfilm.

CHECK PROTECTORS were manufactured in 1870 and consisted of punches which perforated figure holes in paper. These protectors were not certain proof against forgeries. In June 1899, Libanus McLouth Todd completed the model of a check protector in a woodshed at 384 Gregory Street, Rochester, N.Y. He filed his application August 8, 1899, and placed the machine, which he called a "Protectograph," on the market in the fall of that year. The machine forced ink into the paper under pressure, making it part of the fiber of the document. He obtained patent No. 766,853, August 9, 1904. *(Jack W. Speare—Protecting the Nation's Money)*

CHECKMASTER PLAN. *See* Bank: Checkmaster plan

CHEESE

Liederkranz brand cheese of American origin was made in 1892 by Emil Frey in Monroe, N.Y. He was a cheesemaker for the Monroe Cheese Company, which was acquired in 1929 by the Borden Company. The cheese was named for the Liederkranz (wreath of songs) Club, New York City.

CHEESE—*Continued*
Pineapple cheese was made in 1808 by Lewis Mills Norton of Troy, Pa. On April 17, 1810, be obtained a patent on a "vat for forming pineapple cheese."

CHEESE FACTORY
Cheese factory cooperative was established by farmers of Cheshire, Mass., in 1801. On July 20, 1801, a cheese was pressed at the farm of Elisha Brown, Jr., which on August 20 weighed 1,235 pounds. It was placed on a wagon drawn by six horses and on January 1, 1802, presented to President Thomas Jefferson at the White House. *(Agricultural History— Vol. 18 No. 4)*

Cheese factory of consequence was established in Rome, N.Y., by Jesse Williams in 1851. It is referred to as the first permanent system of associated dairying in the United States. The first shipment of milk was received May 10, 1851. *(Benjamin Davis Gilbert—The Cheese Industry of the State of New York)*

CHEMICAL LABORATORY
Chemical laboratory for instruction in chemical analysis and chemistry as applied to the arts was established in Philadelphia in 1836 by James Curtis Booth. Charles Thomas Jackson opened a similar laboratory in Boston in 1836 for instruction and research in analytical chemistry, but it did not last long.

Chemical laboratory in a collegiate institution where instruction was offered to undergraduates was opened at Boylston Hall, Harvard University, Cambridge, Mass., in 1858. Josiah (Joseph) Parsons Cooke, author of numerous chemical books, was in charge of instruction.

CHEMICAL LABORATORY MANUAL was James Woodhouse's *Young Chemist's Pocket Companion*, a 56-page book which contained about a hundred experiments. It was published in 1797 in Philadelphia, Pa. *(Edgar Fahs Smith—James Woodhouse, a Pioneer in Chemistry)*

CHEMICAL MAGAZINE was the *Memoirs of the Columbian Chemical Society of Philadelphia*, which was printed by Isaac Peirce, 3 South Fourth Street, Philadelphia, Pa., in 1813-1814. The society was founded in 1811.

CHEMICAL SOCIETY
Chemical society in the world was the Chemical Society of Philadelphia, founded in 1792 by James Woodhouse. *(Edgar Fahs Smith —James Woodhouse, a Pioneer in Chemistry)*

Chemical society (national) was the American Chemical Society, organized in New York City April 20, 1876, although many meetings to form the society had been held previous to that date. The first president was John William Draper. The society was chartered November 9, 1877, as a non-profit, non-stock corporation of the State of New York "for the advancement of chemistry and the promotion of chemical research." *(Henry Carrington Bolton—Chemical Societies of the Nineteenth Century)*

CHEMICAL TEXTBOOK was Benjamin Rush's *Syllabus of a Course of Lectures on Chemistry* published in 1770 in Philadelphia, Pa. *(Harry Gehman Good—Benjamin Rush and His Services to American Education)*

CHEMICAL WARFARE CHIEF. *See* Army officer: Chemical warfare chief

CHEMISTRY NOBEL PRIZE WINNER. *See* Nobel prize: Nobel prize in chemistry

CHEMISTRY PROFESSOR
Chemistry professor who taught chemistry only, in a regularly appointed position in an educational institution of recognized standing, was Benjamin Rush, one of the signers of the Declaration of Independence. He gave lectures in chemistry at the Philadelphia Medical School, Philadelphia, Pa., as early as 1769. *(Lyman Churchill Newell. Chemical Education in America from the Earliest Days to 1820. Journal of Chemical Education. Vol. 9. April 1932)*

Professorship of applied chemistry was granted by Yale University, New Haven, Conn., to Benjamin Silliman, Jr. in 1846 although the Yale Analytical Laboratory did not open its doors to students until 1847. The Yale Analytical Laboratory was afterwards renamed the Sheffield Scientific School in honor of Joseph Earl Sheffield in recognition of his benefactions to the institution. *(Forris Jewett Moore—A History of Chemistry)*

CHENILLE MANUFACTURING MACHINE was made by William Canter of New York City who obtained patent No. 37,415 on January 13, 1863.

CHESS BOOK was *Chess Made Easy—New Comprehensive Rules For Playing the Game of Chess with Examples from Philidor, Cunningham, etc. to which is prefixed a pleasing account of its origin; some interesting anecdotes of several exalted personages who have been admirers of it; and the Morals of Chess written by the ingenious Dr. Franklin.* It consisted of 106 pages, including 8 pages of advertisements and a frontispiece, and was printed and sold in 1802 by James Humphreys of Philadel-

THE FIRST

THE FIRST

phia, Pa. Evidently it was a reprint of an English edition. *(Alfred C. Klahre—Early Chess in America)*

CHESS CHAMPION of the world (American-born) was Paul Charles Morphy, 20 years old, of New Orleans, La., who won first place at the First Chess Congress held in New York City from October 6, 1857, to November 10, 1857. He visited Europe and won the Grand Tournament of the First National Chess Association in England and France held from July 19, 1858, to August 22, 1858. He returned to New York City, May 11, 1859.

CHESS TOURNAMENT of importance was held October 6, 1857, by the American Chess Congress at the Descoule's Rooms, 764 Broadway, New York City, under the sponsorship of the New York Chess Club. The victor of the Grand Tournament was Paul Morphy, who received the first prize, a silver service consisting of a pitcher, four goblets, and a salver. A national organization, the American Chess Association, was formed October 10, 1857, in New York City. A. B. Meek was elected president of the Congress and Daniel Willard Fiske the secretary. *(Daniel Willard Fiske—Book of the First American Chess Congress)*

CHEVRON. *See* Army insignia: Chevrons

CHEWING GUM
    Chewing gum was the "State of Maine Pure Spruce Gum," manufactured in Bangor, Me., in 1848 by John Curtis and his brother on a Franklin stove. In 1850, they moved to Portland, Me., and made paraffin gums under the brands of "Licorice Lulu," "Four-in-Hand," "Sugar Cream," "Biggest and Best," and "White Mountain"; and also spruce gums, "Yankee Spruce," "American Flag," "Trunk Spruce," and "200 Lump Spruce." *(George Thomas Little—Genealogical and Family History of the State of Maine. Vol. 2)*

    Chewing gum patent was No. 98,304 issued on December 28, 1869, to William Finley Semple of Mount Vernon, Ohio, who claimed the "combination of rubber with other articles, in any proportions adapted to the formation of an acceptable chewing gum."

CHICKEN SHOW. *See* Poultry show

CHIEF ENGINEER (Continental army). *See* Army officer: Chief engineer

CHIEF JUSTICE. *See* Supreme Court (U.S.): Chief justice

CHILD BORN. *See* Births

CHILD DELINQUENCY law (state) was passed April 28, 1909, by Colorado. It defined as guilty, persons "who shall encourage, cause or contribute to the dependency, neglect or delinquency of a child."

CHILD HYGIENE BUREAU was established August 1908 in New York City with Dr. Sara Josephine Baker as director. It was "the first organization established under municipal control to deal with the health of children from birth to legal working age, in so far as a municipal Health Department may regulate and control the conditions of child life and health."

CHILD LABOR LAW
    See also Education: Compulsory education law

    Child labor law (federal) was passed September 1, 1916 (39 Stat.L.675), "an act to prevent interstate commerce in the products of child labor," the provisions of which were to be administered by the Children's Bureau. The government did not have the power to legislate directly in the field of labor so the attempt was made to regulate child labor through its power to legislate on interstate commerce. The act became effective September 1, 1917, but on June 3, 1918, it was declared unconstitutional by the Supreme Court as an invasion of states' rights.

    Child labor law regulating hours of employment was Chapter 60 of the laws of 1842 of Massachusetts, approved by Governor John Davis on March 3, 1842. Massachusetts prohibited children under 12 years of age from working more than 10 hours a day. Connecticut enacted a similar law which prohibited children under 14 years of age working more than 10 hours a day. *(Massachusetts Acts and Resolves. 1842)*

    Child labor law restricting the age of the worker was Pamphlet Law No. 278, approved March 28, 1848, by Governor Francis Rawn Shunk of Pennsylvania. The law prohibited children under 12 years of age from engaging in commercial labor. In 1849, the age limit was raised to 13 years. Similar legislation was enacted in 1853 by Rhode Island, in 1855 by Connecticut, and in 1866 by Massachusetts with age limits respectively of 12, 9, and 10 years.

    Child labor law to include educational provision was Chapter 245 passed by Massachusetts April 16, 1836, effective April 1, 1837. It required all children to attend school at least 3 months of the year, until they came to the age of 15. Manufacturers were not allowed to hire children in their mills for more than 9 months a year, but the children were conveniently transferred from mill to mill so that this legislation

THE FIRST

THE FIRST

CHILD LABOR LAW—*Continued*
was not effective. *(Miriam Elizabeth Laughran
—Historical Development of Child Labor Legislation in the United States)*

CHILD WELFARE CONGRESS. *See*
Children's Welfare Congress (International)

CHILDREN'S BOOK was John Cotton's
catechism *Milk for Babes, Drawn out of the
Breasts of Both Testaments, Chiefly for the
Spiritual Nourishment of Boston Babes in
either England: But may be of like use for any
children,* printed by Stephen Day in Cambridge, Mass., 1641-1645. No first edition has
been located and the reprints (one printed in
London, England, in 1646; and one printed for
Hezekiah Usher in Boston, Mass., by S[amuel]
G[reen], Cambridge Mass.) vary and appear
with different subtitles. *(Paul Leicester Ford
—The New England Primer)*

CHILDREN'S BUREAU (U.S.) was established in the Department of Commerce and
Labor, by act of Congress, April 9, 1912 (37
Stat.L.79) "to investigate and report . . . upon
all matters pertaining to welfare of children and
child life among all classes of our people." The
first chief, Julia Clifford Lathrop, was appointed
June 4, 1912, by President Woodrow Wilson
and confirmed by the Senate. *(James Alner
Tobey—The Children's Bureau)*

CHILDREN'S CHURCH. *See* Church:
Children's church

CHILDREN'S CLINIC. *See* Medical clinic:
Children's clinic

CHILDREN'S COURT. *See* Court: Juvenile court

CHILDREN'S HOSPITAL. *See* Hospital:
Children's hospital

**CHILDREN'S LIBRARY DEPART-
MENT.** *See* Library: Children's department
in a library

CHILDREN'S MAGAZINE. *See* Periodical: Children's magazine

CHILDREN'S PLAYGROUND. *See* Playground for children

**CHILDREN'S WELFARE CONGRESS
(international)** was the International Congress in America for the Welfare of the Child,
held March 10-17, 1908, in Washington, D.C.,
under the auspices of the National Congress of
Mothers. President Theodore Roosevelt addressed the congress.

CHIMES and bells as well as the first tower
clocks were manufactured by Benjamin Hanks,
who came to America in 1699, settling in
Plymouth, Mass.

CHINAWARE
Chinaware for restaurant use was made
by the Greenwood Pottery Company of Trenton,
N.J. in 1862. It combined the best qualities of
both porcelain and earthenware.

Dishes (complete set) made in America
for the Executive Mansion, Washington,
D.C., were ordered by President Woodrow
Wilson and delivered July 31, 1918. The set,
consisting of 1,700 pieces bearing the seal of the
President of the United States, was manufactured by Walter Scott Lenox of Lenox Incorporated, Trenton, N.J.

CHINCHILLA FARM. *See* Animals:
Chinchilla farm

CHINESE BROADCAST. *See* Radio
broadcast: All-Chinese commercial radio program

**CHINESE-DESCENT MARINE OF-
FICER.** *See* Marines: Marine officer of
Chinese descent

CHINESE EMBASSY was under the jurisdiction of Chen Lan-Pin, who presented his
papers as Envoy Extraordinary and Minister
Plenipotentiary to President Rutherford Birchard Hayes, October 4, 1878, in Washington,
D.C. Yung Wing was the associate minister,
a title which was afterward abolished. Accompanied by 34 persons, Chen Lan-Pin landed at
San Francisco, Calif., on July 25, 1878.

CHINESE GRANTED CITIZENSHIP.
See Citizenship: Chinese granted citizenship

CHINESE HOSPITAL. *See* Hospital:
Chinese hospital

CHINESE IMMIGRANTS. *See* Immigration: Chinese immigrants

CHINESE LABOR IMMIGRATION. *See*
Immigration: Chinese labor immigration

**CHINESE LANGUAGE AND LITERA-
TURE LECTURESHIP** was created by
Yale University, New Haven, Conn., in 1877.
Samuel Wells Williams, Commodore Oliver
Hazard Perry's secretary and interpreter in
Japan, was the lecturer.

CHINESE NEWSPAPER. *See* Newspaper; Chinese daily newspaper

CHINESE OFFICER IN MARINES. *See* Marines: Marine officer of Chinese descent

CHINESE PUBLIC SCHOOL. *See* Public school: Public school for Chinese

CHINESE STUDENTS were brought to the United States by the Reverend Samuel Robbins Brown, head of the Morrison School, the first English school in China. Three Chinese arrived April 12, 1847, in New York City and entered the Monson Academy, Monson, Mass. One of them, Yung Wing, entered Yale University, New Haven, Conn., in 1850 and graduated in 1854 with a B.A. degree, becoming the first Chinese to graduate in the United States. *(Yung Wing—My Life in China and America)*

CHINESE TELEPHONE EXCHANGE. *See* Telephone: Telephone switchboard or exchange for Chinese subscribers

CHINESE THEATER. See Theater: Chinese theater

CHINESE THEATRICAL PERFORM-ANCE. *See* Play (drama): Chinese theatrical performance

CHINESE TONG. *See* Tong (Chinese secret society)

CHINESE WOMEN'S CLUB. *See* Women's club: Chinese women's club incorporated

CHIROPODIST was Nehemiah Kenison, who was assisted by his brother and a cousin. They opened an office in 1840 directly opposite the Old South Church on Washington Street, Boston, Mass. They developed instruments and protective dressings which greatly aided in the relief of the pain caused by troublesome corns, etc.

CHIROPODY BOOK. *See* Medical book: Chiropody book

CHIROPODY LAW. *See* Medical legislation: Chiropody law governing the study of chiropody

CHIROPODY SCHOOL
Chiropody school as a regular division of a university opened September 20, 1915, at Temple University, Philadelphia, Pa. The chiropody clinic at the Garretson Hospital, an annex to Temple Hospital, opened April 6, 1915. Four students completed the thirty-four weeks' course June 1916 and received the degree of M.Cp. The course now covers four years and leads to the degree of D.S.C. (Doc-

tor of Surgical Chiropody). Dr. Frank Adoniram Thompson was the first dean of the school, and Dr. W. Ashton Kennedy and Dr. James Richardson Bennie were the first professors of chiropody. *(Pedic Items. May 1915)*

Chiropody school of note was the New York School of Chiropody, organized in 1910 by members of the Pedic Society of the State of New York, incorporated June 3, 1895. On January 1, 1913, it became the First Institute of Podiatry with Dr. Maurice J. Lewi as president. Its first graduating class in 1913 consisted of thirteen men and one woman. On November 16, 1939, it became affiliated with Long Island University, awarding the degree of Pod.D. (Doctor of Podiatry).

CHIROPRACTIC SCHOOL was the Palmer School of Chiropractic, Davenport, Iowa which opened in 1900. It was established by Daniel David Palmer.

CHIROPRACTOR was Daniel David Palmer, who gave the first adjustment treatment of vertebrae on September 18, 1895, to Harvey Lillard in Davenport, Iowa. *(Bartlett Joshua Palmer—Science of Chiropractic)*

CHLORINE WATER PURIFICATION. *See* Water purification: Water supply chemically treated with chlorine compounds

CHLOROFORM was distilled in 1831 by Dr. Samuel Guthrie in Sackets Harbor, N.Y. He called it "Chloric ether," and obtained it by distilling chloride of lime with alcohol in a copper still. He described it in "A New Mode of Preparing a Spirituous Solution of Chloric Ether." It is a colorless liquid known chemically as trichloromethane ($CHCl_3$). *(Edgar Fahs Smith—Chemistry in America)*

CHLOROMYCETIN
Chloromycetin laboratory established exclusively to produce chloromycetin by chemical means was opened on March 13, 1952, by Parke Davis & Company, Holland, Mich. The main processing building was longer than a football field and had a 40-foot ceiling. Chloromycetin was the first antibiotic to be produced commercially by synthesis.

CHLOROPHYLL
Chlorophyll was patented by Dr. Benjamin Grushkin of Philadelphia, Pa., who obtained patent No. 2,120,667 on June 14, 1938, on a "therapeutic agent for use in the treatment of infection." His application was dated December 1, 1937. The patent was assigned to the Lakeland Foundation, Chicago, Ill.

Chlorophyll "a" was synthesized June 27, 1960 by Professor Robert Burns Woodward at

THE FIRST

THE FIRST

CHLOROPHYLL—*Continued*
the Converse Memorial Laboratory, Harvard University, Cambridge, Mass. The chlorophyll molecule is composed of 55 atoms carbon, 72 atoms hydrogen, 5 atoms oxygen, 4 atoms nitrogen, and 1 atom magnesium.

CHOCOLATE MILL was erected beside the Neponset River at Dorchester, Mass., in 1765 and was operated by John Hannan. In 1780 Dr. James Baker purchased the mill, originating the present Walter Baker and Co.

CHOLERA EPIDEMIC. *See* Epidemic: Cholera epidemic

CHOP SUEY was concocted in New York City on August 29, 1896, by Chinese Ambassador Li Hung-Chang's chef, who devised this dish to appeal to both American and Oriental taste. Chop suey was unknown in China at the time. Li Hung-Chang and his suite of 18, attended by 22 servants, 5 valets, 3 cooks and a barber, arrived in New York City, August 28, 1896. He was greeted by President Grover Cleveland. *(Eng Ying Gong—Tong War)*

CHOREOGRAPHIC SCORE COPYRIGHTED. *See* Copyright law: Choreographic score copyrighted

CHRISTIAN SCIENCE church was founded by Mary Baker Eddy in Boston, Mass., in 1879, following her founding of this religion, and her issuing of its textbook, *Science and Health, with Key to the Scriptures* in 1875.

CHRISTMAS CARDS were engraved by Louis Prang at Roxbury, Mass., in 1874 for export to England. They were not introduced to American trade until 1875. *(Museum of the City of New York. Bulletin. Vol. 2. December 1938)*

CHRISTMAS CAROLS ASSOCIATION (national) was the National Christmas Carols Association, organized January 20, 1947, in St. Louis, Mo., with William Henry Danforth as president. The first local club was the St. Louis Christmas Carols Association, organized with nine members in 1911 in St. Louis. The first president was Elizabeth Hitchcock. Numerous groups of carol singers had existed previously and club organization was purely secondary.

CHRISTMAS SAVINGS CLUB. *See* Bank: Christmas savings club

CHRISTMAS SEAL. *See* Seal: Christmas seals of the modern variety

CHRISTMAS TREE, designated as the "Nation's Christmas Tree," was the General Grant Tree, in General Grant National Park, Calif., dedicated May 1, 1926, by Mayor Henry Leonard Suderman of Sanger, Calif., although a Christmas ceremony had been held at high noon Christmas Day 1925. The greatest horizontal diameter of the tree was 40.3 feet at the base, and at 200 feet above the ground, the diameter was about 12 feet. The tree was 267 feet high and 3,500-4,000 years old.

CHRISTOPHER COLUMBUS MONUMENT. *See* Monument: Monument to Christopher Columbus

CHROME TANNING. *See* Leather: Chrome tanned leather successfully manufactured; Leather: Chrome tanning process

CHROMIUM PLATING process (commercial) was invented in 1924 by Dr. Colin Garfield Fink, at Columbia University, New York City. He obtained patent No. 1,581,188 on April 20, 1926. He also received patent No. 1,802,463 on April 28, 1931, on a process of electro-depositing chromium and of preparing baths therefor which he assigned to the Chemical Treatment Co., Inc. *(Allen Gibbs Gray—Modern Electroplating)*

CHROMO was made in 1861 of John Banvard's painting "The Orison"—the interior of the St. Eustace convent in Italy. It was 16 by 24 inches and chromolithographed by Sarony, Major and Knapp. Proofs were $10, prints $5. *(South Dakota Historical Collections. 1942. Vol. 21)*

CHURCH
See also under names of religious organizations or sects, e.g., Buddhist Temple, Catholic Church, Federal Council of Churches, Mormon Temple, etc.; *also* Cathedral

Children's church built to scale and operated by children, was the Children's Church (Unitarian), Milton, Mass., dedicated November 14, 1937, by the Reverend Vivian Towse Pomeroy, pastor of the First Parish Unitarian Church, Milton, Mass. The miniature church was 18 feet by 32 feet, complete with steeple, belfry, organ, spire, and pews 2 feet 8 inches in height. It cost in excess of $5,000. The first pastor was the Reverend Mrs. Dorothy Pomeroy.

Church for the deaf. *See* Deaf—Church service: Church services for the deaf

Church without theology, creed, or dogma was organized by Richard Wolfe of Denver, Colo., in 1912. The First Liberal Church of

Denver, the first of the new sect, was organized in 1922. Wolfe became the first bishop of the Liberal Church of America.

Floating church was moored in the East River at the foot of Pike Street, New York City. It was constructed in 1843 and known as the Floating Church of Our Saviour. The church was organized by the Young Men's Church Missionary Society, an auxiliary of the City Mission Society. The society dissolved in 1844 and deeded the church to the Protestant Episcopal Church Missionary Society for Seamen in the City and Port of New York, an organization that emanated from the original group. The first clergyman was the Reverend Benjamin Clarke Cutler Parker, who was called by the title of "missionary," rather than clergyman. In 1906 the corporate title was changed to Seamen's Church Institute of New York. The work is now conducted in a large building at 25 South Street, New York City.

General Council of Congregational and Christian Churches was formed as the result of a merger of the National Council of Congregational Churches and the General Convention of Christian Churches held in Seattle, Wash., June 25-July 3, 1931. The first executive secretaries were the Reverend Charles Emerson Burton of New York City and the Reverend Warren Hathaway Dennison of Dayton, Ohio.

Mariners' church was built June 4, 1820, by the New York Port Society, as a nonsectarian, interdenominational church. The society was organized in May 1818 and was chartered, April 13, 1819, as the Society for Promoting the Gospel Among Seamen in the Port of New York. The first pastor was the Reverend Ward Stafford, who preached from 1818 to 1821. The society is still active and maintains the church at its headquarters, 524 West 42d Street, New York City.

Universal chapel embracing eight faiths was dedicated April 8, 1956, in the Universalist Church of the Divine Paternity, New York City. On its altar is a globe of the earth representing "human unity" and the symbols of eight religions—Buddhism, Christianity, Confucianism, Hinduism, Judaism, Shinto, Taoism, and Zoroastrianism.

Woman moderator of the General Council of Congregational and Christian Churches was Helen Kenyon of New York City, who was elected June 17, 1948, in Oberlin, Ohio.

CHURCH MILITARY SCHOOL. *See* Military school: Church military school

CHURCH OF ENGLAND
American bishop to become bishop of a British Church of England diocese was the Right Reverend Spence Burton, who was enthroned Bishop of the Church of England, diocese of Nassau, November 1, 1942, at Christ Church Cathedral, Nassau. He was suffragan bishop of Haiti, a missionary district of the Episcopal Church, from May 3, 1939, to September 1, 1942.

Church of England organized in New England was King's Chapel at the corner of Tremont and School Streets, Boston, Mass., built in 1686. The first minister was James Freeman, ordained November 17, 1785. (*Henry Wilder Foote—Annals of King's Chapel from the Puritan Age of New England to the Present Day*)

CHURCH OF JESUS CHRIST OF LATTER DAY SAINTS, more familiarly known as the Mormon Church, was organized on April 6, 1830, in Manchester, N.Y., with 30 members. Joseph Smith, its main organizer, declared that an angel of God had brought him the law. (*History of the Church of Jesus Christ—Church of Jesus Christ*)

CHURCH OF THE UNITED BRETHREN IN CHRIST was formed on Pentecost Sunday, May 18, 1766, at a meeting in Isaac Long's barn, Lancaster, Pa. by the Reverend Martin Boehm and the Reverend Philip William Otterbein. The first conference was held in 1789 at Otterbein's home in Baltimore, Md. Otterbein and Boehm were elected to the office of bishop in September 1800 at a conference. The first general conference at which delegates were regularly elected was held June 6, 1815, in Mount Pleasant, Pa. (*Reverend Daniel Berger—History of the Church of the United Brethren in Christ*)

CHUTE. *See* Postal service: Mail chute

CHUTE-THE-CHUTES. *See* Shoot-the-shutes

CIDER MILL was patented by Isaac Quintard of Stanfield, Conn., who obtained a patent April 5, 1806, on a cider and bark mill.

CIGAR BAND
Cigar band of special interest was prepared for cigars distributed at a dinner given by the Common Council of the City of New York on September 2, 1858, at the Metropolitan Hotel, New York City, to honor Cyrus West Field and the officers of the U.S. steam frigate "Niagara" and the British steamship H.B.M. "Gorgon" who had completed the laying of the Atlantic cable August 5, 1858. About 600 persons attended the dinner. The cigar bands, which were printed in black ink, depicted Field.

THE FIRST

THE FIRST

CIGAR FACTORY of importance was established by Simeon Viets in 1810 in West Suffield, Conn. He employed fifteen women and a foreman. His popular brands were "Windsors" and "Long Nines." *(General Executive Committee—Celebration of the 250th Anniversary of the Settlement of Suffield, Conn.)*

CIGAR LIGHTER PATENT was No. 121,049, granted to Moses F. Gale of New York City on November 21, 1871.

CIGAR ROLLING MACHINE (that was practical) was invented by Oscar Hammerstein of New York City, who obtained patent No. 272,958 on February 27, 1883.

CIGARETTE MANUFACTURING MACHINE was the Hook machine, which was invented by Albert H. Hook of New York City in 1872, but did not come into practical commercial use until 1882. As late as 1875 only 50 million cigarettes were made, according to revenue collection figures. The Hook machine was granted patent No. 184,207 on November 7, 1876. It produced a continuous cigarette of indefinite length, to be cut into separate cigarettes. Tobacco was fed to a ribbon of paper as it was drawn from a spool, the edges passing over a gummed wheel.

CIGARETTE TAX
Cigarette tax was levied by the United States under an act of June 30, 1864 (13 Stat.L.302), but the system of placing stamps on each package was not inaugurated until ordered by an act of July 20, 1868 (15 Stat.L. 155).

Cigarette tax (state) was established April 11, 1921, when Iowa enacted a tax applicable only to cigarettes, cigarette papers, and cigarette tubes. The tax on cigarettes was one mill on each cigarette ($1 per 1,000) and was effective July 4, 1921. This act repealed the then existing law prohibiting the sale of cigarettes in that state. *(Alfred Greher Buehler—General Sales Taxation, Its History and Development)*

CIRCUIT COURT JUSTICE (woman). *See* Judge: Woman associate justice of the Circuit Court of Appeals

CIRCULAR OFFICE BUILDING. *See* Building: Circular office building

CIRCULAR SAW. *See* Saw (circular)

CIRCULAR SCHOOL. *See* School: Circular school building

CIRCULATING LIBRARY. *See* Library: Circulating library

CIRCULATION AUDIT (newspaper). *See* Newspaper audit: Newspaper circulation audit

CIRCUS
See also Equestrian exhibition; Flea circus

Circus was owned by John Bill Ricketts and known as Ricketts' Circus. A building was erected especially for his use at 12th and Market Streets, Philadelphia, Pa., where he gave exhibitions as early as 1792. President George Washington attended Ricketts' Circus, April 22, 1793. Ricketts erected a larger building called the Art Pantheon and Amphitheatre, which opened to the public October 19, 1795, and in 1797 he built an Amphitheatre on Greenwich Street in New York. In 1797 he exhibited in other towns as far north as Albany, N.Y. *(American Antiquarian Society Proceedings. April 1933)*

Circus telecast. *See* Television—Telecast: Circus telecast

Circus to feature an automobile as an attraction was Wheeler, Hatch & Hitchcock's Circus and Royal Hippodrome, which toured New York, Massachusetts, Connecticut, and Rhode Island, in 1864. It exhibited a "tremendous novelty, never seen before, of an ordinary road carriage driven over the common high-ways without the aid of horses or other draught animals, being beyond doubt the most simple, useful and ingenious piece of mechanism ever put into practical use."

CIRCUS TIGHTS. *See* Tights (circus)

CITIZENS' MILITARY TRAINING CAMP. *See* Army camp: Army citizens' military training camp

CITIZENSHIP
See also Immigration

Chinese granted citizenship, after the repeal of the Chinese exclusion act, was Edward Bing Kan of Chicago, Ill., interpreter of the United States Immigration and Naturalization Service, who filed his application December 18, 1943, and was naturalized January 18, 1944, in Chicago. On December 17, 1943, President Franklin Delano Roosevelt signed the Chinese Act (57 Stat.L.600) "to repeal the Chinese exclusion acts, to establish quotas." This made Chinese residents eligible for naturalization and permitted the annual immigration of a quota of 105 Chinese. *(Department of Justice, Immigration and Naturalization Service. Monthly Review. Vol. 1, No. 10. April 1944)*

THE FIRST

THE FIRST

Citizenship (colonial) conferred by special grant was awarded by the General Assembly of Maryland at the session held November 1, 1784, to January 22, 1785, at Annapolis, Md. It provided that "the Marquis de Lafayette and his heirs male for ever, shall be, and they and each of them are hereby deemed, adjudged, and taken to be, natural born citizens of this state, and shall henceforth be entitled to all the immunities, rights and privileges, of natural born citizens thereof." *(Maryland. Acts of 1784. Chapter XII November session. William Paca, Governor)*

Citizenship granted to an alien on foreign soil was conferred December 4, 1942, in the Panama Canal Zone by Thomas Buckman Shoemaker, Assistant Commissioner of the Immigration and Naturalization Service, on Irish-born Private James Alexander Finnell Hoey. The Second War Powers Act of March 27, 1942 (56 Stat.L.176) authorized the Commissioner of Immigration and Naturalization to designate a representative who shall have power to naturalize "any person entitled to naturalization, who while serving honorably in the military or naval forces of the United States is not within the jurisdiction of any court authorized to naturalize aliens."

Indian citizenship statute. *See* Indians: Indian citizenship statute

Japanese granted citizenship was Joseph Heco, naturalized June 30, 1858, in the United States District Court, Baltimore, Md., before the Hon. William Fell Giles. His witnesses were Beverly C. Saunders and Thomas Spicer, clerk of the court. *(Joseph Heco—The Narrative of a Japanese)*

Naturalization act in the American colonies was provided for on March 12, 1664, in the letters patent of Charles II to James, the Duke of York, who was permitted to bring in subjects of the realm as well as "any other subjects who would become subjects." *(Joseph Willard —Naturalization in the American Colonies)*

CITIZENSHIP AND PUBLIC AFFAIRS SCHOOL was opened October 3, 1924, by Syracuse University, Syracuse, N.Y., through the generosity of George Holmes Maxwell. The first dean was William Eugene Mosher.

CITRON fruit grown commercially in any large quantity was raised by Edwin Giles Hart, who planted six thousand trees at La Habra, Calif., in 1925.

CITY (incorporated) in the colonies was Georgeana, now York, Me. Sir Ferdinando Gorges on December 2, 1631, received a grant of 24,000 acres on both sides of the Agamenti-

cus, or York, River and founded a town named after the river on April 10, 1641. It subsequently changed its name to Georgeana when it was incorporated on March 1, 1642. The name was later changed to York, Me. The charter embraced a territory of 21 square miles and the inhabitants were formed into a body politic. This was the first English charter for a city in America. Kittery, Me., was the first and oldest town in the state, whereas Georgeana was a city incorporate and not a town. *(George Alexander Emery—Ancient City of Georgeana and Modern Town of York, Me.)*

CITY (Lilliputian city) was built under the direction of William H. Johnson upon a carefully prepared townsite of five acres, with avenues, electric lights, and water mains, all to a scale of one inch to a foot, in Grant Beach Park, Springfield, Mo., June 6, 1925. Ten thousand children helped to build Tiny Town, which had 1,200 miniature structures, covering every aspect of a modern city. The town was conducted under the manager-commission form of government, the officers being school children. Conceived and constructed as an incentive to building, Tiny Town boosted building permits from a $280 daily average for the 90 days preceding its exhibition to $1,843 per day for the 90 days immediately following. Six years before the townsite was selected, a miniature village was exhibited by Johnson on the floor of the convention hall in Springfield.

CITY COLLEGE. See College: City college

CITY DIRECTORY. *See* Directory: Directory (city)

CITY MANAGER was Charles E. Ashburner of Richmond, Va., who on April 2, 1908, was elected general manager by the City Council of Staunton, Va. His first report covered the period from March 1, 1909, to June 1, 1909. He served until July 1911.

CITY MANAGER PLAN of government was adopted by Sumter, S.C. In June 1912, through a regular election, the voters adopted the commission-city manager form of government. The commission was composed of a mayor and two councilmen, all elected at large. The commission employed a city manager, and active administration of the affairs of the city was entrusted to him. He was, however, accountable to the commission, which was the final authority. Later the commission was composed of a mayor and four councilmen.

CITY MAP. *See* Map: Map of a city

CITY PLANNING INSTRUCTION was offered in 1909 by Harvard University, Cambridge, Mass., under James Sturgis Pray, Pro-

THE FIRST

THE FIRST

CITY PLANNING INSTRUCTION—
Continued
fessor of Landscape Architecture. Registration
commenced September 30, 1909. In the fall of
1929, the Charles Dyer Norton Chair of
Regional Planning was founded by a gift from
James F. Curtis, and a separate School of City
Planning was set up requiring a bachelor's
degree for entrance and giving a Master of City
Planning degree. The first degrees of Master
in Landscape Architecture were conferred on
June 18, 1925, and the first degrees of Master
of City Planning on June 18, 1931.

CIVIC DESIGN CHAIR in a university
was established by the University of Illinois,
Urbana, Ill., in 1912 as part of the landscape
development program inaugurated in 1897 by
Joseph Cullen Blair, in charge of the Department of Horticulture. The first incumbent of
the chair was Professor Charles Mulford Robinson who served as Professor of Civic Design
from September 1, 1913, until his death, December 30, 1917.

CIVIL AERONAUTICS ADMINISTRA-
TION HONORARY LICENSE. *See* Aviation—License: Civil aeronautics administration honorary license

CIVIL AERONAUTICS AUTHORITY
(U.S.) was created by act of Congress
passed June 23, 1938 (52 Stat.L.973), "to create
a Civil Aeronautics Authority and to promote
the development and safety and to provide for
the regulation of civil aeronautics." It was
established as an independent agency composed
of a five-member board named the Civil Aeronautics Authority, an administrator, and a three-
member Air Safety Board.

CIVIL AIR PATROL (U.S.) was organized as a division of the Office of Civilian Defense on December 1, 1941. The first national
commander was Major General John Francis
Curry, appointed December 10, 1941. On April
29, 1943, it was transferred to the War Department by presidential order and became an auxiliary of the Army Air Forces. It was the only
civilian organization permitted to use "U.S."
on its insignia, and the letters appear on a
shoulder emblem to identify the corps as
prisoners of war, if captured, instead of
civilians.

CIVIL DEFENSE DIRECTOR was Paul
J. Larsen, who assumed office on March 1, 1950,
as director of the Office of Civilian Mobilization
of the National Security Resources Board.

CIVIL ENGINEERING COURSE. *See*
Engineering college: Civil engineering course

CIVIL ENGINEERING NATIONAL SO-
CIETY. *See* Engineering society: Civil engineering national society

CIVIL GOVERNMENT IN AMERICA
was the Watauga Commonwealth, an independent civil government. By the treaty of Fort
Stanwix in 1768 the Six Nations agreed to
surrender all the lands between the Ohio and
Tennessee rivers to the English. Inasmuch as
there was some misunderstanding because the
Iroquois had ceded land to which they had no
legal right, the settlers organized a civil government in May 1772 and drew the "Articles of
the Watauga Association," the first written constitution ever adopted by a community of
American-born freemen. The settlers elected a
representative assembly of 13 men, which in
turn elected a committee of 5, John Sevier, James
Robertson, Charles Robertson, Zachariah Isbell,
and John Carter, vested with judicial and executive authority. This was the first free and
independent community established on the
American continent. The area was in North
Carolina and the mountains of Tennessee.
*(Samuel Cole Williams—History of the Lost
of Franklin)*

CIVIL RIGHTS CHAIR was established
at Lafayette College, Easton, Pa., through the
gift of Fred Morgan Kirby. The first lectures
were given in February 1921, by Professor
Herbert Adams Gibbons. *(David Bishop Skillman—The Biography of a College)*

CIVIL SERVICE
Civil Service Commission was appointed
by President Ulysses S. Grant in March 1871
and consisted of George William Curtis,
Alexander Gilmore Cattell, Joseph Medill, D. A.
Walker, E. B. Elliott, Joseph H. Blackfan,
and David C. Cox. An act of Congress of
March 3, 1871 (16 Stat.L.514) authorized the
President to prescribe regulations for admissions of persons into the Civil Service. It
became effective January 1, 1872. Congress refused to make any further appropriations and
despite two direct appeals from President Grant,
Civil Service was abandoned in 1874. The
Pendleton bill reestablishing Civil Service was
approved by President Chester A. Arthur,
January 16, 1883 (22 Stat.L.403). *(Carl Russell Fish—The Civil Service and the Patron-
age)*

Civil Service woman appointee was Mary
Francis Hoyt (later Mrs. Brice J. Moses), who
passed the examination and was appointed on
September 5, 1883, to a $900-a-year clerkship in
the Bank Redemption Agency of the Treasury
Department. She held the position five years.

Woman Civil Service commissioner was
Helen Hamilton Gardener of Washington, D.C.,
who was appointed by President Woodrow
Wilson and sworn in in Washington, D.C., on
April 13, 1920. She used the pen name Helen
Hunt Gardner in her writings.

THE FIRST

THE FIRST

CIVIL WAR

Act that marked the inauguration of the War of 1861-1865 was the firing upon the "Star of the West," a staunch merchant steam vessel chartered by the United States Government to convey supplies and men to reinforce Major Robert Anderson, at Fort Sumter, Charleston Harbor, although the announced destination was Savannah, Ga., and New Orleans, La. She left New York harbor January 5, 1861, and when within two miles of Forts Sumter and Moultrie was fired upon from a detachment at Morris Island on January 9, 1861. Captain John McGowan retired from the scene after seventeen shots had been fired at his ship, only two of which took effect. Major P. F. Stevens ordered Cadet George E. Haynesworth of Sumter, S.C., to pull the lanyard and fire the first shot. *(John Peyre Thomas—Historical Sketch of the South Carolina Military Academy 1783-1892)*

Attack in the Civil War was made on Fort Sumter, S.C. The first gun was fired on the morning of April 12, 1861, by Edmund Ruffin, a Virginian 75 years of age. There were no casualties. *(Chronological Record of the Great Civil War—Caxton Press)*

Bloodshed in the Civil War occurred on April 19, 1861. When President Abraham Lincoln issued his state of insurrection proclamation and call for militia on April 15, 1861, Governor John Albion Andrew of Massachusetts sent five regiments of infantry, a battalion of riflemen, and a battery of artillery to Washington. While passing through Baltimore, they were stoned and fired upon by a mob of citizens. Four Union soldiers were killed and twenty injured. Nine casualties were reported among the mob.

Bloodshed north of the Mason-Dixon line in the Civil War occurred in the battle of Hanover, Pa., June 30, 1863, between Brigadier General Judson Kilpatrick's Third Cavalry Division, Army of the Potomac, and Major General James Ewell Brown Stuart's Cavalry Division, Army of Northern Virginia. About 11,000 troops were in this cavalry and artillery engagement in which the casualties were more than 300. This battle was one of the determining factors that enabled the North to win at Gettysburg, Pa.

Call for Union troops in the Civil War, a call for 75,000 volunteers, was made by President Abraham Lincoln on April 15, 1861, the day after the surrender of Fort Sumter, S.C.

Confederate cruiser to raid Union commerce. *See* Ship: Confederate cruiser to raid Union commerce

Confederate general killed in the Civil War was Robert Selden Garnett, a graduate of the United States Military Academy, who resigned from the United States Army on April 30, 1861, and was appointed a brigadier general of the Confederate States on June 6, 1861. He was killed July 13, 1861, at the battle of Corrick's (Carrick's) Ford, Va., now near Parsons, W.Va. *(Mark Mayo Boatner—A Civil War Dictionary)*

Confederate officer killed in the Civil War was Captain John Quincy Marr of Warrenton, Va., commander of the Warrenton Rifle Guards (designated Company K of the 17th Virginia Infantry Regiment), who was killed June 1, 1861, in a skirmish at Fairfax Court House, Va. Marr was actually a lieutenant colonel, having been commissioned May 2, 1861, but his letter of commission from Governor John Letcher had not been delivered to him.

See also below Civil War: Skirmish in the Civil War

Conflict between iron-clad vessels in the Civil War was that of the "Merrimac" and "Monitor" at Hampton Roads, Va., March 9, 1862, a battle which was won by the Union's "Monitor." *(Le Grand Bouton Cannon—Records of the Ironclads—Monitor and Merrimac—and Incidents of the Fight)*

Naval engagement in the Civil War took place September 14, 1861, at Pensacola, Fla. Lieutenant John Henry Russell, with a detachment of the crew of the U.S.S. "Colorado," descended upon the navy yard at Pensacola at 2:00 A.M. The steamer "Judah" (five guns), lying at anchor, was burned, and the only gun in the yard spiked. There were no Confederate casualties. Three of the Union troops were killed and four wounded. *(Union Army—Federal Publishing Co.)*

Negro regiment in the Civil War was the First Regiment, South Carolina Volunteers, organized in July and August 1862 by Major General David Hunter. There being no authority at that time for its muster into federal service, it was disbanded, then reorganized in October 1862 and mustered into federal service at Buford, S.C., January 31, 1863. Its designation was changed February 8, 1864, to the 33d United States Colored Infantry. *(Records in Adjutant General's Office. War Department)*

Regiment to respond to President Abraham Lincoln's proclamation of April 15, 1861, was the Ringgold Light Artillery of Reading, Pa., known as "The First Defenders," commanded by Dr. John Keys. They reported to Governor Eli Slifer at Harrisburg, Pa., April 16, 1861. Their first engagement was September 24, 1861, at Hanging Rocks, W.Va. The other Pennsylvania regiments did not arrive in Harrisburg until April 17, 1861.

THE FIRST

THE FIRST

CIVIL WAR—*Continued*
Pennsylvania regiments were the first to arrive at Washington, D.C. *(Samuel Clarke Farrar —The 22nd Pennsylvania Cavalry and the Ringgold Battalion)*

Serious engagement in the Civil War took place on Bull Run Creek, Va., July 21, 1861. The Confederate forces under General Joseph Eccleston Johnston defeated the Union forces under General Irvin McDowell. *(James Ford Rhodes—History of the United States from the Compromise of 1850 to the Final Restoration of Home Rule in the South in 1877)*

Skirmish in the Civil War took place on June 1, 1861, at Fairfax Court House, Va. Fifty men of Company B, 2d United States Cavalry, under Lieutenant Charles H. Tompkins, were sent out to reconnoiter. They discovered a force much larger than their own and retreated. By exceeding his specific orders Tompkins frustrated a much larger movement which had been planned. One Union soldier was killed and four injured, while the Confederates suffered one killed and fourteen wounded. The action at Philippi, W.Va., which has often been regarded as the first Civil War land battle, occurred June 3, 1861. The United States forces under Brigadier General Thomas Armstrong Morris routed the Confederate forces under Colonel George A. Porterfield. *(Union Army—Federal Publishing Co.)*

Union soldier killed by enemy action in the Civil War was Thornberry Baily Brown. On May 22, 1861, while engaged in obtaining recruits, he was fired upon by Confederate pickets at Fetterman, near Grafton, W.Va. He was given a military funeral and buried in a temporary cemetery on upper Maple Avenue in Fetterman. In 1900 Reno Post No. 7, G.A.R., Grafton, erected a shaft to Brown's memory on Pearl Street in Grafton, and in 1928 the Betsy Ross Tent Daughters of the Union Veterans erected a monument in Fetterman on the spot where Brown fell.

CIVIL WAR MONUMENT. *See* Monument: Monument to commemorate the Civil War

CIVIL WORKS ADMINISTRATION (U.S.) was established November 9, 1933, with an allocation of $400 million. The first administrator was Harry Lloyd Hopkins. *(U.S. Federal Civil Works Administration—Rules and Regulations. 1933)*

CIVILIAN CONSERVATION CORPS (U.S.) was authorized by Act of Congress (48 Stat.L.22), "an act for the relief of unemployment through the performance of useful public work, and for other purposes," signed by President Franklin Delano Roosevelt, March

31, 1933. On April 5, 1933, Robert Fechner of Boston was appointed first director. Enrollment began on April 5 and the first camp was set up April 10, 1933. By July 4, the enrollment of all units, including veterans, was complete. The peak registration for the first period was 311,230. The first camp was Camp Roosevelt, near Luray, Va., opened April 17, 1933.

CLAIMS COURT. *See* Court: Conciliation tribunal for small claims

CLARINET made exclusively of metal was manufactured by Charles Gerard Conn of Elkhart, Ind., who obtained patent No. 410,072 on August 27, 1889, on a "clarionet." Previously, all clarinets had been made of wood. Conn's clarinet was made with double metal walls in the old Albert system.

CLAY PIGEON TARGET. *See* Trapshooting: Clay pigeon target

CLEARING HOUSE. *See* Bank: Clearing house

CLEARING HOUSE (stocks and bonds). *See* Brokerage: Clearing house for stocks and bonds

CLIMATOLOGY PROFESSOR was Robert De Courcy Ward, appointed in 1910 by Harvard University, Cambridge, Mass. He was assistant in meteorology, 1892-1895; instructor, 1895-1896; instructor in climatology, 1896-1900; asistant professor, 1900-1910; and professor, 1910-1931.

CLINCHER TIRE. *See* Automobile tire: Clincher tire

CLINIC. *See* Medical clinic

CLINICAL INSTRUCTION. *See* Medical instruction: Clinical instruction and bedside demonstration

CLIPPER FOR CUTTING HAIR was manufactured by George Henry Coates of Worcester, Mass., in 1876. His product was so superior to those imported from England and France that he received an initial manufacturing order for 5,000 clippers.

CLIPPER SHIP. *See* Ship: Clipper ship

CLIPPING BUREAU. *See* Press clipping bureau

THE FIRST

CLOCK

Alarm clock was made by Levi Hutchins of Concord, N.H., in 1787. It was 29 inches high and 14 inches wide and had a pine case with a mirror in the door. The alarm rang at a specified time and could not be set or altered.

Banjo clock patent was obtained by Simon Willard of Boston, Mass., on February 8, 1802, for "an improvement in a time-piece."

Brass clock works were invented in 1837 by Chauncey Jerome of the Jerome Clock Company, Bristol, Conn. (later the New Haven Clock Company). Jerome's production of standardized parts of pierced brass plates from steel dies enabled him to sell an eight-day metal clock for $4 whereas one-day wooden clocks sold for $12.

Clock (one-day back-wind alarm clock) in a metal case was made in 1876 by the Seth Thomas Clock Company of Thomaston, Conn. The clock case was patented October 24, 1876, (No. 183,725) by Seth E. Thomas of New York City.

Clock patent was granted to Eli Terry of East Windsor, Conn., on November 17, 1797, on an equation clock. The clock had two minute hands, one of which showed the mean or true time, while the "other together with the striking part and hour hand showed the apparent time, as divided by the sun according to the table of the variation of the sun and clock for each day of the year." (*Penrose Robinson Hoopes—Connecticut Clockmakers of the Eighteenth Century*)

Clock to operate by atomic power was the Atomicron, made by the National Company, Inc., Malden, Mass., and exhibited October 2, 1956, at the Overseas Press Club, New York City. It was 84 inches high, 22 inches wide, and 18 inches deep, and was priced at $50,000. Its "pendulum" was the cesium atom, which oscillates at a never-changing frequency of 9,192,631,830 megacycles a second.

Clock to strike the hours was constructed in 1754 by Benjamin Banneker, a Negro, at Elkridge Landing, near Baltimore, Md. At the age of 23, and without any tools except a jack-knife, and without ever having seen anything similar but a sun dial and a watch, Banneker constructed this clock, made of wood, which kept time for more than 20 years. Banneker later became distinguished as a scientist. (*Journal of Negro History. Vol. 3. April 1918*)

Electric watch was made by the Hamilton Watch Company, Lancaster, Pa., and introduced to the public on January 3, 1957. The movement is powered by a small energy cell guaranteed to operate the watch for a year. It has no mainspring and has 35 per cent fewer parts than an automatic or self-winding watch.

Electronic wrist watch (called "Accutron") was produced by the Bulova Watch Company in its plant at Jackson Heights, New York City, and placed on sale October 25, 1960. In place of mainspring, hairspring, and related gears the watch has a precision tuning fork vibrating exactly 360 times per second, transistorized electronic circuitry, and a miniature power cell to move the hands and maintain timekeeping accuracy (less than one minute per month is lost or gained).

Self-winding clock was made by Benjamin Hanks of Litchfield, Conn., who made a "clock or machine that winds itself up by help of the air and will continue to do so without any other aid or assistance." On October 6, 1783, he applied for a fourteen-year exclusive patent right from Connecticut.

Watch (eight-day) was manufactured in 1850 by Aaron Lufkin Dennison. It was regarded, however, as impractical and inferior to the one-day watch. It was made in the factory of the American Horologe Company of Roxbury, Mass., later the Waltham Watch Company, Waltham, Mass. (*Charles Walden Moore—Timing a Century, History of the Waltham Watch Company*)

Watch made by machinery was placed on the market in 1838 by James and Henry Pitkin of Hartford, Conn., the manufacturers. The movements were ¾ plate, slow train, and about the diameter of the modern 16-size. The factory was moved to New York, but in 1841 was closed down, being unable to meet the competition of the imported Swiss watches.

Watch movement to be electrically wound and synchronized was made by H. Chester Pond in Chicago in the fall of 1885. In the summer of 1886, 50 of these movements were made and set up in New York City as a system. A high-grade master clock transmitted an hourly signal to the various self-winding or "subsidiary" clocks, correcting them hourly, and thereby maintaining in each clock location the same high degree of time accuracy that was inherent in the master clock.

Watchmaker was Luther Goddard who in 1809 opened a shop in Shrewsbury, Mass., his birthplace. He was aided by a law which forbade the importation of clocks and watches, and so was able to develop a small business. In reality, he assembled more watches from imported parts than he actually constructed. The real beginning of the watch industry came in 1849, when the American Horologe Company was formed in Roxbury, Mass., by three

CLOCK—*Continued*
men, Aaron L. Dennison of Boston, who was an experienced watchmaker; Edward Howard of Bingham, Mass., who was skilled in making machinery for watches; and Samuel Curtis, who financed the enterprise, which later became the Waltham Watch Company. *(Henry G. Abbott—History of the Watch Factories of America)*

CLOCK LOCK. *See* Lock: Lock ("clock")

"CLOSE-UP" MOVING PICTURE. *See* Moving picture: Moving picture "close-up"

CLOTH
Cloth mill was built in 1638 by John Pearson in Rowley, Mass. According to Captain Edward Johnson's book, *Wonder-Working Providences of Sion's Savior in New England*, published in London in 1654, "the Lord brought over the zealous affected and judicious servant of His, Master Ezekiel Rogers, who with an holy and humble people, made his progress to the northeastward and erected a town about six miles from Ipswich, called Rowley—they were the first people that set upon making cloth in this western world."

Gingham factory. *See* Gingham factory

Hair cloth. *See* Hair cloth

Jeans, fustians, everlastings, and coatings were made commercially by Samuel Wetherill, Jr., of Philadelphia, Pa. Prior to April 3, 1782, his products were sold at his dwelling house and factory on what was then South Alley, between Market and Arch Streets.

Sail cloth factory was the Boston Sail Cloth Factory, Boston, Mass., established in 1788. It was 2 stories high and 180 feet long. In 1789, 30 women and girls worked 26 looms and turned out 40 yards each a week.

CLOTH-COVERED BUTTON. *See* Button: Cloth-covered buttons

CLOTURE RESOLUTION (SENATE). *See* Congress (U.S.)—Senate: Senate cloture resolution

CLUB WOMAN was Anne Hutchinson, the founder of the Antinomian party in the New England colonies. She left England and arrived in Boston, Mass., on September 18, 1634. She organized groups of women who met at her house and led them in the discussion of secular and theological questions. Her influence became so great and her views so pronounced that she was brought to trial on November 17, 1637, in Cambridge and was

banished from the territory of Massachusetts. She left for Rhode Island in March 1638, accompanied by 70 followers. *(Edith Roelker Curtis—Anne Hutchinson)*

CLUBS. *See* Societies; *also* specific headings, as Canoe club, Tennis club, etc.

COACH (professional trainer). *See* Sports: Sports trainer (professional)

COACH (railroad). *See* Railroad car: Railroad coach

COACH SERVICE. *See* Stage coach intercity service

COACHING as a pastime was brought to the United States in 1875 by Colonel Delancey Astor Kane. A tallyho was built by Holland and Holland of London, England, and imported to New York. The first trip, May 1, 1876, started from the Hotel Brunswick, Fifth Avenue and 26th Street, New York City, and ended at the Arcubarius Hotel, Pelham, N.Y. The interest in the tallyho lasted 35 years. Some coaches had been imported earlier.

COACHING CLUB to encourage four-in-hand driving was the Coaching Club formed by nine men December 3, 1875, at the Knickerbocker Club, New York City. The officers were William Jay, president; James Gordon Bennett, vice-president; and William P. Douglas, secretary and treasurer. The first meet, at which six coaches participated was held April 22, 1876. *(Reginald William Rives—The Coaching Club)*

COAL
Anthracite coal was discovered accidentally in 1791 by Philip Ginter, a hunter, near Sharp Mountain, Carbon County, Pa. It was regarded as a species of black stone. Its value was not appreciated fully as the coal was difficult to kindle and produced such a high heat that it endangered the old-time boilers, which were designed principally for burning wood. *(Fred Brenckman—History of Carbon County, Pa.)*

Anthracite coal burned experimentally was used by Judge Jesse Fell in his home in Wilkes-Barre, Pa., February 11, 1808, much to the surprise of the populace, which regarded the coal as valueless. *(Wilkes-Barre—The Diamond City)*

Anthracite coal used commercially was successfully burned in 1812 in a heating furnace at White and Hazard's Fairmount Nail and Wire Works near Philadelphia, Pa. The coal was supplied by Colonel George Shoemaker of Pottsville, Pa., who loaded nine

THE FIRST

THE FIRST

wagons from his mine at Centreville, Pa. A second wagonload was sold to Mellon & Bishop of the Delaware County Rolling Mill. The remaining seven loads were given away because no one would buy hard coal. *(William Jasper Nicolls—Story of American Coals)*

Anthracite coal used in smelting iron ore was used in a furnace in 1837 by the Lehigh Coal and Navigation Company at Mauch Chunk, Pa. The anthracite coal used was approximately 80 per cent of the fuel consumed. On August 27, 1838, another blast furnace was erected in which anthracite was used exclusively. *(Walter Rogers Johnson—Notes on the Use of Anthracite)*

Coal is said to have been discovered by Father Louis Hennepin in 1673-1680 while on his exploration trips. It is asserted that he noticed coal on the bluffs of the Illinois River not far from Ottawa and La Salle, Ill. *(Louis Hennepin—A Discovery of a Large Rich and Plentiful Country in the North America)*

Coal hydrogenation chemicals pilot plant (large) designed specifically for converting coal into chemicals was opened May 8, 1952, in Institute, W.Va., by the Carbide and Carbon Chemicals Company. Coal is received, pulverized, and mixed with oil to form a paste, then converted under heat and pressure in combination with hydrogen gas into liquid chemical intermediate products. The $11 million plant has a capacity of 300 tons of coal a day. Some of the principal products are cresols, higher phenols, naphthalene, and aromatic hydrocarbon.

Coal pipeline loops (experimental) were built as a test at Library, Pa., on May 23, 1950, by the Research and Development Division of the Pittsburgh Consolidation Coal Company, Pittsburgh, Pa. Three other pipelines were also built. They had as their purpose the study of variables in the process of the delivery of solids by pipeline.

Coal pipeline unit (demonstration) began functioning on November 1, 1951, near Cadiz, Ohio, on the property of the Hanna Coal Division of the Pittsburgh Consolidation Coal Company. It carried approximately 9,000 tons daily through a 12¾-inch pipe. A fine size of coal was mixed with water to form a slurry, and this mixture was pumped through the pipeline under pressure.

Commercial coal pipeline was completed September 12, 1956, and placed in commercial operation June 4, 1957. It extended 108 miles from the Georgetown Preparation Plant of the Hanna Coal Company, a division of the Pittsburgh Consolidation Coal Company, near Cadiz, Ohio, to the Eastlake Power Station of the Cleveland Illuminating Company, Eastlake, Ohio. The pipeline, 10¾ inches in diameter, was originally designed to move an equal mixture of coal and water at the rate of 150 tons of coal per hour.

COAL-BURNING LOCOMOTIVE. *See* Locomotive: Locomotive to burn coal (practical, American-made)

COAL CARS. *See* Railroad car: Coal cars with roller bearings

COAL MINE designed for 100 per cent mechanical operation was the Butler Consolidated Coal Company's Wildwood mine, Wildwood, Pa., which opened in October 1930. The drilling, crushing, loading, screening of sizes, mechanical cleaning, dumping, and transportation operations were accomplished mechanically. Rubber conveyor belts carried the coal.

COAL MINING CORRESPONDENCE COURSE. *See* Correspondence school

COAL OIL FACTORY to manufacture coal oil from coal tar was started in 1853 by the U.S. Chemical Manufacturing Company in Waltham, Mass. The light fractions from this coal oil distillation were called "coal oil," and used for illuminating purposes. The oil made in connection with picric acid, benzol, and other products from coal tar was named "Coup Oil" by Luther Atwood, the inventor. When Edwin Drake demonstrated, in 1859, that petroleum could be secured by drilling, the coal oil industry died a natural death. *(Samuel Dana Hayes—History and Manufacture of Petroleum Products)*

COALING STATION (naval). *See* Navy: Naval coaling station on foreign soil

COAST GUARD (U.S.)
Coast Guard was created by an act of January 28, 1915 (38 Stat.L.800), "an act to create the Coast Guard by combining therein the existing Life Saving Service and the Revenue Cutter Service." The Revenue Cutter Service had been organized by an act of August 4, 1790 (1 Stat.L.145), "an act to provide more effectually for the collection of the duties imposed by law on goods, wares and merchandise imported into the United States and on the tonnage of ships and vessels." The Life Saving Service had been authorized by an act of June 18, 1878 (20 Stat.L.163), "an act to organize the Life Saving Service." The motto of the Coast Guard is *Semper Paratus* (Always Ready).

Coast Guard air station. *See* Aviation: Coast Guard air station

THE FIRST

THE FIRST

COAST GUARD (U.S.)—*Continued*
Coast Guard aviation unit. *See* Aviation: Coast Guard aviation unit

Coast Guard commandant was Alexander V. Fraser, who served in the Revenue Cutter Service from February 1, 1842, to November 15, 1848. John Canfield Spencer, Secretary of the Treasury, appointed him Commandant. His first report was submitted January 9, 1844. The Revenue Cutter Service was absorbed into the Coast Guard in 1915.

Coast Guard officers' training school was established July 31, 1876, by the Revenue Cutter Service aboard the schooner "Dobbin," based at New Bedford, Mass. Its complement was 3 officers, a surgeon, 6 warrant officers, 17 men, and 8 cadets.

Coast Guard Women's Reserve (called "SPARS," from the initials of the Coast Guard motto, "Semper Paratus—Always Ready") was authorized November 23, 1942, and placed under the command of Lieutenant Commander Dorothy Constance Stratton. She assumed office November 24, 1942, became commander on January 1, 1944, and captain on February 1, 1944. The first recruit was Dorothy Edith Lorne Tuttle, who enlisted on December 7, 1942, as a yeoman third class.

Inland U.S. Coast Guard station was opened November 3, 1881, when four surfmen were employed on Station No. 10 of the Ninth Life Saving District (embracing Lake Erie and Lake Ontario) at Louisville, Ky., near the falls of the Ohio River. The station was commanded by Captain William M. Devan. The first rescue was made November 7, 1881, when the 1,603-ton steamer "City of Baton Rouge" of St. Louis, Mo., valued at $125,000, with 26 persons on board was stranded on the left-hand reef of the falls. The vessel was finally floated off the rocks on November 24, 1881.

Navy Cross to a Coast Guard officer. *See* Medal: Navy Cross awarded to a Coast Guard officer in World War II

Vice Admiral in the Coast Guard was Russell Randolph Waesche, Commandant of the United States Coast Guard, who was appointed Vice Admiral on March 24, 1942.

COAST SURVEY was authorized by act of Congress of February 10, 1807 (2 Stat.L.413), "an act to provide for surveying the coasts of the United States," which appropriated a sum not exceeding $50,000.

COAST SURVEY BOOK was Captain Lawrence Furlong's *The American Coast Pilot,* containing the courses and distance from Boston to all the principal harbours, capes and headlands included between Passamaquady and the Capes of Virginia with directions for sailing into, and out of, all the principal ports and harbours, with the sounding on the coast . . . , 121 pages, printed March 1796 in Newburyport, Mass., by [Edward March] Blunt and [Angier] March.

COAST SURVEY SUPERINTENDENT was Ferdinand Rudolph Hassler, who was formally appointed August 3, 1816, by Alexander James Dallas, Secretary of the Treasury. Hassler received $3,000 a year and $2,000 for personal expenses in the field. The U.S. Coast Survey was authorized February 10, 1807, but the first appropriation was made July 10, 1832 (4 Stat.L.570) an "act to carry into effect the act to provide for a survey of the coast of the United States." The appropriation was not to exceed $20,000. *(Centennial Celebration of the U.S. Coast and Geodetic Survey)*

COAST-TO-COAST PAVED ROAD. *See* Road: Coast-to-coast paved road

COASTAL SHIPPING SERVICE. *See* Shipping: Coastal shipping service

COAT
Tuxedo coat is said to have been introduced from England by Griswold Lorillard, who wore a tailless dress coat and waistcoat of scarlet satin at the Tuxedo Club, Tuxedo Park, N.Y., on October 10, 1886. *(Edwin Clark Kent—Story of Tuxedo Park)*

COAXIAL CABLE. *See* Cable (telegraph): Coaxial cable

COBRA
King cobra snakes born in captivity in the United States were hatched July 4, 1955, at the New York Zoological Park (Bronx Zoo), New York City. The parent snakes were mated March 10, 1955, and on April 25, 1955, 41 eggs were laid. Nine eggs hatched, the first on July 4 and the last on July 12, 1955. The infant cobras were mottled white and brown and felt leathery to the touch.

COCKTAIL is said to have been served in 1776 by Betsy Flanagan, a barmaid at Halls Corners, Elmsford, N.Y., who decorated the bar with tail feathers. An inebriate called for a glass of "those cocktails," so she prepared a mixed drink, and inserted one of the feathers.

COCKTAIL (oyster). *See* Oyster cocktail

COD LIVER OIL was described in Thomas Morton's *New English Canaan* in 1635. A "great store of traine oyle is mayd of the livers

THE FIRST

of the Codd, and is a commodity that without question will enrich the inhabitants of New England quicly and is therefore a principall commodity." His report was published in 1637 in a book printed by Jacob Frederick Stam in Amsterdam, Holland.

CODE CONVERTER. *See* Telegraph: Telegraph code converter

CODEBALL was played May 11, 1929, at the Lake Shore Athletic Club, Chicago, Ill. The game is a combination of golf and soccer football and was invented by Dr. William Edward Code of Chicago. A 6-inch ball, weighing 12 ounces, capable of withstanding a 600-pound pressure is used. Codeball-in-the-court is played in an enclosed court and codeball-on-the-green is played in the open. Both games were adopted by the Amateur Athletic Union of the United States at St. Louis, Mo., on November 18, 1929

CODIFICATION BOARD (United States) was created by act of June 19, 1937 (50 Stat.L.304), "an act to amend the Federal Register Act (49 Stat.L.500) approved July 26, 1935." Its purpose was "to supervise and coordinate the form, style, arrangement and indexing of codifications to be prepared by each agency of the administrative branch of the Federal Government which is empowered by Congress to exercise rule-making power." The board consisted of six members. The first chairman was Major Bernard Reilly Kennedy appointed June 19, 1937. The first codification was filed July 1, 1938.

COEDUCATIONAL COLLEGE. *See* College: Coeducational college

COEDUCATIONAL MEDICAL SCHOOL. *See* Medical school: Coeducational medical school

COFFEE MILL PATENT was granted April 3, 1829, to James Carrington, Wallingford, Conn.

COFFEE PERCOLATOR PATENT was No. 51,741, granted to James H. Nason of Franklin, Mass., on December 26, 1865.

COG RAILROAD. *See* Railroad: Cog railroad

COIL STAMPS. *See* Postage stamp: Postage stamps in coils

COIN. *See* Money

COIN BOX for street cars was invented about 1870 by Thomas Loftin Johnson in Louisville, Ky. He rose from clerk to owner of a

THE FIRST

street railway in Indianapolis and a large stockholder in railroad companies in New York, Cleveland, and Detroit. *(Thomas Loftin Johnson—My Story)*

COIN-OPERATED MAILBOX. *See* Postal service: Coin-operated mailbox

COIN-OPERATED TELEVISION RECEIVER. *See* Television receiver: Coin-operated television receiver

COIN-OPERATED VENDING MACHINE. *See* Vending machine: Vending machine (coin operated) to dispense postage stamps

COIN TELEPHONE. *See* Telephone: Coin telephone

COKE used successfully as a blast-furnace fuel was demonstrated in 1835 by William Firmstone at the Mary Ann Furnace in Huntingdon County, Pa.

COLD STORAGE PLANT operated by mechanical refrigeration was opened in 1881 by the Mechanical Refrigerating Company at Boston, Mass. *(Department of Agriculture Yearbook. 1900. "The Influence of Refrigeration on the Fruit Industry." William A. Taylor)*

COLLAPSIBLE TUBE. *See* Tube: Collapsible tube

COLLAR
Collar (detached) was made in 1825 in Troy, N.Y., by Hannah Lord Montague, who, tired of washing her husband's shirts merely because the collar was dirty, took scissors and performed the amputation which created a new style in men's apparel. *(Rutherford Hayner—Troy and Rensselaer County, N.Y.)*

Paper collar was invented by Walter Hunt of New York City, who obtained patent No. 11,376, July 25, 1854. He used a thin white cotton muslin and coated both sides with a very thin white paper, a layer of paste interposed between them. The collars were then varnished with a colorless bleached shellac which made them proof against perspiration; they could be wiped clean with a damp cloth.

COLLAR FACTORY for the manufacture of men's linen collars and shirt bosoms as a special business was established by Orlando Montague and Austin Granger, under the firm name of Montague and Granger, in Troy, N.Y., in 1833. *(Arthur James Weise—Troy's One Hundred Years. 1789-1889)*

COLLAR MANUFACTURER

COLLAR MANUFACTURER of detachable collars was Ebenezer Brown who started in Troy, N.Y., in 1829. He hired a number of women to make, wash, and iron the collars, giving in payment merchandise from his retail store, located at 285 River Street. These collars, which were known as "string collars" because they were tied about the neck with a string, were placed in paper boxes sixteen or more inches in length, and were sold in his store. *(Arthur James Weise—Troy's One Hundred Years. 1789-1889)*

COLLEGE

For Chairs, Courses, Departments, Professorships, Special colleges, and the like, see under name of specific subject or profession or type of school, e.g., Agricultural school, Biography course, Language instruction, Law School, Normal school, Political Economy chair, etc.

For college sports, see under name of game or sport, e.g., Baseball, Boat race, etc.

See also Degrees (academic and honorary): Bachelor of Arts degree

Catholic college was Georgetown College, Washington, D.C., established January 23, 1789 and opened November 15, 1791. The first student to register was William Gaston of Newberne, N.C. Authority to grant degrees was authorized by act of Congress of March 1, 1815 (6 Stat.L.152). *(Coleman Nevils—Miniatures of Georgetown)*

Catholic college for women was the College of Notre Dame of Maryland, Baltimore, Md., which opened on September 2, 1895. It was incorporated April 2, 1896. The first commencement was held June 14, 1899, when 4 bachelor of arts and 2 bachelor of literature degrees were awarded to six women. Charles Joseph Bonaparte, a grandnephew of Napoleon, was the commencement speaker, his subject being "The Significance of the Bachelor's Degree."

City college was the College of Charleston, Charleston, S.C., which was founded in 1770, chartered March 19, 1785, and opened in 1790. The Reverend Robert Smith was the first principal and served until 1797. On December 20, 1837, it became a municipal university under municipal control and opened April 1, 1838, with sixteen students. The first president was the Reverend Dr. William Theophilus Brantley, pastor of the Baptist Church, who was appointed February 2, 1838, and who served until his death in 1845. *(Roscoe Huhn Eckelberry—History of the Municipal University)*

Coeducational college was Oberlin Collegiate Institute, Oberlin, Ohio, which opened December 3, 1833, with 44 students, 29 men and 15 women. It was incorporated February 2,

1834. The first commencement was held October 29, 1834. Equal status was not granted to women, however, until September 6, 1837, when four women—Elizabeth Smith Prall of New York City, Caroline Mary Rudd of Huntington, Conn., Mary Hosford of Oberlin, Ohio, and Mary Fletcher Kellogg of Jamestown, N.Y.—and 30 men matriculated. In 1841, the first 3 of these women graduated with the B.A. degree, having pursued a classical course equivalent to that at Yale. On March 21, 1850, the name of the school was changed to Oberlin College. It was the first school to advocate the abolition of slavery and to accept Negro men and women on equal terms with white students.

College was Harvard College, established in 1636. On September 8, 1636, the General Court of Massachusetts Bay appropriated £400 and in 1637 appointed twelve of the principal men of the colony "to take orders for a college at New Towne," and the name Cambridge was adopted. Reverend John Harvard, who died September 24, 1638, left the college about £800 and 300 books, and the name of the college was changed in his honor. The first building, erected in 1637, was known as "The Indian Collidge." The first commencement was held September 23, 1642. Nathaniel Eaton was appointed the first Master of the College. The first president was Henry Dunster, who served from August 27, 1640, to October 24, 1654. *(Samuel Atkins Eliot—A Sketch of the History of Harvard College)*

College charter granted by a governor or acting governor with only the assent of his council was issued October 22, 1746, to twelve trustees of the College of New Jersey (now Princeton University), Princeton, N.J., by Governor John Hamilton, President of His Majesty's Council. The college opened the fourth week of May 1747. The first commencement was held November 9, 1748. Reverend Jonathan Dickinson was the first president. *(John Maclean—History of the College of New Jersey)*

College charter granted by the Crown under the Seal of the Privy Council was "their Majesties Royal College of William and Mary," the charter for which was granted February 8, 1693. The first president of the college was Dr. James Blair, who was "created and established the first president during his natural life." *(Bulletin—College of William and Mary. No. 3. June 1930)*

See also College: College proposed

College classes to combat the influence of communism were instituted December 4, 1935, by St. Joseph's College, Philadelphia, Pa. More than 1,200 students registered for the courses, the only charge being a registration fee of one dollar. College credits were not given but certificates of completion were issued. The president of the college was the Very Reverend Thomas Joseph Higgins.

THE FIRST

College comprehensive senior examination program was adopted on May 26, 1913, by the faculty of Whitman College, Walla Walla, Wash. Beginning with the class of 1914 every student who has graduated from Whitman College has passed successfully an examination, oral, or oral and written, given by a committee of the faculty in his department and covering the entire field of study in his major subject. The written examinations run from six to ten hours and the orals from one to three. *(Edward Safford Jones—Comprehensive Examinations in American Colleges)*

College cooperative. *See* Cooperative: College cooperative store

College course without Greek or Latin was established in 1824 by Geneva College (now Hobart College), Geneva, N.Y. The course, known as the "English Course," was designed "for the practical business of life by which the Agriculturist, the Merchant and the Mechanic may receive a practical knowledge of what genius and experience have discovered, without passing through a tedious course of Classical studies." The first course diploma, in English, was awarded in 1827 to Henry Smith Attwater. *(Journal of Higher Education. October 1933)*

College daily. *See* Newspaper: College daily

College degree. *See* Degrees (academic and honorary)

College entrance "certified school plan" in which admission was based upon the examination of preparatory schools rather than upon the individual was "the Michigan System," originated by Henry Simmons Frieze and introduced in September 1871 at the University of Michigan, Ann Arbor, Mich. A student who graduated from a regularly approved school was admitted without the necessity of taking individual examinations.

College entrance requirement, other than Greek, Latin, and arithmetic, was geography, which was required in 1807 for admission to Harvard College, Cambridge, Mass. *(Clarence Frank Birdseye—Individual Training in Our Colleges)*

College extension courses granting college credits were offered January 1, 1893, by the University Extension Division in the Class-Study Department of the University of Chicago, Chicago, Ill., "with credit . . . given in the books of the University to properly qualified students who completed any course of instruction." Twenty-five academic or secondary school courses and forty college courses were given. Admission requirements were the same

THE FIRST

as those to other parts of the university. The first director of the Extension Division was George Henderson. *(Thomas Wakefield Goodspeed—History of the University of Chicago)*

College for women was Mount Holyoke Seminary, South Hadley, Mass., chartered February 11, 1836, and opened November 8, 1837, as the Mount Holyoke Female Seminary with 80 students who paid $64 a year for tuition and board. They were required to do cooperative household tasks. The first principal was Mary Lyon, who served until 1849. Eunice Caldwell was the associate principal and Mary W. Smith and Amanda A. Hodgman were the teachers. The first graduation was held on August 23, 1838. The four girls who graduated were Martha A. Abbott, Sarah Brigham, Abigail Moore, and Persis C. Woods. In 1893, the name was changed to Mount Holyoke College.

College for women to affiliate with a university was the H. Sophie Newcomb Memorial College, established October 11, 1886, in New Orleans, La. Dr. Brandt Van Blarcom Dixon was the first dean and served from October 11, 1886, until he retired at the end of the 1918-1919 session. The college affiliated with Tulane University, New Orleans, La., in October 1887.

College library building. *See* College: Library building (university)

College magazine. *See* Periodical: College magazine

College medical clinic. *See* Medical clinic: College medical clinic

College museum. *See* Museum: College museum

College named after George Washington was Washington College in Washington College, Tenn. It was founded in 1780 by the Reverend Samuel Doak, and on April 24, 1783, it was chartered as Martin Academy by North Carolina (Tennessee was then a part of North Carolina). A second charter was received March 31, 1785, from the "Lost State of Franklin." A third charter, its present one, received July 8, 1795, changed the name to Washington College. The Reverend Dr. Doak was the first president of the new institution and served until 1818. The name, Washington College, was proposed to the legislature of "Territory of the United States South of the River Ohio" by General John Sevier. *(Howard Ernest Carr—Washington College)*

College orchestra. *See* Orchestra: College orchestra

COLLEGE—*Continued*
College principally for war veterans
(G.I.'s) was Champlain College, Plattsburg,
N.Y., opened September 16, 1946. It was operated by the Associated Colleges of Upper New
York, a corporation created by legislative act
effective April 1, 1946. Two other colleges of
the corporation were established, Mohawk, College, Utica, N.Y., opened October 16, 1946, and
Sampson College, Sampson, N.Y., opened October 23, 1946. The president was Asa Smallidge Knowles. The deans of faculty were Dr.
William H. Tenney of Champlain, Dr. Robert
G. Dawes of Mohawk and Dr. C. M. Louttit
of Sampson.

College proposed was the College of William and Mary in 1617. In 1618, the London
Company set aside 10,000 acres and on July 31,
1619, the General Assembly at Virginia petitioned to have workmen sent for "erecting of
the university and college" at Henrico, Va.
However it was not incorporated as the College
of William and Mary, Williamsburg, Va., until
February 8, 1693, and instruction was begun
about 1696. The first graduation exercises were
held in 1700. James Blair was the first president. The college was second to Harvard College in actual operation.

College summer school was established at
Mount Union College, Alliance, Ohio. Lewis
Miller of Akron, Ohio, presented the idea to
the faculty in February 1870 and the summer
school was started as a part of a four-term
system in June 1870.

College to confer medals as prizes was
the College of William and Mary at Williamsburg, Va. In 1770 Lord Botetourt, Governor
of Virginia, presented two gold medals, one to
be awarded to the best student in philosophy,
the other in classics.

**College to dispense with the system of
credits, hours, points, grades, etc.,** was
Olivet College, Olivet, Mich. A new system was
proposed by its president, Joseph Brewer, and
was put in operation October 1, 1934. The
college is divided into a Junior and a Senior
Division. Candidates for the degree of Bachelor
of Arts are required to pass both a preliminary
examination and a final examination and to have
had at least three years of instruction. Lectures
are at all times open to all members of the
college without distinction. Although tutors are
assigned to guide the student's course, the
responsibility for acquiring an education is
the student's.

**College to grant women absolutely equal
rights** with men was Mount Union College,
Alliance, Ohio, a Methodist Episcopal school,
founded by the Reverend Orville Nelson Hartshorn on October 20, 1846, as Mount Union

Seminary. Women were granted degrees and
permitted to stand on the platform on commencement day, a privilege not generally accorded elsewhere. The first non-sectarian college
of high rank to grant equal privileges was
Antioch College, Yellow Springs, Ohio (chartered May 14, 1852, opened October 5, 1853).
Its first graduating class, July 1, 1857, had three
women. Horace Mann was the first president.
(Herald of Gospel Liberty. February 10, 1916)

College to have a full faculty consisting of
a president, six professors, usher, and writing
master was the College of William and Mary,
Williamsburg, Va. On February 27, 1729, the
college realty was transferred from the trustees
to the faculty.

**College to prohibit discrimination because
of race, religion, or color** was Cooper Union
for the Advancement of Science and Art, New
York City, whose deed of trust, dated April 29,
1851, prohibited discrimination in the acceptance
of students for reasons of race, creed, or color.
Peter Cooper was the first president.

**College to receive a coat-of-arms from the
College of Heralds** was the College of William and Mary at Williamsburg, Va., which
was granted the seal May 14, 1694.

Dean of men was Benjamin Harrison
Brown, Professor of Physics and Chemistry at
Whitman College, Walla Walla, Wash., who
was appointed in 1901. At the same time,
Dr. Louis Francis Anderson, Professor of
Greek, was appointed Dean of Women.
(Stephen Beasley Linnard Penrose—Whitman)

"Dean of the faculty" was Martha Carey
Thomas, one of the four women Ph.D.'s in the
world at that time, appointed at the January
1884 meeting of the trustees of Bryn Mawr
College, Bryn Mawr, Pa.

**Educational institution exclusively for
women,** that offered courses and granted degrees equivalent to those in the best colleges
for men, was Elmira College of Elmira, N.Y.
It was originally chartered in 1852 as Auburn
Female University, but opened in 1855 as the
Elmira Female College. The first class of 17
graduated with the A.B. degree in 1859. From
the first, Elmira was "subject to the visitation
of the Regents of the University of the State
of New York, in the same manner and to the
same extent as the other colleges of the state."
The first chairman of the executive committee
was Samuel Robbins Brown. The first president
was Dr. Augustus Woodruff Cowles, who served
for 35 years. *(Addresses Made upon the Occasion of the Seventy-Fifth Anniversary—June 6,
1930—of the Founding of Elmira College)*

THE FIRST

Elective system of study was introduced by the College of William and Mary, Williamsburg, Va. In 1779 students were permitted to choose the subjects which they cared to pursue. *(Bulletin of the College of William and Mary in Virginia)*

Graduate school for women was Bryn Mawr College, Bryn Mawr, Pa., which was organized in 1884. The formal opening of the college took place October 23, 1885. From the first Bryn Mawr has offered graduate work leading to M.A. and Ph.D. degrees. The first class graduated June 6, 1889, and consisted of 24 candidates for bachelor's degrees.

Group insurance for college students. *See* Insurance: Group insurance policy for college students

Honor examination system. *See* Honor system

Honors course offered by a university was held September 1882 at the University of Michigan, Ann Arbor, Mich. The courses enabled students to take required work for two years and then under faculty committee direction to proceed within a limited range of subjects in a sort of specialized course. Students who exhibited a thorough knowledge in their special fields were given bachelor's degrees or master's degrees upon passing a cumulative examination and completing a thesis.

Inter-collegiate Association of Amateur Athletes of America. *See* Inter-collegiate Athletic Association

Inter-continental system of study was introduced by Boston University, Boston, Mass. which entered into reciprocal agreement on February 11, 1875, with the National University, Athens, Greece, and the Royal University, Rome, Italy. Students could attend these universities without paying tuition and have their credits applied towards degrees at Boston University. *(Bostonia. Vol. 13)*

Italian instruction in a college. *See* Language instruction: Italian instruction in a college

"Junior Year Abroad" was instituted by the University of Delaware, Newark, Del. On July 7, 1923, Professor Raymond Watson Kirkbride took a group of eight students to France for work at the University of Paris. The courses were given by Sorbonne professors.

Lettermen's club. *See* College "Lettermen's club"

Masonic college was the Masonic College of Missouri, opened for enrollment May 12,

THE FIRST

1844, near Philadelphia, Marion County, Mo. Tuition in the college was $15 a session ($10 for the preparatory department); board and washing $25. Two sessions of five months each were offered. The maximum cost was not to exceed $85 a year for the college and $75 a year for the preparatory department. From 1847 to the close of the college year 1859, the college was located at Lexington, Mo. The first president was J. Worthington Smith, A.M., who was also professor of moral philosophy. *(First Annual Catalogue. Masonic College of Missouri. September 30, 1845.)*

Negro land grant college was the Alcorn Agricultural and Mechanical College, which was established by the state of Mississippi in 1871 at Rodney, Miss. The original name was Alcorn University. Mississippi received scrip for 210,000 acres under the Morrill Act of 1862 which it disposed of for $188,928. Three fifths of the sum went to Alcorn University and the remaining two fifths towards the support of the University of Mississippi. *(Survey of Land Colleges and Universities—Department of Education. Bulletin No. 9. 1930)*

Negro university was Lincoln University, which was chartered by act of the Legislature of Pennsylvania April 29, 1854, as Ashmun Institute in Chester County, Pa., to give theological, classical, and scientific training to Negroes. It was named after Jehudi Ashmun, the reorganizer of the colony of Liberia. It opened January 1, 1857. The first president was John Pym Carter who served three years. The charter was amended April 4, 1866, changing the name to Lincoln University. *(Survey of Negro Colleges and Universities—Department of Education. Bulletin No. 7. 1928)*

Negro university (Catholic) was Xavier University, New Orleans, La., which conferred five A.B. degrees on June 6, 1928. It opened September 27, 1915, as a high school and the first diplomas were issued June 15, 1917. A two-year normal department was opened September 24, 1917, the first diplomas being awarded June 24, 1919, to eleven graduates. The college department opened September 13, 1925, with Sister Mary Frances as the first dean. The first president was the Reverend Edward Brunner, S.S.J.

Negro university to establish undergraduate, graduate, and professional schools was Howard University, Washington, D.C., founded November 20, 1866, as the Howard Theological Seminary. On January 8, 1867, the name was changed to Howard University. On May 1, 1867, the normal department and the preparatory department opened in a leased frame structure with five students, children of the trustees. It was incorporated March 2, 1867, by act of Congress (14 Stat.L.438), which authorized the establishment of the normal and preparatory,

COLLEGE—*Continued*
collegiate, theological, medical, law, and agricultural departments. The first president was the Reverend Charles Brandon Boynton, who was elected January 8, 1867, and who served until August 27, 1867. The first Negro president was Dr. Mordecai Wyatt Johnson of Charleston, W.Va., who took office July 1926. (*Walter Dyson—Howard University*)

Non-denominational college was Blount College, Knoxville, Tenn. (now the University of Tennessee), chartered September 10, 1794. The charter provided that the college "take effectual care that students of all denominations may and shall be admitted to the equal advantages of a liberal education and to the emoluments and honors of the college, so that they shall receive a like, fair, generous and equal treatment during their residence therein." The first president was Samuel Carrick. The next non-denominational college was Union College, Schenectady, N.Y., chartered February 25, 1795. It was required that the majority of the twenty-four trustees of Union College "shall not at any time be composed of persons of the same religious sect or denomination." The Reverend John Blair Smith assumed office as the first president on December 8, 1795.

Planetarium owned by a university. *See* Planetarium: Planetarium owned by a university

School for the higher education of women was started by Emma Hart Willard in 1814 in her home in Middlebury, Vt., as the Middlebury Female Seminary. In 1819 she moved to Waterford, N.Y., and established the Waterford Academy. She had hoped for state aid but no funds were appropriated. However the citizens of Troy, N.Y., provided funds for a building and in 1821 she moved to Troy and opened the Troy Female Seminary. The name was later changed and the school is now known as the Emma Willard School. Prior to the opening of Emma Willard's first school, girls were taught the merest rudiments of reading and writing, and accomplishments such as painting, embroidery, French, and singing.

State college for women was established in Columbus, Miss., by act of the Mississippi legislature, March 12, 1884. The original name of the college was the Mississippi Industrial Institute and College. The name was changed by act of the legislature in 1920 to the Mississippi State College for Women, since the word "industrial" was misleading. The first session began October 22, 1885; the first graduation exercises took place in June 1889, at which time ten A.B. degrees were conferred. The first president was Dr. Richard Watson Jones.

State university chartered was the University of Georgia, Athens, Ga. Although it was chartered on January 27, 1785, it was not opened to students until 1801. The first state university actually opened was the University of North Carolina (Chapel Hill, N.C.) on February 13, 1795. (*Elwood Patterson Cubberley and Edward Charles Elliot—State and County School Administration*)

State university supported by a direct property tax was the University of Michigan, Ann Arbor, Mich. Act No. 59, Laws of Michigan, approved March 15, 1867, assessed all taxable property one twentieth of a mill on each dollar of taxable property, for the use, aid and maintenance of the University of Michigan. The funds paid to the university in 1867 were $15,398.30.

State university to grant equal privileges to women was Indiana University, Bloomington, Ind. Sarah Parke Morrison, who was graduated in 1869, was the first woman to enter the school and the first to receive a degree from it. (*Samuel Bannister Harding—Indiana University 1820-1904*)

Technical college for women was Simmons College of Boston, Mass., which was chartered in 1899 by the provisions of the will of John Simmons, a Boston merchant who died in 1870. The college opened in 1902 and the first class graduated June 13, 1906. Thirty-two B.S. degrees were conferred. The first president was Henry Lefavour.

"Unit Cost Plan" was adopted by Rollins College of Winter Park, Fla. The plan, by which the operating expenses of the college are divided by the estimated number of students in order to ascertain the individual cost for each student, was recommended by President Hamilton Holt and was adopted in September 1933. Each student was required to pay $1,350 to cover the cost of board, room, and tuition for the year.

University extension summer meeting was held by the Society for the Extension of University Teaching at the University of Pennsylvania, Philadelphia, Pa., from July 5, 1893, to August 2, 1893. Edward T. Devine was director. Courses were offered in American history, European history, botany, biology, English literature, pedagogy, sanitation, harmony, sociology, political economy, and university extension organization. (*University Extension—October 1893*)

University founded by a federal land grant was Ohio University, Athens, Ohio, which was chartered February 18, 1804, and opened June 1, 1808, with three students. Governor Edward Tiffin presided at the first trustees' meeting. The first president was the Reverend Jacob Lindley. A contract dated October 27, 1787, between the Ohio Company of Associates and the Federal Government provided that the rental derived from the townships of land should be set aside for the support of a university.

University legally designated as a university was the University of the State of Pennsylvania; the name of the institution was changed on November 27, 1779, from the College of Philadelphia by the Pennsylvania legislature. Since 1791, the name has been University of Pennsylvania. It is a privately endowed institution, not a state university. Whether it was a university in fact before it was designated as one, and whether it was the first institution to merit being called a university, are questions of definition.

University on the Pacific coast was Willamette University, Salem, Ore., organized with the election of a board of trustees on February 1, 1842. The school opened August 13, 1844, with five students as the Oregon Institute, offering only elementary work. It was chartered January 12, 1853, as a university by the Oregon Territorial Legislature. The first officers under the new charter were elected March 19, 1853. The Oregon Institute was continued as a preparatory school. *(Willamette University Alumnus—January 1927)*

University to adopt the preceptorial system was Princeton University, Princeton, N.J., which originated the system in 1905 under President Woodrow Wilson. Forty-seven new men were added to the staff with the rank of assistant professor and the special function of "preceptor." *(Varnum Lansing Collins—Princeton)*

University west of the Allegheny Mountains was the Transylvania Seminary, which was chartered in 1783 and located near Danville, Ky. The first classes were held at the home of the Reverend David Rice. It was moved in 1789 to Lexington, Ky., and consolidated with the Kentucky Academy. In 1915 its name was changed from Transylvania University to Transylvania College. *(The Register of the Kentucky State Historical Society—Vol. 33. No. 105. October 1935)*

Woman college president was Frances Elizabeth Willard, professor of science at the Northwestern Female College, Evanston, Ill. When the reorganization took place and the name was changed to the Evanston College for Ladies in February 1871, she became president. All the members of the faculty and all the trustees were women. On June 25, 1873, the College for Ladies became the Woman's College of Northwestern University and Miss Willard became the dean of the Woman's College, which post she occupied until June 16, 1874. *(Lydia Jones Trowbridge—Frances Willard of Evanston)*

Woman college professor, accorded the same privileges as men professors, was Rebecca Mann Pennell, Professor of Physical Geography, Drawing, Natural History, Civil History and Didactics, appointed in September 1852 by Antioch College, Yellow Springs, Ohio. She conducted classes when the college opened on October 5, 1853. In other institutions, women were not permitted to attend faculty meetings at that time.

Woman coxswain of a men's collegiate varsity team. *See* Woman: Woman coxswain of a men's collegiate varsity team

Woman dean of a graduate school was Dr. Frieda Wunderlich, elected January 4, 1939, as Dean of the Graduate Faculty of Political and Social Science organized under the New School for Social Research, New York City. Her term of office began September 15, 1939.

Woman professor at a first-class medical school was Dr. Florence Rena Sabin, who served at Johns Hopkins University School of Medicine, Baltimore, Md., as Special Fellow in Anatomy 1901-1902, Assistant in Anatomy 1902-1903, Associate in Anatomy 1903-1905, Associate Professor of Anatomy 1905-1917, and Professor of Histology 1917-1925. She was the first woman to teach there and was the first woman member of the National Academy of Sciences.

Women's college (chartered) to confer on women "all such honors, degrees, and licenses as are usually conferred in colleges and universities" was Wesleyan College in Macon, Ga. The charter, 1836, called the new college "The Georgia Female College." The first class of 11 women graduated July 16, 1840. The name was changed in 1843 to Wesleyan Female College, later to Wesleyan College. The first president was George Foster Pierce. The first graduate (alphabetically) was Miss Catherine E. Brewer. The first class was examined for graduation by the president of Emory College and by the governor of the state. (It is also claimed that the first chartered women's college was the Elizabeth Female Academy, Washington, Miss., named in honor of Elizabeth Roach. It opened in November 1818, was chartered on February 17, 1819, and remained in operation until 1843.) *(Thomas Woody—A History of Woman's Education in the United States)*

Women's volunteer college unit to serve overseas was the Smith College Relief Unit of Smith College, Northampton, Mass., which sailed August 12, 1917, on the S. S. "Rochambeau." The unit consisted of 18 members, 17 of whom were graduates from the classes of 1888 to 1914, under the direction of Mrs. Harriet Boyd Hawes. *(Ruth Louise Gaines—Ladies of Grécourt)*

COLLEGE ACADEMIC COSTUME STANDARDIZATION was advocated by Gardner Cotrell Leonard of Albany, N.Y., in "The Cap and Gown in America," an article in the December 1893 issue of *University Magazine*. On May 16, 1895, a commission composed of representatives from colleges and universities assembled at Columbia University, New York City, and drew up a code, now subscribed to by 95 per cent of the colleges and universities. A Bureau of Academic Costume was chartered July 2, 1902 at Albany, N.Y., by the Regents of the University of the State of New York "to maintain a register of statutes, codes, and usages, designs and descriptions of the articles of academic costume and regalia with their correct color, materials, qualities, sizes, proportions and the arrangement thereof. . . ."

COLLEGE ALUMNI ASSOCIATION
College alumni association established for any considerable period without suspending operations was the Society of Alumni of Williams College, Williamstown, Mass., formed September 1821. The first president was Dr. Asa Burbank of the class of 1797, and the first secretary was Charles Augustus Dewey of the class of 1811.

College alumni association secretary (full time paid position) was established June 30, 1897, by the University of Michigan, Ann Arbor, Mich., to foster service on the part of the alumni for the university. This office was supported by the regular alumni organization. The first secretary was Ralph C. McAllister.

COLLEGE "LETTERMEN'S CLUB" for sports was established January 29, 1904, at the University of Chicago, Chicago, Ill., by Amos Alonzo Stagg. It was known as the "order of the 'C.'" Since then practically all colleges and high schools have established similar organizations. The practice of awarding blankets to lettermen who had completed their competition was initiated by Amos Alonzo Stagg at the University of Chicago following the football season of 1904. This practice has also been widely copied.

COLLEGE LITERARY SOCIETY
College literary society was the Cliosophic Society, founded at Princeton University, Princeton, N.J., in 1765. (*Charles Richard Williams—The Cliosophic Society, Princeton University*)

College literary society (coeducational) was the Alethezetean Society of Antioch College, Yellow Springs, Ohio, founded in December 1853. The society was disbanded in 1855 by vote of the faculty.

COLLEGE MAGAZINE. *See* Periodical: College magazine

COLLEGE OF SURGEONS. *See* Medical society: American College of Surgeons

COLLEGE SELF-GOVERNMENT ORGANIZATION was the Bryn Mawr Self-Government Association, chartered February 23, 1892, by the trustees, subjecting student conduct outside the classrooms at Bryn Mawr, Pa., to student rulings.

COLLEGE STUDENT
College student to work his way through college was Zechariah Brigden, fourteen years old, who graduated from Harvard College, Cambridge, Mass., in 1657. He earned money by "ringing the bell and waytinge."

COLONIAL CITIZENSHIP. *See* Citizenship: Citizenship (colonial) conferred by special grant

COLONIAL ELECTION. *See* Election: Accredited colonial election; Election law: Fraudulent election law (colonial)

COLONIAL GOVERNMENT
Colonial council in America was held in Jamestown, Va., on May 13, 1607, and consisted of Bartholomew Gosnold, Edward Maria Wingfield, Christopher Newport, John Smith, John Ratcliffe, John Martin, and George Kendall. Edward Wingfield was chosen the first president for a year. King James I placed the names of the officers in a sealed box which was not to be opened until the colonists arrived in America. (*Edward Lewis Goodwin—Colonial Church in Virginia*)

Colonial government union was the United Colonies of New England, organized May 10, 1643, in Boston, Mass., by the colonies of Connecticut, Massachusetts, New Haven, and Plymouth for "a firm and perpetual league of friendship and amity for offence and defence, mutual advice and succor, upon all occasions, both for preserving and propagating the truth and liberties of the gospel, and for their own mutual safety and welfare." A board of 8 commissioners, 2 from each colony, formed the "consocation." Issues could be referred to the general courts for appeal, if not approved by 6 votes. John Winthrop of Massachusetts was the first president. Massachusetts, the largest colony, gradually withdrew since it did not have proportional representation. (*Herbert Levi Osgood—American Colonies in the Seventeenth Century*)

Government on the Pacific coast was authorized by the people of Willamette Valley at Champoeg, Ore., May 2, 1843, when Americans and Canadians met in a field to consider the report of the Committee of Twelve on Organizations, appointed February 2, 1843. A

THE FIRST

THE FIRST

committee of nine was chosen on July 5, 1843, to report a plan of civil government. An executive committee of three, Alanson Beers, David Hill, and Joseph Gale, was appointed for the year ending May 14, 1844. (A second executive committee, P. G. Stewart, Osborne Russell, and W. J. Bailey, served from May 14, 1844 to June 12, 1845.) The first governor was George Abernethy, who served from June 12, 1845, to March 3, 1849, when the United States took over jurisdiction of the Oregon territory. (*John B. Horner—Oregon, Her History, Her Great Men and Her Literature*)

Independent government in any of the American colonies was formed in March 1776 in Charleston, S.C. John Rutledge was elected president, Henry Laurens, vice president, and William Henry Drayton, chief justice. An army and navy were created, privy council and assembly were elected, and the issue of $600,000 of paper money was authorized, as well as the issue of coin. (*The Centennial of the Incorporation of Charleston, S.C.*)

COLONIAL MISSIONARY SOCIETY. *See* Missionary society: Missionary society (colonial)

COLONIAL PATENT. *See* Patent: Patent granted by the colonies

COLONIAL POST OFFICE. *See* Post office: Post office (colonial)

COLONIAL POSTMASTER GENERAL. *See* Postmaster: Postmaster general (colonial)

COLONIAL REBELLION. *See* Rebellion: Rebellion (colonial)

COLONIAL SUFFRAGE. *See* Woman suffrage: Colony to grant suffrage to women

COLONIAL TREATY. *See* Treaty: Colonial treaty with the Indians

COLONIAL WARFARE. *See* War (colonial)

COLONIST
Civilian settlement west of the Allegheny Mountains, other than forts and outposts, was led by Dr. Thomas Walker, a physician, and five companions, Ambrose Powell, Colby Chew, William Tomlinson, Henry Lawless, and John Hughes. They started from Charlottesville, Va., on March 6, 1750, for the Loyal Land Company of Virginia and on April 23, 1750, reached Barbourville, Ky., where they built a house which was completed April 30, 1750.

Colonial white settlement (north of Florida) was on Neutral Island at Calais, Me., on the St. Croix River at the head of Passamaquoddy Bay. It was founded in 1604 by Pierre du Guast, Sieur de Monts, the French explorer. (*Isaac Case Knowlton—Annals of Calais, Me.*)

Colonists to reach the Pacific coast left New York City on September 6, 1810, on the S.S. "Tonquin," a 290-ton vessel captained by Jonathan Thorn. They rounded Cape Horn, December 25, 1810, landing April 12, 1811, at Cape Disappointment, Wash., a promontory at the mouth of the Columbia River. The enterprise was sponsored by John Jacob Astor. (*Elizabeth Louisa Gebhard—Life and Ventures of the Original John Jacob Astor*)

English settlement in America (permanent) was established by the colonists who were sent out by the London Company on December 19, 1606, from Blackwell, England, and who arrived at Jamestown, Va., on May 13, 1607. One hundred and five colonists arrived on the "Susan Constant," 100 tons, under Captain Christopher Newport; the "Godspeed," 40 tons, under Captain Bartholomew Gosnold; and the "Discovery," 20 tons, under Captain John Ratcliffe.

Permanent white settlement in America was founded on September 8, 1565, by Don Pedro Menéndez de Avilés at St. Augustine, Fla. He left Cadiz, Spain, on July 28, 1565, and sighted land off the Florida coast August 28, 1565, St. Augustine's day. (*Herbert Eugene Bolton—The Spanish Borderlands*)

Women to cross the continent were Narcissa Prentiss Whitman and Eliza Hart Spalding, who crossed the continental divide, South Pass, Wyoming on July 4, 1836. They reached Fort Walla Walla, Wash., September 1, 1836, accompanied by their husbands, Marcus Whitman, M.D., and the Reverend Henry Harmon Spalding, Presbyterian missionaries sent by the American Board of Commissioners for Foreign Missions. (*Washington Historical Quarterly January, 1917*)

COLOR MOVIES. *See* Moving Picture: Colored moving pictures

COLOR ORGAN. *See* Organ: Color organ

COLOR PHOTORADIO. *See* Radio facsimile transmission: Color photoradio news photograph transmitted by radio for publication

COLOR PLATE IN A BOOK. *See* Book: Book with color plates

COLOR PLATES. *See* Book: Book with color plates

COLOR TALKING FILM. *See* Moving picture: Talking picture entirely in color

COLOR TELEVISION. *See under* Television—Telecast

COLORED COMMUNITY OF CATHO-LIC NUNS. *See* Catholic nuns: Catholic nuns (colored community)

COLORED NEWSPAPER SUPPLE-MENT. *See* Newspaper: Newspaper Sunday comic section

COLORSCOPE public demonstration was made in New York City June 5, 1930. The colorscope, invented by Harold Horton Sheldon of New York University, and Dr. Walter Arthur Schneider, is a photoelectric cell which reacts to colored light beams. It gives off infinitesimal electric currents capable of operating relays, which will start or stop machinery, operate graph needles, or perform other laboratory or shop service. It matches colors more exactly than is possible by the human eye.

COLUMBUS MONUMENT. *See* Monument: Monument to Christopher Columbus

COMB of ivory was made at Centerbrook, Conn., by Andrew Lord in 1789. He cut the plates and teeth with a handsaw.

COMB-CUTTING MACHINE was invented by Phineas Pratt of Connecticut, who received a patent April 12, 1799, on a "machine for making combs." Phineas Pratt and Abel Pratt cut the plates with handsaws and the teeth with circular saws operated by a windmill and waterpower at Ivoryton, Conn. The firm is now Pratt, Read & Company. *(Perry Walton—Comb Making in America)*

COMB FACTORY on a commercial scale was undertaken by Enoch Noyes of West Newbury, Mass., in 1759. His combs were made from animal horns flattened out with their original color untouched. *(Perry Walton—Comb Making in America)*

COMBAT INFANTRY BADGE. *See* Medal: Combat infantry badge

COMBUSTION ENGINE. *See* Engine: Internal combustion engine

COMIC BOOKS. *See* Periodical: Comic books

COMIC CHARACTER MONUMENT. *See* Monument: Monument to a comic character

COMIC HISTORY. *See* History: Comic history

COMIC OPERA. *See* Opera: Opera (comic)

COMIC SECTION IN A NEWSPAPER. *See* Newspaper: Newspaper Sunday comic section

COMIC WEEKLY. *See* Periodical: Comic weekly

COMMANDER-IN-CHIEF OF THE CONTINENTAL NAVY. *See* Naval officer: Commander-in-chief of the Continental navy

COMMEMORATIVE COINAGE. *See* Money: Commemorative coinage

COMMEMORATIVE POSTAGE STAMP. *See* Postage stamp: Commemorative postage stamps

COMMERCE AND LABOR DEPART-MENT (U.S.) was authorized by act of February 14, 1903 (32 Stat.L.825), an "act to establish the Department of Commerce and Labor." The first secretary was George Bruce Cortelyou of New York, appointed February 16, 1903. The act of March 4, 1913 (37 Stat.L. 736) created the Department of Labor and changed the name of the Department of Commerce and Labor to the Department of Commerce. The Secretary of Commerce and Labor, William Cox Redfield, became the Secretary of Commerce and served until March 5, 1921. William Bauchop Wilson was made Secretary of Labor and served until November 1, 1919.
See also Commerce Department (U.S.)

COMMERCE CASE decided under the Constitution by the Supreme Court was the case of *Thomas Gibbons* vs *Aaron Ogden,* the opinion on which was written by Chief Justice John Marshall in February 1824. The decision determined that navigation from one state to another was interstate commerce and ruled, "This court is therefore of opinion that the decree of the Court of New York for the trial of Impeachments and the Correction of Errors, affirming the decree of the Chancellor of that State, which perpetually enjoins the said Thomas Gibbons, the appellant, from navigating the waters of the State of New York with the steam boats the 'Stoudinger' and the 'Bellona,' by steam or fire, is erroneous, and ought to be reversed, and the same is hereby

THE FIRST

reversed." *(Henry Wheaton—Reports of Cases Argued and Adjudged in the Supreme Court of the United States, February Term. 1824)*

COMMERCE COURT (U.S.). *See* Court: Commerce court (U.S.)

COMMERCE DEPARTMENT (U.S.)
See also Commerce and Labor Department (U.S.)

Commerce Department (U.S.) was established on March 4, 1913, by act of Congress which authorized the division of the Department of Commerce and Labor into two departments. The Secretary of Commerce and Labor, William Cox Redfield, became the first Secretary of Commerce on March 5, 1913 and served until March 5, 1921.

Foreign and Domestic Commerce Bureau was created by the act of August 23, 1912 (37 Stat.L.409) which provided that all duties of the Bureau of Manufactures and the Bureau of Statistics should be exercised by the Bureau of Foreign and Domestic Commerce.

COMMERCIAL ARTIST. *See* Artist: Artist successful in commercial art

COMMERCIAL CORPORATION. *See* Corporation: Commercial corporation

COMMERCIAL HIGH SCHOOL
Commercial high school was established in Pittsburgh, Pa., in 1868, graduating a class of fourteen in 1869. A school report covering the period 1869-1873 contains the following statement: "In August 1868, the Central Board decided to try the experiment of extending the usefulness of the school by creating a Normal Department and a Commercial Department. In the Commercial School the course of study embraces the same studies as are pursued in the best Commercial Colleges, and a diploma is issued to those who sustain a satisfactory examination."

COMMERCIAL MUSEUM. *See* Museum: Commercial museum

COMMERCIAL POLICY EXECUTIVE COMMITTEE, composed of representatives of the various departments, agencies and commissions of the government which are particularly concerned with trade relations with other countries, was organized November 21, 1933. George Nelson Peek, Agricultural Adjustment Administrator, was designated head of this committee as special assistant to the President on American trade policy.

THE FIRST

COMMERCIAL RATING AGENCY. *See* Business: Commercial rating agency

COMMISSION FORM OF GOVERNMENT originated in Galveston, Tex., in 1901 as an emergency measure following the flood. The legislature granted Galveston a charter on April 19, 1901, and the system went into operation on September 18, 1901. Under this form, large powers both legislative and executive are vested in a single group of officers, elected by the whole body of voters within the city without regard to political party. *(Ernest Smith Bradford—Commission Government in American Cities)*

COMMODITY CREDIT CORPORATION (U.S.) was created by Executive Order No. 6340 dated October 16, 1933, in order to carry out efficiently and effectively the provisions of the emergency legislation approved and passed by Congress during 1932 and 1933. The Board of Directors consisted of eight members, with Lynn Porter Talley as president. The corporation was given authority to buy, sell, and deal in agricultural and other commodities and to loan and borrow thereon; to assist in crop reduction and marketing programs; and to store, handle and process commodities of all kinds in connection with relief plans.

COMMON CARRIER LICENSE. *See* Automobile license (federal): Common carrier license

COMMON PRAYER BOOK. *See* Book: Book of common prayer

COMMUNICATIONS COMMISSION. See Federal Communications Commission

COMMUNICATIONS SATELLITE. *See* Rocket: Communications satellite

COMMUNION CUP
Individual communion cups to replace the single chalice were introduced May 1894 by the Central Presbyterian Church, Rochester, N.Y. One of the elders, Dr. Charles Forbes, urged the adoption of individual cups.

COMMUNIST LABOR PARTY OF AMERICA was formed August 31, 1919, in Chicago, Ill., to stand by the principles laid down by the Third Internationale formed in Moscow, Russia. The party adopted the emblem of a scythe and hammer surrounded by a wreath of wheat, and the motto "Workers of the World Unite." On September 1, 1919, the party held a convention in Chicago which was attended by 140 delegates, representing 58,000 party members.

THE FIRST

THE FIRST

COMMUNIST PARTY OF AMERICA was formed September 2, 1919, in Chicago, Ill. Members of the party adopted as an emblem the figure of earth in the center in white with gold lines and a red flag across the face bearing the inscription "All power to the workers." Their program was the seizure of political power, the overthrow of capitalism, and the destruction of the bourgeois state.

COMMUNISTIC SOCIETY
Communistic non-religious settlement was made at New Harmony, Ind., in 1825, by Robert Owen and his associates, who purchased for approximately $150,000 the development of George Rapp and his Rappites. It had about 1,000 members and existed until May 1827. *(Jacob Schneck and Richard Owen—The History of New Harmony, Ind.)*

Communistic society was a monastic group established in the colony of Ephrata, eight miles from Lancaster, Pa., in 1733 by Johann Conrad Beissel. A convent for sisters was similarly established. *(Julius Friedrich Sachse—The German Sectarians of Pennsylvania)*

COMMUNITY CHORUS. *See* Music: Community chorus

COMMUNITY FOREST. *See* Forest: Community forest

COMMUNITY HOSPITAL. *See* Hospital: Community hospital

COMMUNITY TELEVISION ANTENNA SYSTEM. *See* Television: Community television antenna system

COMMUNITY TRUST was the Cleveland Foundation, Cleveland, Ohio, established January 2, 1914, by resolution passed by the board of directors of the Cleveland Trust Company, Cleveland, Ohio. A temporary survey committee was formed in February 1914 which served until 1917 conducting certain important community surveys. The first distribution committee of the foundation was appointed in May 1917 with Dr. James De Long Williamson as chairman. The first director of the Cleveland Foundation was Dr. Raymond Moley, serving under the Distribution Committee from 1919 to 1923. The community trust plan was conceived by Frederick Harris Goff, then president of the Cleveland Trust Company.

COMPANY NURSE. *See* Nurse: Nurse employed by an industrial organization

COMPARATIVE PHILOLOGY CHAIR. *See* Philology chair: Comparative philology chair

"COMPARTMENTIZER" FREIGHT CARS. *See* Railroad car: "Compartmentizer" freight cars

COMPASS. *See* Gyro compass; Radio compass

COMPENSATION (workmen's) *See* Insurance: Workmen's compensation insurance law (federal); Insurance (workmen's compensation law (state); Workmen's compensation

COMPOSER. *See* Musician: Composer

COMPOSER OF AN AMERICAN OPERA. *See* Opera: Opera by an American composer

COMPOSERS', AUTHORS', AND PUBLISHERS' ASSOCIATION. *See* Music society: Music society for the literary protection of composers and authors

COMPOSOGRAPH PHOTOGRAPH. *See* Newspaper: Composograph photograph

COMPOTYPE was designed and patented on October 20, 1925, by Clifton Chisholm of Cleveland, Ohio, who obtained patent No. 1,557,-754 on an "embossing machine." He assigned the patent to the Multigraph Sales Company of Cleveland, Ohio. The machine embosses characters on an aluminum strip from which printed material is produced.

COMPOUND LOCOMOTIVE. *See* Locomotive: Duplex compound locomotive

COMPRESSED AIR. *See* Air (compressed)

COMPRESSED PILL. *See* Pill: Compressed pills or tablets

COMPRESSED YEAST. *See* Yeast: Compressed fresh yeast

COMPTOMETER. *See* Adding machine. Adding machine absolutely accurate at al. times

COMPTROLLER
Comptroller of the Currency was Hugh McCulloch, who served from May 9, 1863, to March 8, 1865, when he resigned to accept appointment as Secretary of the Treasury. His office was authorized February 25, 1863 (12 Stat.L.665). The term was five years at $5,000 a year. *(Thomas P. Kane—The Romance and Tragedy of Banking)*

THE FIRST

Comptroller of the United States Treasury was Nicholas Eveleigh of South Carolina, who served from September 11, 1789, to April 16, 1791. The office was authorized September 2, 1789 (1 Stat.L.65).

COMPTROLLER GENERAL of the United States was John Raymond McCarl, appointed by President Warren Gamaliel Harding on June 27, 1921. He served from July 1, 1921, to June 30, 1936. His office was authorized by act of June 10, 1921 (42 Stat.-L.23). The term was fifteen years without eligibility for reappointment and the salary was $10,000 per annum.

COMPULSORY EDUCATION LAW. *See* Education: Compulsory education law

COMPUTER
Electronic computer was the Electronic Numerical Integrator and Computer (ENIAC), designed and built under the direction of J. Presper Eckert, Jr., and John W. Mauchly of the Moore School of Electrical Engineering at the University of Pennsylvania, Philadelphia, Pa. Completed in 1946, the ENIAC subsequently was used at the Ordnance Department of the U.S. Army at Aberdeen, Md. It was housed in a room 30 by 50 feet, contained approximately 18,000 vacuum tubes, and required 130 kilowatts per hour.

Electronic computer (commercial) was the Univac I, manufactured by the Remington Rand Corporation, Philadelphia, Pa. It was demonstrated and dedicated at the U.S. Bureau of the Census at Philadelphia on June 14, 1951. It could retain a maximum of 1,000 separate numbers; accept information contained on magnetic tape at the rate of more than 10,000 characters per second; and add, subtract, multiply, divide, sort, and collate, and take square and cube roots as needed.

Electronic computer to employ Thin-Film memory was the Univac 1107, built by the Sperry Rand Corporation at St. Paul, Minn., and announced December 9, 1960. Its operational speed was measured in billionths of a second (nanoseconds), compared to speeds in most other computers measured in millionths of a second (microseconds). The computer consisted of a ferromagnetic film a few millionths of an inch thick formed by the deposit of vapors of iron, nickel, cobalt, or other materials on a suitable surface, such as a thin glass plate, a process generating incredible magnetic qualities which may be employed as computer memory. Memory could be accessed more than a million times a second.

Mobile computer center was established by Remington Rand Univac, a division of the Sperry Rand Corporation, New York City,

THE FIRST

which equipped a motor van with a Univac Solid-State 90 computer. The first assignment was undertaken on March 27, 1961, for the Douglas Aircraft Corporation, Charlotte, N.C.

Solid-state electronic computer was developed by Remington Rand Univac, a division of the Sperry Rand Corporation at the company's Philadelphia, Pa., laboratories in 1958 and built at Ilion, N.Y. This computer, because of solid-state elements such as transistors, Ferractor amplifiers, and magnetic cores used in its construction, weighed only 3,500 pounds and occupied only 275 square feet of floor space. Though it had 100 times the capacity and 10 times the speed of the first electronic computer, it occupied about ⅙ the space.

COMPUTER PUMP. *See* Pump: Computer pump

COMPUTING MACHINE. *See* Adding machine

COMPUTING SCALE. *See* Scale: Computing scales

CONCEALED BED. *See* Bed: "Concealed bed"

CONCENTRATED MILK. *See* Milk: Concentrated milk

CONCERT. *See* Music: Concert

CONCHOLOGY REPORT by an American to appear in the United States was Thomas Say's *Descriptions of Land and Fresh-Water Shells of the United States,* which was published in Philadelphia, Pa., in 1817 in an American edition of William Nicholson's *British Encyclopedia, or Dictionary of Arts and Sciences.* It consisted of 15 pages and 4 plates which were published in the second volume, and reprinted separately. *(Harry Bischoff Weiss and Grace M. Ziegler—Thomas Say)*

CONCILIATION COURT. *See* Court: Conciliation tribunal for small claims

CONCORDANCE OF THE BIBLE. *See* Bible concordance

CONCRETE BARGE. *See* Ship: Concrete barge

CONCRETE BRIDGE. *See* Bridge: Concrete arch highway bridge; Bridge: Concrete cantilever bridge

CONCRETE MONOLITHIC BUILDING. *See* Building: Monolithic concrete building

THE FIRST

CONCRETE ROAD. *See* Road: Concrete road

CONDENSED MILK. *See* Milk: Condensed milk (commercial)

CONDUCTOR-COMPOSER (woman). *See* Musician: Woman conductor-composer

CONDUIT. *See* Water conduit: Drinking water conduit

CONE (ice cream). *See* Ice cream cone

CONFECTIONERY MACHINE for making "suckers," more familiarly known by the trade name "lollipops," supposed to be an exclusive name used by the Bradley-Smith Company of New Haven, Conn., was manufactured by the Racine Confectioners' Machinery Company, Racine, Wis., in 1908. Its capacity at that time was forty lollipops a minute, a rate which manufacturers felt would produce more suckers in a week than they could sell in a year.

CONFEDERATE COINAGE. *See* Money: Confederate coinage

CONFEDERATE CRUISER. *See* Ship: Confederate cruiser

CONFEDERATE CURRENCY. *See* Money: Confederate currency

CONFEDERATE FLAG. *See* Flag: Confederate States flag

CONFEDERATE GENERAL KILLED. *See* Civil war: Confederate general killed in the Civil War

CONFEDERATE STATES CONGRESS. *See* Congress of the Confederate States

CONFEDERATE STATES CONSTITUTION. *See* Constitution of the Confederate States of America

CONFEDERATE STATES PRESIDENT. *See* President of the Confederate States

CONFEDERATE STATES SEAL. *See* Seal: Seal of the Confederate States of America

CONFEDERATE STATES WHITE HOUSE. *See* Building: "White House of the Confederacy"

THE FIRST

CONFERENCE
Conference of American Republics was the General Congress of South American States assembled March 14, 1826, at Panama. Convoked by Simón Bolívar, who sent invitations in December 1824, it was attended by delegates from Mexico, Colombia, Peru and Central America. Richard Clough Anderson and John Sargeant were appointed delegates from the United States in July 1825, but their appointment was not confirmed until December 6, 1825, and the conference adjourned before they reached it.

Conference of great powers to be held on American soil and affecting American interests was the Conference on the Limitation of Armaments which assembled in Washington, D.C., November 12, 1921, to February 6, 1922, at Memorial Continental Hall. Nine nations took part in the Conference: the United States, Great Britain, France, Italy, Japan, China, Holland, Belgium, and Portugal. The American delegation consisted of Secretary of State Charles Evans Hughes, Senators Oscar Wilder Underwood and Henry Cabot Lodge, and Elihu Root.

Interstate legislative conference. *See* Legislative conference (interstate)

Pan American Conference in the United States opened in Washington, D.C., on October 2, 1889. It was called the First International Conference of American States and was initiated by James Gillespie Blaine, Secretary of State under President Benjamin Harrison. Ten nations signed an arbitration treaty. *(Russell Herman Conwell—Life and Public Service of James G. Blaine)*

CONGREGATION (Jewish). *See* Jewish congregation: Jewish congregation

CONGREGATIONAL CHURCH
Congregational Church was founded in 1620 by 102 Pilgrim Separatists under the leadership of William Brewster, William Bradford, and Edward Winslow, upon their arrival at Plymouth, Mass. Ralph Smith was the first pastor. *(Albert Elijah Dunning—Congregationalists in America)*

Congregational Church council or synod met at Mr. Shepard's church, Cambridge (Newtowne) Mass., August 30, 1637, to condemn the preachings of Anne Hutchinson's party. Eighty-two errors of Mrs. Hutchinson's party were enumerated and condemned. The synod adjourned September 22, 1637. *(Williston Walker—A History of the Congregational Churches in the United States)*

Congregational woman minister. *See* Woman: Woman ordained a minister

THE FIRST

THE FIRST

CONGRESS (Continental). *See* Continental congress: Continental Congress

CONGRESS of the Confederate States held its first provisional session in Montgomery, Ala., from February 4, 1861, to March 16, 1861. The President of the Senate was Alexander Hamilton Stephens of Georgia, the president pro tempore Robert Mercer Taliaferro Hunter of Virginia, and the Secretary of the Senate, James H. Nash of South Carolina. The House of Representatives under the permanent constitution met in Richmond, Va., February 18, 1861. Emmet Dixon of Georgia was elected clerk, and Thomas Salem Bocock of Virginia, speaker. The session adjourned April 21, 1862.

CONGRESS OF THE UNITED STATES Cabinet officer to address a joint session of Congress. *See* Cabinet of the United States: Cabinet officer to address a joint session of Congress

Congress in which 1,000 bills were introduced was the Twenty-second Congress, held from December 5, 1831, to July 16, 1832 (226 days) and December 3, 1832, to March 2, 1833 (91 days). There were 976 bills and 24 joint resolutions introduced (of which 462 were passed); 175 public acts and 16 resolutions; and 270 private acts and 1 resolution.

Congress of the United States met in New York City from March 4, 1789, to September 29, 1789. The 13 states were represented by 26 senators and 65 representatives. The largest number of representatives from any state was 10, from Virginia. The first quorum of the House of Representatives met April 1, 1789, when 30 members were present, and the first Senate quorum assembled on April 6, 1789. The final session in New York City was held August 12, 1790, when the capital was moved to Philadelphia, Pa. The first session was held in Philadelphia December 6, 1790, and the final session on May 14, 1800. The act of April 24, 1800 (2 Stat.L.55) provided for the removal of the government to Washington, D.C., and on November 17, 1800, the second session of the Sixth Congress convened there. On February 27, 1801, Congress assumed jurisdiction over the District of Columbia.

Congress to appropriate a billion dollars was the Fifty-second Congress (March 4, 1891 to March 3, 1893), which appropriated $507,376,-397.52 in the first session for the fiscal year 1893 and $519,535,293.31 in the second session for the fiscal year 1894. The first session was held from December 7, 1891, to August 5, 1892 (251 days) and the second session was from December 5, 1892, to March 3, 1893 (89 days). The appropriations included appropriations for the postal service, payable from postal revenues, and estimated permanent annual appropriations, including sinking-fund requirements.

Congressional act was "An Act to regulate the Time and Manner of administering certain Oaths" which was approved by President George Washington on June 1, 1789 (1 Stat.L. 23).

Congressional act declared unconstitutional by the Supreme Court of the United States was the act of September 24, 1789 (1 Stat.L.80, sec.13). This section authorized the Supreme Court to issue writs of *mandamus* "in cases warranted by the principles and usages of law, to any courts appointed, or persons holding office, under the authority of the United States." In a suit for a *mandamus* to the Secretary of State, the Court held that it had no jurisdiction, since the statute purported to extend it to cases not named in the Constitution.

Congressional hearing witness (woman). *See* Woman: Woman Congressional hearing witness

Congressional investigation was authorized March 27, 1792, when the House of Representatives by a vote of 44 to 10 resolved "that a committee [of seven] be appointed to inquire into the causes of the failure of the late expedition under Major General [Arthur] St. Clair; and that the said committee be empowered to call for such persons, papers and records as may be necessary to assist their inquiries." The committee decided that his defeat on the Ohio-Indiana border on November 4, 1791 "can in no respect be imputed to his conduct either at any time before or during the action." (*Annals of Congress—Second Congress, First Session*)

Congressional library. *See* Library: Library of Congress

Congressional opening session to be televised. See Television—Telecast: Congressional opening session to be televised

Congressional proceedings report. *See* Senate journal

Congressional session in air-conditioned Senate and House chambers was the second session of the Seventy-fifth Congress, which opened November 15, 1937.

Joint meeting of the Senate and the House of Representatives was held Monday April 6, 1789, in the Senate Chamber, New York City. The House of Representatives attended the opening and the counting by the Senate of the electoral votes for President and Vice President. The electoral votes were cast as follows: George Washington 69, John Adams 34, Samuel Huntingdon 2, John Jay 9, John Hancock 4, Robert H. Harrison 6, George Clin-

THE FIRST

THE FIRST

CONGRESS OF THE UNITED STATES
—*Continued*

ton 3, John Rutledge 6, John Milton 2, James Armstrong 1, Edward Telfair 1, and Benjamin Lincoln 1. Only ten states voted. Rhode Island, North Carolina, and New York did not vote. The first presidential election was held Wednesday, January 7, 1789, and on Wednesday, February 4, 1789, the electors elected the President and Vice President.

Nullification proceedings. *See* Nullification proceedings

Officer to preside over both of the branches of Congress was Schuyler Colfax of Indiana, who served as Speaker of the House of Representatives in the 38th, 39th, and 40th Congresses (March 4, 1863, to March 3, 1869) and who as Vice President under President Ulysses Simpson Grant (March 4, 1869, to March 3, 1873) presided over the Senate.

President elected by the House of Representatives. *See* President: President elected by the House of Representatives

Prime Minister of England to address the Congress of the United States was Ramsay MacDonald, who delivered a short talk before the Senate on October 7, 1929.

Reigning queen to address a joint session of Congress was Queen Wilhelmina of the Netherlands, who made a brief address on August 6, 1942.

Special session was held May 15, 1797, in Philadelphia, Pa. President John Adams had issued a proclamation on March 25, 1797, for convening the Senate and the House of Representatives to consider the difficulty with France. (*Annals of Congress—Fifth Congress, First Session*)

Woman lobbyist. *See* Woman: Woman lobbyist

Woman private citizen to address the House of Representatives and the Senate was Mme. Chiang Kai-shek of China, who spoke before both houses on February 18, 1943. (Reigning Queen Wilhelmina of the Netherlands, however, was the first woman to address a joint session of Congress.)

Woman witness at a congressional hearing. *See* Woman: Woman congressional hearing witness

CONGRESS (U.S.)—HOUSE OF REPRESENTATIVES

Brawl in the House of Representatives took place in Philadelphia, Pa., January 30, 1798, during the presidential administration of John Adams. Matthew Lyon of Vermont had an argument with Roger Griswold of Connecticut and spat in Griswold's face. A resolution was introduced to expel Lyon. Lyon acted as his own attorney and defended himself in the proceedings, which lasted from January 30 to February 12, 1798, and occupied practically all the attention of the House. The resolution was carried, 52 to 44, but Lyon was not expelled, the measure requiring a two-thirds vote. (*Annals of Congress—Fifth Congress, Second Session*)

Committee of the House of Representatives was the Committee on Elections, a standing committee, appointed April 2, 1789, to determine the eligibility and rights of admission of those who had been elected. It was resolved "that a committee be appointed to prepare and report such standing rules and orders of proceedings as may be proper to be observed." (*Chester Harvey Rowell—A Historical and Legal Digest of all the Contested Election Cases in the House of Representatives*)

Congressional committee headed by a woman was the District of Columbia Affairs Committee, of which Mary Teresa Norton of Jersey City, N.J., became the chairman on December 15, 1931. She served until June 22, 1937, when she became the chairman of the House Committee on Labor.

Congressional standing committee headed by a Negro was the Committee on Expenditures in the Executive Departments to which William Levi Dawson of Chicago, Ill., was appointed on January 18, 1949.

Congressman. *See* Congressman (U.S.)

Contested election in the House of Representatives was between David Ramsay and William Loughton Smith of South Carolina. Smith took his seat April 13, 1789. On April 15, 1789, Ramsay presented a petition that Smith be declared ineligible, on the ground that he had not been "seven years a citizen of the United States," as he had studied abroad during that period. The dispute was referred to the Committee on Elections on April 18, 1789, which ruled that Smith was entitled to his seat. (*Matthew St. Clair Clarke and David A. Hall—Cases on Contested Elections in Congress, published by the House of Representatives, 1834*)

Filibuster of "dilatory tactics" occurred June 11, 1790, when Elbridge Gerry of Massachusetts and William Loughton Smith of South

THE FIRST

Carolina made long speeches in the House of Representatives during consideration of the resolution to change the seat of government. *(Annals of Congress—First Congress, Second Session)*

Foreign clergyman to open the House of Representatives with prayer was the Reverend Abraham de Sola, D.D., LL.D., Professor of Oriental History, McGill University, Montreal, Canada, who delivered the invocation January 9, 1872.

Gag rule was adopted May 26, 1836, by the House of Representatives, which voted 117 to 68 that "And, whereas it is extremely important and desirable that the agitation of this subject should be finally arrested, for the purpose of restoring tranquility to the public mind, your committee respectfully recommend the adoption of the following additional resolution: Resolved that all petitions, memorials, resolutions, propositions, or papers, relating in any way, or to any extent whatever, to the subject of slavery, or the abolition of slavery, shall without being either printed or referred, be laid upon the table, and that no further action whatever shall be had thereon." *(Register of Debates in Congress. Vol. 12)*

Girl page was Gene Cox, 13, daughter of Representative Edward Eugene Cox of Georgia, who served on the first day of the Seventy-sixth Congress convening January 3, 1939, and received a check for $4 for her services.

House of Representatives met in New York City, Wednesday, March 4, 1789, and was attended by 4 delegates from Massachusetts, 3 from Connecticut, 4 from Pennsylvania, 1 from Virginia, and 1 from South Carolina. Meetings were constantly called and adjourned inasmuch as no quorum was present. The first quorum gathered Wednesday, April 1, 1789, and the first business transacted was the balloting for Speaker of the House. Frederick Augustus Conrad Muhlenberg of Pennsylvania was elected. John Beckley was elected clerk. The first session of Congress held in Washington, D.C., convened from November 17, 1800 to March 3, 1801, the second session of the Sixth Congress.

Jewish rabbi to open the House of Representatives with prayer was Rabbi Morris Jacob Raphall, rabbi of Congregation B'nai Jeshurun, New York City, who delivered the invocation on February 1, 1860 (first session of the Thirty-sixth Congress). *(Congressional Globe. Feb. 2, 1860. p. 648)*

Joint meeting of the Senate and the House of Representatives. *See* Congress of the United States: Joint meeting of the Senate and the House of Representatives

THE FIRST

Officer to preside over both of the branches of Congress. *See* Congress of the United States: Officer to preside over both of the branches of Congress

Negro preacher to deliver a sermon in the House of Representatives was the Reverend Dr. Henry Highland Garnet, pastor of the 15th Street Presbyterian Church, Washington, D.C. The Chaplain of the House, the Reverend William Henry Channing, extended an invitation to him to preach a sermon commemorating the triumph of the Union Army and the deliverance of the country from chattel slavery. Dr. Garnet delivered his sermon on Sunday, February 12, 1865, to a crowded chamber. He was, incidentally, the first Negro allowed in the House, as previously Negroes had been forbidden to enter the grounds. *(James McCune Smith—Sketch of the Life and Labors of the Rev. Henry Highland Garnet)*

President elected by the House of Representatives. *See* President: President elected by the House of Representatives

Speaker of the House of the first Congress, 1789-1791, was Frederick Augustus Conrad Muhlenberg. *(Hubert Bruce Fuller—Speakers of the House)*

CONGRESS (U.S.)—SENATE
Broadcast from the Senate chamber, Washington, D.C., was made March 4, 1929, in connection with the inauguration ceremonies of President Herbert Clark Hoover and Vice President Charles Curtis. The retiring Vice President, Charles Gates Dawes, and the incoming Vice President, Charles Curtis, were both heard.

Contested election in the Senate was that of Abraham Alfonse Albert Gallatin of Pennsylvania. He presented his credentials as senator-elect on February 28, 1793. No action was taken during the Second Congress, but on December 2, 1793, a petition was presented alleging that he had not been a citizen of the United States for the nine years required by the Constitution. The case began February 20, 1794, and on February 28, 1794, the Federalist Senate declared his election void. *(John Austin Stevens—Albert Gallatin)*

Loud-speaker in the Senate, Washington, D.C., was installed for the impeachment proceedings of Federal Judge Harold Louderback, Judge of the United States District Court for the northern district of California, held in the Senate from May 15, 1933 to May 24, 1933. He was acquitted.

Officer to preside over both of the branches of Congress. *See* Congress of the United States: Officer to preside over both of the branches of Congress

CONGRESS (U.S.)—SENATE—*Continued*

President pro tempore of the United States Senate was John Langdon of New Hampshire, who held office on April 6, 1789, to count the vote for President and Vice President, a quorum of the Senate then appearing for the first time. John Adams, Vice President, appeared on April 21, 1789, and took his seat as President of the Senate. *(Clara Hannah Kerr —The Origin and Development of the United States Senate)*

Senate met in New York City, March 4, 1789. The only members present were Senators John Langdon and Paine Wingate of New Hampshire; William Samuel Johnson and Oliver Ellsworth of Connecticut; William Maclay and Robert Morris of Pennsylvania; Caleb Strong of Massachusetts; and William Few of Georgia. Various sessions were called but adjourned as no quorum was present. The first session of the Senate at which there was a quorum was held April 6, 1789, at which meeting John Langdon of New Hampshire was elected president pro tempore.

Senate cloture resolution was proposed by Senator Thomas Staples Martin of Virginia and passed March 8, 1917, by a vote of 76 to 3: "If at any time a motion, signed by sixteen senators, to bring to a close the debate upon any pending measure is presented to the Senate, the presiding officer shall at once state the motion to the Senate, and one hour after the Senate meets on the following calendar day but one, he shall lay the motion before the Senate. . . ." If it is passed by a two-thirds vote, debate is limited to one hour per individual. The resolution was first invoked November 15, 1919, by a vote of 78 to 16 on the Versailles Treaty discussion. *(U.S. Senate Journal— Sixty-fourth Congress, Second Session)*

Senate filibuster took place February 11-21, 1811, when discussion was held on the Bank of the United States. The filibuster was not continuous as other business was transacted during the period. The charter was approved in an "act to incorporate the subscribers to the Bank of the United States," February 25, 1791 (1 Stat.L.191). *(Annals of the Congress of the United States—Eleventh Congress, Third Session)*

Senate filibuster (continuous) extended from February 18, 1841, to March 11, 1841. The topic was the dismissal of the printers of the Senate (Twenty-seventh Congress) and the election of a public printer.

Senate hearing in which women, other than members of Congress, were permitted on the floor was held on November 22, 1929. Two women employees of the Tariff Commis-

sion, Ruth Peterson and Evelyn Southworth, testified as experts during the tariff debate on rayon.

Senate session to which the public was admitted was the trial of Abraham Alfonse Albert Gallatin, senator from Pennsylvania. It was argued that he had not been a citizen of the United States for the required nine years. On February 11, 1794, it was resolved "that the doors of the Senate be opened, and continue open, during the discussion upon the contested election of Albert Gallatin." A motion was passed February 20, 1794, during the second session of the Third Congress that the Senate chamber "be provided with galleries which shall be permitted to be open every morning so long as the Senate shall be engaged in their legislative capacity, unless in such cases as may in the opinion of the Senate require secrecy." *(Henry H. Gilfry—Precedents. Decision on Points of order, with Phraseology, in the United States Senate)*

Senate special session was held for one day, March 4, 1791, at the Senate Chamber, Philadelphia, Pa., and was summoned by President George Washington to nominate the several officers necessary to put the federal government into operation in the newly admitted state of Vermont, the supervisors of the several districts within the United States, and the officers for an additional military establishment of the United States. *(Annals of Congress— Second Congress, First Session)*

Senatorial controversy in which no candidates were seated after a recount followed the election of November 2, 1926, in Pennsylvania. William Bauchop Wilson, a Democrat, was defeated by William Scott Vare, a Republican, who presented his credentials as senator-elect for the term beginning March 4, 1927. The Senate, on December 6, 1929, by a vote of 58 to 22 decided that Vare was not entitled to the senatorial seat. He was not permitted to qualify and was unseated on December 6, 1929. Governor John Stuchell Fisher of Pennsylvania appointed Joseph Ridgway Grundy, a Republican, to the vacant seat. Grundy served from December 11, 1929, to December 1, 1930.

CONGRESSIONAL APPORTIONMENT under the Constitution was authorized by act of April 14, 1792 (1 Stat.L.253), an "act for apportioning representatives among the several states according to the first enumeration." The first apportionment was made in 1793 based on the first decennial census (1790) and provided for 106 representatives, one for every 33,000 of population. The first Congress consisted of 65 representatives, one for every 30,000.

CONGRESSIONAL CAUCUS

Congressional caucus was held secretly in 1800 by the Federalist party at the instiga-

THE FIRST

tion of Alexander Hamilton, who desired the reelection of President John Adams. The Democratic-Republicans later held a caucus and nominated Thomas Jefferson. Adams and Jefferson each received 73 electoral votes, whereupon the election was turned over to the House of Representatives, which, after 37 ballots between February 11 and 17, 1801, elected Thomas Jefferson of Virginia as President and Aaron Burr of New York as Vice President. *(Theodore Wells Cousens—Politics and Political Organizations in America)*

Congressional caucus (open, not secret) was held February 29, 1804, by the Democratic-Republicans, who nominated Thomas Jefferson of Virginia for President. Jefferson was elected, receiving 162 of the 176 electoral votes. George Clinton was elected Vice President.

CONGRESSIONAL CEMETERY. *See* Cemetery: Congressional cemetery

CONGRESSIONAL DIRECTORY published by the United States Government was authorized by act of February 14, 1865 (13 Stat.L.568) and published in 1865 for the first session of the Thirty-ninth Congress. Compiled by Benjamin Perley Poore, it contained, in addition to a roster of congressmen, information about Washington banks, insurance companies, hotels, express offices, churches, railroads, steamboats, mails, etc. It contained 57 pages. *(Benjamin Perley Poore—Perley's Reminiscences)*

CONGRESSIONAL HEARING WITNESS (woman). *See* Woman: Woman Congressional hearing witness

CONGRESSIONAL LIBRARY. *See* Library: Library of Congress

CONGRESSIONAL MEDAL. *See* Medal: Medal of honor

CONGRESSMAN (U.S.)
See also Senator (U.S.)

Catholic congressman was Thomas Fitz-Simons of Pennsylvania, who was elected as a Federalist to the First, Second, and Third Congresses. He served from March 4, 1789, to March 3, 1795. Charles Carroll of Maryland, who was a Catholic, also served in the First Congress. *(American Catholic Historical Society of Philadelphia. Records 1889. Vol. 2)*

Congressman elected by the prohibitionists was Kittel Halvorson, born in Telemarken, Norway, who was elected as the candidate of the Farmers' Alliance and the prohibitionists.

THE FIRST

He served as a representative from Minnesota from March 4, 1891, to March 3, 1893, in the Fifty-second Congress.

Congressman elected who served time in prison was Matthew Lyon, a Vermont anti-Federalist, who was a member of Congress from March 4, 1797, to March 3, 1801, and March 4, 1803, to March 3, 1811. He served a four-month term and was fined $1,000 for publishing a letter critical of the government, in violation of the Sedition Act of 1798. He was reelected while still in prison. In 1840 a bill was enacted which refunded the fine to his heirs.

Congressman of Asian ancestry was Dalip Singh Saund, a Democrat, representing the 29th district of California, who was born in Amritsar, India. He was elected to the Eighty-fifth Congress on November 6, 1956, and reelected in 1958 and 1960.

Congressman of Japanese ancestry elected to the House of Representatives was Daniel Ken Inouye, 34, Democrat, who was elected July 28, 1959, by Hawaii, the fiftieth state. He was sworn in on August 24, 1959, by Sam Rayburn, Speaker of the House. Inouye lost an arm fighting in World War II.

Congressman to die was Theodoric Bland of Virginia, born March 21, 1742, who died June 1, 1790, in New York City. He was buried in Trinity Churchyard, New York City. His body was reinterred in the Congregational Cemetery, Washington, D.C., on August 31, 1828.

Congressman who had been a President of the United States was John Quincy Adams. He served as President from March 4, 1825, to March 3, 1829, and represented the Plymouth, Mass., district in Congress as a Whig from March 4, 1831, to February 23, 1848, when he died. He served in the Twenty-second and the eight succeeding Congresses, 17 years less 10 days. *(John Quincy Adams—The Diary of John Quincy Adams)*

Congressmen (brothers) to serve simultaneously were the Washburn brothers, each representing a different state: Israel Washburn, Jr., of Maine (Whig, Thirty-second—Thirty-third Congresses, Republican, Thirty-fourth—Thirty-sixth Congresses, March 4, 1851, to January 1, 1861); Elihu Benjamin Washburne of Illinois (spelled with an *e*) (Whig, Thirty-third and eight succeeding Congresses, March 4, 1853, to March 6, 1869); and Cadwallader Colden Washburn of Wisconsin (Republican, Thirty-fourth—Thirty-sixth Congresses, March 4, 1855, to March 3, 1861). The three brothers served simultaneously as congressmen from March 4, 1855, to January 1,

CONGRESSMAN (U.S.)—*Continued*
1861. Another brother, William Drew Washburn of Minnesota (Republican, Forty-sixth—Forty-eighth Congresses) served from March 4, 1879, to March 3, 1885.

Congresswoman elected to the United States House of Representatives was Jeannette Rankin. She was elected as a Republican by Montana and served from March 4, 1917, to March 4, 1919, and from January 3, 1941, to January 3, 1943. She was the first representative to vote twice against entry into war, on April 6, 1917 and December 8, 1941. *(Annabel Paxton—Women in Congress)*

Congresswoman elected to serve in the place of her husband was Mae Ella Nolan of the 5th district of California. She was a Republican and filled the vacancy in the House of Representatives caused by the death of her husband, John Ignatius Nolan. She served from January 23, 1923, to March 3, 1925.

Congresswoman to head a committee. *See* Congress (U.S.)—House of Representatives: Congressional committee headed by a woman

Congresswoman to preside over the House of Representatives was Alice Mary Robertson of Oklahoma. At a special session of the Sixty-seventh Congress on June 20, 1921, Representative David Walsh of Massachusetts asked her to take the chair. She merely announced the vote, which was 209 yeas and 42 nays on an appropriation of $15,000 for a commission to represent the United States at the Peruvian Centennial of Independence exhibition. *(Chronicles of Oklahoma. Vol. 10)*

Congresswoman to vote twice against the entry of the United States into war was Mrs. Jeannette Rankin of Montana whose votes were cast April 6, 1917, and December 8, 1941.

Duel between congressmen. *See* Duel: Duel between congressmen

Jewish congressman was Israel Jacobs, who was elected by Pennsylvania to sit in the Second Congress. He served from March 4, 1791, to March 3, 1793. (As there were two men named Israel Jacobs from Pennsylvania, this statement may be open to contradiction; confusion exists as to which one served.) The next Jewish congressman was Lewis Charles Levin, representative from Pennsylvania, elected as a candidate of the American Party to the Twenty-ninth, Thirtieth, and Thirty-first Congresses. He served from March 4, 1845, to March 3, 1851.

Mother and son simultaneously elected to Congress were Ohio Republicans elected November 4, 1952, to serve in the Eighty-third Congress beginning January 3, 1953. Oliver Payne Bolton, 35, represented Ohio's Eleventh District. His mother, Frances Payne Bolton, 67, represented Ohio's Twenty-second District, and had served since February 27, 1940, having been elected to fill the vacancy caused by the death of her husband, Chester Castle Bolton.

Negro congressman in the House of Representatives was Joseph Hayne Rainey of Georgetown, S.C. He was sworn in December 12, 1870, to fill the vacancy caused by the action of the House of Representatives in declaring the seat of Benjamin Franklin Whittemore vacant. Rainey served ten years, in the Forty-first—Forty-fifth Congresses, until March 3, 1879.

Negro congressman from the North was Oscar Stanton De Priest, a Republican, of Chicago, Ill., who served in the House of Representatives from March 4, 1929, to January 3, 1935.

Negro congressman to head a committee. *See* Congress (U.S.)—House of Representatives: Congressional standing committee headed by a Negro

Roman Catholic priest to serve in Congress was Gabriel Richard, 56 years old, who served as a Delegate from Michigan Territory in the Eighteenth Congress from March 4, 1823, to March 3, 1825. He was ordained a priest in France on October 15, 1790, and served as a missionary in Detroit, Mich.

Socialist congressman was Victor Louis Berger of Wisconsin, who served from March 4, 1911, to March 3, 1913, in the Sixty-second Congress. He was elected to the Sixty-sixth and Sixty-seventh Congresses, but was not permitted to hold a seat therein. He was elected to the Sixty-eighth, Sixty-ninth and Seventieth Congresses and served from March 4, 1923, to March 3, 1929. *(Victor L. Berger —Voice and Pen of Victor L. Berger)*

CONSCIENCE FUND was started in 1811 during President James Madison's administration by an unknown person who claimed to have defrauded the government and the Treasury of $5. Other deposits in that year increased the total to $250. No further deposits were received until 1827, when $6 was forwarded. Nothing was received in 1848. The largest amount collected in one year was received in 1950 when $370,285.47 was sent in. For statistical and accounting purposes, funds are listed as "Miscellaneous Receipts."

THE FIRST

THE FIRST

CONSCIENTIOUS OBJECTOR TO RECEIVE A MEDAL OF HONOR. *See* Medal: Medal of Honor awarded to a conscientious objector

CONSCIENTIOUS OBJECTORS to refuse to aid the country in time of war were led by Ann Lee. She and eight of her sect of Shakers left Liverpool, England, on the "Mariah," May 19, 1774, arrived in New York City, August 6, 1774, and settled in Watervliet, N.Y., in 1776. Because of religious reasons, she and a group of Shakers refused to aid the colonies in the War for Independence with the result that they were accused of treason and imprisoned in the old fort in Albany, N.Y. They were placed in jail without the formality of a trial. Her disciples were released prom prison on December 20, 1780. Ann Lee was transferred to the Poughkeepsie, N.Y. jail and was released shortly thereafter. *(The Life and Gospel Experience of [Mother] Ann Lee. Canterbury, Md.)*

See also Shakers

CONSCIENTIOUS OBJECTORS' CAMP (class IV-3) was the Patapsco Camp-Civilian Public Service Camp, Relay Post Office, Md., opened May 15, 1941, when 26 men of various faiths and beliefs arrived. The director was Dr. Ernest Atkins Wildman, professor of chemistry, Earlham College, Richmond, Ind. Members worked in the neighboring Patapsco State Park and in the State Forestry Nursery. Similar camps were later opened by the National Service Board for Religious Objectors.

CONSCRIPTION
Colonial conscription legislation was enacted April 18, 1637, in Boston, Mass., by the Massachusetts Bay legislature, which provided "there shalbee 160 men pvided to be chosen out of the severall townes according to the portion underwritten," to be used in the war against the Pecoit Indians. The conscription call was as follows: Boston 26, Salem 18, Ipswich 17, Saugust 16, Watertowne 14, Dorchester 13, Charlestown 12, Roxberry 10, Newetowne 9, Newberry 8, Hingham 6, Waymothe 5, Meadfoarde 3, and Marbleheade 3. *(Nathaniel B. Shurtleff—Records of the Governor and Company of the Massachusetts Bay of New England 1628-1641)*

Conscription was authorized by the act of May 8, 1792 (1 Stat.L.270), "effectually to provide for the National Defense by establishing a uniform militia throughout the United States." Every free able-bodied white male citizen between the ages of 18 and 45 was required to be enrolled in the militia of the United States and to supply himself with a gun and no fewer than 24 cartridges suited to the bore of his musket. There was no penalty for non-observance. This law left the militia in the command of the states.

Peacetime conscription bill was passed September 14, 1940 (Senate: 47 for, 35 against; House: 232 for, 124 against) and called for a total of 900,000 selectees to be trained in any given year. Registration was required of all men who attained the age of 21 and who had not reached the age of 36 on October 16, 1940. The drawing of numbers was made October 29, 1940, in Washington, D.C. The call for the first 75,000 men was made November 15, 1940. Dr. Clarence Addison Dykstra was confirmed as director of the draft on October 15, 1940. The first number, No. 158, was drawn by Secretary of War Henry Lewis Stimson.

Wartime conscription bill was passed March 3, 1863 (12 Stat.L.731), "an act for enrolling and calling out the national forces, and for other purposes." It required men 20 to 45 years of age to be enrolled April 1, 1863, by provost marshals. Exemptions could be bought for $300. The first draft call was made July 7, 1863. A conscription bill had been passed November 10, 1814, by the Senate and another on December 9, 1814, by the House, but no compromise bill was enacted as the Treaty of Peace signed December 24, 1814, at Ghent, Belgium, terminated the war of 1812.

CONSERVATION CORPS. *See* Civilian conservation corps (U.S.)

CONSTITUTION
Constitution to state "the foundation of authority is in the free consent of the people" was the "fundamental orders," the first constitution of Connecticut, drawn by Roger Ludlow and adopted January 14, 1639, in Hartford, Conn., by representatives of Wethersfield, Windsor, and Hartford. Ludlow was influenced by a sermon delivered May 31, 1638, by Thomas Hooker at Center Church, Hartford, Conn. *(James Hammond Trumbull—Public Records of the Colony of Connecticut Prior to the Union with the New Haven Colony)*

Constitution of the Continental Congress. See Articles of Confederation

State constitution. *See* State: State constitution

CONSTITUTION OF THE CONFEDERATE STATES OF AMERICA, adopted March 11, 1861, contained this preamble: "We the people of the Confederate States, each State acting in its sovereign and independent character, in order to form a permanent federal government, establish justice, insure domestic tranquility, and secure the blessings of liberty to ourselves and our posterity—invoking the favor and guidance of Almighty God—do ordain and establish this constitution for the Confederate States of America." It was adopted at

Montgomery, Ala. *(Confederate States of America—The Statutes at Large of the Provisional Government of the Confederate States of America . . .)*

CONSTITUTION OF THE UNITED STATES

Constitution (federal) was signed September 17, 1787, at the conclusion of the Constitutional Convention which first met at Philadelphia, Pa., on May 25, 1787. The convention was scheduled for May 14, 1787, but a quorum of seven states was not present until May 25, 1787, on which date the delegates elected George Washington president of the convention and William Jackson secretary. Sessions were held on 87 of the 116 days between May 25 and September 17. Of the original 55 delegates, only 41 remained to the conclusion. Three refused to sign the Constitution. The ninth state to ratify the Constitution, thus making it binding for the 13 former colonies, was New Hampshire, whose legislature approved by a vote of 57 to 47 on June 21, 1788.

Constitution of the United States was first published in a newspaper in the September 19, 1787, *Pennsylvania Packet and Daily Advertiser*, Philadelphia, Pa., published by [John] Dunlap and [David C.] Claypoole.

Printed copies of the Constitution of the United States of America, consisting of a preamble and seven articles, were printed from plates engraved by Jacob Shallus, assistant clerk of the Pennsylvania Assembly, who received $30 for the work. Sixty proof sheets were printed August 1-3, 1787, and laid before the Constitutional Convention on August 6, 1787. The constitution was adopted September 17, 1787, and ratified by the necessary nine states by June 21, 1788, but was not declared in effect until March 4, 1789.

State to ratify the federal Constitution. *See* State: State to ratify the federal Constitution

CONSTITUTIONAL AMENDMENT (U.S.)

See also Declaration of rights

Constitutional amendment submitted to the states for repeal was offered by the Blaine repeal resolution to void the Eighteenth Amendment. The bill was passed by the Senate, February 16, 1933, by a vote of 63 to 23, and by the House on February 20, 1933, which concurred by 289 to 121. The amendment was proposed to conventions of the states by the Seventy-second Congress on February 20, 1933. The first state to ratify was Michigan, April 10, 1933. The amendment was declared ratified December 5, 1933, by a proclamation of the Secretary of State, after the thirty-sixth state had ratified it. (Amendments to the Consti-

tution are not repealed, but are nullified by other amendments to set aside their provisions.)

Constitutional amendments, known as the "Bill of Rights," were drawn up by James Madison and were declared in force on December 15, 1791, having been passed by both Houses and ratified by the required number of states. Originally twelve amendments were passed by both houses, but two of them failed to secure the requisite number of state ratifications. The first of the ten amendments established religious freedom, freedom of speech and press, and the right to assemble and to petition. The amendments were submitted to the states by the First Congress on September 25, 1789. The first state to ratify was New Jersey, which acted on November 20, 1789. *(Francis Newton Thorpe—Constitutional History of the American People)*

Income tax amendment to the Constitution. *See* Tax: Income tax amendment to the Constitution

Woman suffrage amendment. *See* Woman suffrage: Woman suffrage amendment approved by Congress

CONSTITUTIONAL UNION PARTY

was organized May 9, 1860, at a convention held in Baltimore, Md., the occasion on which the party may be said to have been definitely organized. This was the party's first and only convention. The platform declared for "the Constitution of the Country, the Union of the States and the Enforcement of the Laws." The delegates nominated John Bell of Tennessee for president and Edward Everett of Massachusetts for vice president. They received twelve electoral votes as compared with 180 cast for Abraham Lincoln, the Republican nominee, in the election of November 6, 1860.

CONSULAR SERVICE. *See* Diplomatic service: Consul

CONSUMERS' ADVISORY BOARD (U.S.) was authorized June 16, 1933 (48 Stat.L.195) under the National Industrial Recovery Act. It was organized June 26, 1933. The first chairman was Mrs. Charles Cary Rumsey.

CONSUMERS' COOPERATIVE SOCIETY. *See* Cooperative: Consumers' cooperative society

CONSUMERS' COUNSEL (U.S.) was authorized June 16, 1933, under the Agricultural Adjustment Act. Frederic Clemson Howe was appointed the first counsel.

THE FIRST

CONSUMPTIVES' HOSPITAL. *See* Hospital: Tuberculosis hospital

CONTACT LENS. *See* Lens: Contact lenses

CONTEMPORARY NOVELS COURSE. *See* Novel course: Course on the contemporary novel

CONTESTED ELECTION (Congress). *See* Congress (U.S.)—House of Representatives: Contested election; Congress (U.S.) —Senate: Contested election

CONTINENTAL CONGRESS
See also President of the Continental Congress

Continental Congress assembled at Carpenter's Hall, Philadelphia, Pa., on Monday, September 5, 1774, and consisted of 44 delegates from 11 colonies. Delegates from Georgia and North Carolina did not attend until later sessions. The Congress adjourned October 26, 1774, recommending another session to begin May 10, 1775, at Philadelphia, Pa. *(Journals of the Continental Congress from 1774 to 1789)*

Continental Congress to be opened with prayer was held on September 7, 1774. The Reverend Jacob Duché, an Episcopalian, rector of Christ Church, appeared in his canonicals attended by his clerk. The morning service of the Episcopal Church was read, the clerk making the responses. The Psalter for the seventh day of the month includes the 35th Psalm, wherein David prays for protection against his enemies: "Plead my cause, O Lord, with them that strive with me; fight against them that fight against me." The rector concluded with an appeal so heartfelt that Congress gave him a vote of thanks. The session opened at 9 A.M. at Carpenter's Hall, Philadelphia, Pa. *(Thatcher's Military Journal)*

CONTINENTAL CONGRESS CONSTITUTION. *See* Articles of Confederation

CONTINENTAL CONGRESS LOTTERY. See Lottery: Lottery held by the Continental Congress

CONTINENTAL CONGRESS MEDAL. *See* Medal: Medal awarded by the Continental Congress

CONTINENTAL CONGRESS PENSION ACT. *See* Pension: Pension act of the Continental Congress

THE FIRST

CONTINENTAL CONGRESS PRESIDENT. *See* President of the Continental Congress

CONTINENTAL MONEY. *See* Money: Continental money

CONTINENTAL NAVY COMMANDER. *See* Naval officer: Commander-in-chief of the Continental Navy

CONTINUATION SCHOOL
Apprentice continuation school supported by a board of education from public funds was established in Cincinnati, Ohio, on August 30, 1909. Classes were conducted in the third story of a building at Twelfth and Jackson Streets. Tool apprentices were given the opportunity of a technical education along practical lines.

Continuation school established by state law was the Racine Continuation School, Racine, Wis., which opened November 3, 1911, to offer evening instruction to adults as well as to children from 14 to 16 years of age who had permits to work. It was authorized under Chapter 616 approved July 7, 1911, "an act relating to education in industrial, commercial, continuation and evening schools."

CONTRACEPTIVE CLINIC. *See* Medical clinic: Contraceptive clinic (state)

CONTRACT CARRIER LICENSE. *See* Automobile license (federal): Contract carrier license

CONVENT
Catholic convent to admit colored women as sisters was the Sisters of Loretto, Loretto, Ky. The Reverend Charles Nerinck in May 1824 admitted five Negro women to the novitiate who followed the same community exercises as the other sisters, but who lived apart from the white sisters.

Convent permanently established was in New Orleans, La., in a two-story frame building, with six apartments on each floor, occupied August 6, 1727, by the Ursulines. On August 9, 1727, the Holy Sacrifice of the Mass was offered for the first time. The Superioress was Mother Marie (Tranchepain) of St. Augustine. *(Reverend Henry Churchill Semple—The Ursulines in New Orleans and Our Lady of Prompt Succor)*

CONVENTION (POLITICAL) BROADCAST. *See* Radio broadcast: Political convention broadcast

THE FIRST

CONVENTION (POLITICAL) TELE-CAST. *See* Television—Telecast: Political convention to be televised

CONVEYOR BELT SYSTEM. *See* Belt conveyor system

CONVICT LABOR LAW. *See* Labor law: Convict labor law

COOK BOOK
    Cook book was *The Compleat House-wife: or Accomplished Gentlewoman's Companion. Being a collection of upwards of Five Hundred of the most approved Receipts fit either for private Families, or such Publick-Spirited Gentlewomen as would be beneficent to their poor Neighbours.* It was modeled after one printed by Mrs. E. Smith in England. It was published in 1742 in Williamsburg, Va., by William Parks. *(Lawrence Counselman Wroth—William Parks)*

    Cook book of American authorship was Amelia Simmons' *American Cookery, or the Art of Dressing Viands, Fish, Poultry and Vegetables, and the Best Modes of Making Puff-Pastes, Pies, Tarts, Puddings, Custards and Preserves, and All Kinds of Cakes, from the Imperial Plumb to Plain Cake—Adapted to This Country, and All Grades of Life.* It was printed by Hudson and Goodwin in Hartford, Conn., in 1796 for the author and contained 46 pages.

COOKING EXPERIMENT (electric). *See* Electric cooking experiment

COOKING SCHOOL was the New York Cooking School, which was opened in November 1876 by Juliet Corson at her residence in St. Mark's Place, New York City. In 1875, she gave cooking instruction in the Ladies' Cooking Class of the free Training School for Women, New York City.

COOPERATIVE
    College cooperative store was the Harvard Co-operative Society, Cambridge, Mass., the constitution for which was presented February 28, 1882. On March 15, 1882, it had 400 subscribers. The plan was proposed by Charles Hayden Kip. Frank Bolles was the first president. Merchandise was sold below prevailing retail prices to members. The store was managed by students of the university. *(Norman Scott Brien Gras—Harvard Co-operative Society—Past and Present 1892-1942)*

    Consumers' cooperative society was organized in 1830 in New York City by William Bryan, treasurer of a cooperative in Brighton, England. He established a store in New York

THE FIRST

City which sold articles to members at prices generally below those prevailing at retail outlets.

    Cooperative cheese factory. *See* Cheese factory: Cheese factory cooperative

    Cooperative operated entirely by women was the Montgomery Farm Women's Cooperative Market, Bethesda, Md., incorporated August 1932 by 29 women. The following year, they built a market valued at about $50,000, the mortgage on which was paid off in January 1945.

    Cooperative state law was an "act to authorize the formation of mechanics' and laboring men's cooperative associations," Act No. 288 of Michigan, approved and effective March 20, 1865, which allowed "any ten or more persons, who shall be desirous of uniting as mechanics and laboring men, in any cooperative association" to incorporate.

    Group hospital-medical cooperative. *See* Insurance: Group hospital-medical cooperative

COOPERATIVES CONVENTION was held in Springfield, Ill., September 25-27, 1918, under the auspices of the Co-operative League of America. Dr. James Peter Warbasse, president of the league, presided over the 185 delegates. *(Report of the Proceedings of the First American Co-operative Convention Held at Springfield, Ill., September 25, 26, 27, 1918, under the Auspices of the Co-operative League of America)*

COPLEY MEDAL. *See* Medal: Copley Medal awarded to an American

COPPER COINS. *See* Money: Copper coins

COPPER MINE known to have been worked was the Simsbury mine at Granby, Conn., with a history dating back to 1705. A company to mine the ore was formed in 1709 by John Winthrop, the younger, and was the first mining company chartered. The mine was also known as the Granby mine and was worked for several years by convicts in the Newgate prison established there. In 1737 the copper obtained from this mine was used in the manufacture of the "Granby coppers," among the earliest colonial coins minted. The mine was worked spasmodically until 1773. *(Charles Burr Todd—In Olde Connecticut)*

COPPER REFINERY FURNACE (to operate by the use of gaseous fuel) was constructed in 1878 by William Franklin Durfee for the Wheeler and Wilson Company in Ansonia, Conn.

THE FIRST

THE FIRST

COPPER TUBE. *See* Brass and copper seamless tubes

COPYRIGHT
Book entered for copyright. *See* Book: Book entered for copyright

Choreographic score copyrighted was presented in Labanotation (the Rudolf von Laban notation system) on microfilm by Hanya Holm, New York City, and registered February 25, 1952, as an unpublished dramatic-musical composition. It was a complete score of her choreography for Cole Porter's musical comedy *Kiss Me Kate*, which opened December 30, 1948, at the Century Theater, New York City.

Motion picture film copyrighted consisted of 47 successive frames showing Fred Ott sneezing. The copyright was recorded as follows: "Edison Kinetoscopic Record of a Sneeze, January 7, 1894. Entered in the name of W. K. L. Dickson, under No. 2,887, January 9, 1894." On August 28, 1882, pictures in silhouette showing motion had been copyrighted by Edweard J. Muybridge. They could not be projected but could be arranged to simulate movement when viewed in an electrical tachyscope.
See also Moving Picture: Moving picture "close-up"

COPYRIGHT LAW
Copyright law securing benefit of copyright was passed May 15, 1672, by the General Court of Massachusetts assembled in Boston, Mass., which granted John Usher, a book seller, the privilege of publishing on his own account a revised edition of *The General Laws and Liberties of the Massachusetts Colony.* It was ordered "that for at least seven years, unless he shall have sold them all before that time, there shall be no other or further impression made by any person thereof in this jurisdiction." The penalty for violation of the copyright was treble the whole charges of printing and paper.

Copyright law of the United States was an act (1 Stat.L.124) "for the encouragement of learning by securing the copies of maps, charts and books to the authors and proprietors of such copies during the times therein mentioned." The bill was signed by the Speaker and the President of the Senate, May 25, 1790, laid before President George Washington on May 27, 1790, and signed May 31, 1790. Rights were granted only to citizens of the United States, a policy which continued until 1891. Protection was extended over a 14-year period, renewal rights being granted only if the author was still alive.

Copyright law (state) was "an act for the encouragement of literature and genius," passed during the session of the General Court of Assembly of the Governor and Company of the State of Connecticut, held in Hartford, Conn., January 8-February 7, 1783. The law gave authors sole right of publication for 14 years with power of renewal. Massachusetts passed a law March 17, 1783, for 21-year period. Both laws extended rights only to other states having reciprocal legislation. *(Richard Rogers Bowker —Copyright, Its History and Its Law)*

International copyright agreement was the Platt-Simonds Copyright Act, passed March 4, 1891 (26 Stat.L.1107), effective July 1, 1891. Citizens of Switzerland, France, Belgium, and Great Britain were thus enabled to obtain copyright protection in the United States. The United States was represented by Boyd Winchester at the Berne International Copyright Convention, September 9, 1886, but did not become a signatory to the convention. *(Thorvald Solberg—The United States and International Copyright)*

COPYRIGHTED BOOK. *See* Book: Book entered for copyright

COPYRIGHTS REGISTRAR OF THE UNITED STATES was Thorvald Solberg, who served from July 1, 1897, to April 22, 1930.

CORAL REEF BARRIER (copy) of importance on exhibition was installed in the American Museum of Natural History, New York City, under the direction of Dr. Roy Waldo Miner. Its construction occupied five years and the reef, weighing forty tons, was completed in July 1934.

CORD TIRE. *See* Automobile tire: Cord tire; Bicycle tire: Bicycle tire (cord)

CORK for steam pipe covering was manufactured in the United States in 1894 by Stone & Duryea of Brooklyn, N.Y. The company moved to Bridgeport, Conn., in 1896 and the following year produced cork covering for cold pipe lines. It was succeeded by the Nonpareil Cork Manufacturing Company, which in turn was purchased by the Armstrong Cork Company in 1904.

CORK CENTER BASEBALL. *See* Baseball: Cork center baseball

CORK JACKET. *See* Life preserver of cork

CORK MANUFACTURER is said to have been William King, who opened a factory in Brooklyn, N.Y., where he produced cork products from 1850 to 1860.

CORKBOARD (IMPREGNATED) was made in 1900 by the Armstrong Cork Company of Pittsburgh, Pa. It was produced in a specially constructed plant in Beaver Falls, Pa. The business grew rapidly until the "composition" corkboard gave way entirely to pure corkboard insulation.

CORKBOARD PATENT to be issued on pure corkboard was No. 456,068, granted to John T. Smith of Brooklyn, N.Y., on July 14, 1891. Manufacture was begun in Brooklyn, in 1894 by Stone and Duryea. Cork covering was produced first, and then the manufacture of pure corkboard followed within a very few years. *(Pearl Edwin Thomas—Cork Insulation)*

CORKSCREW PATENT, No. 27,615, was granted on March 27, 1860, to M. L. Byrn of New York City. It covered a gimlet screw with a "T" handle.

CORN
Shipment of hybrid seed corn was sold to Samuel Ramsay, Jacobsburg, Ohio, on April 13, 1916, by Funk Brothers Seed Co., Bloomington, Ill. The price was $15 a bushel.

CORN HUSKING CHAMPIONSHIP CONTEST (national) was held December 1, 1924, on a farm near Alleman, Polk County, Iowa. There were six contestants. The winner was Fred Stanek of Webster County, Iowa, who husked 1,891 pounds, a net of 1,705 pounds, or 24.3 bushels, in 80 minutes.

CORNCOB PIPE. *See* Pipe: Corncob pipe commercial manufacture

CORNSTALK PAPER BOOK. *See* Book: Book on cornstalk paper

CORNSTARCH
Cornstarch patent was No. 2,000, issued March 22, 1841, to Orlando Jones of City Road, England, "for operating on farinaceous matters to obtain starch and other products," especially flour or powder produced from rice.

Starch made commercially from Indian corn was made by Thomas Kingsford, who produced a small quantity in 1842 in Jersey City, N.J. In 1846, he and his son, Thomas, Jr., erected a small cornstarch plant in Bergen, N.J., and a larger one in Oswego, N.Y., in 1848.

CORNSTONE, or Maizolith, a product harder than the hardest wood and several times stronger than the strongest wood, was first made at the Iowa State College, Ames, Iowa, in 1922. It is made principally from corncobs

or cornstalks by means of specially designed machinery. It ranges in color from golden tan to ebony and is used principally as a structural material when great strength as compared with weight is desired, and when great abrasion and impact must be withstood. It has a specific gravity of 1.5 and modulus of rupture of about 35,000 pounds.

CORPORATION
Commercial corporation was the New York Fishing Company, which was chartered January 8, 1675, by the Governor and Council of New York acting for the Duke of York "for settleing a fishery in these parts." Shares of the capital stock were £10 each. *(New York Council—Minutes III, part 2:10)*

Corporate body of more than temporary duration, excluding town incorporations, was the President and Fellows of Harvard College, Cambridge, Mass., chartered May 30, 1650. It consisted of seven persons; Henry Dunster, president; five fellows, Samuel Mather, Samuel Danford, Jonathan Michell, Comfort Starr, and Samuel Eaton; and Thomas Danford, treasurer. *(Nathaniel Bradstreet Shurtleff—Records of the Governor and Company of the Massachusetts Bay in New England. Vol. 4)*

Corporation incorporated with a capitalization of $1 billion was the United States Steel Corporation. It was incorporated on February 25, 1901, and was ready for business on April 1, 1901, with an authorized capitalization of $1.4 billion. The original member companies were the Carnegie Company, Federal Steel Company, National Steel Company, National Tube Company, American Steel and Wire Company of New Jersey, American Tin Plate Company, American Steel Hoop Company, American Sheet Steel Company, Lake Superior Consolidated Iron Mines, and American Bridge Company. The first president was Charles M. Schwab.

Corporation to earn more than $1 billion in one year was the General Motors Corporation, Detroit, Mich. The corporation's forty-seventh annual report, for the year ending December 31, 1955, showed a net income of $1,189,477,082.

CORPORATION COURSE
Industrial corporation course was entitled "Private Corporations; Origin, history and present status of joint stock concerns, including railroads." It was offered by Dr. Amos Griswold Warner, lecturer on Political and Economic Science, at the University of Nebraska, Lincoln, Neb., in 1888-1889.

CORPORATION TAX. *See* Tax: Corporation tax

THE FIRST

THE FIRST

CORRESPONDENCE SCHOOL to achieve distinction was started through the initiative of Thomas Jefferson Foster, proprietor and editor of the Shenandoah *Herald,* who issued a course in coal mining as a means of educating workmen and safeguarding lives through a knowledge of the fundamentals of mine developing and operating. The first student of this organization, which is now known as the International Correspondence Schools, with headquarters at Scranton, Pa., was enrolled October 16, 1891. Instruction is now offered in a great variety of subjects. *(International Correspondence Schools Field Staff Training Course —International Textbook Press)*

See also Forestry correspondence course; Home study courses; Blind correspondence school

CORRUGATED LIFEBOAT. *See* Lifeboat: Lifeboat (corrugated)

CORRUGATED PAPER. *See* Paper: Corrugated paper

CORRUPT ELECTION PRACTICES LAW. *See* Election law: Corrupt election practices law

CORSET manufactured by a factory as a health item rather than a fashion article was made July 1874 by Warner Brothers, McGraw, N.Y., a partnership of Dr. Ira DeVer Warner and Dr. Lucien Calvin Warner. The corset combined three garments in one—a corset, a skirt supporter, and self-adjusting pads—and had shoulder straps. *(Lucien C. Warner— Always Starting Things Through Seventy Eventful Years)*

COSMIC RAY was discovered in 1925 by Robert Andrews Millikan at the California Institute of Technology, Pasadena, Calif. The formal announcement of the discovery was made on November 11, 1925, before the National Academy of Sciences assembled in convention at Madison, Wis. *(Robert Andrews Millikan—Cosmic Rays)*

COSTUME MUSEUM. *See* Museum: Costume museum

COTTON
Cotton acreage reduction payment was made July 28, 1933, to William E. Morris of Nueces County, Tex., who was presented with a check for $517 by President Franklin Delano Roosevelt for having plowed under 47 acres of his cotton crop. In addition, he was given an option on 23½ bales of cotton at 6 cents a pound.

Cotton crop commercially produced entirely by machinery, from planting to baling, with the exception of a few incidental hours of hand labor, was grown during the year 1944 on 28 acres owned by Hopson Planting Company of Clarksdale, Miss. The soil was prepared, crop-seeded and cultivated by machines, weeds eradicated by flame, and the crop harvested with a mechanical picker.

Cotton exported to England consisted of eight bales from Charleston, S.C., which were seized by the custom house in England in 1764 on the grounds that the American colony could not have produced so much.

Cotton fabric used on a road. *See* Road: Cotton fabric used on a road

Cotton goods to be trademarked were made by the Beverly Cotton Manufactory, Beverly, Mass. On June 6, 1788, it was enacted "that all goods which may be manufactured by the said corporation, shall have a label of lead affixed to one end thereof, which shall have the same impression as the seal of the corporation, and that if any person shall knowingly use a like seal or label with that used by said corporation, by annexing same to any cotton or cotton and linen goods, not manufactured by said corporation with a view of vending or distributing thereof, as the proper manufacture of said corporation, every person so offending shall forfeit and pay treble the value of said goods to be sued for and recovered for the use of said corporation, by action of debt, in any court of record proper to try the same."

COTTON-BALE METALLIC TIE was invented by Frederick Cook of New Orleans, La., who obtained patent No. 19,490, March 2, 1858, on "a friction clasp or buckle for attaching the ends of iron ties or hoops for fastening cotton bales and other packages so that the ties are prevented from slipping by the friction against a certain portion of the buckle."

COTTON-BOLL WEEVIL, which has been so destructive to cotton crops, was introduced into the United States from Central America about 1892, probably through Brownsville, Tex. The weevil is a species of beetle which because of its small size and immunity to most insecticides has become a serious problem.

COTTON GIN, which separated the seed from the cotton, was invented in 1792 by Eli Whitney of Mulberry Grove (near Savannah), Ga.., who applied for a patent on June 20, 1793. His model was stolen and was manufactured by dishonest interests, before Whitney received a patent on March 14, 1794, on "a machine for ginning cotton." Whitney formed a partnership with Phineas Miller and manufactured cotton gins. The invention was

THE FIRST

THE FIRST

COTTON GIN—*Continued*
so valuable that redress was unobtainable, and his patent was not renewed because of the power exerted by those who had been enriched by his invention. (*Denison Olmsted—Memoir of Eli Whitney, Esq.*)

COTTON MILL
Cotton mill (see rival claim—next paragraph) was established in Beverly, Mass., between August 1788 and July 1789 by a company of proprietors known as the Beverly Cotton Manufactory. The company was incorporated on February 3, 1789, and was visited October 30, 1789, by George Washington. The spinning jenny spun 60 threads at one time and the carding machine carded 40 pounds of cotton a day. (*Edwin Martin Stone—History of Beverly*)

Cotton mill was established on James Island, near Charleston, S.C., by Frances Ramage, widow of a South Carolina planter, in 1789. It was used in the weaving and spinning of cotton or linen yarns. An account of the mill is contained in the *City Gazette or Daily Advertiser* of Charleston, S.C., of February 24, 1789. (*South Carolina Historical and Genealogical Magazine. Vols. 8 and 9*)

Cotton mill in the world in which the whole process of cotton manufacturing from spinning to weaving was carried on by power was that of the Boston Manufacturing Company, Waltham, Mass., incorporated February 23, 1813, with a capitalization of $100,000. The mill was erected later the same year in Waltham, whence it took its better known name, The Waltham Company. Labor was paid a fixed wage and various groups were departmentalized. Nathan Appleton, Francis Cabot Lowell, and Patrick Tracy Jackson were the prime sponsors of this organization. The machinery was constructed by Paul Moody. (*Edmund Lincoln Sanderson—Waltham as a Precinct of Watertown and as a Town*)

Cotton mill to spin cotton yarn successfully was started on December 20, 1790, by Samuel Slater in Pawtucket, R.I. It was 40 feet long, 26 feet wide, and 2 stories high, with an attic. Power was obtained from the old fulling mill waterwheel in Ezekiel Carpenter's clothier's shop on the east bank of the Blackstone River at the southwest abutment of Pawtucket Bridge. Alexander Hamilton in his report as Secretary of the Treasury made on December 5, 1791 said, "The manufactory at Providence has the merit of being the first in introducing into the United States the celebrated cotton mill, which not only furnishes materials for the manufactory itself but for the supply of private families, for household manufacturing." (*Frederick Lewis Lewton—Samuel Slater and the Oldest Cotton Machinery in America*)

COTTON PICKER (mechanical) of importance was the Rust Cotton Picker, a horse-drawn picker, built by John Daniel Rust in Weatherford, Tex., in 1928. In 1929 it was rebuilt into a self-propelled model powered by a model "T" motor; in 1935, a tractor model was built and tested; and in 1937 an improved model picked thirteen bales of cotton in one day.

COTTON SPINNING JENNY was put into operation by Daniel Jackson, a coppersmith, of Providence, R.I., in 1786. At first it was set up in a private house, but was afterward removed to the upper room in the Market House where it was operated. (*Edward Field—History of Rhode Island and Providence Plantations*)

COTTON THREAD. *See* Thread: Cotton thread

COTTON TWINE FACTORY was established in 1839 by Jacob Sloat of Sloatsburg, N.Y. The mill was opened in 1815 and produced cloth until 1839. Sloat invented a dressing and produced as much as 6,000 pounds a week of cotton twine in 1839.

COTTONSEED HULLING MACHINE was invented by John Lineback of Salem, N.C., and patented by him on March 31, 1814.

COTTONSEED OIL was produced in 1768 through the efforts of Dr. Otto, a Moravian, of Bethlehem, Pa. He was able to get nine pints of oil from a bushel and a half of cotton seed.

COTTONSEED OIL MILL was established in Petersburg, Va., in 1829 by Francis Follet.

COUNCIL (colonial). *See* Colonial government: Colonial council in America

COUNTESS
American woman to become a countess was Sarah Thompson, whose father, Benjamin Thompson, an American physicist, born in North Woburn, Mass., was created a count of the Holy Roman Empire in 1791 by Charles Philip Frederick, Duke of Bavaria. The daughter was received as the Countess of Rumford with the privilege of residing in any country she chose and receiving half of her father's pension of 2,000 florins. (*George Edward Ellis—Memoir of Sir Benjamin Thompson, Count Rumford, With Notices of His Daughter*)

COUNTRY CLUB
Country club to remain in existence eighty years was the Country Club of Brookline,

THE FIRST

Mass., organized September 13, 1882, and incorporated November 7, 1882. Its purpose was the encouragement of athletic exercise and the establishment and maintenance of places for reading rooms and social meetings. In 1882, Clyde Park, the estate of Francis E. Bacon, was leased for five years, and in 1887 it was purchased. In 1883, the Myopia Club, organized in Winchester in 1879, was absorbed by the Country Club. *(Frederic Haines Curtiss and John Heard—The Country Club, 1882-1932)*

COUNTRY DAY SCHOOL was the Country School for Boys of Baltimore, a private school (now the Gilman Country School for Boys, Roland Park, Baltimore, Md.) which was opened September 1897. The first headmaster was Frederick Winsor.

COUNTY LIBRARY. *See* Library: County library

COUPLER (railroad). *See* Railroad coupler

COURT

Bicycle traffic court. *See* Bicycle traffic court

Commerce court (U.S.) was established by act of Congress, June 18, 1910 (36 Stat.L.539). A presiding judge and five associates were appointed by President William Howard Taft for terms that extended from one to five years. The court was organized February 8, 1911, and opened February 15, 1911, in Washington, D.C. Appeal of its decisions could be made only to the Supreme Court. Because of various abuses, the court was abolished December 31, 1913. *(Walker Downer Hines—United States Commerce Court)*

Conciliation tribunal for small claims was the Conciliation Branch of the Municipal Court of Cleveland, established March 15, 1913, in Cleveland, Ohio. The first case was filed March 17, 1913, and was heard by Judge Dan B. Cull on March 24, 1913. The complainant could not be represented by counsel but had to present his own case. Strict rules of evidence and procedure were waived. The judgment rendered had the same force and effect, and was as binding, as a judgment rendered in any court of record. *(American Judicature Society —Bulletin No. 8. April 1915)*

Court of claims was established by an act "to establish a court for the investigation of claims against the United States" (10 Stat.L. 612), signed February 24, 1855, by President Franklin Pierce. It required the appointment of three judges with life tenure by the President with the consent of the Senate. President

THE FIRST

Pierce appointed Isaac Blackford of Indiana and John James Gilchrist of New Hampshire on March 3, 1855, and George P. Scarborough of Virginia on May 8, 1855. The judges received $4,000 annually. The court was organized May 11, 1855, with Judge Gilchrist as presiding judge. It was reorganized by act of March 3, 1863 (12 Stat.L.765). Until March 3, 1887, it was the only court in which cases could be prosecuted against the government.

Domestic relations court was established in Buffalo, N.Y., in 1909 by Simon Augustine Nash, Judge of Police Court, who privately heard domestic relations cases in his chambers instead of in open court. Chapter 570, Laws of New York State, approved May 29, 1909, established the City Court of Buffalo, and the domestic relations division was opened January 1, 1910. *(Station Probation Commissoin, Buffalo. 1928)*

Governor removed from office by a state supreme court. *See* Governor: Governor removed from office by a state supreme court

Juvenile court in the world was the Juvenile Court of Cook County, known as the Chicago Juvenile Court, authorized April 21, 1899, and opened July 1, 1899, with Richard Stanley Tuthill as judge. On March 3, 1913, cases involving girls were tried by a woman judge, Mary Margaret Bartelme. During the first year about 2,300 children's cases were heard. *(Timothy David Hurley—Origin of Illinois Court Law)*

Night court in the world was opened in New York City on September 1, 1907. The first night session of a magistrates' court, the Jefferson Market Court at Ninth Street and Sixth Avenue, was presided over by Charles Nathan Harris. Sessions were held from 8 P.M. to 3 A.M. until September 1, 1910, when cases against men were transferred to Yorkville Court, 153 East 57th Street. Cases against women were held in the same building as before. On June 28, 1911, the closing hour of both sessions was fixed at 1 A.M. On April 21, 1919, the sessions of the Women's Court were changed to day sessions. *(Records in City Magistrates' Courts. New York City)*

Small debtors' court established by state law was authorized March 15, 1913, by Chapter 20, Laws of Kansas, to take effect April 30, 1913. Plaintiffs and defendants appeared without legal representation. Judges served without fee, pay, or award and were not required to be lawyers. Appeals could be taken to the district court. Cases were tried involving not more than $20. The first court was at Topeka, Kan., with W. H. Kemper as judge. *(William Franklin Willoughby—Principles of Judicial Administration)*

COURT—*Continued.*
State Supreme Court composed entirely of women was the Special Supreme Court of Texas appointed by Governor Pat Morris Neff on January 8, 1925. When an application for writ of error in the case of *W. T. Johnson, et al.* vs. *J. M. Darr, et al.,* from El Paso County (a Woodmen of the World case) reached the Supreme Court of Texas, the three members thereof found themselves disqualified to consider it and immediately certified their disqualifications to the governor as required by law. Thereupon the governor appointed Hortense Ward of Houston as Special Chief Justice, and Hattie L. Henenberg of Dallas and Ruth Brazzil of Galveston as Special Associate Justices to hear and determine the cause of action. They were sworn in January 8, 1925. The case was finally decided by the Special Supreme Court on May 23, 1925, affirming the judgment of the Court of Civil Appeals.

Supreme Court. *See* Supreme Court (U.S.)

United States case tried before the Permanent Court of Arbitration at the Hague. *See* Arbitration: Arbitration proceeding

Woman clerk of a state supreme court. *See* Woman: Woman clerk of a state supreme court

COURT MARTIAL
Court martial trial was held August 24, 1676, in Newport, R.I., by Governor Walter Clarke, Deputy Governor John Crayton, and assistants. Edmund Calverly was the Attorney General. Quanpen, an Indian sachem also known as Sowagonish, was found guilty of participation in King Philip's War against the colonists and ordered shot on August 26. Others who had participated in the war were sentenced to various penalties. *(Record of a Court Martial held at Newport, R.I., in August and September 1676 for the Trial of Indians charged with being engaged in Philip's designs)*

Court martial trial at which enlisted men were allowed to sit as members of the court was convened at 8:30 A.M., on February 1, 1949, in Heidelberg, Germany. Pfc. Andrew D. Byrd of Orlando, Fla., and Pfc. Oscar B. Gannon of Hanging Rock, Ohio, charged with premeditated murder of a German civilian and assault on another on December 31, 1948, in a brawl, were tried by a military court of 4 sergeants and 6 officers. They were convicted on February 3, 1949, of manslaughter and sentenced to serve seven years at hard labor and to receive dishonorable discharges.

Court martial trial in the United States at which enlisted men were allowed to sit as members of the court was convened February 3, 1949, at Fort Bragg, N.C., and consisted of 4 sergeants and 5 officers. Rudy F. Johnson, 19, was convicted of escaping from the guardhouse and sentenced to six months at hard labor and fined $50 a month for six months. On the same day, a trial was held at First Army Headquarters on Governors Island, N.Y. It consisted of 3 sergeants and 5 officers. Private Thomas F. Quinn of Brooklyn, N.Y., 21, was convicted of absence without leave and theft of government and private property and sentenced to one year at hard labor and a dishonorable discharge.

Court martial trial of an officer for collaborating with his captors was held September 23, 1954, at Fort Sheridan, Ill. A court of 8 colonels and 3 lieutenant colonels sentenced Lieutenant Colonel Harry Fleming, reserve officer, of Racine, Wis., to "involuntary discharge" for collaborating with Communists during the Korean War. On February 8, 1957, the United States Court of Military Appeals upheld the conviction and agreed with the court martial and military board of review.

Military court martial was held January 20, 1778, in Cambridge, Mass. Colonel David Henley, commanding officer of the American troops in Cambridge, was accused "of a general tenor of language and conduct heinously criminal as an officer, and unbecoming a man, of the most indecent, violent, vindictive severity against unarmed men, and of intentional murder." The trial was concluded on February 25, 1778, when Henley was found not guilty. Brigadier General John Glover was the presiding officer at the trial. *(Proceedings of a General Court-Martial, held at Cambridge, on Tuesday the 20th of January and continued by several adjournments to Wednesday, the 25th of February 1778; upon the trial of Colonel David Henley)*

COURT TENNIS. *See* Tennis: Court tennis

COW. *See* Animals: Cows

COWCATCHER. *See* Locomotive cowcatcher

COXSWAIN (woman). *See* Woman: Woman coxswain of a men's collegiate varsity team

CQD DANGER SIGNAL. *See* Radio distress signal

CRACKER
Cracker (sweet) of American manufacture was introduced to the public in 1865 by Belcher & Larrabee of Albany, N.Y., in competition with the English varieties which were im-

ported in increasing quantities. These crackers were of the sweetened variety. Soda crackers and salt crackers had been made previously.

Hard water crackers were made by hand in 1801 by Josiah Bent in his home in Milton, Mass. They were made from the best winter wheat and pure cold water and baked in ovens heated by bundles of hardwood fagots. Bent peddled them around the country and in 1827 sold his business, which became Bent & Company. *(Albert Kendall Teele—The History of Milton, Mass.)*

Meat biscuit was invented by Gail Borden, Jr., of Elizabethport, N.Y., who manufactured a desiccated soup bread formed of the concentrated extract of alimentary animal substances combined with vegetable flour or meal and baked as flat, brittle cakes. Hot water and seasoning added to the biscuit produced a soup. Borden obtained patent No. 7,066 on July 30, 1850, on a "preparation of portable soup bread."
See also Medal: Medal awarded to an American food producer

CRACKER BAKERY was that of Theodore Pearson of Newburyport, Mass., which started in 1792. His products appealed chiefly because they kept better than bread.

CRAFT LABOR UNION. *See* Labor union: Craft labor union (local)

CRANBERRY CULTIVATION was attempted about 1820 by Captain Henry Hall of Dennis, Barnstable County, Mass. Cranberries grew wild and, most likely, were eaten by the Pilgrims.

CRANBERRY TREATISE was B. Eastwood's *A Complete Manual for the Culture of the Cranberry, with a Description of the Best Varieties,* published in 1856 by C. M. Saxton & Co., New York City. It contained 120 pages and described the location of patches, preparation of soils, planting vines, diseases, picking, etc.

CRANE
Automobile wrecking crane was devised in 1917 by Robert E. Manley, who later formed the Manley Manufacturing Company, York, Pa., which in 1928 was absorbed by the American Chain and Cable Company, Inc. The wrecking car had a tilting beam which permitted adjustment of height and overhang to suit various conditions and a swivel nose which permitted direct pull from any angle. The crane had six leverages and speeds and two sets of controls so that it could be operated from either side of the car.

Crane was manufactured by the Yale and Towne Manufacturing Company, Stamford, Conn., in 1883 for the Pittsburgh Bessemer Steel Company. This machine was a two-ton full-revolving, self-propelling steam crane mounted on a four-wheel standard gage truck.

Wrecking crane was built by the Industrial Brownhoist Corporation, Bay City, Mich., in 1883. It had a capacity of twenty tons, and was mounted on a non-propelling car to operate on a standard gage track. In 1886 an adaptation of the revolving crane was developed. This was a fifteen-ton steam railway type crane in which the crane proper was mounted at one end of the car and the boiler at the other.

CRANIOSCOPY BOOK was Dr. Samuel George Morton's *Crania Americana; or A Comparative View of the Skulls of Various Aboriginal Nations of North and South America to Which Is Prefixed an Essay on the Varieties of the Human Species,* published in 1839 by J. Dobson, Philadelphia, Pa. It was a tall folio containing a 5-page preface, 297 pages of text, and 4 blank sheets. It had 71 full pages of lithograph plates.

CRAPS was introduced in New Orleans, La., about 1813 by Bernard Xavier Philippe de Marigny de Mandeville, who had seen the game played in France as "hazards." As the nickname for a Creole was Johnny Crapaud, the game became known as Crapaud's game which later was abbreviated to Craps. Mandeville lost a fortune at the game. He owned considerable property through which he was obliged to cut a street and sell lots on both sides to obtain funds to pay his debts. Maps show this street named Craps Street, later changed to Burgundy Street. *(Edward Laroque Tinker—The Palingenesis of Craps)*

CREAM SEPARATOR
Centrifugal cream separator was made in 1879 by David M. Weston and Edward Burnett of Boston, Mass., whose experience was obtained with sugar centrifugals. The first machine was used on the Deerfoot Farm, Southborough, Mass. It made 1,600 revolutions a minute and had a 26-inch bowl. The machine had to be stopped to draw off the cream and skim milk after separation.

Centrifugal cream separator patent was No. 195,515 granted September 25, 1877, to Wilhelm C. L. Lefeldt and Carl G. O. Lentsch of Schoeningen, Germany, on an "improvement in centrifugal machines for creaming milk." It consisted of an electric rotator which forced the heavy milk to the base of the pan.

Continuous flow centrifugal cream separator was invented by Carl Gustaf Patrik de Laval of Stockholm, Sweden, who applied for

CREAM SEPARATOR—*Continued*
a patent on July 31, 1879, which was granted October 4, 1881, No. 247,804. The first machine of this type used in the United States was put in operation in 1881 by Theodore Augustus Havemeyer, sugar refiner and Jersey stock breeder, on his farm at Mahwah, N.J.

CREAMERY (commercial) was established by Alanson Slaughter at Wallkill, N.Y., in 1861.

CREDIT INSURANCE. *See* Insurance: Credit insurance

CREDIT PROTECTIVE GROUP was the Merchants' Vigilance Association, formed in 1842 by importers and commission houses in New York City. The association distributed reports prepared by Sheldon P. Church. William C. Dusenbury, who later formed the Mercantile Agency of Woodward & Dusenbury, was the secretary.

CREDIT REPORT BOOK was prepared by Sheldon P. Church and published anonymously in 1844 in New York City. It was distributed to subscribers only and contained commercial information about merchants in southern and midwestern states.

CREDIT UNION ACT. *See* Federal credit union act

CREDIT UNION ASSOCIATION was founded by Alphonse Desjardins in Manchester, N.H., on December 16, 1908. It was known as "La Caisse Populaire Ste. Marie" and was chartered April 6, 1909. Ninety-nine per cent of the depositors were French. *(Edson Leone Whitney—Cooperative Credit Societies, Credit Unions in America and Foreign Countries)*

CREDIT UNION LAW was sponsored by Pierre Jay, first bank commissioner of Massachusetts, and was passed by the Massachusetts legislature. It was approved May 21, 1909, by Governor Eben Sumner Draper. *(Chapter 419 —Acts of 1909—Massachusetts)*

CREMATION was that of Henry Laurens, who was born in Charleston, S.C., in 1724 and who died on December 8, 1792. He was a staunch patriot, and after the Revolutionary War became one of the ministers to make arrangements for peace. His will read as follows: "I solemnly enjoin it upon my son as an indispensable duty that, as soon as he conveniently can after my decease, he cause my body to be wrapped in twelve yards of tow cloth, and burnt until it is entirely consumed, and then, collecting my ashes, deposit them wherever he may see proper." *(Cobb—Quarter Century of Cremation in North America)*

CREMATORY
Crematory was erected by Francis Julius LeMoyne on his own grounds in Washington, Pa., in 1876. It was the first and the only crematory in the United States until 1884. The first incineration was of the body of Baron Joseph Henry Louis de Palm on December 6, 1876. LeMoyne died of diabetes on October 14, 1879, and two days later was cremated in his own crematory. *(Howard Atwood Kelly and Walter Lincoln Burrage—Dictionary of American Medical Biographies)*

Crematory (state) was authorized by Chapter 341 of New York State on May 21, 1888, when $20,000 was appropriated to build and equip a crematory on Swinburne Island in New York harbor. It was built by Dr. Miles Lewis Davis of Lancaster, Pa. In 1889, those buried at the Quarantine cemetery (Sequine's Point) were disinterred and cremated. *(New York Quarantine Commissioners—Annual Report 1889)*

CREPE was produced in France in 1912 and was introduced into New York City in the same year by Haas Bros., who registered the name "Crepe Georgette" in the United States Patent Office on December 30, 1913, and commenced production in the United States.

CREPE PAPER. *See* Paper: Crepe paper

CRICKET CLUB
Cricket club was the Boston Cricket Club, founded in 1809 in Boston, Mass. The first president was Andrew Allen.

Cricket club to own its own clubhouse was the Germantown Cricket Club, which in 1854 occupied "Belfield," the home of William Wister, in Germantown, Pa. *(Site and Relic Society of Germantown—Reports)*

CRICKET TOURNAMENT
Cricket game played by a college team is said to have been played at Haverford College, Haverford, Pa. The game was introduced in 1836 by William Carvill, the college gardener. The bats and balls were of home manufacture.

Cricket match was held in New York City, on the site of Fulton Market, on May 1, 1751, between the Londoners and the New Yorkers. The New Yorkers made 80 and 86 and the Londoners 43 and 47. Cricket had been played by local teams on the same site about five years earlier. *(William Rotch Wister—Some Reminiscences of Cricket in Philadelphia Before 1861)*

International cricket tournament was held October 3, 4, 5, 1859, in Hoboken, N.J., between the All-England team, captained by

THE FIRST

George Parr, and the St. George's Cricket Club of New York, captained by J. Wisden. The American team was weak at bat and the English team won in one inning and sixty-four runs. A second game was played October 10, 1859, at Philadelphia, Pa., the English winning by seven wickets. The English team played two games in the United States and two in Canada. *(Henry Chadwick—American Cricket Manual)*

CRIME PREVENTION AND DETECTION

Crime prevention commission for interstate cooperation was the New Jersey Commission on Interstate Cooperation, established by Senate Joint Resolution No. 3, introduced and sponsored by Senator Joseph Gustave Wolber. The joint resolution was passed and signed March 12, 1935, by Governor Harold Giles Hoffman and the commission was immediately organized with Judge Richard Hartshorne as the first chairman. The commission consisted of 15 members, 5 each appointed by the Senate, the Assembly, and the Governor. The commission was responsible for developing cooperation between states on various problems such as crime control, motor vehicles, conflicting taxation, labor problems, agriculture, etc.

Interstate crime pact was effected between New York and New Jersey and signed September 16, 1833, in New York City by Benjamin Franklin Butler, Peter Augustus Jay, Henry Seymour, Theodore Frelinghuysen, James Parker, and Lucius Quintius Cincinnatus Elmer. Article 6 related to criminal process for New Jersey and article 7 for New York. The New Jersey legislature ratified the pact on February 26, 1834, and New York on February 5, 1834. The pact was ratified by act of Congress, June 28, 1834. *(U.S. Laws 1834—Chapter 126)*

National conference on crime was held October 11-12, 1935, in Trenton, N.J., with a roster of official delegates from 41 states and from the Federal Government. Its purpose was to develop reciprocal legislation and interstate compacts between states and to curb crime throughout the country. The conference developed a permanent organization composed of one official representative from each state in the union and one from the Federal Government and established for the purpose of carrying out the recommendations of the conference.

CRIMINAL ALIEN INVESTIGATION BUREAU. *See* Police: Police bureau of criminal alien investigation

CRIPPLES

Hospital for crippled children. *See* Hospital: Crippled childrens' hospital (state)

THE FIRST

Kindergarten for crippled children was opened at the Alta Settlement House, Cleveland, Ohio in 1900.

Orthopedic hospital. *See* Hospital: Orthopedic hospital

Private school for cripples was planned in 1861 by a Miss Cornelia and Dr. James Knight. It was opened May 1, 1863, at the Hospital for the Ruptured and Crippled, New York City, under the auspices of the New York Society for the Relief of the Ruptured and Crippled, incorporated March 27, 1863. *(Fenwick Beekman—Hospital for the Ruptured and Crippled)*

Public school for cripples was the Tilden School, Chicago, Ill., opened in 1900, with Emma Haskell as teacher. A horsedrawn wagon was used to transport the children.

CROIX DE GUERRE. *See* Medal: Croix de Guerre

CROPS. *See* Agriculture: Crop limitation law; Agriculture: Crop surplus destruction

CROQUET LEAGUE was the National Croquet League, organized February 12, 1880, in Philadelphia, Pa. The first president was George Washington Johnson of the Lemon Hill Croquet Club. David Evans of the Pennsylvania Croquet Club was elected secretary and treasurer. Representatives from eighteen clubs attended to standardize the game. Wickets were reduced in size and the balls reduced in diameter.

CROSSING GATE (railroad). *See* Railroad crossing gate patent

CROSSWORD PUZZLE was prepared by Arthur Wynne and was published in the supplement of the New York (Sunday) *World* of December 21, 1913.

CROSSWORD PUZZLE BOOK was the *Crossword Puzzle Book,* published by Simon and Schuster, Inc., New York City, on April 18, 1924. It was edited by (Albert) Prosper Buranelli, F. Gregory Hartswick, and Margaret Petherbridge. It was an anthology of fifty puzzles from the New York *World.*

CROUP REPORT. *See* Medical Book: Croup report

CRUISE SHIP. *See* Ship: Cruise ship to circumnavigate the world

CRUSHER (stone). *See* Stone crusher

CRYOTRONS were developed by Dudley Allen Buck at the Massachusetts Institute of Technology, Cambridge Mass., and publicly reported on February 6, 1957. A cryotron is a superconductive switch designed for use in digital computers. A switching circuit containing large numbers of cryotrons operates at about four degrees above absolute zero.

CRYPTOGRAPHY BOOK was *A Dictionary to enable any two persons to maintain a correspondence with a secrecy, which is impossible for any other person to discover,* a 48-page pamphlet published anonymously in 1805 in Hartford, Conn. *(James D. Volts and David Shulman—A Bibliography of Cryptography)*

CRYPTOGRAPHY CHART was P. R. Wouves' *A Syllabical and Steganographical Table,* a chart 27 by 19¼ inches, with a list of syllables and words in English and French intended for secret correspondence. It contained 62 alphabetical columns, 6138 two-letter combinations, numbered from 1 to 99 so that words could be converted into numerical figures. It had two title pages, one in English and one in French, and was published in 1797 by Benjamin Franklin Bache in Philadelphia, Pa.

CRYSTAL CHANDELIER. *See* Glass crystal chandelier

CUMULATIVE BOOK INDEX MONTHLY. *See* Book index: Monthly cumulative index of books

CURB EXCHANGE. *See* Brokerage: Curb exchange

CURFEW BELL was introduced by Wilhelm Kieft, the third governor of New Netherlands (New York). In 1638 he instituted the custom of ringing the church bell nightly at nine o'clock to announce the hour of resting; every morning and evening to call persons to and from labor; and on Thursdays to summon prisoners to court. *(Edmund Bailey O'Callaghan —History of New Netherland, or New York Under the Dutch)*

CURIUM. *See* Element: Element 96

CURLING CHAMPIONSHIP (national) competition was held March 28-30, 1957, at the Stadium, Chicago, Ill. The men's national curling championship was won by the Hibbing Curling Club, Hibbing, Minn. The team con-

sisted of Harold Lauber, skip; Louis Lauber, Peter Beasy, Matt Brklich, and Irwin Akin, alternate. Ten teams competed. Hibbing won 8 games and lost 1 game. Second place was won by the Chicago, Ill., Curling Club and the Minot, N.D., Curling Club.

CURLING CLUB was the Orchard Lake Curling Club, organized in the winter of 1831-1832, near the present site of Pontiac, Mich. Lacking genuine curling stones, the club improvised wooden blocks sawed from hickory and shaped with axe and chisel. *(T. Williamson—Curling in Detroit and Vicinity)*

CURLING RINK
Indoor curling rink devoted exclusively to curling was opened December 19, 1920, by the Country Club, Brookline, Mass. *(Frederic Curtiss and John Heard—The Country Club 1882-1932)*

CURRENCY COMPTROLLER. *See* Comptroller: Comptroller of the currency

CURRENCY LEGISLATION. *See* Money: Bimetallism

CUSTOMHOUSE in colonial America was established in Yorktown, Va. It was built about 1706 by Richard Ambler, who occupied it as "Collector of Ports for Yorktown in 1720." At this period Yorktown was the port of entry for New York, Philadelphia, and other northern cities. A tombstone in Hampton, Va., badly obliterated but decipherable, reads "Peter Heyman, Collector of his Majesty's custom, died April 29, 1700." He is presumed to have been one of the early collectors of customs at Yorktown. *(Records in Bureau of Customs. Treasury Department, Washington, D.C.)*

CUSTOMS COURT JUDGE (Negro). *See* Judge: Negro judge of a Customs Court (U.S.)

CUT GLASS. *See* Glass: Cut glass

CUTLERY FACTORY
Cutlery factory of importance was the Green River Works of John Russell and Company, Greenfield, Mass., established about 1833 for the manufacture of chisels and table cutlery. It developed into the J. Russell Cutlery Company and had a branch office in New York City in 1840. *(Francis McGee Thompson—History of Greenfield, Mass.)*

Cutlery factory for the manufacture of pocket cutlery was started at Lakeville, Conn., by the Holley Manufacturing Company in 1845.

CUTLERY SHEARS were made in Elizabethport, N.J. in 1825 by Rochus Heinisch.

CYCLOTRON. *See* Physics: Cyclotron

CYLINDER PAPER-MAKING MACHINE. *See* Paper-Making machinery: Paper-making machine (cylinder)

CYLINDER PRINTING PRESS. *See* Printing press: Cylinder printing press

CYSTOSCOPIC PHOTOGRAPHS IN COLOR. *See* Photograph: Cystoscopic photographs in color

CZECH LANGUAGE NEWSPAPER. *See* Newspaper: Czech language newspaper

DACRON
Dacron men's suits were introduced May 8, 1951, by Hart, Schaffner & Marx Co. They were made of 8-8½ ounce fabric, consisting of 55 per cent dacron and 45 per cent worsted, produced by Deering, Milliken & Co., New York City, under the brand name of Visa.

DAGUERROTYPE. *See* Photograph: Photograph taken in the United States

DAILY NEWSPAPER. *See* Newspaper: Daily newspaper

DAIRY DIVISION OF THE BUREAU OF ANIMAL INDUSTRY. *See* Animal industry bureau (U.S.): Dairy division

DAIRY LEGISLATION (state) was enacted by Massachusetts, "an act to punish fraud by the sale of adulterated milk," chapter 222, signed May 30, 1856, by Governor Henry Joseph Gardner.

DAIRY SCHOOL of collegiate rank with an organized course was offered by the College of Agriculture, University of Wisconsin, Madison, Wis., opened January 3, 1890, to supplement courses in testing milk and farm churning. The first instructor in charge of dairying was Professor John Wright Decker. The first year the organized course was attended by only ten students, but the following year seventy registered from nine states and Canada. Dairy certificates were awarded to those who passed the full course and had been in practical charge of a creamery or cheese factory for two seasons of not less than seven months each, one of which followed the period of completing the course.

DAIRYMEN'S ASSOCIATION. *See* Agricultural society: Agricultural society for dairymen

DAM
Needle-type dam was constructed in 1900 under the supervision of B. F. Thomas at Louisa, Ky. It is located on the Levisa Fork of the Big Sandy River, just below the junction of Tug River. This needle dam was built from the West Virginia side to the Kentucky side and creates a pool some forty miles long.

Rock-filled dam was built at Castlewood, Colo., for the Denver Land and Water Company, and opened in November 1890. The upstream and downstream faces of the dam were built of dry or mortar rubble masonry. The core of the dam consisted of loosely dumped rock. The maximum height of the dam above the valley floor was about 70 feet, and the length about 600 feet. There was a spillway, located near the center of the dam, consisting of an opening 4 feet deep and 100 feet long. The outlets through the structure consisted of 8 twelve-inch cast iron pipes, placed in pairs, at four different elevations, with valves in a chamber built inside the dam. The reservoir capacity was about 3,400 acre feet.

Steel dam was the Ash Fork Dam in Johnson Canyon, four miles east of Ashfork, Ariz., which was built in 1898 by the Atchison, Topeka and Santa Fe Railway Company. It is built of steel with masonry abutments. The west abutment is 84 feet long, 16 feet high. The steel portion is 184 feet long. Height of the spillway crest above present reservoir bottom is 30 feet; lowest bedrock to spillway crest is 46 feet; width of canyon at stream bed is 40 feet; top of dam (exclusive of spillway) is 300 feet. Water spills over the crest of the dam are designed as an overflow weir. The capacity of this reservoir at spillway crest is 96.7 acre feet. Area of surface at spillway crest is 7.1 acres. This canyon drains about 30 square miles. Water flow is intermittent in the stream bed. *(Edward Wegmann—The Design and Construction of Dams)*

DANCE COURSE with collegiate credit was approved November 11, 1926, by the Board of Regents, and offered in the Department of Physical Education of Women, University of Wisconsin, Madison, Wis. Margaret Newell H'Doubler (Mrs. Wayne Claxton) was appointed chairman of the course, known as the dance major. The department offered work in the dance in the summer of 1917 without collegiate credit.

DANCE MARATHON began Saturday, March 30, 1923, at 6:57 P.M., at the Audubon Ballroom, New York City, and continued until Sunday March 31, 1923, 9:57 P.M., when Alma Cummings concluded 24 hours of continuous dancing. She danced the fox trot, one-step, and waltz, and tired out six partners.

THE FIRST

THE FIRST

DANGER SIGNAL (CQD). *See* Radio distress signal: Radio distress signal

DAVIS CUP TENNIS MATCH. *See* Tennis match: Lawn tennis matches for the Davis cup

DAYLIGHT SAVING, sponsored by the National Daylight Saving Association, was put into operation in the United States on Easter Sunday, March 31, 1918, when clocks were set one hour ahead. The measure was introduced by Senator William Musgrave Calder of New York on April 17, 1917, but was defeated. It was later passed without a roll call on June 27, 1917.

"DEAD LETTER" OFFICE. *See* Postal service: Dead letter office

DEAF—ASSOCIATION
National social organization for the hard of hearing was the American Association for the Hard of Hearing formed February 27, 1919, in New York City. The first annual meeting was held in New York City March 12, 1920. The name was changed to the American Society for the Hard of Hearing on June 5, 1935, at a meeting held in Cincinnati, Ohio.

DEAF—BONE BANK
National temporal bone bank center for ear research was established in January 1961 at the Department of Otolaryngology, University of Chicago, Chicago, Ill.

DEAF—CHURCH SERVICE
Church service telecast in sign language. *See* Television—Telecast: Church service televised in sign language

Church services for the deaf were held by an Episcopal priest, the Reverend Thomas Gallaudet (son of Thomas Hopkins Gallaudet) on October 3, 1852, in the small chapel of New York University, New York City. Oral services were held in the morning, sign services in the afternoon. On September 11, 1854, St. Ann's Church for Deaf-Mutes was incorporated and property purchased in 1859. The first services in the new church building were held August 7, 1859. *(Thomas Gallaudet—Sermon preached at the 25th Anniversary—Oct. 7, 1879)*

Ordained deaf clergyman was the Reverend Henry Winter Syle, a deacon in 1876 and a priest in 1883. He founded All Souls' Church for the Deaf, Philadelphia, Pa., in 1885.

Prayers in the sign language of the deaf were offered in 1817 at the American Institution for the Deaf, Hartford, Conn., by the Reverend Thomas Hopkins Gallaudet, a Congregational clergyman and teacher of the deaf.

DEAF—HEARING AID
Electrical hearing aid produced commercially was the Acousticon, invented by Miller Reese Hutchinson of New York City in 1901. On April 27, 1880, Francis D. Clarke and M. G. Foster secured patent No. 226,902 on a "device for aiding the deaf to hear" which made its own electricity and operated by bone conduction.

Hearing aid of interest other than ear trumpets was the Audiphone, a fan-like device held against the teeth, patented September 23, 1879, by Richard S. Rhodes of River Park, Ill., who obtained patent No. 219,828.

Transistorized hearing aid was manufactured by the Sonotone Corporation, Elmsford, N.Y., and offered for sale December 29, 1952. It weighed 3½ ounces and measured 3 by ¾ by 19/32 inches.

DEAF—LIP READING TOURNAMENT. *See* Lip reading tournament (national)

DEAF—SCHOOL
Institution in the world for the higher education of the deaf was the National Deaf Mute College, Washington, D.C., a department of the Columbia Institution for the Instruction of the Deaf, Dumb, and Blind, incorporated February 16, 1857 (11 Stat.L.161). On April 8, 1864, the Columbia Institution for the Deaf was authorized by a special act of Congress (13 Stat.L.45) to confer degrees. The first degree was an honorary Master of Arts conferred June 1864. The first graduate received his diploma in 1866. The name of the institution was changed to the Columbia Institution for the Deaf, as the education of the blind was transferred elsewhere. The name of the advanced department was changed in 1894 to Gallaudet College in honor of Thomas Hopkins Gallaudet, who was the first principal of the first school for the deaf in America. Dr. Edward Miner Gallaudet (son of Thomas Hopkins Gallaudet), served as president of Gallaudet College from 1864 to 1910. *(Henry Winter Syle—A Biographical Sketch of Thomas Hopkins Gallaudet)*

Instruction for the deaf was given by the Reverend John Stanford, Chaplain to the Humane and Criminal Institutions, in 1807 in the Almshouse, New York City. This instruction continued for about a year. Ten years later a meeting was held at his home to organize the New York Institution for the Deaf, now the New York School for the Deaf, which opened in 1818. *(Fred de Land—The Story of Lip Reading)*

Lip reading instruction for the deaf was given by Sarah Warren Keeler, a teacher at the Institution for the Improved Instruction of

THE FIRST

Deaf Mutes in New York City, who advertised lip-reading lessons for adults in 1882. She lectured on the subject in 1884 and published her method in 1894.

Lip reading school for adults (successful) was established by Lillie Eginton Warren in 1890 in New York City. In 1895 she published *Defective Speech and Deafness,* a 116-page book, and on April 28, 1903, obtained patent No. 726,484 on a "means for teaching of the facial expressions which occur in speaking."

Lip reading tournament. *See* Lip reading tournament (national)

Lip reading was first referred to in print in Dr. William Thornton's essays *On the Mode of Teaching the Deaf, or Surd, and Consequently Dumb, to Speak,* which appeared in the *Transactions of the American Philosophical Society,* Philadelphia, 1793.

Oral instruction for the deaf (known as visible speech) was used by the Horace Mann School in Boston, Mass., in 1871. Alexander Graham Bell instructed the teachers of this school in the system which his father, Alexander Melville Bell, was advocating. Visible speech was phonetic writing invented by Alexander Melville Bell to show graphically any sound made by the human voice, and used to facilitate pronunciation of foreign languages. In appreciation of his services the Boston School Committee provided a fund of $500 to pay for the services of Alexander Graham Bell during the spring of 1871. Oral instruction had been used in England in the eighteenth century.

Oral school for the deaf (still existing) was the Clarke School for the Deaf, which was founded in 1867 in Northampton, Mass. The nucleus of this school was a small experimental school in Chelmsford, Mass., founded by Harriet Rogers in 1865. Miss Rogers was appointed principal. John Clarke, philanthropist, gave $50,000. An oral school was started at Cobbs, Chesterfield County, Va., in 1815 by Colonel William Bolling with John Braidwood as instructor, but it lasted only two years.

School for the deaf (permanent) was the Connecticut Asylum for the Education and Instruction of Deaf and Dumb Persons, Hartford, Conn., which opened April 15, 1817, with seven pupils. It was incorporated May 1816. A grant of $5,000 was made by the Connecticut legislature October 1816. On May 5, 1819, the name was changed to the American Asylum. The school was financed through the generosity of a few men, one of whom, Dr. Mason Fitch Cogswell, had a deaf daughter,

THE FIRST

Alice. Thomas Hopkins Gallaudet, the first principal, inaugurated the system of teaching with the collaboration of the Frenchman Laurent Clerc. Sign language and finger spelling were the only means of communication. *(Henry Winter Syle—A Biographical Sketch of Rev. Thomas Hopkins Gallaudet)*

DEAF—STUDENTS' MAGAZINE

Magazine for deaf students was the *Deaf Mute Casket,* a four-page monthly printed in a school for the deaf by the deaf and edited by William D. Cooke. It was published in 1851 by the State School for the Blind and the Deaf in Raleigh, N.C.

DEAF—TRANSMISSION

Visible and oral communication by the deaf over distance was accomplished October 13, 1940, when Bertha O'Donnell and Adele Costa conversed in sign language through two-way television sets at W2USA, New York World's Fair Amateur Television Booth, and W2HID, 220 East 42nd Street, New York City, eight miles away.

DEAN OF MEN. *See* College: Dean of men

DEAN OF THE FACULTY. *See* College: Dean of the faculty

DEAN (WOMAN) OF A GRADUATE SCHOOL. *See* College: Woman dean of a graduate school

DEATH PENALTY. *See* Capital punishment: Death penalty was first abolished

DEATH PENALTY FOR KIDNAPPING. *See* Kidnapping: Death penalty for kidnapping

DEBATE (radio). *See* Radio broadcast: Debate over the radio

DEBT

Public debt of the United States to exceed $100 million was $127,334,933.74 on January 1, 1816. The first to exceed $500 million was $524,176,412.13 on July 1, 1862. The first to exceed $1 billion was $1,119,772,138.63 on July 1, 1863. *(Treasury Department—Bureau of Statistics—Public Debt of the United States 1791-1896)*

DEBT LEGISLATION (federal) exempt-

ing debtors from prison on processes issuing from a United States court amounting to less than $30 was "an act for the relief of persons imprisoned for debt" passed May 28, 1796 (1 Stat.L.482). On February 28, 1839, an act of Congress (5 Stat.L.321) prohibited

DEBT LEGISLATION (federal)—*Cont.*
imprisonment for debt by a United States court in states in which imprisonment for debt had been abolished.

DEBTORS' COURT. *See* Court: Small debtors' court established by state law

DEBTORS' PRISON to be abolished by law was that of Kentucky, which passed "an act to abolish imprisonment for debt" on December 17, 1821. The act repealed all laws authorizing *capias ad satisfaciendum.* *(Chapter 229—Acts Passed at First Session Thirtieth General Assembly, Frankfort, Ky.)*

DECALCOMANIAS or transfer papers were imported in 1862 and used as playthings. The first commercial production for decorating buggies, sleighs, bicycles, sewing machines, etc., was undertaken in Philadelphia, Pa., in 1890 by Thomas Burke, who established the National Decalcomania Company. The company was incorporated in 1922 and is still manufacturing on the original site.

DECATHLON CHAMPION (American). *See* Olympic games: American decathlon champion

DECIMAL SYSTEM OF MONEY. *See* Money: Decimal system of money

DECK CHAIR. *See* Chair: Steamer chair

DECKED SHIP. *See* Ship: Decked ship

DECLARATION OF INDEPENDENCE (American)
Declaration of Independence was formally made on July 12, 1774, in the First Presbyterian Church in Carlisle, Pa., at a meeting of freeholders and freemen from the several townships. Various resolutions were passed. The Reverend John Montgomery presided. *(Conway Phelps Wing—History of the First Presbyterian Church of Carlisle)*

Declaration of Independence by a colony was made on April 12, 1776, when the Provincial Congress in session at Halifax, N.C., by unanimous action empowered the delegates to the Continental Congress to concur with delegates of other provinces in declaring independence from Great Britain. The Mecklenburg (N.C.) Declaration of Independence had been previously adopted on May 20, 1775, in Charlotte, Mecklenburg County, N.C., by citizens who formally declared independence from Great Britain. Less drastic actions of similar nature were advocated by Patrick Henry and others. *(William Henry Hoyt—The Mecklenburg Dec-*

laration of Independence. See also conflicting statement by *James Hall Moore—Defense of the Mecklenburg Declaration of Independence)*

Declaration of Independence was first ordered "to be fairly engrossed on parchment" on July 19, 1776, and was signed in Philadelphia on August 2, 1776, by 50 members of the original 56 who voted for its adoption. The other 6 signed at various later times. The last signer was Thomas McKean, who originally voted for it, but had left Philadelphia to join the army and was permitted to sign as late as 1781.

Declaration of Independence was first printed July 5, 1776, in Philadelphia, Pa., by John Dunlop in a folio broadside and distributed the same day. On July 4, Congress, acting as a Committee of the Whole, approved the Declaration and ordered that it be printed and that copies be "sent to the several assemblies, conventions and committees or counsels of safety and to the several commanding officers of the Continental troops that it be proclaimed in each of the United States and at the head of the army."

Declaration of Independence was first published in a newspaper on July 6, 1776. It was reprinted in Vol. II, No. 228, of the *Pennsylvania Evening Post* of Philadelphia, Pa.

Declaration of Independence was first read publicly on July 8, 1776, when Colonel John Nixon, delegated by the High Sheriff of Philadelphia, read it in the old State House yard (Independence Square). The "Liberty Bell" with the prophetic inscription "Proclaim liberty throughout all the land unto all the inhabitants thereof" was rung to call the citizens together to hear the reading. *(Harold Donaldson Eberlein and Cortland Van Dyke Hubbard—Diary of Independence Hall)*

Declaration of Independence was signed first by John Hancock of Massachusetts, President of the Continental Congress, on July 4, 1776, in Philadelphia, Pa. It was also signed by Charles Thomson, secretary (but not a delegate). The parchment copy was signed by the delegates on August 2, 1776. *(John Sanderson—Biography of the Signers of the Declaration of Independence)*

DECLARATION OF RIGHTS was passed on October 14, 1774, and was known as the "Declaration and Resolves of the First Continental Congress." It agreed, "That they [the colonists] are entitled to life, liberty and property; and they have never ceded to any foreign power whatsoever a right to dispose of either without their consent." It was enacted in Philadelphia, Pa. *(Journals of the Continental Congress—1774-1789)*

THE FIRST

DECORATION. *See* Medal

DECORATION DAY. *See* Holiday: Decoration day

DEEP FREEZE LOCKER. *See* Locker: Public locker plant

DEFENSE COMMAND (U.S.). *See* Air defense command (U.S.)

DEFENSE DEPARTMENT (U.S.) was formed on September 17, 1947, when the War and Navy departments were combined with James Vincent Forrestal as chief. He was sworn in September 17, 1947, by Supreme Court Justice Frederick Moore Vinson. The following day John Laurence Sullivan was sworn in as Secretary of the Navy and William Stuart Symington as Secretary for Air. Kenneth Claiborne Royall had been sworn in nine weeks previously as Secretary of the Army. The department was granted cabinet status and was authorized by the National Security Act of July 26, 1947 (61 Stat.L.495).

DEGREES (academic and honorary)

American awarded honorary degrees from three of England's leading universities was Ambassador Robert Worth Bingham, recipient of an honorary LL.D. (Doctor of Laws) from London University on November 25, 1933, and from Cambridge University on October 22, 1934; and an honorary Litt.D. (Doctor of Letters) from Oxford University on November 21, 1936.

Anthropology doctorate was conferred March 9, 1892, by Clark University, Worcester, Mass., on Alexander Francis Chamberlain for his 84-page thesis on "The Language of the Mississagua Indians." *(American Anthropologist. Vol. 16. p. 337)*

Bachelor of Arts degree was conferred September 23, 1642, by Harvard College, Cambridge, Mass., on nine graduates: Tobias Barnard, Samuel Bellingham, Nathaniel Brewster, John Bulkley, George Downing, William Hubbard, Henry Saltonstall, John Wilson, and Benjamin Woodbridge.
See also College: College

Bachelor of Music degree was granted December 23, 1873, by Adrian College, Adrian, Mich., to Mattie Pease Lowrie, who completed a four-year course in vocal and instrumental music and theory. A Master of Music degree was authorized for musicians of recognized ability who paid the regular fee and passed the required examination.

THE FIRST

Bachelor of Sacred Music degree was conferred June 10, 1953, by the Hebrew Union College Jewish Institute of Religion, New York City, on seven men who had completed the course.

Degree awarded a ventriloquist's dummy was conferred August 28, 1938, by the School of Speech of Northwestern University, Evanston, Ill., on Charlie McCarthy during the regular Edgar Bergen-Charlie McCarthy hour in the Chicago studios of the National Broadcasting Company. The degree of "Master of Innuendo and Snappy Comeback" was conferred by the dean, Ralph Dennis.

Degree conferred by radio was granted June 9, 1925, by the State University of Iowa, Iowa City, Iowa, to Clifford L. Lideen of Burlington, Iowa. The university broadcast the conferring of his B.A. dergee. He was forced to leave the university in 1922 because of illness and completed his work through broadcasts given by station WOI, Ames, Iowa.

Doctor of Laws honorary degree was awarded July 21, 1773, by Harvard College, Cambridge, Mass., to John Winthrop, Doctor of Laws *pro meritas. (Henry Herbert Edes— John Winthrop, the First Recipient from Harvard College of the Degree of Doctor of Laws)*

Doctor of Medicine. *See* Physician

Doctor of Military Science degree was created by New York University, New York City, and conferred April 11, 1930, upon General John Joseph Pershing, the first recipient of such a degree in the United States.

Doctor of Music degree was conferred July 24, 1849, by Georgetown University, Washington, D.C., on Professor Henry Dielman of Mount St. Mary's, Emmitsburg, Md. The degree was awarded *honoris causa* at exercises attended by President Zachary Taylor. *(John Gilmary Shea—Memorial of the First Centenary of the Georgetown College)*

Doctor of Philosophy degree was awarded in 1861 by Yale University, New Haven, Conn., to three graduates, Eugene Schuyler, James Morris Whiton, and Arthur Williams Wright. The degree had been authorized July 24, 1860. *(Paul Monroe—Cyclopedia of Education)*

Doctor of Philosophy degree awarded to a Negro was granted to Edward Alexander Bouchet by Yale University, New Haven, Conn., in 1876. He was also the first Negro to be elected to Phi Beta Kappa, the national scholastic fraternity. He was graduated from Yale in 1874. His thesis was entitled "Measuring Refractive Indices."

DEGREES (academic and honorary)—*Cont.*

Doctor of Philosophy degree **awarded to a woman** was granted by Boston University Boston, Mass., June 6, 1877 to Helen Magill (Mrs. Andrew Jackson White). The title of her dissertation was "The Greek Drama." She received her A.B. degree in 1875 from Swarthmore. *(Institute of Women's Professional Relations. Greensboro, N.C.)*

Doctor of Philosophy degree awarded to a woman by a women's college was granted on June 21, 1882, by Smith College, Northampton, Mass., to Kate Eugenia Morris (later Mrs. Charles Morris Cone). The subject of her dissertation in history was the German electoral college.

Doctor of Philosophy in Accounting degree was conferred June 12, 1939, on John Wood McMahan at the annual commencement of the University of Illinois, Urbana, Ill.

Doctor of Sacred Theology degree was granted to Increase Mather in 1692 by Harvard College, Cambridge, Mass. Two tutors, John Leverett and William Brattle, were awarded the Bachelor of Sacred Theology degree.

Doctor of Science degree earned by a woman was awarded to Caroline Willard Baldwin (later Mrs. Charles T. Morrison) on June 20, 1895, by Cornell University, Ithaca, N.Y. The title of her dissertation was "A Photographic Study of Arc Spectra."

Doctor of Social Science degree was awarded to Helen Rankin Jeter in 1924 by the School of Social Science Administration of the University of Chicago, Chicago, Ill. Her thesis, "The Chicago Juvenile Court," was published by the Children's Bureau of the United States Department of Labor.

Honorary degree awarded a Negro woman by a southern white college was a Doctor of Humanities degree awarded Mary McLeod Bethune on February 21, 1949, by Rollins College, Winter Park, Fla.

Honorary degree granted George Washington was the degree of "Doctor of Laws, the Law of Nature and Nations, and the Civil Law," conferred by the Governing Board of Harvard College, April 3, 1776, in Cambridge, Mass. *(Publications. Colonial Society of Massachusetts. Vol. 7)*

Husband and wife awarded honorary degrees by an American university were Vice President and Mrs. John Nance Garner, recipients of Doctor of Laws degree from Baylor University, Waco, Tex., on November 21, 1936.

Law degree of LL.M. (Master of Laws) was conferred June 29, 1864, at the 110th annual commencement of Columbia University, held at the Academy of Music, New York City. It was also granted in 1865, but not again (by Columbia University) until 1894, after which it was conferred at intervals. During the last few years, however, it has been conferred regularly. *(Alfred Zantzinger Reed —Training for the Public Profession of Law)*

Master of Arts degree in Sacred Music was conferred June 6, 1956, by the Hebrew Union School of Education and Sacred Music, New York City, on two students who had concluded thirty full sessions and submitted approved theses. The recipients were Cantor Ben William Belfer of Rockville Centre, N.Y., and Cantor Arthur M. Wolfson of Temple Emanuel, New York City.

Master of Hebrew Literature degree awarded a woman was granted May 28, 1939, by the Jewish Institute of Religion, New York City to Helen Hadassah Levinthal, the first Jewish woman to graduate from a recognized theological college, having completed the full rabbinical course.

DELINQUENCY LAW. *See* Child delinquency law (state)

DELIVERY TUNNEL (freight). *See* Tunnel: Freight delivery tunnel system

DEMAND NOTE. *See* Money: Demand notes

DEMOCRATIC CARTOON. *See* Cartoon: Democratic cartoon

DEMOCRATIC NATIONAL CONVENTION was held May 21-23, 1832 in Baltimore, Md., under the name, "Republican Delegates from the Several States." Twenty-one states and the District of Columbia sent delegates who nominated Andrew Jackson for President and Martin Van Buren for Vice President. While the present Democratic Party was officially known at the time as the "Republican Party"—a name which had come down from the time of Jefferson—it was becoming popularly known as the Democratic-Republican Party. In the early national conventions "Democrat" and "Republican" were often used interchangeably, but in 1840 the word "Republican" was dropped entirely and the official title became the "Democratic National Convention," although even then speakers employed the name "Republican" when referring to what is now the Democratic Party. *(Frank Richardson Kent—The Democratic Party)*

THE FIRST

DEMOCRATIC NEWSPAPER. *See* Newspaper: Democratic newspaper

DE MOLAY, ORDER OF. *See* Freemasons: Order of De Molay

DEMOUNTABLE TIRE-CARRYING RIM. *See* Automobile tire: Demountable tire-carrying rim

DENTAL BOOK
Book for dental hygienists (text) was *Mouth Hygiene,* compiled and edited by Dr. Alfred Civilion Fones and associate editors Robert Hallock Wright Strang and Edward Cameron Kirk. It was a course of instruction for dental hygienists and consisted of 530 pages with 278 illustrations and 7 plates. It was published by Lea & Febiger, Philadelphia and New York, in 1916.

Book on dental surgery was Dr. James Edmund Garretson's *A Treatise on the Diseases and Surgery of the Mouth, Jaws and Associate Parts,* a 700-page book published in 1869 by J. B. Lippincott & Co., Philadelphia, Pa.

Book on dental technics of value was *The Manual of Operative Technics—A Practical Treatise On the Elements of Operative Dentistry* published in Chicago, Ill., in 1894 by Thomas Edwin Weeks, Professor of Operative Dentistry and Dental Anatomy in the College of Dentistry, University of Minnesota, Minneapolis, Minn.

Book on dentistry (strictly American) was Richard Cort Skinner's *A Treatise on the Human Teeth, Concisely Explaining Their Structure and Cause of Disease and Decay,* published in 1801 by Johnson and Stryker, New York City. It contained 26 pages and sold for 30 cents. *(Fielding Hudson Garrison— An Introduction to the History of Medicine)*

Book on dentistry to become popular was Josiah Foster Flagg's *The Family Dentist; Containing a Brief Description of the Structure, Formation, Diseases and Treatment of the Human Teeth,* printed and published in 1822 in Boston, Mass., by Joseph W. Ingraham. It contained 82 pages.

Dental textbook was *A System of Dental Surgery in three parts: 1. Dental surgery as a science; 2. Operative dental surgery; 3. Pharmacy connected with dental surgery,* by Samuel Sheldon Fitch, a surgeon dentist of Philadelphia, Pa. The work, which contained 568 pages, was published in 1829 in New York City by G. & C. H. Carvill.

THE FIRST

Orthodontia treatise to be printed was *An Essay On The Importance of Regulating the Teeth of Children Before the Fourteenth Year; or the Period of Life when the Second Set of Teeth Become Perfectly Developed,* by Solyman Brown, M.D., which was printed in 1841 in New York City. *(Bernhard Wolf Weinberger—Orthodontics)*

DENTAL CHAIR which provided such necessary conveniences as a head rest and changes in height and position of the seat and back was designed by M. Waldo Hanchett of Syracuse, N.Y., who received patent No. 5,711, on August 15, 1848. *(History of Dental and Oral Science in America)*

DENTAL CODE OF ETHICS was proposed July 28, 1865, by Dr. John Allen at the Fifth Annual Convention of the American Dental Association held in Chicago, Ill.

DENTAL CORPS (U.S. Army)
Army Dental Corps Major General was Major General Robert H. Mills, Director of the Dental Division, whose appointment was made possible by War Department Special Orders No. 280, October 7, 1943. The date of his rank was September 17, 1943.

Dental Corps commissions were authorized by act of Congress of March 3, 1911 (36 Stat.L.1054) which limited commissions to first lieutenant. The act of June 3, 1916 (39 Stat. L.173) permitted the ranks of captain and major; the act of October 6, 1917 (40 Stat.L. 397) the ranks of lieutenant colonel and colonel; the act of January 29, 1938 (52 Stat.L.8) the rank of brigadier general for the Director of the Dental Division, one of the assistants to the Surgeon General.

Dental Corps of the U.S. Army was authorized by the Army Reorganization Act, February 2, 1901 (31 Stat.L.752), "an act to increase the efficiency of the permanent military establishments of the United States." It authorized the employment of contract dental surgeons "not to exceed one to every 30,000 of said army, and not to exceed 30 in all." The first three contract dental surgeons were Drs. John Sayre Marshall, Robert T. Oliver, and Robert W. Morgan, named by the Surgeon General on February 11, 1901.

Dentist officially employed in the U.S. Army was Dr. W. H. Ware, an enlisted man in the Medical Department, who served as a dental surgeon in the U.S. Army in the Philippine Islands in 1898.

DENTAL CORPS (U.S. Navy)
Admiral in the Dental Corps (U.S. Navy) was Dr. Alexander Gordon Lyle, appointed a rear admiral on March 13, 1943.

THE FIRST

THE FIRST

DENTAL CORPS (U.S. Navy)—*Continued*

Dental Corps of the U.S. Navy was authorized by act of Congress of August 12, 1912 (37 Stat.L.344), which provided for not more than 30 dental surgeons to be part of the Medical Department of the U.S. Navy and to provide professional service for navy personnel. They received the rank of lieutenant, junior grade.

DENTAL DISPENSARY

Dental dispensary was the City Dispensary for the Medical Relief of the Poor, New York City, which opened February 1, 1791. It was incorporated April 8, 1795. Isaac Roosevelt was the first president. From February 1, 1791, to November 23, 1791, 310 patients were admitted. The fee for extractions and filling cavities with silver or lead foil was 50 cents; filling cavities with gold or a good set of front teeth cost $1.

DENTAL DRILL (electric). *See* Drill: Dental drill (electric)

DENTAL LEGISLATION

Legislation (state) regarding dental hygienists was the Public Acts of the State of Connecticut, passed by the January 1915 session, Chapter 316, Section 12, and approved May 19, 1915. The first examination for dental hygienists was given by the State Board in June 1918 as no hygienists had applied for license prior to that date.

Legislation (state) regarding dental surgery was passed December 31, 1841, by Alabama. It provided that from and after the first Monday of December 1842, there should be "medical boards of the state to examine and to issue a license to applicants to practice dental surgery under the same rules and regulations, and subject to the same restrictions as those who apply for license to practice medicine."

DENTAL MAGAZINE

Dental journal to be published was *The American Journal of Dental Science, Devoted to Original Articles, Reviews of Dental Publications, etc.,* 24 pages, which made its appearance July 1839. The publishing committee consisted of Dr. Eleazar Parmly, Dr. Elisha Baker, and Dr. Solyman Brown. Dr. Chapin Aaron Harris was the first editor. It was published in New York City.

Orthodontia magazine was the *International Journal of Orthodontia,* edited by Dr. Martin Dewey. The first issue was published January 1915 in St. Louis, Mo., and contained 44 pages. The title was changed to the *American Journal of Orthodontics and Oral Surgery in* January 1938.

DENTAL MALLET

Dental mallet was invented by Dr. William Gibson Arlington Bonwill of Philadelphia, Pa., who obtained patent No. 170,045 on November 16, 1875, on "electro-magnetic dental pluggers" used to impact gold into cavities. He conceived the idea of a vibrating mallet on February 27, 1867, while watching the "sounder" of a telegraph key in operation at the Continental Hotel in Philadelphia. (*Dental Cosmos. December 1875. Vol. 17, No. 12*)

DENTAL SCHOOL

Dental assistants' and nurses' course was given by the Ohio College of Dental Surgery, Cincinnati, Ohio, from October 3, 1910, to May 1, 1911. The tuition fee was $75. The course was introduced by Henry Tomlinson Smith, the dean. (*Ohio College of Dental Surgery, 1911-1912 Annual Announcement*)

Dental college was the Baltimore College of Dental Surgery, organized in Baltimore, Md., in 1839 with Chapin Aaron Harris, Horace Henry Hayden, Henry Willis Baxley, and others on the faculty. The college was incorporated February 1, 1840, and the first degrees were conferred March 9, 1841 on Robert Arthur and R. Covington Mackall. (*Van Broadus Dalton—The Genesis of Dental Education in the United States*)

Dental hygienists' course was inaugurated by Dr. Alfred Civilion Fones who established the Fones Clinic, Bridgeport, Conn. The course started November 17, 1913, with 33 women, 27 of whom graduated June 5, 1914.

Dental school permanently established by a university, and the first associated with a medical school, was the Harvard School of Dental Medicine, Boston, Mass., established July 17, 1867. The first commencement exercises were held March 10, 1869, and the Doctor of Dental Medicine degree (D.M.D.) was awarded to six dentists. Dr. Nathan Cooley Keep was the first dean.

DENTAL SOCIETY

Dental society (local) was the Society of Surgeon-Dentists of the City and State of New York, which was formed December 3, 1834, with Dr. Eleazar Parmly as the first president and Dr. Solyman Brown as the first corresponding secretary. This was a local society, as was the Dental Association of Western New York. (*American Journal of Dental Science. Vol. 1*)

Dental society of importance was the American Society of Dental Surgeons, organized August 18, 1840, at a meeting held at the American Hotel, New York City. The first officers were Dr. Horace Henry Hayden of Baltimore, Md., president; Dr. Josiah Foster

THE FIRST

THE FIRST

Flagg of Boston, Mass., Dr. Eleazer Parmly of New York City, and Dr. Emile B. Gardette, vice presidents. The society disbanded in 1856. *(Journal American Dental Association. Vol. 27. March 1940)*

Orthodontists' society was the American Society of Orthodontists, founded June 1900 in St. Louis, Mo. The first annual meeting was held June 11, 12, 13, 1901, in St. Louis. The constitution was adopted June 15, 1901. The first president was Dr. Edward Hartley Angle of St. Louis. The society was incorporated February 23, 1917, in Pennsylvania, and the name changed April 21, 1937, to the American Association of Orthodontists.

DENTIST

Dentist who was a native-born American was Josiah Flagg, who, at the age of 18, practiced dentistry in 1782 in Boston, Mass. In 1785 he advertised as follows: "Dr. Flagg transplants teeth, cures ulcers and eases them from pain without drawing; fastens those that are loose; mends teeth with foil or gold to be as lasting and useful as the sound teeth . . . sells, by wholesale and retail, dentifrices, tinctures, chew-sticks, mastics, teeth and gum brushes, suitable for every age, complaint and climate, with directions for their use." *(Charles Rudolph Edward Koch—History of Dental Surgery)*

Woman dentist to maintain a dental office independently was Dr. Emeline Roberts Jones, who commenced practice in Danielsonville (now Danielson), Conn., in May 1855 as an assistant to her husband, Dr. Daniel Albion Jones. In 1859, she became his partner and in 1864 carried on independently when her husband died. *(James McManus—Record of Connecticut Dentists)*

Woman dentist to obtain a D.D.S. degree from a dental college was Lucy B. Hobbs (Mrs. Taylor), who graduated February 21, 1866, from the Ohio College of Dental Surgery, Cincinnati, Ohio. She was required to attend only one college session because of credits allowed for previous practice. (Licenses to practice dentistry were not compulsory.) She was elected a member of the Iowa State Dental Society on July 1865, the first woman member of a dental society. *(Dental Cosmos. November 1910)*

DENTISTRY

Amalgam for filling teeth was introduced by Messrs. Crawcour and Sons, who advertised it in the August 12, 1834, New York *Commercial Advertiser* as "Royal Mineral Succedaneum for filling decayed teeth without the slightest pain, heat or pressure." They paid little attention to caries and filled all cavities without treatment. Their work was unsatisfactory and they were obliged to flee the country.

Anesthetic in dentistry. *See* Anesthesia: Anesthetic in dentistry

Dental assistants' and nurses' course. *See* Dental school: Dental assistants' and nurses' course

Dental association. *See* Dental society: Dental society

Dental hygienists' book. *See* Dental book: Book for dental hygienists (text)

Dental hygienists' course. *See* Dental school: Dental hygienists' course

Gold crown tooth was made by Dr. William Newton Morrison, corresponding secretary of the Missouri State Dental Association, who described his process in the May 1869 issue of the *Missouri Dental Journal*.

Gold inlay was described by William H. Taggart, a Chicago dentist, before the New York Odontological Society, January 15, 1907. He invented the method of casting gold inlays by the inverted pattern procedure, using the ancient principle of the "disappearing core." *(Dental Cosmos. November 1907)*

Gold used for the filling of dental cavities was advocated by Dr. Robert Arthur. In 1855 he discovered the cohesive property of annealed gold foil, a discovery which practically revolutionized the dental profession. He described it in an article, "Sponge Gold," in the *Dental News Letter* of October 1854 published in Philadelphia, Pa., and in an 86-page book, *A Treatise on the Use of Adhesive Gold Foil,* published in 1857 in Philadelphia.

Patent for a gold crown was No. 144,182 granted November 4, 1873, to Dr. John B. Beers of San Francisco, Calif., on "artificial crowns for teeth." The technique of preparing the hollow metal crown or shell is described in the September 1880 *Dental Cosmos,* published by S. S. White Dental Manufacturing Company, Philadelphia, Pa.

Patent for artificial teeth was granted on March 9, 1822, to Charles M. Graham of New York City.

Porcelain teeth were introduced about 1785, owing principally to the efforts of Dr. John Greenwood of New York City. He advertised "artificial teeth set in so firm (without drawing stumps or causing the least pain) as to eat with them, and so exact as not to be distinguished from natural." Greenwood also invented the foot-power drill. One of his patients was George Washington. *(Dental Items of Interest—November 1943)*

THE FIRST

DEPARTMENT STORE. *See* Business: Department store

DEPARTMENTAL POSTAGE STAMPS. *See* Postage stamp: Departmental postage stamps

DEPARTMENTS (U.S.) *See* specific departments, e.g. Agriculture department, Interior department

DEPORTATION was effected by the Plymouth Colony in 1628. Thomas Morton, residing at Mare Mount (Merry Mount), Mass., with a licentious group and also accused of supplying guns to the Indians, was deported because of the general disapproval of his actions. He was sent to England June 9, 1628, in the custody of John Oldham. *(Massachusetts Historical Collections. III. Governor Bradford's Letter Book)*

DEPOSIT GUARANTY ACT. *See* Bank legislation: Bank guaranty legislation

DEPOSIT INSURANCE CORPORATION. *See* Federal deposit insurance corporation

DEPRESSED TROUGH ROAD. *See* Road: Road with a depressed trough

DERBY HAT. *See* Hat: Derby hat

DERMATOLOGY CHAIR. *See* Medical instruction: Dermatology chair

DERMATOLOGY TREATISE. *See* Medical book: Dermatology treatise

DESERT HOMESTEAD ACT. *See* Homestead act: Homestead act (desert)

DESIGN PATENT. *See* Patent: Design patent

DESK with roll top was invented about 1850 by Abner Cutler, who formed the Cutler Desk Company of Buffalo, N.Y. The original patent showed the top very similar to the roll top of today. Flexible wooden curtains had been used previously. Cutler improved upon their manufacture by using a strong fabric held between an outer row of moldings and an inner row of soft wood slats, which made it possible to operate rolls six feet long and four feet wide.

DESK TELEPHONE. *See* Telephone: Desk telephone

THE FIRST

DETECTIVE (woman). *See* Police: Woman detective

DETECTIVE STORY to achieve popularity was Edgar Allan Poe's "The Murders in the Rue Morgue," published April 1841 in *Graham's Magazine*, Philadelphia, Pa. *(Graham's Magazine. Vol. 18, No. 4)*

DETECTOR CAR. *See* Railroad car: Rail detector car

DETERGENT
Synthetic detergent for use in the home was Dreft, marketed October 10, 1933. It was a sodium alkyl sulfate made from chlorosulfonic acid and a fatty alcohol by the Procter & Gamble Company, Cincinnati, Ohio.

DETONATING FUSE. *See* Fuse: Textile-wrapped detonating fuse

DEUTERIUM. *See* Water: Heavy water

DIAGNOSTIC BACTERIOLOGY LABORATORY. *See* Bacteriology laboratory: Bacteriology diagnostic laboratory

DIAL TELEPHONE. *See* Telephone: Dial telephone service coast-to-coast without the aid of operators

DIAL TIME RECORDER. *See* Time recorder: Dial time recorder

DIAMOND
Diamonds in a meteorite were found in June 1891 by Dr. George Augustus Koenig, professor of mineralogy and geology at the University of Pennsylvania, Philadelphia, Pa., while cutting a meteorite found at Canon Diablo, Arizona. In various cavities, he found small black diamonds of little commercial value which cut through polished corundum. *(Science. July 8, 1892)*

Diamonds in actual rock, peridotite, were found in the United States in the matrix at Murfreesboro, Pike County, Ark., in 1906. *(American Institute of Mining Engineers— Transactions 1909—Vol. 39. George Frederick Kunz—Diamonds in Arkansas)*

Pilot plant for the actual production of man-made diamonds was established by the General Electric Company in 1955. Scientists of the General Electric Research Laboratory, Schenectady, N.Y., announced on February 15, 1955, that they had succeeded in making diamonds 1/16 inch by subjecting carbonaceous compounds to pressures of 1,500,000 pounds per square inch at temperatures up to 5,000° Fahrenheit. They used a special pressure vessel in a large hydraulic press.

THE FIRST

THE FIRST

DIATHERMY MACHINE for medical use that was practical was constructed by Dr. Willis Rodney Whitney, director of research for the General Electric Company, Schenectady, N.Y., in December 1928. Albert B. Page first used the set February 19, 1929, at the Ellis Hospital, Schenectady, N.Y., and the first patient was treated February 23, 1929, by Dr. Charles Milton Carpenter. *(Science. May 2, 1930)*

DICE. *See* Craps

DICTATOR (baseball). *See* Baseball dictator

DICTIONARY
Agricultural dictionary published in the United States was Samuel Deane's *The New England Farmer; or, georgical dictionary: containing a compendious account of the ways and methods in which the most important art of husbandry, in all its branches is, or may be practised to the greatest advantage in this country,* a 335-page double-column book, published in 1790 by Isaiah Thomas in Worcester, Mass. It was copyrighted September 13, 1790, in the Third Massachusetts District.

Bohemian-American dictionary was the *Dictionary of Bohemian and English Languages,* compiled by Karel Jonas and published in Racine, Wis., in 1876. It contained 626 pages. *(Fanny S. Stone—Racine, Belle City of the Lakes)*

Dictionary compiled by a woman was *The Language of Fashion,* edited by Mary Brooks Picken, published February 2, 1940, in New York City. It contained 8,000 terms and 600 illustrations relating to wearing apparel.

Dictionary published in the United States was *The Royal Standard English Dictionary; the First American Dictionary, Carefully Revised and Corrected, from the Fourth British Edition,* by William Perry, lecturer in the Academy at Edinburgh, which was printed in 1788 in Worcester, Mass., by and for Isaiah Thomas. It sold for 7 shillings and contained 596 pages, of which pages 73-359 contained the dictionary proper and an appendix of "Scripture Proper Names." There were 38 lines to a page, double column, and the definitions usually consisted of only one line, the same line as the word itself. The dictionary was dedicated to the American Academy of Arts and Sciences. *(The Worcester Magazine. February 1788)*

Hebrew dictionary was Clement Clarke Moore's *A Compendious Lexicon of the Hebrew Language in Two Volumes; Volume 1,* containing an explanation of every word which occurs in the Psalms with notes; Volume 2, being a lexicon and grammar of the whole language, printed and sold in 1809 by [Isaac] Collins and Perkins, New York City.

Indian-English dictionary was *A Key into the Language of America, or an help to the language of the natives in that part of America called New England; together with briefe observations of the customes, manners and worships, etc., of the aforesaid natives,* by "Roger Williams of Providence in New England." Williams prepared it on shipboard en route to Southampton, England, and it was published by Gregory Dexter, London, England, in 1643. *(James Ernst—Roger Williams)*

Law dictionary. *See* Law dictionary (American)

Military dictionary was *A Military Dictionary, or explanation of the several systems of Discipline of different kinds of troops, infantry, artillery and cavalry, the principles of fortification and all the modern improvements in the science of tactics . . .,* by William Duane, a retired lieutenant colonel, published in 1810 in Philadelphia, Pa. It contained 748 pages.

Mongolian-English English-Mongolian dictionary was *Mongolian Vocabulary (Modern Khalkha Language),* compiled by Dorothy A. Troxel of the Army Map Service and published in January 1953 as Army Technical Manual TM 30-537.

Phonetic dictionary was the *Phonetic Dictionary of the English Language adapted to the present state of literature and science, with pronouncing vocabularies of classical, scriptural and geographical names,* 776 pages, compiled by Daniel S. Smalley and published by Longley Brothers, phonetic publishers, Cincinnati, Ohio, in 1855.

Pocket dictionary was William Perry's *The Royal Standard English Dictionary, in which the words are . . . rationally divided into syllables, accurately accented, their parts of speech properly distinguished . . .,* 12mo, 596 pages, printed in 1788 by Isaiah Thomas, Worcester, Mass. It was dedicated to the American Academy of Arts and Sciences, and was based upon a British edition.

Rhyming dictionary was *A Rhyming Dictionary, containing all the perfect rhymes of a different orthography, and allowable rhymes of a different sound, throughout the language, with authorities for the usage of them from our best poets,* published in 1823 by F. & R. Lockwood, New York City. It was an American edition of John Walker's *A Dictionary*

THE FIRST

THE FIRST

DICTIONARY—*Continued*
of the English language answering at once the purposes of rhyming, spelling and pronouncing on a plan not hitherto attempted, first published in London, England, in 1775.

DIDACTICS COURSE
  Didactics course in a college was offered in 1853 as an elective to the sophomore course at Antioch College, Yellow Springs, Ohio. The college was opened October 5, 1853. Professor Rebecca Mann Pennell, in charge of the course, was elected to a professorship September 15, 1852.

DIES FOR COINS. *See* Money: Dies for coins

DIESEL ELECTRIC FREIGHT LOCO-MOTIVE. *See* Locomotive: Diesel electric freight locomotive; Locomotive: Diesel electric locomotive

DIESEL ELECTRIC TOWBOAT. *See* Ship: Tugboat (diesel electric)

DIESEL ENGINE
  See also under Engine; Locomotive

  Diesel engine automobile trip was made by Clessie Lyle Cummins of the Cummins Engine Company, Columbus, Ind., with a stock model engine weighing 1,200 pounds, delivering 50 h.p. at 1,000 r.p.m. with four cylinders of 4½ by 6 inch bore, installed in a seven-passenger Packard sedan. He left Indianapolis, Ind., January 3, 1930, and arrived in New York City January 6, 1930, covering 792 miles at a total fuel cost of $1.38.

  Diesel engine speed record (official) was made March 20, 1930, by Clessie Lyle Cummins of the Cummins Engine Company, Columbus, Ind., in a Packard roadster chassis equipped with a four-cylinder marine-type diesel engine with a bore and stroke of 4½ by 6 inches and piston displacement of 381.5 cubic inches. The car was stripped of fenders, windshield, and spare tires and fitted with a fabric cover over the driver's compartment. Cummins averaged 80.398 miles per hour in the test at Daytona Beach, Fla.

  Streamlined all-steel diesel motor train. *See* Railroad: Streamlined all-steel diesel motor train

DIESEL ENGINE TRACTOR. *See* Automobile tractor: Diesel engine tractor

DIME. *See* Money: Silver coins

DINER. *See* Lunch wagon

DINING CAR. *See* Railroad car: Dining car

DIOCESE (Catholic). *See* Catholic diocese

DIPLOMATIC SERVICE
  Ambassador, according to the records of the Department of State, was Thomas Francis Bayard, who was appointed ambassador extraordinary and plenipotentiary to Great Britain on March 30, 1893. His letter of credence was dated April 14, 1893, and he arrived at his post on June 10, 1893 and presented his credentials on June 22, 1893. He left his post on March 17, 1897, and his letter of recall dated March 31, 1897, was presented by his successor on April 22, 1897. (*Charles Callan Tansill*—*The Foreign Policy of Thomas F. Bayard*)

  Ambassador to Canada was Ray Atherton, who was nominated as Ambassador Extraordinary and Plenipotentiary on November 18, 1943. He held this office until his resignation and mandatory retirement on August 31, 1948. Previously, on July 7, 1943, he had been confirmed as Envoy Extraordinary and Minister Plenipotentiary of the United States to Canada and to Denmark.

  Ambassador to England was John Adams, who on June 1, 1785, was introduced by the Marquis of Carmarthen to the King of England as ambassador extraordinary from the United States of America to the Court of London. The first minister plenipotentiary to England was Thomas Pinckney of South Carolina, who was appointed on January 12, 1792. Adams, however, is not listed as an ambassador by the State Department, which reckons 1893 as the year of the first appointment of the first ambassador. (*Samuel Willard*—*John Adams, A Character Sketch*)

  Ambassador to Nepal was Henry Endicott Stebbins of Milton, Mass., appointed August 29, 1959. The nomination was approved September 9, 1959. Previously the United States Ambassador to India had served as envoy to Nepal.

  Ambassador to the Union of Soviet Socialist Republics was William Christian Bullitt, who served from November 21, 1933, until August 25, 1936. The first Soviet representative to the United States was Alexander Antonovich Troyanovsky, who was accredited as Russian ambassador from January 8, 1934, to June

THE FIRST

22, 1938. Recognition of the U.S.S.R. was effected November 16, 1933, between President Franklin Delano Roosevelt and Maksim Maksimovich Litvinov, the People's Commissar for Foreign Affairs.

Ambassador (woman) was Eugenie Anderson of Red Wing, Minn., who was nominated October 12, 1949, and sworn in October 28, 1949, as ambassador to Denmark.

American legation in which a woman assumed charge was the American Legation at Stockholm, Sweden. Frances Elizabeth Willis, Third Secretary of the American Legation at Stockholm, assumed charge while Minister John Motley Morehead was on furlough. She became ex-officio American Chargé d'Affaires ad interim October 12, 1932, until October 29, 1932. Edwin S. Crocker, 2d, Second Secretary of the Legation, who had also been absent from Stockholm, returned on October 29, 1932, and succeeded Miss Willis as Chargé d'Affaires ad interim.

Chief executive-elect of a foreign country to serve in a diplomatic position in Washington, D.C., was Dr. Enrique Olaya Hererra, who arrived April 20, 1930. He was sworn in August 7, 1930, as President of Colombia. Previously, he had served as Colombian Ambassador to the United States.

Consul general was appointed by authority of the act of August 18, 1856 (11 Stat.L.57), which passed the House on August 15 and the Senate on August 16. The act went into effect August 18, 1856.

Consul to California was Thomas Oliver Larkin, who was appointed consul to Monterey, Calif., on May 1, 1843, and special agent on October 17, 1845. His resignation from the position of consul was dated August 17, 1846. His successor as special agent was appointed on August 2, 1849. *(Reuben Lukens Underhill —From Cowhides to Golden Fleece)*

Consul to die in service was Colonel William Palfrey, Paymaster General of the Continental Armies, who was elected consul to Paris, France, on November 4, 1780, by the Continental Congress at a salary of $1,500 a year. He received his commission November 9, 1780. He sailed for his post in France on the "Shillala," an armed ship of sixteen guns, which stopped en route at the port of Wilmington, Del., on December 23, 1780, and was lost at sea after it passed the Delaware capes. *(Jared Sparks—The Library of American Biography, Vol. 7—2nd Series)*

Consul under the Department of State was Major Samuel Shaw of Massachusetts. Having been appointed Consul to Canton,

THE FIRST

China, on January 1, 1786, prior to the ratification of the Constitution, he was nominated on February 9, 1790, and confirmed the following day as consul of the United States of America at Canton, China. *(Tracy Hollingsworth Lay—The Foreign Service of the U.S.)*

Consular officer detailed for duty in the Department of Foreign Affairs of the Continental government was Thomas Barclay of Pennsylvania, who was appointed vice consul to Paris, France, on January 21, 1781, at a salary of $1,000 a year. Upon the formation of the United States Government, President George Washington appointed him consul to Morocco on March 31, 1791. *(American Foreign Service Journal—April 1929)*

Consuls of the United States appointed after the adoption of the Constitution were Joseph Fenwick of Maryland; Nathaniel Barrett, Sylvanus Bourne, Burrell Carnes, and William Knox of Massachusetts; John Marsden Pintard of New York; and James Maury and Fulwar Skipwith of Virginia, all of whom were appointed June 7, 1790.

Foreign service committee was formed November 29, 1775, when the Continental Congress voted "that a committee of five be appointed for the sole purpose of corresponding with our friends in Great Britain, Ireland and other parts of the world." The members of this secret Committee of Correspondence were William Samuel Johnson of Connecticut, John Jay of New York, John Dickinson of Pennsylvania, Benjamin Harrison of Virginia and Benjamin Franklin of Pennsylvania, who was the chairman. *(Secret Journals of the Acts and Proceedings of Congress—Vol. 2)*

Foreign Service of the United States was created on July 1, 1924, by the Rogers bill (43 Stat.L.140), approved May 24, 1924, when the diplomatic and consular services were merged under the Department of State.

Jewish ambassador was Oscar Solomon Straus, who was appointed Envoy Extraordinary and Minister Plenipotentiary to Turkey on March 24, 1887. He presented his letter of recall, June 16, 1889. He was reappointed June 3, 1898. He left on leave of absence December 20, 1899, and his letter of recall was presented by his successor March 29, 1901. On May 17, 1909, he was again appointed Ambassador Extraordinary and Plenipotentiary to Turkey and in September 1910 he left the post. His successor presented his letter of recall on August 28, 1911. *(William Willard Howards— Oscar S. Straus in Turkey)*

Jewish diplomatic representative was Manuel Mordecai Noah, who represented the United

THE FIRST

THE FIRST

DIPLOMATIC SERVICE—*Continued*
States as Consul to Tunis from 1813 to 1816.
He was a consul with diplomatic powers.
(Isaac Goldberg—Major Noah, American-Jewish Pioneer)

Korean embassy was received by President
Chester Alan Arthur on September 18, 1883,
at the Fifth Avenue Hotel, 23rd Street, New
York City. Min Yong Ik, the ambassador,
presented his credentials. He was accompanied
by Hong Yong Sik, the vice-ambassador, and
by his secretary, the foreign secretary, and
five attachés. The Koreans were dressed in
court robes and dropped upon their knees as
they salaamed President Arthur and Secretary
of State Frederick Theodore Frelinghuysen.

Minister plenipotentiary was Benjamin
Franklin, who was elected by the Continental
Congress on September 14, 1778, to the court
of France. The Department of State accredits
Thomas Jefferson of Virginia, who was ap-
pointed on March 10, 1785, as the first minister
plenipotentiary after the Revolutionary War.
He sailed July 5, 1785, on the "Ceres" and
served until October 1789. He left Yarmouth,
England, October 22, 1789, and arrived at
Norfolk, Va., November 23, 1789. *(Journals
of the Continental Congress—Vol. 12)*

**Ministers plenipotentiary to South and
Central America** were appointed on January
27, 1823, by President James Monroe. His
appointments were Caesar Augustus Rodney of
Delaware to Argentina, Herman Allen of
Vermont to Chile, and Richard Clough Ander-
son of Kentucky to Colombia. *(Records in
Department of State, Washington, D.C.)*

Naval attaché. *See* Naval officer: Naval
attaché

Negro consul was Ebenezer Don Carlos
Bassett, who was made Consul General to
Haiti, where he served from April 16, 1869, to
November 27, 1877.

**Negro delegate to the United Nations
from the United States** was Edith Spurlock
Sampson, who was appointed August 24, 1950,
alternate delegate to the fifth General Assembly. Her first assignment, on September 28,
1950, was to the Social, Humanitarian and Cultural Committee.

Pan American delegates (American) were
Caesar Augustus Rodney, Theodore Bland and
John Graham, who were appointed in July 1817
by President James Monroe "to obtain information of the actual condition and political pros-
pects of the Spanish provinces which were con-
tending for independence." They served at
Buenos Aires, Argentina, from February 1818
until April 30, 1818. *(House Document 2,
Fifteenth Congress—2nd Session)*

**Representative of a foreign country to the
United States** was Conrad Alexandre Gérard
of France, who arrived in July 1778. He was
styled Minister Plenipotentiary and also bore a
commission as Consul General. *(Maryland
Historical Magazine—1920—Vol. 15)*

**Woman ambassador from a foreign coun-
try** was Her Excellency Shrimati Vijaya
Lakshmi Pandit, ambassador of India, who
presented her letter of credence to President
Harry S. Truman on May 12, 1949.

**Woman career diplomat advanced to the
rank of ambassador** was Frances Elizabeth
Willis, who after 25 years in the foreign service
was sworn in as ambassador to Switzerland on
August 10, 1953, at a ceremony in the State
Department, Washington, D.C.

**Woman diplomat to represent the United
States in the capacity of a minister** was Ruth
Bryan Owen, who was appointed by President
Franklin Delano Roosevelt on April 12, 1933, as
Envoy Extraordinary and Minister Plenipoten-
tiary to Denmark and Iceland. Her nomination
was confirmed by the Senate on April 12, 1933,
without even the customary formality of refer-
ence to a committee. Ruth Bryan Owen (Mrs.
Börge Rohde) was the eldest daughter of
William Jennings Bryan. *(Ruth Bryan Owen—
Leaves from a Greenland Diary)*

Woman legation secretary was Lucille
Atcherson of Columbus, Ohio. She was appointed on December 4, 1922, and was recommissioned as Foreign Service Officer of Class 8
on July 1, 1924, serving thereafter as Secretary
of Legation at Berne, Switzerland, and at
Panama, R.P. On May 24, 1924, the diplomatic
and consular services were amalgamated into
the American Foreign Service.

Woman vice consul in the American Foreign Service was Pattie Hockaday Field of
Denver, Colo. She was appointed Foreign
Service Officer unclassified on March 20, 1925,
and as American Vice Consul. She was assigned to Amsterdam, Holland, September 2,
1925. She resigned June 27, 1929.

DIRECT-LIFT AIRCRAFT. *See* Helicopter: Helicopter (direct-lift aircraft)

DIRECTORY (city) was *Macpherson's Directory for the City and Suburbs of Philadelphia Extending to Prime Street, Southward;
and Maiden Street, Northward; and From the
River Delaware to Tenth Street Westward,*
published October 1, 1785, by John Macpherson.
It was printed by Francis Bailey at Loick's
Head, 65 Market Street, Philadelphia, Pa., and
contained 6,250 names, of which 686 were subscribers. William Bradford of Philadelphia also

published a directory of that city the same year. It contained 83 pages, 43 names to the page, making a total of 3,569 names. *(American Collector. August 1926)*

See also Congressional directory; Postal directory; Telephone directory

DIRIGIBLE. *See* Aviation—Airship: Dirigible

DIRIGIBLE BALLOON RACE. *See* Balloon race: Dirigible balloon race

DIRIGIBLE PASSENGER TRANSFER TO AN AIRPLANE. *See* Aviation—Passenger: Dirigible passenger transfer to an airplane

DISBARRED LAWYER. *See* Lawyer: Lawyer disbarred

DISCIPLES OF CHRIST church was organized August 17, 1809, in Washington, Pa., when a group of Presbyterians headed by Thomas Campbell formed themselves into a religious association, the Christian Association of Washington. On May 4, 1811, a church was established in Brush Run, Pa., with Thomas Campbell as elder. Alexander Campbell, his son, was licensed to preach the gospel. John Dawson, George Sharp, John Foster, and William Gilchrist were chosen as deacons. No attempt at forming a separate and distinct denomination was made until 1823, when Alexander Campbell and several members of the Brush Run Church founded a church in Wellsburg, W.Va. The first convention of the Disciples of Christ was held August 1827, when the Mahoning Association met at New Lisbon, Ohio, and appointed Walter Scott as the general evangelist to go into Ohio to preach and establish churches. The first general convention was held in Cincinnati, Ohio, October 24, 1849, at which time the American Christian Missionary Society was organized *(Walter Wilson Jennings—Origin and Early History of the Disciples of Christ)*

DISCOVERY
American to land by air at the South Pole and the first American to set foot and plant a flag at the South Pole was Rear Admiral George John Dufek who, with a party of six as part of Operation Deepfreeze commanded by Admiral Richard Evelyn Byrd and undertaken in connection with the International Geophysical Year 1957-1958, landed October 31, 1956, in the "Que Será Será," a Navy R4D transport plane. Dufek was in charge of logistic support for the scientific body of the expedition.

Discovery of Antarctica was made November 18, 1820, by Captain Nathaniel Brown Palmer in the "Hero," a sloop of 44 tons, with a crew of six men including the captain and the

mate. He sailed from Stonington, Conn., July 25, 1820, and returned May 8, 1821. His discovery was made at a point near latitude 64° S and longitude 60° W. *(John Randolph Spears—Captain Nathaniel Brown Palmer. An Old Time Sailor of the Sea)*

Discovery of land on the United States Pacific Coast by actual contact with it was made by Juan Rodríguez Cabrillo, who landed September 28, 1542, at what is now known as Ballast Point, San Diego, Calif. He left Navidad, Mexico, on June 27, 1542. The Pacific Ocean had been discovered by Europeans previously, however—Balboa and Magellan, among others. *(George Montague Wheeler—Report upon U.S. Geographical Surveys West of the 100th Meridian)*

Discovery of New England by an Englishman was made by Captain Bartholomew Gosnold, who with his crew of 31 landed at South Dartmouth, near New Bedford, Mass., on May 15, 1602. Gosnold township, Mass., comprising the Elizabeth Islands, was named in his honor. Gosnold left Falmouth, England, on March 26, 1602 in the "Concord" and landed on the southern Maine coast, near Cape Porpoise. *(Massachusetts Historical Society—Collections. Vol. VIII. 1843)*

Discovery of the Mississippi River by a European was made by Hernando de Soto, who in May 1541 with his crew of adventurous Spaniards, arrived at a village called Chisca, where they erected a huge cross. Shortly afterwards De Soto died and was buried in the "Father of Waters," the first European to be buried in the Mississippi. In 1519 Alonso Alvarez de Pineda, who was sent out by Francisco de Garay, governor of Jamaica, entered the mouth of the river, which he called the Rio de Espíritu Santo. *(John Dawson Gilmary Shea—Discovery and Exploration of the Mississippi Valley)*

Discovery of the North Pole was made on April 6, 1909, by Robert Edwin Peary, accompanied by Matthew Alexander Henson, a Negro assistant, and four Eskimos, who reached 90° N.

Northwest passage, between the Atlantic and the Pacific Oceans, was charted in the period from June to September 1957 by three United States Coast Guard cutters ("Bramble," "Spar," and "Storis") led by the "Labrador," a Canadian ice patrol ship, through Beloit Strait between Boothia Peninsula and Somerset Island. The commanding officer was Commander Harold L. Wood.

DISCRIMINATION LAW. *See* Army exclusion law

THE FIRST

DISCRIMINATION LAW (labor). *See* Labor law: Labor discrimination law (state)

DISCRIMINATORY LAW (alien). *See* Alien discriminatory law

DISCUS THROWING as a competitive event was revived in 1896 at the Olympic Games in Athens, Greece. Robert Garrett of Princeton University, representing the United States, won with a record throw of 95 feet 7½ inches. *(The Olympic Games 776 B.C.—1896 A.D.—Official Report)*

DISEASE (distinctly American) was tularemia, an epizootic of wild rabbits and other animals, which was recognized in 1910 in ground squirrels of Tulare County, Calif., by Dr. George Walter McCoy. He and Dr. Charles Willard Chapin named the organism *Bacterium tularense*. Dr. Edward Francis of the U.S. Public Health Service was awarded a gold medal by the American Medical Association for his research in this disease. *(Journal of American Medical Association. April 25, 1925)*

DISHES. *See* Chinaware: Dishes (complete set) made in America for the Executive Mansion

DISPENSARY. *See* Hospital: Dispensary

DISPENSARY (dental). *See* Dental dispensary: Dental dispensary

DISPENSATORY. *See* Medical book: Dispensatory

DISSECTION ESSAY. *See* Medical book: Dissection essay

DISTILLING BOOK was Michael August Krafft's *American Distiller, or The Theory and Practice of Distilling, according to the latest discoveries and improvements, including its most important methods of constructing stills and of rectification*, dedicated to Thomas Jefferson. It contained 219 pages and 6 plates and was printed in 1804 by Thomas Dobson, Philadelphia, Pa. The preface was dated May 25, 1804, Bristol, Pa.

DISTINGUISHED FLYING CROSS. *See* Medal: Distinguished flying cross

DISTINGUISHED SERVICE CROSS. *See* Medal: Distinguished service cross

DISTINGUISHED SERVICE MEDAL. *See* Medal: Distinguished service medal

THE FIRST

DISTINGUISHED SERVICE MEDAL (Navy). *See* Medal: Distinguished service medal (Navy)

DISTRESS SIGNAL. *See* Radio distress signal: Radio distress signal

DISTRICT ATTORNEY (woman). *See* Woman: Woman district attorney of the U.S.

DISTRICT LAND OFFICE. *See* Land grant: District land office

DISTRICT NURSE. *See* Nurse: District nurse

DIVING SUIT (practical) for submarine diving was invented by Leonard Norcross of Dixfield, Me., who obtained a United States patent on June 14, 1834, on a "water-dress." It consisted of an airtight rubber dress to which was attached a brass cap or helmet resting on the shoulders. The cap was connected to an air pump on the boat by means of a rubber hose. The feet were weighted with heavy lead shot. *(Niles Register. September 27, 1834)*

DIVINITY DEGREE. *See* Degrees (academic and honorary): Doctor of sacred theology degree

DIVINITY PROFESSOR was Edward Wigglesworth, appointed January 24, 1722, to the Thomas Hollis Professorship of Divinity at Harvard College, Cambridge, Mass. He served until his death, January 16, 1765.

DIVINITY SCHOOL. *See* Theological school: Theological school

DOCK
State-owned docks were acquired by California by act approved April 24, 1863, chapter 306, "an act to provide for the improvement and protection of the wharves, docks and water front in the city and county of San Francisco." Three commissioners, one elected by the state, one elected by San Francisco, and one appointed by the Senate and Assembly at a joint session, formed the Board of State Harbor Commissioners "to construct new wharves, to keep in good repair sea-walls, embankments, wharves, piers, landings and thoroughfares for the advancement of commerce." The first meeting of the board was held November 4, 1863, in San Francisco. Robert E. C. Stearns was the first secretary.

DOCTOR (Navy). *See* Naval officer: Naval doctor

DOCTOR OF MEDICINE. *See* Physician

THE FIRST

DOCTOR'S DEGREE. *See* Degrees (academic and honorary)

DOCUMENT (printed). *See* Printing: Document printed in America

DOCUMENTS CATALOG. *See* Index of government publications

DOG LICENSE
Dog license law (state) was "an act for the better protection of lost and strayed animals and for securing the rights of the owners thereof," passed March 8, 1894, by New York State, Chapter 115. It authorized the American Society for the Prevention of Cruelty to Animals to carry out the provisions of the law and collect a $2 annual fee for dogs in cities with populations over 1,200,000. Unlicensed dogs were to be destroyed if not redeemed within forty-eight hours. Nonresidents and exhibitors were not required to obtain licenses for their dogs.

DOG RACE. *See* Greyhound racing association

DOG RACE TRACK on which an imitation rabbit was used was erected by Owen P. Smith at Emeryville, Calif., and opened February 22, 1920. It was about 300 yards around and was designed by R. S. Hawley. A car was run through a housing which covered the trolley and track; the car had a slot on the track side through which the arm carrying the rabbit extended.

DOG SHOW of importance was held at the Hippodrome (Gilmore's Garden), 26th Street and Madison Avenue, New York City, May 8, 1877, under the auspices of the Westminster Kennel Bench Show of Dogs. Charles Lincoln was superintendent of this show at which there were 1,191 entries. Dog shows were often held as features at fairs and circuses. A successful dog show was held May 12, 1862, at Barnum's American Museum, New York City.

DOG SLED MAIL. *See* Postal service: International dog sled mail

DOG SLED RACE
Dog sled race on an Olympic demonstration program was held February 6-7, 1932, when the United States and Canada entered 13 teams. Contestants were required to cover the course of 25.1 miles on two consecutive days. First place was won by Emile St. Goddard of Canada, but the United States teams won 7 of the 12 points. The race was held at Lake Placid, N.Y.

DOGS TRAINED TO GUIDE THE BLIND. *See* Animals: Dogs trained to guide the blind

THE FIRST

DOLLAR. *See* Money: Fifty-dollar gold pieces

DOLLAR MARKS to be made in type were cast in 1797 by [Archibald] Binny & [James] Ronaldson, type-founders of Philadelphia, who started in business on November 1, 1796. *(Daniel Berkeley Updike—Printing Types)*

DOMESTIC AIR MAIL CONTRACTOR. *See* Air mail service: Air mail contractor (domestic)

DOMESTIC RELATIONS COURT. *See* Court: Domestic relations court

DOOR (revolving) was invented by Theophilus Van Kannel of Philadelphia, Pa., who obtained patent No. 387,571 on August 7, 1888, on a "storm door structure."

DOUBLE-DECK BRIDGE. *See* Bridge: Double-deck bridge

DOUBLE-DECK BUS. *See* Automobile bus: Bus with a double deck

DOUBLE-DECK CAR. *See* Railroad car: Double-deck railroad coaches

DOUBLE-DECK ELEVATOR. *See* Elevator: Double-deck elevator

DOUBLE-DECK STEAMBOAT. *See* Ship: Steamboat (double decked)

DOUBLE EAGLE COINAGE. *See* Money: Double eagle coinage

DOUGHNUT CUTTER was invented by John F. Blondel of Thomaston, Me., who obtained patent No. 128,783 on July 9, 1872. A spring pushed the dough out of a center tube to provide the hole.

DRAFT LEGISLATION. *See* Conscription

DRAGOON REGIMENT. *See* Army: Cavalry unit

DRAMA. *See* Play (drama); Theater

DRAMA (FULL-LENGTH MELODRAMA) BROADCAST. *See* Radio broadcast: Drama (full-length melodrama) broadcast

DRAMA TELECAST FOR A FULL HOUR. *See* Television—Telecast: Play to be televised as a full-hour program

THE FIRST

DRAMA TO WIN A PULITZER PRIZE.
See Play (drama): Drama to win a Pulitzer prize

DRAMATIC CRITICISM COURSE. *See*
Theatrical school: Theater and dramatic criticism course

DRAWBACK LEGISLATION was Sections 3 and 4 of the Tariff Act of July 4, 1789 (1 Stat.L.26), which became effective August 1, 1789. Dutiable merchandise imported into the United States which was reexported within a year was entitled to a refund of 99 per cent of the duty paid. In lieu of a drawback of the duties imposed on the importation of salt employed and expended in the fish industry, an allowance of five cents was granted on the exportation of every quintal of dried fish, and on every barrel of pickled fish or salted provision. From August 1, 1789, to December 31, 1790, drawback to the amount of $10,582 was allowed on dried and pickled fish.

DREDGE. *See* Ship: Dredge (seagoing hopper)

DRIED BLOOD SERUM. *See* Blood bank: Blood serum (human) (dried)

DRIED MILK. *See* Milk: Dried milk patent

DRILL
Dental drill was invented in 1790 by John Greenwood of New York City. It was adapted from the spinning wheel, power being obtained by means of a foot treadle. *(Dental Items of Interest. November 1943)*

Dental drill (electric) was invented by George F. Green of Kalamazoo, Mich., who obtained patent No. 159,028 on January 26, 1875, on "electro-magnetic dental tools" used for sawing, filing, dressing, and polishing teeth. He claimed the application to dental instruments of an electro-magnetic motor. The patent was assigned to Samuel S. White of Philadelphia, Pa. The engines were too heavy and the batteries too expensive for general use.

Oil drill seagoing rig (for drilling in over 100 feet of water) was built in the Beaumont Yard of Bethlehem Steel Company for the C. G. Glasscock Drilling Company. The rig can drive piles with a force of 827 tons and can pull a pile with the force of 942 tons. It was placed in service March 24, 1955.

Percussion rock drill was patented March 27, 1849, by Joseph James Couch, who received patent No. 6,237 on "improved machinery for drilling rocks." The drill was driven by steam power and acted independently of gravity. The

THE FIRST

machine was stationary and the drill was thrown against the rock, the tool being seized at the end of the blow by means of friction-grips.

DRILL MANUAL. *See* Military drill manual

DRINKING STRAW. *See* Straws (artificial) for drinking

DRIVE-IN BANK. *See* Bank: "Autobank" complete service

DRIVE-IN SERVICE STATION. *See* Automobile service station: Drive-in service station

DRIVE-IN THEATER. *See* Moving picture theater: Drive-in moving picture theater

DRIVE-UP MAIL BOX. *See* Postal service: Mail box (drive-up)

DRIVING COURSE. *See* Automobile driving course

DROUGHT recorded occurred in New England in 1727. After the first week of April, with the exception of two showers in May, rain did not fall until June. *(Sidney Perley— Historic Storms of New England)*

DRUG LEGISLATION. *See* Pure food law: Pure food and drug legislation

DRUG MILL was established in 1812 in Philadelphia, Pa., by Charles V. Hagner who used water power for grinding, performing in one day work which previously would have required months of hand powdering in mortars. His first task of importance was the grinding of several tons of cream of tartar for which Dr. Haral, a druggist, paid him three cents a pound. *(Philadelphia College of Pharmacy and Science—The First Century of the Philadelphia College of Pharmacy)*

DRUGGIST to fill prescriptions other than his own was Jonathan Roberts, who served from May 1754 to May 19, 1755, as apothecary in the Pennsylvania Hospital, Philadelphia, Pa. Previously apothecaries had made up their own remedies only. *(Benjamin Franklin—Some Account of the Pennsylvania Hospital From Its First Beginning of the Fifth Month, called May, 1754)*

DRY GAS METER. *See* Gas: Gas meter (dry)

DRY ICE. *See* Ice: Dry ice

THE FIRST

DRY LAUNDRY SERVICE. *See* Laundry service: Rough dry laundry service

DRYDOCK
Drydock was constructed by Robert Fulton in 1805 in front of his foundry on the corner of Green and Morgan Streets, in Jersey City, N.J. He managed it until his death, February 24, 1815. A block of ground was sold to him by the Associates of the Jersey Company for $1,000, allowing him five years on the purchase money without interest. The deed was dated November 3, 1804. A drydock had been authorized by Charlestown, Mass., October 30, 1677, to be constructed by James Russell, John Heyman, Samuel Ballard, and John Phillips. On May 30, 1679, it was voted that the drydock be rate free for thirty years and that no other drydock be authorized for the same period provided it was kept in "good repair." The Charlestown dock, however, was never built. (*Records of the Governor and Company of the Massachusetts Bay. Vol. 5. May 30, 1679.*)

Drydock authorized for the United States Government was approved February 25, 1799 by an act (1 Stat.L. 622) which provided that "two docks, for the convenience of repairing the public ships and vessels, be erected in suitable places, under direction of the President of the United States, and that the sum of $50,000 be appropriated towards effecting this object, to be paid out of the monies in the Treasury of the United States, not otherwise appropriated." On December 15, 1802, an appropriation of $100,000 was made, but drydocks were not constructed as the amount was insufficient.

Federal drydocks were constructed at Boston, Mass., and Norfolk, Va., under authority of act of Congress of March 28, 1827 (4 Stat.L. 243). They were designed by Colonel Loammi Baldwin of Boston, Mass., who was hired by Secretary of the Navy Samuel Southard. The drydocks were founded upon piles and were built entirely of stone faced with cut granite. Construction of the Boston drydock was started June 1827, the cornerstone laid May 21, 1829, and the drydock turned over to the commandant September 9, 1833. It cost $677,089.98. The Norfolk drydock was begun November 1827 and completed March 15, 1834. It cost $943,676.73. (*American Society of Civil Engineers. Transactions. Vol. 41. June 1899*)

National ship in a federal drydock was the "Delaware," which docked June 17, 1833, at the Norfolk Dry Dock, Portsmouth, Va. The "Constitution" was received at the Boston Dry Dock, June 24, 1833. Both ships docked before the drydocks were completed. (*Charles Beebe Stuart—Naval Dry Docks of the United States*)

Timber drydock was erected at Buffalo, N.Y., in 1840 for Great Lakes ships. The ex-

THE FIRST

cavation was lined entirely with wood secured to poles driven in the bottom and upon the slopes of the sides, and faced with longitudinal timbers forming steps or altars upon the sides. The first timber drydock on the Atlantic coast was erected in 1854 at Boston, Mass., by J. E. Simpson and Co. The first construction cost for these drydocks was small, but they did not prove practical for long periods as they deteriorated rapidly. (*American Society of Civil Engineers Transactions. Vol 41. June 1899*)

DRYDOCK PATENT was issued on December 13, 1816, to John Adamson of Boston, Mass. A floating drydock was erected a few years later in Weehawken Cove, Hoboken, N.J., for the drydocking and repairing of canal boats. The patent was extended fourteen years by act of Congress, March 2, 1831 (6 Stat.L.458) (*Sven Anderson—Floating Drydocks*)

DUAL ELEVATOR. *See* Elevator: Dual elevator

DUAL SEWAGE SYSTEM. *See* Sewage: Sewage "dual system"

DUCK STAMP. *See* Revenue stamp

DUCTILE TUNGSTEN. *See* Tungsten: Ductile tungsten

DUDE RANCHING COURSE. *See* Recreational ranching course

DUEL
Duel of which there is any record took place on June 18, 1621, between two servingmen, Edward Leister and Edward Dotey, both servants of Stephen Hopkins, one of the leaders of the Plymouth Colony. Governor William Bradford's decision was rendered as follows: "The Second Offense is the first Duel fought in New England, upon a Challenge at Single Combat with Sword and Dagger between Edward Dotey and Edward Leister, Servants of Mr. Hopkins; Both being wounded, the one in the Hand, the other in the Thigh; they are adjudg'd by the whole Company to have their Head and Feet tied together, and so to lie for 24 hours, without Meat or Drink; which is begun to be inflicted, but within an Hour, because of their great Pains, at their own and their Master's humble request, upon Promise of better Carriage, they are Released by the Governor."

Duel between congressmen was held on the famous Bladensburg, Md., dueling field in 1808, when George Washington Campbell of Tennessee shot Barent Gardenier of New York through the body. Gardenier had accused Congress of being under the influence of France, which Campbell denied, at the same time assail-

DUEL—*Continued*
ing Gardenier with a torrent of personal abuse.
Gardenier challenged him to a duel, was
wounded, and after his recovery returned to
his attacks with more animosity than before.
(Campbell served in Congress from October
17, 1803, to March 3, 1809; Gardenier served
from March 4, 1807, to March 3, 1811.)
(Edward L. Merritt—Barent Gardenier)

**Duel in which a future President of the
United States participated** took place on May
30, 1806, at Harrison's Mills on the Red River,
Logan County, Ky. Andrew Jackson shot and
killed Charles Dickinson in a duel, one of a
hundred duels and brawls in which Jackson is
said to have participated. They stood twenty-
four feet apart, pistols downward. Dickinson
fired first and the shot broke a couple of Jackson's ribs and grazed his breastbone. Despite
the injury, Jackson fired and killed Dickinson.
Jackson served as President of the United
States from March 4, 1829, to March 3, 1837.

DUELING LEGISLATION (state) was
an "act to prevent the evil practice of duelling"
passed by the Fourth General Assembly held
at Knoxville, Tenn., and signed November 10,
1801, by Governor Archibald Roane. *(Chapter
32—Act of Tennessee—1801)*

DUGONG. *See* Aquatic mammals: Dugong

DUMMY (football). *See* Football dummy

DUMMY AWARDED A DEGREE. *See*
Degrees (academic and honorary): Degree
awarded a ventriloquist's dummy

DUNKARD. *See* Baptist church: German
Baptists

DUPLEX COMPOUND LOCOMOTIVE.
See Locomotive: Duplex compound locomotive (Mallet)

DUPLEX TELEGRAPH. *See* Telegraph:
Duplex telegraph (practical)

**DUPLICATE   AUCTION   BRIDGE
CHAMPIONSHIP.** *See* Auction bridge
championship (duplicate)

DUTCH REFORMED CHURCH. *See* Reformed church (Dutch)

DWARF exhibited was a man, 53 years of
age, 22 inches high, who was shown at the
house of Widow Bignall, next door to King's
Head Tavern, a little above Mr. Hancock's
wharf in Boston, Mass. Admission was one
shilling. His appearance was advertised in the
Massachusetts *Spy*, August 22, 1771.

DYNAMITE was manufactured in San
Francisco, Calif., in 1866, in what is now
Golden Gate Park, at the approximate location
of "Portals of the Past," by Julius Bandmann,
using the Nobel patents, under the name of
Bandmann Neilson & Company. In 1867 the
Giant Powder Company grew out of this con-
cern. *(Arthur Pine Van Gelder and Hugo
Schlatter—History of the Explosives Industry
in America)*

DYNAMO
Dynamo that was successful was "Jumbo
No. 1," a direct-current steam dynamo, which
was built in 1881 at the Edison Machine
Works, Goerck Street, New York City. It
weighed 27 tons, of which the armature
weighed 6 tons. Its capacity was 700 sixteen-
candlepower lamps when the armature was
air-cooled. *(Eric Hodgins and Frederick Alexander Magoun—Behemoth, the Story of
Power)*

**Dynamo for a direct-current outdoor light-
ing system** was built in 1875 at Cornell Uni-
versity, Ithaca, N.Y., by Professor William
Arnold Anthony and a graduate student,
George Sylvanus Moler. It was exhibited at the
Philadelphia Centennial in 1876 and was made
from designs of the original Gramme machine.
It was used to supply the current to light the
Cornell campus in 1875.

"E PLURIBUS UNUM." *See* Money: Coin
(state) to use "E Pluribus Unum"

EAGLE SCOUT. *See* Boy Scouts of America: Boy scout to become an eagle scout

EARMUFF was invented in 1873 by
Chester Greenwood of Farmington, Me., who
commenced manufacturing them commercially
the following year. He obtained patent No.
188,292, March 13, 1877, on his "ear mufflers."

EARTH SATELLITE. *See* Rocket: Satellite placed in orbit

EARTHQUAKE
Earthquake of consequence was felt on
August 31, 1886, throughout the eastern part
of the United States. In Charleston, S.C.,
41 lives were lost and property to the extent
of $5 million damaged. The epicenter was
15 miles northwest of Charleston. The loss of
lives in the entire area was about 100. In
Charleston, 90 per cent of 6,956 brick buildings
were damaged and about 95 per cent of 14,000
chimneys were broken off at the roof. *(Clarence Edward Dutton—Ninth Annual Report of
the United States Geological Survey)*

Earthquake description is contained in
Governor William Bradford's *History of the*

THE FIRST

Plymouth Plantation. The earthquake occurred Friday, June 1, 1638, at 2 P.M. at Plymouth, Mass., and is described in part as follows: "However, it was very terrible for ye time; and as ye men were set talking in ye house, some women and others were without ye doors, and ye earth shooke with ye violence as they could not stand without catching hold of ye posts and pails yt stood next them, but ye violence lasted not long. And about halfe an hower, or less, came an other noyse & shaking, but neither so loud nor strong as ye former, but quickly passed over, and so it ceased." In 1638 several Indians described to Roger Williams an earthquake which occurred in 1558 at Providence. No accurate record exists prior to this date, although it is evident that there must have been many earlier earthquakes. *(U.S. Coast and Geodetic Survey—Earthquake History of the United States.)*

EAST-WEST RAILROAD SERVICE. *See* Railroad: Railroad to run west, out of Chicago

EASTER EGG ROLL was held April 2, 1877, at the Capitol grounds, Washington, D.C., during President Rutherford Hayes' administration. The custom was carried on by later Presidents until discontinued by President Franklin Delano Roosevelt in 1942. It was reinstated on April 6, 1953, during the administration of President Dwight David Eisenhower.

ECLIPSE OF THE SUN MOTION PICTURE. *See* Moving picture: Moving picture of an eclipse of the sun

ECONOMIC COOPERATION ADMINISTRATION

Economic Cooperation Administration was authorized April 3, 1948 (62 Stat.L.137) "to promote world peace and the general welfare, national interest, and foreign policy of the United States through economic, financial and other measures necessary to the maintenance of conditions abroad in which free institutions may survive and consistent with the maintenance of the strength and stability of the United States." The first administrator was Paul Gray Hoffman, who was sworn in April 9, 1948, at $20,000 a year. On April 19, 1949, $1.15 billion was authorized for the April-June 1949 period and $4.28 billion for the fiscal year commencing July 1, 1949. The first European Recovery Program relief purchases totaled $21 million for Italy, France, Greece, Austria, and the Netherlands.

Industrial guaranty contract of investment of American capital in ERP (European Recovery Program) countries was made October 27, 1948, between Godfrey L. Cabot, Inc., Boston Mass., and the Export-Import Bank of Washington, D.C., as agent of the Economic Cooperation Administrator, under the guaranty

THE FIRST

provisions of the Foreign Assistance Act of 1948 (62 Stat.L.137). The amount of the guaranty was $850,000, later increased to $2,025,000. Cabot Carbon Limited erected a plant at Ellesmere Port, England, which on July 27, 1950, produced carbon black, used for the compounding of natural and synthetic rubber. A prior contract was canceled with another company which did not proceed with an investment in Italy.

ECONOMICS ASSOCIATION was the American Economic Association, founded September, 9, 1885, in Saratoga, N.Y. The purpose of the association was to encourage "economic research and freedom of economic discussion." The first president was Francis Amasa Walker. *(American Economic Association—Publication No. 1)*

ECONOMICS COURSE. *See* Business economics course

ECONOMICS MAGAZINE devoted exclusively to economics was the *Quarterly Journal of Economics,* published in Boston, Mass., for Harvard University. The first number appeared in October 1886.

EDITOR (newspaperwoman). *See* Woman: Woman newspaper editor

EDITORIAL APOLOGY (newspaper). *See* Newspaper: Newspaper editorial apology

EDUCATION

Chair in education permanently established was created by the University of Iowa, Iowa City, in 1873, and was called "Philosophy and Education." The Normal Department, established 1855, was absorbed by the Collegiate Department of Education in 1873. A temporary department of education had been created by New York University in New York City in 1832.

Compulsory education law was passed by Massachusetts June 14, 1642. It stated: "This Court, taking into consideration the great neglect of many parents and masters in training up their children in learning and labor and other impl(o)yments which may be profittable to the common wealth, so hereupon order and decree, that in every towne the chosen men appointed for managing the prudentiall affayers of the same shall henceforth stand charged with the care of the redresse of this evil . . . . and for this end . . . . they shall have power to take account from time to time of all parents and masters, and of their children, concerning their calling and impl(o)yment of their children." *(Records of the Governor and Company of Massachusetts Bay. Vol. 2)*

THE FIRST

THE FIRST

EDUCATION—*Continued*

Compulsory school attendance law (state) was Chapter 240, Acts of 1852 approved May 18, 1852, by Governor George Sewall Boutwell of Massachusetts. It prescribed that children must attend school "between the ages of eight and fourteen years" for twelve weeks in the year, six of which must be consecutive.

State board of education was established by Massachusetts on April 30, 1837 (Chapter 241, Section 1, Laws of Massachusetts, 1837). The first secretary of the board, later designated as commissioner, was Horace Mann. He was appointed June 29, 1837, and received $1,000 a year. *(Massachusetts Statutes. General Laws and Resolves Relating to Public Instruction)*

War Orphans Education Law was enacted June 29, 1956 (70 Stat.L.411), "to establish an educational assistance program for children of servicemen who died as a result of a disability or disease incurred in line of duty during World War One, World War Two, or the Korean conflict." It authorized the Veterans Administration to pay subsistence up to $110 a month not in excess of 36 months to a son or daughter between the ages of 18 and 23. The first recipient was George A. Turner, 19, of Brooklyn, N.Y., who enrolled at the University of Oklahoma, Norman, Okla. He was the son of William G. Turner, who died in 1954 at the age of 43 from a disability incurred during the Normandy invasion.

EDUCATION DEPARTMENT (U.S.)

Department of Education (U.S.) was created by act of March 2, 1867 (14 Stat.L.434), an "act to establish a Department of Education," an agency "for the purpose of collecting such statistics and facts as shall show the condition and progress of education in the several states and territories, and of diffusing such information respecting the organization and management of school systems and methods of teaching as shall aid the people of the United States in the establishment and maintenance of efficient school systems and otherwise promote the cause of education." The first commissioner of education was Henry Barnard, appointed March 14, 1867, by President Andrew Johnson. He served until March 17, 1870. The act of July 28, 1868 (15 Stat.L.106), effective June 30, 1869, abolished the Department of Education and established the Office of Education in the Department of the Interior. *(Darrell Hevenor Smith—Bureau of Education)*

Secretary of Health, Education and Welfare. *See* Cabinet of the United States: Secretary of Health, Education and Welfare

EDUCATIONAL ASSOCIATION

Educational association (local) was the Middlesex County Association for the Improvement of Common Schools, organized May 1799 in Middletown, Conn., by the Reverend William Woodbridge, who served as its first president. *(American Journal of Education. July 1856)*

Educational association (national) was the American Institute of Instruction, formed at a preliminary meeting March 15-19, 1830, and organized August 19-21, 1830, at a convention at Boston, Mass., attended by delegates from fifteen states. A constitution was adopted August 24, 1830, and the association was incorporated March 4, 1831. The first president was Francis Wayland, Jr., president of Brown University. *(The Introductory Discourse and Lectures Delivered in Boston Before the Convention of Teachers and Other Friends of Education)*

EDUCATIONAL BOOK was the Reverend Samuel Read Hall's *Lectures to Teachers on School Keeping*, which was published in 1829 in Boston, Mass., by Richardson, Lord and Holbrook. Ten thousand copies were purchased by the State of New York. *(David Brainard Hall—The Halls of New England)*

EDUCATIONAL ENDOWMENT in America was made by Benjamin Syms (or Symmes), "Founder of the first Free School in the American Colonies" in 1634. He donated "two hundred acres of land on Poquoson River with the milk and increase of eight cows for the maintenance of a learned and honest man to keep upon the said grounds a free school." The school became known as the Syms-Eaton Academy, located in Hampton, Va. In 1805 the name was changed to the Hampton Academy. *(James Luther Kibler—Historic Virginia Landmarks)*

EDUCATIONAL MAGAZINE

Educational magazine was the *Juvenile Mirror or Educational Magazine* published in New York City. It was edited by Albert Picket and John W. Picket. The first issue appeared August 1811. It lasted less than a year.

Educational magazine to achieve success was the *Academician*, a sixteen-page semimonthly published from February 7, 1818, to January 29, 1820, in New York City. It was edited by Albert Picket and John W. Picket, president and corresponding secretary, respectively, of the Incorporated Society of Teachers, which published the magazine. It offered advice and comments on teaching, and cost $3 a year.

EDUCATIONAL TRUST FUND established by a municipality was created by Burlington, N.J., in 1682. The Assembly provided that a valuable tract of land situated in the Delaware River above Burlington, and known as Matinicunk Island, "remain to and for the use of the town of Burlington . . . for the maintaining of a school for the education of youth. (*Francis Bazley Lee—New Jersey as a Colony and a State*)

EGG INCUBATOR PATENT. *See* Incubator (eggs) patent

EGG ROLL. *See* Easter egg roll

EGYPTIAN ANTIQUITIES COLLECTION was imported in 1835 by Colonel Mendes I. Cohen of Baltimore, Md. It was not publicly displayed until 1884, when it was bequeathed to Johns Hopkins University, Baltimore. (*New-York Historical Society Quarterly Bulletin. April 1920*)

EIGHT-DAY WATCH. *See* Clock: Watch (eight-day)

EIGHT-ENGINED AIRPLANE. *See* Aviation—Airplane: Airplane with eight engines

EIGHT-HOUR-DAY LAW. *See* Labor law: Eight-hour day

EINSTEINIUM. *See* Element: Element 99

ELASTIC WEBBING was produced by power machinery in the plant of the Russell Manufacturing Company of Middletown, Conn., in 1841, through the efforts of Henry Griswold Hubbard. The concern was incorporated in 1834 with a capital stock of $40,000, nine tenths of which was owned by Samuel Russell and Samuel D. Hubbard. Originally the company manufactured non-elastic webbing, a venture which was not profitable. The elastic webbing, however, proved very successful. (*Middletown, Conn.—Mercantile Publishing Company.*)

ELECTION
See also Election law; Suffrage; Voting machine

Accredited colonial election in America was held on May 18, 1631, when John Winthrop was elected Governor of Massachusetts. It is believed that in 1619 the Virginia Assembly was selected by means of votes.

Election contested in the House of Representatives. *See* Congress of the United States—House of Representatives: Contested election

Election contested in the Senate. *See* Congress of the United States—Senate: Contested election

Election day uniformly observed was authorized by act of January 23, 1845 (5 Stat.L.721), "an act to establish a uniform time for holding elections for electors of President and Vice President in all the states of the Union." "The Tuesday next after the first Monday in the month of November of the year in which they are to be appointed" was selected. The first election under the act was held November 7, 1848.

Election in defiance of the Royal Courts was held April 11, 1640, in Wethersfield, Conn. Matthew Mitchell was elected recorder. The King's Court at Hartford refused to recognize the election and penalized Wethersfield five pounds and the recorder forty nobles. The fines were not paid.

Federal election in the United States was authorized on Saturday, September 13, 1788, by the Constitutional Convention which "Resolved that the first Wednesday in January next (January 7, 1789) be the day for appointing electors in the several states, which, before the said day, shall have ratified the said Constitution, that the first Wednesday in February (February 4) next be the day for the electors to assemble in their respective states, and vote for a President; and that the first Wednesday in March next (March 4) be the time, and the present seat of Congress (New York City) the place for commencing the proceedings under the said Constitution."

Mayor elected by popular vote in a city was Cornelius Van Wyck Lawrence, a Democrat, who defeated Gulian Crommelin Verplanck, a Whig, in the three-day election held April 8-10, 1834, in New York City. There were 34,988 votes cast, of which 17,573 were for Lawrence, 17,393 for Verplanck, and 22 for others. Seven other municipal officers were also elected. Previously mayors had been chosen by a board of the Common Council.

Negro voter. *See* Election law: Negro to vote under authority of the Fifteenth Amendment

Presidential election. *See* Presidential election

Printed ballot was authorized by the "act to regulate the general elections within this commonwealth" enacted February 15, 1799, by Pennsylvania. Section ten provided that "every elector may deliver written or printed tickets." The ballots were prepared by political parties and were known as "vest pocket tickets." They contained only the names of the issuing party's candidates. (*Eldon Cobb Evans—History of the Australian Ballot System in the United States*)

Woman whose vote was recorded. *See* Woman: Woman whose vote was recorded

ELECTION LAW
Absentee voting law for military personnel. *See* Army vote

Absentee voting law (state) was enacted by Vermont on November 24, 1896. It provided that a person, by showing a certificate that he was qualified to vote in the state, could vote for state officers at any election booth in the state. *(Helen Mitchell Rocca—A Brief Digest of the Laws Relating to Absentee Voting and Registration)*

Australian ballot system was adopted by Kentucky in February 1888 and approved by Governor Simon Bolivar Buckner on February 24, 1888. It applied only to the city of Louisville. The first state to adopt the Australian ballot was Massachusetts, which enacted legislation May 30, 1888. Allen Thorndike Rice advocated this system of voting in 1886. *(Eldon Cobb Evans—History of the Australian Ballot System in the United States.)*

Corrupt election practices law (federal) was passed January 26, 1907 (34 Stat.L.864). It prohibited corporations from contributing toward campaign funds in national elections of President, Vice President, senators, and representatives. An act passed March 4, 1909 (35 Stat.L.1088), effective January 1, 1910, further prohibited national banks and corporations from making financial contributions to campaign funds in connection with any election to any political office.

Corrupt election practices law (state) was passed by New York State and signed by Governor Theodore Roosevelt on April 4, 1890, (Chapter 94, New York State Corrupt Practices Act of 1890), "an act to amend title five of the Penal Code Relating to Crimes Against the Elective Franchise." Candidates were required to file itemized expense accounts of campaign expenditures under penalty of imprisonment and loss of office. *(James Kern Pollock, Jr.—Party Campaign Funds)*

Fraudulent election law (colonial) was passed May 22, 1649, by the General Court in Warwick, R.I., and provided that "no one should bring in any votes that he did not receive from the voters' own hands, and that all votes should be filed by the Recorder in the presence of the Assembly." A committee of four freemen was authorized to determine violations of the law and "to examine parties and present to this court what they find in the case." *(Samuel Greene Arnold—History of the State of Rhode Island and Providence Plantations)*

Fraudulent election law (state) was passed by the legislature of California and signed by Governor Frederick Low on March 26, 1866. It was an "act to protect the elections of vol-

untary political associations, and to punish frauds therein" (Chapter 359—Statutes of California—16th Session). *(Charles Edwin Merriam and Louisa Overacker—Primary Elections)*

Negro to vote under authority of the Fifteenth Amendment (March 30, 1870) was Thomas Peterson-Mundy of Perth Amboy, N.J., who voted March 31, 1870, in Perth Amboy, N.J., in a special election for ratification or rejection of a city charter. The charter was adopted and he was appointed to the committee to revise the charter.

Preferential ballot system originated in the city of Grand Junction, Colo. The charter which contained the preferential ballot provision was adopted September 14, 1909, and the first election was held thereunder on November 2, 1909. Opposite the name of each candidate were three columns headed "First Choice," "Second Choice," and "Third Choice." Any person receiving more than half of all the votes cast for first choice was elected; if no one received more than half of the first choices, the lowest candidate was dropped and first and second choices were added together. If any remaining candidate received a majority of the combined votes, he was elected, but if not, then the lowest candidate was again dropped, and all choices for each candidate then added together, and the person receiving the largest total vote was elected. In case of a tie, priority in choice determined election.

Primary election law was passed by Minnesota April 20, 1899 (Chapter 349). It applied to candidates for city and county offices, judges, and elective members of school, library, and park boards in counties having a population of 200,000 or more. Hennepin County was the only one that had the required population when the law went into effect. *(William Watts Folwell—History of Minnesota)*

Primary election (state-wide) was held September 4, 1906, in Wisconsin. The law authorizing the election had been passed in 1903, Chapter No. 451, and published June 3, 1903. The first governor nominated and elected under the primary system was James Ole Davidson. The Minnesota primary law of 1899 antedated the Wisconsin primary law, but was limited in its application to counties of 200,000 population or over.

Proportional representation election was held November 2, 1915, in Ashtabula, Ohio. On August 10, 1915, the Hare system was authorized under Ashtabula's manager-plan charter adopted November 3, 1914. As seven council members were to be elected, the votes were so counted that each group consisting of one seventh of all the voters secured a representative. *(National Municipal Review. January 1916)*

THE FIRST

Registration law (state) was enacted by Massachusetts (Chapter 74) and signed March 7, 1801, by Governor Caleb Strong. *(Joseph Pratt Harris—Registration of Voters in the United States)*

ELECTIVE SYSTEM OF STUDY. *See* College: Elective system of study

ELECTORAL COLLEGE. *See* Presidential electoral college

ELECTRIC ALTERNATOR in parallel successfully operated was installed in 1896 by the Hartford Electric Light Company in its station at Hartford, Conn. It was used in connection with a water-power unit.

ELECTRIC ARC LIGHTS. *See* Electric lighting: Electric arc lights

ELECTRIC ATTACHMENT PLUG (separable) was invented by Harvey Hubbell of Bridgeport, Conn., who obtained patent No. 774,250, November 8, 1904. The plugs were first manufactured by Harvey Hubbell, Inc., Bridgeport, Conn.

ELECTRIC AUTOMOBILE. *See* Automobile: Electric storage battery automobile

ELECTRIC BELL was invented by Joseph Henry in 1831. He was the first to insulate iron for the magnetic coil and the first to work out the differing functions of two entirely different kinds of electro-magnets, the one surrounded by numerous coils of no great length, the other surrounded by a continuous coil of very great length. Joseph Henry's invention of 1831 increased the lifting power of the magnet from 9 pounds to 3,500 pounds. Every electrical dynamo or motor uses the electro-magnet in practically the same form in which Henry left it. *(William Bower Taylor—Historical Sketch of Henry's Contribution to the Electro-Magnetic Telegraph)*

ELECTRIC BLANKET. *See* Blanket: Electronic blanket

ELECTRIC BLOCK SYSTEM. *See* Railroad signal system: Railroad signal system (automatic electric block)

ELECTRIC BRIDGE TABLE to shuffle and deal the cards by electricity was patented November 29, 1932, by Laurens Hammond of Chicago, Ill., who obtained patent No. 1,889,729 for a "card table with an automatic dealing device." The unshuffled cards are placed in a sliding drawer which starts the mechanism and delivers thirteen cards to each player. The entire mechanism is concealed in the table. The

THE FIRST

table was manufactured by the Hammond Clock Company of Chicago, Ill., which marketed it in 1932.

ELECTRIC CAR. *See* Street car: Electric cars commercially operated

ELECTRIC CELL. *See* Photoelectric cell

ELECTRIC COMPANY
Electric company was the Edison Electric Light Company, 65 Fifth Avenue, New York City, incorporated October 15, 1878, and organized October 24, 1878. Three thousand shares with a par value of $100 each were issued for the express purpose of financing Thomas Alva Edison in his invention of the incandescent lamp. The Edison Electric Illuminating Company was incorporated December 17, 1880, with a capitalization of $1 million dollars for the purpose of furnishing electric light in New York City. The first president of the company was Dr. Norvin Green, who was chosen December 20, 1880.

Electric company organized to produce and sell electricity was the California Electric Light Company, Inc., San Francisco, Calif., organized June 30, 1879. In September 1879 it furnished current from a central generating station for lighting Brush arc light lamps.

Electric station (central) to supply light and power was the Edison Electric Illuminating Company of 257 Pearl Street, New York City, which opened on Saturday evening, September 4, 1882. It had one engine, which generated power for 800 electric light bulbs. Within fourteen months, the service had 508 subscribers and 12,732 bulbs. *(Francis Trevelyan Miller—T. A. Edison)*

Three-wire central station incandescent electric lighting plant was the Edison Electric Illuminating Company, Sunbury, Pa., incorporated April 30, 1883. Operations were begun on July 4, 1883. Two 110-volt direct current generators were connected in series, raising the distribution voltage to 220 volts. This increase in voltage allows more current (amperes) to be transported over a given size of wire for a given distance, or allows an equal amount of current to be transported over a given size of wire for a greater distance than is possible when lower voltages are used. The station was constructed by Thomas Alva Edison who served in the triple capacity of chief electrical engineer, mechanical expert, and superintendent of construction.

ELECTRIC COOKING EXPERIMENT was performed by Benjamin Franklin, on the banks of the Schuylkill River, Philadelphia, Pa., in 1749. In a letter sent to Peter Collinson, Franklin stated: "A turkey is to be killed for our dinner by the electrical shock and roasted

ELECTRIC COOKING EXPERIMENT
—*Continued*
by the electrical jack, before a fire kindled by the electrified bottle; when the healths of all the famous electricians in England, Holland, France and Germany are to be drank in electrified bumpers, under the discharge of guns from the electrical battery." The letter was dated April 29, 1749. (*I. Bernard Cohen—Benjamin Franklin's Experiments*)

ELECTRIC DENTAL DRILL. *See* Drill: Dental drill (electric)

ELECTRIC DYNAMO. *See* Dynamo: Dynamo

ELECTRIC ELEVATED RAILROAD. *See* Elevated railroad: Electric elevated railroad

ELECTRIC ELEVATOR. *See* Elevator: Electric elevator successfully operated

ELECTRIC ENGINE USED BY A RAILROAD. *See* Railroad: Railroad to use an electric engine

ELECTRIC EXECUTION. *See* Execution: Electrocution experiment

ELECTRIC-EYE CAMERA. *See* Camera: Photo-finish camera (electric eye) installed at a race track

ELECTRIC EYE FOR HIGH JUMPING STANDARDS. *See* High jumping standards

ELECTRIC FAN was invented by Dr. Schuyler Skaats Wheeler who in 1882 placed a fan or propeller on the shaft of an electric motor. In 1904 the Franklin Institute awarded him the John Scott medal for this invention.

ELECTRIC FLATIRON was invented by Henry W. Seely of New York City, who received patent No. 259,054, on June 6, 1882.

ELECTRIC FREIGHT LOCOMOTIVE. *See* Locomotive: Electric freight locomotive

ELECTRIC GENERATOR
Hydrogen-cooled turbine generator was built by the General Electric Company, Schenectady, N.Y., and installed in the Millers Ford station of the Dayton Power and Light Company, Ohio. The generator was put into commercial operation October 12, 1937. It had a capacity of 25,000 kilowatts.

Hydrogen-cooled turbine generator for outdoor installation was built by the General Electric Company, Schenectady, N.Y., for the

city of Glendale, Calif., at a cost of $391,669. It went into operation April 11, 1941. The normal rating of the turbo-generator was 20,000 kilowatts. The generator unit was located on an open deck and served with a traveling gantry crane.

Mercury boiler turbine was installed at the Dutch Point Station of the Hartford Electric Light Company, Hartford, Conn., and placed in service September 7, 1923. It generated about 1,500 kilowatts.

ELECTRIC HOME AND FARM AUTHORITY, INC., was authorized by Executive order No. 6,514, December 19, 1933. It was incorporated January 17, 1934, under the laws of the State of Delaware with a capital of $1 million "to encourage the fullest possible utilization of the present productive capacity of industries—to avoid undue restriction of production." The directors of the corporation named in the executive order were Dr. Arthur Ernest Morgan, chairman, Dr. Harcourt Alexander Morgan, and David Eli Lilienthal. The first sale of electric ranges, refrigerators, and water heaters financed by the Electric Home and Farm Authority, Inc., was held at Tupelo, Miss., May 21, 1934. The corporation was dissolved and a new one incorporated August 1, 1935, under the laws of the District of Columbia.

ELECTRIC LIGHT PLANT MUNICIPALLY OWNED. *See* Electric power plant: Municipally owned electric power pant

ELECTRIC LIGHT SOCKET with pull chain was patented August 11, 1896 (No. 565,451), by Harvey Hubbell of Bridgeport, Conn. The sockets were manufactured by Harvey Hubbell, Inc., Bridgeport, Conn.

ELECTRIC LIGHTING
Electric arc lights for public street lighting were made by Charles Francis Brush and were used in the Public Square, Cleveland, Ohio, April 29, 1879. Twelve lamps of the carbon variety—two carbon points slightly separated—were used. The current jumped from carbon to carbon giving off "a dazzling white light." Women complained about these lamps because they lighted their complexions to disadvantage. (*Thomas Commerford Martin and Stephen Leidy Coles—Story of Electricity*)

Electric incandescent lamp of practical value was invented on October 21, 1879, by Thomas Alva Edison of Menlo Park, N.J. After thirteen months of experimenting, he discovered carbonized cotton filaments and produced a light bulb which would burn forty hours in a vacuum inside a glass bulb. The first demonstration was held on December 20, 1879. Patent papers on this invention were applied for on November 4, 1879, and were granted Januar

27, 1880 (No. 223,898). The first public demonstration was held December 31, 1879. The Pennsylvania Railroad Company ran special trains to Menlo Park, N.J., to enable the public to view the demonstration. *(William Andrew Durgin—Electricity in Its Development)*

Electric incandescent lamp factory was the Edison Lamp Works, Menlo Park, N.J., opened October 1, 1880. More than 130,000 bulbs had been manufactured by April 1, 1882, when the factory moved to Harrison, N.J.

Electric indirect lighting demonstration was made in Chicago, Ill., in October 1908 by Augustus Darwin Curtis before the Illuminating Engineering Society and the Ophthalmological Society. *(Jacob L. Stair—The Lighting Book)*

Electric lamp bulb frosted on the inside with sufficient strength for commercial handling was invented by Marvin Pipkin of the Incandescent Lamp Department of the General Electric Company at Nela Park, Ohio. On June 29, 1925, he applied for a patent, which was granted October 16, 1928 (No. 1,687,510). Inside-frosted bulbs have a number of distinct advantages over outside-frosted bulbs, among which are less absorption of light and less collection of dust. Pipkin found that bulbs frosted by previous methods were weak because the etched surface was made up of minute sharp-angled pits or depressions, and that he could strengthen the bulb by changing these into rounded pits by treating the bulb with a weaker etching solution, or by using the strong solution for a shorter period of time.

Electric light for household illumination was probably used by Professor Moses Gerrish Farmer at 11 Pearl Street, Salem, Mass. In July 1859 he arranged in his parlor a series of lamps, the current for which was generated by a galvanic battery of some three dozen six-gallon jars in his cellar. He invented an incandescent lamp which consisted of a strip of sheet platinum operating in air. *(John White Howell and Henry Schroeder—The History of the Incandescent Lamp)*

Electric light from a power plant in a residence was generated by an independent plant installed in the home of James Hood Wright in Fort Washington, N.Y., before December, 1881. Other residences which were equipped with local generating power plants were those of William Henry Vanderbilt and John Pierpont Morgan of New York City.

Electric light in a store was installed in the Philadelphia, Pa., establishment of John Wanamaker on December 26, 1878, in the "Grand Depot." Twenty-eight arc lamps were used, eight dynamos supplying the current.

Electric sterilamp was introduced in March 1938 by the Lamp Division of the Westinghouse Electric and Manufacturing Company, Bloomfield, N.J. It was designed to reduce the germ population of the air by bactericidal ultraviolet radiation.

Electric traffic signal light. *See* Traffic light: Electric traffic signal lights

Electrically lighted elevator. *See* Elevator: Elevator with an electric light

Electrically lighted train. *See* Railroad: Electrically lighted train

Glass light bulb machine was invented by Benjamin D. Chamberlin of Washington, D.C., who received patent No. 1,551,935, September 1, 1925, for an "apparatus for gathering glass and the treatment thereof on blowpipes," assigned to the Hartford-Empire Company, Hartford, Conn. He filed his application on April 23, 1909, serial No. 491,812. The first commercial machine was the result of several individuals' work and went into regular use about 1914 at the main plant of the Corning Glass Works, Corning, N.Y.

Hotel to install electric lights. *See* Hotel: Hotel to install electric lights

Klieglight lighting unit for the motion picture industry was invented by John Hugh Kliegl and Anton Tiberius Kliegl and placed in use in 1911. Two 35-ampere arcs operating in series were equipped with an automatic arc-feed arrangement, using the then new white flame carbons. It gave four times as much light as other available sources. They were first used by the Carlton Motion Picture Laboratory, Coney Island, N.Y.; the Lubin Manufacturing Co., Philadelphia, Pa., and the Thomas A. Edison, Inc., Decatur Avenue Studio, New York City. The name was not adopted until later.

Mercury vapor lamp was invented by Peter Cooper Hewitt of New York City, who received eight patents on September 17, 1901. It consisted of an elongated vacuum glass tube having a mercury electrode at one end and an iron electrode at the other end, the light being obtained from the gas or vapor of the mercury, through which an electric current passed. The lamps lack red rays. The lamps were manufactured by the Cooper Hewitt Electric Company in New York City in December 1902. *(Electrical World and Engineer. April 27, 1901)*

Photograph taken by incandescent electric light. *See* Photograph: Photograph taken by incandescent electric light

ELECTRIC LIGHTING—*Continued*

School completely irradiated with germicidal lamps. *See* School: School completely irradiated with germicidal lamps

School to have all classroom lights controlled by electric eyes. *See* School: School to have all classroom lights controlled by electric eyes

Sewing machine lamp holder. *See* Sewing machine: Sewing machine lamp holder

Ship (steamboat) with electric lights. *See* Ship: Steamboat to employ electric lights; Ship: Steamboat to successfully employ electricity for arc lamps

Sodium vapor lamps were installed June 13, 1933, on the Balltown Road, near Schenectady, N.Y., by the General Electric Company and the New York Power and Light Corporation. The lamps were monochromatic and glowed in one color, giving two and a half times the light output of incandescent lamps of the same wattage. The lamp wattage is about 80 to 90 watts and the light output about 4,000 lumens, which is the equivalent of the 400 candlepower Mazda lamp consuming 215 watts.

Street light of an automatic system in which the lights individually turn themselves on and off was installed in New Milford, Conn., on March 2, 1949, by the Connecticut Light and Power Co., New Milford, Conn. The electronic device used in each street light was a joint development of the General Electric Company and the Connecticut Light and Power Company. The installation of 190 photoelectric controlled street lights on approximately 7 miles of street was completed in November 1949.

Street lighting (electric) by a municipality was undertaken by Wabash, Ind., which appropriated $100 on February 2, 1880, to the Brush Electric Light Company of Cleveland, Ohio, to install a light on the dome of the courthouse. On March 31, 1880, four lights, each over 4,000 candlepower, were placed on a staff above the courthouse, and on April 8, 1880, a further payment of $1,800 was authorized.

Theater lighted by electric lights. *See* Theater: Theater lighted by electricity

ELECTRIC LOCOMOTIVE. *See* Locomotive: Electric locomotive

ELECTRIC LOCOMOTIVE HEADLIGHT. *See* Locomotive headlight: Electric locomotive headlight

ELECTRIC MAGNET was invented by Joseph Henry, who, in June 1828, exhibited one closely wound with silk-covered wire about $1/30$ inch in diameter, before the Albany Institute, Albany, N.Y. *(Ellis H. Crapper—Electric and Magnetic Circuits)*

ELECTRIC METER, indicating the amount of electrical energy dispensed or applied, was invented by Oliver B. Shallenberger of Rochester, Pa., who obtained patent No. 388,003 on August 14, 1888. Commercial production of the meters was started in August 1888 by the Westinghouse Electric and Manufacturing Company, Pittsburgh, Pa.

ELECTRIC MOTOR

Electric motor (single-phase alternating current) of variable speed was first used in 1901 in interurban service. In 1907 the first steam railroad adopted it.

ELECTRIC ORGAN. *See* Organ: Electric organ

ELECTRIC PORTABLE TYPEWRITER. *See* Typewriter: Electric portable typewriter

ELECTRIC POWER LINE COMMERCIAL CARRIER. *See* Electric transmission: Electric power line commercial carrier

ELECTRIC POWER PLANT

Alternating current hydroelectric power plant to operate over a long distance was built by the Willamette Falls Electric Company at Willamette Falls, Oregon City, Ore., and operated two 300 h.p. Stilwell & Bierce waterwheels belted to a single-phase generator rated at 720 kilowatts. On June 2, 1889, it supplied current to Portland, Ore., a distance of 13 miles. *(Oregon Historical Quarterly. Vol. 31. No. 1. March 1930)*

Alternating current power plant was placed in operation in Great Barrington, Mass., on March 6, 1886, and commercially operated on March 20, 1886. The transformers were built by William Stanley in the Great Barrington laboratory and were successfully operated for a considerable time, but an accident disabled the generators and the plant was discontinued. *(Charles James Taylor—History of Great Barrington)*

Alternating current power plant commercially successful was built in Buffalo, N.Y., in November 1886, by the Westinghouse Electric and Manufacturing Company, Pittsburgh, Pa. The station, located on Wilkerson Street, Buffalo, was placed in operation on November 30, 1886, by the Brush Electric Light Company. *(Edward Dean Adams—Niagara Power)*

Atomic electric generating station (full scale) devoted exclusively to peaceful uses is the Shippingport Atomic Power Station, Shippingport, Pa., whose reactor attained criticality December 2, 1957. The plant produced its full rated capacity of 60,000 net kilowatts on December 23, 1957. It consists of a single pressurized water-type reactor and its associated systems, four steam generators heated by the reactor, a single turbine-generator and associated systems, a radioactive waste disposal system, laboratory, shops, and administrative facilities. The station was designed to supply an initial electrical output of 60,000 kilowatts net, enough to provide for the residential needs of a city of 250,000 people. To allow for increased output from future nuclear fuel loadings, the turbine generator was designed with a capacity of 1,000,000 kilowatts. President Dwight David Eisenhower broke ground for the station by remote control from Denver, Colo., on September 6, 1954, and formally dedicated the plant by remote control from Washington, D.C., on May 26, 1958.

Electric power from nuclear energy. *See* Atomic energy: Electric power from nuclear energy

Electric power generated from atomic energy to be sold commercially was delivered by the Atomic Energy Commission at West Milton, N.Y., to the Niagara Mohawk Power Corporation, which supplied power on July 18, 1955, to homes and industry at three mills per kilowatt hour. The power was obtained from a reactor, the prototype of the reactor used in the submarine "Seawolf." A capacity of about 10,000 kilowatts was integrated with the regular current.

Electric power generated from atomic energy to illuminate an entire town was obtained from the Utah Power and Light Company's station at Arco, Idaho, on July 17, 1955. At 11:28 P.M. the station released steam from a borax reactor into a turbine which drove a 3,500 kilowatt-capacity generator to supply current for 1,200 inhabitants of Arco. The power, which lasted only one hour, was the sole source of the town's light. The news was withheld until August 11, 1955, when it was announced at the Atoms for Peace Conference at Geneva, Switzerland.

Hydroelectric power plant was opened September 30, 1882, in Appleton, Wis. A single dynamo of 180 lights, each of ten candle power, was erected. Incandescent lighting was furnished. (*Thomas Commerford Martin— Forty Years of Edison Service*)

Hydroelectric power plant (commercial) to furnish arc lighting service was the Grand Rapids Electric Light and Power Co., Grand Rapids, Mich., organized March 22, 1880, in-

corporated March 30, 1880, and placed in operation July 23, 1880. The first president and organizer was William T. Powers. The first generating equipment was a 16-arclight Brush generator installed in the factory of the Wolverine Chair Company, which was driven by a waterwheel to supply power to the factory. Seven organizations were supplied with electric light. In September 1880, a larger generator was installed at a different site and on August 1, 1881, a new building was occupied from which current was generated to supply street lighting. This plant furnished arc lighting service for the first four years of its operations. (*Michigan History Magazine— 1939*)

Hydroelectric power plant (county-owned) was placed in operation by the people of Crisp County, Ga., on August 1, 1930. The plant is fourteen miles southwest of Cordele on the Flint River and was built under government license. Emmet Stephen Killebrew was the chief engineer. It has a capacity of 14,000 h.p. and produces 47 million kilowatt hours per annum. (*America's First County-Owned Hydro-Electric Power Plant—Crisp County Power Commission*)

Hydroelectric power plant to produce a million kilowatts was Boulder Dam, Boulder City, Nevada, which reached this production peak in June 1943. The Bureau of Reclamation of the Department of the Interior awarded a contract on March 11, 1931, for a concrete arch-gravity type dam. The dam was dedicated September 30, 1935, by President Franklin Delano Roosevelt. The first of its four generators (N-2) was placed in operation October 26, 1936, to serve the Los Angeles area. In 1947 its name was changed to Hoover Dam.

Hydroelectric power plant to use a storage battery making it possible to supply the peak load requirements from waterpower that would otherwise have gone to waste during the periods of relatively small demands was installed by the Hartford Electric Light Company, Hartford, Conn., in 1896.

Hydroelectric power plant to use water pumped into a reservoir was constructed in 1927 by the Connecticut Light and Power Company, Waterbury, Conn., at Rocky River, Conn. The first pumping commenced February 1928. Two 8,100 h.p. centrifugal pumps drove water into a reservoir 10 miles long and 1¼ miles wide at its widest point. The water was stored and then used for generating electricity as needed in a 33,000 h.p. turbine. (*Transactions American Institute of Electrical Engineers. October 1928*)

Mobile electric power plant was delivered January 10, 1944, by the General Electric Company, Schenectady, N.Y., to the U.S. Navy

THE FIRST

ELECTRIC POWER PLANT—*Continued*
Bureau of Yards and Docks, Navy Yard, Philadelphia, Pa. It consisted of six specially built railway cars housing a complete steam-turbine generating plant as well as the switchgear and transformer apparatus for controlling and distributing the 10,000 kilowatts of electric power it is capable of generating. The boilers are fired by oil. The unit has no motive power of its own but can be hauled over the rails at speeds up to 40 miles an hour and can be placed in operation within 24 hours.

Municipally owned electric power plant was purchased in 1882 by Fairfield, Iowa. It supplied 13 street lights, and 6 Brush arc lamps of 2,000 candlepower which were situated on a 185-foot tower. City operation was supervised by Al Robb and James McQuiston. The illumination cost $70 annually per arc. A windstorm blew the tower down May 9, 1883.

Rotary converter power plant was operated by the Chicago Edison Company, Chicago, Ill., on May 16, 1896, for the purpose of inaugurating a 2,500-volt alternating transmission from the company's station at Harrison Street at the river, to its station at 27th Street and Wabash Ave.

Warship propelled by electricity. *See* Ship: Warship propelled by electricity

Wind turbine to generate energy for an alternating current central power system was placed in service at Grandpa's Knob, Vt., on October 19, 1941, when it was phased into the Central Vermont Public Service Corporation's system. Synchronized operation continued for two hours during which a maximum output of 800 kilowatts was delivered. The wind velocity indicated by the anemometers at this load was 26 miles an hour. Palmer Cosslet Putnam was the inventor. (*Power. June 1941*)

ELECTRIC PRINTING PRESS. *See* Printing press: Printing press operated by electricity

ELECTRIC PROCESS WELDING. *See* Welding by the electric process

ELECTRIC RAZOR. *See* Razor: Electric dry shaver

ELECTRIC SAWMILL. *See* Sawmill: Electrically driven sawmill

ELECTRIC SELF-STARTER. *See* Automobile electric self-starter

ELECTRIC SEWING MACHINE. *See* Sewing machine: Electric sewing machine

THE FIRST

ELECTRIC SHAVER. *See* Razor: Electric dry shaver

ELECTRIC SIGN
Animated-cartoon electric sign was displayed April 28, 1937, by Douglas Leigh on the front of a building on Broadway, New York City. It contained 2,000 bulbs and presented a 4-minute show depicting a cavorting horse, ball-tossing cats, etc.

Electric sign flasher installed was the "Motogram," placed in service on the four sides of the New York *Times* building, New York City, on November 6, 1928, with the flashing of election returns. The system was invented by Francis E. J. Wilde of Meadowmere Park, N.Y., who obtained patent No. 1,626,900 on May 3, 1927, on an "electric sign control" designed "to permit changing of sign without interruption." It was installed by the Motogram Corporation, New York City, and was 360 feet long and 5 feet high. It had 14,800 lamps, 88,000 soldered connections, 1,386,000 feet of wire, and 39,000 contact brushes which created 21,925,664 lamp flashes an hour.

Electric sign (large) was designed and constructed by the Edison General Electric Company and installed in June 1892 on the wall of a nine-story building near Broadway and 23rd Street, New York City. The sign occupied a surface area 60 by 68 feet and was composed of 107 galvanized iron boxes varying in height from 3 to 6 feet. The front of each box was cut out to form the desired letter. Inside the boxes were 1,457 16-candlepower Edison bulbs in red, blue, green, and white frosted. The sign read:
"BUY HOMES ON / LONG ISLAND / SWEPT BY OCEAN BREEZES / MANHATTAN BEACH / ORIENTAL HOTEL / MANHATTAN HOTEL / GILMORE'S BAND / BROCK'S FIREWORKS." Current was supplied by the Edison Electric Illuminating Company. The sign was illuminated from dusk to 11 P.M. One line went on at a time, until all the lights were on, then all the lights went out. (*Electrical World. Vol. 20. No. 2. July 16, 1892*)

Neon tube advertising sign was installed on a marquee at the Cosmopolitan Theatre, Fifty-ninth Street and Columbus Circle, New York City, in July 1923. This sign advertised the theatrical production "Little Old New York," in which Marion Davies played the leading role. A United States patent on this tube was granted to George Claude of Paris. It was applied for on November 9, 1911 and issued on January 19, 1915 (No. 1,125,476).

ELECTRIC STARTING GATE (race track) was invented by Clay Puett, who installed a two-stall working model on May 8, 1939, at Hollywood Park, Inglewood, Calif. The first full-size gate was used at Bay

THE FIRST

Meadows Race Track, San Francisco, Calif., October 7, 1939. The gates were equipped with a bomb-release type of lock operated by solenoids. The front doors when closed formed a "V" and opened outward by means of springs.

ELECTRIC STORAGE BATTERY AUTOMOBILE. See Automobile: Electric storage battery automobile

ELECTRIC STOVE
See also Electric cooking experiment

Electric range was invented by George B. Simpson of Washington, D.C., who received patent No. 25,532 on September 20, 1859, on an "electrical heating apparatus" which he termed an electro-heater. Heat was generated by passing currents of electricity over a coil or coils of platina or other metallic wire.

Electric stove was a one-ring spiral coiled conductor invented by William S. Hadaway, Jr. of New York City, who obtained patent No. 563,032 June 30, 1896. It provided a uniform surface distribution of heat.

ELECTRIC TATTOO MACHINE. See Tattoo: Electric tattoo machine

ELECTRIC TAXICAB. See Automobile: Electric taxicabs

ELECTRIC THIRD RAIL SYSTEM. See Railroad: Railroad operated by an electric third rail system

ELECTRIC TOASTER
Electric toaster of the household automatic pop-up type was marketed in June 1926 by the McGraw Electric Company, Minneapolis, Minn., under the trademark "Toastmaster." One lever lowered the bread into the toaster and another wound the timer. It received one slice of toast at a time. The retail price was $13.50.

ELECTRIC TORPEDO. See Torpedo: Underwater torpedo operated by electric current

ELECTRIC TRAFFIC SIGNAL LIGHT. See Traffic light: Electric traffic signal lights

ELECTRIC TRANSMISSION
Alternating current power transmission installation was made in 1890 at Telluride, Colo., by the Westinghouse Electric and Manufacturing Company. A 100 h.p., 88⅓ cycle, single phase, 3,000 volt generator was driven by water power. A three-mile transmission line was erected and a single-phase synchronous motor was installed at the end of the line. The motor

THE FIRST

lacked a starting torque, and a necessary adjunct was a starting motor to bring the unloaded synchronized motor to its normal speed. *(Francis Ellington Leupp—George Westinghouse)*

Electric power line commercial carrier was placed in operation December 6, 1922, by the Utica Gas and Electric Company, Utica, N.Y. The plant was built by the General Electric Company, Schenectady, N.Y., and consisted of the transmitters, the power lines, and the associated receivers. The transmission lines carry both voices and power. A single power line can carry several different carrier frequencies simultaneously, making possible distant supervisory control of various types of electric equipment.

Substation with a rotary converter completely unattended was the Rowena Substation of the Detroit Edison Company, Detroit, Mich., which went into service in April 1914. It consisted of a 500-kilowatt General Electric rotary converter, three 175-kilowatt step-down transformers, and the necessary equipment for balancing direct-current machine voltage against bus voltage at Rowena. Included also were the typical devices to protect against alternating current failure, direct current failure, reverse current, and overspeed. This equipment acted to convert three-phase alternating current at 4,600 volts to direct current at 250 volts. This station was fed and controlled from another substation about a mile distant, which was attended, and known as Station "I" (now called the Elizabeth Substation).

Three-phase alternating high frequency current transmission for any considerable distance by a utility company was operated in March 1893 from the Rainbow Hydroelectric Station on the Farmington River to the State Street station of the Hartford Electric Light Company, Hartford, Conn. The power transmitted was 300 kilowatts, between 4,000 and 5,000 volts.

ELECTRIC TROLLEY. See Street car: Electric cars commercially operated

ELECTRIC TURNSTILE. See Turnstile (electric)

ELECTRIC VOTE RECORDER. See Voting machine: Electric vote recorder

ELECTRIC WASHING MACHINE. See Washing machine: Complete self-contained electric washing machine

ELECTRIC WATCH. See Clock: Electric watch

ELECTRIC WELDING. *See* Welding by the electric process

ELECTRICAL CONTRACT by a city with the federal government for electrical power was signed by J. P. Nanney, mayor of Tupelo, Miss., and Arthur Ernest Morgan, chairman of the Tennessee Valley Authority on November 11, 1933, and went into effect February 7, 1934. The contract was for twenty years, and by it the city agreed to purchase electricity from TVA and to sell it to its customers at rates agreed upon with the Authority. The electricity costs the city of Tupelo about 5½ mills per kilowatt hour.

ELECTRICAL ENGINEERING COURSE *See* Engineering college: Electrical engineering course

ELECTRICAL HEARING AID. *See* Deaf —Hearing aid: Electrical hearing aid

ELECTRICAL JOURNAL. *See* Periodical: Electrical journal

ELECTRICAL SHOW was held in Philadelphia, Pa., September 2-October 11, 1884, and was known as the Electrical Exhibition and National Conference of Electricians. It was sponsored by the Franklin Institute and was held in the Pennsylvania Railroad Station, 32d and Market Streets. There were 216 exhibitors and 282,779 paid admissions. *(Official Catalogue of the International Electrical Exhibition—1884)*

ELECTRICALLY PROPELLED SHIP. *See* Ship: Electrically propelled ship of the U.S. Navy

ELECTRICALLY WOUND CLOCK. *See* Clock: Watch movement to be electrically wound

ELECTROBASOGRAPH was invented by Dr. Russell Plato Schwartz of the University of Rochester Medical School, Rochester, N.Y., who exhibited it June 12, 1933, at the American Medical Association convention, Milwaukee, Wis. It was designed "to record the walking gait of individuals, to distinguish between actual and spurious limps in damage claims for injuries."

ELECTROCUTION EXPERIMENT. *See* Execution: Electrocution experiment

ELECTROCUTOR (insect). *See* Insect electrocutor patent

ELECTRO-MAGNETIC TELEGRAPH. *See* Telegraph: Telegraph (electro-magnetic)

ELECTRON MICROSCOPE. *See* Microscope: Electron microscope

ELECTRON TUBE to enable man to see in the dark was invented by Dr. Vladimir Kosma Zworykin and Dr. George Arthur Morton and described January 2, 1936, at the American Association for the Advancement of Science meeting, St. Louis, Mo. The device was sensitive to ultraviolet and infrared rays. Light rays from moving pictures were converted into electrons.

ELECTRONIC BLANKET. *See* Blanket: Electronic blanket

ELECTRONIC COMPUTER. *See* Computer: Electronic computer

ELECTRONIC RANGE. *See* Stove: Electronic range for domestic use

ELECTRONIC TELEVISION SYSTEM. *See* Television: Electronic television system

ELECTRONIC WRIST WATCH. *See* Clock: Electronic wrist watch

ELECTROPHOTOGRAPHY. *See* Radio facsimile transmission

ELECTRO-THERAPEUTIC BOOK was Dr. Alfred Charles Garratt's *Electro-Physiology and Electro-Therapeutics, showing the best methods for the medical uses of electricity,* 712 pages, published in 1860 by Ticknor and Fields, Boston, Mass.

ELECTROTYPE
Electrotype was produced from a wood engraving in 1839 in New York City by Joseph Alexander Adams. The electrotype was made by an impression taken in an alloy of soft metal, bismuth probably being the chief ingredient. Electrotypes were first published in 1840 in *Mapes Magazine. (Robert Francis Salade— Handbook of Electrotyping and Stereotyping)*

Electrotype manufacturing for commercial purposes was started in 1846 by John W. Wilcox in Boston, Mass. *(Robert Francis Salade —Handbook of Electroplating and Stereotyping)*

ELEMENT
Element 87, francium (symbol Fr, atomic weight 223), was discovered by Drs. Fred Allison and Edgar Jackson Murphy of the Alabama Polytechnic Institute at Auburn in samples of pollucite and lepidolite ores. The discovery was announced in a letter dated January 11, 1930, published in the *Physical Review. (Physical Review. Vol. 35. No. 3. February 1, 1930)*

THE FIRST

Element 93, neptunium (symbol Np, atomic weight 237), was discovered at the University of California at Berkeley by Professor Edwin Mattison McMillan and Philip Hauge Abelson and announced June 8, 1940.

Element 94, plutonium (symbol Pu, atomic weight 242), was discovered in 1940 at the University of California at Berkeley by Drs. Glenn Theodore Seaborg and Edwin Mattison McMillan, who received the 1951 Nobel prize in chemistry.

Element 95, americium (symbol Am, atomic weight 243), was discovered by Glenn Theodore Seaborg, Ralph Arthur James, Leon Owen Morgan, and Albert Ghiorso late in 1944 and announced November 16, 1945. It was formed by intense neutron bombardment of plutonium in the chain reacting uranium-graphite structures at Clinton, Tenn., and Hanford, Wash.

Element 96, curium (symbol Cm, atomic weight 242), was discovered by Glenn Theodore Seaborg, Ralph Arthur James, and Albert Ghiorso in the summer of 1944 and announced November 16, 1945. It was obtained by the helium-ion bombardment of plutonium, element 94, in the sixty-inch cyclotron of the Crocker Radiation Laboratory of the University of California at Berkeley.

Element 97, berkelium (symbol Bk, atomic weight 249), was identified by Stanley Gerald Thompson, Albert Ghiorso, and Glenn Theodore Seaborg in December 1949. It was produced by the bombardment of milligram amounts of americium with helium ions accelerated in the sixty-inch cyclotron of the Crocker Radiation Laboratory of the University of California at Berkeley. It was the fifth element produced by the cyclotron's atomic particle bombardment.

Element 98, californium (symbol Cf, atomic weight 249), was identified and produced by Stanley Gerald Thompson, Albert Ghiorso, Kenneth Street, Jr., and Glenn Theodore Seaborg in January 1950 and announced March 17, 1950. It does not exist in nature and was produced by the bombardment of microgram amounts of curium with helium ions accelerated in the sixty-inch cyclotron of the Crocker Radiation Laboratory of the University of California at Berkeley.

Element 99, einsteinium (symbol E, atomic weight 253), was identified by Albert Ghiorso, Stanley Gerald Thompson, Bernard George Harvey, and G. Bernard Rossi in December 1952. It was obtained by the bombardment of uranium 238, element 92, with a beam of positively charged nitrogen atoms from the sixty-inch cyclotron at the University of California at Berkeley. It was found in the debris of a

THE FIRST

thermonuclear explosion carried out by the University of California Radiation Laboratory, the Argonne National Laboratory, and the Los Alamos Scientific Laboratory.

Element 100, fermium (symbol Fm, atomic weight 255), was identified by Albert Ghiorso and others early in 1953 in the debris of a thermonuclear explosion carried out by the University of California Radiation Laboratory, the Argonne National Laboratory, and the Los Alamos Scientific Laboratory.

Element 101, mendelevium (symbol Mv, atomic weight 256), was discovered by Albert Ghiorso, Bernard George Harvey, Gregory Robert Choppin, Stanley Gerald Thompson, and Glenn Theodore Seaborg in February 1955 and announced April 30, 1955. It was obtained by the bombardment of einsteinium with helium ions in the sixty-inch cyclotron at the University of California at Berkeley.

Element 102, nobelium (symbol No, atomic weight 253), was discovered by Swedish, British, and American scientists who bombarded curium, element 96. The discovery was announced July 9, 1957, by the Argonne National Laboratory, Lemont, Ill.

Element 103, lawrencium, was produced on February 14, 1961, at the Lawrence Radiation Laboratory of the University of California, Berkeley, Calif., by Albert Ghiorso, Torbjørn Sikkeland, Almon E. Larsh, and Robert M. Latimer, who bombarded a target consisting of three millionths of a gram of californium, element 98, with boron ions of approximately 60 million electron volts energy. When a californium nucleus captures one of the boron nuclei, a new nucleus of 103 protons is instantaneously formed.

ELEPHANT. *See* Animals: Elephant

ELEVATED RAILROAD

Electric elevated railroad, and the first commercial electric line, was operated at the Chicago Railway Exposition in June 1883 by the Electric Railway Company of the United States. "The Judge," a 15 h.p. electric locomotive, hauled the trains on a 3-foot gauge track around the outer edge of a gallery of the main exhibition building, curving sharply at either end on a radius of 56 feet. The total length of the track was 1,553 feet. The trial trip was made June 2, 1883, but the line was not permitted to operate until June 9. It ceased operating June 23, having run 118¾ hours. It made 1,588 trips, carried 26,805 passengers, and ran 446.24 miles. *(Thomas Commerford Martin and Joseph Wetzler—The Electric Motor and Its Application)*

ELEVATED RAILROAD—*Continued*

Elevated railroad was opened for traffic on July 2, 1867, in New York City. Charles T. Harvey received authority for its construction and built the first half-mile test section on single columns along the curb line of Greenwich Street, between Battery Place and Dey Street. The speed of the cars was from 12 to 15 miles an hour. The line was unsuccessful and was sold at a sheriff's sale. It was reorganized February 14, 1870, and placed in operation with steam power. Service was extended as far north as the New York Central Railroad Passenger station at 29th Street and 9th Avenue. (*The Industrial Museum of New York. Vol. 1-2— Museum of the Peaceful Arts*)

ELEVATOR

Double-deck elevator was installed January 1932 by the Otis Elevator Company in the Sixty Wall Tower, Inc., building, New York City. It serves 30 floors and travels at a speed of 1,000 feet a minute. Eight double-decked cars were installed which stopped at two floors at the same time. The building was formally opened May 13, 1932.

Dual elevator, with two cars operated separately on different levels in the same shaftway, was made and placed in regular service by the Westinghouse Electric and Manufacturing Company in its main office building in East Pittsburgh, Pa., in 1931. The upper elevator is an express. When it is on the main floor, the local is in the basement. Precautions have been taken to prevent a collision in the shaft. The service was announced on January 13, 1931. (*Westinghouse News Service*)

Electric elevator successfully operated was installed in 1889 by Otis Brothers & Company for the Demarest Building, Fifth Avenue and 33d Street, New York City.

Electronic signal control elevator commercial installation was completed by the Otis Elevator Company during April 1948 at the Universal Pictures Building, New York City, after several years of experiment and development. Eight elevators, four local and four express, serve the building's twenty-two stories. When a passenger touches a landing button, the call is registered by an electronic tube, the light of which indicates that the call is registered. The stopping of the cars in response to these calls, the canceling of the calls as they are answered, and the operation of the cars are all controlled by means of electronic circuits.

Elevator was a platform-type elevator which was made by Henry Waterman in 1850 in his shop on Duane Street, New York City. The elevator was installed in a building owned by Hecker and Brother, millers, 203 Cherry Street, New York City, who used it to hoist barrels upstairs in their mill.

Elevator in a hotel was installed in the six-story Fifth Avenue Hotel, New York City, which opened on August 23, 1859. The elevator operated on the principle of an Archimedean screw. It was viewed and inspected by Albert Edward, Prince of Wales, on October 11, 1860.

Elevator in an office building was installed in the original Equitable Life Assurance Society building, located on lower Broadway, New York City, in 1868.

Elevator patent, for a vertical-geared hydraulic electric elevator, was No. 123,761, granted February 20, 1872, to Cyrus W. Baldwin of Boston, Mass. The elevator was installed in the Stephens Hotel, at 11th Street, near Broadway, New York City.

Elevator (suspended) was a steam hoist which was installed in 1866 in the St. James Hotel, New York City.

Elevator with an electric light was installed in the Blue Mountain House, Blue Mountain Lake, N.Y., on July 12, 1882. The hotel was operated by M. T. Merwin.

Elevator with completely enclosed car for conveying passengers to the upper floor of a building was installed in 1857 by Elisha Graves Otis in the store of E. V. Haughwout, at the corner of Broadway and Broome Streets, New York City.

Elevator with safety devices to prevent falling of the car in case the ropes should break was made by Elisha Graves Otis in 1853 and exhibited by him the same year at the Crystal Palace Exposition in New York City. The first was delivered September 20, 1853 to Benjamin Newhouse, 275 Hudson Street, New York City.

Grain elevator operated by steam in the transfer and storage of grain for commercial purposes was designed by Robert Dunbar and made by Jewett & Root for Joseph Dart, Buffalo, N.Y., in 1842. The first cargo of corn was unloaded June 22, 1843, from the "South America." (*Publications Buffalo Historical Society—1879*)

ELKS. *See* Benevolent and Protective Order of Elks

EMANCIPATED SLAVE. *See* Slavery: Slave emancipated

EMANCIPATION ACT (state) was passed July 2, 1777, by Vermont, which embodied the following provision in its constitution: "No male person, born in this country, or brought

THE FIRST

here from over sea, ought to be holden by law, to serve any person as a servant, slave or apprentice, after he arrives to the age of twenty-one years, nor female, in like manner, after she arrives and to the age of eighteen years, unless they are bound by their own consent, after they arrive at such age, or bound by law, for the payment of debts, damages, fines, costs, or the like."

EMANCIPATION PROCLAMATION (preliminary) was made by President Abraham Lincoln on September 22, 1862. He issued a further proclamation on January 1, 1863, freeing the slaves in all states then in rebellion except in certain districts in Louisiana and Virginia occupied by Federal troops. *(Henry Watson Wilbur—President Lincoln's Attitude Toward Slavery and Emancipation)*

EMBALMING BOOK was the *History of Embalming, and of Preparations in Anatomy, Pathology and Natural History; including an account of a new process for embalming,* 264 pages, by Jean Nicolas Gannal, published in 1840 in Philadelphia, Pa., by Judah Dobson. It was a translation by Richard Harlan, M.D., with notes and additions of Gannal's book, published in French in 1838 in Paris.

EMBARGO ACT was passed December 22, 1807 (2 Stat.L.451), by vote of 82 to 44. The act, "laying an embargo on all ships and vessels in the ports and harbors of the United States," required all American ships to refrain from international commerce. It was approved December 22, 1807, by President Thomas Jefferson. The act was repealed March 1, 1809. A later act substituted non-intercourse with England and France. *(Annals of Congress. Tenth Congress, First Session)*

EMBOSSED BIBLE. *See* Bible: Bible for the blind in embossed form

EMBOSSED INLAID LINOLEUM. *See* Linoleum: Embossed inlaid linoleum

EMBOSSING PRESS was a standing hand lever press built in New York City in 1838 by Bernard Sheridan. An object placed between the descending die and the bed was given a raised surface when pressure was applied. The press sold for $200.

EMERGENCY COUNCIL (U.S.). *See* National emergency council (U.S.)

EMERGENCY HOUSING CORPORATION (U.S.) was authorized October 28, 1933, through the powers delegated to the Administrator under the act of June 16, 1933, which created the Public Works Administration.

THE FIRST

The corporation was organized November 18, 1933, under Delaware laws and was composed of five officers and five directors. The president of the corporation was Harold Le Claire Ickes, Administrator of Public Works. The Federal Housing Administration was created by the National Housing Act approved June 27, 1934 (48 Stat.L.1246) "to encourage improvement in housing standards and conditions, to provide a system of mutual mortgage insurance." Its first administrator was James Andrew Moffett, appointed for the four-year term at an annual salary of $10,000.

EMERGENCY RELIEF ADMINISTRATION. *See* Federal Emergency Relief Administration

EMPLOYEES' TIME RECORDER. *See* Time recorder

EMPLOYER'S LIABILITY ACT (federal). *See* Insurance: Employer's liability act (federal)

EMPLOYMENT SERVICE

Employment service (U.S.) as a distinct and separate unit of the Department of Labor was inaugurated under an order promulgated January 3, 1918, by the Secretary of Labor in pursuance of an act approved October 6, 1917 (40 Stat.L.376). Previously the employment service had functioned under authority of an act to establish a Division of Information in the Bureau of Immigration (section 40, Immigration Act of February 20, 1907, 34 Stat.L. 909) and by the provisions of the organic act creating the Department of Labor (March 4, 1913, 37 Stat.L.783).

Employment service (U.S.E.S.) was created June 6, 1933 (48 Stat.L.113), "to provide for the establishment of a national employment system and for cooperation with the states in the promotion of such a system." The first director was William Frank Persons, who received $8,500 annually. Within ten weeks, 3,220 local offices opened which registered 9 million people. It was, in turn under the Department of Labor, the Social Security Board, and the War Manpower Commission.

Municipal employment office was authorized by Seattle, Wash., on March 5, 1894, by a vote of 2,058 for and 523 against. John Lamb, the first labor commissioner, opened an office April 1, 1894, in a rough board shanty containing one small room. The following year larger quarters were obtained in the City Hall. *(Seventh Annual Report of Labor Commissioner —Seattle, Wash.)*

State employment service was created April 28, 1890, in Ohio by act of legislature amending section 308 of the Revised Statutes.

EMPLOYMENT SERVICE—*Continued*
Authorization was given to establish public employment offices in cities of the first and second class, Cincinnati, Cleveland, Columbus, Dayton, and Toledo. The first office was opened June 4, 1890, in Toledo, with Charles W. Murphy as superintendent. The Commissioner of Labor Statistics, under whom the system of five offices was set up during the year 1890, was John McBride. (*Ohio Bureau of Labor Statistics—1890—Fourteenth Annual Report*)

ENCLAVE
Enclave was established at Fairhope, Baldwin County, Ala., by the Fairhope Industrial Association, Inc., composed of seven men who purchased 135 acres in the town for $771 on January 5, 1895, and an additional 200 acres for $250 at a later date. The association was succeeded by the Fairhope Single Tax Corporation, incorporated August 9, 1904, which owns about 4,000 acres, three fourths of which is under lease. The association pays all taxes, and leaseholders pay only rent for the land.

Municipal enclave of economic ground rent was authorized by the Collierville Enclave Act passed by Collierville, Shelby County, Tenn. Governor Hill McAlister signed the bill April 21, 1933, and it took effect immediately. The bill was drawn up by Abe D. Waldauer, City Attorney for Collierville, and approved by Mayor J. T. Patrick. (*Chapter 523 Private Acts of the General Assembly of Tennessee for 1933.*)

ENCLOSED CABIN AIRSHIP. *See* Aviation—Airship: Airship with an enclosed cabin

ENCLOSED CAR (elevator). *See* Elevator: Elevator with completely enclosed car

ENCLOSURE FOR ANIMALS (pound). *See* Pound (enclosure for animals)

ENCYCLOPEDIA
Agricultural encyclopedia. *See* Agricultural encyclopedia

American encyclopedia was the *Encyclopedia Americana*, edited by Francis Lieber. The set consisted of thirteen volumes, the first of which was issued in 1829 and the thirteenth in 1833. It was published in Philadelphia, Pa.

Encyclopedia printed in the United States was a reproduction of the third edition of the *Encyclopaedia Britannica*, originally published in Edinburgh between the years 1788 and 1797. The American reprint, however, was not called "Encyclopaedia Britannica," but "Encyclopaedia; or a Dictionary of Arts, Sciences, and Miscellaneous Literature." It consisted of eighteen volumes and was completed in 1798 by

Thomas Dobson in Philadelphia, Pa. The first volume appeared in 1790 and contained 799 pages and 31 plates.

ENDLESS CHAIN TRACTOR. *See* Automobile tractor: Endless chain tractor

ENDOWED LECTURE SERIES. *See* Lecture series (endowed)

ENDOWED SCHOOL. *See* School: Endowed school

ENDOWMENT (educational). *See* Educational endowment

ENDOWMENT (social service). *See* Social service endowment

ENDURANCE RUN (motorcycle). *See* Motorcycle endurance run

ENGINE
See also

Diesel engine	Locomotive
Electric motor	Motor
Fire engine	Steam engine
Gas engine	

Diesel engine built for commercial service was a two-cylinder 60 h.p. unit built in September 1898 in the plant of the St. Louis Iron and Marine Works, St. Louis, Mo. The engine, which drove a direct-current generator, was erected and operated in the Second Street plant of the Anheuser Busch, Inc., brewery and was the first diesel engine in the world to be placed in commercial service. Adolphus Busch bought Dr. Rudolf Diesel's American patent rights in 1897 for a sum of approximately $250,000. The next engines were built for the Diesel Motor Company of America, which was formed by Busch. These engines were built in the plant of the Hewes and Philips Iron Works, Newark, N.J., about 1900, and were of one size. They had an 11 by 20 inch cylinder which when running 200 r.p.m. was intended to develop 20 h.p. (*Lacey Harvey Morrison—Diesel Engines*)

Diesel engine in a submarine was the Vickers air injection type, four cycle, four cylinder, non-air starting and non-reversing units. Two were placed in the Submarines E-1 and E-2, built by the New London Ship and Engine Company of Groton, Conn., and commissioned on February 14, 1912. (*American Society of Naval Engineers Journal. Vol. 37. August 1925*)

Internal combustion engine was invented by Captain Samuel Morey of Orford, N.H., who received a patent April 1, 1826, "on a gas or vapor engine." His engine had two cylinders,

THE FIRST

180-degree cranks, poppet valves, a carburetor, an electric spark, and a water cooling device. He employed the vapor of spirits of turpentine and common air. A small tin dish contained the spirits, and the only heat he used was from a common table lamp. By means of a crank and flywheel, a rotary movement was obtained, as in the steam engine. (*Katherine Goodwin and Charles Edgar Duryea—Captain Samuel Morey*)

Multi-engine hydroplane. *See* Aviation—Airplane: Hydroplane with a multi-engine

Outboard motor (commercially successful) was developed in Milwaukee, Wis., in 1909 by Ole Evinrude. It was a single cylinder two-port two-cycle battery-ignited engine, developing 1½ h.p. at about 1,000 r.p.m. It weighed 46 pounds. (*Journal of the Society of Automotive Engineers. January 1931*)

Outboard twin-cylinder motor (light) was developed in Milwaukee, Wis., in 1921 by Ole Evinrude. This was the two-port two-cycle Elto, which developed 2½ h.p. at 1,400 r.p.m. It weighed 47 pounds.

ENGINEER (Army). *See* Army officer: Chief engineer

ENGINEER (Navy). *See* Naval officer: Naval officer to become an engineer

ENGINEER (woman). *See* Woman: Woman automotive engineer

ENGINEER CORPS. *See* Army: Army Engineering Department; Army: Engineer Corps

ENGINEERING BOOK was a translation of Louis André de la Mamie de Clairac's *L'Ingénieur de Campagne; or Field Engineer.* It contained 256 pages and a variety of copperplates. It was translated by Major Lewis Nicola and was published in 1776 by R[obert] Aitken, Philadelphia, Pa.

ENGINEERING COLLEGE
Aeronautical engineering. *See* Aviation—School: Aeronautical engineering course

Civil engineering course in a college was given in 1819 at Norwich University, now located in Northfield, Vt. The university was founded August 6, 1819, as the American Literary, Scientific and Military Academy by Captain Alden Partridge in Norwich, Vt. Courses in civil engineering included the construction of roads, canals, locks, and bridges, and architecture. The name was changed November 6, 1834, to Norwich University. In March 1866 the buildings were destroyed by fire and the college was moved to Northfield, Vt.

THE FIRST

Electrical engineering course in a college was established September 21, 1883, by the College of Engineering, Cornell University, Ithaca, N.Y. A four-year course was given, leading to the degree of Bachelor of Science. Instruction was given in the theory of electricity; the construction and testing of telegraph lines, cables, and instruments; dynamo machines; civil and mechanical engineering, etc. Dr. Andrew White pledged his own resources for the school.

Engineering college was the Rensselaer School, Troy, N.Y., founded November 5, 1824, and opened January 3, 1825. It was incorporated March 21, 1826. The first class of ten students graduated April 26, 1826, with the degree of A.B. The first C.E. degree was awarded in October 1835. Amos Eaton was senior professor and the first director. He served from November 1824 to May 10, 1842. The name of the school was changed to Rensselaer Institute on April 26, 1832, and to Rensselaer Polytechnic Institute on April 8, 1861.

ENGINEERING LABORATORY (mechanical). *See* Mechanical engineering laboratory

ENGINEERING SOCIETY
Civil engineering national society was the American Society of Civil Engineers, founded as the American Society of Civil Engineers and Architects, November 5, 1852, in New York City for "the advancement of the sciences of engineering and architecture in their several branches, the professional improvement of its members, the encouragement of intercourse between men of practical science, and the establishment of a central point of reference and union for its members." The name of the society was shortened later. The first president was James Laurie and the first secretary was Robert Bennett Gorsuch.

Engineering society of importance was the Boston Society of Civil Engineers, organized at an informal meeting April 26, 1848, at the United States Hotel, Boston, Mass. The first regular meeting was held July 3, 1848. The society was incorporated April 24, 1851, for the purpose of "promoting science and instruction in the department of civil engineering." The first officers were James Fowle Baldwin, president; George Dexter Minot, vice president; John Harrison Blake, secretary; and William Pearce Parrott, treasurer. Attempts had been made to form engineering societies in 1836 by engineers of the Cincinnati & Charleston Railroad, in 1839 by engineers in Baltimore, Md., and in 1841 in Albany, N.Y., but these sporadic attempts were not successful.

Mechanical engineering national society was the American Society of Mechanical Engineers, founded February 16, 1880, by 40 men from 8 states who met at the office of the *Amer-*

ENGINEERING SOCIETY—*Continued*
ican Machinist, New York City, and elected
Alexander Lyman Holley chairman. An organi-
zation meeting was held April 7, 1880, at the
Assembly Hall of Stevens Institute of Technol-
ogy, Hoboken, N.J. The first president was
Robert Henry Thurston. The first annual meet-
ing was held November 4-5, 1880, in New York
City. *(William Frederick Durand—Robert
Henry Thurston, Biography)*

**Woman elected to the American Society of
Civil Engineers** was Nora Stanton Blatch,
elected as a Junior on March 6, 1906. The
grade of Junior was a temporary one, and the
first woman elected as an Associate Member
(which is one of the two grades of corporate
membership) was Elsie Eaves, elected on
March 14, 1927.

ENGLISH ACTOR OF NOTE. *See* Actor:
English actor of note

ENGLISH BIBLE. *See* Bible: Bible printed
in English

ENGLISH CHANNEL SWIMMER
(American woman). *See* Woman: American woman to swim the English Channel

ENGLISH GRAMMAR. *See* Grammar:
English grammar

ENGLISH GRAND OPERA. *See* Opera:
Grand opera sung in English

ENGLISH NOVEL COURSE. *See* Novel
course: Lecture course on the English novel

ENGLISH SETTLEMENT. *See* Colonist:
English settlement

**ENGLISH STEAM PACKET TO AR-
RIVE IN THE UNITED STATES.** *See*
Ship: Packet line

ENGRAVER of record to practice his art
in the American colonies was Peter Pelham.
In 1727 he produced the first mezzotint engrav-
ing, a picture of Cotton Mather. *(David Mc-
Neely Stauffer—American Engravers upon
Copper and Steel)*

ENGRAVING
Engraving was a woodcut made about
April 22, 1669, by John Foster, of the Reverend
Richard Mather prior to his death. Foster cut
away from the surface of a flat wooden block
those parts which were to appear white in the
print, leaving the actual design in raised outline on the block. The print was five by six
inches. *(Carl W. Drepperd—Early American
Prints)*

Engraving of any artistic merit was a copperplate portrait of Increase Mather, made in
1701 by Thomas Emmes, which was used as a
frontispiece to a sermon, "The Blessed Hope,"
published in Boston, Mass., in 1701 by Timothy
Green for Nicholas Boone. *(Arthur Mayger
Hind—History of Engraving and Etching)*

Half-tone engraving was made by Stephen
Henry Horgan and appeared in the New York
Daily Graphic, March 4, 1880. It depicted a
"Scene in Shantytown, N.Y." A screen gradated
from transparency to opacity was the basis of
the invention. *(Inland Printer—March-April
1924)*

Historical print engraved in America was
*A Prospective Plan of the Battle Fought Near
Lake George,* which presented a bird's-eye view
of the march of troops shown at the left, the
camp and battle at the right, and Forts William
Henry and Edward in the upper right hand
corner. It was an engraving in line, colored by
hand, by Thomas Johnston after Samuel Blodget, and printed by Richard Draper, in Boston,
Mass., in 1755.

Wood engraving made with an engraving
tool, the burin, making use of the intaglio
"white line," was a tobacco stamp made by
Alexander Anderson in June 1793 in New York
City. The following year, he made a wood
engraving for a book, *The Looking-Glass for
the Mind; or Intellectual Mirror* by William
Durell, translated from Arnaud Berquin's *L'Ami
des Enfants.* *(Everet Augustus Duyckinck—A
Brief Catalogue of Books Illustrated with Engravings by Dr. Alexander Anderson with a
Biographical Sketch of the Artist)*

**ENGRAVING AND PRINTING BU-
REAU (U.S.)** began operations August 28,
1862. Signatures were to be engraved in facsimile and the seal of the treasury imprinted on
the notes after they had been delivered to the
engravers. Certain stamps, notes, and bills were
printed by individuals under contract. The act
of February 25, 1862 (12 Stat.L.346) authorized
the Bureau. *(Laurence Frederick Schmeckebier
—The Bureau of Engraving and Printing)*

ENTOMOLOGIST
Federal entomologist was Townend Glover, commissioned June 14, 1854. He was the
"expert for collecting statistics and other information on seeds, fruits and insects of the
United States." His first report, which appeared under the imprint of the Patent Office,
was *Insects Injurious and Beneficial to Vegetation* printed in 1854. *(Charles Richards Dodge
—The Life and Entomological Work of the
Late Townend Glover)*

State entomologist (not official, but so
designated) to be appointed was Asa Fitch.
The New York State Legislature on April 15,

THE FIRST

THE FIRST

1854, made an appropriation of $1,000 to pay for an examination and description of the insects of New York State, particularly those injurious to vegetation. The New York State Agricultural Society, through its executive committee, meeting at the Astor House, New York City, on May 4, 1854, appointed Asa Fitch to do this work and instructed him at that time to make his first report relative to injurious insects affecting fruits. The report appeared in the Agricultural Society Report for 1855. *(Journal of the N.Y. State Agricultural Society. 1854-1855)*

ENTOMOLOGY BOOK (comprehensive) was Thomas Say's *American Entomology, or Descriptions of the Insects of North America,* three volumes, published in Philadelphia, Pa., by Samuel Augustus Mitchell. The first volume was published in 1824, the second in 1825, and the third in 1828. Each contained 18 plates. In 1817 a portion of Volume I, containing 6 plates and 38 pages, was published.

ENTOMOLOGY MAGAZINE devoted to applied entomology was the *Practical Entomologist,* the first issue of which was published in Philadelphia, Pa., in October 1865 by the Entomological Society of Philadelphia. The original editors were Ezra Townsend Cresson, Augustus Radcliffe Grote, and James W. McAllister. The magazine ceased publication after two years. The Entomological Society was founded in 1859 and incorporated in 1862. It changed its name to the American Entomological Society on February 23, 1867.

ENTOMOLOGY PROFESSOR was Hermann August Hagen, who served at Harvard University, Cambridge, Mass., from 1870 to 1893.

ENVELOPE
Envelope folding and gumming machine was patented on February 8, 1898, by John Ames Sherman of Worcester, Mass., who received patent No. 598,716 on a "mechanism for folding and sealing envelopes." It reduced the cost of a completely gummed envelope ready for market from 60 cents to 8 cents per 1,000.

Envelope folding machine that proved practical commercially was patented on January 21, 1853, No. 9812, by Dr. Russell L. Hawes of Worcester, Mass. It was not self-gumming but nevertheless it enabled three girls to produce the finished product at the rate of about 25,000 envelopes in ten hours. *(U. S. Envelope Co.— An Early History of the Envelope)*

Envelope machine patent was No. 6,055, granted on January 23, 1849, to Jesse K. Park and Cornelius S. Watson of New York City on "an improvement in machines for making en-

velopes." Other patents on improved machines were granted shortly thereafter with the result that this patent had but little value.

Envelope with an outlook or window was patented by Americus F. Callahan of Chicago, Ill., who obtained patent No. 701,839 on June 10, 1902. It was first manufactured in July 1902 by the U.S. Envelope Company of Springfield, Mass., to which company the patent was leased.

Stamped envelope (U.S.) *See* Postage stamp: Stamped envelopes (U.S.)

ENVELOPE MANUFACTURER was a Mr. Pierson of New York City, who manufactured envelopes in a little store on Fulton Street in 1839. Prior to the manufacture of envelopes, letters were folded and the name and address written on the blank side.

EPIDEMIC
Cholera epidemic occurred in 1832. Individual cases are said to have developed in several cities, but the real force of the epidemic was manifested in the larger cities like New York, Boston, Philadelphia, etc. The first case in New York City appeared June 28, 1832, and from July 5, 1832, to August 29, 1832, 5,835 cases developed, of which 2,251 resulted in death. On July 21, 1832, New York City reported 311 cases and 100 deaths. *(Edward Warren—Sketch of the Progress of the Malignant or Epidemic Cholera)*

Influenza epidemic occurred in 1733 and was most serious in Philadelphia and New York City. About three fourths of the entire population was affected. *(James Thacher—American Medical Biography. 1828)*

Poliomyelitis epidemic occurred in Vermont, when 123 cases appeared in Rutland and Wallingford between June 17, 1894 and September 1, 1894. *(New York Medical Record. December 1, 1894)*

Smallpox epidemic of importance occurred in 1616-1617 and almost swept away the New England Indians from the Penobscot to Narragansett Bay. Smallpox broke out about May 26, 1721, principally affecting Boston, Mass., and the larger cities. The death rate varied from 12 per cent to 24 per cent of the population. *(Reginald Heber Fitz—Zabdiel Boylston, Inoculator and the Epidemic of Small Pox in Boston in 1721)*

EPIDEMIOLOGIST was Noah Webster In 1796, he published *A Collection of Papers on the Subject of Bilious Fevers, Prevalent in the United States for a Few Years Past,* which was printed in New York City by Hopkins, Webb & Co., and, in 1799, a two-volume work, *A Brief*

EPIDEMIOLOGIST—*Continued*
History of Epidemics and Pestilential Diseases; with the Principal Phenomena of the Physical World, which Precede and Accompany Them, and Observations Deduced from the Facts Stated, which was published by Hudson and Goodwin, Hartford, Conn.

EPISCOPAL CATECHISM. *See* Protestant episcopal catechism

EPISCOPAL CATHEDRAL. *See* Cathedral: Episcopal cathedral

EPISCOPAL CHURCH. *See* Church of England; Protestant Episcopal Church

EQUAL RIGHTS PARTY was formed in San Francisco, Calif., September 20, 1884, at a convention of the Woman's Rights Party of Female Suffragettes. Belva Ann Bennett Lockwood of the District of Columbia was nominated as the presidential candidate and Marietta Lizzie Bell Stow of California as the vice presidential candidate.

EQUESTRIAN EXHIBITION in America was given by John Sharp in Boston, Mass., in 1771. He gave other exhibitions in Salem, Mass., and other cities. A Mr. Pool was the first rider to introduce a clown to the American public. He advertised in the *Pennsylvania Packet* on August 15, 1785, that he would mount three horses and while standing on the saddles would leap a hurdle at full speed.

EQUESTRIAN STATUE (bronze). *See* Monument: Bronze equestrian statue

ERASER ATTACHED TO A PENCIL. *See* Pencil: Pencil with an attached eraser

ESCALATOR
Escalator was manufactured by the Otis Elevator Company of New York City in 1900 and placed on exhibit at the Paris Exposition the same year. It was returned to the United States and installed in 1901 in the Eighth Street building of Gimbel Brothers, Philadelphia, Pa. The trade-mark "Escalator" was registered May 29, 1900, and was renewed by the Otis Elevator Company in 1930.

Escalator patent was obtained by Nathan Ames of Saugus, Mass., who obtained patent No. 25,076 on August 9, 1859, on an improvement in revolving stairs. Steps or stairs were arranged upon an inclined endless belt or chain.

ESKIMO CHICKEN (ptarmigan). *See* Birds: Ptarmigan (Eskimo chicken)

ESKIMO PIE, an ice cream confection containing a normally liquid material frozen to a substantially hard state and encased in a chocolate covering to maintain its original form during handling, was invented by Christian K. Nelson of Onawa, Iowa, who obtained patent No. 1,404,539 on January 24, 1922. Subsequent patents which have also been issued are controlled by the Eskimo Pie Corporation of New York City.

ESPERANTO
Esperanto, a new artificial universal language, was proposed by Dr. Lazaro Ludovico Zamenhof, a Russian physician, in 1887. An attempt was made to introduce it into the United States but it received little favor.

Talking picture in Esperanto. *See* Moving picture: Talking picture in Esperanto

ESPERANTO CLUB
Esperanto club was the Esperanto Association, organized February 16, 1905, at Boston, Mass. John Fogg Twombly was the first secretary.

Esperanto club (national organization) was the Esperanto Association of North America, organized September 7, 1908, at Chautauqua Lake, N.Y. George Brinton McClellan Harvey was the first president.

Esperanto Congress in the United States was the Sixth International Congress of Esperantists, held August 14-20, 1910, in Washington, D.C. It was attended by about three hundred delegates from thirty-five nations.

ESPERANTO COURSE carrying college credit was offered by Clark University, Worcester, Mass., on September 16, 1908. Dr. Robert Mowry Bell taught the course, which offered "a brief outline of the grammar, and some practice in reading the new universal language."

ESPERANTO MAGAZINE was *L'Amerika Esperantisto,* "a monthly journal of Esperanto, the international language," published October 1906 at Oklahoma City, Okla. It contained 16 pages and a cover. Subscription was $1 a year.

ETCHER of skill was William Dunlap, whose success in 1830 inspired others to practice the art of etching. *(William Dunlap—History of the Rise and Progress of the Arts of Design in the United States)*

ETHER FOR CHILDBIRTH. *See* Anesthesia: Ether administered in childbirth

ETHICAL CULTURE SOCIETY was the New York Society for Ethical Culture founded in New York City in May 1876 by Dr. Felix

THE FIRST

Adler. Additional groups were formed and in 1886 the American Ethical Union was organized. *(Horace James Bridges—Aspects of Ethical Religion, Essays in Honor of Felix Adler on the Fiftieth Anniversary of His Founding of the Ethical Movement, 1876, by His Colleagues)*

ETHYL GASOLINE. *See* Gasoline: Ethyl gasoline

EUCHARISTIC CONGRESS (international). *See* International Eucharistic congress

EUTHANASIA SOCIETY was the National Society for the Legalization of Euthanasia, formed January 14, 1938, in New York City with Reverend Charles Francis Potter as president, Dr. Harold Hays, secretary, and Charles Edward Nixdorff, treasurer. The society was incorporated as the Euthanasia Society of America on November 30, 1938.

EVANGELICAL AND REFORMED CHURCH was organized June 26, 1934, in Cleveland, Ohio, by the merging of the Reformed Church in the United States, organized by John Philip Boehm, October 15, 1725, in Falkner Swamp, Montgomery County, Pa., and the Evangelical Synod of North America, organized October 15, 1840, in Mehlville, St. Louis County, Mo. The first president of the new group was Dr. George Warren Richards, president of the Theological Seminary of the Reformed Church, Lancaster, Pa.

EVANGELICAL ASSOCIATION COUNCIL met at the house of John Walter, Bucks County, Pa., November 3, 1803, to found a separate ecclesiastical organization. The fourteen representatives present ordained Jacob Albright.

EVANGELICAL CHURCH was founded in 1800 by Jacob Albright. The first annual conference was held in Lebanon County, Pa., in November 1807. Albright was elected bishop. *(Ammon Stapleton—Flashlights on Evangelical History)*

EVANGELICAL CHURCH BUILDING was the Evangelical Church erected in 1816 in New Berlin, Pa. It was dedicated March 2, 1817. The Reverend John Dreisbach preached the dedicatory sermon. The church was 34 by 38 feet.

EVANGELICAL CHURCH GENERAL CONFERENCE convened on the property of Abraham Eyer, at the house of Martin Dreisbach, in Buffalo Valley, Union County, Pa., October 14-17, 1816, at which time the denomination took the name Evangelical Association. Twelve delegates attended.

THE FIRST

EVANGELICAL CONFERENCE was held at the house of Samuel Becker, November 15, 1807, in Mühlbach, Dauphin County (now Kleinfeltersville, Lebanon County), Pa. It was attended by all the officers of the church, 5 itinerant ministers, 3 local preachers, and 20 class leaders and exhorters. Jacob Albright was elected Bishop and George Miller an elder.

EVANGELICAL UNITED BRETHREN CHURCH was formed November 16, 1946, in Johnstown, Pa., by approximately 500 delegates representing 4,832 churches who united the Church of the United Brethren in Christ and the Evangelical Church. There were 9 active bishops. Bishop Arthur Raymond Clippinger of Dayton, Ohio was the senior bishop.

EVAPORATED MILK. *See* Milk: Evaporated milk

EVENING SCHOOL. *See* School: Evening school

EVOLUTION law (state), prohibiting the teaching of the theory of evolution, was proposed by John Washington Butler, passed by the Tennessee legislature, and signed March 23, 1925, by Governor Austin Peay. It provided that "it shall be unlawful for any teacher in any of the universities, normal and all other public schools of the state which are supported in whole or in part by the public school funds of the state to teach any theory that denies the story of the Divine creation of man as taught in the Bible, and to teach instead that man has descended from a lower order of animals." The first conviction under the act was that of John Thomas Scopes, who appealed the decision of the court. The Attorney General entered a *nolle prosse* which ended the proceedings. *(John Thomas Scopes vs. State of Tennessee, 154— Tenn. 105—1926)*

EXCESS PROFITS TAX. *See* Tax: Excess profits tax

EXCHANGE. *See* Brokerage

EXCHANGE AND SECURITIES COMMISSION. *See* Securities and exchange commission (U.S.)

EXCISE TAX. *See* Tax: Excise tax (federal)

EXCLUSION LAW. *See* Army exclusion law

EXECUTION
See also Capital punishment

    Army execution. *See* Army Execution

EXECUTION—*Continued*

Electrocution experiment was performed in Philadelphia, Pa., by Benjamin Franklin who described his findings in 1773 in a letter to Barbeau Dubourg and Thomas Francois Dalibard. Current from six Leyden jars was used to electrocute chickens, a ten-pound turkey, and a lamb.

Electrocution of a human being was that of William Kemmler, alias John Hart, on August 6, 1890, at Auburn Prison, Auburn, N.Y. The electric chair used was invented by Dr. Alphonse David Rockwell. An autopsy was performed three hours after the execution under the direction of Dr. Carlos Frederick MacDonald. The execution was in accordance with the law governing first-degree murder. Kemmler had been convicted of the murder of Matilda Ziegler, a crime committed on March 29, 1889. (*Report of Carlos F. MacDonald, M.D. on the Execution by Electricity of William Kemmler, Alias John Hart*)

Execution (federal) for slave trading took place at the Tombs prison, New York City, on February 21, 1862, when Nathaniel Gordon, a native of Portland, Me., was hanged. He was tried and convicted of piracy under the law of May 15, 1820, which defined slave trading as piracy. Gordon was the captain of the "Erie," a ship transporting 890 Negroes, 600 of whom were boys and girls, to a slave market. The U.S. "Mohican" stopped his ship about 50 miles off the African coast, released the captives in Liberia, and brought Gordon's ship to New York City, where his trial was held.

Execution (federal) for the killing of a Federal Bureau of Investigation agent took place at Sing Sing Prison, Ossining, N.Y., August 12, 1954, when Gerhard Puff was electrocuted. He was convicted of the killing of FBI agent Joseph Brock in a gun battle in New York City on July 26, 1952. Puff was wanted for participating in the November 23, 1951, robbery of $62,650 from the Johnson County National Bank and Trust Company of Prairie Village, Kan. He was confined fifteen months in the death house and his execution was postponed five times pending various appeals.

Execution for treason. *See* Treason: Citizen of the United States to be tried for treason, convicted, and hanged

Execution for treason in peacetime. *See* Treason: Execution for treason in peacetime

Execution in America was that of John Billington, one of the signers of the Pilgrims' compact, who was hanged in Plymouth, Mass., September 30, 1630. He was "arraigned, and both by grand and petie jurie found guilty of

willful murder, by plaine and notorious evidence, and was for the same accordingly executed. This, as it was ye first execution amongst them, so was it a matter of great sadness unto them. He way-laid a young man, one John Newcomin (about a former quarele), and shote him with a gune, whereof he dyed." (*Joseph Dillaway Sawyer—History of Pilgrims and Puritans*)

Execution of a woman took place at Sing Sing Prison, Ossining, N.Y., March 20, 1899, when Martha M. Place of Brooklyn, N.Y. was electrocuted for the murder, on February 7, 1898, in Brooklyn, N.Y., of her step-daughter Ida.

Execution of civilians. *See* Treaty: Treaty violation

Lethal gas execution was that of a Chinese, Gee Jon, on February 8, 1924, in Carson City, Nev. Gee Jon was convicted of killing a rival tong man. Lethal gas as a means of execution had been adopted by Nevada on March 28, 1921.

Witchcraft execution. *See* Witchcraft execution

EXECUTIVE COMMERCIAL POLICY COMMITTEE. *See* Commercial policy executive committee

EXECUTIVE ORDER (presidential). *See* Presidential executive order

EXHIBITION. *See* Fair

EXPEDITION
See also Discovery

Arctic expedition was made by Elisha Kent Kane and crew, who left New York City, May 31, 1853, in the "Advance." They arrived at Cape Constitution, where they remained for 21 months, being unable to free the boat which had become frozen in the ice pack. As disease broke out on board, the crew made a 1,000-mile trek to the nearest Eskimo village. (*William Elder— Biography of Elisha Kent Kane*)

Arctic expedition to seek the northwest passage for the £20,000 reward offered by Parliament for proofs of its existence, sailed March 1753 from Philadelphia, Pa. Captain Charles Swaine made a voyage in the "Argo," a sixty-ton schooner. He encountered ice off Cape Farewell, and entered Hudson's Strait in the latter part of June 1753. He returned in

November 1753. He made a second voyage the following year. *(Justin Winsor—A Narrative and Critical History of America)*

Astronomical expedition. *See* Astronomical expedition

Botanic scientific expedition. *See* Botanic scientific expedition

Expedition of Englishmen to cross the Alleghany Mountains began August 27, 1650, from Fort Henry, at the falls of the Appomattox River, Va., and returned September 4, 1650. The party consisted of Captain Abraham Wood and his servant Henry Newcombe; Edward Bland, merchant, and his servant Robert Farmer; Elias Pennant and Sackford Brewster; and two guides, Oyeocker, a Nottaway werowance (chief), and Pyancha, an Appamattuck war captain. *(Clarence Walworth Alvord and Lee Bidgood—First Explorations of the Trans-Alleghany Region by the Virginians)*

Expedition across the continent to the Pacific coast was undertaken by Captains Meriwether Lewis and William Clark, who left St. Louis, Mo., May 14, 1804, reached the mouth of the Columbia River November 8, 1805, and returned to St. Louis on September 23, 1806. The expedition consisted of 9 Kentucky men, 14 Army men, 2 French voyageurs, and a Negro servant. *(Elliot Coues—History of the Expedition Under the Command of Lewis and Clark)*

Exploration of the Grand Canyon of the Colorado, by a white man was made by Major John Wesley Powell, who left Green River City, above the head of the Colorado proper, on May 24, 1869, and emerged from the lower end of the Grand Canyon, August 29, 1869, with 5 of the 9 men who had started with him. The following year he was appointed chief of the U.S. Topographical and Geological Survey of the Colorado River of the West. (The discovery of the Grand Canyon was reported by Spanish explorers in 1540, and described by the Sitgreaves expedition in 1851, and in 1858 by the War Department, which explored navigable waters from the south, but which stopped at the foot of the canyon. *(John Wesley Powell—First Through The Grand Canyon)*

Naval expedition (colonial). *See* Navy: Naval expedition (colonial)

Polar expedition of which a woman was a member was the Peary Expedition. Josephine Peary, wife of the North Polar explorer Robert Edwin Peary, sailed with her husband June 6, 1891, in the "Kite." This expedition did not reach the Pole. The expedition which left on the "Roosevelt," July 6, 1908, located the North Pole on April 6, 1909, but the discovery was not announced until September 6, 1909. Both expeditions started from New York City. *(Josephine Diebitsch Peary—My Arctic Journal; A Year Among Ice Fields and Eskimos)*

Scientific expedition was outfitted by the Commonwealth of Massachusetts in 1761. John Winthrop, a physicist, went to Newfoundland in a vessel in the Provincial Service. His expenses were defrayed by the colonial government, and he observed for the second time the transit of Mercury. *(John Winthrop—Two Letters on the Parallax and Distance of the Sun)*

Scientific expedition fitted out by the United States Government was authorized by Congress May 14, 1836 (5 Stat.L.29). An appropriation of $150,000 was made for a surveying and exploring expedition to the Pacific Ocean and the South Sea. Instructions were received August 11, 1838. The expedition left Hampton Roads, Va., August 18, 1838, with Lieutenant Charles Wilkes in command, to explore the South Seas, and returned to New York City June 10, 1842. The explorers saw the Antarctic continent on January 16, 1840. *(Charles Wilkes—Narrative of the U.S. Exploring Expedition)*

EXPEDITIONARY FORCE (U.S.) *See* American expeditionary force: American Expeditionary Force

EXPERIMENT STATION (agricultural). *See* Agricultural experiment station: State agricultural experiment station

EXPERT INFANTRYMAN'S BADGE. *See* Medal: Expert Infantryman's Badge

EXPLOSION (atomic bomb). *See* Atomic bomb: Atomic bomb explosion

EXPLOSION TELECAST. *See* Television—Telecast: Atomic explosion telecast

EXPORT
See also under specific subjects, e.g., Animals, Cotton, Furs, Meat, etc.

Export report by the federal government covered the fiscal year ending September 30, 1791. The exports for the year amounted to $19,012,041, of which $18,500,000 was for domestic merchandise and $512,041 for foreign goods. The imports for the same period amounted to $29,200,000, an excess of imports over exports of $10,187,959.

THE FIRST

EXPORT—*Continued*

Exports from the United States to exceed the imports were for the fiscal year ending September 30, 1811, and amounted to an excess of $7,916,832 over imports. The exports of domestic merchandise were $45,294,042, and for foreign merchandise $16,022,790, making a grand total of exports of $61,316,832 whereas the imports amounted to $53,400,000.

EXPORT-IMPORT BANK. *See* Bank: Export-import bank

EXPOSITION. *See* under specific type of exposition, e.g., Automobile show, Aviation —Expositions and Meets, Dog show, Fair, etc.

EXPOSURE METER. *See* Photography: Camera exposure meter

EXPRESS SERVICE was organized February 23, 1839, by William Frederick Harnden of Boston, Mass., who arranged for delivery service between Boston and New York. The service was advertised to begin on March 4, 1839. The first shipment was a few suitcases. Shipments were made via the Boston and Providence Railway and Long Island Sound Steamboat. (*Alexander Lovett Stimson—History of Express Companies and the Origin of American Railroads*)

EXTENSION COURSE. *See* College: College extension courses

EXTENSION SUMMER MEETING. *See* College: University extension summer meeting

EXTENSION TRAINING WORK (agricultural). *See* Agricultural appropriation

EXTINGUISHER. *See* Fire extinguisher

EXTRADITION

Extradition was established by the New England Confederation of 1643, which provided for the extradition of criminals between the provinces of Massachusetts, Connecticut, Plymouth, and New Haven.

Extradition treaty with a foreign country was the Treaty of Amity, Commerce and Navigation (8 Stat.L.116), popularly known as the Jay Treaty, with Great Britain, signed in London, England, November 19, 1794. Article XXVII provided for the apprehension and delivery of persons charged with certain crimes. The signatory for the United States was John Jay, and for Great Britain, William Wyndham Grenville, Baron Grenville of Wotton, one of His Majesty's Privy Council and His Maj-

THE FIRST

esty's Principal Secretary of State for Foreign Affairs. (*Treaties and Other International Acts of the United States of America—Document 16*)

EYE

Artificial eyes were manufactured by Pierre Gougelman in 1851 at Van Dam Street, New York City, from glass imported from France. The business is conducted by his descendants under the name of Mager & Gougelman, Inc. It was originally believed that artificial eyes offered their wearers new vision.

Eye bank was opened May 9, 1944, through the efforts of Dr. Richard Townley Paton of the Manhattan Eye, Ear and Throat Hospital and Dr. John McLean of the New York Hospital. These hospitals cooperated to establish the joint project at the New York Hospital, New York City. Nineteen other hospitals in the metropolitan area offered cooperation in obtaining and sending eyes to the bank.

Eye conservation class for the education of school children with seriously defective vision opened April 3, 1913, at the Thornton Street School, Boston, Mass. Helen L. Smith was the teacher.

Identification system, based upon the pattern formed by the veins and arteries of the retina of the human eye and the relation of the four veins—the superior temporal, the inferior temporal, the superior nasal, and the inferior nasal—with their various branches, was devised by Dr. Isidore Goldstein, ophthalmic surgeon of Mount Sinai Hospital, New York City, in collaboration with Dr. Carleton Simon, former Deputy Police Commissioner of New York. The system was presented before the annual convention of the International Association of Chiefs of Police, July 7, 1935, in Atlantic City, N.J.

EYE INFIRMARY. *See* Hospital: Eye infirmary

EYEGLASS BIFOCALS. *See* Lens: Bifocal contact lens; Lens: Eyeglass bifocals

FACSIMILE BROADCAST. *See* Radio facsimile transmission: Facsimile high-speed transmission

FACSIMILE TRANSMISSION. *See* Radio facsimile transmission

FACTORY

Air-conditioned factory to be built was the Gray Manufacturing Company's Gastonia, N.C., plant, erected in 1905 with an air-conditioning system manufactured by Stuart W. Cramer of

THE FIRST

Charlotte, N.C. This equipment drew in fresh air from out-of-doors, filtered and washed it, heated or cooled it, corrected any variation in humidity, and completely changed the air in the factory about five times an hour.

Air-conditioned factory with temperature and humidity control was the Brooklyn, N.Y., plant of the Sackett-Wilhelms Lithographing and Publishing Company, which in 1902 installed a 30-ton fan-cooled dehumidifying unit designed by Willis Haviland Carrier. Its primary purpose was to check the expansion and contraction of paper caused by varying weather conditions. *(Margaret Ingels—Father of Air Conditioning, Willis Haviland Carrier)*

Factories operated by the United States Government in peacetime were a jersey cloth mill formerly operated by the Famb Knitting Company and a fairly large hall called Forester's Hall at Millville, Mass., in which the Federal Emergency Relief Administration of Massachusetts established sewing and stock rooms. The project was started June 4, 1934, by authority of Joseph P. Carney, Emergency Relief Administrator of Massachusetts, who detailed Thomas E. Wye as factory supervisor to organize and start the project. The products were not sold but were distributed to different welfare divisions of the cities and towns in Massachusetts.

Factory-built building. *See* Building: Building built inside a factory

Steam-heated factory was the Burlington Woolen Company at Winooski River, Burlington, Vt., built in 1846. The factory, sold at auction October 20, 1852, was described in an advertisement in the Burlington *Free Press:* "The factory building and dye houses were heated by steam conducted through iron pipes in the most modern and approved manner. This modern and up to date mill was built six years ago." The mill is now owned by the American Woolen Company, Inc.

Windowless factory was erected in Fitchburg, Mass., in 1930. The plant, one story high and consisting of one room, was illuminated by hundreds of 1,000-watt electric lamps containing a small percentage of healthful ultraviolet rays. The walls and ceilings were painted orange, blue, green, and white to increase visibility, and the floors were jet black. The building also lacked skylights. It was ventilated by a system that circulated fresh air of the proper temperature which had been washed, heated, and humidified throughout the building. Ten million cubic feet of air were changed every ten minutes. The walls were soundproof as cork pads were used to reduce the noise inside. The building was constructed by the

THE FIRST

Austin Company of Cleveland, Ohio, for the Simonds Saw and Steel Company at a cost of $1,500,000.

FACTORY INSPECTION LAW. *See* Labor law: Factory inspection law

FACTORY MUTUAL INSURANCE. *See* Insurance: Mutual fire insurance company

FACTORY STANDARDIZATION OF PRODUCTION by the United States Government was required in 1813, when a contract specifying interchangeable parts was drawn up between the United States Government (Callender Irvine, Commissary General of the United States) and Colonel Simeon North of Berlin, Conn., on April 16, 1813, in Middletown, Conn. The contract, for 20,000 pistols at $7 each to be produced within 5 years, stipulated that "component parts of the pistols are to correspond so exactly that any limb or part of one pistol may be fitted to any other pistol of the 20,000." Colonel North established his pistol manufactory in 1810 in Staddle Hill, a suburb of Middletown. The factory produced about 10,000 pistols a year. *(Simeon Newton Dexter North —Simeon North, First Official Pistol Maker of the United States)*

FAIR

Agricultural fair was held October 1, 1810, in Pittsfield, Mass. It was promoted by Elkanah Watson and was known as the Berkshire Cattle Show. There were 383 sheep, 20 bulls, and 15 yoke of oxen entered for premiums amounting to $70. After the fair, there was a grand procession a half mile long of sixty yoke of prime oxen. *(Elkanah Watson— History of the Rise, Progress and Existing State of the Berkshire Agricultural Society)*

Annual fair was authorized by the director and council of New Netherlands on September 30, 1641. They "ordained that henceforth there shall be held annually at Fort Amsterdam a Cattle Fair on the 15th of October; and a fair for Hogs on the 1st of November. Whosoever hath any things to sell or to buy can regulate himself accordingly." *(Laws and Ordinances of New Netherlands 1638-1674)*

Industrial exposition of an international character was held in New York City in 1853, modeled after the World's Fair (1851) of London, England. On March 11, 1852, the "Association for the Exhibition of the Industry of all Nations" was chartered. On March 17, 1852, the directors elected Theodore Sedgwick president. The exposition was held at Reservoir Square, 40th-42d Streets between Fifth and Sixth Avenues, in a specially erected two-story building with an area of 249,691 square feet. The exposition was opened by

THE FIRST

FAIR—*Continued*
President Franklin Pierce, July 14, 1853. The
building was destroyed by fire October 5, 1858.
(Illustrated Record of the Exposition)

Manufacturers' fair was held October 24,
1828, under the auspices of the American
Institute in the Masonic Hall, New York
City. The American Institute in the City of
New York was incorporated May 2, 1829,
to encourage and promote domestic industry
in the United States in agriculture, commerce,
manufacuring, and the arts. *(New York As
It Is in 1833)*

Woman's World Fair was held in Chicago, Ill., April 18-25, 1925, at which time
women's progress was shown in seventy industries. At the World's Fair of 1893 in
Chicago, Ill., women's handicraft had been
featured only at the sewing exhibit. The
Woman's World Fair was officially opened by
Mrs. Calvin Coolidge.

**FAIR TRADE ADVERTISING COM-
MITTEE.** *See* Advertising organization

FAIR TRADE LAW. *See* Price regulation
law

FALLOUT SHELTER. *See* Building:
House with a built-in nuclear bomb shelter

FAN (electric). *See* Electric fan

FARM (agricultural experiment farm). *See*
Agricultural experiment station: Agricultural experiment farm

FARM BOARD (federal) met July 15,
1929, and consisted of eight members appointed by the President and confirmed by
the Senate, in addition to the Secretary of
Agriculture, who was an ex officio member.
It was organized "to protect, control and
stabilize the currents of interstate and foreign commerce" by minimizing speculation,
by preventing inefficient and wasteful distribution, by encouraging farmers' organizations,
and by preventing surpluses through orderly
production. The Agricultural Marketing Act
(46 Stat.L.11) passed by Congress June 15,
1929, authorized $500 million to be used as
a revolving fund. The board was later designated as the Farm Credit Administration.
*(U.S. Federal Farm Board—First Annual
Report)*

FARM BOOK. *See* Agricultural book:
Agricultural book

FARM BUREAU, a department of a city
chamber of commerce working in combination
with the cooperative agencies—the U.S. Depart-

THE FIRST

ment of Agriculture, the state college of agriculture, county and local farmers' organizations
—was the Broome County Farm Bureau, established March 20, 1911, in Binghamton, N.Y.
John H. Barron began work in Broome County,
N.Y., as an agent of the U.S. Department of
Agriculture, cooperating with the State College
of Agriculture at Cornell University, the Binghamton Chamber of Commerce, and the Delaware, Lackawanna and Western Railway. The
agent was given an office with the Chamber of
Commerce and made manager of a new department of this organization which was called a
farm bureau. On May 24, 1913, an act appropriating $25,000 for assisting the farm bureaus
was passed by New York State, the first state
to pass an act of this kind. *(William Allison
Lloyd—Status and Results of County Agent
Work)*

**FARM CREDIT ADMINISTRATION
(U.S.)** was authorized March 27, 1933, by
executive order of President Franklin Delano
Roosevelt under power granted by the Seventy-
third Congress, special session "Economy Act."
The administration "to provide a complete
and coordinated credit system for agriculture
by making available to farmers long-term and
short-term credit" was organized by executive
order No. 6,084, March 27, 1933, with Henry
Morgenthau, Jr., as the first administrator.
Several agencies were grouped under this
department.

FARM JOURNAL. *See* Agricultural journal

FARM LOAN BOARD (federal) was
created in the Department of the Treasury to
administer the Federal Farm Loan Act, approved July 17, 1916 (39 Stat.L.360). The first
federal land bank was chartered March 1, 1917,
and the first national farm loan association
March 27, 1917. The first farm loan commissioner was George William Norris, who took
the oath of office August 7, 1916. Executive
Order No. 6084 of March 27, 1933, effective
May 27, 1933, transferred its functions to the
Farm Credit Administration. *(U.S. Federal
Loan Bureau—First Annual Report from Organization to November 30, 1937)*

FARM SOCIETY. *See* Agricultural society

FARMER LABOR PARTY was organized
at a convention assembled June 12, 1920, in
Chicago, Ill., and emanated from the National
Labor Party, which was formed in 1919. The
first presidential candidate was Parley Parker
Christensen of Utah and the vice presidential
candidate, Maximilian Sebastian Hayes of
Ohio. They received approximately 265,000
votes.

FARMERS' INSTITUTE
Farmers' institute held by a land grant
agricultural college off its campus was spon-

THE FIRST

sored by Iowa State College, Ames, Iowa, at Cedar Falls, Iowa, on December 20, 1870. The institute course continued five days and consisted of day and evening lectures on stock breeding and management, fruit culture, farm accounts, and kindred topics, conducted by George William Jones, professor of mathematics; James Mathews, professor of pomology; and Adonijah Strong Welch, president of the college. Other institutes were held the same year at Council Bluffs, Washington, and Muscatine, Iowa. *(Homestead and Western Farm Journal. December 1870)*

Farmers' institute sponsored by a college was held November 14, 1868, by the Kansas State Agricultural College, now the Kansas State College of Agriculture and Applied Science, at the Riley County Courthouse, Manhattan, Kan. Local arrangements for the institute were made by the Riley County Agricultural Society.

Farmers' institute sponsored by a state was held by the Massachusetts State Board of Agriculture in Springfield, Mass. The institute opened December 8, 1863, and continued for four days. Lectures and discussions pertaining to agriculture occupied the meetings. *(Jay Brownlee Davidson—A Study of the Extension Service)*

FARRIERS' COURSE IN A COLLEGE was presented in 1930 by Jack MacAllan at the Michigan State College, East Lansing, Mich., as part of a course in horse management. It was open only to students enrolled either in the sixteen-week short course or the four-year course in the School of Agriculture. In 1946, a special farriers' course was offered under Jack MacAllan in the winter term to those who wished to train as specialists.

FARRIER'S GUIDE was *The Husband-Man's Guide, in Four Parts—Part first, containing many excellent rules for setting and planting. Part second, choice physical receipts for divers dangerous distempers in men, women and children. Part third, the experienced farrier. Part fourth containing rare receipts.* The book contained 107 pages and was printed in Boston, Mass., in 1710 by John Allen for Eleazer Phillips.

FASHION PLATE. *See* Periodical: Magazine containing a fashion plate

FASHION SHOW TELECAST. *See* Television—Telecast: Fashion show telecast

FASTENING
Hookless fastening was invented by Whitcomb L. Judson of Chicago, Ill., who obtained patent No. 557,207 on March 31, 1896 (on a

THE FIRST

fastening for shoes) comprising two metal chains which could be fastened together by movement of a slider. They were first manufactured in 1893 by the Automatic Hook and Eye Company of Meadville, Pa., through the efforts of Colonel Lewis Walker.

Hookless fastening for universal use was invented about 1906 by Gideon Sundback of Hoboken N.J., who obtained patent No. 1,063,378 on April 29, 1913 on "separable fasteners." This fastener has been improved upon by patents No. 1,219,881 and No. 1,243,458, which Sundback obtained on March 20, 1917, and October 16, 1917, respectively. These patents are controlled by the Hookless Fastener Company of Meadville, Pa., manufacturers of the Talon Slide Fastener. *(Talon Hookless Fastener Co.)*

Hooks and eyes were successfully manufactured in 1836 in Waterbury, Conn., by Holmes & Hotchkiss. *(Henry Bronson—History of Waterbury)*

FATHER'S DAY. *See* Holiday: Father's day

FATHOMETER, a device to measure the depth of water, was invented by Herbert Grove Dorsey of the U.S. Coast and Geodetic Survey, who received patent No. 1,667,540 on April 24, 1928. By means of a series of electrical sounds and light signals, the depth of water could be easily ascertained.

FEATURE MOVING PICTURE. *See* Moving picture: Foreign feature film exhibited

FEDERAL ALCOHOL CONTROL ADMINISTRATION was authorized December 4, 1933, by executive order No. 6,474 issued by President Franklin Delano Roosevelt. Joseph Hodges Choate, Jr., was appointed director, Harris Emanuel Willingham assistant director, and Edward George Lowry, Jr., counsel.

FEDERAL BOARD OF MEDIATION AND CONCILIATION. *See* Arbitration: Federal board of mediation and conciliation

FEDERAL BUILDING. *See* Building: Building erected by the government in Washington, D.C.

FEDERAL BUREAU OF INVESTIGATION TRAINING SCHOOL. *See* Police: Police training school

FEDERAL CEMETERY. *See* Cemetery: Federal cemetery in the United States to contain graves of both Union and Confederate soldiers; Cemetery: National cemeteries

FEDERAL COMMUNICATIONS COMMISSION

Federal Communications Commission was created by act approved June 19, 1934 (48 Stat.L.1064) to provide for the regulation of interstate and foreign commerce by wire or radio and to centralize these duties and responsibilities with a view to more effective supervision of communication. A committee of seven was appointed July 11, 1934. The first chairman was Eugene Octave Sykes, who served until March 11, 1935. Successors to the original committee were to be appointed for seven years, unless appointed to fill an unexpired term.

Federal Communications Commission woman member was Frieda B. Hennock, named by President Harry S. Truman to succeed Commissioner Clifford Judkins Durr, who resigned. She was sworn in July 6, 1948, in Washington, D.C.

International broadcasting license. *See* Radio license: International broadcasting license

FEDERAL COUNCIL OF THE CHURCHES OF CHRIST IN AMERICA

was organized in Philadelphia, Pa., December 2, 1908. The first president of the Council was Bishop Eugene Russell Hendrix of the Methodist Episcopal Church. The first executive secretary was Elias Benjamin Sanford. The constitution of the council, which had been ratified prior to the first meeting by the constituent denominations, provided for approximately four hundred official members named directly by the cooperating denominations. They were appointed to attend the first meeting held December 2, 1908, in Philadelphia, and were designated as charter members. (*Elias Benjamin Sanford—Origin and History of the Federal Council of the Churches of Christ in America*)

FEDERAL CREDIT UNION ACT

was approved June 26, 1934 (48 Stat.L.1216) "to establish a Federal Credit Union System, to establish a further market for securities of the United States and to make more available to people of small means credit for provident purposes through a national system of cooperative credit, thereby helping to stabilize the credit structure of the United States." Charter No. 1 was granted to the Morris Sheppard Federal Credit Union of Texarkana, Tex., named in honor of the sponsor of the law, which held its organization meeting, October 1, 1934.

See also Bank legislation

FEDERAL CROP INSURANCE CORPORATION

was established by the Federal Crop Insurance Act, part of the Agricultural Adjustment Act of 1938 (52 Stat.L.72), approved February 16, 1938, to provide for insuring wheat yields against natural hazards such as drought, flood, hail, winter-kill, lightning, insect infestation and plant diseases. The directors were Milburn Lincoln Wilson, Jesse Washington Tapp, and Rudolph Martin Evans. Roy M. Green was manager of the corporation. The first application was signed May 18, 1938, by M. L. Purvines, Panhandle, Tex., and the first indemnity payment was made April 14, 1939, to John F. Biggs, Floydada, Floyd County, Tex., a payment of $129.32 to compensate him for the total loss of his share in a 52-acre wheat crop.

FEDERAL DEPOSIT INSURANCE CORPORATION

was created June 16, 1933 (48 Stat.L.162) by the Banking Act of 1933, "to provide for the safer and more effective use of the assets of banks, to regulate interbank control, to prevent the undue diversion of funds into speculative operations." The management of the corporation was vested in a board of three directors, one of whom was the Comptroller of the Currency. The first board was composed of chairman Walter Joseph Cummings of Chicago, Elbert Gladstone Bennett of Salt Lake City, and James Francis Thaddeus O'Connor, Comptroller of the Currency. The first official meeting of the board of directors was held September 11, 1933. The system went into effect January 1, 1934. The first payment was one of $125,000 to 1,789 depositors of the Fond du Lac State Bank of East Peoria, Ill. The bank suspended business May 28, 1934, and receivership became final on June 25, 1935. Lydia Lobsiger, a widow, received the first insurance check, covering her deposit, July 3, 1934.

See also Bank legislation

FEDERAL EMERGENCY RELIEF ADMINISTRATION

was created by the Federal Emergency Relief Act of 1933 (48 Stat. L.55), approved May 12, 1933, "to provide for cooperation by the federal government with the several states and territories, and the District of Columbia in relieving the hardships and suffering caused by unemployment." The Federal Emergency Relief Administration became operative ten days after approval of the act. The first Federal Emergency Relief Administrator was Harry Lloyd Hopkins, appointed by the President with the advice and consent of the Senate. He took office May 22, 1933.

FEDERAL FARM BOARD. *See* Farm board (federal)

FEDERAL FARM CREDIT ADMINISTRATION (U.S.) *See* Farm Credit Administration (U.S.)

THE FIRST

FEDERAL FARM LOAN BOARD. *See* Farm loan board (federal)

FEDERAL FISH HATCHERY. *See* Fish hatchery (federal)

FEDERAL FISH PROTECTION OF-FICE. *See* Fish protection: Fish protection office (federal)

FEDERAL FOREIGN AID BILL was "an act for the relief of the citizens of Venezuela" (2 Stat.L.730), enacted May 8, 1812. An appropriation of $50,000 was made to enable the President to obtain such provisions as he should deem advisable for the relief of the citizens of Venezuela "who have suffered by the late earthquake."

FEDERAL FREE TRADE POLICY. *See* Free Trade Policy (federal)

FEDERAL GRANT-IN-AID TO STATES FOR ROADS. *See* Road: Federal grant-in-aid to states for roads

FEDERAL HIGHWAY. *See* Road: Federal highway

FEDERAL HOME LOAN BANK BOARD was established July 22, 1932, by the Federal Home Loan Bank Act (47 Stat.L.725) for the purpose of establishing and supervising the Federal Home Loan Banks as a permanent credit reserve system for savings and loan associations and similar local thrift and home financing institutions and for savings banks and insurance companies making long-term home mortgage loans. The board consisted of five members, Franklin William Fort, chairman, Dr. John Matthew Gries, William Edward Best, Nathan Adams, and Morton Bodfish, who took the oath of office and held the first meeting August 9, 1932.

FEDERAL JUDGE IMPEACHED. *See* Impeachment: Impeachment of a federal judge

FEDERAL LABOR ADVISORY BOARD. *See* Labor: Labor advisory board (federal)

FEDERAL LAW COMPILATION. *See* Law book: Law book containing the federal laws

FEDERAL MOTOR CARRIER LEGISLATION. *See* Automobile legislation: Federal motor carrier legislation

FEDERAL NARCOTIC SANATORIUM. *See* Narcotic: Narcotic sanatorium (federal) for drug addicts

THE FIRST

FEDERAL PENITENTIARY. *See* Prison: Penitentiary building (national)

FEDERAL PLAY PRESENTATION. *See* Play (drama): Theatrical presentation sponsored by the federal government

FEDERAL RADIO COMMISSION. *See* Radio commission (U.S.)

FEDERAL REGISTER. *See* Periodical: Magazine of the United States government

FEDERAL RESERVE SYSTEM. *See* Bank: Federal reserve system

FEDERAL ROAD AGENCY. *See* Road: Federal road agency

FEDERAL SAVINGS AND LOAN ASSOCIATION was authorized by the Home Owners Loan Act of June 13, 1933 (48 Stat. L.128), to provide a convenient place for the investment of small or large sums and to lend money on first mortgages on homes in the area in which the association is located. The first association was the First Federal Savings and Loan Association of Miami, Fla., which received Charter No. 1 on August 8, 1933. The Federal Savings and Loan Insurance Corporation, created June 27, 1934 (48 Stat.L.1255), was organized to insure investors against loss up to $5,000, which amount was later increased by law to $10,000.

FEDERAL SECURITY AGENCY was established by the President's Reorganization Plan 1 on April 25, 1939 (53 Stat.L.1424), to place under one administration the agencies which had as their major purpose the promotion of social and economic security, educational opportunity, and health. The units were the U.S. Employment Service, the Office of Education, the Public Health Service, the National Youth Administration, the Social Security Board, and the Civilian Conservation Corps. The first administrator was Paul Vories McNutt who took office on July 13, 1939, and who served until September 13, 1945. His salary was $12,000 a year. On April 11, 1953, the Federal Security Agency became the Department of Health, Education and Welfare.

FEDERAL SHIP. *See* Ship: Ship constructed by the federal government

FEDERAL SURPLUS RELIEF CORPORATION was incorporated under the laws of the state of Delaware, October 4, 1933. The incorporators were Federal Emergency Relief Administrator Harry Lloyd Hopkins, president; Secretary of Agriculture Henry Agard Wallace, vice president; and Federal Emergency

FEDERAL SURPLUS RELIEF COR-PORATION—Continued

Administrator of Public Works Harold Le Claire Ickes, treasurer. (*U.S. Agriculture Department—Surplus Marketing Administration—First Report October 4, 1933 to December 31, 1934*)

FEDERAL TRADE COMMISSION

Federal Trade Commission came into existence September 26, 1914, by Act of Congress (38 Stat.L.717), "an act to create a Federal Trade Commission, to define its powers and duties." The commission was organized to regulate commerce and prohibit unlawful means of obtaining trade March 16, 1915, when five commissioners, George Rublee, Edward Nash Hurley, Will H. Parry, Joseph Edward Davies, and William Julius Harris, were appointed, each at an annual salary of $10,000. (*Gerald Carl Henderson—The Federal Trade Commission*)

Federal Trade Commission trade practice conference was held October 3, 1919, in Omaha, Neb., for the creamery industry. Representatives from six states met with Commissioner William Byron Colver to discuss unfair practice complaints in the industry.

FEDERAL TRANSPORTATION CO-ORDINATION. See Transportation coordination: Transportation coordination (federal)

FEDERAL WOMEN EMPLOYEES. See Woman: Women to become federal government employees

FEDERAL WORKS AGENCY was established by President Franklin Delano Roosevelt July 1, 1939, under authority of act of April 25, 1939 (53 Stat.L.1427, Reorganization Plan No. 1), as a consolidation of five governmental public works units, the Public Buildings Administration, the Public Roads Administration, the Public Works Administration, the Works Projects Administration, and the United States Housing Authority. The first Federal Works Administrator was John Michael Carmody, who received $12,000 per annum.

FEDERATION OF ORGANIZED TRADES AND LABOR UNIONS. See Labor union: Labor union of importance

FELLOWSHIP

Fellowship awarded a woman was the Sage Fellowship in Entomology and Botany, granted June 19, 1884, to Harriet Elizabeth Grotecloss by Cornell University, Ithaca, N.Y. The fellowship had a stipend of $400 per year payable in six installments and provided free tuition for graduate study.

Fellowship (graduate) awarded by a women's college was offered the graduating class of Bryn Mawr College, Bryn Mawr, Pa. The first award was made June 6, 1889, to Emily Greene Balch of Boston, Mass., for "prosecuting sociological studies."

Resident fellowship for women awarded by a women's college was offered by Bryn Mawr College, Bryn Mawr, Pa., which established five resident fellowships in 1884, prior to the actual opening of the college. The recipients, who received free tuition, a furnished room, and $350 annually, were Jane M. Bancroft, in history; Katherine Augusta Gage, in Greek; Mary Gwinn, in English; Effie A. Southworth, in biology and Ella C. Williams, in mathematics.

FELT HAT. See Hat: Soft felt hats for women

FELT manufacturing mechanical process was invented by Thomas Robinson Williams of Newport, R.I. in 1820. The wool is carded and placed in layers until the desired thickness is obtained, the outside rolls being the finest in texture. The mass is placed between rollers, partly immersed in water, and is beaten, pressed, and given an oscillating movement at the same time. Dyeing and finishing complete the process.

FENCING

Fencing champion to win three titles in one year was Charles G. Bothner of the New York Athletic Club, who won three amateur fencing titles—foil, épee, and saber—on May 1, 1897, at the Fencers Club, New York City.

Fencing league (national) was the Amateur Fencers League of America, organized May 6, 1891. The first officers were Dr. Graeme M. Hammond, president; Charles Tatham, vice president; and W. Scott O'Connor, secretary and treasurer, all of New York City. The first competition was held in 1892. The winners were W. Scott O'Connor of the Fencers Club (men's foils) and Dr. B. F. O'Connor and R. O. Haubold of the New York Athletic Club (dueling swords and sabers, respectively).

Intercollegiate fencing championship competition was held by the International Fencing Association on May 5, 1894, at the Racquet & Tennis Club, New York City. Harvard defeated Columbia five matches to four and won the silver challenge cup. Yale, the only other entry in the competition, withdrew after an accident to one of the team. Fitzhugh Townsend of Columbia had the highest individual score.

International fencing championship competition was held at the Racquet Club, Washington, D.C., on November 18-19, 1921. The

United States team defeated Great Britain 13 to 3 the first day. The U.S. team lost 10 to 4 on the second day. The finals were held November 21, 1921 at the Hotel Astor, New York City, the score being 8 to 8. The United States won 25 of the 46 matches to win the Colonel Robert M. Thompson International Trophy.

FENCING BOOK was Edward Blackwell's *A Compleat System of Fencing; or the art of defence, in the use of the small sword; wherein the most necessary parts thereof are plainly laid down; chiefly for gentlemen, promoters and lovers of that science in North America*, printed in 1734 by William Parks, Williamsburg, Va. It was based on Henry Blackwell's *The English Fencing Master*, published in London in 1705. (*Robert William Henderson—Early American Sport*)

FERMIUM. *See* Element: Element 100

FERRIS WHEEL was invented in 1892 by George Washington Gale Ferris, stimulated by a prize for an attraction like the Eiffel Tower of Paris. It was erected on the Midway at the Columbian Exposition in Chicago, Ill., in 1893. It consisted of 36 cars, each capable of holding 60 passengers. The highest point of the wheel was 264 feet. The total weight of the wheels and cars was 2,100 tons, of the levers and machinery 2,200 tons, and of the passengers per trip 150 tons. (*Cassier's Magazine, July 1894. "The Ferris and Other Big Wheels"*)

FERRYBOAT
Double-deck ferryboat was launched October 25, 1888, at the Delmater Iron Works, Newburgh, N.Y. She was called the "Bergen" and plied across the Hudson River from New York City to Hoboken, N.J. She was 203 feet in length and 62 feet wide with a 10-foot draft, and was first piloted by Captain G. Beckwith.

Double-deck ferryboat with the propeller-type steel hull was the "Hamburg," built in 1891 by Thomas S. Marvel & Company of Newburgh, N.Y. She weighed 1,266 tons gross, 833 tons net, was 219 feet long, 40 feet wide, with a 16-foot draft, and cost $180,843.02. Passengers could not be taken on or discharged from the upper deck. In 1905 the ferry was altered so that both the upper and lower levels could be used for receiving and discharging passengers. The ferry plied between Hoboken, N.J., and New York City. (*Harry J. Smith and John M. Emery—The Romance of the Hoboken Ferry*)

Ferry (aerial). *See* Bridge: Aerial ferry

Ferryboat built exclusively for motor vehicle transportation was the "Governor Moore," a diesel-electric ferry placed in service November 8, 1926. She was built by the New

York Shipbuilding Company of Camden, N.J., from plans conceived by Eads Johnson. Five other boats were built in 1926, each with capacity for 46 automobiles. The boats, which were operated by Electric Ferries, Inc., originally plied between 23rd Street, New York City, and Edgewater, N.J., and 23rd Street, New York City, and Weehawken, N.J. (*Motorship. December 1932*)

Municipally owned ferryboats were placed in operation in New York City, October 25, 1905, between Whitehall Street, Manhattan and St. George, Staten Island. They were under the jurisdiction of the Department of Docks up to July 1, 1918. (*Records in Department of Plants and Structures, New York City*)

Steam-propelled ferryboat was the "Juliana," operated October 11, 1811, by John Stevens and his son, Robert Livingston Stevens. She plied between Hoboken, N.J., and New York City.

Steel-hull ferryboat was the "Lackawanna," built in 1881 at Newburgh, N.Y. by Ward Stanton at a cost of $76,000. She weighed 822 gross tons, 645 net tons, and was 200 feet long, 35 feet wide, with a 13-foot draft. The boat plied between Hoboken, N.J., and New York City. (*Harry J. Smith and John M. Emery—The Romance of the Hoboken Ferry*)

Streamlined ferryboat was the "Kalakala" (the name is taken from Chinook, is pronounced Kah-lock'ah-lah, and means "Flying Bird"). She was 276 feet long, had a beam of 55 feet 8 inches and a draft of 13 feet, and was designed to carry 2,000 passengers and 110 automobiles. She was 97.75 per cent steel in construction and was built at the Lake Washington Shipyards at Houghton, Wash. She was first placed in commercial operation on July 4, 1935, by the Puget Sound Navigation Company, Seattle, Wash., between Seattle and Bremerton, Wash., on Puget Sound, under the command of Captain Wallace H. Mangan.

FERTILIZER (artificial) was developed by Professor James Jay Mapes of Newark, N.J., who experimented in 1847 with fertilizers on his 20-acre farm at Newark, N.J. He applied for a patent in 1849 on a superphosphate of lime made from charred bone (waste products of sugar refineries) to which were added sulphate of ammonia and Peruvian guano. Patent No. 26,196 was granted November 22, 1859. (*Chemical Industries. October 1937*)

FERTILIZER LAW (state) was passed March 16, 1871 (Chap. 35) by Delaware. The law was unworkable and was amended April 8, 1881 (Chap. 348) and several times later.

FEVER THERAPY INTERNATIONAL CONFERENCE. *See* Medical congress: Fever Therapy International Conference

FEVER TREATISE (typhus). *See* Medical book: Typhus fever treatise

FIBERGLAS. *See* Suture: Fiberglas sutures

FIBERGLAS AUTOMOBILE. *See* Automobile: Plastic laminated fiberglas body sports car

FICTION MAGAZINE. *See* Periodical: All-fiction pulp magazine

FIELD HOSPITAL. *See* Hospital: Army field hospital

FIELD HOSPITAL AUTOMOBILE (X-ray). *See* Automobile: Field hospital automobile with X-ray equipment

FIELD RANGE. *See* Army field range

FIELDING CAGE. *See* Baseball batting and fielding cage

FIFTY-DOLLAR GOLD PIECES. *See* Money: Fifty-dollar gold pieces minted by the United States

FIGHT. *See* Prize fight

FIGHTER AIRPLANE. *See* Aviation—Airplane: Fighter airplane

FIGURE GLASS (stained). *See* Glass: Stained figure glass

FIGURE SKATING. *See* Skating tournament: Figure skating international championship tournament

FIGURE SKATING CHAMPION. *See* Ice skating champion: American world figure skating champion

FIGURE SKATING OLYMPIC CHAMPIONSHIP. *See* Olympic games: Figure skating Olympic champion

FILE FACTORY
File factory (hand cutting) to manufacture files was started by Broadmeadow & Company in Pittsburgh, Pa., in 1829. The files were made by hand. With this exception, file making in the United States was practically unknown until 1839.

File factory (machine cutting) to attain success was the Nicholson File Company, which was organized in Providence, R.I., in 1864 to manufacture files by machine. This company used a machine for cutting files which was patented by William Nicholson of Providence, R.I., April 5, 1864 (patent No. 42,216).

FILE MANUFACTURING MACHINE was invented by Morris B. Belknap in 1812 in Greenfield, Mass. As far as is known, the machine was not a success.

FILIBUSTER. *See* Congress (U.S.)—House of Representatives: Filibuster of "dilatory tactics"; Congress (U.S.)—Senate: Senate filibuster

FILM. *See* Photographic film

FILM CAMERA. *See* Camera: Roll film camera

FILM DEVELOPING MACHINE. *See* Photography: Film developing machine

FILTRATION (WATER) SYSTEM. *See* Water purification: Municipal filtration system

FINANCE COMPANY. *See* Automobile finance company; Business: Installment finance company

FINANCIAL CORNER. *See* Brokerage: Financial "corner"

FINANCIAL NEWS AGENCY. *See* News agency: Financial news agency

FINE ARTS DEPARTMENT
Fine arts department in a college was the School of Fine Arts, Yale University, New Haven, Conn., established in 1864. In 1869, John Ferguson Weir was appointed Professor of Painting and Design and the school formally opened with four students. Certificates were given to those who completed the three-year course, until 1891, when upon the fulfillment of more advanced requirements Josephine Miles Lewis received a Bachelor of Fine Arts (B.F.A.) degree.

Fine arts department in a college to grant degrees was the College of Fine Arts, Syracuse University, Syracuse, N.Y., established June 24, 1873. Dr. George Fisk Comfort was the first dean of the College of Fine Arts.

FINE ARTS SOCIETY. *See* Art organization: Art organization

FINGERPRINT SOCIETY

Fingerprint society (international) was the International Association for Criminal Identification, formed October 9, 1915, in Oakland, Calif. Harry Howard Caldwell of the Oakland Police Department was the first president. A. J. Renoe of Washington, D.C., was the first secretary. On June 11-14, 1918, the word "criminal" was eliminated from the title. *(Dr. Henry Pelousz de Forest—Evolution of Dactyloscopy in the United States)*

FINGERPRINTING

Community to fingerprint its citizens was Oskaloosa, Iowa, which acted upon the suggestion made by Police Chief Howard Ray Allgood on May 21, 1934. Although registration was not compulsory, a Personal Identification Bureau was established through which most of the town's residents had their fingerprints recorded.

Federal penitentiary fingerprinting was undertaken November 2, 1904, by the Bureau of Criminal Identification at the United States Penitentiary at Leavenworth, Kan. This work was carried on until October 1, 1924, when it was taken over by the Federal Bureau of Investigation.

Fingerprint conviction was obtained by the New York Police Department, which arrested Caesar Cella, alias Charles Crispi, for burglary on March 8, 1911. Latent fingerprints found at the scene of the crime were introduced as evidence. He was convicted and sentenced to the New York County Penitentiary by Judge Otto Alfred Rosalsky in General Sessions Court, New York City, on May 19, 1911.

High school to fingerprint its students was the Watertown Senior High School, Watertown, S.D. The fingerprinting was started on October 19, 1936, as an outgrowth of a talk by a member of the Federal Bureau of Investigation.

International exchange of fingerprints between the United States and Europe was made July 6, 1905, when the St. Louis (Mo.) Metropolitan Police Department obtained the fingerprints of John Walker, alias Captain John Pearson, a frequent offender, from New Scotland Yard, London, England. The prints were later forwarded to New Orleans, La., and introduced as part of his criminal record.

Police department to adopt the fingerprinting system was the St. Louis (Mo.) Metropolitan Police Department, which on October 28, 1904, adopted the Henry method to fingerprint persons arrested on serious charges. John M. Shea was the first to qualify as a fingerprint expert connected with any police service.

He became associated with the St. Louis Metropolitan Police Department, May 1, 1899, and was appointed Superintendent of the Bertillon System, September 14, 1903. He remained in office until his death, July 17, 1926. *(Charles Edward Chapel—Fingerprinting, A Manual of Identification)*

State prison to take fingerprints of its prisoners was Sing Sing Prison, Ossining, N.Y., which commenced taking impressions on March 3, 1903.

FIRE

Fire in a mine was chronicled by the Reverend Charles Beatty in 1765. He reported that a fire had been burning at least a year in a coal mine known as "Spot Hill," the opening of which was somewhere between the Point Bridge and the Smithfield Street Bridge, on the south side of the Monongahela river in that part of Pittsburgh now known as Mt. Washington. *(Pittsburgh and the Pittsburgh Spirit —Pittsburgh Chamber of Commerce)*

Fire of great destructive force took place in New York City on December 16, 1835, when six hundred buildings were demolished, entailing a loss of over $20 million. *(Martha Joanna Reade Lamb—History of the City of New York)*

Fire of serious consequence in America occurred on November 27, 1676, when there "burned down to the ground 46 dwelling houses, besides other buildings, meeting house, etc." in Boston Mass. On August 8, 1679, also in Boston, 80 dwellings and 70 commercial buildings were destroyed, the damage amounting to almost a million dollars. *(Reverend William Hubbard—A General History of New England from the Discovery to 1680)*

Oil well fire. *See* Oil: Oil well fire

Theater destroyed by fire. *See* Theater: Theater destroyed by fire

FIRE ALARM SYSTEM (electric) was invented by William Francis Channing of Boston, Mass., and Moses Gerrish Farmer of Salem, Mass., who on May 19, 1857, received patent No. 17,355 for "a magnetic electric fire-alarm." The first city to adopt this system was Boston, which on June 1851 voted $10,000 to test the device.

FIRE BRICK. *See* Brick: Fire brick

FIRE DEPARTMENT

Fire department composed entirely of women was the Ashville Fire Department, Ashville, N.Y. In February 1943, 13 women

FIRE DEPARTMENT—*Continued*
replaced the male members who were serving
in the armed forces or were working elsewhere.
They served without pay, operated a 500-gal-
lon-per-minute pumper, and were proficient in
rescue work and other fire department procedures.

Fire department established by municipal
action was organized in 1659 by Peter
Stuyvesant, governor of New Amsterdam, later
New York. He distributed 250 leather buckets
and a supply of ladders and hooks which he
imported from Holland. A tax of one guilder
for every chimney was imposed for the maintenance of this equipment. The fire alarm was
given by the twirling of a rattle, with the result that the firemen became known as the
"Rattle Watch." In 1669 the city appointed a
"Brent-Master," who seems to have been the
first fire chief in this country. (*Industrial Fire
Chief—Foamite-Childs Corporation*)

Fire department to be paid was authorized
in 1697 by New York City. Two fire wardens
were authorized for every ward. A penalty of
three shillings was imposed upon owners for
neglecting to remedy defective flues and
hearths. If a fire resulted after warning, the
fine was forty shillings. Half of the fee went
to the wardens and half to the city.

Fire department to be paid a salary was
established by Cincinnati, Ohio, on April 1,
1853, through the efforts of Miles Greenwood.
Members of the company received $60 a year,
lieutenants $100, captains $150, pipemen and
drivers $365. The chief engineer received
$1,000 a year and assistant engineers $300.
(*Charles Theodore Greve—Centennial History
of Cincinnati and Representative Citizens*)

FIRE ENGINE
Fire engine made in this country was built
in 1654 by Joseph Jencks, an iron maker of
Lynn, Mass. He made a contract with the
Selectmen of Boston for an "Ingine" to carry
water in case of fire. It was a clumsy pump
worked by relays of men at the handles. Its
cistern was supplied with water by lines of
bucket passers. (*Arthur Wellington Brayley
—History of Boston Fire Department*)

Fire engine that was practical was the
"Uncle Joe Ross," invented by Alexander Bonner Latta and manufactured by Latta, Shawk
& Company in 1852 in Cincinnati, in the shops
of John H. McGowan. It took nine months to
build, cost $10,000, and was tested on January
1, 1853, the date it went into service. It
weighed five tons, was drawn by four horses
and its own power, and had a square fire-box,
like that of a locomotive boiler, with a furnace
open at the top, upon which the chimney was
placed. It ran on three wheels, the front one

revolving in the center of the car. It threw
from one to six streams of water. In a single
stream 1¾ inches in diameter it threw water
a distance of 240 feet. Its adoption was due
principally to the efforts of Miles Greenwood.
(*History of the Cincinnati Fire Department*)

Steam fire engine was designed and built
by Paul Rapsey Hodge, C.E., and publicly
tested March 27, 1841, at the City Hall, New
York. It was 14 feet long and weighed about
8 tons. It had two small wheels under the
boiler in front and two huge wheels at the rear.
Two horses were required to draw it on level
ground. It was placed in service by Pearl
Hose No. 28. It was too heavy and was abandoned because sparks poured from its stacks.

FIRE ESCAPES for tenements were required by New York State, April 17, 1860
(Laws of New York 1860—Chapter 470). A
serious fire in Elm Street, New York City,
February 2, 1860, in which 20 persons were
suffocated or burned to death showed the necessity for this legislation.

FIRE EXTINGUISHER using vaporized
chemical was manufactured by the Pyrene
Manufacturing Company, Newark, N.J., and
introduced in 1905. The first model had a
single action pump, which had to be tilted down
after each stroke, in order to suck up liquid
for the next discharge stroke.

FIRE EXTINGUISHER PATENT was
awarded to Alanson Crane of Fortress Monroe,
Va., who obtained United States patent
No. 37,610, February 10, 1863.

FIRE HOSE of rubber-lined cotton web
to replace riveted leather hose was invented
by James Boyd of Boston, Mass., who obtained
a patent May 30, 1821, on a "new and useful
improvement in the mode of manufacturing
fire engine hose." In 1819 he established James
Boyd & Sons in Boston, Mass., and manufactured Boyd's Patent Double Fire Engine Hose.

FIRE INSURANCE. *See* Insurance: Fire
insurance company

FIRE LOOKOUT TOWER. *See* Forest
fire: Forest fire lookout tower

FIRE PATROL
Fire patrol was "The Philadelphia Society
for the Protection of Movable Property in
Time of Fire," organized in Philadelphia in
1819, to prevent theft and to salvage articles
in fires. The company had large baskets in
which to place the articles saved and had
vehicles for carrying the baskets away.

Fire patrol to receive a salary was organized in New York City in 1835 and consisted of four men, each of whom was paid a salary of $250 a year to protect property from theft and damage during fires.

FIRE PREVENTION LEGISLATION

was enacted March 17, 1631, by Cambridge (Newtowne) Mass., as the result of a fire the previous day in Boston, Mass., which spread to an adjoining house. The legislation provided that "no man there shall build his chimney with wood, nor cover his house with thatch." *(Thomas Prince—A Chronological History of New England in the Form of Annals)*

FIREARM. *See* Ordnance; Pistol

FIREBOAT

Fireboat was used in New York City in 1800. It was a flat-bottom boat shaped like a scow and had a sharp bow and square stern. It was powered by twelve men who used oars. A hand-operated pump was mounted on the boat, which was stationed at the foot of Roosevelt Street on the East River, and patrolled the docks and waterfront of New York City. Two of these fireboats, called "floating engines," were imported from England at a cost of $4,000 each. They arrived in New York City on September 28, 1800. They were in the charge of Thomas Howell and were inspected on November 10, 1800. *(Our Firemen—New York City)*

Fireboat with two-way radio equipment was placed in service in 1925 by Boston, Mass. Bids on four transmitting and receiving radio stations, one land station and three on boats, were opened August 29, 1923. The boats were licensed March 17, 1924, and assigned the call letters WEY. *(Annual Report of the Fire Department and Wire Division of the City of Boston for the year ending January 31, 1924)*

FIREPROOF BUILDING. *See* Building: Building of fireproof construction

FIREPROOF HOTEL. *See* Hotel: Fireproof hotel

FIREPROOF SAFE. *See* Safe: Safe (fireproof)

FIREWORKS BOOK was *A System of Pyrotechny, comprehending the theory and practice with the application of chemistry, designed for exhibition and for war, adapted to the military and naval officer, the man of science and the artificer.* The book contained 612 pages, and a 44-page introduction. It was written by James Cutbush, acting professor of chemistry and mineralogy at the U.S. Military Academy, and published by Clara F. Cutbush in Philadelphia, Pa., in 1825.

FIREWORKS LEGISLATION

Fireworks legislation enacted by a large city was Section I (1557-a) passed by Cleveland, Ohio, July 18, 1908. It provided that "no person, firm or corporation shall within the city, sell, offer for sale or have in his or its possession or custody any toy pistol, squib, rocket, cracker, Roman candle or fire balloon or other combustibles, or fireworks" under penalty of a $100 fine or 30 days imprisonment, or both. The Board of Public Service was permitted to give pyrotechnic displays when directed by the Council.

Fireworks legislation (state) was Act No. 14, Public Laws of 1929, passed March 29, 1929, by Michigan. It prohibited the use of fireworks by the general public but allowed displays by approved or licensed operators. Other states had partially restrictive laws.

"FIRST AID" EMERGENCY ORGANIZATION was the Humane Society of Philadelphia, Philadelphia, Pa., which was organized in 1780. The society was incorporated January 23, 1793. Its object, according to the charter, was the "recovery of drowned persons, and of those whose animation may be suspended from other causes, as breathing air contaminated by burning charcoal, hanging, exposure to the choke-damp of wells, drinking cold water while warm in summer, strokes of the sun, lightning, swallowing laudanum, etc."

"FIRST AID" INSTRUCTION was given at the annual encampment of the New York State militia at Peekskill, N.Y., in 1885. The idea was proposed by George Ryerson Fowler. *(William Francis Campbell—In Memoriam Dr. George Ryerson Fowler)*

FIRST EDITIONS CATALOG. *See* Bookseller's catalog

FISH AND FISHERIES COMMISSIONER of the United States was Spencer Fullerton Baird, who served without pay from March 8, 1871, to August 17, 1887. An appropriation of $5,000 was made March 3, 1871 (16 Stat. L.503) for expense in "prosecuting the inquiry authorized by law into the cause of the decrease of the food fishes of the coast and lakes." The first full-time salaried commissioner was Marshall McDonald, who served from February 18, 1888, to September 1, 1895. The office was known as the United States Fish Commission until 1903, when it was made the Bureau of Fisheries in the Department of Commerce and Labor. In 1913 when the departments were separated, the Bureau of Fisheries was placed under the jurisdiction of the Department of Commerce.

FISH COMMISSION (state) was authorized by Massachusetts on May 16, 1856, "to ascertain, and report to the next General Court, such facts respecting the artificial propagation of fish, as may tend to show the practicability and expediency of introducing the same into this Commonwealth, under the protection of law." The commission consisted of R. A. Chapman, chairman, Henry Wheatland, and N. E. Atwood. It ceased to function when the task was completed. *(Report of Commissioners Appointed under Resolve of 1856, Chapter 58, Concerning the Artificial Propagation of Fish)*

FISH HATCHERY
Fish hatchery to breed salmon was an experimental laboratory established in 1864 under the supervision of James B. Johnson. He imported from Europe salmon eggs which were hatched in his New York City laboratory.

Fish hatchery (federal) was established at Bucksport, Me., in 1872 for the propagation of Atlantic salmon. It was a joint activity, with the cooperation of the states of Maine, Massachusetts, and Connecticut, and was a continuation of experiments initiated by these agencies in 1871. It was under the supervision of Charles Grandison Atkins and was permanently established at East Orland, Me. It has continued in operation under the Bureau of Fisheries of the federal government up to the present time. *(Records in Bureau of Fisheries. Department of Commerce. Washington, D.C.)*

Fish-hatching steamer (federal). *See* Ship: Fish-hatching steamer (federal)

Goldfish hatchery successfully operated was established in the summer of 1899 by Eugene Curtis Shireman at Martinsville, Ind. The hatchery, which started with 200 goldfish, now breeds about 40 million goldfish annually. It contains 1,500 acres and has over 600 ponds and 350 acres under water. It was incorporated in 1924 as Grassyfork, Inc.

FISH PROTECTION
Fish legislation was an act for "preserving fish in fresh water ponds" enacted May 28, 1734, by New York City. Fishing by hoop-net, draw-net, purse-net, catching-net, cod-net, bley-net or with any other engine, machine, arts, ways and means whatsoever, other than by angling with angle-rod, hook and line only was subject to a fine of twenty shillings.

Fish protection office (federal) was authorized by act of February 9, 1871 (16 Stat.L.594). It empowered President Ulysses Simpson Grant to appoint "from among the civil officers or employees of the Government, one person of proved scientific and practical acquaintance with the fishes of the coast to

be Commissioner of Fish and Fisheries to serve without additional salary." The first commissioner was Spencer Fullerton Baird, appointed March 8, 1871.

FISH WARDEN. *See* Game warden

FISHERMAN'S BOAT RACE. *See* Boat race: Fisherman's boat race

FISHERY (commercial) is believed to have been established at Medford, Mass. On April 17, 1629, the colonists were given instructions to let the fish "be well saved with the said salt, and packed up in hogsheads; and send it home by the 'Talbot' or 'Lion's Whelpe.'" The industry flourished and on May 28, 1639, received "salt, lines, hooks, knives, boots, etc., for the fishermen." Fishing had also been attempted elsewhere by the first colonists. *(Charles Brooks—History of the Town of Medford)*

FISHES
See also Aquatic mammals

Goldfish industry is believed to have had its inception in 1878 when Rear Admiral Daniel Ammen, U.S.N., presented a group of goldfish that had been brought over from Japan to the United States Fish Commission, now the Bureau of Fisheries. *(Bureau of Fisheries—Economic Circular No. 68)*

FISHING BOOK. *See* Fishing treatise

FISHING CLUB of more than temporary existence was the Schuylkill Fishing Company, founded in 1732 in Philadelphia, Pa., with a limited membership of twenty-five. *(William Milnor, Jr.—An Authentic History of the Schuylkill Fishing Company of the State in Schuylkill from Its Establishment on that Romantic Stream near Philadelphia in the Year 1732 to the Present Time)*

FISHING (FLY CASTING) TOURNAMENT. *See* Fly casting tournament

FISHING LINE FACTORY was established in 1859 in Harlem, New York City, by Henry Hall, who manufactured linen and silk lines. The company moved to Astoria, Long Island, N.Y., later operating under the trade name Henry Hall and Sons. *(Forest and Stream—Vol. 12 February 13, 1879)*

FISHING MAGAZINE was the *American Angler*, issued October 15, 1881. It contained twelve pages, was published in Philadelphia, Pa., and was edited by William Charles Harris. It was increased to sixteen pages and issued monthly until January 21, 1882. On January 28, 1882, it became a weekly.

FISHING ROD of telescoping steel tubes was made by Everett Horton of Bristol, Conn., who obtained patent No. 359,153 on March 8, 1887, on a fishing rod in "tubular metallic sections."

FISHING TREATISE was a 22-page report, *A Discourse Utter'd In Part at Ammauskeeg Falls in the Fishing Season 1739*, by Joseph Seccombe ("Fluviatulis Piscator"), parish minister in Kingston, N.H., published in 1743 in Boston, Mass., by Samuel Kneeland and Timothy Green. It was dedicated "to the honourable Theodore Atkinson, Esq., and others, the worthy patrons of the fishing at Ammauskeeg."

FIVE-CENT STORE. *See* Business: Five-cent store

FIVE-MASTED TOPSAIL SCHOONER. *See* Ship: Schooner (five-masted)

FLAG
Air Force flag was approved March 26, 1951, by General Hoyt Sanford Vandenberg, Chief of Staff, as the ceremonial flag of the United States Air Force. It is an ultramarine blue flag with a center design showing the coat of arms and the encircling thirteen white stars on the seal of the Department of the Air Force. On a scroll attached to the bottom of the shield are the words "United States Air Force."

American flag was formally adopted by Congress on June 14, 1777, as the National Standard, and except for the adding of a new star for each new state and changes in the arrangement of the stars, the flag displayed today is the same as the first flag. Claims have been made that the first flag was made by Betsy Ross in her little shop at 239 Arch St., Philadelphia, Pa., at the request of George Washington, Robert Morris, and Colonel George Ross, for the Continental Congress. (*George Henry Preble—Our Flag—Origin and Process of the Flag of the United States of America*)

American flag displayed on a man-of-war was flown in Portsmouth Harbor, N.H., when a group of young women made a flag of cloth from their own and their mothers' gowns which they presented to Captain John Paul Jones, who raised it to the mast of his ship, the "Ranger," on July 4, 1777. (*Ezra Green—Diary of Ezra Green, M.D.*)

American flag flown in battle was carried September 3, 1777, by a detachment of light infantry and cavalry under General William Maxwell which met an advance guard of British and Hessian troops under Generals Richard Howe, Charles Cornwallis and Wilhelm von Knyphausen at Cooch's Bridge, Delaware. (The August 3, 1777 Fort Stanwix flag was not the Stars and Stripes.)

American flag flown in battle on the Pacific was carried by the frigate "Essex," commanded by Captain David Porter. The "Essex" sailed around Cape Horn and was the first American ship of war in the Pacific. She entered the Pacific Ocean March 5, 1813, and docked March 15, 1813, at Valparaiso, Chile. Her first prize on this cruise was the "Nereyda," a Peruvian cruiser which was captured March 25, 1813. The "Nereyda's" armament was thrown overboard and she was dispatched to Callao with a letter to the Viceroy of Peru. (*George Henry Preble—First Cruise of the U.S. Frigate Essex*)

American flag flown in World War I over a band of fighting Americans was flown at the Pérignon Barracks, Toulouse, France, on September 30, 1914. Although the United States was neutral at the time, the American flag was carried by American members of the French Foreign Legion who were ready to entrain for the front. (*Paul Ayres Rockwell—American Fighters in the Foreign Legion*)

American flag flown over a fortress of the Old World was flown on April 27, 1805, when Lieutenant Presley Neville O'Bannon of the U.S. Marines raised the colors over the Tripolitan fortress at Derne, on the north coast of Africa. (*James Alfred Moss—The Flag of the U.S.*)

American flag made of American bunting to fly over the Capitol, Washington, D.C., was hoisted February 24, 1866. It was 21 feet by 12 feet and was made by the United States Bunting Company, Lowell, Mass. It was presented to the Senate by the company.

American flag on the high seas was carried by Captain Thomas Thompson of the American sloop "Raleigh," who, on September 4, 1777, was engaged in an encounter with a British vessel.

American flag over a schoolhouse was flown in May 1812 over the log schoolhouse at Catamount Hill, Colrain, Mass. It was cut and made by Rhoda Shippee, Mrs. Lois Shippee, Mrs. Sophia Willis, and Mrs. Stephen Hale at the home of Captain Amasa Shippee, who instructed the women in the arrangement of the stars and stripes. (*Harlan Hoyt Horner—The American Flag*)

American flag raised in Japan was flown September 4, 1856, at Shimoda, on the southern tip of Izu Peninsula, southwest of Yokohama, by Townsend Harris, American Consul General. The treaty of Yedo (Tokyo), signed July 29, 1858, opened Japan to the outside world. (*Carl*

THE FIRST

FLAG—*Continued*
Crow—He Opened the Door of Japan; Town-send Harris and the Story of His Amazing Adventures)

American flag saluted by a foreign nation was flown from the top mast of the "Ranger." The "Ranger" sailed for France, November 1, 1777, with dispatches of Burgoyne's surrender. On February 14, 1778, the "Ranger," commanded by Captain John Paul Jones, saluted the French flag in the harbor of Quiberon, France, with 13 guns, which salute was returned by Admiral La Motte Piquet with 9 guns, the same salute authorized by the French court to be given an admiral of Holland or of any other republic. *(Henry Ernest Dunnack—The Maine Book)*

American flag saluted by a foreigner was flown at St. Eustatius, Dutch West Indies, on November 16, 1776, when Governor Johannes de Graeff saluted the "Andrea Doria," which was flying the Continental Union flag. The brig was captained by Nicholas Biddle, who had been sent to St. Eustatius to tranport arms and ammunition for the American army. *(Schuyler Hamilton—History of the National Flag of the United States of America)*

Army flag (official) was established by executive order No. 10,670, signed June 12, 1956, by President Dwight David Eisenhower. On June 13, 1956, Vice President Richard Milhous Nixon presented a silk flag at the Capitol Building, Washington, D.C., to Secretary of the Army Wilber Marion Brucker, who passed it to General Maxwell Davenport Taylor, Army Chief of Staff, who handed it to the Third Infantry Regiment from Fort Meyer, Va. Although the army had been established 181 years previously and had served in seven major wars and 145 campaigns, this was its first official flag. The flag bears on a field of white the old War Department seal in blue above a red scroll bearing the inscription "United States Army," and beneath the scroll the date "1775."

Confederate States flag legally established was the "Stars and Bars," adopted by the Convention of Confederated States at Montgomery, Ala., on March 4, 1861, the same day Lincoln became President of the United States. It was designed by Major Orren Randolph Smith of Louisburg, N.C., and was reported to the convention by William Porcher Miles, president of North Carolina College. The original flag consisted of three bars and a field of seven stars, one for each of the Confederate States at that time. A star was added for each additional seceding state. Later this design was changed since it resembled the national flag. *(George Henry Preble—History of the Flag of the U.S.A.)*

THE FIRST

Flag around the world. *See* Ship: Ship to carry the U.S. flag around the world

Flag at the North Pole. *See* Discovery: Discovery of the North Pole

Flag displayed from the right hand of the Statue of Liberty in honor of an individual was flown on June 13, 1927, designated as Lindbergh Day, in honor of Charles Augustus Lindbergh's flight. The flag was hoisted to the peak of the right arm of the Statue of Liberty in unison with the raising of the Post Flag and the discharge of the Morning Gun at Governors Island, and was lowered in unison with Post Retreat ceremonies.

Naval vessel of the United States to display the American flag around Cape Horn. *See* Ship: Naval vessel of the United States to display the American flag around Cape Horn

President's flag, with the President's seal in bronze upon a blue background and a large white star in each corner, was adopted May 29, 1916, by executive order No. 2390 of President Woodrow Wilson. Previously other Presidents had had flags but they were more or less individual emblems. President Harry S. Truman, by executive order No. 9646 of October 25, 1945, made several further changes and increased the number of stars to 48, one for each state. The flag now has 50 stars as decreed by executive order No. 10,860 of February 9, 1960, effective July 4, 1960. *(10 Federal Register 13391)*

Ship to carry the United States flag around the world. *See* Ship: Ship to carry the United States flag around the world

Vice President's flag was established February 7, 1936, by executive order No. 7285. It contains the seal of the United States and a blue star in each corner, on a field of white. The Navy had previously created a flag for the Vice President, but its use by other departments was optional.

FLAG DAY. *See* Holiday: Flag Day

FLAG LEGISLATION
    Flag act officially to establish the American flag was passed April 4, 1818 (3 Stat. L.415), "an act to establish the flag of the United States." It authorized a flag with thirteen horizontal stripes, alternate red and white representing the thirteen original states, and a union of twenty white stars in a blue field, one star to be added to the flag for each new state on the Fourth of July succeeding such admission.

THE FIRST

Legislation authorizing changes in the American flag was passed by Congress on January 13, 1794 (1 Stat.L.341), an "act making an alteration in the flag of the United States" and providing "that from and after the first day of May 1795, the Flag of the United States be fifteen stripes, alternate red and white; and that the union be fifteen stars, white, in a blue field." The change was made so that Vermont and Kentucky would be represented on the flag. A law was passed on April 4, 1818 (3 Stat.L.415) reducing the number of stripes to thirteen to represent the original thirteen states as in the first American flag made, and providing one star for each state. A new star was to be added on the Fourth of July following the admission of each new state.

FLAG MONUMENT. See Monument: Monument to the American flag

FLASHER. See Electric sign: Electric sign flasher

FLASHLIGHT was manufactured by the American Electric and Novelty Manufacturing Company of New York City which started in business in 1896. The first flashlight was produced about 1898. The model was a crude affair, and consisted only of a paper tube with metal fittings, a rough brass stamping used for a reflector, without any lens, and a spring contact switch. The lamp was handmade, as was also the battery. The company later changed its name to the American Eveready Company and subsequently became a part of the National Carbon Company, Inc.

FLASHLIGHT LAMP. See Photography: Photographic flashlight lamps

FLATIRON (electric). See Electric flatiron

FLEA CIRCUS was an "Extraordinary Exhibition of the Industrious Fleas" at 187 Broadway, New York City, which opened January 1835. Admission was 50 cents and performances were given from 11 A.M. to 3 P.M. and from 5 P.M. to 9 P.M. A cold spell forced the exhibit to close to enable the exhibitor "to fill up the vacancies that grim death had made." It was reopened January 20, 1835, for one week. (New York Commercial Advertiser. January 20, 1835)

FLEA LABORATORY was opened January 1, 1939, at the University of California's Hooper Foundation for Medical Research, San Francisco, Calif. It was a flea-tight, rodent-tight, two-story concrete building, air conditioned at a constant temperature. The first director was Dr. Karl Friedrich Meyer.

THE FIRST

FLEET (warship). See Ship: Warship

FLICKER, a series of successive drawings bound together in book form which appeared to show animation, was patented by Henry Van Hoevenbergh of Elizabeth, N.J., who obtained patent No. 258,164, May 16, 1882, on an "optical toy." On June 20, 1882 he obtained patent No. 259,950 on an improvement combining two or more series of superposed leaves. Alternate leaves were indented and cut.

FLIGHT. See Aviation—Flights; Aviation—Flights (transatlantic); Aviation—Flights (transcontinental); Aviation—Flights (transpacific); Aviation—Flights (world)

FLIGHT SURGEON (U.S. Army). See Army Officer: Flight surgeon

FLINT GLASS FACTORY. See Glass factory: Flint glass factory

FLOATING CHURCH. See Church: Floating church

FLOATING HOSPITAL. See Hospital: Floating hospital

FLOATING SEAPLANE RAMP. See Aviation: Floating seaplane ramp

FLOATING TABLEAUX PARADE. See Parade: Parade with float tableaux

FLOATING THEATER (showboat). See Theater: Showboat

FLOOD of which there is any known record was that of the Mississippi River in 1543. When Fernando De Soto was making an exploratory trip, he noted that on March 18, 1543, the Mississippi River began overflowing its banks and continued until it reached its height on April 20, 1543. By the end of May, the flood had receded. There had doubtless been many previous floods but no records exist of them. (Garcilaso de la Vega—La Florida del Inca)

FLOOR TILES. See Tile: Wall and floor tiles

FLORAL MAGAZINE. See Horticultural magazine

FLORAL SOCIETY. See Horticultural society

FLOUR MILL

Flour mill equipped with elevators conveyors, drills, and a "hopper boy" was designed by Oliver Evans in 1789. With this equipment the mill could be operated by one man instead of the four who were needed in the old-fashioned mills. The mill had an endless belt conveyor with buckets spaced a foot apart on the belt, each bucket holding a quart of grain.

Flour rolling mill was invented by John Stevens of Neenah, Wis., whose patent application of December 28, 1877, on a "grain crushing mill" was granted March 23, 1880, No. 225,770. His method increased production 70 per cent and produced a superior flour which sold for $2 more a barrel. *(State Historical Society of Wisconsin—Proceedings 1907)*

FLOWERS

Tetraploid flower produced by the use of chemicals was publicly exhibited by David Burpee of the W. Atlee Burpee Company, Philadelphia, Pa., on January 29, 1940, at the New York City Flower Show. A marigold was treated with colchicine, a chemical extracted from the roots of the fall crocus, with the result that it was one and a half times as large in diameter as the Guinea Gold from which it started.

FLUORESCENT ILLUMINATED CAR.
See Railroad car: Car with fluorescent lighting

FLUORESCENT mineral exhibit was
opened April 26, 1929, at the Academy of Natural Sciences of Philadelphia, Pa. Carbon arc lamps with Corning filters were used by Samuel George Gordon, associate professor of minerals, to activate a display of minerals.

FLUOROGRAPH. *See* X-ray

FLUORSPAR commercial mining was at-
tempted in 1837 at Trumbull, Conn. It was used with magnetic iron pyrite in the smelting of copper ores and sold for $60 a ton. *(Charles Upham Shepard—A Report on the Geological Survey of Connecticut)*

FLY CASTING TOURNAMENT

Fly casting tournament was held June 18, 1861, in Utica, N.Y., by the New York State Sportsmen's Association. The "throwing the fly" competition was won by George Lennebacker of Utica, N.Y.

Indoor fly casting tournament was held March 15-20, 1897, under the auspices of the Sportsmen's Association at Madison Square Garden, New York City. Competitions were

held in casting for distance, casting for accuracy and distance, bass fly casting, etc. *(Score Book of the First Indoor Fly Casting Tournament of the Sportsmen's Association)*

FLYING CROSS. *See* Medal: Distinguished Flying Cross

FLYING MEDICAL CLINIC. *See* Medical clinic: Flying medical clinic

FLYING-WING BOMBER. *See* Aviation
—Airplane: Bomber with the Flying Wing design

FOG DISPOSAL UNIT was accepted by
test on March 29, 1949, by the Los Angeles Airport, Los Angeles, Calif. It consisted of 392 oil burners installed alongside runways. During World War II, the system was used in England and known as "FIDO," Fog Investigation and Disposal Operation.

FOLDING BED. *See* Bed: Folding bed manufacture

FOLDING MACHINE to fold paper for
books and newspapers was invented by Cyrus Chambers, Jr., of Kennet Square, Pa., who obtained patent No. 15,842 on October 7, 1856. It was for plain three-fold right-angle work and delivered a sixteen-page folded signature to the packing box. It was installed in the Bible printing house of Jasper Harding & Son, Philadelphia, Pa.

FOLDING THEATER CHAIR. *See*
Chair: Folding theater chair

FOOD LEGISLATION. *See* Pure food
law: Pure food and drug legislation

"FOOD-O-MAT." *See* Business: "Food-O-Mat"

FOODSTUFFS PRODUCER to achieve
great commercial success was Henry John Heinz, who in 1869 opened a factory at Sharpsburg, Pa. His first product was grated and prepared horse-radish. His company, known as the H. J. Heinz Company, manufactures several hundred varieties of products. *(The Romance of the 57—H. J. Heinz Co.)*

FOOTBALL

Football with a rubber covering was made by the W. J. Voit Rubber Corporation, Los Angeles, Calif., in March 1936. The ball, which does not soak up water, is otherwise identical with conventional leather-covered footballs. It is also cheaper and longer-lasting.

THE FIRST

Football with a rubber covering used in a major collegiate game was used October 13, 1951, at Grant Field, Atlanta, Ga., in a game in which Georgia Tech defeated Louisiana State University 25 to 7.

FOOTBALL BOOK was *American Football,* by Walter Camp, published in 1891 by Harper and Brothers, New York City.

FOOTBALL CLUB
Football association (professional) was the American Professional Football Association, formed in Canton, Ohio, on September 17, 1920, by eleven clubs representing the following cities: Chicago, Decatur, and Rock Island, Ill.; Hammond and Muncie, Ind.; Rochester, N.Y.; Akron, Canton, Cleveland, Dayton, and Masillon, Ohio.

Football club was the Oneida Football Club, which was organized in 1862 by Gerrit Smith Miller at Epes Sargent Dixwell's School in Boston, Mass. The members played all comers from 1862 to 1865. They were never defeated nor was their goal line crossed. *(Winthrop Saltonstall Scudder—An Historical Sketch of the Oneida Football Club of Boston 1862-1865)*

Intercollegiate football association was the Intercollegiate Football Association organized at the Massasoit House, Springfield, Mass., November 23, 1876, with Columbia, Harvard, and Princeton as its three charter members (Rutgers and Yale joined later). The association standardized the number of men on each team (15) and the area of the field (140 by 70 yards). *(Frank Presbrey—Athletics at Princeton)*

FOOTBALL DUMMY for tackling purposes was improvised by Amos Alonzo Stagg at Yale University, New Haven, Conn., in the fall of 1889. He used an old gymnasium mat for the purpose. *(Amos Alonzo Stagg and Wesley Winans Stout—Touchdown)*

FOOTBALL GAME
Army-Navy football game was played November 29, 1890, at West Point, N.Y. The Army captain was Dennis Michie, '92, and the Navy captain was Charles Rulf Emerich, '91. The score was Navy 24, Army 0. *(Dean Hill —Football thru the Years)*

Football game at night was played September 29, 1892, at the Mansfield Fair, Mansfield, Pa., between the Mansfield Teachers College and the Wyoming Seminary of Kingston, Pa. Twenty electric lights of 2,000 candlepower were used with a Thompson & Huston

THE FIRST

Dynamo Machine. The game lasted 70 minutes, but only one half was played, neither team scoring.

Football game between Negro colleges was played January 1, 1897, at Brisbine Park, Atlanta, Ga., between Atlanta University and Tuskegee Normal and Industrial Institute. Atlanta won 10-0. Atlanta's captain was George F. Porter, and Tuskegee's captain was Clarence Matthews. *(Atlanta University Bulletin—January 1897)*

Football game (collegiate) broadcast. *See* Radio broadcast: Football game (collegiate) broadcast

Football game played in the United States to be broadcast in England was the Yale-Harvard game of November 22, 1930, played at New Haven, Conn. Harvard won with a score of 13-0. The game was broadcast by the British Broadcasting Corporation.

Football game televised. *See* Television—Telecast: Football game (collegiate) to be televised; Television—Telecast: Football game (professional) to be televised

Indoor football game was played by the Springfield (Mass.) Young Men's Christian Association against the Yale Consolidated Team, a team which had five of the Yale varsity players on it. The game was played as part of a three-day winter carnival at Madison Square Garden, New York City, after the close of the 1891 season. The score was 16-10 in favor of Yale. The Springfield team led 10-6 until the end of the game, when Hefflinger evened the score. In the try for goal, the ball struck the post, bounding back into the field of play. Josh Hartwell caught the ball as then allowed and charged to the five-yard line, where an additional touchdown was made, making the score 16-10. *(Amos Alonzo Stagg and Wesley Winans Stout—Touchdown)*

Indoor football game (large) was played in the Chicago Coliseum, 63rd Street, Chicago, Ill., on Thanksgiving Day, November 26, 1896. The game was played between teams representing the University of Chicago and the University of Michigan. Chicago won 7 points to Michigan's 6. The gate receipts were approximately $10,000. *(Amos Alonzo Stagg and Wesley Winans Stout—Touchdown)*

Intercollegiate football championship was won in the fall of 1876 by Yale under the captaincy of Eugene Voy Baker, '77. Although not a member of the Intercollegiate Football Association, Yale played and defeated Columbia, Harvard, and Princeton. The standing of the teams was Yale 2, Princeton 2, Harvard 1, Columbia 0.

FOOTBALL GAME—*Continued*

Intercollegiate football contest in the world was played at New Brunswick, N.J., on November 6, 1869. Captain William Stryker Gummere, '70 of Princeton (later Chief Justice of New Jersey), challenged Captain William Leggett of Rutgers to a friendly game. Each team consisted of 25 men. Rutgers won with a score of 6 goals to Princeton's 4. Each goal constituted a game. Six games decided the match, which lasted one hour.

International football game was played December 6, 1873, at New Haven, Conn. The Yale team defeated the Eton (England) team with a score of 2 goals to 1.

Midwestern football team to play on the Pacific coast was that of the University of Chicago, Chicago, Ill. The game was played on December 25, 1894, at San Francisco, Calif. against Leland Stanford, Jr. University. The score was 24-4 in favor of the Chicago team.

Professional football game was played September 3, 1895, at Latrobe, Pa., between the Latrobe Young Men's Christian Association and the Jeannette (Pa.) Athletic Club, the former winning 12-0. Latrobe's captain was Harry Ryan and Jeannette's captain was "Posie" Flowers. The regular quarterback being unable to play, John K. Brallier of Indiana, Pa., was paid $10 and expenses. The following year four men were paid and in 1897 the entire team was paid.

Rugby contest (international) was held May 14, 1874, at Jarvis Field, Cambridge, Mass., between Harvard and McGill (Montreal, Canada) Universities. The games were played under the Harvard rules and Harvard won three games, the first two lasting about five minutes and the third about twelve minutes. It was considered a game under the Harvard rules as soon as either team scored. McGill arrived with eleven men and Harvard with fifteen, four of whom were dropped to equalize the teams. A second match was played the following day and a third match was played in the fall in Montreal.

FOOTBALL GOAL POST

Football goal post was used in the contest between McGill University (Montreal, Canada) and Harvard University, played at Cambridge, Mass., May 14, 1874. At this game, admission was charged, the first instance in which an admission fee was charged at a collegiate sporting event. The proceeds were used for lavishly entertaining the McGill team.

Football goal posts of collapsible folding metal were manufactured by Fisher Metal Parts Manufacturing Company, New York City, and were installed in June 1936 at the Yankee Stadium, New York City.

FOOTBALL RULES were formulated at a meeting held October 18, 1873, in New York City and attended by delegates from Columbia, Princeton, Rutgers, and Yale.

FOOTBALL UNIFORM NUMERALS sewn on the players' uniforms to enable the spectators easily to distinguish the players were used by the University of Pittsburgh, Pittsburgh, Pa., on December 5, 1908, for the game against Washington and Jefferson. The score was 14-0 in favor of Washington and Jefferson.

FOREIGN AFFAIRS DEPARTMENT. (U.S.) *See* State department (U.S.)

FOREIGN AID BILL. *See* Federal foreign aid bill

FOREIGN AND DOMESTIC COMMERCE BUREAU (U.S.) *See* Commerce department (U.S.): Foreign and domestic commerce bureau

FOREIGN FEATURE FILM. *See* Moving picture: Foreign feature film exhibited

FOREIGN MISSIONARY SOCIETY. *See* Missionary society: Foreign missionary society

FOREIGN NEWSPAPER. *See* under Newspaper

FOREIGN SERVICE. *See* Diplomatic service: Foreign service of the United States

FOREIGN SERVICE SCHOOL was the School of Comparative Jurisprudence and Diplomacy of George Washington University, Washington, D.C., which opened November 15, 1898. It was discontinued as a separate school in 1913, the courses being given, however, in Columbian College until September 1928, when training in foreign service and governmental theory and administration was reestablished as a separate branch under the School of Government.

FOREIGN SERVICE WOMEN INTERRED IN ARLINGTON CEMETERY. *See* Cemetery: Foreign Service women interred in the Arlington National Cemetery

FOREIGN SQUADRON AIRPLANE FLIGHT. *See* Aviation—Flights (transatlantic): Transatlantic foreign squadron flight to the United States.

FOREIGN TREATY. *See* under Treaty

FOREST
Community forest was established in 1710 in Newington, N.H. An area of 110 acres of pine trees was set aside as a "town forest." *(U.S. Department of Agriculture—Community Forests)*

FOREST FIRE
Forest fire drenched by man-made rain, produced by seeding cumulus clouds with dry ice, was attacked October 29, 1947, at Concord, N.H. Seeders of the General Electric Company, Schenectady, N.Y., flew over the burning area in "rain-making" planes and caused rain to fall. The experiment was Project Cirrus, a joint weather research program of the United States Army Signal Corps and the Office of Naval Research. General rain caused by natural conditions followed, so it was impossible to determine the extent of man-made rainfall.

Forest fire lookout tower was a log cabin with flat roof erected by M. G. Shaw Lumber Company, Greenville, Maine, on Squaw Mountain, southwest of Moosehead Lake. The first watchman was William Hilton of Bangor, Maine, whose service started June 10, 1905.

FOREST HORSE. *See* Horse: Forest horse

FOREST MANAGEMENT on a professional scale was begun in 1891 in Asheville, N.C., on the Biltmore estate of George Washington Vanderbilt.

FOREST PLANTING (federal). *See* Forest service: Federal planting of forests

FOREST RESERVE
Forest reserve (national) was the Yellowstone Park Timberland Reserve, which was so designated by act of Congress on March 30, 1891 (26 Stat.L.1565), signed by President Benjamin Harrison. It was placed under the administration of the Land Office of the Department of the Interior. *(Jenks Cameron—The Development of Government Forest Control in the United States)*

Forest reserve (state) was the New York State Forest Preserve, designated May 15, 1885. Legislation prohibiting the sale of state lands in certain counties in the Adirondack area was passed February 6, 1883. Essentially this forest reserve is a state park, and in it logging and other commercial forms of exploitation are prohibited.

FOREST SERVICE
Aircraft owned by the Forest Service of the Department of Agriculture was placed in service August 17, 1938, at the Oakland, Calif., airport. It was a 450 h.p. green-coated fire-

fighting plane with a cruising speed of 175 m.p.h. and flying range of 700 miles. It had a service ceiling of 22,000 feet and could carry a full load of 1,250 pounds.

Federal planting of forests was begun in 1891 in cooperation with private individuals in the sand hills of Nebraska. A small plantation of jack and Norway pines was established four miles west of Swan, Neb., for the purpose of holding the sand in place by the use of shelterbelts. The land was acquired under authority of the act of March 3, 1891 (26 Stat. L.1095), "an act to repeal timber culture laws, and for other purposes."

Forest commission (state) (permanent) was the Board of Forestry of California authorized by "act to create a state board of forestry," passed March 3, 1885. The first meeting was held April 1, 1885, in San Francisco, Calif. James V. Coleman was elected chairman; Charles M. Chase, treasurer; and Sands W. Forman, secretary. Dr. Albert Kellogg was the other member of the original board. New York State on May 15, 1885, authorized a state forestry commission which held its first meeting September 23, 1885.

Forest service aerial patrol was established by the Department of Agriculture on June 1, 1919. Two patrols a day were operated out of March Field, Riverside, Calif. Five routes were covered, for each of which there was one airplane. The expense was borne mainly by the Army. From June 1 to October 30, the airplanes flew 2,457 hours, and covered 202,009 miles. The patrol was discontinued October 31, 1919.

Forest Service (U.S.) was organized as the Division of Forestry and received permanent statutory recognition by the act of June 30, 1886 (24 Stat.L.103). Dr. Bernhard Eduard Fernow was the first chief and served until 1898. By the act of March 2, 1901 (31 Stat.L.929), the Division of Forestry became the Bureau of Forestry. The act of February 1, 1905 (33 Stat.L.628), signed by President Theodore Roosevelt, provided for the transfer of Forest Reserves from the Department of the Interior to the Department of Agriculture, opened natural resources of the forests to legitimate use, and stabilized principles of reserving for public purposes the federally owned forest lands. The Appropriation Act of March 3, 1905 (33 Stat. L.872) designated the old Bureau of Forestry as the Forest Service, which is the present organization. *(Bernhard Eduard Fernow—Division of Forestry—Department of Agriculture—1897 Yearbook)*

Forestry inquiry commission (state) was appointed by Wisconsin under act of March 23, 1867, relating to the growth of forest trees.

FOREST SERVICE—*Continued*

The state agricultural society and the state horticultural society were each authorized to appoint one person, these two to appoint a third, to constitute a committee "to inquire and make report in detail" on "increasing the growth and preservation of forest and other trees." The first commissioners were Increase Allen Lapham, Joseph Gillett Knapp, and Hans Crocker, who published a 104-page report in 1867 entitled *Report on the Disastrous Effects of the Destruction of Forest Trees.*

FORESTRY LEGISLATION

Colonial forestry legislation was the act of March 29, 1626, passed by the Plymouth Colony, which required the approval of the governor and the council to sell or transport lumber out of the colony. (*Jay P. Kinney— Forest Legislation in America Prior to March 4, 1789*)

Federal forestry legislation was the act of February 25, 1799 (1 Stat.L.622), which authorized the President to direct a sum "not exceeding $200,000 to be laid out in the purchase of growing or other timber, or of lands on which timber was growing, suitable for the navy." On December 19, 1799, a tract of 350 acres on Grover's Island, Ga., was purchased for $7,500. (*Jenks Cameron—The Development of Governmental Forest Control in the United States*)

Federal forestry supervision was attempted August 15, 1876. An appropriation for this purpose had been provided by an amendment to the act making appropriations for the legislative, executive, and judicial expenses of the government for the year ending June 30, 1877. The total appropriation for the Division of Forestry for the fiscal year 1877, March 3, 1877 (19 Stat.L.360), was only $10,000 ($2,000 for salaries and $8,000 for the "purpose of enabling the Commissioner of Agriculture to experiment and to continue an investigation and report upon the subject of forestry and the collection and distribution of valuable economic forest-tree seeds and plants." Dr. Franklin Benjamin Hough was placed in charge of the survey on August 30, 1876. (*Michigan Political Science Association. Publications. Vol. 5*)

FORESTRY SCHOOL

Forestry correspondence course in tree surgery was started in 1914 by the Davey Tree Expert Company to prepare the men who intended to join to the Davey Institute of Tree Surgery of Kent, Ohio. (*The Davey Bulletin. Vol. XVII. No. 1A. January 1, 1929*)

Forestry course in a university was established in 1881 by the University of Michigan, Ann Arbor, Mich., as one of seven main subjects given in the curriculum of a newly estab-

lished School of Political Science. It was given for four successive years, then discontinued until the reestablishment of the Department of Forestry in 1902. Lectures, however, had been given on forestry and tree culture at Yale University in 1873, and at Cornell University in 1874

Forestry school dealing exclusively with problems of forestry was the Biltmore Forest School of Biltmore, N.C., a private institution, opened by Dr. Carl Alvin Schenck, September 1, 1898. Instruction was largely given by Dr. Schenck in class, and later in field work and on extensive tours both in the western part of this country and in European countries. The school ran until 1912, when Dr. Schenck returned to Germany.

Forestry school of collegiate character for training men in forestry was established September 19, 1898, at Cornell University, Ithaca, N.Y., as the New York State College of Forestry. It was under the leadership of Dr. Bernhard Eduard Fernow as Director and Dean. The law under which this school was established was signed by Governor Frank Swett Black on April 8, 1898. New York was therefore the first state to establish a forestry course. The Forest Engineer degree (F.E.) was awarded in 1900 to Ralph Clement Bryant. The activities of the school were suspended in 1903.

Forestry school to give scientific training in the care and preservation of trees was a department of the Davey Tree Expert Company, Kent, Ohio, incorporated February 9, 1909. The school technically is not a forestry school, but has devoted itself to shade trees and the specialized methods of caring for them. The first president was John Davey, who served from February 9, 1909, to November 8, 1923.

FORESTRY SOCIETY

National forestry association was the American Forestry Association, organized September 10, 1875, in Chicago, Ill. The first president was Robert Douglas and the first secretary was Professor Henry H. McAfee, professor of Horticulture and Forestry, Iowa State College. Douglas immediately resigned and Dr. John Aston Warder was elected in his place. The American Forestry Congress (organized in Cincinnati, Ohio, April 25, 1882) merged with the American Forestry Association at a meeting held June 29, 1882, in Rochester, N.Y. It was incorporated January 25, 1897. (*American Forestry Association—American Conservation*)

State forestry association was the Minnesota Forestry Association, organized January 12, 1876, in St. Paul, Minn., to promote the planting of forest trees. E. F. Drake was president and Leonard B. Hodges, secretary. On March 2, 1876, the state appropriated $2,500 to carry on the work (Chapter 110).

THE FIRST

THE FIRST

FORK brought to America was in a leather case with a bodkin and knife. Governor John Winthrop of Massachusetts introduced it into this country about 1630, following the style which Queen Elizabeth of England had introduced despite the flaming denunciations of many eminent clergymen.

FORTY-HOUR-WEEK LAW (federal). *See* Labor law: Forty-hour-week law (federal)

FOUNDRY (type). *See* Type foundry

FOUNTAIN PEN that was practical was invented by Lewis Edson Waterman and was manufactured in 1884 by the L. E. Waterman Company in New York City. The first year about 200 fountain pens were manufactured. They were originally manufactured by hand. Waterman also invented the machinery to produce fountain pens in commercial quantities. (*Pens—L. E. Waterman Co.*)

FOUNTAIN PEN PATENT was awarded on May 20, 1830, to D. Hyde of Reading, Pa.

FOUR-MASTED SCHOONER. See Ship: Schooner (four-masted)

FOURDRINIER PAPER-MAKING MACHINE. *See* Paper-making machinery: Paper-making machine (cylinder)

FOX HUNTING CLUB was the Gloucester Fox Hunting Club, composed of residents of Philadelphia, Pa., and Gloucester County, N.J. A group of 27 dog owners met October 29, 1766, in Philadelphia, Pa., and decided to hold a meeting on December 13, 1766, to formulate rules for the club, which began its activities January 1, 1767. John Massey, huntsman, was appointed to keep the dogs. The club dissolved in 1818. (*William Milnor, Jr.—Memoirs of the Gloucester Fox Hunting Club near Philadelphia*)

FOXHOUND ASSOCIATION was the Masters of Fox Hounds Association, formed February 14, 1907, in New York City. The first president was W. Austin Wadsworth and the first secretary Henry G. Vaughan.

FOXHOUND MASTER (American) to become a Master of Foxhounds in England was Robert Early Strawbridge of Philadelphia, who on May 1, 1913, became Master of Fox Hounds of the Cottesmore Hounds, Oakham, Rutland, England and served until May 1, 1915.

FRACTIONAL CURRENCY. *See* Money: Paper money fractional currency

FRANCIUM. *See* Element: Element 87

FRANKING PRIVILEGE. *See* Postal service: Mail franking privilege

FRATERNAL GROUP INSURANCE. *See* Insurance: Fraternal group insurance

FRATERNITY CATALOG was published in 1830 by the Kappa Alpha Society, founded November 26, 1825, at Union College, Schenectady, N.Y.

FRATERNITY (Greek letter)
Fraternity house was occupied in 1839 by the Williams Chapter (Alpha Chapter of Massachusetts) of the Kappa Alpha Society at Williams College, Williamstown, Mass. The chapter was founded October 29, 1833, and used various quarters until 1839, when it hired a frame structure two stories high, an annex to the residence of Captain James Meachem. The first floor supplied space for the social gatherings and a banquet room. A winding stair led to the second story, planned expressly for the secret meetings.

Fraternity west of the Alleghenies was Beta Theta Pi, founded August 8, 1839, at Miami University, Oxford, Ohio.

Inter-fraternity council was the National Interfraternity Conference composed of 26 fraternities which met November 17, 1909, at the University Club, New York City, to discuss matters of general interest and welfare.

Professional fraternity was Theta Xi, founded April 29, 1864, at the Rensselaer Polytechnic Institute, Troy, N.Y. Membership was confined to students of engineering and science. The fraternity was an offspring of Sigma Delta, a local society at Rensselaer Polytechnic Institute. (*William Raimond Baird—Baird's Manual of American College Fraternities*)

Scholastic fraternity was Phi Beta Kappa, founded December 5, 1776, at William and Mary College, Williamsburg, Va., with a nucleus of 50 members. In December 1779 it authorized the establishment of branches at Yale and Harvard. (*Oscar McMurtrie Voorhees—History of Phi Beta Kappa*).

Scholastic fraternity chapter established at a Negro university was formed April 4, 1953, by Phi Beta Kappa at Fisk University, Nashville, Tenn. Goodrich Cook White, president of the United Chapters of Phi Beta Kappa, presented the charter to eight charter members and two foundation members, both Fisk alumni. On April 8, 1953, a chapter was established at Howard University, Washington, D.C.

FRATERNITY (Greek letter)—*Continued*
Scholastic fraternity Negro member. *See* Degrees (academic and honorary): Doctor of Philosophy degree awarded to a Negro

Social fraternity was Kappa Alpha, established November 26, 1825, at Union College, Schenectady, N.Y. The first initiation was held December 3, 1825. The first presiding officer was David White. *(Kappa Alpha Record—Centennial Edition 1825-1925)*

FRATERNITY MAGAZINE
Fraternity journal which has had a continuous existence and which has always possessed the features and aims of the current fraternity periodical is the *Beta Theta Pi*. It was a monthly, first published December 15, 1872, in Alexandria, Va., and edited by the Reverend Charles Duy Walker, professor at Virginia Military Institute.

FRAUDULENT ELECTION LAW. *See* Election law: Fraudulent election law

FRAUDULENT USE OF THE MAILS. *See* Postal service: Postal fraud order

FREE LUNCH
Free lunch was dispensed by Pierre Maspero of the City Exchange, St. Louis Street, New Orleans, La., in the fall of 1838. *(Herbert Asbury—The French Quarter)*

Free lunches to aid convalescents were provided by a kitchen which the New York Diet Kitchen Association opened on April 24, 1873, at 410 East 23rd Street, New York City, for the relief of the destitute sick. Beaf tea, soup, milk-cooked rice, eggs, and oatmeal were served. The first officers were Mrs. A. H. Gibbons, president; Mrs. William C. (Flora Payne) Whitney, secretary; and Mrs. Charles L. Tiffany, treasurer.

FREE MAIL DELIVERY. *See* Postal service: Free city delivery of mail

FREE PORT was opened February 1, 1937, at Stapleton, Staten Island, N.Y., under authority of act of Congress, "an act to provide for the establishment, operation and maintenance of foreign-trade zones in ports of entry of the United States, to expedite and encourage foreign commerce, and for other purposes," approved June 18, 1934 (48 Stat.L.998). The port embraced an 18-acre tract around New York Municipal Piers Nos. 12, 13, 15, and 16, and was operated as a public utility by the Department of Docks, New York City, under the supervision of the U.S. Customs Service. Foreign merchandise was admitted in bond without payment of import duties. The first superintendent was Dock Commissioner John McKenzie.

FREE PUBLIC LIBRARY. *See* Library: Free public library

FREE SOIL PARTY was organized at the National Free Soil Convention in Buffalo, N.Y., August 9-10, 1848. In the election of 1848 the party's presidential candidate was Martin Van Buren of New York and the vice presidential candidate, Charles Francis Adams of Massachusetts. Van Buren received 291,263 popular votes as compared with 1,360,099 cast for Zachary Taylor, the Whig candidate. The Free Soil Party was formed by the antislavery element of the Democratic Party and was supported by the Liberty Party. The party's slogan was "Free Soil, Free Speech, Free Labor, Free Men."

FREE TRADE POLICY (federal) was in effect from 1775 to 1780, but imports were taxed by the various states. Trade was free in Massachusetts during 1774-1781, in South Carolina 1776-1783, in Maryland and Connecticut 1776-1780. Although there were no federal restrictions, this period was extremely complicated and taxes were different in practically every state. *(William Hill—First Stages of the Tariff Policy of the United States. American Economic Association Journal. November 1893)*

FREEDMEN'S BANK. *See* Bank: Freedmen's bank

FREEDMEN'S BUREAU (U.S.) was created by act of Congress, March 3, 1865 (13 Stat.L.507), signed by President Abraham Lincoln. Its existence was scheduled to have terminated in one year but was extended to June 30, 1872. Its object was to establish schools and better the conditions of the Negro. The first commissioner was General Oliver Otis Howard, who took office May 15, 1865. His salary was $3,000 a year. *(Paul Skeels Peirce—Freedmen's Bureau)*

FREEDOM MEDAL. *See* Medal: Medal of Freedom

FREEMASONRY BOOK. *See* Masonic book

FREEMASONRY MAGAZINE. *See* Masonic magazine

FREEMASONS

Ancient Arabic Order of Nobles of the Mystic Shrine was established June 16, 1871, at Masonic Hall, 114 East 13th St., New York City. It was founded by Dr. Walter Millard Fleming and Professor Albert Leighton Rawson. The first temple, Mecca, was instituted in New York City, September 26, 1872. Only Masons are eligible for membership.

Grotto began in a committee in Hamilton Lodge (Masonic) No. 120, Hamilton, N.Y. It was formed for frolic, with Le Roy Fairchild as its moving spirit. The first formal organization was effected September 10, 1889. The ritual was written by R. R. Riddell and George Beal. A central governing committee known as the Supreme Council of the Mystic Order of Veiled Prophets of the Enchanted Realm was instituted June 13, 1890, at Hamilton, N.Y., with Thomas Lemuel James, New York City, in the chair as Grand Monarch. The first charter was granted June 13, 1890, to Druid Grotto No. 1, changed July 5, 1890, to Mokanna.

Knights Templar Grand Encampment was held January 22, 1814, in New York City, at which time De Witt Clinton was elected Grand Master, a position which he filled until 1827. The first reference to Knights Templar in the United States is found in the *Independent Journal* of New York, December 28, 1785.

Mason known to arrive in America was John Skene (or Skeen) of Burlington, N.J. He was a member of a Lodge in Aberdeen, Scotland, came to New Jersey in 1682, and later became Deputy Governor of West Jersey.

Mason (native born) was Jonathan Belcher, a citizen of Boston, Mass., who was made a Mason in England in 1704. Belcher became Royal Governor of the Colony of Massachusetts Bay (1730 to 1741) and Royal Governor of New Jersey in 1745. (*Massachusetts Historical Society Collections Vol. 6*)

Masonic college. *See* College: Masonic college

Masonic Grand Lodge was organized at Williamsburg, Va., October 13, 1778, when the Grand Lodge of Virginia was established with Right Worshipful John Blair, Past-Master of Williamsburg Lodge No. 6, as the first Grand Master. (*Melvin Maynard Johnson—The Beginnings of Freemasonry in America*)

Masonic lodge to work under a regular charter was St. John's Lodge, established July 30, 1733, in Boston, Mass. It was organized by Henry Price. The first written records of an American Masonic lodge are found in an account book of St. John's Lodge, Philadelphia, Pa., indicating that the lodge existed as early as 1730. Such a lodge had no warrant as we understand the term today, but was merely an assembly of Masons who foregathered according to ancient custom.

Military Masonic lodge was formed at Crown Point, N.Y., under authority granted April 13, 1759, by Provincial Grand Master

Jeremy Gridley of Massachusetts. Abraham Savage, master of the first lodge in Boston, Mass., served as the first master.

Negro Mason was initiated on March 6, 1775, in an Army lodge (No. 441) stationed at Castle William under General Thomas Gage in or near Boston, Mass. It operated under Irish constitutions. When the British evacuated Boston, Prince Hall and his fellow members were given a permit to meet as a lodge. Under it, African Lodge No. 1 was formed July 3, 1776. On June 30, 1784, after the Revolution, Prince Hall and others applied to the Grand Lodge of England for a warrant, which was issued September 29, 1784, to African Lodge No. 459, with Prince Hall as Master. The first meeting under the charter was held May 6, 1787, in Boston, Mass. The lodge was not recognized by American masonry. (*Harry E. Davis—A History of Freemasonry Among Negroes in America*)

See also Masonry: Negro Masonic Grand Lodge (not Free and Accepted Masons)

Negro Masonic lodge was the Alpha Lodge of New Jersey, No. 116 Free and Accepted Masons, the warrant for which was granted at the Annual Communication of the Grand Lodge in Trenton, N.J., January 19, 1871. The first regular communication was held January 31, 1871. The first Worshipful Master was Nathan Mingus. (*Harold Van Buren Voorhis—Negro Masonry in the United States*)

Order of De Molay was founded by Frank Sherman Land and nine young men in Kansas City, Mo., in 1919. It is an organization for boys whose male relatives are Masons. The seven cardinal precepts of De Molay are Love of Parents, Reverence, Patriotism, Cleanliness, Courtesy, Comradeship, and Fidelity.

Provincial Grand Master (Masonic) was Daniel Coxe, who was deputized on June 5, 1730. His deputation included New York, New Jersey and Pennsylvania. He visited the Grand Lodge of England, January 29, 1731, and was received as the "Provincial Grand Master of North America." He was a Justice of the Supreme Court of the Province of New Jersey.

FREEZER (ice cream). *See* Ice cream freezer

FREIGHT CAR. *See* under Railroad car

FREIGHT DELIVERY TUNNEL. *See* Tunnel: Freight delivery tunnel system

FREIGHT GLIDER. *See* Glider: Glider commercial freight service

THE FIRST

THE FIRST

FREIGHT LOCOMOTIVE. *See* Locomotive: Diesel electric freight locomotive; Locomotive: Electric freight locomotive

FREIGHT RAILROAD STATION. *See* Railroad station: Railroad station (passenger and freight)

FREIGHT TRANSPORTATION RAILROAD. *See* Railroad: Railroad for freight transportation

FREIGHT YARD (RAILROAD) FULLY AUTOMATIC. *See* Railroad: Railroad freight yard fully automatic

FRENCH AND INDIAN WAR. *See* War (colonial): Bloodshed in the French and Indian war

FRENCH GRAMMAR. *See* Grammar: French grammar

FRENCH INDO-CHINA WAR. *See* War (French Indo-China): American civilian pilot wounded in Indo-China

FRENCH INSTRUCTION. *See* Language instruction: French instruction

FRENCH NEWSPAPER. *See* Newspaper: French newspaper

FREQUENCY MODULATION. *See* Radio license: Frequency modulation

FRESCO PAINTING COURSE. *See* Art course: Art course

FRICTION MATCH. *See* Match: Friction matches

FRIGATE. *See* Ship: Frigate

FROG JUMPING JUBILEE was held at Angels Camp, Calaveras County, Calif., May 19-20, 1928. Fifty-one frogs were entered in the contest. "The Pride of San Joaquin," a frog owned by Louis R. Fischer of Stockton, Calif., was the winner with a jump of 3 feet 4 inches. The affair, an annual one, is sponsored by the Angels Boosters Club and is held in commemoration of Mark Twain's famous story, "The Celebrated Jumping Frog of Calaveras County."

FRONTIER DAY. *See* Holiday: Frontier day

FROZEN BREAD. *See* Bread: Frozen bread

FRUIT CULTURE TREATISE was *A Treatise on the Culture and Management of Fruit Trees; in which a new method of pruning and training is fully described. Together with observations on the diseases, defects and injuries in all kind of fruit and forest trees,* by William Forsyth, published for J. Morgan in 1802 in Philadelphia, Pa. The book also contained *An Introduction and Notes Adapting the Rules of the Treatise to the Climates and Seasons of the United States* by William Cobbett.

FRUIT SPRAYING was done in 1878 when an apple grower in Niagara County, N.Y., sprayed his apple trees with Paris green for the control of canker worms. (*U.S. Department of Agriculture. 1925 Yearbook*)

FRUIT TREE PATENT. *See* Patent: Fruit tree patent

FUEL OIL LOCOMOTIVE. *See* Locomotive: Locomotive to use oil fuel

FUGITIVE SLAVE LAW. *See* Slavery: Fugitive slave law

FULLER'S EARTH was discovered by John Olson in 1891 in Benton, Ark. It was used in cleansing (fulling) cloth, wool, and fur, and later in the bleaching, clarifying, or filtering of fats, greases, and oils. It was imported in 1878 and used for refining edible oils and petroleum. (*Charles Lathrop Parsons—Fuller's Earth*)

FULLING MILL. *See* Wool: Fulling mill

FUNERAL (Catholic). *See* Catholic funeral

FUNERAL PARLOR. *See* Mortuary

FUR-BEARING ANIMALS. *See* Animals: Fur-bearing animals

FUR TRADING POST was established by the Pilgrims of Plymouth Colony in Augusta, Me., in 1628. Trade was carried on with the Norridgewock Indians. The pelts were principally exported to England although some were retained for protection against the cold. (*James William North—History of Augusta*)

FURNACE (blast). *See* Iron: Iron blast furnace

FURNITURE CASTER PATENT. *See* Caster

FURS exported were shipped on the S.S. "Fortune" on December 13, 1621. Robert Cushman returned to England with a cargo valued at $2,450 consisting of furs, sassafras, clapboards, and wainscot. The boat was captured by the French and the cargo seized. *(Albert Christopher Addison—The Romantic Story of the Mayflower Pilgrims)*

FUSE

Cordeau-Bickford detonating fuse was introduced in 1913 by the Ensign-Bickford Company, Simsbury, Conn., which started to manufacture it in 1915. It is a detonating fuse consisting of a lead tube carefully drawn to a uniform size, filled with trinitrotoluene (TNT). It functions at a speed of 17,000 feet a second.

Safety fuse was manufactured in 1836 by (Richard) Bacon, (William) Bickford, (Joseph) Eales & Company, Simsbury, Conn., on a spinning bench machine with traveling jennies which drew and twisted the yarn. Powder was fed to the center of the twisting strands and the resulting fuse lengths were afterwards "countered" and coated with waterproof compounds. The machine was imported from England.

Textile-wrapped detonating fuse was manufactured in 1936 by the Ensign-Bickford Company, Simsbury, Conn. It was known as "Primacord" and consisted of a core of pentaerythrite tetranitrate enclosed in textile wrappings suitably protected by waterproof coverings. It had a velocity of detonation of approximately 20,000 feet per second.

FUTURITY RACE. *See* Horse race: Futurity race

GI COLLEGE. *See* College: College principally for war veterans

GAG RULE. *See* Congress (U.S.)—House of Representatives: Gag rule

GAGE. *See* Wire gage

GALLSTONE OPERATION. *See* Surgical operation: Gallstone operation

GAMBLING LEGISLATION. *See* Blue law: Blue law regulating gambling

GAMBLING LEGISLATION (colonial) was passed March 22, 1630, in Boston, Mass.: "It is . . . ordered that all persons whatsoever that have cards, dice or tables in their houses, shall make away with them before the next court under pain of punishment." *Nathaniel*

Bradstreet Shurtleff—Records of the Governor and Company of the Massachusetts Bay in New England.

GAME LAW

Game law (colonial) was passed March 24, 1629, by Virginia and provided that "no . . . hides or skins whatever be sent or carried out of this colony upon forfeiture of thrice the value, whereof the half to the informer and the other half to public use."

Game law (national) was approved May 19, 1796 (1 Stat.L.470) "to regulate the trade and intercourse with the Indian tribes and to preserve peace on the frontiers." The penalty for crossing the line to hunt or destroy game within Indian territory was a fine of $100 and six months in jail. A later treaty with the Indians signed in 1832 is generally regarded as the first national game law.

Game law (state) was passed by Massachusetts in 1817. Other states quickly followed but as there was some difference regarding the hunting seasons and importation of birds, feathers, etc., an act was passed by Congress on March 4, 1909 (35 Stat.L.1138) prohibiting the transportation of birds, parts, etc. On March 4, 1913 (37 Stat.L.847) the first law regulating the shooting of migratory birds was passed, which became known as the McLean Law.

Hunting license fee (state) was required by law of 1864, Chapter 426, passed April 30, 1864, by New York. Deer hunters in Suffolk County were obliged to pay $10 for a license, the money to be "paid over to the overseers of the poor of such town for the benefit of the poor thereof."

GAME MANAGEMENT CHAIR was established by the University of Wisconsin, Madison, Wis., in August 1933, at which time Aldo Leopold was appointed Professor of Game Management. The primary aim was to provide facilities for graduate research and a clearinghouse for the development of game production as a new use for Wisconsin land. Although this was the first chair, it was not the first venture in game management by a university. Michigan had established a School of Conservation in 1927 and Iowa had set up a Director of Game Research in 1932.

GAME MANUFACTURING COMPANY to make games and children's books was the McLoughlin Company, organized in New York City in 1828 by John McLoughlin. In 1850 his sons, John and Edmund, were taken into partnership and the firm name became McLoughlin Brothers. In 1920, the company confined its activities to manufacturing books and moved to Springfield, Mass.

GAME PRESERVE

Game preserve was established by Judge John Dean Caton of Ottawa, Ill., about 1860, on his own estate. The preserve was well stocked with all kinds and species of American native game.

Game preserve appropriation (federal) assisting state wildlife restoration projects was "an act to provide that the United States shall aid the states in wildlife restoration projects" (50 Stat.L.917), passed September 2, 1937. A million dollars was appropriated June 16, 1938 (52 Stat.L.736). The federal government pays 75 per cent of the costs and the state 25 per cent. The first project was Utah's Fish and Game Commission's plan to stabilize the water levels on some 2,000 acres of land bordering Great Salt Lake, approved July 23, 1938 by the U.S. Fish and Wildlife Service.

GAME PROTECTION SOCIETY was

the New York Sportsmen's Club, founded May 20, 1844, in New York City. B. J. Meserole was president and James McGay, secretary. On March 10, 1873, it became the New York Association for the Protection of Game. (*Forest and Stream—December 26, 1889*)

GAME WARDEN (salaried game and fish warden) was William Alden Smith,

of Grand Rapids, Mich., appointed for a four-year term at $1,200 annually and expenses under Act No. 28, Public Acts of Michigan, approved March 15, 1887, "an act to provide for the appointment of a game and fish warden and to prescribe his powers and duties to enforce the statutes of this state for the preservation of moose, wapiti, deer, birds and fish." Wisconsin approved Act No. 456 on April 12, 1887, authorizing appointment of four game wardens for two-year terms at an annual salary of $600 with a maximum of $250 for expenses. Only two wardens were appointed by Wisconsin in 1887.

GARAGE

Completely automatic push-button controlled garage was the Park-O-Mat Garage, opened December 5, 1951, in Washington, D.C., by Parking Services, Inc. It had no ramps, no aisles, and no lanes and needed but one attendant. A car could be parked or returned in 50 seconds. The garage was an open building with sixteen floors and two basement levels. Two elevators parked 72 cars on a lot 25 by 40 feet. It was not necessary for the attendant to enter the cars. The "vehicle parking apparatus" was patented October 14, 1947, by Richard L. Sinclair of Los Angeles, Calif., who obtained patent No. 2,428,856.

Garage (public) was established in Boston, Mass., on May 24, 1899, by W. T. McCullough, as the Back Bay Cycle and Motor

Company. He advertised its opening as a "stable for renting, sale, storage and repair of motor vehicles." (*Horseless Age. July 1889*)

Hydraulic lift parking device was the Sky-Park, manufactured by Simmons Industries, Inc., Albany, N.Y., the first unit being installed in October 1954 in Washington, D.C. A rigid central column with two hydraulically-powered platforms operated by push-button control raised automobiles, singly or doubly, thus providing double the parking space.

GARBAGE COLLECTION

City to discontinue garbage collection because of the installation of waste disposing units was Jasper, Ind., which discontinued service August 1, 1950. The reduction of taxes by a corresponding amount helped homeowners amortize the cost of their disposal units.

GARBAGE DISPOSAL. *See* Incinerator

GARDEN (botanic). *See* Botanic garden

GARDENER'S MANUAL was the *Young Gardener's Assistant, containing a catalogue of garden and flower seeds, with practical directions under each head, for the cultivation of culinary vegetables and flowers, also directions for cultivating fruit trees, the grape vine, etc.,* by Thomas Bridgeman, published in 1835 in New York City.

GAS

Gas company was the Gas Light Company of Baltimore, incorporated February 5, 1817. An ordinance was passed permitting Rembrandt Peale and others to manufacture and distribute gas "to provide for more effectually lighting the streets, squares, lanes and alleys of the city of Baltimore." Coal gas was used. The first street was lighted on February 17, 1817. The first engineer of the company was David Pugh. (*Baltimore Gas and Electric News. February 1929*)

Gas light in the White House, Washington, D.C., was turned on December 29, 1848, during the administration of President James Knox Polk.

Gas lights for display were introduced in Philadelphia, Pa., in August 1796. The inflammable gas was manufactured by Michael Ambroise & Company on Mulberry Street between Eighth and Ninth Streets, Philadelphia. The light showed "a grand fire-work by means of light composed of inflammable air." The lights were disposed so as to form an Italian parterre and Masonic figures and emblems. The jets of light were made to issue from orifices in pipes

THE FIRST

bent into the requisite shapes. The gas was not used for illuminating purposes. *(John Fanning Watson—Annals of Philadelphia)*

Gas lights (street) were installed on Pelham Street in front of the residence of David Melville of Newport, R.I. in 1806. He patented his apparatus for making coal gas March 18, 1813, about which time several important installations were made. *(American Gas Light Journal—Vol. 1)*

Gas meter (dry) to record the amount of gas used was a "gasometer" patented October 17, 1834, by James Bogardus of New York City. It operated on the principle of a bellows, alternately being filled with gas and emptied, the pulsations being counted on a register.

Gas ordinance (city) authorized the Gas Light Company of Baltimore, Md., to lay pipes in Baltimore. It was approved June 19, 1816, by Mayor Edward Johnson and by William Patterson and Henry Payson, presidents of the first and second branch of the City Council, respectively. *(Gas Age. July 1, 1916)*

Gas storage tank (waterless) was completed about February 3, 1925, and put into service on February 10, 1925, by the Northern Indiana Gas and Electric Company in Michigan City, Ind. It was 105 feet in diameter, and 160 feet high, with a capacity of 1 million cubic feet of gas. The top section did not slide up and down; instead a steel piston inside the shell rose and fell as the amount of gas varied. The walls of the holder were made of steel plates 20 feet long and 32 inches wide.

Helium gas. *See* Helium

Municipal gas plant was acquired by Wheeling, W.Va., which appointed a board of trustees on June 23, 1871, to operate the gas works. It was incorporated March 18, 1850, as the Wheeling Gas Company and received a city franchise on April 13, 1850. The company was organized with a capital stock of $50,000, the city subscribing $15,000. After considerable litigation, the city acquired the gas plant in 1871. *(Charles A. Wingerter—History of Greater Wheeling and Vicinity)*

Natural gas corporation was the Fredonia Gas Light & Water Works Company, organized in Fredonia, N.Y., in 1865. *(Brief History of the Natural Gas Industry—Zwetsch Heinzelmann & Co.)*

Natural gas for manufacturing was used in Olean, N.Y., in 1870 and in Tidioute, Pa., an oil town. The first use of natural gas in iron working occurred at the Leechburg, Pa.,

THE FIRST

works of Rogers and Burchfield Iron Mill, where it was extensively used in 1873 in both iron and puddle mill furnaces.

Natural gas used as an illuminant was tried in Fredonia, N.Y., in 1824. A pipeline was laid from the well to a hall where a reception was tendered to Lafayette. The illumination by the gas was regarded as a great curiosity. In 1821 a well, dug to the depth of 27 feet near a gas spring, supplied sufficient gas for 30 lamps. It was later walled up because its odor was offensive.

Pipeline (long distance) for natural gas was a two-inch pipe five miles in length, extending from Newton Wells to Titusville, Pa. It was completed on August 1, 1872.

Theater lighted by gas. *See* Theater: Theater lighted by gas

Water gas plant was built in 1874 in Phoenixville, Pa. It was the first apparatus of the superheated generator type and was covered by three patents granted August 13, 1872 (Nos. 130,381; 130,382; 130,383) to Thaddeus Sobieski Coulincourt Lowe of Norristown, Pa., the inventor and originator of water-gas production. *(O. E. Norman—Romance of the Gas Industry)*

Water gas production which was practical, and its first successful commercial use, began with Thaddeus Sobieski Coulincourt Lowe of Norristown, Pa., who obtained patent No. 167,847 September 21, 1875, for an "improvement in processes and apparatus for the manufacture of illuminating or heating gas."

GAS (carbide). *See* Acetylene

GAS COMMISSION (state) was established by Massachusetts, Chapter 314, Acts of 1885, approved June 11, 1885, by Governor George Dexter Robinson. In 1885 a commission, now the Department of Public Works, was established by Massachusetts to regulate the industry, to supervise the issue of capital stock, to reduce after complaint and hearing the price of gas and electricity to consumers, and to require gas companies to file annual returns with the commission. The Department of Public Utilities which assumed these duties was quasi-judicial in character.

GAS ENGINE was invented by Stuart Perry of New York City, who received patent No. 3,597, May 25, 1844. He invented both air and water-cooled types and used turpentine gases as fuel.

GAS MASK

Gas mask resembling the modern type was patented by Lewis Phectic Haslett of Louisville, Ky., who received patent No. 6,529 on June 12, 1849, on an "inhaler or lung protector." It had a filter of woolen fabric or other porous substance to purify the air, remove dust, etc.

Gas mask with a self-contained breathing apparatus was patented on July 2, 1850, by Benjamin J. Lane of Cambridge, Mass., who received patent No. 7,476 on a "respiring apparatus."

GAS PIPELINE. *See* Gas: Pipeline (long distance)

GAS-POWERED STREET CAR. *See* Street car: Gas-powered street car

GAS PRODUCTION COURSE. *See* Oil and gas production course

GAS REFRIGERATOR. *See* Refrigerator: Gas refrigerator (household)

GAS REGIMENT. *See* Army: Gas regiment

GAS TURBINE AUTOMOBILE. *See* Automobile: Gas turbine automobile

GAS TURBINE BUS. *See* Automobile bus: Gas turbine bus

GAS TURBINE ELECTRIC LOCOMOTIVE. *See* Locomotive: Gas turbine-electric locomotive .

GAS TURBINE HELICOPTER. *See* Helicopter: Gas turbine helicopter (turborotor)

GAS TURBINE PROPELLER-DRIVEN AIRPLANE. *See* Aviation-Airplane: Gas turbine propeller-driven airplane

GASOLINE

Aviation gasoline (100 octane) obtained by the catalytic cracking method was commercially produced June 6, 1936, by the Socony-Vacuum Oil Company, Inc., Paulsboro, N.J., which used the process invented by Eugene Houdry.

Cracking process used to obtain gasoline from crude petroleum was invented by William M. Burton of Chicago, Ill., who obtained patent No. 1,049,667 on January 7, 1913, on the "manufacture of gasoline." His method of treating the residue of the paraffin group of petroleum by distillation and condensation of the vapors was used by the Standard Oil Company of Indiana.

Ethyl gasoline was marketed in Dayton, Ohio, February 2, 1923. Tetraethyl lead, made from alcohol and lead, was found to influence the combustion rate of gasoline, by Thomas Midgley, Jr., of the General Motors Research Laboratories, Dayton. During the seven years of experimenting in the development of ethyl gasoline at least 33,000 compounds were tested to determine their anti-knock effect. *(Information about Ethyl Gasoline—Ethyl Gasoline Corporation)*

GASOLINE AUTOMOBILE. *See* Automobile: Automobile (gasoline-electric combination)

GASOLINE PUMP. *See* Pump: Gasoline pump

GASOLINE TAX

Gasoline tax (federal) was enacted June 6, 1932, by the Revenue Act of 1932 (47 Stat.L. 266) which placed a tax of one cent a gallon on gasoline and other motor fuel.

Gasoline tax (state) was levied February 25, 1919, when Oregon (chapter 159) placed a tax of 1 cent a gallon on all motor fuel. The funds collected were used for road construction and maintenance. *(Oregon. Laws of 1919)*

GASOLINE TRACTOR. *See* Automobile tractor: Gasoline tractor

GASOLINE TRAIN. *See* Railroad: Gasoline-driven, stainless steel, air-conditioned, pneumatic-tire, two-car train

GASTROENTEROLOGY BOOK. *See* Medical book: Gastroenterology treatise

GAZETTEER

American gazetteer was compiled by Jedidiah Morse and was printed in 1795 in Boston, Mass., by Isaiah Thomas and Ebenezer T. Andrews. It was titled *American Universal Geography, or a View of the Present State of All the Empires, Kingdoms, States and Republics in the Known World, and of the United States of America in Particular*. It contained 7,000 different subjects, "exhibiting in alphabetical order a much more full and accurate account than has been given of States, Provinces, Counties, Cities, Towns, etc."

Gazetteer of the world was *Lippincott's Pronouncing Gazetteer of the World*, which was published in 1854 by Lippincott, Grambo and Company of Philadelphia, Pa. It contained 1,364 pages.

GEM-CUTTING MACHINE (or lapidary) was invented by Abel Buell of Killingworth, Conn., in 1766. He claimed that his "method of grinding and polishing crystals and other stones of great value, all the growth of the Colony" would effect a great saving in money. *(Lawrence Counselman Wroth—Abel Buell of Connecticut)*

GENE PHOTOGRAPH. *See* Photograph: Photograph of genes

GENEALOGY
Genealogical collective work was Farmer's *Genealogical Register of the First Settlers of New England*, published in 1829 by John Farmer in Lancaster, Mass.

Genealogy of an American family was a 24-page pamphlet published in Hartford, Conn., in 1771 by Ebenezer Watson. It was *The Genealogy of the Family of Mr. Samuel Stebbins and Mrs. Hannah Stebbins, His Wife from the Year 1707 to 1771 with their names, time of their births, marriages, and deaths of those that are deceased.* In *The Memoirs of Captain Roger Clap*, 38 pages, published by Bartholomew Green in Boston, Mass., in 1731, there was a 10-page supplement by James Blake, Jr., containing "a short account of the author and his family. Written by one that was acquainted therewith." Clap's family consisted of his wife and their six children.

GENERAL. *See* Army officer: General

GENERAL COUNCIL OF CONGREGATIONAL AND CHRISTIAN CHURCHES. *See* Church: General council of Congregational and Christian churches

GEODETIC SURVEY was undertaken by Simeon Borden and completed by him in 1841. In 1830 he made an apparatus for measuring the base line of the trigonometrical survey required by Massachusetts. The apparatus was 50 feet long and was enclosed in a tube. It was also fitted with four compound microscopes, everything being adjustable to permit movement in any direction. *(American Philosophical Society Proceedings. Vol. II. 1841-1843)*

GEOGRAPHER OF THE UNITED STATES was Thomas Hutchins, appointed under an ordinance of May 20, 1785. He was the first and only incumbent of this office. He was in charge of the surveys of the public land and was known as the "Geographer of the United States." *(Thomas Donaldson—The Public Domain)*

GEOGRAPHY was Jedidiah Morse's *Geography Made Easy being a short but comprehensive system of that useful and agreeable*

science, a 214-page duodecimo published in 1784 in New Haven, Conn., by Meigs, Bowen and Dana.

GEOGRAPHY SCHOOL was the Clark Graduate School of Geography, Clark University, Worcester, Mass., which opened in the fall of 1921. Dr. Wallace Walter Atwood, president of the university, was appointed Director of the Clark Graduate School of Geography and Professor of Physical and Regional Geography.

GEOLOGICAL MAP. *See* Geology book: Geology book

GEOLOGICAL SOCIETY (national) was the American Geological Society, founded in 1819 at Yale College, New Haven, Conn. The society functioned until 1828. The first president was William Maclure. *(Herman Le Roy Fairchild—The Beginning of Geologic Science)*

GEOLOGICAL SURVEY
Geological survey appropriation (U.S.) was authorized June 28, 1834 (4 Stat.L.702), when Congress appropriated $5,000 to be applied to geological and mineralogical survey and research. The funds were used in making a geological survey of the country between the Missouri and the Red Rivers. George William Featherstonhaugh was in charge of the survey.

Geological survey director (U.S.) (under the Department of Interior) was Clarence King, nominated March 21, 1879, confirmed April 3, 1879. He entered upon his duties May 24, 1879, and received a salary of $6,000 a year. His office was created by an "act making appropriations for sundry civil expenses of the government for the fiscal year ending June 30, 1880, and for other purposes," approved March 3, 1879 (20 Stat.L.394). *(U.S. Geological Survey—The United States Geological Survey, Its Origin, Development, Organization and Operations)*

Geological survey (state) completed at state expense was undertaken by Edward Hitchcock, 1830-1833, for Massachusetts. *(George Perkins Merrill—Contributions to the History of American Geology)*

GEOLOGY
Woman graduate in geology was Lou Henry (Mrs. Herbert Hoover), who completed the geology course at Leland Stanford, Jr., University, Palo Alto, Calif. She received her degree in 1898, three years after Herbert Hoover received his A.B. degree in geology. With her husband she translated Agricola's *De Re Metallica.*

GEOLOGY BOOK

Geology book of importance was *Observations on the Geology of the United States* which was read by William Maclure on January 20, 1809 before the American Philosophical Society. It was published in revised form in 1817 in Philadelphia, Pa., and contained the first geological map of the eastern United States and one of the first geological maps in the United States.

Geology textbook was *The Index to the Geology of the Northern States* by Amos Eaton which was published in 1818 in Leicester, Mass. (*John Milton Nickles—Geological Literature on North America 1785-1918*)

GEORGE WASHINGTON MONUMENT. *See* Monument: Monument to George Washington

GEORGETTE CREPE. *See* Crepe

GERMAN BAPTIST. *See* Baptist church: German Baptists

GERMAN BIBLE. *See* Bible: Bible printed in German

GERMAN BOOK

German book printed in America was Johann Conrad Beissel's *Das Büchlein vom Sabbath*, printed in Philadelphia, Pa., in 1728 by Andrew Bradford. (*Oswald Seidensticker—First Century of German Printing in America 1728-1830*)

German book printed in German type in America was *Der Hoch-Deutsche Amerikanische Calender, auf das Jahr nach der Gnadenreichen Geburth Unseres Herrn und Heylandes Jesu Christi 1739 . . . zum ersten mal herausgegeben*, published in 1739 by Christoph Saur in Germantown, Pa. (Philadelphia). It contained 36 pages.

GERMAN INSTRUCTION. *See* Language instruction: German instruction

GERMAN NEW CHURCH SOCIETY. *See* Swedenborgian or New Church Temple

GERMAN NEWSPAPER. *See* Newspaper: German newspaper

GIANT exhibited as a theatrical attraction was Patrick Magee, "just arrived from Ireland," who went on exhibition October 6, 1825, at 13 Park, Park Exchange, New York City, from 7 A.M. until 10 P.M. A charge of 25 cents was made to see the giant, "conspicuous for the masculine beauty of his form and his surprising strength."

GIANT PANDA. *See* Animals: Giant panda

GILT BUTTONS. *See* Button: Gilt buttons to be commercially manufactured

GIN (cotton). *See* Cotton gin

GINGHAM FACTORY was opened in Clinton, Mass., by Erastus Brigham Bigelow in 1846. It was named Lancaster Mills and was capitalized at $500,000. On April 10, 1845, Bigelow received patent No. 3,987 for his invention of gingham manufacturing machinery. Previously, all gingham had been made by hand at home. (*Andrew Elmer Ford—History of the Origin of Clinton, Mass. 1653-1865*)

GIRDER BRIDGE (cast iron). *See* Bridge: Cast iron girder bridge

GIRL PAGE. *See* Congress (U.S.)—House of Representatives: Girl page

GIRL SCOUTS organization was the Girl Guides, founded March 12, 1912, in Savannah, Ga., by Juliette Gordon Low. They wore a blue uniform similar to the English Girl Guides. The name was changed to Girl Scouts in 1913 and a khaki uniform adopted. On June 10, 1915, the organization was incorporated under the laws of the District of Columbia and the First Annual Convention and National Council was formed. The first Girl Guide was Mrs. Low's niece, Daisy Gordon. (*Mildred Mastin Pace—Juliette Low*)

GIRLS' HIGH SCHOOL. *See* High school: High school for girls

GLASS

Cut glass made from pressed blanks was manufactured in 1902 by Henry Clay Fry, who organized the H. C. Fry Glass Company, Rochester, Pa. The glass was pressed into a mold, the marks of the iron plunger remaining on the inside of the glass. Previously, cut glass had been blown.

Glass skyscraper. *See* Building: Bronze and glass skyscraper

Invisible glass installation was made in September 1935 at Marcus & Co., New York City. The glass window was bent at several different radius points. Mirrors flanked the window opening. The glass was covered by patent No. 1,911,881 granted May 30, 1933, to Gerald Brown of London, England, on a "means for nullifying or reducing window reflections," and patent No. 2,003,735 on June 4, 1935 to Gerald Brown and Edward Pollard of London on a "display window."

THE FIRST

Milk bottle. *See* Bottle: Milk bottle

Photosensitive glass was made in November 1937 by the Corning Glass Works, Corning, N.Y., and announced publicly ten years later, on June 1, 1947. It is a crystal clear glass in which submicroscopic metallic particles can be formed by exposure to ultraviolet light and subsequent heat treatment. Exposure through photographic negatives permits development of positive images within the glass in a variety of colors. The image is believed to be as permanent as the glass itself. Photosensitive glass is believed to be the most durable photographic medium extant.

Plate glass was manufactured about 1853 by James N. Richmond in the factory which he established in 1850 in Cheshire, Mass., for the production of window glass. The plate glass was about a half inch in thickness and sold for 50 cents a square foot. To make 600 square feet of glass, one day's work, 2,800 pounds of sand, 500 pounds of soda ash and 800 pounds of lime were used. The factory operated about nine months a year, until 1856 when it went out of business. *(Ellen M. Raynor and Emma L. Petitclerc—History of the Town of Cheshire, Mass.)*

Plate glass produced on a large scale was manufactured in 1883 by the New York City Plate Glass Company in Creighton, Pa. The company was capitalized for $600,000 but was refinanced a few months later and the name changed to the Pittsburgh Plate Glass Company. *(Pittsburgh Plate Glass Company—Its Foundation and Growth)*

Sheet glass drawing machine was invented in 1899 by Irving Wightman Colburn, who obtained patent No. 696,007 on March 25, 1902. It was installed in 1899 in an experimental factory on Frankford Avenue, Philadelphia, Pa. The glass was not transparent.

Stained figure glass was made in 1844 by William Jay Bolton and John Bolton for Christ Church, Pelham Manor, N.Y., consecrated September 25, 1843. It depicted "The Adoration of the Magi," over which was the legend "Behold the Lamb of God, which taketh away the sins of the world." It was placed in a window above the altar.

Wire glass was invented by Frank Schuman of Philadelphia, Pa., in 1892. He obtained patent No. 483,020 on September 20, 1892. While the glass was still plastic, he pressed a wire netting into it, smoothing the abrased surface. This glass was better able to withstand heat and shattering.

THE FIRST

GLASS BEAD was manufactured about 1608 in Jamestown, Va., for trade and commerce with the Indians. The London Company later sent Captain William Norton, accompanied by four Italians and two servants, to the disbanded Jamestown glass factory which they revived on July 25, 1621. The work was of short duration because of the Indian massacre of 1622.

GLASS BLOWING MACHINE was patented (No. 534,840) February 26, 1895, by Michael Joseph Owens of Toledo, Ohio. It operated five molds which circulated around the machine, each one surrounding the melted glass, which was placed in its proper position on the end of a pipe and simultaneously revolved so as to make a perfect article without seams or roughness.

GLASS CRYSTAL CHANDELIER consisted of "six lights and shower upon shower of rainbow casting prisms." It was cut by William Peter Eichbaum at Bakewell's, Pittsburgh, Pa., in 1810 and made in a ten-pot furnace. It sold for $300 to a Mr. Kerr, who hung it in his hostelry.

GLASS DRESS of spun glass was made in 1893 for Georgia Cayven, who ordered twelve yards of glass cloth at $25 a yard from the E. D. Libbey Glass Company, Toledo, Ohio, which produced it at its exhibit at the World Columbian Exposition, Chicago, Ill. The cloth was made into a dress, but was not practical for wearing purposes.

GLASS FACTORY

Flint glass factory that was successful was founded in 1807 by George Robinson and Edward Ensel. It was located on the Monongahela River at the foot of Ross Street, Pittsburgh, Pa. The first furnace held six 20-inch pots. The factory was sold to Bakewell & Page in 1808, and the name was later changed to Bakewell, Pears & Company.

Glass factory was established in Jamestown, Va., in October 1608. German and Polish mechanics were imported, eight in number, to start the new industry. The factory remained in operation spasmodically for about seven years and was then disbanded, owing principally to the fact that the workmen found it more profitable to grow tobacco to supply England's trade.

Glass factory west of the Allegheny Mountains was established in 1794 by Abraham Alfonse Albert Gallatin, later Secretary of the United States Treasury, at what is now the site of New Geneva, Pa., about 90 miles south of Pittsburgh on the Monongahela River. It was an eight-pot window glass factory, with wood for fuel. The firm made its own alkali from wood ashes for making the

THE FIRST

THE FIRST

GLASS FACTORY—*Continued*
glass. The name Gallatin & Company was subsequently changed to the New Geneva Glass Works. (*Henry Adams—Life of Albert Gallatin*)

Window glass factory of importance was the Boston Crown Glass Company of Boston, Mass. It was chartered in 1787 and the manufacture of crown window glass began in 1792. The glass was blown through a pipe into a huge bulb, which was opened, flared out into a disc and then cut into panes. The legislature gave this company the sole right to manufacture glass in Massachusetts for a fifteen-year period and exempted the company from taxes and the workmen from military duty. (*Arthur E. Frowle—Flat Glass*)

GLASS INSURANCE. *See* Insurance: Plate glass insurance

GLASS LIGHT BULB MACHINE. *See* Electric lighting: Glass light bulb machine

GLASS-LINED TANK CAR. *See* Railroad car: Glass-lined tank car

GLASS SLIDES. *See* Magic lantern slides

GLASS WINDOWLESS STRUCTURE. *See* Building: All-glass windowless structure

GLASS WOOL and the machinery for its manufacture was invented by Games Slayter and John H. Thomas of Newark, Ohio, who obtained four patents on October 11, 1938. On November 1, 1938, the Owens-Corning Fiberglas Corporation was founded by the Owens-Illinois Glass Company and the Corning Glass Works to market the product, used extensively for industrial equipment and building insulation.

GLIDER
Amphibious seaplane glider was the XL-Q-1, manufactured by the Bristol Aeronautical Corporation, New Haven, Conn., and flown January 16, 1943, at the Navy Yard, Philadelphia, Pa. It was designed as a troop transport and cargo carrier by the National Aircraft factory under Commander Ralph Stanton Barnaby at the Navy Yard. The glider was taken aloft behind a Catalina seaplane and released. It had an all-wood body, was 40 feet long, with a 72-foot wing span, and carried 12 men and equipment.

Glider (all plywood-plastic) built entirely of wood and other non-strategic materials was Model BM-5, built by Bowlus Sailplanes, Inc., San Fernando, Calif. Mock-up tests were begun December 1, 1941, an Army Air Force contract

was obtained January 20, 1942, and the prototype was flown May 1942. The contract was terminated prior to delivery of the finished models and construction thereon was suspended.

Glider commercial freight service was inaugurated April 24, 1946, by Winged Cargo, Inc., of Philadelphia, Pa. Colonel Fred Paul Dollenberg took off from Northeast Airport, Philadelphia, in a DC-3 Air Liner which towed a Waco glider at the end of a nylon tow-rope. The plane carried 5,000 pounds of freight and the glider 3,500 pounds. The average speed of the flight was 150 miles per hour. The first stop was at Miami, Fla., others at Havana, Cuba, and San Juan, Puerto Rico. Paul Myers Aubin piloted the glider.

Glider flight was made by John Joseph Montgomery on March 17, 1884, from a hillock south of the valley of Otay, Calif. The weight of the first glider was only 30 pounds and that of its rider 130 pounds. It traveled about 600 feet. Although Montgomery did not receive full recognition for his work at the time, probably because of lack of publicity, he nevertheless gained the title of "The Father of Gliding."

Glider flight indoors in "dead air" was made on March 2, 1930. Harry Kuchins, a member of the St. Louis Glider Club, flew a glider inside the St. Louis Terminal building at a Boy Scout circus. The glider was the one which had been used by Colonel Charles Augustus Lindbergh in June 1929.

Glider released from a dirigible was piloted by Lieutenant Ralph Stanton Barnaby of the U.S. Navy. The glider was cast loose on January 31, 1930, at Lakehurst, N.J., from the "Los Angeles," commanded by Lieutenant Commander Herbert Victor Wiley, at an altitude of 3,000 feet. (*Records in Office of Naval Intelligence. Washington, D.C.*)

Glider towed across the continent was piloted by Captain Frank Monroe Hawks. On March 30, 1930, he took off from Lindbergh Field, San Diego, Calif., across San Diego Bay from the Naval Flying base in a glider designed for the Texas Company by Professor Roswell Earl Franklin of the University of Michigan. The glider was attached by a tow line to a plane piloted by J. D. ("Duke") Jernigin, Jr. Stops were made at Tucson, Ariz.; Sweetwater, Tex.; Tulsa, Okla.; East St. Louis, Ill.; Columbus, Ohio; and Buffalo, N.Y. The glider landed April 6, 1930, at Van Cortlandt Park, New York City. Flying time was 36 hours, 47 minutes. (*Frank Monroe Hawks— Once to Every Pilot*)

Glider towed by an autogiro. *See* Autogiro: Autogiro to tow a glider

THE FIRST

Glider two-way conversation. *See* Radio telephone: Two-way conversation between a glider and the land

Glider with cambered wings was invented in 1895 by Octave Chanute, who made about 2,000 glider flights without accident in 1896 and 1897 from his base at Miller's Station (near Chicago), Ill. *(Indiana Magazine of History. September 1936. Vol. 32, No. 3)*

Powered soaring glider commercially licensed was the "Dragonfly," designed by William Hawley Bowlus and built by the Nelson Aircraft Corporation, San Fernando, Calif., which was licensed by the Civil Aeronautics Administration on October 15, 1946. It was a strut-braced high wing monoplane with a 47-foot, 4-inch wing span. It had a 4-cylinder 2-cycle pusher engine developing 25 h.p. at 3,900 r.p.m.

Rocket glider flight that was successful was made at Atlantic City, N.J., on June 4, 1931, by William G. Swan. The 200-pound glider was equipped with pontoons. When it was up in the air, the pilot turned on a switch and the rocket ignited. He made a 1,000-foot hop at a 100-foot altitude. The next day, June 5, 1931, he made an 8-minute flight at an altitude of 200 feet, using the full power of 12 rockets.

Seaplane glider to be piloted in the air was loosed from a seaplane on March 15, 1930, at Port Washington, Long Island, N.Y. The first seaplane glider pilot was Frank Monroe Hawks, whose achievement was duplicated later the same day by Robert Atwater flying a German-built converted glider.

GLIDER LICENSE. *See* Aviation—License: Glider pilot's license

GLIDER PILOT COMBAT MEDAL. *See* Aviation—Aviator: Pilot to receive the Congressional Medal of Honor

GLOBE FACTORY to produce terrestrial and celestial globes was started in 1813 by James Wilson in Bradford, Orange County, Vt. A large globe was made in 1811 by Ira H. Hill of St. Albans, Vt., for the Fairfield Academy of St. Albans. *(Abby Maria Hemenway—Vermont Historical Gazetteer)*

GLOBULAR MAP. *See* Map: Globular map

GLOVE (baseball). *See* Baseball glove

GLOVES manufactured in commercial quantities in the United States were made in 1809, when Talmadge Edwards of Johnstown,

THE FIRST

N.Y., hired a few operators to help him in producing gloves. As the demand was larger than the capacity of his small shop, he employed stitchers who performed their work at home. *(Daniel Walter Redmond—The Leather Glove Industry in the United States)*

GLUCOSE made from potato starch was obtained in 1831 by Samuel Guthrie in a refinery at Sackets Harbor, N.Y. *(Benjamin Silliman, Jr.—America's Contributions to Chemistry)*

GLUE FACTORY (animal products) was established in 1807 at Boston, Mass., by Roger Upton. It was absorbed by the American Glue Company of Boston, Mass., and later taken over by the Peter Cooper Corporation, Gowanda, N.Y.

GOAL POSTS (football). *See* Football goal post

GOAT SHOW (of milch goats) was held September 15-27, 1913, at Exhibition Park, Rochester, N.Y., in connection with the sixth annual Rochester Industrial Exposition. Pedigreed goats were exhibited at the show, sponsored by the Standard Milch Goat Breeders' Association of North America, a group which was formed May 24, 1913, and which changed its name on September 22, 1913, to the New York Milch Goat Breeders' Association.

GOLD
Deposit of gold bullion. *See* Money: Deposit of gold bullion

Gold discovered in California was found near the San Fernando Mission in 1842, but no importance was attached to the discovery. On January 24, 1848, James Wilson Marshall found a nugget on property owned by John Augustus Sutter in a mill race on a branch of the Sacramento River near Coloma, Calif. This was the discovery which started the gold rush of the "Forty-niners" to California. *(John Shertzer Hittell—Marshall's Gold Discovery)*

Gold nugget was found in the Reed Mine, Cabarrus County, North Carolina, in 1799. For several years its nature was not known. The nugget was the size of a "small smoothing iron." Later one was found weighing 28 pounds. Gold in limited quantities was discovered elsewhere, however. In 1782, Thomas Jefferson described a lump of ore of about 4 pounds, found 4 miles below the falls on the north side of the Rappahannock in Virginia, which yielded 17 pennyweight of gold. *(U.S. Geological Survey. Annual Report. Vol. XVI. pt. 3. 1894—George F. Becker)*

GOLD CROWN TOOTH. *See* Dentistry: Gold crown tooth

GOLD FILLINGS. *See* Dentistry: Gold used for the filling of dental cavities

GOLD INLAY. *See* Dentistry: Gold inlay

GOLD (money). *See* Money: Gold coinage

GOLD LEAF in roll form was patented on April 5, 1892, by Walter Hamilton Coe of Providence, R.I., who obtained patent No. 472,252. It was made by the W. H. Coe Manufacturing Company of Providence, in rolls 67 feet in length, 1/250,000 inch thick, varying in width from 1/16 inch to 3 1/4 inches. *(Bookbinding Magazine. Sept. 1932)*

GOLDFISH HATCHERY. *See* Fish hatchery: Goldfish hatchery

GOLDFISH INDUSTRY. *See* Fishes: Goldfish industry

GOLF BOOK was *Golf in America,* a practical manual by James Parrish Lee, published May 25, 1895, by Dodd, Mead and Company, New York City.

GOLF CHAMPION
Golf champion (American born) to win the United States Amateur Golf Championship was Herbert M. Harriman of the Meadow Brook Golf Club, Hempstead, Long Island, N.Y., who on July 8, 1899, defeated Findlay S. Douglas, the defending champion, by a score of 3-2. Ninety-eight entrants participated in the tournament, the fifth United States Championship, which was played at the Onwentsia Club, Lake Forest, Ill. Harriman's scores were 81 and 82.

Golf champion (American born professional) to win the United States Open Tournament was John J. McDermott, who won the play-off of a triple tie on June 26, 1911, at the Chicago Golf Club, Wheaton, Ill., with a score of 80, four above par.

Golf champion to hold the four highest golf titles at one time was Robert Tyre (Bobby) Jones, who won the British Open Championship at Hoylake, England, June 20, 1930; the British Amateur at St. Andrews, Scotland, May 31, 1930; the United States Open at Minneapolis, Minn., July 12, 1930; and the United States Amateur at Philadelphia, Pa., September 27, 1930.

Golf champion to win the United States National Amateur Tournament two years in succession was Robert Tyre (Bobby) Jones

of Atlanta, Ga., who won the amateur championship September 27, 1924, at the Merion Cricket Club, Ardmore, Pa., and September 5, 1925, at the Oakmont Country Club, Pittsburgh, Pa. He again became a two-year champion by winning on August 27, 1927, at the Minikahda course, Minneapolis, Minn., and on September 15, 1928, at the Brae Burn course, West Newton, Mass.

Golf champion to win the United States Open and the Professional was Gene Sarazen, who won the United States Open Golf Championship July 15, 1922, at the Skokie Country Club, Glencoe, Ill., with a score of 288 for 72 holes, defeating 320 starters. He won the Professional Golfers' Tournament at the Oakmont Country Club, Oakmont, Pa., on August 18, 1922, winning a diamond medal and a purse of $500. *(Gene Sarazen—Thirty Years of Championship Golf)*

Holes-in-one by a father and son in the same game were shot by Charles H. Calhoun, Sr. and Jr., on August 24, 1932, at the third hole of the Washington Golf Club, Washington, Ga., while the two were playing in a foursome.

Woman golfer (American born) to win the British Women's Amateur Golf Tournament was Babe Didrikson Zaharias, who defeated Jacqueline Gordon on June 12, 1947, at Kullane, Scotland to win the championship.

GOLF CLUB
Golf association (national) of importance was the United States Golf Association, formed in New York City on December 22, 1894, by the following charter members: Newport Golf Club, Newport, R.I.; Shinnecock Hills Golf Club, Southampton, Long Island, N.Y.; the Country Club, Brookline, Mass.; St. Andrews Golf Club, Mount Hope, N.Y.; and the Chicago Golf Club, Wheaton, Ill. Officers for 1894-1896 were President Theodore A. Havemeyer of the Newport Golf Club, Secretary Henry O. Tallmadge of the St. Andrews Golf Club, and Treasurer Samuel L. Parrish of the Shinnecock Hills Golf Club.

Golf club was formed in Charleston, S.C., in 1786. In 1793, the officers were Dr. Purcell, president; Edward Penman, vice president; James Gardner, treasurer and secretary. *(South Carolina and Georgia Almanac for 1793)*

Intercollegiate Golf Association was formed in January 1897 by representatives from Columbia, Harvard, Princeton, and Yale. The first tournament was held May 13-14, 1897, at the Ardsley Casino Golf Club, Ardsley-on-Hudson, N.Y. The team championship was won by Yale; the individual championship by Louis Pintard Bayard, Jr., of Princeton's class of 1898.

THE FIRST

GOLF CLUBS (or golf sticks)

Golf clubs (or golf sticks) are mentioned in an account of the estate of William Burnet, governor of New York and Massachusetts, who died in 1729. Among his possessions were "Nine Golf clubs, one iron ditto and seven dozen balls." *(Esther Singleton—The Furniture of Our Forefathers)*

Steel shaft for a golf club was invented by Arthur F. Knight of Schenectady, N.Y., who obtained patent No. 976,267 on November 22, 1910, on a golf club with tapered and tempered steel tubing.

GOLF COURSE

Eighteen-hole golf course was designed and constructed by Charles Blair Macdonald, for the Chicago Golf Club, at Wheaton, Ill. It was opened for play in 1893.

Golf course (nine holes) was completed at Brenton's Point, near Newport, R.I., in 1890. *(Herbert Warren Wind—The Story of American Golf)*

Midget golf course is said to have been built in 1929 by John Garnet Carter near Chattanooga, Tenn. The greens were made of a compound of cottonseed hulls dyed green. Carter patented the name "Tom Thumb," which was the trade name of a midget golf course system which was leased and sold as an amusement game device. Small golf courses with fewer than nine holes and courses with short holes, however, had been established previously. The "Tom Thumb" system presented hazards, obstacles, etc. The game was played exclusively with a putter.

GOLF MAGAZINE

was *Golfing*, a weekly published in 1894 in New York City by William L. Dudley, editor and publisher. It contained 32 pages and cover, and sold for 10 cents a copy or $4 a year.

GOLF TEE

was invented by George F. Grant of Boston, Mass., who obtained patent No. 638,920, December 12, 1899, on a wooden tee with a tapering base portion and a flexible tubular concave shoulder to hold the golf ball.

GOLF TOURNAMENT

Amateur golf tournament (official) under the rules of the United States Golf Association was played on October 12, 1895, at the Newport Country Club, Newport, R.I. There were thirty-two entries. The winner was Charles Blair Macdonald and the runner-up Charles E. Sands. *(Charles Blair Macdonald—Scotland's Gift—Golf)*

Amateur golf tournament (unofficial) was played on the old Grey Oaks course of the St. Andrews Golf Club, Yonkers, N.Y., on

THE FIRST

October 13, 1894. Thirty-two contestants played an 18-hole match. The winner was Lawrence B. Stoddard of St. Andrews Golf Club, one up, and the runner-up was Charles Blair Macdonald of Chicago, Ill.

Intercollegiate golf tournament. *See* Golf club: Intercollegiate golf association

International golf match for the Walker Cup was held at the National Golf Links of America, Southampton, N.Y., August 28-29, 1922. The United States team obtained 8 points, 5 points in the singles and 3 points in the foursomes; while the team from Great Britain obtained 4 points, 3 points in the single and 1 point in the foursomes. The cup was presented by George Herbert Walker, president of the United States Golf Association.

National championship stroke-play golf match was held on September 3-4, 1894, at the Newport (R.I.) Country Club. The championship was won by W. G. Lawrence with a score of 188. The runner-up was Charles Blair Macdonald, whose score was 189.

Open championship (official) golf tournament was held on October 4, 1895, at the Newport (R.I.) Country Club, and was won by Horace Rawlins with a score of 173 for 36 holes. There were 11 entries. The runner-up was Willie Dunn.

Professional Golfers Association tournament was won on October 14, 1916, at the Siwanoy Golf Club, Mount Vernon, N.Y., by James ("Long Jim") Barnes of the Whitemarsh Country Club, Philadelphia, Pa., who defeated runner-up Jock Hutchinson at medal play, one up. Barnes won the Rodman Wanamaker trophy, $500, a diamond-studded gold medal, and custody of a huge silver cup.

Professional open championship match under the rules of the United States Golf Association was held June 14, 15, and 17, 1901, at the Myopia Hunt Club, Hamilton, Mass. Willie Anderson and Alex Smith tied for first place with 331 for 72 holes. An 18-hole play-off was won by Anderson 85 to 86.

Women's tournament golf championship (amateur—unofficial) was won by Mrs. Charles R. Brown in November 1895 at the Meadow Brook Golf Club, Westbury, Long Island, N.Y. There were 13 entries. Mrs. Brown scored 132 for 18 holes. The runner-up was Nan C. Sargent.

GOOSE (snow). *See* Birds: Snow goose

GORILLA. *See* Animals: Gorilla born in captivity

GOTHIC-STYLE BUILDING. *See* Building: Building in all-Gothic architecture

GOVERNMENT BUREAU OF STANDARDS. *See* Standards bureau (U.S.)

GOVERNMENT—CABINET. *See* Cabinet of the United States

GOVERNMENT—CONGRESS. *See* Congress of the United States; Congress (U.S.) —House of Representatives; Congress (U.S.)—Senate

GOVERNMENT DEPARTMENTS. *See* under title of departments, as Commerce; Interior; Labor; Treasury; etc.

GOVERNMENT EMPLOYEE (woman) *See* Woman: Women to become federal government employees

GOVERNMENT EMPLOYMENT SERVICE. *See* Employment service: Employment service (U.S.)

GOVERNMENT INSURANCE. *See* Insurance: Government insurance

GOVERNMENT MINT. *See* Mint (U.S.): Mint of the United States

GOVERNMENT-OPERATED FACTORY. *See* Factory: Factories operated by the United States Government

GOVERNMENT OPERATION OF RAILROADS. *See* Railroad: Government operation of railroads

GOVERNMENT PRINTING OFFICE
Government Printing Office was created as an independent establishment by an act of Congress of June 23, 1860 (12 Stat.L.118) to provide printing and binding for Congress and the federal departments, bureaus, and independent offices. On February 19, 1861 (12 Stat.L.132) $135,000 was appropriated for the purchase of the printing plant of Joseph T. Crowell, Washington, D.C. It was purchased March 2, 1861, and began to function March 4, 1861. The first Superintendent of Public Printing was John Dougherty Defrees of Indiana, appointed March 23, 1861, by President Abraham Lincoln. (*Robert Washington Kerr—History of Government Printing Office*)

Superintendent of Documents under the Government Printing Office was authorized by act of January 12, 1895 (28 Stat.L.610) to take charge of the preparation of official catalogs and indexes of the government, and the distribution and sales of government publications. F. A. Crandall, the first superintendent, served from March 26, 1895, to November 17, 1897. Sales were small to the end of the fiscal year

June 30, 1895, but from June 30, 1895, to June 30, 1896, 3,581 publications were sold yielding a revenue of $889.09.

GOVERNMENT PUBLICATIONS INDEX. *See* Index of government publications

GOVERNMENT RECLAMATION SERVICE. *See* Reclamation service (federal)

GOVERNOR
Brothers to serve simultaneously as governors of their respective states were Governor Levi Lincoln, Jr., a Whig, who was sworn in as governor of the Commonwealth of Massachusetts on May 27, 1825, and who served until January 21, 1834, and Governor Enoch Lincoln, a Whig, who served as governor of Maine from January 4, 1827, until his death, October 8, 1829.

Catholic governor was Edward Douglass White, who resigned from the United States House of Representatives on November 15, 1834, and served as Governor of Louisiana from 1835 to 1839. He returned to the House of Representatives and served from March 4, 1839, to March 3, 1843. He died April 18, 1847, and was buried in St. Joseph's Catholic Cemetery at Thibodaux, La.

Governor granted almost dictatorial power was Paul Vories McNutt of Indiana. The Democratically controlled legislature empowered him in February 1933 to organize the state government, then scattered in 168 boards and commissions, into nine departments, Executive, State, Audit, Treasury, Law, Education, Public Works, Commerce, and Industry. He was authorized to hire and fire all state employees and to raise or lower salaries as he saw fit. His power was limited by legislative appropriations and by the authority of the courts to review and void his decisions.

Governor impeached. See Impeachment: Impeachment and removal from office of a state governor

Governor of a territory and a state was John White Geary, who served as governor of the Kansas territory from September 9, 1856, to March 4, 1857, and as governor of Pennsylvania from January 15, 1867, to January 21, 1873.

Governor removed from office by a state supreme court decision was William Augustus Barstow, Democrat, of Wisconsin, who served the term from January 2, 1854, to January 7, 1856. He was installed for a second term on January 7, 1856. On March 20, 1856, the supreme court held that Coles Bashford, Republican, was entitled to the office because of irregularities in the election charged to Barstow. On March 21, 1856, Barstow resigned, and the lieutenant-governor, Arthur MacArthur, was sworn in. MacArthur withdrew from office March 25, 1856. The state assembly recognized Bashford on March 27, 1856.

Governor to appoint two United States senators in one year for interim terms was Governor Robert Crosby of Nebraska, who appointed Eve Bowring (sworn in April 26, 1954) to replace Senator Dwight Palmer Griswold (deceased April 12, 1954) and Samuel Williams Reynolds (sworn in July 7, 1954) to replace Senator Hugh Alfred Butler (deceased July 1, 1954). Hazel Hempel Abel was elected to fill out the remaining time in Griswold's term and Roman Lee Hruska was elected to fill out the remaining time in Butler's term.

Gubernatorial election in which two brothers were the opposing candidates was held November 2, 1886, in Tennessee. Robert Love Taylor, the Democratic candidate, received 125,151 votes, defeating his brother, Alfred Alexander Taylor, the Republican candidate, who obtained 109,837 votes. Robert Love Taylor served as governor from January 17, 1887, to January 19, 1891, and from January 21, 1897, to January 16, 1899. Alfred Alexander Taylor defeated Albert Houston Roberts on November 2, 1920, and served as governor of Tennessee from January 15, 1921, to January 16, 1923.

Impeachment proceedings against a state governor. *See* Impeachment: Impeachment proceedings against a state governor

Jewish governor was David Emanuel of Georgia, who served from March 3, 1801, to November 7, 1801, after the resignation of Governor James Jackson. It is not entirely clear whether he became governor by virtue of the fact that he was president of the senate when Governor Jackson resigned, or whether he was regularly elected. The first Jewish governor elected for a full term was Moses Alexander of Idaho, a Democrat, who served from January 4, 1915, to January 6, 1919, as the eleventh governor of Idaho. *(American Jewish Historical Society Publication No. 17)*

Native-born governor of New England was Josiah Winslow of Plymouth, Mass. He was elected governor of Massachusetts in 1673

and served until his death in 1680. *(Joseph Dillaway Sawyer—History of Pilgrims and Puritans)*

Negro governor (acting) was Pinckney Benton Stewart Pinchback, who was lieutenant governor of Louisiana from 1871 to 1872. During Governor Henry Clay Warmoth's impeachment, he acted as governor of Louisiana, from December 11, 1872, to January 14, 1873.

Negro governor appointed by the President of the United States was William Henry Hastie, whose appointment by President Harry S. Truman as governor of the Virgin Islands was confirmed by the Senate on May 1, 1946. He was inaugurated May 7, 1946, at Charlotte Amalie, V.I.

Woman governor of a state was Nellie Tayloe Ross who was elected governor of Wyoming on November 4, 1924, to fill the unexpired term of her husband, William Bradford Ross. She assumed her duties on January 5, 1925. Miriam Amanda ("Ma") Ferguson of Texas was inaugurated governor of Texas on January 10, 1925.

GRADUATE FELLOWSHIP. *See* Fellowship: Fellowship (graduate) awarded by a women's college

GRADUATE SCHOOL. *See* College: Graduate school for women

GRAIN ELEVATOR. *See* Elevator: Grain elevator operated by steam

GRAIN STABILIZATION CORPORATION was authorized February 10, 1930, under act of Congress (46 Stat.L.15) approved June 15, 1929. It was organized in February 1930 and was composed of 28 members. The first president was George Sparks Milnor.

GRAMMAR
English grammar by an American was *A Short English Grammar, an Accidence to the English Tongues,* by Hugh Jones, professor of mathematics at the College of William and Mary. It was published in London, England in 1724. *(Rollo La Verne Lyman—English Grammar in American Schools Before 1850)*

English grammar by an American published in America was Samuel Johnson's *The First Easy Rudiments of Grammar, Applied to the English Tongue. By one who is extremely desirous to promote good literature in America, and especially a right English Education. For the Use of schools.* It was published in 1765, in New York City by "J. Holt, near the Exchange in Broad Street." The

THE FIRST

GRAMMAR—*Continued*
grammar consisted of 36 pages. Dr. Johnson was the first president of King's College (now Columbia University). *(Charles Evans—American Bibliography)*

French grammar written and printed in America was *A New French and English Grammar, wherein the principles are methodically digested, with useful notes and observations, explaining the terms of grammar, and further improving its rules* by John Mary, instructor at Harvard College. It was printed in 1784 by J[ohn] Norman, Boston, Mass., and sold by the author.

Hebrew grammar was *A Grammar of the Hebrew Tongue,* by Judah Monis, an instructor, in Hebrew at Harvard College, published in 1735 in Boston, Mass. It was dedicated to "His Excellency Jonathan Belcher, Esq: Governour in Chief of His Majesty's Province of the Massachusetts Bay in New England, and the Rest of the Honourables and the Reverend Overseers of Harvard College, and to the Reverend Mr. Benjamin Wadsworth, President and the Rest of the Honourable and Reverend Corporation of Said College." *(Lee Max Friedman—Early American Jews)*

Indian grammar was John Eliot's *The Indian Grammar Begun; or, An Essay to Bring the Indian Language into Rules, for the Help of Such as Desire to Learn the Same, for the Furtherance of Gospel Among Them,* published in Cambridge, Mass., in 1666 by Marmaduke Johnson. It was written in the language of the Massachusetts Indians.

Latin grammar textbook was *A Short Introduction to the Latin Tongue. For the use of the lower forms in the Latin School. Being the Accidence abbridg'd and compiled in that most easy and accurate method, wherein the famous Mr. Ezekiel Cheever taught and which he found the most advantageous by seventy years' experience.* It was prepared by Ezekiel Cheever, master of the Boston Latin School, and published in 1709 in Boston, Mass., by "B[artholomew] Green for Benj. Eliot at his shop under the Town-house." It contained 64 pages and was 3 by 6 inches. *(Elizabeth Porter Gould—Ezekiel Cheever, Schoolmaster)*

GRAMMAR INSTRUCTION IN A COLLEGE was offered in 1795 at the University of North Carolina, Chapel Hill, N.C. "The English language [was] taught grammatically on the basis of Webster's and South's *Grammar.*" *(Kemp Plummer Battle—History of the University of North Carolina)*

GRAND AMERICAN TRAPSHOOT TOURNAMENT. *See* Trapshooting tournament

THE FIRST

GRAND ARMY OF THE REPUBLIC. *See* War veterans' society: Grand Army of the Republic

GRAND CANYON EXPLORATION. *See* Expedition: Exploration of the Grand Canyon of the Colorado

GRAND JURY FOREMAN (woman). *See* Jury: Woman grand jury foreman

GRAND MASTER (Masonic). *See* Freemasons: Provincial grand master (Masonic)

GRAND OPERA IN ENGLISH. *See* Opera: Grand opera sung in English

GRANGE. *See* Agricultural society: Agricultural society of national importance

GRANITE was quarried in Quincy, Mass., in 1820 for the Bunker Hill Monument, Boston, Mass. About 9,000 tons in blocks 2 feet 6 inches square and 12 feet long were transported by the Granite Railway Company from the Quincy quarry to the wharf at Charlestown, Mass.

GRAPHITE was produced commercially in 1840 at Ticonderoga, N.Y., and became the center of the graphite industry of the United States. Graphite occurs associated with igneous and metamorphic rocks.

GRAPHOPHONE. *See* Phonograph: Phonograph that was practical

GREAT LAKES COMMERCIAL VESSEL. *See* Ship: Great Lakes commercial vessel

GREAT LAKES TO THE GULF WATERWAY. *See* Canal: Great Lakes to the Gulf waterway

GREAT POWERS CONFERENCE. *See* Conference: Conference of great powers

GREAT SEAL OF THE UNITED STATES GOVERNMENT. *See* Seal: Great Seal of the United States Government

GREEK COLLEGE AND ORPHANAGE was the Monastery of St. Stephanos in Gastonia, N.C., dedicated September 18, 1932, by Archbishop Athenagaros of the Greek Orthodox Church in North and South America to the "oncoming generations of Greek youth."

GREEK DAILY NEWSPAPER. *See* Newspaper: Greek newspaper

THE FIRST

GREEK LETTER SOCIAL SOCIETY. *See* Fraternity (Greek letter): Social fraternity

GREEK ORPHANAGE. *See* Greek college and orphanage

GREEK ORTHODOX CHURCH was the Holy Trinity Church, 1222 N. Dorgenois Street, New Orleans, La., founded in 1867. The first pastor was Paisios Ferentinos. *(Seraphim G. Canoutas—Hellenism in America)*

GREEK PLAY. *See* Play (drama): Greek play

GREEK TESTAMENT. *See* Bible: Greek Testament

GREENBACK LABOR PARTY (formed by members of the Labor Reform and old Greenback party) was organized February 22, 1878, in Toledo, Ohio. The first national convention was held June 9-10, 1880, in Chicago, Ill., and the first presidential candidate was James Baird Weaver of Iowa.

GREENBACK PARTY (or Independent Party) was organized November 25, 1874, in Indianapolis, Ind., and the first convention was held there, May 17, 1876. The first presidential candidate was Peter Cooper of New York, who received 81,737 votes in the 1876 election. Samuel Fenton Cary of Ohio was the vice presidential candidate. The party platform advocated the payment of the national debt of the government in greenbacks.

GREENHOUSE was erected by James Beekman in New York City in 1764. It is claimed that Andrew Faneuil erected a glass house at Boston, Mass., prior to 1737. *(Florists' Exchange. 1859)*

GREYHOUND RACING ASSOCIATION was the International Greyhound Racing Association, formed March 3, 1926, in Miami, Fla., to systematize efforts and to conduct the races on the highest possible standard. The association is incorporated as a nonprofit organization. The first high commissioner was Owen P. Smith.

See also Dog race track

GROTTO. *See* Freemasons: Grotto

GROUP HOSPITAL INSURANCE PLAN. *See* Insurance: Group hospital insurance plan

GROUP INSURANCE. *See* Insurance: Group insurance policy

THE FIRST

GUANO was imported from Peru in 1832 for fertilizer use. Guano is the deposits of droppings and bodies of dead birds and bats, and occurs in caves or above ground in districts where there is little or no rain. *(American Fertilizer Handbook—1936)*

GUARANTY BANK BILL. *See* Bank legislation: Bank guaranty legislation

GUERNSEY CATTLE. *See* Animals: Cattle (Guernsey cattle)

GUERNSEY CATTLE CLUB. *See* Cattle club: Cattle club (Guernsey cattle)

GUIDED MISSILE CRUISER. *See* Ship: Guided missile cruiser

GUIDED MISSILE DESTROYER. *See* Ship: Guided missile destroyer

GUIDED MISSILE SUBMARINE. *See* Submarine: Submarine expressly designed and built to fire guided missiles

GUM. *See* Chewing gum

GUN. *See* Ordnance; Pistol

GUNPOWDER MILL. *See* Ordnance: Gunpowder mill

GUTTA PERCHA was imported from Calcutta in 1840 by William Bartlett as supercargo of the "Mary Parker." Bartlett presented a whip made of gutta percha to William Rider of New York City, who organized William Rider and Brothers to handle the new commodity. Improvements of processes were constantly made. On June 1, 1852, John Rider obtained patent No. 8,992 on "vulcanized rubber," and in 1855 the North American Gutta Percha Company, New York City, was formed by the Rider brothers with a capitalization of $500,000. *(United States Magazine. April 15, 1855)*

GYMNASIUM to offer systematic instruction was started by the Round Hill School, Northampton, Mass., which was opened October 1, 1823, by John Green Cogswell and George Bancroft. Charles Beck was the instructor in Latin and gymnastics. Gymnastics was scheduled from 5 P.M. to 7 P.M. *(Old and New—July 1872)*

GYMNASTICS BOOK was *Gymnastics for Youth; or a practical guide to healthful and amusing exercises for the use of schools,* by Johann Christoph Friedrich Guts Muths, translated from the original work in German, but

GYMNASTICS BOOK—*Continued*
erroneously credited to Christian Gotthelf Salz-
mann. It was published in 1802 by William
Duane, Philadelphia, Pa. It was illustrated
with copper plates and contained 432 pages.

GYMNASTICS INSTRUCTION
Gymnastics instruction at a college was
offered in 1826 at Harvard University, Cambridge, Mass. Charles Theodore Christian
Follen, professor of German, was appointed
superintendent of the gymnasium. He introduced Friedrich Ludwig Jahn's system of
gymnastics. *(Fred Eugene Leonard—A Guide
to the History of Physical Education)*

Gymnastics instruction at a college for
women was offered in 1862 by Mount Holyoke College, South Hadley, Mass. The first
teacher of gymnastics was a Miss Evans. During the first year, the course was optional, and
the instruction was given "in the long store-
room over the wood and coal shed at the
northwest corner of the court." A gymnasium
was erected in 1865. Courses in calisthenics,
however, had been introduced in 1835, but were
replaced by the Dio Lewis system of gymnastics.
*(Persis Harlow McCurdy—The History of
Physical Training at Mount Holyoke College.
American Physical Education Review. March
1909)*

GYRO COMPASS
Gyro compass installed on an American
naval vessel was placed on the U.S.S. "Delaware" and tested at sea August 28, 1911. The
installation consisted of a master gyro compass, employing the meridian seeking properties
of a pendulous gyro. The master compass was
designed to be installed in a protected station,
with repeaters which followed the movements
of the master located suitably for steering and
taking bearings.

GYRO PILOT. *See* Shipping: Automatic
steering gear

GYROSCOPE
See also Aviation— Gyroscope automatic stabilization; Ship—Gyro stabilizer

Gyroscopes (commercially manufactured)
were made by the Holbrook Apparatus Company, Hartford, Conn., in June 1857. They
were made of iron, sold for $2, and used as
toys.

GYRO-STABILIZED AMERICAN LIN-
ER. *See* Ship: Gyro-stabilized American
liner

HABEAS CORPUS
Habeas corpus suspension order was issued May 3, 1861, by President Abraham

Lincoln authorizing the commander of the military forces on the coast of Florida to suspend
the writ of habeas corpus, if necessary. John
Merryman was arrested May 25, 1861, by the
military authorities and was refused the writ
of habeas corpus. There was considerable
agitation and on September 15, 1863, Lincoln
issued a proclamation to the effect that in times
of military strife, the writ of habeas corpus
could be suspended. *(Henry Jarvis Raymond—
Lincoln, His Life and Times)*

Habeas corpus writ in America was obtained about 1707 in behalf of the American
historian Robert Beverley.

HAFLINGER HORSE. *See* Horse: Haf-
linger horse

HAGUE ARBITRATION CASE. *See* Arbi-
tration: Arbitration proceeding

HAIL INSURANCE. *See* Insurance: Hail
insurance

HAIR CLIPPERS. *See* Clipper for cutting
hair

HAIR CLOTH was manufactured at Rah-
way, N.J., in 1813, the process for which was
covered by patents granted to William Shotwell
and Arthur Kinder of New York City on
July 23, 1813. It was called Taurine cloth and
was a coarse fabric made from the hair of
cattle with a mixture of wool.

HALF CENT. *See* Money: Half cent of the
United States

HALF-TONE ENGRAVING. *See* Engrav-
ing: Half-tone engraving

HALL OF FAME
Hall of fame (baseball) was conceived in
1935, erected at Cooperstown, N.Y., during 1938,
and dedicated June 12, 1939, as the National
Baseball Museum and Hall of Fame. On
January 29, 1936, the first group of five was
elected to the Baseball Hall of Fame: Ty Cobb,
Babe Ruth, John Peter ("Honus") Wagner,
Christy Mathewson, and Walter Johnson.

Hall of fame (national) was National
Statuary Hall, formerly the Hall of the United
States House of Representatives in the Capitol
at Washington, D.C., which was established by
act of Congress of July 2, 1864 (13 Stat.L.347).
Each state was invited to contribute marble or
bronze statues of its most distinguished citizens.

Hall of fame (university) was the Hall of
Fame, which was dedicated May 30, 1901, on
the University Heights campus of New York

THE FIRST

University, New York City. Twenty-nine tablets were unveiled. The oration was delivered by Senator Chauncey Mitchell Depew. The idea originated with Dr. Henry Mitchell MacCracken, chancellor of the university, who was aided in the project by a $250,000 endowment from Helen Miller Gould (Mrs. Finley Johnson Shepard). *(Robert Underwood Johnson—Your Hall of Fame)*

Walk of fame. *See* Walk of fame

HAMMER (pneumatic) was invented by Charles Brady King of Detroit, Mich., in 1890. Brady applied for a patent on May 19, 1892; it was granted January 30, 1894 (No. 513,941). The hammer was exhibited at the World's Columbian Exposition in Chicago, Ill., in 1893.

HAMMERED IRON. *See* Iron: Hammered iron

HANDBALL national championship match for amateurs was staged at the Jersey City Handball Club, Jersey City, N.J., on January 7-8, 1897, and was won by Michael Eagan.

HANGING RAILROAD BRIDGE. *See* Bridge: Hanging railroad bridge

HARD PORCELAIN. *See* Porcelain (hard)

HARD WATER CRACKER. *See* Cracker: Hard water crackers

HARNESS RACE. *See* Horse race: Harness horse race (Hambletonian) for three-year-olds; Horse race: Harness race driver to win the Hambletonian four times

HAT
    Derby hat was manufactured by James Henry Knapp of Knapp and Gilliam of South Norwalk, Conn., in 1850. The first derbies were sold to New York jobbers, Henderson and Bird, who sold one and a half dozen each of brown and black to a retail store on Broadway and Ninth Street, New York City. An English clerk suggested "Derby" (pronounced "darby"), after the famous English horse race, as the name of the hat, which, through a difference in pronunciation, became known as "derby."

    Soft felt hats for women were introduced in New York City in 1851 by John Nicholas Genin. Prior to this women wore bonnets. When Lajos (Louis) Kossuth, the Hungarian patriot, arrived in New York City on December 5, 1851, on board the "Mississippi," Genin took low-crowned soft black hats and fastened the left side of the brim of each to the crown

THE FIRST

and ornamented it with a black feather, starting a new style in honor of the distinguished visitor. *(John Nicholas Genin—An Illustrated History of the Hat)*

    Straw hats were made in June 1798 by twelve-year-old Betsey Metcalf (later Mrs. Baker) of Providence, R.I. She plaited seven strands of oat straws into braid which she fashioned into bonnets and trimmed with ribbons. The hats were lined with pink satin and sold for $1 to $1.25. *(Harper's Magazine October 1864)*

HAT BLOCKING AND SHAPING MACHINE was patented by Rudolph Eickemeyer and G. Osterheld of Yonkers, N.Y. Patent No. 52,661 was granted on April 3, 1866.

HAT FACTORY is believed to have been established in Danbury, Conn., in 1780 by Zadoc Benedict. He employed one journeyman and two apprentices whose total output was about eighteen hats a week. They were fur hats made from rabbit or beaver fur, and sold for $6 to $10 apiece. They are described as being "without elegance, being heavy, rough and unwieldy." *(James Montgomery Bailey—History of Danbury)*

HATCHERY. *See* Fish hatchery: Fish hatchery

HAY FEVER BOOK. *See* Medical book: Hay fever book

HEAD TAX (immigration). *See* Immigration: Immigration head tax

HEADLIGHT
    Automatic headlight control was the "Autronic-Eye," developed by the Guide Lamp Division of General Motors Corporation, Anderson, Ind., and offered to the public on January 25, 1952. Headlights automatically dimmed at the approach of an oncoming car and flashed back to bright when traffic passed.

HEADLIGHT (locomotive). *See* Locomotive headlight: Electric locomotive headlight

HEALTH BOARD
    See also Public health

    Health board (local) was appointed by Governor Thomas Sim Lee in 1792 for Baltimore, Md. Dr. John Ross was appointed quarantine physician for land and Dr. John Worthington for sea. On September 12 and 17, 1793, a quarantine was proclaimed against Philadelphia, Pa., which had a yellow fever epidemic

THE FIRST

THE FIRST

HEALTH BOARD—*Continued*
and Governor Lee interdicted all direct commerce. Beginning April 24, 1795, the Board of Health was elected instead of appointed. *(John Russel Quinan—Medical Annals of Baltimore from 1608-1880)*

Health board (municipal) armed with sufficient powers for all emergencies was the Metropolitan Board of Health established in New York City by act of New York State Legislature passed February 26, 1866 (19th section, Chapter 74, Laws of 1866), "an act to create a Metropolitan Sanitary District and Board of Health for the preservation of life and health therein, and to prevent the spread of disease therefrom." The first meeting of the board was held March 5, 1866, and presided over by Jackson Smith Schultz. The other members of the board were Drs. James Crane, Willard Parker, and John Osgood Stone.

Health board (state) was the Massachusetts State Board of Health and Vital Statistics established in 1869 by an "act to establish a State Board of Health" (Chapter 420—Acts of 1869, approved June 21, 1869). The first chairman was Henry Ingersoll Bowditch and the first secretary George Derby. Seven persons were appointed to serve terms ranging from one to seven years so that one term expired every year. The normal term of office was seven years.

Health board (state) to regulate quarantine was a joint city and state board of health "to establish quarantine for the protection of the state," authorized by Louisiana (Section 2 of Act No. 336) and approved March 15, 1855, by Governor Paul Octave Hebert. The board consisted of nine "competent citizens," six appointed by the governor with the consent of the senate and three elected by the council of New Orleans. The first president of the health board was Dr. A. Forster Axson.

HEALTH DEPARTMENT (U.S.) *See* Cabinet of the United States: Secretary of Health, Education and Welfare

HEALTH INSTRUCTION in connection with the schools was undertaken by New York City in October 1902, when the Board of Estimate and Apportionment voted $30,000. The work was undertaken in cooperation with the Henry Street Nursing Service, New York City. Nurses were assigned to certain schools so that the children would not be absent from school for minor illnesses. The first staff of municipal school nurses in the United States was employed in November 1902 by the New York City Department of Health. *(Lillian D. Wald—The House on Henry Street)*

HEALTH INSURANCE. *See* Insurance: Health insurance company

HEALTH LABORATORY
Health laboratory (municipal) was established January 1, 1888, in Providence, R.I., although some experimental work had been undertaken in December 1887. Dr. Charles Value Chapin was in charge. Dr. Gardner Taber Swarts was the medical inspector.

Health laboratory (state) for the examination of sputa to diagnose diseases for physicians was established September 1, 1894, in Providence, R.I., by the Rhode Island Department of Public Health. The laboratory was supervised by Drs. Gardner Taber Swarts and Jay Perkings. During the first six months, 115 tests were made.

HEALTH MUSEUM not connected with another institution was the Cleveland Health Museum, Cleveland, Ohio, opened November 12, 1940, to give accurate understanding of the body and knowledge of how it functions and how to care for it. The museum was incorporated December 28, 1936. The first director was Dr. Bruno Gebhard.

HEALTH ORDINANCE prohibiting spitting on the sidewalks or in other public places was passed May 12, 1896, by the New York City Department of Health. *(Sanitary Code of the Board of Health of the Health Department of the City of New York)*

HEALTH SOCIETY for the promotion of national health, composed of physicians and laymen, was the National Tuberculosis Association, organized June 6, 1904, in Atlantic City, N.J. It had about 400 members. The first annual meeting was held May 18-19, 1905, in Washington, D.C. The first president was Dr. Edward Livingston Trudeau.

HEARING AID. *See* Deaf: Hearing aid

HEART (artificial). *See* Artificial heart

HEART OPERATION. *See* Surgical operation: Heart operation in which the deep freezing technic was employed

HEATER. *See* Stove

HEATING SYSTEM
Heating system from a central station was installed in Lockport, N.Y., in 1877 by Birdsall Holly. He dug a trench and ran a steam line for a distance of 100 feet from his house to an adjoining property and found that the heat was not lost by being carried through pipes. He formed the Holly Steam Combination Company, Ltd.; the first plant was located at Elm and South Streets, Lockport, N.Y. The company is now operated by the New York State Electric and Gas Corporation, Lockport division.

THE FIRST

Heating system (steam) was installed by Walworth & Nason in 1844 in Boston, Mass. James Jones Walworth and Joseph Nason organized a company for the purpose of "warming and ventilating buildings by means of steam and hot water apparatus." They had formed a company in New York City in 1841 and established a plant in Boston in 1842. At first they used hot water for the system, converting to steam in 1844. The company is now known as the Walworth Company. *(W. C. Mattox— Walworth Manufacturing Company: Its History and Traditions)*

HEAVY WATER. *See* Water: Heavy water

HEBREW BIBLE. *See* Bible: Hebrew bible

HEBREW BOOK published in America was *"Abne Yehoshua"* (Stones of Joshua) by Joshua Ben Mordecai ha-Cohen Falk, published in 1860 in New York City. It consisted of 108 pages.

HEBREW DICTIONARY. *See* Dictionary: Hebrew dictionary

HEBREW GRAMMAR. *See* Grammar: Hebrew grammar

HEBREW LITERATURE DEGREE. *See* Degrees (academic and honorary): Master of Hebrew Literature degree awarded a woman

HEBREW TYPE was used in Stephen Day's (Steeven Daye's) *The Whole Book of Psalmes, Faithfully Translated into English Metre . . .* , issued in 1640 by the Cambridge Press, Cambridge, Mass.

HEEL (rubber). *See* Rubber: Rubber heel

HELICOPTER

Aerocycle was built by De Lackner Helicopters, Inc., Mount Vernon, N.Y., and tested at Camp Kilmer, N.J., by the U.S. Army, which bought twelve on December 29, 1955. The aerocycle weighs about 200 pounds, carries a load of about 300 pounds, has a top speed of 65 m.p.h. and a range of about 150 miles. Handlebars control the ascent and descent, the pilot steering by leaning in the direction he wants to go. The machine has helicopter blades, rises vertically, and is powered by a 41 h.p. outboard motor mounted above pontoons.

THE FIRST

Gas-turbine helicopter (turborotor) was the U.S. Navy K-225, built by the Kaman Aircraft Corporation, Bloomfield, Conn., and tested December 10, 1951, at Bradley Field, Windsor Locks, Conn. It was powered by a Boeing 502-2 gas turbine developing 175 h.p. for continuous operation; the turbine was manufactured by the Boeing Airplane Company, Seattle, Wash.

Helicopter air mail. *See* Air mail service: Helicopter air mail delivery

Helicopter battalion. *See* Army: Helicopter battalion

Helicopter commercially designed was the S-51, a four-passenger helicopter, designed and built by the Sikorsky Aircraft Division of the United Aircraft Corporation, Bridgeport, Conn., which made its initial flight February 16, 1946. It received its Approved Type Certificate from the Civil Aeronautics Authority on March 26, 1946. It cruises at 80 miles an hour and has a range of 150 miles with pilot, 3 passengers and 70 pounds of baggage.

Helicopter (direct-lift aircraft) that was successful was the VS-300, constructed in October-November 1939 by Vought-Sikorsky Aircraft, Stratford, Conn. A flight of 15 minutes and 3 seconds was made July 18, 1940, by Igor Ivan Sikorsky at Stratford, Conn., with a single main rotor, powered by a 70 h.p. Franklin engine. The helicopter had three auxiliary tail rotors for control, one turning in a vertical plane for rudder control and the other two turning in a horizontal plane on outriggers on either side of the tail.

Helicopter fully operated by remote control was the HTK-1, built by the Kaman Aircraft Corporation, Bloomfield, Conn. In July 1953, at Windsor Locks, Conn., it took off and landed; flew backward, sideward, and forward; and hovered at varying altitudes, speeds, and distances in compliance with commands from a remote control station. The signals were sent by radio from a ground station to controls in the drone.

Helicopter licensed for commercial use by the Civil Aeronautics Administration was a Bell 47B able to cruise at speeds of 1 to 100 miles an hour; fly forward, backward, or sideways; ascend or descend vertically or hover stationary. License No. 1 was granted March 8, 1946, to the New York *Journal-American,* New York City, which used the helicopter for news coverage and photo delivery.

Helicopter passenger service was instituted by New York Airways Inc., on July 9, 1953, at 9:15 A.M., with two passengers flying between La Guardia Airport and Idlewild Airport, both

THE FIRST

THE FIRST

HELICOPTER—*Continued*
in New York City. Twelve passengers were
transported the first day. The captain was Jack
S. Gallagher and the flight attendant was Neils
Johnson. (Freight service had been inaugurated
October 1, 1947, by Los Angeles Airways, Inc.,
which carried mail in the San Fernando Valley,
Calif.)

**Helicopter pilot awarded a Medal of
Honor.** See Medal: Medal of Honor awarded to a helicopter pilot

**Helicopter rescue of an American pilot be-
hind enemy lines** was effected in Korea on
September 4, 1950, by First Lieutenant Paul
Van Boven of San Mateo, Calif., and hospital
corpsman Corporal John Fuentz of Kansas City,
Mo., who rescued Captain Robert Earl Wayne
of Garden City, Long Island, N.Y., shot down
on his ninety-fifth mission.

**Helicopter to deliver material across a
picket line** was used on March 9, 1947, by
the Cornell-Dubilier Electric Corporation, New
Bedford, Mass. Seven hourly landings were
made with supplies of raw materials. The
helicopter was hired from the New England
Helicopter Service.

**Helicopter with a fully servo-controlled
intermeshing rotor** was the K-125, built by
the Kaman Aircraft Corporation, Bloomfield,
Conn. It made its initial flight in January 1947
at Windsor Locks, Conn.

Helicopter with a twin-engine was the
XHJD-1, built by the McDonnell Aircraft
Corporation, St. Louis, Mo., and tested March
1946, at the Lambert-St. Louis Municipal Airport. Two 450 h.p. Pratt and Whitney Wasp
Jr. engines, mounted midway on the pylons
extending from the fuselage, turned two 40-
foot blade rotors in opposite directions. The
helicopter could carry a 3,000-pound load, operating on either one or both of the engines. It
could take off or land vertically, hover motion-
less, fly forward, backward, or sideways. The
span from rotor tip to rotor tip was 81 feet.

President to fly in a helicopter. See President (United States): President to fly in a
helicopter

Ram-jet helicopter was the "Little Henry,"
built by the McDonnell Aircraft Corporation,
St. Louis, Mo., for the U.S. Air Force and
tested May 5, 1947, by Charles Raymond Wood,
Jr., at Lambert Field, St. Louis. It weighed
310 pounds and had a two-blade rotor, two tip

ram-jets weighing 10 pounds each, a small
rudder, and an open steel tube structure supporting the pilot, fuel tanks, and controls. It
had a 50 m.p.h forward speed and a 300-pound
lifting capacity.

Twin gas-turbine helicopter (turborotor)
was the HTK-1 helicopter, built by the Kaman
Aircraft Corporation, Bloomfield, Conn., and
flown March 26, 1954, at Bloomfield. It had two
190 h.p. Boeing 502-2 gas turbines manufactured
by the Boeing Airplane Company, Seattle,
Wash. They produced 380 h.p. and could be
used separately or simultaneously.

HELICOPTER FLIGHT
Helicopter flight of importance was made
June 16, 1922, by Henry Adler Berliner at College Park, Md., before representatives of the
U.S. Bureau of Aeronautics. The machine
raised itself three times to the height of seven
feet. It had two lifting propellers in the front,
the forward motion being obtained by tilting a
propeller in the rear of the fuselage.

Helicopter flight (cross country) was made
in a two-place army helicopter which took off
May 13, 1942, from Stratford, Conn. It flew
at low altitudes and landed at Wright Field,
Dayton, Ohio (761 miles), May 17, 1942, making sixteen stops en route. Actual flying time
was 16 hours 10 minutes. Charles Lester Morris, test pilot of Sikorsky Aircraft Division
of the United Aircraft Corporation, was the
pilot.

Helicopter flight from water was made
April 17, 1941, by Igor Ivan Sikorsky at Stratford, Conn., in a Vought-Sikorsky helicopter
mounted on rubber bags so that it could land
and take off on either land or water.

Helicopter flight of one-hour duration was
made April 15, 1941, by Igor Ivan Sikorsky,
who hovered aloft in a Vought Sikorsky VS-
300 for 1 hour 5 minutes 14.5 seconds over
Sniffen's Point, Stratford, Conn. The main lift
was supplied by a three-bladed propeller 28 feet
in diameter. On May 6, 1941, the helicopter
hovered over a tennis court for 1 hour 32 minutes 26.1 seconds.

**Helicopter pilot awarded a Medal of Hon-
or.** *See* Medal: Medal of Honor awarded
to a helicopter pilot

Helicopter refueling flight (successful) was
accomplished at Fort Rucker, Ala., August 14,
1956, when an Army twin-rotary H-21 helicopter
manufactured by the Vertol Aircraft Corporation, Morton, Pa., was refueled from a fixed-
wing tanker.

THE FIRST

Helicopter transatlantic flight was made by the U.S. Air Force Air Rescue Service in two H-19 (S-55) helicopters which left Westover Air Force Base, Mass., July 15, 1952, and arrived at the U.S. Air Force base at Wiesbaden, Germany, on August 4, 1952, in 51 hours and 55 minutes elapsed flight time. Leader of the flight was Captain Vincent Howard McGovern of Springfield, N.J., who with co-pilot Harry Celestine Jeffers of Newark, Ohio, piloted the project ship "Hop-A-Long." The accompanying aircraft, "Whirl-O-Way," was piloted by First Lieutenant Harold W. Moore of Cincinnati, Ohio, and copiloted by Major George Okie Hambrick of Carter, Okla. The 3,410-mile Atlantic crossing was made in 42 hours and 25 minutes. (*American Helicopter. August 1952*)

Transcontinental non-stop helicopter flight was made from Miramar Naval Air Station, San Diego, Calif., on August 23, 1956, to Washington, D.C., a distance of 2,610 miles in 31 hours and 40 minutes, by a twin-rotored H21. Refueled several times in flight and while hovering over El Paso, Tex., and Shreveport, La., the helicopter landed August 24, 1956. The crew consisted of Major Hugh Gaddis of Tulsa, Okla., Warrant Officer Joseph E. Givens of Stanford, Ky., Captain James E. Bowman of Amboy, Ind., Specialist Robert M. Price of St. Louis, Mo., and Pfc. Carl D. Herrington of Tulsa, Okla. The helicopter, produced by the Vertol Aircraft Corp., of Morton, Pa., weighed 3,300 pounds.

HELIPORT

Military heliport was the Fort Eustis Heliport, Felker Field, Fort Eustis, Va., dedicated December 7, 1954. The field was named for Warrant Officer Alfred Charles Felker, a graduate of the first Army helicopter pilot course who was killed in an airplane flight in February 1953. The heliport was built in the shape of a huge wheel with 600-foot runways forming the spokes and a circular taxiway composing the rim. The first commanding officer was Lieutenant Colonel Robert C. Spiedel, Jr.

HELIUM

Helium was discovered as a constituent of natural gas in 1905 by Professor Hamilton Perkins Cady and Dr. David Ford McFarland of the University of Kansas. They tested the residuum from a gas well at Dexter, Cowley County, Kan., and found that it had a 1.84 per cent helium content. (*American Chemical Society, Proceedings, 1906. On the Occurrence of Helium in Natural Gas*)

Helium-filled balloon. *See* Balloon: Balloon filled with helium gas

THE FIRST

Helium plant of the United States was the United States Production Plant, Fort Worth, Texas, completed in April 1921 under the cognizance of the Navy Department. It used the Linde Air Products Company process and was operated by that company. The Bureau of Mines assumed the supervision of this plant, July 1, 1925, and operated it until 1929 when it was closed on account of insufficient gas supply. (*Willard A. Pollard—Public Works of the Navy—Bulletin No. 31—United States Helium Production Plant*)

Helium plants (experimental) were those of the Linde Air Products Company, the Air Reduction Company, and the Jeffries-Norton Corporation, erected in 1917 and operated under the Bureau of Mines, Department of the Interior. One of these plants was erected at Petrolia, Tex., and the other two at Fort Worth, Tex. About 200,000 cubic feet of helium was produced by them in their experimental runs of which 147,000 cubic feet, compressed in steel cylinders, was on the dock at New Orleans, La., ready for shipment to France when the armistice was signed. (*Andrew Stewart—Production of Helium for Use in Airships—Bureau of Mines —1919*)

HEMOPHILIA TREATISE. *See* Medical book: Hemophilia treatise

HEMP EXPORTATION was made to England in 1730. It consisted of fifty hundredweight of hemp raised in New England and Carolina, and three hundredweight from Virginia.

HERBAL BOOK was Samuel Stearns' *The American Herbal or Materia Medica wherein the virtues of the mineral, vegetable and animal productions of North and South America are laid open*, printed in 1801 in Walpole, N.H., by D[avid] Carlisle for Thomas and Thomas and the author. It contained 360 pages.

HERD BOOK for livestock was the *American Herd Book, containing pedigrees of short horn cattle to which is prefixed a concise history, of English and American short horns*, 240 pages, edited by Lewis Falley Allen and published in 1846 in Buffalo, N.Y.

HEREDITY CLINIC. *See* Medical clinic: Heredity clinic

HERESY TRIAL of a bishop was held in 1925. William Montgomery Brown, Protestant Episcopal Bishop of Arkansas, author of *Communism and Christianity*, was deposed for heresy at New Orleans, La., on October 12, 1925. The deposition was imposed by the Right Reverend Ethelbert Talbot, D.D., presiding officer of the House of Bishops of the Protestant Episcopal

HERESY TRIAL of a bishop—*Continued*
Church. The Secretary of the House, Dr.
Charles Laban Pardee, drew a line through
Brown's name on the record. He was not ex-
communicated.

HERO FUND COMMISSION. *See* Carnegie hero fund commission

HEROINE. *See* Woman: Heroine

HIGH-DEFINITION TELEVISION. *See*
Television—Telecast: High-definition television

HIGH JUMP over seven feet was made June
29, 1956, at the Coliseum, Los Angeles, Calif.,
by Charles Dumas, a nineteen-year-old Compton
College freshman, who jumped 7 feet and ⅝
inch and was credited with 7 feet and ½ inch.

HIGH JUMPING STANDARDS using
electric eye detectors were constructed by
Lyle Hudson Bennett Peer of the General
Electric Research Laboratory and others, and
were used May 31, 1941, at the Schenectady
Patrolmen's Association interscholastic track
meet, Schenectady, N.Y. A series of four
parallel beams of light, one inch apart, recorded the height of each jump.

HIGH SCHOOL
Commercial high school. *See* Commercial
high school

County high school was the Dickinson
County Community High School, Chapman,
Kan., opened in September 1889. The first
building was constructed entirely of limestone
at a cost of $12,000. Enrollment the first year
was 137. S. M. Cook, who taught mathematics, Latin, and Greek, was the first principal.

High school was opened in May 1820 in
Boston, Mass., known as the English Classical
School. The name was changed in 1824 to the
English High School. Admittance was open to
boys at least twelve years of age who were re-
quired to be "well acquainted with reading,
writing, English grammar in all its branches,
and arithmetic, as far as simple proportions."
(*Josiah Quincy—Municipal History of the
Town and City of Boston*)

High school aviation course. *See* Aviation
—School: High school aviation course

High school business school. *See* Business
school: Business high school

High school for girls was established in
1826 in Boston, Mass., but was abolished in
1828. Instead the course of study in the elementary schools was advanced. (*Alexander
James Inglis—The Rise of the High School in
Massachusetts*)

High school to fingerprint its students. *See*
Fingerprinting: High school to fingerprint
its students

Junior high schools were the McKinley
and the Washington High Schools of Berkeley,
Calif., authorized December 21, 1909, based on
the recommendations made November 30, 1909,
by Frank Forest Bunker. They were known
as "introductory high schools." The McKinley
School housed the seventh, eighth, and ninth
grade pupils in a separate building with a reorganized curriculum and a separate administration, and opened the new term January 2, 1910,
with Charles Louis Biedenbach as principal.
The Washington High School opened on the
same date with G. W. Monroe as principal.
(*Frank Forest Bunker—The Junior High
School Movement—Its Beginnings*)

Public high school to specialize in the
performing field was the School of Performing Arts, a division of the Metropolitan Vocational High School, New York City, opened
September 13, 1948. Dr. Franklin J. Keller
was the first principal. The school is conducted
on the usual secondary school basis. However,
half the time is given to practical work in the
arts (music, dance, theater, and broadcasting)
and the other half to college preparatory academic courses, with a diploma at the end of
three years to those who have come from junior
high schools and at the end of four years of
study to those who have come from eight-year
elementary schools.

Vocational high school for girls was the
Trade School for Girls, Boston, Mass., opened
July 1904 as a summer experiment in training.
Subjects taught were plain sewing, advanced
sewing, dressmaking, millinery, machine operat-
ing, trade design, and domestic science. Florence
M. Marshall was principal.

HIGH SCHOOL LEGISLATION authorizing night classes was enacted by Ohio (Section XVI of Act passed by the Legislature of
Ohio, March 16, 1829). Accordingly there were
opened in Cincinnati, Ohio, in November 1840,
three evening schools for boys. In 1855, schools
for girls were also opened. (*Paul Monroe—
Cyclopedia of Education*)

HIGHWAY. *See* Road

HIGHWAY LEGISLATION (colonial). *See* Road: Highway legislation (colonial)

HIGHWAY TRAFFIC BUILDING. *See* Building: Building devoted entirely to highway traffic

HIGHWAY TUNNEL. *See* Tunnel: Subaqueous highway tunnel

HILL CLIMBING CONTEST. *See* Automobile hill climbing contest; Motorcycle hill climbing contest

HILLSIDE SHRINE (religious). *See* Religious hillside shrine

HINDU WOMAN TO RECEIVE A DOCTOR OF MEDICINE DEGREE. *See* Physician: Hindu woman to receive a doctor of medicine degree

HISTORICAL PRINT ENGRAVING. *See* Engraving: Historical print engraved in America

HISTORICAL SOCIETY

Historical society (general) was the American Historical Association, founded September 10, 1884, in Saratoga, N.Y., for the "promotion of historical studies, the collection and preservation of historical manuscripts." Its first report was transmitted to Congress June 16, 1890, and was published as Senate Miscellaneous Document No. 170. The first president was Andrew Dickson White. The society was incorporated by act of Congress January 4, 1889. (*American Historical Association. Papers. Vol. 1*)

Historical society (national) was the American Antiquarian Society, founded in Worcester, Mass., by Isaiah Thomas, the first printer of Worcester. Incorporated October 24, 1812, it was the first national historical society and had the first great American historical collection. The first meeting was held November 19, 1812, at the Exchange Coffee House, Boston, Mass. The first president was Isaiah Thomas, and the first vice presidents were Aaron Bancroft and Timothy Bigelow.

Historical society (state) was the Massachusetts Historical Society, organized August 26, 1790, in Boston, Mass., by five persons under the leadership of the Reverend Jeremy Belknap. Their next meeting, held on January 24, 1791, was attended by ten people. The main purpose of the society, incorporated February 19, 1794, was to gather manuscript material to be preserved and used for its publication for general use and to establish a library which would carry on the founders' plan. (*Massachusetts Historical Society. Collections. Vol II and III*)

HISTORY

American history of importance written by a woman was a three-volume narrative history of the Revolutionary War entitled *History of the Rise, Progress, and Termination of the American Revolution, Interspersed with Biographical, Political and Moral Observation,* by Mercy Otis Warren. It was published in Boston, Mass., in 1805. *(Alice Brown—Mercy Warren)*

Business history chair. *See* Business history chair

Comic history of the United States was *A Diverting History of John Bull and Brother Jonathan,* a 135-page book, by Hector Bull-Us [James Kirke Paulding], published in 1812 in New York City by Inskeep and Bradford.

History of New England published in the colonies was *New England's Memoriall, or a Brief Relation of the Most Memorable and Remarkable Passages of the Providence of God, Manifested to the Planters of New England in America: With Special Reference to the First Colony Therefore, Called New Plimouth,"* published by Nathaniel Morton, secretary to the court for the Jurisdiction of New-Plymouth. It was printed in 1669 in Cambridge, Mass. by "S. G[reen] and M. J[ohnson]," for John Usher of Boston, Mass. Edward Johnson's *A History of New-England From the English Planting in the yeere 1628 untill, the yeere 1652, Declaring the Form of Their Government, Civil, Military and Ecclesiastique,* a 236-book also known as *The Wonder-Working Providence of Sions Saviour in New England,* was published in London, England, in 1654.

Political history was *A Political and Civil History of the U.S.A. from the year 1763 to the close of the administration of President Washington in March, 1797 including a summary view of the political and civil state of the North American colonies, prior to that period,* by Timothy Pitkin. It was published in two volumes by Hezekiah Howe and Durrie and Peck in 1828 at New Haven, Conn.

Printing history. *See* Printing history

Theater history. *See* Theater history

HISTORY INSTRUCTION

American history chair was established by the University of Pennsylvania, Philadelphia, Pa., in 1850. The first incumbent was William Bradford Reed, who remained in the post until 1856.

Ancient and modern history chair was the McLean professorship endowed in 1823 under

THE FIRST

THE FIRST

HISTORY INSTRUCTION—*Continued*
the will of John McLean. It was established
at Harvard College, Cambridge, Mass., in 1838.
The first incumbent was Professor Jared
Sparks (1838-1849).

**History course (integrated) in a women's
college** was given by Professor Woodrow
Wilson at Bryn Mawr College, Bryn Mawr,
Pa., in 1885. The histories of Greece and
Rome were taken as representative of ancient
history, and of France and England as representative of medieval and modern history. The
object was to "keep the student mindful of the
broad views of history in which the events in
the lives of individual nations stand related."
*(Herbert Baxter Adams—The Study of History
in American Colleges and Universities)*

History seminar was established by the
University of Michigan at Ann Arbor, in 1869,
under the leadership of Charles Kendall Adams.
*(Andrew Ten Brook—American State Univer-
sities and the University of Michigan)*

School of modern history affiliated with a
college was established at the College of William and Mary, Williamsburg, Va., in 1803.

**HISTORY OF MEDICINE DEPART-
MENT.** *See* Medical instruction: History of
Medicine Department

HISTORY OF SCIENCE SOCIETY. *See*
Science association: History of science society

HOCKEY
Hockey game telecast. *See* Television—
Telecast: Hockey game to be televised

**Hockey team (U.S.) to win the Stanley
Cup** was the Seattle (Wash.) Metropolitans
of the Pacific Coast League of Canada, which
defeated the Montreal Canadiens of the National Hockey League on March 21, 24, and 27,
1917, winning three of the four games played
to decide the series.

Negro player in organized hockey was
Arthur Dorrington, who signed with the Atlantic City Seagulls of the Eastern Amateur
League on November 15, 1950, and played for
them in 1950 and 1951.

HOIST. *See* Crane: Crane

HOLD-UP OF AN ARMORED CAR. *See*
Automobile robbery: Armored commercial
car hold-up

HOLDING COMPANY authorization
(state) was enacted by New Jersey on April
4, 1888, "an act concerning corporations of
this state, and of other states, doing business
in this state." It provided that it was "lawful
for any corporation of this state, or of any
other state, doing business in this state and authorized by law to own and hold shares of
stocks and bonds of corporations of other
states, to own and hold and dispose thereof
in the same manner and with all the rights,
powers and privileges of individual owners of
shares of the capital stock and bonds or other
evidences of indebtedness of corporations of
this state."

HOLE-IN-ONE GOLF CHAMPION. *See*
Golf champion: Holes-in-one by a father
and son

HOLIDAY
Arbor Day celebration was held on April
10, 1872, in Nebraska. Governor Julius Sterling
Morton suggested the holiday and helped celebrate it by causing trees to be planted throughout the state. Arbor Day did not become a
legal holiday in Nebraska until April 22, 1885,
Morton's birthday.

Armistice Day was celebrated simultaneously in many cities on November 11, 1919.
Two California redwood trees were planted in
Lafayette Square, opposite the White House,
Washington, D.C., in the presence of cabinet
officers, General Pershing and other military and
federal officials.

Decoration Day celebration was held May
30, 1868. Two years after the Civil war, April
26, 1866, the women of Columbus, Miss., strewed
flowers on the graves of both the Confederate
and Union soldiers at Friendship Cemetery. In
May 1868, Adjutant General Norton Parker
Chipman suggested to National Commander
John Alexander Logan of the Grand Army of
the Republic that this organization inaugurate
the custom of spreading flowers on the graves
of Union soldiers at periodic intervals. General
Logan appointed May 30, 1868, as the date "for
the purpose of strewing with flowers or otherwise decorating the graves of comrades who
died in defense of their country during the
late rebellion and with the hope that it will be
kept up from year to year." The custom of
decorating graves of soldiers, however, had
often been locally observed previously.

Father's Day celebration was held on June
19, 1910. The idea originated with Mrs. John
Bruce Dodd, and the holiday was launched by
the Ministerial Association and the YMCA of
Spokane, Wash.

Flag Day remembrance took place in 1877.
The Government requested that the flag be

THE FIRST

THE FIRST

flown from all public buildings on June 14, 1877, in commemoration of the 100th anniversary of the adoption of the American flag. Flag Day was made a legal holiday by Pennsylvania on May 7, 1937 (Act No. 155). It established June 14 as Flag Day and provided that the holiday be celebrated on Monday when it falls on Sunday.

Frontier Day holiday was celebrated by Cheyenne, Wyo. The first Cheyenne Frontier Day celebration was held at the Fair Grounds, Cheyenne, on Thursday, September 23, 1897. From a one-day exhibition, the show has grown to a five-day spectacle of ranch and range sports, Indian games and dances, military maneuvers by soldiers of the U.S. Army and races requiring the utmost skill in horsemanship. Other cities had similar celebrations under different names. *(Cheyenne Frontier Days—Cheyenne Chamber of Commerce)*

Indian Day observance was held on May 13, 1916, sponsored by the Society of American Indians. The purpose was to recognize and honor the American Indian and to improve his condition. Indian Day is not a universal holiday. The states that have an Indian population of over 10,000 are Arizona, California, Minnesota, Montana, New Mexico, New York, North Dakota, Oklahoma, South Dakota, Washington, and Wisconsin.

Labor Day holiday was inaugurated December 28, 1869, by the Knights of Labor, an organization formed in Philadelphia, Pa. Annual observance was sponsored by the American Federation of Labor which resolved in convention at Chicago, Ill., on October 7, 1884 "that the first Monday in September be set aside as a laborer's national holiday."

Labor Day holiday (federal) was officially declared by act of Congress of June 28, 1894 (28 Stat.L.96), "an act making Labor Day a legal holiday." It designated the first Monday in September a legal holiday for federal employees and for the District of Columbia. There are no national holidays created for the nation as each state declares for its own jurisdiction the holidays to be observed, either by legislative enactment or by executive proclamation.

Labor Day holiday parade was held September 5, 1882, in New York City under the auspices of the Central Labor Union. Ten thousand workmen, accompanied by bands of music, paraded carrying placards, "Less Work and More Pay"; "Less Hours More Pay"; "Labor Pays All Taxes"; "Labor Creates All Wealth"; "To the Workers Should Belong the Wealth"; "The Laborer Must Receive and Enjoy the Full Fruit of His Labor," etc. *(American Federationist—October 1897)*

Labor Day law (state) making Labor Day a state holiday was passed February 21, 1887, by Oregon. Colorado passed a similar law March 15, 1887, and New York, May 6, 1887.

Mardi Gras of New Orleans, La., had its inception in 1827 when a group of young men returned from Paris and introduced the French carnival idea. Mardi Gras is always on the Tuesday before Ash Wednesday, the day which marks the beginning of the Lenten season.

Maritime Day was established by joint resolution of Congress, May 20, 1933 (48 Stat. L.73) as May 22, the anniversary of the sailing of the steamship "Savannah" from Savannah, Ga., on May 22, 1819. The resolution authorized and requested the President "annually to issue a proclamation calling upon the people of the United States to observe National Maritime Day by displaying the flag."

Memorial Day. *See above* Decoration Day

Mother-in-Law Day was celebrated March 5, 1934, at Amarillo, Tex. The honored mother was Mrs. W. F. Donald, the mother-in-law of Gene Howe, part owner and editor of the Amarillo *Daily News* and the Amarillo *Globe,* who was responsible for the celebration.

Mother's Day was suggested by Miss Anna Jarvis, of Philadelphia, Pa., at a public meeting in 1907. She proposed wearing a carnation on the second Sunday of May. The first city to adopt the plan was Philadelphia which designated May 10, 1908, as the first Mother's Day. Mother's Day received national recognition May 12, 1914.

National holiday was April 30, 1889, authorized by act of Congress March 21, 1889 (25 Stat.L.980), to observe the centennial of the inauguration of George Washington. The day was "hereby declared to be a national holiday throughout the United States." A committee of five senators and five representatives of the Fifty-first Congress was appointed to arrange an appropriate celebration in Congress on December 11, 1889, at which Chief Justice Melville Weston Fuller was the guest speaker.

Navy Day was suggested by Mrs. William Hamilton to the Secretary of the Navy, and celebrated October 27, 1922, the anniversary of the birth of President Theodore Roosevelt. Celebrations in commemoration were held in various parts of the United States.

Saturday half holiday was inaugurated by George Westinghouse, the inventor and manufacturer of the airbrake, who established the

THE FIRST

HOLIDAY—*Continued*
custom in his factory in Pittsburgh, Pa., in
June 1871. *(Francis Ellington Leupp—George
Westinghouse, His Life and Achievements)*

Thanksgiving Day designated by presidential proclamation was November 26, 1789.
On October 3, 1789, President George Washington issued a proclamation appointing November 26, 1789, as a day of general thanksgiving for the adoption of the Constitution.
(Howard Sylvester Jackson Sickel—Thanksgiving)

Thanksgiving Day celebration (nationwide, colonial) was held Thursday, December 18, 1777, commemorating the surrender of
Lieutenant General John Burgoyne on October
17, 1777, at Schuylerville, N.Y. On October 31,
1777, the Continental Congress appointed
Samuel Adams, Richard Henry Lee, and Daniel
Roberdeau to draft a recommendation "to set
apart a day of thanksgiving for the signal success lately obtained over the enemies of the
United States." The resolution was accepted
November 1, 1777, and on November 7, 1777, it
was voted "that a duplicate of the recommendation of Congress to the several states to
set apart a day of thanksgiving signed by the
president be sent to the respective states, and
to General Washington and General Gates."
*(Journals of the Continental Congress 1774-1789.
Volume 9)*

Thanksgiving Day national proclamation
was made on October 3, 1863, by President
Abraham Lincoln, who set the fourth Thursday in November, a date which has since been
generally nationally observed. Special thanksgiving days had been previously set aside for
specific occasions of thanks. On April 10,
1862, Lincoln requested the nation "to implore
spiritual consolation . . . at their next weekly
assemblages in their accustomed places of
pubic worship." On July 15, 1863, he designated
Thursday, August 6, 1863, "to subdue the anger
which has produced and so long sustained a
needless and cruel rebellion."

Thanksgiving Day sermon (west of the
Alleghenies) was given by the Reverend Charles
Beatty, a Presbyterian minister, on November
26, 1758. He delivered a sermon entitled "A
Clarion of Calvinism," at Duquesne (now Pittsburgh), Pa.

Thanksgiving Day service was held August 9, 1607, at Phippsburg, Me., by colonists
on "The Gift of God" and the "Mary and
John" under the leadership of George Popham,
who landed at "St. Georges Illand." Services
were held by the Reverend Richard Seymour,
"gyvinge God thanks for our happy metinge &
saffe aryval into the country." *(Henry Otis
Thayer—The Sagahadoc Colony)*

THE FIRST

HOLY MASS (Catholic). *See* Catholic
Mass

HOLY ORDERS. *See* Catholic holy orders

HOME LOAN BANK BOARD. *See* Federal home loan bank board

HOME OWNERS' LOAN CORPORATION was authorized by the Home Owners'
Loan Act of 1933, approved by President Franklin Delano Roosevelt, June 13, 1933 (47 Stat.
L.736), "to grant long term mortgage loans at
low interest rates to those in urgent need of
funds for the protection, preservation or recovery of their homes who were unable to procure
the needed financing through normal channels."
The Federal Home Loan Bank Board, consisting
of five members, was organized under the
Federal Home Loan Bank Act, approved July
22, 1932, to establish and supervise the twelve
Federal Home Loan Banks according to the
provisions of the act. Franklin Fort was appointed chairman of the Federal Home Loan
Bank Board on July 22, 1932. The Federal
Home Loan Bank System is a permanent system
which makes loans to members of home financing institutions for home financing purposes. The Home Owners' Loan Corporation
was a temporary emergency corporation loaning
directly to home owners who were threatened
with foreclosure and were unable to obtain the
money for refinancing through private channels.

"HOME RUN KING." *See* Baseball player:
Baseball "home run king"

HOME STUDY COURSE of a serious nature was offered by the Literary and Scientific
Circle of the Chautauqua Institution which was
organized August 10, 1878. In harmony with
the plan of the first work of the Assembly, the
correspondence School of Theology was organized and in 1881 received its charter. On
March 30, 1833, the Chautauqua College of
Liberal Arts was given a charter by the legislature of the State of New York, conferring
full authority to grant diplomas and to confer
the usual college and university degrees.
See also Chautauqua organization

HOMEOPATHIC COLLEGE. *See* Medical school: Homeopathic college

HOMEOPATHIC HOSPITAL. *See* Hospital: Homeopathic hospital

HOMEOPATHIC MAGAZINE. *See* Medical periodical: Homeopathic magazine

HOMEOPATHIC MEDICAL SOCIETY.
See Medical Society: Homeopathic medical
society

THE FIRST

HOMEOPATHY was brought to New York City in 1825 by Dr. Hans Burch Gram. In 1828 Gram was elected a member of the New York Medical and Philosophical Society, and in 1829 became its president. *(Thomas Lindsley Bradford—The Pioneers of Homeopathy)*

HOMEOPATHY TREATISE. *See* Medical book: Homeopathic treatise

HOMES (institutional). See Old Age Home for pioneers; Soldiers' homes (national)

HOMESTEAD under the Homestead Act was taken by Daniel Freeman, a Union soldier, on January 1, 1863, near Beatrice, Neb.

HOMESTEAD ACT
Homestead act was "an act to secure homesteads to actual settlers on the public domain," passed by both houses of Congress on May 19, 1862, and approved on May 20, 1862 (12 Stat.L. 392) by President Abraham Lincoln. It went into effect on January 1, 1863. Under this law any man or woman of twenty-one could secure title to 160 acres of public land by living on it for five years, making certain improvements, and paying fees of approximately $18.

Homestead act (desert) was enacted on March 3, 1875 (18 Stat.L.497), "to sell the desert land in Lassen County, Calif., at $1.25 an acre." This act differed from the Homestead Act of May 20, 1862 (12 Stat.L.392) in that the owner was not required to reside on the land and that he could purchase four times the quantity of land permitted under the Homestead Act.

HONOLULU SQUADRON FLIGHT. *See* Aviation—Flights (transpacific): Honolulu squadron flight

HONOR SYSTEM of conducting examinations was introduced by the College of William and Mary, Williamsburg, Va., in 1779, *(Bulletin of the College of William and Mary in Virginia)*

HONORS COURSE. *See* College: Honors course

HOOKLESS FASTENER. *See* Fastening: Hookless fastening

HOOKS AND EYES. *See* Fastening: Hooks and eyes

HORIZON CURVATURE PHOTOGRAPH. *See* Photograph: Photograph showing the lateral curvature of the horizon

THE FIRST

HORMONE. *See* Pituitary hormone

HORSE
Forest horse born in the United States was Pepin, sired by Charlemagne and foaled by Siegling, May 18, 1956, at the Chicago Zoological Park, Brookfield, Ill. This extinct forest breed was recreated by crossing over three hundred Iceland ponies, Shetland ponies, Dartmoor ponies, Norwegian duns, Hanover coach horses, feral horses from Patagonia, and Koniks of Poland. The first forest horses were imported into the United States in 1955.

Haflinger horse was imported by Tempel Smith of Spring Grove, Ill., who imported 17 horses (10 mares, 3 stallions, 2 fillies, and 2 colts) on August 18, 1958. They arrived in New York Harbor from Austria. The Haflinger is compactly built, longer than tall, with a height of 140-150 centimeters at the withers.

Horse farm operated by the United States Government was the United States Morgan Horse Farm, Middlebury, Vt., established in 1907 on 400 acres donated by Colonel Joseph Battell of Middlebury, Vt. The first 270 acres of land were deeded to the United States by Battell, February 1, 1907. Horse breeding under the Bureau of Animal Industry began in December 1904, a cooperative enterprise with the Colorado Experiment Station to develop an American utility horse. *(U.S. Department of Agriculture—The Preservation of Our Native Types of Horses—Circular 137)*

Horse (Morgan horse) was named after its owner, Justin Morgan. It was foaled in 1789 in Randolph, Vt., and got by True Briton, also known as Beautiful Bay. It died in 1821. *(Joseph Battell—The Morgan Horse and Register)*

Horse (Percheron horse) importation was attempted by Edward Harris of Moorestown, N.J., in 1839. Four horses were obtained from France, but only a mare survived the trip. Two stallions and two mares were subsequently imported, one of the stallions (Diligence) being credited with 400 foals. *(Ellis McFarland—Brief History of the Percheron Horse)*

Horse race. *See* Horse race

Horse show. *See* Horse show

Horse (thoroughbred) is claimed to be Bulle Rock, who was imported into Virginia in 1730. He was foaled in 1717 and was a son of Darley Arabian and the mare Byerly Turk. It is also claimed that the first thoroughbred horse was Spark, who was presented to Lord Baltimore by the Prince of Wales, the father

HORSE—*Continued*
of George III. Lord Baltimore gave Spark
to Governor Samuel Ogle of Maryland about
1750. (*John Gilmer Speed—The Horse in
America*)

Horse to pace better than 2:00 was Star
Pointer, in harness at Readville, Mass., on
August 28, 1897. The time was one mile in
1:59¼. (*Hamilton Busbey—The Trotting and
the Pacing Horse in America*)

**Horse to trot a mile in less than two
minutes** was Lou Dillon, which established a
record of 1:58½ on August 24, 1903, at Readville, Mass. She was driven by Millard F.
Sanders at a paced trial with a pacemaker in
front. (*Henry Troth Coates—A Short History
of the American Trotting and Pacing Horse*)

Horse to win a million dollars in races
was Citation, a six-year-old of Calumet Farms,
which won the $100,000 Hollywood Gold Cup
Handicap at Hollywood Park, Inglewood, Calif.,
on July 14, 1951, bringing his total earnings
from 1947 to 1951 to $1,085,760.

Horse to win the triple crown, the "Big
Three," for three-year-olds, was Sir Barton.
In 1919 he won a total of $57,275—on May 1,
$20,825 in the Kentucky Derby, Churchill
Downs, Ky.; on May 14, $24,500 in the Preak-
ness, Pimlico, Md., and on June 11, 1919, $11,950
in the Belmont Stakes, Belmont Park, Long
Island, N.Y. At Belmont a new track record
was set for the mile and three furlong course.

Horse (trotting horse) was Messenger, a
gray horse 15 hands 3 inches high, foaled in
1780. He was imported from England and
arrived at Philadelphia, Pa., in May 1788. He
was buried with military honors January 28,
1808. (*John Hervey—Messenger, The Great
Progenitor*)

**Horse whose total purses exceeded
$100,000** was Miss Woodford, foaled 1880.
She won 37 of 48 races between 1882 and 1886
for a purse of $118,270.00. The mare was the
entry of the Dwyer Brothers (Michael and
Philip).

Horses were imported into the colonies
about April 17, 1629, by the Massachusetts
Bay Colony. The agreement made by Mat-
thewe Cradock, first governor of the company,
required that "such cattle, both horses, mares,
cowes, bulls, and goates, as are shipped by Mr.
Cradock, are to bee devyded in equall halfes
twixt him & the Companie." (*Nathaniel Bradstreet Shurtleff—Records of the Governor and
Company of the Massachusetts Bay in New
England. Vol. 1*)

HORSE BREEDING SOCIETY was the
Massachusetts Society for Encouraging the
Breed of Fine Horses, formed in Boston, Mass.,
in 1810. Annual trials and competitions were
held October 23-25, at the Washington course,
Boston, Mass. Rules provided that "every driver
shall be dressed at starting neatly with a jockey
cap, silk jacket with sleeves." etc.
See also Animal breeding society

HORSE CAR. *See* Street car: Street car

HORSE FARM. *See* Horse: Horse farm

HORSE RACE
See also Horse; Jockey

**American-bred horse to win a major race
abroad** was Prioress, a four-year-old bay
mare, winner of the Cesarewitch Handicap at
Newmarket, England on October 13, 1857.
There were 37 starters, of whom 3 tied. In the
run-off after the regular daily program, Prioress
won by a length and a half (4 minutes 15
seconds for the 2 mile 468 yard course). The
odds were 100 to 1. Her owner was Richard
Ten Broeck. (*Spirit of the Times—November
7, 1857*)

**American-bred horse to win the English
Derby** was Iroquois, a three-year-old, owned
by Pierre Lorillard, winner of the Epsom
Derby at Epsom Downs, England, on June 1,
1881. There were fourteen competitors. Fred
Archer was the jockey.

Filly to win the Kentucky Derby was
Regret, Harry Payne Whitney's chestnut filly.
She ran the mile and a quarter in 2:05⅗ on
May 8, 1915, to win the forty-first Kentucky
Derby. There were sixteen starters.

Futurity race was held October 10, 1843,
at Nashville, Tenn., and known as the Peyton
Stakes. Out of thirty nominations, only four
faced the starter. Four one-mile heats were
held. Glumbalditch, a filly owned by Thomas
Kirkham of Nashville, Tenn., won the third
and fourth heat, thereby winning the race and
a purse of $35,000. She was later renamed
Peytona.

**Harness horse race (Hambletonian) for
three-year-olds** was won by Guy McKinney,
a four-year old, winner of $45,868.42 of the
$73,451.32 purse in 2:05¼ at the initial stake,
August 30, 1926, at the New York State Fair,
Syracuse, N.Y. The horse was owned by Henry
B. Rea of Pittsburgh, Pa., and driven by Nat
Ray. The first driver to win the Hambletonian
twice was Benjamin Franklin White, who won
August 16, 1933, with Mary Reynolds and on
August 12, 1936 with Rosalind (at Goshen,
N.Y.) (*Elizabeth Sharts—Cradle of the Trotter*)

THE FIRST

Harness race driver to win the Hamble-tonian four times was Benjamin Franklin White, who won the eighteenth stake on August 11, 1943, at the Empire City Track, Yonkers, N.Y. There were 11 starters and 8 recalls. White won on Volo Song, a bay colt owned by W. H. Strang. His other victories were on Mary Reynolds in 1933, Rosalind in 1936, and The Ambassador in 1942, all at Goshen, N.Y.

Horse race run on a regular basis was held on the Newmarket Course, Hempstead Plains, Long Island, N.Y., in 1665, when Governor Richard Nichols, the first English governor of New York, established the course. He issued the order to measure off a mile course on the level prairie near the village and gave a cup to reward the owner of the swiftest running horse, "not so much for the divertisement of youth as for encouraging the bettering of the breed of horses, which through neglect has been impaired." *(Farmer's Home Journal. August 1930)*

Horse race (American Derby) was held at Washington Park Club, Chicago, Ill., on June 28, 1884. The race for three-year-olds was won by Modesty (Isaac Murphy, jockey) whose time for the 1½ mile course was 2:42¾. He won $10,700 in a field of twelve. *(Goodwin's Annual Turf Guide for 1884)*

Horse race in which the British Royal Silks participated was the third running of the Washington, D.C., International, the seventh race, at Laurel, Md., on November 3, 1954. Queen Elizabeth II entered Landau, a three-year-old carrying the royal purple, gold, and scarlet silks. The jockey was Willie Snaith. The horse finished last. The $50,000 first prize in the $65,000 event was won by Eddie Arcaro riding Fisherman.

Horse race (Kentucky Derby) was run May 17, 1875, at the Churchill Downs Course at Louisville, Ky. There were fifteen starters. Aristides (jockey, O. Lewis) won a $2,850 purse covering the mile and a half course in 2:37¾. Volcano was second, Verdigris, third.

Horse race of a thousand miles started 5:30 P.M., June 13, 1893, at Chadron, Neb., each contestant being allowed two race horses, one to ride and one to follow. The destination was Chicago, Ill., via Long Pine, Oneill, and Wausa, Neb.; Sioux City, Galva, Fort Dodge, Iowa Falls, Waterloo, Manchester, and Dubuque, Iowa; and Freeport, De Kalb, and Chicago, Ill. The winner, John Berry on Poison, arrived June 27, 1893, at 9:30 P.M., followed on June 28, by Emmet Albright at 11:15 A.M., and Joe Gillespie at 1:31 P.M.

THE FIRST

Horse race prohibition legislation was enacted June 4, 1674, by Massachusetts. It provided "that whatsoeuer p'son shall run a race with any horse in any street or Comon road shall forfeite fiue shillings in Mony forthwith to be leuied by the Constable or set in the stockes one houre if it be not payed." *(David Pulsifer—Records of the Colony of New Plymouth in New England)*

Horse to win a $100,000 purse in one race was Whichone, a two-year-old, son of Chicle and Flying Witch, winner of the Fortieth Belmont Futurity at Belmont Park Race Track, Elmont, Long Island, N.Y., on September 14, 1929. The time was 1:19⅗ for 6¾ furlongs (approximately ⅞ mile). The purse was $105,730. Harry Payne Whitney was the owner and Sonny Workman the jockey. There were seventeen starters in the race.

Jockey. *See* Jockey

Race track at which more than $5,000,000 was bet in one day was Belmont Park, Long Island, N.Y. On September 22, 1945, bets amounting to $5,016,745 were placed by 46,614 people, setting four records: a world mark for a daily double—$210,982; a world record for betting in one day—$5,016,745; a national record for a jumping race—$404,230; and a New York mark for a single race—$769,171.

Steeplechase. *See* Steeplechase

Three-hundred-mile endurance run was held on October 15, 1919, from Fort Ethan Allen, Burlington, Vt., to Camp Devens, Mass. Ramela, owned by W. R. Brown, president of the Arab Club, and ridden by Albert W. Harris of Chicago, Ill., won the $1,000 prize and the United States Mounted Service challenge cup. The horse won 23 34/60 points of a possible 25, covering the distance in 51 hours 26½ minutes. Kingfisher was second and won the $500 prize. There were fourteen starters. Points were determined by rating the condition of the horses, the food consumption, etc. Entrants were required to cover sixty miles a day and were ridden not less than ten hours and not more than fifteen hours a day, carrying weights from 200 to 245 pounds.

Trotting course was established at Jamaica, Long Island, N.Y., in 1825 by the New York Trotting Club. On May 16, 1825, the main race was won by Screwdriver.

Trotting futurity was the Spirit of the Times stake, a sweepstake for three-year-old trotting colts and fillies in 1866. The entrance fee was $250, of which $100 was paid on registration and $150 before the race. A one-mile harness race was held October 12, 1869,

HORSE RACE—*Continued*
at Prospect Park Pleasure Grounds, Brooklyn,
N.Y. Seventeen horses were entered. The race
was won by Isaiah Rynder's Aberdeen (son of
Hambletonian and Widow Machree) in 2 minutes and 46 seconds. The first prize was $2,000,
the second prize $500, and third prize $250.
(*Spirit of the Times. November 16, 1867, and
October 16, 1869*)

HORSE REGISTER
Horse pacing register was the *American
Race-Turf Register, Sportsman's Herald and
General Stud Book; containing the pedigrees
of the most celebrated horses, mares, and geld-
ings that have distinguished themselves as pacers
on the American turf,* 602 pages, by Patrick
Nisbett Edgar, published in 1833 in New York
City.

Trotting register was John Hankins Wallace's *American Trotting Register, containing
all that is known of the pedigrees of trotting
horses, their ancestors and descendants, with
a full record of all published performances in
which a mile was trotted or paced in 2.40 or
less, from the earliest dates till the close of
1868,* a 504-page book published in 1871 in
New York City.

HORSE SHOW
Horse show was the Upperville Colt and
Horse Show, Upperville, Va., established in
1853 by Colonel Richard Hunter Dulany. Shows
were held annually in June until the Civil War.
The first show after the war was held November
10, 1869. Fairs have been held every year
since.

Horse show of national scope was held at
Madison Square Garden, New York City, October 22-26, 1883, by the National Horse Show
Association of America. There were 187 exhibitors wth 623 entries. Cornelius Fellowes was
president of the association from its organization in 1883 until 1909.

**HORSEBACK RIDER (WOMAN) TO
MAKE A SOLO CONTINENTAL TRIP.**
See Woman: Woman horseback rider to
make a solo transcontinental trip

HORSEBLANKETS. *See* Blanket: Horseblankets

**HORSESHOE MANUFACTURING MA-
CHINE** was patented on November 23, 1835
by Henry Burden of Troy, N.Y., who received
subsequent patents in 1843, 1857 and 1862. His
machine produced a completed horseshoe from a
rod of iron that was fed into it. It produced
shoes more rapidly and uniformly than the hand
production method which had been used prior

to this invention. (*Margaret Burden Proudfit—
Henry Burden, His Life, and a History of His
Inventions*)

**HORSESHOE PITCHERS' ASSOCIA-
TION (national)** was the Grand League of
the American Horseshoe Pitchers Association
organized May 16, 1914, in Kansas City, Kan.
Rules were standardized. Pegs were raised to
8 inches and spaced 38½ feet apart. Ringers
counted 5 points and leaners 3 points. The first
championship tournament was held October 23,
1915, in Kellerton, Iowa. Frank Jackson won
the championship winning 24 out of 25 games.

**HORSESHOE PITCHING CONTEST
(international)** open to all was held in Bronson, Kan., in 1909. Frank Jackson of Blue
Mound, Kan., was awarded the World's
Championship belt with miniature horseshoes
attached to it.

HORTICULTURAL MAGAZINE was the
Floral Magazine and Botanical Repository,
published May 1832 in Philadelphia, Pa., by
D[avid] & C[uthbert] Landreth, nurserymen
and seedsmen. Publication ceased after 80
pages and 31 colored lithograph prints had
been issued.

HORTICULTURAL SOCIETY
Horticultural society was the New York
Horticultural Society, founded in 1818 and
incorporated March 22, 1822. It existed about
fifteen years.

Horticultural society (permanent) was the
Pennsylvania Horticultural Society, organized
November 24, 1827, in Philadelphia, Pa., with
a membership of 53. Horace Binney was the
first president. The first exhibition open to
the public was held June 6, 1829. It is the
oldest horticultural society still in existence.
(*James Boyd—History of the Pennsylvania
Horticulture Society*)

HOSE (fire). *See* Fire hose

HOSE (nylon). *See* Nylon: Nylon hose

HOSPITAL
Ambulance ship. *See* Ship: Ambulance
ship

Animal hospital. *See* Veterinary hospital

Army Field Hospital was a tent hospital
established by Brigadier General Bernard John
Dowling Irwin of the Army Medical Corps at
Shiloh, Tenn., prior to the battle of April 6-7,
1862, when the Union army suffered more than
13,000 casualties.

Babies' hospital designed exclusively for infants was the Babies Hospital of the City of New York, which was chartered on June 23, 1887. The hospital opened in a house at 161 East 36th Street, New York City, with a total of eight beds. *(Twenty-Fifth Annual Report—Babies Hospital of the City of New York)*

Cancer home for incurables (free) was established in a room in a flat on Scammel Street, New York City, on September 15, 1896, by Rose Hawthorne Lathrop (later Sister Mary Alphonsa, O.D.) afterward assisted by Alice Huber (later Sister Mary Rose, O.D.). They organized the Servants of Relief for Incurable Cancer and on May 1, 1899, opened St. Rose's Free Home for Incurable Cancer in New York City, with accommodations for fifteen patients. On June 1, 1901, a building in the country was acquired which carried on the work under the name of Rosary Hill Home at Sherman Park (now Hawthorne), N.Y.

Cancer hospital was the New York Cancer Hospital, 106th Street and Central Park West, New York City. The hospital had its beginning at a preliminary meeting held February 7, 1884, at the residence of Mrs. Elizabeth Hamilton Cullum and was incorporated May 31, 1884, "to establish, maintain and conduct a cancer hospital." It was opened for patients December 7, 1887, and by special act of March 6, 1899, of the legislature, its name was changed to the General Memorial Hospital for the Treatment of Cancer and Allied Diseases. On March 22, 1916, a court order was obtained to drop "General" from the title, effective April 26, 1916, and its name became the Memorial Hospital for the Treatment of Cancer and Allied Diseases. The first attending surgeons were Dr. James Bradbridge Hunter, Dr. Clement Cleveland and Dr. William Tillinghast Bull. The first president was John E. Parsons. The hospital is now located at 444 East 68th Street, New York City. *(Milestones of Memorial Hospital)*

Cancer hospital (municipal) was the New York City Cancer Institute on Welfare Island, New York City, dedicated August 1, 1923. The first patient was admitted August 23, 1923. Dr. Isaac Levin was the first director.

Children's hospital was established in 1854 in New York City and was known as "The Nursery and Child's Hospital." It originated from a society founded by Sarah Platt Doremus and Mrs. Cornelius Du Bois "for the maintenance and care of the children of wet-nurses, and the daily charge of infants whose parents labor away from home." *(106th Annual Report —New York Nursery and Child's Hospital, 1928)*

Chinese hospital was the Chinese Hospital, Jackson Street, San Francisco, Calif., opened

April 18, 1925. The first board of directors included B. S. Seid, president; B. S. Fong, vice president; Yee Y. Ng, secretary; and Chow King, treasurer.

Community hospital was the Community Hospital, Elk City, Okla., established by Dr. Michael Abraham Shadid. The organization meeting was held October 20, 1929. The hospital was dedicated August 13, 1931. *(Michael Abraham Shadid—A Doctor for the People)*

Consumptive hospital. *See* Hospital: Tuberculosis hospital

Crippled children's hospital (state) was the Gillette State Hospital for Crippled Children, St. Paul, Minn., authorized April 23, 1897 (Chapter 289, Laws of 1897) by "an act to provide for the care and treatment of crippled and deformed children." Five thousand dollars was appropriated. The hospital was named in honor of Dr. Arthur Jay Gillette.

Dispensary established for the specific purpose of furnishing free medicine to the needy was the Philadelphia Dispensary, instituted on April 12, 1786, by Bishop William White. It was chartered April 15, 1796 and was governed by twelve managers elected annually. It was not, however, the first to do free out-patient work, as the Pennsylvania Hospital treated indigent outpatients as early as December 13, 1752. The Philadelphia Dispensary affiliated with the Pennsylvania Hospital in 1922. *(Thomas George Morton and Frank Woodbury—The History of the Pennsylvania Hospital)*

Eye hospital (permanent) was the New York Eye Infirmary, a two-room hospital on the second floor at 45 Chatham Street, New York City, which was opened August 14, 1820, and incorporated March 29, 1822. The chief surgeons were Dr. Edward Delafield and Dr. John Kearney Rodgers. The first officers were William Few, president; Henry I. Wyckoff, first vice president; John Hone, second vice president; John Delafield, treasurer; and James I. Jones, secretary. By January 1, 1822, the infirmary had treated 1,120 cases and cured 801. On April 30, 1864, the name was changed to the New York Eye and Ear Infirmary. *(Alvin Allace Hubbell—Development of Ophthalmology in America)*

Eye infirmary was established in New London, Conn., in 1817 by Elisha North. He studied at the University of Pennsylvania Medical School but did not obtain his M.D. degree. In appreciation of his interest and effort in behalf of medicine, he was later awarded an M.D. degree in Connecticut. *(Johns Hopkins Hospital Bulletin. October 1908)*

HOSPITAL—*Continued*

Floating hospital was the "Emma Abbott," which made her trial trip July 19, 1875. It was known as the "poor children's yacht" and was operated by St. John's Guild, New York City (organized October 19, 1866 and incorporated December 14, 1877). The ship served until 1902, when it was replaced with a more modern ship. In the summer of 1873, the Guild hired a barge and gave two excursions for sick children, and in 1874 eighteen similar excursions, accommodating 15,202 sick children and mothers. So noticeable was the health benefit that the Guild decided to operate its own floating hospitals. (*St. John's Guild—Sixty-seventh Annual Report*)

Group hospital-medical cooperative. *See* Insurance: Group hospital-medical cooperative

Homeopathic hospital was the Homeopathic Hospital of Pennsylvania, Philadelphia, Pa., incorporated September 20, 1850. Vincent L. Bradford was the first president. In 1852, a hospital with thirty beds was opened which served for about two years.

Hospital completely devoted to the study of the atom in the treatment of cancer was the Argonne Cancer Research Hospital, Chicago, Ill., operated for the Atomic Energy Commission by the University of Chicago as part of the university's South Side Cancer Research Center. The hospital, which was opened March 13, 1953, contained eight floors, two of which were underground. Bed space was limited to two floors to accommodate 56 patients. Other floors were devoted to equipment and laboratories. The first director was Dr. Leon Orris Jacobson. The cost of the building and equipment was about $4,000,000.

Hospital for the military and naval forces was the Army and Navy Hospital, Hot Springs, Ark., opened for the reception of patients on January 17, 1887. The appropriation was authorized by act of Congress of June 30, 1882 (22 Stat.L.121). The hospital had five separate buildings which were connected by verandas. (*Charles Cutter—Guide to the Hot Springs of Arkansas*)

See also above Army field hospital; *and* below Marine hospital; Naval hospital

Hospital in America was the Pennsylvania Hospital, opened in Philadelphia February 11, 1752 through the efforts of Benjamin Franklin and Dr. Thomas Bond. A temporary hospital was erected in 1751 in a private house on High (now Market) Street. The care of the sick, however, had been undertaken earlier by both secular and religious agencies. St. Augustine, Fla., set aside six beds in a home for the poor in 1565; the Dutch West India Company on

December 20, 1656, appointed Master Jacob Hendrickszen Varrevanger surgeon in New Amsterdam to look after the sick; the Ursulines of New Orleans, La., opened an infirmary without restrictions July 17, 1734, with Sister Xavier Herbert as the chief infirmarian. (*Thomas George Morton and Frank Woodbury —The History of the Pennsylvania Hospital*)

Hospital ship. *See* Ship: Hospital ship of the U.S. Navy

Inebriates' asylum was the United States Inebriate Asylum, "for the reformation of the poor and destitute inebriates," incorporated April 15, 1854, and organized May 15, 1854, in Binghamton, N.Y., by Dr. James Edward Turner. In 1857 the name was changed to the New York State Inebriate Asylum. The cornerstone was laid September 24, 1858. John D. Wright was president of the corporation. N. A. Prince was registrar and Dr. James Edward Turner, treasurer. (*James Edward Turner—History of the First Inebriate Asylum in the World*)

Insane detention home is credited to the Religious Society of Friends, which erected it in 1709 in Philadelphia, Pa. The opening of the Pennsylvania Hospital in February 1752 inaugurated a new epoch in the treatment of the insane in this country. They were received as patients, mentally diseased, and were to be subjected to such treatment as their cases required with a view to their ultimate restoration to reason, instead of being confined as malefactors.

Insane hospital (state) for the care of the mentally disordered and insane was the Public Hospital for Persons of Insane and Disordered Minds, incorporated in Williamsburg, Va., in 1768. It was opened October 12, 1773, and received as its first patient Zachariah Mallory of Hanover County, Va. The hospital was maintained by the colony from the beginning and later became known as the Eastern State Hospital. (*Eastern State Hospital—Annual Report*)

Interracial hospital was the Provident Hospital, Chicago, Ill., incorporated January 23, 1891, and opened May 4, 1891, with a grand-opening party. Although primarily for Negroes, there was no racial barrier as to the admission of patients or staff appointments of physicians. Frank Billings was chief consulting physician; Christian Fenger, chief consulting surgeon; and Drs. Ralph N. Isham and Daniel Hale Williams, attending surgeons. A nursing school, the Provident Hospital Training School Association, was connected with the hospital. (*Helen Buckler—Doctor Dan, Pioneer in American Surgery*)

Jewish hospital was Mount Sinai Hospital in New York, organized and incorporated in

THE FIRST

1852 as the Jews' Hospital for "benevolent, charitable and scientific purposes." The founder and first president was Sampson Simson. The first patients were received June 5, 1855, in a small building (25 beds) on West 28th Street, New York City. Julius Raymond was the first superintendent. Dr. Mark Blumenthal was the attending and resident physician. On April 17, 1866, a special act of the New York legislature changed the name to Mount Sinai Hospital of the City of New York.

Leper hospital was the Louisiana Leper Home, Carville, La., founded in 1894 by an act of the Louisiana legislature. It consisted of a plantation of about 200 acres, on which were seven cottages, an elevated pavilion, dining hall, kitchen, and quarters for the Sisters of Charity of the order of St. Vincent de Paul, four of whom took care of the lepers. The home accommodated 25 patients, and was controlled by a Board of Officers. The president was M. D. Lagan and the resident physician was Dr. Elihu Morgan Hooper. The home was purchased by the Federal Government from the state of Louisiana, January 3, 1921, to be operated by the U.S. Public Health Service under the Treasury Department. It was reopened June 8, 1921, and was known as the United States Marine Hospital or the National Leper Home. It accommodated over 300 persons. Surgeon Oswald Evans Denney was appointed Medical Officer in Charge. The Sisters of Charity continued to furnish the nursing care. (*Public Health Reports—Reprint No. 1,440*)

Marine hospital (U.S.) was authorized by act of Congress of July 16, 1798 (1 Stat.L.605), an "act for the relief of sick and disabled seamen" which empowered the President to appoint medical officers at ports and elsewhere to give medical treatment to disabled seamen. Funds were obtained by a tax of 20 cents a month deducted from the pay of those employed on American vessels. On January 20, 1798, the Virginia legislature authorized the governor to offer its Marine Hospital (built in 1787). On April 20, 1801, Governor James Monroe of Virginia deeded the Norfolk Naval Hospital, Norfolk, Va., to the United States. (*Richard Cranston Holcomb—A Century with the Norfolk Naval Hospital*)

Military hospital on the modern pavilion plan was proposed in August 1861 by Dr. Alpheus Benning Crosby, division surgeon on the staff of General Charles Pomeroy Stone, to Surgeon Charles Stuart Tripler. A hospital was built in Poolesville, Md., which on October 21, 1861, was ready to receive the wounded from the battle of Ball's Bluff, Va. (*Josiah Whitney Barstow—In Memoriam, A Tribute to the Memory of Alpheus Benning Crosby, M.D.*)

THE FIRST

Narcotic sanatorium. *See* Narcotic: Narcotic sanatorium (federal) for drug addicts

Naval hospital was authorized by act of Congress "establishing Navy hospitals," February 26, 1811 (2 Stat.L.650), which appropriated $50,000. On April 2, 1827, the cornerstone was laid for the first naval hospital at Portsmouth, Va. One wing was ready for occupancy in July 1830, and the building was completed and dedicated in 1833.
See also above Hospital for military and naval forces

Negro hospital and asylum, founded by whites solely for Negroes, was chartered December 24, 1832, as the "Georgia Infirmary, for the relief and protection of aged and afflicted Negroes," of Savannah, Ga. The organization meeting was held at the Exchange, January 15, 1833, and the first president was Richard F. Williams. (*Short History of the Georgia Infirmary—1933*)

Orthopedic hospital was the Hospital for Ruptured and Crippled, opened May 1, 1863, in New York City by the New York Society for the Relief of the Ruptured and Crippled, organized December 18, 1862 and incorporated April 13, 1863. Dr. James Knight was the resident physician and surgeon. During the first year, treatment was given to 828 patients. The hospital's name was changed in 1940 to the Hospital for Special Surgery.

Psychiatric ward associated with a general hospital fulfilling the function of actual therapeutic treatment, besides detention, was Pavilion F of Albany Hospital, Albany, N.Y., opened in 1901 "for the detention and care of persons afflicted with nervous mental disorders." The first patient was admitted February 1902. Dr. Jesse Montgomery Mosher was placed in full charge of the pavilion. (*Albert Deutsch—The Mentally Ill in America*)

Tuberculosis home for the care of consumptives was the Channing Home, Boston, Mass., opened May 1857 through the benevolence of Harriet Ryan. The home accommodated twelve patients and was not a sanatorium. It also accommodated patients with other chronic diseases.

Tuberculosis hospital to provide medical and surgical care for needy consumptives on a free, nation-wide, nonsectarian basis, was the National Jewish Hospital, Denver, Colo., which opened December 10, 1899, with 58 beds, under the auspices of the B'nai Brith. It was incorporated October 31, 1900. An attempt had been made by the Jewish Hospital Association of Colorado (incorporated April 8, 1890) to establish a hospital earlier. The cornerstone was

HOSPITAL—*Continued*
laid October 9, 1892, but the funds raised were not sufficient to build the hospital. (*Milton Louis Anfenger—The Birth of a Hospital*)

Tuberculosis hospital (municipal) for consumptive poor was the Branch Hospital (now Hamilton County Tuberculosis Hospital) under the jurisdiction of the Cincinnati Hospital (now Cincinnati General Hospital) which opened July 8, 1897, in Cincinnati, Ohio, with a capacity of 20 beds. John Fehrenbach was the superintendent and Dr. Benjamin Lyle the chief physician.

Tuberculosis hospital operated by the government for consumptives was opened at Fort Stanton, N.M., on April 27, 1899. The first patient was received November 18, 1899. It was suggested and established by Walter Wyman. It was not exclusively for men in military service but afforded care and treatment to all beneficiaries of the U.S. Public Health Service, most of whom at that time were seamen.

Tuberculosis preventorium for children was established in 1909 in Lakewood, N.J. through the efforts of Nathan Straus.

Tuberculosis sanatorium (modern) inaugurating present methods of treating tuberculosis, was the Trudeau Sanatorium, sometimes called the Adirondack Cottage Sanatorium, a one-room cottage 14 by 18 feet with two cot beds, heated by a wood stove, built at Saranac Lake, N.Y., for Dr. Edward Livingston Trudeau at a cost of $400. It was opened February 1, 1885. (*Edward Livingston Trudeau—An Autobiography*)

Tuberculosis sanatorium (private) was the Mountain Sanatorium for Pulmonary Diseases, opened in 1875 in Asheville, N.C., by Dr. William Gleitsmann. (*Philadelphia Medical and Surgical Reporter—February 1876*)

Tuberculosis sanatorium (state) was the Massachusetts Hospital for Consumptives and Tuberculosis Patients, Rutland, Mass., completed September 23, 1898. It received its first patient October 3, 1898. Dr. Walter John Marcley was the first medical director. (*State Sanatorium at Rutland, Mass.—Annual Report 1899*)

Vaccine institution. *See* Vaccine institution

Veterinary hospital. *See* Veterinary hospital

Women's hospital in the world, founded by women for the exclusive use of women, was

the Woman's Hospital of New York City. On February 10, 1855, a constitution was adopted by thirty women who termed themselves the Woman's Hospital Association. The Woman's Hospital was opened with 40 beds on May 4, 1855, in a hired building at Madison Avenue and 29th Street, New York City, with Dr. James Marion Sims as Resident Surgeon. The present building on 110th Street, between Columbus and Amsterdam Avenues, New York City, was opened December 5, 1906. (*James Riddle Goffe—Historical Sketch of the Woman's Hospital in the State of New York*)

Women's infirmary staffed by women physicians was the New York Infirmary for Women and Children, New York City, incorporated December 13, 1853 "to provide for poor women the medical advice of competent physicians of their own sex." A one-room infirmary was opened in Tompkins Square. On May 12, 1857, a hospital was opened. The physicians were Dr. Elizabeth Blackwell, Dr. Emily Blackwell, Dr. Marie Elizabeth Zakrzewska.

HOSPITAL AMBULANCE SERVICE. *See* Ambulance: Hospital ambulance service

HOSPITAL AUTOMOBILE (field). *See* Automobile: Field hospital automobile with X-ray equipment

HOSPITAL INSURANCE. *See* Insurance: Health insurance law (state)

HOSPITAL-MEDICAL COOPERATIVE. *See* Insurance: Group hospital-medical cooperative

HOSPITAL PHARMACOPOEIA. *See* Pharmacopoeia: Pharmacopoeia prepared by a hospital staff

HOSPITAL RECORD system was introduced at the Bellevue Training School for Nurses, New York City, in 1874 by the head nurse, Linda Richards. The superintendent of the school was Sister Helen of All Saints' Hospital. Record was made of symptoms, diagnosis, medication, temperature, and pulse rate for all patients in the hospital. (*David Allyn Gorton—History of Medicine*)

HOSPITAL SHIP. *See* Ship: Hospital ship of the U.S. Navy

HOSPITALIZATION GROUP INSURANCE. *See* Insurance: Group hospital insurance plan

HOSTEL (youth). *See* Youth hostel

THE FIRST

HOTEL

Airplane take-off from a hotel roof. *See* Aviation: Airplane take-off from a hotel roof

Airship to land on a roof. *See* Aviation—Airship: Airship to land on a roof

Bibles in hotel rooms. *See* Bible: Bibles in hotel rooms

Fireproof hotel was the Palmer House, Chicago, Ill., opened in November 1873 by Potter Palmer. The building cost approximately $2 million, the land $1 million and the furnishings $500,000. It replaced the Palmer House opened October 1, 1870, and destroyed by fire October 8, 1871. A new Palmer House was completed in 1925.

Hotel definitely recognized as a modern first-class hotel was the Tremont House in Boston, Mass., which celebrated its opening with an elaborate dinner on October 16, 1829. It contained 170 rooms; the rate was $2 a day, including four meals. Travelers were permitted to rent a single room instead of having to double up with strangers. (Previously when a guest retired for the night he did not know whom he might find beside him in the morning. Frequently three or four slept in one bed "spoon fashion." Women were sometimes "roomed" with men.) Other innovations at the Tremont House were a key for each room, a wash bowl, a pitcher, and a free cake of soap for every guest, gas lights, and a fine supply of running water in the eight "bathing rooms" in the basement. *(Jefferson Williamson—The American Hotel)*

Hotel (airport). *See* Aviation—Airport: Airport hotel

Hotel built for strictly hotel purposes was the City Hotel, of seventy rooms, opened in 1794 on Broadway, just below Wall Street, New York City. *(Jefferson Williamson—The American Hotel)*

Hotel exclusively for women was the Martha Washington Hotel, New York City, opened March 2, 1903. It had 416 rooms.

Hotel to establish a heliport was the Western Hills Hotel, Fort Worth, Tex. The heliport, 150 feet by 190 feet, surfaced with asphalt paving, was formally opened May 20, 1953, with 250 members of the national Aviators Writers Association present. It was privately owned but was intended for public use and was licensed by the city of Fort Worth on May 20, 1953, and approved by the Civil Aeronautics Administration. It was built by the E. M. Moore Construction Co., Fort Worth.

THE FIRST

Hotel to install bathrooms and toilets was the Tremont House, Boston, Mass., designed by Isaiah Rogers, which opened October 16, 1829. It covered 12,849 square feet and contained 170 rooms. It had eight water-closets, "privies," and eight bathing-rooms in the basement, to which there was a separate entrance. The kitchen and laundry had running cold water. Each of the two cisterns in the attic contained three hogsheads of rain-water, one for the baths and the other for various outlets. The plumbers were Thomas Philpott and Thomas Pollard. The cornerstone of the hotel was laid July 4, 1828, by Samuel Turell Armstrong, president of the Massachusetts Charitable Mechanic Association. *(Description of the Tremont House, Boston, 1830)*

Hotel to install electric lights was the Prospect House, Blue Mountain Lake, N.Y. In 1881 the electric installation was made, but the lights were not entirely dependable. On October 12, 1882, the Duke of Veranga and his party arrived after dark, to celebrate Columbus Day. As they were shown to their rooms the lights went out, but after a slight delay the lights went on again. The hotel was owned by Howard M. Durant and operated by George Tunnicliffe. The name was later changed to "The Eutowana."

Hotel to install radio reception with two selective channels was Hotel Statler of Boston, Mass., which on May 10, 1927, broadcast programs free to guests from a central control room. Thirteen hundred rooms were originally equipped with individual headsets. Later, loud speakers were placed in the rooms.

Hotel with all foam rubber mattresses, pillows, and furniture cushions was the Western Hills Hotel, Fort Worth, Tex., partially opened on July 11, 1951, and completed and formally opened on October 7, 1951. It cost approximately $2 million and had 200 rooms, no two of which were furnished alike.

HOTEL ADMINISTRATION COLLEGE COURSE

was offered by Cornell University, Ithaca, N.Y., in the fall of 1922, and included courses in accounting, administration, economics, engineering, food preparation, housekeeping, languages, etc. The course required four years and led to a B.S. degree. Professor Howard Bagnall Meek was the first Professor of Hotel Administration. *(Cornell University—Announcement of Department of Hotel Administration)*

HOTEL ELEVATOR. *See* Elevator: Elevator in a hotel

HOTHOUSE. *See* Greenhouse

HOUSE. *See* Building

THE FIRST

HOUSE OF DAVID was established on May 1, 1903, in Benton Harbor, Mich., by Benjamin Purnell as a commonwealth according to apostolic plan. The first church building was opened on May 1, 1903, and the first minister was Benjamin Purnell.

HOUSE OF REPRESENTATIVES (U.S.). *See* Congress (U.S.)—House of Representatives

HOUSING CORPORATION (U.S.). *See* Emergency housing corporation (U.S.)

HUBBARD MEDAL. *See* Medal: National Geographic Society gold medal

HULLING MACHINE. *See* Cottonseed hulling machine

HUMAN BLOOD (dried). *See* Blood bank: Blood serum (human) (dried)

HUMAN INFECTING VIRUS TO BE CRYSTALLIZED. *See* Virus: Virus (human- or animal-infecting virus to be crystallized)

HUMAN PICK-UP BY AN AIRPLANE. *See* Aviation: Airplane human pick-up

HUMANE SOCIETY
Humane association national organization was the American Humane Association, which was organized October 9, 1877, in Cleveland, Ohio, adopted its constitution on November 14, 1878, in Baltimore, Md., and was incorporated under the laws of the District of Columbia November 12, 1903, as a federation of societies for the prevention of cruelty to animals, with the primary purpose of preventing cruelty in the transportation of livestock. The first president was Edwin Lee Brown of Chicago, Ill., and the first secretary was Abraham Firth of Massachusetts.

Humane society was the American Society for the Prevention of Cruelty to Animals, founded in New York City by Henry Bergh, formerly of the American Legation at St. Petersburg, Russia, who was appalled by the beatings which droshky-moujiks administered to their horses. When he returned to the United States he organized the A.S.P.C.A., incorporated April 10, 1866, patterned after the Royal S.P.C.A. of London. *(Chapter 469, Laws of New York 1866)*

HUMANIST SOCIETY was established January 13, 1929, in Hollywood, Calif., "to humanize religion, disseminate science, stimulate thought and promote good will." The

THE FIRST

first director was the Reverend Theodore Curtis Abell. The first Humanist National Assembly was held in New York City, October 10-11, 1934.

HUMORIST (woman). *See* Woman: Woman humorist

HUNGARIAN DAILY NEWSPAPER. *See* Newspaper: Hungarian daily newspaper

HUNTING LICENSE. *See* Game law: Hunting license fee (state)

HURRICANE recorded occurred August 15, 1635, when a cyclonic storm ravaged the Plymouth colony vicinity. *(Thomas Morton—New England Canaan)*

HUSBAND AND WIFE AWARDED DEGREES. *See* Degrees (academic and honorary): Husband and wife awarded honorary degrees

HUSBANDMAN'S GUIDE. *See* Agricultural book: Agricultural book

HUSBANDRY. *See* Animal industry bureau (U.S.): Animal husbandry federal appropriation

HUSKING CHAMPIONSHIP. *See* Corn husking championship contest (national)

HYBRID SEED CORN. *See* Corn: Shipment of hybrid seed corn

HYDRAULIC ELEVATOR. *See* Elevator: Elevator patent for a vertical-geared hydraulic electric elevator

HYDRAULIC-LIFT PARKING GARAGE. *See* Garage: Hydraulic-lift parking garage

HYDRO-ELECTRIC POWER STATION. *See* Electric power plant: Hydroelectric power plant

HYDROGEN BOMB. *See* Atomic bomb: Atomic fusion (thermonuclear) bomb

HYDROGEN-COOLED TURBINE GENERATOR. *See* Electric generator: Hydrogen-cooled turbine generator

HYDROPHOBIA BOOK. *See* Medical book: Hydrophobia book

HYDROPLANE. *See* Aviation—Airplane: Hydroplane

THE FIRST

HYDROPONICS. *See* Soilless culture of plants

HYDROTHERAPY BOOK. *See* Medical book: Hydrotherapy book

HYDROTHERAPY CHAIR was established in the Department of Materia Medica, College of Physicians and Surgeons, Columbia University, New York City in 1907. Dr. Simon Baruch was appointed Professor of Hydrotherapy in March 1907 and served until May 1913.

HYGIENE BUREAU. *See* Child hygiene bureau

HYGIENE INSTRUCTION

Hygiene and physical education professorship was established by the trustees of Amherst College, Amherst, Mass., in 1860. Dr. John Worthington Hooker, the original incumbent, resigned after less than a year of service and was succeeded by Dr. Edward Hitchcock of the class of 1849, who served continuously from 1861 until his death on February 16, 1911. *(Edward Hitchcock—A Report of Twenty Years' Experience in the Department of Physical Education and Hygiene in Amherst College)*

Hygiene and public health school was established in 1916 at Johns Hopkins University, Baltimore, Md., under an endowment from the Rockefeller Foundation "for the advancement of knowledge and the training of investigators, teachers, officials and other workers" in the general field of hygiene and public health. This school was opened October 1, 1918, with Dr. William Henry Welch as its first director.

Hygiene lectures. *See* Medical instruction: Hygiene lectures

Physiology and hygiene courses offered by a liberal arts college were given in 1853 at Antioch College, Yellow Springs, Ohio. The college opened October 5, 1853. Instruction was supervised by Professor Rebecca Mann Pennell and Acting Professor John Wesley Hoyt, M.D.

School Department of Hygiene to aid in instructing children in the fundamental laws of health and generally to improve health conditions was established in Boston, Mass., in 1907. The department was in charge of physical training and athletics, as well as the newly organized nursing program. Physical culture, however, had been introduced in 1864, and Boston had ruled as early as 1853 that "every scholar shall have daily in the forenoon and afternoon some kind of physical exercise."

THE FIRST

HYGIENE PROFESSOR. *See* Medical instruction: Public hygiene professor

HYGIENISTS' TEXTBOOK. *See* Dental book: Book for dental hygienists (text)

HYMN BOOK. *See* Music book: Hymn book

ICE

Commercial transportation of ice was effected in 1799. The ice was cut on Canal Street, New York City, and shipped to Charleston, S.C.

Dry ice manufactured commercially was made by the Prest-Air Devices Company of Long Island City, N.Y., in 1925, through the efforts of Thomas Benton Slate. Dry ice is solid carbon dioxide. When compressed and cooled, it changes to a liquid, then to a solid. Its temperature is 109 degrees below zero. It does not melt but turns to gas. Dry ice was first used by Schrafft's, 181 Broadway, New York City, in July 1925 to keep ice cream from melting. The first large sale of dry ice was made later in the year to the Breyer Ice Cream Company of New York City.

Export of ice was shipped in August 1805 by Frederick Tudor, who sent 130 tons on the brig "Favorite" from Boston to the West Indies (Martinique). His business increased and in 1833 he commenced making shipments to Madras, Bombay, and Calcutta, India. *(Business Historical Society — Bulletin. February 1935)*

ICE CREAM

Ice cream was made commercially by Mr. Hall of 76 Chatham Street (now Park Row), New York City, who advertised it on June 8, 1786. A record of a purchase for "a cream machine for ice" is contained in George Washington's expense ledger under date of May 17, 1784. *(Grover Dean Turnblow and Lloyd Andrew Raffeto—Ice Cream)*

Ice cream wholesale dealer was Jacob Fussel, a milk dealer in Baltimore, Md. In 1851, as a means of using up his surplus cream, he started manufacturing ice cream, which sold at 60 cents a quart.

ICE CREAM CONE

Ice cream cone is said to have originated at the Louisiana Purchase Exposition in St. Louis, Mo., in 1904. Charles E. Menches, a young ice cream salesman, gave an ice cream sandwich, as well as flowers, to the young lady he was escorting. Lacking a vase for the flowers, she took one of the layers of the sandwich and rolled it in the form of a cone to act

ICE CREAM CONE—Continued

as a vase. The remaining layer was also rolled similarly, with the result that the ice cream cone was invented.

Ice cream cone-rolling machine was invented by Carl Rutherford Taylor of Cleveland, Ohio, who obtained patent No. 1,481,813 on January 29, 1924, on a "machine for spinning or turning a waffle."

ICE CREAM FREEZER

ICE CREAM FREEZER was patented by William G. Young of Baltimore, Md., who received patent No. 5,601, May 30, 1848, on an "improvement in ice cream freezers."

ICE CREAM SODA

ICE CREAM SODA is supposed to have been introduced by Robert M. Green, the founder of Robert M. Green & Sons, manufacturers of soda fountains in Philadelphia, who added ice cream to plain soda water. The first demonstration of the new beverage was made at the Semi-Centennial Celebration at Franklin Institute, Philadelphia, Pa., in the summer of 1874.

ICE CREAM SUNDAE

ICE CREAM SUNDAE is said to have originated about 1897 in the Red Cross Pharmacy, State Street, Ithaca, N.Y., directly opposite the barroom of the Ithaca Hotel. As the barroom was closed on Sunday, thirsty patrons went to the drug store where a distinctive drink was sold as a sundae.

ICE LOADING MACHINERY

ICE LOADING MACHINERY for icing refrigerator railway cars was operated in May 1917 by the William Metz Ice Company of Pittsburgh, Pa. The machines were manufactured by the Thomas Wright Company, Inc., of Jersey City, N.J. Wright obtained patent No. 1,059,511, April 22, 1913, on a "body elevating mechanism." It consisted of a truck with an extension top adjustable to any position to enable ice to be placed in the uppermost section of the car, making it possible for one man to do all the loading without the help of assistants.

ICE SKATING CHAMPION

American world figure skating champion was Tenley Albright of Newton Center, Mass., who won the title February 15, 1953, at Davos, Switzerland. She was seventeen years old.

ICE SKATING CLUB

Ice skating club was the Skaters' Club of the City and County of Philadelphia, formed December 21, 1849, at Stigman's Hotel, Philadelphia, Pa. It was formally organized on January 4, 1850. The first election was held January 8, 1850; the officers elected were James Page, president; Josiah Evans, vice president; William H. Jones, secretary; and Edward W. Bushnell, treasurer. (Nigel Bruce—Ice-Skating)

ICE SKATING RINK (indoor). See Skating rink: Ice skating rink (indoor)

ICE YACHT

ICE YACHT was built by Oliver Booth at Poughkeepsie, N.Y., in 1790 and consisted of a square box mounted on three runners covered with iron, a sail, a rudder post, and a wooden tiller.

ICE YACHT CLUB

ICE YACHT CLUB was the Poughkeepsie Ice Yacht Club of Poughkeepsie, N.Y., which was organized in 1861. Regattas and races were held on the Hudson River.

ICEBOX. See Refrigerator

ICONOSCOPE. See Television: Electronic television system

IDENTIFICATION BUREAU (police). See Police: Police bureau of identification

IDENTIFICATION SYSTEM BASED ON THE EYES. See Eye: Identification system

ILLUMINATED AIRWAYS. See Aviation: Airways illumination

ILLUMINATING GAS. See Gas: Natural gas used as an illuminant

ILLUSTRATED BIBLE. See Bible: Bible in folio size to be illustrated

ILLUSTRATED NEWSPAPER. See Newspaper: Illustrated daily newspaper

ILLUSTRATED WEEKLY. See Periodical: Illustrated weekly

IMMIGRATION

Alien registration was authorized under the Alien Registration Act of 1940 (54 Stat.L. 670), approved June 28, 1940, "to amend certain provisions of law with respect to the admission and deportation of aliens; to require the fingerprinting and registration of aliens." The registration was conducted by the Alien Registration Division of the Immigration and Naturalization Service. Earl Grant Harrison was the director in charge of registration. During the period August 27, 1940, to December 26, 1940, the number of non-citizens who registered was 4,741,971.

Border patrol. See Border patrol: Border patrol organization

THE FIRST

Chinese immigrants were two men and a woman who arrived in San Francisco, Calif., in 1848, on the brig "Eagle." *(Dr. Harley Farnsworth McNair—The Chinese Abroad)*

Chinese labor immigration was arranged through the efforts of William Kelly of Pittsburgh, Pa., who in 1854 induced twelve Chinese to work in his foundries. The Chinese were willing to work for extremely low wages.

Chinese labor immigration act restricting the admission of Chinese laborers was passed May 6, 1882, suspending Chinese immigration for a ten-year period and forbidding naturalization. A treaty between China and the United States, concluded November 17, 1880, approved May 5, 1881, by the Senate, was signed May 9, 1881 by President Chester Alan Arthur. Ratifications were exchanged July 19, 1881, and proclaimed October 5, 1881 (22 Stat.L.826). It was agreed that the United States could "regulate, limit or suspend" the immigration of Chinese labor, but not prohibit it altogether. The Chinese exclusion acts were repealed December 17, 1943 (57 Stat.L.600).

Citizenship granted to an alien on foreign soil. *See* Citizenship: Citizenship granted to an alien on foreign soil

Immigration act requiring the recording of data pertaining to the arrival of aliens in the United States was the act of June 25, 1798 (1 Stat.570), which required the master or commander of a vessel to make a written report to the customs officer in charge of the port of entry, giving the names of all arriving aliens, and other prescribed data pertaining to them. *(Records in Bureau of Immigration. Department of Labor. Washington, D.C.)*

Immigration bureau superintendent was William D. Owen, whose appointment on June 15, 1891, was confirmed by the Senate December 16, 1891. His salary was $4,000 a year. The office of Superintendent of Immigration authorized by act of March 3, 1891 (26 Stat.L. 1085) was under the Treasury Department at that time. Owen resigned March 20, 1893.

Immigration head tax was levied in accordance with the federal law of August 3, 1882 (22 Stat.L.214). Each immigrant was required to pay fifty cents. In 1903 the fee was $2, in 1907, $4, and in 1918, $8.

Immigration quota act was the act of May 19, 1921 (42 Stat.L.5), which became effective on June 3, 1921, and as amended on May 11, 1922 (42 Stat.L.540), was effective until July 1, 1924. It limited immigration to 3 per cent of the number of foreign-born persons of any given nationality in the United States as shown

THE FIRST

in the 1910 census. Not more than 20 per cent of any country's quota was permitted to arrive in one month.

Japanese to enter the United States was Nakahama Manjiro, a fifteen-year-old boy, shipwrecked and rescued by American sailors, who in 1841 brought him to Fairhaven, Mass., where he attended school for six years. He returned to Japan and was beaten for having left his country. When Perry went to Japan in 1853, Manjiro acted as interpreter. *(Biographical Dictionary of Japan)*

Naturalization act. *See* Naturalization act

Refugee to arrive under the Refugee Relief Act of 1953 (67 stat.L.400), enacted August 7, 1953, "for the relief of certain refugees and orphans, and for other purposes" was Stamatoula Roumanis, a twelve-year-old Greek girl, who arrived at Idlewild Airport, New York City, on January 1, 1954.

IMMUNOLOGY SOCIETY. *See* Medical society: Immunology society

IMPEACHMENT
Impeachment was that of Nicolas More, who in 1685 was Chief Justice of Philadelphia. He fell under such displeasure that the assembly presented articles of impeachment against him to the council; among other offenses he was charged with "assuming to himself an unlimited and arbitrary power in office." *(Pennsylvania Magazine of History and Biography. Vol. 4)*

Impeachment and removal from office of a state governor was that of William Woods Holden, the thirty-ninth governor of North Carolina. On December 20, 1870, impeachment proceedings were brought against him in which he was charged with "high crimes and misdemeanors." The trial was conducted by Chief Justice Richmond Mumford Pearson. On March 22, 1871, he was ordered to be removed from office, two thirds of the state Senate having found him guilty of six of the eight charges brought against him. *(Trial of William Woods Holden, Governor of North Carolina. Published in 1871 by order of the Senate of North Carolina.)*

Impeachment of a federal judge was that of Judge John Pickering, Judge of the United States District Court for the district of New Hampshire, who was convicted and removed from office for drunkenness, profanity, and violence on the bench. The vote was 19 guilty, and 7 not guilty. The trial was held from March 3, 1803, to March 12, 1804. *(Annals of the Congress of the United States. Eighth Congress. Vols. 13-14. "Impeachment of John Pickering")*

THE FIRST

THE FIRST

IMPEACHMENT—*Continued*

Impeachment proceedings against a Justice of the Supreme Court of the United States were instituted in 1804 when, for political reasons, the Democratic party brought charges against Samuel Chase. The trial was held from November 30, 1804, to March 1, 1805. Chase was acquitted, and served until his death, June 19, 1811, at the age of seventy. (*Charles Warren—The Supreme Court in U.S. History*)

Impeachment proceedings against a President of the United States were instituted against Andrew Johnson, the seventeenth President. The House of Representatives on February 24, 1868, voted to impeach him because he had dismissed Edwin McMasters Stanton, Secretary of War, and declared several laws unconstitutional. The charges were usurpation of the law, corrupt use of the veto power, interference at elections, and misdemeanors. The trial was held in the Senate from March 13 to May 16, with Chief Justice of the United States Salmon Portland Chase presiding. Fifty-four senators took oaths as jurors. Johnson was acquitted. The vote was 35 to 19 against Johnson, one short of the necessary two thirds. (*David Miller De Witt—The Impeachment and Trial of Andrew Johnson*)

Impeachment proceedings against a state governor were brought against Charles Robinson, the first governor of Kansas. He was indicted for treason and conspiracy on a charge by the pro-slavery party. He was acquitted in 1862 by the federal grand jury, and completed his term as governor. (*Frank Wilson Blackmar —Charles Robinson, the First Free-state Governor of Kansas*)

Impeachment proceedings against a United States Senator were instituted against William Blount, United States Senator from Tennessee, who served from August 2, 1796, until July 8, 1797, when he was expelled. The trial was held from December 17, 1798, to January 14, 1799, when the Vice President announced the decision of the High Court of Impeachment that the charges were dismissed for want of jurisdiction. Blount was accused of entering into a conspiracy with British officers to divert part of Louisiana from Spain to England, "a high misdemeanor, entirely inconsistent with his public trust and duty as a Senator." While the trial was in progress in Washington, Blount was elected by Tennessee to serve in the State Senate, and at the opening session (December 3, 1797) was chosen president of the State Senate. (*Marcus Joseph Wright—Some Account of the Life and Services of William Blount*)

IMPERFORATED STAMPS. *See* Postage stamp: Imperforated ungummed sheet of postage stamps

IMPREGNATED CORKBOARD. *See* Corkboard (impregnated)

IMPREGNATION

Impregnation (artificial) resulted from experiments by Dr. Gregory Pincus of Clark University, Worcester, Mass., conducted at Harvard University, Cambridge, Mass., in November 1939 under the auspices of the Dazian and Josiah Macy, Jr., Foundation. Pincus produced a rabbit (born in October 1939) by removing an egg from the ovary of a female rabbit and fertilizing it with a salt solution. The egg was then transferred to the uterus of a second rabbit which acted as an "incubator." He exhibited the young rabbit November 1, 1939, at the twelfth annual Graduate Fortnight at the New York Academy of Medicine.

Impregnation (human) by means of artificial insemination was made in 1866 by Dr. James Marion Sims, gynecologist and chief of the Woman's Hospital, New York City. Sims gave fifty-four other injections in 1866 and 1867.

"IN GOD WE TRUST." *See* Money: Coin to use "In God We Trust"

INAUGURAL BALL. *See* Presidential inaugural ball

INAUGURATION (presidential). *See* President: President inaugurated

INCANDESCENT LAMP. *See* Electric lighting: Electric incandescent lamp

INCINERATOR that was successful was established in 1897 in St. Louis, Mo., by a private contractor who had a contract with the city for the collection and disposal of garbage. The Merz process was used. The water was drained off, cans, bottles, and rags were taken out, and grease was extracted by means of naphtha. (*American Society of Civil Engineers. Transactions. Vol. LIV. Pt. E*)

See also Crematory

INCLINED RAILWAY. *See* Railroad: Inclined railway

INCOME TAX. *See* Tax: Federal income tax

INCORPORATED CITY. *See* City (incorporated)

INCUBATOR AMBULANCE SERVICE. *See* Ambulance: Incubator ambulance service

THE FIRST

INCUBATOR (EGGS) PATENT was No. 3,019, awarded March 30, 1843, to Napoleon E. Guerin of New York City for a "mode of distributing steam heat, purifying air, etc." and hatching chickens by artificial heat.

INCUBATOR FOR INFANTS was constructed by order of Dr. Allan M. Thomas by Dr. William Champion Deming, in charge of the maternity ward of the State Emigrant Hospital, Ward's Island, New York City, in 1888. It was called a "hatching cradle" and was three feet square and four feet high and built in two sections, one of which contained 15 gallons of water. The first child placed in it was Edith Eleanor McLean, who weighed two pounds and seven ounces when born on September 7, 1888. (*Morning Journal—October 14, 1888*)

INDELIBLE PENCIL. *See* Pencil: Indelible pencil

INDEPENDENCE DECLARATION. *See* Declaration of Independence

INDEPENDENT CHRISTIAN CHURCH. *See* Universalist Church of America (Independent Christian Church, Universalist)

INDEPENDENT PARTY. *See* Greenback party

INDEX OF BOOKS. *See* Book index: Monthly cumulative index of books

INDEX OF GOVERNMENT PUBLICATIONS was *A Descriptive Catalogue of the Government Publications of the U.S.—Sept. 5, 1774-March 4, 1881,* compiled by order of Congress. The work was given to Benjamin Perley Poore on March 1, 1883, and finished in 1885. It was arranged chronologically with a general index and was published by the Government Printing Office, Washington, D.C.

INDEX OF NEWSPAPERS. *See* Newspaper index

INDIAN CHURCH
Indian church in New England was established in Natick, Mass., by John Eliot in 1660. Six other praying towns were established before 1674. (*Daniel Gookin—Historical Collections of the Indians in New England*)

Indian church organized by Indians was the First American Church, incorporated October 10, 1918, with its principal seat of government and place of business at El Reno, Canadian County, Okla., by Mack Haag and

THE FIRST

Sidney White Crane of the Cheyenne tribe of Indians; Charles W. Dailey, George Pipestem and Charles N. Moore of the Otto tribe; Frank Eagle of the Ponca tribe; William Peawa and Manwat of the Comanche tribe; Kiowa Charlie of the Kiowa tribe; and Apache Ben of the Apache tribe—all residents of the state of Oklahoma.

INDIAN CORN. *See* Maize

INDIAN DAY. *See* Holiday: Indian day

INDIAN-ENGLISH DICTIONARY. *See* Dictionary: Indian-English dictionary

INDIAN GRAMMAR. *See* Grammar: Indian grammar

INDIAN-LANGUAGE BIBLE. *See* Bible: Bible in an Indian language

INDIAN-LANGUAGE MONTHLY. *See* Periodical: Indian-language monthly

INDIAN MEDAL. *See* Medal: Indian medals

INDIAN NEWSPAPERS. *See* Newspaper: Indian newspaper

INDIAN PLAY. *See* Play (drama): Play about an Indian

INDIAN PRIMER. *See* Primer: Primer in an American Indian dialect

INDIAN RESERVATION
Indian reservation (federal) was established by the United States Government in 1786, but the first official notice of the removal of Indians residing east of the Mississippi to reservations west of that river was contained in the act of March 26, 1804 (2 Stat.L.283), "erecting Louisiana into two territories, and providing the temporary government thereof." Reservations established by executive order without an act of Congress were not held to be permanent before the general allotment act of February 8, 1887 (24 Stat.L.388), an "act to provide for the allotment of lands . . . severally to Indians on the various reservations, and to extend the protection of the laws of the United States and the territories over the Indians."

Indian reservation (state) was established on August 29, 1758, when the New Jersey Legislature appropriated 1,600 acres of a tract of 3,044 acres in Indian Mills, Evesham township, Burlington County, N.J., to be used as a reservation for the Indians of New Jersey.

INDIAN RESERVATION—*Continued*
Governor Francis Bernard named the tract
Brotherton. About two hundred Indians, prob-
ably Lenapes and Unamis, located on it and
John Brainard was appointed superintendent. In
1801, the land was sold and the Indians moved
to the Lake Oneida Reservation. (*William
Nelson—Indians of New Jersey*)

INDIAN SCHOOL
Indian school (boarding) on a reservation
was the Yakima Agency Boarding School,
opened November 1860 with twenty-five pupils,
in the buildings of old Fort Simco on the
Yakima Reservation, Wash., under provision of
Article 5 of the treaty with the "Yakima"
Nation of June 8, 1855, proclaimed April 18,
1859 (12 Stat.L.951). James H. Wilbur was
appointed superintendent of teaching September
1, 1860.

Indian school of prominence was opened
November 1, 1879, at the old Army Barracks,
Carlisle, Pa., with 147 students. It was supported by private funds until March 3, 1881,
when Congress appropriated $1,000 to pay Cap-
tain Richard Henry Pratt's salary as director
(21 Stat.L.501). The school work did not go
above the eighth grade, but useful trades were
taught. Students were assisted under the outing
system to continue their studies under the
supervision of the school. At the end of the
first year 196 students were enrolled—139 boys
and 57 girls. (*Eadle Keatah Toh. Vol. 1. No. 7.
November 1880*)

Indian school (permanent) in America
was established in 1720 in Williamsburg, Va.,
through the generosity of Robert Boyle, the
eminent English scientist and formulator of
"Boyle's Law." To house the school the Braf-
ferton Building was erected at the college of
William and Mary in 1723. The building was
named after Boyle's estate in Yorkshire, which
provided revenue from rents to support the
school. (*James Luther Kibler—Historic Virginia Landmarks*)

INDIAN TREATY. *See* Treaty: Treaty
entered into by the United States with Indian
tribes

INDIANS
Catholic beatification of an American Indian. *See* Catholic beatification: Catholic
beatification of an American Indian

Indian Affairs Commissioner (U.S.) was
Elbert Herring, appointed July 10, 1832, under
the act of July 9, 1832, an "act to provide for
the appointment of a Commissioner of Indian
Affairs" (4 Stat.L.564), at a salary of $3,000.
He was subject to the President and the
Secretary of War and had "the direction and

management of all Indian affairs and of all
matters arising out of Indian relations." He
served until July 4, 1836. (*Bureau of American
Ethnology—Handbook of American Indians
North of Mexico*)

Indian Affairs Commissioner (U.S.) who
was an Indian was Brigadier General Ely
Samuel Parker (Do-Ne-Ho-Geh-Weh), a
chief of the Tonawanda Seneca tribe, who was
appointed Commissioner of Indian Affairs on
April 21, 1869, by President Ulysses Simpson
Grant. He served until December 1871. (*Buf-
falo Historical Society. Publication No. 23,
1919. Arthur Caswell Parker—The Life of
General Ely Samuel Parker, Last Grand
Sachem of the Iroquois and General Grant's
Military Secretary*)

Indian chief (white woman). *See* Woman:
White woman to become an Indian chief

Indian citizenship statute was enacted June
2, 1924 (43 Stat.L.253). It provided that "all
non-citizen Indians born within the territorial
limits of the United States be, and they are
hereby declared to be, citizens of the United
States."

Indian convert (Protestant) to Christianity
was Manteo, who was baptized into the Church
of England and into the Protestant Christian
faith on August 13, 1587. He was invested by
Sir Walter Raleigh with the power of Baron
or Lord of Roanoke (and of Dasamonguepeuk)
by members of what is now regarded as the
"lost colony." There were, however, baptisms
of Indians by the Roman Catholic priests in
Florida prior to this time. (*Hakluyt's Voyages.
Vol. VI*)

Indian league of nations in America was
the Iroquois Confederacy, which was also known
as the "Five Nations" and later as the "Six
Nations." The league was composed of the
following Indian tribes: Senecas, Cayugas,
Onondagas, Mohawks, Oneidas, and later the
Tuscaroras (in 1715). According to tradition
the Confederacy was formed by Hiawatha about
the beginning of the fifteenth century. (*Lewis
Henry Morgan—League of the Ho-dé-no-sau-
nee, or Iroquois*)

Indian massacre of white people was at
Jamestown, Va., on March 22, 1622, when 347
white people out of a population of 1,240 were
slain.

Indian preacher of Christianity was Hiacoomes. Thomas Mayhew taught him how to
read and write. He was ordained August 22,
1670, by John Eliot and John Cotton, and
preached to his countrymen in a small church
in Martha's Vineyard, Mass. (*Charles Edward
Banks—The History of Martha's Vineyard*)

THE FIRST

THE FIRST

Indian scalping by white men took place February 20, 1725. An Indian-hunting party of New Hampshire volunteers ran across a band of ten sleeping Indians and scalped them all. The hunting party entered Dover in triumph with the ten scalps stretched on hoops and elevated on poles. A bounty of £100 for each scalp was paid in Boston out of the public treasury. Individual scalps had been brought in earlier. *(Jeremy Belknap—History of New Hampshire)*

Indian senator. *See* Senator (U.S.): Indian senator

Indian tribal constitution under the Indian Reorganization Act of June 18, 1934 (48 Stat.L.984) was signed October 28, 1935, in the office of the Secretary of the Interior, Harold Le Claire Ickes, in Washington, D.C. The signatories of the constitution affecting the Flathead Reservation at Dixon, Mont., were Roy E. Courville, chairman of the election board; Joseph R. Blodgett, president of the Tribal Council; Luman W. Shotwell, superintendent and ex-officio secretary of the Tribal Council; Martin Charlo of the Confederated Salish Tribe; and Paul Koos-ta-ta, chief of the Kootenai Tribe.

Indian Vice President. *See* Vice president of the United States: Indian Vice President

Indian war. *See* War (colonial): French and Indian war battle

Paper money issued by the American Indians. *See* Money: Paper money issued by the American Indians

Vaccination legislation for Indians. *See* Vaccination legislation: Vaccination legislation for Indians

INDIGO was planted and harvested in South Carolina prior to 1690, when a petition was presented by Governor Seth Sothell to the Lords Proprietors asking that the inhabitants of South Carolina might be allowed to "pay their rents in the most valuable and merchantable produce of their lands" and enumerating such products as silk, cotton, rice, and indigo.

INDUSTRIAL ACCIDENT REPORT. *See* Accident report: Industrial accident reports

INDUSTRIAL ADVISORY BOARD (federal). *See* Industry: Industrial advisory board (federal)

INDUSTRIAL AND LABOR RELATIONS SCHOOL was the New York State School of Industrial and Labor Relations, Cornell University, Ithaca, N.Y., opened for registration on November 2, 1945. Edmund Ezra Day was president of the university and Irving McNeil Ives dean of the school. The first semester began November 5, 1945.

INDUSTRIAL CAMOUFLAGE COURSE. *See* Art course: Industrial camouflage course

INDUSTRIAL CORPORATION COURSE. *See* Corporation course: Industrial corporation course

INDUSTRIAL EXPOSITION. *See* Fair: Industrial expositon

INDUSTRIAL INSURANCE. *See* Insurance: Group insurance policy

INDUSTRIAL MUSEUM. *See* Museum: Industrial museum

INDUSTRIAL ORGANIZATION NURSE. *See* Nurse: Nurse employed by an industrial organization

INDUSTRIAL RECOVERY ACT
Code under the National Industrial Recovery Act was the tentative code of the cotton textile trade which was submitted to President Franklin Delano Roosevelt June 16, 1933, and approved July 9, 1933. It became effective July 17, 1933.

Compliance board under the National Industrial Recovery Act was announced as officially established by Office Order No. 40, issued October 26, 1933, and signed by Alva Brown, Executive Officer, National Recovery Administration. It consisted of the National Compliance Director, one member of the Industrial Advisory Board, and one member of the Labor Advisory Board. The board undertook to further attempts at adjustment, recommend exceptions, and remove the Blue Eagle, the official insignia for full compliance, when and where necessary. General Hugh Samuel Johnson acted as first director of the Compliance Board, then designated Colonel Robert Wentworth Lea to act temporarily, until November 24, 1933, when William Hammatt Davis was officially appointed director.

Conviction under a National Industrial Recovery Code was obtained December 2, 1933, against the Hercules Gasoline Filling Stations, Inc., 711 Bedford Ave., Brooklyn, N.Y. The defendants pleaded guilty to working their employees in excess of the hours allowed by the

INDUSTRIAL RECOVERY ACT—*Cont.*
Petroleum Code, and failing to display their
gasoline prices properly. The case was tried
before Judge Clarence G. Galston in the United
States District Court of the Eastern District of
New York. As the defendants pleaded guilty,
there was no decision on the merits of the case.
They were fined a total of $400. The defendants
had not signed the Petroleum Code. The decision showed that the signing of an NRA code
was not a requisite to its binding force upon the
members of an industry. (*United States Law
Week. December 5, 1933*)

Industrial Recovery Act (national) was
passed by Congress June 16, 1933 (48 Stat.L.
195), and signed by President Franklin Delano
Roosevelt. Its purpose was "to encourage national industrial recovery, to foster fair competition, and to provide for the construction of
certain useful public works, and for other
purposes." General Hugh Samuel Johnson was
appointed by Executive Order No. 6,173 as the
first administrator June 17, 1933, and served
until October 15, 1934. On May 27, 1935, the
Supreme Court of the United States declared
the act unconstitutional, holding that the code-
making provisions of the act constituted an invalid delegation by Congress of its legislative
authority to persons wholly unconnected with
the legislative functions of the government.
(*U.S. National Recovery Administration—Bulletin No. 1*)

**Postage stamps commemorating the Na-
tional Recovery Act** were sold August 15,
1933, in Washington, D.C., by Postmaster
General James Aloysius Farley, who went behind the grille at the Post Office and sold 100
NRA stamps to Recovery Administrator Hugh
Samuel Johnson.

**State to place all its employees under the
blanket code of the National Recovery Act
Code** was West Virginia. On July 27, 1933,
Governor Herman Guy Kump issued an executive order decreeing that all state departments,
boards, agencies, and commissions should adjust
their work in conformity with President Franklin Delano Roosevelt's program.

**INDUSTRIAL RESEARCH LABORA-
TORY** was the General Electric Research
Laboratory, Schenectady, N.Y., opened in
September 1900. It was supervised by Dr.
Willis Rodney Whitney, former instructor at
the Massachusetts Institute of Technology,
who was appointed by Edwin Wilbur Rice,
Jr., vice president and technical director of
the General Electric Company. (*Laurence
Ashley Hawkins—Adventure into the Un-
known, the First Fifty Years of the General
Electric Research Laboratory*)

INDUSTRIAL SCHOOL. *See* Manual
training: Industrial school

INDUSTRY
Industrial Advisory Board (federal) was
authorized by President Franklin Delano Roosevelt, June 16, 1933, under the National Industrial Recovery Act. He stated that "it will be
responsible that every affected industrial group
is fully and adequately represented in an
advisory capacity and any interested industrial
group will be entitled to be heard through
representatives of its own choosing." The
Board was organized June 26, 1933, and was
at first composed of seven members. The first
chairman was Walter Clark Teagle.

Prisoners (federal) employed in industry.
See Prison: Prisoners (federal) employed in
industry

INEBRIATES' ASYLUM. *See* Hospital:
Inebriates' asylum

INFANTILE PARALYSIS EPIDEMIC.
See Epidemic: Poliomyelitis epidemic

INFANTRYMAN'S BADGE (EXPERT).
See Medal: Expert Infantryman's Badge

INFLUENZA EPIDEMIC. *See* Epidemic:
Influenza epidemic

INFORMATION SERVICE (U.S.) was
created by the National Emergency Council as
a directing center for all government activities
under authority of Executive Order No. 6433-A
and in conformity with statement issued by the
White House, December 6, 1933. During the
organization period from January 18, 1934, to
March 7, 1934, Sarah Lee Fain served as chief.
The office was officially opened March 15, 1934,
with Harriet Maria Root as chief.

INFRA-RED PHOTOGRAPH. *See* Photograph: Infra-red photograph

INGRAIN CARPETS. *See* Carpet loom:
Carpet power loom to weave ingrain carpets

INHERITANCE TAX. *See* Tax: Inheritance tax

INITIATIVE AND REFERENDUM legislation was South Dakota's Joint Resolution
No. 101, passed January 27, 1897, by the House
and February 27, 1897, by the Senate. The
amendment was submitted to the voters November 8, 1898, and passed with 23,816 votes for
the amendment and 16,483 against the amendment. On June 2, 1902, Oregon adopted an
amendment to the state constitution authorizing
both initiative and referendum on legislation, by
popular vote. (*Charles Austin Beard and Birl
Earl Shultz—Documents on the Initiative,
Referendum and Recall*)

THE FIRST

INK

Ink was manufactured by the Thaddeus Davids Ink Company, established by Thaddeus Davids in New York City in 1825. The ink was bottled in various sizes and sold at retail. The first year only a few hundred bottles were manufactured. (*Thaddeus Davids—History of Ink*)

Ink paste was invented by Frank Buckley Cooney of Minneapolis, Minn., who obtained patent No. 1,479,533 on January 1, 1924. The paste, known as Cooney's Ink Paste, was manufactured February 10, 1923, by the Standard Ink Manufacturing Company, Minneapolis, Minn. The inventor sold rights to manufacture to the American Crayon Co.

Invisible ink used in diplomatic correspondence was employed by Silas Deane in 1776. As a member of the Committee of Secret Correspondence, organized November 29, 1775, "for the sole purpose of corresponding with our friends in Great Britain, Ireland, and other parts of the world," he left Philadelphia, Pa., March 5, 1776, and arrived in France on May 4, 1776, with instructions to purchase military supplies on credit. His correspondence with John Jay was interlined with invisible ink, invented by Sir James Jay in 1776. Deane sent the first authentic account which Congress received of the determination of the British Ministry to reduce the colonies to unconditional surrender. The writing was done with a solution of tannic acid. To make the ink visible, the paper was sponged with ferrous sulphate or copperas. The iron in the copperas combined with the tannic acid to form a dark compound easily visible.

Printer's ink. *See* Printer's Ink

INLAID LINOLEUM (embossed). *See* Linoleum: Embossed inlaid linoleum

INOCULATION. *See* Vaccination

INSANE DETENTION HOME. *See* Hospital: Insane detention home

INSANE HOSPITAL. *See* Hospital: Insane hospital (state)

INSANE PATIENT'S MAINTENANCE ACT

is found in the records of the Upland Court, Delaware County, Pa., in 1676. The act reads: "Jan Cornelissen of Amesland, Complayning to ye Court that his son Erick is bereft of his naturall Senses and is turned quyt madd and yt; he being a poore man is not able to maintaine him; Ordered: that three or four persons bee hired to build a little blockhouse at Amesland for to put in the said madman, and at the next Court, order will be taken yt; a small Levy be Laid for to pay for the building of ye house and the maintaining of ye said madman according to the laws of ye Government."

INSECT ELECTROCUTOR PATENT

was No. 974,785, granted November 8, 1910, to William M. Frost of Spokane, Wash.

INSECT MONUMENT. *See* Monument: Monument to an insect

INSEMINATION. *See* Impregnation: Impregnation (human) by means of artificial insemination

INSPECTOR, NAVAL (woman). *See* Naval officer: Woman naval inspector

INSTALLMENT SALES LAW

to protect consumers in practically all types of time-sales was signed by Governor William Averell Harriman of New York on April 17, 1957, to become effective October 1, 1957. It placed a limit on credit service charges, required all charges to be clearly itemized, and prohibited fine print in the contracts.

INSULATING BRICK. *See* Brick: Brick insulating

INSURANCE

Accident insurance company was the Travelers Insurance Company of Hartford, Conn., chartered June 17, 1863, through the efforts of James Goodwin Batterson. The charter provided for the issuance of accident insurance to cover travel accidents only. In 1864 this was amended to include accidents of every description.

Accident insurance policy was issued by the Travelers Insurance Company of Hartford, Conn., to James Bolter of Hartford for $1,000 in 1864. The policy covered only the period he spent walking from the post office to his home on Buckingham Street. The premium was two cents. The agreement was oral.

Accident insurance policy (printed) was issued on April 1, 1864, by the Travelers Insurance Company of Hartford, Conn., to James Goodwin Batterson and covered only accidents of travel. The first policy covering general accidents, also issued to Batterson, was policy No. 1164, dated July 1, 1864.

Aircraft liability and property damage insurance was issued by the Travelers Insurance Company of Hartford, Conn., to a New York manufacturer in 1919.

INSURANCE—*Continued*

Automobile compulsory insurance act (state) was "an act requiring owners of certain motor vehicles and trailers to furnish security for their civil liability on account of personal injury caused by their motor vehicles and trailers" (Chapter 346, Acts of Massachusetts), approved May 1, 1925, which became effective January 1, 1927. Automobiles were required to carry $5,000 and $10,000 liability.

Automobile insurance policy was issued by the Travelers Insurance Company of Hartford, Conn., on February 1, 1898, to Dr. Truman J. Martin of Buffalo, N.Y. The premium was $11.25 covering $5,000 to $10,000 liability.

Baby sitters' insurance policy was issued on January 26, 1950, by the American Associated Insurance Companies, St. Louis, Mo., and covered sitters available through the Missouri State Employment Service who were bonded up to $2,500 each for fraud and dishonesty.

Boiler insurance company was the Hartford Steam Boiler Inspection and Insurance Company, of Hartford, Conn., chartered in June 1866. The first president of the company was Enoch Roberts. The first policy was issued February 14, 1867. (*Austin J. Lilly—The Institution of Insurance*)

Bonding company (exclusive) was the American Surety Company, New York City, incorporated December 7, 1881. It began business April 15, 1884.

Bonding law (state) for the bonding of all officers, deputies, and state employees was enacted by North Dakota (Chapter 194, sections 199-200A), approved March 1, 1913, effective January 1, 1914. The law was declared unconstitutional in 1914. Another law was passed (Chapter 158) and approved March 5, 1919. The premiums were 25 cents a year for each $100 of the required bond. A State Bonding Fund was created which in the first year showed a net income of $63,172.04. The fund was under the State Commissioner of Insurance. A. L. Carey was the first commissioner. The first claim was filed August 4, 1919, by Riggin Township, Benson County, for $1,000 for misappropriations of funds, and paid February 4, 1920.

Credit insurance was attempted in New York State in 1887, but the first company which operated for any length of time was the U.S. Credit System Company of New York, organized in 1889. (*Saul Benton Ackerman and Joseph William Neuner—Credit Insurance*)

Department store to sell insurance. *See* Business: Department store to sell insurance

Employer's Liability Act (federal) was passed June 11, 1906 (34 Stat.L.232), but was declared unconstitutional by the Supreme Court in the Employer's Liability Cases (1908) (207 U.S. 463, 52 L.Ed. 297, 28 S.C.R.141) because its provisions extended to include the employees of interstate carriers even when such employees were not themselves engaged in any of the processes of interstate commerce. A revised act was passed April 22, 1908 (35 Stat.L.65).

Federal Deposit Insurance Corporation. *See* Federal Deposit Insurance Corporation

Fire and tornado insurance fund (state) was established by Chapter 159 of the laws of North Dakota and began to function July 1, 1919. For the first five months, the gross income was $28,908.78 and the losses paid were $3,773.32. The net income, after expenses were paid, amounted to $24,143.70. The first loss was $1,500, paid on October 23, 1919, to Conway, S.D., No. 64, to compensate for damage caused by an overheated furnace. The law provided that no policy over $100,000 could be written. When necessary, additional insurance was obtained from private companies. (*Frederick Ludwig Hoffman—Windstorm and Tornado Insurance*)

Fire insurance agent is said to have been John Copson of High Street, Philadelphia, Pa., who inserted an advertisement on May 25, 1721, in the *American Weekly Mercury* to the effect that he would open an office for insurance on "vessels, goods and merchandise." (*John A. Fowler—History of Insurance in Philadelphia for Two Centuries*)

Fire insurance company was organized in 1735 in Charleston, S.C., as "The Friendly Society for the Mutual Insurance of Houses Against Fire," and received subscriptions beginning January 1, 1735. This company issued policies and conducted business over a period of about six years, as evidenced by advertisements and notices in the *South Carolina Gazette* from November 15, 1735, to February 19, 1741. On November 18, 1740, there was a conflagration which consumed half the town and probably ruined the society, as the last advertisement, which appeared on February 19, 1741, stated that "the bonds given by the members will be put in suit unless paid."

Fire insurance company to receive a charter was the Philadelphia Contributionship for the Insurance of Houses from Loss by Fire, Philadelphia, Pa. This was granted by the Lieutenant Governor and Proprietaries of the province of Pennsylvania on February 20, 1768, and was subsequently confirmed by

THE FIRST

George III, King of England, upon the advice of his Privy Council at the Court of St. James, London. On April 13, 1752, twelve directors and a treasurer had been elected, sixteen years before the charter was obtained. The first name subscribed to the Deed of Settlement or Articles of Association was that of James Hamilton, the Lieutenant Governor of the Province under the Proprietaries. The first private name was that of Benjamin Franklin. At the first meeting of the directors, held May 11, 1752, a seal for the company "was ordered, being four Hands united." The marks were of lead, mounted upon a wooden shield, and were put up on all houses insured. The first fire insurance policy was issued on June 1, 1752, to John Smith of Philadelphia, who for £1 insured his house valued at £1,000. Smith was the first treasurer of the company. (*At the Sign of the Hand-in-Hand—Philadelphia Contributionship for the Insurance of Houses*)

Fire insurance joint-stock company was the American Fire Insurance Company, organized February 28, 1810, in Philadelphia, Pa. The first president was Captain William Jones, who later became Secretary of the Navy under President James Madison. The first secretary of the company was Edward Fox. (*American Fire Insurance Company—Fire Insurance in America*)

Fraternal group insurance of consequence was issued in 1869 by the Metropolitan Life Insurance Company, New York City, to the Hildise Bund, an organization of German-American wage-earners, which collected weekly premiums from its members. The premiums are said to have amounted at one time to about $7,500 a week.

Government insurance was enacted by the Plymouth Colony in 1636. The legislation provided that "if any [man] shalbee sent forth as a souldier and shall returne maimed, hee shalbee maintained competently by the Collonie of New Plymouth during his life." The act applied particularly to the soldiers engaged in the Pequot Indian War concluded on November 20, 1637. (*David Pulsifer—Records of the Colony in New England—Laws 1623-1682*)

Group hospital insurance plan was effected by Baylor University Hospital, Dallas, Tex., on December 21, 1929. The plan was inaugurated by Dr. Justin Ford Kimball, executive vice president of Baylor University. The first group insured was the Dallas Public School teachers.

Group hospital-medical cooperative was the Group Health Association, Inc., Washington, D.C., authorized February 24, 1937. The clinic opened November 1, 1937.

THE FIRST

Group insurance contract of importance was made on July 1, 1912, between Montgomery Ward & Company of Chicago, Ill., and the Equitable Life Assurance Society of the United States, whereby 3,000 persons were insured as a group for approximately $6 million without medical examination.

Group insurance policy was written by William J. Graham of the Equitable Life Assurance Society of the United States on June 1, 1911, under one blanket contract. Without medical examination, 121 employees of the Pantasote Leather Company of Passaic, N.J., were insured as a group for $87,030. Each employee was given insurance protection amounting to a year's salary and a funeral benefit of $100.

Group insurance policy for college students covering medical, surgical, and hospital expenses was issued February 1, 1936, by the Ocean Accident and Guarantee Corporation, Ltd., to Vassar College, Poughkeepsie, N.Y. The plan was sponsored by the college for voluntary participation and 565 students were included at a premium of $12 each for the year. Known as the Students' Reimbursement Plan, it was organized and managed by A. W. G. Dewar, Inc., of Boston, Mass., whose Tuition Refund Plan in 1929 had first introduced the insurance of school fees in American private schools.

Hail insurance on growing tobacco crops was written in 1880 by the Tobacco Growers' Mutual Insurance Company of North Canaan, Conn., incorporated in Connecticut, March 24, 1880. This company went out of business in 1887. (*U.S. Department of Agriculture—Bulletin No. 912*)

Hail insurance law (state) was enacted by the legislature of North Dakota in 1911 and approved by Governor John Burke, March 18, 1911. The number of policies issued the first year was 1,011, representing risks of about a million dollars. The losses during the first year exceeded the premiums by nearly 18 per cent, and the losses, as adjusted, had to be prorated at 70 per cent. (*North Dakota Hail Insurance Department—Annual Report—1912*)

Health insurance company was the Massachusetts Health Insurance Company of Boston, Mass., organized April 21, 1847. It was incorporated in 1847 under Chapter 214 of the Massachusetts General Law. The company existed for a very short period. (*George Edwin McNeill—A Study of Accidents and Accident Insurance*)

Health insurance law (state) was the Rhode Island Cash Sickness Compensation act, approved April 29, 1942, effective May 10, 1942. It required employers to collect

INSURANCE—*Continued*
1 per cent from employees after June 1, 1942,
on salaries up to $3,000 paid in any calendar
year, and granted benefits ranging from $6.75
to $18 a week. The board members super-
vising the fund were Chairman Mortimer W.
Newton, Arthur P. Patt, and Tom Howick.

Insurance agency was opened by Israel
Whelan in New York City in 1804. He was
a representative of the Phoenix Fire Office
of London, England. *(Harry Chase Brearley
—History of the National Board of Fire
Underwriters)*

Insurance board (state) was the New
Hampshire Insurance Department, established
July 1, 1851, by New Hampshire Laws (1851,
Chapter 1111), which authorized the governor
to appoint three suitable persons, residents of
the state, for a term of one year, whose duty
it was to examine personally each year the
affairs of all insurance companies and report
to the legislature. The first board consisted of
Albert S. Scott, Jacob E. Ela, and Timo Hoskins. *(Edwin Wilhite Patterson—The Insurance Commissioner in the United States)*

Insurance department (state) charged
with the execution of the laws relating to
insurance was the New York Insurance De-
partment which was established in 1859, by
Chapter 366, approved April 15, 1859, effective
January 1, 1860. The first superintendent was
William Barnes, appointed January 11, 1860.
*(First Annual Report of the Superintendent
of the Insurance Department, New York
State)*

Insurance policy to be illustrated was issued April 8, 1947, by the Allstate Insurance
Company, Chicago, Ill.

Insurance rate standardization was effected
July 18, 1866, in New York City by the National Board of Fire Underwriters, an organization of seventy-five fire insurance companies.
The first annual meeting was held February
20, 1867, in New York City, and the first president was James McLean. *(Harry Chase
Brearley—History of the National Board of
Fire Underwriters)*

Insurance regulation (state) was enacted
by Massachusetts, Chapter 46, approved February 13, 1799, "an act in addition to an act
entitled, 'an act to incorporate sundry persons
by the name of the Massachusetts Fire Insurance Company.'" It required that the company
"shall, when and as often required by the legislature of the Commonwealth, lay before them
such a statement of their affairs as the said
legislature may deem it expedient to require,
and submit to an examination hereon under
oath."

Insurance service offered by a newspaper
to its subscribers was instituted by the
St. Louis *Star*, St. Louis, Mo., on April 14,
1919. Policies on a deferred payment plan
were also offered. The first policy was furnished by the American Bonding and Casualty
Company of Sioux City, Iowa, and was a
peculiar affair resembling an old-style theatre
program.

Life insurance by a general insurance company was offered by the Insurance Company
of North America, organized in Philadelphia,
Pa., on December 10, 1792, with a capital of
$600,000 and chartered on April 14, 1794. The
first policy was issued on December 15, 1792.
Only six policies were written in five years,
and in 1804 the life insurance feature was discontinued. The first president was John Maxwell Nesbitt and the first secretary, Ebenezer
Hazard. *(Joseph Brotherton Maclean—Life
Insurance)*

Life insurance company was the "Corporation for the Relief of Poor and Distressed
Presbyterian Ministers and of the Poor and
Distressed Widows and Children of Presbyterian Ministers," incorporated January 11,
1759, Philadelphia, Pa. The first officers were
the Reverend Robert Cross, president; William
Allen, treasurer; and Francis Alison, secretary.
The first policy was issued May 22, 1761, to
Francis Alison. Survivor annuities were
granted at the death of the policy holder, the
beneficiary receiving £10 to £35 for the duration of his life. The annual premium required
was one fifth of the annuity.

Marine insurance law (state) was enacted
in Massachusetts in 1818 (Chapter 120, Acts of
1818, approved February 16, 1818). An act was
passed defining the powers, duties, and restrictions of insurance companies. It applied only
to companies writing marine insurance and provided for annual publication by the president
and directors of the amount of their stock, the
risks against which they meant to insure, and
the amounts of the single risks. They were
also required to report to the legislature whenever so directed and were forbidden to write in
any risk a sum exceeding 10 per cent of the
capital stock of the company.

Mutual fire insurance company for insuring factories was the Manufacturers' Mutual
Fire Insurance Company of Rhode Island, located in Providence, R.I., and incorporated
October 31, 1835. The first policy was issued
December 3, 1835, to Zachariah Allen for
$2,500 at a cash premium deposit rate of 60
cents a year. At the expiration of the policy
a 51 per cent dividend was declared, resulting
in an insurance cost of 29.4 cents per $100
for the year. *(Journal of American Insurance.
Vol. 1. No. 2)*

THE FIRST

THE FIRST

Mutual liability insurance company was the American Mutual Liability Insurance Company, Boston, Mass., incorporated March 30, 1887, formally organized April 21, 1887, and opened for business October 1, 1887, when twenty-two policies were written covering liability of employers to injured workmen. The rate was 30 cents per $100 of payroll. The first officers were William Croad Lovering, president; Josiah Caleb Bartlett, first manager; Sydney Augustus Williams, secretary; and Charles Edward Hodges, bookkeeper and clerk.

Mutual life insurance company to be chartered was the New England Mutual Life Insurance Company of Boston, Mass., which was chartered April 1, 1835. The first president was Judge Willard Phillips. The company was not actually organized for business until December 1, 1843. The first policy was issued February 1, 1844.

Mutual life insurance company to operate was the Mutual Life Insurance Company of New York, which was chartered on April 12, 1842. The first policy was issued February 1, 1843, to Thomas N. Ayres. The first president was Morris Robinson. Policy holders were entitled to a share in the management through the election of directors. All profits belonged to the policy holders. *(Shepherd Bancroft Clough —A Century of American Life Insurance—A History of the Mutual Life Insurance Company of New York—1843-1943)*

Non-forfeiture insurance law (state) was enacted by Massachusetts in 1861 (Chapter 186, Acts of 1861, approved April 10, 1861). It was sponsored by Commissioner Elizur Wright. This law required domestic companies to use four fifths of the reserve to continue a policy as extended term insurance beyond the date of lapse. In event of death during the term period, the company had the right to deduct from the claim the premiums that would have been paid had the policy continued in force, plus interest.

Non-forfeiture insurance policy was issued by the New York Life Insurance Company of New York City, August 13, 1860, about eight months prior to the enactment of the "nonforfeitable" legislation in Massachusetts. This plan was not made retroactive. Although this was the first policy issued providing for nonforfeiture, non-forfeiture had in fact been granted for some time prior thereto, but was not provided in the policy.

Numerical system of insurance rating was originated by the New York Life Insurance Company of New York City about 1903. Values were assigned to various factors affecting the insurability of an applicant for insurance so as to aid a company in determining under

its rules whether the applicant was insurable, and if insurable, at what rates of premium, i.e., whether the life is "standard" or "substandard," and if the latter to what extent.

Plate glass insurance was written by the United States Plate Glass Insurance Company of Philadelphia, Pa., incorporated April 12, 1867, with an original capital of $20,000. The first president was John Van Dusen.

Savings bank life insurance was launched by act of the Massachusetts legislature, June 26, 1907. The plan was originated by Louis Dembitz Brandeis, then a Boston lawyer, and later Associate Justice of the United States Supreme Court. The first savings bank to establish an insurance department was the Whitman Savings Bank in Whitman, Mass. The department was established June 18, 1908, and the first policy written June 22, 1908. Savings bank life insurance is legal reserve insurance that is sold "over the counter" by certain mutual savings banks. No solicitors are employed. Savings and Insurance Banks may now insure residents of Massachusetts or persons regularly employed therein in amounts up to $5,000 per each issuing bank. However, the total insurance on any one life may not exceed $38,000, exclusive of dividends and group insurance. As long as premiums are paid a policy is still effective even if the insured moves elsewhere. *(General Laws— Massachusetts. Chapter 178, section 6)*

Social security. *See* Social security act (U.S.)

Substandard life insurance policy was issued July 1, 1896, by the New York Life Insurance Company of New York City. A substandard policy is one issued on a life which because of a medical impairment, hazardous occupation, or some other reason is "substandard" and therefore not insurable at "standard" or normal rates of premium.

Teachers' death benefit. *See* Teachers' death benefit

Teachers' pension fund. *See* Teachers' pension funds

Teachers' sick benefit fund. *See* Teachers' sick benefit fund

Title guaranty insurance company was the Real Estate Title Insurance and Trust Company, organized in Philadelphia, Pa., on March 31, 1876. It offered security against errors in titles. The original capital was $250,000, half of which was paid in. The first president was Joshua H. Morris and the first secretary, Joseph S. Siddall.

INSURANCE—*Continued*
Unemployment insurance act passed by a state was enacted by Wisconsin, January 28, 1932, and signed by Governor Philip La Follette. Every employer of ten or more men was required to put 2 per cent of the payroll aside until a fund accrued equaling $75 per eligible worker, which the employee could draw against in time of unemployment at the rate of $10 a week for a maximum of ten weeks. The first payment was made August 17, 1936. The chairman of the Industrial Commission which regulated the department was Voyta Wrabetz.

War Risk Insurance Bureau was established by act of Congress, September 2, 1914 (38 Stat.L.711), to insure American vessels against war risks. The act was amended on June 12, 1917, and October 6, 1917, to provide yearly renewable term insurance against total disability and death to those in active military or naval service. Provision was made for policy conversion to other forms of life insurance. The bureau was under the general direction of the Secretary of the Treasury and directly supervised by William C. De Lanoy. *(U.S. Veterans Bureau—Laws Governing the Organization and Administration of the Bureau of War Risk Insurance)*

Workmen's compensation insurance law (federal) was approved May 30, 1908 (35 Stat.L.556). It became effective August 1, 1908, and was applicable to certain classes of federal employees in the United States: artisans or laborers in any manufacturing establishment, arsenal, or navy yard and employees in the construction of river and harbor fortifications, in hazardous employment on construction work in the reclamation of arid lands, and in hazardous employment under the Isthmian Canal Commission.

Workmen's compensation insurance law (state) to go into effect was passed by Wisconsin, May 3, 1911 (Chapter 50) and went into effect the same date. Washington passed a compensation insurance law (Chapter 74) which was approved on March 14, 1911, but which did not go into effect until October 1, 1911. New Jersey also passed a law (Chapter 95) which was approved April 4, 1911, and which went into effect July 4, 1911. Laws which were later declared unconstitutional had, however, been passed previously: Maryland, 1902; Montana, 1909; New York, 1910.

INSURANCE BOOK
Insurance proposal of importance published in America was *Ways and Means for the Inhabitants of Delaware to Become Rich, wherein the several growths and products of these countries are demonstrated to be a sufficient fund for a flourishing trade*, 65 pages, printed in Philadelphia, Pa., in 1725, by S.

Keimer. The author was Francis Rawle, who advocated the establishment by the legislature of an insurance office in Philadelphia for the purpose of providing marine insurance for merchants. *(Philadelphia Contributionship—Franklin and Fires)*

INSURANCE MAGAZINE was *Tuckett's Monthly Insurance Journal*, published in 1852 in Philadelphia, Pa. *(Journal of American Insurance. Vol. 1, no. 3)*

INSURANCE TREATISE on the law of insurance was a reprint of the English *A System of the Law of Marine Insurances; with three chapters on bottomry, on insurance on lives and on insurances against fire*, by Sir James Alan Park, published in Philadelphia, Pa., in 1789.

INSURED BANK PAYMENTS. *See* Bank: Bank payments to depositors of a closed insured bank

INTEGRATED HISTORY COURSE. *See* History instruction: History course (integrated) in a women's college

INTELLIGENCE TEST used in a school for the feeble-minded was the Binet-Simon Test. It was introduced in August 1908 by Dr. Henry Herbert Goddard, director of research in the New Jersey Training School for Feeble-Minded Boys and Girls in Vineland, N.J., to determine the degree of subnormality of children in the institution. *(Alfred Binet and Théodore Simon—The Development of Intelligence in Children)*

INTER-AMERICAN HIGHWAY APPROPRIATION. *See* Road: Inter-American highway appropriation

INTERCOLLEGIATE AIR MEET. *See* Aviation—Expositions and Meets: Intercollegiate air meet

INTERCOLLEGIATE ATHLETIC ASSOCIATION of importance was the Intercollegiate Association of Amateur Athletes of America, organized in Saratoga, N.Y., in June 1876, when a track meet was held. The charter members were Amherst, Bowdoin, Brown, City College of New York, Columbia, Cornell, Dartmouth, Harvard, Pennsylvania, Princeton, Trinity, Union, Wesleyan, Williams, and Yale. A preliminary meeting was held in Saratoga, N.Y., December 4, 1875. In 1873 James Gordon Bennett offered a cup to the best track athlete, the contestants for which were the members of the crews who participated in the Springfield, Mass., rowing races. The Association was formed as a result of these meetings.

THE FIRST

INTERCOLONIAL WAR. *See* War (colonial): Intercolonial war

INTERCONTINENTAL SYSTEM OF STUDY. *See* College: Intercontinental system of study

INTERFRATERNITY COUNCIL. *See* Fraternity (Greek letter): Interfraternity council

INTERIOR DEPARTMENT (U.S.)
Interior Department secretary was Thomas Ewing of Ohio, who was appointed by President Zachary Taylor on March 8, 1849, and who served until July 23, 1850.

Interior Department (U.S.) was created by act of March 3, 1849 (9 Stat.L.395), titled "an act to establish the Home Department."

INTERLOCKING MACHINE (railroad). *See* Railroad signal system: Railroad signal system of interlocking signal apparatus

INTERMEDIATE RANGE BALLISTIC MISSILE. *See* Rocket: Intermediate range ballistic missile

INTERNAL COMBUSTION ENGINE. *See* Engine: Internal combustion engine

INTERNAL REVENUE ACT was passed by Congress, March 3, 1791 (1 Stat.L.202). It established fourteen revenue districts, one for each state, and placed a tax on distilled spirits varying from 11 to 30 cents a gallon.

INTERNAL REVENUE COLLECTOR (woman). *See* Woman: Woman internal revenue collector

INTERNAL REVENUE COMMISSIONER was George Sewall Boutwell of Massachusetts, who served from July 17, 1862, to March 4, 1863, under the U.S. Bureau of Internal Revenue in the Treasury Department. The Bureau was created by act of Congress July 1, 1862 (12 Stat.L.432). The first Commissioner of the Revenue was Tench Coxe of Pennsylvania, who was assistant to the Secretary of the Treasury in charge of internal revenue from September 11, 1789, to May 8, 1792. He was designated Commissioner of the Revenue on May 8, 1792.

INTERNAL REVENUE TAX. *See* Tax: Internal revenue tax

THE FIRST

INTERNATIONAL AGREEMENTS, INSTITUTIONS, AND EVENTS. *See* under specific subjects, e.g., Automobile race, Copyright law, Hospital, Weights and measures standardization

INTERNATIONAL EUCHARISTIC CONGRESS in America met in Chicago, Ill., June 20-24, 1926. Although this was the twenty-eighth international session, it was the first in the United States. Cardinal John Bonzano was installed as the Papal Legate to preside for Pope Pius XI. Services were held at the Cathedral of the Holy Name, Chicago.

INTERNATIONAL SKI MEET. *See* Ski meet (international)

INTERNATIONAL YACHT RACE. *See* Yacht race: Yacht race (international)

INTERRACIAL HOSPITAL. *See* Hospital: Interracial hospital

INTERSTATE CARRIER ARBITRATION. *See* Arbitration: Interstate carrier arbitration law

INTERSTATE COMMERCE ACT establishing the Interstate Commerce Commission was approved February 4, 1887 (24 Stat.L.379), and was popularly known as the Cullom Act. Its terms, effective April 5, 1887, provided for the appointment of five commissioners from January 1, 1887, for terms of 2, 3, 4, 5, and 6 years. Its principal objects were "to secure just and reasonable charges for [railroad] transportation; to prohibit unjust discrimination in the rendition of like services under similar circumstances and conditions; to prevent undue preferences to persons, corporations or localities; to inhibit greater compensation for shorter than for longer distances over the same lines; and to abolish combinations for the pooling of freights." The commission was organized March 31, 1887, and started to function April 5, 1887, with 38 persons on the payroll. The first commissioners were Aldace Freeman Walker, Augustus Schoonmaker, Walter Lawrence Bragg, Thomas McIntyre Cooley, and William Ralls Morrison, appointed March 22, 1887, by President Grover Cleveland. *(Isaiah Leo Sharfman—The Interstate Commerce Commission)*

INTERSTATE COMMERCE COMMISSION MEDAL. *See* Medal: Interstate commerce commission medal of honor

INTERSTATE CRIME PACT. *See* Crime: Interstate crime pact

THE FIRST

THE FIRST

INTERSTATE LEGISLATIVE CONFERENCE. *See* Legislative conference (interstate)

INTERSTATE RAILROAD. *See* Railroad: Interstate railroad

INTERURBAN STREET CAR. *See* Street car: Interurban street car line

INVESTITURE OF ORDERS. *See* Knighthood

INVESTMENT FINANCE COMPANY. *See* Business: Installment finance company

INVESTMENT TRUST. *See* Brokerage: Investment trust

INVISIBLE GLASS. *See* Glass: Invisible glass installation

INVISIBLE INK. *See* Ink: Invisible ink

IRISH MAGAZINE was *The Shamrock or Hibernian Chronicle,* published December 15, 1810, in New York City. It was edited by Edward Gillespy. Publication was suspended three times. On June 18, 1814, it was revived as *The Shamrock.* *(Apollinaris William Baumgartner—Catholic Journalism)*

IRON
Angle iron was rolled in 1819 by Samuel Leonard at the Union Rolling Mill, on the Monongahela River, at Pittsburgh, Pa. The mill had four puddling furnaces.

Anthracite coal used in smelting iron ore. *See* Coal: Anthracite coal used in smelting iron ore

Cast iron bridge. *See* Bridge: Cast iron bridge

Cast iron pipes used in a city waterworks system were installed by Philadelphia, Pa., in 1817. The pipeline was 400 feet long and 4½ inches in diameter. The pipes were imported from England and were so much superior to the old wooden water pipes that the Watering Committee decided, according to its report of January 23, 1817, to adopt them. In 1818 the committee resolved to make all future installations with cast iron pipe.

Exportation of iron was made in 1650. In "1650—Sam Hutchinson, merchant, shipped on the 'Charles' 3½ tunne, 172 bars of iron for acco. of Ri. Hutchinson, of London." This iron was probably made in Lynn, Mass. *(Stephen Lincoln Goodale—Chronology of Iron and Steel)*

Hammered iron was made in 1842 at the Weymouth Iron Works on the Great Egg Harbor River, N.J., founded in 1754. The iron was hammered at the forge by two great trip hammers operated by waterpower. Stephen Colwell received a medal from the Academy of Natural Sciences for developing the machinery used in this plant.

Iron blast furnace successfully to use anthracite coal was the Pioneer furnace in Pottsville, Pa., which was blown October 19, 1839, by Benjamin Perry. About twenty-eight tons of foundry iron were produced a week. The furnace was built by William Lyman of Boston, Mass.

Iron bridge. *See* Bridge

Iron casting is credited to Joseph Mallinson of Dusboro, Pa., who introduced it in 1739 and received a grant of 200 acres of unimproved land in recognition of his services. *(James Moore Swank—History of the Manufacture of Iron)*

Iron castings (malleable) were produced in Newark, N.J., July 4, 1826, by Seth Boyden. At first, the iron was melted in crucibles, with lime used as a flux and heated in charcoal or hard coal fires.

Iron-clad ships. *See* Ship: Iron-clad naval vessels

Iron foundry. *See* Brass and iron foundry

Iron hull ship. *See* Ship: Iron vessel

Iron lifeboat. *See* Lifeboat: Lifeboat (corrugated)

Iron mill to puddle and roll iron was the Plumstock Rolling Mill on Redstone Creek between Connellsville and Brownsville, Pa., in Fayette County, put into operation September 15, 1817, by Isaac Meason. It was wrecked by floods in 1824 and was not rebuilt. *(Western Pennsylvania Historical Survey—Guide to Historical Places in Western Pennsylvania)*

Iron patent was No. 3,605, granted January 6, 1844, to S. Broadmeadow of Woodbridge, N.J., for a process "to obtain malleable iron direct from iron ore."

Iron pile lighthouse. *See* Lighthouse: Iron pile lighthouse

Iron rail. *See* Railroad track: Railroad rails of iron

THE FIRST

THE FIRST

Iron slitting mill, for slitting nailrods, was established in Milton, Mass., in March 1710 by Jonathan Jackson.

Iron sloop yacht. *See* Ship: Iron sloop yacht

Iron steamship. *See* Ship: Iron steamship

Iron window sash. *See* Sash: Wrought iron window sash installation

Iron wire suspension bridge. *See* Bridge: Iron wire suspension bridge

Iron works was erected at Falling Creek, Va. (near Richmond), in 1619 by the Virginia Company. It operated only a short time, however, because of Indian troubles, and its charter was revoked in 1624. John Berkeley was in charge of operations. *(Transactions American Institute of Mining Engineering. Vol. XX)*

Iron works (successful) was constructed in 1643 by John Winthrop, Jr., and ten others. It was known as the Company of Undertakers for the Iron Works and was established near the Saugus River, near Lynn, Mass. It produced eight tons of iron per week from the neighboring bog ore. A forge was later installed. *(Robert Charles Winthrop—Life and Letters of John Winthrop, Governor of the Massachusetts Bay Company at Their Emigration to New England 1630)*

Iron yacht. *See* Ship: Iron sloop yacht

Rolling mill was the Sarum ironworks, established in 1746 by John Taylor in Chester, Pa. Three stacks worked full blast.

Wrought iron beams used in a building. *See* Building: Building in which wrought iron beams were used

IRON LUNG RESPIRATOR. *See* Respirator (iron lung)

IROQUOIS CONFEDERACY. *See* Indians: Indian league of nations

IRRIGATION LEGISLATION (federal) was the act of July 26, 1866 (14 Stat.L.251), which ruled that control of waterways was a matter of state control subject to "local customs, laws and decisions of the court." *(Ray Palmer Teele—Irrigation in the United States)*

ISLAND PRISON (military). *See* Prison: Military prison of the United States

ISLAND TERRITORIAL ACQUISITION. *See* Territorial expansion: Island territory

ISOTOPE

Radioactive isotope medicine was phosphorus 32, artificially produced in a 37-inch cyclotron. It was administered December 24, 1936, to a 28-year-old woman with chronic leukemia by Dr. John Hunsdale Lawrence, director of the Donner Laboratory at the University of California at Berkeley.

Radioactive isotopes exported were produced from phosphorus 31 at the Oak Ridge National Laboratory, Oak Ridge, Tenn., and flown to San Francisco, Calif., for further flight to Canberra, Australia, where they arrived September 11, 1947. They were a by-product of a chain-reacting uranium pile and were used in the Australian commonwealth's X-ray and medical laboratory. (The Oak Ridge National Laboratory was operated by the Union Carbide Corporation for the United States Atomic Energy Commission.)

ITALIAN INSTRUCTION. *See* Language instruction: Italian instruction in a college

ITALIAN NEWSPAPER. *See* Newspaper: Italian newspaper

ITALIAN OPERA. *See* Opera: Opera (Italian)

IVORY COMB. *See* Comb

JAI-ALAI, the pelota game, was played at the Louisiana Purchase Exposition, St. Louis, Mo., in 1904 in the Jai-Alai Building—not on the World's Fair grounds but near the main entrance. *(Badminton Magazine. Vol. 51. 1919)*

JAIL. *See* Prison

JAPANESE AMBASSADOR to the United States was Niimi Buzennokami. He and his staff of 74 men left Japan, January 22, 1860, on the U.S.S. "Powhatan" under Captain Josiah Tattnall and arrived in San Francisco, Calif., March 9, 1860. They arrived in Washington, D.C., via Panama on April 25, 1860, and were received by President James Buchanan, April 28, 1860. They arrived in New York City, May 28, 1860. On June 13, 1860, the party went back to Japan on board the American battleship "Niagara" via the Cape of Good Hope. The first Japanese legation was established in Washington, D.C., in October 1870, and on January 7, 1906, the legation was raised to the rank of embassy. E. Hicki was appointed chargé d'affaires *ad interim,* and was suc-

JAPANESE AMBASSADOR—*Continued*
ceeded by Shuzo Aoki, who was appointed the
first Japanese Ambassador Plenipotentiary on
April 24, 1906. *(Masakiyo Yanagawa—First
Japanese Mission to America)*

**JAPANESE AMERICAN CONGRESS-
MAN.** *See* Congressman (U.S.): Congress-
man of Japanese ancestry elected to the
House of Representatives

JAPANESE CITIZEN. *See* Citizenship:
Japanese granted citizenship

JAPANESE IMMIGRANT. *See* Immigration: Japanese to enter the United States

JAPANESE LAWYER. *See* Lawyer:
Japanese lawyer

JAPANESE MIDSHIPMAN. *See* Naval
academy: Japanese midshipman in the U.S.
Naval Academy

JAZZ MUSIC COMPOSER. *See* Musician:
Composer of jazz music

JEANS AND FUSTIANS (cloth). *See*
Cloth: Jeans, fustians, everlastings, and coatings

JELLY PETROLEUM. *See* Petroleum
jelly

JENNY (cotton). *See* Cotton spinning
jenny

JERSEY CATTLE. *See* Cattle club: Cattle club (Jersey cattle)

JET ACE. *See* Aviation—Aviator: American ace (jet)

JET PROPELLED AIRPLANE. *See*
Aviation—Airplane: Jet propelled airplane

JEWELERS' SUPPLY HOUSE of importance was established in 1794 by Nehemiah
Dodge, silversmith, goldsmith, and watch re-
pairer, in a shop on North Main Street, Providence, R.I. In addition to his retail business he
sold gold plate made of a thin sheet of gold
united with a thicker sheet of copper to manufacturing jewelers.

JEWISH COLLEGE
Jewish college was Maimonides College,
Philadelphia, Pa., which opened October 28,
1867. It was sponsored by the Hebrew Edu-

cational Society of Philadelphia and the Board
of Delegates of American Israelites. It offered a five-year course leading to Bachelor
and Doctor of Divinity degrees. Tuition was
$100, and board and lodging $200 per year.
Of the eight students approved for matriculation the first year, only two remained the
entire year. Dr. Marcus Jastrow was provost,
and the Reverend Isaac Leeser, professor of
homiletics, belles lettres, and comparative theology, was president of the faculty. The college closed in 1873. *(Bertram Wallace Korn—
Eventful Years and Experiences)*

Jewish college of liberal arts and sciences
under Jewish auspices was the Yeshiva College, Amsterdam Avenue and 186th Street, New
York City, chartered March 29, 1928, by the
Board of Regents of the University of the
State of New York. The cornerstone was laid
May 1, 1927. The first graduating class, consisting of 19 members, received B.A. degrees on
June 16, 1932. The college offers courses leading to the degrees of B.A. and B.S. and awards
honorary degrees of Doctor of Laws and Doctor
of Humane Letters. The first president was Dr.
Bernard Revel. On November 16, 1945, it became Yeshiva University and was authorized to
establish new graduate and undergraduate
schools and to confer 15 kinds of degrees.

Jewish college to train men for the rabbinate was Hebrew Union College, established October 3, 1875, in Cincinnati, Ohio,
through the efforts of Dr. Isaac Mayer Wise,
who served as president from 1875 to 1900. The
first graduation was held July 11, 1883, when
Israel Aaron, Henry Berkowitz, Joseph Krauskopf and David Philipson were ordained.

Jewish non-sectarian college was Dropsie
College for Hebrew and Cognate Learning of
Philadelphia, Pa., chartered June 6, 1907. The
college was founded in accordance with the will
of Moses Aaron Dropsie, who directed "that in
the admission of students there shall be no distinction on account of creed, color or sex." The
first president of the college was Dr. Cyrus
Adler. *(Dropsie College Register. 1918-1919)*

JEWISH CONGREGATION
Jewish congregation was Shearith Israel
(Remnant of Israel) established in 1655 in New
Amsterdam (later New York City) by Sephar-
dic Jews who had fled from the inquisition in
Portuguese Brazil. Saul Brown was the first
rabbi. The foundation stones of the first synagogue were laid on Thursday, September 8,
1729, and the building was consecrated April 8,
1730. The building was located on Mill Street,
now South William Street. The present synagogue is located at Central Park West and
Seventieth Street, New York City. *(David de
Sola Pool—The Mill Street Synagogue)*

THE FIRST

Jewish congregation (Ashkenazic) was Congregation Rodeph Shalom of Philadelphia, Pa., founded October 10, 1802. (*Edward Davis —History of Rodeph Shalom*)

Jewish congregation (Reform) was the Reformed Society of Israelites, organized November 21, 1824, by twelve members of the Congregation Beth Elohim of Charleston, S.C. This body desired a modified form of worship and started a new congregation. The organization lasted eight years and was without a rabbi, because of lack of funds.. (*David Philipson— Reform Movement in Judaism*)

Jewish congregation to call a woman to exercise a rabbi's function was Temple Beth Israel, Meridian, Miss., which installed Mrs. Paula Ackerman, widow of Rabbi William Ackerman, on January 26, 1951, as spiritual leader with the duties and authority of a rabbi.

Jewish mobile synagogue was the Circuit Riding Rabbi Bus dedicated March 27, 1955, at the Amity Country Club, Charlotte, N.C. It was placed in operation April 4, 1955, in North Carolina communities and was the project of the North Carolina Association of Jewish Men. The first rabbi was Harold A. Friedman. The bus was equipped with desks, blackboards, maps, a projection machine, a record player, and a library.

JEWISH PRAYER BOOK published in the United States was *Prayers for Shabbath, Rosh-Hashanah and Kippur, or the Sabbath, the beginning of the year and the Day of Atonements; with the Amidah and Musaph of the Moadim, or Solemn Seasons according to the order of the Spanish and Portuguese Jews,* translated by Isaac Pinto and printed for him in 1766 (the year 5526 according to the Hebrew calendar) by John Holt, New York City. The book contained 196 pages.

JEWS

See also under

Army officer	Normal school
Cemetery	Physician
Congressman	Play
(U.S.)	Senator (U.S.)
Diplomatic	Sunday school
service	Supreme Court
Governor	(U.S.)
Hospital	Women's club
Naval officer	

Jew known to have arrived in America was Jacob Barsimson, who landed at New Netherlands on August 22, 1654. He left the Netherlands on the "Pearboom" (or "Peartree") on July 8, 1654, and paid 36 guilders for his passage. A month later, twenty-three more Jews arrived, but were temporarily denied admission by Governor Peter Stuyvesant as

THE FIRST

"hateful enemies and blasphemers of the name of Christ." They were later allowed to enter provided "the poor among them should not become a burden to the Dutch West Indies Company or the community, but be supported by their own nation." (*Charles Daly—Settlement of Jews in North America*)

Jew to win all the rights and perform all the duties of citizenship was Asser Levy of New Amsterdam. The Council of New Amsterdam passed a law denying Jews the privilege of standing guard and keeping watch, compulsory for all other citizens, and taxed them for the exemption. Asser Levy and Jacob Barsimson objected to the discrimination and a decision was rendered against them. They appealed and on April 20, 1657, equal privilege was granted. (*Leon Huhner—Asser Levy, A Noted Jewish Burgher of New Amsterdam*)

Jewish fraternal society was the B'nai B'rith (Sons of the Covenant), founded October 13, 1843, in New York City by Henry Jones and eleven others. Jones was appointed chairman. The first lodge was formed on November 12, 1843, at which time Isaac Dittenhoefer was elected president.

Jewish Rabbinical Conference met in Cleveland, Ohio, October 17, 1855. Isidor Kalisch, who preached reform Judaism, was instrumental in assembling this meeting, the purpose of which was "to better the spiritual conditions of the Jews in America; to strip the Jewish divine services of heathenism and idolatrous customs; to weed out senseless and useless prayers, and to establish a uniform divine service throughout the land."

Jewish woman cantor. *See* Cantor: Jewish woman cantor

JOCKEY
See also Horse race

Jockey (American-born) to win 3,000 races was Eddie Arcaro, who won the third race, riding Ascent, at Arlington Park, Chicago, Ill., on June 24, 1952. In twenty-one years, he rode 15,327 mounts which won $12,265,455.

Jockey to ride 400 winners in one year was Willie Shoemaker, a twenty-two-year-old of Arcadia, Calif., who brought in his 485th winner, Mercenary, at Santa Anita Park, Arcadia, Calif., on December 31, 1953, in 255 days of riding. He beat the 1952 record of Tony De Spirito by 95 winners.

Jockey to win 4,000 races was English-born Johnny Longden, who on Fleet Driver won his 4,000th race on May 15, 1952, at Hollywood Park, Inglewood, Calif.

JOCKEY—*Continued*
Jockey to win seven races in one day
was Joseph Sylvester, who on October 18, 1930,
at Ravenna, Ohio, won seven out of eight races,
with purses totaling $1,800, and third place in
the third race.

Jockey to win the Kentucky Derby four
times was Eddie Arcaro, who at Churchill
Downs, Ky., won $47,500 in 1938 on Lawrin;
$61,725 in 1941 on Whirlaway; $64,850 in 1945
on Hoop, Jr.; and $111,450 on May 1, 1948, on
Citation.

Jockey to win the national riding championship four times was Willie Shoemaker,
who was champion in 1950, 1953, 1954, and
1958.   On December 31, 1958, he won four
races at Santa Anita Park, Arcadia, Calif.,
including the $17,650 Los Feliz Stakes, scoring
347 victories for the year.

Jockey to win the triple crown twice was
Eddie Arcaro, who rode Whirlaway in 1941 and
Citation in 1948 to win the "Big Three": the
Kentucky Derby at Churchill Downs, Ky., the
Preakness at Pimlico, Md., and the Belmont
Stakes at Belmont Park, Elmont, N.Y. The
combined purses amounted to $150,410 in 1941,
and $324,090 in 1948. The date of the last event
was June 12, 1948, at Belmont Park.

JOURNAL. *See* Periodical

JOURNALISM COURSE
History of journalism course was offered
in 1879-1880 at the University of Missouri, Columbia, Mo. Professor David R. McAnnally,
Jr., for five years taught "the history of journalism . . . lectures with practical explanations
of daily newspaper life. The *Spectator,* the
London *Times,* the New York *Herald*."

Journalism course was given in 1869 by
Professor Willard Fiske at Washington Uni-
versity, later Washington and Lee University,
Lexington, Va. The idea was introduced by
General Robert Edward Lee. A knowledge of
phonography (shorthand) and telegraphy and
practical experience in the university printing
office were required. *(Horatio Stevens White—
A Sketch of the Life and Labors of Professor
Willard Fiske)*

Journalism school offering a degree in
journalism was opened September 14, 1908, at
the University of Missouri, Columbia, Mo.
Enrollment for the school year 1908-1909 was
97: 84 men and 13 women. The first degree,
a B.S.J. (Bachelor of Science in Journalism),
was awarded in 1909 to Charles Arnold. The
following year 5 men and 1 woman were graduated. The first dean was Walter Williams,
whose title was Dean and Professor of the
History and Principles of Journalism.

JUDGE
Impeachment proceedings. *See* Impeachment: Impeachment of a federal judge

Negro judge of a Circuit Court of Appeals was William Henry Hastie, former
governor of the Virgin Islands, who was
unanimously confirmed by the Senate on July
19, 1950, for a recess appointment to the Third
Judicial Circuit (Pennsylvania, New Jersey,
Delaware, and the Virgin Islands). He was
sworn in by Chief Judge John Biggs, Jr., in
Philadelphia, Pa.

Negro judge of a Customs Court (U.S.)
was Irving Charles Mollison of Chicago, Ill.,
sworn in and inducted as a judge of the United
States Customs Court on November 3, 1945, in
New York City.

Negro judge of a District Court (U.S.)
was Judge James Benton Parsons of the
Illinois Supreme Court, whose appointment
as a federal district judge for northern Illinois was confirmed on August 30, 1961 by
the U.S. Senate.

Supreme Court judge. *See* Supreme Court
(U.S.)

Woman associate justice of a state supreme court was Florence Ellinwood Allen
of Cleveland, Ohio, who was elected on December 16, 1922, to the Ohio Supreme Court.
*(Florence Ellinwood Allen—This Constitution
of Ours)*

Woman associate justice of the Circuit
Court of Appeals was Florence Ellinwood
Allen, appointed by President Franklin Delano
Roosevelt to fill the vacancy brought about by
the death of Judge Smith Hickenlooper. She
was sworn in April 9, 1934. The oath was
administered by Presiding Judge Charles
Moorman in the presence of his two associates
on the bench, Judge Xen Hicks of Knoxville,
Tenn., and Judge Charles Caspar Simons of
Detroit, Mich. She served in the sixth Judi-
cial Court.

Woman associate justice on the federal
bench was Genevieve Rose Cline of the U.S.
Customs Court, New York, who was appointed
on May 4, 1928, by President Calvin Coolidge.

Woman judge (Negro) was Jane Matilda
Bolin, who on July 22, 1939, was appointed
judge of the Court of Domestic Relations by
Mayor Fiorello La Guardia of New York
City.

Woman judge of a juvenile court was
Kathryn Sellers, judge of the Juvenile Court
of the District of Columbia, Washington.

THE FIRST

D.C., who was appointed October 15, 1918, and reappointed for a second term on March 6, 1925, and who served until her successor was confirmed by the Senate on February 15, 1934. From 1913 to 1923 Mary Margaret Bartelme was assistant to the judge of the Juvenile Court of Cook County, Chicago, Ill., but she was not appointed as a judge of the Juvenile Court until later.

Woman judge to sentence a man to death was Florence Ellinwood Allen, a judge of the Court of Common Pleas of the County of Cuyahoga, Cleveland, Ohio. She tried Frank Motto, who had been indicted on a charge of murder in the first degree, and who, after being convicted by a jury on May 14, 1921, was sentenced by Judge Allen to be electrocuted August 20, 1921. The sentence was carried out.

JUDGE ADVOCATE. *See* Air Force officer: Judge Advocate General of the U.S. Air Force; Army officer: Judge Advocate; Naval officer: Judge Advocate of the Navy

JUMP. *See* High jump

JUNCTION TRANSISTOR. *See* Transistor: Junction transistor

JUNIOR CHAMBER OF COMMERCE. *See* Chamber of Commerce: Junior chamber of commerce

JUNIOR HIGH SCHOOL. *See* High school: Junior high schools

"JUNIOR YEAR ABROAD." *See* College: "Junior year abroad"

JURY

Jury composed of women was ordered by the Generall Provinciall Court at the session held September 22, 1656, at Patuxent, Md. The jury was cómposed of seven married women and four single women who tried Judith Catchpole for the murder of her child. The order read: "Whereas Judith Catchpole being brought before the Court upon Suspicion of Murdering a Child which She is accused to have brought forth, and denying the fact or that She ever had Child, the Court hath ordered that a Jury of able women be Impannelled and to give in their Verdict to the best of their Judgment whether She the said Judith hath ever had a Child or not." The jury's verdict was "not guilty" and the court ordered that "the said Judith Catchpole be acquitted of that charge unless further evidence appear." *(Maryland Archives. Vol. 10)*

Mixed jury (white and Negro) was the Grand Jury that indicted Jefferson Davis. The Petit Jury in this case was the second mixed jury. Davis, his wife, and their four children were captured at Irwinville, Ga., May 10, 1865, by Lieutenant Colonel Benjamin Dudley Pritchard, commanding the Fourth Michigan Cavalry. Davis was placed in jail and indicted for treason. In 1867 he was released on bond. The case was finally brought to trial on December 3, 1868, in the Circuit Court of the United States at Richmond, Va., before Judges Salmon Portland Chase and John Curtiss Underwood. The case was dismissed because of President Andrew Johnson's general amnesty proclamation, December 25, 1868. The charge was dropped by the District Attorney on February 15, 1869. *(John William Jones— Memorial Volume of Jefferson Davis)*

Woman grand jury foreman was Julia Isabelle Sims of Newark, N.J., who served on the Federal Grand Jury in the United States District Court for the District of New Jersey in session at Newark from April 6, 1937, to October 19, 1937. Judge William Clark, judge of the United States District Court, District of New Jersey, presided.

JURY SCHOOL

Jury school was opened January 16, 1937, by Federal Judge William Clark, United States District Court, District of New Jersey, in the Post Office Building, Newark, N.J. The first class was attended by 150 men and women. About 2,500 persons, mostly women, attended the course, designed to acquaint citizens with courtroom procedure and duties of jurors in considering evidence. The school was disbanded December 10, 1937.

JUSTICE. *See* Judge; Supreme Court of the United States

JUSTICE DEPARTMENT (U.S.) was created June 22, 1870, by an act (16 Stat.L.162) to establish a Department of Justice with the Attorney General as its head. The office of the Attorney General was created by act of September 24, 1789 (1 Stat.L.73). The department was organized July 1, 1870, and all the law offices of the government placed under one head. *(Albert George Langeluttig— The Department of Justice of the United States)*

JUSTICE OF THE SUPREME COURT (impeachment proceedings). *See* Impeachment: Impeachment proceedings against a justice of the Supreme Court of the United States

JUTE CULTURE was introduced by the U.S. Department of Agriculture in 1869-1870. A quantity of seed was imported from France and India and planted from the Carolinas to Texas. *(Charles Richards Dodge—Fiber Investigations, 1896. Report No. 8)*

THE FIRST

JUVENILE COURT. *See* Court: Juvenile court

JUVENILE COURT JUDGE (woman). *See* Judge: Woman judge of a juvenile court

JUVENILE REFORMATORY. *See* Prison: Reformatory for juvenile delinquents under legislative control

KAPOK was commercially introduced by the Netherlands, May 1, 1893, at the formal opening of the World's Columbian Exposition, Chicago, Ill. *(Stephen J. Zand—Kapok)*

KARAKUL SHEEP. *See* Animals: Sheep (Karakul fur sheep)

KEEDOOZLE STORE. *See* Business: Keedoozle store

KENAF FIBER planting of commercial importance was attempted in July 1951 at Belle Glade, Fla., by the American Kenaf Fiber Corporation. One and a half million pounds were harvested that year and sold at 30 cents a pound to the Commodity Credit Corporation for the Munitions Board. Kenaf is a ten-foot plant whose soft fibers are a substitute for jute and burlap. *(Fortune. December 1951)*

KENNEL SHOW. *See* Dog show

KENTUCKY DERBY. *See* Horse race: Horse race (Kentucky Derby)

KEROSENE. *See* Oil: Oil (kerosene)

KETTLE (brass). *See* Brass kettles

KIDNAPPING
Death penalty for kidnapping was mandated by the Circuit Court of Kansas City, Mo., on July 27, 1933. Walter H. McGee was found guilty by a jury of having kidnapped Mary McElroy, daughter of the City Manager of Kansas City. The prosecutor was Assistant County Prosecutor Michael W. O'Hern. The congressional act of May 18, 1934 (48 Stat.L. 781), "whosoever shall knowingly transport or cause to be transported in interstate or foreign commerce . . . shall be convicted of death" was held to apply to kidnapping.

Kidnapping is recorded in a letter dated July 8, 1524, addressed to Francis I, king of France, by Giovanni da Verrazano, the Florentine explorer. It chronicled his discoveries in America and was sent from Dieppe, France. Verrezano relates that in 1524 his crew "tooke a childe [Indian] from . . . [an] olde woman

THE FIRST

to bring into France, and going about to take . . . [a] young woman which was very beautiful and of tall stature, they could not possibly, for the great outcries that she made, bring her to the sea; and especially having great woods to pass through and being farre from the ship, we purposed to leave her behinde, beareing away the childe only." *(James Carson Brevoort—Verrazano the Navigator)*

Kidnapping for ransom occurred July 1, 1874, in Germantown, Pa. Charles Brewster Ross, a four-year-old, was kidnapped and held for $20,000 ransom. *(Edward Dean Sullivan— The Snatch Racket)*

KIDNEY TRANSPLANTING. *See* Surgical operation: Kidney transplanting

KILN (brick). *See* Brick kiln

KINDERGARTEN
American kindergarten was established in Boston, Mass., in 1868 by Elizabeth Palmer Peabody who employed the Friedrich Froebel system of education as used in Germany. *(Nina Catherine Vandewalker—The Kindergarten in American Education)*

Free kindergarten was the Florence Kindergarten, which opened January 3, 1876, in Florence, Mass., in the home of its founder, Samuel Lapham Hill. The school is now known as the Hill Institute. *(Hill Institute Bulletin. 1930-1931)*

Kindergarten for crippled children. *See* Cripples: Kindergarten for crippled children

Kindergarten for the blind was established by the Perkins Institution and Massachusetts School for the Blind in Roxbury, Mass. The kindergarten was authorized March 15, 1887, and was incorporated as a separate department of the school on March 30, 1887. The kindergarten was dedicated April 19, 1887, and was opened May 2, 1887, with ten children. The plan was proposed by Michael Anagnos, who became the first director. *(First Annual Report of the Kindergarten for the Blind. September 30, 1887)*

Nursery school was established in New York City in 1827 by the Infant School Society of the City of New York founded May 23, 1827, "to relieve parents of the laboring classes from the care of their children while engaged in the vocations by which they live, and provide for the children a protection from the weather, from idleness and the contamination of evil example besides affording them the means of early and efficient education." Children from 18 months to 5 years of age were accommodated, 448 receiving attention in two years. Joanna Bethune was the first directress and Hannah L. Murray, the first treasurer.

Public school kindergarten that was successful was authorized August 26, 1873, by the St. Louis, Mo., Board of Education and opened September 1873 with an enrollment of 42 in the Des Peres School. Susan Elizabeth Blow was the teacher. Dr. William Torrey Harris was the superintendent of schools. *(Annual Report of the Board of Education of St. Louis for the Year 1878-1879)*

KINDERGARTEN MANUAL was Edward Wiebé's *The Paradise of Childhood: A Manual for Self-Instruction in Friedrich Froebel's Educational Principles, and a Practical Guide to Kinder-Gartners* printed in 1869 by Milton Bradley & Company, Springfield, Mass. It was intended primarily for kindergarten teachers. Much of the material was translated from the German of Froebel, Marenholtz, Goldammer, and Morgenstern. The manual contained 86 pages and 74 full page plates of illustrations.

KING
King and Queen of England to visit the United States. *See* Visiting celebrities: King and Queen of England

King born in the United States was Bhumibol Adulyadej (Phumiphon Aduldet), King of Thailand, born December 5, 1927, at Mt. Auburn Hospital, Cambridge, Mass. He was crowned May 5, 1950, as King Rama IX. He was the son of Prince Mahidol.

King (reigning) to visit the United States. *See* Visiting celebrities: King (reigning) to visit the United States

KING COBRA SNAKES. *See* Cobra: King cobra snakes

KLIEGLIGHT LIGHTING UNIT. *See* Electric lighting: Klieglight lighting unit

KNIFE (Bowie). *See* Bowie knife

KNIGHTHOOD
Knighthood conferred in America was awarded Major General Jeffery Amherst for his campaign against the French and for his capture of Montreal on September 8, 1760. He was awarded the thanks of Parliament and on May 26, 1761, George III made him a Knight of the Bath, Sir Charles Cotterel-Dormer serving as his proxy. Major Robert Monckton, Governor of New York, conferred the award in a special ceremony October 25, 1761, at Staten Island, N.Y. *(Lawrence Shaw Mayo— Jeffery Amherst)*

Knighthood conferred on a native-born American was awarded at Windsor Castle, London, England, on June 28, 1687, by King James II to William Phips [Phipps] for his fair distribution of thirty-four tons of silver, gold and jewels valued at $1,350,000 which he salvaged from a Spanish ship sunk near the Bahama Islands that had lain in the sea for forty-four years. His share amounted to $72,000. He was born February 2, 1651, at Pemaquid (now Bristol), Me. *(Alice Lounsberry—Sir William Phipps)*

Knighthood conferred on a native-born American for military leadership was awarded on September 23, 1745, to Sir William Pepperell, noted American general. He was made a Baronet by Great Britain because of his military exploit on April 29, 1745, when he undertook the siege and reduction of Louisburg, a French fortress on the island of Cape Breton, Nova Scotia, built at a cost of $6 million. The siege lasted forty-nine days and the fortress capitulated June 16, 1745. *(Massachusetts Historical Society—Pepperell Papers)*

KNIGHTS OF COLUMBUS originated under a special charter granted by Connecticut on March 29, 1882. It was founded as a fraternal benefit association for Catholic men by the Reverend Michael Joseph McGivney and nine parishioners of St. Mary's Roman Catholic Church in New Haven, Conn., on January 16, 1882.

KNIGHTS OF LABOR. *See* Labor union: Organization to admit workmen other than craft workmen

KNIGHTS OF PYTHIAS brotherhood was founded in Washington, D.C., by Justus Henry Rathbone and twelve associates on February 19, 1864, Washington Lodge No. 1 being the first lodge organized. The Grand Lodge of the District of Columbia was formed April 8, 1864, with Joseph Theophilus Kirk Plant as grand chancellor. The Supreme Lodge of the Knights of Pythias of the World was convened August 11, 1868, in Washington, D.C., and the constitution adopted November 10, 1868, in Wilmington, Del. It was incorporated August 5, 1870, in the District of Columbia. The order is founded on the classical story of Damon and Pythias and advocates toleration in religion, obedience to law, and loyalty to government. *(Joseph Dame Weeks—History of the Knights of Pythias)*

KNIGHTS TEMPLAR. *See* Freemasons: Knights Templar Grand Encampment

KNITTING MACHINE (power) was put into operation in 1832 in Cohoes, N.Y., by Egberts and Bailey. The firm consisted of Egbert Egberts, Timothy Bailey, and his brother,

KNITTING MACHINE (power)—*Cont.*
Joshua Bailey, and was in operation until 1843 when the partnership dissolved. Timothy Bailey continued in the old plant dividing his time between manufacturng knit goods and knit-goods machinery. (*Arthur Haynsworth Masten—History of Cohoes N.Y.*)

KNOW-NOTHING PARTY. *See* American party

KONEL metal alloy was announced on September 9, 1929, by Dr. Erwin Foster Lowry of the research department of the Westinghouse Electric and Manufacturing Company of Pittsburgh, Pa. While the konel was red-hot, a test hammer "bounced off" the new metal, whereas steel would have been deformed under similar conditions. Konel is a combination of cobalt and nickel, from which it derives its name, and ferrotitanium, and is used among other things as a substitute for platinum in radio tubes.

KOREAN CONFLICT. *See* War (Korean)

KOREAN EMBASSY. *See* Diplomatic service: Korean embassy

KU KLUX KLAN was established in 1865 in Pulaski, Tenn., as a social order, but became an organization for enforcing white supremacy by means of intimidation and violence, at the time the Negro was granted suffrage. The first grand wizard was General Nathan Bedford Forrest. Several attempts have been made to reorganize the Klan. (*Stanley Fitzgerald Horn —Invisible Empire*)

LABADIST COMMUNITY was established at Bohemia Manor, Md., in 1683, by the followers of Jean de Labadie, who held many tenets similar to those of the Dutch Reformed Church. The first Labadists were P. Vorstman and J. Shilders, who arrived September 23, 1679, in New Netherlands on the "Charles." (*Jasper Danckaerts—Journal of our Voyage to New Netherland begun in the name of the Lord and for His Glory, the 8th of June 1679 and undertaken in the small flute-ship called the "Charles"*)

LABEL (union label). *See* Labor union label

LABEL PATENT. *See* Patent: Label patent

LABOR
See also Labor law

Chinese labor immigration. *See* Immigration: Chinese labor immigration

Labor Advisory Board (federal) was authorized June 16, 1933, under the National Industrial Recovery Act, which empowered the President to set up such administrative agencies as might be necessary to effectuate the purpose of the act. It was organized June 20, 1933, and was composed of nine members. The first chairman was Leo Wolman.

Labor anti-discrimination commission (state) was the New York State Commission Against Discrimination, appointed July 1, 1945, "to formulate policies to eliminate and prevent discrimination in employment because of race, creed, color or national origin, either by employers, labor organizations, employment agencies or other persons." It consisted of five commissioners at $10,000 a year whose terms ranged from one to five years, to be replaced upon expiration by appointments for five-year periods. The first chairman was Henry C. Turner. The commission was authorized by act of March 12, 1945 (chapter 118), signed by Governor Thomas Edmund Dewey.

Labor Board (national) was authorized August 5, 1933, under authority of the National Industrial Recovery Act (48 Stat.L.195), June 16, 1933, "to encourage national industrial recovery, to foster fair competition and to provide for the construction of certain public works." The board was organized August 5, 1933, and was originally composed of seven members. It ceased to exist July 9, 1934. The first chairman was Senator Robert Ferdinand Wagner. Its purpose was to mediate disputes or controversies between employers and employees arising through different interpretations of the President's Reemployment Agreement.

Labor bureau (federal) was authorized by act of June 27, 1884 (23 Stat.L.60), "an act to establish a Bureau of Labor." The first chief of the bureau, established in the Department of Interior, was Carroll Davidson Wright, whose title was Commissioner of Labor. He received $3,000 per annum. He was appointed January 31, 1885, by President Chester Alan Arthur and served until January 31, 1905. (*Gustavus Adolphus Weber—Bureau of Labor Statistics, U.S. Department of Labor*)

Labor bureau (state) was the Massachusetts Bureau of Statistics of Labor, established by Chapter 102, Acts of 1869, approved June 23, 1869, by Governor William Claflin. The duties of the bureau, under a chief and deputy, were "to collect, assort, systematize and present in annual reports to the Legislature . . . statistical details relating to all departments of labor in the Commonwealth." Henry Kemble Oliver was appointed chief July 31, 1869. George E. McNeill was the first deputy. (*Charles Ferris Gettemy—Massachusetts Bureau of Statistics*)

THE FIRST

Labor congress (national) was the First Industrial Congress of the United States, which convened in New York City October 12, 1845. William E. Wait of Illinois was elected president. Although a few local meetings had been called "national organizations," this was the first national congress of importance. Annual meetings were held regularly until 1856. (*New York Times, June 7, 1856*)

Labor Day. *See* Holiday: Labor Day holiday

Labor Relations Act (national) was approved July 5, 1935 (49 Stat.L.449), "to diminish the causes of labor disputes burdening or obstructing interstate and foreign commerce, to create a National Labor Relations Board, and for other purposes." The board consisted of Joseph Warren Madden, chairman, John Michael Carmody, and Edwin Seymour Smith, appointed August 24, 1935, and confirmed by the Senate August 27, 1935. The first meeting was held September 4, 1935.

National Mediation Board was created by an act to amend the Railway Labor Act approved June 21, 1934 (48 Stat.L.1185), to take the place of the U.S. Board of Mediation provided for by the act of May 20, 1926 (44 Stat.L.577). The new Board was organized July 21, 1934, "to avoid any interruption to commerce or to the operation of any carrier engaged therein, . . to provide for the prompt and orderly settlement of all disputes concerning rates of pay, rules or working conditions." Dr. William Morris Leiserson was the first chairman.

Strike. *See* Strike

Woman labor delegate to a national convention. *See* Woman: Woman labor delegate to a national convention

LABOR DAY. *See* Holiday: Labor Day holiday

LABOR DEPARTMENT (U.S.)
See also Commerce and Labor Department (U.S.)

Labor Department (U.S.) was the Department of Labor, created by act of Congress of March 4, 1913 (37 Stat.L.736). The first secretary was William Bauchop Wilson. In 1913 the department was given cabinet rank. Earlier, the congressional act of June 13, 1888 (25 Stat.L.182) had authorized a Department of Labor under a Commissioner of Labor who received $5,000 per annum.

Native-born Secretary of Labor was William Nuckles Doak, who was appointed by

THE FIRST

President Herbert Hoover and sworn in December 9, 1930. He was the first secretary who was not a member of the American Federation of Labor, and the first secretary from any state except Pennsylvania. (He was born in Virginia.) (*Roger Ward Babson—Washington and the Depression Including the Career of W. N. Doak*)

Woman Secretary of Labor was Frances Perkins (Mrs. Paul Caldwell Wilson), who served from March 4, 1933, to June 30, 1945, the only cabinet member to serve throughout the terms of Franklin Delano Roosevelt's administration.

Women's Bureau of the Labor Department was permanently organized by act of Congress on June 5, 1920 (41 Stat.L.987), "an act to establish in the Department of Labor, a bureau to be known as the Women's Bureau." Its purpose was to formulate standards and policies to promote the welfare of wage-earning women, improve their working conditions, increase their efficiency, and advance their opportunities for profitable employment." The first director was Mary Anderson, who received an annual compensation of $5,000. (*Gustavus Adolphus Weber—The Women's Bureau*)

LABOR LAW
Child labor law. *See* Child labor law: Child labor law (federal)

Convict labor law was Act 29 of the Laws of Virginia, passed March 2, 1642, by the "Grand Assemblie at James Citty." It stated: "Be it also enacted that no person or persons whatsoever for any offence already committed or to be committed shall be hereafter adjudged to serve the collony." (*William Waller Hening—Statutes at Large of Virginia*)

Eight-hour day was advocated by local unions, such as the Machinists and Blacksmiths Union, the Molders Union, etc., in 1860. The first unified action was taken on August 20, 1866, in Baltimore, Md., by the National Labor Union at its first congress, which was attended by 77 delegates from 13 states. Industry, however, did not accede to the terms.

Eight-hour day for government laborers and mechanics was authorized by act of Congress of June 25, 1868 (15 Stat.L.77), signed by President Andrew Johnson. It provided, among other things, that "eight hours shall constitute a day's work for all laborers, workmen, and mechanics who may be employed by or on behalf of the Government of the United States."

Factory inspection law was passed April 30, 1879, by Massachusetts, Chapter 305, Acts of 1879. It provided that the governor appoint

THE FIRST

THE FIRST

LABOR LAW—*Continued.*
two or more of the District Police to act as
inspectors of factories and public buildings.
(*Public Document No. 52—Report of the Chief
of the Massachusetts District Police for the
year ending December 31, 1885, including the
result of the Inspection of Factories and Public
Buildings*)

Forty-hour-week law (federal) was the
Public Contract Act of 1936 "to provide conditions for the purchase of supplies and the making of contracts by the United States" (49
Stat.L.2036), approved June 30, 1936. Workers
on government contracts over $10,000 (after
September 28, 1936) were required to receive
overtime compensation at the rate of not less
than time and one half for hours worked in
excess of forty, also overtime in excess of
eight hours in any one day, if such compensation yielded a greater amount than on the
weekly forty-hour basis. Workers were not
to be paid less than the prevailing minimum
wage of industry and locality. The act was
known as the [David Ignatius] Walsh-[Arthur
Daniel] Healy Act.

Labor discrimination law (state) prohibiting the employer from discriminating in matters of employment against members of trade
unions was "an act in relation to the employment of labor by corporations," Chapter 222,
Laws of 1894 of New Jersey, approved May
15, 1894. Violation was subject to a fine not
to exceed $500 or three months' imprisonment.

**Labor law prohibiting the employment of
women** was "An act providing for the health
and safety of persons employed in coal mines,"
passed and approved by Illinois, May 28, 1879,
effective July 1, 1879. It prohibited the employment of women in mines in Illinois. (*Session Laws of Illinois of 1879. Section 6, page
206*)

**Labor law regulating the working hours
of women** was passed by Ohio, March 29,
1852 (Ohio Laws, Volume 50, page 187). It
regulated "the hours of manual labor of children
under eighteen, and women." This law fixed
ten hours per day as the maximum number of
working hours. It was repealed in 1887, when
a new code relative to women and children was
adopted.

Labor Relations Act (national) *See* Labor: Labor Relations Act (national)

Minimum wage law was enacted by Massachusetts, June 4, 1912 (Acts and Resolves,
1912, Chapter 706, pages 780-4), to take effect
July 1, 1913. It established a Minimum Wage
Commission of three, one of whom might be a
woman, to be appointed by the governor with

the advice of the Council. Although Massachusetts passed the first act, Oregon in advance
of all other states set up an administrative body
to carry out the provisions of an act of February 17, 1913, which provided for the appointment, within thirty days, of a Welfare Commission to consist of three members, one representing the employer, one the employee and
one the public (Sessions Laws of Oregon, 1913,
Chapter 62, pages 92-9). (*Department of
Labor—Development of Minimum Wage Laws
in the United States 1912-1927*)

National Mediation Board. *See* Labor: National Mediation Board

Ten-hour-day law was section 20 of Chapter 488, Laws of 1847 of New Hampshire,
which stated that "in all contracts relating to
labor, ten hours actual labor shall be taken to
be a day's work unless otherwise agreed by the
parties." It was passed July 9, 1847, by a majority of 144, and went into effect September
15, 1847. As a result of the bargaining provision, the law was ineffective. (*Florence Pat-
teson Smith—Chronological Development of
Labor Legislation for Women in the United
States*)

Women's equal employment legislation
was passed by Illinois and approved by Governor John McAuley Palmer on March 22, 1872.
The act, which went into effect July 1, 1872, provided that "no person shall be precluded or debarred from any occupation or employment (except military) on account of sex; Provided that
this act shall not be construed to affect the eligibility of any person to an elective office.
Nothing in this act shall be construed as requiring any female to work on streets or roads,
or serve on juries. All laws inconsistent with
this act are hereby repealed." (*Public Laws of
the State of Illinois. 27th General Assembly,
1871-72*)

LABOR ORGANIZATION. *See* Labor
union: Labor organization

LABOR PAPER was *The Man*, published in
New York City, February 18, 1834, by George
Henry Evans. He advocated free homesteads,
equal rights for women, and abolition of all
laws governing collection of and imprisonment
for debt. The *Daily Sentinel,* published February 15, 1830, in New York City was sym-
pathetic to labor.

LABOR PARTY (political)
See also Farmer Labor Party; Greenback
Labor Party

Labor party (national) was the Labor
Reform Party, which was formed at a national
convention held at Columbus, Ohio, February

THE FIRST

THE FIRST

22, 1872. The presidential candidate was David Davis of Illinois, who received but one electoral vote in the 1872 election. Joel Parker of New Jersey was the vice presidential candidate. Both candidates declined to run, but received popular votes nevertheless. (*Harry Edward Pratt—David Davis*)

Labor party (state) was the Workingmen's Party, which was organized in Philadelphia, Pa., in July 1828. The first convention was held on August 25, 1828. Only local Pennsylvania candidates were nominated at a meeting which was held in October of the same year. (*Philadelphia Gazette. August 27, 1828*)

LABOR REFORM PARTY. *See* Labor party (political): Labor party (national)

LABOR RELATIONS SCHOOL. *See* Industrial and labor relations school

LABOR-SAVING DEVICE approved by a labor organization was the Autoplate stereotype plate-making machine, invented by Henry Alexander Wise Wood, which was approved in 1900 by the Stereotypers' Union. It dispensed with the handling of large quantities of molten metal type containing poisonous antimony and lead.

LABOR UNION

See also Trade association, and under specific profession, e.g., Actors' union, Librarians' union, etc.

Craft labor union contract between employers and organized labor was effected in 1799 by the Federal Society of Journeymen Cordwainers (shoemakers) of Philadelphia, Pa. After a strike of ten weeks, the employers acceded to their demands. (*Augusta Emile Galster—Labor Movement in the Shoe Industry*)

Craft labor union (local) was that of Philadelphia shoemakers. They organized in 1792, but the union existed for so short a period that its name is not even known. The shoemakers again organized in Philadelphia in 1794 and formed the Federal Society of Journeymen Cordwainers. They maintained their existence as such until the date of their trial in 1806 for conspiracy. (*John Rogers Commons—History of Labour in the United States.*)

Labor organization was authorized on October 18, 1648, when the "shoomakers of Boston" were permitted "to assemble and meete together in Boston, at such time and times as they shall appoynt, who being so assembled, they, or the greatest number of them, shall have

powre to chuse a master and two wardens, with fowre or six associats, a clarke, a sealer, a searcher, and a beadle. . . ." Similar permission was also extended to coopers. (*Nathaniel Bradstreet Shurtleff—Records of the Governor and Company of the Massachusetts Bay in New England*)

Labor organization to admit workmen other than craft workmen was the Noble Order of the Knights of Labor, a secret society which admitted "sojourners" on October 20, 1870. It was founded in Philadelphia, Pa., on December 9, 1869, by six men, one of whom was Uriah Smith Stevens, a tailor, who became its first Master Workman. Membership was originally restricted to garment cutters. Six candidates were proposed and elected on December 30, 1869. The first regular officers were elected January 6, 1870. The first annual report, on January 5, 1871, showed 69 members. (*Terence Vincent Powderly—Thirty Years of Labor 1859-1889*)

Labor union legalization (state) was "an act relative to persons combining and encouraging other persons to combine," Chapter 28, Laws of 1883, of New Jersey, approved February 14, 1883. It provided that combinations organized to persuade workers to enter or leave employment were not unlawful.

Labor union of importance was the American Federation of Labor, which was organized in Pittsburgh, Pa., in 1881 under the name of "The Federation of Organized Trades and Labor Unions." It adopted the present title December 8, 1886, in Columbus, Ohio, at a meeting attended by 25 officers of national craft unions representing over 300,000 members. (*George Gorham Groat—An Introduction to the Study of Organized Labor in America*)

Labor union to nominate its own political candidates was the Mechanics Union, which nominated candidates for the New York State Assembly in 1784.

Labor union to nominate its own political candidates and win an election was the New York Working Men's Party, whose candidate, Ebenezer Ford, president of the Carpenter's Union, was elected to the New York State Assembly on November 7, 1829. Ford polled 6,166 votes. A meeting to form a Mechanic and Working Men's Ticket was held April 28, 1829. (*Working Man's Advocate. November 7, 1829*)

Union organization of trades in a city was the Mechanics Union of Trade Associations, which was organized in Philadelphia, Pa., in 1827. Invitations to join were sent to "those trades who are as yet destitute of trade societies." They were also urged to "organize and

THE FIRST

LABOR UNION—*Continued*

send delegates as soon as possible." (*Earl Everett Cummins—Labor Problem in the United States*)

Woman labor delegate. *See* Woman: Woman labor delegate

Women's labor organization was the United Tailoresses Society of New York, a protective association formed by tailoresses in 1825 in New York City. In June 1831 they went on strike for an increase in wages. About 600 women remained out four or five weeks.

Women's labor organization (national) was the Daughters of St. Crispin, an organization of women shoe operators. Their first convention was held at Lynn, Mass., July 28, 1869. The first president was Carrie Wilson of Lynn, Mass., and the first secretary was Allie Jacques, also of Lynn. When five thousand male shoe operators struck at Lynn in March 1860, their ranks were augmented by a thousand women shoe workers.

LABOR UNION LABEL was adopted by the Cigar Makers' International Union and first came into use in San Francisco, Calif., in 1874. The label was adopted to combat the menace to free native labor of the Chinese coolies that were being brought into the state of California. This label was furnished free to all native manufacturers. The present blue label of the Cigar Makers' International Union was adopted in 1880 at the thirteenth cenvention of the organization held in Chicago, Ill. This label is issued free of charge to all manufacturers who operate strictly union factories. In 1869, the Carpenters' Eight Hour League of San Francisco stamped the lumber produced by planing mills working eight hours to differentiate it from that produced by the ten-hour mills. (*I. M. Ornburgh—History of Union Labels, Shop Cards and Service Buttons*)

LABORATORY. *See* under specific type of laboratory, e.g., Chemical laboratory, Health laboratory, Zoological laboratory.

LABORATORY MANUAL (chemical). *See* Chemical laboratory manual

LACROSSE ASSOCIATION (intercollegiate) was the Intercollegiate Lacrosse Association, organized March 11, 1882, in Princeton, N.J., with Columbia, Harvard, New York University, and Princeton as charter members. Each college team was scheduled to play one game with every other member. George William Gilmore of Princeton was president and Dunbar Ferdinand Haasis of Columbia vice president. (*Frank Presbrey—Athletics at Princeton—A History*)

THE FIRST

LAFAYETTE ESCADRILLE AVIATOR KILLED. *See* Aviation—Aviator: American aviator killed while a pilot in the Lafayette Escadrille

LAGER BEER. *See* Beer: Lager beer

LAMINATED AUTOMOBILE. *See* Automobile: Plastic laminated fiberglas body sports car

LAMP

Electric lamp. *See* Electric lighting

Oil lamp for burning kerosene was developed in 1857 by A. C. Ferris and Company, later the Tarentum Oil, Salt and Coal Company.

LAND ANNEXATION. *See* Territorial expansion: Annexation of territory

LAND BANK. *See* Bank: Joint stock land bank

LAND GRANT

District land office opened July 2, 1800, in Steubenville, Ohio, with David Hoge as the first registrar. It was established under the act of May 10, 1800, which also authorized other district land offices in Cincinnati, Chillicothe, and Marietta, Ohio.

Land grant was authorized by the act of the Continental Congress of August 14, 1776. The act offered to make citizens of deserters from the British army (Hessians and British) and tendered each deserter, or his heirs, to be held by him or them in absolute property, fifty acres of unappropriated land in certain states. On August 27, 1776, a similar act was passed offering terms to officers to encourage them to desert the British forces.

Land grant college. *See* College: Negro land grant college

Land grant legislation. *See* Agricultural land grant

Land grant to schools by the Continental Congress was authorized by an ordinance of May 20, 1785: "There shall be reserved the lot No. 16 of every township for the maintenance of public schools within said township." This applied to the Western Reserve and other unsurveyed lands to the west. A new system of surveying was established, the land being laid out in townships 6 miles square and the townships subdivided into 36 numbered sections, each a mile square. Section No. 16 was popularly known as the "school section."

Land subsidy for internal improvements was granted April 30, 1802 (2 Stat.L.173), "an act to enable the people of the eastern division of the territory northwest of the river Ohio to form a constitution and state government, and for the admission of such state into the union on an equal footing with the original states." It authorized Ohio to appropriate one twentieth of the net proceeds of the funds received from the sale of public lands to the laying out and making of public roads.

Railroad land grant of importance was authorized by act of September 20, 1850 (9 Stat.L.466), "an act granting the right of way and making a grant of land to the states of Illinois, Mississippi and Alabama in aid of the construction of a railroad from Chicago to Mobile." Illinois received 2,595,133 acres of land, which were transferred to the Illinois Central Railroad Company. The Illinois Central Railroad broke ground on December 23, 1851, and completed the first 60-mile section on May 16, 1853, from La Salle to Bloomington, Ill. *(Howard Gray Brownson—History of the Illinois Central Railroad to 1870)*

Special land grant to an individual was the act of May 17, 1796 (1 Stat.L.464), "an act providing for the sale of the lands of the United States in the territory northwest of the River Ohio, and above the mouth of the Kentucky River." Congress granted Ebenezer Zane three tracts of land in Ohio, each one mile square, to operate ferries—one on the Muskingum River, one on the Sciota, and one on the Hockhocking. These grants were confirmed and patented to Zane on February 14, 1800, in return for his activities in opening Zane's "trail" or "trace" in 1797, about two hundred miles long from Wheeling, W.Va., through Ohio to Maysville, Ky., then known as Limestone.

Special land grant to a foreigner was enacted on March 3, 1803 (2 Stat.L.236), and authorized the Secretary of War to issue land warrants to Major General Lafayette for 11,520 acres which at his option were to be located, surveyed, and patented in conformity with the provisions of the act regulating the grants of land appropriated for military services.

State aid to railroads. *See* Railroad: State aid to railroads

University founded by a federal land grant. *See* College: University founded by a federal land grant

LAND MINES or "booby traps" were invented by Captain Gabriel Jones Rains and were used against the Seminole Indians in 1840. They were also employed in the retreat from

Yorktown, May 3, 1862, by Rains' Brigade under Major General John Bankhead Magruder, but "land torpedoes" were not considered "a proper or effective method of war" and were outlawed. They were permitted at river defenses where use of torpedoes was "clearly admissible." *(Douglas Southall Freeman—Lee's Lieutenants)*

LAND OFFICE was established in 1789 by Oliver Phelps and Nathaniel Gorham, who purchased 2,600,000 acres in the "Great American Wilderness" at Canandaigua, N.Y., for resale to settlers. William Walker was the agent. *(Charles Francis Milliken—History of Ontario County)*

LAND PRE-EMPTION ACT (federal) was enacted March 3, 1801 (2 Stat.L.112), giving the right of pre-emption to certain persons who had contracted with John Cleves Symmes, or his associates, for lands lying along the Miami River. These persons were living upon the lands once within the Symmes tract but were not included in the patent for the reduced area, which he finally obtained. Settlers received preference over persons desiring to purchase and hold for investment or speculation. *(Thomas Corwin Donaldson—The Public Domain)*

LAND RESERVATION. *See* Forest reserve

LAND SALE ORDINANCE (general) for the sale of national land, was passed May 20, 1785, and provided for the sale of land in the Northwest Territory. *(Burke Aaron Hinsdale—The Old Northwest)*

LANDSCAPE ARCHITECT. *See* Architect: Landscape architect

LANDSCAPE ARCHITECTURE COURSE. *See* Architectural school: Landscape architecture course

LANGUAGE INSTRUCTION
Foreign language course broadcast. *See* Radio broadcast: Foreign language course broadcast

French instruction was offered in 1733 at Harvard College, Cambridge, Mass. Louis Langloiserie was appointed instructor. *(Benjamin Pierce—A History of Harvard University)*

German instruction in a college was given by William Creamer, at the University of Pennsylvania, Philadelphia, Pa., from 1754 to July 11, 1755.

THE FIRST

THE FIRST

LANGUAGE INSTRUCTION—*Continued*
Italian instruction in a college was given at the College of William and Mary, Williamsburg, Va., in 1799 by Carlo Bellini, professor of modern languages. (*William and Mary Quarterly. October 1905*)

Modern language school in a college was established by the College of William and Mary, Williamsburg, Va., in 1779. (*Bulletin of the College of William and Mary in Virginia*)

LANTERN SLIDE. *See* Magic lantern slides (glass plate)

LAPIDARY. *See* Gem-cutting machine

LARYNGOLOGICAL SOCIETY (national). *See* Medical society: Laryngological society (national)

LARYNGOLOGY CLINIC. *See* Medical clinic: Laryngology clinic

LARYNGOLOGY INSTRUCTION. *See* Medical instruction: Laryngology instruction

LARYNGOLOGY MAGAZINE. *See* Medical periodical: Laryngology magazine

LARYNGOPHONE (throat microphone) commercially manufactured was made by the Western Electric Company, New York City, in 1941, sale being confined exclusively to the armed forces of democratic powers. Patents were not applied for on the newer models. (*Philips Technical Review, January 1940. Vol. 5. No. 1*)

LATERAL CURVATURE OF THE HORIZON PHOTOGRAPH. *See* Photograph: Photograph showing the lateral curvature of the horizon

LATHE used for fashioning irregular forms was a profile lathe, patented by Thomas Blanchard of Middlebury, Conn., on September 6, 1819, a "machine for manufacturing gun stocks." The lathe did the work of thirteen operators and made possible a great reduction in woodworking prices. (*Asa Holman Waters —Biographical Sketch of Thomas Blanchard*)

LATIN BOOK written in New England was *Responsio ad totam quaestionum syllogen a clarissimo viro domino Guilielmo Apollonio, ecclesiae middleburgensis pastore, propositam,* written by John Norton and published in 1648 in London, England. The preface was by John Cotton.

LATIN GRAMMAR. *See* Grammar: Latin grammar textbook

LAUNDRY
Commercial power laundry came into existence in 1851 when the Contra Costa Laundry was established in Leona Heights, Oakland, Calif. A 10 h.p. donkey engine bought from a ship captain served as a crude form of washing machine. (*California Journal of Development. Vol. 25. July 1935*)

Laundry was established in 1835 by Independence Starks, a manufacturer of Troy, N.Y., at 66 North Second Street, to wash and press the products of his own factory and of near-by collar makers. (*Arthur James Weise —Troy, One Hundred Years 1789-1889*)

Rough dry laundry service was started by W. M. Barnes in 1892 in Philadelphia, Pa. and in 1893 in Pittsburgh, Pa.

Washing machine for public use (washateria). *See* Washing machine: Washing machine for public use

LAW BOOK
Compilation of colonial laws was *The Book of the General Lauues and Libertyes concerning the inhabitants of the Massachusets, collected out of the records of the General Court for the several years wherein they were made and established and now revised by the same Court and disposed into an Alphabetical order and published by the same Authoritie in the General Court held at Boston the fourteenth of the first month Anno 1647.* The work was published in Cambridge, Mass., in 1648 and sold by Hezekiah Usher in Boston, Mass.

Law book published was William Penn's *The Excellent Privilege of Liberty and Property being the birth-right of the free-born subjects of England. Containing 1. Magna Charta, with a learned comment upon it. 2. The confirmation of the charters of the Liberties of England and of the Forrest, made in the 35th year of Edward the first. 3. A statute made the 34 Edw. 1. commonly called De Tallageo non concedendo; wherein all fundamental laws, liberties and customs are confirmed. With a Comment upon it. 4. An abstract of the pattent granted by the king to William Penn and his heirs and assigns for the province of Pennsylvania. 5. And lastly, the charter of liberties granted by the said William Penn to the freemen and inhabitants of the province of Pennsylvania and territories thereunto annexed, in America.* A 16mo book containing 83 pages, it was printed by William Bradford in Philadelphia, Pa., in 1687.

Law book containing the federal laws of the United States was *Acts passed at a Congress of the United States of America, begun and held at the City of New York, on Wednesday the fourth of March 1789, being the acts passed at the first session of the First*

Congress of the United States, to wit, New Hampshire, Massachusetts, Connecticut, New York, New Jersey, Pennsylvania, Delaware, Maryland, Virginia, South Carolina and Georgia, which eleven states ratified the Constitution of Government for the United States. The book contained 486 pages and was published in Hartford, Conn., in 1791 by [Barzillai] Hudson & [George] Goodwin.

Law book containing the federal laws of the United States of more than one session of Congress (without regard to whether or not they had been subsequently repealed prior to publication) was *The Laws of the United States of America. Vol 1. Containing the Federal Constitution; the Acts of the Three Sessions of the First Congress; The Treaties Existing Between the United States and the Foreign Nations, and the Several Indian Tribes. Also the Declaration of Independence and Sundry Resolves and Ordinances of Congress Under the Confederation. The whole collated with and corrected by the original rolls in the Office of the Secretary of State, agreeably to a resolve of Congress, passed February 18, 1791.* To which is added a complete index, 592 pages, printed in 1791 and sold by Francis Childs & John Swaine, New York City.

Law book (text) was George Caines' *An Enquiry into the Law-Merchant of the United States; or Lex Mercatoria Americana; on Several Heads of Commercial Importance,* a 648-page book published in 1802 by Abraham and Arthur Stansbury, New York City.

Law compilation of federal session laws (without regard to validity at time of publication) was *Acts passed at a Congress . . . begun and held . . . March 4-September 29, 1789, First Congress, First session . . . ,* printed in 1789, in New York City and Philadelphia, Pa., by three independent publishers.

Law compilation of United States laws codifying the laws in force was *The Public Statutes at Large of the United States of America, from the organization of the government in 1789 to March 3, 1845, arranged in chronological order with references to the matter of each act and to the subsequent acts on the same subject, and copious notes of the decisions of the Courts of the United States construing those acts and upon the subjects of the laws with an index to the contents of each volume. . . .* The first volume, containing 777 pages, was published in 1845 in Boston, Mass., by Charles C. Little and James Brown. It was edited by Richard Peters. Publication was authorized by act of March 3, 1845 (5 Stat.L. 798, "a resolution to authorize the Attorney General to contract for copies of a proposed edition of the laws and treaties of the United States."

LAW CODIFICATION (state) was the Louisiana Code of 1825, *A System of Penal Law, Divided into Code of Crimes and Punishments, Code of Procedure, Code of Evidence, Code of Reform and Prison Discipline, Beside a Book of Definitions.* On March 14, 1822, the legislature appointed L. Moreau Lislet, Edward Livingston, and Pierre Derbigny to remodel the code of 1808. The code was approved April 12, 1824 and promulgated June 13, 1825. (*Charles Havens Hunt—Life of Edward Livingston*)

LAW DEGREES. *See* under Degrees (academic and honorary)

LAW DICTIONARY (American) was John Bouvier's *A Law Dictionary Adapted to the Constitution and Laws of the United States of America and of the Several States of the American Union With References to the Civil and Other Systems of Foreign Law.* It was published in two volumes in Philadelphia, Pa., in 1839. (*Frederick Charles Hicks—Materials and Methods of Legal Research*)

LAW DIGEST was *An Abridgement of the Laws of the United States or a complete digest of all such acts of Congress as concern the United States at large, to which is added an appendix containing all existing treaties, the Declaration of Independence, the Articles of Confederation, the rules and articles for the government of the army and the ordinance for the government of the territory north-west of Ohio.* It was edited by William Graydon and published in Harrisburg, Pa., in 1803; it contained 650 pages.

LAW MAGAZINE
Law magazine was the *American Law Journal,* which was published in Baltimore, Md., from 1808 to 1817. It was edited by John Elihu Hall. (*Henry Simpson—The Lives of Eminent Philadelphians*)

Law review editor (woman). *See* Woman: Woman editor-in-chief of a law review

LAW REPORTS were Ephraim Kirby's *Reports of Cases Adjudged in the Superior Court of the State of Connecticut from the year 1785 to May 1788 with some determinations in the Supreme Court of Errors,* published in 1789 by Collier and Adam, Litchfield, Conn. It consisted of 456 pages of text, 12 pages of index, and a 5-page list of subscribers. Volume 1 of Harris and McHenry's *Maryland Reports,* published in 1809, reported cases as far back as 1658. (*Western Reserve and Northern Ohio Historical Tract No. 58. January 1883*)

LAW SCHOOL
Doctor of Laws honorary degree. *See* Degrees (academic and honarary): Doctor of Laws honorary degree

LAW SCHOOL—*Continued*

Law instruction in a college was offered by King's College (now Columbia University), New York City, in 1755. The fourth year of study was described as containing among other things "the Chief Principles of Law and Government together with History, Sacred and Profane." (*Edwin Grant Dexter—A History of Education in the United States*)

Law school was opened in Litchfield, Conn., in 1784 by Judge Tapping Reeve. He conducted it alone in a building near his home. The session was from fourteen to eighteen months, for which a tuition fee of $100 was charged for the first year and $60 for the balance of the course. From ten to twenty students were enrolled the first year. Reeve conducted the school alone until 1798. (*Samuel Herbert Fisher—Litchfield Law School*)

Law school in a college was established in 1779 at the College of William and Mary, Williamsburg, Va. Professors did not receive a stipulated amount from the college but were paid by the students attending the course. The first professor was George Wythe, who was appointed to the Professorship of Law and Police on December 4, 1779. (*Chamber of Commerce of the United States—A Historic Old Virginia Pilgrimage*)

Law school of collegiate rank permanently organized was the Harvard College School of Law, Cambridge, Mass., which was opened in 1817. Courses in law, however, had been given previously at Harvard College as well as in many other colleges. The General Assembly of Maryland in 1812 authorized the College of Medicine of Maryland to establish a Faculty of Law. David Hoffman was elected professor of law but no regular school of instruction in law was opened until 1823. (*Josiah Quincy—History of Harvard University*)

Law school (university) to admit women was the St. Louis Law School, now the School of Law, Washington University, St. Louis, Mo. In 1869, two women students matriculated. Only one was graduated from the school (Phoebe W. Couzins of St. Louis, on June 15, 1871) although both eventually became members of the bar.

LAWN TENNIS. *See* Tennis: Lawn tennis

LAWYER

Attorney of the United States. *See* Attorney of the United States

Japanese lawyer to receive legal training in the United States was Takeo Kikuchi, who received an LL.B. degree from Boston University, Boston, Mass., on June 5, 1877.

Japanese woman lawyer was K. Elizabeth Ohi, admitted to practice in Illinois, June 10, 1937. She received the degrees of LL.B. February 6, 1937, and J.D., June 25, 1938, from the John Marshall Law School, Chicago, Ill.

Lawyer disbarred was Thomas Lechford, who was engaged by William and Elizabeth Cole in the summer of 1639 for the prosecution of an action against Mrs. Cole's brother, Francis Doughty of Taunton, Mass. On September 3, 1639, Lechford was disbarred by the General Court of Massachusetts. The records state that "M. Thomas Lechford, for going to the Jewry, pleading with them out of Court, is debarred from pleading any man's cause hereafter, unless his owne, and admonished not to presume to meddle beyond what hee shalbee called to by the Courts." Lechford was pardoned, but a year later was again disbarred for the same offense, and again pardoned. (*Massachusetts Historical Society Collections. 4th Series. Vol. 6. Boston. 1863*)

Lawyers admitted to the Supreme Court of the United States were Elias Boudinot of New Jersey, Thomas Hartly of Pennsylvania, and Richard Harrison of New York, who were admitted on February 5, 1790. The requirements for admittance were "membership for three years past in the Supreme Court of the State in which they respectively belong, and that their private and professional character shall appear to be fair." (*Charles Warren—Supreme Court in United States History*)

Negro lawyer formally admitted to the bar was Macon B. Allen, who passed his legal examination in Worcester, Mass., and was admitted May 3, 1845. He had practiced for two years previously in Maine, where no license was required. (*John Daniels—In Freedom's Birthplace*)

Negro lawyer to practice before the United States Supreme Court was John S. Rock, who was admitted to practice on February 1, 1865. His admittance was moved by Senator Charles Sumner of Massachusetts. Chief Justice Salmon Portland Chase presided. (*The Independent. Vol. 17. No. 845. February 9, 1865*)

Negro woman lawyer was Charlotte E. Ray, admitted to the Supreme Court of the District of Columbia, April 23, 1872. She received an LL.B. degree from the School of Law, Howard University, Washington, D.C.

Negro woman lawyer to practice before the United States Supreme Court was Violette Neatly Anderson of Chicago, Ill., who was admitted January 29, 1926.

THE FIRST

Public defender's office. *See* Public defender's office

Woman lawyer was Arabella A. Mansfield of Mount Pleasant, Iowa, who was admitted to practice law in June 1869. She had studied in a law office and at home. Section 1610 of the Iowa Code of 1851, effective July 1, prevented women from being admitted to the bar by statute providing admission to "any white male person. . . ." The section was repealed by an act approved January 5, 1853. The court held that "the affirmative declaration that male persons may be admitted is not an implied denial to the right of females." Mrs. Mansfield was admitted to practice and on March 8, 1870, the words "white male" were omitted from the statute. *(Green Bag. January 1890)*

Woman lawyer graduated from a law school was Ada H. Kepley of Effingham, Ill., who was graduated from the Union College of Law, Chicago, Ill., on June 30, 1870. *(Records in the Clerk's Office. Supreme Court of the United States. Washington, D.C.)*

Woman lawyer to become a member of the American Bar Association was Mary Florence Lathrop, who was admitted in 1917. She received her LL.B. degree from the University of Denver, Denver, Colo.

LAWYERS' ASSOCIATION
Lawyers' association (national) was the American Bar Association, organized August 21, 1878, at an informal meeting in Saratoga, N.Y., proposed by Judge Simeon Eben Baldwin. At the close of the meeting, the membership consisted of 291 lawyers from 29 states. The first president was James Overton Broadhead of St. Louis, Mo. *(James Grafton Rogers— Fifty Years of the American Bar Association)*

Lawyers' association (state) was the New York Bar Association, New York City, which operated from 1747 to 1770. Its purpose was to develop collective opinion on the economic issues prior to the Revolutionary War and to control admission to practice. *(Charles Warren—A History of the American Bar)*

LEAD was mined and smelted in 1620 near Falling Creek, Va., to supply the local demand for bullets and shot. Mining operations ceased after John Berkeley and twenty workmen were massacred by Indians in May 1622. *(William Henry Pulsifer—Notes for a History of Lead)*

LEAD PENCIL FACTORY. *See* Pencil factory

LEAD (white). *See* White lead manufacturer

THE FIRST

LEAGUE OF AMERICAN WHEELMEN. *See* Bicycle society: Bicycle society (national organization)

LEAGUE OF NATIONS (Indian). *See* Indians: Indian league of nations

LEAGUE OF NATIONS representative (unofficial) was Grace Abbott, Chief of the Children's Bureau of the Department of Labor, who was appointed in an unofficial capacity on October 13, 1922, by President Warren Gamaliel Harding to attend the League's Advisory Committee on the Traffic in Women and Children.

LEAPING SUBMARINE. *See* Submarine: Leaping submarine

LEATHER
Chrome tanned leather successfully marketed was produced in 1890 by Robert Herman Foerderer of Philadelphia, Pa., who devised a method by which the fibrous and gelatinous matter in the natural article could be prepared to receive tanning agents, then another method to overcome the brittle effect. He registered his trademark, a horseshoe with seven nails, each nail standing for a letter of his trade name, "Vici Kid."

Chrome tanning process for tanning hides and skins through the action of a metallic salt was invented by Augustus Schultz of New York City, who filed patent papers on May 31, 1883. He was granted patents No. 291,784 and No. 291,785 for tawing hides and skins on January 8, 1884. His process enabled leather to be tanned thinner and stronger than by vegetable tanning.

Leather-splitting machine to split leather to any thickness was invented by Samuel Parker of Billerica, Mass., who received patents on July 9, 1808, and April 26, 1809, on "currying and finishing leather." This invention doubled the use of leather.

Leather tanning in America is credited by many to the American Indians. The first of the known white tanners was Experience Miller who came to Plymouth, Mass., on the "Ann" in 1623. *(Romance of Leather—American Leather Producers, Inc.)*

Leather tanning by the "oil tan" method of preparing buckskin and other leathers was originated by Talmadge Edwards in Johnstown, N.Y., in 1810.

Patent leather was tanned in 1819 in Newark, N.J., by Seth Boyden at the tannery which he had established in 1813. At first, the

THE FIRST

THE FIRST

LEATHER—*Continued*
varnish was dried in the sun, but later it was dried in a warm room. Still later, in 1820, he made an oven to hold sixteen skins.

LEATHER BELTING. See Belts of leather

LECTURE SERIES (endowed) was given in 1866 at the Union Theological Seminary, New York City, by Professor Arnold Guyot, Ph.D., LL.D., on "The First Chapter of Genesis." A committee of the Board of Directors founded the Morse Lectureship on the Relationship of the Bible to Any of the Sciences, named in memory of the founder's father, Samuel Finley Breese Morse, on May 20, 1865. On May 8, 1865, an endowed series known as the Elias P. Ely Lectureship on the Evidences of Christianity had been established by the same institution, but lectures were not given until 1867. The Reverend Albert Barnes, D.D., LL.D., was the lecturer.

LECTURER
Lecturer of royal blood to speak for personal profit was Prince Vilhelm of Sweden, who toured the country twice, arriving in New York City on January 5, 1927, and again on October 3, 1927. He was the second son of King Gustaf V of Sweden.

LEG (artificial) patent was No. 4,834, granted to Benjamin F. Palmer of Meredith, N.H., on November 4, 1846. The leg had a pliable joint that worked noiselessly and preserved its contour in all positions. Artificial legs had been used previously. Howland & Co., of Brookfield, Mass., exhibited one in 1837 at the Massachusetts Charitable Mechanics Association.

LEGATION. *See* Diplomatic service

LEGION. *See* War veterans' society: American legion

LEGION OF MERIT MEDAL. *See* Medal: Legion of Merit Medal

LEGISLATIVE ASSEMBLY in America met at the Old Church in Jamestown, Va., on July 30, 1619. The men sat with their hats on. It was decided that the new governor, Sir George Yeardley, was to summon a "General Assembly" elected by the inhabitants, every free man voting. The assembly was to consist of 22 members, 2 from each borough. The speaker was Master John Pory. The session was opened with prayer by a Mr. Bucke. *(John Esten Cooke —Virginia)*

LEGISLATIVE CONFERENCE (interstate) assembled in Washington, D.C., Feb-

ruary 3, 1933, under the auspices of the American Legislators' Association. The conference was attended by 100 state legislators and tax experts from 32 states who discussed double taxation, overlapping and conflicting of federal and state taxes, etc. Only the legislators were entitled to vote.

LEGISLATOR (state)
Husband and wife simultaneously elected to both chambers of a state legislature were Richard Lewis Neuberger, state senator, and Maurine Brown Neuberger, state representative, both Democrats, elected to the Oregon legislature November 7, 1950. Richard Neuberger had served previously as state senator, having been elected November 2, 1948, to represent the 13th district. *(Richard Lewis Neuberger—Adventures in Politics)*

Negro legislator (state) to represent a constituency where the majority were white was Bishop Benjamin William Arnett of the African Methodist Episcopal Church, Greene County, Ohio, who served in the lower house of the Ohio State Legislature from 1885 to 1887. He served in the sixty-sixth session, which convened January 6, 1885, and adjourned May 4, 1885, and the sixty-seventh, which convened January 4, 1886, and adjourned May 19, 1886. *(Booker Taliaferro Washington—The Story of the Negro)*

Negro representatives to sit in any state legislature were Edwin Garrison Walker and Charles Lewis Mitchell of Boston, Mass., who in 1866 were elected to the Massachusetts House of Representatives.

Negro woman state legislator was Crystal Bird Fauset of Philadelphia, Pa., elected November 8, 1938, to the Pennsylvania House of Representatives. Her term of office began December 1, 1938, and she was sworn in and assumed her seat January 3, 1939.

Woman speaker of a state house of representatives was Mrs. Minnie Davenport Craig of Esmond, N.D. On January 3, 1933, she was elected Speaker of the North Dakota House of Representatives. She was a Republican and served for one session from January 3, 1933, to March 31, 1933.

LEGISLATURE
Legislature with two chambers convened in Massachusetts in 1644. "An Act of the Generall Court at Boston, March 7/17, 1644," established one house for magistrates and another for deputies. *(Records of the Governor and Company of Massachusetts Bay. Vol. 2)*

Unicameral legislature (state), after the formation of the United States, was adopted by constitutional amendment by Nebraska on

THE FIRST

November 6, 1934. A body of 43 members replaced a House of 100 and a Senate of 33. The first president was Walter Herman Jurgensen and the speaker was Charles Joseph Warner. The first session was opened January 5, 1937, by United States Senator George William Norris. The first bill, passed January 21, 1937, appropriated $10,000 for mileage, postage, and incidental expenses for the members. All states adopted bicameral systems at the formation of the United States, except Pennsylvania, Georgia, and Vermont, which changed after 4, 12, and 58 years, respectively. (*Harrison Boyd Summers—Unicameral Legislatures*)

LENS

Achromatic lenses were made in 1844 in Cambridgeport, Mass., by Alvan Clark. (*William Wallace Payne—The Life and Achievements of Alvan Clark*)

Bifocal contact lens was developed by Newton K. Wesley, O.D., of the Eye Research Foundation and the Plastic Contact Lens Company, Chicago, Ill., and officially introduced in May 1958. Distant-vision prescriptions were ground in the center of the lens, and reading prescriptions were ground on the outer circle. The cost of a pair varied from $200 to $400.

Contact lenses were imported for commercial purposes in New York City in 1924 from Jena, Germany, where they were manufactured by Carl Zeiss, Inc. The lenses were ground, rather than blown. They were thin saucer-shaped shells of optical glass which were worn under the eyelid in direct contact with the eye itself.

Eyeglass bifocals were invented by Benjamin Franklin, who, annoyed at having to carry two pairs of glasses, fashioned a single pair of glasses each lens of which consisted of two parts with different focusing powers. On May 23, 1785, from Passy, France, he wrote to George Whatley, "I have only to move my eyes up and down as I want to see distinctly far or near." Inasmuch as ordinary spectacles in the colonies cost as much as $100 each, his invention did not receive a ready popular response. (*Nathan Gerson Goodman—The Ingenious Dr. Franklin*)

Lens to provide zoom effects without requiring the camera to be moved toward or away from the object televised was the Zoomar lens invented by Dr. Frank Gerard Back of New York City, who received patent No. 2,454,686 on November 23, 1948, on a "varifocal lens for cameras" adjustable for close-ups or long-distance shots. It was demonstrated April 16, 1947, by the National Broadcasting Company in New York City.

THE FIRST

Plastic lens for cataract patients was fitted March 18, 1952, at Wills Eye Hospital, Philadelphia, Pa., by Dr. Warren Snyder Reese, who performed the [Frederick Thomas] Ridley operation, the insertion of a plastic lens approximately 8 mm. in diameter.

LEOPARD. *See* Animals: Leopard

LEPER HOSPITAL. *See* Hospital: Leper hospital

LEPERS' CHURCH (Protestant). *See* Protestant church: Protestant church for lepers

LETHAL GAS EXECUTION. *See* Execution: Lethal gas execution

LETTER

Letter descriptive of America was probably written by Christopher Columbus, admiral of the ocean fleet, who sailed August 3, 1492, from the harbor of Palos, Spain, with three small caravels and about 90 men, and returned 224 days later, on March 14, 1493, to Lisbon, Portugal, where he dispatched two letters of identical content, one to Raphael Sanchez and the other to Luis de Santangel. (*The First Letter of Christopher Columbus to the Noble Lord Raphael Sanchez Announcing the Discovery of America*)

Letters written in English in America which have been recorded are claimed to be the four letters of Ralph Lane, the first commander of Raleigh's first colony, which were written on August 12, 1585, from Porte Ferdynando. The letters were not published until 1860. (*Francis Lister Hawks—History of North Carolina*)

LETTER BOX. *See* Postal service: Mail box

LETTER-CARRIER'S UNIFORM. *See* Postal service: Letter-carrier's uniform

LETTER TO ENCIRCLE THE WORLD. *See* Postal service: Letter to encircle the world by commercial airmail

LETTERMEN'S CLUB (college). *See* College "Lettermen's club"

LEVEES were built along the Mississippi River at New Orleans, La., in 1724. They extended 18 miles above and 18 miles below New Orleans, but they were rudimentary dikes compared with the present mighty embankments. Sieur le Blond de la Tour, a Knight of St. Louis and chief engineer of the colony, began construction of a levee in 1718. It was completed in 1727. (*Henry Rightor—Standard History of New Orleans*)

THE FIRST

THE FIRST

LEWISITE was developed in February 1918 by Dr. Winford Lee Lewis, Washington, D.C. Production of this explosive compound of chloro-vinyl-dichloro-arsine was undertaken at Nela Park, Cleveland, Ohio, in the autumn of 1918 and amounted to ten tons a day in November 1918.

LIBERAL ARTS RADIO COURSE. See Radio instruction: Radio college course

LIBERAL REPUBLICAN PARTY convention was held in Cincinnati, Ohio, on May 1, 1872, at which meeting the party was formed. Horace Greeley of New York was the presidential candidate and Benjamin Gratz Brown of Missouri was the vice presidential candidate. In the election held November 5, 1872, Greeley (who was also the Democratic candidate) received 2,834,079 votes, as compared with 3,597,132 cast for Ulysses Simpson Grant, the Republican candidate. (Proceedings of Liberal Republican Party Convention. 1872)

LIBERTY ACT (religious). See Religious liberty act (colonial)

LIBERTY LOAN. See Loan: Liberty loan subscriptions

LIBERTY PARTY. See Anti-slavery party

LIBERTY SHIP. See Ship: Liberty ship

LIBRARIAN
Librarian to be paid for his services was Louis Timothee, a young French immigrant, who was hired November 14, 1732, and received three pounds sterling every trimester. He worked every Wednesday from two to three o'clock and every Saturday from ten to four in the Library Company of Philadelphia, the library which was started in 1731 by Benjamin Franklin. (George Maurice Abbot—A Short History of the Library Company of Philadelphia)

Librarian of Congress was John Beckley of Virginia, clerk of the House of Representatives, appointed January 29, 1802. He served until his death, April 8, 1807. His salary was not to exceed $2 per diem for every day of necessary attendance. The Library of Congress was established by authority of the act of April 24, 1800 (2 Stat.L.56) appropriating $5,000 "for the purchase of such books as may be necessary for the use of both Houses of Congress." Until 1815, when George Watterston was appointed, the librarians were the clerks of the House of Representatives. (Lucy Salamanca—Fortress of Freedom)

LIBRARIANS' CONVENTION was held September 15-17, 1853, at the University of the City of New York, New York City. It was

called to order by Charles Folsom of the Boston Athenaeum and was attended by 82 delegates from 47 libraries in 13 states. Charles Coffin Jewett, librarian of the Smithsonian Institution, served as president.

LIBRARIANS' UNION affiliated with the American Federation of Labor was the Library Employes' Union No. 15,590 of New York City, chartered May 15, 1917. The first secretary was May Walker and the first president was Tilloah Squires. The union was suspended November 20, 1929.

LIBRARY
Book-wagon traveling library was started at the Washington County Free Library, Hagerstown, Md. Mr. Thomas, the janitor, drove a wagon through the county, making three trips a week beginning in April 1905. The wagon had shelves on the outside so that the books were visible. The inside of the wagon had been used for gathering eggs, butter, and country produce prior to library use. (Mary Lemist Titcomb—The Story of the Washington County Free Library)

Business library supported by taxes was a branch of the Newark Public Library opened October 1, 1904, at 16 Academy Street, Newark, N.J. The first librarian of the business branch was Sarah B. Ball. John Cotton Dana was librarian of the Newark Public Library. The budget for the year 1904 was approximately $1,500.

Children's department in a library is said to be that of the Minneapolis Public Library, opened in December 1889. The children's books were separated from those of the adults. In 1892 children were served from a special desk in the lower corridor in a separate room. In the fall of 1893 a children's department was opened, the whole corridor being equipped for their sole use.

Circulating library in America was set up by the Library Company of Philadelphia, organized in 1731 by Benjamin Franklin through his society, the Junto. The instrument of association of the company was dated July 1, 1731. The first meeting was held November 8, 1731, at the house of Nicholas Scull. Fifty persons contributed forty shillings each for purchasing the first parcel of books and ten shillings per annum charges. The first books were ordered March 31, 1732. An agreement to hire Louis Timothee as librarian was made November 14, 1732. (George Maurice Abbot—A Short History of The Library Company of Philadelphia)

County library successfully conducted was the Brumback Library of Van Wert County, Van Wert, Ohio, which was organized in 1898. Actual work throughout the county was started in 1901, when the present building was opened to the public. Funds were secured from the County Commissioners through a tax levy.

Free public library was the Juvenile Library of Dublin, N.H., established in 1822.

Free public library (town supported) maintained by a public tax and controlled and managed by vote of the town was established in Peterborough, N.H., April 9, 1833.

Library was established in Charleston, S.C., in 1698 through the efforts of Thomas Bray (later representative in Maryland of the Bishop of London), who in 1696 forwarded religious books to the clergy. In 1700, Charleston passed an act "for securing the Provincial Library of Charlestown, by which commissioners and trustees were appointed for its preservation." *(Edward McCrady—History of South Carolina Under the Proprietary Government, 1670-1719)*

Library building used exclusively as a library was a frame house erected by James Logan on the west side of Sixth Street, between Chestnut and Walnut streets, Philadelphia, Pa., in 1725. It was available to the public for reading purposes by written permission from James Logan. On March 8, 1745, he turned over this property and 2,000 books to the city, but the library did not start to function as a public library until November 8, 1760. Upon the death in 1776 of his son, William Logan, who was the first librarian, the library was closed for several years. On March 31, 1792, the Loganian Library was incorporated with the Library Company of Philadelphia. *(Austin Kayingham Gray—First American Library)*

Library building (university) was the library of the University of South Carolina, Columbia, S.C., completed May 6, 1840. The first librarian of the university was Elisha Hammond, who began to serve in 1805. The first librarian in the separate building was Dr. Thomas Park.

Library for seamen was inaugurated March 1829 by the American Seamen's Friend Society of New York City, which supplied traveling libraries to ships soon after its organization May 5, 1828, when Smith Thomson was elected president. Loan libraries were placed on board American ships, Coast Guard, and naval vessels, and in life-saving stations.

Library newspaper room was the [Michael Hodge] Simpson Annex of the Newburyport Public Library, Newburyport, Mass., dedicated April 28, 1882. On March 26, 1870, William

Cleaves Todd offered the library $300 annually for the purchase of newspapers and magazines, and supplemented the grant until it amounted to $400. He established a $10,000 fund for the same purpose, increasing it on April 12, 1900, to $15,000.

Library of Congress was established by act of April 24, 1800 (2 Stat.L.56), which appropriated $5,000 "for the purchase of such books as may be necessary for the use of Congress at the said city of Washington and for fitting up a suitable apartment for containing them and for placing them therein." The first library catalog, dated April 1802, listed 964 volumes and 9 maps.

Library of Congress catalog. *See* Library catalog: Catalog of the Library of Congress

Library of Congress librarian. *See* Librarian: Librarian of Congress

Mechanics' library was opened in New York City in 1820 by the General Society of Mechanics and Tradesmen of the City of New York and was known as the "Apprentice's Library." The name was changed in 1898 to the "Free Library of the General Society of Mechanics and Tradesmen." The Free Quakers in 1820 opened an apprentices' library at Carpenters Hall, Philadelphia, Pa., holding the first public meeting and adopting a constitution on February 28, 1820. The library was opened June 3, 1820, at 100 Chestnut Street, Philadelphia. Horace Binney was the first president and Daniel B. Smith, the secretary. *(One Hundred and Forty-fifth Annual Report—General Society of Mechanics and Tradesmen of the City of New York; also Watson's Annals of Philadelphia)*

Mercantile library was the Mercantile Library Association of the City of New York, organized at 49 Fulton Street, New York City, November 9, 1820, with 150 sponsors in attendance. The constitution was adopted November 27, 1820. The library was founded to assist clerks and others engaged in mercantile business to enjoy the use of reading facilities. It opened February 12, 1821. Its present building is located at 17 East 47th Street, New York City. The first president was Lucius Bull, who served from November 27, 1820, to December 17, 1823. *(Mercantile Library Association of the City of New York—First Annual Report. November 6, 1821)*

Youth's library was established in January 1803 in Salisbury, Conn., through the generosity of Caleb Bingham of Boston, a native of Salisbury. He donated 150 volumes, the nucleus of the Bingham Library for Youth.

LIBRARY CATALOG

Catalog of the Library of Congress was *A Catalogue of Books, Maps, and Charts, Belonging to the Library of the Two Houses of Congress,* printed in 1802 by William Duane, Washington, D.C.

Union catalog of books in libraries in the United States was begun in 1901, when the Librarian of Congress authorized the exchange of Library of Congress printed catalog cards for cards printed by other libraries for books for which no Library of Congress cards were available. The catalog combines all holdings of the Library of Congress together with the holdings of over 600 other libraries in one author alphabet. More than 15,000,000 card entries have been made, 9,000,000 of which represent books located in libraries in the United States and Canada other than the Library of Congress.

Union catalog of books in a state library was undertaken in 1909 by the California State Library, Sacramento, Calif. At first cards for periodical files only were collected. The catalog was later extended to include books as well as periodicals in California libraries. *(Robert Bingham Downs—Union Catalogs in the United States)*

LIBRARY CHAIR endowed in a library school was the Melvil Dewey Professorship of Library Service, established by trustees' vote of April 4, 1938, as of July 1, 1938, at the Columbia University School of Library Service, New York City, through an endowment of $150,000 made by the Carnegie Corporation of New York. The first incumbent was Ernest James Reece, Professor of Library Service. *(Columbia University Quarterly. June 1938)*

LIBRARY LAW enacted by a state was Chapter 861 of the Laws of 1849 of New Hampshire, approved July 7, 1849, "an act providing for the establishment of public libraries." It provided that "the inhabitants of any school district in any city or town, and of any city or town not divided into school districts, in this Commonwealth, may, at any meeting called for that purpose, raise money for the purchase of libraries, in the same manner as school districts may raise money for erecting and repairing school houses in their respective districts . . . and that every public library established under provision of this act shall be open to the free use of every inhabitant of this town." *(William Frederick Yust—Library Legislation)*

LIBRARY LOAN made by a state library to a community was made on February 8, 1892, by the New York State Library. The law of April 27, 1892 (Chapter 378, section 36) permitted the loan of books for a period not exceeding six months to libraries or communi-

ties not yet having a public library, provided they were available to the public without charge for either reference or circulation. *(New York State Library—76th Annual Report for Year Ending September 30, 1893)*

LIBRARY SCHOOL. *See* Library training (systematic)

LIBRARY SOCIETY

Library association (national) was the American Library Association, organized October 6, 1876, at a meeting in Philadelphia, Pa., attended by 103 librarians. The association was incorporated December 10, 1879, under the laws of Massachusetts. The first president was Dr. Justin Winsor, and the first secretary was Melvil Dewey. Executive offices are maintained in Chicago, Ill. The first annual convention was held September 4, 1877, in New York City.

Library society (local) was the New York Library Club, formed June 18, 1885, at a meeting held at Columbia University, New York City, "to promote acquaintance and fraternal relations among librarians and those interested in library work and advance the interests of the libraries of New York and its vicinity." On September 11, 1885, the executive committee selected the first permanent officers—Richard Rogers Bowker, president, and C. Alexander Nelson, secretary. The first general meeting was held November 12, 1885.

State librarians' society was the National Association of State Libraries, formed November 16, 1898, in Washington, D.C. William Elmer Henry of Indiana was chairman and Pauline L. Jones of Tennessee was secretary.

State library society was the New York Library Association "to promote library interests of the state of New York," organized by forty-three persons on July 11, 1890, at the New York State Library, Albany, N.Y. The first president was Melvil Dewey and the first secretary-treasurer was George B. Gallup.

Woman to become president of the American Library Association was Theresa Hubbell West Elmendorf of the Buffalo (N.Y.) Public Library, who served from May 24, 1911, to July 2, 1912. *(Bulletin of the American Library Association. Vol. 6, No. 4)*

LIBRARY TRAINING (systematic)

was introduced by the School of Library Economy at Columbia University, New York City, which opened January 5, 1887, through the efforts of Melvil Dewey. The school was transferred on April 1, 1889, to Albany, N.Y., and its name changed to the New York State Library School. It was placed under the direction of the University of the State of New

York. The first session was held April 10, 1889. The first public commencement and conferring of degrees took place July 8, 1891. The first summer session was held from July 7 to August 10, 1896. In 1926 the school was returned to Columbia University, where it was united with the Library School of the New York Public Library to form the School of Library Service, Columbia University. It is a charter member of the Association of American Library Schools. *(School of Library Economy, Columbia University—First Annual Report)*

LIBRETTO published was Andrew Barton's *The Disappointment, or The Force of Credulity,* a two-act comic opera satire with prologue and epilogue, published in 1767 in New York City. It depicted the popular notion of the time concerning the treasure supposed to have been buried by Blackbeard, the pirate. *(Oscar George Theodore Sonneck—Early Opera in America)*

LICENSE (aviation). *See* Aviation—License

LICENSE PLATES (automobile). *See* Automobile license plates

LIE DETECTOR used as evidence in a court of law for consideration by a jury was the Keeler Polygraph, invented by Leonarde Keeler of the Scientific Crime Detection Laboratory, Northwestern University School of Law, Chicago, Ill. Keeler conducted a test February 2, 1935, in Portage, Wis., and produced graphs of the test in the case of *Wisconsin State* vs. *Cecil Loniello and Tony Grignano.* Both defendants were found guilty of assault and sentenced by Judge Clayton F. Van Pelt of the Circuit Court of Columbia County, Wis. Tests of a similar nature, however, had been used in minor civil and criminal cases as early as 1924, when blood pressure readings were made with a Tycos sphygmomanometer. *(Journal of Criminal Law and Criminology. July 1935)*

LIEDERKRANZ CHEESE. *See* Cheese: Liederkranz brand cheese

LIFE INSURANCE. *See* Insurance: Life insurance

LIFE PRESERVER
Life preserver of cork was invented by Napoleon E. Guerin of New York City, who obtained patent No. 2,359 on November 16, 1841, on "an improvement in buoyant dresses or life-preservers." It was a jacket or waistcoat containing 18 to 20 quarts of rasped or grated cork.

Life preserver of cork approved by the Board of Supervising Inspectors was the "Neversink Cork Jacket," formed of granu-

lated cork compressed under pressure. It was invented by David Kahnweiler of New York City and tested in 1872 in the Potomac River. Patent No. 192,832 was issued on July 10, 1877. Life preservers of this type, used on board the S.S. "San Francisco" of the Pacific Mail Steamship Company, saved the lives of 287 persons when the ship was wrecked in the Pacific Ocean in 1877.

LIFEBOAT
Lifeboat was built in Nantucket, Mass., by William Raymond under the supervision of Captain Gideon Gardner and was completed in 1807. It was built for the Humane Society of the Commonwealth of Massachusetts and cost $1,433.11. An additional $160 was used for a shed in Cohasset, Mass., where the lifeboat remained until 1813. *(John Cameron Lamb—The Life Boat and Its Work)*

Lifeboat (corrugated) was patented by Joseph Francis of New York City, who obtained patent No. 3,974 on March 26, 1845, on "making boats and other vessels of sheet iron and other materials." His "life car," built in 1850 by Stillman, Allen & Company, New York City, was 33 feet long and made of four sheets of hard rolled copper pressed into shape. It was used to rescue 201 persons on January 12, 1850, from the British ship "Ayreshire," wrecked off Squan Beach, Monmouth County, N.J. *(Life Saving Appliances of Joseph Francis)*

Lifeboat race. *See* Boat race: International boat race

LIFESAVING MEDAL. *See* Medal: Lifesaving medal

LIFESAVING SERVICE
Lifesaving service was introduced in 1871 by Sumner Increase Kimball. An act of Congress of June 18, 1878 (20 Stat.L.163), an "act to organize the Life Saving Service," formally authorized the Life Saving Service as a separate and distinct service in the Treasury Department. This service and the Revenue Cutter Service were merged on January 28, 1915, to form the Coast Guard.

"First Aid" Emergency Organization. *See* "First Aid" Emergency Organization

LIFESAVING STATIONS FOR DISTRESSED MARINERS were established in 1787 by the Humane Society of the Commonwealth of Massachusetts (incorporated February 23, 1791). Huts were erected at a cost of $40 each at Scituate Beach, Nantucket, Mass., and at the west end of Lovell's Island, Mass. *(Mark Antony De Wolfe Howe—The Humane Society of the Commonwealth of Massachusetts, 1785-1916)*

LIFTBRIDGE. *See* Bridge: Rolling lift bridge

LIGATURES. *See* Suture: Silk suture

LIGHT BEAM COMMUNICATION from a dirigible was made May 19, 1932, from the U.S. Navy dirigible "Los Angeles." The ship "fired" a searchlight beam at a 30-inch target atop the General Electric building at Schenectady, N.Y. As long as the light beam was on the target, communication was maintained.

LIGHT (electric). *See* Electric lighting: Electric incandescent lamp

LIGHT-WEIGHT BRICK. *See* Brick: Light-weight brick

LIGHTER-THAN-AIR AIRSHIP. *See* Aviation—Airship: Airship (lighter-than-air)

LIGHTHOUSE
See also Lightship

Iron pile lighthouse was built between 1847 and 1849 at Minot's Ledge, Mass., by William Henry Swift. The lamp was lit January 1, 1850, by Isaac Dunham, the keeper. The lighthouse was swept away in the gale of April 16, 1851, and two keepers were lost at sea. A lightship was placed in service in 1854. Construction of the stonework for a new lighthouse started July 1, 1855. It was completed June 29, 1860, and the light placed in operation November 15, 1860. *(Edward Rowe Snow— The Story of Minot's Light)*

Lighted beacon on the Pacific coast was the Spanish lighthouse, erected in 1855 at Ballast Point on Point Loma, San Diego, Calif.

Lighthouse in America was a conical masonry tower erected by the Province of Massachusetts in 1716 on Little Brewster Island at the entrance to Boston Harbor at a cost of £2,285 17s 8½d. The lighthouse was authorized by act of July 23, 1715, and the light was first kindled September 14, 1716. Spermaceti oil was used. A levy of a penny per ton was placed on all incoming and outgoing vessels except those engaged in coastal service. The lighthouse was rebuilt in 1783 and is still in service. The first lighthouse keeper was George Worthylake.

Lighthouse built after American independence was located at Cape Henry, Va., at the entrance of Chesapeake Bay. On August 7, 1789, an act (1 Stat.L.53) was passed "for the establishment and support of lighthouses, beacons, buoys and public piers," and on March

31, 1791, a contract for the erection of the Cape Henry Lighthouse was made with John McComb, Jr., It was finished in 1792. The first lighthouse keeper was Laban Goffigan. Fish oil was used for illumination. Then followed, in order, whale oil, colza oil, lard oil, kerosene, gas, and finally electricity.

LIGHTING BLACKOUT. *See* Blackout: Blackout lighting demonstration

LIGHTNING (artificial) demonstration of 10 million volts of man-made lightning was conducted June 10, 1932, in Pittsfield, Mass., by the General Electric Company. Five million volts had been the previous maximum voltage attained in the laboratory.

LIGHTNING DEMONSTRATION showing the relationship between lightning and electricity was made June 15, 1752, in Philadelphia, Pa., by Benjamin Franklin. His letter to Peter Collison, dated October 19, 1752, describing his experiments, was read before the Royal Society of London in December 1752. *(Benjamin Franklin—New Experiments and Observations on Electricity Made in Philadelphia in America)*

LIGHTNING OBSERVATORY was erected during the summer of 1935 on top of the Pittsfield Works, the General Electric Company's building in Pittsfield, Mass. It was built almost entirely of metal and enclosed a circular area 14 feet in diameter. Within was a light-proof room seven feet square which contained a periscope with a brilliantly silvered area reflecting lightning flashes from any direction and sending their images to a mirror set at an angle of 45 degrees. A twelve-lens motor-operated high-speed camera recorded on a moving strip of film any flash of lightning within range.

LIGHTNING ROD was invented in 1749 by Benjamin Franklin, who installed it on his house at 141 Market Street, Philadelphia, Pa. He described his experiments in his "Opinions and Conjectures concerning the Properties and Effects of the Electrical Matter, and the means of preserving Buildings, Ships, etc., from Lightning, arising from Experiments and Observations made at Philadelphia, 1749." *(Oliver Joseph Lodge—Lightning Conductors and Lightning Guards)*

LIGHTSHIP was placed in the Elizabeth River off Craney Island, Va., on July 14, 1820. The displacement was seventy tons. The ship was built at a cost of $6,000. *(Records in Bureau of Lighthouses. Department of Commerce. Washington, D.C.)*

LILLIPUTIAN CITY. *See* City (Lilliputian)

THE FIRST

LIME was manufactured on January 27, 1662, in Providence, R.I. Thomas Hackelton was granted liberty by the town to burn lime at a certain place on the commons. On October 27, 1665, the town ordered that the lime rocks about the limekiln should remain in common ownership. *(Sidney Smith Rider—The Lands of Rhode Island)*

LIMITED SERVICE ARMY CAMP. *See* Army camp: Army camp for "limited service"

LINEN THREAD FACTORY (successful) was established in Paterson, N.J., in 1865 by William Barbour and Sons of Lisburn, Ireland. The mill was driven by water power. The thread was used principally by shoe manufacturers and harness makers.

LINOLEUM
Embossed inlaid linoleum was introduced in 1925 by the Armstrong Cork & Insulation Company of Lancaster, Pa. The company manufactured the linoleum and then placed it under an embossing press in which parts of the design were compressed, so that the tile blocks or other portions of the pattern stood out in relief. *(A Story of Floors—Armstrong Cork Co.)*

Linoleum was manufactured in 1873 by the American Linoleum Manufacturing Company, Richmond, Staten Island, N.Y. *(Frederick Walton—The Infancy and Development of Linoleum Floorcloth)*

Linoleum machine (fully automatic) for manufacturing straight-line linoleum was installed in 1911 by Congoleum-Nairn, Inc. at its Kearny, N.J., plant. *(Frederick Walton—The Infancy and Development of Linoleum Floorcloth)*

LINOTYPE MACHINE. *See* Typesetting machine: Linotype machine

LINOTYPE-SET BOOK. *See* Book: Book set by linotype

LION. *See* Animals: Lion

LIP READING INSTRUCTION FOR THE DEAF. *See* Deaf—School: Lip reading instruction for the deaf

LIP READING TOURNAMENT (national) was held June 23, 1926, in Philadelphia, Pa., during the seventh annual meeting of the American Federation of Organizations for the Hard of Hearing.

LIQUID AIR. *See* Air (liquid)

THE FIRST

LIQUID FIRE EXTINGUISHER. *See* Fire extinguisher

LIQUID FUEL ROCKET. *See* Rocket: Liquid fuel rocket flight

LIQUID HEAT in actual installation was employed in the laboratories of the Pierce Foundation, Summit, N.J., on January 7, 1942. The system was operated by Orion O. Oaks, director of Heating, Ventilating and Sanitation Research of the John B. Pierce Foundation. Liquid heat is the designation given to the utilization of a chemical which, among other novel characteristics, has a boiling point of 800 degrees F. and still is fluid at 40 degrees below zero.

LIQUID SOAP. *See* Soap: Soap in liquid form

LIQUOR BOARD MEMBER (woman). *See* Woman: Woman state liquor board member

LIQUOR REFORM MOVEMENT was undertaken by the Dutch Reformed Church on Manhattan Island in 1623. It maintained a strong position against liquor, particularly with regard to excessive use. *(Edward Tanjore Corwin—Manual of the [Dutch] Reformed Church in America)*

LIQUOR STORES (state) were established by Pennsylvania in 1933. An act was passed by a special session of the legislature and signed by Governor Gifford Pinchot on November 29, 1933. On January 2, 1934, 90 stores were opened in various parts of the state, stocked and ready to do business.

LITERACY qualification for voting was required by Massachusetts. An amendment was passed May 1, 1857, by a vote of 23,833 for and 13,746 against, providing that "no person shall have the right to vote, or to be eligible to office under the constitution of this commonwealth, who shall not be able to read the constitution in the English language, and write his name," excepting those unable to qualify because of physical disability or those over sixty years of age. *(Chapter 20. Laws of 1857. Massachusetts)*

LITERARY SOCIETY (college). *See* College literary society

LITERATURE PRIZE WINNER (Nobel Prize). *See* Nobel Prize: Nobel Prize in literature

THE FIRST

THE FIRST

LITHOGRAPH was "A Water Mill," by Bass Otis of Philadelphia, Pa., published July 1819 in the *Analectic Magazine*. *(Harry Twyford Peters—America on Stone)*

LITHUANIAN CHURCH was St. Casimir's Lithuanian Church, Plymouth, Pa., organized October 27, 1889. The first pastor was the Reverend Alexander Burba.

LIVESTOCK-MARKET PAPER was the *Drover's Journal* published by Harvey L. Goodall at the Chicago Union Stock Yards, Chicago, Ill. The first issue was dated January 11, 1873. On January 19, 1877, it became a daily.

LOAN
See also Bonds

Liberty loan subscriptions were taken from May 2, 1917, to June 15, 1917, during which time approximately 4,000,000 people subscribed for $3,035,226,850 in bonds to yield 3½ per cent. The first loan was authorized by act of April 24, 1917 (40 Stat.L.35), "an act to authorize an issue of bonds to meet expenditure for the national security and defense, and for the purpose of assisting in the prosecution of the war, to extend credit to foreign governments and for other purposes." A subscription of $2,000,000,000 was required.

Loan for war purposes by a central governmental agency was negotiated with France by the Continental Congress. A resolution of December 23, 1776, authorized the loan of $181,500 (1,000,000 livres), which was used for the purchasing of supplies and construction of cruisers. The length of the loan was indefinite. Bonds were sold at par. The rate of interest was 5 per cent payable annually. The loan was received on June 4, 1777. The final redemption was made on December 31, 1793, when the balance due was merged into the general account of the French debt. *(Rafael Arroyo Bayley—The National Loans of the United States from July 4, 1776 to June 30, 1880)*

Loan to the United States was negotiated by Alexander Hamilton, who obtained, from the Bank of New York and the Bank of North America, between September 13, 1789, and February 17, 1790, $191,608.81, inclusive of $8.81 overcharge in their interest account. It was known as the Temporary Loan of 1789 and was obtained without authority of law. The money was used to pay salaries of the President, senators, representatives and officers of the first Congress during the first session under the Constitution. The interest rate was 6 per cent. The final redemption of the loan was made June 8, 1790.

State loan was authorized December 10, 1690, by the Massachusetts Bay Colony, which issued tax anticipation certificates which did not have a maturity date or bear interest. They were not redeemable in metal and were not considered legal tender.

War loan made by the United States government to a war ally was a loan of $200,-000,000 at 3.5 per cent made to Great Britain on April 25, 1917.

LOAN ASSOCIATION (building and loan). *See* Building and loan association

LOBBYIST (woman). *See* Woman: Woman lobbyist

LOBOTOMY (prefrontal). *See* Surgical operation: Lobotomy (prefrontal)

LOCK
Lock ("clock") superseding the keyhole lock and the first double locks (two locks within one case) were invented in 1851 by Linus Yale of Newport, N.Y., who obtained patent No. 8,071, May 6, 1851, on a lock and key. *(Henry Robinson Towne—Locks and Builders' Hardware)*

Mortised lock was introduced in 1835 by Philos Blake and Eli Whitney Blake of Blake Brothers, Westville, Conn.

Time-lock was manufactured by [James] Sargent & [Halbert] Greenleaf, Rochester, N.Y., and installed May 1874 on the vault of the First National Bank of Morrison, Ill. James Sargent of Rochester, N.Y., obtained patent No. 165,878 on July 20, 1875, on a "time-lock" and patent No. 195,539 on September 25, 1877, on "combined time-locks, and bolt-works for safes."

LOCK STITCH SEWING MACHINE. *See* Sewing machine: Lock stitch sewing machine

LOCKER
Locker (coin vender) was invented by Willis S. Farnsworth of Petaluma, Calif., who received patent No. 985,989 on March 7, 1911, which he assigned to the Coin Controlled Lock Co. He also secured a patent jointly with Wm. H. Reed on a coin receptacle "magazine-hinge and conveyor" on the same date which bore No. 985,990. The insertion of a coin in a slot provided a key to open and close the locker.

Public locker plant was established in 1903 by A. G. Eames of the Chico Ice and Cold Storage Company, Chico, Calif. Individual lockers each with a lock and key, were rented to the public. The company was purchased in 1913 by the Union Ice Company of San Francisco, Calif.

LOCKS (canal). *See* Canal locks

LOCOMOTIVE

Diesel electric freight locomotive was constructed by the New York Central Lines in January 1928. It was placed in operation in June 1928. A diesel oil-electric passenger locomotive was first used in March 1929.

Diesel electric locomotive was No. 1000, a 300 h.p. locomotive placed in service December 17, 1924, by the Central Railroad of New Jersey at the Bronx terminal, New York City. The diesel engine was built by the Ingersoll-Rand Company, Phillipsburg, N.J., the electrical components by the General Electric Company, Elmira, N.Y., and the locomotive structure by the American Locomotive Company, Schenectady, N.Y. The locomotive remained in service until 1957.

Duplex compound locomotive (Mallet) was built in 1904 at the Schenectady, N.Y., plant of the American Locomotive Company for the Baltimore and Ohio Railroad. The engine, locomotive No. 2400, used bituminous fuel and had a driving-wheel diameter of 56 inches. Its weight on drivers was 334,500 pounds.

Electric freight locomotive was built by the Pullman Car Company at Pullman, Ill., in 1888 for the Ansonia, Derby and Birmingham Electric Line, now a part of the Connecticut Company and thus a part of the New Haven System. The locomotive weighed 17.5 tons and was capable of hauling a train weighing about 35 tons at less than 10 miles an hour. The first trial took place May 1, 1888. (*Along the Line. Vol. 6. No. 2. September 1929)*

Electric locomotive made a trial round-trip on April 29, 1851, on the Washington branch of the Baltimore and Ohio Railroad from Washington, D.C., to Bladensburg, Md., five miles each way. It was designed by Charles Grafton Page of Salem, Mass. It was 15 feet long, 6 feet wide, and had a platform truck of four wheels under the forward end, and two 5-foot driving wheels under the rear end. It attained a speed of 19 miles an hour. It was operated by "galvanism" storage batteries, but was not practical as it did not run any appreciable distance. (*Edward Hungerford—Story of the Baltimore and Ohio Railroad)*

Gas turbine-electric locomotive was track-tested November 15, 1948, at Erie, Pa. It was built by the American Locomotive Company for the Union Pacific Railroad Company and publicly demonstrated June 16, 1949. The locomo-

tive weighed 500,000 pounds and had a continuous tractive effort of 68,500 pounds at 20.4 miles per hour. It was 83 feet 7½ inches long inside of knuckles. Power from the generator was supplied to 8 traction motors, each of which drove an axle. It was geared for 79 miles an hour, the locomotive carrying enough fuel for 12 hours of operation at 4,500 h.p. The gas turbine power was rated at 4,800 h.p.

Gas turbine propane-fueled locomotive was placed in service on June 8, 1953, by the Union Pacific Railroad to haul freight between Los Angeles, Calif., and Las Vegas, Nev. It delivered 4,800 h.p., more than three diesel units operated together. The locomotive was built by the General Electric Company. Propane burns without leaving carbon-like deposits on the turbine blades.

Locomotive bid was solicited by the Baltimore and Ohio Railroad Company in a series of advertisements which first appeared January 4, 1831, in the Baltimore, Md., *American.* For the most approved engine of American manufacture $4,000 was offered, and $3,500 for the one adjudged the next best. The "York," built by Phineas Davis of York, Pa., was selected. It weighed 3.5 tons and attained velocity by gearing, a spur wheel and pinion being on one of the axles of the wheels.

Locomotive built in the United States to pull passengers was the "Tom Thumb," designed and built by Peter Cooper in Baltimore, Md. It weighed 6 tons and had a 30-inch driving wheel. Its gauge was 4 feet 8½ inches. On Saturday, August 28, 1830, it carried 26 passengers 13 miles over the tracks of the Baltimore and Ohio Railroad in 1 hour and 15 minutes. It returned with 30 passengers in 61 minutes, including a 4-minute stop to take on water. Another American locomotive, the "Best Friend," built at the West Point Foundry for use on the Charleston and Hamburg Railroad, made its initial trip November 2, 1830, but it was derailed. (*Edward Hungerford—The Story of the Baltimore and Ohio Railroad)*

Locomotive for railroad use was the "Stourbridge Lion" built by Foster, Rastrick & Co. of Stourbridge, England. The diameter of the driving wheel was 48 inches. The gauge was 4 feet 3 inches. Horatio Allen was sent to England by the Delaware and Hudson Railroad Company to purchase it. The engine weighed 7 tons and traveled at the speed of 10 miles an hour. Its first run in the United States took place on August 9, 1829, on the tracks of the Delaware and Hudson between Carbondale, a coal mining center, and Honesdale, the canal terminus in Pennsylvania. The centenary of this run was celebrated at Honesdale, Pa., and Mrs. Russell D. Lewis of Orange, N.J., a granddaughter of Horatio Allen, the first engineer of the "Stourbridge Lion," unveiled a statue in commemoration of the event.

LOCOMOTIVE—*Continued*
Locomotive (super-giant) to carry the weight of 1,000,000 pounds on drivers was the Class EL-2B No. 125, a 6,800 h.p. electric locomotive built by the General Electric Company, Erie, Pa., and placed in operation on January 27, 1948, by the Virginian Railway Company, Norfolk, Va., between Roanoke, Va., and Mullens, W.Va. It had 16 driving axles and an over-all length of 150 feet 8 inches.

Locomotive to attain the proved speed of 112.5 miles an hour was the New York Central's famous locomotive 999, the "Empire State Express," built at the West Albany shops of the New York Central and Hudson River Railroad. The time was clocked May 10, 1893.

Locomotive to burn coal (practical, American-made) was the "York," built at York, Pa., invented by Phineas Davis, a watchmaker. Its first trial took place on February 19, 1831. It was the first locomotive which had coupled wheels and a double instead of a single pair of drivers. The only accident in which it was involved occurred on September 27, 1835, when as the result of a defective track Phineas Davis was killed riding on the locomotive. (*John C. Jordan—An Historical Citizen—The Career of Phineas Davis*)

Locomotive to pull a train on a track was a steam locomotive which was built by John Stevens October 23, 1824. When he was 76 years old Stevens designed a locomotive which he operated on a circular track 220 feet in circumference on his estate at Hoboken, N.J. It was moved by means of a large gear wheel engaging a toothed rack placed on the ties between the rails. To keep it from running off the track—the wheels had no flanges—little horizontal friction rollers, fixed to posts like table legs on the underside chassis, pressed and rolled along the inner vertical face of the wooden beams used for rails. The locomotive could pull a 1,000-pound load at 12 miles an hour. (*Carl Weaver Mitman—The Beginning of the Mechanical Transport Era in America*)

Locomotive to use oil fuel was the "Young America," an eight-wheeled wood-burning locomotive equipped with an oil-burner from a San Francisco steamboat in 1879 by the Central Pacific Railroad. The fuel supply consisted of one barrel of crude oil mounted on a tender and connected to the burner with five hose lines.

Locomotive with a cab for the engineer and crew was the "Samuel D. Ingham," built in 1835-1836 in Philadelphia, Pa., for the Beaver Meadow Railroad (now the Lehigh Valley). It was of the eight-wheel type and had a peculiar valve motion, the reversing being done by a block sliding on the valve seats. It was designed by Andrew Eastwick. Abner Houston was the engineer, and Stephen Maxwell and

"Squire Longshore" were the spragmen who pressed the brake blocks against the wheels to lessen speed.

Locomotive with a four-wheeled front truck was the "Experiment," designed by John Bloomfield Jervis for the Mohawk & Hudson River Railroad, the first railroad operated in New York State, and later a part of the New York Central. The "Experiment" was tried out in August 1832.

Locomotive with six or eight driving wheels, the axles of which were placed parallel to each other, was patented by Ross Winans on October 1, 1834. Winans was also the first to introduce eight-wheel cars in railroading. The first car was the "Columbus," which was first used by the Baltimore and Ohio Railroad Company July 4, 1831. (*John Langdon Sullivan—On the Baltimore Rail-road Carriage Invented by Ross Winans*)

Narrow gauge locomotive was constructed in Philadelphia by the Baldwin Locomotive Works. It was known as Engine No. 1, the "Montezuma," and was first used by the Denver and Rio Grande Western Railroad Company on July 3, 1871. It had a 3-foot gauge, a length of 30 feet, and a total weight of 25,000 pounds.

Race between a locomotive and a horse-drawn vehicle took place on August 25, 1830, between Relay and Baltimore, Md., a distance of 9 miles. The horse won as the "Tom Thumb," the locomotive of the Baltimore and Ohio Railroad, driven by Peter Cooper, was involved in an accident.

Rack-rail diesel-electric locomotive was built by the General Electric Company, Schenectady, N.Y., for the Manitou and Pike's Peak Railway, the highest cog railroad in the world, and placed in service July 16, 1939. It pushed the 50-passenger car up the 16 per cent grade, and on the downward trip backed down the grade in front of the car. Dynamic braking assisted in holding the car at a safe speed in descending the steep slopes.

Streamlined electric engine was No. 4800, type GG1, placed in service by the Pennsylvania Railroad Company on January 28, 1935, in a test run between Washington, D.C., and Philadelphia, Pa. The engine was 79½ feet long, of all-steel construction, and weighed 230 tons. It operated on an 11,000-volt, 25-cycle, single-phase system, the current fed by overhead wires through a pantograph. The electric engine was placed in passenger service February 10, 1935.

Streamlined steam locomotive was introduced by the New York Central Lines December 14, 1934, between Albany, N.Y., and Karner,

THE FIRST

N.Y. It was named the "Commodore Vanderbilt," after the founder of the New York Central Lines and was 96 feet long and weighed
228 tons. It developed 4,075 h.p. and was built
in West Albany, N.Y.

LOCOMOTIVE BOOSTER was used on
a New York Central locomotive in July, 1918.
This is a device to aid the locomotive when
starting and on grades.

LOCOMOTIVE COWCATCHER was invented by Isaac Dripps and used in 1833 on the
Camden & Amboy Railroad between Bordentown and Hightstown, N.J. It consisted
originally of a small attachment on two wheels
with projecting points, but since the prongs
impaled animals a heavy bar at right angles to
the rails replaced it. (*John Elfreth Watkins—
The Camden and Amboy Railroad*)

LOCOMOTIVE HEADLIGHT
Electric locomotive headlight was patented by Leonidas G. Woolley of Mendon,
Mich., who obtained patent No. 241,112 on May
3, 1881. It was a polygonal lamp-frame suspended in position by a series of opposing
springs which neutralized the jarring.

Locomotive illumination was devised by
Horatio Allen for the Charleston and Hamburg Railroad in 1831. He placed a little square
flat car, about five feet long, in front of the
locomotive and spread a layer of sand several
inches deep, on top of which he built a fire of
pinewood knots. The device was impractical
because of the frequent fires ignited by sparks
blowing into and against the cars when the train
was in motion. (*Horatio Allen—The Railroad
Era, the First Five Years of Its Development*)

Talking headlight was installed November
6, 1934, on a Union Pacific six-car streamlined
train, and was demonstrated the following day
at Schenectady, N.Y. The operator on the train
aimed the beacon of his projector at a concave
mirror on the platform which enabled persons
aboard the train to speak over the beam of light
to those on the platform. The installation was
made by the General Electric Company of
Schenectady, N.Y. The talking headlight was
used principally to demonstrate the effectiveness
of such a communication system on railroads,
even in daylight.

LOCOMOTIVE STEAM WHISTLE was
made by the Rogers Locomotive and Machine
Works, Paterson, N.J., and used October 6,
1837, on "The Sandusky," a locomotive with a
four-wheeled truck under the forward part of
the engine. The whistle was so overworked on
its run from Paterson, N.J., to New Brunswick, N.J., on the Paterson and Hudson River
Railroad that it affected the supply of steam.
The locomotive was sold to the Mad River and

THE FIRST

Lake Erie Railroad Company for $6,750 and on
October 14, 1837, was packed in boxes and
shipped by schooner. (*Charles Frederick Carter
—When Railroads Were New*)

**LOG ROLLING (BIRLING) NATION-
AL CHAMPIONSHIP** was held Septem-
ber 9, 1898, on the lagoon at the Trans-Missis-
sippi Exposition, Omaha, Neb., on "Lumbermen's Day," by the Lumbermen's Association of
America. There were six entries. The winner
was Tommy Fleming of Eau Claire, Wis.

LOGANBERRY was introduced in 1881 by
Judge James Harvey Logan in Santa Cruz,
Calif., and given to the public in 1893 by the
University of California. The loganberry is a
cross between a California wild blackberry and
a red raspberry. (*Edward James Wickson—
California Fruits and How to Grow Them*)

LOGIC BOOK was William Brattle's
*Compendium Logicae Secundum Principia, D.
Renati Cartesii Plerumque Efformatum, et
Catechistice Propositum* published in Boston,
Mass., in 1735. It was published in Latin and
contained 64 pages.

LOLLIPOP MACHINE. *See* Confectionery machine

LONG DISTANCE TELEPHONE CALL.
See Telephone : Long distance telephone call

LOOKOUT (forest fire). *See* Forest fire:
Forest fire lookout tower

LOOP THE LOOP (airplane). *See* Aviation—Flights : Airplane loop the loop

LOOP THE LOOP (autogiro). *See* Autogiro: Autogiro to loop the loop publicly

**LOOP THE LOOP CENTRIFUGAL
RAILWAY** was invented by Edwin Prescott of Arlington, Mass., who obtained patent
No. 609,164 August 16, 1898, on a roller coaster,
and patent No. 667,455, February 5, 1901, on a
centrifugal railway. It was known as Boyton's
Centrifugal Railway and was installed at Coney
Island, N.Y., in 1900. It had a 75-foot incline
and a 20-foot wide loop.

LOTTERY
Lottery of importance was held on June
26, 1614, by the Virginia Company. The first
Great Prize was 4,500 crowns. This method of
obtaining funds was used by the colonies
and the Continental Congress.

Lottery held by the Continental Congress
was held April 10, 1777, in Philadelphia, Pa.,
for the purpose of obtaining funds. On No-

LOTTERY—*Continued*
vember 1, 1776, a lottery was approved and a
committee appointed which rendered a report,
November 18, 1776. Seven managers were appointed to conduct the lottery. Treasury bank
notes were awarded as prizes payable at the end
of five years. Funds were obtained by lottery
by the individual colonies at various times prior
to this national lottery.

Lottery legislation (national) hostile to
lotteries was the act of March 2, 1827 (4
Stat.L.238), which provided "that no postmaster or assistant postmaster shall act as agent
for lottery offices or under any color of purchase, or otherwise, send lottery tickets; nor
shall any postmaster receive free of postage or
frank lottery schemes, circulars or tickets."

LOUD-SPEAKER IN U.S. SENATE
See Congress (U.S.)—Senate: Loud-speaker

LOUISIANA PURCHASE. *See* Territorial
expansion: Annexation of territory

**LUCITE (polymethyl methacrylate) pro-
duction (commercial)** was begun by E. I.
du Pont de Nemours & Company, Wilmington,
Del., on May 21, 1936. Lucite is a plastic which
is low in moisture absorption, highly non-conducting, and crystal clear, and which possesses
the interesting property of bending light rays
as they pass through it.

LUNCH (free). *See* Free lunch

LUNCH WAGON was introduced in Providence, R.I., in 1872 by Walter Scott. He drove
a wagon to a location on Westminster Street
where he sold coffee, sandwiches, pies, and
cakes. This was the first "lunch car" or "Night
Owl," the forerunner of the dining lunch cars.
In order to comply with Board of Health
regulations and to secure running water, the
operators of the wagons obtained desirable
vacant sites where they hooked up to a water
supply. Individual wagons were constructed
until 1887, when they were commercially manufactured in Providence, R.I., by Ruel B. Jones
who also operated a chain of lunch wagons.
(*Franklin Pierce Rice—Dictionary of Worcester*)

LUNG REMOVAL. *See* Surgical operation: Lung removal

LUTHERAN CHURCH
American Lutheran Church was organized
in Toledo, Ohio, August 11, 1930, through the
merger of the Lutheran Synod of Buffalo (organized June 25, 1845), the Evangelical Lutheran Synod of Iowa and other states (organized August 24, 1854), and the Evangelical
Lutheran Joint Synod of Ohio and other states
(organized September 14, 1818).

Lutheran Church building was dedicated
by the Reverend Johannes Campanius at Christina (Tinicum Island), near the present site
of Essington, Pa., September 4, 1645. Governor Johan Printz had erected Fort Göteborg
and a small blockhouse in which Campanius
had conducted services previous to the erection
of the church.

Lutheran pastor was Reorus Torkillus
from Mölndal, Sweden, who came over on the
"Kalmar Nyckel" ("Key of Kalmar") with
Governor Peter Hollander Ridder, landing on
April 17, 1640, at Fort Christina, Del. He died
of the plague in 1643. (*Christopher Ward—
New Sweden on the Delaware*)

Lutheran pastor ordained in America was
Justus Falckner, ordained in Gloria Dei Church
at Wicaco, Philadelphia, Pa., November 24,
1703, with Andrew Rudman, Erick Biörck, and
Andrew Sandel as officiating clergymen. (*Julius
Friedrich Sachse—Justus Falckner*)

Lutheran services in English were held in
1694 in Germantown and Philadelphia by Heinrich Bernhard Koester. The first Lutheran
synod in America, the "Evangelical Lutheran
Ministerium of Pennsylvania and adjacent
states," was held on August 26, 1748, through
the efforts of Henry Melchior Muehlenberg.

LYCEUM was organized by Josiah Holbrook in Millbury, Mass., in October 1826. Its
purpose was to afford adults an opportunity
for mutual improvement through association
and study, stimulate an interest in the schools,
and contribute to the training of teachers and
the dissemination of knowledge through libraries and museums. The American Lyceum
Association was organized May 4, 1831, in New
York City by delegates from Maine, Massachusetts, and New York. The Millbury Lyceum became the Millbury Lyceum No. 1,
branch of the American Lyceum. (*Centennial
History of Millbury, Mass.*)

LYNCH LAW (state) was an anti-lynching statute approved December 20, 1893, by
Georgia, "an act to prevent mob violence in
this state, to prescribe a punishment for the
same, to provide a means for carrying this act
into effect, to punish a failure to comply with
its requirements, and for other purposes" (No.
347 Part 1—Title 10, Misc.). Violators were
guilty of a felony punishable by imprisonment
of one to twenty years. If death resulted, a
murder charge could be instituted.

MACADAM ROAD. *See* Road: Macadam
road

MACARONI FACTORY was established
by Antoine Zerega in Brooklyn, N.Y., in 1848.
It consisted of a small mill with crude mechanical equipment for grinding raw materials.

THE FIRST

MACHINE GUN. *See* Ordnance: Machine gun

MACHINE GUN IN AIRPLANE. *See* Aviation—Airplane: Airplane outfitted with a machine gun

MACHINE PATENT. *See* Patent: Machine patent

MADSTONE is supposed to have come from Chicago, Ill., in 1804. It was sold by Dr. Parker to Benjamin Milam of Winona, Miss., who used it to perform "miraculous cures." A madstone is a light porous stone of greenish color said to possess the property of drawing poison from the bite of a dog.

MAGAZINE. *See* Periodical; *also* magazines under specific languages, occupations, religious and fraternal organizations, sciences, sports, trades, e.g., Agricultural magazine, Book trade magazine, Catholic magazine, Masonic magazine, Welsh magazine

MAGIC LANTERN SHOW
Magic lantern feature show was "Miss Jerry," previewed October 9, 1894, at the Carbon Studio, New York City. Alexander Black was the author, scenario writer, director, camera man, and titler. The leads were taken by Blanche Bayliss, who played Jerry, William Courtenay as the hero, and Ernest Hastings as the villain. Slides were shown at the rate of five a second.

MAGIC LANTERN SLIDES (glass plate) known as Hyalotypes were invented by Frederick Langenheim of Philadelphia, Pa., who obtained patent No. 7,784 November 19, 1850, on an "improvement in photographic pictures on glass."

MAGICIAN'S ADVERTISEMENT. *See* Advertisement: Magician's advertisement

MAGNESIUM commercially produced from sea water was extracted on January 21, 1941, by the Dow Chemical Company, Freeport, Tex. It sold for approximately 23 cents a pound.

MAGNESIUM AIRPLANE. *See* Aviation—Airplane: Jet magnesium airplane

MAGNET. *See* Electric magnet

MAGNETIC TAPE RECORDER. *See* Tape Recorder: Magnetic tape recorder

MAIL BOX. *See* Postal service: Mail box

THE FIRST

MAIL CAR. *See* Railroad Car: Mail car (steel)

MAIL CHUTE. *See* Postal service: Mail chute

MAIL FRANKING PRIVILEGE. *See* Postal service: Mail franking privilege

MAIL-ORDER HOUSE. *See* Business: Mail-order house

MAIL SERVICE. *See* Air mail service; Postal service

MAIL WAGON (automobile). *See* Automobile mail wagon

MAIZE, or Indian corn, produced in quantity by people of English blood, of which there is any authentic record, was grown on a 40-acre tract planted in the Jamestown colony, Va., in 1609. Maize is indigenous to America, and records of its growth and use were made by both Columbus and Verrezano. (*Philip Alexander Bruce—Institutional History of Virginia in the 17th Century*)

MAIZOLITH. *See* Cornstone

MAJOR GENERAL. *See* Army officer: Major general

MALLET (dental). *See* Dental mallet: Dental mallet

MALLET LOCOMOTIVE. *See* Locomotive: Duplex compound locomotive (Mallet)

MALTED MILK. *See* Milk: Malted milk

MANGANESE STEEL. *See* Steel: Manganese steel

MANILA PAPER. *See* Paper: Manila paper

MANUAL BLOCK RAILROAD SIGNAL SYSTEM. *See* Railroad signal system: Railroad signal system (manual block)

MANUAL FOR KINDERGARTENS. *See* Kindergarten manual

MANUAL TRAINING
Industrial school on the Fellenberg plan was established in 1819 in Derby, Conn., by Josiah Holbrook. The boys paid a portion of their tuition by laboring on the farm. In 1824,

MANUAL TRAINING—*Continued*
with the cooperation of the Reverend Truman Coe, Holbrook established an "Agricultural Seminary." Neither of these enterprises was successful. (*History of Agricultural Education in the United States—U.S. Department of Agriculture. Miscellaneous Publication No. 36*)

Industrial school for girls was organized in Lancaster, Mass., the funds being obtained by subscription undertaken in April 1854. The school was incorporated as a state institution, August 27, 1856, with Bradford K. Pierce as the first superintendent. This school was administered by the Department of Public Welfare.

Manual training institute was the Fellenberg Manual Labor Institute opened in 1829 in Greenfield, Mass., by James Henry Coffin. (*John Cunningham Clyde—Life of James H. Coffin*)

Manual training school entirely financed by public taxes was the Baltimore Manual Training School, established in Baltimore, Md., in 1884 under authority of municipal ordinance of October 20, 1883. Instruction and practice were given in the use of tools embracing the fields of carpentry, wood-turning, pattern-making, chipping and filing, forge work, molding, soldering and brazing, etc.

School to offer courses in manual training was organized in Talbot County, Md., in 1750 by the Reverend Thomas Bacon, who named it "A Charity Workers' School." It opened December 1, 1751, with an enrollment of six boys. It was financed through funds from a series of concerts given in Maryland and Virginia. (*Oswald Tilghman—History of Talbot County, Md.*)

Vocational high school. *See* High school: Vocational high school for girls

MANUFACTURERS' ASSOCIATION of diversified industries (national) was the National Association of Manufacturers of the United States, organized on January 22, 1895, at a convention held in Cincinnati, Ohio. The first president elected was Thomas P. Dolan.

MANUFACTURERS' FAIR. *See* Fair: Manufacturers' fair

MAP
Automobile road map was published and distributed in 1914 by the Gulf Oil Company, Pittsburgh, Pa. William B. Akin conceived the idea and 10,000 maps were distributed showing roads and routes in Allegheny County, Pa.

Geological map. *See* Geology book: Geology book

Globular map published showing the western hemisphere and the first map to use the description "America" was printed in April 1507 at St. Dié in the Vosges Mountains of Alsace. It was designed in twelve connected globular segments, presumably intended to be cut out, mounted on heavy paper, and shaped into globular form. It was made by Martin Waldseemüller, a German cartographer, from a single wood block 9½ by 15 inches. *See also* "America"

Map made in the United States published in a book appeared in the Reverend William Hubbard's *The Present State of New England being a narrative of the troubles with the Indians in New England, from the first planting thereof in the year 1607 to 1677*, published by John Foster, Boston, Mass., in 1677. It was a topographical woodcut folding map and was known as the "Wine Hills' Map" since the English edition had "Wine Hills" instead of the "White Hills" of New Hampshire. It bore the inscription "Being the first that ever was here cut, and done by the best Pattern that could be had, which being in some places defective, it made the other less exact, yet doth it sufficiently shew the Scituation of the Countrey and conveniently well the distance of places." The name of the cartographer is unknown. (*Emerson David Fite and Archibald Freeman—A Book of Old Maps*)

Map of a city within the present limits of the United States is a line engraving map of St. Augustine, Fla., which appeared in *Expeditis Francisco Draki Eqvitis Angli in Indias Occidentalis—1588*. This illustrated map may not have been the first, but it is the earliest known.

Map of the United States engraved in America was a wall map, 41 by 46.5 inches, made by Abel Buell in New Haven, Conn., in 1783, after the Treaty of Peace. It was a line engraving, and was advertised for sale in the *Connecticut Journal* of March 31, 1784: "As this Map is the effect of the compiler's long and unwearied application, diligence and industry, and as perfection has been the great object of his labors, and it being the first ever compiled, engraved, and finished by any one man, and an American, he flatters himself, that every patriotic gentleman, and lover of geographical knowledge, will not hesitate to encourage the improvement of his country. Every favour will be most gratefully acknowledged, by the public's most obedient and very humble servant." (*Leonard Mackall—Abel Buell*)

Relief map was of the Island of San Domingo, made in 1871, by Edwin Eugene

THE FIRST

Howell. In 1876, he made a relief map of the Grand Canyon of the Colorado as part of the Government Exhibit at the Philadelphia Centennial Exposition, Philadelphia, Pa.

Road map was *A Survey of the Roads of the United States of America* published in 1789 in New York City by Christopher Colles. It contained 86 plates and detailed the routes near New York City.

Road map for public use was printed in *Tulley's Almanac* of 1698 published in Boston, Mass., by John Tulley. The almanac showed a list of towns, roads, and distances from Boston. Later editions gave the names of the tavern keepers.

War map to appear in America was published in the December 24, 1733, issue of John Peter Zenger's *New York Weekly Journal*. A map of the harbor and fortifications of Louisburg, Nova Scotia, were shown. *(Willard Grosvenor Bleyer—History of American Journalism)*

MAPPING CAMERA. *See* Camera: Aerial camera (nine-lens) for large-scale mapping

MARATHON DANCE. *See* Dance marathon

MARATHON RACE (annual) was the American Marathon Race, 26 miles and 385 feet, from Hopkinton, Mass. (through Ashland, Framingham, Natick, Wellesley, and Newton) to Exeter Street, Boston, Mass., on April 19, 1897. It was won by John J. McDermott of the Pastime Athletic Club of New York City whose time was 2 hours, 55 minutes, and 10 seconds. *(Boston Daily Globe, April 20, 1897)*

MARBLE BUILDING of importance was the Bank of the United States, Philadelphia, Pa., incorporated February 25, 1791. The building was designed by Samuel Blodget, although he was not an architect, and built in 1791.

MARBLE QUARRY was operated in 1785 by Isaac Underhill on land owned by Reuben Bloomer in Dorset, Vt. The quarry was first worked for stone for fire jambs, chimney backs, hearths and lintels. A quarry was also opened in Rutland, Vt., in 1785. Marble used before 1785 had been obtained from exposed marble ledges. *(Report of Marble, Slate and Granite Industries of Vermont—George H. Perkins, state geologist)*

MARBLE STATUARY GROUP executed by an American was "The Chanting Cherubs" designed in 1830 by Horatio Greenough for James Fenimore Cooper. The subject was sug-

THE FIRST

gested by a portion of a Raphael painting but incurred hostility because of the nudity of the figures. *(Henry Theodore Tuckerman—A Memorial of Horatio Greenough)*

MARDI GRAS. *See* Holiday: Mardi Gras of New Orleans

MARGARINE. *See* Oleomargarine

MARIAN CONGRESS. *See* Servite church: Marian congress

MARINE BATTLE. *See* War (colonial): Marine engagement in battle

MARINE HOSPITAL. *See* Hospital: Marine hospital (U.S.)

MARINE INSURANCE LAW (state). *See* Insurance: Marine insurance law (state)

MARINERS' CHURCH. *See* Church: Mariners' church

MARINES

American Marines were organized on November 10, 1775, under authority of the Continental Congress. They were called "The First and Second Battalions of American Marines," and were commanded by 1 colonel, 2 lieutenant colonels, 2 majors, etc. The Marines were under the jurisdiction of the War Department until April 30, 1798, when Congress created the Navy Department. The present U.S. Marine Corps was created by act of July 11, 1798 (1 Stat.L.594), "an act for the establishing and organizing a Marine Corps," which authorized 1 major, 4 captains, 16 first lieutenants, 12 second lieutenants, 48 sergeants, 48 corporals, 32 drums and fifes, and 720 privates, including enlisted men. *(Clyde Hill Metcalf—History of the U.S. Marine Corps)*

Marine aviator was Lieutenant Alfred Austell Cunningham, assigned for training and instruction to the Navy Aviation Camp, Annapolis, Md., on July 9, 1912.

Marine corps was organized in 1740 when three regiments were recruited in New York to serve under the British flag. They wore green swallowtail coats faced with red, white waistcoats and buff trousers, crossed white belts and three-cornered hats. *(Richard Strader Collum—History of the U.S. Marine Corps)*

Marine engagement in battle. *See* War (colonial): Marine engagement in battle

Marine officer of Chinese descent in the U.S. Marine Corps was Wilbur Carl Sze, commissioned a second lieutenant on December

THE FIRST

MARINES—*Continued*
15, 1943. He was born in Washington, D.C., and at the age of five went to China, where he remained eleven years before returning to the United States.

Negro commissioned officer in the regular U.S. Marine Corps was John Earl Rudder, a midshipman in the regular Naval Reserve Officers' Training Corps at Purdue University, Lafayette, Ind., who was commissioned June 8, 1948, as a second lieutenant. He served as an enlisted man in the Marine Corps Reserve from July 24, 1943, to June 26, 1946.

Woman marine was Lucy Brewer, alias George Baker and Louisa Baker, who concealed her sex and served on board the "Constitution" in its battle with the "Guerriere," August 19, 1812. (*Lucy Brewer—Affecting Narrative*)

Woman marine major was Ruth Cheney Streeter of Morristown, N.J., appointed January 29, 1943. She was advanced to lieutenant colonel November 22, 1943, and to colonel February 1, 1944.

Woman marine reserve was Mrs. Opha May Johnson, who enrolled August 12, 1918, as a private and was assigned to duty as a clerk at Headquarters, Quartermaster Corps, U.S. Marine Corps, Washington, D.C. She was appointed sergeant (provisional) September 11, 1918, and was honorably discharged February 28, 1919.

MARITIME DAY. *See* Holiday: Maritime day

MARITIME DISTINGUISHED SERVICE MEDAL. *See* Medal: Distinguished Service Medal (Merchant Marine)

MARITIME MUSEUM. *See* Museum: Maritime museum

MARKETS, OFFICE OF (U.S.). *See* Agriculture department (U.S.): Office of markets

MARRIAGE. *See* Wedding

MARRIAGE COURSE in a college was given by Professor Ernest Rutherford Groves in 1924 at the University of North Carolina, Chapel Hill, N.C. (*Ernest Rutherford Groves—Marriage*)

MASK. *See* Baseball catcher's mask; Gas mask

MASONIC BOOK was printed and published by Benjamin Franklin in Philadelphia in

THE FIRST

1734. It was advertised from May 9 to May 30, 1734, in the *Pennsylvania Gazette*. It was an American edition of Anderson's *Constitutions of the Freemasons; containing the History, Charges, Regulations, etc., of that most Ancient and Right Worshipful Fraternity.*

MASONIC COLLEGE. *See* College: Masonic college

MASONIC MAGAZINE was *Free-Masons Magazine and General Miscellany*, a monthly, published April 1811 by Levis and Weaver, Philadelphia, Pa. It was edited by George Richards. (*American Lodge of Research—Transactions. Vol. 3*)

MASONRY
Freemasons. *See* Freemasons

Negro Masonic Grand Lodge (not Free and Accepted Masons) was the Provincial Grand Lodge organized June 24, 1791, in Boston, Mass., with Prince Hall as Grand Master.

MASS (Catholic). *See* Catholic Mass

MASSACRE. *See* Indians: Indian massacre of white people

MASTER'S DEGREE. *See under* Degrees (academic and honorary)

MASTOID OPERATION. *See* Surgical operation: Mastoid operation

MASTSHIP. *See* Ship: Ship equipped with a masthead sea anchorage for a dirigible

MATADOR. *See* Bull fight

MATCH
"Book matches" were made by the Diamond Match Company at its Barberton, Ohio, factory in 1896 under patent No. 483,166 granted September 27, 1892, to Joshua Pusey of Lima, Pa. (*Herbert Manchester—Fifty Years of Match Making*)

Friction matches were made in Springfield, Mass., in 1834 in a small establishment in the "L" of the Frederick Chapin house on Chicopee Street, Chicopee (then a part of Springfield). Daniel M. Chapin and Alonzo Dwight Phillips of East Hartford produced matches which were known as the Chapin-Phillips matches. The business was finally sold to Byam and Carlton of Boston, Mass., and the product was thereafter known as the Boston Match. Previous to 1834 the only match in use had been a slender sulphur splint which was ignited by being drawn quickly through a double fold of sandpaper.

Match patent on phosphorous friction matches was patent No. 68 on "manufacturing of friction matches" awarded on October 24, 1836, to Alonzo Dwight Phillips of Springfield, Mass. The constituents of the "head" were chalk, phosphorus, glue, and brimstone. (*Herbert Manchester—The Romance of the Match*)

MATERIA MEDICA BOOK. *See* Medical book: Therapeutics and materia medica book

MATERNITY BOOK was *Letters to Married Women on Nursing and the Management of Children* by Dr. Hugh Smith, published in 1792 in Philadelphia, Pa., by Mathew Carey. It contained 167 pages (15 chapters), devoted to birthmarks, miscarriages, mother's milk, suckling, weaning, etc. It was printed from the sixth London edition.

MATINEE IDOL. *See* Actor: Matinee idol

MATRON (prison). *See* Prison: Prison matrons

MAYOR (woman). *See* Woman: Woman mayor

MEASURES STANDARDIZATION. *See* Weights and measures standardization

MEASURING MACHINE. *See* Caliper (screw)

MEAT
Beef export was from Savannah, Ga., in 1755 when 40 barrels of beef were shipped out; in 1770, 639 barrels of beef and 4,985 pounds of tallow were exported.

Beef exported to England was shipped October 1, 1875, by Timothy C. Eastman of New York City. It was known as "dead meat" and was sampled by Queen Victoria. (*Rudolf Alexander Clemen—History of the American Livestock and Meat Industry*)

Railroad shipments of dressed beef. *See* Railroad: Railroad shipments of dressed beef (year-round long-distance)

MEAT BISCUIT. *See* Cracker: Meat biscuit

MEAT INSPECTION LEGISLATION (federal) was approved August 30, 1890 (26 Stat.L.414) and provided for the inspection of salted pork and bacon intended for export, and the inspection of export swine, cattle, sheep, and other ruminants. (*Ulysses Grant Houck—Bureau of Animal Industry*)

MEAT PACKER was William Pynchon, who established a warehouse at Warehouse Point, Springfield, Mass., in 1636. He dealt in mutton, tallow, and wool, but his chief business was pork packing. He also sold beaver skins. Competition was keen and "merchants encreased so many that it became little worth, by reason of their out-buying one another, which caused them to live on husbandry." (*Proceedings of Connecticut Valley Historical Society. Vol. 2*)

MECHANICAL COTTON PICKER. *See* Cotton picker (mechanical)

MECHANICAL ENGINEERING LABORATORY for research work was established at Stevens Institute of Technology at Hoboken, N.J., in 1874. It was proposed by Robert Henry Thurston, professor of mechanical engineering, who on January 30, 1874, outlined the usefulness of the laboratory to the community in a letter which he sent to the trustees of the school. (*William Frederick Durand—Robert Henry Thurston, a Biography*)

MECHANICAL ENGINEERS' SOCIETY. *See* Engineering society: Mechanical engineering society (national)

MECHANICS' LIBRARY. *See* Library: Mechanics' library

MECHANICS TEXTBOOK was *The Elements of Analytical Mechanics*, 445 pages, by William Holmes Chambers Bartlett, professor of natural and experimental philosophy at the United States Military Academy, published by A. S. Barnes & Co., New York City, in 1853.

MECHANIZED SHOOTING GALLERY. *See* Shooting gallery (mechanized)

MEDAL
Agriculture Department distinguished service gold medal was awarded November 12, 1947, to five individuals—Dr. Hugh Hammond Bennett, William Ashby Jump, and Milburn Lincoln Wilson of Washington, D.C., Dr. James Fitton Couch of Wyndmoor, Pa., and Lewis B. Holt of Clearwater, Idaho—and to two units, the Northern Regional Research Laboratory, Peoria Penicillin Group, Peoria, Ill., and the Orlando Florida Laboratory, Orlando, Fla.

Agriculture Department distinguished service gold medal presented to a woman was awarded May 25, 1950, to Lucy Maclay Alexander of Beltsville, Md., "for outstanding achievement in applying fundamental scientific principles to meat and poultry cookery; for relating cooking shrinkage to chemical composition and to method of producing and processing for market; for formulating precise,

MEDAL—*Continued*
practical directions for cooking meat and poultry; and for designing and sponsoring a practical meat thermometer."

Air Force Medal of Honor for action in the Korean War was awarded posthumously to Major Louis J. Sebile of Chicago, Ill., who was killed August 5, 1951, in an F-51 Mustang which he dived into the ground amid a group of enemy armored vehicles near Hamchang, Korea. The award was presented to his widow, Mrs. Elizabeth J. Sebile, on August 24, 1951, at March Air Force Base, Riverside, Calif., by General Hoyt Sanford Vandenberg, Chief of Staff of the Air Force.

Air Mail Flyer's Medal of Honor was presented to Mal Bryan Freeburg, December 13, 1933, by President Franklin Delano Roosevelt. On April 12, 1933, while Freeburg was flying a tri-motor plane, an outward propeller broke and the vibration loosened a motor, which lodged in a wing strut and damaged the landing gear. He flew over the Mississippi River, banked his plane and shook the motor free so that it would fall in the river and not endanger anyone. He then flew 25 miles to an emergency field and landed safely. The Air Mail Flyer's Medal was authorized February 14, 1931 (46 Stat.L.1110).

Air Medal (U.S.) awarded to a woman was presented to Second Lieutenant Elsie S. Ott, Army Nurse Corps, at Bowman Field, Louisville, Ky., March 26, 1943, by Brigadier General Fred S. Borum, First Troop Carrier Command, "for meritorious achievement while participating in an aerial flight." She served as nurse for five patients evacuated from India to Washington, D.C., January 17-23, 1943.

Albert Medal presented to a native-born American was awarded June 10, 1884, to James Buchanan Eads for his plan for deepening the Mississippi River as far as the mouth of the Ohio River by jetties. The Albert Medal was established in 1862 in memory of Prince Albert, consort of Queen Victoria, and was awarded by the (British) Society for the Encouragement of Arts, Manufactures and Commerce for distinguished merit in promoting arts, manufactures or commerce. (*Louis How —James B. Eads*)

Bronze Star was established by Executive Order No. 9419 dated February 4, 1944. It was authorized for those who while serving in any capacity with the Army, Navy, Marine Corps or Coast Guard distinguished themselves on or after December 7, 1941, "by heroic or meritorious achievement or service, not involving participation in aerial flight." Airmen were eligible but not for deeds performed in the air. The ribbon worn with the medal is red with a vertical blue stripe in the center. Both the blue stripe and the ribbon ends are piped in white.

Bronze Star presented to a woman was awarded to First Lieutenant Cordelia E. Cook, an Army nurse of Fort Thomas, Ky., who served in direct support of combat operations from November 1943 to January 1944, when she was wounded. Despite her wounds, she carried on her hospital duties. The award was presented in May 1944 by Major General Geoffrey Keys of the Fifth Army. Lieutenant Cook also received the Purple Heart, thus qualifying as the first woman in World War II to win two decorations.

"Campaign medal" was the "Dewey Medal," authorized by act of Congress of June 3, 1898 (30 Stat.L.746), to be presented to all officers and men under the command of Commodore George Dewey, who on May 1, 1898, participated in the Battle of Manila Bay. Unlike medals suspended from ribbons, this bronze medal is suspended from a bar which bears the design of an American eagle with its wings spread over the sea.

Chaplain to win a Congressional Medal of Honor. *See* Naval officer: Chaplain to win a Congressional Medal of Honor

College to confer medals as prizes. *See* College: College to confer medals as prizes

Combat decoration for Army personnel who participate in a combat parachute jump, a combat glider landing, or an initial assault landing on a hostile shore, was authorized December 22, 1944, for action after December 7, 1941. It is a bronze Indian arrowhead one quarter of an inch high, worn in a vertical position with the point upward on the service ribbon indicating the theater in which it was earned.

Combat infantry badge was authorized November 4, 1943, to be awarded to those "whose conduct in combat is exemplary, or whose combat action occurs in a major operation."

Congressional Medal of Honor. *See below* Medal of Honor

Copley Medal awarded to an American was presented to Benjamin Franklin in 1753 for his "curious experiments and observations on electricity." The medal, the highest distinction given by England for scientific research, was awarded by the Royal Society of London. (*Bernard Fay—Franklin, the Apostle of Modern Times*)

Croix de Guerre awarded to a Negro in the American army was given to Private Henry Johnson, 369th Infantry, 93d Division, on May

THE FIRST

24, 1918, with the following citation: "Being on double sentry duty at night, was attacked by twelve Germans. He shot one and seriously wounded two others with his bayonet. Even though he had been three times wounded at the beginning of the action by revolver bullets and grenades, he went to the assistance of his wounded comrade, who was about to be carried off by the enemy, and continued the combat until he put the Germans to flight. It was a splendid example of courage and energy." (*Emmett Jay Scott—American Negro in the World War*)

Distinguished Flying Cross was authorized July 2, 1926 (44 Stat.L.789), "for heroism or extraordinary achievement while participating in an aerial flight," to be awarded to members of the Air Corps of the Army of the United States, including the National Guard and the organized reserves since April 6, 1917. The medal is a bronze four-blade propeller in the form of a cross superimposed on an enchased block. The first presentation was made June 11, 1927, to Charles Augustus Lindbergh for his solo Atlantic flight.

Distinguished Flying Cross in the Korean War was awarded to First Lieutenant Robert Earl Wayne on July 14, 1950, by Advanced Headquarters, Fifth Air Force (General Orders No. 2).

Distinguished Service Cross (Army) was authorized by Congress July 9, 1918 (40 Stat. L.870), for persons who "while serving in any capacity with the Army of the United States distinguish themselves by extraordinary heroism in connection with military operations against an armed enemy." The cross is of bronze with an eagle in the center. Below the eagle is a scroll bearing the inscription "For Valor." On the reverse, the name of the recipient is engraved within a wreath. The ribbon is a broad band of blue, bordered on both edges by narrow bands of red and white.

Distinguished Service Cross awarded to an animal was authorized under General Orders 79 of the 3rd Infantry Division dated October 24, 1943, and conferred by Major General Lucian Truscott on Chips, a half-shepherd and half-husky dog owned by Mr. and Mrs. Edward Wren of Pleasantville, N.Y., for "courageous action in singlehandedly eliminating a dangerous machine-gun nest and causing surrender of the crew." The award, however, was rescinded February 3, 1944, in General Orders 17 of the unit, as the award of decorations to animals was prohibited by a War Department circular of January 19, 1944.

Distinguished Service Medal (Army) was authorized by act of Congress approved July 9, 1918 (40 Stat.L.870), for persons who while serving in any capacity with the Army of the

THE FIRST

United States distinguish themselves by exceptionally meritorious service in a duty of great responsibility. The medal bears the coat of arms of the United States in bronze surrounded by a circle of dark blue enamel bearing the inscription "For Distinguished Service." The name of the recipient is inscribed on the reverse on a scroll upon a trophy of flags and weapons. It is worn suspended from a white ribbon separated from red ends by a narrow blue band.

Distinguished Service Medal (Army) awarded to a woman was presented to Oveta Culp Hobby, director of the Women's Army Corps, on December 31, 1944. It was formally presented to her by Secretary of War Henry Lewis Stimson in his office in Washington, D.C., in the presence of General George Catlett Marshall, Chief of Staff, and General Henry Harley Arnold, General of the Army.

Distinguished Service Medal awarded to a woman was presented to Evangeline Booth, commander of the Salvation Army, on October 19, 1919, by Major General David Carey Shanks as personal representative of President Woodrow Wilson and Secretary of War Newton Diehl Baker.

Distinguished Service Medal (Merchant Marine) was authorized April 11, 1942 (56 Stat.L.217), "to provide decorations for outstanding conduct or service in the line of duty" to persons who, on or after September 3, 1939, have distinguished themselves serving in the American Merchant Marine. The first presentation was made by President Franklin Delano Roosevelt at the White House in the presence of Rear Admiral Emory Scott Land, chairman of the United States Maritime Commission and administrator of the War Shipping Administration, on October 8, 1942, to Edwin Fox Cheney, Jr., of Yeadon, Pa., who, on March 12, 1942, had swum under blazing oil to save six shipmates from the torpedoed tanker "John D. Gill."

Distinguished Service Medal (Navy) was authorized by act of Congress dated February 4, 1919 (40 Stat.L.1056), for presentation to persons who while in the Naval Service of the United States since April 6, 1917, have distinguished themselves by "exceptionally meritorious service to the government in a duty of great responsibility." The medal is gold, bronze and enamel. The obverse has the picture of an American eagle surrounded by a blue enameled band bearing the inscription "United States of America and Navy." The reverse is a trident encircled by olive branches around which is a band of blue enamel on which is inscribed "For Distinguished Service." It is worn suspended from a blue ribbon with a stripe of gold. On November 11, 1920, the Secretary of the Navy approved 150 awards.

MEDAL—*Continued*
Doctor to receive a congressional medal.
See Physician: Doctor to receive a medal
from Congress

Expert Infantryman's Badge of the U.S.
Army was awardèd March 29, 1944, at Fort
Bragg, N.C., to Technical Sergeant Walter L.
Bull of the 100th Division by Lieutenant General Lesley James McNair, commanding general
of the Army Ground Forces. The badge, three
inches long and a half inch wide, consists of a
miniature silver rifle mounted on an infantry
blue field with a silver border.

Indian medals known to be presented by
the colonists to friendly Indians were authorized in Virginia by the Act of 1661 which authorized "silver and plated placques to be worn
by the Indians when visiting the settlements."
One of these has a crude representation of a
tobacco plant and scrolls, above which is "Ye
King Of" on the obverse, while on the reverse
is a similarly engraved plant and the word
"Patomeck" with the "e" overlined. The surface
edges were engraved to represent scrolls and
foldings while the medal was holed for suspension. On December 2, 1662, an act "prohibiting the entertainment of Indians without
badges" was passed by the Assembly at James
City, Va. (*Harrold Edgar Gillingham—Indian
and Military Medals*)

**Interstate Commerce Commission Medal
of Honor** was a bronze medal awarded December 5, 1905, to George H. Poell of Grand
Island, Neb. On June 26, 1905, while a fireman on the St. Joseph and Grand Island Railway, he climbed out on the pilot of his engine
and rescued a child on the tracks. Poell was
seriously injured and one foot had to be ampu-
tated. The medal was authorized by act of
Congress of February 23, 1905 (33 Stat.L.743)
for presentation to those "who shall hereafter,
by extreme daring, endanger their own lives in
saving, or endeavoring to save lives from any
wreck, disaster or grave accident, or in preventing or endeavoring to prevent" accidents. Four
degrees were established: chief commander,
commander, officer, and legionnaire.

Legion of Merit Medal was authorized
July 20, 1942 (56 Stat.L.662), in four degrees
for presentation to the personnel of the armed
forces of this and friendly foreign nations,
who since the proclamation of an emergency by
the President on September 8, 1939, had distinguished themselves by meritorious conduct
in the performance of outstanding services.
The first presentation was made to Captain
Ralph B. Praeger for services in the Philippine Islands, December 1941-March 1942. The
award was presented posthumously in 1943.

**Legion of Merit Medal awarded to a for-
eign national** was presented on November 7,
1942, when the Legion of Merit, Degree of
Commander, was conferred upon General Amaro
Soares Bittencourt, military attaché of the
Brazilian Embassy at Washington, D.C. The
presentation was made at the U.S. Army parade
grounds at the Air Force Technical Training
Command, Miami Beach, Fla. An announcement
of the award was made October 22, 1942, at a
luncheon given in honor of the recipient. The
first Legion of Merit, Degree of Chief Commander, presentation was made in China on
July 7, 1943, to Generalissimo Chiang Kai-shek,
Commander in Chief of the Chinese Military
forces, by Lieutenant General Joseph W. Stilwell.

**Legion of Merit Medal awarded to a
Women's Army Corps member** was presented to Lieutenant Colonel Westray Battle
Boyce on September 27, 1944, for outstanding
services in the North African Theatre of
Operations from August 12, 1943, to August 8,
1944, in obtaining maximum utilization of WAC
personnel, etc.

Lifesaving medal awarded by the Treasury Department was authorized by act of June
20, 1874 (18 Stat.L.127), to "persons who
should thereafter endanger their own lives in
saving or endeavoring to save the lives of
others from the perils of the sea within the
United States or upon any American vessel."
It was awarded in two classes, a gold medal
worn from a red ribbon and a silver medal
worn from a blue ribbon. The first award was
a silver medal to Lucian M. Clemons, keeper of
the United States Lifesaving Service Station at
Marblehead, Ohio, on June 19, 1876, for saving
men from the schooner "Consuelo" on May 1,
1875.

**Medal awarded by the Continental Con-
gress** was granted to General George Washington for his exploit of March 17, 1776, in
compelling the British forces to evacuate Boston, Mass. The date of the resolution authorizing the medal was March 25, 1776. It was
struck in Paris, and showed the profile of
George Washington on the obverse. The reverse
showed George Washington and his officers
on horseback viewing the town of Boston in
the distance with the British fleet in view under
sail. Although this medal, the first authorized,
was granted in 1776, it was not presented to
Washington until 1786. (*Joseph Floumond
Loubat—Medallic History of the U.S.A.—
1776-1876*)

**Medal awarded by the Continental Con-
gress to a foreigner** was a silver medal presented to Lieutenant Colonel François Louis
Teisseidre de Fleury who commanded the first
of the storming parties in the assault upon
Stony Point, July 15, 1779. He was the first

THE FIRST

THE FIRST

man to enter the main fort and strike the British flag with his own hands. Fleury, who had been in the French military service, joined the Continental army in 1777. The date of the congressional resolution was July 26, 1779, and the presentation was made October 1, 1779.

Medal awarded to an American food producer was the Great Council Medal, which was awarded in 1851 to Gail Borden at the Great International Exposition in London, England for his invention of the meat biscuit. A one-pound meat biscuit contained a nutrient value of five pounds of meat and ten ounces of flour and retained its original flavor and value for years. The biscuit was eagerly accepted by explorers, travelers, troops, etc., who needed rations packed as compactly as possible. (*The Borden Eagle. 1922*)

See also Cracker: Meat biscuit

Medal of Freedom was established on July 6, 1945, by executive order of President Harry S. Truman for award to civilians for a meritorious act or service against an enemy or enemies on or after December 7, 1941, and for which an award of another United States medal or decoration is considered inappropriate. It is not awarded to a member of the armed forces of the United States or for service performed within the continental limits of the United States. The obverse depicts the head of "Freedom." In the lower portion in an arc is the inscription "Freedom." On the reverse is the "Liberty Bell" without carriage, within a circle composed of the words "United States of America." The ribbon has five red and four white stripes alternating.

Medal of Freedom awarded to a woman was presented to Anna Rosenberg, a member of the Advisory Board of the Office of War Mobilization and Reconversion, on October 29, 1945, by Secretary of War Robert Porter Patterson in his office in Washington, D.C.

Medal of Honor action took place February 13-14, 1861, at Apache Pass, Arizona, when Colonel Bernard John Dowling Irwin, assistant surgeon, "voluntarily took command of troops and attacked and defeated the hostile Indians (Chiricahua) he met on the way." This action occurred before the medal was authorized on July 12, 1862. The award was made January 21, 1894.

Medal of Honor (Army) was authorized July 12, 1862 (12 Stat.L.623), to be given in the name of Congress "to such non-commissioned officers and privates as shall most distinguish themselves by their gallantry in action and other soldier-like qualities during the present insurrection." The first award was made to six members of a raiding party of twenty who in 1862 penetrated the Confederate lines for more than two hundred miles and destroyed bridges and tracks between Chattanooga and Atlanta. A congressional act of March 3, 1863 (12 Stat.L.751), authorized the award to commissioned officers. It is conferred upon those who have distinguished themselves in actual conflict with the enemy by gallantry and intrepidity at the risk of life beyond the call of duty. (*Theophilus Francis Rodenbough —Uncle Sam's Medal of Honor*)

Medal of Honor awarded in the Korean War was presented on September 30, 1950, by President Harry S. Truman to Major General William Frische Dean of Berkeley, Calif., commanding general of the 24th Infantry Division, who at the battle for Taejon on July 20-21, 1950, personally and alone attacked an enemy tank while armed with only a hand grenade. Other recipients at the ceremony were Private First Class Melvin L. Brown of Mahaffey, Pa., and First Lieutenant Frederick F. Henry of Clinton, Okla. Posthumous awards were also made to Sergeant Charles W. Turner of Boston, Mass., and Master Sergeant Travis E. Watkins of Gladewater, Texas.

Medal of Honor awarded in World War II was presented on February 10, 1942, by Major General Walter H. Frank, commander of the Third Air Force, at Tampa, Fla., to Alexander Ramsey Nininger posthumously for Second Lieutenant Alexander Ramsey ("Sandy") Nininger, Jr., for heroism in action in the vicinity of Abucay, Bataan, Philippine Islands, on January 12, 1942.

Medal of Honor awarded to a conscientious objector was presented on October 12, 1945, by President Harry S. Truman to Private First Class Desmond T. Doss of Lynchburg, Va., for outstanding bravery as a medical corpsman on Okinawa in specific acts between April 29 and May 21, 1945.

Medal of Honor awarded to a helicopter pilot was conferred posthumously upon Lieutenant (Junior Grade) John Kelvin Koelsch of Hudson, N.Y., on April 8, 1955, and presented to his next of kin on August 3, 1955. On July 3, 1951, Koelsch and Aviation Machinist Mate George M. Neal volunteered, took off without fighter escort, and rescued James V. Wilkins in North Korea. The helicopter was shot down and the three men were captured a few days later. Koelsch died of malnutrition and dysentery in a Korean prisoner of war camp on October 16, 1951.

Medal of Honor awarded to a Jewish soldier was conferred upon Sergeant Leopold Karpeles of Springfield, Mass., of Company E, 57th Massachusetts Infantry, who while color bearer rallied the retreating troops at the Battle of the Wilderness, Va., on May 6, 1864, and induced them to check the enemy's advance. The award was authorized July 12, 1864, and the date of issue was April 30, 1870.

MEDAL—*Continued*

Medal of Honor awarded to a Marine was presented to Sergeant John Mackie by Commander Henry Rolando under authorization of General Order No. 17 dated July 10, 1862. During the attack on Fort Darling at Drewrys Bluff, James River, Va., on May 15, 1862, Mackie rallied the Marine Guard on the U.S.S. "Galena" after the entire Third Division manning four 10-inch Dahlgren guns and 100-pound rifles was killed or wounded. He cleared the deck and resumed the action without awaiting orders.

Medal of Honor awarded to a Marine in the Korean War was presented to Lieutenant Henry Alfred Commiskey of Hattiesburg, Miss., who on September 20, 1950, near Yongdungpo, outside Seoul, Korea, armed with a pistol, killed seven enemy soldiers in hand-to-hand combat. The medal, the thirtieth medal award of the Korean War, was presented on August 1, 1951, by President Harry S. Truman at the White House, Washington, D.C.

Medal of Honor awarded to a member of the Naval Service was authorized by act of Congress, December 21, 1861 (12 Stat.L.330), which authorized 200 medals for gallantry in action and other seaman-like qualities during the Civil War. The first awards were made to 36 recipients by General Order No. 11 of April 3, 1863. The first heroic deed for which the Medal of Honor was awarded was performed by John Williams, captain of the maintop of the U.S.S. "Pawnee" during an attack on Matthias Point on June 26, 1861.

Medal of Honor awarded to a Nisei (American of Japanese parentage) in U.S. service was conferred upon Private First Class Sadao S. Munemori of Co. A, 100th Infantry Battalion, 442nd Combat Team, for action near Seravezza, Italy, on April 5, 1945, when he knocked out two machine guns with grenades and saved the life of two of his companions by diving on an exploding grenade. The medal was presented posthumously on March 13, 1946, to his mother, Mrs. Nawa Munemori.

Medal of Honor awarded to a Nisei in the Korean War was awarded August 26, 1953, to Sergeant Hiroshi Hershey Miyamura of Gallup, N.M., for his heroism in covering the retreat of his squad on April 25, 1951, and holding a position at Imjin River while he was attached to the Third Regiment of the Seventh Division. He was captured and held a prisoner for twenty-eight months. He was repatriated from a prisoner of war camp in Korea to Freedom Village, Korea, where the award was made by Brigadier General Ralph Osborne. The medal was presented on October 27, 1953, by President Dwight David Eisenhower at ceremonies held at the White House, Washington, D.C.

Medal of Honor awarded to a pilot. *See* Aviation—Aviator: Pilot to receive the Congressional Medal of Honor

Medal of Honor awarded to a soldier who already had received a Distinguished Service Cross in World War II was presented to Gerry Kisters of Bloomington, Ind., by President Franklin Delano Roosevelt on June 21, 1943, for heroism in the Sicily campaign. The Distinguished Service Cross had been awarded to him by General George Catlett Marshall in May 1943, for bravery in Africa.

National Aeronautics and Space Administration Distinguished Service Medal was presented by President John Fitzgerald Kennedy in Washington, D.C., on May 8, 1961, to astronaut Alan Bartlett Shepard, Jr., for making America's first space flight. Shepard's flight, 302 miles down the Atlantic missile range from Cape Canaveral, Florida, at an altitude of 115 miles, was made on May 5, 1961.

See also Astronauts: Space flight by an American astronaut

National Geographic Society gold medal was the Hubbard medal, presented December 15, 1906, in Washington, D.C., by President Theodore Roosevelt to Commander Robert Edwin Peary for Arctic explorations. (On December 15, 1909, Peary also received a medal for his discovery of the North Pole on April 6, 1909.) The Hubbard medal was first awarded to a woman on January 30, 1934, when the designee was Anne Morrow Lindbergh, copilot and radio operator of the Charles A. Lindbergh Aerial Survey. The medal was presented to Mrs. Lindbergh on March 31, 1934, in Washington, D.C., by Dr. Gilbert Grosvenor, president of the National Geographic Society.

National Geographic Society special gold medal was presented by President Herbert Clark Hoover at Constitution Hall, Washington, D.C., on June 21, 1932, to Amelia Earhart Putnam (Mrs. George Palmer Putnam) who on May 20-21, 1932, was the first woman to achieve a solo transatlantic flight.

National Institute of Arts and Letters gold medal was awarded posthumously on November 20, 1909, to Augustus Saint-Gaudens for his meritorious achievements in sculpture. (*American Academy of Arts and Letters—Public Meeting of the American Academy and the National Institute of Arts and Letters at the Fine Arts Society, New York, November 20, 1909. . .*)

Navy Cross awarded to a Coast Guard officer in World War II was presented on June 4, 1942, to Lieutenant Maurice D. Jester in command of the 165-foot Coast Guard "Icarus"

THE FIRST

off the Carolina coast which sank an enemy submarine, captured the commanding officer, his first mate and thirty-one members of the crew and brought them as prisoners to Charleston, S.C.

Navy Expert Pistol Shot Medal awarded to a woman was presented to Ensign Rosalie Thorne of the Bureau of Aeronautics who qualified August 4, 1943, as a pistol expert by making 211 out of a possible 240 points.

Navy-Marine Corps medal for heroism awarded to a woman was presented on August 7, 1953, to Staff Sergeant Barbara Olive Barnwell, of Pittsburgh, Pa., U.S. Marine Corps Reserve, by General Lemuel Cornick Shepherd, Jr., Commandant of the U.S. Marine Corps, in Washington, D.C. She saved Private First Class Frederick G. Romann from drowning on June 7, 1952, at Onslow Beach, Camp Lejeune, N.C.

Navy Unit Commendation decoration for heroism in action against the enemy and for extremely meritorious military service not involving combat, but not sufficient to justify award of the Presidential Unit Citation, was established December 20, 1944. Members of units winning this award (for performing as a unit service of a character comparable to that which would merit the award of a Silver Star Medal or a Legion of Merit to an individual) are entitled to wear a ribbon having a wide myrtle-green stripe in the center with smaller cardinal red, Spanish yellow, and royal blue stripes extending to the edge in that order on either side. The first award of the Navy Unit Commendation to a ship or unit was granted on March 11, 1945, to the light cruiser "Helena": "Her brave record of combat achievement is evidence of the 'Helena's' intrepidity and the heroic fighting spirit of her officers and men." The "Helena" was lost July 1943 in Kula Gulf.

Order of the Purple Heart, a decoration for "military merit," was established by George Washington on August 7, 1782, at Newburgh, N.Y., and was the first honor badge for enlisted men and noncommissioned officers. The first recipients of this honor "for singularly meritorious action" were Sergeants Daniel Bissell, William Brown, and Elijah Churchill of Connecticut regiments, decorated May 9, 1783. They were entitled "to wear on facings over the left breast, the figure of a heart in purple cloth or silk, with narrow lace or binding."

Order of the Purple Heart awarded in the Korean War was presented by Major General Edgar Erskine Hume, chief surgeon of the Far East Command, on July 8, 1950, in Tokyo, Japan, to Sergeant Leroy Deans, 22, of Alice, Tex., for an eye injury received June 28, 1950, when a Han River bridge was blown up.

THE FIRST

Order of the Purple Heart awarded to a nurse was conferred on Captain Annie G. Fox "for outstanding performance of duty and meritorious acts of extraordinary fidelity and essential service" during the attack on Hickam Field, Hawaii, on December 7, 1941.

Pilot to receive the Congressional Medal of honor. *See* Aviation—Aviator: Pilot to receive the Congressional Medal of Honor.

Platinum medal made by the United States Mint was presented to President Herbert Hoover on December 1, 1932, by the George Washington Bicentennial Commission of which he was chairman. The medal was made in the Federal Mint in Philadelphia, Pa., and was three inches in diameter. It contained enough platinum for 120 wedding rings.

Presidential citation in peacetime was awarded August 8, 1958, to the 116-man crew of the submarine "Nautilus" which made a 1,830-mile underwater crossing of the North Pole on August 3, 1958, under the command of William Robert Anderson.

Presidential citation to an entire division was made March 15, 1945, to the 101st Airborne Division, the heroes of Bastogne, by General Dwight David Eisenhower, somewhere on the western front. From December 18 to December 27, 1944, the division withstood tremendous odds. (*Samuel Lyman Atwood Marshall—Bastogne, the First Eight Days*)

Recipient of the four highest decorations awarded by the United States was Lieutenant Colonel William Joseph ("Wild Bill") Donovan, who received the Medal of Honor, the Distinguished Service Cross, and the Distinguished Service Medal for meritorious conduct in combat in 1918 in France and the National Security Medal on April 4, 1957, for his service as director of the Office of Strategic Services from June 13, 1942, to October 1, 1945.

Reserve Officers Association medal was presented on January 15, 1953, to President Harry S. Truman, who retired as a colonel after thirty years of service. The medal, with two clusters, was presented in the Rose Garden of the White House by Brigadier General Fred Marshall Warren of Fort Thomas, Ky., vice president of the association.

Silver Star Army Medal awarded to a civilian was presented by General Douglas MacArthur to Vern Haugland, Associated Press correspondent, on October 3, 1942. He was a passenger on an army airplane forced to descend in New Guinea. After forty-three days in the jungle, he reached civilization.

MEDAL—*Continued*

Silver Star Medal awarded to a civilian by the U.S. Navy in World War II, presented to Tony Duenas, a Guam native, was approved March 3, 1945. The second award, approved May 22, 1945, was made to Donald H. Russell of Orange, Conn., for gallantry aboard the carrier "Franklin" when it was hit off Kyushu. He was a technician assigned to keep the Corsair planes in fighting condition. The presentation was made by Rear Admiral Monroe Kelly.

Soldier to receive seven decorations at one time was Llewellyn M. Chilson of Berwyn, Pa., a technical sergeant in the 45th Division, who was presented with the Distinguished Service Cross with two Oak Leaf clusters, the Silver Star and one Oak Leaf cluster, the Legion of Merit and the Bronze Star by President Harry S. Truman on December 6, 1946, in Washington, D.C.

Soldier to win the three highest ranking decorations for valor in combat was Maurice Lee Britt of Lonoke, Ark., who received the Silver Star for action at Acerno, Italy, September 1943; the Medal of Honor for action November 7-12, 1943, at Mount Rotundo, Italy; and the Distinguished Service Cross for heroism in action on January 24, 1944, near Campo Morto, Italy. He also received the Purple Heart with three Oak Leaf clusters, the Military Cross of the British Empire, the Combat Infantryman Badge, and a Distinguished Unit Badge awarded his unit, the Third Battalion.

Soldier's Medal awarded to a woman was conferred on nurse Edith Greenwood June 21, 1943, for heroism in saving the lives of her patients in a fire in a station hospital near Yuma, Ariz., on April 17, 1943.

Soldier's Medal awarded to a Women's Army Corps member was presented November 17, 1943, to Private Margaret Helen Maloney of Rochester, N.Y., by Major General Everett Strait Hughes at Allied Headquarters, Algiers, for rescuing Private Kenneth J. Jacobs from a pool of burning gasoline.

Woman to have her likeness on a medal issued by the United States Mint was Nellie Tayloe Ross. The obverse of the three-inch medal showed her profile and the date when she became Director of the Mint, 1933. The reverse, with the seal of the Mint at the top, showed her seated with assay balances, coins, bullion, and coining press. The medal was designed by John Ray Sinnock and was issued in June 1935.

MEDIATION. *See* Labor: National mediation board

MEDIATION AND CONCILIATION BOARD (federal). *See* Arbitration: Federal Board of Mediation and Conciliation

MEDIATION AND CONCILIATION BOARD (state). *See* Arbitration: State board of mediation and arbitration

MEDICAL ALMANAC. *See* Almanac: Patent medicine almanac

MEDICAL BOOK

Anatomy book was *A Compendious System of Anatomy* (an extract from the American edition of the *Encyclopaedia Britannica*) which was published in 1792 by Thomas Dobson in Philadelphia, Pa. It contained 438 pages and 12 anatomical plates and was divided into six parts covering osteology, the muscles, the abdomen, the thorax, the brain and nerves, and the senses.

Anatomy book (American) was *A System of Anatomy for the Use of Students of Medicine,* by Dr. Caspar Wistar, professor of anatomy at the medical school of the University of Pennsylvania from 1808 to 1818. The book contained 422 pages and was published in 1811 by Thomas Dobson in Philadelphia, Pa.

Aviation medicine book was *Aviation Medicine,* 241 pages, by Dr. Louis Hopewell Bauer, commandant of the School of Aviation Medicine. The book was published by Williams & Wilkins Co., Baltimore, Md., in 1926.

Bacteriology textbook was *Bacteria,* by Dr. Antoine Magnin, translated from the French by George Miller Sternberg, M.D., Surgeon of the United States Army. The 227-page book was published in 1880 by Little, Brown & Co., Boston, Mass. (*Martha L. Sternberg—George Miller Sternberg*)

Bronchitis treatise was published in 1846 by Horace Green, Professor of Theory and Practice of Medicine at the New York Medical College, and was entitled *Treatise on the Diseases of the Air Passages comprising an Inquiry into the History, Pathology, Causes and Treatment of those affections of the Throat called Bronchitis, Chronic Laryngitis, Clergyman's Sore Throat.* (*Johann Hermann Baas—Outlines of the History of Medicine*)

Chiropody book was *Surgical and Practical Observations on the Diseases of the Human Foot* by Issachar Zacharie, published in 1860 in New York City.

Croup report (printed) was published in 1781 by H[ugh] Gaine, New York City. It consisted of a report made to William Hunter, M.D., by Richard Bayley, Surgeon, N.Y., en-

THE FIRST

titled "Cases of the Angina Trachealis with the Mode of Cure." He reported that his observances dated from April 1774.

Dermatology treatise was *The Atlas of Skin Diseases* by Dr. Louis Adolphus Duhring, professor of skin diseases at the medical school of the University of Pennsylvania. The first section was published in 1876 in Philadelphia, Pa.

Dispensatory was the *American Dispensatory, Containing the Operations of Pharmacy, Together With the Natural, Chemical, Pharmaceutical and Medical History of the Different Substances Employed in Medicine,* by John Redman Coxe. It was printed in 1806 in Philadelphia, Pa., by A. Bartram for Thomas Dobson. It was a simplified arrangement of Dr. Duncan's *Edinburgh New Dispensatory,* and contained 787 pages and 6 plates.

Dispensatory (American) was the *Dispensatory of the United States of America,* 1092 pages, published in 1833 in Philadelphia, Pa., by Grigg and Elliot. It was prepared by Dr. George Bacon Wood, professor of materia medica and pharmacy, and Dr. Franklin Bache, professor of chemistry, at the Philadelphia College of Pharmacy.

Dissection essay appeared in 1750. It was a report by Dr. John Bard and Dr. Peter Middleton who in 1750 in New York City dissected the body of Hermanus Carroll, a criminal executed for murder. (*Dr. James Thacher—American Medical Biography. 1828*)

Gastroenterology treatise was *An Experimental Inquiry into the Principles of Nutrition and the Digestive Processes,* a 48-page graduation thesis submitted by John Richardson Young at the University of Pennsylvania, Philadelphia, Pa. It was published by Eaken & Mecum, Philadelphia, Pa., in 1803.

Hay fever book was Morrill Wyman's *Autumnal Catarrh—Hay Fever,* published in 1872 by Hurd & Houghton, New York City. It was dedicated to Jeffries Wyman, professor of anatomy, Harvard University School of Medicine, and contained 173 pages and 3 maps. Hay fever was known as "Catarrhus Autumnalis."

Hemophilia treatise was prepared by Dr. John Conrad Otto of Philadelphia, Pa., who stated that the hemorrhagic tendency was transmitted through the females to the males but that the females were not susceptible themselves. His report appeared in 1803 in the *Medical Repository & Review of American Publications on Medicine and Surgery,* and was entitled "An Account of an Haemorrhagic Disposition Existing in Certain Families."

THE FIRST

The magazine was published in New York City. (*Francis Randolph Packard—History of Medicine in the U.S.*)

Homeopathic treatise was Christian Friedrich Samuel Hahnemann's *Geist der Homöopathischen Heil-Lehre,* translated by Dr. Hans Birch Gram and published as a 24-page pamphlet entitled *The Characteristics of Homöopathia.* The book was issued in December 1825 by J. & J. Harper, New York City.

Hydrophobia book was James Thacher's *Observations on Hydrophobia, Produced by the Bite of a Mad Dog or Other Rabid Animal,* published in 1812 by Joseph Avery at Plymouth, Mass.

Hydrotherapy book in English was Dr. Simon Baruch's *The Uses of Water in Modern Medicine,* published in 1892 in Detroit, Mich., by George S. Davis. It was published in two volumes of 115 pages and 228 pages.

Medical book for army medical use was *A Journal of the Practice of Medicine, Surgery and Pharmacy in the Military Hospitals of France, published by order of the King.* Reviewed and digested by M. De Horne, under the inspection of the Royal Society. Only one volume appeared. The 120-page octavo book, printed in 1790 by J. M. McLean & Co., New York City, was translated from the French by Joseph Browne. The French edition consisting of seven volumes was published from 1782 to 1788.

Medical encyclopedia was the *American Cyclopedia of Practical Medicine and Surgery; A Digest of Medical Literature,* edited by Isaac Hays, surgeon to Wills' Hospital and physician to the Philadelphia Orphan Asylum, published by Carey, Lea & Blanchard, Philadelphia, Pa. Only two volumes of the work were published, covering "A to Azygores": Volume 1, 1834, 560 pages, and Volume 2, 1836, 589 pages.

Medical jurisprudence treatise (authoritative) was Theodoric Romeyn Beck's *Elements of Medical Jurisprudence,* a two-volume work published in 1823 in Albany, N.Y.

Medical pamphlet in America was published on January 21, 1677. It was a treatise on smallpox entitled *Brief Rule to Guide the Common People of New England how to Order themselves and theirs in the Small Pocks or Measles.* It was published in Boston, Mass., by Thomas Thacher and consisted of a single sheet of 15½ by 10½ inches. (*Fielding Hudson Garrison—History of Medicine*)

Mental diseases book was *Medical Inquiries and Observations upon the Diseases of the Mind,* by Benjamin Rush, published in Phila-

MEDICAL BOOK—*Continued*
delphia, Pa., in 1812. (*William Staughton—An Eulogium in Memory of the Late Dr. Benjamin Rush*)

Neurasthenia book was George Miller Beard's *A Practical Treatise on Nervous Exhaustion (Neurasthenia); Its symptoms, nature, sequences and treatment.* It contained 198 pages and was published in 1880 by M. Wood & Company, New York City. Beard's first article on this subject appeared April 29, 1869, in the *Boston Medical and Surgical Journal.*

Neurology textbook was Dr. William Alexander Hammond's *The Diseases of the Nervous System,* divided into five sections covering diseases of the brain, spinal cord, cerebro-spinal system, nerve cells, and peripheral nerves. It was published in 1871 in New York City and was edited by Dr. Thaddeus M. B. Cross. The book consisted of Hammond's lectures delivered at the New York State Hospital for Diseases of the Nervous System and Bellevue Hospital Medical College, New York City.

Obstetrics book was Samuel Bard's *A Compendium of the Theory and Practice of Midwifery,* a 239-page book published in 1807 by Collins & Perkins, New York City.

Ophthalmology book was *A Treatise on the Diseases of the Eye; Including the Doctrines and Practice of the Most Eminent Modern Surgeons, and Particularly those of Professor [George Joseph] Beer,* by Dr. George Frick, Ophthalmic Surgeon to the Baltimore General Dispensary, Baltimore, Md. It was published by Fielding Lucas, Jr., and printed by John D. Toy in Baltimore, Md., in 1823.

Pathology textbook was *A Treatise on Pathological Anatomy* which was published in Philadelphia, Pa., in 1829. It contained 460 pages. The author was William Edmonds Horner, who in 1831 was appointed professor of anatomy in the medical school of the University of Pennsylvania, Philadelphia, Pa.

Pediatrics book was *The Maternal Physician; A Treatise on the Nurture and Management of Infants, from the Birth until Two Years Old, Being the Result of Sixteen Years' Experience in the Nursery,* published in Philadelphia, Pa., in 1810 by "An American Matron."

Pediatrics book of importance was Dr. Luther Emmett Holt's *The Care and Feeding of Children, a Catechism for the Use of Mothers and Children's Nurses,* 66 pages, published in 1894 by D. Appleton & Company, New York City. It was dedicated to Mrs. Chapin,

"the founder of the first training school for nurses of infants in America." (*Robert Luther Holt and L. Emmett Holt, Jr.—L. Emmett Holt, Pioneer of a Children's Century*)

Pediatrics monograph was Charles Caldwell's *An Attempt to Establish the Original Sameness of Those Phenomena of Fever, (Principally confined to Infants and Children) Described by Medical Writers Under the Several Names of Hydrocephalus Internus, Cynanche Trachealis and Diarrhoea Infantum,* a thesis presented May 17, 1796, for a degree at the University of Pennsylvania Medical School, Philadelphia, Pa. It was published in Philadelphia, Pa., by Thomas Dobson. (*Transactions of the American Pediatric Society. Vol. 9. 1897*).

Pharmacopoeia. *See* Pharmacopoeia

Surgery manual was *Plain, Concise Practical Remarks on the Treatment of Wounds and Fractures; to which is added a short appendix on camp and military hospitals; principally designed for the use of young military surgeons in North America,* 92 pages, printed in 1775 by John Holt, New York City. The author was Dr. John Jones, professor of surgery in King's College (now Columbia University), New York City. (*American Journal of Surgery—December 1934*)

Therapeutics and materia medica book was *Discourses on the Elements of Therapeutics and Materia Medica,* published in 1817 in Philadelphia, Pa., by Nathaniel Chapman. (*Samuel David Gross—Lives of Eminent American Physicians and Surgeons*)

Tuberculosis circular. *See* Tuberculosis circular

Typhus fever treatise was Elisha North's *History of the Typhus Petechialis, or the Malignant petechial or Spotted Fever, as it appeared in Goshen, Conn., during the winter 1807-1808 with such remarks as may tend to elucidate its nature and to establish the best method of care,* which appeared in 1809 in *The Philadelphia Medical Museum,* published in Philadelphia, Pa. (*Philadelphia Medical Museum. Volume 6*)

MEDICAL CHEMISTRY COURSE. *See* Medical instruction: Medical chemistry course (systematic)

MEDICAL CLINIC
Birth control clinic was opened on October 16, 1916, at 46 Amboy Street, Brooklyn, N.Y., by Fania Mindell, Ethel Byrne, and Margaret Sanger. A dodger circular announcing its

THE FIRST

opening was printed in English, Yiddish, and Italian. (*Margaret Sanger—My Fight for Birth Control*)

Cancer clinic (traveling) was established on February 14, 1946, by the Oklahoma Division, American Cancer Society of Oklahoma City, Okla. A school bus was remodeled to convey equipment and instruments necessary for establishing four examination rooms which were presided over by an internist, a dermatologist, a gynecologist, and a surgeon. All services were rendered free of charge and both physicians and nurses serving on the staff donated both time and expenses. Clinics were usually set up in church classrooms. The first clinic was set up in Tonkawa, Kay County, Okla.

Cancer prevention clinic for children was the Kate Depew Strang Foundation Prevention Clinic opened January 3, 1947, in the Prevention Clinic of Memorial Hospital, New York City.

Children's clinic was established in 1862 by the Medical Faculty of the University of the City of New York under the leadership of Dr. Abraham Jacobi. (*Solomon Robert Kagan—Leaders of Medicine*)

College medical clinic was established in 1840 by Dr. Willard Parker, Professor of Surgery in the College of Physicians and Surgeons, New York City. He opened a dispensary where out-patients were brought to be examined and treated in the presence of the medical students. Clinics were held one day a week, but the service was later extended. (*John Call Dalton—History of the College of Physicians and Surgeons*)

Contraceptive clinic (state) was opened March 15, 1937, in Raleigh, N.C., when the North Carolina State Board of Health officially introduced a program setting up contraceptive clinics for indigent married women in the regular maternity and child health services as locally administered. The director was Dr. George Marion Cooper of the Division of Preventive Medicine. Roberta Pratt, a Raleigh nurse, was employed to cooperate with the health officers.

Flying medical clinic left the United States in January 1930 to attend the Pan American Medical Association convention in Panama City, Panama. It was composed of physicians who demonstrated the latest methods in surgery and medicine in local hospitals in Guatemala, Nicaragua, Panama, Colombia, Venezuela and other Central American countries. The first demonstration of an operation was made on January 25, 1930, by Dr. Fred Houdlett Albee.

THE FIRST

Heredity clinic was opened November 12, 1941, by the Department of Human Heredity, a research unit of the Laboratory of Vertebrate Genetics, University of Michigan, Ann Arbor, Mich., under the direction of Dr. Lee Raymond Dice. It secured data on the role that heredity plays and furnished advice to families about matters in which heredity is a factor.

Laryngology clinic was established in March 1863 by the Medical Faculty of the University of the City of New York under the supervision of Dr. Louis Elsberg. (*Laryngoscope. Vol. 15. 1905*)

Medical clinic (general) of importance was opened by the Johns Hopkins Medical School, Baltimore, Md., in October 1889. The Johns Hopkins Hospital was opened in May 1889. Sir William Osler, Regius Professor of Medicine at Oxford, was the first Physician-in-Chief of the Johns Hopkins Hospital and Professor of Medicine at the Johns Hopkins Medical School. In this dual role, he was the director of the medical clinic, but he was without that title. (*William Henry Welch—Johns Hopkins Medical School*)

Ophthalmology clinic was opened by the Fifth Avenue Hospital, New York City, in September 1932. The clinic was devoted to the treatment of ocular muscle imbalances (including some types of cross-eye). The clinic was under the direction of Le Grand Haven Hardy, M.D., Director of Eye Service.

MEDICAL COLLEGE. *See* Medical school: Medical college

MEDICAL CONGRESS

Cancer institute (convention) was attended by 530 persons, September 7-8, 1936, at the University of Wisconsin, Madison, Wis. The Wisconsin Alumni Research Foundation made available the necessary funds to finance the institute. Dr. William Shainline Middleton, dean of the medical school, served as chairman. The institute was opened by Dr. Glenn Frank, president of the University of Wisconsin. The conference emphasized the need for cooperation between medical authorities and public health departments to reduce cancer incidence.

Fever Therapy International Conference was held March 29-31, 1937, at the College of Physicians and Surgeons, Columbia University, New York City, and attended by physicians from sixteen countries.

Mental Hygiene International Congress opened May 4, 1930, in Washington, D.C., with Dr. William Alanson White presiding. The sessions were attended by 3,000 persons from 53 countries, workers in mental hygiene and related fields.

MEDICAL CORPS (Army). *See* Army: Medical corps

MEDICAL ENCYCLOPEDIA. *See* Medical book: Medical encyclopedia

MEDICAL INSTRUCTION
See also Medical school

Anatomy lectures (scientific) to medical students were given by Dr. William Shippen at the College of Philadelphia, Pa., from 1762 to 1765. Public lectures on anatomy were given in Boston, Mass., in 1789 by John Jeffries, but public opinion was so much against his policy of dissecting that at the second lecture a mob invaded the lecture room and carried off the body of a convict on which he was demonstrating. Further lectures were stopped as a result of public animosity. (*Casper Wistar— Eulogium on Dr. William Shippen*)

Bacteriology courses in a college were given by the Hygienic Laboratory of the University of Michigan, Ann Arbor, Mich. The laboratory was established in 1887, and the first class in bacteriology was instituted by Dr. Victor Clarence Vaughan and Dr. Frederick George Novy in January 1889. Classes were in session four hours daily for three months. In 1890-1891 bacteriology became a required course for medical students.

Bacteriology lectures in a medical school were given in 1885 by Harold Clarence Ernst at the Harvard Medical School, Cambridge, Mass. (*Journal of Medical Research—1903*)

Clinical instruction and bedside demonstration were introduced in 1818 by Alexander Hodgdon Stevens. It is said that in his operations as surgeon of the New York Hospital he often purposely avoided the neatness deemed so essential by other surgeons, in order to show his students that it was not essential to the recovery of the patient, provided the surgeon's skill and rapidity of manipulation were great enough. (*John Glover Adams—Discourse Commemorative of the Life and Character of Alexander Hodgdon Stevens, M.D., LL.D*)

Dermatology chair was founded by Harvard University, Cambridge, Mass., in 1871, when Dr. James Clarke White was made Professor of Dermatology. He was a lecturer in the medical school, 1863-64; adjunct professor of chemistry, 1866-71; instructor in medical chemistry, 1871-72. He was the first president of the American Dermatological Association founded in 1876.

History of Medicine Department with a full salaried professor and staff was the In-

stitute of the History of Medicine, inaugurated October 18, 1929, by Johns Hopkins University, Baltimore, Md. Dr. William Henry Welch was the first Professor of the History of Medicine and Dr. Stephen d'Irsay was Associate. (*Bulletin of the Johns Hopkins Hospital Vol. 46. 1930*)

Hygiene lectures offered by a college were delivered in 1818 by Dr. James Jackson, Hersey Professor of the Theory and Practice of Physic, at Harvard College, Cambridge, Mass. The committee decided on October 8, 1818, "that he be required to deliver a number of lectures on subjects relating to the care and preservation of health, and that they be this year delivered to the members of the two upper classes, at the hour appointed on Friday for a public lecture to those classes."

Instruction for nurses. *See* Nursing school: Instruction for nurses

Laryngology instruction was offered regularly by the Medical Department of the University of the City of New York in the autumn of 1861. Dr. Louis Elsberg was a Lecturer on the Laryngoscope and Diseases of the Throat and Larynx 1863-1864. From 1869 to 1873 he was Clinical Professor of Diseases of the Throat and from 1873 to 1881 Professor of Diseases of the Throat and Laryngology. (*Transactions. American Laryngological Association. Vol. 1. 1879*)

Medical chemistry course (systematic) was offered in 1871 by Dr. Edward Stickney Wood, Assistant Professor of Chemistry, at the Harvard Medical School, Cambridge, Mass.

Medical jurisprudence course was given by Dr. James Stringham, Professor of Medical Jurisprudence at the College of Physicians and Surgeons, Columbia University, New York City, from 1813 to 1817. Prior to this appointment, he served as Professor of Chemistry.

Medical research chair in an American university was the John Herr Musser chair, established in 1910 by the School of Medicine, University of Pennsylvania, Philadelphia, Pa. The first incumbent was Professor Richard Mills Pearce. (*Medical Research and Education. 1913*)

Midwifery professor was Dr. John Van Brugh Tennent, appointed Professor of Midwifery at King's College (now Columbia University), New York City, in 1767. He held this post until his death in 1770.

THE FIRST

Ophthalmology course (regular) was established in 1823 at the Ophthalmic Clinic, Baltimore General Dispensary, University of Maryland, Baltimore, Md.

Ophthalmology professor was Elkanah Williams, who was appointed by the Miami Medical College of Cincinnati, Ohio, in 1865.

Orthopedics chair was established by Bellevue Hospital Medical College, New York City, in 1861. The first incumbent was Dr. Lewis Albert Sayre. (*New England Medical Monthly.* June 1884)

Pathology chair was established at Harvard University, Cambridge, Mass., in 1847 when John Barnard Sweet Jackson was appointed Professor of Pathological Anatomy and Curator of the Warren Museum. The professorship was endowed by George Cheyne Shattuck in 1854. The first chair of modern pathology (after the field had been revolutionized by Louis Pasteur and his successors) was established in 1883 by Johns Hopkins University, Baltimore, Md. The first incumbent was Professor William Henry Welch.

Pediatrics professor was Dr. Abraham Jacobi, who lectured in 1857 at the College of Physicians and Surgeons (now the College of Physicians and Surgeons of Columbia University), New York City, and became Clinical Professor of Pediatrics in 1870. He held the post until 1899. (*Medical Life.* October 1926)

Plastic surgery professor in any medical school or hospital was Dr. Joseph Eastman Sheehan who was appointed in 1926 to that post by the New York Postgraduate Medical School and Hospital, New York City. (*Joseph Eastman Sheehan—A Manual of Reparative Plastic Surgery*)

Psychiatric institute, organized for research and the training of physicians, was the Pathological Institute, New York City, established by Chapter 545 of the Laws of 1896 of New York State, passed May 12, 1896, effective July 1, 1896. Dr. Ira Van Gieson was appointed the first director and served until June 1901. It was reorganized by Dr. Adolf Meyer, who took office December 1902. The name was changed to the New York State Psychiatric Institute and Hospital by a decision of the State Commission in Lunacy and announced in the report for the year 1908-1909, but the name was first used officially in the commission's handbook for 1909. In 1927, it became the Psychiatric department of the Columbia University-Presbyterian Hospital Medical Center and was housed in a new building dedicated December 3-4, 1929.

THE FIRST

Public hygiene professor was Dr. Thomas Bevan, appointed in 1868 by Northwestern University, Chicago, Ill. In 1869, the title was changed to Professor of Hygiene, and the chair was held by Dr. Bevan until 1875. From 1858 to 1867 the departments of pathology and public hygiene were combined.

State medicine and public hygiene professorship was established in 1882 by Northwestern University, Chicago, Ill. The first incumbent was Dr. Oscar Coleman De Wolf.

MEDICAL JOURNAL. *See* Medical periodical: Medical magazine

MEDICAL JURISPRUDENCE BOOK. *See* Medical book: Medical jurisprudence treatise

MEDICAL JURISPRUDENCE COURSE. *See* Medical instruction: Medical jurisprudence course

MEDICAL LEGISLATION
Blood grouping test laws (state) were passed by New York State in 1935. Two bills, amending the civil practice act and the inferior criminal courts act, to empower the court to order the making of blood tests, were introduced by Assemblyman Charles H. Breitbart on January 9, 1935, as well as a bill on February 15, 1935, to amend the domestic relations law. The three bills, Chapter 196, 197 and 198, laws of 1935, were signed by Governor Herbert Henry Lehman on March 22, 1935, to take effect immediately.

Chiropody law governing the study of chiropody was passed in New York City in 1895. It is difficult to ascertain which was the first school established, for the law required only the passing of an examination and demanded no prescribed course of study. For this reason many individuals "coached" prospective applicants for licenses, and those "schools" that did exist taught the theory of chiropody as a side-line of beauty culture.

Law (state) requiring marriage license applicants to undergo medical tests was enacted by New York. Chapter 640, Laws of 1938, "to amend the domestic relations law in relation to examinations and serological tests of applicants for a marriage license and effectual duration of the license for preventing the spread of syphilis," was signed April 12, 1938, by Governor Herbert Henry Lehman. The bill, known as the Demond-Breitbart Law, became effective July 1, 1938.

Law (state) requiring serological blood tests of pregnant women was Chapter 133, Laws of 1938, New York, the [Jeremiah F.]

MEDICAL LEGISLATION—*Continued*
Twomey-[William Allan] Newell bill signed
by Governor Herbert Henry Lehman on March
18, 1938, on which date it became effective.

Law to license the practice of medicine
was New Jersey's law of September 26, 1772.
The act was effective for a five-year period.
It authorized a licensing board consisting of
two judges of the Supreme Court of New
Jersey and a third individual appointed by
them, and forbade the practice of medicine
without a license. Very severe fines were imposed upon violators, but the law did not apply
to those who drew teeth, bled patients, or
gave medical assistance for which they received no fee or compensation.

Law to regulate the practice of medicine
(actually enforced) was an "act to regulate
the practice of Physick and Surgery in the City
of New York," passed June 10, 1760. It provided that "no person whatsoever shall practice
as a physician or surgeon . . . before he shall
first have been examined in physick or surgery and approved of and admitted by one of
His Majesty's Council, the Judges of the Supreme Court, the King's Attorney General and
the Mayor of the City of New York for the
time being or by any three or more of them."
Violators were subject to a penalty of five
pounds, one half of which went to the informer and the remainder to the poor funds.

Law to regulate the practice of medicine
(colonial) was enacted May 3, 1649, in
Massachusetts. "Physicians, chirurgians, midwives or others" were forbidden "to exercise
or put forth any act contrary to the known
rules of art, nor exercise any force, violence,
or cruelty upon or towards the bodies of any,
whether young or old." The act was "not intended to discourage the lawful use of their
skill but to encourage and direct them in the
right use thereof and to inhibit and restrain the
presumptious arrogance of such as . . . exercise violence upon . . . bodies." (*Colonial Laws
of Massachusetts*)

Medical law was passed by Virginia, October 21, 1639, an "act to compel physicians and
surgeons to declare on oath the value of their
medicines." (*William Waller Hening—Statutes
at Large. Vol. 1*)

Premature baby health law was passed
March 5, 1935, by Chicago, Ill., requiring
physicians to report the birth of all premature
babies within an hour after birth. A supple-
mental item was added to the official birth certificate to show whether or not a baby was
born prematurely.

Sterilization legislation. *See* Sterilization
legislation

MEDICAL PAMPHLET. *See* Medical
book: Medical pamphlet

MEDICAL PERIODICAL
Allergy magazine was the *Journal of Allergy*, published November 1929 in St. Louis,
Mo. It was edited by Dr. Harry Louis Alexander and the first issue contained 112 pages.

Homeopathic magazine was the *American
Journal of Homeopathia*, 48 pages, issued February 1835. It was edited by Drs. John F.
Gray and Amos Gerald Hull and published by
Moore and Payne, New York City. Subscription was $4 a year. Only four issues were
printed, February, April, June, and August,
1835.

Laryngology magazine was the *Archives of
Laryngology*, a 108-page quarterly, published in
New York City in March 1880. It was edited
by Dr. Louis Elsberg of New York City, Dr.
George Morewood Lefferts of New York City,
Dr. Jacob Solis-Cohen of Philadelphia, Pa., and
Dr. Frederick Irving Knight of Boston, Mass.

Medical magazine was published in New
York City on August 8, 1797, and was called
The Medical Repository, a "depository of facts
and reasonings relative to Natural History,
Agriculture and Medicine." It was published
quarterly and appeared until 1824. It was also
the first scientific periodical published in the
United States. The first editor was Dr. Samuel
Latham Mitchill, who continued in this capacity
for sixteen years. Drs. Edward Miller and
Elihu Hubbard Smith were also active in the
founding of this journal.

**Medical periodical devoted to diseases of
women and children** was the *American Jour-
nal of Obstetrics and Diseases of Women and
Children*, a quarterly, started May 1868 in
New York City. It was edited by Dr. Emil
Jacob Noeggerath and Dr. Benjamin Frederick
Dawson. The first issue contained 96 pages,
including an article by Dr. Abraham Jacobi on
"The Pathology and Treatment of the Different
Forms of Croup."

Negro medical journal was the *Medical
and Surgical Observer*, 32 pages and cover,
published in Jackson, Tenn., in December 1892.
It appeared regularly for eighteen months.
The first editor was Vandahurst Lynk, M.D.

Optometry magazine was *The Optician*, a
16-page monthly, edited and published by Frederick Boger, New York City, January 1891.
Subscription was 50 cents a year. In May
1892, the name was changed to *The Optician
and Allied Interests* and, in October 1892,
to *The Optician and Jeweler.*

THE FIRST

Osteopathy magazine was the *Journal of Osteopathy*, which was started in May 1894 by the American School of Osteopathy in Kirksville, Mo. The first editor was Dr. Jenette Hubbard Bolles.

Physiology magazine. *See* Physiology magazine

MEDICAL RESEARCH CHAIR. *See* Medical instruction

MEDICAL "ROGUES' GALLERY" listing medical quacks, manufacturers of spurious "cure-alls," peddlers of nostrums, "inventors" of diet, exercise, and other worthless systems, and others who prey on the ill and the gullible was started in January 1930 by the New York City Department of Health and is said to be the first of its kind in the world. The "gallery" was compiled by the National Better Business Bureau, Inc., at the suggestion of Special Deputy Health Commissioner Edward Fisher Brown.

MEDICAL SCHOOL

See also Medical instruction

Coeducational medical school was the Boston University School of Medicine, which was founded in 1873 (originally as a homeopathic school). When the New England Female Medical College was merged with it in 1874, the Boston University School of Medicine became the first coeducational medical school in the world.
See also Medical School: Women's medical school

Homeopathic college was the Homeopathic Medical College of Pennsylvania, Philadelphia, Pa., incorporated April 8, 1848. Preliminary instruction was given October 16, 1848. The regular course started with fifteen students on November 6, 1848, and concluded on March 1, 1849. Six students graduated at the commencement exercises March 29, 1849. Dr. Walter Williamson was the dean of the college.

Homeopathic school was the North American Academy of the Homeopathic Healing Art, founded April 10, 1835, in Allentown, Pa. The cornerstone was laid May 27, 1835. Chartered on June 17, 1836, the school was known as the Allentown Academy. The degree of "Doctor of Homoeopathia" was conferred upon graduates. Instruction was in German. Constantine Hering, who came to Philadelphia in 1832 from Germany, became the first president and principal instructor.

Institute for research. *See* Research institute

THE FIRST

Medical college was the College of Philadelphia Department of Medicine, now the University of Pennsylvania School of Medicine, which was established in Philadelphia, Pa., on May 3, 1765, principally through the efforts of Dr. William Shippen, Jr., and Dr. John Morgan, who became Professor of the Theory and Practice of Physick and Professor of Anatomy and Surgery, respectively. The school was started in a wooden building known as Surgeons' Hall. The first commencement was held June 21, 1768, and the first medical diplomas (Bachelor of Medicine) issued in America were presented to the ten members of the graduating class.

Medical college on the Pacific coast was the Medical Department of the University of the Pacific, opened at Santa Clara, Calif., in 1858 by Dr. Elias Samuel Cooper. (*University of the Pacific—1859 Announcement of Lectures*)

Medical school professor (woman). *See* College: Woman professor at a first-class medical school

Medical summer school was opened at the Medical College of South Carolina, Columbia, S.C., in 1853 by John Julian Chisholm. (*Centennial Memorial of the Medical College of the State of South Carolina*)

Naval medical school was the Naval Laboratory and Department of Instruction opened August 1, 1893, at the United States Naval Hospital, Brooklyn, N.Y. The first director was Henry M. Wells, appointed August 21, 1893, with the relative rank of captain.

Naval medical school (unofficial) was authorized May 19, 1823, and opened at the Navy Yard Hospital, Philadelphia, Pa., under the direction of Dr. Thomas Harris of the Pennsylvania Hospital, Philadelphia, Pa., who taught naval hygiene, military surgery, customs and usage of the naval service, etc. The Secretary of the Navy appropriated $400 for the support of the school, the expenses being paid by Dr. Harris from his own income. The school was discontinued by order of January 31, 1843.

Osteopathy school was the American School of Osteopathy, chartered in Kirksville, Mo., on May 10, 1892. It opened October 3, 1892, in a little frame cottage. It had an enrollment of about twenty students. Eighteen diplomas were granted to the first graduating class on March 2, 1894. Its purpose, according to the articles of incorporation, was "to improve our system of surgery, midwifery, and treatment of general diseases—the adjustment of the bones is the leading feature of this school." The founders were Dr. Andrew Taylor Still and Dr. William Smith. (*Andrew Taylor Still —Autobiography*)

MEDICAL SCHOOL—*Continued*
Women's medical school was the Boston Female Medical School, which was organized through the initiative of Samuel Gregory on November 1, 1848, with twelve pupils. The first lecturer was Enoch C. Rolfe, M.D. It later became the New England Female Medical College. In 1874 it was absorbed by the Boston University School of Medicine, which thus became the first coeducational medical school in the world. *(James Read Chadwick—The Study and Practice of Medicine)*
See also Medical school: Coeducational medical school

Women's medical school (still in existence as an independent institution), the Women's Medical College of Pennsylvania, was organized in 1850. The first class was graduated on December 30, 1851.

MEDICAL SOCIETY
American College of Surgeons was incorporated November 25, 1912, in Springfield, Ill., and was organized in Washington, D.C., May 5, 1913, "to elevate the standard of surgery, to establish a standard of competency and of character for practitioners of surgery, and to educate the public and the profession to understand that the practice of surgery calls for special training." The first annual convocation for the admission of fellows took place in Chicago, Ill., November 13, 1913. Dr. John Miller Turpin Finney of Baltimore, Md., was the first president. *(American College of Surgeons. Yearbook. 1913)*

"First aid" emergency organization. *See* "First aid" emergency organization

Homeopathic medical society was the Hahnemann Society, organized April 10, 1833, in Philadelphia, Pa., by Drs. Carl Ihm, George H. Bute, Charles F. Matlack, Constantine Hering, and William Wesselhoeft.

Immunology society was the American Association of Immunologists, organized in Minneapolis, Minn., June 19, 1913, with Dr. Gerald Bertram Webb as temporary chairman. The first annual meeting was held June 22, 1914, in Atlantic City, N.J. The original conception of the society was to bring together vaccine therapists, but in 1915 it developed into a scientific organization covering the whole field of immunology. Its purpose was to study problems of immunology and its application to clinical medicine.

Laryngological society (national) was the American Laryngological Association, founded June 3, 1878, in Buffalo, N.Y. The first president was Dr. Louis Elsberg; the first secretary and treasurer was Dr. George Morewood Lef-

ferts. The first annual meeting was held June 10, 1879, in New York City. *(American Laryngological Society. Transactions. 1879)*

Laryngological society (state) was the Laryngological Society of New York, organized in New York City in October 1873. Robert Fulton Weir was president; Clinton Wagner, vice president; and Woolsey Johnson, secretary. *(Fieldng Hudson Garrison—An Introduction to the History of Medicine)*

Medical society was founded in Boston, Mass., prior to 1735, and functioned until 1741. It was not very effective and was only local in character.

Medical society (national) of real permanence was the American Medical Association, which was organized May 5, 1847, in Philadelphia, Pa., in the Hall of the Academy of Natural Sciences. It was an outgrowth of the National Medical Association which had been organized a year before, on May 5, 1846. Dr. Jonathan Knight was the first president. This meeting was the first national convention of the medical profession. Two hundred and fifty delegates attended, representing twenty-two states, twenty-eight medical schools and forty medical societies.

Medical society (state) of consequence was the Massachusetts Medical Society, which was incorporated in Boston November 1, 1781. The charter was signed by Samuel Adams as President of the Senate, and by John Hancock as Governor of the Commonwealth. *(Samuel Abbott Green—History of Medicine in Massachusetts)*

Negro doctor to become a member of a medical association. *See* Physician: Negro doctor to become a member of a medical association

Negro medical society was the Medico-Chirurgical Society of the District of Columbia, organized April 24, 1884, in Washington, D.C. The first president was Dr. Robert Reyburn. The society was incorporated January 15, 1895. *(William Montague Cobb—The First Negro Medical Society)*

Woman member of the Association of American Physicians was Dr. Helen Brooke Taussig, who was elected May 3, 1950, at the sixty-third annual meeting held in Atlantic City, N.J.

Woman physician admitted to the American Institute of Homeopathy, Philadelphia, Pa., was Dr. Mercy Bisbee Jackson, who was

THE FIRST

accepted in 1871. (*Egbert Cleave—Biographical Cyclopedia of Homeopathic Physicians and Surgeons*)

Woman physician elected a member of the American Medical Association was Dr. Sarah Hackett Stevenson, who graduated from the Woman's Medical College of Chicago in 1874. She was elected to membership in the A.M.A. in 1876 at the Philadelphia meeting, having been sent there as a delegate from the Illinois State Medical Society. (*Sarah Hackett Stevenson—The Physiology of Woman Embracing Girlhood, Maternity and Mature Age*)

Woman president of a major medical society was Dr. Emma Sadler Moss of the Charity Hospital, New Orleans, La., who was elected president of the American Society of Clinical Pathologists on October 13, 1955, at the thirty-fourth annual meeting.

Woman president of a state medical society was Dr. Leslie Swigart Kent of Eugene, Ore., who was elected president of the Oregon Medical Society at a meeting held September 18, 1948, in Medford, Ore.

Women members of the American College of Surgeons were Dr. Alice Gertrude Bryant of Boston, Mass., a graduate (1890) of the Woman's Medical College of New York, and Dr. Florence West Duckering, also of Boston, a graduate (1901) of Tufts College Medical School, who became fellows of the society when 1,065 candidates were admitted at the second annual convocation held June 22, 1914, in Philadelphia, Pa.

Women's medical society was the Female Medical Educational Society of Boston, Mass., organized November 23, 1848, with six members "to provide and promote the education of midwives, nurses and female physicians, and to diffuse among women generally a knowledge of physiology and the principles and means of preserving and restoring health." Timothy Gilbert was president; Samuel Gregory, secretary; and John P. Jewett, treasurer. Membership was not confined to the professions.

MEDICATED PLASTER. *See* Adhesive and medicated plaster

MEDICINE

See also branches of medicine; phrases beginning with the word Medical (Medical books, Medical school); names of drugs; hospitals and types of hospitals; and names of diseases

Blood bank. *See* Blood bank

Bone bank was established in April 1946 by Dr. Leonard Franklin Bush and Dr. Clarence

THE FIRST

Zent Garber at the New York Orthopaedic Hospital and Dispensary, New York City, and by Dr. Philip Duncan Wilson at the Hospital for Special Surgery, New York City.

Tissue bank, applying the freeze-dried principle to the storage of human tissue grafts, was undertaken in 1954 at the United States Naval Medical School, National Naval Center, Bethesda, Md. It was under the supervision of Lieutenant Commander George William Hyatt. Tissues were procured for storage in a centralized unit.

MEDICINE BALL was invented by Robert Jeffries Roberts, physical education director of the Boston Young Men's Christian Association, in 1895, and first used in Boston, Mass. (*Benjamin Deane Brink—The Body Builder, Robert J. Roberts*)

MEDICINE (PATENT) ADVERTISEMENT. *See* Patent medicine advertisement

MEDIUM. *See* Spiritualist

MELODEON PATENT was No. 6,543 granted to C. Austin of Concord, N.H., on June 19, 1849. The melodeon was a small kind of reed organ and employed a suction bellows worked by treadles which drew the air through the reeds.

MELONS and cantaloupes were grown in Germantown, Pa., at the residence of E. B. Gardette on Wissahickon Avenue. The seed was brought over from Tripoli by Commodore James Barron in 1818.

MEMBER OF PARLIAMENT (American-born woman). *See* Woman: American-born woman to become a member of Parliament

MEMORIAL DAY. *See* Holiday: Decoration day

MEMORIAL STAMP. *See* Postage stamp: Memorial stamp

MENDELEVIUM. *See* Element: Element 101

MENNONITES

Mennonite church meeting-house was built in 1708 on the east side of Germantown Avenue, above Herman Street, Germantown, Pa. It was succeeded in 1770 by a stone building which is still in use. The first minister was William Rittenhouse (Rittinghuysen), who served for two years. (*John Thompson Faris—Old Churches and Meeting Houses In and Around Philadelphia*)

THE FIRST

MENNONITES—*Continued*
Mennonites arrived October 6, 1683, on the "Concord" from Crefeld, Germany. Thirteen families were induced to come to America through the generosity of William Penn who offered them land in Germantown, Pa., and freedom from religious persecution.

MENTAL DISEASES BOOK. *See* Medical book: Mental diseases book

MENTAL HYGIENE INTERNATIONAL CONGRESS. *See* Medical congress: Mental hygiene international congress

MERCANTILE LIBRARY. *See* Library: Mercantile library

MERCHANT MARINE
Merchant Marine Distinguished Service Medal. *See* Medal: Distinguished Service Medal (Merchant Marine)

Merchant Marine officer to hold the rank of rear admiral was Albert Borland Randall, commissioned Rear Admiral in the U.S. Naval Reserve as of February 1, 1942. He was appointed Commandant of the U.S. Maritime Service effective March 31, 1943. He was released from active duty on April 30, 1945, because of poor health, and died December 1, 1945.

MERCHANT MARINE ACADEMY
Merchant Marine Academy (U.S.) at Kings Point, N.Y., was dedicated September 30, 1943, when President Franklin Delano Roosevelt's message was read to 5,000 guests. The dedicatory address was delivered by Captain Edward Macauley, Maritime Commissioner. The course of instruction was 18 months. Previously, training had been held aboard ship and in temporary shore establishments.

Merchant Marine Cadet Corps (U.S.) was established March 15, 1938, following the passage of the Merchant Marine Act of June 29, 1936 (49 Stat.L.1985). The first class, started January 28, 1942, had an enrollment of 74 cadets. The first B.S. degree was awarded June 21, 1950, to 220 graduates. Degrees were subsequently awarded retroactively to all classes beginning with the class of December 1947. (*Irving Crump—Our Merchant Marine Academy*)

MERCHANT SHIP. *See* under Ship

MERCURY BOILER TURBINE. *See* Electric generator: Mercury boiler turbine

MERCURY VAPOR LAMP. *See* Electric lighting: Mercury vapor lamp

THE FIRST

MERGER (railroad). *See* Railroad: Railroad merger

MERINO SHEEP. *See* Animals: Sheep (Merino sheep)

MERRY-GO-ROUND. *See* Carrousel

MESH STEEL FLOORING BRIDGE. *See* Bridge: Bridge with open mesh steel flooring

METAL CARTRIDGE. *See* Ordnance: Metal cartridge

METAL PURCHASED FOR COINAGE. *See* Money: Metal purchased for coinage

METAL SKATE. *See* Skate (all-metal)

METEORIC DISPLAY. *See* Astronomy: Meteoric display

METEORITE
Meteorite containing a diamond. *See* Diamond: Diamonds in a meteorite

Meteorite known to have struck a woman crashed through the roof of a house at Sylacauga, Ala., on November 30, 1954, and struck Mrs. Elizabeth Hodges. It was a sulphide meteorite, weighed eight and a half pounds, and was seven inches long at its longest.

Photograph on which a meteor was found. *See* Photograph: Photograph (taken in the United States) on which a meteor was found.

METER (electric). *See* Electric meter

METHODIST
Methodist bishop was Francis Asbury, who was appointed in 1784 by Thomas Coke, to whom the title really belonged. They were known as the joint bishops of the Church in North America. Bishop Asbury was elected by the first General Conference, called the "Christmas Conference," which met December 24, 1784, in the Light Street Church, Baltimore, Md. (*Ezra Squier Tipple—Francis Asbury*)

Methodist missionary was Ebenezer Brown, sent out by the Methodist Missionary Society. In 1819 he was assigned a residence in New Orleans, La., to preach to the French people of Louisiana. (*Christian Advocate. January 1899*)

Methodist missionary bishop was Francis Burns. In September 1834 he sailed to Liberia with the Reverend John Seys. At the Liberia

THE FIRST

Annual Conference, January 1858, Burns was elected the first bishop. He returned to the United States and was ordained October 14, 1858, at the Genesee Conference by Bishops Janes and Baker.

Methodist preacher was Philip Embury who arrived August 11, 1760, in New York City on the "Perry," which carried seventy passengers, half of whom were Methodists. With the assistance of Barbara Heck, he organized the first Methodist Society in America in 1776. (*New York Mercury. August 18, 1760*)

Negro Methodist minister of an all-white congregation was the Reverend Simon Peter Montgomery of Pineville, S.C., who assumed the pulpit of the Old Mystic Methodist Church, Old Mystic, Conn., on October 2, 1955.

Negro minister with two white congregations was the Reverend Joseph Reed Washington, who on June 3, 1958, served as minister of the Methodist Church of Newfield and the Congregational Church of West Newfield, Maine, three miles apart.

METHODIST CHAPEL, or meeting house, was the Wesley Chapel, 42 by 60 feet, at 42 John Street, New York City, dedicated by Philip Embury, the first minister, October 30, 1768. It was a small frame house, one and a half stories high, built in antique Dutch style. It accommodated 700 people. (*Jesse Lee—A Short History of the Methodists in the United States*)

METHODIST COLLEGE was Cokesbury College, Abingdon, Md., named in honor of the two bishops, Thomas Coke and Francis Asbury. The building was 108 feet long, 40 feet wide, and 3 stories high. The first headmaster was the Reverend Mr. Heath. The foundation sermon was delivered June 5, 1785, and the building was opened December 6, 1787. (*George W. Archer—An Authentic History of Cokesbury College*)

METHODIST CONFERENCE was held July 16, 1773, in Philadelphia, Pa. It was called together by Thomas Rankin. In 1773 there were 1,160 Methodists in America whose spiritual care was administered by ten preachers. (*J. B. Eakeley—Lost Chapters Recovered from the Early History of American Methodism*)

METHODIST EPISCOPAL CHURCH

African Methodist Episcopal church was established April 9, 1816, in Philadelphia, Pa., by Bishop Richard Allen, who led the Negro Methodists to separate from the white church because of disturbances due to color discrimination. The first general convention of the

THE FIRST

African Methodist Episcopal Church was held in Philadelphia, Pa., April 9-11, 1816. Richard Allen was ordained April 11, 1816 as the first bishop by General Conference, and consecrated by five regularly ordained ministers. (*Richard Robert Wright—Centennial Encyclopedia of the African Methodist Episcopal Church.*)

Scandinavian Methodist Episcopal Church was organized in Cambridge, Wis., in April 1851 by the Reverend Christian B. Willerup with an initial membership of fifty-two. The Church was incorporated May 3, 1851, and a stone building, costing $4,000, was dedicated in the summer of 1852. This church is the oldest Methodist Episcopal church built by Scandinavians in this or any other country.

METRIC SYSTEM LEGALIZATION. *See* Weights and measures standardization

MEXICAN WAR. *See* War (Mexican)

MEZZOTINT. *See* Engraver

MICA

Mica was obtained from the Ruggles mine, Isinglass Mountain, Grafton, N.H., in 1803. (*United States Geological Survey—Douglas B. Sterrett—Some Deposits of Mica in the United States.*)

Synthetic mica commercial production was undertaken by the Synthetic Mica Corporation, Caldwell Township, N.J., and offered for sale May 17, 1956, under the trade name of Synthamica. It was a chemically pure synthetic fluor-phlogopite mica capable of withstanding sustained temperatures as high as 2000° Fahrenheit without physical or electrical failure. Research on synthetic mica was begun in 1947 by the Bureau of Mines in Norris, Tenn.

MICROBIOLOGY LABORATORY (devoted exclusively to the field) was the Institute of Microbiology, Rutgers University, New Brunswick, N.J., dedicated June 7, 1954. The cost of the building was approximately $3,050,-000 and of the equipment $450,000. Classroom and seminar instruction was offered to graduate students. The first director was Dr. Selman Abraham Waksman.

MICROCARD

Book on microcards was Fremont Rider's *The Scholar and the Future of the Research Library*, put on microcards by the Microcard Corporation, La Crosse, Wis., in the fall of 1947. The 236-page book was reproduced on 3 by 5 inch cards containing about 80 pages to a card. These cards were not offered for sale but were given away to various individuals and institutions.

MICROFILM

Book series microfilmed was *A Short Title Catalogue of Books Printed in England, Scotland and Ireland and of English Books Printed Abroad 1475-1640*, compiled by [Alfred William] Pollard and [Gilbert Richard] Redgrave, 609 pages, published in London in 1926. It was microfilmed by University Microfilms, Ann Arbor, Mich., in 1935 from negatives made by the British Museum.

Check photographing device. *See* Check photographing device

Magazine on microfilm offered to subscribers was *Newsweek*, published in New York City, which offered a microfilm and microcard service to subscribers on June 1, 1949, for $15 a year. The microcard editions were printed on 3 by 5 inch cards. The microfilm editions were on 35mm reels in 100-foot lengths, 26 issues to a roll. Both editions were available in March and September of each year.

Microfilm machine to project enlarged images on ceilings for the use of bedridden patients was made by University Microfilms, Ann Arbor, Mich., and Argus Cameras, Inc., Ann Arbor, Mich., in 1945. The first machine was installed on March 21, 1946, at the Percy Jones Hospital, Battle Creek, Mich.

Microfilm reading device was invented by Bradley Allen Fiske of Washington, D.C., who applied for a patent on November 17, 1920, and received patent No. 1,411,008 on March 28, 1922, on a "reading machine." It was known as a "Fiskeoscope" and could be carried in the pocket. A 2½-inch newspaper column was reduced to ¼ inch and 100,000 words were contained on a 40-inch tape.

Microfilms of U.S. Government publications or documents offered as a regular service was offered by University Microfilms, Ann Arbor, Mich., in April 1952. The price was $900 for *Hearings, Reports, Committee Prints for the 82nd Congress*.

Newspaper to microfilm its current issues was the New York *Herald Tribune*, which began the service with the issue of January 1, 1936.

Newspaper to microfilm its past issues was the New York *Times*, whose microfilms of the issues from 1914 to 1927 were received in November 1935.

MICROGROOVE RECORD. *See* Phonograph record: Long-playing microgroove records

MICROPALEONTOLOGY COURSE. *See* Paleontology course

MICROPHONE (carbon). *See* Radio microphone

MICROPHONE (throat microphone). *See* Laryngophone

MICROSCOPE

Electron microscope was invented by Dr. Vladimir Kosma Zworykin of the RCA Laboratory, Camden, N.J., and was first publicly demonstrated by Dr. Ladislaus Morton on April 20, 1940, at the American Philosophical Society convention, Philadelphia, Pa. The instrument was ten feet high, weighed about a thousand pounds and magnified up to 100,000 diameters.

Microscope for examining structure of materials with ability to block dangerous radiations from radioactive specimens was built by the American Optical Company's division, Buffalo, N.Y., and installed in September 1951 at the Knolls Atomic Power Laboratory, Schenectady, N.Y., which is operated by the General Electric Company for the Atomic Energy Commission. The microscope includes a camera, periscopes, and an illuminating system to permit light to get in and out through the thick walls of the test chamber.

MICROWAVE TELEVISION STATION. *See* Television station: Microwave television station

MIDGET. *See* Dwarf

MIDGET GOLF COURSE. *See* Golf course: Midget golf course

MIDWIFERY PROFESSOR. *See* Medical instruction: Midwifery professor

MIGRATORY DUCK STAMP. *See* Revenue stamp

MILESTONES were set by the directors of an insurance company known as The Philadelphia Contributionship for the Insurance of Houses from Loss by Fire. On February 17, 1761, they agreed "to apply their fines (a forfeiture of one shilling for not meeting precisely at the hour appointed, and two shillings for total absence) in purchasing Stones to be erected on the Road leading from Philadelphia toward Trenton, the distance of a mile one from another with the Number of miles from Philadelphia, to be cut in each stone, and Tho. Wharton and Jacob Lewis are requested to Contract for the same." On May 15, 1764, at 5 o'clock in the morning, the two men started

THE FIRST

at Front and Market Streets, taking with them the Surveyor General of the Province, and at the distance of every mile planted one of the stones. Within four chains from the edge of the Delaware River, they planted the 29th milestone, and having gained by accurate measurement two miles in the estimated distance, they gave the two additional stones, numbered 30 and 31, to be planted on the Jersey side of the road to New York. (*At the Sign of the Hand-in-Hand—Philadelphia Contributionship for the Insurance of Houses from Loss by Fire*)

MILITARY ACADEMY (U.S.). *See* Army school

MILITARY AIRPLANE. *See* Aviation: Airplane in actual military operation

MILITARY BICYCLE CORPS. *See* Bicycle corps (military)

MILITARY COURT MARTIAL. *See* Court martial

MILITARY DECORATION. *See under* Medal

MILITARY DICTIONARY. *See* Dictionary: Military dictionary

MILITARY DRILL MANUAL
   Military drill manual was Baron von Steuben's *Regulations for the Order and Discipline of the Troops of the United States,* 154 pages, printed in 1779 in Philadelphia, Pa., by [Melchior] Styner and [Charles] Cist.

   Military drill manual devoted to field strategy was Roger Stevenson's *Military Instructions for Officers detached in the field, containing a scheme for forming a corps of a partisan, illustrated with plans of the manoeuvres necessary in carrying on the Petite Guerre.* The 232-page book was printed in 1775 by Robert Aitken, Philadelphia, Pa.

MILITARY EXECUTION. *See* Army execution

MILITARY HELIPORT. *See* Heliport: Military heliport

MILITARY HOSPITAL. *See* Hospital: Army field hospital; Hospital: Military hospital

MILITARY INSIGNIA. *See* Army insignia

MILITARY LEADER of the Puritan settlers was Miles Standish, one of the Mayflower

THE FIRST

Pilgrims, who in 1621 was unanimously chosen military captain of the colony. (*Tudor Jenks—Captian Myles Standish*)

MILITARY MASONIC LODGE. *See* Freemasons: Military masonic lodge

MILITARY ORDER OF FOREIGN WARS. *See* War veterans' society: Military order of foreign wars

MILITARY ORGANIZATION
   See also War veterans' society

   Military organization in an American colony was the Ancient and Honorable Artillery Company. It was chartered in Boston, Mass., on March 13, 1638, at which time it assumed legal rights. At the first elections, June 1638, Captain Robert Keayne was elected commander; Daniel Haugh (Howe), lieutenant; and Joseph Weld, ensign. (*Zacheriah Gardner Whitman—History of the Ancient and Honorable Artillery Company*)

   Military organization (anti-British) was the Light Horse of the City of Philadelphia, Pa., organized November 17, 1774, by twenty-eight gentlemen, three of whom were members of the Committee of Correspondence of the first Congress of America, to resist the aggressions of the British crown. They elected their officers, and all swore to uphold the interests of the American colonists. The present First Troop Philadelphia City Cavalry is the continuation of the Light Horse of Philadelphia. (*Philadelphia City Cavalry First Troop—History of the First Troop—Philadelphia City Cavalry from its Organization 1774 to 1874*)

MILITARY PRISON (U.S.). *See* Prison: Military prison of the United States on an island

MILITARY RADIO CAR. *See* Radio car (military)

MILITARY SCHOOL
   Church military school was the Catonsville Military Academy, founded in 1845 by Libertius Van Bokkelen in Catonsville, Md., and affiliated with St. Timothy's Protestant Episcopal Church.

   Military school was the American Literary, Scientific and Military Academy founded by Captain Alden Partridge in Norwich, Vt., August 6, 1819. The students (cadets) were required to "dress in uniforms" and received instruction in fencing, military drawing, topography, "the Laws of Nations, Military Law . . . the construction of Marine Batteries, Artillery duty, the Principles of Gunnery . . .

MILITARY SCHOOL—Continued
etc." The first class entered September 4, 1820.
The first cadet enrolled was Cyril Pennock of
Hartford, Vt. No specific time for completing
the course was required, but the enrollment
period varied from one to six years according
to the student's ability. The name was changed,
November 6, 1834, to Norwich University. In
March 1866, the buildings were destroyed by fire
and the school was removed to Northfield, Vt.

State military school was the Virginia
Military Institute, Lexington, Va., established
as an independent school at the Lexington
Arsenal by act of March 29, 1839. It was
governed by a board of visitors, appointed by
the governor, subject to approval by the state
senate. The first corps of 28 cadets was mustered into service November 11, 1839, and later
increased by three others. The first superintendent was Professor (later Major General)
Francis Henney Smith who served until January
1, 1890. (Virginia Military Institute Catalogue.
Vol. 15. No. 3)

MILITARY SCIENCE DEGREE. See
Degrees (academic and honorary): Doctor of
military science degree

MILITARY SERVICE FOR NEGROES.
See Army: Law (federal) authorizing military service for Negroes

MILITARY TRAINING CAMP. See
Army camp: Army Citizens' Training Camp

MILITARY UNIFORM. See Army uniform

MILITIA (naval). See Navy: Naval militia
(state)

MILK
Acidophilus milk was devised early in 1920
by Dr. Leo Frederick Rettger and Harry Chep-
lin at Yale University, New Haven, Conn.
Commercial production was undertaken by the
Fairlea Farms Company, Orange, Conn., in
February 1922 under the supervision of Dr.
Rettger.

Concentrated milk was "Sealtest," which
was sold November 30, 1950, by the Clover
Dairy Company, Wilmington, Del., as a test.
Two parts of water were added to one part
fluid milk. The Clover Dairy Company was a
division of the National Dairy Products Corporation.

Condensed milk (commercial) was produced in 1851 by Gail Borden of Brooklyn,
N.Y., who applied for a patent on May 14,
1853, which was granted August 19, 1856—
patent No. 15,553 on an "improvement in con-
centration of milk." The patent office doubted

the value of the invention. The first condensery
was established at Wolcottville, Conn., in 1856.
It was not successful and another attempt was
made at Burrville, Conn., in May 1857, but
that was also a failure. A third attempt was
made with an enlarged factory at Wassaic,
N.Y., in June 1861. This venture was successful and later developed into the Borden Company, with factories throughout the country.
(The Borden Eagle. January 1922)

Dried milk patent was obtained by Samuel
R. Percy of New York City who obtained
patent No. 125,406, April 9, 1872, on a "process for the simultaneous atomizing and desic-
cating of fluids and solid substances" (spray
drying of various liquid products). It was
never used commercially in its original form.

Evaporated milk was produced by John
B. Meyenberg of St. Louis, Mo., who received
patent No. 308,421 on November 25, 1884, for an
"apparatus for preserving milk." On February
14, 1885, Meyenberg formed the Helvetia Milk
Condensing Co., of Highland, Ill. Evaporated
milk is milk from which approximately 60 per
cent of the water has been removed by evaporation. (Theodore R. Gamble—Seventy-Five
Years of the Pet Milk Company)

Malted milk was invented in 1882 or 1883
by William Horlick of Racine, Wis., who
coined the name in 1886. It was originally
known as "Diastoid." He dried whole milk and
combined it with extract of wheat and malted
barley in powder or tablet form. This was the
first whole dried milk that would keep.

Milk delivery in glass bottles was made in
1878 in Brooklyn, N.Y., by Alexander Campbell.

Milk pasteurized commercially was processed in Bloomville, N.Y., in 1895 by the
Sheffield Farms Company of New York City.
It was flash pasteurization, very slow, and quite
expensive on account of the large quantity of
ice used. Lewis Benjamin Halsey used two
Champion coolers, one for the heating medium
and the other for the cooling.

MILK BOTTLE. See Bottle: Milk bottle

MILK INSPECTORS were required by
Massachusetts under law of April 6, 1859. An
Inspector of Milk was appointed August 10,
1859, by Boston, Mass., "to prosecute before
the proper tribunal all such violations as shall
come to his knowledge."

MILK SALE REGULATIONS were passed
by the New York City Department of Health
in 1896. The sale of milk without a permit

THE FIRST

was prohibited. This regulation has since been generally adopted by health authorities. The Department of Health, in June 1906, was also the first to organize a group of milk inspectors to undertake the inspection of dairies located beyond the political boundaries of the city which offer milk for sale in the city.

MILK STATION (municipal) to insure clean, raw, tuberculin-tested milk for children during July and August and to raise the standard of the milk supply was established in 1897 in Rochester, N.Y., through the efforts of Dr. George Washington Goler. *(John Walter Kerr—History, Development and Statistics of Milk Charities in the United States)*

MILK TESTER of value for determining the percentage of butterfat in milk and cream was invented in 1890 by Stephen Moulton Babcock, professor of agricultural chemistry, University of Wisconsin, Madison, Wis. He did not apply for a patent. Prior to this invention, the amount of butterfat in milk and cream was determined by a method that could be used only in a chemical laboratory and was entirely unsuitable for use in a creamery or milk plant. *(University of Wisconsin—Agricultural Experiment Station—Bulletin No. 24 July 1890—A New Method for the Estimation of Fat in Milk, Especially Adapted to Creameries and Cheese Factories)*

MILKING PLATFORM (rotating) was invented by Henry W. Jeffers and housed on November 13, 1930, in the lactorium of the Walker Gordon Laboratory Company, Inc., at Plainsboro, N.J. It permitted 1,680 cows to be milked in seven hours by means of a revolving platform that brought them into position with the milking machines. It was called a "Rotolactor." *(Walker Gorden News)*

MILL. *See* Cotton mill; Silk: Silk mill; Windmill

MIMEOGRAPH was invented by Thomas Alva Edison of Menlo Park, N.J., who obtained patent No. 180,857 August 8, 1876, on a "method of preparing autographic stencils for printing." On February 17, 1880, he obtained patent No. 224,665 for an improved model.

MIMEOGRAPHED DAILY NEWSPAPER. *See* Newspaper: Mimeographed daily newspaper

MINE BARRAGE was the invention of David Bushnell, who conceived the idea of floating kegs containing explosives which would ignite upon contact with ships. In August 1777, he attached a series of mines together in Black Point Bay, near New London, Conn. Members of the crew of the British frigate "Cerberus," commanded by Captain J. Symons (or Sim-

THE FIRST

mons), noticed a rope alongside their ship. They hauled it in, not realizing that a mine was attached to the other end. They hoisted the mine on board and it exploded, killing three of the crew and blowing a fourth into the water. The mines were equipped with a gunlock with hammer which exploded upon collision contact. *(Royal Bird Bradford—History of Torpedo Warfare)*

MINE (coal). *See* Coal mine

MINE FIRE. *See* Fire: Fire in a mine

MINE (land). *See* Land mines

MINE LAYER. *See* Ship: Mine layer; Ship: Navy vessel constructed as a mine layer; Ship: Navy vessel equipped to lay mines

MINE (torpedo). *See* Torpedo: Torpedo mine

MINERAL EXHIBIT (fluorescent). *See* Fluorescent mineral exhibit

MINERAL SEGREGATION by flotation, the process that causes particles of the same metal to cling together, was demonstrated by Francis Edward Elmore in 1898. Employment of the law of gravitation was the main principle of the process. The first commercial operation was begun in 1911 by James M. Hyde in the Butte and Superior Mining Company's plant at Butte, Mont.

MINERAL WATER BOTTLER. *See* Bottler of mineral water

MINERALOGY INSTRUCTION (systematic) was given in 1786 by Dr. Benjamin Waterhouse at the Rhode Island College, Providence, R.I. *(Benjamin Waterhouse—A Journal of a Young Man of Massachusetts)*

MINERALOGY MAGAZINE was the *American Mineralogical Journal*, founded by Archibald Bruce, the first number of which was printed in New York City in January 1810. This was followed by three other issues, the last of which appeared in 1814. These four numbers, comprising 270 pages, constitute the first and only volume that was published.

MINES BUREAU (U.S.) was established in the Department of the Interior, by act of Congress (36 Stat.L.369), an "act to establish in the Department of the Interior, a Bureau of Mines," approved May 16, 1910, and effective July 1, 1910. The first director was Dr. Joseph Austin Holmes. On July 1, 1925, the Bureau

MINES, BUREAU (U.S.)—*Continued* was transferred to the Department of Commerce. *(Fred Wilbur Powell—Bureau of Mines)*

MINES SCHOOL was opened November 15, 1864, in the basement of the Columbia University building on East 49th Street, New York City. The first professor of mines and metallurgy was Thomas Egleston, who was appointed February 1, 1864. It was through his efforts that the plan of the school was proposed and carried out. *(Joshua Lawrence Chamberlin—Universities and Their Sons)*

MINIATURE BOOK. *See* Book: Miniature book

MINIATURE GOLF. *See* Golf course: Midget golf course

MINIATURE TELEVISION TUBE. *See* Television tube: Miniature tube

MINIMUM WAGE LAW. *See* Labor law: Minimum wage law

MINING SECURITIES EXCHANGE. *See* Brokerage: Exchange to specialize in mining securities

MINING TUNNEL. *See* Tunnel: Mining tunnel (large)

MINISTER (diplomatic). *See* Diplomatic service

MINISTER PLENIPOTENTIARY. *See* Diplomatic service: Minister plenipotentiary

MINISTER (religious). *See* under specific religious denominations

MINKS. *See* Animals: Fur-bearing animals

MINSTREL SHOW TROUPE was the Virginia Minstrels, organized by Daniel Decatur Emmett. Performances were given at the Chatham Theatre, New York City (constructed in 1842) which was located on Chatham Street between Roosevelt and James Streets. Frank Brower played the bones, Richard Pelham the tambourine, Daniel Emmett the violin, and William Whitlock the banjo. On January 31, 1843, they played at a benefit performance at the Chatham Theatre and on February 6, 1843, they were engaged to appear at the Bowery Amphitheatre. They wore white trousers, striped calico shirts, long blue calico swallow-tail coats. Their popular songs included "Old Dan Tucker," "Happy Uncle Tom," and "The Raccoon Hunt." *(Carl Wittke—Tambo and Bones)*

MINT (U.S.)
See also Money

Assay office building (federal). *See* Assay office building (federal)

Mint of the United States was at Philadelphia. Robert Morris as head of the Finance Department of the United States Government laid a plan for American money coinage before Congress on January 15, 1782. Through his efforts and the cooperation of Thomas Jefferson and Alexander Hamilton, an act "establishing a mint and regarding the coins of the United States" (1 Stat.L.246) was approved by both houses and signed by George Washington on April 2, 1792. The mint was built the same year. The cornerstone was laid July 31, 1792.

Mint (U.S.) director was David Rittenhouse, who was appointed by President George Washington April 14, 1792, and who remained in charge of the mint at Philadelphia until June 1795, when he resigned because of illness. *(Jesse Paul Watson—The Bureau of the Mint)*

Private mint authorized by the United States Government was the Moffat Assay Office, Mt. Ophir, Mariposa County, Calif., built in 1850 by John L. Moffat. The mint manufactured $50 hexagonal gold ingots used as legal tender to replace gold dust and nuggets. Beginning on February 20, 1851, the ingots were made under the supervision of the United States Assayer, and on July 3, 1852, Congress passed an "act to establish a branch of the mint of the United States in California" (10 Stat.L.11). Augustus Humbert of New York was appointed United States Assayer to place the government stamp upon the ingots produced by Moffat and Company. In 1852 it became the United States Assay Office. *(Newell D. Chamberlain—The Call of Gold)*

Woman Director of the Mint was Nellie Tayloe Ross, who assumed office May 3, 1933. *(Records in Office of Director of Mint, Treasury Department—Washington, D.C.)*

MISSILE. *See* Rocket

MISSILE MAIL. *See* Air mail service: Missile mail (official)

MISSION (California). *See* California mission

MISSIONARY
Methodist missionary. *See* Methodist: Methodist missionary

THE FIRST

Negro missionary to the Indians was John Marrant, of New York, ordained May 15, 1785, as a Methodist minister in London, England. Among his converts were the king of the Cherokees and his daughter. (*William Aldridge—A Narrative of the Lord's Wonderful Dealings with John Marrant, a Black*)

MISSIONARY SOCIETY

Foreign missionary society was the American Board of Commissioners for Foreign Missions organized June 29, 1810, by the General Association of Massachusetts at its annual meeting in Bradford, Mass. The board received its charter in 1812 from Massachusetts.

Foreign missionary society organized by women to send unmarried missionaries to the Orient was the Woman's Union Missionary Society of America for Heathen Lands, organized November 1860 in Boston, Mass., by Ellen H. B. Mason (Mrs. Francis B. Mason) and nine other women. In May 1861, a similar society was formed in Philadelphia, Pa., which united with the former to form the Woman's Union Missionary Society for Heathen Lands, which received its charter April 11, 1861. The first president was Sarah B. Doremus (Mrs. Thomas C. Doremus). The first missionary was Sarah H. Marston, who sailed November 1861 for Tounghoo, Burma.

Missionary society (colonial) was the New England Protestant Missionary Society, chartered July 1649 by the British Parliament to propagate the gospel. Missionary work among the Indians, however, had been carried on earlier by John Eliot, John Cotton, Henry Dunster, and others.

Missionary society organized in the United States was the Society for the Propagation of Christian Knowledge Among the Indians of North America, which was founded in 1762 in the Massachusetts Bay Colony. The Archbishop of Canterbury persuaded King George III to cancel the charter, fearing it might become a non-Episcopal channel of influence.

MISSISSIPPI RIVER RAILWAY BRIDGE. *See* Bridge: Railway bridge across the Mississippi River

MOBILE COMPUTER CENTER. *See* Computer: Mobile computer center

MOBILE POWER PLANT (electric). *See* Electric power plant: Mobile electric power plant

MOBILE TELEPHONE. *See* Telephone: Mobile telephone

THE FIRST

MOBILE TELEVISION STATION. *See* Television—Mobile unit: Mobile television unit

MODEL SCHOOL. *See* School: Model school

MODELS' TRAINING SCHOOL, for the systematic training of young women to be models and mannequins, was officially opened in 1928 in Chicago, Ill., and was known as *L'École de Mannequins,* the School of Modeling. Training was based upon the principles of mental control over physical action and expressions of bodily movements, a correct understanding of balance, poise, and control towards grace, and personality development for a definite purpose.

MODERATOR OF THE UNITED PRESBYTERIAN CHURCH. *See* Presbyterian church: Moderator of the United Presbyterian Church

MODERN LANGUAGE SCHOOL. *See* Language instruction: Modern language school

MOHAIR was commercially manufactured by the Arlington Mills, Lawrence, Mass., in 1872.

MOLAY, DE, ORDER OF. *See* Freemasons: Order of De Molay

MOLDED PLYWOOD AIRPLANE. *See* Aviation—Airplane: Molded plywood airplane

MOLYBDENUM

Molybdenum centrifugal casting was made November 4, 1958, when a hollow molybdenum cylinder $4\frac{1}{2}$ inches wide and 8 inches long was cast at the Albany Metallurgy Research Center of the U.S. Bureau of Mines, Albany, Ore. The cast metal weighed about 10 pounds. Although molybdenum had previously been arc-melted in water-cooled copper crucibles to form cylindrical ingots, this was the first reported production of a shaped casting obtained from poured metal.

MONARCH TO VISIT THE UNITED STATES. *See* Visiting celebrities: Absolute monarch

MONEY

Bill bearing the portrait of a woman was the one-dollar silver certificate, series of 1886, delivered by the Bureau of Engraving and Printing to the United States Treasurer during September 1886. It had a portrait of

MONEY—*Continued*
Martha Washington. The reverse was in green, covered with ornamental lathe work. Each certificate carried the signature of the Register and the United States Treasurer. (The following individuals' names were used: William Starke Rosecrans and J. Fount Tillman, Registers; Conrad N. Jordan, James W. Hyatt, James N. Huston, Enos H. Nebeker and Daniel N. Morgan, Treasurers.)

Bill to depict both the face and the reverse side of the Great Seal of the United States was the one-dollar silver certificate, series of 1935, issued December 18, 1935. The steel plates from which the bills were printed did not carry the signature of the Secretary of the Treasury or the Treasurer. The signatures were printed in a blank space on the face of bills at the same time that the bills were numbered and sealed.

Coin bearing the portrait of a foreign monarch was the Isabella silver quarter issued for the World's Columbian Exposition in Chicago, Ill. The coin was authorized March 3, 1893 (27 Stat.L.586) and issued in June 1893. It bore on its obverse a crowned bust of Queen Isabella, facing left, with the year "1893" to the right in the field. About the center design was the inscription "United States of America." On the reverse, a spinner was pictured kneeling to the left, holding a distaff in her left hand and a spindle in her right. Below was the inscription "Columbian Quar. Dol."

Coin bearing the portrait of a living person was the 1921 Alabama Centennial commemorative half dollar, of which 70,000 were struck at the mint at Philadelphia, Pa. The obverse showed the heads of William Wyatt Bibb, the first governor of Alabama, and Thomas Erby Kilby, governor in office at the time of the centennial. The reverse depicted an American eagle.

Coin bearing the portrait of a living President was the 1926 Sesquicentennial half dollar, the obverse of which bore the heads of Presidents George Washington and Calvin Coolidge. The reverse depicted the original Liberty Bell. The net coinage was 141,120 pieces, struck at the mint at Philadelphia, Pa.

Coin bearing the portrait of a Negro was the fifty-cent silver commemorative, honoring Booker Taliaferro Washington, authorized August 7, 1946. The first coin was presented to President Harry S. Truman on December 17, 1946. The obverse showed the head of Booker T. Washington and the reverse a stylized Hall of Fame, under which were the words "From Slave Cabin to Hall of Fame." Centered under this wording was a slave cabin, to the left of which was "In God We Trust," and to the

right, "Franklin County, Va." Around the rim was "Booker T. Washington Birthplace Memorial—Liberty."

Coin bearing the portrait of a President was the 1909 Lincoln penny, a copper cent, designed by Victor David Brenner and based on a photograph of President Abraham Lincoln taken in 1864 by Mathew B. Brady.

Coin (state) to use "E Pluribus Unum" as a motto was the New Jersey cent issued in 1786, the obverse of which showed a horse's head above a plow with the date of coinage and the name of the state in Latin, "Nova Caesarea." The reverse showed a heart-shaped shield of the United States and the national motto "E Pluribus Unum."

Coin to use "In God We Trust" was the two-cent piece of 1864. Salmon Portland Chase, Secretary of the Treasury, addressed a letter to the Director of the Mint at Philadelphia stating that our coinage should bear a motto expressing in the fewest words that no nation can be strong except in the strength of God. Congress established the motto by act of April 22, 1864 (13 Stat.L.54), which authorized the Director of the Mint to fix the shape, mottoes, and devices to be used. On July 11, 1955, Congress enacted a law (69 Stat.L.290) to provide that "all United States currency (and coins) shall bear the inscriptions 'In God We Trust.'" (*American Journal of Numismatics. Vol. 35. 1901. Boston*)

Coin (United States) to use "E Pluribus Unum" as a motto was the half eagle, authorized by act of April 2, 1792 (1 Stat.L.248) and coined in 1795. The obverse showed the draped bust of Liberty facing right, with long, loose hair, and a liberty cap; above, "Liberty" and fifteen stars; below, "1795." The reverse displayed an eagle, bearing the shield of the United States on its breast; arrows in right claw and olive branch in left; in beak, a scroll inscribed "E Pluribus Unum"; above the head sixteen stars; beneath, an arch of clouds. The coin had a reeded edge and weighed 135 grains.

Coins manufactured for a foreign government by the United States Mint were authorized January 29, 1874 (18 Stat.L.6) and provided for ten million pieces of "un centavo" of the nominal value of $100,000 and two million pieces of "dos y medio centavos" (nominal value, $50,000), the charge to equal the expenses, including labor and use of machinery. They were manufactured for Venezuela in 1876. The bill provided that their production was not to interfere with the required coinage for the United States. (*Report of the Director of the Mint for the Fiscal Year Ending June 30, 1876*)

THE FIRST

Coins produced by steam power were coined in 1836 on a machine invented by M. Thonnelier of France in 1833. Previously all the work at the mint had been done by hand or horsepower.

Commemorative coinage was the Columbian silver half dollar authorized by the act of August 5, 1892 (27 Stat.L.389) for the World's Columbian Exposition held in Chicago, Ill. It was first issued in November 1892. The Isabella silver quarter, also issued for the same exposition, was authorized by the act of March 3, 1893 (27 Stat.L.586).

Confederate coinage was a silver half dollar produced at the New Orleans mint in 1861. Only four pieces were minted. On the obverse was the Confederate shield with a liberty cap and a wreath of sugar cane and cotton branches. On the reverse side was the regular United States die. (*John Smith Dye—Coin Encyclopedia*)

Confederate currency was issued under the Confederate States Act of March 9, 1861, at Mobile, Ala., in denominations of $50, $100, $500, and $1,000. The $50 note featured three Negroes in a field, two of them hoeing; the $100 note a train of cars at a depot, at the right, and Liberty standing, at the left; the $500 note showed a rural scene with cattle wading in a brook; and the $1,000 note showed busts of Jackson and Calhoun.

Continental coin was the copper Fugio or Franklin cent, designed by Benjamin Franklin and authorized July 6, 1787. One side showed thirteen circles linked together to form a circle around the edge; a small circle in the middle bore the words "United States" around it and in the center "We are one." The other side showed a dial with hours on the face and a meridian sun above; on the left was the word "Fugio" ("I fly") and on the right the year 1787; below the dial were the words "Mind Your Business." A contract for the manufacture of 300 tons of the coins was awarded James Jarvis, who manufactured them in New Haven, Conn. The dies were made by Abel Buell, also of New Haven.

Continental money was a $3,000,000 issue of which $2,000,000 was issued on June 22, 1775, and $1,000,000 on July 25, 1775. A second issue of $3,000,000 was authorized November 29, 1775. The largest share of the original issue, $434,244, was given to Massachusetts; seconded by $372,208 awarded to Pennsylvania. Only twelve states were granted money. Georgia was not included as she was not represented in the Congress. (*William F. De Knight—History of the Currency of the Country and of the Loans of the United States*)

THE FIRST

Copper cents minted by a state were issued by Vermont. On June 15, 1785, the state granted authority to Reuben Harmon, Jr., to make these coins for two years, beginning July 1, 1785. The copper coins were to be one third of an ounce each, troy weight. Harmon established a mint at Rupert, Vt., where he lived. In October 1785 Connecticut authorized the coinage of 10,000 pounds of copper cents. The mint at New Haven was operated by Samuel Bishop and John Goodrich of New Haven and Joseph Hopkins of Waterbury, Conn. (*Sylvester Sage Crosby—The Early Coins of America*)

Copper coins were made from copper obtained from the Simsbury mine in Granby, Conn., by John Higley in 1737. They were stamped upon planchets of the pure copper, and, in consequence, were in demand by goldsmiths for alloy. The obverse side showed a standing deer, facing left, occupying the whole field, with the legend, "Value me as you please." The reverse side showed three hammers, each bearing a crown upon the head with the legend "I am good copper—1737." (*Richard H. Phelps—Newgate of Connecticut*)

Copper coins made by the United States Mint were one cent and half cent issues, of which there were four designs, the "chain cent," the "wreath cent," the "flowing hair," and the "liberty cap," which were authorized by congressional act "establishing a mint regulating the coins of the United States" (1 Stat.L.246), approved April 2, 1792. The cent equaled 1/100 part of a dollar and contained eleven pennyweights of copper, while the half cent contained five pennyweights of copper. This issue was discontinued by act of February 21, 1857. (*Guttag Bros.—Coins of the Americas*)

Decimal system of money, with the dollar as a unit, was adopted July 6, 1785, by the Continental Congress, which established "that the money unit of the United States of America be one dollar; that the smallest coin be of copper, of which two hundred shall pass for one dollar; that the several pieces shall increase in a decimal ratio." On August 8, 1786, it was voted "that the standard of the United States of America for gold and silver, shall be eleven parts fine and one part alloy." (*Journals of the Continental Congress, 1774-1789*)

Demand notes were issued under the authority of an act of Congress of July 17, 1861 (12 Stat.L.259), which provided that each note should be signed by the First or Second Comptroller or the Register of the Treasury and countersigned by such officer or officers as might be designated by the Secretary of the Treasury. (*Laurence Frederick Schmeckebier—The Bureau of Engraving and Printing*)

MONEY—*Continued*

Demonetization of silver (abolishing bimetallism and making gold the sole monetary standard) was effected by the act of February 12, 1873 (17 Stat.L.424), known as "the Crime of '73," which stopped the coinage of the old standard silver dollar of 412½ grains and authorized the coinage of the trade dollar of 420 grains for export. The trade dollar, not intended for circulation in the United States, but inadvertently made legal tender up to $5, was deprived of its legal tender feature by joint resolution of July 22, 1876 (19 Stat.L.215) and dropped from the list of coins March 3, 1887 (24 Stat.L.635). (*John Smith Hanson—Coin and Currency*)

Deposit of gold bullion for coinage was made by Moses Brown, a merchant of Boston, Mass., on February 12, 1795. It was of gold ingots worth $2,276.72 which were paid for in silver coins. (*George Greenlief Evans—Illustrated History of the U.S. Mint*)

Deposit of silver for coinage was made by the Bank of Maryland on July 18, 1794. It consisted of coins of France worth $80,715.73 as silver bullion. The first return of American silver coins to the Treasury was made on October 15, 1794.

Dies for coins in America were made in 1652 by Joseph Jencks at the Iron Works of Lynn, Mass., for the General Court of Massachusetts which established a minthouse in Boston on May 27, 1652. The dies were for silver coins worth three, six and twelve pence, "forme flatt," with "N.E. Anno 1652" and a Roman numeral denoting the value on the obverse side. On the reverse were "Massachusetts" and a pine tree. The date was not changed annually. John Hull was the mint master. (*Noble Foster Hoggson—Epochs in American Banking*)

Double eagle coinage ($20) was authorized by act of Congress on March 3, 1849 (9 Stat. L.397), an "act to authorize the coinage of gold dollars and double eagles." The first double eagles were coined in 1850.

Fifty-dollar gold pieces were manufactured on February 20, 1851, by the Moffat Assay Office, Mt. Ophir, Mariposa County, Calif. They were octagonal with an eagle in the center surrounded by "United States of America," above the eagle "887 thous" indicating the fineness of the gold, and at the bottom "50 D C." On the reverse a number of radii extended from a center in which was stamped in small figures "50." Around the edge was "The United States Assayer." (*Newell D. Chamberlain—Call of Gold*)

Fifty-dollar gold pieces minted by the United States government were coined June

15, 1915, for the Panama Pacific International Exposition. They were designed by Robert Aitken and about three thousand were produced at the mint at San Francisco, Calif. Half were octagonal and half were round. The main design was a bust of Minerva with crested helmet.

Gold certificates were authorized by the act of Congress of March 3, 1863 (12 Stat.L. 709). Gold certificates of one- and two-year notes, and of compound interest notes, and certificates under the fifth section of the act were used for clearing house purposes soon after the passage of the national bank act. They were issued November 13, 1865, and were authorized to be received at par in payment of duties. (*John Jay Knox—United States Notes*)

Gold coinage was authorized April 2, 1792 (1 Stat.L.248) when eagles ($10), half-eagles ($5), and quarter-eagles ($2.50) were authorized. On March 3, 1849, the coinage of double-eagles ($20) and one-dollar gold pieces was authorized, and on February 21, 1853, three-dollar gold pieces were authorized. The minting of the one-dollar and three-dollar gold pieces was discontinued September 26, 1890 (26 Stat. L.485). (*David Kemper Watson—History of American Coinage*)

Gold price fixed by Congress was $19.39 an ounce, authorized on April 2, 1792 (1 Stat. L.248), which value remained firm except for the period between August 1814 and February 1817. On June 28, 1834 (4 Stat.L.700) the value of an ounce of gold was raised to $20.67, which price remained firm until May 29, 1933, except during the panics of 1837 and 1857 and from February 25, 1862, to January 1, 1879.

Gold standard abrogation was authorized by the House May 29, 1933, and by the Senate June 3, 1933. The bill was signed by President Franklin Delano Roosevelt June 5, 1933 (48 Stat.L.112), and provided that all obligations which gave the obligee the right to require payment in gold or any particular kind of currency were against public policy and that payment could be made dollar for dollar in any currency that was legal tender at the time of payment. Previous to this legislation, President Roosevelt had issued an order on April 5, 1933, forbidding the hoarding of gold and on April 20, 1933, had placed an embargo on gold exports which was modified on August 28, 1933, to permit the exportation of mined gold.

Half cent of the United States was authorized by the act of April 2, 1792 (1 Stat.L.246). The obverse depicted "Liberty" facing left, over the date 1793. The reverse bore the inscription "United States of America" and a wreath of olive branches enclosing "half cent," below which was 1/200. It was size 14, weighed

THE FIRST

132 grains, and was designed by the engraver Robert Scot. On the edge appeared "Two hundred for a dollar." Coinage was discontinued by act of February 21, 1857.

Metal purchased for coinage was six pounds of old copper at one shilling and three pence per pound which was coined and delivered to the Treasurer in 1793.

Mint. *See* Mint (U.S.)

Nickel or five-cent piece was authorized May 16, 1866 (14 Stat.L.47). It weighed 77.16 grains and was composed of 75 per cent copper and 25 per cent nickel. The obverse side showed a United States shield surmounted by a cross, an olive branch pendant at each side; back of the base of the shield were two arrows, only the heads and feathers visible; beneath "1866"; above in the field, "In God We Trust." The reverse showed the figure "5" within a circle of thirteen stars and rays, and "United States of America."

Notes wholly engraved and printed at the Bureau of Engraving and Printing, Washington, D.C., were those of the fractional currency authorized by the act of March 3, 1863 (12 Stat.L.711). Over three million sheets of this currency with a monetary value of over $13,000,000 had been printed by November 26, 1864. (*Laurence Frederick Schmeckebier—The Bureau of Engraving and Printing*)

Paper money in America was issued by the colonists. On February 3, 1690, Massachusetts established a provincial bank and issued money in denominations from two shillings to five pounds to pay the soldiers who served in the war with Quebec. Other states also issued paper money without any basis so that in 1780 the ratio of paper to silver was 40 to 1. (*Adolphus M. Hart—History of Issues of Paper Money in the American Colonies*)

Paper money fractional currency was issued from August 21, 1862, to May 27, 1863, in denominations of 5 cents, 10 cents, 25 cents, and 50 cents. The bills were originally issued with perforated edges, but later were cut plain. They were also known as "postage currency" as they depicted postage stamps. They were receivable in payment for all dues to the United States less than five dollars and were exchangeable for United States notes by any assistant treasurer or designated United States Depository in sums not less than five dollars.

Paper money issued by the American Indians is believed to have been issued about 1840 or 1850 by the Arapahos in Oregon. A later specimen bears the following inscription: "Office of Discount at Arrapahos Way in the

THE FIRST

Far West. The President and Directors of the Oregon State Bank promise to pay five dollars on demand." The only known specimen of paper money of the Cherokee Nation in Oklahoma is a one-dollar note, on which is inscribed in ink, June 18, 1862," and #592. It reads in part, "Lewis Ross—Cherokee Nation" and is payable "in notes of the Confederate States at Tahlequah." It also bears numerous Cherokee symbols.

Paper money issued by the Government of the United States was authorized by the acts of July 17, 1861 (12 Stat.L.259), and August 5, 1861 (12 Stat.L.313), the amount authorized being $50,000,000. The notes were first issued March 10, 1862. The denominations were $5 (Hamilton), $10 (Lincoln), and $20 (Liberty). They were called "demand notes" because they were payable on demand at certain designated subtreasuries. They were not legal tender when first issued but afterwards were made so by act of March 17, 1862 (12 Stat.L. 370). (*American Institute of Banking—Study Course*)

Paper money of the present small size was issued on July 10, 1929. At that time there was outstanding a total of $4,997,000,000 in old size currency, about 823,000,000 pieces.

Return of coins to the treasury took place on July 31, 1795 and consisted of 744 half eagles. The first return of eagles took place on September 22, 1795, and consisted of 400 pieces. The first return of silver coins to the treasury took place on October 15, 1794. (*George Greenlief Evans—Illustrated History of the U.S. Mint*)

Scrip money to be self-liquidating was issued March 8, 1933, by the Franklin Chamber of Commerce, Franklin, Ind. The method of liquidating was that of placing a two-cent stamp on each dollar every time it circulated. Twenty-four hundred dollars of scrip was issued, of which nine hundred dollars was paid out. The full amount would have been paid had the banks not reopened.

Silver coins were the half dollar, quarter dollar, dime, and half dime authorized April 2, 1792 (1 Stat.L.248). Other coins were authorized as follows: three-cent piece March 3, 1851; trade dollar February 12, 1873; twenty-cent piece March 3, 1875 (18 Stat.L.478); Columbian half dollar August 5, 1892; and Columbian quarter dollar March 3, 1893. The three-cent piece and half dime were discontinued February 12, 1873, the trade dollar March 3, 1887, and the twenty-cent piece May 2, 1878. (*David Kemper Watson—History of American Coinage*)

Silver dollar was coined in Philadelphia, Pa., at the mint in 1794, under the act of April

MONEY—*Continued*
2, 1792 (1 Stat.L.246), which established the mint and provided for the coinage of silver dollars. Under this act, all gold and silver coins struck at the mint were full tender. *(Alonzo Barton Hepburn—History of Coinage and Currency in the United States)*

Silver half dimes were authorized April 2, 1792, and coined at the mint in Philadelphia, Pa., on October 9, 1792. George Washington in his November 6, 1792, address to Congress reported: "There has been a small beginning in the coinage of silver half dimes; the want of small coins in circulation calling the first attention to them." *(John Smith Dye—Coin Encyclopedia)*

Trade dollar was authorized by act of February 12, 1873 (17 Stat.L.427) and was not intended for circulation in the United States, but for export to China. When its coinage was authorized it was inadvertently made legal tender to the amount of five dollars, but this was repealed July 22, 1876 (19 Stat. L.215). The trade dollar was discontinued March 3, 1887. *(Monetary Units and Coinage Systems of the Principal Countries of the World—Director of the Mint, Treasury Department)*

Trade tokens were issued in 1789 by William and John Mott, manufacturers and dealers in watches and jewelry, Water Street, New York City. They were smaller in size than the ordinary copper cent and beautifully engraved. On the obverse was a regulator supported by two columns, and surmounted by a small eagle. The inscription read, "Motts, N.Y. Importers, Dealers, Manufacturers of Gold and Silver Ware." On the reverse was an eagle, with expanded wings, facing to the left, holding an olive branch in one talon and three barbed arrows in the other, the shield of the United States upon its breast. The date "1789" was above the eagle, while below was the inscription, "Watches, Jewelry, Silver Ware, Chronometers, Clocks." *(Charles Ira Bushnell—An Arrangement of Tradesmen's Cards, Political Tokens; also Election Medals, etc.)*

Treasury notes. *See* Bonds

Wooden money was issued at Tenino, Wash., in February 1932. When the Citizens Bank of Tenino closed its doors December 5, 1931, the town was without ready cash to do business. The Tenino Chamber of Commerce, through three trustees and the State Supervisor of Banking, devised the assignment of scrip. By this plan a depositor could assign to the Chamber a certain amount of his own proven deposit in exchange for a similar amount of scrip which the Chamber guaranteed to redeem when the liquidation paid them the necessary

funds. The first scrip was printed on lithographed sheets in denominations of 25 cents, 50 cents, $1, $5, and $10 by the *Thurston County Independent* in December 1931. In February 1932 wooden money in denominations of 25 cents, 50 cents, and $1 was printed on three-ply sitka spruce wood. Red cedar and Port Orford cedar were used afterward.

MONEY ORDER SYSTEM. *See* Postal service: Money order system

MONKEY TRAINED TO PERFORM. *See* Animals: Monkey trained to perform

MONOLITHIC CONCRETE BUILDING. *See* Building: Monolithic concrete building

MONOPLANE. *See* Aviation—Airplane: Monoplane (American)

MONOTYPE. *See* Typesetting machine: Monotype

MONUMENT
Bronze equestrian statue was Clark Mills' statue of General Andrew Jackson unveiled January 8, 1853, at Lafayette Park, Washington, D.C. It was cast from cannons captured by Jackson in the War of 1812. *(Charles Edwin Fairman—Art and Artists of the Capitol of the United States)*

Bronze statue. *See* Bronze statue

Marble statuary group. *See* Marble statuary group

Monument by a woman ordered by the U.S. Government was a life size model of Abraham Lincoln. An act of Congress of July 28, 1866 (14 Stat.L.370) authorized the Secretary of Interior to enter into contract with the sculptor Vinnie Ream (later Mrs. Richard Leveridge Hoxie). A contract was signed August 30, 1866, to pay her $10,000, half upon presentation of the model in plaster and the balance upon completion of the marble statue. The statue was unveiled January 25, 1871, in the Rotunda of the U.S. Capitol.

Monument to a bird was unveiled October 1, 1913, at Salt Lake City, Utah. It was designed by Mahonri Young, a grandson of Brigham Young, to commemorate the sea gulls from the Great Salt Lake which attacked a devouring horde of black crickets, or grasshoppers, which were destroying the wheat fields of the Mormon settlers in May 1848.

Monument to a comic character was the "Popeye" statue in Popeye Park, Crystal City,

THE FIRST

THE FIRST

Tex., unveiled March 26, 1937, during the Second Annual Spinach Festival. It was six feet tall, made of concrete, and colored to represent Elzie Crisler Segar's cartoon character "Popeye."

Monument to a woman financed by women was dedicated May 10, 1894, to "Mary, the Mother of Washington" over the grave of Mary Ball Washington, Fredericksburg, Va. The National Mary Washington Memorial Association, chartered February 22, 1890, raised a fund of $11,500 to replace a neglected monument, the cornerstone of which had been laid May 7, 1833. The new monument, a forty-foot monolith on bases and plinth ten feet high, was designed and built by a Mr. Crawford. The cornerstone was laid October 21, 1893. *(Susan Riviere Hetzel—The Building of a Monument)*

Monument to an American poet was a full length bronze statue of Fitz-Greene Halleck. It was the work of Wilson MacDonald and was presented to New York City by a committee of private citizens. It was unveiled in Central Park, New York, May 15, 1877, ten years after the death of Halleck, by President Rutherford Birchard Hayes. *(William Cullen Bryant—Life and Writings of Fitz-Greene Halleck)*

Monument to an insect was dedicated December 11, 1919, at Enterprise, Ala. It was erected by the citizens of Enterprise, Coffee County, Ala., "in profound appreciation of the Boll Weevil and what it has done as the herald of prosperity." The deadly destruction of the weevil had caused the farmers to diversify their crops with the result that their income shortly jumped to triple the amount received in the best cotton years.

Monument to Christopher Columbus was the Columbus Monument, dedicated October 12, 1792, in Baltimore, Md., three hundred years after his discovery of this continent. *(Maryland Historical Magazine—September 1906)*

Monument to commemorate the Civil War was a plain brownstone shaft designed by Nelson Augustus Moore and dedicated in Kensington, Conn., on July 25, 1863, two years before the end of the war, at a cost of $350. It was "erected to commemorate the death of those who perished in suppressing the Southern Rebellion," and finally carried the names of sixteen men. *(Connecticut Magazine—September-October 1900)*

Monument to George Washington was a cairn-like monument, 54 feet in circumference at its base and 15 feet high. The monument was built by Isaac C. Lutz in Boonsboro, Md., on July 4, 1827. The wall of the monument was composed of huge stones, many weighing

upwards of a ton. A flight of steps ran to the top, which was also used as an observation tower. There is some dispute as to whether or not this cairn should be called a monument. It was completed before the Baltimore monument which had been started several years earlier. *(Historical Sketch of the First Monument to Washington—Washington County Historical Society)*

Monument to George Washington (city or state) was the Washington monument of Baltimore, Md., the cornerstone of which was laid on July 4, 1815, with Masonic ceremony. The monument was not completed until October 19, 1829. The Baltimore monument has a shaft 180 feet high and is surmounted by a 16-foot statue of George Washington. The site was donated by General John Eager Howard and the funds were raised by lottery.

Monument to George Washington (national) was the Washington Monument in Washington, D.C., completed in 1884. It is a white marble obelisk 555 feet in height and 55 feet square at the base. The cornerstone was laid July 4, 1848. The capstone with the aluminum tip was set in place December 6, 1884. The monument was dedicated February 21, 1885, by George Winthrop, who had delivered the formal address at the cornerstone ceremonies thirty-seven years earlier. The public was admitted to the monument October 9, 1888.

Monument to the American flag was dedicated June 14, 1927, the 150th anniversary of the United States adoption of the Stars and Stripes as the national banner, at Schenley Park, Pittsburgh, Pa. It was designed by Harvey A. Schwab, dedicated by William T. Kerr, founder of the American Flag Day Association, and unveiled by Florence Bent of the Bellefield High School, Pittsburgh, Pa.

Monument to the memory of the soldiers and sailors of the Spanish-American war was unveiled in Monroeville, Ohio, on Thursday, September 29, 1904.

Monument to the "Unknown Soldier" (national) was built to honor the large number of unidentified American soldiers who lost their lives in World War I. The "Unknown Soldier" was buried on November 11, 1921, in the National Cemetary at Arlington, Va. President Warren Gamaliel Harding, accompanied by practically every prominent government officer, attended the services and the unveiling of the national shrine.

National monument was the Devils Tower, a massive fluted column of volcanic rock 865 feet tall in the Black Hills at Belle Fourche River, Wyoming. The base of this gray igneous rock is 1,700 feet in diameter. Presi-

MONUMENT—*Continued*
dent Theodore Roosevelt signed a bill on September 24, 1906, establishing 1,153 acres as a national monument.

National monument dedicated to a Negro was the George Washington Carver National Monument, authorized July 14, 1943, officially established June 14, 1951, and dedicated July 14, 1953. It consists of 210 acres about two and a half miles southwest of Diamond in Newton County, Mo. It is administered by the National Park Service of the United States Department of the Interior.

Obelisk to be brought to the United States was loaded in Alexandria June 12, 1880, and arrived in New York City July 20, 1880, on the U.S.S. "Dessoug" under Commander Henry Honeychurch Gorringe, U.S.N. A hole was cut in the starboard bow of the ship to accommodate the massive object. William Henry Vanderbilt bore the expenses of its removal. The obelisk was 90 feet high, and weighed 443,000 pounds. It was built in Heliopolis, Egypt, between 1591 and 1565 B.C. and was removed about 22 B.C. to Alexandria, where it stood until it was brought to the United States. It was presented to the United States by the Khedive of Egypt and was erected on its pedestal in Central Park, New York City, January 22, 1881. On February 22, 1881, it was officially presented to the City of New York by William Maxwell Evarts, Secretary of State, on behalf of the United States Government and received by William Russell Grace, Mayor of New York City. It is popularly known as "Cleopatra's Needle." (*Henry Honeychurch Gorringe—Egyptian Obelisks*)

Statue cast by the United States Government was a bronze of Admiral David Glasgow Farragut. On January 28, 1875, George Maxwell Robeson, Secretary of the Navy, awarded a $20,000 contract to the sculptor Vinnie Ream (later Mrs. Richard Leveridge Hoxie). It was cast at the Washington Navy Yard, Washington, D.C., and the mechanical work was performed by artisans employed by the Government. It was accepted April 25, 1881, by President James Abram Garfield. The base of the monument is formed of three tiers of uncut granite, the lower tier measuring 20 feet. The figure is of heroic size, standing in an easy position with one foot resting upon a pulley block around which a cable is coiled. In the hands is a telescope. The statue is located at Farragut Square, Washington, D.C.

Statue of a woman in National Statuary Hall, the Capitol, Washington, D.C., was the figure of Frances Elizabeth Willard, educator, editor, and temperance reformer, erected by Illinois and dedicated February 17, 1905.

Statue officially sanctioned by Rome was the figure of Our Lady of Prompt Succor—

the Patroness of Louisiana—which was blessed by Archbishop Janssens in the name of Pope Leo XIII on November 10, 1895, at the Ursulines Convent, New Orleans, La.

Statue presented by a foreign country to America was Liberty Enlightening the World, popularly called the Statue of Liberty, which stands on Liberty Island (formerly Bedloe Island) in New York harbor. The statue, designed by the French sculptor Frédéric Auguste Bartholdi, was a gift of the people of France in commemoration of the hundredth anniversary of American independence. The right hand and torch of the statue were exhibited at the Centennial Exhibition in Philadelphia in 1876. The statue was put in place in 1885 and unveiled on October 28, 1886. It is 151 feet high and stands on a granite pedestal 155 feet high which was provided by popular subscription in the United States.

Statue to commemorate literary characters was the Tom Sawyer and Huck Finn statue, a bronze group by Frederick Cleveland Hibbard, donated by Mr. and Mrs. George Addison Mahan and their son, Daniel Dulany Mahan. It was erected on a base of red granite on May 27, 1926, at Hannibal, Mo.

MOON PHOTOGRAPH. *See* Photograph: Celestial photograph

MORAVIAN to come to America was George Boehnisch, an Evangelist, who accompanied a group of Schwenkfelders to Pennsylvania. He arrived September 22, 1734.

MORAVIAN BISHOP was David Nitschmann who came to Georgia in 1736. He was the first bishop of the Renewed Unitas Fratrum and was consecrated on March 13, 1735, in Germany, by Bishop Daniel Ernst Japlonsky with the written concurrence of Bishop Christian Sitkovius of Lissa. Nitschmann ordained Anton Seiffert, the first pastor of the Savannah group, which was the first ordination by a Protestant bishop in America.

MORAVIAN CHURCH was built in 1735 in Savannah, Ga., where General James Edward Oglethorpe had given six hundred acres of land for a colony of Moravians. Their leader was Bishop August Gottlieb Spangenberg. (*Adelaide Lisetta Freis—The Moravian Church*)

MORAVIAN EASTER SERVICE was probably held in Bethlehem, Pa., in 1742 though it is possible that an earlier service was held either in Savannah, Ga., or in Nazareth, Pa. A group of Moravians had lived temporarily in Nazareth before settling permanently in Bethlehem in 1741.

THE FIRST

MORGAN HORSE. *See* Horse: Horse (Morgan horse)

MORMON CHURCH. *See* Church of Jesus Christ of Latter Day Saints

MORMON TEMPLE was built in Kirtland, Ohio, in 1834, by Joseph Smith and was dedicated on March 27, 1836. Joseph Smith, who was the first prophet and founder of the church which became known as the Church of Jesus Christ of Latter Day Saints, claimed that an angel visited him in 1820 in Manchester, N.Y. He started the new cult with fifty families. They moved to Kirtland, Ohio, where they resided for about seven years. Opposition to the cult increased and they were again obliged to move westward. Joseph Smith and his brother, Hyrum Smith, were murdered June 27, 1844, in Carthage, Ill.

MORTISED LOCK. *See* Lock: Mortised lock

MORTUARY to operate on the cooperative plan was the Collingwood Memorial, Toledo, Ohio, which opened September 15, 1930. The expenses of operation were divided equally by the concerns using the building, thereby enabling funeral services to be provided more cheaply.

MOSAIC CONCRETE PREFABRICATED WALLS. *See* Building: Building with prefabricated walls of mosaic concrete

MOSAIC PAVEMENT. *See* Road: Mosaic pavement

MOSQUE of importance was the Islamic Center, Washington, D.C., whose cornerstone was laid January 11, 1949. It has a minaret 160 feet above the street level from which calls to prayer may be announced through a loudspeaker. A colonnade cloister joins the mosque to two wings which house an institute containing a library, a museum, classrooms for study, and administration offices. An auditorium accommodates three hundred persons in the basement of the mosque. The first director was Dr. Mahmoud Hoballah.

MOTHER-IN-LAW DAY. *See* Holiday: Mother-in-law day

MOTHER'S DAY. *See* Holiday: Mother's day

MOTION PICTURE. *See* Moving picture

MOTION PICTURE STUDIO. *See* Moving picture "studio"

THE FIRST

MOTOR BOAT
Motor boat was invented by James Rumsey and exhibited by him in September 1784 on the Potomac River, in the presence of George Washington. It worked against the stream by mechanical means. He subsequently gave his attention to steam as a motive power and in March 1786 propelled a boat on the Potomac by a steam engine which produced motion by the force of a stream of water thrown out by a pump at the stern. In December 1787 the experiment was successfully repeated on a larger scale. (*Ella May Turner—James Rumsey, Pioneer in Steam Navigation*)

Motor boat pleasure craft was produced in 1885 by F. W. Ofeldt and manufactured by the Gas Engine and Power Company, New York City. The boat contained a 2 h.p. engine, propelled by naphtha, which developed a speed of 5 to 7 knots. She was 21 feet long, had a 64-inch beam, and a draught of 22 inches.

Storage battery motor boat was the "Magnet" which was operated by one motor revolving a two-blade screw 18 inches in diameter. The battery was of 56 storage cells. A 10-hour charge ran the boat for 60 to 70 miles at a speed of 10 miles an hour. The "Magnet" was built in Newark, N.J., in 1888 and was owned by Anthony and Frederick Reckenzaun. She was 28 feet long, with a 6-foot beam, and was 3 feet deep amidships.

MOTOR BOAT ENGINE. *See* Engine: Outboard twin-cylinder motor (light)

MOTOR BOAT RACE. *See* Boat race: Motor boat race under organized rules

MOTOR BUS. *See* Automobile bus

MOTOR (electric). *See* Electric motor: Electric motor (single-phase alternating current)

MOTOR TRUCK. *See* Automobile truck

MOTORCYCLE
Motorcycle (practical) was manufactured by the E. R. Thomas Motor Company of Buffalo, N.Y., in 1900. A single-cylinder gasoline engine was attached to the transverse bar of an ordinary bicycle and a flat belt ran to a concentric pulley on the rear wheel.

Motorcycle (steam-driven) was a two-wheeled vehicle invented by William A. Austin of Winthrop, Mass., in 1868. The steam boiler was suspended amidships. The vehicle had a very limited traveling radius because of the small amount of steam generated.

MOTORCYCLE—Continued

Motorcycle (twin-cycle) was an "Indian," made in 1905 in Springfield, Mass. It had a spring-front fork, battery ignition, and a gravity feed oiling system. The machine was started by pedaling. The gas tank was mounted on the rear fender.

Motorcycle with built-in gas engine especially designed was manufactured in Springfield, Mass., by George M. Hendee, who formed the Hendee Manufacturing Company, which began to market the "Indian Motorcycle" in 1901. Previously, motorcycles had been ordinary bicycles to which motors were attached. In 1901, three motorcycles were built, and in 1902 production was increased to 143. The motors were made by the Aurora Machine Co., Aurora, Ill, and were assembled to the frames in Springfield, Mass., where they were built. The machines were first publicly demonstrated June 1, 1901, in a hill-climbing exhibition.

MOTORCYCLE ASSOCIATION was the

Federation of American Motorcyclists, organized September 7, 1903, at Manhattan Beach, N.Y. The first president was R. G. Betts of the New York Motor Cycle Club. About 200 delegates attended the first meeting.

MOTORCYCLE ENDURANCE RUN

was held July 4-5, 1902, covering a distance of 254 miles from Boston to New York City, through South Framingham, Worcester, Warren, Springfield, Hartford, Meriden, New Haven, Bridgeport, and Greenwich. Of the thirty-two entries, thirty-one started and thirteen finished, and seven made a perfect score of 1,000 points.

MOTORCYCLE HILL-CLIMBING

CONTEST was staged in Riverdale, N.Y., on May 30, 1903, and was won by Glenn Hammond Curtiss, who received a gold medal from the New York Motorcycle Club. The race created quite a sensation because it was not believed that a motorcycle had much power.

MOTORCYCLE RACE

Motorcycle race (300 miles) was held July 4, 1914, at Dodge City, Kan., on a two-mile dirt track about two and a half miles from the city. Of the 36 starters, 18 finished, 6 completing 150 laps. The first-place prize of two gold medals and $600 was won by Glen R. ("Slivers") Boyd of Denver, Colo., in an "Indian" motorcycle. His time was 4 hours, 24 minutes, and 58 seconds, with an average of 67.92 miles per hour.

Motorcycle to exceed 200 miles an hour was ridden by Wilhelm Herz, who rode a measured mile over the salt flats at Wendover, Utah, on August 4, 1956, at a speed of 210 miles an hour.

MOTORCYCLE TRIP

Motorcycle transcontinental trip was made by George A. Wyman of San Francisco, Calif., on a Yale-California motorcycle built by L. W. Leavitt and Company, San Francisco. Wyman left San Francisco May 16, 1903, and arrived in New York City July 6, 1903. The motorcycle was a 3½ h.p. single-cylinder machine with a belt drive. (Motorcycle Magazine. August 1903)

Motorcycle transcontinental trip by women was made by Adelina and Augusta Van Buren, who left New York City on July 5, 1916, and arrived in San Diego, Calif., on September 12, 1916, via Buffalo, Chicago, Omaha, Denver, and Salt Lake City.

MOTTO OF THE UNITED STATES

—"In God We Trust"—was authorized by act of July 30, 1956 (70 Stat.L.732), a joint resolution "to establish a national motto of the United States" signed by President Dwight David Eisenhower.

MOURNING STAMP. See Postage stamp:
Mourning stamp

MOVABLE CHURCH was the Chapel of

the Transfiguration (Episcopal), which was consecrated June 3, 1899, at Conanicut Island, R.I. It was 27 feet long and 18 feet wide and contained 14 benches, 20 chairs, a platform and an altar. The interior, including the pews, prayer desk and altar, was made of oak. The church was built on a wooden chassis with four wheels and was drawn from place to place by horses. The first preacher was the Reverend Charles E. Preston of St. Matthew's Church. The first service was held April 23, 1899. (Charles E. Preston—The First Movable Church)

MOVING PICTURE
See also
Moving picture actor   Moving picture studio
Moving picture cen-   Moving picture the-
sorship   ater
Moving picture pro-
jector

Airplane moving picture show. See Aviation: Airplane moving picture show

Animated cartoon was James Stuart Blackton's Humorous Phases of Funny Faces, containing about 8,000 drawings showing a man rolling his eyes and blowing smoke at a girl, a dog jumping over a hoop, etc. The final scene was a chalk-type drawing which the artist started as a sketch of one object, but which ended as a sketch of another. The film was released by Vitagraph in 1906. (Journal of the Society of Motion Picture Engineers. September 1933)

THE FIRST

Animated cartoon in color was *The Debut of Thomas Kat,* the story of a kitten, taught by his mother to catch mice, who confidently and tragically tackled a rat. The cartoon was produced by the Bray Pictures Corporation, New York City, and was released in 1916 by Paramount. The drawings were made on transparent celluloid, the colors painted on the reverse side, and then photographed with a regular color camera. The Brewster color process was used.

Animated cartoon in color (Technicolor) of feature length with sound was Walt Disney's *Snow White and the Seven Dwarfs,* based on Grimm's fairy tale, first exhibited December 21, 1937, at the Carthay Circle Theatre, Los Angeles, Calif. The running time was 75 minutes.

Animated cartoon (present technique) was *The Artist's Dream,* also known as *The Dachshund,* released June 12, 1913, by Pathé Frères. The cartoon showed John Randolph Bray drawing a dachshund. The dog ate sausages until he exploded. It was produced by John Randolph Bray of New York City, who filed an application for a patent on January 9, 1914, which was granted August 11, 1914, No. 1,107,193.

Animated cartoon talking picture was Walt Disney's *Steamboat Willie,* produced in Hollywood, Calif., depicting the antics of Mickey Mouse. It was shown September 19, 1928, at the Colony Theatre, New York City.

Animated cartoon (technical), visualizing "unseeable" phenomena such as the flow of invisible gases, radio waves, etc., was produced in 1916 by the Bray Pictures Corporation of New York City.

Animated photographic picture projection before a theater audience was shown February 5, 1870, at the Ninth Annual Entertainment of the Young Men's Society of St. Mark's Evangelical Lutheran Church of Philadelphia, at the Academy of Music, Philadelphia, Pa., by Henry Renno Heyl. Heyl used his "Phasmatrope," a converted projecting lantern in front of which was a revolving disc containing sixteen openings near the edge on which photographic plates were placed. The first plate showed dancers who appeared to move as the revolving wheel showed successive motions. The pictures were continuous and did not change. (*Motion Picture Magazine, November 1914*)

Animated three-dimensional cartoon in Technicolor (modern) was Walt Disney's *Melody,* distributed by RKO Radio Pictures. Its world premiere took place May 28, 1953, at the Hollywood Theatre and the Downtown Paramount Theatre, Los Angeles, Calif.

THE FIRST

Colored moving pictures were exhibited December 11, 1909, at the Madison Square Garden Concert Hall, New York City. They were run through red and green screens at about twice the present speed and were very hard on the eyes. The presentation was of about ten minutes' duration and was composed of short subjects and views. The pictures used the Kinemacolor films of Charles Urban and G. Albert Smith of England. American rights to manufacture were acquired by Gilbert Henry Aymer and James Klein Bowen, both of Allentown, Pa., who formed the Kinemacolor Company of America. In September 1895 Thomas Alva Edison exhibited colored moving pictures at the Cotton States Exposition, Atlanta, Ga. One of them was "Annabelle, the Dancer." The film was hand-colored at West Orange, N.J., in 1894.

Foreign feature film exhibited was *Queen Elizabeth,* shown to an invited audience July 12, 1912, at the Lyceum Theatre, New York City, and commercially exhibited August 12, 1912, at the Powers Theater, Chicago, Ill. It was a four-reel feature made in France which starred Sarah Bernhardt as Queen Elizabeth and Lou Tellegen as Robert Devereux, Earl of Essex. It was released by Famous Players Film Co., of which Adolph Zukor was president and Daniel Frohman managing director.

Magic lantern show. *See* Magic lantern show: Magic lantern feature show

Motion picture film copyrighted. *See* Copyright: Motion picture film copyrighted

Moving picture camera. *See* Camera: Moving picture camera (portable)

Moving picture "close-up" was made February 2, 1893, at the Edison studio, West Orange, N.J., by William Kennedy Laurie Dickson and showed Fred Ott sneezing. (*Antonia and William Kennedy Laurie Dickson—Edison's Invention of the Kineto-Phonograph*)

Moving picture contract. *See* Moving picture actor: Actor to have an exclusive contract

Moving picture film. *See* Photographic film: Moving picture film (commercial)

Moving picture film exhibition was held May 9, 1893, before 400 persons at the Department of Physics, Brooklyn Institute, Brooklyn, N.Y. Thomas Alva Edison's Kinetograph was used. An optical lantern projector showed moving images of a blacksmith and his two helpers passing a bottle and forging a piece of iron. Each film strip had 700 images, each image

MOVING PICTURE—*Continued*
being shown 1/92 second. The equipment which was to have provided sound accompaniment failed to operate at this showing. (*Scientific American. May 20, 1893*)

Moving picture for training soldiers utilized by the U.S. Army was *School of the Soldier*, produced by the Bray Pictures Corporation of New York City at West Point, N.Y., in 1917.

Moving picture from an airplane was taken February 16, 1912, by Frank Trenholm Coffin in a hydroplane over Governors Island on a flight over lower Manhattan, New York City, to the Statue of Liberty, Bedloe Island. Still photographs were shown on a full page of the New York *Times* of February 18, 1912.

Moving picture of a complete grand opera was Fortune Gallo's production of Leoncavallo's *Pagliacci*, shown February 20, 1931, at the Central Park Theatre, Seventh Avenue and 59th Street, New York City. A symphony orchestra of 75 was featured with the San Carlo Grand Opera Company of 150. The part of Nedda was sung by Alba Novella, Canio by Fernando Bertini, Tonio by Mario Vaili, and Silvio by Giuseppe Interranti.

Moving picture of a real pugilistic encounter taken at night was made by the Biograph Company November 3, 1899, at the Coney Island Athletic Club, Coney Island, N.Y. Illumination was furnished by four hundred arc lamps over the ring. The contestants were James (Jim) Jackson Jeffries and Tom Sharkey. The bout was a bona fide fight of twenty-five rounds. Jeffries won on points. Sharkey was not knocked out. George Silver was the referee.

Moving picture of a staged prize fight was made by the Kinetoscope Exhibition Company in its "Black Maria" studio, West Orange, N.J., in July 1894, and showed Michael Leonard defeating Jack Cushing. The pictures were shown in six peep machines, each showing one round of the fight, at 83 Nassau Street, New York City.

Moving picture of an eclipse of the sun taken from a dirigible was taken from the U.S. Navy dirigible "Los Angeles" on January 24, 1925, when it was about 4,500 feet in the air at a point about 18¾ miles east of Monauk Point, Long Island, N.Y. The total eclipse of the sun (2 minutes and 4.6 seconds) was recorded by four astronomical cameras, two moving picture cameras, and one spectrograph. (*United States Naval Observatory Publications. Vol. 13*)

Moving picture of an eclipse of the sun taken from an airplane was made April 28, 1930, by Lieutenant Leslie Edward Gehres and Chief Photographer J. M. F. Haase of the U.S. Navy, flying approximately 18,000 feet over Honey Lake, Calif. The flight was sponsored by the United States Naval Observatory. The totality of the eclipse was 1½ seconds. An attempt to take similar pictures had been made September 10, 1923, at Santa Catalina, Calif., by Captain Albert Ware Marshall, Lieutenant Ben Harrison Wyatt, and Chief Photographer J. M. F. Haase of the U.S. Navy, but the pictures were of little value as it was cloudy. (*Popular Astronomy. Oct. 1930*)

Moving picture of the inside of a living heart (of a dog) showing the opening and closing of the mitral valve (a structure often crippled by rheumatic fever) was made at Montefiore Hospital, New York City, by Dr. Elliott Samuel Hurwitt, Dr. Adrian Kantrowitz, and Anatol Herskovitz (photographer). The official title of the 9½-minute color film was *A Cinematographic Study of the Function of the Mitral Valve in Situ*, and it was first shown October 16, 1951, at the clinical session of the New York Academy of Medicine Post Graduate Fortnightly held at Montefiore Hospital.

Moving picture of the planets was made of Mars in October 1926 and of Jupiter in September 1927 by William Hammond Wright at the Lick Observatory, Mt. Hamilton, Calif., with the aid of the Crossley telescope. Exposures were made every three minutes, so that at the rate of 32 frames a minute, movement of the planets took as many seconds on the screen as it does hours in the sky. The photographs were taken in several colors, ranging from ultra-violet to infra-red. They illustrated the alterations in the appearance of the planets when the color by which they are viewed is changed.

Moving picture of the sun (other than of eclipses) was taken by Robert Raynolds McMath at the McMath-Hulbert Observatory of the University of Michigan at Lake Angelus, Pontiac, Mich., on June 19, 1934, with the Spectroheliokinematograph. The pictures, which showed solar prominences or sunspots in motion as well as activity in connection with sunspot groups, were first shown publicly before the American Astronomical Society on September 10, 1934, at Connecticut College New London, Conn.

Moving picture on film shown on a screen was exhibited by Woodville Latham, who demonstrated his "Pantoptikon" at 35 Frankfort Street, New York City, on April 21, 1895. A continuous roll of film, with hole perforations on the sides for spokes of the sprocket, reeled in front of an electric light contained in a

THE FIRST

magic-lantern type projector. A bout of four minutes' duration between "Young Griffo" and "Battling (Charles) Barnett" was staged May 5, 1895, by Otway Latham on the roof of Madison Square Garden, New York City. The film was exhibited May 20, 1895, at 153 Broadway, New York City, after which it was shown in a tent at Surf Avenue, Coney Island, N.Y., for the rest of the summer.

Moving picture premiere telecast. *See* under Television—Telecast

Moving picture presented simultaneously in major cities throughout the world was *On the Beach,* an adaptation of the novel by Nevil Shute, which had its premiere December 17, 1959, at the Astor Theatre, New York City, and seventeen other cities. The 134-minute film was produced by Stanley Kramer and written by John Paxton. It starred Gregory Peck, Ava Gardner, Fred Astaire, and Anthony Perkins.

Moving picture with a plot was *The Great Train Robbery,* produced by the Edison Company in the fall of 1903. It was staged and directed by Edwin S. Porter. The scenes were filmed in New Jersey. The cast included George Barnes, Broncho Billy Anderson (Max Aronson), Marie Murray, A. C. Abadie, and others. The film was printed on tinted celluloid: yellow for the dancehall, bluish green for the woods. (*Terry Ramsaye—A Million and One Nights*)

Moving picture with scent was *Behind the Great Wall,* a travelogue of modern China, presented December 8, 1959, at the De Mille Theatre, New York City. The film depicted a tiger hunt, fishing with cormorants, a May Day parade in Peiping, and other scenes. The scent was forced through ceiling vents by the Aromarama process.

Newsreel was the Pathé Weekly, later known as Pathé News, which was first operated in November 1910. H. C. Hoagland was the editor. Moving pictures of historic events had, however, been taken earlier. Films of the McKinley inaugural parade of 1896, the funeral procession in Colon, Cuba, of the "Maine" victims in 1898, the embarkation of Theodore Roosevelt's Rough Riders, etc., had been made. (*International Photographer. Vol. 5. No. 8. September 1933*)

Newsreel in color was a Warner Brothers-Pathé Newsreel taken January 1, 1948, of the Tournament of Roses and the Rose Bowl Game, Pasadena, Calif. It was made by Cinecolor process and released January 5, 1948.

Peep show in which film was used in a vending machine or cabinet was exhibited by Andrew M. Holland of the Holland Brothers at

THE FIRST

1155 Broadway, New York City, on April 14, 1894. The machine was invented by Thomas Alva Edison, who utilized the film prepared by George Eastman. The films were made in the Edison laboratories. The pictures were viewed directly, and not reflected, and were visible to only one person at a time. Annie Oakley, Sandow, Buffalo Bill, Ruth St. Denis and other celebrities were shown. (*Frederick William Wile—A Century of Industrial Progress*)

Peep show machine was patented by Samuel D. Goodale of Cincinnati, Ohio, who obtained patent No. 31,310 on February 5, 1861, on a stereoscope machine. It was called "The Mutoscope" and was operated by hand. Pictures were placed on leaves fastened by one edge to an axis in such a way that they stood out like spokes. As the shaft revolved, different images were seen in motion.

Photographic attempt to show motion was made by Dr. Coleman Sellers of Philadelphia, Pa., who obtained patent No. 31,357, February 5, 1861, on the "Kinematoscope," an "improvement in exhibiting stereoscopic pictures of moving objects." A series of still pictures with successive stages of action was mounted on blades of a paddle and viewed through slits passed under the lens of a stereoscope revolved at right angles. The pictures were not reflected on a screen, and were visible only in the cabinet. The whole of the picture was not seen at once, but only by degrees as the cylinder revolved. (*International Photographer. February 1933*)

Serial moving picture was *The Adventures of Kathlyn,* issued by [William N.] Selig's Polyscope Company, Chicago, Ill., on December 29, 1913. The first installment was a two-part drama, "The Unwelcome Throne," in three reels. Twelve other installments of two reels each followed. Kathlyn Williams was the featured actress and F. J. Grandon the director. The film was adapted by Gilson Willets from Harold MacGrath's story which appeared in the Hearst newspapers in 1913 and which was published in book form by the Bobbs-Merrill Company, Indianapolis, Ind., in 1914.

Six-reel feature-length comedy was *Tillie's Punctured Romance,* released December 21, 1914, by the Alco Film Corporation. It took four weeks to produce. The director was Mack Sennett and the stars were Marie Dressler, Mabel Normand, Charles Chaplin and Mack Swain. (*Moving Picture World. November 14, 1914*)

Sound-on-film moving picture was Dr. Lee De Forest's "Phonofilm," demonstrated March 12, 1923, for the press and on April 4, 1923, before the New York Electrical Society at the Engineering Society's building, New

MOVING PICTURE—*Continued*
York City. Pictures were shown with music, but no voices were heard. The pictures were later shown to an invited audience April 15, 1923, at the Rivoli Theatre, New York City. Presented on the film were "The Gavotte" (a man and woman dancing to old-time music); "The Serenade" (four musicians playing on wind, percussion, and string instruments); and an Egyptian dancer. The sound occupied a narrow margin of the film on which the pictures appeared.

Talking picture was presented on August 5, 1926, at an invitation performance at the Warner Theatre, New York City. On August 6, a gala premiere was held at which seats sold for $10, plus tax. The film depicted Will Hays, who welcomed Vitaphone; Mischa Elman, who played "Humoresque"; Marion Talley, who sang "Caro Nome"; Giovanni Martinelli, who sang an aria from *I Pagliacci;* and several other short features. The feature picture was "Don Juan," a film of 10,018 feet, in which John Barrymore, Mary Astor, Warner Oland, Estelle Taylor, Myrna Loy, and other well-known stars took part. The musical score was played by the New York Philharmonic Orchestra of 107 men. The picture was directed by Alan Crosland. The film itself had no sound recorded on it but was synchronized with disc phonograph records (Vitaphone) of the musical score.

Talking picture entirely in color was Warner Brothers' Vitaphone Technicolor film *On With the Show,* exhibited May 28, 1929, at the Winter Garden, New York City. The cast included Betty Compson, Joe E. Brown, and Ethel Waters. It was directed by Alan Crosland and was based on a story by Humphrey Pearson.

Talking picture in Esperanto was a four-minute film made July 13, 1929, in the Paramount studio, New York City. The actors were Germaine Chomette and Henry W. Hetzel. Donald E. Parrish, secretary for the United States section of the Universal Esperanto Association with headquarters in Geneva, Switzerland, delivered an address and salutation to accompany the film at the twenty-second annual convention of the Esperanto Society of North America. The film was exported to sixteen countries.

Talking picture of more than 6,000 feet was *The Lights of New York,* which was produced by Warner Brothers and released July 21, 1928. The principal players were Helene Costello, Mary Carr, Cullen Landis, Gladys Brockwell, and Wheeler Oakman. A gala performance was presented at midnight on Friday, July 6, 1928, at the Strand Theatre, New York City. The sound was on film (Vitaphonic). The picture was based on an original story by F. Hugh Herbert and Murray Roth.

Talking picture taken outdoors (full length) was *In Old Arizona,* a Fox Movietone with sound recorded on the film. It was an all-talking drama, 8,724 feet, and was released January 20, 1929. Nine tenths of the entire production was taken on location in Zion National Park and Bryce Canyon, in Utah; on the Mohave desert; and at the old mission of San Fernando in California. It was directed by Raoul Walsh and Irving Cummings and featured Edmund Lowe, Warner Baxter, and Dorothy Burgess.

Talking pictures of presidential candidates were taken August 11, 1924, by Theodore W. Case and Lee De Forest, of President Calvin Coolidge on the grounds of the White House and of Senator Robert Marion La Follette on the steps of the Capitol, Washington, D.C. John William Davis was photographed at Locust Valley, N.Y. The newsreel was shown in various theaters in September 1924.

Technicolor motion picture really successful was *The Toll of the Sea,* released December 3, 1922, at the Rialto Theatre, New York City. The process was developed by Dr. Herbert Thomas Kalmus, president and general manager of Technicolor Motion Picture Corporation from its inception until 1959.

Three-dimensional feature moving picture was *Bwana Devil,* produced, directed, and written by Arch Oboler (Arch Oboler Productions) and released by United Artists in 1953. It was a Natural Vision-Magnetic Sound Track picture requiring Polaroid viewers. It opened February 18, 1953, at Loew's State Theatre, New York City, and featured Robert Stack, Barbara Britton, Nigel Bruce, and Ramsay Hill. It was the story of a British engineer who tracked two man-eating lions that had disrupted the construction of the first railroad in East Africa at the turn of the century.

Three-dimensional feature moving picture in color produced by a major studio was *The House of Wax,* starring Vincent Price, first exhibited April 10, 1953, at the Paramount Theatre, New York City. It was a remake of the 1933 *Mystery of the Wax Museum. The House of Wax* was in Warnercolor and was seen through Polaroid viewers.

Three-dimensional feature moving picture produced and released by a major company was *Man in the Dark,* which had its world premiere at the Globe Theatre, New York City, on April 8, 1953. It was produced by Columbia Pictures in sepia and starred Edmond O'Brien and Audrey Totter.

X-ray moving pictures. *See* X-ray: X-ray moving pictures

THE FIRST

MOVING PICTURE ACTOR

Actor to have an exclusive contract for a single appearance in a moving picture was James John Corbett, engaged by the Kinetoscope Exhibition Company to appear in a six-round fight, one minute each round, with Pete Courtney of Trenton, N.J., in August 1894. (*Terry Ramsaye—A Million and One Nights*)

Moving picture actor and son to receive "Oscars" were Walter Huston, as the best supporting actor, and his son, John Huston, as the best director, for *The Treasure of Sierra Madre*. (The film also received the best screen play award.) The presentations were made in Hollywood, Calif., on March 24, 1949, by the Academy of Motion Picture Arts and Sciences.

Moving picture actors to receive "Oscars," the award of the Academy of Motion Picture Arts and Sciences, were Emil Jannings (*The Last Command, The Way of All Flesh*) and Janet Gaynor (*Seventh Heaven, Street Angel, Sunrise*), who received "Oscars" in Hollywood, Calif., on May 16, 1929, "for the best acting in pictures released in Los Angeles, Calif., between August 1, 1927, and July 31, 1928." Ten similar awards and two special awards were presented to others for excellence in allied fields, such as cinematography, art direction, engineering effects, direction, etc.

Moving picture actress depicted on a postage stamp was Grace Kelly, whose marriage to Prince Rainier III of Monaco on April 19, 1956, was commemorated by a series of eight Monacan stamps (1, 2, 3, 5, 15, 100, 200, and 500 francs), sold only on the wedding day.

Moving picture star was Max Aronson, known as Broncho Billy, Max Anderson, and G. M. Anderson. His first film appearance was in 1903 in *The Great Train Robbery*. (*Terry Ramsaye—A Million and One Nights*)

Moving picture star (female) was Florence Lawrence, whose first performance in films was in 1907 for the Edison company. She then worked for the Vitagraph Company. In 1909 she went to the Biograph Company and was featured as "The Biograph Girl." Later she became known as "The IMP Girl," working for the Independent Moving Picture Company.

Negro to win an "Oscar" from the Academy of Motion Picture Arts and Sciences was Hattie McDaniel, who played Scarlett O'Hara's "mammy" in the movie adapted from Margaret Mitchell's *Gone With the Wind*. The award was presented February 29, 1940, in Hollywood, Calif., for the best performance by a "supporting actress."

Stunt actor was Frederick Rodman Law, a steeplejack, who staged a parachute jump

THE FIRST

from the Statue of Liberty on Bedloe Island in New York Harbor on February 2, 1912, for Pathé News. On April 14, 1912, he jumped from the Brooklyn Bridge, and on November 12, 1912, from a dynamited balloon into the Hudson River.

MOVING PICTURE CENSORSHIP

Moving picture censorship board (national) was the National Board of Censorship of Motion Pictures, organized March 1909 (by the People's Institute of New York City founded May 15, 1897, by Charles Sprague Smith, its first executive chairman). Producing companies agreed to prorate a review charge among their member companies on the basis of $3.50 for a negative reel of 1,000 feet. The fund was applied to the office expense of the board. In 1916, the name was changed to the National Board of Review of Motion Pictures.

Moving picture censorship board (state) was the State Board of Censors created in Pennsylvania by act of June 19, 1911. No appropriation was made until April 4, 1913, when $7,500 was provided. Censors were appointed February 1, 1914. Ohio approved an act May 3, 1913, providing for a motion picture censorship board of three, who were appointed in 1913. Kansas approved an act March 13, 1913, effective April 1, 1913, but no provisions to enforce it were made until 1915. The United States Supreme Court in February 1915 held the Ohio and Kansas censorship laws unconstitutional.

Moving picture censorship regulation (federal) was the act of July 31, 1912 (37 Stat.L. 240) "to prohibit the importation and the interstate transportation of films or other pictorial representations of prize fights." The penalty for violation was not more than $1,000, or one year at hard labor, or both.

MOVING PICTURE MACHINE

Machine to show animated pictures was the Zoëtrope, the Wheel of Life, patented April 23, 1867, No. 64,117, by William E. Lincoln of Providence, R.I., who assigned it to Milton Bradley & Company, Springfield, Mass. It consisted of a horizontal wheel with a series of animated drawings showing successive steps at right angles to the circumference. The drawings were viewed through a slit and when the wheel revolved appeared to show animation.

MOVING PICTURE PROJECTOR

Moving picture projector patent was awarded O. B. Brown of Malden, Mass., who obtained patent No. 93,594 on August 10, 1869, on an "optical instrument." It combined the principles of the phenakistoscope and the magic lantern.

Moving picture projector (portable) was invented by Dr. Herman Adolf De Vry and

MOVING PICTURE PROJECTOR—
Continued
produced in 1913 in Chicago, Ill. It weighed approximately 26 pounds, cost $200, and was known as "the projector in a suit case."

MOVING PICTURE "STUDIO" was a frame cabin covered with black roofing paper located on the Edison lot in West Orange, N.J., in 1892. The structure was built so that it could be pivoted to enable the stage to secure the maximum sunlight. It was a "revolving photographic building" and was completed February 1, 1893, at a cost of $637.67. It was nicknamed "Black Maria."

MOVING PICTURE THEATER
  Drive-in moving picture theater was opened June 6, 1933, on a ten-acre plot on Admiral Wilson Boulevard, Camden, N.J., by Richard Milton Hollingshead, Jr., and Willis Warren Smith of Riverton, N.J. Two shows were presented nightly on a screen 40 by 50 feet. Nine rows of inclined planes with aisles 45 feet deep accommodated five hundred cars. The sound equipment was supplied by the RCA-Victor Company, Camden, N.J.

  Moving picture theater was the Electric Theater, 262 South Main Street, Los Angeles, Calif., a circus front tent-show called a "black top," which was opened April 2, 1902, by Thomas Lincoln Tally. Among the first pictures shown were *The Capture of the Biddle Brothers* and *New York in a Blizzard*. The show lasted about one hour; the admission was ten cents. (*Frederick William Wile—A Century of Industrial Progress*)

  Theater built especially for the rear projection of moving pictures was the Trans-Lux Theatre at 58th Street and Madison Avenue, New York City, which was opened March 14, 1931. The first rear projection screen of theater size had been installed March 11, 1927, for the opening night of the Roxy Theatre, New York City. It was a Trans-Lux screen 18 by 22 feet which at first was used only for silhouette work, because the lens of the projector was imperfect.

  Theater in the world devoted exclusively to the exhibition of motion pictures was the "Nickelodeon," which was opened in June 1905 by Harry Davis in an empty store at 433-435 Smithfield Street, Pittsburgh, Pa. It had 96 seats taken from Davis's theaters. Among the first films shown were *Poor But Honest* and *The Baffled Burglar*. A profit of over a thousand dollars was netted the first week. John Paul Harris was general manager and Isaac Lisbon manager.

MOVING PICTURE TRAILER. *See* Television—Telecast: Moving picture trailer to be televised

MOVING SIDEWALK. *See* Sidewalk (traveling): Two-way moving walk

MOVING STAIRWAY. *See* Escalator

MOWER (horsepower) was patented on December 4, 1812, by Peter Gaillard of Lancaster, Pa. (*Robert L. Ardrey—American Agricultural Implements*)

MULE. *See* Animals: Mule

MULTIGRAPH was invented by Harry Christian Gammeter of Cleveland, Ohio, who obtained patent No. 722,404, March 10, 1903, on a "duplicating machine." It was the first successful machine designed to simplify the printing processes, so that the ordinary layman could print from type, either with ribbon or ink. Commercial manufacture was undertaken December 12, 1902, by the American Multigraph Sales Company of Cleveland, Ohio.

MULTIPLE TELEPHONE SWITCHBOARD. *See* Telephone: Multiple common battery switchboard

MUNICIPAL BATHHOUSE. *See* Bathhouse: Bathhouse owned and operated by a municipality

MUNICIPAL CANCER HOSPITAL. *See* Hospital: Cancer hospital (municipal)

MUNICIPAL FILTRATION SYSTEM. *See* Water purification: Municipal filtration system

MUNICIPAL MILK STATION. *See* Milk station (municipal)

MUNICIPAL RAILROAD. *See* Railroad: Municipal railroad

MUNICIPAL STADIUM. *See* Stadium: Municipal stadium

MUNICIPAL THEATER. *See* Theater: Municipal theater

MUNICIPAL UNIVERSITY. *See* College: City college

MURDER TRIAL TELECAST. *See* Television—Telecast: Murder trial to be televised

MUSEUM
  College museum was the College of Charleston Museum, Charleston, S.C. The old Charleston museum building was torn down

and the museum moved to the College of Charleston, where it was greatly enlarged and rechristened the College of Charleston Museum. On August 29, 1850, the City Council ratified an "Ordinance to provide for the appointment of a Curator for the Museum of the College of Charleston" and on November 25, 1850, Francis Simmons Holmes was elected. On December 28, 1850, he was appointed Professor of Geology and Paleontology at the College and on May 6, 1855, Professor of Natural History. (*Charleston Museum Bulletin*)

Commercial museum was the Philadelphia Commercial Museum organized by city ordinance approved June 15, 1894. It was developed by Dr. William Powell Wilson, who conceived the idea of the institution and who served as its director and executive head from the first meeting of the Board of Directors on June 20, 1894, until his death May 12, 1927. The Philadelphia Commercial Museum is composed of the Museum proper, the department of Visual Education, the Foreign Trade Bureau, the Library, and the Exhibition Hall with its convention hall. (*Report of the Philadelphia Commercial Museum—A Resolution in Memory of William P. Wilson, Sc.D.*)

Costume museum was the Museum of Costume Arts, New York City, incorporated April 28, 1937, to develop "cultural education in connection with those arts and industries which function in conjunction with design in form of apparel and accessories by applying to this field the ways and means now commonly used or applied by fine arts and industrial museum associations and foundations and musical societies of various kinds in their respective fields."

Health museum. *See* Health museum

Industrial museum was established by the Association for the Establishment and Maintenance for the People of the City of New York of a Museum of Peaceful Arts. It was incorporated February 26, 1914, and the name was changed in 1931 to the New York Museum of Science and Industry.

Maritime museum devoted exclusively to maritime affairs worldwide in scope was the Mariners' Museum, Newport News, Va., established June 2, 1930, by Archer Milton Huntington. The first board of trustees was composed of Mr. Huntington, Anna Hyatt Huntington, Homer Lenoir Ferguson, Charles Franklin Bailey, and Frederick Henry Skinner.

Museum devoted exclusively to atomic energy was the American Museum of Atomic Energy, Oak Ridge, Tenn., opened to the public on March 19, 1949, the anniversary of the removal of the security fence from the city of Oak Ridge. The museum is operated for the Atomic Energy Commission as a service to the public by the Oak Ridge Institute of Nuclear Studies, a nonprofit educational organization.

Museum devoted exclusively to paper-making was the Dard Hunter Paper Museum of the Massachusetts Institute of Technology, Cambridge, Mass., which opened June 5, 1939. The curator was Dr. Dard Hunter who personally collected the material in every paper-making country of the world over a period of about forty years.

Museum especially constructed as a museum and art gallery was Peale's Baltimore Museum and Gallery of the Fine Arts, operated by Rembrandt Peale, son of Charles Willson Peale. It was a three-story building at 225 North Holliday Street, Baltimore, Md., and was designed by Robert Cary Long, Sr. The opening was advertised for August 15, 1814. The building was sold in 1830 to the City of Baltimore, which used it as its first City Hall.

Museum to install refrigerated vaults with automatic temperature control for the preservation of valuable specimens of furs and similar articles was the University of California Museum of Vertebrate Zoology, Berkeley, Calif. The museum was thus equipped when it was moved into the Life Science Building in March 1930.

Outdoor museum (or nature trail) was established in 1925 by Dr. Frank Eugene Lutz at the Station for the Study of Insects located in the Ramapo Mountains in Tuxedo Park, N.Y. This nature trail was developed under the auspices of the American Museum of Natural History, New York City, with the cooperation of the Palisades Interstate Park Commission. It consisted of two trails, each a half mile long, the Training Trail and the Testing Trail, which were posted with signs describing the trees, shrubs, flowering plants, insects, etc.

Public museum in America was the Charleston Museum of Charleston, S.C. It was organized on January 12, 1773, at the annual anniversary meeting of the Charleston Library Society. The first curators of the museum were Charles Cotesworth Pinckney, Esquire; Thomas Heyward, Esquire; Alexander Baron, Physician; and Peter Fayssoux, Physician. In 1915 the museum was incorporated as the Charleston Museum. (*Charleston Museum Quarterly. Vol. 1. No. 1. 1923.*)

Wax works museum. *See* Wax works museum

MUSIC

Chamber music organization was the Mendelssohn Quintette Club of Boston, Mass. Its first concert was given at Chickering Hall, December 14, 1849.

Community chorus was established in 1912 in Rochester, N.Y., by Harry Barnhart, who appeared by permission of the mayor of Rochester at a band concert at the Convention Hall, where he introduced the idea of community singing.

Concert reported was "a concert of music on sundry instruments" held at six o'clock at Mr. (Peter) Pelham's "great room" near the Sun Tavern in Boston, Mass., on December 30, 1731. Tickets were five shillings. (*Boston News-Letter. Dec. 16-23, 1731*)

Libretto. *See* Libretto

Long distance telephone concert was held March 31, 1877, at Steinway Hall, New York City. Music played in Philadelphia, Pa., was heard by means of Elisha Gray's so-called "Transmission of Music by Telegraph." The audience heard "Home Sweet Home," "The Last Rose of Summer," "Yankee Doodle," and other songs.

Music convention was attended by ninety-six men and forty-two women singing-teachers from ten states and was held August 16-25, 1838, in Boston, Mass. Colonel Asa Barr of New Braintree, Mass., was president.

Music festival is claimed to have been given to celebrate the signing of the Treaty of Ghent, between the United States and England, on December 25, 1814. The news reached Boston, Mass., February 13, 1815, and a concert of sacred music was played February 16, 1815, at the Reverend Dr. Baldwin's, in Boston, Mass. The first part of Haydn's *Creation*, parts of Handel's *Judas Maccabeus*, the Dettingen *Te Deum, Ode to St. Cecilia's Day*, and the *Hallelujah Chorus* were presented. (*William Arms Fisher—Music Festivals in the United States*)

Music printed in a magazine was "The Hill Tops, a New Hunting Song" printed in the April 1774 issue of the *Royal American Magazine or Universal Repository of Instruction and Amusement*, published by Isaiah Thomas, in Boston, Mass.

Music publishers (exclusive) were [John C.] Moller & [Henri] Capron of Philadelphia, Pa., established in 1790. They also had a music store and offered musical instruction. (*Robert A. Gerson—Music in Philadelphia*)

Musical comedy broadcast. *See* Radio broadcast: Musical comedy broadcast

Musical comedy telecast. *See* Television—Telecast: Musical comedy telecast (one-hour)

Musical instrument. *See* under specific instruments

Musical instrument dealer was Michael Hillegas, who opened a shop in Philadelphia, Pa., in 1759. On December 13, 1759, he advertised instruments, music, and musical supplies in the *Pennsylvania Gazette*. Musical instruments, however, had been sold previously and were advertised for sale at a dancing school in Boston, Mass., in 1716. (*William Arms Fisher—One Hundred and Fifty Years of Music Publishing in the United States*)

Musical play to win a Pulitzer prize. *See* Play (drama): Musical play to win a Pulitzer prize

Opera telecast. *See* Television—Telecast: Opera telecast

Operetta telecast. *See* Television—Telecast: Operetta to be televised

Orchestral song printed contained parts for a first viol, a second viol, a first clarinet, a second clarinet, E-flat horns, etc., and was tipped in after page 186 of the *Massachusetts Magazine* published in Boston, Mass., in March 1791. The song was "The Death Song of an Indian Chief," by Hans Gram of Boston. It was based upon *Ouabi*, an Indian tale in four cantos by "Philenia, a lady of Boston" (Sarah Wentworth Apthorp Morton). (*John Tasker Howard—Our American Music*)

Patriotic American song was "The Liberty Song" (In Freedom We're Born) published by John Mein and John Fleming in July 1768 in Boston, Mass. The lyrics were by John Dickinson, set to the tune of "Hearts of Oak" by William Boyce of London. The words were published in the Boston *Gazette* of July 18, 1768. (*Frank Moore—Songs and Ballads of the American Revolution*)

Program theme song. *See* Radio broadcast: Program theme song

Public school opera studio. *See* Public school: Public school opera studio

Radio concert from an airplane. *See* Radio broadcast: Radio concert from an airplane

THE FIRST

Saengerfest was held in Cincinnati, Ohio, in 1849. It was the first meeting of the several midwestern German singing societies and as a result the North American "Sängerbund" was formed. Only one concert was given. The choir consisted of 118 singers.

Secular song by a native American composer was "My Days Have Been So Wondrous Free," composed in 1759 by Francis Hopkinson. It was based on a poem by Thomas Parnell. Despite its popularity, it was not published until the twentieth century.

Secular song hit with words and music by an American was "The Ministrel's Return From the War," by John Hill Hewitt, composed in Greenville, S.C., in 1825. It was published in 1827 by James L. Hewitt & Co., Boston, Mass., but was not copyrighted as its importance was not anticipated. *(Harry Dichter and Elliott Shapiro—Early American Sheet Music)*

Singing contest in America took place in 1790 in Dorchester, Mass., between the singers of the First Parish of Dorchester and the singing society of Stoughton. The Stoughtonians commenced with Jacob French's "Heavenly Vision," the author of which was their fellow townsman. When they finally sang Handel's "Hallelujah Chorus" without books the Dorchestrians gave up the contest and gracefully acknowledged defeat. *(The Old Stoughton Musical Society—An Historical and Informative Record of the Oldest Choral Society in America)*

Symphony. *See* Symphony

Taps. *See* Taps

War song was "Chester," composed in 1778 by William Billings of Boston, Mass. The song was published in Billings' *The Singing Master's Assistant, or Key to Practical Music,* printed by Draper and Folsom, Boston, in 1778. "Chester" contains the following chorus: "Let tyrants shake their iron rod;/ And Slav'ry clank her galling chains, / We fear them not; / We trust in God, / New England's God forever reigns." *(American Mercury. May 1928)*

War song of the Confederate States to achieve popularity was "I Wish I Was In Dixie's Land" (now known as "Dixie"), written and composed by Daniel Decatur Emmett, a Northerner, expressly for Bryant's Minstrels, who performed at 472 Broadway, New York City. It was announced as a plantation song and dance. According to some sources it was based on a song of lament of slaves owned by a Dutch tobacco planter named Dixye, who was unable to harvest tobacco in

THE FIRST

Harlem, New Amsterdam (New York) and who sold his slaves to a farmer in Piedmont County, South Carolina. The song was first introduced by Emmett on April 4, 1859, at Mechanics Hall, New York City. It was published by Firth Pond & Co., New York City. The song was sung at the inauguration of Jefferson Davis as President of the Confederate States on February 18, 1861.

MUSIC BOOK

Hymn book was Stephen Day's (Steeven Daye's) *The Whole Booke of Psalmes, Faithfully Translated into English Metre whereunto is prefixed a discourse declaring not only the lawfullness, but also the necessity of the heavenly ordinance of singing scripture psalmes in the Churches of God,* 296 pages, published July 1640 in Cambridge, Mass.

Hymn book with music was the ninth edition of *The Psalms, Hymns & Spiritual Songs of the Old and New Testament; Faithfully Translated into English Meetre. For the Use, Edification and Comfort of the Saints in publick and private especially in New England,* 420 pages, printed in 1798 by Bartholomew Green and J. Allen, Boston, Mass., for Michael Perry. The book contained thirteen tunes.

Music book by a native American was *Urania; or a Choice Collection of Psalm-Tunes, Anthems, and Hymns, in Two, Three and Four parts; the whole peculiarly adapted to the use of churches and private families—to which are prefix'd the plainest and most necessary rules of Psalmody,* by James Lyon, A.B. It was published in 1761 in Philadelphia and contained 198 songs in its 220 pages.

Music book printed from type to be published in the United States was *The Psalms of David, with the ten commandments, creed, Lord's prayer &c. In Metre, also the catechism, confession of faith, liturgy &c.,* printed by James Parker, New York City, in 1767. It contained 150 psalms translated from the Dutch for the use of the Reformed Protestant Dutch Church of the City of New York. The type for the music notes was obtained from Amsterdam, Holland.

Music book printed with bars was *The Grounds and Rules of Musick Explained; or, an Introduction to the art of singing by note. Fitted to the Meanest Capacities. Recommended by Several Ministers,* by the Reverend Thomas Walter of Roxbury, Mass. It was an oblong book containing nineteen pages of songs with the reverse pages blank, and was printed in 1721 by J[ames] Franklin, Boston, Mass.

Music composition book was *The New England Psalm-Singer or American Chorister*

THE FIRST

THE FIRST

MUSIC—*Continued*
containing a number of psalm tunes, anthems, and canons in four and five parts, composed by William Billings. It was printed by Edes and Gill, Boston, Mass., in 1770, consisted of 112 pages, and sold for eight shillings. (*Louis Charles Elson—History of American Music*)

Ragtime instruction book was Ben Harney's *Rag-Time Instructor,* published by M. Witmark & Sons, New York City, in 1897. It was "the only work published giving full instructions how to play rag-time music on the piano," contained twelve pages, and cost fifty cents. Harney was the composer of "Mister Johnson Turn Me Loose," "You've Been a Good Old Wagon, But You've Done Broke Down," etc. (*Isaac Goldberg—Tin Pan Alley*)

Secular song book was Alexander Reinagle's *A Selection of the Most Favorite Scots Tunes,* published in August 1787 by Thomas Dobson, Philadelphia, Pa.

Secular song book by a native American composer was Francis Hopkinson's *Seven Songs for the Harpsichord or Forte Piano,* which was dedicated to George Washington and published in 1788 by Thomas Dobson, Philadelphia, Pa. It was advertised in the *Federal Gazette*: "These songs are composed in an easy familiar style, intended for young practitioners on the harpsichord or forte piano, and is the first work of this kind attempted in the U.S."

Vocal instruction book was *A Very Plain and Easy Introduction to the Art of Singing Psalm-tunes; with the cantus or trebles of twenty-eight psalm-tunes, contrived in such a manner as that the learner may attain the skill of singing them, with the greatest ease and speed imaginable,* by John Tufts, pastor of Newburyport, Mass. It was printed by J[ames] F[ranklin] for S. Gerrish in Boston, Mass., in 1721. Letters took the place of notes on the staff. F, S, L, were used for fa, sol, la, etc. (*Frank Johnson Metcalf—American Writers and Compilers of Sacred Music*)

MUSIC DEGREES. *See* under Degrees (academic and honorary)

MUSIC INSTRUCTION
College music chair was established at Harvard University, Cambridge, Mass., on August 30, 1875, when John Knowles Paine was appointed Professor of Music. On March 29, 1862, he had been appointed instructor in music and on June 2, 1873, assistant professor. He served until his death, April 25, 1906.

Music instruction (public school) was conducted by Lowell Mason in November 1837 at the Hawes School, South Boston, Mass. On August 28, 1838, the school board voted that a committee on music be instructed to contract with a teacher of vocal music for the several public schools of Boston. Lowell Mason was appointed and served from 1838 to 1841. He was in charge of four assistants. (*Edward Bailey Birge—History of Public School Music in the United States*)

Music school authorized to confer degrees was established about 1835 by Oramel Whittlesey in Salem, Conn. It was successively known as Mr. Whittlesey's Music School, Music Vale Seminary, and the Normal Academy of Music. The first degree was conferred about 1849. (*Frances Hall Johnson—Music Vale Seminary 1835-1876*)

Musical pedagogy school was the Boston Academy of Music, Boston, Mass., founded January 8, 1833. Samuel Atkins Eliot was the first president. The faculty consisted of Lowell Mason and George James Webb. The Pestalozzian method of teaching vocal music in classes was advocated.

State Supervisor of Music was Paul Eugene Beck, appointed July 1, 1915, by Pennsylvania. He served until August 1921.

MUSIC MAGAZINE
Music magazine was the *American Musical Magazine,* which was published in May 1786 in New Haven, Conn. It was issued regularly and was a collection of tunes and hymns. It was published and sold by Amos Doolittle and Daniel Read. The first issue of six pages contained the selection "The Seasons Moralized." (*Frank Luther Mott—History of American Magazines*)

Music magazine published in Braille was *The Musical Review for the Blind,* the first issue of which appeared in January 1930. It was published by the American Braille Press for War and Civilian Blind.

MUSIC SOCIETY
Music society for the literary protection of composers and authors was the American Society of Composers, Authors and Publishers, which was formed February 13, 1914, in New York City. The object of the society was to protect the copyrighted musical compositions of its members against illegal public performance for profit and other forms of infringement, and to collect license fees in respect of authorized performances in public amusement establishments for distribution among its members. The society is an unincorporated voluntary association and is affiliated with similar societies functioning in some twenty-five foreign countries. George Maxwell was the first president.

Music society of importance (local) was the St. Cecilia Society of Charleston, S.C., organized in 1737 as an amateur concert society. It was formally organized in 1762 and with the exception of a few years has given annual concerts and balls ever since.

MUSIC SUPERVISOR (state). *See* Music instruction: State Supervisor of Music

MUSICAL INSTRUMENTS. *See* under specific instrument

MUSICIAN

Composer (native-born American) was Francis Hopkinson, one of the signers of the Declaration of Independence, who graduated in 1757 from the College of Philadelphia. His first important song was "My Days Have Been So Wondrous Free," composed in 1759, and is one of the earliest secular compositions extant. In 1763, his *A Collection of Psalm Tunes, with a few anthems and hymns, some of them entirely new, for the use of the United Churches of Christ Church and St. Peter's Church in Philadelphia* was printed by W. Dunlop, Philadelphia, Pa. (*Quarterly Magazine of the International Musical Society. Vol. 5*)

Composer of jazz music was William Christopher Handy, the Negro composer of the "Memphis Blues," which he wrote in 1912. He was known as the "father of the blues," having composed numerous other pieces in the same idiom, among them "St. Louis Blues" and "Beale Street Blues." (*John Tasker Howard—Our American Music*)

Musician (native-born American) to achieve European fame was Louis Moreau Gottschalk, who in 1852 gave concerts in the leading music centers of the world. He exhibited a fondness for music at the age of four and when but six years old played an organ in church. In April 1845 he appeared in Paris, in 1846-47 in Italy, and in 1850 in Switzerland. (*Graham's Magazine. January 1853*)

Negro-song popularizer was Johann Christian Gottlieb Graupner, the "father of Negro songs." On December 30, 1799, at the Federal Street Theatre, Boston, Mass., he sang "The Gay Negro Boy" in the second act of *Oroonoko*. He accompanied himself on the banjo. He was well received and thereafter he specialized in popularizing Negro songs. (*Memorial History of Boston. Vol. 4. 1883*)

Orchestra leader to conduct without using a baton was George James Webb, who instituted this practice in Boston in 1843.

Woman conductor-composer to write an opera and conduct it in a major opera house was Ethel Leginska (Ethel Legins) whose opera *Gale* was sung November 23, 1935, by the Chicago City Opera Company, Chicago, Ill. It was a one-act arrangement of a Cornish legend adapted from "The Haunting" (1922) by Mrs. Catharine Amy Dawson-Scott. It was performed by an all-American cast including John Charles Thomas, Frank Forest, Julia Peters, and Helen Bertush.

MUSKET. *See* Ordnance: Muskets

MUSTARD was manufactured by Benjamin Jackson, who established the Globe Mills on Germantown Road, Philadelphia, Pa., and sold his product in glass bottles with his label on them. He advertised in the *Pennsylvania Chronicle*, February 15, 1768, that he was "the original establisher of the mustard manufactory in America, and . . . at present the only mustard manufacturer on the continent. I brought the art with me into the country."

MUTINY (Naval officer condemned). *See* Naval officer: Naval officer condemned for mutiny

MUTUAL INSURANCE. *See* Insurance: Mutual fire insurance company

MYSTERY RAILROAD EXCURSION. *See* Railroad excursion: Railroad excursion (mystery)

MYSTIC SOCIETY PARADE. *See* Parade: Street parade held by a mystic society

NAIL CUTTING AND HEADING MACHINE was patented December 12, 1796 by George Chandler of Maryland.

NAIL MACHINE (wire) was built under the supervision of Major Thomas Norton by Adolph and Felix Brown of New York City and used in 1851 by William Hassall of New York City.

NAILS

Nails were cold cut in 1777 and were manufactured by Jeremiah Wilkinson of Cumberland, R.I. "They were first cut by a pair of shears from an old chest lock and afterward headed in a smith's vice. Sheet iron was afterward used and the process extended to small nails." (*Samuel Greene Arnold—History of the State of Rhode Island*)

Steel-cut nails were manufactured in 1883 by the Riverside Iron Works of Wheeling, W.Va.

NARCOTIC

Narcotic prohibition act (federal) was Section 1 of the act of February 9, 1909 (35 Stat.L.614): "After the first day of April 1909, it shall be unlawful to import into the United States, opium in any form or any preparation or derivative thereof . . . other than smoking opium for medicinal purposes."

Narcotic regulation (federal) was enacted by Congress as part of the McKinley Tariff Act on October 1, 1890 (26 Stat.L.567). This act provided for an internal revenue tax of $10 a pound upon all smoking opium manufactured in the United States for smoking purposes, and limited the manufacture to United States citizens. It further provided for the bonding of manufacturers, the keeping of books, rendering of returns, etc. (*Records in Bureau of Narcotics, Treasury Department, Washington, D.C.*)

Narcotic regulation (state) was adopted March 10, 1933, by Nevada.

Narcotic sanatorium (federal) for drug addicts was the United States Narcotic Farm at Lexington, Ky., which covered 11 acres of a 1,050 acre plot. The cornerstone was laid July 29, 1933, and the building was dedicated May 25, 1935, by Surgeon General Hugh Smith Cumming of the United States Public Health Service. The first occupants were received on May 29, 1935. Dr. Lawrence Kolb was the first director.

Narcotic sanatorium for minors offering full-scale long-term treatment was the Riverside Hospital, North Brother Island, New York City, which was converted for the purpose in November 1951. The first patients were received on July 1, 1952. The first superintendent was Dr. Jerome Louis Leon.

Narcotic tariff was enacted by the Tariff Act of August 30, 1842 (5 Stat.L.558), which placed a levy of 75 cents a pound on opium. Prior to this act, opium was exempted from duty by the act of July 14, 1832 (4 Stat.L.583), and the act of March 2, 1833 (4 Stat.L.629).

NARROW GAUGE LOCOMOTIVE. *See* Locomotive: Narrow gauge locomotive

NATIONAL ACADEMY OF SCIENCES. *See* Science association: National academy of sciences

NATIONAL ADVISORY COMMITTEE FOR AERONAUTICS. *See* Aviation: Advisory committee for aeronautics (national)

NATIONAL AERONAUTICS AND SPACE ADMINISTRATION. *See* Space Agency (U.S.)

NATIONAL AERONAUTICS AND SPACE ADMINISTRATION DISTINGUISHED SERVICE MEDAL. *See* Medal: National Aeronautics and Space Administration Distinguished Service Medal

NATIONAL ANTHEM was the "Star-Spangled Banner" designated by act of Congress (46 Stat.L.1508) approved by President Herbert Hoover, March 3, 1931. The words were written by Francis Scott Key while a prisoner on the British warship "Supreme" during the British attack on Fort McHenry, Baltimore, Md., September 13, 1814. The verses were set to the air of "Anacreon in Heaven." The song was originally known as "The Defense of Fort McHenry," and printed on a handbill September 15, 1814, without the name of Francis Scott Key. (*Veterans of Foreign Wars—The Star Spangled Banner*)

NATIONAL ARCHERY ASSOCIATION. *See* Archery club: Archery association (national)

NATIONAL ASSOCIATION OF BASEBALL PLAYERS. *See* Baseball league: Baseball league of importance

NATIONAL ASSOCIATION OF MANUFACTURERS. *See* Manufacturers' association

NATIONAL ASSOCIATION OF PROFESSIONAL BASEBALL LEAGUES. *See* Baseball league: Baseball league association

NATIONAL BANK. *See* Bank: National bank

NATIONAL BANKING SYSTEM. *See* Bank legislation: National banking system

NATIONAL BIBLIOGRAPHIC SOCIETY. *See* Bibliography Society (national)

NATIONAL CEMETERY. *See* Cemetery: National cemeteries

NATIONAL CHRISTMAS CAROLS ASSOCIATION. *See* Christmas carols association (national)

NATIONAL COLORED CONVENTION. *See* Negro: National colored convention

THE FIRST

NATIONAL EMERGENCY COUNCIL (U.S.) was authorized November 17, 1933, under Executive Order No. 6433A "for the purpose of coordinating and making more efficient and productive the work of the numerous field agencies." Frank Comerford Walker was appointed the executive director. He was also appointed executive secretary of the executive council of twenty-three members which was established July 11, 1933. *(United States National Emergency Council—Informational Handbook)*

NATIONAL GEOGRAPHIC SOCIETY GOLD MEDAL. *See* Medal: National Geographic Society gold medal

NATIONAL GRANGE OF THE PATRONS OF HUSBANDRY. *See* Agricultural society: Agricultural society of national importance

NATIONAL HALL OF FAME. *See* Hall of fame: Hall of fame (national)

NATIONAL HOLIDAY. *See* Holiday: National holiday

NATIONAL INDUSTRIAL RECOVERY ACT. *See* Industrial recovery act

NATIONAL INSTITUTE OF ARTS AND LETTERS. *See* Arts and letters society: Arts and letters society (national)

NATIONAL INSTITUTE OF SOCIAL SCIENCES. *See* Social science society (national)

NATIONAL LABOR BOARD. *See* Labor: Labor advisory board (federal)

NATIONAL LABOR PARTY. *See* Labor party (political): Labor party (national)

NATIONAL LABOR RELATIONS BOARD. *See* Labor: Labor Relations Act (national)

NATIONAL LEAGUE. *See* Baseball: National league

NATIONAL MEDIATION BOARD. *See* Labor: National mediation board

NATIONAL PARK. *See* Park: Park (national)

NATIONAL PIKE. *See* Road: Federal highway

THE FIRST

NATIONAL PLANNING BOARD (U.S.) to advise on preparation of a comprehensive program of public works was organized July 30, 1933, and was composed of three members: Frederic Adrian Delano, chairman, Wesley Clair Mitchell, and Charles Edward Merriam. The board was later abolished and its work delegated to other committees. *(United States National Resources Commission—National Planning)*

NATIONAL PROHIBITION SOCIETY. *See* Temperence society: Women's temperence society (national)

NATIONAL RADIO CONFERENCE. *See* Radio conference: National radio conference

NATIONAL RESEARCH COUNCIL. *See* Science association: National research council

NATIONAL SECURITY COUNCIL
    National Security Council was established by the National Security Act of 1947 (61 Stat. L.497), July 26, 1947, to advise the President with respect to the integration of domestic, foreign, and military policies relating to the national security. The Council is composed of the President, the Vice President, the Secretary of State, the Secretary of Defense, the director of the Foreign Operations Administration, and the director of the Office of Defense Mobilization. The Council staff is headed by a civilian executive secretary appointed by the President.

    National Security Council meeting held outside Washington, D.C., was held September 13, 1954, in Denver, Colo.

    Vice President to preside at a National Security Council. *See* Vice President of the United States: Vice President to preside at a National Security Council

NATIONAL SOLDIERS' HOME. *See* Soldiers' homes (national)

NATIONAL STATUARY HALL MONUMENT TO A WOMAN. *See* Monument: Statue of a woman in National Statuary Hall

NATIONAL TUBERCULOSIS ASSOCIATION. *See* Health society

NATIONAL UNION FOR SOCIAL JUSTICE originated November 1934 in Royal Oak, Mich. The first national convention was held August 14, 1936, at the Public Auditorium, Cleveland, Ohio, and the vote was 8,153 to 1 to support William Lemke and Thomas Charles O'Brien as candidates for President and Vice President of the United States.

THE FIRST

NATIONAL UNITARIAN CONVENTION. *See* Unitarian church convention (national): National organization of the Unitarian Churches of the United States and Canada

NATIONAL WOMAN'S RIGHTS CONVENTION. *See* Woman suffrage: Woman suffrage associations (national)

NATURAL CEMENT ROCK. *See* Cement: Natural cement rock

NATURAL COLOR PHOTOGRAPH. *See* Photograph: Photograph in natural colors taken in the air

NATURAL GAS. *See* under Gas

NATURAL SCIENCE SUMMER SCHOOL. *See* Science school: Natural science summer school

NATURALIZATION ACT
Naturalization act of the United States Government was that of March 26, 1790 (1 Stat.L.103), authorizing courts of record to "entertain the applications" of alien free white persons who had resided in the United States for two years or more, one year of which should be in a particular state, on proof of good character and on their taking an oath or affirmation to support the Constitution.

Naturalization act (colonial). *See* Citizenship naturalization act

NATURE TRAIL. *See* Museum: Outdoor museum

NAUTICAL ALMANAC. *See* Almanac: Nautical almanac

NAUTICAL SCHOOL
See also
Naval Academy
Naval Officers Training School
Naval War College

Nautical municipal school was opened January 11, 1875, in New York City on board the "St. Mary." The officers were Commander Robert Lees Phythian, Lieutenant Commander George Henry Wadleigh, Lieutenants George Washington De Long and William Henry Jaques, all U.S. Naval Academy graduates. From July 22, 1875, to October 8, 1875, a Long Island Sound cruise was conducted. The school was authorized by Chapter 288, Laws of New York State, passed April 24, 1873, and was supported by state funds.

THE FIRST

Nautical school was established May 29, 1827 in Nantucket, Mass., and was known as Admiral Sir Isaac Coffin's Lancasterian School. It was conducted by William Coffin, Jr. and Miss A. Meach and was located in a wooden schoolhouse. Courses on shipboard to train sailors had been offered previously.

Nautical state school was established by Massachusetts, Chapter 402, Act of June 11, 1891, an "act to establish a Nautical Training School" which authorized three commissioners to serve one, two and three years for the Massachusetts Nautical Training School. On February 17, 1891, legislation authorized the governor to petition the United States Secretary of the Navy for a suitable vessel, and on October 28, 1892, the steam sloop "Enterprise" was transferred to Massachusetts.

NAVAL ACADEMY
See also
Chaplains' school
Nautical School
Naval Officers Training School
Naval War College

Japanese midshipman in the United States Naval Academy was Zun Zow Matzmulla, admitted December 8, 1869, under act of Congress, July 27, 1868 (15 Stat.L.261), authorizing the Secretary of the Navy "to receive for instruction not exceeding six persons to be designated by the government of the Empire of Japan." Matzmulla completed the course in 1873 and stood 28th in a class of 29.

Naval Academy (U.S.) was established on a nine-acre site at Windmill Point, Fort Severn, Annapolis, Md., transferred on August 15, 1845, by the War Department to the Navy Department for the purpose of establishing a naval school. It was known as the Naval School and officially opened October 10, 1845. The first superintendent was Commander Franklin Buchanan, appointed September 3, 1845. The first class was graduated in July 1846. On July 1, 1850, the name was changed to the U.S. Naval Academy and graduation exercises were held June 10, 1854. The academy was transferred to Newport, R.I., May 9, 1861 and was returned to Annapolis, Md., September 9, 1865, when Rear Admiral David Dixon Porter assumed charge. *(James Russell Soley—Historical Sketch of the U.S. Naval Academy)*

Negro midshipman in the United States Naval Academy was James Henry Conyers of South Carolina, who attended from September 21, 1872, to November 11, 1873. He did not graduate. *(Annual Register of U.S. Naval Academy, 1874-1875)*

Negro midshipman in the United States Naval Academy to graduate was Wesley Anthony Brown of Washington, D.C., who graduated June 3, 1949, and received his commission as ensign.

NAVAL "ACE." *See* under Aviation—Aviator

NAVAL AIR TRAINING SCHOOL. *See* Aviation—School: Naval air training school

NAVAL ATTACHÉ. *See* Naval officer; Naval attaché

NAVAL CHAPLAIN. *See* Naval officer: Naval chaplain

NAVAL CHAPLAINS' SCHOOL. *See* Chaplains' school: Naval chaplains' school

NAVAL COALING STATION. *See* Navy: Naval coaling station on foreign soil

NAVAL DOCTOR. *See* Naval officer

NAVAL ENGAGEMENT IN THE CIVIL WAR. *See* Civil War: Naval engagement in the Civil war

NAVAL EXPEDITION (colonial). *See* Navy: Naval expedition (colonial)

NAVAL HOSPITAL. *See* Hospital: Naval hospital

NAVAL INSPECTOR (woman). *See* Naval officer: Woman naval inspector

NAVAL MAIL SERVICE. *See* Postal service: Navy mail service

NAVAL MILITIA. *See* Navy: Naval militia (state)

NAVAL NURSES' CORPS. *See* Navy: Naval nurses' corps

NAVAL OFFICER
Admiral in the Dental Corps. *See* Dental Corps (U.S. Navy): Admiral in the Dental Corps (U.S. Navy)

Admiral in uniform to ride in an airplane. *See* Aviation—Passenger: Admiral in uniform to ride in an airplane

Admiral killed in action in World War II was Rear Admiral Isaac Campbell Kidd, staff aide to Admiral Husband Edward Kimmel,

Commander in Chief of the United States Fleet, killed December 7, 1941, in the Japanese attack on Pearl Harbor, Hawaii.

Admiral who was Jewish was Rear Admiral Adolph Marix, who was advanced to the rank of rear admiral by President William Howard Taft on July 4, 1908. He entered the service as midshipman on September 26, 1864, served as master, lieutenant, lieutenant-commander, and commander.

Captain in the U.S. Navy who was a woman was Captain Sue Sophia Dauser, superintendent of the Nurse Corps, U.S.N., who received the rank of captain on February 26, 1944 and served until November 9, 1945. Previously, she had held the relative rank of captain authorized by Public Law No. 828, the Pay Bill, effective December 22, 1942. She entered the service on September 15, 1917, when she was appointed a Naval Reserve Nurse.

Captain in the U.S. Navy who was Jewish was Uriah Phillips Levy, whose rank of captain was effective March 29, 1844. He joined the service as a sailing master on October 21, 1812, became a lieutenant on March 5, 1817, and a commander on February 9, 1837. (*American Jewish Historical Society—Publications—1909*)

Chaplain to win a Congressional Medal of Honor was Lieutenant Commander Joseph Timothy O'Callahan, who received the award from President Harry S. Truman on January 23, 1946, at Washington, D.C., for his heroism on board the aircraft carrier "Franklin" when it was bombed off Kobe, Japan, in March 1945.

Commander-in-chief of the Continental Navy was Esek Hopkins, who served from December 22, 1775, to January 2, 1778. (*Edward Field—Esek Hopkins, Commander-in-Chief of the Continental Navy During the American Revolution*)

Commander of a combat ship who was a Negro was Lieutenant Commander Samuel L. Gravely, Jr., of Richmond, Va., who on January 31, 1961, assumed command of the destroyer escort U.S.S. "Falgout," one of the vessels of Escort Sqaudron 5 on duty with the barrier Pacific force.

Judge advocate of the Navy was William Eaton Chandler of New Hampshire, who on March 6, 1865, was appointed by President Abraham Lincoln to be Solicitor and Naval Judge Advocate General under act of March 2, 1865 (13 Stat.L.468). His salary was $3,500 a year. (*Leon Burr Richardson—William E. Chandler, Republican*)

NAVAL OFFICER—*Continued*
Naval attaché was Lieutenant Commander French Ensor Chadwick. He was sent to London, England, November 15, 1882, and he remained there until April 3, 1889. *(French Ensor Chadwick—The American Navy)*

Naval chaplain was William Balch, a Congregationalist. He received his commission from President John Adams on October 30, 1799, and served until May 10, 1801.

Naval chaplain (Continental navy) known to have served was the Reverend Benjamin Parks, a Congregationalist, appointed October 28, 1788, with the relative rank of lieutenant. It is possible that others preceded him but their identities are unknown.

Naval chaplain killed in action was Chaplain John L. Lenhart, who was commissioned chaplain on February 27, 1847. At that time chaplains did not hold naval rank and were known simply as chaplains. On March 8, 1862, the Confederate iron-clad "Merrimac" encountered the Union frigate "Cumberland" off Hampton Roads, Va. The "Merrimac" crushed the "Cumberland" by driving her iron prow through the side of the "Cumberland," at the same time pouring in a fire of shells. Chaplain Lenhart died with his sinking ship.

Naval chaplain who was Catholic was the Reverend Charles Henry Parks, who was commissioned chaplain U.S. Navy on April 30, 1888, with the relative rank of lieutenant. He resigned January 25, 1900, with the rank of lieutenant. Actual rank was not given chaplains until March 3, 1899.

Naval chaplain who was Jewish was the Reverend David Goldberg of Corsicana, Texas, who was appointed chaplain, U.S. Navy, with the rank of lieutenant junior grade on October 30, 1917. He was the only Jewish chaplain who served in World War I. He was advanced to lieutenant commander on January 1, 1938, and retired March 1, 1941. *(Clifford Merrill Drury—U.S. Navy Chaplains 1778-1945)*

Naval doctor was Dr. Joseph Harrison, appointed in 1775 in Philadelphia, Pa., to serve on the "Alfred." *(John Cropper Wise—Evolution of the Naval Medical Service and the Naval Medical School)*

Naval medical officer to write a book was Edward Cutbush, whose *Observations on the Means of Preserving the Health of Soldiers and Sailors; and on the Duties of the Medical Department of the Army and Navy; with remarks on hospitals and their internal arrangement* was printed by Thomas Dobson, Philadelphia, Pa., in 1808. It contained 336 pages

and a 14-page supplement by Dr. Benjamin Rush. *(Annals of Medical History. Vol. 5. No. 4)*

Naval nurses' corps (woman member) to receive the Distinguished Service Medal was Captain Sue Sophia Dauser, who received the decoration December 14, 1945, from Secretary of the Navy James Forrestal.

Naval officer commissioned was Captain Hopley Yeaton of New Hampshire appointed March 21, 1791, by George Washington to command "a cutter in the service of the United States of America."

Naval officer condemned for mutiny was Midshipman Philip Spencer, son of the Secretary of War, who with Boatswain Samuel Cromwell and Seaman Elisha Small was hanged December 1, 1842, from the yardarm of the U.S.S. "Somers," a brig of war, while at sea in the West Indian waters. They were convicted, at a court martial held on shipboard, of conspiring to organize a mutiny, murder the officers, and turn the ship into a pirate cruiser. The commander of the "Somers" was Alexander Slidell Mackenzie, who was exonerated at a court of inquiry and court martial of charges. *(Case of the "Somers" Mutiny—Report at Courtmartial of A. S. Mackenzie held at the Navy Yard, Brooklyn, N.Y.)*

Naval officer designated Commander, Aircraft Battle Force was Henry Varnum Butler, whose appointment was made March 5, 1935, effective April 1, 1935, with the rank of vice admiral.

Naval officer killed in the Spanish-American war. *See* Spanish-American war: Naval officer killed in the Spanish-American war

Naval officer to become a commodore was John Barry, senior officer in the navy, who was appointed in 1794 after the reorganization of the navy. *(Martin Ignatius Joseph Griffin—History of Commodore John Barry)*

Naval officer to become "Admiral of the Navy" was Admiral George Dewey, who served from March 3, 1899, until his death, January 16, 1917. The rank was conferred by act of Congress, passed March 2, 1899 (30 Stat.L.995).

Naval officer to become an admiral was David Glasgow Farragut, who received his appointment on July 25, 1866. Previously by act of Congress, on July 16, 1862 (12 Stat.L. 583) Farragut had been given the rank of rear admiral, and on December 13, 1864, he had received the title of vice admiral. The office of vice admiral was authorized by act of December 21, 1864 (13 Stat.L.420), an "act to establish the grade of Vice Admiral." The pay was $7,000 at sea, $6,000 on shore duty and $5,000 when awaiting offices. On July 25, 1866 (14 Stat.L. 231), the Navy was authorized to have 10 rear admirals, 1 vice admiral, and 1 admiral. *(Joel Tyler Headley—Farragut and Our Naval Commanders)*

Naval officer to become an engineer in the U.S. Navy was Charles Haynes Haswell. He was commissioned February 19, 1836, by Secretary of the Navy Mahlon Dickerson, and appointed to design steam-power equipment. *(American Society of Civil Engineers—Transactions 1908. Vol. 61)*

Naval officers to wear the five-star insignia as Admirals of the Fleet were Ernest Joseph King, William Daniel Leahy, and Chester William Nimitz, whose appointments were ratified December 15, 1944, by the Senate. The grade of fleet admiral of the U.S. Navy was established by Public Law No. 482 approved by Act of Congress, December 14, 1944.

Naval surgeon of the U.S. Navy was Dr. George Balfour, who was ordered in 1801 to take charge of the first Marine Hospital established in Norfolk, Va. He entered the Army, April 11, 1792, and was transferred to the Navy, March 9, 1798. He resigned on April 12, 1804, to enter private practice. *(Richard Cranston Holcomb—A Century with the Norfolk Naval Hospital)*

Negro commissioned officer in the Naval Reserve was Bernard Whitfield Robinson, a medical student at Harvard University, Cambridge, Mass., who was commissioned June 18, 1942.

Negro commissioned officer in the regular U.S. Navy was Ensign John Lee of Indianapolis, Ind., who was commissioned March 15, 1947 and assigned to the U.S.S. "Kearsarge."

Negro nurse in the Navy Reserve Nurse Corps was Phyllis Mae Daley, a registered nurse of New York City, who was sworn in March 8, 1945, as an ensign at the office of the Naval Officer Procurement, New York City.

Surgeon General of the Navy was Dr. William Maxwell Wood, appointed Chief of Medical Bureau and Surgery, June 28, 1869. He served until October 25, 1871, although he had been placed on the retired list for age on May 27, 1871. The Naval Appropriations Act of March 3, 1871 (16 Stat.L.532) provided that the chief of the bureau have the title Surgeon General *(Annals of Medical History. Vol. 6. No. 4)*

Woman doctor in the regular U.S. Navy was Dr. Frances Lois Willoughby of Pitman, N.J., appointed a lieutenant commander on October 15, 1948. During World War II, women were accepted in the Navy Medical Corps Reserve on a temporary basis.

Woman medical officer assigned to a naval vessel was Lieutenant Commander Bernice Rosenthal Walters, Medical Corps, U.S. Naval Reserve, of New York, who was assigned on March 8, 1950, to the Hospital Ship U.S.S. "Consolation," reporting for duty on July 13, 1950. She entered the U.S. Naval Reserve on July 12, 1943, and served during World War II at the U.S. Naval Shipyards, Boston, Mass.; the U.S. Naval Air Station, Weymouth, Mass.; and the U.S. Naval Hospital, Bainbridge, Md.

Woman naval inspector was Jean Hales of Berkeley, Calif., appointed August 24, 1942, by the Twelfth Naval District as junior inspector of engineering to test bars of metal to determine yield and tensile strength.

Woman naval officer commissioned in the U.S. Naval Reserve was Mildred Helen McAfee, who accepted an appointment as Lieutenant Commander on August 3, 1942, to serve as Director of the Women's Reserve, U.S. Naval Reserve, nicknamed WAVES (Women Accepted for Volunteer Emergency Service). The oath of office was administered by Secretary of the Navy Frank Knox. Miss McAfee, on November 13, 1943, became the first woman line officer to hold the rank of captain.

Woman physician in the Medical Corps Reserve of the U.S. Navy was Dr. Hulda Thelander of San Francisco, Calif., who received a direct commission as a Lieutenant Commander MC-V (S) U.S.N.R. on April 19, 1944, in accordance with the existing laws. She was assigned to Headquarters, U.S. Marine Corps, Department of the Pacific, San Francisco, Calif.

Woman to preside as law officer of a General Court Martial in the Navy was Lieutenant Commander Mary Lou McDowell of Annandale, Va., appointed February 11, 1957. She presided in March 1957.

Women sworn into the regular U.S. Navy took their oaths of office as administered by Rear Admiral George Lucius Russell on July 7, 1948, in Washington, D.C. They were Frances Teresa Devaney, Ruth Flora, Kay Louise Langdon, Wilma Juanita Marchal, Doris Roberta Robertson, and Edna Earle Young, all of whom were transferred from the Naval Reserve.

NAVAL OFFICERS' TRAINING SCHOOL

See also

Naval Academy; Naval War College

THE FIRST

THE FIRST

NAVAL OFFICERS' TRAINING SCHOOL—*Continued*

Naval officers' training school was established in Boston, Mass., December 10, 1815, at the Navy Yard, Charlestown. It was under the guidance of Commodore William Bainbridge, whose courage as a naval leader had been demonstrated in the war with Tripoli.

NAVAL PATROL BOMBER. *See* Aviation—Airplane: Naval patrol bomber

NAVAL POST OFFICE. *See* Post office: Naval post office aboard a naval vessel

NAVAL RADIO STATION. *See* Radio station: Naval radio station

NAVAL SEAPLANE TENDER. *See* Ship: Seaplane tender designed and built for the U.S. Navy

NAVAL SHIP. *See* Ship

NAVAL UNIFORM. *See* Navy: Naval uniforms (standardized)

NAVAL WAR COLLEGE

Naval War College was at Coaster's Harbor Island, Newport, R.I., and was established October 6, 1884, by General Order No. 325 of the Secretary of the Navy. Commander Stephen Bleecker Luce had been appointed superintendent on September 13, 1884. The college opened September 3, 1885, with a one-month course for a class of eight. Naval officers were offered an eleven-month course in military science, the art of naval warfare, and marine international law. On January 11, 1889, the college was consolidated with the Torpedo Station on Goat Island in Newport harbor. (*Albert Gleaves—Life and Letters of Rear Admiral Stephen B. Luce*)

NAVEL ORANGES. *See* Oranges (seedless navel)

NAVIGATION ACT

Navigation Act affecting the American colonies was passed by the British Parliament in 1651 by which all merchandise for the English-American plantations were exempted from duty for three years on the condition that no colonial vessel be suffered to lade any goods of the growth of the plantations and carry them to a foreign port. Except for intercolonial trade all goods were to be carried in English bottoms.

Navigation Act (U.S.) was approved July 20, 1789 (1 Stat.L.27). It imposed a duty on the tonnage of vessels. (*Lloyd Milton Short—The Bureau of Navigation, Its History, Activities and Organization*)

NAVIGATION BUREAU (U.S.) was established under the Treasury Department by act of Congress, July 5, 1884 (23 Stat.L.118), and permanently organized July 1, 1885. The Bureau was directed by the Deputy Commissioner of Navigation appointed by the President. (*Lloyd Milton Short—The Bureau of Navigation, Its History, Activities and Organization*)

NAVY

Air squadron of jets (U.S. Navy) was Fighter Squadron 17-A, which received its first jet airplane, a McDonnell FH-1 Phantom, at the Naval Air Station, Quonset Point, Rhode Island, on July 23, 1947. On May 5, 1948, at the close of three days of operations aboard the U.S.S. "Saipan," the squadron became the first U.S. Navy jet squadron to qualify aboard a carrier.

American sailor to lose his life in World War I. *See* World War I: American sailor to lose his life in World War I

Armor plate contract (U.S. Navy). *See* Armor plate contract (U.S. Navy)

Atomic submarine division was Atomic Submarine Division 102, formed March 31, 1958, at New London, Conn. under command of Commander Robert Glennwood Black, who served from March 31 to July 1, 1958, when he was replaced by Captain Eugene Parks Wilkinson. The division consisted of the atomic submarines "Nautilus," "Sea Wolf," and "Skate," and the conventional submarines "Hardhead," "Bang," and "Halfbreak."

Bureau of Medicine and Surgery of the U.S. Navy was authorized by act of Congress, August 31, 1842 (5 Stat.L.579). It was organized in 1842 by Dr. William Paul Crillon Barton, who served as Chief from September 2, 1842, to April 1, 1844. He was the first chief and the senior surgeon of the Navy at the time of his death. (*Military Surgeon. Vol. 46*)

Naval coaling station on foreign soil was completed by the Navy in Lower California, Mexico, in April 1901.

Naval expedition (colonial) was undertaken in 1613 against a French settlement in Nova Scotia. It consisted of eleven vessels carrying a total of fourteen light guns, commanded by Samuel Argall of Virginia. Argall captured Mount Desert, St. Croix and Port Royal, Nova Scotia. (*Massachusetts Historical Society Proceedings. November 1884*)

Naval fleet was authorized on October 13, 1775, when the Continental Congress authorized two cruisers, one of 10 guns and another of

14 guns, and appointed a Marine Committee, consisting of John Adams, John Langdon, and Silas Deane, from its members to be in complete control of naval affairs. Although open hostilities began April 19, 1775, no consideration was given to protection by sea until October 5, 1775, when news was received that a British naval fleet would arrive. The Continental Navy was organized December 22, 1775, and consisted of two 24-gun frigates, the "Alfred" (Captain Dudley Saltonstall) and the "Columbus" (Captain Abraham Whipple) and two 14-gun brigs, the "Andrea Doria" (Captain Nicholas Biddle) and the "Cabot" (Captain John Burroughs Hopkins), and the schooners "Hornet," (10 guns), "Wasp" (8 guns) and the "Fly" (8 guns). Esek Hopkins was commissioned commander of the fleet and received $125 a month. Sailors received $8 a month.

Naval legislation standardizing nomenclature for naval vessels was a congressional resolution passed March 3, 1819 (3 Stat.L.538), a "resolution declaring the manner in which the vessels comprising the Navy of the United States shall be named." It provided that the Secretary of the Navy shall name ships of the first class for states, of the second class for rivers, and of the third class for cities and towns."

Naval man to reenlist while under the North Pole was James Robert Sordelet, U.S.N., of Fort Wayne, Ind., electrician's mate first class on the submarine "Nautilus," who reenlisted on August 3, 1958.

Naval militia (state) was the Massachusetts Naval Battalion, organized under Executive Order of March 18, 1890, carried into effect by General Order No. 6, A.G.O. Massachusetts of the same date authorizing the formation of four companies to be lettered A, B, C, and D. The companies were formed March 25, 1890, with Thomas A. DeBlois, William M. Paul, William M. Wood and John W. Weeks, all of Boston, commanding companies A, B, C, and D, respectively. On May 7, 1890, John Codman Soley, a graduate of the United States Naval Academy, was commissioned Lieutenant Commander of the Naval Battalion.

Naval nurses' corps was established May 13, 1908 (35 Stat.L.146). Navy nurses received the same pay allowances, emoluments and privileges as the nurse corps (female) of the Army. The first superintendent was Esther Voorhees Hasson, who served from August 18, 1908, to January 16, 1911.

Naval protection was afforded by the Revenue Cutter Service, which was organized August 4, 1790 (1 Stat.L.145), under an act of Congress, approved by President George Wash-

ington. It operated under the general direction of the Secretary of the Treasury. For six years and eleven months the revenue cutters formed the only armed force of the United States afloat. Commissions were granted March 21, 1791, to captains to command "a cutter in the Service of the United States of America" under the United States Revenue Cutter Service (now Coast Guard).

Naval uniforms (standardized) were adopted by the Marine Committee on September 5, 1776. The uniform of captains in the Navy consisted of a coat of blue with red lapels, slashed cuffs, a stand-up collar, flat yellow buttons, blue breeches, and a red waistcoat with yellow lace. The sailors or mariners were to have green coats faced with white, round cuffs, slashed sleeves and pockets, with buttons around the cuff, a silver epaulet on the right shoulder, shirt collars turned back, buttons to match the facings, white waistcoats and breeches edged with green, black gaiters, and garters. The men were also to have green shirts, "if they can be procured."

Navy Day. See Holiday: Navy day

Navy Department (U.S.) was established by act of Congress approved April 30, 1798 (1 Stat.L.553). The conduct of naval affairs was under the Secretary for the Department of War under act of Congress approved April 7, 1789.
See also below Secretary of the Navy

Navy yard acquired after the establishment of the Navy Department, April 30, 1798, was the Portsmouth Navy Yard, N.H., which was purchased June 12, 1800, from William Dennet and his wife for $5,500. It embraced 58.18 acres and had previously been used in the building of men-of-war.

Podiatry Section of the Navy was established on November 3, 1953, under the Navy Medical Service Corps. The first podiatrist assigned was Ensign Richard Stuart Gilbert of New York City, who was assigned to the Naval Training Center, Bainbridge, Md., on June 3, 1954.

Prize money awarded by the U.S. Navy was granted to the U.S.S. "Delaware," commanded by Captain Stephen Decatur, Sr., which captured the French schooner "Croyable" in June 1798 off the Delaware Capes during the undeclared naval war with France (1798-1801). By act of Congress, June 28, 1798 (1 Stat.L. 574), cases involving captured ships were tried in U.S. District Courts. The act provided that after condemnation the part accruing to the United States was to be paid into the public treasury, and the amount due the officers

THE FIRST

NAVY—*Continued*
and crews to be distributed among them in the proportions which the President should direct. Prize money, however, had been awarded as early as the Revolution to men on the vessels of the Continental and state navies and privateers.

Secretary of the Navy was Benjamin Stoddert of Maryland, who was appointed by President John Adams, May 18, 1798. He was commissioned May 21, 1798, entered upon his duties June 18, 1798, and served until March 3, 1801. George Cabot of Massachusetts had been nominated on May 1, 1798, and commissioned May 3, 1798, but on May 11, 1798, had declined to serve. Appointments were made under the act of April 30, 1798 (1 Stat.L.553), which established the Navy Department (*Henry Cabot Lodge—Life and Letters of George Cabot*)

Shot fired by the American Navy in World War I. *See* World War I. Shot fired by the American Navy in World War I

Task force to fight undersea craft was Alfa, which consisted of an aircraft carrier with group of antisubmarine aircraft, a helicopter squadron, destroyers, shore-based patrol planes, and submarines. The task force was created March 24, 1958, under the command of Rear Admiral John Smith Thach and placed in operation in April 1958.

NAVY "ACE." *See* under Aviation—Aviator

NAVY DAY. *See* Holiday: Navy day

NAVY DENTAL CORPS. *See* Dental Corps (U.S. Navy): Dental Corps of the U.S. Navy

NAVY DISTINGUISHED SERVICE MEDAL. *See* Medal: Distinguished Service Medal (Navy)

NAVY "E" AWARD
Army-Navy "E" awards were made to 20 war production plants, the first presentation ceremonies being held August 10, 1942. The award was granted to 4,283 concerns, approximately 5 per cent of those engaged in war work. In July 1942, the Navy "E," the Army "A," and the Army-Navy Munitions Board "star" awards were all merged into the Army-Navy "E."

Navy "E" certificates of meritorious service were granted to fourteen companies on July 25, 1941, by the Bureau of Ordnance, U.S. Navy.

THE FIRST

Navy "E" certificates of meritorious service presented to an institution of higher learning was awarded by Lieutenant Holman Faust to Dr. Clarence Addison Dykstra, University of Wisconsin, Madison, Wis., on June 1, 1942, in recognition of the university's contribution of more men to naval aviation than any other similar institution.

NAVY EXPERT PISTOL SHOT MEDAL. *See* Medal: Navy expert pistol shot medal awarded to a woman

NAVY MAIL SERVICE. *See* Postal service: Navy mail service

NAVY RESERVE NURSE CORPS. *See* Navy: Naval nurses' corps

NAVY SHIP. *See* under Ship

NAVY TORPEDO STATION. *See* Torpedo: Torpedo manufacturing station

NAVY UNIT COMMENDATION DECORATION. *See* Medal: Navy Unit Commendation decoration

NAVY YARD. *See* Navy: Navy yard

NEEDLE-TYPE DAM. *See* Dam: Needle-type dam

NEEDLES (machine made) for sewing were manufactured by the Excelsior Needle Company of Wolcottville, Conn., which was organized March 2, 1866, with $20,000 capital. By means of the cold swaging process, needles of a uniform size and shape were made at a cost very much lower than that of the crude needles previously made. (*Samuel Orcutt—History of Torrington, Conn.*)

NEGRO
See also under names of churches, civil and military positions, organizations, professions, scholarships, schools, sports, etc.

National colored convention assembled at Bethel Church, Philadelphia, Pa., on September 15, 1830, to better the condition of the Negro. It was attended by delegates from seven states. Bishop Richard Allen was elected the first president.

Negro college graduate was John Brown Russwurm, one of thirty-two men graduates who completed the four-year course at Bowdoin College, Brunswick, Me., in 1826. Three years later, Russwurm received his A.M. from Bowdoin.

THE FIRST

THE FIRST

NEON TUBE ADVERTISING SIGN. *See* Electric sign: Neon tube advertising sign

NEOPRENE. *See* Rubber: Synthetic rubber (neoprene)

NEPTUNIUM. *See* Element: Element 93

NERVOUS DISEASES RESEARCH INSTITUTE. *See* Research institute: Institute for research in nervous diseases

NETWORK TELEVISION DISTANCE DEMONSTRATION. *See* Television—Telecast: Television network demonstration (distant)

NEURASTHENIA BOOK. *See* Medical book: Neurasthenia book

NEUROLOGICAL INSTITUTE. *See* Research institute: Institute for research in nervous diseases

NEUROLOGY TEXTBOOK. *See* Medical book: Neurology textbook

NEUTRALITY PROCLAMATION was made by President George Washington on April 22, 1793: "Whereas it appears that a state of war exists between Austria, Prussia, Sardinia, Great Britain and the United Netherlands on the one part and France on the other" citizens of the United States will be "liable to punishment or forfeiture under the law of nations by committing, aiding or abetting hostilities against any of the said powers."

NEUTRALITY REGULATION, governing the actions of citizens, was passed by act of Congress, June 5, 1794 (1 Stat.L.381). The act provided that any citizen who "accepts and exercises a commission to serve a foreign prince, state, colony, district or people, with whom the United States are at peace shall be fined not more than $2,000 and imprisoned not more than three years." The first conviction was that of Isaac Williams of Norwich, Conn., who accepted a commission in a French armed vessel and served against Great Britain. He was tried in September 1799, in the Circuit Court of the United States for the Connecticut District, at Hartford, Conn., found guilty under two counts, and sentenced to a fine of $1,000 and imprisonment for four months, on each charge. (*Francis Wharton—State Trials of the United States*)

NEW CHURCH TEMPLE. *See* Swedenborgian or New Church Temple

NEW YORK STOCK EXCHANGE. *See* Brokerage: Stock exchange

NEWS AGENCY
Financial news agency was the Kiernan Financial News Agency, established in 1869 by John James Kiernan at 21 Wall Street, New York City. In 1882, the service was extended to include results of athletic contests, arrivals of steamships, commodity quotations abroad, etc.

News agency for gathering news was established in Boston, Mass., about 1811. Local papers were issued weekly and the current news was discussed at the coffee houses, the principal one of which was Gilbert's Coffee House and Marine Diary. In 1814, Samuel Topliff became the owner of this establishment the name of which he changed to the Merchant's Reading Room. The local newspapers published news "from Mr. Topliff's correspondent." Topliff kept a record of the news for his own patrons and supplied the papers with news articles which he collected from his correspondents in foreign countries. (*Ethel Stanwood Bolton—"Memoir of Samuel Topliff" in Topliff's Travels*)

Teletypesetter circuit operated by a news agency. *See* Teletypesetter: Teletypesetter circuit operated by a news agency

NEWS CORRESPONDENT
Negro news correspondent was Joel Augustus Rogers, who was sent to Addis Ababa, Ethiopia, by the Pittsburgh, Pa., *Courier*, in October 1935. He returned April 21, 1936.

Negro news correspondent accredited to the White House was Harry McAlpin, representing the Atlanta, Ga., *Daily World* and the press service of the Negro Newspaper Publishers Association. He attended his first White House press conference February 8, 1944.

Negro news correspondent admitted to the House of Representatives and Senate press gallery was Percival L. Prattis, representative of *Our World*, New York City, who was accredited on February 3, 1947.

Washington correspondent of importance was James Gordon Bennett (the elder), whose articles first appeared January 2, 1828, in the New York *Enquirer*, later the *Courier and Enquirer*. (*Oliver Carlson—The Man Who Made News*)

White House reporter was William W. (Bill) Price, employed by the Washington, D.C., *Star* from April 24, 1897, to February 17, 1917. Starting with President Theodore Roosevelt's administration (1901-1909), he interviewed celebrities at the Executive Mansion, instead of at Capitol Hill.

NEWS CORRESPONDENT—*Continued*
Woman news correspondent accredited to the White House was Mrs. Emily Edson Briggs, correspondent for the Philadelphia, Pa., *Press,* who used the pseudonym "Olivia" for her "Olivia Letters," published January 1866 to January 7, 1882, during the administration of Presidents Johnson, Grant, Hayes, and Garfield. (*Emily Edson Briggs—The Olivia Letters*)

Woman news reporter at a political convention was Mary Ashton Rice Livermore, one of the editors of the *New Covenant,* who covered the Republican National Convention, May 12-18, 1860, at the Chicago Wigwam, Chicago, Ill., which nominated Abraham Lincoln. (*Edith Horton—A Group of Famous Women*)

NEWS DISPATCH BY CABLE. *See* Cable (telegraph) : News dispatch by cable

NEWS DISPATCH BY TELEGRAPH. *See* Telegram: News dispatch by telegram

NEWS DISPATCH BY TELEPHONE. *See* Telephone: News dispatch by telephone

NEWS PHOTOGRAPH. *See* Photograph: News photographs of distinction

NEWSBOY was Barney Flaherty, a ten-year-old who answered the advertisement, "To the Unemployed—A number of steady men can find employment by vending this paper. A liberal discount is allowed to those who buy to sell again," inserted in the New York *Sun,* New York City, on September 4, 1833, by Benjamin Day, the publisher.

NEWSPAPER
Abolition newspaper was the *Philanthropist,* published and edited by Charles Osborn, which appeared in Mt. Pleasant, Ohio, on August 29, 1817. It published "An Appeal to Philanthropists" by Benjamin Lundy, which is said by some to be the most powerful abolition appeal ever made. (*Ohio State Archaeological and Historical Society. Publications. Vol. 31*)

Arabic daily newspaper in the United States was *Al-Hoda,* founded February 22, 1898, in Philadelphia, Pa., as a weekly by Naoum Anthony Mokarzel. On August 25, 1902, it started publication as a daily in New York City. Mokarzel was editor-in-chief and owner until his death in 1932.

Chinese daily newspaper was the *Chung Sai Yat Po* (The Chinese Western Daily Paper) of San Francisco, Calif., the first issue of which appeared February 16, 1900. It was

15 by 22 inches and consisted of four pages. The founder of the paper was Ng Poon Chew, Litt.D., who was the president and managing editor until his death, March 13, 1931.

College daily was the *Yale News,* which was published in New Haven, Conn., on January 28, 1878. In that issue it was stated that the paper would be published daily during the college term.

Colored comic section. *See* below Newspaper Sunday comic section

Composograph photograph in a newspaper was published November 25, 1925 in the *Evening Graphic,* New York City. It purported to depict a scene in the private chambers of Justice Morschauser at White Plains, N.Y., showing Alice Jones and her husband, Leonard Kip Rhinelander. A model was used and the photograph was pasted in true perspective to form a composite layout.

Constitution of the United States first published in a newspaper. *See* Constitution of the United States: Constitution of the United States was first published in a newspaper

Czech language newspaper was the *Slovan Amerikansky,* a small folio weekly sheet edited by Frank Korizek and first issued January 1, 1860, in Racine, Wis. (*Fanny S. Stone—Racine, Belle City of the Lakes*)

Daily newspaper was the *Pennsylvania Packet and Daily Advertiser,* published by David C. Claypoole and John Dunlap in Philadelphia, Pa., which appeared September 21, 1784, as a daily. It sold for four pence a copy. Previously, it had been the *Pennsylvania Packet and General Advertiser,* founded in 1771 as a weekly. The claim of being the first daily newspaper is also made for the *Pennsylvania Evening Post and Daily Advertiser,* whose title was changed in 1783 from the *Pennsylvania Evening Post and Public Advertiser.* It originally appeared on Tuesday, Thursday, and Saturday as a tri-weekly from June 24, 1775, until January 7, 1779, when it became a semi-weekly. Benjamin Towne was editor and publisher.

Declaration of Independence first published in a newspaper. *See* Declaration of Independence: Declaration of Independence was first published

Democratic newspaper using the word "Democratic" in its title was the Philadelphia, Pa., *Democratic Press,* published three times

THE FIRST

a week from March 27, 1807 until June 29, 1807, when it appeared as a daily, *The Democratic Press for the Country*. The editor was John Binns. (*Pennsylvania Historical Commission—A Checklist of Pennsylvania Newspapers*)

European edition of an American newspaper was the Paris edition of the New York *Herald*, published October 4, 1887. It consisted of four six-column pages, the last page being devoted to advertisements. (*Al Laney—Paris Herald, The Incredible Newspaper*)

French daily newspaper was the *Courrier Français* of Philadelphia, Pa., established April 15, 1794. It became a tri-weekly August 24, 1795, but was restored to a daily October 26, 1795. It was discontinued July 3, 1798.

French daily newspaper (successful) was the *Courrier des États Unis*, which appeared June 10, 1851 in New York City with Paul Arpin as editor. It was originally started as a weekly by E. William Hoskin, the founder and first editor, and the first issue appeared March 1, 1828.

French newspaper was the *Courier de l'Amérique* of Philadelphia, published from July 27, 1784, to October 26, 1784.

German daily newspaper was the *New Yorker Staats-Zeitung* published in New York City on January 26, 1850. It had originally been a weekly paper, the first issue of which appeared December 24, 1834. The first editor was Gustav Adolf Neumann.

German newspaper was published on May 6, 1732 by Benjamin Franklin in Philadelphia, Pa., and was entitled *Philadelphische Zeitung*. It was a small sheet printed in German, four pages, 6½ by 9 inches, text in double columns and in Roman type. The second issue appeared on Saturday, June 24, 1732. Christopher Sauer's German newspaper *Der Hoch-Deutsch Pennsylvanische Geschichts-Schreiber, oder Sammlung wichtiger Nachrichten aus dem Natur-und-Kirchen-Reich*, "The High German Pennsylvania Recorder of Events or Collection of Important News from the Kingdom of Nature and of the Church," which is generally credited as the first newspaper, was first published on August 20, 1739. (*Pennsylvania Magazine of History and Biography. April 1902. "The First German Newspaper in America"*)

Greek newspaper was the *Atlantis*, issued March 3, 1894, from 2 Stone Street, New York City as a four-page weekly of tabloid size, and afterwards two and three times a week. On January 3, 1905, it became a full-sized four-page daily. It was the first Greek publication in America and the first publication in the world to use typesetting machinery for the Greek alphabet. Its founder and first editor was Solon John Vlasto.

Hungarian daily newspaper was the *Amerikai Magyar Népszava*, published October 18, 1904, in New York City. Its founder and editor-in-chief was Geza David Berko. It was originally established in March 1899 as a weekly, and then was issued twice a week until October 18, 1904, when it became a daily.

Illustrated daily newspaper was the New York *Daily Graphic*, which was published in 1873 and sold for five cents a copy. Zinc plate etchings were issued. The first issue appeared on Tuesday, March 4, 1873.

Illustrated tabloid was the *Illustrated Daily News* of New York City, which appeared on June 26, 1919. It was published by Robert Rutherford McCormick and Joseph Medill Patterson. (*Willard Grosvenor Bleyer—History of American Journalism*)

Index. *See* Newspaper index

Indian newspaper was the *Cherokee Phoenix*, a weekly newspaper in English and Cherokee published from February 21, 1828, to October 1835 in New Echota, Ga. (the capital of the Cherokee nation). The Cherokee alphabet was invented by Sequoyah, son of Mastahangan. The paper was edited by Elias Boudinot, a Cherokee who was educated at the foreign mission school in Cornwall, Conn., at the instance of the philanthropist whose name he was allowed to adopt. (*Frederick Webb Hodge—Handbook of American Indians*)

Insurance service offered by a newspaper. *See* Insurance: Insurance service offered by a newspaper

Italian newspaper was *Il Progresso Italo-Americano*, issued in New York City in September 1880. The first owner and editor was Charles Barsotti.

Labor newspaper. *See* Labor paper

Livestock market paper. *See* Livestock-market paper

Mimeographed daily newspaper was the *Kellogg Daily Reminder*, published July 25, 1923, by Eaton's Letter Shop, Kellogg, Idaho. The founder and first editor was Marson M. Eaton, Jr. The first issue was only one sheet printed on both sides.

NEWSPAPER—*Continued*
Negro newspaper edited by Negroes for Negroes was *Freedom's Journal*, a four-page weekly published in New York City from March 16, 1827, to March 28, 1829, and edited by John Brown Russworm and Samuel E. Cornish. (*Frederick German Detweiler—The Negro Press in the United States*)

Newspaper was a broadside. One of the earliest of the broadsides and in some ways the most important was *The Present State of the New English Affairs*. It was published "to prevent false reports" in 1689 by Samuel Green in Cambridge, Mass., and consisted of a single sheet printed in two columns, newspaper style, folio size, 8 by 14½ inches. (*Isaiah Thomas—History of Printing in America*)

Newspaper advertisement. *See* Advertisement: Advertisement

Newspaper advertisement printed on aluminum foil appeared in the *Sentinel,* Milwaukee, Wis., on March 18, 1958. It was a lamination of Reynolds aluminum foil on one side and paper on the other. The foil side was printed in seven colors at the gravure plant of the Reynolds Metal Company in St. Louis, Mo., while the paper side was printed by the *Sentinel* in one color and black.

Newspaper association was the American Newspaper Publishers Association, organized November 17, 1886, in Detroit, Mich. The call was made by William Henry Brearley of the Detroit *News.* The first convention was held February 16-17, 1887, in Rochester, N.Y., and was attended by fifty-one delegates.

Newspaper cartoon. *See* Cartoon: Newspaper cartoon

Newspaper colored supplement was issued by the New York City *World* Sunday, November 19, 1893, and consisted of a four-page section, the outside pages of which were printed in five colors. Two half-page drawings in color featured "A Scene in Atlantic Gardens, Saturday Night" and "The Cathedral at Eleven O'Clock Mass." The inside pages were printed in black.

Newspaper daily railroad delivery service was instituted by the *Morning News* of Dallas, Tex., on October 1, 1885, when a special train was leased on the Texas and Pacific Railway to carry newspapers from Dallas to Fort Worth, Texas.

Newspaper delivery train was operated by the International Great Northern Railroad over the Galveston, Houston and Henderson

Railroad, in 1883 to deliver the Galveston *News* to subscribers located between Galveston and Houston, Tex. The *News* paid $500 a month for the exclusive lease of the train.

Newspaper editorial apology appeared in the *American Weekly Mercury* of April 20, 1721. It stated: "N.B. In our last week's *Mercury* [April 13] No. 70, there is an account inserted from a private Letter sent to Boston, dated the 20th of September last, That the Government of Pennsilvania is Surrendered to the Crown, etc. These are to give Notice that we have now Letters from London, of a later Date, by which we find that the said Report concerning the Province of Pennsilvania is false and groundless and therefore was both by them and us too rashly inserted." This newspaper was published in Philadelphia, Pa.

Newspaper printed on a train was the *Weekly Herald,* a single sheet printed on both sides, approximately 7 by 8 inches. It was issued by Thomas Alva Edison and distributed on the train between Port Huron and Detroit, Mich. The first known issue was dated Port Huron, Mich., February 3, 1862.

Newspaper printed on pine-pulp paper was the *Soperton News,* Soperton, Ga., of March 31, 1933, a four-page six-column newspaper. The pines were grown in Treutlen County, Ga., and the paper was obtained from the Charles Holmes Herty-Savannah Pulp and Paper Laboratory, now the Herty Foundation Laboratory.

Newspaper printed on pine-pulp paper in color was the *News* of Dallas, Tex., a daily, which printed a pine-paper edition March 31, 1937.

Newspaper printed on wood-pulp paper was the Boston *Morning Journal* of Boston, Mass., published January 15, 1863. It was a four-page, eight-column newspaper and sold for three cents a copy.

Newspaper published at sea was the illustrated *Atlantic Telegraph,* printed on board the cable-laying "Great Eastern," captained by James Anderson. It sold for five shillings for the series. Issues were published Saturday, July 29, 1865, August 5, 1865 and August 12, 1865. (*Isabella Field Judson—Cyrus W. Field —His Life and Work*)

Newspaper published at sea (daily) to carry world news was the *Cunard Daily Bulletin,* inaugurated by Guglielmo Marconi in October 1902 on the S.S. "Campania" and the S.S. "Lucania," at that time "the crack liners of the fleet." The news was obtained from the wireless stations at Poldhu, Cornwall, England, and Glace Bay, Canada.

THE FIRST

Newspaper published at sea (radio news service) was the *Transatlantic Times,* a four-page newspaper, which was issued on November 15, 1899, on board the American liner "St. Paul," by Guglielmo Marconi and two engineers. It sold for a dollar a copy, and the proceeds were donated to the Seaman's Fund. The news was obtained by wireless from the Needles Station, Isle of Wight.

Newspaper published by soldiers in the field was the *United States American Volunteer,* published May 21, 1861, at De Soto, Mo., by members of Company A, Fifth Regiment, Missouri Volunteers, commanded by Captain Nelson Cole. The issue consisted of a single page, the reverse being the first page of the abandoned *Jefferson County Herald.*

Newspaper published on the Pacific coast was the *Oregon Spectator,* a semi-monthly issued in Oregon City, Ore., February 5, 1846. Its slogan was "Westward the star of empire takes its way." The newspaper was published by the Oregon Printing Association and was nonpolitical. The first editor was Colonel William G. T'Vault. The first California newspaper was the *Californian,* published August 15, 1846 in Monterey, Calif., by Robert Semple and the Reverend Walter Colton. (*John B. Horner—Oregon History and Early Literature*)

Newspaper published south of the Potomac River was the *Virginia Gazette,* containing "the freshest advices both Foreign and Domestick." It was established by William Parks and began its regular publication in Williamsburg, Va., August 5, 1736. It was a single sheet folded so as to have four pages. The subscription price was fifteen shillings a year.

Newspaper published west of the Alleghenies was the *Pittsburgh Gazette,* which was first issued on July 29, 1786. It was founded by John Scull and Joseph Hall and was printed in a log house on the Monongahela River, Pittsburgh, Pa. (*Pittsburgh and the Pittsburgh Spirit—Pittsburgh Chamber of Commerce*)

Newspaper publisher was Benjamin Harris, "the father of American newspapers." His paper, *Publick Occurrances, Both Foreign and Domestic,* issued from the London Coffee House, Boston, Mass., was printed by R. Pierce, on September 25, 1690. It was promptly suppressed because of certain "reflexions" distasteful to Governor Simon Bradstreet of Massachusetts. Harris had intended to issue it monthly "or if any Glut of Occurrances happen, oftener," but only the one issue appeared. It was a one-sheet paper folded to present four pages, containing news in double columns. The

THE FIRST

last page was blank. There were no advertisements. (*George Emery Littlefield—Early Massachusetts Press*)

Newspaper room (library). *See* Library: Library newspaper room

Newspaper rotogravure sections were simultaneously instituted by seven newspapers on March 29, 1914, when an eight-page supplement showing thirteen masterpieces of the Altman Collection in the Metropolitan Museum of Art, New York City, was included with the New York *Times,* the Boston *Sun-Herald,* the Philadelphia *Public Ledger,* the Chicago *Tribune,* the Cleveland *Plain Dealer,* the St. Louis *Post-Dispatch,* and the Kansas City *Star.*

Newspaper serial story in an American newspaper appeared in Samuel Keimer's *Pennsylvania Gazette* in Philadelphia in 1729. It was entitled "Religious Courtship" and was written by Daniel Defoe, author of *Robinson Crusoe.* It was reprinted from his book of the same title published in 1722 in London.

Newspaper (successful) was the Boston *News-Letter,* the first issue of which was dated April 17-24, 1704. The editor was John Campbell, a New England postmaster, who earned the distinction of being America's first vendor of news. It was printed by Bartholomew Green in a back room of his home. The page size was 7½ by 12½ inches. The text was set in small pica type. The paper was without competition for fifteen years and reached a circulation of 300 copies.

Newspaper Sunday comic section was published by the New York *World* in 1893. The drawings were made by Richard Felton Outcault and depicted a humorous set of characters under the title of "Hogan's Alley." On November 18, 1894, the newspaper published the first of his six-box cartoon series "The Origin of a New Species," and later "The Yellow Kid." This was the first successful colored section.

Newspaper to appear on Sunday was the Sunday *Monitor,* Baltimore, Md., published by Philip Edwards, which appeared December 18, 1796. It consisted of four pages, 10¼ by 17 inches.

Newspaper to be microfilmed. *See* Check photographing device

Newspaper to insert an aluminum foil sheet to be used as a household wrapping was the *Sentinel,* Milwaukee, Wis., whose April 2, 1957, issue contained an insert featuring an advertisement of the Aluminum Corporation of America.

THE FIRST

NEWSPAPER—*Continued*
Newspaper to microfilm its current issues.
See Microfilm: Newspaper to microfilm its
current issues

Newspaper to microfilm its past issues.
See Microfilm: Newspaper to microfilm its
past issues

Newspaper to use an airplane. *See* Aviation—Airplane: Airplane used by a newspaper

**Newspaper with perfumed advertising
page** was issued March 25, 1937, by the
Daily News, Washington, D.C. It contained a
page advertisement of the Peoples Drug Stores
featuring flowers.

Newspaper wrappers. *See* Postal service;
Newspaper wrappers

Norwegian-American newspaper was *Nord-
lyset* ("The Northern Light"), first published
July 29, 1847, in Muskego, Wis. James De
Noon Reymert was the first editor.

Penny daily newspaper was *The Cent,*
which was published in Philadelphia, Pa., in
1830 by Dr. Christopher Columbus Conwell, but
the first successful penny paper was the New
York *Sun,* published by Benjamin Henry Day,
which appeared on September 3, 1833. *(George
Henry Payne—History of Journalism in the
United States)*

Periodicals on microfilm. *See* Microfilm:
Magazine on microfilm offered to subscribers

Political newspaper of national importance
was the *Gazette of the United States,* the political organ of Alexander Hamilton, edited by
John Fenno. The first issue appeared in New
York City, April 11, 1789. When the government moved its headquarters to Philadelphia,
the *Gazette* followed. The first issue printed in
Philadelphia was that of April 14, 1790. The
New York Weekly Journal was established November 5, 1733, by John Peter Zenger as a
political organ to expose Governor Cosby.
Zenger was arrested and imprisoned November
17, 1734, defended by Andrew Hamilton, a
Philadelphia lawyer, and acquitted. His news-
paper is often termed the first political paper.
*(Merritt Way Haynes—Student's History of
Printing)*

Radio facsimile newspaper was transmitted
by KSTP, St. Paul, Minn., on December 17,
1937. It consisted of a roll of sensitized paper
nearly five inches wide, with perforations at
the sides, which issued from a receiving set.

THE FIRST

Radio facsimile newspaper (daily) was
transmitted December 7, 1938, by the *Post-
Dispatch,* St. Louis, Mo., over Station
W9XZY on an ultra high frequency. Nine
pages, each 8½ inches long, four columns to
a page, printed in seven-point type, issued from
a receiving set. About fifteen minutes was
required to transmit each page.

Religious weekly newspaper. *See* Religious
publication: Religious weekly newspaper

Spanish newspaper was *El Redactor,* published July 1, 1827, in New York City. The
first editor was Juan José de Lerena.

**Three-dimensional newspaper advertise-
ment.** *See* Advertisement: Three-dimensional newspaper advertisement

**Trademark controversy involving a news-
paper.** *See* Trademark lawsuit: Trademark
controversy involving a newspaper

Transoceanic newspaper was the *Daily
Mail,* a weekly digest of the London, England,
Daily Mail, dated January 5, 1944. It was
made up and edited in London, microfilmed, and
flown to New York City, where it was enlarged
and printed. It contained twelve pages, 9 by 12
inches, four columns wide.

Ukrainian daily newspaper was the
Ukrainian Daily News, established January 31,
1920, in New York City. The first editor was
M. Tkach.

Woman newspaper editor. *See* Woman:
Woman newspaper editor

Yiddish daily newspaper was the *Yiddishes-Tageblatt* or "Jewish Daily News," which
was founded in New York City in 1885 by
Kasriel Hersch Sarasohn.

NEWSPAPER AUDIT
Newspaper circulation audit was made by
a group of advertisers who organized the Association of American Advertisers to verify
circulation figures. On August 21, 1914, the
Audit Bureau of Circulations was formed in
Chicago, Ill., with headquarters in that city
as a cooperative, non-profit-making organization.
Membership was composed of advertisers, advertising agencies, and publishers. Of the
twenty-five directors, four were from daily
newspapers, two from magazines, two from
business papers, two from farm papers, two
from advertising agencies, and thirteen from
among advertisers.

NEWSPAPER INDEX separately published was *The Index to the New York Times
for 1865,* published in 1866 by Henry J. Ray-

mond & Company, New York City. It contained 182 pages. Earlier indexes had been printed primarily for staff use.

NEWSPAPER PRINTING PRESS. *See* Printing press: High-speed newspaper printing and folding machine

NEWSPAPER SYNDICATE
Newspaper syndicate to supply articles, stories, etc., was started on November 8, 1884, but was postponed until November 15, 1884, by Samuel Sidney McClure of New York City, who organized the McClure Syndicate. Because the syndicate offered larger payment than individual newspapers, a better class of writers endeavored to write for the daily press, their articles being syndicated throughout the country. (*Samuel Sidney McClure—My Autobiography*)

Press syndicate facsimile transmission. *See* Radio facsimile transmission: Press syndicate facimile transmission direct to newspaper offices

Syndication of newspaper material was attempted by Moses Yale Beach of New York City, who printed President John Tyler's message, delivered December 7, 1841, to the second session of the Twenty-seventh Congress. Sales were made to the Albany, N.Y., *Advertiser;* the Troy, N.Y., *Whig;* the Salem, Mass., *Gazette;* the Boston, Mass., *Times;* etc. Each newspaper printed its own name in the blank space provided for that purpose. (*Alexander Gurdon Abell—Life of John Tyler*)

NEWSREEL. *See* Moving picture: Newsreel

NEWSREEL THEATER. *See* Theater: Newsreel theater

NIAGARA FALLS
Person to cross Niagara Falls on a tightrope was Jean François Gravelet, a Frenchman, better known by his professional name, Émile Blondin, whose first exhibition took place on June 30, 1859, before a crowd of five thousand people. Wearing pink tights and a spangled tunic of yellow silk, he crossed a cable about 2 inches in diameter strung 151 hundred feet high. The rope was stretched below the suspension bridge with a series of parallel ropes alongside. In 1859 and 1860, Blondin gave a series of "ascensions." He carried a man on his back across the cable, trundled over a loaded wheelbarrow, and walked across in a sack. On July 14, 1859, dressed as an ape, he pushed a wheelbarrow across. He usually carried a long pole which aided him to balance himself and which could also serve as a guard in case he fell since it would be supported by the parallel ropes

and thus prevent him from falling into the river. (*George Washington Holley—The Falls of Niagara*)

Person to go over Niagara Falls in a barrel was Anna Edson Taylor, who, on October 24, 1901, went over the Horseshoe Falls on the Canadian side in a barrel 4½ feet high and 3 feet in diameter. A leather harness and cushions were placed inside the barrel to protect her.

Person to go over Niagara Falls in a rubber ball was Jean Lussier, who made the descent July 4, 1928, in a ball of his own construction weighing 750 pounds and costing $1,485. It was equipped with oxygen tanks and reinforced with cushions. It was set adrift from a launch and went over the Horseshoe Falls. (*Wide World Magazine. Vol. 26. No. 370. January 1929*)

Utilization of Niagara Falls waterpower was made in 1757 by Chabert Joncaire, who dug a ditch so that the water would operate an overshot waterwheel to drive a crude sawmill. In 1879, the water turned a small dynamo which fed sixteen arc lights in Prospect Park. In Niagara Falls, N.Y., on December 1881, an arc light machine was installed in a papermill on the cliff.

Utilization of Niagara Falls waterpower (large scale) was made by the Niagara River Hydraulic Tunnel Power and Sewer Company, incorporated March 31, 1886. The name was changed to the Niagara Falls Power Company November 11, 1889. The Cataract Construction Company, incorporated June 13, 1889 under the general laws of the state of New Jersey, was the agent of the Niagara Falls Power Company in building and putting the project into operation. It ceased to exist in 1899. Ground was broken October 4, 1890. On October 24, 1893, a contract was executed with the Westinghouse Electric and Manufacturing Company of Pittsburgh, Pa., for three 5,000 h.p. generators delivering two-phase currents at 2,200 volts, 25 cycles. The first 5,000 h.p. turboalternator unit was completed within eighteen months. On August 26, 1895, power was first transmitted commercially, the current being employed by the Pittsburgh Reduction Company in the reduction of aluminum ore. Buffalo received its first power for commercial purposes November 15, 1896. The three 5,000 h.p. generators at first installed were changed to 11,000 volt machines after twenty-five years of service and these are still in use. Prior to the installation of the 5,000 h.p. generators, 1,000 h.p. was the capacity of the largest generator. (*Edward Dean Adams—Niagara Power*)

NICKEL COIN. *See* Money: Nickel

NICKEL PLATING was invented by William H. Remington of Boston, Mass., who obtained patent No. 82,877 on October 6, 1868, on a "process of electroplating with nickel." He used a solution prepared by dissolving refined nickel in nitric acid, then precipitating the nickel by the addition of carbonate of potash, washing the precipitate with water, dissolving it in a solution of sal-ammoniac, and filtering it.

NICKEL SILVER SPOONS. *See* Spoons: Nickel silver spoons

"NICKELODEON." *See* Moving picture theater: Theater in the world devoted exclusively to the exhibition of motion pictures

NIGHT BASEBALL GAME. *See* Baseball game: Baseball game at night

NIGHT-COACH BUS. *See* Automobile bus: Bus night coach

NIGHT COURT. *See* Court: Night court

NO-HIT BASEBALL GAME. *See* Baseball game: No-hit nine-inning baseball game

NO-RUN NINE-INNING BASEBALL GAME. *See* Baseball game: No-run nine-inning game

NOBEL PRIZE
  Husband and wife in the United States to receive a joint Nobel Prize award were Dr. Carl Ferdinand Cori and Dr. Gerty Theresa Cori of the Washington University School of Medicine, St. Louis, Mo., who discovered how sugar in the human system is converted into glycogen through an enzyme or biological catalyst called phosphorylase. The award was announced October 23, 1947. A co-sharer of the medicine award was Dr. Bernardo Alberto Houssay of the Buenos Aires Institute of Biology and Experimental Medicine for work on the relation between the pancreas and the pituitary gland.

  Negro to win the Nobel Peace Prize was Dr. Ralph Johnson Bunche, whose mediations in 1949 between Israel and its warring Arab neighbors resulted in an armistice settlement. On December 10, 1950, at Oslo, Norway, he received the Nobel Medal and diploma and a cash award equivalent to $31,674,08.

  Nobel Peace Prize awarded an American woman was granted to Jane Addams of Chicago, Ill., who received the award jointly with Dr. Nicholas Murray Butler, president of Columbia University, New York City. It was

accepted for them at Oslo, Norway on December 10, 1931, by Hoffman Phillips, United States Minister to Norway. Jane Addams was the second woman recipient, the 1905 award having been made to Bertha von Suttner of Austria.

  Nobel Prize awarded to an American was granted in 1906 to President Theodore Roosevelt for his service in the cause of peace in concluding the treaty between Russia and Japan at the end of the Russo-Japanese War.

  Nobel Prize in chemistry awarded to an American was granted in 1914 to Theodore William Richards of Harvard University, Cambridge, Mass., "in recognition of his accurate determination of the atomic weight of a large number of chemical elements." The prize of 146,900 Swedish kroner. was presented November 12, 1915, in Stockholm.

  Nobel Prize in literature awarded to an American was granted in 1930 to Sinclair Lewis "for his great and living art in painting life, with a talent for creating types with wit and humor."

  Nobel Prize in medicine and physiology awarded to an American was granted in 1912 to Dr. Alexis Carrel of the Rockefeller Institute for Medical Research "for his work on vascular ligature and on the grafting of blood vessels and organs."

  Nobel Prize in physics awarded to an American was granted in 1907 to Albert Abraham Michelson of the University of Chicago "for his optical instruments of precision, and the spectroscopic and metrologic investigations which he carried out by means of them." (*Scientific Monthly, January 1939*)

NOBELIUM. *See* Element: Element 102

NOMINATING CONVENTION. *See* Political convention: Nominating convention (state)

NON-DENOMINATIONAL COLLEGE. *See* College: Non-denominational college

NON-ELECTRONIC DEVICE FOR OBSERVING IN TOTAL DARKNESS. *See* Camera: Non-electronic device for observing in total darkness

NON-FORFEITURE INSURANCE POLICY. *See* Insurance: Non-forfeiture insurance policy

NON-RELIGIOUS COMMUNISTIC SETTLEMENT. *See* Communistic Society: Communistic non-religious settlement

THE FIRST

NON-SKID TIRE. *See* Automobile tire: Non-skid tire

NORMAL SCHOOL
See also College

Normal school established exclusively for the preparation of teachers was the Concord Academy, Concord, Vt., opened on March 11, 1823 by the Reverend Samuel Read Hall, who conducted it as a teachers' seminary until 1830.

Normal school instruction course given at a university was offered December 1, 1841 when Alfred Saxe was appointed Professor of Normal Instruction at Wesleyan University, Middletown, Conn., for a term of two years "to prepare teachers more perfectly for the business of instruction." No tuition charge was made for the course, which was a one-year program of study.

Normal school instruction offered by a college was given at the "model school" established at Lafayette College, Easton, Pa., by Dr. George Junkin, who paid $2,230.22 of his own money to erect a three-story building known as West College. A commemorative marble dial was inserted at the laying of the cornerstone on July 4, 1838, to give the latitude, longitude, and magnetic variations of the college. *(David Bishop Skillman—The Biography of a College)*

Normal school (state) was the Normal School, Lexington, Mass., which opened July 3, 1839, with only three pupils. Cyrus Pierce was the first principal. Edmund Dwight of Boston offered $10,000 on condition that the Commonwealth appropriate the same amount to be expended by the Board of Education in qualifying teachers for common schools. On April 19, 1838, the council appropriated the $10,000 to be used as required. On December 15, 1853, the school moved to Framingham, Mass., where it is now located. *(Samuel Joseph May—Memoir of Cyrus Pierce, First Principal of the First State Normal School in the United States)*

Normal school (state) at which students actually conducted classes was the Oswego Training School for Primary Teachers, Oswego, N.Y., established May 1, 1861, with an enrollment of nine students. Dr. Edward Austin Sheldon who served from 1861 to 1897 was the first principal. The first class, 39 students, was graduated in 1862. On March 4, 1863, the New York legislature passed "an act for the support of a training school for primary teachers" which appropriated $3,000 for two years calculated on an attendance of 50 pupils. On April 7, 1866, New York passed the Normal School Act, and on March 27, 1867, acquired the school as a state normal school and changed its

THE FIRST

name to the Oswego State Normal and Training School. *(Ned Harland Dearborn—The Oswego Movement in American Education)*

Teachers' training school (Jewish) was Gratz College, Philadelphia, Pa., which offered a series of general lectures in 1895. Nine trustees were elected February 17, 1895. They selected from their number Moses Aaron Dropsie as president, Charles Joseph Cohen as treasurer, and David Sulzberger as secretary. Regular instruction did not commence until 1897.

Woman principal of a normal school was Anna Callender Brackett, who on January 5, 1863, took charge of the St. Louis Normal School, St. Louis, Mo. Sarah M. Platt acted as her assistant. Miss Platt and Miss Ann J. Forsyth were temporarily in charge of the school until the principalship was granted to Miss Brackett. *(Report of the St. Louis Public Schools. 1862-1863)*

NORTH POLE. *See* Aviation—Flights; Discovery; Expedition

NORTHERN LIGHTS. *See* Aurora borealis

NORTHWEST PASSAGE. *See* Discovery: Northwest passage

NORTHWEST TERRITORY. *See* Territorial expansion: Acquisition of land by the federal government

NORWEGIAN-AMERICAN NEWSPAPER. *See* Newspaper: Norwegian-American newspaper

NOVEL
American novel published in America was *The Power of Sympathy or the Triumph of Nature Founded in Truth,* dedicated "to the young ladies of America." It was printed in 1789 in Boston, Mass., by Isaiah Thomas & Co., and sold at the company's bookstore, 45 Newbury Street. Publication was announced in the *Independent Chronicle* of January 21, 1789. It appeared in two volumes of 138 and 158 pages. The story deals with seduction. The author used the nom de plume "Philenia." Authorship is attributed to Mrs. Sarah Wentworth Apthorp Morton of Boston, Mass., and to William Hill Brown. *(Emily Pendleton and Milton Ellis—Philenia, or the Life and Works of Sarah Wentworth Morton)*

American novel republished in England was Royall Tyler's *The Algerine Captive; or the Life and Adventures of Doctor Updike Underhill; Six Years a Prisoner among the Algerines,* originally published in 1797 in Walpole, N.H.

THE FIRST

NOVEL—*Continued*
Novel by a Negro was William Wells Brown's *Clotel, or the President's Daughter, a Narrative of Slave Life in the United States,* the story of an efficient colored woman represented as the housekeeper of Thomas Jefferson. In the novel one of the woman's two daughters drowns herself in the Potomac River to elude pursuing slavers. The book was published in London, England, in 1853, and reprinted with slight changes in 1864 in Boston, Mass., under the title of *Clotelle, A Tale of the Southern States.* It was published by James Redpath of Boston, Mass., contained 104 pages, and sold for ten cents.

Novel to win the Pulitzer prize in letters was *His Family,* by Ernest Poole, published in 1917 by the Macmillan Company, New York City. It was about Roger Gale, a New York man, and his three daughters, Edith, Deborah, and Laura. The award was announced June 3, 1918, by President Nicholas Murray Butler of Columbia University, New York City.

Novel written in America was *Adventures of Alonso: Containing Some Striking Anecdotes of the Present Prime Minister of Portugal* (Sebastião José de Carvalho e Mello, Marquis de Pombal) by "A Native of Maryland, some years resident in Lisbon." The work is attributed to Thomas Atwood Digges of Warburton Manor, Md. The original edition consisted of two volumes, 148 pages and 129 pages, and was printed for John Bew in London in 1775. The book was also the first American novel to be translated; it was published in Leipzig in 1787 by Schwickert as *Alonzo's Abenteur* [*Abentheur*], in two parts. (*American Literature. Vol. 12. No. 4. January 1941*)

NOVEL COURSE
Course on the contemporary novel, exclusively, was given by Professor William Lyon Phelps at Yale University, New Haven, Conn., in the academic year 1895-96. The course was called "Modern Novels" and was elected by 250 juniors and seniors.

Lecture course on the English novel offered by a university was given in 1889 by Professor Felix Emmanuel Schelling at the University of Pennsylvania, Philadelphia. It consisted of two one-hour lectures known as "English Literature 2." (*Catalogue of the University of Pennsylvania, 1889-1890*)

NUCLEAR BOMB SHELTER. *See* Building: House with a built-in nuclear bomb shelter

NUCLEAR ENGINEERING COLLEGE COURSE fully organized was established by the North Carolina State College of Agriculture and Engineering of the University of

THE FIRST

North Carolina, Raleigh, under the direction of Dr. Clifford Keith Beck, head of the physics department. The first students were accepted and enrolled June 12, 1950.

NUCLEAR FISSION. *See* Atomic energy: Self-sustaining nuclear chain reaction demonstration

NUCLEAR REACTOR. *See* Atomic reactor

NUCLEAR UNDERGROUND BLAST. *See* Atomic bomb: Atomic bomb underground explosion

NUDIST ORGANIZATION was the American League for Physical Culture, organized by three men, December 5, 1929, in New York City. The first nudist summer camp was that of the American League at Central Valley, N.Y., which opened in June 1930. There were approximately thirty members at the first summer camp.

NUGGET. *See* Gold: Gold nugget

NULLIFICATION PROCEEDINGS to offset federal congressional legislation were the Kentucky Resolutions introduced by John Breckinridge. They were adopted by the Lower House of Kentucky on November 10, 1798, and by the Upper House on November 13, 1798, and approved by Governor James Garrard on November 16, 1798. Objection was taken to the "act concerning aliens," June 25, 1798 (1 Stat. L.570) and an "act for the punishment of certain crimes against the United States," July 14, 1798 (1 Stat.L.596). (*Edward Payson Powell—Nullification and Secession in the United States*)

NUMBERING SYSTEM OF INSURANCE RATING. *See* Insurance: Numerical system of insurance rating

NUNS. *See* Catholic nuns

NURSE
Army Medical Specialist Corps male officer. *See* Army Officer: Army medical specialist corps male officer

Army Nurse Corps (female). *See* Army Nurse Corps (female)

Army nurse (male). *See* Army Officer: Male nurse

District nurse was employed by the Woman's Branch of the New York City Mission Society, New York City in 1877. (*William Raymond Jelliffe—One Hundred Years of City Mission and Tract Society*)

THE FIRST

Naval nurses. *See* Naval officer: Naval nurses' corps (woman member); Navy: Naval nurses' corps

Nurse appointed to a university professorship was Mary Adelaide Nutting, who was appointed Professor of Household Administration, Teachers College, Columbia University, New York City, and who served from 1906 to 1910. From 1910 to 1923, she served as Professor of Nursing Education, and from 1923 to 1925 as Professor of Nursing Education at the Helen Hartley Foundation. She retired July 1, 1925, and was appointed Professor Emeritus of Nursing Education.

Nurse employed by an industrial organization to attend to the health of its employees, was Ada Stewart, who was employed by the Vermont Marble Company of Proctor, Vt., in 1896.

Nurses' registration law (state) was ratified March 3, 1903, by North Carolina (Chapter 359, Public Laws of 1903). It provided voluntary registration with the county clerk of the Superior Court of any licensed trained nurse, after January 1, 1904, and for an examining and licensing board composed of two physicians and three registered nurses.

Order of the Purple Heart awarded to a nurse. *See* Medal: Order of the Purple Heart awarded to a nurse

NURSERY SCHOOL. *See* Kindergarten: Nursery school

NURSES' CORPS (naval). *See* Navy: Naval nurses' corps

NURSES' MAGAZINE was *The Nightingale*, "a paper in the interests of the methodical nursing of the sick," which appeared March 6, 1886, in New York City. The first issue consisted of four pages. It was a monthly, subscription $2 a year, edited by Sarah [Sara] E. Post of the Graduate Training School for Nurses, Bellevue Hospital, New York City.

NURSES' SOCIETY

Nurses' society (local) was the Philomena Society, organized November 24, 1885, in New York City. It disbanded in 1887. (*Historical Sketch of the American Nurses Association*)

Society for superintendents of nursing schools was the American Society of Superintendents of Training Schools for Nurses, founded at the Hall of Columbus, Chicago, Ill., June 15-17, 1893. The first officers were Anna Alston, president, L. Darche, secretary, and L. L. Drown, treasurer. The first national convention was held January 10, 1894, in New

THE FIRST

York City. (*First and Second Annual Convention of American Society of Superintendents of Training Schools for Nurses*)

NURSING SCHOOL

Army School of Nursing was authorized May 25, 1918, by Secretary of War Newton Diehl Baker, as a division of the Surgeon General's Office under the Medical Department of the Army. The first class of 402 graduates completed the course at Walter Reed Hospital, Washington, D.C., on June 16, 1921. A three-year course of study was prescribed, but advanced credits were offered to graduates of approved courses. The first dean of the school was Annie Warburton Goodrich. The school was discontinued August 12, 1931, by Secretary of War Patrick Jay Hurley.

Instruction for nurses (systematic) was given by Dr. Valentine Seaman of the New York Hospital, New York City, who gave lectures on anatomy, physiology, the care of children, and midwifery from 1798 to 1817. The first class consisted of 24 nurses. (*Minnie Goodnow—Nursing History in Brief*)

School for nurses to award a diploma was the School of Nursing of the Woman's Hospital of Philadelphia, chartered March 22, 1861. The first diploma was awarded in 1865. The first nurse known to have received the diploma was Harriet N. Phillips.

Training school for Negro nurses was the Spelman Seminary, Atlanta, Ga., founded in 1881 by Sophia Booker Packard and Harriet E. Giles of Boston, Mass., as the Atlanta Baptist Female Seminary. In 1884, the name was changed to the Spelman Seminary and in 1924 to Spelman College, the name by which it is now known. A nurses' training department was established in 1886 in a two-room frame building set apart for an infirmary and known as the Everts Ward. The first nurse received her certificate in 1888.

University school of nursing established as an integral part of a university was the School of Nursing, University of Minnesota, Minneapolis, authorized by the Board of Regents October 1, 1908, and established March 1, 1909, through the efforts of Dr. Richard Olding Beard. The first director of the school was Bertha Erdmann. The first graduation took place June 13, 1912, four students completing the training.

NUT AND BOLT FACTORY was established by Micah Rugg and Martin Barnes, in Marion, Conn., in 1840, although they began making bolts and nuts for the market in 1838 in Rugg's blacksmith shop. Their factory was a one-story wooden building, 30 feet by 20 feet,

NUT AND BOLT FACTORY—*Continued* designed especially to carry on the business started two years before. They employed six operators and the capacity production was 500 bolts a day. Prior to 1838, when they started making bolts commercially, these articles were hammered out and hand-finished by a blacksmith as needed from time to time. (*W. R. Wilbur—History of the Bolt and Nut Industry of America*)

NUT AND BOLT MACHINE was invented by David Wilkinson of Rhode Island who obtained a patent December 14, 1798. The first machine of importance for trimming the heads of nuts and bolts was invented by Micah Rugg who obtained patent No. 2,766, August 31, 1842.

NYLON
Nylon was invented by Dr. Wallace Hume Carothers, who on February 16, 1937, obtained patent No. 2,071,250, which was assigned to E. I. du Pont de Nemours & Company, Inc. The patent covered synthetic linear condensation polymers capable of being drawn into pliable strong fibers as well as the process for making them.

Nylon bristle filament production for toothbrushes began at Arlington, N.J., on February 24, 1938, by E. I. du Pont de Nemours & Company, Inc.

Nylon hose was placed on sale May 15, 1940, at stores throughout the country.

Nylon stretch yarn was introduced from Switzerland by Heberlein Patent Corporation, New York City. The first licensee to process Helanca stretch yarn was the Duplan Corporation, New York City, which supplied yarn to the Marion Knitting Company, the Chester H. Roth Company, and the Interwoven Stocking Company, which introduced men's stretch socks in August 1952.

Nylon yarn manufacture (commercial) was begun by E. I. du Pont de Nemours & Company, Inc., at Seaford, Del., on December 15, 1939. The yarn was distributed to hosiery mills, which knitted it into women's hosiery. This was the first use of nylon for apparel. Nylon stockings went on sale commercially for the first time in May 1940.

OAT-CRUSHING MACHINE was patented November 30, 1875, by Asmus J. Ehrrichson of Akron, Ohio, who obtained patent No.170,536, on "an improvement in oatmeal machines." A hopper with a perforated bottom and a series of horizontal knives were the basis of his invention. It converted hulled kernels of oats into a cereal meal, thus superseding the old method of crushing grain with burrs or millstones

which produced a product of inferior quality and reduced the grain to a fine flour of less value than the coarse meal.

OBELISK. *See* Monument: Obelisk to be brought to the United States

OBJECTORS (conscientious). *See* Conscientious objectors

OBSERVATION CAR. *See* Railroad car: Railroad car with an observation dome

OBSERVATION CARS (super dome). *See* Railroad car: Observation cars (super dome)

OBSERVATORY
See also Planetarium

Observatory (astronomical) connected with an institution of learning was built in 1830 by Joseph Caldwell, president of the University of North Carolina, Chapel Hill. It contained a meridian transit telescope, a zenith telescope, a refracting telescope, an astronomical clock, a sextant, a reflecting circle and a Hadley's quadrant. The observatory was completed in 1831, having been built with Caldwell's own funds at a cost of $430.29. Caldwell was eventually reimbursed by the trustees of the college. (*Kemp Plummer Battle—History of the University of North Carolina*)

Observatory (lightning). *See* Lightning observatory

Observatory (national) was established by the Navy on December 6, 1830, in Washington, D.C. The first instrument installed was a thirty-inch portable transit which was made by Richard Patten of New York. Lieutenant Louis Malesherbes Goldsborough was appointed the first officer in charge of the observatory and served until 1833.

OBSTETRICS BOOK. *See* Medical book: Obstetrics book

OCCUPATIONAL THERAPY COURSE in a college was given in 1913 by the Milwaukee-Downer College of Milwaukee, Wis. The subjects included psychology, physiology, sociology, design, metal work, leather work, and textile craft. Two students enrolled. The form of treatment called occupational therapy "includes any occupation, mental or physical, which is definitely prescribed and guided for the distinct purpose of contributing to, or hastening recovery from diseases or injury."

OCCUPATIONAL THERAPY TREATMENT (systematic) was given by Susan Edith Tracy, author of *Studies in Invalid Occu-*

pation, at the Training School for Nurses of the Adams Nervine Asylum, Jamaica Plain, Boston, Mass., which had been established under the will of Seth Adams, who died December 7, 1873. The school was incorporated March 16, 1877, and the first patients admitted in April 1880.

OCEAN-GOING BROKERAGE OFFICE. *See* Brokerage: Ocean-going brokerage office

OCEAN MAIL CONTRACTS. *See* Postal service: Ocean mail contracts

OCEAN PIER. See Pier

OCEANOGRAPHY INSTITUTION was the Scripps Institution of Oceanography of the University of California, located at La Jolla, Calif. It developed from the Scripps Institution for Biological Research of the University of California, which was established in 1912. The present name of the institution was adopted in October 1925. Its investigations cover the circulation of the waters in the ocean and the interrelation of the sea and the atmosphere, the chemistry of ocean water, the sediments on the sea floor, and marine organisms in their manifold interrelations with one another and with other conditions in the sea. (*University of California Register. 1929-1930*)

ODD FELLOWS LODGE was Washington Lodge No. 1 established April 26, 1819 in Baltimore, Md. It was organized by Thomas Wildey, and acted under a charter obtained from the Duke of York Lodge of England. In 1821, Wildey organized the Grand Lodge of Maryland and the Grand Lodge of the United States, and became Grand Master of the Grand Lodge of Maryland and the Grand Sire of the Grand Lodge of the United States. (*James L. Ridgley—History of American Odd Fellowship*)

OFFICE BUILDING ELEVATOR. *See* Elevator: Elevator in an office building

OFFICE OF MARKETS (U.S.). *See* Agriculture department (U.S.): Office of markets

OFFICERS' RESERVE CORPS. *See* Army: Reserve Officers Training Corps

OFFICERS' TRAINING CAMP FOR NEGROES. *See* Army camp for training Negro officers

OFFICERS' TRAINING SCHOOL (Coast Guard). *See* Coast Guard (U.S.): Coast Guard officers' training school

OFFICERS' TRAINING SCHOOL (naval). *See* Naval officers' training school

OFFSHORE RADAR WARNING STATION. *See* Radar: Offshore radar warning station

OIL
Offshore oil wells successfully drilled in the ocean were drilled at Summerland, Santa Barbara County, Calif., in 1896.

Oil company was the Pennsylvania Rock Oil Company, incorporated December 30, 1854, in New York City by George H. Bissell of New Haven, Conn., with a capital stock of $250,000 (10,000 shares at $25). George Henry Bissell and Jonathan G. Eveleth were the two principal trustees. (*Paul Henry Giddens—Beginnings of the Petroleum Industry*)

Oil exported. *See* Petroleum exported to Europe

Oil (kerosene) from bituminous shale and cannel coal for illuminating purposes was obtained by Dr. Abraham Gesner, who secured U.S. patent No. 12,612 on March 27, 1855, covering his process. The product was called "kerosene" and was manufactured by the North American Kerosene Gaslight Company at Newton Creek, Long Island, N.Y. Gesner obtained patents No. 11,203, 11,204, and 11,205 on June 27, 1854, on a process for obtaining kerosene by heat distillation. (*Raymond Foss Bacon and William Allen Hamor—American Petroleum Industry*)

Oil pipeline of importance to transport crude petroleum successfully was completed October 9, 1865, by Samuel Van Syckel of Titusville, Pa. It was about five miles long and extended from Miller's Farm on Oil Creek to Pithole, Pa. Wrought iron pipes 2 inches in diameter were laid underground in 15-foot sections. Two pumping stations supplied the power. (*David Talbot Day—Handbook of the Petroleum Industry*)

Oil pipeline within the oil regions was laid in 1862 by Barrows & Co., under the direction of J. L. Hutchins at the James Tarr farm at Oil Creek, Pa., a distance of 2½ miles to the Humboldt refinery at Plumer, Pa., on Cherry Run. The pipeline had a two-inch diameter; the sockets were of lead. It was completed February 19, 1863, but was abandoned because of leakage. (*Titusville Morning Herald. March 6, 1866*)

Oil refinery was started by Dr. Samuel M. Kier, a druggist of Pittsburgh, Pa., to refine petroleum. He built a small refinery in 1855 using the oil, which he called "Kier's Rock Oil," for medicinal purposes. A little later, he distilled the oil in his drug store with laboratory equipment, bottled the product, and sold it for

THE FIRST

OIL—*Continued*
fifty cents a half-pint. He also discovered that the light fractions from the crude oil would burn and the heavy fractions or bottoms were good for cleaning wool. (*Charles E. Bowles—The Petroleum Industry*)

Oil refinery (commercial) was erected by William Barnsdall and William Hawkins Abbott in Oil Creek Valley, Pa., June 1860. The only product saved was the kerosene. The small amount of gasoline manufactured was run into Oil Creek. The kerosene was sold in competition with whale oil and rock oil for use in lamps. In 1864 this refinery and some oil property on the Parker farm were sold for $50,000 to Jonathan Watson, William F. Hansell, Standish F. Hansell, Charles B. Keen, John C. Gillett, and Henry E. Rood, who organized an oil company.

Oil spring of record in America was marked on a map of territory near Cuba, N.Y. in 1627 by François Dollier de Casson and René de Brehant de Galinée, missionaries of the Order of St. Sulpice. The map was sent by them to Jean Talon, Intendant of Canada. A description of the oil spring is contained in a letter written by the Franciscan missionary Joseph de la Roche d'Allion dated July 18, 1627, reproduced in Gabriel Sagard-Théodat's *Histoire du Canada et Voyages que les Frères Mineurs Recollets y ont Faicts pour la Conversion des Infidelles* published in 1636.

Oil tank cars were introduced by Charles P. Hatch of the Empire Transportation Company, Philadelphia, Pa., in 1864-1865 and used on the Oil Creek Railroad, the Warren and Franklin Railroad, etc. Cars with three wooden tanks containing 3,500 gallons were used, but rain dissolved the glue coating and caused leakage. Later, riveted iron tanks mounted horizontally were used. On September 1, 1865, Amos Densmore used two wooden tanks, one on each end over the trucks of a flat-car, and shipped oil from Miller's Farm to New York City over the Atlantic and Great Western Railroad. The shipment consisted of two cars, each car with two tanks, and each tank containing about 40 barrels.

Oil well commercially productive was discovered August 27, 1859, at Titusville, Pa. It produced from a depth of 69½ feet about 400 gallons a day. E. B. Bowditch and Edwin Laurentine Drake of the Seneca Oil Company, organized March 23, 1858, bored through the rock at Titusville in a section known as Oil Creek. William A. Smith and his son, Samuel B. Smith, were to do the work. Edwin Drake was the first to tap petroleum at its source and to offer proof of the occurrence of oil in reservoirs beneath the earth's surface. (*Raymond Foss Bacon and William Allen Hamor—American Petroleum Industry*)

THE FIRST

Oil well drilled by torpedoes, as an experiment, was the Ladies' well on Watson Flats near Titusville, Pa., on January 21, 1865. The method had been advocated in 1862 by Colonel Edward A. L. Roberts of New York City, who received patent No. 47,458 on April 25, 1865, on "exploding torpedoes in artesian wells." (*Charles Austin Whiteshot—The Oil Well Driller*)

Oil well fire occurred April 17, 1861, when the Little and Merrick well on the Buchanan farm near Rouseville, Pa., at Oil Creek, caught fire, shortly after it gushed. It burned for three days and nineteen persons lost their lives. The well produced about 3,000 barrels a day.

Oil well (flowing) was drilled unintentionally in 1818 at the mouth of Troublesome Creek, on the Big South Fork of the Cumberland River, 28 miles southeast of Monticello, Ky., by Martin Beatty, who was seeking brine. The drillers, Marcus Huling and Andrew Zimmerman, searching for salt, drilled a five-inch hole with pole and auger to a depth of 536 feet. The oil had no known value and sand was thrown down the well to plug it up. The "Devil's Tar," as Beatty called the oil, was allowed to flow into the Cumberland River and covered its surface for a distance of 35 miles. The oil became ignited and an enormous conflagration ensued which destroyed trees along the banks of the river and the salt works. (*Augusta Phillips Johnson—A Century of Wayne County, Kentucky, 1800-1900*)

OIL AND GAS PRODUCTION COURSE at an institute of collegiate character was offered by the School of Engineering, University of Pittsburgh, Pittsburgh, Pa., in the university year 1912-1913. The course was given by Professor Roswell Hill Johnson.

OIL FUEL LOCOMOTIVE. *See* Locomotive: Locomotive to use oil fuel

OIL LAMP. *See* Lamp: Oil lamp

OIL TAN LEATHER. *See* Leather: Leather tanning by the "oil tan" method

OIL TANKER. *See* Ship: Oil tanker

OILCLOTH FACTORY (successful) was erected in 1845 in Winthrop, Me., by Ezekiel Bailey. It was known as C. M. Bailey Sons & Company and within ten years did an annual business of $200,000. (*David Thurston—History of Winthrop*)

OILED SILK PATENT was granted February 1, 1793, to Ralph Hodgson, Lansingburg, N.Y., on "manufacturing oiled silk and linen."

THE FIRST

OKAPI. *See* Animals: Okapi

OLD AGE COLONY was dedicated October 23, 1936, at Roosevelt Park, Millville, N.J., by Senator Arthur Harry Moore. The project, which was completed January 1, 1937, contained seven houses for couples which rented for $7 a month; six houses for single people, which rented for $5; and a community house. The city of Millville supplied the land, which had been taken over for taxes; the WPA supplied $34,571. The city collected rent and agreed to keep the houses in repair. Residents received $15 monthly from the state under the Old Age Assistance Act. The plan was originated by Effie Morrison, Deputy Director of Cumberland County Welfare Board, and was realized through William H. J. Ely, state WPA administrator, and George R. Swinton, WPA Director for Cumberland, Atlantic and Cape May counties.

OLD AGE HOME FOR PIONEERS was the Home for Aged and Infirm Arizona Pioneers, Prescott, Ariz., authorized by Chapter 23, Session Laws of the 25th Legislative Assembly of the Territory of Arizona, approved March 10, 1909. Residents of Arizona not less than thirty-five years or over sixty years of age, citizens of the United States for at least five years prior to the date of application, who were active in the development in Arizona and who were unable to provide themselves with the necessities and comforts of life because of adverse circumstances or failing health, could apply for admission. It was opened for guests February 6, 1911. The first superintendent was Major A. J. Doran.

OLD AGE PENSION. *See* Pension: Old age pension laws (state)

OLEOMARGARINE
Oleomargarine legislation (federal) was "an act defining butter, also imposing a tax upon and regulating the manufacture, sale, importing and exporting of oleomargarine," passed August 2, 1886 (24 Stat.L.209). It placed a $600 tax on manufacturers, $400 on wholesalers, and $48 on retailers, and levied a manufacturing stamp tax of two cents a pound.

Oleomargarine legislation (state) was "an act for the protection of dairymen and to prevent deception in sales of butter," passed June 5, 1877 (Chapter 415) by New York State.

Oleomargarine manufacturer (successful) was Alfred Paraf of New York City, who organized the Oleo-Margarin Manufacturing Company in 1871. On April 8, 1873, he obtained patent No. 137,564 on his process for purifying and separating fats. *(Henry Augustus Mott—The Complete History and Process of the Manufacture of Artificial Butter)*

THE FIRST

Oleomargarine patent was No. 110,626, granted January 3, 1871, to Henry W. Bradley, Binghamton, N.Y., on a "compound for culinary use," composed of lard, vegetable butter, or shortening.

OLYMPIC GAMES
American athlete to win four prizes in one year at the Olympic Games was Jesse Owens. In the Olympic Games held in Germany in 1936, he won the 100-meter run (10.3 seconds) on August 3; the broad jump (26 feet, 5⅜ inches) on August 4; the 200-meter run (20.7 seconds) on August 5; and the 400-meter relay (39.9 seconds) on August 9. The relay team consisted of Jesse Owens, Ralph Metcalfe, Foy Draper, and Frank Wykoff. *(John Kieran and Arthur Daley—The Story of the Olympic Games)*

American athlete to win ten prizes at the Olympic Games was Ray Ewry, who won the standing high jump and the standing broad jump at the games held in Paris in 1900, in St. Louis in 1904, in Athens in 1906 and in London in 1908. At the Paris and St. Louis Games, he won the hop, step and jump. *(John Kieran and Arthur Daley—The Story of the Olympic Games)*

American decathlon champion was Harold M. Osborne of the Illinois Athletic Club, who won 7,710.775 points on July 12, 1924, at the Olympic Games, Paris. The ten events in the decathlon are the 100-meter dash, the 400-meter run, the 1,500-meter run, the 110-meter hurdle, the broad jump, the high jump, the shot put, the discus throw, the pole vault, and the javelin throw.

Dog-sled race on an Olympic demonstration program. *See* Dog Race: Dog-sled race on an Olympic demonstration program

Figure skating Olympic champion (American) was Richard (Dick) Button of Englewood, N.J., who earned the title February 5, 1948, at the Fifth Winter Olympic Games, St. Moritz, Switzerland.

Olympic celebration in the United States was the Third Olympiad, held in St. Louis, Mo., May 14, 1904, to August 1, 1904. The games were first awarded to Chicago, Ill., but later they were given to St. Louis to be staged in connection with the World's Fair. The games were not popular as there were few entrants other than Americans in the fourteen events. In the field competitions, the American athletes made a clean sweep of all the events with the exception of lifting the bar and throwing the 56-pound weight.

Olympic competition winner was James Brendan Connolly of the Suffolk Athletic Club

THE FIRST

THE FIRST

OLYMPIC GAMES—*Continued*
of South Boston, Mass., who represented the
United States in the hop, skip and hop contest
on April 6, 1896, at the Olympiad in Athens,
Greece. His jump of 45 feet exceeded that of
his nearest competitor by 3 feet, 3 inches. The
American team of ten men won nine of the
twelve track events.

Olympic Games basketball championship
was won by a team from the United States,
which defeated a Canadian team, 19-8, on
August 14, 1936, in Berlin, Germany. The
United States was the gold medalist, Canada
the silver medalist, and Mexico the bronze
medalist.

Ski tournament (international). *See* Ski
tournament (international)

Winter Olympic Games competition was
held at Lake Placid, N.Y., during which 335
athletes from 17 nations participated. Governor
Franklin Delano Roosevelt of New York opened
the games on February 4, 1932.

**Woman (American) to win an Olympic
competition** was Ethelda Bleibtrey, who, at
the Seventh Olympiad, held in Antwerp, Belgium, won the 100-meter free style swim (1
minute, 13 3/5 seconds) on August 25, 1920,
and the 300-meter free style swim (4 minutes,
34 seconds) on August 26, 1920. (*Bill Henry—
An Approved History of the Olympic Games*)

**Woman slalom Olympic champion (Amer-
ican)** was Gretchen Fraser of Vancouver,
Wash., who won second place on February 5,
1948, in the Alpine Combination in the Olympic
ski race at the Fifth Winter Olympic Games,
St. Moritz, Switzerland.

**ONE-STOP TRANSCONTINENTAL
FLIGHT.** *See* Aviation—Flights (transcontinental): Transcontinental flight in 24 hours
flying time

ONE-WAY TRAFFIC. *See* Traffic regulation: One-way traffic regulation

OPEN AIR POST OFFICE. *See* Post
office: Open air post office

OPEN HEARTH FURNACE. *See* Steel:
Open hearth furnace

**OPEN MESH STEEL FLOORING
BRIDGE.** *See* Bridge: Bridge with open
mesh steel flooring

OPEN SEA BRIDGE. *See* Bridge: Bridge
with piers sunk in the open sea

OPERA
Grand opera sung in English was *Der
Freischutz* ("The Free Shooter"), in three acts,
billed as *The Wild Huntsman of Bohemia.* It
was presented at the Park Theatre, New York
City, on March 2, 1825. The music was by
Karl Maria von Weber and the libretto by
Johann Friedrich Kind. Mr. Lee appeared as
Baron Ottocar; Mr. Woodhull as Conrad; Mr.
Clarke as Caspar; Mr. Keene as Wilhelm.
The opera commenced at 6:45 P.M. and at its
conclusion was followed by a farce, "A Row-
land for an Oliver."

Moving picture of a complete grand opera.
See Moving Picture: Moving picture of a
complete grand opera

Negro prima donna of an opera company
was Caterina Jarboro, who appeared July 22,
1933, as Aida, the Ethiopian slave, in Giuseppe
Verdi's opera *Aida,* presented by Alfredo
Salmaggi's Chicago Opera Company at the
New York Hippodrome, 6th Avenue and 43rd
Street, New York City.

Negro singer of the Metropolitan Opera
was Marian Anderson, contralto, who was the
fortune teller Ulrica in Giuseppe Verdi's *Un
Ballo in Maschera* ("The Masked Ball"), a
three-act opera presented January 7, 1955, at
the Metropolitan Opera House, New York City.

**Negro to sing a white role with a white
cast in an opera company** was Robert Todd
Duncan, a baritone of Washington, D.C., who
first appeared as Tonio in *I Pagliacci* on September 28, 1945, and as Escamillo in *Carmen*
on September 30, 1945, in the New York City
Opera Company's presentation at the City Center
of Music and Drama, New York City. Both
operas were included in the 1945 fall season
(September 27 to December 17). *I Pagliacci*
was performed five times and *Carmen* seven.

Opera at the Metropolitan Opera House,
New York City, was Charles François Gounod's
Faust, sung in Italian on October 22, 1883.
Augusto Vianesi was the conductor. Faust was
sung by Italo Campanini, Mephistopheles by
Franco Novara, Valentin by Giuseppe Del
Puente, Wagner by Ludovico Contini, Siebel by
Sofia Scalchi, Marthe by Louise Lablache and
Marguerite by Christine Nilsson. (The opera,
however, had been performed in the United
States in 1863.)

Opera broadcast in its entirety was
presented Thursday May 19, 1921 at 8:15 P.M.
during Music Week from the Auditorium, Denver, Colo. A municipal chorus of 150 voices
presented *Martha* over station 9ZAF (now
KLZ). Martha was sung by Ruth Hammond
Theiss, Nancy by Florence Lamont Abramowitz,

THE FIRST

Plunkett by L. R. Hinman, Lionel by Robert H. Edwards, and the Sheriff of Richmond by B. H. Gilbert.

Opera broadcast in its entirety by a professional cast was Camille Saint-Saëns *Samson et Dalila,* broadcast Monday, November 14, 1921, the opening night of the season of the Chicago Opera Company, over station KYW, Chicago, Ill., from the Chicago Auditorium. Lucien Muratore was Samson, Marguerite D'Alvarez was Dalila. Giorgio Polacco conducted.

Opera broadcast in its entirety by the Metropolitan Opera Company was Humperdinck's opera *Hansel and Gretel,* presented on December 25, 1931, through the National Broadcasting Company, New York City. Editha Fleischer was Hansel; Queena Mario was Gretel; Karl Riedel conducted.

Opera broadcast in part from the stage of the New York City Metropolitan Opera Company was heard on January 13, 1910, when Enrico Caruso and Emmy Destinn sang arias from *Cavalleria Rusticana* and *I Pagliacci* which were "trapped and magnified by the dictograph directly from the stage and borne by wireless Hertzian waves over the turbulent waters of the sea to transcontinental and coastwise ships and over the mountainous peaks and undulating valleys of the country." The microphone was connected by telephone wire to the laboratory of Dr. Lee De Forest. (*New York Times. January 14, 1910*)

Opera broadcast over a national network from an American opera house was the third act garden scene from Gounod's *Faust,* which was broadcast January 21, 1927, from the stage of the auditorium in Chicago by the Chicago Civic Opera Company. The "Flower Song," "Le Roi de Thule," the "Invocation" and Marguerite's song at the window were sung by Edith Mason, soprano (Marguerite); Charles Hackett, tenor (Faust); Vanni-Marcoux, bass (Mephistopheles); Richard Bonelli, baritone (Valentin); and others. Fifteen microphones were used to pick up the opera from various places in the opera house. Giorgio Polacco was the director.

Opera by an American composer was *The Archers, or the Mountaineers of Switzerland,* which was performed in New York City on April 18, 1796. It dealt with the exploits of William Tell. The libretto was by William Dunlap and the music by Benjamin Carr.

Opera by an American composer (important) was *Leonora* a lyrical drama in three acts with a libretto by Joseph Reese Fry and music by William Henry Fry, which was performed June 4, 1845, at the Chestnut Street

THE FIRST

Theatre, Philadelphia, Pa. The plot was based on Bulwer-Lytton's *The Lady of Lyons.* It was sung in English and had a chorus of seventy-five and an orchestra of fifty. (*Genealogical Society of Pennsylvania—Publications Vol. 14. October 1943*)

Opera by an American composer performed at the Metropolitan Opera House of New York was *The Pipe of Desire,* by Frederick Shepherd Converse, which was produced March 18, 1910. The libretto was by George Edward Barton. The cast included Riccardo Martin as Iolan; Louise Homer, Naoia; Clarence Whitehill, the Old One; Leonora Sparkes, the First Sylph; Lillia Snelling, the First Undine; Glenn Hall, the First Salamander; and Herbert Witherspoon, the First Gnome. The opera had been previously produced in Boston in 1906.

Opera (comic) to be prepared for the American stage was Andrew Barton's *The Disappointment, or The Force of Credulity,* a satirical comedy in two acts with a prologue and epilogue, inspired by "the infrequency of dramatic compositions in America, the necessity of contributing to the entertainment of the city, and to put a stop (if possible) to the foolish and pernicious practice of searching after supposed hidden treasures." The satire was directed against the seekers of the treasure supposed to have been buried by the pirate Blackbeard. The opera contained eighteen songs and was arranged with seven scenes in the first act and five in the second. A performance was scheduled to take place on April 20, 1767, in Philadelphia, Pa., but at the last moment the work was withdrawn for fear of offending. (*George Overcash Seilhamer—History of American Theatre*)

Opera composed by a woman performed at the Metropolitan Opera House was *Der Wald,* in one act, by Ethel Mary Smyth, performed March 11, 1903, in New York City. Alfred Hertz was conductor. Johanna Gadski sang Roschen and Georg Anther was Heinrich. Others in the opera were Luisa Reuss-Belce, David Bispham, Robert Blass, Adolph Mühlmann, and Eugene Dufriche.

Opera house municipally owned was the War Memorial Opera House of San Francisco, Calif., which was opened on October 15, 1932, with a performance of *Tosca* by the San Francisco Opera Company.

Opera (Italian) to be produced in the United States in Italian, with Italian singers, was Gioacchino Antonio Rossini's *Il Barbiere di Siviglia,* performed on November 29, 1825, at the Park Theatre, New York City. The libretto was by Cesare Sterbini. The singers were Manuel de Populo Vicente, De Rosich,

THE FIRST

THE FIRST

OPERA—*Continued*
Manuel Crivelli, Maria Felicita Garcia, and
Manuel Garcia, Jr. The orchestra of 25 musicians was conducted by Nathaniel De Luce.
Performances were given at 7:30 P.M. The
prices were listed as follows: boxes, $2.00;
orchestra, $1.00; and gallery, 25 cents. Twenty-
three performances were given. The largest
receipts for a single performance were $1,962
and the smallest $250.

Opera of a serious nature produced in
America was James Hewitt's *Tammany, or
The Indian Chief*, based on the book by Mrs.
Anne Julia Kemble Hatton. The opera was
produced on March 3, 1794, by Charles Ciceri
under the auspices of the Tammany Society by
the Old American Company at the John Street
Theatre, New York City.

**Opera performed by a professional visiting
troupe** was *The Beggar's Opera*, a three-act
burlesque by John Gay, performed December 3,
1750, by the Walter Murray and Thomas Kean
Company at the Nassau Street Theater, New
York City. Entertainment was presented between the acts. *(Phoebe Fenwick Gaye—John
Gay)*

Opera performed in America was Colley
Cibber's ballad opera *Flora, or Hob in the
Well*, presented Tuesday, February 18, 1735,
at the Courtroom, Charleston, S.C. It was
advertised in the *South Carolina Gazette* and
was shown with a pantomime entertainment
billed as *The Adventure of Harlequin Scaramouche*. *(Oscar George Theodore Sonneck—
Early Opera in America)*

**Opera singer (American) to sing in an
Italian opera in Italian** was Julia Wheatley,
who sang in Rossini's *Eduardo e Cristina* on
November 25, 1834, at the Italian Opera House,
New York City.

**Opera singer to sing two major roles on
the same day** at the Metropolitan Opera
House, New York City, was Hermann Jadlowker, who on March 22, 1911, sang the role
of Turiddu in Mascagni's *Cavalleria Rusticana*
and substituted for Riccardo Martin as Canio
in Leoncavallo's *I Pagliacci*.

Opera telecast. *See* Television—Telecast:
Opera (complete) to be televised

**Orchestra used in conjunction with an
opera.** *See* Orchestra: Orchestra used in
conjunction with an opera

Pay television opera. *See* Television—Telecast: Pay television presentation of an opera

OPERATION (abdominal). *See* Surgical
operation: Abdominal operation

OPERETTA TELECAST. *See* Television
—Telecast: Operetta to be televised

OPHTHALMOLOGY BOOK. *See* Medical
book: Ophthalmology book

OPHTHALMOLOGY CLINIC. *See* Medical clinic: Ophthalmology clinic

OPHTHALMOLOGY PROFESSOR. *See*
Medical instruction: Ophthalmology professor

OPTOMETRY INSTRUCTION
Optics and optometry courses offered by
a university were given at Columbia University,
New York City, in 1910, following enactment
of legislation by New York State on March 31,
1909 (Chapter 134) which required licenses for
optometrists. The work in optometry was given
by Andrew Jay Cross and Frederic Albert Woll.
Members of the university departments of
physics and mathematics gave instruction in
those subjects to the optometry students.

Optometry school was the Northern Illinois College of Ophthalmology and Otology,
Chicago, Ill., founded in 1872. The first president was Dr. James D. McFatrick. The name
was changed to the Northern Illinois College of
Optometry in 1929.

OPTOMETRY LEGISLATION (state)
was signed April 13, 1901 (Chapter 269, Laws
of 1901) by Governor Samuel Rinnah Van Sant
of Minnesota. *(George Ole Virtue—Government
of Minnesota)*

OPTOMETRY MAGAZINE. *See* Medical
periodical: Optometry magazine

**ORAL INSTRUCTION FOR THE
DEAF.** *See* Deaf—School: Oral instruction
for the deaf

ORANGES (seedless navel) grown in the
United States were from a dozen budded sap-
plings brought from Bahia, Brazil, in 1871 by
William Saunders, horticulturist of the United
States Department of Agriculture. Two of the
trees, which were secured by Jonathan and
Eliza C. Tibbets in 1873, started the industry
in Riverside, Calif. Other types of oranges,
however, had been grown earlier in Florida.
*(John Raymond Gabbert—History of Riverside,
City and County)*

ORATORIO
Oratorio by an American was John
Knowles Paine's *Oratorio of St. Peter*, per-

formed June 3, 1873, at the City Hall, Portland, Me., by the Haydn Society of Portland, assisted by eminent artists from abroad and the Harvard orchestra of Cambridge, Mass. (41 members). *(Daily Eastern Argus. June 4, 1873)*

Oratorio performance (complete) was a presentation of *The Messiah* on December 25, 1818, by the Handel and Haydn Society, Boylston Hall, Boston, Mass., with a chorus of approximately two hundred singers. The soloists were the Misses Sumner and Bennett, Mr. J. Sharp, and Master White. Benjamin Holt was president of the society and, as was customary, conducted the concert.

ORCHESTRA

College orchestra was founded at Harvard University, Cambridge, Mass., March 6, 1808. The minutes record that "at a meeting held on March 6, 1808, by a number of students of Harvard University, they unanimously agreed to institute a society for their mutual improvement in instrumental music." It was known as the Pierian Sodality, as it was not the custom for any extracurricular activities to assume the name of the college. The orchestra is now known as the Harvard University Orchestra.

Municipal orchestra supported by taxes was the Baltimore Symphony Orchestra, Baltimore, Md., formed in 1915 with a Board of Estimate appropriation of $6,000. It was managed by Frederick R. Huber, who took office July 13, 1915, as the Municipal Director of Music. The first concert master was J. C. van Hulsteyn; the first soloist, Mabel Garrison; the first conductor, Gustav Strube. The first concert was presented February 11, 1916.

Orchestra was founded about 1810-1811 in Boston, Mass., by Johann Christian Gottlieb Graupner. This orchestra is believed to have been the original Philharmonic Orchestra. The last concert was given at the Pantheon, Boylston Square, Boston, on November 24, 1824. *(Frederic Louis Ritter—Music In America)*

Orchestra (American) to make a European tour was the Symphony Society of New York, which sailed for Europe April 22, 1920. Under the leadership of Walter Johannes Damrosch, 34 concerts were given in 21 cities in France, Italy, Belgium, Holland, and England. The first concert was given on May 4, 1920, at the Paris Opera House. The last in the tour was given on June 20, 1920, at the Royal Albert Hall, London. The Symphony Society merged with the New York Philharmonic on March 30, 1928, to form the Philharmonic Society of New York with Arturo Toscanini as conductor in chief.

Orchestra in a theater was employed in the Nassau Street Theater, between John Street and Maiden Lane, New York City, in 1750. The

instruments used were German flutes, horns, and drums. The theater, two stories high, opened March 5, 1750, with a presentation of Shakespeare's *King Richard III*. It was illuminated by a chandelier, made of a barrel hoop through which a dozen nails were driven to serve as candle holders. The stage was set five feet above the floor level. *(Thomas Allston Brown —A History of the New York Stage)*

Orchestra used in conjunction with an opera was employed in 1752 when the Kean and Murray Company of London opened the new theatre in Upper Marlborough, Md., with *The Beggar's Opera*.

Radio orchestra was the Detroit News Orchestra, a sixteen-piece symphonic ensemble, which began broadcasting May 28, 1922. It was composed principally of members of the Detroit Symphony Orchestra. Otto Krueger, piccolo player, was conductor and Maurice Warner, first violinist, was concertmaster. The broadcasts were sponsored by the Detroit Bank on station WWJ, Detroit, Mich.

Symphony orchestra was the Collegium Musicum of Bethlehem, Pa., formed in 1744. There were fourteen players—two first violins, two second violins, two violas, two flutes, two trumpets, two French horns, one cello, and one double bass. *(Raymond Walters—Bethlehem, Long Ago and Today)*

ORCHESTRA LEADER. *See* Musician: Orchestra leader to conduct without using a baton

ORCHESTRAL SONG. *See* Music: Orchestral song

ORDER OF DE MOLAY. *See* Freemasons: Order of De Molay

ORDER OF THE PURPLE HEART. *See* Medal: Order of the Purple Heart

ORDINANCE OF SECESSION. *See* Secession: Secession act

ORDNANCE
See also Army armored tank

Airplane outfitted with a machine gun. *See* Aviation—Airplane: Airplane outfitted with a machine gun

Atomic cannon was "Atomic Annie" or "Amazon Annie," a 40-foot, 85-ton cannon, electronically fired at 8:30 A.M., May 25, 1953, at Frenchman Flat., Nev., at a target 7 miles away. A 280-millimeter projectile, 11 inches by

ORDNANCE—*Continued*
3 feet, was loaded by a crew of 9 from the 52nd
Field Artillery Group, Fort Sill, Okla. The
shot produced an 8-second fireball visible 65
miles away despite the bright sunshine. The
charge was touched off by scientists of the
Atomic Energy Commission, 10 miles away, and
the explosion was witnessed from points 3 to 7
miles from the target area by Defense Secretary
Charles Erwin Wilson, Admiral Arthur William Radford, Army Secretary Robert Stevens,
Army Chief of Staff Joseph Lawton Collins,
and 100 congressmen.

Automatic aircraft cannon of 20 milli-
meters was manufactured by the Eclipse
Machine Division of the Bendix Aviation Corporation, Elmira, N.Y., and was delivered to the
U.S. Army, May 16, 1941.

Bazooka rocket gun was produced on June
14, 1942, by the General Electric Company,
Bridgeport, Conn. It consisted of a steel tube,
about 50 inches long and 2½ inches in diameter,
open at both ends. Attached to the tube were
a shoulder stock and front and rear grips for
the gunner, together with sights and an electric
battery which set off the rocket-propelled
charge when the launcher trigger was squeezed.
The rocket was nearly two feet long. The
first sample gun was produced in four days
from plans, development was completed in three
weeks, and production of 5,000 rocket guns
completed within thirty days. It was known
as "Launcher, Rocket AT, M-1."

Cannon (breech loading) was invented by
Benjamin Chambers, Sr., who obtained patent
No. 6,612 on July 31, 1849, on "an improvement
in movable breeches for fire-arms and the locks
and appurtenances of the same." His wooden
model was discovered in an old smithy and is
now in the possession of the Virginia Historical
Society.

Cannon (steel, breech loading, rifled) was
made in 1854 by James Richards Haskell. He
sold twenty-five to the Mexican Government.

Cartridge-loading machinery was invented
by G. Moore Peters of Xenia, Ohio, who received patents No. 321,848 and No. 321,849 on
July 7, 1885, for a round table loading machine,
one of which was later installed at his factory,
the Peters Cartridge Company, King Mills,
Ohio.

Fighter airplane carrying a cannon. *See*
Aviation—Airplane: Fighter airplane carrying a cannon

Gun (revolving) was made by John Gill
of Newberne, N.C., in 1829. It had 14 chambers
and was a percussion gun. It was never

patented. The first patent for this type of gun
was granted to David G. Colburn of Canton
Canal, N.Y., on June 29, 1833.

Gun (rifled) was made in 1834 by Cyrus
Alger. The first perfect bronze cannon was
made by him in 1827 at the South Boston Iron
Company's foundry for the U.S. Ordnance Department.

Gunpowder mill was operated by Edward
Rawson, to whom the General Court of Massa-
chusetts granted 500 acres of land at Pecoit,
Mass., on June 6, 1639, on which to erect it.
(*Arthur Pine Van Gelder and Hugo Schlatter
—History of the Explosives Industry in
America*)

Machine gun was invented by Charles E.
Barnes of Lowell, Mass., who obtained patent
No. 15,315 on July 8, 1856, on an "improved
automatic cannon." It was operated by a crank,
the speed of firing depending upon the speed
with which the crank was turned.

Machine gun (rapid fire) was invented by
Richard Jordan Gatling of Indianapolis, Ind.,
who obtained patent No. 36,836 on November 4,
1862, on "an improvement in revolving battery
guns." The first gun, which fired 250 shots a
minute, was made in Indianapolis. (*Gatling's
System of Fire-Arms, with Official Reports of
Recent Trials and Great Success, Descriptions,
General Directions, etc.*)

Metal cartridge successfully produced was
made by Daniel Baird Wesson of the Smith &
Wesson Company, Springfield, Mass., in 1857,
based upon patent No. 11,496 granted him
August 8, 1854. In 1860, additional patents
were granted on a cartridge in which the
fulminate was enclosed in the hollow annular
projecting case. Metal cartridges revolutionized
the firearms industry and made the breech loading rifle possible.

Muskets produced at a government arsenal
were made in 1795 at the Springfield Armory,
Springfield, Mass., under the direction of
David Ames, the first superintendent, and
Robert Orr, a master armorer. The first
gunlock was filed by Alexander Crawford,
after a struggle of three days. Richard Beebe
stocked it by hand. In the first year 245
muskets were produced.

Pistol. *See* Pistol

Revolving gun turret, used on the iron-
clad "Monitor" which defeated the Confederate
"Merrimac" on March 9, 1862, at Hampton
Roads, Va., was invented by Theodore Ruggles
Timby, who was also the first to advocate
the use of iron in the construction of ships.

THE FIRST

In April 1841 he showed the War Department an ivory model of a revolving battery and filed a caveat in 1843 for "a revolving tower for offensive and defensive warfare to be used on land and water." His idea, which he adapted from the shape of Castle Williams, N.Y., was not accepted until twenty years afterward. He obtained patents No. 35,846 and No. 35,847 on July 8, 1862 for his revolving battery tower. (*Francis Brown Wheeler—The First Monitor and Its Builders*)

Rifle. *See above* Gun (rifled); *and below* Semi-automatic rifle.

Sea coast gun carriage made of wrought iron was constructed in 1855 by James Gilchrist Benton, instructor in ordnance and gunnery at the United States Military Academy. It was immediately adopted by the United States Government. (*James Gilchrist Benton—The Fabrication of Small Arms for the United States Service*)

Semi-automatic rifle adopted as standard by the U.S. Army was the U.S. Rifle Caliber .30, M1, the Garand Semi-Automatic Shoulder Rifle, a service shoulder weapon adopted January 9, 1936. It was invented by John C. Garand of Somerset, Md., who obtained patent No. 1,603,684 on October 19, 1926, on an "automatic gun." (*Julian Sommerville Hatcher—The Book of the Garand*)

Shot tower used by an American manufacturer of ammunition was erected in 1895 by the Peters Cartridge Company at Kings Mills, Ohio. The factory was organized by G. Moore Peters and was incorporated on January 24, 1887.

Submachine gun was the Thompson Submachine Gun ("Tommy Gun"), invented by Brigadier General John Taliaferro Thompson, who organized the Auto-Ordnance Company in 1915 to build light-weight semi-automatic infantry shoulder rifles. The first model was proof-fired at the Warner & Swasey Company, Cleveland, Ohio, where the first gun was built. The gun weighed approximately 10 pounds and had a cyclic rate of fire of between 600 and 800 shots a minute.

Tank (heavy 60-ton) built in the United States for the U.S. Army was constructed by the Baldwin Locomotive Works, Eddystone, Pa., and presented by William Henry Harman, vice president of the company, to Brigadier General Gladeon Marcus Barnes, Army Ordnance Department, on December 8, 1941. It had a 75-millimeter (3-inch) cannon in the turret.

OREGON TRAIL. *See* Road: Overland wagon road across the Rocky Mountains

THE FIRST

ORGAN

Color organ was invented by Bainbridge Bishop of New Russia, N.Y., who obtained patent No. 186,298 on January 16, 1877, on an "attachment for key-board musical instruments" for typifying musical sounds by the display of colors.

Electric organ was built by Hilborne Lewis Roosevelt in 1876, and installed in Chickering Hall, Fifth Avenue and 18th Street, New York City. It was operated by storage batteries. It had 31 ranks, 10 in the great organ, 8 in the swell organ, 5 in the solo organ, 3 in the echo organ, and 5 in the pedal organ.

Organ built in the United States was constructed by Johann Gottlob Klemm (John Clemm) of Philadelphia, Pa., who proposed building an organ on June 1, 1739, for Trinity Church, New York City. His proposition was accepted and in May 1740 the pipe organ was installed in the West Gallery. It had 3 manuals and 26 stops (10 in the great organ, 10 in the choir, and 6 in the swell) and cost about £520. (*Arthur Henry Messiter—A History of the Choir and Music of Trinity Church, New York City*)

Organs imported were brought into the United States in 1700, by the Episcopal Church, Port Royal, Pa., and the Gloria Dei Church (Swedish Lutheran, dedicated July 2, 1700) in Philadelphia, Pa. Priority is claimed for each. (*Bishop William Meade—Old Churches, Ministers and Families of Virginia*)

Pipeless organ was invented by Laurens Hammond, who received patent No. 1,956,350, April 24, 1934, covering 74 claims. The organ was manufactured by the Hammond Clock Company, Chicago, Ill., and was first exhibited at the Industrial Arts Exposition, New York City, on April 15, 1935. The organ consisted of a two-manual console with pedal clavier and a power cabinet. It had neither reeds, pipes nor vibrating parts. It weighed 275 pounds and cost less than one cent an hour to operate.

ORGAN SCHOOL was the Guilmant Organ School, New York City, established in 1899 by Dr. William Crane Carl and Dr. Howard Duffield. The first classes met in the First Presbyterian Church, New York City. The school was named for the French organist Alexandre Guilmant.

ORGANISTS' SOCIETY

Organists' society (national) was the American Guild of Organists, organized April 13, 1896 and incorporated December 17, 1896. One hundred and forty-five organists, called founders, were enrolled by December 31, 1896. The first convention was held December 29-30,

THE FIRST

ORGANISTS' SOCIETY—*Continued*
1914, in New York City. Gerrit Smith was the first warden and Dr. Henry Granger Hanchett, inventor of the third pedal, the first secretary. The first branch chapter was organized in Philadelphia, Pa., on June 10, 1902.

ORPHANAGE
See also Greek College and Orphanage

Orphanage was established in New York City (New Amsterdam) in June 1654. Fifty orphan children were sent from Holland in order to help populate Manhattan Island. They arrived on the "Pereboom" and the "Gelderse Blom." A resolution was passed and signed by Peter Stuyvesant, November 9, 1654, "to hire the house of Mr. [Isaac] Allerton and lodge there the children sent over by the Poormasters." This orphanage also received the orphan children of the early colonists. (*New York Colonial Documents. Vol. 14*)

Orphanage with a continuous existence was founded in Savannah, Ga., by the Reverend George Whitefield in 1740. It was known as the Bethesda Home (house of mercy). The site was selected by James Habersham, the first superintendent. Whitefield was a Church of England curate in the colony, but there is nothing in the records to show that Bethesda was ever sectarian. At first, both boys and girls were admitted. The home, which is now under the care of the Union Society, organized 1750, is known as the Bethesda Home for Boys. Girls are cared for in the Savannah Female Orphan Asylum and the Episcopal Home for Girls.

ORRERY. *See* Planetarium

ORTHODONTIA MAGAZINE. *See* Dental magazine: Orthodontia magazine

ORTHODONTIA TREATISE. *See* Dental book: Orthodontia treatise

ORTHODONTISTS' SOCIETY. *See* Dental society: Orthodontists' society

ORTHOPEDIC HOSPITAL. *See* Hospital: Orthopedic hospital

ORTHOPEDICS CHAIR. *See* Medical instruction: Orthopedics chair

"OSCAR" AWARDS. *See* under Moving picture actor

OSTEOPATHIC PHYSICIAN. *See* Physician: Osteopathic physician

THE FIRST

OSTEOPATHY MAGAZINE. *See* Medical periodical: Osteopathy magazine

OSTEOPATHY SCHOOL. *See* Medical school: Osteopathy school

OSTRICH. *See* Birds: Ostrich farm

OUTBOARD MOTOR. *See* Engine: Outboard motor

OUTDOOR ADVERTISING LEGISLATION (state). *See* Advertising law: Outdoor advertising legislation (state)

OUTDOOR BLACKOUT LIGHTING CONTROL. *See* Blackout: Blackout outdoor light control

OUTDOOR MUSEUM. *See* Museum: Outdoor museum

OUTER SPACE BROADCAST. *See* Radio broadcast: Outer space broadcast

OUTLOOK ENVELOPE. *See* Envelope: Envelope with an outlook or window

OVER-WATER FLIGHT. *See* Aviation—Flights: Over-water round trip flight

OVERLAND MAIL SERVICE. *See* Postal service: Overland mail service

OVERLAND ROAD. *See* Road: Overland wagon road across the Rocky Mountains

OVERSHOES ("Artics"). *See* "Artics"

OXIDIZED CELLULOSE (sponge). *See* Sponge: Oxidized cellulose (sponge)

OYSTER COCKTAIL is attributed to a miner who appeared at a California bar about 1866 and ordered a whiskey cocktail and a plate of California raw oysters. After drinking the cocktail, he placed the oysters in the same glass with some tomato catsup, Worcestershire sauce, and pepper sauce, and ate them with great gusto. The bartender, seizing the idea, marketed a new product which sold for "four bits" per glass and which has since been called oyster cocktail.

OYSTER PROPAGATION (state) began in Rhode Island, which in June 1779 set aside part of the public domain for the cultivation and propagation of oysters. (*William Keith Brooks —The Oyster*)

THE FIRST

PACER. *See* Horse: Horse to pace better than 2:00

PACIFIC AIR MAIL FLIGHT. *See* Air mail service: Pacific air mail flight

PACIFIC CABLE. *See* Cable: Cable across the Pacific Ocean

PACIFIC COAST DISCOVERY. *See* Discovery: Discovery of land on the United States Pacific coast

PACIFIC COAST GOVERNMENT. *See* Colonial government: Government on the Pacific coast

PACIFIC COAST MAIL. *See* Postal service: Overland mail service

PACIFIC COAST NEWSPAPER. *See* Newspaper: Newspaper published on the Pacific coast

PACIFIC COAST UNIVERSITY. *See* College: University on the Pacific coast

PACING REGISTER. *See* Horse register: Horse pacing register

PACKAGE DELIVERY SERVICE. *See* Express service

PACKAGE STORES. *See* Liquor stores (state)

PACKER (meat). *See* Meat packer

PACKET LINE. *See* Ship: Packet line

PAGE (girl). *See* Congress (U.S.)—House of Representatives: Girl page

PAGING SERVICE BY RADIO. *See* Radio paging service

PAINLESS SURGERY DEMONSTRATION. *See* Anesthesia: Painless surgery demonstration

PAINT
  Paint prepared from standard formulas for floors, woodwork, furniture, walls, etc., was manufactured by the Sherwin-Williams Company of Cleveland, Ohio, in 1880. Stains, enamels, varnishes and varnish stains were later produced under uniform production methods.

THE FIRST

  Paint (ready-mixed) was manufactured by the Averill Paint Company of New York City using as a basis patent No. 66,773, granted on July 16, 1867, to D. R. Averill of Newburg, Ohio. The concern went out of business about 1900. It was unable to maintain a "standard" paint.

PAINT SPRAYING DEVICE commercially manufactured was made in 1909 by the De Vilbiss Company of Toledo, Ohio. Employment of the same principle used in the De Vilbiss medical atomizer combined with compressed air started a revolution in painting and spraying. *(Spray Painting System—De Vilbiss Co.)*

PAINTER. *See* Artist

PALEONTOLOGY CHAIR in a college was established by Yale University, New Haven, Conn., in 1866, and was held by Professor Othniel Charles Marsh from that date to 1899. He was the first professor of vertebrate paleontology.

PALEONTOLOGY COURSE
  Micropaleontology course was given by Professor Jesse James Galloway at Columbia University, New York City, starting on September 25, 1924. It covered the principles of paleontology, classification and nomenclature, the use of paleontological literature, and the identification of small forms with the microscope.

PALEONTOLOGY REPORT was prepared in 1713 by the Reverend Cotton Mather and read before the Royal Society of London in 1714. He regarded three teeth and a seventeen-foot thigh bone which were unearthed in Albany, N.Y., in 1705 as the remains of a race of giants. He was elected a member of the Royal Society of London, the first American to receive this distinction. *(Abijah Perkins Marvin—Life and Times of Cotton Mather)*

PAMPHLET PRINTED ON VELLUM. *See* Book: Book (pamphlet) on vellum

PAN AMERICAN CONFERENCE. *See* Conference: Pan American conference

PAN AMERICAN DELEGATES. *See* Diplomatic service: Pan American delegates (American)

PAN AMERICAN UNION was the International Bureau of American Republics, established on April 14, 1890, by the First International Conference of American States, which met at Washington, D.C., from October 2, 1889, to April 19, 1890, and was presided over by James Gillespie Blaine, United States Secretary

THE FIRST

THE FIRST

PAN AMERICAN UNION—*Continued*
of State. The name of the Bureau was changed
by resolution of August 11, 1910, to the Pan
American Union. The first director of the
Bureau was William Eleroy Curtis, who was
appointed August 26, 1890, and who served
until May 17, 1893. *(Bulletin of the Pan American Union. April 1930)*

PANAMA CANAL. *See* Ship: Steamboat
to pass through the Panama Canal

PANDA. *See* Animals: Giant panda

PANORAMA SHOW. *See* Theater: Panorama show

PAPER
Blotting paper. *See* Blotting paper

Corrugated paper was invented by Albert
L. Jones of New York City, who received patent No. 122,023, December 19, 1871, on an
"improvement in paper for packing." His
patent covered corrugated sheets only and made
no mention of backing or facing sheets. Later
a facing sheet was applied to one side, and then
to both sides. making single-face and double-
face corrugated cardboard. Jones assigned his
patent to Thompson & Norris Company of
Brooklyn, N.Y., which was the first manufacturer of corrugated paper in the United States.
Corrugated paper boxes came into use about
1890.

Crepe paper was manufactured in 1890 by
Charles T. Bainbridge's Sons, Brooklyn, N.Y.
It was made of rag paper with only one ratio
of stretch. It was made in a variety of colors
and sold to the trade for fifty cents a roll,
20 inches wide and 10 feet long.

Manila paper was invented by John Mark
and Lyman Hollingsworth of South Braintree,
Mass., partners under the firm name of J. M.
& L. Hollingsworth, who received patent
No. 3,362 on December 4, 1843. They manufactured it from hemp sails, canvas, and rope.
*(Lyman Horace Weeks— History of Paper
Manufacturing)*

Perforated wrapping paper was patented
July 25, 1871, by Seth Wheeler of Albany,
N.Y., who received patent No. 117,355. The
paper was wound into rolls and was torn off at
the perforations. It was claimed that "the
fibers left between the perforations [were] sufficient for holding the sheets together as wound
into a roll."

Sandpaper. *See* Sandpaper patent

Straw paper was made from straw and
grass in 1829 by George A. Shryrock of Phila-

delphia, in the Hollywell mill near Chambersburg, Pa. He also invented a machine for
producing it.

Toilet paper was unbleached pearl-colored
pure manila hemp paper made in 1857 by Joseph
C. Gayetty of New York City, whose name was
watermarked on each sheet. It sold at five
hundred sheets for fifty cents and was known
as "Gayetty's Medicated Paper—a perfectly
pure article for the toilet and for the prevention of piles."

Wallpaper. *See* Wallpaper

Wood-pulp and rag paper for printing
was manufactured by William Orr, of Troy,
N.Y., in 1854. He made paper, the composition
of which was three fourths rag and one fourth
wood fiber, in his Troy paper mill. *(Arthur
James Weise—City of Troy and Its Vicinity)*

Wood-pulp paper was made of basswood
by John Beardsley of Buffalo, N.Y. He exhibited three samples of it on December 26, 1854,
to the editor of the Buffalo *Democrat.*

PAPER BAG MANUFACTURING MACHINE
Paper bag manufacturing machine was invented by William Goodale of Clinton, Mass.,
who obtained patent No. 24,734 on July 12,
1859.

Square-bottom paper bag machinery was
invented by Luther Childs Crowell of Boston,
Mass., who obtained patents No. 123,811 and
123,812 on February 20, 1872, on an "improvement in paper-bag machines." The bags produced by the machine had two longitudinal
inward folds.

PAPER COLLAR. *See* Collar: Paper collar

PAPER-FOLDING MACHINE. *See* Folding machine

PAPER-MAKING MACHINERY
Paper-making machine (cylinder) was
made by Thomas Gilpen in August 1817 and
used in his paper mill at Brandywine, Del. The
mill manufactured the first machine-made paper
in the United States. Previously paper had been
hand made and in small sizes because of limited facilities and molds, but this machine permitted paper to be made in unlimited lengths
and as wide or narrow as desired. *(Joel Munsell—Chronology of Paper and Papermaking)*

Paper-making machine (Fourdrinier) made
in the United States was manufactured in 1829
in South Windham, Conn., by James Phelps

THE FIRST

and George Spafford, who formed the firm of Phelps and Spafford. Aided by Charles Smith, they produced a machine which was set up in May 1829 in the mill of Amos H. Hubbard of Norwich Falls, Conn. The machine had no driers. The paper was run off wet and hung up to dry. The firm name of Phelps and Spafford was changed to Smith, Winchester & Company in 1837, and later to the Smith and Winchester Company.

Paper-making machine (Fourdrinier) imported was purchased in December 1827 by Joseph Pickering and set up in his shop in North Windham, Conn., January 1828 by George Spafford of South Windham, Conn. Henry and Sealy Fourdrinier of London purchased the patent of Nicholas Louis Robert and developed a machine for making paper in an endless web.

PAPER-MAKING MUSEUM. *See* Museum: Museum devoted exclusively to paper-making

PAPER MILL was built in 1690 by William Rittenhouse, Samuel Carpenter, Robert Turner, Thomas Tresse and William Bradford in Germantown, Pa., on a rivulet called Paper Mill Run, about two miles above the junction of the Wissahickon with the Schuylkill. The mill was built on 20 acres of land leased from Samuel Carpenter at an annual rental of five shillings. The paper was made by hand, each sheet separately. Linen rags were pounded into pulp in stone mortars. The production rate was about 250 pounds a day. *(An Historie for Young & Olde About the Beginnings of Paper-making— Eastwood Wire Corporation)*

PAPER MONEY. *See* Money: Paper money

PAPER PATTERNS that were practical for dresses and other garments were manufactured by Ebenezer Butterick in 1863 in Sterling, Mass. Four years later he formed E. Butterick & Company, with offices on lower Broadway, New York City.

PAPER PENCIL. *See* Pencil: Paper pencil

PAPER TWINE machinery was patented December 17, 1895, by George Loomis Brownell of Worcester, Mass., who obtained patent No. 551,615 on a "machine for making paper twine." It twisted strips or ribbons of paper into cord which was as strong as any known steel.

PAPER WATERMARK. See Watermark

THE FIRST

PAPRIKA MILL was the Carolina Paprika Mills, Inc., Dillon, S.C., incorporated March 25, 1941. The president was Robert Robich.

PARACHUTE. *See* Aviation: Parachute

PARACHUTE JUMP COMBAT DECORATION. *See* Medal: Combat decoration

PARACHUTE WEDDING. *See* Wedding: Parachute wedding

PARADE
Automobile parade. *See* Automobile parade

Labor Day parade. *See* Holiday: Labor Day holiday parade

Parade with float tableaux was held in Mobile, Ala., on the evening of Mardi Gras day, February 24, 1868. The Order of Myths produced the first pageant. Next day followed the Infant Mystics and their pageant, then the Knights of Revelry. These are the original mystic societies of the South, and all still parade in Mobile's pageants. *(History of Mardi Gras—Mobile Carnival Association)*

Street parade held by a mystic society was held by the Cowbellian de Rakian Society, organized on December 31, 1830, in Mobile, Ala. The peculiar feature of this society and those which followed later was that absolute secrecy was maintained about their membership, the members never appearing except in costume and in mask. Parades were held annually on New Year's Eve, the first, December 31, 1830, being an impromptu raid on a hardware store staged by a score of young bloods, who were led, according to tradition, by Michael Krafft. On March 5, 1867 Mobilians abandoned the New Year's eve celebration in favor of daylight parades which were held on Mardi Gras, literally Fat Tuesday or Shrove Tuesday, the day preceding Ash Wednesday and the penitential season of Lent as observed in Catholic and Episcopal liturgy. *(Erwin Craighead—Mobile: Facts and Tradition)*

PARCEL POST. *See* Postal service: Parcel post service

PARCEL POST DOMESTIC AIR SERVICE. *See* Air mail service: Parcel post domestic air service

PARCEL POST STAMPS. *See* Postage stamp: Parcel-post stamps

PARENT-TEACHER ASSOCIATION (national) was the National Congress of Mothers organized February 17, 1897, in Wash-

PARENT - TEACHER ASSOCIATION (national)—*Continued*
ington, D.C., by Alice McLellan Birney and Phoebe Apperson Hearst at a meeting attended by 2,000 persons. At the annual meeting of March 9, 1908, the name was changed to the National Congress of Mothers and Parent-Teacher Associations. On May 9, 1924, the name was changed to the National Congress of Parents and Teachers.

PARISH (Catholic). *See* Catholic parish

PARK
Park land purchased by a city was Elm Park, containing 27 acres, which was sold to Worcester, Mass., on March 17, and March 20, 1854, by Levi Lincoln and John Hammond.

Park (national) was the Yellowstone National Park, Wyo., authorized March 1, 1872 (17 Stat.L.32), by "an act to set aside a certain tract of land (2,142,720 acres) lying near the headwaters of the Yellowstone River as a public park." The first superintendent was Nathaniel Pitt Langford. Yellowstone Park now consists of 2,213,205 acres in the following states: Wyoming, 2,039,216 acres; Montana, 142,501 acres; Idaho, 31,488 acres. Hot Springs National Park in Arkansas, consisting of 911 acres with 46 hot springs, was established as a reservation by an act of Congress on April 20, 1832 (4 Stat.L.505). It was not until March 4, 1921 (41 Stat.L.1407) that it was designated as the Hot Springs National Park. Therefore, although it is the oldest national park, it was not the first one to be so called.

Park (national) containing an active volcano was the Lassen Volcanic National Park in the Sierra Nevada Mountains in California. It was established by an act of Congress approved August 9, 1916 (39 Stat.L.443). It contains 104,526 acres, including the famous Lassen Peak, 10,453 feet high. This is the only active volcano in continental United States.

Park (national) east of the Mississippi and the only one located on an ocean is the Acadia National Park, on the island of Mount Desert, about a mile south of Bar Harbor, Me. It was established by President Wilson, July 8, 1916 (39 Stat.L.1785), as the Sieur de Monts National Monument and February 26, 1919 (40 Stat.L.1178), as the Lafayette National Park. The name was changed January 19, 1929 (45 Stat.L.1083), to Acadia National Park. It contains 27,871 acres. *(George Bucknam Dorr —Acadia National Park, Its Origin and Background)*

State park was the Yosemite Valley park in California, an area embracing the valley itself and the Mariposa Grove of Big Trees some miles south of it. It was granted to the

state of California by act of Congress, June 30, 1864 (13 Stat.L.325), but actual control of the area and its development were delayed some ten years by the adverse claims of settlers in the area. The Yosemite National Park was created in 1890, and in 1905 the California State Legislature passed an act of retrocession by which the valley and grove were returned to the federal government to be included in the national park. *(Carl Parcher Russell—One Hundred Years in Yosemite)*

Underseas park (federal) was the Key Largo Coral Reef Preserve, 21 miles long and 3½ miles wide, lying in the Atlantic Ocean off Key Largo, Fla., established March 15, 1960 by presidential proclamation No. 3,339 of President Dwight David Eisenhower. This wildlife refuge contains 40 of the 52 known coral species. Previously, it had been the John Pennekamp Coral Reef State Park, the title to which had been obtained December 3, 1959, by the Florida Board of Parks and Historic Monuments. *(Federal Register. March 19, 1960)*

PARK SERVICE (national) was created by act of August 25, 1916 (39 Stat.L.535), "to establish a National Park Service, and for other purposes" to promote and regulate the use of the Federal areas known as national parks, monuments and reservations. A director at $4,500 per annum was appointed by the Secretary of the Interior. *(Jenks Cameron— The National Park Service)*

PARKING GARAGE. *See* Garage: Hydraulic-lift parking garage

PARKING METER (automatic) was the Park-O-Meter, which was installed in Oklahoma City, Okla., on July 16, 1935, by the Dual Parking Meter Company of Oklahoma City. Twenty-foot spaces were painted on the pavement and a nickel-in-the-slot parking meter was installed at each space so that it would be opposite the hood of the car parked there. The machines, devised by Carlton Cole Magee, were sold outright to the city, funds being obtained from their earnings.

PARLIAMENT MEMBER (American-born woman). *See* Woman: American-born woman to become a member of Parliament

PARLIAMENTARY RULES OF ORDER were Thomas Jefferson's *A Manual of Parliamentary Practice, for the Use of the Senate of the United States,* a 199-page book, printed in 1801 by Samuel Harrison Smith in Washington, D.C.

PARLOR CAR. *See* Railroad car: Parlor car

PARTIES, POLITICAL. *See* under name of specific party

PARTRIDGE PROPAGATION. *See* Birds: Partridge propagation

PASSENGER CAR. *See* Automobile

PASSENGER CONVEYOR. *See* Sidewalk (traveling): Sidewalk (traveling)

PASSENGER STATION (railroad). *See* Railroad station: Railroad station

PASSPORT
   Passport recorded in the Passport Division of the State Department is dated July 8, 1796. The passport was issued to Francis Maria Barrere, "a citizen of the United States having occasion to pass into foreign countries about his lawful affairs," and was signed by Thomas Pickering, Secretary of State. *(American Passport: Its History—State Department. Washington, D.C.)*

   Passport division chief (woman). *See* Woman: Woman passport division chief

   Passport fee was levied under the Internal Revenue Act of July 1, 1862 (12 Stat.L.472), "to provide internal revenue to support the government and to pay interest on the public debt." It fixed a fee of $3 for "every passport issued in the office of the Secretary of State." Prior to this time, consuls in foreign countries charged a fee, not exceeding $1, for passports which they issued, but passports which were issued in the United States were gratis.

   Passport photographs were required by a regulation effective November 20, 1914.

PASTE INK. *See* Ink: Ink paste

PASTELLIST was Henrietta Johnston, whose artistic endeavors were produced between 1707 and 1720. She worked with colored chalk; her subjects were principally colonial women of South Carolina. In 1718 she executed her best piece of work, a likeness of "His Excellency Robert Johnson Captain General, Governor and Commander-in-Chief in and over His Majesty's Province of Carolina." She also has the honor of being the first American woman painter. *(The Antiquarian. September 1928)*

PASTEURIZED MILK. *See* Milk: Milk pasteurized commercially

PATENT
   Design patent was issued November 9, 1842, to George Bruce of New York City,

under authority of an act of August 29, 1842 (5 Stat.L.544). Design patent No. 1 was on a type face. Design patent No. 2 was on a design impressed on metal and was issued on February 24, 1843, to Waterman L. Ormsby of Bristol, Conn.

   English patent granted to a resident of America was No. 401, issued November 25, 1715, to "Thomas Masters, Planter of Pennsylvania, for an invention found out by Sibylla his wife for cleaning and curing the Indian Corn growing in several colonies in America." *(Records in the Patent Office, London, England)*

   Fruit tree patent was plant patent No. 7, which was issued February 16, 1932, to James E. Markham, and assigned to the Stark Bros. Nurseries & Orchards Company of Louisiana, Mo. The patent was obtained on a peach tree, the fruit of which ripens later than ordinary peaches.

   Label patent was issued August 1, 1874, to the Baltimore Pearl Hominy Company of Baltimore, Md. Label patent No. 1 was for a breakfast hominy label to be attached to the sack, barrel, or box in which the hominy was to be sold.

   Machine patent granted by the colonies was issued March 6, 1646, to Joseph Jencks by Massachusetts: "The Cort, considring ye necessity of raising such manufactures of engins of mils to go by water, for speedy dispatch of much worke with few hands, & being sufficiently informed of ye ability of ye petitionr to pforme such workes, grant his petition, (yt no othr pson shall set up or use any such new invention or trade for fourteen yeares, without ye licence of him, ye said Joseph Jenkes,) so farr as concernes any such new invention, & so as it shalbe always in ye powr of this Corte to restraine ye exportation of such manufactures, & ye prizes of them, to moderation, if occasion so require." *(Nathaniel Bradstreet Shurtleff— Records of the Governor and Company of the Massachusetts Bay in New England)*

   Negro to obtain a patent was Henry Blair of Glenross, Md., who obtained a patent on October 14, 1834, on a corn planter. Two years later, on August 31, 1836, he was also given a patent on a cotton seed planter.

   Numbering system for patents was introduced July 13, 1836. Previous to that 9,957 unnumbered patents had been issued. Patent No. 1 under the consecutive numbering system was issued July 13, 1836 to John Ruggles of Thomaston, Me., for "traction wheels for locomotive steam-engine for rail and other roads." Ruggles was chairman of the Committee on Patents of the United States Senate.

PATENT—*Continued*
Patent granted by the colonies was
awarded to Samuel Winslow in 1641 by Massachusetts for a new method of extracting salt:
"Whereas Samuel Winslow hath made a proposition to this Court to furnish the contrey
with salt at more easy rates then otherwise can
bee had, & to make it by a meanes & way
which hitherto hath not bene discovered, it is
therefore ordered, that if the said Samuel shall,
within the space of one yeare, set upon the said
worke, hee shall enjoy the same, to him & his
associates, for the space of ten yeares, so as
it shall not bee lawfull to any other pson to
make salt after the same way during the said
yeares; pvided, nevthelesse, that it shall bee
lawfull for any pson to bring in any salt, or
to make salt after any othrway, dureing the
said tearme." (*Nathaniel Bradstreet Shurtleff
—Records of the Governor and Company of
the Massachusetts Bay in New England. Vol.
1*)

**Patent granted by the United States gov-
ernment** was issued to Samuel Hopkins of
Vermont on July 31, 1790, for a process of
making potash and pearl ashes. The document
bore the signatures of George Washington,
President; Thomas Jefferson, Secretary of
State; and Edmund Randolph, Attorney General. Only three patents were issued that year.
In May 1802 the Patent Office was organized
and Dr. William Thornton was made Superintendent "to have charge of the issuing of
patents." In 1833 the head of the Patent Office
wanted to resign because "everything seems
to have been done," althou^h only about 9,000
patents had been issued. By 1960 nearly 3
million had been granted. (*George Whitfield
Evans—The Birth and Growth of the Patent
Office*)

Patent granted jointly to a father and son
was awarded August 2, 1791, to Samuel Briggs,
Sr. and Jr. of Philadelphia, Pa., on a machine
for making nails.

Patent law (national) was an "act to promote the progress of useful arts," approved
April 10, 1790 (1 Stat.L.109). The board in
charge of granting patents styled itself the
"Patent Board," the "Patent Commission," or
the "Commissioners for the Promotion of Useful Arts." Its first members were Thomas
Jefferson, Secretary of State; Henry Knox,
Secretary of War; and Edmund Randolph, Attorney General. The responsibility for administering the patent laws was given to the Department of State. (*U.S. Department of Commerce—The Story of the American Patent
System 1790-1940*)

Patent re-issue was granted January 9,
1838, to Julius Hatch of Great Bend, Pa. Patent reissue No. 1 was on a "machine for sowing
plaster, ashes, seed and other separable sub-

stances," which had been patented August 17,
1835. A re-issue is an amended claim and does
not extend the life of a patent.

Patentee to obtain more than one patent
from the United States Patent Office was
Samuel Mulliken of Philadelphia, Pa., who was
granted four patents on March 11, 1791. They
were on a "machine for threshing grain and
corn," a "machine for breaking and swingling
hemp," a "machine for cutting and polishing
marble," and a "machine for raising a nap on
cloths."

Plant patent was awarded to Henry F.
Bosenberg of New Brunswick, N.J., on August
18, 1931. Plant patent No. 1 covered a climbing rose named "New Dawn" which blooms
successively throughout the season instead of
in June only as does its parent "Dr. Van Fleet."
The application for the patent was filed on
August 6, 1930.

President who had received a patent. *See*
President: President who had received a patent

Print patent was issued March 7, 1893, to
the H. J. Heinz Company of Pittsburgh, Pa.
The application was filed October 31, 1892.
Print patent No. 1 was for "Heinz's Preserves,
Celery Sauce, Ketchup" in the shape of a
pickle with three designs in circles. A patented
print cannot be used as a trademark but only
in advertisements.

Woman granted a patent. *See* Woman:
Woman granted a patent

PATENT COMMISSIONER was Henry
Leavitt Ellsworth, who was appointed on June
15, 1835, by President Andrew Jackson. Prior
to that time the Patent Office had been directed
by the Superintendent of Patents. Ellsworth resigned on April 30, 1845, to act as land agent
in Lafayette, Ind. for the purchase and settlement of public lands. (*Henry Leavitt Ellsworth
—A Digest of Patents Issued by the United
States from 1790 to January 1, 1839*)

PATENT EXAMINER
Woman patent examiner was Anna R. G.
Nichols of Melrose, Mass., a clerk in the United
States Patent Office, who satisfactorily passed
a scientific examination and took office July 1,
1873 as an assistant examiner in the Patent
Office.

PATENT LEATHER. *See* Leather: Patent leather

PATENT LIST was the *Official Gazette of
the U.S. Patent Office,* issued weekly, which
gave the numbers, titles, and claims of the pat-

ents issued during the week immediately preceding together with the names and addresses of the patentees. The first issue was dated January 3, 1872.

PATENT MEDICINE ADVERTISEMENT appeared in the 1692 *Boston Almanack* printed by Benjamin Harris and John Allen: "That Excellent Antidote against all manner of Gripings called Aqua anti torminales, which if timely taken, it not only cures the Griping of the Guts, and the Wind Cholick; but preventeth that woful Distemper of the Dry Belly Ach; With printed directions for the use of it. Sold by Benjamin Harris at the London-Coffee House in Boston. Price three shillings the half pint Bottle."

PATENT MEDICINE ALMANAC. *See* Almanac: Patent medicine almanac

PATHOLOGICAL DIVISION (animal industry bureau). *See* Animal industry bureau (U.S.): Pathological division

PATHOLOGY CHAIR. *See* Medical instruction: Pathology chair

PATHOLOGY TEXTBOOK. *See* Medical book: Pathology textbook

PATRIOTIC AMERICAN SONG. *See* Music: Patriotic American song

PATROL. *See* Border patrol; Fire patrol

PATROL BOMBER (naval). *See* Aviation —Airplane: Naval patrol bomber

PATROL WAGON (police). *See* Automobile police patrol wagon

PATROLMAN (border). *See* Border patrol: Border patrolman

PATTERNS (paper). *See* Paper patterns

PAVEMENT. *See* Road: Mosaic pavement

PAWNBROKING ORDINANCE was passed July 13, 1812, by New York City. *(Minutes of the Common Council of the City of New York 1784-1831)*

PAY STATION (telephone). *See* Telephone: Pay station telephone service

PAY TELEVISION. *See* Television— Telecast: Pay television

PAYMASTER (U.S. Army). *See* Army officer: Paymaster

PEACE PRIZE (Nobel). *See* Nobel prize: Nobel prize

PEACE SOCIETY was the New York Peace Society, which was organized August 16, 1815. David Low Dodge was its first president. Similar societies were formed elsewhere and on May 8, 1828, the New York Peace Society became a member of a national organization called the American Peace Society, which held its first annual meeting May 13, 1829, in New York City. *(Edson Leone Whitney— Centennial History of the American Peace Society)*

PEACETIME CONSCRIPTION BILL. *See* Conscription: Peacetime conscription bill

PEARL BUTTON. *See* Button: Buttons of fresh water pearl

PEDAGOGY BOOK. *See* Teaching methods book

PEDAGOGY CHAIR
  Pedagogy chair (permanent) in a college requiring the occupant to give all his time to the subject was established by the University of Michigan, Ann Arbor, Mich., in 1879. The first incumbent was Professor William Harold Payne. The professorship was called the Science and the Art of Teaching. Although this was the first Chair of Pedagogy, it was not the first attempt at instruction in pedagogy, as Brown University had given instruction in the subject in 1850, and Antioch College had offered an elective course in the subject in 1853.

PEDIATRICS BOOK. *See* under Medical book

PEDIATRICS PROFESSOR. *See* Medical instruction: Pediatrics professor

PEEP SHOW. *See* Moving picture: Peep show

PEEP SHOW MACHINE. *See* Moving picture: Peep show machine

PEGGING MACHINE (shoe). *See* Shoe pegging machine

PELLAGRA EXPERIMENT. *See* Public health: Pellagra experiment

PELOTA. *See* Jai-alai

THE FIRST

THE FIRST

PEN
See also Fountain pen

Ball-point pen patent was No. 392,046, awarded October 30, 1888, to John J. Loud of Weymouth, Mass., on a pen having a spheroidal marking-point capable of revolving in all directions. The application was filed February 4, 1888.

Steel pen patent was obtained by Peregrine Williamson of Baltimore, Md., on November 22, 1809, on "a metallic writing pen."

Steel pens commercially produced were manufactured by Richard Esterbrook, who in 1858 established a factory in Camden, N.J. He produced steel pens which met with great success. His company is still producing pens and is now known as the Esterbrook Steel Pen Manufacturing Company.

PENCIL
Indelible pencil was invented by Edson P. Clark of Northampton, Mass., who obtained patent No. 56,180 on July 10, 1866. It had a "filling composed of silver, black lead, calcined gypsum and lampblack or asphaltum" which was shellacked to the groove in the wood.

Paper pencil was invented by Frederick E. Blaisdell of Philadelphia, Pa., who obtained patent No. 549,952 on November 19, 1895, as well as patent No. 550,212 on the same date on a machine for manufacturing paper pencils.

Pencil with an attached eraser was patented by Hyman L. Lipman of Philadelphia, Pa., who received patent No. 19,783 on March 30, 1858. The pencil had a groove at one end into which was "secured a piece of prepared rubber, glued in at one end."

PENCIL FACTORY was established by William Monroe of Concord, Mass., in June 1812. He manufactured about thirty lead pencils of unfinished cedar, unpolished, very thin, with square leads, which he sold to Benjamin Adams, a hardware dealer of Union Street, Boston, Mass. Adams then contracted to purchase all the pencils Monroe could produce.

PENITENTIARY. *See* Prison: Penitentiary building (national)

PENNY DAILY NEWSPAPER. *See* Newspaper: Penny daily newspaper

PENNY RESTAURANT. *See* Restaurant: Penny restaurant

PENSION
Old age pension laws (state) were enacted March 5, 1923, by Montana and Nevada, whose respective governors signed their pension measures the same hour on the same day. Montana, however, had the first statewide mandatory system. It granted pensions of $25 a month to people who were over seventy years of age and who had been citizens and residents of the state for the previous fifteen years. The funds were derived from the counties. (*Abraham Epstein—Challenge of the Aged*)

Pension act was passed by the Plymouth Pilgrims, who enacted a regulation in 1636 providing that whosoever should set forth as a soldier and return maimed should be competently maintained by the colony for the rest of his life. (*David Pulsifer—Records of the Colony of New Plymouth in New England. Vol. II. p. 106*)

Pension act of the Continental Congress was passed August 26, 1776. It provided "that every commissioned officer, non-commissioned officer, and private soldier who shall have lost a limb in any engagement, or be so disabled in the service of the United States of America as to render him incapable afterwards of getting a livelihood, shall receive, during his life or the continuance of such disability, one half of his monthly pay from and after the time that his pay as an officer or soldier ceases." As the resources of the Continental Congress were meager, the states were asked to make the payment: "That it be recommended to the assemblies or legislative bodies of the several States to cause payment to be made of all such half pay or other allowances as shall be adjudged due to the persons aforenamed on account of the United States." (*William Henry Glasson—History of Military Pension Legislation in the United States*)

Pension for a President. *See* President (United States): Pension for Presidents

Pension to the widow of a President was authorized by an "act granting a pension to Mary Lincoln," July 14, 1870 (16 Stat.L.653). She received $3,000 per annum. An act of February 2, 1882 (22 Stat.L.647) increased the annual pensions to $5,000 for the three widows then living, and made a special grant of $15,000 to Mrs. Lincoln.

Pensions paid by the United States Government were those paid under the act of September 29, 1789 (1 Stat.L.95) which took up the obligation of paying the pensions granted under the provisions of the pension laws enacted by the Continental Congress and appropriated money for payments to invalids who were wounded and disabled during the Revolutionary War for one year from March 4,

1789. The act of July 16, 1790 (1 Stat.L.121), continued the payment of pensions for one year from March 4, 1790. The act of April 30, 1790 (1 Stat.L.121), provided for pensions to those wounded or disabled in the line of duty and the act of March 23, 1792 (1 Stat.L.245), provided for pensions of those suffering wounds or disabilities known to be of service origin. The act of March 18, 1818 (3 Stat.L. 410), was the first universal service pension act and was not limited to those who could prove their disabilities to be of service origin. (*William Henry Glasson—History of Military Pension Legislation in the United States*)

Pensions paid by the United States Government to workers in private industry were mailed July 13, 1936, when checks totaling $901.56 were sent to eighteen retired railroad employees, in accordance with the Railroad Retirement Act of August 29, 1935 (49 Stat.L. 967), which appropriated $46,685,000 "to establish a retirement system for employees of carriers subject to the Interstate Commerce Act, and for other purposes."

Teachers' pensions. *See* Teachers' pension fund

PENSIONS COMMISSIONER (U.S.) was James L. Edwards, appointed under the provisions of the act of March 2, 1833 (4 Stat.L.622). He served as Commissioner of Pensions under the War Department from March 3, 1833, to November 1850, and received $2,500 a year. Previously he had been a clerk in the office of the Secretary of War and had been in charge of pension work since 1816.

PEOPLE'S PARTY (formed by members of the Farmers' Alliance and other industrial unions) was organized at a national convention held in Cincinnati, Ohio, May 19, 1891. At the second national convention, held July 2-5, 1892, in Omaha, Neb., James Baird Weaver of Iowa was nominated as the presidential candidate and James Gaven Field of Virginia for vice president. The People's Party developed later into the Populist Party.

PERAMBULATOR. *See* Baby carriage

PERCHERON HORSE. *See* Horse: Horse (Percheron horse) importation

PERCOLATOR. *See* Coffee percolator patent

PERCUSSION ROCK DRILL. *See* Drill: Percussion rock drill

PERFORATED PAPER (wrapping). *See* Paper: Perforated wrapping paper

PERFORATED POSTAGE STAMP. *See* Postage stamp: Perforated postage stamps

PERFUMED ADVERTISING PAGE. *See* Newspaper: Newspaper with perfumed advertising page

PERIODICAL
See also magazines under specific languages, occupations, religious and fraternal organizations, sciences, sports, trades, e.g., Agricultural magazine, Book trade magazine, Catholic magazine, Welsh magazine

All-fiction pulp magazine was the October 1896 *Argosy*, 192 pages, size 7 by 10 inches. It was an outgrowth of an 8-page illustrated weekly for boys and girls edited by Frank Andrew Munsey entitled *The Golden Argosy*, which was first issued December 2, 1882, bearing the date December 9, 1882. *The Golden Argosy* became the *Argosy* on December 1, 1888. It was published in New York City.

Children's magazine was published in Hartford, Conn., by [Barzillai] Hudson and [George]Goodwin, and was called the *Children's Magazine: Calculated for the Use of Families and Schools*. Only four issues were printed from January to April 1789, each containing 48 pages, an "abridgement of geography, essays on morality, religion, manners, etc., familiar letters, dialogues and select pieces of poetry."

Children's magazine with literary merit was *The Juvenile Miscellany,* founded by Lydia Maria Frances Child in 1826. It was a bimonthly and appeared from September 1826 to January 1829. It was published by Putnam & Hunt in Boston, Mass. The first issue contained 108 pages. (*Letters of Lydia Maria Child*)

College magazine was the Yale *Literary Cabinet,* published November 15, 1806, in New Haven, Conn. It was an 8-page bi-weekly and was edited by three college seniors. It sold for $1 a year and continued for a year only. (*Four Years at Yale—Anonymous.* Henry Holt & Co. 1871)

Comic books containing colored cartoons which had been published previously in newspapers were published in 1904 by Cupples & Leon, New York City. The books were 10 inches high and 15 inches long, contained 40 pages, and retailed for 75 cents. The titles of some of the books were *Alphonse and Gaston and Their Friend Leon,* by Frederick Burr Opper; *Happy Hooligan,* by Frederick Burr Opper; *The Naughty Adventures of Vicious Mr. Jack,* by James Swinnerton; *Tigers,* by James Swinnerton; *The Katzenjammer Kids;* and *Lulu and Leander.*

PERIODICAL—*Continued*

Comic weekly was *The John Donkey,* 16 pages, published by G. B. Zieber & Company of Philadelphia, Pa., from January 1, 1848, to October 21, 1848. It cost 6 cents a copy or $3 a year. It was edited by Thomas Dunn English and George G. Foster and was illustrated by Felix Octavius Carr Darley and Henry Louis Stephens.

Electrical journal was *The Electro-Magnetic and Mechanics Intelligencer,* which appeared on January 18, 1840. This was the first magazine printed on a printing press operated by electricity. It was printed in New York City on a press "propelled by electro-magnetism." The editor of the magazine and the inventor of the electrical printing press was Thomas Davenport.

Illustrated weekly was *Brother Jonathan, a Weekly Compend of Belles Lettres and the Fine Arts, Standard Literature and General Intelligence,* issued January 1, 1842. It consisted of 28 pages and a 32-page supplement containing the installment "Adventures of Tom Stapleton," by John M. Moore. It was founded by Benjamin Henry Day and Nathaniel Parker Willis and was published by Wilson & Company, New York City. It was not the first magazine, however, to contain an illustration.

Indian-language monthly was the *Siwinowe Kesibwi* ("The Shawnee Sun"), printed February 24, 1835, at the press of Jotham Meeker, a missionary at the Shawnee Baptist Mission in Kansas. The first issue was dated March 1835. Johnston Lykins, a Baptist missionary, was editor. *(Kansas Historical Quarterly. Vol. 2. No. 4. November 1933)*

Magazine containing a fashion plate was *The Port Folio,* published by Bradford and Inskeep, Philadelphia, Pa., and Inskeep and Bradford, New York City. The June 1809 issue contained two engravings, one page showing a full dress and one showing the front and back views of "Fontarabian robes of Saragossa brown net."

Magazine for the blind was the *Student's Magazine, a Periodical for the Blind,* published January 1837 by the Pennsylvania Institution for the Instruction of the Blind, Philadelphia, Pa. Embossed raised capital letters were used. It was a monthly and cost $3 a year. *(Pennsylvania Institution for the Instruction of the Blind. Sixth Annual Report. 1839)*

Magazine for women to continue publication for more than five years was the *Ladies' Magazine,* which was founded in Boston, Mass., in 1828 by Sarah Josepha Hale *(Frederic Hudson—Journalism in the United States)*

Magazine of the United States Government was the daily *Federal Register,* issued March 14, 1936. The masthead was decorated with the eagle shield and a Latin motto "Littera Scripta Manet" ("The Written Word Endures"). It was published in Washington, D.C. by the National Archives under Federal Register Act approved July 26, 1935 (49 Stat.L. 500), and contained 16 two-column pages. The Administrative Committee consisted of the Archivist or Acting Archivist, an officer of the Attorney General, and the Public Printer or Acting Public Printer. The magazine publishes federal laws, orders and reports and is not limited in scope like the *Congressional Record.*

Magazine published for mental patients was the *Illuminator,* written and published in 1843 by patients in Pennsylvania Hospital, Philadelphia, Pa. The first issue appeared April 1, 1843, and contained 24 three-column pages, each in Spencerian handwriting. Volume 1 consisted of three issues, April, May, and June; volume 2 contained two issues, July and August.

Magazine published in America was *The American Magazine, or a Monthly View of the Political State of the British Colonies,* the first issue probably appearing February 13, 1741, in Philadelphia, Pa. It was published by Andrew Bradford and edited by John Webbe. The first number contained 50 pages. It was published monthly for three months. It appeared probably about three days prior to Benjamin Franklin's *The General Magazine and Historical Chronicle for All the British Plantations in America. (Lyon Norman Richardson—A History of Early American Magazines)*

Magazine to contain a phonograph record was the November 1955 issue of *Pageant,* published in New York City, which went on sale October 10, 1955. It contained a 78-revolution-per-minute acetate recording of "If You Don't Want My Love," sung by Jaye P. Morgan to the accompaniment of Hugo Winterhalter's orchestra. Approximately 1,100,000 copies were issued.

Music printed in a magazine. *See* Music: Music printed in a magazine

Photo-engraved magazine was the *Literary Digest,* published in New York City, October 25, 1919. It consisted of 80 pages and cover. The material was typewritten and photoengraved. A strike of printers at the time made it impossible to issue regularly printed numbers without great difficulty.

Quarterly magazine was *The American Review of History and Politics and General Repository of Literature and State Papers,*

THE FIRST

edited by Robert Walsh and published in Philadelphia, Pa. The first issue, January 1811, contained 200 pages and a 60-page appendix. Subscription was $6 a year to be paid on the delivery of the second number of every year. The last issue was published October 1812.

Sectarian magazine was *The Arminian Magazine,* which appeared from January 1789 to December 1790. It was edited by Methodist Bishops Thomas Coke and Francis Asbury and published in Philadelphia, Pa., by William Prichard and Peleg Hall. (*Lyon Norman Richardson—History of Early American Magazines*)

Sectarian magazine printed in rotogravure was *Catholic Missions,* issued October 1, 1934, by the Society for the Propagation of the Faith, New York City. It was issued quarterly and sold for a penny a copy. Its editor was the Right Reverend Monsignor William Quinn.

Spanish magazine published by students was *El Estudiante Comercial,* founded in 1917 at the High School of Commerce, New York City. Philip Leonard Green was its first director and Irving B. Simon its first editor.

Trade journal was the *Rail-road Advocate,* published bi-weekly from July 4, 1831, to June 14, 1832, in Rogersville, Tenn., by "an association of gentlemen." The first issue contained 8 pages measuring 12½ by 9¾ inches. Its main objects were "to advocate railroads and other internal improvements that would connect East Tennessee with markets for its surplus produce" and "end its isolation from the rest of the country," and to collect and publish "all the information that can be collected on this interesting subject."

PERIODICAL INDEX was *An Alphabetical Index to Subjects Treated in the Reviews and Other Periodicals to Which No Indexes Have Been Published,* which was edited by William Frederick Poole and issued in 1848 by George Palmer Putnam, New York City. This was the forerunner of the famous *Poole's Index to Periodical Literature.*

PERISCOPE was invented by Thomas Doughty, acting chief engineer of the United States Navy in 1864. During Nathaniel Prentiss Banks' Red River expedition Doughty was on the turreted monitor "Osage." Annoyed by bushwhackers and snipers who could not be seen, yet did deadly work, Doughty rigged up a sheet iron tube extending from a few feet above the deck to the engine room below, with openings near the top and bottom, and by an arrangement of mirrors he could see the shore.

THE FIRST

When attacked, he would signal the gunners to fire. Admiral David Dixon Porter officially thanked him for his invention.

PERITONITIS
Peritonitis preventive (successful) was amniotic fluid, first used to prevent postoperative peritonitis and adhesions in 1922 by Dr. Herbert Lester Johnson of Boston, Mass. The first fluid was of human origin, from caesarean operations, but the widespread use of this new principle of preventive medicine resulted in a commercial preparation known as Amniotic Fluid Concentrate, made from bovine amniotic fluid.

PERMALLOY was developed June 7, 1913, at the Bell Telephone Laboratories, New York City, by Gustaf Waldemar Elmen. It was first applied commercially in 1924 when it was used in the New York-Azores submarine telegraph cable and increased the transmission rate from 300 to 2,000 letters a minute. Permalloy was used in the form of a thin tape, six-thousandths of an inch thick, which was wound around the conductor. Its extraordinarily high magnetic permeability at very low magnetizing forces permitted the high inductance necessary for high-speed transmission.

PETROLEUM EXPORTED TO EUROPE was shipped in barrels on the "Elizabeth Watts," a 224-ton brig captained by Charles Bryant. On November 12, 1861, Messrs. Peter Wright and Sons of Philadelphia chartered this brig from Messrs. Edmund A. Sander and Co., and the shipment was made from Philadelphia, Pa., to London, England. Since it was not easy to recruit a crew (the men would not work above a cargo of oil), a crew was shanghaied. (*James Dodds Henry—Thirty-five Years of Oil Transport*)
See also Oil

PETROLEUM JELLY was manufactured in 1870 by Robert Augustus Chesebrough who coined the word "Vaseline" and registered it May 14, 1878, as a trademark to identify his particular brand. On May 10, 1880, he organized the Chesebrough Manufacturing Company, New York City, of which he became president, holding this office until May 6, 1909.

PETROLEUM REFINING COURSE of a collegiate grade was offered by the School of Mines, University of Pittsburgh, Pittsburgh, Pa., in the university year 1922-1923 under the direction of Dr. Warren Fred Faragher.

PEWTER BUTTON. See Button: Pewter or block tin buttons

PHARMACIST
Pharmacist (woman) was Elizabeth Marshall (1768-1836), a daughter of Charles

PHARMACIST—*Continued*
Marshall, who served as president of the Philadelphia College of Pharmacy (1821-1824). She became manager of the apothecary originally established by her grandfather, Christopher Marshall, in 1729 in Philadelphia, Pa. She served from 1804 until 1825, when the store was sold.

Pharmacist (woman graduate) was Susan Hayhurst of St. Michael's, Md., who graduated March 16, 1883, from the Philadelphia College of Pharmacy, Philadelphia, Pa., with the Ph.G. degree. The subject of her thesis was "Dispensary Work." She graduated on February 28, 1857, from the Female Medical College of Pennsylvania, receiving an M.D. degree. She was also the first woman physician to graduate from a pharmacy college.

PHARMACOPOEIA
Pharmacopoeia was the 32-page work of Dr. William Brown, Physician-General to the Hospitals of the United States, written especially for army usage and published in Philadelphia, Pa., in 1778 for the use of the Military Hospital of the U.S. Army located at Lititz, Pa. It was entitled *Pharmacopoeia simpliciorum et efficaciorum, in usum nosocomii militaris,* etc., and was printed entirely in Latin. The size of the type page was 4¼ by 2½ inches.

Pharmacopoeia (general) was *The Pharmacopoeia of the United States of America.* It was published December 15, 1820, in both English and Latin by Wells & Lilly of Boston, Mass., and copyrighted by Ewer & Bedlington of Boston. It consisted of 274 pages printed on rather porous paper, 6 by 10 inches, and was recommended by the New York County Medical Society. The chairman in charge of the work was Dr. Lyman Spalding, who had proposed the work on January 8, 1817, to the medical society. (*Dr. James Alfred Spalding—Dr. Lyman Spalding*)

Pharmacopoeia prepared by a hospital staff was the *"Pharmacopoeia Nosocomii neoeboracensis, or the Pharmacopoeia of the New York Hospital,"* published under the authority of the physicians and surgeons of that institution, to which was added an appendix containing a general dosage table. The work consisted of 180 pages prepared by Dr. Valentine Seaman and Dr. Samuel Latham Mitchill. It was printed by A. Paul and published in 1816 by Collins & Company, New York City.

Pharmacopoeia prepared by a medical association for the use of its members was authorized October 3, 1805, by the Massachusetts Medical Society, Boston, Mass. It contained 286 pages and was edited by Dr. James Jackson and Dr. John Collins Warren. It was pub-

lished in 1808 in Boston, Mass., as *The Pharmacopoeia of the Massachusetts Medical Society.*

PHARMACY COLLEGE
Pharmacy college was the Philadelphia College of Apothecaries, established February 23, 1821, at a meeting presided over by Stephen North at Carpenters' Hall, Philadelphia, Pa. Charles Marshall was elected president of the college on March 27, 1821. On April 23, 1821, Dr. Samuel Jackson was appointed Professor of Materia Medica and Pharmacy, and Dr. Gerardt Troost Professor of Chemistry. The first class was held November 9, 1821. The school was incorporated March 30, 1822, at which time it was renamed the Philadelphia College of Pharmacy. The Ph.G. degree was conferred November 28, 1826, on three graduates, Charles Hazard Dingee, Charles H. McCormick, and William Sharp. They completed two full courses. (This was not the first time, however, that degrees had been granted to pharmacists. The University of Pennsylvania on April 5, 1821, had awarded honorary Master of Pharmacy degrees to sixteen practicing apothecaries.) (*Joseph Winters England—The First Century of the Philadelphia College of Pharmacy*)

Pharmacy college to make analytical chemistry a required course was the Maryland College of Pharmacy (now part of the University of Maryland), Baltimore, Md. The chair of Analytical Chemistry was established on March 20, 1872, and Dr. William Simon was the first professor appointed thereto. The Maryland College of Pharmacy was incorporated January 27, 1841. The first graduation took place June 19, 1842, when three students received degrees.

PHARMACY LEGISLATION (state) requiring graduation from a pharmacy course was enacted May 3, 1904, by New York, effective January 1, 1905 (Chapter 554). Four years of practical experience and two years of schooling in pharmacy were required.

PHARMACY MAGAZINE was *The Journal of the Philadelphia College of Pharmacy,* which appeared in December 1825. Its first editor was Daniel B. Smith, who served from 1825 to 1828. The magazine contained 32 pages of "original and selected papers on subjects connected with pharmacy and chemistry," and sold for 25 cents.

PHARMACY PROFESSOR
Pharmacy professor was Dr. Samuel Powel Griffitts, appointed Professor of Materia Medica and Pharmacy in 1789 at the Medical School of the College of Philadelphia, Pa. He continued in 1791, when the school merged with the University of Pennsylvania, and served until 1796.

Pharmacy professorship in which the holder gave full time to instructing the students in the theory and practice of pharmacy was established in 1844 by the Maryland College of Pharmacy (now part of the University of Maryland), Baltimore, Md. David Stewart was appointed to the chair of Theory and Practice of Pharmacy, which he held from April 24, 1844, to April 28, 1846. *(Eugene Fauntleroy Cordell—University of Maryland 1807-1907)*

PHARMACY SOCIETY (national) was the American Pharmaceutical Association, organized October 6, 1852, in Philadelphia, Pa. Daniel B. Smith was elected president and William Procter, Jr., corresponding secretary. The first annual meeting was held in Boston, Mass., August 24, 1853. A preliminary meeting, held October 15, 1851, at the New York College of Pharmacy, New York City, led to the organization of the association.

PHILATELIC AGENCY. *See* Postal service: Philatelic agency

PHILOLOGICAL SOCIETY

National philological society was the American Philological Association, organized in New York City on November 13, 1868, to promote the advancement and diffusion of philological knowledge. The first convention was held July 27, 1869, in Poughkeepsie, N.Y., and the first president was William Dwight Whitney. *(American Philological Transactions. Vol. 50. 1919)*

PHILOLOGY CHAIR

Comparative philology chair was established by Lafayette College, Easton, Pa., in 1856. The first professor was Francis Andrew March.

PHILOSOPHY DEGREE. See Degrees (academic and honorary): Doctor of philosophy degree

PHONETIC BIBLE. *See* Bible: Phonetic Bible

PHONETIC DICTIONARY. *See* Dictionary: Phonetic dictionary

PHONOGRAPH

Phonograph was invented by Thomas Alva Edison of Menlo Park, N.J., who secured patent No. 200,521 on February 19, 1878, on a "phonograph or speaking machine." His original idea had been to invent a telegraph repeater, directions for the building of which he had given to one of his mechanics, John Kreusi, on August 12, 1877. The first cylinder, operated by a hand crank, was wrapped in tin foil with which two needles fastened to diaphragms made contact. The first verse recorded on the

new instrument was "Mary had a little lamb." A clock spring motor and wax-like record were invented some ten years later.

Phonograph that was practical was the Graphophone, manufactured by Bell & Tainter. On May 4, 1886, Chichester Bell and Charles Sumner Tainter received United States patent No. 341,214, a fundamental and basic patent, "for recording and reproducing speech and other sounds." Patents No. 341,212 on "reproducing sounds from phonograph records" and No. 341,213 on "transmitting and recording sounds by radiant energy" were also received on May 4, 1886, jointly with Alexander Graham Bell.

Phonograph with an automatic record-changer was introduced by the Victor Talking Machine Company, Camden, N.J., in March 1927. It played twelve ten-inch records or twelve twelve-inch records and stopped automatically after the last record had been played.

Phonograph with an enclosed horn in the cabinet was the Victor Victrola, manufactured August 22, 1906, by the Victor Talking Machine Co., Camden, N.J. It was in a mahogany cabinet (4 feet high, 20 inches wide, and 22 inches deep), cost $200, and was advertised September 1906.

PHONOGRAPH RECORD

Long-playing microgroove records that were successful were made by Columbia Records, Bridgeport, Conn., a division of the Columbia Broadcasting System, Inc., and introduced to the public on June 21, 1948, at the Waldorf-Astoria Hotel, New York City. The records were made of non-breakable Vinylite plastic and were played at a speed of 33⅓ revolutions per minute. One side of a 12-inch record played for 23 minutes, compared to 4 minutes on one side of a standard 78 rpm record.

Magazine to contain a phonograph record. *See* Periodical: Magazine to contain a phonograph record

Phonograph record of a stage performance by the original cast was a ten-inch single-face disc record of "Old Folks At Home" ("Swanee River"), sung in Act I of the spectacular military operetta *When Johnny Comes Marching Home,* recorded in 1904 and released as No. M2931 by the Victor Talking Machine Company, Camden, N.J. The libretto was by Stanislaus Stange, the music by Julian Edwards, and the production by the Whitney Opera Company of which F. C. Whitney was the proprietor and manager. W. H. Thompson took the role of Major William Walker and Miss Quinn was Kate Pemberton.

PHONOGRAPH TRADE MAGAZINE

was *The Phonogram,* "official organ of the phonograph companies of the United States," edited by V. H. McRae, which was published monthly in New York City from January 1891 to January 1893. The first issue contained an article by Thomas Alva Edison entitled "How Sound Is Reproduced."

PHOTOELECTRIC CELL

Photoelectric cell or tube was publicly demonstrated on October 21, 1925, by the Westinghouse Electric and Manufacturing Company at the Electrical Show at Grand Central Palace in New York City. At this demonstration the photoelectric cell, which is sensitive to light, was used to count objects as they interrupted a light beam in passing, to open doors as a person or car approached, and to perform similar functions.

Photoelectric cell installed commercially for operating doors was in Wilcox's Pier Restaurant, West Haven, Conn. The Stanley Works of New Britain, Conn., had completed the installation on June 19, 1931, of the "magic eye" which provided fully automatic control and operation of swinging doors between the main dining room and kitchen.

PHOTO-ENGRAVED MAGAZINE. *See* Periodical: Photo-engraved magazine

PHOTO-FINISH CAMERA. *See* Camera: Photo-finish camera

PHOTOGRAPH

Aerial photograph was "Boston as the Eagle and the Wild Goose See It," taken October 13, 1860, by Samuel Archer King (navigator) of Providence, R.I., and J. W. Black (photographer) of Boston, Mass., in a balloon, "The Queen of the Air," held by a cable 1,200 feet above the city. Eight pictures were taken, only one of which was good. Wet plates were used which were prepared in the balloon before each exposure.

Celestial photograph was a daguerrotype of the moon taken December 18, 1839, by John William Draper, professor of chemistry at New York University, New York City. He exposed the plate twenty minutes. The image was one inch in diameter. He presented the photographs on March 23, 1840, to the Lyceum of Natural History of New York City. *(George Frederick Barker—Memoir of John William Draper)*

Color photo sent by radio. *See* Radio facsimile transmission: Color photoradio news photograph transmitted by radio for publication

Composograph photograph. *See* Newspaper: Composograph photograph

Cystoscopic photographs in color publicly exhibited were shown March 11-12-13, 1940, at the Postgraduate Surgical Assembly of the Southeastern Surgical Congress, Birmingham, Ala. The pictures were taken by Drs. Edgar Garrison Ballenger, Harold Paul McDonald and Reese Clinton Coleman of Atlanta, Ga., and were printed in the *Southern Surgeon,* June 1940.

Infra-red photograph of a large group of people taken in the dark with a short exposure was made in the Eastman Kodak Research Laboratories in Rochester, N.Y., on October 7, 1931. A photograph was taken with a one-second exposure, in apparently total darkness, of a group of fifty visitors to the laboratories. The room was flooded with invisible infra-red rays, and a new photographic emulsion sensitive to infra-red was used.

News photographs of distinction were made by Mathew B. Brady of New York City who, with the permission of President Abraham Lincoln and the U.S. Secret Service, had followed the Union Army and photographed it in action. He took more than 7,000 pictures, 2,000 of which were purchased by the Government for $25,000. Brady's studio at Broadway and Fulton Streets in New York City was opened in 1844 as Brady's Daguerrian Miniature Gallery. *(Roy Meredith—Mathew B. Brady—Mr. Lincoln's Camera Man)*

Passport photograph. *See* Passport: Passport photographs

Photograph bounced off a satellite was a photograph of President Dwight David Eisenhower which on August 18, 1960, was beamed 1,000 miles up to the satellite Echo I from a "dish" antenna by the Collins Radio Co., Cedar Rapids, Iowa. It was received on standard Associated Press Wirephoto equipment by the Alpha Corporation near Dallas, Texas.

Photograph bounced off the moon was received on January 28, 1960, at Washington, D.C., having been transmitted by the U.S. Navy from Hawaii.

Photograph from an airplane was taken by Major H. A. ("Jimmie") Erickson on January 10, 1911, in a Curtiss biplane piloted by Charles Hamilton over San Diego, Calif.

Photograph from an airplane at night was taken November 20, 1925, over Rochester, N.Y., by Lieutenant George Goddard in cooperation with the Eastman Kodak Company, which supplied a photometer by which the intensity of

THE FIRST

light was measured. The photographs were taken from a 3,000-foot altitude and showed about three square miles of the city's area. A light bomb was dropped which made a flash lasting but one twentieth of a second.

Photograph in color of the earth from outer space was taken December 1, 1959, from the nose cone of a Thor missile launched from Cape Canaveral, Fla. The camera was found February 16, 1960, in the data capsule on the beach of Mayaguana Island, Bahama Islands, approximately 1,700 miles from the take-off point.

Photograph in natural colors taken in the air was made by Melville Bell Grosvenor, Assistant Chief of Illustrations Division of the *National Geographic Magazine,* in July 1930, and published in the September 1930 issue.

Photograph of a beam of 1 billion-volt X-rays, made by William Morris and Hubert Luckett in October 1946, showed the rays emanating from the betatron of the General Electric Company, Schenectady, N.Y. The beam does not cause a glowing of the air through which it passes, but was made visible to the camera by the placement of a fluorescent screen in its path. The camera exposure was made through a three-foot concrete wall in which an opening was made for the lens.

Photograph of a President (in office) was made of President James Knox Polk on February 14, 1849, by Mathew B. Brady in New York City. Former President John Quincy Adams sat for three photographs on November 13, 1843, while in Cincinnati, Ohio.

Photograph of a star (other than the sun) was that of Vega which was made at the Harvard College Observatory, Cambridge, Mass., July 17, 1850, by Whipple, a professional photographer, under the direction of William Cranch Bond, the first director of the observatory. A 15-inch telescope was used as a camera lens and the daguerrotype plate was set up at the eye end.

Photograph of a stellar spectrum showing the dark lines was one of Vega, Alpha Lyrae, made in 1872 by Dr. Henry Draper at Hastings-on-Hudson, N.Y. *(George Frederick Barker—Memoir of Henry Draper)*

Photograph of a total solar eclipse was taken August 7, 1869, by Professor Edward Charles Pickering at Mt. Pleasant, Iowa. Using a portrait lens, he made the first successful photographs of the corona. The eclipse crossed America diagonally from Alaska to North Carolina. *(Samuel Alfred Mitchell—Eclipses of the Sun)*

THE FIRST

Photograph of genes, the particles which transmit physical characteristics from one generation to another, was taken by Drs. Daniel Chapin Pease and Richard Freligh Baker at the University of Southern California, Los Angeles, Calif., and announced January 7, 1949. The tissue sections were magnified 120,000 times.

Photograph sent by radio across the continent. *See* Radio facsimile transmission: Photograph sent by radio across the continent (commercial)

Photograph showing action (not moving pictures) was taken in 1872 on a stock farm of Leland Stanford at Palo Alto, Calif., by Eadweard Muybridge. He used a series of twelve clocks for breaking electric circuits connected with camera shutters, thus taking a series of photographs at regular intervals, in rapid succession, of a race horse in action.

Photograph showing air in motion across aerofoils or wings of airplanes was taken by Colonel Rutherford B. Harts during the winter of 1918-1919 at Bolling Field, Washington, D.C., under the auspices of the Division of Military Aeronautics and the Invention Secretary of the General Staff of the U.S. Army. Three miles of film showed that no flying power whatever is exerted for about 30 per cent of a flight on the wings of an aircraft by the air flow produced by the air screws and that rarefication, which produces the lifting power of an airplane, is not continuous but is exerted in intermittent or pulsating air waves. *(Aerial Age Weekly. June 2, 1919)*

Photograph showing motion. *See* Moving picture: Photographic attempt to show motion

Photograph showing the lateral curvature of the horizon taken in the United States was made by Captain Albert William Stevens from the gondola of the stratosphere balloon "Explorer 11," sent up November 11, 1935, by the National Geographic Society and the U.S. Army Air Corps. The photograph was made from an altitude of 72,395 feet or 13.71 miles above sea level. It was the first photograph of the horizon taken from such a great altitude; the first photograph the line of sight of which was entirely in the stratosphere; and the first photograph showing the extreme top of the "dust sphere" which marks the dividing line between the lower atmosphere with its clouds and dust and the stratosphere, which is clear. The balloon took off from Rapid City, S.D., and landed 8 hours and 13 minutes later at White Lake, S.D.

Photograph taken by incandescent electric light was the portrait of Charles Batchelor, made in December 1879 in Menlo Park, N.J.

PHOTOGRAPH—*Continued*
Photograph taken in the United States was a daguerrotype, a form of image recording invented by Louis Jacques Mande Daguerre of France on August 19, 1839. The first published description of the method appeared in the London *Globe*, which arrived in the United States on September 20, 1839, on the "British Queen." Among those who are credited with taking the first daguerrotype are Samuel Finley Breese Morse, Amasa Holcomb, Robert Cornelius (a Philadelphia lamp maker), and Joseph Saxton (a balance-maker at the Philadelphia mint). Dr. John William Draper took a picture of his sister Dorothy Catherine Draper which is believed to be the first daguerrotype portrait.

Photograph (taken in the United States) on which a meteor was found was taken on August 10, 1889, by the Harvard College Observatory, Harvard University, Cambridge, Mass. The photograph of the meteor showed a straight dense line. The exposure, 13 hours and 50 minutes, was taken by a Gundlach camera strapped to an 11-inch telescope. (*Annals Harvard College Observatory. Vol. 87, part 3*)

Photograph to gain world fame was a daguerrotype panorama of Niagara Falls, N.Y., taken in July 1845 by William and Frederick Langenheim of the Philadelphia Daguerrotype Establishment, Philadelphia, Pa., from a site near the Clifton House on the Canadian side. Sets were made and presented to Louis Jacques Mande Daguerre, President James Knox Polk, Queen Victoria, the kings of Prussia, Saxony and Wurtemberg, and the Duke of Brunswick. (*Beaumont Newhall—Photography 1839-1939*)

Photograph transmitted by wire or wireless. *See* Radio facsimile transmission

Photographs sent by radio across the Atlantic. *See* Radio facsimile transmission: Photograph sent by radio across the Atlantic

Photographs taken under the sea which were successful were obtained by John Ernest Williamson at Chesapeake Bay, Va., in 1913 with the use of the Williamson Submarine Tube and Photosphere. (*John Ernest Williamson—Twenty Years Under the Sea*)

Photographs taken under the sea in natural colors were made for the *National Geographic Magazine* off the Tortugas of the Florida Keys, on July 16, 1926, and were published in the January 1927 issue of the magazine. The work was carried out by Dr. William Harding Longley of Goucher College and Charles Martin, Chief of the National Geographic Society's photographic laboratory. The camera used in making these autochromes was inclosed in a brass case with a plate glass window in front of the lens. A supplementary hood was fitted

above the regulation reflector and by means of an acute-angle mirror the photographer was able to focus his instrument.

Portrait (life-size) of a human in a newspaper was a photograph of Larry Quinn, a 14-pound, 7-ounce baby, 21½ inches high, published November 14, 1935, in the *Call-Bulletin*, San Francisco, Calif. The infant was born November 12, 1935, at Mary's Help Hospital, San Francisco, Calif.

Satellite to transmit photographs. *See* Rocket: Satellite to transmit photographs

Ultraviolet pictures of the sun were taken March 13, 1959, by a camera at an altitude of 123 miles from an Aerobee-Hi research rocket at White Sands, N.M., under the direction of the U.S. Naval Research Laboratory. A camera with spectroscopic mirrors reflected out the visible light of the sun, leaving only the Lyman-Alpha radiation to fall on the special film.

X-ray photograph. *See* X-ray

PHOTOGRAPHIC COPYING MACHINE. *See* Photostat: Photographic copying machine

PHOTOGRAPHIC FILM
Celluloid photographic film and the process for producing it were invented by the Reverend Hannibal Williston Goodwin of Newark, N.J., who applied for a patent on May 2, 1887, and received patent No. 610,861 on September 13, 1898, on "nitro cellulose transparent flexible photographic film pellicles." He received an order from Thomas Alva Edison for one roll at $2.50 on September 2, 1889.

Moving picture film (commercial) was manufactured March 26, 1885, by the Eastman Dry Plate & Film Company of Rochester, N.Y., which was also the first to produce, manufacture, and market films in continuous strips on reels. (*The Home of Kodak—Eastman Kodak Co.*)

Roll film for cameras was patented by David Henderson Houston of Cambria, Wis., who obtained patent No. 248,179 October 11, 1881 for a "photographic apparatus." He had a camera with a receptacle or box at its inner end containing a "roll of sensitized paper or any other suitable tissue, such as gelatine or any more durable material that may be discovered, and an empty reel, upon which the sensitized band is wound as rapidly as it has been acted upon by the light." The purpose of the camera was "to facilitate taking a number of photographic views successively in a short time."

Transparent paper strip photographic film was invented in February 1884 by George Eastman of Rochester, N.Y., who obtained patent No. 306,594 on October 14, 1884. The film consisted of paper coated with an insoluble sensitive gelatin emulsion.

"V" mail film. *See* Postal service: "V" mail film

PHOTOGRAPHIC GLASS SLIDES. *See* Magic lantern slides (glass plate)

PHOTOGRAPHIC PAMPHLET was François Fauvel-Gouraud's *Description of the Daguerrotype Process, or a Summary of M. Gouraud's Public Lectures, According to the Principles of M. Daguerre, with a Description of a Provisory Method for Taking Human Portraits,* sixteen pages and cover, printed in 1840 in Boston, Mass., by Dutton and Wentworth.

PHOTOGRAPHIC PATENT
Aerial photography patent was No. 510,758, awarded December 12, 1893 to Cornele Berrien Adams of Augusta, Ga., on a "method of photogrammetry." By means of photographs of the same tract taken from different points a topographic effect was obtained.

Photographic patent was No. 1,582, granted to Alexander S. Wolcott of New York City on May 8, 1840, for "a method of taking likenesses by means of a concave reflector and plates so prepared that luminous or other rays will act thereon."

PHOTOGRAPHY
Camera exposure meter was invented in 1931 by William Nelson Goodwin, Jr., of the Weston Electrical Instrument Corporation, Newark, N.J., who obtained patent No. 1,407,147, February 21, 1932, on a thermal ammeter. The first one, manufactured in February 1932, was called the Photronic Photoelectric Cell, although popularly known as a camera exposure meter. It contained a dial calculating device for translating brightness values into camera aperture settings. It required no battery for its operation, as it changed light energy directly into electrical energy.

Demonstration of rapid aerial photography was made September 5, 1925, before the U.S. General Staff and Command School. Lieutenant George W. Goddard, Director of Photography of the Air Corps Technical School, U.S. Army, took photographs of the Fort Leavenworth area in the "Flying Laboratory." These were developed and finished and dropped to the ground within eight minutes from the time of exposure. A photographic transmitting set sent the picture to Governors Island,

where it was in the hands of General Charles Pelot Summerall within twenty-seven minutes after it had been taken in Kansas, 1,700 miles away. Copies were also sent to General William Sidney Graves in Chicago, Ill., and General Charles Thomas Menoher in San Francisco, Calif.

Film developing machine (fully automatic) was the Photomaton, invented by Anatol M. Josepho, who constructed the first model in a loft building on 125th Street, New York City. He applied for a patent March 13, 1925; patent No. 1,656,522 was issued January 17, 1928, on an apparatus for developing photographic film strips. It is said that the inventor received a million dollars for this invention. The first Photomaton studio was opened to the public at 1659 Broadway, New York City, in September 1926.

Photographic flashlight lamps, fireless, smokeless, odorless, and noiseless, similar to incandescent lamp bulbs, were made by the General Electric Company of Schenectady, N.Y., on August 1, 1930, under patent No. 1,776,637, awarded on September 23, 1930, to Johannes Ostermeier of Althegnenberg, Germany, for a "flash lamp." A small filament in the bulb, when connected to a source of electricity, becomes heated and ignites the foil and oxygen causing a flash of light of high intensity and short duration. The bulb, a No. 20, was the size of a 150-watt incandescent bulb.

PHOTORADIOGRAPHY. *See* Radio facsimile transmission

PHOTOSENSITIVE GLASS. *See* Glass: Photosensitive glass

PHOTOSTAT
Photographic copying machine known by the trade name "Photostat" was commercially manufactured in 1910 by the Eastman Kodak Company, Rochester, N.Y., under the supervision of John S. Greene of the Photostat Corporation. It photographed the subject to be copied directly upon a roll of sensitized paper and eliminated the necessity for the use of any glass plate or film negative. It was capable of making a print 11½ by 14 inches. The process was not new, but was simplified.

PHOTOTELEGRAPHY. *See* Radio facsimile transmission

PHOTOTRANSISTOR. *See* Transistor: Phototransistor

PHRENOLOGIST of importance to visit the United States was Johann Gaspar Spurzheim, an associate of Dr. Franz Joseph Gall,

THE FIRST

THE FIRST

PHRENOLOGIST—*Continued*
the German physician who originated the theory of phrenology. Spurzheim arrived in New York City on August 6, 1832. On August 20 he went to Boston, Mass., to give a series of eighteen lectures at Athenaeum Hall, and on September 17 to Cambridge, Mass., for an additional series. He died on November 10, 1832. His funeral was attended by the Boston Medical Association as a group, and the oration was delivered by Charles Follen, Professor of German Literature, Harvard University.

PHRENOLOGY BOOK was the *Outlines of Phrenology* by Johann Gaspar Spurzheim, M.D., of the universities of Vienna and Paris, and a licentiate of the Royal College of Physicians of London. It was published in 1832 by Marsh, Capen & Lyon, Boston, Mass. It was divided into three sections covering general principles of phrenology, special facilities of the mind, and the usefulness of phrenology.

PHRENOLOGY MAGAZINE was published by Nathan Allen in October 1838 in Philadelphia, Pa. It was entitled the *American Phrenological Journal and Miscellany* and enjoyed a good circulation until its discontinuance in January 1911. *(William Lewis Montague—Biographies of Recent Alumni of Amherst)*

PHYSICAL CULTURE. *See* Health instruction

PHYSICAL CULTURE DEPARTMENT established by a university on a par with other departments was at the University of Chicago, Chicago, Ill. Amos Alonzo Stagg was made Assistant Professor and Director of the Department of Physical Culture and Athletics and a regular member of the faculty in 1892. In 1901 he was granted a full professorship. Previously, in the East, Midwest, and South, athletics had been under the control of a student athletic association and on the Pacific coast under what is now known as the Associated Students. After the establishment of the department, the coaching of all athletic teams at the University of Chicago was done by members of the department. An Athletic Fund was established with the gate receipts placed in the hands of the comptroller of the university, but disbursed only with the consent of the director of the department.

PHYSICAL EDUCATION PROFESSORSHIP. *See* Hygiene instruction: Hygiene and physical education professorship

PHYSICIAN
See also individual specialties under Medical instruction

American-born doctor who had graduated from a medical school abroad was Dr. William Bull, of Charleston, S.C. He had received his degree from Leyden University, Leyden, Netherlands, on August 18, 1734. The title of his thesis was "Colica pictonum."

Capitol physician was Dr. George Wehnes Calver, a retired rear admiral, who reported for duty at the Capitol, Washington, D.C., on December 8, 1928, in response to a resolution, H.R. 253 of the 70th Congress, passed December 4, 1928, requesting the Secretary of the Navy to detail a medical officer to be in attendance at the sessions of Congress. His title was "the attending physician."

Chinese woman to receive a doctor of medicine degree was Dr. Mary Stone (Shih Mai-yu), who graduated from the Medical School of the University of Michigan, Ann Arbor, Mich., on June 22, 1896. She founded the Women's Hospital at Kiukiang, China, under the auspices of the Methodist Foreign Mission and served as its head for twenty-five years.

Doctor in New England was Dr. Samuel Fuller, one of the signers of the Compact on board the "Mayflower" on November 21, 1620. He arrived December 21, 1620. For some time he was the sole physician in the colony. In a letter dated June 28, 1630, written at Salem, Mass., to Governor William Bradford, he described one of the customary treatments, in which he "let some twenty of these people blood." *(Mayflower Descendants. Vol. 7. 1905)*

Doctor in the colony of Virginia was Lawrence Bohune, who arrived in the first half of 1610. He was the first physician of the London Company. He was killed on March 19, 1622, on board the "Margaret and John" when the vessel was attacked by Spanish ships. *(Wyndham Bolling Blanton—Medicine in Virginia in the 18th Century)*

Doctor to receive a bachelor of medicine degree was John Archer, who graduated with nine others on June 21, 1768, from the University of Pennsylvania, Philadelphia, Pa. His name was the first alphabetically and he was therefore known as the first graduate. Four of these ten graduates returned to the university three years later (1771) and received the degree of doctor of medicine. Three years had to elapse before this M.D. degree could be obtained. At King's College, New York City (now Columbia University), the first M.D. degree was awarded in 1770. This school required only one year to elapse before a student could return and get his M.D. degree. At both schools, the applicant for the higher degree was required to write a thesis in Latin or an inaugural dissertation and defend it satisfactorily before the faculty in order to obtain the degree.

THE FIRST

Doctor to receive a medal from Congress was Frederick Henry Rose of the British Navy. In April 1858, in Jamaica, yellow fever broke out on the U.S.S. "Susquehanna." Rose offered his services and sailed to New York with the stricken crew. On May 11, 1858, Congress authorized a gold medal to be presented to him (11 Stat.L.369) "for kindness and humanity to officers and crew of the U.S.S. 'Susquehanna.'"

Doctor to receive an honorary medical degree was Daniel Turner, who received a degree of honorary doctor of medicine from Yale University, New Haven, Conn., on September 11, 1723, as a reward for valuable monetary contributions to the college. It was awarded by the Reverend Timothy Woodbridge, rector pro tempore. Turner never practiced in America. *(Annals of Medical History. 1919. Vol. 2. No. 4)*

Hindu woman to receive a doctor of medicine degree was Anandibai Joshee, who arrived in the United States on June 4, 1883, and graduated from the Woman's Medical College of Pennsylvania, Philadelphia, Pa., on March 11, 1886, at the age of 21. She returned to her native city, Poona, India, where she died February 26, 1887. *(Pundita Ramabai Sarasvati—The High-Caste Hindu Woman)*

Jewish doctor was Jacob Lumbrozo, who settled in Maryland, January 24, 1656. He was a native of Lisbon, Portugal. He died in May 1666. *(Dr Solomon Robert Kagan— Contributions of American Jews to Medicine)*

Naval doctor. *See* Naval officer: Naval doctor

Naval medical officer. *See* Naval officer: Naval medical officer to write a book

Negro doctor was James Derham of Philadelphia, who settled in New Orleans, La., before 1790. Dr. Benjamin Rush said of him: "I thought I could give him information concerning the treatment of diseases, but I learned more from him than he could expect from me." *(John Andrew Kenney—The Negro in Medicine)*

Negro doctor to become a member of a medical association was Dr. John Vancerlle De Grasse, who was admitted to the Massachusetts Medical Society in 1854. He graduated from Bowdoin and the Hampton Medical College, and practiced in New York City. *(Massachusetts Medical Society—A Catalogue of Its Officers and Fellows)*

Negro woman awarded a medical degree was Rebecca Lee, who received an M.D. degree on March 1, 1864, from the New England

THE FIRST

Female Medical College, Boston, Mass. She completed a seventeen-week course to earn the Doctress of Medicine degree. Prior to May 28, 1856, the College had been known as the Female Medical Education Society. *(Frederick Clayton Waite—History of the New England Female Medical College 1848-1874)*

Ophthalmologist of note was Dr. Edward Delafield, who in 1864 became the first president of the American Ophthalmological Society. In 1818 he formulated a plan to establish the New York Eye Infirmary, which opened in 1820 in two rooms at 45 Chatham Street, treating 436 patients in the first seven months. *(Alvin Allace Hubbell—The Development of Ophthalmology in America)*

Orthopedics chair. *See* Medical instruction: Orthopedics chair

Osteopath (woman) was Jenette Hubbard Bolles, who graduated March 1, 1894, from the American School of Osteopathy, Kirksville, Mo. Two other women who graduated at the same time, Mamie B. Carter and Lou J. Kern, share the distinction.

Osteopathic physician was Dr. Andrew Taylor Still of Macon, Mo., who cured a case of "flux" on June 22, 1874. He was instrumental in founding both a college and a magazine devoted to osteopathy. *(Missouri Historical Review. Vol. 19)*

Pediatrics professor. *See* Medical instruction: Pediatrics professor

Physiologist. *See* Physiologist

Surgeon general (Army). *See* Army officer: Surgeon general

Surgeon general (Navy). *See* Naval officer: Surgeon general of the Navy

Surgeon to substitute radium treatment for surgery for the treatment of cancer was Dr. Robert Abbe, who published his conclusions in the June 1904 *Yale Medical Journal.* He held professorships of surgery in the Women's Medical College and the New York Post Graduate School of New York City. *(City College Alumnus. January 1929)*

Woman appointed "personal physician to the President" was Dr. Janet Graeme Travell (Mrs. John Powell) of New York City, whose appointment was announced January 26, 1961, by President John Fitzgerald Kennedy.

Woman assistant army surgeon. *See* Army officer: Woman assistant army surgeon

PHYSICIAN—*Continued*
Woman doctor commissioned in the regular Army. *See* Army officer: Woman doctor commissioned in the regular Army

Woman physician was Dr. Elizabeth Blackwell, a native of Bristol, England, who came to the United States in her youth and received her M.D. degree from the Medical Institution of Geneva, N.Y., on January 23, 1849, having attended "two full courses of Medical Lectures." On October 20, 1847, the entire medical class decided "that the application of Elizabeth Blackwell to become a member of our class meets our entire approval." The school is now the College of Medicine, Syracuse University. *(Elizabeth Blackwell—Pioneer Work in Opening the Medical Profession to Women)*

Woman physician admitted to the American Institute of Homeopathy. *See* Medical society: Woman physician admitted to the American Institute of Homeopathy

Woman physician elected a member of the American Medical Association. *See* Medical society: Woman physician elected a member of the American Medical Association

Woman physician in the Medical Corps of the U. S. Navy. *See* Naval officer: Woman physician in the Medical Corps Reserve of the U. S. Navy

Woman surgeon was Dr. Mary Harris Thompson, who received her M.D. degree in 1863 from the New England Medical College, Boston, Mass. In May 1865 she founded the Mary Thompson Hospital in Chicago, Ill., to care for widows and children of the poor, to sustain a free dispensary, and to train competent nurses. The hospital had fourteen beds. It was destroyed by fire October 9, 1871, but the patients were removed to another location and operation resumed the same day. The hospital is now the Women's and Children's Hospital, Chicago, Ill.

Woman's infirmary staffed by women physicians. *See* Hospital: Woman's infirmary staffed by women physicians

PHYSICS
Cyclotron, spiral atom smasher, was developed by Professor Ernest Orlando Lawrence, University of California, Berkeley, in 1934, to study the nuclear structure of the atom. A magnetic whirling machine using an 80-ton magnet produced 10-million- to 15-million-volt rays, and sent a stream of high energy bullets from the nuclei of helium gas atoms or alpha particles in the form of a beam of light a foot from the machine. Professor Lawrence was assisted by Dr. Milton Stanley Livingston. *(Wilfred Basil Mann—The Cyclotron)*

National physics association was the American Physical Society for the advancement and diffusion of the knowledge of physics, formed May 20, 1899, at Columbia University, New York City, by physicists from 17 institutions. The first officers were Henry Augustus Rowland, president; Albert Abraham Michelson, vice president; Ernest Merritt, secretary; and William Hallock, treasurer. The first year 59 fellows were admitted.

Positron, a positively charged particle with the same mass and energy as the electron, was recognized in 1934 by Dr. Carl David Anderson at the California Institute of Technology, Pasadena. While working with cosmic rays, he noticed a line which curved in the wrong direction, a trailing vapor in a "cloud expansion chamber." In 1936 Anderson received a Nobel Prize in physics.

Radioactive substance produced synthetically was radium E, made by Dr. John Jacob Livingood of the University of California, Berkeley, on February 4, 1936. Radium E is one of the intermediary products in the slow deterioration of radium. Synthetic radium E was obtained through the bombardment of common inert bismuth with deuterons at an energy of approximately 5½ million volts. Radiobismuth made synthetically is theoretically identical with natural radium E.

PHYSICS NOBEL PRIZE WINNER. *See* Nobel Prize: Nobel Prize in physics

PHYSIOLOGICAL LABORATORY was established in the Sheffield Scientific School at Yale University, New Haven, Conn., in 1874 under the direction of Russell Henry Chittenden. (Two rooms had been set aside in the Harvard Medical School, Boston, Mass., in 1871 for experimental medicine. Dr. Oliver Wendell Holmes was professor of physiology and anatomy.)

PHYSIOLOGICAL RESEARCH LABORATORY OF THE U.S. ARMY AIR CORPS. *See* Aviation: Physiological research laboratory of the U.S. Army Air Corps

PHYSIOLOGICAL SOCIETY
Physiological society was the American Physiological Society, organized February 11, 1837, in Boston, Mass., by 124 men and 39 women who signed the constitution. The object was to acquire and diffuse a knowledge of the laws of life and of the means of promoting human health and longevity. Dues were $1.00 per year. The first monthly meeting was held March 7, 1837. The first officers were William Andrus Alcott, president; David Campbell, corresponding secretary; John Kilton, recording secretary; and Nathaniel Perry,

treasurer. This was a local organization. (*Bulletin of Institute of History of Medicine, October 1937. Vol. 5. No. 8*)

Physiological society (national organization) was the American Physiological Society, organized in New York City on December 30, 1887 with Silas Weir Mitchell of Philadelphia as president and Henry Newell Martin, professor of biology at Johns Hopkins University, as · secretary. Their proceedings, the *American Journal of Physiology,* were first published on January 3, 1898.

PHYSIOLOGIST of note was Dr. William Beaumont, whose *Experiments and Observations on the Gastric Juice and the Physiology of Digestion* was published in 1833 in Plattsburg, N.Y. He achieved fame ·by his treatment of Alexis St. Martin, who was shot in the stomach on June 6, 1822 at Fort Mackinac trading post. Dr. Beaumont was able to watch the digestive process through the aperture in the stomach wall and to find by experiment the effect of different foods and medicines. He found that gastric juices were secreted only when there was food in the stomach and that simple irritation of the mucous membrane would not initiate a flow of gastric juices. (*Jesse Shire Myer—Life and Letters of Dr. William Beaumont*)

PHYSIOLOGY AND HYGIENE COURSE. *See* Hygiene instruction: Physiology and hygiene courses

PHYSIOLOGY AND MEDICINE NOBEL PRIZE WINNER. *See* Nobel Prize: Nobel Prize in medicine and physiology

PHYSIOLOGY MAGAZINE was *The American Journal of Physiology,* 144 pages, the first issue of which was dated February 1898. It was published by Ginn and Company, Boston, Mass.

PIANO
Piano was made by John Harris. It was called a spinet and was described in the *Boston Gazette* of September 18, 1769. It had only three or four octaves and differed from the modern piano in that it had no hammers to strike the strings. Instead, each jack was provided with a little spur of goose-quill which plucked the thin wire, almost as a mandolin player plucks a string with a pick. (*Alfred Dolge—Pianos and Their Makers*)

Piano frame of iron, designed to resist the tremendous tension of the modern piano without allowing the wires to deflect from pitch, was made in 1837 in Boston, Mass., by Jonas

Chickering. (*Richard Green Parker—A Tribute to the Life and Character of Jonas Chickering*)

Piano patent was granted James Sylvanus McLean of New Jersey, on May 27, 1796, for an "improvement in piano fortes."

PIANO PLAYER
Piano player was invented by John McTammany, Jr., of Cambridge, Mass., who filed a caveat September 7, 1876, and received patent No. 242,786 on June 14, 1881, on a "mechanical musical instrument." He constructed a mechanism for automatic playing of organs using narrow sheets of perforated flexible paper which governed the notes to be played.

Piano player (completely automatic) to be manufactured was the Angelus, made by the Wilcox & White Company, Meriden, Conn., in February 1897. It was invented by Edward H. Leveaux of Surrey, England, who obtained a British patent on February 27, 1879, and who filed an application for a U.S. patent on August 29, 1881. U.S. patent No. 247,993 was granted to Leveaux on October 4, 1881, for an "apparatus for storing and transmitting motive power."

Pneumatic piano player that was practical was the "Pianola," invented in 1896 by Edwin S. Votey, of Detroit, Mich., who applied for a patent January 25, 1897; No. 650,285 was granted on May 22, 1900. His original model was larger than the piano to which it was attached. The patent was for an attachment of practical and economical construction which could be applied to and removed from any piano.

PIANO WIRE. *See* Wire: Piano wire

PICK-UP BY AIRPLANE. *See* Aviation: Airplane human pick-up

PIER
Ocean pier was built by Colonel George W. Howard of Washington, D.C., at Atlantic City, N.J., in 1881. It was known as Howard's Pier and extended 650 feet seaward from the foot of Kentucky Avenue. On July 12, 1882, it was finally completed. It was destroyed in September 1882 by a severe storm and was rebuilt to 865 feet, but was again destroyed and washed away by a severe storm on January 9, 1884.

Ocean pier of steel was erected at Atlantic City, N.J. It was half a mile long, devoted exclusively to amusements, and was opened to the public on June 18, 1898. It was owned by the Atlantic Steel Pier Company, of which Kennedy Crossan was president. The pier was designed by Frank A. Souder and built by John T. Windram, architect.

"PIGGY-BACK" RAILROAD OPERA-TION. *See* Railroad: "Piggy-back" railroad operation

PILE BRIDGE. *See* Bridge: Pile bridge

PILE DRIVER
Pile driver was patented March 10, 1791, by John Stone of Concord, Mass., who obtained his patent on "driving pile for bridges."

Steam pile driver patent was No. 5,172 awarded June 26, 1847, by the U.S. Patent Office to James Nasmyth of Patricroft, England, on a "steam pile driver."

PILL
Compressed pills or tablets commercially manufactured, were made in 1863-1864 by Jacob Dunton, a wholesale druggist of Philadelphia, Pa., who employed a machine in their manufacture. The formulas that were sold in tablet form consisted principally of simple chemicals such as potassium chlorate, ammonium chloride, etc. Dunton sold his products to dispensing druggists and did not attempt to market them under his own name until 1869. His entire production from 1869 to 1876 was less than that now made daily in the laboratories of this country. *(Journal of the American Pharmaceutical Association. 1914. p. 820)*

Patented pills were introduced in 1796 by Samuel Lee, Jr., of Conn., and known as Lee's Windham Pills and Lee's New London Bilious Pills. On April 30, 1796, he obtained a patent on a "composition of bilious pills."

PILOT (automatic). *See* Aviation: Automatic pilot

PILOT LICENSE. *See* Aviation—License: Pilot's license

PILOT TO RECEIVE THE CONGRESSIONAL MEDAL OF HONOR. *See* Aviation—Aviator: Pilot to receive the Congressional Medal of Honor

PIN
Machine for manufacturing pins that was practical was invented by John Ireland Howe of Derby, Conn., who obtained a patent on it June 22, 1832. The machine was exhibited at the American Institute Fair in New York, and Howe received a silver medal for his contribution to manufacturing. In December 1835, he formed the Howe Manufacturing Company, New York City. He obtained patent No. 2,013 on March 24, 1841, for an improved model.

Machine "for sticking pins into paper" was patented September 30, 1841, No. 2,275, by Samuel Slocum of Poughkeepsie, N.Y. A sliding hopper deposited the pins in grooves.

Pins manufactured with a solid head were made in 1838 by Samuel Slocum of Rhode Island, who invented the machine to manufacture them. He did not obtain a patent on it. One man tending two machines could produce 100,000 pins in eleven hours. He formed the firm of Slocum, Jilson & Company, Poughkeepsie, N.Y., in 1839. His products were known as "Poughkeepsie pins." *(Journal of American Institute—June 1839)*

Safety pin was invented by Walter Hunt of New York City who obtained patent No. 6,281, April 10, 1849. Within the short period of three hours, he conceived the idea, made a model, and sold his patent rights for $100. The pins were manufactured in New York City.

PINBALL GAME
Pinball game machine was the "Whoopee Game," manufactured in 1930 by In & Outdoor Games Company, Chicago, Ill. It was 24 inches wide, 48 inches long, and had adjustable legs. It sold for $175. The fee for playing was five cents for ten balls. The game was modeled after the children's game known as "Bagatelle."

Pinball game machine (toy) was the Caille "Log Tavern" built in 1910 by Adolph Caille of Caille Brothers Company, Detroit, Mich. The machine, which was placed flat on a table, had a slightly inclined board with pins on it. Marbles were shot up the board through an alley to top position, and would then roll down into scoring positions.

Pinball legislation enacted by a major city prohibiting the machines was the ordinance, approved June 19, 1939, by Atlanta, Ga., entitled "an ordinance to prohibit the operation of pin ball machines and similar machines in the city of Atlanta," signed by Mayor William Berry Hartsfield. The act, effective July 1, 1939, provided that any person convicted of a violation of this ordinance be subject to a fine not to exceed $20 and a sentence to the public works of the city for a period of thirty days, any part of either one or both at the discretion of the recorder.

"PINCH HITTER." *See* Baseball player: Baseball "pinch hitter"

PINE PAPER NEWSPAPER. *See* Newspaper: Newspaper printed on pine-pulp paper

PINEAPPLE CHEESE. *See* Cheese: Pineapple cheese

PINNACE. *See* Ship

PIPE

Corncob pipe commercial manufacture was undertaken in 1869 by Henry Tibbe of Washington, Mo., who used plaster of paris to fill uneven surfaces in the pipe. He obtained patent No. 205,816 on July 9, 1878 on a "smoking pipe made of corn-cob, in which the interstices are filled with a plastic self-hardening cement."

PIPELESS ORGAN. *See* Organ: Pipeless organ

PIPELINE

Pipeline (gas). *See* Gas: Pipeline (long distance)

Pipeline (interstate) to transport ethylene, a petroleum chemical used in the manufacture of plastics and synthetic rubber, was constructed between Lake Charles, La., and Orange, Tex., a distance of 30 miles, and placed in operation September 6, 1958. This 6⅝-inch pipeline transported ethylene to the E. I. du Pont de Nemours & Company plant at Orange, on September 6, 1958, and to the Spencer Chemical Company, also at Orange, on September 9, 1958.

Pipeline (oil). *See* Oil: Oil pipeline of importance

PIRATE
on the Atlantic seaboard was Dixie Bull, who looted Bristol, Me., in 1632. Previously, he had received a grant of land at York, Me. In June 1632, while Bull was in Penobscot Bay, a French pinnace arrived and seized his shallop and stock of "coats, ruggs, blanketts, bisketts, etc." Angered at this, he revenged himself by in turn becoming a pirate.

PISTOL

Government contract for pistols was authorized May 4, 1798, when Congress appropriated $800,000 for guns, pistols, etc. The first contract was made March 9, 1799, with Simeon North, Berlin, Conn., for 500 horse pistols at $6.50 each. A second contract for 1,500 additional pistols of the same type was signed February 6, 1880. *(Simeon Newton Dexter North—Simeon North, First Official Pistol Maker of the United States)*

Pistol with a revolving barrel was invented in 1830 by Samuel Colt while on the S.S. "Corlo." With a pocket knife he whittled a wood model. He obtained a patent from England in 1835 and patent No. 138 from the United States on February 25, 1836, on "an improvement in revolving fire-arms." He formed the Patent Arms Manufacturing Company of Paterson, N.J., capitalized at $230,000, which

was incorporated March 5, 1836. The first revolvers commercially manufactured were .34-caliber Texas models.

Revolver that was self-cocking was the "Rider model," which was invented by John Rider and manufactured in 1856 by E. Remington and Sons of Ilion, N.Y.

PISTOL SHOOTING TOURNAMENT (international). *See* Revolver shooting tournament (international)

PISTON AUTOMOBILE. *See* Automobile: Free piston automobile

PITCHER (baseball). *See* Baseball player: Baseball pitcher

PITUITARY HORMONE

Pituitary hormone isolated in chemically pure crystalline form was announced July 23, 1937 in *Science* by Drs. Abraham White, Hubert Ralph Catchpole and Cyril Norman Hugh Long of the Laboratories of Physiological Chemistry and Physiology, Yale University School of Medicine, New Haven, Conn.

Polypeptide hormone synthesized was oxytocin, a protein-like compound made up of eight amino acids which stimulates uterine contractions and starts the flow of milk. Dr. Vincent du Vigneaud, biochemist, Cornell University Medical College, New York City, and his co-workers isolated oxytocin and synthetically reproduced the hormone. The announcement of the synthesis was made in the fall of 1953. On November 2, 1955, Dr. du Vigneaud was awarded the Nobel Prize in chemistry for this and other work on the chemistry and metabolism of sulfur compounds.

PLAGUE. *See* Epidemic

PLANET. *See* Astronomy: Planet

PLANET (photographed in moving pictures). *See* Moving picture: Moving picture of the planets

PLANETARIUM
See also Observatory

Planetarium open to the public was the Adler Planetarium and Astronomical Museum, presented to the city of Chicago by Max Adler, at a cost of $1,000,000. Under the direction of Professor Philip Fox, the museum was opened to the public on May 10, 1930. The planetarium is a complex instrument for reproducing on an elaborate scale the planets of the solar system

THE FIRST

PLANETARIUM—*Continued*
and the 5,400 stars visible to man. *(Philip Fox— Adler Planetarium and Astronautical Museum; an Account of the Optical Planetarium and a Brief Guide to the Museum)*

Planetarium or orrery was imported from England in 1732 and was presented by Thomas Hollis to Harvard College, Cambridge, Mass. It was built by Joseph Page and was "a very costly orrery, an instrument that this, or any other part of America, as far as we can learn, has never before been favored with." *(Boston News-Letter. September 14, 1732)*

Planetarium or orrery built in America to represent the motion of the celestial bodies was constructed in 1743 by Thomas Clap, president of Yale College, New Haven, Conn. In the center was a globe 3 inches in diameter, from which 12 wooden arms about 7 feet long extended. The sun, planets, satellites, etc., were represented. The orrery was operated by hand as it had no gear work. *(American Magazine and Historical Chronicle. January 1744)*

Planetarium owned by a university was the Morehead Planetarium, University of North Carolina, Chapel Hill, opened May 10, 1949. It was the gift of John Motley Morehead. The first director was Dr. Roy Kenneth Marshall.

PLANK ROAD. *See* Road: Plank road

PLANNING BOARD (U.S.). *See* National planning board (U.S.)

PLANT PATENT. *See* Patent: Plant patent

PLANT QUARANTINE. *See* Quarantine: Plant quarantine legislation

PLASTER (adhesive and medicated). *See* Adhesive and medicated plaster

PLASTIC
Expandable polystyrene production (commercial) was undertaken by the Koppers Company, Kobuta, Pa., in 1954, with 17 tons valued at $20,000. Full production was not attempted until April 1958. Polystyrene is produced in small beads, which when heated in molds expand to take the shape of the enclosure.

Thermosetting man-made plastic was developed in 1906 by Dr. Leo Hendrik Baekeland of Yonkers, N.Y., who succeeded in controlling the reaction of phenol and formaldehyde. This reaction was explained in patent No. 942,699, granted December 7, 1909, on "an improvement in methods of making insoluble condensation products of phenol-formaldehyde," commonly referred to as the "heat and pressure" patent.

THE FIRST

PLASTIC AIRPLANE. *See* Aviation—Airplane: Plastic bonded airplane

PLASTIC AUTOMOBILE. *See* Automobile: Plastic laminated fiberglas body sports car

PLASTIC CARPETING. *See* Carpeting: Carpeting of tufted plastic

PLASTIC GLIDER. *See* Glider: Glider (all plywood-plastic)

PLASTIC LENS. *See* Lens: Plastic lens

PLASTIC LICENSE PLATE. *See* Automobile license plates: Plastic license plate tabs

PLASTIC SURGERY PROFESSOR. *See* Medical instruction: Plastic surgery professor

"PLATE FULCRUM" RAILWAY TRACK SCALE. *See* Scale: Platform scale

PLATE GLASS. *See* Glass: Plate glass

PLATE GLASS INSURANCE. *See* Insurance: Plate glass insurance

PLATFORM (national political party). *See* Political platform (national)

PLATFORM ELEVATOR. *See* Elevator: Elevator

PLATFORM SCALE. *See* Scale: Platform scale

PLATINUM MEDAL. *See* Medal: Platinum medal

PLATOON SCHOOL was the Central School, Bluffton, Ind., established September 1899, under the direction of William Wirt. The curriculum was arranged so that specific time was allotted to study, work, and play. In September 1902, the system was extended to the three elementary schools in the city. *(Roscoe David Case—The Platoon School in America)*

PLATYPUS. *See* Aquatic mammals: Platypus (duck-billed)

PLAY (drama)
See also Theater

Anti-vivisection play, *Woven Dreams,* written by Nina Halvey, winner of the Inter-

THE FIRST

national Humanitarian prize of 1931, was presented October 4, 1932, in Philadelphia, Pa., under the auspices of the American Anti-Vivisection Society.

Aquatic play was *The Pirate's Signal, or The Bridge of Death,* presented July 4, 1840, at the Bowery Theatre, New York City. At the end of the fifth act, at the upper entrance of the stage, a full rigged ship floated on water down to the footlights, turned and went up the stage and off at the upper entrance. *(Thomas Allston Brown—A History of the New York Stage)*

Benefit performance was given January 7, 1751, at the Theatre on Nassau Street, New York City, for Walter Murray, one of the managers. It was advertised in the December 31, 1750, issue of the *Weekly Post-Boy:* "By his Excellency's Permission (for the benefit of Mr. Murray). On Monday, the seventh of January, will be performed, a comedy, called, 'A Bold Stroke For A Wife,' (being the last time of its being perform'd this season) to which will be added, an Entertainment called 'The Devil To Pay, Or, The Wives Metamorphos'd' . . ."

Broadway play telecast. *See* Television—Telecast: Play to be televised with its original Broadway cast

Burlesque show of importance was *The Black Crook,* an original magical and spectacular drama in four acts by Charles M. Barras, with the scene laid in and around the Hartz Mountains about 1600. It opened September 12, 1866, at Niblo's Garden, New York City, with the "Great Parisienne Ballet Troupe." Betty Regal of the Grand Opera, Paris, was the prima donna and soloist. It closed January 4, 1868, after playing 475 performances and grossing $1,300,000. *(Arthur Hornblow—A History of the Theatre in America)*

Chinese theatrical performance in America was offered by the Tong Hook Tong Dramatic Company under the management of Mr. Li-keoon, Norman Assing and Tong Chick at the American Theatre, Sansome Street, San Francisco, Calif., on October 18, 1852. The company consisted of 123 performers and musicians who were shareholders in the theatrical enterprise. The performance consisted of (1) "The Eight Genii Offering Their Congratulations to the High Ruler Yuk Hwang on His Birthday," (2) "Too Tsin Made High Minister by the Six States," (3) "Parting at the Bridge of Parkew of Kwan Wanchang and Tsow," and (4) "Defeated Revenge."

Drama broadcast. *See* Radio broadcast: Drama broadcast

THE FIRST

Drama (full length melodrama) broadcast. *See* Radio broadcast: Drama (full length melodrama) broadcast

Drama to win a Pulitzer prize was Jesse Lynch Williams' *Why Marry?,* a three-act comedy produced by Selwyn & Co., which opened December 25, 1917, at the Astor Theatre, New York City. It starred Nat C. Goodwin as Uncle Everett, Lotus Robb as Jean, Edmund Breese as John, and Harold West as Rex. It was originally written as a novel in 1914 entitled *And So They Were Married.* The Pulitzer award was announced June 3, 1918, by President Nicholas Murray Butler, president of Columbia University.

Greek play produced in Greek was *Oedipus Tyrannus* by Sophocles. It was presented at Harvard University, Cambridge, Mass., in May 1881. George Riddle played the part of Oedipus.

Hebrew professional acting troupe was the Hebrew Opera and Dramatic Company, which gave performances at the Bowery Garten Theater, 113 Broadway, New York City. An advertisement of August 12, 1882, stated that a performance would be given for the benefit of ten poor Russian immigrant families. *Die Hexe* was presented, the part of the eighty-year-old witch being taken by the seventeen-year-old comic Leon Golubok. *(George Clinton Densmore Odell—Annals of the New York Stage. Vol. 11)*

Musical comedy broadcast. *See* Radio broadcast: Musical comedy broadcast

Musical play to win a Pulitzer prize was the two-act comedy *Of Thee I Sing,* by George Simon Kaufman, Morrie Ryskind, George Gershwin, and Ira Gershwin, awarded a Pulitzer prize on May 2, 1932. It was produced by Sam H. Harris at the Music Box Theatre, New York City, on December 26, 1931, and starred Victor Moore as Alexander Throttlebottom and William Gaxton as John P. Wintergreen. It played for 441 performances.

Native American play successfully acted on a regular stage by an established company was Royall Tyler's *The Contrast,* in five acts, produced April 16, 1787, at the John Street Theatre, New York City, by the American Company under the management of [Lewis] Hallam and [John] Henry. It depicted the contrast between meretricious standards of the fashionable world and simple, straightforward ideals of the true American. The play was published in 1790 for Thomas Wignell in Philadelphia, Pa., by Prichard & Hall. *(Dramatic Magazine. May 1880)*

PLAY (drama)—*Continued*
Play about an Indian written by an American was James Nelson Barker's *The Indian Princess, or La Belle Sauvage,* a three-act operatic melodrama, based on Captain John Smith's *General History of Virginia,* which was produced April 6, 1808, at the Chestnut Street Theatre, Philadelphia, Pa. *(Democratic Press. April 5, 1808)*

Play acted by professional players was given at the New Theatre, December 6, 1732 in New York City. It was George Farquhar's *The Recruiting Officer. (Arthur Hornblow— A History of the American Theatre)*

Play given by non-professional actors was *Ye Bare and Ye Cubb,* by Philip Alexander Bruce, performed August 27, 1665, at Accawmack, Va. The actors, Cornelius Watkinson, Philip Howard, and William Darby were summoned to appear in court on November 16, 1665, "in those habilements that they then acted in and give a draught of such verses or other speeches and passages which were then acted by them." They were found not guilty of sedition and Edward Martin "who had informed on them" was ordered "to pay all the expenses of the presentment." *(Jennings Cropper Wise— Ye Kingdome of Accawmack)*

Play of note written by an American and acted in America was *Gustavus Vasa,* a tragedy by Benjamin Colman. Harvard students gave a performance of it in 1690 in Cambridge, Mass. *(Oscar Wegelin—Early American Plays)*

Play performed 1,000 times was *The Gladiator,* a five-act blank verse tragedy set in Rome and other parts of Italy about 73 B.C. It was written by Dr. Robert Montgomery Bird and was first performed September 26, 1831, at the Park Theatre, New York City, with Edwin Forrest as Spartacus. By 1853, it had been performed 1,000 times. *(Clement Edgar Foust—The Life and Dramatic Works of Robert Montgomery Bird)*

Play televised. *See* Television—Telecast: Play to be televised

Printed American play was Governor Robert Hunter's *Androboros,* a biographical ("biographical") farce in three acts, "viz, the senate, the consistory and the apotheosis," printed in 1714 by William Bradford in New York City ("Monoropolis"). The work consisted of three preliminary leaves, 27 pages, quarto size. "Androboros" means "man-eater" and "Monoropolis" means "Fool's town (otherwise, New York City)." *(Frank Pierce Hill— American Plays Printed 1714-1830)*

Puppet show. *See* Puppet show

Puppet show televised. *See* Television—Telecast: Puppet show to be televised

Shakespearean play given in America is supposed to have been *King Richard III,* which was presented at the Nassau Street Theatre, New York City on March 5, 1750, by Walter Murray and Thomas Kean. The play was "altered" by Colley Cibber. The performance began at 6:30 P.M. Admission to the pit was 5 shillings and to the gallery 3 shillings.

Theatrical presentation sponsored by the federal government was *The Family Upstairs,* produced January 30, 1934, by a cast of players operating under the Civil Works Administration at the Central School of Business and Arts, New York City. An appropriation of $28,000 for wages only was made January 12, 1934. The project was under the direction of Margaret Smith. Other plays were also presented later the same day. By March 25, 1934, 864,000 persons had witnessed 576 performances of 17 plays in 107 schools, clubs, and museums.

Vaudeville show. *See* Vaudeville

Wild West show. *See* Wild West show

PLAYER PIANO. *See* Piano player: Piano player

PLAYGROUND for children was erected in Boston, Mass., in 1886 in the yard of the Children's Mission. "Three piles of yellow sand" were brought there. The first Boston school appropriation for playgrounds was made in 1899.

PLAYOFF BASEBALL SERIES. *See* Baseball game: Baseball playoff series

PLAYWRIGHT (professional) was William Dunlap, who wrote or adapted sixty-three dramatic pieces. His first comedy, *Modest Soldier, or Love in New York* was written in a few weeks in 1787. Five years previously, Dunlap had written *The History of The American Theatre. (William Dunlap—The Diary of William Dunlap)*

PLOW
Cast steel for plows. *See* Steel: Cast steel for plows

Plow for pulverizing the soil was patented by George Page of Washington, D.C., who received patent No. 5,218 on August 7, 1847. Page designed a revolving single disk on the side of a peculiar form of plow. *(Robert L. Ardrey—American Agricultural Implements)*

THE FIRST

Plow patent was granted June 26, 1797, to Charles Newbold, a farmer of Burlington County, N.J. This plow was the first cast-iron plow to be used. It was of solid cast-iron (excepting handles and beam) and consisted of a bar, sheath, and moldplate. The invention did not meet with great success as farmers believed that the iron poisoned the land, reduced fertility, and promoted the growth of weeds, and that the point would soon wear off. *(Agriculture of the United States in 1860—U.S. Census Office)*

Plow with interchangeable parts was patented by John Jethro Wood of Poplar Ridge, N.Y., September 1, 1819. His plow substituted cast-iron for the wooden moldboard, landside, and standard. In this it was similar to the plow which had been patented in 1797 by Charles Newbold. *(Robert L. Ardrey—American Agricultural Implements)*

Submarine cable plow was patented January 12, 1937, by Chester S. Lawton of Ridgewood, N.J., and Captain Melville H. Bloomer of Halifax, Nova Scotia, Canada, who obtained patent No. 2,607,717, which they assigned to the Western Union Telegraph Company. The plow digs a trench in the bed of the ocean and simultaneously feeds cable into the furrow. The plow can be used in depths as great as half a mile. The first transatlantic cable of a high-speed permalloy was buried June 14, 1938.

PLUG (electric). *See* Electric attachment plug

PLUMBING
State plumbing legislation, enacted May 30, 1881, by Illinois, was "an act for the regulation and inspection of tenement and lodging houses or other places of habitation." In cities of 50,000 population, plumbers were required to receive a written certificate of instruction from the commissioner or commissioners before commencing work on buildings and to proceed according to plan. Violations were punishable by a fine of not less than $100 for the first offense and $10 a day for non-compliance.

PLUTONIUM. *See* Element: Element 94

PLUTONIUM PRODUCTION BY AN ATOMIC REACTOR. *See* Atomic reactor: Atomic reactor to produce plutonium

PLYWOOD
Douglas fir plywood commercial production was undertaken by the Portland Manufacturing Company, Portland, Ore., in 1905 at St. Johns, Ore. Plywood contains an odd number of veneer sheets bonded together, with the grain of each at right angles to the one above

THE FIRST

and below. Laminated sheets, all having the grain in the same direction, had been made earlier.

PLYWOOD AIRPLANE (molded). *See* Aviation—Airplane: Molded plywood airplane

PLYWOOD GLIDER. *See* Glider: Glider (all plywood-plastic)

PNEUMATIC HAMMER. *See* Hammer (pneumatic)

PNEUMATIC PLAYER PIANO. *See* Piano player: Pneumatic piano player

PNEUMATIC SUBWAY. *See* Subway: Pneumatic subway

PNEUMATIC TIRE. *See* Automobile tire: Pneumatic tire; Bicycle tire: Bicycle tire (pneumatic)

POCKET DICTIONARY. *See* Dictionary: Pocket dictionary

PODIATRIST. *See* Chiropodist

POEM by an American to receive recognition at home and abroad was "Thanatopsis," written in 1810 by William Cullen Bryant. Washington Irving received recognition as the first American author. In both cases, the contemporaries were many, but the fame rests with these two men. This subject is one of constant dispute with those who prefer other authors. *(Parke Godwin—A Biography of William Cullen Bryant)*

POET
See also Author

American poet recognized as such was Benjamin Tompson. He graduated from Harvard College, Cambridge, Mass., in 1662 and produced many poems. His principal work, the first collection of American poems published in America, was *New Englands Crisis, or a Brief Narrative of New Englands Lamentable Estate at present, compar'd with the former (but few) years of Prosperity. Occasioned by many unheard of Crueltyes practised upon the Persons and Estates of its united Colonyes, without respect of Sex, Age or Quality of Persons, by the Barbarous Heathen thereof.* This work, a 31-page book of poems about King Philip's War, was published in 1676 in Boston, Mass. It was printed and sold by John Foster. Tompson's selection of subject matter was of greater importance than his literary style. *(Howard Judson Hall—Benjamin Tompson—His Poems)*

THE FIRST

THE FIRST

POET—*Continued*

Negro poet to be employed to teach creative writing by a Negro university was James Weldon Johnson, author of *God's Trombones, The Book of American Negro Spirituals,* etc. He was appointed in January 1932 by Fisk University, Nashville, Tenn., to the Adam K. Spence Chair of Creative Literature and Writing, founded in memory of a Fisk professor who had taught those subjects. *(James Weldon Johnson—Along This Way, the Autobiography of James Weldon Johnson)*

Negro poetess was Phillis Wheatley (Phillis Peters), born 1753, whose first poem was published in 1770. Her first book was published in London in 1773 and dedicated to the Countess of Huntingdon. *(Charles Fred Heartman—Phillis Wheatley (Phillis Peters) Poems and Letters)*

POETRY ANTHOLOGY. *See* Anthology (American)

POETRY BOOK. *See* Book: Profane poetry translation prepared in the colonies to be published

POETRY COLLECTION BY AN AMERICAN. *See* Poet: American poet

POET'S MONUMENT. *See* Monument: Monument to an American poet

POLAR EXPEDITION. *See* Expedition: Arctic expedition

POLARIS MISSILE. *See* Ship: Ship to fire a Polaris missile

POLE VAULTER

Pole vault jump indoors over 16 feet was made February 2, 1962, by John Uelses, a Marine corporal, at the Millrose games, New York City. Uelses cleared the bar at 16 feet and ¼ inch. The next night, at the Boston Athletic Association games, Boston, Mass., he exceeded his record by ½ inch.

Pole vaulter to clear the bar at 15 feet, Cornelius Warmerdam of the San Francisco Olympic Club, established this record on April 13, 1940, in Berkeley, Calif. In 33 meets, 8 indoors and 25 outdoors, he duplicated or bettered this mark 43 times from 1940 through 1944.

POLICE

See also Border patrol; Fingerprinting; Secret Service

Police bureau of criminal alien investigation was started by the New York City Police Department December 23, 1930. The purpose was to bring to the attention of the United States Immigration authorities the undesirable aliens who are subject to deportation under the Immigration Law, either because of their criminal records or their illegal entry into the United States. *(Spring 3100. New York Police Department Magazine. April 1932)*

Police bureau of identification was established by Captain Michael Patrick Evans on January 1, 1884, for the Chicago Police Department. At its inception, only photographs were used. On June 1, 1887, the Bertillon system of identification was adopted and on November 1, 1904, the Sir E. R. Henry system of fingerprinting was added. Evans was in charge of the Bureau of Identification from the time of its organization until the time of his death, October 6, 1931.

Police car radio. *See* Radio broadcast: Radio police system (two-way three-way)

Police department to adopt the fingerprinting system. *See* Fingerprinting: Police department to adopt the fingerprinting system

Police patrol wagon (automobile). *See* Automobile police patrol wagon

Police training school of the Federal Bureau of Investigation, U.S. Department of Justice, was initiated on July 29, 1935. The courses, similar to those given in the training school for newly appointed special agents of the Bureau, provide a program of training for local and state law enforcement officials and include subjects under the following headings: Scientific and technical; Statistics, records and report writing; Firearms training and first aid; Investigations, enforcement and regulatory procedure; Police administration and organization. The course of training lasts for a period of twelve weeks and is given without cost to those enrolled. The first class consisted of twenty-three representatives of local and state law enforcement agencies.

Police uniforms were authorized by the Common Council of New York, July 8, 1693, which ordered that the mayor should provide the police "with a coat of ye citty livery, with a badge of ye citty arms, shoes and stockings, and charge it to ye account of the city." *(Augustine E. Costello—Our Police Protectors)*

Policewoman on the aerial force was Cora Sterling, who was given a special commission as Seattle's first aerial policewoman by Mayor Charles Louis Smith. Her appointment to the aerial force was made July 13, 1934, and the commission by the Seattle Police Force was given in December 1934. She was only twenty years old and the holder of a Transport License.

THE FIRST

THE FIRST

Policewoman to be appointed was Marie Owen, a patrolman's widow. In 1893 she was appointed to the Detroit Bureau of Police by Morgan A. Collins, Superintendent of Police.

Prohibition enforcement officer. *See* Prohibition: Prohibition enforcement officers

Radio system (police). *See* Radio broadcast: Radio police system (two-way three-way)

State police were the Texas Rangers, who were authorized by the General Council of the Provisional Government of Texas to organize three Ranger companies in 1835. On November 9, 1835, G. W. Davis was commissioned to raise twenty more men for this new service. *(Walter Prescott Webb—Texas Rangers)*

Traffic police squad was the famous old "Broadway Squad" of New York City, organized in 1860. This was the first unit of the Police Department to have special functions in the field of traffic regulation. The members of the squad were stationed on the sidewalks along Broadway, from Bowling Green to 59th Street, at the intersections of the cross streets. It was their purpose to escort pedestrians across the streets and to stop traffic while so doing. The pavement of Broadway was of cobble stones and most of the traffic consisted of slow-moving horse-drawn vehicles.

Woman chief of police was Dolly Spencer, who was appointed in 1914 by the Mayor of Milford, Ohio.

Woman detective was Isabella Goodwin, who was appointed as acting detective sergeant, first grade, on March 1, 1912, by the police department of New York City. She had served as a police matron since May 15, 1896. On October 31, 1924, she retired.

POLIOMYELITIS EPIDEMIC. *See* Epidemic: Poliomyelitis epidemic

POLIOMYELITIS VACCINE. *See* Vaccine: Poliomyelitis vaccine

POLITICAL CONVENTION
National committee of a political organization was formed May 22, 1848, at the Democratic convention held May 22-26, in Baltimore, Md. At the convention, Lewis Cass of Michigan was nominated for President and William Orlando Butler of Kentucky for Vice President. They received 1,220,544 popular votes (127 electoral votes). The Whig party candidates, Zachary Taylor and Millard Fillmore, were elected (1,360,099 popular votes, 163 electoral votes).

National nominating convention presided over by a Negro, held by a major political party, met in the Exposition Building, Chicago, Ill., on June 3, 1884. John Roy Lynch, a Negro, three times congressman from Mississippi, was nominated for temporary chairman of the Republican party by Henry Cabot Lodge. The nomination was supported by Theodore Roosevelt and George William Curtis, and was carried by a vote of 424 for Lynch to 384 for Powell Clayton. John Brooks Henderson was the permanent chairman. The convention nominated James Gillespie Blaine for President and General John Alexander Logan for Vice President. *(Proceedings of the Eighth Republican National Convention Held at Chicago, Ill., June 3, 4, 5 and 6, 1884)*

Negro delegate to a national political convention was Frederick Douglass of Rochester, N.Y., who attended the National Loyalists' Loyal Union convention at Philadelphia, Pa., on September 6, 1866. He paired with Theodore Tilton of New York City in the street parade. *(Frederick Douglass—Life and Times of Frederick Douglass)*

Nominating convention (state) assembled at Utica, N.Y., in 1824 for the purpose of nominating candidates for governor and lieutenant governor. The number of delegates corresponded with the number of representatives in the assembly. De Witt Clinton was nominated by the Democratic-Republican party and was elected November 3, 1824. He served as governor from January 1, 1825 to February 11, 1828, when he died. He had previously served as governor from January 1, 1818 to December 31, 1822.

Political convention broadcast. *See* Radio broadcast: Political convention broadcast

Political convention telecast. *See* Television—Telecast: Political convention to be televised

Political nominating caucus was held by the Democratic-Republican Party in New York City on September 15-16, 1812. President James Madison was nominated for a second term, and Elbridge Gerry of Massachusetts was nominated for the vice presidency, the latter office being vacant as a result of the death of George Clinton of New York. The Federalists nominated De Witt Clinton of New York and Jared Ingersoll of Pennsylvania. In the election, Madison received 128 electoral votes against 89 for Clinton and was elected President. Gerry received 131 electoral votes against 86 for Ingersoll. The votes were counted February 10, 1813.

Political nominating caucus attended by party leaders to designate presidential candi-

POLITICAL CONVENTION—*Continued*
dates was held February 25, 1804, by the
Democratic-Republicans in Washington, D.C.
Thomas Jefferson of Virginia was nominated
for a second term as President and George
Clinton of New York was nominated to serve
as Vice President. The Federalists did not
hold a caucus but supported Charles Cotesworth Pinckney of South Carolina for President and Rufus King of New York for Vice
President. In 1800, certain leaders met in
secret session.

**Presidential candidate to fly to a political
convention.** *See* Presidential candidate:
Presidential candidate to fly to a political
convention

**Presidential candidate to make a speech
of acceptance at a nominating convention.**
See Political convention: Presidential candidate to make a speech of acceptance at a
nominating convention

**Presidential convention (national) ad-
dressed by a woman** was the Republican National Convention in Cincinnati, Ohio, at
which Sara Andrews Spencer spoke on June 15, 1876,
against the disfranchisement of women and
presented a memorial of the National Woman
Suffrage Association stating "that the right
to use the ballot inheres in the citizens of the
United States."

Two-thirds rule, requiring a candidate for
nomination to receive two thirds of the votes of
the delegates, was adopted by the Democratic-
Republican Convention, May 21-22, 1832, at
the Athenaeum, Baltimore, Md. Robert Lucas
of Ohio was chairman of the convention, which
nominated Andrew Jackson for President and
Martin Van Buren for Vice President. It was
resolved "that the delegates from each state be
entitled to as many votes in the selection of the
candidates for the office of Vice President of
the United States as such state may be entitled
to in the Electoral College for the choice of
this officer equally to the apportionment bill,
recently passed by Congress; and that two
thirds of the whole number of the votes given
be required for a nomination, and on all questions therewith." *(Proceedings of a Convention of Republican Delegates from the several
states in the Union, for the purpose of nominating a candidate for the office of the Vice
President of the United States)*

Unit rule was adopted by the Whig Convention at Harrisburg, Pa., December 4, 1839.
The state delegates selected a committee of
three from their membership which was to assemble with other committees from other states
similarly selected to form a Committee of the
Whole. The state delegates meeting separately
gave instructions to the members of their committee, who later voted as a unit in the Com-

mittee of the Whole. At the 1840 convention,
the first at which the unit rule was applied,
the final vote for presidential nominee was 148
for William Henry Harrison of Ohio, 90 votes
for Henry Clay, and 16 votes for Winfield
Scott. John Tyler of Virginia was nominated
for Vice President. *(Joseph Bucklin Bishop—
Presidential Nominations and Elections)*

POLITICAL ECONOMY COURSE
College chair of political economy was established at Columbia College, New York City,
in 1818. Professor John McVickar occupied
the chair of Moral Philosophy and Political
Economy from 1818 to 1825.

Political economy chair, exclusively devoted to that subject, was established at Harvard University, Cambridge, Mass., in 1871.
The first professor was Charles Franklin
Dunbar.

Political economy course was given at the
College of William and Mary of Williamsburg,
Va., in 1784.

POLITICAL HISTORY. *See* History:
Political history

POLITICAL MACHINE that was well organized was the Albany Regency, made up of a
group of Democrats who, from 1820 to 1854,
exercised a controlling influence over the politics of New York State. Their headquarters
were in Albany, N.Y., but their power extended
into national politics. Prominent among them
were Martin Van Buren, William Learned
Marcy, Silas Wright, and John Adams Dix.

POLITICAL NEWSPAPER. *See* Newspaper: Political newspaper

POLITICAL NOMINATING CAUCUS.
See Political convention: Political nominating caucus

POLITICAL PARTIES. *See*

American Party	Equal Rights
Anti-Masonic	Party
Party	Farmer Labor
Anti-Monopoly	Party
Party	Free Soil Party
Anti-Slavery	Greenback Labor
Party	Party
Communist Labor	Greenback Party
Party of Amer-	Labor Party
ica	Liberal Republi-
Communist Party	can Party
of America	National Union
Constitutional	for Social Justice
Union Party	People's Party
Democratic Na-	Progressive Party
tional Conven-	Prohibition Party
tion	Quids

THE FIRST

Republican Party	Socialist Party
Silverites	Union Labor
Single Tax	Party
Social Democracy	Union Party
of America	Union Reform
Party	Party
Social-Democratic	United Christian
Party of	Party
America	United Labor
Socialist Labor	Party
Party of North	Whig Party
America	

POLITICAL PLATFORM (national) was adopted May 11, 1832, by a group of 295 Democratic-Republican delegates from sixteen states and the District of Columbia who assembled in Washington, D.C., and drew up a list of resolutions for a platform. At the convention, on December 12, 1831, in Baltimore, Md., Henry Clay was nominated for President and John Sergeant for Vice President. *(Proceedings of National Republican Convention of Young Men Assembled May 7, 1832 at Washington, D.C.)*

POLITICAL SCIENCE SOCIETY

Political and social science society (national) was the American Academy of Political and Social Science, organized in Philadelphia, Pa., December 14, 1889, for the purpose of promoting the political and social sciences. The first president was Professor Edmund Janes James; the first corresponding secretary, Roland Post Falkner; the first treasurer, Stuart Wood. The first annual meeting was held in Philadelphia, March 21, 1890. The academy was incorporated April 4, 1891.

Political science association was the American Political Science Association founded in New Orleans, La., December 30, 1903, for the encouragement of the scientific study of politics, public law, administration, and diplomacy. The first president was Professor Frank Johnson Goodnow. *(American Political Science Association. Proceedings. Vol. 1)*

POLO

Intercollegiate indoor polo championship was won by Princeton University, which defeated Yale University, 10½-½, on March 18, 1922, at Squadron A Armory, New York City. Each team consisted of three players.

International polo series was played at Newport, R.I., August 25, 1886, between teams representing England and America. England won the series of two games with scores of 10-4 and 14-2. The American team consisted of Captain Thomas Hitchcock, Raymond Belmont, Foxhall P. Keene and W. K. Thorne. *(Frank Gray Griswold—The International Polo Cup)*

THE FIRST

Polo was introduced by James Gordon Bennett upon his return from England in 1876. He imported polo balls, mallets, etc. The horses were brought up from Texas by Harry Blassan, a New York riding master. The first polo games were played in Dickel's Riding Academy, at the northeast corner of Fifth Avenue and 39th Street, New York City. On Thursday, May 11, 1876, a team captained by James Gordon Bennett played Lord Mandeville's team at Jerome Park, Westchester County, New York. *(Thomas Francis Dale—Polo, Past and Present)*

Polo game played outdoors at night took place on July 2, 1931, at Homewood Field, Baltimore, Md., between the Maryland Polo Club and the 110th Field Artillery. The first game was played with four men on each side. Homewood Field was amply lighted for the event.

POLO CLUB

Polo association (national) was the United States Polo Association, formed June 6, 1890, in New York City, by the Meadow Brook Club (Westbury, L.I.), Philadelphia Country Club (Bala, Pa.), Rockaway Hunting Club (Cedarhurst, L.I.) and the Westchester Polo Club (Newport, R.I.). The first chairman was H. L. Herbert and the first secretary-treasurer was Douglas Robinson.

Polo club was the Westchester Polo Club, organized in New York City in 1876. Matches were played at the Jerome Park race track in Westchester County, New York. *(Newell Bent—American Polo)*

POLYGAMY LEGISLATION (federal), enacted July 1, 1862 (12 Stat.L.501), was "an act to punish and prevent the practice of polygamy in the territories of the United States and other places, and disapproving and annulling certain acts of the legislative assembly of the territory of Utah." Little effort was made to enforce it. The first important legislation was the act of March 22, 1882 (22 Stat.L.30), the [George Franklin] Edmunds law, which defined simultaneous marriages as bigamy and prescribed loss of citizenship as an additional penalty for bigamists. It legitimized children born in polygamy before January 1, 1883.

POLYMETHYL METHACRYLATE PRODUCTION. *See* Lucite (polymethyl methacrylate) production (commercial)

POLYPEPTIDE HORMONE SYNTHESIZED. *See* Pituitary hormone: Polypeptide hormone synthesized

POLYSTYRENE (expandable). *See* Plastic: Expandable polystyrene production (commercial)

PONTIFF TO HAVE VISITED THE UNITED STATES. *See* Visiting celebrities: Pontiff

PONTOON BRIDGE. *See* Bridge: Pontoon bridge

PONY EXPRESS MAIL. *See* Postal service: Pony Express Mail

POOL. *See* Swimming pool in the White House

POORHOUSE (state) to be replaced by a state home was closed by Delaware in 1933. On October 11, 1933, the State Welfare Home at Smyrna, Del., replacing three almshouses, was dedicated by Governor Clayton Douglass Buck. The first guests were admitted September 25, 1933, prior to the dedication. Dr. Alan Victor Gilliland was the first superintendent and served from August 1, 1933 to June 1, 1943. *(Delaware State Board of Welfare—Annual Report 1934)*

POPCORN was introduced to the English colonists at their first Thanksgiving dinner February 22, 1630, by Quadequina, brother of Massasoit. As his contribution to the dinner he offered a deerskin bag containing several bushels of the "popped" corn.

POPULAR VOTE FOR PRESIDENT. *See* Presidential popular vote

POPULIST PARTY. *See* People's party

PORCELAIN (hard) to be manufactured successfully was made about 1825 by William Ellis Tucker at the American China Manufactory at the southwest corner of Sixth and Chestnut Streets, Philadelphia, Pa. *(Walter Alden Dyer—Early American Craftsmen)*

PORCELAIN TEETH. *See* Dentistry: Porcelain teeth

PORPOISES. *See* Aquatic Mammals: Porpoise

PORT (free). *See* Free port

PORTABLE TYPEWRITER. *See* Typewriter: Portable typewriter

PORTLAND CEMENT. *See* Cement: Cement

POSITRON. *See* Physics: Positron

POST OFFICE
Airplane post office was Flagship Station 1, officially opened and dedicated May 15, 1938, by Mrs. Franklin Delano Roosevelt during National Air Mail Week. It consisted of an American Airlines sleeper plane which, with wings removed, was set up as a special post office on Pennsylvania Avenue, Washington, D.C. Stamps were to have been sold in the plane, but this was found impractical and a station was set up in an adjoining building. The plane was exhibited and viewed by 78,636 people during the week it was open.

Colonial post office. *See* Postal service: Parliamentary act to establish a post office

Naval post office aboard a naval vessel was established August 20, 1908, on the U.S.S. "Nebraska."

Open air post office was opened October 1, 1917, in St. Petersburg, Fla. It had a roof, but no sides or enclosing walls. A lobby 18 feet wide extended around three sides of the building. The floor was made of pink natural colored stone resembling sandstone.

Post office act. *See* Postal service: Parliamentary act to establish a post office

Post office building (U.S.) built for that purpose was the Custom House and Post Office in Newport, R.I., built in 1829 and occupied in 1830. An act of Congress approved May 24, 1828 (4 Stat.L.303), authorized the erection of the building. The title to the site was vested in the government on November 12, 1828.

Post office (colonial) for the collection of mail was established by order of the General Court of Massachusetts on November 5, 1639, in Boston at the house of Richard Fairbanks for "all letters which are brought from beyond the seas, or are to be sent thither." He was allowed a penny for the transmission of each letter and was accountable to the authorities in charge of the colony.

Post Office Department of the United States was temporarily established by act of September 22, 1789 (1. Stat.L.70), which also created the office of Postmaster General. The act of February 20, 1792 (1. Stat.L.234) was the first to provide in detail for the Post Office Department and the postal service generally. The Post Office Department became an executive department by act of June 8, 1872 (17 Stat.L.283), although it had been known as a department for many years. The change of status was made during the term of Postmaster General John Angel James Creswell of Maryland, who served from March 5, 1869, to March 17, 1873.

THE FIRST

Post office fully mechanized was opened October 20, 1960, in Providence, R.I. A $20,-000,000 experimental installation designated Project Turnkey and built by Intelex Systems, Inc., a subsidiary of the International Telephone and Telegraph Corporation, was leased to the Post Office Department for twenty years. Letters were electronically faced and canceled and automatically transported to 300 destination bins at the rate of 18,000 per hour.

POSTAGE METER. *See* Postal service: Postage meter

POSTAGE STAMP

Adhesive stamps were used by the City Despatch Post, established February 15, 1842, by Alexander M. Greig, with principal office at 46 William Street, New York City. They were engraved by Rawdon, Wright & Hatch, New York City, and printed in sheets of 42. They were a 3-cent denomination and sold for $2.50 a hundred stamps. Local delivery service was authorized by act of Congress July 2, 1836 (5 Stat.L.80), "an act to change the organization of the Post Office Department." On August 1, 1842, the City Despatch Post was acquired by the United States government for $1,200 and was named the United States City Despatch Post. Alexander Greig was appointed a clerk in the new service and served until November 24, 1844.

Air mail stamps were issued May 13, 1918, and consisted of three denominations, 6-cent orange, 16-cent green, and 24-cent carmine, rose and blue, all with airplanes depicted on them.

Books of postage stamps were issued April 16, 1900, as follows: books containing twelve 2-cent stamps, priced at 25 cents; twenty-four 2-cent stamps, 49 cents; and forty-eight 2-cent stamps, 97 cents. (*Records in Division of Stamps. Post Office Department, Washington, D.C.*)

Commemorative postage stamps issued by the Post Office Department was the Columbian series of 1893, which depicted incidents in the discovery of America by Columbus. The stamps were of sixteen denominations and ranged in value from 1 cent to $5. They were issued January 2, 1893, with the exception of the 8-cent stamp which was issued March 3, 1893.

Departmental postage stamps were authorized by act of Congress of March 3, 1873 (17 Stat.L.542), to be issued July 1, 1873, but they were placed in use May 24, 1873. The various departments had special colors assigned to them: Agriculture, yellow; Executive, carmine; Interior, vermilion; Justice, mauve; Navy, blue; Post Office, black; State, green; Treasury, brown; War, dull rose. The denomina-

THE FIRST

tions were 1 cent, 2 cents, 3 cents, 6 cents, 7 cents, 10 cents, 12 cents, 15 cents, 24 cents, 30 cents, and 90 cents.

Imperforated ungummed sheet of postage stamps was the Byrd stamp souvenir sheet made for the National Stamp Exhibition at Rockefeller Center, New York City. The stamps were issued on February 10, 1934 and contained six 3-cent blue "Little America" stamps.

Memorial stamp was the Lincoln 2-cent memorial issue commemorating the 100th anniversary of the birth of Abraham Lincoln and placed on sale February 12, 1909. This stamp was red, the size and shape of the regular issue of postage stamps. It depicted a profile of the head of Lincoln from Saint-Gaudens' statue in an oval with the words "1809 Feb. 12 1909" on a ribbon below. (*Records in Office of Third Assistant Post Master General—Post Office, Washington, D.C.*)

Mourning stamp was the 15-cent black postage stamp issued June 17, 1866, which depicted President Abraham Lincoln. A 10-cent and a 12-cent black stamp showing portraits of George Washington were issued on July 1, 1847, and July 1, 1851, but these were not "mourning" stamps.

Moving picture actress depicted on a postage stamp. *See* Moving picture actor: Moving picture actress depicted on a postage stamp

Negro depicted on a U.S. postage stamp was the educator Booker Taliaferro Washington, whose likeness was placed on the 10-cent stamp issued April 7, 1940.

Parcel-post stamps were the series of 1912-1913, placed on sale January 1, 1913, with the inauguration of the parcel post service. The issue consisted of twelve red stamps, from 1 cent to $1, prepared in three groups of four stamps each. The working personnel of the Postal Service was depicted on the first group, the transportation of mail on the second group, and the manufacturing and agricultural interests of the country on the third group. Five parcel-post postage-due green stamps from 1 cent to 25 cents were also issued at the same time.

Perforated postage stamps were contracted for February 6, 1857, and were delivered to the government February 24, 1857. The designs were the same as the 1851-1855 issue with the addition of three new values, the 24-cent portrait of Washington, the 30-cent profile bust of Franklin, and the 90-cent portrait of Washing-

POSTAGE STAMP—*Continued*
ton. The stamps were printed by Toppan, Carpenter and Co. of Philadelphia, Pa. Previously imperforate stamps had been used.

Postage stamp in two colors produced by the rotary process at the Bureau of Engraving and Printing, Washington, D.C., was the 3-cent International Red Cross issue released November 21, 1952, in New York City. Two colors, red and blue, appeared on a white stamp.

Postage stamp of the United States having the same design as that of another country (Canada) was issued June 26, 1959. The inscriptions, denominations, and sizes differed, however. The denomination of the United States stamp was 4 cents, that of the Canadian stamp 5 cents. The design featured two interlocking links superimposed on a map of the Great Lakes with the St. Lawrence leading from them toward the sea. Within the left link was a maple leaf, Canada's emblem, and within the right link was a bald eagle, the United States emblem. The stamps commemorated the opening of the St. Lawrence Seaway.

Postage stamp on which was inscribed the name of a living American was the issue of 1927, a 10-cent blue stamp which pictured the "Spirit of St. Louis," Colonel Charles Augustus Lindbergh's airplane, in flight, with "Lindbergh Air Mail" above it. In the background to the left appeared the coast line of the North American continent with the words, "New York" in small dark letters, and to the right the coast line of Europe showing Ireland, Great Britain, and France, with the word "Paris" in small dark letters. A dotted line connected the two cities showing the route of the flight. The stamp was first placed on sale June 18, 1927, in St. Louis, Detroit, Little Falls, Minn., and Washington, D.C. The issue included special booklets of six stamps which represent the first and only air mail stamps issued in this form. Rules provide that no living American may be shown on postage stamps.

Postage stamp to bear the likeness of a Vice President of the United States issued by a foreign country was a green 2-sucre postage stamp issued by Ecuador on May 15, 1958. It bore the likeness of Vice President Richard Milhous Nixon and the flags of the United States and Ecuador.

Postage stamps commemorating the National Recovery Act. *See* Industrial recovery act: Postage stamps commemorating the National Recovery Act

Postage stamps depicting scenes were the series of 1869, issued from March 1, 1869, to April 9, 1870. The designs were furnished by the National Bank Note Company of New

York City, which received a contract on December 12, 1868, for furnishing the stamps. There were ten denominations. The 2-cent stamp depicted a post horse and rider, the 3-cent a locomotive, the 12-cent a steamboat, the 15-cent the landing of Columbus, and the 24-cent the signing of the Declaration of Independence. The 1-cent, 6-cent, and 90-cent stamps carried portraits of Franklin, Washington, and Lincoln respectively; the 10-cent and 30-cent stamps pictured an eagle resting on a shield.

Postage stamps depicting the American eagle were the 1-cent carrier's stamps in blue issued November 17, 1851.

Postage stamps in coils were issued February 18, 1908, and were coarsely perforated, 8½ holes to two centimeters. They were printed by the Bureau of Engraving and Printing, Washington, D.C., for the Post Office Department. In 1902, sheets of 400 stamps were cut into strips of 20 and spliced together into rolls which were prepared for vending and affixing machines by commercial organizations. These stamps were perforated on two sides only, either horizontally or vertically, two sides being imperforate.

Postage stamps issued by the Post Office Department were authorized by act of Congress of March 3, 1847 (9 Stat.L.201), and first placed on sale in New York City on July 1, 1847. The issue consisted of two stamps, a 5-cent red-brown stamp depicting Benjamin Franklin, and a 10-cent black stamp bearing the likeness of George Washington. They were printed by Rawdon, Wright, Hatch and Edson of New York City. They were withdrawn from use on June 30, 1851. The issue consisted of 3,712,200 of the 5-cent denomination and 891,000 of the 10-cent denomination. The Bureau of Engraving and Printing began the printing of stamps with the 1894 issue of the "triangle" design stamps. (*Post Office Department—A Description of United States Postage Stamps*)

Postage stamps to picture a woman were the Columbian commemorative stamps of 1893. Queen Isabella was depicted on three varieties which were placed on sale January 2, 1893. The 5-cent stamp (35,248,250 issued) was in chocolate brown and depicted "Columbus Soliciting the Aid of Isabella"; the $1 stamp (55,050 issued) was in rose salmon and showed "Isabella Pledging Her Jewels"; and the $4 stamp (26,350 issued) was in carmine, with portraits of Columbus and Isabella. Women were also shown as characters in group scenes in this set, but their identity was not given. The first American woman's portrait on a stamp was that of Martha Washington on an 8-cent dark lilac stamp issued December 6, 1902. The portrait was after the painting by Gilbert Stuart.

THE FIRST

Postage stamps to picture an airplane were the 20-cent parcel post stamps issued on December 16, 1912, aud placed on sale January 1, 1913.

Postage stamps to picture the coat of arms of the United States were the 10-cent yellow stamps and the 30-cent blue and carmine stamps of the issue of 1869 on sale from March 1, 1869 to April 9, 1870.

Precanceled stamps printed on rotary presses at the Bureau of Engraving and Printing were issued April 21, 1923. This initial order embraced 1-cent stamps of the 1923 series. One-cent precanceled stamps in coils were first issued January 7, 1924. Prior to the addition of precanceling devices to rotary presses, the Bureau of Engraving and Printing precanceled 1-cent stamps in sheets for a limited number of post offices with electrotype plates containing 400 stamps each. The records indicate that Bureau precanceled stamps of this style were first issued to the New Orleans, La., Augusta, Me., and Springfield, Mass., post offices in January 1917.

Public exhibition of postage stamps was held from May 10, 1876, to November 10, 1876 in the United States Building at the Centennial Exhibition at Fairmount Park, Philadelphia, Pa. It was arranged by John Walter Scott. The first important exhibit by collectors opened March 11, 1889, at the Eden Musee, New York City; 31 exhibitors showed 272 sheets of stamps from 161 countries valued in excess of $200,000.

Sheet of postage stamps to contain more than one variety of stamps was placed on sale May 9, 1936, in a temporary post office at Grand Central Palace, New York City, during the Third International Philatelic Exposition, May 9-May 17. The sheet consisted of four purple ungummed imperforate 3-cent stamps—one of the San Diego Exposition issue of 1935, one Texas Centennial issue of 1936, one Connecticut Tercentenary issue of 1935, and one Michigan Centenary issue of 1935—surrounded by a white border on which was lettered "Printed by the Treasury Department, Bureau of Engraving and Printing" at the left; "Under Authority of James A. Farley, Postmaster General" at the top; "In Compliment to the Third International Philatelic Exhibition of 1936" at the right; and "New York, N.Y., May 9-17, 1936," at the lower edge. About two thirds of the total issue of 2,809,039 sheets was sold during the exposition.

Stamp collecting agency. *See* Postal service: Philatelic agency

Stamped envelopes issued to commemorate an event were the 3-cent green stamped envelopes printed on a Hartford press set up in

THE FIRST

the Post Office Department in the Government Building at the Centennial Exposition in Philadelphia, Pa., between May 10 and November 10, 1876. (*Annual Report of the Third Assistant Postmaster General for the Fiscal Year Ending June 30, 1876*)

Stamped envelopes (U.S.) were issued in June 1853, under act of August 31, 1852 (10 Stat.L.141) and were manufactured by George F. Nesbitt & Company of New York City under a contract dated October 25, 1852. They showed the profile of George Washington in an oval, the value above, and "cents" below. They were printed on white and buff paper. The first series included a 3-cent red, a 6-cent red and green, and a 10-cent green. (*Thomas Doane Perry—Guide to the Stamped Envelopes and Wrappers of the United States*)

POSTAGE STAMP CATALOG was compiled by A. C. Kline, 824 Walnut Street, Philadelphia, Pa., in 1862. It listed 1,500 varieties of stamps and was published in Philadelphia. Its title was *The Stamp Collector's Manual, Being a complete guide to the collectors of American and Foreign postage and despatch stamps.*

POSTAL CAR (steel). *See* Railroad car: Mail car (steel)

POSTAL CARD was issued May 1, 1873, under act of Congress of June 8, 1872 (17 Stat. L.304). A 1-cent stamp printed on the upper right hand corner showed a profile of the Goddess of Liberty looking to the left and surrounded by a lathe-work border with the words "U.S. Postage" inserted above, and "One Cent" below. The body of the card was light buff, the printing velvet brown. The size of the card was 3 x 5⅛ inches. The cards were made by the Morgan Envelope Company, Springfield, Mass. The first known cancellation was May 12, 1873.

POSTAL DIRECTORY was *A List of Post Offices in the United States with the Names of the Postmasters on the first of July 1855, also the Principal Regulations of the Post Office Department,* compiled by Daniel Tompkins Leech of the Post Office Department and printed by George S. Gideon, Washington, D.C., in 1855. It contained 146 pages of directory, 48 pages of regulations, and 6 pages of miscellaneous material.

POSTAL FRAUD ORDER. *See* Postal service: Postal fraud order

POSTAL ROUTE. *See* Postal service: Postal route

POSTAL SAVINGS BANK. *See* Bank: Postal savings bank

POSTAL SAVINGS STAMPS were issued December 22, 1910. Five denominations were issued in accordance with the authority conferred upon the Post Office Department by act of Congress of June 25, 1910 (36 Stat.L.814) establishing postal savings depositories. Their use was discontinued on September 23, 1914. (*Edwin Walter Kemmerer—Postal Savings, An Historical and Critical Study of the Postal Savings System of the United States.*)

POSTAL SERVICE

Airplane mail pick-up. *See* Air mail service: Airplane mail pick-up

Autogiro mail delivery. *See* Air mail service: Autogiro mail

Automobile mail wagon. *See* Automobile mail wagon

Balloon flight carrying mail. *See* Balloon: Balloon flight carrying mail

Coin-operated mailbox was the "Mailomat," combining a postage meter with a United States letter box. Manufactured by Pitney-Bowes, Inc., Stamford, Conn., the first machine was installed at the General Post Office, New York City, on May 17, 1939. It was covered by patent No. 2,290,920, granted July 28, 1942, to Linden A. Thatcher of Stamford, Conn. Coins are dropped in slots, the desired stamp denomination is dialed, and the letter is inserted in a letter slot. The machine does the rest automatically—prints meter stamp with postmark and date of mailing and holds the letter for scheduled collection. It provides postage from 1 cent to 33 cents, including airmail, special delivery, etc. It obviates the need of ordinary adhesive stamps, operates day or night as "a selfservice postoffice," and speeds mail because metered mail needs no post office "facing," canceling, or postmarking.

Collection and delivery of mail in automobiles owned by the government were made October 19, 1914, in Washington, D.C.

Dead letter office of the Post Office Department was organized in 1825 in Washington, D.C.

Dirigible transfer of mail to a train. *See* Aviation—Airship: Dirigible transfer of mail to a train

Free city delivery of mail was authorized by act of March 3, 1863 (12 Stat.L.705). City delivery service was placed in operation July 1, 1863, in 49 cities with 440 carriers at an annual cost of $300,000. On January 3, 1887, free delivery service was extended to cities of

over 50,000 population and permitted in places having a population of at least 10,000 and postal receipts of $10,000.

Highway Post Office Service was approved July 11, 1940. The first route was established February 10, 1941, between Washington, D.C., and Harrisonburg, Va. Mail was transported in large bus-type vehicles equipped with facilities for sorting, handling and dispatch of mail.

International air mail. *See* Air Mail Service: International air mail

International dog sled mail left Lewiston, Me., on December 20, 1928, with Alden William Pulsifer, postmaster of Minot, Me., in charge and arrived January 14, 1929, at Montreal, Canada. A regular 8-foot mushing sled weighing 200 pounds was pulled by 6 blackhead Eskimo dogs. They averaged 9 miles an hour (7 to 8 on bare ground) and covered from 40 to 60 miles a day. The mail pouch contained 385 letters which were placed in government stamped canceled envelopes. The trip was not an official one. The sled returned to Lewiston on February 2, 1929, having passed through 118 cities, and having covered 600 miles, of which 90 per cent was bare of snow.

Jet-propelled airplane to transport mail. *See* Air mail service: Jet-propelled airplane to transport mail

Letter-carriers' uniforms were authorized by act of Congress of July 27, 1868 (15 Stat.L.197), which authorized the Postmaster General "to prescribe a uniform dress to be worn by the letter-carriers." On October 31, 1868, Postmaster General Alexander Williams Randall approved a standard uniform.

Letter to encircle the world by commercial air mail was dispatched from New York City on April 19, 1937. It was routed via San Francisco, Hong Kong, Penang, Amsterdam, and Brazil and was returned to New York on May 25, 1937.

Mail box was invented in 1810 by Thomas Brown, who was governor of Florida from 1849 to 1853. His mail boxes consisted of a series of numbered pigeonholes with glass fronts which enabled people to see whether there was any mail for them in their respective boxes.

Mail box (drive-up) to enable automobilists to post letters without moving from the seat of their cars was installed in July 1927 at Houston, Tex. The box had metal handles 8 to

THE FIRST

THE FIRST

10 inches long and was tilted 4 inches. The boxes were known as "courtesy collection boxes."

Mail chute (such as those used in office buildings, hotels, apartment houses, and other structures at which mail is dropped from the upper stories) was installed in 1883 in the Elwood Building, Rochester, N.Y., after plans prepared by James Goold Cutler, the architect of the building, who received patent No. 284,-951, on September 11, 1883. The device was later developed and suited to the requirements of the Post Office and public use by Joseph Warren Cutler, under a series of about thirty patents issued to him.

Mail delivery by steamboats was authorized by act of Congress of February 27, 1813 (2 Stat.L.805). The Postmaster General was granted the power to transport mail "in any steamboats or boats . . . the pay not [to] be at a greater rate, taking into consideration distance, expedition and frequency, than is paid for carrying the mail by stages on the post road, or roads, adjacent to the course of such steamboats."

Mail franking privilege was granted to members of Congress and private soldiers in service on November 8, 1775. Regulations of January 9, 1776, provided that soldiers' mail was to be franked by the officer in charge. On April 3, 1800 (2 Stat.L.19), free franking of mail during her natural life was granted to Martha Washington. (*Edward Stern—History of Free Franking of Mail in the United States*)

Missile mail (official). *See* Air mail service: Missile mail (official)

Money order system was established on November 1, 1864, in order to promote public convenience and insure safety in the transfer by mail of small sums of money. Foreign service was authorized July 27, 1868. The first agreement was made with Switzerland effective September 1, 1869. Service was extended to Great Britain on October 2, 1871 and to Germany on October 1, 1872. (*United States Official Postal Guide—Post Office Department*)

Navy mail service was established May 27, 1908, when an appropriation was made for the year ending June 30, 1909 (35 Stat.L.417), to designate enlisted men of the Navy as naval mail clerks and assistant naval mail clerks to receive $500 and $300 extra respectively. The U.S.S. "Illinois," "Prairie," and "Rhode Island" were the first vessels afforded postal facilities, naval post offices having been established thereon August 15, 1908.

Newspaper wrappers were issued in October 1861 under act of February 27, 1861 (12

Stat.L.167), in manila and buff, bearing a 1-cent blue stamp with the head of Franklin. In 1863 a 2-cent wrapper was added, bearing a black stamp with the head of Jackson.

Ocean mail contracts were authorized by act of March 3, 1845 (5 Stat.L.732, chap. 43), "to provide for the transportation of the mail between the United States and foreign countries." The first contract was made in 1847, with the Ocean Navigation Company, for the transportation of United States mail once a month between the ports of New York City, Southampton, England, and Bremen, Germany, the compensation to be $16,666 for each round trip. The "Washington," pioneer of American ocean steamers, started this service June 1, 1847. The contract expired June 1, 1857.
See also Shipping: Ship subsidy

Overland mail service to the Pacific Coast was begun on September 15, 1858, by the Overland Mail coaches, the old John Butterfield stage line. Stages left Tipton, Mo., and San Francisco, Calif., simultaneously every Monday and Thursday. The route was operated under government contract authorized by act of March 3, 1857 (11 Stat.L.189), for six years at a cost not to exceed $300,000 per annum for a semi-monthly service, $450,000 for a weekly service, and $600,000 for a semi-weekly service. The contract was signed on September 16, 1857, at $600,000 a year for six years, for semi-weekly trips in both directions, in "good four-horse post coaches or spring wagons suitable for the convenience of passengers as well as safety and security of the mails." The specified running time for the 2,800 miles was to be not more than 25 days. The first trips were made in a few hours less than 24 days. (*Le Roy R. Hafen—Overland Mail, 1849-1869*)

Parcel post convention was negotiated with Jamaica, British West Indies, July 22, 1887 (25 Stat.L.1393), and upon the adoption of the treaty, a feathered fan was sent to Mrs. Grover Cleveland by Jamaica officials.

Parcel post service was authorized August 24, 1912 (37 Stat.L.559), when appropriations were made for the service that started January 1, 1913. Previously the weight limit of mail had been four pounds. The rates of the parcel post service depended upon the weight of the package and the distance carried.

Parliamentary act to establish a post office in the American colonies was passed in April 1692. A royal patent had been granted to Thomas Neale, February 17, 1691, by the sovereigns William and Mary, with "full power and authority to erect, settle and establish within the chief parts of their Majesties' colonies and plantations in America, an office or offices for the receiving and dispatching of letters and

THE FIRST

THE FIRST

POSTAL SERVICE—*Continued*
pacquets, and to receive, send and deliver the
same under such rates and sums of money as
the planters shall agree to give, and to hold and
enjoy the same for the term of 21 years."
Neale did not come to America but named
Andrew Hamilton as postmaster general, an
appointment which was confirmed April 4,
1692, by the British Postmaster General.

Philatelic agency of the Post Office Department was placed in operation December 1,
1921, under Percy Warder Gibbon. Sales for
the fiscal year were $20,906.50.

Pony Express mail left St. Joseph, Mo.,
and Sacramento, Calif., simultaneously April
3, 1860, carried by Henry Wallace riding west
and John Roff riding east. The westbound
packet was delivered in ten days, the eastbound
in eleven and a half. (According to some accounts, the first rider westward was William
(Billy) Richardson or John Frey, and the
first rider eastward was Samuel Hamilton, who
rode 20 miles in 59 minutes.) The route was
through Fort Kearney, Fort Laramie, Fort
Bridger, Salt Lake City, Camp Floyd, Carson
City, Washoe Silver Mines, and Placerville.
Until the service was discontinued on October
24, 1861, a rider left St. Joseph at noon and
Sacramento at 8 A.M. every day except Sunday.
It was a private enterprise under a charter
granted by the state of Kansas to the Central
Overland and Pike's Peak Express Co. The
charge was $5 a half ounce. *(Waddell F.
Smith—Story of the Pony Express)*

Postage canceling machine patent was issued to J. C. W. Maas and Carl Fisher of
Hamburg, Germany, who received U.S. patent
No. 75,638 on March 17, 1868 on a "machine
for stamping letters."

Postage meter was officially set at Stamford, Conn., November 16, 1920. Although the
idea of metered mail originated in 1900 when
the American Postage Meter Company of Chicago, Ill., was organized for that purpose, it
was not until September 1, 1920, that the Post
Office Department approved of it. The Acting
Assistant Postmaster General informed the
Pitney Bowes Postage Meter Company of
Stamford, Conn., that its machine would be
acceptable to the Department. About $2,000,000
was spent on research and development of the
machine. *(Metered Mail—Postage Meter Co.)*

Postal directory. *See* Postal directory

Postal fraud order was authorized by the
act of Congress of June 8, 1872 (17 Stat.L.322).
The act granted the postmaster general, in cases
in which fraud was practiced, the right to

stamp mail, registered mail, and money orders
"fraudulent" and return them to the sender
instead of making the delivery to the addressee.

Postal route was between New York City
and Boston, Mass. On December 10, 1672,
Governor Francis Lovelace of New York announced that monthly service would be inaugurated January 1, 1673. The first trip was
made January 22, 1673.

Postal service act under the Constitution
was signed by President Washington, February 20, 1792 (1 Stat.L.232). This act set the
rates at 6 cents for letters to be carried not
more than 30 miles, 8 cents between 30 and 60
miles, 10 cents between 60 and 100 miles, and
12½ cents between 100 and 150 miles.

Postmen's uniforms. *See* Postal Service:
Letter-carriers' uniforms

Railroad post office was tested July 7, 1862,
and placed in operation July 28, 1862, on the
Hannibal and St. Joseph (Mo.) Railroad dur-
ing the administration of Postmaster General
Montgomery Blair. The idea was originated by
William Augustine Davis and the mail car
built at Hannibal, Mo. *(J. L. Bittinger—The
Railway Postal Service)*

**Railroad post office for the general distri-
bution of mail** was tested July 1, 1864, regular service commencing August 28, 1864,
on the Chicago & Northwestern Railway between Chicago, Ill., and Clinton, Iowa. George
Buchanan Armstrong, one of the two special
agents commissioned on December 20, 1864, to
superintend postal matters, was appointed general superintendent of the Railway Mail Service on April 4, 1869.

Registration of letters was authorized by
act of Congress of March 3, 1855. The system was placed in operation July 1, 1855.

**Right-hand-drive automobile for the deliv-
ery of mail.** *See* Automobile: Right-hand-
drive automobile for the delivery of mail

Rocket air mail flight. *See* Air mail service: Rocket air mail flight

Rural free delivery was established October
1, 1896. Three routes were designated in West
Virginia, one from Charles Town, one from
Uvilla, and one from Halltown.

Rural free delivery appropriation was made
through the efforts of Thomas Edward Watson, a member of Congress from Georgia, 1891-
1893. Watson was the Populist party's nominee
for Vice President, and later its choice for

THE FIRST

President. Representative Watson's bill was introduced in 1893. (*U.S. Department of Agriculture. Yearbook. 1900—"Free Delivery of Rural Mails." C. H. Greathouse*)

Special delivery service was authorized by act of March 3, 1885 (23 Stat.L.388). The service was established October 1, 1885, and at first was restricted to free delivery offices in towns of 4,000 or more inhabitants. An additional charge of 10 cents a letter was made for this service and a blue special delivery stamp was issued on October 1, 1885. On August 4, 1886, the service was extended to all free delivery offices. (*Louis Melius—American Postal Service*)

Street letter box was invented by Albert Potts of Philadelphia, Pa., who obtained patent No. 19,578 on March 9, 1858, on "a mode of attaching metallic letter-boxes." The box had a center hole through which the shaft of an ordinary cast-iron lamp post was placed. Boxes were erected on August 2, 1858, in Boston and New York City. (*American Gas Light Journal—October 1, 1869*)

"V" mail film was dispatched overseas from New York to London on June 22, 1942. It consisted of a partial roll of film on which there were only 212 individual letters. A complete roll of film contained 1600 letters.

Vending machine (coin operated) to dispense postage stamps. *See* Vending machine: Vending machine (coin operated) to dispense postage stamps

POSTMASTER
Postmaster general appointed from the ranks was Jesse Monroe Donaldson, appointed by President Harry S. Truman on November 24, 1947, to take office December 1, 1947. The son of a postman, he became a letter carrier in 1908 and rose to first assistant postmaster general, an office to which he was appointed July 6, 1945.

Postmaster general (colonial) was Andrew Hamilton, appointed April 4, 1692, by the postmaster general of Great Britain, under an act of Parliament of April 1692 establishing post offices in the American colonies.

Postmaster general of the United States was Samuel Osgood, who was appointed by President George Washington and who served from September 26, 1789, to August 19, 1791. His office was authorized by act of Congress of September 22, 1789 (1 Stat.L.70), which gave the general supervision of the post office to a

THE FIRST

postmaster general under the direction of the President. Other postmasters under Washington's administration were Timothy Pickering, appointed in 1791, and Joseph Habersham, in 1797. (*Daniel Calhoun Roper—The U.S. Post Office*)

Postmaster general of the United States to become a member of the President's cabinet was William Taylor Barry, appointed by President Andrew Jackson, who served from April 6, 1829, to April 30, 1835.

Postmaster general under the Continental Congress was Benjamin Franklin, who was appointed July 26, 1775, by the Second Continental Congress at a salary of $1,000 a year and who served until November 7, 1776. He served the crown as deputy postmaster at Philadelphia, Pa., from 1737 to 1753, and as deputy postmaster general for the colonies from 1753 to 1774. (*Ruth Lapham Butler—Dr. Franklin, Postmaster General*)

Woman postmaster appointed after the adoption of the Constitution was Sarah De Crow, who was made postmaster at Hertford, N.C., on September 27, 1792.

Woman postmaster (colonial) was Mary Katherine Goddard, appointed postmaster at Baltimore, Md., in 1775. She served until November 14, 1789.

POSTMEN'S UNIFORMS. *See* Postal service: Letter-carriers' uniforms

POTATO
Potato is believed by some authorities to have been introduced in December 1621 or January 1622. Imported from Bermuda by Virginia colonists, the first potatoes are said to have been used for food rather than for planting. (*Journal of Heredity. Vol. 16. No. 4. April 1925*)

Potato cultivation was undertaken in 1719 at Londonderry Common Field (now Derry), N.H., by Scotch-Irish immigrants who settled there and planted crops of their native Ireland.

POTATO CHIPS were introduced by a Negro chef about 1865. The first plant constructed for the exclusive manufacture of potato chips was erected in Albany, N.Y., in 1925 by A. A. Walter & Company.

POTTER is believed to have been John Pride of Salem, Mass., who operated a pottery from 1641 to 1647. He made red earthenware from common brick clay. (*Joseph B. Felt—Annals of Salem, Mass.*)

THE FIRST

POTTERY
See also Chinaware

Pottery was established by Dr. Daniel Coxe in Burlington, N.J., in 1680. It produced white and "chiney" ware for the local trade and also for export to Jamaica and Barbados. The factory was sold in 1691. He was Governor of West New Jersey, from 1687 to 1692, but never came to America. *(Francis Bazley Lee— History of Trenton, N.J.)*

Pottery to make sanitary ware was founded in Trenton, N.J., in 1853 by Milington & Astbury. On April 4, 1873, they consolidated with Thomas Maddock & Sons.

POULTRY SHOW was the Grand Show of Domestic Poultry and Convention of Fowl Breeders and Fanciers held November 15th and 16th, 1849, at the Public Garden, Boston, Mass., with 1,423 specimens in 219 cages. More than 10,000 persons attended. *(Report of the Committee of Supervision of the First Exhibition of Domestic Poultry)*

POUND (enclosure for animals) was authorized by section 48, Connecticut Code of 1650, passed May 1650, which decreed "that there shall be one sufficient pound or more made and maintained in every town and village within this jurisdiction, for the impounding of all swine and cattle as shall be found in any cornfield or other inclosure." *(Public Records of the Colony of Connecticut prior to the union with the New Haven Colony)*

POUR-LIP BOTTLE. *See* Bottle: Screwcap bottle with a pour lip

POWDER MILL. *See* Ordnance: Gunpowder mill

POWDERED SOAP. *See* Soap: Soap powder in packages

POWER ALCOHOL PLANT. See Alcohol: Power alcohol plant

POWER LINE CARRIER (electric power). *See* Electric transmission: Electric power line commercial carrier

POWER PLANT (electric). *See* Electric power plant

POWER PRESS. *See* Printing press: Power or steam printing press

POWERED GLIDER. *See* Glider: Powered soaring glider commercially licensed

THE FIRST

PRAYER BOOK (Book of Common Prayer). *See* Book: Book of Common Prayer

PRAYER BOOK (Unitarian). *See* Unitarian prayer book

PREACHER. *See* under name of specific religious denomination

PREACHER (Indian). *See* Indians: Indian preacher

PRECANCELED STAMPS. *See* Postage stamp: Precanceled stamps printed on rotary presses

PRECEPTORIAL SYSTEM (university). *See* College: University to adopt the preceptorial system

PRE-EMPTION LAND ACT. *See* Land pre-emption act (federal)

PREFABRICATED BUILDING. *See* Building: Building with prefabricated walls of mosaic concrete

PREFERENTIAL BALLOT. *See* Election law: Preferential ballot system

PREFRONTAL LOBOTOMY. *See* Surgical operation: Lobotomy (prefrontal)

PREMATURE BABY HEALTH LAW. *See* Medical legislation: Premature baby health law

PREMIUM
Premiums given by publishers were offered between 1870 and 1881 by the *Christian Union,* edited by Henry Ward Beecher. The paper's subscription jumped from 10,000 to 100,000. The premiums usually given to subscribers were chromos.

Premiums given with merchandise were successfully introduced by Benjamin Talbert Babbitt in 1865. When he first introduced wrapped soap, people felt that they were paying for the wrappers, so he printed the word "coupon" on them, and gave a "beautiful lithograph picture" for ten of them. This slowly developed into the operating of a premium department, which carried as many as a thousand different items in stock.

PRESBYTERIAN CHURCH
Moderator of the United Presbyterian Church in the United States was the Reverend Theophilus Mills Taylor, elected May 28, 1958, in Pittsburgh, Pa. Earlier the same day,

this church was formed by a merger of the Presbyterian Church in the United States of America and the United Presbyterian Church of North America. A communion service was held to mark the occasion.

Presbyterian Church was established in 1611 in Virginia. The Reverend Alexander Whitaker was installed as pastor of the church, which was governed by him and a few of the most religious men of the colony.

Presbyterian Church of America was formed June 11, 1936, at a meeting of Presbyterians assembled in Philadelphia, Pa. The first General Assembly was held June 11-14 in Philadelphia and was attended by 35 ministers and 22 elders. The first two of its Presbyteries was established in New York and Philadelphia. The first convener of the New York Presbytery was the Reverend Craig Long and the convener of the Philadelphia Presbytery was Hall McAllister Griffiths.

Woman ordained a minister in the Presbyterian Church was the Reverend Margaret Ellen Towner, ordained October 24, 1956, in her home church in Syracuse, N.Y. She assumed the position of minister of Christian education of the First Presbyterian Church, Allentown, Pa. On May 25, 1954, she received a bachelor of divinity degree from Union Theological Seminary, New York City.

PRESBYTERIAN ELDER (woman). *See* Woman: Woman Presbyterian elder

PRESBYTERIAN GENERAL ASSEMBLY, the governing body of the church, met on May 22, 1789, at the Second Church of Philadelphia.

PRESBYTERIAN PRESBYTERY met in Philadelphia, Pa., in 1705 and was composed of seven ministers—Francis Makemie, John Hampton, George McNish, Samuel Davis, Nathaniel Taylor, John Wilson and Jedidiah Andrews—and thirty-four others. The first known ordination, which took place in 1706, was that of John Boyd, who settled in Freehold, N.J. *(Presbyterian Handbook—1936)*

PRESERVE. *See* Game preserve

PRESIDENT OF A NEGRO COUNTRY TO VISIT THE UNITED STATES. *See* Visiting celebrities: President of a Negro country

PRESIDENT OF A SOUTH AMERICAN COUNTRY BORN IN THE UNITED STATES was Galo Plaza Lasso, president of Ecuador (1948-1952), who was

born in the Greenwich Village section of New York City on February 17, 1906, the son of General Leonidas Plaza, Ecuadoran minister to the United States and later president of Ecuador for two terms.

PRESIDENT OF THE CONFEDERATE STATES of America was Jefferson Davis of Mississippi, who was elected February 9, 1861. He was inducted into office February 18, 1861, and delivered his inaugural address on the steps of the State Capitol at Montgomery, Ala. Alexander Hamilton Stephens of Georgia was sworn in as Vice President February 11, 1861.

PRESIDENT OF THE CONTINENTAL CONGRESS was Peyton Randolph, a delegate from Virginia, who was elected September 5, 1774, the day the Congress assembled. He resigned October 22, 1774, to attend the Virginia State Legislature, and his place was taken on the same day by Henry Middleton of South Carolina. *(Edmund Cody Burnett—The Continental Congress)*

PRESIDENT OF THE REPUBLIC OF TEXAS was Sam Houston, who was elected September 5, 1836, and who took the oath of office on October 22, 1836 in Columbia, Tex. David Gouverneur Burnett served as Provisional President of Texas. Houston served until December 10, 1838, and was succeeded by Mirabeau Buonaparte Lamar. Houston was re-elected and served from December 14, 1841, to December 9, 1844. Upon the admission of Texas on December 29, 1845, as the 28th state of the United States, Houston was elected as a Democrat to the United States Senate where he served from February 21, 1846, to March 3, 1859. *(Rupert Norval Richardson—Texas, the Lone Star State)*

PRESIDENT (United States)
  Brother of a President to receive a cabinet appointment. *See* Cabinet of the United States: Cabinet member who was a brother of a President

  Coin bearing the portrait of a President. *See* Money: Coin bearing the portrait of a President

  Duel in which a future President of the United States participated. *See* Duel: Duel in which a future President of the United States participated

  Legislation passed over a President's veto. *See* Veto: Legislation passed over a President's veto

THE FIRST

THE FIRST

PRESIDENT (United States)—*Continued*
Pension for Presidents was enacted by Congress August 25, 1958. The act provided a pension of $25,000 for former Presidents and $10,000 to their widows.

Pension to the widow of a President. *See* Pension: Pension to the widow of a President

Photograph of a President. *See* Photograph: Photograph of a President

Planet named for an American President. *See* Astronomy: Planet (asteroid) named for an American President

President and President's wife to die during the term for which he had been elected were Warren Gamaliel Harding, who died August 2, 1923, in San Francisco, Calif., and Florence Kling De Wolfe Harding, who died November 21, 1924, in Marion, Ohio. The term for which Harding had been elected was March 4, 1921-March 3, 1925.

President born a citizen of the United States was Martin Van Buren, the eighth President (1837-1841). He was born December 5, 1782 in Kinderhook, N.Y. *(William Lyon Mackenzie—Life and Times of Martin Van Buren)*

President born beyond the boundaries of the original thirteen states was Abraham Lincoln, the sixteenth President (1861-1865). He was born near Hodgenville, Ky., February 12, 1809.

President born on Independence Day was Calvin Coolidge, the thirtieth President (1923-1929). He was born July 4, 1872, in Plymouth, Vt.

President born posthumously was Andrew Jackson, the seventh President (1829-1837). He was born March 15, 1767, in Union County, N.C., a few days after the death of his father.

President buried in the National Cemetery at Arlington, Va., was William Howard Taft, the twenty-seventh President (1909-1913). He was buried March 11, 1930.

President buried in Washington, D.C., was Woodrow Wilson, the twenty-eighth President. He was buried February 5, 1924, in the National Cathedral, the Protestant Episcopal Cathedral of Saints Peter and Paul. *(Josephus Daniels—Life of Woodrow Wilson)*

President elected under the Constitution was George Washington, who was inaugurated in the Federal Building on Wall Street in New York City, and served from April 30, 1789, to March 4, 1797. However, after the adoption of the Articles of Confederation in 1781, the presidents of the sessions of the Continental Congress signed themselves "President of the United States in Congress Assembled." The first president of the Continental Congress was Thomas McKean of Delaware.

President elected by the House of Representatives was Thomas Jefferson, the third President (1801-1809). The electoral vote stood as follows: Thomas Jefferson 73, Aaron Burr 73, John Adams 65, Charles Cotesworth Pinckney 64, and John Jay 1. The House assembled on February 11, 1801, and on the thirty-sixth ballot elected Jefferson. Delaware and South Carolina cast blank ballots, with the result that the vote was 10 states for Jefferson and 4 for Burr. *(Henry Stephens Randall—Life of Thomas Jefferson)*

President elected for a fourth term was Franklin Delano Roosevelt, the thirty-second President (1933-1945). He was also the first President of the United States to be elected for a third term. He had received 27,241,939 popular votes in November 1940, against Wendell Lewis Willkie's 22,304,755, when running for a third term; and 25,603,152 votes in November 1944 against Thomas Edmund Dewey's 22,006,616 when running for a fourth term. He served only a few months of the fourth term, from January 20, 1945, until his death on April 12, 1945.

President elected for two non-consecutive terms was Grover Cleveland, the twenty-second President (1885-1889) and the twenty-fourth President (1893-1897).

President inaugurated in the city of Washington was Thomas Jefferson. He was inducted in the Senate Chamber and sworn in by Chief Justice John Marshall on March 4, 1801. *(Edward Channing—The Jeffersonian System: 1801-1811)*

President inaugurated on January 20, in accordance with the twentieth amendment to the Constitution, was Franklin Delano Roosevelt. The amendment was ratified on February 6, 1933, and President Roosevelt was inaugurated for his second term on January 20, 1937, in Washington, D.C.

President inaugurated on March 5 because March 4 fell on Sunday was James Monroe, the fifth President (1821-1825). He was inaugurated in Washington, D.C., on March 5, 1821. President Zachary Taylor was inaugurated on March 5, 1849, and Rutherford Birchard Hayes on March 5, 1877. Since 1877,

THE FIRST

THE FIRST

whenever March 4 has fallen on a Sunday, the oath of office has been administered in a private ceremony on March 3 or March 4 and repeated in a public ceremony on March 5.

President married in the White House. *See* Wedding: White House wedding of a President

President married while in office was John Tyler, the tenth President (1841-1845). He married Julia Gardiner, daughter of a New York State senator, on June 25, 1844, at the Church of the Ascension, New York City. His first wife, Letitia Christian Polk, whom he married March 29, 1813, died September 10, 1842, in the White House. *(John Robert Irelan—The Republic, or, A History of the United States of America in the Administrations)*

President on television. *See* Television—Telecast: President to appear on television

President to be assassinated was Abraham Lincoln. He attended a performance of *Our American Cousin* on April 14, 1865, at Ford's Theatre, Washington, D.C., where he was shot by John Wilkes Booth. He died the following day, April 15, 1865. *(Thomas Mealey Harris—Assassination of Lincoln, A History of the Great Conspiracy)*

President to become a congressman. *See* Congressman (U.S.): Congressman who had been a President of the United States

President to become a godfather to a member of the English royal family was Franklin Delano Roosevelt. On August 4, 1942, the Duke of Kent, youngest brother of King George VI, served as proxy for President Roosevelt at the christening of his son, Michael George Charles Franklin, Prince George of Kent, born July 4, 1942.

President to become a senator was Andrew Johnson, the seventeenth President (1865-1869). Johnson was an unsuccessful candidate for election to the Senate in 1869 and an unsuccessful independent candidate for election to the House of Representatives in 1872. He was elected in 1875 and served as senator from Tennessee from March 4, 1875, until his death, July 31, 1875. *(Robert Watson Winston—Andrew Johnson, Plebeian and Patriot)*

President to become Chief Justice of the United States after serving as President was William Howard Taft. He was appointed Chief Justice June 30, 1921. He resigned on February 3, 1930, a few weeks before his death. *(Francis McHale—President and Chief Justice, the Life and Public Services of William Howard Taft)*

President to broadcast a presidential message. *See* Radio Broadcast: Presidential message to be broadcast

President to broadcast by radio was President Warren Gamaliel Harding, the twenty-ninth President (1921-1923). His speech at the dedication of the Francis Scott Key Memorial at Fort McHenry, Baltimore, Md., on June 14, 1922, was broadcast by WEAR (now WFBR), Baltimore, Md. His voice was carried over telephone lines to the studio and broadcast from there. His World Court speech on June 21, 1923, at St. Louis, Mo., was transmitted over KSD, St. Louis, and WEAF, New York City. On November 5, 1921, a message from President Harding had been broadcast from Washington, D.C., to 28 countries. It was sent in code over the 25,000 volt RCA station at Rocky Point (near Port Jefferson), L.I., N.Y.

President to broadcast from a foreign country was Franklin Delano Roosevelt, whose speech at Cartagena, Colombia, on July 10, 1934, was relayed to New York and transmitted over the combined WEAF, WJZ, and WABC networks.

President to broadcast from the White House. *See* Radio Broadcast: President to broadcast from the White House

President to broadcast in a foreign language was Franklin Delano Roosevelt, who addressed the French people on November 7, 1942, from Washington, D.C., at the same time that the American Army was taking part in the invasion of French territorial possessions in Africa.

President to celebrate his silver wedding anniversary at the White House was Rutherford Birchard Hayes, the nineteenth President (1877-1881). The Reverend Dr. Lorenzo Dow McCabe of Ohio Wesleyan University, who had united him in marriage with Lucy Webb on December 30, 1852, again performed the ceremony on December 31, 1877. Mrs. Hayes wore her wedding gown of white flowered satin. *(Charles Richard Williams—Life of Rutherford Birchard Hayes)*

President to die in Washington, D.C., was William Henry Harrison, the ninth President, who died in the White House, April 4, 1841. President Harrison served only from March 4, 1841, to April 4, 1841. *(Benjamin Fisk Barrett—A Discourse . . . Suggested by the Death of William Henry Harrison)*

President to face enemy gunfire while in office, and the first President actively to use his authority as Commander-In-Chief was James Madison, the fourth President (1809-

PRESIDENT (United States)—*Continued*
1817). He assumed command August 25, 1814, of Commodore Joshua Barney's battery, known as "Barney's Battery," stationed a half mile north of Bladensburg, Md. *(Mary Barney— A Biographical Memoir of the Late Commodore Joshua Barney)*

President to fly was Theodore Roosevelt, the twenty-sixth President (1901-1909). He was a passenger in a plane piloted by Archibald (Archie) Hoxsey at St. Louis, Mo., on October 11, 1910, more than a year after he had ceased to be President. *(Henry Ladd Smith—Airways—History of Commercial Aviation in the United States)*

President to fly in a helicopter was Dwight David Eisenhower, the thirty-fourth President (1953-1961). On July 12, 1957, he flew in a three-seat Bell Ranger H-47J piloted by Major Joseph E. Barrett from the White House to an undisclosed site chosen for relocation of the White House during an atomic attack drill. He had previously flown in a helicopter while he was Supreme Allied Commander of the North Atlantic Treaty Organization.

President to fly in a twin-engined airplane was Dwight David Eisenhower, who made a 146-mile round-trip flight from Washington, D.C., to his farm at Gettysburg, Pa., on June 3, 1955. The trip to Gettysburg was made in 32 minutes and the return flight in 22 minutes. The airplane, a blue and white Aero Commander 560 (AF-2), was manufactured by the Aero Design and Engineering Company of Bethany, Okla., and cost approximately $70,000. It was flown by Lieutenant Colonel William Grafton Draper. (Before this flight security regulations had required four-engine planes for presidential flights.)

President to fly in an airplane while in office was Franklin Delano Roosevelt, who in January 1943 flew 5,000 miles in a four-engine Boeing Flying Boat from Miami, Florida, to the west coast of French Morocco for the Casablanca conference with British Prime Minister Winston Churchill (January 14-23, 1943).

President to go through the Panama Canal while President was President Franklin Delano Roosevelt. He passed through the canal July 11, 1934, on the U.S.S. "Houston" destined for Hawaii and was greeted at Balboa, Panama, by President Harmodio Arias and Foreign Secretary Arosemena of Panama.

President to hold an airplane pilot's license was Dwight David Eisenhower, who was issued pilot's license No. 93,258 on November 30, 1939, by the Civil Aeronautics Administration. He

learned to fly in 1939 when he was a lieutenant colonel on General Douglas MacArthur's staff in the Philippines.

President to invite the President-elect to discuss governmental problems was Herbert Clark Hoover, the thirty-first President (1929-1933). On November 12, 1932, Hoover invited President-elect Franklin Delano Roosevelt to confer with him with regard to the request made by Great Britain for suspension of payments of her war debt. The instalment due on December 15, 1932, was $95,000,000. Roosevelt, then governor of New York, called on President Hoover on November 22, 1932. *(Vernon Boyce Hampton—Breasting World Frontiers, Herbert Hoover's Achievements)*

President to pitch a ball to open the baseball season was President William Howard Taft. On April 14, 1910, he threw the baseball which opened the American League Washington-Philadelphia game. Washington won 3 to 0. Pitcher Walter Johnson held the visitors to one hit. The crowd, 12,226 paid admissions, broke all previous attendance records.

President to receive fewer popular and electoral votes than an opponent was John Quincy Adams, the sixth President (1825-1829). In the November 1824 elections Andrew Jackson had received 153,544 popular and 99 electoral votes; Adams had received 108,740 popular and 84 electoral votes; and William Harris Crawford and Henry Clay had received 42 and 37 electoral votes, respectively. Since no candidate had a majority of the electoral votes, it devolved upon the House of Representatives to choose from the highest three. In the meantime Crawford had become ill and was practically eliminated, and Clay as fourth agreed to use his influence to have Adams elected provided he would be appointed Secretary of State under Adams. The House of Representatives elected Adams by a vote of 13 states for Adams, 7 for Jackson, and 4 for Crawford.

President to receive the unanimous vote of the presidential electors was George Washington, who received all of the 69 votes cast by the electors from the ten states which voted on February 4, 1789. In the election for the ninth term, 1821-1825, James Monroe of Virginia received 231 of the 232 votes cast by the electors from twenty-four states. The dissenting vote was cast by William Plumer of New Hampshire.

President to reside in Washington, D.C., was John Adams, the second President (1797-1801). On June 3, 1800, he resided at the Union Tavern, Georgetown, D.C., and in November 1800 moved into the President's House, the Executive Mansion.

President to rest in state in the United States Capitol rotunda was Abraham Lincoln who died April 15, 1865. His body was removed to the White House where it remained April 15-18, after which it was removed to the Capitol rotunda, where it was kept April 19-20. On April 21 it was taken to the railroad station where it was conveyed to Springfield, Ill. Lincoln was buried May 4, 1865, in Oakland Cemetery, near Springfield, Ill. *(Ida Minerva Tarbell—Life of Abraham Lincoln)*

President to review the military forces at his residence was Thomas Jefferson. On July 4, 1801, on the White House grounds, he reviewed the Marines, led by the Marine Band.

President to ride in an automobile was Theodore Roosevelt, who rode in a purple-lined Columbia Electric Victoria August 22, 1902, at Hartford, Conn. He was accompanied by Colonel Jacob Lyman Greene. Twenty carriages followed the presidential car during the tour of the city.

President to ride on a railroad train was Andrew Jackson, who on June 6, 1833, took the stagecoach to Ellicott's Mills, where he boarded the Baltimore and Ohio train for Baltimore, Md. on a pleasure trip. John Quincy Adams, however, had made a trip on the same line a few months earlier, but after he had left the presidency.

President to serve as an official of the Confederate States was John Tyler, who became a delegate to the Provisional Congress of the Confederate States on August 1, 1861. He was elected a member of the House of Representatives of the permanent Confederate Congress on November 7, 1861, but died on January 18, 1862, before taking his seat. He had been President of the United States from 1841 to 1845. *(Journals of the Confederate Congress. Vol. 1)*

President to tour the country was George Washington, who traveled through the New England states from October 15 to November 13, 1789. He traveled in a hired coach accompanied by Major William Jackson, his aide-de-camp, and Tobias Lear, his private secretary, six servants, nine horses, and a luggage wagon. He went as far north as Kittery, Me. (then part of Massachusetts). As Rhode Island and Vermont had not joined the new government, he did not visit those states. Washington's first tour of the southern states was made from April 7 to June 12, 1791, during which time he left Mount Vernon, Va., on a 1,887-mile trip through Philadelphia, south through Virginia and the Carolinas into Georgia and back to Mount Vernon.

President to travel underwater in a captured enemy submarine was Harry S. Truman, the thirty-third President (1945-1953). He embarked at Key West, Fla., on November 21, 1946 in the U-2513, a captured German submarine. At sea off Key West, the vessel engaged in exercises during which it submerged. (President Theodore Roosevelt had submerged in the "Plunger," an American submarine, on August 25, 1905.)

President to use a telephone was James Abram Garfield, the twentieth President (1881). He had a telephone installed in 1878 while he was a member of Congress.

President to visit a European country while President was Woodrow Wilson. He left Washington, D.C., December 4, 1918, on the S.S. "George Washington" and arrived at Brest, France, December 13, 1918. He returned to Boston, February 24, 1919. Wilson made a second trip, leaving Hoboken, N.J., March 5 and arriving at Brest, March 13, 1919. He returned to Hoboken July 8, 1919. *(Gerald White Johnson—Woodrow Wilson)*

President to visit a foreign country in wartime was Franklin Delano Roosevelt, who flew from Miami, Fla., to Trinidad, B.W.I., on January 10, 1943, then to Belém, Brazil; Bathurst, Gambia; and Casablanca, Morocco, arriving there on January 14. He returned by plane via Natal, Union of South Africa; Belém; Trinidad; and Miami. He arrived in Washington, D.C., by train on January 31, 1943.

President to visit a foreign country while President was Theodore Roosevelt, who sailed on the U.S.S. "Louisiana" for Panama where he remained from November 14 to 17, 1906, after which he went to Puerto Rico. (While on a fishing trip Grover Cleveland once passed beyond the three mile limit.) *(Harold Howland—Theodore Roosevelt and His Times)*

President to visit Alaska and Canada while President was Warren Gamaliel Harding, who visited Metlakahtla, Alaska, July 8, 1923, and Vancouver, B.C., July 26, 1923. He sailed on the U.S. naval transport "Henderson."

President to visit Hawaii while President was Franklin Delano Roosevelt, who landed July 25, 1934, at Hilo, Hawaii. He was officially welcomed by Governor Joseph Poindexter on board the cruiser U.S.S. "Houston."

President to visit South America while President was Franklin Delano Roosevelt, who stopped off at Cartagena, Colombia, July 10, 1934. Prior to his visit, he received President Enrique Olaya Herrera of Colombia at

PRESIDENT (United States)—*Continued*
a formal visit on board the cruiser U.S.S.
"Houston." President Roosevelt returned President Herrera's visit on July 10.

President who had been a senator was
James Monroe, who served as senator from
Virginia from November 9, 1790, to May 27,
1794, filling the vacancy caused by the death of
William Grayson on March 12, 1790.

President who had received a patent was
Abraham Lincoln. On March 10, 1849, in
Springfield, Ill., he applied for a patent for
"buoying vessels over shoals," a device for
lifting vessels over shoals by means of inflated
cylinders. His application was granted and on
May 22, 1849, he obtained patent No. 6,469.
(Sven Anderson—Floating Drydocks)

**President who had used a telephone for
campaigning** was William McKinley, the
twenty-fifth President (1897-1901). He called
thirty-eight of his campaign managers in as
many states from Canton, Ohio, in 1896 during
the presidential campaign which resulted in his
election.

President who was a bachelor was James
Buchanan, the fifteenth President (1857-1861).

President who was a Catholic was John
Fitzgerald Kennedy, who was inaugurated
January 20, 1961, in Washington, D.C., as
the thirty-fifth President.

President who was a "dark horse" candidate was James Knox Polk, the eleventh
President (1845-1849). His name appeared for
the first time on the eighth ballot at the Democratic convention on May 29, 1844. On the
ninth ballot, amid great confusion, the convention stampeded for him. *(Frank van der Linden
—Dark Horse)*

President whose assassination was attempted was Andrew Jackson. On January
30, 1835, Richard Lawrence snapped two pistols
at President Jackson as he attended the funeral
of Representative Warren Ransom Davis of
South Carolina at the Capitol in Washington,
D.C. Fortunately the weapons missed fire.
(Niles' Weekly Register. February 1835)

President whose grandson became President was William Henry Harrison, the ninth
President (1841). His grandson, Benjamin
Harrison, was the twenty-third President
(1888-1893).

President whose mother lived at the Executive Mansion, Washington, D.C., was
James Abram Garfield, the twentieth President

(March 4, 1881-September 19, 1881). His
mother, Eliza Ballou Garfield, lived in the
White House with her son. *(John Clark Ridpath—The Life and Work of James A. Garfield)*

**President whose mother saw her son inaugurated President of the United States for
a second term** was Franklin Delano Roosevelt, whose mother, Sarah Delano Roosevelt,
saw him take his second oath of office on January 20, 1937.

President whose son became President was
John Adams, the second President (1797-1801),
father of John Quincy Adams, the sixth President (1825-1829).

**President whose wife was not born in the
United States** was John Quincy Adams.
Mrs. Adams was the former Louisa Catherine
Johnson, born February 12, 1775, in London,
England, the daughter of Joshua Johnson of
Maryland, first United States Consul in London. On July 26, 1797, they were married at
the Church of the Parish of All Hollows,
Barking, England. At the time Adams was
United States Minister to Holland.

Presidential address to be televised. *See*
Television—Telecast: Presidential address
televised from the White House.

Presidential airplane was the "Sacred
Cow," a four-engine Skymaster C-54 built at
the Douglas Aircraft Company's Santa Monica,
Calif., plant and delivered June 1944 to the
Air Transport Command. Its first mission outside the United States was to fly Henry Lewis
Stimson, Secretary of War, from Washington,
D.C., to Naples, Italy, a distance of 4,200 miles,
in 24 hours.

**Presidential airplane (turbo-compound
powered)** was the Air Force "Columbine
III," a Lockheed Super Constellation V C 121
E, christened November 24, 1954, at the National Airport, Washington, D.C., by Mrs.
Dwight David Eisenhower. It cruised at 335
m.p.h. and could fly faster than 370 m.p.h. It
was powered by four Wright turbo-compound
3250 h.p. engines turning three-bladed Hamilton
Standard propellers. It had a wing span of 123
feet, a fuselage length of 116 feet, and a maximum gross takeoff weight of 133,000 pounds.
It had accommodations for a crew of 18 and
28 passengers during daytime flight. The first
official trip was made November 24, 1954, from
Washington, D.C., to Augusta, Ga., with British Field Marshal Viscount Bernard Law
Montgomery, and Ellis Slater, George Allen,
Colonel Thomas Belshe and their wives. (Mrs.
Eisenhower had flown in the plane on a trip to
New York City before November 15.)

THE FIRST

Presidential amnesty proclamation. *See* Amnesty

Presidential campaign co-manager (woman). *See* Woman: Woman presidential campaign co-manager

Presidential citation. *See* Medal: Presidential citation

Presidential flag. *See* Flag: President's flag

Presidential impeachment proceedings. *See* Impeachment: Impeachment proceedings against a President of the United States

Presidential inauguration broadcast. *See* Radio broadcast: Presidential inauguration

Presidential message broadcast. *See* Radio broadcast: Presidential message to be broadcast

Presidential news conference filmed for television and newsreels. *See* Television— Telecast: Presidential news conference filmed for television and newsreels

Presidential notification ceremony. *See* Television—Telecast: Presidential nomination notification ceremony to be televised

President's car. *See* Railroad car: President's car

President's child born in the White House. *See* Births: Child born in the White House, Washington, D.C., the offspring of a President

President's flag. *See* Flag: President's flag

President's widow to receive a pension. *See* Pension: Pension to the widow of a President

President's wife to frank mail was Martha Washington. On April 3, 1800, an "act to extend the privilege of franking letters and packages to Martha Washington" (2 Stat.L.19) was passed. This privilege was granted her "for and during her life."

Veto message read by a President. *See* Veto (presidential): Veto message read by a President

Vice President to become President automatically. *See* Vice President: Vice President to become President automatically

THE FIRST

PRESIDENTIAL CANDIDATE

Presidential candidate debate series on television was the Richard Milhous Nixon-John Fitzgerald Kennedy debate series during the 1960 presidential campaign. The first of four debates was held September 26, 1960, in a Chicago studio; the second, October 7, 1960, in a Washington, D.C., studio; the third, October 13, 1960 (Kennedy in New York City, Nixon in Hollywood, Calif.); and the fourth, October 21, 1960, in a New York City studio.

Presidential candidate nominated at a caucus was Thomas Jefferson. The Democratic-Republican Party held a caucus on February 25, 1804, in Washington, D.C., at which Thomas Jefferson of Virginia was unanimously nominated for President, and George Clinton of New York for Vice President. Without holding a caucus, the Federalists supported Charles Cotesworth Pinckney of South Carolina for President and Rufus King of New York for Vice President. At the election in November 1804, Jefferson received 162 electoral votes and Pinckney 14.

Presidential candidate nominated at a national convention was Andrew Jackson. The Democrats at their national convention in Baltimore in 1832 nominated Andrew Jackson of Tennessee for President, and Martin Van Buren of New York for Vice President. *(Edgar Eugene Robinson—The Evolution of American Political Parties)*

Presidential candidate of Negro blood nominated in a political convention was Frederick Douglass of Rochester, N.Y., who received one complimentary vote on June 23, 1888, on the fourth ballot at the Republican convention opened in Chicago, Ill., June 19, 1888. (On June 25, on the eighth ballot, the convention nominated Benjamin Harrison, who was elected as the twenty-third President.) Douglass was later appointed United States Minister to Haiti. *(Official Proceedings of the Republican National Convention Held at Chicago, June 19, 20, 21, 22, 23 and 25, 1888)*

Presidential candidate to broadcast a political speech. *See* Radio broadcast: Presidential candidate to broadcast a political speech

Presidential candidate to campaign and make speeches in a foreign language was James Abram Garfield, who made several political speeches in German. He was elected the twentieth President and was sworn in March 4, 1881. *(Emma Elizabeth Brown—Life and Public Services of James A. Garfield)*

Presidential candidate to fly to a political convention to make an acceptance speech was Franklin Delano Roosevelt, then Governor of New York, who chartered a ten-passenger

THE FIRST

THE FIRST

PRESIDENTIAL CANDIDATE—*Cont.*
tri-motor plane for himself and his party on July 2, 1932, and flew from Albany, N.Y., to Chicago, Ill.

Presidential candidate to make a speech of acceptance at a nominating convention was Franklin Delano Roosevelt, who on July 2, 1932, flew from Albany, N.Y. to Chicago, Ill. to address the Democratic convention.

Presidential candidate to receive the greatest number of popular and electoral votes and yet fail of election was Andrew Jackson on November 2, 1824. He received 153,544 popular and 99 electoral votes, while John Quincy Adams received 108,740 popular and 84 electoral votes, William Harris Crawford 47,136 popular and 41 electoral votes, and Henry Clay 46,618 popular and 37 electoral votes. Since no candidate received a majority of the electoral votes, the decision went to the House of Representatives, which elected Adams after Clay, who in fourth place was out of the running, had thrown his votes to Adams.

Presidential candidate who was a Catholic was Charles O'Conor of New York, who, on September 3, 1872, was nominated at the Democratic convention at Louisville, Ky., by a wing of Democrats who refused to accept the nomination of Horace Greeley made at Baltimore, Md. O'Conor declined the nomination but his name nevertheless was listed and he received approximately 30,000 votes from 23 states. *(American Irish Historical Society. Vol. 27, 1928)*

Talking pictures of presidential candidates. *See* Moving picture: Talking pictures of presidential candidates

Woman presidential candidate was Victoria Claflin Woodhull, who was nominated by the National Radical Reformers at a meeting held May 10, 1872 at Apollo Hall, New York City. She was nominated by Judge Carter of Cincinnati, Ohio. Frederick Douglass was the vice presidential nominee. The National Radical Reformers seceded from the National Woman Suffrage Association, which met May 9-11, 1872 at Steinway Hall, New York City. *(Theodore Tilton—Biographical Sketch of Victoria C. Woodhull)*

PRESIDENTIAL CENSURE was passed
in the form of a resolution by the United States Senate on March 28, 1834, by a vote of 26 to 20. The resolution declared that President Andrew Jackson "in the last executive proceedings in relation to the public revenue, has assumed upon himself authority and power not conferred by the constitution and laws, but in derogation of both." He incurred displeasure by his handling of the Bank of the United States

matter. *(Gales and Seaton—Register of Debates in Congress—23rd Congress—First Session)*

PRESIDENTIAL COMMISSION
President requested by Congress to justify the creation of a presidential committee was John Tyler. The House of Representatives on February 7, 1842, passed a resolution "that the President of the United States inform this House under what authority the commission, consisting of George Poindexter and others, for the investigation of the concerns of the New York Custom House was raised, what were the purposes and objects of said commission . . . and out of what fund the said expenditures have been or are to be paid." Tyler, in a letter, dated February 9, 1842, cited the "authority vested in the President of the United States 'to take care that the laws be faithfully executed and to give to Congress from time to time information on the state of the Union.'"

Presidential commission was appointed by President George Washington to deal with the rebellious elements in Washington and Allegheny counties, Pa. In his proclamation to Congress on August 7, 1794, Washington stated: "I do hereby command all persons, being insurgents as aforesaid, on or before the first day of September next to disperse and retire peacefully to their respective abodes." In his sixth annual address, on November 19, 1794, he declared: "The report of the commissioners marks their firmness and abilities, and must unite all virtuous men, by shewing that the means of conciliation have been exhausted."

PRESIDENTIAL ELECTION
Presidential election in which candidates had been nominated for the vice presidency was held on November 6, 1804. Prior to the adoption of the twelfth amendment to the Constitution on September 25, 1804, the candidate for President receiving the second highest number of votes became Vice President. In 1804 Thomas Jefferson was elected President and George Clinton, Vice President.

Presidential election in which more than one candidate declared for the presidency was the election of 1797. John Adams received 71 electoral votes and was elected President. Thomas Jefferson, his opponent, received 68 electoral votes, and was elected Vice President. In the elections of 1789 and 1793, George Washington was the only avowed presidential candidate. *(Alexander Kelly McClure—Our Presidents and How We Make Them)*

PRESIDENTIAL ELECTORAL COLLEGE invited to an inauguration was the
college which had elected Franklin Delano Roosevelt in 1932. The 531 electors, all but 59 of whom were Democrats, were officially invited to attend the inauguration on March 4, 1933. *(Compton Mackenzie—Mr. Roosevelt)*

THE FIRST

PRESIDENTIAL EULOGY, in which George Washington was termed "first in war, first in peace and first in the hearts of his countrymen," was delivered on December 26, 1799, before both Houses of Congress by Henry Lee of Virginia. *(Henry Lee—Funeral Oration on the Death of General Washington)*

PRESIDENTIAL EXECUTIVE ORDER to be numbered was issued by President Abraham Lincoln on October 20, 1862: "I do hereby constitute a provisional court, which shall be a court of record, for the State of Louisiana, and I do hereby appoint Charles A. Peabody of New York to be a provisional judge to hold said court" Peabody's annual compensation was $3,500. (Lincoln's order was not the first executive order issued by a President; it is the first one in the files of the Department of State.) *(James Daniel Richardson—A Compilation of the Messages and Papers of the Presidents)*

PRESIDENTIAL INAUGURAL BALL was held Thursday, May 7, 1789, at the Assembly Rooms, on the east side of Broadway, a little above Wall Street, New York City. A medallion portrait of President George Washington in profile on a fan was presented as a souvenir to the ladies.

"PRESIDENTIAL MANSION" was No. 1 Cherry Street, the Franklin House, corner of Franklin and Cherry Streets, now Franklin Square, New York City, which was occupied by President and Mrs. George Washington from April 23, 1789, to February 23, 1790. It originally was the home of Samuel Osgood. *(New-York Historical Society Quarterly Bulletin. Vol. 23, 1939)*

PRESIDENTIAL NEWS CONFERENCE ON TELEVISION. *See* Television—Telecast: Presidential news conference filmed for television and newsreels

PRESIDENTIAL POPULAR VOTE was recorded in the election of November 2, 1824, in which 356,038 votes were cast. In 6 states the electors were chosen by the state legislatures, and in 18 states by popular vote (in 13 by general ticket and in 5 by districts). Andrew Jackson received 153,544 votes (99 electoral votes); John Quincy Adams, 108,740 votes (84 electoral votes); William Harris Crawford, 47,136 votes (41 electoral votes); and Henry Clay, 46,618 votes (37 electoral votes). None of the candidates having an electoral majority, the election went, on February 9, 1825, to the House of Representatives, which chose from the highest three. Clay was excluded and his strength went to Adams, who carried 13 of the 24 states and was elected. The candidates represented different factions of the Jeffersonian Republican party. Those

THE FIRST

in the Adams-Clay wing were known as National Republicans, and those in the Jackson wing as Democratic-Republicans or Democrats.

PRESIDENTIAL PROTEST was signed April 15, 1834, by Andrew Jackson. He protested against the Senate resolution censuring the President for his course in the bank controversy.

PRESIDENTIAL SUCCESSION ACT passed March 1, 1792 (1 Stat.L.239). It read: "In case of the removal, death, resignation, or disability of both the President and Vice-President of the United States, the President of the Senate, pro tempore, and in case there shall be no President of the Senate, then the Speaker of the House of Representatives for the time being shall act as President of the United States until such disability be removed or until a President be elected."

PRESS CLIPPING BUREAU was opened at 60 Ann Street, New York City, on April 15, 1884, by Samuel Leavitt. The business was absorbed by Henry Romeike, who had established a similar service in June 1881 in London, England. It was known as Henry Romeike's Press Cuttings.

PRESSING MACHINE (steam-operated) was invented by Adon J. Hoffman, who applied for a patent December 1, 1904, which was granted July 13, 1909, No. 928,199. The machine was equipped with a "buck" or lower pressing surface. The "head" or upper pressing surface was heated by gas and it was necessary to lay a damp press cloth over the goods, as when pressing with a hand iron. The machine was marketed first in 1907 by the United States Hoffman Company of Seattle, Wash.

PRICE REGULATION AGREEMENT *See* Trust: Manufacturers' price regulation agreement

PRICE REGULATION LAW
Price regulation law (colonial) was "an act to prevent monopolies and oppression by excessive and unreasonable prices for many of the necessaries and conveniencies of life, and for preventing engrossers, and for the better supply of our troops in the army with such necessaries as may be wanted," enacted by Rhode Island, at Providence, on December 31, 1776, effective January 8, 1777. The law regulated prices on farm labor, beef, hides, shoes, cotton, sugar, salt, coffee, cheese, butter, beans, peas, potatoes, pork, wool, flannel, towcloths, flax, tallow, rum, molasses, oats, stockings, wheat, rye, Indian corn, salted pork, etc. Fines equivalent to the value of the merchandise were applied equally to the state and to informers.

PRICE REGULATION LAW—*Continued*
Price regulation law (federal) was enacted by the Emergency Price Control Act of 1942, approved January 30, 1942 (56 Stat.L.23), which created the Office of Price Administration as an independent agency under the direction of the Price Administrator. The Office of Price Administration and Civilian Supply was created by Executive Order No. 8,734 on April 11, 1941. Its name was shortened to Office of Price Administration by Executive Order No. 8,875 on August 28, 1941.

Price regulation law (state) was Act No. 128 of Louisiana, "to prohibit unfair commercial discrimination between different sections, communities, cities, or localities in the State of Louisiana or unfair competition therein and providing penalties therefor," approved July 2, 1908, by Governor Jared Young Sanders. It became effective July 29, 1908.

Resale price maintenance law (state) was the California "Fair Trade Act" approved May 8, 1931 (Statutes 1931, chapter 278, effective August 14, 1931), which provided "that the buyer will not resell such commodity except at the price stipulated by the vendor." The title of the act is "an act to protect trade-mark owners, distributors and the public against injurious and uneconomic practices in the distribution of articles of standard quality under a distinguished trade-mark, brand or name."

PRIEST (Catholic). *See* Catholic priest

PRIMA DONNA (Negro). *See* Opera: Negro prima donna of an opera company

PRIMARY ELECTION. *See* Election law: Primary election law

PRIME MINISTER OF ENGLAND TO ADDRESS THE CONGRESS OF THE UNITED STATES. *See* Congress of the United States: Prime Minister of England to address the Congress of the United States

PRIMER
See also School book

Primer in an American Indian dialect was *The Indian Primer; or, The Way of Training Up of Our Indian Youth in the Good Knowledge of God, in the Knowledge of the Scriptures and in an Ability to Read*, by John Eliot. It was printed in the Massachusetts Indian language and was published in Cambridge, Mass., in 1669 by Marmaduke Johnson. A similar edition by Eliot is believed to have been published in 1653-1654 by Samuel Green, Cambridge, Mass., but no known copies are in existence.

Typewriting primer was *Ted and Polly*, by Ralph Haefner, published in November 1933 by the Macmillan Company, New York City, and intended for use in first and second grades by children from five to eight. The material in the book had been tried out two years previously in various schools.

PRINCE OF WALES TO VISIT THE UNITED STATES. *See* Visiting celebrities: Prince of Wales

PRINT PATENT. *See* Patent: Print patent

PRINTED AMERICAN PLAY. *See* Play: Printed American play

PRINTED BALLOT. *See* Election: Printed ballot

PRINTER (woman). *See* Woman: Woman printer

PRINTER'S INK was successfully manufactured in America by Charles Eneu Johnson, who began manufacturing inks in Philadelphia, Pa., in 1804. His concern has been in continuous operation at the same location ever since. It is now part of the United Carbon Company.

PRINTING
Document printed in America (known to have been printed) was the "Oath of a Free Man," printed in March 1639 by the Stephen Day Press, Cambridge, Mass. It was a one-page sheet: "I doe solemnly bind myself in the sight of God, that when I shall be called to give my voice touching any subject of this State, in which Freemen are to deal, I will give my vote and suffrage as I shall judge in mine own conscience may best conduce and tend to the publick weal of the body, without respect of persons, or favour of any man." (*Lawrence Counselman Wroth—The Oath of a Free Man*)

PRINTING HISTORY was Isaiah Thomas's *History of Printing in America, with a Biography of Printers, and an Account of Newspapers*, published in two volumes in 1810 in Worcester, Mass.

PRINTING INSTRUCTION
Printing instruction was given in the social community school founded by Robert Owen in New Harmony, Ind., in 1826. Printing, lithography and engraving were the subjects studied. (*Indiana Magazine of History.—Vol. 33. No.4. December 1937*)

Printing lecture course in a college was "An introduction to the technique of printing," offered February 1911, by the Graduate

THE FIRST

School of Business Administration, Harvard University, Cambridge, Mass. The course was given by Daniel Berkeley Updike. *(Daniel Berkeley Updike—Printing Types, Their History, Forms and Use)*

PRINTING MAGAZINE (professional) was the *Typographic Advertiser,* a quarterly, published by L. Johnson & Co., Philadelphia, Pa., which appeared April 1855.

PRINTING OFFICE (United States). *See* Government printing office

PRINTING PRESS

Cylinder and flat bed combination printing press was manufactured in 1844 by R. Hoe & Co., New York City. It was invented by Robert Hoe, who obtained patent No. 3,551 on April 17, 1844. The circumference of the cylinder was equivalent to the entire travel of the bed forward and backward. The cylinder made one revolution for each impression in printing without stopping.

Cylinder printing press was made by R. Hoe & Co., New York City, in 1831 and was operated by hand power. Later steam was employed. It was used to print the *Temperance Recorder,* a monthly first published on March 6, 1832, in Albany, N.Y., and devoted exclusively to the cause of temperance. *(Merritt Way Haynes—Student's History of Printing)*

High-speed newspaper printing and folding machine, utilizing the gathering cylinder with a rotary folding cylinder, was installed in 1876 on the presses of the Philadelphia, Pa., *Times.* It printed and folded a four-page sheet at the rate of four hundred a minute. The press was shown in operation at the Philadelphia Centennial Exposition in 1876.

Power or steam printing press was made by Daniel Treadwell of Boston in 1822. It was based upon the principle of the Washington hand press. Only three or four were manufactured.

Power printing press capable of fine book work was the Adams Press, invented by Isaac Adams of Boston, Mass., who obtained a patent October 4, 1830, on a "power printing press." He improved it and received an additional patent on the improvements on March 2, 1836.

Printing press was imported from England by the Reverend Jesse (Jose) Glover of Sutton, England, in the summer of 1638 on the "John" of London, together with printers skilled in its operation. Glover contracted with Stephen Day on June 7, 1638, to sail to America. They were accompanied by Day's wife, Rebecca,

THE FIRST

his sons, Stephen and Matthew, and William Boardman. Glover died on board the ship. The press was set in operation in March 1639, at Cambridge, Mass. *(Robert F. Roden—The Cambridge Press)*

Printing press for polychromatic printing was invented by Thomas F. Adams of Philadelphia, Pa., who obtained patent No. 3,744 on September 17, 1844. Different color rollers, operating in parallel, were used to produce linear work.

Printing press for printing "paper hangings" (wall paper) in color was invented by Peter Force of Washington, D.C., who patented it August 22, 1822.

Printing press invented in America was the Columbian Press. In 1816 George E. Clymer of Philadelphia, Pa., devised an iron hand-printing press which was operated by a combination of compound levers instead of a screw to give the downward pressure. *(Wilbur Fisk Cleaver—Five Centuries of Printing)*

Printing press invented in America that was practical and successful was the Washington Press, invented in 1827 by Samuel Rust of New York City. This type of press is still used for taking fine proofs. Rust obtained patents on May 13, 1821, March 2, 1826, and April 17, 1829.

Printing press operated by electricity was invented by Thomas Davenport of Brandon, Vt., and used in 1839 in New York City. An engine weighing less than one hundred pounds operated a rotary printing press. The *Electro-Magnet and Mechanics Intelligencer* issued January 18, 1840, by Davenport was one of the periodicals printed by this press. He obtained patent No. 132 on February 25, 1837 on an "electrical motor."

Printing press to use a continuous web or roll of paper was the Bullock Press, produced by William Bullock of Pittsburgh, Pa., in 1865. It was the first machine built especially for curved stereotype plates. It printed both sides of the sheet, and cut it either before or after printing. U.S. patent No. 38,200 was granted April 14, 1863. The press was first used by the New York *Sun.*

Quadruple newspaper press was constructed in 1887 by R. Hoe & Co., New York City, for the New York *World* plant, where it was installed in 1891. It produced an eight-page newspaper at a running speed of 48,000 per hour or ten, twelve, fourteen or sixteen pages at a running speed of 24,000 an hour. The papers were cut and folded, ready for delivery.

PRINTING PRESS—*Continued*

Rotary printing press with a continuous roll feed to be perfected was produced in 1871 by R. Hoe & Company, New York City, and utilized the first gathering and delivery cylinder patented by Stephen D. Tucker of New York City. The press was installed in the New York *Tribune* plant and produced as many as 18,000 newspapers an hour.

Rotary type printing press was the double cylinder machine invented by Richard March Hoe, of New York City. It was first used in the *Ledger* office in Philadelphia in 1846. The bed was of such length that the form of type passed backward and forward under both cylinders. The central cylinder was placed in a horizontal position. The output was 2,000 sheets per hour for each of four feeders. Patent No. 5,199 was obtained July 24, 1847. *(Robert Hoe—Short History of the Printing Press)*

Rotogravure press was imported in November 1904, by the American Photogravure Company of Philadelphia. It was built in Ramsbottom, England, by John Wood. *(Pennell's 1931 Annual of Photography)*

Sextuple printing press was constructed by R. Hoe & Co., New York City, and installed in 1891 at the New York *Herald* plant. It took 18 months to construct, weighed 58 tons, and was composed of 16,000 pieces. The form and impression cylinders were placed parallel instead of at right angles. It could print and fold 90,000 four-page newspapers an hour.

Web-fed four-color rotary printing press was made in 1890 by Walter Scott & Co., Plainfield, N.J., for the Chicago, Ill., *Inter-Ocean*. It was placed in operation in 1892. Curved stereotype plates, cast to fit the cylinders, were used in printing on a two-page-wide roll of paper.

PRISON

American imprisoned in the Tower of London was Henry Laurens of Charlestown, S.C., President of the Continental Congress from November 1, 1777, to December 10, 1778, who was confined from October 6, 1780, to December 31, 1781, on suspicion of high treason. Laurens sailed from Philadelphia, Pa., on August 13, 1780, on the brigantine "Mercury" en route to Holland to serve as United States Minister and negotiate the Lee-Van Berkel loan and treaty but was captured three weeks later by the British off Newfoundland. He threw his papers overboard, but they were recovered and led to the British declaration of war against Holland on December 20, 1780. Imprisoned in the Tower, he was forced to pay for his room, board, and guard. He was released in exchange for Lord Cornwallis. Laurens, with Benjamin Franklin and John

Jay, drew up the preliminary treaty of peace with Great Britain on November 30, 1782, to terminate the Revolutionary War.

Congressman elected who served time in prison. *See* Congressman (U.S.): Congressman elected who served time in prison

Debtors' prison. *See* Debtors' prison

Federal penitentiary fingerprinting. *See* Fingerprinting: Federal penitentiary fingerprinting

Military prison of the United States on an island was Fort Jefferson, Monroe County, Fla. Construction was begun in 1846 on an island in the Gulf of Mexico, sixty miles from Key West. It was a six-sided masonry structure with a huge courtyard in the center. The sides were 1,000 feet long, 80 feet high, and 60 feet thick. On January 19, 1861, it was garrisoned for the first time by Brevet Major Lewis Golding Arnold, 2d U.S. Artillery, with 4 officers and 62 men. At that time the fort had not been completed and was hardly defensible. A prison for the confinement of U.S. military prisoners was established at Fort Jefferson in 1863. The prison, often called Dry Tortugas, was maintained during the Civil war.

Organization of a prison into "community" groups was tried out in 1914 at Auburn Prison, Auburn, N.Y. A Mutual Welfare League, consisting of prisoners, was created to assume the responsibility of discipline in the prison. *(Louis Newton Robinson—Penology in the United States)*

Penitentiary building (national) authorized to be built was the Federal Penitentiary, Leavenworth, Kansas, authorized March 3, 1891 (26 Stat.L.839). It was completed February 1, 1906. The Federal Penitentiary, Atlanta, Georgia, although authorized in 1899, two years after work had begun at Leavenworth, was completed in January 1902.

Prison was constructed in 1676 in Nantucket, Mass. The Court hired William Bunker on November 16, 1676, to keep the prison for one year and agreed to pay him "foeur pounds, halfe in wheat, the other in other graine."

Prison built for women and managed exclusively by women was the Indiana Reformatory Institution for women and girls, Indianapolis, Ind., which received its first prisoners, seventeen women, on October 8, 1873. The first superintendent was Sarah J. Smith, who served from June 10, 1873, to December 1, 1883. In 1907, the name was changed to the

THE FIRST

Indiana Women's Prison. Since January 1877, members of the Board of Trustees have all been women.

Prison matrons were appointed in 1845 through the efforts of the American Female Guardian Society. Four were assigned to Blackwell's Island, N.Y., and two to the City Prison, New York City.

Prison to have individual cells for prisoners was the Walnut Street prison in Philadelphia, Pa., built in 1773, which was remodeled in 1790 (in accordance with the act of April 5, 1790, of the Pennsylvania General Assembly) to contain twenty-four solitary cells each 6 feet wide, 8 feet long, and 7 feet high. *(Negley King Teeters—The Cradle of the Penitentiary; the Walnut Street Jail at Philadelphia 1773-1835)*

.Prisoners (federal) employed in industry produced cotton duck for mail bags, etc., at the Cotton Duck Mill, United States Penitentiary, Atlanta, Ga., whose first loom started July 11, 1919. The building covered an area of almost three acres. The first year, 386,414 yards of duck were produced. The mill was authorized by act of Congress of July 10, 1918 (40 Stat.L.896), which appropriated $650,000 for equipment and $150,000 as working capital. A wage system for inmates established April 29, 1921, set up a wage fund of 2 cents per yard which was divided among the inmates in proportion to their number of hours of service.

Reformatory for boys (state) was the reformatory school at Westborough, Mass., now the Lyman School for Boys. It was authorized April 9, 1847 (chapter 165). *(Hastings Hornell Hart—Juvenile Court Laws in the United States)*

Reformatory for juvenile delinquents under legislative control was the New York House of Refuge, New York City, opened January 1, 1825, with three boys and six girls. It was under the supervision of the Society for the Reformation of Juvenile Offenders in the City of New York and was incorporated March 29, 1824. The first president was Cadwallader David Colden. On April 9, 1825, the state authorized a grant of $2,000 annually for the next five years. *(First Annual Report of the Managers of the Society for the Reformation of Juvenile Offenders in the City of New York)*

Reformatory (state) conducted for women was the Reformatory Prison for Women, Sherborn, Mass., opened November 7, 1877. By an act of legislature, chapter 181, March 22, 1911, the name was changed to the Reformatory for Women. The first superintendent was Eudora

THE FIRST

Clark Atkinson. She resigned September 1, 1880 and was succeeded by Dr. Eliza Maria Mosher, who had been resident physician from the opening of the institution. In 1925, the part of Sherborn in which the reformatory was located was annexed to the town of Framingham, Mass. *(Massachusetts Bureau of Prisons —Annual Report, 1915)*

State prison to take fingerprints. *See* Fingerprinting: State prison to take fingerprints

PRISON REFORM SOCIETY to bring about changes in prison administration was the Philadelphia Society for Alleviating the Miseries of Public Prisons, formed May 8, 1787, in the German School House on Cherry Street, Philadelphia, Pa., by Philadelphia Quakers. The first president was William White. A similar organization for war prisoners was the Philadelphia Society for Relieving Distressed Prisoners Owing to the War of Independence, organized in 1776. *(Gustave de Beaumont and Charles Alexis Clerel de Tocqueville—Penitentiary System in the United States)*

PRIVATE RAILROAD CAR. *See* Railroad car: Private railroad car

PRIVATE SCHOOL FOR CRIPPLES. *See* Cripples: Private school for cripples

PRIZE FIGHT
American to win distinction in the prize ring was Bill Richmond, a Negro, born in Richmond, Staten Island, N.Y., August 5, 1763, the son of a slave owned by the Reverend Charlton. On July 8, 1805, Richmond knocked out Jack Holmes, alias Tom Tough, in the twenty-sixth round at Cricklewood Green, a short distance from Kilburn Wells, England. On October 8, 1805, he was defeated by Tom Cribb at Hailsham, Sussex. He never fought in the United States. *(Henry Downes Miles—Pugilistica)*

International fight, with bare knuckles, was held on the outskirts of St. Louis, Mo., June 15, 1869. Mike McCoole, American champion, fought Tom Allen of England and won on a questionable foul in the ninth round. *(Alexander Johnston—Ten—And Out)*

Moving picture of a prize fight. *See* Moving picture: Moving picture of a staged prize fight

Negro heavyweight champion of the world was Jack Johnson, who defeated Tommy Burns at Sydney, Australia, on December 26, 1908, in fourteen rounds, technically winning the championship. The actual title was earned July 4, 1910, when he defeated James Jackson (Jim)

PRIZE FIGHT—*Continued*
Jeffries in fifteen rounds at Reno, Nevada. Johnson lost his title April 5, 1915, at Havana, Cuba, to Jess Willard in twenty-six rounds.

Open-air arena especially built for a prize fight was constructed at Carson City, Nevada, for the James John Corbett-Robert Prometheus (Bob) Fitzsimmons fight held March 17, 1897. Fitzsimmons knocked Corbett out in the fourteenth round to win the world heavyweight championship. George Silver was the referee.

Prize fight at which admission tickets sold at $100 was the Joe Louis-Billy Conn world heavyweight championship fight at the Yankee Stadium, New York City, on June 19, 1946. It was promoted by the Twentieth Century Sporting Club, of which Mike Jacobs was president. Louis won in the eighth round. The attendance was 45,266.

Prize fight fatality on record occurred in a bare knuckle fight on September 13, 1842, at Hastings, N.Y. Chris Lilly, an Englishman, knocked out Tom McCoy, an Irish American. McCoy died a short time later.

Prize fight of importance under the Marquis of Queensberry rules was the heavyweight championship fight between John Lawrence Sullivan and James John Corbett on September 7, 1892, at the New Orleans Olympic Club, New Orleans, La., for a purse of $25,000 and an outside bet of $10,000. Corbett won in the twenty-first round. A previous contest under the Marquis of Queensberry rules had been held August 29, 1885, at Chester Park, Cincinnati, Ohio, between Sullivan and Dominick F. McCaffery of Pittsburgh, Pa. "Six rounds to decide the Marquis of Queensberry glove contest for the championship of the world" were presented. Billy Tate of Toledo, Ohio, was the referee. Sullivan was the winner but "ascribed his failure to knock the youngster out to the latter's get-away tactics and to the restrictions of the Marquis of Queensberry Rules." *(Commercial Gazette—Cincinnati, Ohio. August, 30, 1885)*

Prize fight to attract 100,000 spectators was the Jack Dempsey-Gene Tunney fight held September 23, 1926, at the Sesqui-centennial Stadium, Philadelphia, Pa. The attendance was 120,757 and the gate receipts was $1,895,733. Tunney defeated Dempsey in a ten-round fight under the point system.

Prize fight to gross a million dollars was held July 2, 1921, at Jersey City, N.J. Approximately 75,000 persons paid $1,626,580 in gate receipts to see Jack Dempsey fight Georges Carpentier. Dempsey won "the battle of the century" by a knock-out in the 57th second of

the fourth round. He received $300,000 and Carpentier $200,000 as purses. *(Jack Dempsey—Round by Round)*

Pugilist to hold three titles simultaneously was Henry Jackson Armstrong, who became featherweight champion October 29, 1937, by defeating Petey Sarron, at Madison Square Garden, New York City; welterweight champion by defeating Barney Ross on May 31, 1938, at Madison Square Garden Bowl, Long Island City, N.Y.; and lightweight champion by defeating Lou Ambers at Madison Square Garden, New York City, on August 17, 1938.

Pugilist to win three world championships was Robert Prometheus (Bob) Fitzsimmons, who became middleweight champion by defeating Jack Dempsey (known as "The Nonpareil") in thirteen rounds at New Orleans, La., on January 14, 1891; heavyweight champion by knocking out James John Corbett in fourteen rounds at Carson City, Nev., March 17, 1897; light heavyweight champion by outpointing George Gardner in a twenty-round decision at San Francisco, Calif., November 25, 1903. Prior to this fight, Fitzsimmons had lost the heavyweight championship to James Jackson (Jim) Jeffries, who knocked him out in the eighth round at San Francisco, Calif., on July 25, 1902.

Radio broadcast of a heavyweight championship prize fight. *See* Radio broadcast: Prize fight (heavyweight championship) broadcast

State legislation concerning prize fighting was Louisiana's Act No. 25, Laws of 1890, passed May 12, 1890, "an act defining the crime of prize fighting, and to provide for the punishment thereof in and out of the State of Louisiana." Although prize fighting was prohibited, the act did not "apply to exhibitions and glove contests between human beings, which may take place within the rooms of regularly chartered athletic clubs."

Telecast of a prize fight. *See* Television—Telecast: Prize fight to be televised

Woman licensed as a referee. *See* Woman: Woman prize fight referee (licensed)

PRIZE MONEY AWARDED BY THE U.S. NAVY. *See* Navy: Prize money awarded by the U.S. Navy

PROBATION
Probation legislation for juvenile delinquents was enacted by the state of Massachusetts on June 23, 1869. The law required the governor to appoint a visiting agent at

$2,500 a year to work for the welfare and redemption of the delinquent, rather than for his punishment. The visiting agent or his deputies were directed to visit all children maintained wholly or in part by the Commonwealth of Massachusetts once every three months.

Probation system, without restrictions as to age, in any country in the world, was legally established as a judicial policy by Boston, Mass., in 1878 and Massachusetts in 1880.

PROCEDURE CODE. *See* Law book

PRODUCTION STANDARDIZATION. *See* Factory standardization of production

PROFESSIONAL BASEBALL LEAGUE. *See* Baseball league

PROFESSIONAL CLUB (women's). *See* Women's club: Women's professional club

PROFESSIONAL FRATERNITY. *See* Fraternity (Greek letter): Professional fraternity

PROFESSIONAL GOLF TOURNAMENT. *See* Golf tournament: Professional open championship

PROFESSOR. *See* specific subjects, such as agriculture professor; Chemistry professor, etc.

PROFESSOR (woman). *See* College: Woman college professor

PROGRAM THEME SONG. *See* Radio broadcast: Program theme song

PROGRESSIVE PARTY was organized June 19, 1912, by seceding members of the Republican Party. The first national convention, held August 6, 1912, at the Coliseum, Chicago, Ill., was attended by 1,800 delegates who on August 7, 1912, nominated Theodore Roosevelt of New York for President and Hiram Warren Johnson of California for Vice President. Roosevelt received 4,126,000 popular votes (88 electoral votes); William Howard Taft, the Republican candidate, 3,487,922 (8 electoral votes); and Woodrow Wilson, the Democratic candidate, 6,297,099 (435 electoral votes). The party was nicknamed the Bull Moose party. *(George Edwin Mowry—Theodore Roosevelt and the Progressive Movement)*

PROHIBITION
Prohibition amendment to the Constitution was the eighteenth amendment, which prohibited the manufacture, sale, or transportation of intoxicating liquors within the United

States. The amendment was submitted to the legislatures of the states on December 18, 1917. Mississippi was the first state to ratify it (January 8, 1918) and Nebraska the thirty-sixth (January 16, 1919). On January 29, 1919, the Secretary of State proclaimed the amendment effective as of January 16, 1920.

Prohibition bureau (federal) was authorized by act of Congress of March 3, 1927 (44 Stat.L.1381) "to create a Bureau of Customs and a Bureau of Prohibition in the Department of the Treasury." The prohibition amendment became part of the Constitution on January 29, 1919, but did not become effective until January 16, 1920. The first commissioner was John Franklin Kramer, of Mansfield, Ohio, appointed November 17, 1919, by Secretary of the Treasury Carter Glass.

Prohibition enforcement officers were authorized by proclamation of Sir Francis Wyatt, Governor of Virginia, on June 21, 1622: "We do ordaine an officer for that purpose to be sworne in every plantacion, to give information of all such, as shalbe so disordered: the moiety of the forfeitures to be given the sd officer so informing, or for default in him to any other that shall informe, and the other to the publique Threasury." *(William and Mary College Quarterly Historical Magazine. Vol. 7. Series 2. No. 4. October 1927)*

Prohibition law (national) forbidding the sale of intoxicating liquors, except for export, was the Wartime Prohibition Act passed November 21, 1918 (40 Stat.L.1050). The prohibition of the sale of liquor containing more than one half of one per cent was enacted by act of Congress passed October 28, 1919 (41 Stat.L. 305), the [Andrew John] Volstead Prohibition Act.

Prohibition state was Tennessee, which passed an "act to repeal all laws licensing tippling houses" on January 26, 1838. It provided that "all persons convicted of the offense of retailing spirituous liquors shall be fined at the discretion of the court" and that the fines and forfeitures be used for the support of common schools.

Prohibition vote which showed the House of Representatives with a dry majority was taken on December 22, 1914. The congressmen voted 197 to 189 in favor of a resolution to provide a constitutional amendment banning the manufacture and sale of intoxicating beverages. The resolution, offered by Representative Richmond Pearson Hobson of Alabama, failed to win the necessary two-thirds majority.

Repeal of prohibition amendment. *See* Constitutional amendment (U.S.): Constitutional amendment submitted to the states for repeal

THE FIRST

THE FIRST

PROHIBITION PARTY (national) was organized on September 12, 1869, at a convention in Chicago, Ill, attended by 194 delegates from 9 states. The party was organized because neither of the major political parties had put a prohibition plank in its platform. The first national convention met in Columbus, Ohio, February 22, 1872, and nominated James Black of Pennsylvania and John Russell of Michigan as the Prohibition candidates for President and Vice President respectively. The platform advocated prohibition, woman suffrage, a direct popular vote for President and Vice President, a sound currency, the encouragement of immigration and a reduction of transportation rates. Black received 5,608 votes in the 1872 election, as compared with Grant, who received 3,597,132 votes. The organ of the party was *The Voice*, a magazine published in Chicago, the first issue of which appeared September 25, 1884.

PROHIBITION REFORM MOVEMENT. *See* Liquor reform movement

PROHIBITIONIST CONGRESSMAN. *See* Congressman (U.S.): Congressman elected by the prohibitionists

PROJECTION OF PICTURES ON A SCREEN. *See* Moving picture: Animated photographic picture projection before a theater audience

PROJECTOR (portable). *See* Moving picture projector: Moving picture projector (portable)

PRONGHORN ANTELOPE. *See* Animals: Pronghorn antelope

PROPAGANDA COURSE (college) was given by Professor Harold Dwight Lasswell of the Department of Political Science, University of Chicago, Chicago, Ill. in 1927 and was entitled "Political Opinion and Propaganda."

PROPANE-FUEL LOCOMOTIVE. *See* Locomotive: Gas turbine propane-fueled locomotive

PROPELLER BLADE (hollow steel). *See* Aviation: Propeller blade of hollow steel

PROPELLER RESEARCH TUNNEL. *See* Wind tunnel: Propeller research tunnel

PROPELLER (twin-screw). *See* Ship: Steamboat with a twin-screw propeller

PROPERTY DAMAGE INSURANCE. *See* Insurance: Aircraft liability and property damage insurance

PROPERTY TAX. *See* Tax: Property tax law (colonial)

PROPORTIONAL REPRESENTATION ELECTION LAW. *See* Election law: Proportional representation

PROSTITUTE is recorded as "this goodly creature of incontinency" in Thomas Morton's *New English Canaan,* published in England in 1637. Morton was condemned by the Pilgrim fathers of the Plymouth colony as "the lord of misrule." In 1627, the Pilgrims, incensed at the licentiousness of his group at "Merry Mount," in what is now Quincy, Mass., cut down a Maypole he erected "upon the festival day of Philip and Jacob" when he regaled the natives with a "barrel of excellent beer." *(Thomas Morton—New English Canaan—Third Book— Chapter IX and XIII)*

PROTACTINIUM OXIDE. *See* Chemical element to be isolated in the United States

PROTESTANT CHILD BORN IN AMERICA. *See* Births: White child of French Protestant parentage

PROTESTANT CHURCH
Protestant church west of Pennsylvania was built in 1772-1773 at Schoenbrunn, Ohio. The first communion service was held June 9, 1772, but the church was not finished until September 19, 1772. A larger church was built and was dedicated October 24, 1773. The Reverend David Zeisberger was the first preacher. *(Joseph E. Weinland—The Romantic Story of Schoenbrunn)*

Protestant church for lepers was the Community Church dedicated at Carville, La., June 14, 1915. The sermon was "A merry heart doeth good like a medicine." The church was served by ministers who came in turn from Baton Rouge and New Orleans, La., a different minister coming each week for several years. There was no settled pastor until the summer of 1922 when the Reverend Henry Thomas Cousins was called.

Reformed Dutch Church Negro pastor was the Reverend Dr. James Joshua Thomas, who on November 14, 1954, was installed as minister of the Mott Haven Reformed Church, the Bronx, New York City.

PROTESTANT EPISCOPAL BISHOP
Negro suffragan in the Episcopal church was the Reverend Edward Thomas Demby, who was appointed suffragan among the Negroes in Arkansas and the southwest on September 29, 1918. Suffragans or assistants, unlike diocesans, are not in full charge of a diocese.

THE FIRST

Protestant Episcopal bishop was Samuel Seabury, consecrated November 14, 1784, at Aberdeen, Scotland, by the Scottish bishops Robert Kilgour, Arthur Petrie, and John Skinner. He was rector of St. James Church, New London, Conn., and Bishop of Rhode Island and Connecticut from his consecration until his death on February 25, 1796.

Protestant Episcopal bishop consecrated in the United States was the Reverend Thomas John Claggett, founder of the Trinity Episcopal Church, Upper Marlboro, Md. He was consecrated September 17, 1792, at Trinity Church, New York City, by the Bishops Seabury, White, Provoost, and Madison. *(George Burwell Utley—The Life and Times of Thomas John Claggett)*

Protestant Episcopal bishop (Negro) of the American church was the Reverend Samuel David Ferguson, who was elected to the House of Bishops of the Protestant Episcopal Church in 1884. He was consecrated June 24, 1885, at Grace Church, New York City, as the successor of the Missionary Bishop of Liberia.

PROTESTANT EPISCOPAL CATECHISM

Episcopal catechism published after the separation of the American synod from the British church was *The ABC with the Church of England Catechism. To which are annexed, prayers used in the academy of the Protestant Episcopal Church in Philadelphia. Also a Hymn on the Nativity of our Saviour; and another for Easter-day* (12 pages, printed in 1785 by Young, Stewart and M'Cullough, Philadelphia, Pa.) Only the verses of the hymns were printed. On page 6 instead of the words "king" and "him," dotted lines were printed so that the title of the head of government could be written in.

See also Book: Book of Common Prayer

PROTESTANT EPISCOPAL CHURCH

Christian religious service in English on the Pacific coast was the Holy Communion from the Book of Common Prayer of the Church of England conducted by the Reverend Francis Fletcher of Sir Francis Drake's ship the "Pelican" on June 24, 1579, St. John the Baptist's Day, at Drakes Bay, Calif. Drake named the place Nova Albion, Latin for New England. A 57-foot marble cross commemorates the event in Golden Gate Park, San Francisco, Calif.

Protestant Episcopal church was established in 1607. The Reverend Robert Hunt celebrated the Eucharist for the first time in America at Cape Henry, Va., on May 9, 1607. The event was reported as follows: "We did hang an awning (which is an old saile) to three or four trees, to shadow us from the sunne,

THE FIRST

our walles were railes of wood, our seats unhewed trees till we cut plankes; our Pulpit a bar of wood nailed to two neighboring trees." The first parish was started June 21, 1607, at Jamestown. *(Edward Lewis Goodwin—The Colonial Church in Virginia)*

PROTESTANT INDIAN CONVERT. *See* Indians: Indian convert (Protestant)

PROTESTANT SCHOOL FOR GIRLS. *See* School: School for Protestant girls

PROVINCIAL COUNCIL (Catholic). *See* Catholic provincial council

PSYCHIATRIC ASSOCIATION was the Association of Medical Superintendents of American Institutions for the Insane, formed October 16, 1844, in Philadelphia, Pa., by thirteen members. The first president was Samuel B. Woodward, the first vice president Samuel White, and the first secretary-treasurer Thomas Story Kirkbride. The name of the association was changed in 1892 to the American Medico-Psychological Association and in 1921 to the American Psychiatric Association.

PSYCHIATRIC INSTITUTE. *See* Medical instruction: Psychiatric institute

PSYCHIATRIC WARD. *See* Hospital: Psychiatric hospital

PSYCHOLOGICAL SOCIETY

Psychological society (national organization) was the American Psychological Association, organized July 8, 1892, at Clark University, Worcester, Mass., and incorporated January 2, 1925, in Washington, D.C. Professor Granville Stanley Hall was the first president and Dr. Joseph Jastrow the first secretary and treasurer. The first scientific meeting was held December 27, 1892, at the University of Pennsylvania, Philadelphia, Pa. The official statement of purpose in the certificate of incorporation read: "The object of this society shall be to advance psychology as a science." *(Psychological Review. Vol. 1)*

PSYCHOLOGY LABORATORY was established at Johns Hopkins University, Baltimore, Md., in 1881 by Granville Stanley Hall. It was discontinued in 1888 when Dr. Hall was appointed president of Clark University. A larger laboratory was established in 1904 by Professor George Malcolm Stratton, also at Johns Hopkins University.

PSYCHOLOGY MAGAZINE was the *American Journal of Psychology,* a quarterly first published in Baltimore, Md., in November 1887 under the editorship of Granville Stanley Hall. The subscription price was $3 a year.

PSYCHOLOGY PROFESSOR was James McKeen Cattell, who was appointed professor of psychology at the University of Pennsylvania, Philadelphia, and who served from 1888 to 1891.

PTARMIGAN (Eskimo chicken). *See* Birds: Ptarmigan (Eskimo chicken)

PUBLIC ACCOUNTANT. *See* Accountant

PUBLIC AFFAIRS SCHOOL. *See* Citizenship and public affairs school

PUBLIC ART COMMISSION. *See* Art commission (public)

PUBLIC BATH AND WASHHOUSE. *See* Bathhouse: Public bath and washhouse

PUBLIC BATHS LEGISLATION. *See* Bathhouse: Legislation concerning public baths

PUBLIC BUILDING (federal). *See* Building: Building erected in the United States for public use

PUBLIC BUILDINGS ADMINISTRATION was established as a part of the Federal Works Agency under the provisions of Reorganization Plan 1, section 303, pursuant to the provisions of the Reorganization Act of 1939, approved April 3, 1939 (53 Stat.L.561). The first commissioner was Winchester Englebert Reynolds, who served from July 1, 1939, to July 1, 1949. Congress enacted Public Law 152, which became effective July 1, 1949, creating the General Services Administration and Reynolds continued as Commissioner of the Public Buildings Service, GSA, until July 1, 1954.

PUBLIC DEBT. *See* Debt: Public debt of the United States to exceed $100,000,000

PUBLIC DEFENDER'S OFFICE was created by Los Angeles County, Calif., on June 13, 1913. The first public defender was Walton J. Wood, who assumed his duties on January 7, 1914. His salary was $200 a month. He had three deputies, one secretary, and one assistant secretary.

PUBLIC DOCUMENTS CATALOG. *See* Index of government publications

PUBLIC GARAGE. *See* Garage (public)

PUBLIC HEALTH
Medical system of inspection of school children was established by the Board of Health, Boston, Mass., in 1894. Eighty inspec-

tors examined pupils sent to them by teachers, and advised with regard to medical and surgical treatment. They also provided for exclusion and isolation in cases of contagious diseases and imposed the conditions of readmission to school. In June 1915, this work was transferred to the School Committee, which commenced to function November 22, 1915. *(Dr. Burke—Hygiene in the Boston Public School. National Education Association. 1909)*

Pellagra experiment of note was made by Dr. Joseph Goldberger of the United States Public Health Service at the Mississippi State Penitentiary, eight miles east of Jackson, Miss. Twelve convicts agreed to submit to a restricted diet test in exchange for an offer of pardon made by Governor Earl LeRoy Brewer. The test was held from February 4, 1915, to April 19, 1915. Six of the eleven convicts (one was excused) developed pellagra, confirming conclusions that a deficiency of vitamin B "P-P" (pellagra preventative) in the diet caused the disease. *(Joseph Goldberger—Experimental Pellagra in the Human Subject Brought About by a Restricted Diet)*

Public health school. *See* Hygiene instruction: Hygiene and public health school

Public health service (U.S.) was established by the act of July 16, 1798 (1 Stat.L. 605-6), and provided that after September 1, 1798, the master of every American ship arriving from a foreign port should pay to the Collector of Customs the sum of twenty cents a month for each seaman, which amount he was authorized to deduct from the seaman's wage. This act referred only to merchant seamen. The money collected was spent for health service only in the district in which it was collected. The Public Health Service was reorganized under the act of June 29, 1870 (16 Stat.L.169). Dr. John Maynard Woodworth was appointed supervising surgeon in April 1871. The department was placed under the Secretary of the Treasury.

Public health service (U.S.) assistant surgeon general (woman) was Lucile Petry (Mrs. Nicholas Charles Leone) of Lewisburg, Ohio, appointed June 7, 1949, with the pay, privileges, and gold braid of an admiral. She took office the same day.

PUBLIC HYGIENE PROFESSOR. *See* Medical instruction: Public hygiene professor

PUBLIC LIBRARY. *See* Library

PUBLIC MUSEUM. *See* Museum: Public museum

THE FIRST

PUBLIC SCHOOL
See also High School; School

Public school classes for epileptic children were organized January 1935 in a small school building in Detroit, Mich. In 1936, the courses were transferred to the White School, designated the White Special School, one of the divisions of Special Education of the Detroit Public Schools. The first teachers were Alice Mortimore and Edith Sargent.

Public school for Chinese supported by a municipality was established September 1859 in the basement of the Chinese Chapel, San Francisco, Calif. James Denman was the superintendent of schools. The school had an enrollment of 67 boys and 8 girls, but it had an average attendance of only 12. The school was suspended in June 1860, but later opened as an evening school. *(William Warren Ferrier—Ninety Years of Education in California)*

Public school for cripples. *See* Cripples: Public school for cripples

Public school kindergarten. *See* Kindergarten: Public school kindergarten

Public school music instruction. *See* Music instruction: Music instruction (public school)

Public school opera studio for stage, radio and screen was at the Los Angeles Junior College, part of the school system of Los Angeles, Calif., which offered courses in October 1937 under the direction of Dr. Hugh Strelitzer. Instruction was not individual, but in groups.

Public school supported by direct taxation or by assessment on the inhabitants of the town was established by vote of Dorchester, Mass., on May 20, 1639: "It is ordered the 20th of May 1639, that there shall be a rent of twenty pounds a year for ever imposed upon Tomsons Island to be paid by every person that hath property in the said island according to the proportion that any such person shall from time to time enjoy and possess there." *(Committee of the Dorchester Antiquarian and Historical Society—History of the Town of Dorchester, Mass.)*

Public school with a continuous existence, the Boston Public Latin School for boys, was established February 13, 1635. The first schoolmaster was Philemon Pormort. Originally its purpose was training for the ministry and its objective was to enable students to "obtain a knowledge of the Scriptures and by acquaintance with the Ancient Tongues qualify them to discern the true sense and meaning of the original, however corrupted by false glosses."

THE FIRST

The school was originally supported by voluntary contributions. *(Henry Fitch Jenks—The Boston Public Latin School)*

PUBLIC SPEAKING DEPARTMENT in
a university was established December 1892 at the University of Michigan, Ann Arbor, with Thomas Clarkson Trueblood as professor of elocution and oratory from 1892 to 1908. Similar courses had been given in 1887 but without departmental status.

PUBLIC WORKS ADMINISTRATION
(U.S.) was authorized June 16, 1933, by President Franklin Delano Roosevelt. Full organization was not effective until July 8, when Harold Le Claire Ickes, Secretary of the Interior, was appointed Administrator of the Public Works Administration. The Special Board of Public Works was composed of nine members and the first chairman of the board was Harold Le Claire Ickes.

PUBLICITY MAN. *See* Theatrical advance publicity man

PUBLISHER (denominational). *See* Book publisher

PUBLISHER (newspaper). *See* Newspaper: Newspaper publisher

PUBLISHING SOCIETY was the Seventy-
Six Society, organized September 5, 1854, in Philadelphia, Pa. Its *Collections* dealt solely with subjects pertaining to the American Revolution. Henry J. Williams was president; Henry Penington, secretary; and William Duane, treasurer. Other societies published tracts, religious papers, etc., but in conjunction with other activities and interests

PUGILIST. *See* Prize fight

PULITZER PRIZE IN LETTERS. *See*
Novel: Novel to win the Pulitzer prize in letters

PULL-CHAIN ELECTRIC SOCKET. *See*
Electric light socket

PULLMAN CAR. *See* Sleeping car

PULP NEWSPAPER. *See* Newspaper: Newspaper printed on pine-pulp paper

PULP PAPER. *See* Paper: Wood-pulp paper

PUMP
Computer pump was marketed by the Wayne Company, Fort Wayne, Ind., on Novem-

THE FIRST

PUMP—*Continued*
ber 1, 1932. The pump was invented by Robert Joseph Jauch, Ivan Richard Farnham, and Ross Harper Arnold, who received patent No. 1,888,533 on November 22, 1932, on a "liquid dispensing apparatus." The pump accurately computes and indicates exact quantity delivered in gallons and the price in dollars and cents as delivery is made. Total gallons dispensed and cash received are recorded by two totalizers.

Gasoline pump was manufactured in a barn by Sylvanus F. Bowser of Fort Wayne, Ind., in 1885. The first pump and tank were delivered September 5, 1885, to Jake D. Gumper of Fort Wayne. The tank had marble valves and wooden plungers and had a capacity of one barrel. Bowser's invention, for which patent No. 372,250 was issued on October 25, 1887, to Sylvanus F. Bowser and Augustus Bowser, Fort Wayne, Ind., became popular and he organized S. F. Bowser and Co., Inc., of Fort Wayne.

Independent single direct-acting steam power pump was invented in 1840 by Henry Rossiter Worthington of New York City, who obtained patent No. 3,677, July 24, 1844, on a steam engine auxiliary for the purpose of supplying a steam boiler with water. The following year, with William H. Baker as partner, he started the firm of Worthington and Baker at Brooklyn, N.Y., now the Worthington Pump and Machinery Corporation, Harrison, N.J.

PUMPING PLANT. *See* Water: Water pumping plant

PUNCHBOARDS were manufactured by Charles A. Brewer & Sons, Chicago, Ill. They were patented January 17, 1905 (No. 780,086) as "vending devices" by Charles A. Brewer and Clinton G. Scannell of Chicago, Ill.

PUPPET SHOW to which admission was charged was held February 12, 1738, in Mr. Holt's room (a room 39 feet long, 19 feet wide, and 9 feet high) at Broad and Pearl Streets, New York City. The show was entitled *The Adventures of Harlequin and Scaramouche, or The Spaniard Trick'd.* Admission was five shillings. (*New York Gazette. January 29-February 6, 1738*)

PUPPET SHOW TELECAST. *See* Television—Telecast: Puppet show to be televised

PURE FOOD LAW
Pure food and drug legislation (national) to prevent the importation of adulterated drugs was passed June 26, 1848 (9 Stat.L.237), an "act to prevent the importation of adulterated and spurious drugs and medicines." It was enforced by the Treasury Department through the Customs Service. Although it has never been

THE FIRST

repealed, it has been superseded by the Federal Food and Drug Act of June 30, 1906 (34 Stat.L.768), effective January 1, 1907. (*U.S. Compiled Statutes—1901. Vol. 2*)

Pure food and drug legislation (state) was "an act to prevent the adulteration of food or drugs," passed May 28, 1881, by New York to take effect August 27, 1881. Violators were guilty of a misdemeanor, subject to a fine up to $50 for the first offense and not exceeding $100 for each subsequent offense. Laws prohibiting the adulteration of specific products had been passed earlier however.

PURPLE HEART. *See* Medal: Order of the Purple Heart

PUSHBALL played with a huge six-foot ball, was invented by M. G. Crane of Newport, Mass., in 1894. It found favor the following year at Harvard, but never became a major sport.

PUZZLE (crossword). *See* Crossword puzzle

PYTHIAN BROTHERHOOD. *See* Knights of Pythias

QUACKS. *See* Medical rogues' gallery

QUADRANT that was practical was invented in 1730 by Thomas Godfrey, who called it a "reflecting quadrant." It was used on vessels plying between the West Indies and the Colonies in 1731-1732. The invention was credited to John Hadley of England but the Royal Society sent £200 to Godfrey to make amends. (*Pennsylvania Magazine of History and Biography. Vol. 51. 1927*)

QUADRUPLE NEWSPAPER PRESS. *See* Printing press: Quadruple newspaper press

QUADRUPLETS DELIVERED BY CAESARIAN OPERATION. *See* Births: Quadruplets delivered by Caesarean operation

QUADRUPLETS TO COMPLETE A COLLEGE COURSE were the Keys sisters, Leota, Mary, Mona, and Roberta, who received B.A. degrees from Baylor University, Waco, Tex., on May 31, 1937. They were born June 4, 1914.

QUAKERS
Quakers' annual meeting was held in Scituate, Mass., in 1660. The first monthly meeting is believed to have been held in Sandwich, Mass., on June 25, 1672. It is possible

THE FIRST

that earlier meetings were held but no records of them have been preserved. *(Allen Clapp Thomas—History of the Friends in America)*

Quakers to arrive in America were two women, Ann Austin and Mary Fisher, who landed at Boston, Mass. July 11, 1656, from Barbados. They were subject to rigid examination and five weeks' imprisonment to ascertain if they were witches before admittance to the colony. The examining officers searched their trunks and their books "were by an order of council burned in the market place by the hangman." *(Allen Clapp Thomas—History of the Friends in America)*

QUARANTINE
Plant quarantine legislation (national) was the act of August 20, 1912 (37 Stat.L.315), directed against dangerous plant diseases and injurious insect pests "new to or not theretofore widely prevalent or distributed within and throughout the United States." The quarantine provisions of Section 7 of the act became immediately effective as to the white-pine blister rust, potato wart, and Mediterranean fruit fly. Except as noted, the act did not become effective until October 1, 1912. The first quarantine under the authority of this act, directed against white-pine blister rust, was issued September 16, 1912. *(Leland Ossian Howard— A History of Applied Entomology)*

Plant quarantine legislation (state) was passed by California, March 4, 1881. Quarantine rules and regulations for the protection of fruit and fruit trees covering both intrastate and interstate shipments were issued November 12, 1881. The quarantine was particularly designed against an insect known as Phylloxera vastatrix, which in 1873 attacked the cultivated grapevines in the Sonoma Valley, and against the San Jose scale and codling moth, which in 1875 had caused serious damage to tree fruits. *(Records in California Department of Agriculture—Sacramento, Calif.)*

Quarantine legislation (colonial) was passed by the General Court of Massachusetts March 1647. An epidemic, which raged in Barbados and the other islands of the West Indies and took over 6,000 lives, caused the Court to publish an order that all ships which came from the West Indies should stay at the Castle at the entrance to the harbor and not land any passengers or goods without a license from three of the council, under a severe penalty. A like penalty was imposed upon any person visiting such quarantined vessel without permission. The act was repealed May 2, 1649. The first Quarantine Act passed by the General Assembly of Pennsylvania was "An act to prevent sickly vessels coming into this government," passed November 27, 1700. *(Pennsylvania Statutes at Large. Vol. 2. p. 80)*

THE FIRST

Quarantine legislation (national) was passed by Congress on February 25, 1799 (1 Stat.L.619). It was "an act respecting quarantines and health laws" requiring federal officers to aid and assist the enforcement of state and municipal regulations.

Ship permitted to enter port without stopping for quarantine. *See* Ship: Ship permitted to enter port without stopping for quarantine procedure

QUARRY. *See* Marble quarry

QUARTER DOLLAR. *See* Money: Silver coins

QUARTERLY MAGAZINE. *See* Periodical: Quarterly magazine

QUARTERMASTER (U.S. Army). *See* Army officer: Quartermaster

QUARTZ MERCURY ARC LAMP. *See* Electric lighting: Mercury vapor lamp

QUEEN TO VISIT THE UNITED STATES. *See* Visiting celebrities: Queen to visit the United States

QUETZAL BIRD. *See* Birds: Quetzal bird

QUIDS were organized during President Thomas Jefferson's administration and were led from 1804 to 1808 by John Randolph of Roanoke, Va. They believed in extreme states' rights and were also opposed to Jefferson's attempts to acquire West Florida. They ran James Monroe against James Madison in 1808. The name is derived from the Latin *tertium quid* (a third thing), indicating separation from both existing political parties, or from both administration and opposition forces. *(James Albert Woodburn—Political Parties and Party Problems in the United States)*

QUININE
Quinine was manufactured in 1822 by John Farr and Abraham Kunzi in Philadelphia, Pa.

Quinine sulphate was manufactured commercially in 1823 by Powers and Weightman of New York City. *(Samuel Hazzard Cross— Quinine-Production and Marketing)*

Synthetic quinine was produced April 10, 1944, by Dr. Robert Burns Woodward and Dr. William von Eggers Doering at the Converse Memorial Laboratory, Harvard University, Cambridge, Mass. It consists of 20 atoms carbon, 24 atoms hydrogen, 2 atoms oxygen, and 2 atoms nitrogen.

QUINTUPLETS. *See* Births: Quintuplets

QUONSET HUT. *See* Building: Building known as a Quonset hut

QUOTA ACT (immigration). *See* Immigration: Immigration quota act

RABBINICAL CONFERENCE. *See* Jews: Jewish rabbinical conference

RABBINICAL SCHOOL. *See* Jewish college: Jewish college to train men for the rabbinate

RACE
  See under specific subjects:

Automobile	Lifeboat
Aviation	Locomotive
Bicycle	Motorboat
Boat	Motorcycle
Camel	Ship
Dog	Yacht
Horse	

RACE TRACK STARTING GATE (electric). *See* Electric starting gate

RACE TRACK TO INSTALL AN ELECTRIC EYE CAMERA. *See* Camera: Photofinish camera

RACING SHELL. *See* Ship: Racing shell

RACK-RAIL DIESEL-ELECTRIC LOCOMOTIVE. *See* Locomotive: Rack-rail diesel-electric locomotive

RADAR
  Battleship equipped with radar was the U.S.S. "New York," which was tested during battle maneuvers at sea in the months of January, February and March of 1939. This radar set operated on a wave length of a meter and a half, detecting destroyers at a distance of approximately eight miles. The first set to be installed on the "New York" was constructed at the Naval Research Laboratory at Washington, D.C.; the first contract was awarded in October 1939 to the Radio Corporation of America for the manufacture of six sets of aircraft detection equipment.

  Off-shore radar warning station was built by the Bethlehem Steel Company's shipbuilding division at Fore River, Quincy, Mass., for the Continental Air Defense Command. The keel was laid January 10, 1955, and the station was launched May 20, 1955. Known as a Texas Tower, it served as a weather collecting and reporting station, and consisted of a triangular 6,000-ton platform resting on three legs 87 feet

above the water level. It was turned over to the First Naval District of the U.S. Navy on December 2, 1955.

  Passenger ship equipped with radar was the flagship "New York" of the Hamburg-American Line. Two circular appendages 3 feet in diameter were installed atop the pilot house of the ship. The equipment was placed in service February 26, 1938.

  Radar detection of airplanes was accomplished June 24, 1930, by Dr. Albert Hoyt Taylor and Leo C. Young of the Naval Aircraft Radio Laboratory, Anacostia, D.C., who noted that airplanes, even though above the transmitter and receiver, rather than between them, reflected radio waves.

  Radar for commercial and private planes was developed by Howard Hughes and the electronic engineers of the Hughes Aircraft Corporation, Culver City, Calif., and demonstrated May 1, 1947, at Culver City on a TWA (Transcontinental & Western Air, Inc.) plane. A brilliant red light on the instrument panel and a horn in the cockpit warned the pilot whenever he came too close to an obstacle.

  Radar installation aboard a commercial carrier. *See* Ship: Radar installation aboard a commercial carrier

  Radar observations were made September 27, 1922, by Dr. Albert Hoyt Taylor and Leo C. Young of the Naval Aircraft Radio Laboratory, Anacostia, D.C., who reported to the U.S. Navy that radio detection equipment placed on any two ships could detect the passage of any vessel between them despite fog, darkness, or smoke screen, and that tall buildings reflected radio signals.

  Radar signal bounced off the sun was transmitted on April 7, 1959, at Stanford University, Stanford, Calif., by Professor Von Russel Eshleman, Lieutenant Colonel Robert Charles Barthle, and Dr. P. B. Gallagher, who used a 40,000 watt transmitter. The signals reached the sun's corona about a half million miles above the visible part of the sun. The signals required 1,000 seconds for transmission in both directions. The signals consisted of a series of dots and dashes which were detected by an electronic computer even though they were much weaker than the radio noise from the sun.

  Radar signal to the moon was beamed by the Army Signal Corps on January 10, 1946, from the Evans Signal Laboratories, Belmar, N.J. The experiment was supervised by Lieutenant Colonel John H. De Witt. An echo was received 2.4 seconds later which consisted of a 180-cycle note of a quarter-second duration.

THE FIRST

Radar used to detect enemy airplanes was employed at Pearl Harbor, Hawaii. At 7:20 A.M., December 7, 1941, Private Joseph L. Lockard of Williamsport, Pa., reported to his superiors that he heard the approach of planes. The planes were assumed to be friendly, proper precautions were not taken, and a great disaster resulted. On February 8, 1942, Lockard received the Distinguished Service Medal and was sent to Officer Training School, Fort Monmouth, N.J.

RADIATION-COOLED HOUSE. *See* Building: Solar-heated and radiation-cooled house

RADIO ADVERTISING

Radio advertising contract for frequency modulation broadcasts was signed December 9, 1940, by the Longines Watch Company and provided for the broadcasting of Longines time signals by W2XOR, New York, for twenty-six weeks beginning January 1, 1941. On April 1, 1941, the experimental license was replaced with commercial license W71NY, and the station was operated from 8:30 A.M. to 11:30 P.M. on a frequency of 47,100 kilocycles.

Radio-advertising course. *See* Radio instruction: Radio-advertising course

RADIO BEACONS were originally known as radio fog signals. The first successful radio beacons, which sent out signals by radio in all directions around the horizon, as do lighthouses by means of light beams, were established by the United States Lighthouse Service at three stations in the approaches to New York Harbor—on the Ambrose Channel Lightship, Fire Island Lightship, and Sea Girt Lighthouse, N.J. They were placed in regular operation May 1, 1921. Tests of radio fog signal transmitting sets leading to the installation of these stations were begun in 1916-1917 at Navesink Light Station, Atlantic Highlands, N.J., by the Lighthouse Service and the Bureau of Standards. The tests were interrupted when the United States entered World War I but were resumed in the fall of 1919 and lasted until September 1920. (*George Rockwell Putnam—Radio Beacons*)

RADIO BROADCAST

Advertising or commercial radio broadcast was sponsored by the Queensboro Realty Corporation, Jackson Heights, New York City, on August 28, 1922, over station WEAF, the experimental station of the American Telephone and Telegraph Company, New York City. The commercial rate was $100 for ten minutes. H. M. Blackwell spoke for ten minutes about Hawthorne Court, a dwelling in Jackson Heights.

All-Chinese commercial radio program was broadcast April 22, 1940, by KSAN, San

THE FIRST

Francisco, Calif. Thomas Tong, of the Golden Star Radio Company, San Francisco, was the director and the sponsor.

Baseball game broadcast with a play-by-play description was aired August 5, 1921, by KDKA, Pittsburgh, Pa., the field being connected by wire to the broadcasting station. The National League Pittsburgh Corsairs defeated Philadelphia, 8-5, at Pittsburgh, for their third straight victory.

Baseball World Series broadcast was effected by WJZ of the Westinghouse Electric and Manufacturing Company, Newark, N.J., which broadcast a play-by-play account of the National League New York Giants-American League New York Yankees series October 5, 1921, to October 13, 1921. The series was won by the Giants, who won five of the scheduled nine games. The Yankees won three games.

Chain broadcast was accomplished October 7, 1922, when WJZ and WGY transmitted a World Series game from the field. Ordinary telegraph lines from Newark, N.J., and Schenectady, N.Y., were connected with the Polo Grounds, New York City, where a single microphone connected to these lines completed the requirements. It was not possible to transmit highest and lowest frequencies. Graham McNamee was the announcer. On January 4, 1923, WEAF of New York City and WNAC of Boston, Mass., had repeater points, and amplifiers were provided for faithful reproduction and transmission of both music and speech.

Coast-to-coast hook-up took place February 8, 1924, when General John Joseph Carty, vice president and chief of research of the Bell Telephone system, spoke from the meeting of the Bond Men's Club at the Congress Hotel, Chicago, Ill. It is estimated that the speech—broadcast by WJAR, Providence, R.I.; WEAF, New York City; WCAP, Washington, D.C.; WMAQ, Chicago, Ill.; KLX, Oakland, Calif.; and KTO, San Francisco, Calif.—was heard by 50,000,000 people.

Cooperative radio show was "Thirty Minutes in Hollywood," broadcast October 10, 1937, by KHJ, Hollywood, Calif., over the Mutual Broadcasting System. It was broadcast for 26 weeks in 72 cities, the cost being borne by 48 commercial sponsors on a pro rata cost basis. The orchestra was conducted by Tommy Tucker; the masters of ceremony were George Jessel and Norma Talmadge (Mrs. George Jessel). The guest star on the first program was Eddie Cantor.

Debate over the radio was held May 23, 1922, over station WJH of the White and Boyer Company, Washington, D.C. The affirmative, "Resolved, That daylight saving is

RADIO BROADCAST—*Continued*
an advantage," was taken by Calvin Ira Kephart, representing the Miller Debating Society and the negative by Thomas E. Rhodes, representing the Alvey Debating Society, both of the National University Law School, Washington, D.C. The audience was requested to act as judge.

Degree conferred by radio. *See* Degrees (academic and honorary): Degree conferred by radio

Dinner broadcast round-the-world was broadcast by short wave from 2XAF, Schenectady, N.Y., on April 20, 1927, to London, Paris, Honolulu, and Tokyo. The dinner was held at the Waldorf-Astoria Hotel, New York City, and was broadcast by WEAF, New York City. The toastmaster was Dr. George Edgar Vincent, president of the Rockefeller Foundation, and the principal speaker was Dr. James Rowland Angell, fourteenth president of Yale University. The broadcast opened an appeal by Yale University for $20,000,000.

Double radio wedding. *See* Wedding: Double radio wedding

Drama broadcast from a regular stage with full scenery and a cast in costume was *Roses and Drums,* a dramatic story of the unsuccessful Union attempt in 1864 to capture Jefferson Davis and free the Union prisoners from Libby Prison. It was presented by WABC, New York City, September 24, 1933.

Drama broadcast from a ship at sea was heard over the WABC Columbia network, July 1, 1933, when an air version of a new motion picture was presented from the main salon of the Furness-Bermuda liner "Queen of Bermuda" on a week-end cruise to the mid-Atlantic. The picture from which the radio version was prepared was *Lady for a Day,* adapted from the short story by Damon Runyon.

Drama (full-length melodrama) broadcast was *The Wolf,* by Eugene Walter, broadcast August 3, 1922, by WGY, Schenectady, N.Y. The 2½-hour performance was directed by Edward H. Smith.

Election returns broadcast took place on August 31, 1920, when WWJ of Detroit, Mich., broadcast the results of congressional and county primaries. On November 2, 1920, Leo H. Rosenberg of KDKA of Pittsburgh, Pa., broadcast the results of the Harding-Cox presidential election. (An experimental station, the De Forest Radio Laboratory in the Highbridge section of the Bronx, New York City, broadcast bulletins from the New York *American* on the results of the Wilson-Hughes election for approximately six hours beginning after

dark on November 7, 1916. The broadcasters signed off about 11 P.M., with the announcement that Hughes had been elected.)
See also below Radio broadcast: News program

Football game (collegiate) broadcast was presented November 25, 1920, by WTAW of College Station, Tex. The game was played on Thanksgiving Day between Texas University and the Agricultural and Mechanical College of Texas at College Station. At that time, the station was operating under an experimental license and had the call letters 5XB. A spark transmitter was used and the transmission was in code. This was the first play-by-play broadcast of a football game.

Football game (collegiate) coast-to-coast broadcast was presented October 28, 1922, by WEAF, New York City, from Stagg Field, Chicago, Ill. The Princeton Tigers defeated the Chicago Maroons 21-18. Long distance telephone lines carried the announcer's voice to New York City, from where it was broadcast. In addition to broadcasting, the station equipped a truck at Park Row, New York City, with a public address system.

Football game played in the United States to be broadcast in England. *See* Football game: Football game played in the United States to be broadcast in England

Foreign language course broadcast took place on March 21, 1924, when WJZ, New York City, operating on a 455-meter wave length, offered French lessons in cooperation with the Berlitz School of Languages.

Musical comedy broadcast with specially composed music, was *The Gibson Family,* sponsored by Procter and Gamble Company of Cincinnati, Ohio, and introduced over the National Broadcasting Company network, September 15, 1934. The comedy was composed by Arthur Schwartz and the lyrics were written by Howard Dietz. The musical comedy was booked for a thirty-nine-week period and was broadcast from WEAF, New York City.

Network broadcast received on the Pacific Coast was the speech of President Calvin Coolidge on October 23, 1924, at the dedication of the Chamber of Commerce of the United States building, Washington, D.C. The 45-minute speech was broadcast by 23 stations, including stations in Los Angeles, Calif.; Portland, Ore.; and Seattle, Wash.

Network sponsored broadcast was "The Eveready Hour" broadcast February 12, 1924, from station WEAF, New York City, to

THE FIRST

WCAP, Washington, D.C., and WJAR, Providence, R.I., under the sponsorship of the National Carbon Company.

News program was broadcast August 31, 1920, by station 8MK, owned by the Detroit, Mich., *News.* The call letters were changed later to WWJ. The station had begun operating on August 20, 1920.
See also above Radio broadcast: Election returns broadcast *and also* Radio Station: Commercial radio station

News program (cooperative) was broadcast in November 1937 by Fulton Lewis, Jr., from WOL, Washington, D.C., under the direction of William B. Dolph. Individual sponsors in different cities bore the expenses on a cooperative basis.

News program (daily) was broadcast September 1, 1922, by WBAY, American Telegraph and Telephone Company, New York City, between 4:30 P.M. and 5:30 P.M. It was known as "The Radio Digest" and was edited by George F. Thompson. Questions and answers concerning radio were also broadcast.

Opera broadcast. *See* Opera: Opera broadcast

Outer space broadcast was made December 19, 1958, when a tape recording of the voice of President Dwight David Eisenhower delivering his Christmas greetings was broadcast on frequencies of 107.97 and 107.94 megacycles from a rocket revolving around the earth.

Police broadcast was made by WIL, St. Louis, Mo., September 4, 1921.

Political convention broadcast took place on June 10, 1924, when the Republican convention assembled at Cleveland, Ohio, nominated Calvin Coolidge of Massachusetts and Charles Gates Dawes of Illinois for President and Vice President respectively. Graham McNamee was the announcer for the program, which was carried by fifteen stations of the National Broadcasting Company from Boston, Mass., to Kansas City, Mo.

Political speech by a President on radio was made by Calvin Coolidge on February 12, 1924, at the thirty-eighth annual Lincoln Day dinner of the National Republican Club held at the Hotel Waldorf Astoria, New York City. He discussed tax reduction, oil, and other problems. About 5,000,000 heard his speech over stations WJZ and WEAF, New York City; WGY, Schenectady, N.Y.; WCAR, Washington, D.C.; and WJAR, Providence, R.I.

President to broadcast. *See* President (United States): President to broadcast by radio

THE FIRST

President to broadcast from the White House was Calvin Coolidge, whose address on George Washington's birthday, transmitted from his study in the White House, Washington, D.C., on February 22, 1924, was heard on 42 stations from coast to coast.

Presidential inauguration was broadcast March 4, 1925, from Washington, D.C., over 24 stations. Calvin Coolidge and Charles Gates Dawes took the oath as President and Vice President, respectively. On March 4, 1921, Harold W. Arlin of KDKA, Pittsburgh, Pa., who had received an advance copy of President Warren Gamaliel Harding's inaugural address, read it at the same time that President Harding was delivering it. Harding's 41-minute address was carried by 24 stations and heard by an audience estimated at 22,800,000.

Presidential message to be broadcast was heard on December 6, 1923, when President Calvin Coolidge delivered his message to a joint session of Congress held in the House of Representatives, Washington, D.C. It was broadcast by KSD, St. Louis, Mo.; WCAP, Washington, D.C.; WDAF, Kansas City, Mo.; WEAF, New York City; WFAA, Dallas, Tex.; and WJAR, Providence, R.I. His voice was received over telephone wires. On March 4, 1925, he broadcast his inaugural address.
See also President (United States): President to broadcast by radio

Prize fight broadcast was the Jack Dempsey-Billy Miske fight at Benton Harbor, Mich., broadcast September 6, 1920, by WWJ, Detroit, Mich. Miske was knocked out in the third round of the scheduled ten-round fight.

Prize fight broadcast from the ringside was presented December 22, 1920, from Madison Square Garden, New York City. Joe Lynch of New York City defended his bantamweight title against Peter Herman of New Orleans in a fifteen-round fight.

Prize fight (heavyweight championship) broadcast was the Jack Dempsey-Georges Carpentier fight on July 2, 1921 at Boyle's Thirty Acres, Jersey City, N.J., in which Carpentier was knocked down in the fourth round. The fight was broadcast by Major J. Andrew White through WJY, Hoboken, N.J.

Program theme song was broadcast October 21, 1921, by Billy Jones and Ernie Hare. It was the theme song introducing "The Happiness Boys" program.

Radio broadcast demonstration was made by Nathan B. Stubblefield in 1892. He was the first person to transmit the voice by air without the aid of wires. He gave a public exhibition

RADIO BROADCAST—_Continued_
of his invention on January 1, 1902; and on
May 30, 1902, in Fairmont Park, Philadelphia,
Pa., his voice was heard a mile away from the
transmitter. He obtained patent No. 887,357 on
May 12, 1908, but because of his idiosyncrasies
he did not permit knowledge of his invention to
be spread abroad. Inability to obtain a fabulous
sum for his invention, as well as fear of im-
parting its secret before the patent was granted,
deprived him of the fame which by right of
priority should have been his. *(Kentucky
Progress Magazine. Vol. II. No. 7)*

Radio broadcast from a moving train, of a
regular program on a national network, was
made by WABC, at 9 P.M., March 27, 1932,
from a Baltimore and Ohio train. Pick-up
points were at Beltsville, Md., and Laurel, Md.
The transmitter was operated on a frequency of
1542 kilocycles, employing high percentage modulation and running on fifty watts power.
Belle Baker and Jack Denny's orchestra were
featured on the program.

Radio broadcast from a tape recording.
See Tape recording: Radio broadcast from
a tape recording

Radio broadcast heard in both the Arctic
and the Antarctic regions was effected September 23, 1934, by W2XAF, the short-wave
station of the General Electric Company, Schenectady, N.Y. Admiral Richard Evelyn Byrd
with his second expedition at Little America
heard the program sent to Rockwell Kent, who
was near Labrador, broadcast by the New York
Coffee House.

Radio broadcast sent from an airplane was
dispatched August 27, 1910, by James A. Macready from an airplane above the racetrack,
Sheepshead Bay, N.Y. The message was "Another chapter in aerial achievement is hereby
written in the receiving of this first message
ever recorded from an airplane in flight."
(United States Air Services. March 1926)

Radio broadcast (two-way) from an airplane was accomplished August 14, 1924,
in New York City by WJZ. A conversation
was broadcast between Major William Nicholas
Hensley, Commandant of Mitchel Field, in a
plane, with Major Lester Durand Gardner on
the ground in Central Park, New York City.
(Aviation. September 8, 1924)

Radio concert from an airplane was broadcast April 14, 1922, from a Fokker airplane
over New York City. The plane was piloted by
Belvin W. Maynard, an ordained Baptist minister. Jeanette Vreeland, a lyric soprano, sang
to raise money for the Veterans Mountain
Camp, Tupper Lake, N.Y., a home for tubercular ex-service men. She was introduced by

Thais Magrane, chairman of the American
Legion Auxiliary. The program was relayed by
telephone to the camp's New York offices at the
Hotel Astor.

Radio police system (two-way three-way)
from headquarters to the cars, cars to headquarters, and from car to car, was installed by
Radio Engineering Laboratories, Inc., Long
Island City, N.Y., which contracted with Eastchester Township, N.Y., on May 8, 1933, to
install one transmitter and receiver for police
headquarters (20 watts, W2XCT) and two for
police cars (4.5 volts, W2XCS and W2XEL).
The cars were placed in operation July 10, 1933,
and were under the direction of Sergeant William E. Robinson. (On October 22, 1932, Bay-
onne, N.J., made formal application for a
construction permit; it was granted December
22, 1932, but the installation was not completed
until July 31, 1933.)

Radio program broadcast was sent by
Professor Reginald Aubrey Fessenden on December 24, 1906, from Brant Rock, Mass. The
general call "CQ" was heard, followed by a
song, the reading of verse, a violin solo, a
speech, and an invitation to report on the kind
of reception. A 40 h.p. steam engine driving a
35 kilowatt, 125 cycle alternator, with rotary
spark at a frequency of 250 per second was
used. The antenna consisted of a single straight
tube, 36 inches outside diameter, 429 feet high,
in 8-foot sections bolted together. *(Gleason
Leonard Archer—History of Radio to 1926)*

Radio program simultaneously transmitted
over 24 AM and FM stations, and telecast over
5, was presented on March 20, 1948, when a
sustaining feature, the NBC Symphony, was
broadcast. The first commercial program similarly aired was "The Voice of Firestone" on
March 22, 1948. The New York City outlet was
WNBC.

Recorded coast-to-coast broadcast was
made on May 6, 1937, by Herbert Morrison,
who described the explosion of the dirigible
Hindenburg at Lakehurst, N.J. The recording
was flown to New York City. It was broadcast
over both the Red and Blue networks of the
National Broadcasting Company, from New
York City.

Religious service broadcast was made January 2, 1921, when the Calvary Episcopal
Church of Pittsburgh, Pa., broadcast its services through KDKA. The preacher was the
Reverend Edwin Jan Van Etten.

Round the world broadcast was accomplished in one eighth of a second on June 30,
1930, by a series of radio relays. Clyde Decker
Wagoner spoke into a short-wave microphone
from W2XAD, Schenectady, N.Y. His voice

THE FIRST

was relayed to Holland, to Java, to Australia, across the Pacific Ocean to North America, and back to Schenectady.

Senate chamber broadcast. *See* Congress (U.S.)—Senate: Broadcast from the Senate chamber

Ship-at-sea broadcast from an ocean liner was made March 25, 1930, from the 49,746-ton German steamship "Europa" in quarantine in New York Harbor. Speeches made in the chart room were sent out by short wave, received on the New Jersey coast, and rebroadcast by stations WEAF and WJZ, New York City.

Ship launching broadcast was presented April 7, 1925, when several stations broadcast the launching of the airplane carrier U.S.S. "Saratoga," christened by Mrs. Curtis Dwight Wilbur, wife of the Secretary of the Navy, at the New York Shipbuilding Corporation Yard, on the Delaware River, Camden, N.J.

Singer to broadcast was Eugenia H. Farrar, whose voice was broadcast by Lee De Forest December 16, 1907, from the Brooklyn Navy Yard, Brooklyn, N.Y., on the occasion of the departure of Admiral Robley Dunglison Evans ("Fighting Bob Evans") on a cruise with the fleet.

Speaker to address an organization by radio was Dr. Weir Carlyle Ketler, president of Grove City College, Grove City, Pa., who addressed the Rotary Club of New Castle, Pa., twenty-five miles away, on April 20, 1920. The talk was received by Station 8HA, which amplified it to the audience. Rex Patch of New Castle, Pa., was in charge of the radio reception and amplification. *(Radio News, May 1920)*

Stereophonic sound program broadcast by separately owned stations was broadcast November 5, 1955, from 6:30 P.M. to 8 P.M. by KYW, Cleveland, Ohio, of the Westinghouse Broadcasting Company and WFLN of the Franklin Broadcasting Corporation from the High Fidelity Music Show at the Benjamin Franklin Hotel, Philadelphia, Pa. It was entitled "Sounds of Tomorrow" and was a cooperative undertaking. Listeners were advised to tune in KYW on AM and WFLN on FM, and arrange their sets about twelve feet apart with equal volume to obtain the stereophonic sound.

Submarine (submerged) broadcast was made December 7, 1930, from the submarines 0-4 and 0-8 cruising ten miles off New London, Conn., in Long Island Sound. The broadcast by short wave was rebroadcast from 1:30 P.M. to 2:00 P.M. by station WEAF of New

THE FIRST

York City. Lieutenant Norman S. Ives described the mechanics of submarines to the accompaniment of the submerging sounds of the 0-4. Lieutenant George C. Hern in the interior of the 0-3 underwater was heard later. The announcers were George Hicks and James Wallington.

Tennis match broadcast was the Davis Cup match between Australia and Great Britain, broadcast August 4, 1921, from the Allegheny Country Club, Sewickley, Pa., by KDKA, Pittsburgh, Pa.

Transatlantic broadcast (not experimental) was sent in code January 19, 1903, between Cape Cod, Mass., and Cornwall, England. Greetings were exchanged between King Edward VII and President Theodore Roosevelt.

Transatlantic broadcast of a voice was that of Dr. Harry Phillips Davis, vice president of the Westinghouse Electric and Manufacturing Company, Pittsburgh, Pa., broadcast December 31, 1923, by KDKA, Pittsburgh, via short wave. It was received by 2AZ, a station operated by the Metropolitan Vickers Company, Manchester, England, and rebroadcast to London.

Transatlantic radio message of the regular westward service was sent by Privy Councillor Lord Avebury, formerly Sir John Lubbock, to the New York *Times* from Clifden, Ireland, via Glace Bay, Nova Scotia, October 17, 1907, on regular Marconi transatlantic service. The message sent in code was:

IB Lr Sn Dh & 53 Collect D, PR, Land Lines London Via Marconi Wireless Glace Bay N. S., Oct. 17.

Times, New York

"This message marks opening transatlantic wireless handed Marconi Company for transmission Ireland Breton limited 50 words only send one many messages received Times signalize event quote Trust introduction wireless more closely unite people states Great Britain who seem form one Nation though under two Governments and whose interests are really identical. Avebury Marshall 12:10 A.M. Oct. 17."

Transatlantic radio signal was sent from Poldhu, Cornwall, by Guglielmo Marconi and was received at St. Johns, Newfoundland. The letter "S" was repeatedly sent by Morse code at stated time intervals and was faintly received by Percy Wright Paget, and by G. S. Kempon, December 11, 1901, and again on December 12, 1901.

Weather broadcasts for the United States government were made April 26, 1921, by Station WEW, St. Louis, Mo.

THE FIRST

THE FIRST

RADIO BROADCAST—Continued

Yacht race broadcast was made in code October 16, 17 and 20, 1899, off Sandy Hook, N.J. The "Columbia" under Commander John Pierpont Morgan of the New York Yacht Club defeated the "Shamrock" under Sir Thomas Lipton of the Royal Ulster Yacht Club, in three races held for the International Yacht Race trophy (eleventh contest). The news was transmitted to coast stations and relayed by land wires to the Associated Press. *(Oliver Gramling—AP. The Story of News)*

RADIO CAR (military) was designed in

1911 by Colonel Royal Page Davidson at Lake Geneva, Wis., and was equipped with telescopic masts for radio broadcasting. Current for the operation of the radio was generated by the automobile motor. The radio car was also equipped with rapid-fire machine guns and two powerful electric searchlights with helix shutters for flashlight signaling.

RADIO CHURCH was established November 27, 1921, when services of the Radio Church of America were broadcast by Walter J. Garvey from his home, 2000 University Avenue, the Bronx, New York City. Hospitals, military installations, and radio operators were alerted to the program. The sermon was preached by Richard Jay Ward, assisted by Dr. M. H. Leventhal. Solos were sung by Clara Brookhurst and Adele Lauriat Barrow.

RADIO COMMISSION (U.S.) was created on February 23, 1927 (44 Stat.L.1162), and consisted of five members, Henry Adams Bellows, Admiral William Hannum Grubb Bullard, U.S.N. Ret., Orestes Hampton Caldwell, John Forrest Dillon, and Eugene Octave Sykes, who were granted authority to license broadcasting stations for one year, to determine to whom licenses should be granted and to fix wave lengths and hours of operation. The organization meeting was held March 15, 1927. On March 15, 1928, this authority was placed under the Secretary of Commerce, the commission becoming an appellate body. *(Laurence Frederick Schmeckebier—The Federal Radio Commission)*

RADIO COMPASS on a naval airplane was used July 7, 1920, when a Curtiss F-5-L naval seaplane flew from Norfolk, Va., to the battleship "Ohio," ninety-five miles at sea, and returned, guided entirely by radio signals.

RADIO CONFERENCE

National Radio Conference convened in Washington, D.C., on February 27, 1922. It was called by Secretary of Commerce Herbert Clark Hoover to discuss regulations necessary for the industry and was attended by government officials, radio representatives, and radio amateurs.

RADIO CONTEST was held by the United Wireless Telegraph Company in Philadelphia, Pa., February 23, 1910. The American Morse telegraphic code was used in a test of speed and accuracy in receiving and transmitting signals. The winner was Robert F. Miller of the United Wireless Company; Harvey Williams of Western Union was the runner-up.

RADIO DISTRESS SIGNAL

Radio distress signal was the CQD signal which was established January 7, 1904, by General Order Circular #57 of the Marconi Company to become effective February 1, 1904. The CQ really meant "Stop sending and listen" while the D was later interpreted as "Danger." The popular interpretation of the call was "Come quick—danger." The SOS distress signal was adopted November 22, 1906, at the International Radio Telegraphic Convention in Berlin, Germany, and superseded the CQD call in July 1908.

Radio distress signal (CQD) from an American ship was sent December 7, 1903, by Ludwig Arnson from the "Kroonland" of the Red Star line bound from Antwerp to New York City. Heavy seas struck the rudder and broke the tiller on which the steering engine was mounted, leaving the ship out of control. The call, sent out 130 miles west of Fastnet on the Irish coast, was received by the British H.M.S. "Kent," which arrived about two hours later and towed the disabled ship to Queenstown (now Cobh), Ireland.

Radio SOS from an American ship was transmitted by Theodore D. Haubner, operator of the Clyde liner "Arapahoe," a single screw freight and passenger steamer of some 3,000 tons bound for Charleston and Jacksonville, from New York City. Her engines were disabled twenty-one miles southeast of Diamond Shoals, off Cape Hatteras, at 3:45 P.M. August 11, 1909. Both the SOS and the CQD signals were sent. The SOS was first heard and acknowledged by R. J. Vosburg, wireless operator at station HA, at Cape Hatteras. Foreign registry ships had used SOS signals earlier.

RADIO FACSIMILE TRANSMISSION

Check sent by radio across the Atlantic Ocean was transmitted on April 20, 1926. It was drawn by General James Guthrie Harbord in London, England against the Bankers Trust Company of New York City to the amount of $1,000 payable to the Radio Corporation of America.

Color photoradio news photograph transmitted by radio for publication was a photograph of President Harry S. Truman, Generalissimo Josef Stalin, and Prime Minister Clement Richard Attlee, taken at the Potsdam Conference in Germany and transmitted on

August 3, 1945, by radiotelephoto to Washington, D.C. A one-shot camera exposed three negatives simultaneously. From the negatives, three black and white prints were made and each placed on a cylinder representing one of the three basic colors, red, blue, and yellow.

Drawing sent by radio across the Atlantic was a sketch of Ambassador Alanson Bigelow Houghton, drawn April 30, 1926, by Augustus John, which was transmitted from London, England, to the New York *Times,* New York City, on May 2, 1926, in 58 minutes.

Facsimile broadcast in ultra high frequencies was made December 19, 1933, by station W9XAF, Milwaukee, Wis., on frequencies of 42,000-56,000 kilocycles and 60,000-86,000 kilocycles.

Facsimile high-speed transmission was demonstrated October 21, 1948, by the Radio Corporation of America at the Library of Congress, Washington, D.C., using "Ultrafax," a system capable of transmitting a million words a minute. The first message was handwritten by Brigadier General David Sarnoff, president and chairman of the board of RCA. Margaret Mitchell's *Gone With the Wind,* 457,000 words, 1,047 pages, was transmitted from WNBW, Washington, D.C., to the Library of Congress, a distance of three miles, in 2 minutes and 21 seconds.

Facsimile transmitted to a moving train as a public demonstration was sent June 4, 1946, by Robert Emmet Hannegan, Postmaster General of the United States, from the law library in the Capitol, Washington, D.C., and received on a test car moving from Baltimore, Md., to Washington, D.C., on the Baltimore and Ohio Railroad. The message, "What hath God wrought," written and signed by Margaret Truman, daughter of President Harry S. Truman, was the same as the telegraph message inaugurating commercial service over the same route. It was sent over WCBM, Baltimore, Md.

Photograph sent by radio across the Atlantic was a picture of Charles Evans Hughes, Secretary of State, transmitted on July 6, 1924, from the RCA Laboratories, New York City, by phototelegraphy to New Brunswick, N.J., then by radio to Brentwood, England, by wire to London, England, whence it was relayed back by wire to Carnarvon, Wales, then by radio to Riverhead, Long Island, N.Y., and by wire to New York City, where it was recorded in the same room from which it was originally transmitted. It was not recorded in England as there were no recording sets there at that time.

Photograph sent by radio across the Atlantic as a public demonstration was

transmitted on November 30, 1924, from the Marconi offices in the Strand, London, England, and were received at 66 Broad Street, New York City. Pictures were sent of President Calvin Coolidge; Prime Minister Stanley Baldwin; Secretary of Foreign Affairs Austen Chamberlain; Secretary of State Charles Evans Hughes; the Prince of Wales; Owen D. Young; the Oxford team winning a relay race at Cambridge; the steamship "Reclamation" aground in the Thames River; and a photograph of the Chinese proverb "One picture is worth ten thousand words." The pictures were published December 1, 1924, in the New York *Herald Tribune.* Other pictures were sent of Queen Alexandría; Ambassador Frank Billings Kellogg; and of Donald Gordon Ward, sending the pictures from London.

Photograph sent by radio across the Atlantic from Europe was a photograph of Pope Pius XI, transmitted June 11, 1922, from Rome by Dr. Arthur Korn, a German physicist. It was published in the New York *World* on Sunday, June 11, 1922. The picture, a half-tone 7 by 9½ inches, was received 40-minutes after transmission by Chief Radioman Edmund H. Hansen, U.S.N., at Bar Harbor, Me. Light falling on a selenium cell produced a group of shaded dots which formed a half-tone. (*Terry and Elizabeth M. Korn—Trailblazer to Television*)

Photograph sent by radio across the Atlantic inaugurating commercial service was transmitted from London, England, on April 30, 1926, at 7 P.M. New York Daylight Saving Time. A photograph of the Pilgrims' Society dinner addressed to the New York *Times* was transmitted in 1 hour and 25 minutes and reproduced in the May 1, 1926, issue. The operation was under the direction of Richard Howland Ranger. Three other photographs were transmitted. The following day, ten pictures were transmitted from London, among them four fashion plates. Transmission from New York to London commenced at midnight April 30, 1926. On May 1, 1926, nine pictures were sent.

Photograph sent by radio across the continent was a photograph of President Calvin Coolidge's inauguration on March 4, 1925, taken in Washington, D.C. One picture was sent every twelve minutes, the actual time for transmission being seven minutes. Nine photographs were sent to New York, Chicago, and San Francisco by the American Telegraph and Telephone Company.

Photograph sent by radio across the continent (commercial) was sent April 18, 1925, from San Francisco, Calif., and received in New York City by the American Telegraph and Telephone Company. The photograph, taken

RADIO FACSIMILE TRANSMISSION
—Continued
in Culver City, Calif., showed Marion Davies receiving a gift of a make-up box from Louis Burt Mayer of Metro-Goldwyn Mayer Pictures.

Photograph sent overland by radio to a distant point was transmitted March 3, 1923, from radio station NOF, Anacostia, D.C., to the *Evening Bulletin,* Philadelphia, Pa. Photographs were transmitted of President Warren Gamaliel Harding, Secretary of Commerce Herbert Clark Hoover, Governor Gifford Pinchot of Pennsylvania, and others. *(Philadelphia Evening Bulletin. March 3, 1923)*

Photographs sent over a city telephone were transmitted on October 3, 1922, by Charles Francis Jenkins from 1519 Connecticut Avenue, Washington, D.C., to United States Navy Radio Station NOF at Anacostia, D.C., in the presence of Commander Albert Hoyt Taylor, U.S.N., and James Clark Edgerton of the Post Office Department. The signals were recorded on a photographic plate at 5502 Sixteenth Street, N.W., Washington, D.C. *(Charles Francis Jenkins—Vision by Radio, Radio Photographs)*

Press syndicate facsimile transmission direct to newspaper offices was an 8 by 10 inch air view of an American Airlines Curtiss Condor transport plane which had crashed in the Adirondack Mountains, 10 miles from Newhouseville, N.Y., on a flight from Cleveland, Ohio, to Boston, Mass. The facsimile was transmitted to newspapers in 24 cities by the Wirephoto service of the Associated Press on January 1, 1935. The picture was transmitted simultaneously to the newspapers over a leased wire in eight minutes.

Radio facsimile broadcasting on the regular broadcast band was instituted February 4, 1938 by WHO (Central Broadcasting Company), Des Moines, Iowa. The facsimile was on 1,000 kilocycles from 12:00 (midnight) to 12:36 A.M.

Radio facsimile long distance transmission of a medical subject was made on May 28, 1925, when the American Telegraph and Telephone Company transmitted stethogram and electrocardiogram pictures or graphs showing heart beats from its New York office to Chicago, Ill. Dr. James Richard Greer of Chicago diagnosed the charts, his report being heard by the American Medical Association in convention at the Steel Pier, Atlantic City, N.J. *(Journal. American Medical Association. June 13, 1925. Vol. 84. No. 24)*

Radio facsimile newspaper. *See* Newspaper radio facsimile newspaper

Radio facsimile patent was No. 785,803, awarded March 28, 1905, to Cornelius D. Ehret of Rosemont, Pa., for "the art of transmitting intelligence." He also received patent No. 785,804 the same day for "a system of transmitting intelligence."

Transpacific and transcontinental facsimile transmission was made May 6, 1925, from Honolulu, Hawaii, to Kahuku by wire; to Marshall, Calif., by radio; to Bolinas, Calif., by radio; to Riverhead, Long Island, N.Y., by radio; to New York City, by wire—a total distance of 5,136 miles. Pictures of war games, of Major General John Leonard Hines, of Rear Admiral Robert Edward Coontz, and of Governor Wallace Rider Farrington were transmitted by Alfred J. Koenig, using the transmitter designed by Captain Richard Howland Ranger.

RADIO FOG SIGNAL. *See* Radio Beacons

RADIO IMPULSE TRANSMISSION
(wireless) was accomplished by Joseph Henry in Princeton, N.J., in December, 1840. Current obtained from a group of Leyden jars was passed through a wire which by means of a magnetized needle produced a vibration on another line about one hundred feet away. The lines were not connected with each other; the transmission was the result of induction.

RADIO INSTRUCTION
Radio-advertising course in a college was instituted by the School of Business and Civic Administration of the City College of New York September 29, 1930, under the direction of Frank Atkinson Arnold, director of development of the National Broadcasting Company. Lectures on the technique of broadcasting as applied to the preparation of programs, both sponsored and sustaining, were given. The class consisted of 62 students.

Radio college course was a four-year combined program in liberal arts and radio with full college credit leading to the degree of Bachelor of Arts, offered by New York University in September 1939 in the Washington Square College of Arts and Science. The course consisted of writing for radio, speaking on the radio, the use of music on the radio, announcing, the planning of radio programs, production, news broadcasting, broadcasting of special events, etc.

RADIO LEGISLATION (national) was
the Wireless Ship Act of June 24, 1910 (36 Stat.L.629), effective July 1, 1911, which required wireless equipment on all passenger vessels carrying fifty or more persons as passengers or crew.

RADIO LICENSE

Experimental radio license issued by the Department of Commerce following the International Radio Convention and Radio Act of 1912 (37 Stat.L.302), August 13, 1912, was serial No. 1, granted St. Joseph's College, Philadelphia, Pa. (3XJ, 2 kilowatts).

Frequency modulation (FM) construction permit was granted August 18, 1937, to W1XOJ, the Yankee Network, Inc., Paxton, Mass. It went on the air with scheduled programs in May 1939 and subsequently operated with the highest output power (50 kilowatts) granted previous to World War II. Call letters were changed to W43B, and later to WGTR, the present call letters. The programs are fed from the studios in Boston, Mass., by an FM circuit.

Frequency modulation transmitter to receive a commercial license was W47NV, Nashville, Tenn., which operated on a frequency of 44,700 kilocycles with a power of 20,000 watts, licensed to cover a 16,000 square mile radius. It began operations March 1, 1941, with full commercial status and presented the commercial of Standard Candy Company, Nashville, Tenn.

International broadcasting license issued by the Federal Communications Commission was granted October 15, 1927, to the Experimenter Publishing Company, New York City. The frequency was 9700 kilocycles and the power 500 watts. The station was taken over in 1929 and subsequently moved to Boston, Mass., where it was operated as W1XAL by the World Wide Broadcasting Corporation.

Radio license issued in the United States was granted George Hill Lewis of Cincinnati, Ohio, in 1911.

Radio station licensed was KDKA, Pittsburgh, Pa., licensed October 27, 1920. At that time broadcasting was not recognized as such. When broadcasting stations received licenses, WBZ, of the Westinghouse Electric and Manufacturing Company, Springfield, Mass., a 1500-watt station operating on 360 meters, was awarded license No. 224 on September 15, 1921, by the Bureau of Navigation, Department of Commerce.

RADIO MAGAZINE was *Modern Electrics*, published April 1908 by Hugo Gernsback, Modern Electrics Publication, New York City. The first issue contained 36 pages and cover. Subscription was one dollar a year.

RADIO MICROPHONE (carbon) for radio broadcasting was employed by Dr. Lee De Forest in 1907 in his laboratory at the Parker

Building, 19th Street and Fourth Avenue, New York City. It was of the ordinary telephone variety. *(Georgette Carneal—A Conqueror of Space, an Authorized Biography of the Life and Work of Lee De Forest)*

RADIO ORCHESTRA. *See* Orchestra: Radio orchestra

RADIO PAGING SERVICE was instituted October 15, 1950, in the New York City area by Aircall, Inc., New York City. The first call was for a doctor who was on a golf course twenty-five miles away. An experimental license was issued by the Federal Communications Commission on September 8, 1948, for station K2XAQ, operating on five frequencies in the 72-73 megacycle range. On October 18, 1949, license KEA627 was granted for operation in the New York City area on 43.58 megacycles. Subscribers equipped with six-ounce Aircall pocket radio receivers could hear their call numbers repeated in numerical sequence on the air at least once per minute within a thirty-mile area.

RADIO PATENT of importance was patent No. 465,971, granted December 29, 1891, to Thomas Alva Edison of Menlo Park, N.J., on a "means for transmitting signals electrically." In the patent, he claimed that "signalling between distant points can be carried on by induction without the use of wires connecting such distant points." His application was filed May 23, 1885.

RADIO RECEIVER

Hotel to install radio reception. *See* Hotel: Hotel to install radio reception

Radio receiver advertised was the Telimco (an acronym of The Electro Importing Company), a $7.50 outfit announced in a one-inch advertisement in the January 13, 1906, issue of the *Scientific American* inserted by Hugo Gernsback of the Electro Importing Company of New York. The advertisement offered a "complete outfit comprising one inch spark coil, balls, key, coherer with auto decoherer and sounder, 50 ohm relay, 4 cell dry battery, send and catch wires and connections with instructions and diagrams. Will work up to one mile. Unprecedented introduction prices. Agents wanted. Illustrated pamphlet."

Radio receiver with an auxiliary silicon unit to convert the rays of the sun into electrical power was the Sun Power Pak, made by the Admiral Corporation, Chicago, Ill., which was first developed in October 1955 and offered for sale on April 16, 1956. The radio weighed 5¼ pounds and contained 6 transistors in place of vacuum tubes. It was 2⅞ inches thick, 8¾ inches high and 10⅜ inches long and cost $59.95. It was operated by six ordinary

THE FIRST

THE FIRST

RADIO RECEIVER—*Continued*
flashlight batteries lasting from 700 to 1,000 hours. The auxiliary Sun Power Pak, which converted energy into power, cost $185 additional. It had a 32 silicon "solar cell element" to pick up rays from the sun or from an incandescent bulb.

Transistor radio receiver mass produced was the Regency Radio, manufactured by the Regency Division of Industrial Development Engineering Associates, Inc., Indianapolis, Ind. The first shipments to dealers were made in October 1954. The receiver was 3 inches by 5 inches by 1¼ inches and weighed 12 ounces. It had no tubes but instead contained four transistors. It was powered entirely by a 22½ volt B battery.

RADIO SEXTANT was made by the Collins Radio Company, Cedar Rapids, Iowa, and announced publicly July 14, 1954, although it had been used in February 1952 as a secret device on naval ships. It determines the sun's position automatically and continuously through reception of microwave energy emitted from the sun.

RADIO SOCIETY was the Wireless Association of America, formed in New York City, November 1908, with Dr. Lee De Forest as president, Dr. John Stone, vice president, William Mauver, Jr., secretary, and Hugo Gernsback, chairman and business manager. There were no dues and no obligations. Within a few months, more than three thousand members were enrolled.

RADIO STATION
  All-local network was formed May 15, 1950, by five local stations: WARL, Arlington, Va., 1000 watts; WGAY, Silver Spring, Md., 1000 watts; WPIK, Alexandria, Va., 1000 watts; WBCC, Bethesda, Md., 250 watts; and WFAX, Falls Church, Va., 250 watts. The time on all five stations was offered at $300 an hour.

  Commercial radio station was 8MK (now WWJ, Detroit, Mich.), which instituted daily service on August 20, 1920, with the program "Tonight's Dinner." Local election returns were broadcast August 31, 1920. KDKA, Pittsburgh, Pa., offered a semi-weekly broadcast from November 2, 1920, to December 1, 1920. KDKA was licensed October 27, 1920.

  Municipal radio station was WRR, Dallas, Tex. (50 watts), established in 1920 to broadcast fire alarms. So that owners of radio receivers could check to determine whether they were tuned to the station, phonograph records were played. In 1925, the station began selling time to sponsors.

  Municipal school-owned ultra-high frequency radio station to receive a license from the Federal Communications Commission was station WBOE, Cleveland, Ohio, granted license No. 1, November 21, 1938, to operate (500 watts, 41,500 kilocycles). Regular classroom lessons and music were broadcast Monday through Friday from 8:30 A.M. to 4:30 P.M. The station became an FM station in February 1941.

  Naval radio station was established in 1903 at the Highlands of Navesink, N.J. Chief Radioman Jack Scanlin was in charge.

  Negro network was the National Negro Network, formed January 20, 1954. The first program was "The Story of Ruby Valentine," starring Juanita Hall, broadcast January 25, 1954, on forty stations. It was sponsored five days a week alternately by Philip Morris & Co., Ltd., and Pet Milk Company. The New York outlet was WOV.

  Radio station operating a 50-kilowatt transmitter was 2XAG, Schenectady, N.Y., using the 379.5 meter wave band, the same length as WGY, Schenectady, N.Y. The station was tested July 25, 1925, and placed in operation July 29, 1925.

  Radio station operating a 100-kilowatt transmitter was 2XAG, Schenectady, N.Y., which was granted a thirty-day permit to operate between the hours of 1 and 2 A.M. It went on the air August 4, 1927. Harry Hadenwater was in charge of broadcasting.

  Radio station owned and operated by Negroes was WERD, 1,000 watts, Atlanta, Ga., opened October 3, 1949. It was owned by Radio Atlanta, Inc., of which Jesse Bee Blayton was president.

  Radio station with 500,000-watt power was KDKA, Pittsburgh, Pa., authorized to use call letters W8XAR from June 12, 1936, to May 1, 1938, to test high power equipment (50 kw to 500 kw) from 1 A.M. to 6 A.M. on an experimental basis.

  Sea-going radio broadcasting station was the 5,800-ton, 338-foot Coast Guard cutter "Courier," commissioned February 15, 1952, at Hoboken, N.J., and dedicated March 4, 1952, by President Harry S. Truman at a pier on the Potomac River, Washington, D.C. The ship had a 150,000 watt medium wave transmitter and two 35,000 watt short wave transmitters. It was used to broadcast the Department of State's "Voice of America" program to Eurasian areas. The first official test was made April 2, 1952, off the coast of Colombia, South America, and the first broadcast from European waters

September 7, 1952, off the island of Rhodes, Greece. The "Courier" was a 1945 Navy cargo ship converted and equipped at a cost of over $2 million. The first captain was Oscar Cottman Buckingham Wev.

RADIO TELEPHONE
See also Telephone

Military portable super-regenerative receiver and transmitter, known as the "Walkie-Talkie," was built in 1933 at the Signal Corps Engineering Laboratories, Fort Monmouth, N.J. The personnel principally concerned with this project were John Hessel, radio mechanic; C. W. Hayhurst, mechanical design engineer and John Reid, shop mechanic. Commercial production was undertaken in 1934 by the Allen D. Cardwell Company, Brooklyn, N.Y.

Radio telephone communication between the ground and an airplane took place July 2, 1917, at Langley Field, Va., where speech of good volume and quality was received from a transmitting plane two miles away. On July 4, 1917, speech from the ground was received by L. M. Clement of the Western Electric Company in a plane several miles away. On August 18, the first two-way communication was established between a plane and the ground, and on August 20, 1917, between two planes, all at Langley Field.

Radio telephone communication (one way) was established April 4, 1915, by Bell System engineers from Montauk Point, Long Island, N.Y., to Wilmington, Del., a distance of 250 miles.

Radio telephone marine demonstration of wireless telephony was held on board the steamer "Bartholdi" on the Potomac River, March 20, 1902. The apparatus and equipment used were the inventions of Nathan B. Stubblefield of Murray, Ky.

Radio telephone service (commercial) was inaugurated July 16, 1920, between Los Angeles and Santa Catalina Island, Calif. The radio link to telephone land lines was between Long Beach, Calif., and the town of Avalon on the island. The service was maintained by the Bell Telephone System for three years until it was replaced by cable because "speechscrambling" devices had not yet been developed and the messages could be picked up by anyone capable of tuning a receiving set.

Radio telephone ship-to-shore commercial service was inaugurated December 8, 1929, when Walter Sherman Gifford, president of the American Telephone and Telegraph Company, lifted a receiver in New York City and spoke to Commodore Harold A. Cunningham

of the S.S. "Leviathan." The first personal call was made by William Hector Rankin, a New York advertising man, to Sir Thomas Lipton, aboard the liner. The rate varied from $7 to $11 a minute, depending upon the zone. *(The Magic of Communication. American Telephone and Telegraph Co.)*

Radio telephone ship-to-shore conversation took place May 6, 1916, over the regular telephone network to demonstrate a way of mobilizing the telephone and telegraph in case of war. Captain Lloyd Horwitz Chandler of the battleship "New Hampshire," while at sea off Hampton Roads, Va., reported and received orders from Secretary of the Navy Josephus Daniels and Admiral William Shepherd Benson in Washington, D.C.

Transatlantic radio telephone message was transmitted October 21, 1915, from Arlington, Va., to Paris. The voice of B. B. Webb was heard by Herbert E. Shreeve and Austen M. Custis of the American Telephone and Telegraph Company, and by Lieutenant Colonel Ferrie of the French Government at the receiving station installed in the Eiffel Tower by Bell System engineers.

Transcontinental radio telephone demonstration was given September 29, 1915, when speech was transmitted from New York City to Arlington, Va., and thence by radio telephone to Mare Island at San Francisco, Calif., 2,500 miles away, and also to Honolulu that night.

Two-way conversation between a glider and the land was effected August 12, 1932 at 2:40 P.M. over the WEAF radio network by Jack O'Meara, a gliding champion, who was circling over the Empire State Building, New York City, in the "Chanute," at an altitude of more than 5,000 feet, and Edward Thorgeson, a radio announcer. A test message was sent August 9, 1932, over Coney Island and Manhattan, New York City.

Two-way radio conversation between a brakeman in a caboose of a moving freight train and an engineer in the cab of a locomotive, a mile and a quarter away, was demonstrated June 15, 1927, by engineers of the General Electric Company, Schenectady, N.Y. Caboose and engine carried identical apparatus, a transmitter and a receiver. Communication was established at either end of the train by the simple act of removing a receiver and pressing a button.

Two-way radio conversation between a submerged submarine and another vessel was held October 5, 1919, between the U.S. submarine H-2, commanded by Lieutenant Commander Clark Withers, and the destroyer

RADIO TELEPHONE—*Continued*
"Blakely." The submarine was submerged in the Hudson River off 96th Street, New York City.

Two-way radio equipped bus was placed in service by the Arnold Lines (the Washington, Virginia and Maryland Coach Company, Inc.) on September 8, 1945. Tests were made July 8, 1945 and a permanent Federal Communications Commission license to operate was granted November 13, 1945.

Two-way radio in an automobile was installed by the Chalmers-Detroit Company in an automobile of its manufacture in March 1910 in New York City. The sending set contained two storage cells, a ten-inch spark coil, two Leyden jars and a high and low voltage battery, a seven-foot aerial, etc. Successful demonstrations were made from the moving automobile in Central Park, New York City, to the Terminal Building, 42nd Street and Park Avenue, New York City, at distances varying from one to three miles. (*Scientific American. May 14, 1910*)

RADIO TELEVISION. *See* Television

RADIO TUBE
Radio tube made of metal was announced April 1, 1935, by the General Electric Company, Schenectady, N.Y. Metal tubes are smaller than the less sturdy conventional glass tubes and provide their own shielding. They are particularly advantageous in the field of short-wave reception as the metal shell is a better heat conductor and radiator than glass.

Three-element vacuum tube was announced to the public by Dr. Lee De Forest at the October 20, 1906, meeting of the American Institute of Electrical Engineers held in New York City. The first three-element tube (filament and two plate electrodes), described as an amplifier of feeble electrical currents, was patented by Dr. De Forest, January 15, 1907, No. 841,387. The first public description of the grid electrode tube was contained in another one of his patents, No. 879,532, February 18, 1908. The name "audion" was given to the tube by Clifford D. Babcock. (*Georgette Carneal— A Conqueror of Space, an Authorized Biography of the Life and Work of Lee De Forest*)

RADIOACTIVE ISOTOPE (medicine). *See* Isotope: Radioactive isotope medicine

RADIOACTIVE SUBSTANCE PRODUCED SYNTHETICALLY. *See* Physics: Radioactive substance produced synthetically

RADIOGRAPH. *See* X-ray

RADIOPHOTOGRAPHY. *See* Radio facsimile transmission

RAG PAPER. *See* Paper: Wood pulp and rag paper

RAGTIME INSTRUCTION BOOK. *See* Music book: Ragtime instruction book

RAIL-DETECTOR CAR. *See* Railroad car: Rail-detector car

RAILROAD
See also

Railroad accident	Railroad legislation
Railroad apprentice school	Railroad passenger
	Railroad signal system
Railroad car	tem
Railroad charter	Railroad station
Railroad commission (state)	Railroad technical report
Railroad coupler	Railroad track
Railroad crossing gate patent	Railroad train robbery
Railroad excursion	Railroad treatise
Railroad guide	

Air-conditioned train was installed by the Baltimore and Ohio Railroad Company, which began this service on the "Columbian" on Sunday, May 24, 1931, in both directions between Washington and New York. The westbound train left New York City at 3:57 P.M. and the eastbound train left Washington at 4 P.M. Each train was made up of the following cars, all of which were air-conditioned and air-cooled: individual-seat smoking car, individual-seat coach, lounge car, colonial dining car, one Pullman parlor car, and one observation sunroom parlor car. The train was drawn by one of the "President" series of twenty locomotives. (*The First Air Conditioned Train in History— B. & O. Railroad*)

Air-rail passenger service. *See* Aviation: Air-rail passenger transcontinental service

Cog railroad in the world was the Mount Washington Cog Railway, which ran to the summit of Mount Washington, N.H. The railway was invented by Sylvester Marsh of Littleton, N.H. Work was begun in May 1866 and the first public demonstration was made at the base on August 29, 1866, on a half-mile section. The railway was completed in July 1869 at a cost of $139,500. (*Guy Roberts and Frank Hunt Burt—Mt. Washington; Its Past and Present*)

Daily railroad service to the Pacific coast, with a change at Omaha, was established in 1887. On November 17, 1889, through service without a change was inaugurated between

Chicago and Portland, Ore., and between Chicago and San Francisco, Calif., by the Union Pacific Railroad Company. This train was the "Overland Limited."

Dirigible transfer of mail to a train. *See* Aviation—Airship: Dirigible transfer of mail to a train

Electrically lighted train was the "Pennsylvania Limited" of the Pennsylvania Railroad Company, placed in service June 1887, between Chicago and New York. Steam from the engine was carried to a turbine in the forward compartment of the baggage car where it drove an electric generator supplying current to the entire train. (*Pennsylvania Railroad Information Bulletin. June 1928*)

Gasoline-driven, stainless steel, air-conditioned, pneumatic-tire, two-car train was built by the Edward G. Budd Manufacturing Co. of Philadelphia, Pa., in 1933 and was delivered to the Texas and Pacific Railway Company at Dallas, Tex., November 4, 1933. The over-all weight was 104,000 pounds. The car was equipped with two 240 h.p. engines. It was placed in service between Fort Worth and Texarkana, Tex., making one round trip a day, a total distance of 490 miles.

Government operation of railroads began January 1, 1918. A proclamation was made by President Woodrow Wilson, December 26, 1917, and William Gibbs McAdoo, Secretary of the Treasury, was appointed director general. The railroads were returned to private ownership March 1, 1920.

Inclined railway was erected in 1764 at Lewiston, N.Y., by British soldiers under the command of Captain John Montresor, for transporting supplies between the Niagara portage and the lower Niagara River, three hundred feet below. The road consisted of two sets of parallel logs laid up the banks on stone piers from the ship wharf below to the portage above. The logs were deeply grooved to receive the wheels of two cradle cars. The cars were joined by heavy ropes passed around a revolving drum to balance when one car was at the bottom, and the other at the top. Originally, the road was used solely for military purposes by the troops, but later it was used for transporting merchandise.

International railroad was the Atlantic and St. Lawrence Railroad, construction of which began July 4, 1846. The first trains ran from Portland, Me., to Montreal, Canada on July 18, 1853, covering 292 miles in less than 12 hours. On August 5, 1853, the line was leased to the Grand Trunk Railway of Canada for 999 years. (*Edward Everett Chase—Maine Railroads*)

Interstate railroad was the Petersburg Railroad, chartered by special act of the General Assembly of Virginia on February 10, 1830, and by special act of the North Carolina Legislature on January 1, 1831. It was opened in 1833 from Petersburg, Va., to Blakely, N.C., a distance of 59 miles along the north bank of the Roanoke River. On November 21, 1898, it became part of the system now known as the Atlantic Coast Line Railroad Company.

Loop the loop railway. *See* Loop the loop centrifugal railway

Municipal railroad was the Cincinnati Southern Railway, whose regular passenger service began July 23, 1877, between Cincinnati, Ohio, and Ludlow and Somerset, Ky. Freight service started August 13, 1877. Construction was authorized by the Ohio legislature, May 4, 1869, with an "act to authorize cities of the first class to build railroads and to lease or operate the same." Freight service between Cincinnati and Chattanooga, Tenn., was inaugurated February 21, 1880, and through passenger trains on March 5, 1880. The railroad was leased on October 12, 1881, to the Cincinnati, New Orleans and Texas Pacific Railway Company for five five-year periods. (*Henry Paine Boyden—The Beginnings of the Cincinnati Southern Railway*)

Newspaper delivery train. *See* Newspaper: Newspaper delivery train

"Piggy-back" railroad operation began January 5, 1885, on the Long Island Rail Road Company when a produce train, consisting of eight flat cars for carrying farmers' wagons, eight cars to carry their horses, and a coach for teamsters, left Albertson's Station, Long Island, N.Y., and arrived at Long Island City at 6:30 A.M. At 7 A.M., a ferry carried the wagons across the East River to New York City.

Pullman sleeping car. *See* Sleeping car: Pullman sleeping car

Railroad bridge. *See* Bridge: Railway bridge

Railroad car. *See* Railroad car

Railroad for commercial transportation of passengers and freight was the Baltimore and Ohio Railroad Company. It was incorporated in the state of Maryland February 28, 1827. The incorporation was confirmed by the state of Virginia, March 8, 1827. Stock was subscribed to provide funds for its execution April 1, 1827. The first board of directors was elected April 23, 1827, with Philip E. Thomas as president. The company was or-

RAILROAD—*Continued*
ganized April 24, 1827. Construction began at Baltimore, Md., July 4, 1828. The first passenger revenue was obtained January 7, 1830. Tickets were 9 cents each or three tickets for 25 cents for a ride from Pratt Street to the Carrollton Viaduct. Passengers rode at first primarily for the novelty and experience. (*The Fair of the Iron Horse—B. & O. Railroad*)

Railroad for freight transportation was a tramroad built in 1809 by John Thompson for Thomas Leiper to carry stone from his quarries on Crum Creek to Ridley Creek, Pa., a distance of about three fourths of a mile. Wooden rails rested on sleepers eight feet apart. The cars had grooved wheels and were pulled by horses. The service was in operation for 19 years.

Railroad for freight transportation to celebrate its centenary was the Granite Railway Company of Massachusetts, which was incorporated by Massachusetts on March 4, 1826, for the "conveyance of stone and other property" with a capital of $1,000,000. The first president was Thomas Handasyd Perkins. Work on the road was begun April 1, 1826, and was completed October 7, 1826. The tracks were five-foot gauge, and the rails were pine, a foot deep and covered with oak plate and then with flat bars of iron. The cost was about $50,000. The railroad was constructed by Gridley Bryant and was used to carry heavy blocks of granite for the building of the Bunker Hill Monument from the quarries at Quincy, Mass., to the docks about three miles away at Milton, Mass. It was also the first American railroad to cover the wooden rails with iron plates.

Railroad freight yard fully automatic was the Elgin, Joliet and Eastern Railway Company's Kirk Yard at Gary, Ind., which began operating under manual control on January 25, 1952 and changed to fully automatic operation on December 17, 1954. Radar and electronic brain circuits were used to sort out and assemble freight cars by destination, weigh them automatically, and couple them into trains. The equipment was installed by the General Railway Signal Company, Rochester, N.Y. (*Modern Railroads. October 1953*)

Railroad merger of importance was the agreement of May 17, 1853, in which ten companies consolidated under the title of New York Central Railroad Company with an aggregate capital of $23,085,000. On April 2, 1853, an act was passed by the New York legislature "to authorize the consolidation of certain railroad companies." Thirteen directors were selected on July 6, 1853, and on August 1, 1853, the company began to operate under its own officers. The equipment consisted of 187

first class passenger coaches; 55 second class coaches; 65 baggage, mail and express cars; and 1,702 freight cars. There were 298 miles of main line, 236 miles of branch line, and 29 miles of leased road.

Railroad operated by an electric third rail system was the Lackawanna & Wyoming Valley Railroad Company (Laurel Company), which commenced operations in Scranton, Pa., May 25, 1903. After the system had been tried out successfully in Scranton, the elevated railway in New York City was electrified with a third rail.

Railroad shipments of dressed beef (year-round, long-distance) were made in 1877 by Gustavus Franklin Swift of Swift & Company, who shipped meat from Chicago in ten refrigerated cars built to his own specifications. The beef was hung from racks, and the floor was covered with boxes and cases.

Railroad to be completely equipped with diesel-electric engines was the New York, Susquehanna and Western Railroad. The first diesel unit was placed in service December 27, 1941, and on May 25, 1945, the last of a fleet of 16, completely dispensing with other types of engines, was put in operation. The diesels were built by the American Locomotive Company, New York City, and the General Electric Company, Schenectady, N.Y.

Railroad to carry troops was the Baltimore and Ohio Railroad Company, which on June 30, 1831, transported Brigadier General George H. Steuart, First Division Maryland Guards, and about a hundred volunteer troops to Sykes Mills (now Sykesville), Md., where they quelled a riot of railroad workmen by arresting about fifty of them who were striking for back pay due.

Railroad to install gasoline-mechanical cars in regular service was the Pennsylvania Railroad Company, which placed them in operation in February 1923 on the Berwick, Flemington and Bustleton branches in the Philadelphia district. These cars superseded local passenger trains whose operation was unprofitable. They were replaced in 1926 by gasoline-electric cars.

Railroad to install track water tanks for trains to take water on the run was the Pennsylvania. A track tank was placed in the northbound track at Sang Hollow on the Pittsburgh division during the early months of 1870. In the same year a 1,200-foot tank was put down in the southbound track at the same location. In the same year, the New York Central installed track tanks between Montrose and Albany.

THE FIRST

THE FIRST

Railroad to run trains to Washington, D.C., was the Baltimore and Ohio Railroad· On July 1, 1835, the president, directors, and other officers of the road made a trial run from Baltimore to Washington and back. *(The Story of the Centenary Pageant of the B & O. Railroad Co.)*

Railroad to run west of the Mississippi River was the Pacific Railway of Missouri, incorporated March 12, 1849. Ground was broken at St. Louis, Mo., on July 4, 1851. On December 2, 1852, Charles Williams, the chief machinist of the company, made a test run; on December 9, 1852, the president and director of the company with a company of fifty officials and friends rode a distance of five miles in ten minutes to Cheltenham Sulphur Springs, where a party was held. The return trip was made in the afternoon. On December 23, 1852, the railroad began its passenger service. The name was changed to the Missouri Pacific Railway Company on October 20, 1876. (It is now part of the Missouri Pacific Lines.)

Railroad to run west, out of Chicago, was the Galena and Chicago Union Railroad, a constituent company of the Chicago and North Western Railway, whose first train was hauled by "The Pioneer," a ten-ton wood-burning locomotive, which left Chicago, Ill., on October 25, 1848, for Oak Park, 5 miles away. The North Western rails reached the Missouri River at Council Bluffs in 1867, and when the last spike was driven by Senator Leland Stanford for the Union Pacific at Promontory, Utah, May 10, 1869, service between the East and the West coast was available for the first time. The western roads were the Chicago & North Western, the Union Pacific, and the Central Pacific, now a part of the Southern Pacific.

Railroad to use an electric engine for a short distance in place of steam engines was the Baltimore and Ohio, which ran its first train with an electric engine through the Baltimore tunnel for a distance of 3.6 miles, supplanting the steam engine for that distance. The regular use of electric engines for freight trains for this distance was begun on August 4, 1894, and for passenger trains on May 1, 1895. *(Baltimore and Ohio 69th Annual Report for Year Ending June 30, 1895)*

Railroad tunnel. *See* Tunnel: Railroad tunnel

State aid to railroads was granted by Illinois, which was empowered by Congress on March 2, 1833 (2 Stat.L.662), to sell land it had acquired from the federal government for canal land on March 2, 1827 (2 Stat.L.234), and to use the proceeds to aid in the construction of railroads. This grant did not become effective and was not used by the state.

State-owned railroad was the Philadelphia and Columbia Railway, constructed under the act of March 24, 1828, P.L. 221 Section 5, Pennsylvania, which authorized and required the canal commissioners to build a railroad from Philadelphia to Columbia by way of Lancaster, and extending to the west end of York. The first locomotive trip was made April 2, 1834, from Lancaster to Columbia. This line was completed in 1834 from Philadelphia to Pittsburgh, in four divisions, the first of which was the Columbia Railroad. The construction and regulation of this road was imposed upon the Pennsylvania Board of Canal Commissioners who built and operated it until August 1, 1857, when the Pennsylvania Railroad purchased it from the state and the road came under private management and control. *(Slason Thompson—Short History of American Railroads)*

Streamlined all-steel diesel motor train was the "Zephyr," 196 feet long, and 208,061 pounds in weight, built by the Edward G. Budd Manufacturing Company of Philadelphia, Pa., for the Chicago, Burlington and Quincy Railroad for service between Kansas City, Mo., and Lincoln, Neb. It was driven by a Winton 600 h.p. high-compression two-cycle, 8 inch by 10 inch, eight-in-line diesel-electric motor. The first trip, on November 11, 1934, was a run from Lincoln to Kansas City, via Omaha, and back the same day.

Streamlined light-weight high-speed three-car passenger train was operated by the Union Pacific System, March 2, 1934, west from Omaha, Neb. It was designed by E. E. Adams, vice president, who conducted the research and development work under the direction of Carl Raymond Gray and William Martin Jeffers, president and executive vice president, respectively, of the Union Pacific System. The train was constructed of aluminum alloys having three times the strength of steel and therefore requiring one third of the material to obtain equivalent strength. The train was tubular in shape. The equipment was designed for a maximum speed of 110 miles an hour, with a sustained speed on straight and level track of 90 miles an hour. The train of three cars weighed 80 tons, the weight of one old-style Pullman sleeping car. The train was fully air-conditioned; windows were sealed and forced ventilation was used to heat the train in winter, to cool it in summer, and to filter all dirt and dust from the air as it was brought into the train.

Streamlined Pullman train (six cars) was the Union Pacific "Streamliner—M-10001" which left Los Angeles, Calif., October 22, 1934, at 10 P.M. and drew into Grand Central Terminal, New York City, at 9:55 A.M. October 25, 1934, covering 3,259 miles in 56 hours and 55 minutes. The average speed was a trifle under 60 miles an hour. The train was

RAILROAD—*Continued*

constructed of aluminum alloy for strength and lightness and streamlined into a smooth, low-slung tube. It was powered by a 900 h.p. V-type diesel of 12 cylinders which provided energy for the four electrical traction motors. The train was made up of the power car, a combination mail-baggage car, 3 Pullman sleeping cars, and a coach-buffet.

Streamlined railroad train was invented by the Reverend Samuel R. Calthorp of Roxbury, Mass., who obtained patent No. 49,227, on August 8, 1865, on an "air resister train." He gave "to the exterior surface of a railway train a form tapering from the center of the train toward either end, for the purpose of diminishing the atmosphere resistance." The front and rear ends of the train were pointed, and the wheels were enclosed in casing, the only projection being the smokestack. The tender was attached to the locomotive by an accordion hood.

Switchback railway was invented by La Marcus Adna Thompson and put in operation in June 1884 by the L. A. Thompson Scenic Railway Company at Coney Island, N.Y. It was 450 feet long. The cars started from a peak and ran down grade, the momentum carrying the cars up an incline. The passengers got out, the attendants pushed the train over a switch to a higher point on a second track, and the passengers returned. The highest drop was only thirty feet. Thompson obtained patent No. 310,966 on January 20, 1885, on a roller coasting structure and patent No. 332,762 on December 22, 1885 on a gravity switch-back railway. (*Oliver Pilat and Jo Ranson—Sodom by the Sea, History of Coney Island*)

Telegraph in railroading. *See* Telegraph: Telegraph in railroading

Telephone service (commercial station) on railroad trains for passengers. See Telephone: Commercial telephone service on railroad trains for passengers

Telephone used by a railroad company. *See* Telephone: Telephone used by a railroad company

Transcontinental through sleeping car. *See* Sleeping car: Transcontinental through Pullman sleeping car service

RAILROAD ACCIDENT occurred July 25, 1832, on the Granite Railway, Quincy, Mass. Four visitors, after seeing the process of transporting large and weighty loads of stone, were invited to ascend the inclined plane in one of the vacant returning cars. The cable chain

snapped and they were precipitated over a cliff, a distance of 30 to 40 feet. One man was killed and the others seriously injured. (*Granite Railway Company—The First Railroad in America*)

RAILROAD APPRENTICE SCHOOL for railway mechanics was established by the New York Central Railroad at Elkhart, Ind., in 1872.

RAILROAD AUTO TRUCKING SERVICE. *See* Automobile trucking service

RAILROAD BRAKE PATENT. *See* Brake: Railroad brake patent

RAILROAD BRIDGE. *See* Bridge: Railway bridge

RAILROAD BUS. *See* Automobile bus: Bus operated by a railroad

RAILROAD CAR

Air-conditioned car was tried in 1854 by the New York and Erie Railroad, which installed a funnel-shaped opening at the top and sides of a railroad car to catch the air, which was then passed through a water tank underneath the car to the interior of the car. In winter, the air was heated by a stove. An opening in the rear of the car enabled the air to escape. (*Scientific American. Vol. 9. No. 28. March 25, 1854*)

Air-conditioned cars were installed by the Atchison, Topeka and Santa Fe Railway Company. Fifteen new dining cars were built in 1914, cars No. 1441 to No. 1455, in service on the "California Limited" between Chicago, Ill., and Los Angeles, Calif. The system was known as the Duntley Air Washer and consisted of a motor-driven spray wheel partially submerged in ice water. Fresh air was drawn through the spray and delivered into the car by means of a fan and air ducts along the deck of the car. This system was successful inasmuch as it washed the air and lowered the temperature of the cars a few degrees, but the capacity was inadequate.

Car with a center aisle was "The Columbus," introduced July 4, 1831, by the Baltimore and Ohio Railroad Company. It was designed by Ross Winans and built at Baltimore, Md. It was feared that it would become one long spittoon. (*William Henry Brown—History of the First Locomotive in America*)

Car with an observation dome was placed in service July 23, 1945, by the Chicago, Burlington & Quincy Railroad. It was a standard Budd stainless steel coach into which a

THE FIRST

THE FIRST

"Vista Dome" was built at the Burlington's Aurora, Ill., shops. The Vista Dome car had three decks, an upper deck in the center with a curved double glass roof, an intermediate deck at the usual floor level, and a lower deck beneath the dome section. The Vista Dome section was 19½ feet long and extended the full width of the car. It seated 24 passengers, their heads and shoulders above the normal roofline of the train.

Car with fluorescent lighting was New York Central coach 1472, placed in service September 2, 1938. The "Twentieth Century Limited" streamliner used the first fluorescent tail sign June 15, 1938.

Chapel car was the "Evangel," dedicated May 23, 1891, in Cincinnati, Ohio. The dedicatory address was delivered by Dr. Wayland Hoyt. The car was fitted out for religious services and was used on the Northern Pacific Railroad's tracks. Experimental services were held in St. Paul and Minneapolis, Minn., and after several months of prospecting work, the car was committed for the winter to the Reverend and Mrs. E. G. Wheeler, who conducted services in it on the Pacific coast.

Coal cars with roller bearings were placed in service on the Wheeling and Lake Erie Railroad in December 1925. There were two 50-ton hopper cars, the trucks of which were placed under the existing car bodies by the Timken Roller Bearing Company. The cars were placed in coal service operating between mines in Ohio and Lake Erie. (*William C. Sanders—Railway Roller Bearings*)

"Compartmentizer" freight cars were developed jointly by the Western Pacific Railroad Company and the Pullman Standard Car Company and placed in service on September 12, 1952, between Chicago, Ill., and San Francisco, Calif. Four gates were installed in each car to separate the contents into sections and to prevent shifting and crushing.

Complete train of coal cars with roller bearings was placed in service during the early part of January 1930 by the Pennsylvania Railroad Company and consisted of 100 hopper cars of 70 tons capacity each. The cars were used between the Cresson Division and the eastern seaboard. The trucks, made by the Timken Roller Bearing Company, were placed under the regular standard cars.

Dining car ever operated in the world was the "Delmonico," built in 1868 by the Pullman Palace Car Company, Pullman, Ill., and placed in service between Chicago, Ill., and St. Louis, Mo., by the Chicago & Alton Railroad Company. The Philadelphia, Wilmington and Baltimore Railroad in 1863 operated two remodeled day refreshment coaches, 50 feet long,

fitted with an eating bar, steam box, etc., on the Philadelphia-Baltimore run. Food prepared at the terminals was sold. (*First in All Travel Conveniences—Chicago & Alton Traffic Department*)

Dining car (all-electric) was the "Cafe St. Louis," built in Chicago, Ill., and placed in service March 9, 1949, between Chicago and St. Louis, Mo., by the Illinois Central Railroad. It has a self-contained electric power unit which develops approximately 50,000 watts, supplying the power for two broilers, two ranges, hot food table, coffee urn, plate and cup warmers, deep fry kettle, dish washer, glass washer, mixers and fruit juice extractors, refrigerators, garbage disposal system, etc.

Double-deck railroad coaches were built by Richard Imlay in August 1830 and used on the Baltimore and Ohio Railroad. The "Improved Passenger Cars" accommodated 12 passengers, while outside seats at the end accommodated 6 persons, including the driver. On top of the carriages was a double sofa which accommodated twelve additional passengers. An iron framework supported an awning which protected those on the upper deck. The coaches were placed in service between Baltimore, Md., and Ellicott's Mill, Md.

Freight car (Adapto Car) was built by the American Car and Foundry Division of ACF Industries, Inc., at Berwick, Pa., and placed in service on July 24, 1956, by the Chicago, Rock Island and Pacific Railroad Company between St. Louis, Mo., and Wichita, Kan. Sections of various shapes and sizes were made to fit above the chassis of a flat car. The sections could be removed with their contents to allow reuse of the car without the delay generally attendant upon unloading.

Glass-lined tank car for transporting milk was built in 1910 by the Pflaudler Company, Rochester, N.Y., for the Whiting Milk Company, Boston, Mass. It was used on the Boston and Maine Railroad to collect milk from the country for city consumption.

Mail car (steel) was built by the Standard Steel Car Company, Pittsburgh, Pa., and exhibited May 4-13, 1905, at the International Railway Congress, Washington, D.C. It was lighted with acetylene gas and lined with fireproof composite board. The inside length was 65 feet 2 inches. It was framed of steel posts and girders, covered with steel plates, and insulated with hair felt. It was placed in service June 7, 1905, by the New York, Salamanca and Chicago Railroad Company. (*Erie Railroad Employes' Magazine. July 1905*)

Observation cars (super dome) were built by the Pullman-Standard Car Manufacturing

RAILROAD CAR—Continued

Company, Chicago, Ill., in 1952. Ten cars were placed in service January 1, 1953, by the Chicago, Milwaukee, St. Paul and Pacific Railroad (Milwaukee Railroad). They were 85 feet over-all, 10 feet wide, 15 feet 6 inches from top to rail. The dome section contained 625 square feet of curved safety glass in sections 3 feet wide and 5 feet high. The laminated glass consisted of polished plate glass and layers of plastic.

Oil tank cars. *See* Oil: Oil tank cars

Parlor car was the "Maritana" built by George Mortimer Pullman and placed in operation in 1875. The chairs were "richly upholstered," fitted with adjustable backs, and revolved on swivels.

Passenger car (ACF-Talgo) was built by the American Car and Foundry Division of ACF Industries, Inc., Berwick, Pa., for export to Spain. A complete train was tested on March 3, 1949. Coach height was 4 feet lower than that of conventional coaches. Floors were 3 feet closer to the rails than those of conventional coaches. The train weighed two thirds less than trains then in use as it was made of aluminum and other light-weight material. It used about 40 per cent less fuel, and cost 45 per cent less than conventional equipment.

Passenger car (ACF-Talgo for use in the United States) was built by the American Car and Foundry Division of ACF Industries, Inc., Berwick, Pa., and completed on April 22, 1955. The first train was the "Jet Rocket," placed in service on February 11, 1956, by the Chicago, Rock Island and Pacific Railroad Company between Peoria and Chicago, Ill.

President to ride on a railroad train. *See* President: President to ride on a railroad train

President's car, owned by the government for the exclusive use of the President of the United States, is U.S. Car No. 1, formerly known as the "Ferdinand Magellan," built in 1942 by the Association of American Railroads. It was purchased for a nominal fee by the government and assigned to the White House. It weighs 285,000 pounds, is built on extra heavy trucks, and is sheathed throughout with armor plate ⅝ inch thick. It has bullet-proof glass 3 inches thick in all of the windows and doors. The car has a lounge-observation compartment, a dining room seating 12 persons, a special galley where all the meals are prepared, and 4 bedrooms. It carries no identification marks other than the presidential seal on the brass-railed rear platform. (A private car was built for President Abraham Lincoln, but it was never accepted by him or assigned to the White

House. It was, however, used to bear his remains from Washington, D.C., to Springfield, Ill.)

Private railroad car was outfitted for Jenny Maria Lind Goldschmidt (Jenny Lind, the "Swedish Nightingale"), who made her first appearance September 11, 1850, at Castle Garden, New York City. The car was used on her tour of the country.

Pullman sleeping car. *See* Sleeping car: Pullman sleeping car

Pullman train completely equipped with roller bearings was the "Pioneer Limited" of the Chicago, Milwaukee, St. Paul and Pacific Railroad. Regular service was inaugurated May 21, 1927, between Chicago, Ill., and St. Paul-Minneapolis, Minn., a distance of 421 miles. *(The Military Engineer. September 1930)*

Rail detector car was invented by Dr. Elmer Ambrose Sperry and tested June 13, 1928, at Beacon, N.Y. It enabled railroads to locate internal flaws in railroad tracks. It was demonstrated September 13, 1928, near Poughkeepsie, N.Y., before representatives of the American Railway Association and various railroads. The first car, car No. 101, which traveled at 10 miles an hour, enabled only one rail to be examined at a time.

Rail detector car in commercial service was placed in service by the Wabash Railroad on November 15, 1928, at Montpelier, Ohio. It was a double unit car, with one unit for towage and one for equipment. The first test, 155 miles, required 14 consecutive days and revealed 14 defects a day.

Railroad coach modeled after those in use in England was built at the Old Colony South Boston (Boston, Mass.) shops for the Fall River Line, and placed in service on May 19, 1847.

Railroad shipments of dressed beef. *See* Railroad: Railroad shipments of dressed beef

Refrigerator car patent was No. 71,423, granted to J. B. Sutherland of Detroit, Mich., November 26, 1867, and covered an insulated car constructed with ice bunkers in each end and ventilated by air admission above the ice and gravity circulation. "Hanging flaps," created and maintained constant circulation in the car by means of differences of temperature in the air. The air was admitted at the top, passed through the ice chamber, and then discharged into the cooling room near the bottom to reduce its temperature. *("Railway Refrigeration." Ice and Refrigeration. September 1891)*

Refrigerator car shipment of fresh fruit was made by Parker Earle of Cobden, Ill., who in 1866 built and shipped chests of strawberries on the Illinois Central Railroad. The chests had three layers of board and were airtight and watertight. They held 100 pounds of ice and 200 quarts of strawberries, which brought $2.00 a quart. In 1872, Earle shipped a full carload from Anna, Ill., to Chicago, Ill. *(Carlton Jonathan Corliss—Main Line of Mid-America)*

Sleeping car. *See* Sleeping car

Steel passenger railroad coach was built in 1902 by the Pennsylvania Railroad Company in its shop at Altoona, Pa. It was completed in December 1903. It had a steel underframe and superstructure, a composite roof, and wooden window frames and sills. On December 23, 1907, the first all-steel passenger railroad coach was completed.

Train with fluorescent lights was the "General Pershing Zephyr," a stainless steel streamlined train operated by the Chicago, Burlington and Quincy Railroad. Its first run, on April 30, 1939, was between St. Louis, Mo., and Kansas City, Mo. Coaches, parlor-lounge, dining car, rear car, dressing rooms, and lavatories were all equipped with fluorescent lights. *(Railway Age. April 29, 1939)*

RAILROAD CHARTER was granted by New Jersey on February 6, 1815, when "an act to incorporate a company to erect a rail-road from the river Delaware, near Trenton, to the river Raritan, at or near New Brunswick" was passed in Trenton, N.J. The railroad, advocated by John Stevens of Hoboken, N.J., was not completed. James Ewing, Pearson Hunt and Alner Reeder were appointed to receive subscriptions (not more than 5,000 shares at $100).

RAILROAD COACH. *See* Railroad car: Railroad coach

RAILROAD COMMISSION (state) was established July 1, 1869, under chapter 408 of the Acts of 1869 by the state of Massachusetts. It is now the Department of Public Works. The first three commissioners appointed were James C. Converse, Edward Appleton, and Charles Francis Adams, Jr.

RAILROAD COUPLER with which every railroad car in the United States, Canada, and Mexico is equipped was invented by Eli Hamilton Janney of Alexandria, Va., who obtained

patent No. 138,405 on an "improvement in car-couplings" on April 29, 1873. *(Carl Weaver Mitman—The Beginning of the Mechanical Transport Era in America)*

RAILROAD CROSSING GATE PATENT was No. 68,306, which was awarded August 27, 1867, to J. Nason and J. F. Wilson of Boston, Mass.

RAILROAD (elevated). *See* Elevated railroad: Elevated railroad

RAILROAD EXCURSION

Railroad excursion (mystery) was run by the Missouri Pacific Railroad May 21, 1932. The trip was from St. Louis to Arcadia, Mo., a distance of 92 miles, but the passengers were not told in advance where they were going. The round trip fare was $2.50, which included a barbecue at Arcadia.

Railroad excursion rates originated in 1849 when Josiah Perham of Boston, Mass., persuaded railroads to grant a one-day excursion rate to Boston to persons desirous of viewing the panorama of the Saguenay, St. Lawrence, and Niagara Falls exhibited in Boston. The low rates stimulated travel. *(Charles Frederick Carter—When Railroads Were New)*

Railroad excursion (transcontinental) of an organization was made by the Boston Board of Trade, which left Boston May 23, 1870, in 8 Pullman cars pulled by the locomotives "Meteor" and "William Penn." The excursionists carried their own printing press and published a daily newspaper titled "Trans-Continental." They arrived at San Francisco, Calif., on May 31, 1870, and returned to Boston on July 2, 1870.

RAILROAD GUIDE

Railroad guide was *The Traveller's Guide Through the State of New York, Canada, etc., embracing a general description of the city of New York; the Hudson River Guide, and the fashionable tour to the springs and Niagara Falls: with steam-boat, rail-road, and stage routes, accompanied by correct maps* (72 pages, published in 1836 by J. Disturnell, New York City.) It contained a folded map of New York State and one of the Hudson River vicinity; a list of canal routes; stage and railroad routes from Albany to Buffalo, Albany to Boston, etc.; a list of railroads, cemeteries, monuments, colleges, museums, hotels, amusements, etc.; and a general description of New York City.

Railroad guide that printed the time schedule of the arrival and departure of trains at the various stops along the route and at the terminal points was Doggett's *United States Railroad and Ocean Steam Navigation Guide, illustrated with a map of the United States,*

RAILROAD GUIDE—*Continued*
showing the working lines of Railroad, published September 1847 by John Doggett, Jr., of New York City. It contained 132 pages, and a folding map. It sold for 12½ cents.

RAILROAD LAND GRANT. *See* Land grant: Railroad land grant of importance

RAILROAD LEGISLATION
Railroad legislation (federal) was the Safety Appliance Act, passed March 2, 1893 (27 Stat.L.531), "an act to promote the safety of employees and travelers upon railroads by compelling common carriers engaged in interstate commerce to equip their cars with automatic couplers and continuous brakes and their locomotives with driving wheel brakes, and for other purposes."

Railroad legislation (state) was passed by the state of Georgia, March 5, 1856 (General Law 103). The state law making railroad companies liable for injuries caused by negligence to employees and others was "an act to define the liability of the several railroad companies of this state for injuries to persons or property, to prescribe in what counties they may be sued, and how served with process." (*John W. Duncan*—*Acts of the General Assembly of the State of Georgia passed in Milledgeville at Bi-ennial Session in November, December, January, February and March 1855-1856*)

RAILROAD LOCOMOTIVE. *See* Locomotive

RAILROAD MAGAZINE. *See* Periodical: Trade journal

RAILROAD MOTOR-COACH TRUCKING. *See* Automobile trucking service

RAILROAD PASSENGER
Railroad honeymoon trip was made by Mr. and Mrs. Henry L. Pierson of Ramapo, N.Y., who on January 15, 1831, while in Charleston, S.C., on their wedding trip, took a ride on the South Carolina Railroad from Charleston, S.C., to Hamburg, S.C., six miles away. The locomotive was "The Best Friend of Charleston" and Nicholas W. Darrell was the engineer. (*Charles Frederick Carter—When Railroads Were New*)

RAILROAD POST OFFICE. *See* Postal service: Railroad post office

RAILROAD SIGNAL SYSTEM
Railroad interlocking machine was placed in service at Spuyten Duyvil, N.Y., in 1874 by the New York Central & Hudson River Rail-

road. Levers, operated from a central location, controlled an arrangement of switch and signal appliances, providing a safe path for the movement of trains through switches, junctions, grade crossings, and terminal stations, and over drawbridges.

Railroad signal system (automatic electric block) was invented by Thomas S. Hall of Stamford, Conn., in 1867 and was installed on the New York and Harlem Railroad. Hall obtained patent No. 103,875 on June 7, 1870 for his electro-magnetic railway signal apparatus. The wheels of the locomotive struck a lever fastened to the rail and this in turn set the signal at danger until the train was out of the block.

Railroad signal system (manual block) was installed in 1863 between Philadelphia (Kensington), Pa., and Trenton, N.J., on the Philadelphia and Trenton Railroad, a division of the Camden and Amboy Railroad, now a part of the Pennsylvania Railroad System. Installation was made by Robert Stewart, Superintendent of Telegraph and Train Dispatcher of the Camden and Amboy Railroad, under instructions of Ashbel Welch, President of the Camden and Amboy Railroad. The system was extended to New Brunswick, N.J. in 1864.

Railroad signal system of continuous cab signals was used by the Pennsylvania Railroad. On July 11, 1923, cab signals were installed experimentally in locomotives hauling trains between Lewiston Junction and Sunbury, Pa. These cab signals, located on the locomotives where the engineman and fireman can readily see them, are actuated by electric currents in track circuits of the track on which the locomotive is located. This is accomplished by coding the electric circuits to reflect the conditions on the track ahead of the locomotive.

Railroad signal system of interlocking signal apparatus operated by compressed air was installed by the Union Switch and Signal Company in 1883 at Bound Brook, N.J., at the crossing of the Central Railroad of New Jersey with the Pennsylvania railroad.

RAILROAD STATION
Railroad station (passenger and freight) was the Baltimore and Ohio Railroad depot on Poppleton Street, south of Pratt Street, Baltimore, Md. The original two-story building, erected in 1830, still stands, part of it being used by the freight agent as an auxiliary office and the remainder as an adjunct to the company's printing plant. (*First Passenger and Freight Station—Baltimore and Ohio Railroad Co.*)

Union passenger station was the Union Station at Indianapolis, Ind., opened September 20, 1853, for the trains of five railroad companies. The depot was 100 feet wide and 420 feet long, and contained five tracks inside and through the depot, two tracks outside and north of the depot. The building contract was let in May 1852. The constructing engineer was Colonel T. A. Morris. Edwards and Copeland were the general contractors. The depot was owned and operated by the Indianapolis Union Railway Company, which ran the union station, the union tracks, and the Indianapolis Belt Railroad.

RAILROAD TECHNICAL REPORT was William Strickland's *Reports on Canals, Railways, Roads and Other Subjects made to the Pennsylvania Society for the Promotion of Internal Improvement,* a 51-page pamphlet containing 72 engraved plates, published in 1826 by H. C. Carey and I. Lea, Philadelphia, Pa.

RAILROAD TIMETABLE. *See* Timetable (railroad)

RAILROAD TRACK
Manganese steel for railroad tracks. *See* Steel: Manganese steel for railroad tracks

Railroad rails of Bessemer steel were rolled at the North Chicago rolling mill May 24, 1865, from ingots made at the experimental steel works at Wyandotte, Mich. The rails were rolled in Chicago, Ill., and their manufacture witnessed by members of the American Iron and Steel Association who were assembled in conference at Chicago.

Railroad rails of iron were rolled in 1844 at the Mount Savage Rolling Mill, Allegany County, Md., and weighed 42 pounds a yard. Five hundred tons of the inverted "U" type rails were rolled in 1844. They were laid between Mount Savage and Cumberland, Md., a distance of approximately nine miles. This rolling mill also produced "T" rails, which weighed 50 pounds a yard. *(James Walter Thomas and Thomas John Chew Williams—History of Allegany County, Md.)*

Railroad rails of steel were used by the Pennsylvania Railroad. The rails, which weighed 56 pounds a yard, were placed in service in 1864 between Altoona and Pittsburgh, Pa.

Railroad rails of "T" shape were invented in 1830 by Robert Livingston Stevens, president and engineer of the Camden and Amboy Railroad. They were made of malleable iron, weighed 36 pounds a yard, and were used by his railroad. Their adoption was very slow as the type of rail then preferred was the flat rail which was nailed to the ties. *(Robert Henry Thurston—History of the Growth of the Steam Engine)*

Railroad track (practical) was made of wood laid on a steep grade of one and a half

inches to the yard, in Philadelphia, Pa., and was 180 feet in length. On July 31, 1809, a carriage with four grooved wheels was placed on the track at the lower end and a single horse walking on the loose dirt between the tracks pulled 10,696 pounds up the slope. *(Du Pont Magazine. June 1925)*

Railway track scale. *See* Scale: Railway track scale

RAILROAD TRAIN ROBBERY
Railroad train robbery of a disabled train took place on May 5, 1865, when an Ohio and Mississippi railroad train en route from St. Louis, Mo., to Cincinnati, Ohio, overturned at North Bend, Ohio, fourteen miles from Cincinnati, and was robbed by looters.

Railroad train robbery of a train in motion took place on October 6, 1866, when Frank Sparks, John Reno, and Simeon Reno boarded an Ohio and Mississippi Railroad baggage and express car while it was getting into motion and threw off two safes, one containing $15,000 and the other $30,000. The latter was recovered. The bandits were arrested, freed on bail, and never tried, although later convicted of other crimes and punished. *Robert William Shields— Seymour, Indiana, and the Famous Story of the Reno Gang*

RAILROAD TREATISE was John Stevens' *Documents Tending to Prove the Superior Advantages of Rail-ways and Steam-Carriages Over Canal Navigation,* printed in 1812 by T. and J. Swords, 160 Pearl Street, New York City. Stevens proposed to build a railroad from Albany to Buffalo, N.Y., laying the track on wooden stringers capped with wrought iron plate. *(Magazine of History. Extra No. 54)*

RAILROAD TUNNEL. *See* Tunnel: Railroad tunnel

RAIN (man-made) to drench a forest fire. *See* Forest fire: Forest fire drenched by man-made rain

RAM-JET HELICOPTER. *See* Helicopter: Ram-jet helicopter

RANGE (army field range). *See* Army field range

RANGE (electric). *See* Electric stove: Electric range

RANSOM KIDNAPPING. *See* Kidnapping: Kidnapping for ransom

RAT EXTERMINATION (city-wide) to avert bubonic plague was accomplished in San Francisco, Calif., in 1907-1908 by the Public

THE FIRST

RAT EXTERMINATION—*Continued*
Health Service, which saved the city and perhaps the nation by destroying the rats and ground squirrels which carry plague-bearing fleas. *(San Francisco—Citizens' Health Committee Report—March 31, 1909)*

RATE STANDARDIZATION (insurance). *See* Insurance: Insurance rate standardization

RATING AGENCY (commercial). *See* Business: Commercial rating agency

RATTLESNAKE MEAT in cans was packed in March 1931 by George Kenneth End of Arcadia, Fla. On April 9, 1931, canned rattlesnake meat was served at a dinner to American Legionnaires at the Hillsboro Hotel, Tampa, Fla. End founded and became president of the Floridian Products Corporation, which made its first sale of canned rattlesnake May 22, 1931.

RAY (cosmic). *See* Cosmic ray

RAYON
Rayon was commercially produced by the American Viscose Company in Marcus Hook, Pa., on December 19, 1910. Production in 1911 amounted to 362,000 pounds. The patents were acquired from the General Artificial Silk Company, Lansdowne, Pa., which started in 1901. The term "rayon" was adopted in 1924 to replace "artificial silk" and similar names. *(Mois Herban Avran—The Rayon Industry)*

Rayon patent on spinning of artificial silk from cellulose acetate was granted William H. Walker, Newton, Mass., Dr. Arthur D. Little, Brookline, Mass., and Harry S. Mork, Boston, Mass., who obtained joint patent No. 709,922, September 30, 1902, "on making cellulose esters." They also received patent No. 712,200, October 28, 1902, on artificial silk, which they assigned to the Chemical Products Company, Boston, Mass.

RAZOR
Electric dry shaver was manufactured by Schick, Inc., Stamford, Conn., and delivered March 18, 1931. Colonel Jacob Schick obtained patents on a "shaving implement" on November 6, 1928 (No. 1,721,530).

Safety razor was the Star Safety Razor, made by Kampfe Brothers, New York City in 1880. It consisted of a short portion of a hand-forged blade of a barber's straight razor inserted in a frame with full safety features.

Safety razor to be successfully marketed was invented by King Camp Gillette. In 1895 he invented a razor equipped with a flexible and

THE FIRST

movable blade which could be thrown away. The blades were punched out of thin steel instead of being forged. The original Gillette Company was incorporated September 28, 1901. Twenty people paid $250 each for 500 shares of stock. In 1903 only fifty-one razors were sold. In 1906 the first dividend was paid, amounting to $130,000. *(Gillette's Decade of Development—Gillette Safety Razor Co.)*

READING DEVICE (microfilm). *See* Microfilm: Microfilm reading device

REAPER
Reaper patent was granted to Richard French and John F. Hawkins of New Jersey on May 17, 1803. *(R. L. Ardrey—American Agricultural Implements)*

Reaper that actually worked was invented by Henry Ogle in 1826. It consisted of a straight scythe blade which moved against a series of triangular fingers, and cut the grain, which fell upon a collecting board. *(Merritt Finley Miller—The Evolution of Reaping Machines)*

Reaper that was practical was built by Cyrus Hall McCormick, who obtained a patent on June 21, 1834. His father, Robert McCormick, had also experimented with reapers but was unsuccessful and abandoned the work. The younger McCormick, using a new principle, built a reaper which he demonstrated in 1831 at a public trial in a field near Walnut Grove, Va. The owner of the field feared that the machine would rattle the heads off his wheat and stopped the demonstration. Another neighbor, whose ground was more level, invited McCormick to his field, and there the machine worked splendidly, cutting six acres of wheat in half a day—as much as six men would have done. The reaper was very difficult to popularize and it was not until 1841 that McCormick was able to sell two machines. *(Herbert Newton Casson—The Romance of the Reaper)*

REAR-FACING AIRPLANE SEATS. *See* Aviation: Airline to install rear-facing passenger seats

REBELLION
See also
Civil War
Revolutionary War
War

Insurrection of Negro slaves. *See* Slavery: Insurrection of Negro slaves

Rebellion against the federal government. *See* War: Rebellion against the federal government

THE FIRST

Rebellion (colonial) was attempted in 1607 at the Jamestown colony, Va. George Kendall, one of the original first council appointed in England, "was put off from being of the Council, and committed to prison; for that it did manyfestly appear he did practize to sew discord between the President and Council." He was shot to death for mutiny. *(Edward Maria Wingfield—A Discourse of Virginia)*

Rebellion of colonists against the English was led by Marcus Jacobson, "The Long Finne," who claimed to be the son of the Swedish general Konigsmark. He advocated an uprising against the English and was trapped and turned over to the English commandant. On December 20, 1669, he was condemned for insurrection in the first trial by jury in Delaware. He was lashed in public, branded with the letter "R," and sold in chains as a slave in Barbados for having opposed the governmental authority of Governor Francis Lovelace.

RECLAMATION SERVICE (federal) was the United States Reclamation Service, a bureau of the Department of Interior, created by act of Congress of June 17, 1902 (32 Stat.L.389) for reclamation of arid and semiarid lands. It was an outgrowth of the United States Geological Survey, authorized on March 30, 1888 (25 Stat.L.63). *(Institute for Government Research. United States Reclamation Service—Its History, Activities and Organization)*

RECONSTRUCTION FINANCE CORPORATION was created by the Reconstruction Finance Corporation Act, approved January 22, 1932 (47 Stat.L.5), "to provide emergency financial facilities for financial institutions, to aid in financing agriculture, commerce and industry, and other purposes." The act authorized the corporation to create, in any of the twelve Federal Land Bank Districts, intermediate credit corporations to assist farm stockmen. Interest at 7 per cent was charged for the loans, which included all costs of inspection. The original capital of the corporation was set at $500,000,000. It was authorized to have up to three times its subscribed capital outstanding. The corporation was organized February 2, 1932 and managed by the United States Secretary of the Treasury and six directors.

RECORDED RADIO PROGRAM. *See* Radio broadcast: Recorded coast-to-coast broadcast

RECORDING DEVICE FOR TELEPHONE CONVERSATIONS. *See* Telephone: Telephone recording devices

RECREATIONAL RANCHING COURSE in a college, often referred to unofficially as a dude ranching course, was offered by the Col-

THE FIRST

lege of Agriculture of the University of Wyoming, Laramie. The first bachelor of science degree awarded by the College of Agriculture for the completion of the optional program known as "recreational ranching" was conferred June 6, 1938 on Donald Ellsworth Smith, who completed the four-year course.

RECUMBENT CHAIR. *See* Chair: Recumbent chair patent

RED CROSS SOCIETY. *See* American Red Cross

REFEREE (woman). *See* Woman: Woman prize fight referee (licensed)

REFERENDUM. *See* Initiative and referendum

REFINERY. *See* Copper refinery furnace; Oil refinery; Sugar refinery

REFLECTING TELESCOPE. *See* Telescope: Reflecting telescope

REFORM CONGREGATION (Jewish). *See* Jewish Congregation: Jewish congregation (reform)

REFORMATORY. *See* Prison

REFORMED CHURCH (Dutch) was established in 1628 in New Amsterdam, N.Y., under the West India Company and the Church of Holland. *(Edward Tanjore Corwin—Manual of the Reformed Church in America)*

REFRIGERATED CAR. *See* Railroad car: Refrigerator car patent; Railroad car: Refrigerator car shipment of fresh fruit

REFRIGERATION (mechanical). *See* Cold storage plant

REFRIGERATOR
See also Ice cream freezer

Gas refrigerator (household) to be successfully introduced into the American market was the Electrolux, which was sponsored in 1926 by the Electrolux Refrigerator Sales Company of Evansville, Ind. A tiny gas flame and a tiny flow of water in the refrigerator took the place of all moving parts, circulating a liquid refrigerant which was hermetically sealed in

THE FIRST

REFRIGERATOR—*Continued*
rigid steel. The first patent issued to the Electrolux Servel Corporation on an absorption refrigerating apparatus was No. 1,609,334, granted December 7, 1926, to Baltzar Carl von Platen and Georg Munters of Stockholm, Sweden.

Household refrigerating machine patent was No. 630,617, granted to Albert T. Marshall of Brockton, Mass., on August 8, 1899, for "an automatic expansion-valve for refrigerating apparatus." *(E. H. Parfitt—Home Refrigerator)*

Ice-making machine of the vapor compression type to be made in commercial quantities was invented in 1834 by Jacob Perkins, an American living in London, who obtained British patent No. 6,662, on August 14, 1834, on an "apparatus for producing ice and cooling liquids." Perkins showed that vapors or gases which do not ordinarily exist in liquid state may be liquefied upon being subjected to high pressure. *(James Ambrose Moyer and Raymond Underwood Fittz—Refrigeration)*

Mechanical refrigerator patent was No. 8,080, granted Dr. John Gorrie of Apalachicola, Fla., May 6, 1851, on an "improvement in the process for the artificial production of ice." At a dinner on July 14, 1850, at the Mansion House, Apalachicola, Gorrie produced blocks of ice the size of bricks. He installed his system in the United States Marine Hospital in Apalachicola.

Refrigerator was invented in 1803 by Thomas Moore of Baltimore, Md. It consisted of two boxes, one inside the other, separated by insulating material. Ice and food were stored in the inner box. Licenses were granted for manufacture, but permission was extended without charge to the poor. The invention was described in a 28-page pamphlet, "An essay on the most eligible construction of ice houses, also, a description of the newly invented machine, called the Refrigerator."

REFRIGERATOR CAR. *See* Railroad car: Refrigerator car patent; Railroad car: Refrigerator car shipment of fresh fruit

REFUELING IN AIR. *See* Aviation: Refueling attempt in mid-air

REFUGE (bird). *See* Bird refuge

REFUNDING ACT (federal) was approved August 4, 1790 (1 Stat. L.138), "an act making provision for the [payment of the] debt of the United States," which provided that state, domestic, and foreign debts be consolidated and refinanced by three classes of bonds.

THE FIRST

REFUSE DISPOSAL. *See* Incinerator

REGATTA. *See* Boat race; Yacht race

REGIMENT TO RESPOND TO LINCOLN'S PROCLAMATION. *See* Civil war: Regiment to respond to President Lincoln's proclamation

REGIMENTAL JEWISH CHAPLAIN. *See* Army officer: Regimental Jewish chaplain

REGISTRATION LAW (state). *See* Election law: Registration law (state)

REGISTRATION OF ALIENS· *See* Immigration: Alien registration

REGISTRATION OF LETTERS. *See* Postal service: Registration of letters

REGULATION OF TRAFFIC (printed regulations). *See* Traffic regulation pamphlet: Printed traffic regulations

REINDEER. *See* Animals: Reindeer

RELIEF ADMINISTRATION (federal). *See* Federal emergency relief administration; Federal surplus relief corporation

RELIEF MAP. *See* Map: Relief map

RELIGIOUS HILLSIDE SHRINE similar to those in European Catholic countries was "The Way of the Cross," built in New Ulm, Minn., in 1884. Connected with the shrine are the Loretto Hospital and the St. Alexander Home for the Aged.

RELIGIOUS LIBERTY ACT (colonial) passed by an established legislature was the Tolerance Act of Maryland enacted in April 1649. It ordered toleration for all who professed faith in Jesus Christ and subscribed to the orthodox interpretation of the Trinity but prescribed the death penalty for Aryan heretics, atheists, and Jews. It stated that "Whatsoever person or persons within this province and the islands thereunto belonging shall from henceforth blaspheme God or deny our Saviour Jesus Christ to be the Son of God, or shall deny the Holy Trinity, the Father, Son and Holy Ghost, or the Godhead of any of these said persons of the Trinity, or the unity of the Godhead, shall be punished with death and forfeiture of all his or her lands and goods to the Lord Proprietary."

THE FIRST

THE FIRST

RELIGIOUS PUBLICATION
Religious journal was *The Christian History,* published weekly in Boston, Mass., by Samuel Kneeland and Timothy Green for Thomas Prince, Jr., editor, from March 5, 1743, to February 23, 1745.

Religious review was *The Herald of Gospel Liberty,* which was issued September 1, 1808, by the Reverend Elias Smith. In the beginning it was issued "every other Thursday" and in 1816 it was issued only on "the first of every other month." It was published in Portsmouth, N.H

Religious weekly newspaper in the world with a continuous publication record was *The Religious Remembrancer.* It was first issued in Philadelphia, Pa., on September 4, 1813, by John Welwood Scott. In 1840 the name was changed to *The Christian Observer.* In 1869 the offices were moved to Louisville, Ky., where it is still published. *(Christian Observer—Converse and Co.)*

RELIGIOUS ROTOGRAVURE MAGAZINE. *See* Periodical: Sectarian magazine printed in rotogravure

RELIGIOUS SERVICE BROADCAST. *See* Radio broadcast: Religious service broadcast

RELIGIOUS SERVICE TELECAST. *See* Television—Telecast: Religious services to be televised

RELIGIOUS SOCIETY OF FRIENDS. *See* Quakers: Quakers to arrive in America

RELIGIOUS TRACT SOCIETY. *See* Tract society: Tract society

REPORTER (woman) accredited to the White House. *See* News correspondent: Woman news correspondent accredited to the White House

REPUBLICAN CARTOON. *See* Cartoon: Republican cartoon

REPUBLICAN PARTY
Republican Party meeting (local) was held on February 22, 1854, when the anti-slavery factions of the Whig and Free Democratic parties of Michigan held a preliminary organization meeting. The name "Republican" was suggested by Alvan Earle Bovay at a meeting in Ripon, Wis., on March 20, 1854; at a previous meeting in Ripon, on February 28, the new party had been organized in protest against the Kansas-Nebraska bill. The first convention formally organized under the name of "Republican Party" met in Strong, Me., on August 7, 1854.

Republican Party meeting (national) was held in Pittsburgh, Pa., February 22, 1856, in response to a call issued on January 17, 1856, by David Wilmot of Pennsylvania, Lawrence Bainard of Vermont, William W. White of Wisconsin, A. P. Stone of Ohio, and J. Z. Goodrich of Massachusetts. The purpose of the meeting was to perfect the national organization and to arrange for a national convention of the new party to nominate candidates for President and Vice President for the coming election. *(Frank C. Harper—Pittsburgh of Today)*

Republican Party national convention was held at Music Fund Hall, Philadelphia, Pa., on June 17, 1856; at that convention the first Republican National platform was adopted. The first presidential candidate was John Charles Fremont and the vice presidential candidate William Lewis Dayton.

RESALE PRICE MAINTENANCE LAW. *See* Price regulation law: Resale price maintenance law

RESEARCH COUNCIL. *See* Science association: National research council

RESEARCH INSTITUTE
Anatomy research institute was the Wistar Institute of Anatomy and Biology, which was established in Philadelphia, Pa., on July 20, 1891, by General Isaac Jones Wistar through a $20,000 fund in memory of Caspar Wistar. It was incorporated April 22, 1892. The first building was dedicated on May 21, 1894. *(Methods and Problems of Medical Education. Seventeenth series. Rockefeller Foundation)*

Institute for research in nervous diseases was the Neurological Institute of New York, incorporated April 5, 1909, which opened its hospital October 1, 1909, in New York City. The first superintendent was Alexander H. Candlish.

RESEARCH LABORATORY (industrial). *See* Industrial research laboratory

RESERVATION. *See* Bird reservation: Indian reservation

RESERVE (forest). *See* Forest reserve: Forest reserve

RESERVE OFFICERS ASSOCIATION MEDAL. *See* Medal: Reserve Officers Association medal

THE FIRST

RESERVE OFFICERS TRAINING CORPS. *See* Army: Reserve Officers Training Corps

RESIDENT FELLOWSHIP. *See* Fellowship: Resident fellowship for women awarded by a women's college

RESPIRATOR (iron lung) was invented by Professor Philip Drinker and Louis Agassiz Shaw, who made the original model in April 1927, adapted only for laboratory use. It consisted of a cheap galvanized iron box with a bed made from "garage creepers" and two household vacuum cleaners with hand-operated valves as the source of alternate positive and negative pressure. The Consolidated Gas Company of New York donated $7,000 to Harvard University, Cambridge, Mass., and a second model was manufactured which was first used October 12, 1928, at the Children's Hospital, Boston, Mass., on a little girl suffering from respiratory failure caused by infantile paralysis. The machine was manufactured by Warren E. Collins, Inc., Boston, Mass. (*Journal of the American Medical Association. May 18, 1929*)

RESTAURANT
Cafeteria. *See* Cafeteria

Penny restaurant where most items were sold for one cent was opened by Bernarr Adolphus Macfadden at 487 Pearl Street, New York City, in the winter of 1900. In 1901 he opened a larger one and continued opening branches until thirty were in operation in 1906. They were known as the Macfadden Physical Culture Restaurants.

Restaurant with an automatic arrangement for vending food was the Automat Restaurant, which was opened by the Horn & Hardart Baking Company at 818 Chestnut Street, Philadelphia, Pa., on June 9, 1902. The mechanism was imported from Germany, the patents having been acquired there from their Swedish originators. These original mechanisms differed materially from those used in the Automat restaurants of today, which are of the company's own patent and manufacture.

Self-service restaurant was opened September 4, 1885, at 7 New Street, New York City, opposite the New York Stock Exchange. It was called the Exchange Buffet.

RESTAURANT CHINA. *See* Chinaware

RETAIL PRICE LAW (state). *See* Price regulation law: Price regulation law (state)

REVENUE BUREAU. *See* Internal revenue act

THE FIRST

REVENUE COLLECTOR (woman). *See* Woman: Woman internal revenue collector

REVENUE CUTTER. *See* Ship: Revenue cutter

REVENUE STAMP printed by the Post Office Department was the "Federal duck stamp," a one-dollar stamp required of all waterfowl hunters over sixteen years of age, to be attached to game licenses as required by the Migratory Bird Conservation Act of March 16, 1934 (48 Stat.L.451). The stamp went on sale August 14, 1934, and was the same size as the special delivery postage stamps. It depicted a male and female mallard coming to rest on a marshland and was drawn by Jay Norwood ("Ding") Darling, chief of the Bureau of Biological Survey of the Department of Agriculture. Stamps of this class, as well as all other revenue stamps, had previously been issued by the Treasury Department. Although sold through the Post Office Department, the proceeds went to the Department of Agriculture where 10 per cent was used for the expense of printing and selling the stamps and the balance to lease or purchase marsh areas for waterfowl sanctuaries.

REVIVAL MEETING of importance was known as "The Great Awakening" and was inspired by the Reverend Jonathan Edwards, noted theologian and metaphysician, pastor of the Congregational Church, Northampton, Mass. He was instrumental in bringing about the wave of religious hysteria which swept the country from 1735 to 1740.

REVOLUTIONARY WAR
Armed conflict in the Revolutionary War was a skirmish at Lexington, Mass., April 19, 1775, between the Minutemen under Captain John Parker and the British Regulars under Major John Pitcairn.

Incident in the Revolutionary War occurred December 13, 1774, when Major John Sullivan of the Granite State Volunteers, later a major general in the Continental Army, and 400 patriots attacked Fort William and Mary at New Castle, N.H., in Portsmouth Harbor. They bound the commander of the fort and frightened the soldiers away, capturing one hundred casks of powder and small arms. This attack took place some four months before the battle of Lexington. (*Thomas Coffin Amory—The Military Services and Public Life of Major General John Sullivan*)

Martyr in the Revolutionary War was Christopher Snider, an eleven-year-old boy, who was killed February 22, 1770, in Boston, Mass., when Ebenezer Richardson fired upon a mob which attacked his house because he had removed the marks set against the house

THE FIRST

of Theophilus Lille, who had violated the merchants' agreement against importing. Sammy Gore was also shot by Richardson but did not die. On the day of the funeral, shops and schools closed. Richardson was convicted of murder and sentenced to two years in prison. (*Boston Evening Post, February 26, 1770*)

Naval battle of the Revolution took place June 12, 1775, when Captain James Moore of the British schooner "Margaretta" arrived in the harbor of Machias, Me., and ordered the citizens to take down a liberty pole which they had erected. The citizens, led by Jeremiah and John O'Brien, set out in a confiscated sloop, "Unity," and in a hand-to-hand encounter captured the "Margaretta," confiscated her cannons, captured the crew, and marched them overland to Cambridge, Mass., where they were turned over to General Washington. The American loss was four killed and eight wounded. (*Andrew Magoun Sherman—Life of Captain Jeremiah O'Brien.*)

REVOLVER. *See* Pistol: Revolver

REVOLVER SHOOTING TOURNAMENT (international) was held June 16, 1900, between teams representing the United States and France. Each contestant had 30 shots at targets placed at 150 feet and 52½ feet. The American team won by 61 points. Out of a possible score of 6,000 points, the Americans received 4,889 and the Frenchmen 4,828 points. The contest was held at the shooting range in Armbruster Park, Greenville, N.J., and Gastinne-Renett's pistol range, Paris. The scores were cabled to the opposing teams.

REVOLVING DOOR. *See* Door (revolving)

REVOLVING GUN. *See* Ordnance: Revolving gun turret

RHINOCEROS. *See* Animals: Rhinoceros

RHODES SCHOLAR
Negro to win a Rhodes scholarship was Alain Le Roy Locke of Pennsylvania, who "attended Hertford [Oxford University] 1907-1910, read Philosophy." He received his A.B. degree in 1908 from Harvard University. (*Rhodes Scholarships. Records of Past Scholars*)

Rhodes Scholars took up their residence at Oxford University, England, in 1904. Under the last will of Cecil Rhodes, dated July 1, 1899, annual awards of three-year scholarships at Oxford were available to two American students from each state. Until World War 1, one man was appointed from each state each year for two years, and all appointments were omitted

THE FIRST

the third year. During World War I the awards were suspended. Later the system was changed so that now the United States is divided into six districts of six states each and two of seven states, from which thirty-two scholars are chosen each year, four from each district. The total number of scholars in residence at one time is the same under the two systems. (*Laurence Alden Crosby—Oxford of Today: A Manual for Prospective Rhodes Scholars*)

RHUBARB was shipped from London, England on January 11, 1770, by Benjamin Franklin to John Bartram in Philadelphia, Pa.

RHYMING DICTIONARY. *See* Dictionary: Rhyming dictionary

RICE was imported by Sir William Berkeley, governor of Virginia, in 1647. He directed that a half bushel of seeds be planted. The yield was sixteen bushels. (*Amory Austin—Rice, Its Cultivation, Production and Distribution in the United States and Foreign Countries*)

RIDING CHAMPION (jockey). *See* Jockey: Jockey to win the national riding championship four times

RIFLE. *See* Ordnance: Gun (rifled); Ordnance: Semi-automatic rifle

RIFLE ASSOCIATION
Rifle association (national) was the National Rifle Association, organized and chartered November 24, 1871, in New York City with thirty-five members. The first shooting meet was held April 25, 1873, at Creedmoor, Long Island, N.Y. Nine regiments of the New York National Guard, one regiment of the New Jersey National Guard, the U.S. Engineers, and a squad of regular servicemen from Governors Island competed. The first officers of the association were president, General Ambrose Everett Burnside; vice president, Colonel William Conant Church; secretary, Captain George Wood Wingate; corresponding secretary, Frederick M. Peck; and treasurer, General John Blackburne Woodward.

Rifle tournament (international) of consequence was held September 26, 1874, at Creedmoor, Long Island, N.Y., between an American team commanded by Colonel George Wood Wingate, and an Irish team, commanded by Captain Arthur Blennerhassett Leech, which was the challenger. Each team was composed of six men who fired fifteen shots each at targets at a distance of 800, 900, and 1,000 yards. The targets had square bull's-eyes and scores were rated at 4, 3, and 2 according to position. The maximum score possible was

RIFLE ASSOCIATION—*Continued*

1,080 points. The Americans represented by the Amateur Rifle Club of New York used American breechloaders and won the contest, 934 to 931 points. Captain Leech of the Irish team presented a cup to the National Rifle Association. In 1875 Princess Louise on behalf of Queen Victoria presented the association with the Wimbledon Cup, which has been the trophy since that date. *(A. H. Weston—The Rifle Club and Range)*

RIM (automobile). *See* Automobile tire: Demountable tire-carrying rim

RIVET production (commercial) was attempted by Josiah Gilbert Pierson, who invented a "cold-header machine" on which he obtained a patent on March 23, 1794. His heading machine was a massive affair, with a heavy framework anchored to the floor. A large flywheel was provided and operated on the toggle principle. His factory was located on the present site of the New York Produce Exchange.

RIVETLESS CARGO VESSEL. *See* Ship: Rivetless cargo vessel

ROAD

Brick pavement was laid in Charleston, W.Va., in 1870 by a private citizen at his own expense. In 1873 the city extended the paving to include several streets.

Brick pavement on a rural road was the 7.93-mile project begun in 1893 on the Wooster Pike, now U.S. Route 42, leading out of Cleveland, Ohio. An eight-foot brick pavement was laid on a six-inch broken stone base and edged with stone curbs. Completed in 1895, it extended from the York Road to the Lunn Road, then in the countryside outside the city.

Coast-to-coast paved road was the Lincoln Highway. Carl G. Fisher proposed a 3,300-mile highway and on July 1, 1913, the Lincoln Highway Association was formed with Henry Bourne Joy as president. The proclamation of the opening of the road from New York City to San Francisco, Calif., was made September 10, 1913. The highway traversed thirteen states—New York, New Jersey, Pennsylvania, Ohio, Indiana, Illinois, Iowa, Nebraska, Colorado, Wyoming, Utah, Nevada, and California—and cost about $10,000,000. The first complete coast-to-coast run over the official route was made by Neil Patterson. The association disbanded December 31, 1927.

Concrete road was built in Bellefontaine, Ohio, in 1892 on the west side of Main Street. A strip 10 feet wide and 220 feet long was put down. In 1893-1894 the remainder of Main

Street and also Columbus, Opera, and Court Streets were paved on the four sides of the public square.

Concrete rural road was laid in Wayne County, Mich., in the spring of 1909. One mile of concrete pavement 18 feet wide and 6½ inches deep was laid on Woodward Road between Six Mile and Seven Mile Roads near Detroit.

Cotton fabric used on a road was placed on a short stretch of experimental bituminous double surface pavement on Route 2 between Chapin and Prosperity, Newberry County, S.C. in 1926. The fabric, classed as Cider Duck, was laid on the road in longitudinal strips overlapping each other two or three inches, after a coat of tar prime had been applied. Hot asphalt was then applied and covered with coarse sand and crushed rock.

Electronic highway system was conceived by Dr. Vladimir Kosma Zworykin at the RCA Laboratories, David Sarnoff Research Center, Princeton, N.J. Demonstrations were given in June 1953 with a controlled miniature car and on June 3, 1960, with a standard automobile. Wire cables buried under the pavement conveyed impulses to electronic circles in the automobiles in order to reduce speed automatically and thus prevent collisions.

Federal grant-in-aid to states for roads was the Federal Aid Road Act, "to provide that the United States shall aid the states in the construction of rural post roads, and for other purposes," passed July 11, 1916 (39 Stat.L. 355). For the fiscal year ending June 30, 1917, $5,000,000 was appropriated, which amount was increased $5,000,000 every year until the appropriation in 1921 was $25,000,000. The first project was in Contra Costa County, Calif., between the Alameda-Contra Costa boundary and the city limits of Richmond, Calif. Bids were opened June 26, 1916, and the contract awarded July 10, 1916, for the 2.55 miles. The work cost $53,938.85, of which $24,246.56 was the federal appropriation. The project statement was submitted September 1, 1916, and approved October 18, 1916, by David Franklin Houston, Secretary of Agriculture.

Federal highway built with funds from the national treasury was the Great National Pike, also known as the Cumberland Road, built in sections from 1806 to 1840 between Cumberland, Md., and Vandalia, Ill. A Congressional act of March 29, 1806 (2 Stat.L.357) "to regulate the laying out and making a road from Cumberland, in the state of Maryland, to the state of Ohio" appropriated $30,000. The first construction contracts were let April 16 and May 8, 1811. The last appropriation was made May 25, 1838 (5 Stat.L.228), the total appropriation being $6,821,246. In 1856, the road

THE FIRST

was turned over to the states through which it passed. Some of the money obtained from the sale of public lands, however, was appropriated for state road work. (*Thomas B. Searight—The Old Pike*)

Federal road agency, known as the Office of Road Inquiry, was established in the Department of Agriculture by statute approved March 3, 1893 (27 Stat.L.737) "to make inquiries in regard to the systems of road management throughout the United States, to make investigations in regard to the best method of road making, to prepare publications on this subject suitable for distribution." General Roy Stone was appointed head of the new organization as Special Agent and Engineer for Road Inquiry.

Highway legislation (colonial) was Act No. 50, passed by the Virginia legislature at the September 4, 1632, session at James City. It provided that "Highways shall be layd out in such convenient places as are requisite accordinge as the Governor and Counsell or the Commissioners for the monthlie corts shall appoynt, or accordinge as the parishoners of every parish shall agree." (*William Waller Hening—The Statutes at Large being a Collection of all the Laws of Virginia from the First Session of the Legislature in the Year 1619. Vol. 1*)

Highway planning surveys (nation-wide) were authorized by Congress in the Hayden-Cartwright Act (48 Stat.L.993), approved June 18, 1934. The surveys were designed to obtain traffic volume and load-weight and other information needed for the rational planning of a nation-wide system of interstate highways. The surveys were to be made by the Bureau of Public Roads of the United States Department of Agriculture, in cooperation with the several state highway departments.

Inter-American highway appropriation was made by Congress March 26, 1930 (46 Stat.L.115), when $50,000 was authorized for extending a route through the Central American republics connecting Panama City, Panama, with the United States.

Law regarding state aid for roads was "an act to provide for the more permanent improvement of the public roads of this state," passed April 14, 1891, by New Jersey and signed by Governor Leon Abbett. It placed the administration of state aid under the direction of the president of the State Board of Agriculture, who served without fee or reward for two and a half years. On March 29, 1892, the act was amended and provided for the appointment of a Commissioner of Public Roads. The first commissioner was Edward Burroughs, appointed May 17, 1894, by Governor George

THE FIRST

T. Werts. (*First Annual Report of the Commissioner of Public Roads for the year ending December 31, 1894*)

Macadam road was the Lancaster Turnpike, 62 miles long, connecting Philadelphia and Lancaster, Pa. Work was begun in February 1793 by the Philadelphia and Lancaster Turnpike Railroad Company, chartered April 9, 1792, of which William Bingham was the first president. The road was completed December 1795 at an approximate cost of $7,500 a mile, a total of $465,000, which was provided by individual investors. The first two miles of the road were surfaced with coarse gravel. The remainder, surfaced with "pounded" or broken stone, was 24 feet in width, 18 inches deep in the center, and 12 inches deep at the edge. Paralleling the main stone-surfaced road was a summer or side road 13 feet in width which was used in good weather as it was easier on the horses' feet than the angular crushed stone.

Mosaic pavement similar to old mosaics was laid on Canal Street, New Orleans, La. The mosaic effect was secured by mixing chipped metronite, crown point spar, and mica with the cement, then pouring the mixture into diamond-shaped brass-stripped forms, sanding it down, and polishing it. The work was completed on February 4, 1930, and was part of the project referred to as the "Beautification of Canal Street."

Overland wagon road across the Rocky Mountains to the Pacific Coast was the Oregon Trail. It followed Indian and buffalo trails, and was blazed by many, but it may be considered to date from 1842 when John Charles Fremont made a survey of it for the government prior to the great covered wagon expeditions. The Oregon Trail began at Westport Landing or Independence Landing on the Missouri River, followed the Sante Fe trail for a short distance, then extended for some 2,000 miles across Missouri, Kansas, Nebraska, Wyoming, Idaho, and Oregon to Vancouver on the north side of the Columbia River, in what is now the state of Washington.

Plank road was completed July 18, 1846 by the Salina and Central Square Plank Road Company between Syracuse and Central Square, N.Y. Trenches were dug slightly below the level of the road and a single track of hemlock planks about 4 inches thick and 8 feet long was placed at right angles to the road. The track was covered with dirt as protection against horses' hoofs.

Road pavement was laid at Pemaquid, Me., in 1625. It consisted of stones, rocks, and cobblestones. (*John Henry Cartland—Twenty Years at Pemaquid*)

ROAD—*Continued*

Road with a depressed trough was constructed on the Meridian Highway No. 2 between Temple and Belton, Tex., at a cost of approximately $50,000 a mile. It was opened to traffic on December 15, 1925, but did not prove satisfactory. *(Records in State Highway Department. Austin, Tex.)*

Route numbering system (nation-wide) was adopted March 2, 1925, by the Joint Board of State and Federal Highway officials appointed by the Secretary of Agriculture. To eliminate confusion caused by the motley array of signs in various localities the board adopted the familiar U.S. shield numbered marker.

Sheet asphalt pavement was laid on William Street, Newark, N.J., on July 29, 1870, by Professor Edward Joseph De Smedt of the American Asphalt Pavement Company, New York City. It was known as French asphalt pavement. On May 31, 1870, De Smedt obtained patents (Nos. 103,581 and 103,582) which he assigned to the New York Improved Anthracite Coal Company. *(Scientific American. March 5, 1870)*

State road appropriation of a specific sum was made by Kentucky on December 19, 1795, when $2,000 was appropriated for the purpose of opening a wagon road from Crab Orchard to Cumberland Gap. *(Lewis Collins—History of Kentucky)*

State road authorization was made by Kentucky December 14, 1793, when Daniel Weisiger, Bennett Pemberton, and Nathaniel Sanders were appointed "commissioners to receive subscriptions in money, labor or property, to raise a fund for clearing a wagon road from Frankfort, Ky., to Cincinnati, Ohio."

Stone pavement was laid in New York City in 1657 on the street now known as Stone Street.

Synthetic rubber in an asphaltic concrete resurfacing mixture was used in Akron, Ohio, on September 7, 1948, when work commenced on the resurfacing of one mile on Exchange Street. Seven to eleven pounds of rubber powder were used to each ton of asphaltic concrete. A small test section was resurfaced in 1947.

Toll road was the Little River Turnpike in Virginia, which led from Alexandria to Snicker's (Snigger's) Gap, a pass through the Blue Ridge Mountains, leading into the Shenandoah Valley in the northwest part of the state. The General Assembly in October 1785 appointed nine commissioners to erect a chain of toll gates to collect tolls to "keep in repair the

said roads." The receipts were to be applied to clearing and repairing this road and the road between Alexandria and Georgetown. The road was not surfaced and by 1795 was so completely worn out that complainants charged that the road needed "an artificial bed of pounded or broken stone." *(Joseph Austin Durrenberger—Turnpikes)*

Walk of fame. *See* Walk of fame

ROAD MAP. *See* Map: Automobile road map; Map: Road map

ROBBERY (bank). *See* Bank robbery

ROBOT PILOTLESS AIRPLANE. *See* Aviation—Airplane: Transatlantic robot pilotless airplane

ROCK DRILL. *See* Drill: Percussion rock drill

ROCK-FILLED DAM. *See* Dam: Rock-filled dam

ROCK WOOL FACTORY was the Crystal Chemical Works, Alexandria, Ind., opened June 1, 1897, by Charles Corydon Hall, who melted limestone rock in a specially designed water-jacketed cupola. The rock was blown by steam pressure into fine wool-like threads for use as insulating material. The Johns Manville Corporation acquired the works in 1929.

ROCKET

Air-to-air rocket was the "Mighty Mouse," created by the Navy's Bureau of Ordnance for use by interceptor planes to destroy bombers. The rocket, which was placed in production in October 1951, was 4 feet long, weighed 18 pounds, and had a diameter of 2.75 inches. The rockets could be fired one at a time or in salvos of 6, 12, 18, or 24.

American satellite to reach the moon was the Ranger IV, launched April 23, 1962, at 3:50 P.M. E.S.T. from the Atlantic Missile Range, Cape Canaveral, Fla. It was launched by an Atlas-Agena B, 102 feet high with a 16-foot base diameter and a lift-off weight of 275,000 pounds. It traveled an estimated 229,541 miles and impacted the moon at 7:49:53 A.M. E.S.T. on April 26, 1962. The velocity at lunar impact was 5,963 miles per hour.

Animals fired into space and rescued from a rocket were Able and Baker, two one-pound female monkeys, one a rhesus, the other a spider monkey, who survived a fifteen-minute flight in separate containers in the nose cone of a Jupiter rocket launched on May 28, 1959, from Cape Canaveral, Fla. The cone was shot 300 miles into space and recovered about ninety minutes after firing off the island of Antigua, about 1,500 miles away, by U.S. Navy frogmen from the tug "Kiowa." A previous attempt made December 13, 1958, had been unsuccessful.

Ballistic missile was the Corporal, fired May 22, 1947, at White Sands Proving Grounds, N.M. It responded accurately to guidance commands and reached a range of 63 miles.

Communications satellite was a 26½-inch magnesium sphere, Echo I, launched by a Thor Delta rocket, 92 feet high, with a 112,000-pound lift-off weight, launched August 12, 1960, at 5:39 A.M. from Cape Canaveral, Fla. The satellite went into orbit at 7:45 A.M. after the three stages of the rocket had been fired successfully. A taped message was transmitted from Goldstone, Calif., bounced off the satellite, and received by the Bell Telephone laboratory at Holmdel, N.J.

Intermediate range ballistic missile was a Jupiter, fired May 31, 1957, from the Atlantic Missile Range, Cape Canaveral, Fla. The firing was conducted by the Jet Propulsion Laboratories and the Army Ballistic Missile Agency.

Liquid fuel rocket flight was made March 16, 1926, at Auburn, Mass., under the direction of Professor Robert Hutchins Goddard. Pressure was produced internally by an outside pressure tank, and after launching by an alcohol heater on the rocket. The rocket traversed 184 feet in 2.5 seconds, making speed along the trajectory about 60 miles an hour. The flight was reported to the Smithsonian Institution, May 5, 1926. Working under a grant from Clark University, Worcester, Mass., Professor Goddard, as early as 1920, demonstrated the lifting force of rockets using liquid oxygen and ether. (*Smithsonian Institution. Miscellaneous Collection. Vol. 95*)

Liquid fuel rocket patent was No. 1,103,503, granted July 14, 1914, to Professor Robert Hutchins Goddard of Worcester, Mass. It covered what was later termed a "rocket motor."

Rocket cone recovery was accomplished August 8, 1957, when the cone of a Jupiter-C ballistic missile, fired from the Atlantic Missile Range, Cape Canaveral, Fla., was recovered. It was fired by the Army Ballistic Missile Agency and the Jet Propulsion Laboratories.

Rocket patent was granted Andrew Lanergan of Boston, Mass., who on June 21, 1859, received patent No.24,468 on an "improvement in exhibition rockets."

Rocket to attain a 100-mile altitude was a captured German V-2 rocket fired July 30, 1946, from the White Sands Proving Grounds, N.M. It descended 69 miles north of the launching platform, having attained an altitude of 104 miles.

Rocket to exceed a 150-mile altitude was a Viking XI, a test missile released by the Navy containing instruments to record weather conditions. On May 24, 1954, it rose to a height of 158 miles over the White Sands Proving Grounds, N.M.

Rocket to intercept a low-flying airplane was a Hawk missile, fired in May 1958, which engaged an F80 jet target flying at treetop level at the White Sands Proving Grounds, N.M.

Rocket to intercept a supersonic target missile was a Nike Hercules missile, fired in November 1958, which destroyed a supersonic target missile traveling faster than 1,500 miles per hour at an altitude greater than 60,000 feet.

Rocket to intercept an airplane was a Nike, fired November 27, 1951, at the White Sands Proving Grounds, N.M., at an aerial target. The missile detonated about 25 feet from the target, which was flying at a range of about 15 miles, an altitude of 33,000 feet, and a speed of 300 miles an hour.

Rocket to reach outer space was a two-stage rocket—a Wac Corporal set in the nose of a German V-2—fired February 24, 1949, from the White Sands Proving Grounds, N.M., by a team of scientists under Dr. Wernher Von Braun. It reached an altitude of 250 miles.

Rocket with an atomic warhead was an MB-I, known as the "Genie," fired July 19, 1957, at Yucca Flat, Nev. It was an air-to-air rocket and contained a built-in guidance mechanism. It was made by the Douglas Aircraft Company, Santa Monica, Calif., and was fired from a jet F89 Scorpion.

Satellite placed in orbit by the United States was Explorer 1 (1958 Alpha), launched January 31, 1958, from Cape Canaveral, Fla., by a Jupiter C Army missile. It was a bullet-shaped tubular rocket 80 inches long and weighed 30.8 pounds (weight of satellite proper, 18.13 pounds; final stage of rocket after burnout, 12.67 pounds). The satellite was airborne at 10:48:16 A.M. and went into orbit around the earth at 10:55 A.M. E.S.T., traveling at a speed ranging from 18,000 to 19,000 miles an hour.

THE FIRST

THE FIRST

ROCKET—*Continued*
Satellite placed in orbit by an all-solid propellant rocket was Explorer IX (1961 Delta), launched February 16, 1961, from the National Aeronautics and Space Administration Wallops Station at Wallops Island, Va. The satellite weighed 80 pounds. It contained a 15-pound sphere and 65-pounds of ejection, inflation, telemetry, and other equipment. Its velocity at perigee was 17,866 miles per hour and at apogee 13,976 miles per hour.

Satellite placed in solar orbit to investigate interplanetary space between the orbits of Earth and Venus was Pioneer V (1960 Alpha), launched March 11, 1960, from Cape Canaveral, Fla. It was launched by a three-stage Thor-Able IV rocket, 90 feet high and 8 feet in diameter with a lift-off weight of approximately 105,000 pounds. The payload was a 26-inch sphere plus four vanes covered by 4,800 solar cells with a total weight of 94.8 pounds, including approximately 40 pounds of instruments. The satellite orbited the sun in 311.6 days. Its velocity at the third-stage burnout was 24,689 miles per hour. It was 74.9 million miles from the sun in perigee and 92.3 million miles in apogee. The last message was received on June 26, 1960, when it was 22.5 million miles from earth and had transmitted data for 138.9 hours.

Satellite to transmit photographs of the earth was Explorer VI (1959 Delta), launched August 7, 1959, from the Atlantic Missile Range, Cape Canaveral, Fla. The pictures, received in Hawaii, took 40 minutes to transmit. They were released September 28, 1959, by the U.S. National Aeronautics and Space Administration. They depicted a crescent shape of part of the earth in sunlight taken about 19,500 miles over Mexico from a position facing the Pacific Ocean. The velocity of the satellite at perigee was 23,031 miles per hour. The perigee was 156 miles and the apogee 26,357 miles. The lift-off weight of the Thor-Able rocket was 105,000 pounds and the payload weight was 142 pounds, which included four solar vanes or paddles, each carrying 2,000 solar cells.

Ship from which a long-range rocket was launched. *See* Ship: Ship from which a long-range rocket was launched

Ship to fire a Polaris missile. *See* Ship: Ship to fire a Polaris missile

Space capsule recovered from an orbiting satellite was located August 11, 1960, in the Pacific Ocean. It was recovered from Discoverer XIII (1960 Theta), a satellite launched from Vandenberg Air Force Base, Calif., on August 10, 1960, by means of a Thor-Agena rocket 78 feet high with an 8-foot base and

a lift-off weight of approximately 108,500 pounds. The 350-pound capsule, 27 by 33 inches, was ejected from the satellite during its 17th polar orbit at a height of 200 miles over latitude 70° north. The descent of the capsule was slowed down by a parachute, which opened at about 50,000 feet. It was recovered by a Navy frogman, Boatswain's Mate third class Robert W. Carroll of Keene, N.H., who dived from a helicopter which took off from the U.S. Navy's "Haiti Victory."

Space capsule recovered in mid-air from an orbiting satellite was a 300-pound capsule ejected from the satellite Discoverer XIV (1960 Kappa) and retrieved on August 19, 1960. The capsule dropped back to earth by parachute and was snatched at 8,000 feet by a U.S. Air Force C-119 aircraft, piloted by Captain Harold E. Mitchell, about 360 miles southwest of Honolulu, Hawaii. Discoverer XIV was launched on August 18, 1960, from Vandenberg Air Force Base, Calif. The launch vehicle was a Thor-Agena rocket 78 feet high with an 8-foot base diameter and a lift-off weight of approximately 108,500 pounds. Its velocity was 17,658 miles per hour.

Submarine to fire a Polaris missile. *See* Submarine: Submerged submarine to fire a Polaris missile

ROCKET AIR MAIL FLIGHT. *See* Air mail service: Rocket air mail flight

ROCKET AIRPLANE. *See* Aviation—Airplane: Rocket airplane (military)

ROCKET GLIDER FLIGHT. *See* Glider: Rocket glider flight

ROCKET GUN. *See* Ordnance: Bazooka rocket gun

ROCKET SLED
Rocket-driven sled on rails was tested March 19, 1954, by Air Force Lieutenant Colonel John Paul Stapp, chief of the Aero Medical Field Laboratory of the Holloman Air Development Center at the Holloman Air Force Base, Alamogordo, N.M. It was known as the "abrupt deceleration vehicle" and was designed by Northrop Aircraft, Inc., to determine the effect upon fliers of bailing out at very high altitudes at supersonic speeds. Six rockets propelled the sled at 421 miles per hour. Later experiments increased the speed to over 3,000 miles per hour. The sled moved along heavy rails mounted in concrete. It was halted by water scooped in vents in the bottom of the sled. The water trough was 5 feet wide and 18 inches deep.

THE FIRST

ROCKING CHAIR. *See* Chair: Rocking chair

ROCKING TREADLE SEWING MACHINE. *See* Sewing machine: Sewing machine equipped with a rocking treadle or double treadle

ROD (brass). *See* Brass rod

RODENT EXTERMINATION. *See* Rat extermination (city-wide) to avert bubonic plague

RODEO competition was held July 4, 1888, at the racetrack at Prescott, Ariz. Juan Leivas was awarded a medal "for roping and tieing steer." With a 100-yard start, his time was 1.175 seconds. This rodeo developed into an annual competition.

ROLL FILM CAMERA. *See* Camera: Roll film camera

ROLL FILM FOR CAMERAS. *See* Photographic film: Roll film for cameras

ROLL-ON ROLL-OFF CARRIER. *See* Ship: Roll-on roll-off carrier

ROLL-TOP DESK. *See* Desk

ROLLER-BEARING COAL CAR. *See* Railroad car: Coal cars with roller bearings

ROLLER-BEARING PULLMAN TRAIN. *See* Railroad car: Pullman train completely equipped with roller bearings

ROLLER SKATE
Ball-bearing skate patent was patent No. 308,990, awarded to Levant M. Richardson of Chicago, Ill., on December 9, 1884.

ROLLER SKATING. *See* Skating: Roller derby

ROLLER SKATING RINK. *See* Skating rink: Roller skating rink (public)

ROLLING LIFT BRIDGE. *See* Bridge: Rolling lift bridge

ROLLING MILL (flour). *See* Flour mill: Flour rolling mill

ROLLING MILL (iron). *See* Iron: Iron mill to puddle and roll iron; Iron: Rolling mill

THE FIRST

ROMAN CATHOLIC CHURCH. *See* entries beginning with the word *Catholic*

ROOFING TILE (brick). *See* Tile: Brick roofing tile

ROOT BEER was manufactured by Charles Elmer Hires, a student at the Jefferson Medical College, Philadelphia, Pa., in cooperation with Dr. William Simpson and Dr. Henry Leffman in 1866. In 1869 Hires opened a drug store in Philadelphia and placed a sign over his fountain: "Hires Root Beer 5c." In 1876, he started a national business selling root beer.

ROPE SKI TOW. *See* Ski tow (rope)

ROPING MACHINE. *See* Spinning, carding, and roping machines

ROSE TOURNAMENT. *See* Tournament of Roses

ROSICRUCIAN SOCIETY. *See* Ancient Mystical Order Rosae Crucis

ROTARY CLUB was founded February 23, 1905, in Chicago by a lawyer, Paul Percy Harris, who induced three friends of his—a coal dealer, a tailor, and a mining engineer—to join. Meetings were held in each member's place of business in rotation, so that each could obtain some knowledge of the others' businesses. A national association was formed by a convention of sixteen clubs in August 1910 in Chicago. An international association was formed in August 1912 in Duluth, Minn., to provide charters for Winnipeg, Canada, and London, England. The constitution was revised at the Los Angeles convention, June 6, 1922, and "Rotary International" adopted as the new name. (*Paul Percy Harris—This Rotarian Age*)

ROTARY CONVERTER POWER PLANT. *See* Electric power plant: Rotary converter power plant

ROTARY CRANK (bicycle). *See* Bicycle: Bicycle with a rotary crank

ROTARY MOTION WASHING MACHINE. *See* Washing machine: Rotary motion washing machine

ROTARY PRESS. *See* Printing press: Rotary type printing press

ROTOGRAVURE PRESS. *See* Printing press: Rotogravure press

ROTOGRAVURE SECTARIAN MAGA-ZINE. *See* Periodical: Sectarian magazine printed in rotogravure

ROTOGRAVURE SECTIONS (newspaper). *See* Newspaper: Newspaper rotogravure sections

ROTOLACTOR. *See* Milking platform (rotating)

ROTOR SHIP. *See* Ship: Rotor ship

ROTOR WINDMILL. *See* Windmill: Windmill driven by rotor power

ROUGH DRY LAUNDRY SERVICE. *See* Laundry: Rough dry laundry service

ROUTE NUMBERING SYSTEM. *See* Road: Route numbering system

ROWING
Boat race. *See* Boat race

College to feature rowing as a sport was Yale, which in 1844 held races between various classes and students.

Racing shell. *See* Ship: Racing shell

Transatlantic trip by rowboat was accomplished by George Harpo and Frank Samuelson, who left Battery Park, New York City, June 7, 1896, and arrived at the Scilly Isles, off the coast of England, fifty-four days later.

Woman coxswain of a men's collegiate varsity team. *See* Woman: Woman coxswain of a men's collegiate varsity team

ROYAL ARCANUM was founded in Boston, Mass., June 23, 1877, by Darius Wilson. It is a fraternal mutual assessment beneficiary and benevolent society with the motto "Mercy, Virtue and Charity." (*Royal Arcanum Supreme Council. Official Bulletin 1893. Vol. 1*)

RUBBER
Football with a rubber covering. *See* Football: Football with a rubber covering

Rubber company was the Roxbury India Rubber Company of Roxbury, Mass., which manufactured various rubber products in 1832. It was incorporated February 11, 1833, by Lemuel Blake, Luke Baldwin, Edwin M. Chaffee, and Charles Davis, Jr. Inasmuch as the rubber was affected by heat and cold and had a disagreeable odor, the company was unable to create an outlet for its products.

Rubber company west of the Allegheny mountains was founded in 1870 by Dr. Benjamin Franklin Goodrich in Akron, Ohio. (*Wonder Book of Rubber—Goodrich Rubber Co.*)

Rubber heel was made in Lowell, Mass., by Humphrey O'Sullivan. He obtained a patent on January 24, 1899, No. 618,128, on a "safety-heel."

Rubber patent was granted to Jacob Frederick Hummel of Philadelphia, Pa., on April 29, 1813 on a "varnish of elastic gum to render water-proof" shoes and other objects.

Rubber patent of importance was No. 240, granted to Charles Goodyear on June 17, 1837, for a method of destroying the adhesive properties of rubber by superficial application of nitric acid with copper, or bismuth, etc. (*Bradford Kinney Peirce—Trials of an Inventor; Life and Discoveries of Charles Goodyear*)

Rubber shoe manufacturer was Leverett Candee, who established the L. Candee Shoe Factory in Hamden, Conn., in 1842. He used the Goodyear vulcanizing patent. Prior attempts had been made in 1823 and 1831 to manufacture rubber footwear out of gum elastic, but the shoes were not serviceable. They melted, and produced offensive odors.

Rubber tire patent was No. 5,104, awarded May 8, 1847, to Robert William Thomson of Adelphi, Middlesex County, England, on "an improvement in carriage wheels." It was granted on the application of elastic bearings around the rims of carriage wheels. This was based on a similar patent obtained June 10, 1846 (No. 10,990) in England.

Synthetic rubber was made by Lucas Petrou Kyrides and Dr. Richard Blair Earle in 1913 for the Hood Rubber Company, East Watertown, Mass. They prepared a number of polymerized hydrocarbons having rubber-like qualities, of which dimethyl butadiene had the most likely commercial possibilities. (*Chemical and Engineering News. October 10, 1943*)

Synthetic rubber (neoprene) was produced April 10, 1930, by Dr. Arnold M. Collins, who isolated chloroprene and observed its polymerization. In 1931, it was commercially manufactured in Deepwater, N.J., by the Du Pont Company.

Synthetic rubber produced on a commercial scale in competition with natural rubber was Du Prene, manufactured by the Du Pont company, Wilmington, Del., November 2, 1931. Chemists working under Dr. Elmer K. Bolton

THE FIRST

discovered that vinylacetylene could be treated by chemical reaction with other substances to produce a chemical called chloroprene from which synthetic rubber was made. The first commercial production of various articles made from Du Prene began in May 1932, when the Manhattan Rubber Manufacturing Division of Raybestos-Manhattan, Inc., of Passaic, N.J., made oil hose from Du Prene and offered it for sale to oil companies. Experimental tires were made of this material in February 1934 by the Dayton Rubber Manufacturing Company of Dayton, Ohio.

Vulcanized rubber was successfully produced by Charles Goodyear of New York City who obtained patent No. 3,633 on June 15, 1844, on an "improvement in india-rubber fabrics." *(Ralph Frank Wolf—India Rubber Man; the Story of Charles Goodyear)*

RUBBER-BALL CROSSING OF NIAGARA FALLS. *See* Niagara Falls: Person to go over Niagara Falls in a rubber ball

RUBBER-LINED COTTON HOSE. *See* Fire hose: Fire hose of rubber-lined cotton

RUBBERS ("Artics"). *See* "Artics"

RUGBY CONTEST (international). *See* Football game: Rugby contest (international)

RULES OF ORDER. *See* Parliamentary rules of order

RUNNER
Runner (American) to run a mile in less than four minutes was Don Bowden of the University of California, who on June 1, 1957, ran the mile in 3 minutes and 58.7 seconds at the Pacific Amateur Athletic Union Meet at Stockton, Calif. He was the eleventh man in the world to better the four-minute mile.

Runner to run a mile under four minutes (in the United States) was Jim Bailey, a University of Oregon student from Australia, who ran the mile on May 5, 1956, in 3 minutes and 58.6 seconds at the Los Angeles Coliseum, Los Angeles, Calif.

RUNNING CHAMPIONSHIP (cross-country). *See* Sports: Cross-country championships

RUNNING MEET (intercollegiate). *See* Track meet (intercollegiate)

RURAL FREE DELIVERY. *See* Postal service: Rural free delivery

THE FIRST

RUSSIAN SETTLEMENT was established March 15, 1812, at Cazadero, 18 miles north of Bodega Bay on the Russian River in California. The party consisted of 95 Russians and 80 Aleut hunters from Sitka, Alaska. Under the command of Ivan Alexandrovich Kuskof they built Fort Rumiantzof, consisting of 9 buildings in an area 300 by 280 feet, surrounded by a 12-foot stockade surmounted by spikes, and 50 other buildings outside the stockade. The fort was dedicated September 11, 1812. On April 15, 1839, the Russians decided to abandon it, and it was sold to John Augustus Sutter for $30,000. The bill of sale, signed by the Russian American Company, was delivered on December 12, 1841, by Commandant Alexander Rotcheff and registered at Yerba Buena the next day. The Russians evacuated the fort in December and sailed from San Francisco on January 1, 1842. The Spaniards called the settlement Fuerto de los Rusos, the Americans, Fort Ross. *(California Historical Society Quarterly. September 1933. Vol. 12. No. 3)*

SOS. *See* Radio distress signa: Radio SOS from an American ship

SACCHARIN was discovered by Constantine Fahlberg working under the direction of Professor Ira Remsen at Johns Hopkins University, Baltimore, Md. Fahlberg submitted an article "On the Liquid Toluenesulphochloride" on February 27, 1879, to the *American Chemical Journal. (American Chemical Journal. Vol. 1. No. 2-3. June 1879)*

SACRED THEOLOGY DEGREE. *See* Degrees (academic and honorary): Doctor of Sacred Theology degree

SAENGERFEST. *See* Music: Saengerfest

SAFE DEPOSIT VAULT was opened June 5, 1865, by the Safe Deposit Company of New York, 140-146 Broadway, New York City. Four vaults were located on the ground floor of the building and were constantly guarded. One of the vaults was devoted exclusively to the reception of deposits of valuable articles for which the rates ranged from $1.50 to $2.50 per year for every $1,000 represented. The three other vaults contained individual safe deposit vaults the rate on which varied from $30 to $40 annually. Each subscriber was provided with an individual key to open his vault box.

SAFE (fire-proof) worthy of the name was the "Salamander Safe," invented by Charles A. Gayler of New York City, who obtained a patent April 12, 1833 on a "fire-proof iron chest." It consisted of two chests, one within the other with a space between to "inclose air or any non-conductors of heat."

THE FIRST

SAFETY CONGRESS

Safety congress, together with a public exhibition of safety appliances, was held January 28, 1907, under the auspices of the American Institute of Social Science at the American Museum of Natural History, New York City.

Safety congress (national) was the Co-operative Safety Congress held September 30-October 5, 1912, in Milwaukee, Wis. At the second congress, September 23-25, 1913, in New York City, the name was changed to the National Council for Industrial Safety and, on October 13-15, 1914, in Chicago, Ill., at the third congress, to the National Safety Council.

SAFETY FUSE. See Fuse: Safety fuse

SAFETY PIN. See Pin: Safety pin

SAFETY RAZOR. See Razor: Safety razor

SAIL CLOTH FACTORY. See Cloth: Sail cloth factory

SAILING VESSEL. See Ship

SAILORS' CHURCH. See Church: Mariners' church

SAILORS' LIBRARY. See Library: Library for seamen

SAINT (Catholic) who was an American citizen was Frances Xavier Cabrini, born July 15, 1850, in Italy. She came to the United States in 1889 and became a citizen. She died December 22, 1917, was declared venerable in November 1937, and was beatified November 13, 1938. On June 13, 1946, she was voted upon favorably and on July 7, 1946, Pope Pius XII participated in the formal rites held at St. Peter's Cathedral, Rome, at which she was canonized. *(Lucille Papin Borden—Francesca Cabrini)*

SAINT LAWRENCE SEAWAY. See Canal: Saint Lawrence Seaway

SALES MACHINE. See Vending machine

SALES TAX. See Tax: Sales tax (state)

SALMON CANNERY. See Canning: Salmon cannery

SALMON HATCHERY. See Fish hatchery: Fish hatchery

SALT

Salt well drilled west of the Alleghenies, was bored, tubed, rigged, and operated by David Ruffner and his brother Joseph in 1808 at the Great Buffalo Lick, six miles above Charleston, W.Va., on the Big Kanawha. They started drilling on November 1, 1807, and on January 15, 1808, had an ample flow of brine. With the most primitive instruments they bored through forty feet of rock before they were successful.

Salt works was established in America in 1630 by Governor John Harvey of Virginia, who designed and established a factory for obtaining salt by evaporation of sea water. The factory was erected at Accomac on the eastern shore of Chesapeake Bay. *(Geoffrey Martin—Salt and Alkali Industry)*

SALT TRUST. See Trust: Trust

SALT WATER AQUARIUM. See Aquarium: Aquarium (inland salt water)

SALUTE (complimentary) fired by Great Britain in honor of an officer of the United States and virtually the first salute to the United States, was fired May 8, 1783. General George Washington and Governor George Clinton boarded the British ship "Ceres," commanded by Sir Guy Carleton, in New York Harbor to arrange for the British evacuation and were saluted on their arrival. When they departed, seventeen guns were fired in honor of Washington's rank. New York was evacuated by the British November 25, 1783. *(Magazine of American History. Annual 1880. Vol. 5. p. 108)*

SALVATION ARMY

Salvation army, which had been founded by William Booth in London, England, in 1865 under the name of the East London Mission and later had changed its name to the Christian Mission, started in the United States in March 1880. Commissioner George Scott Railton and seven black-coated women arrived on the "Australia," landed at the Battery, New York City, March 10, 1880, and proceeded to Castle Garden, New York City, where the first services were held. Services were held also between performances of *Uncle Tom's Cabin* at Harry Hill's Gentleman's Sporting Theatre, as well as at street meetings. *(George Scott Railton—Twenty-one Years' Salvation Army)*

Woman commander of the Salvation Army was General Elizabeth Booth, daughter of the Army's founder, who was elected its fourth general on September 3, 1934, in London, England on the fourth ballot. She was 69 years of age.

SANATORIUM (narcotic). See Narcotic: Narcotic sanatorium (federal) for drug addicts

THE FIRST

SANCTUARY (bird). *See* Bird sanctuary

SAND BLASTING, the process of cleaning, engraving, cutting, and boring glass, stone, metal, and other hard substances, was invented by Benjamin Chew Tilghman of Philadelphia, who received patent No. 108,408 on October 18, 1870, for "cutting and engraving stone, metal, glass, etc." with "sand used as a projectile."

SANDPAPER PATENT was granted to Isaac Fischer, Jr., of Springfield, Vt., on June 14, 1834. His invention was covered by four different patents all issued on the same date.

SANITARY DISTRICT was the Sanitary District of Chicago, Ill., authorized November 5, 1889, by referendum vote to construct and operate the sewage system for the protection of the public water supply. A special election of trustees was held December 12, 1899, at which Murray Nelson was chosen president; Lyman Edgar Cooley, chief engineer; and Charles Bary, secretary. The first business meeting was held on January 18, 1890.

SANITARY FAIR STAMPS. *See* Seal: Seals for raising funds

SANITARY WARE. *See* Pottery: Pottery to make sanitary ware

SANTA CLAUS SCHOOL was opened September 27, 1937, in Albion, N.Y., with an enrollment of six students for the one-week course. It was conducted by Charles Willis Howard to train men to play the part of Santa Claus.

SARDINE CANNERY. *See* Canning: Sardine cannery

SARRUSOPHONE was manufactured in 1921 by C. G. [Charles Gerard] Conn Company, Ltd., Elkhart, Ind. It is an instrument of the oboe class with a metal tube.

SASH
Wrought iron window sash installation of importance was made in 1929 by the Mesker Brothers Iron Company of St. Louis, Mo., which placed 70,000 square feet of sash in the new plant of the Pittsburgh Plate Glass Company in Crystal City, Mo.

SATELLITE. *See* Photograph: Photograph bounced off a satellite; Rocket

SATURDAY HALF-HOLIDAY. *See* Holiday: Saturday half-holiday

THE FIRST

SAVINGS AND LOAN ASSOCIATION (federal). *See* Federal savings and loan association

SAVINGS BANK. *See* Bank: Savings bank

SAVINGS BANK LIFE INSURANCE. *See* Insurance: Savings bank life insurance

SAVINGS GROUP. *See* Bank: Savings group

SAVINGS STAMP (postal). *See* Postal savings stamps

SAW (circular) is supposed to have been produced by Benjamin Cummins in Bentonsville, N.Y., about 1814. His saws were originally used for cutting the teeth of clock wheels, and were later used for cutting wood. (*Edward Henry Knight—Mechanical Dictionary*)

SAWMILL
Band sawmill was operated in 1867 by Hoffman Brothers of Fort Wayne, Ind., who employed a band saw forty feet in length, the ends of which were joined so as to revolve continuously. The saw blades, from four to five inches wide, were obtained from Sweden. Jacob Rosecrans Hoffman of Fort Wayne, Ind., obtained patent No. 92,191, July 6, 1869, on a "sawmill."

Electrically driven sawmill to operate successfully was designed and operated in 1896 by the Allis-Chalmers Manufacturing Company for the American River Land and Lumber Company, Folsom, Calif.

Sawmill engine that was portable was built in 1858 by Francis Wedge, designer for the H. & F. Blandy Company of Zanesville, Ohio. It was horizontal and mounted on a horizontal boiler.

SAXOPHONE production was undertaken in 1888 by Charles Gerard Conn, Elkhart, Ind. The instruments were made of brass, had two octave keys, and descended only to B-flat. Originally they were used only by military bands.

SCALE
Automatic computing pendulum-type scales were invented by Allen De Vilbiss, Jr. of Toledo, Ohio, who applied for a patent on the fan-type automatic computing scale on January 24, 1899. The patent was granted May 22, 1900, No. 649,915. In 1899 he organized the De Vilbiss Scale Company, which later developed into the Toledo Scale Company of Toledo, Ohio. This company was the first to produce an adjustable automatic indicator controller for

SCALE—*Continued*
bringing the hand to a quick stop. It was also
the first to produce a commercially successful
computing scale of the gravity type; first to
invent and patent a cylinder type platform scale,
replacing the hanging cylinder type scale; first
to produce a commercially successful automatic
dial portable scale; first to produce auto truck
scales having the lever pivots all on the same
plane to permit the use of a shallow pit; first
to produce a double-pendulum counterbalance
with a floating fulcrum; first to produce a built-
in, automatic, electric lighting system with a
ribbon switch which does not hold the scale off
zero; and first to produce a device for locking
the pendulum and tare beam lever for safety in
loading the scale.

Computing scales were manufactured by
Edward Canby in a small shop in the rear of
the Callahan Building on Main Street, Dayton,
Ohio. On March 20, 1891, the Computing Scale
Company was incorporated, the first computing
scale company in the world. In 1895 it produced
and brought out the first successful computing
scale.

Platform scale was built in St. Johnsbury,
Vt., in 1830 by Thaddeus Fairbanks. It was
patented June 30, 1831, by Erastus and Thaddeus Fairbanks of St. Johnsbury. Previously,
even-balance and steelyard types of scales had
been used.

Railway track scale was introduced by
E. and T. Fairbanks and Company of St. Johnsbury, Vt., which operated under patent No.
16,381, granted January 13, 1857, to Thaddeus
Fairbanks.

SCALPING (Indian). *See* Indians: Indian
scalping

SCANDINAVIAN METHODIST EPIS-
COPAL CHURCH. *See* Methodist Episcopal Church: Scandinavian Methodist Episcopal Church

SCHOLASTIC FRATERNITY. *See* Fraternity (Greek letter): Scholastic fraternity

SCHOOL
See also Academy; Education; *also* type of
school or subject taught, e.g., Agricultural
school, Army War College, Art course, Commercial high school, Jewish college.

Air-conditioned public elementary school
was the Belaire School, San Angelo, Tex., which
was opened in October, 1955. The school,
containing eight classrooms, was completely air-
conditioned.

Circular school building was St. Patrick
Central High School, Kankakee, Ill., opened
February 6, 1956. It was a two-story building,
200 feet in diameter, which housed classrooms
and a gymnasium unit accommodating 2,000
spectators. It was connected to a small rectangular wing containing the administrative offices
and library. The total cost of the school was
$736,592. Belli and Belli of Chicago, Ill., were
the architects.

Endowed school was the "Free Schoole
in Roxburie," which was established in Roxbury, Mass., in 1645. It was incorporated in
1789 as the "Grammar School in the Easterly
Part of the Town of Roxbury." The school is
still in existence and is known as the Roxbury
Latin School. (*Charles Knapp Dillaway—A
History of the Grammar School, or the Free
Schoole of 1645 in Roxburie*)

Evening school was established in New
Amsterdam (New York City) in 1661. Fees
and regulations for instruction are contained
in a report, *Instructions and Rules for Schoolmaster, Evert Pietersen,* which was drawn up
by the burgomasters on November 4, 1661.
(*Minutes of the Orphan Masters of New Amsterdam*)

Evening school (free, public) developed
in New York City directly and naturally from
the evening school controlled by philanthropic
agencies and partly supported by public funds.
The schools opened in 1833 in New York City
were free, and in a sense public, for they were
supported in part by public funds. (*Paul
Monroe—Cyclopedia of Education. Vol. II*)

Land grant to schools. *See* Land grant:
Land grant to schools

Model school or laboratory school of
practice for teachers was opened October 31,
1838, by Lafayette College, Easton, Pa., and
was known as West College. Its cost of
$2,230.22 was defrayed by President George
Junkin of Lafayette College. (*David Bishop
Skillman—Biography of a College*)

Negro school for freedmen was established
by the American Missionary Association at
Fortress Monroe, Va., on September 17, 1861.
The teacher was Mary S. Peake, a Negro.

Negro school (state) was the Snowden
School of Alexandria, Va. It was authorized
by act of legislature July 11, 1870, and was
under the guidance of William Frank Powell.
Its existence was of short duration.

Public school. *See* Public school

THE FIRST

THE FIRST

School completely irradiated with germicidal lamps was the Cato-Meridian Central School, Cato, N.Y. The lamps, made of special glass to permit ultraviolet bactericidal wave lengths to pass through, were made by the General Electric Company, Schenectady, N.Y., and were installed January 3, 1945. *(American School and University. 1946)*

School for Protestant girls was a boarding school established by Countess Benigna von Zinzendorf at Germantown, Pa., in 1742, exclusively for girls of the Moravian Church. By 1800 this had become a noted seminary. It is now the Moravian College for Women. Earlier, the Ursulines had opened a convent for girls in New Orleans, La.

School for the mentally retarded was the Massachusetts School for the Idiotic and Feeble-Minded Youth, created through the efforts of Dr. Samuel Gridley Howe and established by a legislative resolution, approved May 8, 1848, which appropriated $2,500 a year for three years. The first students were received on October 1, 1848. The school was incorporated April 4, 1850. Later the name was changed to the Massachusetts School for the Feeble-Minded. The institution is now operated as the Walter E. Fernald State School, named for Dr. Walter Elmore Fernald, the first resident superintendent. *(Albert Deutsch—The Mentally Ill in America)*

School in America was established by the Dutch West India Company on Manhattan Island in 1633. (It is possible that instruction given a group of pupils by Pilgrim settlers may have constituted an earlier school.) The Dutch school was established in New Amsterdam (New York City) with Adam Roelantsen as its first master. Instruction was given in Dutch prior to 1775. In 1783 the school became known as the Collegiate School, the oldest school still in existence in the United States. *(Henry Webb Dunshee—History of the School of the Collegiate Reform Dutch Church in the City of New York)*

School to fly an American flag. *See* Flag: American flag over a school house

School to have all classroom lights controlled by electric eyes was the Glenn H. Curtiss Memorial and Central Rural School, Hammondsport, N.Y., which placed the lights in operation on January 4, 1936. Paul William Seagers was the principal. *(American School and University. 1946)*

School to install a teletypesetter. *See* Teletypesetter: Teletypesetter installed in a school

School to operate on the one-class-to-a-room basis was established in 1846 in Quincy, Mass. *(Massachusetts Board of Education. Reports. Vol 10)*

SCHOOL ATTENDANCE LAW. *See* Education: Compulsory school attendance law (state)

SCHOOL COMMITTEE in America was elected in Dorchester, Mass., in 1645. The members were elected for life although the town reserved the right to remove any of them for "weighty reasons." They had charge of everything which pertained to the betterment of the school.

SCHOOL DEPARTMENT OF HYGIENE. *See* Hygiene instruction: School department of hygiene

SCHOOL LAND GRANT. *See* Land grant: Land grant to schools

SCHOOL LAW (compulsory) was passed November 11, 1647, by Massachusetts. It "ordered that every township in this jurisdiction, after the Lord hath increased them to the number of fifty householders, shall then forthwith appoint one within their town to teach all such children as shall resort to him to write and read, whose wages shall be paid either by the parents or masters of such children, or by the inhabitants in general." Towns of one hundred families were required to "set up a grammar school, the master thereof being able to instruct youths so far as they may be fitted for the university." *(Records of Massachusetts Bay Colony. Vol. II)*

See also Education: Compulsory attendance

SCHOOL OF MODERN LANGUAGES. *See* Language instruction: Modern language school

SCHOOL STADIUM. *See* Stadium: School stadium

SCHOOL SUPERINTENDENT

School superintendent (city) was Roswell Willson Haskins, who was appointed "city superintendent of common schools" in 1836 by Buffalo, N.Y. He resigned before the end of the year as the law was imperfect and restrictions hampered his work. In 1837 Louisville, Ky., appointed Samuel Dickinson superintendent with the title "agent of the board."

School superintendent (state) was Gideon Hawley, who was appointed state Superintendent of Common Schools by New York State in 1812. He served from January 14, 1813, until

SCHOOL SUPERINTENDENT—*Cont.*
February 22, 1821. An act was passed April 15 1814 making him secretary of the New York State Board of Regents at a salary of $400 a year. He was removed in 1821 because of political influence (Chapter 249 of 1821), and the Secretary of State was authorized to act ex officio as superintendent. In 1854, New York again created a Superintendent of Public Instruction. (*Proceedings of University Convocation, Albany, N.Y. August 2, 1870*)

SCHOOLBOOK was the *New England Primer* of 1689-90. It was "printed by R. Pierce for, and sold by Benjamin Harris, at the London Coffee-House," Boston, Mass. It was reprinted in 1691 and was used mostly by the Dissenters and the Lutherans.
See also Educational book

SCHOOLHOUSE west of the Allegheny Mountains was started in Schoenbrunn, Ohio, December 22, 1772, and completed July 29, 1773, by Moravian missionaries. The first teacher was the Reverend David Zeisberger. (*Joseph E. Weinland—The Romantic Story of Schoenbrunn*)

SCHOONER. *See* Ship

SCHWENKFELDER to immigrate to America was George Schultz, who arrived at Philadelphia, Pa., in 1731. The Schwenkfelders were a religious sect, followers of the Silesian nobleman Kaspar von Schwenkfeld. (*Samuel Kriebel Brecht—General Records of the Schwenkfelders*)

SCIENCE ADVISORY BOARD was authorized July 31, 1933, under Executive Order No. 6238, to appoint committees to deal with specific problems in the various departments of the federal government. The nine-member board held its first meeting August 21, 1933. The first president was Dr. Karl Taylor Compton, president of the Massachusetts Institute of Technology.

SCIENCE ASSOCIATION
History of science society was organized in Boston, Mass., January 12, 1924, and incorporated under the laws of the District of Columbia, January 30, 1925, "to encourage and maintain active interest in the history of science and the various sciences in particular." The first president was Lawrence Joseph Henderson.

National Academy of Sciences was incorporated by act of Congress approved by President Abraham Lincoln, March 3, 1863 (12 Stat. L.806) with the stipulation that "the Academy shall, whenever called upon by any department of the Government, investigate, examine, experiment, and report upon any subject of sci-

ence or art, the actual expense of such investigations, examinations, experiments, and reports to be paid from appropriations which may be made for the purpose, but the Academy shall receive no compensation whatever for any services to the Government of the United States." The first president of the National Academy of Sciences was Alexander Dallas Bache, who held that position from 1863 to 1867. (*National Academy of Sciences. Report. 1864*)

National Research Council was established in 1916 by the National Academy of Sciences at the request of President Woodrow Wilson "to bring into co-operation existing governmental, educational, industrial and other research organizations, with the object of encouraging the investigation of natural phenomena, the increased use of scientific research in the development of American industries, the employment of scientific methods in strengthening the national defense, and such other applications of science as will promote the national security and welfare." The original membership numbered forty-four, including ten officers of the United States Government assigned by President Wilson. The council held its first meeting September 20, 1916, in New York City. (*Annual Report of the National Academy of Sciences for the Year July 1, 1933-June 30, 1932*)

Scientific society was the Boston Philosophical Society, which was founded by Increase Mather in 1683 in Boston, Mass. He wrote that it was "a philosophical society of agreeable gentlemen who met once a fortnight for a conference upon improvements in philosophy and additions to the stores of natural history." (*Ralph Samuel Bates—Scientific Societies in the United States*)

Scientific society (national organization) was the American Association for the Advancement of Science, organized September 20, 1848, in Philadelphia, Pa., for the purpose of advancing science in every way. The first president was William Charles Redfield. (*American Association for the Advancement of Science— A Brief History of the Association from its Founding in 1848 to 1940*)

Scientific society of importance was the American Philosophical Society, organized 1743 in Philadelphia, Pa., by Benjamin Franklin. On May 14, 1743, he issued a broadside, "A Proposal for Promoting Useful Knowledge Among the British Plantations in America," as a prospectus. The organization was an outgrowth of the Junto, a Philadelphia society which he had organized in 1727. (*American Philosophical Society. Proceedings. Vol. 22*)

Woman elected to the National Academy of Sciences was Dr. Florence Rena Sabin,

THE FIRST

elected on April 29, 1925. At the time she was Professor of Histology at Johns Hopkins University, Baltimore, Md.

SCIENCE MAGAZINE
Science magazine was the *American Journal of Science and Art,* printed in New York City, and issued in July 1818. It was edited by Benjamin Silliman. The first volume of four numbers contained 448 pages. (*American Journal of Science. July 1918. Series 4, Vol. 46*)

Science magazine (popular) to report news of laboratory and workshop in popular terms was *Popular Science Monthly,* published by D. Appleton & Co., New York City, and first issued in May 1872. The first editor was Edward Livingston Youmans. The monthly contained 128 pages and sold for 50 cents. Some of the articles in the first issue were "Early Superstitions of Medicine," "The Study of Sociology," "The Causes of Dyspepsia," "Disinfection and Disinfectants," and "Science and Immortality."

SCIENCE SCHOOL
Natural science summer school was opened on the island of Penikese, Buzzard's Bay, Mass., in 1873, when Professor Louis Agassiz and Professor Nathaniel Southgate Shaler established the Anderson School. Forty-three students attended the first session. (*Jules Marcou—Life, Letters and Works of Louis Agassiz*)

SCIENTIFIC EXPEDITION. *See* Botanic scientific expedition; Expedition: Scientific expedition

SCOUTS. *See* Boy Scouts of America; Girl Scouts

SCREW
Screw factory was established in 1810 by Aborn and Jackson at Bellefonte, R.I. Originally, screw manufacturing was a complicated matter. A blank was forged and the head of the screw was pinched between dies while hot, after which the threads were made by filing.

Screw machine to make the manufacture of pointed screws practical was devised by Cullen Whipple of Providence, R.I., who obtained patent No. 15,502 on June 3, 1856. Prior to this invention, the threaded end of the screw being blunt, it was necessary to bore a hole for its insertion. (*Wood Screws. American Screw Co.*)

Screw patent in connection with a machine for making screws was granted December 14, 1798, to David Wilkinson of Rhode Island.

THE FIRST

SCREW AUGER. *See* Auger (screw auger)

SCREW CALIPER. *See* Caliper (screw)

SCREW CAP BOTTLE WITH A POUR LIP. *See* Bottle: Screw cap bottle with a pour lip

SCREW WRENCH. *See* Wrench: Pipe or screw wrench (practical)

SCRIP MONEY. *See* Money: Scrip money to be self-liquidating

SCULPTOR
Sculptor (American) of merit was Hiram Powers, whose chief works were undertaken from 1835 to 1873. In addition to his statues of Eve, the Greek Slave, Proserpine, Il Penseroso, A Californian, and An American, he made busts of Washington for Louisiana, of Calhoun for South Carolina, and of Daniel Webster for Boston. He made busts also of John Quincy Adams, Andrew Jackson, Chief Justice Marshall, Martin Van Buren, and other distinguished Americans. (*Lorado Taft—History of American Sculpture*)

Sculptor (American) to obtain a federal commission was John Frazee. A federal appropriation for $400 was granted March 2, 1831 (4 Stat.L.474) for a bust of John Jay for the Supreme Court, Washington, D.C. (*Charles Edwin Fairman—Art and Artists of the Capitol of the U.S. of A.*)

Woman sculptor. *See* Monument: Monument by a woman ordered by the U.S. Government; Monument: Statue cast by the U.S. Government; Woman: Woman sculptor honored by membership in the National Academy of Design

SEA BATTLE. *See* Revolutionary war: Naval battle of the Revolution; Spanish American War: Ship captured in the Spanish-American war; War (1812): Frigate action of importance in the war of 1812; World War I: Shot fired by the American Navy in World War I; World War II: Japanese submarine sunk by an American ship.

SEA COAST GUN CARRIAGE. *See* Ordnance: Sea coast gun carriage

SEA WATER CONVERSION PLANT. *See* Water: Sea water conversion plant (practical)

THE FIRST

THE FIRST

SEAL

Christmas seals of the modern variety, sold to raise funds to fight tuberculosis, were designed in 1907 by Emily Perkins Bissell of Wilmington, Del., who proposed the idea, drew the design, and had the seals printed. They were first placed on sale December 9, 1907, in the post office, Wilmington, Del. About $3,000 was realized. (*Leigh Mitchell Hodges—The People Against Tuberculosis*)

Great Seal of the United States Government was designed by William Barton and adopted June 20, 1782. The seal is composed of a spread eagle, the emblem of strength, bearing on its breast an escutcheon with thirteen stripes, alternate red and white. In its right talon is an olive branch, the emblem of peace, and in its left thirteen arrows, emblematic of the thirteen states, ready for war should it be necessary. In its beak is a ribbon bearing the legend "E Pluribus Unum" (From many, one). Over the head of the eagle is a golden light breaking through a cloud surrounding thirteen stars forming a constellation on a blue field. (*History of the Seal of the United States. State Department*)

Great Seal on a bill. *See* Money: Bill to depict both the face and the reverse side of the Great Seal of the United States

Seal of the Confederate States of America was authorized April 30, 1863, at the third session of the first Congress of Confederate States with the resolution "that the seal of the Confederate States shall consist of a device representing an equestrian portrait of Washington (after the statue which surmounts his monument in the capital square at Richmond), surrounded with a wreath composed of the principal agricultural products of the Confederacy (cotton, tobacco, sugar cane, corn, wheat and rice) and having around its margin the words 'The Confederate States of America, twenty-second February, eighteen hundred and sixty-two' with the motto 'Deo vindice.'" (*James M. Matthews, editor—The Statutes at large of the Confederate States of America Passed at the Third Session of the First Congress, 1863*)

Seals for raising funds (forerunners of the modern Christmas seals and tuberculosis stamps) were the Sanitary Fair Stamps. Eight days after the first gun was fired on Fort Sumter, April 12, 1861, a group of women in Cleveland, Ohio, formed an organization for aiding wounded soldiers. Five days later another group formed in New York City. The idea spread and fairs were held in various parts of the country to raise funds, notably in Chicago, New York, Albany, Boston, and Stamford. Special offices were established in these cities to sell stamps now known as the "Sanitary Fair Stamps."

SEAMEN'S LIBRARY. *See* Library: Library for seamen

SEAPLANE GLIDER. *See* Glider: Seaplane glider

SEAPLANE RAMP (floating). *See* Aviation: Floating seaplane ramp

SEAPLANE TENDER. *See* Ship: Seaplane tender designed and built for the U.S. Navy

SEAT BELT LEGISLATION. *See* Automobile legislation: Automobile seat belt safety legislation

SEATRAIN. *See* Ship: Seatrain

SECESSION

Secession act (the Ordinance of Secession) was passed by South Carolina, December 20, 1860, in the following form: "We, the people of the State of South Carolina, in convention assembled, do declare and ordain, that the ordinance adopted by us in convention on the 23d day of May, in the year of our Lord 1788, whereby the Constitution of the United States was ratified, and also all acts and parts of the General Assembly of this State ratifying amendments of the said Constitution, are hereby repealed; and that the Union now subsisting between South Carolina and other States, under the name of the United States of America, is hereby dissolved." On December 24, 1860 the South Carolina delegation in Congress offered its resignation, but it was not accepted by the speaker, and the names of its members were called regularly throughout the entire session. The new state constitution was ratified on April 3, 1861. The vote was 114 yeas and 6 nays. At the close of the Civil War, on May 29, 1865. a provisional government was established. (*David Franklin Houston—A Critical Study of Nullification in South Carolina*)

Secession was first mentioned in Congress on June 4, 1811, when Representative Josiah Quincy of Massachusetts declared, in a debate on the proposal to create a state from the Orleans Territory: "It will be the right of all and the duty of some [of the states] definitely to prepare for a separation; amicably, if they can; violently, if they must." Representative Poindexter of Mississippi called Quincy to order, as did the Speaker of the House; but on appeal the Speaker's decision was reversed, and Quincy was sustained by a vote of 53 ayes to 56 nays on the point of order. (*Edmund Quincy—Life of Josiah Quincy*)

THE FIRST

SECOND ADVENT BELIEVERS General Conference convened October 14-15, 1840, in the Chardon Street Chapel, Boston, Mass. Henry Dana Ward was elected chairman. (*(William Miller—Life of William Miller)*)

SECRET SERVICE

Secret Service (colonial) was organized by Aaron Burr and Major Benjamin Tallmadge in June 1778 for the United Colonies. It was known as the Headquarters Secret Service and developed into the first organized intelligence department of the Army of the United Colonies. On July 4, 1778, General George Washington in a special order made Burr head of the Department for Detecting and Defeating Conspiracies and ordered him "to proceed to Elizabeth Town to procure information of movements of the enemy's shipping about New York." Information about the activities of the British, however, had been secretly gathered previously by patriotic individuals and societies.

Secret Service (federal) under the Treasury Department was created by act of June 23, 1860 (12 Stat.L.102) to suppress counterfeiting in U.S. coins. The act was extended to include counterfeiting of notes, obligations, and securities of the government by act of July 11, 1862 (12 Stat.L.533), and an appropriation act approved July 2, 1864. Since the death of President Lincoln, one of the duties of the Secret Service has been to guard the President and his family. The Federal Bureau of Investigation was created in 1908 under the Department of Justice to supplement the work of the Secret Service.

Secret service (U.S. Army). *See* Army Secret Service Bureau

SECRET SOCIETY (women's). *See* Women's club: Women's secret society

SECTARIAN MAGAZINE. *See* Periodical: Sectarian magazine

SECULAR SONG. *See* Music: Secular song

SECULAR SONGBOOK. *See* Music book: Secular song book

SECURITIES AND EXCHANGE COMMISSION (U.S.) was created pursuant to section 4 of the Securities Exchange Act of 1934, approved by President Franklin Delano Roosevelt June 6, 1934 (48 Stat.L.881). The first meeting was held July 2, 1934, to provide for regulation and control of transactions and practices of security exchanges and over-the-counter markets. Five members were appointed June 30, 1934. The first chairman was James McCauley Landis.

THE FIRST

SEDAN AUTOMOBILE. *See* Automobile: Sedan type automobile

SEED BUSINESS regularly established was organized January 7, 1784, by David Landreth at High Street, Philadelphia, Pa. The location is now covered by the buildings at 1210 and 1212 Market Street. Previously seeds had been imported from Europe. The firm, incorporated in 1904 as the D. Landreth Seed Company, is now a subsidiary of the Robert Buist Company, founded in Philadelphia in 1828.

SEED DISTRIBUTION. *See* Agricultural seed distribution (national)

SEEDING MACHINE PATENT was granted January 25, 1799 to Eliakim Spooner of Vermont on "a machine for planting." The seeds were fed by gravity. The machine was not practical.

SEEDING MACHINE (practical) was invented by Joseph Gibbons of Adrian, Mich., who received patent No.1,731 on August 25, 1840. His machine was a grain drill with cavities to deliver seed and a device for regulating the volume. (*Robert L. Ardrey—American Agricultural Implements*)

SEEDLESS NAVEL ORANGE. *See* Oranges (seedless navel)

SEISMOGRAPH was installed at the Lick Observatory, University of California, Mount Hamilton, Calif., and exhibited at the formal opening of the building June 1, 1888. The equipment consisted of a three-component Ewing seismograph, a Gray seismograph, and a Duplex seismograph. (*Proceedings. Royal Society of London. Vol. 31*)

SELF-GOVERNMENT COLLEGE ORGANIZATION. *See* College self-government organization

SELF-SERVICE RESTAURANT. *See* Cafeteria; Restaurant: Self-service restaurant

SELF-STARTER. *See* Automobile electric self-starter

SELF-WINDING CLOCK. *See* Clock: Self-winding clock

SEMAPHORE TELEGRAPH SYSTEM was invented in 1799, by Jonathan Grout of Belchertown, Mass., who installed a series of towers, each within sight of the next, between Boston and Martha's Vineyard, Mass., ninety miles distant. By means of a combination of

SEMAPHORE TELEGRAPH SYSTEM
—Continued
the semaphore and flag systems, he was able to ask a question and receive an answer within ten minutes. This system did not involve the use of an electric telegraph line.

SEMI-AUTOMATIC RIFLE. *See* Ordnance: Semi-automatic rifle

SEMINARY (Catholic). *See* Catholic seminary

SENATE JOURNAL was the *Journal of the First Session of the Senate of the United States. Begun and Held at the City of New York, March 4, 1789,* published in 1789 in New York City.

SENATE (state)
Woman secretary of a state senate. *See* Woman: Woman secretary of a state senate

Woman state senator was Martha Hughes Cannon, elected to the second session of the Utah Senate November 3, 1896. She served from January 11, 1897, through March 11, 1897, and was reelected to serve in the third session, which convened January 8, 1889, and adjourned March 9, 1899. She was a Democrat and represented the 6th Senatorial District comprising Salt Lake County.

SENATE (U.S.). *See* Congress (U.S.)—Senate

SENATOR (U.S.)
Cabinet appointee rejected by the Senate. *See* Cabinet of the United States: Cabinet appointee rejected by the Senate

Catholic senator was Daniel Carroll, a Federalist of Maryland, who served from March 4, 1789, to March 3, 1791. His brother was John Carroll, the first Catholic Bishop in the United States. *(American Catholic Historical Society. Records. 1941. Vol. 2)*

Father and son senators at the same session were Henry Dodge (father) of Wisconsin and Augustus Caesar Dodge (son) of Iowa who sat together from December 7, 1848, to February 22, 1855 (30th-33rd Congress). Previously, they had served as delegates to the House of Representatives in the 27th and 28th Congresses from March 4, 1841, to March 3, 1845, prior to the statehood of their territories. Henry Dodge served in the Senate until March 3, 1857.

Impeachment proceedings against a senator. *See* Impeachment: Impeachment proceedings against a U.S. Senator

Indian senator was Charles Curtis of Kansas, who served from January 23, 1907, to March 3, 1913, and from March 4, 1915, to March 3, 1929, when he resigned to assume the vice presidency under President Herbert Clark Hoover.

Jewish senator was David Levy Yulee, a Democrat from Florida, who served from July 1, 1845, to March 3, 1851, and from March 4, 1855, to January 21, 1861. Prior to the admission of Florida as a state, he had been a delegate to the 27th and 28th Congresses serving from March 4, 1841, to March 3, 1845. *(American Jewish Historical Society—Publications 1917)*

Negro senator was Hiram Rhodes Revels of Mississippi, who was elected January 20, 1870, by the legislature of Mississippi to the United States Senate for the unexpired term beginning March 4, 1865, and ending March 3, 1871. He was sworn in February 25, 1870.

Senator appointed by a governor was John Walker of Virginia, who was appointed March 31, 1790, by Governor Beverley Randolph. Walker was appointed to the Senate to fill the vacancy caused by the death of William Grayson. He produced his credentials, took his seat April 26, 1790, and served until November 9, 1790, when James Monroe was elected to fill the unexpired term ending March 3, 1791. *(Biographical Directory of the American Congress 1774-1927)*

Senator elected by a write-in vote was J(ames) Strom Thurmond, a Democrat, of South Carolina, who was elected on November 2, 1954, for the term ending January 3, 1961. Thurmond received 139,106 votes, defeating Edgar Brown, the state Democratic Executive Committee nominee, who received 80,956 votes.

Senator elected on an anti-slavery ticket was John Parker Hale of New Hampshire, who was elected June 9, 1846, for the six-year term which began March 4, 1847. Previously, he had served as a Democrat in the House of Representatives from March 4, 1843, to March 3, 1845.

Senator of Asian ancestry was Hiram Leong Fong, a Republican of Chinese-American ancestry, who was elected July 29, 1959, by Hawaii, the fiftieth state. He was sworn in on August 24, 1959, by Vice President Richard Milhous Nixon.

Senator to become President. *See* President: President who had been a senator

Senator to receive a mileage allowance for a trip which he did not make was George Evans of Maine, who served from March 4,

THE FIRST

1841, to March 3, 1847. It was not necessary for him to travel because he was already in Washington, D.C., having served in Congress as a representative from Maine in previous sessions, including the 2nd Session of the 26th Congress, December 7, 1840-March 3, 1841.

Senator to serve three states was James Shields of Illinois, Minnesota, and Missouri. He was elected as a Democrat to serve Illinois in the 33rd Congress for the term commencing March 4, 1849. His election was declared void as he had not been a citizen the requisite number of years. He was reelected for the same term and served October 27, 1849, to March 3, 1855. He represented Minnesota in the 35th Congress and served from May 12, 1858, to March 3, 1859. He was elected by Missouri January 22, 1879, to fill the vacancy caused by the death of Lewis Vital Bogy and served in the 44th Congress from January 27, 1879, to March 3, 1879.

Senator to win a seat which had been occupied by his father and his mother was Russell Long of Louisiana, who was elected November 2, 1948, and sworn in December 31, 1948, for the term expiring January 2, 1951. His father, Huey Pierce Long, was elected November 4, 1930, and took the oath of office January 25, 1932. His mother, Rose McConnell Long, was appointed January 31, 1936, serving until January 2, 1937.

Senator unseated after a recount was Smith Wildman Brookhart, a Republican of Iowa, presumed winner of the November 4, 1924, election. He presented his credentials as a senator-elect for the term commencing March 4, 1925, and served until April 12, 1926, when he was ousted by a Senate vote of 45 to 41. He was succeeded by Daniel Frederic Steck, a Democrat, who served from April 12, 1926, to March 3, 1931, having been found entitled to the senatorial seat.

Senator who had been President. *See* President: President to become a senator

Senators censured were Benjamin Ryan Tillman of South Carolina and John Lowndes McLaurin of South Carolina. Tillman charged that McLaurin had been bribed to vote for the Treaty of Paris terminating the Spanish-American war. McLaurin declared the accusation was "a willful, malicious and deliberate lie" and a fist fight ensued on the Senate floor on February 22, 1902 (Fifty-seventh Congress, 1st Session). Both were censured. They apologized and were permitted to retain their seats. Tillman served as senator from March 4, 1895, to July 3, 1918, and McLaurin from June 1, 1897, to March 3, 1903.

Senators "elected by the people," were chosen November 4, 1913. Section 3, Article 1

THE FIRST

of the Constitution provided for the election of senators by the state legislatures. The Seventeenth Amendment was passed in the House, April 13, 1912, and by the Senate, June 12, 1912. The thirty-sixth state to ratify the amendment was Wisconsin, May 9, 1913, and the amendment was declared in force May 31, 1913. (*Charles Austin Beard—American Government and Politics*)

Vice President elected by the Senate. *See* Vice President of the United States: Vice President elected by the Senate

Woman elected to the Senate was Hattie Ophelia Wyatt Caraway, a Democrat of Jonesboro, Ark., widow of Senator Thaddeus Horatio Caraway. Before being elected she had received a temporary appointment from Governor Garvey Parnell on November 13, 1931, to fill the vacancy caused by the death of her husband. She was elected January 12, 1932, and reelected in 1938, serving until January 3, 1945.

Woman senator elected without having previously served an appointed term was Margaret Chase Smith, a Republican of Maine, who was elected to the 81st Congress on September 13, 1948. She had been elected as a representative to the 76th Congress on June 3, 1940, to fill the vacancy caused by the death of her husband, Clyde Harold Smith.

Woman senator to preside over the Senate was Hattie Wyatt Caraway, Democrat of Arkansas, who on October 19, 1943, opened the proceedings and presided as president pro tempore in the absence of Vice President Henry Agard Wallace (78th Congress, 1st Session). On May 9, 1932 (75th Congress, 1st Session), while Senator Carter Glass held the floor, she had occupied the president's chair for a brief period but no question of procedure arose.

Woman senator to succeed a woman senator was Hazel Hempel Abel, a Republican of Nebraska, who replaced Eve Bowring, also a Republican, on November 8, 1954. Mrs. Abel was elected November 2, 1954, for the balance of a two-month term.

Woman to occupy a seat in the Senate was Rebecca Latimer Felton, a Democrat, who was appointed by Governor Thomas William Hardwick of Georgia to the Senate on October 3, 1922, to fill the vacancy caused by the death of Thomas Edward Watson. She attended two sessions of the Senate (November 21 and November 22, 1922) before a successor was elected.

SEPARATOR. *See* Cream separator

THE FIRST

SERBIAN ORTHODOX CATHEDRAL was the Cathedral of St. Sava, New York City, elevated June 11, 1944, from a pro-cathedral. On the same day Bishop Dionisije [Dionisije Milivojevich] conferred the Gold Cross and the title "Stravrophor" on Rector Doushan Jefta Shoukletovich and elevated him to dean.

SERIAL MOVING PICTURE. *See* Moving picture: Serial moving picture

SERIAL STORY. *See* Newspaper: Newspaper serial story

SERIAL WRITER (woman). *See* Author: Successful woman serial writer

SERMON PRINTED (American) was "The Sin and Danger of Self-Love, a Discourse" based on the text from I Cor. 10:24, "Let no man seek his own; But every man another's wealth." It was delivered December 9, 1621, by Robert Cushman in Plymouth, Mass., in "an assembly of His Majesty's faithful subjects, there inhabiting" and was printed in London, England in 1622. It was reprinted by S. Kneeland, Boston, Mass. in 1724. *(Robert Cushman —The First Sermon Ever Preached in New England)*

SEROLOGICAL BLOOD TESTS. *See* Medical legislation: Law (state) requiring serological blood tests of pregnant women

SERVICE STATION (automobile). *See* Automobile service station: Drive-in service station

SERVITE CHURCH
Marian Congress was held at the Sanctuary of Our Sorrowful Mother, Portland, Ore., August 12-15, 1934, under the auspices of the Servite Fathers. A Marian Congress is similar to a Eucharistic Congress, except that the Blessed Virgin is the object of devotion rather than the Holy Eucharist.

Servite Church in America was established in August 1870 at Menasha, Wis., under the direction of the Very Reverend Austin Morini, O.S.M., a Servite of the Italian Province.

SESSION LAWS (U.S.). *See* Law book: Law compilation of federal session laws

SETTLEMENT BY EUROPEAN COLONISTS. *See* Colonist: Permanent white settlement in America

SETTLEMENT HOUSE was the University Settlement, established by Stanton Coit in 1886 in a Forsythe Street tenement, New York

THE FIRST

City, "to raise not only the standard of living but the standard of living-together." Playgrounds were provided for children, instruction was given in English to foreigners, and other educational programs were established. The idea was that intellectuals would "settle" in a slum area and by living and working with tenement neighbors would be able to help them raise standards.

SEVEN-MASTED STEEL SCHOONER. *See* Ship: Schooner (seven-masted, steel)

SEVENTH DAY ADVENTIST CHURCH was the Adventist church in Washington Center, N.H., which began to keep the seventh day as Sabbath in the spring of 1844. The first Adventist minister to accept the seventh day as the Sabbath was Frederick Wheeler, of the Washington Center Church, in March 1844. The first general conference of Seventh Day Adventists was organized May 21, 1863.

SEVENTH DAY BAPTIST CHURCH. *See* Baptist church: Seventh Day Baptist Church

SEWAGE
Separate system of sewage disposal was started in Memphis, Tenn., under the direction of George Edwin Waring on January 21, 1880. Within four months, a system comprising 18 miles of pipe, with 152 flush-tanks and four-inch connecting drains, was installed. The pipes were for sewage only and were kept constantly cleansed and well ventilated, always being kept half full of water. Six-inch vitrified pipes emptied into larger pipes, which in turn emptied into increasingly larger ones until twenty-inch pipes were used. An independent and separate set of pipes was provided for disposing of storm water. The total cost of twenty miles for the two main sewers, including labor, materials, engineering, superintending, and incidentals, was about $137,000. A similar system was also adopted by Pullman, Ill. (now a part of Chicago, Ill.). *(John Preston Young—History of Memphis, Tenn.)*

Sewage disposal by chemical precipitation was undertaken by Worcester, Mass., in 1890. Six chemical precipitation settling basins, each 66⅔ by 100 by 7 feet were used. The raw sewage was screened and then treated with milk of lime. It was passed through a mixing channel into the six settling basins in series. The detention period was approximately six hours. After being quiescent for a few hours the top water was drawn off, and the sludge run to a six-inch centrifugal pump and discharged into lagoons.

Sewage "dual system" was built in Brooklyn, N.Y., in 1857 by Colonel Julius Adams. The size and capacity were scientifically calcu-

THE FIRST

THE FIRST

lated to care for a rainfall intensity of one inch per hour. *(Leonard Metcalf and Harrison Prescott Eddy—Sewerage and Sewage Disposal)*

Underground comprehensive sewer system (city) was undertaken by Chicago, Ill., in 1856 on the grid pattern. The sewers were of circular cross sections ranging from 3 to 6 feet in diameter and had brick walls 8½ inches thick. Branch sewers were 2 feet in diameter, and the hose drains were 4- and 6-inch pipes or boxes made of wood planks. Manholes were provided every 100 feet and in general the slope or gradient was 1 foot in 500. By June 30, 1860, about 46 miles had been completed. Single uncoordinated sewers had been used earlier.

SEWING MACHINE

Chain-stitch single-thread sewing machine (practical) was invented by James Edward Allen Gibbs of Mill Point, Va., who received patent No. 17,427 on June 2, 1857.

Electric sewing machine was manufactured by the Singer Manufacturing Company in 1889 at its factory, Elizabethport, N.J.

Lock-stitch sewing machine was made in 1832-34 by Walter Hunt of New York, whose machine used two threads, one below the cloth and the other coming down through the cloth, thus interlocking with each other. As he made no attempt to patent his machine until June 27, 1854, his original appplication was refused on the ground of abandonment. Elias Howe obtained patent No. 4,750 on a lock-stitch machine on September 10, 1846.

Sewing machine equipped with a rocking treadle or double treadle was invented by Isaac Merritt Singer of New York City, who obtained patent No. 8,294, August 12, 1851. He used a treadle similar to that employed in the old spinning wheel and attached it by means of a pitman to the handle on the driving gear of the machine.

Sewing machine lamp holder was introduced by the Singer Sewing Machine Company in 1876. It "quite obviated the difficulty experienced by operators when sewing at night" because the lamp would not "jar off the table or upset" and it could "be moved without soiling the fingers." It was patented by Ludwig Martin Nicolaus Wolf of Avon, Conn., who obtained patent No. 138,831 on May 13, 1873, on a "lamp bracket for sewing."

Sewing machine manufacturer who was successful was Isaac Merritt Singer, who began business at 19 Harvard Place, Boston, Mass., in 1851, on a capital of $40 supplied by

George B. Zieber. His first machine was made in eleven days in the machine shop owned by Orson C. Phelps.

Sewing machine motor patent was No. 13,661, which was granted on October 9, 1855, to Isaac Merritt Singer of New York City. It covered a spring and cone pulley device.

Sewing machine patent of which there is any record was granted on February 21, 1842, (No. 2,466) to John James Greenough of Washington, D.C. It was a short-thread machine, the needle being threaded with short lengths of thread as in hand sewing.

Sewing machine to sew curving seams was patented (No. 12,116) by Allen Benjamin Wilson of Watertown, Conn., on December 19, 1854. The machine operated with four-motion feed which made it possible to sew a curved seam on a sewing machine. Wilson received his first patent on a sewing machine on November 12, 1850 (patent No. 7776).

Sewing machine to stitch buttonholes was a machine patented by Charles Miller of St. Louis, Mo., on March 7, 1854. He obtained patent No. 10,609.

SEXTANT (radio). *See* Radio sextant

SEXTUPLE PRINTING PRESS. *See* Printing press: Sextuple printing press

SEXTUPLETS. *See* Births: Sextuplets

SHADE. *See* Venetian blinds

SHAFT-DRIVEN AUTOMOBILE. *See* Automobile: Shaft-driven automobile

SHAKER SOCIETY, a celibate religious community, was founded by Ann Lee of Manchester, England, and eight others who left Liverpool on the "Mariah" and arrived in New York City on August 6, 1774. The first Shaker "Family" was formed in Watervliet, N.Y., in 1776, and the first organized Shaker Community was established in 1788 in New Lebanon, N.Y. New Lebanon became Mount Lebanon in 1861. The ministers were the spiritual leaders of the Society and the Elders of Families. As the rules of the Society stated, "The head of the Shaker Order is Christ, Represented in a Dual Order of Leaders, Ministry, Elders and Trustees." *(Frederick William Evans—Compendium of the Origin, History, Principles, Rules and Regulations, Government, and Doctrines of the United Society of Believers in Christ's Second Appearing)*

SHAKESPEAREAN PLAY. *See* Play (drama) : Shakespearean play

SHAVER (electric). *See* Razor: Electric dry shaver

SHEARS. *See* Cutlery shears

SHEEP. *See* Animals: Sheep

SHEET ASPHALT PAVEMENT. *See* Road: Sheet asphalt pavement

SHEET GLASS. *See* Glass: Sheet glass drawing machine

SHEET MILL. *See* Steel: Continuous sheet steel mill

SHELTER. *See* Air raid shelter; Building: House with a built-in nuclear bomb shelter

SHEPHERD DOG TO GUIDE THE BLIND. *See* Animals: Dogs trained to guide the blind

SHIP

Air-conditioned naval ship (fully conditioned) was the cruiser "Newport News," laid down October 1, 1945, by the Newport News Shipbuilding and Drydock Company, Newport News, Va. She was launched March 6, 1947, christened by Mrs. Homer Lenoir Ferguson, and commissioned January 29, 1949. She had a 75⅙-foot beam, was 716½ feet long, and mounted nine 8-inch guns in three turrets. The first captain was Captain Roland Nesbit Smoot.

Air-conditioned ship was the "Mariposa," 18,152 tons, built for the Matson Navigation Company at the Fore River plant of the Bethlehem Shipbuilding Corporation, Quincy, Mass. The keel was laid May 17, 1930, and the ship launched July 18, 1931. Only the dining room was air-conditioned. She left New York City on January 16, 1932, for the South Seas, Australia, and New Zealand.

Air mail service to a steamer at sea. *See* Air mail service: Air mail service to a steamer at sea

Aircraft carrier wholly designed and built as such was the "Ranger," constructed by the Newport News Shipbuilding and Drydock Company, Newport News, Va. Her keel was laid September 26, 1931, and she was launched February 25, 1933. She was commissioned at Norfolk, Va., and formally delivered June 4, 1934. Her first Captain was Arthur Leroy Bristol.

Aircraft carrier (atomic powered) was the "Enterprise," CVA (N) 65, ordered August 16, 1957, laid down February 4, 1958, launched September 24, 1960, and completed in September 1961. She was 1,101 feet long and 252 feet wide, with a 133-foot beam, a 75,700-ton standard displacement and an 85,350-ton full-load displacement, and a draught of 37 feet. The carrier, built by the Newport News Shipbuilding and Dry Dock Company, Newport News, Va., had a complement of 440 officers and 4,160 enlisted men. She was equipped with eight pressurized water-cooled nuclear reactors and capable of steaming for five years without refueling. Her flight deck was large enough to accommodate four football fields, and her four propellers were the height of two-story buildings. She was christened by Mrs. William Birrell Franke, wife of the Secretary of the Navy.

Aircraft carrier to sail around Cape Horn was the U.S.S. "Oriskany," which passed Cape Horn at 8:30 A.M. on June 29, 1952. She left New York City on March 30, 1952, and arrived at San Diego, Calif., at 6:20 P.M. on July 21, 1952, and at San Francisco, Calif., on August 7, 1952, calls having been made at Rio de Janeiro, Brazil; Valparaiso, Chile; and Callao, Peru. The commanding officer was Captain John Osgo Lambrecht, U.S.N.

Aircraft carrier with an angle deck was the supercarrier U.S.S. "Forrestal," contracted for July 12, 1951, and laid down July 14, 1952. She was launched December 11, 1954, by the Newport News Shipbuilding & Drydock Company at Newport News, Va., and christened by Mrs. James Vincent Forrestal, wife of the first Secretary of Defense, for whom the ship was named. She was commissioned October 1, 1955. The first captain was Captain Roy Lee Johnson. She cost $198,000,000, was 1,045⅞ feet long and 252 feet wide, and carried a crew of 3,500 including her own air group. Her height from keel to top of mast was equal to that of a twenty-five-story building, and her flight deck had an area of nearly four acres.

Airplane flight from a ship. *See* Aviation—Flights: Airplane flight from a ship

Ambulance ship was the U.S.S. "Solace," of 5,700 tons, in service April 14, 1898, and used in naval warfare in the war with Spain. Formerly the S.S. "Creole," she was purchased April 7, 1898. The "Solace" was the creation of Admiral William Knickerbocker Van Reypen. She was fitted out under the terms of the Geneva Convention and was undoubtedly the first designated ambulance ship—used for transporting as well as caring for the sick and wounded—and the first to carry the Geneva Cross flag at the fore. She was removed from the Navy list August 6, 1930, and sold November 6, 1930. The first hospital ship, as dis-

THE FIRST

tinguished from an ambulance ship, was the "Red Rover," converted to a hospital ship in 1862.

Ambulance ship designed and built as a hospital for the transportation of sick and wounded naval men was the U.S.S. "Relief." Congress authorized the construction of the "Relief" August 29, 1916, and the contract for her construction was signed August 29, 1916; on July 4, 1917, her keel was laid, and the frame was erected May 15, 1918. The vessel was launched December 23, 1919, christened by Mrs. William G. Braisted, and delivered to the Navy, December 28, 1920. The over-all length of the "Relief" was 484 feet and she had a displacement of 9,750 tons and a speed of 16 knots. The hospital capacity was 515 beds in 14 wards and 15 officers' rooms.

American army troopship torpedoed by the Germans. See World War I: American army troopship in World War I torpedoed by the Germans

American destroyer torpedoed. See World War II: American destroyer torpedoed

American flag displayed on a man-of-war. See Flag: American flag displayed on a man-of-war

American ship lost in World War I. See World War I: American ship lost in World War I

American ship sunk by a U-boat. See World War II: American ship sunk by a U-boat

Atomic-powered cruiser was the "Long Beach," CG (N) 9, 721 feet long, beam 73 feet, draught 26 feet, 14,000 tons standard, 18,000 tons full load. The cost of construction was about $320 million. The keel was laid December 2, 1957, and the ship christened by Mrs. Craig Hosmer at the launching July 14, 1959, at the Fore River Shipyard of the Bethlehem Steel Company's shipyard at Quincy, Mass. The ship, which had two nuclear reactors, attained a speed of 30 knots.

Atomic-powered merchant ship was the N.S. "Savannah," 595 feet 21,000 tons, authorized July 30, 1956 (70 Stat.L.731). She was built by the New York Shipbuilding Corporation, Camden, N.J., for the U.S. Maritime Commission. The pressurized water power reactor was built by Babcock & Wilcox Co., New York City. The keel was laid May 22, 1958, and the ship christened July 21, 1959, by Mrs. Dwight David Eisenhower.

THE FIRST

Balloon carrier was the U.S.S. "Fanny," an armed transport which John La Mountain used August 3, 1861, to transport a balloon attached to a windlass at the stern. At a height of 2,000 feet, the balloon was used to observe military positions at Fortress Monroe, Va.

Battleship built on the Pacific coast was the "Nebraska," 441 feet 3 inches long, extreme beam 76 feet 3 inches, normal displacement 14,948 tons. The ship was authorized March 3, 1899, and built by the Moran Company, Seattle, Wash. Her keel was laid July 4, 1902, and she was commissioned July 1, 1907. The first captain was R. F. Nicholson.

Battleship equipped with radar. See Radar: Battleship equipped with radar

Battleship of importance was the U.S.S. "Maine," authorized by act of Congress of August 3, 1886 (24 Stat.L.215). She was built at the Brooklyn Navy Yard, Brooklyn, N.Y. Her keel was laid October 17, 1888, and she was launched November 18, 1890. She was commissioned September 17, 1895. Her length was 319 feet, beam 57 feet, mean draft 21 feet 6 inches, displacement 6,682 tons. On the night of February 15, 1898, the "Maine" was mysteriously destroyed by explosion in Havana Harbor, Cuba. Only 16 of the total crew of 354 wholly escaped injury. (*Charles Dwight Sigsbee—The Maine*)

Battleship sunk by an airplane. See Aviation: Battleship sunk by an airplane

Battleship to visit an inland city was the U.S.S. "Mississippi" (length, 375 feet; draft 24.8 feet; extreme breadth 77 feet; displacement 13,000 tons), which sailed 300 miles up the Mississippi River to Natchez, Miss., on May 20, 1909, and departed for New Orleans, May 24, 1909. She was built by William Cramp and Sons, Philadelphia, Pa., and was commissioned February 1, 1908.

Boat race. See Boat race: Intercollegiate boat race

Catamaran. See Catamaran

Child born on a vessel passing through the Panama Canal. See Births: Child born on a vessel passing through the Panama Canal

Clipper ship was the "Ann McKim," built in 1833 for Isaac McKim by Kennard & Williamson of Fells Point, Baltimore, Md. She was 143 feet long, 31 feet wide, and of 493 tons register. The first master was Joseph Martin.

SHIP—*Continued*
Many other claims are made since definitions vary as to what constitutes a clipper ship. (*Arthur Hamilton Clark—The Clipper Ship Era*)

Concrete barge was the barge "Socony 200," which was also the first reinforced steel concrete barge for carrying oil in bulk. She was built to specifications for the Standard Oil Company of New York and was 98 feet long, 31 feet wide, and 9 feet 6 inches deep. The vessel was launched July 27, 1918, and placed in commission August 12, 1918. She was built by the Fougner Shipbuilding Company, Flushing Bay, New York.

Concrete seagoing ship was the "Faith," built by the San Francisco Shipbuilding Company at Redwood City, Calif., and launched March 14, 1918, six weeks after the pouring of the concrete had started. She cost $750,000 and was the first concrete ship to cross the Atlantic Ocean. Her builder and owner was W. Leslie Comyn, president of the San Francisco Shipbuilding Company. The engineers were Allan MacDonald and Victor Poss.

Concrete ship built for the United States Shipping Board Emergency Fleet Corporation was the "Atlantus," launched December 4, 1918, and delivered November 11, 1919. The first ship delivered was the "Polias," launched May 22, 1919, and delivered October 23, 1919. These ships were launched at Brunswick, Ga., and built by the Liberty Shipbuilding Company, Brunswick.

Confederate cruiser built in England, the "Oneto," sailed from Liverpool, England, March 22, 1862, bound for the Bahamas. The ship was transferred to Captain John Newland Maffitt of the Confederate Navy, who took rank as commodore. The guns and stores were sent in another ship which followed.

Confederate cruiser to raid Union commerce was the "Sumter," commanded by Captain Raphael Semmes. The "Sumter" was a merchantman which had been fitted out in 1861 at New Orleans, La., with five small guns. Semmes on the "Sumter" captured eighteen vessels of which eight were burned. (*Raphael Semmes—Memoirs of Service Afloat During the War Between the States*)

Conflict between iron-clad vessels in the Civil War. See Civil War: Conflict between iron-clad vessels in the Civil War

Cruise ship to circumnavigate the world was the Cunard liner "Laconia," which left New York City on November 21, 1922, with 440 passengers on a 130-day cruise and returned March 30, 1923. An earlier world cruise was made by the "Cleveland" of the Hamburg-American Line which departed February 6, 1912, from New York City, rounded Cape Horn and reached Hamburg, Germany, on May 17, 1912, via Honolulu, Yokohama, Kobe, Nagasaki, Hong Kong, Manila, Batavia, Singapore, Rangoon, Calcutta, Colombo, Bombay, Suez, Port Said, Naples, Gibraltar, and Southampton.

Decked ship built in America was completed and launched on the Hudson River in the summer of 1614 by Adrianen Blok, a native of Holland. He named her the "Onrust" (the "Restless"). She was a 16-ton ship, 38 feet on the keel, 44½ feet over-all, and 11 feet in the beam.

Dirigible landing and taking-off from an ocean-going steamship. *See* Aviation—Airship: Dirigible landing and taking off from an ocean-going steamship

Drama broadcast from a ship at sea. *See* Radio broadcast: Drama broadcast from a ship at sea

Dredge (seagoing hopper) was the "General Moultrie," a steam dredge, built by William Colyer, New York City, in 1855. The 365-ton dredge was 150 feet long, 26 feet 8 inches wide, and 10 feet 3 inches in depth. Originally a commercial steamer, it was converted into a dredge by the installation of centrifugal dredging pumps, piping, etc., and the construction of bins in the holds. The machinery was furnished by C. H. De Lamater, New York City. The dredge was used in the Charleston, S.C., harbor.

Electrically propelled ship of the U.S. Navy was the U.S.S. "Jupiter," built as a collier at the Navy Yard, Mare Island, Calif. Her keel was laid October 16, 1911, and she was launched August 24, 1912. She was commissioned April 7, 1913. Her conversion to an aircraft carrier was authorized July 11, 1919 (41 Stat.L.133), when $2,500,000 was appropriated. Her name was changed from "Jupiter" to "Langley" on April 21, 1920.

Federal steamer named for a woman was the "Harriet Lane," named after a niece of President James Buchanan. A side-wheeler of 500 tons with 8 guns, the "Harriet Lane" was 270 feet long with a 22-foot beam. She was designed as a Treasury Department Revenue cutter and was built by William Henry Webb in 1857 in New York City. During the Civil War, she fired a shot, April 12, 1861, near the bow of the steamer "Nashville" to force the "Nashville" to show her true colors—the first shot fired from a U.S. vessel in the war. On January 1, 1863, the "Harriet Lane" was captured in Galveston Bay after desperately resisting boarding parties from four rebel cottonclads. (*Fletcher Pratt—The Navy, a History*)

Ferryboat. *See* Ferryboat

Fireboat. *See* Fireboat

Fish hatching steamer (federal) was the "Fishhawk," authorized by Congress March 3, 1879 (20 Stat.L.383) with an appropriation of $45,000. The vessel was designed by Charles W. Copeland, built by the Pusey and Jones Company of Wilmington, Del., launched December 13, 1879, and turned over to the U.S. Fish Commission on February 23, 1880. She was of 441 gross tonnage and 156 feet 6 inches long overall with a 27-foot beam. The hull below the main deck was iron, sheathed with yellow pine. When commissioned, she was equipped with a very complete hatchery as well as a laboratory, a hoisting engine, dredges, trawls, deep-sea thermometers, etc. Lieutenant Zera Luther Tanner, U.S.N. was the first commanding officer. *(Records in Department of Interior—Bureau of Fisheries, Washington, D.C.)*

Frigate was the "United States," which was built by Joshua Humphreys at what was formerly the "Association Battery," Philadelphia, Pa., and launched May 10, 1797. President John Adams attended the launching. The vessel was of 1,576 tons and was first captained by Commodore John Barry. She was scuttled and sunk April 20, 1861, when the Federal forces abandoned the Norfolk Navy Yard.

Frigate (American-built, steam-driven) to cross the Atlantic Ocean was the U.S. Steam Frigate "Missouri," which left Norfolk, Va., August 5, 1843 with 384 persons. Under the Command of Captain John Thomas Newton, she arrived at Gibraltar, August 25, 1843. The following day she caught fire and became a total loss. *(William Bolton—A Narrative of the Last Cruise of the U.S. Steam Frigate Missouri)*

German ship captured in World War II. *See* World War II: German ship captured in World War II by an American ship

Great Lakes commercial vessel was "Le Griffon," a two-masted armored square rigger built in 1679 by Robert Cavelier, Sieur de La Salle, at Cayuga Creek, near the Niagara River. The keel was laid January 26, 1679. Her first voyage was made August 7, 1679. She was of 60 tons burden and sailed Lakes Erie and Michigan. She sank on September 18, 1679, in a gale in Mackinaw Strait and is believed to be resting in Mississagi Strait, Menitoulin Island, Canada. *(Edward Channing and Marion Florence Lansing—Story of the Great Lakes)*

Guided missile cruiser was the "Boston," CAG 1, converted November 1, 1955, and recommissioned at the U.S. Naval Base, Philadelphia, Pa. The cruiser, 13,600 tons standard,

17,200 tons full load, was laid down June 30, 1941, launched August 26, 1942, at the Bethlehem Steel Company, Quincy, Mass., and commissioned June 30, 1943. Her superstructure was entirely remodeled, one of the two stacks being removed to accommodate twin launchers capable of firing Terrier missiles. The ship was 673½ feet long and had a 71-foot beam and a draught of 26 feet. Captain Charles Bowling Martell was the first commanding officer of the converted cruiser.

Guided missile destroyer was the U.S.S. "Dewey," DLG 14, designed expressly as a guided missile ship and built by the Bath Iron Works Corporation, Bath, Maine. The keel was laid August 10, 1957. The destroyer was launched November 30, 1958, and commissioned December 7, 1959. The first captain was Commander Elmo Russell Zumwalt, Jr.

Gyro compass installed on an American naval vessel. *See* Gyro compass: Gyro compass installed on an American naval vessel

Gyro-stabilized American liner was the S.S. "Mariposa" of the Matson Lines, christened October 16, 1956, in Portland, Ore., by Electa Sevier. She sailed on her maiden voyage on October 26, 1956, from Los Angeles, Calif., to Australia and the South Seas. Fins made by the Sperry Gyroscope Company were built into her hull, below the surface of the sea, to remove up to 90 per cent of the ship roll.

Gyro-stabilized vessel to cross the Atlantic Ocean was the "Conte di Savoia" of the Italian Line, which arrived in New York City on December 7, 1932. The Captain of the "Conte di Savoia" was Antonio Lena.

Gyro stabilizer installed on an American naval vessel was placed on the U.S.S. "Worden" in April 1913 by the Sperry Gyroscope Company, Brooklyn, N.Y.

Hospital ship of the U.S. Navy was the U.S.S. "Red Rover," which had been captured from the Confederate forces on September 20, 1862. On December 26, 1862, she was converted into a hospital ship, and she remained in service until August 12, 1865. The first ambulance ship (used for transporting as well as caring for the sick and wounded) was the U.S.S. "Solace," in service in 1898.

Ice yacht. *See* Ice yacht

Intercollegiate boat race. *See* Boat race: Intercollegiate boat race

Iron-clad naval vessels were the "Benton" and the "Essex" (1,000 tons each), and seven others (of 512 tons each), delivered at St.

SHIP—*Continued.*
Louis, Mo., where they were accepted for the
government by Captain Andrew Hull Foote on
January 15, 1862. They were constructed under
contract with James Buchanan Eads at Mound
City and Cairo, Ill., and added to the Western
Flotilla, also known as the Gunboat Flotilla on
Western Waters, or the Mississippi Squadron,
which was organized October 1, 1862.

Iron-clad turreted vessel in the U.S. Navy
was the U.S.S. "Monitor," designed and built
by John Ericsson, the contract for which was
signed October 4, 1861, by Gideon Welles, Secretary of the Navy. The terms of the contract
provided that the ship was to be completed
within a hundred days. Her keel was laid
October 22, 1861, and she was launched at
Greenpoint, L.I., N.Y., on January 30, 1862.
She was completed February 19, 1862, and the
trial trip and delivery were made to the Navy
on February 20, 1862. She had two 11-inch
guns in the turret which fired a solid shot
weighing 180 pounds. She left New York City,
March 6, 1862, with Lieutenant John Lorimer
Worden in command and arrived at Hampton
Roads, Va., on March 8, 1862, where she participated the next day in the engagement against
the former Federal ship "Merrimac" (renamed
the "Virginia" by the Confederates). (*Ebenezer
Pearson Dorr—A Brief Sketch of the First
Monitor and Its Inventor*)

Iron-clad warship for service at sea was
the "Galena," built by Cornelius Scranton Bushnell and H. L. Bushnell of New Haven, Conn.,
and launched February 14, 1862, at the Maxson
and Fish Yard, Mystic, Conn. The "Monitor,"
a single-turreted vessel was launched January
30, 1862, New York City, but it was not a
sea-going iron-clad, merely a floating battery
for harbor defense.

Iron sloop yacht was the "Vindex," built
in 1871 at Chester, Pa., by Reany, Son and
Company. She was 54 gross tons, 36 net tons,
62.5 feet long, 17.3 feet wide and had a depth
of 7.9 feet and a draught of 8.95 feet. Robert
Center was the first owner. She was abandoned
June 30, 1898. (*Howard Irving Chapelle—History of American Sailing Ships*)

**Iron steamship built for transatlantic serv-
ice** was the "Bangor," constructed by Betts,
Harlan and Hollingsworth at Wilmington, Del.,
for the Bangor Steam Navigation Company and
launched in May 1844. She was 120 feet long
with 231 tons burden. She was schooner rigged,
had three wooden masts, and carried eight sails.
(*Francis Burke Brandt—The Majestic Delaware*)

Iron vessel was the "John Randolph," 122
tons, which was built in 1834 at Savannah, Ga.,
by John Caut for Gazaway Bugg Lamar. The

plates were made by John Laird of Birkenhead,
England, and shipped in sections to Savannah,
where they were riveted together. The vessel
was owned in and operated from Savannah. According to record, the "John Randolph" was not
enrolled until July 2, 1842, although she may
have been enrolled earlier. In 1836 John Caut
also built the "Chatham," 198 tons, which was
enrolled on August 1, 1837, and in 1838 John
Wade built the "Lamar," 196 tons, which was
enrolled on December 4, 1838. These three iron
vessels were all built in Savannah of iron
manufactured in England.

Iron vessel built for the U.S. Navy was an
iron side-wheel steamer, the "Michigan," built
in Erie, Pa., under authority of act of Congress
of September 9, 1841 (5 Stat.L.460). Construction began in 1842 with the building of sections
in Pittsburgh, Pa. These sections were transported to Erie, where the ship was completed
and launched December 5, 1843. The cost of
the ship was $165,000. Her hull was designed
and built by Stockhouse and Tomlinson, Pittsburgh. Her displacement was 685 tons; length
163 feet, 3 inches; breadth 27 feet, 1½ inches;
depth of hold 13 feet, 9 inches. She was renamed the "Wolverine" on June 17, 1905, and
loaned to the city of Erie on July 19, 1927, by
act of Congress of December 21, 1926 (44
Stat.L.923). She was officially stricken from
the Navy list on March 12, 1927.

Iron vessel built of American iron was
the "De Rosset" of 186 tons which was built
in 1839 at Baltimore, Md., by Langley B. Culley. The "De Rosset" was registered at
Baltimore on April 4, 1839. (*Records in Bureau
of Navigation. Department of Commerce.
Washington D.C.*)

Iron vessel (sheet iron) was the steamboat "Codorus," built by John Elgar at York,
Pa., and tested November 14, 1825, on the
Susquehanna River. The sheet iron was riveted
with iron rivets. The 5-ton vessel, built at a
cost of about $3,000, had a 60-foot keel and
a 9-foot beam, and drew about 7 inches of
water. She had a cylindrical 8 h.p. coal-and-
wood-burning engine. The boiler weighed two
tons. The "Codorus" was completed and loaded on an eight-wheeled wagon, to which ropes
were attached, and on November 14, 1825, was
drawn from the foundry west of the
Codorus Creek to the Susquehanna River, 12
miles distant. (*Alexander Crosby Brown—
The Sheet Iron Steamboat Codorus*)

**Japanese submarine sunk by an American
ship.** See World War II: Japanese submarine
sunk by an American ship

Liberty ship in World War II was the
"Patrick Henry," launched September 27, 1941.

THE FIRST

She was built by the Bethlehem-Fairfield Shipbuilding Company, Baltimore, Md., in 244 days and delivered December 30, 1941, at Baltimore, Md., to the United States Maritime Commission, which transferred her to the Lykes Bros. Steamship Company, Inc., of New Orleans, La. She had an over-all length of 441 feet 6 inches, a beam of 57 feet, a depth of 37 feet 4 inches, a total displacement of 14,100 tons, and a general cargo capacity of 9,146 tons. She had single-screw steam reciprocating propulsion and on her first voyage (to Alexandria, Egypt) her average speed was 11.19 knots. She was sponsored by Mrs. Henry Agard Wallace, wife of the Vice President. The first captain was Richard Gailard Ellis.

Lifeboat. *See* Lifeboat

Lightship. *See* Lightship

Mail delivery by steamboat. *See* Postal service: Mail delivery by steamboats

Merchant ship formally blessed at a launching ceremony was the "Rio Hudson" of the Moore-McCormack Lines, Inc., blessed on November 27, 1940, by the Right Reverend Francis Taitt, Bishop of the Pennsylvania Protestant Episcopal Diocese, at the yards of the Sun Shipbuilding and Drydock Company, Chester, Pa. She had a 17,500-ton displacement and carried 197 passengers.

Merchant ship of the United States commanded by a Negro captain was the "Booker T. Washington," a Liberty ship launched by the California Shipbuilding Corporation at Wilmington, Del., September 29, 1942. She was commanded by Captain Hugh Mulzac, the first Negro to hold an unlimited mariner's license. She arrived at her first port, London, England, February 12, 1943. (*John Beecher—All Brave Soldiers; the Story of the S.S. Booker T. Washington*)

Mine layer was a 32-foot steam launch used August 1872 at the Engineer School of Application. She made eight knots and carried a dozen men. (*Henry Larcom Abbot—Material of the Submarine Mining Service of the U.S.A.*)

Motor boat. *See* Motor boat

National ship in a federal drydock. *See* Drydock: National ship in a federal drydock

Naval post office aboard a naval vessel. *See* Post office: Naval post office aboard a naval vessel

Naval ship with a plural name was the destroyer "The Sullivans," launched April 4, 1943,

THE FIRST

at San Francisco, Calif. It was named for the five Sullivan brothers of Waterloo, Iowa—George Thomas, Francis Henry, Joseph Eugene, Madison Abel, and Albert Leo—who enlisted January 3, 1942, and were lost when the cruiser "Juneau" was sunk November 15, 1942, in a battle off Guadalcanal in the Solomon Islands.

Naval vessel of the United States to display the American flag around Cape Horn was the "Essex," commanded by Captain David Porter, which left the Delaware capes on October 27, 1812, with a crew of 287, and 32 marines, and arrived at Valparaiso, Chile, on March 14, 1813. (*David Porter—Journal of a Cruise Made to the Pacific Ocean by Captain David Porter in the United States Frigate "Essex" in the Years 1812, 1813, and 1814*)

Naval vessel of the United States to sail around the Cape of Good Hope to the west coast of the United States was the "Constellation," which left Boston, Mass., December 1840. Stopping first at Rio de Janeiro, she proceeded to the Cape of Good Hope, and thence to China. On the return voyage, she anchored in Monterey Bay, Calif., September 15, 1843.

Naval vessels to sink an enemy submarine in the Atlantic were the U.S.S. "Fanning" and the U.S.S. "Nicholson." On November 17, 1917, at 4:10 P.M. in latitude 57°37' N., longitude 8°12' W., the U.S.S. "Fanning" while in convoy sighted the periscope of a submarine. The "Fanning" headed for the spot and dropped depth charges. The U.S.S. "Nicholson," one of the vessels of the convoy, speeded to the spot and also dropped depth charges. The German submarine U-58 came to the surface. The "Nicholson" fired three shots from her stern while the "Fanning" headed for the submarine and fired her bow gun. After three shots the crew of the submarine came on deck and surrendered. The submarine sank shortly afterwards. The commanding officer of the "Fanning" at the time was Lieutenant Commander Arthur Schuyler Carpenter and the commanding officer of the "Nicholson" was Lieutenant Commander Frank Dunn Berrien.

Navy vessel constructed as a mine layer was the U.S.S. "Terror" (CM-5), whose keel was laid September 3, 1940. She was launched June 6, 1941, at Philadelphia, Pa., and commissioned July 15, 1942. The ship displaced 5,875 tons standard, 8,640 at load speed, and had an over-all length of 454 feet, 10 inches, beam of 60 feet 2 inches. She cruised at 20 knots and mounted four 5-inch 38-caliber dual purpose guns and two twin 40-millimeter anti-aircraft guns.

Navy vessel equipped to lay mines was the cruiser "Baltimore," which was commissioned January 7, 1890. She was built by Wil-

SHIP—*Continued*

liam Cramp & Sons, Philadelphia, Pa., and her keel laid May 5, 1887. She was 252 feet 4 inches long. Her captain was Winfield Scott Schley. The "Baltimore" served during the Spanish-American War as a cruiser. After being decommissioned, she was converted into a mine layer and recommissioned as such on March 8, 1915. During World War I she saw considerable service in this assignment.

Newspaper published at sea. *See* Newspaper: Newspaper published at sea

Ocean-going brokerage office. *See* Brokerage: Ocean-going brokerage office

Oil tanker was the "Charles" of Antwerp, Belgium, which plied between the United States and Europe from 1869 to 1872. She contained 59 iron tanks, arranged in rows at the bottom of her hold in the 'tween decks. Her bulk capacity was 7,000 barrels (794 tons). (*Victor Ross— Evolution of the Oil Industry*)

Packet line, and the best known, was the Black Ball Line, out of New York to Liverpool. It began in 1816 with sailings on the first of each month. The original ships were the "Amity," "Courier," "Pacific," and "James Monroe" of 400 tons each. Additional sailings were added later for the sixteenth of each month. During the first nine years, ships of this line averaged twenty-three days for the transatlantic crossing. (*Arthur Hamilton Clark—The Clipper Ship Era*)

Post office aboard a naval vessel. *See* Post office: Naval post office aboard a naval vessel

Racing shell was "The Harvard," a 6-oared 40-foot rudderless round-bottom white pine boat built in 1857 by James Mackay of Brooklyn, N.Y., for the Harvard Boat Club of Harvard College, Cambridge, Mass. She was 26 inches wide and weighed 50 pounds. (*James Wellman—The Story of the Harvard-Yale Race 1852-1912*)

Radar installation aboard a commercial carrier operated by an American company was installed April 27, 1946, on the S.S. "African Star" of the American South African Line, Inc. and placed in operation on May 1, 1946, at which time the ship made her maiden voyage from New York City. The equipment, supplied by the General Electric Company, Schenectady, N.Y., was known as the "Mariner."

Radio broadcast of a drama from a ship at sea. *See* Radio broadcast: Drama broadcast from a ship at sea

Radio telephone ship-to-shore conversation. *See* Radio telephone: Radio telephone ship-to-shore conversation

Revenue cutter was the "Massachusetts," the keel of which was laid in 1791 in the yard of [William] Searle and [Joseph] Tyler at Newburyport, Mass. She had one deck and two masts and cost $1,440. She was one of ten revenue cutters authorized August 4, 1790 (1 Stat. L.175) at a cost of $10,000 to be paid out of the duties on goods imported. The master was John Foster Williams and the first mate Hezekiah Welch, both of whom were appointed March 21, 1791. (*Horatio Davis Smith—Early History of the U.S. Revenue Marine Service or U.S. Revenue Cutter Service*)

Revenue cutter and Navy cooperation took place July 10, 1798, when the "Governor Jay," 14 tons and 70 men, and the "General Greene," 10 guns and 54 men, of the revenue cutter service were placed under the command of Commodore John Barry of the Navy, who was cruising between Nantucket, Mass., and Cape Henry, Va. (*Horatio Davis Smith—Early History of the U.S. Revenue Marine Service or U.S. Revenue Cutter Service*)

Rivetless cargo vessel was built by the Charleston Dry Dock and Machine Company, Charleston, S.C., for the Texas Oil Company and was launched February 1930. The entire hull was put together by the arc welding process under a new system of dove-tailed lock-notched plates, and only 11,000 pounds of welding wire was used instead of 18,000 pounds of rivets. A 20 per cent to 25 per cent saving in hull construction cost was effected by the use of the welding process. The boat had a ten-foot draft and a cargo capacity of 120 by 23 feet.

Roll-on roll-off carrier especially designed and built was the "Searoad," placed in service September 1, 1955, between Hyannis and Nantucket Island, Mass., by the Searoad Transport Company, Inc., Hyannis, Mass. She was 64 feet long, had a superstructure 14 feet high, and drew only 6½ feet of water. Her 220-h.p. General Motor diesel engine attained a speed of 9 knots. She was built by the Blount Marine Corporation of Warren, R.I., and cost $65,000 to build and $25,000 to equip. The first skipper was Morris Johnson.

Rotor ship to dock in an American port was the "Baden-Baden," which arrived in New York Harbor May 9, 1926, under the command of Captain Peter Callsen. She was equipped with two 45-foot towers, 9 feet in diameter, which rotated at 120 revolutions per minute maximum speed. The ship was invented by Anton Flettner and sailed from Hamburg, Germany, via the Canary Islands. She attained a speed of 9½ knots. (*Anton Flettner—Story of the Rotor*)

THE FIRST

SOS from a ship. *See* Radio distress signal

Schooner built in America was launched at Gloucester, Cape Ann, Mass., in 1714. She was built by Henry Robinson. *(John James Babson—History of Gloucester, Mass.)*

Schooner (five masted) was the "David Dows," built at the Bailey Brothers Shipyard, Toledo, Ohio, and launched April 21, 1881. She had a keel length of 260 feet and a length overall of 275 feet. Her breadth of beam was 37½ feet with an average depth of hold of 18 feet. She had five masts with top masts, 162 feet high, a gross tonnage of 1,418 tons, and a 1,347 net tonnage. She was owned by M. D. Carrington, Toledo, Ohio, and her first captain was Joseph Skeldon. She was lost off Whiting, Ind., on Thanksgiving Day 1889. *(Henry Hall—Report on the Shipbuilding Industry of the U.S.)*

Schooner (four masted) to be built was the "William J. White," which was launched at Bath, Me., in June 1880.

Schooner (seven masted, steel) was the "Thomas W. Lawson," built at Quincy, Mass., by the Fore River Ship and Engine Company for the Coastwise Transportation Company of Boston, Mass. The contract was signed January 25, 1901, and the keel laid November 1, 1901. The ship was launched July 10, 1902. Her overall length was 403 feet 4 inches, her beam 50 feet, and her depth 35 feet 3 inches. Her sail area was 40,617 square feet. The masts alone weighed about 17 tons apiece, excluding the rigging of three tons for each. Her tonnage was 4,914 net and 5,218 gross, and her carrying capacity 8,100 tons.

Schooner (six masted) was the "George W. Wells" built by Holly Marshall Bean at Camden, Me., and launched July 1, 1900. She was 340 feet over-all, with a beam of 48 feet.6 inches, and a depth of 23 feet. She had a net tonnage of 2,745 and cost $125,000. The captain was John G. Crowley. *(Reuel Robinson—History of Camden and Rockport, Maine)*

Seaplane tender designed and built for the U.S. Navy was the U.S.S. "Curtiss," authorized by Congress, July 30, 1937 (50 Stat.L.544). Her keel was laid April 25, 1938, and she was launched April 20, 1940, at the New York Shipbuilding Corporation Yard, Camden, N.J. She was 527 feet 4 inches over-all and had a standard displacement of 8,625 tons. Her contract price was $9,943,000. Three other vessels had been used earlier as seaplane tenders: the U.S.S. "Wright," originally a lighter-than-air craft tender, and the U.S.S. "Jason" and U.S.S. "Langley," both originally fleet colliers.

Seatrain was built in 1928 by the Sun Shipbuilding Company of Chester, Pa., for the Sea-

THE FIRST

train Lines, Inc., which inaugurated a service on January 12, 1929, between New Orleans, La., and Havana, Cuba. Loaded freight cars are hoisted from the railroad rails and placed aboard the seatrain, which accommodates 95 railroad cars. The seatrains have been named after the cities they serve—New York, New Orleans, etc.

Ship (American) attacked by a German submarine was the "Nantucket Chief," from Port Arthur, Tex. (christened "Gulflight" in 1913) a 5,189-ton tanker, 3,262 net tonnage, 360 feet long, which was torpedoed May 1, 1915, off the Scilly Isles.

Ship-at-sea broadcast. *See* Radio broadcast: Ship-at-sea broadcast from an ocean liner

Ship brokerage office. *See* Brokerage: Ocean-going brokerage office

Ship built by the English in the American colonies was the "Virginia of Sagadahock," launched in Maine from the banks of the Sagadahoc River (now the Kennebec) by the Popham colonists in 1607. A ship of 30 tons, she was 30 feet long, had a beam of 13 feet, and drew 8 feet. Moss was used for calking and shirts were used for her sails. *(Henry Ernest Dunnack—The Maine Book)*

Ship built on the Pacific coast was the "Northwest America," a schooner of forty tons, begun June 11, 1788. She was built, launched and equipped at Friendly Cove in King George's Sound (now Nootka Sound) abreast of the village of Nootka, British Columbia. Robert Funter was master. The ship was captured June 9, 1789, by Spain. *(John Meares—Voyages Made in the Years 1788 and 1789 from China to the North West Coast of America)*

Ship built to cross the Atlantic Ocean was a pinnace, a light sailing ship, built by the Huguenots of Jean Ribaut's expedition at Port Royal, S.C., in 1562. In the winter of 1562-1563, about thirty of them endeavored to return to France. They ran out of food and water and killed La Chere, one of their crew, whose "flesh was divided equally among his fellows." They reached the French coast but were rescued by an English ship which took them to Queen Elizabeth. *(Francis Parkman—France and England in North America)*

Ship captured by American forces in the Spanish American War. *See* Spanish American War: Ship captured in the Spanish-American War

SHIP—*Continued*

Ship constructed by the federal government was the "Chesapeake," built at the Navy Yard, Gosport, Va., under an act of March 27, 1794, "to provide a naval armament" (1 Stat.L.350). The President was authorized to obtain six ships by purchase or otherwise, equip and employ four ships to carry 44 guns each and two ships to carry 36 guns each, to protect our commerce from the Algerines. The marine yard was lent to the government by Virginia, and Captain Richard Dale was appointed its superintendent. Construction started in 1794, but as peace was concluded in 1796, the work was discontinued. Work was again undertaken in 1797, after materials on hand had been sold, with Commodore Samuel Barron as superintendent of the yard. The "Chesapeake" was launched in December 1799. *(Edward Phelps Lull—History of the United States Navy Yard at Gosport, Va.)*

Ship equipped with a masthead sea anchorage for a dirigible was the U.S.S. "Patoka." While the "Patoka" rode at anchor on August 15, 1925, off Newport News, Va., the ZR1 "Shenandoah" "landed" and was towed about twenty miles.

Ship equipped with radar. *See* Radar: Passenger ship equipped with radar

Ship from the Atlantic coast to anchor in a California port was the "Otter" of Boston, commanded by Captain Ebenezer Dorr. She carried six guns and twenty-six men and arrived October 29, 1796, at Monterey, where she remained until November 6, 1796. *(Herbert Howe Bancroft—History of California)*

Ship from which a long-range rocket was launched was the airplane carrier "Midway." On September 6, 1947, a captured German V-2 rocket was fired from the flight deck while the ship was several hundred miles off the east coast of the United States. The rocket traveled about six miles. Rear Admiral John Jennings Ballentine commanded the task group of which the U.S.S. "Midway," commanded by Captain Albert Kellogg Morehouse, was the flagship.

Ship launching broadcast. *See* Radio broadcast: Ship launching broadcast

Ship outfitted for hurricane research was the "Crawford," a 125-foot converted cutter, which was placed in service July 3, 1956, by the Oceanographic Institution, Woods Hole, Mass., to study how hurricanes originate. It carried a crew of fourteen and eight scientists. The first captain was David Casiles.

Ship permitted to enter port without stopping for quarantine procedure was the British S.S. "Cameronia," which arrived February 1, 1937, at the port of New York. Ships which complied with certain health requirements were permitted to enter under a system of radio pratique for passenger vessels. During the first six months, 84 vessels of 9 nationalities representing 19 lines used radio pratique 471 times. Originally the arrangement applied only to New York; later it was extended to include Boston, Mass.

Ship to capture an enemy ship after the Revolution was the U.S.S. "Constellation," a 36-gun frigate of 1,265 tons, launched September 7, 1797, at Baltimore, Md. On February 9, 1799, off the island of Nevis, West Indies, the "Constellation," under the command of Commodore Thomas Truxton, met the French frigate "Insurgente," inflicting seventy casualties and suffering only four herself.

Ship to carry the United States flag around the world was the "Columbia," a 212-ton vessel which sailed from Boston, Mass., September 30, 1787, under Captain Kendrick. She was accompanied by the sloop "Washington," under Captain Robert Gray, who exchanged commands with Captain Kendrick, and completed the trip, returning to Boston on August 9, 1790. The trip took three years and covered a distance of 41,899 miles. The crew explored the Queen Charlotte Islands and discovered the straits of Juan de Fuca and the mouth of the Columbia River. *(Rupert Sargent Holland—Historic Ships)*

Ship to circumnavigate the world with but one in the crew was manned by Captain Joshua Slocum. He sailed from Boston, Mass., on April 24, 1895, in a little sloop called "The Spray." She was 36 feet 9 inches long, 14 feet 2 inches wide, and 4 feet 2 inches in depth. Her tonnage was 9 tons net and her cost $553.62. The round trip of 46,000 miles was completed on July 3, 1898, when Captain Slocum sailed into Fairhaven, Mass., harbor, where the ship had been built. *(Captain Joshua Slocum—Sailing Alone Around The World)*

Ship to fire a Polaris missile was the "Observation Island" (EAG 154), commissioned December 5, 1958. She was 563 feet long over-all, had a beam of 76 feet, a full load displacement of 16,100 tons, a draft of 24 feet, and a speed of 20 knots. She was commanded by Captain Leslie Slack. Formerly, she had been the S.S. "Empire State Mariner" (YAG 57), a cargo-type merchant ship. On August 27, 1959, a Polaris missile was launched from the "Observation Island" seven miles off Cape Canaveral, Fla. The missile, fired by compressed air, ignited successfully at 70 feet and sped 700 miles to the target area. It was a solid-propellant two-stage missile, 28 feet long and 4 feet 6 inches in diameter.

Ship-to-shore air mail service. *See* Air mail service: Air mail service from ship to shore

Ship-to-shore commercial telephone service. *See* Radio telephone: Radio telephone ship-to-shore commercial service

Ship to transport fresh orange juice in stainless steel tanks was the S.S. "Tropicana," 8,000 tons, which left Port Canaveral, Fla., on February 16, 1957, and arrived February 19, 1957, at Whitestone, Long Island, N.Y., 56 hours later. The first shipment was made by Fruit Industries, Inc., of Bradenton, Fla., and consisted of 650,000 gallons.

Speed-boat to exceed 200 miles an hour was the jet-powered "Bluebird," piloted by Donald Malcolm Campbell, which averaged 216.2 miles per hour on November 16, 1955, on a measured kilometer course on Lake Mead, Nev. The speed for one leg of the course was 239.5 miles per hour.

Steam-propelled frigate was the "Demologos," or "Fulton, the First," of 2,475 tons, built by Robert Fulton for the U.S. Navy. Her keel was laid June 20, 1814, and she was launched October 29, 1814, without engines, at Brown's Ship Yard, New York City. She was made of wood five feet thick and had a center-wheel propulsion. Her length was 156 feet on deck, breadth of beam 56 feet, and depth 20 feet. She drew 8 feet of water. The hull was built by A. & N. [Adam and Noah] Brown. She cost $320,000. She carried thirty 32-pound carronades and two columbiads, the latter each carrying a 100-pound red-hot ball. The guns were mounted in a battery protected by massive wooden sides. On June 1, 1815, she was propelled by her own steam and machinery. *(Charles Beebe Stuart—The Naval and Mail Steamers of the U.S.)*

Steam whaler was the "Pioneer," whose first trip was made April 28, 1866, to November 14, 1866, under Captain Ebenezer Morgan. She had been converted in 1865 by Thomas W. Williams of New London, Conn., from a government transport. She was crushed in the ice in 1867. *(Clifford Warren Ashley—The Yankee Whaler)*

Steam whaler built as a whale boat was the "Mary and Helen," 420.5 tons, built at Bath, Me., in 1879, registered September 8, 1879, from New Bedford, Mass., under the command of M. V. B. Millard. Her length was 138 feet 2 inches; breadth 30 feet 3 inches; and depth 16.06 feet.

Steamboat was built by William Henry in 1763. He built an engine and model stern-wheel boat which was tested on the Conestoga Creek

at Lancaster, Pa. The trials demonstrated that the invention was unsuccessful. John Fitch invented a successful steam-engine in 1787 and in 1807 Robert Fulton built the "Clermont," which made the first run from New York City to Albany. *(Alex Harris—Biographical History of Lancaster County, Pa.)*

Steamboat built in America to cross the Atlantic Ocean was the "Savannah," a 350-ton full-rigged wooden boat, designed by Daniel Dod of Elizabeth, N.J. She was built at Corlear's Hook, New York, at the shipyards of Crocker and [Francis] Fickett and launched August 22, 1818. She had one inclined direct-acting low-pressure engine of 90 h.p. The trial trip from New York City to Savannah, Ga., was made March 28, 1819. The "Savannah" sailed May 22, 1819, from Savannah, Ga., and arrived at Liverpool, England, June 20, 1819. Steam power was used for only eighty hours during the trip. Moses Rogers was the captain and Steven Rogers the first officer. The ship had 32 staterooms, but no passengers dared make the trip. *(John Elfreth Watkins—The Log of the Savannah—Smithsonian Report 1890)*

Steamboat built on the Pacific coast for the government was the 453-ton side-wheel "Saginaw," built by Peter M. Donahue in 1860 at the Union Iron Works, San Francisco, Calif. The "Saginaw" was wrecked at Ocean Island in the Pacific, October 29, 1870. *(George Henry Read—The Last Cruise of the Saginaw)*

Steamboat (double decked) was the "Washington," built by Captain Henry Miller Shreve at the mouth of Wheeling Creek, Wheeling, Va. (now W.Va.). Her keel was laid September 10, 1815, and she was launched June 4, 1816. She arrived at her first destination, New Orleans, La., on October 7, 1816. Previously, engines had been placed in the hull. Shreve placed the machinery on the deck in a horizontal position, instead of in an upright position. Since that left no room on the deck for passengers, he added another deck. He built two high-pressure engines, 24-inch cylinder, 6-foot stroke, unconnected, each one operating a side wheel, so that the pilot could go ahead on one wheel and reverse on the other, thus turning the boat around in its own length, 148 feet. *(Florence L. Dorsey—Master of the Mississippi)*

Steamboat engine built in America for a screw-propelled vessel was installed in the "Vandalia," launched December 1, 1841, and enrolled April 14, 1842, at the port of Oswego, N.Y. It was designed by John Ericsson and built by Captain Sylvester Doolittle. It had two vertical cylinders, 14 inches in diameter, the stroke of which was 22 inches. Ericsson had previously built two engines which were installed in British ships. The "Vandalia" was

SHIP—*Continued*
91 feet long, her beam was 20 feet 2 inches, and her depth of hold of 8 feet 3 inches. Her displacement was 138 tons. She was the first screw-propelled vessel on the Great Lakes. *(Robert Dollar—One Hundred and Thirty Years of Steam Navigation)*

Steamboat on the Great Lakes was the "Walk-in-the-Water," 135 feet long, 388 tons gross tonnage, built at Black Rock, Buffalo, N.Y., for McIntyre & Stewart and launched April 4, 1818. The first trip was on October 10, 1818, when she left Buffalo, N.Y., with 100 passengers, bound for Detroit, Mich. The "Frontenac," built by Teabout and Chapman, launched September 7, 1816, plied only Lake Ontario.

Steamboat on the Pacific coast was the "Beaver," tested May 16, 1836 under steam at Vancouver, Washington. She entered the Willamette River, Oregon, May 31, 1836, on her maiden voyage, ran down the river under steam, and entered the lower reaches of the Columbia River near Vancouver. She was 101.4 feet long, 20 feet in the beam, with a depth of 11 feet, and a tonnage of 109.12. The engines, built by Bolton & Watt of England, were not installed when the ship left Gravesend, England, on August 27, 1835, shortly after completion. *(Robert Carlton Clark—History of the Willamette Valley, Oregon)*

Steamboat patent was issued by the state of Georgia to Isaac Briggs and William Longstreet on February 1, 1788, through the General Assembly at Augusta, Ga. This was the first and only patent issued by Georgia, authority having been vested by the Articles of Confederation, which were then in effect. The steamboat worked but was not practical. It was equipped with a boiler, two cylinders, and a condenser.

Steamboat service (regular) across the Atlantic was started by the "Great Western" and "Sirius." Both ships arrived in New York City on April 23, 1838, the "Sirius" having completed the trip from London in nineteen days and the "Great Western" from Bristol in fifteen days. They were built by Isambard Kingdom Brunel, the celebrated English engineer. *(New York Albion—April 28, 1838)*

Steamboat service (regular) to California via Cape Horn was established by the Pacific Mail Steamship Company in 1849. The S.S. "California," 1,050 tons, left New York October 6, 1848. She stopped at Rio de Janeiro, Brazil; Valparaiso, Chile; and Callao and Paita, Peru. On February 1, 1849, she arrived at Panama, where she took on 350 passengers. Further stops were made at Acapulco, San Blas, and Mazatlán, Mexico, and at San Diego

and Monterey, Calif. On February 28, 1849, she reached San Francisco, where most of the crew deserted to work in the gold fields. Captain Cleveland Forbes was in command. This trip started a semi-monthly mail service between New York and Panama and a monthly service between Panama and Oregon. *(Theodore Henry Hittell—History of California)*

Steamboat service round-the-world (regular passenger service) was inaugurated by the S.S. "President Harrison" of the Dollar Steamship Line, which sailed from San Francisco, Calif., February 1924. Cruise steamers, however, had made trips previously, usually one trip a year.

Steamboat to carry a man was built by John Fitch. On August 27, 1787, his boat plied up and down the Delaware River at the speed of three miles an hour. The boat was propelled by twelve large wooden paddles, six in tandem fashion along each side of the boat, alternately dipping into and drawing out of the water. The action of the paddles was the same as that used by the Indians in paddling a canoe. *(Carl Weaver Mitman—The Beginning of the Mechanical Transport Era)*

Steamboat to employ electric lights was the "Jeannette," owned by James Gordon Bennett, acquired by act of Congress of February 27, 1879 (20 Stat.L.323), which authorized the Secretary of the Navy "to accept for the purpose of a voyage of exploration by way of Bering Straits the ship 'Jeannette' tendered by James Gordon Bennett for that purpose" at no government expense. She sailed from San Francisco, Calif., July 8, 1879, under command of Lieutenant Commander George Washington De Long, U.S.N. Unsuccessful attempts were made to use an electric system to light the sixty 16-candlepower lamps from October 14 to 30, 1879. On September 16, 1879, the "Jeannette" had begun to drift uncontrollably. On January 19, 1880, she sprang a leak from pressure of ice, and on June 13, 1881, she sank. *(George Washington De Long—The Voyage of the Jeannette)*

Steamboat to employ electric lights successfully was the "Columbia" (length 309 feet; beam, 38 feet 5 inches; hold, 23 feet 3 inches; net tonnage, 1,746 tons) of the Oregon Railway and Navigation Company, built at Chester, Pa. The "Columbia" plied between San Francisco, Calif., and Portland, Ore. An "A" type dynamo, placed in operation on May 2, 1880, illuminated the passenger rooms and main salons. It operated successfully for fifteen years, until a larger dynamo was installed.

Steamboat to make an ocean voyage was the "Phoenix," 100 feet long, built at Hoboken, N.J., by Robert Livingston Stevens with his

THE FIRST

father, John Stevens. On June 10, 1809, she went from New York City to Philadelphia, Pa., by sea, navigating the Atlantic from Sandy Hook, N.J., to Cape May, N.J. under the command of Moses Rogers. *(Richard Cornelius McKay—South Street)*

Steamboat to make regular trips was designed by Robert Fulton. Under his supervision the hull of the "Clermont" was built by Charles Brown, a shipbuilder of New York. A Boulton & Watt engine was installed, and the boat made ready for its trial trip on August 7, 1807. She made a trip to Albany, a distance of 150 miles, in 32 hours and returned in 30 hours. *(Robert Henry Thurston—Robert Fulton, His Life and Its Results)*

Steamboat to pass through the Panama Canal was the craneboat "Alex. La Valley," a self-propelled steamer, on January 7, 1914. Commercial traffic was inaugurated August 15, 1914. The first passage of commercial cargo took place on May 18-19, 1914. The first vessel to make a direct continuous voyage from ocean to ocean through the canal was the tug "Mariner," on May 19, 1914. The first regular merchant vessel to transit the canal in commercial service was the "Ancon," on August 15, 1914. The first merchant vessel to use the canal on a voyage between ports beyond the canal terminal was the "Arizonan," on August 15-16, 1914. The first Army transport to transit the canal was the "Buford," on September 9, 1914, en route from San Francisco, Calif., to Galveston, Tex. *(Darrell Hevenor Smith—The Panama Canal, Its History, Activities and Organizations)*

Steamboat to sail down the Mississippi was the "New Orleans," which left Pittsburgh, Pa., in September 1811 under the ownership and guidance of Nicholas J. Roosevelt. She arrived at New Orleans, La., October 1, 1811. The crew consisted of a captain, engineer, pilot, six sailors, two female servants, a waiter, a cook. Mr. and Mrs. Roosevelt were the only passengers. The "New Orleans" cost $38,000. *(Maryland Historical Society Fund Publications. No. 4. John Hazlehurst Boneval Latrobe—The First Steamboat Voyage on the Western Waters)*

Steamboat with a twin-screw propeller was built by John Stevens at Hoboken, N.J., in 1803. He patented the engine on April 11, 1803, and successfully navigated in New York Harbor in 1804. The boat was 25 feet long and 4 feet wide and had two 5-foot screw propellers with four blades set at an angle of 35°. She was operated by a double direct-acting noncondensing engine with a 4½-inch cylinder and a 9-inch stroke. *(George Henry Preble—A Chronological History of the Origin and Development of Steam Navigation)*

THE FIRST

Steamship passenger line between United States ports and Europe to fly the American flag was the Ocean Steam and Navigation Company, service commencing with the sailing of the "Washington" from New York City on June 1, 1847, for Bremen, Germany, with 120 passengers. The "Washington" had four decks, three masts, and a full-length effigy of George Washington as a figurehead. She was 260 feet long, and had a 39-foot beam and a 31-foot-depth hold. The "Hermann" was later added to the service. *(U.S. Department of Commerce. Trade Promotion Series No.129, Shipping and Shipbuilding Subsidies)*

Steel sailing vessel was the "Dirigo," built by Arthur Sewall & Co., Bath, Me., and launched February 3, 1894. George W. Goodwin was the first captain. The "Dirigo" had a gross tonnage of 3,004 tons, and a net tonnage of 2,855 tons. Her length was 310 feet, her width 45.15 feet, and her depth 25.6 feet. She had two full decks and carried 13,000 square yards of canvas. *(Mark William Hennessy—The Sewall Ships of Steel)*

Steel vessels of the U.S. Navy were the cruisers "Atlanta," "Boston," and "Chicago" and the despatch boat "Dolphin," authorized by Congress March 3, 1883 (22 Stat.L.477). The hulls were built by John Roach and Sons, Chester, Pa., and the machinery at the New York Navy Yard. The "Atlanta" and the "Boston" were 270 feet 3 inches long and 42 feet wide, and had horizontal back-acting engines and cylindrical tubular boilers. The "Chicago" was 325 feet long and 48 feet 2 inches wide. The "Atlanta" was launched October 9, 1884, and commissioned July 19, 1886; the "Boston" was launched December 4, 1884, and commissioned May 2, 1887. *(Report of the Secretary of the Navy for 1883. Volume 1)*

Streamlined steamship to arrive in the United States was the "Arctees," of British registry, which sailed from Nicolaieff, Russia, on April 17, 1934, and arrived at Boston, Mass., on May 14, 1934.

Submarine. *See* Submarine

Telephone communication with a ship at sea. *See* Radio telephone: Radio telephone ship-to-shore conversation

Torpedo boat, worthy of the name, was the "Lightning," built in 1876 at Bristol, R.I., by John Brown Herreshoff and Nathanael Greene Herreshoff. She was 58 feet long and had a speed of about twenty knots. *(U.S. Navy Department. Report of the Secretary. 1902)*

Torpedo boat of importance was the U.S.S. "Cushing," authorized August 3, 1886 (24 Stat.L.215). She was 140 feet long, of

SHIP—*Continued*
steel, with a normal displacement of 116 tons, and was built at a cost of $82,750. Her keel was laid in 1888 by the Herreshoff Manufacturing Company, Bristol, Pa., and she was commissioned April 22, 1890, as seagoing torpedo boat No. 1. (*Lewis Francis Herreshoff—Captain Nat Herreshoff*)

Trading ship sent to China was the "Empress of China," a 360-ton privateer which was commanded by Captain John Green. She left New York February 22, 1784; arrived in Canton, China, August 28, 1784; left China on the return voyage December 28, 1784; and returned to New York May 11, 1785. Her owners made a profit of $30,727 on a $120,000 investment which was financed by Robert Morris, Peter Whiteside, and William Whiteside. (*Foster Rhea Dulles—The Old China Trade*)

Transatlantic trip by rowboat. *See* Rowing: Transatlantic trip by rowboat

Transoceanic newspaper published on a ship. *See* Newspaper: Newspaper published at sea

Troopship torpedoed. *See* World War I: American army troopship in World War I torpedoed by the Germans

Tugboat (diesel electric) was placed in service in 1929 on the Warrior River, Ala., by the Tennessee Coal, Iron and Railroad Company. The power plant included two 550 h.p. diesel engines. Each propeller was driven by a double motor rated at 400 h.p. The length of the tow was limited to seven barges.

Tugboat (steam) was the "Rufus King," built in 1825 by Smith and Dimon for the New York Dry Dock Company to tow vessels to and from the railway at the foot of east Tenth Street, New York City. She was 102 feet long and 19 feet wide and had a square engine of 34-inch cylinder by 4-inch stroke. (*John Harrison Morrison—American Steam Navigation*)

Turbine-propelled ocean-going merchant vessel (constructed in the United States) was the "Governor Cobb," launched April 21, 1906, and delivered October 17, 1906, to the Eastern Steamship Line for service between Boston, Mass., and Saint John, New Brunswick, Canada. She was 2,522 gross tons and 289 feet 1 inch long. The turbine was built by the W. A. Fletcher Company (now owned by the Bethlehem Steel Company) at Hoboken, N.J.

Turbine-propelled ship of the U.S. Navy was the "Chester," a scout cruiser, launched

July 26, 1907, and commissioned April 25, 1908. She was built at the Bath Iron Works Company, Bath, Me. The contract price for the hull and machinery was $1,688,000. The "Chester," which was equipped with four Parsons turbines, had an over-all length of 423 feet 1 inch and a displacement of 3,750 tons. Her trial speed was 26.52 knots.

Turreted frigate in the U.S. Navy was the U.S.S. "Roanoke," originally a wooden screw steam frigate built at the Norfolk Navy Yard under authorization of Act of Congress of April 6, 1854. She was launched December 13, 1855, and made her trial trip in 1857. She was altered to an iron-clad in 1862-1863 by the Novelty Iron Works, New York, and transferred to the New York Navy yard, April 16, 1863. She had three revolving turrets of the Ericsson type and two pilot houses, and her battery on July 9, 1863 consisted of two 15-inch, two 11-inch, and two 150-pounder rifle guns. The alteration was not found satisfactory, the hull not being strong enough to sustain the weight. She was sold in 1883.

Two-way radio between a submarine and a ship. *See* Radio telephone: Two-way radio conversation between a submerged submarine and another vessel

Warship (American built) to enter European waters was the sixteen-gun brig "Reprisal," which on December 4, 1776, under the command of Captain Lambert Wickes, conveyed Benjamin Franklin, who was traveling incognito to Auray, France, to obtain French assistance. On the way over she captured two British vessels, and two others in the Bay of Biscay, one of which was the King's packet plying between Falmouth and Lisbon. This was the first capture by the American colonists of a ship in enemy waters and the first attempt to block and destroy British commerce at the source.

Warship builder was Joshua Humphreys, "father of the American Navy," appointed June 28, 1794, by General Henry Knox as Constructor or Master Builder at an annual salary of $2,000. On March 27, 1794, Congress passed an "act to provide a naval armament" (1 Stat.L.350), which authorized four ships of 44 guns and two of 36 guns. In 1794, Humphreys constructed the first of the naval war vessels, the "Constitution," "Constellation," "Chesapeake," "President," "The United States," and numerous other ships. Humphreys served until October 26, 1801. (*Edward Phelps Lull—History of the United States Navy Yard at Gosport, Va.*)

Warship built on inland waters was the torpedo boat "Ericsson," which was launched on the Mississippi at Dubuque, Iowa, on May

THE FIRST

12, 1894. She was a triple-screw steam vessel of 120 tons and carried three guns and a crew of twenty-three. She cost $113,500.

Warship captured by a commissioned officer of the U.S. Navy was the British warship "Edward." Captain John Barry of the 16-gun brig "Lexington" met her April 17, 1776, off the Virginia coast, captured her, and conveyed her to Philadelphia, Pa. *(William Bell Clark—Gallant John Barry)*

Warship docked in a government drydock. *See* Drydock: National ship in a federal drydock

Warship fleet to circumnavigate the globe left Hampton Roads, Va., on December 16, 1907, under the command of Rear Admiral Robley Dunglison Evans, who relinquished his command on May 9, 1908, to Rear Admiral Charles Stillman Sperry. The fleet left San Francisco, Calif., on July 7, 1908, and returned to Hampton Roads on February 22, 1909, stopping at Honolulu, Auckland, Sydney, Melbourne, Manila, Yokohama, Amoy, Colombo, Suez, and Gibraltar en route. The fleet was made up of the "Connecticut," "Vermont," "Kansas," "Minnesota," "Georgia," "Nebraska," "New Jersey," "Rhode Island," "Louisiana," "Virginia," "Missouri," "Ohio," "Wisconsin," "Illinois," "Kentucky," "Kearsarge," and several auxiliary vessels. *(U.S. Navy—Information Relative to the Voyage of the U.S. Atlantic Fleet Around the World)*

Warship named for a Negro was the U.S.S. "Harmon," a destroyer launched July 25, 1943, at the Fore River Plant of the Bethlehem Steel Company at Quincy, Mass. It was named for Leonard Roy Harmon of Cuero, Tex., a mess attendant, who shielded a shipmate from enemy fire at the Battle of Guadalcanal, November 12-13, 1942, and was posthumously awarded the Navy Cross.

Warship propelled by electricity was the U.S.S. "New Mexico," which was built at the Navy Yard, New York. The keel was laid on October 14, 1915. She was launched April 23, 1917, and commissioned May 20, 1918. The "New Mexico" was 624 feet in length, displaced 30,000 tons, and carried twelve 14-inch guns and twelve 5-inch guns. *(Records in Office of Naval Intelligence. Navy Department. Washington, D.C.)*

Warship regularly commissioned, by authority derived from the United Colonies with definite orders to attack the enemy, was the schooner "Hannah," commanded by Captain Nicholson Broughton of Marblehead, Mass. His order was dated September 2, 1775. The

THE FIRST

crew consisted of a detachment of soldiers from the Essex County Regiment of Marblehead, Mass.

Warship to circumnavigate the globe was the U.S.S. "Vincennes," a 16-gun sloop of war of 700 tons burden, which left New York, August 31, 1826, for the Pacific by way of Cape Horn, under the command of Commander William Bolton Finch (afterwards known as William Compton Bolton). She returned in 1829 by way of the Cape of Good Hope, arriving at New York on June 8, 1830. *(Early Voyages of American Vessels to the Orient. Vol. 36. U.S. Naval Institute. Proceedings)*

Warship with propelling machinery below the waterline and out of reach of hostile shot was the screw-warship "Princeton," which was designed by John Ericsson in 1841. Her length on deck was 164 feet; beam 30½ feet; displacement 954 tons. Her wooden hull was built at the U.S. Navy Yard under the supervision of Captain Robert Field Stockton and the machinery by Merrick and Towne, Philadelphia, Pa. She was launched December 10, 1843, at the Navy Yard, Philadelphia, Pa., and cost $212,615.00. She carried two long 225-pound wrought iron guns and twelve 42-pound carronades. On February 28, 1844, while the ship was on a demonstration run, one of her guns exploded, killing several of the distinguished visitors. *(Samuel John Bayard—A Sketch of the Life of Commodore Robert F. Stockton)*

Whaleback steamer to cross the Atlantic was the S.S. "Charles W. Wetmore," which sailed from Duluth, Minn., on June 11, 1891, with a cargo of grain for Liverpool, England. She was 265 feet long and 38 feet in the beam, with a 24-foot hold, a net tonnage 1,075 and a dead capacity of 3,000 tons.

Woman to sail solo across the Atlantic Ocean was Ann Davidson, who in a 23-foot sailboat, the 'Felicity Ann," left Plymouth, England, on May 18, 1952, and arrived at Miami, Fla., on August 12, 1953. She made stops en route at Douarnenez, France; Vigo, Spain; Gilbraltar; and Dominica, Antigua, Nevis, St. Thomas, and Nassau, British West Indies.

Yacht was the "Jefferson," a 22-ton sloop. She was constructed in Salem, Mass., in 1801 by Christopher Turner for Captain George Crowninshield. She was 35 feet 10 inches long and 12 feet 4 inches wide, and had a 6-foot depth. She was rigged first as a schooner, afterward as a sloop. *(Arthur Hamilton Clark—History of Yachting)*

SHIP SUBSIDY. *See* Shipping: Ship subsidy

SHIPPING

Automatic **steering gear** for ships, or Gyro-Pilot, called "Metalmike," was installed on the "John D. Archibold" of the Standard Oil Company of New Jersey and tested April 7, 1922.

Coastal shipping service was established in 1831 by Thomas Lowery Servoss. He outfitted five packet ships that ran regularly between New York and New Orleans.

Embargo. *See* Embargo act

Ship subsidy was established "to provide for the transportation of the mail between the United States and foreign countries, and for other purposes." The act (5 Stat.L.739), approved March 3, 1845, authorized the Postmaster General to make contracts with citizens of the United States for the carrying of mail in American vessels, by American citizens. The rate paid per letter for mail to Mexico and the West Indies was 10 cents a half ounce, 20 cents an ounce, and 5 cents for each additional half ounce; for ports not less than three thousand miles away the rate was 24 cents a half ounce, 48 cents an ounce, and 15 cents for each additional half ounce. (*Royal Meeker—History of Shipping Subsidies*)
See also Postal Service: Ocean mail contracts

United States Shipping Board was established by the Shipping Act of September 7, 1916 (39 Stat.L.728) "to regulate carriers by water in the foreign and interstate commerce of the U.S." On December 22, 1916, five commissioners were nominated, Bernard Nadel Baker, William Denman, John A. Donald, John Barber White and Theodore Brent, all of whose nominations were confirmed by January 23, 1917. (*Darrell Hevenor Smith and Paul Vernon Betters—The United States Shipping Board*)

SHIRT FACTORY of importance was established in Boston, Mass., in 1848 by Oliver Fisher Winchester.

SHOE

Rubber shoe manufacturer. *See* Rubber: Rubber shoe manufacturer

Shoe was manufactured in 1628 by Thomas Beard, who came over on the "Mayflower." Prior to that date shoes were imported from England. The colonists also learned from the Indians how to make moccasins, which were so well liked that as early as 1650 they were exported to England.

SHOE MANUFACTURING MACHINE was the McKay stitching machine, which revolutionized shoe manufacturing methods. It

was invented by Lyman Reed Blake of Abington, Mass., who obtained patents No. 29,561 and 29,775, July 6, 1858. The upper was lasted upon the insole by means of tacks driven through the insole and clinched against the steel bottom of the last. The outsole was then attached to the insole and upper by the McKay sewing machine, which made a chain-stitch through and through to the inside of the shoe. The surface of the insole was then covered by a lining. The machine was introduced in the factory of William Porter & Sons, Lynn, Mass., in 1861. It was probably operated by foot power. (*Frederic Augustus Gannon—Short History of American Shoemaking*)

SHOE MEASURING STICK was introduced as early as 1657. A dispute arose in court with regard to sizes and the court was informed that William Newman of Stamford, Conn., "hath an instrument in his hand, which he brought out of England, which is thought to be right to determine the question between the buyer and the seller." The court "did ordain that the said instrument should be procured and sent to New Haven."

SHOE PEG was invented by Joseph Walker of Hopkinton, Mass., in 1818. Prior to his invention, all shoe soles were sewn.

SHOE PEGGING MACHINE was operated by Charles D. Bigelow at his shop in Jacob Street, New York City, in the "Swamp" district, in 1852.

SHOOT-THE-CHUTES was built by Captain Paul Boyton in 1894 at Coney Island, N.Y. (*Edo McCullough—Good Old Coney Island*)

SHOOTING GALLERY (mechanized) that was fully automatic was invented in 1890 by Charles Wallace Parker of Abilene, Kan., whose first sale was made to Leon Brownie of Houston, Texas.

SHOOTING STAR. *See* Astronomy: Meteoric display

SHORTENING

Shortening made by the hydrogenation process from vegetable oils was introduced as Crisco by the Procter & Gamble Company, Cincinnati, Ohio, on August 15, 1911. It was a creamy-white all-vegetable shortening, odorless and tasteless, made from cottonseed oil.

SHORTHAND BOOK was printed in 1728 by S. Keimer in Philadelphia, Pa., and was offered as a premium to anyone purchasing three shillings' worth of useful books. (*Charles Evans—American Bibliography*)

THE FIRST

SHORTHAND MAGAZINE was the
American Phonographic Journal, 16 pages, edited and published by Dyer & Webster, Philadelphia, Pa., which appeared in July 1848. It sold for 10 cents an issue or $1.00 a year. The first volume contained only eight issues, none being published in November and December 1848 or January and February 1849. It resumed publication in March 1849 (Vol. 2, No. 1), with E. Webster as the publisher.

SHORTHAND REPORT of a trial was
made by John Llywellin, Clerk of the Council, who was instructed by Lord Baltimore to record the proceedings held in the Provinciall Court, St. Johns, Md., on November 15, 1681. The Justices Tailoor, Stevens, and Diggens found Josias Fendall guilty of mutiny on March 26, 1681, and sentenced him to pay "40,000 pounds of Tobacco for a fine, Be kept in safe custody at [his] own proper costes and charges until [he] shall have paid the same and after the same is paid to be for ever banished out of this Province." *(Maryland Archives—Vol. 5)*

SHORTHORN CATTLE AUCTION
SALE. *See* Animals: Cattle (shorthorn) public auction sale

SHOT-PUT
Shot-put toss over 60 feet was made May 8, 1954, when Parry O'Brien, formerly of the University of Southern California, tossed the sixteen-pound shot 60 feet 5¼ inches at the University of California at Los Angeles-Southern California Pacific Coast Conference dual meet held in Los Angeles.

SHOT TO LAND ON AMERICAN
SOIL. *See* World War I: Shots to land on American soil

SHOT TOWER. *See* Ordnance: Shot tower

SHOULDER PATCH. *See* Army insignia:
Shoulder sleeve insignia

SHOVEL
See also Steam shovel

Shovel (steel) was manufactured in 1774 by Captain John Ames in West Bridgewater, Mass.

SHOW. *See*

Automobile show	Horse show
Baby show	Magic lantern show
Dog show	Milch goat show
Exposition	Poultry show
Fair	Theater

SHOWBOAT. *See* Theater: Showboat

THE FIRST

SHOWERS IN PUBLIC BATHS. *See*
Bathhouse: Public baths with showers

SHREDDED WHEAT BISCUIT. *See*
Breakfast food: Shredded wheat biscuits

SHRINERS. See Freemasons

SIAMESE TWINS
Siamese twins were first brought to Boston, Mass., by Robert Hunter on August 16, 1829. They were known as Chang and Eng (Bunker). They were born April 15, 1811, in Bangesau, Siam, of a Chinese father and a Sino-Siamese mother. They were joined at the waist by a cartilaginous band about four inches long and eight inches in circumference. They grew to be about 5 feet 2 inches in height, and, since they faced in the same direction, could walk, run and swim. They were exhibited throughout the United States and later in Europe. They were married in April 1843 to the Misses Sarah and Adelaide Yates. Chang had ten children and Eng nine children. They died within three hours of each other on January 17, 1874.

Siamese twins separated successfully by surgery were pygopagus twins whose lower intestines were connected and whose lower spinal bone structure and dural membrane were joined. The twins, Carolyn Anne and Catherine Anne, daughters of Ashton and Rosa Mouton, were born in Lafayette, La., on July 22, 1953. On September 17, 1953, fifteen doctors worked 2¼ hours at the Ochsner Foundation Hospital, New Orleans, La., to separate them, and on October 14, 1953, they were discharged from the hospital.

Siamese twins to survive a separation operation and live for one year were Nancy and Ellen, born December 14, 1952, in Cleveland, Ohio. They were joined at the base of the breastbone by a band of tissue ½ inch wide and 1½ inches long. The separation operation was performed by Dr. Jac Sidney Geller at the Mount Sinai Hospital, Cleveland, Ohio. The operation was a superficial one—the cutting of a layer of skin or cartilage that joined the babies at the chest.

SIDEWALK (traveling)
Sidewalk (traveling) was installed at the Columbian Exposition in Chicago in 1893 to convey passengers from one part of the fairgrounds to the other. It traveled at two speeds, three and six miles an hour, and accommodated 5,610 persons.

Sidewalk (traveling) in a railroad station was placed in operation May 24, 1954, by the Hudson and Manhattan Railroad Company at its Erie station, Jersey City, N.J. It cost

SIDEWALK (traveling)—*Continued*
$75,000. Made of rubber and canvas, it was 227 feet long and 5½ feet wide, and traveled up a 10 per cent grade at 1½ miles per hour.

Two-way moving walk was placed in service January 30, 1958 at Love Field Air Terminal, Dallas, Tex. It consisted of three loops and totaled 1,435 feet of moving walkway. In each loop a continuous rubber carpet was attached to an endless train of wheeled pallets, flexibly interconnected so that they could follow vertical or horizontal curves as required. The walk was also known as a moving sidewalk and passenger conveyor.

SIEVE
Sieve was produced in 1768 in Philadelphia, Pa., by John Sellers. His sieves were used principally by millers.

Wire sieves were manufactured commercially in 1834 by Edwin Gilbert of Gilbert, Bennett & Company at Georgetown, Conn. *(One Hundred Years of Progress—Gilbert and Bennett Manufacturing Co.)*

SIGHT-SEEING BUS. *See* Automobile bus: Automobile sight-seeing bus

SIGN FLASHER. *See* Electric sign: Electric sign flasher

SIGN-LANGUAGE RELIGIOUS SERVICE. *See* Deaf—Church service: Prayers in the sign language of the deaf

SIGNAL CORPS (U.S. Army). *See* Army: Signal corps

SIGNAL LIGHT (electric). *See* Traffic light: Electric traffic signal lights

SILK
Silk culture was started about 1623 in Virginia. The Colonial Assembly directed the planting of mulberry trees. In 1656 an act was passed in which silk was described as the most profitable commodity for the country, and "a penalty of ten pounds of tobacco . . . imposed upon every planter who should fail to plant at least ten mulberry trees for every hundred acres of land in his possession." *(Linus Pierpont Brockett—Silk Industry in America)*

Silk dyers to achieve success were Edward Vallentine and Lewis Leigh, who emigrated from England in 1838. They began business at Gurleyville, Conn., and achieved fame by producing a permanent black. *(Albert Henry Heusser—History of the Silk Dyeing Industry in the U.S.)*

Silk exportation took place in 1735 when eight pounds of raw silk was exported from Savannah to England. The Trustees of Georgia reported in 1736: "The raw silk from Georgia, organized by Sir Thomas Lombe, was made into a piece of silk and presented to the queen." This entry appears in the manuscript book of the trustees. It is possible that some silk may have been sent previously from Virginia, where silk cultivation was first introduced. *(Letter from the Secretary of the Treasury Regarding the Growth and Manufacture of Silk. Washington, D.C., February 7, 1828)*

Silk loom of importance was the "Gem Silk Loom," built in 1887 by the Knowles Loom Works, Worcester, Mass. On April 23, 1887, three 40-inch, 20-harness, 4 by 4 box loom machines were ordered by the Empire Silk Company, Paterson, N.J. Crepes, chiffons or fancy pattern material requiring up to twenty harnesses could be woven on this loom.

Silk mill was erected for the Mansfield Silk Company by Rodney and Horatio Hanks in Mansfield, Conn., in 1810 in a building 12 by 12 feet. An effort was made to make sewing silk and twist by the machinery they had invented and manufactured.

Silk power loom, the figure or pattern of the cloth being made on a chain, was invented by William Crompton of Taunton, Mass., who obtained patent No. 491 on November 25, 1837, on a figure power loom. *(American Silk Journal. Thumbnail History of the Broad Silk Industry in the United States. November 1931)*

Silk suture. *See* Suture: Silk suture

Silk thread. *See* Thread: Silk thread; Thread: Silk thread on spools

SILO (of record) was constructed by Fred L. Hatch in 1873 in McHenry County, Ill. *(Thomas Ross Pirtle—History of the Dairy Industry)*

SILVER BULLION DEPOSIT. *See* Money: Deposit of silver for coinage

SILVER COIN. *See* Money: Silver coins

SILVER DEMONETIZATION. *See* Money: Demonetization of silver

SILVER DOLLAR. *See* Money: Silver dollar

SILVER HALF-DIME. *See* Money: Silver half dimes

THE FIRST

THE FIRST

SILVER HALF-DOLLAR. *See* Money: Silver coins

SILVER MILL to treat silver ore successfully and the first reducing mill to treat ore-bearing quartz was established by the Washoe Gold and Silver Mining Company, No. 1, near Virginia City, Nev., formed March 1860. The mill, operated by water power, was built by Almarin B. Paul, who began the construction work May 25, 1860, and completed it August 9, 1860. It consisted of 24 stamps which began to crush ore on August 11, 1860. *(Department of the Interior. Monographs of the U.S. Geological Survey. 1883. Vol. 4)*

SILVER MINE was the Silver Hill Mine, discovered in 1838 about ten miles from Lexington, N.C. The company was incorporated January 7, 1839, for $500,000. *(Richard Cowling Taylor—Reports on the Washington Silver Mine)*

SILVER PLATING FACTORY (successful) was Rogers Brothers, Hartford, Conn., established in 1847 by three brothers, William, Asa, and Simeon S. Rogers. In 1862, their factory was moved to Meriden, Conn., and they associated themselves with the Meriden Britannia Company, which in 1898 was succeeded by the International Silver Company. Silverplate consists of a hard metal which is plated or coated with silver. The base metal is usually nickel-silver, a combination of copper, zinc, and nickel. Prior to the introduction of silverplated ware, silverware had been made from coin silver.

SILVER STAR. *See* Medal: Silver star

SILVER WIRE SUTURE. *See* Suture: Silver wire suture

SILVERITES, who favored silver as monetary standard, held their first national convention in St. Louis, Mo., July 22, 1896, and endorsed the Democratic candidates, William Jennings Bryan for President, and Arthur Sewall for Vice President. The temporary chairman of the convention was Francis Griffith Newlands of Nevada, and the permanent chairman was William Pope St. John of New York. *(Wayne Cullen Williams—William Jennings Bryan)*

SIMPLIFIED SPELLING. *See* Spelling reform advocate

SIMULCAST. *See* Television—Telecast: Simulcast presented regularly by a sponsor

SINGER OF OPERA IN ITALIAN. *See* Opera: Opera (Italian)

SINGING CONTEST. *See* Music: Singing contest

SINGING TELEGRAM. *See* Telegram: Singing telegram

SINGLE-PHASE ALTERNATING CURRENT MOTOR. *See* Electric motor: Electric motor (single-phase alternating current)

SINGLE TAX
City to adopt the single tax for local revenue purposes was Hyattsville, Md., which operated under this system from July 1892 to March 1893. The Maryland legislature empowered the Board of Commissioners to make such deductions or exceptions from or addition to the assessment made by the assessors as they might deem just. The acts were declared unconstitutional and the law abrogated. *(Arthur Nichols Young—History of the Single Tax Movement in the United States)*

Single tax national conference assembled September 1, 1890, in New York City and adopted a platform September 3. Five hundred delegates from thirty states formed a national organization, the Single Tax League of the United States, with a national committee composed of one member from each state, and an executive committee of which William T. Croasdale was the chairman. The first noted advocate of a single tax, on land, was Henry George, who in 1871 propounded the idea in *Our Land and Our Land Policy. (Joseph Dana Miller—Single Tax Year Book)*

Single tax political ticket was presented to the voters of Delaware in 1896. In September a full state ticket was drawn up, with Dr. Louis N. Slaughter nominated for governor. In the election of November 6, 1896, the single tax party polled only 855 votes. The symbol or device of the party was "The Earth." *(Arthur Nichols Young—The History of the Single Tax Movement in the United States)*

SINGLE-THREAD SEWING MACHINE. *See* Sewing machine: Chain-stitch single-thread sewing machine

SIT-DOWN STRIKE. *See* Strike: Modern sit-down strike

SIX-DAY BICYCLE RACE. *See* Bicycle race: International six-day bicycle race

SIX-MASTED SCHOONER. *See* Ship: Schooner (six-masted)

SIX-REEL COMEDY. *See* Moving picture: Six-reel feature-length comedy

SKATE (all-metal) was marketed by Everett Hosmer Barney. In 1864 he commenced business in Springfield, Mass., as Barney & Berry. On November 29, 1904, the firm was incorporated under the laws of the state of Massachusetts. In 1919, the capital stock was purchased by the Winchester Repeating Arms Company, which in 1922 moved the manufacturing business to its plant in New Haven. Barney was the first to conceive and execute the idea of fastening shoes to skates by means of metal clamps. He obtained patent No. 52,301, covering his invention of a screw clamp skate, on January 16, 1866.

SKATING
Roller derby was the Transcontinental Roller Derby, which opened August 13, 1935, at the Coliseum, Chicago, Ill., under the direction of Leo A. Seltzer. Fifty contestants, paired two to a team, endeavored to skate and race a distance equal to that from New York to California.

SKATING CHAMPION
Figure skating Olympic champion. *See* Olympic Games: Figure skating Olympic champion

Skating champion (ice) was Charles June of Newburgh, N.Y., who defeated recognized English contestants in 1849.

SKATING RINK
Ice skating rink (indoor) was built by Thomas L. Rankin at Madison Square Garden, New York City in 1879. It had 6,000 square feet of surface. On February 12, 1879, a gala carnival was presented.

Roller skating rink (public) was opened at Newport, R.I., in 1866 under the auspices of James Leonard Plimpton of Boston, Mass., the inventor of the Plimpton skate. The skating rink was located in the Atlantic House, corner of Bellevue Avenue and Pelham Street on the site later occupied by the Elks' Home.

SKATING TOURNAMENT
Figure skating international championship tournament was held March 20, 1914, at the Arena Ice Rink, New Haven, Conn., under the rules of the Skating Union of America. The ladies' championship was won by Theresa Weld of the Skating Club of Boston, Mass., the men's by Norman Scott of the Winter Club of Montreal, Canada. Other events were pair skating to music and waltzing.

SKEE BALL ALLEY was built in 1914 by the National Skee Ball Company of Coney Island, N.Y., and the first battery was operated by William A. Norwood in April 1914 at Coney Island.

SKEET
College skeet tournament was held November 12, 1928, in Princeton, N.J. A five-man team from Yale defeated Princeton 221 to 202. Bob Rosien of Yale scored a perfect fifty.

National skeet tournament sponsored by the National Skeet Association was won by Lovell S. Pratt of Indianapolis, Ind., who led a field of 114 in Solon, Ohio, on August 31, 1935, to win the national all-bore with a score of 244 out of a possible 250. Second place was won by Phip Conway of Green Village, N.J., with 242 points. The women's title was won by Esther Abbie Ingalls of Hot Springs, Va., with a score of 95 out of 100.

SKI CLUB
Ski club association was the Central Organization, formed by ten clubs in 1891. The first meeting and tournament were held at Ishpeming, Mich., January 16, 1891. The National Ski Association of America was formed at Ishpeming, February 21, 1904, with Carl Tellefsen of Ishpeming as president.

Ski club (local) was the Nansen Ski Club of Berlin, N.H., formed January 15, 1882.

Ski club (local) that was active was the Aurora Ski Club, organized January 19, 1886, by twenty-eight men at Red Wing, Minn., with Christ Boxrud as the first president. Its first ski classic was held February 8, 1887, with two great Norwegian skiers, Mikkel and Torjus Hemmestvedt, participating.

SKI JUMP (steel) was built in November 1908 at Chippewa Falls, Wis. It was 98 feet high with a concrete foundation above the ground to make it 100 feet. In 1910, the national ski tournament was held on this jump.

SKI MEET (international) of importance was held February 10-13, 1932, at Lake Placid, N.Y., during the Olympic Games. Finland and Sweden each won an event and Norway two events.

SKI TOW (rope) was built by Robert Royce and placed in operation January 28, 1934, at Woodstock, Vt. About 900 yards of ⅞-inch manila rope was spliced together, passed over pulleys and around a wheel attached to a tractor, and extended up the hill 300 yards. (*Ski Bulletin. Vol. 4. No. 7 February 2, 1934*)

SKIMOBILE was invented in 1937 by George Morton of Goodrich Falls, N.H., and a 3,000 foot section was placed in operation December 27, 1938, by Cranmore Skimobiles Inc., at North Conway, N.H. One hundred and fifty toy cars, each seating one or two persons, were conveyed up a wide wood and steel trestle by a 6,000-foot endless steel cable, ⅞ inch in diameter, which was propelled by electric motors. On August 1, 1939, another 2,000-foot unit was added to propel 60 cars from the halfway station to the summit of Cranmore Mountain. The system had a capacity of 1,000 passengers per hour. The vertical lift from bottom to top was 1,367 feet.

SKIN GRAFTING. *See* Surgical operation: Skin grafting

SKY-TRAIN FLIGHT. *See* Aviation—Flights: Sky-train international round-trip flight

SKYSCRAPER. *See* Building: Building known as a skyscraper

SKYWRITING
Skywriting was accomplished over New York City on November 28, 1922, by Captain Cyril Turner, Royal Air Force, who wrote "Hello, U.S.A." The following month skywriting was employed commercially.

Skywriting at night was exhibited by Andy Stinis of the Skywriting Corporation of America over New York City on September 18, 1937, when he wrote "Green River" for Oldtyme Distillers, Inc. The material used was the same as in the daytime and showed only when the moon was bright.

SLALOM OLYMPIC CHAMPION. *See* Olympic Games: Woman slalom Olympic champion (American)

SLANDER PROCEEDINGS were instituted September 17, 1607, by John Robinson who accused Edward Maria Wingfield, the first governor of the Jamestown, Va., colony "of having said he, with others, consented to run awaye with the shallop to Newfoundland." A verdict was rendered in favor of Robinson. (*Edward Maria Wingfield—A Discourse of Virginia*)

SLATE used for roofing material was obtained from Delta, Pa., and Cardiff, Md., in 1734 by William and James Reese. (*Mining World. July 30, 1910*)

SLAVERY
Anti-slavery book was published in Boston in 1833 by Allen & Ticknor. It was written by Lydia Maria Francis Child and entitled *An Appeal in Favor of That Class of Americans Called Africans.*

Anti-slavery magazine was *The Emancipator*, issued from April 30, 1820, to October

31, 1820. It was edited and published by Elihu Embree in Jonesboro, Tenn. It was a monthly and cost $1.00 a year

Anti-slavery newspaper. *See* Newspaper: Abolition newspaper

Anti-slavery senator. *See* Senator (U.S.): Senator elected on an anti-slavery ticket

Anti-slavery society. *See* Abolition society

Fugitive slave law (federal) was passed February 12, 1793 (1 Stat.L.302). It provided for the return of fugitives from justice and from labor: "No person held to service or labor in one state, under the laws thereof, escaping into another, shall, in consequence of any law or regulation therein, be discharged from such service or labor, but shall be delivered up on claim of the party to whom such service or labor may be due."

Insurrection of Negro slaves occurred in 1739 in South Carolina where they greatly outnumbered the whites. The riot was promptly quelled by Lieutenant Governor William Bull. (*South Carolina Historical and Genealogical Magazine. January 1900*)

Law regulating slavery was one of several "Acts and Orders made at the General Court of Election held at Warwick, R.I., this 18th day of May, anno 1652." It contained the following provision: "No blacke mankind or white . . . [may be] forced by covenant bond or otherwise to serve any man or his assignes longer than ten years, or until they come to be 24 years of age, if they be taken in under 14, from the time of their coming within the Liberties of the Collonie, and at the end or terme of ten years . . . [are to be set] free, as is the manner with the English servants. And that man that will not let them goe free, or shall sell them away elsewhere, to that end that they may be enslaved to others for a long time, he or they shall forfeit to the Collonie forty pounds."

Law (state) abolishing slavery was "an act for the gradual abolition of slavery," chapter 881, passed by the Pennsylvania Legislature March 1, 1780. (*Pennsylvania 10 Stat. L.67*)

Non-importation of slaves act was passed June 13, 1774, by the Rhode Island General Assembly in Newport, R.I. It provided that "No Negro or mulatto slave shall be brought in to this colony, and in case any slave shall be brought in, he or she shall be, and are hereby, rendered immediately free, so far as respects personal freedom, and the enjoyment of private property, in the same manner as the

THE FIRST

THE FIRST

SLAVERY—*Continued*
native Indians." *(Records of the Colony of Rhode Island and Providence Plantations. Vol. 7)*

Slave emancipated was Elizabeth Freeman, ("Marm Bett"), owned by Colonel Ashley of Sheffield, Mass., in 1780. Mrs. Ashley endeavored to strike her sister with a red hot poker. The slave interfered, received the blow, and ran away. Judge Theodore Sedgwick of Stockbridge, Mass., defended her in a trial in Great Barrington, Mass. He granted her freedom. She died in 1829 and was buried in the Sedgwick plot.

Slavery protest of importance was made February 18, 1688, by the German Friends at a meeting in Germantown, Pa. They protested against the "traffic in the bodies of men" and considered the question of the "lawfulness and unlawfulness of buying and keeping Negroes." Some of the protestants were Francis Daniel Pastorius, Dirck op den Graeff, Abraham op den Graeff, and Gerhard Hendricks. *(Rufus Matthew Jones—The Quakers in the American Colonies)*

Slaves were introduced in Jamestown, Va., in August 1619 by a Dutch man-of-war which sold twenty "Negars," to the planter colonists as slaves.

SLED (rocket). *See* Rocket sled: Rocket-driven sled on rails

SLED RUN. *See* Bobsled run

SLEEPING BERTHS (airplane). *See* Aviation: Airplane sleeping berths

SLEEPING CAR
Pullman sleeping car was "Old No. 9," built by Ben Field and George Mortimer Pullman in 1859 in Chicago, Ill., and placed in service September 1, 1859, on the Chicago and Alton Railroad between Bloomington, Ill., and Chicago, Ill. It was a reconstructed day coach, little more than half the length of present coaches. Except for wheels and axles, it was constructed almost entirely of wood. The roof was flat and so low that a tall man was likely to bump his head. The seats were adamantine. Two small wood-burning stoves furnished heat. The illumination was furnished by candles. There was a small lavatory at each end. The drinking faucet supplied water to a non-enclosed wash basin. There were ten upper and ten lower berths with mattresses and blankets but not sheets. The upper berth was suspended about half-way between the floor and ceiling at night, and by day was drawn up to the ceiling by pulleys. *(Pullman Company—Pullman Progress)*

Pullman sleeping car made entirely of steel was manufactured in 1907 and complied with the regulations of the Hudson and Manhattan Railroad System which specified that no combustible equipment be used in the Hudson River tubes. The 74-foot-long car, which was manufactured in Pullman, Ill., had a steel-sheeted exterior and electric light obtained from an axle device. It had a low pressure vapor heat system. *(Pullman Company—Evolution of the Pullman Car)*

Pullman sleeping car that was comfortable was "The Pioneer," built by George Mortimer Pullman in 1865 in Chicago, Ill., at a cost of $18,000. It rested on sixteen wheels, an experiment later abandoned in favor of twelve, the present standard. The car was longer, higher, and wider than its predecessors and had the first raised upper deck and folding upper berth. It was heated by hot air furnaces under the floor, lighted with candles, and ventilated through deck windows. It was fully carpeted, and the seats were covered with French plush upholstery. *(Pullman Company—A Pioneer's Centennial)*

Sleeping car was used in 1836 by the Cumberland Valley Railroad between Harrisburg and Chambersburg in Pennsylvania. It included four sleeping sections, each section with three bunks. No bedding was provided, and it was common for persons traveling to carry shawls which they drew over themselves when lying down in their clothes on the bunks.

Sleeping car patent was granted to Henry B. Myer of Buffalo, N.Y., on September 19, 1854 (No.11,699), for a "mode of converting the backs of car seats into beds or lounges."

Transcontinental through Pullman sleeping car service (standard, daily, without change of cars) was inaugurated March 30, 1946, between New York City and Los Angeles, Calif. The "Imperial Forest," an all-room sleeping car of the Twentieth Century Limited left at 5:30 P.M. and arrived at Los Angeles April 3, 1946, 11:50 A.M., attached to the Santa Fe Chief. The hook-up and transfer were made at Chicago, Ill. Similar service started from Los Angeles. The first car arriving in New York City was the Pullman "Moencopi." This service was discontinued April 27, 1958.

SLEEVE INSIGNIA (U.S. Army). *See* Army insignia: Shoulder sleeve insignia

SLICING MACHINE was patented November 4, 1873, by Anthony Iske of Lancaster, Pa., who obtained patent No. 144,206 on a "machine for slicing dried beef." It employed an oblique knife in a vertical sliding frame.

SLITTING MILL (iron). *See* Iron: Iron slitting mill

SMALL CLAIMS COURT. *See* Court: Small debtors' court established by state law

SMALL DEBTORS' COURT. *See* Court: Small debtors' court established by state law

SMALLPOX EPIDEMIC. *See* Epidemic: Smallpox epidemic

SMALLPOX INOCULATION. *See* Vaccination for smallpox

SMOKE SCREEN used for concealing the movement of troops and ships was invented in 1923 by Thomas Buck Hine. It was first demonstrated publicly on September 5, 1923, during naval bombing tests off Cape Hatteras, N.C.

SNAKE (cobra). *See* Cobra: King cobra snakes

SNOW
  Artificial snow from a natural cloud was produced November 13, 1946, by Vincent Joseph Schaefer of the General Electric Company who flew in an airplane over Mt. Greylock, Mass. He dispensed small dry-ice pellets over a tract about three miles long from a height of about 14,000 feet. Snow fell an estimated 3,000 feet, but because of the dry condition of the atmosphere beneath the cloud it evaporated before reaching the ground. Previously, on July 12, 1946, Schaefer had produced snow in a coldchamber.

SNOW CRUISER (automobile) for antarctic travel was designed by the staff of the Research Foundation of the Armour Institute of Technology, Chicago, Ill., under the direction of Dr. Thomas Charles Poulter. Built at a cost of $150,000, it was 55 feet 8 inches long and 19 feet 10½ inches wide and contained living quarters, a combination galley and darkroom, a two-way radio station, an engine room, a scientific laboratory, a machine shop, and a control room. It moved for the first time under its own power October 22, 1939, in Chicago. On October 24, the Snow Cruiser was driven to Boston, Mass., where it arrived November 12, 1939, to sail November 15, 1939. on the "North Star" for the Antarctic.

SNOW GOOSE. *See* Birds: Snow goose

SNOW-MELTING APPARATUS
  Snow-melting apparatus was patented by Nicholas H. Borgfeldt of New York City, who obtained patent No. 88,693 on April 6, 1869. The device combined a sieve and a

heated surface. A mass of snow was subdivided into flakes by a sieve and then melted by a heated surface.

  Snow-melting apparatus (practical) with pipe imbedded in the sidewalk was tested December 8, 1946, and in actual operation during a blizzard on December 26, 1946. Best & Company, a department store in New York City, installed a system of fifteen coils comprising 4,530 feet of pipe. A solution of about 67 per cent water and 33 per cent Zerex by volume was circulated as protection against freezing temperatures as low as 5 degrees below zero.

SNOWSHOE production for commercial purposes was undertaken in 1862 in Norway, Me., by Alanson Millen Dunham, Jr. *(Charles Foster Whitman—History of Norway)*

SOAP
  Cakes of soap of uniform weight and individually wrapped were manufactured by Jessie Oakley of Newburgh, N.Y., about 1830. Cakes had been sold to grocers in large blocks from which pieces were cut as desired. Oakley prepared one-pound packages. *(Ignatius Valerius Stanley Stanislaus and P. B. Meerbott—American Soap Maker's Guide)*

  Soap in liquid form was patented August 22, 1865, by William Sheppard of New York City, who was granted patent No. 49,561. It was made by mixing one pound of common soap with one hundred pounds of ammonia solution or spirits of hartshorn. The soap was dissolved in water or by steam to the consistency of molasses.

  Soap powder in packages was introduced by Benjamin Talbert Babbitt about 1845. Rather than remelt the waste shavings of soap, he packaged the shavings in boxes ranging in contents from 1½ to 2 pounds. This innovation met with instantaneous success at laundries and hotels.

  Soap to float was made in 1878 by the Procter & Gamble Company, Cincinnati, Ohio. It was known as "White Soap" until October 1879, when it was renamed "Ivory Soap." A trademark was obtained July 18, 1879, and on December 21, 1882, the slogan "99 ⁴⁴/₁₀₀% Pure" was introduced.

SOAP MANUFACTURER to render fats in his plant for soap stock was William Colgate, who opened a factory in 1806 at 6 Dutch Street, New York City. He had learned his trade at 50 Broadway, New York City, in the plant of John Slidell & Company. *(Ignatius Valerius Stanley Stanislaus and P. B. Meerbott —American Soap Maker's Guide)*

THE FIRST

THE FIRST

SOCIAL DEMOCRACY OF AMERICA PARTY was formed by the Brotherhood of the Cooperative Commonwealth organized by Julius Augustus Wayland and members of the American Railway Union. The first national convention was held June 7, 1898 in Chicago, Ill.

SOCIAL-DEMOCRATIC PARTY OF AMERICA was formed in 1898 by Eugene Victor Debs, Victor Louis Berger, and Seymour Stedman, dissenters from the Social Democracy of America party. The first convention was held in Rochester, N.Y., January 27, 1900. Eugene Victor Debs was the presidential candidate and Job Harriman the vice presidential nominee. The party received a popular vote of less than 100,000 compared with 7,200,000 cast for William McKinley of Ohio, the Republican candidate.

SOCIAL FRATERNITY. *See* Fraternity (Greek letter) : Social fraternity

SOCIAL REGISTER published was the *Society List and Club Register for the Season of 1886-7,* compiled by the Society List Publishing Company, New York City. It cost $3 and contained 381 pages, 276 pages being devoted to a list of marriages, deaths, subscription balls, and a directory of clubs and names, and 105 pages to advertisers and advertisements.

SOCIAL SCIENCE DOCTORATE. *See* Degrees (academic and honorary): Doctor of Social Science degree

SOCIAL SCIENCE SOCIETY (national) was the American Social Science Association, founded in 1865 and incorporated by act of Congress of January 28, 1899 (30 Stat.L.804). An outgrowth of it was the National Institute of Social Sciences, organized in 1912 as a department, Hamilton Wright Mabie serving as president from October 1912 to October 1915. The first annual meeting was held March 20, 1914 in New York City. The federal charter was amended by act of Congress, June 16, 1926 (44 Stat.L.751). Since then the National Institute of Social Sciences has operated as the main organization.

SOCIAL SECURITY ACT (U.S.) was approved by President Franklin Delano Roosevelt August 14, 1935 (49 Stat.L.620). It authorized the appointment of a Social Security Board of three members. The first appointments were those of John Gilbert Winant, chairman (6 years) ; Arthur Joseph Altmeyer (4 years) ; and Vincent Morgan Miles (2 years). The board administered grants-in-aid to the states which approved plans for assistance to the needy aged, the blind, and dependent children; approved state unemployment compensation laws for tax credit and for administrative grants; and administered a federal system of old-age benefits. The first unemployment compensation law approved by the Board was enacted November 15, 1935, by the District of Columbia. Several groups of unemployment insurance cards were issued simultaneously so that it is not known to whom the first social security card was issued. The first beneficiary of monthly social security payments was Ida M. Fuller of Ludlow, Vt., who received check No. 00-000-001 for $22.54, dated January 31, 1940. Payments of various amounts had been made previously to individuals who did not have sufficient quarters of coverage or who did not qualify for monthly benefits.

SOCIAL SERVICE ENDOWMENT was the White-Williams Foundation, established in February 1800 as the Magdalen Society, a Home for Girls, for the purpose of "providing more normal opportunities of development and inculcating good habits." The society was incorporated March 23, 1802. On September 16, 1918, the corporate name was amended to the White-Williams Foundations for Girls, and again to the White-Williams Foundation, by decree of July 6, 1920. *(Frederick Paul Keppel —The Foundation)*

SOCIALIST CONGRESSMAN. *See* Congressman (U.S.): Socialist congressman

SOCIALIST LABOR PARTY OF NORTH AMERICA was formed July 4, 1874, as the Social Democratic Workmen's Party of North America. The name was changed in December 1877. The first national convention was held in Newark, N.J., on December 26, 1877. Simon Wing of Boston, Mass., and Charles Horatio Matchett of New York, the party's first presidential and vice presidential candidates, received 21,512 votes in the election held November 8, 1892. Grover Cleveland, the Democratic candidate, received 5,550,000 votes.

SOCIALIST PARTY was formed March 25, 1900, in Indianapolis, Ind., by a group of secessionists from the Socialist Labor Party, led by Morris Hillquit, who united with the Social-Democratic Party led by Eugene Victor Debs and Victor Louis Berger. The first national convention was held in Indianapolis, May 1, 1904.

SOCIETIES. *See* under names or types of organizations, e.g., academic, athletic, charitable, fraternal, professional, religious, scientific, service.

SOCIETY FOR THE RELIEF OF FREE NEGROES UNLAWFULLY HELD IN BONDAGE. *See* Abolition society

SOCIETY OF THE CINCINNATI. *See* War veterans society: Society of the Cincinnati

SOCIOLOGICAL SOCIETY

Sociological society (national) was the American Sociological Society, organized in Baltimore, Md., in December 1905, for the "encouragement of sociological research and discussion, and the promotion of intercourse between persons engaged in the scientific study of society." The first president was Lester Frank Ward. The first annual meeting was held in Providence, R.I., December 27-29, 1906. (*American Sociological Society. Papers and Proceedings 1906. Vol 1*)

SOCIOLOGY PROFESSOR was Albion Woodbury Small, appointed Professor and Head of the Department of Sociology at the University of Chicago, Chicago, Ill., effective October 1, 1892. Small held the position until his retirement on October 1, 1925. (He was also Dean of the Graduate School of Arts and Literature from 1905 to 1923.) A course in sociology had been offered at Bryn Mawr in 1892 by Franklin Henry Giddings, Associate Professor of Political Science.

SOCIOLOGY TREATISE was *A Treatise on Sociology; Theoretical and Practical* (292 pages), by Henry Hughes of Mississippi published in Philadelphia, Pa., in 1854. (*Mississippi Valley Historical Association Proceedings, 1914-1915*)

SODA FOUNTAIN

Ornamented soda fountain was made of white Italian marble and produced in 1858 by Gustavus D. Dows of Lowell, Mass. Typically American in design, it was adorned with spread eagles perched on the syrup cocks. In 1862, Dows invented the double-stream draft arm and cock, which allowed the use of a large or small stream. In 1863, Dows embarked on the manufacture of these fountains, which he sold for $225 each. His first patent was No. 99,170, which he obtained January 25, 1870.

Soda fountain patent was granted April 24, 1833, to Jacob Ebert of Cadiz, Ohio, and George Dulty of Wheeling, W.Va. (*Journal of the Franklin Institute. Vol. 16*)

SODA (ice cream). *See* Ice cream soda

SODA WATER

Soda water was prepared by Townsend Speakman of Philadelphia, Pa., who carbonated water for Dr. Philip Syng Physick. In 1807 Speakman added fruit juices to make it more palatable. The first soda water was dispensed regularly to patients from fountains at $1.50 a month for one glass a day.

Soda water commercially bottled was a carbonated water prepared in 1835 by Elias Durand at Philadelphia, Pa. (*First Century of the Philadelphia College of Pharmacy*)

SODA WATER MACHINE MANUFACTURER was John Matthews, who opened an establishment in New York City in 1834 exclusively for the manufacture of soda water apparatus. Various types of machines for making carbonated beverages had been made previously, however.

SODIUM REACTOR. *See* Atomic reactor: Sodium reactor (experimental)

SODIUM VAPOR LAMPS. *See* Electric lighting: Sodium vapor lamps

SOFT FELT HATS FOR WOMEN. *See* Hat: Soft felt hats for women

SOFTBALL (indoor baseball game) was played November 30, 1887, at the Farragut Boat Club, Chicago, Ill. The game was invented by George W. Hancock. A broomstick was used for the bat and a boxing glove for the ball. The game was named "softball" by Walter C. Hakanson. (*George W. Hancock—Indoor Baseball Guide*)

SOIL CONFERENCE. *See* Agricultural soil conference

SOILLESS CULTURE OF PLANTS

Commercial hydroponicum built on the roof of a building was erected in 1936 in Seattle, Wash., by George O. Brehm.

Commercial hydroponicum (large) was established in Montebello, Calif., on December 5, 1935, by Ernest Walfrid Brundin and Frank Farrington Lyon, who installed a circulating system. They obtained patent No. 2,062,755 on December 1, 1936, on a "system of water culture" and incorporated the company October 19, 1937, as the Chemi-Culture Company.

Commercial production of plants in water instead of soil was undertaken by the firm of Vetterle and Reinelt of Capitola, Calif., in February 1934. They constructed a greenhouse 100 by 33 feet, with 100 tanks. The first planting consisted of about 2,000 begonias, which, as a result of exact regulation of humidity and food supply, grew more rapidly than if soil-planted. On October 12, 1935, tomato plantings were made which grew to 15 feet in height within six or eight months.

Hydroponic description was William Frederick Gericke's "Aquaculture, A Means of Crop Production," published December 1929 in

SOILLESS CULTURE OF PLANTS—
—*Continued*
the *American Journal of Botany* (Vol. 16. No. 10, p. 862). The term "hydroponics" for soilless crop production was first used in Gericke's article "Hydroponics—Crop Production in Liquid Culture Media," published February 12, 1937, in *Science* (Vol. 85. No. 2198. p. 177). Previously, crops had been grown in sand beds, mounted over nutrient solutions held in tanks. (*A. H. Phillips—Gardening Without Soil*)

Private soilless garden to grow vegetables and flowers was created in 1931 by William Frederick Gericke at his home in Berkeley, Calif. (*New York Times Mid-Week Pictorial. October 8, 1932*)

SOLAR BATTERY. *See* Battery: Solar battery

SOLAR ENERGY BATTERY. *See* Battery: Solar energy battery

SOLAR-HEATED BUILDING. *See* Building: Commercial building heated by the sun; Building: Solar-heated and radiation-cooled house

SOLAR MOTION PICTURES. *See* Moving picture: Moving picture of the sun

SOLAR ORBIT. *See* Rocket: Satellite placed in solar orbit

SOLDIER VOTE. *See* Army vote

SOLDIERS' HOMES (national) put into operation in 1867 were the Eastern Home, Togus, Me.; the Central Home, Dayton, Ohio; and the Northwestern Home, Milwaukee, Wis. These were authorized by act of Congress of March 21, 1866 (14 Stat.L.10), an "act to incorporate a national military and naval asylum for the relief of the totally disabled officers and men of the volunteer forces of the United States." (*Records in Bureau of National Homes. Veterans Administration Bureau. Washington, D.C.*)

SOLDIERS' MEDAL. *See* Medal: Soldiers' medal

SOLICITOR GENERAL of the United States was Benjamin Helm Bristow, who was appointed October 4, 1870, by President Ulysses Simpson Grant and who served to November 12, 1872. (*David Willcox. Memorial of B. H. Bristow*)

SOLO AIRPLANE FLIGHT AROUND THE WORLD. *See* Aviation—Flights (world): World solo airplane flight

SONG. *See* National anthem; *also* under Music

SORORITY
See also Women's club: Women's secret society

Negro sorority was the Alpha Kappa Alpha sorority, founded January 15, 1908, at Howard University, Washington, D.C., by Ethel Hedgeman Lyle. The first officers were Lucy Slowe, president; Ethel Hedgeman Lyle, vice president; Marie Woolfolk, secretary; and Anna Brown, treasurer. On January 29, 1913, the sorority was incorporated in the District of Columbia.

Sorority (women's Greek-letter society) was Kappa Alpha Theta which was founded January 27, 1870, at Indiana Asbury University, now De Pauw University, in Greencastle, Ind. Kappa Kappa Gamma Sorority of Monmouth, Ill., was organized in March 1870, but was not brought to public notice until October 13, 1870. (*William Raimond Baird—American College Fraternities*)

SOS. *See* Radio distress signal

SOUND-ABSORBING MATERIAL (rigid insulating board) perfected for use in buildings was invented by Carl Gebhard Muench of St. Paul, Minn., who obtained patent No. 1,153,512 on September 14, 1915, on a "thermo non-conductor" known as "Insulite." The invention consisted of a rigid thermal insulation with groundwood screenings as a fiber source. The first board machine built to make a fibrous board in one thick continuous layer was installed in International Falls, Minn., where production was started May 15, 1914. Sugar cane bagasse was also found to be a satisfactory fiber for making insulation board and its manufacture was begun on August 10, 1921 in Marrero, La., by the Celotex Corporation of Chicago, Ill., under the trade name of "Celotex."

SOUND MECHANISM TO CREATE SPEECH SOUNDS. *See* Voice mechanism: Voice mechanism capable of creating the complex sounds of speech

SOUND-ON-FILM MOVING PICTURE. *See* Moving picture: Sound-on-film moving picture

SOUP COMPANY to introduce and market "finished" or "liquid" soups was the Franco-American Food Company of New York City, which was organized in November 1886 by Alphonse Biardot and his sons, Ernest and Octava.

THE FIRST

THE FIRST

SOUSAPHONE was manufactured by the C. G. [Charles Gerard] Conn Company, Ltd., Ekhart, Ind., from designs suggested by John Philip Sousa. The first model was the "bell up" type. The first "bell front" instrument, such as those used today, was made in 1908.

SOUTH POLE FLIGHT. *See* Aviation—Flights: South Pole flight

SOUTH POLE LANDING. *See* Discovery: American to land by air at the South Pole

SOYBEAN PROCESSING PLANT (commercially successful) was built by Augustus Eugene Staley in Decatur, Ill., in 1922. The beans were run through an expeller, the oil removed to within 4 per cent, and the residue or cake sold to the feed industry for use in commercial feeds or to farmers, who mixed the meal with other ingredients as a protein supplement.

SPA opened to the public was deeded to the colony of Virginia in 1756 by Thomas Fairfax, sixth Baron Fairfax, "to be forever free to the publick for the welfare of suffering humanity." (George Washington had visited the mineral springs on March 18, 1748.) The spa was located in Bath, Berkeley County, Va. (now Berkeley Springs, Morgan County, W.Va.) and was chartered in October 1776. The water, which has a temperature of 110 degrees, has been discovered to be radioactive. *(Bulletin of the History of Medicine. Vol. 11. No. 2. February 1942)*

SPACE AGENCY (U.S.) was the National Aeronautics and Space Administration, authorized by the National Aeronautics and Space Act of July 29, 1958 (72 Stat.L.426). It was controlled by a civilian administrator, who received a salary of $22,500, and a deputy administrator, who received $21,500. On August 19, 1958, Thomas Keith Glennan was sworn in as administrator and Hugh Latimer Dryden as deputy administrator.

SPACE CABIN was the space cabin simulator, a hermetically sealed cabin with equipment which supplied oxygen, removed waste products by chemical means, and recirculated body moisture to cool the cabin. It was used at the School of Aviation Medicine, U.S. Air Force, Randolph Air Force Base, Tex. Simulated in the cabin were the same climatic conditions that an astronaut would meet in the sealed cabin of a rocket ship in space. The first person to spend twenty-four hours within the cabin, living in outer-space conditions, was Dalton F. Smith of New Orleans, La., an aeromedical technician, who was observed through glass ports from 3 P.M. on March 31, 1956, to 3 P.M. on April 1, 1956.

SPACE FLIGHT. *See* Astronauts: Space flight by an American astronaut

SPACE ORBIT CAPSULE. *See* Rocket: Space capsule recovered from an orbiting satellite

SPANISH-AMERICAN WAR
 Army officer killed in battle in the Spanish-American war was Captain Allen Kissam Capron, who was killed in action on June 24, 1898, at Las Guásimas, Cuba.

 Balloon destroyed by enemy gunfire. *See* Balloon: Balloon destroyed by enemy gunfire

 Naval officer killed in the Spanish-American war was Ensign Worth Bagley, executive officer of the U.S.S. "Winslow," commanded by Lieutenant John Baptiste Bernadou. The "Winslow," which had been sent to the wharves at Cárdenas, Cuba, for a closer inspection of the docks, was fired upon May 11, 1898, simultaneously by a shore battery and a Spanish gunboat. *(John Randolph Spears—Our Navy in the War with Spain)*

 Ship captured in the Spanish-American war was the Spanish "Buena Ventura," which was taken April 22, 1898, by the gunboat "Nashville." Spain declared that war existed with the United States on April 24, three days after United States Minister Stewart Lyndon Woodford's passports had been returned to him. On April 25 Congress declared that a state of war had existed since April 21. Sentiment against Spain was inflamed by the destruction of the battleship "Maine," which had blown up mysteriously on February 15 in the harbor of Havana, Cuba, with a loss of about 260 American crewmen. *(French Ensor Chadwick—Relations of the United States and Spain)*

 Soldier killed in the Spanish-American war was George Burton Meek, who lost his life in action on board the torpedo boat "Winslow" May 11, 1898. A monument was erected to his memory in the McPherson Cemetery, Clyde, Ohio. *(Records in Office of Naval Records and Library. Department of the Navy)*

 Spanish-American land engagement took place June 24, 1898, at Las Guásimas, Cuba, in which the 1st Cavalry, the 10th Cavalry, and the Rough Riders, all unmounted, took part. Juragua was captured and eleven Spanish dead were left on the field. Sixteen Americans were killed and fifty-two wounded. *(Herbert Howland Sargent—Campaign of Santiago de Cuba)*

SPANISH-AMERICAN WAR MONUMENT. See Monument: Monument to the memory of the soldiers and sailors of the Spanish-American war

THE FIRST

THE FIRST

SPANISH MAGAZINE PUBLISHED BY STUDENTS. *See* Periodical: Spanish magazine published by students

SPANISH NEWSPAPER. *See* Newspaper: Spanish newspaper

SPARROW. *See* Birds: Sparrows

SPARS. *See* Coast Guard (U.S.): Coast Guard women's reserve

SPEAKER (House of Representatives). *See* Congress (U.S.)—House of Representatives: Speaker of the House

SPECIAL DELIVERY SERVICE. *See* Postal service: Special delivery service

SPECTROPHOTOMETER was invented by Professor Arthur Cobb Hardy of Wellesley, Mass., who received patent No. 1,987,441 on January 8, 1935, on a "photometric apparatus." This electronic device detected 2,000,000 different shades of color and produced for permanent records a chart of each color. The patent was assigned to the General Electric Company, Schenectady, N.Y., which sold the first machine May 24, 1935. *(Journal of the Optical Society of America—Feb. 1929)*

SPECULATORS (ticket). *See* Ticket speculators

SPEED-BOAT. *See* Ship: Speed-boat to exceed 200 miles an hour

SPEED LAW. *See* Traffic regulation: Traffic law

SPEEDING ARREST. *See* Automobile speeding arrest

SPELLING BOOK was printed by Stephen Day in 1643 in Cambridge, Mass.

SPELLING REFORM ADVOCATE was Benjamin Franklin, who in 1768 wrote *A Scheme for a New Alphabet and Reformed Mode of Spelling; with Remarks and Examples.* He advocated dropping C, J, Q, W, X, and Y from the alphabet and substituting six other characters so "that there be no distinct sounds in the language without letters to express them." *(Noah Webster—Dissertations on the English Language)*

SPERM WHALE. *See* Whale: Sperm whale

SPERMACETI CANDLE FACTORY. *See* Candle factory

SPINAL ANESTHESIA REPORT. *See* Anesthesia: Spinal anesthesia report

SPINET. *See* Piano

SPINNING (brass). *See* Brass spinning

SPINNING, CARDING, AND ROPING MACHINES were manufactured in 1786 by Hugh Orr with the help of Robert Barr and Alexander Barr in their workshop in Bridgewater, Mass. On November 16, 1786, the Senate granted them £200 for their ingenuity and afterwards granted them a further compensation of six tickets in the land lottery of that period. *(Nahum Mitchell—History of the Early Settlement of Bridgewater, Mass.)*

SPINNING JENNY. *See* Cotton spinning jenny

SPIRITUALIST was John D. Fox of Hydeville, Wayne County, N.Y., whose house in 1848 was the mecca of the curious who wanted to hear spirit knockings and rappings. Fox's daughters, Margaret and Catherine, continued his work and acted as mediums. *(Buffalo Medical Journal. March 1851)*

SPITTING LEGISLATION. *See* Health ordinance

SPLIT-SCREEN IMAGE. *See* Television —Telecast: Split-screen image

SPLITTING MACHINE (leather). *See* Leather: Leather-splitting machine

SPOILS SYSTEM was introduced by President Andrew Jackson as a reward to Simon Cameron of Pennsylvania and other supporters for their political assistance. Jackson served as President from March 4, 1829, to March 3, 1837. *(Thomas Edward Watson—Life and Times of Andrew Jackson)*

SPONGE
Oxidized cellulose (sponge) was made in 1936 by Dr. William Orlin Kenyon of the Tennessee Eastman Company, Kingsport, Tenn., a division of the Eastman Kodak Company, Rochester, N.Y.

Oxidized cellulose (sponge) for medical and surgical use was marketed by Parke Davis & Company, Detroit, Mich., under the trademark "Oxycel," on June 5, 1946. It is a hemostatic material in the form of surgical dressings, which, when left in contact with incised body tissues, convert to an absorbable form. *(Industrial and Engineering Chemistry. Vol. 41. January 1949)*

THE FIRST

SPOONS

Nickel silver spoons were manufactured by Robert Wallace of Wallingford, Conn., in 1835. Spoons previously had been made of silver or pewter. Nickel silver or German silver consisted of two parts copper, one part nickel, and one part zinc fused together.

SPORTS

See also under names of specific games and sports, e.g., Baseball, Boat race, Polo; *also* under Radio; Television—Telecast

Amateur athletic competition (inter-club) was held September 27, 1879, by the National Association of Amateur Athletes of America at the New York Athletic Club's grounds in Mott Haven, N.Y. Twenty games were on the program. *(Frederick William Janssen—A History of American Amateur Athletics and Aquatics)*

Amateur indoor athletic games were held November 11, 1868, by the New York Athletic Club at the Empire Skating Rink at 63rd Street and Third Avenue, New York City.

Amateur outdoor athletic games were held October 21, 1871, by the New York Athletic Club on its grounds at 130th Street and the Harlem River. This site was used afterwards for the foundations of the Harlem Bridge.

Athletic club was the New York Athletic Club, which was organized September 8, 1868, at the Knickerbocker Cottage, Sixth Avenue and 28th Street. The club was incorporated April 4, 1870.

Cross country championships were run November 6, 1883, under the auspices of the New York Athletic Club. *(New York Athletic Club, 1929)*

Sports trainer (professional) was Bob Rogers, who was engaged by the New York Athletic Club on May 1, 1883. Previous to this he was with the London Athletic Club.

Sports writer. *See* Author: Sports writer

SPORTS BOOK of importance was *The Sportsman's Companion, or, an essay on shooting; illustratiously shewing in what manner to fire at birds of game, in various directions and situations—and, directions to gentlemen for the treatment and breaking their own pointers and spaniels.* The book was published in 1783 in New York City.

SPORTS MAGAZINE was the *American Turf Register and Sporting Magazine*, published in Baltimore, Md., by John Stuart Skin-

THE FIRST

ner. The first issue appeared in September 1829 and contained 56 pages. Its purpose was "to serve as an authentic record of the performances and pedigrees of the bred horse." *(Benjamin Perley Poore—Biographical Sketch of John Stuart Skinner)*

SPORTS TROPHY

Negro to win the James E. Sullivan Memorial Trophy, the top award for United States amateur athletes, presented annually since 1930 by the Amateur Athletic Union, was Malvin Greston (Mal) Whitfield of the Los Angeles Athletic Club, a half-miler, who was the first choice on 252 of 657 ballots cast by a nation-wide tribunal of sports authorities and tabulated on December 30, 1954. Whitfield set the Olympic record for 800 meters in London in 1948 and held the world 880-yard record and the 600-yard indoor record.

SPOTTED FEVER TREATISE. *See* Medical book: Typhus fever treatise

SPRAYING DEVICE. *See* Paint spraying device

SPRING MANUFACTURER was Edward Lucian Dunbar, whose factory in Bristol, Conn., opened in 1845, and who specialized in coiled clock springs. They were tempered by a process invented by Silas Burnham Terry. At the time, weights were generally used in clocks, except smaller clocks, in which imported springs were used.

SPRING (oil). *See* Oil: Oil spring

SPRING WINDING MACHINE, in which the size of the spring helix was determined solely by the angle at which the wire was forced between guides, was developed and built in 1892 by Clinton S. Marshall of the Washburn and Moen Manufacturing Company, Worcester, Mass.

SPRINKLER

Sprinkler to be used was the perforated pipe system invented by James Bichens Francis. The first installation was made in 1852 at the plant of the Proprietors of the Locks and Canals on the Merrimack River at Lowell, Mass. *(American Academy of Arts and Sciences, Proceedings. Vol. 28)*

Sprinkler head was invented by Henry S. Parmelee of New Haven, Conn., who obtained patent No. 154,076, August 11, 1874. It consisted of a perforated head containing a valve which was held closed against water pressure by a heavy spring made of low fusing material. *(Gorham Dana—Automatic Sprinkler Protection)*

SPRINKLER—*Continued*

Sprinkler system patent was No. 131,370, granted to Philip W. Pratt of Abington, Mass., September 17, 1872. The system operated by means of a valve to which cords and fuses were attached. When the cords and fuses melted, the valve opened, releasing a stream of water.

SPUN GLASS DRESS. *See* Glass dress of spun glass

SPY. *See* World War I: German spy to receive a death sentence from the American forces during World War I

SQUASH CLUB

Squash tennis organization (national) was the National Squash Tennis Association, formed by fourteen charter members March 20, 1911, at the Harvard Club of New York City. The officers were John W. Prentiss, president; Josiah O. Low, vice president; Dr. Alfred Stillman, secretary, and C. M. Bull, treasurer. (*National Squash Tennis Association Official Handbook 1912*)

SQUASH RACQUETS CHAMPION

Squash racquets champion to win the U.S.A. Squash Racquets Singles championship was John A. Miskey of the Overbrook Golf Club, Philadelphia, Pa., who won the championship in 1907.

Woman to win the U.S.A. Women's Squash Racquets Singles championship was Eleanora R. Sears of the Harvard Club, Boston, Mass., who won at the Round Hill Club, Greenwich, Conn., January 16-19, 1928. Forty players entered. Miss Sears won three of four matches with Miss A. Boyden of Boston, Mass.

SQUASH TOURNAMENT sponsored by the National Squash Tennis Association was held at the Harvard Club, New York City, April 8, 9, 10, 1911. Forty entries from thirteen clubs played. The champion was Dr. Alfred Stillman, 2d, who defeated J. W. Prentiss on April 10, 1911, by scores of 15-5 and 17-15.

STABILIZED AIRPLANE. *See* Aviation—Airplane: Airplane (commercial) stabilized

STADIUM

Cement stadium was the Harvard Stadium, Cambridge, Mass., constructed by the Aberthaw Construction Company, Boston, Mass., under the direction of Professor Lewis Jerome Johnson and Joseph Ruggles. The general architectural design was worked out by George Bruns de Gersdorff. The outer walls measured 527 by 420 feet and were divided into 37 reinforced concrete sections. The stadium was completed in the spring of 1904. Its capacity was 40,000.

The colonnade was added in 1910 and the steel stands in 1929. The first football game played there was the Harvard-Dartmouth game of November 14, 1903, won by Dartmouth, 11-0.

Municipal stadium was the Golden Gate Park Stadium, San Francisco, Calif., completed in 1907. It was oval shaped and covered a 30-acre field. It had two entrances, one on the north and one on the south side, through tunnels 20 feet wide and 10 feet high under a ¾-mile trotting track 60 feet wide which encircled the stadium. Bicycle races were held November 29, 1906, before completion.

School stadium was built in Tacoma, Wash., and was dedicated June 10, 1910. It was 250 feet wide at the narrowest point next to the curve and 400 feet wide at the open ends. It cost $150,000, of which $100,000 was borne by the School District and $50,000 was obtained through the sale of five-year passes at $10 each. Frederick Heath was the architect and L. A. Nicholson the engineer.

STAGE COACH INTER-CITY SERVICE was inaugurated November 9, 1756, between Philadelphia, Pa., and New York City by John Butler, Francis Holman, John Thompson, and William Waller.

STAINED GLASS. *See* Glass: Stained figure glass

STAINLESS STEEL HYDROPLANE. *See* Aviation—Airplane: Hydroplane of stainless steel

STAIRWAY (moving). *See* Escalator

STAMP. *See* Postage stamp

STAMP ACT REPUDIATION was made on November 23, 1765, by the Court of Frederick County, Frederick, Md. The British Stamp Act levied by England under King George III had placed a tax of one shilling on every pack of playing cards, ten shillings on every pair of dice, etc. These twelve "immortal judges" strenuously opposed England's impost legislation by declaring that "all proceedings shall be valid and effectual without the use of stamps." (*Souvenir of Historic Frederick—Marken and Bielfeld, Inc.*)

STAMP CATALOG. *See* Postage stamp catalog

STAMP (trading). *See* Trading stamp

STAMPED ENVELOPE. *See* Postage stamp: Stamped envelopes (U.S.)

THE FIRST

STANDARD TIME. *See* Time (standard)

STANDARDIZATION OF PRODUC-TION. *See* Factory standardization of production

STANDARDS BUREAU (U.S.) was established by act of Congress of March 3, 1901 (31 Stat.L.1449), effective July 1, 1901, which made the office of Standards, Weights and Measures a separate bureau. The first director was Samuel Wesley Stratton. Prior to this, the office of Standard Weights and Measures was a unit of the United States Coast and Geodetic Survey in the Treasury Department. On July 1, 1913, it became the National Bureau of Standards under the Department of Commerce.

STAR PHOTOGRAPH. *See* Photograph: Photograph of a star

"STAR SPANGLED BANNER." *See* National anthem

STARTING GATE (electric). *See* Electric starting gate

STATE
Noncontiguous overseas state was Hawaii, 2,090 miles across the Pacific from San Francisco, Calif. Voted into the Union by Congress March 12, 1959 (323 for, 89 against), Hawaii was admitted as the fiftieth state by proclamation of President Dwight David Eisenhower on August 21, 1959. A star was added to the American flag on July 4, 1960.

Noncontiguous state was Alaska, which was admitted as the 49th state on January 3, 1959, by proclamation of President Dwight David Eisenhower (73 Stat.L.c16). Alaska had become a territory August 24, 1912 (37 Stat.L.512). A constitution was approved by popular vote on April 24, 1956. It was ratified by the United States Congress on July 7, 1958 (72 Stat.L.339). Voters approved statehood on August 26, 1958, and the first state election was held November 25, 1958.

State admitted to the Union after the ratification of the Constitution by the original thirteen colonies was Vermont, on March 4, 1791. Statehood was authorized by Act of Congress of February 18, 1791 (1 Stat.L.191). Vermont was formed from the New Hampshire Grants, over which both New York and New Hampshire claimed jurisdiction. In 1777 it had declared herself an independent commonwealth, the Republic of Vermont, and elected Thomas Chittenden as the first governor. He was also the first state governor, serving to 1797. (*Hinland Hall—History of Vermont*)

THE FIRST

State admitted to the Union on the Pacific coast was California on September 9, 1850. The first state governor was Peter Hardeman Burnett, a Democrat, who served from 1849 to 1851. (*Hubert Howe Bancroft—History of California*)

State admitted to the Union west of the Mississippi River was Missouri, on August 10, 1821. The first governor of the new state was Alexander McNair, a Democrat, who served from 1820 to 1824. (Louisiana, the 18th state, admitted April 30, 1812, is both east and west of the Mississippi.) (*Perry Scott Rader—The History of Missouri*)

State constitution was that of Massachusetts, which was adopted on May 16, 1775, by the Provincial Congress of Massachusetts. The motto of the state was *Ense petit placidam sub libertate quietem*—"With the sword she seeks peace under liberty." The constitution was temporary. A new constitution was framed in Boston, September 1, 1779, and was completed March 2, 1780. It was ratified by a two-thirds vote. John Hancock served as the first governor under it. (*James Quayle Dealey—Our State Constitutions*)

State re-admitted to the Union after the Civil War was Tennessee, on July 24, 1866. A new constitution was adopted on January 9, 1865, and ratified on February 22, 1865. (*James Welch Patton—Unionism and Reconstruction in Tennessee 1860-1869*)

State to abolish both entail and primogeniture was Georgia, whose constitution of February 5, 1777, abrogated those two bulwarks of the ancient regime. (*Virginius Dabney—Liberalism in the South*)

State to provide universal manhood suffrage. *See* Suffrage: State to provide universal manhood suffrage

State to ratify the federal Constitution was Delaware, on December 7, 1787. The constitution was ratified December 6, 1787, and signed December 7, 1787, by all thirty members of the convention. Thomas Collins, who was president of Delaware at that time, automatically became the first state governor. (*George Herbert Ryden—Delaware, the First State in the Union*)

State to repudiate a debt was Mississippi in 1842. The sovereign state of Mississippi sold $5,000,000 worth of bonds in June 1838 to pay for 50,000 shares in the Union Bank of Mississippi. The bank became hopelessly insolvent in 1840, and in 1842 the legislature denied that the state was under legal or moral obligation to pay the bonds in question. (*William Amasa Scott—The Repudiation of State Debts*)

STATE—*Continued*
  State to secede from the Union. *See* Secession: Secession act

States admitted to the Union simultaneously were North and South Dakota. The Admission Act was signed February 22, 1889, by President Grover Cleveland. Each state held a constitutional convention beginning July 4, 1889 and both held the ratifying election October 1, 1889. President Benjamin Harrison signed the proclamations of admission without knowing which was which. Both states were admitted to the Union November 3, 1889. The first governor of North Dakota was John Miller, and of South Dakota Arthur Calvin Mellette, both Republicans. Washington and Montana were admitted by the same enabling act, but the proclamations were not signed until a few days later.

STATE ATLAS. *See* Atlas

STATE BOUNDARY DECISION. *See* Supreme Court (U.S.) decision: Supreme Court decision in a state boundary case

STATE CAPITOL. *See* Capitol

STATE COLLEGE FOR WOMEN. *See* College: State college for women

STATE COLLEGE OF AGRICULTURE. *See* Agricultural school: Agricultural college (state) to be chartered

STATE DEPARTMENT (U.S.)
  Consul under the Department of State. *See* Diplomatic service: Consul

State Department (U.S.) was established by an "act for establishing an executive department to be denominated the Department of Foreign Affairs," approved July 27, 1789 (1 Stat.L.28). The name was ordered changed to the Department of State by act approved September 15, 1789 (1 Stat.L.68).

State Department (U.S.) Negro official was Dr. Ralph Johnson Bunche, who was appointed January 4, 1944, as Divisional Assistant, Division of Political Studies, Department of State. On July 1, 1946, Dr. Bunche went on leave without pay from the Department of State to work with the United Nations. On March 23, 1947, he was transferred from the Department of State to the United Nations.

State Department (U.S.) Secretary was Thomas Jefferson, who was appointed by President George Washington. John Jay, who served as Secretary for Foreign Affairs for the Continental Congress from December 21, 1784, was

held over without appointment or commission and continued, though not officially, to superintend the department under the Constitution until Thomas Jefferson took office as Secretary of State on March 22, 1790. (*Gaillard Hunt—The Department of State of the United States*)

Woman Acting Assistant Secretary of State was Florence Kirlin of Indiana, who assumed the post on September 3, 1955, and served through November 30, 1955, during the absence of Thruston Ballard Morton, Assistant Secretary of State for Congressional Relations.

STATE LAW CODE. *See* Law codification (state)

STATE LEGISLATOR. *See* Legislator (state)

STATE MEDICINE AND PUBLIC HYGIENE PROFESSORSHIP. *See* Medical instruction: State medicine and public hygiene professorship

STATE MILITARY SCHOOL. *See* Military school: State military school

STATE PARK. *See* Park: State park

STATE POLICE. *See* Police: State police

STATE REFORMATORY FOR BOYS. *See* Prison: Reformatory for boys (state)

STATE TAX. *See under* Tax

STATE THEATER. *See* Theater: State-owned theater

STATE UNION CATALOG. *See* Library catalog: Union catalog of books by a state library

STATE UNIVERSITY. *See* College: State university chartered

STATISTICAL BOARD (central). *See* Central statistical board (U.S.)

STATISTICAL SOCIETY of importance was the American Statistical Association, organized November 27, 1839, in Boston, Mass., "to collect, preserve and diffuse statistical information in the different departments of human knowledge." A constitution was adopted December 11, 1839, and the association incorporated February 5, 1841. The first president was Richard Fletcher, who served from December 1839 to January 1844. The first annual meeting was held February 5, 1840 in Boston. (*John Korene—History of Statistics*)

THE FIRST

STATUARY GROUP. *See* Marble statuary group

STATUE. *See* Bronze statue; Monument

STATUS OF FORCES TREATY. *See* Treaty: Status of forces treaty

STEAM AUTOMOBILE. *See* Automobile: Steam automobile

STEAM BATHS. *See* Bathhouse: Steam baths for curing disease

STEAM DISTRIBUTION PLANT of importance was the New York Steam Corporation, 16 Cortlandt Street, New York City, formed July 26, 1880. The first boiler plant was erected in the block bounded by Cortlandt, Dey, Greenwich, and Washington Streets, and contained 48 boilers of 250 h.p. each. It had a chimney 225 feet high. On September 19, 1881, the company was consolidated with the Steam Heating and Power Company of New York, a smaller organization. The first distribution of steam from a central plant in New York City was made March 3, 1882, to the United Bank Building, 88-92 Broadway. Within nine months, the service had been extended to sixty-two customers. (*New York Steam Corporation—Fifty Years of New York Steam Service*)

STEAM-DRIVEN MOTORCYCLE. *See* Motorcycle: Motorcycle (steam-driven)

STEAM ELEVATOR. *See* Elevator: Elevator (suspended)

STEAM ENGINE
  Steam engine was imported from England. It was brought over by Josiah Hornblower, who has been recognized as America's first steam engineer. Hornblower left London on the S.S. "Irene" June 6, 1753, and arrived in New York City September 9, 1753. The engine was delivered to the copper mine of Colonel John Schuyler in New Barbadoes Neck, now North Arlington, N.J., September 25, 1753. Its only use was to pump water from the mine. It was assembled, installed, and placed in service on March 12, 1755. (*Leonor Fresnel Loree—First Steam Fire Engine in America*)

  Steam engine that was practical was manufactured by Oliver Evans of Philadelphia in 1795. In 1799 he introduced a high-pressure engine which because of its lightness and cheapness was ideally suited to the needs of the simple colonial industries. (*Journal of the Franklin Institute. July 1886*)

STEAM FIRE ENGINE. *See* Fire engine: Steam fire engine

THE FIRST

STEAM FRIGATE. *See* Ship: Frigate

STEAM-HEATED BUILDING. *See* Building: Building heated by steam

STEAM-HEATED FACTORY. *See* Factory: Steam-heated factory

STEAM HEATING SYSTEM. *See* Heating system: Heating system (steam)

STEAM LOCOMOTIVE. *See* Locomotive: Streamlined steam locomotive

STEAM-OPERATED AMPHIBIOUS VEHICLE was the "Orukter Amphibolos," or "amphibious digger," invented in 1805 by Oliver Evans of Philadelphia, Pa. He had been commissioned by the Philadelphia Board of Health to manufacture a scow, and he built a steam vehicle 30 feet long and 12 feet wide which was equipped with wheels so that it could be operated either on land or water. It was also equipped with a chain of buckets which brought up mud when it was employed as a scow. In July 1805 he propelled it a distance of about a mile and a half, from his shop to the Schuylkill River. There, by means of a stern paddle wheel, it was navigated down to the Delaware junction. (*Greville Bathe and Dorothy Bathe—Oliver Evans*)

STEAM PRESSING MACHINE. *See* Pressing machine

STEAM-PROPELLED FERRYBOAT. *See* Ferryboat: Steam-propelled ferryboat

STEAM-PROPELLED FRIGATE. *See* Ship: Steam-propelled frigate

STEAM SHOVEL was invented in 1838 by William S. Otis of Philadelphia, Pa., who obtained patent No. 1,089 on February 24, 1839, on a crane for excavating and removing earth. It was first used on the Western Railroad in Massachusetts. (*Civil Engineer and Architect's Journal. April 1843*)

STEAM THRESHING MACHINE. *See* Thresher: Threshing machine to employ steam

STEAM TRACTOR. *See* Automobile tractor: Steam tractor

STEAM TUGBOAT. *See* Ship: Tugboat (steam)

STEAM TURBINE. *See* Turbine: Steam turbine

STEAM WHALER. *See* Ship: Steam whaler

STEAM WHISTLE (locomotive). *See* Locomotive steam whistle

STEAMBOAT. *See* under Ship

STEAMBOAT INSPECTION SERVICE (U.S.) was established by act of Congress, July 7, 1838 (5 Stat.L.304) for the "better security of the lives of passengers on board of vessels propelled in whole or in part by steam." Inspectors were appointed by district judges of U.S. Courts and received $5 for each inspection. They gave the owners a certificate stating the age of the boat and soundness of the vessel. An annual inspection was required. (*Lloyd Milton Short—Steamboat Inspection Service*)

STEAMER CHAIR. *See* Chair: Steamer chair

STEAMSHIP. *See* under Ship

STEEL
Armor plate contract (U.S. Navy). *See* Armor plate contract (U.S. Navy)

Bessemer steel converter used commercially was erected by the Eureka Iron and Steel Works in 1864 in Wyandotte, Mich., on the site of what is now the public library. The steel was made in a 2½-ton experimental converter by William Franklin Durfee by means of the Kelly-pneumatic process.

Bessemer steel track. *See* Railroad track: Railroad rails of Bessemer steel

Building of pressed structural steel. *See* Building: Building of pressed structural steel

Cast steel for plows was made by William Woods at the steel works of Jones and Quigg, Pittsburgh, Pa., in 1846. The plows were made by John Deere at Moline, Ill. (*James Moore Swank—History of the Manufacture of Iron in All Ages*)

Continuous sheet steel mill was designed by John Butler Tytus and built by the American Rolling Mill Company, Ashland, Ky., in 1922. The mill consisted of an arrangement of machines that passed sheet steel through a series of mills in a tandem train at a high speed. The process replaced the older and much slower methods. Operations began in 1924.

Manganese steel was manufactured in 1892 by the Taylor Iron and Steel Company in High Bridge, N.J.

Manganese steel for railroad tracks was manufactured August 28, 1894, by William Wharton, Jr. and Co., Inc., in High Bridge, N.J. The first rail frog with a cast manganese steel plate was installed at Fulton Street and Boerum Place, Brooklyn, N.Y.

Open hearth furnace for the manufacture of steel by the Siemens-Martin process was built in 1868 by Frederick J. Slade for Cooper Hewitt & Company, owners of the New Jersey Steel & Iron Company, Trenton, N.J. The furnace was ready for operation in December, 1868. (*James Moore Swank—History of the Manufacture of Iron in All Ages*)

Ski slide (steel). *See* Ski jump (steel)

Steel was manufactured in May 1728 by Samuel Higley of Simsbury, Conn., and Joseph Dewey of Hebron, Conn. In May 1728 Higley employed three workmen in a "curious art, by which to convert, change and transmute common iron into good steel, sufficient for any use" and requested a ten-year monopoly from the state. (*Report of the United States Commissioner of Patents, 1850*)

Steel-frame building. *See* Building: Steel-frame building; Building: Steel-frame residence

Steel mill to install an electrical machine was the Edgar Thomson Works of the Carnegie Steel Company, Braddock, Pa. A two-light arc machine, operated by belt drive from a line shaft, was installed in the blast furnace machine shop in 1882. (The Homestead Works of Carnegie Steel Company as well as other plants in the East also claim to have been first.) The first installation of electric-motor-driven rolls was made in the Edgar Thomson Works of the Carnegie Steel Company in No. 3 Mill in October 1905.

Vacuum-cast steel was poured July 2, 1957 by the Bethlehem Steel Corporation, Bethlehem, Pa., in the form of a 93,900-pound ingot, 78 inches in diameter. Vacuum-cast steel is melted in either an electric or open-hearth furnace and poured into ingots, its gases having been entrapped by vacuum-stream degassing with equipment designed by the F. J. Stokes Corporation, Philadelphia, Pa.

STEEL ANALYSIS LABORATORY was established in 1862 by William Franklin Durfee. He designed the machinery to test the Kelly process for making steel on a large scale and supervised the making of the first Bessemer steel in America at Wyandotte, Mich., by the Kelly-pneumatic process. (*Journal of the Iron and Steel Institute. Vol. 56. 1899*)

THE FIRST

STEEL BOILER PLATE. *See* Boiler plates

STEEL BRIDGE. *See* Bridge: Steel arch bridge

STEEL-CUT NAILS. *See* Nails: Steel-cut nails

STEEL DAM. *See* Dam: Steel dam

STEEL FISHING ROD. *See* Fishing rod

STEEL-FRAME BUILDING. *See* Building: Building of pressed structural steel

STEEL-HULL FERRYBOAT. *See* Ferryboat: Steel-hull ferryboat

STEEL HYDROPLANE. *See* Aviation—Airplane: Hydroplane

STEEL MAIL CAR. *See* Railroad car: Mail car (steel)

STEEL PASSENGER RAILROAD COACH. *See* Railroad car: Steel passenger railroad coach

STEEL PEN. *See* Pen: Steel pen patent

STEEL PIER. *See* Pier: Ocean pier of steel

STEEL POSTAL CAR. *See* Railroad car: Mail car (steel)

STEEL PROPELLER BLADE (hollow). *See* Aviation: Propeller blade of hollow steel

STEEL PULLMAN SLEEPING CAR. *See* Sleeping car: Pullman sleeping car

STEEL RAIL. *See* Railroad track: Railroad rails of steel

STEEL RAILWAY BRIDGE. *See* Bridge: Railway all-steel bridge

STEEL SAILING VESSEL. *See* Ship: Steel sailing vessel

STEEL SCHOONER. *See* Ship: Schooner (seven-masted, steel)

STEEL SHAFT GOLF CLUB. *See* Golf clubs (or golf sticks): Steel shaft for a golf club

THE FIRST

STEEL SHOVEL. *See* Shovel: Shovel (steel)

STEEL TRAPS. *See* Traps: Steel animal traps

STEEPLE. *See* Building: Building with a high steeple

STEEPLECHASE was held October 26, 1869, at Jerome Park, Westchester County, New York, by the American Jockey Club. Seven horses participated. The race was won by Oysterman, Jr., a five-year-old, owned by Colonel D. McDaniel. Between 15,000 and 20,000 spectators witnessed the inaugural race.

STEERING GEAR (automobile). *See* Automobile: Automobile with left-hand steering

STELLAR SPECTRUM PHOTOGRAPH. *See* Photograph: Photograph of a stellar spectrum showing the dark lines

STENOGRAPHY BOOK. *See* Shorthand book

STENOTYPE device for printing a legible text in the English alphabet at a high reporting speed was invented by John Celinergos Zachos of New York City, who received patent No. 175,892 on April 11, 1876, on a "typewriter and phonotypic notation." The type is fixed on eighteen shuttle bars, two or more of which may be simultaneously placed in position. The impression is given by a plunger common to all the bars.

STEREOPHONIC SOUND PROGRAM BROADCAST BY SEPARATELY OWNED STATIONS. *See* Radio broadcast: Stereophonic sound program broadcast by separately owned stations

STEREOSCOPE was invented by Oliver Wendell Holmes, the poet, in 1861. In the instrument devised by Holmes (which he did not attempt to patent) two pictures, separated by a partition, were placed side by side and viewed through two lenticular prisms which slightly magnified the images and combined them into one to give the effect of depth. (*John Torrey Morse—Letters of O. W. Holmes*)

STEREOTYPE
See also Labor-saving device approved by a labor organization

Automatic plate-casting and finishing machine for stereotype printing was invented by Henry Alexander Wise Wood. It was called the Autoplate and was adopted by the New York *Herald* in 1900. This stereotyping machine

THE FIRST

STEREOTYPE—*Continued*
greatly increased the speed at which newspapers could be printed. *(The Reorganization and Reconstruction of the Newspaper Printing Press. American Society of Mechanical Engineers. February 7, 1929)*

Autoplate stereotype plate-making machine. *See* Labor-saving device approved by a labor organization

Curved stereotype plate was cast by Charles Craske in 1854 in New York City for a Hoe rotary press and used by the New York *Tribune*. On August 31, 1861, full pages of the *Tribune* were printed from curved plates. *(George Adolf Kubler—A Short History of Stereotyping)*

Stereotype printing attempt was made in 1745 in Philadelphia, Pa., by Benjamin Mecom, a nephew of Benjamin Franklin. He commenced casting plates for the New Testament but never finished the task. *(John Luther Ringwalt—Encyclopedia of Printing)*

Stereotyped book. *See* Book: Stereotyped book

Stereotypers (successful) were David and George Bruce who established the firm of D. & G. Bruce in New York City in 1813. They designed machinery and molds patterned after those in use in England and had them cast in New York City. The business remained in the family until 1895, when it was sold. *(Robert Francis Salade—Handbook of Electrotyping and Stereotyping)*

STERILAMP. *See* Electric lighting: Electric sterilamp

STERILIZATION LEGISLATION was enacted by Indiana, March 9, 1907 (Indiana Ch. 215) for eugenic, punitive, and therapeutic reasons, and was entitled "an act to prevent the procreation of criminals, idiots, imbeciles and rapists." One hundred and twenty operations were performed under the law. The constitutionality of the law was challenged, and on May 11, 1921, the Supreme Court of Indiana, in the case of *Williams v. Smith*, held it unconstitutional because it denied the appellee due process of law. A sterilization bill had been passed by the Pennsylvania legislature on March 21, 1905, but was vetoed by Governor Samuel Whitaker Pennypacker. *(Jacob Henry Landman—Human Sterilization)*

STETHOSCOPE
Electrical stethoscope (portable) to amplify the sounds of the human body was demonstrated simultaneously to five hundred doctors by the Western Electric Company Incorporated,

THE FIRST

of New York City, on June 10, 1924, at the Municipal Pier, Chicago, Ill. It was developed by Western Electric in cooperation with Bell System engineers and Dr. Horatio Burt Williams, professor of physiology, Columbia University, New York City. The stethoscope was first marketed in October 1925. *(Western Electric News. November 1925)*

STEWARDESS (air). *See* Aviation: Air stewardess

STOCK EXCHANGE. *See* Brokerage: Stock exchange

STOCK QUOTATION BOARD
Automatic electric stock quotation board was manufactured in 1929 by the Teleregister Corporation, Stamford, Conn., and placed in operation May 21, 1929, at Sutro & Co., New York City. The device could record one hundred quotations a minute.

Stock quotation boards were of slate and were manufactured by Mount and Robertson of New York City in 1889.

STOMACH WASHING with a tube or syringe was accomplished by Dr. Philip Syng Physick in 1800 in Philadelphia, Pa. His procedure is described in his *Account of a New Mode of Extracting Poisonous Substances from the Stomach* which appeared in the *Eclectic Report and Analytic Review*, Vol. 3, p. 111-13, 1813. *(Charles Caldwell—A Discourse Commemorative of Philip Syng Physick, M.D.)*

STONE BRIDGE. *See* Bridge: Stone bridge

STONE CRUSHER of value was built by Eli Whitney Blake of New Haven, Conn., who obtained patent No. 20,542, June 15, 1858, on an "improvement in machines for crushing stones." Blake's stone crusher had upright convergent jaws, one fixed and one movable. The stones descended by gravity into pits and were sorted by screens. The device was first used in 1859 in Hartford, Conn., on a road construction job.

STONE PAVEMENT. *See* Road: Stone pavement

STORAGE BATTERY AUTOMOBILE. *See* Automobile: Electric storage battery automobile

STORAGE BATTERY BOAT. *See* Motor boat: Storage battery motor boat

STORAGE TANK (gas). *See* Gas: Gas storage tank (waterless)

THE FIRST

STORY (detective). *See* Detective story

STOVE
See also Electric cooking experiment; Electric stove

Electronic range for domestic use was introduced at a press conference at the Hotel Pierre, New York City, on October 25, 1955, by the Tappan Stove Company, Mansfield, Ohio. A 220-volt electric current produced microwaves which cooked eggs in 22 seconds, bacon in 90 seconds, frozen broccoli in 4½ minutes and a 5-pound roast in 30 minutes. The cost of the range was $1,200.

Stove for heating was a cast iron wood-burning open box which stood out from the chimney and caused heat from its back and sides to be thrown into the room. The stove, invented in 1742 by Benjamin Franklin, was called the "Pennsylvania fireplace." It is now known as the "Franklin stove." Smoke escaped over the top of a flat chamber behind the fire, and passed downward between it and the real back of the stove, then into the chimney. Franklin would not patent his invention. The stoves were manufactured by Robert Grace, the master of Warwick furnace in Chester County, Pa. *(Benjamin Franklin. An Account of the New Invented Pennsylvania fire-places wherein their construction and manner of operation is particularly explained; their advantage above every other method of warming rooms demonstrated)*

STOVE PATENT was granted June 11, 1793, to Robert Haeterick of Pennsylvania. His name is spelled in various ways in the early records.

STOWAWAY (aeronautical). *See* Aviation: Aeronautical stowaway

STRATOLINER COMMERCIAL FLIGHT. *See* Aviation—Flights: Stratoliner commercial flight

STRATOVISION. *See* Television—Telecast: Stratovision flight

STRAW HAT. *See* Hat: Straw hats

STRAW PAPER. *See* Paper: Straw paper

STRAWS (artificial) for drinking were made from paraffined manila paper rolled by hand by Marvin Chester Stone of Washington, D.C., in 1886. He obtained patent No. 375,962, January 3, 1888. Rye straws had been used previously but they proved unsatisfactory as they were generally unclean and cracked. Artificial drinking straws were made by hand until 1905, when

THE FIRST

the first machine to manufacture them successfully was made by the Marvin C. Stone Estate.

STREAMLINED ELECTRIC ENGINE. *See* Locomotive: Streamlined electric engine

STREAMLINED FERRYBOAT. *See* Ferryboat: Streamlined ferryboat

STREAMLINED STEAM LOCOMOTIVE. *See* Locomotive: Streamlined steam locomotive

STREAMLINED STEAMSHIP. *See* Ship: Streamlined steamship

STREAMLINED TRAIN. *See* Railroad: Streamlined railroad train

STREET CAR
Aluminum street car in which the metal was used not only for the body and under-frame but also for the trucks was placed in service December 2, 1926, by the Cleveland Railway Company. The total weight for the car was 30,300 pounds, of which 6,647 pounds were aluminum. The first use of aluminum in subway car construction occurred on October 27, 1904, when the Interborough Rapid Transit Company of New York City used aluminum in 300 subway motor cars and trailers for interior finish work, moldings, window panels, etc. *(Electric Railroad Journal. April 1930)*

Cable car was invented by Eleazer A. Gardner of Philadelphia, Pa., who obtained patent No. 19,736, March 23, 1858, on an "improvement in tracks for city railways." An underground tunnel, having a series of pulleys inside, housed the cable.

Cable street car put into service in the world was August 1, 1873 on Clay Street Hill, San Francisco, Calif. The car was invented by Andrew Smith Hallidie, who obtained patent No. 110,971 on January 17, 1871, on an "endless-wire rope way." *(Edgar Myron Kahn—Cable Car Days in San Francisco)*

Double-deck street car was operated July 4, 1892, on a trial trip in San Diego, Calif. The upper deck, reached by a winding stairway at each end of the car, was on the roof, with longitudinal seats facing outward, accommodating 12 on each side, and roofed over by a canopy. There were no sides or enclosures on the upper deck other than a railing.

Electric cars commercially operated were those of the Baltimore and Hampden Line, a third-rail system which began operation on one line only on August 10, 1885, in Baltimore, Md.

THE FIRST

STREET CAR—*Continued*

The line continued in service for more than a year. The first cars were run over the Hampden Branch of the Baltimore Union Passenger Railway Company, which later became a part of the United Railways and Electric Company of Baltimore, Md.

Electric street car successfully run with current generated by a stationary dynamo was invented by Stephen Dudley Field of New York City in 1874. In this system the current was carried by one of the rails to a wheel of the car, and thence to the motor. From this it flowed back through another wheel, which was insulated from the first one, to the other rail, and thence returned to the dynamo. Field filed a caveat on May 21, 1879, and obtained patent No. 229,991 on July 13, 1880, on "propelling railway cars by electro-magnetism." It covered his claim for an electric tramway motor, the current to be supplied by a stationary source of power and connected with the rails.

Gas-powered street car was No. 13 (later changed to No. 85), which was operated in 1873 in Providence, R.I., from the car barns to Olneyville Square. Henry Thompson was the conductor. It had a gas and air engine, compressed by separate pumps, designed by George B. Brayton of Boston, Mass., who obtained patent No. 125,166 on April 2, 1872, on "a pumping engine for condensing air and gas, and a reservoir for containing such agents."

Interurban street car line was established by Charles Lewis Henry, who organized the Union Traction Company, which ran its first car June 1, 1898, between Anderson, Ind., and Alexandria, Ind. The first conductor was Hadley Clifford.

Light-weight one-man street car was designed by Charles O. Birney and built by the American Car Company of St. Louis, Mo. The first one-man Birney cars were placed in operation in Fort Worth, Tex., November 1916. The safety features included a single front door for both entrance and exit, and a controller by means of which the power was thrown off, sand automatically applied to the tracks, and the brakes set when the operator failed to keep his hand in place. The door could not be opened or the step lowered until the brakes were set.

Municipally owned street cars were operated December 28, 1912, in San Francisco, Calif. The Municipal Railway (an overhead trolley system) began operation with ten cars on Geary Street from Kearney Street to Thirty-third Avenue and Park. Thomas A.

THE FIRST

Cashin was superintendent. Mayor James Rolph, Jr., acted as motorman on the first car. (*Financial Report of the Geary Street Municipal Railway of San Francisco—December 28, 1912—December 31, 1913*)

Street car was the "John Mason," a horse-drawn conveyance designed, constructed, and completed in 1832 by John Stephenson in Philadelphia, Pa., and placed in service in New York City by the New York and Harlem Railway. Named for a prominent New York banker who organized the railway company, the "John Mason" was equipped with iron wheels and drawn over iron rails laid in the center of the pavement. Lank O'Dell was the first driver. The car, which accommodated thirty passengers, was divided into three nonconnecting compartments with seats for ten in each. The three doors opened outward. The first door bore on its panel the name "New York," the second "Yorkville," and the third "Harlaem." The car made its first appearance in New York City November 14, 1832, when municipal officials took the first trip. Public transportation service began November 26, 1832. The tracks were laid along Fourth Avenue from Prince Street to Fourteenth Street. The fare was 12½ cents. In November 1835 a double track running north to Yorkville was completed. (The "John Mason" was the first horse-drawn street car, but horses had been used earlier to pull trains on railroad track lines.)

Street car coin box. *See* Coin box

Street car company was the New York and Harlem Railway, Inc., New York City, incorporated April 25, 1831, "to construct a single or double railroad." It was capitalized for $350,000 and received a thirty-year franchise December 22, 1831, from the Common Council. The first secretary was John Mason, who later became president.

Street car tracks which were tieless, soundless, and shockless were laid in New Orleans, La. The roadway was paved with 8 inches of concrete base and 3 inches of wearing surface, the top of which was 1½ inches of the finest oil asphalt. The line was officially completed February 4, 1930.

Street cars with clear-vision windows affording an unobstructed view of wide areas were placed in operation by the Pittsburgh Railways Company of Pittsburgh, Pa., in 1929. A new seating arrangement was introduced at the same time.

Trackless trolley system was built and placed in operation September 11, 1910, by

THE FIRST

Charles Mann between "Bungalow Land" in Laurel Canyon, Calif., and the terminal point of the Los Angeles Pacific Electric Railway Company, Los Angeles, Calif., a distance of a mile and a half. Two automobile buses were used. On top of the buses were trolley poles making contact with overhead wires. (*John Anderson Miller—Fares, Please*)

Transfers (printed) were invented by John Harry Stedman of Rochester, N.Y., who obtained U.S. patent No. 481,210 on August 23, 1892. They were 1⅞ by 2½ inches and were first used on October 31, 1892 in Rochester, N.Y.

STREET CLEANING MACHINE of importance was employed by Philadelphia, Pa., on December 15, 1854. It consisted of "a series of brooms on a cylinder about two feet six inches wide, attached to two endless chains, running over an upper and lower set of pulleys, which are suspended on a light frame of wrought iron behind a cart, the body of which is near the ground. As the cart wheels revolve, a rotary motion is given to the pulleys conveying the endless chains, and series of brooms attached to them; which being made to bear on the ground successively sweep the surface and carry the soil up an incline or carrier plate, over the top of which it is dropped into the cart." (*Philadelphia Public Ledger. December 16, 1854*)

STREET CLEANING SERVICE was instituted in 1757 by Benjamin Franklin in Philadelphia, Pa. He offered a bill to the Philadelphia Assembly and reported: "After some inquiry, I found a poor industrious man who was willing to undertake keeping the pavement clean by sweeping it twice a week, carrying off the dirt from before the neighbors' doors, for the sum of six pence per month, to be paid by each house."

STREET GAS LIGHT. *See* Gas: Gas lights (street)

STREET LETTER BOX. *See* Postal service: Street letter box

STREET PARADE. *See* Parade: Street parade held by a mystic society

STREPTOMYCIN was isolated from a culture of a soil microbe known as *Streptomyces griseus* by Dr. Selman Abraham Waksman and his students (Albert Schatz, Elizabeth Bugie, Doris Jones, and H. Christine Reilly) of the New Jersey Agricultural Experiment Station, Rutgers University, New Brunswick, N.J., in January 1944. It was first manufactured commercially by Merck & Co., Rahway, N.J., in September 1944. This antibiotic is active

THE FIRST

against both Gram-positive and Gram-negative bacteria as well as upon acidfast bacteria of which the organism that causes tuberculosis is the most important. It is used to control certain diseases caused by Gram-negative bacteria as well as Gram-positive diseases which are resistant to penicillin.

STRIKE

Anti-sit-down strike decision (federal) was rendered by the Supreme Court of the United States on February 27, 1939, in the case of National Labor Relations Board, petitioner, against Fansteel Metallurgical Corporation, North Chicago, Ill., whose employees were on strike from February 17 to February 26, 1937. Chief Justice Charles Evans Hughes wrote the opinion, Justices McReynolds, Butler, Stone and Roberts concurring, Justices Black and Reed dissenting.

Anti-sit-down strike legislation (state) was Act No. 210, an act "prohibiting the conspiring of three or more persons unlawfully to occupy, hold and possess certain buildings against the will and without the consent of the lessee thereof," passed April 9, 1937, by Vermont. The bill was introduced by Senator Ernest Walter Dunklee of Windham, Vt., and provided for penalties of not more than two years' imprisonment or a $1,000 fine.

Helicopter to deliver across a picket line. *See* Helicopter: Helicopter to deliver material across a picket line

Modern sit-down strike occurred in the packing plant of George A. Hormel and Company, Austin, Minn., on November 13, 1933, when striking employees seized control. The Industrial Commission of Minnesota, of which Niels Henriksen Debel was chairman, held mediation hearings November 16-18, 1933, and rendered a decision on December 8, 1933, affecting the specific issues involved. Various forms of stay-in strikes, slow-down strikes, and refusal-to-work strikes, however, had been attempted previously.

Strike took place in New York City in 1741 when the master bakers protested against municipal regulation of the price of bread. They were tried and convicted of unlawfully combining, but no sentence was passed. (*Selig Perlman—History of Trade Unionism in the United States*)

Strike in which federal troops were called in peacetime was that of railroad employees which began July 16, 1877. In response to requests for aid from several governors, including Henry Mason Mathews of West Virginia, John Lee Carroll of Maryland, and John Hartranft of Pennsylvania, President Rutherford Birchard Hayes called out federal troops. In eight days,

STRIKE—*Continued*
he received nine calls for assistance from governors. On January 29, 1834, President Andrew Jackson ordered troops to put down a "riotous assembly" among laborers on the Chesapeake and Ohio canal.

Strike in which the militia was called occurred in Paterson, N.J., July 21, 1828, when the Godwin Guards of the national militia were required to keep peace during a strike brought about by the changing of dinner hours from twelve to one in the factories. The strikers were defeated but afterwards the noon dinner hour was again established. (*Harry Lawrence Harris and John T. Hilton—History of the Second and Fifth Regiment*)

Strike in which women participated was that of the "female weavers" of Pawtucket, R.I., who went on strike in 1824 with the male workmen. (*Florence Peterson—Strikes in the United States 1880-1936*)

Strike of women operatives occurred at the Dover Manufacturing Company, Dover, N.H., in 1828, when about four hundred women went on strike against a wage cut and a ten-hour day in the needlework trades. (*Ruth Delzell—The Early History of Women Trade Unionists of America*)

Strike settlement mediated by the United States Department of Labor was the dispute of the Railway Clerks of the New York, New Haven and Hartford Railroad. Commissioners of Conciliation had not yet been appointed, but the Secretary of Labor assigned the dispute to Glossbrenner Wallace William Hanger, Chief Statistician of the Bureau of Labor Statistics, who entered the case May 24, 1913, and effected a settlement June 2, 1913.

Union strike benefit was authorized May 31, 1786, at the home of Henry Myers, Philadelphia, Pa. Twenty-six members of the Typographical Society in protest against a wage reduction agreed "that we will support such of our brethren as shall be thrown out of employment on account of their refusing to work for less than $6 per week." They won their demands. (*George A. Tracy—History of the Typographical Union*)

STROBORADIOGRAPH was made by General Electric's General Engineering Laboratory, Schenectady, N.Y., in cooperation with the Detroit Arsenal, Center Line, Mich., and the General Electric X-ray Department, Milwaukee, Wis., in 1956 and announced on August 14, 1956. Used with the X-ray betatron, operating at five million to fifteen million volts, it can take still pictures of the inside of an engine operating at normal speed under load conditions. From still pictures spliced

at graduated intervals, X-ray motion pictures of the complete cycle of an engine can be studied to detect flaws or improve design.

STRUCTURAL STEEL BUILDING. *See* Building: Building of pressed structural steel

STUDENTS' FEDERATION (international) was the Pan American Student League, founded in New York City in 1920 to promote inter-American understanding among the younger generation throughout the Americas. The first United States delegate to the International Council and first president of the council was Philip Leonard Green. The first secretary was J. Antonio Reyes of Peru.

STUDIO. *See* Moving picture studio

STUNT ACTOR. *See* Moving picture actor: Stunt actor

SUBAQUEOUS HIGHWAY TUNNEL. *See* Tunnel: Subaqueous highway tunnel

SUB-MACHINE GUN. *See* Ordnance: Submachine gun

SUBMARINE
American ship sunk by a U-boat. *See* World War II: American ship sunk by a U-boat

Atomic-powered submarine was the "Nautilus" SS(N) 571, built by the Electric Boat Company, a division of the General Dynamics Corporation, Groton, Conn., under the supervision of Captain Hyman George Rickover. President Harry S. Truman participated in the keel-laying ceremony on June 14, 1952. The submarine, launched January 21, 1954, on the Thames River at Groton and christened by Mrs. Dwight David Eisenhower, was commissioned September 21, 1954, tested under nuclear power January 17, 1955, and completed April 22, 1955. Her crew consisted of 11 officers and 85 enlisted men. The first commander was Eugene Parks Wilkinson. The steam turbines were powered by a liquid-cooled atomic reactor. The "Nautilus" was 323¼ feet over-all, 2,975 tons light, 3,200 tons standard, and 3,747 tons submerged.

Atomic-powered turbine electric-drive submarine was the "Tullibee," SSB(N) 597, 273 feet long, 2,000 tons light, 2,175 tons submerged, whose keel was laid May 26, 1958. She was launched April 27, 1960, at the Thames River plant of the General Dynamics Corporation's Electric Boat Company at Groton, Conn., and christened by Ann Davidson. The vessel was commissioned at Groton November 9,

1960. She carried a crew of 60 men and 6 officers. All other submarines utilized reduction gears. The torpedo tubes of the "Tullibee" were located amidships rather than in the bow.

Ballistic missile submarine was the atomic-powered "George Washington," SSB(N) 598, laid down November 7, 1957, launched June 9, 1959, and commissioned December 30, 1959, at Groton, Conn., on the Thames River. She was christened by Ellie Mae Anderson, wife of Robert Bernerd Anderson, Secretary of the Treasury. The cost of construction was approximately $110 million. The first commander was James Butler Osborn. The submarine was 380 feet long and had a 5,400-ton displacement light, 5,600 tons standard, and 6,700 tons submerged. She went on her patrol duty November 15, 1960 from Charleston, S.C. and returned January 21, 1961, having traveled 67 days underwater. She was equipped with 16 vertical Polaris missile tubes to be fired below the surface.

Cargo submarine to cross the Atlantic Ocean and the first to cross in time of war, was the German submarine "Deutschland," which landed at Chesapeake Bay July 9, 1916, after a sixteen-day voyage from the island of Heligoland. The submarine unloaded her cargo at Baltimore, Md., left on August 1 with a supply of metal and rubber, and arrived in Germany on August 23, after running the British blockade. She was 315 feet long and had a 31-foot beam. Captain Paul König was in command. *(Paul König—Voyage of the "Deutschland")*

Diesel engine in a submarine. *See* Engine: Diesel engine in a submarine

Guided missile launched from a nuclear-powered submarine was a Regulus I launched March 25, 1960, from the "Halibut," SSG (N) 587, off Oahu, Hawaii. The missile was guided over its simulated target on Lehua Island, 120 miles away, before landing, about 15 minutes after launching, at Bonham Air Force Base, Kauai, 20 miles beyond the target.

Japanese submarine sunk by an American ship at sea. *See* World War II: Japanese submarine sunk by an American ship

Leaping submarine was the U.S.S. "Pickerel," SS-524, commissioned April 4, 1949, at Portsmouth, N.H. The submarine's first sea trials took place between April 4 and July 25, 1949. The first commanding officer was Commander Paul Richard Schratz. The "Pickerel" surfaced from a depth of 150 feet with a 48 degree up-angle during a routine

training exercise off Oahu, Hawaii. Her bow seemed to leap up out of the water. She set a record by snorkeling from Hong Kong to Honolulu, a distance of 5,200 miles, in 21 days (April 1950).

Naval vessels to sink an enemy submarine. *See* Ship: Naval vessels to sink an enemy submarine

Nuclear warhead fired from a Polaris submarine was fired May 6, 1962, from the U.S.S. "Ethan Allen," submerged off Christmas Island in the Pacific test area. The missile sped skyward in a parabolic trajectory and then exploded. It carried a force estimated at 500,000 tons of TNT.

President to travel underwater in a submerged submarine. *See* President (United States): President to travel underwater in a captured enemy submarine

Streamlined submarine of the U.S. Navy was the U.S.S. "Nautilus" (N-2, formerly the V-6) built at the Navy Yard, Mare Island, Calif. Her keel was laid August 2, 1927, she was launched March 15, 1930, and she was commissioned July 1, 1930. Her length was 349 feet, extreme beam 33 feet 3 inches, mean draft 15 feet 9 inches, displacement 2,730 tons. She carried 2 six-inch 53-caliber guns. (An atomic submarine with the same name was constructed later.)

Submarine built for use in war was the "American Turtle," built in 1776 by David Bushnell of Saybrook, Conn. The vessel, which was large enough to accommodate one operator, had a 24-inch two-bladed wooden screw propeller, operated by hand, that enabled her to travel forward or in reverse at three knots. A crank operated the rudder aft. Water was admitted for descent and forced out with a hand pump for surfacing. Another screw, on the bottom, moved the submarine vertically. On September 7, 1776, Ezra Lee used the craft and attached a torpedo time bomb to the hull of Admiral Howe's flag-ship, the sixty-four gun "Eagle," in New York Harbor. An explosion resulted but no serious damage occurred as the bomb drifted away from the ship. *(Connecticut Historical Society—Collections Vol. 11)*

Submarine built on the Great Lakes was the "Peto," constructed from prefabricated parts by the Manitowoc Shipbuilding Company, Manitowoc, Wis. The keel was laid June 18, 1941. She was launched April 30, 1942, accepted November 21, 1942, by Commander Rudolph Frank Hans of the Ninth Naval District, and commissioned the next day.

SUBMARINE—*Continued*
Submarine captured and boarded on the high seas was the German submarine U-505, which was attacked June 4, 1944, by airplanes and ships under the command of Captain Daniel V. Gallery of the aircraft carrier U.S.S. "Guadalcanal." The submarine was boarded by Lieutenant (j.g.) Albert Leroy David and eight crewmen from the destroyer U.S.S. "Pillsbury" (DE 133), commanded by George W. Cassleman. The "Guadalcanal" towed the U-505 more than 1,700 miles. *(Daniel V. Gallery—Twenty Million Tons Under The Sea)*

Submarine contract of the U.S. Navy for $150,000 was awarded to the John P[hillip] Holland Torpedo Boat Company of New York City by Navy Secretary Hilary Abner Herbert on March 13, 1895. Construction was started at the Columbian Iron Works, Baltimore, Md. The keel was laid June 20, 1896, and the submarine launched August 7, 1897. The submarine, 85 feet 3 inches in length and 11 feet 6 inches in extreme breadth, with a displacement of 168 tons, was known as the "Plunger." The project was abandoned and all expenses and advances returned to the government when the contract was canceled in April 1900. A new contract for another submarine was signed November 7, 1900.

Submarine crossing of the North Pole under water was accomplished August 3, 1958, by the "Nautilus" under the command of Commander William Robert Anderson. The atomic-powered submarine, carrying 116 persons (14 officers, 98 crewmen, and 4 civilian scientists), traveled 8,146 miles at a speed of 20 knots. She left Pearl Harbor, Hawaii, July 23, 1958; crossed the Pacific Ocean through the Bering Strait; surfaced and went under the ice cap at Point Barrow, Alaska, on August 1, 1958, at 11:15 P.M., E.D.T. Traveling 1,830 miles under the ice in 96 hours, she arrived under the North Pole August 3, 1958. The "Nautilus" then continued her voyage, reaching Iceland August 7, 1958. The expedition was designated "Northwest Passage."
See also Navy: Naval man to reenlist while under the North Pole

Submarine disaster occurred March 25, 1915, when the F-4, commanded by Lieutenant Alfred L. Ede, sank with a loss of twenty-one men while approximately one and a half miles out of Honolulu Harbor, Hawaii.

Submarine expressly designed and built to fire guided missiles was the U.S.S. "Grayback," ordered June 19, 1952, laid down July 1, 1954, launched July 2, 1957, and commissioned March 7, 1958, at Mare Island, Calif. The "Grayback," designed to fire Regulus I and Regulus II missiles, was completed July 31, 1958. She was 322½ feet long, 1,740 tons

light, 2,287 tons surface, and 3,638 tons submerged and carried a crew of 85 officers and men.

Submarine fitted with an internal combustion engine was the "Argonaut," invented by Simon Lake and built by the Columbian Iron Works and Dry Dock Company of Baltimore, Md., in 1897. A working model had been built by Lake in 1894. He patented the engine on April 7, 1896 (No. 557,835) and the submarine vessel on April 20, 1897 (No. 581, 213). The "Argonaut" was also the first submarine to salvage sunken objects of value. On December 16, 1897, a demonstration was given on the Patapsco River during which twenty-two representatives of newspapers made short descents ranging from an hour and a half to four hours.

Submarine jet propulsion device patent was obtained by Fritz Zwicky of Pasadena, Calif., who filed his application on October 23, 1944, and was granted patent No. 2,461,797 on February 15, 1949, on a "reaction propelled device for operation through water." The patent was assigned to the Aerojet Engineering Corporation, Azusa, Calif., which constructed, tested, and demonstrated the device in September 1943 in the company research laboratory at Pasadena, Calif.

Submarine powered by a liquid metal-cooled atomic reactor was the U.S.S. "Seawolf," SSN-575, ordered July 19, 1952, laid down September 15, 1953, and launched July 21, 1955, at Groton, Conn., under the sponsorship of Mrs. William Sterling Cole. The "Seawolf," which was completed March 30, 1957, had a displacement of 3,260 tons light, 3,495 tons standard surface, and 4,110 tons submerged. She had a complement of 94. A prototype of the power plant was built by the General Electric Company at West Milton, N.Y. The first commanding officer was Richard Boyer Laning, U.S.N.

Submarine (submerged) broadcast. *See* Radio broadcast: Submarine (submerged) broadcast

Submarine that was practical and able to submerge was the Holland No. 9, built by the John P[hilip] Holland Torpedo Boat Company of New York City. Launched March 17, 1898, she submerged off Staten Island, remaining under water 1 hour and 40 minutes. Her over-all length was 53 feet 11 inches, her diameter 10 feet 3 inches; her equipment included a dynamite gun and one torpedo tube. The vessel was purchased by the U.S. Navy on April 11, 1900, for $150,000 (though the actual cost was greater) and placed in commission October 12, 1900.

Submarine to sink a man-of-war in actual warfare was the "Hunley," named after her designer. On the night of February 17, 1864, Lieutenant George Dixon of the Confederate "Hunley" succeeded in approaching the U.S.S. "Housatonic," a new ship of 1,400 tons displacement, which was awash off Charleston, S.C., and sank her by exploding a torpedo under her bottom. The wave thrown up by the explosion swamped the submarine (because her forward hatch was open) and killed her crew. The submarine was built by [Horace L.] Hunley, McClintock & Watson in the shops of Parks & Lyons, Mobile, Ala., in 1863. The interior height of the vessel was 5 feet, her breadth 4 feet, her speed 4 knots. Her propeller was operated by eight men using hand power. There were no provisions for storage of air. (*John Thomas Scharf—History of the Confederate States Navy, from Its Organization to the Surrender of Its Last Vessel*)

Submarine with closed-circuit television. *See* Television: Submarine with closed-circuit television

Submarine with two nuclear reactors was the "Triton," SSR(N) 586, built by the Electric Boat Company, Groton, Conn. The submarine was launched August 19, 1958, completed May 19, 1959, and commissioned November 10, 1959. She was 447 feet long, 37 feet wide, and had a draught of 25 feet. She displaced 5,650 tons light, 5,900 tons standard, and 7,750 tons submerged. She had a cruising range of 110,000 miles and a complement of 148 officers and crew. Her initial trip to sea was made September 28, 1959. The first captain was Edward Latimer Beach. The two water-cooled nuclear reactors were built by the General Electric Company. Each reactor provided current for a propeller.

Submerged circumnavigation of the earth was accomplished by the U.S.S. "Triton," SSR(N) 586, which left New London, Conn., February 16, 1960, crossed the equator February 24, 1960, and completed the submerged navigation April 25, 1960, having traveled 41,500 miles in 84 days. She returned to New London on May 11, 1960. The hull of the submarine was submerged during the entire trip but the upper portion broached the surface twice. The nuclear-powered "Triton" was 447 feet long and had a 37-foot beam; she was 5,650 tons light, 5,900 tons standard, and 7,750 tons submerged. She carried a crew of 13 officers and 135 men and was commanded by Captain Edward Latimer Beach. The "Triton" was laid down May 21, 1956, launched August 19, 1958, and commissioned November 10, 1959.

Submerged submarine to fire a Polaris missile was the U.S.S. "George Washington," commanded by Commander James Butler Osborn, which submerged 90 feet about 30 miles

off Cape Canaveral, Fla., on July 20, 1960, and fired a Polaris missile at 1:39 P.M. and a second one at 4:32 P.M. The 28-foot two-stage rocket traveled 1,150 statute miles eastward in less than 14 minutes.

Telephone message from a submarine. *See* Radio telephone: Two-way radio conversation between a submerged submarine and another vessel

Underwater telecast from a submarine. *See* Television—Telecast: Underwater telecast from a submarine

SUBMARINE CABLE PLOW. *See* Plow: Submarine cable plow

SUBMARINE-ESCAPE TRAINING TANK
Submarine-escape training tank was placed in operation August 15, 1930, at the U.S. Submarine Base, New London, Conn. It was a cylindrical "water tower" column 100 feet deep, with a spiral stairway winding around it and an abutting elevator shaft. Candidates entered the tank through locks at various depths, wearing the submarine-escape lung, and climbed up a rope, hand over hand, in order to slow down their ascent sufficiently to let their bodies become gradually adjusted to the decrease in pressure.

Women to take the submarine-escape test and receive certificates were Ensigns Eleanor MacDonald and Glenn Huckstep (Nurses Corps), U.S.N.R., who received certificates July 12, 1943, from Lieutenant George W. Albin, Jr., at the Submarine-Escape Training Tank, New London, Conn.

SUBMARINE "LUNG" was the result of the combined efforts of two naval officers, Lieutenant Charles Bowers Momsen and Chief Gunner Clarence Louis Tibbals, and a civilian, Frank M. Hobson, civil engineer of the Naval Bureau of Construction and Repairs. Momsen and Tibbals, who tested the device May 10, 1929, by escaping from it in depths of water as great as 206 feet, were rewarded with the Distinguished Service Cross. Hobson received a year's pay for his part in the invention, which consisted of an oxygen bag with a canister of soda lime and tubes similar to those of an army gas mask. The Navy put the invention to test under actual conditions on August 30, 1929, on the Thames River at New London, Conn. Twenty-six officers and men came out of the after-hatch of the submerged submarine S-4.

SUBMARINE TELEGRAPH CABLE. *See* Cable: Submarine telegraph cable

SUBWAY

Bank to operate a window in a subway station. *See* Bank: Bank to operate a window in a subway station

Municipal subway, and the first shallow subway built under city streets for street railway transportation as distinguished from a deep tunnel, was the Tremont Street Subway, Boston, Mass., construction of which was begun on March 28, 1895. The section between Public Gardens and Park Street was opened for traffic September 1, 1897, and the section to North Station September 3, 1898. The subway was built by the City of Boston at a cost of $4,369,000 and leased to the Boston Elevated Railway at an annual rental of 4½ per cent of construction cost.

Pneumatic subway was invented by Alfred Ely Beach and was known as the Beach Pneumatic Underground Railway of New York City. The company was incorporated for freight traffic on June 1, 1868, and for passenger traffic on May 3, 1869, with a capital stock of $5,000,000. The system was opened to the public on February 26, 1870. The tunnel was 312 feet long and ran from the west curb line of Broadway at Warren Street down the middle of Broadway to a point south of Murray Street. It consisted of a circular tube 9 feet in diameter built of iron plates for 60 feet on the curves and brick masonry the rest of the way. The cars, which were well upholstered, carried 22 persons. They were propelled by a rotary blower which drove a blast of air through the tunnel against the rear of the car, carrying it along "like a sailboat before the wind." *(James Walker—Fifty Years of Rapid Transit)*

Subway (rapid transit) was the Interborough Rapid Transit route in New York City from Brooklyn Bridge north under Lafayette Street, 4th and Park Avenues, west along 42nd Street to Broadway, and north to 145th Street. The line was opened October 27, 1904. Trains had run under ground before 1904, but the Interborough Rapid Transit Company established the first rapid transit subway.

Train to run automatically without conductors or motormen was placed in operation January 4, 1962, between Grand Central station and Times Square station in the New York City subway system. The train carried a motorman who stood by without performing any duties—a safety measure demanded by the transport workers' union, then involved in a labor dispute with the New York City Transit Authority.

SUCTION VACUUM CLEANER. *See* Vacuum cleaner: Suction-type vacuum cleaner

SUFFRAGE

State to provide universal manhood suffrage without restriction as to property or wealth was Vermont. The state constitution agreed upon at a general convention held July 28, 1777, at Windsor, Vt., permitted all freemen (natural born citizens over twenty-one years of age) to elect officers and be elected to office.

Suffrage for women. *See* Woman suffrage

SUGAR

Sugar and glucose from cornstarch were manufactured by the Union Sugar Company, New York City. The process was based on patent No. 42,727, dated May 10, 1864, for a "sugar produced from corn and beets." The patent was granted to Frederick W. Gossling and assigned to Gossling, Henry F. Briggs, and Leman Bradley of Buffalo, N.Y. Gossling also received patent No. 45,561 on December 20, 1864, for a new and improved compound sugar made by a combination of cane sugar or cane syrup with corn syrup.

Sugar beets were grown about 1830 at Ensfield, Pa., by the Beet Sugar Society of Philadelphia, of which James Donaldson was president. The first mill was the Northampton Beet Sugar Company, erected by David Lee Child in Northampton, Mass., in 1838 (incorporated March 10, 1837). In 1839, 1,300 pounds of sugar was produced from beets low in sucrose content. In 1839 the company received a $100 premium from the Massachusetts Agricultural Society and a silver medal at the Massachusetts Charitable Mechanics Association's exhibition. The factory did not operate after 1840. *(Franklin Stewart Harris—The Sugar Beet in America)*

Sugar cane was brought to Louisiana by Jesuit priests in 1751 from Hispaniola (Santo Domingo). It was used for making taffia, a kind of rum. Sugar was made from sugar cane in St. Bernard Parish, La., in 1791 by Antonio Méndez. The sugar industry started with the work of Étienne de Bore, who in 1794 planted cane and in 1795 harvested a crop of sugar which sold for $12,000. At his death, his wealth was estimated at $300,000, all from sugar. *(William Carter Stubs—Sugar Cane; Experiments in Cultivation. Second Series No. 66. Bulletin of the Agricultural Experiment Station. Louisiana State University and A.&M. College)*

Sugar refinery (practical) was opened in New Orleans, La., in 1791 by Antonio Méndez. Attempts had been made in 1759, 1764, 1765, and 1766, but because the exact crystallization point and the proper use of lime were not then known, the mills were unsuccessful and were abandoned. The first commercial mill began operation in New Orleans in 1795. *(Henry Rightor—Standard History of New Orleans, Louisiana)*

SULFANILAMIDE

Sulfanilamide was produced in December 1930 at the Jackson Laboratory of E. I. du Pont de Nemours & Company, Wilmington, Del., for use as a diazo component in an experimental disperse azo dye for cellulose acetate fibers. Acetanilide reacted with chlorosulfonic acid, and the reaction was followed by amidation and hydrolysis. Sulfanilamide was not used in medicine until about five years later.

Sulfanilamide as a treatment for infections of streptococcic origins was used in 1935 by Dr. Ashley Weech of Babies Hospital, New York City, but was not reported. Dr. Perrin Hamilton Long of Johns Hopkins Hospital, Baltimore, Md., obtained a sample from E. I. du Pont de Nemours & Company, Inc., on September 9, 1936, and a one-pound vial on November 9, 1936. Dr. Long and Eleanor Bliss reported on their use of the drug—in treating a seven-year-old child with erysipelas—to the Southern Medical Association, Baltimore, Md., on November 17, 1936. *(Journal of the American Medical Association. January 2, 1937. Vol. 108. No. 1)*

SULPHATE OF QUININE. *See* Quinine: Quinine sulphate

SULPHUR DEPOSIT was discovered in the United States in 1869 in a salt dome in Calcasieu Parish, La. It was later developed as the Sulphur Dome of the Union Sulphur Company. Sulphur was first extracted from a well in the dome in October 1895 by Herman Frasch of Cleveland, Ohio. On October 20, 1891, he received patents No. 461,429 and 461,431 on "mining sulphur" and No. 461,430 on "an apparatus for mining sulphur." Sulphur was melted in the ground and pumped to the surface in a liquid state to congeal in bins or blocks.

SULPHUR MINE (offshore) was the Grand Isle offshore mine, 2,000 feet beneath the bottom of the Gulf of Mexico, about seven miles off the Louisiana coast. The mine was operated by means of a steel structure equipped with boilers, generators, and drilling rigs situated in 50 feet of water. The deposit was discovered by the Humble Oil and Refining Company and the mine built and operated by the Freeport Sulphur Company. The first sulphur was obtained on March 14, 1960.

SULPHURIC ACID was produced by John Harrison in 1793 in a little shop at Third and Green Streets, Philadelphia, Pa. At first the acid was concentrated in fragile glass retorts. Later, platinum containers were used instead. The business founded by Harrison, known as Harrison Brothers & Company, was purchased in 1917 by E. I. du Pont de Nemours & Company, Inc., of Wilmington, Del.

SUMMER SCHOOL (college). *See* College: College summer school

SUN-HEATED BUILDING. *See* Building: Commercial building heated by the sun

SUN (moving picture). *See* Moving picture: Moving picture of the sun

SUN-POWERED AUTOMOBILE. *See* Automobile: Sun-powered automobile

SUNDAE (ice cream). *See* Ice cream sundae

SUNDAY COMIC SECTION. *See* Newspaper: Newspaper Sunday comic section

SUNDAY NEWSPAPER. *See* Newspaper: Newspaper to appear on Sunday

SUNDAY SCHOOL

Jewish Sunday School was established under the auspices of the Hebrew Sunday School Society of Philadelphia, Pa., organized March 4, 1838, by Rebecca Gratz for "the religious instruction and general improvement of children of the Jewish faith." The first meeting of the board of the society was held February 4, 1838. The Sunday school began with fifty pupils.

Sunday School was opened in Christ Church, Savannah, Ga., in 1736 by John Wesley and was under the leadership of Charles Delamotte. Before the Sunday evening services Wesley instructed between thirty and forty children and heard them recite their catechism. Prior to this, religious instruction had been given to children individually and in small groups which hardly merited the designation of "school." *(William Bacon Stevens—History of Georgia. Vol. 1. p. 341)*

SUPERINTENDENT OF DOCUMENTS. *See* Government printing office: Superintendent of documents

SUPERVISOR OF MUSIC. *See* Music instruction: State Supervisor of Music

SUPREME COURT (state). *See* Court:
State supreme court composed entirely of women

SUPREME COURT (U.S.)
Associate Justice of the Supreme Court to become Chief Justice was Edward Douglass White, who was appointed Associate Justice March 12, 1894, and Chief Justice December 12, 1910. He took his seat December 19, 1910, and served until May 2, 1921, shortly before his death on May 19, 1921. However, White was not the first man who had served as an Associate Justice to be appointed Chief Justice. In 1795 President Washington appointed John Rutledge as Chief Justice, and Rutledge actually served during one session of the Court before the appointment was rejected by the Senate. Rutledge had been appointed as one of the original five Associate Justices in 1789, but had delayed taking his seat until 1790 and had resigned in 1791.

See below Chief Justice whose nomination was not confirmed

Associate Justice of the Supreme Court who was Jewish was Louis Dembitz Brandeis, who was appointed on January 28, 1916, by President Woodrow Wilson. The nomination was confirmed by the Senate, June 1, 1916, and Brandeis was sworn in June 3, 1916. (*Alpheus Thomas Mason—Brandeis, Lawyer and Judge in the Modern State*)

Chief Justice of the Supreme Court was John Jay of New York, who was appointed by President George Washington on September 24, 1789. His appointment was confirmed on September 26, 1789, and he served until June 29, 1795. (*William Jay—Life of John Jay*)

Chief Justice of the Supreme Court who was Catholic was Roger Brooke Taney of Frederick, Md., who was appointed by President Andrew Jackson March 28, 1836, to succeed John Marshall. (*Bernard Christian Steiner —Life of Roger Brooke Taney*)

Chief Justice whose nomination was not confirmed was John Rutledge of South Carolina, who was appointed Chief Justice by President George Washington and who served from July 1, 1795, to December 15, 1795, on which date the Senate rejected the nomination. He presided at the August 1795 term. He had been an Associate Justice from September 26, 1789 to March 5, 1791.

Congressional act declared unconstitutional by the Supreme Court. *See* Congress of the United States: Congressional act declared unconstitutional by the Supreme Court of the United States

Lawyers admitted before the bar of the Supreme Court. *See* Lawyer: Lawyers admitted to the Supreme Court of the United States

Members of a family admitted simultaneously to practice in the Supreme Court of the United States were William Henry Faust, Mrs. William Henry Faust, and William Henry Faust, Jr., of Indianapolis, Ind., who were admitted March 1, 1940.

Negro clerk of the Supreme Court was William Thaddeus Coleman, Jr., of Philadelphia, Pa., who was appointed by Justice Felix Frankfurter on September 1, 1948. His service terminated on August 31, 1949.

Negro lawyer to practice before the Supreme Court. *See* Lawyer: Negro lawyer to practice in the United States Supreme Court

Negro page of the Supreme Court was Charles Vernon Bush, fourteen, of Washington, D.C., whose service commenced September 27, 1954, for the session opening October 4, 1954.

President to become a Chief Justice. *See* President (United States): President to become Chief Justice of the United States

Supreme Court Justice impeachment proceedings. *See* Impeachment: Impeachment proceedings against a Justice of the Supreme Court of the United States

Supreme Court Justice who was nominated but who did not serve was Robert Hanson Harrison of Maryland, who was nominated by President George Washington on September 24, 1789, and whose appointment was confirmed by the Senate on September 26, 1789. Harrison declined the appointment on October 1, 1789. He also declined a later appointment as Chancellor of Maryland.

Supreme Court of the United States consisted of Chief Justice John Jay of New York (1789-1795), and Associate Justices John Rutledge of South Carolina (1789-1791), William Cushing of Massachusetts (1789-1810), James Wilson of Pennsylvania (1789-1798), John Blair of Virginia (1789-1796), and Robert Hanson Harrison of Maryland (1789-1790). The appointments were made by President George Washington, September 24, and confirmed by the Senate on September 26, 1789. The Judiciary Act of 1789, which implemented the clause in the Constitution providing for the Supreme Court, was passed September 24, 1789 (1 Stat. L.73). It provided for six members—a chief justice and five associate justices—four of whom were to constitute a quorum. The first

THE FIRST

session began February 1, 1790, in the Royal Exchange Building on Broad Street, New York City, and lasted ten days, terminating on February 10. Two sessions were held each year beginning the first Monday of February and of August. Richard Wenman was the first Crier of the Court, and John Tucker of Massachusetts, appointed February 3, 1790, was the first clerk.

Woman admitted to practice before the Supreme Court of the United States was Belva Ann Bennett Lockwood, who was admitted on March 3, 1879. The bill admitting women passed the House of Representatives February 21, 1878, and the Senate February 7, 1879. It was titled an "act to relieve certain legal disabilities of women" (20 Stat.L.292) and was signed February 15, 1879, by President Rutherford Birchard Hayes. It provided that any women member of the bar of good moral character who had practiced for three years before a state supreme court was eligible for admittance to practice before the Supreme Court of the United States.

SUPREME COURT (U.S.) DECISION
Supreme Court commerce case. *See* Commerce case

Supreme Court decision between states was the result of a bill in equity between New York and Connecticut in the term which began August 5, 1799. Chief Justice Oliver Ellsworth presided. The decision read: "As the state of New York was not a party to the suit, nor interested in the decision of these suits, an injunction ought not to issue." (4 Dallas 1). *(James Brown Scott—Judicial Settlement of Controversies Between States of the American Union)*

Supreme Court decision establishing the power of the United States as greater than that of the individual state was made February 20, 1809, when Chief Justice John Marshall rendered an opinion sustaining the federal power and ordered a mandamus issued to carry a previous decree into effect. Judge Richard Peters of the United States District Court of Pennsylvania had decreed that certain prize money be paid to a Mr. Olmstead of Connecticut for his capture of a British sloop during the Revolutionary War. The state of Pennsylvania refused to recognize Olmstead's claim or to award the prize money. As the state militia was called out to stop the United States Marshal from serving his order, the United States Marshal summoned a posse of 2,000 men, but delayed service in order to avoid bloodshed. The power of the federal government was later recognized. In the case of the United States versus Judge Peters (5 Cranch 1150), it was decided that the legislature of a state cannot annul the judgment or determine the jurisdiction of a United States Court.

THE FIRST

Supreme Court decision in a state boundary case was made in 1846 when Chief Justice Taney ruled that a bill "should be dismissed upon the ground that this court under the Constitution of the United States have not the power to try such a question between states, or redress a wrong, even if the wrong is proved to have been done." On March 16, 1832, Rhode Island, the complainant, had petitioned the Supreme Court to settle a boundary controversy with Massachusetts. (Reports United States Supreme Court 7 Peters 651; 11 Peters 226; 12 Peters 657; 12 Peters 755; 13 Peters 23; 14 Peters 210, 15 Peters 233; 4 Howard 591.) *(James Brown Scott—Judicial Settlement of Controversies Between States of the American Union)*

Supreme Court decision that reversed the decision of a state supreme court was rendered in 1813. The Virginia Court of Appeals in the case of *Fairfax's Devisee* v. *Hunter's Lessee* held the confiscation of Lord Fairfax's estate by Virginia in the Revolutionary War illegal. A writ of error was obtained and the case was argued as *Martin v. Hunter's Lessee.* The court in 1816 unanimously sustained the validity of the 25th section of Chapter 20 of the act of September 24, 1789 (1 Stat.L.73) which established the judicial system and established for all time the right of the Supreme Court to review the determinations of the highest state courts in cases involving the Constitution, and federal laws or treaties. *(Henry Wheaton—Reports of Cases Argued and Adjudged in the Supreme Court of the United States)*

SURETY COMPANY. *See* Insurance

SURGEON. *See* Physician

SURGEON (army). *See* Army officer: Air surgeon; Army officer: Woman assistant army surgeon

SURGEON GENERAL (army). *See* Army officer: Surgeon general

SURGEON GENERAL (navy). *See* Naval officer: Surgeon General of the Navy

SURGERY MANUAL. *See* Medical book: Surgery manual

SURGICAL OPERATION
Abdominal operation of the kind called ovariotomy, the surgical removal of an ovarian tumor, was performed by Dr. Ephraim McDowell upon Jane Todd Crawford on December 13, 1809 at Danville, Ky. The operation was performed without an anesthetic. She was 45 years of age at the time of the operation,

SURGICAL OPERATION—*Continued*

and lived to be 78. *(Mary Thompson Young Valentine—Biography of Ephraim McDowell)*

Anesthesia. *See* Anesthesia

Appendicitis operation (appendectomy) was performed in Davenport, Iowa, January 4, 1885, by Dr. William West Grant, on Mary Gartside, aged 22. Dr. Grant was the first physician deliberately to open the abdomen and sever the appendix from the cecum, on a diagnosis of perforation of the appendix. The operation was the first successful appendectomy. The patient lived until 1919, when she died of a quite different illness. *(Colorado Medicine. August 1933)*

Artificial aortic valve was made by Dr. Charles Anthony Hufnagel of the Georgetown University Medical Center, Georgetown University Hospital, Washington, D.C., and successfully fitted on a 30-year old patient on September 11, 1952. It was made of Flexiglas and contained a float three fourths of an inch in diameter which rose and slipped into one of three sockets in the side of the valve sleeve on the heart's upbeat, when blood was forced into the aorta.

Caesarean operation (successful) was performed by Dr. Jessee Bennett, on his wife Elizabeth Hog Bennett, on January 14, 1794, in Edom, Kanawha Valley, Virginia. Bennett had asked Dr. Alexander Humphreys of Staunton, Va., to assist in performing the operation but because of the slight chance of success Humphreys had declined. Dr. Bennett performed the operation with the assistance of two Negroes, who held the patient. She was placed on a table made of two planks laid on a couple of barrels and was given laudanum in lieu of an anesthetic *(Virginia Medical Monthly. Vol. 55. No. 10. January 1929)*

Epileptic case treated by elevation of the skull cap was demonstrated on November 2, 1933, by Dr. Karl Winfield Ney, Professor of Neurosurgery at the New York Medical College and Flower Hospital in New York City, before the members of the Eastern Homeopathic Medical Association and Clinical Congress held at the Flower Hospital. The top of the patient's skull was cut through almost all the way around, lifted slightly, and then replaced.

Gallstone operation was performed June 15, 1867, by Dr. John Stough Bobbs, "the father of cholecystotomy," in Indianapolis, Ind., on Mary E. Wiggins (Mrs. Burnsworth) of McCordsville, Ind., and reported to the Indiana Medical Society, May 19-20, 1868. *("Lithotomy of the Gall Bladder." Transactions of the Indiana State Medical Society, 1868)*

Heart operation for the relief of angina pectoris was performed February 13, 1935, by Dr. Claude Schaeffer Beck, Associate Professor of Surgery at Western Reserve University, on a patient at the Lakeside Hospital, Cleveland, Ohio. Dr. Beck resected one of the pectoral (chest) muscles and fastened the cut end to the heart-wall, to provide an additional source of blood for the heart. *(Annals of Surgery. Vol. 102. November 1935)*

Heart operation in which the deep freezing technique was employed was a 58-minute operation performed September 2, 1952, by Dr. Floyd John Lewis, Associate Professor of Surgery at the Medical School of the University of Minnesota, Minneapolis, Minn. The patient was a five-year-old girl, whose body temperature (except in her head) was reduced to 79 degrees. She recovered and left the hospital on the eleventh post-operative day. *(Surgery. Vol. 33. No. 1)*

Heart operation in which the elective cardiac arrest technique was employed was performed in May 1956 on a seventeen-month-old boy at the Cleveland Clinic, Cleveland, Ohio, by Dr. Donald Brian Effler and a task force of fifteen doctors and nurses. Potassium citrate arrested the heart beat, and the right ventricle was slit open, the blood being fed back into an artery in the chest by by-passing the heart.

Kidney transplanting, from one human to another, was performed by Dr. Richard Harold Lawler of the Little Company of Mary Hospital, Chicago, Ill., on June 17, 1950, in a 45-minute operation witnessed by 40 visiting surgeons and doctors. Dr. James Ward West removed a healthy kidney from a woman who had died. Dr. Lawler transplanted the kidney in the renal pedicle of a patient from whom a polycystic left kidney had been removed.

Lobotomy (prefrontal), the cutting of nerve pathways in the frontal lobe of the brain, was performed by Doctors James Winston Watts and Walter Freeman on September 14, 1956, at the George Washington University Hospital, Washington, D.C., on a 63-year-old female patient. *(Walter Freeman and James Winston Watts—Psychosurgery)*

Lung removal was performed April 5, 1933, at the Barnes Hospital, St. Louis, Mo., by Dr. Evarts Graham of St. Louis, who removed the left lung of a patient. Seven ribs were also removed for the purpose of allowing the soft tissues of the chest wall to collapse against the bronchial stump and therefore to obliterate as much as possible of the pleural cavity.

Lung removal carried out according to pre-operative plans was performed July 24, 1933, by Dr. William Francis Reinhoff, Jr., on

THE FIRST

Doris Yost, a three-year-old girl, at the Johns Hopkins Hospital, Baltimore, Md. She left the hospital September 13, 1933.

Lung tumor operation in which the patient was under hypnosis was performed on a 25-year-old woman at Cedars of Lebanon Hospital, Los Angeles, Calif., in January 1955. The hypnosis was performed by Dr. Milton Jacob Marmer, an anesthesiologist of Beverly Hills, Calif. The operation was reported at the 105th annual meeting of the American Medical Association at Chicago, Ill., on June 12, 1956.

Mastoid operation was performed June 15, 1859, at the Brooklyn City Hospital, Brooklyn, N.Y., by Dr. Joseph Chrisman Hutchison and described by him at the April 1865 meeting of the Medical Society of Kings County, Brooklyn. His report, entitled, "Otitis; Perforating of Mastoid Process with a Trephine," appeared in the *Transactions of the Medical Society of Kings County* (Vol. 2, No. 31, April 1865) and in the *Buffalo Medical and Surgical Journal* (Vol. 3, October 1865).

Mitral valve exposure (prolonged) in a human patient and corrective surgery were carried out on July 3, 1952, by Dr. Forest Dewey Dodrill at the Harper Hospital, Detroit, Mich., on a 41-year-old man. The Michigan Heart was used as a substitute for the lower left ventricle.

Painless surgery operation. *See* Anesthesia: Painless surgery demonstration

Siamese twins separated successfully by surgery. *See* Siamese twins: Siamese twins separated successfully by surgery

Skin grafting was suggested in 1847 by Dr. Frank Hastings Hamilton of Buffalo, N.Y. In 1854 he reported a case in which he had successfully grafted skin on a large raw surface of a man's leg injured by a heavy stone that had fallen on it. (*Howard Atwood Kelly and Walter Lincoln Burrage—Dictionary of American Medical Biography*)

Surgical operation telecast. *See* under Television—Telecast

Surgical operation under anesthesia. *See* Anesthesia

Suture of the human heart (successful) was accomplished July 9, 1893 at the Provident Hospital, Chicago, Ill., on James Cornish, whose internal mammary artery had been damaged by a knife wound. Dr. Daniel Hale Williams sutured the pericardium. The operation,

THE FIRST

which was witnessed by six doctors, was not described until March 27, 1897, in the *Medical Record.*

SURPLUS RELIEF CORPORATION. *See* Federal surplus relief corporation

SURVEY BOOK. *See* Coast survey book

SURVEY OF PUBLIC LANDS was authorized by the Ordinance of 1785, passed by the Continental Congress on May 20, 1785. The first surveys were made in the Seven Ranges in the Western Reserve. The Ordinance of 1785 provided for the division of all public lands into townships six miles square, numbered east and west from Primary Meridians and north and south from Base Lines. This rectangular system of surveying prevails throughout the United States except in the original thirteen states and in Maine, Vermont, Kentucky, Tennessee, and West Virginia.

SURVEYOR was Thomas Hariot (Harriot), surveyor and historian of Sir Walter Raleigh's first colony, who landed in 1585 in Virginia. He remained a year under Sir Ralph Lane, the first governor, and returned to England in July 1586 with the fleet commanded by Sir Richard Grenville. He published his observations in London in 1588 as *A Briefe and True Report of the New Found Land of Virginia, of the Commodities There Found and to be Raysed, As Well Merchantable, As Others for Victuall, Building and Other Necessarie Uses For Those That Are and Shalbe the Planters There. . . .*

SUSPENDED ELEVATOR. *See* Elevator: Elevator (suspended)

SUSPENSION BRIDGE. *See* Bridge: Suspension bridge

SUTURE
Fiberglas sutures were used by Dr. Roy Philip Scholz of St. Louis, Mo., on July 19, 1939, in a mastoid operation. The caliber of the suture was that of #00 silk. It had a carrying strength of 7.4 pounds. (*American Journal of Surgery. June 1942. Vol. 56*)

Silk suture and ligatures, used in place of catgut in operations, were used in 1882 by Dr. William Stewart Halsted of Baltimore, Md. He advocated black silk and introduced its use in 1889 at the Johns Hopkins Hospital, Baltimore. (*Johns Hopkins Hospital Reports. March 1891. p. 306*)

Silver wire suture (in place of silk thread) was used by Dr. James Marion Sims of Montgomery, Ala., who reported his experiments in

SUTURE—*Continued*
an article, "On the Treatment of Vesico-vaginal Fistula," in the *American Journal of the Medical Sciences,* January 1852. Sims had begun his experiments December 9, 1845. He performed a vesico-vaginal fistula operation on June 21, 1849. The suture was removed on the eighth day after the operation. (*American Journal of Surgery. June 1942. Vol. 56*)

SWEDENBORGIAN OR NEW CHURCH
German Swedenborgian Society was organized in Baltimore, Md., in 1855 by the Reverend Arthur Otto Brickman, a former Lutheran, who preached in both English and German.

Swedenborgian or New Church Temple was erected at the southwest corner of Exeter and Baltimore streets, Baltimore, Md. in 1799. The brick structure was built with funds supplied by citizens of the community. The first church service was held Sunday, January 5, 1800. The New Church group in Baltimore was led by Robert Carter, a member of the Virginia Colonial Council, which began meeting in 1792. The first incorporated organization was formed in 1798. The first New Church ministers ordained in America were the Reverend Ralph Mather, formerly of England, and the Reverend John Hargrove, a former preacher of the Methodist Episcopal Church and the Baltimore City Registrar. Hargrove became the first pastor. The first General Convention met in Philadelphia, Pa., in 1817. Hargrove was chosen as the first president. (*John Ellis—The New Church*)

SWEDES arrived in America in 1638. Peter Minuit led an expedition that sailed from Gothenburg, Sweden, on November 20, 1637, in two Dutch vessels, "Kalmar Nyckel" (The Key of Kalmar) and "Vogel Grip" (Bird Grip), with Jan Hendricksen van de Waeter as skipper. The expedition landed in March 1638 at "The Rocks" on the Christina River (the site of Wilmington, Del.). Fort Christina was named by Minuit in honor of the Swedish queen. The Swedes bought out the Dutch interests and in 1643 Johan Printz, the first Swedish governor, arrived.

SWEDISH MAGAZINE was *Skandinavia,* first published January 15, 1847, in New York City. Only eight issues of the magazine were published. (*Adolph Benson—Swedes in America 1638-1938*)

SWEET CRACKER. *See* Cracker: Cracker (sweet)

SWIMMER
American to swim the English Channel was Henry F. Sullivan of Lowell, Mass., who swam from Dover, England to Cape Gris-Nez, France, a distance of 56 miles, in 27 hours and 23 minutes on August 5-6, 1923. Sullivan was the fourth man to swim the channel.

American woman to swim the English Channel. *See* Woman: American woman to swim the English Channel

SWIMMING CHAMPIONSHIP (amateur open) meet was held on September 30, 1877, on the Harlem River by the New York Athletic Club.

SWIMMING POOL in the White House, Washington, D.C., was built by popular subscription. It is located in the west terrace of the mansion and is 50 feet long and 15 feet wide, with a depth ranging from 4 to 8 feet. The pool is lined with aquamarine terra cotta and has a six-foot wainscot of pale green terra cotta. The water is both filtered and sterilized. The pool was built under the direction of Lieutenant Colonel Ulysses Simpson Grant III, Director of Public Buildings, and was formally accepted by President Franklin Delano Roosevelt on June 2, 1933.

SWIMMING SCHOOL was opened July 23, 1827 in Boston, Mass. A boat beyond the Toll House conveyed the students to the Mill Dam, where the school was located. It was open from 5.30 A.M to 7 A.M.; from 9 A.M to 1 PM.; and from 4 P.M. to 8 P.M. The method of instruction was described as follows: "A belt is placed about the bodies, under the arms, attached to a rope and pole, by which the head and body are kept in the proper position in the water, while the pupil is learning the use of his limbs."

SWITCHBACK RAILROAD. *See* Railroad: Switchback railway

SWITCHBOARD (telephone). *See* Telephone: Telephone switchboard or exchange

SWORD SWALLOWER was Senaa Samma, "an Indian juggler from Madras and late from London," who performed at St. John's Hall, New York City, on November 11, 1817. Admission was one dollar, children half-price. On November 25, 1817, Samma swallowed "a sword manufactured by Mr. William Pyle of New York as a substitute for the one lately stolen from him by some villain." (*Columbian. New York City. November 26, 1817*)

SYMPHONY
Symphonic work by an American composer was the Symphony in C minor, Opus 23, by John Knowles Paine, presented in January 1876 in Boston, Mass., by Theodore Thomas and his orchestra.

Symphonic work to call for an airplane propeller was the *Ballet Mécanique,* by George Antheil, which he composed in 1922 at the age of twenty-two. It was first presented in

THE FIRST

the United States April 10, 1927, at Carnegie Hall, New York City. The score called for player-pianos and other mechanical contraptions, among them an airplane propeller. *(George Antheil—Bad Boy of Music)*

Symphony on a Negro folk theme was the Symphony No. 1 (the Negro Folk Symphony), composed by the Negro conductor William Levi Dawson. It was first presented on November 14, 1934, by the Philadelphia Orchestra under the direction of Leopold Stokowski at the Academy of Music, Philadelphia, Pa.

SYMPHONY ORCHESTRA. *See* Orchestra

SYNDICATE. *See* Newspaper syndicate: Newspaper syndicate

SYNTHETIC DETERGENT. *See* Detergent: Synthetic detergent

SYNTHETIC MICA. *See* Mica: Synthetic mica

SYNTHETIC RUBBER. *See* Rubber: Synthetic rubber

SYNTHETIC RUBBER AUTOMOBILE TIRE. *See* Automobile tire: Synthetic rubber tire

SYNTHETIC VITAMIN. *See* Vitamin: Synthetic vitamin

TABLOID. *See* Newspaper: Illustrated tabloid

TABULATING MACHINE was invented by Dr. Herman Hollerith of New York City, who received patent No. 395,782, January 8, 1889, on a system of recording separate statistical items pertaining to the individual by means of holes, or combinations of holes, punched in cards, and then counting or tallying such statistical items either separately or in combination by means of electrical counters operated by electromagnets, the circuits being controlled by the perforated cards. The first extensive use of the electric tabulating system was in the compilation of the statistics of population for the eleventh United States census in 1890.

TACONITE
Taconite project established for large-scale commercial production was the E. W. Davis Works at Silver Bay, Minn., built by the Reserve Mining Company, Duluth, Minn., and owned jointly by the Armco Steel Corpo-

THE FIRST

ration and the Republic Steel Corporation. Full production began September 13, 1956. Taconite is a hard ferruginous rock containing 25 per cent to 30 per cent iron. The rock is crushed, ground, and processed by magnetic separation, and small pellets containing 62½ per cent iron are produced. The processing plant began preliminary operations in the fall of 1955. Its capacity was rated at 3,750,000 tons of iron ore pellets annually.

TALKING ANIMATED CARTOON. *See* Moving picture: Animated cartoon talking picture

TALKING BOOK for the blind was a collection of eight phonograph records of patriotic documents. The Declaration of Independence and the Constitution of the United States comprised four double-faced records, and Washington's Farewell Address to the Continental Army and letter to the Congress of the United States made up the other four. This collection, intended for reproduction on a specially designed phonograph, was issued in July 1934 by the American Foundation for the Blind, New York City.

TALKING HEADLIGHT. *See* Locomotive headlight: Talking headlight

TALKING MOVING PICTURE. *See* under Moving picture

TALLYHO. *See* Coaching

TANK. *See* Ordnance: Tank (heavy 60-ton)

TANK CAR. *See* Railroad car: Glass-lined tank car

TANK CAR (oil). *See* Oil: Oil tank cars

TANK DISCHARGER (airplane). *See* Aviation: Airplane tank discharger

TANK (military). *See* Army armored tank

TANKER. *See* Ship: Oil tanker

TANNER. *See* Leather: Leather tanning

TANNING (leather). *See* Leather

TAPE (adhesive). *See* Adhesive and medicated plaster

TAPE MEASURE PATENT was granted to Alvin J. Fellows of New Haven, Conn., July 14, 1868, No. 79,965. The tape measure was enclosed in a circular case with a spring click lock to hold the tape at any desired point.

TAPE RECORDER

Magnetic tape recorder was the Wireway, announced January 27, 1948, by the Wire Recording Corporation of America. It was a lightweight portable wire-recorder with a built-in oscillator. It retailed at $149.50.

Magnetic tape recorder (commercial) of sound and picture was manufactured by the Ampex Corporation, Redwood City, Calif., and demonstrated simultaneously in Redwood City and Chicago, Ill., on April 14, 1956. The tape, 2 inches wide, moved at a speed of 15 inches a second. A single 14-inch reel accommodated a 65-minute recording. The Columbia Broadcasting System purchased three of the video tape recorders at $75,000 each in 1956.

TAPE RECORDING

Radio broadcast from a tape recording was made by WQXR, Interstate Broadcasting Company, New York City, from 6:30 P.M. to 7 P.M. August 26, 1938, using Millertape, the invention of James Arthur Miller of the Miller Broadcasting System, New York City. A sapphire stylus engraved a 15-minute program on 1,000 feet of tape. Editing and cutting were possible on this sound tape transmission.

Video recording on magnetic tape of high definition was made on October 3, 1952, when the electronics division of Bing Crosby Enterprises, Inc., Los Angeles, Calif., using a Video Tape Recorder, recorded images on magnetic tape, rewound the tape, and immediately reproduced the picture through a standard television monitor tube. A one-inch tape with twelve tracks, one for sound and eleven for pictures, was used. The cost was one third that of photographic processes.

Video recording on magnetic tape in color was the "Betty Feezor Show," recorded from 11:00 to 11:30 A.M. and shown from 1:00 to 1:30 P.M., on September 5, 1958, by WBTV, Charlotte, N.C.

Video recording on magnetic tape televised coast-to-coast was the Jonathan Winters show, televised October 23, 1956, by WRCA-TV, New York City. The process was developed by the Radio Corporation of America for National Broadcasting Company television. Instead of film the system utilized instantaneous tape with pictures that could be played back immediately after recording. The telecast was shown in full compatible color and also in black-and-white.

TAPESTRY. *See* Carpeting (velvet)

TAPS (military signal) was played in its present form about the first week of July 1862. General Daniel Butterfield wrote the music on the back of a torn envelope he had been carrying around with him and whistled the tune to Oliver Willcox Norton, bugler and aide-de-camp of General Strong Vincent, commander of the 83rd Regiment Pennsylvania Volunteers of the Army of the Potomac. They were resting in camp at Harrison's Landing on the James River in Virginia, immediately after the seven days of fighting near Richmond. (*Julia Lorrilard Butterfield—A Biographical Memorial of General Daniel Butterfield*)

TARIFF

Import duty treaty. *See* Treaty: Treaty with a foreign nation to provide for mutual reduction of import duties

Narcotic tariff. *See* Narcotic: Narcotic tariff

Tariff commission was authorized June 7, 1882 (22 Stat.L.64). Nine tariff commissioners at ten dollars a day and expenses were appointed from civil life to investigate tariff questions relating to agriculture, commerce, manufacturing, mining, and mercantile and industrial interests. The first chairman was John Lord.

Tariff for protection rather than primarily for revenue was the "act to regulate the duties on imports and tonnage," passed April 27, 1816 (3 Stat.L.310).

Tariff legislation passed by Congress after the adoption of the Constitution was the Tariff Act of July 4, 1789 (1 Stat.L.24), an "act for laying a duty on goods, wares and merchandises imported into the United States," effective August 1, 1789. The main purpose was the collection of revenue, but protection was also extended to certain industries which the government wished to encourage, such as glass and earthenware. The act was signed by George Washington and was to continue in force until July 1796. It laid specific duties on some articles and ad valorem duties on others, equivalent to an 8½ per cent ad valorem rate, with drawback, up to 1 per cent of the duties on all articles exported within twelve months except distilled spirits other than brandy and geneva.

Tariff to prevent the importation of obscene literature and pictures was the Tariff Act of August 30, 1842 (5 Stat.L.566), an "act to provide revenue from imports. . . ." Section 28 stated: "The importation of all indecent and obscene prints, paintings, lithographs, engravings and transparencies is hereby prohibited . . . and all invoices and packages whereof any such article shall compose a part are . . . liable . . . to be seized and forfeited . . . and the said articles shall be forthwith destroyed."

TARIFF REFUND. *See* Drawback legislation

TATTOO

Electric tattoo machine was employed by Samuel F. O'Reilly in 1875 on the Bowery, New York City. The electric tattoos were called "tattaugraphs." *(Albert Parry—Tattoo)*

Tattoo shop was opened in 1846 by Martin Hildebrandt at Oak Street between Oliver and James Streets, New York City.

Tattooed man exhibited was James F. O'Connell, whose appearance at the Franklin Theatre, Chatham Square, New York City, on October 21, 1849, was advertised as follows in the New York *Herald*: "The manager has at an enormous expense engaged Mr. J. F. O'Connell, the wonderful 'Tattooed Man' who will go through a variety of performances peculiar to himself, and perfectly original."

TAURINE CLOTH. *See* Hair cloth

TAX

See also Cigarette tax; Gasoline tax; Tobacco: Tobacco tax (colonial); Tobacco: Tobacco tax for internal revenue

Bachelor tax was levied by Missouri which on December 20, 1820 (effective January 1, 1821), placed a one-dollar tax "on every unmarried free white male, above the age of 21 years and under 50 years." *(Missouri Territorial Laws. 1820. Chapter 299. Vol. 1)*

Chain stores tax (state) was levied by Indiana (Chapter 207 of the acts of 1929). This statute, commonly referred to as the Indiana Chain Store Tax Law, was signed March 16, 1929, by Governor Harry Leslie, and became effective July 1, 1929. Under the statute, owners were required to pay an annual license fee of $3 to operate a store in Indiana. The tax on two to five stores under the same management, supervision, or ownership was $10, for each additional store; on stores in excess of five but not in excess of ten, $15 for each additional store; on stores in excess of ten but not in excess of twenty, $20 for each additional store; on all stores in excess of twenty, $25 plus a 50-cent filing fee for each additional store. An amendment to this act (Chapter 271, Acts of 1933) was signed March 11, 1933, by Governor Paul Vories McNutt, requiring owners of stores in excess of twenty to pay $150 for each additional store.

Corporation tax was passed by act of Congress August 5, 1909 (36 Stat.L.112). The act taxed all corporations with an income over $5,000. The law was passed prior to the adoption of the U.S. income tax amendment.

Excess profits tax was passed by act of Congress of March 3, 1917 (39 Stat.L.1000), an "act to provide increased revenue to defray the expenses of the increased appropriation for the army and navy and the extension of fortifications." Under the act the profits of all corporations in excess of from 7 to 9 per cent of the capital were taxed. The rates were progressive: 20 per cent on excess profits up to 15 per cent; 35 per cent on the excess from 15 to 25 per cent; 45 per cent on the excess from 25 per cent to 33 per cent; and 60 per cent on the excess above 33 per cent. The act was repealed by section 214 of the Revenue Act of 1917, approved October 3, 1917 (40 Stat.L.308).

Excise tax (federal) was enacted March 3, 1791. It was "an act repealing, after the last day of June next, the duties heretofore laid upon distilled spirits imported from abroad, and laying others in their stead; and also upon spirits distilled within the United States" (1 Stat.L.199). It imposed a tax on distilled spirits from 11 cents to 30 cents a gallon in accordance with alcoholic content prior to removal from distilleries.

Federal income tax was imposed by the act of August 5, 1861 (12 Stat.L.292), effective January 1, 1862, which imposed a 3 per cent tax on incomes exceeding $800, to be paid prior to June 30, 1862. Income from federal and foreign bonds was assessed at other rates. The income tax lists were open to public inspection by "all persons who may apply to inspect the same." This was interpreted in such a way as to eliminate idle curiosity seekers. The tax was collected at a progressive rate based upon income. The tax was rescinded in 1872 with other Civil War taxes. An income-tax law was passed August 27, 1894 (28 Stat.L.553) as part of the tariff act, but it was declared unconstitutional. *(Joseph Jerome Klein—Federal Income Taxation)*

Federal tax levied directly upon the states was a direct pro rata tax upon the sixteen states authorized by act of Congress of July 14, 1798 (1 Stat.L.597), "an act to lay and collect a direct tax within the United States." It was levied upon dwellings, land, and slaves. The amount to be collected was $2,000,000, which was apportioned to the states in direct ratio to the population. The Constitution gives Congress "power to lay and collect taxes, duties, imposts and excises, to pay the debts and provide for the common defense and general welfare of the United States."

Income tax amendment to the Constitution (the 16th) was proposed to the legis-

TAX—*Continued*
latures of the several states by the 61st Congress on July 12, 1909, and was declared to have been ratified by a proclamation of Secretary of State Philander Chase Knox on February 25, 1913 (37 Stat.L.1785). This amendment gave Congress power "to lay and collect taxes on incomes, from whatever source derived, without apportionment among the several states, and without regard to any census or enumeration." The income tax went into effect March 1, 1913.

Inheritance tax (colonial) was levied by Virginia in 1687 when the Colony of Virginia provided that the governor of the colony should collect a fee of a cask and two hundred pounds of tobacco for impressing probates and letters testamentary or letters of administration with the public seal, without which they were invalid. *(William John Shultz—American Public Finance and Taxation)*

Inheritance tax (federal) was a part of the Internal Revenue Law of July 1, 1862 (12 Stat.L.432), which assessed a tax on legacies and distributive shares of personal property.

Inheritance tax (state) was Chapter 72, "relating to collateral inheritance," passed by Pennsylvania on April 7, 1826 to become effective May 1, 1826. It was signed by Governor John Andrew Shulze. It established a 2.5 per cent collateral inheritance tax. The surviving spouse, the parents, and the descendants of the decedent were exempted.

Internal revenue tax was imposed March 3, 1791 (1 Stat.L.199), effective July 1, 1791. It levied taxes on distilled spirits and on carriages. Subsequent early modifications of the act of 1791 imposed taxes on retail dealers in distilled spirits, and on refined sugar, snuff, property sold at auction, snuff mills, legal instruments, and bonds. On July 9, 1798 (1 Stat. L.584) a direct tax was placed on real estate. The receipts for the fiscal year 1792 from internal revenue netted the government $208,942.81

Property tax law (colonial) was passed May 14, 1634, and signed by Governor William Bradford of the Massachusetts colony: "It is further ordered that in all rates and public charges, the towns shall have respect to levy each man according to his estate, and with consideration of all other his abilities, whatsoever, and not according to the number of persons."

Sales tax (state) was approved May 3, 1921, by West Virginia, to become effective July 1, 1921. The funds collected were used largely in place of funds from a tax on

corporate net income. The rate was one-fifth of one per cent on the gross income of banks, street railroads, telephones, telegraph, express, and electric light and power retailers, and two-fifths of one per cent on timber, oil, coal, natural gas, and other minerals. Payments could be made to the state quarterly or annually. *(Robert Murray Haig and Carl Shoup —The Sales Tax in the American States)*

State university supported by a direct property tax. *See* College: State university supported by a direct property tax

Tax on the American colonies without their consent was levied in 1672 when the British Parliament passed a law imposing a duty on sugar, tobacco, ginger, coconuts, indigo, logwood fustic, wool, and cotton.

TAX APPEALS BOARD MEMBER (woman). *See* Woman: Woman tax appeals board member

TAXICAB (electric). *See* Automobile: Electric taxicabs

TAXIDERMY METHOD (sculptural) was devised by Carl Ethan Akeley in 1902. He mounted skins on specially constructed forms, lifelike and true in all details to the living animals. His first important work, "The Four Seasons," representing four groups of Virginia deer and their appropriate surroundings in spring, summer, autumn, and winter, was prepared for the Field Museum of Natural History, Chicago, Ill.

TEA SHRUB was planted at Middleton Barony, S.C., in 1802 by the French botanist François André Michaux.

TEACHERS' CONVENTION
  Teachers' convention (national) was attended by representatives of state teachers' associations who met in the Hall of the Controllers of the Public Schools in Philadelphia, Pa., on August 26, 1857, and organized the National Teachers Association "to elevate the character and advance the interest of the profession of teaching and to promote the cause of popular education in the United States." John L. Enos was chairman and W. E. Sheldon secretary. At the convention held in Cleveland, Ohio, on August 15, 1870, the name was changed to the National Education Association.

Teachers' convention (state) was held in January 1831 at Utica, N.Y., and was advertised as the "State Convention of Teachers and Friends of Education."

THE FIRST

THE FIRST

TEACHERS' DEATH BENEFIT was in operation for a short time beginning in 1869 in New York City under the New York City Teachers Mutual Life Assurance Association. Upon the death of a member, the membership was required to contribute a dollar to pay funeral expenses.

TEACHERS' INSTITUTE was held at Hartford, Conn., in October 1839 when twenty-six men teachers attended a six-week course sponsored by Henry Barnard and received the "opportunity of critically reviewing the studies which they will be called upon to teach, with a full explanation of all the principles involved." Among the authorities who gave instruction were Charles Davies, higher mathematics, and Thomas Hopkins Gallaudet, composition and school government. (*Bernard Christian Steiner—Life of Henry Barnard*)

TEACHERS' PENSION FUND was set up in New York City under authority of Chapter 296, Laws of New York State, passed April 14, 1894, which provided for a public school teachers' retirement fund. The resources were to come from deductions made from the pay of the teachers because of absence. Regular salaries were not assessed.

TEACHERS' SICK BENEFIT FUNDS were established in 1887 in both New York City and Brooklyn. The two organizations were the New York City Teachers Mutual Benefit Association and the Brooklyn Aid Association. Dues based on salary were obtained from teachers. (*Frederick Albert Cleveland—Teachers' Pension Systems in the United States*)

TEACHERS' TRAINING SCHOOL. *See* Normal school

TEACHING CHAIR. *See* Education: Chair in education; Pedagogy chair: Pedagogy chair (permanent)

TEACHING METHODS BOOK was Christopher Dock's *Schul-ordnung; or A Simple and Thoroughly Prepared School-Management clearly setting forth not only in what manner children may best be taught in the branches usually given at school, but also how they may be well instructed in the knowledge of godliness.* The book was completed August 3, 1750, but not published until twenty years later. The preface was dated March 27, 1770. It was originally written in German and was printed by Christopher Saur in Germantown, Pa. (*Marian Groves Brumbaugh—Life and Work of Christopher Dock*)

TECHNICAL ANIMATED CARTOON. *See* Moving picture: Animated cartoon (technical)

TECHNICAL COLLEGE FOR WOMEN. *See* College: Technical college for women

TECHNICAL INSTITUTE was the Gardiner Lyceum, Gardiner, Me., founded by Robert Hallowell Gardiner in 1822 "for the purpose of giving to farmers and mechanics such a scientific education as would enable them to become skillful in their professions." Courses were offered in arithmetic, algebra, geometry, trigonometry, mensuration of surfaces and solids, bookkeeping, surveying, navigation, mechanics, hydrostatics, pneumatics, chemistry, natural philosophy and "the higher branches of mathematics and natural history." The first lecturer was Benjamin Hale. (*Society for the Promotion of Engineering Education—A Study of Technical Institutes. February 1931*)

TECHNICOLOR MOTION PICTURE. *See* Moving picture: Technicolor motion picture

TEE (golf). *See* Golf tee

TEETH. *See* Dentistry

TELAUTOGRAPH was manufactured in 1881. Patent No. 491,347, was issued to Elisha Gray of Highland Park, Ill., on February 7, 1893.

TELECAST. *See* Television—Telecast

TELEGRAM
News dispatch telegram was "One o'clock. There has just been made a motion in the House to go into committee of the whole on the Oregon question. Rejected. Ayes 79—Nays 86." It was sent from Washington, D.C., to the Baltimore *Patriot,* Saturday afternoon, May 25, 1844.

Singing telegram was introduced by the Postal Telegraph Cable Company, New York City, on February 10, 1933. The service continued unofficially until September 1933, when it was given the official sanction of the Metropolitan Division, New York, as a "commercial service."

Telegram dispatched from an aerial station was sent from the balloon "Enterprise" on June 18, 1861, to President Abraham Lincoln by Professor Thaddeus Sobieski Coulincourt Lowe, who acknowledged his indebtedness "for the opportunity of demonstrating the availability of the science of aeronautics in the military service of the country." Lowe made his first official ascent July 24, 1861, and saw the movements of the Confederate troops after the battle of Manassas, Va. Again, he detected a Confederate maneuver to attack the troops of General

TELEGRAM—*Continued*
Heintzelman, who was separated from the main force at Fair Oaks. And on May 24, 1862, he directed artillery fire from his balloon, the first use of a balloon for such a purpose.

Telegram inaugurating commercial service was sent May 24, 1844, by Professor Samuel Finley Breese Morse from the United States Supreme Court room in the Capitol, Washington, D.C., to Alfred Vail at the Mount Clare station of the Baltimore and Ohio Railroad Company, Baltimore, Md. Vail retransmitted it to Morse. The message, "What hath God wrought," was selected from the twenty-third verse of the twenty-third chapter of Numbers by Annie Ellsworth, daughter of the Commissioner of Patents.

Transcontinental telegram was sent October 24, 1861, by Stephen Johnson Field, Chief Justice of California, to President Abraham Lincoln. The Mayor of San Francisco, Calif., also sent a message to Mayor Fernando Wood of New York City on the same date.
See also Telegraph: Telegraph line to the Pacific coast

TELEGRAPH
Army field telegraph used in warfare was employed May 24, 1862, in the Peninsula campaign during the Civil War. A wire several miles long extended from the headquarters of General George Brinton McClellan to an advance guard at Mechanicsville, Va., commanded by General George Stoneman, chief of cavalry in the Army of the Potomac. (*Military Affairs. Vol. 18. No. 4. Winter 1954*)

Duplex telegraph (practical) was invented by Thomas Alva Edison of Newark, N.J., who obtained patent No. 480,567 on August 9, 1892, in the United States and earlier patents in England, France, Italy, Austria-Hungary, and Russia. The telegraph was "to enable two operators to simultaneously send over one wire in one direction, by reversal of a battery current in one instance and increasing and decreasing the strength of the current in the other instance, and the connections are so arranged that the party at the receiving station can signal to the sender to repeat in case of inaccuracy."

Photographs sent over a city telegraph. *See* Radio facsimile transmission: Photographs sent over a city telephone

Semaphore telegraph system. *See* Semaphore telegraph system

Telegraph was constructed in 1827 by Harrison Gray Dyar, who operated a two-mile telegraph system at the racecourse at

Long Island City, New York. Iron wire attached to glass insulators on wooden posts enabled the current to produce a red mark on litmus paper at the receiving station. The lapse of time between the sparks indicated the different letters. (*George Bartlett Prescott—History, Theory and Practice of the Electric Telegraph*)

Telegraph appropriation (federal) was made by Congress on March 3, 1843 (5 Stat.L.618). A sum of $30,000 was appropriated "to test the practicability of establishing a system of electro-magnetic telegraphs by the United States."

Telegraph cable. *See* Cable

Telegraph call boxes were installed June 22, 1872, in Brooklyn, N.Y., by the American District Telegraph Company. Each metal box contained "a Seth Thomas clock movement supported upon a circular iron base . . . [with] two break wheels . . . attached to the clockwork, either of which could be brought into circuit by means of a switch." One wheel was notched for the even number and the other for the odd, the former indicating messenger and the latter fire. The idea was conceived by Edward A. Calahan, who obtained patent No. 127,844 on June 11, 1872 and No. 129,526 on July 16, 1873. (*Telegraph and Telephone Age. February 16, 1911*)

Telegraph code converter was the Trak Code Converter, made by CGS Laboratories, Inc., Stamford, Conn., and announced to the public in the October 1954 issue of *Wire and Radio Communications Magazine.* Incoming International Morse Code signals were converted by a teleprinter which recorded at speeds up to 600 words a minute. The converter, which cost $14,850, was housed in a relay rack 19 inches long and 54 inches high.

Telegraph company was the Magnetic Telegraph Company, incorporated February 4, 1847, under the laws of Maryland. The first meeting was held January 14, 1846. The first president was Amos Kendall. An office was erected at 10 Wall Street for the reception of messages. The rental for the New York office was $250 a year, Philadelphia $150, Baltimore $150, and Washington $50. At first messages were sent by pigeons across the Hudson River from Jersey City, N.J., to New York City; later a lead pipe, enclosing a covered wire saturated with pitch, was laid under the river. The rates from Baltimore to Washington were ten cents for the first ten words, and one cent for each additional word. The rates from New York to Washington were fifty cents for the first ten words and five cents for each additional word.

THE FIRST

Telegraph convention (national) was held July 17, 1850, at the Telegraph Office, New York City. Henry O'Rielly was appointed president and L. W. Jerome secretary. (*American Telegraph Magazine. Vol. 1. April-May-June 1853*)

Telegraph (electro-magnetic) was invented by Joseph Henry, who exhibited it in 1831 at the Albany Academy, Albany, N.Y. The device was fourteen inches long. At each excitation of the electric magnet, one end of a compass rod or needle remained in contact with a limb of the soft iron core. Near the opposite end of the compass rod was a small stationary office-bell. When the current was reversed, the compass rod moved back to the opposite limb of the electro-magnet. Signals were transmitted by means of the electro-magnet through more than a mile of wire. The invention was not put to practical use; it merely demonstrated the possibility of transmitting signals. (*William Bowers Taylor—An Historical Sketch of Henry's Contribution to the Electro-Magnetic Telegraph*)

Telegraph in railroading was used September 22, 1851, when Charles Minot, superintendent of the Erie Railroad, telegraphed fourteen miles to Goshen, N.Y., to delay a train so that his train would not have to wait. Trains were run on the interval system.

Telegraph line to the Pacific coast was placed in operation October 24, 1861, when United States Supreme Court Justice Stephen Johnson Field of California sent the first message to President Abraham Lincoln. On October 25, 1861, telegrams were exchanged between Mayor Fernando Wood of New York City and Mayor H. F. Teschemacher of San Francisco, Calif. Rates during the first week were one dollar a word between San Francisco and the Missouri River. Later the rates were reduced: ten words from San Francisco to New York cost $6, and each additional word 75 cents.

Telegraph station was opened in Washington, D.C., in 1844 under the direction of Samuel Finley Breese Morse. The station was located between Seventh and Eighth streets and E and F Streets. (*National Intelligencer. May 22, 1844*)

Telegraph ticker to operate at high speed was installed November 1929 in the Bankers Club of America, 120 Broadway, New York City. It printed five hundred characters a minute. It operated on only one transmitting wire, instead of two, as did the old tickers.

Telegraph ticker to print letters of the alphabet was patented by Royal Earl House of New York City, who obtained patent

THE FIRST

No. 4,464 on April 18, 1846, on a "magnetic letter printing telegraph." The ticker was first publicly exhibited in 1844 at the American Institute Fair, New York City. It was extensively used for about ten years until superseded by new models.

Telegraph ticker used by a brokerage concern was installed December 29, 1867, in the office of David Groesbeck & Company, a member of the New York Stock Exchange, New York City, by the Gold and Stock Telegraph Company, New York City. A rental of $6 a week was charged for the service, which was operated by Daniel Drew. (*Edmund Clarence Stedman—The New York Stock Exchange*)

Telegraph ticker which successfully printed type was invented by David Edward Hughes of Louisville, Ky., who received patent No. 14,917 on May 20, 1856. He had sold his rights to the Commercial Company for $100,000 on November 1, 1855.

Telegraphic communication system in which dots and dashes represented letters was invented by Alfred Vail of Morristown, N.J., in September 1837. On January 8, 1838, the message "A patient waiter is no loser" was transmitted. On January 24, 1838, in a public demonstration given at New York University, New York City, the message "Attention the Universe. By Kingdom's Right Wheel" was transmitted through a circuit of ten miles. Previously, words had been assigned numbers, marks being acutely angulated lines like the letter V or V in reverse, which appeared on cylinders at the receiving station.

Woman telegrapher. *See* Woman: Woman telegrapher

TELEPHONE

Air-to-ground public telephone service began September 15, 1957, in the Chicago-Detroit area when about 20 airplanes were equipped for the two-way service. The rates varied from $1.50 to $4.25 for a 3-minute call, depending on the location of the airplane and the telephone on the ground.

Automatic telephone system patent was issued December 5, 1879 (No.22,458), to Daniel Connolly of Philadelphia, Thomas A. Connolly of Washington, D.C., and Thomas J. McTighe of Pittsburgh, who had applied for a patent on September 10, 1879. The system employed a single line wire, a battery of cells located at each telephone, and a dial switching mechanism for each line. The system could accommodate only a few lines and was not commercially applied.

TELEPHONE—*Continued*

Automatic telephone system (successful) was invented by Almon B. Strowger, who filed application for a patent March 12, 1889. During 1891 and 1892 twenty machines were made by the Union Model Works. In May 1892 A. E. Keith started the installation of the first automatic exchange at La Porte, Ind. This exchange was formally opened to the public November 3, 1892. The first exchange equipped with a rotating dial was an interior system in the City Hall of Milwaukee, Wis., which was installed during 1896. *(Harry Hughes Harrison —An Introduction to the Strowger System of Automatic Telephony)*

Coin telephone was invented by William Gray of Hartford, Conn., who received patent No. 408,709 on August 13, 1889, on a "coin-controlled apparatus for telephones." He had filed his application August 13, 1888. The first machine in commercial use was installed in the Hartford Bank in 1889 under the supervision of Ellis Benjamin Baker, superintendent of the Southern New England Telephone Company. In 1891 Gray, with Amos Whitney and Francis Pratt, incorporated the Gray Telephone Pay Station Company (now the Gray Manufacturing Company) and installed the telephones in stores on a rental basis. The company rented out pay phones for 25 per cent of the take. Ten per cent of the take went to the place of business in which the telephones were installed and 65 per cent to the telephone company. *(J. Leigh Walsh—Pioneers in Telegraphy)*

Commercial telephone service on railroad trains for passengers was placed in operation August 15, 1947, simultaneously on the Baltimore and Ohio Railroad Company's "Royal Blue" and the Pennsylvania Railroad Company's "Congressional Limited" between New York City and Washington, D.C. Two-way telephone conversation was carried on in the same way as ordinary telephone calls.

Common battery (non-multiple) switch-board was placed in operation January 9, 1894, in Lexington, Mass., by the New England Telephone and Telegraph Company.

Desk telephone, supplementing the wall telephone box, was used in 1886.

Dial telephone service coast-to-coast without the aid of operators was commercially inaugurated November 10, 1951, with a conversation between Mayor M. Leslie Denning of Englewood, N.J., and Mayor Frank P. Osborn of Alameda, Calif. Three digits were added to the number to be dialed. Conversation took place eighteen seconds after the dialing. Raymond J. Neiligan was the manager of the Englewood, N.J. exchange.

International telephone conversation was held July 1, 1881, when service was inaugurated by the National Bell Telephone Company of the State of Maine between Calais, Me., and St. Stephen, New Brunswick, two points separated by the St. Croix River, the international boundary line between the United States and Canada.

Interstate telephone call took place May 17, 1877, when a call was made from New Brunswick, N.J., to Dr. Alexander Graham Bell at Chickering Hall, New York City.

Long-distance telephone call was made March 27, 1884, by branch managers of the American Bell Telephone Company in Boston, Mass., and New York City. "The words were heard as perfectly as though the speakers were standing close by, while no extra effort was needed at the other end of the line to accomplish the result." *(Boston Journal. March 27, 1884)*

Mobile long-distance car-to-car telephone conversation was made September 11, 1946, when a reporter on the Houston (Texas) *Post* telephoned a reporter on the St. Louis (Mo.) *Globe Democrat.*

Mobile telephone commercial service was inaugurated June 17, 1946, by the Southwestern Bell Telephone Company, St. Louis, Mo. Installations were completed in the automobiles of two subscribers, the Monsanto Chemical Company and Henry L. Perkinson, a contractor. Conversation was possible with any Bell Telephone System or connecting company telephone.

Mobile telephone conversation overseas from a moving vehicle was made July 16, 1946, by Roger Pierce from St. Louis, Mo., to Honolulu, Hawaii.

Mobile telephone conversation with commercial equipment over commercial communication lines between an airplane in flight and a moving automobile was accomplished on October 9, 1947, by executives of the Hercules Powder Company, Wilmington, Del., from an airplane 2,000 feet in the air to an automobile about five miles west of Wilmington, Del., on the Lancaster Pike (Route 41).

Mobile telephone news dispatch transmitted from a moving car was sent May 15, 1946, by Richard Everett of the St. Louis (Mo.) *Star-Times.*

Mobile transatlantic telephone conversation between two telephone-equipped automobiles was made June 26, 1947, by United States Ambassador James Clement Dunn from

THE FIRST

Milan, Italy to Vincent R. Impellitteri, president of the New York City Council, on the occasion of Marconi Day at the Milan Fair.

Multiple common battery switchboard was put in service in the fall of 1897 by the Ohio Valley Telephone Company in Louisville, Ky.

News dispatch by telephone was sent from Salem, Mass., February 12, 1877, to the Boston *Globe,* Boston, Mass. by Bell telephone. The *Globe* reported: "This special dispatch to the *Globe* has been transmitted by telephone in the presence of twenty people who have thus been witnesses to a feat never before attempted—the sending of news over the space of sixteen miles by the human voice."

Pay station telephone service began June 1, 1880, in the office of the Connecticut Telephone Company, Yale Bank Building, State and Chapel Streets, New Haven, Conn. The toll was given to an attendant.

Photographs sent over a city telephone. *See* Radio facsimile transmission: Photographs sent over a city telephone

President to use a telephone. *See* President (United States): President to use a telephone

President who had used a telephone for campaigning. *See* President (United States): President who had used a telephone for campaigning

Radio telephone. *See* Radio telephone

Round-the-world telephone conversation was held on April 25, 1935, between Walter Sherman Gifford, president of the American Telephone Company, in his office in New York City, and T. G. Miller, a company vice president, who was in an office about fifty feet away. The call was routed by telephone (over 23,000 miles of wire) and radio through San Francisco, Java, Amsterdam, and London and back to New York.

Telecast over telephone wires. *See* Television—Telecast: Telecast over telephone wires

Telephone cable service (deep sea) was established April 11, 1921 between Key West, Fla., and Havana, Cuba. It was officially opened by President Warren Gamaliel Harding. President Harding, at the Pan American Building, Washington, D.C., conversed with President Mario García Menocal of Cuba, at Havana.

Telephone company answering service was the Ohio Bell Telephone Co., which marketed a recording machine and offered service at

THE FIRST

$12.50 a month, plus a $15 installment fee. As many as twenty 30-second messages could be recorded on a cylinder, which could then be cleaned and used again. The service was offered to the public in March 1951.

Telephone concert. *See* Music: Long-distance telephone concert

Telephone conversation (commercial) using electricity generated by the sun's rays took place October 4, 1955, at Americus, Ga., over the lines of the Southern Bell Telephone and Telegraph Company. The current was supplied by a solar battery developed by the Bell Telephone Laboratories. The aluminum housing of the battery, less than a yard square, contained 432 silicon cells cushioned in oil and covered with glass. The first call, over a distance of about fourteen miles, was made to Gene Summerford by George Mathews, who said, "Hello, Gene. This is George Mathews. How many bales of cotton do I have in your warehouse?"

Telephone conversation over out-of-door wires took place on October 9, 1876, between Alexander Graham Bell in Boston and Thomas Augustus Watson in Cambridge, Mass. The private telegraph wire of the Walworth Manufacturing Company from Boston to Cambridge, a distance of two miles, was used. Parallel accounts of the conversation as recorded by both Bell and Watson were published in the Boston *Advertiser* in answer to the skeptics who did not believe that the telephone was as reliable as the telegraph. *(Thomas A. Watson—The Birth and Babyhood of the Telephone)*

Telephone conversation over the transoceanic telephone cable was held September 25, 1956, when Cleo Frank Craig, chairman of the board of the American Telegraph and Telephone Company in New York City spoke to Dr. Charles Hill, Her Majesty's Postmaster General, at Lancaster House, London, England. The cable, designed to carry 36 conversations at the same time, was the joint undertaking of the Bell System, the British Post Office (which operates telephone service in Great Britain), and the Canadian Overseas Telecommunications Corporation. The first commercial service began with a conversation between Samuel H. Berlin of New York City and John Blackburn Batley of England. The rate was $12 for a three-minute call. The transatlantic cable—between Clarenville, Newfoundland, and Oban, Scotland, a distance of about 2,250 miles—was laid by the "Monarch" from June 22, 1955, to September 26, 1955.

Telephone for domestic use was installed in April 1877 at the home of Charles Williams, Jr., of Somerville, Mass., at the corner of

TELEPHONE—*Continued*
Arlington and Lincoln Streets. Williams also had a telephone installed at the same time in his office at 109 Court Street, Boston, Mass.

Telephone message (distinguishable) was "Come here, Watson, I want you" spoken into the telephone on March 10, 1876, by Alexander Graham Bell and received by Thomas Augustus Watson, on another floor in Bell's home at 5 Exeter Place, Boston, Mass.

Telephone message from a submarine under water to shore was sent January 6, 1898, by the submarine inventor, Simon Lake, submerged at the bottom of the Patapsco River. Lake telephoned the mayor of Baltimore, Md., William Talbot Malster, at his office in the City Hall. Afterwards, Lake called others in Washington, D.C., and New York City by telephone from his submarine. (*American Shipbuilder. Feb. 9, 1899*)

Telephone patent was No. 174,465, issued March 7, 1876, to Alexander Graham Bell of Salem, Mass. His application for an "improvement in telegraphy" was filed February 14, 1876. (*Catherine Dunlop Mackenzie—Alexander Graham Bell, the Man Who Contracted Space*)

Telephone recording devices were authorized by the Federal Communications Commission on June 30, 1948. They were required to have a tone-warning device producing a distinctive "beep" signal at regular intervals in order to let those taking part in the conversation know that their voices were being recorded. Recording devices had been used previously, however, by government and business.

Telephone switchboard or exchange was put in operation on May 17, 1877. It was located at 342 Washington Street, Boston, Mass., where Edwin Thomas Holmes was operating an electrical burglar alarm business. Holmes' office was connected by wire to a number of banks and similar institutions, and the telephones were placed in the offices of a few of his subscribers and connected to these wires. The first switchboard was connected with the telephones of six subscribers when the service began. It served as a telephone system by day and as a burglar alarm system at night. The telephones were connected only in the daytime. (*Herbert Newton Casson—History of the Telephone*)

Telephone switchboard or exchange (commercial) was installed on January 28, 1878, in New Haven, Conn., and served twenty-one subscribers. For the first six weeks the exchange was not operated at night. The first operator was George Willard Coy of New Haven. The first regularly employed boy oper-

ator was Louis Herrick Frost. "Ahoy-ahoy" was the first experimental shout, instead of "hello." (*Telephone Almanac—American Telephone and Telegraph Co.*)

Telephone switchboard or exchange for Chinese subscribers was established in 1894 by Loo Kum Shu in the Chinatown district of San Francisco, Calif. It was operated by three Chinese men who handled all the calls. The exchange is now the "China" central office of the Pacific Telephone and Telegraph Company and is located on Washington Street, east of Grant Avenue, San Francisco. The original number of subscribers was 100, a total which had increased by 1946 to over 2,000. At first all calls were made by name, but later the number system was adopted.

Telephone switchboard or exchange (multiple) was installed in Chicago, Ill., in January 1879.

Telephone switchboard with Braille markings and devices to enable the blind to operate it by touch and sound was designed by the Western Electric Company and installed by the New York Telephone Company on April 1, 1928, in the New York Institute for the Education of the Blind, the Bronx, New York City. The first operator was Frances Sievert, who held the position for over twenty-five years.

Telephone transatlantic wedding. *See* Wedding: Transatlantic telephone wedding

Telephone used by a railroad company was installed by the Pennsylvania Railroad Company. On May 21, 1877, Alexander Graham Bell sent his associate, Gardiner Greene Hubbard, and his mechanical expert, Thomas Augustus Watson, to Altoona, Pa., to give the telephone a trial test in the Pennsylvania Railroad Company shops. The demonstration was successful, and a permanent installation was made.

Toll line commercial telephone service was instituted on April 2, 1879, between Springfield, Mass., and Holyoke, Mass., by the District Telephone Company.

Transatlantic telephone service (commercial) was established between New York and London. It was inaugurated on January 7, 1927, when Walter Sherman Gifford, President of the American Telephone and Telegraph Company, in New York, talked to Sir George Evelyn Pemberton Murray, Secretary of the British Post Office, in London. Thirty-one commercial calls were made the first day. The charge was $75 for a three-minute conversation.

THE FIRST

Transcontinental telephone demonstration was held January 25, 1915. On that date Alexander Graham Bell, calling from New York City and using a model of the first telephone, again spoke the words "Come here, Watson, I want you." Thomas Augustus Watson, in San Francisco, about three thousand miles away, responded. Later Mayor John Purroy Mitchel of New York City talked with Mayor James Rolph, Jr., of San Francisco. Commercial service was inaugurated April 7, 1915, the toll being $20.70 for the first three minutes and $6.75 for each minute thereafter.

Underground cable long distance telephone conversation was held February 26, 1914, between Boston, Mass., and Washington, D.C.

TELEPHONE DIRECTORY was issued February 21, 1878, by the New Haven District Telephone Company, New Haven, Conn. It listed about fifty names.

TELEPHONE OPERATOR

Woman telephone operator was Emma M. Nutt, who went to work for the Telephone Despatch Company, Boston, Mass., on September 1, 1878. Miss Nutt was hired by Edwin Thomas Holmes. Previously, operators had all been men.

TELESCOPE

Reflecting telescope was manufactured by Amasa Holcomb of Southwick, Mass., about 1826. The first one, made to order for John A. Fulton of Chillicothe, Ohio, was 14 feet long with a 10-inch aperture and 6 eye pieces magnifying from 90 to 960 times. Telescopes were later made in four standard sizes. *(Elias Loomis—The Recent Progress of Astronomy, Especially the United States)*

Telescope lens two hundred inches in diameter was molded by the Corning Glass Works, Corning, N.Y. On December 2, 1934, molten glass at 2,700 degrees Fahrenheit was poured into a ceramic mold the construction of which had required several months. The temperature of the glass was lowered a degree or two a day during a period of eleven months; after this cooling period, the glass was removed to room temperature. The twenty-ton disc was shipped on March 26, 1936, to the California Institute of Technology for grinding and polishing before installation in a telescope at the Mount Palomar Observatory, on Palomar Mountain, San Diego County, Calif. The lens was ground and polished over a period of eleven years and completed October 3, 1947. The first test pictures were taken in December 1947. The telescope and observatory were officially dedicated on June 3, 1948, at which time the instrument was named the Hale telescope in honor of the late Dr. George Ellery Hale, who had conceived and promoted it. The telescope was first used on February 1, 1949, to observe the con-

THE FIRST

stellation of Coma Berenices (area 57), near the north pole of the Milky Way, and objects six sextillion (six billion trillion) miles away. *(David Oakes Woodbury—Glass Giant of Palomar)*

Telescope patent was No. 8,509, granted to Alvan Clark of Cambridge, Mass., November 11, 1851, for a combination of a glass and a sliding tube.

TELESCOPIC FISHING ROD. *See* Fishing rod

TELETYPE SERVICE

Teletype service (commercial) was inaugurated November 20, 1931, by the American Telegraph and Telephone Company. Messages typed on tape were transmitted automatically to a central office and retransmitted to their destinations. The charges were based on the time required to transmit each message, not on the number of words. On December 1, 1931, the teletype systems of the Postal Telegraph Company and the Western Union Telegraph Company cooperated in "Timed Wire Service" so that a patron of one service could transmit to a patron of the other service.

TELETYPESETTER

Teletypesetter was manufactured by the Teletypesetter Corporation, Chicago, Ill., and sold in October 1932 to a job printing plant in Detroit, Mich. The teletypesetter consists of two units: a perforator for preparing a paper tape and an operating unit for attachment to either a Linotype or Intertype machine. As the tape is automatically fed into the operating unit, the keys of the linecasting machine are depressed and lines of type steadily produced at a speed impossible to match by manual operation.

Teletypesetter circuit operated by a news agency was established April 23, 1951, in Charlotte, N.C., by the Associated Press. The first message was "Greetings. This is the opening of the first teletypesetter circuit." Messages were sent by means of tape, which was perforated by machine and fed into a transmitter. At the receiving stations, a reperforating machine fed the tape into a monitor printer, which prepared the type for publication.

Teletypesetter installed in a school was placed on a Model 8 Linotype at the Empire State School of Printing, Ithaca, N.Y. The installation was made July 5, 1933, by the Teletypesetter Corporation, Chicago, Ill.

TELEVISION

See also

Television—Mobile unit	Television license
	Television receiver
Television—Telecast	Television station
	Television tube

TELEVISION—*Continued*
College credit course in television was
offered by the School of Speech, Marquette
University, Milwaukee, Wis. The course, entitled "Introduction to Television," began in
the fall of 1951. Fourteen students registered
for instruction in programing, administrative
duties, and coordination of writing, staging, directing, and acting. The course was conducted
by Colby Lewis, assistant program manager of
WTMJ-TV, Milwaukee.

Community television antenna system was
placed in operation in December 1949 in Astoria, Ore., by Le Roy Edward Parsons. There
were three subscribers.

Electronic television system using the
pick-up device known as the Iconoscope, which
displaced the mechanical system by means of
motor-driven scanning disks, was invented by
Vladimir Kosma Zworykin of Wilkinsburg,
Pa., who obtained patent No. 2,141,059 on
December 20, 1938. The patent covered forty
claims and was assigned to the Westinghouse
Electric and Manufacturing Company, East
Pittsburgh, Pa. Zworykin's application was
filed December 29, 1923.

Municipal television film unit organized
to produce films for presentation on commercial stations was established February 15, 1949,
by the Municipal Broadcasting System of the
City of New York. The first television supervisor was Clifford Evans.

Submarine with closed-circuit television
was the "Tullibee," SSB (N) 597, commissioned November 9, 1960. The keel was laid
May 26, 1958, and the submarine launched
April 27, 1960, at Groton, Conn. The "Tullibee" was 273 feet long and had a displacement of 2,600 tons when submerged. She
carried a crew of 60 men and 6 officers.

**Television eyewitness allowed to testify
in a federal court** was Mrs. Sophie Eisenberg of Brooklyn, N.Y., who testified in United
States Federal Court, New York City, before
Judge Irving Robert Kaufman. On March 16,
1947, while viewing a hockey game between
the Montreal Canadiens and the New York
Rangers televised from Madison Square Garden, New York City, Mrs. Eisenberg saw Emile
(Butch) Bouchard, captain of the Canadiens,
hit Jonas Walvisch, a spectator from New York
City. The spectator lost his $75,000 lawsuit
against the player which was tried January 29,
1951.

TELEVISION—MOBILE UNIT
Mobile television unit for outdoor events
consisted of two large motor vans containing
television control apparatus and a microwave
transmitter. The unit was completed by the

RCA Manufacturing Company, Camden, N.J.,
and turned over to the National Broadcasting
Company (W2XBT), New York City, on
December 12, 1937. The telecasts were relayed
by microwave to a tower transmitter in the
Empire State Building, New York City, and
rebroadcast from there.

Mobile television units (color) were
placed in operation January 1, 1954, by the
National Broadcasting Company's station
WNBT, New York City. Two three-color
mobile units with complete audio-video control
were housed in an automobile van 35 feet long,
8 feet wide, and 10 feet 7 inches high.

TELEVISION—TELECAST
Airplane telecast (network) was made December 17, 1948, with a 20-watt transmitter
from an Air Force C-47 airplane cruising over
Washington, D.C., to an Air Force receiver in
the Smithsonian Institution and from there
relayed to a mobile unit and to the transmitter
of WNBW, Washington, D.C. The occasion
was the formal installation of the Wright
brothers' airplane in the Smithsonian Institution.
Previously television programs had been relayed
by Westinghouse-Martin stratovision airplanes.

**Art auction televised on a coast-to-coast
circuit** was held April 27, 1960, for the benefit of the Museum of Modern Art's Thirtieth
Anniversary Fund. It originated at the Parke-
Bernet Galleries, New York City, and was seen
in New York City, Chicago, Dallas, and Los
Angeles through TNT Theatre Network Television.

Atomic explosion telecast was made February 1, 1951, by KTLA, Los Angeles, Calif.
A camera on Mount Wilson telecast a blast at
Frenchman Flats, Nev., 300 miles away. The
explosion was part of "Operation Ranger."

Atomic explosion telecast on a network
was made April 22, 1952, from News Nob,
Nev., by KTLA, Los Angeles, Calif. The
image was relayed to the Atomic Energy Commission's station a quarter of a mile away;
then 46 miles to Charleston Peak; 140 miles to
another station; 125 miles to Mount San Antonio; and finally 23 miles to the KTLA transmitter on Mount Wilson. The explosion was
part of "Operation Tumbler Snapper."

**Auction of federal property to be tele-
vised** was carried by closed circuit to six
cities (Boston, Chicago, Columbus, New York,
Philadelphia, and St. Louis) on October 7, 1959.
Nine auctioneers conducted an eight-hour sale
that brought $2,800,000 from the disposal of
objects ranging from cartridge belts to cranes
to Eisenhower jackets at the Philadelphia Naval
Shipyard, the Air Force Depot at Shelby, Ohio,
and the Army Engineer Depot at Granite City,

THE FIRST

Ill., from which the telecast emanated. More than 3,500 miles of coaxial cable were used.

Audience participation telecast was a program of charades presented on August 7, 1941, by station WNBT, New York City.

Baseball game (collegiate) televised was the Columbia-Princeton game played May 17, 1939, at Baker Field, New York City. The game lasted ten innings and was won by Princeton, 2-1. It was telecast by station W2XBS, New York City. Bill Stern was the announcer.

Baseball games (major league) televised were two National League games played at Ebbets Field, Brooklyn, N.Y., August 26, 1939, between the Cincinnati Reds and the Brooklyn Dodgers. Station W2XBS, New York City, televised the games, using two cameras alternately, according to the play. Leo Durocher, manager of the Dodgers, William McKechnie, manager of the Reds, and several players appeared during the intermission of the double-header.

Baseball games televised in color were the two games of a National League doubleheader played August 11, 1951, at Ebbets Field, Brooklyn, N.Y., between the Brooklyn Dodgers and the Boston Braves. The games were televised by WCBS-TV of the Columbia Broadcasting System. Walter Ranier (Red) Barber and Connie Desmond were the announcers. The Dodgers won the first game, 8-1, and the Braves the second game, 8-4.

Baseball World Series game televised was the opening game of the 1947 series, played on September 30, 1947, between the New York Yankees of the American League and the Brooklyn Dodgers of the National League at the Yankee Stadium, New York City. The game was transmitted to three stations (WABD, WCBS, WNBT) in New York City and to all the video outlets along the Eastern seaboard. The entire series was telecast under the joint sponsorship of the Ford Motor Company and the Gillette Safety Razor Company at a cost of $65,000. The Yankees won the first game, 5-3, and the series, 4 games to 3. The play-by-play descriptions were given by Bob Edge, Bob Stanton, and Bill Slater.

Baseball World Series game televised in color was the opening game of the 1955 series, played on September 28, 1955, between the New York Yankees of the American League and the Brooklyn Dodgers of the National League at the Yankee Stadium, New York City. The game was televised by WRCA-TV. The Yankees won, 6-5.

THE FIRST

Basketball game to be televised was played February 28, 1940, at Madison Square Garden, and televised by station W2XBS, New York City. Fordham University played the University of Pittsburgh. Pittsburgh won the game, 50-37. A game between Georgetown University and New York University followed. New York University won, 50-27. Both games were televised.

Birth (human) to be televised (closed circuit) was shown in color June 14, 1951, as part of the American Medical Association meeting at Atlantic City, N.J. Two thousand physicians and their families watched the birth of Michael Gallagher, who weighed 9 pounds 12 ounces.

Birth (human) to be televised for the public was shown December 2, 1952, by KOA, Denver, Colo., and televised over forty-nine stations of the National Broadcasting Company. Gordon Campbell Kerr, who weighed 5 pounds 7 ounces, was delivered by Caesarian section in the hospital delivery room of the Colorado General Hospital of the University of Colorado Medical School, Denver. The telecast was part of the "March of Medicine" program presented in conjunction with the annual clinical meeting of the American Medical Association.

Book review to be televised was Ernest Boyd's review on May 3, 1938, over station W2XBS, New York City, of Sidney Spencer's *The Greatest Show on Earth.* The program, which combined photographs and text to explain the economic problems of mankind, opened with a telecast of the reviewer and featured numerous pick-ups of photographs from the book.

Cabinet session to be televised was recorded at the White House, Washington, D.C., on October 25, 1954. The telecast showed a special meeting assembled to hear the report of Secretary of State John Foster Dulles on agreements signed in Paris. All the members of President Dwight David Eisenhower's cabinet were present. (Vice President Richard M. Nixon did not attend, however.) The report was broadcast and telecast over the ABC, NBC, and CBS radio and television networks.

Catholic mass (midnight) to be televised was transmitted December 24, 1948, from St. Patrick's Cathedral, New York City, by stations WNBT-TV, WJZ-TV, and WCBS-TV.

Catholic mass televised from a studio was celebrated June 10, 1953, by the Reverend Albert William Low, assistant superintendent of schools for the Roman Catholic Archdiocese, Boston, Mass., at an altar built in WBZ-TV,

TELEVISION—TELECAST—_Continued_
Boston. The telecast was permitted by the Most Reverend Richard James Cushing, archbishop of Boston.

Church service televised in sign language was conducted by the Reverend Floyd F. Possehl, who read the Scriptures and preached a sermon in sign language from St. Matthew's Lutheran Church for the Deaf, Jamaica, Long Island, N.Y., on December 5, 1948, over WPIX, New York City.

Circus telecast was a program featuring the Ringling Brothers-Barnum and Bailey circus. The three-hour show was televised April 25, 1940 from Madison Square Garden, New York City, by station W2XBS, New York City.

Color and black-and-white telecast to be sponsored was a program in the "Dragnet" series, presented December 24, 1953, by WNBT-TV, New York City, of the National Broadcasting Company. Jack Webb was featured as Detective Joe Friday and Ben Alexander as Detective Frank Smith.

Color coast-to-coast live telecast was transmitted November 3, 1953, from the Colonial Theatre, New York City, by WNBT-TV, New York City. The program, which starred Nanette Fabray, was sent in compatible color over the radio relay circuit system of the Bell Telephone Company and received by fourteen-inch receivers at Burbank, Calif.

Color coast-to-coast telecast from the west coast was made January 1, 1954, when the Tournament of Roses parade at Pasadena, Calif., was presented over the National Broadcasting Company network. The program was seen in color in twenty-one cities and in black and white in other cities. Don Ameche was the host and Roy Neal and James Wallington were the announcers.

Color commercial televised on a local show was commissioned on March 9, 1954, by Castro Decorators, Inc., New York City, in a contract with WNBT, New York City, for spot announcements.

Color network telecast in compatible color was transmitted June 7, 1953, from Symphony Hall, Boston, Mass. It was seen in color in Washington, D.C., and in black and white elsewhere. The program was a puppet show, "St. George and the Dragon," featuring Kukla, Fran and Ollie (Fran Allison and Burr Tillstrom), with Arthur Fiedler conducting the Boston "Pops" orchestra. The operetta score was composed by John Fascinato.

Color program (commercial) was presented by sixteen sponsors on June 25, 1951, at 4:35 P.M. by the Columbia Broadcasting System station in New York City and fed to Boston, Philadelphia, Baltimore, and Washington, D.C. Some of the performers were Arthur Godfrey, Faye Emerson, Sam Levenson, Robert Alda, Ed Sullivan, Isabel Bigley, and Garry Moore.

Color program (commercial) to be presented daily was Ivan T. Sanderson's "The World Is Yours," first seen on the Columbia Broadcasting System network on June 26, 1951, from 4:30 to 5:00 P.M.

Color telecast by a local station was presented December 18, 1953, by WPTZ-TV, Philadelphia, Pa. Color film-clips of the Walt Disney Technicolor film _The Living Desert_ were shown, and also a color commercial for Fels & Company's product Felso. The images were also visible in black and white.

Color telecast on a closed circuit local station was presented October 30, 1953, by WPTZ-TV, Philadelphia, Pa.

Color television demonstration of high-definition electronically scanned images was given for the press September 3, 1940, over station W2XAB of the Columbia Broadcasting System, New York City. The telecast was made from the high-power transmitter atop the Chrysler Building, New York City. It had a 343-line quality and used the 4.5 megacycle band, the same frequency required for ordinary black-and-white images. The images were received in black and white, but a color disk placed in front of the receiver tube enabled the audience at the station to view the pictures in color. The apparatus was invented by Dr. Peter Carl Goldmark, Columbia Broadcasting System's chief television engineer.

Color television demonstration (public) was given June 27, 1929, in the Bell Telephone Laboratories, New York City. Some of the objects shown in color were an American flag, a watermelon, and a bunch of roses. The images were of low definition and were mechanically scanned. The equipment demonstrated utilized three complete systems of photoelectric cells, amplifiers, and glow tubes. Each system had screens: red, blue, or green. A system of mirrors superposed the three monochromatic images to make one picture in color.

Commercial filmed by a camera operated by atomically generated electricity was produced at West Milton, N.Y., on July 18, 1955, and televised July 24, 1955, on the General Electric Summer Theatre. The three-minute commercial was produced by George Blake Enterprises, Inc., and supervised by Karl M. Fischer through Batten, Barton, Durstine and Osborne, Inc., New York City, for the General

Electric Company. Nuclear energy generated the electricity produced at the West Milton power plant.

Congressional opening session to be televised was the joint session of the Eightieth Congress that met on January 3, 1947. The proceedings were televised by the major networks.

Demonstration of home reception of television was given in New York City on August 20, 1930, when a half-hour program broadcast from two stations was received on screens placed in a store in the Hotel Ansonia at Broadway and 73d Street, in the Hearst Building at Eighth Avenue and 57th Street, and in a residence at 98 Riverside Drive. On these screens appeared the images of performers talking and singing in the studios of the Jenkins W2XCR television station at Jersey City, N.J., and the de Forest W2XCD station at Passaic, N.J. The distance, approximately six miles, was the greatest over which pictures had been transmitted by television. Harry Hershfield, cartoonist, was master of ceremonies, introducing George Jessel, Arthur ("Bugs") Baer, Health Commissioner Shirley Wilmotte Wynne, Benny Rubin, Diana Seaby, and other entertainers. Sets had been installed in homes earlier, however. On January 13, 1928, the Radio Corporation of America and the General Electric Company installed three home sets in Schenectady, N.Y. The images were transmitted over a wave length of 37.8 meters and the sound sent simultaneously over a wave length of 379.5 meters. The picture was 1½ inches square. The television receiver's elements were a light source, a scanning device, and a synchronizing system.

Department store sales demonstrations (large-scale) were staged at Gimbel Brothers, Philadelphia, Pa., from October 24 to November 14, 1945, inclusive, with RCA-Victor equipment. A preview was held October 23, 1945. Approximately 25,000 people viewed the demonstrations at the auditorium and at twenty telesites scattered at strategic locations on the seven floors of the department store. Eleven daily demonstrations of about ten minutes each were given showing millinery, home furnishings, shoes, scarves, furs, nursery furniture, toys, curtains, interior decorating, and hair styling.

Fashion show telecast was presented May 17, 1939, by WNBT-TV, New York City, in cooperation with the Swiss Fabric Group and the Ostrich Feather Group from the Ritz-Carlton Hotel, New York City. Renee Macready was the fashion coordinator.

Football game (collegiate) to be televised was played at Randall's Island, New York City, September 30, 1939, between Fordham Univer-

sity and Waynesburg College and televised by station W2XBS, New York City. Fordham won, 34-7.

Football game (professional) to be televised was transmitted on October 22, 1939, from Ebbets Field, Brooklyn, N.Y., by W2XBS of the National Broadcasting Company, New York City. The Brooklyn Dodgers defeated the Philadelphia Eagles, 23-14.

Football game televised in color on a network was transmitted September 29, 1951, by channel 2 of the Columbia Broadcasting System from Franklin Field, Philadelphia, Pa. The Golden Bears of the University of California defeated the Quakers of the University of Pennsylvania, 35-0.

High-definition telecast was made June 29, 1936, by W2XBS from the Empire State Building, New York City, at the rate of 30 pictures per second with the 343-line screen. On July 7, 1936, David Sarnoff, president of the Radio Corporation of America and Major General James Guthrie Harbord, chairman of the board of RCA, opened for invited guests a program in which Henry Hull, Graham McNamee, Ed Wynn and members of the Water Lily Ensemble appeared as performers. A fashion show and a film were also presented.

Hockey game to be televised was played February 25, 1940, at Madison Square Garden, New York City, between the New York Rangers and the Montreal Canadiens and televised by W2XBS, New York City. The Rangers won, 6-2.

Husband and wife to broadcast a religious program were Dr. Norman Vincent Peale, minister of the Marble Collegiate Church, New York City, and Mrs. Ruth Peale, who on October 1, 1952, began a television series entitled "What's Your Trouble?" The program was produced by the Broadcasting and Film Commission of the National Council of the Churches of Christ in the United States and presented on the Columbia Broadcasting System.

Jewish temple services (complete) to be televised were shown November 4, 1951, from Temple Israel of the City of New York, by WPIX, New York City. Rabbi William Franklin Rosenblum preached the sermon. Cantor Harold Orbach, of Temple Israel, New Rochelle, N.Y., conducted the musical portions. This service, as well as three others on successive Saturdays, was arranged by the Radio and Television Division of the American Jewish Committee.

King and queen to be televised were King George VI and Queen Elizabeth of England, who, on June 10, 1939, visited the New York

TELEVISION—TELECAST—*Continued*
World's Fair, New York City, during "British Week." They were pictured visiting the exhibits.

Live telecast from a non-contiguous foreign country was transmitted November 13, 1955, by CMQ, Havana, Cuba. A five-minute aerial view of Havana was televised from an airplane to CMQ and thence relayed by airplanes to WIOD, Miami, Fla., for telecasting on Dave Garroway's show "Wide Wide World" on the National Broadcasting System network.

Medical intracity color telecast was shown December 6-9, 1949, by WMAR-TV, Baltimore, Md., from the Johns Hopkins Hospital, Baltimore, over a closed circuit of the Columbia Broadcasting System to a clinical session of the American Medical Association at the National Guard Armory, Washington, D.C. The telecast was arranged by Georgetown University and George Washington University.

Medical symposium televised coast to coast on a closed circuit was shown September 23, 1954, on large-screen (11 by 14 feet) projection units in twenty-three cities by Box Office Television, Inc., through the cooperation of the American College of Physicians and the Wyeth Laboratories, Philadelphia, Pa. About 5,000 physicians at the Columbia Auditorium, Louisville, Ky., viewed the telecast, which originated in New York City. The post-graduate symposium dealt with hypertension.

Missing persons telecast was made October 3, 1943, by the Missing Persons Bureau of the Police Department of the City of New York on W2XWV, the DuMont station in New York City.

Moving picture premiere festivities to be televised were presented December 19, 1939, on W2XBS of the National Broadcasting Company on the occasion of the New York opening of *Gone With the Wind*. Two cameras, one on the sidewalk outside the Capitol Theatre, New York City, and the other in the lobby, recorded interviews with celebrities. Ben Grauer was the master of ceremonies. The film, based on Margaret Mitchell's novel, was produced by David Oliver Selznick. It starred Clark Gable and Vivien Leigh.

Moving picture premiere performance to be televised was a presentation of a two-reel short *Patrolling the Ether,* which was televised April 10, 1944, simultaneously by WNBT of New York City, WRGB of Schenectady, N.Y., and WPTZ of Philadelphia, Pa. The film depicted the wartime activities of the radio intelligence division of the Federal Communications Commission in tracing illegal and espionage radio

transmitters. It was produced by Metro-Goldwyn-Mayer and released April 22, 1944, twelve days after its premiere on television.

Moving picture premiere performance to be televised (feature-length foreign film) was a presentation on WNBT, New York City, on January 1, 1948, of *African Journey,* a French film featuring Victor Francen and Harry Baur. English dialogue was dubbed in on the sound track.

Moving picture premiere performance to be televised (major film) was a presentation of *The Constant Husband* by the National Broadcasting Company on a coast-to-coast network from WNBT-TV, New York City, on November 6, 1955. The picture was a London Films production starring Rex Harrison and Margaret Leighton. It was directed by Sir Alexander Korda.

Moving picture trailer to be televised was shown September 20, 1946, on WNBT-TV, New York City. It advertised a Columbia Pictures film, *The Jolson Story.*

Murder trial to be televised was the trial of Harry Washburn, held December 5-9, 1955, in the District Court, Waco, Tex., with Judge Drummond William Bartlett presiding. The defense and prosecution had agreed to the placing of a camera on a balcony, and the entire 25-hour proceedings were televised by KWTX-TV, Waco, as a public service to the community. Washburn was convicted of the automobile bomb slaying of his former mother-in-law.

Musical comedy (full-length) written especially for television was *The Boys from Boise,* produced by the Charles M. Storm Company for *Esquire* magazine on September 28, 1944, over WABD, New York City. The program was directed by Ray Nelson.

Musical comedy telecast (one-hour) was a performance of "Topsy and Eva—Television Edition," presented July 25, 1939, by W2XBS of National Broadcasting Company, New York City. The entertainers who appeared on the program were the Duncan sisters, Billy Kent, Florence Auer, Winfield Hoeney, Edwin Vail, the Southernaires, and the Chansonettes.

Newsreel telecast presented daily was the 20th Century-Fox Movietone News telecast, first presented on February 16, 1948, over the National Broadcasting Company's east coast network. The program was sponsored by the R. J. Reynolds Tobacco Company.

Opera (complete) to be televised was presented December 23, 1943, by WRGB of the

THE FIRST

General Electric Company, Schenectady, N.Y. The presentation was Humperdinck's *Hansel and Gretel.*

Opera (complete) to be televised from the Metropolitan Opera House was Giuseppe Verdi's *Otello,* a three-and-a-half-hour performance on November 29, 1948, sponsored by the Texas Company over WJZ-TV, New York City. It starred Licia Albanese, Ramon Vinay, Leonard Warren, Martha Lipton, John Garris, and Nicola Moscona and was conducted by Fritz Busch. Milton Cross was the commentator. The telecast was also seen at network outlets in Philadelphia, Pa., Baltimore, Md., Washington, D.C., and Boston, Mass.

Opera (major) televised in color was Bizet's *Carmen* presented October 31, 1953, by the NBC-TV Opera Theatre in compatible color in a one-hour program transmitted by WNBT-TV, New York City. It was sung in English. Vera Bryner was Carmen; Robert Rounseville, Don José; and Warren Galjour, Escamillo. Peter Herman Adler was the director.

Opera telecast was presented by members of the Metropolitan Opera Company, on March 10, 1940, over W2XBS, New York City. A condensed version of the first act of Ruggiero Leoncavallo's *I Pagliacci* was televised from a Radio City studio. Edward Johnson, general manager of the Metropolitan Opera Company, was the master of ceremonies, and Francis St. Leger conducted. In the cast were Armand Tokatyan (tenor), Hilda Burke (soprano), Richard Bonelli (baritone), George Cehanovsky (baritone), and Alessio de Paolis (tenor).

Opera written for television was *Amahl and the Night Visitors,* by Gian-Carlo Menotti, first televised December 24, 1951, by the National Broadcasting Company from WNBT, New York City. The program was sponsored by Hallmark Greeting Cards. Thomas Schippers was the conductor and Chet Allen, a twelve-year-old boy soprano, the featured singer The opera tells the story of the Three Wise Men and the miraculous cure of a crippled boy.

Opera written for television on commission for a commercial sponsor was *The Parrot,* presented by the Armstrong Cork Company of Lancaster, Pa., from WNBT, New York City, on March 24, 1953. Darrell Peter composed the score. The book, by Frank P. De Felitta, told the story of an eccentric old lady who willed her money to a parrot. The opera was directed by Garry Simpson. Six singers participated in the twenty-three minute show.

Operetta to be televised was Gilbert and Sullivan's *Pirates of Penzance,* presented June 20, 1939, from 8:30 to 9:30 P.M. by W2XBS,

THE FIRST

New York City. The program starred Margaret Daum and Ray Heatherton. Harold Sanford was the conductor.

Outdoor scenes to be televised were viewed in the offices of the Bell Telephone Laboratories, New York City, on July 12, 1928. Scenes enacted in the open air were almost as clear as those taken in specially designed studios.

Pay television system was Phonovision, demonstrated January 1, 1951, by the Zenith Radio Corporation, Chicago, Ill., KS2KSBS, under authority of the Federal Communications Commission. A scrambled radio signal was transmitted for reception only by those with the "key signal" sent to their home sets by a telephone circuit. At 4 P.M., *April Showers,* with Jack Carson, was shown; at 7 P.M. *Welcome Stranger,* with Bing Crosby; and at 9 P.M. *Homecoming,* with Clark Gable and Lana Turner. A charge of $1.00 was made for each full-length feature program. During the first four weeks, 2,561 sales were made. The test was limited to 300 families chosen from 51,000 applicants by the National Opinion Research Council of the University of Chicago.

Pay television presentation of a moving picture shown simultaneously in theaters was a presentation of Paramount's *Forever Female,* starring William Holden, Ginger Rogers, and Paul Douglas, transmitted on November 28, 1953, to 70 Telemeter receiving sets in Palm Springs, Calif. The picture, directed by Pat Duggan, was based upon James Matthew Barrie's play *Rosalind.* It was presented simultaneously at the Plaza Theatre in Palm Springs. The telecast fee, $1.35, was placed in a coin-box attached to each set.

Pay television presentation of a sporting event was the closed circuit coast-to-coast telecast of the Jersey Joe Walcott-Rocky Marciano fight at the Municipal Stadium, Philadelphia, Pa., on September 23, 1952. Marciano won the heavyweight title by a knockout in 43 seconds of the 13th round. The telecast was viewed by 40,379 persons in 49 theaters located in 31 cities. Ticket sales totaled $504,645.

Pay television presentation of an opera was a performance of *Carmen,* televised on a closed circuit December 11, 1952, from the Metropolitan Opera House, New York City. The opera was shown in 31 theaters located in 27 cities to a total audience of about 70,000. Prices for tickets ranged from $1.20 to $7.20. Fritz Reiner was the conductor. Richard Tucker starred as Don José, Nadine Conner as Micaela, Rise Stevens as Carmen, and Robert Merrill as Escamillo.

Phase-contrast cinemicrography film (American-made) telecast was a presentation of *The Birth of a Plant,* televised February

TELEVISION—TELECAST—Continued
28, 1954, by KPIX-TV, San Francisco, Calif.
The film process, which utilizes a system of
optics that permits ordinarily invisible objects
to be seen, was the invention of Colonel Arthur T. Brice of Ross, Calif., who produced
the plant reproduction film under the supervision of Dr. Ralph Emerson, professor of
botany, University of California, Berkeley,
Calif.

Play to be televised was *The Queen's
Messenger*, by J. Hartley Manners, presented
on September 11, 1928, by radio station WGY
of the General Electric Company, Schenectady,
N.Y. The telecast was under the direction of
Mortimer Stewart, with Izetta Jewell (Mrs.
Hugh Miller) and Maurice Randall as the principal performers, assisted by Joyce Evans and
William J. Toniski. The performance went
out on three wave lengths, the picture on 379.5
meters and 21.4 meters, and the voices on 31.96
meters. Several semicommercial 24-line receivers were set up in the WGY studios.

Play to be televised as a full-hour program
was *The Donovan Affair*, by Owen Davis,
presented June 29, 1939, by W2XBS, New
York City, of the National Broadcasting Company. The cast included William Harrigan,
Laura Baxter, Henry Wadsworth, Matt Briggs,
and Horace Braham.

**Play to be televised with its original Broad-
way cast** was Rachel Crothers' comedy
Susan and God, presented on June 7, 1938, over
W2XBS, operating on channels of 46.5 megacycles for the picture and 49.75 for sound. The
play was produced by the Radio Corporation
of America in cooperation with John Golden,
the Broadway producer. Featured in the cast
were Gertrude Lawrence, Paul McGrath, and
Nancy Coleman, then playing in *Susan and God*
at the Plymouth Theater, New York City.
Exact replicas of the stage settings were built
for the telecast from the National Broadcasting
Company's studio in the RCA building, New
York City.

Political campaign telecast was presented
on October 11, 1932, when the Democratic National Committee broadcast a television show
from the studios of the Columbia Broadcasting System, 485 Madison Avenue, New York
City.

Political convention to be televised was
the twenty-second Republican Convention, June
24-29, 1940, in Philadelphia, Pa., at which
Wendell Lewis Willkie of New York and
Charles Linza McNary of Oregon were nominated for President and Vice President. The
telecast was made by W2XBS of the National
Broadcasting Company, New York City, 49.75
megacycles.

President to appear on television was
Franklin Delano Roosevelt, who spoke at the
Federal Building on the exposition grounds
overlooking the Court of Peace at the opening
session of the New York World's Fair, Flushing, Long Island, on April 30, 1939, over
WNBT of National Broadcasting Company,
New York City. Two NBC mobile vans were
used, one containing a transmitter and the other
handling the pick-up. Burke Crotty was the producer of the 3½ hour show. The show began
with a view of the World's Fair Trylon and
the Perisphere. The images were carried on
45.25 megacycles and the sound on 49.75 megacycles.

President to appear on television in color
was Dwight David Eisenhower, colorcast while
delivering the commencement address at the
graduation exercises of the United States
Military Academy at West Point, N.Y., on
June 7, 1955.

**President to discuss state affairs with
cabinet members on television.** *See* Cabinet
of the United States: Cabinet conference telecast; Television—Telecast: Cabinet session to
be televised

**Presidential address televised from the
White House** was presented October 5, 1947,
when President Harry S. Truman's speech
about food conservation and the world food
crisis was televised from Washington, D.C.,
and relayed to New York City, Philadelphia,
and Schenectady. The President proposed meat-
less Tuesdays, and eggless and poultryless
Thursdays.

**Presidential candidate debate series on tele-
vision.** *See* Presidential candidate: Presidential candidate debate series on television

**Presidential news conference filmed for
television and newsreels** was held January 19,
1955, in the treaty room of the State Department building, Washington, D.C. President
Dwight David Eisenhower held a 33-minute
conference. The film was cut to 28 minutes and
25 seconds plus introductory and closing remarks, certain sections having been omitted.
The television film was recorded by the National Broadcasting Company on a pooled basis
with the Columbia Broadcasting System, the
American Broadcasting System, and the Du-
Mont Network. The cost was prorated.

**Presidential news conference to be tele-
vised live** was held January 25, 1961, in the
auditorium of the State Department building,
Washington, D.C. President John Fitzgerald
Kennedy answered 31 questions in 38 minutes.
The conference was also broadcast on radio.
President Eisenhower's news conferences
were filmed and recorded for use later the
same day.

Presidential nomination notification ceremony to be televised by remote pick-up was transmitted on Wednesday, August 22, 1928, from the New York State Assembly Chamber at Albany, where the Democratic candidate, Alfred Emanuel Smith, was notified of his nomination. The pictures were transmitted from Schenectady, N.Y., and relayed by short wave over 2XAF and 2XAD by the General Electric Company. This was the first remote televised pick-up.

Prize fight (heavyweight championship bout) to be televised was shown June 19, 1946, by WNBT-TV, New York City, and transmitted to Washington, D.C., by coaxial cable. Joe Louis defended his title against Billy Conn at the Yankee Stadium, New York City. Louis won by a knockout in the eighth round.

Prize fight in a "studio" was televised on September 1, 1954, from Philadelphia, Pa. Two six-round bouts were substituted for a fifteen-round welterweight fight between Johnny Saxton of New York City and Kid Gavilan of Camaguey, Cuba, scheduled to take place at the Connie Mack Stadium but postponed because of illness. The televised fights were held at the Met, a small club with about 5,000 seats. No admission was charged. George Justine of Philadelphia defeated Ellwood Davis of Philadelphia, and Bobby Bell of Youngstown, Ohio, fought a draw with Ike Chestnut of New York City. Each fighter received $1,500.

Prize fight televised coast-to-coast was the middleweight fight between Dave Sands, the British Empire champion, and Carl ("Bobo") Olson, held October 3, 1951, at the Stadium, Chicago, Ill., and televised by the Columbia Broadcasting System. Sands, an Australian who had achieved victory in 88 of his previous 98 fights, defeated Olson in the ten-round contest.

Prize fight televised in color was the Joe Giardello-Willie Troy fight held March 19, 1954, at Madison Square Garden, New York City, and televised by WNBT, New York City. Troy was knocked out in the seventh round of a scheduled ten-round fight.

Prize fight to be televised was the Lou Nova-Max Baer fight, shown June 1, 1939, by WNBT-TV, New York City, from the Yankee Stadium, New York City. Sam Taub was the announcer. Referee Frank Fullam halted the bout in the eleventh round and awarded the decision to Nova. About 300 persons saw the telecast in the smoking room of the New Amsterdam Theatre, and about 20,000 saw it in stores and dealer display rooms.

Programs regularly televised were begun May 11, 1928, on a three-times-a-week schedule

from the General Electric Station, WGY, Schenectady, N.Y. The image consisted of 24 scanning lines repeated 20 times a second.

Puppet show to be televised was a two-minute symbolic one-act play with puppet characters produced August 21, 1928, by WOR, Newark, N.J., a radio station then owned by L. Bamberger & Co. of Newark. In the play a character symbolizing "Creative Genius" produced an apparatus which brought forth "The Spirit of Television," a winged sprite holding a globe. Sight and sound were synchronized, the narrator and musical accompaniment being heard through earphones.

Religious services to be televised were produced March 24, 1940, by W2XBS, of the National Broadcasting Company, New York City. Dr. Samuel McCrea Cavert of the Federal Council of the Churches of Christ in America officiated at Protestant Easter services at 11:30 A.M. The Westminster Choir, directed by Dr. John Finley Williamson, provided the musical selections. At 12:30 Msgr. Fulton John Sheen of the Catholic University of America officiated at a Roman Catholic Easter service with the Paulist Choristers directed by Father William Joseph Finn. Other Easter services were televised from the Hollywood Bowl, Hollywood, Calif., and from Central Park, New York City.

Sales meeting televised on a closed circuit was presented by the Bulova Watch Company on January 9, 1940, from WNBT-TV, New York City, and shown to convention delegates in a reception room. Milton Biow acted as the master of ceremonies for the fifty-minute program, which featured moving pictures, visual charts, and sales presentations.

Simulcast presented regularly by a sponsor was the Lowell Thomas news commentary program sponsored by the Sun Oil Company, and first presented on February 21, 1940, on W2XBS-TV, New York City, and radio station WJZ, New York City, at 6:45 P.M.

Speaker to address an organization by television was Dr. Peter Irving Wold, president of the Fortnightly Club, Schenectady, N.Y., who conducted a meeting of the club from the television station at the General Electric Laboratory on April 1, 1930. The members were assembled at the home of Dr. Ernst Fredrik Werner Alexanderson in Schenectady.

Split-screen image, showing two pictures from different points of origin side by side on the same kinescope picture tube, was exhibited December 8, 1948, by the National Broadcasting Company at the Television Broadcasters Association Clinic held at the Waldorf-Astoria

THE FIRST

THE FIRST

TELEVISION—TELECAST—*Continued*
Hotel, New York City. The telecast showed
John Cameron Swayze, in New York City,
interviewing Representative Karl Earl Mundt
of South Dakota, in Washington, D.C.

Sports event televised in color was the
$15,000 Molly Pitcher Handicap, a mile-and-
one-sixteenth race for three-year-olds and upwards, run July 14, 1951, at the Monmouth
Park Jockey Club, Oceanport, N.J. The seven-
horse race was won by Marta. The jockey was
Conn McCreary. The race was televised by
the Columbia Broadcasting System.

Standard broadcast station to transmit a
television image was Hugo Gernsback's station WRNY, Coytesville, N.J., which on August 13, 1928, transmitted a 1½-inch square
image of the face of Mrs. John Geloso. The
image was viewed at Philosophy Hall, New
York University, New York City, by 500 persons. It was magnified by a lens to twice the
size.

Stockholders' annual meeting televised on a
closed circuit was the April 16, 1957, meeting
of the American Machine and Foundry Company, televised in New York City and
Chicago, Ill. Shareholders witnessed the proceedings in which they themselves participated
on screens at the Blackstone Hotel, Chicago,
and at the Hotel Sheraton-Astor, New York
City. Executives in both cities were questioned
by stockholders.

Stockholders' meetings televised coast-to-
coast simultaneously were transmitted October 29, 1959, from Minneapolis, Minn., and
from New York, Chicago, Los Angeles, San
Francisco, Boston, and Buffalo. By means of
a closed circuit, stockholders in each city were
able to ask questions of two General Mills
officials—Gerald S. Kennedy, chairman, and
Charles Heffelfinger Bell, president—who presided at the meetings in New York City and
Minneapolis, respectively.

Stratovision flight during which a television signal was transmitted was made April
30, 1948. It consisted of the test pattern of
WMAR, Baltimore, Md. On a December 9,
1945 flight, only a frequency modulation sound
signal was transmitted.

Stratovision flight public demonstration
was made June 23, 1948 when at 8:55 P.M. an
airplane flying 25,000 feet in the air in the
vicinity of Pittsburgh, Pa., rebroadcast the television program of the Republican National Convention at Philadelphia, Pa., from WMAR-TV,
in Baltimore, Md. Reception was obtained in
nine states over an area 525 miles in diameter.

Stratovision flight test was made December 9, 1945, at Middle River, Md., under the
direction of Charles Edward Nobles of the
Westinghouse Electric Corporation, Baltimore,
Md., in conjunction with the Glenn L. Martin
Company. William Smith, a test pilot, flew
an airplane in the stratosphere from which
telecasts were made. A license to conduct experiments had been granted October 24, 1945,
by the Federal Communications Commission.

Stratovision World Series telecast was
made October 11, 1948, when the sixth game
of the World Series between the Boston Braves
of the National League and the Cleveland Indians of the American League, played at Boston,
Mass., was transmitted from a stratovision plane
flying at 25,000 feet over the Pittsburgh, Pa.,
area.

Surgical operation televised coast-to-coast
was transmitted June 10, 1952, from the Wesley
Memorial Hospital, Chicago, Ill., in connection
with the 101st annual meeting of the American
Medical Association at the Palmer House, Chicago, Ill. Shown on television was an 8-
minute period during a 3½-hour duodenal ulcer
operation performed on a 60-year-old man by
Dr. Samuel Julian Fogelson. The program was
sponsored by Smith, Kline and French Laboratories, Inc., and presented by the National
Broadcasting Company.

Surgical operation televised on a closed
circuit was shown February 27, 1947, at a
meeting of the Johns Hopkins Medical and
Surgical Association held at the Johns Hopkins
Hospital, Baltimore, Md. The operation was
one of four on the heart and one on the sym-
pathetic nerve trunk along the vertebral column
televised to ten receivers in four classrooms.
The first two operations were performed by
Dr. Alfred Blalock. (*Bulletin. Johns Hopkins
Hospital. September 1947*)

Surgical operation televised on a closed
circuit in color was presented on June 6, 1949,
by the Columbia Broadcasting System. An
appendectomy performed by Dr. David Bacharach Allman, surgical director of the Atlantic
City Hospital, Atlantic City, N.J., was shown
at the annual session of the American Medical
Association convention at Atlantic City. The
field sequential type of color television was
shown by means of the equipment of the Smith,
Kline and French Laboratories, Inc., made by
the Zenith Radio Corporation and the Webster-
Chicago Corporation. Ten television receivers,
each with a tube 12 by 14 inches, were used.

Surgical operation televised on a coast-to-
coast closed circuit in color was transmitted
December 7, 1951, over a closed circuit of the
Columbia Broadcasting System by KNXT-TV,
Los Angeles, Calif. Dr. John Clifton Jones

THE FIRST

operated on the constricted aorta of Richard D. Russell, 20, of Pacoima, Calif., at the Los Angeles County Hospital, Los Angeles. Surgeons in New York questioned Dr. Jones while the operation was in progress. Neither the beginning nor the end of the operation was shown in the one-hour telecast.

Surgical operation televised on a local program for the general public was transmitted March 16, 1952, by WPTZ, Philadelphia, Pa. Dr. Isador Schwaner Ravdin, who performed a 2½-hour peptic ulcer operation at the University of Pennsylvania Hospital, Philadelphia, was observed in action for ten minutes.

Symphonic concerts to be televised were transmitted March 20, 1948, by the Columbia Broadcasting System and the National Broadcasting Company. Eugene Ormandy at 5 P.M. conducted the Philadelphia Symphony Orchestra in a concert televised by WCAU-TV, Philadelphia, Pa., on CBS. Arturo Toscanini at 6:30 P.M. conducted the NBC Symphony Orchestra in an all-Wagner concert televised by WNBT, New York City.

Telecast images received in an airplane were sent on May 21, 1932, to a Western Air Express trimotor airplane in flight over Los Angeles, Calif. The images were transmitted by W6XAO of the Don Lee Broadcasting System, Los Angeles. A 150-watt transmitter on ultra high frequency of 44.500 kilocycles under the direction of Harry R. Lubcke, director of television, transmitted at the rate of 15 pictures per second with the 80-line screen. The telecast, originating about 10 miles away, was shown for 5 minutes on a screen 8 inches in diameter.

Telecast (long-distance) received in an airplane was sent October 17, 1939, from W2XBS of the National Broadcasting Company, New York City. An airplane flying high above Washington, D.C., intercepted the ultra short waves which came on a straight line from New York City.

Telecast of an object in motion was made June 13, 1925, from radio station NOF, Bellevue, D.C., and received at the laboratory of Charles Francis Jenkins, 1519 Connecticut Avenue, Washington, D.C., where it was viewed by Curtis Dwight Wilbur, Secretary of the Navy; George Kimball Burgess, Director of the Bureau of Standards; Stephen Brooks Davis, Acting Secretary of Commerce; and others. The apparatus used was "Vision-by-Radio," invented by Jenkins. The image transmitted was a small model windmill with blades in motion.

Telecast of image and sound transmitted over any considerable distance was demonstrated

THE FIRST

April 7, 1927. Secretary of Commerce Herbert Clark Hoover, in Washington, D.C., was both seen and heard by a large group gathered in the auditorium of the Bell Telephone Laboratories, New York City.

Telecast originating live in three countries was presented on June 27, 1955, on the National Broadcasting Company's network program "Wide Wide World" under the sponsorship of the Ford Motor Company and the Radio Corporation of America. Pictures were shown of a fiesta-time bullfight in Tijuana, Mexico; the opening night of the Shakespeare Festival at Stratford, Ontario, Canada; and events in Washington, D.C.; Denver, Colo.; San Francisco, Calif.; and New York City.

Telecast produced for a tri-city gathering was accomplished December 8, 1939, when International Rotary leaders assembled at the General Electric Station, W2XB, Schenectady, N.Y., were seen and heard simultaneously at Rotary dinners in Albany, Troy, and Schenectady, N.Y.

Telecast (public) over telephone wires was a presentation of the bicycle races at Madison Square Garden, New York City, by the National Broadcasting Company on May 20, 1939. The images were transmitted from Madison Square Garden to the National Broadcasting Company studio at Radio City, New York City, via the Circle telephone exchange at Ninth Avenue and 50th Street. When the images were received at the studio over telephone wire, they were conveyed over a coaxial cable to the transmitter in the tower of the Empire State Building, from which they were telecast.

Telecast received from England was transmitted June 18, 1959, from London to Montreal, Canada, via cable and relayed by the Canadian Broadcasting Company to the National Broadcasting Company in New York City, from where it was sent out over the entire NBC network. The film showed the departure from London of Queen Elizabeth and Prince Philip to the St. Lawrence Seaway ceremonies. Motion Picture Facsimile process used in the telecast was developed by the BBC. Each frame required eight seconds for transmission. The film was seen two hours and twenty-one minutes after the recording.

Telecast transmitted to Canada was presented January 20, 1953, over a 66-mile microwave link between Buffalo, N.Y., and Toronto, Ontario. The lines of the American Telegraph and Telephone Company were linked with the Bell Telephone Company of Canada. The first live show, a "Studio One" play, was televised on CBLT, Toronto, by the Canadian Broadcasting System.

TELEVISION—TELECAST—*Continued*

Telecast using coaxial cable was transmitted June 10, 1936, from Radio City, New York City, to the transmitter atop the Empire State Building, New York City, a distance of approximately 1½ miles. The first intercity telecast was transmitted October 5, 1936, from New York City to Philadelphia, Pa. The first coast-to-coast telecast was transmitted September 4, 1951, from New York City to San Francisco, Calif.

Television network demonstration (long distance) was given February 1, 1940, when members of the Federal Communications Commission at General Electric station W2XB, Schenectady, N.Y., witnessed a program televised from New York City, approximately 130 miles distant. The program, which was received at a relay station on the 44-50 megacycle band by means of a rhombic antenna supported by four 128-foot towers, was rebroadcast to the Schenectady-Albany district.

Television theater. *See* Theater: Television theater

Television wedding. *See* Wedding: Television wedding

Tennis tournament to be televised was the Eastern Grass Court championship matches which opened August 9, 1939, at the Westchester Country Club, Rye, N.Y. Station W2XBS, New York City, used a telescopic lens in addition to the iconoscope to obtain close-ups of important points.

Tennis tournament to be televised in color was the Davis Cup match at the West Side Tennis Club, Forest Hills, N.Y., on August 26, 1955, between Australia and the United States. The match was televised by WNBT of the National Broadcasting Company.

Track meet (intercollegiate) to be televised was the 19th annual Intercollegiate A.A.A.A. track and field championship meet at Madison Square Garden, New York City, televised March 2, 1940, by W2XBS. Twenty-three colleges participated in the various events: dashes, runs, relays, high hurdles, shot-put, pole vault, weight throwing, broad jumps, and high jumps. New York University won, with 27 points.

Transcontinental telecast by means of an orbiting satellite was accomplished April 24, 1962, when the Massachusetts Institute of Technology's Lincoln Laboratory field station at Camp Parks, Calif., transmitted to the two-year-old orbiting balloon Echo I waves which were bounced back to earth and received at Millstone Hill, Westford, Mass. The pictures were of poor quality but were recognizable.

Transcontinental telecast received on the east coast was transmitted from the War Memorial Opera House, San Francisco, Calif., on September 4, 1951, at 10:30 P.M. by a pool of the four networks to 94 of the 107 television stations then in operation. The telecast was transmitted by microwave relays to Omaha, Neb., and then by coaxial cables to stations in the East, North, and South. Secretary of State Dean Acheson introduced President Harry S. Truman, who made an address from the War Memorial Opera House in conjunction with the signing of the Japanese Peace Treaty.

Transcontinental telecast received on the west coast was the Columbia Broadcasting System program "Crusade For Freedom," transmitted from WCBS-TV, New York City, on September 23, 1951. General Lucius DuBignon Clay was chairman of the program.

Transoceanic television image was received February 8, 1928, at Hartsdale, N.Y., by Robert M. Hart, owner of short wave station W2CVJ. The sound vision, a picture of Mrs. Mia Howe, was sent across the ocean from station 2 KZ, Purley, England, two kilowatt power, by John Logie Baird of the Baird Television Development Company of London, England, using short radio waves.

Transoceanic television program was transmitted July 10, 1962, from Andover, Me., bounced off the 170-pound orbiting relay satellite Telstar, and received at various stations in Europe and the United States. The following day, July 11, a telecast from Pleumeur-Bodou, France, was received by means of the 380-ton horn-shaped antenna at Andover. The satellite was launched July 10, 1962, from Cape Canaveral, Fla.

Two-way demonstration of television in a theater was given April 9, 1930. On that date persons separated by a considerable distance were for the first time able to talk to and see each other as if they were on opposite sides of the same table. The two ends of the circuit were located in New York City, one in the auditorium of Bell Telephone Laboratories, 463 West Street, and the other at the American Telephone and Telegraph Company, 195 Broadway. The images appeared on a foot-square screen.

Underwater telecast from a submarine was made April 10, 1947, from the U.S.S. "Trumpetfish" at the Brooklyn Navy Yard, New York City, by WNBT, New York City. It was relayed by coaxial cable to WTTG, Washington, D.C.; WPTZ, Philadelphia, Pa.; and WRGB, Schenectady, N.Y. Three cameras were installed in the submarine; another

THE FIRST

camera, on the dock, filmed the submarine as it submerged, conducted a simulated torpedo attack, and finally surfaced.

Unscheduled event to be televised as it occurred was a fire in an abandoned barracks, on Ward's Island, N.Y., on November 15, 1938, recorded by a National Broadcasting Company mobile television unit (W2XBT). The unit had been assigned to record pictures of a swimming pool when the fire was discovered.

Variety talent show series with an all-Negro cast was "Happy Pappy," first televised on April 1, 1949 over WENR-TV, Chicago, Ill. The program featured Ray Grant as master of ceremonies, the Four Vagabonds, the Modern Modes, and guests.

Video recording on magnetic tape. *See* Tape recording: Video recording on magnetic tape

Visible and oral communication by the deaf over distance. *See* Deaf—Transmission: Visible and oral communication by the deaf over distance

Weather map telecast from a land sending station to a land receiving station was sent August 18, 1926, from radio station NAA, Arlington, Va., and received at the Weather Bureau Office, Washington, D.C. The demonstration was arranged by the Jenkins Laboratory, Washington, D.C. *(Monthly Weather Review. October 1926. Vol. 54)*

Weather map telecast to a transatlantic steamer was sent by the Radiomarine Corporation station, New York City, on June 20, 1930, to the S.S. "America," nearly 3,000 miles distant.

X-ray fluoroscopy television discussion was televised December 5, 1950, on the "Johns Hopkins Science Review" from WAAM, Baltimore, Md. over the DuMont Television Network. Dr. Russell Hedley Morgan, radiologist-in-chief of the Johns Hopkins Hospital, Baltimore, showed an X-ray fluoroscopic image of a patient with a chest wound. Dr. Paul Chesley Hodges in Chicago and Dr. Walter Sinnett in New York City viewed the closed circuit telecast simultaneously in their respective cities and participated in the consultation.

TELEVISION LICENSE

Commercial television license was granted to station W2XBS of the National Broadcasting Company, New York City, on July 1, 1941. Operations were required four hours a week, but approximately fifteen hours a week were presented.

THE FIRST

Construction permit for a commercial television station was granted June 17, 1941, to WNBT of the National Broadcasting Company, New York City, to operate on 50,000-56,000 kilocycles. A license to cover this construction permit was also granted June 17, 1941, effective July 1, 1941.

Television license was issued February 25, 1928, by the Federal Radio Commission to the [Charles Francis] Jenkins Laboratories for the operation of a television broadcast station at 1519 Connecticut Avenue, N.W., Washington, D.C., using the call letters W3XK. In 1929 the station was authorized to move its transmitter to a location between Silver Spring and Wheaton, Md. The station ceased to operate on October 31, 1932.

TELEVISION RECEIVER

Coin-operated television receiver was the "Tradio-Vision," manufactured by Tradio, Inc., Asbury Park, N.J., and publicly exhibited November 7, 1946, in New York City. The receiver, housed in a metal cabinet 16 inches high, 8 inches deep, and 9 inches wide, contained 20 tubes and a 5-inch cathode tube which reflected a 500-line image on a mirror on the lid. The apparatus was designed to operate upon insertion of a 25-cent piece.

Television receiver to permit two audiences to see and hear two different programs at the same time was the "Duoscopic," publicly demonstrated January 7, 1954, in New York City and Chicago, Ill., by the Allen B. Du Mont Laboratories, Inc. Two superimposed images were projected onto the screen by two cathode ray tubes set at right angles. The images were visible through polaroid glasses. Contrast controls were separate, and two separate systems were used to carry sounds through personalized ear-pieces. Each speaker could be turned off independently, and one image could be seen, if the viewer desired, as in standard sets.

Television receivers to project large images (up to 9 by 12 feet) were installed in April 1955 in seven of the Sheraton Hotels. The receivers, Fleetwood model FL-1001 Television Projectors built by the Fleetwood Corporation, Toledo, Ohio, were 4 feet high, 2 feet wide, and 3 feet deep and weighed 400 pounds. They were mounted on rubber-tired casters so that they could be moved easily. They were designed to show closed-circuit programs in ballrooms, conference rooms, and places of assembly.

TELEVISION STATION

All-color station to televise live local programs was WNBQ-TV, channel 5, Chicago, Ill., which began operations on April 15, 1956. Three color studios were equipped with five color cameras and two color-film projector chains for 16mm and 35mm films. The station

TELEVISION STATION—*Continued*

had begun operations on January 7, 1949, with black-and-white telecasts and had begun the conversion to color on November 3, 1955.

City to have two educational television channels was Pittsburgh, Pa. The Metropolitan Pittsburgh Educational Station was granted a permit to operate WQED, channel 13, on May 13, 1953. The first community-supported educational television station, WQED went on the air April 1, 1954. A second channel, WQEX, channel 16, was granted on July 16, 1958.

Commercial television station west of the Mississippi River was KTLA, Hollywood, Calif., which began operations January 22, 1947, at 8:30 P.M. from a converted garage. Dick Lane was the announcer.

Illegal television station closed by the Federal Communications Commission was operated by the Tube Division of Sylvania Electric Products, Inc., at Emporium, Pa., and closed October 19, 1950. A station with a 90-foot tower on top of Whittemore Mountain had televised programs from WJAC-TV, Johnstown, Pa., without authorization.

Microwave television station was KTRE-TV, Lufkin, Tex., owned by the Forest Capital Broadcasting Company, which began operations August 31, 1955, on channel 9 (very high frequency). Signals from KPRC-TV, Houston, Tex., channel 2, were deflected to booster equipment at the bottom of a tower at Coldspring, 60 miles away. There the signals were amplified and sent to the next relay tower, at Carmona, 30 miles away, where they were again amplified and sent to Lufkin, 30 miles away. Richman Lewin was vice president and general manager of KTRE-TV.

Noncommercial educational television station was KUHT, Houston, Tex., which broadcast test patterns May 12, 1953, and began programing May 25, 1953, from 5 P.M. to 9 P.M. five days a week over channel 8, on very high frequency. The formal dedication ceremonies took place June 8, 1953. The station was licensed jointly by the University of Houston and the Houston Public School system on April 14, 1952. John Schwarzwalder was director.

State-wide and state-supported educational television network was officially opened August 9, 1956, by Governor James Elisha Folsom of Alabama. WAIQ, Andalusia, Ala. (channel 2) was joined to WBIQ, Birmingham, Ala. (channel 10) and WTIQ, Munford, Ala. (channel 7) to reach 90 per cent of the state of Alabama. Programs were supplied by the

University of Alabama, Alabama Polytechnic Institute, and the Greater Birmingham Area Educational Television Association, Inc.

Television stations to share the same time and frequency were KSBW-TV, Salinas, Calif., and KMBY-TV, Monterey, Calif. On February 19, 1953, both stations were granted licenses. A protest was filed, but the licenses were declared valid on June 26, 1953, and both stations began telecasting officially on September 11, 1953, from the same transmitter atop Mount Toro, Calif. The hours were divided equally on alternate nights, each station transmitting alone on alternate Sundays.

Ultra high frequency commercial television station was KPTV (channel 27), Portland, Ore., which began regular commercial program service October 1, 1952.

Ultra high frequency television station to operate on a regular daily basis was KC2XAK, Bridgeport, Conn., which began operating December 29, 1949, on 530 megacycles. Programs received via microwaves from WNBT, New York City, were rebroadcast on the ultra high frequency band. The transmitter, located on Success Hill, Stratford, Conn., was completed on November 15, 1949.

TELEVISION TUBE

Miniature tube was the "peanut tube," an N-type tube, 2 inches high and ⅝ inch in diameter, operated on a single dry cell. The tube was created by Howard W. Weinhart of Elizabeth, N.J., who filed his application July 14, 1919, and obtained patent 1,550,768 on August 25, 1925, on an "electric discharge device." The patent was assigned to the Western Electric Company, Inc., New York City.

Rectangular television tube (practical) was announced to the trade July 10, 1949, by the Kimble Glass Company, subsidiary of Owens-Illinois in Toledo, Ohio. The bulb faces of the tube were approximately 12 by 16 inches. The tube sold for approximately $12. The first deliveries were made October 1, 1949.

TELLURIUM. *See* Tungsten: Tungsten and tellurium

TEMPERANCE LAW (colonial) was signed March 5, 1623, by Governor Sir Francis Wyatt of Virginia and thirty-two others. It provided that "the proclamations for swearing and drunkenness set out by the Governor and Counsell are confirmed by this assembly, and it is further ordered that the churchwardens shall be sworne to present them to the commanders of every plantation and that the forfeitures shall be collected by them to be for publique uses." *(William Waller Hening— Statutes at Large. Vol. 1)*

TEMPERANCE SOCIETY

Anti-Saloon League was founded by Howard Hyde Russell and fifteen members of the Oberlin Temperance Alliance who formed the Ohio Anti-Saloon League on May 24, 1893, in Oberlin, Ohio. The first meeting was held in the Oberlin College library building. The original purpose of the society was to force the Ohio saloons out of business and to preach the benefits of temperance. On June 23, 1893, the Anti-Saloon League of the District of Columbia was formed in Washington, D.C., with Major Samuel Hamilton Walker as the first president. The constitution was adopted July 7, 1893.

Anti-Saloon League (national organization) was the Anti-Saloon League of America, formed December 17-18, 1895, at the Calvary Baptist Sunday School, Washington, D.C., by a coalition of the Anti-Saloon League of the District of Columbia, the Anti-Saloon League of Ohio, and forty-five other local temperance organizations. The first officers were Hiram Price, president; the Reverend Luther Barton Wilson, first vice president; Archbishop John Ireland, second vice president; James Lithgow Ewin, recording secretary; and F. W. Walsh, treasurer.

Liquor reform movement. *See* Liquor reform movement

Temperance organization (local) was formed in 1789 by the farmers of Litchfield County, Conn. Their pledge read in part: "We do hereby associate and mutually agree that hereafter we will carry on our business without the use of distilled spirits as an article of refreshment, either for ourselves or for those whom we employ; and that, instead thereof, we will serve our workmen with wholesome food and the common simple drinks of our production." *(Litchfield (Conn.) Enquirer. September 26, 1833)*

Temperance society (union) was the Union Temperate Society of Moreau and Northumberland, organized April 13, 1808, at a meeting in Saratoga Springs, N.Y., by Dr. Billy James Clark, who became secretary. Sidney Berry was the president, Ichabod Hawley vice president, and Thomas Thompson treasurer. The members agreed not to drink, except at public dinners, under a penalty of 25 cents for each offense and 50 cents for intoxication. Total abstinence was not demanded until 1836. *(Jacob Hilton Durkee—History of the World's Temperate Centennial Congress)*

Women's temperance society (national) was the National Woman's Christian Temperance Union organized in the Second Presbyterian Church, Cleveland, Ohio, November 18, 19 and 20, 1874. The society was incorporated

March 1, 1883. The first president was Mrs. Annie T. Wittenmyer of Philadelphia Pa., who served from November 18, 1874, to October 29, 1879. At a convention in Detroit, Mich., October 31-November 3, 1883, the World Woman's Christian Temperance Union was organized. The first convention was held November 10-11, 1891, in Boston, Mass.

Women's temperance society (state) was the New York Women's State Temperance Society, founded April 20, 1852, at a convention held in Rochester, N.Y., principally through the efforts of Susan Brownell Anthony. Approximately five hundred women attended. *(Standard Encyclopedia of the Alcohol Problem. Vol. 5)*

TEN-HOUR-DAY LAW. *See* Labor law: Ten-hour-day law

TENEMENT HOUSE. *See* Building: Tenement house

TENNESSEE VALLEY AUTHORITY CONTRACT. *See* Electrical contract

TENNIS
See also Squash

Court tennis was introduced in Boston, Mass., in 1876 by Hollis Hunnewell. The game is played with a curiously shaped racket on a court (usually enclosed) 110 feet long and 38 feet wide, with an elaborate lay-out. There are only about a dozen such courts in the United States.

Lawn tennis was introduced in March 1874 by Mary Ewing Outerbridge, who imported rackets and other equipment from Bermuda. It is said that customs officials were unable to determine under what section of the Tariff Act the equipment belonged, and after a week's indecision permitted it to enter "duty free." A court was laid out in 1874 at the Staten Island Cricket and Baseball Club, to which Miss Outerbridge's family belonged. The first players were members of the family. Within seven years tennis had become popular, and on May 21, 1881, her brother Eugenius H. Outerbridge organized the United States Lawn Tennis Association, to which thirty-three tennis clubs sent delegates. General Robert Shaw Oliver of the Albany Tennis Club was elected the first president. *(Malcolm Douglass Whitman—Tennis, Origin and Mysteries)*

TENNIS MATCH
See also Squash tournament

Intercollegiate court tennis match was played May 4, 1954, at the Racquet and Tennis Club, New York City. Yale defeated Princeton

TENNIS MATCH—*Continued*
2-1: James Laughlin of Yale defeated Ken-
ley Webster, Charles Watson of Yale defeated
Gary Nash, and Dozier Gardner of Princeton
defeated Robert Easton of Yale. On May 23,
1954, at Manhasset, Long Island, N.Y., Yale
defeated Harvard 4-3 for the challenge bowl
donated by James H. Van Alen.

Intercollegiate lawn tennis match was held
June 7-8, 1883, at Hartford, Conn., on the
grounds of Trinity College. Joseph Sill Clark
of Philadelphia, Pa., won the singles. The
doubles were won by Clark and Howard Augustus Taylor of New York City. The winners represented Harvard.

Lawn tennis champions who were brothers
were Carr Baker Neel and Samuel R. Neel of
Chicago, Ill., who on August 18, 1896, won the
United States Lawn Tennis Association outdoor
men's doubles championship at Newport Casino,
Newport, R.I., defeating Robert D. Wrenn and
M. G. Chace, 6-3, 1-6, 6-1, 3-6, 6-1.

Lawn tennis matches for the Davis Cup
(international lawn tennis challenge trophy)
were held at the Longwood Cricket Club,
Brookline, Mass., August 8-10, 1900, under the
auspices of the United States Lawn Tennis
Association. The Davis Cup was first won by
an American team consisting of Malcolm
Douglass Whitman, Dwight Filley Davis, and
Holcombe Ward, all of Harvard, who won
three matches to none, ten sets to one, and
seventy-six games to fifty against England. The
tournament called for one doubles and four
singles matches. The United States won the
first three matches (rain spoiled the other two)
and was declared victorious. *(Stephen Wallis
Merrihew—The Quest of the Davis Cup)*

**Lawn tennis national championship match-
es** were held at the Newport Casino, Newport, R.I., August 31, 1881. The singles were
won by Richard D. Sears, and the doubles by
Clarence Monroe Clark and Frederick W.
Taylor.

Lawn tennis tournament of national scope
was held September 1, 1880, at the Staten Island
Club, New Brighton, Staten Island, N.Y.
Twenty-three entrants competed for the first
prize, a silver cup valued at about a hundred
dollars.

**National tennis tournament of the United
States Lawn Tennis Association in which a
Negro woman competed** was held at the
West Side Tennis Club, Forest Hills, N.Y.
in August 1950. On August 29, 1950, Althea
Gibson, a Negro player of New York City,

was eliminated by Louise Brough of Beverly
Hills Calif., the Wimbledon champion, who
won 6-1, 3-6, 9-7.

**Professional lawn tennis contest (inter-
national)** was begun at the Newport Casino,
Newport, R.I., on August 29, 1889. George
Kerr, an Irish professional, defeated Thomas
Pettit, 6-3, 6-1, 6-1. Pettit won 6-4, 2-6, 6-3, 6-4
on September 21, 1889, at Springfield Mass.
The third match was held at the Longwood
Cricket Club, Brookline, Mass., on September
25, 1889, and Kerr won 6-3, 3-6, 6-4. *(Amer-
ican Lawn Tennis—November 20, 1927)*

Tennis match broadcast. *See* Radio Broadcast: Tennis match broadcast

Tennis tournament telecast. *See* Television
—Telecast: Tennis tournament to be televised

**Women's national championship lawn ten-
nis matches** were held at the Philadelphia
Cricket Club, Philadelphia, Pa., in 1887, and
won by Ellen F. Hansell The first women's
doubles championship was played in 1890 and
won by Ellen and Grace Roosevelt.

TENNIS PLAYER
**Lawn tennis champion to win four major
titles** within a year was John Donald Budge
of Oakland, Calif., who won the Australian title
January 29, 1938, at Adelaide, Australia; the
French title June 11, 1938, at Auteuil, France;
the British title July 1, 1938, at Wimbledon,
England; and the American title September 24,
1938, at Forest Hills, N.Y. *(John Donald
Budge—Budge On Tennis)*

**Negro tennis player to participate in a
United States Indoor Lawn Tennis Association championship tournament** was Dr. Reginald Weir of New York City, who won his first
match on March 11, 1948, and was eliminated
on March 13, 1948. The tournament was held
in New York City.

TENNIS SOCIETY
Tennis society (national) was the United
States Lawn Tennis Association, formed May 21,
1881, at the Fifth Avenue Hotel, New York City.
It formulated the rules of play, standardized
the height of the net and the size of the ball,
and ruled on such matters as the service line
and the size of the court. The first officers
were Robert Shaw Oliver of the Albany Tennis
Club, president; Samuel Campbell of the Orange
Lawn Tennis Club, vice president; and Clarence
M. Clark of the Young American Cricket Club,
secretary and treasurer.

TERMINAL (air). *See* Aviation—Airport:
Air terminal (not located at an airport)

THE FIRST

TERRA COTTA. *See* Brick: Terra cotta

TERRAMYCIN was publicly announced by Chas. Pfizer & Co., Inc., Brooklyn, N.Y., in the January 27, 1950, issue of *Science* magazine. Terramycin, an antibiotic used in the treatment of some urinary tract infections and certain types of pneumonia and dysentery, was isolated from Indiana soil. *(Science. Vol. 3. p 85. January 27, 1950)*

TERRITORIAL EXPANSION
Acquisition of land by the federal government from various states took place between 1781 and 1802. New York was the first state to cede territory to the government (1781). Other states soon followed—Virginia in 1784, Massachusetts in 1785, Connecticut in 1786, and other states later. The ceded territory was established on July 13, 1787, as the Northwest Territory. Arthur St. Clair was appointed the first governor of this territory in October 1787. The first territorial legislature assembled on September 24, 1799. This territory was later formed into states, the first of which was Ohio, admitted to the Union February 19, 1803. *(Charles Moore—The Northwest Under Three Flags)*

Annexation of territory was the Louisiana Purchase, a tract of land bought from France on April 30, 1803, for $15,000,000. It covered 1,171,931 square miles and included the entire Mississippi Valley from the Mississippi River to the Rocky Mountains and from the Gulf of Mexico to Canada. This territory included the present states of Louisiana, Arkansas, Missouri, Iowa, North and South Dakota, Nebraska, Kansas, Oklahoma; part of Colorado and Wyoming; and most of Montana and Minnesota. The treaty was arranged by Robert R. Livingston, minister at Paris, and James Monroe, who had been sent by President Thomas Jefferson as a special envoy to assist Livingston. On November 30, 1803, Spain ceded her claims to the territory to France, and on December 20, 1803, France formally delivered the colony to the American representatives. *(James Alexander Robertson—Louisiana Under the Rule of Spain, France and the United States, 1785-1807)*

Island territory added to the United States was the Hawaiian Islands, which were formally annexed on August 12, 1898, at the request of the Hawaiian people. The treaty was signed June 16, 1897, by John Sherman, Secretary of State, for the United States. A joint congressional resolution to provide for the annexation was passed July 7, 1898 (30 Stat.L. 751). *(John Roy Musick—Hawaii, Our New Possession)*

Non-contiguous territory added to the United States was Alaska, which was purchased from Russia on June 20, 1867, for $7,200,000.

THE FIRST

General Lovell Harrison Rousseau, the first military governor of the territory, took formal possession of Alaska in October 1867.

TETRAPLOID FLOWER. *See* Flowers: Tetraploid flowers

TEXAS PRESIDENT. *See* President of the Republic of Texas

TEXTBOOK printed in America was Thomas Dilworth's *A New Guide to the English Tongue*, a reader, speller, and grammar combined, published in London, England, in 1740 and reprinted by Franklin's press in 1747 in Philadelphia, Pa. It went through twenty-six editions before 1792. Dilworth was one of the first to provide word lists for spelling. Prior to this time, spelling had been taught incidentally with reading, the Bible being used as an advanced reader. *(Stuart Grayson Noble—The History of American Education)*

TEXTILE MACHINERY PATENT was granted February 14, 1794, on a carding and spinning machine, to James Davenport, who established the Globe Mills, Philadelphia, Pa.

TEXTILE SCHOOL
Textile school in a college was one of six departments of the Clemson Agricultural College, Clemson, S.C. It was established in 1899, six years after the opening of the college. The first textile graduates, five in number, received degrees in textile engineering on June 6, 1904. The first director of the textile school was J. H. M. Beaty.

TEXTILE - WRAPPED DETONATING FUSE. *See* Fuse: Textile-wrapped detonating fuse

THANKSGIVING DAY. *See* Holiday: Thanksgiving day

THEATER
Baby show. *See* Baby show

Ballet. *See* Ballet

Chinese theater was the theater of "Celestial John," on Telegraph Hill, fronting Dupont Street, San Francisco, Calif., which opened December 23, 1852. It consisted of one vast pit or parquet and had a seating capacity of 1,400. There were no tiers of boxes. No scenery was used.

Drama broadcast. *See* Radio broadcast: Drama broadcast

Exhibition. *See* Fair

THEATER—*Continued*
Flea circus. *See* Flea circus

Minstrel show. *See* Ministrel show troupe

Moving picture theater. *See* Moving picture theater

Municipal theater was the Academy of Music of Northampton, Mass., which was accepted by the City of Northampton as a gift from Edward Hutchinson Robbins Lyman on February 9, 1893. Visiting companies and traveling troupes offered their presentations there. The first stock company was that of Jessie Bonstelle and Bertram Harrison, who played from 1912 to 1917. *(Constance D'Arcy Mackay—Little Theatre in the United States)*

Municipally owned and operated summer theater-in-the-round was the Playhouse in the Park, Fairmount Park, Philadelphia, Pa., which opened June 30, 1951, with a performance of *Goodbye My Fancy* starring Conrad Nagel and Sylvia Sidney. Profits from performances went to the city. The theater is housed in a tent containing 1,072 seats encircling a stage 68½ feet in circumference.

Newsreel theater was the Embassy, on Broadway and 46th Street, New York City, which opened November 2, 1929.

Orchestra in a theater. *See* Orchestra: Orchestra in a theater

Panorama show was *Jerusalem,* exhibited in 1790 at Lawrence Hyer's Tavern, 62 Chatham Street, New York City, "between the Gaol and the Tea Water Pump." It was open from ten in the morning until ten at night, and according to advertisements in the *Daily Advertiser,* the sight was "most brilliant by candlelight." *(George Clinton Densmore Odell—Annals of the New York Stage)*

Showboat or floating theater was a keel boat converted by Noah Miller Ludlow in 1817 at a cost of $200. It left Nashville, Tenn., October 20, 1817, and was used on the Cumberland, Ohio, and Mississippi Rivers. The first dramatic pieces presented were David Garrick's *The Honeymoon* and *The Lying Valet,* which were performed November 15, 1817. *(Noah Miller Ludlow—Dramatic Life As I Found It)*

Showboat of importance was "The Floating Palace," a flat scow with a superstructure which plied the Mississippi River in 1852. It was operated by Spalding and Rogers. The dress circle had 1,100 cane bottom chairs, the family circle 500 cushioned settees, and the

gallery 900 seats. It was heated by steam. *(Gleason's Pictorial Drawing Room Companion. February 19, 1853)*

State-owned theater operated as an integral part of a state school system was the Washington State Theatre, authorized April 15, 1936, and sponsored by the Department of Public Instruction, State of Washington, in connection with the Seattle Repertory Playhouse, Seattle, Wash. The first play presented was William Shakespeare's *The Comedy of Errors,* produced November 2, 1936. Traveling troupes visited schools offering Shakespearian, classic, and significant modern plays. The first director of the theater was Burton Wakeley James.

State-owned theater dedicated to its own drama was the Playmakers Theatre, Chapel Hill, N.C., opened November 23, 1925. About twenty new full-length and one-act plays are presented annually by members of the four playwriting courses of the University of North Carolina.

Television theater to be licensed was the Massachusetts Television Institute, Boston, Mass., which opened July 13, 1938, with a 45-minute show witnessed by 200 people who had paid a 25-cent admission fee. Sound accompanied the black-and-white images appearing on a screen 9 x 12 inches. The show featured specialty acts—vocal, instrumental, and dance numbers—performed in a room above the auditorium and transmitted by wire.

Television theater demonstration took place May 22, 1930, at the R.K.O. Proctor Theatre, Schenectady, N.Y. The theater orchestra was led by conductor John Gamble, who was not in the theater but in a laboratory a few miles away. The musicians followed Gamble's life-size television image, which was flashed on a six-foot screen. The projection was from the rear of the screen. Gamble listened to their music by telephone. Merrill Trainer was the master of ceremonies. Other performers were Matilda Biglow Russ, soprano, and Frank Camadine, harmonica player. The demonstration was arranged by Dr. Ernst Fredrik Werner Alexanderson, consulting engineer of the General Electric Company and the Radio Corporation of America, to show the possibilities of television as a medium of theater entertainment. The telecast was made by the General Electric Company, Schenectady, N.Y., on a wave length of 92 meters.

Television theater demonstration of a sports event on a full-size screen took place at the Paramount Theatre, New York City, on April 14, 1948, when a boxing match in Brooklyn, N.Y., was televised by WPIX, New York City, on a special wave length. The images were relayed from Brooklyn to the Daily News Building and thence to the Paramount Theatre.

THE FIRST

Theater was built in 1718 by William Levingston at Williamsburg, Va. He acquired the lots from the Trustees of Williamsburg on November 5, 1716, and in December 1716 contracted with Charles Stagg, dancing master, and Mary Stagg, his wife, to act and teach others how to act in the playhouse he would erect for the acting of comedies, drolls, and stage plays. In 1718 Governor Alexander Spotswood entertained a number of guests at the theater.

Theater building (permanent) was the Southwark Theatre, on South Street above Fourth, Philadelphia, Pa., built by David Douglass, which opened November 21, 1766, with Lewis Hallam of the American Company in *The Gamester*. The walls and the first story were built of brick. The building was used as a hospital in the Revolutionary War and was partly destroyed by fire in 1821. *(John Fanning Watson—Annals of Philadelphia)*

Theater destroyed by fire was the Federal Street Theatre, Boston, Mass., which suffered a $60,000 loss on February 2, 1798.

Theater lighted by electricity was the Bijou Theatre, 545 Washington Street, Boston, Mass., which was lighted by an Edison isolated plant on December 11, 1882. Six hundred and fifty lamps were used. The proscenium was surrounded with 192 lights, and 140 were used in the borders. Colliers' Standard Opera Company presented Gilbert and Sullivan's *Iolanthe, or the Peer and the Peri*. *(Boston Evening Transcript. December 12, 1882)*

Theater lighted by gas was the Chatham Garden and Theatre, which was situated at what is now 80 to 90 Chatham Street, New York City. Gas lighting had been used previously in theaters, but as a novelty rather than as illumination. The New York *Post* and *Mirror* on May 9, 1825, stated that the whole theater was lighted by gas, "which sheds a clear soft light over the audience and stage." The illumination "elicited the loudest plaudits from all present."

Theater provided with scientific air distribution to furnish comfortable conditions throughout was the Metropolitan Theatre, Los Angeles, Calif., equipped in 1921 by the Carrier Engineering Corporation with a system to distribute air from various parts of the theater.

Theater school. *See* Theatrical school

Theater to employ women ushers was the Majestic Theatre, 59th Street and Central Park West, New York City, on December 16, 1903. They wore black dresses with red satin sashes over one shoulder.

THE FIRST

Therapeutic theater to treat psychiatric cases by "psycho-dramatic shock treatment" was instituted by Dr. Jacob L. Moreno in Beacon, N.Y., in 1937. The treatment was designed to enable the psychiatric worker to achieve a clearer understanding of the patient's mental processes. None but interested participants and doctors were privileged to see the re-enactment of cases. *(Jacob L. Moreno—Psychodrama)*

Vaudeville. *See* Vaudeville

Wax works museum. *See* Wax works museum

Wild west show. *See* Wild west show

THEATER HISTORY of importance was *A History of the American Theatre* by William Dunlap, published in 1832 in New York City by J. & J. Harper. It contained 430 pages.

THEATRICAL ADVANCE PUBLICITY MAN was Robert Upton, who left London in October 1750 for New York City to prepare the way for the Hallam Company. Instead, he joined the [Walter] Murray and [Thomas] Kean Company then performing in New York City. *(George Overcash Seilhamer—History of the American Theatre)*

THEATRICAL SCHOOL

Public high school to specialize in the performing field. *See* High school: Public high school to specialize in the performing field

Theater and dramatic criticism course to award a Ph.D. degree was established by the Department of Drama, Yale University, New Haven, Conn., on September 24, 1934. The first degrees were awarded to George Riley Kernodle, John Huber McDowell, and Virginia More Roediger on June 23, 1937. The normal minimum time required for the course was four full years of study and research. The first professor of the history of the drama was Allardyce Nicoll.

Theatrical school devoted exclusively to training for the professional stage was the Lyceum School of Acting in New York City, which was founded by Franklin Haven Sargent on October 1, 1884. It was renamed the American Academy of Dramatic Arts in 1890.

Theatrical school sponsored by an institution of higher learning in association with a professional theater was the Mohawk Drama Festival and Institute of the Theater, which offered its first courses on July 2, 1935, at Union College, Schenectady, N.Y. Seventy students enrolled in the intensive eight-week course covering history, theory, and practice. The director was Dr. Thomas Herbert Dickinson.

THEATRICAL SCHOOL—*Continued*
Four plays were presented: *The Merry Wives of Windsor, Lysistrata, Rip Van Winkle,* and *Master of the Revels.* The course concluded August 24, 1935, when twenty-five certificates of meritorious achievement were awarded. The school was chartered by the Regents of the University of the State of New York in 1938.

THEME SONG. *See* Radio broadcast: Program theme song

THEOLOGICAL BIBLIOGRAPHY. *See* Bibliography: Bibliography of theological and biblical literature

THEOLOGICAL SCHOOL
    Theological school was founded by the Dutch Reformed Church in 1784 with the appointment of Dr. John Henry Livingston of the Collegiate Church of New York City as professor of theology. In 1810 Livingston went to New Brunswick, N.J., under an agreement whereby the school was to share the campus of Queen's College (later Rutgers). The school, named the New Brunswick Theological Seminary, has been closely associated with the adjacent institution. The seminary campus today is surrounded by the buildings of Rutgers—The State University. The two institutions are not corporately connected, however, and have always retained separate identities.

    Theological school (non-sectarian) was the Divinity School of Harvard College, Cambridge, Mass., organized as a separate department in 1816 although the faculty of the Divinity School was not appointed until 1819. Six students graduated in 1817. Degrees were not conferred by the Divinity School until 1870. Theology had been taught since the opening of Harvard College.

    Theological school to admit women as students was the Boston University School of Theology, Boston, Mass., formed March 30, 1871, when the Boston Theological Seminary united with Boston University. The first woman student matriculated on September 25, 1872. The first B.D. degree awarded to a woman was granted to Anna Oliver on June 7, 1876.

    Theological school to present regular courses by scholars representing different denominations was the Boston Theological Seminary, Boston, Mass., which opened September 1867 with Catholic, Methodist, and Presbyterian professors, as well as members of other faiths.

THEOLOGICAL TREATISE of importance was *Vier kleine doch ungemeine und sehr nützliche Tractätlein,* by Francis Daniel Pastorius published in 1690 in Germantown, Pa.

It contained an outline of the saints, an account of the bishops and saints, and a review of the church councils and the bishops and patriarchs of Constantinople. *(Marion Dexter Learned— The Life of Francis Daniel Pastorius)*

THEOSOPHICAL SOCIETY was the American Theosophical Society, founded November 17, 1875, by Helena Petrovna Blavatsky and Colonel Henry Steele Olcott in New York City. The society later was incorporated in Adyar, Madras, India, the city which was made the international headquarters of the society. The national headquarters of the American section of the organization is now in Wheaton, Ill. Theosophy is not a religion but a "synthesis of the principles underlying all religions and science." Its object is to form a nucleus of the Universal Brotherhood of Humanity, without distinctions of race, creed, sex, caste or color; to encourage the study of comparative religion, philosophy, and science; and to investigate the unexplained laws of nature and the powers latent in man. *(Theosophical Society in America—Inaugural Address)*

THERAPEUTIC THEATER. *See* Theater; Therapeutic theater

THERAPEUTICS AND MATERIA MEDICA BOOK. *See* Medical book: Therapeutics and materia medica book

THERAPY (OCCUPATIONAL) COURSE. *See* Occupational therapy course

THERMIT used to break up ice jams was employed on February 24, 1925, when a 250,000-ton ice jam in the St. Lawrence River at Waddington, N.Y., was moved in a few hours after the reaction of three thermit charges of ninety pounds each. Thermit is a mixture of finely powdered aluminum metal and oxide of iron. When properly ignited, it reacts vigorously, generating very high temperatures and producing extremely hot liquid iron. This method of using thermit in ice-breaking work was first applied by Howard Turner Barnes, Professor of Physics at McGill University, Montreal, Canada. *(Howard Turner Barnes—Ice Engineering)*

THERMONUCLEAR BOMB. *See* Atomic bomb: Atomic fusion (thermonuclear) bomb

THERMOSETTING PLASTIC. *See* Plastic: Thermosetting man-made plastic

THESIS DIRECTORY was a broadside, "A List of Theses at the Commencement of Harvard College," published in 1642 by Stephen Day, Cambridge, Mass. No copy is known to exist. *(Sidney Arthur Kimber—The Story of an Old Press)*

THE FIRST

THIRD PARTY QUIDS. *See* Quids

THIRD TERM PRESIDENT. *See* President (United States): President elected for a fourth term

THORIUM-URANIUM REACTOR. *See* Atomic reactor: Thorium-uranium reactor (privately owned)

THOROUGHBRED HORSE. *See* Horse: Horse (thoroughbred)

THREAD
Cotton thread was made in Pawtucket, R.I., in 1793 by Hannah Wilkinson (Mrs. Slater), who conceived the idea of twisting fine Surinam cotton yarn on spinning wheels. She manufactured No. 20 two-ply thread, which proved superior to the linen thread then in use.

Non-twisted sewing thread (and the first non-twisted nylon sewing thread) was made commercially available in February 1946 by Belding Hemingway Corticelli, Putnam, Conn. It was called "Monocord" and "Nymo."

Silk thread was manufactured in 1819 at Mansfield, Conn., by Rodney Hanks and Horatio Hanks.

Silk thread on spools was produced in 1849 by General Merritt Heminway. Previous to this, silk thread had been sold in skeins. The spools at first contained twelve yards of thread, and later fifty and a hundred yards. The factory in which this thread was manufactured was started in 1822 in Watertown, Conn., by Bishop & Heminway, incorporated in 1842 under the name of M. Heminway and Sons.

THREE-BALL BILLIARD MATCH. *See* Billiard match: Billiard three-ball match on a six-by-twelve carom table

THREE-CENT PIECE. *See* Money: Silver coins

THREE-DIMENSIONAL FEATURE MOVING PICTURE. *See* Moving picture: Three-dimensional feature moving picture

THREE-DIMENSIONAL NEWSPAPER ADVERTISEMENT. *See* Advertisement: Three-dimensional newspaper advertisement

THREE-ELEMENT VACUUM TUBE. *See* Radio tube: Three-element vacuum tube

THREE-MOTOR AIRPLANE. *See* Aviation—Airplane: Three-motor airplane

THE FIRST

THREE-WIRE CENTRAL STATION INCANDESCENT ELECTRIC LIGHTING PLANT. *See* Electric company: Three-wire central station incandescent electric lighting plant

THRESHER
Threshing machine to employ steam was patented by John A. Pitts and Hiram Abial Pitts of Winthrop, Me., who received patent No. 542 on December 29, 1837, on a "machine for threshing or cleaning grain." The machine separated grain from the straw and chaff.

THROAT CLINIC. *See* Medical clinic: Laryngology clinic

THROAT MICROPHONE. *See* Laryngophone

TICKER. *See* Telegraph: Telegraph ticker to operate at high speed

TICKET SPECULATORS plied their trade in New York City in September 1850. Prior to the first appearance of Jenny Lind at Castle Garden, September 11, 1850, Phineas Taylor Barnum auctioned the seats, charging 25 cents admission to the auction. The first ticket was sold to John Nicholas Genin for $225. One thousand tickets sold for $10,141. Jenny Lind donated her share of the $17,864 gross receipts of the first performance to New York charities. Premiums were exacted by those who sold their tickets. *(Rodman Gilder—The Battery)*

TICKETS (airplane commutation). *See* Aviation: Airplane commutation tickets

TIE (cotton-bale metallic fastening). *See* Cotton-bale metallic tie

TIGHTROPE
Tightrope crossing of Niagara Falls. *See* Niagara Falls: Person to cross Niagara Falls on a tightrope

Woman tightrope performer was Madame Adolphe of Paris, who, accompanied by Monsieur Godau, appeared June 1, 1819, at the Anthony Street Theatre, New York City.

TIGHTS (circus) are believed to have been introduced in 1828 by Nelson Hower, a bareback rider in the Buckley and Wicks Show, as the result of a mishap. The performers wore

THE FIRST

TIGHTS—*Continued*
short jackets, knee breeches and stockings, but
Hower's costume failed to arrive and he appeared for the show in his long knit underwear.
(*Billboard. September 6, 1930*)

TILE
Brick roofing tile was manufactured in
1735 by Hüster, a German tile maker in Montgomery County, Pa. (*W. G. Worcester—Geological Survey of Ohio*)

Wall and floor tiles were manufactured in
1845 by Abraham Miller, 7th and Zane Streets,
Philadelphia, Pa. In 1810 he had succeeded
Andrew Miller, who had conducted a pottery
in Sugar Alley since 1791. (*Heinrich Ries and
Henry Leighton—History of the Clay-working
Industry in the United States*)

TIMBER DRYDOCK. *See* Drydock: Timber drydock

**TIMBER TRESTLE PIER OF LATTICE
CONSTRUCTION.** *See* Bridge: Timber
trestle pier of lattice construction

TIMBERLAND RESERVATION. *See*
Forest reserve: Forest reserve (national)

TIME-LOCK. *See* Lock: Time-lock

TIME RECORDER
Autograph time recorder was patented by
Benjamin Frederick Merritt of Newton, Mass.,
who received patent No. 375,087 on December
20, 1887. The recorder was manufactured by
the Chicago Time Register Company, now a
part of the International Business Machines
Corporation.

Card time recorder was invented by Daniel
M. Cooper of Rochester, N.Y., who received
patent No. 528,223 on October 30, 1894. The
pressing of a lever recorded the time on specially printed cards divided by horizontal lines
into seven equal spaces for the days of the
week. The recorder, known as the "Rochester,"
was manufactured by the Willard and Frick
Manufacturing Company.

Dial time recorder was invented in 1888
by Dr. Alexander Dey of Glasgow, Scotland,
who obtained patent No. 411,586 on September
24, 1889. Employees' numbers appeared around
the circumference of a large ring on the front
of the machine. A pivoted pointer-arm pressed
into a guide hole printed the time opposite the
number on a prepared sheet inside the machine.
In 1893 Alexander Dey, with his two brothers,
John and Robert, who conducted a department
store in Syracuse, N.Y., formed the Dey Patents Company of Syracuse, which later changed
its name to the Dey Time Register Company.

THE FIRST

Employees' time recorder was invented by
Willard L. Bundy of Auburn, N.Y., who obtained patent No. 393,205 on November 20, 1888.
A key bearing the workman's number inserted
in the mechanism printed both the number and
the time on a paper tape. Bundy formed the
Bundy Manufacturing Company, now a division of the International Business Machines
Corporation.

TIME (standard) was suggested for the
United States by Charles Ferdinand Dowd of
Saratoga Springs, N.Y., in 1870 but was not
adopted at the time. The question was again
brought forward in 1879, but the change did
not meet with popular approval. On the initiative of the American Railway Association in
1883, Standard Time was adopted in the United
States. At noon on November 18, 1883, the
telegraphic signals sent out daily from the
Naval Observatory at Washington, D.C. were
changed to the new system. (*Charles North
Dowd—Charles F. Dowd, A.M., Ph.D., A Narrative of His Services in Originating and Promoting the System of Standard time*)

TIMETABLE (railroad)
Railroad timetable was advertised in the
Baltimore, Md., *American*, May 20, 1830, by the
Baltimore and Ohio Railroad Company. It was
announced that on May 24, 1830, passenger
transportation would be effected between Baltimore, Md., and Ellicott's Mills, Md., and that a
brigade of train coaches would leave the company's depot on Pratt Street, Baltimore, at
7 A.M., 11 A.M., and 4 P.M. and would return
from Ellicott's Mills at 9 A.M., 1 P.M., and
6 P.M. The price for the 26-mile trip was 75
cents. Because of a shortage of cars, passengers were obliged to return in the same coach
and had to book passage for the whole trip.
When additional cars were available, passengers
could use any car and engage passage for a
shorter distance, if desired.

TIN CAN. *See* under Canning; Cans

TIN FACTORY, for the manufacture of
black plate, as well as tin and terne plate,
was established in 1874 by Rogers and Burch-
held in Leechburg, Pa.

TINTYPE CAMERA. *See* Camera: Tintype camera

TINWARE MANUFACTURERS
Successful tinware manufacturers were La-
lance and Grosjean, who in 1860 established a
factory at Woodhaven, Long Island, N.Y., for
the manufacture of deeper tinware, such as milk
pans, wash bowls, dishpans, etc.

Tinware manufacturers are said to have
been Edward and William Pattison, brothers
who settled in Berlin, Conn., about 1740

and manufactured culinary vessels and household articles made of sheet tin. Exact data as to the extent of their manufacturing activities have not been definitely determined, but it is known that they peddled their wares from house to house. *(Timothy Dwight—Travels in New England and New York)*

TIRE. *See* Automobile tire: Bicycle tire

TIRE CHAIN. *See* Automobile tire chain

TISSUE BANK. *See* Medicine: Tissue bank

TISSUE PAPER. *See* Paper: Toilet paper

TITANIUM
Titanium mill for rolling and forging titanium was opened November 2, 1957, in Toronto, Ohio, by the Titanium Metals Corporation of America, owned by the National Lead Company and the Allegheny Ludlum Steel Corporation.

Titanium plant fully self-contained and fully integrated was opened June 1, 1951, in Henderson, Nev., by the Titanium Metals Corporation of America. Titanium ore was converted at the plant to titanium sponge, which was melted and cast into ingots of titanium metal.

TITLE GUARANTY INSURANCE COMPANY. *See* Insurance: Title guaranty insurance company

TOASTER. *See* Electric toaster: Electric toaster

TOBACCO
Cigarette tax. *See* Cigarette tax

Tobacco cultivation was undertaken at Jamestown, Va., in 1612 by John Rolfe, the husband of Pocahontas. Rolfe had arrived from England with 107 other settlers on May 13, 1607. *(Ralphe Hamor—A True Discourse of the present estate of Virginia and the successes of the Affaires there till the 18 of June 1614)*

Tobacco tax (colonial) was authorized October 3, 1632, by the Massachusetts Court of Assistants and General Court, which ruled in Boston "that no person shall take any tobacco publicly, under pain of punishment; also that everyone shall pay 1d. for every time he is convicted of taking tobacco in any place, and that any Assistant shall have power to receive evidence and give order for the levying of it, as also to give order for the levying of the officer's charge. This order to begin the tenth of

November next." *(Nathaniel Bradstreet Shurtleff—Records of the Governor and Company of the Massachusetts Bay in New England)*

Tobacco tax for internal revenue was levied by an act of Congress of July 1, 1862 (12 Stat. L.432) but did not go into effect until September 1, 1862. The first federal tax on tobacco was levied in 1794, but after two years it was abandoned. A similar attempt was made in 1812 and lasted until 1816, when the tax was repealed. *(Meyer Jacobstein—Tobacco Industry in the United States)*

TOILET PAPER. *See* Paper: Toilet paper

TOKEN MONEY. *See* Money: Trade tokens

TOLL BRIDGE. *See* Bridge: Toll bridge

TOLL COLLECTOR (automatic) was placed in service November 19, 1954, at the Union Toll Plaza (in the Newark-Irvington-Union area) on the Garden State Parkway of New Jersey. Two machines went into operation at the extreme right lane for each direction of traffic to provide the correct change. Coins were deposited in a wire-mesh hopper. A green light flashed when the 25-cent toll was received, and an audible alarm sounded to signal evaders.

TOLL ROAD. *See* Road: Toll road

"TOMMY GUN." *See* Ordnance: Submachine gun

TONG (Chinese secret society) organized was the Kwong Dock Tong of San Francisco, about 1870. The first tong war broke out in 1873 as a result of an attack made on Ming Long of the Kwong Dock Tong by Low Sing, a member of the Suey Sing Tong. The dispute arose in connection with the slave-girl traffic. At Ross Valley and Waverly Place, San Francisco, the two factions met by appointment and began shooting. Six members of the Kwong Dock Tong were wounded—three of the six died—and one of the Suey Sing Tong men was killed. *(Eng Ying Gong and Bruce Grant—Tong War)*

TOOL FACTORY devoted exclusively to the manufacture of machinists' tools was established in 1838 by John H. Gage in the Water Street shop of the Nashua Manufacturing Company, Nashua, N.H. *(Edward Everett Parker—History of the City of Nashua, N.H.)*

TOOTHBRUSH with synthetic bristles was Dr. West's Miracle Tuft Toothbrush, made of Du Pont "Exton," a product synthesized from elementary substances. The brush was introduced to the retail trade during September 1938.

TOOTHPICK MANUFACTURING MACHINE PATENT was No. 123,790, granted February 20, 1872, to Silas Noble and James P. Cooley of Granville, Mass. The machine made it possible for "a block of wood, with little waste, at one operation, [to] be cut up into toothpicks ready for use."

TORNADO of which there is any record occurred at New Haven, Conn., June 10, 1682, about 2:30 P.M. *(John Park Finley—Tornadoes)*

TORNADO AND FIRE INSURANCE FUND. *See* Insurance: Fire and tornado insurance fund (state)

TORPEDO
Airplane torpedo was invented by Bradley Allen Fiske of the U.S. Navy, who obtained patent No. 1,032,394, July 16, 1912, on a "method of and apparatus for delivering submarine torpedoes from airships." The torpedo, held rigidly in place, its bow pointing in the same direction as the airplane, was dropped under its own power.

Torpedo manufacturing station was established in 1869 on Goat Island, in Newport Harbor, under the supervision of the Bureau of Ordnance of the Navy Department. The purpose of the station was to instruct naval officers in the manufacture of torpedoes. Commander Edmund O. Matthews was ordered on June 9, 1869, to report for duty and in September 1869 he took possession of Goat Island and commenced the erection of the necessary buildings. *(Records in Office of Naval Records and Library, Navy Department. Washington, D.C.)*

Torpedo mine attack in the Civil War was made July 7, 1861, by the Confederates at Acquia Creek on the Potomac. Two large casks, connected by a piece of manila rope about twenty-five fathoms long, and kept at surface by cork floats, were floated down the river in an attempt to destroy the "Pawnee," commanded by Commander Stephen Clegg Rowan. The attempt failed. The first attack that destroyed a war vessel was made in the Yazoo River, December 12, 1862, on the U.S. "Cairo," an armored river gunboat of 512 tons, under the command of Lieutenant Commander Thomas Oliver Selfridge. A large demijohn placed in a wooden box was anchored in the channel and exploded by means of a friction fuse. The first Confederate loss was a torpedo boat destroyed February 17, 1864, off Charleston, S.C.

Torpedoes used for oil drilling. *See* Oil: Oil well drilled by torpedoes

Underwater torpedo operated by electric current was invented by Samuel Colt of Hartford, Conn., who wrote President John

Tyler on June 19, 1841, that he could sink ships by mines. He sank the gunboat "Boxer" in New York harbor on July 4, 1842, and the 300-ton brig "Volta" on October 18, 1842. On April 13, 1843, in the presence of President Tyler and his cabinet, General Winfield Scott, and other officials, Colt blew up a schooner on the Potomac River by an electric mine from a distance of five miles. His invention was a combination of Robert Fulton's stationary torpedo and Professor Robert Hare's galvanic current.

TORPEDO BOAT. *See* Ship: Torpedo boat

TOTALISATOR to record race track bets and odds was invented by Sir George Julius, an Australian engineer, and installed in 1931 by the American Totalisator Company, Inc., Baltimore, Md., at the Hialeah Race Track, Miami, Fla. It was known as "the totalizer" and "the Julius" and was first used January 14, 1932.

TOUR OF THE WORLD
Passenger to fly around the world on commercial airlines in less than 100 hours was Major Horace C. Boren of Dallas, Tex., who arrived at New York International Airport, Idlewild, N.Y., on June 25, 1953, having completed a world flight in 99 hours and 16 minutes. Boren stopped at nineteen airports on his 21,000-mile flight.

Tour of the world made by a woman traveling alone was made by Elizabeth Cochrane (Nellie Bly). She made the tour in 72 days, 6 hours, 11 minutes, and 14 seconds, as a stunt for the New York *World* in 1889-90. She left New York City, Thursday, November 14, 1889, sailed from Hoboken, N.J., on the "Augusta Victoria" for Southampton, went around the world, and returned to New York on the Chicago express January 25, 1890, spending 56 days, 12 hours and 41 minutes in actual travel. *(Nellie Bly—Around the World in 72 Days)*

TOURNAMENT OF ROSES, originally called "The Battle of Flowers," was held January 1, 1890, at Pasadena, Calif., under the auspices of the Valley Hunt Club. In the afternoon, amateur sports contests were held. The first college football contest, held January 1, 1902, was a game between the University of Michigan and Stanford University. The University of Michigan won 49-0. Football games have been a regular annual event since January 1, 1916, when Washington State College defeated Brown University, 14-0. Since 1897 the tournament has been conducted by a non-profit organization known as the Pasadena Tournament of Roses Association, Limited. *(Pasadena Tournament of Roses Association—Tournament of Roses)*

THE FIRST

THE FIRST

TOW ROPE (ski). *See* Ski tow (rope)

TOWN NAMED FOR GEORGE WASHINGTON was the town of Forks of Tar River, N.C., which changed its name to Washington in 1775. The town was originally formed November 20, 1771, by James Bonner, who owned all the land on which it was situated. It was incorporated April 13, 1782. Washington, Ga., incorporated January 23, 1780, was the first town incorporated under the name of Washington.

TOYERY was opened September 24, 1932, at the New York University Community Center, New York City. The first director was Mrs. Ida Cash. At the toyery old toys were repaired for distribution to children.

TRACK. *See* Railroad track

TRACK MEET (intercollegiate)
Track meet (intercollegiate) was held in Saratoga, N.Y., July 20-21, 1876, under the auspices of the Intercollegiate Association of Amateur Athletes of America. The participating teams represented Bowdoin, City College of New York, Columbia, Dartmouth, University of Pennsylvania, Princeton, Wesleyan, Williams, and Yale. A silver cup was awarded annually to the winning team. Permanent possession of the trophy was granted to the college with the greatest number of victories in fourteen years. The first meet was won by Princeton with four firsts and four seconds. The cup was given permanently to Harvard, which won eight of the first fourteen meets.

Track meet (intercollegiate) to be televised. *See* Television—Telecast: Track meet (intercollegiate) to be televised

TRACKLESS TROLLEY SYSTEM. *See* Street car: Trackless trolley system

TRACT SOCIETY
Tract society was the Massachusetts Society for Promoting Christian Knowledge, instituted in Boston, Mass., September 1, 1803, at the suggestion of Samuel Phillips and Professor D. Tappan.

Tract society (national) was the American Tract Society, organized May 11, 1825, in New York City. The first president was Sampson Vryling Stoddard and the first secretary, the Reverend William Allen Hallock. The society, still in existence, was the outgrowth of a combination of about fifty large and small tract societies. The society is evangelical in principle, interdenominational in character, interracial in purpose, and international in scope. It was organized to minister to all classes and conditions of people, in many languages, through the medium of the printed page.

TRACTOR. *See* Automobile tractor

TRADE ASSOCIATION was the American Brass Association, which was organized in Naugatuck Valley, Conn., in February 1853. Headquarters were opened in Waterbury, Conn. Originally, in 1853, the object of the association was to regulate prices, but in 1856 it attempted to regulate production. The association ceased to function in 1869. Local associations had been formed earlier by various groups. *(William Gilbert Lathrop—The Brass Industry in Connecticut)*

TRADE COMMISSION (federal). *See* Federal Trade Commission

TRADE DOLLAR. *See* Money: Trade dollar

TRADE JOURNAL. *See* Periodical: Trade journal

TRADE REGISTER was *Aitken's General American Register, and the Gentleman's and Tradesman's Complete Annual Account Book and Calendar for . . . 1773.* Printed by J. Crukshank for R. Aitken in Philadelphia, Pa., in 1772-73, it contained 110 unnumbered pages and included a calendar, an account book for the year, and space for memoranda. Aitken's prefatory letter stated: "The intercourse and connection of the several colonies with each other is enlarging . . . so that it becomes a matter of some consequence to every inhabitant to be acquainted with the public offices and officers . . . in all the . . . provinces on the continent."

TRADE TOKENS. *See* Money: Trade tokens

TRADEMARK LAWSUIT
Trademark controversy involving a newspaper was tried before Judge Nathan Sandford, Chancellor of New York State, who decided on January 31, 1825, that the *National Advocate* of New York City was not entitled to an injunction to restrain the *New York National Advocate* in the case of Thomas Snowden vs. Mordecai M. Noah, John D. Brown, and others. *(Samuel M. Hopkins—Reports of Cases Argued and Determined in the Court of Chancery of the State of New York)*

TRADEMARK (U.S.) was registered under the act of July 8, 1870. During that year there were 121 registrations under the law, the first thereof (No. 1) under date of October 25,

THE FIRST

TRADEMARK (U.S.)—*Continued*

1870, by the Averill Chemical Paint Company of New York City on a "trade-mark for liquid paint." This law was declared unconstitutional and void.

See also Cotton: Cotton goods to be trademarked

TRADING POST. *See* Fur trading post

TRADING SHIP. *See* Ship: Trading ship sent to China

TRADING STAMP was originated in 1891 by Thomas Alexander Sperry, who in 1896 organized the Sperry & Hutchinson Company of Bridgeport, Conn. The company was incorporated in 1900. (*Twenty-Fifth Anniversary —Sperry & Hutchinson Co.*)

TRAFFIC COURT (bicycle). *See* Bicycle traffic court

TRAFFIC LIGHT

Electric traffic signal lights were installed August 5, 1914, at Euclid Avenue and East 105th Street, Cleveland, Ohio, by the American Traffic Signal Company under the direction of Safety Director Alfred A. Benesch. Cross arms, fifteen feet above the ground, were equipped with red and green lights and buzzers. Two long buzzes permitted Euclid Avenue traffic to proceed, and one long buzz, 105th Street traffic.

TRAFFIC LINES to designate lanes were painted in white on River Road, near Trenton, Wayne County, Mich., in the fall of 1911 under the direction of Edward Norris Hines (a road commissioner for Wayne County), who called his idea a "center line safety stripe." A machine was later developed which cut the painting cost.

TRAFFIC POLICE. *See* Police: Traffic police squad

TRAFFIC REGULATION

One-way traffic regulation appears to have been issued in New York City on December 17, 1791, when a regulation incidental to a performance at the John Street Theatre requested that "Ladies and Gentlemen will order their Coachmen to take up and set down with their Horse Heads to the East River, to avoid Confusion."

Traffic law was passed June 27, 1652, by New Amsterdam (New York City): "The Director General and Council of New Netherland in order to prevent accidents do hereby ordain that no Wagons, Carts or Sleighs shall be run, rode or driven at a gallop within this city of New Amsterdam, that the drivers and

THE FIRST

conductors of all Wagons, Carts and Sleighs within this city (the Broad Highway alone excepted) shall walk by the Wagons, Carts or Sleighs and so take and lead the horses, on the penalty of two pounds Flemish for the first time, and for the second time double, and for the third time to be arbitrarily corrected therefor and in addition to be responsible for all damages which may arise therefrom." (*Minutes of the Common Council of the City of New York, 1675-1676*)

Traffic policemen. *See* Police: Traffic police squad

TRAFFIC REGULATION COURSE

Air traffic regulation course was endowed in 1934 by Godfrey Lowell Cabot, who created the James Jackson Cabot Professorship of Air Traffic Regulation and Air Transportation at Norwich University, Northfield, Vt. Lectures have been given at intervals since the establishment of the course.

Graduate course in traffic engineering and administration was established August 16, 1937, at Harvard University, Cambridge, Mass., under the direction of Miller McClintock.

Teacher training course in "Training Traffic Safety" was offered at the Pennsylvania State College during the 1936 summer session under the guidance of Amos Earl Neyhart, administrative head of the Institute of Public Safety, Pennsylvania State College, State College, Pa. This course included both classroom techniques and road instruction procedures.

TRAFFIC REGULATION PAMPHLET

Printed traffic regulations were *Rules For Driving*. The regulations, printed in a four-page pamphlet 3¼ by 6¼ inches in size, were put into effect October 30, 1903, by the New York City Police Department.

TRAILER BANK. *See* Bank: Trailer bank

TRAILER CHURCH was Saint Paul's Wayside Cathedral, which was placed in operation October 1, 1937, by the Diocese of Southern Ohio Protestant Episcopal Church under the direction of Bishop Henry Wise Hobson. It was designed by Norman R. Sturgis and built by the Aerocar Company, Detroit, Mich. The exterior was of sheet metal with a backing of Masonite painted gun-metal gray. The roof was covered with a silver-finish fabric. The church was equipped with a removable altar, an organ, an amplification unit, and sound moving-picture apparatus. It seated about 25 people.

TRAILER (moving pictures). *See* Television—Telecast: Moving picture trailer to be televised

THE FIRST

TRAIN. *See* Railroad; Railroad car

TRAIN NEWSPAPER. *See* Newspaper: Newspaper printed on a train

TRAIN ROBBERY. *See* Railroad train robbery

TRAINER (aviation). *See* Aviation: Aviation trainer (jet)

TRAINING SCHOOL. *See* Army School: Army training school; Naval officers' training school; Police: Police training school; etc.

TRAITOR to the American cause was William Demont (Dement) who, on February 29, 1776, was appointed adjutant in Colonel Robert Magraw's battalion. He notified the British of the position of Fort Washington, Mount Washington (now in New York City). Demont's act enabled Sir William Howe to conquer the fort on November 16, 1776. The British force of 8,900 men captured 2,818 officers and men, 43 guns, 2,800 muskets, etc. Demont, a member of the Fifth Pennsylvania Battalion, deserted on November 2, 1776, and gave his plans to Lieutenant General Earl Percy. *(Empire State Society of the Sons of the American Revolution—Fort Washington)*

TRANSATLANTIC FLIGHT. *See* Aviation—Flights (transatlantic)

TRANSCONTINENTAL AIR MAIL. *See* Air mail service: Air mail transcontinental flight

TRANSCONTINENTAL AIR RACE. *See* Aviation—Races: Transcontinental air race

TRANSCONTINENTAL FLIGHT. *See* Aviation—Flights (transcontinental)

TRANSCONTINENTAL HORSEBACK TRIP. *See* Woman: Woman horseback rider to make a solo transcontinental trip

TRANSCONTINENTAL TRIPS. *See* under Automobile transcontinental trip; Bicycle trip; Railroad excursion

TRANSCRIPTION (radio). *See* Radio broadcast: Recorded coast-to-coast broadcast

TRANSFER PAPERS. *See* Decalcomanias

THE FIRST

TRANSFERS (street car). *See* Street car: Transfers (printed)

TRANSISTOR

Junction transistor was invented by Dr. William Shockley of the Bell Telephone Laboratories, Murray Hill, N.J., and announced on July 5, 1951. It consisted of a tiny sandwich of germanium treated so that its alternate layers had different electrical properties. It occupied only about one four-hundredths of a cubic inch.

Phototransistor, a transistor operated by light rather than electric current, was invented by Dr. John Northrup Shive of the Bell Telephone Laboratories, Murray Hill, N.J., and announced on March 30, 1950. It was composed of a midget disk of germanium with only a single collector wire. Light focused on one side of the disk controlled the flow of current to the opposite side, the side to which the wire was attached.

Transistor was invented at the Bell Telephone Laboratories, Murray Hill, N.J., by Drs. John Bardeen and Walter Houser Brattain, and demonstrated on June 30, 1948. The essential element of the device was a tiny wafer of germanium, a semiconductor. Transistors occupy a fraction of the space required for vacuum tubes needed to do a comparable electronic task and operate on greatly reduced amounts of power.

Transistors produced commercially for a specific product were made in October 1951 by the Western Electric Company, Allentown, Pa., for long-distance dialing equipment of the Bell Telephone System. In 1948 experimental transistors had been manufactured and distributed to military and civilian engineering organizations for early circuit development work.

TRANSISTOR RADIO RECEIVER. *See* Radio receiver: Transistor radio receiver

TRANSISTORIZED HEARING AID. *See* Deaf—Hearing aid: Transistorized hearing aid

TRANSOCEANIC NEWSPAPER. *See* Newspaper: Transoceanic newspaper

TRANSPACIFIC FLIGHT. *See* Aviation—Flights (transpacific)

TRANSPARENT PAPER STRIP PHOTOGRAPHIC FILM. *See* Photographic film: Transparent paper strip photographic film

THE FIRST

TRANSPARENT-TOP AUTOMOBILE.
See Automobile: Transparent-top automobile

TRANSPORT AIRPLANE. See Aviation
—Airplane: Transport airplane designed
especially for trans-oceanic service

TRANSPORTATION COORDINATION
Transportation coordination (federal) was
undertaken by the act of June 16, 1933 (48
Stat.L.211). Joseph Bartlett Eastman, a member
of the Interstate Commerce Commission, was
appointed coordinator June 16, 1933. His office
was created the same day, by the enactment of
the Emergency Railroad Transportation Act,
"to relieve the existing national emergency in
relation to interstate railroad transportation."
(Public Act No. 68.—73d Congress)

TRAPS
Steel animal traps commercially manufactured were made in 1855 by Sewell Newhouse of the Oneida Community, N.Y. He
made them in eight different sizes intended
to trap animals ranging from the house rat
to the grizzly bear and sold them principally
to Indians. Various types of traps had been
made earlier by Newhouse and by others, but
they had been devised for individual use and
were not marketed. Newhouse was the author
of The Trapper's Guide: A Manual of Instructions for Capturing All Kinds of Fur-Bearing
Animals and Curing Their Skins.

TRAPSHOOTING
Clay pigeon target was invented by
George Ligowsky of Cincinnati, Ohio, who
obtained patent No. 231,919 on September 7,
1880, on a concave slotted "flying target."

Trapshooting intercollegiate association
was the Intercollegiate Shooting Association,
formed March 25, 1898, at the Fifth Avenue
Hotel, New York City, by Columbia, Cornell,
Harvard, Pennsylania, Princeton, and Yale. The
first officers were president, H. R. Lunt of
Harvard; secretary, Oglesby Paul; and treasurer, C. B. Spears. The first meet was held at
the New Haven Shooting Club, New Haven,
Conn., on May 7, 1898. Clay pigeons were used.

TRAPSHOOTING TOURNAMENT
Trapshoot (Grand American) with clay
targets was held at Interstate Park, Queens,
Long Island, New York, June 12, 1900, and
won by Rolla O. (Pop) Heikes, of Dayton,
Ohio, who scored 91 targets out of a possible
100 from a distance of 22 yards. There were
74 entries. Walter S. Beaver of Berwyn, Pa.,
was the first shooter to win the Grand American
from the extreme distance of 25 yards. On
August 25, 1933, he broke 99 out of 100 targets.

Trapshoot (Grand American) with live
birds was held in March 1893 at Dexter

THE FIRST

Park, Jamaica, New York, with 21 entries.
R. A. Welch won, and killed 23 out of 25 birds
from 23 yards. (Robert A. Welch—First Annual Grand American Handicap Program)

TRAVELERS AID was instituted in 1851
when Bryan Mullanphy of St. Louis died and
left approximately one third of his fortune of
more than $1,000,000 in a trust fund, to be
administered by the City Council for the purpose
of assisting, while they were in St. Louis, those
who were "traveling to the west." In 1885
William Collins and Edward Prior, of the
Society of Friends, paid the salary of the first
employed worker among travelers. (Travelers
Aid Manual. National Association of Travelers
Aid Societies)

TRAVELERS AID SOCIETY
Travelers Aid Society (national) was the
National Association of Travelers Aid Societies,
which developed from the Travelers Aid Society of the City of New York. The New York
society, founded in 1904, cooperated in
forming the National Travelers Aid Society in
1917. In May 1920, the name was changed from
National Travelers Aid Society to National
Association of Travelers Aid Societies and in
1923 articles of incorporation were secured
under the new name. (Travelers Aid Manual.
National Association of Travelers Aid Societies)

TRAVELERS' CHECKS. See Check:
Travelers' checks

TRAVELING SIDEWALK. See Sidewalk
(traveling)

TREADMILL was completed September 7,
1822 in a specially constructed building for the
New York City Prison. By means of the treadmill, which was designed to be operated by 8
to 16 persons, 40 to 50 bushels of Indian corn
were ground daily. The wheel was 5 feet 2
inches in diameter. The treadmill was placed in
operation September 23, 1822, in a two-story
building 60 feet in length and 30 feet wide,
with a garret which served as a granary. Isaac
Collins, one of the managers of the Society for
the Prevention of Pauperism, and Stephen
Greelet are credited with suggesting the treadmill to Stephen Allen, then mayor of New
York. (James Hardie—History of the Tread-
Mill)

TREASON
American colonist hanged for treason was
Jacob Leisler, who in 1689 led an insurrection
against Governor Francis Nicholson of New
York "for the preservation of the Protestant
religion" and in behalf of the sovereigns William and Mary. Through trickery the aristo-
cratic party regained power and in a manifestly

THE FIRST

unfair trial convicted Leisler of treason and on May 16, 1691, hanged him from a scaffold erected in City Hall Park. *(Jared Sparks—Library of American Biography)*

Citizen of the United States to be tried for treason, convicted, and hanged was William Bruce Mumford, a retired gambler. During the Civil War Captain Theodorus Bailey was sent by Admiral David Glasgow Farragut to New Orleans, La., where he hoisted the American flag over the mint on April 28, 1862. After the troops left, Mumford tore down the flag. On May 1, General Benjamin Franklin Butler arrived in New Orleans with 2,000 troops and took possession of the St. Charles Hotel. A crowd gathered in front of it, among them Mumford who boasted of his exploit in humbling the "old rag of the United States." Mumford was tried under the direction of the provost marshal of the district of New Orleans and hanged on June 7, 1862. *(James Parton—General Butler in New Orleans)*

Execution for treason in peacetime was the electrocution of Julius and Ethel Rosenberg, husband and wife, on June 19, 1953 at Sing Sing Prison, Ossining, N.Y. The Rosenbergs were the first native-born Americans executed for espionage by order of a civilian court. They were sentenced April 5, 1951, by Judge Irving Robert Kaufman of the United States District Court, Southern District.

Treason trial (colonial) was held May 7, 1634, when the Virginia Assembly heard complaints against Sir John Harvey, Governor of Virginia, who had assumed his duties March 24, 1630. Opposition to his rule increased and on April 28, 1635, he was accused of treason and thrust out of the government. Captain John West assumed the governorship until the wishes of the king could be ascertained. Harvey was returned to England, where his case was considered. On April 2, 1636, he returned to assume his post, which he held until November 1639.

TREASURY DEPARTMENT (U.S.)
Secretary of the Treasury was Alexander Hamilton of New York, who was appointed by President George Washington on September 11, 1789, and who served until February 1, 1795. *(Henry Jones Ford—Alexander Hamilton)*

Treasurer of the United States was Michael Hillegas, who held office from July 29, 1775, to September 11, 1789. On July 29, 1775, Hillegas and George Clymer were appointed joint treasurers of the United Colonies. On September 6, 1777, additional compensation was "allowed to Michael Hillegas, Esq., Treasurer of the United States, from the 6th day of August 1776 when Mr. Clymer resigned the office of joint treasurer"

THE FIRST

to become a delegate to the Continental Congress. Hillegas remained in office after the organization of the Treasury Department (September 2, 1789 (1 Stat.L.65) until September 11, 1789, when Samuel Meredith assumed office. *(Emma St. Clair Whitney—Michael Hillegas, and His Descendants)*

Treasury Department lifesaving medal. *See* Medal: Lifesaving medal

Treasury Department (U.S.) was organized September 2, 1789 by act of Congress (1 Stat.L.65) under the Secretary of the Treasury. The Sub-Treasury Act of July 4, 1840 (5 Stat.L.385), an "act to provide for the collection, safe-keeping, transfer and disbursement of the public revenue" provided for sub-treasuries in New York City, Boston, Charleston, and St. Louis, a mint in Philadelphia, and a branch mint in New Orleans. The first Sub-Treasury was established in 1846 in Wall Street, New York City, pursuant to the provisions of the act of August 4, 1846 (9 Stat.L.59), an "act to provide for the better organization of the Treasury, and for the collection, safe-keeping, transfer, disbursement of the public revenue."

Treasury surplus returned and apportioned among the several states was authorized by Section 13 of the act of June 23, 1836 (5 Stat.L.55). Twenty-six states received a total of $28,101,644.91, distributed in proportion to their respective representation in the Senate and House and given in three installments. This money was to remain on deposit until Congress directed otherwise, but no effort to secure its return has been made.

Woman assistant treasurer of the United States was Marion Glass Bannister, appointed July 26, 1933, by President Franklin Delano Roosevelt.

Woman treasurer of the United States was Georgia Neese Clark of Richland, Kan., nominated June 3, 1949 by President Harry S. Truman and confirmed June 9, 1949.

TREASURY NOTES. *See* Bond: Treasury notes (interest bearing)

TREATY
Colonial treaty with the Indians was a defensive alliance made April 1, 1621, on Strawberry Hill, Plymouth, Mass., between Massasoit, war chief of the Wampanoags, and the Pilgrims in behalf of King James I. The agreement in all its parts was kept by both parties for more than half a century. *(Henry William Elson—United States, Its Past and Present)*

THE FIRST

THE FIRST

TREATY—*Continued*
International treaty for the protection of wild birds. *See* Bird legislation (international)

Status of Forces treaty was the March 27, 1941, Leased Naval and Air Bases Agreement between the United States and the United Kingdom. A similar treaty, the North Atlantic Status of Forces Treaty, became effective August 23, 1953.

Treaty between the United States Government and a nation with which it had been at war was the armistice with Great Britain. Preliminary articles of peace were signed November 30, 1782, in Paris, France. Hostilities ceased January 20, 1783. The treaty was proclaimed by the Continental Congress April 11, 1783. The definite treaty of peace was signed in Paris September 3, 1783, by David Hartley, plenipotentiary of Great Britain, and Benjamin Franklin and John Adams of the United States. The treaty was ratified and proclaimed January 14, 1784. (*Treaties, Conventions, International Acts, Protocols and Agreements Between the United States of America and other Powers 1776-1909*)

Treaty entered into by the United States was signed with France on February 6, 1778. The plenipotentiary of France was Conrad Alexandre Gérard; the United States plenipotentiaries were Benjamin Franklin, Silas Deane, and Arthur Lee (*John Bassett Moore—History and Digest of International Arbitrations*)
See also United States: Nation to recognize the independence of the United States

Treaty entered into by the United States after the treaty of peace with Great Britain of September 3, 1783, was concluded with Prussia and signed at the Hague, September 10, 1785, by Benjamin Franklin, John Adams, and Thomas Jefferson for the United States. The treaty was ratified by Congress on May 17, 1786 (8 Stat.L.84) and the ratifications exchanged in October 1786.

Treaty entered into by the United States with Indian tribes was a treaty with the Delaware Nation, signed September 17, 1778 (7 Stat.L.13). The signers were Andrew and Thomas Lewis, Commissioners for and in behalf of the United States; and Captain White Eyes, Captain Pipe, and Captain John Kill Buck on behalf of the Delawares. This treaty, agreed upon at Fort Pitt (now Pittsburgh), contained the following provisions: (1) all offenses were to be mutually forgiven; (2) peace and friendship were to be perpetual; in case of war, each party was to assist the other; (3) the United States was to have free passage to forts and towns of former enemies, and such warriors as could be spared were to join the troops of the United States; (4) neither party was to inflict punishment without an impartial trial; (5) an agent was to be appointed by the United States to trade with the Delaware Nation; (6) the United States was to guarantee all territorial rights granted by former treaties and to allow a representative in Congress on certain conditions. (*Records in Office of Indian Affairs. Department of the Interior. Washington, D.C.*)

Treaty (federal) signed by a woman was the Charter of the United Nations, signed June 26, 1945, at San Francisco, Calif., by Virginia Crocheron Gildersleeve, a delegate to the United Nations Conference on International Organization.

Treaty signed by a woman ambassador was the treaty of friendship, commerce, and navigation between the United States and Denmark, signed in Copenhagen, Denmark, on October 1, 1951, by Eugenie Anderson, United States Ambassador to Denmark, and Ole Bjorn Kraft, Denmark's Minister of Foreign Affairs.

Treaty violation occurred October 15, 1565. On that date Pedro Menéndez de Avilés, the Spanish navigator, captured French Huguenot settlers in Florida, who surrendered under a truce. Instead of granting them the customary amnesty which was expected, Menéndez put them to death. (*Francisco López de Mendoza Grajales—Memoir of the Happy Result and Prosperous Voyage of the Fleet commanded by the illustrious captain General Pedro Menéndez de Avilés which sailed from Cadiz on the morning of Thursday June 28th for the coast of Florida and arrived there on the 28th of August 1565*)

Treaty with a Far Eastern country was the Treaty of Amity and Commerce with Siam, concluded March 20, 1833 (the last day of the fourth month of the Siamese year 1194, called Pi-Marông-chat-tava-sôk, or the year of the Dragon). One copy was in Siamese, and one in English, with a Portuguese and a Chinese translation annexed. Edmund Roberts was the envoy of the United States. Ratifications were exchanged April 14, 1836, in Bangkok (the royal city of Sia-Yut'hia) and the treaty proclaimed June 24, 1837, by President Martin Van Buren.

Treaty with a foreign nation to provide for mutual reduction of import duties was the Convention with France, Regarding Claims and Regarding Duties on Wines and Cottons, signed in Paris, July 4, 1831 (8 Stat.L.430). The ratifications were exchanged February 2, 1832, and proclaimed July 13, 1832 (1832 ch. 199) (*Treaties and Other International Acts of the United States of America. Volume 3*)

Treaty with a South American country was the treaty or general convention of Peace,

THE FIRST

Amity, Navigation and Commerce which was signed at Bogotá, Colombia, October 3, 1824, between the United States and the Republic of Colombia. (The Republic of Colombia then included Venezuela and Ecuador.) The treaty was submitted to the Senate on February 22, 1825, and ratified March 7, 1825. It was ratified by Colombia March 26, 1825. The treaty was proclaimed May 31, 1825. The plenipotentiaries who signed the treaty were Richard Clough Anderson, Minister Plenipotentiary of the United States to the Republic of Colombia, and Pedro Gual, Secretary of State and Foreign Relations of Colombia. (*Treaties and Other International Acts of the United States of America. Department of State. Washington, D.C.*)

TREATY ADVISORY BOARD was the Inter-Departmental Advisory Board on Reciprocity Treaties, established in July 1933, as a continuation and enlargement of a committee set up in March 1933 by arrangement between the heads of certain departments and other establishments of the government for the purpose of making studies more or less similar to those of the Advisory Board. Neither the board nor the committee which it succeeded was authorized by act of Congress. The duties of the board included the investigation of subjects suggested for inclusion in or regulation by treaties under contemplation or negotiation, the drafting of such treaties, and informal negotiations with foreign representatives or experts.

TREE (Christmas). *See* Christmas tree

TREE PATENT. *See* Patent: Fruit tree patent

TREE-PLANTING (federal). *See* Forest service: Federal planting of forests

TREE SURGERY COURSE. *See* Forestry school: Forestry correspondence course

TRESTLE PIER (timber). *See* Bridge: Timber trestle pier of lattice construction

TRIBAL CONSTITUTION (Indian). *See* Indians: Indian tribal constitution

TRIBUNAL (arbitration). *See* Arbitration: Arbitration tribunal

TRIFLUOROETHYL VINYL ETHER. *See* Anesthesia: Trifluoroethyl vinyl ether

"TRIPLE CROWN." *See* Horse: Horse to win the triple crown; Jockey: Jockey to win the triple crown twice

THE FIRST

TRIPLE PLAY (baseball). *See* Baseball game: Triple play unassisted

TROMBONE was used in the liturgical services conducted at the obsequies for a child whose remains were interred November 15, 1754, at Bethlehem, Pa. Trombones were used March 30, 1755 in the Easter services. (*William C. Reichel—Something About Trombones*)

TROPHY (aeronautical). *See* Aviation: Aeronautical trophy

TROTTER. *See* Horse: Horse to trot a mile in less than two minutes; Horse: Horse (trotting horse)

TROTTING COURSE. *See* Horse race: Trotting course

TROTTING REGISTER. *See* Horse register: Trotting register

TRUANCY legislation (state) was "an act to provide for the care and instruction of idle and truant children," enacted by New York on April 12, 1853 (Chapter 185). A $50 fine was levied against parents whose children between the ages of five and fourteen were absent from school.

TRUCK (automobile). *See* Automobile truck

TRUCK-DRIVING TRAINING SCHOOL. *See* Automobile school: Truck-driving training school

TRUSS BRIDGE. *See* Bridge: Iron truss bridge

TRUST
Anti-trust law (national), passed July 2, 1890 (26 Stat.L.209), was an "act to protect trade and commerce against unlawful restraints and monopolies." Section One provided that "every contract combination in the form of trust or otherwise, or conspiracy, in restraint of trade or commerce among the several states, or with foreign nations, is hereby declared to be illegal." The act is popularly known as the Sherman Act.

Anti-trust law (state) was Act. No. 79, an act "to prevent monopolies in the transportation of freight, and to secure free and fair competition in the same," approved February 23, 1883, by Alabama. The first general law was Chapter 257, passed March 9, 1889, by Kansas "to declare unlawful trusts and combinations in restraint of trade and products, and to provide penalties therefor."

TRUST—*Continued*

Blue-sky laws were passed by Kansas on March 10, 1911, "for the regulation and supervision of investment companies and providing penalties for the violation thereof." *(Chapter 133. Laws of 1911. Kansas)*

Cartel listed by that name was the Pacific Coast Gasolene Cartel. The cartel was an agreement entered into by companies selling 95 per cent of the gasoline in the states of California, Washington, Oregon, Arizona, and Nevada, and the territories of Hawaii and Alaska. The agreement was approved by the Secretary of the Interior as Oil Administrator on February 13, 1934. A committee of seven persons was chosen to manage the activities of the cartel. The first chairman was Ralph Kenneth Davies of San Francisco, director of the Standard Oil Company of California, elected February 24, 1934. The government representative on the board was William Herbert Eaton. The cartel became effective March 1, 1934, but was abandoned before the end of the month.

Community trust. *See* Community trust

Investment trust. *See* Brokerage: Investment trust

Manufacturers' price regulation agreement was signed by the coopers of New York City on December 17, 1679. The coopers agreed upon "ye Rate and Prizes of Caske, this is to Say, for euery Dry halfe Baril one shilling Six Pence. . . ." The agreement concluded: "And Wee, ye Under Written, Doo Joyntly and Seavorally Bind ourselves, that for Euery one that shall sell any cask Beefore mentioned under the Rate or Prizes aboue, Sd., that for euery Such Default ffiuety Shillinges he or they shall pay for vse of the poore, as Wittnes our hands, this 17th Day of December, 1679." Twenty-one coopers signed the agreement. Their action was condemned and they were brought to trial in the Council Chamber, January 8, 1680. The compact was annulled and the following verdict issued: "They are adjudged guilty, all that have signed the Contract, and are To pay each 50s, & either of them in publick employ to be dismist. The paym't to be to the Church or pious uses."

Trust was the salt trust organized November 10, 1817, by the salt manufacturers of Kanawha, W.Va. It went into active operation on the first day of January 1818, at the Kanawha Salt Company. It was formed for the purpose of controlling the quantity of salt manufactured, the method of manufacture, the packing, and the production. The company disbanded January 1, 1822. *(Phil. Conley—West Virginia Encyclopedia)*

Trust company. *See* Bank: Trust company

Trust fund (educational). *See* Educational trust fund

TUBE

Collapsible tube was invented by John Rand who received patent No. 2,252 on September 11, 1841, on a "mode of preserving paints, and other fluids, by confining them in close metallic vessels so constructed as to collapse with slight pressure, and thus force out the paint or fluid confined therein through proper openings for that purpose." The tubes, molded of lead and used to hold oil colors, were provided with caps to keep them airtight.

Machine designed to produce collapsible tubes was built in 1873 at Philadelphia, Pa., under the direction of August Herman Wirz. Wirz had seen tube-making machines in operation when he was United States Commissioner at the Industrial Exposition in Vienna and had brought over the plans. The first machine-made tubes produced in the United States were used for cucumber jelly.

TUBE (electron). *See* Electron tube

TUBELESS AUTOMOBILE TIRE. *See* Automobile tire: Tubeless automobile tires

TUBERCULOSIS CIRCULAR was issued in July 1889 by the New York City Department of Health through the efforts of Dr. Hermann Michael Biggs.

TUBERCULOSIS HOSPITAL. *See* Hospital: Tuberculosis hospital

TUBERCULOSIS LABORATORY

Tuberculosis diagnostic community laboratory where specimens of sputum could be examined was authorized December 13, 1893, and opened by the New York City Department of Health under the direction of Dr. Hermann Michael Biggs. The laboratory administered sputum examinations, reporting and registration (compulsory by institutions, and voluntary by physicians), official supervision of isolation, terminal disinfection, provision of hospital facilities, and public education. *(American Review of Tuberculosis—July 1929)*

Tuberculosis research laboratory was the Saranac Laboratory, established in 1894 by Dr. Edward Livingston Trudeau in a room in his home at Saranac Lake, N.Y.

TUBERCULOSIS SANATORIUM. *See* Hospital: Tuberculosis sanatorium (modern)

THE FIRST

TUBERCULOSIS SCHOOL

Outdoor school for tubercular children was the Meeting Street School, Providence, R.I., opened January 27, 1908, as the Fresh Air School. A temporary teacher was appointed, but after three months Marie E. Powers was assigned to the school as teacher and principal. Dr. Ellen R. Stone was the superintendent. Twenty children were in the first class, which comprised grades one through eight. Hot lunches furnished by the school supplemented lunches brought by the children.

TUBERCULOSIS SOCIETY

Tuberculosis society was the Pennsylvania Society for the Prevention of Tuberculosis, founded April 10, 1892, in Philadelphia, Pa., by Lawrence Francis Flick.

TUBERCULOSIS TEST (cattle). *See* Animals: Cattle tuberculosis test

TUBERCULOSIS VACCINE. *See* Vaccine: Tuberculosis vaccine

TUBULAR PLATE GIRDER BRIDGE. *See* Bridge: Tubular plate girder bridge

TUFTED PLASTIC CARPETING. *See* Carpeting: Carpeting of tufted plastic

TUGBOAT. *See* Ship: Tugboat

TULAREMIA. *See* Disease (distinctly American)

TUNG trees (*Aleurites fordii*) successfully grown for tung oil were planted in 1905 by the United States Plant Introduction Garden, Chico, Calif. The seeds had been forwarded by David Fairchild, Chief of the Division of Plant Exploration and Introduction, United States Department of Agriculture, who had received them from L. S. Wilcox, United States Consul-General at Hankow, China.

TUNGSTEN

Ductile tungsten was produced in 1908 by Dr. William David Coolidge of the General Electric Company, Schenectady, N.Y., who used high temperatures to draw the tungsten into fine filaments for incandescent lamps. Coolidge reported his findings in the May 17, 1910, issue of the *Journal of the American Institute of Electrical Engineers* and obtained patent No. 1,082,933 on December 30, 1913, on "tungsten and method of making the same, for use as filaments of incandescent electric lamps."

Tungsten and tellurium were found in 1819 in a bismuth mine in Huntington, Conn. The mine was owned by Ephraim Lane. Tungsten, a ferruginous metal known to mineralogists as

THE FIRST

"wolfram," was found in the state of yellow oxide while tellurium was found in the metallic state. (*American Journal of Science. Vol. 1*)

TUNNEL

Freight delivery tunnel system was put into operation in Chicago, Ill., August 15, 1906, but the whole underground network was not completed until September 1, 1907. The completed system was placed in operation January 2, 1908. The original franchise was granted February 20, 1899, to the Illinois Telephone and Telegraph Company, and by an amendatory ordinance was extended to include mail delivery. This franchise was acquired by the Illinois Tunnel Company on July 20, 1903. A new franchise was given to the Chicago Tunnel Company on July 19, 1932.

Mining tunnel (large) was started as early as 1824 by the Lehigh Navigation Company. This was the "Hacklebernie" anthracite coal-mine tunnel near Mauch Chunk, Pa. It was driven by hand with black powder. Work stopped in 1827, when 790 feet had been penetrated. The opening was 16 feet wide and 8 feet high. In 1846 work was resumed and the length extended to 2,000 feet. (*Henry Sturgis Drinker —Tunneling*)

Railroad tunnel was built in 1831 near Johnstown, Pa., by the Allegheny Portage Railroad, the first railroad to go west of the Allegheny Mountains. The tunnel, driven through slate, was 901 feet long, 25 feet wide, and 21 feet high. It was lined throughout with masonry 18 inches thick. Construction began on April 12, 1831, and was completed March 18, 1834. The tunnel extended from Hollidaysburg, Pa., to Johnstown, Pa., a distance of 36⅔ miles. The engineer was Solomon White Roberts. (*David William Brunton and John Allen Davis —Modern Tunneling*)

Subaqueous highway tunnel was the Washington Street Tunnel beneath the Chicago River, Chicago, Ill., authorized July 17, 1866, by the Board of Public Works. The total length of the tunnel and approaches was 1,520 feet. The contract price was $328,500, but the final cost was $512,709. The tunnel had two roadways, each 11 feet high and 13 feet wide, and a separate footway 10 feet high and 10 feet wide. Work was started November 30, 1866, and the tunnel completed in 1869. The tunnel was lowered in 1907 to provide a clear draft of 27 feet in the Chicago River. The tunnel was closed to automobile traffic until 1911.

Subaqueous railroad tunnel to a foreign country was the St. Clair Railway tunnel between Port Huron, Mich., and Sarnia, Ontario, Canada, which was opened for freight traffic September 19, 1891, and for passenger

THE FIRST

THE FIRST

TUNNEL—*Continued*
traffic December 7, 1891. The tunnel has been equipped with electricity since May 17, 1908. It is still in use. Its length from portal to portal is 6,025 feet. The original cost was $2,700,000. It was designed and built under the supervision of Joseph Hobson, Chief Engineer of the Grand Trunk Railway, now the Canadian National Railways.

Tunnel was built as part of the Schuylkill Navigation Company's canal above Auburn, Pa., at the Orwigsburg landing. Job Samson and Solomon Fudge were the contractors. Construction began in 1818, and the tunnel was opened to traffic in 1821. Cut through red shale, it was 20 feet wide, 18 feet high from the canal bottom, and 450 feet long. It was arched for about 75 feet inward from each portal. In 1834 it was shortened to half its length. It was shortened once more in 1845. In 1856 it was again shortened "until nothing remained but air."

Tunnel under the Hudson River was that of the Hudson and Manhattan Railroad System, going from Jersey City, N.J., to Morton Street, New York City. It was officially opened February 25, 1908. Two single-track tubes, approximately 5,700 feet long, with a minimum inside diameter of 15 feet 3 inches, were built under the river. (*Railroad Age Gazette. 1909—Vol. 47*)

Twin-tube subaqueous vehicular tunnel was the Holland Tunnel between New York City and Jersey City. Actual construction began October 12, 1920. The tunnel was opened for public operation November 13, 1927, and on April 21, 1930, all operation was turned over to the Port of New York Authority as agent for the states of New York and New Jersey. The tunnel consists of twin tubes 9,250 feet long. The part below the river is 5,480 feet in length. The tunnel accommodates 1,900 motor vehicles an hour. The air in the tubes is changed 42 times an hour, at the rate of 3,761,000 cubic feet a minute. The chief engineer was Clifford Milburn Holland. (*New York State Bridge and Tunnel Commission— The Holland Tunnel, the Underground Highway Which Joins a Continent to a City*)

Vehicular tunnel to a foreign country was the Detroit-Windsor tunnel under the Detroit River between Detroit, Mich., and Windsor, Ontario, opened for traffic November 3, 1930. It connects Canada with the United States and has a capacity of 1,000 motor cars per hour each way. (The Ambassador Bridge from Detroit to Canada was opened November 11, 1929. Ferries also ply between the two cities, adding a third mode of international travel between Detroit and Canadian border cities.)

Water supply tunnel. *See* Water conduit: Water supply tunnel for a city

Wind tunnel. *See* Wind tunnel

TURBINE
See also Electric generator

Gas turbine to pump natural gas was installed by the Mississippi River Fuel Corporation of St. Louis, Mo., at Wilmar, Ark., on May 13, 1949. The unit was later moved to Bonne Terre, Mo., and placed in operation January 19, 1951.

Gas turbine used by an electrical utility company was a General Electric turbine placed in service July 29, 1949, in the Belle Isle station of the Oklahoma Gas and Electric Company, Oklahoma City, Okla. The unit attains full capacity in seventeen minutes.

Steam turbine operated by a public utility to produce electricity was a 1,500 kilowatt steam turbine installed in April 1901 by the Hartford Electric Light Company, Hartford, Conn., at its Pearl Street Station. The turbine, manufactured by the Westinghouse Electric and Manufacturing Company, East Pittsburgh, Pa., began to generate electricity in October 1901.

Steam turbine generator of large capacity for commercial service was a 5,000-kilowatt Curtis turbine built by the General Electric Company, Schenectady, N.Y., for the Fiske Street station of the Commonwealth Edison Company, Chicago, Ill. The turbine required one tenth the space of the reciprocating engine it replaced, weighed one eighth as much, and cost only one third as much. It operated with steam at 175 pounds per square inch at 375 degrees Fahrenheit and developed 6,700 h.p. It was factory tested March 4, 1903, and placed in service on October 2, 1903.

Turbine successfully operated by water power was invented in 1844 by Uriah Atherton Boyden and installed in the cotton mills of the Appleton Company at Lowell, Mass. It was an improvement on the turbine waterwheel invented by the French engineer Fourneyron and utilized approximately 80 per cent of the power expended.

TURBINE AUTOMOBILE. *See* Automobile: Gas turbine automobile

TURBINE (GAS) PROPELLER-DRIVEN AIRPLANE. *See* Aviation—Airplane: Gas turbine propeller-driven airplane

TURBINE (mercury boiler). *See* Electric generator: Mercury boiler turbine

THE FIRST

TURBINE-PROPELLED OCEAN-GOING MERCHANT VESSEL. *See* Ship: Turbine-propelled ocean-going merchant vessel

TURBINE PROPELLER LIGHT-AIR-PLANE. *See* Aviation—Airplane: Turbine propeller light-airplane

TURBINE (wind). *See* Electric power plant: Wind turbine

TURKISH BATH. *See* Bathhouse: Turkish bath

TURNPIKE. *See* Road

TURNSTILE (electric) with ratchet was used at the Philadelphia Centennial, Philadelphia, Pa., which opened May 10, 1876. When a person desired entrance, the attendant released the brake by foot-pressure. The number of turns was registered on a machine in the central office.

TURRETED SHIP. *See* Ship: Turreted frigate in the U.S. Navy

TUXEDO COAT. *See* Coat: Tuxedo coat

TWENTY-CENT PIECE. See Money: Silver coins

TWINE. *See* Cotton twine factory

TWINE (PAPER) MACHINERY. *See* Paper twine machinery

TWINS (Siamese). *See* Siamese twins

TWO-THIRDS RULE. *See* Political convention: Two-thirds rule

TYPE. *See* Dollar marks; Hebrew type

TYPE FOUNDRY
Type foundry in America was that belonging to Abel Buell, who cast his first font on April 1, 1769, at Killingworth, Conn. It is said that the statue of King George III which was torn down in New York was brought to Buell's foundry to be cast into type. (*Lawrence Counselman Wroth—Abel Buell of Connecticut*)

Type foundry to be permanently established in America was that of Christopher Sauer (or Sower) II, erected in Germantown, Pa., in 1771. The founding equipment was imported from Germany. (*Felix Reichmann—Christopher Sower, Sr. 1694-1758*)

THE FIRST

TYPE SPECIMEN BOOK of an American type foundry is said to be that of [Archibald] Binny & [James] Ronaldson. It was printed in 1809 by Fry and Kammerer and titled *A Specimen of Metal Ornaments cast at the Letter Foundry of Binny & Ronaldson, Philadelphia.* Type sizes were not shown, but about 100 ornaments were illustrated. In 1812 Binny & Ronaldson published *A Specimen of Printing Types,* in which type faces were shown. (*Daniel Berkeley Updike—Printing Types*)

TYPESETTING MACHINE
Linotype machine was invented by Ottmar Mergenthaler of Baltimore, Md., who obtained patent No. 304,272 on August 26, 1884, on a "matrix making machine."

Linotype machine used commercially was a blower machine installed July 1, 1886, by the Mergenthaler Linotype Company in the New York *Tribune* printing plant and used to cast type for the July 3, 1886, newspaper. The machine had a keyboard assembling mechanism, a mechanism for casting a full line of type in a single bar, and a matrix lifting and distributing device. When the matrix was released from a vertical tube which resembled a pipe of an organ, it was carried by air blast along an inclined chute to its place in the assembling line of matrices.

Monotype machine for casting new type, letter by letter, from matrices which are used over and over, was invented by Tolbert Lanston of Washington, D.C., who received five patents, No. 364,521 to No. 364,525 inclusive, on June 7, 1887.

Photo-engraving high-speed process for making half-tones, line plates, or combination plates was developed by the Dow Chemical Company in cooperation with the American Newspaper Publishers Association Research Institute, Inc., Easton, Pa. By means of this process a machine could produce zinc or magnesium plates in about one fifth the conventional time. The first commercial machine was placed in operation in February 1954 by the *Patriot-Ledger,* Quincy, Mass.

Photographic type-composing machine was the Photon (Higonnet-Moyroud) machine, which was manufactured by Photon, Inc., under license from the Graphic Arts Research Foundation, Inc. in April 1953. The machine, operated from a standard typewriter keyboard at full electric-typewriter speed, delivers film negatives instead of type. The first book set by the Photon process was *The Wonderful World of Insects,* by Albro Tilton Gaul, offered for sale to the public on February 26, 1953, by Rinehart & Co., New York City. The first copy was presented to Dr. Karl Taylor Compton, chairman of the

TYPESETTING MACHINE—*Continued*

Corporation of the Massachusetts Institute of Technology, on February 5, 1953, by Dr. Vannevar Bush, a director of the Graphic Arts Research Foundation, Inc., Boston, Mass.

Typesetting machine that actually operated was a machine invented by Timothy Alden of New York City, who obtained patent No. 18,175 on September 15, 1857. The type was arranged in cells around the circumference of a horizontal wheel. As the wheel revolved, several receivers also started to rotate. The desired type was picked up and dropped in proper order in a line.

Typesetting machine patent was No. 2,139 issued June 22, 1841, to Adrien Delcambre and James Hadden Young of Lisle, France, on a "machine for setting type." The machine had keys like a piano, with push-type levers. The type fell by gravity.

Typesetting machine to dispense with metal type was the Intertype Fotosetter Photographic Line Composing Machine, manufactured by the Intertype Corporation, Brooklyn, N.Y., and installed at the plant of Stecher-Traung Lithograph Corporation, Rochester, N.Y., in 1949. The machine was exhibited at the Sixth Educational Graphic Arts Exposition held at the International Amphitheater, Chicago, Ill., on September 11, 1950.

TYPEWRITER

Electric portable typewriter was manufactured by Smith-Corona, Inc., Syracuse, N.Y., announced October 9, 1956, and placed on sale February 4, 1957. It weighed about 19 pounds.

Portable typewriter was the Blickensderfer, which was patented April 12, 1892, by George C. Blickensderfer of Stamford, Conn. (patent No. 472,692).

Typewriter was patented July 23, 1829, by William Austin Burt of Mount Vernon, Mich., who received a patent on his invention of a "typographer." The first letter written on the machine was sent by John P. Sheldon, editor of the *Michigan Gazette,* Detroit, Mich., to Martin Van Buren, Secretary of State, on May 25, 1829. (*Horace Eldon Burt—William Austin Burt*)

Typewriter that successfully typed was a "Chirographer," invented by Charles Thurber of Norwich, Conn., who received patent No. 3,228 on August 26, 1843. It was known as "Thurber's Patent Printer" and was proposed as an aid for the blind. The inking was effected by a roller. The machine lacked speed and did not meet with great success. (*The Weekly Mirror. October 19, 1844*)

Typewriter that was practical was invented in 1867 by Christopher Latham Sholes, who also coined the word "type-writer." The machine was patented June 23, 1868 (No. 79,-265) and was known commercially as "The Type-Writer." This machine had a movable carriage, a lever for turning paper from line to line, and a converging type bar. The keyboard —similar to that of a piano—had two rows of black walnut keys with letters painted in white. The machine had all the letters in capitals, figures from 2 to 9, a comma, and a period. It was originally manufactured by E. Remington & Sons of Ilion, N.Y., under contract dated March 1, 1873. The first machine was completed September 12, 1873. A few years later they sold their typewriter business to Wyckoff, Seamans & Benedict, who afterwards organized the Remington Typewriter Company. (*Herkimer County Historical Society—The Story of the Typewriter*)

Typewriter to produce a line of writing visible as it was being typed was invented by Herman L. Wagner of Brooklyn, N.Y., who obtained patent No. 497,560 on May 16, 1893. This machine went through an experimental period with the Wagner Typewriter Company and then was sold to John T. Underwood, who had been associated with his father in the ribbon and carbon business of John Underwood & Company. The Underwood Typewriter Company, incorporated in March 1895, undertook the manufacture of Wagner's machine in New York City.

TYPEWRITER RIBBON

Typewriter "copy" ribbon for manifold work was patented January 24, 1888, by Jacob L. Wortman of Philadelphia, Pa. The patent was No. 376,764.

Typewriter ribbon patent was No. 349,026, which was granted September 14, 1886, to George K. Anderson of Memphis, Tenn.

TYPEWRITING PRIMER. *See* Primer: Typewriting primer

TYPEWRITING SCHOOL was opened

by D. L. Scott-Browne at 737 Broadway, New York City, in 1878.

TYPEWRITTEN BOOK MANUSCRIPT

was the manuscript of *The Adventures of Tom Sawyer,* by Mark Twain (Samuel Langhorne Clemens). It was typed on a Remington typewriter in 1875. *Life on The Mississippi* was also typewritten the same year. Mark Twain did not publicize these facts as he did not want to write testimonials or explain the operation of the machine to inquirers. (*Herkimer County Historical Society—The Story of the Typewriter 1873-1923*)

THE FIRST

TYPHUS FEVER TREATISE. *See* Medical book: Typhus fever treatise

UKRAINIAN NEWSPAPER. *See* Newspaper: Ukrainian daily newspaper

ULTRASONIC BURGLAR ALARM. *See* Burglar alarm: Burglar alarm operated by ultrasonic or radio waves

UMBRELLA is believed to have been used in Windsor, Conn., in 1740. It produced a riot of merriment and derision, the neighbors parading after the user, carrying sieves balanced on broom handles.

UMPIRE. *See* Baseball umpire

UNCLE SAM CARTOON. *See* Cartoon: Uncle Sam cartoon

UNDERGROUND CITY SEWER. *See* Sewage: Underground comprehensive sewer system (city)

UNDERSEA PHOTOGRAPH. *See* Photograph: Photographs taken under the sea

UNDERSEAS PARK (federal). *See* Park: Underseas park

UNDERWATER TORPEDO. *See* Torpedo: Underwater torpedo operated by electric current

UNEMPLOYMENT INSURANCE. *See* Insurance: Unemployment insurance act

UNICAMERAL LEGISLATURE. *See* Legislature: Unicameral legislature (state)

UNIFORM. *See* Army uniform; Navy: Naval uniforms; Police: Police uniforms

UNION CATALOG OF BOOKS. *See* Library catalog: Union catalog of books

UNION DEPOT. *See* Railroad station: Union passenger station

UNION LABEL. *See* Labor union label

UNION LABOR PARTY was formed in Cincinnati, Ohio, February 22, 1887, and on May 15, 1888, held its first convention there. Two hundred and seventy-four delegates represented twenty-five states. Alson Jennes Streeter of Illinois was nominated for President and Samuel Evans of Texas for Vice Presi-

THE FIRST

dent. Evans declined and Charles E. Cunningham of Arkansas replaced him. The party received 146,935 votes in the election of 1888, which was won by Benjamin Harrison.

UNION PARTY was organized June 18, 1936. The first convention, held August 15, 1936, in Cleveland, Ohio, nominated William Lemke for President and Thomas Charles O'Brien for Vice President. The ticket was supported by liberals, the National Union of Social Justice, and Dr. Francis Everett Townsend of the Townsend organization, among others.

UNION REFORM PARTY held its first convention in Baltimore, Md., September 3, 1900. Seth Hockett Ellis of Ohio was nominated for President and Samuel T. Nicholson of Pennsylvania for Vice President. They received fewer than 6,000 votes, as compared with 7,200,000 cast for William McKinley of Ohio, the Republican candidate, in the election of November 6, 1900. The platform had been adopted March 1, 1899, in Cincinnati, Ohio.

UNIT COMMENDATION DECORATION (U.S. Navy). *See* Medal: Navy Unit Commendation decoration

UNIT COST PLAN (college). *See* College: Unit cost plan

UNIT RULE. *See* Political convention: Unit rule

UNITARIAN CHURCH CONVENTION (national) assembled in New York City, April 5, 1865, at the call of the American Unitarian Association, and elected Governor John Albion Andrew of Massachusetts as its president. The convention was attended by 379 lay delegates who represented 150 congregations. (*Joseph Henry Allen—A History of the Unitarian Movement Since the Reformation*)

UNITARIAN MINISTER
Unitarian minister was James Freeman, who was ordained minister by the congregation of King's Chapel, Boston, Mass., on November 18, 1787. The first church to adopt the Unitarian name was the Society of Unitarian Christians, Philadelphia, Pa., organized June 12, 1796, under the leadership of Joseph Priestley, LL.D. The first worship in a Unitarian church building took place February 14, 1813. (*Earl Morse Wilbur—Our Unitarian Heritage*)

Woman ordained to the Unitarian ministry was Celia C. Burleigh, who was given a parish in Brooklyn, Conn., October 5, 1871. (*George Willis Cooke—Unitarianism in America*)

UNITARIAN PRAYER BOOK was *A Liturgy, Collected Principally From the Book of Common Prayer, for the use of the first Episcopal Church in Boston; together with the Psalter or Psalms of David,* compiled by the Reverend James Freeman and printed in 1785 by Peter Edes of Boston, Mass., for King's Chapel, Boston.

UNITARIAN SOCIETY
National organization of the Unitarian Churches of the United States and Canada was the American Unitarian Association, organized May 25, 1825, in the vestry of the Federal Street Church, Boston, Mass. The Reverend Aaron Bancroft, D.D., was the first president of the association, the Reverend Ezra Stiles Gannett, secretary, and Lewis Tappan, treasurer. The first anniversary was observed June 30, 1826, at Pantheon Hall, Boston.

Woman moderator of the Unitarian Church was Dr. Aurelia Henry Reinhardt, a member of the Oakland Unitarian Church, Oakland, Calif., who served as moderator of the Unitarian Churches of America from 1940 to 1942.

UNITED BRETHREN CHURCH. *See* Church of the United Brethren in Christ

UNITED CHRISTIAN PARTY was organized in Rock Island, Ill., and was devoted to the inculcation of religious and moral ideas as controlling forces in politics. The party held its first convention May 2, 1900, at which time Silas Comfort Swallow of Pennsylvania was nominated for President and John Granville Woolley of Illinois for Vice President. The candidates withdrew and Jonah Fitz Randolph Leonard of Iowa was nominated for President and David H. Martin of Pennsylvania for Vice President. The party's popular vote in the election of November 6, 1900, was only 1,060, as compared with 7,200,000 cast for William McKinley, the Republican candidate.

UNITED COLONIES OF NEW ENGLAND. *See* Colonial government: Colonial government union

UNITED LABOR PARTY was formed at a convention in Cincinnati, Ohio, May 16, 1888, composed of secessionists from the Union Labor Party. Robert Hall Cowdrey of Illinois was nominated for President and William H. T. Wakefield of Kansas for Vice President. In the popular election held November 6, 1888, in which Benjamin Harrison, the Republican candidate, was elected President, Cowdrey received 2,818 votes.

UNITED NATIONS CONFERENCE ON INTERNATIONAL ORGANIZATION was held in San Francisco, Calif., from April

25, 1945, to June 26, 1945, when the charter was signed. It was attended by representatives from fifty nations. The United Nations moved into temporary headquarters at Hunter College, New York City, on March 21, 1946; to Lake Success, N.Y., on August 16-19, 1946; and later to permanent headquarters in New York City.

UNITED NATIONS NEGRO DELEGATE FROM THE UNITED STATES. *See* Diplomatic service: Negro delegate to the United Nations from the United States

UNITED STATES
See also specific bureaus and departments

Nation to recognize the independence of the United States was France. A Treaty of Amity and Commerce and a Treaty of Alliance were signed by the United States and France in Paris on February 6, 1778. Benjamin Franklin, Silas Deane, and Arthur Lee represented the United States, and the Count de Vergennes represented France. These pacts were the first public agreements of the United States with a foreign power.

See also Treaty: Treaty entered into by the United States

"United States" as a name, instead of "United Colonies," was first authorized on September 9, 1776, by the Second Continental Congress: "That in all continental commissions and other instruments where heretofore the words, 'United Colonies' have been used, the style be altered, for the future, to the 'United States.'" The colonies were first definitely proclaimed to be united in a resolution adopted by the Second Continental Congress on June 7, 1775: "On motion, resolved, that Thursday, the 20th of July next, be observed throughout the Twelve United Colonies as a day of humiliation, fasting and prayer." Georgia not having sent delegates to the First and Second Continental Congresses, only twelve colonies were represented.

UNITED STATES AIR DEFENSE COMMAND. *See* Air defense command (U.S.)

UNITED STATES AMATEUR GOLF CHAMPION. *See* Golf champion: Golf champion (American-born)

UNITED STATES ARMY AIRPLANE. *See* Aviation—Airplane: Airplane purchased by the United States Government

UNITED STATES CIVIL AIR PATROL. *See* Civil air patrol (U.S.)

THE FIRST

UNITED STATES CONSTITUTION. *See* Constitution of the United States

UNITED STATES EMPLOYMENT SERVICE. *See* Employment service: Employment service (U.S.)

UNITED STATES FOREIGN SERVICE. *See* Diplomatic service

UNITED STATES GOLF ASSOCIATION. *See* Golf Club: Golf association (national)

UNITED STATES GOVERNMENT BUILDING. *See* Building: Building erected by the Government in Washington, D.C.

UNITED STATES GOVERNMENT MAGAZINE. *See* Periodical: Magazine of the United States Government

UNITED STATES INFORMATION SERVICE. *See* Information service (U.S.)

UNITED STATES LABOR ADVISORY BOARD. *See* Labor: Labor advisory board (federal)

UNITED STATES MAP. *See* Map: Map of the United States

UNITED STATES MORGAN HORSE FARM. *See* Horse: Horse farm operated by the United States Government

UNITED STATES NATIONAL AMATEUR GOLF CHAMPION. *See* Golf champion: Golf champion to win the United States National Amateur Tournament two years in succession

UNITED STATES NAVAL RESERVE Negro flier. *See* Aviation—Aviator: Negro flier of the United States Naval Reserve

UNITED STATES OPEN GOLF TOURNAMENT CHAMPION. *See* Golf champion: Golf champion (American-born professional) to win the United States Open Tournament

UNITED STATES SEAL. *See* Seal: Great Seal of the United States Government

UNITED STATES SHIPPING BOARD. *See* Shipping: United States Shipping Board

UNIVERSAL CHAPEL. *See* Church: Universal chapel embracing eight faiths

THE FIRST

UNIVERSALIST CHURCH OF AMERICA (Independent Christian Church, Universalist) held its first meetings in 1774 but was not formally organized until January 1, 1779, when the articles of association were signed by thirty-one men and thirty women led by the Reverend John Murray. Reverend Murray, "father of the organized Universalist church," was made the first minister. A church built in Winthrop Sargent's garden, Water Street, Gloucester, Mass., was dedicated December 25, 1780. It contained thirty box pews. *(Richard Eddy—Universalism in America)*

UNIVERSITY. *See* College

UNKNOWN SOLDIER MEMORIAL. *See* Monument: Monument to the "Unknown Soldier" (national)

USHER (woman). *See* Theater: Theater to employ women ushers

"V" MAIL. *See* Postal service: "V" mail film

VACATION FUND to send poor children to the country was established in 1847 by the Reverend William Augustus Muhlenberg, rector of the Church of the Holy Communion, New York City. *(Anne Ayres—Life and Work of W. A. Muhlenberg)*

VACCINATION for smallpox with cowpox, as originated in England by Dr. Edward Jenner, was introduced by Dr. Benjamin Waterhouse, Harvard professor of the theory and practice of medicine, Cambridge, Mass., who inoculated his son, Daniel Oliver Waterhouse, on July 8, 1800. Inoculation from human smallpox pustules had been introduced in America by Dr. Zabdiel Boylston of Boston, Mass. On June 26, 1721, Boylston inoculated his six-year-old son, Thomas, and two Negro servants. In 1721 and 1722 Boylston inoculated 247 individuals, the acceptance of inoculation due in large measure to the efforts of Cotton Mather, the Boston divine, who persistently advocated the practice. *(Benjamin Waterhouse—A Prospect of Exterminating the Small-pox; being the history of Variolae-Vaccine or Kine-pox, as it appeared in England with an account of a series of inoculations performed in Massachusetts)*

VACCINATION LEGISLATION
Vaccination legislation for Indians was the act of May 5, 1832 (4 Stat.L.514), "an act to provide the means of extending the benefits of vaccination, as a preventive of the smallpox, to the Indian tribes, and thereby, as far as possible, to save them from the destructive ravages of that disease." An appropriation of $12,000 was made. Physicians were paid $6 a day for their services.

VACCINATION LEGISLATION—*Cont.*

Vaccination legislation (national) was the act of February 27, 1813 (2 Stat.L.806) to encourage vaccination. It authorized the President to appoint a vaccine agent to furnish vaccine through the Post Office to any citizen of the United States who might apply for it. The act was repealed May 4, 1822 (3 Stat.L.677). *(John Walter Kerr—Vaccination—U.S. Public Health Bulletin. No.52)*

Vaccination legislation (state) was Chapter 116, "an act to diffuse the benefits of inoculation for the Cow-Pox," enacted March 6, 1810, by Massachusetts, which required "every town, district and plantation to choose "three or more suitable persons, whose duty it shall be to superintend the inoculation of the inhabitants . . . with the cow-pox." The towns of Milton and Bedford offered free inoculations. A committee chosen July 8, 1809, authorized Dr. Amos Holbrook to charge a 25-cent fee for his services. He inoculated the entire population of Milton, 337, and pledged that the people "are for ever secure against Small Pox." *(Independent Chronicle. Boston, Mass. December 25, 1809)*

VACCINE

Anthrax vaccine for humans was developed in 1948 by Dr. George Green Wright of the Biological Laboratory of the United States Army Chemical Laboratory.

Poliomyelitis vaccine was produced by Dr. Maurice Brodie, of New York City, in February 1933. The vaccine was obtained from the spinal cords of rare Indian monkeys that had been infected with poliomyelitis. The spinal cords were excised and an emulsion made of them. This emulsion was treated with formalin which kills all viruses during the process of preparation.

Tuberculosis vaccine (effective) produced in this country was developed in 1928 by Dr. William Hallock Park, director of the research laboratory of the Health Department of New York City and professor of preventive medicine at New York University, New York City. The vaccine was manufactured at the research laboratories of the Department of Health and first used in January 1928. *(Wade Wright Oliver—The Man Who Lived for Tomorrow)*

Yellow fever vaccine for human immunization was developed by Drs. Wilbur Augustus Sawyer, Wray Devere Marr Lloyd, and Stuart Fordyce Kitchen and publicly announced April 28, 1932, at a meeting of the American Societies for Experimental Biology, Philadelphia, Pa. The work was sponsored by the Rockefeller Foundation. The first test vaccinations were made in May 1931. *(Journal of Experimental Medicine. June 1, 1932 Vol. 55. No. 6)*

VACCINE INSTITUTION for the propagation of the smallpox virus and free distribution of the vaccine to the poor was opened by Dr. James Smith in Baltimore, Md., on March 25, 1802. *(John Russel Quinan—Medical Annals of Baltimore from 1608 to 1880)*

VACUUM CLEANER

Motor-driven vacuum cleaner was invented by John S. Thurman of the General Compressed Air and Vacuum Machinery Company, St. Louis, Mo., who obtained patent No. 634,042 on October 3, 1899, on a "pneumatic carpet renovator." He obtained patents No. 663,943 on December 18, 1900; No. 665,983 on January 15, 1901; and No. 668,559 on December 10, 1901.

Suction-type vacuum cleaner was invented by Ives W. McGaffey of Chicago, Ill., who obtained patent No. 91,145, June 8, 1869, on a "sweeping machine," a light hand-powered suction device for surface cleaning.

VACUUM TUBE. *See* Radio tube: Three-element vacuum tube

VALETERIA was made by the United States Hoffman Machinery Corporation and displayed September 19, 1951, in the lobby of the Bulkley Building, Cleveland, Ohio. The clothes-pressing device had a control unit equipped with a telephone and a series of lockers in which garments could be hung. It was designed to open doors, accept payments, and give correct change without any manual aid. It was based on the invention of Ross L. Timms of Akron, Ohio.

VANDERBILT CUP RACE. *See* Automobile race: Vanderbilt cup race

VAPOR LAMP. *See* Electric lighting: Sodium vapor lamps

VAPORIZED CHEMICAL FIRE EXTINGUISHER. *See* Fire extinguisher

VARIETY SHOW. *See* Vaudeville

VARNISH manufacturer to produce varnish exclusively was Christian Schrack, a carriage maker, who opened a shop in 1815 in Philadelphia, Pa. Furniture had previously been finished with shellac or oil. *(George Baugh Heckel—The Paint Industry)*

VASELINE. *See* Petroleum jelly

VAUDEVILLE originated in 1883 in Boston, Mass., when Benjamin Franklin Keith opened a small museum next to the old Adams

THE FIRST

House in Washington Street which he called the "Gaiety Museum." One of its principal attractions was "Baby Alice," a midget.

VAULT. *See* Safe deposit vault

VECTOLITE was manufactured by the General Electric Company in West Lynn, Mass., on February 27, 1935. Vectolite is a non-metallic, light-weight, non-conducting magnetic material, a sintered combination of iron rust and cobalt oxide mixed in desired proportion in powdered form. It was known as "sintered oxide" until April 7, 1945, when the trade name was changed to Vectolite.

VEHICULAR TUNNEL. *See* under Tunnel

VELOCIPEDE. *See* Bicycle: Bicycle velocipedes

VELLUM BOOKS. *See* Book: Book on vellum

VELVET CARPETING. *See* Carpeting: Carpeting (velvet)

VENDING MACHINE

Vending machine to operate automatically without the aid of plungers or indicators was produced by the Pulver Company, Inc., Rochester, N.Y., in 1897. The machine dispensed gum for a penny a package.

Vending machine (coin operated) to dispense postage stamps was manufactured in 1892 by the United States Postage Stamp Delivery Company, Boston, Mass., of which Carroll Davidson Wright was president. It was a quartered-oak case 20 inches high, 9¾ inches wide, and 5⅝ inches deep. It delivered a capsule containing four cents' worth of stamps and a coupon upon insertion of a nickel. The coupon bore manufacturers' advertisements and was redeemable for one cent in purchases of a manufacturer's products at a ratio of one coupon to every ten cents in cash.

Vending machine law was ordinance No. 4,431 of Omaha, Neb., approved May 10, 1898, by Mayor Frank Edward Moores. All vending machines were subject to a $5 permit fee.

Vending machine to sell from bulk was the Automatic Clerk, a wooden cabinet six feet high, which dispensed hot peanuts in bags. The machine was equipped with a heater and a weighing device. It was invented in 1897 by T. S. Wheatcraft of Rush, Pa. *(New York Herald. December 5, 1897)*

THE FIRST

VENETIAN BLINDS

Venetian blind patent was granted to John Hampson of New Orleans, La., who obtained patent No. 2,223 on August 21, 1841 on a "manner of retaining in any desired position the slats of Venetian Blinds."

Venetian blinds are said to have been installed in 1761 in St. Peter's Church, Third and Pine Streets, Philadelphia, Pa.

VESSEL. *See* Ship

VETERANS' BUREAU was established under the act of August 9, 1921 (42 Stat.L. 147). The act provided that all forms of veterans' relief previously delegated to the Federal Board for Vocational Education, the U.S. Public Health Service, and the Bureau of War Risk Insurance should be delegated to one bureau to be known as the U.S. Veterans' Bureau and to be directly responsible to the President of the United States. The Veterans' Administration was created by Executive Order 5398, dated July 21, 1930, under authorization of the act of Congress approved July 3, 1930 (46 Stat.L.1016).

VETERANS' ORGANIZATION. *See* War veterans' society

VETERINARY CORPS (army). *See* Army: Army veterinary corps

VETERINARY HOSPITAL was opened by Charles C. Grice in 1830 on Pearl Street, New York City. A fair beginning was made after much labor, patient waiting, and perseverance. After a few years, Grice moved to White Street, where he remained about fourteen years; then he moved to his last residence, 122 Macdougal Street. Grice graduated from the Royal Veterinary College of England in 1826, and came to America in 1830. He was the first graduate of veterinary medicine to practice his profession in the United States. *(American Veterinary Review. Vol. 26. June, 1902)*

VETERINARY SCHOOL

Veterinary college was the Boston Veterinary Institute, Boston, Mass., incorporated April 28, 1855. The first president was Daniel Denison Slade, M.D. Courses were given in anatomy, physiology, chemistry, pharmacy, the theory and practice of medicine and surgery, etc. *(American Veterinary Review. Vol. 1. No. 1. January 1877)*

Veterinary college of importance was the New York College of Veterinary Surgeons, New York City, incorporated April 6, 1857. It did not go into active operation until 1865. The course of study, which embraced comparative

VETERINARY SCHOOL—*Continued*
anatomy, was given in two sections of five months each. The tuition fee was $135, of which amount $5 was for matriculation fees, $100 for lecture fees, $5 for the dissecting room fee, and $25 for the diploma. The president of the school was Eben Mason. The school had professors of histology, anatomy, physiology, theory and practice, surgical pathology, and operative surgery. (*Annual Announcement of the New York College of Veterinary Surgeons. 1867-1868*)

Veterinary department of collegiate character in a university was the Department of Veterinary Science of Cornell University, Ithaca, N.Y., which offered courses by Professor James Law, October 7, 1868.

Veterinary school (state) was established May 23, 1879, by the Board of Trustees of Iowa State College at Ames, Iowa. Lectures were given on veterinary anatomy, physiology, materia medica, pathology, disease and treatment, surgery, sanitary science, and practice. The first class of the veterinary school graduated in 1880. In 1876 Dr. Milliken Stalker was granted the professorship of agriculture and veterinary science. The Iowa School was the first veterinary school in the United States to inaugurate a four-year course and the first to require as prerequisites for entrance a high school and college course. (*Charles Henry Stange—History of Veterinary Medicine at Iowa State College*)

VETO (presidential)
Legislation passed over a President's veto was S. 66 (28th Congress, 2d session), "an act relating to revenue cutters and steamers." It provided that no revenue cutter could be built without prior appropriation. President John Tyler vetoed the bill on February 20, 1845, arguing that a contract for two revenue cutters had already been let, one to a firm in Richmond, Va., and another to a Pittsburgh, Pa., contractor. The bill was reconsidered by the Senate and House on March 3, 1845. The Senate passed it without debate over the veto, 41 to 1, and the House by a vote of 127 to 30. (*Benjamin Perley Poore—Veto Messages of the Presidents*)

Veto by a President of the United States was exercised by George Washington on April 5, 1792, when he vetoed a bill for the apportionment of representation. (*Edward Campbell Mason—The Veto Power*)

Veto message read by a President in person was the veto of the Patman Bonus Bill (H.R. Bill No. 3896) read by President Franklin Delano Roosevelt, May 22, 1935, to a joint session of Congress, Washington, D.C. The Bonus Bill, introduced by Representative Wright Patman of Texas, provided for the

immediate payment to veterans of the 1945 face value of their adjusted service certificates. Within an hour after the veto, the House voted to override the veto 322 to 98 (the original vote on the measure had been 318 to 90). The following day the Senate voted 54 to 40 to override the veto (the original vote had been 55 to 33). A two-thirds vote of both houses is necessary to override a veto.

VICE CONSUL (woman). *See* Diplomatic service: Woman vice consul

VICE PRESIDENT OF THE UNITED STATES
Indian Vice President was Charles Curtis of Kansas, who served under President Herbert Clark Hoover from March 4, 1929, to March 4, 1933. (*Don Carlos Seitz—From Kaw Tepee to Capitol*)

Postage stamp issued by a foreign country to bear the likeness of a Vice President of the United States. *See* Postage stamp: Postage stamp to bear the likeness of a Vice President of the United States issued by a foreign country

Vice President elected by the Senate was Richard Mentor Johnson, who was chosen by the Senate on February 8, 1837, as no candidate had received a majority of the electoral votes. He served from March 4, 1837, to March 4, 1841, as Vice President under Martin Van Buren. (*William Emmons—Authentic Biography of Col. Richard M. Johnson of Kentucky*)

Vice President sworn in on foreign soil was William Rufus de Vane King, a Democrat, the running-mate of Franklin Pierce in the 1852 campaign. King took the oath of office March 4, 1853, in Havana, Cuba, where he had gone for his health. The oath was administered by William L. Sharkey, United States Consul in Havana. The privilege was extended to King by a special act of Congress. King's term of office was of short duration; he died April 17, 1853, in Cahawba, Ala. (*U.S. Senate—Obituary Addresses—William R. King. 1853*)

Vice President to be nominated specifically for the vice presidency was George Clinton, who ran with Thomas Jefferson in the 1804 election. He served under Jefferson from 1805 to 1809, and under James Madison from 1809 to 1812. Prior to the ratification of the twelfth amendment to the Constitution on September 24, 1804, the presidential candidate receiving the second highest number of votes became Vice President.

Vice President to become President automatically on the death of a President was John Tyler, the tenth President. Tyler suc-

THE FIRST

ceeded William Henry Harrison, who died on April 4, 1841. Harrison served from March 4, 1841, to April 4, 1841, and Tyler from April 4, 1841, to March 4, 1845. *(Oliver Perry Chitwood—John Tyler, Champion of the Old South)*

Vice President to die in office was George Clinton, who served under President Thomas Jefferson from March 4, 1805, to March 4, 1809, and under President James Madison from March 4, 1809, to April 20, 1812, when he died in Washington, D.C. William Harris Crawford acted as president pro tempore of the United States Senate for the unexpired portion of Clinton's term. *(Gouverneur Morris—Oration in Honor of the Memory of George Clinton)*

Vice President to leave the United States while the President was away was Vice President John Nance Garner, who sailed from Seattle, Wash., on October 16, 1936, for Japan on the "President Grant," while President Franklin Delano Roosevelt was aboard the U.S.S. "Houston" on vacation. Under the act of succession of January 19, 1886 (24 Stat.L. 2), Secretary of State Cordell Hull acted as President until the President's return. Technically the President was on United States soil as he was on a naval vessel.

Vice President to marry in office was Alben William Barkley, who was married to Elizabeth Jane Rucker (widow of Carleton Sturtevant Hadley) on November 18, 1948, at St. John's Methodist Church, St. Louis, Mo., by the Reverend Abea Godbolt and Bishop Ivan Lee Holt, Methodist Bishop of Missouri.

Vice President to preside at a National Security Council meeting was Richard Milhous Nixon, who presided over the final session of a meeting held in Washington, D.C., on July 14, 1953. On August 13, 1953, he presided over an entire meeting.

Vice President to preside over a cabinet meeting was Richard Milhous Nixon, who presided as chairman of a meeting held on July 22, 1955.

Vice President to resign before the expiration of his term of office was John Caldwell Calhoun, who served as Vice President under President John Quincy Adams from March 4, 1825, to March 4, 1829, and under President Andrew Jackson from March 4, 1829 to December 28, 1832, when he resigned. He had been elected senator from South Carolina on December 12, 1832, to fill the vacancy caused by the resignation of Robert Young Hayne. *(John Stilwell Jenkins—Life of John Caldwell Calhoun)*

THE FIRST

Vice President to serve under two Presidents was George Clinton, who served under President Thomas Jefferson from March 4, 1805, to March 4, 1809, and under President James Madison from March 4, 1809, until his death on April 20, 1812 in Washington, D.C.

Vice President's flag. *See* Flag: Vice President's flag

Vice President's widow to receive a pension was Lois I. Kimsey Marshall, widow of Thomas Riley Marshall, who died June 1, 1925. The act of January 25, 1929 (45 Stat.L.2041) awarded her an annual allowance of $3,000 and instructed the Secretary of the Interior to place her name on the pension roll.

VICE PRESIDENTIAL CANDIDATE

Negro vice presidential candidate was Frederick Douglass, nominated May 10, 1872, by the National Woman Suffrage Association convention, assembled at Apollo Hall, New York City, under the name of the National Radical Reformers. About 500 delegates attended from twenty-six states and four territories. The presidential nominee was Victoria Claflin Woodhull. *(Frederick Douglass—Life and Times of Frederick Douglass)*

Vice presidential nominee to decline nomination was John Langdon of New Hampshire. The congressional caucus of the Republican Party, which was held in Washington, D.C., May 12, 1812, nominated him as its vice presidential candidate. He received 64 of the 82 votes cast. James Madison, the presidential nominee, received 82 votes. Despite his nomination, Langdon declined to run, and a second caucus was held at which Elbridge Gerry was nominated. Gerry received 74 of the 77 votes for Vice President. *(Lawrence Shaw Mayo—John Langdon of New Hampshire)*

Vice presidential nominee to die before the meeting of the electoral college was James Schoolcraft Sherman, candidate on the 1912 Republican ticket headed by William Howard Taft. He was Vice President from March 4, 1909, to October 12, 1912. In June 1912, he was renominated as the Republican vice presidential candidate. The notification speech was made August 21, 1912, at Utica, N.Y., by Senator George Sutherland of Utah. Sherman died on October 30, 1912, before the election. Nicholas Murray Butler was the substitute for whom the electoral college cast its Republican votes. *(James Schoolcraft Sherman—Speech Accepting the Republican Nomination for Vice President of the United States)*

VIDEO RECORDING ON MAGNETIC TAPE. *See* Tape recording: Video recording on magnetic tape

THE FIRST

THE FIRST

VILLAGE IMPROVEMENT SOCIETY

with a continued existence was the Laurel Hill Association of Stockbridge, Mass., founded by Mary Gross Hopkins. Laurel Hill was presented to the town in 1834 by Theodore Sedgwick. The society was organized August 24, 1853, and incorporated September 5, 1853, "to improve and ornament the streets and public parts of Stockbridge, by planting and cultivating trees and doing such other acts as shall tend to improve and beautify the village." (*Frederick N. Evans—Town Improvement*)

VINEYARD (successful) was established on August 28, 1798, by John James Dufour on a tract of land consisting of about 630 acres situated twenty-five miles from Lexington, Ky. He called it "The First Vineyard." Dufour was one of the pioneer viticulturists and founder of Swiss vineyards in America. Attempts to establish vineyards had been made as early as 1619 in Virginia. (*Liberty Hyde Bailey—Sketch of the Evolution of Our Native Fruits*)

VINYL ETHER. *See* Anesthesia: Trifluoroethyl vinyl ether

VIRUS

Virus (human- or animal-infecting virus) to be crystallized was the poliomyelitis virus, which was crystallized by Dr. Carlton Everett Schwerdt of the Virus Laboratory, University of California, Berkeley. The achievement was announced November 3, 1955, at the meeting of the National Academy of Sciences held at the California Institute of Technology, Pasadena.

Virus obtained in crystalline form was the tobacco mosaic virus crystallized by Dr. Wendell Meredith Stanley at the Rockefeller Institute for Medical Research, Princeton, N.J. The research was reported in *Science* magazine, June 28, 1935.

Virus separated into component parts, which on reconstruction yielded a material as effective as it was in its original form, was the tobacco virus, which causes a disease in tobacco and many other plants. The research was performed by Drs. Heinz Ludwig Fraenkel-Conrat and Robley Cook Williams of the Virus Laboratory of the University of California at Berkeley early in 1955, and first reported on June 10, 1955.

VISIBLE SPEECH TRAINING. *See* Deaf—School: Oral instruction for the deaf

VISITING CELEBRITIES

Absolute monarch to visit the United States was King Prajadhipok of Siam. He arrived in New York City in April 1931, accompanied by his wife, Queen Rambai Barni, and the royal entourage. President Herbert Clark Hoover received him April 29, 1931. The

visitors crossed into United States territory on April 19, 1931, at Portal, N.D., from Canada. The king had visited the United States when he was a prince, arriving September 22, 1924, in New York City from England.

King and Queen of England to visit the United States were King George VI and Queen Elizabeth, who crossed the international border at 10:39 P.M. on June 7, 1939, at the Suspension Bridge Station, Niagara Falls, N.Y. They visited New York City and Washington, D.C., and recrossed the border at 5:22 A.M. on June 12, 1939, bound for Halifax, Nova Scotia, whence they sailed June 15, 1939.

King (reigning) to visit the United States was David Kalakaua, King of the Sandwich Islands (Hawaii), elected February 12, 1874, by a vote of 39 to 6 to succeed William C. Lunalilo, who died February 3, 1874. He embarked November 17, 1874, on the U.S.S. "Benicia" and was received at the White House, Washington, D.C., by President Ulysses Simpson Grant on December 15, 1874. Congress tendered him a reception on December 18, 1874. He arranged for a treaty of reciprocity, which was concluded January 30, 1875, ratifications being exchanged in Washington, D.C., on June 3, 1875 (19 Stat.L.625). He returned to his country on February 15, 1875, on the U.S.S. "Pensacola."

Lecturer of royal blood to speak for personal profit. *See* Lecturer: Lecturer of royal blood to speak for personal profit

Pontiff who had visited the United States was Eugenio Pacelli (Pope Pius XII). He visited America while Papal Secretary of State, arriving October 8, 1936, and returned November 7, 1936. His headquarters were at "Inisfada," which was the Long Island mansion of the Papal Duchess Genevieve Garvan Brady and is now a seminary of the Jesuit order.

President of a Negro country to visit the United States was President Edwin Barclay of Liberia, who addressed the U.S. Senate May 27, 1943, the day following his arrival. On October 14, 1943, President Elie Lescot of Haiti, former Minister to the United States, arrived for a brief visit.

Prince of Wales to visit the United States was Albert Edward (later King Edward VII), who left Plymouth, England, July 10, 1860, and arrived in Detroit, Mich., on September 20, 1860, from Hamilton, Ontario, Canada. He was received by Moses Wisner, Governor of Michigan, and Mayor Christian Buhl of Detroit. He sailed from Portland, Me., October 20, 1860. He traveled through Canada and the United States as Baron Renfrew. He became King of Great Britain and Ireland and Emperor of India on

THE FIRST

January 22, 1901. *(Kinahan Cornwallis—Royalty in the New World, or The Prince of Wales in America)*

Queen to visit the United States was Queen Emma, widow of King Kamehameha IV, of the Sandwich Islands (Hawaii), who arrived August 8, 1866, in New York City from England on the Cunard "Java" and was received on August 14, 1866, by President Andrew Johnson and introduced to his official family. *(Gilson Willets—Inside History of the White House)*

VITAMIN
Synthetic vitamin was vitamin D commercially manufactured in 1927 by Mead, Johnson and Company, Evansville, Ind., and marketed in the spring of 1928. It was made by exposing a solution of ergosterol to ultraviolet light. *(Charles Everett Bell—"Physiology of the Sterols, Including Vitamin D." Physiological Reviews. Vol. 15. No. 1. January 1935)*

Synthetic vitamin K was made by Dr Louis Frederick Fieser of the Harvard University Department of Chemistry, Cambridge, Mass., on August 1, 1939. A report was submitted to the September 10, 1939, meeting of the American Chemical Society in Boston, Mass.

Vitamin E, the anti-sterility vitamin, was first recognized by Dr. Herbert McLean Evans with Dr. Katherine Cott Bishop in 1922. Dr. Evans, Dr. Oliver Hudleston Emerson, and Gladys Anderson Emerson of the Institute for Experimental Biology of the University of California, Berkeley, were the first to reduce it to a pure substance, alpha tocopherol. Announcement of the process was made at the American Chemical Society meeting at San Francisco, Calif., on August 20, 1935. This was published as "The Isolation from Wheat Germ Oil of an Alcohol, Alpha Tocopherol, Having the Properties of Vitamin E," by H. M. Evans, O. H. Emerson, and G. A. Emerson in the *Journal of Biological Chemistry* of February 1936. *(Science 1922)*

VITROLITE was manufactured in 1907 in Parkersburg, W.Va., by the Meyercord-Carter Company. It was an opaque structural flat glass made originally in white. The first important installation was made in 1907 on the walls of the subway stations of the Interborough Rapid Transit System, New York City. About that time color was first utilized in firing-on colored designs for brewery signs, etc. In 1922, colors were added to the vitrolite itself by the introduction of coloring material into the sand, soda ash, lime and other ingredients. The Meyercord-Carter Company was purchased in 1935 by the Libbey-Owens-Ford Glass Company.

THE FIRST

VIVISECTION of animals to show the process of life was performed about 1855 by Dr. John Call Dalton. He introduced the methods of vivisection in classroom demonstrations. In 1859 he published his *Treatise on Human Physiology,* and in 1860 he became Professor of Physiology and Microscopic Anatomy at the Long Island College Hospital. *(James Joseph Walsh—History of Medicine in New York)*

VIVISECTION PLAY. *See* Play (drama): Antivivisection play

VIVISECTION SOCIETY. *See* Anti-vivisection society

VOCAL INSTRUCTION BOOK. *See* Music book: Vocal instruction book

VOCATIONAL AGRICULTURAL SCHOOL. *See* Agricultural school: Vocational agricultural school

VOCATIONAL GUIDANCE CHAIR in an American university was established in 1914 by Indiana University, Bloomington. The first professor was Robert Josselyn Leonard, who served from June 1914 to April 1918.

VOCATIONAL HIGH SCHOOL FOR GIRLS. *See* High school: Vocational high school for girls

VOICE MECHANISM
Voice mechanism capable of creating the complex sounds of speech in an intelligible manner was "Pedro, the Voder," designed by Homer Walter Dudley, Robert Richard Riesz, and Stanley Sylvester Alexander Watkins of the Bell Telephone Laboratories, New York City, and publicly exhibited June 5, 1938, at the Franklin Institute, Philadelphia, Pa.

VOLCANO in eruption in America for which a date can be estimated occurred at Cinder Cone in the Lassen Peak district in California about 1694. On November 22, 1842, Mount Saint Helens, and on November 13, 1843, Mount Rainier (Tacoma), both in the state of Washington, were in eruption. Professor George Davidson of the United States Coast Survey in 1843 and John Shertzer Hittell in 1858 saw Mount Baker, also in Washington, in eruption. *(Israel Cook Russell—Volcanoes of North America)*

VOLCANO IN A NATIONAL PARK. *See* Park: Park (national) containing an active volcano

VOLLEY BALL was developed in 1895 as a game by Physical Director William George Morgan of the Young Men's Christian Asso-

VOLLEY BALL—*Continued*
ciation, Holyoke, Mass. The game, at first called mintonette, was played with a basketball bladder over a rope. Later, a light-weight leather-covered ball was adopted, and an 8-foot net substituted for the rope. Rules were local until 1900, when the Young Men's Christian Association Physical Directors' Association Volley Ball Committee developed standard rules. The first rules were published in the *Physical Education Magazine*, July 1896. (*Winged Acorn, November 1932*)

VOTE (army). *See* Army vote

VOTERS' QUALIFICATIONS. *See* Literacy qualification for voting

VOTING. *See* Election; Election law

VOTING MACHINE
Electric vote recorder was patented by Thomas Alva Edison, then of Boston, Mass., who received patent No. 90,646, June 1, 1869, on an "electrographic vote recorder." By means of the device a legislator could register his "aye" or "no" vote by turning a switch to the right or to the left.

Voting machines for use in federal elections were approved by Congress, February 14, 1899 (30 Stat.L.836). The bill was signed by President William McKinley, February 14, 1899. It provided that "all votes for representatives in Congress must be by written or printed ballot, or voting machines, the use of which has been duly authorized by the state."

Voting machines were authorized for use in New York State on March 15, 1892, by an act (Chapter 127) "to secure independence of voters at town meetings, secrecy of the ballot and provide for the use of Myers' automatic ballot cabinet." Later legislation extended the use of the machine to cities. The machines were first used on April 12, 1892, at Lockport, N.Y., where 3,271 votes were cast for mayor and other town officials. The machine was invented by Jacob H. Myers and manufactured by the American Ballot Machine Company, which was later absorbed by the Automatic Voting Machine Corporation of Jamestown, N.Y. (*T. David Zuckerman—The Voting Machine*)

VOTING MACHINE COMMISSION (state) was authorized by New York, Chapter 450, May 17, 1897, "an act relating to the use of voting machines," which provided that three commissioners should be appointed by the Governor, "one of whom shall be an expert in patent law and two of whom shall be mechanical experts." The term of the commissioners was five years. The first commissioners were Robert Henry Thurston, Philip Tell Dodge,

and Palmer Chamberlaine Ricketts, appointed June 16, 1897. Ricketts declined and Harry de Berkeley Parsons was appointed June 28, 1897.

VULCANIZED RUBBER. *See* Rubber: Vulcanized rubber

WAFFLE IRON PATENT was No. 94,093, issued August 24, 1869, to Cornelius Swarthout of Troy, N.Y.

WAGE LAW. *See* Labor law: Minimum wage law

WAGON (lunch). *See* Lunch wagon

WALK OF FAME was originated in the autumn of 1929 by Hamilton Holt, president of Rollins College, Winter Park, Fla., who gave the college 22 stones from the former homes, birth places, and resting places of world-famous men and women from all parts of the world. The stones were set between Carnegie Hall and Knowles Hall and along a walk leading past Carnegie Hall. They are of various sizes, shapes and textures, and follow no pattern. Some 700 stones have been placed, without any design, along both sides of the pathways.

WALKIE-TALKIE. *See* Radio telephone: Military portable

WALL TILE. *See* Tile: Wall and floor tiles

WALLPAPER
Wallpaper was manufactured in 1739 by Plunket Fleeson of Philadelphia, Pa. Wooden blocks stamped the design on sheets of paper which were joined together. A paint brush was used to apply the color. In August 1739 Fleeson advertised in the *Pennsylvania Gazette* the sale of "bedticks, choice live geese feathers, blankets, as well as paperhangings." (*Nancy Vincent McClelland—Historic Wallpapers From Their Inception to the Introduction of Machinery*)

Wallpaper printing press. *See* Printing press: Printing press for printing "paper hangings"

WAR
See also

Civil War	War (1812)
Revolutionary War	War (Korean)
Spanish-American	War (Mexican)
War	War (Quemoy)
War (colonial)	World War I
War (French Indo-	World War II
China)	

Battle fought by United States troops, after the formation of the Union, was the

THE FIRST

Miami Expedition. On October 19, 1790, Colonel John Hardin, under Brigadier General Josiah Harmar, led 400 troops against 150 Indians in the territory of the United States, northwest of Ohio. Because of poor leadership, insufficient training, and unworkable guns, the attack culminated in a retreat. The force was composed principally of militia lacking the training of the federal troops. (*American State Papers. Military Affairs. Vol. I*)

Bloodshed in the new world caused by Europeans occurred in 1493 when Columbus and his men attempted to land in the dominion of Mayobanex (cacique of the Ciguaneyes of Haiti). Repulsed by the natives, the Europeans used force and wounded several of them.

Rebellion against the federal government took place in 1786 when Daniel Shays organized an armed force in Massachusetts which threatened public order by overthrowing courts and committing other acts of violence. On December 5, 1786, the rebels seized Worcester. By February 1787, however, they were completely routed. The uprising was caused by economic discontent—the depreciation of paper money, the insistence of creditors on being paid in silver money, and the imprisonment of debtors.

WAR (colonial)

Bloodshed in the French and Indian war occurred May 28, 1754, on an isolated mountainside a few miles east of Uniontown, Pa. George Washington, at the head of several companies of Virginia militia, appeared on the Monongahela and overtook a French reconnoitering party from Fort Duquesne. Jumonville, the French commander, was slain and his force captured. (*Winthrop Sargent—History of Braddock's Campaign*)

Colonial warfare between England and France for the possession of North America occurred in 1613 at Mount Desert, Me. Father Pierre Biard, Superior of Saint Sauveur, who sailed March 12, 1613, from France on the ship "Jonas," established a French Jesuit settlement of colonists at Mount Desert. The settlement was attacked by an English expedition under the command of Captain Samuel Argall, whose aim was to suppress piracy and to defend England's title to the country founded on the discovery of the Cabots. A brief description of the conflict records that an English "vessel and forty soldiers landed at a place called Mount Desert in Nova Scotia, near St. John's River, or Tweed, possessed by the French; they killed some French, took away their guns and dismantled the Fort." (*A Description of the Province of New Albion—1648*)

French and Indian war battle took place on July 3, 1754, at Fort Necessity, located on the Great Meadows, nine miles east of Uniontown, Pa. Lieutenant Colonel George Washington, commanding 400 Virginia and South Carolina provincial troops, opposed the French commander Coulon de Villiers and his army of 1,600 French regulars, French Canadian Militia, and Indians. (*Fort Necessity Memorial Association—A Young Colonel from Virginia and the Blow He Struck for American Independence in the Year 1754*)

THE FIRST

Indian war of importance fought by English colonists took place on May 27, 1607, at which time about 200 Indians were repulsed by English settlers in Virginia under Captain Edward-Maria Wingfield. It is recorded that he "was shot clean through his beard" by an Indian. (*John Fiske—Old Virginia and Her Neighbors*)

Intercolonial war in America started September 20, 1565, when Pedro Menéndez de Avilés and 400 Spaniards proceeded overland to the St. Johns River, in Florida, and surprised and captured Fort Caroline (at St. John's Bluff, near the present site of Jacksonville) without the loss of a man. They had sailed from Cadiz, Spain, June 28, 1565, and arrived off the Florida coast August 28, 1565. The French, commanded by René Goulaine de Laudonnière, lost 140 men in the attack. Ground had been broken June 30, 1564, for Fort Caroline, named for King Charles IX of France. After its capture, Menéndez changed the name to San Mateo. (*Florida Historical Association Quarterly. Vol. 12. No. 2. October 1933*)

Marine engagement in battle took place on March 4, 1776, when Captain Samuel Nicholas and approximately 200 marines captured Fort Nassau in the Bahamas. Nicholas was assisted by 50 sailors under Lieutenant Thomas Weaver of the "Cabot." The assault was a surprise attack and the fort was unprepared. It surrendered without conflict. Large military stores were captured—about 100 cannon, 15 mortars, 5,400 shells, 11,000 rounds of ammunition, etc.—and brought back to New London, Conn., on April 8, 1776. This naval expedition, which left the Delaware Capes on February 17, 1776, was under the command of Esek Hopkins of the "Alfred."

WAR (1812)

Defeat in history of a British squadron was brought about by Oliver Hazard Perry, American naval officer, in the War of 1812. In the beginning of the action of September 10, 1813, Perry's short-range guns prevented success on his part, and his ship was battered to a hulk, with only a handful of capable men left. Perry went to a sister ship, the "Niagara," renewed the fight, and had the satisfaction of seeing the British strike colors. This action took place at Put-in Bay, Lake Erie. (*Charles Judson Dutton—Oliver Hazard Perry*)

WAR (1812)—*Continued*

Frigate action of importance in the War of 1812 took place August 19, 1812, when the "Constitution," commanded by Captain Isaac Hull met the British frigate "Guerrière," commanded by Captain James Richard Dacres. The "Constitution," which was built in Boston, Mass., in 1797, rated as a frigate of 1,576 tons, with an armament of 44 guns. The "Guerrière" was a 38-gun frigate. Within a quarter of an hour the mizzen-mast of the "Guerrière" was shot away, and her spars, sails and rigging torn to shreds. The contest was one-sided. On March 3, 1813, an award of $50,000 was made by Congress (2 Stat.L.818) to Hull for the capture of the "Guerrière."

President to face enemy gunfire while in office. *See* President (United States): President to face enemy gunfire while in office

Prisoners in the War of 1812 were taken by Lieutenant William Learned Marcy, who captured a corps of Canadian militia at St. Regis, N.Y., on October 22-23, 1812. Their flag was the first trophy of the kind captured during the war.

War declaration was made by Congress on June 18, 1812 (2 Stat.L.755) against the United Kingdom of Great Britain and Ireland and the dependencies thereof. The following day, President James Madison issued a proclamation to that effect.

WAR (French Indo-China)

American civilian pilot wounded in Indo-China was Paul Robert Holden of Greenleaf, Kan., who was wounded in the right thigh and arm by 37mm. anti-aircraft shells over Dien Bien Phu on April 24, 1954. Holden was flying a C-119 Flying Boxcar for the Civil Air Transport to deliver supplies to the French. His co-pilot, Wallace Abbott Buford, of Kansas City, Kan., managed to land the plane safely in French territory. Buford was killed May 7, 1954, near Dien Bien Phu.

WAR (Korean)

American pilot to destroy an enemy airplane in the Korean War was First Lieutenant William G. Hudson of the 68th Fighter Squadron (all-weather), who shot down a YAK-9 on June 26, 1950, while flying an F-82 airplane over Kimpo to provide cover for the evacuation of Kimpo.

American tank crew to cross the 38th parallel in Korea was a patrol of the First Cavalry Division which crossed into the Kaesong Area, about eighty-five miles south of the Red capital of Pyongsang, at 3:14 P.M. on October 7, 1950. The crew members were Sergeant Homer Lee of Evansville, Ind.; Private First Class James Emerich of Sutton,

W.Va.; Sergeant Walter Hill of Fairmont, N.D.; Sergeant Charles Gissendanner of Autaughville, Ala.; and Corporal Clarence Johnson of Taylorsville, N.C.

Korean War hero buried in Arlington Cemetery, Arlington, Va., was Second Lieutenant Howell Garrone Thomas, Jr., of Washington, D.C., who served in Company L of the Twenty-first Infantry Regiment. Thomas was buried August 14, 1950, with ceremonies attended by Secretary of the Army Frank Pace, Jr., Chief of Staff Joseph Lawton Collins, Major General Thomas Wade Herren, commander of the Washington Military District, two Korean embassy officials, and other federal representatives.

Soldier killed in the Korean War was Private Kenneth Shadrick, 19, of Skin Fork, W.Va., a member of a bazooka squad, who was killed July 5, 1950, near Sojong, Korea, by a bullet fired from an enemy tank.

South Korean combat mission involving an exchange of fire occurred on June 27, 1950, between Communist forces and an F-80C aircraft from the 8th Fighter-Bomber Group of the Fifth Air Force, which was based at Itazuke Air Base in southern Japan. A few visual reconnaissance missions had been flown June 26, 1950.

WAR (Mexican)

Mexican war shots were fired at La Rosia, Mexico, April 25, 1846. General Zachary Taylor sent Captain Seth Barton Thornton with a squadron of dragoons into enemy territory. Thornton and fifty cavalrymen were taken prisoners. Lieutenant George Thompson Mason was the first officer killed. (*George Lockhart Rives—The United States and Mexico*)

WAR (Quemoy)

American casualty of the Red Chinese bombardment of Quemoy, in Formosa Strait, was Army Specialist third class George W. Johnston of Springdale, Pa., who was wounded in the left arm September 3, 1958. Johnston was attached to the U.S. Military Assistance Advisory Group.

WAR BOND issued by the federal government, exclusive of the refunding of the Revolutionary War debts, was authorized on March 14, 1812, for the purchase of ordnance and equipment and the enlargement of the army in preparation for the impending War of 1812. The amount authorized was $11,000,000. Bonds were issued to the amount of $8,134,700 and sold exclusively in the United States. (*William F. De Knight—History of the Currency of the Country and of the Loans of the United States from the Earliest Period to June 30, 1900*)

See also Bond

THE FIRST

THE FIRST

WAR COLLEGE. *See* Army school; Army war college; Naval war college

WAR CRIMINAL PROCEEDINGS were held in Washington, D.C., from August 23, 1865, to November 4, 1865. Captain Henry Wirz, superintendent of the Confederate prison at Andersonville, Ga., accused of conspiring to torture, injure, and murder federal prisoners, was tried under thirteen separate specifications by a military commission presided over by General Lewis Wallace, U.S. Volunteers. Wirz was sentenced on November 6, 1865, to be hanged. The sentence was carried out November 10, 1865. He was buried in Mount Olivet Cemetery, Washington, D.C.

WAR DEPARTMENT (U.S.)
See also National defense department (U.S.)

Aeronautical division. *See* Aviation: Aeronautical Division of the U.S. War Department

War Department (U.S.) was authorized by an "act to establish an executive department to be denominated the Department of War," approved August 7, 1789 (1 Stat.L.49). The department superseded a similar department established prior to the adoption of the Constitution. The act of 1789 authorized the appointment of a Secretary of War at a salary of $3,000 a year. The first Secretary was Henry Knox of Massachusetts, appointed by President Washington on September 11, 1789. The appointment was confirmed and Knox was commissioned. He entered on his duties on September 12, 1789. *(Lurton Dunham Ingersoll— History of the War Department of the United States)*

WAR LOAN. *See* Loan: Loan for war purposes; Loan: War loan made by the United States government to a war ally

WAR MAP. *See* Map: War map

WAR ORPHANS EDUCATION LAW. *See* Education: War orphans education law

WAR RISK INSURANCE BUREAU. *See* Insurance: War risk insurance bureau

WAR SONG. *See* Music: War song

WAR VETERANS' COLLEGE. *See* College: College principally for war veterans

WAR VETERANS' SOCIETY
American Legion was organized in Paris, France, February 15-16, 1919, but the first caucus was not held until March 15, 1919. The adoption of the name was moved by Maurice Kirby Gordon of Madisonville, Ky. The Legion was incorporated by act of Congress of September 16, 1919, "to uphold and defend the Constitution of the United States; to maintain law and order; to foster and perpetuate one hundred per cent Americanism; to preserve our memories of incidents in the Great War; to inculcate a sense of individual obligation to the community, state and nation; to safeguard and transmit to posterity the principles of justice, freedom and democracy; to consecrate and sanctify our comradeship by our devotion to mutual helpfulness." The first national convention was held in Minneapolis, Minn., November 10-12, 1919. *(Richard Seelye Jones—A History of the American Legion)*

Grand Army of the Republic post was established in Decatur, Illinois, on April 6, 1866. The organization was founded principally through the efforts of Dr. Benjamin Franklin Stephenson, surgeon, and the Reverend William J. Rutledge, chaplain, both of the 14th Illinois Infantry. The first state convention was held on July 12, 1866, in Springfield, Ill. At the first national convention, held November 20, 1866, in Indianapolis, Ind., Stephen Augustus Hurlbut was elected commander-in-chief.

Military Order of Foreign Wars was founded in New York City on December 27, 1894, by veterans and descendants of veterans of one or more of the five wars waged between the United States and foreign powers. Membership was restricted to commissioned officers and their lineal descendants. The National Commandery was instituted on March 11, 1896.

Society of the Cincinnati was instituted May 10, 1783, and organized May 13, 1783, when the constitution was completed, at the Verplanck house, near Fishkill, N.Y. Final organization was effected June 9, 1783, on which date New York and Massachusetts organized the first two of the thirteen state societies. Membership was limited to officers who had served three years in the Continental army or who had been honorably discharged for disability. George Washington was elected the first president-general in 1783; he remained in office until his death and was succeeded by Major General Alexander Hamilton. Major General Henry Knox was secretary-general and Major General Alexander McDougall was treasurer-general. The first general meeting was held May 7, 1784, in Philadelphia, Pa. The Society in France was organized January 7, 1784, in Paris. The name was derived from Lucius Quinctius Cincinnatus, the distinguished Roman who, called from the plough, "left all to save the republic." *(Alonzo Norton Lewis— Historical Sketches of the Venerable and Illustrious Order of the Cincinnati)*

WAR VETERANS' SOCIETY—*Continued*

Veterans of Foreign Wars of the United States, composed of Army, Navy, and Marine Corps veterans who served in time of war in theaters of operation, was formed August 18-20, 1913, in Denver, Colo. (under the temporary name of Army of the Philippines, Cuba and Puerto Rico) with Rice W. Means as the first commander-in-chief. It was an amalgamation of three separate groups: the American Veterans of Foreign Service (organized September 23, 1899, in Columbus, Ohio); the Army of the Philippines (organized December 12, 1899, in Denver as the Colorado Society of the Philippines); and the American Veterans of Foreign Service (organized September 10-12, 1903, in Altoona, Pa.). The society organized in Altoona was a combination of the Philippine War Veterans (organized October 13, 1901, in Pittsburgh, Pa.) and the American Veterans of the Philippines and China Wars (organized July 24, 1902, in Philadelphia, Pa.).

World War II veterans' society officially recognized by Congress was the American Veterans of World War II, chartered July 23, 1947. Eleven groups with a membership of about 1,700 amalgamated on December 12, 1944, in Kansas City, Mo. The first national commander was Elmo Woodrow Keel.

WARDEN. *See* Game warden

WAREHOUSE legislation was passed by Congress on August 6, 1846 (9 Stat.L.53). This act permitted the storage of imported merchandise in warehouses owned or leased by the federal government, duty free, the duty to be paid upon withdrawal of the merchandise within a specified time of not more than one year. The act of March 28, 1854 (10 Stat.L.271) extended bonded storage privileges to private warehouses approved by the Secretary of the Treasury—warehouses having proper customs officers in charge or having joint custody with customs officers of all merchandise.

WARSHIP. *See* Ship

WARTIME CONSCRIPTION BILL. *See* Conscription: Wartime conscription bill

WASHHOUSE AND PUBLIC BATHS. *See* Bathhouse: Public bath and washhouse

WASHING MACHINE

Complete, self-contained electric washing machine was a Thor machine, which was put on the market in 1907 by the Hurley Machine Company of Chicago, Ill. Patent No. 966,677 was granted August 9, 1910, to Alva J. Fisher of Chicago, Ill., on a "drive mechanism for washing machines."

Rotary motion washing machine was made in 1859 by Hamilton Erastus Smith of Philadelphia, Pa., who obtained patent No. 21,909, October 26, 1858. A crank, turned by hand, caused a perforated cylinder within a wooden shell to revolve. Smith continued to improve his machine and in 1863 secured patent protection on the first self-reversing-motion attachment to the machine.

Washing machine for public use was installed by J. F. Cantrell in a "washateria" in Fort Worth, Tex., on April 18, 1934. Four electric washing machines were rented by the hour to those who wished to do their laundry. Hot water and electricity were supplied, but users were obliged to furnish their own soap.

Washing machine patent was granted March 28, 1797, to Nathaniel Briggs of New Hampshire for an "improvement in washing cloaths."

WASHINGTON (college named for George Washington). *See* College: College named for George Washington

WASHINGTON CORRESPONDENT. *See* News correspondent: Washington correspondent of importance

WASHINGTON MONUMENT. *See* Monument: Monument to George Washington

WASHINGTON (town named for George Washington). *See* Town: Town named for George Washington

WATCH. *See* Clock: Watch

WATER

Cast iron pipes used in a city water works. *See* Iron: Cast iron pipes used in a city water works

Community to fluoridate its municipal water in order to reduce tooth decay was Grand Rapids, Mich. Fluoridation started January 25, 1945, with the addition of one part of fluoride ion to each million parts of water passing through the water treatment plant.

Heavy water, D_2O, was identified by Harold Clayton Urey in the autumn of 1931 and subsequently named deuterium. The first public scientific announcement of the discovery of the hydrogen atom of double weight was made at the Christmas meeting of the American Association for the Advancement of Science in New Orleans, La., December 29, 1931.

THE FIRST

Irrigation legislation (federal). *See* Irrigation legislation (federal)

Municipal water supply system was built in Boston, Mass., by the Water Works Company in 1652. A series of wooden pipes was used to convey the water from nearby springs to a central reservoir, which was only twelve feet square.

Sea water conversion plant (practical) was opened May 8, 1961, by the Office of Saline Water, U.S. Department of the Interior, at Freeport, Tex., and dedicated June 21, 1961, by President John Fitzgerald Kennedy, who pressed a switch installed in his office at Washington, D.C. The plant was set up to produce about a million gallons of water a day at a cost of $1 to $1.25 per 1,000 gallons.

Soda water. *See* Soda water machine manufacturer

Track water tanks. *See* Railroad: Railroad to install track water tanks

Water pumping plant to supply water for municipal purposes was installed in Bethlehem, Pa., May 27, 1755. The water was pumped into the water tower through wooden pipes. The pumping plant was constructed by Hans Christopher Christiansen. (*Joseph Mortimer Levering—History of Bethlehem, Pa.*)

WATER CONDUIT

Drinking water conduit placed under water was built in 1848 by the Water Department of Boston, Mass. It was constructed on the shore, floated into place, and sunk into a prepared trench below the surface of the channel under Dover Street Bridge, Warren Avenue Bridge, Chelsea Street South Bridge, and Chelsea Street North Bridge. The wooden tunnels were approximately 4 feet 8½ inches in diameter and some 50 feet or more in length. Inside were laid cast-iron water pipes 20 inches in diameter to carry drinking water from Boston proper to the South Boston, Charlestown, and Chelsea sections of Boston. All these pipes were in use before 1852.

Water supply tunnel for a city was the Chicago Lake Tunnel, which extended 10,587 feet under Lake Michigan to an inlet crib. It was 5 feet in diameter. Ellis Sylvester Chesbrough was the city engineer at the time of construction. The work was contracted for October 28, 1863, by Dull and Gowan of Philadelphia, Pa., and cost $380,784.60. Construction was started March 17, 1864. The tunnel was completed December 6, 1866, but water was not let into it until March 25, 1867. The pumping station with the standpipe tower still stands at the intersection of Michigan Boulevard and

THE FIRST

Chicago Avenue, having escaped destruction during the fire of 1871. (*The Tunnels and Water System of Chicago*)

WATER CURES were introduced by Russell Thacher Trall, who opened a hydropathic institute and physiological school on November 1, 1853, at 15 Laight Street, New York City.

WATER GAS PLANT. *See* Gas: Water gas plant

WATER POWER

Water power development grant was established in 1620 by Ferdinando Gorges on that part of the Piscataqua River known as the Newwichawanick River at South Berwick, Me. Gorges obtained a grant from the English Crown which gave him the right to develop the territory lying between the 40th and 48th parallels north latitude, from sea to sea. The grant required him to develop water power. He constructed a log dam, erected a grist mill, and sent some of the meal to England as proof that he was conforming to the agreement in the charter. The water power has been in use ever since the grant to Gorges in 1620.

WATER POWER CANAL. *See* Canal: Canal for creating water power

WATER PURIFICATION

Municipal filtration system for the bacterial purification of a water supply was the Lawrence Filter, Lawrence, Mass., designed by Hiram Francis Mills. It was an open filter of 2¾ acres and was completed in September 1893. Water from the Merrimack River was purified by slow sand filtration. (*Maurice B. Dorgan—History of Lawrence, Mass.*)

Water purification by filtration dates from 1870, when an English-type slow sand filter was built at Poughkeepsie, N.Y. The plans were prepared by James Pugh Kirkwood and the filter was erected in 1872-1873. (*George Chandler Whipple—History of Water Purification. American Society of Civil Engineers. Transactions 1922*)

Water supply chemically treated with chlorine compounds for drinking water (on a practical scale) was the water supply of Jersey City, N.J., in 1908 under the supervision of George Arthur Johnson. The Jersey City Water Supply Company opened the Boonton reservoir September 26, 1908. (*George C. Bunker—"The Use of Chlorine in Water Purification." Journal of the American Medical Association. January 5, 1929*)

WATER SKI ASSOCIATION (national) was the American Water Ski Association, formed in April 1939 at Trenton, N.J. The first president was Dan Hains of Bayville, N.Y.

THE FIRST

WATER SKI TOURNAMENT (national) was held at Jones Beach State Park, Long Island, N.Y., on June 22, 1939. Bruce Parker of Garden City, N.Y., won the men's championship and Esther Yates of Amityville, N.Y., the women's championship. The events included the slalom, jumping, and trick riding.

WATER VELOCIPEDE PATENT. *See* Bicycle patent: Water velocipede patent

WATERLESS GAS STORAGE TANK. *See* Gas: Gas storage tank (waterless)

WATERMARK was the single word "company," which was formed in the paper manufactured in 1690 by William Rittenhouse in his mill on Paper Mill Run or rivulet, Germantown, Pa. Afterwards he used several other watermarks to distinguish his paper. (*Mennonite Quarterly Review—Vol. 16. No. 2*)

WAX WORKS MUSEUM was opened by James Wyatt in New York City in June 1749. The figures were imported from England and exhibited from June to December 1749 at the Sign of the Dolphin, Privateer, near the Work-House. Effigies were shown of George II and Frederick, Prince of Wales, "both dressed in Royal Robes . . . as when sitting in the Parliament House," the Duke of Cumberland "in his Regimentals," Miss Peggy [Woffington], "the present famous actress," nuns, friars, British and Hungarian-Bohemian royal personages, etc.

WEATHER BROADCAST. *See* Radio broadcast: Weather broadcasts

WEATHER BUREAU (U.S.) was authorized by act of Congress on February 9, 1870 (16 Stat.L.369), which assigned meteorological duties to the Signal Corps of the War Department. The first weather observations were made November 1, 1870, from reports gathered by telegraph from twenty-four sources. Official forecasts were distributed by telegraph by the Division of Telegrams and Reports for the Benefit of Commerce and Agriculture, as well as by the Signal Corps. The first chief was Brigadier General Albert James Myer of the U.S. Army, who had been Chief Signal Officer since 1860. Myer took over the direction of the weather service upon its organization and served until his death on August 24, 1880. The Weather Department was transferred to the Department of Agriculture on July 1, 1891, and the name changed to the Weather Bureau. (*William Babcock Hazen—History of the Signal Service*)

WEATHER MAP (television). *See* Television—Telecast: Weather map telecast

WEATHER OBSERVATIONS systematically recorded were made by Dr. John Lining

THE FIRST

of Charleston, S.C., who took daily observations at 6:30 A.M., 3 P.M., and 10 P.M. in January 1738. He recorded temperature, rainfall, atmospheric pressure, humidity, wind direction and force, and the state of the weather, and, as a physician, he studied the effect of the weather on the human body, communicating his reports to the Royal Society of London. (*Philosophical Transactions of the Royal Society of London. 1743*)

WEBBING (elastic). *See* Elastic webbing

WEDDING
Airplane wedding took place on May 31, 1919, in a Handley-Paige bombing plane with two twelve-cylinder motors. The plane was flying about 2,000 feet over Ellington Field, Houston, Tex. at the "Flying Frolic" air show. About 10,000 spectators were present at the field. Marjorie Dumont of Yorkville, Ind., and Lieutenant R. W. Meade of Cincinnati, Ohio, were married by Lieutenant J. E. Reese, Chaplain, of Nevan, Ohio. The best man was C. R. Henriques, and the matron of honor was Laura Troy. The pilot of the bomber was Lieutenant E. W. Kilgore.

American woman married to a former king of England was Wallis Warfield Simpson of Baltimore, Md., who was married by the Reverend Robert Anderson Jardine on June 3, 1937, at Monts, France, to Edward Albert Christian George Andrew Patrick David, Duke of Windsor [Edward VIII]. He acceded to the throne of England on January 20, 1936, and abdicated on December 11, 1936, without having been formally crowned. (*Robert Anderson Jardine—At Long Last*)

Balloon wedding was held October 19, 1874, over Cincinnati, Ohio. The Reverend H. B. Jeffries married Mary Walsh and Charles M. Colton.

Double radio wedding took place December 22, 1922, at Grand Central Palace, New York City, in connection with the American Radio Exposition. The Reverend B. F. Saxon of the 61st Street Methodist Church, New York City, officiated at the ceremony uniting Margaret Girstner and Joseph Woorn of Brooklyn, N.Y., and Helen Koller and John Brunschweyler of New York City. Each couple was presented with a hundred dollars. The ceremony, witnessed by 4,000 spectators, was broadcast by station WEAF, New York City.

Parachute wedding was performed August 25, 1940, at the World's Fair, New York City. The Reverend Homer Tomlinson of the Church of God, Jamaica, N.Y., performed the marriage ceremony for Arno Rudolphi and Ann Hayward. The minister, the bride and groom, the best man, the maid of honor, and four musicians were all suspended in parachutes.

THE FIRST

President married while in office. *See* President (United States): President married while in office

Silver wedding anniversary of a President in the White House. *See* President (United States): President to celebrate his silver wedding anniversary in the White House

Television wedding was held October 14, 1928, in the radio studio at Des Plaines, Ill. Cora Dennison and James Fowlkes of Kansas City, Mo., were married by the Reverend Gustave A. Klenle of St. Luke's Evangelical Church. The ceremony was telecast.

Transatlantic telephone wedding took place December 2, 1933, when Bertil Hjalmar Clason in Detroit, Mich., and Sigrid Sophia Margarete Carlson in Stockholm, Sweden, were married by Judge John Dennis Watts of the Wayne County Common Pleas Court in Detroit. The ceremony was relayed from Detroit through New York to a Maine radio station, whence it was sent to Scotland to be relayed through London to Stockholm.

Vice President to marry in office. *See* Vice President of the United States: Vice President to marry in office

Wedding abroad of a soldier in the American Expeditionary Force was solemnized July 14, 1917, in London, England. The first war bride was Kate Lewis (Mrs. William Lewis).

Wedding broadcast was that of Bertha Annie McCunn of Pitcairn, Pa., and George Albert Carver of Swissvale, Pa., transmitted November 7, 1922, from the Motor Square Garden, Pittsburgh, Pa., as part of the Electrical Expositon. The ceremony took place in a sound-proof glass booth at the Exposition; the wedding march was played at station KDKA, East Pittsburgh, Pa., about seven miles away. The minister was the Reverend J. Hankey Cololaugh of the Presbyterian Church of Pitcairn, Pa. Adia McCunn was the bridesmaid and Carl F. Carver the best man.

Wedding in New England was that of Governor Edward Winslow and Susanna, the widow of William White, on May 22, 1621. The Governor's first wife, Elizabeth Barker, whom he had married in Holland in 1618, died March 24, 1621. William White died February 21, 1621. *(William Franklin Atwood—The Pilgrim Story)*

Wedding in the United States Occupation Forces in Korea took place November 17, 1945, in the Immaculate Conception Cathedral, Seoul, Korea. First Lieutenant James Richardson Burrows of Oswego, S.C., attached to the

THE FIRST

24th Corps Military Police, married Second Lieutenant Virginia Elizabeth Reynolds of Detroit, Mich., an army nurse. The ceremony was performed by Colonel Philip James Newman, Catholic chaplain of the 24th Corps.

Wedding in Virginia was that of Anne Burras, maid of Mistress Forrest, to John Laydon, in 1609. The maid and her mistress were the first women colonists in America, arriving in 1608. No women came over with the original Jamestown settlers in 1607.

White House wedding took place March 29, 1812, when Mrs. Lucy Payne Washington was married to Justice Thomas Todd of the United States Supreme Court. Mrs. Washington was a sister of Mrs. James Madison and the widow of George Steptoe Washington, a nephew of George Washington. *(National Intelligencer. March 31, 1812)*

White House wedding of a President was Grover Cleveland's marriage to his ward, Frances Folsom, June 2, 1886. Cleveland served as President of the United States from March 4, 1885, to March 4, 1889, and from March 4, 1893, to March 4, 1897.

WEEVIL (cotton-boll). *See* Cotton-boll weevil

WEIGHTS AND MEASURES STANDARDIZATION

Act legalizing the employment of the metric system was approved July 28, 1866 (14 Stat.L.339). The act provided that it "shall be lawful throughout the United States of America to employ the weights and measures of the metric system."

International Bureau of Weights and Measures was established by the International Metric Convention at Sèvres, France, on May 20, 1875. The Bureau is maintained by assessed contributions of the signatory governments and is the repository for the International Prototype Meter, the International Prototype Kilogram, and secondary standards.

National organization to improve systems of weights, measures, and moneys was the American Metrological Society, formed December 30, 1873, at Columbia University, New York City, by Wolcott Gibbs, Frederick Augustus Porter Barnard, and Hubert Anson Newton.

Standards bureau. *See* Standards bureau (U.S.)

Weights and measures standardization was established by section 21 of the act of March 2, 1799 (1 Stat.L.643), which required the surveyor of customs of each port to stand-

WEIGHTS AND MEASURES STAND-ARDIZATION—*Continued*
ardize his measures to comply with the customs clause requiring "all duties, imposts, and excises [to] be uniform throughout the United States."

WELDING by the electric process was invented by Professor Elihu Thomson of Lynn, Mass., who obtained patent No. 347,140 on August 10, 1886, on "an apparatus for electric welding." *(Franklin Institute Journal. Vol. 229. 1940)*

WELFARE SECRETARY (U.S.). *See* Cabinet of the United States: Secretary of Health, Education and Welfare

WELL (oil). *See* Oil: Oil well

WELSH MAGAZINE was *Cymro Americaidd,* a semi-monthly first published in 1832 in Welsh in New York City. J. A. Williams was the editor. Later, an English section was added.

WEST POINT. *See* Army school: Army school

WHALE
Sperm whale was captured in 1711 at sea by a Nantucket, Mass., whaler. This was the beginning of an industry which in 1846 numbered over 700 whaling vessels.

WHALEBACK STEAMER. *See* Ship: Whaleback steamer to cross the Atlantic

WHALING
Whale-killing machine (electric) was patented by Dr. Albert Sonnenberg and Philip Rechten of Bremen, Germany, who obtained U.S. patent No. 8,843 on March 30, 1852.

Whaling expedition set sail from Nantucket, Mass., about 1715. Six sloops, of thirty to forty tons burden each, returned with cargoes amounting to 600 barrels of oil and 11,000 pounds of bone, the total value of which was £1,100 sterling. There were whaling trips by single boats and it is possible that prior expeditions may have sailed, but early records of their activities have not been preserved. *(Alexander Starbuck—History of the American Whale Fishery)*

Whaling (systematic) was undertaken March 7, 1644, by Southampton, Long Island, N.Y., which ordered the town divided into four wards of eleven persons each to attend to the driftwhales cast ashore. Two persons from each ward were employed to cut up the whales

so that each and every inhabitant obtained an equal portion. A whaling franchise was granted a Mr. Whiting in 1647 for the waters between Stonington and Montauk Point. *(George Rogers Howell—The Early History of Southampton)*

WHEAT (shredded). *See* Breakfast food: Shredded wheat biscuits

WHIG PARTY held its first convention in Albany, N.Y., on February 3, 1836. William Henry Harrison of Ohio was unanimously nominated for President and Francis Granger of New York was designated as the candidate for Vice President. This was a state convention attended by delegates from 32 of the 52 counties. Ohio held a state convention in Columbus on February 22-23, 1836. In the election of November 8, 1836, Harrison received 73 electoral votes, compared with 170 electoral votes (762,000 popular votes) cast for Martin Van Buren, a Democrat, the successful candidate.

WHIPS were manufactured commercially in 1801 by Titus Pease in Little River (village), Westfield, and Thomas Rose, Mundale, Westfield, Mass. In 1808 Joseph Jokes of Westfield used hickory wood shafts and put a strip of horsehide at the end fastened to the stock by a "keeper." *(Clifton Johnson—Hampden County 1636-1936)*

WHIST TOURNAMENT. *See* Bridge whist tournament: Duplicate bridge tournament

WHISTLE (locomotive). *See* Locomotive steam whistle

WHITE HOUSE. *See* under Birth; Building; Gas; News correspondent; Swimming pool; Wedding

"WHITE HOUSE OF THE CONFEDERACY." *See* Building: "White House of the Confederacy"

WHITE LEAD manufacturer was Samuel Wetherill of Philadelphia, Pa., who began production in 1789. The white lead was used primarily in paint and to some extent for medicinal purposes. *(William Henry Pulsifer—Notes for a History of Lead)*

WHITE RATS. *See* Actors' union

WHITE SETTLEMENT. *See* Colonist: Colonial white settlement (north of Florida)

WILD BIRD SANCTUARY. *See* Bird sanctuary

WILD WEST SHOW was prepared by William Frederick Cody, more familiarly known as "Buffalo Bill," and presented in North Platte, Neb., as part of a Fourth of July celebration in 1883. The following year, Cody commercialized the show and exhibited it in various parts of the United States. The first commercial showing was held in Omaha, Neb.

WILDLIFE PROTECTION SOCIETY. *See* Game protection society

WILDLIFE RESTORATION PROJECT. *See* Game protection society

WIND TUNNEL
Full-scale wind tunnel for testing airplanes was placed in operation May 27, 1931, at the Langley Research Center of the National Advisory Committee for Aeronautics, Langley Field, Va. It was used to test airplanes to determine flying characteristics. The jet of air in the tunnel, 30 feet high and 60 feet wide, was moved by two propellers 35 feet 5 inches in diameter up to a speed of 110 miles an hour. Each propeller was driven by a 4,000 h.p. electric motor. In 1936 a new tunnel was constructed with air speed up to 600 miles an hour.

High-speed jet wind tunnel was completed June 29, 1929, at the Langley Field Laboratory of the National Advisory Committee for Aeronautics, Langley Field, Va. Preliminary design work was begun November 14, 1928. A wind speed of approximately 600 miles an hour was attained, permitting the testing of airfoils at this speed. The tunnel has since been deactivated.

Propeller research tunnel was completed in the summer of 1927 at the Langley Field Laboratory of the National Advisory Committee for Aeronautics, Langley Field, Va. Preliminary work commenced April 28, 1925. The tunnel permitted the full-scale testing of engines and propellers, engine nacelles, wing combinations, and fuselages. It had an air stream 20 feet in diameter which traveled at speeds up to 110 miles an hour.

Wind tunnel of variable air density for testing airplanes was conceived by Dr. Max Michael Munk and completed in April 1923 at the Langley Field Laboratory of the National Advisory Committee for Aeronautics, Langley Field, Va. Air was compressed to twenty times its normal pressure and, by means of a propeller, moved past wing models at a speed as high as 80 miles an hour. By increasing the air pressure twenty times it was possible to obtain results equivalent to those that would be obtained if the model were twenty times the size.

WIND TURBINE. *See* Electric power plant: Wind turbine

WINDMILL
Windmill was erected in 1632 in Cambridge, Mass. As "it would not grind but with a westerly wind," it was moved in August 1632 to Copp's Hill (Boston Neck), Boston, Mass. *(John Winthrop—History of New England from 1630 to 1649)*

Windmill driven by rotor power was erected and tested in July 1933 in West Burlington, N.J., to determine the amount of rotor power needed to turn or spin the windmill and to measure the force. The first driving unit, a duralumin rotor 90 feet high and 22 feet wide, built like a cylinder, was revolved by a motor at 60 revolutions a minute. The combination of the turning and the wind produced the force tending to make the cylinder rotate along the ground. The principle involved was similar to that used by Anton Flettner in his rotor ship. Original plans were to have a series of cylinders mounted on 30-foot-gauge cars run around a circular track one-half mile in diameter. The rotor project was sponsored by the Madaras Rotor Power Corporation, Detroit, Mich., with the support of public utility companies.

WINDOW ENVELOPE. *See* Envelope: Envelope with an outlook or window

WINDOW GLASS. *See* Glass factory: Window glass factory

WINDOW SASH. *See* Sash: Wrought iron window sash installation

WINDOWLESS FACTORY. *See* Factory: Windowless factory

WINDOWLESS STRUCTURE. *See* Building: All-glass windowless structure

WINGLESS AUTOGIRO. *See* Autogiro: Autogiro (wingless direct control)

WINTER OLYMPIC GAMES. *See* Olympic games: Winter olympic games competition

WIRE
Barbed wire was made in 1873 by Joseph Farwell Glidden of De Kalb, Ill., who obtained patent No. 157,124 for this invention November 24, 1874. He filed his application October 27, 1873, and started manufacturing on November 1, 1873, in De Kalb, Ill. The barbs were cut from sheet metal and were inserted between two wires which were twisted considerably more than is the practice today. *(Wrought Iron Record. Vol. I. No. 4. Wrought Iron Research Association)*

THE FIRST

WIRE—*Continued*

Brass wire was manufactured in 1840 by Edwin Hodges of West Torrington, Conn., but was not commercially successful. In 1841 the Wolcottville Brass Company was founded with a capital investment of $56,000 and was the first to manufacture brass wire successfully. (*Samuel Orcutt—History of Torrington, Conn.*)

Legislation (state) requiring wires to be placed underground was enacted June 14, 1884 (chapter 534), by New York State. It required that "all telegraph, telephonic and electric light wires and cables in any incorporated city having a population of 500,000 or over . . . be placed under the surface of the streets, lanes and avenues." It also specified that telegraph poles be removed prior to November 1, 1885.

Piano wire was produced at the factory of Ichabod Washburn, Grove Street, Worcester, Mass., in 1850. This plant was later part of the Washburn and Moen Manufacturing Company, afterwards absorbed by the American Steel and Wire Company.

Wire-cutting machine and automatic straightener was invented in 1866 by John Adt who established a small plant in Wolcottville, Conn. Before this invention, wire had been straightened by being drawn between two corrugated wooden blocks or through holes in several wooden blocks. The cutting off was done by hand. Adt's machine did the work mechanically. The concern which he founded was absorbed in 1895 by the F. B. Shuster Company of New Haven, Conn.

Wire rope factory was erected in Saxonburg, Pa., in 1841 by John Augustus Roebling, who also had to create the machinery to make the rope. A small building was erected to house the machinery for splicing wire and winding it on large reels for running out. Separate strands, seven in number, were laid up and then twisted into the larger rope. The twisting machine was out in the open and operated by hand power. (*Hamilton Schuyler—The Roeblings*)

Woven wire fence industry owes its creation to John Wallace Page, who in 1883 erected on his own farm in Lenawee County, Mich., a fence with horizontally and vertically interlaced wires. This type of fence found such demand among Page's neighbors that he opened a factory in Adrian, Mich.

WIRE BRIDGE. *See* Bridge: Iron wire suspension bridge; Bridge: Wire cable suspension aqueduct bridge; Bridge: Wire suspension bridge for general traffic

THE FIRST

WIRE-DRAWING MACHINE (brass). *See* Brass wire-drawing and tube-making machinery

WIRE GAUGE for standardizing the sizes of drawn wire, was a "V" type gauge developed in 1849 by Ichabod Washburn of Worcester, Mass. It was used by the Washburn and Moen Manufacturing Company (afterwards part of the American Steel and Wire Company) and was the foundation for the present steel wire gauge.

WIRE GLASS. *See* Glass: Wire glass

WIRE NAIL MACHINE. *See* Nail machine (wire)

WIRE SIEVE. *See* Sieve: Wire sieves

WIRE RECORDER was invented in the late 1930's by Marvin Camras, a student at the Armour Institute of Technology, Chicago, Ill., who obtained U.S. patents No. 2,351,003 to 2,351,011 on June 13, 1944. The recorder was used experimentally in 1939 and in 1940. In 1941 several models were used by the U.S. Navy.

WIRELESS. *See* Radio broadcast; Radio receiver; etc.

WITCHCRAFT EXECUTION of record was that of Achsah Young of Massachusetts, who was hanged as a witch on May 27, 1647. (*Justin Winsor—Memorial History of Boston*)

WOLFRAM. *See* Tungsten: Tungsten and tellurium

WOMAN

See also under names of the armed services, colleges, decorations, government departments, medals, occupations, organizations, schools, societies, sports, etc.

American-born woman to become a member of Parliament in Great Britain was Lady Astor, whose maiden name was Nancy Witcher Langhorne. She was elected to represent the Plymouth constituency. She took her oath as a member of the House of Commons on December 1, 1919. (*Nancy Witcher Langhorne Astor—My Two Countries*)

American woman to swim the English Channel was Gertrude (Trudy) Ederle, who accomplished the feat on August 6, 1926. She swam from Gris-Nez, France, to Kingsdown (Dover), England in 14 hours and 34 minutes.

THE FIRST

American woman to swim the English Channel from both coasts was Florence Chadwick of San Diego, Calif., who on August 8, 1950, swam from Gris-Nez, France, to Dover, England, in 13 hours and 28 minutes, and on September 10, 1951, from Dover to Sangatte, France, in 16 hours and 22 minutes.

Bible translation by a woman. *See* Bible: Bible translation by a woman

Heroine publicly rewarded was Hannah Duston. During an attack on Haverhill, Mass., on March 16, 1697, Indians killed her one-week-old baby by dashing it against a tree and captured her and Mary Neff, the child's nurse, as well as murdering or capturing 39 other persons and destroying six houses. The prisoners were brought to the Indian camp at which Samuel Leonardson, a young boy who had been captured on March 30, 1695, at Worcester, Mass., was held prisoner. Hannah Duston, on April 29, 1697, killed ten Indians with a tomahawk, scalping them as proof of her deed. The Great and General Court of Massachusetts on June 8, 1697, voted "that Thomas Durstan [sic] in behalf of his wife shall be allowed and paid out of the publick treasury twenty-five pounds; and Mary Neff, the sum of twelve pounds ten shillings and the young man (named Samuel Lenerson [sic] concerned in the same action the like sum of twelve pounds ten shillings." *(George Wingate Chase—The History of Haverhill)*

Monument to a woman financed by women. *See* Monument: Monument to a woman financed by women

White woman to become an Indian chief was Harriet Maxwell Converse, who was made a chief of the Six Nations Tribe on September 18, 1891, at the Tonawanda Reservation, N.Y., in a ceremony known as "The Condolence." In recognition of her services to the Indians she was given the name Ga-is-wa-noh, meaning "the watcher." In 1884, Mrs. Converse had been adopted as a member of the Seneca tribe in appreciation of her efforts in their behalf. *(American Scenic and Historic Preservation Society. 10th Annual Report. 1905)*

Woman automotive engineer was Marie Luhring, draftsman for the International Motor Company, who received the Master of Engineering degree from Cooper Union, New York City, June 5, 1922. On April 9, 1920, she was elected an associate member of the Society of Automotive Engineers, becoming the first woman member. *(Journal of the Society of Automotive Engineers. June 1920)*

Woman clerk of a state supreme court was Grace F. Kaercher (later Mrs. Davis) of

THE FIRST

Ortonville, Minn., elected November 7, 1922. She was the first woman to be elected to a state office in Minnesota. She was reelected for four-year terms in 1926, 1930, 1938, and 1942. Her salary was $4,500 a year.

Woman congressional hearing witness was Elizabeth Cady Stanton, who addressed the District Committee of the United States Senate January 20, 1869, in a plea to save women of the District of Columbia from being debarred from voting. *(Carrie Chapman Catt and Nettie Rogers Shuler—Woman Suffrage and Politics)*

Woman coxswain of a men's collegiate varsity team was Sally Stearns, who led the shell of Rollins College, Winter Park, Fla., on May 27, 1936, against Marietta College and on June 1, 1936, against Manhattan College. The crew raced only twice in 1936, losing to Marietta by four lengths and winning from Manhattan by a half-length.

Woman District Attorney of the United States was Annette Abbott Adams, who served in the Northern California District from July 25, 1918, to June 26, 1920.

Woman editor-in-chief of a law review was Mary Honor Donlon, who edited the November 1919, January 1920, and March 1920 issues of the *Cornell Law Quarterly* of the Cornell Law School, Ithaca, N.Y.

Woman granted a patent was Mary Kies of South Killingly, Conn., who obtained a patent on May 5, 1809, for "a new and useful improvement in weaving straw with silk or thread." *(George Larkin Clark—History of Connecticut)*

Woman horseback rider to make a solo transcontinental trip was Nan Jane Aspinwall, who left San Francisco, Calif., September 1, 1910, carrying a letter from Mayor Patrick Henry McCarthy to Mayor William Jay Gaynor of New York City. She covered 4,500 miles in 301 days, 108 of which were spent traveling. She arrived in New York City on July 8, 1911.

Woman humorist was Frances Miriam Berry Whitcher, who used the nom de plume "Frank" in 1846 in Joseph Clay Neal's *Saturday Gazette*. Her "Widow Bedott" papers, republished in book form in 1855, sold over 100,000 copies. *(Walter Blair—Native American Humor)*

Woman internal revenue collector was Mabel Gilmore Reinecke, who served from June 1, 1923, to March 31, 1929, as Collector of

WOMAN—*Continued*
Internal Revenue for the First District of Illinois. She was appointed by President Warren Gamaliel Harding.

Woman labor delegate to a national convention of the American Federation of Labor was Mary Burke, who represented the Retail Clerks' Union of Findlay, Ohio, at the convention held in Detroit, Mich., December 8-13, 1890.

Woman labor delegate to the British Trades Union was Sara Agnes McLaughlin Conboy, who was elected in 1920 as a fraternal delegate of the American Federation of Labor. She was the first woman organizer of the United Textile Workers of America.

Woman lobbyist of more than local influence was Dorothea Lynde Dix, who in the 1840's and 1850's championed the care of the indigent insane. On June 23, 1848, she presented a memorial to Congress for a grant of 5,000,000 acres for "the relief and support of the indigent insane in the United States." By courtesy of Congress, a special alcove in the Capitol Library was set apart for her use, where she could converse with members. *(Francis Tiffany—Life of Dorothea Lynde Dix)*

Woman mayor was Susanna Medora Salter, elected mayor of Argonia, Kan., on April 4, 1887. Her name was submitted without her knowledge by the Woman's Christian Temperance Union, and she did not know that she was a candidate until she went to the polls and found her name listed on the ballot. Although only twenty-seven years of age, she received a two-thirds majority of the votes. She served one year for one dollar.

Woman newspaper editor was Ann Franklin, Benjamin Franklin's sister-in-law, who became editor of the Newport *Mercury*, Newport, R.I., upon the death of her son, James Franklin, Jr., August 22, 1762. The first number had appeared June 12, 1758, under the editorship of the son. At his death, she took charge of the newspaper and printing plant. She edited the paper until her death, April 16, 1763. *(Bulletin No. 65. Newport Historical Society. April 1928)*

Woman of American descent to become a queen was Countess Geraldine Apponyi of Hungary (born August 6, 1915), who married King Zog (Ahmed Zogu) of Albania on April 27, 1938, at the Royal Palace, Tirana, Albania. The marriage was proclaimed by Heqmet Delvina, vice president of the Albanian parliament. The countess was the daughter of Virginia Gladys Stewart, who married Count Julius Apponyi. *(Antoinette de Szinyei-Merse —Ten Years, Ten Months, Ten Days)*

Woman ordained a minister was the Reverend Antoinette Brown Blackwell, who was ordained September 15, 1853, at the Congregational Church, South Butler, N.Y. *(Harriot Kesia Hunt—Glances and Gimpses)*

Woman passport division chief was Ruth Bielaski Shipley, appointed by Secretary of State Frank Billings Kellogg. She assumed office June 1, 1928.

Woman Presbyterian elder, as finally permitted by the General Assembly at Cincinnati, Ohio, on May 31, 1930, was Sarah E. Dickson of the Wauwatosa Presbyterian Church of Milwaukee, Wis., elected June 2, 1930. She served until January 1, 1934.

Woman presidential campaign co-manager was Ruth Hanna McCormick Simms, daughter of Mark Hanna, who was made a co-manager on December 2, 1939, of Thomas Edmund Dewey's campaign. J. Russel Sprague, Republican leader of Nassau County, N.Y., was the other co-manager.

Woman printer was Dinah Nuthead of Annapolis, Md., who petitioned the Assembly on May 5, 1696, for license to print and carry on the printing trade of her deceased husband, William Nuthead. *(Lawrence Counselman Wroth—A History of Printing in Colonial Maryland 1686-1776)*

Woman prize fight referee (licensed) was Belle Martell of Van Nuys, Calif., granted a license (No. 209), on April 30, 1940, by the California State Athletic Commission. She also held an announcer's license and a timekeeper's license. Her first assignment was a complete show of eight bouts in San Bernardino, Calif., on May 2, 1940. She retired the following month, on June 24, 1940, after an assignment in Los Angeles, Calif.

Woman sculptor honored by membership in the National Academy of Design was Mary Evelyn Beatrice Longman, who was elected in 1919. Her first important work was a male statue, "Victory," placed in Festival Hall at the 1904 St. Louis Exposition. For this statue she was awarded a silver medal.

Woman secretary of a national political party was Dorothy McElroy Vredenburgh of Alabama, who was appointed secretary of the Democratic National Committee on February 29, 1944, by chairman Robert Emmet Hannegan. She was secretary at the Democratic national convention, July 19-21, 1944, in Chicago, Ill.

Woman secretary of a state senate was Fern Ale, who served as secretary of the Senate of Indiana, Indianapolis, during the session

THE FIRST

of 1927, beginning January 6 and adjourning March 7. She also served as secretary of the special meeting of the Senate immediately following the regular adjournment of the legislature. This special meeting, called for the impeachment of a judge, lasted several days.

Woman secretary to a Vice President of the United States was Lola M. Williams, who served as secretary to Vice President Charles Curtis when he assumed office on March 4, 1929. Previously, she had been his secretary five years while he was Senator from Kansas.

Woman state budget commissioner was Jean Wetterau Wittich of Minneapolis, Minn. She served as Budget Commissioner of the state of Minnesota from March 16, 1931, to May 16, 1933.

Woman state committee chairman of a major political party was Mary Teresa Norton, who was elected Chairman of the Democratic State Committee of New Jersey at the state convention held in Trenton, May 22, 1934. Mrs. Norton was at the time of her election a member of the U.S. House of Representatives from the 13th District, New Jersey.

Woman state liquor board member was Jeanie Rumsey Sheppard, appointed April 12, 1933, by Governor Herbert Henry Lehman to New York's Alcoholic Beverage Control Board established to license, regulate, and control the sale of all alcoholic beverages.

Woman tax appeals board member was Annabel Matthews, whose appointment by President Herbert Clark Hoover was confirmed by the Senate on February 14, 1930. She served from February 18, 1930 to June 1, 1936.

Woman telegrapher was Sarah G. Bagley, who was in charge of the Lowell, Mass., office of the New York and Boston Magnetic Telegraph Association when the line opened February 21, 1846, between Boston and Lowell. *(James D. Reid—The Telegraph in America)*

Woman to compile a dictionary. *See* Dictionary: Dictionary compiled by a woman

Woman to have her name placed on the cornerstone of a United States Government building was Nellie Tayloe Ross, Director of the Mint. The building was the United States Depository, Fort Knox, Ky., completed during the early part of April 1936. No formal dedication ceremonies were held.

Woman to undergo astronaut tests was Jerrie Cobb of Oklahoma City, Okla., who passed a series of 75 examinations conducted

THE FIRST

February 15-21, 1960, at the Lovelace Foundation, Albuquerque, N.M. The tests were the same as those given to male astronauts. In August 1960 she underwent additional examinations which included psychological, psychiatric, and isolation tests.

Woman whose vote was recorded was the widow of Josiah Taft of Uxbridge, Mass., who in 1756 voted her approval of levying a town tax. She was granted this privilege because her son, Bazaleel, was a minor. *(Henry Chapin—Address Delivered at the Unitarian Church in Uxbridge, Mass. in 1864)*

Women to become federal government employees were Sarah Waldrake and Rachael Summers, employed in 1795 by the Mint in Philadelphia, Pa., at fifty cents a day as adjusters to weigh gold coins.

Women ushers. *See* Theater: Theater to employ women ushers

WOMAN SUFFRAGE

Colony to grant suffrage to women was New Jersey. A new constitution, adopted on July 2, 1776, provided "that all the inhabitants of this Colony of full age who are worth 50 Pounds Proclamation money, with clear estate in the same, and have resided within the county in which they claim a vote for twelve months immediately preceding the election" were entitled to vote at the general election. In 1790 this was interpreted to mean both men and women, but on November 16, 1807, the General Assembly passed laws providing that only free white male citizens could exercise the franchise.

Convention (national) of women advocating woman suffrage was the National Woman's Rights Convention held at Brinley Hall, Worcester, Mass., October 23-24, 1850, "to consider the question of woman's rights, duties and relations." The convention was called to order by Sarah H. Earle of Worcester. The officers elected were Paulina W. Davis of Providence, R.I., president, and William H. Channing of Boston, Mass., and Sarah Tyndale of Philadelphia, Pa., vice presidents.

Convention of women advocating woman suffrage was held in the Wesleyan Chapel, Seneca Falls, N.Y., July 19-20, 1848. The convention was assembled through the initiative of Lucretia Mott and Elizabeth Cady Stanton. A Declaration of Sentiments was read and a series of resolutions adopted, one of them calling for woman suffrage. *(National American Woman Suffrage Association—Victory—How Women Won It)*

State to grant suffrage to women after the adoption of the United States Constitution was

WOMAN SUFFRAGE—*Continued*
Wyoming, which became a state on July 10,
1890. Women had voted in Wyoming territory from the beginning. The first territorial
legislature, which convened on October 12,
1869, had voted on December 10, 1869, to extend the vote to women. New Jersey women
had the privilege of voting for a time under
the constitution adopted July 2, 1776, but the
constitutional provision was re-interpreted in
1807 as limiting the right to vote to free white
male citizens. *(Carrie Chapman Catt and
Nettie Rogers Shuler—Woman Suffrage and
Politics)*

Woman suffrage advocate, better known
as America's first feminist, was Margaret
Brent, a niece of Lord Baltimore. She came
to America in January 1638 and was the first
woman of Maryland to own property in her
own name. On June 24, 1647, she demanded a
voice and vote for herself in the colonial assembly by virtue of her position as Governor
Leonard Calvert's secretary. She was ejected
from the meetings. She protested and demanded a "place and voyce." At the death of
Calvert, she was his executrix and became
acting governor and presided over the General Assembly. She was refused a voice in
the affairs of the government as "it would
set a bad example to ye wives of ye colony."
(National Republic. May 1930)

**Woman suffrage amendment approved by
Congress** for submission to the states was
passed by the House of Representatives May
21, 1919, and by the Senate on June 4, 1919.
It was ratified by Illinois, Wisconsin, and
Michigan on June 10, 1919. Tennessee was the
thirty-sixth state to ratify the amendment, on
August 18, 1920, completing the necessary
three quarters of the states to put the amendment into effect. On August 26, 1920, Secretary of State Bainbridge Colby signed the
Proclamation of the Woman Suffrage Amendment to the Constitution, giving public notice
that the Nineteenth Amendment had been
formally adopted, and was in effect. Woman
suffrage amendments had been presented to
Congress at intervals beginning in 1868 without success.

**Woman suffrage association (internation-
al)** was the International Woman Suffrage
Alliance, which was organized in Washington,
D.C., in February 1902 at a meeting of the
National American Woman Suffrage Association. The first international convention of the
Alliance was held in Berlin in 1904, in conjunction with the quinquennial convention of
the International Council of Women.

Woman suffrage associations (national)
stemmed from the American Equal Rights
Association, which had been organized in 1866,
when the Fourteenth Amendment to the Constitution was up for ratification. The consti-

tution of the Association, adopted May 10,
1866, in New York City, advocated the right
of suffrage irrespective of race, color, or sex.
Lucretia Mott was president and Susan
Brownell Anthony secretary. In 1869 the
American Equal Rights Association split over
the question of equal suffrage for Negroes,
one faction forming the American Woman
Suffrage Association led by Lucy Stone and
Julia Ward Howe, and the other forming the
National Woman Suffrage Association led by
Elizabeth Cady Stanton and Susan B. Anthony.
Some twenty years later the two were reunited
to form the National American Woman Suf-
frage Association.

Woman suffrage book was a reprint of
*A Vindication of the Rights of Women, with
Strictures on Political and Moral Subjects* by
Mary Wollstonecraft Godwin, 276 pages,
printed in 1792 in Philadelphia, Pa., by William Gibbons. The author's name was erroneously spelled "Woolstonecraft." Another
edition, 340 pages, was published in Boston,
Mass., by Peter Edes with a slight subtitle
variation. The book was originally published
in England in 1790 and was dedicated to
Charles Maurice de Talleyrand-Périgord,
formerly bishop of Autun.

WOMEN'S ARMY AUXILIARY CORPS.
See Army auxiliary corps: Women's Army
Auxiliary Corps (WAAC)

**WOMEN'S AUXILIARY FERRYING
SQUADRON**
Women's Auxiliary Ferrying Squadron
(WAFS) was established September 10, 1942,
by the Air Transport Command. It consisted
of women pilots with Civil Service status who
ferried Army aircraft to domestic airfields
and overseas bases.

**WOMEN'S BUREAU (Labor Depart-
ment).** *See* Labor department (U.S.): Wom-
en's bureau

WOMEN'S CLUB
Chinese women's club incorporated was
the Chinese Women's Association, Inc., New
York City, organized March 29, 1932, and
incorporated June 10, 1936. The first president was Theodora Chan Wang.

Jewish women's organization (national)
was the National Council of Jewish Women
formed in Chicago, Ill., in January 1894. The
first president was Hannah Greenebaum Solomon and the first secretary was Sadie American.

Women's club was the Female Charitable
Society of Wiscasset, Me., which held its first
meeting on November 18, 1805, at the home
of "Tempe" Lee, wife of Judge Silas Lee, a
member of Congress. Thirty women were

THE FIRST

present and were admitted as members. A total of $78 was subscribed. The first president was Sally Sayward Wood, Maine's first woman novelist. (*Daughters of the American Revolution Magazine. May 1920*)

Women's club federation was the General Federation of Women's Clubs organized March 20, 1890, at Madison Square Garden, New York City. The first convention was held April 23, 1890, and the constitution adopted April 24, 1890. The first officers were Charlotte Emerson Brown, president; Mary Wright Sewall, vice president; Phoebe Apperson Hearst, treasurer; Mary B. Temple, corresponding secretary; Jane Cunningham Croly ("Jennie June"), recording secretary; and Kate Tanett Woods, auditor. (*Jane Cunningham Croly—History of the Woman's Club Movement in America*)

Women's professional club was "Sorosis," founded in New York City, March 21, 1868, by Jane Cunningham Croly ("Jennie June") and a few of her friends. The first officers were Alice Carey, president; Mrs. Croly, vice president; Kate Fields, corresponding secretary, and Charlotte Beebee Wilbour, treasurer and recording secretary. (*Jane Cunningham Croly—History of the Woman's Club Movement in America*)

Women's secret society was organized May 15, 1851, at Wesleyan College, Macon, Ga., as the Adelphean Society with sixteen charter members whose motto was "We live for one another." The original founder was Eugenia Tucker Fitzgerald. The name was changed to Alpha Delta Phi Sorority in 1904, at which time the society had 60 active members and 3,000 alumnae. In 1913 it changed its name to the Alpha Delta Pi Sorority. (*The Adelphean of Alpha Delta Pi. Vol. 1. No. 1*)
See also Sorority

WOMEN'S COLLEGE. *See* under College

WOMEN'S HOSPITAL. *See* Hospital: Woman's hospital

WOMEN'S LABOR LEGISLATION. *See* Labor law: Women's equal employment legislation

WOMEN'S LABOR ORGANIZATION. *See* Labor union: Women's labor organization (national)

WOMEN'S RIGHTS CONVENTION. *See* Woman suffrage: Convention of women advocating woman suffrage

WOMEN'S STRIKE. *See* Strike: Strike of women operatives

THE FIRST

WOMEN'S WORLD'S FAIR. *See* Fair: Woman's world fair

WOOD DRYDOCK. *See* Drydock: Timber drydock

WOOD ENGRAVING. *See* Engraving: Wood engraving made with an engraving tool

WOOD FIBER OR PULP PAPER. *See* Paper: Wood pulp and rag paper

WOODCUT. *See* Engraving: Engraving

WOODEN MONEY. *See* Money: Wooden money

WOODEN RAILROAD BRIDGE. *See* Bridge: Wooden railroad bridge of a purely truss type

WOODEN TRACK (bicycle). *See* Bicycle race track of wood

WOOL

Fulling mill was established in Rowley, Mass., in 1643 and operated by emigrants from Yorkshire, England.

Wool carding machine was built by John and Arthur Scholfield in Newburyport, Mass., and installed in a mill in Byfield, Mass., in 1793. It was 25 inches wide and had a single cylinder, 33 inches in diameter. It carried two workers and strippers, a fancy, and a 14-inch doffer cover with card clothing sheets. A fluted cylinder of 13 inches was arranged behind the doffer. (*Arthur Harrison Cole—The American Wool Manufacture*)

Worsted mill was established in 1695 in Boston, Mass., by John Cornish. The spinning was done by farmers, who called for clean top wool, from which the noil had been removed, and brought back spun worsted. An appraisal of Cornish's estate revealed "two pairs of combs, four looms and tackling, and two dye furnaces."

Worsted mill operated by water power and the first operated on a strictly commercial basis was the Hartford Woolen Manufactory, Hartford, Conn., which was organized on April 15, 1788. A capital of 1,250 pounds was raised by subscription in nearby towns, the largest contributor being Jeremiah Wadsworth. A bounty of one penny per pound was given for all yarn spun in the factory before June 1, 1789, as a means of encouraging the new industry. Water power had previously been used in fulling mills.

WOOL (glass). *See* Glass wool

WORKINGMEN'S PARTY. *See* Labor party (political): Labor party (state)

WORKMEN'S COMPENSATION
Workmen's compensation agreement was made January 26, 1695, by Captain William Kidd, commander of the "Adventure Galley" of 787 tons burden. One fourth of the booty captured was to be distributed among the crew. According to the agreement, "If any man should Loose a Leg or Arm in ye said service, he should have six hundred pieces of Eight, or six able slaves; if any man should loose a joynt on ye said service, he should have a hundred pieces of eight." *(Harold Tom Wilkins—Captain Kidd and His Skeleton Island)*

Workmen's compensation insurance. *See* Insurance: Workmen's compensation insurance law

Workmen's compensation lawsuit involving the rights of an injured servant against his master was the case of *James Murray* vs. *South Carolina Railroad Company*, which was tried before Judge Belton O'Neall at the July Extra Term, 1838, of Barnwell County, S.C. The trial resulted in a verdict of $1,500 in favor of the plaintiff. The defendant appealed and the case was heard by the Court of Errors of South Carolina in Charleston in February 1841. The court reversed the decision and granted a new trial. The decision was written by Judge Josiah James Evans. *(Mc-Mullan Law Reports. Vol. I. p. 251)*

WORKS PROGRESS ADMINISTRATION
Works Progress Administration was created by Presidential Executive Order No. 7034, May 6, 1935, under the Emergency Relief Appropriation Act of 1935, approved April 8, 1935 (49 Stat.L.115) to "provide relief, work relief and to increase employment by providing for useful projects." Harry Lloyd Hopkins, appointed May 6, 1935, was the first administrator.

Works Progress Administration Federal Art Project Gallery was officially opened December 28, 1935, in New York City "to provide an outlet for the showing of work by artists on the projects, and at the same time to enable the public and cooperating sponsors to see for themselves the results of the federal art program." A large part of the work exhibited was allocated to tax-free and tax-supported institutions which paid for the cost of the material used.

WORLD BANK. *See* Bank: World bank

WORLD FLIGHT. *See* Aviation—Flights (world): World flight

WORLD SERIES BASEBALL GAME. *See* Baseball game: World Series baseball games to gross a million dollars

WORLD TOUR BY A WOMAN TRAVELING ALONE. *See* Tour of the world: Tour of the world made by a woman traveling alone

WORLD WAR I
Air combat of an American organization in World War I took place April 14, 1918. Alan Winslow and Douglas Campbell shot down two German single-seaters almost directly over the Squadron Aerodrome at Toul, France.

Air squadron. *See* Aviation: Air squadron

Airplane bombing raid by an American air unit. *See* Aviation—Airplane Bombing: Airplane bombing raid by an American air unit

American Army casualty in World War I was First Lieutenant Louis J. Genelba, Medical Corps, who received a shell wound July 14, 1917, while serving with the British Army at the front southwest of Arras, France. *(United States Battle Monuments Commission—American Armies and Battlefields in Europe)*

American Army division to cross the Rhine River into the American sector of the American Army of Occupation was the First Division, which passed over the pontoon bridge at Coblentz on the morning of December 13, 1918. Lieutenant Donald McClure, commanding officer of Company M, Eighteenth Infantry, First Division, led the advance with his company of infantry. In daily marching order down the Moselle River from Luxembourg to the river's confluence with the Rhine, regiments, battalions, and companies rotated in the advance. On November 26, 1918, the American Army crossed the Moselle into Rhenish Prussia.

American Army soldiers killed in combat in World War I were Corporal James B. Gresham of Evansville, Ind., and Privates Thomas F. Enright of Pittsburgh, Pa., and Merle D. Hay of Glidden, Iowa, members of Company F, 16th Infantry, First Division. They met death when the Germans raided the 16th Infantry's trenches near Bathelémont, France, on the nights of November 2-3, 1917. On November 3, 1917, General Bordeaux of the French Army commended their heroism and sacrifice.

American Army soldiers killed in World War I were Lieutenant William T. Fitzsimons and enlisted men Rudolph Rubino, Jr.,

THE FIRST

Oscar Le Tugo, and Leslie G. Woods, of U.S. Army Base Hospital No. 5, then operating No. 11 General Hospital, British Expeditionary Force, Dannes-Camiers, France. They were killed at 11 P.M. September 4, 1917, when enemy bombs exploded. *(Carlisle Barracks—In Memoriam—The Medical Department of the U.S. Army in the World War)*

American Army troopship in World War I torpedoed by the Germans was the S.S. "Tuscania" carrying 119 officers and 2,037 men. It was torpedoed and sunk, by the German Undersea Boat No. 77, February 15, 1918, off the north coast of Ireland, with a loss of 183 men.

American aviator shot down. *See* Aviation—Aviator: American aviator shot down in World War I

American combatant casualty in World War I was Corporal Bouligny, serving in the French Army, who was shot through the knee November 15, 1914. Bouligny was wounded while attacking a German outpost installed at the cemetery surrounding the mausoleum erected to Napoleon's soldiers who fell at the battle of Craonne in 1814.

American combatant to die in World War I was Edward Mandell Stone of Chicago, Ill. He was wounded February 17, 1915, and he died February 27, 1915. Living in Paris, he enlisted in the French Foreign Legion and was assigned to the second regiment. He served at Champagne and in the Aisne until mortally wounded. He was posthumously awarded the Croix de Guerre and the military medal.

American division in the trenches in World War I and the first in battle was the First Division, which entered the line October 21, 1917, in the Lunéville sector, near Nancy, France. Each unit was attached to a corresponding French unit. *(Records in Adjutant General's Office. War Department. Washington, D.C.)*

American flag flown in World War I. *See* Flag: American flag flown in World War I over a band of fighting Americans

American sailor to lose his life in World War I was John E. Eopolucci, who was killed when the steamship "Aztec" was torpedoed and sunk April 1, 1917. The sinking occurred five days before the War Risk Insurance Act went into effect.

American ship lost in World War I was the "William P. Frye," a steel sailing vessel of 3,374 gross tons, built in 1901 and owned by Arthur Sewall & Company of Maine. She cleared from Seattle, Wash., November 4, 1914,

THE FIRST

bound for Queenstown, Falmouth, or Plymouth, for orders, with a cargo consisting solely of 186,950 bushels of wheat. She was sunk January 28, 1915, by the German cruiser "Prinz Eitel Friedrich." *(Henry Ernest Dannack—Maine Book)*

American shot fired in World War I was fired at 6:05 A.M. October 23, 1917, by Battery C of the 6th Field Artillery. Sergeant Alexander Arch of South Bend, Ind., was in command of the crew that fired the shot.

American to sail to Europe to enlist in World War I was Denis Patrick Dowd, Jr., of Sea Cliff, Long Island, N.Y. He enlisted August 6, 1914, fought with the French Foreign Legion, was transferred to a line regiment when the battered Legion was withdrawn, was wounded, and upon recovery was transferred to the Lafayette Escadrille. He died August 11, 1916, when his plane crashed in a nose dive at Buc, near Paris, the day before he was to fly to the front. His body lies in the Memorial Cemetery of the Lafayette Escadrille in the Parc du Villeneuve l'Étang near St. Cloud, France. *(James Norman Hall and Charles Bernard Nordhoff—The Lafayette Flying Corps)*

American troop contingent to arrive in France was Base Hospital 4, which sailed from New York City on May 8, 1917. The group arrived at Liverpool, England, on May 18, 1917, and at Rouen, France, on May 25, 1917.

American troops to land in England in World War I were members of a group of 40 regular army officers, 17 reserve officers, 2 marine corps officers, 67 enlisted men, 36 field clerks, 20 civilians, 3 interpreters, and 3 correspondents. The group left New York City May 28, 1917, on the "Baltic" and docked at Liverpool, England, June 8, 1917. After spending some days in consultation with British authorities, they reached Paris June 13, 1917. General John Joseph Pershing was in command.

American troops to land in France in World War I were the members of the First Division, 346 officers and 11,607 men, who sailed from America on June 14, 1917, on the S.S. "Tenadores," and disembarked at St. Nazaire, France, June 26, 1917. The first group to land was Company K, 28th Infantry. Major General William Luther Sibert was the commanding general of the First Division from June 8 to December 14, 1917. *(Henry Russell Miller—The First Division)*

German spy to receive a death sentence from the American forces during World War I was Lothar Witzke, alias Pablo Waberski. On Friday August 16, 1918, he was brought to Fort Sam Houston, where a court-

WORLD WAR I—*Continued*
martial found him guilty and sentenced him to be hanged. On November 2, 1918 the death sentence was approved by Major DeRosey Carroll Cabell, commanding officer. On November 11, 1918, the armistice was signed and President Wilson gave orders that Witzke was not to be executed until he personally reviewed the findings. On May 27, 1920, the President confirmed the sentence but commuted it to "confinement at hard labor for the term of his natural life." On November 22, 1923, President Coolidge pardoned Witzke on the understanding that he leave the United States and never return. On November 29, 1923, Witzke sailed for Berlin.

Naval ace in World War I. *See* Aviation—Aviator: Naval ace in World War I

Night-flying scout group. *See* Aviation: War night-flying scout group

Pilot to receive the Congressional Medal of Honor. *See* Aviation—Aviator: Pilot to receive the Congressional Medal of Honor

Ship (American) attacked by a German submarine. *See* Ship: Ship (American) attacked by a German submarine

Shot fired by the American Navy in World War I was fired on April 7, 1917, at Guam Island. Commander William Alden Hall, U.S.N., in command of a prize crew, left the U.S.S. "Supply" about 6:30 A.M. (Guam time) and proceeded to the port town of Piti with orders to follow the Governor's Aide, who had boarded the interned German cruiser "Cormoran" under a flag of truce to demand its surrender. A German launch with a cutter in tow was sighted and a shot was fired across her bow by Corporal Michael B. Chickie, U.S.M.C. As the launch disregarded the warning, a second Marine was ordered to fire. After several shots the launch hove to and was ordered to Piti to surrender to the authorities there.

Shot fired by the American Navy in World War I against a known German submarine was fired on April 19, 1917, by the S.S. "Mongolia," a merchant ship captained by Emery Rice. Lieutenant Bruce Richardson Ware, U.S.N., of Massachusetts, was in command of the naval gun crew aboard the ship. The submarine submerged, and the result of the shot could not be ascertained.

Shots to land on American soil in World War I were fired July 21, 1918, by the German submarine U-156 at the tugboat "Perth Amboy" and four barges loaded with stone off Nauset Bluffs, Orleans, Mass. About seventy or eighty shots were fired three miles off shore. A few shots landed at Meeting House Pond, Mass. (*Henry Johnson James—German Subs in Yankee Waters*)

United States declaration of war against Germany (World War I) was made on April 6, 1917, and against Austria-Hungary on December 7, 1917. The United States was the thirteenth country to declare war against the Central Powers.

WORLD WAR II
Admiral killed in action in World War II. *See* Naval officer: Admiral killed in action in World War II

Air hero was Second Lieutenant George S. Welch of Wilmington, Del., who during the attack on December 7, 1941, shot down four Japanese airplanes at Oahu, Hawaiian Islands. He was awarded the Distinguished Service Cross at Wheeler Field, Hawaii, on December 16, 1941, and was congratulated by President Franklin Delano Roosevelt at the White House, Washington, D.C., on May 25, 1942. In thirty-three months he shot down eighteen enemy aircraft.

American bombardier over German-occupied territory was Bernard L. Bell, who, while assigned to a British group, flew in a Boston bomber escorted by Spitfires in a raid over Hazebrouck, France, June 29, 1942.

American bombing mission in the Orient took place December 9, 1941, when B-17 airplanes of the 19th Bombardment Group attacked enemy ships off the east coast of Vigan, Luzon, Philippine Islands.

American bombing mission over enemy-occupied territory in Europe took place July 4, 1942, when six American crews manned A-20 Boston bombers of the Royal Air Force. They were accompanied by six British-manned Bostons in a daylight attack against Nazi airfields at Alkmaar, Haamstede, and Valkenburg, in the Netherlands. Enemy planes, installations, and personnel were gunned and bombed.

American destroyer torpedoed was the "Kearny," under the command of Lieutenant Commander Anthony Leo Danis, which was attacked October 17, 1941, 350 miles southwest of Iceland. Eleven of the crew were killed, two were seriously wounded, and eight sustained minor wounds. The "Kearny" arrived at Iceland on October 19, 1941.

American destroyer torpedoed and sunk while on convoy duty in the North Atlantic was the "Reuben James," under the command of Lieutenant Commander Heywood Lane Edwards, on October 30, 1941. About 115 of the crew of 160 were reported dead or missing.

American expeditionary force to land in Africa was the 41st Engineers General Service Regiment, which landed June 17, 1942, at

Port Takoradi, Gold Coast, Africa. The first man to land was Private Napoleon Edward Taylor of Baltimore, Md., orderly of Major Charles S. Ward.

American expeditionary force to land on the European continent arrived January 26, 1942, in Ireland and was greeted by Sir Archibald Sinclair, British Air Minister. The first officer to land was Major General Russell Peter Hartle. The first enlisted man to land was Private Milburn Henke of Hutchinson, Minn.

American general killed in World War II was Major General Herbert Arthur Dargue, killed December 12, 1941, in an airplane which crashed en route to the Pacific area.

American general missing in action in World War II was Major General Clarence Leonard Tinker, missing in action off Midway, June 7, 1942, and declared dead June 7, 1943. He was posthumously awarded the Distinguished Service Medal on November 10, 1942.

American general wounded in action in World War II was Brigadier General Clinton Albert Pierce, commander of the 26th cavalry Philippine scouts, Fort Stotenburg, Philippine Islands, who was wounded February 4, 1942, at Bataan Peninsula while opposing the Japanese at Lingayen Gulf. He was subsequently held as a prisoner of war by the Japanese at Taiwan Camp, Formosa.

American offensive in the Pacific area was undertaken August 7, 1942, at Guadalcanal, Solomon Islands, by the Marines under Lieutenant General Alexander Archer Vandergrift. (*Richard Tregaskis—Guadalcanal Diary*)

American pilot to shoot down a German fighter plane in World War II (a victory which was confirmed) was Second Lieutenant Sam F. Junkin of Natchez, Miss., who shot down a Focke-Wulf-190 ship over Dieppe, France, in a Commando-Ranger raid on August 19, 1942. Junkin was wounded and jumped from his disabled plane. He was picked up by a returning Commando barge. On the same date a similar plane was shot down by Frank A. Hill of the 31st Fighter Group, but it was listed as "probably destroyed" since observers did not see the plane hit the ground or explode in the air, or see the pilot bail out.

American ship sunk by a U-boat was the "Robin Moor," 4,985 tons, operated by the Robin Line of New York, which sailed May 6, 1941, from New York City for Cape Town, South Africa, with eight passengers and a crew of thirty-eight under Captain Edward Myers. She was sunk May 21, 1941, in the South Atlantic, 400 miles south of the Cape Verde Islands and 900 miles due west of Monrovia, Liberia.

American to land on French soil in World War II was Corporal Franklin M. Koons of Swea City, Iowa, one of the Rangers, who accompanied Lieutenant Colonel Lord Lovat's Commandos on the Dieppe raid August 19, 1942. Koons destroyed a German 155-millimeter gun and was awarded the British Military Medal for "conspicuous gallantry and admirable leadership" on October 2, 1942.

Bombing on continental American soil occurred September 9, 1942, at Mount Emily, Oregon. One bomb crater was found, possibly caused by a Japanese plane or pilotless balloon.

German ship captured in World War II by an American ship was the "Busko," a 60-ton trawler, formerly Norwegian, which was captured at Mackenzie Bay, Greenland, on September 12, 1941, by the Coast Guard cutter "Northland," captained by Commander Carl Christian von Paulsen. The "Busko" had entered U.S. waters without proper documentation and had radioed weather reports and other information to Germany. After being captured the ship was sent under the escort of the Navy-manned U.S.S. "Bear" to Boston, Mass., where her crew—20 men and 1 woman —was held without bail. (*Rex Ingraham— First Fleet*)

Japanese attack in World War II was made Sunday, December 7, 1941, against Pearl Harbor, Hawaii. The United States loss was five battleships, three destroyers, a minelayer, and a target vessel sunk, as well as many ships damaged. About 400 airplanes were destroyed. American casualties of the sneak attack totaled 2,117 killed, 1,272 wounded, and 960 missing.

Japanese submarine sunk by an American ship was hit by a four-inch gun of the U.S.S. "Ward" on December 7, 1941, at Pearl Harbor, Hawaii.

Naval ace. *See* Aviation—Aviator: Naval ace in World War II

Sea battle fought solely by air power was the Battle of the Coral Sea, which took place May 4-8, 1942. American planes took off from carriers 180 miles away from each other. The Japanese loss was 39 ships, the United States loss the aircraft carrier "Lexington."

WORLD WAR BABY. *See* Births: World War baby

WORSTED MILL. *See* Wool: Worsted mill

WOUND CHEVRON. *See* Army insignia: Wound chevron

WOVEN WIRE FENCE INDUSTRY. *See* Wire: Woven wire fence industry

WRAPPING PAPER (perforated). *See* Paper: Perforated wrapping paper

WRECKING CRANE. *See* Crane: Wrecking crane

WRENCH
Pipe or screw wrench (practical) was the Stillson wrench, invented by Daniel C. Stillson of Somerville, Mass., who obtained patent No. 184,993 on December 5, 1876. In 1869 Stillson had whittled a model out of wood.

Wrench patent was obtained August 17, 1835, by Solyman Merrick of Springfield, Mass.

WRESTLING
Intercollegiate wrestling association was formed April 7, 1905, at the University of Pennsylvania, Philadelphia, through the efforts of Leonard Mason, an instructor in gymnastics, who visited other eastern universities to seek members. The first tournament, held April 7, 1905, in the gymnasium of the University of Pennsylvania, was witnessed by over a thousand spectators. Yale won, Columbia was second, Princeton third, and Pennsylvania fourth.

WRITER. *See* Author; Playwright (professional); Poet

WROUGHT IRON. *See* Bridge: Wrought iron lattice girder railroad bridge; Building: Building in which wrought iron beams were used; Sash: Wrought iron window sash installation

X-RAY
Fluoro-record reflector camera which made X-ray pictures in one-sixth the time previously required was announced November 18, 1950, by the Fairchild Camera & Instrument Corp., Jamaica, N.Y. The camera was used for gastro-intestinal surveys.

Photograph of a beam of 1 billion-volt X-rays. *See* Photograph: Photograph of a beam of 1 billion-volt X-rays

X-ray machine in the United States was exhibited January 18, 1896, at the Casino Cham-

bers, New York City. Viewers were charged 25 cents admission to see the "Parisian sensation."

X-ray moving picture process by which pictures could be taken over a considerable period of time without danger of overexposing the patient to radiation was developed by Dr. Russell Hedley Morgan of Johns Hopkins Hospital, Baltimore, Md., and demonstrated on February 1, 1951.

X-ray moving pictures (successful) of the action of the human heart, stomach, diaphragm, lungs, etc., were made with an amateur motion picture camera set in front of a fluoroscopic screen by Drs. William Holmes Stewart, William Joseph Hoffman, and Francis Henshall Ghiselin, all of New York City. The pictures were exhibited October 2, 1937, at a convention of the American Roentgen Ray Society held in New York City.

X-ray of the entire body of a living person made by one exposure was taken by Dr. William James Morton of New York City in April 1897. The film was a coated single sheet 3 feet by 6 feet. The apparatus employed was a 12-inch induction coil whose primary was supplied from the 117-volt Edison current. At a revolution of the break wheel (the rate was 5,000 a minute), the coil afforded a free discharge of sparks across a 5-inch air gap. The Crookes tube employed was an ordinary focus tube; its vacuum at the start corresponded to a spark of 2 inches and gradually rose until at the end it corresponded to 8 inches. The distance of the tube from the sensitive film, made by the Eastman Kodak Company, Rochester, N.Y., was 4 feet 6 inches. The tube was run steadily for the first ten minutes; then the current was turned off several times a minute to allow it to cool. The total time consumed, including stoppages, was thirty minutes. The heavier regions of the body, such as the pelvis, spine, and thighs, were underexposed, while the thinner portions, such as the hands, were overexposed. (*Electrical Engineer. May 19, 1897*)

X-ray photograph was made January 12, 1896, by Dr. Henry Louis Smith, professor of physics and astronomy, Davidson College, Davidson, N.C. Smith obtained the hand of a corpse, fired a bullet into it, and then took a 15-minute exposure which, when developed, revealed the exact location of the bullet.

X-ray photograph of the entire body taken in a one-second exposure made under ordinary clinical conditions available to the average hospital or average radiographer, and the first in which a selective filter was used, was a full-length, full-size, one-piece radiograph of a living human body taken July 1, 1934, by Arthur Wolfram Fuchs of the Eastman Kodak

Company, Rochester, N.Y. The size of the film was 32 by 72 inches. The radiograph was exhibited by the Chicago Roentgen Society at the Century of Progress Exposition, Chicago, Ill.

X-ray photograph showing the complete arterial circulation in an adult individual was completed July 16, 1936, in Rochester, N.Y., by Dr. Edmond John Faris of the Wistar Institute of Anatomy and Biology, Philadelphia, Pa., and Arthur Wolfram Fuchs of the Medical Division, Eastman Kodak Company, Rochester, N.Y. A radio-opaque medium was injected into the arteries of a cadaver by Faris. Fuchs made several entire-body radiographs on film 32 by 72 inches, employing the following technical factors: 70 kilovolts, 10 milliamperes, 30 seconds of exposure at a distance of 12 feet. Ultra-speed X-ray intensifying screens, 32 by 72 inches, were also used in a large cassette made to accommodate the film and screen.

X-RAY FIELD HOSPITAL AUTOMOBILE. *See* Automobile: Field hospital automobile with X-ray equipment

"Y" BRIDGE. *See* Bridge: "Y" bridge

YACHT. *See* Ship: Yacht

YACHT CLUB was the New York Yacht Club, organized July 30, 1844, by four yachting enthusiasts in the cabin of John Cox Stevens' schooner "Gimcrack." The first regular election of officers was held March 17, 1845, at which time Stevens was elected commodore, a post which he held until 1855. In 1846 a club house was erected at the Elysian Fields, Hoboken, N.J. It was towed to Glen Cove, Long Island, N.Y., in 1904 and officially reopened July 6, 1904. In 1848 the Secretary of the Navy allowed the vessels of the club—sloops and schooners—to proceed from port to port in the United States without entering or clearing at the Custom House, provided that they did not transport merchandise for pay (Act of August 7, 1848). The signal of the club was a pointed burgee, with a five-pointed white star in the center and two red stripes crossing on a field of blue. The Boston Yacht Club, founded in 1835, with Captain R. B. Forbes as commodore, was chiefly a fishing organization. It went out of existence in 1837. (*Charles A. Peverelly—Book of American Pastimes*)

YACHT (ice). *See* Ice yacht

YACHT RACE
See also Boat race

Regatta of importance was held by the New York Yacht Club, New York City, July 16, 1845. The following contestants entered

the competition: the "Cygnet," 45 tons; the "Sybil," 42 tons; the "Spray," 37 tons; the "Newburg," 33 tons; the "Minra," 30 tons; the "Coquille," 27 tons; the "Gimcrack," 25 tons; the "Lancet," 20 tons; and the "Ada," 17 tons. The yachts raced in the waters of New York from Robbin's Reef to Bay Ridge, thence to Stapleton, thence to the Southwest Spit buoy, and then back to the starting point.

Yacht race across the Atlantic Ocean was held December 11, 1866. An agreement was entered into October 27, 1866, by which three contestants each put up a $30,000 purse, the winner to receive $90,000. The competing yachts were the "Henrietta," 205 tons, owned by James Gordon Bennett, Jr.; the "Vesta," 201 tons, owned by Pierre Lorillard; and the "Fleetwing," 212 tons, owned by George Osgood. The "Henrietta" was the winner, making the trip in 13 days and 22 hours. (*Charles A. Peverelly—Book of American Pastimes*)

Yacht race (international) was held August 22, 1851, under the auspices of the Royal Yacht Squadron around the Isle of Wight, a distance of 53 miles. The race was won by an American yacht, "America," owned by a syndicate headed by Commodore John Cox Stevens of the New York Yacht Club. She was designed by George Steers and built by William Henry Brown of New York. She was 101 feet 9 inches over all, and 90 feet 3 inches at the water line. She had a beam of 23 feet 11 inches. Her foremast measured 79 feet 6 inches and her mainmast 81 feet. Her total sail area was 5,263 square feet. She carried three sails—jib, foresail, and mainsail. She was planked with white oak and coppered below the water line. The "America" covered the course in 10 hours and 37 minutes, defeating 14 other contestants. She received a trophy valued at 100 pounds sterling and known as the Queen's Cup, in honor of Queen Victoria. (*Herbert Lawrence Stone and Alfred Fullerton Loomis—Millions for Defense, a Pictorial History of the Races for the America's Cup*)

Yacht race (international) broadcast. *See* Radio broadcast: Yacht race broadcast

"YANKEE DOODLE" verses were written in 1755 by Dr. Richard Shuckburgh, regimental surgeon of General Braddock, to accompany an ancient tune. The verses were written at Fort Crailo, Albany, N.Y., in derision of the "homely clad colonials," but later the song was taken up by the colonists themselves. The song was played at Yorktown at the surrender of Cornwallis. It was the first patriotic song to achieve national popularity. (*Burton Alva Konkle—Benjamin Chew*)

YARN (stretch). *See* Nylon: Nylon stretch yarn

YEAST
Compressed fresh yeast was introduced in 1868 by Charles Fleischmann, whose firm, Gaff, Fleischmann & Company, manufactured it in Riverside, near Cincinnati, Ohio.

Yeast preparation patent was No. 40,451, which was granted on November 3, 1863, to J. T. Alden of Cincinnati, Ohio, on "an improvement in the preparation of yeast."

YELLOW FEVER VACCINE. *See* Vaccine: Yellow fever vaccine for human immunization

YIDDISH NEWSPAPER. *See* Newspaper: Yiddish daily newspaper

YIDDISH PROFESSORSHIP was established on February 11, 1952, at Columbia University, New York City. The first incumbent was Uriel Weinreich, Associate in Yiddish Language, Literature and Culture.

YOUNG MEN'S CHRISTIAN ASSOCIATION
Young Men's Christian Association was organized on December 29, 1851, in Boston, Mass. (On December 9, 1851, a YMCA had been organized in Montreal, Canada.) The YMCA was patterned after a similar organization started in London on June 6, 1844. The first international convention was held in Boston, June 7, 1854. The first well-equipped gymnasium was opened in New York City in 1869 and in the same year the first separate boys' department was opened in Salem, Mass. *(Samuel Lowry—Historical Sketch of the Progress of the Young Men's Christian Associations in North America)*

Young Men's Christian Association for Negro members was organized in Washington, D.C., in 1853 by Anthony Bowen and Jerome Johnson, who served respectively as president and secretary. The first paid secretary was William Alphaeus Hunton, a Negro, who received $800 a year for his services from the Norfolk, Va., YMCA in January 1888. *(Addie Waite Hunton—William Alphaeus Hunton)*

YOUNG MEN'S HEBREW ASSOCIATION
was founded on March 22, 1874, in New York City. It was incorporated on September 15, 1875. The first president was Lewis May, who served from May 3, 1874, to February 15, 1876.

YOUNG WOMEN'S CHRISTIAN ASSOCIATION
originated as a local organization in Boston, Mass., in 1866. The first president

was Mrs. Henry Fowle Durant. In 1858 an organization called "The Ladies Christian Association" was formed in New York City, and a branch of this group was later called the YWCA. In 1871 the local eastern associations met in national convention in Hartford, Conn., and in 1886 a central group met in Lake Geneva, Wis. These two national organizations came together as the YWCA of the U.S. of A. of which the present National Board is the executive body. The first president of the national YWCA was Grace Hoadley Dodge of New York City and the first convention of the present national organization was held in New York City December 5-6, 1906.

YOUNG WOMEN'S HEBREW ASSOCIATION
was organized on February 6, 1902, in New York City. Mrs. Israel Unterberg was the founder and the first president. The first building used by the organization was at 1584 Lexington Avenue, New York City. *(Young Women's Hebrew Association—Annual Report 1903)*

YOUTH HOSTEL
was opened December 27, 1934, in Northfield, Mass., as headquarters of the American Youth Hostels, Inc., incorporated March 15, 1934, in Hartford, Conn. The organization was the eighteenth group in the International Youth Hostels. Isabel and Monroe Smith were appointed directors of the American group. *(The Knapsack. November 1935)*

YOUTH'S LIBRARY. *See* Library: Youth's library

ZINC
Underground mill for the separation of zinc and lead by the flotation process was completed in 1929 at the New Jersey Zinc Company's mine under Battle Mountain at Gilman, Colo. The mine is air-conditioned and fireproof and has its own water system, an elevator, and 100 miles of steel track. Ore is hauled to a central point at the 450-foot level, where it is ground into small particles to enable the flotation milling process to separate the ore into zinc and lead concentrates.

Zinc was produced in 1835-1836 by John Hitz in the Arsenal at Washington, D.C. *(Heinrich Oscar Hofman—Metallurgy of Zinc and Cadmium)*

Zinc commercial production was undertaken at the Pennsylvania and Lehigh Zinc Company Mill, which was erected in Bethlehem, Pa., October 13, 1853, by Samuel Wetherill. The company was incorporated May 2, 1855. The zinc was obtained from calamine ores. *(Joseph Mortimer Levering—History of Bethlehem, Pa.)*

THE FIRST

Zinc patent for the process of reducing zinc ore was No. 16,362, granted to Samuel Wetherill of Bethlehem, Pa., on January 6, 1857. On February 20, 1855, Wetherill received patent No. 12,418 for an apparatus for separating zinc white, and on November 13, 1855, patent No. 13,806 for the process of making zinc white. He patented a zinc white furnace on September 30, 1856 (No. 15,830). On January 7, 1868, he obtained patent No. 73,146 for the process of manufacturing white oxide of zinc.

Zinc sheet mill was erected in Bethlehem, Pa., and the first production begun in March 1865. (*Clifford Dyer Holley—Lead and Zinc in the United States*)

ZIONIST SOCIETY
Zionist national organization was the United American Zionists, formed October 22, 1897, in New York City by ten local societies. The first convention was held July 4, 1898, in New York City. Local Zionist societies, Chovevi (Hovevai) Zion or Hibat Zion (Love of Zion) groups, without political aims, had been formed as early as 1882 and had advocated Palestine colonization.

"ZIPPER." *See* Fastening: Hookless fastening

ZOOLOGICAL GARDEN
Barless zoological garden of naturalistic rock construction was started in 1915 at the City Park Zoo, Denver, Colo., and was completed in 1918 at a cost of $60,000. The materials used were colored concrete and steel. This "Mountain Habitat" was designed and supervised by Victor Borcherdt, the director

THE FIRST

of the zoo. This barless zoo was not a pit, the floors of the enclosures being on ground level or above the outside walkway.

Zoological garden was the Philadelphia Zoological Garden, Philadelphia, Pa., which was under the management of the Zoological Society of Philadelphia. The society was incorporated March 21, 1859. The garden was opened to the public July 1, 1874. Feature attractions were the bear pit and the lion house. (*Roger Conant—Official Illustrated Guide to the Philadelphia Zoological Garden*)

ZOOLOGICAL LABORATORY (U.S.)
Zoological laboratory (U.S.) for the study of parasites of man was started August 16, 1902, by the Public Health Service simultaneously with the appointment of Dr. Charles Wardell Stiles as chief of the division of zoology at the Hygienic Laboratory (now the National Institute of Health), Washington, D.C.

Zoological laboratory (U.S.) for the study of the parasites of livestock was opened August 1, 1886, in Washington, D.C., in the Bureau of Animal Industry of the Department of Agriculture. Dr. Cooper Curtice, the first person placed in charge of the work by the federal government, entered the service August 1, 1886. The appellation "zoological laboratory" was not applied, however, until June 3, 1891, when Dr. Charles Wardell Stiles was placed in charge, with Dr. Albert Hassall as his assistant. In 1901, the laboratory received the classification of a division. Dr. Brayton Howard Ransom was put in charge of the division June 1, 1903.

"ZOOM" LENS. *See* Lens: Lens to provide zoom effects

Index by Years

To obtain a complete account of the various items, the reader should consult the main body of the text. The **boldface** type shows the alphabetical heading under which each item may be found. If an item appears in the text under a general heading, the specific heading is noted below after the general heading.

1007

Births—child born of European parents on American soil—Snorro

1493

Letter—letter descriptive of America— dispatched—March 14
War—bloodshed in the new world

1507

"America"—used as a geographical designation—April
Map—globular map published showing the western hemisphere—Alsace

1524

Kidnapping—recorded in letter—July 8

1526

Catholic Mass—Catholic Mass—June

1540

Baptism—Ocmulgee River, Ga.—March

1541

Discovery—discovery of the Mississippi River by a European—H. de Soto—May

1542

Discovery—discovery of land on the United States Pacific Coast—J. R. Cabrillo—landed—Sept. 28

1543

Flood—Mississippi River—March 18

1562

Ship—ship built to cross the Atlantic Ocean

1564

Artist—artist to arrive in America—Jacques Le Moyne de Morgues—Florida

1565

Billiards—brought to America—St. Augustine, Fla.
Births—white child born of French Protestant parentage—Fort Caroline, Fla.
Catholic Parish—founded—St. Augustine, Fla.—Sept. 8
Catholic Settlement—St. Augustine, Fla.
Colonist—permanent white settlement in America—St. Augustine, Fla.
Treaty—treaty violation—Oct. 15
War (colonial)—intercolonial war—Spain vs. France—Sept. 20

1579

Book—book of Common Prayer used—June 24
Protestant Episcopal Church—Christian religious service in English—San Francisco, Calif.—Francis Fletcher—June 24

1585

Artist—English artist—John White
Letter—letters written in English—Aug. 12
Surveyor—Thomas Hariot—landed

1587

Beer—brewed—Virginia
Births—child born of English parents in America—Virginia Dare—Aug. 18
Indians — Indian convert (Protestant) — Manteo—Aug. 13

1588

Map—map of a city—St. Augustine, Fla.

1602

Discovery—discovery of New England by an Englishman—B. Gosnold—landed—South Dartmouth, Mass.—May 15

1604

Colonist—colonial white settlement (north of Fla.)—Calais, Me.

1607

Catholic Bishop—visited Florida
Colonial Government—colonial council in America—Jamestown, Va.—May 13
Colonist — English settlement in America —Jamestown, Va.—May 13
Holiday — Thanksgiving Day service — Phippsburg, Me.—Aug. 9
Protestant Episcopal Church — Protestant Episcopal Church—established—first Eucharist—May 9
Rebellion—rebellion (colonial)—led by George Kendall—Jamestown, Va.
Ship—ship built by the English in the American colonies—launched—Maine
Slander Proceedings—instituted—John Robinson—Jamestown, Va.—Sept. 17
War (colonial)—Indian war of importance fought by English colonists—Virginia—May 27

1608

Bottle—blown
Glass Bead—manufactured—Jamestown, Va.
Glass Factory—glass factory—established—Jamestown, Va.—Oct.

1609

Animals—sheep—imported—Jamestown, Va.
Maize—Indian corn grown—Jamestown, Va.
Wedding—wedding in Virginia—Anne Burras and John Laydon

1610

Physician—doctor in the colony of Virginia —Lawrence Bohune—arrived

1611

Presbyterian Church—Presbyterian Church —established—Virginia

1612

Tobacco— tobacco—cultivation—Jamestown, Va.

1613

Navy—naval expedition (colonial)—Samuel Argal
War (colonial)—colonial warfare between England and France for the possession of North America

1614

Lottery—of importance—Virginia—June 26
Ship—decked ship—launched—New York— "Onrust"—A. Blok

1616

Epidemic—smallpox epidemic

1617

College—college proposed — Henrico, Va.

1619

Blue Law—blue law—enacted—Virginia
Iron—iron works—erected —Falling Creek, Va.
Legislative Assembly — Jamestown, Va.— July 30
Slavery—slaves — introduced — Jamestown, Va.—Aug.

1620

Congregational Church — Congregational Church founded—Plymouth, Mass.
Lead—mined—Falling Creek, Va.
Physician—doctor in New England — Dr. Samuel Fuller—arrived—Mass.—Dec. 21
Water Power — water power development grant—South Berwick, Me.

1621

Duel—duel—E. Leister and E. Dotey—Plymouth, Mass.—June 18
Furs—exported—Robert Cushman—Massachusetts—Dec. 13
Military Leader—Miles Standish—Massachusetts
Sermon Printed (American)—delivered— Plymouth, Mass. — Robert Cushman — [published—Boston, Mass.—1724]
Treaty—colonial treaty with the Indians— Plymouth, Mass.—April 1
Wedding—wedding in New England—Edward Winslow and Susanna White—May 22

1622

Indians—Indian massacre of white people Jamestown, Va.—March 22
Potato—introduced—Jan.
Prohibition—prohibition enforcement officers —authorized—Virginia—June 21

1623

Breach of Promise Suit—Virginia—June 14
Leather—leather tanning—Plymouth, Mass. —Experience Miller
Liquor Reform Movement—New York City
Silk—silk culture—started
Temperance Law (colonial)—Virginia— March 5

1624

Animals—cows—imported—Massachusetts— March
Blue Law—blue law regulating gambling— Virginia

1625

Road—road pavement—laid—Pemaquid, Me.

1626

Book—profane poetry translation prepared in the colonies to be published—Virginia
Forestry Legislation—colonial forestry legislation—March 29

1627

Oil—oil spring — recorded — Cuba, N.Y.— July 18

1628

Deportation—Thomas Morton — deported— June 9
Fur Trading Post — established — Augusta, Me.
Reformed Church (Dutch) — established — New York City—1628
Shoe — manufactured — Massachusetts — Thomas Beard

1629

Agriculture—crop limitation law—enacted— Virginia—Oct. 16
Apples—imported—John Winthrop
Brick Kiln—established—Salem, Mass.
Fishery (commercial) — established — Medford, Mass.—April 17
Game Law—game law (colonial)—enacted— Virginia—March 24
Horse—horses—imported

1630

Execution—execution in America—John Billington—hanged—Plymouth, Mass.—Sept. 30
Fork—introduced — Massachusetts — John Winthrop
Gambling Legislation (colonial)—enacted— Boston, Mass.—March 22
Popcorn—introduced
Salt—salt works—established—Virginia

1631

Election — accredited colonial election — Massachusetts—May 18
Fire Prevention Legislation—enacted—Cambridge, Mass.—March 17

1632

Pirate—Dixie Bull—looted Bristol, Me.
Road — highway legislation (colonial) — James City, Va.—Sept. 4
Tobacco—tobacco tax (colonial) — Mass. — enacted—Oct. 3
Windmill—windmill — erected —Cambridge, Mass.

1633

Building—brick building—New York City
School—school in America—New York City

1634

Bridge—bridge—erected—Dorchester, Mass.
Club Woman—Anne Hutchinson—arrived— Boston, Mass.—Sept. 18
Educational Endowment—established—Virginia—Benjamin Syms
Tax—property tax law (colonial)—enacted —Massachusetts—May 14
Treason—treason trial (colonial)—Virginia —May 7

1635

Cod Liver Oil—described
Hurricane—recorded — Plymouth, Mass.— Aug. 15
Public School—public school with a continuous existence—established—Feb. 13

1636

College—college — Harvard College—Cambridge, Mass.—established—Sept. 8
Insurance—government insurance—enacted —Plymouth Colony
Meat Packer—Wm. Pynchon—warehouse— Springfield, Mass.
Pension—pension act—Massachusetts—Pilgrims

1637

Club Woman—Anne Hutchinson—banished —Massachusetts—Nov. 17
Congregational Church — Congregational Church council—Cambridge, Mass.—Aug. 30
Conscription—colonial conscription legislation—enacted—Boston, Mass.—April 18
Prostitute—recorded

1638

Almanac— almanac—published—Cambridge, Mass.
Cloth—cloth mill—John Pearson—Rowley, Mass.
Curfew Bell—introduced—New York City
Earthquake—earthquake description—Plymouth, Mass.—June 1
Military Organization—military organization — Ancient and Honorable Artillery Company—Boston, Mass.—chartered — March 13
Swedes—arrived—Delaware—March

1639

Agriculture—crop surplus destruction—Virginia—Jan. 6
Autopsy—autopsy—Salem, Mass.—Sept.
Baptist Church — Baptist Church — established—Providence, R.I.
Bookseller — of importance — Hezekiah Usher—Cambridge, Mass.

Canal—canal for creating water power—construction ordered—Dedham, Mass.—March 25

Constitution—constitution — "fundamental orders"—Connecticut—Jan. 14

Lawyer—lawyer disbarred — Thomas Lechford—Massachusetts—Sept. 3

Medical Legislation—medical law—Virginia —Oct. 21

Ordnance—gunpowder mill—Pecoit, Mass.—land grant—June 6

Post Office—post office (colonial)—established—Boston, Mass.—Nov. 5

Printing—document printed in America — *Oath of a Free Man*—Cambridge, Mass.—March

Printing Press—printing press — imported —Cambridge, Mass.—March

Public School—public school supported by direct taxation—established—May 20

1640

Author—woman author—Anne Bradstreet —poems published

Book—book (full size) — published — Cambridge, Mass.

Election—election in defiance of the Royal Courts — Wethersfield, Conn.—April 11

Hebrew Type—used—Cambridge, Mass.

Lutheran Church—Lutheran pastor—Reorus Torkillus—landed—April 17

Music Book — hymn book — published— Cambridge, Mass.

1641

Children's Book—published—*Milk for Babes* —Cambridge, Mass.

Fair—annual fair — authorized — New York City—Sept. 30

Patent—patent granted by the colonies — Mass.—Samuel Winslow

Potter—John Pride—Salem, Mass.

1642

City (incorporated) — Georgeana, Me. — March 1

College—college — Harvard College, Cambridge, Mass.—commencement—Sept. 23

Degrees (academic and honorary)—Bachelor of Arts degree—conferred—Harvard College—Cambridge, Mass.—Sept. 23

Education — compulsory education law — enacted—Mass.—June 14

Labor Law—convict labor law — enacted — March 2

Thesis Directory—published — Cambridge, Mass.

1643

Catholic Priest—native Catholic priest — joined Jesuit order

Colonial Government—colonial government union—organized—Boston, Mass.—May 10

Dictionary—Indian-English dictionary—published

Extradition—extradition—agreement— New England Confederation

Iron—iron works (successful)—constructed —John Winthrop, Jr.

Spelling Book—published—Cambridge, Mass.

Wool—fulling mill — established—Rowley, Mass.

1644

Branding Legislation—enacted—Connecticut —Feb. 5

Legislature—legislature with two chambers —Massachusetts—March 7

Whaling—whaling (systematic)—Southampton, L.I.—undertaken—March 7

1645

Brass and Iron Foundry — opened — Joseph Jencks—Lynn, Mass.

Lutheran Church—Lutheran Church building—dedicated—Essington, Pa.—Sept. 4

School—endowed school—established—Roxbury, Mass.

School Committee — elected — Dorchester, Mass.

1646

Bounty—authorized—James City, Va.—Oct. 5

Patent—machine patent—granted—Massachusetts—Joseph Jencks—March 6

1647

Quarantine—quarantine legislation (colonial)—enacted—Massachusetts—March

Rice—imported—Virginia

School Law (compulsory)—enacted—Nov. 11

Witchcraft Execution—Achsah Young — Massachusetts—May 27

Woman Suffrage—woman suffrage advocate —Margaret Brent—demanded vote—June 24

1648

Labor Union—labor organization — authorized—Boston, Mass.—Oct. 18

Latin Book—written in New England—published—London, England

Law Book—compilation of colonial laws— published—Cambridge, Mass.

1649

Election Law—fraudulent election law (colonial)—enacted—Warwick, R.I.—May 22

Medical Legislation—law to regulate the practice of medicine (colonial)—enacted— Massachusetts—May 3

Missionary Society—missionary society (colonial)—chartered—July

Religious Liberty Act (colonial)—established—Maryland—April

1650

Corporation—corporate body — Cambridge, Mass.—May 30
Expedition—expedition—of Englishmen to cross the Allegheny Mountains—commenced—Aug. 27
Iron—exportation of iron
Pound (enclosure for animals)—authorized —Connecticut—May

1651

Navigation Act—enacted

1652

Money—dies for coins in America—mint established—Boston, Mass.—May 27
Slavery—law regulating slavery—enacted— Warwick, R.I.—May 18
Traffic Regulation—traffic law — enacted — New York City—June 27
Water—municipal water supply system— built—Boston, Mass.

1654

Bridge—toll bridge — erected — Rowley, Mass.
Fire Engine—fire engine—manufactured— Lynn, Mass.—Joseph Jencks
Jews—Jew—arrived—New York City—Jacob Barsimson—Aug. 22
Orphanage—orphanage—established — New York City—June

1655

Jewish Congregation—Jewish Congregation —Shearith Israel—New York City—established

1656

Cemetery—Jewish burial plot — New York City
Jury—jury composed of women—Patuxent, Md.—Sept. 22
Physician—Jewish doctor—Jacob Lumbrozo —Maryland—Jan. 24
Quakers—Quakers to arrive in America— Massachusetts—July

1657

Autopsy—autopsy and verdict of a coroner's jury—recorded—Maryland—Sept. 24
College Student—college student to work his way through college—Z. Brigden
Jews—Jew to win all the rights and perform all the duties of citizenship—Asser Levy —April 20
Road—stone pavement—laid—New York City
Shoe Measuring Stick—introduced

1659

Fire Department—fire department established by municipal action—New York City

1660

Indian Church—Indian church — Natick, Mass.
Quakers—Quakers' annual meeting—Scituate, Mass.

1661

Bible—Bible in an Indian language—John Eliot — New Testament — Cambridge, Mass.
Medal—Indian medals—authorized—Virginia
School—evening school—established — New York City

1662

Book Auction—authorized—New York City —April 18
Lime—manufactured—Providence, R.I.—Jan. 27
Poet—American poet—Benjamin Tompson —graduated—Cambridge, Mass.

1663

Bible—Bible in Indian language—published —John Eliot
Book Binder—John Ratliffe—Massachusetts

1664

Citizenship—naturalization act—New York —March 12

1665

Book—book privately printed — *Communion of Churches*—Cambridge, Mass.
Horse Race—horse race—on a regular basis Hempstead Plains, N.Y.
Play (drama)—play given by non-professional actors—Accomac (Accawmack), Va.—Aug. 27

1666

Brokerage — financial "corner"—New York City
Grammar—Indian grammar — published — Cambridge, Mass.

1669

Engraving—engraving—wood cut — John Foster—April 22
History—history of New England — *New England's Memoriall* — published — Cambridge, Mass.
Primer—primer in an American Indian dialect — *Indian Primer* — published — Cambridge, Mass.
Rebellion—rebellion of colonists against the English—Marcus Jacobson—condemned— —Dec. 20

1670

Indians—Indian preacher — Hiacoomes—ordained—Aug. 22

1671

Baptist Church — Seventh Day Baptist Church—organized—Newport, R.I.

1672

Copyright Law—copyright law—passed—Massachusetts—May 15
Tax—tax on the American colonies without their consent

1673

Coal—coal—discovered—Louis Hennepin
Governor — native-born governor of New England—Josiah Winslow—elected
Postal Service—postal route—New York and Boston—service commenced—Jan. 22

1674

Horse Race—horse race prohibition legislation—Massachusetts

1675

Catholic Holy Orders—conferred—St. Augustine, Fla.—Aug. 24
Corporation—commercial corporation—New York—Jan. 8

1676

Court Martial—court martial trial—Newport, R.I.—Aug. 24
Fire—fire of serious consequence—Boston, Mass.—Nov. 27
Insane Patient's Maintenance Act—Upland Court, Delaware County, Pa.
Prison—prison — constructed — Nantucket, Mass.

1677

Map—map made in the United States published in a book—Boston, Mass.
Medical Book—medical pamphlet—published—Boston, Mass.

1679

Ship—Great Lakes commercial vessel—"Le Griffon"—sailed—Aug. 7
Trust—manufacturers' price regulation agreement—New York City—Dec. 17

1680

Pottery—pottery—established — Burlington, N.J.

1681

Shorthand Report—of a trial—St. John's, Md.—Nov. 15

1682

Educational Trust Fund—created—Burlington, N.J.
Freemasons—Mason—arrived—John Skene—Burlington, N.J.
Tornado—recorded—New Haven, Conn.—June 10

1683

Architect—landscape architect — John Reid arrived—New York City—Dec. 19
Bible Concordance—published—Cambridge, Mass.
Labadist Community — established — Bohemia Manor, Md.
Mennonites—Mennonites — arrived — Philadelphia, Pa.—Oct. 6
Science Association—scientific society—Boston Philosophical Society founded

1685

Impeachment—impeachment—Nicolas More—Philadelphia, Pa.

1686

Church of England—Church of England organized in New England

1687

Knighthood—knighthood conferred on a native-born American—William Phips—June 28
Law Book—law book—William Penn—published—Philadelphia, Pa.
Tax—inheritance tax (colonial)—Virginia

1688

Slavery—slavery protest—Philadelphia, Pa.—Feb. 18

1689

Newspaper—newspaper — broadside — published—Cambridge, Mass.
Schoolbook—*New England Primer*—published—Boston, Mass.

1690

Indigo—planted—South Carolina
Loan — state loan — authorized — Massachusetts—Dec. 10
Money—paper money—issued—Massachusetts—Feb. 3
Newspaper — newspaper publisher — *Publick Occurrances*—published — Boston, Mass.—Sept. 25
Paper Mill—built—William Rittenhouse—Philadelphia, Pa.
Play (drama)—play of note written by an American and acted in America—performed—Cambridge, Mass.

Theological Treatise—F. D. Pastorius—published—Philadelphia, Pa.

Watermark—William Rittenhouse—Philadelphia, Pa.

1691

Treason—American colonist hanged for treason—Jacob Leisler — hanged — New York City—May 16

1692

Degrees (academic and honorary)—Doctor of Sacred Theology degree -- granted — Cambridge, Mass.

Patent Medicine Advertisement—*Boston Almanack*

Postal Service—parliamentary act to establish a post office

Postmaster—postmaster general (colonial) —Andrew Hamilton—appointed—April 4

1693

College—college charter granted by the crown—College of William and Mary—Feb. 8

College—college proposed—College of William and Mary—incorporated—Feb. 8

Police—police uniforms—authorized—New York City—July 8

1694

Ancient Mystical Order Rosae Crucis — established—Philadelphia, Pa.

College—college to receive a coat-of-arms from the College of Heralds—May 14

Lutheran Church—Lutheran services in English—Philadelphia, Pa.

1695

Wool—worsted mill—Boston, Mass.

Workmen's Compensation—workmen's compensation agreement—Jan. 26

1696

Book—book intended for circulation in the English colonies—printed

Woman—woman printer—Dinah Nuthead—Annapolis, Md.—petition—May 5

1697

Bridge—stone bridge—Germantown, Pa.

Fire Department—fire department to be paid —New York City

Woman—heroine—publicly rewarded—Hannah Duston—captured—Haverhill, Mass.

1698

Capitol—statehouse—Williamsburg, Va.

Library—library—established — Charleston, S.C.

Map—road map for public use—printed—John Tulley—Boston, Mass.

1699

Chimes—chimes and bells—manufactured—Benjamin Hanks—Plymouth, Mass.

1700

Organ—organs imported—Port Royal and Philadelphia, Pa.

1701

Engraving—engraving of any artistic merit —Thomas Emmes — published — Boston, Mass.

1703

Business Manual—*Young Secretary's Guide*—published—Boston, Mass.

Lutheran Church—Lutheran pastor ordained in America—Justus Falckner—ordained—Nov. 24

1704

Advertisement—advertisement—Boston, Mass. —*News-Letter*—May 1

Freemasons—Mason (native born)—Jonathan Belcher

Newspaper—newspaper (successful) — Boston, Mass. *News-Letter*—April 17

1705

Book—miniature book—*A Wedding Ring*—published—Boston, Mass.

Copper Mine—worked—Granby, Conn.

Presbyterian Presbytery—assembled—Philadelphia, Pa.

1706

Customhouse—Yorktown, Va.

1707

Artist—woman painter

1708

Mennonites—Mennonite church meetinghouse—built—Philadelphia, Pa.

1709

Copper Mine—company formed—Granby, Conn.

Grammar—Latin grammar textbook—published—Boston, Mass.

Hospital—insane detention home—erected—Philadelphia, Pa.

1710

Agricultural Book — agricultural book — *The Husbandman's Guide* — published — Boston, Mass.

Farrier's Guide—published—Boston, Mass.

Forest—community forest—Newington, N.H.

Iron—iron slitting mill—established—Milton, Mass.

1711

Whale—sperm whale—captured

1712

Calico—printery — established — Boston, Mass.

1713

Book Auction Catalog—book auction catalog—announced—May 18

Paleontology Report — prepared — Cotton Mather

1714

Play (drama)—printed American play—*Androboros*—published—New York City

Ship—schooner built in America—launched—Gloucester, Mass.

1715

Book—Book of Common Prayer (in the Mohawk Indian language)—New York City

Indians—Indian league of nations—Tuscaroras joined

Lighthouse—lighthouse authorized—Massachusetts—July 23

Patent—English patent granted to a resident of America—Thomas Masters—Nov. 25

Whaling—whaling expedition—sailed—Nantucket, Mass.

1716

Animals—lion—exhibited—Boston, Mass.—Nov. 26

Lighthouse—lighthouse — erected — Little Brewster Island, Mass.—Sept. 14

Theater—theater—land leased—William Levingston—Nov. 5

1717

Book Auction Catalog—book auction printed catalog—sale—July 2

1718

Theater—theater—built—Williamsburg, Va.

1719

Arithmetic—arithmetic—printed in the colonies

Aurora Borealis—recorded—Dec. 11

Potato—potato cultivation—Derry, N.H.

1720

Indian School—Indian school (permanent)—established—Williamsburg, Va.

1721

Animals—camel imported—Boston, Mass.—advertised—Oct. 2

Art Commission (public)—work ordered—Prince Georges County, Md.—Sept. 5

Insurance—fire insurance agent—John Copson—Philadelphia, Pa.—advertised—May 25

Music Book—music book printed with bars—published

Music Book—vocal instruction book—John Tufts—Boston, Mass.—published

Newspaper—newspaper editorial apology—*American Weekly Mercury* — published — April 20

Vaccination for smallpox—inoculations introduced—Zabdiel Boylston—June 26

1722

Art Commission (public)—work completed—Prince George's County, Md.—Nov. 26

Divinity Professor—E. Wigglesworth—appointed—Cambridge, Mass.—Jan. 24

1723

Baptist Church—German Baptists—immersion—Philadelphia—Dec. 25

Physician—doctor to receive an honorary medical degree—Daniel Turner—Sept. 11

1724

Grammar—English grammar by an American—Hugh Jones—published—London

Levees—built—New Orleans, La.

Sermon Printed (American)—Robert Cushman—reprinted—Boston, Mass.

1725

Indians—Indian scalping—New Hampshire—Feb. 20

Insurance Book—insurance proposal — *Ways and Means* . . .—published — Philadelphia, Pa.

Library—library building—used exclusively as a library—Philadelphia, Pa.

1726

Bibliography—bibliography of theological and biblical literature—published—Boston, Mass.

Book—book of folio size—*Compleat Body of Divinity* . . .—published—Boston, Mass.

1727

Convent—convent—permanently established New Orleans, La.—mass offered—Aug. 9

Drought—recorded—New England—April

Engraver—mezzotint—Peter Pelham

1728

Botanic Garden—John Bartram—Philadelphia, Pa.

German Book—German book printed in America—J. C. Beissel—published—Philadelphia, Pa.

Shorthand Book—published

Steel—steel—manufactured—Simsbury, Conn.

1729

Arithmetic — American arithmetic — Isaac Greenwood—published

Catholic Nuns—nun who professed her vows in the United States—Sister St. Stanislas Hachard — New Orleans, La. — vows — March 15

College—college to have a full faculty—William and Mary—Williamsburg, Va.

Golf Clubs (or golf sticks)—golf clubs (or golf sticks)—mentioned

Jewish Congregation—Jewish congregation—foundation stones of synagogue—laid—Sept. 8

Newspaper—newspaper serial story—*Pennsylvania Gazette*

1730

Algebra Book—algebra book—*Arithmetic*—Pieter Venima — published — New York City

Freemasons—Provincial Grand Master (Masonic)—Daniel Coxe—deputized—June 5

Hemp Exportation—to England

Horse—horse (thoroughbred)—imported—Bulle Rock

Jewish Congregation—Jewish congregation—synagogue consecrated—April 8

Quadrant—invented—Thomas Godfrey

1731

Catholic Nuns—nun who was born in the United States—Mary Turpin

Library—circulating library—formed—Philadelphia, Pa.—July 1

Music—concert—Boston, Mass.—Dec. 30

Schwenkfelder—George Schultz—arrived—Philadelphia, Pa.

1732

Fishing Club—Schuylkill Fishing Company —founded—Philadelphia, Pa.

Librarian—librarian—to be paid for his service—Louis Timothee—hired—Nov. 14

Newspaper — German newspaper — *Philadelphische Zeitung*—published—May 6

Planetarium—planetarium or orrery—imported—Cambridge, Mass.

Play (drama)—play acted by professional players—New York City—Dec. 6

1733

Animals—bear (white)—exhibited—Jan. 18

Communistic Society—communistic society—J. C. Beissel—Lancaster, Pa.

Epidemic—influenza epidemic

Freemasons—Masonic lodge to work under a regular charter—St. John's Lodge, Boston, Mass.—established—July 30

Language Instruction—French instruction—Cambridge, Mass.

Map—war map—published—New York City —Dec. 24

Newspaper—political newspaper—*New York Weekly Journal*—established—J. P. Zenger—Nov. 5

1734

Advertisement—magician's advertisement—New York City—March 18

Fencing Book—*A Compleat System on Fencing*—published—Williamsburg, Va.

Fish Protection—fish legislation—New York City—May 28

Masonic Book — *Constitutions of the Freemasons*—published—Philadelphia, Pa.

Moravian—George Boehnisch — arrived — Sept. 22

Physician—American-born doctor—graduated from a medical college abroad—William Bull—Aug. 18

Slate—for roofing material—obtained—Delta, Pa. and Cardiff, Md.

1735

Agricultural Experiment Station—agricultural experiment farm—Savannah, Ga.

Book—translated classic published—Philadelphia, Pa.

Grammar — Hebrew grammar — *Grammar of the Hebrew Tongue* — published — Boston, Mass.

Insurance—fire insurance company—organized—Charleston, S.C.—subscriptions received—Jan. 1

Logic Book—*Compendium Logicae*—published —Boston, Mass.

Medical Society—medical society—Boston, Mass.

Moravian Bishop—David Nitschmann—consecrated—Germany—March 13

Moravian Church—built—Savannah, Ga.

Opera—opera performed in America—Charleston, S.C.—Feb. 18

Revival Meeting—of importance—Jonathan Edwards

Silk—silk exportation—from Savannah, Ga.

Tile—brick roofing tile—manufactured—Montgomery County, Pa.

1736

Moravian Bishop — David Nitschmann — arrived—Georgia

Newspaper—newspaper published south of the Potomac River—*Virginia Gazette*—Williamsburg, Va.—Aug. 5

Sunday School — Sunday school — Christ Church—Savannah, Ga.

1737

Greenhouse — erected — Andrew Faneuil—Boston, Mass.

Money—copper coins — minted — Granby, Conn.

Music Society—music society of importance (local)—Charleston, S.C.—organized

1738

Puppet Show—New York City—Feb. 12

Weather Observations—weather observations systematically recorded—John Lining—Charleston, S.C.—Jan.

1739

Astronomer—astronomer of note in the American colonies—John Winthrop—sunspot observations—April 19

German Book—German book printed in German type in America — published — Philadelphia, Pa.

Iron — iron casting — Joseph Mallinson — Dusboro, Pa.

Slavery—insurrection of Negro slaves—South Carolina

Wallpaper — wallpaper — manufactured — Philadelphia, Pa.

1740

Bookplate—Nathaniel Hurd—Boston, Mass.

Marines — Marine corps — organized — New York

Organ—organ built in the U.S.—installed—Trinity Church—New York City

Orphanage—orphanage with a continuous existence—founded—Bethesda Home—Savannah, Ga.

Tinware Manufacturers—tinware manufacturers—Berlin, Conn.

Umbrella—used—Windsor, Conn.

1741

Periodical—magazine published in America—*American Magazine*—Philadelphia, Pa.—Feb. 13

Strike—strike—New York City

1742

Cook Book — cook book — published — Williamsburg, Va.

Moravian Easter Service—Bethlehem, Pa.

School—school for Protestant girls—established—Philadelphia, Pa.

Stove—stove—for heating—invented—Benjamin Franklin

1743

Advertisement—advertisement to occupy a half-page — New York — *Weekly Journal* — July 18

Automaton—automaton—imported—May 3

Bible—Bible printed in German—published—Philadelphia, Pa.

Fishing Treatise—published—Boston, Mass.

Planetarium—planetarium or orrery built in America—New Haven, Conn.

Religious Publication — religious journal — *The Christian History* — Boston, Mass. — March 5

Science Association—scientific society of importance—American Philosophical Society—organized

1744

Orchestra—symphony orchestra—Bethlehem, Pa.

1745

Carillon—carillon — installed — Old North Church—Boston, Mass.

Knighthood—knighthood conferred on a native-born American for military leadership—Sir William Pepperell—Sept. 23

Stereotype—stereotype printing — Benjamin Mecom—Philadelphia, Pa.

1746

College—college charter granted by a governor or acting governor with only the assent of his council—Princeton, N.J.—Oct. 22

Iron—rolling mill—established—Chester, Pa.

1747

Lawyers' Association (state)—New York Bar Association—formed

Textbook printed in America—Thomas Dilworth—*A New Guide to the English Tongue*—reprinted—Philadelphia, Pa.

1748

Candle Factory—Newport, R.I.

College—college charter granted by a governor or acting governor with only the assent of his council—first commencement—Nov. 9

Lutheran Church—Lutheran services in English—Lutheran synod—held—Aug. 26

1749

Academy—Academy and College of Philadelphia—founded
Electric Cooking Experiment—Benjamin Franklin—Philadelphia, Pa.
Lightning Rod—invented—Benjamin Franklin—Philadelphia, Pa.
Wax Works Museum — opened — James Wyatt—New York City—June

1750

Colonist—civilian settlement west of the Allegheny Mountains—Barbourville, Ky.—April 23
Medical Book—dissection essay—New York City
Opera—opera performed by a professional visiting troupe—*Beggar's Opera*—New York City—Dec. 3
Orchestra—orchestra in a theater—New York City
Play (drama)—Shakespearean play—*King Richard III*—New York City—March 5
Teaching Methods Book — *Schul-ordnung* — completed—Aug. 3
Theatrical Advance Publicity Man—Robert Upton—arrived—New York City

1751

Academy—Academy and College of Philadelphia—Philadelphia, Pa.—opened—Aug. 13
Animals—monkey trained to perform—exhibited—New York City—Feb. 25
Cricket Tournament—cricket match—New York City—May 1
Manual Training—school to offer courses in manual training—opened—Dec. 1
Play (drama)—benefit performance—New York City—Jan. 7
Sugar—sugar cane—imported—Louisiana

1752

Catholic Nuns—nun who was born in the United States—Mary Turpin—profession of faith—Jan. 31
Hospital—hospital in America—Pennsylvania Hospital—opened—Philadelphia, Pa.—Feb. 11
Insurance—fire insurance company to receive a charter—Philadelphia Contributionship for the Insurance of Houses—first policy—June 1
Lightning Demonstration—Benjamin Franklin—Philadelphia, Pa.—June 15
Orchestra—orchestra used in conjunction with an opera—*Beggar's Opera*—Upper Marlborough, Md.

1753

Arbitration—colonial arbitration law—enacted—New Haven, Conn.—Oct. 11
Expedition—Arctic expedition to seek the northwest passage for the £20,000 reward—Charles Swaine—sailed—March

Medal—Copley Medal awarded to an American—Benjamin Franklin
Poet—Negro poetess—Phillis Wheatley—born
Steam Engine—steam engine—imported—North Arlington, N.J.—Sept. 25

1754

Cartoon—newspaper cartoon—"Join or Die"—published—Philadelphia, Pa.—May 9
Clock—clock to strike the hours—constructed—Benjamin Banneker—Elkridge Landing, Md.
Druggist—Jonathan Roberts—Philadelphia, Pa.—May
Language Instruction—German instruction—William Creamer—Philadelphia, Pa.
Trombone—used—Bethlehem, Pa.—Nov. 15
War (colonial)—bloodshed in the French and Indian war—Uniontown, Pa.—May 28
War (colonial)—French and Indian war battle—Fort Necessity, Pa.—July 3

1755

Animals—cattle exportation—Savannah, Ga.
Engraving—historical print engraved in America—printed—Boston, Mass.
Law School—law instruction in a college—King's College (Columbia University)—New York City
Meat—beef export—Savannah, Ga.
Steam Engine—steam engine—in service—March 12
Water—water pumping plant—municipal purposes—installed—Bethlehem, Pa.—May 27
"Yankee Doodle"—verses written—Richard Shuckburgh

1756

Spa—opened to public—Bath, Va.
Stage Coach Inter-City Service—New York and Philadelphia, Pa.—Nov. 9
Woman—woman whose vote was recorded—Uxbridge, Mass.

1757

Academy—Academy and College of Philadelphia—Philadelphia, Pa. — graduation — May 17
Niagara Falls—utilization of Niagara Falls waterpower
Street Cleaning Service—instituted—Benjamin Franklin—Philadelphia, Pa.

1758

Holiday—Thanksgiving Day sermon—west of the Alleghenies—Charles Beatty—Pittsburgh, Pa.—Nov. 26
Indian Reservation — Indian reservation (state)—established—New Jersey—Aug. 29

1759

Comb Factory—established—West Newbury, Mass.

Freemasons—military masonic lodge—Crown Point, N.Y.—April 13

Insurance—life insurance company—incorporated—Philadelphia, Pa.—Jan. 11

Music—musical instrument dealer—Michael Hillegas

Music—secular song — composed — Francis Hopkinson

1760

Agricultural Book—agricultural book distinctly American—published—Jared Eliot —Boston, Mass.

Chair—rocking chair — invented — Benjamin Franklin

Medical Legislation—law to regulate the practice of medicine (actually enforced)— New York City—June 10

Methodist—Methodist preacher—Philip Embury—arrived—New York City—Aug. 11

1761

Bridge—pile bridge—constructed—York, Me.

Expedition—scientific expedition—John Winthrop

Insurance—life insurance company—first policy issued—May 22

Knighthood—knighthood conferred in America—Jeffery Amherst—Staten Island, New York—Oct. 25

Music Book—music book by a native American—Urania—published—Philadelphia, Pa.

Venetian Blinds—venetian blinds—installed —St. Peter's Church—Philadelphia, Pa.

1762

Caricature — published — Nathaniel Hurd— Boston, Mass.

Medical Instruction—anatomy lectures (scientific—William Shippen—Philadelphia, Pa.

Missionary Society—missionary society organized in the U.S.—founded—Massachusetts

Woman — woman newspaper editor — Ann Franklin—Newport Mercury—Newport, R.I. —Aug. 22

1763

Prize Fight—American to win distinction in the prize ring—Bill Richman—born—Aug. 5

Ship—steamboat—built—William Henry

1764

Cotton—cotton exported—Charleston, S.C.

Greenhouse — erected — James Beekman— New York City

Milestones — erected — Philadelphia, Pa.— May 15

Railroad—inclined railway—erected—Lewiston, N.Y.

1765

Chocolate Mill—established — Dorchester, Mass.

College Literary Society—college literary society—Princeton, N.J.

Fire—fire in a mine—Pittsburgh, Pa.

Grammar—English grammar by an American published in America—Samuel Johnson—published—New York City

Medical School — medical college — established—Philadelphia, Pa.—May 3

Stamp Act Repudiation—Frederick, Md.— Nov. 23

1766

Actor—matinee idol—John Henry—debut— Philadelphia, Pa.—Oct. 6

Church of the United Brethren in Christ— formed—Lancaster, Pa.—May 18

Fox Hunting Club—Gloucester Fox Hunting Club—organized—Philadelphia, Pa.—Oct. 29

Gem-Cutting Machine—lapidary—invented— Abel Buell—Killingworth, Conn.

Jewish Prayer Book published in the United States—New York City

Theater — theater building (permanent) — opened—Philadelphia, Pa.—Nov. 21

1767

Libretto—published—The Disappointment— New York City

Medical Instruction—midwifery professor— Dr. J. V. B. Tennent—appointed—New York City

Music Book—music book printed from type —The Psalms of David—printed—New York City

Opera—opera (comic) — scheduled — Philadelphia, Pa.—April 20

President (U.S.)—President born posthumously—Andrew Jackson—March 15

1768

Arbitration—arbitration tribunal—New York City—May 3

Artist—artist successful in commercial art— Matthew Pratt

Botany Professor—Adam Kuhn—appointed —Philadelphia, Pa.

Chamber of Commerce—Chamber of Commerce (state)—formed—New York City— April 5

Cottonseed Oil—produced—Dr. Otto—Bethlehem, Pa.

Hospital—insane hospital (state)—Williamsburg, Va.—incorporated

Insurance—fire insurance company to receive a charter—Philadelphia, Pa.—Feb. 20

Medical School—medical college—College of Philadelphia—commencement—June 21

Methodist Chapel — Wesley Chapel — New York City—dedicated—Oct. 30

Music—patriotic American song—by John Dickinson — published — Boston, Mass.—July

Mustard—manufactured—Benjamin Jackson —Philadelphia, Pa.—advertised—Feb. 15

Physician—doctor to receive a bachelor of medicine degree — graduation — Philadelphia, Pa.—June 21

Sieve—sieve—produced—John Sellers—Philadelphia, Pa.

Spelling Reform Advocate—Benjamin Franklin—Philadelphia, Pa.

1769

California Mission—dedicated—San Diego, Calif.—July 16

Chemistry Professor—chemistry professor—Benjamin Rush—Philadelphia, Pa.

Piano—piano—John Harris—spinet described —Boston, Mass.—Sept. 18

Type Foundry—type foundry—Killingworth, Conn.—April 1

1770

Chamber of Commerce—Chamber of Commerce (state)—incorporated—New York City—March 13

Chemical Textbook — published — Benjamin Rush—Philadelphia, Pa.

College—college to confer medals as prizes —Williamsburg, Va.

Music Book—music composition book—*New England Psalm-Singer*—William Billings—Boston, Mass.

Revolutionary War—martyr in the Revolutionary War—Christopher Snider—killed—Boston, Mass.—Feb. 22

Rhubarb—shipped from London, England, to Philadelphia, Pa.

Teaching Methods Book—*Schul-ordnung*—Christopher Dock—Germantown, Pa.

1771

Dwarf—exhibition advertised—Boston, Mass. —Aug. 22

Equestrian Exhibition—John Sharp—Boston, Mass.

Genealogy—genealogy—of American family —Ebenezer Watson—Hartford, Conn.

Type Foundry—type foundry to be permanently established in America—Christopher Sauer II—Germantown, Pa.

1772

Civil Government in America—Watauga Commonwealth—North Carolina—Tennessee

Medical Legislation—law to license the practice of medicine—New Jersey—Sept. 26

Protestant Church—Protestant church—west of Pennsylvania—Schoenbrunn, Ohio communion service—June 9

Schoolhouse—west of the Allegheny Mountains—Schoenbrunn, Ohio—started—Dec. 22

Trade Register—*Aitken's General American Register*—Philadelphia, Pa.

1773

Baptist Church—Baptist church (Negro)—established—Silver Bluff, S.C.

Degrees (academic and honorary)—doctor of laws honorary degree—John Winthrop —Cambridge, Mass.

Execution—electrocution experiment—Benjamin Franklin

Hospital—insane hospital (state)—Williamsburg, Va.—opened—Oct. 12

Methodist Conference — Philadelphia, Pa.—July 16

Museum — public museum — organized — Charleston, S.C.—Jan. 12

Schoolhouse—west of the Allegheny Mountains — completed — Schoenbrunn, Ohio—July 29

1774

Conscientious Objectors — landed — New York City—Aug. 6

Continental Congress—Continental Congress —assembled—Philadelphia, Pa.—Sept. 5

Continental Congress — Continental Congress to be opened with prayer—Philadelphia, Pa.—Sept. 7

Declaration of Independence—declaration of independence — formally made — Carlisle, Pa.—July 12

Declaration of Rights—Philadelphia, Pa.—Oct. 14

Military Organization — military organization (anti-British) — organized—Philadelphia, Pa.—Nov. 17

Music—music printed in a magazine—Boston, Mass.—April

President of the Continental Congress—Peyton Randolph—elected—Philadelphia, Pa.—Sept. 5

Revolutionary War—incident in the Revolutionary War—New Castle, N.H.—Major John Sullivan—Dec. 13

Shaker Society—arrived—New York City—Aug. 6

Shovel—shovel (steel)—manufactured—John Ames—West Bridgewater, Mass.

Slavery—non-importation of slaves act—enacted—Rhode Island—June 13

1775

Abolition Society—organized—Philadelphia, Pa.—April 14

Architectural Book — architectural book printed in America—Philadelphia, Pa.

Army—army engineering department—Continental Army—authorized—June 16

Army Insignia—special insignia—authorized —Boston, Mass.—July 5

Army Officer — adjutant general — Horatio Gates—June 17

Army Officer — chief engineer — Richard Gridley—June 17

Army Officer—general (Continental Army) —George Washington—appointed—June 15

Army Officer — judge advocate — William Tudor—July 29

Army Officer — major general — Artemas Ward—June 17

Army Officer — paymaster general — James Warren—June 27

Army Officer—quartermaster—Thomas Mifflin—Aug. 14

Army Officer—surgeon general of the Continental Army — Benjamin Church — July 27

Declaration of Independence (American)— declaration of independence by a colony— Charlotte, N.C.—May 20

Diplomatic Service—foreign service committee—Nov. 29

Free Trade Policy (federal)—in effect

Freemasons—Negro Mason—initiated—Boston, Mass.—March 6

Marines — American marines — organized — Nov. 10

Medical Book—surgery manual—*Plain, Concise Practical Remarks*—John Jones—published—New York City

Military Drill Manual—military drill manual devoted to field strategy—published

Money—continental money — issued—June 22

Naval Officer—commander-in-chief of the Continental Navy — Esek Hopkins—Dec. 22

Naval Officer—naval doctor—Joseph Harrison—appointed

Navy—naval fleet—authorized—Oct. 13

Navy—naval fleet—Continental Navy organized—Dec. 22

Novel—novel written in America—*Adventures of Alonso*—published—London, England

Postal Service — mail franking privilege — granted—Nov. 8

Postmaster—postmaster general under the Continental Congress—Benjamin Franklin —appointed—July 26

Postmaster — woman postmaster (colonial) —M. K. Goddard—Baltimore, Md.

President (U.S.)—President whose wife was not born in the United States—L. C. J. Adams—born—Feb. 12

Revolutionary War—armed conflict in the Revolutionary War — Lexington, Mass.— April 19

Revolutionary War — naval battle of the Revolution—Machias, Me.—June 12

Ship — warship regularly commissioned — "Hannah"—Sept. 2

State—state constitution—adopted—Massachusetts—May 16

Town Named for George Washington — Washington, N.C.

Treasury Department (U.S.)—treasurer of the U.S.—Michael Hillegas—July 29

United States — "United States" — colonies united—June 7

Army—brevet—authorized—July 20

Army Execution — Thomas Hickey — New York City—June 27

Army Officer—chaplain (Catholic) of the Continental army—appointed—Jan. 26

Cocktail—introduced—Elmsford, N.Y.

Colonial Government—independent government in any of the American colonies— Charleston, S.C.—March

Declaration of Independence (American)— Declaration of Independence—by a colony —Halifax, N.C.—April 12

Declaration of Independence (American)— Declaration of Independence was first ordered "to be fairly engrossed on parchment"—Philadelphia, Pa.—July 19

Declaration of Independence (American)— Declaration of Independence was first printed—John Dunlop—Philadelphia, Pa.— July 5

Declaration of Independence (American)— Declaration of Independence was first published—Philadelphia, Pa.—July 6

Declaration of Independence (American)— Declaration of Independence was first read publicly on July 8

Declaration of Independence (American)— Declaration of Independence was signed first—Philadelphia, Pa.—July 4

Degrees (academic and honorary)—honorary degree granted George Washington—Cambridge, Mass.—April 3

Engineering Book—published—Philadelphia, Pa.

Flag—American flag saluted by a foreigner —Governor de Graeff—Nov. 16

Fraternity (Greek letter)—scholastic fraternity—Phi Beta Kappa—Williamsburg, Va. —founded—Dec. 5

Ink — invisible ink — used — Committee of Secret Correspondence

Land Grant—land grant—Continental Congress—Aug. 14

Loan—loan for war purposes—authorized— Dec. 23

Lottery—lottery held by the Continental Congress—report rendered—Nov. 18

Medal—medal awarded by the Continental Congress—to George Washington—resolution—March 25

Navy—naval uniforms (standardized)—Sept. 5

Pension — pension act of the Continental Congress—Aug. 26

Price Regulation Law—price regulation law (colonial)—enacted—Rhode Island—Dec. 31

Prison Reform Society—Philadelphia Society for Relieving Distressed Prisoners Owing to the War of Independence— formed

Shaker Society—Shaker "family"—formed— Watervliet, N.Y.

Ship—warship (American built) to enter European waters — "Reprisal" — sailed — Dec. 4

Ship—warship captured by a commissioned officer of the U.S. Navy—"Edward"—captured by John Barry—April 17

Submarine—submarine built for use in war—"American Turtle" — built — Saybrook, Conn.

Traitor—to the American cause—William Demont—Nov. 2

United States—"United States" authorized—Sept. 9

War (colonial)—marine engagement in battle—Fort Nassau, Bahamas—March 4

Woman Suffrage—colony to grant suffrage to women—New Jersey—July 2

1777

Army—brevet conferred upon an American —Walter Stewart—Nov. 19

Army Officer—chaplain killed in action—John Rosbrugh—Trenton, N.J.—Jan. 2

Articles of Confederation—adopted—Philadelphia, Pa.—Nov. 15

Catholic Funeral—Catholic funeral attended by the U.S. Continental Congress—Philadelphia, Pa.—Sept. 17

Emancipation Act (state)—Vermont—July 2

Flag—American flag—formally adopted—Philadelphia, Pa.—June 14

Flag—American flag displayed on a man- of-war—Portsmouth Harbor, N.H.—July 4

Flag—American flag flown in battle—Cooch's Bridge, Del.—Sept. 3

Flag—American flag on the high seas—"Raleigh"—Sept. 4

Holiday—Thanksgiving Day celebration (nation-wide, colonial)—Dec. 18

Loan—loan for war purposes—from France —received—June 4

Lottery—lottery held by the Continental Congress—Philadelphia, Pa.—April 10

Mine Barrage—David Bushnell—New London, Conn.—Aug.

Nails—nails—cold cut—Jeremiah Wilkinson —Cumberland, R.I.

Price Regulation Law—price regulation law (colonial)—effective—Rhode Island—Jan. 8

State—state to abolish both entail and primogeniture—Georgia—Feb. 5

Suffrage—state to provide universal manhood suffrage—Vermont—July 28

1778

Arbitration—state arbitration law—Maryland —Dec. 15

Arsenal—Springfield, Mass.—April

Articles of Confederation—ratified—South Carolina—Feb. 5

Blockade—across Hudson River

Court Martial—military court martial—commenced—Cambridge, Mass.—Jan. 20

Diplomatic Service—minister plenipotentiary —to France—Benjamin Franklin—Sept. 14

Diplomatic Service—representative of a foreign country to the U.S.—C. A. Gérard—July

Flag—American flag saluted by a foreign nation—France—Feb. 14

Freemasons—Masonic grand lodge—organized—Williamsburg, Va.—Oct. 13

Music—war song—Chester—published—Boston, Mass.

Pharmacopoeia—pharmacopoeia — William Brown—published—Philadelphia, Pa.

Secret Service—secret service (colonial)—organized—June

Treaty—treaty entered into by the United States—France—Feb. 6

Treaty—treaty entered into by the United States with Indian tribes—Sept. 17

United States—nation to recognize the independence of the United States—France —Feb. 6

1779

Army — Army engineering department — "Corps of Engineers" — established — March 11

Army Uniform—standardized—Oct.

College—elective system of study—Williamsburg, Va.

College—university legally designated as a university—University of Pennsylvania

Honor System—College of William and Mary—Williamsburg, Va.

Language Instruction — modern language school—in a college—Williamsburg, Va.

Law School—law school in a college—Williamsburg, Va.

Medal—medal awarded by the Continental Congress to a foreigner—F. L. T. de Fleury—July 26

Military Drill Manual—military drill manual —published—Philadelphia, Pa.

Oyster Propagation—Rhode Island—June

Universalist Church of America (Independent Christian Church Universalist)—organized—Jan. 1

1780

Arts and Science Society—arts and science society (national)—chartered—May 4

Astronomical Expedition—observed eclipse —Penobscot Bay—Oct. 27

Diplomatic Service—consul to die in service —William Palfrey—Dec.

"First Aid" Emergency Organization—Humane Society of Philadelphia—organized

Hat Factory—established—Danbury, Conn.

Prison—American imprisoned in the Tower of London—Henry Laurens

Slavery—law (state) abolishing slavery—Pa.—March 1

Slavery—slave emancipated—"Marm Bett"—Sheffield, Mass.

Universalist Church of America (Independent Christian Church Universalist)—church dedicated—Gloucester, Mass.—Dec. 25

1781

Bank—bank chartered by Congress—organized—Nov. 1

Diplomatic Service—consular officer detailed for duty in the Department of Foreign Affairs—Thomas Barclay—Jan. 21

Medical Book—croup report (printed)—published—Richard Bayley—New York City

Medical Society—medical society (state)—of importance — Massachusetts Medical Society—incorporated—Nov. 1

Territorial Expansion—acquisition of land by the federal government—New York ceded territory

1782

Almanac—nautical almanac—Samuel Stearns —published—Dec. 29

Bank—bank chartered by Congress—opened for business—Jan. 7

Bible—Bible printed in English—Robert Aitken—Philadelphia, Pa.

Cloth—jeans, fustians, everlastings, and coatings—manufactured commercially—Philadelphia, Pa.

Dentist—dentist—native-born—Josiah Flagg —opened office—Boston, Mass.

Medal—Order of the Purple Heart—established—Newburgh, N.Y.—Aug. 7

Mint (U.S.)—Mint of the United States—proposed—Robert Morris

President (U.S.)—President born a citizen of the U.S.—Martin Van Buren—Kinderhook, N.Y.—Dec. 5

Seal—Great Seal of the United States Government—adopted—June 20

Treaty—treaty between the United States Government and a nation with which it had been at war—signed in France—Nov. 30

1783

Clock — self-winding clock — patent applied for—Oct. 6

College—university west of the Allegheny Mountains—Transylvania—chartered

Copyright Law — copyright law (state) — Connecticut

Salute (complimentary)—New York harbor —May 8

Sports Book of importance—*Sportsman's Companion*—published—New York City

Treaty—treaty between the United States Government and a nation with which it had been at war—treaty with Great Britain—proclaimed—April 11

War Veterans' Society—Society of the Cincinnati—organized—May 13

1784

Author—woman author to make writing a profession—Hannah Adams—first book published

Balloon—balloon flight—Edward Warren—Baltimore, Md.—June 23

Botanic Scientific Expedition—left Ipswich, Mass.—July 19

Catholic Work—by an American—published —Annapolis, Md.

Citizenship—citizenship (colonial) conferred by special grant—Maryland

Geography — published — Jedidiah Morse — New Haven, Conn.

Grammar—French grammar—John Mary—published—Boston, Mass.

Labor Union—labor union to nominate its own political candidates — Mechanics Union—New York State

Law School—law school—Tapping Reeve —Litchfield, Conn.

Map—map of the United States—engraved —advertised—Hartford, Conn.—March 31

Methodist—Methodist bishop—Francis Asbury—Dec. 24

Motor Boat—motor boat—invented—James Rumsey

Newspaper — daily newspaper—*Pennsylvania Packet and Daily Advertiser*—Philadelphia, Pa.—Sept. 21

Newspaper—French newspaper—*Courier de l'Amérique*—Philadelphia, Pa.—July 27

Political Economy Course—political economy course—Williamsburg, Va.—College of William and Mary

Protestant Episcopal Bishop—Protestant Episcopal bishop—Samuel Seabury—consecrated—Nov. 14

Seed Business — established — Philadelphia, Pa.—Jan. 7

Ship—trading ship sent to China—"Empress of China"—Feb. 22

State Department (U.S.)—State Department (U.S.) Secretary—John Jay—Dec. 21

Theological School—theological school—New York City

Treaty—treaty between the United States Government and a nation with which it had been at war—ratified and proclaimed—Jan. 14

War Veterans' Society—Society of the Cincinnati—general meeting—Philadelphia, Pa. —May 7

1785

Agricultural Society—agricultural society—Philadelphia Society for the Promotion of Agriculture—organized—March 1

Animals — mule — George Washington received jackasses from Spain—Oct. 26

Botany Book—botany book strictly American—printed—Philadelphia, Pa.

Church of England—Church of England—organized in New England—first minister ordained

College—state university chartered—Athens, Ga.—Jan. 27

Dentistry—porcelain teeth—introduced

Diplomatic Service — ambassador to England—John Adams—June 1

Diplomatic Service—minister plenipotentiary —Thomas Jefferson—appointed—March 10

Directory (city) — published — Philadelphia, Pa.—Oct. 1

Shaker Society—organized Shaker commu-
nity—New Lebanon, N.Y.
Ship — ship built on the Pacific coast —
"Northwest America"—begun—June 11
Ship — steamboat patent — Isaac Briggs —
Georgia—Feb. 1
Wool—worsted mill operated by water pow-
er—Hartford, Conn.

1789

Army—medical corps—Richard Allison ap-
pointed surgeon—Sept. 29
Attorney General—attorney general—E. J.
Randolph—Sept. 26
Attorney of the United States — Samuel
Sherburne, Jr.—appointed—Sept. 26
Bibliography—bibliography of Americana in
English—published
Book Publisher of denominational books—
New York City—May
Cabinet of the United States—cabinet—April
30
Catholic Diocese—established — Baltimore,
Md.—April 6
Catholic Magazine — Catholic magazine —
published—Boston, Mass.—April 23
College—Catholic college—Georgetown Col-
lege — established — Washington, D.C. —
Jan. 23
Comb — of ivory — manufactured — Center-
brook, Conn.
Comptroller—Comptroller of the United
States Treasury — Nicholas Eveleigh—
served—Sept. 11
Congress of the United States—Congress of
the U.S.—New York City—March 4
Congress of the United States—congression-
al act—June 1
Congress of the United States—congression-
al act declared unconstitutional by the
Supreme Court of the U.S.—Sept. 24
Congress of the United States—joint meet-
ing of the Senate and the House of Rep-
resentatives—April 6
Congress (U.S.)—House of Representatives
—committee of the House of Representa-
tives—appointed—April 2
Congress (U.S.)—House of Representatives
—contested election—April 13
Congress (U.S.)—House of Representatives
—House of Representatives—assembled—
March 4
Congress (U.S.)—House of Representatives
—Speaker of the House—F. A. Muhlen-
berg
Congress (U.S.) — Senate — president pro
tempore of the United States Senate—
John Langdon—April 6
Congress (U.S.) — Senate — senate — senate
meeting—New York City—March 4
Congressman (U.S.)—Catholic congressman
—served—March 4
Constitution of the United States—printed
copies of the Constitution—Constitution
declared in effect—March 4
Constitutional Amendment (U.S.)—constitu-
tional amendments—submitted to the
states—Sept. 25

Cotton Mill — cotton mill — established —
Charleston, S.C.
Drawback Legislation—tariff act—July 4
Flour Mill—flour mill—of importance—de-
signed—Oliver Evans
Holiday—Thanksgiving Day—designated by
presidential proclamation — Oct. 3 — for
Nov. 26
Horse—horse (Morgan horse)—foaled—
Randolph, Vt.
Insurance Treatise—English reprint—pub-
lished—Philadelphia, Pa.
Internal Revenue Commissioner — Tench
Coxe—Commissioner of Revenue—Sept.
11
Justice Department (U.S.)—office of Attor-
ney General created—Sept. 24
Land Office—"Great American Wilderness"
—Canandaigua, N.Y.
Law Book—law compilation of federal ses-
sion laws—published
Law Reports—E. Kirby—Reports of Cases
—published—Litchfield, Conn.
Lighthouse—lighthouse built after American
independence—legislation—Aug. 7
Loan—loan to the United States—negotiated
by Alexander Hamilton—Sept. 13
Map—road map—published—New York City
Money—trade tokens — issued — "Motts,
N.Y."—New York City
Navigation Act—navigation act (U.S.)—ap-
proved—July 20
Newspaper—political newspaper—Gazette of
the United States—New York City—April 11
Novel—American novel published in Amer-
ica—The Power of Sympathy—published—
Boston, Mass.
Pension—pensions paid by the United States
Government—authorized—Sept. 29
Periodical—children's magazine — published
—Hartford, Conn.
Periodical—sectarian magazine — Arminian
Magazine — published — Philadelphia, Pa.—
Jan.
Pharmacy Professor—pharmacy professor—
S. P. Griffiths—Philadelphia, Pa.
Post Office—Post Office Department of the
United States—established—Sept. 22
Postmaster — postmaster general of the
United States—Samuel Osgood—Sept. 26
Presbyterian General Assembly—Philadel-
phia, Pa.—May 22
President (U.S.)—President elected—George
Washington—inaugurated—April 30
President (U.S.)—President to receive the
unanimous vote of the presidential electors
—George Washington
President (U.S.)—President to tour the
country—George Washington—Oct. 15
Presidential Inaugural Ball—New York City
—May 7
"Presidential Mansion"—New York City—
April 23
Senate Journal—published—New York City
Senator (U.S.)—Catholic senator—Daniel
Carroll—March 4

State Department (U.S.)—State Department (U.S.)—established—July 27

Supreme Court (U.S.)—Chief Justice of the Supreme Court—John Jay—Sept. 24

Supreme Court (U.S.)—Supreme Court Justice who was nominated but who did not serve—R. H. Harrison—Sept. 24

Supreme Court (U.S.)—Supreme Court of the United States—appointments made

Tariff—tariff legislation—enacted—July 4

Temperance Society—temperance organization (local)—formed—Litchfield County, Conn.

Treasury Department (U.S.)—Secretary of the Treasury—Alexander Hamilton—Sept. 11

Treasury Department (U.S.)—Treasury Department (U.S.)—organized—Sept. 2

War Department (U.S.)—War Department (U.S.)—authorized—Aug. 7

White Lead Manufacturer—Samuel Wetherill—Philadelphia, Pa.

1790

Actor—actor of American birth—appeared—March 13

Bible — Catholic Bible — printed—Philadelphia, Pa.

Birds—partridge propagation—Beverly, N.J.

Bond—bonds—of the U.S. Government—authorized—Aug. 4

Book — book entered for copyright — Pennsylvania—June 9

Button—pewter or block tin buttons—manufactured—Waterbury, Conn.

Catholic Bishop—Catholic bishop appointed to serve in the U.S.—John Carroll—consecrated—Dorset, England—Aug. 15

Census—census of the United States—authorized—March 1—enumerated—Aug. 1

Coast Guard (U.S.)—Coast Guard—revenue cutter service—organized—Aug. 4

Congress of the United States—Congress of the United States—first session in Philadelphia, Pa.—Dec. 6

Congress (U.S.)—House of Representatives —filibuster of "dilatory tactics"—June 11

Congressman (U.S.)—congressman to die— Theodoric Bland—June 1

Copyright Law—copyright law of the U.S. —enacted—May 31

Cotton Mill—cotton mill to spin cotton yarn successfully—Pawtucket, R.I.—Dec. 20

Dictionary—agricultural dictionary—*The New England Farmer* — published — Worcester, Mass.

Diplomatic Service—consul under the Department of State—Samuel Shaw—Feb. 9

Diplomatic Service—consuls of the United States appointed after the adoption of the constitution

Drill—dental drill—invented—John Greenwood

Historical Society—historical society (state) —Massachusetts Historical Society — organized—Aug. 26

Ice Yacht—built — Oliver Booth — Poughkeepsie, N.Y.

Lawyer—lawyers admitted to the Supreme Court of the United States—Feb. 5,

Medical Book—medical book for army medical use—published—New York City

Music—music publishers (exclusive)—Moller & Capron—Philadelphia, Pa.

Music—singing contest—Dorchester, Mass.

Naturalization Act — naturalization act — of the U.S. Government—March 26

Navy—naval protection—organized—Aug. 4

Patent—patent granted by the United States Government—Samuel Hopkins—July 31

Patent — patent law (national) — enacted— April 10

Physician—Negro doctor—James Derham— Philadelphia, Pa.

President (U.S.)—President who had been a senator—James Monroe—Nov. 9

Prison — prison to have individual cells — Philadelphia, Pa.

Refunding Act (federal)—approved—Aug. 4

Senator (U.S.) — senator appointed by a governor — John Walker — Virginia — appointed—March 31

Ship—revenue cutter—"Massachusetts"—authorized—Aug. 4

Ship—ship to carry the U.S. flag around the world—returned—Boston, Mass.—Aug. 9

State Department (U.S.)—State Department (U.S.) Secretary — Thomas Jefferson — took office—March 22

Supreme Court (U.S.)—Supreme Court of the U.S.—first session—New York City— Feb. 1

Theater — panorama show—"Jerusalem" — New York City

War—battle fought by United States troops —Ohio—Oct. 19

1791

Academy—University of Pennsylvania—first trustees meeting—Nov. 8

Army Officer—Chaplain of the U.S. Army— John Hurt—March 4

Attorney General—opinion by a U.S. Attorney General—decision—Aug. 21

Bank—Bank of the United States — chartered—Feb. 25

Bible—Bible in folio size to be illustrated— published—Worcester, Mass.

Carpet Factory — carpet mill — founded — Philadelphia, Pa.

Coal — anthracite coal—discovered—Carbon County, Pa.

College—Catholic college—Georgetown College — opened — Washington, D.C.—Nov. 15

Congress (U.S.) — Senate — senate special session—Philadelphia, Pa.—March 4

Congressman (U.S.)—Jewish congressman— Israel Jacobs—March 4

Constitutional Amendment (U.S.)—Constitutional amendments—"Bill of Rights"— Dec. 15

Countess—American woman to become a countess—Sarah Rumford

Dental Dispensary — dental dispensary — New York City—opened—Feb. 1

Export—export report—fiscal year ending Sept. 30

Internal Revenue Act—enacted—March 3

Law Book—law book containing the federal laws of the United States of more than one session of Congress—published—New York City

Law Book—law book containing the federal laws of the United States—published—Hartford, Conn.

Lighthouse—lighthouse built after American independence—contract for Cape Henry Lighthouse—March 31

Marble Building—of importance—Philadelphia, Pa.

Masonry (Negro)—Masonic Grand Lodge (not Free and Accepted Masons)—Boston, Mass.—organized—June 24

Music—orchestral song—published—Boston, Mass.

Naval Officer—naval officer commissioned—Hopley Yeaton—appointed—March 21

Patent—patent granted jointly to a father and son—Philadelphia, Pa.—Aug. 2

Patent—patentee to obtain more than one patent—Philadelphia, Pa.—March 11

Pile Driver—pile driver—patented—John Stone—Concord, Mass.—March 10

President (U.S.)—President to tour the country—to southern states—April 7

Ship — revenue cutter — "Massachusetts" — keel laid—Newburyport, Mass.

State—state admitted to the Union—Vermont—March 4

Sugar—sugar refinery — opened — New Orleans, La.

Tax—excise tax (federal)—enacted

Tax—internal revenue tax—imposed—March 3

Traffic Regulation—one-way traffic regulation—New York City—Dec. 17

1792

Agriculture Professor—Columbia College—New York City—July 9

Army Officer—paymaster—Caleb Swan—appointed—May 9

Brokerage—stock exchange—predecessors—May 17

Building—building erected by the Government in Washington, D.C.—White House—cornerstone laid—Oct. 13

Building—building erected in the United States for public use—U.S. Mint—cornerstone laid—July 31

Chemical Society—chemical society—founded—Philadelphia, Pa.

Circus—circus—J. B. Ricketts—Philadelphia, Pa.

Congress of the United States—congressional investigation—March 27

Congressional Apportionment—authorized—April 14

Conscription—conscription — authorized — May 8

Cotton Gin—invented—Eli Whitney—Mulberry Grove, Ga.

Cracker Bakery—Newburyport, Mass.

Cremation—Charleston, S.C.—Dec. 8

Diplomatic Service—ambassador to England —Thomas Pinckney—minister plenipotentiary to England—Jan. 12

Glass Factory—window glass factory—production began—Boston, Mass.

Health Board—health board (local)—Baltimore, Md.

Insurance—life insurance—Philadelphia, Pa.—organized—Dec. 10

Labor Union—craft labor union (local)—organized—Philadelphia, Pa.

Lighthouse—lighthouse built after American independence — completed — Cape Henry, Va.

Maternity Book — published — Philadelphia, Pa.

Medical Book—anatomy book—published

Mint (U.S.)—mint (U.S.) director—David Rittenhouse—appointed—April 14

Mint (U.S.)—Mint of the United States—established—April 2

Money—coin (United States) to use "E Pluribus Unum"—authorized—April 2

Money—copper coins made by the United States Mint—authorized—April 2

Money—gold coinage—authorized—April 2

Money—gold price fixed by Congress—April 2

Money—half cent of the United States—authorized—April 2

Money—silver coins—authorized—April 2

Money—silver dollar—authorized—April 2

Money — silver half dimes — authorized — April 2

Monument—monument to Christopher Columbus—Baltimore, Md.—dedicated—Oct. 12

Postal Service—postal service act—established—Feb. 20

Postmaster—woman postmaster appointed after the adoption of the Constitution—Sarah De Crow—Hertford, N.C.—Sept. 27

Presidential Succession Act — enacted — March 1

Protestant Episcopal Bishop — Protestant Episcopal bishop consecrated in the United States—T. J. Claggett—New York City—Sept. 17

Road—macadam road—Lancaster Turnpike Railroad Company—chartered—April 9

Veto (presidential)—veto—by a President—George Washington—April 5

Woman Suffrage—woman suffrage book—*A Vindication of the Rights of Women*—published

1793

African Church—founded—Richard Allen—Philadelphia, Pa.

Alfalfa—description published—Wilmington, Del.

Animals—sheep (merino sheep) — William Foster—smuggled

Anthology (American) — published — Litchfield, Conn.

Balloon—balloon flight in which a presidential order was carried—Philadelphia, Pa.—Jan. 9

Broadcloth—produced—Pittsfield, Mass.

Canal—canal—built—South Hadley Falls, Mass.

Capitol (of the United States)—cornerstone laid—Sept. 18

Catholic Priest—Catholic priest ordained in the United States—S. T. Badin—May 25

Congress (U.S.)—Senate—contested election—Feb. 28

Deaf—School—lip reading was first referred to in print—Philadelphia, Pa.

Engraving—wood engraving made with an engraving tool — Alexander Anderson — New York City—June

"First Aid" Emergency Organization—Humane Society of Philadelphia—incorporated—Jan. 23

Money—metal purchased for coinage

Neutrality Proclamation—George Washington—April 22

Oiled Silk Patent—Ralph Hodgson—Lansingburg, N.Y.—Feb. 1

Road—state road authorization—Kentucky—Dec. 14

Slavery—fugitive slave law (federal)—enacted—Feb. 12

Stove Patent—Robert Haeterick—June 11

Sulphuric Acid—produced—John Harrison—Philadelphia, Pa.

Thread—cotton thread—made—Pawtucket, R.I.

Wool—wool carding machine—built—Newburyport, Mass.

1794

African Church — dedicated — Philadelphia, Pa.—July 29

Arsenal—national arsenal—Springfield, Mass.—April 2

Ball Bearing—commercial installation—Lancaster, Pa.—Oct. 30

Book—best seller novel—published—Philadelphia, Pa.

Capital Punishment—death penalty was first abolished—Pennsylvania—April 22

College—non-denominational college—chartered—Knoxville, Tenn.—Sept. 10

Congress (U.S.)—Senate—contested election—case commenced—Feb. 20

Congress (U.S.)—Senate—Senate session to which the public was admitted—Feb. 11

Extradition—extradition treaty with a foreign country—England—Nov. 19

Flag Legislation — legislation authorizing changes in the American flag—enacted—Jan. 13

Glass Factory—glass factory west of the Allegheny Mountains—established—A. A. Gallatin

Historical Society—historical society (state)—Massachusetts Historical Society—incorporated—Feb. 19

Hotel—hotel built—City Hotel—New York City

Insurance—life insurance—Insurance Company of North America—Philadelphia, Pa.—chartered—April 14

Jewelers' Supply House—Nehemiah Dodge—Providence, R.I.

Money—deposit of silver for coinage—July 18

Money—silver dollar—coined—Philadelphia, Pa.

Naval Officer—naval officer to become a commodore—John Barry—appointed

Neutrality Regulation—enacted—June 5

Newspaper—French daily newspaper—*Courrier Français*—April 15

Opera—opera of a serious nature—*Tammany*—New York City—March 3

Presidential Commission—presidential commission—George Washington

Rivet—commercial production—J. G. Pierson—patent—March 23

Ship—ship constructed by the federal government — "Chesapeake" — authorized — March 27

Ship—warship builder—Joshua Humphreys—appointed—June 28

Surgical Operation — Caesarean operation (successful)—Jessee Bennett—Edom, Va.—Jan. 14

Textile Machinery Patent—James Davenport—Philadelphia, Pa.—Feb. 14

1795

Belt Conveyor System—belt conveyor system—described—Oliver Evans—Philadelphia, Pa.

Book—book printed on American paper with American-made plates and bound in America—*Elegiac Sonnets*

Business Publication—*New York Prices Current*—New York City

Catholic Priest—Catholic priest to receive his full theological training in the U.S.—ordained bishop—March 18

College—college named after George Washington—Washington College, Tenn.—name changed—July 8

College—non-denominational college—Union College, Schenectady, N.Y.—chartered—Feb. 25

College—state university chartered—University of North Carolina opened—Feb. 13

Dental Dispensary—dental dispensary—City Dispensary—New York City—incorporated—April 8

Gazetteer—American gazetteer — Jedidiah Morse—published—Boston, Mass.

Grammar Instruction in a College—University of North Carolina—Chapel Hill, N.C.

Money—coin (United States) to use "E Pluribus Unum"—issued

Money—deposit of gold bullion—Feb. 12

Money—return of coins—gold eagles—July 31

Ordnance — muskets — manufactured — Springfield Armory—Springfield, Mass.

Road—state road appropriation of a specific sum—Kentucky—Dec. 19

Steam Engine—steam engine that was practical—Oliver Evans—Philadelphia, Pa.

Supreme Court (U.S.)—Chief Justice whose nomination was not confirmed—John Rutledge

Woman—women to become federal government employees—Philadelphia, Pa.

1796

African Church—Bethel African Methodist Episcopal Church—incorporated—March 28

Animals—elephant — arrived — New York City—April 13

Bathhouse—steam baths for curing disease —Samuel Thomson

Bridge—suspension bridge—Westmoreland County, Pa.

Coast Survey Book—published—Newburyport, Mass.—March

Cook Book—cook book of American authorship—published—Hartford, Conn.

Debt Legislation (federal)—enacted—May 28

Epidemiologist—Noah Webster—published report—New York City

Game Law—game law (national)—approved —May 19

Gas—gas lights for display—introduced—Philadelphia, Pa.—Aug.

Hospital—dispensary—Philadelphia Dispensary—chartered—April 15

Land Grant—special land grant—May 17

Medical Book—pediatrics monograph—published — Charles Caldwell — Philadelphia, Pa.

Nail Cutting and Heading Machine—patented—George Chandler—Dec. 12

Newspaper—newspaper to appear on Sunday—*Monitor*—Baltimore, Md.—Dec. 18

Opera—opera by an American composer—*The Archers*—New York City—April 18

Passport—passport—recorded—State Department—July 8

Piano—piano patent—J. S. McLean—May 27

Pill—patented pills

Ship—ship from the Atlantic coast to anchor in a California port—"Otter"—arrived—Monterey, Calif.—Oct. 29

Unitarian Minister—Unitarian minister—Society of Unitarian Christians organized—June 12

1797

Architectural Book—architectural book distinctly American — printed — Greenfield, Mass.

Army Officer—Judge Advocate of the U.S. Army—Campbell Smith—began service—March 3

Chemical Laboratory Manual—James Woodhouse—published—Philadelphia, Pa.

Clock—clock patent—Eli Terry—Nov. 17

Congress (U.S.)—special session—May 15

Congressman (U.S.)—congressman elected who served time in prison—Matthew Lyon —served—March 4

Cryptography Chart—published—Philadelphia, Pa.

Dollar Marks—cast—Philadelphia, Pa.— Binny & Ronaldson

Impeachment — impeachment proceedings against a United States Senator—William Blount—expelled—July 8

Medical Periodical—medical magazine— *Medical Repository*—New York—Aug. 8

Novel—American novel republished in England—Royall Tyler—*The Algerine Captive*

Plow — plow patent — Charles Newbold — June 26

President (U.S.)—President to reside in Washington, D.C.—John Adams—inaugurated

President (U.S.)—President whose son became President—John Adams—inaugurated

Presidential Election—presidential election in which more than one candidate declared—John Adams—elected

Ship—frigate—"United States"—launched—Philadelphia, Pa.—May 10

Ship—ship to capture an enemy ship after the Revolution—"Constellation"—launched Sept. 7

Washing Machine—washing machine patent —Nathaniel Briggs—March 28

1798

Alien Discriminatory Law—enacted—July 6

Author—author—professional—C. B. Brown —novel announced—April 28

Congress (U.S.)—House of Representatives —brawl—Philadelphia, Pa.—Jan. 30

Encyclopedia—encyclopedia—printed in the U.S.—Philadelphia, Pa.

Hat—straw hats—made—Betsey Metcalf— Providence, R.I.

Hospital—marine hospital (U.S.)—authorized—July 16

Immigration—immigration act — enacted — June 25

Marines—American Marines—Navy Department created

Marines—American Marines—United States Marine Corps—created—July 11

Music Book—hymn book with music—published—Boston, Mass.

Navy—Navy Department (U.S.)—established

Navy—navy yard—acquired — Portsmouth, N.H.

Navy—prize money awarded by the U.S. Navy—authorized—June 28

Navy—Secretary of the Navy — Benjamin Stoddert—May 21

Nullification Proceedings—Kentucky Resolutions

Nursing School—instruction for nurses—New York City

Nut and Bolt Machine—David Wilkinson—patent—Dec. 14

Pistol—government contract for pistols—authorized—May 4

Public Health—public health service (U.S.) —authorized—July 16

Screw—screw patent—David Wilkinson—patent—Dec. 14

Ship—Revenue cutter and Navy cooperation

Tax—federal tax levied directly upon the states—authorized—July 14

Theater—theater destroyed by fire—Boston, Mass.—Feb. 2

Vineyard (successful)—established—Lexington, Ky.—Aug. 28

1799

Astronomy—meteoric display — "shooting stars"—recorded—Nov. 12

Aviation—aeronautical patent—Moses McFarland—Oct. 28

Comb-Cutting Machine—patented—April 12

Drydock—drydock authorized for the United States Government—approved—Feb. 25

Educational Association—educational association (local)—Middletown, Conn.—organized—May

Election—printed ballot—authorized—Pennsylvania—Feb. 15

Forestry Legislation—federal forestry legislation—Feb. 25

Gold — gold nugget — found — Cabarrus County, N.C.

Ice—commercial transportation of ice—from New York City

Insurance—insurance regulation (state)—Mass.—Feb. 13

Labor Union—craft labor union contract—Philadelphia, Pa.

Language Instruction—Italian instruction in a college—Williamsburg, Va.

Musician—Negro-song popularizer—J. C. G. Graupner—Dec. 30

Naval Officer — naval chaplain — William Balch—commissioned—Oct. 30

Presidential Eulogy—delivered—Dec. 26

Quarantine—quarantine legislation (national)—enacted—Feb. 25

Seeding Machine Patent—Eliakim Spooner —Jan. 25

Semaphore Telegraph System—invented—J. Grout—Belchertown, Mass.

Ship—ship to capture an enemy ship after the Revolution—"Constellation" vs. "Insurgente"—Feb. 9

Supreme Court Decision—supreme court decision between states—New York and Connecticut—commenced—Aug. 5

Swedenborgian or New Church—Swedenborgian or New Church Temple—erected —Baltimore, Md.

Weights and Measures Standardization—weights and measures standardization—enacted—March 2

1800

Axe—manufacturing plant—erected—Johnstown, N.Y.

Bankruptcy Act—enacted—April 4

Bible—Greek testament—printed—Worcester, Mass.

Book—book with color plates

Congress (U.S.)—House of Representatives —House of Representatives—first session —Washington, D.C.—Nov. 17

Congressional Caucus—congressional caucus —secretly held—Federalist Party

Evangelical Church—founded

Fireboat—fireboat—used—New York City

Land Grant—district land office—opened—Steubenville, Ohio—July 2

Library—Library of Congress — authorized —April 24

President (U.S.)—President's wife to frank mail—Martha Washington—authorization —April 3

Social Service Endowment — established — White-Williams Foundation — Philadelphia, Pa.

Stomach Washing—P. S. Physick—Philadelphia, Pa.

Swedenborgian or New Church—Swedenborgian or New Church Temple—church service—Baltimore, Md.—Jan. 5

Vaccination for smallpox—Benjamin Waterhouse—Cambridge, Mass.—July 8

1801

Blowpipe—invented—Robert Hare — Philadelphia, Pa.

Booksellers' Association — American Company of Booksellers—organized — New York City—June 7

Bridge—suspension bridge—design patented —James Finley

Building—building erected by the Government in Washington, D.C.—first New Year's reception—Jan. 1

Cheese Factory—cheese factory cooperative —Cheshire, Mass.

Congress of the United States—Congress of the United States—assumed jurisdiction over the District of Columbia—Feb. 27

Cracker — hard water crackers — manufactured—Milton, Mass.

Dental Book—book on dentistry — R. C. Skinner—New York City

Dueling Legislation (state)—enacted—Tennessee—Nov. 10

Election Law — registration law (state) — enacted—Massachusetts—March 7

Governor—Jewish governor—David Emanuel—Georgia—March 3

Herbal Book—published—Samuel Stearns—American Herbal—Walpole, N.H.

Hospital—marine hospital (U.S.)—Norfolk Naval Hospital deeded to U.S.—April 20

Land Pre-emption Act (federal) — enacted —March 3

Naval Officer—naval surgeon of the U.S. Navy—George Balfour

Parliamentary Rules of Order—Thomas Jefferson—published—Washington, D.C.

President (U.S.)—President elected by the House of Representatives—Thomas Jefferson—Feb. 11

President (U.S.)—President inaugurated in the city of Washington—Thomas Jefferson—March 4

President (U.S.)—President to review the military forces—Thomas Jefferson—Washington, D.C.—July 4

Ship — yacht — constructed — "Jefferson"—Salem, Mass.

Whips—manufactured—Titus Pease—Westfield, Mass.

1802

Animals — leopard — exhibited — Boston, Mass.—Feb. 2

Animals—sheep (merino sheep)—imported

Army—engineer corps—established—March 16

Army School—army school—Military Academy of the United States—authorized—March 16

Army School—army school graduate (Jewish) — S. M. Levy — graduated — West Point, N.Y.—Oct. 11

Army School—army school graduates—commissioned—Oct. 12

Astronomer — astronomer to acquire fame after the Revolution—Nathaniel Bowditch

Book Fair—New York City—June 1

Brass—rolled—Abel Porter & Co.—Waterbury, Conn.

Button — gilt buttons to be commercially manufactured—Waterbury, Conn.

Chess Book—*Chess Made Easy*—published—Philadelphia, Pa.

Clock—banjo clock patent—Simon Willard —Boston, Mass.—Feb. 8

Fruit Culture Treatise—William Forsyth—published—Philadelphia, Pa.

Gymnastics Book — *Gymnastics For Youth* — published—Philadelphia, Pa.

Jewish Congregation—Jewish congregation (Ashkenazic)—founded—Philadelphia, Pa. —October, 10

Land Grant—land subsidy for internal improvements—April 30

Law Book—law book (text)—*Lex Mercatoria Americana*—published—New York City

Librarian — Librarian of Congress — John Beckley—appointed—Jan. 29

Library Catalog—catalog of the Library of Congress—published—Washington, D.C.

Social Service Endowment—White-Williams Foundation—incorporated—March 23

Tea Shrub—planted—Middleton, S.C.

Vaccine Institution—organized — Baltimore, Md.—March 25

1803

Apple Parer — invented — Moses Coats — Downington, Pa.—Feb. 14

Bird Banding—bird banding—J. J. Audubon —Montgomery County, Pa.

Botany Book—botany book (elementary work)—published—Philadelphia, Pa.

Camp Meeting—Logan County, Ky.

Evangelical Association Council—assembly —Bucks County, Pa.

History Instruction—school of modern history—College of William and Mary—Williamsburg, Va.

Impeachment — impeachment of a federal judge—John Pickering—trial—March 3

Land Grant—special land grant to a foreigner—enacted

Law Digest—*An Abridgement of the Laws* — published—Harrisburg, Pa.

Library — youth's library—Salisbury, Conn. —Jan.

Medical Book — gastroenterology treatise—published—Philadelphia, Pa.

Medical Book—hemophilia treatise—J. C. Otto—published—New York City

Mica—mica—mined—Grafton, N.H.

Reaper—reaper—patented—Richard French and J. F. Hawkins—May 17

Refrigerator — refrigerator — invented — Thomas Moore—Baltimore, Md.

Ship—steamboat with a twin-screw propeller —patented—John Stevens—Hoboken, N.J. —April 11

Territorial Expansion—annexation of territory—Louisiana Purchase

Tract Society—tract society—Massachusetts Society for Promoting Christian Knowledge—instituted—Boston, Mass.—Sept. 1

1804

Agricultural Encyclopedia — *Domestic Encyclopedia*—published—Philadelphia, Pa.

Banana Importation—from Cuba

Book—book printed in the Indiana Territory

Book Index—general catalog of books — published—Boston, Mass.—Jan.

Bridge—pontoon bridge—Lynn, Mass.

Cemetery—congressional cemetery — Washington, D.C.

College—university founded by a federal land grant—Ohio University—chartered—Feb. 18

Congressional Caucus—congressional caucus (open, not secret)—Washington, D.C.— Feb. 29

Distilling Book — *American Distiller* — published—Philadelphia, Pa.

Expedition—expedition across the continent to the Pacific coast—Lewis and Clark—left—St. Louis, Mo.—May 14

Impeachment—impeachment of a federal judge—Joseph Pickering—impeached

Impeachment — impeachment proceedings against a Justice of the Supreme Court of the U.S.—Samuel Chase—Nov. 30

Indian Reservation—Indian reservation (federal)—official notice of removal—act of March 26

Insurance—insurance agency—Israel Whelan—New York City

Madstone—purchased — Benjamin Milam—Winona, Ill.

Pharmacist—pharmacist (woman) — Elizabeth Marshall—Philadelphia, Pa.

Political Convention — political nominating caucus attended by party leaders—Washington, D.C.—Feb. 25

Presidential Candidate—presidential candidate nominated at a caucus—Thomas Jefferson—Washington, D.C.—Feb. 25

Presidential Election — presidential election in which candidates had been nominated for the vice presidency—Nov. 6

Printer's Ink—successfully manufactured—C. E. Johnson—Philadelphia, Pa.

Quids—organized

Ship—steamboat with a twin-screw propeller —navigated—John Stevens

1805

Art Organization—art organization—of importance—established—Philadelphia, Pa.—Dec. 26

Cryptography Book — published—Hartford, Conn.

Drydock — drydock — constructed—Robert Fulton—Jersey City, N.J.

Expedition—expedition across the continent to the Pacific coast—reached mouth of Columbia River—Nov. 8

Flag—American flag flown over a fortress of the Old World—Tripoli—April 27

History—American history of importance written by a woman—M. O. Warren—published—Boston, Mass.

Ice—export of ice—to West Indies—Aug.

Prize Fight—American to win distinction in the prize ring—Bill Richmond—winner—July 8

Steam-Operated Amphibious Vehicle — Oliver Evans—Philadelphia, Pa.—July

Vice President of the United States—vice president to be nominated—George Clinton—served—March 4

Women's Club — women's club — Female Charitable Society — Wiscasset, Me.—organized

1806

Art Organization—art organization—Pennsylvania Academy of Fine Arts—incorporated—March 28

Births—child born in the White House, Washington, D.C. — J. M. Randolph — Jan. 17

Cathedral—cathedral—cornerstone laid—Baltimore, Md.—July 7

Cider Mill — patented — I. Quintard—Stanfield, Conn.—April 5

Duel—duel in which a future President of the United States participated—Andrew Jackson—May 30

Expedition—expedition across the continent to the Pacific coast—returned to St. Louis, Mo.—Sept. 23

Gas—gas lights (street)—David Melville—Newport, R.I.

Medical Book—dispensatory—*American Dispensatory*—published—Philadelphia, Pa.

Periodical—college magazine — *Literary Cabinet*—Yale—New Haven, Conn.—published—Nov. 15

Road — federal highway — Great National Pike—Cumberland, Md.—commenced

Soap Manufacturer—soap manufacturer to render fats in his plant—William Colgate —New York City

1807

Animals—sheep (Merino sheep) exhibition —Pittsfield, Mass.

Coast Survey—authorized—Feb. 10

College—college entrance requirement, other than Greek, Latin, and arithmetic—Harvard—Cambridge, Mass.

Deaf—School—instruction for the deaf — New York City

Embargo Act—enacted—Dec. 22

Evangelical Church — annual conference — Lebanon County, Pa.—Nov.

Evangelical Conference — Kleinfeltersville, Pa.—Nov. 15

Glass Factory—flint glass factory—successful—Pittsburgh, Pa.

Glue Factory (animal products)—established —Roger Upton—Boston, Mass.

Lifeboat — lifeboat — built—William Raymond—Nantucket, Mass.

Medical Book—obstetrics book — Samuel Bard—published—New York City

Newspaper — Democratic newspaper — *Democratic Press*—published—Philadelphia, Pa.—March 27

Ship—steamboat to make regular trips—Robert Fulton — "Clermont"—trial trip—New York City—Aug. 7

Soda Water—soda water—prepared—Townsend Speakman—Philadelphia, Pa.

1808

Bible — Bible translated into English in America—copyrighted—Sept. 12

Bible Society — Bible society — organized—Philadelphia, Pa.—Dec. 12

Brushes—manufactured—Medford, Mass.

Catholic Diocese — became Archdiocese — Baltimore, Md.—April 8

Cheese — pineapple cheese—manufactured—Troy, Pa.

Coal—anthracite coal burned experimentally —Jesse Fell—Wilkes-Barre, Pa.—Feb. 11

College — university founded by a federal land grant — opened — Athens, Ohio — June 1

Duel—duel between congressmen—Bladensburg, Md.

Law Magazine — law magazine — *American Law Journal*—published—Baltimore, Md.

Leather — leather-splitting machine — patented—Samuel Parker—Billerica, Mass.—July 9

Naval Officer — naval medical officer to write a book — Edward Cutbush — published—Philadelphia, Pa.

Orchestra—college orchestra—Harvard University — Cambridge, Mass. — formed — March 6

Pharmacopoeia—pharmacopoeia prepared by a medical association—published—Boston, Mass.

Play (drama)—play about an Indian—by an American—J. N. Barker—*The Indian Princess* —produced—Philadelphia, Pa.—April 6

Religious Publication — religious review — *Herald of Gospel Liberty*—published—Portsmouth, N.H.—Sept. 1

Salt — salt well — west of the Allegheny Mountains — operated — Charlestown, W.Va.—Jan. 15

Temperance Society — temperance society (union) — organized — Saratoga Springs, N.Y.—April 13

1809

Catholic Magazine—Catholic magazine in English—issued—Detroit, Mich.—Aug. 31

Clock — watchmaker — Luther Goddard — Shrewsbury, Mass.

Cricket Club—cricket club—founded—Boston, Mass.

Dictionary—Hebrew dictionary—C. C. Moore —published—New York City

Disciples of Christ—church — organized — Washington, Pa.—Aug. 17

Geology Book—geology book—of importance —William Maclure—Philadelphia, Pa.

Gloves—commercial manufacture—Talmadge Edwards—Johnstown, N.Y.

Medical Book—typhus fever treatise—Elisha North—published—Philadelphia, Pa.

Pen—steel pen patent—Peregrine Williamson—Baltimore, Md.—Nov. 22

Periodical—magazine containing a fashion plate—*The Port Folio*—June

President (U.S.)—President born beyond the boundaries of the original thirteen states— Abraham Lincoln — Hodgenville, Ky. — Feb. 12

Railroad—railroad for freight transportation —Thomas Leiper—Crum Creek, Pa. to Ridley Creek, Pa.

Railroad Track—railroad track (practical)— used—Philadelphia, Pa.—July 31

Ship—steamboat to make an ocean voyage— "Phoenix"—sailed—New York City to Philadelphia, Pa.—June 10

Supreme Court (U.S.) Decision—Supreme Court decision establishing the power of the United States—Feb. 20

Surgical Operation—abdominal operation— Ephraim McDowell—Danville, Ky.—Dec. 13

Type Specimen Book—showing ornaments— published—Philadelphia, Pa.

Vice President of the United States—vice president to serve under two presidents— George Clinton—second term—March 4

Woman—woman granted a patent—Mary Kies—South Killingly, Conn.—May 5

1810

Actor—English actor of note—G. F. Cooke —debut—New York City—Nov. 21

Agricultural Journal—agricultural journal— *Agricultural Museum* — published — Georgetown, D.C.—July 4

Auger (screw auger)—manufactured—Walter French—Seymour, Conn.

Carpet Factory—carpet mill to make ingrain carpets—Frederick City, Md.

Cheese—pineapple cheese—L. M. Norton— patent—April 17

Cigar Factory—of importance—West Suffield, Conn.

Colonist—colonists to reach the Pacific coast —left New York City—Sept. 6

Dictionary—military dictionary — William Duane—published—Philadelphia, Pa.

Fair—agricultural fair — Pittsfield, Mass.— Oct. 1

Glass Crystal Chandelier—Pittsburgh, Pa.

Horse Breeding Society—Massachusetts Society for Encouraging the Breed of Fine Horses—formed—Boston, Mass. — annual trials—Oct. 23

Insurance—fire insurance joint-stock company—American Fire Insurance Company —organized—Philadelphia, Pa.—Feb. 28

Irish Magazine—*The Shamrock*—published— New York City—Dec. 15

Leather—leather tanning by the "oil tan" method—Talmadge Edwards—Johnstown, N.Y.

Medical Book—pediatrics book—*The Maternal Physician*—published—Philadelphia, Pa.

Mineralogy Magazine—*American Mineralogical Journal*—published—New York City— Jan.

Missionary Society—foreign missionary society—organized—Bradford, Mass. — June 29

Orchestra—orchestra — founded — J. C. G. Graupner

Poem by an American—to receive recognition—"Thanatopsis"—W. C. Bryant

Postal Service—mail box—invented—Thomas Brown

Printing History—Isaiah Thomas—*History of Printing*—published—Worcester, Mass.

Screw—screw factory — established — Bellefonte, R.I.

Silk—silk mill—Mansfield, Conn.

Vaccination Legislation—vaccination legislation (state) — enacted — Massachusetts— March 6

1811

Boat Club—boat club—Knickerbocker Boat Club—New York City—organized

Colonist—colonists to reach the Pacific coast —April 12

Congress (U.S.)—Senate—senate filibuster— Feb. 11

Conscience Fund—started

Disciples of Christ—church established— Brush Run, Pa.—May 4

Educational Magazine—educational magazine—*Juvenile Mirror*—published—New York City

Export—exports from the United States to exceed the imports—fiscal year ending Sept. 30

Ferryboat — steam-propelled ferryboat — "Juliana"—Hoboken, N.J. and New York City—operation—Oct. 11

Hospital—naval hospital—authorized — Feb. 26

Masonic Magazine—*Free-Masons Magazine*—published—Philadelphia, Pa.—April

Medical Book—anatomy book (American)—Caspar Wistar—*A System of Anatomy*—published—Philadelphia, Pa.

News Agency—news agency—established—Boston, Mass.

Periodical—quarterly magazine — *American Review of History*—published—Philadelphia, Pa.—Jan.

Secession—secession was first mentioned in Congress—Josiah Quincy—June 4

Ship—steamboat to sail down the Mississippi —"New Orleans"—from Pittsburgh, Pa.—arrived—New Orleans, La.—Oct. 1

1812

Army School—army school graduate killed —in military action—George Ronan—Chicago, Ill.—Aug. 15

Bond—treasury notes (interest bearing)—authorized—June 30

Bridge—"Y" bridge—authorized—Zanesville, Ohio—Jan. 21

Canning Book—François Appert—published —New York City

Coal—anthracite coal used commercially—Philadelphia, Pa.

Drug Mill—established—C. V. Hagner—Philadelphia, Pa.

Federal Foreign Aid Bill—enacted

File Manufacturing Machine—invented—Morris B. Belknap—Greenfield, Mass.

Flag—American flag over a schoolhouse—Colrain, Mass.—May

Historical Society—historical society (national)—American Antiquarian Society—Worcester, Mass.—incorporated—Oct. 24

History—comic history of the United States —J. K. Paulding—published—New York City

Marines—woman marine—Lucy Brewer—in battle—Aug. 19

Medical Book—hydrophobia book—James Thacher—*Observations on Hydrophobia*—published—Plymouth, Mass.

Medical Book—mental diseases book—*Medical Inquiries*—Benjamin Rush—published—Philadelphia, Pa.

Mower (horsepower)—patented—Peter Gaillard—Lancaster, Pa.—Dec. 4

Pawnbroking Ordinance — enacted — New York City—July 13

Pencil Factory—William Monroe—Concord, Mass.—June

Political Convention—political nominating caucus—New York City—Sept. 15-16

Railroad Treatise—John Stevens—published —New York City

Russian Settlement—established—Cazadero, Calif.—March 15

School Superintendent—school superintendent (state)—Gideon Hawley—New York —appointed

Ship—naval vessel of the United States to display the American flag around Cape Horn—"Essex"—sailed—Oct. 27

Type Specimen Book—published—Binny & Ronaldson—Philadelphia, Pa.

Vice President of the United States—Vice President to die in office—George Clinton —died—April 20

Vice Presidential Candidate—vice presidental nominee to decline nomination—John Langdon—May 12

War (1812)—frigate action of importance in the War of 1812—Aug. 19

War (1812)—prisoners in the War of 1812—captured—St. Regis, N.Y.—Oct. 22-23

War (1812)—war declaration—June 18

War Bond—issued by the federal government—authorized—March 14

Wedding—White House wedding—Todd-Washington—March 29

1813

Army Officer—surgeon general of the U.S. Army—James Tilton—June 11

Book—stereotyped book — published — New York City—June

Chemical Magazine—printed—Philadelphia, Pa.

Cotton Mill—cotton mill in the world in which the whole process of cotton manufacturing from spinning to weaving was carried on by power—Waltham, Mass.—incorporated—Feb. 23

Craps—introduced—New Orleans, La.

Diplomatic Service—Jewish diplomatic representative—M. M. Noah—Consul to Tunis

Factory Standardization of Production—contract—Middletown, Conn.—April 16

Flag—American flag flown in battle on the Pacific — "Essex" — docked — Valparaiso, Chile

Gas—gas lights (street)—patent—David Melville—March 18

Globe Factory—terrestrial and celestial globes—James Wilson—Bradford, Vt.

Hair Cloth—manufactured—Rahway, N.J.

Medical Instruction—medical jurisprudence course—James Stringham—Columbia University—New York City

Postal Service—mail delivery by steamboats —authorized—Feb. 27

Religious Publication — religious weekly newspaper—*The Religious Remembrancer*—published—Philadelphia, Pa.—Sept. 4

Rubber—rubber patent—J. F. Hummel—Philadelphia, Pa.—April 29

School Superintendent—school superintendent (state)—Gideon Hawley—New York—served—Jan. 14

Ship—naval vessel of the United States to display the American flag around Cape Horn—arrived—Valparaiso, Chile—March 14

Stereotype—stereotypers —successful — New York City

Supreme Court Decision—Supreme Court decision that reversed the decision of a state supreme court

Vaccination Legislation—vaccination legislation (national)—enacted—Feb. 27

War (1812)—defeat in history of a British squadron—O. H. Perry—Sept. 10

1814

Bible—Hebrew Bible—*Biblia Hebraica*—published—Philadelphia, Pa.

Building—building in all-Gothic architecture—Trinity Episcopal Church—New Haven, Conn

College—school for the higher education of women—Middlebury, Vt.

Conscription—wartime conscription bill—passed by Senate—Dec. 9

Cottonseed Hulling Machine—patented—J. Lineback—Salem, N.C.—March 31

Freemasons—Knights Templar Grand Encampment—New York City—Jan. 22

Museum—museum especially constructed as a museum and art gallery—Baltimore, Md.—Aug. 15

President (U.S.)—President to face enemy gunfire while in office—James Madison—Bladensburg, Md.—Aug. 25

Saw (circular)—produced—Benjamin Cummins—Bentonsville, N.Y.

Ship—steam-propelled frigate—"Demologos"—launched—New York City—Oct. 29

1815

Monument—monument to George Washington (city or state)—cornerstone laid—Baltimore, Md.—July 4

Music—music festival—Boston, Mass.—Feb. 16

Naval Officers' Training School—naval officers' training school—established—Boston, Mass.—Dec. 10

Peace Society—New York Peace Society—organized—New York City—Aug. 16

Railroad Charter—New Jersey—Feb. 6

Ship—steam-propelled frigate—"Demologos"—propelled by own steam—June 1

Ship—steamboat (double decked)—"Washington"—keel laid—Wheeling, W. Va.—Sept. 10

Varnish manufacturer — exclusively—Christian Schrack—Philadelphia, Pa.

1816

American Language—book on Americanisms — John Pickering — published — Boston, Mass.

Army Officer—paymaster—Pay Department—organized—April 24

Bank—savings bank—Bank for Savings—New York City—conceived—Nov. 29

Bank—savings bank actually to receive money on deposit—Philadelphia Saving Fund Society—Philadelphia, Pa.—opened—Dec. 2

Bank—savings bank to become a corporation—Provident Institution for Savings—Boston, Mass.—chartered—Dec. 13

Bible Society—Bible society (national organization)—New York City—May 11

Boiler Plates — manufactured — Coatesville, Pa.

Bridge — iron wire suspension bridge—Schuylkill River

Coast Survey Superintendent—F. R. Hassler—appointed—Aug. 3

Debt—public debt of the United States to exceed $100 million

Drydock Patent—John Adamson—Boston, Mass.—Dec. 13

Evangelical Church General Conference—Buffalo Valley, Pa.—Oct. 14-17

Gas—gas ordinance (city)—Baltimore, Md.—June 19

Methodist Episcopal Church—African Methodist Episcopal Church — established — Philadelphia, Pa.—April 9

Pharmacopoeia—pharmacopoeia prepared by a hospital staff—published—New York City

Printing Press—printing press invented in America—G. E. Clymer—Columbian press—Philadelphia, Pa.

Ship—packet line—Black Ball Line—New York City to Liverpool, England

Ship—steamboat (double decked)—arrived—New Orleans, La.—Oct. 7

Tariff—tariff for protection—enacted—April 27

Theological School—theological school (nonsectarian)—Harvard College—Cambridge, Mass.

1817

Bank—savings bank to become a corporation—opened—Feb. 19

Brokerage — stock exchange — New York Stock Exchange—new organization

Canal—canal of importance—Erie Canal—authorized—April 15

Conchology Report — published — Philadelphia, Pa.

Deaf—Church Service—prayers in the sign language of the deaf—Hartford, Conn.

Deaf—School—school for the deaf—permanent—Connecticut Asylum for the Education and Instruction of Deaf and Dumb Persons—Hartford, Conn.—opened—April 15

Diplomatic Service—Pan American delegates (American)—appointed—July

Evangelical Church Building—Evangelical Church—dedicated—New Berlin, Pa.—March 2

Game Law—game law (state)—Massachusetts

Gas—gas company—Gas Light Company—Baltimore, Md.—incorporated—Feb. 5

Hospital—eye infirmary—established—New London, Conn.

Iron—cast iron pipes used in a city waterworks system—installed—Philadelphia, Pa.

Iron—iron mill to puddle and roll iron—Brownsville, Pa.—operated—Sept. 15

Law School—law school of collegiate rank—permanently organized—Harvard College School of Law—Cambridge, Mass.

Medical Book—therapeutics and materia medica book—Nathaniel Chapman—published—Philadelphia, Pa.

Newspaper — abolition newspaper —*Philanthropist*—published—Mt. Pleasant, Ohio

Paper-Making Machinery — paper-making machine (cylinder)—manufactured—Brandywine, Del.

Sword Swallower — Senaa Samma — New York City—Nov. 11

Theater—showboat—left Nashville, Tenn.—Oct. 20

Trust—trust—salt trust—organized—Nov. 10

1818

Army—medical corps—organized—April 14

Army Officer—Surgeon General of the U.S. Army—Joseph Lovell—began service—April 18

Cement—natural cement rock—discovered—Fayetteville, N.Y.

Chair Factory—established—Lambert Hitchcock—Riverton, Conn.

College—women's college (chartered)—college opened—Elizabeth Female Academy—Washington, Miss.—Nov.

Educational Magazine—educational magazine to achieve success—*Academician*—published—New York City—Feb. 7

Flag Legislation—flag act—enacted—April 4

Geology Book—geology textbook—Amos Eaton—published—Leicester, Mass.

Horticultural Society—horticultural society—New York Horticultural Society—founded—New York City

Insurance—marine insurance law (state)—Massachusetts—enacted—Feb. 16

Medical Instruction—clinical instruction and bedside demonstration—introduced—A. H. Stevens—New York City

Medical Instruction — hygiene lectures — James Jackson—Harvard College—Cambridge, Mass.—Oct. 8

Melons—melons and cantaloupes—grown—Germantown, Pa.

Oil—oil well (flowing)—Martin Beatty—Monticello, Ky.

Oratorio—oratorio performance (complete) —*Messiah*—Boston, Mass.—Dec. 25

Pension—pensions paid by the United States government—universal service pension act —enacted—March 18

Political Economy Course—college chair of political economy—Columbia University—New York City

Science Magazine—science magazine—*American Journal of Science*—published—New York City—July

Ship—steamboat built in America to cross the Atlantic ocean—"Savannah"—launched —New York City—Aug. 22

Ship—steamboat on the Great Lakes—"Walk-in-the-Water" — sailed — Buffalo, N.Y.—Oct. 10

Shoe Peg—invented—Joseph Walker—Hopkinton, Mass.

Tunnel—tunnel—Auburn, Pa.—construction commenced

1819

Agricultural "Board" (state)—authorized—New York—April 7

Agricultural Journal—agricultural journal to attain prominence—*American Farmer*—published—Baltimore, Md.—April 2

Aviation—Parachute —parachute jump from a balloon—New York City—Aug. 2

Bank—savings bank actually to receive money on deposit—chartered—Feb. 25

Bicycle—bicycle velocipedes — driven—New York City—May 21

Bicycle .Patent — bicycle patent — W. K. Clarkson—New York City—June 26

Canal—canal of importance—first boat between Rome and Utica, N.Y.—Oct. 22

Canning—canning—introduced—Ezra Daggett

Church—mariners' church—New York City —chartered—April 13

College — women's college (chartered) — Elizabeth Female Academy—Washington, Miss.—chartered—Feb. 17

Engineering College—civil engineering course in a college—Norwich University—Northfield, Vt.—founded—Aug. 6

Fire Patrol—fire patrol—Philadelphia Society for the Protection of Movable Property in Time of Fire—organized—Philadelphia, Pa.

Geological Society (national)—American Geological Society—founded—New Haven, Conn.

Iron—angle iron—rolled—Samuel Leonard—Pittsburgh, Pa.

Lathe—patented—Thomas Blanchard—Middlebury, Conn.—Sept. 6

Leather—patent leather—tanned—Seth Boyden—Newark, N.J.

Lithograph — Bass Otis — published—Philadelphia, Pa.

Manual Training—industrial school—Fellenberg plan—Derby, Conn.

Methodist—Methodist missionary—Ebenezer Brown—New Orleans, La.

Military School—military school— Norwich, Vt.—founded—Aug. 6

Navy—naval legislation standardizing nomenclature for naval vessels—enacted—March 3

Odd Fellows Lodge — established — Baltimore, Md.—April 26

Plow—plow with interchangeable parts—J. J. Wood—Poplar Ridge, N.Y.—patented—Sept. 1

Ship—steamboat built in America to cross the Atlantic Ocean—"Savannah"—sailed—Savannah, Ga.—May 22

Thread—silk thread—manufactured—Mansfield, Conn.

Tightrope—woman tightrope performer—performance—New York City—June 1

Tungsten—tungsten and tellurium—found—Huntington, Conn.

1820

Agricultural "Board" (state)—organized—New York—Jan. 20

Census—states to exceed 1,000,000 in population—New York, Virginia, and Pennsylvania

Church—mariners' church—built—New York City—June 4

Cranberry Cultivation—Dennis, Mass.

Discovery—discovery of Antarctica—N. B. Palmer—Nov. 18

Felt Manufacturing Mechanical Process—invented—T. R. Williams

Granite—quarried—Quincy, Mass.

High School—high school—English Classical School—opened—Boston, Mass.—May

Hospital—eye hospital (permanent)—New York City—opened—Aug. 14

Library—mechanics' library—opened—New York City

Library — mercantile library — organized — New York City—Nov. 9

Lightship—Craney Island, Va.—July 14

Military School—military school—first class enrolled—Norwich, Vt.—Sept. 4

Pharmacopoeia—pharmacopoeia (general)—published—Boston, Mass.—Dec. 15

Political Machine—Albany Regency

Slavery—anti-slavery magazine—*The Emancipator*—published—Jonesboro, Tenn.—April 30

Tax—bachelor tax—Missouri—Dec. 20

1821

Actor—actor to receive curtain applause—Edmund Keene—Boston, Mass.

Cathedral—cathedral—Baltimore, Md.—dedicated—May 31

College Alumni Association—college alumni association—Williams College—Williamstown, Mass.—Sept.

Debtors' Prison—abolished—Kentucky—Dec. 17

Discovery—discovery of Antarctica—expedition returned—May 8

Fire Hose—of rubber-lined cotton web—patented—James Boyd—Boston, Mass.—May 30

Odd Fellows Lodge—grand lodges organized

Pharmacy College—pharmacy college—Philadelphia College of Apothecaries organized—Philadelphia, Pa.—Feb. 23

President (U.S.)—president inaugurated on March 5—James Monroe

State—state admitted to the Union west of the Mississippi River—Missouri—Aug. 10

Tunnel—tunnel—Auburn, Pa.—opened to traffic

1822

Bank—trust company—Farmer's Fire Insurance and Loan Company—New York City—incorporated—Feburary 28

Building—building of fireproof construction—Charleston, S.C.

Dental Book—book on dentistry to become popular—J. F. Flagg—*The Family Dentist*—published—Boston, Mass.

Dentistry—patent for artificial teeth—C. M. Graham—New York City—March 9

Horticultural Society—horticultural society—New York Horticultural Society—New York City—incorporated—March 22

Hospital—eye hospital (permanent)—New York City—incorporated—March 29

Library—free public library—Juvenile Library—Dublin, N.H.

Printing Press—power or steam printing press—manufactured—Daniel Treadwell—Boston, Mass.

Printing Press—printing press for printing "paper hangings"—patented—Peter Force—Washington, D.C.—Aug. 22

Quinine—quinine— manufactured — Philadelphia, Pa.

Technical Institute — Gardiner Lyceum — Gardiner, Me.

Treadmill—completed—New York City—Sept. 7

1823

Birth Registration—birth registration law (state)—passed—Georgia—Dec. 19

Congressman (U.S.)—Roman Catholic priest to serve in Congress—Gabriel Richard—Michigan Territory—took office—March 4

Dictionary—rhyming dictionary—published—New York City

Diplomatic Service—ministers plenipotentiary to South and Central America—appointed—Jan. 27

Gymnasium—to offer systematic instruction—Round Hill School — Northampton, Mass.—opened—Oct. 1

Medical Book—medical jurisprudence treatise (authoritative)—T. R. Beck—published—Albany, N.Y.

Medical Book — ophthalmology book — George Frick—published—Baltimore, Md.

Medical Instruction—ophthalmology course (regular)—established—Baltimore, Md.

Medical School—naval medical school (unofficial)—authorized—Philadelphia, Pa.—May 19

Normal School—normal school established exclusively for the preparation of teachers — Concord Academy — Concord, Vt. — opened—March 11

Quinine — quinine sulphate — manufactured commercially—New York City

1824

Britannia Ware—produced—Isaac Babbitt—Taunton, Mass.

College—college course without Greek or Latin—Hobart College—Geneva, N.Y.

Commerce Case—decided under the Constitution—Feb.

Convent—Catholic Convent to admit colored women as sisters—Loretto, Ky.—May

Engineering College—engineering college—Rensselaer School—Troy, N.Y.—founded —Nov. 5

Entomology Book (comprehensive) *American Entomology* — published—Philadelphia, Pa.

Gas—natural gas used as an illuminant—Fredonia, N.Y.

Jewish Congregation—Jewish congregation (reform)—Reformed Society of Israelites —organized—Charleston, S.C.—Nov. 21

Locomotive—locomotive to pull a train—John Stevens—Hoboken, N.J.—Oct. 23

Political Convention—nominating convention (state)—assembled—Utica, N.Y.

President (U.S.)—President to receive fewer popular and electoral votes than an opponent—J. Q. Adams—elected—Nov. 2

Presidential Candidate—presidential candidate to receive the greatest number of popular and electoral votes yet fail of election—Andrew Jackson—Nov. 2

Presidential Popular Vote—Nov. 2

Prison—reformatory for juvenile delinquents under legislative control—New York City —incorporated—March 29

Strike—strike in which women participated —Pawtucket, R.I.

Treaty—treaty with a South American country—signed—Oct. 3

Tunnel—mining tunnel (large)—commenced —Mauch Chunk, Pa.

1825

Annual—*Le Souvenir*—published — Philadelphia, Pa.

Archery Club — archery club — founded — United Bowmen—Philadelphia, Pa.

Art Organization—artists' society of importance—organized—New York City—Nov. 8

Atlas—issued by a state—South Carolina

Bottler of Mineral Water—E. M. Durand—Philadelphia, Pa.

Brick — fire brick — manufactured — Woodbridge, N.J.

Canal—canal of importance—Erie Canal—New York—opened—Oct. 26

Canning—canning—patent—Jan. 19

Collar—collar—made—Troy, N.Y.

Communistic Society—communistic non-religious settlement—New Harmony, Ind.

Congressman (U.S.)—congressman who had been a President of the United States—J. Q. Adams—served as congressman—March 4

Cutlery Shears—manufactured—R. Heinisch —Elizabethport, N.J.

Engineering College—engineering college—Rensselaer School—Troy, N.Y.—opened—Jan. 3

Fireworks Book—*A System of Pyrotechny*—published—Philadelphia, Pa.

Fraternity (Greek Letter)—social fraternity —Kappa Alpha—Schenectady, N.Y.—established—Nov. 26

Giant—theatrical attraction—New York City —exhibited—Oct. 6

Homeopathy—introduced—H. B. Gram—New York City

Horse Race—trotting course—established—Jamaica, N.Y.

Ink—ink—manufactured—Thaddeus Davids —New York City

Labor Union—women's labor organization—United Tailoresses Society—formed—New York City

Law Codification (state)—Louisiana—promulgated—June 13

Medical Book—homeopathic treatise—C. F. S. Hahnemann — published — New York City—Dec.

Music—secular song hit—composed—J. H. Hewitt—Greenville, S.C.

Opera — grand opera sung in English—*Der Freischutz*—presented—New York City—March 2

Opera — opera (Italian) — *Il Barbiere di Siviglia*—produced—New York City— Nov. 29

Pharmacy Magazine—*The Journal of the Philadelphia College of Pharmacy*—published —Philadelphia, Pa.—Dec.

Porcelain (hard)—successfully manufactured —W. E. Tucker—Philadelphia, Pa.

Postal Service—dead letter office—organized

President (U.S.)—President whose son became president—J. Q. Adams—inaugurated

Prison—reformatory for juvenile delinquents under legislative control—New York City —opened—Jan. 1

Ship—iron vessel (sheet iron)—"Codorus" tested—Nov. 14

Ship — tugboat (steam) — "Rufus King" — built—New York City

Theater—theater lighted by gas—Chatham Garden—New York City—newspaper account—May 9

Tract Society—tract society (national)—
American Tract Society—organized—New
York City—May 11

Trademark Lawsuit—trademark controversy
involving a newspaper

Unitarian Society—national organization of
the Unitarian Churches of the United
States and Canada—organized—Boston,
Mass.—May 25

1826

Actor—American actor to appear abroad—
J. H. Hackett—New York City—professional appearance

Animals—rhinoceros—exhibited—New York
City—Sept. 13

Arcade—cornerstone laid—Philadelphia, Pa.
—May 3

Art Organization—artists' society of importance—National Academy of Design—authorized—Jan. 18

Belting—sold — Pliny Jewell — Hartford,
Conn.

Button—cloth-covered button—made by
hand—Easthampton, Mass.

Conference—conference of American Republics—Panama—March 14

Engineering College—engineering college—
Rensselaer School—Troy, N.Y.—incorporated—March 21

Engine—internal combustion engine—patented—Samuel Morey—Orford, N.H.—
April 1

Gymnastics Instruction—gymnastics instruction at a college—Harvard University—
Cambridge, Mass.

High School—high school for girls—established—Boston, Mass.

Iron—iron castings (malleable)—produced—
Newark, N.J.—July 4

Lyceum—organized—Josiah Holbrook—Millbury, Mass.—Oct.

Negro—Negro college graduate—J. B. Russwurm—Bowdoin College—Brunswick, Me.

Periodical—children's magazine with literary merit—*Juvenile Miscellany*—published—
Boston, Mass.—Sept.

Printing Instruction—printing instruction—
Robert Owen—New Harmony, Ind.

Railroad—railroad for freight transportation
to celebrate its centenary—Granite Railway Company—Quincy, Mass.—road completed—Oct. 7

Railroad Technical Report—William Strickland—published—Philadelphia, Pa.

Reaper—reaper that actually worked—invented—Henry Ogle

Ship—warship to circumnavigate the globe
"Vincennes"—left—New York City—
August 31

Tax—inheritance tax (state)—Pennsylvania
—effective—May 1

Telescope — reflecting telescope — manufactured — Amasa Holcomb — Southwick,
Mass.

1827

Actor—American actor to appear abroad—
J. H. Hackett—London, England—April 5

Anarchist—Josiah Warren—opened "time
store"—Cincinnati, Ohio

Anti-Masonic Party—formed—New York

Ballet—presented—Bowery Theater — New
York City—Feb. 7

Drydock — federal drydocks — authorized—
March 28

Governor—brothers to serve simultaneously
as governors of their respective states—
Enoch Lincoln (Maine)—1827-1829—Levi
Lincoln (Massachusetts)—1825-1834

Holiday—Mardi Gras of New Orleans, La.

Horticultural Society—horticultural society
(permanent)—Pennsylvania Horticultural
Society—organized — Philadelphia, Pa. —
Nov. 24

Kindergarten—nursery school—established—
New York City—Infant School Society—
founded—May 23

Labor Union—union organization of trades
in a city—Mechanics Union of Trade Associations—organized—Philadelphia, Pa.

Lottery—lottery legislation (national)—enacted—March 2

Monument—monument to George Washington—Boonsboro, Md.—July 4

Music—secular song hit—J. H. Hewitt—
"The Minstrel's Return"—published—Boston, Mass.

Nautical School — nautical school — established—Nantucket, Mass.—May 29

Newspaper — Negro newspaper — *Freedom's
Journal*—published—New York City—March
16

Newspaper—Spanish newspaper—*El Redactor*
—published—New York City—July 1

Ordnance—gun (rifled)—Cyrus Alger—Boston, Mass.—bronze cannon—made

Printing Press—printing press invented in
America that was practical and successful
—Samuel Rust—Washington Press—New
York City

Railroad—railroad for commercial transportation of passengers and freight—Baltimore and Ohio Railroad Company—incorporated—Feb. 28

Swimming School—opened—Boston, Mass.
July 23

Telegraph—telegraph — constructed — H. G.
Dyar—New York City

1828

Belts of Leather—used in transmitting power—Paul Moody—Lowell, Mass.

Brake Patent—brake patent—Robert Turner
—Ward, Mass.—Aug. 29

Electric Magnet—invented—Joseph Henry—
Albany, N.Y.—June

Fair—manufacturers' fair—New York City
—Oct. 24

Game Manufacturing Company—John Mc-
Loughlin—New York City

Cooperative—consumers' cooperative society
—organized—New York City

Educational Association—educational association (national)—formed—Boston, Mass.
—March 15-19

Etcher—of skill—William Dunlap

Fountain Pen Patent—D. Hyde—Reading,
Pa.—May 20

Fraternity Catalog—Kappa Alpha Society—
published—Schenectady, N.Y.

Geological Survey—geological survey (state)
—begun—Massachusetts

Locomotive—locomotive built in the U.S. to
pull passengers—"Tom Thumb"—Baltimore, Md.—Aug. 28

Locomotive—race between a locomotive and
a horse-drawn vehicle—Relay, Md. to Baltimore, Md.—Aug. 25

Marble Statuary Group—Horatio Greenough

Negro—national colored convention—Philadelphia, Pa.—Sept. 15

Newspaper — penny daily newspaper — The
Cent—Philadelphia, Pa.

Observatory — observatory (astronomical)
connected with an institution of learning—
Joseph Caldwell—Chapel Hill, N.C.

Observatory—observatory (national)—Washington, D.C.—Dec. 6

Parade—street parade held by a mystic society—Mobile, Ala.—Dec. 31

Pistol—pistol—with a revolving barrel—invented—Samuel Colt

Printing Press—power printing press capable of fine book work—patented—Isaac
Adams—Boston, Mass.—Oct. 4

Railroad — interstate railroad — chartered —
Petersburg Railroad

Railroad—railroad for commercial transportation of passengers and freight—Baltimore and Ohio Railroad Co.,—passenger
revenue received—Jan. 7

Railroad Car—double-deck railroad coaches
—used—Baltimore, Md.

Railroad Station — railroad station — (passenger and freight)—erected—Baltimore,
Md.

Railroad Track—railroad rails of "T" shape
—invented—R. L. Stevens

Scale — platform scale — built — Thaddeus
Fairbanks—St. Johnsbury, Vt.

Ship—warship to circumnavigate the globe—
"Vincennes"—returned—New York City—
June 8

Soap—cakes of soap of uniform weight and
individually wrapped — manufactured —
Jessie Oakley—Newburgh, N.Y.

Sugar—sugar beets—grown—Ensfield, Pa.

Timetable (railroad) — railroad timetable —
advertised—Baltimore, Md.—May 20

Veterinary Hospital—opened—C. C. Grice—
New York City

1831

Animals—cattle (Guernsey cattle)—imported
—Boston, Mass.

Anti-Masonic Party—presidential candidate
nominated at convention—Baltimore, Md.
—Sept. 26

Bank Robbery—New York City

Brass Wire Drawing and Tube Making
Machinery—imported—Waterbury, Conn.

Building and Loan Association—Oxford
Provident Building Association — organized—Frankford, Pa.—Jan. 3

Cabinet of the United States—cabinet member who was a Catholic—R. B. Taney—
Attorney General

Chloroform — distilled — Samuel Guthrie —
Sackets Harbor, N.Y.

Congress of the United States—Congress in
which 1,000 bills were introduced

Congressman (U.S.)—Congressman who had
been a President of the United States—
J. Q. Adams—served—March 4

Curling Club—organized—Pontiac, Mich.

Electric Bell—invented—Joseph Henry

Glucose—from potato starch—Samuel Guthrie—Sackets Harbor, N.Y.

Locomotive—locomotive bid — advertised —
Baltimore, Md.—Jan. 4

Locomotive—locomotive to burn coal (practical, American-made) — "York" — York,
Pa.—Phineas Davis—Feb. 19

Locomotive Headlight—locomotive illumination—devised—Horatio Allen

Periodical—trade journal — Rail-road Advocate—published—Rogersville, Tenn.—July 4

Play (drama)—play performed 1,000 times—
The Gladiator—New York City—opened

Printing Press—cylinder printing press—
made—R. Hoe & Co.—New York City

Railroad—railroad to carry troops—Baltimore and Ohio Railroad—to Sykesville,
Md.—June 30

Railroad Car—car with a center aisle—"Columbus" — introduced — Baltimore, Md. —
July 4

Railroad Passenger—railroad honeymoon
trip—Charleston, S.C. to Hamburg, S.C.—
Mr. & Mrs. H. L. Pierson—Jan. 15

Reaper—reaper that was practical—C. H.
McCormick—Walnut Grove, Va.

Scale—platform scale—patented—June 30

Sculptor—sculptor (American) to obtain a
federal commission—John Frazee—appropriation—March 2

Shipping — coastal shipping service — New
York City to New Orleans, La.

Street Car — street car company — incorporated—New York City—April 25

Teachers' Convention—teachers' convention
(state)—Utica, N.Y.—Jan.

Telegraph — telegraph (electro-magnetic) —
exhibited—Joseph Henry—Albany, N.Y.

Treaty—treaty with a foreign nation to provide for mutual reduction of import duties
—with France—signed—July 4

Tunnel—railroad tunnel—built—Johnstown,
Pa.

1832

"America" (the song)—publicly sung—Boston, Mass.—July 4

Democratic National Convention — Baltimore, Md.—May 21-23

Education—chair in education—New York University—New York City

Epidemic—cholera epidemic

Guano—imported—from Peru

Horticultural Magazine — *Floral Magazine* — published—Philadelphia, Pa.—May

Hospital — Negro hospital and asylum — Georgia Infirmary—chartered—Dec. 24

Indians — Indian Affairs Commissioner (U.S.)—Elbert Herring—appointed—July 10

Knitting Machine (power)—operated—Cohoes, N.Y.

Locomotive—locomotive with a four-wheeled front truck—"Experiment"—tested—New York—Aug.

Park — park (national)—Hot Springs National Park—Arkansas—established as a reservation—April 20

Phrenologist — of importance—to visit the U.S. — J. G. Spurzheim — arrived — New York City—Aug. 6

Phrenology Book—*Outlines of Phrenology*—published—Boston, Mass.

Pin—machine for manufacturing pins—patented—J. I. Howe—Derby, Conn.—June 22

Political Convention — two-thirds rule — adopted—Baltimore, Md.—May 21

Political Platform (national) — adopted — Washington, D.C.—May 11

Presidential Candidate — presidential candidate nominated at a national convention—Andrew Jackson—Baltimore, Md.

Railroad Accident — Granite Railway — Quincy, Mass.—July 25

Rubber — rubber company—Roxbury, Mass.

Sewing Machine—lock stitch sewing machine — invented — Walter Hunt — New York City

Street Car—street car—John Stephenson — service commenced — New York City — Nov. 26

Theater History—of importance—William Dunlap—*A History of the American Theatre*—published—New York City

Treaty—treaty with a foreign nation to provide for mutual reduction of import duties —France—proclaimed—July 13

Vaccination Legislation—vaccination legislation for Indians—enacted—May 5

Vice President of the United States—Vice President to resign—J. C. Calhoun—resigned—Dec. 28

Welsh Magazine — *Cymro-Americaidd* — published—New York City

1833

Animals — cattle importation of purebred shorthorns — company organized — Chillicothe, Ohio—Nov. 2

Annunciator—patented — Seth Fuller—Boston, Mass.—Dec. 26

Army—cavalry unit — organized—Jefferson Barracks, Mo.—Aug.

Avocado—planted—Santa Barbara, Calif.

Book—book for the blind—*Gospel of St. Mark* —published—Philadelphia, Pa.

Building — tenement house —built— New York City

Collar Factory—to produce shirts and collars—Troy, N.Y.

College—coeducational college—Oberlin Institute—opened—Dec. 3

Crime Prevention and Detection—interstate crime pact — signed — New York City— Sept. 16

Cutlery Factory—cutlery factory—of importance—Greenfield, Mass.

Drydock—national ship in a federal drydock — "Delaware" — Portsmouth, Va. — June 17

Horse Register — horse pacing register — *American Race-Turf Register* — published— New York City

Hospital—Negro hospital and asylum— Savannah, Ga.—organization meeting—Jan. 15

Library — free public library (town supported)—Peterborough, N.H.—April 9

Locomotive Cowcatcher — used — Camden and Amboy Railroad—Bordentown, N.J. and Hightstown, N.J.

Medical Book — dispensatory (American) *Dispensatory of the United States of America*—published—Philadelphia, Pa.

Medical Society—homeopathic medical society — Hahnemann Society—organized—Philadelphia, Pa.—April 10

Music Instruction—musical pedagogy school — Boston Academy of Music — Boston, Mass.—founded—Jan. 8

Newsboy—Barney Flaherty—New York City—Sept. 4

Newspaper — penny daily newspaper—successful—New York *Sun*—appeared—Sept. 3

Ordnance—gun (revolving)—patent — D. G. Colburn—Canton Canal, N.Y.—June 29

Pensions Commissioner (U.S.)—J. L. Edwards—appointed—March 2

Physiologist—of note—William Beaumont—Plattsburg, N.Y.—observations published

President (U.S.)—President to ride on a railroad train—Andrew Jackson

Rubber—rubber company—Roxbury India Rubber Co.—incorporated—Feb. 11

Safe (fire-proof)—patented—C. A. Gayler—New York City—April 12

School—evening school (free, public)—New York City—opened

Ship—clipper ship — "Ann McKim" — built —Baltimore, Md.

Slavery—anti-slavery book—L. M. F. Child —*An Appeal in Favor* . . . published—Boston, Mass.

Soda Fountain—soda fountain patent—Jacob Ebert—Cadiz, Ohio—April 24

Treaty—treaty with a Far Eastern country —Siam—March 20

1834

Baseball Book—*The Book of Sports*—published—Boston, Mass.

Boat Club—boat club association of amateur clubs—formed—New York City

Book Trade Magazine—book trade magazine
—published—New York City—Jan. 1

Brass Kettles—made—Coe Brass Company
—Torrington, Conn.

Cabinet of the United States—cabinet appointee rejected by the Senate—R. B.
Taney

College—coeducational college—Oberlin Collegiate Institute—first commencement—
Oct. 29

Dental Society—dental society (local)—
formed—New York City—Dec. 3

Dentistry—amalgam for filling teeth—introduced—New York City—Aug. 12

Diving Suit—(practical) for submarine diving—patented — Leonard Norcross — Dixfield, Me.—June 14

Drydock—federal drydocks—Norfolk, Va.
drydock—completed—March 15

Election—mayor elected by popular vote in
a city—C. V. W. Lawrence—New York
City—Apr. 8

Gas—gas meter (dry) — patented — James
Bogardus—New York City—Oct. 17

Geological Survey—geological survey appropriation (U.S.)—authorized—June 28

Labor Paper—*The Man* — published — New
York City—Feb. 18

Locomotive—locomotive with six or eight
driving wheels—patented—Ross Winans—
Oct. 1

Match—friction matches—manufactured commercially—Chicopee, Mass.

Medical Book—medical encyclopedia—*American Cyclopedia of Practical Medicine*—published—Philadelphia, Pa.

Methodist—Methodist missionary bishop—
Francis Burns—sailed for Liberia

Money—gold price fixed by Congress—gold
price raised—June 28

Mormon Temple — built — Joseph Smith —
Kirtland, Ohio

Opera—opera singer (American) to sing in
an Italian opera in Italian—Julia Wheatley—New York City—Nov. 25

Ordnance—gun (rifled)—Cyrus Alger

Patent—Negro to obtain a patent—Henry
Blair—Glenross, Md.—Oct. 14

Presidential Censure—Senate resolution—
March 28

Presidential Protest—signed—Andrew Jackson—April 15

Railroad—state-owned railroad—Philadelphia
and Columbia Railway—locomotive trip—
Lancaster, Pa. to Columbia, Pa.—April 2

Refrigerator—ice-making machine—invented
—Jacob Perkins

Sandpaper Patent—Isaac Fischer—Springfield, Vt.—June 14

Ship—iron vessel—"John Randolph"—built
—Savannah, Ga.

Sieve—wire sieves—manufactured commercially—Georgetown, Conn.

Soda Water Machine Manufacturer—John
Matthews—New York City

Tunnel—railroad tunnel—Hollidaysburg to
Johnstown, Pa.—completed—March 18

1835

Bible—Bible for the blind in embossed form
—New York City

Bowie Knife—invented—James Bowie

Bridge—cast iron bridge—Brownsville, Pa.

Coke—used successfully as a blast-furnace
fuel—Huntingdon County, Pa.

Egyptian Antiquities Collection—imported—
M. I. Cohen—Baltimore, Md.

Fire—fire of great destructive force—New
York City—Dec. 16

Fire Patrol—fire patrol to receive a salary—
New York City

Flea Circus—opened—New York City—Jan.

Gardener's Manual — *Young Gardener's Assistant*—published—New York City

Governor—Catholic governor—E. D. White

Horseshoe Manufacturing Machine — patented—Henry Burden—Troy, N.Y.—Nov.
23

Insurance—mutual fire insurance company—
Manufacturers' Mutual Fire Insurance
Company—Providence, R.I.—incorporated
—Oct. 31

Insurance—mutual life insurance company
to be chartered—New England Mutual
Life Insurance Company—Boston, Mass.
—chartered—April 1

Laundry—laundry—established — Independence Starks—Troy, N.Y.

Lock — mortised lock — Blake Brothers —
Westville, Conn.

Locomotive—locomotive with a cab—"Samuel D. Ingham"—built—Philadelphia, Pa.

Medical Periodical—homeopathic magazine—
American Journal of Homeopathia—published
—New York City—Feb.

Medical School—homeopathic school—North
American Academy of the Homeopathic
Healing Art—Allentown, Pa.—founded—
April 10

Music Instruction—music school authorized
to confer degrees—established — Salem,
Conn.

Patent Commissioner—H. L. Ellsworth—appointed—June 15

Periodical—Indian-language monthly—*Shawnee Sun*—Feb. 24

Police—state police—Texas Rangers—organized

President (U.S.)—President whose assassination was attempted—Andrew Jackson,
—Jan. 30

Railroad—railroad to run trains to Washington, D.C.—Baltimore and Ohio Railroad—
July 1

Sculptor—sculptor (American) of merit—
Hiram Powers

Soda Water—soda water commercially bottled—Philadelphia, Pa.—Elias Durand

Spoons—nickel silver spoons—manufactured
—Robert Wallace—Wallingford, Conn.

Wrench—wrench patent—Solyman Merrick
—Springfield, Mass.—Aug. 17

Zinc—zinc—produced—Washington, D.C.

1836

Agricultural Seed Distribution (national)—H. L. Ellsworth

Animals—cattle (shorthorn) public auction sale—Chillicothe, Ohio—Oct. 29

Chemical Laboratory—chemical laboratory for instruction in chemical analyses—Philadelphia, Pa.

Child Labor Law—child labor law to include educational provision—enacted—Massachusetts—April 16

College—college for women—Mount Holyoke Seminary—South Hadley, Mass.—chartered—Feb. 11

College—women's college (chartered)—Wesleyan College, Macon, Ga.

Colonist—women to cross the continent—crossed continental divide—South Pass, Wyo.—July 4

Congress (U.S.)—House of Representatives—gag rule—adopted—May 26

Cricket Tournament—cricket game played by a college team—Haverford College—Haverford, Pa.

Expedition—scientific expedition fitted out by the United States Government—authorized—May 14

Fastening — hooks and eyes — successfully manufactured—Waterbury, Conn.

Fuse—safety fuse—manufactured—Simsbury, Conn.

Match—match patent—phosphorous friction matches — A. D. Phillips — Springfield, Mass.—Oct. 24

Medical School—homeopathic school—North American Academy of the Homoepathic Healing Art—Allentown, Pa.—incorporated—June 17

Money—coins produced by steam power

Mormon Temple—Kirtland, Ohio—dedicated March 27

Naval Officer—naval officer to become an engineer—C. H. Haswell—commissioned—Feb. 19

Patent—numbering system for patents—introduced—July 13

Pistol—pistol—with a revolving barrel—patent—Samuel Colt—Feb. 25

Postage Stamp—adhesive stamps—local delivery service authorized—July 2

President of the Republic of Texas—Sam Houston—took oath—Columbia, Tex.—Oct. 22

Railroad Guide—railroad guide—*The Traveller's Guide . . . .*—New York

School Superintendent—school superintendent (city)—R. W. Haskins—Buffalo, N.Y.

Ship—steamboat on the Pacific coast—"Beaver" — tested — Vancouver, Washington—May 16

Sleeping Car—sleeping car—Harrisburg to Chambersburg, Pa.

Supreme Court (U.S.)—Chief Justice of the Supreme Court who was Catholic—R. B. Taney—appointed—March 28

Treasury Department (U.S.)—treasury surplus returned and apportioned among the several states—authorized—June 23

Whig Party—state convention—Albany, N.Y.—Feb. 3

1837

Blind—state school for the blind—opened—Columbus, Ohio—July 4

Carpet Loom—carpet power loom—patented—E. B. Bigelow—West Boylston, Mass.—April 20

Child Labor Law—child labor law to include educational provision—Massachusetts—effective—April 1

Clock—brass clock works—invented—Chauncey Jerome—Bristol, Conn.

Coal—anthracite coal used in smelting iron ore—Mauch Chunk, Pa.

College—city college—became municipal university—Charleston, S.C.

College—coeducational college—Oberlin Collegiate Institute—equal status granted to women—Sept. 6

College—college for women—Mount Holyoke Seminary opened—Nov. 8

Education—state board of education—Massachusetts—established—April 30

Fluorspar—commercial mining — Trumbull, Conn.

Locomotive Steam Whistle—used—"The Sandusky"—Oct. 6

Music Instruction—music instruction (public school)—Hawes School—South Boston, Mass.—Nov.

Periodical—magazine for the blind—*Student's Magazine*—published—Philadelphia, Pa.

Physiological Society—physiological society—American Physiological Society—organized—Boston, Mass.—Feb. 11

Piano—piano frame of iron—Jonas Chickering—Boston, Mass.

Rubber — rubber patent of importance — Charles Goodyear—June 17

Silk—silk power loom—patented—William Crompton—Taunton, Mass.—Nov. 25

Telegraph—telegraphic communication system in which dots and dashes represented letters—invented — Alfred Vail — Morristown, N.J.—Sept.

Thresher—threshing machine to employ steam—patented—Dec. 29

Treaty—treaty with a Far Eastern country—proclaimed—June 24

Vice President of the United States—Vice President elected by the Senate—R. M. Johnson—Feb. 8

1838

Astronomical Observations Book—J. M. Gillis—*Astronomical Observations*—published—Washington, D.C.

Brake Patent—railroad brake patent—E. Morris—Bloomfield, N.J.—Sept. 19

Bridge—wooden railroad bridge of a purely truss type—built—Alberton, Md.

Bunting—manufactured—M. H. Simpson—Saxonville, Mass.

Caster — for furniture — patented — Blake—New Haven, Conn.—June 30

Clock—watch made by machinery—marketed—James and Henry Pitkin

College—city college—opened as municipal university—Charleston, S.C.—April 1

College—college for women—Mount Holyoke Seminary—graduation—Aug. 23

Embossing Press—built—B. Sheridan—New York City

Expedition—scientific expedition fitted out by the United States Government—started—Hampton Roads, Va.—Aug. 18

Free Lunch—free lunch—Pierre Maspero—New Orleans, La.

History Instruction—ancient and modern history chair — Harvard College — Cambridge, Mass.

Music—music convention—Boston, Mass.—Aug. 16-25

Normal School—normal school instruction—Lafayette College—cornerstone laid—July 4

Patent—patent re-issue—Julius Hatch—Great Bend, Pa.—Jan. 9

Phrenology Magazine—*American Phrenological Journal* — published — Nathan Allen—Philadelphia, Pa.—Oct.

Pin—pins manufactured with a solid head—Poughkeepsie, N.Y.

Prohibition — prohibition state — legislation enacted—Tennessee—Jan. 26

School—model school — opened — Lafayette College—Easton, Pa.—Oct. 31

Ship—steamboat service (regular) across the Atlantic—arrived New York City—April 23

Silk—silk dyers—Gurleyville, Conn.

Silver Mine—discovered—Lexington, N.C.

Steam Shovel—invented—W. S. Otis—Philadelphia, Pa.

Steamboat Inspection Service (U.S.)—established—July 7

Sugar — sugar beets — Northampton Beet Sugar Company—erected—Northampton, Mass.

Sunday School—Jewish Sunday School—organized—Hebrew Sunday School Society—Philadelphia, Pa.—March 4

Telegraph—telegraphic communication system in which dots and dashes represented letters—message sent—Jan. 8

Tool Factory—established—Nashua, N.H.—John H. Gage

Workmen's Compensation—workmen's compensation lawsuit—South Carolina—July

1839

Anti-Slavery Party — convention — Warsaw, N.Y.—Nov. 13

Baseball Game—baseball—Abner Doubleday—Cooperstown, N.Y.

Building—building with a high steeple—commenced—New York City—Oct. 17

Cotton Twine Factory—Sloatsburg, N.Y.

Cranioscopy Book—Crania Americana—published

Dental Magazine—dental journal—*American Journal of Dental Science*—published—New York City—July

Dental School—dental college—Baltimore College of Dental Surgery—organized—Baltimore, Md.

Electrotype—electrotype—produced — New York City

Envelope Manufacturer—Mr. Pierson—New York City

Express Service—organized—W. F. Harnden—Boston, Mass.—Feb. 23

Fraternity (Greek Letter)—fraternity house—Kappa Alpha Society—Williams College—Williamstown, Mass.

Fraternity (Greek Letter)—fraternity west of the Alleghenies—Beta Theta Pi—Miami University—Oxford, Ohio—founded—Aug. 8

Horse—horse (Percheron horse)—importation—Moorestown, N.J.

Iron—iron blast furnace—anthracite coal—Pottsville, Pa.—furnace blown—Oct. 19

Law Dictionary (American)—John Bouvier *A Law Dictionary*—published—Philadelphia, Pa.

Military School—state military school—Virginia Military Institute—Lexington, Va.—established—March 29

Normal School—normal school (state)—Normal School—Lexington, Mass.—opened—July 3

Photograph—celestial photograph—of the moon—J. W. Draper—New York City—Dec. 18

Photograph—photograph taken in the United States—daguerrotype

Political Convention—unit rule—adopted—Harrisburg, Pa.—Dec. 4

Printing Press—printing press operated by electricity — used — Thomas Davenport — New York City

Ship—iron vessel built of American iron—"De Rosset"—built—Baltimore, Md.

Statistical Society—of importance—American Statistical Association—Boston, Mass.—organized—Nov. 27

Steam Shovel—patented—W. S. Otis—Philadelphia, Pa.—Feb. 24

Teachers' Institute—Hartford, Conn.—Oct.

1840

Beer—lager beer—manufactured—John Wagner—Philadelphia, Pa.

Bowling Tournament—bowling match—New York City—Jan. 1

Bridge—cast iron girder bridge—Erie Canal

Bridge—timber trestle pier of lattice construction—commenced—Shuman's Station, Pa.—June

Chiropodist — Nehemiah Kenison — Boston, Mass.

College—women's college (chartered)—Wesleyan College, Macon, Ga.—first class graduated—July 16

Dental School—dental college—Baltimore College of Dental Surgery—Baltimore, Md.—incorporated—Feb. 1

Dental Society—dental society of importance —American Society of Dental Surgeons—organized—New York City—Aug. 18

Drydock—timber drydock—erected—Buffalo, N.Y.

Embalming Book—*History of Embalming*—published—Philadelphia, Pa.

Expedition—scientific expedition fitted out by the United States Government—saw Antarctic continent—Jan. 16

Graphite—commercial production—Ticonderoga, N.Y.

Gutta Percha—imported—New York City

Land Mines—used against Seminole Indians

Library—library building (university)—Columbia, S.C.—completed—May 6

Medical Clinic—college medical clinic—established—Willard Parker—New York City

Money—paper money issued by the American Indians—Oregon

Nut and Bolt Factory—Marion, Conn.

Periodical—electrical journal—*The Electro-Magnetic and Mechanics Intelligencer*—published—New York City—Jan. 18

Photographic Pamphlet—published—Boston, Mass.

Photographic Patent—photographic patent—Alexander S. Wolcott—New York City—May 8

Play (drama)—aquatic play—*The Pirate's Signal*—presented—New York City—July 4

Pump — independent single direct-acting steam power pump — invented — H. R. Worthington—New York City

Radio Impulse Transmission (wireless)—Joseph Henry—Princeton, N.J.—Dec.

Second Advent Believers General Conference—Boston, Mass.—Oct. 14-15

Seeding Machine (practical) — patented — Joseph Gibbons—Adrian, Mich.—Aug. 25

Treasury Department (U.S.)—Treasury Department (US.)—Sub-Treasury act—July 4

Wire—brass wire — manufactured — Edwin Hodges—West Torrington, Conn.

1841

Advertising Agency—V. B. Palmer—Philadelphia, Pa.

Anesthesia—anesthetic—(general) — used — C. W. Long—Jefferson, Ga.

Anti-Slavery Party—Liberty Party national convention—New York City—May 12

Botanist — botanist — prominent landscape gardener—A. J. Downing

Brick—fire brick to withstand high heat—Mount Savage, Md.

Bridge—tubular plate girder bridge—James Millholland

Business—commercial rating agency—Mercantile Agency—New York City—established—Aug. 1

Carpet Loom—carpet power loom to weave ingrain carpets—Lowell Manufacturing Company—Lowell, Mass.

Chair—recumbent chair patent—H. P. Kennedy—Philadelphia, Pa.

Congress (U.S.)—Senate—senate filibuster (continuous)—began—Feb. 18

Cornstarch—cornstarch patent—O. Jones—March 22

Dental Book—orthodontia treatise—Solyman Brown—published—New York City

Dental Legislation—legislation (state) regarding dental surgery—enacted—Alabama —Dec. 31

Detective Story—to achieve popularity—E. A. Poe—*Murders in the Rue Morgue*—published—Philadelphia, Pa.—April

Elastic Webbing — produced — Middletown, Conn.

Fire Engine—steam fire engine—tested—P. R. Hodge—New York City—March 27

Geodetic Survey—completed—Simeon Borden

Immigration—Japanese to enter the United States — Nakahama Manjiro — Fairhaven, Mass.

Life Preserver—life preserver of cork—patented—N. E. Guerin—New York City—Nov. 16

Newspaper Syndicate—syndication of newspaper material—M. Y. Beach—New York City—Dec. 7

Normal School—normal school instruction course given at a university—Middletown, Conn.—Dec. 1

Pin—machine "for sticking pins into paper" —patented—Samuel Slocum—Poughkeepsie, N.Y.—Sept. 30

President (U.S.)—President to die in Washington, D.C.—W. H. Harrison—April 4

President (U.S.)—President whose grandson became President—W. H. Harrison—served

Senator (U.S.)—senator to receive a mileage allowance for a trip which he did not make—George Evans—March 4

Ship—iron vessel built for the U.S. Navy—"Michigan"—authorized—Sept. 9

Ship—steamboat engine built in America for a screw-propelled vessel—installed—"Vandalia"—launched—Dec. 1

Statistical Society—American Statistical Association—incorporated—Feb. 5

Torpedo—underwater torpedo operated by electric current—invented—Samuel Colt—Hartford, Conn.

Tube—collapsible tube — patented — John Rand

Typesetting Machine—typesetting machine patent—June 22

Venetian Blinds—venetian blind patent—John Hampson—New Orleans, La.—Aug. 21

Vice President of the United States—Vice President to become President automatically—John Tyler—April 4

Wire—wire rope factory—erected—J. A. Roebling—Saxonburg, Pa.

1842

Bridge—wire suspension bridge for general traffic—Schuylkill River—Jan. 2

Business School—business school—Eastman Commercial College—Rochester, N.Y.

Cable—cable—laid—S. F. B. Morse—New York Harbor

Child Labor Law—child labor law regulating hours of employment—Massachusetts —March 3

Coast Guard (U.S.)—Coast Guard commandant—appointed—Feb. 1

College—university on the Pacific coast—organized—Salem, Ore.—Feb. 1

Cornstarch—starch made commercially from Indian corn—Thomas Kingsford—Jersey City, N.J.

Credit Protective Group - - formed — New York City

Elevator—grain elevator operated by steam —Robert Dunbar—Buffalo, N.Y.

Expedition—scientific expedition fitted out by the United States Government—returned to New York City—June 10

Gold—gold discovered in California—San Fernando Mission

Insurance—mutual life insurance company to operate—Mutual Life Insurance Co.—New York City—chartered—April 12

Iron—hammered iron—Great Egg Harbor River, N.J.

Minstrel Show Troupe—performances—New York City

Narcotic—narcotic tariff—enacted—August 30

Naval Officer—naval officer condemned for mutiny—hanged—Dec. 1

Navy—Bureau of Medicine and Surgery—authorized—Aug. 31

Nut and Bolt Machine—patented—Micah Rugg—Aug. 31

Patent—design patent—George Bruce—New York City—Nov. 9

Periodical—illustrated weekly—*Brother Jonathan*—published—New York City—Jan. 1

Postage Stamp—adhesive stamps—issued—City Despatch Post—New York City—Feb. 15

Presidential Commission — President requested by Congress to justify the creation of a presidential committee—John Tyler—Feb. 7

Prize Fight—prize fight fatality—Hastings, N.Y.—Sept. 13

Road—overland wagon road across the Rocky Mountains—Oregon Trail

Rubber—rubber shoe manufacturer—Leverett Candee—Hamden, Conn.

Sewing Machine—sewing machine patent—J. J. Greenough—Washington, D.C.—Feb. 21

State—state to repudiate a debt—Mississippi

Tariff—tariff to prevent the importation of obscene literature and pictures—enacted—Aug. 30

Volcano—eruption—reported—Nov. 22

1843

Almanac—patent medicine almanac — published—Batavia, N.Y.

Book Index—book index—published—**New York City**

Church—floating church—New York City

Colonial Government—government on the Pacific coast—Oregon—May 2

Diplomatic Service—consul to California— T. O. Larkin—appointed—May 1

Horse Race—futurity race—Nashville, Tenn. —Oct. 10

Incubator (Eggs) Patent—N. E. Guerin— New York City—March 30

Insurance—mutual life insurance company to be chartered—organized for business—Dec. 1

Insurance—mutual life insurance company to operate—policy issued—Feb. 1

Musician—orchestra leader to conduct without using a baton—G. J. Webb—Boston, Mass.

Paper—manila paper—patented — Hollingsworth—South Braintree, Mass.—Dec. 4

Periodical—magazine published for mental patients — *Illuminator* — Philadelphia, Pa.— April 1

Ship—frigate (American-built, steam-driven) to cross the Atlantic Ocean—"Missouri"— left Norfolk, Va.—Aug. 5

Ship—iron vessel built for the U.S. Navy— "Michigan"—launched—Dec. 5

Ship—naval vessel of the United States to sail around the Cape of Good Hope to the west coast of the United States—"Constellation"—returned—Monterey Bay, Calif.— Sept. 15

Ship—warship with propelling machinery below the waterline—"Princeton"—launched —Dec. 10

Telegraph—telegraph appropriation (federal)—enacted—March 3

Typewriter — typewriter that successfully typed—patented—Charles Thurber—Norwich, Conn.—Aug. 26

1844

Anesthesia—anesthetic in dentistry—Horace Wells—Hartford, Conn.—Dec. 11

Book Review—book review editor—S. M. F. Ossoli—New York City—Dec.

Bridge Whist Rule Book—*The Whist Player's Hand Book*—published—Philadelphia, Pa.

Coast Guard (U.S.)—Coast Guard commandant—first report submitted—Jan. 9

College—Masonic college—opened—Philadelphia, Mo.—May 12

Credit Report Book—prepared—S. P. Church —New York City

Game Protection Society—New York Sportsmen's Club— formed—New York City— May 20

Gas Engine—patented—Stuart Perry—New York City—May 25

Glass—stained figure glass—installed—Pelham Manor, N.Y.

Baking Soda — manufactured — New York City

Building—building with a high steeple—Trinity Church—New York City—dedicated—May 21

Capital Punishment—death penalty was first abolished—Michigan—May 4

Cellulose Nitrate Patent—Dec. 5

Chemistry Professor—professorship of applied chemistry—Benjamin Silliman—New Haven, Conn.

College—college to grant women absolutely equal rights—Mount Union College, Alliance, Ohio—founded—Oct. 20

Electrotype — electrotype manufacturing — J. W. Wilcox—Boston, Mass.

Factory—steam-heated factory—built—Burlington, Vt.

Gingham Factory—opened—E. B. Bigelow—Clinton, Mass.

Herd Book—published—Buffalo, N.Y.

Leg (artificial) patent—B. F. Palmer — Meredith, N. H.—Nov. 4

Medical Book—bronchitis treatise— Horace Green—published—New York City

Newspaper—newspaper published on the Pacific Coast—*Oregon Spectator*—Oregon City, Ore.—Feb. 5

Printing Press—rotary type printing press—used—*Ledger*—Philadelphia, Pa.

Prison—military prison of the United States on an island—construction started—Fort Jefferson, Fla.

Railroad—international railroad—from Portland, Me.—construction—July 4

Road—plank road — completed — Syracuse, N.Y.—July 18

School—school to operate on the one-class-to-a-room basis — established — Quincy, Mass.

Senator (U.S.)—Senator elected on an anti-slavery ticket—J. P. Hale—New Hampshire—June 9

Steel—cast steel for plows—manufactured—William Woods—Pittsburgh, Pa.

Supreme Court (U.S.) Decision—Supreme Court decision in a state boundary case—Justice R. B. Taney

Tattoo—tattoo shop—Martin Hildebrandt—New York City

Telegraph—telegraph company — Magnetic Telegraph Company—first meeting—Jan. 14.

Telegraph—telegraph ticker to print letters of the alphabet—patented—R. E. House—New York City—April 18

Treasury Department (U.S.)—Treasury Department (U.S.) — sub-treasury — established

War (Mexican)—Mexican war shots—April 25

Warehouse legislation — enacted—Aug. 6

Woman—woman telegrapher—S. G. Bagley —Lowell, Mass.—Feb. 21

1847

Army Insignia—chevrons—authorized

Bread—bread from unbolted flour—introduced—Sylvester Graham

Bronze Statue (full length)—Mount Auburn, Cambridge, Mass.—Ball Hughes

Capital Punishment—death penalty was first abolished—Michigan—effective—March 1

Chinese Students—arrived—New York City —April 12

Fertilizer (artificial) — developed — J. J. Mapes—Newark, N.J.

Insurance—health insurance company—Massachusetts Health Insurance Company—organized—Boston, Mass.—April 21

Labor Law—ten-hour day law—New Hampshire—July 9

Lighthouse—iron pile lighthouse built—Minot's Ledge, Mass.—commenced

Medical Instruction—pathology chair—established—Harvard University—Cambridge, Mass.

Medical Society—medical society (national) —of permanence—American Medical Association—organized—Philadelphia, Pa.— May 5

Newspaper—Norwegian-American newspaper —*Nordlyset*—Muskego, Wis.

Pile Driver—steam pile driver patent—awarded—James Nasmyth

Plow—plow for pulverizing the soil—patented—George Page—Washington, D.C.— August 7

Postage Stamp—postage stamps issued by the Post Office Department—authorized—March 3

Printing Press—rotary type printing press—patented—July 24

Prison—reformatory for boys (state)—Westborough, Mass.—authorized—April 9

Railroad Car—railroad coach—placed in service—May 19—Boston, Mass.

Railroad Guide—railroad guide that printed the time schedule—*United States Railroad and Ocean Steam Navigation Guide*—published—New York City

Rubber—rubber tire patent—R. W. Thomson—May 8

Ship—steamship passenger line between United States ports and Europe to fly the American flag—Ocean Steam and Navigation Company—New York City—service —June 1

Silver Plating Factory—Rogers Brothers—Hartford, Conn.

Surgical Operation—skin grafting—F. H. Hamilton—Buffalo, N.Y.

Swedish Magazine—*Skandinavia*—published—New York City—Jan. 15

Telegraph—telegraph company — Magnetic Telegraph Co.—incorporated—Feb. 4

Vacation Fund—established—W. A. Muhlenberg—New York City

1848

Arts and Science Society—woman elected to the American Academy of Arts and Sciences—Maria Mitchell—May 30

Baby Carriage—manufactured—Charles Burton—New York City

Bible—phonetic Bible—published—Philadelphia, Pa.

Bloomers—introduced—Seneca Falls, N.Y.—July 19

Building—building constructed wholly of cast iron—James Bogardus—New York City

Cable (telegraph)—submarine telegraph cable to be insulated with gutta percha—Brooklyn, N.Y.—May

Chewing Gum—chewing gum—manufactured Bangor, Me.

Child Labor Law—child labor law restricting the age of the worker—enacted—Pennsylvania—March 28

Dental Chair—patented—M. W. Hanchett—Syracuse, N.Y.—Aug. 15

Election—election day—uniformly observed —Nov. 7

Engineering Society—engineering society—of importance—Boston Society of Civil Engineers — Boston, Mass. — organized—April 26

Free Soil Party—National Free Soil Convention—organized—Buffalo, N.Y.—Aug. 9-10

Gas—gas light in the White House—Washington, D.C.—Dec. 29

Gold—gold discovered in California—Marshall discovery—Coloma, Calif.—Jan. 24

Ice Cream Freezer—patented—W. G. Young —Baltimore, Md.—May 30

Immigration—Chinese immigrants — arrived —San Francisco, Calif.

Macaroni Factory—Antoine Zerega—Brooklyn, N.Y.

Medical School—homeopathic college—Homeopathic Medical College—Philadelphia, Pa.—incorporated—April 8

Medical School—women's medical school—Boston Female Medical School—Boston, Mass.—organized—Nov. 1

Medical Society—women's medical society—organized—Boston, Mass.

Monument—monument to George Washington (national)—cornerstone laid—July 4

Periodical—comic weekly—*John Donkey*—published—Philadelphia, Pa.—Jan. 1

Periodical Index—published—W. F. Poole—New York City

Political Convention—national committee of a political organization—Baltimore, Md.—May 22-26

Pure Food Law—pure food and drug legislation (national)—enacted—June 26

Railroad—railroad to run west, out of Chicago—Chicago and North Western Railway—Oct. 25

School—school for the mentally retarded—opened—Massachusetts—Oct. 1

Science Association—scientific society (national organization)—American Association for the Advancement of Science—organized—Philadelphia, Pa.—Sept. 20

Senator (U.S.)—father and son senators at the same session—Henry Dodge and A. C. Dodge—Dec. 7

Ship—steamboat service (regular) to California via Cape Horn—left—New York City—Oct. 6

Shirt Factory—O. F. Winchester—Boston, Mass.

Shorthand Magazine—*American Phonographic Journal*—published—Philadelphia, Pa.

Spiritualist—J. D. Fox—Hydeville, N.Y.

Water Conduit—drinking water conduit—built—Boston, Mass.

Woman Suffrage—convention of women advocating woman suffrage—Seneca Falls, N.Y.—July 19-20

1849

Army Officer—chaplain (Catholic) of the U.S. Army—served—Sept. 28

Business Economics Course—University of Louisiana—New Orleans, La.

Clock — watchmaker — American Horologe Company—Roxbury, Mass.—formed

Degrees (academic and honorary)—Doctor of Music degree—conferred—Georgetown University—Washington, D.C.—July 24

Disciples of Christ—general conference—Cincinnati, Ohio—Oct. 24

Drill—percussion rock drill—patented—J. J. Couch—March 27

Envelope—envelope machine patent—New York City—Jan. 23

Gas Mask—gas mask—patented—L. P. Haslett—Louisville, Ky.—June 12

Ice Skating Club—ice skating club—formed —Philadelphia, Pa.—Dec. 21

Interior Department (U.S.)—Interior Department secretary—Thomas Ewing—appointed—March 8

Interior Department (U.S.)—Interior Department (U.S.)—created—March 3

Library Law enacted by a state—New Hampshire—July 7

Medical School—homeopathic college—graduation—March 29

Melodeon Patent—C. Austin—Concord, N.H. —June 19

Money—double eagle coinage—authorized—March 3

Money—gold coinage — double-eagles and one-dollar gold pieces authorized—March 3

Music—chamber music organization—Mendelssohn Quintette Club—Boston, Mass.—concert—Dec. 14

Music—saengerfest—Cincinnati, Ohio

Ordnance—cannon (breech loading)—patented—Benjamin Chambers—July 31

Photograph—photograph of a President (in office)—J. K. Polk—New York City—Feb. 14

Physician — woman physician — Elizabeth Blackwell — graduated — Geneva, N.Y. — Jan. 23

Pin—safety pin—patented—Walter Hunt—New York City—April 10

Poultry Show—Boston, Mass.—Nov. 15-16

President (U.S.)—President who had received a patent—Abraham Lincoln—May 22

Railroad—railroad to run west of the Mississippi River—incorporated—March 12

Railroad Excursion—railroad excursion rates—Boston, Mass.

Ship—steamboat service (regular) to California via Cape Horn—from New York City—arrived—San Francisco, Calif.—Feb. 28

Tattoo—tattooed man—J. F. O'Connell—exhibited

Thread—silk thread on spools—M. Heminway

Wire Gauge — developed — I. Washburn—Worcester, Mass.

1850

Adding Machine—adding machine to employ depressible keys—patented—D. D. Parmelee—New Paltz, N.Y.—Feb. 5

Billiard Book—*Billiards Without A Master*—published—New York City

Birds—sparrows—imported—Brooklyn, N.Y.

Catholic Bishop—native bishops of the South—ordained—Mobile, Ala.—Aug. 15

Clock—watch (eight-day)—manufactured—A. L. Dennison—Roxbury, Mass.

Cork Manufacturer—William King—Brooklyn, N.Y.

Cracker—meat biscuit—patented—Gail Borden—July 30

Desk with roll top—invented—Abner Cutler—Buffalo, N.Y.

Elevator—elevator—platform type—installed—Henry Waterman—New York City

Gas Mask—gas mask with a self-contained breathing apparatus—patented—B. J. Lane—Cambridge, Mass.—July 2

Hat—derby hat—manufactured—South Norwalk, Conn.

History Instruction—American history chair—established—University of Pennsylvania—Philadelphia, Pa.

Hospital — homeopathic hospital — Homeopathic Hospital of Pennsylvania—Philadelphia, Pa.—incorporated—Sept. 20

Ice Skating Club—ice skating club—formally organized—Philadelphia, Pa.—Jan. 4

Land Grant—railroad land grant of importance

Lighthouse—iron pile lighthouse—operated—Minot's Ledge, Mass.—Jan. 1

Magic Lantern Slides (glass plate)—patented—F. Langenheim—Philadelphia, Pa.—Nov. 19

Medical School—women's medical school (still in existence as an independent institution)—organized

Mint (U.S.)—private mint authorized by the United States Government—Moffat Assay Office—Mt. Ophir, Calif.

Money—double eagle coinage—double eagles coined

Museum—college museum—Charleston Museum—Charleston, S.C.—F. S. Holmes—elected curator—Nov. 25

Newspaper—German daily newspaper—*New Yorker Staats-Zeitung* — published — New York City—Jan. 26

Photograph—photograph of a star (other than the sun)—Vega—Cambridge, Mass.—July 17

Railroad Car—private railroad car—used—Jenny Lind

School—school for the mentally retarded—incorporated—Boston, Mass.—April 4

State—state admitted to the Union on the Pacific Coast—California—Sept. 9

Telegraph—telegraph convention (national)—New York City—July 17

Ticket Speculators—New York City—Sept.

Wire—piano wire—manufactured—Ichabod Washburn—Worcester, Mass.

Woman Suffrage—convention (national) of women advocating woman suffrage—National Woman's Rights Convention—Worcester, Mass.—Oct. 23-24

1851

Aviation—Airship — airship bombing — suggested—John Wise

Brass and Copper Seamless Tubes—manufactured—Somerville, Mass.

Brass Spinning—H. W. Hayden—Waterbury, Conn.—Dec. 16

Cemetery—national cemeteries—Mexico City National Cemetery

Cheese Factory—cheese factory of consequence—Rome, N.Y.

College—college to prohibit discrimination because of race, religion, or color—Cooper Union—New York City—April 29

Deaf—Students' Magazine — magazine for deaf students—*Deaf Mute Casket*—published—Raleigh, N.C.

Engineering Society—engineering society—of importance—Boston Society of Civil Engineers—incorporated—April 24

Eye—artificial eyes — manufactured — Pierre Gougelman—New York City

Fire Alarm System (electric)—tested—Boston, Mass.

Hat—soft felt hats for women—introduced—J. N. Genin—New York City

Ice Cream—ice cream wholesale dealer—Jacob Fussel—Baltimore, Md.

Insurance—insurance board (state)—established—New Hampshire—July 1

Laundry—commercial power laundry—Oakland, Calif.

Lock — lock ("clock") — patented — Linus Yale, Newport, N.Y.—May 6

Locomotive—electric locomotive—trial trip—Washington, D.C. to Bladensburg, Md.—April 29

Medal—medal awarded to an American food producer—Gail Borden

1852

1853

Envelope—envelope folding machine—patented—R. L. Hawes—Worcester, Mass.—Jan. 21

Expedition—arctic expedition—E. K. Kane—left—New York City—May 31

Fair—industrial exposition—New York City—opened—July 14

Fire Department—fire department to be paid a salary—established — Cincinnati, Ohio—April 1

Fire Engine—fire engine that was practical—tested—Cincinnati, Ohio—Jan. 1

Glass—plate glass—manufactured—J. N. Richmond—Cheshire, Mass.

Horse Show—horse show—Upperville, Va.

Hospital—women's infirmary staffed by women physicians—New York Infirmary for Women and Children—incorporated—Dec. 13

Hygiene Instruction—physiology and hygiene courses—at a college—Antioch College—Yellow Springs, Ohio

Librarians' Convention—New York City—Sept. 15-17

Mechanics Textbook—*The Elements of Analytical Mechanics* — published — New York City

Medical School—medical summer school—Medical College of South Carolina—Columbia, S.C.

Money — gold coinage — three-dollar gold pieces authorized—Feb. 21

Monument—bronze equestrian statue—Andrew Jackson statue unveiled—Washington, D.C.—Jan. 8

Pharmacy Society (national) — American Pharmaceutical Association—annual meeting—Boston, Mass.—Aug. 24

Postage Stamp—stamped envelopes (U.S.)—issued—June

Pottery—pottery to make sanitary ware—founded—Trenton, N.J.

Railroad—railroad merger—of importance—New York Central Railroad Company—May 17

Railroad Station—union passenger station—Union Station—Indianapolis, Ind.—opened—Sept. 20

Trade Association—American Brass Association—organized

Truancy legislation (state)—enacted—New York—April 12

Vice President of the United States—Vice President sworn in on foreign soil—W. R. D. King—Havana, Cuba—March 4

Village Improvement Society—Laurel Hill Association—Stockbridge, Mass. — organized—Aug. 24

Water Cures—introduced—R. T. Trall—New York City—Nov. 1

Woman—woman ordained a minister—A. B. Blackwell—South Butler, N.Y.—Sept. 15

Young Men's Christian Association—Young Men's Christian Association for Negro members—organized—Washington, D.C.

Zinc—zinc commercial production—Bethlehem, Pa.—mill erected—Oct. 13

1854

Accordion Patent—Anthony Faas—Jan 13

Agricultural School — agricultural college (state) to be chartered—Farmers High School of Pennsylvania—incorporated—April 13

Alfalfa—introduced—California

American Party—organized

Assay Office Building (federal)—erected—New York City

Baby Show—Springfield, Ohio—Oct. 5

Bank—clearing house—charter adopted—June 6

Billiard Match—billiard match—of importance—Syracuse, N.Y.—May 13

Blanket—blanket factory—Burleigh Blanket Mills—So. Berwick, Me.

Book—book (pamphlet) on vellum—published—Cambridge, Mass.

Bridge — railway suspension bridge — completed—Niagara Falls, N.Y.

Building—building in which wrought iron beams were used—New York City

Chair—folding theater chair—patented—A. H. Allen—Boston, Mass.—Dec. 5

Chinese Students—college graduate—Yung Wing—Yale University — New Haven, Conn.

Collar—paper collar—patented—Walter Hunt—New York City—July 25

College—Negro university—Chester County, Pa.—chartered—April 29

Cricket Club—cricket club to own its own clubhouse—Germantown, Pa.

Entomologist—federal entomologist—Townend Glover—commissioned—June 14

Entomologist—state entomologist—Asa Fitch—appointed—New York—May 4

Gazetteer—gazetteer of the world—*Lippincott's Pronouncing Gazetteer of the World*—published—Philadelphia, Pa.

Hospital—children's hospital—Nursery and Child's Hospital—established—New York City

Hospital—inebriates' asylum—United States Inebriate Asylum—organized—Binghamton, N.Y.—May 15

Immigration—Chinese labor immigration—William Kelly—Pittsburgh, Pa.

Manual Training—industrial school for girls—organized—Lancaster, Mass.

Oil—oil company—Pennsylvania Rock Oil Company—incorporated—Dec. 30

Ordnance—cannon (steel, breech loading, rifled)—J. R. Haskell

Ordnance—metal cartridge—patented—D. B. Wesson—Springfield, Mass.—Aug. 8

Paper—wood-pulp and rag paper—manufactured—William Orr—Troy, N.Y.

Paper—wood-pulp paper—of basswood—exhibited—Buffalo, N.Y.—Dec. 26

Park — park land — purchased—Worcester, Mass.—March

Physician—Negro doctor to become a member of a medical association—J. V. De Grasse—Massachusetts Medical Society

Publishing Society—Seventy-Six Society—organized—Philadelphia, Pa.—Sept. 5

Railroad Car—air-conditioned car—tested

Republican Party—Republican Party meeting (local)—Feb. 22

Sewing Machine—sewing machine to sew curving seams—patented—A. B. Wilson—Watertown, Conn.—Dec. 19

Sewing Machine—sewing machine to stitch buttonholes—patented—Charles Miller—St. Louis, Mo.—March 7

Ship—turreted frigate in the U.S. Navy—authorized—April 6

Sleeping Car—sleeping car patent—H. B. Myer—Buffalo, N.Y.—Sept. 19

Sociology Treatise—Henry Hughes—published—Philadelphia, Pa.

Stereotype—curved stereotype plate—cast—Charles Craske—New York City

Street Cleaning Machine—used—Philadelphia, Pa.—Dec. 15

1855

Agricultural School — agricultural college (state) to be chartered—Farmers High School of Pennsylvania—reincorporated—Feb. 22

Agricultural School — agricultural college (state) to open—Agricultural College of Michigan — Lansing, Mich. — chartered — Feb. 12

American Party—national convention—Philadelphia, Pa.—June 5

Billiard Match—billiard three-ball match on a six-by-twelve carom table—San Francisco, Calif.—April 30

Bohemian American Church—opened—St. Louis, Mo.—April 20

Book Trade Magazine—successful book trade magazine—published—New York City—Sept. 1

Bridge—railway suspension bridge—Niagara Falls—train crossed—March 8

Calliope—patented—J. C. Stoddard—Worcester, Mass.—Oct. 9

Carpeting—carpeting (velvet)—manufactured—John Johnson—Newark, N.J.

College—educational institution exclusively for women—Elmira Female College—opened

Congressman (U.S.)—Congressmen (brothers) to serve simultaneously—Washburn brothers—March 4

Court—court of claims—established—Feb. 24

Dentist—woman dentist—E. R. Jones—Danielson, Conn.

Dentistry—gold used for the filling of dental cavities

Dictionary—phonetic dictionary—published—Cincinnati, Ohio

Health Board—health board (state) to regulate quarantine—Louisiana

Hospital — Jewish hospital — Mount Sinai Hospital—New York City—received patients—June 5

Hospital—women's hospital—Woman's Hospital—New York City—opened—May 4

Jews—Jewish Rabbinical Conference—Cleveland, Ohio—Oct. 17

Lighthouse—lighted beacon on the Pacific coast—San Diego, Calif.

Oil—oil (kerosene)—from bituminous shale—patent—A. Gesner—March 27

Oil—oil refinery—S. M. Kier—Pittsburgh, Pa.

Ordnance—sea coast gun carriage—constructed

Postal Directory — published — Washington, D.C.

Postal Service—registration of letters—authorized—March 3

Printing Magazine (professional) *Typographic Advertiser*—published—Philadelphia, Pa.—April

Sewing Machine—sewing machine motor patent—I. M. Singer—New York City—Oct. 9

Ship—dredge (seagoing hopper)—"General Moultrie"—built—New York City

Ship—turreted frigate in the U.S. Navy—"Roanoke"—launched—Norfolk, Va.—Dec. 13

Swedenborgian Or New Church—German Swedenborgian Society—organized—Baltimore, Md.

Traps—steel animal traps—commercially manufactured — S. Newhouse — Oneida Community, N.Y.

Veterinary School—veterinary college—Boston Veterinary Institute—Boston, Mass.—incorporated—April 28

Vivisection—of animals—J. C. Dalton

Warehouse legislation—privileges extended to private warehouses—March 28

1856

Animals—camels imported for commercial purposes—Indianola, Tex.—May 14

Blotting Paper — manufactured — Joseph Parker & Son—New Haven, Conn.

Borax—discovered—Tuscan Springs, Calif.—Jan. 8

Bridge—railway bridge across the Mississippi River—Rock Island, Ill.—Davenport, Iowa—completed—April 21

Camera—tintype camera—patented—H. L. Smith—Feb. 19

Cranberry Treatise—published—New York City

Dairy Legislation (state)—enacted—Massachusetts—May 30

Diplomatic Service — consul general — appointment authorized—Aug. 18

Fish Commission (state)—authorized—Massachusetts—May 16

Flag—American flag raised in Japan—flown—Sept. 4

Folding Machine—patented—Cyrus Chambers—Kennet Square, Pa.—Oct. 7

Governor—governor of a territory and a state—J. W. Geary—Kansas territory

Governor—governor removed from office by a state supreme court—W. A. Barstow—Mar. 20

Milk—condensed milk (commercial)—patented—Gail Borden—Brooklyn, N.Y.—Aug. 19

Ordnance—machine gun—patented—Charles E. Barnes—Lowell, Mass.—July 8

Philology Chair — comparative philology chair—Lafayette College—Easton, Pa.

Pistol — revolver — self-cocking — invented —John Rider

Railroad Legislation — railroad legislation (state)—enacted—Georgia—March 5

Republican Party—Republican Party meeting (national)—Feb. 22—Pittsburgh, Pa.

Republican Party—Republican Party national convention—Philadelphia, Pa.—June 17

Screw — screw machine — patented — Cullen Whipple—Providence, R.I.—June 3

Sewage—underground comprehensive sewer system (city)—Chicago, Ill.

Telegraph—telegraph ticker which successfully printed type — patented — D. E. Hughes—Louisville, Ky.—May 20

1857

Agricultural School — agricultural college (state) to open—Agricultural College of Michigan—Lansing, Mich.—opened—May 13

Bed—box spring—imported—New York City

Brick Machine—installed—Henry Martin—Hartford, Conn.

Bustle—patented—Alexander Douglas—New York City

Cable (Telegraph)—cable across the Atlantic Ocean was paid out—Aug. 6

Chess Champion—P. C. Morphy—New York City

Chess Tournament—of importance—New York City—Oct. 6

College—college to grant women absolutely equal rights—non-sectarian—Antioch College, Yellow Springs, Ohio—graduation—July 1

Deaf—School—institution in the world for the higher education of the deaf—National Deaf Mute College—Washington, D.C.—incorporated—Feb. 16

Elevator—elevator with completely enclosed car—installed—E. G. Otis—New York City

Fire Alarm System (electric)—patented—May 19

Gyroscope — gyroscopes—(commercially manufactured)—Hartford, Conn.

Horse Race—American-bred horse to win a major race abroad—Prioress—Newmarket, England—Oct. 13

Hospital—tuberculosis home for the care of consumptives—Channing Home—Boston, Mass.—opened—May

Hospital—women's infirmary staffed by women physicians—New York Infirmary for Women and Children—New York City —opened—May 12

Lamp—oil lamp—developed

Literacy qualification for voting—enacted—Massachusetts—May 1

Medical Instruction—pediatrics professor—Abraham Jacobi—lectured—New York City

Paper — toilet paper — manufactured — J. C. Gayetty—New York City

Postage Stamp—perforated postage stamps —used—Feb. 24

President (U.S.)—President who was a bachelor—James Buchanan—served

Scale—railway track scale—patented—Thaddeus Fairbanks—St. Johnsbury, Vt.—Jan. 13

Sewage — sewage "dual system" — built — Brooklyn, N.Y.

Sewing Machine—chain-stitch single-thread sewing machine (practical)—patented—J. E. A. Gibbs—Mill Point, Va.—June 2

Ship—federal steamer named for a woman—"Harriet Lane"—built—New York City

Ship—racing shell—"The Harvard"—built—James Mackay—Brooklyn, N.Y.

Teachers' Convention—teachers' convention (national)—Philadelphia, Pa.—Aug. 26

Typesetting Machine—typesetting machine—patented — Timothy Alden — New York City—Sept. 15

Veterinary School—veterinary college of importance—New York College of Veterinary Surgeons—New York City—incorporated—April 6

Zinc—zinc patent—Samuel Wetherill—Bethlehem, Pa.—Jan. 6

1858

"Artics"—patented—T. C. Wales—Dorchester, Mass.—Feb. 2

Baby Carriage Factory—Leominster, Mass.

Baseball Game—baseball series—July 20

Baseball Rules—baseball rules—standardizing the game—passed—New York City—May

Burglar Alarm—burglar alarm—installed—Edwin Holmes—Boston, Mass.—Feb. 21

Cable (Telegraph)—cable across the Atlantic Ocean was completed—Aug. 5

Cable (Telegraph)—news dispatch by cable —published—New York City—*Sun*—Aug. 27

Chemical Laboratory—chemical laboratory in a collegiate institution—Harvard University—Cambridge, Mass.

Cigar Band—cigar band of special interest—C. W. Field—New York City—Sept. 2

Citizenship—Japanese granted citizenship—Joseph Heco—June 30

Cotton-Bale Metallic Tie—patented—Frederick Cook—New Orleans, La.—March 2

Hospital—inebriates' asylum — cornerstone laid—Sept. 24

Medical School—medical college on the Pacific coast—Medical Department of the University of the Pacific—opened—Santa Clara, Calif.

Pen—steel pens commercially produced—Richard Esterbrook—Camden, N.J.

Pencil—pencil with an attached eraser—patented—H. L. Lipman—Philadelphia, Pa.—March 30

Physician—doctor to receive a medal from Congress—F. H. Rose—authorized—May 11

Postal Service—overland mail service—to Pacific coast—Tipton, Mo. and San Francisco, Calif.—Sept. 15

Postal Service—street letter box—erected—Boston, Mass. and New York City—Aug. 2

Postal Service—street letter box—patented—Albert Potts—Philadelphia, Pa.—March 9

Sawmill—sawmill engine — portable—built—Zanesville, Ohio

Shoe Manufacturing Machine—patented—L. R. Blake—Abington, Mass.—July 6

Soda Fountain—ornamented soda fountain—produced—G. D. Dows—Lowell, Mass.

Stone Crusher—patented—E. W. Blake—New Haven, Conn.—June 15

Street Car—cable car—patent—E. A. Gardner—Philadelphia, Pa.—March 23

Washing Machine—rotary motion washing machine—patented—H. E. Smith—Philadelphia, Pa.—Oct. 26

1859

Agricultural School — agricultural college (state) to be chartered—Farmers High School of Pennsylvania—opened—Feb. 16

Balloon—balloon flight carrying mail—John Wise—Lafayette, Ind.—Aug. 17

Baseball Game—baseball series—spectators charged admission—New York—July 20

Baseball Game — intercollegiate baseball game—Pittsfield, Mass.—July 1

Billiard Match—billiard match to attain international prominence—Detroit, Mich.—April 12

Blind—school for the blind to adopt the Braille system—St. Louis, Mo.

Boat Race—intercollegiate regatta—Worcester, Mass.—July 26

Bridge—wrought iron lattice girder railroad bridge—Schenectady, N.Y.

Cricket Tournament—international cricket tournament—Hoboken, N.J.—Oct. 3-5

Electric Lighting—electric light—for household illumination—M. G. Farmer—Salem, Mass.—July

Electric Stove—electric range—invented—G. B. Simpson—Washington, D.C.

Elevator—elevator in a hotel—Fifth Avenue Hotel—New York City—Aug. 23

Escalator—escalator patent—Nathan Ames—Saugus, Mass.—Aug. 9

Fishing Line Factory—Henry Hall—New York City

Insurance—insurance department (state)—authorized—New York—April 15

Milk Inspectors—authorized—Massachusetts—April 6

Music—war song of the Confederate States "Dixie" sung—New York City—April 4

Niagara Falls—person to cross Niagara Falls on a tight-rope—J. F. Gravelet (Émile Blondin)—June 30

Oil—oil well commercially productive—discovered—Titusville, Pa.—Aug. 27

Paper Bag Manufacturing Machine—paper bag manufacturing machine—patented—William Goodale—Clinton, Mass.—July 12

Public School—public school for Chinese—supported by a municipality—established—San Francisco, Calif.—Sept.

Rocket—rocket patent—Andrew Lanergan—Boston, Mass.—June 21

Sleeping Car—Pullman sleeping car—in service—Bloomington, Ill. and Chicago, Ill.—Sept. 1

Surgical Operation—mastoid operation—J. C. Hutchison—New York City—June 15

Washing Machine—rotary motion washing machine—produced

Zoological Garden — zoological garden — Philadelphia Zoological Garden—Philadelphia, Pa.—society incorporated—March 21

1860

Baseball Team—baseball team to tour—Brooklyn Excelsiors—June 30

Billiard Match—intercollegiate billiard match—Worcester, Mass.—July 25

Congress (U.S.)—House of Representatives—Jewish rabbi to open the House of Representatives with prayer — M. J. Raphall—Feb. 1

Consitutional Union Party—organized—Baltimore, Md.—May 9

Corkscrew Patent—M. L. Byrn—New York City—March 27

Electro-Therapeutic Book—*Electro-Physiology and Electro-Therapeutics*—published—Boston, Mass.

Fire Escapes for tenements—required—legislation—New York—April 17

Game Preserve—game preserve—J. D. Caton—Ottawa, Ill.

Government Printing Office—Government Printing Office—authorized—June 23

Hebrew Book—*Abne Yehoshua*—published—New York City

Hygiene Instruction—hygiene and physical education professorship—established—Amherst College—Amherst, Mass.

Indian School—Indian school (boarding) on a reservation—Yakima Reservation, Wash.—opened—Nov.

Insurance—non-forfeiture insurance policy—New York Life Insurance Company—New York City—Aug. 13

Japanese Ambassador—arrived—San Francisco, Calif.—March 9

Labor Law—eight-hour day—advocated

Medical Book—chiropody book—*Surgical and Practical Observations. . .*—I. Zacharie—published—New York City

Missionary Society—foreign missionary society organized by women—Boston, Mass. Nov.

News Correspondent—woman news reporter at a political convention—M. A. R. Livermore—Republican National Convention—May 12-18

Newspaper — Czech language newspaper — *Slovan Amerikansky* — published — Racine, Wis.—Jan. 1

Oil—oil refinery (commercial)—Oil Creek Valley, Pa.—June

Photograph — aerial photograph — taken — Boston, Mass.—Oct. 13

Police — traffic police squad — organized — New York City

Postal Service—Pony Express mail—St. Joseph, Mo. and Sacramento, Calif.—April 3

Secession — secession act — enacted — South Carolina—Dec. 20

Secret Service—Secret Service (federal)—authorized—June 23

Ship—steamboat built on the Pacific coast for the government—"Saginaw"—built—San Francisco, Calif.

Silver Mill—to treat silver ore successfully—formed—Virginia City, Nev.—March

Tinware Manufacturers—successful tinware manufacturers—Woodhaven, L.I., N.Y.

Visiting Celebrities—Prince of Wales—arrived—Detroit, Mich.—Sept. 20

1861

Army—law (state) conferring military privileges and duties on the Negro—Tennessee —June 28

Army Balloon Corps—formed—Oct. 1

Army Secret Service Bureau—inaugurated

Book Trade Magazine — book collectors' magazine—*The Philobiblion*—published—New York City

Building—"White House of the Confederacy"—occupied—Montgomery, Ala.—Feb. 18

Camp for Boys'—Milford, Conn.—Aug.

Chromo—made

Civil War—act that marked the inauguration of the War of 1861-1865—firing upon "Star of the West"—Jan. 9

Civil War—attack in the Civil War—Fort Sumter, S.C.—April 12

Civil War—bloodshed in the Civil War—Baltimore, Md.—April 19

Civil War—call for Union troops in the Civil War—April 15

Civil War—Confederate general killed in the Civil War—R. S. Garnett—July 13

Civil War—Confederate officer killed in the Civil War—J. Q. Marr—Fairfax Court House, Va.—June 1

Civil War—naval engagement in the Civil War—Pensacola, Fla.—Sept. 14

Civil War—regiment to respond to President Abraham Lincoln's proclamation—April 16

Civil War—serious engagement in the Civil War—Bull Run Creek, Va.—July 21

Civil War—skirmish in the Civil War—Fairfax Court House, Va.—June 1

Civil War—Union soldier killed by enemy action in the Civil War—T. B. Brown—May 22

Congress of the Confederate States—House of Representatives under permanent constitution — assembled — Richmond, Va. — Feb. 18

Congress of the Confederate States—provisional session—Montgomery, Ala.—Feb. 4

Constitution of the Confederate States of America—adopted—March 11

Creamery—established—A. Slaughter—Wallkill, N.Y.

Degrees (academic and honorary)—Doctor of Philosophy degree — awarded — Yale University—New Haven, Conn.

Flag — Confederate States flag — adopted — Montgomery, Ala.—March 4

Fly Casting Tournament—fly casting tournament—Utica, N.Y.—June 18

Government Printing Office—Government Printing Office—began to function—March 4

Habeas Corpus—habeas corpus suspension order—May 3

Hospital—military hospital on the modern pavilion plan—Poolesville, Md.—Oct. 21

Ice Yacht Club—formed—Poughkeepsie, N.Y.

Insurance — non-forfeiture insurance law (state) — Massachusetts — approved — April 10

Medal—Medal of Honor action—Apache Pass, Ariz.—Feb. 13-14

Medal—Medal of Honor awarded to a member of the Naval Service—authorized—Dec. 21

Medical Instruction—laryngology instruction—New York City

Medical Instruction—orthopedics chair—New York City

Money—Confederate coinage—minted—New Orleans, La.

Money—Confederate currency—authorized—Mobile, Ala.—March 9

Money—demand notes—authorized—July 17

Money—paper money issued by the government of the United States—authorized

Moving Picture—peep show machine—patented—S. D. Goodale—Cincinnati, Ohio—Feb. 5

Moving Picture—photographic attempt to show motion—Coleman Sellers—Philadelphia, Pa.—Feb. 5

Newspaper—newspaper published by soldiers in the field—*United States American Volunteer*—May 21

Normal School—normal school (state) at which students actually conducted classes —Oswego Training School for Primary Teachers — Oswego, N.Y. — established—May 1

Nursing School—school for nurses to award a diploma—Philadelphia, Pa.—chartered—March 22, 1861

Oil—oil well fire—Oil Creek, Pa.—April 17

Petroleum Exported to Europe—Philadelphia, Pa.—Nov. 12

Postal Service—newspaper wrappers—authorized—Feb. 27

President of the Confederate States—Jefferson Davis—elected—Feb. 9

President (U.S.)—President to serve as an official of the Confederate States—John Tyler—delegate—Aug. 1

School—Negro school for freedmen—established—Fortress Monroe, Va.—Sept. 17

Seal—seals for raising funds—organization founded

Ship—balloon carrier—"Fanny"—used—Aug. 3

Ship—Confederate cruiser to raid Union commerce—"Sumter" — fitted out — New Orleans, La.

Stereoscope—invented—O. W. Holmes

Tax—federal income tax—law enacted—Aug. 5

Telegram—telegram dispatched from an aerial station—T. S. Lowe—June 18

Telegram—transcontinental telegram—Oct. 24

Telegraph—telegraph line to the Pacific coast—in operation—Oct. 24

Torpedo—torpedo mine — attack — Potomac River—July 7

1862

Agricultural Land Grant—bill signed by Abraham Lincoln—July 2

Agriculture Bureau—agriculture bureau—Commissioner of Agriculture—I. Newton —appointed—July 1

Agriculture Bureau—agriculture bureau scientific publication—published—Oct. 15

Army—law (federal) authorizing military service for Negroes—signed—Abraham Lincoln—July 17

Army Ambulance Corps—army ambulance corps—established—Aug. 2

Army Officer—chaplain (Catholic) appointed by the President—June 13

Army Officer—chaplain (Jewish) of the U.S. Army—appointed—J. Frankel—Sept. 10

Brokerage—exchange to specialize in mining securities—San Francisco, Calif.—Sept. 11

Cathedral — Episcopal cathedral — begun — Faribault, Minn.

Cemetery—national cemeteries—authorized—July 17

Chinaware—chinaware for restaurant use

Civil War—conflict between iron-clad vessels in the Civil War—Hampton Roads, Va.—March 9

Civil War—Negro regiment in the Civil War —organized—July-Aug.

Decalcomanias—imported

Emancipation Proclamation (preliminary)—Abraham Lincoln—Sept. 22

Engraving and Printing Bureau (U.S.)—operations commenced—Aug. 28

Execution—execution (federal) for slave trading—Nathaniel Gordon—New York City—Feb. 21

Football Club—football club—Oneida Football Club—Boston, Mass.—organized

Gymnastics Instruction—gymnastics instruction at a college for women—Mount Holyoke College—South Hadley, Mass.

Homestead Act—homestead act—enacted—May 20

Hospital—Army Field Hospital — Shiloh, Tenn.—established

Hospital—orthopedic hospital—Hospital for Ruptured and Crippled—society organized —New York City

Impeachment — impeachment proceedings against a state governor—Charles Robinson—Kansas—acquitted

Internal Revenue Commissioner—G. S. Boutwell—served—July 17

Land Mines—used in Civil War—May 3

Medal—Medal of Honor (Army)—authorized—July 12

Medal—Medal of Honor awarded to a Marine—John Mackie

Medical Clinic—children's clinic—established —New York City

Money—paper money fractional currency—issued

Naval Officer—naval chaplain killed in action J. L. Lenhart—March 8

Naval Officer—naval officer to become an admiral—D. G. Farragut—became rear-admiral—July 16

Newspaper—newspaper printed on a train— T. A. Edison—*Weekly Herald*—Feb. 3

Oil—oil pipeline within the oil regions—laid —Oil Creek, Pa.

Ordnance—machine gun (rapid fire)—patented—R. J. Gatling—Indianapolis, Ind.—Nov. 4

Ordnance—revolving gun turret—patented—T. R. Timby—July 8

Passport—passport fee—authorized—July 1

Polygamy Legislation (federal)—authorized —July 1

Postage Stamp Catalog—A. C. Kline—Philadelphia, Pa.—published

Postal Service—railroad post office—tested—July 7

Presidential Executive Order to be numbered—Abraham Lincoln—Oct. 20

Ship—Confederate cruiser built in England— "Oneto"—left Liverpool, England—March 22

Ship—hospital ship of the U.S. Navy—"Red Rover"—converted—Dec. 26

Ship — iron-clad naval vessels — accepted—Jan. 15

Ship—iron-clad turreted vessel in the U.S. Navy—"Monitor"—launched — Greenpoint, N.Y.—Jan. 30

Ship—iron-clad warship for service at sea— "Galena"—launched—Mystic, Conn.—Feb. 14

Snowshoe—commercial production—A. M. Dunham—Norway, Me.

Steel Analysis Laboratory—W. F. Durfee—Wyandotte, Mich.

Taps (military signal)—Daniel Butterfield—July

Tax—federal income tax—law effective—Jan. 1

Tax—inheritance tax (federal)—authorized—
July 1

Telegraph—army field telegraph used in
warfare—Mechanicsville, Va.—May 24

Tobacco—tobacco tax for internal revenue—
authorized—July 1

Torpedo—torpedo mine attack—to destroy
war vessel—Yazoo River—Dec. 12

Treason—citizen of the United States to be
tried for treason, convicted, and hanged—
W. B. Mumford—New Orleans—hanged—
June 7

1863

Amnesty—proclamation—Abraham Lincoln
—Dec. 8

Army—Signal Corps—authorized—March 3

Army Officer—chaplain (Negro) of the U.S.
Army—H. M. Turner—commissioned

Bank—national bank—under national banking law—opened—June 29

Bank—national bank chartered—Philadelphia, Pa.—June 20

Bank Legislation—national banking system
—created—Feb. 25

Bathhouse — Turkish bath — opened — New
York City—Oct. 6

Book—book on vellum—published—Philadelphia, Pa.

Catholic Church—Catholic parish church for
Negroes — Baltimore, Md. — purchased —
Oct. 10

Charity Board (state)—Massachusetts—established—April 29

Chenille Manufacturing Machine—patented
—Jan. 13

Civil War—bloodshed north of the Mason-
Dixon line—June 30

Civil War—Negro regiment in the Civil War
—in federal service—Jan. 31

Comptroller—Comptroller of the Currency—
H. McCulloch—appointed—May 9

Congress of the United States—officer to
preside over both of the branches of Congress—March 4—House of Representatives

Conscription—wartime conscription bill—
passed—March 3

Cripples—private school for cripples—opened
New York City—May 1

Dock—state owned docks—authorized—California—April 24

Farmers' Institute—farmers' institute sponsored by a state—opened—Springfield,
Mass.—Dec. 8

Fire Extinguisher Patent—Alanson Crane—
Fortress Monroe, Va.—Feb. 10

Habeas Corpus—habeas corpus suspension
order—proclamation suspending habeas
corpus during military strife—Abraham
Lincoln—Sept. 15

Holiday—Thanksgiving Day national proclamation—Abraham Lincoln—Oct. 3

Homestead — awarded — Daniel Freeman —
Beatrice, Neb.—Jan. 1

Hospital—orthopedic hospital—Hospital for
the Ruptured and Crippled—New York
City—opened—May 1

Insurance—accident insurance company—
Travelers Insurance Company—Hartford,
Conn.—chartered—June 17

Medal—Medal of Honor (Army)—authorized for commissioned officers—March 3

Medal—Medal of Honor awarded to a member of the Naval Service—April 3

Medical Clinic—laryngology clinic—established—New York City—March

Money—gold certificates—authorized—March 3

Money—notes wholly engraved and printed
at the Bureau of Engraving and Printing
—Washington, D.C.—authorized—March 3

Monument—monument to commemorate the
Civil War—dedicated—Kensington, Conn.
—July 25

Newspaper—newspaper printed on wood-
pulp paper—*Morning Journal*—Boston, Mass.
—Jan. 15

Normal School—woman principal of a normal school—A. C. Brackett—St. Louis,
Mo.—Jan. 5

Oil—oil pipeline within the oil regions—completed—Oil Creek, Pa.—Feb. 19

Paper Patterns—Ebenezer Butterick—Sterling, Mass.

Physician—woman surgeon—M. H. Thompson—graduated—New England Medical
College—Boston, Mass.

Pill—compressed pills or tablets—commercially manufactured—Jacob Dunton—Philadelphia, Pa.

Postal Service—free city delivery of mail—
authorized—March 3

Railroad Signal System—railroad signal system (manual block)—installed—Philadelphia, Pa. to Trenton, N.J.—Philadelphia
and Trenton Railroad

Science Association—National Academy of
Sciences—incorporated—March 3

Seal—seal of the Confederate States of
America—authorized—April 30

Water Conduit—water supply tunnel for a
city—contract—Chicago, Ill.—Oct. 28

Yeast—yeast preparation patent—J. T. Alden—Cincinnati, Ohio—Nov. 3

1864

Army Ambulance Corps—Army Ambulance
Corps established by congressional action
—authorized—March 11

Army Officer—woman assistant army surgeon—M. E. Walker—March 11

Army Vote—tabulated

Boiler Legislation—state boiler inspection
law passed—Connecticut—July 9

Borax—commercial production—Borax Lake,
Calif.

Business—chain store organization—Great
American Tea Company—originated

Camel Race—Sacramento, Calif.—April 7

Canning — salmon cannery — Washington,
Calif.

Catholic Church—Catholic parish church for
Negroes — dedicated — Baltimore, Md.—
Feb. 21

Cigarette Tax—cigarette tax—federal—enacted—June 30

Circus—circus to feature an automobile as an attraction

Deaf—School—institution in the world for the higher education of the deaf—Columbia Institution for the Deaf—authorized to confer degrees—April 8

Degrees (academic and honorary)—Law Degree of LL.M. (Master of Laws)—conferred—Columbia University—New York City—June 29

File Factory—file factory (machine cutting) to attain success—Nicholson File Company—Providence, R.I.—organized

Fine Arts Department—fine arts department in a college—School of Fine Arts—Yale University—New Haven, Conn.—established

Fish Hatchery—fish hatchery—to breed salmon—established—James B. Johnson—New York City

Fraternity (Greek Letter)—professional fraternity—Theta Xi—founded—Troy, N.Y.—April 29

Game Law—hunting license fee (state)—New York—April 30

Hall of Fame—hall of fame (national)—National Statuary Hall—Washington, D.C.—established—July 2

Insurance—accident insurance policy

Insurance—accident insurance policy (printed)—Travelers Insurance Company—Hartford, Conn.—issued—April 1

Knights of Pythias—founded—Washington, D.C.—J. H. Rathbone—Feb. 19

Medal—Medal of Honor awarded to a Jewish soldier—Leopold Karpeles—July 12

Mines School—opened—Columbia University—New York City—Nov. 15

Money—coin to use "In God We Trust"—authorized—April 22

Naval Officer—naval officer to become an admiral—D. G. Farragut—vice-admiral—Dec. 13

Novel—novel by a Negro—*Clotelle*—published—Boston, Mass.

Oil—oil tank cars—introduced

Park—state park—Yosemite Valley park—granted by act of Congress

Periscope—invented—Thomas Doughty

Physician—Negro woman awarded a medical degree—Rebecca Lee—Boston, Mass.—March 1

Physician—ophthalmologist of note—Edward Delafield — became president of American Opthalmological Society

Postal Service—money order system—established—Nov. 1

Postal Service—railroad post office for the general distribution of mail—service commenced—Chicago, Ill. to Clinton, Iowa—Aug. 28

Railroad Track—railroad rails of steel—Altoona, Pa. to Pittsburgh, Pa.

Skate (all-metal)—marketed—E. H. Barney—Springfield, Mass.

Steel—Bessemer steel converter—used commercially—Eureka Iron and Steel Works—Wyandotte, Mich.

Submarine—submarine to sink a man-of-war—"Hunley"—Feb. 17

Sugar—sugar and glucose from cornstarch—patent—F. W. Gossling—May 10

Torpedo—torpedo mine attack—Confederate loss—near Charleston, S.C.—Feb. 17

Water Conduit—water supply tunnel for a city—construction started—Chicago, Ill.—March 17

1865

Advertising Law—outdoor advertising legislation (state)—New York—passed—March 28

Advertising Magazine—*Advertising Agency Circular*—published—New York City

Animals—cattle importation law (U.S.)—passed—Dec. 18

Architectural School—architectural school—of college rank—Massachusetts Institute of Technology—Boston, Mass.—opened—Feb. 20

Army Officer—major (Negro)—M. R. Delany—Feb. 8

Bank—freedmen's bank—chartered—March 3

Bank—national bank failure—Attica, N.Y.—April 14

Bathhouse—bathhouses owned and operated by a municipality—Boston, Mass.—built

Billiard Ball of composition material resembling ivory—patented—J. W. Hyatt—Oct. 10

Coffee Percolator Patent—Dec. 26

Congress (U.S.)—House of Representatives—Negro preacher to deliver a sermon in the House of Representatives—H. H. Garnet—Feb. 12

Congressional Directory—authorized—Feb. 14

Cooperative—cooperative state law—enacted—Michigan—March 20

Cracker—cracker—manufactured — Albany, N.Y.

Dental Code of Ethics—proposed—Chicago, Ill.—July 28

Entomology Magazine—*Practical Entomologist*—published—Philadelphia, Pa.—Oct.

Freedmen's Bureau (U.S.)—authorized—March 3

Gas—natural gas corporation—organized—Fredonia, N.Y.

Ku Klux Klan—established—Pulaski, Tenn.

Lawyer—Negro lawyer to practice before the United States Supreme Court—J. S. Rock—admitted—Feb. 1

Linen Thread Factory (successful)—established—Paterson, N.J.

Medical Instruction—ophthalmology professor—Elkanah Williams—appointed—Cincinnati, Ohio

Money—gold certificates—issued—Nov. 13

Naval Officer—judge advocate of the Navy—W. E. Chandler—appointed—March 6

Newspaper—newspaper published at sea—*Atlantic Telegraph*—published—July 29

Nursing School—school for nurses to award a diploma — Philadelphia, Pa. — diploma awarded

Oil—oil pipeline of importance—completed —Pithole, Pa.—Oct. 9

Oil—oil well drilled by torpedoes—Titusville, Pa.—Jan. 21

Potato Chips—introduced

Premium—premiums given with merchandise —introduced—B. T. Babbitt

President (U.S.)—President to be assassinated—Abraham Lincoln—April 14

President (U.S.)—President to rest in state in the United States Capitol rotunda—Abraham Lincoln—April 15

Printing Press—printing press to use a continuous web or roll of paper—William Bullock—Pittsburgh, Pa.

Railroad—streamlined railroad train—patented—S. R. Calthorp—Roxbury, Mass.—Aug. 8

Railroad Track—railroad rails of Bessemer steel—Wyandotte, Mich.—May 24

Railroad Train Robbery—railroad train robbery of a disabled train—North Bend, Ohio—May 5

Safe Deposit Vault—opened—New York City—June 5

Sleeping Car—Pullman sleeping car that was comfortable—"The Pioneer"—built—Chicago, Ill.

Soap—soap in liquid form—patented—William Sheppard—New York City—Aug. 22

Social Science Society (national)—American Social Science Association—founded

Unitarian Church Convention (national)—assembled—New York City—April 5

War Criminal Proceedings—Henry Wirz trial—Aug. 23 to Nov. 4—Washington, D.C.

Zinc—zinc sheet mill—erected—Bethlehem, Pa.

1866

Animals—fur-bearing animals—raised commercially—Oneida County, N.Y.

Army Officer—General of the U.S. Army—U. S. Grant—appointed—July 25

Automobile—steam automobile—invented—H. A. House—Bridgeport, Conn.

Baseball Player—baseball pitcher—to curve a ball—W. A. Cummings

Bicycle—bicycle with a rotary crank—patented—Nov. 20

Births—sextuplets—born—Bushnell family—Chicago, Ill.—Sept. 8

Cans—can (tin) with a key opener—patented —J. Osterhoudt—New York City—Oct. 2

College—Negro university to establish undergraduate, graduate, and professional schools—Washington, D.C.—Nov. 20

Dentist—woman dentist to obtain a D.D.S. degree—from a dental college—L. B. Hobbs—graduated—Cincinnati, Ohio—Feb. 21

Dynamite — manufactured — San Francisco, Calif.

Election Law—fraudulent election law (state)—enacted—California—March 26

Elevator—elevator (suspended)—installed—St. James Hotel—New York City

Flag—American flag made of American bunting to fly over the Capitol, Washington, D.C.—hoisted—Feb. 24

Hat Blocking and Shaping Machine—patented—Yonkers, N.Y.—April 3

Health Board—health board (municipal) armed with sufficient powers—established —New York City—Feb. 26

Humane Society—humane society—American Society for the Prevention of Cruelty to Animals—incorporated—New York City

Impregnation—impregnation (human) by means of artificial insemination—J. M. Sims

Insurance—boiler insurance company—Hartford Steam Boiler Inspection and Insurance Company—Hartford, Conn.—chartered—June

Insurance—insurance rate standardization—New York City—July 18

Irrigation Legislation (federal)—enacted—July 26

Labor Law—eight-hour day—unified action —Baltimore, Md.—Aug. 20

Lecture Series (endowed)—Union Theological Seminary—New York City

Legislator (state)—Negro representatives to sit in any state legislature—elected—Massachusetts

Money—nickel—coinage authorized—May 16

Monument—monument by a woman ordered by the U.S. Government—statue of Abraham Lincoln—authorized—Vinnie Ream—July 28

Naval Officer—naval officer to become an admiral—D. G. Farragut—appointed—July 25

Needles (machine made)—Excelsior Needle Company—Wolcottville, Conn.—organized —March 2

Newspaper Index separately published—New York City

Oyster Cocktail—originated

Paleontology Chair—in a college—Yale University—New Haven, Conn.

Pencil—indelible pencil—patented—E. P. Clark—Northampton, Mass.—July 10

Play (drama)—burlesque show—of importance—"Black Crook"—opened—New York City—Sept. 12

Political Convention—Negro delegate to a national political convention—Frederick Douglass—Philadelphia, Pa.—Sept. 6

Postage Stamp—mourning stamp—issued—June 17

Railroad—cog railroad—Mount Washington, N.H.—construction began—May

Railroad Car—refrigerator car shipment of fresh fruit—Parker Earle

Railroad Train Robbery—railroad train robbery of a train in motion

Root Beer—manufactured—C. E. Hires—Philadelphia, Pa.

Ship—steam whaler—"Pioneer"—April 28

Skating Rink—roller skating rink (public)—opened—Newport, R.I.

Soldiers' Homes (national)—authorized—March 21

State—state re-admitted to the Union—Tennessee—July 24

Tunnel—subaqueous highway tunnel—Washington Street Tunnel—Chicago, Ill.—commenced—Nov. 30

Visiting Celebrities—queen to visit the United States—Queen Emma—Hawaii—arrived—New York City—Aug. 8

War Veterans' Society—Grand Army of the Republic — established — Decatur, Ill.—April 6

War Veterans' Society—Grand Army of the Republic—national convention—Indianapolis, Ind.—Nov. 20

War Veterans' Society—Grand Army of the Republic — state convention — Springfield, Ill.—July 12

Water Conduit—water supply tunnel for a city—Chicago Lake Tunnel—Chicago, Ill.—completed—Dec. 6

Weights and Measures Standardization—act legalizing the employment of the metric system—approved—July 28

Wire—wire-cutting machine and automatic straightener—invented—John Adt—Wolcottville, Conn.

Woman Suffrage—woman suffrage associations (national)—American Equal Rights Association — constitution adopted — New York City—May 10

Yacht Race—yacht race across the Atlantic Ocean—Dec. 11

Young Women's Christian Association—originated—Boston, Mass.

1867

Agricultural Society—agricultural society of national importance—organized—Washington, D.C.—Dec. 4

Bank—national bank failure—receivership terminated—Attica, N.Y.—Jan. 2

Blanket—blanket robe and carriage lap robe business — successfully undertaken — Sanford, Me.

Brick—terra cotta factory — successful — Louisville, Ky.

Cartridge Belt Patent—Anson Mills—Aug. 20

College—Negro university to establish undergraduate, graduate, and professional schools—incorporated—March 2

College—state university supported by a direct property tax—authorized—Michigan—March 15

Deaf—School—oral school for the deaf (still existing)—Clarke School for the Deaf—Northampton, Mass.—founded

Dental Mallet—dental mallet—idea conceived—W. G. A. Bonwill—Philadelphia, Pa.—Feb. 27

Dental School—dental school permanently established by a university — Harvard School of Dental Medicine—Boston, Mass.—established—July 17

Education Department (U.S.)—Department of Education (U.S.)—authorized—March 2

Elevated Railroad—elevated railroad—New York City—opened for traffic—July 2

Forest Service—forestry inquiry commission (state)—authorized—Wisconsin—March 23

Governor—governor of a territory and a state—J. W. Geary—served—Jan. 15

Greek Orthodox Church — Holy Trinity Church—New Orleans, La.—founded

Insurance—boiler insurance company—Hartford, Conn.—policy issued—Feb. 14

Insurance—insurance rate standardization—annual meeting—Feb. 20

Insurance—plate glass insurance—United States Plate Glass Insurance Company—Philadelphia, Pa.—incorporated—April 12

Jewish College—Jewish college—Maimonides College—Philadelphia, Pa.—established—Oct.

Moving Picture Machine—machine to show animated pictures—Zoëtrope—patented—W. E. Lincoln — Providence, R.I. — April 23

Paint—paint (ready-mixed)—patented—D. R. Averill—Newburg, Ohio—July 16

Railroad Car—refrigerator car patent—J. B. Sutherland—Detroit, Mich.—Nov. 26

Railroad Crossing Gate Patent—Boston, Mass.—Aug. 27

Railroad Signal System—railroad signal system (automatic electric block)—invented—T. S. Hall—Stamford, Conn.

Sawmill—band sawmill—operated—Hoffman Brothers—Fort Wayne, Ind.

Soldiers' Homes (national)—opened

Surgical Operation—gallstone operation—J. S. Bobbs—Indianapolis, Ind.—June 15

Telegraph—telegraph ticker used by a brokerage concern—installed—New York City—Dec. 29

Territorial Expansion—non-contiguous territory—Alaska—acquired—June 20

Theological School—theological school to present regular courses by scholars representing different denominations—Boston Theological Seminary—Boston, Mass.

Water Conduit—water supply tunnel for a city—Chicago, Ill.—operated—March 25

1868

Animals—cattle exportation to Great Britain

Benevolent and Protective Order of Elks—founded—New York City—Feb. 16

Bicycle School—for velocipede riding—opened—New York City—Dec. 5

Business—department store—Zion's Co-Operative Mercantile Institution—Salt Lake City, Utah

Cattle Club—cattle club (Jersey cattle)—formed—Newport, R.I.—July

Cigarette Tax—cigarette tax—stamps on packages—legislation enacted—July 20

Commercial High School—commercial high school—established—Pittsburgh, Pa.—Aug.

Education Department (U.S.)—Department of Education (U.S.)—act abolished Department of Education and established Office of Education in the Department of the Interior

Elevator—elevator in an office building—installed—New York City

Farmers' Institute—farmers' institute sponsored by a college—Manhattan, Kan.—Nov. 14

Holiday—Decoration Day—celebration—May 30

Impeachment — impeachment proceedings against a President of the United States—Andrew Johnson—Feb. 24

Kindergarten — American kindergarten — opened—Boston, Mass.

Labor Law—eight-hour day for government laborers and mechanics—authorized—June 25

Medical Instruction—public hygiene professor—Thomas Bevan — appointed — Northwestern University—Chicago, Ill.

Medical Periodical—medical periodical devoted to diseases of women and children—*American Journal of Obstetrics*—published New York City—May

Motorcycle — motorcycle (steam-driven) — W. A. Austin—Winthrop, Mass.

Nickel Plating—patented—W. H. Remington—Boston, Mass.—Oct. 6

Parade—parade with float tableaux—Mobile, Ala.—Feb. 24

Philological Society—national philological society—American Philological Association—organized—New York City—Nov. 13

Postal Service—letter-carriers' uniforms—approved—Oct. 31

Postal Service—money order system—foreign service authorized—July 27

Postal Service—postage canceling machine patent—March 17

Railroad Car—dining car—"Delmonico"—built

Sports—amateur indoor athletic games—New York City—Nov. 11

Sports—athletic club—New York Athletic Club—New York City—organized—Sept. 8

Steel—open hearth furnace—built—Trenton, N.J.

Subway—pneumatic subway—Beach Pneumatic Underground Railway—incorporated—June 1

Tape Measure Patent—A. J. Fellows—New Haven, Conn.—July 14

Typewriter—typewriter that was practical—patented—C. L. Sholes—June 23

Veterinary School—veterinary department of collegiate character—Cornell University—Ithaca, N.Y.—courses—Oct. 7

Women's Club—women's professional club—"Sorosis" — founded — New York City—March 21

Yeast—compressed fresh yeast—introduced—Cincinnati, Ohio

1869

Agricultural Society—agricultural society for dairymen—organized—Oct. 27

Air Brake—patented—George Westinghouse—April 13

Baseball Team—baseball team to receive a regular salary—Cincinnati, Ohio

Bicycle Patent—water velocipede patent—Oct. 5

Blind—school for the Negro blind—Raleigh, N.C.—opened—Jan. 4

Boat Race—international boat race—London, England—Aug. 17

Brokerage—woman brokerage office owner—V. C. Woodhull—New York City

Building—apartment house with a modern lay-out—erected—New York City

Cathedral — Episcopal cathedral—Cathedral of Our Merciful Saviour—completed—Faribault, Minn.

Cattle Club—cattle club (Jersey cattle)—annual meeting—New York City—April 5

Celluloid—patented—June 15

Chewing Gum—chewing gum patent—W. F. Semple—Dec. 28

College—state university to grant equal privileges to women—Indiana University—Bloomington, Ind.—S. P. Morrison—graduated

Congress of the United States—officer to preside over both of the branches of Congress—Schuyler Colfax—Senate—March 4

Dental Book—book on dental surgery—J. E. Garretson—*A Treatise on the Diseases and Surgery of the Mouth*—published—Philadelphia, Pa.

Dentistry—gold crown tooth—process described—W. N. Morrison—May

Diplomatic Service—Negro consul—E. D. C. Bassett—to Haiti—served—April 16

Expedition—exploration of the Grand Canyon of the Colorado—J. W. Powell—May 24-Aug. 29

Foodstuffs Producer—H. J. Heinz—Sharpsburg, Pa.

Football Game—intercollegiate football contest—Rutgers-Princeton—New Brunswick, N.J.—Nov. 6

Health Board—health board (state)—Massachusetts—authorized—June 21

History Instruction—history seminar—University of Michigan—Ann Arbor, Mich.

Holiday—Labor Day holiday—inaugurated—Philadelphia, Pa.—Dec. 28

Horse Race—trotting futurity—New York City—Oct. 12

Indians—Indian Affairs Commissioner (U.S.) who was an Indian—E. S. Parker—appointed—April 21

Insurance—fraternal group insurance—of consequence—Metropolitan Life Insurance Company—New York City

Journalism Course — journalism course — Washington and Lee University—Lexington, Va.

Jute Culture—introduced

Kindergarten Manual—Edward Wiebé—*Paradise of Childhood*—published—Springfield, Mass.

Labor—labor bureau (state)—Massachusetts Bureau of Statistics of Labor—authorized —June 23

Labor Union—labor organization to admit workmen other than craft workmen—Noble Order of the Knights of Labor—organized—Philadelphia, Pa.—Dec. 9

Labor Union—women's labor organization (national) — convention — Lynn, Mass. — July 28

Law School—law school (university) to admit women—St. Louis Law School—St. Louis, Mo.

Lawyer—woman lawyer—A. A. Mansfield—Mount Pleasant, Iowa—June

Moving Picture Projector—moving picture projector patent—O. B. Brown—Malden, Mass.—Aug. 10

Naval Academy—Japanese midshipman in the United States Naval Academy—Z. Z. Matzmulla—admitted—Dec. 8

Naval Officer—Surgeon General of the Navy W. M. Wood—appointed Chief of Medical Bureau and Surgery—June 28

News Agency—financial news agency—Kiernan Financial News Agency—established —New York City

Philological Society—national philological society—American Philological Association — convention — Poughkeepsie, N.Y.— July 27

Photograph—photograph of a total solar eclipse—Mt. Pleasant, Iowa—August 7

Pipe—corncob pipe commercial manufacture —Henry Tibbe—Washington, Mo.

Postage Stamp—postage stamps depicting scenes—issued—March 1

Postage Stamp—postage stamps to picture the coat of arms of the United States— issued—March 1

Postal Service—money order system—foreign service agreement with Switzerland effective—Sept. 1

Prize Fight—international fight, with bare knuckles—St. Louis, Mo.—June 15

Probation—probation legislation for juvenile delinquents — enacted — Massachusetts — June 23

Prohibition Party (national)—organized— Chicago, Ill.—Sept. 12

Railroad—municipal railroad — construction authorized—Ohio—May 4

Railroad—railroad to run west, out of Chicago—last spike driven—Union Pacific— Promontory, Utah—May 10

Railroad Commission (state)—established— Massachusetts—July 1

Ship—oil tanker—"Charles"

Snow-Melting Apparatus—snow-melting apparatus—patented—N. H. Borgfeldt—New York City—April 6

Steeplechase—New York City—Oct. 26

Sulphur Deposit—discovery—Calcasieu Parish, La.

Teachers' Death Benefit—New York City

Torpedo—torpedo manufacturing station— Goat Island, Va.

Vacuum Cleaner—suction-type vacuum cleaner—patented—I. W. McGaffey—Chicago, Ill.—June 8

Voting Machine—electric vote recorder— T. A. Edison—Boston, Mass.—patented— June 1

Waffle Iron Patent—Cornelius Swarthout— Troy, N.Y.—Aug. 24

Woman—woman congressional hearing witness—E. C. Stanton—Jan. 20

Woman Suffrage—state to grant suffrage to women—Wyoming Territory—Dec. 10

1870

Baking Powder Manufacturer—B. T. Babbitt

Boardwalk—completed—Atlantic City, N.J. —June 26

Brokerage—clearing house for stocks and bonds — organized — Philadelphia, Pa. — Aug.

Canoe Club—New York Canoe Club— founded

Cartoon—Democratic cartoon—donkey emblem used—New York City—Jan. 15

Cement—cement—imported

Check Protectors—manufactured

Coin Box—for street cars—invented—T. L. Johnson—Louisville, Ky.

College — college summer school — Mount Union College—Alliance, Ohio

Congressman (U.S.)—Negro congressman— sworn in—J. R. Rainey—Dec. 12

Election Law—Negro to vote under authority of the Fifteenth Amendment—March 31

Entomology Professor—H. A. Hagen—Harvard University—Cambridge, Mass.

Farmers' Institute—farmers' institute held by a land grant agricultural college off its campus—Iowa State College—Cedar Falls, Iowa—Dec. 20

Gas—natural gas for manufacturing—used— Olean, N.Y.—Tidioute, Pa.

Japanese Ambassador—Japanese legation— established—Washington, D.C.—Oct.

Justice Department (U.S.) — authorized — June 22

Labor Union—labor organization to admit workmen other than craft workmen— Noble Order of the Knights of Labor— permitted membership—Oct. 20

Lawyer—woman lawyer graduated from a law school—A. H. Kepley—June 30

Medical Instruction — pediatrics professor— Abraham Jacobi—New York City

Moving Picture—animated photographic picture projection before a theater audience— Academy of Music—Philadelphia, Pa.— Feb. 5

Pension—pension to the widow of a President—Mary Lincoln—authorized—July 14

Petroleum Jelly—manufactured—R. A. Chesebrough

Premium—premiums given by publishers—
Christian Union

Public Health—public health service (U.S.)
—reorganization act—June 29

Railroad—railroad to install track water
tanks—Pennsylvania Railroad

Railroad Excursion — railroad excursion
(transcontinental) of an organization—
Boston Board of Trade—left Boston, Mass.
for San Francisco, Calif.—May 23

Railroad Signal System—railroad signal system (automatic electric block)—patented
—T. S. Hall—Stamford, Conn.—June 7

Road — brick pavement — laid — Charleston,
W.Va.

Road—sheet asphalt pavement—laid—Newark, N.J.

Rubber—rubber company west of the Allegheny Mountains

Sand Blasting—patented—B. C. Tilghman—
Oct. 18

School — Negro school (state) — Snowden
School—Alexandria, Va.—authorized—July
11

Senator (U.S.)—Negro senator—H. R.
Revels—Mississippi—sworn in—Feb. 25

Servite Church—Servite Church in America
—established—Menasha, Wis.—Aug.

Soda Fountain—crnamented soda fountain—
patent—G. D. Dows—Jan. 25

Solicitor General of the United States—B. H.
Bristow—appointed—Oct. 4

Sorority—sorority (women's Greek letter society)—Kappa Alpha Theta—founded—
Greencastle, Ind.—Jan. 27

Subway—pneumatic subway—Beach Pneumatic Underground Railway—opened—
Feb. 26

Time (standard)—suggested—C. F. Dowd—
Saratoga Springs, N.Y.

Tong (Chinese secret society)—Kwong
Dock Tong—San Francisco, Calif.—organized

Trademark—registered—Oct. 25

Water Purification—water purification by filtration—Poughkeepsie, N.Y.

Weather Bureau (U.S.)—authorized—Feb.
9

1871

Band Wagon—used—B. T. Babbitt

Baseball League—baseball league of impor-
tance—National Association of Base-Ball
Players—organized—New York City—
March 17

Baseball Player—professional baseball player—A. J. Reach

Benevolent and Protective Order of Elks—
Grand Lodge incorporated—March 10

Carrousel — carrousel patent — Willhelm
Schneider—Davenport, Iowa—July 25

Cement — cement — patent—D. O. Saylor—
Allentown, Pa.—Sept. 26

Cigar Lighter Patent—M. F. Gale—New
York City—Nov. 21

Civil Service—Civil Service Commission—
authorized—March 3

College—college entrance "certified school
plan"—introduced—Ann Arbor, Mich.—
Sept.

College—Negro land grant college—established—Rodney, Miss.

College—woman college president—F. E.
Willard—Feb.

Deaf—School—oral instruction for the deaf
—Horace Mann School—Boston, Mass.

Fertilizer Law (state)—enacted—Delaware
—March 16

Fish and Fisheries Commissioner—S. F.
Baird—served—March 8

Fish Protection—fish protection office (federal)—authorized—Feb. 9

Freemasons—Ancient Arabic Order of Nobles of the Mystic Shrine—established—
New York City—June 16

Freemasons—Negro Masonic lodge—Alpha
Lodge—New Jersey—warrant granted—
Jan. 19

Gas—municipal gas plant—acquired—Wheeling, W.Va.—June 23

Holiday—Saturday half holiday—inaugurated—George Westinghouse—Pittsburgh,
Pa.

Horse Register—trotting register—J. H.
Wallace — *American Trotting Register* —
published—New York City

Impeachment—impeachment and removal
from office of a state governor—W. W.
Holden—North Carolina—March 22

Law School—law school (university) to admit women—St. Louis Law School—St.
Louis, Mo.—woman graduate—June 15

Lifesaving Service—introduced—S. I. Kimball

Locomotive — narrow gauge locomotive —
used—Denver and Rio Grande Western
Railroad Company—July 3

Map—relief map—made—E. E. Howell

Medical Book—neurology textbook—W. A.
Hammond—*The Diseases of the Nervous
System*—published—New York City

Medical Instruction — dermatology chair —
J. C. White—Harvard University—Cambridge, Mass.

Medical Instruction — medical chemistry
course (systematic)—E. S. Wood—Harvard Medical School, Cambridge, Mass.

Medical Society—woman physician admitted
to the American Institute of Homeopathy
— Philadelphia, Pa. — M. B. Jackson—
accepted

Monument—monument by a woman ordered
by the U.S. Government—unveiled—Washington, D.C.—Jan. 25

Oleomargarine—oleomargarine manufacturer
(successful)—Alfred Paraf—New York
City

Oleomargarine — oleomargarine patent — H.
W. Bradley—Binghamton, N.Y.—Jan. 3

Oranges (seedless navel)—imported—from
Brazil

Paper—corrugated paper—patented—A. L.
Jones—New York City—Dec. 19

Paper—perforated wrapping paper—patented
—Seth Wheeler—Albany, N.Y.—July 25

Political Economy Course—political economy chair—C. F. Dunbar—Harvard University—Cambridge, Mass.

Printing Press—rotary printing press—produced—R. Hoe & Co.—New York City

Rifle Association—rifle association (national)—organized—New York City—Nov. 24

Ship—iron sloop yacht—"Vindex"—built—Chester, Pa.

Sports—amateur outdoor athletic games—New York Athletic Club—New York City—Oct. 21

Street Car—cable street car—patent—A. S. Hallidie—Jan. 17

Theological School—theological school to admit women—Boston University School of Theology — Boston, Mass. — formed — March 30

Unitarian Minister—woman ordained to the Unitarian ministry—C. C. Burleigh—Oct. 5

1872

Adding Machine—adding machine to print totals and subtotals—patented—E. D. Barbour—Boston, Mass.—Nov. 19

Air Brake—"triple air brake"—patented—George Westinghouse, Jr.—Schenectady, N.Y.—March 5

Bird Refuge—authorized by a state—Oakland, Calif.—Feb. 14

Burglar Alarm—burglar alarm system—installed—New York City

Business—mail-order house—A. M. Ward—Chicago, Ill.

Cigarette Manufacturing Machine—invented—A. H. Hook—New York City

Civil Service—Civil Service Commission—law on regulation of admissions effective—Jan. 1

Congress (U.S.)—House of Representatives—foreign clergyman to open the House of Representatives with prayer—Abraham de Sola—invocation—Jan. 9

Doughnut Cutter—patented—J. F. Blondel—Thomaston, Me.—July 9

Elevator—elevator patent, for a vertical-geared hydraulic electric elevator—C. W. Baldwin—Boston, Mass.—Feb. 20

Fish Hatchery—fish hatchery (federal)—established—Bucksport, Me.

Fraternity Magazine—fraternity journal—Beta Theta Pi—published—Alexandria, Va.—Dec. 15

Freemasons—Ancient Arabic Order of Nobles of the Mystic Shrine—Mecca temple—instituted—New York City—Sept. 26

Gas—pipeline (long distance)—completed—Newton Wells to Titusville, Pa.—Aug. 1

Governor—Negro governor (acting)—P. B. S. Pinchback—Louisiana—Dec. 11

Holiday—Arbor Day—celebration—Nebraska—April 10

Labor Law—women's equal employment legislation—enacted—Illinois—March 22

Labor Party (political)—labor party (national)—Labor Reform Party—formed—Columbus, Ohio—Feb. 22

Lawyer—Negro woman lawyer—C. E. Ray—Washington, D.C.—April 23

Liberal Republican Party—convention—Cincinnati, Ohio—May 1

Lunch Wagon—introduced—Walter Scott—Providence, R.I.

Medical Book—hay fever book—Morrill Wyman—Autumnal Catarrh — published — New York City

Milk—dried milk patent—S. R. Percy—New York City—April 9

Mohair — commercial manufacture — Arlington Mills—Lawrence, Mass.

Naval Academy—Negro midshipman in the United States Naval Academy—J. H. Conyers—Sept. 21

Optometry Instruction—optometry school—Northern Illinois College of Ophthalmology and Otology—founded—Chicago, Ill.

Paper Bag Manufacturing Machine—square-bottom paper bag machinery—patented—L. C. Crowell

Park—park (national)—Yellowstone National Park—authorized—March 1

Patent List—Official Gazette — published — Washington, D.C.—Jan. 3

Pharmacy College—pharmacy college to make analytical chemistry a required course—Maryland College of Pharmacy—Baltimore, Md.—March 20

Photograph—photograph of a stellar spectrum showing the dark lines—Vega—Henry Draper—Hastings-on-Hudson, N.Y.

Photograph — photograph showing action (not moving pictures)—taken—Eadweard Muybridge—Palo Alto, Calif.

Post Office—Post Office Department of the United States—became executive department officially—act of June 8

Postal Service—postal fraud order—authorized—June 8

President (U.S.)—President born on Independence Day—Calvin Coolidge

Presidential Candidate—presidential candidate who was a Catholic—nominated—Charles O'Conor—Sept. 3

Presidential Candidate—woman presidential candidate—V. C. Woodhull—nominated—New York City—May 10

Prohibition Party (national)—national convention—Columbus, Ohio—Feb. 22

Railroad Apprentice School—established—Elkhart, Ind.

Science Magazine—science magazine (popular)—Popular Science Monthly—published—May

Ship—mine layer—used

Sprinkler—sprinkler system patent—P. W. Pratt—Abington, Mass.—Sept. 17

Street Car—gas-powered street car—patented—April 2

Telegraph—telegraph call boxes—installed—Brooklyn, N.Y.—June 22

Toothpick Manufacturing Machine Patent—Silas Noble and J. P. Cooley—Feb. 20

Vice Presidential Candidate—Negro vice presidential candidate—Frederick Douglass—nominated—New York City—May 10

Water Purification—water purification by filtration—filter erected—Poughkeepsie, N.Y.

1873

Animals—cattle (Aberdeen—Angus) importation—George Grant—Victoria, Kan.

Army School—Army school graduate (Negro)—H. O. Flipper—admitted

Balloon—balloon Atlantic crossing attempt—Brooklyn, N.Y.—Oct. 6

Book Catalog—*The Uniform Trade List Annual*—published—New York City

Brass Rod—drawn—Coe Brass Co.—Torrington, Conn.

Celluloid—celluloid trademark registered—Jan. 14

Degrees (academic and honorary)—Bachelor of Music degree—awarded—M. P. Lowrie—Adrian, Mich.—Dec. 23

Dentistry—patent for a gold crown—J. B. Beers—San Francisco, Calif.—Nov. 4

Earmuff—invented — Chester Greenwood—Farmington, Me.

Education—chair in education—established—University of Iowa—Iowa City, Iowa

Fine Arts Department—fine arts department in a college to grant degrees—College of Fine Arts—Syracuse University—Syracuse, N.Y.—established—June 24

Free Lunch—free lunches to aid convalescents—N. Y. Diet Kitchen Assn.—opened—April 24

Football Game—international football game—New Haven, Conn.—Dec. 6

Football Rules—formulated—New York City—Oct. 18

Gas—natural gas for manufacturing—used in iron working—Leechburg, Pa.

Hotel—fireproof hotel—Palmer House—Chicago, Ill.—opened

Kindergarten—public school kindergarten—authorized—St. Louis, Mo.—Aug. 26

Linoleum—linoleum—manufactured —American Linoleum Manufacturing Company—Richmond, S.I., N.Y.

Livestock-Market Paper—*Drover's Journal*—published—Chicago, Ill.—Jan. 11

Medical School—coeducational medical school—Boston University School of Medicine—Boston, Mass.—founded

Medical Society — laryngological society (state)—organized—Oct.

Money—demonetization of silver—bimetallism abolished—Feb. 12

Money—trade dollar—authorized—Feb. 12

Newspaper—illustrated daily newspaper—New York City—*Daily Graphic*—published—March 4

Oratorio—oratorio by an American—J. K. Paine— "Oratorio of St. Peter" — performed—Portland, Me.—June 3

Patent Examiner—woman patent examiner—A. R. G. Nichols—Melrose, Mass.—July 1

Postage Stamp — departmental postage stamps—authorized—March 3

Postal Card—issued—May 1

Prison—prison built for women and managed exclusively by women—Indianapolis, Ind.

Railroad Coupler—patented—E. H. Janney—Alexandria, Va.—April 29

Rifle Association—rifle association (national)—shooting meet—April 25

Science School—natural science summer school—opened

Silo (of record)—constructed—F. L. Hatch—McHenry County, Ill.

Slicing Machine—patented—Anthony Iske—Lancaster, Pa.—Nov. 4

Street Car—cable street car—in service—San Francisco, Calif.

Street Car—gas powered street car—operated—Providence, R.I.

Tube—machine designed to produce collapsible tubes—built—A. H. Wirz—Philadelphia, Pa.

Weights and Measures Standardization—national organization to improve systems of weights, measures, and moneys—American Metrological Society—formed—New York City—Dec. 30

Wire—barbed wire — manufactured—J. F. Glidden—De Kalb, Ill.

1874

Adhesive and Medicated Plaster—adhesive and medicated plaster with a rubber base—successfully manufactured—East Orange, N.J.

Agriculture Department (state)—state department of agriculture—created—Georgia—Feb. 28

Baseball Team—baseball teams to travel beyond the confines of the U.S.—exhibition—England—July 30

Bridge—steel arch bridge—St. Louis, Mo.—opened—July 4

Caliper (screw)—constructed—Ithaca, N.Y.

Cartoon—Republican cartoon—elephant emblem—used—New York City—Nov. 7

Chautauqua Organization—Fair Point, N.Y.—Aug. 4

Christmas Cards—engraved—Louis Prang—Roxbury, Mass.

Corset—manufactured as a health item—McGraw, N.Y.

Football Game—rugby contest (international)—Harvard-McGill — Cambridge, Mass.—May 14

Football Goal Post—football goal post—used—Cambridge, Mass.—May 14

Gas—water gas plant—built—Phoenixville, Pa.

Greenback Party (or Independent Party)—organized—Indianapolis, Ind.—Nov. 25

Hospital Record — system — introduced — Bellevue Training School for Nurses—New York City

Ice Cream Soda—introduced—R. M. Green—Philadelphia, Pa.

Kidnapping—kidnapping for ransom—C. B. Ross—Germantown, Pa.—July 1

Labor Union Label—adopted—Cigar Makers' International Union—San Francisco, Calif.

Typewritten Book Manuscript — S. L. Clemens—*Adventures of Tom Sawyer*

Visiting Celebrities—king (reigning) to visit the United States—David Kalakaua—returned—Feb. 15

Weights and Measures Standardization—International Bureau of Weights and Measures—established—May 20

1876

Agricultural Experiment Station—state agricultural experiment station—work began—Jan. 1

Animals—cattle exportation to Great Britain—large shipment—William Colwell—Boston, Mass.

Baseball League—National League—formed—Feb. 2

Baseball Player—baseball player to hit over .400—Ross Barnes

Bible—Bible translation by a woman—J. E. Smith—published—Hartford, Conn.

Bridge—cantilever bridge—Kentucky River

Canning—sardine cannery—successful—Eastport, Me.

Carpet Loom—carpet power loom to weave Axminster carpets—Yonkers, N.Y.—invented

Carpet Sweeper—patented—M. R. Bissell—Grand Rapids, Mich.—Sept. 19

Cattle Club—cattle club (Guernsey cattle)—formed—Farmington, Conn.—March 1

Chemical Society—chemical society (national)—American Chemical Society—organized—New York City—April 20

Cigarette Manufacturing Machine—patented—A. H. Hook—New York City—Nov. 7

Clipper for Cutting Hair—manufactured—G. H. Coates—Worcester, Mass.

Clock—clock (one-day back-wind alarm clock)—Thomaston, Conn.

Coaching—first tallyho trip—New York City—May 1

Coaching Club—first meet—April 22

Coast Guard (U.S.)—Coast Guard officers' training school—New Bedford, Mass.—established—July 31

Cooking School—New York Cooking School—opened—New York City—Nov.

Crematory—crematory—Washington, Pa.

Degrees (academic and honorary)—Doctor of Philosophy degree awarded to a Negro—E. A. Bouchet—Yale University—New Haven, Conn.

Dictionary—Bohemian-American dictionary—published—Racine, Wis.

Ethical Culture Society—New York Society for Ethical Culture—founded—New York City—May

Football Club—intercollegiate football association—Springfield, Mass.—Nov. 23

Football Game—intercollegiate football championship

Forestry Legislation—federal forestry supervision—attempted—Aug. 15

Forestry Society—state forestry association—Minnesota—organized—St. Paul, Minn.—Jan. 12

Greenback Party (or Independent Party)—convention—Indianapolis, Ind.—May 17

Insurance—title guaranty insurance company—Philadelphia, Pa.—organized—March 31

Intercollegiate Athletic Association—organized—Saratoga, N.Y.—June

Kindergarten—free kindergarten — Florence Kindergarten—Florence, Mass.—opened—Jan. 3

Library Society—library association (national)—American Library Association—organized—Philadelphia, Pa.—Oct. 6

Medal—lifesaving medal—of Treasury Department—awarded—L. M. Clemons—June 19

Medical Book—dermatology treatise—L. A. Duhring—*Atlas of Skin Diseases*—published—Philadelphia, Pa.

Medical Society—woman physician elected a member of the American Medical Association—S. H. Stevenson

Mimeograph—patented—T. A. Edison—Menlo Park, N.J.—Aug. 8

Organ—electric organ—installed—New York City

Political Convention—presidential convention (national) addressed by a woman—S. A. Spencer—Cincinnati, Ohio—June 15

Polo—polo—introduced—J. G. Bennett—New York City

Polo Club — polo club — organized — New York City

Postage Stamp—public exhibition of postage stamps—Philadelphia, Pa.—May 10

Postage Stamp—stamped envelopes issued to commemorate an event—issued—Philadelphia, Pa.—May 10

Printing Press—high-speed newspaper printing and folding machine—installed—*Times*—Philadelphia, Pa.

Sewing Machine — sewing machine lamp holder—introduced

Ship—torpedo boat—worthy of the name—"Lightning"—built—Bristol, R.I.

Stenotype—patented—J. C. Zachos—New York City—April 11

Symphony—symphonic work by an American composer—J. K. Paine—presented—Boston, Mass.—Jan.

Telephone—telephone conversation over out-of-door wires — Boston to Cambridge, Mass.—Oct. 9

Telephone—telephone message—distinguishable—Boston, Mass.—March 10

Telephone—telephone patent—A. G. Bell—March 7

Tennis—court tennis—introduced—Boston, Mass.—Hollis Hunnewell

Track Meet (intercollegiate)—track meet (intercollegiate)—Saratoga, N.Y.—July 20-21

Turnstile (electric)—used—Philadelphia, Pa.—May 10

Wrench—pipe or screw wrench (practical)—patented — D. C. Stillson — Somerville, Mass.—Dec. 5

1877

Army School—army school graduate (Negro)—H. O. Flipper—June 15

Bicycle Factory—established—Pope Manufacturing Co.—Hartford, Conn.

Bicycle Magazine—*American Bicycling Journal*—published—Boston, Mass.

Bridge—cantilever bridge—completed—Kentucky River

Cabinet of the United States—Confederate to serve in the cabinet—D. M. Key—served—March 12

Carpet Loom—carpet power loom to weave Axminster carpets—patented—Jan. 16

Catamaran—patented—N. G. Herreshoff—Providence, R.I.—April 10

Cattle Club—cattle club (Guernsey cattle)—American Guernsey Cattle Club—permanent organization—New York City—Feb. 7

Chemical Society—chemical society (national)—American Chemical Society—chartered—Nov. 9

Chinese Language and Literature Lectureship—S. W. Williams—Yale University—New Haven, Conn.

Cream Separator—centrifugal cream separator patent—Sept. 25

Degrees (academic and honorary)—Doctor of Philosophy degree awarded to a woman—Helen Magill—Boston University—Boston, Mass.

Dog Show—of importance—New York City—May 8

Easter Egg Roll—Washington, D.C.—April 2

Heating System—heating system from a central station—installed—Lockport, N.Y.

Holiday—Flag Day—remembrance—June 14

Humane Society—humane association national organization—American Humane Association—organized—Cleveland, Ohio—Oct. 9

Lawyer—Japanese lawyer—Takeo Kikuchi—Boston University—Boston, Mass.—June 5

Library Society—library association (national)—annual convention—New York City—Sept. 4

Life Preserver—life preserver of cork approved by the Board of Supervising Inspectors—patented—David Kahnweiler—New York City—July 10

Monument—monument to an American poet—Fitz-Green Halleck statue unveiled—New York City—May 15

Music—long distance telephone concert—from Philadelphia, Pa.—heard in New York City—March 31

Nurse — district nurse — employed — New York City

Occupational Therapy Treatment—Training School for Nurses—Boston, Mass.—incorporated—March 16

Oleomargarine — oleomargarine legislation (state)—enacted—New York—June 5

Organ—color organ—patented—Bainbridge Bishop—New Russia, N.Y.—Jan. 16

President (U.S.)—President to celebrate his silver wedding anniversary at the White House—R. B. Hayes—Dec. 31

Prison—reformatory (state) conducted for women—Reformatory Prison for Women—Sherborn, Mass.—opened—Nov. 7

Railroad — municipal railroad — Cincinnati Southern Railway—regular service—Cincinnati, Ohio—Somerset, Ky.—July 23

Railroad—railroad shipments of dressed beef (year round, long-distance)—G. F. Swift—Chicago, Ill.

Royal Arcanum—founded—Boston, Mass.—June 23

Socialist Labor Party of North America—national convention—Newark, N.J.—Dec. 26

Strike—strike in which federal troops were called in peacetime—July 16

Swimming Championship (amateur open)—New York City—Sept. 30

Telephone—interstate telephone call—New Brunswick, N.J. to New York City—May 17

Telephone—news dispatch by telephone—*Globe*—Boston, Mass.—Feb. 12

Telephone—telephone for domestic use—installed—Somerville, Mass.—April

Telephone—telephone switchboard or exchange—Boston, Mass.—May 17

Telephone—telephone used by a railroad company—tried—Altoona, Pa.—May 21

1878

Aviation—Airship—dirigible — flight scheduled—July 3

Baseball Catcher's Mask—patented—F. W. Thayer—Feb. 12

Baseball Game—triple play unassisted—by player in organized baseball—Paul Hines—May 8

Bibliography Course—University of Michigan—Ann Arbor, Mich.

Bicycle Society—bicycle club—formed—Boston, Mass.—Feb. 11

Bridge—railway all-steel bridge—Glasgow, Mo.—contract signed—Oct. 12

Chinese Embassy—Oct. 4

Copper Refinery Furnace—to use gaseous fuel—Ansonia, Conn.

Electric Company—electric company—Edison Electric Light Company—New York City—incorporated—Oct. 15

Electric Lighting—electric light in a store—installed—Philadelphia, Pa.—Dec. 26

Fishes—goldfish industry

Fruit Spraying—Niagara County, N.Y.

Greenback Labor Party—organized—Toledo, Ohio—Feb. 22

Home Study Course—Chautauqua, N.Y.—organized—Aug. 10

Humane Society—humane association national organization — American Humane Association—constitution adopted—Baltimore, Md.—Nov. 14

Lawyers' Association—lawyers' association (national)—American Bar Association—organized—Saratoga, N.Y.—Aug. 21

Lifesaving Service—lifesaving service—authorized—June 18

Medical Society—laryngological society (national)—American Laryngological Association—founded—Buffalo, N.Y.—June 3

Milk—milk delivery in glass bottles—Alexander Campbell—Brooklyn, N.Y.

Newspaper—college daily—*Yale News*—published—New Haven, Conn.—Jan. 28

Phonograph—phonograph—patented—T. A. Edison—Menlo Park, N.J.—Feb. 19

Pipe—corncob pipe commercial manufacture—Henry Tibbe—patent—July 9

President (U.S.)—President to use a telephone—J. A. Garfield—while in Congress

Probation—probation system, without restrictions as to age—established—Boston, Mass.

Soap—soap to float—manufactured—Cincinnati, Ohio

Telephone—telephone switchboard or exchange (commercial) — installed — New Haven, Conn.—Jan. 28

Telephone Directory—issued—New Haven, Conn.—Feb. 21

Telephone Operator—woman telephone operator—E. N. Nutt—Boston, Mass.—Sept. 1

Typewriting School — opened — New York City

1879

Air (compressed)—for tunnel construction—Hoboken, N.J.—New York City

Archaeological Society—archaeological society (national)—founded—Boston, Mass.—May 10

Archery Club—archery association (national) — formed — Crawfordsville, Ind.—Jan. 23

Automobile Patent—filed—G. B. Selden—Rochester, N.Y.—May 8

Bottle—milk bottles—manufactured—L. P. Whiteman—Cumberland, Md.

Bridge — hanging railroad bridge — Canon City, Colo.—built

Bridge—railway all-steel bridge—Glasgow bridge—opened

Business — five-cent store—opened — F. W. Woolworth—Utica, N.Y.—Feb. 22

Cash Carrier System — installed — Lowell, Mass.—Feb.

Cash Register—patented—J. J. Ritty—Dayton, Ohio—Nov. 4

Christian Science—M. B. Eddy—Boston, Mass.

Cream Separator—centrifugal cream separator—Boston, Mass.

Deaf—Hearing Aid—hearing aid of interest—Audiphone—patented—R. S. Rhodes—River Park, Ill.—Sept. 23

Electric Company—electric company organized to produce and sell electricity—California Electric Light Company, Inc.—San Francisco, Calif.

Electric Lighting—electric arc lights—used for street lighting—C. F. Brush—Cleveland, Ohio—April 29

Electric Lighting—electric incandescent lamp—of practical value—invented—T. A. Edison—Menlo Park, N.J.—Oct. 21

Geological Survey—geological survey director (U.S.)—Clarence King—confirmed—April 3

Indian School—Indian school of prominence—Carlisle, Pa.—opened—Nov. 1

Journalism Course—history of journalism course—University of Missouri—Columbia, Mo.

Labor Law—factory inspection law—enacted—Massachusetts—April 30

Labor Law—labor law prohibiting the employment of women—Illinois—effective—July 1

Library Society—library association (national)—American Library Association—incorporated—Dec. 10

Locomotive—locomotive to use oil fuel—"Young America"

Medical Soceity—laryngological society (national)—annual meeting—June 10

Pedagogy Chair—pedagogy chair (permanent)—University of Michigan—Ann Arbor, Mich.

Photograph—photograph taken by incandescent electric light—Menlo Park, N.J.—Dec.

Saccharin — discovered — Baltimore, Md. —

Senator (U.S.)—senator to serve three states—James Shields—elected—Missouri—Jan. 22

Ship—fish hatching steamer (federal)—"Fishhawk"—authorized—March 3

Ship—steam whaler built as a whale boat—"The Mary and Helen"—built—Bath, Me.

Ship—steamboat to employ electric lights—"Jeannette"

Skating Rink—ice skating rink (indoor)—built—T. L. Rankin—New York City

Sports—amateur athletic competition (interclub)—New York City—Sept. 27

Supreme Court (U.S.)—woman admitted to practice before the Supreme Court of the United States—B. A. B. Lockwood—March 3

Telephone—automatic telephone system patent—Dec. 5

Telephone—telephone switchboard or exchange (multiple)—installed—Chicago, Ill.

Telephone—toll line commercial telephone service—instituted—Springfield, Mass. and Holyoke, Mass.—April 2

Veterinary School—veterinary school (state)—Iowa State College—Ames, Iowa—May 23

1880

Archaeological Society—archaeological society (national)—Archaeological Institute of America — annual meeting — Boston, Mass.—May 15

Bicycle Society—bicycle society (national organization)—formed—Newport, R.I.

Canoe Association—formed—Lake George, N.Y.

Cattle Club—cattle club (Jersey cattle)—incorporated—May 25

Census—city to exceed 1,000,000 in population—New York City

Census—state to exceed 5,000,000 in population—New York

Croquet League—National Croquet League—formed—Feb. 12

Deaf—Hearing Aid—electrical hearing aid—bone conduction device patented—April 27

Electric Company—electric company—Edison Electric Illuminating Company—incorporated—Dec. 17

Electric Lighting—electric incandescent lamp factory—Menlo Park, N.J.—Oct. 1

Electric Lighting—street lighting (electric) by a municipality—in operation—March 31

Electric Power Plant—hydroelectric power plant (commercial)—Grand Rapids Electric Light and Power Co.—Grand Rapids, Mich.—organized—March 22

Engineering Society—mechanical engineering national society—American Society of Mechanical Engineers — founded — New York City—Feb. 16

Engraving—half-tone engraving—S. H. Horgan—*Daily Graphic*—New York City—March 4

Flour Mill—flour rolling mill—patented—John Stevens—Neenah, Wis.—March 23

Greenback Labor Party—national convention—Chicago, Ill.—June 9

Insurance—hail insurance—Tobacco Growers' Mutual Insurance Company—North Canaan, Conn.

Medical Book — bacteriology textbook — A. Magnin — *Bacteria* — published — Boston, Mass.

Medical Book—neurasthenia book—G. M. Beard—*A Practical Treatise on Nervous Exhaustion*—published—New York City

Medical Periodical—laryngology magazine —*Archives of Laryngology*—published—New York City

Newspaper—Italian newspaper—*Il Progresso Italo-Americana*—published—New York City —Sept.

Occupational Therapy Treatment—Adams Nervine Asylum—Boston, Mass.—patients admitted—April

Paint—paint prepared from standard formulas—manufactured—Cleveland, Ohio

Railroad—municipal railroad—freight service began—Feb. 21

Razor—safety razor—manufactured—Kampfe Brothers—New York City

Salvation Army—landed—New York City—March 10

Sewage—separate system of sewage disposal —started—Memphis, Tenn.—Jan. 21

Ship—schooner (four masted)—"William J. White"—launched—Bath, Me.—June

Ship—steamboat to employ electric lights successfully—"Columbia"—dynamo operated

Steam Distribution Plant—New York Steam Corporation—New York City—formed

Telephone—pay station telephone service—New Haven, Conn.—June 1

Tennis Match—lawn tennis tournament of national scope—Staten Island, N.Y.—Sept. 1

Trapshooting—clay pigeon target—patented —G. Ligowsky—Cincinnati, Ohio—Sept. 7

1881

Air Brush Patent—L. L. Curtis—Cape Elizabeth, Me.—Oct. 25

American Red Cross—organized—Washington, D.C.—May 21

Architect—woman architect—L. B. Bethune —Buffalo, N.Y.

Business School—business collegiate school —Wharton School of Commerce and Finance—Philadelphia, Pa.—established

Catholic Student—pontifical college—M. A. Corrigan—became archbishop—March 4

Coast Guard (U.S.)—inland U.S. Coast Guard station—opened—Louisville, Ky.—Nov. 3

Cold Storage Plant—operated by mechanical refrigeration—Boston, Mass.

Cream Separator—continuous flow centrifugal cream separator—used—Mahwah, N.J.

Dynamo—dynamo—successful — "Jumbo" — built—New York City

Electric Lighting—electric light from a power plant in a residence—installed—Fort Washington, N.Y.

Ferryboat — steel-hull ferryboat — "Lackawanna"—built—Newburgh, N.Y.

Fishing Magazine—*American Angler*—published—Philadelphia, Pa.—Oct. 15

Forestry School—forestry course in a university—University of Michigan—Ann Arbor, Mich.

Horse Race—American-bred horse to win the English Derby—Iroquois—June 1

Hotel—hotel to install electric lights—Prospect House—Blue Mountain Lake, N.Y.

Immigration—Chinese labor immigration act —proclaimed

Insurance—bonding company (exclusive)— American Surety Company—New York City—incorporated—Dec. 7

Labor Union—labor union of importance— American Federation of Labor—organized —Pittsburgh, Pa.

Locomotive Headlight—electric locomotive headlight — patented — L. G. Woolley — Mendon, Mich.—May 3

Loganberry — introduced — J. H. Logan — Santa Cruz, Calif.

Monument—statue cast by the United States Government—D. G. Farragut statue—accepted—April 25

Nursing School—training school for Negro nurses—Spelman Seminary—Atlanta, Ga. —founded

Photographic Film—roll film for cameras— patented—D. H. Houston—Cambria, Wis. Oct. 11

Piano Player—piano player—patented—J. McTammany—Cambridge, Mass.—June 14

Piano Player—piano player (completely automatic)—patented—Oct. 4

Pier—ocean pier—built—G. W. Howard—Atlantic City, N.J.

Play (drama)—Greek play—*Oedipus Tyrannus*—produced—Harvard University—Cambridge, Mass.

Plumbing—state plumbing legislation—enacted—Illinois—May 30

President (U.S.)—President whose mother lived at the Executive Mansion—J. A. Garfield—served—March 4

Presidential Candidate—presidential candidate to campaign and make speeches in a foreign language—J. A. Garfield

Psychology Laboratory—established—Johns Hopkins University—Baltimore, Md.

Pure Food Law—pure food and drug legislation (state)—enacted—May 28

Quarantine — plant quarantine legislation (state)—enacted—California—March 4

Ship — schooner (five masted) — "David Dows"—launched—Toledo, Ohio—April 21

Telephone—international telephone conversation—July 1

Tennis Match—lawn tennis national championship matches—Newport, R.I.—Aug. 31

Tennis Society—tennis society (national)—United States Lawn Tennis Association—formed—New York City—May 21

1882

Accountants' Society—accountants' society—organized—New York City—July 28

Army Officer—general to become a rear admiral—appointed—May 16

Baseball Team—professional league baseball team to win three pennants in succession—Chicago, Ill.—Cubs

Bicycle Trip—bicycle trip of 100 miles sponsored by a club—Worcester to Boston, Mass.

College—honors course—University of Michigan—Ann Arbor, Mich.

Cooperative — college cooperative store — Cambridge, Mass.—Feb. 28

Country Club—country club to remain in existence eighty years—formed—Brookline, Mass.—Sept. 13

Deaf—School—lip reading instruction for the deaf—S. W. Keeler—New York City

Degrees (academic and honorary)—Doctor of Philosophy degree awarded to a woman by a women's college—K. E. Morris—Northampton, Mass.

Electric Company—electric station (central) to supply light and power—Edison Electric Illuminating Company—New York City—opened—Sept. 4

Electric Fan—invented—S. S. Wheeler

Electric Flatiron—patented—H. W. Seely—New York City—June 6

Electric Power Plant—hydroelectric power plant—opened—Appleton, Wis.—Sept. 30

Electric Power Plant—municipally owned electric power plant—purchased—Fairfield, Iowa

Elevator—elevator with an electric light—Blue Mountain Lake, N.Y.—July 12

Flicker—patented—H. Van Hoevenbergh—Elizabeth, N.J.—May 16

Forestry Society—national forestry association—American Forestry Congress and American Forestry Association—merged—June 29

Holiday—Labor Day holiday parade—New York City—Sept. 5

Hospital—hospital for the military and naval forces—authorized—June 30

Immigration—Chinese labor immigration act—enacted—May 6

Immigration—immigration head tax—authorized—Aug. 3

Knights of Columbus—chartered—Connecticut—March 29

Lacrosse Association (intercollegiate)—Intercollegiate Lacrosse Association—organized—Princeton, N.J.—March 11

Library—library newspaper room—Newburyport, Mass.—dedicated—April 28

Medical Instruction—state medicine and public hygiene professorship—Northwestern University—Chicago, Ill.

Milk—malted milk—invented—William Horlick—Racine, Wis.

Naval Officer—naval attaché—F. E. Chadwick—served—Nov. 15

Play (drama)—Hebrew professional acting troupe—New York City—Aug. 12

Ski Club—ski club (local)—Nansen Ski Club—Berlin, N.H.

Steam Distribution Plant—first distribution from central plant—March 3

Steel—steel mill to install an electrical machine—Braddock, Pa.

Suture—silk suture—used—W. S. Halsted—Baltimore, Md.

Tariff—tariff commission—authorized—June 7

Theater — theater lighted by electricity — Bijou Theatre—Boston, Mass.—Dec. 11

1883

Anti-Vivisection Society—organized—Philadelphia, Pa.—Feb. 23

Baseball Game—baseball game at night—Fort Wayne, Ind. June 2

Bible School—Missionary Training College—opened—New York City

Cigar Rolling Machine—patented—Oscar Hammerstein—New York City—Feb. 27

Civil Service—civil service woman appointee—M. F. Hoyt—appointed

Crane—crane — manufactured — Stamford, Conn.

Crane—wrecking crane—Bay City, Mich.

Deaf—Church Service—ordained deaf clergyman—H. W. Syle

Diplomatic Service—Korean embassy—received

Electric Company—three-wire central station incandescent electric lighting plant—Edison Electric Illuminating Company—Sunbury, Pa.—incorporated—April 30

Elevated Railroad—electric elevated railroad —Chicago, Ill.

Engineering College—electrical engineering course—in a college—established—Cornell University—Ithaca, N.Y.—Sept. 21

Glass—plate glass produced on a large scale —New York City Plate Glass Company —Creighton, Pa.

Horse Show—horse show of national scope —New York City—Oct. 22-26

Jewish College—Jewish college to train men for the rabbinate—first graduation—July 11

Labor Union — labor union legalization (state)—New Jersey—Feb. 14

Manual Training—manual training school entirely financed by public taxes—Baltimore Manual Training School—Baltimore, Md.—authorized

Medical Instruction—pathology chair—modern pathology—Johns Hopkins University —Baltimore, Md.

Nails—steel-cut nails—manufactured—Riverside Iron Works—Wheeling, W.Va.

Newspaper—newspaper delivery train—operated—Galveston, Tex. to Houston, Tex.

Opera—opera at the Metropolitan Opera House—New York City—*Faust*

Pharmacist—pharmacist (woman graduate) —Susan Hayhurst — Philadelphia, Pa.—graduated—March 16

Postal Service—mail chute—patented—J. G. Cutler—Rochester, N.Y.—Sept. 11

Railroad—state aid to railroads—granted—Illinois—March 2

Railroad Signal System—railroad signal system of interlocking signal apparatus operated by compressed air—installed—Bound Brook, N.J.

Ship—steel vessels of the U.S. Navy—authorized—March 3

Sports—cross country championships—New York Athletic Club—New York City—Nov. 6

Sports—sports trainer (professional)—Bob Rogers—New York Athletic Club—New York City—engaged—May 1

Temperance Society—women's temperance society (national)—World Woman's Christian Temperance Union—formed

Tennis Match—intercollegiate lawn tennis match—Hartford, Conn.—June

Time (standard)—signals sent out—Naval Observatory—Washington, D.C.—Nov. 18

Trust—anti-trust law (state)—enacted—Alabama—Feb. 23

Vaudeville—originated—B. F. Keith—Boston, Mass.

Wild West Show—W. F. Cody—North Platte, Neb.—July 4

Wire—woven wire fence industry—J. W. Page—Lenawee County, Mich.

1884

Adding Machine—adding machine absolutely accurate at all times—"Comptometer"—constructed—Chicago, Ill.—Nov.

Animal Industry Bureau (U.S.)—Bureau of Animal Industry—authorized—May 29

Anti-Monopoly Party—formed—Chicago, Ill. —May 14

Anti-Vivisection Society—annual meeting—Philadelphia, Pa.—Jan. 30

Baseball Game—baseball series world championship—won by Providence team

Baseball Player—baseball pitcher to pitch three no-hit games—Larry Corcoran—June 27

Baseball Player—Negro baseball player—M. F. Walker—Toledo, Ohio

Bicycle Trip—bicycle trip around the world —started—San Francisco, Calif.—April 22

Bullfight—bullfight—Dodge City, Kan.—July 4

College—"dean of the faculty"—Bryn Mawr, Pa.

College—state college for women—established—Columbus, Miss.—March 12

Electrical Show—Philadelphia, Pa.

Equal Rights Party—formed—San Francisco, Calif.—Sept. 20

Fellowship—fellowship awarded a woman—Sage Fellowship in Entomology and Botany—granted—H. E. Grotecloss—June 19

Fellowship—resident fellowship for women awarded by a women's college—Bryn Mawr College—Bryn Mawr, Pa.

Fountain Pen—practical—invented—L. E. Waterman—New York City

Glider—glider flight—J. J. Montgomery—Otay, Calif.—March 17

Historical Society—historical society (general)—American Historical Association—founded—Saratoga, N.Y.—Sept. 10

Horse Race—horse race (American Derby) —Chicago, Ill.—June 28

Hospital—cancer hospital—New York Cancer Hospital—New York City—organized —Feb. 7

Insurance—bonding company (exclusive)—began business—April 15

Labor—labor bureau (federal)—authorized —June 27

Leather—chrome tanning process—patented —Augustus Schultz—New York City—Jan. 8

Manual Training—manual training school entirely financed by public taxes—Baltimore Manual Training School—Baltimore, Md.—established

Medal—Albert Medal presented to a native-born American—J. B. Eads—June 10

Medical Society—Negro medical society—Medico-Chirurgical Society—organized—Washington, D.C.—April 24

Milk — evaporated milk — patented—J. B. Meyenberg—Nov. 25

Monument—monument to George Washington (national)—Washington Monument—Washington, D.C.—completed—Dec. 6

Naval War College—naval war college—established—Newport, R.I.—Oct. 6

Navigation Bureau (U.S.) — authorized—July 5

Newspaper Syndicate—newspaper syndicate to supply articles—S. S. McClure—New York City—Nov.

Photographic Film—transparent paper strip photographic film—patented—George Eastman—Rochester, N.Y.—Oct. 14

Police—police bureau of identification—established—Chicago, Ill.—Jan. 1

Political Convention—national nominating convention presided over by a Negro—J. R. Lynch—Chicago, Ill.—June 3

Press Clipping Bureau—Samuel Leavitt—New York City—April 15

Railroad—switchback railway — operated—Coney Island, N.Y.—June

Religious Hillside Shrine—built—New Ulm, Minn.

Roller Skate—ball-bearing skate patent—L. M. Richardson—Chicago, Ill.—Dec. 9

Telephone—long-distance telephone call—Boston-New York City—March 27

Theatrical .School—theatrical school—Lyceum School of Acting—New York City—founded—Oct. 1

Typesetting Machine—linotype machine—patented—Ottmar Mergenthaler — Baltimore, Md.—Aug. 26

Wire—legislation (state) requiring wires to be placed underground—New York State—enacted—June 14

1885

Bank—savings group—to teach children to save—organized—Long Island City, N.Y.

Bankers' Association—bankers' association formed by a state group—July 23

Baseball Batting and Fielding Cage—built—New Haven, Conn.

Baseball Team—baseball team (Negro professional)—organized—New York City

Biology—biology course (general) offered in a college—Bryn Mawr, Pa.

Bird Protection Agency (federal)—Economic Ornithology Division—July 1

Bookseller's Catalog—of first editions—New York City

Building—building known as a skyscraper—completed—Chicago, Ill.

Clock—watch movement to be electrically wound—Chicago, Ill.

College—graduate school for women—formal opening—Bryn Mawr, Pa.—Oct. 23

College—state college for women—opened—Columbus, Miss.—Oct. 22

Economics Association—American Economic Association—founded—Saratoga, N.Y..—Sept. 9

"First Aid" Instruction—Peekskill, N.Y.

Forest Reserve—forest reserve (state)—New York State Forest Preserve—designated—May 15

Forest Service—forest commission (state)—permanent— authorized — California — March 3

Gas Commission (state)—authorized—Massachusetts—June 11

History Instruction—history course (integrated) in a women's college—Bryn Mawr College—Bryn Mawr, Pa.

Hospital—tuberculosis sanatorium (modern)—Saranac Lake, N.Y.—opened—Feb. 1

Index of Government Publications—published

Legislator (state)—Negro legislator (state)—B. W. Arnett—served—Ohio

Library Society—library society (local)—New York Library Club—formed—New York City

Medical Instruction—bacteriology lectures—Harvard Medical School — Cambridge, Mass.

Monument—monument to George Washington (national)—Washington, D.C.—dedicated—Feb. 21

Motor Boat—motor boat pleasure craft—manufactured—New York City

Naval War College—naval war college—opened—Sept. 3

Navigation Bureau (U.S.)—permanently organized—July 1

Newspaper—newspaper daily railroad delivery service—*Morning News*—Dallas, Tex.—Oct. 1

Newspaper—Yiddish daily newspaper—published—New York City

Nurses' Society—nurses' society (local)—Philomena Society—organized—New York City—Nov. 24

Ordnance — cartridge-loading machinery — patented—G. M. Peters—Xenia, Ohio—July 7

Photographic Film—moving picture film (commercial)—manufactured — Rochester, N.Y.—March 26

Postal Service—special delivery service—authorized—March 3

President (U.S.)—President elected for two non-consecutive terms—Grover Cleveland—began first term

Prize Fight—prize fight of importance under the Marquis of Queensberry rules—Cincinnati, Ohio—Aug. 29

Protestant Episcopal Bishop — Protestant Episcopal bishop (Negro)—S. D. Ferguson—consecrated—New York City—June 24

Pump—gasoline pump—manufactured—S. F. Bowser—Fort Wayne, Ind.

Railroad—"piggy-back" railroad operation—Long Island Rail Road Company

Restaurant—self-service restaurant—opened—New York City—Sept. 4

Street Car—electric cars commercially operated—Baltimore, Md.—Aug. 10

Surgical Operation—appendicitis operation (appendectomy) — performed — W. W. Grant—Davenport, Iowa—Jan. 4

1886

Accountants' Society—accountants' society to become a national organization—American Association of Public Accountants—formed—New York City—Dec. 22

Aluminum—aluminum—C. M. Hall—invented process—Feb. 23

Arbitration—State Board of Mediation and Arbitration—organized—New York State—June 1

Automobile Tractor—endless chain tractor—patented—Charles Dinsmoor—Warren, Pa.—Nov. 2

Automobile Tractor—steam tractor—manufactured—San Leandro, Calif.

Biblical Students Summer Conference—D. L. Moody—Northfield, Mass.—July 7

Birds — ostrich farm — established— South Pasadena, Calif.

Boat Race—fisherman's boat race—Boston, Mass.—May 1

Brokerage—stock exchange at which more than a million shares were traded in one day—New York City—Dec. 15

Catholic Priest—Negro Catholic priest—ordained to work in the U.S.—Augustus Tolton—ordained—April 24

Coat — tuxedo coat — introduced — Tuxedo Park, N.Y.—Oct. 10

Earthquake—of consequence—Aug. 31

Economics Magazine—*Quarterly Journal of Economics*—published—Boston, Mass.—Oct.

Electric Power Plant—alternating current power plant—operated—Great Barrington, Mass.—March 6

Electric Power Plant—alternating current power plant commercially successful—built—Buffalo, N.Y.—Nov.

Forest Service—Forest Service (U.S.)—Division of Forestry—statutory recognition—June 30

Governor—gubernatorial election in which two brothers were the opposing candidates R. L. Taylor—A. A. Taylor—Tennessee—Nov. 2

Horse—horse whose total purses exceeded $100,000

Money—bill bearing the portrait of a woman—Martha Washington—Sept.

Monument—statue presented by a foreign country—Statue of Liberty—Liberty Island (Bedloe Island), N.Y.—unveiled—Oct. 28

Newspaper—newspaper association—American Newspaper Publishers Association—organized—Nov. 17

Nurses' Magazine—*Nightingale* — published—New York City—March 6

Oleomargarine — oleomargarine legislation (federal)—enacted—Aug. 2

Phonograph—phonograph that was practical—patented—May 4

Physician—Hindu woman to receive a doctor of medicine degree—Anandibai Joshee—graduated—March 11

Playground—for children—Children's Mission—Boston, Mass.

Polo—international polo series—Newport, R.I.—England vs U.S.—Aug. 25

Postal Service—special delivery service—extended to all free delivery offices—Aug. 4

Settlement House—University Settlement—established—New York City

Ship—battleship of importance—authorized—Aug. 3

Ship—torpedo boat of importance—"Cushing"—authorized—Aug. 3

Ski Club—ski club (local) that was active—Aurora Ski Club—Red Wing, Minn.—organized—Jan. 19

Social Register—published—New York City

Soup Company—Franco-American Soup Co.—organized—New York City

Telephone—desk telephone—used

Typesetting Machine—linotype machine used commercially — installed — *Tribune* — New York City—July 1

Typewriter Ribbon—typewriter ribbon patent—G. K. Anderson—Memphis, Tenn.—Sept. 14

Wedding—White House wedding of a President—Grover Cleveland—June 2

Welding—by the electric process—patented—Elihu Thomson—Lynn, Mass.—Aug. 10

Zoological Laboratory (U.S.) — zoological laboratory (U.S.) for the study of the parasites of livestock—opened—Washington, D.C.—Aug. 1

1887

Accident Report—industrial accident reports—required—Massachusetts—Sept. 1

Accountants' Society—accountants' society to become a national organization—American Association of Public Accountants—incorporated—Aug. 20

Adding Machine—adding machine absolutely accurate at all times—patented—D. E. Felt—Chicago, Ill.—Oct. 11

Armor Plate Contract (U.S. Navy)—June 1

Bacteriology Laboratory—bacteriology laboratory—Brooklyn, N.Y.—incorporated—Feb. 21

Bauxite—discovered—Floyd County, Ga.

Bicycle Trip—bicycle trip around the world—returned—San Francisco, Calif.—Jan. 4

Book—book set by linotype—*Tribune Book of Open Air Sports*—published—New York City

Brewery to remain in business for 200 years—Philadelphia, Pa.—incorporated

Building — steel-frame building — Tacoma Building—Chicago, Ill.—completed

College—college for women to affiliate with a university—New Orleans, La.

Diplomatic Service—Jewish ambassador—O. S. Straus—appointed—March 24

Esperanto—proposed—L. L. Zamenhof

Fishing Rod—of telescoping steel tubes—patented—Everett Horton—Bristol, Conn.—March 8

Game Warden (salaried game and fish warden)—authorized—Michigan—March 15

Holiday—Labor Day law (state)—enacted—Oregon—Feb. 21

Hospital—babies' hospital designed exclusively for infants—Babies Hospital of the City of New York—incorporated—June 23

Hospital — cancer hospital — opened—New York City—Dec. 7

Hospital—hospital for the military and naval forces—Army and Navy Hospital—Hot Springs, Ark.—opened—Jan. 17

Insurance—credit insurance—attempted—New York State

Insurance—mutual liability insurance company—American Mutual Liability Insurance Company—Boston, Mass.—opened—Oct. 1

Interstate Commerce Act—enacted—Feb. 4

Kindergarten—kindergarten for the blind—established by Perkins institution—opened—Roxbury, Mass.—May 2

Library Training (systematic)—introduced—Columbia University—New York City—Jan. 5

Newspaper—European edition of an American newspaper—*Herald*—Oct. 4

Newspaper—newspaper association—convention—Rochester, N.Y.—Feb.

Photographic Film—celluloid photographic film—invented—H. W. Goodwin—Newark, N.J.

Physiological Society—physiological society (national organization)—American Physiological Society—organized—New York City—Dec. 30

Postal Service—parcel post convention—negotiated with Jamaica, B.W.I.—July 22

Printing Press—quadruple newspaper press—constructed—New York City

Psychology Magazine—*American Journal of Psychology* — published — Baltimore, Md.—Nov.

Railroad—daily railroad service to the Pacific coast—established

Railroad—electrically lighted train—in service—Pennsylvania Railroad Co.—June

Ship—navy vessel equipped to lay mines—"Baltimore"—keel laid—May 5

Silk—silk loom—of importance—"Gem Silk Loom" built—Worcester, Mass.

Ski Club—ski club (local) that was active—first ski classic—Feb. 8

Softball—indoor baseball game—played—Chicago, Ill.—Nov. 30

Teachers' Sick Benefit Funds—established—New York City

Tennis Match—women's national championship lawn tennis matches—Philadelphia, Pa.

Time Recorder—autograph time recorder—patented—B. F. Merritt—Newton, Mass.—Dec. 20

Typesetting Machine—monotype—patented—T. Lanston—Washington, D.C.—June 7

Union Labor Party—formed—Cincinnati, Ohio—Feb. 22

Woman—woman mayor—S. M. Salter—Argonia, Kan.—April 4

1888

Adding Machine—adding machine successfully marketed—patented—Aug. 21

Agricultural School—vocational agricultural school—established—St. Paul, Minn.—Oct. 18

Aluminum—aluminum—commercial production—Pittsburgh Reduction Company—Pittsburgh, Pa.

Arbitration—interstate carrier arbitration law—enacted—Oct. 1

Bank—bank for Negroes operated by Negroes—chartered—Richmond, Va.—March 2

Bank—bank for Negroes privately operated by Negroes — organized — Washington, D.C.—Oct. 17

Baseball Team—baseball teams to go on a world tour—Oct. 20

Camera — roll film camera—patented—G. Eastman

Corporation Course—industrial corporation course—University of Nebraska—Lincoln, Neb.

Crematory—crematory (state) — authorized—New York—May 21

Door (revolving)—patented—T. Van Kannel—Philadelphia, Pa.—Aug. 7

Election Law—Australian ballot system—adopted—Kentucky—Feb. 24

Electric .Meter—patented—O. B. Shallenberger—Rochester, Pa.—Aug. 14

Ferryboat—double-deck ferryboat—launched—"Bergen"—Newburgh, N.Y.—Oct. 25

Health Laboratory—health laboratory (municipal)—Providence, R.I.—established—Jan. 1

Holding Company authorization (state)—enacted—New Jersey—April 4

Incubator for Infants—constructed—New York City

Locomotive—electric freight locomotive—built—Pullman, Ill.—tested—May 1

Monument—monument to George Washington (national)—Washington, D.C.—opened to public—Oct. 9

Motor Boat—storage battery motor boat—"Magnet"—built—Newark, N.J.

Naval Officer—naval chaplain who was Catholic—C. H. Parks

Pen—ball-point pen patent—J. J. Loud—Weymouth, Mass.—Oct. 30

Presidential Candidate—presidential candidate of Negro blood nominated—Frederick Douglass—Chicago, Ill.—June 23

Psychology Professor—J. M. Cattell—Philadelphia, Pa.

Rodeo—competition—Prescott, Ariz.—July 4

Saxophone—manufactured—Elkart, Ind.

Seismograph—exhibited—Lick Observatory—Mount Hamilton, Calif.—June 1

Ship—battleship of importance—"Maine"—keel laid—Oct. 17

Ship—torpedo boat of importance—"Cushing"—keel laid—Bristol, Pa.

Straws (artificial)—for drinking—patented—M. C. Stone—Washington, D.C.—Jan. 3

Time Recorder—dial time recorder—invented—Alexander Dey

Time Recorder—employees' time recorder—patented—W. L. Bundy—Auburn, N.Y.—Nov. 20

Typewriter Ribbon—typewriter "copy" ribbon—patented—J. L. Wortman—Philadelphia, Pa.—Jan. 24

Union Labor Party—convention—Cincinnati, Ohio—May 15

United Labor Party—formed—Cincinnati, Ohio—May 16

1889

Agriculture Bureau—agriculture bureau—made an executive department—Feb. 9

Agriculture Department (U.S.)—Secretary of the Department of Agriculture—N. J. Colman—appointed—Feb. 13

Aluminum—aluminum—C. M. Hall—patented process—April 2

Bacteriology Laboratory—bacteriology laboratory — Hoagland Laboratory — New York City—opened—Feb.

Bank—bank for Negroes operated by Negroes—opened—Richmond, Va.—April 3

Bicycle—bicycle with a back pedal brake—patented—Dec. 24

Brokerage—investment trust—New York City

Business School—business high school—authorized—Washington, D.C.—June 11

Clarinet—made of metal—patented—Aug. 27

Conference—Pan American Conference—Washington, D.C.—Oct. 2

Electric Power Plant—alternating current hydroelectric power plant to operate over a long distance—June 2

Elevator—electric elevator successfully operated—installed—New York City

Fellowship—fellowship (graduate) awarded by a women's college—Bryn Mawr College—Bryn Mawr, Pa.—June 6

Football Dummy—used—New Haven, Conn.

Freemasons — Grotto — formed — Hamilton, N.Y.—Sept. 10

High School—county high school—Dickinson County Community High School—opened—Chapman, Kan.

Historical Society—historical society (general)—American Historical Association—incorporated—Jan. 4

Holiday—national holiday—April 30

Library—children's department in a library —Minneapolis Public Library—Minneapolis, Minn.

Lithuanian Church—organized—Plymouth, Pa.—Oct. 27

Medical Clinic—medical clinic (general)—Johns Hopkins Medical School—Baltimore, Md.—opened—Oct.

Medical Instruction—bacteriology courses in a college—University of Michigan—Ann Arbor, Mich.—Jan.

Niagara Falls—utilization of Niagara Falls waterpower (large scale)—Cataract Construction Company incorporated—June 13

Novel Course—lecture course on the English novel—University of Pennsylvania—Philadelphia, Pa.

Photograph—photograph (taken in the U.S.) on which a meteor was found—Cambridge, Mass.—Aug. 10

Political Science Society—political and social science society (national) — American Academy of Political and Social Science —organized—Philadelphia, Pa.—Dec. 14

Railroad—daily railroad service to the Pacific coast—through service without a change—Nov. 17

Sanitary District—Chicago, Ill.—authorized —Nov. 5

Sewing Machine—electric sewing machine —manufactured — Singer Manufacturing Company—Elizabethport, N.J.

State—states admitted to the Union simultaneously—North and South Dakota—Nov. 3

Stock Quotatiton Board—stock quotattion boards—manufactured—New York City

Tabulating Machine — patented — Herman Hollerith—New York City—Jan. 8

Telephone—automatic telephone system (successful)—A. B. Strowger—patent application—March 12

Telephone—coin telephone—patented—William Gray—Aug. 13

Tennis Match—professional lawn tennis contest (international)—Newport, R.I.—Aug. 29

Time Recorder—dial time recorder—patented —A. Dey—Sept. 24

Tour of the World—tour of the world made by a woman traveling alone—E. Cochrane (Nellie Bly)—started—Nov. 14

Trust—anti-trust law (state)—general law—enacted—Kansas—March 9

Tuberculosis Circular—issued—New York City—July

1890

Animal Husbandry—animal husbandry professor—J. A. Craig—University of Wisconsin—Madison, Wis.

Architect—woman architect—L. B. Bethune —elected to membership in American Institute of Architects—Sept. 15

Baseball Team—women's baseball team

Building — steel-frame residence — built—Brooklyn, N.Y.

Business School—business high school—opened—Washington, D.C.—Sept. 22

Button—buttons of fresh water pearl—Muscatine, Iowa

Dairy School—of collegiate rank—University of Wisconsin—Madison, Wis.—Jan. 3

Dam—rock-filled dam—Castlewood, Colo.—opened—Nov.

Deaf—School—lip reading school for adults —established—New York City

Decalcomanias — manufactured — Thomas Burke—Philadelphia, Pa.

Election Law—corrupt election practices law (state)—New York State—enacted—April 4

Electric Transmission—alternating current power transmission—Telluride, Colo.

Employment Service — state employment service—Ohio—April 28

Execution—electrocution of a human being —Auburn Prison—Auburn, N.Y.—Aug. 6

Football Game—Army-Navy football game —West Point, N.Y.—Nov. 29

Golf Course—golf course (nine holes)—completed—Newport, R.I.

Hammer (pneumatic)—invented—C. B. King —Detroit, Mich.

Leather—chrome tanned leather successfully marketed—R. H. Foerderer—Philadelphia, Pa.

Library Society—state library society—Albany, N.Y.

Meat Inspection Legislation (federal)—enacted—Aug. 30

Milk Tester—of value—invented—S. M. Babcock

Narcotic—narcotic regulation (federal)—enacted—Oct. 1

Navy—naval militia (state)—Massachusetts —organized—March 18

Niagara Falls—utilization of Niagara Falls waterpower (large-scale)—ground broken —Oct. 4

Pan American Union—established—Washington, D.C.—April 14

Paper—crepe paper—manufactured—Brooklyn, N.Y.

Polo Club—polo association (national)—U.S. Polo Association — formed — New York City—June 6

Prize Fight—state legislation concerning prize fighting—Louisiana — enacted—May 12

Sewage—sewage disposal by chemical precipitation—Worcester, Mass.

Ship—battleship of importance — "Maine" launched—Nov. 18

Ship—navy vessel equipped to lay mines— "Baltimore"—commissioned—Jan. 7

Ship—torpedo boat of importance—"Cushing" — commissioned — Bristol, Pa.—April 22

Shooting Gallery (mechanized)—invented— C. W. Parker—Abilene, Kan.

Single Tax—single tax national conference— New York City—Sept. 1

Tour of the World—tour of the world made by a woman traveling alone—E. Cochrane (Nellie Bly)—returned—New York City —Jan. 25

Tournament of Roses—Pasadena, Calif.— Jan. 1

Trust—anti-trust law (national)—enacted— July 2

Woman—woman labor delegate to a national convention—M. Burke—Detroit, Mich.— Dec. 8-13

Woman Suffrage—state to grant suffrage to women—Wyoming—July 10

Women's Club—women's club federation— General Federation of Women's Clubs— New York City—March 20

1891

Animal Industry Bureau (U.S.)—pathological division—established—April 1

Automobile—electric storage battery automobile—designed—William Morrison

Bathhouse—public baths with showers— opened—New York City—Aug. 17

Bicycle Race—international six-day bicycle race—New York City—Oct. 18-24

Bicycle Tire — bicycle tire (pneumatic) — manufactured—New York City—April

Billboard Standardization—Associated Bill Posters and Distributors of the U.S. and Canada—formed—Chicago, Ill.—July 15

Bridge Whist Organization—of importance —formed—Milwaukee, Wis.—April 14

Bridge Whist Tournament—duplicate whist tournament—Milwaukee, Wis.

"Carborundum"—invented—E. G. Acheson —Monongahela City, Pa.

Catholic Priest—Negro Catholic priest ordained in the United States—C. R. Uncles —Baltimore, Md.—Dec. 19

Chair — steamer chair — introduced — New York City—H. Conried

Check—travelers' checks—devised—M. F. Berry

Congress of the United States—congress to appropriate a billion dollars—Washington, D.C.

Congressman (U.S.)—congressman elected by the prohibitionists—Kittel Halvorson— served

Copyright Law — international copyright agreement—enacted—March 4

Corkboard Patent—J. T. Smith—New York City—July 14

Correspondence School—to achieve distinction — Scranton, Pa. — student enrolled — Oct. 16

Diamond—diamonds in a meteorite—G. A. Koenig—June

Expedition—polar expedition of which a woman was a member—Peary Expedition —sailed—New York City—June 6

Fencing—fencing league (national)—Amateur Fencers League of America—organized—New York City—May 6

Ferryboat—double-deck ferryboat with the propeller type steel hull—"Hamburg"— built

Football Book — American Football — Walter Camp—published—New York City

Football Game—indoor football game—New York City

Forest Management — professional scale — Asheville, N.C.

Forest Reserve—forest reserve (national)— Yellowstone Park Timberland Reserve— designated—March 30

Forest Service—federal planting of forests— Swan, Neb.

Fuller's Earth—discovered—Benton, Ark.

Hospital — interracial hospital — Provident Hospital—Chicago, Ill.—opened—May 4

Immigration—immigration bureau superintendent—W. D. Owen—appointed—June 15

Medical Periodical—optometry magazine—*The Optician*—published—New York City—Jan.

Nautical School—nautical state school—established—Massachusetts—June 11

People's Party—organized—Cincinnati, Ohio—May 19

Phonograph Trade Magazine—*The Phonogram*—published—New York City—Jan.

Printing Press—sextuple printing press—installed—New York City

Radio Patent—of importance—T. A. Edison—Dec. 29

Railroad Car—chapel car—"Evangel"—dedicated—May 23

Research Institute—anatomy research institute—Wistar Institute of Anatomy and Biology—established—Philadelphia, Pa.—July 20

Road—law regarding state aid for roads—New Jersey—April 14

Scale — computing scales — manufactured — Dayton, Ohio—Computing Scale Company incorporated—March 20

Ship—whaleback steamer to cross the Atlantic—"Charles W. Wetmore"—sailed—Duluth, Minn.—June 11

Ski Club—ski club association—Ishpeming, Mich.—Jan. 16

Temperance Society—women's temperance society (national) — World Woman's Christian Temperance Union—convention—Nov. 10

Trading Stamp—originated—T. A. Sperry

Tunnel—subaqueous railroad tunnel to a foreign country—Port Huron, Mich. to Sarnia, Ontario—opened—Sept. 19

Woman—white woman to become an Indian chief—H. M. Converse

1892

Acetylene—manufactured—T. L. Willson—Spray, N.C.—May 4

Addressograph—invented—J. S. Duncan

Alligator Farm — established — Anastasia Island, Fla.

Animals — cattle tuberculosis test — Villa Nova, Pa.—March 3

Arabic Magazine — published — New York City

Attorney General—assistant attorney general (state) who was a woman—E. L. Knowles—Montana

Automobile Tire—pneumatic tire patent—Dec. 20

Automobile Tractor—gasoline tractor—manufactured

Bacteriology Laboratory—bacteriology diagnostic laboratory—as part of work of health department—New York City

Baseball Player—baseball "pinch hitter"—played—Brooklyn, N.Y.—June 7

Baseball Player—baseball player to catch a ball dropped from the Washington Monument, Washington, D.C.—Aug. 29

Basketball — basketball — invented — James Naismith

Basketball—basketball played at a women's college — Smith College — Northampton, Mass.

Basketball — basketball team (college) — formed—Alliance, Ohio—Dec.

Basketball Rules—basketball rule book—published—Springfield, Mass.

Basketball Rules—basketball rules—Springfield, Mass.

Bicycle Tire—bicycle tire (cord)—patented J. F. Palmer—Chicago, Ill.—June 7

Bottle Cap — crown cork — invented — W. Painter

Canal Locks—of concrete—Hennepin canal—Chicago to Rock Island, Ill.—commenced—July

Cheese — Liederkranz brand cheese — produced—Monroe, N.Y.

College Self-Government Organization — Bryn Mawr, Pa.—chartered—Feb. 23

Cotton-Boll Weevil—introduced—Texas

Degrees (academic and honorary)—anthropology doctorate—conferred—Worcester, Mass.—March 9

Electric Sign—electric sign (large)—installed New York City

Ferris Wheel—invented—G. W. G. Ferris

Football Game—football game at night—Mansfield, Pa.—Sept. 29

Glass—wire glass—patented—Frank Schuman—Philadelphia, Pa.—Sept. 20

Gold Leaf—in roll form—patented—W. H. Coe—Providence, R.I.—April 5

Hospital — tuberculosis hospital — National Jewish Hospital—Denver, Colo.—cornerstone laid—Oct. 9

Laundry—rough dry laundry service—W. M. Barnes—Philadelphia, Pa.

Library Loan—made by a state library to a community—New York—Feb. 8

Matches—"book matches"—patented

Medical Book—hydrotherapy book—Simon Baruch—*The Uses of Water*—published—Detroit, Mich.

Medical Periodical—Negro medical journal—*Medical and Surgical Observer*—published—Jackson, Tenn.—Dec.

Medical School—osteopathy school—American School of Osteopathy—Kirksville, Mo.—incorporated—May 10

Money — commemorative coinage — authorized—Aug. 5

Money—silver coins—Columbian half dollar authorized—Aug. 5

Moving Picture "Studio" — built — West Orange, N.J.

Physical Culture Department—University of Chicago—Chicago, Ill.

Printing Press—web-fed four-color rotary printing press—used—*Inter-Ocean*—Chicago, Ill.

Prize Fight—prize fight of importance under the Marquis of Queensberry rules—Sullivan-Corbett—New Orleans, La.—Sept. 7

Psychological Society—psychological society (national organization)—American Psychological Association—organized—Worcester, Mass.—July 8

Public Speaking Department—in a university —University of Michigan—Ann Arbor, Mich.—Dec.

Radio Broadcast—radio broadcast demonstration—N. B. Stubblefield

Research Institute—anatomy research institute—incorporated—April 22

Road—concrete road—built—Bellefontaine, Ohio

Single Tax—city to adopt the single tax for local revenue purposes—Hyattsville, Md. —July

Sociology Professor—A. W. Small—University of Chicago—Chicago, Ill.—Oct. 1

Spring Winding Machine—built—Worcester, Mass.

Steel — manganese steel — manufactured — Taylor Iron and Steel Co.—High Bridge, N.J.

Street Car—double-deck street car—operated —San Diego, Calif.—July 4

Street Car—transfers (printed)—patented— J. H. Stedman—Rochester, N.Y.

Telegraph — duplex telegraph (practical) — patented—T. A. Edison—Newark, N.J.— Aug. 9

Telephone — automatic telephone system (successful)—exchange opened—La Porte, Ind.—Nov. 3

Tuberculosis Society—tuberculosis society— Pennsylvania Society for the Prevention of Tuberculosis—founded—Philadelphia, Pa. —April 10

Typewriter—portable typewriter—patented— G. C. Blickensderfer—Stamford, Conn.— April 12

Vending Machine—vending machine (coin operated) to dispense postage stamps— manufactured—Boston, Mass.

Voting Machine—voting machines were authorized—New York—March 15

1893

Addressograph—manufactured—July 26

Aquarium—aquarium (inland salt water)— Chicago, Ill.

Automobile—foreign automobile exhibited— Chicago, Ill.

Aviation—Expositions and Meets—air conference (international) — Chicago, Ill. — Aug. 1-4

Aviation—Magazine—aviation magazine— Aeronautics—published New York City

Bicycle Race Track of Wood—opened—San Francisco, Calif.—July 1

Bicycle Tire—bicycle tire (cord)—exhibited —Philadelphia Cycle Show—Philadelphia, Pa.—Feb.

Births—child born in the White House, Washington, D.C., the offspring of a President—Esther Cleveland—Sept. 9

Bowling Magazine — Gut Holz — published — New York City—Aug. 9

Breakfast Food—shredded wheat biscuits— patented—Aug. 1

Bridge—concrete arch highway bridge— erected—Philadelphia, Pa.

Catholic Apostolic Delegate—arrived—Jan. 24

College—college extension courses—Chicago, Ill.—Jan. 1

College—university extension summer meeting—Philadelphia, Pa.—July 5

College Academic Costume Standardization —advocated—Albany, N.Y.—Dec.

Diplomatic Service—ambassador—State Department—T. F. Bayard—to Great Britain —March 30

Electric Transmission—three-phase alternating high frequency current transmission —March

Fastening—hookless fastening—commercial manufacture—Meadville, Pa.

Ferris Wheel—erected—Chicago, Ill.

Glass Dress—of spun glass—manufactured

Golf Course—eighteen-hole golf course— opened—Wheaton, Ill.

Horse Race—horse race of a thousand miles —from Chadron, Neb. to Chicago, Ill.— completed—June 27

Kapok—commercially introduced—Chicago, Ill.—May 1

Library—children's department in a library —Minneapolis Public Library—Minneapolis, Minn.—separate room

Locomotive—locomotive to attain the proved speed of 112.5 miles an hour—"999"— tested—May 10

Lynch Law (state)—enacted—Georgia—Dec. 20

Medical School—naval medical school— Brooklyn, N.Y.—opened—Aug. 1

Money—coin bearing the portrait of a foreign monarch—Isabella silver quarter— authorized—March 3

Money — silver coins — Columbian quarter dollar—authorized—March 3

Monument—monument to a woman financed by women—Fredericksburg, Va.—cornerstone laid—Oct. 21

Moving Picture—moving picture "close-up" —West Orange, N.J.—Feb. 2

Moving Picture—moving picture film exhibition—Brooklyn, N.Y.—May 9

Newspaper—newspaper colored supplement New York World—Nov. 19

Newspaper—newspaper Sunday comic section —published—New York World

Nurses' Society—society for superintendents of nursing schools—formed—Chicago, Ill. —June 15-17

Patent—print patent—issued—H. J. Heinz Co.—Pittsburgh, Pa.—March 7

Photographic Patent—aerial photography patent—awarded—C. B. Adams

Police — policewoman to be appointed — Marie Owen—Detroit, Mich.

Postage Stamp — commemorative postage stamps—issued—Columbia series—Jan. 2

Postage Stamp—postage stamps to picture a woman—Columbian series—Jan. 2

Postal Service—rural free delivery appropriation

President (U.S.)—President elected for two non-consecutive terms—Grover Cleveland —began second term

Railroad Legislation — railroad legislation (federal)—Safety Appliance Act—enacted —March 2

Road—brick pavement on a rural road— Cleveland, Ohio

Road—federal road agency—established— March 3

Sidewalk (traveling)—sidewalk (traveling)— installed—Chicago, Ill.

Surgical Operation—suture of the human heart (successful)—D. H. Williams—Chicago, Ill.—July 9

Telautograph — patented — Elisha Gray — Highland Park, Ill.—Feb. 7

Temperance Society—Anti-Saloon League— Ohio Anti-Saloon League—formed—Oberlin, Ohio—May 24

Theater — municipal theater — Academy of Music—Northampton, Mass.—Feb. 9

Trapshooting Tournament — trapshoot (Grand American) with live birds — Jamaica, N.Y.—March

Tuberculosis Laboratory—tuberculosis diagnostic community laboratory—authorized —New York City—Dec. 13

Typewriter—typewriter to produce a line of writing visible as it was being typed— patented—H. L. Wagner—Brooklyn, N.Y. —May 16

Water Purification—municipal filtration system—Lawrence, Mass.—Sept.

1894

Agricultural Appropriation—by a state— New York—May 12

Antitoxin Laboratory — established — New York City—Sept.

Baseball Player—baseball player to hit four home runs in one game—Bobby Lowe— Boston, Mass.—May 30

Bicycle Corps (military)—organized—Lake Geneva, Wis.

Carbide Factory—established—Spray, N.C.

Ceramics School—established—Ohio State University—Columbus, Ohio

Communion Cup — individual communion cups—Rochester, N.Y.—May

Copyright—motion picture film copyrighted —Fred Ott—Jan. 9

Cork—for steam pipe covering—manufactured—New York City

Dental Book—book on dental technics— T. E. Weeks—published—Chicago, Ill.

Dog License—dog license law (state)—New York—March 8

Employment Service—municipal employment office—authorized—Seattle, Wash.—March 5

Epidemic—poliomyelitis epidemic—Vermont —June 17-Sept. 1

Fencing—intercollegiate fencing championship competition—New York City—May 5

Football Game—midwestern football team to play on the Pacific coast—San Francisco, Calif.—Dec. 25

Golf Club—golf association (national)— United States Golf Association—formed— New York City—Dec. 22

Golf Magazine—Golfing—published—W. L. Dudley

Golf Tournament—amateur golf tournament (unofficial)—Yonkers, N.Y.—Oct. 13

Golf Tournament—national championship stroke-play golf match—Newport, R.I.— Sept. 3

Health Laboratory — health laboratory (state)—Providence, R.I.—Sept. 1

Holiday—Labor Day holiday (federal)—enacted—June 28

Hospital—leper hospital—Louisiana Leper Home—Carville, La.

Labor Law—labor discrimination law (state) —New Jersey—May 15

Magic Lantern Show—magic lantern feature show—New York City—Oct. 9

Medal — Medal of Honor action — award made—Jan. 21

Medical Book—pediatrics book of importance—The Care and Feeding of Children— L. E. Holt—published—New York City

Medical Periodical—osteopathy magazine— Journal of Osteopathy—Kirksville, Mo.— May

Medical School—osteopathy school—graduation—March 2

Monument—monument to a woman financed by women — Fredericksburg, Va. — dedicated—May 10

Moving Picture—moving picture of a staged prize fight—West Orange, N.J.—July

Moving Picture—peep show—using film— New York City—April 14

Moving Picture Actor—actor to have an exclusive contract—James Corbett

Museum—commercial museum—Philadelphia Commercial Museum—organized—Philadelphia, Pa.—June 15

Newspaper—Greek newspaper—Atlantis—issued—New York City—March 3

Nurses' Society—society for superintendents of nursing schools — convention — New York City—Jan. 10

Physician—osteopath (woman)—J. H. Bolles —graduated—Kirksville, Mo.—March 1

Public Health—medical system of inspection of school children—Boston, Mass.

Pushball—game invented—M. G. Crane— Newport, Mass.

Railroad—railroad to use an electric engine —Baltimore, Md.—Aug. 4

Research Institute—anatomy research institute—building dedicated—May 21

Ship—steel sailing vssel—"Dirigo"—launched —Bath, Me.—Feb. 3

Ship—warship built on inland waters— "Ericsson"—launched—Dubuque, Iowa— May 12

Shoot-the-Chutes — built — Paul Boyton — Coney Island, N.Y.

Steel—manganese steel for railroad tracks— High Bridge, N.J.—manufactured—Aug. 28

Supreme Court (U.S.)—Associate Justice of the Supreme Court to become Chief Justice—E. D. White—appointed—March 12

Teachers' Pension Fund — enacted — New York City—April 14

Telephone—common battery (non-multiple) switchboard—Lexington, Mass.—Jan. 9

Telephone—telephone switchboard or exchange for Chinese subscribers—established—San Francisco, Calif.

Time Recorder—card time recorder—patented—D. M. Cooper—Rochester, N.Y.—Oct. 30

Tuberculosis Laboratory—tuberculosis research laboratory—established—Saranac Lake, N.Y.

War Veterans' Society—Military Order of Foreign Wars—founded—New York City—Dec. 27

Women's Club—Jewish women's organization (national)—National Council of Jewish Women—formed—Chicago, Ill.—Jan.

1895

Air (liquid)—practical—C. E. Tripler—New York City

Animal Industry Bureau (U.S.)—dairy division—organized—July 1

Automobile—automobile regularly made for sale—Duryea Motor Wagon Co.—Springfield, Mass.

Automobile Catalog—Duryea Motor Wagon Co.—Springfield, Mass.

Automobile Club—American Motor League —organized—Chicago, Ill.—Nov.

Automobile Company—Duryea Motor Wagon Co.—Springfield, Mass.—incorporated —Sept. 21

Automobile Magazine—*The Horseless Age* —published—New York City—Nov.

Automobile Patent—G. B. Selden—Rochester, N.Y.—Nov. 5

Automobile Race — automobile race — Chicago, Ill. to Waukegan, Ill.—Nov. 28

Automobile Tire—pneumatic tire—manufactured—Hartford, Conn.

Bathhouse — legislation concerning public baths—New York—April 18

Bowling Tournament—bowling convention— New York City—Sept. 9

Bridge — rolling lift bridge — opened — Chicago, Ill.—Feb. 4

Cafeteria—opened—Chicago, Ill.

Canal Locks—of concrete—Hennepin canal —Rock Island, Ill.—opened—April 17

Catholic Apostolic Delegate — Francesco Satolli created cardinal—Nov. 29

Chiropractor—D. D. Palmer—Davenport, Iowa—treatment—Sept. 18

College—Catholic college for women—College of Notre Dame of Maryland—Baltimore, Md.—opened—Sept. 2

Degrees (academic and honorary)—Doctor of Science degree earned by a woman— C. W. Baldwin—Cornell University, Ithaca, N.Y.—June 20

Enclave—enclave—Fairhope, Ala.—Jan. 5

Football Game—professional football game —Latrobe, Pa.—Sept. 3

Glass Blowing Machine—patented—M. J. Owens—Toledo, Ohio—Feb. 26

Glider—glider with cambered wings—invented—Octave Chanute—Miller's Station, Ill.

Golf Book—*Golf in America*—J. P. Lee— published—New York City—May 25

Golf Tournament—amateur golf tournament (official)—Newport, R.I.—Oct. 12

Golf Tournament—open championship (official)—Newport, R.I.—Oct. 4

Golf Tournament—women's tournament golf championship—Westbury, N.Y.—Nov.

Government Printing Office—Superintendent of Documents—authorized—Jan. 12

Manufacturers' Association—National Association of Manufacturers—organized—Cincinnati, Ohio—Jan. 22

Medical Legislation—chiropody law governing the study of chiropody—enacted—New York City

Medicine Ball—invented—R. J. Roberts— Boston, Mass.

Milk — milk pasteurized commercially — Bloomville, N.Y.

Monument—statue officially sanctioned by Rome—blessed—New Orleans, La.—Nov. 10

Moving Picture—moving picture on film shown on a screen—demonstrated—New York City—April 21

Niagara Falls—utilization of Niagara Falls waterpower (large scale)—power transmitted commercially—Aug. 26

Normal School—teachers' training school (Jewish) — Gratz College — Philadelphia, Pa.—trustees elected—Feb. 17

Novel Course—course on the contemporary novel—W. L. Phelps—Yale University— New Haven, Conn.

Ordnance — shot tower — erected — Kings Mills, Ohio

Paper Twine machinery—patented—G. L. Brownell—Worcester, Mass.—Dec. 17

Pencil—paper pencil—patented—F. E. Blaisdell—Philadelphia, Pa.—Nov. 19

Razor—safety razor to be successfully marketed—invented—K. C. Gillette

Ship—battleship of importance—"Maine"— commissioned—Sept. 17

Ship—ship to circumnavigate the world with but one in the crew—Joshua Slocum— sailed—Boston, Mass.—April 24

Submarine—submarine contract of the U.S. Navy—J. P. Holland—March 13

Subway — municipal subway — construction commenced—Boston, Mass.—March 28

Temperance Society — Anti-Saloon League (national organization) — Anti-saloon League of America—formed—Washington, D.C.—Dec. 17-18

Volley Ball—developed—W. G. Morgan— Holyoke, Mass.

1896

Accountancy Law (state)—enacted—New York—April 17

Accountant — certified public accountant — Frank Broaker—Dec. 1

Actors' Union—Actors' National Protective Union—chartered—Jan. 4

Automobile Accident—New York City—May 30

Automobile Race—automobile race on a track—Cranston, R.I.—Sept. 7

Aviation—Airplane—airplane (heavier-than-air) to make any long sustained flight—under its own power—S. P. Langley—May 6

Basketball—basketball intercollegiate game —New Haven, Conn.—Dec. 10

Bicycle Race—intercollegiate bicycle race— New York City

Bicycle Race—women's six-day bicycle race —New York City—Jan. 6-11

Book Review—book review newspaper supplement — published — New York City — Oct. 10

Camouflage — treatise published — A. H. Thayer—New York City

Carrousel—carrousel with the jumping horse mechanism — invented — C. W. Parker — Leavenworth, Kan.

Carrousel — portable carrousel — manufactured—Abilene, Kan.

Chop Suey—concocted—New York City—Aug. 29

College—Catholic college for women—College of Notre Dame of Maryland—Baltimore, Md.—incorporated—April 2

Discus Throwing—Olympic Games—Athens, Greece

Election Law—absentee voting law (state)— Vermont—enacted—Nov. 24

Electric Alternator—in parallel—installed— Hartford, Conn.

Electric Light Socket—with pull chain—patented — Harvey Hubbell — Bridgeport, Conn.—Aug. 11

Electric Power Plant—hydroelectric power plant to use a storage battery—Hartford, Conn.

Electric Power Plant—rotary converter power plant—opened—Chicago, Ill.—May 16

Electric Stove—electric stove—patented—W. S. Hadaway—New York City—June 30

Fastening—hookless fastening — patented— W. L. Judson—Chicago, Ill.—March 31

Flashlight—manufactured—New York City

Football Game—indoor football game (large) —Chicago, Ill.—Nov. 26

Health Ordinance prohibiting spitting—enacted—New York City—May 12

Hospital—cancer home for incurables (free) —established—New York City—Sept. 15

Insurance—substandard life insurance policy—New York City—July 1

Match — "book matches" — manufactured — Barberton, Ohio

Medical Instruction — psychiatric institute— authorized—May 12

Milk Sale Regulations—enacted—New York City

Niagara Falls—utilization of Niagara Falls waterpower (large scale)—first power to Buffalo, N.Y.—Nov. 15

Nurse—nurse employed by an industrial organization—Proctor, Vt.

Oil—offshore oil wells successfully drilled in the ocean—Summerland, Calif.

Olympic Games—Olympic competition winner—J. B. Connolly

Organists' Society—organists' society (national)—American Guild of Organists—organized

Periodical—all-fiction pulp magazine—*Argosy*—published—Oct.

Physician—Chinese woman to receive a doctor of medicine degree—Mary Stone—Ann Arbor, Mich.—June 22

Postal Service—rural free delivery—established—West Virginia—Oct. 1

President (U.S.)—President who had used a telephone for campaigning—William McKinley—Canton, Ohio

Rowing—transatlantic trip by rowboat— George Harpo and Frank Samuelson—left —New York City—June 7

Sawmill—electrically driven sawmill—Folsom, Calif.

Silverites—national convention—St. Louis, Mo.—July 22

Single Tax—single tax political ticket—Delaware

Submarine—submarine contract of the U.S. Navy—"Plunger" keel laid—June 20

Telephone — automatic telephone system (successful)—rotating type dial exchange opened—Milwaukee, Wis.

Tennis Match—lawn tennis champions who were brothers

Volley Ball—rules published—*Physical Education Magazine*—July

War Veterans' Society—Military Order of Foreign Wars—National Commandery instituted—March 11

X-Ray — X-ray machine — exhibited—New York City—Jan. 18

X-Ray — X-ray photograph—taken—H. L. Smith—Davidson College—Davidson, N.C.

1897

Accountants' Society—accountants' society formed by a state group—New York State Society of Certified Public Accountants—formed—March 30

Automobile—electric taxicabs—introduced— New York City

Basketball—basketball intercollegiate five-man team game—New Haven, Conn.

Book—best seller other than a text or purely theological work—*In His Steps*—published

Breakfast Food—breakfast foods introduced —C. W. Post

College Alumni Association—college alumni association secretary (full time paid position)—Ann Arbor, Mich.—June 30

Copyrights Registrar of the United States— Thorvald Solberg—took office—July 1

Country Day School—opened—Baltimore, Md.—Sept.

Fencing—fencing champion to win three titles in one year—C. G. Bothner—New York City—May 1

Fly Casting Tournament—indoor fly casting tournament—New York City—March 15-20

Football Game—football game between Negro colleges—Atlanta, Ga.—Jan. 1

Forestry Society—national forestry association — American Forestry Association — incorporated—Jan. 25

Golf Club—Intercollegiate Golf Association —tournament—Ardsley-on-Hudson, N.Y. —May 13-14

Handball—national championship match for amateurs—Jersey City, N.J.—Jan. 7-8

Holiday—Frontier day—celebrated—Cheyenne, Wyo.—Sept. 23

Horse—horse to pace better than 2:00—Star Pointer—Readville, Mass.

Hospital — crippled children's hospital (state)—St. Paul, Minn.—authorized— April 23

Hospital—tuberculosis hospital (municipal) for consumptive poor — opened — Cincinnati, Ohio—July 8

Ice Cream Sundae—originated—Ithaca, N.Y.

Incinerator—established—St. Louis, Mo.

Initiative and Referendum—enacted—South Dakota—Jan. 27

Marathon Race (annual)—Hopkinton, Mass. to Boston, Mass.—April 19

Milk Station (municipal)—Rochester, N.Y. —established

Music Book—ragtime instruction book— *Rag-Time Instructor*—published—Ben Harney—New York City

News Correspondent—White House reporter—W. W. Price—Washington, D.C. *Star* —April 24

Parent-Teacher Association (national)—National Congress of Mothers—organized— Washington, D.C.—Feb. 17

Piano Player—piano player (completely automatic)—manufactured—Meriden, Conn.

Piano Player—pneumatic piano player—invented—E. S. Votey—Detroit, Mich.

Prize Fight—open-air arena especially built for a prize fight.—Carson City, Nev.

Rock Wool Factory—opened—Alexandria, Ind.—June 1

Senate (state)—woman state senator—M. H. Cannon—served—Jan. 11

Submarine—submarine contract of the U.S. Navy—"Plunger"—completed

Submarine—submarine fitted with an internal combustion engine—"Argonaut"—Simon Lake — patent — Baltimore, Md.— April 20

Subway—municipal subway — first section opened—Sept. 3

Telephone—multiple common battery switchboard—Louisville, Ky.

Vending Machine—vending machine—to operate automatically—Rochester, N.Y.

Vending Machine—vending machine to sell from bulk—invented—T. S. Wheatcraft—Rush, Pa.

Voting Machine Commission (state)—authorized—New York—May 17

X-Ray—X-ray of the entire body of a living person—New York City—April

Zionist Society—Zionist national organization—United American Zionists—formed— New York City—Oct. 22

1898

Advertisement—automobile advertisement

Advertising Law — advertising legislation (state)—enacted—New York—April 30

American Expeditionary Force—American Expeditionary Force — landed — Manila, P.I.—July 1

Automobile—armored car—designed—R. P. Davidson—Lake Geneva, Wis.—May

Automobile Driver (woman)—G. D. Mudge —drove a Waverly Electric

Automobile Truck — designed — Pittsburgh, Pa.

Balloon—balloon destroyed by enemy gun fire—Santiago, Cuba—July 1

Book Index—monthly cumulative index of books — published — Minneapolis, Minn.— Feb.

Cancer Laboratory—New York State Pathological Laboratory—established—Buffalo, N.Y.—May

Carrousel—carrousel with the jumping horse mechanism—completed—C. W. Parker

Dam—steel dam—built—Ashfork, Ariz.

Dental Corps (U.S. Army)—dentist officially employed in the U.S. Army—W. H. Ware

Engine—diesel engine built for commercial service—St. Louis, Mo.—Sept.

Envelope—envelope folding and gumming machine — patented — J. A. Sherman— Worcester, Mass.—Feb. 8

Foreign Service School—School of Comparative Jurisprudence and Diplomacy—George Washington University — Washington, D.C.—opened—Nov. 15

Forestry School—forestry school dealing exclusively with problems of forestry—Biltmore Forest School—Biltmore, N.C.— opened—Sept. 1

Forestry School—forestry school of collegiate character—established—Cornell University—Ithaca, N.Y.—Sept. 19

Geology—woman graduate in geology—Lou Henry—Leland Stanford, Jr. University— Palo Alto, Calif.

Hospital—tuberculosis sanatorium (state)— Massachusetts Hospital for Consumptives and Tuberculosis Patients—Rutland, Mass. —completed—Sept. 23

Initiative and Referendum—South Dakota— amendment passed—Nov. 8

Insurance—automobile insurance policy—issued—Hartford, Conn.—Feb. 1

Library—county library — organized — Van Wert, Ohio

Library Society—state librarians' society— Washington, D.C.—Nov. 16

Log, Rolling (Birling) National Championship—Omaha, Neb.—Sept. 9

Radio Broadcast—yacht race broadcast—Sandy Hook, N.J.—Oct. 16

Refrigerator—household refrigerating machine patent—A. T. Marshall—Brockton, Mass.—Aug. 8

Rubber—rubber heel—patented—Humphrey O'Sullivan—Lowell, Mass.—Jan. 24

Social Science Society (national)—American Social Science Association—incorporated—Jan. 28

Textile School—textile school in a college—Clemson Agricultural College—Clemson, S.C.—established

Tunnel—freight delivery tunnel system—franchised—Feb. 20

Union Reform Party—platform adopted—Cincinnati, Ohio—March 1

Vacuum Cleaner—motor-driven vacuum cleaner—patented—J. S. Thurman—St. Louis, Mo.—Oct. 3

Voting Machine—voting machines for use in federal elections—authorized—Feb. 14

1900

Advertisement—automobile advertisement—in a national magazine—March 31

Army War College—maintenance appropriation—May 26

Astronomer—woman astronomer employed in the U.S. Naval Observatory—Washington, D.C.—July 20

Automobile Bus—automobile sightseeing bus—built—New York City

Automobile Show—New York City—Nov. 3-10

Baseball League — American League — formed—January 29

Bond—bonds payable specifically in U.S. gold coins—authorized—March 14

Chiropractic School — opened — Davenport, Iowa

Corkboard (impregnated)—manufactured — Pittsburgh, Pa.

Cripples—kindergarten for crippled children—opened—Cleveland, Ohio

Cripples—public school for cripples—opened—Chicago, Ill.

Dam — needle-type dam — constructed — Louisa, Ky.

Dental Society — orthodontists' society — founded—St. Louis, Mo.—June

Escalator—escalator—manufactured — New York City

Industrial Research Laboratory—opened—Schenectady, N.Y.—Sept.

Labor-Saving Device approved by a labor organization—Stereotypers' union

Motorcycle—motorcycle (practical)—manufactured—Buffalo, N.Y.

Newspaper—Chinese daily newspaper—*Chung Sai Yat Po*—San Francisco, Calif.—Feb. 16

Piano Player—pneumatic piano player—patented—E. S. Votey—Detroit, Mich.—May 22

Postage Stamp—books of postage stamps—issued—April 16

Restaurant — penny restaurant — opened—New York City

Revolver Shooting Tournament (international)—Greenville, N.J.—June 16

Scale—automatic computing pendulum-type scales—patented—A. De Vilbiss—Toledo, Ohio—May 22

Ship—schooner (six masted)—"George W. Wells"—launched—Camden, Me.—July 1

Social-Democratic Party of America—convention—Rochester, N.Y.—Jan. 27

Socialist Party—formed—Indianapolis, Ind.—March 25

Stereotype—automatic plate-casting and finishing machine for stereotype printing—used—New York City

Tennis Match—lawn tennis matches for the Davis Cup—Brookline, Mass.—Aug. 8-10

Trapshooting Tournament — trapshoot (Grand American) with clay targets—Interstate Park, N.Y.—June 12

Union Reform Party—convention—Baltimore, Md.—Sept. 3

United Christian Party—organized—Rock Island, Ill.

1901

Architectural School—landscape architecture course for women—Groton, Mass.—Sept. 15

Army Nurse Corps (female)—superintendent appointed—D. H. Kinney—March 15

Army War College—authorized—Nov. 27

Automobile—automobile to exceed the speed of a mile a minute—A. C. Bostwick—Brooklyn, N.Y.—Nov. 16

Automobile—shaft-driven automobile—constructed—Ardmore, Pa.

Automobile Hill Climbing Contest—Peekskill, N.Y.—Sept. 9

Automobile Legislation—state motor car legislation—enacted—Conn.—May 21

Automobile License Plates — automobile license plates—law effective—N.Y.—April 25

Automobile Race—automobile race (long distance)—New York City to Buffalo, N.Y.—Sept. 9-14

Aviation—Flights—airplane flight—Bridgeport, Conn.—Aug. 14

Baseball League—baseball league association—National Association of Professional Baseball Leagues — organized — Chicago, Ill.—Sept. 5

Bicycle Race—paired six-day bicycle race—New York City—Dec. 9-14

Bowling Tournament—bowling tournament sponsored by the American Bowling Congress—Chicago, Ill.—Jan. 8-11

Catholic Mass—Catholic Mass for night-workers—New York City—May 5

College—dean of men—B. H. Brown—Walla Walla, Wash.

College—woman professor at a first-class medical school—F. R. Sabin—Baltimore, Md.

Commission Form of Government—Galveston, Texas—Sept. 18

Corporation—corporation incorporated with a capitalization of $1 billion—U.S. Steel Corp.

Dental Corps (U.S. Army)—Dental Corps of the U.S. Army—authorized—Feb. 2

Dental Society — orthodontists' society — American Society of Orthodontists—annual meeting—June 11

Electric Lighting—mercury vapor lamp—patented—P. C. Hewitt—Sept. 17

Electric Motor—electric motor (single-phase alternating current) — used — interurban service

Forest Service — Forest Service (U.S.)—Division of Forestry became Bureau of Forestry—March 2

Golf Tournament—professional open championship—Hamilton, Mass.—June 14

Hall of Fame—hall of fame (university)—dedicated—New York City—May 30

Hospital—psychiatric ward—Albany Hospital—Albany, N.Y.—opened

Library Catalog—union catalog of books—Library of Congress—Washington, D.C.

Loop-the-Loop Centrifugal Railway—centrifugal railway patented—Edwin Prescott—Feb. 5

Motorcycle—motorcycle with built-in gas engine—manufactured—Springfield, Mass.

Navy—naval coaling station on foreign soil—Mexico—April

Niagara Falls—person to go over Niagara Falls in a barrel—A. E. Taylor—Oct. 24

Optometry Legislation—state—Minnesota—April 13

Radio Broadcast—transatlantic radio signal—G. Marconi—Dec. 11

Ship—schooner (seven masted, steel)—keel laid—Nov. 1

Standards Bureau (U.S.) — established — March 3

Turbine—steam turbine—operated by a public utility—Hartford, Conn.—April

1902

Arbitration—arbitration proceeding—protocol signed—May 22

Cable (telegraph)—cable across the Pacific Ocean—paid out—Dec. 14

Cancer Research Fund—New York City—established

Envelope—envelope with an outlook or window—patented—A. F. Callahan—Chicago, Ill.—June 10

Factory—air-conditioned factory with temperature and humidity control—Brooklyn, N.Y.

Glass—cut glass—made from pressed blanks—manufactured—H. C. Fry—Rochester, Pa.

Glass—sheet glass drawing machine—patented—I. W. Colburn—March 25

Health Instruction—in connection with the schools—New York City—Oct.

Initiative and Referendum—enacted by Oregon—June 2

Motorcycle Endurance Run—Boston to New York City—July 4-5

Moving Picture Theater—moving picture theater—Electric Theater—Los Angeles, Calif.—April 2

Newspaper—Arabic daily newspaper—Al-Hoda—New York City—Aug. 25

Newspaper—newspaper published at sea (daily)—Cunard Daily Bulletin—Oct.

Organists' Society—organists' society (national)—branch chapter organized—Philadelphia, Pa.—June 10

Postage Stamp—postage stamps in coils—for vending machines—issued

President (U.S.)—President to ride in an automobile—T. Roosevelt—Hartford, Conn.—Aug. 22

Radio Broadcast—radio broadcast demonstration — public demonstration — N. B. Stubblefield—Jan. 1

Radio Telephone—radio telephone marine demonstration — "Bartholdi" — Potomac River—N. B. Stubblefield—March 20

Railroad Car—steel passenger railroad coach—built—Altoona, Pa.

Rayon—rayon patent—Sept. 30

Reclamation Service (federal)—created—June 17

Restaurant — restaurant with an automatic arrangement for vending food—Philadelphia, Pa.—Automat—opened—June 9

Senator (U.S.)—senators censured

Ship — schooner (seven masted, steel) — "Thomas W. Larson"—launched—Quincy, Mass.—July 10

Taxidermy Method (sculptural)—devised—C. E. Akeley

Tournament of Roses—football game

Woman Suffrage—woman suffrage association (international)—organized—Washington, D.C.—Feb.

Young Women's Hebrew Association—organized—New York City—Feb. 6

Zoological Laboratory (U.S.) — zoological laboratory (U.S.) for the study of parasites of man—Washington, D.C.—Aug. 16

1903

Animals—pronghorn antelope—bred and reared in captivity—born—Denver, Colo.

Architectural School — landscape architecture course for women—Groton, Mass.—certificates awarded—June 10

Army War College—cornerstone laid—Washington, D.C.—Feb. 21

Automobile Electric Self-Starter—automobile electric self-starter patent—C. J. Coleman—New York City—Nov. 24

Automobile School—automobile school—established—Y.M.C.A.—Boston, Mass.

Automobile Transcontinental Trip—transcontinental automobile trip—by a nonprofessional driver—H. N. Jackson—San Francisco to New York City—completed—July 26

Aviation—Airplane—airplane to receive national acclaim—Kitty Hawk, N.C.—Dec. 17

Bank—bank president (Negro woman)—M. L. Walker—Richmond, Va.—July 28

Bird Reservation (national)—established—Pelican Island, Fla.—March 14

Boycott Law—enacted—Ala.—Sept. 26

Bridge—suspension bridge of importance having steel towers—New York City—Williamsburg Bridge—opened—Dec. 19

Cable (telegraph)—cable across the Pacific Ocean—completed—Jan. 1

Cable (telegraph)—cable across the Pacific Ocean between Honolulu, Midway, Guam, and Manila—completed—July 3

Commerce and Labor Department (U.S.)—authorized—Feb. 14

Fingerprinting—state prison to take fingerprints—Ossining, N.Y.—March 3

Horse—horse to trot a mile in less than two minutes—Lou Dillon—Readville, Mass.—Aug. 24

Hotel—hotel exclusively for women—Martha Washington Hotel—opened—March 2

House of David—established—Benton Harbor, Mich.

Humane Society—humane association national organization—American Humane Association—incorporated—Nov. 12

Insurance—numerical system of insurance rating—New York Life Insurance Co.—New York City

Locker—public locker plant—established—Chico, Calif.

Motorcycle Association — Federation of American Motorcyclists — organized — Manhattan Beach, N.Y.—Sept. 7

Motorcycle Hill Climbing Contest—Riverdale, N.Y.—May 30

Motorcycle Trip—motorcycle transcontinental trip—from San Francisco to New York City—completed—July 6

Moving Picture—moving picture with a plot —The Great Train Robbery—filmed—New Jersey

Moving Picture Actor — moving picture star—Max Aronson

Multigraph—patented — H. C. Gammeter — Cleveland, Ohio—March 10

Nurse — nurses' registration law (state) — North Carolina—enacted—March 3

Opera—opera composed by a woman performed at the Metropolitan Opera House —New York City—E. M. Smyth—March 11

Political Science Society—political science association — American Political Science Association—founded—Dec. 30

Prize Fight — pugilist to win three world championships — Bob Fitzsimmons—Nov. 25

Radio Broadcast — transatlantic broadcast (not experimental) — from Cape Cod, Mass.—Jan. 19

Radio Distress Signal — radio distress (CQD) signal from an American ship—"Kroonland"

Radio Station—naval radio station — established—Navesink, N.J.

Railroad—railroad operated by an electric third rail system—Scranton, Pa.—May 25

Railroad Car — steel passenger railroad coach—completed—Altoona, Pa.

Theater—theater to employ women ushers — Majestic Theatre — New York City—Dec. 16

Traffic Regulation Pamphlet—printed traffic regulations — Rules for Driving — effective —Oct. 30—New York City

Turbine—steam turbine generator of large capacity for commercial service—Chicago, Ill.—Oct. 2

1904

"American"—recommended as an adjective—Aug. 3

Animal Industry Bureau (U.S.) — animal husbandry federal appropriation — approved—April 23

Arts and Letters Society—arts and letters society (national)—founded—April 23

Automobile—automobile with a circulating lubrication system

Automobile Race—Vanderbilt Cup Race—Hicksville, N.Y.—Oct. 8

Automobile Tire Chain — patented — H. D. Weed—Canastota, N.Y.—Aug. 23

Automobile Trucking Service—automobile inter-city trucking service—Oct. 29

Balloon — balloon circular flight — Oakland, Calif.—Aug. 3

Bibliography Society (national) — Bibliographical Society of America—organized—S. Louis, Mo.—Oct. 18

Boat Race—motor boat race under organized rules—New York City—June 23

Border Patrol — border patrolman — J. D. Milton—served

Buddhist Temple — established — Los Angeles, Calif.—July 15

Business—installment finance company—organized—Rochester, N.Y.—April 7

Carnegie Hero Fund Commission — established—March 12

College "Lettermen's Club" — established—Chicago, Ill.—Jan. 29

Electric Attachment Plug (separable)—patented — Harvey Hubbell — Bridgeport, Conn.—Nov. 8

Fingerprinting—federal penitentiary fingerprinting — U.S. Penitentiary — Leavenworth, Kan.—Nov. 2

Fingerprinting—police department to adopt the fingerprinting system—St. Louis, Mo. —Oct. 28

Health Society—National Tuberculosis Association — organized—Atlantic City, N.J. —June 6

High School—vocational high school for girls—Boston, Mass.—opened—July

Ice Cream Cone — ice cream cone — introduced—Louisiana Purchase Exposition—St. Louis, Mo.

Jai-Alai — introduced — Louisiana Purchase Exposition—St. Louis, Mo.

Library—business library supported by taxes —Newark, N.J.

Locomotive — duplex compound locomotive (Mallet)—built—Schenectady, N.Y.

Monument—monument to the memory of the soldiers and sailors of the Spanish-American war—unveiled—Sept. 29

Newspaper — Hungarian daily newspaper—published—Oct. 18

Olympic Games—Olympic celebration—St. Louis, Mo.—May 14

Periodical—comic books—published — New York City

Pharmacy Legislation (state) — enacted — New York—May 3

Phonograph Record—phonograph record of a stage performance by the original cast—recorded

Physician — surgeon to substitute radium treatment—Robert Abbe—report—June

Printing Press — rotogravure press — imported—Nov.

Radio Distress Signal—radio distress signal —CQD—established—Jan. 7

Rhodes Scholar — Rhodes scholars — appointed

Ski Club—ski club association—National Ski Association of America—formed—Ishpeming, Mich.—Feb. 21

Socialist Party — national convention—Indianapolis, Ind.—May 1

Stadium — cement stadium — Harvard Stadium—Cambridge, Mass.—completed

Street Car—aluminum street car—aluminum used—Oct. 27

Subway—subway (rapid transit)—opened—New York City—Oct. 27

Travelers Aid Society—Travelers Aid Society (national)—Travelers Aid Society—formed—New York City

Health Society—National Tuberculosis Association—national convention—Washington, D.C.—May 18-19

Helium—discovered as natural gas constituent

Library—book-wagon—traveling library

Medal — Interstate Commerce Commission Medal of Honor—awarded—G. H. Poell—Grand Island, Neb.

Monument—statue of a woman in National Statuary Hall—Washington, D.C. — dedicated—Feb. 17

Motorcycle—motorcycle (twin-cycle)—manufactured—Springfield, Mass.

Moving Picture Theater — theater in the world devoted exclusively to the exhibition of motion pictures—Pittsburgh, Pa. —June

Newspaper—Greek newspaper—*Atlantis*—daily —New York City—Jan. 3

Pharmacy Legislation (state)—New York —effective—Jan. 1

Plywood—Douglas fir plywood—commercial production—St. Johns, Ore.

Punchboards—patented — C. A. Brewer — Chicago, Ill.—Jan. 17

Radio Facsimile Transmission — radio facsimile patent—C. D. Ehret—March 28

Railroad Car—mail car (steel)—exhibited—Washington, D.C.—May 4

Rotary Club—founded—Chicago, Ill.—Feb. 23

Sociological Society—sociological society (national)—American Sociological Society —organized—Baltimore, Md.—Dec.

Tung—trees planted—Chico, Calif.

Wrestling—intercollegiate wrestling association—formed—Philadelphia, Pa. — April 7

1905

Automobile Race—transcontinental automobile race (for a time record)—New York City to Portland, Ore.—started—May 8

Aviation — Legislation—aviation legislation (state) —Tennessee enacted tax on aircraft

Bridge — aerial ferry — operated — Duluth, Minn.—April 9

Bridge—concrete cantilever bridge—Marion, Iowa

College—university to adopt the preceptorial system—Princeton, N.J.

Esperanto Club—Esperanto club—Esperanto Association—organized—Boston, Mass.— Feb. 16

Factory—air-conditioned factory—Gastonia, N.C.

Ferryboat—municipally owned ferryboats—operated—New York City—Oct. 25

Fingerprinting — international exchange of fingerprints—St. Louis, Mo.—July 6

Fire Extinguisher—using vaporized chemical—manufactured—Newark, N.J.

Forest Fire — forest fire lookout tower — Greenville, Me.—watchman service began —June 10

Forest Service — Forest Service (U.S.) — name changed—designated—March 3

1906

Archaeological Society—archaeological society (national)—Archaeological Institute of America—incorporated—May 26

Automobile Bus—bus with a double deck—imported

Automobile Tire—demountable tire-carrying rim—patent applied for—May 21

Aviation—Airship—woman airship passenger —M. P. Miller—Franklin, Pa.—Aug. 11

Balloon Race—balloon cup race—for James Gordon Bennett Aeronautic Cup—Sept. 30

Bank—bank open day and night—opened—New York City—May 1

Cabinet of the United States—cabinet member who was Jewish—O. S. Straus—appointed—Dec. 12

College—technical college for women—Simmons College—Boston, Mass.—first graduation—June 13

Diamond—diamonds in actual rock—Murfreesboro, Ark.

Election Law—primary election (state-wide) —Wisconsin—Sept. 4

Engineering Society—woman elected to the American Society of Civil Engineers—N. S. Blatch—March 6

Esperanto Magazine—*L'Amerika Esperantisto* —published—Oklahoma City, Okla.—Oct.

Fastening—hookless fastening for universal use—invented—Gideon Sundback—Hoboken, N.J.

Insurance—Employer's Liability Act (federal)—enacted—June 11

Japanese Ambassador—legation raised to embassy—Jan. 7

Medal—National Geographic Society gold medal—Hubbard medal—presented—R. E. Peary—Washington, D.C.—Dec. 15

Monument—national monument—established —Devils Tower, Wyo.—Sept. 24

Moving Picture—animated cartoon—"Humorous Phases of Funny Faces"—released

Nobel Prize—Nobel Prize—awarded to an American—Theodore Roosevelt

Nurse—nurse appointed to a university professorship—M. A. Nutting—Columbia University—New York City

Phonograph—phonograph with an enclosed horn in the cabinet—manufactured—Camden, N.J.—Aug. 22

Plastic—thermosetting man-made plastic— developed—L. H. Baekeland—Yonkers, N.Y.

President of a South American Country Born in the United States—Galo Plaza Lasso—born—New York City—Feb. 17

President (U.S.)—President to visit a foreign country while President—Theodore Roosevelt—Panama—Nov. 14

Radio Broadcast—radio program broadcast —R. A. Fessenden—Dec. 24

Radio Distress Signal—radio distress signal —S.O.S.—adopted—Nov. 22

Radio Receiver—radio receiver advertised— New York City—Jan. 13

Radio Tube—three-element vacuum tube— announced—Lee De Forest—New York City—Oct. 20

Ship—turbine-propelled ocean-going merchant vessel—"Governor Cobb"—launched —April 21

Sociological Society—sociological society (national)—American Sociological Society —annual meeting—Providence, R.I.—Dec. 27-29

Tunnel—freight delivery tunnel system— Chicago, Ill.—Aug. 15

1907

Almanac—almanac bibliography—published —Washington, D.C.

Army War College—opened—Washington, D.C.—June 20

Arts and Letters Society—woman elected to the National Institute of Arts and Letters—J. W. Howe

Automobile — automobile with left-hand steering—manufactured—Detroit, Mich.

Aviation—Aeronautical Division of the U.S. War Department—authorized—Aug. 1

Balloon Race—balloon cup race—St. Louis, Mo.—Oct. 21

Bank—national bank branch legally operated —Moss Point, Miss.—chartered—March 14

Building—building of pressed structural steel —Tuxedo Park, N.Y.

Court—night court—opened—New York City —Sept. 1

Dentistry—gold inlay — described — W. H. Taggart—Jan. 15

Election Law—corrupt election practices law (federal)—Jan. 26

Foxhound Association—Masters of Fox Hounds Association—formed—New York City—Feb. 14

Holiday—Mother's Day—suggested — Anna Jarvis

Horse—horse farm operated by the U.S. Government—Middlebury, Vt. — deeded— Feb. 1

Hydrotherapy Chair—Simon Baruch—appointed Professor of Hydrotherapy— March

Hygiene Instruction—School Department of hygiene—established—Boston, Mass.

Insurance—savings bank life insurance—authorized—Massachusetts—June 26

Jewish College—Jewish non-sectarian college—Dropsie College—chartered—June 6

Moving Picture Actor—moving picture star (female)—Florence Lawrence

Nobel Prize—Nobel Prize in physics—A. A. Michelson

Radio Broadcast—singer to broadcast—E. H. Farrar—Dec. 16

Radio Broadcast—transatlantic radio message of the regular westward service—to New York City—Oct. 17

Radio Microphone (carbon)—used—Lee De Forest—New York City

Radio Tube—three-element vacuum tube— patented—Lee De Forest—Jan. 15

Railroad Car—steel passenger railroad coach —all-steel coach—completed—Altoona, Pa. —Dec. 23

Rat Extermination (city-wide) to avert bubonic plague—San Francisco, Calif.

Rhodes Scholar—Negro to win a Rhodes scholarship—A. L. R. Locke

Safety Congress — safety congress — New York City—Jan. 28

Seal—Christmas seals of the modern variety, sold to raise funds—designed—E. P. Bissel—Wilmington, Del.—sold—Dec. 9

Senator (U.S.) — Indian senator — Charles Curtis—served—Jan. 23

Ship—battleship built on the Pacific coast— "Nebraska"—commissioned—July 1

Ship—turbine-propelled ship of the U.S. Navy—"Chester"—launched—July 26

Ship—warship fleet to circumnavigate the globe—sailed—Hampton Roads, Va.—Dec. 16

Sleeping Car—Pullman sleeping car made entirely of steel—manufactured—Pullman, Ill.

Squash Racquets Champion—squash racquets champion—J. A. Miskey

Stadium—municipal stadium — completed — San Francisco, Calif.

Sterilization Legislation—Indiana—enacted —March 9

1909

Automobile—production of more than 100,-000 passenger cars in one year

Automobile Race—transcontinental automobile race—left New York City—June 1

Automobile Transcontinental Trip—transcontinental automobile trip by a woman—left New York City—June 9—arrived San Francisco—Aug. 6

Aviation—Airplane—airplane purchased by the U.S. Government—accepted—Aug. 2

Aviation—Airplane—airplane sold commercially—Hammondsport, N.Y.

Aviation—Airplane—monoplane (American)—flown—Mineola, N.Y.—Dec. 9

Aviation—Aviator—Army aviator to solo—F. E. Humphreys—College Park, Md.—Oct. 26

Aviation—Flights—inter-city airplane flight—B. D. Foulois—July 30

Aviation—Passenger—woman airplane passenger—flight—College Park, Md.—Oct. 27

Aviation—Races—airplane race won by an American in Europe—G. H. Curtiss—Aug.

Balloon Race — dirigible balloon race — St. Louis, Mo.—Oct. 4-9

Bank—Christmas savings club—originated—Carlisle, Pa.

Baseball—cork center baseball—patented—B. S. Shibe—June 15

Baseball Game—baseball game at night by a regular league team—Grand Rapids, Mich.—July 8

Baseball Game—triple play unassisted in a modern major league game—Neal Ball—Cleveland, Ohio—July 19

Bed—"concealed bed"—manufactured—San Francisco, Calif.

Bird Banding Society—formed—New York City—Dec. 8

Bowling Tournament—gold medal award to a perfect-score bowler—roll-off—Pittsburgh, Pa.—March 11

Bridge—double-deck bridge—of importance—opened—New York City—March 30

Child Delinquency law (state)—enacted—Colorado—April 28

City Planning Instruction—offered—Cambridge, Mass.

Continuation School—apprentice continuation school—established—Cincinnati, Ohio—Aug. 30

Court—domestic relations court—established—Buffalo, N.Y.

Credit Union Association—Manchester, N.H.—chartered—April 6

Credit Union Law—enacted—Massachusetts—May 21

Discovery—discovery of the North Pole—R. E. Peary—April 6

Election Law—preferential ballot system—Grand Junction, Colo.—Sept. 14

Engine—outboard motor—developed—Ole Evinrude—Milwaukee, Wis.

Forestry School—forestry school to give scientific training in the care and preservation of trees—Davey Tree Expert Co.—incorporated—Feb. 9

Fraternity (Greek letter)—inter-fraternity council—New York City—Nov. 17

High School—junior high schools—authorized—Berkeley, Calif.—Dec. 21

Horseshoe Pitching Contest (international)—Bronson, Kan.

Hospital—tuberculosis preventorium for children—Lakewood, N.J.

Library Catalog—union catalog of books in a state library—Sacramento, Calif.

Medal—National Institute of Arts and Letters gold medal—awarded—Nov. 20

Money—coin bearing the portrait of a President

Moving Picture—colored moving pictures—exhibited—New York City—Dec. 11

Moving Picture Censorship—moving picture censorship board (national)—organized

Narcotic—narcotic prohibition act (federal)—enacted—Feb. 9

Nursing School—university school of nursing—established—March 1

Old Age Home For Pioneers—Prescott, Ariz.—authorized—March 10

Paint Spraying Device—commercially manufactured—De Vilbiss Co.—Toledo, Ohio

Plastic—thermosetting man-made plastic—patented — L. H. Baekeland — Yonkers, N.Y.—Dec. 7

Postage Stamp—memorial stamp—issued—Feb. 12

Pressing Machine (steam-operated)—patent granted—A. J. Hoffman—July 13

Radio Distress Signal—radio SOS from an American ship—transmitted—Aug. 11

Research Institute—institute for research in nervous diseases—Neurological Institute—New York City—opened—Oct. 1

Road—concrete rural road—laid—Wayne County, Mich.

Ship—battleship to visit an inland city—Natchez, Miss.—May 20

Tax—corporation tax—enacted—Aug. 5

Tax—income tax amendment to the Constitution—proposed to states—July 12

1910

Air Rights Lease—New York Central Railroad Co.—New York City—Feb.

Automobile — automobile (gasoline-electric combination)—used

Automobile Race Track—automobile speedway (board track)—Playa del Rey, Calif.—opened—April 7

Automobile Tire—cord tire—B. F. Goodrich Co.—Akron, Ohio

Aviation—airplane merchandise shipment—Dayton, Ohio to Columbus, Ohio—Nov. 7

Aviation—Airplane Bombing—airplane bombing experiment—Hammondsport, N.Y.—June 30

Aviation—Airport—airport municipal legislation—Modesto, Calif.—ratified—Sept. 14

1911

Aviation—airplane to land on the White House lawn—H. N. Atwood—Washington, D.C.

Aviation—**Airplane**—hydroplane — that was successful—"Flying Fish"—flown—Jan. 26

Aviation—**Airplane**—naval airplane — delivered

Aviation — Airplane Bombing — airplane bombing experiment with explosives — Jan. 7-25

Aviation—**Flights**—hydroplane flight to and from a ship—Glenn Curtiss—Feb. 17

Aviation—**Flights (transcontinental)**—transcontinental airplane flight—left—Sheepshead Bay, N.Y.—C. P. Rodgers—Sept. 17

Aviation—**Flights (transcontinental)**—transcontinental airplane flight (east-bound)—left—Los Angeles, Calif.—Oct. 19

Aviation — Legislation — aviation legislation (state)—enacted—Connecticut—June 8

Aviation—**License**—pilot's license issued by the Aero Club of America—G. H. Curtiss —June 8

Aviation—**License**—woman aviator to pass the test of the Aero Club of America— Harriet Quimby—Aug. 1

Aviation—**Races**—inter-city airplane race— New York City to Philadelphia, Pa.—Aug. 5

Bank—postal savings bank—initiated—Jan. 3

Boy Scouts of America—boy scout uniformed troop—organized—Troy, N.Y.

Cemetery—federal cemetery in the U.S. to contain graves of both Union and Confederate soldiers—Springfield, Mo.—March 3

Congressman (U.S.)—Socialist congressman —V. L. Berger—March 4

Continuation School — continuation school established by state law—opened—Racine, Wis.—Nov. 3

Court — commerce court (U.S.) — opened— Feb. 15

Dental Corps (U.S. Army)—Dental Corps commissions—authorized—March 3

Electric Lighting—klieglight lighting unit— used

Farm Bureau—city department—established —Binghamton, N.Y.—March 20

Fingerprinting—fingerprint conviction—New York City—May 19

Golf Champion—golf champion (American born professional) to win the United States Open Tournament—J. J. McDermott—Wheaton, Ill.—June 26

Gyro Compass—gyro compass installed on an American naval vessel—"Delaware"— tested—Aug. 28

Insurance — group insurance policy — New York City—June 1

Insurance—hail insurance law (state)—enacted—North Dakota—March 18

Insurance—workmen's compensation insurance law (state) — enacted—Wisconsin— May 3

Library Society—woman to become president of the American Library Association —T. H. W. Elmendorf—May 24

Linoleum — linoleum machine (fully automatic)—installed—Kearny, N.J.

Locker—locker (coin vender) — patented — W. S. Farnsworth—Petaluma, Calif.

Mineral Segregation—commercial operation —Butte, Mont.

Moving Picture Censorship—moving picture censorship board (state)—enacted—Pennsylvania—June 19

Old Age Home for Pioneers — Prescott, Ariz.—opened—Feb. 6

Opera—opera singer to sing two major roles on the same day—Herman Jadlowker— Metropolitan Opera House—New York City—March 22

Photograph—photograph from an airplane— H. A. Erickson—Jan. 10

Printing Instruction—printing lecture course in a college—Cambridge, Mass.—Feb.

Radio Car (military) — designed — R. P. Davidson—Lake Geneva, Wis.

Radio License—radio license—G. H. Lewis —Cincinnati, Ohio

Ship — electrically propelled ship of the United States Navy—"Jupiter"—keel laid —Oct. 16

Shortening—shortening made by the hydrogenation process—introduced—Cincinnati, Ohio—Aug. 15

Squash Club — squash tennis organization (national) — formed — New York City — March 20

Squash Tournament — New York City — April 8-10

Traffic Lines—painted in white — Trenton, Mich.

Trust—blue-sky laws—Kansas—March 10

Woman—woman horseback rider to make a solo transcontinental trip—N. J. Aspinwall—arrived New York City—July 8

1912

Advertising Organization — investigation work commenced—March

Aviation—airplane fatality (woman) — Julie Clark—Springfield, Ill.—June 17

Aviation—airplane take-off from a hotel roof—Silas Christoferson—Portland, Ore.

Aviation—**Airplane**—airplane outfitted with a machine gun—flown—College Park, Md. —May 7

Aviation—**Expositions and Meets**—aeronautic international exposition — New York City—May 9-18

Aviation — Flights — airplane catapulted — Washington, D.C.—Nov. 12

Aviation—**Flights** — over-water round-trip— to Catalina Island, Calif.—May 10

Aviation—**Flights (transcontinental)**—transcontinental airplane flight (eastbound)— R. G. Fowler—landed—Feb. 8

Aviation—**Parachute**—parachute jump from an airplane — Jefferson Barracks, Mo. — March 1

Aviation—**Passenger**—admiral in uniform to ride in an airplane—B. A. Fiske—New York City—May 10

Boy Scouts of America—Boy Scout to become an eagle scout—A. R. Eldred— Oceanside, N.Y.

1913

Dental School—dental hygienists' course—Bridgeport, Conn.—A. C. Fones—started—Nov. 17

Eye—eye conservation class—Boston, Mass.—April 3

Farm Bureau— state appropriation — New York—May 24

Fastening—hookless fastening for universal use—patented — Gideon Sundback — April 29

Foxhound Master (American)—in England—R. E. Strawbridge—May 1

Fuse—Cordeau-Bickford detonating fuse—introduced—Simsbury, Conn.

Gasoline—cracking process used to obtain gasoline from crude petroleum—W. M. Burton—Chicago, Ill.—Jan. 7

Goat Show (of milch goats)—Rochester, N.Y.—Sept. 15-27

Ice Loading Machinery—patent—April 22

Insurance—bonding law (state)—North Dakota—enacted—March 1

Labor Department (U.S.)—Labor Department (U.S.)—created

Labor Law—minimum wage law—Massachusetts—effective—July 1

Medical Society—American College of Surgeons — organized — Washington, D.C.—May 5

Medical Society — immunology society — American Association of Immunologists—organized—Minneapolis, Minn.—June 19

Monument—monument to a bird—Salt Lake City, Utah—Oct. 1

Moving Picture—animated cartoon (present technique)—"The Artist's Dream"—released

Moving Picture—serial moving picture—issued—Chicago, Ill.—Dec. 29

Moving Picture Projector—moving picture projector (portable)—produced—H. A. De Vry—Chicago, Ill.

Occupational Therapy Course—Milwaukee, Wis.

Permalloy—developed—G. W. Elmen—New York City—June 7

Photograph—photographs taken under the sea—Chesapeake Bay, Va.

Postage Stamp—parcel-post stamps—placed on sale—Jan. 1

Postage Stamp—postage stamps to picture an airplane—on sale—Jan. 1

Postal Service—parcel post service—started—Jan. 1

Public Defender's Office—created—Los Angeles, Calif.

Road—coast-to-coast paved road—Lincoln Highway—Lincoln Highway Association—formed

Rubber—synthetic rubber — manufactured—L. P. Kyrides and R. B. Earle—East Watertown, Mass.

Senator (U.S.)—senators "elected by the people"—seventeenth amendment in effect—May 31

Ship—gyro stabilizer installed on an American naval vessel—"Worden"—April

Strike—strike settlement—mediation settlement—June 2

Tax—income tax amendment to the Constitution—effective—March 1

Tungsten—ductile tungsten—patented—W. D. Coolidge—Dec. 30

War Veterans' Society—Veterans of Foreign Wars of the United States—formed—Denver, Colo.—Aug. 18-20

1914

Auction Bridge Championship (duplicate)—Lake Placid, N.Y.—July 9

Automobile Bus—bus with cross seats—New York City—double deck buses—March 17

Automobile Tire—non-skid tire—patented April 14

Aviation—air service of the United States Army—created—July 18

Aviation—hydroplane commercial line service—St. Petersburg and Tampa, Fla.—Jan. 1

Aviation — Airplane — hydroplane with a multi-engine—christened—June 22

Aviation—School—airplane flying school operated by a woman—San Antonio, Tex.

Aviation—School—naval air training school—opened—Pensacola, Fla.—Dec. 1

Bank—bank established in a foreign country—Nov. 10

Bank—federal reserve system — formally opened—Nov. 16

Bird Banding—bird banding by federal authorities

Community Trust — organized — Cleveland, Ohio—Jan. 2

Dental School—dental hygienists' course—graduation—June 5

Electric Transmission—substation with a rotary converter completely unattended—Detroit, Mich.

Federal Trade Commission—Federal Trade Commission—created—Sept. 26

Flag—American flag flown in World War I over a band of fighting Americans—Sept. 30

Forestry School—forestry correspondence course in tree surgery—Kent, Ohio

Holiday—Mother's Day—national recognition—May 12

Horseshoe Pitchers' Association (national)—organized—Kansas City, Kan.—May 16

Insurance—War Risk Insurance Bureau—established—Sept. 2

Map—automobile road map—published—Pittsburgh, Pa.

Medical Society—women members of the American College of Surgeons—A. G. Bryant and F. W. Duckering—June 22

Motorcycle Race — motorcycle race (300 miles)—Dodge City, Kan.—July 4

Moving Picture—animated cartoon (present technique)—patent—J. R. Bray—August 11

Moving Picture—six-reel "feature"-length comedy — *Tillie's Punctured Romance*—released—Dec. 21

Museum—industrial museum—New York City—incorporated—Feb. 26

Music Society—music society for the literary protection of composers and authors—American Society of Composers, Authors and Publishers—formed—New York City—Feb. 13

Newspaper—newspaper rotogravure sections

Newspaper Audit — newspaper circulation audit—Audit Bureau of Circulations—Chicago, Ill.—formed—Aug. 21

Nobel Prize—Nobel prize in chemistry—T. W. Richards

Organists' Society—organists' society (national)—convention — New York City—Dec. 29

Passport—passport photographs—required—Nov. 20

Police—woman chief of police—Dolly Spencer—Milford, Ohio

Postal Service—collection and delivery of mail in automobiles—government owned—Oct. 19

Prison—organization of a prison—"community groups"—Auburn, N.Y.

Prohibition—prohibition vote—dry majority—Dec. 22

Public Defender's Office—W. J. Wood assumed duties—Los Angeles, Calif.

Railroad Car—air-conditioned cars—built

Rocket—liquid fuel rocket patent—R. H. Goddard—July 14

Ship—steamboat to pass through the Panama Canal—"Alex La Valley"—Jan. 7

Skating Tournament—figure skating international championship tournament — New Haven, Conn.—March 20

Skee Ball Alley—built—Coney Island, N.Y.—April

Social Science Society (national)—annual meeting—New York City—March 20

Telephone—underground cable long distance telephone conversation—Boston, Mass., to Washington, D.C.—Feb. 26

Traffic Light—electric traffic signal lights—installed—Cleveland, Ohio—Aug. 5

Vocational Guidance Chair—Indiana University—Bloomington, Ind.

World War I—American combatant casualty in World War I—Corporal Bouligny—Nov. 15

World War I—American to sail to Europe to enlist in World War I—D. P. Dowd, Jr.—enlisted—Aug. 6

1915

Automobile—field hospital automobile with x-ray equipment—used—May

Automobile Bus—bus with a double-deck body and chassis made in the U.S.—New York City

Automobile Bus—bus with cross seats—single-deck buses—New York City—Aug. 27

Automobile Electric Self-Starter—automobile electric self-starter, applied commercially—patented—Aug. 17

Automobile Finance Company—organized—New York City—Feb.

Automobile Race Track—automobile race track (asphalt covered)—opened—Cranston, R.I.—Sept. 18

Aviation—Advisory Committee for Aeronautics (national)—approved—March 3

Aviation—Airship—airship of the U.S. Navy—contract—June 1

Chamber of Commerce—Junior Chamber of Commerce—organized—St. Louis, Mo.—Oct. 13

Chiropody School—chiropody school as a regular division of a university—opened—Philadelphia, Pa.—Sept. 20

Coast Guard (U.S.)—Coast Guard—created—Jan. 28

College — Negro university (Catholic) — Xavier University — opened as a high school—Sept. 27

Dental Legislation—legislation (state) regarding dental hygienists—Connecticut—enacted—May 19

Dental Magazine—orthodontia magazine—published—St. Louis, Mo.—Jan.

Election Law—proportional representation election—Ashtabula, Ohio—Nov. 2

Federal Trade Commission—Federal Trade Commission—organized—March 16

Fingerprint Society—fingerprint society (international) — formed — Oakland, Calif.—Oct. 9

Girl Scouts—incorporated—June 10

Governor—Jewish governor — full term—Moses Alexander—served—Jan. 4

Horse Race—filly to win the Kentucky Derby—Louisville, Ky.—May 8

Horseshoe Pitchers' Association (national)—championship tournament—Kellerton, Iowa—Oct. 23

Money—fifty-dollar gold pieces minted by the United States—San Francisco, Calif.—June 15

Music Instruction — State Supervisor of Music—P. E. Beck—appointed—Pennsylvania—July 1

Nobel Prize—Nobel prize in chemistry—presented—T. W. Richards—Nov. 12

Ordnance—submachine gun—Auto-Ordnance Company—organized—J. T. Thompson

Protestant Church—Protestant church for lepers—dedicated—Carville, La.—June 14

Public Health—pellagra experiment—Jackson, Miss.—Joseph Goldberger—Feb. 4

Radio Telephone—radio telephone communication (one way)—Montauk Point, N.Y. to Wilmington, Del.—April 4

Radio Telephone—transatlantic radio telephone message—from Arlington, Va. to Paris, France—Oct. 21

Radio Telephone — transcontinental radio telephone demonstration—New York City to San Francisco—Sept. 29

Ship—ship (American) attacked by a German submarine—"Nantucket Chief"—torpedoed—May 1

Ship—warship propelled by electricity—"New Mexico"—keel laid—Oct. 14

Sound-Absorbing Material—C. G. Muench—St. Paul, Minn.—patent—Sept. 14

Submarine—submarine disaster—Hawaii—March 25

Telephone—transcontinental telephone demonstration—New York City to San Francisco—Jan. 25

World War I—American combatant to die in World War I—E. M. Stone—Feb. 27

World War I—American ship lost in World War I—"William P. Frye"—sunk—Jan. 28

Zoological Garden—barless zoological garden of naturalistic rock construction—started—Denver, Colo.—City Park Zoo

1916

Army—Army Veterinary Corps—established

Army—Reserve Officers Training Corps—authorized—June 3

Army—Reserve Officers Training Corps Units—authorized—Oct. 21

Aviation—airplane in actual military operation—Mexico—March

Aviation—Coast Guard aviation unit—authorized—Aug. 29

Aviation—Aviator—American aviator killed while a pilot in the Lafayette Escadrille—V. E. Chapman—June 23

Aviation—Aviator — American aviator shot down in World War I—H. C. Balsley—June 18

Aviation—Flights—airplane to fly a distance exceeding 500 miles—Chicago, Ill. to Hornell, N.Y.—Ruth Law—Nov. 19

Bird Legislation (international)—Migratory Bird Treaty—signed—Aug. 16

Child Labor Law—child labor law (federal)—enacted—Sept. 1

Corn—shipment of hybrid seed corn—Bloomington, Ill.—April 13

Dental Book—book for dental hygienists (text)—*Mouth Hygiene*—published

Farm Loan Board (federal)—authorized—July 17

Flag—President's flag—adopted—May 29

Golf Tournament—Professional Golfers Association tournament—Siwanoy Golf Club—Mount Vernon, N.Y.—Oct. 14

Holiday—Indian Day—observance—May 13

Hygiene Instruction—hygiene and public health school—established—Baltimore, Md.

Medical Clinic—birth control clinic—opened—New York City—Oct. 16

Motorcycle Trip—motorcycle transcontinental trip by women—completed—New York City to San Diego, Calif.—Sept. 12

Moving Picture—animated cartoon in color—produced—New York City

Moving Picture—animated cartoon (technical)—produced—New York City

Orchestra—municipal orchestra supported by taxes—Baltimore, Md.—first concert—Feb. 11

Park—park (national) containing an active volcano—Lassen Volcanic National Park—established—Aug. 9

Park—park (national) east of the Mississippi—Acadia National Park — established—July 8

Park Service (national)—created—Aug. 25

Radio Beacons—tested—Navesink Light Station—Atlantic Highlands, N.J.

Radio Telephone—radio telephone ship-to-shore conversation—May 6

Road—federal grant-in-aid to states for roads—enacted—July 11

Science Association — National Research Council—meeting—New York City—Sept. 20

Shipping—United States Shipping Board—established—Sept. 7

Street Car—light-weight one-man street car—built—St. Louis, Mo.

Submarine—cargo submarine to cross the Atlantic Ocean—"Deutschland"—landed—Baltimore, Md.—July 9

Supreme Court (U.S.)—associate justice of the Supreme Court who was Jewish—L. D. Brandeis—appointed—Jan. 28

Tournament of Roses—football game annual event

1917

Agricultural Soil Conference—Washington, D.C.—June 13-22

Army—gas regiment—authorized—Aug. 15

Army Balloon School — established — St. Louis, Mo.—April 6

Army Camp—army camp for training Negro officers—DesMoines, Iowa—June 15

Army Officer—regimental Jewish chaplain—commissioned—Nov. 15

Aviation—Airship—airship of the U.S. Navy—tested—Pensacola, Fla.—April

Aviation—Airship—airship of the U.S. Navy that was successful—tested—May 30

Bank—joint stock land bank—chartered—Sioux City, Iowa—April 24

Baseball Game—double no-hit nine-inning baseball game—Chicago, Ill.—May 2

Bowling Tournament—bowling tournament for women—St. Louis, Mo.—March 17

Child Labor Law—child labor law (federal)—effective—Sept. 1

College — Negro university (Catholic) — Xavier University — normal department opened—Sept. 24

College—women's volunteer college unit to serve overseas—Smith College Relief Unit

Congress (U.S.)—Senate—Senate cloture resolution—enacted—March 8

Congressman (U.S.)—congresswoman elected—Jeannette Rankin—served—March 4

Congressman (U.S.) — congresswoman to vote twice against the entry of the United States into war—Jeannette Rankin—first vote—April 6

Crane—automobile wrecking crane—R. E. Manley—York, Pa.

Daylight Saving—legislation enacted—June 27

Employment Service—employment service (U.S.)—authorized—Oct. 6

Helium — helium plants (experimental) — erected—**Texas**

Lewisite — developed—Washington, D.C.— W. L. Lewis—Feb.

Locomotive Booster—used—New York Central R.R.—July

Marines—woman marine reserve—O. M. Johnson, enrolled—Aug. 12

Medal—Croix de Guerre awarded to a Negro—Henry Johnson—May 24

Medal—Distinguished Service Cross (Army) —authorized—July 9

Medal—Distinguished Service Medal (Army)—authorized—July 9

Novel—novel to win the Pulitzer prize in letters—*His Family*—award announced—June 3

Nursing School—Army School of Nursing—authorized—May 25

Photograph—photograph showing air in motion—Washington, D.C.

Postage Stamp—air mail stamps—issued—May 13

President (U.S.)—President to visit a European country while President—Woodrow Wilson—sailed—Dec. 4

Prohibition—prohibition amendment to the Constitution—first state to ratify amendment—Mississippi—Jan. 8

Prohibition—prohibition law (national)—enacted—Nov. 21

Protestant Episcopal Bishop—Negro suffragan—E. T. Demby—appointed—Sept. 29

Railroad—government operation of railroads —Jan. 1

Ship—concrete barge—"Socony 200"—launched —New York City—July 27

Ship — concrete seagoing ship—"Faith"—launched—Redwood City, Calif.—March 14

Ship—concrete ship built for the United States Shipping Board — "Atlantus" — launched—Dec. 4

Ship — warship propelled by electricity — "New Mexico"—commissioned—May 20

Woman—woman District Attorney of the United States—A. A. Adams—served—July 25

World War I—air combat of an American organization in World War I—Toul, France—April 14

World War I—American Army division to cross the Rhine River—Coblentz—Dec. 13

World War I—American Army troopship in World War I torpedoed by the Germans— "Tuscania"—Feb. 15

World War I—German spy to receive a death sentence from the American forces during World War I—condemned—Aug. 16

World War I—shots to land on American soil—Orleans, Mass.—July 21

Zoological Garden—barless zoological garden of naturalistic rock construction—completed—Denver, Colo.

1919

Actors' Union—strike called—Aug. 7

Air Mail Service—air mail service to a steamer at sea—Aug. 14

Air Mail Service—air mail transcontinental service—first section opened—New York City to Cleveland—July 1

Air Mail Service—international air mail— between Seattle, Wash. and Victoria, B.C. —March 3

Army Officer—General of the Armies of the U.S.—J. J. Pershing—confirmed—Sept. 4

Automobile—armored commercial car completely protected—construction started—Minneapolis, Minn.—March

Aviation — aeronautical stowaway—arrived July 6

Aviation—Airplane—three motor airplane —flown—Garden City, N.Y.—July 24

Aviation — **Airport** — airport municipally owned—Tucson, Ariz.—Nov. 20

Aviation—Airship—airship (lighter-than-air) —arrived—New York City—July 6

Aviation—Airship—airship to land on a roof —Cleveland, Ohio.—May 23

Aviation—Aviator—pilot to receive the Congressional Medal of Honor—posthumously presented—May 29

Aviation—Flights—New York-Chicago nonstop flight—April 19

Aviation—Flights (transatlantic)—transatlantic hydroplane flight—left New York City—May 8

Aviation — **Flights (transatlantic)** — transatlantic non-stop flight from America—Alcock and Brown—left—June 14

Aviation—Parachute—parachute—"free parachute" jump—Dayton, Ohio—April 28

Aviation—Races—transcontinental air race— left San Francisco, Calif.—Oct. 8

Biography Course—biography department— in a college—Northfield, Minn.

Caterpillar Club—Caterpillar Club member— John Boettner—July 21

College — Negro university (Catholic) — Xavier University—normal school diplomas awarded—June 20

Communist Labor Party of America—organized—Chicago, Ill.—Aug. 31

Communist Party of America—organized— Chicago, Ill.—Sept. 2

Congress (U.S.)—Senate—Senate cloture resolution—invoked—Nov. 15

Deaf—Association—national social organization for the hard of hearing—formed— New York City—Feb. 27

Federal Trade Commission—Federal Trade Commission trade practice conference— Omaha, Neb.—Oct. 3

Forest Service—forest service aerial patrol— established—June 1

Freemasons—Order of De Molay—founded F. S. Land—Kansas City, Mo.

Gasoline Tax—gasoline tax (state)—Oregon —Feb. 25

Holiday—Armistice Day—celebrated—Nov. 11

Horse—horse to win the triple crown—Sir Barton

Horse Race—three-hundred-mile endurance run—Burlington, Vt. to Camp Devens, Mass.—Oct. 15

Insurance—aircraft liability and property damage insurance—Hartford, Conn.

Insurance—fire and tornado insurance fund (state) — North Dakota—in operation—July 1

Insurance—insurance service offered by a newspaper—*Star*—St. Louis, Mo.—April 14

Medal—Distinguished Service Medal awarded to a woman—Evangeline Booth

Medal—Distinguished Service Medal (Navy) —authorized—Feb. 4

Monument—monument to an insect—dedicated—Enterprise, Ala.—Dec. 11

Newspaper—illustrated tabloid — *Illustrated Daily News*—New York City—June 26

Periodical—photo-engraved magazine—*Literary Digest*—New York City—Oct. 25

Prison — prisoners (federal) employed in industry—Atlanta, Ga.—July 11

Prohibition—prohibition bureau (federal)—amendment enacted—Jan. 29

Prohibition—prohibition law (national)—Volstead Prohibition Act—enacted—Oct. 28

Radio Telephone—two-way conversation between a submerged submarine and another vessel—Oct. 5

Ship—ambulance ship, designed and built as a hospital—"Relief"—launched—Dec. 23

Ship—concrete ship built for the United States Shipping Board—"Atlantus"—delivered—Nov. 11

War Veterans' Society—American Legion—organized—Paris, France—Feb. 15-16

Wedding—airplane wedding—Houston, Texas—May 31

Woman—American-born woman to become a member of Parliament—Lady Astor—Dec. 1

Woman—woman editor-in-chief of a law review—M. H. Donlon—*Cornell Law Quarterly*—Nov.

Woman—woman sculptor honored by membership in the National Academy of Design—M. E. B. Longman

Woman Suffrage—woman suffrage amendment approved by Congress—June 4

1920

Air Mail Service—air mail transcontinental service — combination airplane-railroad—Sept. 8

Air Mail Service—international air mail—regular service under contract—commenced—Oct. 14

Arbitration—state arbitration law (modern) —passed—New York—April 19

Army Camp—Army Citizens' Military Training Camp—authorized—June 4

Army Officer—Chaplain (chief) of the U.S. Army—appointed—July 15

Army Officer—Chemical Warfare Chief—served—July 16

Army Officer—woman with rank corresponding to major—rank conferred—June 4

Astronomer—astronomer to measure the size of a fixed star—Dec. 13

Astronomy—planet (asteroid) named for an American President—discovered—March

Automobile—armored commercial car completely protected—in service—St. Paul, Minn.—Feb. 1

Aviation—Coast Guard air station—established—Morehead City, N.C.—March 24

Aviation—hydroplane commercial line service (international)—Key West, Fla.—Nov. 1

Aviation—Airplane—airplane used by a newspaper—Baltimore, Md.—Sept. 1

Aviation—Aviator—Naval ace in World War I—received Distinguished Service Medal

Aviation—Expositions and Meets—intercollegiate air meet—Mitchel Field, N.Y.—May 7

Aviation—Flights—New York-Alaska flight —left Mitchel Field, N.Y.—July 15

Baseball "Dictator"—K. M. Landis—elected —Nov. 12

Baseball Game—triple play unassisted in a World Series—Cleveland, Ohio—Oct. 10

Cabinet of the U.S.—woman sub-cabinet member—A. A. Adams—appointed—June 26

Civil Service—woman Civil Service commissioner—H. H. Gardener—sworn in—Washington, D.C.

Curling Rink—indoor curling rink—opened —Brookline, Mass.—Dec. 19

Deaf—Association—national social organization for the hard of hearing—annual meeting—March 12

Dog Race Track—imitation rabbit used—Emeryville, Calif.—opened—Feb. 22

Farmer Labor Party—organized—Chicago, Ill.—June 12

Football Club—football association (professional)—formed—Canton, Ohio—Sept. 17

Labor Department (U.S.)—Women's Bureau—permanently organized—June 5

Milk—acidophilus milk — devised — L. F. Rettger and Harry Cheplin—New Haven, Conn.

Newspaper—Ukrainian daily newspaper—*Ukrainian Daily News*—established—Jan. 31

Olympic Games—woman (American) to win an Olympic competition—Ethelda Bleibtrey

Orchestra—orchestra (American) to make a European tour—Symphony Society of New York—sailed—April 22

Postal Service—postage meter—set—Stamford, Conn.—Nov. 16

Prohibition—prohibition amendment to the Constitution—effective—Jan. 16

Prohibition—prohibition bureau (federal)—amendment effective—Jan. 16

Radio Broadcast—election returns broadcast —Detroit, Mich.—Aug. 31

Radio Broadcast—football game (collegiate) broadcast—College Station, Texas—Nov. 25

Radio Broadcast—news program—Detroit, Mich.—Aug. 31

Radio Broadcast—prize fight broadcast— WWJ—Detroit, Mich.—Sept. 6

Radio Broadcast—prize fight broadcast from the ringside—New York City—Dec. 22

Radio Broadcast—speaker to address an organization by radio—W. C. Ketler—Grove City, Pa.—April 20

Radio Compass—on a naval airplane—used —Norfolk, Va.—July 7

Radio License—radio station licensed—Pittsburgh, Pa.—Oct. 27

Radio Station—commercial radio station— WWJ—Detroit, Mich. — daily service— Aug. 20

Radio Station—municipal radio station— Dallas, Tex.

Radio Telephone—radio telephone service (commercial)—Los Angeles and Catalina Island, Calif.—July 16

Ship—ambulance ship designed and built as a hospital—"Relief"—delivered—Dec. 28

Students' Federation (international)—Pan American Student League—founded—New York City

Tunnel—twin-tube subaqueous vehicular tunnel—New York City and Jersey City, N.J.—construction begun—Oct. 12

Woman—woman labor delegate to the British Trades Union—S. A. M. Conboy—elected

Woman Suffrage—woman suffrage amendment approved by Congress—ratification formally announced—Aug. 26

1921

Air Mail Service—air mail transcontinental flight—San Francisco, Calif. to New York City—Feb. 22

Army Camp — Army Citizens' Military Training Camp—established

Aviation—battleship sunk by an airplane— near Hampton Roads, Va.—July 21

Aviation—Flights (transcontinental)—transcontinental flight in 24 hours flying time —San Diego, Calif. to Jacksonville, Fla.— Feb. 21

Balloon—balloon filled with helium gas— Hampton Roads, Va.—Dec. 1

Blind—correspondence school for the blind to offer instruction in the Braille system —Winnetka, Ill.—Aug.

Budget Bureau (U.S.)—created—June 10

Cartoon—cartoon awarded a Pulitzer prize appeared—New York *World*—Aug. 5

Cigarette Tax—cigarette tax (state)—levied —Iowa—April 11

Civil Rights Chair — established — Easton, Pa.—Feb.

Comptroller General of the U.S.—J. R. McCarl—appointed—June 27

Conference—conference of great powers— Washington, D.C.—Nov. 12

Congressman (U.S.) — congresswoman to preside over the House of Representatives —A. M. Robertson—June 20

Engine — outboard twin-cylinder motor (light) — Ole Evinrude — developed—Milwaukee, Wis.

Execution—lethal gas execution—adopted— Nevada—March 28

Fencing — international fencing championship competition — Washington, D.C. — Nov. 18-19

Geography School—Clark University, Worcester, Mass.

Helium—helium plant of the United States —Fort Worth, Texas

Hospital—leper hospital—reopened—June 8

Immigration — immigration quota act — enacted—May 19

Judge—woman judge to sentence a man to death—F. E. Allen—Aug. 20

Money—coin bearing the portrait of a living person — Alabama Centennial commemorative half-dollar

Monument — monument to the "Unknown Soldier" (national)—"Unknown Soldier" buried—Arlington, Va.—Nov. 11

Nursing School—Army School of Nursing— graduation

Opera — opera broadcast in its entirety — *Martha*—Denver, Colo.—May 19

Opera—opera broadcast in its entirety by a professional cast—*Samson et Dalila*—Chicago, Ill.—Nov. 14

Postal Service—philatelic agency—in operation—Dec. 1

President (U.S.) — President to become Chief Justice of the United States—W. H. Taft—appointed—June 30

Prize Fight—prize fight to gross a million dollars—Jersey City, N.J.—July 2

Radio Beacons—placed in regular operation —May 1

Radio Broadcast—baseball game broadcast with a play-by-play description — Pittsburgh, Pa.

Radio Broadcast — baseball world series broadcast—Oct. 5-13

Radio Broadcast — police broadcast — St. Louis, Mo.—Sept. 4

Radio Broadcast—prize fight (heavyweight championship) broadcast — Jersey City, N.J.—July 2

Radio Broadcast — religious service broadcast—Pittsburgh, Pa.—Jan. 2

Radio Broadcast—tennis match broadcast— Sewickley, Pa.—Aug. 4

Radio Broadcast — weather broadcasts — St. Louis, Mo.—April 26

Radio Church—New York City—Nov. 27

Sarrusophone—manufactured—Elkhart, Ind.

Tax—sales tax (state)—enacted—West Virginia—May 3

Telephone—telephone cable service (deep sea)—opened—Key West, Fla.—April 11

Theater—theater provided with scientific air distribution—Los Angeles, Calif.

Veterans' Bureau—established—Aug. 9

1922

Aquatic Mammals—platypus (duck-billed)—exhibited—New York City—July 15

Arbitration Association—arbitration association—Arbitration Society of America—formed—New York City—May 15

Aviation—sermon from an airplane—B. W. Maynard—April 16

Aviation—Flights—airplane to exceed the speed of 200 miles an hour—L. J. Maitland—Oct. 14

Aviation—Flights (transcontinental)—transcontinental dirigible flight (non-rigid dirigible)—left Newport News, Va.—Sept. 14

Aviation—Parachute—aviator to bail out of a disabled airplane—H. R. Harris—Dayton, Ohio—Oct. 20

Aviation—Passenger—woman airplane passenger (transcontinental)—left San Francisco, Calif.—Oct. 5

Blind—correspondence school for the blind to offer instruction in the Braille system—Winnetka, Ill.—incorporated—Jan. 2

Carillon—carillon (modern)—blessed—Gloucester, Mass.—July 2

Cartoon—cartoon awarded a Pulitzer prize—May 21

Catholic Nuns (cloistered community) —founded—Baltimore, Md.—April 24

Cornstone—produced—Ames, Iowa

Diplomatic Service—woman legation secretary—Lucille Atcherson—appointed—Dec. 4

Electric Transmission — electric power line commercial carrier — Utica, N.Y.—operation—Dec. 6

Eskimo Pie — patented — C. K. Nelson — Onawa, Iowa—Jan. 24

Golf Champion—golf champion to win the United States Open and the Professional—Gene Sarazen—Aug. 18

Golf Tournament—international golf match—Southampton, N.Y.—Aug. 28-29

Helicopter Flight—helicopter flight—College Park, Md.—June 16

Holiday—Navy Day—celebrated—Oct. 27

Hotel Administration College Course—Cornell University—Ithaca, N.Y.

Judge—woman associate justice of a state supreme court — F. E. Allen — Cleveland, Ohio—Dec. 16

League of Nations representative (unofficial)—Grace Abbott—Oct. 13

Microfilm Machine—microfilm reading device—patented—B. A. Fiske—March 28

Moving Picture — Technicolor motion picture—released—New York City—Dec. 3

Orchestra—radio orchestra—Detroit, Mich.—May 28

Peritonitis — peritonitis preventive (successful)—used—H. L. Johnson — Boston, Mass.

Petroleum Refining Course — University of Pittsburgh — Pittsburgh, Pa. — W. F. Faragher

Polo—intercollegiate indoor polo championship—Princeton-Yale—New York City—March 18

President (U.S.)—President to broadcast by radio—W. G. Harding—Baltimore, Md.—June 14

Radar—radar observations—Anacostia, D.C.—Sept. 27

Radio Broadcast—advertising or commercial radio broadcast—New York City—Aug. 28

Radio Broadcast — chain broadcast — New York City—Oct. 7

Radio Broadcast—debate over the radio—Washington, D.C.—May 23

Radio Broadcast—drama (full-length melodrama) broadcast—Schenectatdy, N.Y.—Aug. 3

Radio Broadcast—football game (collegiate) coast-to-coast broadcast—New York City

Radio Broadcast—news program (daily)—New York City—Sept. 1

Radio Broadcast—radio concert from an airplane—New York City—April 14

Radio Conference—National Radio Conference—Washington, D.C.—Feb. 27

Radio Facsimile Transmission—photograph sent by radio across the Atlantic from Europe—June 11

Radio Facsimile Transmission—photographs sent over a city telephone—Washington, D.C.—Oct. 3

Senator (U.S.)—woman to occupy a seat in the Senate — R. L. Felton — appointed — Oct. 3

Ship — cruise ship to circumnavigate the world—"Laconia"—New York City—start—Nov. 21

Shipping—automatic steering gear—installed—April 7

Skywriting — skywriting — Cyril Turner — New York City—Nov. 28

Soybean Processing Plant—A. E. Staley—Decatur, Ill.

Steel—continuous sheet steel mill—built—Ashland, Ky.

Vitamin—vitamin E—recognized—Berkeley, Calif.

Wedding — double radio wedding — New York City—Dec. 22

Wedding—wedding broadcast — Pittsburgh, Pa.—Nov. 7

Woman — woman automotive engineer — Marie Luhring — graduated — New York City—June 5

Woman—woman clerk of a state supreme court—G. F. Kaercher—elected—Nov. 7

1923

Animals—chinchilla farm—established—Los Angeles, Calif.—Feb. 22

Automobile Tire—balloon tire production—on regular basis--Akron, Ohio—April 5

Automobile Trucking Service—automobile trucking service—Baltimore, Chesapeake and Atlantic Railway—Jan. 8

Aviation—airways illumination—Aug. 21

Aviation—refueling attempt in mid-air—Coronado, Calif.—L. H. Smith and J. F. Richter—June 27

Aviation—Airship—dirigible (American-built rigid)—Lakehurst, N.J.—launched—Aug. 20

Aviation—Flights (transcontinental)—transcontinental non-stop flight—left New York City—May 2

Baseball Game—World Series baseball games to gross a million dollars—New York City —Oct. 10-15

Book—book (of size) completed entirely by one man—Dard Hunter—Chillicothe, Ohio

Business History Chair—established—Cambridge, Mass.

Camera—moving picture camera (portable) —manufactured—Davenport, Iowa

Catholic Seminary—for Negro priests— opened—Bay St. Louis, Miss.—Sept. 16

College—"Junior Year Abroad"—Newark, Del.—first group tour—July 7

Congressman (U.S.)—congresswoman elected to serve in the place of her husband— M. E. Nolan—Calif.—served—Jan. 23

Dance Marathon—New York City

Electric Generator—mercury boiler turbine —Hartford, Conn.—Sept. 7

Electric Sign—neon tube advertising sign— installed—New York City—July

Gasoline—ethyl gasoline—marketed—Dayton, Ohio—Feb. 2

Hospital—cancer hospital (municipal)—New York City Cancer Institute—New York City—Aug. 1

Ink—ink paste—manufactured—Minneapolis, Minn.—Feb. 10

Moving Picture—moving picture of an eclipse of the sun taken from an airplane— attempted—Santa Catalina, Calif.—Sept. 10

Moving Picture—sound-on-film moving picture—Lee De Forest—New York City

Newspaper—mimeographed daily newspaper —*Kellogg Daily Reminder*—published—Kellogg, Idaho—July 25

Pension—old age pension laws (state)—enacted—Montana and Nevada—March 5

Postage Stamp—precanceled stamps printed on rotary presses—issued—April 21

President (U.S.)—President and President's wife to die during the term for which he had been elected—W. G. Harding—died— Aug. 2

President (U.S.)—President to visit Alaska and Canada while President—W. G. Harding

Radio Broadcast—chain broadcast—with repeater points—New York City and Boston, Mass.—Jan. 4

Radio Broadcast—presidential message to be broadcast—Calvin Coolidge—Dec. 6

Radio Broadcast—transatlantic broadcast of a voice—Pittsburgh, Pa.—Dec. 31

Radio Facsimile Transmission—photograph sent overland by radio to a distant point— Anacostia, D.C. to Philadelphia, Pa.— March 3

Railroad—railroad to install gasoline-mechanical cars—Pennsylvania Railroad— Feb.

Railroad Signal System—railroad signal system of continuous cab signals—Pennsylvania Railroad—July 11

Smoke Screen—demonstrated—Cape Hatteras, N.C.—Sept. 5

Swimmer—American to swim the English Channel—H. F. Sullivan—Aug. 5-6

Wind Tunnel—wind tunnel of variable air density—Langley Field, Va.—April

Woman—woman internal revenue collector —M. G. Reinecke—served—June 1

1924

Air Mail Service—air mail transcontinental through regular service—New York City to San Francisco—July 1

Automobile Bus—bus operated by a railroad —company incorporated—July 23

Aviation — Airship — dirigible merchandise shipment—arrived—Lakehurst, N.J.—Oct. 15

Aviation—Flights (transcontinental)—transcontinental airship voyage—left—Lakehurst, N.J.—Oct. 7

Aviation—Flights (transcontinental)—transcontinental flight within 24 hours—left— New York City—June 23

Aviation—Flights—(world)—world flight— begun — Seattle, Wash. — April 6 — completed—Sept. 28

Border Patrol—border patrol organization— established—June 1

Bowler—bowler to roll two perfect games— —Frank Caruana—Buffalo, N.Y.

Cellophane—manufactured—Buffalo, N.Y.

Chromium Plating process (commercial)— invented—New York City

Citizenship and Public Affairs School— opened—Syracuse, N.Y.—Oct. 3

Corn Husking Championship Contest (national)—Alleman, Iowa—Dec. 1

Crossword Puzzle Book—published—New York City—April 18

Degrees (academic and honorary)—Doctor of Social Science degree—awarded—H. R. Jeter—Chicago, Ill.

Diplomatic Service—Foreign Service of the United States—created—July 1

Execution — lethal gas execution — Carson City, Nev.—Feb. 8

Governor—woman governor of a state— N. T. Ross—Wyoming—elected

Ice Cream Cone—ice cream cone-rolling machine—patented—C. R. Taylor—Cleveland, Ohio—Jan. 29

Indians—Indian citizenship statute—enacted —June 2

Ink—ink paste—patented—F. B. Cooney— Minneapolis, Minn.—Jan. 1

Lens—contact lenses—imported—New York City

Locomotive—diesel electric locomotive—in service—Dec. 17

Marriage Course in a college—University of North Carolina—Chapel Hill, N.C.—E. R. Groves

Moving Picture—talking pictures of presidential candidates—Washington, D.C.—Aug. 11

Olympic Games—American decathlon champion—H. M. Osborne—Paris, France—July 12

Paleontology Course — micropaleontology course—Columbia University—New York City

Postage Stamp—precanceled stamps printed on rotary presses—one-cent precanceled stamps issued—Jan. 7

President (U.S.)—President buried in Washington, D.C.—Woodrow Wilson—Feb. 5

Radio Broadcast—coast-to-coast hook up—J. J. Carty—Feb. 8

Radio Broadcast—foreign language course broadcast—New York City—March 21

Radio Broadcast—network broadcast received on the Pacific Coast—Oct. 23

Radio Broadcast—network sponsored broadcast—New York City—Feb. 12

Radio Broadcast—political convention broadcast—Cleveland, Ohio—June 10

Radio Broadcast—political speech by a President on radio—Calvin Coolidge—New York City—Feb. 12

Radio Broadcast—President to broadcast from the White House—Calvin Coolidge—Washington, D.C.—Feb. 22

Radio Broadcast—radio broadcast (two-way) from an airplane—Aug. 14

Radio Facsimile Transmission—photograph sent by radio across the Atlantic—C. E. Hughes—New York City—July 6

Radio Facsimile Transmission—photograph sent by radio across the Atlantic as a public demonstration—London, England to New York City—Nov. 30

Science Association—history of science society—organized—Boston, Mass.—Jan. 12

Ship—steamboat service round-the-world (regular passenger service)—inaugurated—San Francisco, Calif.—Feb.

Stethoscope—electrical stethoscope (portable)—exhibited—Chicago, Ill.—June 10

1925

Air Mail Service—air mail long-distance night service—July 1

Arbitration—federal arbitration law — approved—Feb. 12

Atheism Society—American Association for the Advancement of Atheism—incorporated—Nov. 16

Aviation—Airship—airship with an enclosed cabin—flown—June 3

Billboard Standardization—Outdoor Advertising Association of America—formed—Kansas City, Mo.—Oct. 16-20

Caterpillar Club—woman caterpillar club member—I. McFarland—jumped—Cincinnati, Ohio—June 28

Citron — commercially grown — La Habra, Calif.

City (Lilliputian city)—Springfield, Mo.—June 6

City Planning Instruction—Master in Landscape Architecture — degree conferred—June 18

College — Negro university (Catholic) — Xavier University — college department opened—Sept. 13

Compotype—patented—Oct. 20

Cosmic Ray—discovered—R. A. Millikan—Pasadena, Calif.

Court—State Supreme Court composed entirely of women — Texas — appointed — Jan. 8

Degrees (academic and honorary)—degree conferred by radio—State University—Iowa City, Iowa—June 9

Diplomatic Service—woman vice consul—P. H. Field—appointed—March 20

Electric Lighting—glass light bulb machine —patented—B. D. Chamberlin—Sept. 1

Evolution law (state)—enacted—Tennessee —March 23

Fair—Woman's World Fair—Chicago, Ill.—April 18-25

Fireboat — fireboat with two-way radio equipment—in service—Boston, Mass.

Gas—gas storage tank (waterless)—in service—Michigan City, Ind.—Feb. 10

Golf Champion—golf champion to win the United States National Amateur Tournament two years in succession—R. T. Jones

Governor—woman governor of a state—N. T. Ross—Wyoming—assumed office—Jan. 5

Helium—helium plant of the United States —Bureau of Mines assumed charge—Fort Worth, Texas—July 1

Heresy Trial of a bishop—W. M. Brown—New Orleans, La.—Oct. 12

Hospital—Chinese hospital — opened — San Francisco, Calif.—April 18

Ice—dry ice—manufactured commercially—Long Island City, N.Y.

Insurance—automobile compulsory insurance act (state) — enacted — Massachusetts—May 1

Linoleum—embossed inlaid linoleum—introduced—Lancaster, Pa.

Moving Picture—moving picture of an eclipse of the sun taken from a dirigible—Montauk Point, L.I., N.Y.—Jan. 24

Museum—outdoor museum (or nature trail) —established—Tuxedo Park, N.Y.

Newspaper—composograph photograph in a newspaper—published—New York City—Nov. 25

Photoelectric Cell—photoelectric cell—demonstrated—New York City—Oct. 21

Photograph—photograph from an airplane at night—Rochester, N.Y.—Nov. 20

Photography—demonstration of rapid aerial photography—Fort Leavenworth, Kan.—Sept. 5

Potato Chips—exclusive manufacturing plant —Albany, N.Y.

Psychological Society—psychological society (national organization)—American Psychological Association — incorporated — Jan. 2

Radio Broadcast—presidential inauguration —Calvin Coolidge—Washington, D.C.

Radio Broadcast—ship launching broadcast
—Camden, N.J.—April 7

Radio Facsimile Transmission—photograph
sent by radio across the continent—Washington, D.C.—March 4

Radio Facsimile Transmission—photograph
sent by radio across the continent (commercial)—San Francisco, Calif.

Radio Facsimile Transmission—radio facsimile long distance transmission of a medical subject—New York City—May 28

Radio Facsimile Transmission—transpacific
and transcontinental facsimile transmission
—May 6

Radio Station—radio station operating a 50-kilowatt transmitter—Schenectady, N.Y.—operated—July 29

Railroad Car—coal cars with roller bearings
—placed in service—Dec.

Road—road with a depressed trough—opened—Texas—Dec. 15

Road—route numbering system (nationwide)—adopted—March 2

Science Association—woman elected to the
National Academy of Sciences—F. R.
Sabin—April 29

Ship—ship equipped with a masthead sea
anchorage for a dirigible—Newport News,
Va.—Aug. 15

Television—Telecast—telecast of an object
in motion—Bellevue, D.C.—June 13

Television Tube—miniature tube—patented
—H. W. Weinhart—Elizabeth, N.J.—Aug.
25

Theater—state-owned theater dedicated to
its own drama—Chapel Hill, N.C.—opened
—Nov. 23

Thermit—used to break up ice jams—Waddington, N.Y.—Feb. 24

1926

Air Mail Service—air mail contractor (domestic)—service—Pasco, Wash., and Elko,
Nev.—April 6

Arbitration—federal arbitration law—effective—Jan. 1

Aviation—Airplane Bombing—airplane bombing in the United States—Williamson
County, Ill.—Nov. 12

Aviation—Flights—North Pole flight—R. E.
Byrd—May 9

Aviation — Legislation — aviation legislation
(national) dealing with the operation of
civil aircraft—passed—May 20

Book Club—Book-of-the-Month Club—established—New York City—April

Book Course — instruction — Winter Park,
Fla.—Sept. 22

Catholic Church—Catholic church raised to
the dignity of a Basilica—Lackawanna,
N.Y.

Christmas Tree—official tree—General Grant
National Park, Calif.—May 1

Dance Course—collegiate credit—University
of Wisconsin—Madison, Wis.—approved
—Nov. 11

Electric Toaster — electric toaster — household-type—marketed—June

Ferryboat—ferryboat built exclusively for
motor vehicle transportation—service—
Nov. 8

Greyhound Racing Association — International Greyhound Racing Association—
formed—Miami, Fla.—March 3

Horse Race—harness horse race (Hambletonian) for three-year-olds — Syracuse,
N.Y.—Aug. 30

International Eucharistic Congress in America—Chicago, Ill.—June 20-24

Lawyer—Negro woman lawyer to practice
before the United States Supreme Court
—V. N. Anderson—admitted—Jan. 29

Lip Reading Tournament (national)—Philadelphia, Pa.—June 23

Medal—Distinguished Flying Cross—authorized—July 2

Medical Book — aviation medicine book —
Aviation Medicine — published — Baltimore,
Md.

Medical Instruction—plastic surgery professor — J. E. Sheehan — appointed — New
York City

Money—coin bearing the portrait of a living
President—Sesquicentennial half dollar

Monument—statue to commemorate literary
characters—erected—Hannibal, Mo.—May
27

Moving Picture—moving picture of the
planets—Mt. Hamilton, Calif.—Oct.

Moving Picture—talking picture—presented
—New York City—Aug. 5

Ordnance—semi-automatic rifle—patented—
J. C. Garand—Oct. 19

Photograph—photographs taken under the
sea in natural colors—Tortugas, Fla.—July
16

Prize Fight—prize fight to attract 100,000
spectators—Dempsey-Tunney fight—Philadelphia, Pa.—Sept. 23

Radio Facsimile Transmission—check sent
by radio across the Atlantic—received—
New York City—April 20

Radio Facsimile Transmission — drawing
sent by radio across the Atlantic—received
—New York City—May 2

Radio Facsimile Transmission—photograph
sent by radio across the Atlantic inaugurating commercial service—received—
New York City—April 30

Refrigerator—gas refrigerator (household)
—marketed—Evansville, Ind.

Road—cotton fabric used on a road—Newberry County, S.C.

Rocket—liquid fuel rocket flight—Auburn,
Mass.—March 16

Senator (U.S.)—senator unseated after a recount—S. W. Brookhart—April 12

Ship—rotor ship—docked—New York City
—May 9

Street Car—aluminum street car—operated
—Cleveland, Ohio—Dec. 2

Television—Telecast—weather map telecast
—Arlington, Va.—Aug. 18

Woman—American woman to swim the
English Channel—Gertrude Ederle—Aug.
6

1927

Automobile—automobile to exceed the speed of 200 miles an hour—Daytona Beach, Fla.—March 29

Automobile Robbery—armored commercial car hold-up—Pittsburgh, Pa.—March 11

Aviation—air control municipal board—created—San Diego, Calif—Dec. 19

Aviation—Airplane—airplane equipped with radio to cross the Atlantic Ocean—flight commenced—Roosevelt Field, N.Y.—June 29

Aviation—Airport—air passenger international station—opened—Key West, Fla.—Oct. 28

Aviation—Flights—airplane night scheduled passenger flight—April 1

Aviation — Flights (transatlantic) — transatlantic solo flight—C. A. Lindbergh—left—New York City—May 20

Aviation—Flights (transpacific)—California-Hawaii flight—left—Oakland, Calif.—June 28

Aviation—License—pilot's license granted to a woman by the U.S. Department of Commerce—P. F. Omlie—June 30

Aviation—License—pilot's license issued by the U.S. Department of Commerce—W. P. MacCracken—April 6

Balloon Flight—balloon flight to exceed an altitude of 40,000 feet—ascended—Scott Field, Ill.—H. C. Gray—May 4

Boat Race—international lifeboat race—New York City—Sept. 7

Brick — light-weight brick — developed — Madison, Wis.

Business History Chair—N. S. B. Gras—appointed — Harvard University — Cambridge, Mass.

Check Photographing Device—commercial manufacture undertaken—May 1

Electric Power Plant—hydroelectric power plant to use water pumped into a reservoir—Rocky River, Conn.

Electric Sign—electric sign flasher—patent—May 3

Engineering Society—woman elected to the American Society of Civil Engineers—Associate Member—Elsie Eaves—March 14

Flag—flag displayed from the right hand of the Statue of Liberty—in honor of an individual—June 13

Hotel—hotel to install radio reception—Hotel Statler—Boston, Mass.—May 10

Jewish College—Jewish college of liberal arts and sciences under Jewish auspices—Yeshiva College—New York City—cornerstone laid—May 1

King—king born in the United States—King Rama IX—Cambridge, Mass.—Dec. 5

Lecturer—lecturer of royal blood to speak for personal profit—Prince Vilhelm—arrived—New York City—Jan. 5

Medal — Distinguished Flying Cross — presented—C. A. Lindbergh—June 11

Monument—monument to the American flag—dedicated—Pittsburgh, Pa.—June 14

Moving Picture Theater—theater built especially for the rear projection of moving pictures—rear projection screen installed—New York City—March 11

Opera—opera broadcast over a national network from an American opera house—Chicago, Ill.—Jan. 21

Phonograph—phonograph with an automatic record-changer—introduced—Camden, N.J.

Postage Stamp—postage stamp on which was inscribed the name of a living American—C. A. Lindbergh—sold—June 18

Postal Service—mail box (drive-up)—installed—Houston, Tex.

Prohibition—prohibition bureau (federal)—authorized—March 3

Propaganda Course (college)—University of Chicago—Chicago, Ill.

Radio Broadcast—dinner broadcast round-the-world—Schenectady, N.Y.—April 20

Radio Commission (U.S.)—created—Feb. 23

Radio License—international broadcasting license—granted—Oct. 15

Radio Station—radio station operating a 100-kilowatt transmitter—Schenectady, N.Y.—Aug. 4

Radio Telephone—two-way radio conversation between a brakeman in a caboose of a moving freight train and an engineer in the cab of a locomotive—June 15

Railroad Car—Pullman train completely equipped with roller bearings—service began—May 21

Respirator (iron lung)—invented—Philip Drinker and L. A. Shaw

Submarine—streamlined submarine of the U.S. Navy—"Nautilus"—keel laid—Aug. 2

Symphony—symphonic work to call for an airplane propeller—*Ballet Mécanique*—produced—New York City—April 10

Telephone—transatlantic telephone service—(commercial)—Jan. 7

Television—Telecast—telecast of image and sound—April 7

Tunnel—twin-tube subaqueous vehicular tunnel—Holland Tunnel—opened—Nov. 13

Vitamin—synthetic vitamin—D—commercial manufacture—Evansville, Ind.

Wind Tunnel—propeller research tunnel—Langley Field, Va.—completed

Woman—woman secretary of a state senate—Fern Ale—Indiana—Jan. 6

1928

Air Mail Service—air mail service from ship to shore—Aug. 13

Army Armored Car Unit—organized

Autogiro—autogiro — flown — Philadelphia, Pa.—Dec. 19

Automobile Bus—coast to coast through bus line—New York City to Los Angeles, Calif.—Sept. 11

Aviation—airplane diesel engine—manufactured—Detroit, Mich.

Aviation—Airship—dirigible transfer of mail to a train—June 15

Aviation—Passenger—woman airplane passenger to cross the Atlantic ocean—Amelia Earhart—started—June 17

Aviation—Passenger—woman Zeppelin passenger (paying)—Clara Adams—started—Lakehurst, N.J.—Oct. 29

Baseball Player — baseball player to score more than 4,000 hits—Ty Cobb

Book—book on cornstalk paper—printed—New York City—June

Building—air-conditioned office building—San Antonio, Texas—opened—Jan. 1

Caterpillar Club—father and son Caterpillar Club members—P. F. Collins—jumped—Nov. 19

College — Negro university (Catholic) — Xavier University — degrees conferred—June 6

Cotton Picker (mechanical)—built—Weatherford, Texas

Diathermy Machine—constructed—Schenectady, N.Y.

Electric Lighting—electric lamp bulb frosted on the inside—patented—Marvin Pipkin—Oct. 16

Electric Sign—electric sign flasher—New York City—operated—Nov. 6

Fathometer — patented — H. G. Dorsey — April 24

Frog Jumping Jubilee—Angels Camp, Calif. —May 19-20

Jewish College—Jewish college of liberal arts and sciences under Jewish auspices—New York City—chartered—March 29

Judge—woman associate justice on the federal bench—G. R. Cline—appointed—May 4

Locomotive—diesel electric freight locomotive—operated—New York Central—June

Models' Training School—Chicago, Ill.—opened

Moving Picture—animated cartoon talking picture — *Steamboat Willie*—exhibited—New York City—Sept. 19

Moving Picture—talking picture of more than 6,000 feet—*The Lights of New York*—released—July 21

Niagara Falls—person to go over Niagara Falls in a rubber ball—Jean Lussier—July 4

Photography — film developing machine — (fully automatic) — patented — A. M. Josepho—New York City—Jan. 17

Physician—Capitol physician—G. W. Calver —Washington, D.C.—Dec. 8

Postal Service—international dog sled mail —started—Lewiston, Me.—Dec. 20

Railroad Car — rail detector car — tested—Beacon, N.Y.—June 13

Railroad Car—rail detector car in commercial service—Montpelier, Ohio—Nov. 15

Respirator (iron lung) — improved model used—Children's Hospital—Boston, Mass. —Oct. 12

Ship—cruise ship to circumnavigate the world—"Laconia"—returned to New York City—March 30

Ship—seatrain—built—Chester, Pa.

Skeet—college skeet tournament—Princeton, N.J.—Nov. 12

Squash Racquets Champion—woman to win the U.S.A. Women's Squash Racquets Singles championship—Greenwich, Conn. —Jan. 16-19

Telephone — telephone switchboard with Braille markings—New York City—April 1

Television—Telecast—outdoor scenes to be televised—New York City—July 12

Television—Telecast—play to be televised—*Queen's Messenger* — Schenectady, N.Y. — Sept. 11

Television—Telecast — presidential nomination notification ceremony to be televised —Aug. 22

Television—Telecast — programs regularly televised—Schenectady, N.Y.—May 11

Television — Telecast — puppet show to be televised—*Creative Genius*—Newark, N.J.—Aug. 21

Television — Telecast — standard broadcast station to transmit a television image—Coytesville. N.J.—Aug. 13

Television—Telecast — transoceanic television image—received—Hartsdale, N.Y.—Feb. 8

Television License — television license—issued—Washington, D.C.—Feb. 25

Vaccine—tuberculosis vaccine—(effective)—produced—W. H. Park—New York City

Vitamin—synthetic vitamin—marketed

Wedding—television wedding—Des Plaines, Ill.—Oct. 14

Woman—woman passport division chief—R. B. Shipley—assumed office—June 1

1929

Air Mail Service—air mail service between North and South America—May 14

Air Mail Service—airplane mail pick-up—demonstrated—Washington, D.C.—Oct. 1

Animals—dogs trained to guide the blind—"The Seeing Eye" incorporated—Jan. 9

Animals—reindeer—born—May 31

Automobile — automobile (new type gasoline-electric combination)—Aug. 30

Automobile Bus—bus night coach—in service—July

Aviation — air-rail passenger transcontinental service—inaugurated—June 14

Aviation — airplane commutation tickets — Newark-Boston—sold—May 1

Aviation—airplane "fly-it-yourself" system—Kansas City, Kan.—Sept. 15

Aviation—airplane high-speed tank to test airplanes—designed—Washington, D.C.

Aviation—airplane moving picture show—Oct. 8

Aviation—ambulance air service—organized —New York City—Oct. 21

Aviation—automatic pilot — tested — Trow Sebree—Oct. 8

Aviation—aviation trainer—sold—Binghamton, N.Y.

Aviation—Airport—airport hotel—opened—Oakland, Calif.—July 15

Aviation—Airship—dirigible made completely of metal—tested—Grosse Ile, Mich.

Aviation — Flights — airplane endurance flight exceeding 400 hours—St. Louis, Mo. —landed—July 30

Aviation — Flights — all blind flight — J. H. Doolittle—Sept. 24

Aviation—Flights—South Pole flight—R. E. Byrd—Nov. 28

Aviation — License — glider pilot's license (honorary)—issued—Nov. 7

Aviation — Passenger — dirigible passenger transfer to an airplane — Cleveland, Ohio —Aug. 29

Aviation — School — high school aviation course—New York City—Sept.

Births—child born in an airplane—Miami, Fla.—Oct. 28

Bridge—bridge of flowers—Shelburne and Buckland, Mass.

Brokerage — curb exchange — to transact more business than the stock exchange— New York City—June 15

Brokerage — ocean-going brokerage office— opened—Aug. 15

Cabinet of the United States—cabinet member convicted of a crime—A. B. Fall— Oct. 25

Codeball—played—Chicago, Ill.—May 11

Congress of the United States—Prime Minister of England to address the Congress of the United States—Ramsay MacDonald —Oct. 7

Congress (U.S.)—Senate — broadcast from the Senate chamber—Washington, D.C.— March 4

Congress (U.S.)—Senate—senate hearing in which women, other than members of Congress, were permitted on the floor — Washington, D.C.—Nov. 22

Congress (U.S.)—Senate—senatorial controversy in which no candidates were seated after a recount—Dec. 6

Congressman (U.S.) — Negro congressman from the North—O. S. De Priest—served —March 4

Farm Board (federal)—assembled—July 15

Fireworks Legislation—fireworks legislation (state)—enacted—Michigan—March 29

Fluorescent mineral exhibit — Philadelphia, Pa.—April 26

Golf Course—midget golf course—Chattanooga, Tenn.

Horse Race—horse to win a $100,000 purse in one race—Whichone—Belmont Park, Elmont, N.Y.—Sept. 14

Hospital — community hospital — Elk City, Okla.—organization meeting—Oct. 20

Humanist Society—established—Hollywood, Calif.—Jan. 13

Insurance—group hospital insurance plan — effected—Dallas, Tex.—Dec. 21

Konel—metal alloy—announced—Pittsburgh Pa.—Sept. 9

Medical Instruction—History of Medicine Department—inaugurated—Baltimore, Md. Oct. 18

Medical Periodical—allergy magazine—*Journal of Allergy*—published—St. Louis, Mo.— Nov.

Money—paper money of the present small size—issued—July 10

Moving Picture—talking picture entirely in color—*On with the Show*—exhibited—New York City—May 28

Moving Picture—talking picture in Esperanto—New York City—July 13

Moving Picture—talking picture taken outdoors (full length)—*In Old Arizona*—released—Jan. 20

Moving Picture Actor — moving picture actors to receive "Oscars"—May 16

Nudist Organization—American League for Physical Culture — New York City — organized—Dec. 5

Radio Telephone — radio telephone ship-to-shore commercial service — inaugurated— Dec. 8

Sash—wrought iron window sash installation—St. Louis, Mo.

Ship—tugboat (diesel electric)—operated— Warrior River, Ala.

Soilless Culture of Plants—hydroponic description—W. F. Gericke—published—December

Stock Quotation Board—automatic electric stock quotation board — installed — New York City—May 21

Street Car—street car with clear-vision windows—Pittsburgh, Pa.

Submarine "Lung"—tested—May 10

Tax—chain stores tax (state)—Indiana—enacted—March 16

Telegraph — telegraph ticker to operate at high speed—installed—New York City— Nov.

Television—Telecast—color television demonstration (public) — New York City — June 27

Theater—newsreel theater—Embassy—New York City—opened—Nov. 2

Vice President of the United States—Indian Vice President—Charles Curtis—March 4

Vice President of the United States—Vice President's widow to receive a pension— L. I. K. Marshall—authorized

Walk of Fame—originated—Winter Park, Fla.

Wind Tunnel—high-speed jet wind tunnel— Langley Field, Va.—completed—June 29

Woman—woman secretary to a Vice President of the United States—L. M. Williams—March 4

Zinc—underground mill for the separation of zinc and lead—Gilman, Colo.

1930

Animals—cow flown in an airplane — St. Louis, Mo.—Feb. 18

Astronomy—planet—found beyond Neptune —Pluto discovered—Feb. 18

Automobile Tractor—diesel engine tractor assembled—Columbus, Ind.

Aviation — air stewardess—first flight—May 15

Aviation—Airport — airport to receive an AI-A rating—Pontiac, Mich.—Feb. 11

Aviation — Airship — dirigible for private commercial operation—delivered—May 22

Aviation — Airship — dirigible landing and taking off from an ocean-going steamship —July 31

Aviation—Flights—airplane catapulted from a dirigible—May 20

Aviation — Flights — New York-Bermuda flight—April 1

Aviation—Flights—New York-Panama non-stop flight—Nov. 9

Aviation—Flights (transatlantic) — transatlantic non-stop flight from Europe to the United States—landed—Sept. 2

Aviation—Flights (transcontinental)—transcontinental airplane flight by a woman—Laura Ingalls—Oct. 5-9

Aviation—Flights (transcontinental)—transcontinental regularly scheduled through air service—began—Oct. 25

Aviation—License — glider pilot's license—issued by N.A.A.—Oct. 7

Births — child born on a vessel passing through the Panama Canal—June 2

Bobsled Run—of international specifications —North Elba, N.Y.—opened—Dec. 25

Bowler—woman bowler to obtain a perfect score—Emma Fahning — Buffalo, N.Y.—March 4

Brokerage—stock order from a Zeppelin—Aug. 8

Catholic Canonization of North Amercans—June 30

Check Photographing Device — patented — Feb. 25

Coal Mine—100 per cent mechanical operation—Wildwood, Pa.—opened

Colorscope—demonstrated—New York City —June 5

Degrees (academic and honorary)—Doctor of Military Science degree—conferred—J. J. Pershing—New York City—April 11

Diesel Engine — diesel engine automobile trip—completed—Jan. 6

Diesel Engine—diesel engine speed record (official)—Daytona Beach, Fla. — March 20

Diplomatic Service—chief executive-elect of a foreign country—in a diplomatic position in Washington, D.C.—became President of Colombia—Aug. 7

Electric Power Plant—hydroelectric power plant (county-owned) — operated — Crisp County, Ga.—Aug. 1

Element—element 87—francium—announced

Factory—windowless factory — erected — Fitchburg, Mass.

Farriers' Course in a College — Michigan State College—East Lansing, Mich.

Football Game—football game played in the United States to be broadcast in England —New Haven, Conn.—Nov. 22

Glider—glider flight indoors—St. Louis, Mo. —March 2

Glider—glider released from a dirigible—R. S. Barnaby—Lakehurst, N.J.—Jan. 31

Glider—glider towed across the continent—F. M. Hawks—landed—April 6

Glider—seaplane glider — Port Washington, L.I., N.Y.—March 15

Golf Champion—golf champion to hold the four highest golf titles—R. T. Jones—Philadelphia, Pa.—Sept. 27

Grain Stabilization Corporation—authorized —Feb. 10

Jockey—jockey to win seven races in one day—Joseph Sylvester—Ravenna, Ohio

Labor Department (U.S.)—native-born Secretary of Labor—W. N. Doak—appointed —Dec. 9

Lutheran Church — American Lutheran Church—organized—Toledo, Ohio — Aug. 11

Medical Clinic—flying medical clinic—left U.S. for Panama City, Panama—Jan.

Medical Congress—Mental Hygiene International Congress — Washington, D.C. — May 4

Medical "Rogues' Gallery" — started—New York City—Jan.

Milking Platform (rotating) — Plainsboro, N.J.—Nov. 13

Mortuary — cooperative plan—Toledo, Ohio —Sept. 15

Moving Picture — moving picture of an eclipse of the sun taken from an airplane —Honey Lake, Calif.—April 28

Museum—maritime museum — established—Newport News, Va.—June 2

Museum—museum to install refrigerated vaults—Berkeley, Calif.—March

Music Magazine—music magazine published in Braille—Jan.

Nobel Prize—Nobel Prize in literature — awarded—Sinclair Lewis

Photograph—photograph in natural colors taken in the air—published—Sept.

Photography—photographic flashlight lamps —patented—Sept. 23

Pinball Game—pinball game machine—manufactured—Chicago, Ill.

Planetarium—planetarium open to the public — Adler Planetarium — Chicago, Ill.—opened—May 10

Police—police bureau of criminal alien investigation—New York City—Dec. 23

President (U.S.)—President buried in the National Cemetery at Arlington, Va.—W. H. Taft—March 11

Radar—radar detection of airplanes—anacostia, D.C.—June 24

Radio Broadcast—round the world broadcast—Schenectady, N.Y.—June 30

Radio Broadcast — ship-at-sea broadcast from an ocean liner — "Europa"—March 25

Radio Broadcast — submarine (submerged) broadcast—New London, Conn.—Dec. 7

Radio Instruction—radio-advertising course —New York City—Sept. 29

Railroad Car—complete train of coal cars with roller bearings—in service—Jan.

Road — inter-American highway appropriation—March 26

Road—mosaic pavement—New Orleans, La. —completed—Feb. 4

Rubber—synthetic rubber (neoprene)—produced—April 10

Ship — air-conditioned ship — "Mariposa"—keel laid—Quincy, Mass.—May 17

Ship — rivetless cargo vessel — launched — Charleston, S.C.—Feb.

Street Car—street car tracks which were tieless, soundless, and shockless—New Orleans, La.—completed—Feb. 4

Submarine — streamlined submarine of the U.S. Navy—"Nautilus" — commissioned — Mare Island, Calif.—July 1

Submarine-Escape Training Tank — submarine-escape training tank—New London, Conn.—operated—Aug. 15

Sulfanilamide—sulfanilamide — produced — Wilmington, Del.

Television — Telecast — demonstration of home reception of television—New York City—Aug. 20

Television—Telecast—speaker to address an organization by television—P. I. Wold—Schenectady, N.Y.—April 1

Television—Telecast—two-way demonstration of television in a theater—April 9

Television—Telecast—weather map telecast to a transatlantic steamer—New York City —June 20

Theater—television theater demonstration—Schenectady, N.Y.—May 22

Tunnel—vehicular tunnel to a foreign country—Detroit, Mich.—opened—Nov. 3

Veterans' Bureau—Veterans' Administration —authorized—July 3

Woman—woman Presbyterian elder—S. E. Dickson—Milwaukee, Wis.—June 2

Woman—woman tax appeals board member —Annabel Matthews—served—Feb. 18

1931

Animals—cattle (Africander cattle)—arrived —New York City—Dec. 11

Anthropology Laboratory—Sante Fe, N.M. opened—Sept. 1

Autogiro—autogiro manufactured with a closed cabin—flown—Philadelphia, Pa.—Oct. 21

Autogiro—autogiro to land on the White House lawn—J. G. Ray—Washington, D.C.—April 22

Autogiro—autogiro to land packages on a moving ship—April 30

Autogiro—autogiro with side-by-side seating arrangement—tested—Philadelphia, Pa.—April 17

Autogiro—transcontinental autogiro flight—J. M. Miller—arrived—May 28

Automobile Tractor—diesel-powered tractor —manufactured—Peoria, Ill.

Aviation—airplane high-speed tank to test airplanes—completed—May

Aviation—Airplane—airplane (commercial) stabilized—built—New York City

Aviation—Flights (transpacific)—transpacific non-stop flight—landed—Wenatchee, Wash. —Oct. 5

Aviation—License—glider license awarded a woman—Maxine Dunlap—Feb. 5

Aviation—License—glider license Class "C" —R. S. Barnaby—Feb. 5

Aviation—Parachute—parachute jump from an autogiro—Caldwell, N.J.—Nov. 15

Aviation—Races—airplane race (of importance) in which both men and women were contestants—completed—Cleveland, Ohio—Aug. 31

Baha'i House of Worship—opened—Wilmette, Ill.—May 1

Baseball Player—woman baseball pitcher—Chattanooga, Tenn.—April 1

Cable (telegraph)—coaxial cable—patented—Dec. 8

Church—General Council of Congregational and Christian Churches—Seattle, Wash.—June 25

City Planning Instruction—Master in City Planning—degree conferred—June 18

Congress (U.S.)—House of Representatives —congressional committee headed by a woman — M. T. Norton—became chairman—Dec. 15

Elevator—dual elevator — installed — East Pittsburgh, Pa.

Glider—rocket glider flight—Atlantic City, N.J.—June 4

Hospital—community hospital — Elk City, Okla.—dedicated—Aug. 13

Medal—Air Mail Flyer's Medal of Honor—authorized—Feb. 14

Moving Picture—moving picture of a complete grand opera—*Pagliacci*—Feb. 20

Moving Picture Theater—theater built especially for the rear projection of moving pictures—New York City—opened—March 14

National Anthem—"Star-Spangled Banner" —officially designated—March 3

Nobel Prize—Nobel Peace Prize awarded an American woman—Jane Addams

Opera—opera broadcast in its entirety by the Metropolitan Opera Company—New York City—Dec. 25

Patent—plant patent—issued—H. F. Bosenberg—New Brunswick, N.J.—Aug. 18

Photoelectric Cell—photoelectric cell installed commercially—West Haven, Conn. —June 19

Photograph—infra-red photograph—Rochester, N.Y.—Oct. 7

Play (drama)—musical play to win a Pulitzer prize—*Of Thee I Sing*—opened—New York City—Dec. 26

Polo—polo game played outdoors at night—Baltimore, Md.—July 2

Price Regulation Law—resale price maintenance law (state)—California—enacted—May 8

Railroad—air-conditioned train—installed—B.&O. R.R.—May 24

Rattlesnake Meat—canned—Arcadia, Fla.

Razor—electric dry shaver—manufactured—Stamford, Conn.

Rubber—synthetic rubber (neoprene)—commercial production—Deepwater, N.J.

Senate (U.S.)—woman elected to the Senate H. O. W. Caraway—Arkansas—temporary appointment—Nov. 13

Ship — air-conditioned ship — "Mariposa" — launched—July 18

Ship—aircraft carrier—"Ranger"—keel laid —Newport News, Va.—Sept. 26

Soilless Culture of Plants—private soilless garden—Berkeley, Calif.

Teletype Service—teletype service (commercial)—begun—Nov. 20

Visiting Celebrities—absolute monarch—to visit the U.S.—King Prajadhipok of Siam —April 19

Water—heavy water—identification publicly announced—H. C. Urey—New Orleans, La.—Dec. 29

Wind Tunnel—full-scale wind tunnel for testing airplanes—Langley Field, Va.—operated—May 27

Woman—woman state budget commissioner —J. W. Wittich—Minnesota—March 16

1932

Autogiro—autogiro to loop the loop publicly —demonstrated—Cleveland, Ohio—August 27

Aviation—Airport—airport manager (woman)—appointed — Port Bucyrus, Ohio — May 28

Aviation—Flights—all-blind solo flight by the U.S. Army—Dayton, Ohio—May 7

Aviation—Flights (transatlantic) — transatlantic solo flight by a woman—A. E. Putnam—landed—May 21

Aviation—Flights (transatlantic) — transatlantic solo westward flight—J. A. Mollison —landed—Aug. 19

Aviation—Flights (transcontinental)—transcontinental non-stop flight by a woman—A. E. Putnam—Aug. 24

Bank—savings bank with a half-billion dollar deposit—New York City

Baseball Manager—baseball manager to win pennants in both leagues—J. V. McCarthy

Baseball Player—baseball player to hit four consecutive home runs in one game—Lou Gehrig—Philadelphia, Pa.—June 3

Bobsled Competition—four-man bob-team competition—Lake Placid, N.Y.—Feb. 14-15

Bobsled Competition—two-man bob-team competition—Lake Placid, N.Y.—Feb. 9-10

Cooperative—cooperative operated entirely by women—Bethesda, Md.

Diplomatic Service—American legation in which a woman assumed charge—F. E. Willis—Oct. 12

Dog Sled Race—dog sled race on an Olympic demonstration program—Lake Placid, N.Y.—Feb. 6-7

Electric Bridge Table—patented—Laurens Hammond—Chicago, Ill.—Nov. 29

Elevator—double-deck elevator — installed—New York City—Jan.

Federal Home Loan Bank Board—established—July 22

Gasoline Tax—gasoline tax (federal)—enacted—Washington, D.C.—June 6

Golf Champion—holes-in-one by a father and son—Washington, Ga.—Aug. 24

Greek College and Orphanage—dedicated—Gastonia, N.C.—Sept. 18

Home Owners' Loan Corporation—Federal Home Loan Bank Act—approved—July 22

Insurance—unemployment insurance act—by a state—enacted—Wisconsin—Jan. 28

Jewish College—Jewish college of liberal arts and sciences under Jewish auspices—B. A. degrees conferred—June 16

Light Beam Communication from a dirigible —Schenectady, N.Y.—May 19

Lightning (artificial)—demonstrated—Pittsfield, Mass.—June 10

Medal—National Geographic Society special gold medal—presented—A. E. Putnam—June 21

Medal—platinum medal—presented to H. C. Hoover—Dec. 1

Medical Clinic — ophthalmology clinic — opened—New York City—Sept.

Money—wooden money — issued — Tenino, Wash.—Feb.

Olympic Games—winter Olympic Games competition—Lake Placid, N.Y.—began—Feb. 4

Opera—opera house municipally owned—San Francisco, Calif.—opened—Oct. 15

Patent—fruit tree patent—issued—Louisiana, Mo.—Feb. 16

Photography—camera exposure meter—patented—W. N. Goodwin—Newark, N.J.—Feb. 21

Play (drama)—anti-vivisection play— *Woven Dreams* — presented — Philadelphia, Pa. — Oct. 4

Poet—Negro poet to be employed to teach creative writing—J. W. Johnson—Nashville, Tenn.—Jan.

President (U.S.)—President to invite the President-elect—to discuss governmental problems—H. C. Hoover—Nov. 12

Presidential Candidate—presidential candidate to fly to a political convention—F. D. Roosevelt—July 2

Presidential Candidate—presidential candidate to make a speech of acceptance at a nominating convention—F. D. Roosevelt—Chicago, Ill.—July 2

Pump—computer pump — marketed — Fort Wayne, Ind.—Nov. 1

Radio Broadcast—radio broadcast from a moving train, of a regular program on a national network—March 27

Radio Telephone—two-way conversation between a glider and the land—New York City—Aug. 12

Railroad Excursion — railroad excursion (mystery)—May 21

Reconstruction Finance Corporation—created —Jan. 22

Senator (U.S.)—woman elected to the Senate—H. O. W. Caraway—Jan. 12

Senator (U.S.)—woman senator to preside over the Senate—H. O. W. Caraway—May 9

Ship—gyro-stabilized vessel to cross the Atlantic Ocean—arrived—Dec. 7

Ski Meet (international)—Lake Placid, N.Y.—Feb. 10-13

Teletypesetter — teletypesetter — manufactured—Chicago, Ill.

Television—Telecast — political campaign telecast—New York City—Oct. 11

Television—Telecast—telecast images received in an airplane—Los Angeles, Calif.—May 21

Totalisator—used—Miami, Fla.—Jan. 14

Toyery—opened—New York City—Sept. 24

Vaccine—yellow fever vaccine for human immunization—announced—April 28

Women's Club—Chinese women's club incorporated—organized New York City—March 29

1933

Agricultural Adjustment Administration—approved—May 12

Autogiro—autogiro to tow a glider—Valley Stream, N.Y.—May 23

Aviation—airplane sleeping berths—used—Oct. 5

Aviation—Aviator—woman aviator to fly across the Atlantic Ocean east to west—A. J. Mollison—left Pendine, Wales—July 22

Aviation—Flights—airplane to exceed the speed of 300 miles per hour—J. R. Wedell—Glenview, Ill.—Sept. 4

Aviation—Flights — all-blind cross-country test—College Park, Md. to Newark, N.J.—March 21

Aviation—Flights (transatlantic) — transatlantic foreign squadron flight to the United States—arrived—Chicago, Ill.—July 15

Aviation—Flights (transcontinental)—transcontinental flight made by Negroes in their own plane—arrived—Los Angeles, Calif.—July 19

Aviation—Flights (world)—world solo airplane flight—returned—July 22

Bank Legislation—bank guaranty legislation—enacted—June 16

Baseball Player—baseball player to hit a home run in an All-Star game—Babe Ruth—July 6

Blood Bank—blood serum (human) (dried)—prepared—Dec. 21

Bridge—bridge with open mesh steel flooring—Seattle, Wash.—opened—April 7

Bridge—bridge with piers sunk in the open sea—San Francisco, Calif.—construction began—Jan. 5

Cabinet of the United States—father and son to occupy the same cabinet posts—H. A. Wallace (son)—served

Cabinet of the United States—full cabinet sworn in at the same time and place—Washington, D.C.—March 4

Cabinet of the United States—woman cabinet member—Frances Perkins—served—March 4

Canal—Great Lakes to the Gulf waterway—tow arrived—Chicago, Ill.—June 21

Central Statistical Board (U.S.)—created—July 27

Civil Works Administration (U.S.)—established—Nov. 9

Civilian Conservation Corps (U.S.)—authorized—March 31

College—"Unit Cost Plan"—adopted—Winter Park, Fla.—Sept.

Commercial Policy Executive Committee—organized—Nov. 21

Commodity Credit Corporation (U.S.)—created—Oct. 16

Congress (U.S.)—Senate—loud-speaker—installed

Constitutional Amendment (U.S.)—Constitutional amendment submitted to the states for repeal—Feb. 20

Consumers' Advisory Board (U.S.)—authorized—June 16

Consumers' Counsel (U.S.)—authorized—June 16

Cotton—cotton acreage reduction payment—made—July 28

Detergent—synthetic detergent—for home use—marketed—Oct. 10

Diplomatic Service—ambassador to the Union of Soviet Socialist Republics—W. C. Bullitt—Nov. 21

Diplomatic Service—woman diplomat to represent the United States in the capacity of a minister—R. B. Owen—appointed—April 12

Electric Home and Farm Authority, Inc.—authorized—Dec. 19

Electric Lighting—sodium vapor lamps—installed—Schenectady, N.Y.—June 13

Electrical Contract—by a city with the federal government—Tupelo, Mass.—signed—Nov. 11

Electrobasograph—exhibited publicly—Milwaukee, Wis.—June 12

Emergency Housing Corporation (U.S.)—authorized—Oct. 28

Employment Service—employment service (U.S.E.S.)—created—June 6

Enclave—municipal enclave of economic ground rent—Collierville, Tenn.—April 21

Farm Credit Administration (U.S.)—authorized—March 27

Federal Alcohol Control Administration—authorized—Dec. 4

Federal Deposit Insurance Corporation—created—June 16

Federal Emergency Relief Administration—created—May 12

Federal Savings and Loan Association—authorized—June 13

Federal Surplus Relief Corporation—incorporated—Oct. 4

Game Management Chair—established—University of Wisconsin—Madison, Wis.—Aug.

Glass—invisible glass installation—patent—May 30

Governor—governor granted almost dictatorial power—P. V. McNutt—Indiana—Feb.

Holiday—Maritime Day—established—May 20

Home Owners' Loan Corporation—authorized—June 13

Industrial Recovery Act—code under the National Industrial Recovery Act—effective—July 17

Industrial Recovery Act—compliance board under the National Industrial Recovery Act—established—Oct. 26

Industrial Recovery Act—conviction under a National Industrial Recovery Code—New York City—Dec. 2

Industrial Recovery Act—Industrial Recovery Act (national)—enacted—June 16

Industrial Recovery Act—postage stamps commemorating the National Recovery Act—sold—Washington, D.C.—Aug. 15

Industrial Recovery Act—state to place all its employees under the blanket code of the National Recovery Act Code—West Virginia—July 27

Industry—Industrial Advisory Board (federal)—authorized—June 16

Kidnapping—death penalty for kidnapping—mandated—Kansas City, Mo.—July 27

Labor—Labor Advisory Board (federal)—authorized—June 16

Labor—Labor Board (national)—authorized—Aug. 5

Labor Department (U.S.)—woman Secretary of Labor—Frances Perkins—March 4

Legislative Conference (interstate)—Washington, D.C.—Feb. 3

Legislator (state)—woman speaker of a state house of representatives—M. D. Craig—North Dakota—elected—Jan. 3

Liquor Stores (state)—established—Pennsylvania—Nov. 29

Medal—Air Mail Flyer's Medal of Honor—presentation—Dec. 13

Mint (U.S.)—woman Director of the Mint—N. T. Ross—May 3

Money—gold standard abrogation—enacted—June 5

Money—scrip money to be self-liquidating—issued—Franklin, Ind.—March 8

Moving Picture Theater—drive-in moving picture theater—Camden, N.J.—June 6

Narcotic—narcotic regulation (state)—adopted—Nevada—March 10

Narcotic—narcotic sanatorium (federal) for drug addicts—cornerstone laid—Lexington, Ky.—July 29

National Emergency Council (U.S.)—authorized—Nov. 17

National Planning Board (U.S.)—organized—July 30

Newspaper—newspaper printed on pinepulp paper—*Soperton News*—Soperton, Ga.—March 31

Opera—Negro prima donna of an opera company—Caterina Jarboro—New York City—July 22

Poorhouse (state)—replaced by a state home—Delaware—state home dedicated—Oct. 11

Presidential Electoral College—invited to an inauguration—March 4

Primer—typewriting primer—*Ted and Polly*—published—New York City

Public Works Administration (U.S.)—authorized—June 16

Radio Broadcast—drama broadcast from a regular stage—"Roses and Drums"—Sept. 24

Radio Broadcast—drama broadcast from a ship at sea—July 1

Radio Broadcast—radio police system (two-way three-way) — operated — Eastchester Township, N.Y.—July 10

Radio Facsimile Transmission — facsimile broadcast in ultra high frequencies—Milwaukee, Wis.—Dec. 19

Radio Telephone—military portable—Walkie-Talkie—built—Fort Monmouth, N.J.

Railroad—gasoline-driven, stainless steel, air-conditioned, pneumatic-tired, two-car train—delivered—Dallas, Texas—Nov. 4

Science Advisory Board—authorized—July 31

Ship—aircraft carrier—"Ranger"—launched—Feb. 25

Strike—modern sit-down strike — Austin, Minn.—Nov. 13

Surgical Operation—epileptic case treated by elevation of the skull cap—demonstrated—New York City—Nov. 2

Surgical Operation—lung removal — performed—St. Louis, Mo.—April 5

Surgical Operation—lung removal carried out according to pre-operative plans—Baltimore, Md.—July 24

Swimming Pool in the White House—formally accepted—June 2

Telegram—singing telegram — introduced — New York City—Feb. 10

Teletypesetter—teletypesetter installed in a school—Ithaca, N.Y.—July 5

Transportation Coordination—transportation coordination (federal)—June 16

Treasury Department (U.S.)—woman assistant treasurer of the United States—M. G. Bannister—appointed—July 26

Treaty Advisory Board—Inter-Departmental Advisory Board—established—July

Vaccine—poliomyelitis vaccine—produced—Maurice Brodie—New York City—Feb.

Wedding—transatlantic telephone wedding—Detroit, Mich.—Dec. 2

Windmill—windmill driven by rotor power—West Burlington, N.J.—tested—July

Woman—woman state liquor board member—J. R. Sheppard—New York—appointed—April 12

1934

Abrasive—boron carbide for commercial use—announced—Sept. 27

Archivist of the United States—appointed—Oct. 10

Autogiro—autogiro (wingless direct control) —flown—Philadelphia, Pa.—Dec. 9

Automobile Driving Course—in a high school—State College, Pa.—Feb. 17

Aviation—floating seaplane ramp (municipally owned)—New York City—launched Aug. 15

Aviation—Aviator—woman aviator to pilot an air-mail transport—Helen Richey— Dec. 31

Aviation—Flights — "airplane train" — New York City—Aug. 2

Aviation—Flights (transcontinental)—transcontinental commercial overnight transport service—inaugurated—Aug. 1

Aviation—Flights (transpacific)—Honolulu squadron flight—left San Francisco—Jan. 10

Bank—bank payments to depositors of a closed insured bank—East Peoria, Ill.— July 3

Bank—Export-Import Bank — Washington, D.C.—organized—Feb. 8

Bank Legislation—bank guaranty legislation —effective—Jan. 1

Bird Sanctuary—for wild birds—Drehersville, Pa.—Aug. 29

Birds—ptarmigan (Eskimo chicken)—hatched —Ithaca, N.Y.—July 24

Birds—snow goose—hatched—Denver, Colo.

Book—book bound with a pre-printed offset cloth—*Portraits and Prayers*—published— New York City

Camera—aerial camera (nine lens) for large-scale mapping—designed

Capital Punishment—capital punishment authorized by federal law—enacted—May 18

College—college to dispense with the system of credits, hours, points, grades, etc.— Olivet, Mich.—Oct. 1

Coral Reef Barrier—(copy)—of importance —installed—New York City—July

Electric Home and Farm Authority, Inc.— incorporated—Jan. 17

Electrical Contact—by a city with the federal government—effective—Feb. 7

Emergency Housing Corporation (U.S.)— Federal Housing Administration—created —June 27

Evangelical and Reformed Church—organized—Cleveland, Ohio—June 26

Factory—factories operated by the United States Government—in peacetime—Millville, Mass.—project started—June 4

Federal Communications Commission—Federal Communications Commission—created June 19

Federal Credit Union Act—authorized— June 26

Federal Deposit Insurance Corporation—effective—Jan. 1

Federal Savings and Loan Association—Federal Savings and Loan Insurance Corporation—created—June 27

Fingerprinting—community to fingerprint its citizens—Oskaloosa, Iowa—May 21

Free Port—legislation enacted—June 18

Holiday—Mother-in-Law Day—celebrated— Amarillo, Texas—March 5

Humanist Society—national assembly—New York City—Oct. 10-11

Indians—Indian tribal constitution—Indian Reorganization Act—June 18

Information Service (U.S.)—opened—March 15

Judge—woman associate justice of the Circuit Court of Appeals—F. E. Allen—sworn in—April 9

Labor—National Mediation Board—created —June 21

Legislature—unicameral legislature (state) —after the formation of the U.S.—Nebraska—Nov. 6

Liquor Stores (state) — Pennsylvania — opened—Jan. 2

Locomotive—streamlined steam locomotive —introduced—New York Central Lines— Dec. 14

Locomotive Headlight—talking headlight— installed—Schenectady—Nov. 6

Medal—National Geographic Society gold medal—A. M. Lindbergh—March 31

Moving Picture—moving picture of the sun —Pontiac, Mich.—June 19

National Union for Social Justice—founded —Royal Oak, Mich.—Nov.

Organ—pipeless organ—patented—Laurens Hammond—April 24

Periodical—sectarian magazine printed in rotogravure—*Catholic Missions*—New York City—Oct. 1

Physics—cyclotron—developed—E. O. Lawrence—Berkeley, Calif.

Physics—positron—recognized—C. D. Anderson—Pasadena, Calif.

Play (drama)—theatrical presentation sponsored by the federal government—*The Family Upstairs*—New York City—Jan. 30

Police—policewoman on the aerial force— Cora Sterling—Seattle, Wash.—appointed —July 13

Postage Stamp—imperforated ungummed sheet of postage stamps—issued—Feb. 10

President (U.S.)—President to broadcast from a foreign country—F. D. Roosevelt— Cartagena, Colombia—July 10

President (U.S.)—President to go through the Panama Canal while President—F. D. Roosevelt—July 11

President (U.S.)—President to visit Hawaii while President—F. D. Roosevelt—July 25

President (U.S.)—President to visit South America while President—F. D. Roosevelt —Cartagena, Colombia—July 10

Radio Broadcast—musical comedy broadcast—with specially composed music— "The Gibson Family"—Sept. 15

Radio Broadcast—radio broadcast heard in both the Arctic and the Antarctic regions —effected—Sept. 23

Railroad—streamlined all-steel diesel motor train—Nov. 11

Railroad—streamlined light-weight highspeed three-car passenger train—started— Omaha, Neb.—March 2

Railroad—streamlined Pullman train (six cars—left Los Angeles, Calif.—Oct. 22

Revenue Stamp printed by the Post Office Department—"Federal duck stamp"—sold —Aug. 14

Road—highway planning surveys nationwide)—authorized—June 18

Salvation Army—woman commander of the Salvation Army—Elizabeth Booth—elected —Sept. 3

Securities and Exchange Commission (U.S.) —created—June 6

Servite Church—Marian Congress—held— Portland, Ore.—Aug. 12-15

Ship—aircraft carrier—"Ranger"—formally delivered—June 4

Ship—streamlined steamship—"Arctees"— arrived—Boston, Mass.—May 14

Ski Tow (rope)—operated—Woodstock, Vt.—Jan. 28

Soilless Culture of Plants—commercial production of plants in water—Capitola, Calif. —Feb.

Symphony—symphony on a Negro folk theme—W. L. Dawson—Philadelphia, Pa. —Nov. 14

Talking Book—for the blind—issued—New York City—July

Telescope—telescope lens two hundred inches in diameter—molding began—Corning, N.Y.—Dec. 2

Theatrical School—theater and dramatic criticism course—to award a Ph.D. degree —Yale University—New Haven, Conn.— Sept. 24

Traffic Regulation Course—air traffic regulation course—endowed—Northfield, Vt.

Trust—cartel—effective—March 1

Washing Machine—washing machine for public use—installed—Fort Worth, Tex.— April 18

Woman—woman state committee chairman —M. T. Norton—New Jersey—May 22

X-Ray—X-ray photograph of the entire body taken in a one-second exposure— Rochester, N.Y.—July 1

Youth Hostel—opened—Northfield, Mass.— Dec. 27

1935

Air Mail Service—autogiro mail delivery direct to a post office—Philadelphia, Pa.— May 25

Air Mail Service—Pacific air mail flight— left San Francisco, Calif.—Nov. 22

Ambulance—incubator ambulance service— used—Chicago, Ill.—March 21

Artificial Heart—invented—New York City

Automobile—automobile to exceed the speed of 300 miles an hour—Sir Malcolm Campbell—Sept. 3

Automobile Legislation—federal motor carrier legislation—Interstate Commerce Act amendment—Aug. 9

Automobile Truck—automobile truck completely streamlined—introduced—Cleveland, Ohio—Sept. 4

Aviation—Airplane—transport airplane designed especially for trans-oceanic service —left San Francisco, Calif.—April 16

Aviation—Aviator—woman aviator to fly solo across the Pacific Ocean—A. E. Putnam—left Honolulu—Jan. 11

Aviation—Flights—airplane flight with an auto slung beneath the fuselage—New York City—Feb. 11

Aviation—Flights—sky-train international round-trip flight—left Key West, Fla.— May 14

Aviation—Flights (transcontinental)—transcontinental non-stop east-west flight by a woman—Laura Ingalls—left New York City—July 10

Aviation—Parachute—parachute tower for training parachute jumpers—built—Hightstown, N.J.—April

Balloon Flight—balloon flight to exceed an altitude of 70,000 feet—Rapid City, S.D.— Nov. 11

Bank—checkmaster plan—introduced—New York City—June 27

Baseball Game—baseball game at night by major league teams—Cincinnati, Ohio— May 24

Bridge—bridge with open mesh steel flooring—steel flooring patent—W. E. Irving— Feb. 12

Brokerage—woman stock exchange member (commodity exchange)—New York City —admitted—Sept. 3

Building—building with prefabricated walls of mosaic concrete—completed—Washington, D.C.—Feb.

Cans—beer in cans—placed on sale—Richmond, Va.—Jan. 24

Casein Fiber—produced—Washington, D.C. —Dec.

College—college classes to combat the influence of communism—instituted—Philadelphia, Pa.—Dec. 4

Crime Prevention and Detection—crime prevention commission for interstate cooperation—N.J.—March 12

Crime Prevention and Detection—national conference on crime—Trenton, N.J.—Oct. 11-12

Electric Power Plant—hydroelectric power plant to produce a million kilowatts— dedicated—Sept. 30

Eye—identification system—announced—Atlantic City, N.J.—July 7

Ferryboat—streamlined ferryboat—"Kalakala"—in service—July 4

Glass—invisible glass installation—New York City—Sept.

Labor—Labor Relations Act (national)—approved—July 5

Lie Detector—used in court—Portage, Wis. Feb. 2

Lightning Observatory—erected—Pittsfield, Mass.

Locomotive—streamlined electric engine— tested—Jan. 28

1936

Fuse — textile-wrapped detonating fuse— manufactured—Simsbury, Conn.

Gasoline—aviation gasoline—produced commercially—Paulsboro, N.J.—June 6

Hall of Fame—hall of fame (baseball)—election—Jan. 29

Insurance—group insurance policy for college students—Vassar College—Poughkeepsie, N.Y.—issued—Feb. 1

Isotope—radioactive isotope medicine—administered—Berkeley, Calif.—Dec. 24

Labor Law—forty-hour-week law (federal) —approved—June 30

Lucite (polymethyl methacrylate) production (commercial)—Wilmington, Del.—May 21

Medical Congress—cancer institute (convention)—Madison, Wisc.—Sept. 7-8

Microfilm—newspaper to microfilm its current issues—New York *Herald Tribune*—Jan. 1

National Union for Social Justice—national convention—Cleveland, Ohio—Aug. 14

Old Age Colony—Millville, N.J.—dedicated —Oct. 23

Olympic Games—American athlete to win four prizes in one year at the Olympic Games—Jesse Owens—Aug. 9

Olympic Games—Olympic Games basketball championship—Berlin, Germany—Aug. 14

Ordnance—semi-automatic rifle—adopted— U.S. Army—Jan. 9

Pension—pensions paid by the United States Government to workers in private industry —mailed—July 13

Periodical—magazine of the United States Government—*Federal Register*—issued— March 14

Physics — radioactive substance produced synthetically—radium E—Berkeley, Calif. —Feb. 4

Postage Stamp—sheet of postage stamps to contain more than one variety—sold—New York City—May 9

Presbyterian Church—Presbyterian Church of America—formed—Philadelphia, Pa.— June 11

Radio Station—radio station with 500,000-watt power—Pittsburgh, Pa.—June 12

School—school to have all classroom lights controlled by electric eyes—Hammondsport, N.Y.—Jan. 4

Soilless Culture of Plants—commercial hydroponicum built on the roof—Seattle, Wash.

Sponge—oxidized cellulose (sponge)—manufactured—W. O. Kenyon — Kingsport, Tenn.

Television—Telecast—high-definition telecast —New York City—June 29

Television—Telecast—telecast using coaxial cable—transmitted—June 10

Theater — state-owned theater — Seattle, Wash.—authorized—April 15

Traffic Regulation Course—teacher training course in "Training Traffic Safety"— State College, Pa.

Union Party—convention—Cleveland, Ohio —Aug. 15

Vice President of the United States—Vice President to leave the United States while the President was away—J. N. Garner—sailed—Seattle, Wash.—Oct. 16

Visiting Celebrities—pontiff—who had visited the U.S.—arrived as Papal Secretary of State—Oct. 8

Woman—woman coxswain of a men's collegiate varsity team—Sally Stearns—Winter Park, Fla.—May 27

Woman—woman to have her name placed on the cornerstone of a United States Government building—N. T. Ross—April

Women's Club—Chinese women's club incorporated—New York City—June 10

X-Ray—X-ray photograph showing the complete arterial circulation — completed— Rochester, N.Y.—July 16

1937

Animals—okapi—imported—New York City —Aug. 4

Aquarium—aquarium for monsters of the deep—ground broken—Marineland, Fla.— May 15

Army Insignia—shoulder sleeve insignia issued to an independent air unit—authorized—July 20

Automobile — automobile-airplane combination—tested—Santa Monica, Calif.—Feb. 20

Automobile — License — common carrier license—effective—Jan. 21

Automobile License Plates—permanent license plates—Connecticut—issued—March 1

Aviation—physiological research laboratory of the U.S. Army Air Corps—Dayton, Ohio—completed—Jan. 1

Bicycle Racer—woman bicycle champion of the National Amateur Bicycle Association —Doris Kopsky—Sept. 4

Blood Bank—blood bank—established—Chicago, Ill.—March 15

Business—Keedoozle store—opened—Memphis, Tenn.—May 15

Church—children's church—dedicated—Milton, Mass.—Nov. 14

Codification Board (United States)—created —June 19

Congress of the United States—congressional session in air-conditioned Senate and House chambers—Washington, D.C.— Nov. 15

Electric Generator—hydrogen-cooled turbine generator—Dayton, Ohio—operated—Oct. 12

Electric Sign—animated-cartoon electric sign —New York City—displayed—April 28

Free Port—Stapleton, N.Y.—opened—Feb. 1

Game Preserve—game preserve appropriation (federal)—enacted—Sept. 2

Holiday—Flag Day—legal holiday—Pennsylvania—established—June 14

Insurance—group hospital-medical cooperative—Group Health Association Inc.—opened—Nov. 1

1938

Euthanasia Society — formed — New York City—Jan. 14

Federal Crop Insurance Corporation—authorized—Feb. 16

Forest Service—aircraft owned by the Forest Service—operated—Oakland, Calif.—Aug. 17

Game Preserve—game preserve appropriation (federal)—approved—July 23

Glass Wool—machinery patented—Oct. 11

Library Chair—in a library school—New York City—endowed—April 4

Medical Legislation—law (state) requiring marriage license applicants to undergo medical tests—enacted—New York—April 12

Medical Legislation—law (state) requiring serological blood tests of pregnant women —enacted—New York—March 18

Merchant Marine Academy—Merchant Marine Cadet Corps (U.S.)—established—March 15

Newspaper — radio facsimile newspaper (daily) — *Post Dispatch* — St. Louis, Mo. — Dec. 7

Nylon—nylon bristle filament production for toothbrushes—Arlington, N.J.—Feb. 24

Post Office—airplane post office—dedicated —May 15—Washington, D.C.

Prize Fight—pugilist to hold three titles simultaneously—H. J. Armstrong—Aug. 17

Radar—passenger ship equipped with radar —"New York"—in service—Feb. 26

Radio Facsimile Transmission—radio facsimile broadcasting on the regular broadcast band—began—Des Moines, Iowa—Feb. 4

Radio Station—municipal school-owned ultra-high frequency radio station—Cleveland, Ohio—licensed—Nov. 21

Railroad Car—car with fluorescent lighting —in service—Sept. 2

Recreational Ranching Course—in a college — Laramie, Wyo. — degree conferred — June 6

Saint (Catholic)—who was a citizen—F. X. Cabrini—beatified—Nov. 13

Ship—seaplane tender designed and built for the U.S. Navy—keel laid—April 25

Skimobile—in operation—North Conway, N.H.—Dec. 27

Tape Recording—radio broadcast from a tape recording—New York City—Aug. 26

Television — electronic television system — patented—V. K. Zworykin—Dec. 20

Television—Telecast—book review to be televised—New York City—May 3

Television—Telecast—play to be televised with its original Broadway cast—*Susan and God*—New York City—June 7

Television—Telecast—unscheduled event to be televised—fire—New York City—Nov. 15

Tennis Player—lawn tennis champion to win four major titles—J. D. Budge—New York City—Sept. 24

Theater—television theater—licensed — Boston, Mass.—July 13

Toothbrush—with synthetic bristles—marketed

Voice Mechanism—voice mechanism capable of creating the complex sounds of speech —publicly exhibited—Philadelphia, Pa.—June 5

Woman—woman of American descent to become a queen—married—King Zog of Albania—April 27

1939

Air Mail Service—air mail transatlantic service—inaugurated—May 20

Air Mail Service—autogiro mail delivery regular service—Philadelphia, Pa.—July 6

Autogiro—autogiro rotary wing aircraft fellowship—student enrolled—New York City —Sept. 8

Automobile — air-conditioned automobile — Packard—exhibited—Chicago, Ill.—Nov. 4

Automobile—miniature automobile manufactured in the U.S.—Crosley—offered for sale—April 28

Aviation—Flights (transatlantic) — Atlantic Ocean scheduled air service—inaugurated —May 20

Aviation—Flights (transatlantic) — transatlantic regular commercial airplane service —began—June 28

Aviation—License—airplane instructor's license—Civil Aeronautics Authority—A. J. Banks—Sept. 27—issued to a woman— E. P. Kilgore—Oct. 13

Aviation—Passenger—woman flown in a U.S. Army plane from one country to another—left New York City—Dec. 7

Aviation—Passenger—woman to fly entirely around the world by commercial heavier-than-air plane—completed trip—June 19

Building—building devoted entirely to highway traffic—completed—Saugatuck, Conn. July 1

Catholic Beatification—Catholic beatification . of an American Indian—Rome, Italy— May 19

College—woman dean of a graduate school— elected—New York City—Jan. 4

Congress (U.S.)—House of Representatives —girl page—served—Washington, D.C.— Jan. 3

Degrees (academic and honorary)—Doctor of Philosophy in Accounting degree—Urbana, Ill.—conferred—June 12

Degrees (academic and honorary)—Master of Hebrew Literature degree awarded a woman—New York City—May 28

Electric Starting Gate (race track)—installed—Inglewood, Calif.—May 8

Federal Crop Insurance Corporation—indemnity payment—J. F. Biggs—Floydada, Tex.—April 14

Federal Security Agency—established—April 25

Federal Works Agency—established—July 1

Flea Laboratory—San Francisco, Calif.— opened—Jan. 1

Hall of Fame—hall of fame (baseball)—dedicated—June 12

Helicopter—helicopter (direct-lift aircraft)—successful—constructed—Stratford, Conn.

Impregnation — impregnation (artificial) — Cambridge, Mass.

Judge—woman judge (Negro)—J. M. Bolin—appointed—New York City—July 22

Locomotive—rack-rail diesel-electric locomotive—in service—July 16

Museum—museum devoted exclusively to paper-making—opened—Cambridge, Mass.—June 5

Nylon—nylon yarn manufacture (commercial)—Seaford, Del.—Dec. 15

Pinball Game—pinball legislation enacted by a major city prohibiting the machines—Atlanta, Ga.—effective—July 1

Postal Service—coin-operated mailbox—installed—New York City—May 17

President (U.S.)—President to hold an airplane pilot's license—D. D. Eisenhower

Public Buildings Administration—approved—April 3

Radar—battleship equipped with radar—"New York"—tested—Jan.

Radio Instruction—radio college course—offered—New York City

Railroad Car—train with fluorescent lights—in service—April 30

Snow Cruiser (automobile)—demonstrated—Chicago, Ill.—Oct. 22

Strike—anti-sit-down strike decision (federal)—Feb. 27

Suture—fiberglas sutures — used — R. P. Scholz—St. Louis, Mo.—July 19

Television—Telecast—baseball game (collegiate) televised—New York City—May 17

Television—Telecast—baseball games (major league) televised—New York City—Aug. 26

Television—Telecast—fashion show telecast—New York City—May 17

Television — Telecast — football game (collegiate) to be televised—New York City—Sept. 30

Television—Telecast—football game (professional) to be televised—Brooklyn, N.Y.—Oct. 22

Television—Telecast—king and queen to be televised—New York City—June 10

Television—Telecast—moving picture premiere festivities to be televised—New York City—Dec. 19

Television—Telecast—musical comedy telecast (one-hour)—New York City—July 25

Television—Telecast—operetta to be televised—New York City—June 20

Television—Telecast—play to be televised as a full-hour program—New York City—June 29

Television—Telecast—President to appear on television—F. D. Roosevelt—April 30

Television—Telecast—prize fight to be televised—New York City—June 1

Television — Telecast — telecast (long distance) received in an airplane—Oct. 17

Television—Telecast—telecast produced for a tri-city gathering—Schenectady, N.Y.—Dec. 8

Television—Telecast—telecast (public) over telephone wires—New York City—May 20

Television—Telecast—tennis tournament to be televised—Rye, N.Y.—Aug. 9

Visiting Celebrities—King and Queen of England—arrived—Niagara Falls, N.Y.—June 7

Vitamin—synthetic vitamin K—produced—Cambridge, Mass.—Aug. 1

Water Ski Association (national)—American Water Ski Association—formed—Trenton, N.J.—April

Water Ski Tournament (national)—Jones Beach State Park, N.Y.—June 22

Woman—woman presidential campaign co-manager—R. H. M. Simms—Dec. 2

1940

Air Defense Command (U.S.) — created — Feb. 26

Air Raid Shelter—air raid shelter—completed—Fleetwood, Pa.—Nov. 1

Aquatic Mammals — born in captivity — Marineland, Fla.—Feb. 14

Archival Administration—American University—Washington, D.C.—training program offered—Sept. 25

Army Officer—brigadier-general (Negro)—B. O. Davis—appointed—Oct. 25

Army Parachute Troops—training started—July 1

Art Course—industrial camouflage course—Kansas City, Mo.—Oct. 15

Automobile Tire—synthetic rubber tire—exhibited—Akron, Ohio—June 5

Aviation—Airplane—naval patrol bomber—launched like a ship—"Mars"—keel laid—Baltimore, Md.—Aug. 22

Aviation—Airplane—plastic bonded airplane—built—Van Nuys, Calif.—July

Aviation—Airport—airport (federally owned and operated)—cornerstone laid—Washington, D.C.—Sept. 28

Aviation—Flights—all blind distance flight by the U.S. Army—New York City to Langley Field, Va.—April 6

Aviation — Flights — stratoliner commercial flight—July 8

Aviation—License—Civil Aeronautics Administration—honorary license—to Orville Wright—Aug. 19

Betatron—betatron—placed in operation—Urbana, Ill.—July 15

Birds—quetzal bird—imported—Oct. 4

Bridge—pontoon bridge of reenforced concrete—Seattle, Wash.—dedicated—July 2

Conscription—peacetime conscription bill—passed—Sept. 14

Deaf—Transmission—visible and oral communication by the deaf over distance—New York City—Oct. 13

Dictionary—dictionary compiled by a woman—*Language of Fashion*—M. B. Picken—published—Feb. 2

Element—element 93—neptunium—discovery announced—June 8

Element—element 94 — plutonium — discovered

Flowers—tetraploid flowers—chemically produced—Philadelphia, Pa.—Jan. 29

Health Museum—Cleveland Health Museum —Cleveland, Ohio—opened—Nov. 12

Helicopter—helicopter (direct-lift aircraft)—successful flight—Stratford, Conn.—July 18

Immigration—alien registration—authorized —June 28

Microscope — electron microscope — demonstrated—Philadelphia, Pa.—April 20

Moving Picture Actor—Negro to win an "Oscar"—Hattie McDaniel — presentation —Feb. 29

Nylon—nylon hose—placed on sale—May 15

Photograph — cystoscopic photographs in color — publicly exhibited— Birmingham, Ala.—March 11-13

Pole Vaulter—pole vaulter to clear the bar at 15 feet—Cornelius Warmerdam—Berkeley, Calif.—April 13

Postage Stamp—Negro depicted on a U.S. postage stamp — B. T. Washington — issued—April 7

Postal Service—highway post office service —approved—July 11

President—President elected for a fourth term—F. D. Roosevelt—elected for third term

Radio Advertising—radio advertising contract for frequency modulation broadcasts —W2XOR—signed—Dec. 9

Radio Broadcast — all-Chinese commercial radio program — KSAN — San Francisco, Calif.—April 22

Ship—merchant ship formally blessed at a launching ceremony — "Rio Hudson" — Chester, Pa.—Nov. 27

Ship—navy vessel constructed as a mine layer—"Terror"—keel laid—Sept. 3

Ship—seaplane tender designed and built for the U.S. Navy — "Curtiss" — launched— Camden, N.J.—April 20

Supreme Court (U.S.)—members of a family admitted simultaneously to practice in the Supreme Court of the United States— Faust family—March 1

Television—Telecast—basketball game to be televised—New York City—Feb. 28

Television—Telecast—circus telecast — New York City—April 25

Television—Telecast—color television demonstration of high definition electronically scanned images — W2XAB—New York City—Sept. 3

Television—Telecast — hockey game to be televised—New York City—Feb. 25

Television — Telecast — opera telecast — W2XBS—New York City—March 10

Television—Telecast — political convention to be televised—Republican convention— Philadelphia, Pa.—June 24-29

Television—Telecast — religious services to be televised—New York City—March 24

Television—Telecast — sales meeting televised—New York City—Jan. 9

Television—Telecast — simulcast presented regularly by a sponsor—Lowell Thomas— New York City—Feb. 21

Television — Telecast — television network demonstration (long distance)—New York City to Schenectady, N.Y.—Feb. 1

Television—Telecast—track meet (intercollegiate) to be televised—W2XBS—New York City—March 2

Unitarian Society—woman moderator of the Unitarian Church—A. H. Reinhardt

Wedding—parachute wedding — New York City—Aug. 25

Woman — woman prize fight referee (licensed)—Belle Martell—April 30

1941

Army Language School—courses begun— San Francisco, Calif.—Nov. 1

Army Officer—air surgeon of the War Department—D. N. W. Grant—appointed— Oct. 24

Automobile—plastic automobile—manufactured—Dearborn, Mich.—Aug.

Aviation—Airplane—naval patrol bomber—launched like a ship—"Mars"—christened —Baltimore, Md.—Nov. 8

Aviation—Airplane—plastic bonded airplane —approved—April 5

Aviation—Airport—air terminal (not located at an airport)—opened—New York City— Jan. 27

Aviation—Airport—airport (federally owned and operated)—opened for traffic—Washington, D.C.—June 16

Aviation—Aviator—American ace in World War II—B. D. Wagner

Aviation—Aviator—woman test pilot—Alma Heflin—Nov. 12

Aviation—Flights—airplane flight (commercially scheduled) over a single route linking four continents—started—New York City—Feb. 1

Aviation—Flights (world)—world flight by a commercial airplane — started — San Francisco, Calif.—Dec. 2

Blackout—blackout lighting demonstration— Lynn, Mass.—May 14

Brokerage—woman to sell securities on the floor of the New York Curb Exchange— Linda Darnell—Nov. 19

Building—building known as a Quonset hut —built—Greenwich, R.I.—Sept.

Business—department store to hold a public art auction—New York City—Nov. 14

Civil Air Patrol (U.S.)—organized—Dec. 1

Congressman (U.S.)—congresswoman to vote twice against the entry of the United States into war—Jeannette Rankin—Dec. 8

Conscientious Objectors' Camp—opened— Relay, Md.—May 15

1942

Citizenship—citizenship granted to an alien on foreign soil—Dec. 4

Coast Guard (U.S.)—Coast Guard Women's Reserve—authorized—Nov. 23

Coast Guard (U.S.)—vice admiral in the Coast Guard—R. R. Waesche—appointed —March 24

Congress of the United States—reigning queen to address a joint session of Congress—Queen Wilhelmina of the Netherlands—Washington, D.C.—Aug. 6

Helicopter Flight—helicopter flight (cross country)—Stratford, Conn. to Dayton, Ohio—started—May 13

Insurance—health insurance law (state)—approved—Rhode Island—April 29

Liquid Heat—system operated—Summit, N.J. —Jan. 7

Medal—Distinguished Service Medal Merchant Marine)—authorized—April 11

Medal—Legion of Merit Medal—authorized —July 20

Medal—Legion of Merit Medal awarded to a foreign national—presentation—Miami Beach, Fla.—Nov. 7

Medal—Medal of Honor awarded in World War II—presented posthumously—A. R. Nininger—Feb. 10

Medal—Navy Cross awarded to a Coast Guard officer in World War II—M. D. Jester—June 4

Medal—Silver Star Army Medal awarded to a civilian—Vern Haugland—Oct. 3

Merchant Marine—Merchant Marine officer to hold the rank of rear admiral—A. B. Randall—commissioned—Feb. 1

Merchant Marine Academy—Merchant Marine Cadet Corps (U.S.)—first class started—Kings Point, N.Y.—Jan. 28

Naval Officer—Negro commissioned officer in the Naval Reserve—B. W. Robinson—commissioned—June 18

Naval Officer—woman naval inspector—Jean Hales—appointed—Aug. 24

Naval Officer—woman naval officer commissioned in the U.S. Naval Reserve— M. H. McAfee—inducted—Aug. 3

Navy "E" Award—Army-Navy "E" awards —presented—Aug. 10

Navy "E" Award—Navy "E" certificates of meritorious service presented to an institution of higher learning—University of Wisconsin—Madison, Wis.—June 1

Ordnance—bazooka rocket gun—produced— Bridgeport, Conn.—June 14

Postal Service—"V" mail film—dispatched— June 22

President (U.S.)—President to become a godfather to a member of the English royal family—F. D. Roosevelt—Aug. 4

President (U.S.)—President to broadcast in a foreign language—F. D. Roosevelt—Nov. 7

Price Regulation Law—price regulation law (federal)—enacted—Jan. 30

Railroad Car—President's car—built

Ship—merchant ship of the United States commanded by a Negro captain—"Booker T. Washington"—launched—Wilmington, Del.—Sept. 29

Ship—navy vessel constructed as a mine layer—"Terror"—commissioned—July 15

Submarine—submarine built on the Great Lakes—"Peto" — launched — Manitowoc, Wis.—April 30

World War II—American bombardier over German occupied territory—B. L. Bell— June 29

World War II—American bombing mission over enemy-occupied territory in Europe— July 4

World War II—American expeditionary force to land in Africa—June 17

World War II—American expeditionary force to land on the European continent— arrived—Ireland—Jan. 26

World War II—American general missing in action in World War II—C. L. Tinker —June 7

World War II—American general wounded in action in World War II—C. A. Pierce —Philippine Islands—Feb. 4

World War II—American offensive in the Pacific area — Guadalcanal, Solomon Islands—Aug. 7

World War II—American pilot to shoot down a German fighter plane—S. F. Junkin—Aug. 19

World War II—American to land on French soil—F. M. Koons—Aug. 19

World War II—bombing on continental American soil—Mount Emily, Ore.—Sept. 9

World War II—sea battle fought solely by air power—Coral Sea—May 4-8

1943

Arts and Letters Society—Negro member of the National Institute of Arts and Letters—W. E. B. Du Bois—elected—Dec. 22

Aviation—airplane human pick-up — Wilmington, Ohio—Sept. 5

Aviation—Airplane—rocket airplane (military)—tested as a glider—Oct. 2

Aviation—Aviator—Negro Army aviator to down an Axis airplane—Charles Hall— July 2

Cabinet of the United States—cabinet officer to address a joint session of Congress— Cordell Hull—Nov. 18

Congress of the United States—woman private citizen to address the House of Representatives and the Senate—Mme. Chiang Kai-shek—Feb. 18

Dental Corps (U.S. Army)—Army Dental Corps Major General—R. H. Mills—appointed—Oct. 7

Dental Corps (U.S. Navy)—admiral in the Dental Corps (U.S. Navy)—A. G. Lyle— appointed—March 13

Diplomatic Service—ambassador to Canada —Ray Atherton—nominated—Nov. 18

Television—Telecast—musical comedy (full-length) written especially for television—presented—New York City—Sept. 28

Wire Recorder—patented—Marvin Camras—Chicago, Ill.—June 13

Woman—woman secretary of a national political party—appointed—Feb. 29

1945

Army Officer—general to be consecrated a bishop—Oct. 11

Atomic Bomb—atomic bomb explosion—Alamogordo Air Base, N.M.—July 16

Atomic Bomb—atomic bomb explosion over enemy territory—Hiroshima, Japan—Aug. 6

Aviation—Airplane—gas turbine propeller-driven airplane—tested—Feb. 11

Aviation—Airplane—jet propelled landing on an aircraft carrier—Nov. 6

Bank—world bank—International Bank for Reconstruction and Development—formed

Bicycle Racer—woman bicycle champion of the National Amateur Bicycle Association to win twice—M. M. Dietz—Aug. 18-19

Business—"Food-O-Mat"—installed — Carlstadt, N.J.—May 24

Element—element 95—americium—announced—Nov. 16

Element—element 96—curium—announced—Nov. 16

Flag—President's flag—48 stars—authorized—Oct. 25

Horse Race—race track at which more than $5,000,000 was bet in one day—Belmont Park, Elmont, N.Y.—Sept. 22

Industrial and Labor Relations School—Ithaca, N.Y.—instruction began—Nov. 5

Judge—Negro judge of a Customs Court (U.S.)—I. C. Mollison—inducted—Nov. 3

Labor—labor anti-discrimination commission (state)—New York—appointed—July 1

Medal—Medal of Freedom—established—July 6

Medal—Medal of Freedom awarded to a woman—Anna Rosenberg—Oct. 29

Medal—Medal of Honor awarded to a conscientious objector—Oct. 12

Medal—Navy Unit Commendation decoration—awarded—"Helena"—March 11

Medal—presidential citation to an entire division—March 15

Medal—Silver Star Medal awarded to a civilian by the U.S. Navy in World War II—approved—March 3

Microfilm—microfilm machine to project enlarged images on ceilings—manufactured—Ann Arbor, Mich.

Naval Officer—naval nurses' corps (woman member)—to receive the Distinguished Service Medal—S. S. Dauser—Dec. 14

Naval Office—Negro nurse in the Navy Reserve Nurse Corps—P. M. Daley—sworn in—March 8

Opera—Negro to sing a white role with a white cast in an opera company—R. T. Duncan—New York City—Sept. 28

Radio Facsimile Transmission—color photo-radio news photograph transmitted by radio for publication—Aug. 3

Radio Telephone—two-way radio equipped bus—in service—Sept. 8

Railroad Car—car with an observation dome—July 23

School—school completely irradiated with germicidal lamps—Cato, N.Y.—lamps installed—Jan. 3

Television—Telecast—department store sales demonstrations (large-scale)—Gimbel Bros.—Philadelphia, Pa.—Oct. 24

Television—Telecast—stratovision flight test—Middle River, Md.—Dec. 9

Treaty—treaty (federal) signed by a woman—Charter of the United Nations—San Francisco, Calif.—V. C. Gildersleeve—June 26

United Nations Conference on International Organization—San Francisco, Calif.—April 25

Water—community to fluoridate its municipal water—Grand Rapids, Mich.—Jan. 25

Wedding—wedding in the United States Occupation Forces in Korea—Nov. 17

1946

Air Mail Service—helicopter airmail delivery—Bridgeport, Conn.—July 5

Air Mail Service—helicopter airmail experimental tests—Burbank, Calif.—July 8

Air Mail Service—jet propelled airplane to transport mail—June 22

Atomic Bomb—atomic bomb dropped from an airplane over water—Bikini Lagoon—June 30

Atomic Bomb—atomic bomb underwater explosion—Bikini Atoll—July 24

Atomic Energy Commission—Atomic Energy Commission—established—Aug. 1

Aviation—Airplane—bomber with the Flying Wing design—flight—June 25

Aviation—Airplane—jet airplane to land on a ship—July 21

Aviation—Airplane—rocket plane—tested—Dec. 8

Aviation—Flights (transcontinental)—transcontinental round-trip airplane flight within one day—June 12

Bank—"autobank" complete service—Chicago, Ill.—Nov. 12

Baseball Game—baseball playoff series—Oct. 1

Blanket—electronic blanket—manufactured—Petersburg, Va.—Oct. 9

College—college principally for war veterans—Plattsburg, N.Y.—Sept. 16

Computer—electronic computer—completed—Philadelphia, Pa.

Evangelical United Brethren Church—formed—Johnstown, Pa.—Nov. 16

Glider—glider commercial freight service—Philadelphia, Pa.—April 24

Glider—powered soaring glider commercially licensed—"Dragonfly"—licensed—Oct. 15

1947

Forest Fire—forest fire drenched by man-made rain—Concord, N.H.—Oct. 29

Glass—photosensitive glass — publicly announced—Corning, N.Y.—June 1

Golf Champion — woman golfer (American born) to win the British Women's Amateur Golf Tournament—B. D. Zaharias—June 12

Helicopter — helicopter to deliver material across a picket line—New Bedford, Mass.—March 9

Helicopter—helicopter with a fully servo-controlled intermeshing rotor — flown — Windsor Locks, Conn.

Helicopter—ram-jet helicopter — tested—St. Louis, Mo.—May 5

Insurance—insurance policy to be illustrated—issued—Chicago, Ill.—April 8

Isotope—radioactive isotopes exported—arrived—Canberra, Australia—Sept. 11

Lens—lens to provide zoom effects—demonstrated—New York City—April 16

Medal — Agriculture Department distinguished service gold medal — awarded — Nov. 12

Medical Clinic—cancer prevention clinic for children — opened—New York City—Jan. 3

Microcard—book on microcards—*The Scholar and the Future of the Research Library*

National Security Council—National Security Council — established — Washington, D.C.—July 26

Naval Officer—Negro commissioned officer in the regular U.S. Navy—John Lee—March 15

Navy—air squadron of jets (U.S. Navy)—Quonset Point, R.I.—July 23

News Correspondent—Negro news correspondent admitted to the House of Representatives and Senate press gallery—P. L. Prattis—accredited—Feb. 3

Nobel Prize—husband and wife in the United States to receive a joint Nobel Prize—C. F. and G. T. Cori—St. Louis, Mo.—award announced—Oct. 23

Postmaster — postmaster general appointed from the ranks—J. M. Donaldson—appointed—Nov. 24

Radar—radar for commercial and private planes—demonstrated—Culver City, Calif.—May 1

Rocket—ballistic missile—fired—May 22

Ship—air-conditioned naval ship—"Newport News"—launched—Newport News, Va.—March 6

Ship—ship from which a long-range rocket was launched—"Midway"—Sept. 6

Telephone—commercial telephone service on railroad trains for passengers — began — Aug. 15

Telephone — mobile telephone conversation with commercial equipment—between an airplane and a moving automobile—Oct. 9

Telephone — mobile transatlantic telephone conversation between two telephone-equipped automobiles—June 26

Telescope—telescope lens two hundred inches in diameter—completed—Oct. 3

Television—Telecast—baseball World Series game televised—New York City—Sept. 30

Television—Telecast — congressional opening session to be televised—Washington, D.C.—Jan. 3

Television—Telecast — Presidential address televised from the White House—H. S. Truman—Washington, D.C.—Oct. 5

Television — Telecast — surgical operation televised on a closed circuit—Baltimore, Md.—Feb. 27

Television — Telecast — underwater telecast from a submarine—New York City—April 10

Television Station — commercial television station west of the Mississippi River—Hollywood, Calif.—Jan. 22

War Veterans' Society—World War II veterans' society officially recognized by Congress—American Veterans of World War II—chartered—July 23

1948

Air Force Officer—Judge Advocate General of the U.S. Air Force—R. C. Harmon—nominated—Sept. 8

Air Mail Service—parcel post domestic air service—began—Sept. 1

Air Mail Service—parcel post international air service—to Europe—began—March 15

Army Auxiliary Corps—woman to become a member of the Women's Army Corps—V. M. Bates—sworn in—Washington, D.C.—July 8

Army Officer—woman army officer—sworn in—M. A. Hallaren—Dec. 3

Aureomycin — aureomycin chlortetracycline—produced—Pearl River, N.Y.

Aviation—Airplane—jet propelled fighter plane (four-engine)—tested—Muroc, Calif.—March 1

Aviation—Flights—airplane to exceed the speed of sound which was piloted by a civilian — H. H. Hoover — Edwards Air Force Base, Calif.—March 10

Aviation—Flights (transatlantic)—jet transatlantic flight west to east—from Mount Clemens, Mich.—July 20

Baseball Player—baseball player to win the Most Valuable Player Award three times—Stan Musial—third time

Betatron — mobile betatron — operated — White Oak, Md.—Nov. 12

Birth Registration—birth registration uniform system for the numbering of birth certificates—approved—Aug. 30

Building—house completely sunheated—occupied—Dover, Mass.—Dec. 24

Cantor—school for cantors — opened—Oct. 16

Church—woman moderator of the General Council of Congregational and Christian Churches—Helen Kenyon—elected—June 17

Economic Cooperation Administration — Economic Cooperation Administration—authorized—April 3

Belt Conveyor System—belt conveyor more than four miles long—installed

Bicycle Trip—bicycle rider to cross the continent in less than three weeks—Eugene McPherson—trip completed—New York City—Sept. 21

Birth Registration—birth registration uniform system for the numbering of birth certificates—began—Jan. 1

Congress (U.S.)—House of Representatives —congressional standing committee headed by a Negro—W. L. Dawson—appointed— Jan. 18

Court Martial—court martial trial at which enlisted men were allowed to sit as members of the court—convened—Heidelberg, Germany—Feb. 1

Court Martial—court martial trial in the United States at which enlisted men were allowed to sit as members of the court— convened—Fort Bragg, N.C.—Feb. 3

Degrees (academic and honorary)—honorary degree awarded a Negro woman—by a Southern white college—M. M. Bethune— Winter Park, Fla.—Feb. 21

Diplomatic Service—ambassador (woman)— Eugenie Anderson—nominated—Oct. 12

Diplomatic Service — woman ambassador from a foreign country—S. V. L. Pandit of India—received—May 12

Electric Lighting—street light of an automatic system—installed—New Milford, Conn.—March 2

Element—element 97—berkelium—identified

Fog Disposal Unit—accepted by test—Los Angeles, Calif.—March 29

Locomotive—gas turbine-electric locomotive —demonstrated—Erie, Pa.—June 16

Microfilm—magazine on microfilm offered to subscribers—*Newsweek*—New York City— June 1

Mosque—of importance—cornerstone laid— Washington, D.C.—Jan. 11

Moving Picture Actor—moving picture actor and son to receive "Oscars"—presented— March 24

Museum—museum devoted exclusively to atomic energy—opened—Oak Ridge, Tenn. —March 19

Naval Academy—Negro midshipman in the United States Naval Academy to graduate —W. A. Brown—June 3

Photograph — photograph of genes — announced—Los Angeles, Calif.—Jan. 7

Planetarium—planetarium owned by a university—opened—Chapel Hill, N.C.—May 10

Public Health—public health service (U.S.) assistant surgeon general (woman)— Lucile Petry—appointed—June 7

Radio Station—radio station owned and operated by Negroes—opened—Atlanta, Ga.—Oct. 3

Railroad Car—dining car (all-electric)— placed in service—March 9

Railroad Car—passenger car (ACF-Talgo)— tested—March 3

Rocket—rocket to reach outer space—fired —White Sands Proving Grounds, N.M.— Feb. 24

Ship—air-conditioned naval ship—"Newport News"—commissioned—Jan. 29

Submarine—leaping submarine—"Pickerel"— commissioned—Portsmouth, N.H.—April 4

Submarine—submarine jet propulsion device patent—Fritz Zwicky—Pasadena, Calif.— Feb. 15

Telescope—telescope lens two hundred inches in diameter—used—Feb. 1

Television—community television antenna system—used—Astoria, Ore.

Television—municipal television film unit— established—New York City—Feb. 15

Television—Telecast—medical intracity color telecast—Johns Hopkins—Hospital—Baltimore, Md.—Dec. 6-9

Television—Telecast — surgical operation televised on a closed circuit in color— presented—Atlantic City, N.J.—June 6

Television—Telecast—variety talent show series with an all-Negro cast—Chicago, Ill. —April 1

Television Station—ultra high frequency television station to operate on a regular daily basis—Bridgeport, Conn.—Dec. 29

Television Tube—rectangular television tube (practical)—announced — Toledo, Ohio — July 10

Treasury Department (U.S.)—woman treasurer of the United States—G. N. Clark— confirmed—June 9

Turbine—gas turbine to pump natural gas— installed—Wilmar, Ark.—May 13

Turbine—gas turbine used by an electrical utility company—in service—July 29

1950

Aviation—Aviator—aviator to down two enemy fighter airplanes in one day in Korea —R. E. Wayne—June 27

Aviation—Aviator—jet plane combat victor in the Korean War—R. J. Brown—Nov. 8

Aviation—Flights (transatlantic)—jet passenger international trip—April 18

Aviation—Flights (transatlantic)—jet transatlantic non-stop flight east to west—D. C. Schilling—Sept. 22

Baseball Manager—baseball manager to guide the same club on three different occasions—Bucky Harris

Basketball—basketball collegiate team to win the National Collegiate Athletic Association trophy—second win—March 28

Basketball—National Basketball Association Negro player—C. H. Cooper—played— Fort Wayne, Ind.—Nov. 1

Civil Defense Director—P. J. Larsen—assumed office—March 1

Coal—coal pipeline loops (experimental)— built—Library, Pa.—May 23

Diplomatic Service—Negro delegate to the United Nations from the United States— E. S. Sampson—appointed—Aug. 24

Kenaf Fiber—planting of commercial importance—Belle Glade, Fla.

Medal—Air Force Medal of Honor for action in the Korean War—L. J. Sebile—presented—Riverside, Calif.—Aug. 24

Medal—Medal of Honor awarded to a Marine in the Korean War—H. A. Commiskey—Aug. 1

Microscope—microscope for examining structure of materials—installed—Schenectady, N.Y.

Moving Picture—moving picture of the inside of a living heart (of a dog)—shown—New York City—Oct. 16

Rocket—air-to-air rocket—"Mighty Mouse" —placed in production

Rocket—rocket to intercept an airplane—White Sands Proving Grounds, N.M.—Nov. 27

Telephone—dial telephone service coast-to-coast without the aid of operators—commercially inaugurated—Nov. 10

Telephone—telephone company answering service—offered—Ohio Bell Telephone Co.

Teletypesetter—teletypesetter circuit operated by a news agency—established—Charlotte, N.C.—April 23

Television—college credit course in television —offered—Marquette University—Milwaukee, Wis.

Television—television eyewitness allowed to testify in a federal court—Sophie Eisenberg—New York City

Television—Telecast—atomic explosion telecast—Feb. 1

Television—Telecast—baseball games televised in color—New York City—Aug. 11

Television—Telecast—birth (human) to be televised (closed circuit)—Atlantic City, N.J.—June 14

Television—Telecast—color program (commercial)—New York City—June 25

Television—Telecast—color program (commercial) to be presented daily—began—June 26

Television—Telecast—football game televised in color on a network—Philadelphia, Pa.—Sept. 29

Television—Telecast—Jewish temple services (complete) to be televised—New York City—Nov. 4

Television—Telecast—opera written for television—*Amahl and the Night Visitors*—New York City—Dec. 24

Television — Telecast — pay television — "Phonovision"—demonstrated — Chicago, Ill.—Jan. 1

Television—Telecast—prize fight televised coast-to-coast—Chicago, Ill.—Oct. 3

Television—Telecast—sports event televised in color—Oceanport, N.J.—July 14

Television—Telecast—surgical operation televised on a coast-to-coast closed circuit in color—Los Angeles, Calif.—Dec. 7

Television—Telecast—telecast using coaxial cable—coast-to-coast transmission—Sept. 4

Television—Telecast—transcontinental telecast received on the east coast—from San Francisco, Calif.—Sept. 4

Television—Telecast—transcontinental telecast received on the west coast—from New York City—Sept. 23

Theater—municipally owned and operated summer theater-in-the-round — opened — Philadelphia, Pa.—June 30

Titanium—titanium plant fully self-contained and fully integrated—opened—Henderson, Nev.—June 1

Transistor — junction transistor — invention announced—Murray Hill, N.J.—July 5

Transistor — transistors produced commercially for a specific product — manufactured—Allentown, Pa.

Treason—execution for treason in peacetime —sentence given—April 5

Treaty—treaty signed by a woman ambassador—Eugenie Anderson—Oct. 1

Valeteria — displayed — Cleveland, Ohio — Sept. 19

X-ray—X-ray moving picture process by which pictures could be taken over a considerable period of time—demonstrated—Feb. 1

1952

Atomic Bomb — atomic fusion (thermonuclear) bomb—detonated—Marshall Islands —Oct. 31

Aviation—Airplane—turbine propeller light-airplane—flown—Wichita, Kan.—Nov. 5

Aviation—Flights—North Pole landing by an airplane at the geographic pole—May 3

Aviation—Flights (transpacific)—jet transpacific non-stop flight—July 29

Baseball Umpire—Negro umpire in organized baseball—E. L. Ashford—Feb. 20

Bread—frozen bread—marketed—Nov. 3

Bull Fight—woman bull fighter (professional)—Patricia McCormick—debut—Jan. 20

Chloromycetin—chloromycetin laboratory—opened—Holland, Mich.—March 13

Coal — coal hydrogenation chemicals pilot plant (large)—opened—Institute, W.Va.—May 8

Congressman (U.S.)—mother and son simultaneously elected to Congress—Nov. 4

Copyright—choreographic score copyrighted —Hanya Holm—New York City—Feb. 25

Deaf—Hearing Aid—transistorized hearing aid—offered for sale—Elmsford, N.Y.—Dec. 29

Element—element 99 — einsteinium—identified

Headlight — automatic headlight control — offered—Jan. 25

Helicopter Flight — helicopter transatlantic flight—began—July 15

Jockey — jockey (American-born) to win 3,000 races—Eddie Arcaro—Chicago, Ill. —June 24

Jockey—jockey to win 4,000 races—Johnny Longden—Inglewood, Calif.—May 15

Lens—plastic lens — for cataract patients—fitted—Philadelphia, Pa.—March 18

Microfilm—microfilms of U.S. Government publications or documents—offered

Catholic Priest—Catholic cardinal whose see was west of the Rockies—J. F. McInytre—elevated—Jan. 12

Catholic Seminarians (Negro) to be ordained to the priesthood by a Negro bishop—St. Louis, Miss.—June 29

Censorship—state board of censorship on literature—authorized—Feb. 19

Congressman (U.S.)—mother and son simultaneously elected to Congress—served—Jan. 3

Degrees (academic and honorary)—Bachelor of Sacred Music degree—conferred—New York City—June 10

Dictionary—Mongolian-English English-Mongolian dictionary—published

Diplomatic Service—woman career diplomat advanced to the rank of ambassador—F. E. Willis—sworn in—Aug. 10

Element—element 100—fermium—identified

Federal Security Agency—became Department of Health, Education and Welfare—April 11

Fraternity (Greek letter)—scholastic fraternity chapter established at a Negro university—Phi Beta Kappa—Fisk University—Nashville, Tenn.—April 4

Helicopter—helicopter fully operated by remote control — built — Windsor Locks, Conn.

Helicopter—helicopter passenger service—began—New York City—July 9

Hospital—hospital completely devoted to the study of the atom in the treatment of cancer—Argonne Cancer Research Hospital—Chicago, Ill.—opened—March 13

Hotel—hotel to establish a heliport—Fort Worth, Tex.—opened—May 20

Ice Skating Champion—American world figure skating champion—Tenley Albright—Feb. 15

Jockey—jockey to ride 400 winners in one year—Willie Shoemaker

Locomotive — gas turbine propane-fueled locomotive—in service—June 8

Medal—Navy-Marine Corps medal for heroism awarded to a woman—B. O. Barnwell—Aug. 7

Medal—Reserve Officers Association medal—presented—H. S. Truman—Jan. 15

Monument—national monument dedicated to a Negro—G. W. Carver monument—dedicated—July 14

Moving Picture—animated three-dimensional cartoon in Technicolor (modern)—*Melody*—premiere—May 28

Moving Picture—three-dimensional feature moving picture—*Bwana Devil*—shown—New York City—Feb. 18

Moving Picture—three-dimensional feature moving picture in color—*The House of Wax*—shown—New York City—April 10

Moving Picture—three-dimensional feature moving picture produced and released by a major company—*Man in the Dark*—premiere—New York City—April 8

Navy—Podiatry Section of the Navy—established—Nov. 3

Ordnance—atomic cannon — electronically fired—Frenchman Flat, Nev.—May 25

Pituitary Hormone—polypeptide hormone synthesized—announced

Railroad Car—observation cars (super dome)—in service—Jan. 1

Road—electronic highway system—demonstrated—Princeton, N.J.—June

Ship—woman to sail solo across the Atlantic Ocean — Ann Davidson — arrived — Miami, Fla.—Aug. 12

Siamese Twins—Siamese twins separated successfully by surgery—Sept. 17

Submarine—submarine powered by a liquid metal-cooled atomic reactor—"Seawolf"—laid down—Sept. 15

Television—Telecast—Catholic mass televised from a studio—Boston, Mass.—June 10

Television—Telecast—color and black-and-white telecast to be sponsored—presented—Dec. 24

Television—Telecast — color coast-to-coast live telecast—New York City—Nov. 3

Television—Telecast—color network telecast in compatible color—Boston, Mass.—June 7

Television—Telecast—color telecast by a local station—Philadelphia, Pa.—Dec. 18

Television—Telecast—color telecast on a closed circuit local station—Philadelphia, Pa.—Oct. 30

Television—Telecast—opera (major) televised in color—*Carmen*—New York City—Oct. 31

Television—Telecast—opera written for television on commission for a commercial sponsor—New York City—March 24

Television—Telecast—pay television presentation of a moving picture shown simultaneously in theaters—Palm Springs, Calif.—Nov. 28

Television—Telecast—telecast transmitted to Canada—from Buffalo, N.Y.—Jan. 20

Television Station—noncommercial educational television station—began programs—Houston, Tex.—May 25

Television Station—television stations to share the same time and frequency—Salinas and Monterey, Calif.—Sept. 11

Tour of the World—passenger to fly around the world on commercial airlines in less than 100 hours—H. C. Boren—arrived—New York City—June 25

Treason—execution for treason in peacetime—Ossining, N.Y.—June 19

Typesetting Machine—photographic type-composing machine — Photon — manufactured

Vice President of the United States—Vice President to preside at a National Security Council meeting—R. M. Nixon—July 14

1954

Air Force Academy (U.S.)—Air Force Academy—authorized—April 1

Air Force Officer—Brigadier General (Negro) in the Air Force—B. O. Davis—Oct. 27

Television Receiver—television receiver to permit two audiences to see and hear two different programs at the same time—demonstrated—Jan. 7

Tennis Match—intercollegiate court tennis match—New York City—May 4

Toll Collector (automatic)—operated—Garden State Parkway, N.J.—Nov. 19

Typesetting Machine—photo-engraving high-speed process for making half-tones—used—Quincy, Mass.—Feb. 26

War (French Indo-China)—American civilian pilot wounded in Indo-China—P. R. Holden—April 24

1955

Air Force Academy (U.S.)—Air Force Academy—temporary headquarters established—Denver, Colo.—July 11

Air Mail Service—helicopter air mail and express service to carry passengers—began—Nov. 22

Aquatic Mammals—dugong — arrived — San Francisco, Calif.—Nov. 16

Army Officer — Army Medical Specialist Corps male officer—Sheldon Saffren—commissioned—Dec. 30

Army Officer—male nurse—E. L. T. Lyon—sworn in—Oct. 6

Automobile—gas turbine automobile operated on city streets—Detroit, Mich.—April 19

Automobile—sun-powered automobile—demonstrated—Chicago, Ill.—Aug. 31

Automobile Legislation—automobile seat belt safety legislation—enacted—Illinois—June 27

Aviation—Airplane—jet magnesium airplane—flown—June 11

Aviation—Flights—airplane to exceed the speed of 800 miles an hour—H. A. Hanes—Palmdale, Calif.—Aug. 20

Aviation—Flights (transcontinental)—transcontinental round-trip solo flight between sunrise and sunset—J. M. Conroy—May 21

Aviation—Parachute—aviator to bail out of an airplane flying at supersonic speed—G. F. Smith—Feb. 26

Bank—bank to operate a window in a subway station for the convenience of subway riders—New York City—opened—Sept. 26

Battery—solar energy battery—shipment—June 1

Building—atom bomb-resistant federal building—dedicated—Washington, D.C. — May 23

Building—solar-heated and radiation-cooled house—used—Tucson, Ariz.—Jan. 15

Cabinet of the United States—cabinet session held at a place other than the seat of the United States Government—Gettysburg, Pa.—Nov. 22

Cantor—Jewish woman cantor—Betty Robbins — first service — Oceanside, N.Y. — Sept. 15

Cobra—king cobra snakes—born in captivity—New York City—July 4

Corporation—corporation to earn more than $1 billion in one year—Detroit, Mich.

Diamond—pilot plant for the actual production of man-made diamonds—production announced—Schenectady, N.Y.—Feb. 15

Drill—oil drill seagoing rig—placed in service—March 24

Electric Power Plant—electric power generated from atomic energy to be sold commercially—July 18

Electric Power Plant—electric power generated from atomic energy to illuminate an entire town—Arco, Idaho—July 17

Element—element 101 — mendelevium — announced—April 30

Helicopter—aerocycle—purchased by U.S. Army—Dec. 29

Horse—forest horse—imported

Jewish Congregation—Jewish mobile synagogue—operated—April 4

Medal—Medal of Honor awarded to a helicopter pilot—J. K. Koelsch—conferred posthumously—April 8

Medical Society—woman president of a major medical society—E. S. Moss—elected—Oct. 13

Methodist—Negro Methodist minister of an all-white congregation—S. P. Montgomery—Old Mystic, Conn.—Oct. 2

Opera—Negro singer of the Metropolitan Opera—Marian Anderson—appeared—New York City—Jan. 7

Periodical—magazine to contain a phonograph record—*Pageant*—New York City—Oct. 10

President (U.S.)—President to fly in a twin-engined airplane—D. D. Eisenhower—June 3

Radar—off-shore radar warning station—launched—May 20

Radio Broadcast—stereophonic sound program broadcast by separately owned stations—presented—Nov. 5

Railroad Car—passenger car (ACF-Talgo for use in the United States)—completed—April 22

School—air-conditioned public elementary school—opened—San Angelo, Tex.

Ship—guided missile cruiser — "Boston"—converted—Philadelphia, Pa.—Nov. 1

Ship—roll-on roll-off carrier—"Searoad"—in service—Sept. 1

Ship—speed-boat to exceed 200 miles an hour—D. M. Campbell—Nov. 16

State Department (U.S.)—woman Acting Assistant Secretary of State—Florence Kirlin—Sept. 3

Stove—electronic range for domestic use—introduced—New York City—Oct. 25

Submarine—submarine powered by a liquid metal-cooled atomic reactor—"Seawolf"—launched—Groton, Conn.—July 21

Surgical Operation—lung tumor operation in which the patient was under hypnosis—performed—Los Angeles, Calif.

Telephone—telephone conversation (commercial) using electricity generated by the sun's rays—Americus, Ga.—Oct. 4

Ship—ship outfitted for hurricane research —"Crawford"—in service—July 3

Space Cabin—D. F. Smith—24 hours within cabin

Stroboradiograph — announced — Schenectady, N.Y.—Aug. 14

Submarine—submerged circumnavigation of the earth—"Triton"—laid down—May 21

Surgical Operation—heart operation in which the elective cardiac arrest technique was employed—performed—Cleveland, Ohio

Surgical Operation—lobotomy (prefrontal) —performed—Washington, D.C.—Sept. 14

Taconite—taconite—large-scale commercial production—began—Sept. 13

Tape Recorder—magnetic tape recorder (commercial) of sound and picture—demonstrated—April 14

Tape Recording—video recording on magnetic tape televised coast to coast—presented—Oct. 23

Telephone—telephone conversation over the transoceanic telephone cable—Sept. 25

Television Station—all-color station to televise live local programs—Chicago, Ill.— April 15

Television Station—state-wide and state-supported educational television network—opened—Alabama—Aug. 9

1957

Air Force Academy (U.S.)—Air Force Academy woman officer—N. M. McCracken—Denver, Colo.—April 26

Air Force Officer—Air Force chairman of the Joint Chiefs of Staff—N. F. Twining —sworn in—Aug. 15

Atomic Reactor—military nuclear power plant—dedicated—Fort Belvoir, Va.—April 29

Atomic Reactor—sodium reactor (experimental)—operated—April 25

Aviation—Aviator—Negro airplane pilot on a scheduled passenger line—P. H. Young —began flights—Feb. 1

Aviation—Flights (world)—jet round-the-world non-stop flight—completed—Jan. 18

Balloon Flight—balloon flight to exceed an altitude of 100,000 feet—D. G. Simons—Crosby, Minn.—Aug. 19

Building—bronze and glass skyscraper—completed—New York City

Building—commercial building heated by the sun — completed — Albuquerque, N.M. — Aug. 1

Clock—electric watch—introduced—Lancaster, Pa.—Jan. 3

Coal—commercial coal pipeline—placed in operation—June 4

Court Martial—court martial trial of an officer for collaborating with his captors—decision sustained—Feb. 8

Cryotrons — publicly reported — Cambridge, Mass.—Feb. 6

Curling Championship (national) — held—Chicago, Ill.—March 28-30

Discovery—northwest passage—charted

Electric Power Plant—atomic electric generating station (full scale)—power generated—Shippingport, Pa.—Dec. 2

Element—element 102—nobelium—announced —July 9

Installment Sales Law—enacted—New York —April 17

Medal—recipient of the four highest decorations awarded by the United States—W. J. Donovan—fourth medal—April 4

Naval Officer—woman to preside as law officer—M. L. McDowell—appointed—Feb. 11

Newspaper—newspaper to insert an aluminum foil sheet—*Sentinel*—Milwaukee, Wis. —April 2

President (U.S.)—President to fly in a helicopter—D. D. Eisenhower—July 12

Rocket—intermediate range ballistic missile —fired—Cape Canaveral, Fla.—May 31

Rocket—rocket cone recovery—accomplished —Aug. 8

Rocket—rocket with an atomic warhead—fired—Yucca Flat, Nev.—July 19

Runner—runner (American) to run a mile in less than four minutes—Don Bowden—Stockton, Calif.—June 1

Ship—aircraft carrier (atomic powered)—"Enterprise"—ordered—Aug. 16

Ship—atomic-powered cruiser—"Long Beach" —keel laid—Dec. 2

Ship—guided missile destroyer—"Dewey"—keel laid—Bath, Me.—Aug. 10

Ship—ship to transport fresh orange juice in stainless steel tanks—"Tropicana"—arrived —New York City—Feb. 19

Steel—vacuum-cast steel — poured — Bethlehem, Pa.—July 2

Submarine — ballistic missile submarine — "George Washington"—laid down—Groton, Conn.—Nov. 7

Submarine—submarine expressly designed and built to fire guided missiles—"Grayback"—launched—Mare Island, Calif.—July 2

Submarine—submarine powered by a liquid metal-cooled atomic reactor—"Seawolf"—completed—March 30

Telephone—air-to-ground public telephone service—began—Sept. 15

Television—Telecast — stockholders' annual meeting televised on a closed circuit—April 16

Titanium—titanium mill—opened—Toronto, Ohio—Nov. 2

Typewriter—electric portable typewriter—placed on sale—Syracuse, N.Y.—Feb. 4

1958

Air Force Academy (U.S.)—Air Force Academy—first cadets received—Colorado Springs, Colo.—Aug. 29

Atomic Reactor—thorium-uranium reactor (privately owned)—Buchanan, N.Y.—construction began—Jan. 28

1959

Rocket—satellite to transmit photographs of the earth—launched—Cape Canaveral, Fla.—Aug. 7

Senator (U.S.)—senator of Asian ancestry—H. L. Fong—elected—July 29

Ship — atomic-powered cruiser — "Long Beach"—launched — Quincy, Mass.—July 14

Ship — atomic-powered merchant ship — "Savannah"—christened—Camden, N.J.—July 21

Ship—guided missile destroyer—"Dewey"—commissioned—Bath, Me.—Dec. 7

Ship—ship to fire a Polaris missile—"Observation Island"—missile launched—Aug. 27

State — noncontiguous overseas state — Hawaii—admitted to the Union—Aug. 21

State — noncontiguous state — Alaska—admitted to the Union—Jan. 3

Submarine — ballistic missile submarine — "George Washington"—launched — Groton, Conn.—June 9

Submarine—submarine with two nuclear reactors—"Triton"—commissioned—Nov. 10

Submarine—submerged circumnavigation of the earth—"Triton" commissioned—Nov. 10

Television—Telecast — auction of federal property to be televised—transmitted—Oct. 7

Television—Telecast — stockholders' meetings televised coast-to-coast simultaneously—transmitted—Oct. 29

Television—Telecast—telecast received from England—transmitted—June 18

1960

Atomic Reactor — atomic reactor for research and development—placed in operation—Richland, Wash.—Nov. 25

Atomic Reactor—atomic reactor system to be patented—J. W. Flora—Canoga Park, Calif.—May 17

Basketball—basketball player (professional) to score more than 15,000 points—Dolph Schayes—Philadelphia, Pa.—Jan. 12

Chlorophyll—chlorophyll "a"—synthesized—R. B. Woodward—Cambridge, Mass.—June 27

Clock—electronic wrist watch—placed on sale—New York City—Oct. 25

Computer—electronic computer to employ Thin-Film memory—announced—Dec. 9

Park—undersea park (federal)—Key Largo Coral Reef Preserve—established—March 15

Photograph—photograph bounced off a satellite—beamed — Cedar Rapids, Iowa—Aug. 18

Photograph—photograph bounced off the moon—received—Washington, D.C.—Jan. 28

Post Office—post office fully mechanized—opened—Providence, R.I.—Oct. 20

Presidential Candidate—presidential candidate debate series on television—Nixon-Kennedy debates

Rocket—communications satellite—launched—Cape Canaveral, Fla.—Aug. 12

Rocket—satellite placed in solar orbit—launched — Cape Canaveral, Fla.—March 11

Rocket—space capsule recovered from an orbiting satellite—located—Pacific Ocean—Aug. 11

Rocket—space capsule recovered in mid-air from an orbiting satellite — retrieved — Aug. 19

Ship—aircraft carrier (atomic powered)—"Enterprise"—launched — Newport News, Va.—Sept. 24

Submarine—atomic-powered turbine electric-drive submarine — "Tullibee"—launched—Groton, Conn.—April 27

Submarine—ballistic missile submarine—"George Washington"—on patrol duty—Nov. 15

Submarine—guided missile launched from a nuclear-powered submarine—"Halibut"—March 25

Submarine—submerged circumnavigation of the earth—"Triton"—completed—April 25

Submarine—submerged submarine to fire a Polaris missile—"George Washington"—July 20

Sulphur Mine (offshore)—Louisiana coast—sulphur obtained—March 14

Television — submarine with closed-circuit television—"Tullibee"—launched — Groton, Conn.—April 27

Television—Telecast—art auction televised on a coast-to-coast closed circuit—transmitted—April 27

Woman—woman to undergo astronaut tests—Jerrie Cobb—Albuquerque, N.M.—Feb. 15-21

1961

Air Raid Shelter—air raid community shelter—completed—Boise, Idaho—July 1

Astronauts—space flight by an American astronaut—Cape Canaveral, Fla.—A. B. Shepard—May 5

Aviation—Flights—airplane to exceed the speed of 4,000 miles an hour—Edwards Air Force Base, Calif.—Robert White—Nov. 9

Cabinet of the United States—cabinet member who was a brother of a President—R. F. Kennedy—took office—Jan. 21

Computer—mobile computer center—assignment undertaken—March 27

Deaf—Bone Bank—national temporal bone center for ear research—established—Chicago, Ill.

Element—element 103—lawrencium — produced—Berkeley, Calif.—Feb. 14

Judge—Negro judge of a District Court (U.S.)—J. B. Parsons—appointment confirmed—Aug. 30

Medal — National Aeronautics and Space Administration Distinguished Service Medal—presented—A. B. Shepard—Washington, D.C.—May 8

Naval Officer—commander of a combat ship who was a Negro—S. L. Gravely—assumed command—Jan. 31

Index by Days of the Month

To obtain a complete account of the various items, the reader should consult the main body of the text. The **boldface** type shows the alphabetical heading under which each item may be found. If an item appears in the text under a general heading, the specific heading is noted below after the general heading.

1937 Aviation—physiological research laboratory of the U.S. Army Air Corps —completed—Dayton, Ohio

1939 Flea Laboratory—opened—San Francisco, Calif.

1948 Moving Picture—newsreel in color— taken—Pasadena, Calif.

1948 Television—Telecast—moving picture premiere performance to be televised (feature-length foreign film) — New York City

1949 Birth Registration—birth registration uniform system for the numbering of birth certificates—system inaugurated

1951 Television—Telecast — pay television — "Phonovision" demonstrated—Chicago, Ill.

1953 Railroad Car—observation cars (super dome)—in service

1954 Immigration—refugee to arrive under the Refugee Relief Act of 1953— Stamatoula Roumanis

1954 Television—Mobile Unit—mobile television units (color)—WNBT, New York City

1954 Television—Telecast — color coast-to-coast telecast from the west coast— Tournament of Roses — Pasadena, Calif.

JANUARY 2

1777 Army Officer—chaplain killed in action—John Rosbrugh—Trenton, N.J.

1797 Business Publication — *New York Prices Current*—earliest known copy

1828 News Correspondent — Washington correspondent of importance—J. G. Bennett—first articles

1842 Bridge — wire suspension bridge for general traffic — opened—Fairmount, Pa.

1867 Bank — national bank failure — First National Bank of Attica, N.Y.—receivership terminated

1893 Postage Stamp—commemorative postage stamps—issued

1893 Postage Stamp — postage stamps to picture a woman—on sale

1908 Tunnel — freight delivery tunnel system—completed—Chicago, Ill.

1910 High School — junior high schools — opened—Berkeley, Calif.

1914 Community Trust — established — Cleveland, Ohio

1918 Army Insignia—wound chevron—authorized

1921 Radio Broadcast — religious service broadcast—Pittsburgh, Pa.

1922 Blind—correspondence school for the blind to offer instruction in the Braille system—incorporated—Winnetka, Ill.

1925 Psychological Society — psychological society (national organization)—American Psychological Association — incorporated

1934 Liquor Stores (state) — opened — Pennsylvania

1936 Electron Tube—described—St. Louis, Mo.

JANUARY 3

1825 Engineering College—engineering college—Rensselaer School—Troy, N.Y. —opened

1831 Building and Loan Association—Oxford Provident Building Association —organized—Frankford, Pa.

1871 Oleomargarine Patent—oleomargarine patent—H. W. Bradley

1872 Patent List—*Official Gazette of the U.S. Patent Office*—issued—Washington, D.C.

1876 Kindergarten — free kindergarten— opened—Florence, Mass.

1888 Straws (artificial) for drinking—patented—M. C. Stone

1890 Dairy School—collegiate rank — University of Wisconsin—Madison, Wis. —opened

1905 Newspaper—Greek newspaper—*Atlantis* —New York City—daily

1911 Bank — postal savings bank — banks opened

1918 Employment Service — employment service (U.S.)—inaugurated

1921 Hospital—leper hospital — purchased by the U.S.—Carville, La.

1933 Legislator (state)—woman speaker of a state House of Representatives—M. D. Craig—elected—North Dakota

1939 Congress (U.S.)—House of Representatives—girl page—served

1945 School — school completely irradiated with germicidal lamps—lamps installed —Cato, N.Y.

1947 Medical Clinic — cancer prevention clinic for children — opened — New York City

1947 Television—Telecast — congressional opening session to be televised — Washington, D.C.

1948 Moving Picture—newsreel in color— released

1953 Congressman (U.S.)—mother and son simultaneously elected to Congress— F. P. Bolton and O. P. Bolton— served

1957 Clock—electric watch — introduced — Lancaster, Pa.

1957 Congressman (U.S.) — Congressman of Asian ancestry—D. S. Saund— sworn in

1959 State—noncontiguous state—Alaska— admitted

1960 Diesel Engine—diesel engine automobile trip—started—Indianapolis, Ind.

JANUARY 4

1827 Governor—brothers to serve simultaneously as governors of their respective states — Levi Lincoln and Enoch Lincoln

1831 Locomotive — locomotive bid—advertised—Baltimore, Md.

1850 Ice Skating Club—ice skating club organized—Philadelphia, Pa.

1869 Blind—school for the Negro blind — opened—Raleigh, N.C.

1885 **Surgical Operation**—appendicitis operation (appendectomy)—W. W. Grant —Davenport, Iowa

1887 **Bicycle Trip**—bicycle trip around the world — completed — San Francisco, Calif.

1889 **Historical Society** — historical society (general)—American Historical Association—first report published

1896 **Actors' Union**—Actors' National Protective Union—chartered

1915 **Governor**—Jewish governor — elected for a full term—served—Moses Alexander—Idaho

1923 **Radio Broadcast** — chain broadcast— with repeater points — WEAF and WNAC—New York City and Boston

1936 **School**—school to have all classroom lights controlled by electric eyes — operated—Hammondsport, N.Y.

1939 **College**—woman dean of a graduate school—Frieda Wunderlich—elected— New York City

1944 **State Department (U.S.)**—State Department (U.S.) Negro official—R. J. Bunche—appointed

1953 **Carpeting**—carpeting of tufted plastic —offered for sale—La Fayette, Ga.

1962 **Subway**—train to run automatically without conductors or motormen— New York City

JANUARY 5

1800 **Swedenborgian or New Church** — Swedenborgian or New Church Temple—service—Baltimore, Md.

1863 **Normal School**—woman principal of a normal school—A. C. Brackett—St. Louis, Mo.

1885 **Railroad**—"piggy-back" railroad operation—Long Island Rail Road Company

1887 **Library Training (systematic)** — instruction—New York City

1895 **Enclave**—enclave — land purchased — Fairhope, Ala.

1903 **Cable**—cable across the Pacific Ocean —from San Francisco, Calif.—opened for public use

1925 **Governor**—woman governor of a state —N. T. Ross—assumed office—Wyoming

1927 **Lecturer**—lecturer of royal blood to speak for personal profit—Prince Vilhelm—arrived

1933 **Bridge**—bridge with piers sunk in the open sea — construction started—San Francisco, Calif.

1937 **Legislature** — unicameral legislature (state)—opened—Nebraska

1944 **Newspaper** — transoceanic newspaper —*Daily Mail*—issued

1948 **Moving Picture**—newsreel in color — exhibited

JANUARY 6

1639 **Agriculture**—crop surplus destruction —ordered—Virginia

1844 **Iron**—iron patent—S. Broadmeadow

1857 **Zinc**—zinc patent—S. Wetherill

1870 **Labor Union**—labor organization to admit workmen other than craft workmen—regular officers elected

1885 **Legislator (state)**—Negro legislator (state)—representing white constituency—B. W. Arnett—served—Ohio

1896 **Bicycle Race**—women's six-day bicycle race—New York City

1898 **Telephone** — telephone message from a submarine under water — Simon Lake—New York City

1927 **Woman**—woman secretary of a state senate—Fern Ale—served—Indiana

1930 **Diesel Engine**—diesel engine automobile trip—completed—New York City

1942 **Aviation — Flights (world)** — world flight by a commercial airplane — "Pacific Clipper"—returned to New York City

JANUARY 7

1751 **Play (drama)**—benefit performance— New York City

1782 **Bank**—bank chartered by Congress— Bank of North America—Philadelphia, Pa.—opened for business

1784 **Seed Business** — organized — David Landreth—Philadelphia, Pa.

1784 **War Veterans' Society** — Society of the Cincinnati—Society in France — organized

1789 **Congress of the United States**—joint meeting of the Senate and the House of Representatives—election meeting

1817 **Bank**—Bank of the United States — second bank opened — Philadelphia, Pa.

1830 **Railroad** — railroad for commercial transportation of passengers and freight — Baltimore, Md. — passenger revenue obtained

1890 **Ship** — navy vessel equipped to lay mines—"Baltimore"—commissioned

1894 **Copyright**—motion picture film copyrighted—Frank Ott

1897 **Handball** — national championship match for amateurs—Jersey City, N.J.

1904 **Radio Distress Signal**—CQD signal— established

1911 **Aviation — Airplane Bombing** — airplane bombing experiment with explosives—San Francisco, Calif.

1913 **Gasoline** — cracking process used to obtain gasoline from crude petroleum —W. M. Burton—Chicago, Ill.

1914 **Public Defender's Office**—W. J. Wood —assumed duties

1914 **Ship**—steamboat to pass through the Panama Canal—craneboat—"Alex. La Valley"

1924 **Postage Stamp** — precanceled stamps printed on rotary presses — one-cent precanceled stamps issued

1927 **Telephone** — transatlantic telephone service—commercial—New York City and London, **England**

1942 **Liquid Heat**—used—Summit, N.J.

1949 **Photograph** — photograph of genes—Los Angeles, Calif.—announced

1954 **Television Receiver** — television receiver to permit two audiences to see and hear two different programs at the same time

1955 **Opera**—Negro singer of the Metropolitan Opera — Marian Anderson—New York City

JANUARY 8

1675 **Corporation**—commercial corporation—New York City—incorporated

1777 **Price Regulation Law**—price regulation law (colonial)—effective—Rhode Island

1783 **Copyright Law**—copyright law (state)—enacted—Connecticut

1833 **Music Instruction**—musical pedagogy school—Boston Academy of Music—founded—Boston, Mass.

1838 **Telegraph** — telegraphic communication system in which dots and dashes represented letters — message transmitted

1853 **Monument**—bronze equestrian statue—unveiled—Washington, D.C.

1856 **Borax**—discovered — Tuscan Springs, Calif.

1867 **College** — Negro university to establish undergraduate, graduate and professional schools — C. B. Boynton elected president

1884 **Leather** — chrome tanning process — patented—Augustus Schultz

1889 **Tabulating Machine**—patented—Herman Hollerith

1901 **Bowling Tournament**—bowling tournament sponsored by the American Bowling Congress—Chicago, Ill.

1918 **Prohibition** — prohibition amendment to the Constitution—first state to ratify—Mississippi

1923 **Automobile Trucking Service** — automobile trucking service—by railroad motor coaches — inaugurated—Maryland

1925 **Court**—state supreme court composed entirely of women—appointed—Texas

1935 **Spectrophotometer**—patented — A. C. Hardy—Wellesley, Mass.

JANUARY 9

1793 **Balloon Flight**—balloon flight in which a presidential order was carried—ascended—Philadelphia, Pa.

1838 **Patent**—patent re-issue—Julius Hatch—Great Bend, Pa.

1844 **Coast Guard (U.S.)** — Coast Guard commandant — A. V. Fraser — report submitted

1861 **Civil War**—act that marked the inauguration of the War of 1861-1865—"Star of the West" fired upon

1872 **Congress (U.S.)—House of Representatives**—foreign clergyman to open the House of Representatives with prayer—Abraham de Sola

1894 **Telephone** — common battery (non-multiple) switchboard — operated — Lexington, Mass.

1929 **Animals**—dogs trained to guide the blind — "Seeing Eye" — Nashville, Tenn.—incorporated

1936 **Ordnance** — semi-automatic rifle — adopted—U.S. Army

1940 **Television—Telecast** — sales meeting televised—New York City

JANUARY 10

1894 **Nurses' Society**—society for superintendents of nursing schools—American Society of Superintendents of Training Schools for Nurses—national convention—New York City

1910 **Aviation — Expositions and Meets** — aviation meet—Los Angeles, Calif.

1911 **Photograph**—photograph from an airplane—San Diego, Calif.

1934 **Aviation — Flights (transpacific)** — Honolulu squadron flight — left San Francisco, Calif.

1943 **President**—President to visit a foreign country in wartime—F. D. Roosevelt—sailed from Miami to Trinidad

1944 **Electric Power Plant**—mobile electric power plant—delivered—Philadelphia, Pa.

1946 **Radar**—radar signal to the moon—beamed—Belmar, N.J.

1951 **Aviation—Flights**—jet passenger trip—Chicago-New York City

1955 **Radar**—off-shore radar warning station—keel laid

JANUARY 11

1759 **Insurance**—life insurance company — Philadelphia, Pa.—incorporated

1770 **Rhubarb** — shipped to the United States from London, England

1860 **Insurance**—insurance department (state) superintendent appointed

1873 **Livestock-Market Paper**—published—Chicago, Ill.

1875 **Nautical School** — nautical municipal school—opened—New York City

1897 **Senate (state)**—woman state senator—served—Utah—M. H. Cannon

1913 **Automobile**—sedan type automobile—officially shown—New York City

1930 **Element**—element 87—francium—announced

1935 **Aviation—Aviator**—woman aviator to fly solo across the Pacific Ocean—start—Honolulu—A. E. Putnam

1938 **Bank**—national bank woman president—F. E. Moulton—elected—Limerick, Me.

1949 **Mosque** — cornerstone laid — Islamic Center—Washington, D.C.

JANUARY 12

1773 **Museum**—public museum — organized

1792 **Diplomatic Service** — ambassador to England—Thomas Pinckney — minister plenipotentiary—appointed

1853 **College** — university on the Pacific coast—Willamette University—incorporated—Salem, Ore.

1876 **Forestry Society**—state forestry association—Minnesota Forestry Association—organized

1895 **Government Printing Office**—Superintendent of Documents—authorized

1896 **X-Ray**—X-ray photograph—H. L. Smith—Davidson, N.C.

1910 **Aviation—Aviator** — aviator (American) to establish an altitude record—Louis Paulhan—Los Angeles, Calif.

1924 **Science Association**—history of science society — organized — Boston, Mass.

1929 **Ship**—seatrain—service inaugurated—New Orleans, La. and Havana, Cuba

1932 **Senator (U.S.)** — woman elected to the Senate—H. O. W. Caraway — elected—Arkansas

1937 **Plow** — submarine cable plow—patented

1942 **Medal** of Honor awarded in World War II—A. R. Nininger

1953 **Catholic Priest** — Catholic Cardinal whose see was west of the Rockies—J. F. McIntyre — elevated to the Sacred College of Cardinals

1960 **Basketball**—basketball player (professional) to score more than 15,000 points—Dolph Schayes—Philadelphia, Pa.

JANUARY 13

1794 **Flag Legislation**—legislation authorizing changes—enacted

1854 **Accordion Patent**—Anthony Faas

1857 **Scale**—railway track scale — patented —T. Fairbanks

1863 **Chenille Manufacturing Machine** — patented—William Canter

1906 **Radio Receiver** — radio receiver advertised — Hugo Gernsback — New York City

1910 **Opera**—opera broadcast in part—from Metropolitan Opera—New York City

1929 **Humanist Society**—established—Hollywood, Calif.

1931 **Autogiro**—autogiro with side-by-side seating arrangement—design planned

1942 **Automobile**—plastic automobile—construction patented — Henry Ford — Dearborn, Mich.

1953 **Business** — department store to sell apartments—Gimbel Brothers—Philadelphia, Pa.

JANUARY 14

1639 **Constitution** — constitution — fundamental orders—Hartford, Conn.

1784 **Treaty**—treaty between the United States Government and a nation with which it had been at war—ratified and proclaimed

1794 **Surgical Operation**—Caesarean operation (successful)—Jessee Bennett—Edom, Va.

1813 **School Superintendent**—school superintendent (state)—Gideon Hawley — New York—served

1846 **Telegraph**—telegraph company—Magnetic Telegraph Company—formed

1873 **Celluloid**—trade-mark registered

1929 **Postal Service** — international dog sled mail—arrived—Montreal, Canada

1932 **Totalisator**—used—Miami, Fla.

1938 **Euthanasia Society**—National Society for the Legalization of Euthanasia—formed—New York City

1943 **President (U.S.)**—President to fly in an airplane while in office—F. D. Roosevelt

JANUARY 15

1782 **Mint (U.S.)**—Mint of the United States—proposed

1831 **Railroad Passenger**—railroad honeymoon trip—Charleston, S.C. to Hamburg, S.C.

1833 **Hospital**—Negro hospital and asylum —Georgia Infirmary — organized — Savannah, Ga.

1847 **Swedish Magazine**—*Skandinavia*—published—New York City

1862 **Ship**—iron-clad naval vessels — accepted—St. Louis, Mo.

1863 **Newspaper** — newspaper printed on wood-pulp paper—Boston *Morning Journal*—Boston, Mass.

1867 **Governor** — governor of a territory and a state—J. W. Geary—Pennsylvania

1870 **Cartoon**—Democratic cartoon — donkey emblem — published—New York City

1882 **Ski Club**—ski club (local)—Nansen Ski Club—Berlin, N.H.—formed

1892 **Basketball Rules**—basketball rules—published—Springfield, Mass.

1907 **Dentistry**—gold inlay — described — W. H. Taggart

1907 **Radio Tube** — three-element vacuum tube—patented—Lee De Forest

1908 **Sorority** — Negro sorority — Alpha Kappa Alpha Sorority — founded — Washington, D.C.

1936 **Building**—all-glass windowless structure—completed—Toledo, Ohio

1953 **Medal**—Reserve Officers Association medal—presented—H. S. Truman

1955 **Building**—solar-heated and radiation-cooled house—built—R. W. Bliss—Tucson, Ariz.—system in operation

JANUARY 16

1840 **Expedition** — scientific expedition fitted out by the United States Government—reached Antarctic

1866 Skate (all-metal)—screw clamp skate —patented—E. H. Barney

1877 Carpet Loom—carpet power loom to weave Axminster carpets—patented— Halcyon Skinner

1877 Organ—color organ—patented—Bainbridge Bishop

1891 Ski Club—ski club association—tournament—Ishpeming, Mich.

1919 Prohibition—prohibition amendment to the Constitution—ratified by thirty-sixth state—Nebraska

1920 Prohibition—prohibition amendment to the Constitution — eighteenth amendment effective

1920 Prohibition—prohibition bureau (federal)—prohibition amendment became effective

1936 Camera — photo-finish camera (electric eye) installed at a race track— Hialeah, Fla.

1937 Jury School—jury school—opened — Newark, N.J.

1942 Army Officer — general appointed from civilian rank—W. S. Knudsen— appointed

1943 Glider—amphibious seaplane glider— flown—Philadelphia, Pa.

1957 Aviation—Flights (world)—jet round-the-world non-stop flight—take-off— Merced, Calif.

JANUARY 17

1806 Births—child born in the White House, Washington, D.C. — J. M. Randolph

1871 Street Car—cable street car—patented —A. S. Hallidie — San Francisco, Calif.

1887 Hospital—hospital for the military and naval forces—Army and Navy Hospital—Hot Springs, Ark.—opened

1905 Punchboards—patented

1928 Photography — film developing machine (fully automatic) — patented — A. M. Josepho

1934 Electric Home and Farm Authority, Inc.—incorporated—Delaware

JANUARY 18

1733 Animals — bear (white) — exhibited —Boston, Mass.

1826 Art Organization—artists' society of importance—New York Drawing Association committee formed for the National Academy of Design

1840 Periodical—electrical journal — published—New York City

1890 Sanitary District—business meeting —Chicago, Ill.

1896 X-Ray—X-ray machine—exhibited— New York City

1934 Information Service (U.S.)—organized—Washington, D.C.

1944 Citizenship—Chinese granted citizenship—E. B. Kan—naturalized—Chicago, Ill.

1949 Congress (U.S.)—House of Representatives — congressional standing committee headed by a Negro—W. L. Dawson

1957 Aviation—Flights (world)—jet round-the-world non-stop flight—landing— Riverside, Calif.

JANUARY 19

1825 Canning—canning—patent

1861 Prison—military prison of the United States on an island—Fort Jefferson, Fla.—garrisoned

1871 Freemasons—Negro Masonic lodge— Alpha lodge—New Jersey—warranted

1886 Ski Club—ski club (local) that was active—Aurora Ski Club—Red Wing, Minn.—organized

1903 Radio Broadcast—transatlantic broadcast (not experimental)—Cape Cod, Mass.

1915 Electric Sign—neon tube advertising sign—patent awarded

1928 Squash Racquets Champion—woman to win the U.S.A. Women's Squash Racquets Singles championship—E. R. Sears—Greenwich, Conn.

1929 Park—park (national) east of the Mississippi—name changed to Acadia National Park

1955 Television — Telecast — presidential news conference filmed for television and newsreels—Washington, D.C.

JANUARY 20

1778 Court Martial—military court martial —Cambridge, Mass.

1783 Treaty—treaty between the United States Government and a nation with which it had been at war—hostilities ceased—England

1809 Geology Book—geology book—of importance—William Maclure—read before American Philosophical Society— Philadelphia, Pa.

1820 Agricultural "Board" (state)—New York State board formed

1869 Woman—woman congressional hearing witness—E. C. Stanton

1885 Railroad—switchback railway—roller coaster patent—L. A. Thompson— Coney Island, N.Y.

1929 Moving Picture—talking picture taken outdoors (full length)—*In Old Arizona*—released

1937 President—President inaugurated on January 20—F. D. Roosevelt

1937 President—President whose mother saw her son inaugurated President of the United States for a second term —F. D. Roosevelt

1947 Christmas Carols Association (national)—organized—St. Louis, Mo.

1952 Bull Fight—woman bull fighter (professional) — Patricia McCormick — debut

1953 **Television—Telecast**—telecast transmitted to Canada—from Buffalo, N.Y.
1954 **Radio Station**—Negro network—National Negro network—formed

JANUARY 21

1677 **Medical Book**—medical pamphlet—published—Boston, Mass.
1781 **Diplomatic Service**—consular officer detailed for duty in the Department of Foreign Affairs—Thomas Barclay —appointed
1789 **Novel**—American novel published in America—*Power of Sympathy*—advertised
1812 **Bridge** — "Y" bridge —authorized — Zanesville, Ohio
1853 **Envelope**—envelope folding machine —patented—R. L. Hawes
1865 **Oil**—oil well drilled by torpedoes
1880 **Sewage**—separate system of sewage disposal—started—Memphis, Tenn.
1894 **Medal** — Medal of Honor action — medal awarded to B. J. D. Irwin
1927 **Opera**—opera broadcast over a national network from an American opera house—Chicago, Ill.
1937 **Automobile License (federal)**—common carrier license—effective
1937 **Legislature** — unicameral legislature (state)—first appropriation bill—Nebraska
1941 **Magnesium** — commercial production —Freeport, Tex.
1954 **Automobile**—gas turbine automobile—publicly introduced—New York City
1954 **Submarine**—atomic-powered submarine—"Nautilus"—launched — Groton, Conn.
1961 **Cabinet of the United States**—cabinet member who was a brother of a President—R. F. Kennedy—took office

JANUARY 22

1673 **Postal Service**—postal route—service began—Boston to New York City
1814 **Freemasons**—Knights Templar Grand Encampment—New York City
1879 **Senator (U.S.)**—senator to serve three states—James Shields—elected
1881 **Monument**—obelisk to be brought to the United States—erected on pedestal—New York City
1895 **Manufacturers Association**—National Association of Manufacturers—organized—Cincinnati, Ohio
1932 **Reconstruction Finance Corporation** —authorized
1947 **Television Station**—commercial television station west of the Mississippi River—Hollywood, Calif.

JANUARY 23

1789 **College**—Catholic College — Georgetown College—established—Washington, D.C.

1793 **"First Aid" Emergency Organization** —Humane Society of Philadelphia—incorporated
1845 **Election**—election day—uniform observation authorized
1849 **Envelope**—envelope machine patent
1849 **Physician**—woman physician—Elizabeth Blackwell—graduated—Geneva, N.Y.
1879 **Archery Club**—archery association (national)—National Archery Association—formed—Crawfordsville, Ind.
1891 **Hospital**—interracial hospital—Provident Hospital—Chicago, Ill.—incorporated
1907 **Senator (U.S.)**—Indian senator — Charles Curtis—served
1917 **Shipping**—United States Shipping Board—nominations of commissioners confirmed
1923 **Congressman (U.S.)**—congresswoman elected to serve in the place of her husband—M. E. Nolan—served
1946 **Naval Officer**—chaplain to win a Congressional Medal of Honor—awarded —J. T. O'Callahan

JANUARY 24

1656 **Physician**—Jewish doctor — Jacob Lumbrozo—Maryland
1722 **Divinity Professor**—Edward Wigglesworth—appointed—Cambridge, Mass.
1838 **Telegraph**—telegraphic communication system in which dots and dashes represented letters—public demonstration
1848 **Gold**—gold discovered in California —J. W. Marshall—Coloma, Calif.
1888 **Typewriter Ribbon**—typewriter "copy" ribbon—patented—J. L. Wortman
1893 **Catholic Apostolic Delegate**—Francesco Satolli—arrived
1899 **Rubber** — rubber heel — Humphrey O'Sullivan—patent
1922 **Eskimo Pie**—C. K. Nelson—patent
1925 **Moving Picture**—moving picture of an eclipse of the sun taken from a dirigible—Montauk Point, L.I., N.Y.
1935 **Cans**—beer in cans—placed on sale—Richmond, Va.
1944 **Medal**—soldier to win the three highest ranking decorations—M. L. Britt —heroism

JANUARY 25

1799 **Seeding Machine Patent**—granted—Eliakim Spooner
1870 **Soda Fountain**—ornamented soda fountain—patented—G. D. Dows
1871 **Monument**—monument by a woman ordered by the United States Government—Lincoln statue unveiled—Washington, D.C.
1890 **Tour of the World**—tour of the world made by a woman traveling alone—Nellie Bly—returned to New York City

1897 **Accountants' Society** — accountants' society formed by a state group—incorporated

1897 **Forestry Society**—national forestry association—American Forestry Association—incorporated

1897 **Piano Player**—pneumatic piano player —patent application

1901 **Ship**—schooner (seven masted, steel) —contract signed

1907 **Arts and Letters Society**—woman elected to the National Institute of Arts and Letters—J. W. Howe

1915 **Telephone**—transcontinental telephone demonstration—New York City to San Francisco, Calif.

1929 **Vice President of the United States**—Vice President's widow to receive a pension—L. I. K. Marshall—authorized

1930 **Medical Clinic**—flying medical clinic —demonstration of operation—F. H. Albee

1945 **Water**—community to fluoridate its municipal water — Grand Rapids, Mich.

1952 **Headlight**—automatic headlight control—Autronic Eye—Anderson, Ind.

1952 **Railroad**—railroad freight yard fully automatic—Gary, Ind.

1959 **Aviation—Flights (transcontinental)**—jet passenger commercial transcontinental service—Los Angeles-New York City

1961 **Television — Telecast** — presidential news conference to be televised live—J. F. Kennedy—Washington, D.C.

JANUARY 26

1679 **Ship**—Great Lakes commercial vessel—"Le Griffon"—keel laid

1695 **Workmen's Compensation** — workmen's compensation agreement—William Kidd

1776 **Army Officer**—chaplain (Catholic) of the Continental Army—L. E. Lotbiniere—appointed

1838 **Prohibition**—prohibition state—legislation enacted—Tennessee

1850 **Newspaper**—German daily newspaper —*New Yorker Staats-Zeitung*—published—New York City

1875 **Drill**—dental drill (electric)—patented —G. F. Green

1907 **Election Law**—corrupt election practices law (federal)—enacted

1909 **Bird Reservation (national)**—Pelican Island—enlarged

1910 **Bank**—postal savings bank—bill introduced—T. H. Carter

1911 **Aviation—Airplane** — hydroplane — flown—G. H. Curtiss—San Diego, Calif.

1942 **World War II**—American expeditionary force to land on the European continent—arrived

1950 **Insurance**—baby sitters' insurance policy—issued—St. Louis, Mo.

1951 **Jewish Congregation**—Jewish congregation to call a woman to exercise a rabbi's function—Meridian, Miss.

1961 **Physician**—woman appointed "personal physician to the President"—J. G. Travell—appointment announced

JANUARY 27

1662 **Lime**—manufactured—Providence, R.I.

1785 **College**—state university chartered—Athens, Ga.

1823 **Diplomatic Service**—ministers plenipotentiary to South and Central America—appointed

1870 **Sorority**—sorority — women's Greek-letter society—Kappa Alpha Theta—founded

1879 **Senator (U.S.)**—senator to serve three states — James Shields — Missouri — served

1880 **Electric Lighting**—electric incandescent lamp—patented—T. A. Edison

1897 **Initiative and Referendum**—legislation passed—House of Representatives—South Dakota

1900 **Social-Democratic Party of America** —convention—Rochester, N.Y.

1908 **Tuberculosis School**—outdoor school for tubercular children — opened — Providence, R.I.

1941 **Aviation—Airport**—air terminal (not located at an airport)—opened—New York City

1948 **Locomotive**—locomotive (super-giant) to carry the weight of 1,000,000 pounds—operated—Norfolk, Va.

1948 **Tape Recorder**—magnetic tape recorder—announced

1950 **Terramycin**—publicly announced

JANUARY 28

1875 **Monument**—statue cast by the United States Government—contract awarded—Vinnie Ream

1878 **Newspaper**—college daily — *Yale News* —published—New Haven, Conn.

1878 **Telephone**—telephone switchboard or exchange (commercial) — installed — New Haven, Conn.

1899 **Social Science Society (national)** — American Social Science Association —incorporated

1907 **Safety Congress** — safety congress—New York City

1908 **Arts and Letters Society** — woman elected to the American Academy of Arts and Letters—J. W. Howe

1915 **Coast Guard (U.S.)**—Coast Guard—created

1915 **World War I**—American ship lost in World War I—"William P. Frye" sunk

1916 **Supreme Court (U.S.)**—Associate Justice of the Supreme Court who was Jewish—L. D. Brandeis—appointed

1932 **Insurance** — unemployment insurance act—enacted—Wisconsin
1934 **Ski Tow (rope)**—operated—Woodstock, Vt.
1935 **Locomotive**—streamlined electric engine — tested — Washington, D.C. to Philadelphia, Pa.
1942 **Merchant Marine Academy**—Merchant Marine Cadet Corps (U.S.)—first class started—Kings Point, N.Y.
1958 **Atomic Reactor**—thorium-uranium reactor (privately owned) — Buchanan, N.Y.—construction began
1960 **Photograph**—photograph bounced off the moon — received — Washington, D.C.

JANUARY 29

1802 **Librarian** — Librarian of Congress — John Beckley—appointed
1874 **Money**—coins manufactured for a foreign government—authorized
1900 **Baseball League** — American League —organized—Philadelphia, Pa.
1904 **College "Lettermen's Club"** — established—Chicago, Ill.
1919 **Prohibition** — prohibition amendment to the Constitution—amendment proclaimed by Secretary of State
1919 **Prohibition**—prohibition bureau (federal)—prohibition amendment became part of the Constitution
1924 **Ice Cream Cone**—ice cream cone-rolling machine—patented—C. R. Taylor
1926 **Lawyer** — Negro woman lawyer to practice before the United States Supreme Court—V. N. Anderson—admitted
1936 **Hall of Fame**—hall of fame (baseball) —players elected—Cooperstown, N.Y.
1940 **Flowers** — tetraploid flower—publicly exhibited—New York City
1943 **Marines** — woman marine major—R. C. Streeter—appointed
1949 **Ship** — air-conditioned naval ship — "Newport News"—commissioned
1951 **Television**—television eyewitness allowed to testify in a federal court—New York City

JANUARY 30

1781 **Articles of Confederation**—adopted by Maryland, last of the thirteen states
1798 **Congress (U.S.) — House of Representatives**—brawl—Philadelphia, Pa.
1835 **President (U.S.)**—President whose assassination was attempted—Andrew Jackson—Washington, D.C.
1862 **Ship**—iron-clad turreted vessel in the U.S. Navy — "Monitor" — launched—Greenpoint, N.Y.
1874 **Mechanical Engineering Laboratory**—for research work—proposed—Stevens Institute of Technology
1884 **Anti-Vivisection Society** — annual meeting—Philadelphia, Pa.
1894 **Hammer (pneumatic)** — patented — C. B. King

1910 **Automobile Race Track**—automobile speedway (board track) — started — Los Angeles, Calif.
1911 **Aviation**—airplane rescue at sea—J. A. D. McCurdy
1925 **Science Association**—History of Science Society—incorporated
1934 **Medal**—National Geographic Society gold medal—Hubbard Medal to a woman—A. M. Lindbergh—Washington, D.C.
1934 **Play (drama)**—theatrical presentation sponsored by the federal government —*The Family Upstairs* — produced — New York City
1942 **Price Regulation Law**—price regulation law (federal)—enacted
1958 **Sidewalk (traveling)**—two-way moving walk—in service—Dallas, Tex.

JANUARY 31

1825 **Trademark Lawsuit**—trademark controversy involving a newspaper—tried
1863 **Civil War**—Negro regiment in the Civil War — First Regiment South Carolina volunteers — mustered into federal service
1871 **Freemasons**—Negro Masonic lodge—Alpha lodge—regular communication
1885 **Labor**—labor bureau (federal)—Commissioner of Labor—C. D. Wright—appointed
1920 **Newspaper** — Ukrainian daily newspaper — *Ukrainian Daily News* — New York City
1930 **Glider**—glider released from a dirigible—piloted—Lakehurst, N.J
1958 **Rocket**—satellite placed in orbit—Explorer I—launched from Cape Canaveral, Fla.
1961 **Naval Officer**—commander of a combat ship who was a Negro—S. L. Gravely

FEBRUARY 1

1788 **Ship** — steamboat patent — Georgia — Isaac Briggs and William Longstreet
1790 **Supreme Court (U.S.)** — Supreme Court of the United States—first session—New York City
1791 **Dental Dispensary**—dental dispensary —opened—New York City
1793 **Oiled Silk Patent**—R. Hodgson
1840 **Dental School**—dental college—incorporated
1842 **Coast Guard (U.S.)** — Coast Guard Commandant — A. V. Fraser — appointed
1842 **College** — university on the Pacific coast — trustees elected — Willamette University—Salem, Ore.
1843 **Insurance**—mutual life insurance company to operate—policy issued
1844 **Insurance** — mutual life insurance company to be chartered—New England Mutual Life Insurance Company —first policy

1860 **Congress (U.S.)—House of Representatives**—Jewish rabbi to open the House of Representatives with prayer—M. J. Raphall

1864 **Mines School**—Thomas Egleston—professor of mines and metallurgy—appointed

1865 **Lawyer**—Negro lawyer to practice before the United States Supreme Court—J. S. Rock

1885 **Hospital** — tuberculosis sanatorium (modern) opened—Saranac Lake, N.Y.

1898 **Insurance**—automobile insurance policy — issued — Travelers Insurance Company—Hartford, Conn.

1904 **Radio Distress Signal**—radio distress signal—CQD signal—effective

1906 **Prison**—penitentiary building (national)—completed—Federal Penitentiary—Leavenworth, Kan.

1907 **Horse**—horse farm operated by the United States Government—property deeded—Middlebury, Conn.

1914 **Moving Picture Censorship** — moving picture censorship board (state)—censors appointed—Pennsylvania

1920 **Automobile**—armored commercial car completely protected — in service—St. Paul, Minn.

1936 **Insurance**—group insurance policy for college students—issued

1937 **Free Port**—opened—Stapleton, N.Y.

1937 **Ship** — ship permitted to enter port without stopping for quarantine procedure — "Cameronia" — New York City

1940 **Television—Telecast** — television network demonstration (long distance)— New York City to Schenectady, N.Y.

1941 **Aviation — Flights** — airplane flight (commercially scheduled) over a single route linking four continents—left—New York City

1942 **Merchant Marine** — Merchant Marine officer to hold the rank of rear admiral—A. B. Randall—commissioned

1944 **Marines** — woman marine major — R. C. Streeter—appointed colonel

1949 **Court Martial**—court martial trial at which enlisted men were allowed to sit as members of the court—Heidelberg, Germany

1949 **Telescope**—telescope lens two hundred inches in diameter—used—Palomar Mountain, Calif.

1951 **Television — Telecast** — atomic explosion telecast—Los Angeles, Calif.

1951 **X-Ray**—X-ray moving picture process by which pictures could be taken over a considerable period of time—demonstrated—Baltimore, Md.

1957 **Aviation — Aviator** — Negro airplane pilot on a scheduled passenger line—P. H. Young

FEBRUARY 2

1798 **Theater**—theater destroyed by fire—Federal Street Theatre — Boston, Mass.

1802 **Animals** — leopard — exhibited — Boston, Mass.

1832 **Treaty**—treaty with a foreign nation to provide for mutual reduction of import duties — ratifications exchanged with France

1834 **College**—coeducational college—Oberlin Collegiate Institute — Oberlin, Ohio—incorporated

1838 **College** — city college — Charleston, S.C.—president appointed

1843 **Colonial Government**—government on the Pacific coast — committee appointed—Champoeg, Ore.

1858 **"Artics"**—patented—T. C. Wales

1876 **Baseball League**—National League—formed

1880 **Electric Lighting** — street lighting (electric) by a municipality—appropriation made—Wabash, Ind.

1892 **Bottle Cap**—crown cork — patented—William Painter

1893 **Moving Picture** — moving picture "close-up"—West Orange, N.J.

1901 **Army Nurse Corps (female)** —authorized

1901 **Dental Corps (U.S. Army)**—Dental Corps of the U.S. Army—authorized

1912 **Moving Picture Actor**—stunt actor—F. R. Law—jumped from Statue of Liberty

1923 **Gasoline**—ethyl gasoline—marketed—Dayton, Ohio

1929 **Postal Service**—international dog sled mail—returned from Montreal

1932 **Reconstruction Finance Corporation**—organized

1935 **Lie Detector**—tested—Portage, Wis.

1940 **Dictionary**—dictionary compiled by a woman—M. B. Picken—published — New York City

1962 **Pole Vaulter**—pole vault jump indoors over sixteen feet—John Uelses—New York City

FEBRUARY 3

1690 **Money**—paper money—issued — Massachusetts

1789 **Cotton Mill**—cotton mill—Beverly Cotton Manufactory — incorporated — Beverly, Mass.

1836 **Whig Party** — state convention — Albany, N.Y.

1860 **Agriculture Bureau**—Agriculture bureau — Superintendent of Agriculture under Department of Interior—T. G. Clemson—took office

1862 **Newspaper**—newspaper printed on a train—Port Huron, Mich.

1894 **Ship**—steel sailing vessel—"Dirigo"—launched—Bath, Me.

1933 **Legislative Conference (interstate)**—meeting—American Legislators' Association—Washington, D.C.

1947 **News Correspondent** — Negro news correspondent admitted to the House of Representatives and Senate press gallery—P. L. Prattis

1949 **Court Martial**—court martial trial at which enlisted men were allowed to sit as members of the court—conviction

1949 **Court Martial**—court martial trial in the United States at which enlisted men were allowed to sit as members of the court—convened—Fort Bragg, N.C.

FEBRUARY 4

1789 **Congress of the United States**—joint meeting of the Senate and the House of Representatives—presidential candidates elected—Continental Congress

1789 **President**—President to receive the unanimous vote of the presidential electors—George Washington

1847 **Telegraph**—telegraph company—Magnetic Telegraph Company — incorporated

1861 **Congress of the Confederate States**—provisional session — Senate — Montgomery, Ala.

1887 **Interstate Commerce Act**—approved

1895 **Bridge** — rolling lift bridge — Van Buren Street bridge—Chicago, Ill.—opened

1913 **Automobile Tire** — demountable tire-carrying rim—patented—L. H. Perlman

1915 **Public Health**—pellagra experiment—Joseph Goldberger

1919 **Medal**—Distinguished Service Medal (Navy)—authorized

1930 **Road**—mosaic pavement — completed —New Orleans, La.

1930 **Street Car**—street car tracks which were tieless, soundless, and shockless —completed—New Orleans, La.

1932 **Olympic Games** — winter Olympic Games competition — Lake Placid, N.Y.

1936 **Physics** — radioactive substance produced synthetically—radium E—produced — University of California — Berkeley, Calif.

1938 **Radio Facsimile Transmission**—radio facsimile broadcasting on the regular broadcast band—Des Moines, Iowa

1942—**World War II** — American general wounded in action in World War II —C. A. Pierce

1944 **Medal**—Bronze Star—established

1957 **Typewriter** — electric portable typewriter—on sale—Syracuse, N.Y.

1958 **Ship**—aircraft carrier (atomic powered) — "Enterprise" — laid down — Newport News, Va.

FEBRUARY 5

1644 **Branding Legislation** — enacted — Connecticut

1777 **State**—state to abolish both entail and primogeniture—Georgia

1778 **Articles of Confederation—first state** to ratify—South Carolina

1790 **Lawyer** — lawyers admitted to the Supreme Court of the United States

1817 **Gas** — gas company — incorporated —Baltimore, Md.

1834 **Crime Prevention and Detection**—interstate crime pact—ratified by New York State

1841 **Statistical Society**—American Statistical Society—incorporated

1846 **Newspaper**—newspaper published on the Pacific coast — *Oregon Spectator*—Oregon City, Ore.

1850 **Adding Machine**—adding machine to employ depressible keys—patented — D. D. Parmelee

1861 **Moving Picture**—peep show machine —patented—S. D. Goodale

1861 **Moving Picture** — photographic attempt to show motion—patented—Coleman Sellers

1870 **Moving Picture** — animated photographic picture projection before a theatre audience—H. R. Heyl

1901 **Loop the Loop Centrifugal Railway** —patent—Edwin Prescott—Arlington, Mass.

1918 **Aviation—Aviator**—Army aviator—to win victory—S. W. Thompson

1924 **President**—President buried in Washington, D.C.—Woodrow Wilson

1931 **Aviation — License** — glider license awarded a woman—M. Dunlap

1931 **Aviation — License** — glider license class "C"—National Aeronautic Association—awarded—R. S. Barnaby

1948 **Olympic Games** — figure skating Olympic champion (American)—Richard Button

1948 **Olympic Games** — woman slalom Olympic champion (American) — Gretchen Fraser

FEBRUARY 6

1778 **Treaty**—treaty entered into by the United States—France

1778 **United States** — nation to recognize the independence of the United States —France

1815 **Railroad Charter** — railroad charter—New Jersey

1857 **Postage Stamp** — perforated postage stamps—contract

1902 **Young Women's Hebrew Association** —organized—New York City

1911 **Old Age Home for Pioneers**—Prescott, Ariz.—opened

1912 **Ship**—cruise ship to circumnavigate the world—"Cleveland"—left New York City

1932 **Dog Sled Race**—dog sled race on an Olympic demonstration program — Lake Placid, N.Y.

1937 **Lawyer** — Japanese woman lawyer — K. E. Ohi—received LL.B. degree

1956 **School** — circular school building — opened—Kankakee, Ill.

1957 **Cryotrons**—publicly reported—D. A. Buck—Cambridge, Mass.

FEBRUARY 7

1818 **Educational Magazine** — educational magazine to achieve success — *Academician*—published—New York City

1827 **Ballet** — presented — Bowery Theatre —New York City

1842 **Presidential Commission** — President requested by Congress to justify the creation of a presidential commission —John Tyler

1877 **Cattle Club**—cattle club (Guernsey cattle) — American Guernsey Cattle Club—permanent organization — New York City

1893 **Teleautograph**—patented—Elisha Gray

1934 **Electrical Contract**—city with government—Tupelo, Miss.—effective

1936 **Flag** — Vice President's flag—established

FEBRUARY 8

1693 **College**—college charter granted by the Crown—Williamsburg, Va.

1693 **College**—college proposed — College of William and Mary—incorporated—Williamsburg, Va.

1802 **Clock** — banjo clock patent — Simon Willard

1837 **Vice President of the United States**—Vice President elected by the Senate—R. M. Johnson—chosen

1865 **Army Officer** — major (Negro)—M. R. Delany—commissioned

1887 **Ski Club**—ski club (local) that was active—Aurora Ski Club tournament —Red Wing, Minn.

1889 **Automobile Tractor**—steam tractor—delivered—San Leandro, Calif.

1892 **Library Loan**—made by a state library to a community—New York

1898 **Envelope**—envelope folding and gumming machine—patented—J. A. Sherman

1910 **Boy Scouts of America**—Boy Scouts of America—incorporated

1911 **Court**—commerce court (U.S.)—organized—Washington, D.C.

1912 **Aviation — Flights (transcontinental)** — transcontinental airplane flight (eastbound)—R. G. Fowler—landed—Jacksonville, Fla.

1924 **Execution**—lethal gas execution—Carson City, Nev.

1924 **Radio Broadcast**—coast-to-coast hookup—J. J. Carty—Chicago, Ill.

1928 **Television — Telecast** — transoceanic television image — received — Hartsdale, N.Y.

1934 **Bank** — Export-Import Bank—organized

1944 **News Correspondent** — Negro news correspondent accredited to the White House—Harry McAlpin

1957 **Court Martial**—court martial trial of an officer for collaborating with his captors—decision sustained

FEBRUARY 9

1790 **Diplomatic Service**—consul under the Department of State—Samuel Shaw—nominated

1799 **Ship**—ship to capture an enemy ship after the Revolution—"Constellation" vs. "Insurgente"

1861 **President of the Confederate States**—Jefferson Davis—elected

1870 **Weather Bureau (U.S.)** — Weather Bureau (U.S.)—authorized

1871 **Fish Protection**—fish protection office (federal)—authorized

1889 **Agriculture Bureau**—agriculture bureau—made an executive department in the federal government

1893 **Theater**—municipal theater — Academy of Music—Northampton, Mass. —accepted as a gift

1909 **Forestry School**—forestry school to give scientific training in the care and preservation of trees—Davey Tree Expert Company — Kent, Ohio — incorporated

1909 **Narcotic** — narcotic prohibition act (federal)—enacted

1918 **Chaplains' School**—Army school for chaplains — organized—Fort Monroe, Va.

1932 **Bobsled Competition**—two-man bob-team competition—Lake Placid, N.Y.

1941 **Aviation — Flights** — airplane flight (commercially scheduled) over a single route linking four continents—"Dixie Clipper" returned—New York City

FEBRUARY 10

1807 **Coast Survey**—authorized

1807 **Coast Survey Superintendent** — U.S. Survey—authorized

1830 **Railroad**—interstate railroad—Petersburg Railroad—chartered

1855 **Hospital**—women's hospital—constitution adopted—New York City

1863 **Fire Extinguisher Patent** — Alanson Crane

1923 **Ink**—ink paste — manufactured—Minneapolis, Minn.

1925 **Gas**—gas storage tank (waterless)—in service—Michigan City, Ind.

1930 **Grain Stabilization Corporation**—authorized

1932 **Ski Meet (international)**—Lake Placid, N.Y.

1933 **Telegram** — singing telegram — introduced—New York City

1934 **Postage Stamp** — imperforated ungummed sheet of postage stamps—issued—New York City

1935 **Locomotive**—streamlined electric engine—Pennsylvania Railroad Company—in passenger service

1941 **Postal Service**—highway post office service—route established—Washington, D.C. to Harrisonburg, Va.

1942 **Medal**—Medal of Honor awarded in World War II—presented posthumously

FEBRUARY 11

1752 Hospital — hospital in America — opened—Philadelphia, Pa.

1794 Congress (U.S.) Senate—Senate session to which the public was admitted —trial of A. A. A. Gallatin

1801 President—President elected by the House of Representatives — Thomas Jefferson—Washington, D.C.

1808 Coal—anthracite coal burned experimentally—Wilkes Barre, Pa.

1811 Congress (U.S.)—Senate—Senate filibuster

1833 Rubber—rubber company—Roxbury India Rubber Company—incorporated

1836 College—college for women — Mount Holyoke Seminary, South Hadley, Mass.—chartered

1837 Physiological Society — physiological society—American Physiological Society—organized—Boston, Mass.

1875 College — inter-continental system of study—introduced—Boston University —Boston, Mass. — reciprocal agreement

1878 Bicycle Society—bicycle club—Boston Bicycle Club—formed—Boston, Mass.

1901 Dental Corps (U.S. Army)—Dental Corps of the U.S. Army—contract—dental surgeons appointed

1916 Orchestra—municipal orchestra supported by taxes—Baltimore, Md.—first concert

1930 Aviation—Airport—airport to receive an A1-A rating—Pontiac, Mich.

1935 Aviation — Flights — airplane flight with an auto slung beneath the fuselage—Floyd Bennett Field, N.Y.

1944 Caterpillar Club—father and son Caterpillar Club members—son jumped —Fairbanks, Alaska

1945 Aviation—Airplane—gas turbine propeller driven airplane—tested—Muroc, Calif.

1952 Yiddish Professorship — established—Columbia University—New York City

1956 Railroad Car—passenger car (ACF Talgo for use in the United States)—in service between Peoria, Ill, and Chicago, Ill.

1957 Naval Officer—woman to preside as law officer—Mary Lou McDowell

1958 Aviation — air stewardess (Negro) — R. C. Taylor—Ithaca, N.Y.—New York City

FEBRUARY 12

1738 Puppet Show—New York City

1775 President—President whose wife was not born in the United States—J. Q. Adams

1793 Slavery—fugitive slave law (federal) —enacted

1795 Money—deposit of gold bullion

1809 President—President born beyond the boundaries of the original thirteen states—Abraham Lincoln—Hodgenville, Ky.

1821 Library—mercantile library — opened —New York City

1855 Agricultural School—agricultural college (state) to open — Agricultural College of Michigan—Lansing, Mich. —incorporated

1865 Congress (U.S.) — House of Representatives—Negro preacher to deliver a sermon in the House of Representatives—H. H. Garnet

1873 Assay Office Building (federal)—under Bureau of Mint—authorized

1873 Money—demonetization of silver—bimetallism—abolished

1873 Money—silver coins—trade dollar authorized

1873 Money—trade dollar—authorized

1877 Telephone — news dispatch by telephone—from Salem, Mass. to Boston. Mass.

1878 Baseball Catcher's Mask—patented—F. W. Thayer

1880 Croquet League — National Croquet League—organized—Philadelphia, Pa.

1899 Bicycle Race—international six-day bicycle race — two-man team event — New York City

1908 Automobile Race — automobile race from New York to Paris—started

1909 Postage Stamp—memorial stamp—on sale

1924 Radio Broadcast—network sponsored broadcast—New York City

1924 Radio Broadcast—political speech by a President on radio—Calvin Coolidge —New York City

1925 Arbitration—federal arbitration law—enacted

1935 Bridge—bridge with open mesh steel flooring—steel flooring patent—W. E. Irving

FEBRUARY 13

1635 Public School—public school with a continuous existence—Boston Public Latin School — established — Boston, Mass.

1741 Periodical — magazine published in America — *American Magazine* — published—Philadelphia, Pa.

1795 College—state university chartered—state university opened — University of North Carolina—Chapel Hill, N.C.

1799 Insurance — insurance regulation (state)—enacted—Massachusetts

1861 Medal — Medal of Honor action — Apache Pass, Ariz.

1875 Births—quintuplets — born — Watertown, Wis.

1889 Agriculture Department (U.S.)—Secretary of the Department of Agriculture—N. J. Colman—appointed

1914 Music Society—music society for the literary protection of composers and authors—formed—New York City

1934 Bank—Export-Import Bank—officers elected

1934 **Trust**—cartel—Pacific Coast Gasoline Cartel—approved

1935 **Surgical Operation** — heart operation for the relief of angina pectoris—C. S. Beck—Cleveland, Ohio

FEBRUARY 14

1778 **Flag**—American flag saluted by a foreign nation — France saluted the "Ranger"

1794 **Textile Machinery Patent** — James Davenport

1803 **Apple Parer**—patented—Moses Coats

1849 **Photograph**—photograph of a President (in office)—J. K. Polk—New York City

1862 **Ship**—iron-clad warship for service at sea — "Galena" — launched — Mystic, Conn.

1865 **Congressional Directory** — publication authorized

1867 **Insurance**—boiler insurance company —policy issued—Hartford, Conn.

1872 **Bird Refuge**—authorized by a state— California

1883 **Labor Union**—labor union legalization (state)—New Jersey—enacted

1899 **Voting Machine**—voting machines for use in federal elections—approved

1903 **Commerce and Labor Department (U.S.)**—authorized

1907 **Foxhound Association** — Masters of Fox Hounds Association — formed— New York City

1912 **Engine**—diesel engine in a submarine —launched—Groton, Conn.

1931 **Medal**—Air Mail Flyer's Medal of Honor—authorized

1932 **Bobsled Competition**—four-man bobteam competition—Lake Placid, N.Y.

1940 **Aquatic Mammals**—porpoise—born in captivity—Marineland, Fla.

1946 **Medical Clinic**—cancer clinic (traveling) — established — Oklahoma City, Okla.

1961 **Element** — element 103 — produced — Berkeley, Calif.

FEBRUARY 15

1768 **Mustard**—advertised—Benjamin Jackson—Philadelphia, Pa.

1799 **Election**—printed ballot — authorized —Pennsylvania

1842 **Postage Stamp** — adhesive stamps — used—City Despatch Post—New York City

1875 **Visiting Celebrities** — king (reigning) to visit the United States — David Kalakaua—returned

1898 **Ship** — battleship of importance — "Maine" — destroyed by explosion — Havana harbor, Cuba

1911 **Court** — commerce court (U.S.) — opened—Washington, D.C.

1918 **World War I** — American Army troopship in World War I torpedoed by the Germans—"Tuscania"

1919 **War Veterans' Society** — American Legion—organized—Paris, France

1933 **Building** — building devoted entirely to highway traffic—Eno Foundation— affiliated with Yale University—New Haven, Conn.

1949 **Submarine**—submarine jet propulsion device patent—Fritz Zwicky — Pasadena, Calif.

1949 **Television**—municipal television film unit—established—New York City

1952 **Radio Station**—sea-going radio broadcasting station — "Courier"—commissioned—Hoboken, N.J.

1953 **Ice Skating Champion** — American world figure skating champion—Tenley Albright

1954 **Bevatron** — in operation — Berkeley, Calif.

1955 **Diamond**—pilot plant for the actual production of man-made diamonds— production announced — Schenectady, N.Y.

1956 **Camera**—non-electronic device for observing in total darkness — built — Cambridge, Mass.

1960 **Woman**—woman to undergo astronaut tests—Albuquerque, N.M.—Jerrie Cobb

FEBRUARY 16

1815 **Music**—music festival—Boston, Mass.

1818 **Insurance** — marine insurance law (state)—enacted—Massachusetts

1857 **Deaf — School** — institution in the world for the higher education of the deaf—National Deaf Mute College— Washington, D.C.—incorporated

1859 **Agricultural School**—agricultural college (state) to be chartered—Pennsylvania State College—opened

1868 **Benevolent and Protective Order of Elks**—organized—New York City

1880 **Engineering Society**—mechanical engineering national society—American Society of Mechanical Engineers — founded—New York City

1887 **Newspaper**—newspaper association— convention—Rochester, N.Y.

1900 **Newspaper**—Chinese daily newspaper —*Chung Sai Yat Po*—published—San Francisco, Calif.

1903 **Commerce and Labor Department (U.S.)**—G. B. Cortelyou — appointed secretary

1905 **Esperanto Club** — Esperanto club — Esperanto Association — organized — Boston, Mass.

1912 **Moving Picture**—moving picture from an airplane—F. J. Coffin—New York City

1932 **Patent**—fruit tree patent—issued

1933 **Constitutional Amendment (U.S.)** — constitutional amendment submitted to the states for repeal—passed by the U.S. Senate

1937 **Nylon** — nylon — patented — W. H. Carothers

1938 **Federal Crop Insurance Corporation** —established

1946 **Helicopter** — helicopter commercially designed—Bridgeport, Conn.

1948 **Television—Telecast** — newsreel telecast presented daily

1957 **Ship**—ship to transport fresh orange juice in stainless steel tanks — left Port Canaveral, Fla.

1960 **Submarine**—submerged circumnavigation of the earth—"Triton"—left New London, Conn.

1961 **Rocket**—satellite placed in orbit by an all-solid propellant rocket—Explorer IX launched—Wallops Island, Va.

FEBRUARY 17

1691 **Postal Service**—parliamentary act to establish a post office—enacted

1761 **Milestones** — planned — Philadelphia, Pa.

1776 **War (colonial)** — marine engagement in battle—New Providence, Bahamas —fleet left Delaware Capes

1817 **Gas**—gas company—street lights lit— Baltimore, Md.

1819 **College**—women's college (chartered) —Elizabeth Female Academy—Washington, Miss.

1864 **Submarine**—submarine to sink a man-of-war—"Hunley"

1864 **Torpedo**—torpedo mine—Confederate torpedo boat destroyed — Charleston, S.C.

1895 **Normal School** — teachers' training school (Jewish) — trustees elected — Gratz College—Philadelphia, Pa.

1897 **Parent-Teacher Association (national)** —National Congress of Mothers—organized—Washington, D.C.

1905 **Monument** — statue of a woman in National Statuary Hall—dedicated— F. E. Willard

1906 **President of a South American Country Born in the United States**—Galo Plaza Lasso—born—New York City

1911 **Aviation—Flights** — hydroplane flight to and from a ship—Glenn Curtiss— San Diego, Calif.

1913 **Labor Law**—minimum wage law—enacted—Oregon

1915 **World War I**—American combatant to die in World War I—E. M. Stone —wounded

1934 **Automobile Driving Course** — State College, Pa.

FEBRUARY 18

1688 **Slavery** — slavery protest — Germantown, Pa.

1735 **Opera** — opera performed—"Flora"— Charleston, S.C.

1804 **College**—university founded by a federal land grant — Ohio University— Athens, Ohio

1834 **Labor Paper** — *The Man*—published— New York City

1841 **Congress (U.S.)—Senate**—Senate filibuster (continuous)

1856 **American Party** — convention—Philadelphia, Pa.

1861 **Building**—"White House of the Confederacy" — used — Jefferson Davis— Montgomery, Ala.

1861 **Congress of the Confederate States**— House of Representatives — session— Richmond, Va.

1861 **President of the Confederate States**— Jefferson Davis — inducted — Montgomery, Ala.

1888 **Fish and Fisheries Commissioner** — salaried commissioner—M. McDonald —served

1908 **Postage Stamp**—postage stamps in coils—issued

1930 **Animals**—cow flown in an airplane— St. Louis, Mo.

1930 **Astronomy** — planet — found beyond Neptune—Pluto

1930 **Woman**—woman tax appeals board member—Annabel Matthews

1943 **Congress of the United States**—woman private citizen to address the House of Representatives and the Senate—Mme. Chiang Kai-shek

1953 **Moving Picture**—three-dimensional feature moving picture—*Bwana Devil*

FEBRUARY 19

1794 **Historical Society**—historical society (state)—Massachusetts Historical Society—incorporated

1817 **Bank**—savings bank to become a corporation — Provident Institution for Savings—Boston, Mass.—opened

1831 **Locomotive**—locomotive to burn coal (practical, American made) tested— York, Pa.

1836 **Naval Officer**—naval officer to become an engineer—C. H. Haswell— commissioned

1856 **Camera**—tintype camera — patented— H. L. Smith—Gambier, Ohio

1862 **Ship**—iron-clad turreted vessel in the U.S. Navy — "Monitor" — completed —Greenpoint, L.I., N.Y.

1863 **Oil**—oil pipeline within the oil regions —completed

1864 **Knights of Pythias**—founded—Washington, D.C.

1878 **Phonograph**—patented—T. A. Edison

1929 **Diathermy Machine**—used—Schenectady, N.Y.

1953 **Censorship**—state board of censorship on literature — approved — Georgia

1953 **Television Station**—television stations to share the same time and frequency —Salinas, Calif.—Monterey, Calif.

1957 **Ship**—ship to transport fresh orange juice in stainless steel tanks—"Tropicana"—arrived—Whitestone, N.Y.

FEBRUARY 20

1725 **Indians** — Indian scalping — by white men—New Hampshire colony

1768 **Insurance**—fire insurance company to receive a charter—Philadelphia, Pa.

1792 **Post Office**—Post Office Department of the United States—provided for by act of Congress

1792 **Postal Service**—postal service act—signed—George Washington

1794 **Congress (U.S.)—Senate** — contested election — A. A. A. Gallatin case started

1809 **Supreme Court (U.S.) Decision**—Supreme Court decision establishing the power of the United States—Chief Justice John Marshall

1862 **Ship**—iron-clad turreted vessel in the U.S. Navy—"Monitor"—delivered to U.S. Navy

1865 **Architectural School** — architectural school of collegiate character—established — Massachusetts Institute of Technology—Boston, Mass.

1867 **Insurance**—insurance rate standardization—National Board of Fire Underwriters — annual meeting — New York City

1872 **Elevator**—elevator patent, for a vertical-geared hydraulic electric elevator —C. W. Baldwin

1872 **Paper Bag Manufacturing Machine**—square-bottom paper bag machinery—patented—L. C. Crowell

1872 **Toothpick Manufacturing Machine Patent**—Silas Noble and J. P. Cooley —Granville, Mass.

1877 **Bridge**—cantilever bridge—completed —Kentucky River

1899 **Tunnel**—freight delivery tunnel system—Chicago, Ill.—franchise granted

1931 **Moving Picture**—moving picture of a complete grand opera—*Pagliacci*

1933 **Constitutional Amendment (U.S.)**—constitutional amendment submitted to the states for repeal—amendment submitted to the states

1937 **Automobile** — automobile-airplane combination—completed—Santa Monica, Calif.

1942 **Aviation — Aviator** — naval ace in World War II—E. H. O'Hare—in southwest Pacific

1952 **Baseball Umpire**—Negro umpire in organized baseball—E. L. Ashford

1962 **Astronauts** — American astronaut to orbit the earth—take-off—Cape Canaveral, Fla.—J. H. Glenn, Jr.

FEBRUARY 21

1828 **Newspaper**—Indian newspaper—*Cherokee Phoenix*—New Echota, Ga.

1842 **Sewing Machine** — sewing machine patent—J. J. Greenough

1846 **Woman** — woman telegrapher—S. G. Bagley—Lowell, Mass.

1853 **Money** — gold coinage — three-dollar gold pieces authorized

1858 **Burglar Alarm** — burglar alarm — installed—Boston, Mass.—E. T. Holmes

1862 **Execution** — execution (federal) for slave trading — Nathaniel Gordon—New York City

1864 **Catholic Church** — Catholic parish church for Negroes—dedicated—Baltimore, Md.

1866 **Dentist**—woman dentist to obtain a D.D.S. degree—L. B. Hobbs—graduated—Cincinnati, Ohio

1878 **Telephone Directory** — issued — New Haven, Conn.

1880 **Railroad**—municipal railroad—freight service between Cincinnati, Ohio, and Chattanooga, Tenn.—inaugurated

1885 **Monument** — monument to George Washington (national)—Washington, D.C.

1887 **Bacteriology Laboratory** — bacteriology laboratory—Hoagland Laboratory—Brooklyn, N.Y.—incorporated

1887 **Holiday**—Labor Day law (state)—enacted—Oregon

1903 **Army War College**—cornerstone laid —Washington, D.C.

1904 **Ski Club**—ski club association — National Ski Association—formed—Ishpeming, Mich.

1921 **Aviation—Flights (transcontinental)** —transcontinental flight within 24 hours flying time—W. D. Coney—San Diego, Calif. to Jacksonville, Fla.

1932 **Photography**—camera exposure meter —patent—W. N. Goodwin

1940 **Television—Telecast** — simulcast presented regularly by a sponsor—Lowell Thomas—New York City

1947 **Camera**—camera to take, develop and print pictures on photographic paper —demonstrated — E. H. Land—New York City

1949 **Degrees (academic and honorary)**—honorary degree awarded a Negro woman — M. M. Bethune — Winter Park, Fla.

FEBRUARY 22

1630 **Popcorn**—introduced to English colonists

1770 **Revolutionary War** — martyr in the Revolutionary War—Boston, Mass.—Christopher Snider killed

1784 **Ship**—trading ship sent to China — "Empress of China" — sailed — New York City

1836 **Whig Party**—state convention — Columbus, Ohio

1854 **Republican Party**—Republican Party meeting (local)

1855 **Agricultural School**—agricultural college (state) to be chartered—Farmers High School of Pennsylvania—reincorporated

1856 **Republican Party**—Republican Party meeting (national)—Pittsburgh, Pa.

1872 **Labor Party (political)**—Labor Party (national) — Labor Reform Party—formed—Columbus, Ohio

1872 **Prohibition Party (national)**—national convention—Columbus, Ohio

1878 **Greenback Labor Party**—organized—Toledo, Ohio

1879 **Business**—five-cent store — opened—Utica, N.Y.

1881 **Monument**—obelisk to be brought to the United States—officially presented to New York City

1887 **Union Labor Party**—formed—Cincinnati, Ohio

1889 **State**—states admitted to the Union simultaneously—North and South Dakota

1890 **Monument**—monument to a woman financed by women—National Mary Washington Memorial Association—incorporated

1898 **Newspaper**—Arabic daily newspaper—*Al-Hoda*—published — Philadelphia, Pa.

1909 **Ship**—warship fleet to circumnavigate the globe—returned—Hampton Roads, Va.

1920 **Dog Race Track**—to use imitation rabbit—opened—Emeryville, Calif.

1921 **Air Mail Service**—air mail transcontinental flight — left San Francisco, Calif. for New York City

1923 **Animals**—chinchilla farm—established —Los Angeles, Calif.

1924 **Radio Broadcast**—President to broadcast from the White House—Calvin Coolidge—Washington, D.C.

FEBRUARY 23

1791 **Life Saving Stations for Distressed Mariners**—Humane Society of Massachusetts—incorporated

1813 **Cotton Mill**—cotton mill in the world in which the whole process of cotton manufacturing from spinning to weaving was carried on by power—Waltham, Mass.

1821 **Pharmacy College**—pharmacy college —College of Apothecaries—organized —Philadelphia, Pa.

1839 **Express Service**—organized—W. F. Harnden—Boston, Mass. to New York City

1883 **Anti-Vivisection Society** — American Anti-Vivisection Society—organized—Philadelphia, Pa.

1883 **Trust**—anti-trust law (state)—enacted —Alabama

1886 **Aluminum** — aluminum — commercial process invented—C. M. Hall

1892 **College Self-Government Organization** —Bryn Mawr Self-Government Association—chartered

1905 **Medal**—Interstate Commerce Commission Medal of Honor—authorized

1905 **Rotary Club**—founded—Chicago, Ill.

1910 **Radio Contest**—Philadelphia, Pa.

1917 **Dental Society**—orthodontists' society —American Society of Orthodontists —incorporated

1921 **Air Mail Service**—air mail transcontinental flight—completed—New York City

1927 **Radio Commission (U.S.)**—created

1929 **Diathermy Machine** — first patient treated—Schenectady, N.Y.

1936 **Air Mail Service**—rocket air mail flight—Greenwood Lake, N.Y.

1942 **Chaplains' School**—naval chaplains' school—Norfolk, Va.

FEBRUARY 24

1839 **Steam Shovel**—patented—W. S. Otis

1835 **Periodical**—Indian-language monthly —*Shawnee Sun*—published

1855 **Court**—court of claims (U.S.)—established

1857 **Postage Stamp**—perforated postage stamps—received by government

1863 **Bank**—national bank—under national banking law—application for charter made—Davenport, Iowa

1866 **Flag**—American flag made of American bunting to fly over the Capitol—hoisted—Washington, D.C.

1868 **Impeachment**—impeachment proceedings against a President of the United States—authorized by House of Representatives—against Andrew Johnson

1868 **Parade**—parade with float tableaux—Mobile, Ala.

1888 **Election Law**—Australian ballot system—election—Louisville, Ky.

1921 **Aviation**—**Flights (transcontinental)**—transcontinental flight in twenty-four hours flying time—W. D. Coney—arrived—Jacksonville, Fla.

1925 **Thermit**—used to break ice jam—Waddington, N.Y.

1934 **Trust** — cartel — chairman — R. K. Davies—elected

1937 **Insurance**—group hospital-medical cooperative—authorized — Washington, D.C.

1938 **Nylon**—nylon bristle filament production for toothbrushes—Arlington, N.J.

1949 **Rocket**—rocket to reach outer space—White Sands Proving Grounds, N.M.

1960 **Submarine**—submerged navigation of the earth — "Triton" — crossed the equator

FEBRUARY 25

1751 **Animals**—monkey trained to perform —exhibited—New York City

1778 **Court Martial**—military court martial —concluded—Cambridge, Mass.

1791 **Bank**—Bank of the United States—Philadelphia, Pa.—incorporated

1795 **College**—non-denominational college—Union College—Schenectady, N.Y.—incorporated

1799 **Drydock**—drydock authorized for the United States Government—approved

1799 **Forestry Legislation**—federal forestry legislation—enacted

1799 **Quarantine** — quarantine legislation (national)—enacted

1804 **Political Convention**—political nominating caucus attended by party leaders—Washington, D.C.

1804 **Presidential Candidate** — presidential candidate nominated at a caucus—Washington, D.C.—Thomas Jefferson,

1819 **Bank**—savings bank actually to receive money on deposit—Philadelphia Saving Fund Society—incorporated

1836 **Pistol**—pistol—patented—Samuel Colt

1837 **Printing Press**—printing press operated by electricity—electrical motor—patent—Thomas Davenport

1862 **Engraving and Printing Bureau (U.S.)** —authorized

1863 **Bank Legislation**—national banking system—created

1863 **Comptroller**—Comptroller of the Currency—office authorized

1870 **Senator (U.S.)**—Negro senator—H. R. Revels—Mississippi—sworn in

1901 **Corporation**—corporation incorporated with a capitalization of $1 billion— United States Steel Corporation

1908 **Air (compressed)**—(for tunnel construction)—tunnel opened—Hoboken, N.J. to New York City

1908 **Tunnel**—tunnel under the Hudson River—opened—New York City to Jersey City

1913 **Tax**—income tax amendment to the Constitution—proclaimed

1919 **Gasoline Tax**—gasoline tax (state)— Oregon

1928 **Television License**—television license —Washington, D.C.

1930 **Check Protecting Device**—patented— G. L. McCarthy

1933 **Ship** — aircraft carrier — "Ranger" — launched—Newport News, Va.

1940 **Television—Telecast**—hockey game to be televised—New York City

1952 **Copyright**—choreographic score copyrighted — Hanya Holm — New York City

FEBRUARY 26

1811 **Hospital**—naval hospital—authorized

1834 **Crime Prevention and Detection**—interstate crime pact—ratified—New Jersey

1866 **Health Board**—health board (municipal) armed with sufficient powers—established—New York City

1870 **Subway**—pneumatic subway—opened —New York City

1895 **Glass Blowing Machine**—patented— M. J. Owens

1908 **Bowling Tournament** — gold medal award to a perfect-score bowler—claim entered

1914 **Museum**—industrial museum — incorporated—New York City

1914 **Telephone**—underground cable long distance telephone conversation—Boston, Mass., to Washington, D.C.

1919 **Park**—park (national) east of the Mississippi—name changed to Lafayette National Park

1935 **Ambulance** — incubator ambulance service—authorized—Chicago, Ill.

1938 **Radar**—passenger ship equipped with radar—"New York"

1940 **Air Defense Command (U.S.)**—created

1944 **Naval Officer**—captain in the U.S. Navy who was a woman—S. S. Dauser—appointed

1949 **Aviation — Flights (world)** — round-the-world non-stop airplane flight—take-off—Fort Worth, Tex.

1953 **Typesetting Machine** — photographic type-composing machine—book set by the Photon process—*The Wonderful World of Insects*

1954 **Typesetting Machine** — photo-engraving high-speed process for making half-tones — in operation — Quincy, Mass.

1955 **Aviation—Parachute**—aviator to bail out of an airplane flying at supersonic speed—Los Angeles, Calif.

FEBRUARY 27

1729 **College**—college to have a full faculty —property transferred to the faculty —Williamsburg, Va.

1813 **Postal Service** — mail delivery by steamboats—authorized

1813 **Vaccination Legislation**—vaccination legislation (national)—enacted

1861 **Postal Service**—newspaper wrappers —authorized

1867 **Dental Mallet** — dental mallet — idea conceived—W. G. A. Bonwill—Philadelphia, Pa.

1879 **Ship** — steamboat to employ electric lights—"Jeannette"—authorized

1883 **Cigar Rolling Machine** — practical — patented—Oscar Hammerstein

1897 **Initiative and Referendum**—passed— Senate—South Dakota

1915 **World War I**—American combatant to die in World War I—E. M. Stone

1919 **Deaf—Association**—national social organization for the hard of hearing— American Association for the Hard of Hearing—formed—New York City

1922 **Radio Conference** — national radio conference—Washington, D.C.

1935 **Vectolite**—manufactured—West Lynn, Mass.

1939 **Strike**—anti-sit-down strike decision (federal)—U.S. Supreme Court

1947 **Television—Telecast**—surgical operation televised on a closed circuit— Baltimore, Md.

FEBRUARY 28

1794 **Congress (U.S.)—Senate** — contested election—election result voided

1810 **Insurance**—fire insurance joint-stock company — American Fire Insurance Company—organized — Philadelphia, Pa.

1820 **Library**—mechanics' library—constitution adopted—General Society of Mechanics and Tradesmen of the City of New York

1822 **Bank**—trust company—Farmer's Fire Insurance and Loan Company—New York City—incorporated

1827 **Railroad** — railroad for commercial transportation of passengers and freight—Baltimore and Ohio Railroad Company—incorporated

1849 **Ship**—steamboat service (regular) to California via Cape Horn—"California"—arrived—San Francisco, Calif.

1874 **Agriculture Department (state)** — state department of agriculture—created—Georgia

1882 **Cooperative**—college cooperative store —Harvard Co-operative Society — Cambridge, Mass.—constitution

1893 **Carborundum**—E. G. Acheson—patent granted

1940 **Television—Telecast**—basketball game to be televised—New York City

1954 **Television—Telecast** — phase-contrast cinemicrography film (American-made) telecast—*The Birth of a Plant*

FEBRUARY 29

1804 **Congressional Caucus**—congressional caucus (open, not secret)—Washington, D.C.

1940 **Moving Picture Actor**—Negro to win an "Oscar"—Hattie McDaniel—award presented

1944 **Woman**—woman secretary of a national political party—appointed

MARCH 1

1642 **City (incorporated)**—Georgeana, Me. —incorporated

1780 **Slavery**—law (state) abolishing slavery—enacted—Pennsylvania

1781 **Articles of Confederation** — formally announced

1785 **Agricultural Society**—agricultural society — Philadelphia Society for the Promotion of Agriculture—organized

1790 **Census**—census of the United States —authorized

1792 **Presidential Succession Act**—enacted

1826 **Actor** — American actor to appear abroad—J. H. Hackett—New York City debut

1847 **Capital Punishment** — death penalty was first abolished—effective—Michigan

1864 **Physician**—Negro woman awarded a medical degree—Rebecca Lee—Boston, Mass.

1869 **Postage Stamp**—postage stamps depicting scenes—on sale

1869 **Postage Stamp**—postage stamps to picture the coat of arms of the United States—on sale

1872 **Park**—park (national) — Yellowstone National Park—authorized

1873 **Typewriter**—typewriter that was practical—contract to manufacture—Ilion, N.Y.

1876 **Cattle Club** — cattle club (Guernsey cattle)—formed—Farmington, Conn.

1883 **Index of Government Publications**— work assigned to B. P. Poore

1883 **Temperance Society** — women's temperance society (national)—National Woman's Christian Temperance Union—organized—Cleveland, Ohio

1894 **Physician**—osteopath (woman)—J. H. Bolles—graduated—Kirksville, Mo.

1899 **Union Reform Party**—platform adopted—Cincinnati, Ohio

1909 **Nursing School**—university school of nursing — established — Minneapolis, Minn.

1912 **Aviation** — **Parachute** — parachute jump from an airplane—Albert Berry —Jefferson Barracks, Mo.

1912 **Police** — woman detective — Isabella Goodwin — appointed — New York City

1913 **Insurance**—bonding law (state)—enacted—North Dakota

1913 **Tax**—income tax amendment to the Constitution—effective

1917 **Farm Loan Board (federal)**—federal land bank chartered

1937 **Automobile License Plates**—permanent license plates—effective—Conn.

1940 **Supreme Court (U.S.)**—members of a family admitted simultaneously to practice in the Supreme Court of the United States—Faust family

1941—**Radio License**—frequency modulation transmitter to receive a commercial license—operation—Nashville, Tenn.

1948 **Aviation—Airplane**—jet propelled fighter plane (four-engine)—tested in flight —Muroc, Calif.

1950 **Civil Defense Director**—P. J. Larsen —assumed office

MARCH 2

1642 **Labor Law**—convict labor law—enacted—Virginia

1799 **Weights and Measures Standardization**—weights and measures standardization—enacted

1817 **Evangelical Church Building**—church dedicated—New Berlin, Pa.

1825 **Opera**—grand opera sung in English —*Der Freischütz*—New York City

1827 **Lottery**—lottery legislation (national) —enacted

1829 **Blind**—school for the blind—New England Asylum for the Blind—Boston, Mass.—incorporated

1831 **Sculptor**—sculptor (American) to obtain a federal commission—appropriation granted

1833 **Pensions Commissioner (U.S.)**—act authorizing appointment

1833 **Railroad**—state aid to railroads—authorized—Illinois

1858 **Cotton-Bale Metallic Tie**—patented—Frederick Cook

1861 **Government Printing Office**—Government Printing Office—printing plant purchased—Washington, D.C.

1866 **Needles (machine made)**—Excelsior Needle Company—incorporated

1867 **College**—Negro university to establish undergraduate, graduate and professional schools—Howard University—incorporated

1867 **Education Department (U.S.)**—Department of Education (U.S.)—created

1888 **Bank**—bank for Negroes operated by Negroes—Richmond, Va.—chartered

1893 **Railroad Legislation**—railroad legislation (federal)—Safety Appliance Act—enacted

1894 **Medical School**—osteopathy school—Kirksville, Mo.—graduation

1899 **Naval Officer**—naval officer to become "Admiral of the Navy"—authorized

1901 **Forest Service**—Forest Service (U.S.)—Division of Forestry became Bureau of Forestry

1903 **Hotel**—hotel exclusively for women—opened—New York City

1925 **Road**—route numbering system (nation-wide)—adopted

1930 **Glider**—glider flight indoors—H. Kuchins—St. Louis, Mo.

1934 **Railroad**—streamlined light-weight high-speed three-car passenger train—operated—Union Pacific System

1940 **Television—Telecast**—track meet (intercollegiate) to be televised—New York City

1949 **Aviation—Flights (world)**—round-the-world non-stop airplane flight—completed—Fort Worth, Tex.

1949 **Electric Lighting**—street light of an automatic system — installed — New Milford, Conn.

MARCH 3

1791 **Internal Revenue Act**—enacted

1791 **Tax**—excise tax (federal)—enacted

1791 **Tax**—internal revenue tax—imposed

1794 **Opera**—opera of a serious nature—*Tammany*—produced—New York City

1797 **Army Officer**—Judge Advocate of the U.S. Army— Campbell Smith—began service

1801 **Governor**—Jewish governor—David Emanuel—Georgia—served

1801 **Land Pre-emption Act (federal)**—enacted

1803 **Impeachment**—impeachment of a federal judge—trial of John Pickering commenced

1803 **Land Grant**—special land grant to a foreigner—enacted

1813 **Army Officer**—surgeon general of the U.S. Army—office established

1819 **Navy**—naval legislation standardizing nomenclature for naval vessels

1833 **Pensions Commissioner (U.S.)**—J. L. Edwards—served

1842 **Child Labor Law**—child labor law regulating hours of employment—approved—Massachusetts

1843 **Telegraph** — telegraph appropriation (federal)—enacted

1845 **Law Book**—law compilation of United States laws—authorized

1845 **Postal Service**—ocean mail contracts—authorized

1845 **Shipping**—ship subsidy—legislation

1845 **Veto (presidential)**—legislation passed over a President's veto—John Tyler

1847 **Postage Stamp**—postage stamps issued by the Post Office Department—authorized

1849 **Interior Department (U.S.)**—Interior Department (U.S.)—office authorized

1849 **Money**—double eagle coinage—authorized

1849 **Money**—gold coinage — double-eagles and one-dollar gold pieces authorized

1851 **Money**—silver coins—three-cent piece—authorized

1853 **Assay Office Building (federal)**—authorized

1855 **Court**—court of claims—judges appointed

1855 **Postal Service**—registration of letters—authorized

1863 **Army**—signal corps—authorized as separate branch of army

1863 **Conscription** — wartime conscription bill—enacted

1863 **Medal**—Medal of Honor (Army)—award authorized for officers

1863 **Money**—gold certificates—authorized

1863 **Money**—notes wholly engraved and printed at the Bureau of Engraving and Printing—authorized

1863 **Postal Service**—free city delivery of mail—authorized

1863 **Science Association**—National Academy of Sciences—chartered

1865 **Bank**—Freedmen's bank—Freedman's Savings and Trust Company—incorporated

1865 **Freedman's Bureau (U.S.)**—created

1871 **Civil Service**—civil service commission—President authorized to regulate admission requirements

1871 **Fish and Fisheries Commissioner**—appropriation made

1873 **Postage Stamp**—departmental postage stamps—authorized

1875 **Homestead Act**—homestead act (desert)—enacted

1875 **Money** — silver coins — twenty-cent pieces authorized

1879 **Geological Survey**—geological survey director (U.S.)—authorized

1879 **Ship**—fish hatching steamer (federal)—"Fishhawk"—authorized

1879 **Supreme Court (U.S.)**—woman admitted to practice before the Supreme Court of the United States—B. A. B. Lockwood

1882 **Steam Distribution Plant**—steam distributed—New York City

1883 **Ship**—steel vessels of the United States Navy—authorized

1885 **Forest Service**—forest commission (state) (permanent) — authorized — California

1885 **Postal Service**—special delivery service—authorized

1891 **Immigration**—immigration bureau superintendent—office authorized

1891 **Prison**—penitentiary building (national)—authorized

1892 **Animals**—cattle tuberculosis test—Villa Nova, Pa.

1893 **Money**—coin bearing the portrait of a foreign monarch—authorized

1893 **Money**—silver coins—Columbian quarter-dollar—authorized

1893 **Road**—federal road agency—Office of Road Inquiry—authorized

1894 **Newspaper**—Greek newspaper—*Atlantis*—published—New York City

1899 **Naval Officer**—naval officer to become "Admiral of the Navy"—George Dewey—served

1899 **Ship**—battleship built on the Pacific coast—"Nebraska"—authorized

1901 **Standards Bureau (U.S.)**—authorized

1903 **Fingerprinting**—state prison to take fingerprints—Ossining, N.Y.

1903 **Nurse**—nurses' registration law (state)—North Carolina

1905 **Forest Service** — Forest Service (U.S.)—Bureau of Forestry designated as the Forest Service

1911 **Cemetery**—federal cemetery in the United States to contain graves of both Union and Confederate soldiers—authorized—Springfield, Mo.

1911 **Dental Corps (U.S. Army)**—dental corps commissions—authorized

1913 **Court**—juvenile court—cases tried by a woman judge—Chicago, Ill.

1915 **Aviation**—Advisory Committee for Aeronautics (national)—established

1917 **Tax**—excess profits tax—enacted

1919 **Air Mail Service**—international air mail—Seattle, Wash., and Victoria, B.C.

1923 **Radio Facsimile Transmission**—photograph sent overland by radio to a distant point—Anacostia, D.C., to Philadelphia, Pa.

1926 **Greyhound Racing Association**—International Greyhound Racing Association—formed—Miami, Fla.

1927 **Prohibition**—prohibition bureau (federal)—authorized

1931 **National Anthem**—"Star Spangled Banner"—designated national anthem

1945 **Medal**—silver star medal awarded to a civilian by the U.S. Navy in World War II—Tony Duenas

1949 **Railroad Car**—passenger car (ACF-Talgo)—tested

MARCH 4

1776 **War (colonial)**—marine engagement in battle—fort captured—New Providence, Bahamas

1789 **Congress of the United States**—Congress of the United States—scheduled—New York City

1789 **Congress (U.S.)—House of Representatives**—House of Representatives—scheduled—New York City

1789 **Congress (U.S.) — Senate** — Senate—scheduled—New York City

1789 **Congressman (U.S.)**—Catholic congressman — Thomas FitzSimons—served

1789 **Constitution of the United States**—printed copies of the Constitution—Constitution declared in effect

1789 **Senator (U.S.)**—Catholic senator—Daniel Carroll—served

1791 **Army Officer**—chaplain of the United States Army—John Hurt—appointed

1791 **Congress (U.S.)—Senate**—Senate special session

1791 **Congressman (U.S.)**—Jewish congressman—Israel Jacobs—served

1791 **State**—state admitted to the Union—after the Constitution—Vermont

1797 **Congressman (U.S.)** — congressman elected who served time in prison—Matthew Lyon—term began

1801 **President**—president inaugurated in the city of Washington—Thomas Jefferson

1809 **Vice President of the United States**—vice president to serve under two presidents — George Clinton — began second term

1823 **Congressman (U.S.)**—Roman Catholic priest to serve in Congress—Gabriel Richard—Michigan Territory—term began

1826 **Railroad**—railroad for freight transportation to celebrate its centenary—Granite Railway Company—incorporated

1829 **Spoils System**—introduced—Andrew Jackson

1831 **Congressman (U.S.)** — congressman who had been a President of the United States—J. Q. Adams—served

1837 **Vice President of the United States**—Vice President elected by the Senate—R. M. Johnson—served

1838 **Sunday School**—Jewish Sunday school—organized—Philadelphia, Pa.

1841 **Senator (U.S.)**—senator to receive a mileage allowance for a trip which he did not make—George Evans—served

1853 **Vice President of the United States**—Vice President sworn in on foreign soil—W. R. D. King—Havana, Cuba

1855 **Congressman (U.S.)** — congressmen (brothers) to serve simultaneously—Washburn brothers

1861 **Flag**—Confederate States flag—adopted—Montgomery, Ala.

1861 **Government Printing Office**—Government Printing Office—purchased printing plant began to function—Washington, D.C.

1863 **Congress of the United States**—officer to preside over both of the branches of Congress—Schuyler Colfax—served

1863 **Normal School**—normal school (state) at which students actually conducted classes—Oswego, N.Y.—state appropriation—enacted

1873 **Newspaper**—illustrated daily newspaper—*Daily Graphic*—published—New York City

1875 **President**—President to become a senator—Andrew Johnson—served in U.S. Senate

1880 **Engraving** — half-tone engraving — published—*Daily Graphic*—New York City

1881 **Catholic Student**—palladium conferred —M. A. Corrigan

1881 **President**—President whose mother lived at the Executive Mansion—J. A. Garfield—inaugurated

1881 **Presidential Candidate** — presidential candidate to campaign and make speeches in a foreign language—J. A. Garfield—inaugurated

1881 **Quarantine**—plant quarantine legislation (state)—enacted—California

1891 **Congress of the United States**—Congress to appropriate a billion dollars—Washington, D.C.

1891 **Congressman (U.S.)** — congressman elected by the prohibitionists—Kittel Halvorson—served

1891 **Copyright Law**—international copyright agreement—Platt-Simonds Copyright Act—enacted

1903 **Turbine**—steam turbine generator of large capacity for commercial service —Chicago, Ill.—tested

1909 **Game Law Department (U.S.)**—game law (state)—act prohibiting the transportation of game

1911 **Congressman (U.S.)**—Socialist congressman—V. L. Berger—served

1913 **Agriculture Department (U.S.)** — Office of Markets—created

1913 **Arbitration**—Federal Board of Mediation and Conciliation—authorized

1913 **Commerce Department (U.S.)**—Commerce Department (U.S.)—established

1913 **Game Law**—game law (state)—McLean law—regulating shooting of migratory birds—enacted

1913 **Labor Department (U.S.)**—Labor Department (U.S.)—created

1917 **Agriculture Department (U.S.)**—Office of Markets—changed to Bureau of Markets

1917 **Congressman (U.S.)**—congresswoman elected—Jeannette Rankin—served

1921 **Park**—park (national)—Hot Springs National Park—designated

1925 **Radio Broadcast**—presidential inauguration—Calvin Coolidge—Washington, D.C.

1925 **Radio Facsimile Transmission**—photograph sent by radio across the continent—Washington, D.C.

1929 **Congress (U.S.)—Senate**—broadcast from the Senate chamber—Washington, D.C.

1929 **Congressman (U.S.)**—Negro congressman from the North—O. S. De Priest —served

1929 **Vice President of the United States**— Indian Vice President—Charles Curtis —served

1929 **Woman**—woman secretary to a Vice President of the United States—L. M. Williams—served

1930 **Bowler**—woman bowler to obtain a perfect score—Emma Fahning—Buffalo, N.Y.

1933 **Cabinet of the United States**—father and son to occupy the same cabinet posts—H. C. Wallace and H. A. Wallace—H. A. Wallace—served

1933 **Cabinet of the United States**—full cabinet sworn in at the same time and place — Washington, D.C. — F. D. Roosevelt

1933 **Cabinet of the United States**—woman cabinet member—Frances Perkins— served

1933 **Labor Department (U.S.)**—woman Secretary of Labor—Frances Perkins —served

1933 **Presidential Electoral College** — invited to attend inaugural ceremony— March 4

1952 **Radio Station**—sea-going radio broadcasting station—"Courier"—dedicated —Washington, D.C.

1954 **Cabinet of the United States**—Negro sub-cabinet member—J. E. Wilkins— appointed

MARCH 5

1623 **Temperance Law (colonial)**—enacted —Virginia

1743 **Religious Publication**—religious journal—*Christian History*—published—Boston, Mass.

1750 **Play (drama)**—Shakespearean play— *King Richard III*—presented—New York City

1813 **Flag**—American flag flown in battle on the Pacific — "Essex" entered Pacific Ocean

1821 **President**—President inaugurated on March 5—James Monroe

1836 **Pistol**—pistol—Samuel Colt— company incorporated

1856 **Railroad Legislation**—railroad legislation (state)—enacted—Georgia

1866 **Health Board**—health board (municipal) armed with sufficient powers— meeting—New York City

1872 **Air Brake**—triple air brake patented— George Westinghouse

1880 **Railroad**—municipal railroad—through passenger trains—Cincinnati, Ohio and Chattanooga, Tenn.

1894 **Employment Service**—municipal employment office — opened — Seattle, Wash.

1913 **Commerce and Labor Department (U.S.)**—W. C. Redfield—became Secretary of Commerce

1923 **Pension**—old age pension laws (state) —enacted—Montana and Nevada

1924 **Bowler**—bowler to roll two perfect games—Frank Caruana—Buffalo, N.Y.

1934 **Holiday** — mother-in-law day — celebrated—Amarillo, Tex.

1935 **Medical Legislation**—premature baby health law—enacted—Chicago, Ill.

1935 **Naval Officer**—naval officer designated Commander, Aircraft Battle Force— H. V. Butler

MARCH 6

1646 **Patent**—machine patent—Joseph Jencks —Massachusetts

1775 **Freemasons**—Negro mason—initiated —Boston, Mass.

1808 **Orchestra**—college orchestra—founded —Cambridge, Mass.

1810 **Vaccination Legislation**—vaccination legislation (state)—enacted—Illinois

1865 **Naval Officer**—Judge Advocate of the Navy—W. E. Chandler—appointed

1886 **Electric Power Plant**—alternating current power plant—Great Barrington, Mass.

1886 **Nurses' Magazine**—*The Nightingale*— published—New York City

1906 **Engineering Society**—woman elected to the American Society of Civil Engineers—N. S. Blatch

1947 **Aviation — Airplane** — jet propulsion four-engine bomber — tested — Muroc, Calif.

1947 **Ship**—air-conditioned naval ship— "Newport News"—launched—Newport News, Va.

MARCH 7

1644 **Legislature** — legislature with two chambers — established — Massachusetts

1644 **Whaling** — whaling (systematic) — Southampton, N.Y.

1801 **Election Law**—registration law (state) —enacted—Massachusetts

1825 **Treaty**—treaty with a South American country—Colombia—ratified

1854 **Sewing Machine**—sewing machine to stitch buttonholes—patented—Charles Miller

1876 **Telephone**—telephone patent—A. G. Bell

1893 **Patent**—print patent—H. J. Heinz Co. —Pittsburgh, Pa.

1911 **Locker** — locker (coin vender) — patented—W. S. Farnsworth

1958 **Submarine**—submarine expressly designed and built to fire guided missiles —"Grayback"—commissioned — Mare Island, Calif.

1959 **Aviation**—**Aviator**—aviator to fly a million miles in a jet airplane—M. C. Garlow

MARCH 8

1849 **Interior Department (U.S.)**—Interior Department secretary—Thomas Ewing —appointed

1855 **Bridge**—railway suspension bridge— Niagara Falls Suspension Bridge— train crossed over

1862 **Naval Officer**—naval chaplain killed in action—J. L. Lenhart

1871 **Fish and Fisheries Commissioner (U.S.)**—S. F. Baird—served

1887 **Fishing Rod**—of telescoping steel tubes—patented—Everett Horton

1894 **Dog License**—dog license law (state) —enacted—New York City

1917 **Congress (U.S.)**—Senate—Senate cloture resolution—enacted

1933 **Money**—scrip money to be self-liquidating—issued

1945 **Naval Officer**—Negro nurse in the Navy Reserve Corps—inducted—P. M. Daley—New York City

1946 **Helicopter**—helicopter licensed for commercial use—license granted to *Journal American*—New York City

MARCH 9

1745 **Carillon**—carillon—shipped from England—to Boston, Mass.

1798 **Naval Officer**—naval surgeon of the U.S. Navy—George Balfour transferred to Navy

1799 **Pistol**—government contract for pistols—Simeon North—Berlin, Conn.

1822 **Dentistry**—patent for artificial teeth— C. M. Graham

1830 **Bank**—trust company—New York Life Insurance and Trust Company—chartered—New York City

1841 **Dental School**—dental college—Baltimore College of Dental Surgery—Baltimore, Md.—degrees conferred

1858 **Postal Service**—street letter box—patented—Albert Potts

1860 **Japanese Ambassador**—staff arrived— San Francisco, Calif.

1861 **Money** — Confederate currency — authorized

1862 **Civil War**—conflict between iron-clad vessels in the Civil War—"Monitor" and "Merrimac"

1862 **Ordnance** — revolving gun turret — "Monitor"—used

1889 **Trust**—anti-trust law (state)—general law—enacted—Kansas

1892 **Degrees (academic and honorary)**— anthropology doctorate — conferred— Worcester, Mass.

1907 **Sterilization Legislation**—enacted—Indiana

1947 **Helicopter**—helicopter to deliver material across a picket line—New Bedford, Mass.

1949 **Railroad Car**—dining car (all-electric) —in service between Chicago, Ill., and St. Louis, Mo.

1954 **Television—Telecast**—color commercial televised on a local show

MARCH 10

1785 **Diplomatic Service**—minister plenipotentiary—appointed after the Revolution—Thomas Jefferson

1791 **Pile Driver**—pile driver—patented—John Stone

1849 **President**—President who had received a patent—Abraham Lincoln made application

1869 **Dental School**—dental school permanently established by a university—graduation—Cambridge, Mass.

1871 **Benevolent and Protective Order of Elks**—Grand Lodge—incorporated

1876 **Telephone**—telephone message—A. G. Bell—Boston, Mass.

1880 **Salvation Army**—landed—New York City

1903 **Multigraph**—patented—H. C. Gammeter

1908 **Children's Welfare Congress (international)**—met—Washington, D.C.

1909 **Old Age Home for Pioneers**—approved—Arizona

1911 **Trust**—blue-sky laws—passed—Kansas

1913 **Bowler**—bowler to make a perfect score of 300 in an American Bowling Congress tournament—William Knox —Toledo, Ohio

1933 **Narcotic**—narcotic regulation (state)—adopted—Nevada

1940 **Television—Telecast**—opera telecast—New York City

1948 **Aviation—Flights**—airplane to exceed the speed of sound which was piloted by a civilian—H. H. Hoover—Edwards Air Force Base, Calif.

MARCH 11

1779 **Army**—Army Engineering Department —formal "Corps of Engineers"—established

1791 **Patent**—patentee to obtain more than one patent—Samuel Mulliken

1823 **Normal School**—normal school established exclusively for the preparation of teachers—Concord Academy—Concord, Vt.—opened

1852 **Fair**—industrial exposition—company chartered

1861 **Constitution of the Confederate States of America** — adopted — Montgomery, Ala.

1864 **Army Ambulance Corps**—Army Ambulance Corps established by congressional action

1864 **Army Officer**—woman assistant army surgeon—M. E. Walker

1882 **Lacrosse Association (intercollegiate)** —Intercollegiate Lacrosse Association —organized—Princeton, N.J.

1886 **Physician**—Hindu woman to receive a doctor of medicine degree—Anandibai Joshee—graduated

1896 **War Veterans' Society**—Military Order of Foreign Wars—National Commandery—instituted

1903 **Opera**—opera composed by a woman performed at the Metropolitan Opera House—*Der Wald*—New York City—E. M. Smyth

1909 **Bowling Tournament**—gold medal award to a perfect-score bowler—roll-off—Pittsburgh, Pa.

1927 **Automobile Robbery**—armored commercial car hold-up—Pittsburgh, Pa.

1927 **Moving Picture Theater**—theater built especially for the rear projection of moving pictures—rear projection screen used—New York City

1930 **President**—President buried in the National Cemetery at Arlington, Va.—W. H. Taft

1940 **Photograph**—cystoscopic photographs in color—publicly exhibited—Birmingham, Ala.

1945 **Medal**—navy unit commendation decoration—to ship—"Helena"—awarded

1948 **Tennis Player**—Negro tennis player to participate in a United States Indoor Lawn Tennis Association championship tournament — Reginald Weir — New York City

1953 **Army Officer**—woman doctor commissioned in the regular Army—F. M. Adams

1960 **Rocket**—satellite placed in solar orbit —Pioneer V (1960 Alpha)—launched —Cape Canaveral, Fla.

MARCH 12

1664 **Citizenship** — naturalization act — in the American colonies—enacted

1755 **Steam Engine**—steam engine—used—North Arlington, N.J.

1804 **Impeachment**—impeachment of a federal judge — John Pickering — impeached

1849 **Railroad**—railroad to run west of the Mississippi River—Pacific Railroad of Missouri—incorporated

1877 **Cabinet of the United States**—Confederate to serve in the cabinet—D. M. Key—served

1884 **College**—state college for women—authorized—Mississippi

1889 **Telephone**—automatic telephone system (successful)—patent application

1894 **Supreme Court (U.S.)**—associate justice of the Supreme Court to become Chief Justice—E. D. White appointed justice

1904 **Carnegie Hero Fund Commission**—established—Andrew Carnegie

1912 **Girl Scouts**—founded—Savannah, Ga.

1920 **Deaf**—Association—national social organization for the hard of hearing—American Association for the Hard of Hearing—annual meeting

1923 **Moving Picture**—sound-on-film moving picture — demonstrated — for the press — Lee de Forest — New York City

1935 **Crime Prevention and Detection** — crime prevention commission for interstate cooperation—joint resolution —enacted—New Jersey

1945 **Labor**—labor anti-discrimination commission (state)—commission authorized—New York

MARCH 13

1638 **Military Organization**—military organization—Ancient and Honorable Artillery Company—chartered

1735 **Moravian Bishop**—David Nitschmann —consecrated at Berlin, Germany

1770 **Chamber of Commerce**—Chamber of Commerce (state) — incorporated — New York

1790 **Actor**—actor of American birth—John Martin—appeared—Philadelphia, Pa.

1852 **Cartoon**—"Uncle Sam" cartoon—published—New York City

1868 **Impeachment**—impeachment proceedings against a President of the United States — against Andrew Johnson — Washington, D.C.

1877 **Earmuff** — patented — Chester Greenwood

1895 **Submarine**—submarine contract of the United States Navy — "Plunger" — John P. Holland Torpedo Boat Co.

1913 **Moving Picture Censorship**—moving picture censorship board (state)—approved—Kansas

1930 **Astronomy** — planet — discovery of Pluto—announced

1942 **Army Officer**—woman with rank corresponding to colonel—J. O. Flikke

1943 **Dental Corps (U.S. Navy)**—admiral in the Dental Corps (U.S. Navy)—A. G. Lyle—appointed

1946 **Medal**—Medal of Honor awarded to a Nisei—presented

1952 **Chloromycetin**—chloromycetin laboratory—opened—Holland, Mich.

1953 **Hospital**—hospital completely devoted to the study of the atom in the treatment of cancer—Argonne Cancer Research Hospital — opened — Chicago, Ill.

1955 **Building**—atom bomb-resistant federal building—occupied—Washington, D.C.

1959 **Photograph** — ultraviolet pictures of the sun—White Sands, N.M.

MARCH 14

1493 **Letter**—letter descriptive of America —dispatched

1794 **Cotton Gin**—patented—Eli Whitney

1812 **War Bond**—authorized

1813 **Ship**—naval vessel of the United States to display the American flag around Cape Horn — arrived — Valparaiso, Chile

1826 **Conference**—conference of American Republics—assembled at Panama

1867 **Education Department (U.S.)** — Department of Education (U.S.)—Commissioner Henry Barnard—appointed

1900 **Bond**—bonds payable specifically in United States gold coins—authorized

1903 **Bird Reservation (national)** — established—Sebastian, Fla.

1907 **Bank**—national bank branch legally operated — chartered — Moss Point, Miss.

1911 **Insurance** — workmen's compensation insurance law (state) — enacted — Washington

1917 **Aviation — Airship** — airship of the United States Navy that was successful—F1—flight

1918 **Ship**—concrete seagoing ship—"Faith" —launched—Redwood City, Calif.

1927 **Engineering Society**—woman elected to the American Society of Civil Engineers—as associate member—Elsie Eaves

1931 **Moving Picture Theater**—theater built especially for the rear projection of moving pictures—opened—New York City

1936 **Periodical**—magazine of the United States Government—*Federal Register*—issued

1960 **Sulphur Mine (offshore)**—off Louisiana coast—sulphur obtained

MARCH 15

1729 **Catholic Nuns**—nun who professed her vows—New Orleans, La.

1767 **President** — President born posthumously—Andrew Jackson—born—Union County, N.C.

1812 **Russian Settlement**—established—Cazadero, Calif.

1830 **Educational Association**—educational association (national)—American Institute of Instruction—formed—Boston, Mass.

1834 **Drydock**—federal drydocks—Norfolk, Va. drydock completed

1855 **Health Board**—health board (state) to regulate quarantine—Louisiana

1867 **College** — state university supported by a direct property tax—approved—Michigan

1875 **Catholic Priest**—Catholic priest to be elevated to the cardinalate—John McCloskey—preconized

1887 **Game Warden**—(salaried game and fish warden)—authorized—Michigan

1887 **Kindergarten** — kindergarten for the blind—authorized—Roxbury, Mass.

1892 **Voting Machine** — voting machines were authorized—New York

1897 **Flycasting Tournament** — indoor fly casting tournament—New York City

1901 **Army Nurse Corps (female)**—Superintendent D. H. Kinney—appointed

1913 **Court**—conciliation tribunal for small claims—established—Cleveland, Ohio

1913 **Court**—small debtors' court established by state law—authorized—Kansas

1919 **War Veterans' Society** — American Legion—caucus—Paris, France

1927 **Radio Commission (U.S.)**—organization meeting

1930 **Glider**—seaplane glider—tested—Port Washington, N.Y.

1930 **Submarine**—streamlined submarine of the U.S. Navy—"Nautilus"—launched—Mare Island, Calif.

1934 **Information Service (U.S.)**—opened

1934 **Youth Hostel** — incorporated — Hartford, Conn.

1937 **Blood Bank**—blood bank—established—Chicago, Ill.

1937 **Medical Clinic** — contraceptive clinic (state)—opened—Raleigh, N.C.

1938 **Merchant Marine Academy** — Merchant Marine Cadet Corps (U.S.)—established—Kings Point, N.Y.

1945 **Medal**—presidential citation to an entire division—awarded

1947 **Naval Officer** — Negro commissioned officer in the regular U.S. Navy—John Lee—commissioned

1948 **Air Mail Service**—parcel post international air service — inaugurated — to Europe

1960 **Park**—underseas park (federal)—Key Largo Coral Reef Preserve established—Key Largo, Fla.

MARCH 16

1697 **Woman** — heroine — captured by Indians—Hannah Duston

1802 **Army**—engineer corps—established

1802 **Army School**—Army school — established—West Point, N.Y.

1827 **Newspaper** — Negro newspaper — *Freedom's Journal* — published — New York City

1829 **High School Legislation**—high school legislation—enacted—Ohio

1871 **Fertilizer Law**—fertilizer law (state)—enacted—Delaware

1877 **Occupational Therapy Treatment** — training school—incorporated

1882 **American Red Cross**—ratification of international agreement by United States

1883 **Pharmacist** — pharmacist (woman graduate)—Susan Hayhurst — graduated

1885 **Bank**—savings group—started—Long Island City, N.Y.

1915 **Federal Trade Commission** — organized

1926 **Rocket**—liquid fuel rocket flight—Auburn, Mass.

1929 **Tax**—chain stores tax (state)—authorized—Indiana

1931 **Woman**—woman state budget commissioner — J. W. Wittich—served—Minnesota

1934 **Revenue Stamp**—printed by the Post Office Department—authorized

1947 **Aviation—Airplane**—twin-engine pressurized airplane—tested—San Diego, Calif.

1952 **Television—Telecast**—surgical operation televised on a local program—Philadelphia, Pa.

MARCH 17

1631 **Fire Prevention Legislation**—enacted—Cambridge, Mass.

1845 **Yacht Club**—New York Yacht Club—regular election—New York City

1852 **Fair**—industrial exposition—directors elected—New York City

1854 **Park**—park land—purchased by a city—Worcester, Mass.

1861 **Money**—paper money issued by the Government of the United States—demand notes—made legal tender

1864 **Water Conduit**—water supply tunnel for a city—construction began—Chicago, Ill.

1868 **Postal Service**—postage canceling machine patent

1871 **Baseball League**—baseball league of importance — National Association of Base-Ball Players—organized

1884 **Glider**—glider flight—J. J. Montgomery—Otay, Calif.

1897 **Prize Fight**—open-air arena especially built for a prize fight—Carson City, Nev.—Corbett-Fitzsimmons fight

1898 **Submarine**—submarine that was practical and able to submerge—"Holland No. 9"—launched

1912 **Camp Fire Girls** — organization — announced—Lake Sebago, Me.

1913 **Court**—conciliation tribunal for small claims—Ohio—court opened

1914 **Automobile Bus**—bus with cross seats—introduced

1917 **Bowling Tournament**—bowling tournament for women—St. Louis, Mo.

1924 **Fireboat** — fireboat with two-way radio equipment — licensed — Boston, Mass.

1950 **Element**—element 98—announced

MARCH 18

1543 **Flood**—recorded—Mississippi River—Fernando De Soto

1734 **Advertisement**—magician's advertisement—published—New York City

1795 **Catholic Priest**—Catholic priest to receive his full theological training in the United States—D. A. Gallitzin—ordained bishop—Baltimore, Md.

1813 Gas—gas lights (street)—David Melville—Newport, R.I.—patent

1818 Pension—pensions paid by the United States Government—universal service pension

1834 Tunnel—railroad tunnel—completed—Hollidaysburg to Johnstown, Pa.

1890 Navy—naval militia (state)—Massachusetts Naval Battalion—organized

1910 Opera—opera by an American composer performed at the Metropolitan Opera House of New York—*Pipe of Desire*—produced

1911 Insurance—hail insurance law (state)—enacted—North Dakota

1922 Polo — intercollegiate indoor polo championship — Princeton-Yale — New York City

1931 Razor—electric dry shaver—manufactured—Stamford, Conn.

1938 Medical Legislation—law (state) requiring serological blood tests of pregnant women — enacted — New York

1948 Birth Registration—birth registration uniform system for the numbering of birth certificates

1950 Basketball—basketball collegiate team to win the National Invitation Tournament and the National Collegiate Athletic Association trophy

1952 Lens—plastic lens—for cataract patients—fitted—Philadelphia, Pa.

1958 Newspaper—newspaper advertisement printed on aluminum foil—Milwaukee *Sentinel*

MARCH 19

1831 Bank Robbery—bank robbery—New York City

1949 Museum—museum devoted exclusively to atomic energy—opened—Oak Ridge, Tenn.

1954 Rocket Sled—rocket-driven sled on rails—tested—Alamogordo, N.M.

1954 Television—Telecast—prize fight televised in color—New York City

MARCH 20

1768 Artist—artist successful in commercial art—Matthew Pratt—sailed from Bristol, England

1833 Treaty—treaty with a Far Eastern country—concluded with Siam

1856 Governor — governor removed from office by a state supreme court—decision against W. A. Barstow

1865 Cooperative—cooperative state law—effective—Michigan

1872 Pharmacy College—pharmacy college to make analytical chemistry a required course — chair of Analytical Chemistry — Maryland College of Pharmacy—Baltimore, Md.

1886 Electric Power Plant — alternating current power plant—commercial operation—Great Barrington, Mass.

1890 Women's Club—women's club federation—General Federation of Women's Clubs—organized—New York City

1891 Scale—computing scales—Computing Scale Company—Dayton, Ohio—incorporated

1897 Basketball—basketball intercollegiate five-man team game — New Haven, Conn.

1899 Execution—execution of a woman—M. M. Place—Ossining, N.Y.

1902 Radio Telephone — radio telephone marine demonstration—N. B. Stubblefield—"Bartholdi"

1911 Farm Bureau—Binghamton, N.Y.

1911 Squash Club—squash tennis organization (national) — National Squash Tennis Association — formed — New York City

1914 Skating Tournament — figure skating international championship tournament—New Haven, Conn.

1925 Diplomatic Service—woman vice-consul—P. H. Field—appointed

1930 Diesel Engine — diesel engine speed record (official)—Daytona Beach, Fla.

1948 Radio Broadcast—radio program simultaneously transmitted—over AM and FM stations, and telecast—NBC Symphony—New York City

1948 Television—Telecast—symphonic concerts to be televised—Philadelphia, Pa.

MARCH 21

1791 Naval Officer—naval officer commissioned—Hopley Yeaton

1791 Navy—naval protection—commissions granted to captains

1791 Ship — revenue cutter — officers appointed

1826 Engineering College — engineering college — Rensselaer School — Troy, N.Y.—incorporated

1850 College—coeducational college—Oberlin College — name adopted — Oberlin, Ohio

1856 Governor—governor removed from office by a state supreme court—W. A. Barstow—resigned

1859 Zoological Garden — zoological garden—Philadelphia Zoological Garden—incorporated

1866 Soldiers' Homes (national) — authorized

1868 Women's Club—women's professional club—"Sorosis"—founded—New York City

1879 Geological Survey—geological survey director (U.S.) — Clarence King — nominated

1889 Holiday—national holiday—authorized for April 30, 1889

1905 Sterilization Legislation — passed by Pennsylvania but vetoed by governor

1924 Radio Broadcast — foreign language course broadcast—New York City

1933 Aviation — Flights — all-blind cross-country test—College Park, Md.

1935 **Ambulance** — incubator ambulance service—inaugurated—Chicago, Ill.

1946 **Microfilm**—microfilm machine to project enlarged images on ceilings—installed—Ann Arbor, Mich.

1946 **United Nations Conference on International Organization** — temporary quarters established—New York City

MARCH 22

1622 **Indians**—Indian massacre of white people—Jamestown, Va.

1630 **Gambling Legislation (colonial)** — enacted—Boston, Mass.

1822 **Horticultural Society**—horticultural society—New York Horticultural Society —incorporated

1841 **Cornstarch** — cornstarch patent — O. Jones

1861 **Nursing School**—school for nurses to award a diploma—School of Nursing —Philadelphia, Pa.—incorporated

1862 **Ship** — Confederate cruiser built in England—sailed from England

1871 **Impeachment**—impeachment and removal from office of a state governor —W. W. Holden—North Carolina—impeached

1872 **Labor Law**—women's equal employment legislation—enacted—Illinois

1874 **Young Men's Hebrew Association** — founded—New York City

1880 **Electric Power Plant**—hydroelectric power plant (commercial)—organized —Grand Rapids, Mich.

1882 **Polygamy Legislation (federal)**—important legislation—enacted

1887 **Interstate Commerce Act** — commissioners appointed

1911 **Opera** — opera singer to sing two major roles on the same day—Herman Jadlowker—Metropolitan Opera House—New York City

1935 **Medical Legislation**—blood grouping test laws (state) — enacted — New York

1948 **Radio Broadcast**—radio program simultaneously transmitted— over AM and FM stations, and telecast—commercial—"The Voice of Firestone"—New York City

MARCH 23

1794 **Rivet**—patent—J. G. Pierson

1802 **Social Service Endowment** — White-Williams Foundation—incorporated

1858 **Street Car**—cable car — patented—E. A. Gardner—Philadelphia, Pa.

1861 **Government Printing Office**—Government Printing Office—J. D. Defrees—Superintendent of Public Printing—appointed

1867 **Forest Service**—forestry inquiry commission (state) authorized—Wisconsin

1880 **Flour Mill**—flour rolling mill—patent —John Stevens—Neenah, Wis.

1910 **Automobile Race Track**—automobile speedway (board track)—trial race—Playa del Rey, Calif.

1925 **Evolution Law (state)** — enacted — Tennessee

MARCH 24

1629 **Game Law**—game law (colonial)—enacted—Virginia

1792 **Artist**—American artist to win distinction—Benjamin West became president of Royal Academy of London

1828 **Railroad**—state-owned railroad—Philadelphia and Columbia Railway—authorized

1880 **Insurance**—hail insurance—company incorporated—North Canaan, Conn.

1887 **Diplomatic Service**—Jewish ambassador—O. S. Straus—appointed

1920 **Aviation**—Coast Guard air station—opened—Morehead City, N.C.

1932 **Radio Broadcast** — radio broadcast from a moving train—WABC

1940 **Television**—**Telecast**—religious services to be televised—New York City

1942 **Coast Guard (U.S.)**—vice admiral in the Coast Guard—appointed

1949 **Moving Picture Actor**—moving picture actor and son to receive "Oscars" —John and Walter Huston—Hollywood, Calif.

1953 **Television** — **Telecast**—opera written for television on commission for a commercial sponsor—New York City

1955 **Drill**—oil drill seagoing rig—placed in service

1958 **Navy**—task force to fight undersea craft—created

MARCH 25

1639 **Canal**—canal for creating water power—Dedham, Mass.

1776 **Medal**—medal awarded by the Continental Congress — authorized for George Washington

1802 **Vaccine Institution**—opened — James Smith—Baltimore, Md.

1813 **Flag**—American flag flown in battle on the Pacific—"Essex"

1867 **Water Conduit**—water supply tunnel for a city—Chicago, Ill.—water received

1890 **Navy**—naval militia (state)—formed—Massachusetts—companies formed

1898 **Trapshooting**—trapshooting intercollegiate association—formed—New York City

1900 **Socialist Party**—formed—Indianapolis, Ind.

1902 **Glass**—sheet glass drawing machine—patented—I. W. Colburn

1915 **Submarine**—submarine disaster—Hawaii

1930 **Radio Broadcast**—ship-at-sea broadcast from an ocean liner—"Europa"

1937 **Newspaper**—newspaper with perfumed advertising page—*Daily News*—Washington, D.C.

1941 **Paprika Mill**—Dillon, S.C.—incorporated

1960 **Submarine**—guided missile launched from a nuclear-powered submarine—Regulus I

MARCH 26

1790 **Naturalization Act**—naturalization act—enacted

1804 **Indian Reservation**—Indian reservation (federal)—removal notice enacted

1819 **Bank**—savings bank—Bank for Savings in the City of New York—chartered

1845 **Adhesive and Medicated Plaster**—adhesive and medicated plaster patent

1845 **Lifeboat**—lifeboat (corrugated)—patented—Joseph Francis

1866 **Election Law**—fraudulent election law (state)—enacted—California

1885 **Photographic Film**—moving picture film (commercial) — manufactured — Rochester, N.Y.

1895 **Government Printing Office**—Superintendent of Documents—F. A. Crandall—served

1930 **Road**—inter-American highway appropriation

1936 **Telescope**—telescope lens two hundred inches in diameter—shipped—Corning, N.Y.

1937 **Monument**—monument to a comic character — unveiled — Crystal City, Tex.

1943 **Medal**—Air Medal (U.S.) awarded to a woman—presented—E. S. Ott

1951 **Flag**—Air Force flag—approved

1954 **Helicopter**—twin gas-turbine helicopter (turborotor)—flown—Bloomfield, Conn.

1956 **Automobile Transcontinental Trip**—gas turbine automobile to make a transcontinental trip—left New York City for Los Angeles, Calif.

MARCH 27

1770 **Teaching Methods Book** — preface dated—Christopher Dock

1792 **Congress of the United States**—congressional investigation—authorized

1794 **Ship**—ship constructed by the federal government—authorized—Gosport, Va.

1807 **Newspaper**—Democratic newspaper—published—Philadelphia, Pa.

1821 **Pharmacy College**—pharmacy college—Charles Marshall elected president Philadelphia College of Pharmacy

1836 **Mormon Temple** — dedicated — Kirtland, Ohio

1841 **Fire Engine**—steam fire engine—tested—New York City

1849 **Drill (percussion rock drill)**—patent—J. J. Couch

1855 **Oil**—oil (kerosene)—patented—Abraham Gesner

1860 **Corkscrew Patent**—patented—M. L. Byrn

1863 **Cripples**—private school for cripples—New York Society for the Relief of the Ruptured and Crippled—incorporated

1867 **Normal School**—normal school (state) at which students actually conducted classes—Oswego, N.Y.—school acquired—New York State

1884 **Telephone**—long distance telephone call—Boston, Mass. to New York City

1917 **Farm Loan Board (federal)**—federal land bank—chartered

1917 **Hockey**—hockey team (U.S.) to win the Stanley Cup—Seattle—Metropolitans

1933 **Farm Credit Administration (U.S.)**—authorized

1933 **Farm Loan Board (federal)**—transferred to Farm Credit Administration

1941 **Treaty**—Status of Forces treaty

1955 **Jewish Congregation**—Jewish mobile synagogue—dedicated

1961 **Computer**—mobile computer center—assignment undertaken — Charlotte, N.C.

MARCH 28

1796 **African Church** — Bethel African Methodist Episcopal Church—Philadelphia, Pa.—incorporated

1797 **Washing Machine**—washing machine patent—Nathaniel Briggs

1806 **Art Organization**—art organization—Pennsylvania Academy of Fine Arts—incorporated

1827 **Drydock**—federal drydocks—authorized

1834 **Presidential Censure**—Senate resolution enacted—Washington, D.C.

1836 **Supreme Court (U.S.)**—Chief Justice of the Supreme Court who was Catholic—R. B. Taney—appointed

1848 **Child Labor Law**—child labor law restricting the age of the worker—approved—Pennsylvania

1854 **Warehouse**—warehouse legislation—privileges extended to private warehouses

1865 **Advertising Law**—outdoor advertising legislation (state)—enacted—New York

1895 **Subway**—municipal subway—construction started—Boston, Mass.

1905 **Radio Facsimile Transmission**—radio facsimile patent—C. D. Ehret

1921 **Execution**—lethal gas execution—authorized—Nevada

1922 **Microfilm Machine**—microfilm reading device—patented—B. A. Fiske

1957 **Curling Championship (national)**—began—Chicago, Ill.

MARCH 29

1626 **Forestry Legislation**—colonial forestry legislation—enacted—Plymouth Colony, Mass.

1806 **Road**—federal highway—Great National Pike—authorized

1812 **Wedding**—White House wedding—Justice Thomas Todd

1822 **Hospital**—eye hospital (permanent)—incorporated — New York Eye Infirmary

1824 **Prison**—reformatory for juvenile delinquents under legislative control—incorporated

1839 **Military School**—state military school—established—Lexington, Va.

1844 **Naval Officer**—Captain in the U.S. Navy who was Jewish—U. P. Levy

1849 **Medical School**—homeopathic college—Homeopathic Medical College of Pennsylvania — graduation — Philadelphia, Pa.

1852 **Labor Law**—labor law regulating the working hours of women—enacted—Ohio

1882 **Knights of Columbus**—chartered

1914 **Newspaper**—newspaper rotogravure sections

1927 **Automobile**—automobile to exceed the speed of 200 miles an hour—Daytona Beach, Fla.

1928 **Jewish College**—Jewish college of liberal arts and sciences under Jewish auspices—Yeshiva College—chartered—New York City

1929 **Fireworks Legislation**—fireworks legislation (state)—enacted—Michigan

1932 **Women's Club**—Chinese women's club incorporated—organized—New York City

1937 **Medical Congress**—Fever Therapy International Conference—New York City

1944 **Medal**—Expert Infantryman's Badge—awarded—Fort Bragg, N.C.

1949 **Fog Disposal Unit**—accepted by test—Los Angeles, Calif.

MARCH 30

1822 **Pharmacy College**—pharmacy college—Philadelphia College of Pharmacy—incorporated—Philadelphia, Pa.

1842 **Anesthesia** — anesthetic (general) — C. W. Long—operation performed—Jefferson, Ga.

1843 **Incubator (Eggs) Patent** — N. E. Guerin

1852 **Whaling**—whale killing machine (electric)—patented

1858 **Pencil**—pencil with an attached eraser—patented—H. L. Lipman

1871 **Theological School**—theological school to admit women—formed—Boston, Mass.

1880 **Electric Power Plant**—hydroelectric power plant (commercial)—incorporated—Grand Rapids, Mich.

1887 **Insurance**—mutual liability insurance company—American Mutual Liability Insurance Company—Boston, Mass.—incorporated

1887 **Kindergarten**—kindergarten for the blind—Roxbury, Mass.—incorporated

1891 **Forest Reserve**—forest reserve (national)—Yellowstone Park Timberland Reserve—designated

1893 **Diplomatic Service**—ambassador—extraordinary and plenipotentiary—T. F. Bayard—appointed to Great Britain

1897 **Accountants' Society** — accountants' society formed by a state group—New York State Society of Certified Public Accountants—formed—New York City

1909 **Bridge**—double-deck bridge—Queensboro Bridge—New York City—opened to traffic

1923 **Dance Marathon**—New York City

1923 **Ship**—cruise ship to circumnavigate the world—"Laconia"—returned—New York City

1930 **Glider**—glider towed across the continent—take-off—San Diego, Calif.—F. M. Hawks

1946 **Sleeping Car**—transcontinental through Pullman sleeping car service—inaugurated—New York City and Los Angeles, Calif.

1950 **Transistor** — phototransistor — invention announced—Murray Hill, N.J.

1956 **Automobile Transcontinental Trip**—gas turbine automobile to make a transcontinental trip—arrived in Los Angeles, Calif., from New York City

1957 **Submarine**—submarine powered by a liquid metal-cooled atomic reactor—"Seawolf"—completed

MARCH 31

1732 **Library** — circulating library — books ordered—Library Company of Philadelphia

1783 **College**—college named after George Washington—new charter received

1784 **Map**—map of the United States—engraved—advertised for sale

1790 **Senator (U.S.)**—senator appointed by a governor—John Walker—Virginia

1791 **Lighthouse**—lighthouse built after American independence—contract for Cape Henry Lighthouse—John McComb, Jr.

1812 **Cemetery** — congressional cemetery — deed recorded

1814 **Cottonseed Hulling Machine**—patented—John Lineback

1870 **Election Law**—Negro to vote under authority of the fifteenth amendment — Thomas Peterson-Mundy — Perth Amboy, N.J.

1876 **Insurance**—title guaranty insurance company — organized — Philadelphia, Pa.

1877 **Music**—long distance telephone concert—New York City

1880 **Electric Lighting** — street lighting (electric) by a municipality—installation made—Wabash, Ind.

1887 Interstate Commerce Act—commission organized

1896 Fastening—hookless fastening—patented—W. L. Judson

1900 Advertisement—automobile advertisement—national—*Saturday Evening Post*—Philadelphia, Pa.

1918 Daylight Saving—in effect

1932 Bank—savings bank with a half-billion dollar deposit — statement — Bowery Savings Bank—New York City

1933 Civilian Conservation Corps (U.S.)—authorized

1933 Newspaper—newspaper printed on pine-pulp paper—Soperton, Ga.

1934 Medal—National Geographic Society gold medal—awarded to a woman—A. M. Lindbergh—Washington, D.C.

1937 Newspaper—newspaper printed on pine-pulp paper in color—Dallas *News*

1956 Space Cabin—space cabin simulator—tested

1958 Navy—atomic submarine division—formed—New London, Conn.

APRIL 1

1621 Treaty—colonial treaty with the Indians—Plymouth, Mass.

1769 Type Foundry—Abel Buell—Killingworth, Conn.

1789 Congress (U.S.)—House of Representatives—first quorum—New York City

1826 Engine—internal combustion engine—patented — Samuel Morey — Orford, N.H.

1826 Railroad—railroad for freight transportation to celebrate its centenary—Quincy, Mass.,—construction started

1827 Railroad — railroad for commercial transportation of passengers and freight—stock offered

1835 Insurance—mutual life insurance company to be chartered—New England Mutual Life Insurance Company—Boston, Mass.

1837 Child Labor Law—child labor law to include educational provision—effective —Massachusetts

1838 College—city college—under municipal control—opened—Charleston, S.C.

1840 Anti-Slavery Party—nominations confirmed

1843 Periodical—magazine published for mental patients—*Illuminator*—Philadelphia, Pa.

1853 Fire Department—fire department to be paid a salary—established—Cincinnati, Ohio

1863 Conscription — wartime conscription bill—enrollment required

1864 Insurance—accident insurance policy (printed)—Hartford, Conn.

1875 Advertising Magazine — *Advertising Agency Circular*—became a weekly

1885 Forest Service—forest commission (state) (permanent) — meeting — San Francisco, Calif.

1891 Animal Industry Bureau (U.S.)—pathological division—established

1894 Employment Service—municipal employment office—authorized — Seattle, Wash.

1909 Narcotic—narcotic prohibition act (federal)—effective

1913 Moving Picture Censorship—moving picture censorship board (state)—Kansas—act effective

1917 World War I—American sailor to lose his life in World War I—J. E. Eopolucci

1927 Aviation — Flights — airplane night scheduled passenger flight—left Boston, Mass.

1928 Telephone—telephone switchboard with Braille markings—New York City

1930 Aviation — Flights — New York-Bermuda flights—L. A. Yancey

1930 Television—Telecast—speaker to address an organization by television—P. I. Wold—Schenectady, N.Y.

1931 Baseball Player—woman baseball pitcher—Jackie Mitchell—engaged

1935 Naval Officer—naval officer designated Commander, Aircraft Battle Force—rank effective

1935 Radio Tube—radio tube of metal—announced—Schenectady, N.Y.

1941 Radio Advertising—radio advertising contract for frequency modulation broadcasts—W2XOR granted commercial license

1946 College—college principally for war veterans—Associated Colleges of Upper New York—authorized

1949 Television—Telecast—variety talent show series with an all-Negro cast—Chicago, Ill.

1954 Air Force Academy (U.S.)—Air Force Academy—authorized

1954 Army—helicopter battalion—activated—Fort Bragg, N.C.

1954 Television Station—city to have two educational television channels—first station in operation—Pittsburgh, Pa.

APRIL 2

1789 Congress (U.S.)—House of Representatives—committee of the House of Representatives—committee on elections—appointed

1792 Building—building erected in the United States for public use—mint authorized

1792 Mint (U.S.)—Mint of the United States—authorized

1792 Money—coin (United States) to use "E Pluribus Unum"—authorized

1792 Money—copper coins made by the United States Mint—authorized

1792 Money—gold coinage—authorized

1792 Money—gold price fixed by Congress

1792 **Money**—half cent of the United States —authorized

1792 **Money**—silver coins—authorized

1792 **Money**—silver dollar—authorized

1792 **Money**—silver half dimes—authorized

1794 **Arsenal**—national armory—Springfield, Mass.

1819 **Agricultural Journal**—agricultural journal to attain prominence—founded—Baltimore, Md.

1829 **Bank Legislation**—bank legislation (state)—New York

1834 **Railroad**—state owned railroad—locomotive trip—from Lancaster to Columbia, Pa.

1872 **Street Car**—gas-powered street car—patented—G. B. Brayton — Boston, Mass.

1877 **Easter Egg Roll**—Washington, D.C.

1879 **Telephone**—toll line commercial telephone service—instituted—Springfield, Mass. and Holyoke, Mass.

1889 **Aluminum**—patented—C. M. Hall

1896 **College**—Catholic college for women —College of Notre Dame of Maryland—Baltimore, Md.—incorporated

1902 **Moving Picture Theater**—opened—Los Angeles, Calif.

1952 **Radio Station**—sea-going radio broadcasting station—"Courier"—broadcast test

1957 **Newspaper**—newspaper to insert an aluminum foil sheet—Milwaukee *Sentinel*

APRIL 3

1776 **Degrees (academic and honorary)**—honorary degree granted George Washington—Cambridge, Mass.

1800 **President**—President's wife to frank mail—authorized

1829 **Coffee Mill Patent**—James Carrington —Wallingford, Conn.

1837 **Blind**—state school for the blind—Ohio Institution for the Blind—authorized

1860 **Postal Service**—Pony Express mail—St. Joseph, Mo. and Sacramento, Calif.

1863 **Medal**—Medal of Honor awarded to a member of the Naval Service—April 3

1866 **Hat Blocking and Shaping Machine**—patented

1889 **Bank**—bank for Negroes operated by Negroes—opened—Richmond, Va.

1913 **Eye**—eye conservation class—opened —Boston, Mass.

1939 **Public Buildings Administration**—approved

1948 **Economic Cooperation Administration** —Economic Cooperation Administration—authorized

APRIL 4

1692 **Postal Service**—parliamentary act to establish a post office—Andrew Hamilton—appointed postmaster

1692 **Postmaster**—postmaster general (colonial)—Andrew Hamilton—appointed

1800 **Bankruptcy Act**—enacted

1818 **Flag Legislation**—flag act—established

1818 **Ship**—steamboat on the Great Lakes — "Walk-in-the-Water" launched — Buffalo, N.Y.

1839 **Ship**—iron vessel built of American iron—"De Rosset"—registered — Baltimore, Md.

1841 **President**—President to die in Washington, D.C.—W. H. Harrison

1841 **Vice President of the United States**—Vice President to become President automatically—John Tyler

1850 **School**—school for the mentally retarded—incorporated—Boston, Mass.

1859 **Music**—war song of the Confederate States—"Dixie" sung—New York City

1870 **Sports**—athletic club—New York Athletic Club—New York City—incorporated

1873 **Pottery**—pottery to make sanitary ware—consolidated

1885 **Agriculture Department (U.S.)**—Secretary of the Department of Agriculture—N. J. Colman—served as Commissioner of Agriculture

1887 **Woman**—woman mayor—S. M. Salter —elected

1888 **Holding Company**—holding company authorization (state)—enacted—New Jersey

1890 **Election Law**—corrupt election practices law (state)—enacted—New York State

1891 **Political Science Society**—political and social science society (national)—American Academy of Political and Social Science—incorporated

1911 **Insurance**—workmen's compensation insurance law (state)—legislation enacted—New Jersey

1913 **Moving Picture Censorship**—moving picture censorship board (state)—Pennsylvania—appropriation

1915 **Radio Telephone** — radio telephone communication (one way)—from Montauk Point, N.Y. to Wilmington, Del

1938 **Library Chair**—established—Columbia University—New York City

1943 **Ship**—naval ship with a plural name — "The Sullivans" — launched — San Francisco, Calif.

1949 **Submarine**—leaping submarine—"Pickerel" commissioned

1953 **Fraternity (Greek Letter)**—scholastic fraternity chapter established at a Negro university—Phi Beta Kappa—Fisk University—Nashville, Tenn.

1955 **Jewish Congregation**—Jewish mobile synagogue—in operation—North Carolina

1957 **Medal**—recipient of the four highest decorations awarded by the United States—W. J. Donovan

1880 **Engineering Society**—mechanical engineering national society—organization meeting—Hoboken, N.J.

1904 **Business**—installment finance company—Fidelity Contract Company—Rochester, N.Y.

1905 **Wrestling** — intercollegiate wrestling association—formed—Philadelphia, Pa.

1906 **Art Organization**—artists' society of importance—Society of American Artists merged with National Academy of Design

1910 **Automobile Race Track**—automobile speedway (board track)—opened—Playa del Rey, Calif.

1913 **Ship**—electrically propelled ship of the United States Navy—"Jupiter"—commissioned

1917 **World War I**—shot fired by the American Navy in World War I—Guam

1922 **Shipping**—automatic steering gear—tested—"John D. Archibold"

1925 **Radio Broadcast** — ship launching broadcast—Camden, N.J.

1927 **Television—Telecast**—telecast of image and sound—transmitted—Washington, D.C. to New York City

1933 **Bridge**—bridge with open mesh steel flooring—opened—Seattle, Wash.

1940 **Postage Stamp**—Negro depicted upon a United States postage stamp—B. T. Washington

1953 **Aviation—Flights** (transatlantic)—jet transatlantic non-stop flight west to east—from Limestone, Me.

1959 **Astronauts**—astronauts—National Aeronautics and Space Administration selection announced

1959 **Radar**—radar signal bounced off the sun

APRIL 8

1730 **Jewish Congregation**—Jewish congregation—Shearith Israel—consecrated—New York City

1795 **Dental Dispensary**—dental dispensary—City Dispensary—New York City—incorporated

1808 **Catholic Diocese**—raised to Archdiocese—Baltimore, Md.

1834 **Election**—mayor elected by popular vote in a city—C. V. Lawrence—New York City

1848 **Medical School**—homeopathic college—Homeopathic Medical College of Pennsylvania—incorporated

1864 **Knights of Pythias**—grand lodge of District of Columbia—formed

1873 **Oleomargarine**—oleomargarine manufacturer (successful)—patent—A. Paraf—New York City

1898 **Forestry School**—forestry school of collegiate character—authorized

1911 **Squash Tournament**—squash tennis tournament—New York City

1918 **Aviation**—air squadron of the United States Army—assigned to front

1935 **Works Progress Administration** — Works Progress Administration — created

1947 **Insurance**—insurance policy to be illustrated—Chicago, Ill.

1953 **Moving Picture**—three-dimensional feature moving picture produced and released by a major company—New York City—*Man in the Dark*

1955 **Medal**—Medal of Honor awarded to a helicopter pilot—J. K. Koelsch

1956 **Church**—universal chapel embracing eight faiths—Universalist Church of the Divine Paternity—New York City—dedicated

APRIL 9

1792 **Road**—macadam road—turnpike company chartered

1816 **Methodist Episcopal Church**—African Methodist Episcopal Church—established—Philadelphia, Pa.

1825 **Prison**—reformatory for juvenile delinquents under legislative control—five-year appropriation enacted—New York

1833 **Library**—free public library (town supported) — established — Peterborough, N.H.

1847 **Prison**—reformatory for boys (state)—authorized—Westborough, Mass.

1872 **Milk**—dried milk patent—S. R. Percy—New York City

1905 **Bridge**—aerial ferry—operated—Duluth, Minn.

1912 **Children's Bureau (U.S.)**—established—Department of Commerce and Labor

1920 **Woman**—woman automotive engineer—Marie Luhring—associate member of Society of Automotive Engineers

1930 **Television—Telecast**—two-way demonstration of television in a theater—New York City

1934 **Judge**—woman associate justice of the circuit court of appeals—F. E. Allen—sworn in

1937 **Strike**—anti-sit-down strike legislation (state)—Vermont

1947 **Atomic Energy Commission**—Atomic Energy Commission—confirmed

1948 **Economic Cooperation Administration**—Economic Cooperation Administration—Administrator P. G. Hoffman sworn in

APRIL 10

1777 **Lottery**—lottery held by the Continental Congress—Philadelphia, Pa.

1790 **Patent**—patent law (national)—enacted

1816 **Bank**—Bank of the United States—second bank authorized

1833 **Medical Society**—homeopathic medical society—Hahnemann Society—organized—Philadelphia, Pa.

1835 **Medical School**—homeopathic school—North American Academy—founded—Allentown, Pa.

1845 **Gingham Factory**—E. B. Bigelow—machinery patent

1849 **Pin**—safety pin—patented—Walter Hunt—New York City

1861 **Insurance** — non-forfeiture insurance law (state)—enacted—Massachusetts

1866 **Humane Society**—humane society—American Society for the Prevention of Cruelty to Animals—incorporated

1872 **Holiday**—Arbor Day celebration—Nebraska

1877 **Catamaran**—patented—N. G. Herreshoff—Providence, R.I.

1892 **Tuberculosis Society**—founded—Philadelphia, Pa.

1927 **Symphony**—symphonic work to call for an airplane propeller — *Ballet Mécanique*—produced—New York City

1930 **Rubber**—synthetic rubber (neoprene)—produced

1933 **Civilian Conservation Corps (U.S.)**—Camp Roosevelt established

1933 **Constitutional Amendment (U.S.)**—constitutional amendment submitted to the states for repeal—first ratification—Michigan

1944 **Quinine**—synthetic quinine—produced—Cambridge, Mass.

1944 **Television**—Telecast—moving picture premiere performance to be televised—*Patrolling the Ether*

1947 **Television** — Telecast — under-water telecast from a submarine—U.S.S. "Trumpetfish"—New York City

1953 **Anesthesia**—trifluorethyl vinyl ether—administered—J. C. Krantz, Jr.—Chicago, Ill.

1953 **Moving Picture**—three-dimensional feature moving picture in color—*The House of Wax*—New York City

APRIL 11

1640 **Election**—election in defiance of the Royal Courts—Wethersfield, Conn.

1783 **Treaty**—treaty between the United States Government and a nation with which it had been at war—proclaimed by Continental Congress

1789 **Newspaper** — political newspaper — *Gazette of the United States* — New York City—published

1803 **Ship** — steamboat with a twin-screw propeller—patented—New York

1816 **Methodist Episcopal Church**—African Methodist Episcopal church—Richard Allen ordained bishop

1831 **Building and Loan Association**—Oxford Provident Building Association—Philadelphia, Pa.—loan made

1876 **Stenotype**—patented—J. C. Zachos—New York City

1921 **Cigarette Tax**—cigarette tax (state)—enacted—Iowa

1921 **Telephone** — telephone cable service (deep sea)—opened—Key West, Fla.

1930 **Degrees (academic and honorary)**—doctor of military science degree—awarded—J. J. Pershing—New York City

1941 **Electric Generator** — hydrogen-cooled turbine generator for outdoor installation—operated—Glendale, Calif.

1941 **Price Regulation Law**—price regulation law (federal)—Office of Price Administration and Civilian Supply created

1942 **Medal**—Distinguished Service Medal (Merchant Marine)—authorized

1947 **Baseball Player**—Negro major league baseball player — Jackie Robinson —

1953 **Cabinet of the United States**—Secretary of Health, Education and Welfare—Oveta Culp Hobby—sworn in

1953 **Federal Security Agency** — changed to Department of Health, Education and Welfare

APRIL 12

1776 **Declaration of Independence (American)** — Declaration of Independence by a colony—Halifax, N.C.

1786 **Hospital** — dispensary — Philadelphia Dispensary—instituted

1799 **Comb Cutting Machine** — patented — Phineas Pratt—Connecticut

1811 **Colonist**—colonists to reach the Pacific coast—landed—Cape Disappointment, Wash.

1824 **Law Codification (state)**—approved—Louisiana

1830 **Bank** — trust company — New York Life Insurance and Trust Company—New York City—organization meeting

1831 **Tunnel**—railroad tunnel—construction began—Hollidaysburg to Johnstown, Pa.

1833 **Safe (fire-proof)** — patented—Charles A. Gayler—New York City

1842 **Insurance**—mutual life insurance company to operate—Mutual Life Insurance Company of New York—chartered—New York City

1847 **Chinese Students** — arrived — New York City

1853 **Bank**—trust company—United States Trust Company of New York—first exclusive trust company — incorporated

1853 **Truancy Legislation (state)**—enacted—New York

1859 **Billiard Match**—billiard match to attain international prominence — Detroit, Mich.

1861 **Civil War**—attack in the Civil War—Fort Sumter, S.C.

1861 **Seal**—seals for raising funds

1867 **Insurance** — plate glass insurance — United States Plate Glass Insurance Company — Philadelphia, Pa. — incorporated

1877 **Baseball Catcher's Mask** — used in game—Lynn, Mass.

1892 **Typewriter** — portable typewriter — Blickensderfer — patented — Stamford, Conn.

1892 **Voting Machine** — voting machines were authorized — used — Lockport, N.Y.

1918 **Aviation**—air squadron of the U.S. Army—first combat action

1926 **Senator (U.S.)**—Senator unseated after a recount—S. W. Brookhart—Iowa

1933 **Diplomatic Service**—woman diplomat to represent the United States in the capacity of a Minister—R. B. Owen—appointed

1933 **Woman** — woman state liquor board member—J. R. Sheppard—appointed —New York State

1938 **Medical Legislation**—law (state) requiring marriage license applicants to undergo medical tests—enacted—New York State

APRIL 13

1759 **Freemasons** — military masonic lodge —formed—Crown Point, N.Y.

1782 **Town Named for George Washington**—Washington, N.C.—incorporated

1796 **Animals** — elephant — arrived — New York City

1802 **Army**—engineer corps—Jonathan Williams—appointed

1808 **Temperance Society**—temperance society (union)—Union Temperate Society — organized — Saratoga Springs, N.Y.

1819 **Church**—mariners' church—New York Port Society—incorporated

1854 **Agricultural School**—agricultural college (state) to be chartered—Farmers High School of Pennsylvania—incorporated

1863 **Hospital**—orthopedic hospital — Hospital for Ruptured and Crippled—New York City—incorporated

1869 **Air Brake**—patented—George Westinghouse—Schenectady, N.Y.

1896 **Organists' Society**—organists' society (national) — American Guild of Organists—organized

1901 **Optometry Legislation (state)**—Minnesota

1904 **Border Patrol** — border patrolman — J. D. Milton—served

1912 **Senator (U.S.)**—senators "elected by the people" — legislation enacted — House of Representatives

1916 **Corn**—shipment of hybrid seed corn —sold—Jacobsburg, Ohio

1920 **Civil Service**—woman Civil Service commissioner — H. H. Gardener—sworn in—Washington, D.C.

1940 **Pole Vaulter**—pole vaulter to clear the bar at 15 feet—Cornelius Warmerdam—Berkeley, Calif.

APRIL 14

1775 **Abolition Society**—Society for the Relief of Free Negroes Unlawfully Held in Bondage — formed — Philadelphia, Pa.

1792 **Congressional Apportionment** — authorized

1792 **Mint (U.S.)**—mint (U.S.) director—David Rittenhouse—appointed

1794 **Insurance** — life insurance—Insurance Company of North America—incorporated

1818 **Army**—medical corps—organized

1863 **Printing Press**—printing press to use a continuous web or roll of paper—patent—William Bullock—Pittsburgh, Pa.

1865 **Bank** — national bank failure — First National Bank—Attica, N.Y.

1865 **President** — President to be assassinated — President Lincoln shot — Washington, D.C.

1890 **Pan American Union** — International Bureau of American Republics

1891 **Bridge Whist Organization** — of importance—formed—Milwaukee, Wis.

1891 **Road** — law regarding state-aid for roads—enacted—New Jersey

1894 **Moving Picture**—peep show—opened —New York City

1894 **Teachers' Pension Fund**—enacted—New York City

1898 **Ship**—ambulance ship—U.S.S. "Solace" —in service

1910 **President**—President to pitch a ball to open the baseball season—W. H. Taft

1912 **Moving Picture Actor**—stunt actor—F. R. Law—jumped from Brooklyn Bridge

1914 **Automobile Tire**—non-skid tire—patented—S. G. Carkhuff—Akron, Ohio

1918 **Aviation — Aviator** — American ace—Douglas Campbell—first victory

1918 **World War I** — air combat of an American organization in World War I—Toul, France

1919 **Aviation — Aviator** — pilot to receive the Congressional Medal of Honor—awarded posthumously—Frank Luke

1919 **Insurance**—insurance service offered by a newspaper—St. Louis *Star*

1922 **Radio Broadcast**—radio concert from an airplane—New York City

1939 **Federal Crop Insurance Corporation** — indemnity payment made — Floydada, Tex.

1948 **Theater** — television theater demonstration of a sports event on a full-size screen—New York City

1956 **Tape Recorder** — magnetic tape recorder (commercial) of sound and picture — demonstrated — Chicago, Ill. and Redwood City, Calif.

APRIL 15

1788 **Wool**—worsted mill operated by water power—Hartford, Conn.

1789 **Congress (U.S.)—House of Representatives**—contested election—W. L. Smith

1794 **Newspaper**—French daily newspaper—*Courrier Français*—Philadelphia, Pa.

1796 **Hospital** — dispensary — Philadelphia Dispensary—incorporated

1802 **Army School**—army school—superintendent Jonathan Williams—served

1817 **Deaf—School**—school for the deaf—Connecticut Asylum—Hartford, Conn.—opened

1834 **Presidential Protest**—signed—Andrew Jackson

1854 **Entomologist** — state entomologist — appropriation—New York

1859 **Insurance** — insurance department (state)—authorized—New York

1861 **Civil War**—call for Union troops in the Civil War—Abraham Lincoln

1865 **President**—President to be assassinated—Abraham Lincoln—died

1865 **President**—President to rest in state in the United States Capitol rotunda—Abraham Lincoln

1884 **Insurance**—bonding company (exclusive)—American Surety Company—New York City—began business

1884 **Press Clipping Bureau**—opened—New York City

1891 **Bridge Whist Tournament**—duplicate whist tournament—Milwaukee, Wis.

1923 **Moving Picture**—sound on film moving picture—demonstration for the public—New York City

1935 **Organ** — pipeless organ — exhibited—Laurens Hammond—New York City

1936 **Theater**—state-owned theater—authorized—Washington

1941 **Helicopter Flight**—helicopter flight of one-hour duration—Stratford, Conn.

1949 **Aviation—Aviator**—Negro flier of the U.S. Naval Reserve—J. L. Brown—commissioned

1956 **Automobile**—free piston automobile—announced—Detroit, Mich.

1956 **Television Station**—all-color station to televise live local programs—WNBQ-TV—Chicago, Ill.

APRIL 16

1787 **Play (drama)**—native American play successfully acted on a regular stage—*The Contrast*—New York City

1813 **Factory Standardization of Production**—Simeon North—Middletown, Conn.

1836 **Child Labor Law**—child labor law to include educational provision—enacted—Massachusetts

1851 **Lighthouse** — iron pile lighthouse — Minot's Ledge, Mass.—swept away in storm

1861 **Civil War**—regiment to respond to President Abraham Lincoln's proclamation—Harrisburg, Pa.

1863 **Ship**—turreted frigate in the U.S. Navy—"Roanoke" transferred to U.S. Navy

1869 **Diplomatic Service**—Negro consul—E. D. C. Bassett—served

1900 **Postage Stamp**—books of postage stamps—issued

1922 **Aviation**—sermon from an airplane—B. W. Maynard

1926 **Book Club**—Book-of-the-Month Club—book selection — distributed — New York City

1935 **Aviation — Airplane** — transport airplane designed especially for transoceanic service—left San Francisco, Calif.

1947 **Army**—Women's Army Medical Specialist Corps—authorized

1947 **Lens**—lens to provide zoom effects—demonstrated—New York City

1956 **Radio Receiver**—radio receiver with an auxiliary silicon unit to convert the rays of the sun into electrical power—Chicago, Ill.

1957 **Television—Telecast** — stockholders' annual meeting televised on a closed circuit—New York City and Chicago

APRIL 17

1629 **Fishery (commercial)**—established—Medford, Mass.

1629 **Horse**—horses — imported — Massachusetts

1640 **Lutheran Church**—Lutheran pastor—Reorus Torkillus—arrived—Wilmington, Del.

1704 **Newspaper**—newspaper (successful)—*News-Letter*—Boston, Mass.—published

1776 **Ship**—warship captured by a commissioned officer of the U.S. Navy—"Edward"

1810 **Cheese**—pineapple cheese—patent—L. M. Norton—Troy, Pa.

1844 **Printing Press**—cylinder and flat bed combination printing press—patented—Robert Hoe

1860 **Fire Escapes**—required for tenements—legislation—New York

1861 **Oil**—oil well fire—Oil Creek, Pa.

1866 **Hospital** — Jewish hospital — name changed to Mount Sinai Hospital

1895 **Canal Locks**—of concrete—opened to traffic—Hennepin Canal

1896 **Accountancy Law (state)**—enacted—New York

1916 **Arts and Letters Society**—arts and letters society (national)—American Academy of Arts and Letters—incorporated

1917 **Daylight Saving**—measure introduced in the U.S. Senate—W. M. Calder—defeated

1931 **Autogiro**—autogiro with side-by-side seating arrangement—tested—Philadelphia, Pa.

1933 **Civilian Conservation Corps (U.S.)**—Camp Roosevelt—opened—Luray, Va.

1935 **Aviation—Airplane**—transport airplane designed especially for trans-oceanic service—Pan American Clipper—arrived—Pearl Harbor, Hawaii

1941 **Helicopter Flight**—helicopter flight from water—I. I. Sikorsky—Stratford, Conn.

1957 **Installment Sales Law**—enacted—New York

APRIL 18

1637 **Conscription** — colonial conscription legislation—enacted—Boston, Mass.

1662 **Book Auction**—authorized—New York City

1789 **Congress (U.S.)**—House of Representatives — contested election dispute decided

1796 **Opera**—opera by an American composer—*The Archers*—performed—New York City

1818 **Army Officer**—Surgeon General of the U.S. Army—Joseph Lovell—began service

1846 **Telegraph**—telegraph ticker to print letters of the alphabet—patented—R. E. House—New York City

1895 **Bathouse**—legislation concerning public baths—enacted—New York

1910 **Aviation—Flights**—night flight—W. R. Brookins—Montgomery, Ala.

1924 **Crossword Puzzle Book**—published—New York City

1925 **Fair**—Woman's World Fair—Chicago, Ill.

1925 **Hospital**—Chinese hospital—opened—San Francisco, Calif.

1925 **Radio Facsimile Transmission**—photograph sent by radio across the continent (commercial)—San Francisco, Calif. to New York City

1934 **Washing Machine**—washing machine for public use—installed—Fort Worth, Tex.

1950 **Aviation—Flights**—jet passenger international trip—Toronto, Canada to New York City

1956 **Baseball Umpire**—baseball umpire (major league) to wear eyeglasses—E. A. Rommel

APRIL 19

1739 **Astronomer**—astronomer of note in the American colonies—John Winthrop—sun spot observations

1775 **Revolutionary War**—armed conflict in the Revolutionary War—Lexington, Mass.

1861 **Civil War**—bloodshed in the Civil War—Baltimore, Md.

1887 **Kindergarten**—kindergarten for the blind—Perkins Institution—Roxbury, Mass.—dedicated

1892 **Automobile**—automobile regularly made for sale—operated—C. E. Duryea—Springfield, Mass.

1897 **Marathon Race (annual)**—Hopkinton, Mass.

1901 **Commission Form of Government**—authorized—Galveston, Tex.

1917 **World War I**—shot fired by the American Navy in World War I against a known German submarine—"Mongolia"

1919 **Aviation—Flights**—New York-Chicago non-stop flight—E. F. White

1920 **Arbitration**—state arbitration law (modern)—effective—New York

1931 **Visiting Celebrities**—absolute monarch —King Prajadhipok—Siam—arrived—Portal, N.D.

1937 **Postal Service**—letter to encircle the world by commercial airmail—dispatched—New York City

1944 **Naval Officer**—woman physician in the Medical Corps Reserve of the U.S. Navy—Hulda Thelander—commissioned

1955 **Automobile**—gas turbine automobile operated on city streets—Detroit, Mich.

1956 **Moving Picture Actor**—moving picture actress depicted on a postage stamp—Grace Kelly

APRIL 20

1564 **Artist**—artist—Jacques Le Moyne—sailed—from France

1657 **Jews**—Jew to win all the rights and perform all the duties of citizenship—Asser Levy

1721 **Newspaper**—newspaper editorial apology—*American Weekly Mercury*

1767 **Opera**—opera (comic)—performance scheduled—Philadelphia, Pa.

1801 **Hospital**—marine hospital (U.S.)—Norfolk Naval Hospital deeded to U.S.

1812 **Vice President of the United States**—Vice President to die in office—George Clinton

1832 **Park**—park (national)—Hot Springs National Park — reservation — established

1837 **Carpet Loom**—carpet power loom—patented—E. B. Bigelow—West Boylston, Mass.

1852 **Temperance Society**—women's temperance society (state)—New York Women's State Temperance Society—founded—Rochester, N.Y.

1855 **Bohemian American Church**—opened —St. Louis, Mo.

1876 **Chemical Society**—chemical society (national)—American Chemical Society—organized—New York City

1899 **Election Law**—primary election law—enacted—Minnesota

1920 **Radio Broadcast**—speaker to address an organization by radio—W. C. Ketler—New Castle, Pa.

1926 **Radio Facsimile Transmission**—check sent by radio across the Atlantic Ocean—London to New York City

1927 **Radio Broadcast**—dinner broadcast round-the-world—Schenectady, N.Y.

1930 **Diplomatic Service**—chief executive-elect of a foreign country—to serve in a diplomatic position at Washington—E. O. Hererra of Colombia—arrived

1940 **Microscope** — electron microscope — demonstrated—Philadelphia, Pa.

1940 **Ship**—seaplane tender designed and built for the United States Navy—"Curtiss"—launched—Camden, N.J.

APRIL 21

1712 **Calico**—printery advertised — Boston, Mass.

1789 **Congress (U.S.)** — Senate — president pro tempore of the United States—Senate—Vice President John Adams—took seat as president of the Senate—New York City

1847 **Insurance**—health insurance company — Massachusetts Health Insurance Company—Boston, Mass.—organized

1856 **Bridge**—railway bridge across the Mississippi River—completed — Glasgow, Mo.

1857 **Bustle**—patented—Alexander Douglas

1869 **Indians**—Indian Affairs Commissioner (U.S.) who was an Indian—E. S. Parker—appointed

1881 **Ship**—schooner (five masted)—"David Dows"—launched—Toledo, Ohio

1887 **Insurance**—mutual liability insurance company—American Mutual Liability Insurance Company—Boston, Mass.—organized

1895 **Moving Picture**—moving picture on film shown on a screen—exhibited—Woodville Latham—New York City

1899 **Court** — juvenile court — authorized—Chicago, Ill.

1906 **Ship**—turbine-propelled ocean-going merchant vessel—"Governor Cobb"—launched

1923 **Postage Stamp**—precanceled stamps printed on rotary presses—issued

1933 **Enclave**—municipal enclave of economic ground rent—authorized—Collierville, Tenn.

1937 **Dental Society**—orthodontists' society—American Society of Orthodontists—name changed to American Association of Orthodontists

APRIL 22

1669 **Engraving** — engraving — woodcut—made—John Foster

1793 **Circus**—circus—attended by George Washington—Philadelphia, Pa.

1793 **Neutrality Proclamation** — George Washington

1794 **Capital Punishment**—death penalty was first abolished—except for first degree murder—Pennsylvania

1856 **Bridge**—railway bridge across the Mississippi River — locomotive and passenger cars test trip—Rock Island, Ill., to Davenport, Iowa

1864 **Money**—coin to use "In God We Trust"—authorized

1876 **Coaching Club**—first meet—New York City

1884 **Bicycle Trip**—bicycle trip around the world—Thomas Stevens — left San Francisco, Calif.

1890 **Ship**—torpedo boat of importance—"Cushing" — commissioned — Bristol, Pa.

1892 **Research Institute**—anatomy research institute—Wistar Institute of Anatomy and Biology—Philadelphia, Pa.—incorporated

1898 **Spanish-American War**—ship captured in the Spanish-American war—"Buena Ventura"

1913 **Ice Loading Machinery**—patent

1920 **Orchestra**—orchestra (American) to make a European tour—Symphony Society of New York—sailed

1921 **Building**—building devoted entirely to highway traffic—Eno Foundation for Highway Traffic Control—incorporated

1931 **Autogiro**—autogiro to land on the White House lawn—J. G. Ray—Washington, D.C.

1940 **Radio Broadcast**—all-Chinese commercial radio broadcast—San Francisco, Calif.

1944 **Television—Telecast**—moving picture premiere performance to be televised—*Patrolling the Ether*—released to theaters

1952 **Television — Telecast** — atomic explosion telecast on a network—Los Angeles, Calif.

1953 **Catholic Bishop**—Catholic bishop (Negro) consecrated in the United States—J. O. Bowers—Bay St. Louis, Miss.

1955 **Railroad Car**—passenger car (ACF-Talgo for use in the United States—completed

APRIL 23

1750 **Colonist**—civilian settlement, west of the Allegheny Mountains—reached Barbourville, Ky.

1789 **Catholic Magazine**—Catholic magazine—*Courier de Boston*—published—Boston, Mass.

1789 **"Presidential Mansion"**—George Washington—New York City

1821 **Pharmacy College**—pharmacy college—Samuel Jackson appointed professor—Philadelphia, Pa.

1827 **Railroad** — railroad for commercial transportation of passengers and freight—board of directors elected—Baltimore, Md.

1838 **Ship** — steamboat service (regular) across the Atlantic—arrived—New York City

1867 **Moving Picture Machine**—machine to show animated pictures—Zoetrope—patented—W. E. Lincoln—Providence, R.I.

1872 **Lawyer**—Negro woman lawyer—C. E. Ray—Washington, D.C.

1890 **Women's Club**—women's club federation—General Federation of Women's Clubs—convention

1897 **Hospital**—crippled children's hospital (state)—authorized—St. Paul, Minn.

1899 **Movable Church**—service — Coanicut Island, R.I.

1904 **Animal Industry Bureau (U.S.)**—animal husbandry federal appropriation—approved

1904 **Arts and Letters Society**—arts and letters society (national)—American Academy of Arts and Letters—founded

1917 **Ship**—warship propelled by electricity — "New Mexico" — launched — New York City

1951 **Teletypesetter**—teletypesetter circuit operated by a news agency—Charlotte, N.C.

1962 **Rocket**—American satellite to reach the moon—Ranger IV—launched—Cape Canaveral, Fla.

1908 **Automobile Transcontinental Trip**—transcontinental family automobile trip requiring only a month—Murdock family—left Los Angeles, Calif.

1917 **Bank**—joint stock land bank—chartered—Sioux City, Iowa

1917 **Loan**—liberty loan subscriptions—authorized

1922 **Catholic Nuns (cloistered community)**—Magdalen Sisters—Baltimore, Md.—founded

1928 **Fathometer**—patented—H. G. Dorsey

1934 **Organ** — pipeless organ — invented—Laurens Hammond—Chicago, Ill.

1946 **Glider**—glider commercial freight service—inaugurated—Philadelphia, Pa.

1954 **War (French Indo-China)**—American civilian pilot wounded in Indo-China

1956 **Brokerage**—visitor to open the New York Stock Exchange—Leonard Ross—New York City

1962 **Television—Telecast** — transcontinental telecast by means of an orbiting satellite—Westford, Mass.

APRIL 24

1783 **College**—college named after George Washington — Washington College, Tennessee—chartered

1800 **Librarian**—librarian of Congress—authorized

1800 **Library**—Library of Congress—authorized

1816 **Army Officer**—paymaster—Pay Department—authorized

1827 **Railroad** — railroad for commercial transportation of passenger and freight —Baltimore and Ohio Railroad Company—organized

1833 **Soda Fountain**—soda fountain patent—Jacob Ebert—Cadiz, Ohio

1844 **Pharmacy Professor**—pharmacy professorship—David Stewart—appointed—Baltimore, Md.

1851 **Engineering Society**—engineering society—Boston Society of Civil Engineers—incorporated

1863 **Dock**—state-owned docks—authorized—California

1873 **Free Lunch**—free lunches to aid convalescents—New York Diet Kitchen Association—opened

1884 **Medical Society**—Negro medical society—organized—Washington, D.C.

1886 **Catholic Priest**—Negro Catholic priest—Augustus Tolton—ordained

1890 **Women's Club**—women's club federation — constitution adopted — New York City

1895 **Ship**—ship to circumnavigate the world with but one in the crew—Joshua Slocum—sailed—Boston, Mass.

1897 **News Correspondent**—White House reporter—W. W. Price—Washington, D.C.

APRIL 25

1831 **Street Car**—street car company—New York and Harlem Railway—incorporated

1846 **War (Mexican)**—Mexican war shots—fired—La Rosia, Mexico

1860 **Japanese Ambassador**—arrived—Washington, D.C.

1865 **Oil**—oil well drilled by torpedoes—patent—E. A. L. Roberts—New York City

1873 **Rifle Association** — rifle association (national)—shooting meet

1881 **Monument**—statue cast by the United States Government—Admiral D. G. Farragut—accepted by President Garfield

1882 **Forestry Society**—national forestry association—American Forestry Congress—held—Cincinnati, Ohio

1901 **Automobile License Plates**—automobile license plates—legislation enacted—New York

1908 **Ship**—turbine-propelled ship of the U.S. Navy—"Chester"—commissioned

1917 **Loan**—war loan made by the United States Government to a war ally—Great Britain

1928 **Animals**—dogs trained to guide the blind—Seeing Eye dog presented

1935 **Telephone**—round-the-world telephone conversation—New York City

1938 **Ship**—seaplane tender designed and built for the United States Navy—"Curtiss"—keel laid—Camden, N.J.

1939 **Federal Security Agency**—established

1939 **Federal Works Agency**—authorized

1940 **Television—Telecast**—circus telecast—New York City

1945 **United Nations Conference on International Organization**—San Francisco, Calif.

1954 **Battery**—solar battery—announced—New York City

1957 **Atomic Reactor**—sodium reactor (experimental)—operated—Santa Susana Mountains, Calif.

1959 **Canal**—Saint Lawrence Seaway—opened

APRIL 26

1790 **Senator (U.S.)**—senator appointed by a governor—John Walker—Virginia—seated

1819 **Odd Fellows Lodge**—established—Baltimore, Md.

1826 **Engineering College**—engineering college—Rensselaer School—Troy, N.Y.—graduation

1848 **Engineering Society**—Boston Society of Civil Engineers—organized—New York City

1921 **Radio Broadcast**—weather broadcasts—St. Louis, Mo.

1929 **Fluorescent Mineral Exhibit**—opened—Philadelphia, Pa.

1957 **Air Force Academy (U.S.)**—Air Force Academy woman officer—N. M. Mc-Cracken

APRIL 27

1805 **Flag**—American flag flown over a fortress of the Old World—Tripoli, Africa

1816 **Tariff**—tariff for protection—enacted

1875 **Catholic Priest**—Catholic priest to be elevated to the cardinalate—John Mc-Closkey—investiture—New York City

1880 **Deaf—Hearing Aid**—electrical hearing aid—bone conduction device—patented

1899 **Hospital**—tuberculosis hospital operated by the government—opened—Fort Stanton, N.M.

1938 **Baseball**—baseball (yellow)—used—Columbia-Fordham—New York City

1938 **Woman**—woman of American descent to become a queen—married—King Zog of Albania

1946 **Ship**—radar installation aboard a commercial carrier—New York City

1960 **Submarine**—atomic-powered turbine electric-drive submarine—"Tullibee"—launched—Groton, Conn.

1960 **Television**—submarine with closed-circuit television—"Tullibee"—launched—Groton, Conn.

1960 **Television—Telecast**—art auction televised on a coast-to-coast closed circuit—New York City

APRIL 28

1798 **Author**—author—C. B. Brown—book announced—New York City

1855 **Veterinary School**—veterinary college—Boston Veterinary Institute—Boston, Mass.—incorporated

1860 **Japanese Ambassador**—received by President Buchanan—Washington, D.C.

1862 **Treason**—citizen of the United States to be tried for treason, convicted, and hanged—W. B. Mumford—New Orleans, La.

1866 **Ship**—steam whaler—"Pioneer"

1882 **Library**—library newspaper room—Newburyport, Mass.—dedicated

1890 **Employment Service**—state employment service—created—Ohio

1896 **Addressograph**—patented—J. S. Duncan—Sioux City, Iowa

1898 **Advertising Law**—advertising legislation (state)—enacted

1909 **Child Delinquency Law (state)**—enacted—Colorado

1919 **Aviation — Parachute** — parachute — jump with army parachute—Dayton, Ohio

1925 **Wind Tunnel**—propeller research tunnel—Langley Field, Va.

1930 **Moving Picture**—moving picture of an eclipse of the sun taken from an airplane—Honey Lake, Calif.

1932 **Vaccine**—yellow fever vaccine for human immunization—announced

1936 **Aviation**—airplane tank discharger—patented — J. H. Hammond, Jr. — Gloucester, Mass.

1937 **Electric Sign**—animated-cartoon electric sign—displayed—Douglas Leigh—New York City

1937 **Museum**—costume museum—Museum of Costume Arts—New York City—incorporated

1939 **Automobile** — miniature automobile — Crosley—offered for sale

APRIL 29

1813 **Rubber**—rubber patent—J. F. Hummel—Philadelphia, Pa.

1851 **College**—college to prohibit discrimination because of race, religion, or color—Cooper Union—New York City

1851 **Locomotive**—electric locomotive—trial trip—Washington, D.C.

1854 **College**—Negro university—Lincoln University—incorporated

1863 **Charity Board (state)**—authorized—Massachusetts

1864 **Fraternity** — professional fraternity — Theta Xi—Troy, N.Y.

1873 **Railroad Coupler**—railroad coupler—patented—E. H. Janney—Alexandria, Va.

1879 **Electric Lighting**—electric arc lights—used—Cleveland, Ohio

1898 **Cancer Laboratory**—appropriations—New York State

1913 **Fastening**—hookless fastening for universal use—patented—Gideon Sundback—Hoboken, N.J.

1918 **Aviation—Aviator**—American Ace of Aces—E. V. Rickenbacker—first victory—Toul, France

1921 **Prison**—prisoners (federal) employed in industry—wage system adopted—Atlanta, Ga.

1925 Science Association—woman elected to the National Academy of Sciences —F. R. Sabin—Baltimore, Md.

1931 **Visiting Celebrities**—absolute monarch—King Prajadhipok of Siam received by President Hoover, Washington, D.C.

1942 **Insurance** — health insurance law (state)—Rhode Island—cash sickness compensation—approved

1943 **Civil Air Patrol (U.S.)**—transferred to War Department

1949 **Aviation—License**—cargo airlines licensed by the Civil Aeronautics Board

1957 **Atomic Reactor** — military nuclear power plant—dedicated—Fort Belvoir, Va.

APRIL 30

1778 Blockade—effected—West Point, N.Y.

1789 **Cabinet of the United States**—cabinet —appointed—George Washington

1789 **President**—President elected—George Washington—inaugurated

1798 **Marines**—American Marines—transferred to Navy Department

1798 **Navy**—Navy Department (U.S.)—established

1798 **Navy**—navy yard—acquired—Portsmouth, N.H.

1802 **Land Grant**—land subsidy for internal improvements—granted

1803 **Territorial Expansion**—annexation of territory—Louisiana Purchase from France

1820 **Slavery**—anti-slavery magazine—*The Emancipator* — published — Jonesboro, Tenn.

1837 **Education**—state board of education— established—Massachusetts

1855 **Billiard Match** — billiard three-ball match on a six-by-twelve carom table —San Francisco, Calif.

1863 **Seal**—seal of the Confederate States of America—authorized

1864 **Game Law**—hunting license fee (state) —enacted—New York

1879 **Labor Law**—factory inspection law— enacted—Massachusetts

1883 **Electric Company**—three-wire central station incandescent electric lighting plant—Sunbury, Pa.—incorporated

1888 **Naval Officer**—naval chaplain who was Catholic—C. H. Parks

1889 Holiday—national holiday—celebrated

1898 **Advertising Law**—advertising legislation (state)—enacted—New York

1913 **Court**—small debtors' court established by state law—effective—Kansas

1926 **Radio Facsimile Transmission**—photograph sent by radio across the Atlantic inaugurating commercial service—transmitted—London, England to New York City

1931 **Autogiro**—autogiro to land packages on a moving ship—New York City

1932 **Animals**—dogs trained to guide the blind—Seeing Eye—incorporated

1939 Railroad Car—train with fluorescent lights—St. Louis, Mo. to Kansas City, Mo.

1939 **Television—Telecast**—President to appear on television—F. D. Roosevelt

1940 **Woman**—woman prize fight referee (licensed)—Belle Martell—Van Nuys, Calif.

1942 **Submarine**—submarine built on the Great Lakes — "Peto" — launched — Manitowoc, Wis.

1948 **Television — Telecast** — stratovision flight—television signal transmitted

1953 **Building**—building for telephone directory compilation and printing— dedicated—Des Plaines, Ill.

1955 **Element**—element 101—mendelevium —announced

MAY 1

1704 **Advertisement**—advertisement—*News-Letter*—Boston, Mass.—published

1751 **Cricket Tournament**—cricket match— New York City

1826 **Tax**—inheritance tax (state)—effective —Pennsylvania

1840 **Blind**—state school for the blind— Ohio Institution for the Blind—Superintendent William Chapin—took office

1843 **Diplomatic Service**—consul to California—appointed—T. O. Larkin

1857 **Literacy qualification for voting**—enacted—Massachusetts

1861 **Normal School**—normal school (state) at which students actually conducted classes—Oswego Training School— Oswego, N.Y.—established

1863 **Cripples**—private school for cripples— opened—New York City

1863 **Hospital**—orthopedic hospital—Hospital for Ruptured and Crippled—New York City—opened

1872 **Liberal Republican Party**—convention —Cincinnati, Ohio

1873 Postal Card—issued

1876 **Coaching**—tallyho trip — New York City

1883 **Sports**—sports trainer (professional) —Bob Rogers—engaged—New York City

1884 **Building**—building known as a skyscraper—construction began—Chicago, Ill.

1886 **Boat Race**—fisherman's boat race— Boston Light

1888 **Locomotive**—electric freight locomotive—tested

1893 **Kapok** — commercially introduced — Chicago, Ill.

1895 **Railroad**—railroad to use an electric engine—Baltimore and Ohio—for passenger service

1897 **Fencing**—fencing champion to win three titles in one year—C. G. Bothner —New York City

1899 **Hospital**—cancer home for incurables (free)—opened—New York City

1903 **House of David**—established—Benton Harbor, Mich.

1904 **Socialist Party**—national convention—Indianapolis, Ind.

1906 **Bank**—bank open day and night—New York City

1913 **Foxhound Master (American)**—R. E. Strawbridge—England

1915 **Ship**—ship (American) attacked by a German submarine—"Nantucket Chief"—torpedoed

1921 **Radio Beacons**—in regular service

1925 **Insurance**—automobile compulsory insurance act (state)—approved—Massachusetts

1926 **Christmas Tree**—National Christmas Tree—dedicated—General Grant National Park, Calif.

1927 **Check Photographing Device**—commercial manufacture—Rochester, N.Y.

1927 **Jewish College**—Jewish college of liberal arts and sciences under Jewish auspices—cornerstone laid

1929 **Aviation**—airplane commutation tickets—placed on sale

1931 **Baha'i House of Worship**—opened—Wilmette, Ill.

1946 **Governor**—Negro governor appointed by the President of the United States—W. H. Hastie—appointed

1946 **Ship**—radar installation aboard a commercial carrier—"African Star"—in operation—New York City

1947 **Radar**—radar for commercial and private planes — demonstrated — Culver City, Calif.

1948 **Jockey**—jockey to win the Kentucky Derby four times—Eddie Arcaro

MAY 2

1829 **Fair**—manufacturers' fair—American Institute—New York City—incorporated

1843 **Colonial Government**—government on the Pacific coast—Champoeg, Ore.

1855 **Zinc**—zinc commercial production—Pennsylvania and Lehigh Zinc Company incorporated

1880 **Ship**—steamboat to employ electric lights successfully—"Columbia"—dynamo operated

1887 **Kindergarten**—kindergarten for the blind—Perkins Institution—Roxbury, Mass.—opened

1887 **Photographic Film**—celluloid photographic film—patent application—H. W. Goodwin

1900 **United Christian Party**—first convention

1917 **Baseball Game**—double no-hit nine-inning baseball game—major league—Chicago, Ill.

1917 **Loan** — liberty loan subscriptions — taken

1923 **Aviation** — Flights (transcontinental)—transcontinental non-stop flight—from Roosevelt Field, N.Y.

1926 **Radio Facsimile Transmission**—drawing sent by radio across the Atlantic—transmitted—London to New York City

MAY 3

1649 **Medical Legislation**—law to regulate the practice of medicine (colonial)—enacted—Massachusetts

1654 **Bridge**—toll bridge—erected—Rowley, Mass.

1743 **Automaton** — imported — New York City

1765 **Medical School**—medical college—established—Philadelphia, Pa.

1768 **Arbitration**—arbitration tribunal—established—New York City

1826 **Arcade**—cornerstone laid—Philadelphia, Pa.

1845 **Bridge**—iron truss bridge—construction began—Pottstown, Pa.

1845 **Lawyer**—Negro lawyer formally admitted to the bar—M. B. Allen—Worcester, Mass.

1851 **Methodist Episcopal Church**—Scandinavian Methodist Episcopal Church—incorporated

1861 **Habeas Corpus**—habeas corpus suspension order—Abraham Lincoln

1862 **Land Mines**—land mines—used

1874 **Young Men's Hebrew Association**—Lewis May—served—New York City

1881 **Locomotive Headlight**—electric locomotive headlight — patented — L. G. Woolley—Mendon, Mich.

1904 **Pharmacy Legislation (state)**—requiring graduation—enacted—New York

1911 **Insurance** — workmen's compensation insurance law (state)—enacted—Wisconsin

1913 **Moving Picture Censorship**—moving picture censorship board (state)—Ohio approved censorship

1921 **Tax**—sales tax (state)—approved—West Virginia

1923 **Aviation**—Flights (transcontinental)—transcontinental non-stop flight—O. G. Kelly and J. A. Macready—arrived—Coronado Beach, Calif.

1927 **Electric Sign**—electric sign flasher—F. E. J. Wilde—patent—Meadowmere Park, N.Y.

1933 **Mint (U.S.)**—woman Director of the Mint—N. T. Ross—assumed office

1938 **Television**—Telecast—book review to be televised—New York City

1944 **Army Officer**—woman officer in the Judge Advocate General's Department—P. L. Propp

1950 **Medical Society**—woman member of the Association of American Physicians—H. B. Taussig—elected—Atlantic City, N.J.

1952 **Aviation**—Flights—North Pole landing by an airplane at the geographic pole

MAY 4

1776 **Ink**—invisible ink—Silas Deane—arrived in France as American agent

1780 **Arts and Science Society**—arts and science society (national)—American Academy of Arts and Sciences—incorporated

1798 **Pistol**—government contract for pistols—authorized—Simeon North

1811 **Disciples of Christ**—church established—Brush Run, Pa.

1845 **Bridge**—iron truss bridge—completed—Pottstown, Pa.

1846 **Capital Punishment**—death penalty was first abolished—enacted—Michigan

1854 **Entomologist** — state entomologist — New York—Asa Fitch—appointed

1855 **Hospital**—women's hospital—opened—New York City

1869 **Railroad** — municipal railroad — construction authorized—Ohio

1886 **Phonograph**—phonograph that was practical—patented

1891 **Hospital**—interracial hospital—Provident Hospital—Chicago, Ill.—opened

1892 **Acetylene**—made—T. L. Willson—Spray, N.C.

1905 **Railroad Car**—mail car (steel)—exhibited—Washington, D.C.

1920 **Orchestra**—orchestra (American) to make a European tour—concert—Paris, France

1927 **Balloon Flight**—balloon flight to exceed an altitude of 40,000 feet—ascended—Scott Field, Ill.—H. C. Gray

1928 **Judge**—woman associate justice on the federal bench—G. R. Cline—appointed

1930 **Medical Congress**—Mental Hygiene International Congress — opened — Washington, D.C.

1942 **World War II**—sea battle fought entirely by air power—Coral Sea

1954 **Tennis Match**—intercollegiate court tennis match—New York City

MAY 5

1696 **Woman**—woman printer—Dinah Nuthead—license application—Annapolis, Md.

1809 **Woman**—woman granted a patent—Mary Kies—South Killingly, Conn.

1832 **Vaccination Legislation**—vaccination legislation for Indians—enacted

1847 **Medical Society**—medical society (national)—American Medical Association—organized—Philadelphia, Pa.

1865 **Railroad Train Robbery** — railroad train robbery of a disabled train—North Bend, Ohio

1881 **Immigration**—Chinese labor immigration act—approved—U.S. Senate

1894 **Fencing**—intercollegiate fencing championship competition—New York City

1901 **Catholic Mass**—Catholic Mass for nightworkers—Church of St. Andrew—New York City

1908 **Army Exclusion Law** — enacted — Rhode Island

1913 **Medical Society**—American College of Surgeons—organized—Springfield, Ill.

1936 **Bottle**—screw cap bottle with a pour-lip—patented—E. A. Ravenscroft—Glencoe, Ill.

1947 **Helicopter**—ram-jet helicopter—tested—St. Louis, Mo.

1956 **Runner**—runner to run a mile under four minutes—Jim Bailey—Los Angeles, Calif.

1961 **Astronauts**—space flight by an American astronaut—Cape Canaveral, Fla.—A. B. Shepard

MAY 6

1732 **Newspaper**—German newspaper—published—Philadelphia, Pa.

1787 **Freemasons**—Negro mason—African lodge meeting under charter

1840 **Library**—library building (university)—completed—Columbia, S.C.

1851 **Lock**—lock ("clock") — patented — Linus Yale—Newport, N.Y.

1851 **Refrigerator**—mechanical refrigerator patent — John Gorrie — Apalachicola, Fla.

1862 **Agricultural School**—agricultural college (state) to be chartered—name of Farmers High School of Pennsylvania changed to Agricultural College of Pennsylvania

1882 **Immigration**—Chinese labor immigration act—suspending immigration—enacted

1887 **Ship**—navy vessel equipped to lay mines—"Baltimore"—keel laid

1891 **Fencing**—fencing league (national)—Amateur Fencers League of America—organized—New York City

1896 **Aviation**—Airplane—airplane (heavier-than-air) to make any long sustained flight—S. P. Langley

1916 **Radio Telephone**—radio telephone ship-to-shore conversation

1925 **Radio Facsimile Transmission**—transpacific and transcontinental facsimile transmission

1935 **Works Progress Administration**—Works Progress Administration—created—H. L. Hopkins appointed administrator

1936 **Aviation**—Flights (transatlantic)—Atlantic Ocean regular commercial airship service—"Hindenburg"—take-off

1937 **Radio Broadcast**—recorded coast-to-coast broadcast—Lakehurst, N.J.

1941 **World War II**—American ship sunk by a U-boat—"Robin Moor"—sailed

1948 **Navy**—air squadron of jets (U.S. Navy)—qualified aboard a carrier

1962 **Submarine** — nuclear warhead fired from a Polaris submarine—"Ethan Allen"—Christmas Island

MAY 7

1634 **Treason**—treason trial (colonial)—Virginia

1784 **War Veterans' Society**—Society of the Cincinnati—first general meeting —Philadelphia, Pa.

1789 **Presidential Inaugural Ball** — New York City

1833 **Monument**—monument to a woman financed by women—cornerstone laid —Fredericksburg, Va.

1898 **Trapshooting**—trapshooting intercollegiate association—meet—New Haven, Conn.

1912 **Aviation—Airplane**—airplane outfitted with a machine gun—flown—College Park, Md.

1920 **Aviation—Expositions and Meets**—intercollegiate air meet—Mitchel Field, Long Island, N.Y.

1932 **Aviation—Flights**—all-blind solo flight by the U.S. Army—A. F. Hegenberger—Dayton, Ohio

1936 **Catholic Mass**—Catholic Mass in an airship over the ocean

1946 **Governor**—Negro governor appointed by the President of the United States —W. H. Hastie—appointment confirmed

MAY 8

1783 **Salute (complimentary)** — fired by Great Britain in honor of George Washington

1787 **Prison Reform Society** — formed — Philadelphia, Pa.

1792 **Army Officer**—paymaster—office authorized

1792 **Conscription** — conscription—authorized by Congress

1812 **Federal Foreign Aid Bill**—enacted

1816 **Bible Society**—Bible society (national organization)—American Bible Society—delegates met—New York City

1821 **Discovery**—discovery of Antarctica—expedition returned

1828 **Peace Society**—New York Peace Society joins American Peace Society

1840 **Photographic Patent** — photographic patent—A. S. Wolcott—New York City

1847 **Rubber** — rubber tire patent — R. W. Thomson—England

1848 **School**—school for the mentally retarded—created—Boston, Mass.

1877 **Dog Show** — of importance — New York City

1878 **Baseball Game** — triple play unassisted—Paul Hines—Providence, R.I.

1879 **Automobile Patent**—filed—G. B. Selden—Rochester, N.Y.

1905 **Automobile Race** — transcontinental automobile race (for a time record)—started—New York City

1915 **Horse Race**—filly to win the Kentucky Derby—Regret—Louisville, Ky.

1917 **World War I**—American troop contingent to arrive in France—sailed—New York City

1919 **Aviation — Flights** (transatlantic) — transatlantic hydroplane flight—left—New York City

1931 **Price Regulation Law**—resale price maintenance law (state)—approved—California

1939 **Electric Starting Gate (race track)**—used—Inglewood, Calif.

1951 **Dacron** — dacron men's suits — introduced—New York City

1952 **Coal** — coal hydrogenation chemicals pilot plant (large)—opened—Institute, W.Va.

1954 **Shot-Put**—shot-put toss over 60 feet —Parry O'Brien—Los Angeles, Calif.

1961 **Medal** — National Aeronautics and Space Administration Distinguished Service Medal — presented — A. B. Shepard—Washington, D.C.

1961 **Water**—sea water conversion plant (practical)—Freeport, Tex.—opened

MAY 9

1607 **Protestant Episcopal Church** — Protestant Episcopal Church—established —Jamestown, Va.

1754 **Cartoon**—newspaper cartoon—*Pennsylvania Gazette*—Philadelphia, Pa.

1792 **Army Officer** — paymaster — Caleb Swan—appointed

1825 **Theater**—theater lighted by gas—New York City—newspaper account

1860 **Constitutional Union Party** — organized—Baltimore, Md.

1863 **Bank Legislation** — national banking system—Comptroller of Currency—Hugh McCulloch—served

1863 **Comptroller**—Comptroller of the Currency—Hugh McCulloch—began service

1893 **Moving Picture**—moving picture film exhibition—T. A. Edison—Brooklyn, N.Y.

1912 **Aviation — Exposition and Meets** — aeronautic international exposition—New York City

1913 **Senator (U.S.)**—senators "elected by the people"—amendment ratified by Wisconsin, 36th state

1926 **Aviation—Flights**—North Pole flight —R. E. Byrd

1926 **Ship** — rotor ship — "Baden-Baden"—arrived—New York City

1932 **Senator (U.S.)** — woman senator to preside over the Senate—H. O. W. Caraway

1936 **Aviation—Flights (transatlantic)**—Atlantic Ocean regular commercial airship service — "Hindenburg"—landed —Lakehurst, N.J.

1936 **Postage Stamp** — sheet of postage stamps to contain more than one variety—on sale—New York City

1939 **Catholic Beatification**—Catholic beatification of an American Indian—Kateri Tekakwitha

1944 **Eye**—eye bank—opened—New York
City
1947 **Bank** — world bank — International
Bank for Reconstruction and Development—loan to France

MAY 10

1643 **Colonial Government** — colonial government union — organized — Boston,
Mass.
1783 **War Veterans' Society** — Society of
the Cincinnati — organized — Fishkill,
N.Y.
1797 **Ship** — frigate — "United States" —
launched—Philadelphia, Pa.
1852 **Catholic Provincial Council**—plenary
session—Baltimore, Md.
1866 **Woman Suffrage**—woman suffrage associations (national)—American Equal
Rights Association—New York City
—constitution adopted
1869 **Railroad**—railroad to run west, out of
Chicago — completed — Promontory,
Utah
1872 **Presidential Candidate**—woman presidential candidate—V. C. Woodhull—
nominated—New York City
1872 **Vice Presidential Candidate**—Negro
vice presidential candidate—Frederick
Douglass — nominated — New York
City
1876 **Postage Stamp**—public exhibition of
postage stamps—Philadelphia, Pa.
1876 **Postage Stamp** — stamped envelopes
issued to commemorate an event —
Philadelphia, Pa.
1876 **Turnstile (electric)** — with ratchet —
used—Philadelphia, Pa.
1879 **Archaeological Society** — archaeological society (national)—Archaeological
Institute of America — formed—Boston, Mass.
1892 **Medical School**—osteopathy school—
American School of Osteopathy—
Kirksville, Mo.—chartered
1893 **Locomotive**—locomotive to attain the
proved speed of 112.5 miles an hour—
time clocked
1894 **Monument**—monument to a woman
financed by women—M. B. Washington—dedication
1898 **Vending Machine** — vending machine
law—enacted—Omaha, Neb.
1908 **Holiday**—Mother's Day—celebrated—
Philadelphia, Pa.
1912 **Aviation—Flights**—over-water round-
trip flight—G. L. Martin
1912 **Aviation—Passenger**—admiral in uniform to ride in an airplane—B. A.
Fiske—New York City
1927 **Aviation—Legislation**—aviation legislation (state) — Connecticut Department of Aviation—authorized
1927 **Hotel**—hotel to install radio reception
—Hotel Statler—Boston, Mass.
1929 **Submarine "Lung"**—tested
1930 **Planetarium** — planetarium opened to
the public—Adler Planetarium—Chicago, Ill.

1942 **Insurance** — health insurance law
(state)—effective—Rhode Island
1949 **Planetarium**—planetarium owned by a
university — Chapel Hill, N.C. —
opened

MAY 11

1752 **Insurance**—fire insurance company to
receive a charter—first meeting of directors—Philadelphia Contributionship
for the Insurance of Houses from
Loss by Fire
1785 **Ship**—trading ship sent to China—
"Empress of China" — returned to
New York City
1816 **Bible Society**—Bible society (national
organization)—American Bible Soci-
ety—formed—New York City
1825 **Tract Society**—tract society (national)—American Tract Society—organized—New York City
1832 **Political Platform (national)**—adopted
—Washington, D.C.
1855 **Court**—court of claims—organized
1858 **Physician**—doctor to receive a medal
from Congress—F. H. Rose—authorization
1875 **Baseball Game** — no-run nine-inning
baseball game—St. Louis, Mo.
1898 **Spanish American War**—naval officer
killed in the Spanish-American war—
Worth Bagley
1898 **Spanish American War**—soldier killed
in the Spanish-American war—G. B.
Meek
1928 **Television—Telecast**—programs regularly televised—Schenectady, N.Y.
1929 **Codeball**—played—Chicago, Ill.
1942 **Blackout**—blackout outdoor light control—Seattle, Wash.
1947 **Automobile Tire**—tubeless automobile
tires—announced—Akron, Ohio
1960 **Submarine**—submerged circumnavigation of the earth—"Triton"—returned
to New London, Conn.

MAY 12

1812 **Vice Presidential Candidate** — vice
presidential nominee to decline nomination—John Langdon
1831 **Bank Robbery**—bank robbery—Edward Smith—sentenced
1841 **Anti-Slavery Party**—Liberty Party—
national convention—New York City
1844 **College**—masonic college — opened—
Philadelphia, Mo.
1857 **Hospital**—women's infirmary staffed
by women physicians—hospital opened
—New York City
1860 **News Correspondent** — woman news
reporter at a political convention—
M. A. R. Livermore—Chicago, Ill.
1873 **Postal Card**—first known cancellation
1890 **Prize Fight**—state legalization concerning prize fighting — enacted —
Louisiana
1894 **Agricultural Appropriation** — New
York

1894 **Ship**—warship built on inland waters — "Ericsson" — launched — Dubuque, Iowa

1896 **Health Ordinance prohibiting spitting** —enacted—New York City

1896 **Medical Instruction**—psychiatric institute—authorized—New York

1908 **Radio Broadcast** — radio broadcast demonstration — N. B. Stubblefield — patent

1914 **Holiday** — Mother's Day — national recognition

1933 **Agricultural Adjustment Administration**—approved

1933 **Federal Emergency Relief Administration**—created

1949 **Diplomatic Service**—woman ambassador from a foreign country—S. V. L. Pandit—received

1953 **Television Station** — noncommercial educational television station—KUHT —Houston, Tex.

MAY 13

1607 **Colonial Government**—colonial council in America—Jamestown, Va.

1607 **Colonist** — English settlement in America (permanent) — arrived — Jamestown, Va.

1821 **Printing Press** — printing press invented in America that was practical and successful—patent—Samuel Rust —New York City

1829 **Peace Society**—American Peace Society—annual meeting — New York City

1854 **Billiard Match** — billiard match — of importance—Syracuse, N.Y.

1857 **Agricultural School**—agricultural college (state) — to open — Agricultural College of Michigan, Lansing, Mich.—opened

1873 **Sewing Machine** — sewing machine lamp holder—patented—M. N. Wolf —Avon, Conn.

1897 **Golf Club**—intercollegiate golf association tournament—Ardsley-on-Hudson, N.Y.

1908 **Navy**—naval nurses' corps—authorized

1916 **Holiday**—Indian Day—observance

1918 **Postage Stamp** — airmail stamps—issued

1942 **Helicopter Flight** — helicopter flight (cross country)—take-off

1949 **Turbine**—gas turbine to pump natural gas—installed—Wilmar, Ark.

1953 **Television Receiver**—city to have two educational television channels—Pittsburgh, Pa.

MAY 14

1634 **Tax**—property tax law (colonial)— Massachusetts

1694 **College**—college to receive a coat-of-arms from the College of Heralds— Williamsburg, Va.

1804 **Expedition** — expedition across the continent to the Pacific coast—Lewis and Clark—left—St. Louis, Mo.

1836 **Expedition** — scientific expedition fitted out by the United States Government—authorized

1852 **College**—college to grant women absolutely equal rights with men—nonsectarian — Antioch College, Yellow Springs, Ohio—chartered

1853 **Milk**—condensed milk (commercial)— Gail Borden—patent application

1856 **Animals**—camels imported for commercial purposes—Indianola, Tex.

1857 **Agricultural School**—agricultural college (state) to open — Agricultural College of Michigan—instruction offered

1874 **Football Game**—rugby contest (international)—Cambridge, Mass.

1874 **Football Goal Post** — football goal post used—Cambridge, Mass.

1878 **Petroleum Jelly** — "vaseline" trademarked

1884 **Anti-Monopoly Party** — formed—Chicago, Ill.

1887 **Accident Report** — industrial accident reports required—Massachusetts

1904 **Olympic Games**—Olympic celebration —St. Louis, Mo.

1908 **Aviation — Passenger** — airplane passenger (official) — first passenger to fly—C. W. Furnas—Fort Myer, Va.

1921 **Judge**—woman judge to sentence a man to death—F. E. Allen—Cleveland, Ohio

1929 **Air Mail Service**—air mail service between North and South America—inaugurated—Miami, Fla.

1931 **Autogiro** — transcontinental autogiro flights—J. M. Miller—started—Philadelphia, Pa.

1934 **Ship**—streamlined steamship — "Arctees"—arrived—Boston, Mass.

1935 **Aviation—Flights**—sky-train international round-trip flight — left — Key West, Fla.

1941 **Blackout** — blackout lighting demonstration—Lynn, Mass.

1942 **Army Auxiliary Corps** — women's army auxiliary corps (WAAC)—authorized

MAY 15

1602 **Discovery**—discovery of New England by an Englishman—B. Gosnold

1672 **Copyright Law**—copyright law—enacted—Massachusetts

1764 **Milestones**—installed — Philadelphia, Pa.

1785 **Missionary**—Negro missionary—John Marrant—ordained

1797 **Congress (U.S.)**—special session

1851 **Women's Club**—women's secret society—Adelphean Society — organized —Macon, Ga.

1854 **Hospital**—inebriates' asylum—United States Inebriate Asylum — founded— Binghamton, N.Y.

1862 **Agriculture Bureau**—Agriculture Bureau made a separate entity

1880 **Archaeological Society** — archaeological national society — Archaeological Institute of America—annual meeting —Boston, Mass.

1885 **Forest Reserve**—forest reserve (state) —New York State Forest Preserve— designated

1888 **Union Labor Party** — convention — Cincinnati, Ohio

1894 **Labor Law**—labor discrimination law (state)—enacted—New Jersey

1914 **Sound Absorbing Material** — production started — International Falls, Minn.

1917 **Army Balloon School** — graduation— St. Louis, Mo.

1917 **Librarians' Union**—Library Employes' Union affiliated with AFL—chartered

1918 **Air Mail Service**—air mail experimental route — flown — Washington, D.C. to New York City

1918 **Ship**—ambulance ship designed and built as a hospital—"Relief"—frame erected

1919 **Air Mail Service**—air mail transcontinental service—Cleveland, Ohio to Chicago, Ill.

1920 **Air Mail Service**—air mail transcontinental service — Chicago, Ill., to Omaha, Neb.

1922 **Arbitration Association** — arbitration association — Arbitration Society of America—formed—New York City

1930 **Aviation** — air stewardess — Ellen Church

1933 **Congress (U.S.)—Senate**—loud-speaker—installed—Senate

1937 **Aquarium**—aquarium for monsters of the deep—ground broken—Marineland, Fla.

1937 **Business**—Keedoozle store — opened —Memphis, Tenn.

1938 **Post Office** — airplane post office — Washington, D.C.

1940 **Nylon**—nylon hose—placed on sale

1941 **Conscientious Objectors' Camp**—Relay Post Office, Md.

1942 **Army Auxiliary Corps**—women's army auxiliary corps (WAAC) — director O. C. Hobby appointed

1946 **Telephone** — mobile telephone news dispatch—St. Louis, Mo.

1950 **Radio Station**—all-local network

1952 **Jockey**—jockey to win 4,000 races— Johnny Longden—Inglewood, Calif.

1958 **Postage Stamp** — postage stamp to bear the likeness of a Vice President of the United States issued by a foreign country—Ecuador

MAY 16

1691 **Treason**—American colonist hanged for treason — Jacob Leisler — New York City

1775 **State**—state constitution — adopted — Massachusetts

1825 **Horse Race**—trotting course—Screwdriver won main event

1856 **Fish Commission (state)**—authorized —Massachusetts

1866 **Money**—nickel—authorized

1882 **Army Officer**—general to become a rear admiral—S. P. Carter—appointed

1882 **Flicker**—Henry Van Hoevenbergh— Elizabeth, N.J.—patent

1888 **United Labor Party**—formed—Cincinnati, Ohio

1893 **Typewriter**—typewriter to produce a line of writing visible as it was being typed — patented — H. L. Wagner — Brooklyn, N.Y.

1895 **College Academic Costume Standardization**—assembled—New York City

1896 **Electric Power Plant**—rotary converter power plant—operated—Chicago, Ill.

1903 **Motorcycle Trip**—motorcycle transcontinental trip—started—San Francisco, Calif.

1910 **Mines Bureau (U.S.)**—authorized

1913 **Agriculture Department (U.S.)** — Office of Markets—chief served—C. J. Brand

1914 **Horseshoe Pitchers Association (national)** — organized — Kansas City, Kan.

1929 **Moving Picture Actor**—moving picture actors to receive "Oscars"—Emil Jannings and Janet Gaynor—Hollywood, Calif.

1938 **Animal Breeding Society**—artificial animal breeding cooperative society— organized—New Jersey

1941 **Ordnance**—automatic aircraft cannon —delivered—Elmira, N.Y.

MAY 17

1757 **Academy**—Academy and College of Philadelphia—seven men graduated

1786 **Treaty**—treaty entered into by the United States after the treaty of peace with Great Britain—with Prussia— ratified

1792 **Brokerage** — stock exchange — New York City

1796 **Land Grant**—special land grant

1796 **Medical Book**—pediatrics monograph —presented—Philadelphia, Pa.

1803 **Reaper**—reaper patented

1853 **Railroad**—railroad merger—of importance—New York Central Railroad Co.

1875 **Horse Race**—horse race (Kentucky Derby)—Louisville; Ky.

1876 **Greenback Party** — convention — Indianapolis, Ind.

1877 **Telephone**—interstate telephone call— from New Brunswick, N.J., to New York City

1877 **Telephone**—telephone switchboard or exchange—operated—Boston, Mass.

1879 **Archaeological Society**—archaeological society (national)—constitution adopted—Archaeological Institute of America

1897 **Voting Machine Commission**—authorized—New York

1908 **Tunnel**—subaqueous railroad tunnel to a foreign country—Port Huron, Mich.—operated by electricity

1912 **Ship**—cruise ship to circumnavigate the world—arrived—Hamburg, Germany

1918 **Aviation**—air squadron (complete)—first flight of De Havilland airplane in France

1930 **Ship** — air-conditioned ship — "Mariposa"—keel laid—Quincy, Mass.

1939 **Postal Service**—coin-operated mailbox —installed—New York City

1939 **Television — Telecast** — baseball game (collegiate) televised—Princeton-Columbia—New York City

1939 **Television — Telecast** — fashion show telecast—New York City

1942 **Helicopter Flight**—helicopter flight (cross-country) — from Stratford, Conn.—landed Dayton, Ohio

1956 **Mica**—synthetic mica—offered for sale —Caldwell Township, N.J.

1960 **Atomic Reactor**—atomic reactor system to be patented—J. W. Flora—Canoga Park, Calif.

MAY 18

1631 **Election**—accredited colonial election —Massachusetts

1652 **Slavery** — law regulating slavery — Warwick, R.I.

1713 **Book Auction Catalog**—book auction catalog—announced—Boston, Mass.

1766 **Church of the United Brethren in Christ**—Lancaster, Pa.

1798 **Navy**—Secretary of the Navy—Benjamin Stoddert—appointed

1852 **Education**—compulsory school attendance law (state)—enacted—Massachusetts

1886 **Arbitration**—state board of mediation and arbitration — authorized — New York State

1905 **Health Society**—National Tuberculosis Association — annual meeting — Washington, D.C.

1914 **Ship**—steamboat to pass through the Panama Canal—first commercial cargo—"Mariner"

1917 **World War I**—American troop contingent to arrive in France—arrived in England on May 18, 1917

1934 **Capital Punishment**—capital punishment authorized by federal law—law enacted

1938 **Federal Crop Insurance Corporation** —first application—Panhandle, Tex.

1953 **Aviation—Aviator**—woman to pilot an airplane faster than the speed of sound—Jacqueline Cochran—Rogers Dry Lake, Calif.

1956 **Horse**—forest horse—foaled—Brookfield, Ill.

MAY 19

1774 **Conscientious Objectors**—left Liverpool, England

1796 **Game Law**—game law (national)—approved

1823 **Medical School**—naval medical school (unofficial) — authorized — Philadelphia, Pa.

1847 **Railroad Car**—railroad coach—English style—in service

1857 **Fire Alarm System (electric)**—patent —Boston, Mass.

1891 **People's Party** — organized — Cincinnati, Ohio

1911 **Fingerprinting**—fingerprint conviction —New York City

1912 **Advertising Organization** — national committee formed

1915 **Dental Legislation**—legislation (state) regarding dental hygienists—enacted —Connecticut

1921 **Immigration**—immigration quota act —enacted

1921 **Opera**—opera broadcast in its entirety —*Martha*—Denver, Colo.

1928 **Frog Jumping Jubilee** — Calaveras County, Calif.

1932 **Light Beam Communication**—from a dirigible—Schenectady, N.Y.

1935 **Aviation—Flight** — sky-train international round-trip flight—return flight from Havana

1959 **Submarine**—submarine with two nuclear reactors—"Triton"—completed

MAY 20

1639 **Public School**—public school supported by direct taxation

1775 **Declaration of Independence (American)**—Declaration of Independence by a colony—Charlotte, N.C.

1785 **Geographer of the United States**—Thomas Hutchins—appointment authority enacted

1785 **Land Grant**—land grant to schools—authorized

1785 **Land Sale Ordinance (general)**—enacted

1785 **Survey of Public Lands**—authorized

1830 **Fountain Pen Patent**—D. Hyde—Reading, Pa.

1830 **Timetable**—railroad timetable—advertised—Baltimore, Md.

1844 **Game Protection Society** — wildlife protection society—New York Sportsmen's Club—founded—New York City

1856 **Telegraph** — telegraph ticker which successfully printed type—patented—D. E. Hughes—Louisville, Ky.

1862 **Homestead Act**—homestead act—enacted

1865 **Lecture Series (endowed)**—Morse lectureship—Union Theological Seminary—New York City

1873 **Army School**—army school graduate (Negro) — H. O. Flipper — became cadet

1875 Weights and Measures Standardization—International Bureau of Weights and Measures—established

1899 Automobile Speeding Arrest—driver arrested for speeding—Jacob German—New York City

1899 Physics—national physics association—American Physical Society—formed—New York City

1904 Carnegie Hero Fund Commission—by-laws adopted

1909 Ship—battleship to visit an inland city—sailed to Natchez, Miss.

1918 Ship—warship propelled by electricity—"New Mexico"—commissioned

1925 Chamber of Commerce—Chamber of Commerce of the United States of America — headquarters dedicated — Washington, D.C.

1926 Aviation—Legislation—aviation legislation (national) dealing with the operaton of civil aircraft—Air Commerce Act—enacted

1926 Labor—National Mediation Board—U.S. Board of Mediation—created

1927 Aviation — Flights (transatlantic) — transatlantic solo flight — take-off — C. A. Lindbergh—New York City

1930 Aviation—Flights—airplane catapulted from a dirigible

1932 Aviation — Flights (transatlantic) — transatlantic solo flight by a woman—A. E. Putnam

1933 Holiday—Maritime Day—established—act of Congress

1939 Air Mail Service—air mail transatlantic service—to Marseilles, France

1939 Aviation—Flights (transatlantic)—Atlantic Ocean scheduled air service—inaugurated—"Yankee Clipper"

1939 Television—Telecast—telecast (public) over telephone wires—publicly displayed—New York City

1951 Aviation—Aviator — American ace (jet)—James Jabara

1953 Hotel—hotel to establish a heliport—Fort Worth, Tex.

1955 Radar—off-shore radar warning station—launched

1956 Atomic Bomb—atomic fusion (thermonuclear) bomb dropped from an airplane—Bikini Atoll

MAY 21

1819 Bicycle—bicycle velocipedes—used—New York City

1829 Drydock—federal drydocks—cornerstone laid—Boston, Mass.

1832 Democratic National Convention—began—Baltimore, Md.

1832 Political Convention—two-thirds rule—enacted—Baltimore, Md.

1846 Building—building with a high steeple—Trinity Church, New York City—dedicated

1861 Newspaper—newspaper published by soldiers in the field—*United States American Volunteer*—De Soto, Mo.

1863 Seventh Day Adventist Church—general conference—organized

1877 Telephone—telephone used by a railroad company—tested—Altoona, Pa.

1881 American Red Cross—organized—Washington, D.C.

1881 Tennis Society—tennis society (national)—United States Lawn Tennis Association—formed—New York City

1888 Crematory—crematory (state)—authorized—New York State

1894 Research Institute—anatomy research institute—Wistar Institute of Anatomy and Biology — building dedicated — Philadelphia, Pa.

1901 Automobile Legislation—state motor car legislation—Connecticut

1906 Automobile Tire—demountable tire-carrying rim—patent application—L. H. Perlman—New York City

1909 Credit Union Law—approved—Massachusetts

1922 Cartoon—cartoon awarded a Pulitzer prize—award made

1927 Railroad Car—Pullman train completely equipped with roller bearings—service commenced

1929 Stock Quotation Board—automatic electric stock quotation board—installed—New York City

1932 Aviation — Flights (transatlantic) — transatlantic solo flight by a woman—A. E. Putnam—arrived—Londonderry, Ireland

1932 Railroad Excursion—railroad excursion (mystery)—St. Louis to Arcadia, Mo.

1932 Television—Telecast—telecast images received in an airplane—Los Angeles, Calif.

1934 Electric Home and Farm Authority, Inc. — first financed sale — Tupelo, Miss.

1934 Fingerprinting—community to fingerprint its citizens—Oskaloosa, Iowa

1936 Lucite—(polymethyl methacrylate)—production (commercial) — Wilmington, Del.

1941 World War II—American ship sunk by a U-boat—"Robin Moor"—sunk—South Atlantic Ocean

1955—Aviation—Flights (transcontinental)—transcontinental round-trip solo flight between sunrise and sunset—Los Angeles, Calif.—New York City

1956 Submarine—submerged circumnavigation of the earth—"Triton" laid down

MAY 22

1621 Wedding—wedding in New England—Edward Winslow

1649 Election Law—fraudulent election law (colonial) — enacted — Warwick, R.I.

1761 Insurance—life insurance company—policy issued—Philadelphia, Pa.

1789 Presbyterian General Assembly — Philadelphia, Pa.

1819 **Ship**—steamboat built in America to cross the Atlantic Ocean—"Savannah" —sailed

1841 **Chair**—recumbent chair patent—H. P. Kennedy—Philadelphia, Pa.

1848 **Political Convention**—national committee of a political organization—formed—Baltimore, Md.

1849 **President**—President who had received a patent—Abraham Lincoln

1861 **Civil War**—Union soldier killed by enemy action in the Civil War—T. B. Brown—killed—Grafton, W.Va.

1900 **Piano Player**—pneumatic piano player — patent — E. S. Votey — Detroit, Mich.

1900 **Scale**—automatic computing pendulum-type scales—patented—A. De Vilbiss, Jr.—Toledo, Ohio

1902 **Arbitration**—arbitration proceeding—Pious Fund Case agreement—signed

1919 **Ship**—concrete ship built for the United States Shipping Board—"Polias"—delivered

1930 **Aviation—Airship**—dirigible for private commercial operation—delivered —Bedford, Mass.

1930 **Theater**—television theater demonstration—Schenectady, N.Y.

1931 **Rattlesnake Meat**—rattlesnake meat in cans—sale—Arcadia, Fla.

1933 **Federal Emergency Relief Administration**—H. L. Hopkins—took office

1933 **Holiday**—Maritime Day—celebrated

1934 **Woman** — woman state committee chairman—M. T. Norton—Trenton, N.J.

1935 **Veto (presidential)** — veto message read by a President—F. D. Roosevelt

1947 **Rocket**—ballistic missile—fired—New Mexico

1958 **Ship**—atomic-powered merchant ship —"Savannah"—keel laid—Camden, N.J.

MAY 23

1785 **Lens**—eyeglass bifocals — described — Benjamin Franklin

1827 **Kindergarten**—nursery school—founded —New York City

1879 **Veterinary School**—veterinary school (state)—established—Ames, Iowa

1891 **Railroad Car**—chapel car—"Evangel" —dedicated—Cincinnati, Ohio

1903 **Automobile Transcontinental Trip**—transcontinental automobile trip—nonprofessional driver—left San Francisco, Calif.

1908 **Aviation—Airship**—airship disaster—J. A. Morrell—Berkeley, Calif.

1919 **Aviation—Airship**—airship to land on a roof—Cleveland, Ohio

1922 **Radio Broadcast**—debate over the radio—WJH—Washington, D.C.

1925 **Court**—state supreme court composed entirely of women—case decided—Texas

1933 **Autogiro**—autogiro to tow a glider—J. M. Miller—Valley Stream, N.Y.

1950 **Coal**—coal pipeline loops (experimental)—tested—Library, Pa.

1955 **Building**—atom bomb-resistant federal building—dedicated—Washington, D.C.

1956 **Automaton**—automaton to operate by long-distance control—manufactured—Schenectady, N.Y.

MAY 24

1828 **Post Office**—post office building (U.S.)—authorized

1844 **Telegram** — telegram inaugurating commercial service—from Washington, D.C.

1862 **Telegraph**—army field telegraph used in warfare—Mechanicsville, Va.

1865 **Railroad Track**—railroad rails of Bessemer steel — rolled — Wyandotte, Mich.

1869 **Expedition**—exploration of the Grand Canyon of the Colorado—J. W. Powell

1870 **Railroad Excursion**—railroad excursion (transcontinental) of an organization—left Boston, Mass.

1873 **Postage Stamp**—departmental postage stamps used

1875 **Bankers' Association**—national bankers' association—American Bankers Association—organized

1879 **Geological Survey**—geological survey director (U.S.)—Clarence King took office

1893 **Temperance Society** — Anti-Saloon League—Ohio Anti-Saloon League formed—Oberlin, Ohio

1899 **Garage (public)**—established—Boston, Mass.

1911 **Library Society**—woman to become president of the American Library Association—T. H. W. Elmendorf

1913 **Farm Bureau** — appropriation — New York State

1913 **Strike**—strike settlement—mediated by United States Department of Labor

1918 **Medal**—Croix de Guerre awarded a Negro—Henry Johnson

1924 **Diplomatic Service**—Foreign Service of the United States—created

1931 **Railroad**—air-conditioned train — Baltimore and Ohio Railroad Company—Washington, D.C. to New York City

1935 **Baseball Game** — baseball game at night by major league teams—Cincinnati, Ohio

1935 **Spectrophotometer** — machine sold — Schenectady, N.Y.

1945 **Business** — "Food-O-Mat" installed—Carlstadt, N.J.

1954 **Rocket**—rocket to exceed a 150-mile altitude — Viking XI — White Sands, N.M.

1954 **Sidewalk (traveling)**—sidewalk (traveling) in a railroad station—Jersey City, N.J.

1959 **Building**—house with a built-in nuclear bomb shelter—exhibited—Pleasant Hills, Pa.

MAY 25

1721 **Insurance** — fire insurance agent — John Copson—Philadelphia, Pa.—advertisement

1793 **Catholic Priest**—Catholic priest ordained in the United States—S. T. Badin—Baltimore, Md.

1804 **Distilling Book**—*American Distiller*—preface dated—Bristol, Pa.

1825 **Unitarian Society**—national organization of the Unitarian Churches of the United States and Canada—organized—Boston, Mass.

1844 **Gas Engine**—patent—Stuart Perry—New York City

1844 **Telegram**—news dispatch telegram—from Washington, D.C.

1863 **Bank**—national bank—National Bank of Davenport—subscriptions opened—Davenport, Iowa

1880 **Cattle Club**—cattle club (Jersey cattle)—American Jersey Cattle Club—incorporated

1895 **Golf Book**—golf book—*Golf in America*—published—New York City

1898 **American Expeditionary Force** — American Expeditionary Force — sailed—San Francisco, Calif.

1903 **Railroad**—railroad operated by an electric third rail system—Scranton, Pa.

1917 **World War I**—American troop contingent to land in France—arrived—Rouen, France

1918 **Nursing School**—Army School of Nursing—authorized

1926 **Catholic Church** — Catholic church raised to the dignity of a Basilica—dedicated—Lackawanna, N.Y.

1935 **Air Mail Service**—autogiro mail delivery direct to a post office—Philadelphia, Pa.

1935 **Narcotic**—narcotic sanatorium (federal) for drug addicts—dedicated—Lexington, Ky.

1937 **Postal Service**—letter to encircle the world by commercial airmail—delivered—New York City

1950 **Medal**—Agriculture Department distinguished service gold medal presented to a woman—L. M. Alexander

1953 **Ordnance**—atomic cannon—electronically fired—Frenchman Flat, Nev.

1953 **Television Station** — noncommercial educational television station—Houston, Tex.—programs telecast

MAY 26

1721 **Epidemic**—smallpox epidemic — Boston, Mass.

1836 **Congress (U.S.)**—House of Representatives—gag rule—adopted

1900 **Army War College** — Washington, D.C.—authorized

1906 **Archaeological Society**—archaeological society (national)—Archaeological Institute of America—incorporated

1908 **Automobile Transcontinental Trip**—transcontinental family automobile trip requiring only a month—Murdock family—reached New York City

1913 **Actors' Union**—Actors' Equity Association—organized

1913 **College**—college comprehensive senior examination program—adopted—Walla Walla, Wash.

1956 **Bank**—trailer bank—opened—Locust Grove, N.Y.

1958 **Submarine**—atomic-powered turbine electric-drive submarine — "Tullibee" keel laid—Groton, Conn.

MAY 27

1607 **War (colonial)**—Indian war of importance fought by English colonists—Virginia

1647 **Witchcraft Execution**—Achsah Young—Massachusetts

1652 **Money**—dies for coins—mint established—Boston, Mass.

1755 **Water** — water pumping plant — for municipal purposes—Bethlehem, Pa.

1796 **Piano**—piano patent—J. S. McLean

1835 **Medical School**—homeopathic school—Allentown, Pa.—cornerstone laid

1896 **Bicycle Race**—intercollegiate bicycle race—New York City

1908 **Postal Service**—navy mail service—established

1920 **World War I**—German spy to receive a death sentence from the American forces during World War I—sentence confirmed but commuted to life imprisonment

1926 **Monument**—statue to commemorate literary characters — erected — Hannibal, Mo.

1931 **Wind Tunnel**—full-scale wind tunnel for testing airplanes—operated—Langley Field, Va.

1935 **Industrial Recovery Act** — industrial recovery act (national)—declared unconstitutional by the Supreme Court

1936 **Woman**—woman coxswain of a men's collegiate varsity team—Sally Stearns—Winter Park, Fla.

1943 **Visiting Celebrities**—president of a Negro country—Edwin Barclay of Liberia—addressed U.S. Senate

MAY 28

1734 **Fish Protection**—fish legislation—enacted—New York City

1754 **War (colonial)**—bloodshed in the French and Indian war—Uniontown, Pa.

1796 **Debt Legislation (federal)**—enacted—exemption from prison

1879 **Labor Law**—labor law prohibiting the employment of women—enacted—Illinois

1881 **Pure Food Law**—pure food and drug legislation (state) — enacted — New York

1917 **World War I**—American troops to land in England—left New York City

1922 **Orchestra**—radio orchestra—Detroit, Mich.

1924 **Border Patrol**—border patrol organization authorized

1925 **Radio Facsimile Transmission**—radio facsimile long distance transmission of a medical subject—New York City

1929 **Moving Picture**—talking picture entirely in color—*On with the Show*—exhibited—New York City

1931 **Autogiro** — transcontinental autogiro flight—J. M. Miller—arrived—San Diego, Calif.—from Philadelphia, Pa.

1932 **Aviation—Airport**—airport manager (woman) appointed—Port Bucyrus, Ohio

1934 **Bank**—bank payments to depositors of a closed insured bank—East Peoria, Ill.—suspended business

1939 **Degrees (academic and honorary)** —Master of Hebrew Literature degree awarded a woman—H. H. Levinthal— New York City

1953 **Moving Picture**—animated three-dimensional cartoon in Technicolor (modern)—Walt Disney—premiere— Hollywood, Calif.

1958 **Presbyterian Church**—moderator of the United Presbyterian Church— elected—T. M. Taylor—Pittsburgh, Pa.

1959 **Rocket**—animals fired into space and rescued from a rocket

MAY 29

1827 **Nautical School** — established — Nantucket, Mass.

1844 **President**—President who was a "dark horse" candidate—J. K. Polk— nominated—Baltimore, Md.

1883 **Baseball Game** — baseball game at night—preliminary test—Fort Wayne, Ind.

1884 **Animal Industry Bureau (U.S.)**—Bureau of Animal Industry—established

1909 **Court**—domestic relations court—authorized—New York

1910 **Aviation—Races**—airplane to race a train—G.H. Curtiss

1916 **Flag**—President's flag—adopted

1918 **American Expeditionary Force**— American Expeditionary Force Air Service chief—M. M. Patrick—appointed

1918 **Aviation—Aviator**—pilot to receive the Congressional Medal of Honor— presentation—Phoenix, Ariz.

1933 **Money**—gold standard abrogation— authorized

1935 **Narcotic**—narcotic sanatorium (federal)—Lexington, Ky.—patients received

1951 **Aviation—Flights**—North Pole flight in a single-engine airplane— C. F. Blair

MAY 30

1650 **Corporation**—corporate body—chartered —Cambridge, Mass.

1806 **Duel**—duel in which a future President of the United States participated —Andrew Jackson—Red River, Ky.

1821 **Fire Hose**—of rubber-lined cotton web — patented — James Boyd — Boston, Mass.

1848 **Arts and Science Society**—woman elected to the American Academy of Arts and Sciences—Maria Mitchell

1848 **Ice Cream Freezer**—patented—W. G. Young—Baltimore, Md.

1856 **Dairy Legislation (state)**—enacted-- Massachusetts

1863 **Bank**—national bank—under banking law — stockholders' meeting—Davenport, Iowa

1868 **Holiday**—Decoration Day—celebrated

1881 **Plumbing**—state plumbing legislation —enacted—Illinois

1888 **Election Law**—Australian ballot system—enacted—Massachusetts

1894 **Baseball Player**—baseball player to hit four home runs in one game— Bobby Lowe—Boston, Mass.

1896 **Automobile Accident** — New York City

1901 **Hall of Fame**—hall of fame (university)—inaugurated—New York City

1903 **Motorcycle Hill Climbing Contest**— Riverdale, N.Y.

1908 **Insurance**—workmen's compensation insurance law (federal)—approved

1911 **Automobile Race**—automobile race on a track (long distance)—Indianapolis, Ind.

1917 **Aviation — Airship** — airship of the United States Navy that was successful—F1-flight—left Chicago, Ill.

1933 **Glass**—invisible glass installation— patent granted

MAY 31

1786 **Strike**—union strike benefit—authorized—Philadelphia, Pa.

1790 **Copyright Law**—copyright law of the United States—signed

1821 **Cathedral**—cathedral—Baltimore, Md. —building dedicated

1825 **Treaty**—treaty with a South American country—proclaimed

1836 **Ship**—steamboat on the Pacific coast —"Beaver"—maiden voyage

1853 **Expedition**—Arctic expedition—E. K. Kane—left New York City

1870 **Railroad Excursion**—railroad excursion (transcontinental) of an organization—arrived—San Francisco, Calif.

1870 **Road**—sheet asphalt pavement—patent —E. J. De Smedt—New York City

1880 Bicycle Society—bicycle society (national organization)—League of American Wheelmen—formed — Newport, R.I.

1884 Animal Industry Bureau (U.S.)—Bureau of Animal Industry—chief appointed—D. E. Salmon

1913 Senator (U.S.)—senators "elected by the people"—amendment in force

1918 Aviation — Aviator — American ace—qualified— Douglas Campbell

1919 Aviation — Flights (transatlantic) — transatlantic hydroplane flight—completed—Plymouth, England

1919 Wedding—airplane wedding—Houston, Tex.

1929 Animals—reindeer—born—North Beverly, Mass.

1937 Quadruplets to Complete a College Course—graduated—Waco, Tex.

1941 High Jumping Standards using electric eye detectors—used—Schenectady, N.Y.

1957 Rocket—intermediate range ballistic missile — Jupiter — fired from Cape Canaveral, Fla.

JUNE 1

1638 Earthquake—earthquake description—Plymouth, Mass.

1752 Insurance—fire insurance company to receive a charter—Philadelphia Contributorship — first policy — Philadelphia, Pa.

1785 Diplomatic Service—ambassador to England—John Adams

1789 Congress of the United States—congressional act—approved

1790 Congressman (U.S.)—congressman to die—Theodoric Bland

1802 Book Fair—New York City

1808 College—university founded by a federal land grant — opened — Athens, Ohio

1815 Ship—steam-propelled frigate—"Demologos"—propelled by own steam

1819 Tightrope—woman tightrope performer—appearance—Mme. Adolphe—New York City

1847 Postal Service—ocean mail contracts—service started

1847 Ship—steamship passenger line between United States ports and Europe to fly the American flag—"Washington" sailed—New York City

1860 Army—signal corps—established

1861 Civil War—Confederate officer killed in the Civil War—J. Q. Marr—Fairfax Court House, Va.

1861 Civil War—skirmish in the Civil War—Fairfax Court House, Va.

1869 Voting Machine—electric vote recorder—patented—T. A. Edison—Boston, Mass.

1880 Telephone — pay station telephone service—New Haven, Conn.

1881 Horse Race—American-bred horse to win the English Derby—Iroquois

1886 Arbitration—state board of mediation and arbitration — organized — New York State

1887 Armor-Plate Contract (U.S. Navy)—award—Bethlehem Iron Company—Bethlehem, Pa.

1887 Police—police bureau of identification—Bertillon system of identification used—Chicago, Ill.

1888 Seismograph—installed—Lick Observatory—Mount Hamilton, Calif.

1897 Rock Wool Factory—opened—Alexandria, Ind.

1898 Street Car—interurban street car line—Anderson, Ind. to Alexandra, Ind.

1901 Motorcycle—motorcycle with built-in gas engine—publicly demonstrated

1903 Zoological Laboratory (U.S.)—zoological laboratory (U.S.)—for the study of the parasites of livestock—B. H. Ransom put in charge of division

1909 Automobile Race — transcontinental automobile race—New York City to Seattle, Wash.—started

1911 Insurance—group insurance policy—Equitable Life Assurance Company—New York City

1915 Aviation — Airship — airship of the United States Navy—DNI—purchase contract

1919 Forest Service—forest service aerial patrol — established — Department of Agriculture

1923 Woman — woman internal revenue collector—M. G. Reinecke—served

1924 Border Patrol—border patrol organization—under Immigration and Naturalization Service—established

1928 Woman — woman passport division chief—R. B. Shipley—took office

1933 Canal—Great Lakes to the Gulf waterway—tow left New Orleans, La.

1939 Television—Telecast—prize fight to be televised—New York City—Lou Nova-Max Baer

1942 Insurance — health insurance law (state)—effective—Rhode Island

1942 Navy "E" Award—Navy "E" certificate of meritorious service presented to an institution of higher learning—University of Wisconsin—Madison, Wis.

1947 Glass — photosensitive glass — announced—Corning, N.Y.

1949 Microfilm—magazine on microfilm offered to subscribers—*Newsweek*—New York City

1951 Titanium—titanium plant fully self-contained and fully integrated — opened—Henderson, Nev.

1953 Aviation—airline to install rear-facing passenger seats—first flight—Burbank, Calif. to New York City

1955 Battery—solar energy battery—shipment made—Chicago, Ill.

1957 Runner—runner (American) to run a mile in less than four minutes—Don Bowden—Stockton, Calif.

JUNE 2

1857 **Sewing Machine**—chain-stitch single-thread sewing machine (practical)—patented—J. E. A. Gibbs—Mill Point, Va.

1883 **Baseball Game**—baseball game at night—Fort Wayne, Ind.

1883 **Elevated Railroad**—electric elevated railroad—Chicago, Ill.

1886 **Wedding**—White House wedding of a President — Grover Cleveland — Frances Folsom

1889 **Electric Power Plant**—alternating current hydroelectric power plant to operate over a long distance—supplied current—Portland, Ore.

1902 **Initiative and Referendum**—Oregon—authorized — constitutional amendment

1924 **Indians**—Indian citizenship statute—enacted

1930 **Births**—child born on a vessel passing through the Panama Canal

1930 **Museum** — maritime museum — Newport News, Va.

1930 **Woman**—woman Presbyterian elder—S. E. Dickson—Cincinnati, Ohio—elected

1933 **Swimming Pool in the White House**—accepted—Washington, D.C.

JUNE 3

1800 **President**—President to reside in Washington, D.C.—John Adams

1820 **Library**—mechanics' library—opened—New York City

1856 **Screw**—screw machine—patent—Cullen Whipple—Providence, R.I.

1861 **Civil War**—skirmish in the Civil War—Philippi, W.Va.

1873 **Oratorio**—oratorio by an American—*Oratorio of St. Peter*—performed—Portland, Me.

1878 **Medical Society**—laryngological society (national)—American Laryngological Association—founded—Buffalo, N.Y.

1884 **Political Convention**—national nominating convention presided over by a Negro—Chicago, Ill.

1891 **Zoological Laboratory (U.S.)**—zoological laboratory (U.S.) for the study of the parasites of livestock—termed Zoological Laboratory—Washington, D.C.

1898 **Medal**—"campaign medal"—"Dewey medal"—authorized

1899 **Movable Church** — Chapel of the Transfiguration —consecrated—Coanicut Island, R.I.

1903 **Election Law**—primary election (statewide)—enacted—Wisconsin

1916 **Army**—Army Veterinary Corps—established

1916 **Army** — Reserve Officers Training Corps—authorized

1916 **Supreme Court (U.S.)**—associate justice of the Supreme Court who was Jewish—L. D. Brandeis—sworn in

1918 **Novel**—novel to win the Pulitzer prize in letters—award announced—New York City

1921 **Immigration**—immigration quota act—effective

1925 **Aviation**—**Airship**—airship with an enclosed cabin—tested—Akron, Ohio

1932 **Baseball Player**—baseball player to hit four consecutive home runs in one game—Lou Gehrig—Philadelphia, Pa.

1937 **Wedding**—American woman married to a former king of England—W. W. Simpson—Monts, France

1949 **Naval Academy**—Negro midshipman in the U.S. Naval Academy to graduate—W. A. Brown

1949 **Treasury Department (U.S.)**—woman treasurer of the United States—G. N. Clark—nominated

1953 **Cabinet of the United States**—cabinet conference telecast—Washington, D.C.

1955 **President**—President to fly in a twin-engined airplane—D. D. Eisenhower

1958 **Methodist**—Negro minister with two white congregations—J. R. Washington—Newfield and West Newfield, Me.

1959 **Air Force Academy (U.S.)** — Air Force Academy—first class graduated—Colorado Springs, Colo.

JUNE 4

1674 **Horse Race**—horse race prohibition legislation—Massachusetts

1777 **Loan**—loan for war purposes received—by a central government

1811 **Secession**—secession was first mentioned in Congress

1816 **Ship**—steamboat (double decked)—"Washington" — launched — Wheeling, Va.

1820 **Church** — mariners' church — built — New York City

1845 **Opera**—opera by an American composer (important)—*Leonora*—presented—Philadelphia, Pa.

1890 **Employment Service**—state employment service—office opened—Toledo, Ohio

1912 **Children's Bureau (U.S.)**—chief J. C. Lathrop appointed

1912 **Labor Law**—minimum wage law—enacted—Massachusetts

1920 **Army Camp**—Army Citizens' Military Training Camp—camps authorized—National Defense Act—enacted

1920 **Army Officer**—chaplain (chief) of the United States Army—office—authorized

1920 **Army Officer**—woman with rank corresponding to major—J. C. Stimson—rank conferred

1931 **Glider**—rocket glider flight—W. G. Swan—Atlantic City, N.J.

1934 **Factory**—factories operated by the United States Government—project commenced—Millville, Mass.
1934 **Ship**—aircraft carrier—"Ranger"—delivered
1935 **Glass**—invisible glass installation—patent
1938 **Aviation—Passenger**—woman to fly entirely around the world by commercial heavier-than-air plane—Marjorie Shuler—left Southampton, England
1942 **Medal**—Navy Cross awarded to a Coast Guard officer in World War II —M. D. Jester
1944 **Submarine**—submarine captured and boarded on the high seas—U-505
1946 **Radio Facsimile Transmission**—facsimile transmitted to a moving train—demonstrated — Baltimore, Md. to Washington, D.C.
1957 **Coal**—commercial coal pipeline—in operation—Eastlake, Ohio

JUNE 5

1730 **Freemasons**—Provincial Grand Master (Masonic)—Daniel Coxe—deputized
1785 **Methodist College**—Cokesbury College—Abingdon, Md.—foundation sermon delivered
1794 **Neutrality Regulation**—enacted
1855 **American Party**—organized—Philadelphia, Pa.
1855 **Hospital** — Jewish hospital — Mount Sinai Hospital—opened—New York City
1865 **Safe Deposit Vault**—opened—New York City
1877 **Lawyer** — Japanese lawyer — Takeo Kikuchi—received LL.B. degree—Boston, Mass.
1877 **Oleomargarine** — oleomargarine legislation (state)—enacted—New York
1914 **Dental School** — dental hygienists' course — Fones Clinic — Bridgeport, Conn.—graduation
1920 **Labor Department (U.S.)**—women's bureau—organized
1922 **Woman**—woman automotive engineer —Marie Luhring—received M.E. degree—New York City
1930 **Colorscope** — public demonstration — New York City
1933 **Money**—gold standard abrogation—enacted
1938 **Voice Mechanism**—voice mechanism capable of creating the complex sounds of speech—exhibited—New York City
1939 **Museum**—museum devoted exclusively to papermaking—opened—Cambridge Mass.
1940 **Automobile Tire**—synthetic rubber tire—exhibited—Akron, Ohio
1946 **Sponge**—oxidized cellulose (sponge) for medical and surgical use—marketed—Detroit, Mich.

JUNE 6

1639 **Ordnance**—gunpowder mill—operated —Edward Rawson—Pecoit, Mass.
1788 **Cotton**—cotton goods to be trademarked — manufactured — Beverly, Mass.
1815 **Church of the United Brethren in Christ**—conference of elected delegates—Mount Pleasant, Pa.
1829 **Horticultural Society** — horticultural society (permanent)—exhibition opened to public
1833 **President**—President to ride on a railroad train—Andrew Jackson
1854 **Bank**—clearing house—New York Clearing House incorporated
1863 **Bank**—national bank—directors elected—National Bank of Davenport, Iowa
1877 **Degrees (academic and honorary)**—Doctor of Philosophy degree awarded to a woman
1882 **Electric Flatiron**—patented—H. W. Seely—New York City
1889 **Fellowship** — fellowship (graduate) awarded by a women's college—Bryn Mawr College, Bryn Mawr, Pa.
1890 **Polo Club**—polo association (national)—United States Polo Association—formed—New York City
1891 **Expedition**—polar expedition of which a woman was a member—Peary Expedition—sailed—New York City
1904 **Health Society**—National Tuberculosis Association — organized — Atlantic City, N.J.
1907 **Jewish College**—Jewish non-sectarian college — Dropsie College — chartered —Philadelphia, Pa.
1925 **City (Lilliputian city)**—built—Springfield, Mo.
1928 **College**—Negro university (Catholic) —Xavier University—New Orleans, La.—degrees conferred
1932 **Gasoline Tax**—gasoline tax (federal)
1933 **Employment Service** — employment service (U.S.E.S.)—created
1933 **Moving Picture Theater** — drive-in moving picture theater — opened — Camden, N.J.
1934 **Securities and Exchange Commission (U.S.)**—created
1936 **Gasoline** — aviation gasoline — produced—Paulsboro, N.J.
1938 **Recreational Ranching Course**—degree conferred—University of Wyoming—Laramie, Wyo.
1941 **Ship**—Navy vessel constructed as a minelayer — "Terror" — launched — Philadelphia, Pa.
1942 **Aviation — Parachute** — nylon parachute jump—Hartford, Conn.
1949 **Television—Telecast**—surgical operation televised on a closed circuit in color—Atlantic City, N.J.
1956 **Degrees (academic and honorary)**—master of arts degree in sacred music —conferred—New York City

JUNE 7

1775 **United States** — "United States" — union proclaimed

1790 **Diplomatic Service**—consuls of the United States appointed after the adoption of the Constitution

1801 **Booksellers' Association** — American Company of Booksellers—organized— New York City

1854 **Young Men's Christian Association**— international convention — Boston, Mass.

1862 **Treason**—citizen of the United States to be tried for treason, convicted, and hanged—W. B. Mumford—hanged— New Orleans, La.

1870 **Railroad Signal System**—railroad signal system (automatic electric block) —patent—T. S. Hall—Stamford, Conn.

1876 **Theological School**—theological school to admit women—B. D. degree awarded—Boston, Mass.

1882 **Tariff**—tariff commission—authorized

1883 **Tennis Match**—intercollegiate lawn tennis match—Hartford, Conn.

1887 **Typesetting Machine**—monotype—patent—Tolbert Lanston — Washington, D.C.

1892 **Baseball Player**—baseball "pinch hitter"—J. J. Doyle—Brooklyn, N.Y.

1892 **Bicycle Tire**—bicycle tire (cord)— patent—J. F. Palmer—Chicago, Ill.

1896 **Rowing**—transatlantic trip by rowboat—left—New York City

1898 **Social Democracy of America**—national convention—Chicago, Ill.

1905 **Railroad Car**—mail car (steel) — in service

1913 **Permalloy**—developed—G. W. Elmen —New York City

1918 **Births**—world war baby—born

1938 **Television—Telecast**—play to be televised with its original Broadway cast— *Susan and God*

1939 **Visiting Celebrities**—King and Queen of England—King George VI arrived —Niagara Falls, N.Y.

1942 **World War II**—American general missing in action in World War II— C. L. Tinker—Midway

1949 **Public Health**—public health service (U.S.) assistant surgeon general (woman)—Lucile Petry—appointed

1953 **Television—Telecast**—color network telecast in compatible color

1954 **Microbiology Laboratory**—dedicated— New Brunswick, N.J.

1955 **Television—Telecast**—President to appear on television in color—D. D. Eisenhower

JUNE 8

1786 **Ice Cream**—ice cream— advertised— New York City

1830 **Ship**—warship to circumnavigate the globe — "Vincennes" — arrived — New York City

1869 **Vacuum Cleaner**—suction-type vacuum cleaner—patented—I. W. McGaffey—Chicago, Ill.

1872 **Postal Card**—authorized

1872 **Post Office**—Post Office Department of the United States—became executive department—act passed

1872 **Postal Service**—postal fraud order— authorized

1911 **Aviation—Legislation**—aviation legislation (state)—enacted—Connecticut

1911 **Aviation—License**—pilot's license issued by the Aero Club of America— awarded—G. H. Curtiss

1917 **World War I**—American troops to land in England—arrived

1921 **Hospital**—leper hospital—reopened— Carville, La.

1940 **Element** — element 93 — neptunium— discovery announced

1948 **Marines**—Negro commissioned officer —J. E. Rudder

1953 **Locomotive** — gas turbine propane-fueled locomotive

1959 **Air Mail Service**—missile mail (official)—landed—Jacksonville, Fla.

JUNE 9

1628 **Deportation**—Thomas Morton—Plymouth Colony

1772 **Protestant Church**—Protestant church —west of Pennslyvania—communion service—Schoenbrunn, Ohio

1783 **War Veterans' Society**—Society of the Cincinnati—organization effected

1790 **Book**—book entered for copyright— *The Philadelphia Spelling Book*—registered—Philadelphia, Pa.

1846 **Senator (U.S.)**—Senator elected on an anti-slavery ticket—J. P. Hale— New Hampshire

1880 **Greenback Labor Party**—national convention—Chicago, Ill.

1902 **Restaurant**—restaurant with an automatic arrangement for vending food —opened—Philadelphia, Pa.

1909 **Automobile Transcontinental Trip**— transcontinental automobile trip by a woman—left New York City for San Francisco, Calif.

1925 **Degrees (academic and honorary)**— degree conferred by radio—University of Iowa—Iowa City, Iowa

1949 **Treasury Department (U.S.)**—woman treasurer of the United States —G. N. Clark—confirmed

1959 **Submarine** — ballistic missile submarine — "George Washington" — launched—Groton, Conn.

JUNE 10

1682 **Tornado** — recorded — New Haven, Conn.

1760 **Medical Legislation**—law to regulate the practice of medicine (actually enforced)—New York City

1809 Ship—steamboat to make an ocean voyage—"Phoenix"—sailed from New York City to Philadelphia, Pa.

1842 Expedition—scientific expedition fitted out by the United States Government —Wilkes expedition—returned to New York City

1851 Newspaper—French daily newspaper (successful)—*Courrier des États Unis* —published—New York City

1854 Naval Academy — naval academy (U.S.)—Annapolis, Md.—first graduation

1879 Medical Society — laryngological society (national)—annual meeting

1884 Medal—Albert Medal presented to a native-born American—J.B. Eads

1902 Envelope—envelope with an outlook or window—patented—A.F. Callahan —Chicago, Ill.

1902 Organists' Society—organists' society (national)—branch chapter formed— Philadelphia, Pa.

1903 Architectural School—landscape architecture course—Lowthorpe School of Architecture—Groton, Mass.—certificates awarded

1905 Forest Fire—forest fire lookout tower — watchman service — Greenville, Me.

1910 Stadium—school stadium—dedicated— Tacoma, Wash.

1915 Girl Scouts—incorporated

1919 Woman Suffrage — woman suffrage amendment approved by Congress— ratified by Illinois, Wisconsin and Michigan

1921 Budget Bureau (U.S.)—authorized

1921 Comptroller General of the United States—office authorized

1924 Radio Broadcast—political convention broadcast — Republican convention — Cleveland, Ohio

1924 Stethoscope — electrical stethoscope (portable)—exhibited—Chicago, Ill.

1932 Lightning (artificial) — demonstrated —Pittsfield, Mass.

1936 Television—Telecast—telecast using coaxial cable — transmitted — New York City

1936 Women's Club—Chinese women's club incorporated—Chinese Women's Association—New York City

1937 Lawyer—Japanese woman lawyer— K. E. Ohi—admitted to practice—Illinois

1939 Television—Telecast—king and queen to be televised—New York City

1952 Television—Telecast—surgical operation televised coast-to-coast—Chicago, Ill.

1953 Degrees (academic and honorary)— Bachelor of Sacred Music degree— conferred—New York City

1953 Television — Telecast — Catholic mass televised from a studio—WBZ-TV— Boston, Mass.

1954 Automobile Bus—gas turbine bus— announced—Detroit, Mich.

1955 Virus—virus separated into component parts—reported—Berkeley, Calif.

JUNE 11

1788 Ship—ship built on the Pacific coas. —commenced—Nootka, B.C.

1790 Congress (U.S.)—House of Representatives—filibuster by "dilatory tactics" —Elbridge Gerry

1793 Stove Patent—Robert Haeterick

1813 Army Officer—Surgeon General—of the United States Army—James Tilton—served

1872 Telegraph—telegraph call boxes—patented—E. A. Calahan

1885 Gas Commission (state)—established —Massachusetts

1889 Business School—business high school —Washington Business High School —Washington, D.C.

1891 Nautical School—nautical state school —established—Massachusetts

1891 Ship—whaleback steamer to cross the Atlantic—"Charles W. Wetmore"— sailed—Duluth, Minn.

1901 Dental Society—orthodontists' society —American Society of Orthodontists —annual meeting—St. Louis, Mo.

1906 Insurance—employer's liability act (federal)—enacted, but declared unconstitutional

1912 Aviation—airplane take-off from a hotel roof—Silas Christoferson—Portland, Ore.

1919 Horse—horse to win the triple crown —Sir Barton—Belmont Park, N.Y.

1922 Radio Facsimile Transmission—photograph sent by radio across the Atlantic from Europe

1927 Medal—Distinguished Flying Cross— presentation to C. A. Lindbergh

1936 Presbyterian Church — Presbyterian Church of America—formed—Philadelphia, Pa.

1938 Baseball Player—major league baseball player to pitch two successive no-hit no-run games—Johnny Vander Meer—Cincinnati, Ohio, and New York City

1944 Serbian Orthodox Cathedral—Cathedral of St. Sava—New York City

1955 Aviation — Airplane — jet magnesium airplane—flown

JUNE 12

1775 Revolutionary War—naval battle of the Revolution — "Margaretta"—Machias, Me.

1796 Unitarian Minister—Society of Unitarian Christians—organized — Philadelphia, Pa.

1800 Navy—navy yard—purchased—Portsmouth, N.H.

1845 **Colonial Government**—government on the Pacific coast—Oregon—first governor—George Abernethy

1849 **Gas Mask**—gas mask—patented—L. P. Haslett—Louisville, Ky.

1880 **Monument**—obelisk to be brought to the United States—loaded at Alexandria, Egypt

1900 **Trapshooting Tournament** — trapshoot (Grand American) with clay targets—Interstate Park, N.Y.

1912 **Senator (U.S.)**—senators "elected by the people"—Senate passed bill

1913 **Moving Picture** — animated cartoon (present technique) — *The Dachshund*—released

1918 **Aviation — Airplane Bombing** — airplane bombing raid by an American air unit

1920 **Farmer Labor Party** — organized — Chicago, Ill.

1933 **Electrobasograph** — exhibited — R. P. Schwartz—Milwaukee, Wis.

1936 **Radio Station** — radio station with 500,000-watt power — Pittsburgh, Pa.

1939 **Degrees (academic and honorary)**—doctor of philosophy in accounting—degree conferred—J. W. McMahan—University of Illinois—Urbana, Ill.

1939 **Hall of Fame**—hall of fame (baseball)—dedicated—Cooperstown, N.Y.

1946 **Aviation—Flights (transcontinental)**—transcontinental round-trip airplane flight within one day—Shooting Star—March Field, Calif., to Andrews Field, Md.

1947 **Golf Champion** — woman golfer (American born) to win the British Women's Amateur Golf tournament—B. D. Zaharias

1948 **Jockey**—jockey to win the triple crown twice—Belmont Park, Elmont, N.Y.

1950 **Nuclear Engineering College Course** —Raleigh, N.C.—students enrolled

1953 **Advertisement** — three-dimensional newspaper advertisement—*Daily Freeman*—Waukesha, Wis.

1956 **Flag**—Army flag (official)—established

JUNE 13

1774 **Slavery**—non-importation of slaves act—enacted—Rhode Island

1825 **Law Codification (state)**—promulgated—Louisiana

1862 **Army Officer**—chaplain (Catholic) appointed by the President—F.E. Boyle

1881 **Ship**—steamboat to employ electric lights—"Jeannette"—sank

1889 **Niagara Falls**—utilization of Niagara Falls waterpower (large scale)—Cataract Construction Company incorporated

1890 **Freemasons**—Grotto—charter granted

1893 **Horse Race**—horse race of a thousand miles—started—Chadron, Neb.

1906 **College**—technical college for women —Simmons College—Boston, Mass.—class graduated

1910 **Aviation — Flights** — airplane round trip—in one day between two cities—C. K. Hamilton—New York City to Philadelphia, Pa.

1912 **Nursing School**—university school of nursing—University of Minnesota—Minneapolis, Minn.—class graduated

1913 **Public Defender's Office**—created—Los Angeles, Calif.

1917 **Agricultural Soil Conference**—of importance—International Congress of Soil Science—Washington, D. C.

1925 **Television—Telecast**—telecast of an object in motion—Washington, D.C.

1927 **Flag**—flag displayed from the right hand of the Statue of Liberty

1928 **Railroad Car**—rail detector car—tested—Beacon, N.Y.

1933 **Electric. Lighting** — sodium vapor lamps—installed—Schenectady, N.Y.

1933 **Federal Savings and Loan Association** —authorized

1933 **Home Owners' Loan Corporation**—authorized

1940 **Aviation—License**—Civil Aeronautics Administration honorary license — authorized

1942 **Army School**—army training school—to teach security troops—opened—Concord, Mass.

1944 **Wire Recorder**—patented — Marvin Camras

JUNE 14

1623 **Breach of Promise Suit**—instituted—Greville Pooley—Charles City County, Va.

1642 **Education**—compulsory education law —Massachusetts

1777 **Flag**—American flag—formally adopted—Philadelphia, Pa.

1834 **Diving Suit**—(practical) for submarine diving—patented—Leonard Norcross —Dixfield, Me.

1834 **Sandpaper Patent**—Isaac Fischer, Jr. —Springfield, Vt.

1854 **Entomologist**—federal entomologist—Townend Glover—commissioned

1881 **Piano Player** — piano player — patented—John McTammany, Jr.—Cambridge, Mass.

1884—**Wire** — legislation (state) requiring wires to be placed underground—New York State

1899 **College**—Catholic college for women —College of Notre Dame of Maryland—Baltimore, Md.—commencement

1901 **Golf Tournament**—professional open championship—under rules of United States Golf Association—Hamilton, Mass.

1915 **Protestant Church**—Protestant church for lepers—dedicated—Carville, La.

1919 **Aviation — Flights (transatlantic) —** transatlantic non-stop flight from America—John Alcock and A. W. Brown—started—St. John's, Newfoundland

1922 **President (U.S.)**—President to broadcast by radio—W. G. Harding—Baltimore, Md.

1927 **Monument**—monument to the American flag—dedicated—Pittsburgh, Pa.

1929 **Aviation**—air-rail passenger transcontinental service—inaugurated

1937 **Holiday**—Flag Day—legal holiday—Pennsylvania

1938 **Chlorophyll**—chlorophyll—patented — Benjamin Grushkin

1942 **Ordnance**—bazooka rocket gun—produced—Bridgeport, Conn.

1951 **Computer**—electronic computer (commercial) — dedicated — Philadelphia, Pa.

1951 **Television—Telecast**—birth (human) to be televised (closed circuit)

1952 **Submarine** — atomic-powered submarine — "Nautilus" — keel laid — Groton, Conn.

JUNE 15

1752 **Lightning Demonstration** — Benjamin Franklin—Philadelphia, Pa.

1775 **Army Officer**—general (Continental Army)—George Washington

1785 **Money**—copper cents minted by a state—Vermont authorized coinage

1835 **Patent Commissioner**—H. L. Ellsworth—appointed

1844 **Rubber**—vulcanized rubber—patented —Charles Goodyear—New York City

1858 **Stone Crusher**—of value—patent—E. W. Blake—New Haven, Conn.

1859 **Surgical Operation**—mastoid operation — performed — Brooklyn, N.Y.— J. C. Hutchison

1867 **Surgical Operation**—gallstone operation—J. S. Bobbs—Indianapolis, Ind.

1869 **Celluloid**—patent—J. W. and I. S. Hyatt—Albany, N.Y.

1869 **Prize Fight**—international fight, with bare knuckles—Mike McCoole—Tom Allen—St. Louis, Mo.

1871 **Law School**—law school (university) to admit women—St. Louis Law School—P. W. Couzins—graduated—St. Louis, Mo.

1876 **Political Convention**—presidential convention (national) addressed by a woman—S. A. Spencer—Cincinnati, Ohio

1877 **Army School**—army school graduate (Negro)—H. O. Flipper—graduated

1891 **Immigration**—immigration bureau superintendent—W. D. Owen—appointment

1893 **Nurses' Society**—society for superintendents of nursing schools—American Society of Superintendents of Training Schools for Nurses—founded—Chicago, Ill.

1894 **Museum**—commercial museum—Philadelphia Commercial Museum—authorized

1901 **Dental Society**—orthodontists' society —American Society of Orthodontists —constitution adopted

1909 **Baseball**—cork center baseball—patented—B. F. Shibe

1915 **Money**—fifty-dollar gold pieces minted by the United States—produced—San Francisco, Calif.

1917 **Army Camp**—army camp for training Negro officers—established—Fort Des Moines—Des Moines, Iowa

1917 **College**—Negro university (Catholic) —diploma issued—New Orleans, La.

1927 **Radio Telephone**—two-way radio conversation between a brakeman in a caboose of a moving freight train and an engineer in the cab of a locomotive—Schenectady, N.Y.

1928 **Aviation—Airship**—dirigible transfer of mail to a train—effected—Belleville, Ill.

1929 **Brokerage**—curb exchange—to transact more business than the New York Stock Exchange—New York Curb

1938 **Baseball Player**—major league baseball player to pitch two successive no-hit no-run games—J. Vander Meer—New York City

1938 **Railroad Car**—car with fluorescent lighting—first fluorescent tail sign—used—"Twentieth Century Limited"

JUNE 16

1775 **Army**—Army engineering department —Continental Army—authorized

1775 **Army Officer**—Paymaster General—separate pay department established

1871 **Freemasons**—Ancient Arabic Order of Nobles of the Mystic Shrine—established—New York City

1890 **Historical Society**—historical society —American Historical Association—report submitted to Congress

1897 **Voting Machine Commission**—commissioners appointed

1900 **Revolver Shooting Tournament (international)**—Greenville, N.J.

1909 **Aviation — Airplane** — airplane sold commercially—G. H. Curtiss—Hammondsport, N.Y.

1921 **Nursing School**—army school of nursing—graduation—Washington, D.C.

1922 **Helicopter**—helicopter flight—of importance — H. A. Berliner — College Park, Md.

1932 **Jewish College**—Jewish college of liberal arts and sciences under Jewish auspices — B.A. degrees conferred — Yeshiva College—New York City

1933 **Bank Legislation**—bank guaranty legislation

1933 **Consumers' Advisory Board (U.S.)**—authorized

1933 **Consumers' Counsel (U.S.)** — authorized

1933 **Federal Deposit Insurance Corporation**—created

1933 **Industrial Recovery Act**—code under the National Industrial Recovery Act —cotton textile code—drawn up

1933 **Industrial Recovery Act** — industrial recovery act (national)—enacted

1933 **Industry** — industrial advisory board (U.S.)—authorized

1933 **Labor**—Labor Advisory Board (federal)—authorized

1933 **Public Works Administration (U.S.)** —authorized

1933 **Transportation Coordination** — transportation coordination (federal) — J. B. Eastman—appointed

1941 **Aviation—Airport** — airport (federally owned and operated) — opened — Washington, D.C.

1949 **Locomotive**—gas turbine-electric locomotive—demonstrated—Erie, Pa.

JUNE 17

1775 **Army Officer** — adjutant general — Horatio Gates—selected

1775 **Army Officer**—chief engineer—Richard Gridley—served

1775 **Army Officer**—major general—Artemas Ward—appointed

1833 **Drydock**—national ship in a federal drydock —"Delaware"— Portsmouth, Va.

1836 **Medical School**—homeopathic school —North American Academy of the Homoeopathic Healing Art—Allentown, Pa.—chartered

1837 **Rubber**—rubber patent of importance —Charles Goodyear—New York City

1856 **Republican Party**—Republican Party national convention—Philadelphia, Pa.

1863 **Insurance**—accident insurance company—Travelers Insurance Company —Hartford, Conn.—chartered

1866 **Postage Stamp**—mourning stamp—issued

1894 **Epidemic** — poliomyelitis epidemic — Rutland, Vt.

1902 **Reclamation Service (federal)**—authorized

1912 **Aviation**—airplane fatality (woman) —Julie Clark killed—Springfield, Ill.

1928 **Aviation—Passenger**—woman airplane passenger to cross the Atlantic Ocean —Amelia Earhart — start—Trepassey, Newfoundland

1933 **Industrial Recovery Act** — industrial recovery act (national)—H. S. Johnson appointed administrator

1939 **Aviation—Passenger**—woman to fly entirely around the world by commercial heavier-than-air plane—Marjorie Shuler—took off—Port Washington, L.I., N.Y.

1941 **Television License**—construction permit—WNBT—New York City

1942 **World War II**—American expeditionary force to land in Africa

1946 **Telephone**—mobile telephone commercial service—inaugurated—St. Louis, Mo.

1947 **Aviation—Flights (world)**—round-the-world civil air service—started—New York City

1948 **Church**—woman moderator of the General Council of Congregational and Christian Churches—Helen Kenyon—elected

1950 **Surgical Operation** — kidney transplanting—Chicago, Ill.

JUNE 18

1621 **Duel**—duel—Plymouth colony — Massachusetts

1812 **War (1812)**—war declaration

1861 **Fly Casting Tournament**—fly casting tournament—Utica, N.Y.

1861 **Telegram**—telegram dispatched from an aerial station—T. S. C. Lowe—Va.

1878 **Coast Guard (U.S.)**—Coast Guard—Life Saving Service—authorized

1878 **Lifesaving Service**—Lifesaving service—authorized

1885 **Library Society**—library society (local)—New York Library Club—formed

1895 **Carbide Factory**—patent—T. L. Willson—Spray, N.C.

1898 **Pier**—ocean pier of steel—Atlantic City, N.J.

1908 **Insurance**—savings bank life insurance —department established — Whitman, Mass.

1910 **Court** — commerce court (U.S.) — authorized

1916 **Aviation—Aviator**—American aviator shot down in World War I—H. C. Balsley—Verdun, France

1918 **Army**—gas regiment—independent action—Toul, France

1925 **City Planning Instruction**—degree of Master in Landscape Architecture—conferred—Harvard University—Cambridge, Mass.

1927 **Postage Stamp**—postage stamp on which was inscribed the name of a living American — "Lindbergh Air Mail"

1931 **City Planning Instruction**—degree of Master in City Planning—conferred—Harvard University — Cambridge, Mass.

1934 **Free Port**—legislation enacted

1934 **Road** — highway planning surveys (nation-wide)—authorized

1936 **Bicycle Traffic Court**—Racine, Wis.

1936 **Union Party**—organized

1941 **Submarine**—submarine built on the Great Lakes—"Peto"—keel laid

1942 **Naval Officer**—Negro commissioned officer in the Naval Reserve—B. W. Robinson—commissioned

1959 **Television—Telecast**—telecast received from England—via Montreal, Canada

JUNE 19

1775 Army Officer—adjutant general—Horatio Gates—commissioned

1816 Gas—gas ordinance (city)—approved—Baltimore, Md.

1841 Torpedo—underwater torpedo operated by electric current—proposed by Samuel Colt to President John Tyler

1849 Melodeon Patent—C. Austin—Concord, N.H.

1876 Medal — lifesaving medal—awarded L. M. Clemons

1884 Fellowship — fellowship awarded a woman — H. E. Grotecloss — Cornell University—Ithaca, N.Y.

1910 Holiday—Father's Day—celebrated—Spokane, Wash.

1911 Moving Picture Censorship—moving picture censorship board (state)—created—Pennsylvania

1912 Progressive Party—organized

1913 Medical Society—immunology society—American Association of Immunologists—organized—Minneapolis, Minn.

1931 Photoelectric Cell—photoelectric cell installed commercially—West Haven, Conn.

1934 Archivist of the United States—national archives established

1934 Federal Communications Commission—created

1934 Moving Picture—moving picture of the sun—Pontiac, Mich.

1937 Codification Board (U.S.)—created—B. R. Kennedy appointed director

1939 Aviation—Passenger—woman to fly entirely around the world by commercial heavier-than-air plane—trip completed—Marseilles, France

1939 Pinball Game — pinball legislation enacted by a major city prohibiting the machines—Atlanta, Ga.

1946 Prize Fight—prize fight at which admission tickets sold at $100—Louis-Conn fight—New York City

1946 Television — Telecast — prize fight (heavyweight championship bout) to be televised—Louis-Conn fight—New York City

1947 Aviation—Flights—airplane to exceed the speed of 600 miles per hour—Albert Boyd—Muroc Air Field, Calif.

1952 Submarine—submarine expressly designed and built to fire guided missiles "Grayback"—ordered

1953 Treason—execution for treason in peacetime—Ossining, N.Y.

JUNE 20

1782 Seal—Great Seal of the United States Government—designed

1814 Ship—steam-propelled frigate—"Demologos"—keel laid

1819 Ship—steamboat built in America to cross the Atlantic Ocean — "Savannah"—arrived—Liverpool, England

1863 Bank—national bank chartered—National Bank of Philadelphia

1867 Territorial Expansion — non-contiguous territory—acquired—Alaska

1874 Medal—lifesaving medal—of Treasury Department—authorized

1894 Museum—commercial museum—Philadelphia Commercial Museum — first directors' meeting—Philadelphia, Pa.

1895 Degrees (academic and honorary)—Doctor of Science degree earned by a woman—C. W. Baldwin—Cornell University—Ithaca, N.Y.

1896 Submarine—submarine contract of the U.S. Navy—keel laid—"Plunger"

1907 Army War College — Washington, D.C.—opened

1919 College—Negro university (Catholic)—diplomas awarded for normal department—New Orleans, La.

1921 Congressman (U.S.)—congresswoman to preside over the House of Representatives—A. M. Robertson

1926 International Eucharistic Congress—in America—Chicago, Ill.

1930 Television — Telecast — weather map telecast to a transatlantic steamer—"America"—New York City

1933 Labor—Labor Advisory Board (federal)—organized

1939 Television—Telecast—operetta to be televised—presented—New York City

JUNE 21

1622 Prohibition — prohibition enforcement officers—Virginia

1768 Medical School — medical college — commencement—College of Philadelphia

1768 Physician—doctor to receive a Bachelor of Medicine degree—College of Philadelphia

1788 Constitution of the United States—printed copies of the Constitution—ratified

1834 Reaper—reaper that was practical—patented—C. H. McCormick

1859 Rocket—rocket patent—Andrew Lanergan—Boston, Mass.

1869 Health Board—health board (state)—authorized—Massachusetts

1875 Catholic Bishop — Catholic bishop (Negro)—J. A. Healy consecrated—Boston, Mass.

1882 Degrees (academic and honorary)—Doctor of Philosophy degree awarded to a woman by a women's college—K. E. Morris—Northampton, Mass.

1905 Automobile Race—transcontinental automobile race (for a time record)—completed—Portland, Ore.

1913 Aviation—Parachute—parachute jump from an airplane by a woman — Georgia Broadwick — Los Angeles, Calif.

1932 Medal—National Geographic Society special gold medal — awarded to a woman—A. E. Putnam—presented

1933 **Canal**—Great Lakes to the Gulf waterway—New Orleans tow arrived at Chicago, Ill.

1934 **Labor**—National Mediation Board — act approved

1943 **Medal**—Medal of Honor awarded to a soldier who already had received a Distinguished Service Cross—presented —Gerry Kisters

1943 **Medal**—soldier's medal awarded to a woman—conferred—Edith Greenwood

1948 **Phonograph Record** — long-playing microgroove records—manufactured— Bridgeport, Conn.

1950 **Merchant Marine Academy** — Merchant Marine cadet corps (U.S.)— first B.S. degree awarded — Kings Point, N.Y.

1961 **Water**—sea water conversion plant (practical) — Freeport, Tex. — dedicated

JUNE 22

1564 **Artist**—artist—reached Florida—Jacques Le Moyne

1775 **Money**—continental money—issued

1832 **Pin**—machine for manufacturing pins —patented—J. I. Howe

1841 **Typesetting Machine**—typesetting machine patent—Adrien Delcambre and J. H. Young

1843 **Elevator**—grain elevator operated by steam—cargo unloaded—Buffalo, N.Y.

1870 **Justice Department (U.S.)**—created

1872 **Telegraph**—telegraph call boxes—installed—New York City

1874 **Physician** — osteopathic physician—A. T. Still

1893 **Diplomatic Service**—ambassador—according to State Department records —T. F. Bayard — presented credentials—Great Britain

1896 **Physician** — Chinese woman to receive a doctor of medicine degree— Mary Stone

1908 **Insurance**—savings bank life insurance—first policy—Whitman Savings Bank—Whitman, Mass.

1909 **Automobile Race** — transcontinental automobile race—completed—Seattle, Wash.

1914 **Aviation—Airplane**—hydroplane with a multi-engine — "America" — christened—Hammondsport, N.Y.

1914 **Medical Society**—immunology society —American Association of Immunologists—annual meeting—Atlantic City, N.J.

1914 **Medical Society**—women members of the American College of Surgeons— A. G. Bryant and F. W. Duckering— admitted

1933 **Canal**—Great Lakes to the Gulf waterway — completion officially celebrated—Chicago, Ill.

1939 **Water Ski Tournament (national)**— Jones Beach State Park, N.Y.

1942 **Postal Service**—"V" mail film—dispatched—New York City to London

1946 **Air Mail Service**—jet propelled airplane to transport mail—from Schenectady, N.Y., to Washington, D.C.

JUNE 23

1784 **Balloon Flight** — balloon flight—Edward Warren—Baltimore, Md.

1836 **Treasury Department (U.S.)**—treasury surplus returned and apportioned among the several states—authorized

1848 **Woman**—woman lobbyist—D. L. Dix —petition to Congress

1860 **Government Printing Office**—Government Printing Office—created independent office

1860 **Secret Service**—secret service (federal)—created

1868 **Typewriter**—typewriter that was practical—patented—C. L. Sholes

1869 **Labor**—labor bureau (state)—Massachusetts Bureau of Statistics of Labor —established

1869 **Probation** — probation legislation for juvenile delinquents — enacted—Massachusetts

1871 **Gas**—municipal gas plant—Wheeling, W.Va.—trustees appointed

1877 **Royal Arcanum** — founded — Boston, Mass.

1887 **Hospital** — babies' hospital designed exclusively for infants — New York City—incorporated

1888 **Presidential Candidate** — presidential candidate of Negro blood nominated —Frederick Douglass—Chicago, Ill.

1904 **Boat Race**—motor boat race under organized rules—New York City

1916 **Aviation—Aviator**—American aviator killed while a pilot in the Lafayette Escadrille—V. E. Chapman

1924 **Aviation — Flights (transcontinental)** — transcontinental flight within 24 hours—R. L. Maugham

1926 **Lip Reading Tournament (national)** —Philadelphia, Pa.

1937 **Theatrical School**—theater and dramatic criticism course—Ph.D. degree awarded—Yale University—New Haven, Conn.

1938 **Aquarium**—aquarium for monsters of the deep—Marineland—formal opening—St. Augustine, Fla.

1938 **Civil Aeronautics Authority (U.S.)**—created

1948 **Television — Telecast** — stratovision flight public demonstration — Pittsburgh, Pa.

JUNE 24

1579 **Book**—book of common prayer—used —San Francisco, Calif.

1579 **Protestant Episcopal Church**—Christian religious service in English — on the Pacific coast—Francis Fletcher —San Francisco, Calif.

1647 **Woman Suffrage** — woman suffrage advocate—Margaret Brent—demanded vote—Maryland

1764 Artist—artist successful in commercial art—Matthew Pratt—sailed from Philadelphia, Pa.

1791 Masonry — Negro Masonic Grand Lodge (not Free and Accepted Masons)—Provincial Grand Lodge—organized—Boston, Mass.

1833 Drydock—national ship in a federal drydock—"Constitution" at drydock—Boston, Mass.

1834 Cabinet of the United States—cabinet appointee rejected by the Senate—R. B. Taney—nominated

1837 Treaty—treaty with a Far Eastern country—proclaimed

1873 Fine Arts Department—fine arts department in a college to grant degrees—College of Fine Arts—Syracuse, N.Y.

1885 Protestant Episcopal Bishop—Protestant Episcopal bishop (Negro)—S. D. Ferguson—consecrated—New York City

1898 Spanish-American War—army officer killed in battle in the Spanish-American war—A. K. Capron—killed—Las Guásimas, Cuba

1898 Spanish-American War — Spanish-American land engagement — Las Guásimas, Cuba

1910 Radio Legislation (national) — Wireless Ship Act—enacted

1930 Radar—radar detection of airplanes—Anacostia, D.C.

1940 Television — Telecast — political convention to be televised—Republican convention—Philadelphia, Pa.

1949 Aviation — License — cargo airlines licensed by the Civil Aeronautics Board—effective

1952 Jockey — jockey (American-born) to win 3,000 races—Eddie Arcaro—Chicago, Ill.

JUNE 25

1798 Immigration — immigration act — requiring reports

1844 President—President married while in office—John Tyler—New York City

1868 Labor Law—eight-hour day for government laborers and mechanics—authorized

1873 College — woman college president—Frances Willard—dean

1910 Bank — postal savings bank — authorized

1910 Postal Savings Stamps—authorized

1931 Church—General Council of Congregational and Christian Churches—formed—Seattle, Wash.

1934 Bank—bank payments to depositors of a closed insured bank—made by Federal Deposit Insurance Company—bank went into receivership

1946 Aviation—Airplane—bomber with the flying wing design — take-off from Hawthorne, Calif.

1951 Television—Telecast—color program (commercial)—New York City

1953 Tour of the World—passenger to fly around the world on commercial airlines in less than 100 hours—H. C. Boren

JUNE 26

1614 Lottery — lottery — of importance — Virginia

1721 Vaccination for smallpox—inoculation from human smallpox—Zabdiel Boylston—Boston, Mass.

1797 Plow—plow patent—granted—Charles Newbold—Burlington County, N.J.

1819 Bicycle Patent—W. K. Clarkson, Jr.—New York City

1847 Pile Driver—steam pile driver patent—awarded—James Nasmyth

1848 Pure Food Law—pure food and drug legislation (national)—enacted

1870 Boardwalk—completed—Atlantic City, N.J.

1907 Insurance—savings bank life insurance—launched—Massachusetts

1911 Automobile Transcontinental Trip—transcontinental automobile group tour—began—Atlantic City, N.J.

1911 Golf Champion — golf champion (American born professional) to win the United States Open Tournament—J. J. McDermott—Wheaton, Ill.

1916 Road — federal grant-in-aid — bids opened

1917 World War I—American troops to land in France — disembarked — St. Nazaire, France

1919 Newspaper—illustrated tabloid—*Illustrated Daily News*—published—New York City

1920 Cabinet of the United States—woman sub-cabinet member—A. A. Adams—appointed

1933 Consumers' Advisory Board (U.S.)—organized

1933 Industry—Industrial Advisory Board (federal)—organized

1934 Evangelical and Reformed Church—organized—Cleveland, Ohio

1934 Federal Credit Union Act—approved

1945 Treaty—treaty (federal) signed by a woman—Charter of the United Nations—San Francisco, Calif.—V. C. Gildersleeve

1947 Telephone—mobile transatlantic telephone conversation between two telephone-equipped automobiles — New York City and Milan, Italy

1950 War (Korean)—American pilot to destroy an enemy airplane in the Korean War—W. G. Hudson

1951 Television—Telecast—color program (commercial) to be presented daily

1959 Canal—Saint Lawrence Seaway—formally opened

1959 Postage Stamp—postage stamp of the United States having the same design as that of another country (Canada)—issued

JUNE 27

1652 **Traffic Regulation**—traffic law—enacted—New Amsterdam

1775 **Army Officer**—paymaster general—James Warren—appointed

1776 **Army Execution**—Thomas Hickey—New York City

1860 **Army**—signal corps—A. J. Myer appointed signal officer

1884 **Baseball Player**—baseball pitcher to pitch three no-hit games—Larry Corcoran—third game

1884 **Labor**—labor bureau (federal)—authorized

1893 **Horse Race**—horse race of a thousand miles—completed—Chicago, Ill.

1917 **Daylight Saving**—legislation enacted

1921 **Comptroller General of the United States**—J. R. McCarl—appointed

1923 **Aviation**—refueling attempt in mid-air—Coronado, Calif.—L. H. Smith

1929 **Television**—Telecast—color television demonstration (public)—New York City

1934 **Emergency Housing Corporation (U.S.)**—Federal Housing Administration—created

1934 **Federal Savings and Loan Association**—Federal Savings and Loan Insurance Corporation—created

1935 **Bank**—checkmaster plan—introduced—New York City

1950 **Aviation**—Aviator—aviator to down two enemy fighter airplanes in one day in Korea—R. E. Wayne

1950 **War (Korean)**—South Korean combat mission—fire exchanged

1955 **Automobile Legislation**—automobile seat belt safety legislation—enacted—Illinois

1955 **Television**—Telecast—telecast originating live in three countries

1960 **Chlorophyll** — chlorophyll "a" — synthesized—R. B. Woodward—Cambridge, Mass.

JUNE 28

1687 **Knighthood** — knighthood conferred on a native-born American—William Phips—London, England

1794 **Ship**—warship builder—Joshua Humphreys—appointed

1798 **Navy**—prize money awarded by the U.S. Navy—act

1832 **Epidemic**—cholera epidemic—case reported—New York City

1834 **Crime Prevention and Detection**—interstate crime pact—ratified

1834 **Geological Survey**—geological survey appropriation (U.S.)—authorized

1861 **Army**—law (state) conferring military privileges and duties on the Negro—enacted—Tennessee

1869 **Naval Officer**—Surgeon General of the Navy—R. M. Wood—appointed

1884 **Horse Race**—horse race (American Derby)—Chicago, Ill

1894 **Holiday**—Labor Day holiday (federal)—declared by act of Congress

1925 **Caterpillar Club**—woman Caterpillar Club member — Irene McFarland — jumped—Cincinnati, Ohio

1927 **Aviation**—Flights (transpacific)—California-Hawaii flight—L. J. Maitland and A. F. Hegenberger—take-off—Oakland, Calif.

1935 **Virus**—virus obtained in crystalline form—reported

1939 **Aviation** — Flights (transatlantic) — transatlantic regular commercial airplane service—undertaken—left Port Washington, N.Y.

1940 **Immigration**—alien registration—authorized

1956 **Atomic Reactor**—nuclear reactor built for private industrial research—Chicago, Ill.—in operation

JUNE 29

1810 **Missionary Society**—foreign missionary society—American Board of Commissioners for Foreign Missions—organized—Bradford, Mass.

1833 **Ordnance**—gun (revolving)—patented—D. G. Colburn—Canton Canal, N.Y.

1837 **Education**—state board of education—Horace Mann—appointed commissioner—Massachusetts

1860 **Lighthouse**—iron pile lighthouse—completed—Minot's Ledge, Mass.

1863 **Bank**—national bank—National Bank of Davenport, Iowa—opened

1864 **Degrees (academic and honorary)**—law degree of LL.M.—conferred—Columbia University — New York City

1870 **Public Health**—public health service (U.S.)—reorganization act enacted

1882 **Forestry Society**—national forestry association—merger of American Forestry Congress and American Forestry Association

1925 **Electric Lighting**—electric lamp bulb frosted on the inside—patent application filed

1927 **Aviation**—Airplane—airplane equipped with radio to cross the Atlantic Ocean—flight take-off—Roosevelt Field, N.Y.

1927 **Aviation** — Flights (transpacific) — California-Hawaii flight—concluded—L. J. Maitland and A. F. Hegenberger

1929 **Wind Tunnel**—high-speed jet wind tunnel — completed — Langley Field, Va.

1936 **Television**—Telecast—high definition telecast—W2XBS—New York City

1939 **Television**—Telecast—play to be televised as a full-hour program—New York City

1942 **World War II**—American bombardier over German occupied territory—B. L. Bell—raid—Hazebrouck, France

1948 **Air Mail Service**—parcel post domestic air service—authorized

1952 **Ship**—aircraft carrier to sail around Cape Horn — "Oriskany" — passed Cape Horn

1953 **Catholic Seminarians (Negro) to be ordained to the priesthood by a Negro bishop**—Bay St. Louis, Miss.

1956 **Education**—war orphans education law—enacted

1956 **High Jump**—over seven feet—Charles Dumas—Los Angeles, Calif.

JUNE 30

1812 **Bond**—treasury notes (interest bearing)—authorized

1831 **Railroad**—railroad to carry troops—Baltimore and Ohio Railroad Company—to Sykes Mills, Md.

1831 **Scale**—platform scale—patented— T. Fairbanks—St. Johnsbury, Vt.

1838 **Caster**—for furniture—patented

1858 **Citizenship**—Japanese granted citizenship—Joseph Heco

1859 **Niagara Falls**—person to cross Niagara Falls on a tightrope—J. F. Gravelet

1860 **Baseball Team**—baseball team to tour —Excelsiors—left Albany, N.Y.

1863 **Civil War**—bloodshed north of the Mason-Dixon line—Hanover, Pa.

1864 **Cigarette Tax**—cigarette tax—levied

1870 **Lawyer**—woman lawyer graduated from a law school—A. H. Kepley—graduated—Union College of Law—Chicago, Ill.

1879 **Electric Company**—electric company organized to provide and sell electricity—California Electric Light Company — organized — San Francisco, Calif.

1882 **Hospital**—hospital for the military and naval forces—appropriation authorized

1886 **Forest Service (U.S.)**—organized

1896 **Electric Stove**—patented—W. S. Hadaway—New York City

1897 **College Alumni Association**—college alumni association secretary (full-time paid position) — established—University of Michigan—Ann Arbor, Mich.

1898 **American Expeditionary Force**—American Expeditionary force—arrived—Manila, Philippines

1899 **Bicycle Racer**—bicycle racer—to attain mile-a-minute speed—C. M. Murphy—Farmingdale, N.Y.

1906 **Pure Food Law**—pure food and drug legislation (national)—Federal Food and Drug Act—enacted

1910 **Aviation—Airplane Bombing**—airplane bombing experiment—G. H. Curtiss—Hammondsport, N.Y.

1911 **Army Officer**—flight surgeon—J. P. Kelly—reported for duty

1921 **President**—President to become Chief Justice of the United States—W. H. Taft—appointed

1927 **Aviation — License** — pilot's license granted to a woman by the U.S. Department of Commerce—P. F. Omlie

1930 **Catholic Canonization** — of North Americans

1930 **Radio Broadcast**—round the world broadcast—C. D. Wagoner—Schenectady, N.Y.

1934 **Securities and Exchange Commission (U.S.)**—five commissioners appointed

1936 **Labor Law** — forty-hour-week law (federal)—enacted

1939 **Aviation — Flights (transatlantic)** — transatlantic regular commercial airplane service — plane landed—Marseilles, France

1946 **Atomic Bomb**—atomic bomb dropped from an airplane over water—Bikini Lagoon

1948 **Telephone**—telephone recording devices—authorized by Federal Communications Commission

1948 **Transistor**—transistor — demonstrated —Murray Hill, N.J.

1951 **Theater**—municipally owned and operated summer theater-in-the-round—Philadelphia, Pa.—opened

1953 **Automobile**—plastic laminated fiberglas body sports car—manufactured —Flint, Mich.

JULY 1

1731 **Library**—circulating library—formed —Philadelphia, Pa.

1791 **Tax**—internal revenue tax—effective

1795 **Supreme Court (U.S.)**—Chief Justice whose nomination was not confirmed John Rutledge—served

1827 **Newspaper**—Spanish newspaper — *El Redactor*—published—New York City

1835 **Railroad**—railroad to run trains to Washington, D.C.—from Baltimore, Md.

1845 **Senator (U.S.)**—Jewish senator—D. L. Yulee—Florida

1847 **Postage Stamp**—postage stamps issued by the Post Office Department

1851 **Insurance**—insurance board (state)—New Hampshire Insurance Department—established

1855 **Lighthouse**—iron pile lighthouse—construction of new lighthouse begun—Minot's Ledge, Mass.

1855 **Postal Service**—registration of letters

1857 **College**—college to grant women absolutely equal rights—nonsectarian—Antioch College, Yellow Springs, Ohio—graduation

1859 **Baseball Game**—intercollegiate baseball game—Amherst and Williams—Pittsfield, Mass.

1862 **Internal Revenue Commissioner**—bureau authorized

1862 **Passport**—passport fee—levied

1862 **Polygamy Legislation (federal)**—polygamy legislation (federal)—enacted

1862 **Tax**—inheritance tax (federal)—enacted

1862 **Tobacco**—tobacco tax for internal revenue—enacted

1863 **Postal Service**—free city delivery of mail—in operation

1864 **Insurance**—accident insurance policy (printed) — issued — Travelers Insurance Company—Hartford, Conn.

1864 **Postal Service**—railroad post office for the general distribution of mail—tested

1869 **Railroad Commission (state)**—railroad commission (state)—established—Massachusetts

1870 **Justice Department (U.S.)**—department organized

1872 **Labor Law**—women's equal employment legislation—effective—Illinois

1873 **Patent Examiner**—woman patent examiner—A. R. G. Nichols—took office

1874 **Kidnapping**—kidnapping for ransom—C. B. Ross—Germantown, Pa.

1874 **Zoological Garden**—zoological garden—opened to public—Philadelphia, Pa.

1879 **Labor Law**—labor law prohibiting the employment of women—effective—Illinois

1881 **American Red Cross**—incorporated

1881 **Telephone** — international telephone conversation—Calais, Me. and St. Stephen, New Brunswick

1885 **Bird Protection Agency (federal)**—section of Division of Entomology—Department of Agriculture

1885 **Navigation Bureau (U.S.)**—permanently organized

1886 **Typesetting Machine**—linotype machine used commercially—installed—*Tribune*—New York City

1891 **Copyright Law**—international copyright agreement—effective

1891 **Weather Bureau** — weather bureau (U.S.) transferred to Department of Agriculture

1893 **Bicycle Race Track of Wood**—used—San Francisco, Calif.

1895 **Animal Industry Bureau (U.S.)**—dairy division—of Bureau of Animal Industry—organized

1896 **Insurance**—substandard life insurance policy—issued—New York Life Insurance Company—New York City

1896 **Medical Instruction**—psychiatric institute—law effective

1897 **Copyrights Registrar of the United States**—Thorvald Solberg—served

1898 **American Expeditionary Force** — American Expeditionary Force — landed—Manila, Philippines

1898 **Balloon**—balloon destroyed by enemy gun fire

1899 **Court**—juvenile court—opened—Chicago, Ill.

1900 **Ship**—schooner (six masted)—"George W. Wells"—launched—Camden, Me.

1901 **Standards Bureau (U.S.)**—effective

1904 **Animal Industry Bureau (U.S.)**—animal husbandry federal appropriation—expenditure

1905 **Bird Protection Agency (federal)**—became Bureau of Biological Survey

1907 **Ship**—battleship built on the Pacific coast—"Nebraska"—commissioned

1910 **Bread**—completely automatic bread plant—opened—Ward Baking Company—Chicago, Ill.

1910 **Mines Bureau (U.S.)**—effective

1911 **Radio Legislation (national)**—effective

1912 **Insurance**—group insurance contract of importance—Montgomery Ward & Company—Chicago

1913 **Labor Law**—minimum wage law—effective

1913 **Road**—coast-to-coast paved road—Lincoln Highway Association—formed

1913 **Standards Bureau (U.S.)**—became National Bureau of Standards under the Department of Commerce

1914 **Agriculture Department (U.S.)**—Office of Markets—combined with Office of Rural Organization

1915 **Music Instruction**—State Supervisor of Music—appointed—Pennsylvania

1919 **Air Mail Service**—air mail transcontinental service—New York City to Cleveland, Ohio

1919 **Insurance**—fire and tornado insurance fund (state)—functioned—North Dakota

1921 **Comptroller General** of the United States—J. R. McCarl—served

1921 **Tax**—sales tax (state) — effective — West Virginia

1924 **Air Mail Service**—air mail transcontinental through regular service—established—New York City to San Francisco, Calif.

1924 **Diplomatic Service**—Foreign Service of the United States—created

1925 **Air Mail Service**—air mail long-distance night service—from New York City to Chicago, Ill.

1925 **Helium**—helium plant of the United States—Bureau of Mines assumed supervision of United States Production Plant—Fort Worth, Tex.

1927 **Aviation–Airplane**—airplane equipped with radio to cross the Atlantic Ocean—landed—France

1929 **Tax**—chain stores tax (state)—effective—Indiana

1930 **Submarine**—streamlined submarine of the United States Navy—"Nautilus"—commissioned

1933 **Radio Broadcast**—drama broadcast from a ship at sea—WABC—New York City

1934 **X-ray**—X-ray photograph of the entire body taken in a one-second exposure Rochester, N.Y.

1938 **Library Chair** — opened — Columbia University School of Library Service—New York City

1939 **Bird Protection Agency (federal)**—transferred to Department of Interior

1939 **Building**—building devoted entirely to highway traffic — completed — Saugatuck, Conn.

1939 **Federal Works Agency**—established

1939 **Pinball Game**—pinball legislation enacted by a major city prohibiting the machines—Atlanta, Ga.—effective

1940 **Army Parachute Troops** — training commenced

1941 **Television License**—commercial television license—W2XBS—New York City

1941 **Television License**—construction permit—effective

1945 **Labor**—labor anti-discrimination commission (state)—appointed—New York

1949 **Air Force Officer**—Air Force Surgeon General—M. C. Grow

1952 **Narcotic** — narcotic sanatorium for minors—patients received—New York City

1954 **Submarine**—submarine expressly designed and built to fire guided missiles —"Grayback"—laid down—Mare Island, Calif.

1961 **Air Raid Shelter**—air raid community shelter—completed—Boise, Idaho

JULY 2

1717 **Book Auction Catalog**—book auction printed catalog—sale

1749 **Catholic Nuns**—nun who was born in the United States—Mary Turpin—began novitiate—New Orleans, La.

1776 **Woman Suffrage**—colony to grant suffrage to women—constitutional right— New Jersey

1777 **Emancipation Act (state)**—enacted— Vermont

1800 **Land Grant**—district land office— opened—Steubenville, Ohio

1829 **Catholic Nuns**—Catholic nuns (colored community) — founded — Baltimore, Md.

1836 **Postage Stamp**—adhesive stamps— local delivery service—authorized

1842 **Ship**—iron vessel—"John Randolph"— enrolled

1850 **Gas Mask**—gas mask with a self-contained breathing apparatus—patented —B. J. Lane—Cambridge, Mass.

1862 **Agricultural Land Grant** — signed— Abraham Lincoln

1864 **Hall of Fame**—hall of fame (national) —National Statuary Hall—authorized

1867 **Elevated Railroad**—elevated railroad— opened for traffic—New York City

1890 **Trust** — anti-trust law (national) — Sherman act—enacted

1902 **College Academic Costume Standardization**—Bureau of Academic Costume —incorporated

1908 **Price Regulation Law (state)**—enacted—Louisiana

1917 **Radio Telephone** — radio telephone communication between the ground and an airplane—Langley Field, Va.

1919 **Aviation**—aeronautical stowaway—left East Fortune, Scotland

1919 **Aviation — Airship** — airship (lighter-than-air)—left East Fortune, Scotland

1921 **Prize Fight**—prize fight to gross a million dollars—Dempsey-Carpentier fight—Jersey City, N.J.

1921 **Radio Broadcast**—prize fight (heavyweight championship) broadcast— Dempsey-Carpentier fight—Jersey City, N.J.

1922 **Carillon**—carillon (modern)—blessed —Gloucester, Mass.

1926 **Medal**—Distinguished Flying Cross— authorized

1931 **Polo**—polo game played outdoors at night—Baltimore, Md.

1932 **Presidential Candidate** — presidential candidate to fly to a political convention—F. D. Roosevelt—Albany, N.Y. to Chicago, Ill.

1932 **Presidential Candidate** — presidential candidate to make a speech of acceptance at a nominating convention— F. D. Roosevelt—Chicago, Ill.

1933 **Aviation — Flights (transatlantic)**— transatlantic foreign squadron flight to the United States — left Orbetello, Italy

1934 **Securities and Exchange Commission (U.S.)**—meeting

1935 **Theatrical School**—theatrical school sponsored by an institution of higher learning — Union College — Schenectady, N.Y.

1940 **Bridge**—pontoon bridge of reenforced concrete—Lake Washington Floating Bridge—Seattle, Wash.—dedicated

1943 **Aviation—Aviator**—Negro Army aviator to down an Axis airplane—Charles Hall—Sicily

1957 **Steel**—vacuum-cast steel — poured — Bethlehem, Pa.

1957 **Submarine**—submarine expressly designed and built to fire guided missiles —"Grayback" — launched — Mare Island, Calif.

JULY 3

1754 **War (colonial)**—French and Indian war battle—Fort Necessity, Pa.

1776 **Freemasons**—Negro mason—African Lodge No. 1—formed—under permit

1819 **Bank**—savings bank—Bank for Savings—opened—New York City

1839 **Normal School**—normal school (state) —opened—Lexington, Mass.

1848 **Engineering Society**—engineering society—Boston Society of Civil Engineers—regular meetings—Boston, Mass.

1871 **Locomotive**—narrow gauge locomotive—constructed—Philadelphia, Pa.

1878 **Aviation—Airship** — dirigible — flight —John Wise—Lancaster, Pa.

1898 **Ship**—ship to circumnavigate the world with but one in the crew—trip completed — Joshua Slocum — Fairhaven, Mass.

1903 **Cable**—cable across the Pacific Ocean between Honolulu, Midway, Guam and Manila—spliced

1913 **Birds**—bird for which a definite crossing of the Atlantic has been recorded—banded—Eastern Egg Rock, Me.
1930 **Veterans' Bureau**—authorized
1934 **Bank**—bank payments to depositors of a closed insured bank—East Peoria, Ill.
1934 **Federal Deposit Insurance Corporation**—payment made
1952 **Surgical Operation**—mitral valve exposure (prolonged) in a human patient and corrective surgery
1956 **Ship**—ship outfitted for hurricane research—"Crawford"—in service

JULY 4

1776 **Declaration of Independence (American)**—Declaration of Independence was signed—Philadelphia, Pa.
1777 **Flag**—American flag displayed on a man-of-war — Portsmouth Harbor, N.H.
1778 **Secret Service**—secret service (colonial)—Aaron Burr appointed chief
1789 **Drawback Legislation**—enacted
1789 **Tariff**—tariff legislation—enacted
1801 **President**—President to review the military forces—Thomas Jefferson—Washington, D.C.
1810 **Agricultural Journal**—agricultural journal—*Agricultural Museum*—published—Georgetown, D.C.
1815 **Monument** — monument to George Washington (city or state)—Washington monument—Baltimore, Md.
1817 **Canal** — canal of importance — Erie Canal—construction started
1826 **Iron**—iron castings (malleable)—produced—Seth Boyden—Newark, N.J.
1827 **Monument** — monument to George Washington—Boonsboro, Md.
1828 **Hotel**—hotel to install bathrooms—Tremont House, Boston, Mass.—cornerstone laid
1828 **Railroad** — railroad for commercial transportation of passengers and freight—Baltimore and Ohio Railroad Company—construction commenced
1831 **Locomotive**—locomotive with six or eight driving wheels—used—Baltimore and Ohio Railroad Company
1831 **Periodical** — trade journal — *Rail-road Advocate*—published—Rogersville, Tenn.
1831 **Railroad Car**—car with a center aisle —"The Columbus"—introduced—Baltimore and Ohio Railroad Company
1831 **Treaty**—treaty with a foreign nation to provide for mutual reduction of import duties—signed—Paris, France
1832 **"America"** (the song)—sung publicly —Boston, Mass.
1836 **Colonist**—women to cross the continent—crossed continental divide—South Pass, Wyo.
1837 **Blind**—state school for the blind—Ohio Institution for the Blind—opened —Columbus, Ohio

1838 **Normal School**—normal school instruction—Lafayette College — cornerstone laid
1840 **Play (drama)**—aquatic play—*The Pirate's Signal*—presented—New York City
1840 **Treasury Department (U.S.)**—Treasury Department (U.S.)—Sub-Treasury Act enacted
1846 **Railroad**—international railroad—Atlantic and St. Lawrence Railroad—construction began—Portland, Me.
1848 **Monument**—monument to George Washington (national)—cornerstone laid—Washington, D.C.
1851 **Railroad**—railroad to run west of the Mississippi River—Pacific Railroad of Missouri—ground broken
1872 **President**—President born on Independence Day—Calvin Coolidge—Plymouth, Vt.
1874 **Bridge**—steel arch bridge—completed —J. B. Eads—St. Louis, Mo.
1874 **Socialist Labor Party of North America**—formed
1883 **Electric Company**—three-wire central station incandescent electric lighting plant — operations started — Sunbury, Pa.
1883 **Wild West Show**—presented—North Platte, Neb.
1884 **Bullfight**—bullfight—Dodge City, Kan.
1888 **Rodeo**—competition—Prescott, Ariz.
1889 **State**—states admitted to the Union simultaneously—constitutional conventions—North Dakota and South Dakota
1892 **Street Car**—double-deck street car—operated—San Diego, Calif.
1902 **Motorcycle Endurance Run**—motorcycle endurance run—Boston, Mass., to New York City
1902 **Ship**—battleship built on the Pacific coast—"Nebraska"—keel laid—Seattle, Wash.
1903 **Cable**—cable across the Pacific Ocean between Honolulu, Midway, Guam, and Manila—official message sent—President Theodore Roosevelt
1908 **Aviation**—aeronautical trophy—won—G. H. Curtiss—Hammondsport, N.Y.
1908 **Naval Officer**—admiral who was Jewish—Adolph Marix
1910 **Prize Fight** — Negro heavyweight champion of the world—Jack Johnson
1911 **Insurance** — workmen's compensation insurance law (state)—New Jersey law became effective
1914 **Motorcycle Race** — motorcycle race (300 miles)—Dodge City, Kan.
1917 **Radio Telephone** — radio telephone communication between the ground and an airplane—received by an airplane
1917 **Ship**—ambulance ship, designed and built as a hospital—"Relief"—keel laid
1921 **Cigarette Tax**—cigarette tax (state)—effective—Iowa

1928 Niagara Falls—person to go over Niagara Falls in a rubber ball—Jean Lussier

1935 Ferryboat — streamlined ferryboat — commercial operation — "Kalakala"— Houghton, Wash.

1942 World War II—American bombing mission over enemy-occupied territory in Europe—Netherlands

1955 Cobra—king cobra snakes—born in captivity—New York City

JULY 5

1775 Army Insignia—special insignia—instituted—Massachusetts

1776 Declaration of Independence (American) — Declaration of Independence was first printed—John Dunlop—Philadelphia, Pa.

1843 Colonial Government—government on the Pacific coast—committee of nine chosen—Champoeg, Ore.

1884 Navigation Bureau (U.S.) — under Treasury Department—authorized

1893 College—university extension summer meeting—Philadelphia, Pa.

1916 Motorcycle Trip—motorcycle transcontinental trip by a woman—left—New York City

1933 Teletypesetter—teletypesetter installed in a school—Empire State School of Printing—Ithaca, N.Y.

1935 Labor—Labor Relations Act (national)—approved

1944 Aviation — Airplane — rocket airplane (military)—flown—Hawthorne, Calif.

1946 Air Mail Service—helicopter airmail delivery—Bridgeport, Conn.

1950 War (Korean)—soldier killed in the Korean War—Kenneth Shadrick

1951 Transistor — junction transistor — invention announced—Murray Hill, N.J.

JULY 6

1776 Declaration of Independence (American)—Declaration of Independence was first published—Philadelphia, Pa.

1785 Money—decimal system of money—adopted

1787 Money — Continental coin — copper Fugio—authorized

1798 Alien Discriminatory Law—enacted

1853 Railroad—railroad merger—New York Central Railroad directors selected

1858 Shoe Manufacturing Machine—patented—L. R. Blake—Abington, Mass.

1899 Automobile License Board—authorized—Chicago, Ill.

1903 Motorcycle Trip—motorcycle transcontinental trip—arrived—New York City

1905 Fingerprinting—international exchange of fingerprints—St. Louis, Mo. and London, England

1908 Expedition—polar expedition of which a woman was a member—Peary expedition—sailed

1919 Aviation — aeronautical stowaway — William Ballantyne—arrived—Hazlehurst Field, L.I., N.Y.

1919 Aviation — Airship — airship (lighter-than-air)—British dirigible R-34 arrived—Roosevelt Field, N.Y.

1924 Radio Facsimile Transmission—photograph sent by radio across the Atlantic—from New York City

1933 Baseball Player—baseball player to hit a home run in an All-Star game—Babe Ruth

1939 Air Mail Service—autogiro mail delivery regular service—Philadelphia, Pa., to Camden, N.J.

1945 Medal—Medal of Freedom — established

1948 Federal Communications Commission —federal communications commission woman member—F. B. Hennock—appointed

JULY 7

1806 Cathedral—cathedral—cornerstone laid —Baltimore, Md.

1838 Steamboat Inspection Service (U.S.) —authorized

1849 Library Law—enacted by a state—New Hampshire

1861 Torpedo—torpedo mine—attack—Potomac River

1862 Postal Service—railroad post office—tested

1863 Conscription — wartime conscription bill—first draft call

1885 Ordnance—cartridge-loading machinery—patented—G. M. Peters—Xenia, Ohio

1886 Biblical Students Summer Conference —organized—Mount Hermon School —Northfield, Mass.

1911 Continuation School — continuation school established by state law—Racine Continuation School — Racine, Wis.—authorized

1920 Radio Compass—on naval airplane—used—Norfolk, Va.

1923 College—"junior year abroad"—instituted—University of Delaware—Newark, Del.

1935 Eyes—identification system — presented —Atlantic City, N.J.

1948 Naval Officer—women sworn into the Regular U.S. Navy

JULY 8

1524 Kidnapping—recorded in letter

1693 Police—police uniforms—authorized—New York City

1776 Declaration of Independence (American) — Declaration of Independence was first read publicly—Philadelphia, Pa.

1795 College—college named after George Washington — Washington, Tenn. — third charter

1934 **President** — President to broadcast from a foreign country—F. D. Roosevelt—Cartagena, Colombia

1934 **President**—President to visit South America while President—F. D. Roosevelt—Cartagena, Colombia

1935 **Aviation—Flight (transcontinental)**—transcontinental non-stop east-west flight by a woman—Laura Ingalls—left—Brooklyn, N.Y.

1949 **Television Tube**—rectangular television tube (practical) — announced—Toledo, Ohio

1962 **Television** — Telecast — transoceanic television program—Andover, Me.

JULY 11

1798 **Marines**—American Marines—United States Marine Corps—created

1862 **Secret Service**—secret service (federal)—act extended to include counterfeiting

1863 **Bank**—national bank chartered—First National Bank of Philadelphia — opened for business—Philadelphia, Pa.

1870 **School**—Negro school (state)—Snowden School—authorized—Alexandria, Va.

1883 **Jewish College**—Jewish college to train men for the rabbinate—graduation—Cincinnati, Ohio

1890 **Library Society**—state library society —organized

1916 **Road**—federal grant-in-aid—act approved

1919 **Prison**—prisoners (federal) employed in industry—United States Penitentiary—Atlanta, Ga.

1919 **Ship**—electrically propelled ship of the United States Navy—"Jupiter"—conversion to aircraft carrier "Langley"—authorized

1923 **Railroad Signal System**—railroad signal system of continuous cab signals—installed—Sunbury, Pa.

1933 **National Emergency Council (U.S.)**—executive council established

1934 **Federal Communications Commission** —committee appointed

1934 **President**—President to go through the Panama Canal while President—F. D. Roosevelt

1940 **Postal Service**—highway post office service—approved

1955 **Air Force Academy (U.S.)**—Air Force Academy—temporary headquarters established—Denver, Colo.

JULY 12

1774 **Declaration of Independence (American)**—Declaration of Independence—Carlisle, Pa.

1859 **Paper Bag Manufacturing Machine**—patented—William Goodale—Clinton, Mass.

1862 **Medal**—Medal of Honor (Army)—authorized

1864 **Medal**—Medal of Honor awarded to a Jewish soldier—Leopold Karpeles—award authorized

1866 **War Veterans' Society**—Grand Army of the Republic—state convention—Springfield, Ill.

1882 **Elevator**—elevator with an electric light—installed—Blue Mountain Lake, N.Y.

1882 **Pier**—ocean pier—completed—Atlantic City, N.J.

1909 **Tax**—income tax amendment to the Constitution—proposed to the states

1912 **Moving Picture**—foreign feature film exhibited—*Queen Elizabeth*—exhibited—New York City

1924 **Olympic Games**—American decathlon champion—H. M. Osborne—Paris, France

1928 **Television—Telecast**—outdoor scenes to be televised—New York City

1943 **Submarine-Escape Training Tank**—women to take the submarine-escape test—certificates awarded—New London, Conn.

1957 **President**—President to fly in a helicopter—D. D. Eisenhower—Washington, D.C.

JULY 13

1787 **Territorial Expansion**—acquisition of land by the federal government—territory established

1812 **Pawnbroking Ordinance** — enacted — New York City

1832 **Treaty**—treaty with a foreign nation to provide for mutual reduction of import duties—with France—proclaimed

1836 **Patent**—numbering system for patents—adopted—patent No. 1 to John Ruggles—Thomaston, Me.

1861 **Civil War**—Confederate general killed in the Civil War—R. S. Garnett—Corrick's Ford, Va.

1875 **Cash Carrier System**—patented—David Brown—Lebanon, N.J.

1880 **Street Car**—electric street car successfully run with current generated by a stationary dynamo—patented—S. D. Field

1929 **Aviation—Flights**—airplane endurance flight exceeding 400 hours—Dale Jackson and Forest O'Brine—St. Louis, Mo.—take-off

1929 **Moving Picture**—talking picture in Esperanto—New York City

1934 **Police**—policewoman on the aerial force—Cora Sterling—appointed—Seattle, Wash.

1936 **Pension**—pensions paid by the United States Government to workers in private industry—mailed

1938 **Theater**—television theater—opened—Massachusetts Television Institute—Boston, Mass.

1939 **Federal Security Agency**—administrator P. V. McNutt took office

1950 **Naval Officer**—woman medical officer assigned to a naval vessel—B. R. Walters

JULY 14

1798 **Tax**—federal tax levied directly upon the states—enacted
1820 **Lightship**—Craney Island, Va.
1832 **Narcotic**—narcotic tariff—opium exempted from duty
1853 **Fair**—industrial exposition—opened by President Franklin Pierce—New York City
1868 **Tape Measure Patent**—A. J. Fellows —New Haven, Conn.
1870 **Pension**—pension to the widow of a President—authorized
1891 **Corkboard Patent**—J. T. Smith— Brooklyn, N.Y.
1911 **Aviation**—airplane to land on the White House lawn—H. N. Atwood— Washington, D.C.
1914 **Rocket**—liquid fuel rocket patent— R. H. Goddard—Worcester, Mass.
1917 **Wedding**—wedding abroad of a soldier in the American Expeditionary Force—London, England
1917 **World War I**—American Army casualty—L. J. Genelba—Arras, France
1950 **Medal**—Distinguished Flying Cross in the Korean War—R. E. Wayne
1951 **Horse**—horse to win a million dollars in races—Citation—Inglewood, Calif.
1951 **Television — Telecast**—sports event televised in color—Oceanport, N.J.
1953 **Monument**—national monument dedicated to a Negro—G. W. Carver— Newton County, Mo.
1953 **Vice President of the United States**— Vice President to preside at a National Security Council meeting—R. M. Nixon
1954 **Radio Sextant** — announced—Cedar Rapids, Iowa
1959 **Ship**—atomic-powered cruiser—"Long Beach"—launched—Quincy, Mass.

JULY 15

1891 **Billboard Standardization**—Associated Bill Posters and Distributors of the United States and Canada—formed— Chicago, Ill.
1904 **Buddhist Temple** — established — Los Angeles, Calif.
1920 **Army Officer**—chaplain (chief) of the U.S. Army—J. T. Axton—appointed
1920 **Aviation—Flights**—New York-Alaska flight—left New York City
1922 **Aquatic Mammals**—platypus (duckbilled)—exhibited—New York City
1922 **Golf Champion**—golf champion to win the United States Open and the Professional — Gene Sarazen — won United States Open—Glencoe, Ill.
1929 **Aviation — Airport** — airport hotel — opened—Oakland, Calif.

1929 **Farm Board (federal)**—organization meeting
1933 **Aviation — Flights (transatlantic)**— transatlantic foreign squadron flight to the United States—Italo Balbo— arrived—Chicago, Ill.
1933 **Aviation—Flights (world)**—world solo airplane flight—W. H. Post—New York City
1940 **Betatron**—operated—University of Illinois—Urbana, Ill.
1942 **Ship**—Navy vessel constructed as a minelayer — "Terror"—commissioned
1952 **Helicopter Flight**—helicopter transAtlantic flight—left for Germany
1954 **Aviation — Airplane** — jet transport commercial airplane built in the United States — tested — Renton, Wash.

JULY 16

1769 **California Mission**—blessed—San Diego, Calif.
1773 **Methodist Conference**—Philadelphia, Pa.
1798 **Hospital**—marine hospital (U.S.)—authorized
1798 **Public Health**—Public Health Service (U.S.)—established
1840 **College**—women's college (chartered) —Wesleyan College, Macon, Ga.—first class graduated
1845 **Yacht Race**—regatta—of importance— New York Yacht Club—New York City
1862 **Naval Officer**—naval officer to become an admiral—D. G. Farragut—appointed rear admiral
1867 **Paint**—paint (ready-mixed)—patented —D. R. Averill—Newburg, Ohio
1877 **Strike**—strike in which federal troops were called in peacetime
1912 **Torpedo**—airplane torpedo—patented —B. A. Fiske
1920 **Army Officer**—chemical warfare chief —A. A. Fries—appointed
1920 **Radio Telephone** — radio telephone service (commercial)—inaugurated— Los Angeles to Santa Catalina Island, Calif.
1926 **Photograph**—photographs taken under the sea in natural colors—Tortugas, Fla.
1934 **Aviation**—floating seaplane ramp (municipally owned)—first passenger-flight docked
1935 **Parking Meter (automatic)**—installed —Oklahoma City, Okla.
1936 **X-ray**—X-ray photograph showing the complete arterial circulation—completed—Rochester, N.Y.
1939 **Locomotive**—rack-rail diesel-electric locomotive—in service—Manitou and Pike's Peak Railway
1945 **Atomic Bomb**—atomic bomb explosion —Alamogordo, N.M.
1946 **Telephone**—mobile telephone conversation overseas—from a moving vehicle—St. Louis, Mo. to Honolulu

1958 **Television Station**—city to have two educational television channels—Pittsburgh, Pa.—second channel granted

JULY 17

1794 **African Church** — opened — Philadelphia, Pa.

1839 **Britannia Ware**—patent—Isaac Babbitt—Boston, Mass.

1850 **Photograph**—photograph of a star—Vega—Cambridge, Mass.

1850 **Telegraph**—telegraph convention (national)—New York City

1861 **Money**—demand notes—authorized

1861 **Money**—paper money issued by the government of the United States—authorized

1862 **Army**—law (federal) authorizing military service for Negroes—signed

1862 **Cemetery** — national cemeteries — authorized

1862 **Internal Revenue Commissioner**—G. S. Boutwell—served

1866 **Tunnel**—subaqueous highway tunnel—Washington Street Tunnel—Chicago, Ill.—construction authorized

1867 **Dental School**—dental school permanently established by a university—Harvard School of Dental Medicine—established—Boston, Mass.

1904 **Carnegie Hero Fund Commission**—L. A. Baumann, Jr. heroic act—Wilkinsburg, Pa.

1916 **Farm Loan Board (federal)**—Federal Farm Loan Act—approved

1933 **Aviation—Flights (transcontinental)**—transcontinental flight made by Negroes in their own plane—left Atlantic City, N.J.

1933 **Industrial Recovery Act**—code under the National Industrial Recovery Act—effective

1953 **Aviation—Aviator**—naval ace in Korea—Guy Bordelon

1954 **Baseball Game**—major league game in which the majority of the players on one team were Negroes—Brooklyn Dodgers

1955 **Electric Power Plant**—electric power generated from atomic energy to illuminate an entire town—Arco, Idaho

JULY 18

1627 **Oil**—oil spring—Cuba, N.Y.—described in letter

1743 **Advertisement**—advertisement to occupy a half-page—*Weekly Journal*—New York City

1794 **Money**—deposit of silver for coinage—Bank of Maryland

1846 **Road**—plank road—completed—Syracuse, N.Y.

1853 **Railroad** — international railroad — trains from Portland, Me. to Montreal, Canada

1866 **Insurance**—insurance rate standardization—effected—New York City

1908 **Fireworks Legislation**—fireworks legislation enacted by a city—Cleveland, Ohio

1914 **Aviation**—air service of the United States Army—aviation section created

1938 **Building**—building devoted entirely to highway traffic—ground broken—Saugatuck, Conn.

1940 **Helicopter**—helicopter (direct-lift-aircraft)—flight—Stratford, Conn.

1955 **Electric Power Plant**—electric power generated from atomic energy to be sold commercially — West Milton, N.Y.

1955 **Television — Telecast** — commercial filmed by a camera operated by atomically generated electricity—produced—West Milton, N.Y.

JULY 19

1776 **Declaration of Independence (American)**—Declaration of Independence was first ordered "to be fairly engrossed on parchment"—Philadelphia, Pa.

1784 **Botanic Scientific Expedition**—started—Ipswich, Mass.

1848 **Bloomers**—introduced—Seneca Falls, N.Y.

1848 **Woman Suffrage**—convention of women advocating woman suffrage—Seneca Falls, N.Y.

1875 **Hospital** — floating hospital — "Emma Abbot"—New York City

1909 **Baseball Game**—triple play unassisted in a modern major league game—Neal Ball—Cleveland, Ohio

1933 **Aviation—Flights (transcontinental)**—transcontinental flight made by Negroes in their own plane—arrived—Los Angeles, Calif.

1939 **Suture**—fiberglas sutures—used—R. P. Scholz—St. Louis, Mo.

1942 **Army Camp**—Army camp for "limited service"—opened—Camp McCoy, Wis.

1950 **Judge**—Negro judge of a Circuit Court of Appeals—W. H. Hastie—Philadelphia, Pa.

1952 **Submarine**—submarine powered by a liquid metal-cooled atomic reactor—"Seawolf"—ordered

1957 **Rocket**—rocket with an atomic warhead—fired—Yucca Flat, Nev.

JULY 20

1776 **Army**—brevet—authorized—J. A. de Franchessin

1789 **Navigation Act**—navigation act (U.S.)—approved

1801 **Cheese Factory**—cheese factory cooperative — Cheshire, Mass. — cheese pressed for Thomas Jefferson

1831 **Cabinet of the United States**—cabinet member who was a Catholic—R. B. Taney

1858 Baseball Game—baseball series—Long Island, N.Y.

1859 Baseball Game—baseball series—admission charged

1868 Cigarette Tax—cigarette tax stamps ordered placed on packages

1875 Agricultural Experiment Station—state agricultural experiment station—authorized—Connecticut

1875 Bankers' Association—national bankers' association—American Bankers Association — national convention — Saratoga, N.Y.

1876 Track Meet (intercollegiate)—Saratoga, N.Y.

1880 Monument—obelisk to be brought to the United States — arrived — New York City

1891 Research Institute—anatomy research institute—Wistar Institute of Anatomy and Biology—Philadelphia, Pa.

1900 Astronomer—woman astronomer employed in the U.S. Naval Observatory —E. A. Lamson—employed

1937 Army Insignia—shoulder sleeve insignia issued to an independent air unit—authorized

1942 Army Auxiliary Corps—women's army auxiliary corps (WAAC) training course—Des Moines, Iowa

1942 Medal—Legion of Merit medal—authorized

1948 Aviation—Flights (transatlantic)—jet transatlantic flight west to east—from Mount Clemens, Mich., to England

1960 Submarine—submerged submarine to fire a Polaris missile—"George Washington"—Cape Canaveral, Fla.

JULY 21

1773 Degrees (academic and honorary)— doctor of laws honorary degree— awarded—John Winthrop—Harvard College—Cambridge, Mass.

1828 Strike—strike in which the militia was called—Paterson, N.J.

1861 Civil War—serious engagement in the Civil War—Bull Run Creek, Va.

1880 Air (compressed) — explosion — Hudson tubes—Hoboken, N.J., and New York City

1918 World War I—shots to land on American soil—Meeting House Pond, Mass.

1919 Caterpillar Club — Caterpillar Club member—jump—John Boettner—Chicago, Ill.

1921 Aviation—battleship sunk by an airplane—near Hampton Roads, Va.

1928 Moving Picture—talking picture of more than 6,000 feet—*The Lights of New York*—released

1930 Veterans' Bureau—Veterans Administration—created

1934 Labor—National Mediation Board—organized

1946 Aviation—Airplane—jet airplane to land on a ship—"FD-I Phantom"—on carrier "Franklin D. Roosevelt"—Cape Henry, Va.

1955 Submarine—submarine powered by a liquid metal-cooled atomic reactor—"Seawolf"—launched—Groton, Conn.

1959 Ship—atomic-powered merchant ship — "Savannah"—christened — Camden, N.J.

JULY 22

1887 Postal Service—parcel post convention—with Jamaica

1896 Silverites — national convention —St. Louis, Mo.

1932 Federal Home Loan Bank Board—established

1932 Home Owners' Loan Corporation— Federal Home Loan Bank Act—approved

1933 Aviation—Aviator—woman aviator to fly across the Atlantic Ocean east to west — A. J. Mollison — left — Pendine, Wales

1933 Aviation—Flights (world)—world solo airplane flight—W. H. Post returned—Floyd Bennett Field—New York City

1933 Opera—Negro prima donna of an opera company—Caterina Jarboro—*Aida*—New York City

1939 Judge—woman judge (Negro)—J. M. Bolin—appointed—New York City

1955 Vice President of the United States— Vice President to preside over a cabinet meeting—R. M. Nixon—Washington, D.C.

JULY 23

1715 Lighthouse—lighthouse—Little Brewster Island, Mass.—authorized

1827 Swimming School—opened—Boston, Mass.

1829 Typewriter — typewriter — patented —W. A. Burt—Mount Vernon, Mich.

1877 Railroad—municipal railroad—service began—Cincinnati, Ohio

1880 Electric Power Plant—hydroelectric power plant (commercial)—Grand Rapids Electric Light and Power Company — Grand Rapids, Mich.— in operation

1885 Bankers' Association—bankers' association formed by a state group— Texas Bankers' Association—organized—Lampasas, Texas

1924 Automobile Bus—bus operated by a railroad—Spokane, Portland and Seattle Transportation Company—incorporated

1933 Aviation—Aviator—woman aviator to fly across the Atlantic Ocean east to west—A. J. Mollison—crash-landed— Stratford, Conn.

1937 Pituitary Hormone—pituitary hormone isolated—announced—Yale University School of Medicine—New Haven, Conn.

1938 **Game Preserve**—game preserve appropriation (federal)—state aid project approved—Utah

1945 **Railroad Car**—car with an observation dome

1947 **Navy**—air squadron of jets—Quonset Point, R.I.

1947 **War Veterans' Society**—World War II veterans' society officially recognized by Congress—American Veterans of World War II—chartered

JULY 24

1844 **Pump**—independent single direct-acting steam power pump—patented—H. R. Worthington—New York City

1847 **Printing Press**—rotary type printing press—patented—R. M. Hoe—New York City

1849 **Degrees (academic and honorary)**—Doctor of Music degree—conferred—Georgetown University—Washington, D.C.

1866 **State**—state re-admitted to the Union—Tennessee

1919 **Aviation—Airplane**—three-motor airplane—flight—Garden City, N.Y.

1933 **Surgical Operation**—lung removal carried out according to pre-operative plans—W. F. Reinhoff, Jr.—Baltimore, Md.

1934 **Birds**—ptarmigan (Eskimo chicken) hatched in captivity—Ithaca, N.Y.

1946 **Atomic Bomb**—atomic bomb underwater explosion—Bikini Atoll

1955 **Television — Telecast —** commercial filmed by a camera operated by atomically generated electricity—televised

1956 **Railroad Car**—freight car (Adapto Car)—in service between St. Louis, Mo. and Wichita, Kan.

JULY 25

1820 **Discovery**—discovery of Antarctica—N. B. Palmer—sailed—Stonington, Conn.

1832 **Railroad Accident**—railroad accident—Granite Railway—Quincy, Mass.

1854 **Collar**—paper collar—patented—Walter Hunt—New York City

1860 **Billiard Match**—intercollegiate billiard match—Worcester, Mass.

1863 **Monument**—monument to commemorate the Civil War—dedicated—Kensington, Conn.

1866 **Army Officer**—general of the United States Army—U.S. Grant—appointed

1866 **Naval Officer**—naval officer to become an admiral—D. G. Farragut—appointed

1871 **Carrousel**—carrousel patent—Willhelm Schneider—Davenport, Iowa

1871 **Paper**—perforated wrapping paper—patented — Seth Wheeler — Albany, N.Y.

1878 **Chinese Embassy**—landed—San Francisco, Calif.

1918 **Woman**—woman district attorney of the United States—A. A. Adams—served

1923 **Newspaper** — mimeographed daily newspaper—*Kellogg Daily Reminder*—published—Kellogg, Idaho

1925 **Radio Station**—radio station operating a fifty-kilowatt transmitter—2XAG—Schenectady, N.Y.

1934 **President**—President to visit Hawaii while President—F. D. Roosevelt—landed—Hilo, Hawaii

1939 **Television—Telecast**—musical comedy telecast (one-hour)—New York City

1941 **Navy "E" Award**—Navy "E" certificates of meritorious service—granted

1943 **Ship**—warship named for a Negro—"Harmon"—launched—Quincy, Mass.

JULY 26

1775 **Postmaster**—postmaster general under the Continental Congress—Benjamin Franklin—appointed

1779 **Medal**—medal awarded by the Continental Congress to a foreigner—resolution—F. L. T. de Fleury

1859 **Boat Race**—intercollegiate regatta—Worcester, Mass.

1866 **Irrigation Legislation (federal)**—enacted

1880 **Steam Distribution Plant**—of importance—New York Steam Corporation—formed—New York City

1893 **Addressograph** — commercial production—Chicago, Ill.

1903 **Automobile Transcontinental Trip**—transcontinental automobile trip—by a nonprofessional driver—from San Francisco, Calif.—arrived New York City

1907 **Ship**—turbine-propelled ship of the U.S. Navy—"Chester"—launched

1923 **President**—President to visit Alaska and Canada while President—W. G. Harding—Vancouver, B.C.

1933 **Treasury Department (U.S.)**—woman assistant treasurer of the United States—M. G. Bannister—appointed

1947 **National Security Council**—National Security Council—established—Washington, D.C.

JULY 27

1775 **Army Officer**—surgeon general of the Continental Army—Benjamin Church—served

1784 **Newspaper** — French newspaper — *Courier de l'Amérique*—published—Philadelphia, Pa.

1789 **State Department (U.S.)**—State Department (U.S.)—Department of Foreign Affairs—created

1868 **Postal Service**—money order system—foreign service authorized

1869 **Philological Society**—national philological society—American Philological Association — convention — Poughkeepsie, N.Y.

1918 **Ship**—concrete barge—"Socony 200"—launched

1933 **Central Statistical Board (U.S.)**—created

1933 **Industrial Recovery Act**—state to place all its employees under the blanket code of the National Industrial Recovery Act Code—West Virginia

1933 **Kidnapping**—death penalty for kidnapping—imposed—Kansas City, Mo.

JULY 28

1777 **Suffrage**—state to provide universal manhood suffrage—Vermont—constitution adopted—Windsor, Vt.

1862 **Postal Service**—railroad post office—placed in operation—Hannibal and St. Joseph, Mo.

1865 **Dental Code of Ethics**—proposed—American Dental Association—Chicago, Ill.

1866 **Monument**—monument by a woman ordered by the U.S. Government—authorized

1866 **Weights and Measures Standardization**—act legalizing the employment of the metric system—approved

1868 **Education Department (U.S.)**—Department of Education (U.S.)—Office of Education established

1869 **Labor Union**—women's labor organization (national)—Daughters of St. Crispin—convention—Lynn, Mass.

1875 **Baseball Game** — no-hit nine-inning baseball game

1882 **Accountants' Society**—Institute of Accountants and Bookkeepers—organized—New York City

1903 **Bank**—bank president (Negro woman)—Saint Luke Penny Savings Bank—Richmond, Va.

1926 **Catholic Church** — Catholic church raised to the dignity of a Basilica—Lackawanna, N.Y.

1933 **Cotton**—cotton acreage reduction payment—payment made

1942 **Postal Service**—coin operated mailbox—patented—L. A. Thatcher—Stamford, Conn.

1959 **Congressman (U.S.)**—congressman of Japanese ancestry elected to the House of Representatives—D. K. Inouye

JULY 29

1773 **Schoolhouse**—west of the Allegheny mountains—completed—Schoenbrunn, Ohio

1775 **Army Officer**—judge advocate—William Tudor—served

1775 **Treasury Department (U.S.)**—Treasurer of the United States—Michael Hillegas—served

1786 **Newspaper**—newspaper published west of the Alleghenies—issued—*Pittsburgh Gazette*—Pittsburgh, Pa.

1794 **African Church**—Bethel AfricanMethodist Episcopal Church — opened — Philadelphia, Pa.

1847 **Newspaper**—Norwegian-American newspaper—*Nordlyset*—Muskego, Wis.

1865 **Newspaper**—newspaper published at sea—*Atlantic Telegraph*—published

1870 **Road**—sheet asphalt pavement—laid—Newark, N.J.

1899 **Bicycle Race**—motorcycle-paced bicycle race—Manhattan Beach Track

1908 **Price Regulation Law**—price regulation law (state)—effective—Louisiana

1933 **Narcotic**—narcotic sanatorium (federal) for drug addicts—cornerstone laid—Lexington, Ky.

1935 **Police** — police training school — of Federal Bureau of Investigation—initiated—Washington, D.C.

1949 **Turbine**—gas turbine used by an electrical utility company — Oklahoma City, Okla.

1952 **Aviation—Flights (transpacific)** — jet transpacific non-stop flight—Anchorage, Alaska, to Japan

1958 **Space Agency (U.S.)**—National Aeronautics and Space Administration—authorized

1959 **Senator (U.S.)**—senator of Asian ancestry—Hiram Fong

JULY 30

1619 **Legislative Assembly** — Jamestown, Va.

1733 **Freemasons**—masonic lodge to work under a regular charter—St. John's lodge—established—Boston, Mass.

1844 **Yacht Club**—New York Yacht Club—organized

1850 **Cracker**—meat biscuit—Gail Borden—patented

1874 **Baseball Team**—baseball teams to travel beyond the confines of the United States — exhibition game — England

1898 **Advertisement**—automobile advertisement—*Scientific American*

1909 **Aviation — Airplane** — airplane purchased by the United States Government—tested—Dayton, Ohio

1909 **Aviation—Flights**—inter-city airplane flight—by a U.S. officer—B. D. Foulois—Fort Myer, Va. to Alexandria, Va.

1929 **Aviation—Flights**—airplane endurance flight exceeding 400 hours—Dale Jackson and Forest O'Brine — St. Louis, Mo.—landed

1933 **National Planning Board (U.S.)**—organized

1937 **Ship**—seaplane tender designed and built for the United States Navy—"Curtiss"—authorized

1946 **Rocket**—rocket to attain a 100-mile altitude — White Sands Proving Grounds, N.M.

1956 **Motto of the United States**—"In God We Trust"—authorized

1956 **Ship**—atomic-powered merchant ship —"Savannah"—authorized

JULY 31

1790 **Patent**—patent granted by the United States Government — issued — Samuel Hopkins

1792 **Building**—building erected in the United States for public use—cornerstone of mint—laid—Philadelphia, Pa.

1792 **Mint (U.S.)**—Mint of the United States—cornerstone laid—Philadelphia, Pa.

1795 **Money**—return of coins—to treasury

1809 **Railroad Track**—railroad track (practical)—Philadelphia, Pa.

1849 **Ordnance**—cannon (breech loading)— patent—Benjamin Chambers

1869 **Labor**—labor bureau (state)—Massachusetts Bureau of Statistics—H. K. Oliver appointed chief

1875 **Animals** — cattle importation law (U.S.)—prohibition enforced

1876 **Coast Guard (U.S.)**—Coast Guard officers' training school—established— New Bedford, Mass.

1912 **Moving Picture Censorship**—moving picture censorship regulation (federal) —enacted

1918 **Chinaware** — dishes (complete set) made in America for the Executive Mansion — delivered — Washington, D.C.

1930 **Aviation** — **Airship** — dirigible landing and taking off from an ocean-going steamship — "Mayflower" — New York City

1933 **Science Advisory Board**—authorized

1954 **Automobile School** — truck-driving training school—Bedford, Pa.—class graduated

AUGUST 1

1787 **Constitution of the United States**— printed copies of the Constitution— proof sheets printed

1789 **Drawback Legislation**—tariff act—effective

1790 **Census**—census of the United States —enumeration

1841 **Business**—commercial rating agency— established—New York City

1842 **Postage Stamp**—adhesive stamps — City Despatch Post acquired by United States

1861 **President**—President to serve as an official of the Confederate States— John Tyler—delegate

1872 **Gas**—pipeline (long distance)—Newton Wells to Titusville, Pa.

1873 **Street Car**—cable streetcar—operated —San Francisco, Calif.

1874 **Patent** — label patent — issued — Pearl Hominy Co.—Baltimore, Md.

1881 **Electric Power Plant**—hydroelectric power plant (commercial)—new station opened—Grand Rapids, Mich.

1886 **Zoological Laboratory (U.S.)**—zoological laboratory (U.S.) for the study of the parasites of livestock—opened —Washington, D.C.

1893 **Aviation—Expositions and Meets**—air conference (international)—Chicago, Ill.

1893 **Breakfast Food**—shredded wheat biscuits—patented

1893 **Medical School**—naval medical school —opened—Brooklyn, N.Y.

1907 **Aviation**—aeronautical division of the United States War Department—authorized

1908 **Automobile Race**—automobile race from New York to Paris—winning car returned to New York City

1908 **Insurance**—workmen's compensation insurance law (federal) — effective

1911 **Aviation—License**—woman aviator to pass the test of the Aero Club of America—Harriet Quimby

1916 **Submarine**—cargo submarine to cross the Atlantic Ocean—"Deutschland"— returned

1923 **Hospital**—cancer hospital (municipal) —New York City Cancer Institute— —New York City—dedicated

1930 **Electric Power Plant**—hydroelectric power plant (county-owned)—operated—Crisp County, Ga.

1930 **Photography**—photographic flashlight lamps— manufactured— Schenectady, N.Y.

1933 **Poorhouse (state)**—superintendent A. V. Gilliland appointed

1934 **Aviation—Flights (transcontinental)** —transcontinental commercial overnight transport service—left Newark, N.J.

1939 **Vitamin**—synthetic vitamin K—made —L. F. Fieser—Cambridge, Mass.

1946 **Atomic Energy Commission**—Atomic Energy Commission—authorized

1950 **Garbage Collection**—city to discontinue garbage collection—Jasper, Ind.

1951 **Medal**—Medal of Honor awarded to a marine in the Korean War—presented —H. A. Commiskey

1953 **Building**—aluminum-faced building— Alcoa Building — completed — Pittsburgh, Pa.

1957 **Building**—commercial building heated by the sun—completed—Albuquerque, N.M.

AUGUST 2

1776 **Declaration of Independence (American)**—Declaration of Independence was first ordered "to be fairly engrossed" on parchment—copy signed

1791 **Patent**—patent granted jointly to a father and son—Samuel Briggs, Sr. and Jr.—Philadelphia, Pa.

1819 **Aviation—Parachute**—parachute jump from a balloon—Charles Guille—New York City

1858 **Postal Service**—street letter box—erected—Boston, Mass., and New York City

1862 **Army Ambulance Corps**—established

1886 **Oleomargarine**—oleomargarine legislation (federal)—enacted

1909 **Aviation — Airplane** — airplane purchased by the United States Government—accepted

1923 **President**—President and President's wife to die during the term for which he had been elected—W. G. Harding and F. K. D. Harding

1927 **Submarine**—streamlined submarine of the U.S. Navy—"Nautilus"—keel laid—Mare Island, Calif.

1934 **Aviation—Flights**—"airplane train"—started—Floyd Bennett Field, N.Y.

1958 **Aviation—Flights**—airplane endurance flight exceeding 1,200 hours—Jim Heth and Bill Burkhart—Dallas, Tex.—take-off

AUGUST 3

1750 **Teaching Methods Book**—completed—Germantown, Pa.

1816 **Coast Survey Superintendent**—F. R. Hassler—appointed

1852 **Boat Race**—intercollegiate boat race—Lake Winnepesaukee, N.H.

1861 **Ship**—balloon carrier—"Fanny"—used—Fortress Monroe, Va.

1880 **Canoe Association**—American Canoe Association—formed — Lake George, N.Y.

1882 **Immigration**—immigration head tax—enacted

1886 **Ship** — battleship of importance—"Maine"—authorized

1886 **Ship**—torpedo boat of importance—"Cushing"—authorized

1904 **American**—as an adjective—official—Secretary of State John Hay

1904 **Balloon**—balloon circular flight—Oakland, Calif.

1922 **Radio Broadcast**—drama (full length melodrama) broadcast — Schenectady, N.Y.

1942 **Naval Officer**—woman naval officer commissioned in the U.S. Naval Reserve—M. H. McAfee—inducted

1945 **Radio Facsimile Transmission**—color photoradio news photograph transmitted by radio for publication—received—Washington, D.C.

1958 **Navy**—naval man to reenlist while under the North Pole—J. R. Sordelet

1958 **Submarine**—submarine crossing of the North Pole under water—"Nautilus"

AUGUST 4

1790 **Bonds**—bonds—of the United States Government—authorized

1790 **Coast Guard (U.S.)**—Coast Guard—Revenue Cutter service organized

1790 **Navy** — naval protection — Revenue Cutter service organized

1790 **Refunding act (federal)**—approved

1790 **Ship** — revenue cutter — "Massachusetts"—authorized

1846 **Treasury Department (U.S.)**—treasury department (U.S.)—sub-treasury—authorized

1874 **Chautauqua Organization**—formed—Fair Point, N.Y.

1886 **Postal Service**—special delivery service—extended to all free delivery offices

1894 **Railroad**—railroad to use an electric engine—for freight service

1921 **Radio Broadcast** — tennis match broadcast—Sewickley, Pa.

1927 **Radio Station**—radio station operating a 100-kilowatt transmitter—2XAG—Schenectady, N.Y.

1930 **Bobsled Run**—North Elba, N.Y.—work begun

1937 **Animals** — okapi — imported — New York City

1942 **President (U.S.)**—President to become a godfather to a member of the English royal family—F. D. Roosevelt

1943 **Medal** — Navy Expert Pistol Shot Medal awarded to a woman—awarded—Rosalie Thorne

1952 **Helicopter Flight**—helicopter transatlantic flight—completed—Germany

1956 **Motorcycle Race**—motorcycle to exceed 200 miles an hour—Wilhelm Herz—Wendover, Utah

AUGUST 5

1736 **Newspaper** — newspaper published south of the Potomac River—*Virginia Gazette*—Williamsburg, Va.

1763 **Prize Fight**—American to win distinction in the prize ring—Bill Richmond—born—Staten Island, N.Y.

1799 **Supreme Court (U.S.) Decision**—Supreme Court decision between states—term began—New York vs. Connecticut

1843 **Ship**—frigate (American-built, steam-driven) to cross the Atlantic Ocean—left Norfolk, Va.

1858 **Cable**—cable across the Atlantic Ocean was completed

1861 **Tax**—federal income tax—law enacted

1870 **Knights of Pythias**—Supreme Lodge—incorporated

1892 **Money**—commemorative coinage—authorized

1892 **Money**—silver coins—Columbian half-dollar—authorized

1909 **Tax**—corporation tax—enacted

1911 **Aviation—Races**—inter-city airplane race—between New York City and Philadelphia, Pa.

1914 **Traffic Light**—electric traffic signal lights—installed—Cleveland, Ohio

1921 **Cartoon**—cartoon awarded a Pulitzer prize—Rollin Kirby—New York City

1921 **Radio Broadcast** — baseball game broadcast with a play-by-play description—Pittsburgh, Pa.

1923 **Swimmer**—American to swim the English Channel—H. F. Sullivan

1926 **Moving Picture**—talking picture—presented New York City

1933 **Labor**—labor board (national)—authorized

1951 **Medal**—Air Force Medal of Honor for action in the Korean War—L. J. Sebile—killed in action

AUGUST 6

1727 **Convent**—convent—permanently established—New Orleans, La.

1774 **Conscientious Objectors** — arrived—New York City

1774 **Shaker Society**—arrived—New York City

1787 **Constitution of the United States**—printed copies of the Constitution—proof sheets delivered to convention

1819 **Engineering College**—civil engineering course—Norwich University—Northfield, Vt.

1819 **Military School** — military school—American Literary, Scientific and Military Academy—Northfield, Vt.

1832 **Phrenologist**—J. G. Spurzheim—arrived—New York City

1846 **Warehouse**—warehouse legislation—enacted

1856 **Calliope**—marine exhibition—on tugboat "Union"

1857 **Cable**—cable across the Atlantic Ocean was paid out

1890 **Execution**—electrocution of a human being — William Kemmler — Auburn, N.Y.

1909 **Automobile Transcontinental Trip**—transcontinental automobile trip by a woman—arrived at San Francisco from New York City

1912 **Progressive Party**—national convention—Chicago, Ill.

1914 **World War I**—American to sail to Europe to enlist in World War I—D. P. Dowd, Jr. enlisted

1926 **Woman**—American woman to swim the English Channel—Gertrude Ederle

1936 **Catholic Mass**—Catholic Mass in an airship over the ocean by an American priest—J. R. Cox

1942 **Congress of the United States**—reigning queen to address a joint session of Congress—Queen Wilhelmina of the Netherlands

1945 **Atomic Bomb**—atomic bomb explosion over enemy territory—Hiroshima, Japan

AUGUST 7

1679 **Ship**—Great Lakes commercial vessel —"Le Griffon"—first voyage

1782 **Medal**—Order of the Purple Heart—established—Newburgh, N.Y.

1789 **Lighthouse** — lighthouse built after American independence — authorized

1789 **War Department (U.S.)**—War Department (U.S.)—authorized

1807 **Ship**—steamboat to make regular trips —"Clermont"—tested

1847 **Plow**—plow for pulverizing the soil—patented—George Page—Washington, D.C.

1854 **Republican Party**—Republican Party meeting (local)—convention—Strong, Me.

1859 **Deaf—Church Service**—church services for the deaf—in St. Ann's Church for Deaf-Mutes—New York City

1869 **Photograph**—photograph of a total solar eclipse—Mt. Pleasant, Iowa

1888 **Door**—door (revolving) — patented—Theophilus Van Kannel—Philadelphia, Pa.

1897 **Submarine**—submarine contract of the U.S. Navy—"Plunger" launched

1916 **Farm Loan Board (federal)**—commissioner G. W. Norris—served

1918 **Aviation**—air squadron (complete)—to cross German lines

1919 **Actors' Union**—strike called

1930 **Diplomatic Service**—chief executive-elect of a foreign country—E. O. Herrera—sworn in as President of Colombia

1941 **Television—Telecast**—audience participation telecast—New York City

1942 **World War II**—American offensive in the Pacific area—Guadalcanal

1953 **Medal**—Navy-Marine Corps medal for heroism awarded to a woman—B. O. Barnwell

1959 **Rocket**—satellite to transmit photographs of the earth—Cape Canaveral, Fla.

AUGUST 8

1679 **Fire**—fire of serious consequence—Boston, Mass.

1786 **Money**—decimal system of money—standards established

1797 **Medical Periodical**—medical magazine —*Medical Repository*—New York City

1839 **Fraternity—(Greek letter)**—fraternity west of the Alleghenies—Beta Theta Pi—Oxford, Ohio

1854 **Ordnance**—metal cartridge—patent—D. B. Wesson—Springfield, Mass.

1865 **Railroad**—streamlined railroad train—patented—S. R. Calthorp—Roxbury, Mass.

1866 **Visiting Celebrities**—queen to visit the United States—Queen Emma of Sandwich Islands — arrived — New York City

1876 **Mimeograph**—patented—T. A. Edison —Menlo Park, N.J.

1899 **Check Protector**—patent application filed—L. M. Todd—Rochester, N.Y.

1899 **Refrigerator**—household refrigerating machine patent—A. T. Marshall — Brockton, Mass.

1900 **Tennis Match**—lawn tennis matches for the Davis Cup—Brookline, Mass.

1930 **Brokerage**—stock order from a Zeppelin—received—Tuckertown, N.J.

1933 **Federal Savings and Loan Association** —created—Miami, Fla.

1950 **Woman**—American woman to swim the English Channel from both coasts —Florence Chadwick

1957 **Rocket**—rocket cone recovery

1958 **Medal**—presidential citation in peacetime

AUGUST 9

1607 **Holiday**—Thanksgiving Day service Phippsburg, Me.

1790 **Ship**—ship to carry the United States flag around the world—returned—Boston, Mass.

1829 **Locomotive**—locomotive for railroad use—"Stourbridge Lion"—tested

1848 **Free Soil Party**—organized—Buffalo, N.Y.

1859 **Escalator**—escalator patent—Nathan Ames—Saugus, Mass.

1860 **Silver Mill**—to treat silver ore successfully—completed — Virginia City, Nev.

1892 **Telegraph**—duplex telegraph (practical)—patented—T. A. Edison—Menlo Park, N.J.

1893 **Bowling Magazine**—*Gut Holz*—issued —New York City

1910 **Washing Machine**—complete, self-contained electric washing machine—patent—A. J. Fisher—Chicago, Ill.

1916 **Park**—park (national) containing an active volcano—Lassen Volcanic National Park—established

1921 **Veterans' Bureau**—established

1932 **Federal Home Loan Bank Board**—meeting

1933 **Central Statistical Board (U.S.)**—organized

1935 **Automobile Legislation**—federal motor carrier legislation—enacted

1936 **Olympic Games**—American athlete to win four prizes at the Olympic games —Jesse Owens—Berlin, Germany

1939 **Television**—**Telecast**—tennis tournament to be televised—Rye, N.Y.

1956 **Television Station** — state-wide and state-supported educational television network—Alabama

AUGUST 10

1821 **State**—state admitted to the Union west of the Mississippi River—Missouri

1859 **Milk Inspectors**—appointed — Boston, Mass.

1869 **Moving Picture Projector**—moving picture projector patent—O. B. Brown —Malden, Mass.

1878 **Chautauqua Organization** — home courses offered

1878 **Home Study Course**—Chautauqua Institution—Chautauqua, N.Y.

1885 **Street Car**—electric cars commercially operated—Baltimore, Md.

1886 **Welding**—welding by the electric process—Elihu Thomson—patent — Lynn, Mass.

1889 **Photograph** — photograph (taken in the United States) on which a meteor was found—Cambridge, Mass.

1911 **Automobile Transcontinental Trip**—transcontinental automobile group tour—arrived—Los Angeles, Calif.

1915 **Election Law**—proportional representation election — authorized — Ashtabula, Ohio

1921 **Sound Absorbing Material** — sugar cane bagasse used—Marrero, La.

1942 **Navy "E" Award**—Army-Navy "E" awards—conferred

1953 **Diplomatic Service**—woman career diplomat advanced to the rank of ambassador—F. E. Willis—sworn in

1957 **Ship** — guided missile destroyer — "Dewey"—keel laid—Bath, Me.

AUGUST 11

1760 **Methodist**—Methodist preacher—Philip Embury—arrived

1860 **Silver Mill**—ore crushed

1868 **Knights of Pythias**—Supreme Lodge convened—Washington, D.C.

1874 **Sprinkler**—sprinkler head—patented—H. S. Parmelee—New Haven, Conn.

1896 **Electric Light Socket**—with pull chain — patented — Harvey Hubbell — Bridgeport, Conn.

1906 **Aviation — Airship** — woman airship passenger—M. P. Miller—Franklin, Pa.

1909 **Radio Distress Signal**—radio SOS from an American ship—"Arapahoe" —received—Cape Hatteras, N.C.

1910 **Pan American Union**—Pan American Union—name adopted

1914 **Moving Picture** — animated cartoon (present technique) — patent — J. R. Bray

1924 **Moving Picture**—talking pictures of presidential candidates — taken — Washington, D.C.

1930 **Lutheran Church**—American Lutheran Church—organized—Toledo, Ohio

1943 **Horse Race**—harness race driver to win the Hambletonian four times—B. F. White

1951 **Television**—**Telecast**—baseball games televised in color—New York City—Brooklyn Dodgers-Boston Braves

1960 **Rocket**—space capsule recovered from an orbiting satellite—Pacific Ocean

AUGUST 12

1585 **Letter**—letters written in English—in America—Ralph Lane

1834 **Dentistry**—amalgam for filling teeth—advertised—New York City

1851 **Sewing Machine** — sewing machine equipped with a rocking treadle or double treadle—patented—I. M. Singer—New York City

1879 **Archery Club** — archery association (national)—tournament—Chicago, Ill.

1882 **Play (drama)**—Hebrew professional acting troupe—advertised—New York City

1898 **Territorial Expansion**—island territory —Hawaii—formally annexed

1912 **Dental Corps (U.S. Navy)**—Dental Corps of the U.S. Navy—authorized

1912 **Moving Picture**—foreign feature film exhibited—commercially—*Queen Elizabeth*—New York City

1917 **College**—women's volunteer college unit to serve overseas—Smith College Relief Unit—sailed

1918 **Air Mail Service**—air mail regular service—established—New York City

1918 **Marines** — woman marine reserve — O. M. Johnson—enrolled

1918 **Ship**—concrete barge—"Socony 200"—commissioned—New York City

1923 **Camera**—moving picture camera (portable)—advertised

1931 **Aviation—License**—glider license class "C"—N.A.A. award to a woman—H. M. Barnaby

1932 **Radio Telephone**—two-way conversation between a glider and the land—New York City

1934 **Servite Church**—Marian Congress—Portland, Ore.

1953 **Ship**—woman to sail solo across the Atlantic Ocean—Ann Davidson—arrived—Miami, Fla.

1954 **Execution**—execution (federal) for the killing of a Federal Bureau of Investigation agent—Gerhard Puff

1960 **Rocket** — communications satellite — launched—Cape Canaveral, Fla.

AUGUST 13

1587 **Indians**—Indian convert (Protestant) —Manteo

1751 **Academy**—Academy and College of Philadelphia—opened

1844 **College**—university on the Pacific coast—Willamette University—Salem, Ore.—opened

1860 **Insurance** — non-forfeiture insurance policy—New York Life Insurance Company—New York City

1872 **Gas**—water gas plant—patent—T. S. C. Lowe—Norristown, Pa.

1877 **Railroad**—municipal railroad—Cincinnati Southern Railway—freight service started

1889 **Telephone**—coin telephone—patented —William Gray—Hartford, Conn.

1911 **Automobile Transcontinental Trip**—transcontinental automobile group tour —concluded—Venice, Calif.

1912 **Radio License**—experimental radio license

1928 **Air Mail Service**—air mail service from ship to shore—from "Ile de France"

1928 **Television—Telecast**—standard broadcast station to transmit a television image—WRNY—Coytesville, N.J.

1931 **Hospital**—community hospital—dedicated—Elk City, Okla.

1935 **Skating**—roller derby—opened—Chicago, Ill.

AUGUST 14

1775 **Army Officer**—quartermaster—Thomas Mifflin—served

1776 **Land Grant**—land grant—authorized by Continental congress

1820 **Hospital**—eye hospital (permanent)— New York Eye Infirmary—opened

1866 **Visiting Celebrities**—Queen to visit the United States — Queen Emma — received by President Johnson

1888 **Electric Meter**—patent—O. B. Shallenberger—Rochester, Pa.

1901 **Aviation — Flights** — airplane flight — Gustave Whitehead — Bridgeport, Conn.

1910 **Esperanto Club**—Esperanto congress in the United States—International Congress of Esperantists—Washington, D.C.

1911 **Aviation**—airplane rescue at sea effected by another airplane—Hugh Robinson

1919 **Air Mail Service**—air mail service to a steamer at sea—"Adriatic"—New York City

1924 **Radio Broadcast** — radio broadcast (two-way) from an airplane—New York City

1931 **Price Regulation Law**—resale price maintenance law (state)—Fair Trade Act—effective—California

1935 **Social Security Act (U.S.)**—approved

1936 **National Union for Social Justice**—national convention—Cleveland, Ohio

1936 **Olympic Games**—Olympic games basketball championship — Berlin, Germany

1950 **War (Korean)**—Korean War hero buried in Arlington Cemetery—H. G. Thomas, Jr.

1956 **Helicopter**—helicopter refueling flight (successful)—Fort Rucker, Ala.

1956 **Stroboradiograph**—announced — Schenectady, N.Y.

AUGUST 15

1635 **Hurricane**—Plymouth colony

1790 **Catholic Bishop**—Catholic bishop appointed to serve in the United States—John Carroll — consecrated — Dorset, England

1812 **Army School**—army school graduate killed—George Ronan—Fort Chicago, Ill.

1814 **Museum** — museum especially constructed as a museum and art gallery —Baltimore, Md.—opened

1845 **Naval Academy** — naval academy (U.S.)—Annapolis, Md.—transferred to Navy Department

1848 **Dental Chair**—patent—M. W. Hanchett—Syracuse, N.Y.

1850 **Catholic Bishop**—native bishops of the South—ordained—Mobile, Ala.

1876 **Forestry Legislation**—federal forestry supervision—attempted

1906 **Tunnel**—freight delivery tunnel system—section opened—Chicago, Ill.

1908 **Postal Service**—navy mail service—established

1911 **Shortening**—shortening made by the hydrogenation process—introduced—Cincinnati, Ohio

1914 **Ship**—steamboat to pass through the Panama Canal—merchant vessel service—"Ancon"

1917 **Army**—gas regiment—U.S. Army—authorized

1925 **Ship**—ship equipped with a masthead sea anchorage for a dirigible—"Patoka"—dirigible "Shenandoah"—Newport News, Va.

1929 **Brokerage**—ocean-going brokerage office—opened—"Ile de France"

1930 **Submarine-Escape Training Tank**—submarine-escape training tank—used —New London, Conn.

1933 **Industrial Recovery Act** — postage stamps commemorating the National Recovery Act — sold — Washington, D.C.

1934 **Aviation** — floating seaplane ramp (municipally owned) — launched — Brooklyn, N.Y.

1936 **Union Party**—convention—Cleveland, Ohio

1937 **Automobile**—automobile-airplane combination—built—Santa Monica, Calif.

1947 **Telephone** — commercial telephone service on railroad trains for passengers—in operation—New York City to Washington, D.C.

1957 **Air Force Officer**—Air Force chairman of the Joint Chiefs of Staff—N. F. Twining—sworn in

AUGUST 16

1815 **Peace Society**—New York Peace Society—organized—New York City

1829 **Siamese Twins** — Siamese twins — Chang and Eng—arrived—Boston, Mass.

1838 **Music** — music convention — Boston, Mass.

1858 **Cable**—cable across the Atlantic Ocean was completed—C. W. Field—Trinity Bay, Newfoundland — messages exchanged

1898 **Loop the Loop Centrifugal Railway**—patented—Edwin Prescott—Arlington, Mass.

1902 **Zoological Laboratory (U.S.)**—zoological laboratory (U.S.) for the study of parasites of man—chief C. W. Stiles appointed

1916 **Bird Legislation (international)**—Migratory Bird Treaty—signed

1918 **World War I**—German spy to receive a death sentence from the American forces during World War I—Lothar Witzke found guilty

1937 **Traffic Regulation Course**—graduate course in traffic engineering and administration—established—Cambridge, Mass.

1946 **United Nations Conference on International Organization**—moved to Lake Success, N.Y.

1957 **Ship**—aircraft carrier (atomic powered)—"Enterprise"—ordered

AUGUST 17

1809 **Disciples of Christ** — organized — Washington, Pa.

1835 **Wrench**—wrench patent — Solyman Merrick—Springfield, Mass.

1859 **Balloon Flight**—balloon flight carrying mail—left Lafayette, Ind.

1869 **Boat Race**—international boat race—London, England

1891 **Bathhouse**—public baths with showers —People's Bath—opened—New York City

1915 **Automobile Electric Self-Starter**—patent—C. F. Kettering—Detroit, Mich.

1938 **Forest Service**—aircraft owned by the Forest Service—in service—Oakland, Calif.

1938 **Prize Fight**—pugilist to hold three titles simultaneously—H. J. Armstrong

AUGUST 18

1587 **Births**—child born of English parents in America—Virginia Dare—Roanoke Island, N.C.

1734 **Physician** — American-born doctor—graduated abroad — William Bull — Leyden, Netherlands

1838 **Expedition**—scientific expedition fitted out by the United States Government —Charles Wilkes — left Hampton Roads, Va.

1840 **Dental Society**—dental society of importance—American Society of Dental Surgeons — organized—New York City

1856 **Diplomatic Service**—consul general—office established

1896 **Tennis Match** — lawn tennis champions who were brothers — National Lawn Tennis Association

1908 **Navy**—naval nurses' corps—Superintendent E. V. Hasson—began service

1913 **War Veterans' Society**—Veterans of Foreign Wars of the United States—formed—Denver, Colo.

1917 **Radio Telephone** — radio telephone communication between the ground and an airplane—two-way communication—Langley Field, Va.

1920 **Woman Suffrage** — woman suffrage amendment approved by Congress—ratification by Tennessee, thirty-sixth state

1922 **Golf Champion** — golf champion to win the United States open and the Professional — Gene Sarazen — won Professional Golfers Tournament — Oakmont, Pa.

1926 **Aviation — Airship** — dirigible made completely of metal—Navy contract signed

1926 **Television — Telecast** — weather map telecast—Arlington, Va., to Washington, D.C.

1931 **Patent** — plant patent — awarded—H. F. Bosenberg—New Brunswick, N.J.

1932 **Aviation — Flights (transatlantic)** — transatlantic solo westward flight — J. A. Mollison—left Portmarnock, Ireland

1937 **Radio License**—frequency modulation (FM) construction permit — Yankee Network, Paxton, Mass.

1945 **Bicycle Racer**—woman bicycle champion of the National Amateur Bicycle Association to win twice — M. M. Dietz—Chicago, Ill.

1958 **Horse**—Haflinger horse—imported

1960 **Photograph**—photograph bounced off a satellite — beamed — Cedar Rapids, Iowa

AUGUST 19

1812 **Marines** — woman marine — Lucy Brewer—served on "Constitution"

1812 **War (1812)**—frigate action of importance in the War of 1812—"Constitution" and "Guerrière"

1856 **Milk** — condensed milk (commercial) patented — Gail Borden — Brooklyn, N.Y.

1918 **Aviation—Airplane**—fighter airplane—Kirkham fighter — tested — Garden City, N.Y.

1929 **Aviation — Airship** — dirigible made completely of metal—tested—Grosse Ile, Mich.

1932 **Aviation — Flights (transatlantic)** — transatlantic solo westward flight—J. A. Mollison—landed—New Brunswick

1940 **Aviation—License**—Civil Aeronautics Administration honorary license — awarded to Orville Wright

1942 **World War II**—American pilot to shoot down a German fighter plane—S. F. Junkin—Dieppe, France

1942 **World War II**—American to land on French soil—F. W. Koons—Dieppe, France

1957 **Balloon Flight**—balloon flight to exceed an altitude of 100,000 feet—D. G. Simons—Crosby, Minn.

1958 **Space Agency (U.S.)**—National Aeronautics and Space Administration—administrators appointed

1958 **Submarine**—submarine with two nuclear reactors—"Triton"—launched

1958 **Submarine**—submerged circumnavigation of the earth—"Triton" launched

1960 **Rocket**—space capsule recovered from an orbiting satellite—Discoverer XIV (1960 Kappa)

AUGUST 20

1866 **Labor Law**—eight-hour day—advocated—unified action—Baltimore, Md.

1867 **Cartridge Belt Patent**—Anson Mills—Fort Bridger, Utah

1887 **Accountants' Society**—accountants' society to become a national organization—American Association of Public Accountants—incorporated

1908 **Post Office**—naval post office aboard a naval vessel—established—"Nebraska"

1910 **Aviation—Aviator**—aviator to fire a gun from an airplane—J. E. Fickel—Sheepshead Bay, N.Y.

1912 **Quarantine**—plant quarantine legislation (national)—enacted

1917 **Radio Telephone** — radio telephone communication between the ground and an airplane—conversation between two planes established

1920 **Radio Station**—commercial radio station—daily service — WWJ — Detroit, Mich.

1923 **Aviation—Airship**—dirigible (American-built rigid) — ZRI — launched — Lakehurst, N.J.

1930 **Television—Telecast** — demonstration of home reception of television—New York City

1948 **Birth Registration**—birth registration uniform system for the numbering of birth certificates

1955 **Aviation—Flights**—airplane to exceed the speed of 800 miles an hour—H. A. Hanes—Palmdale, Calif.

AUGUST 21

1791 **Attorney General**—opinion by a U.S. Attorney General—Philadelphia, Pa.

1841 **Venetian Blinds**—venetian blind patent—John Hampson—New Orleans, La.

1862 **Money**—paper money fractional currency—issued

1878 **Lawyers' Association**—lawyers' association (national)—American Bar Association—organized—Saratoga, N.Y.

1888 **Adding Machine** — adding machine successfully marketed — patented — W. S. Burroughs—St. Louis, Mo.

1912 **Boy Scouts of America**—Boy Scout to become an eagle scout—A. R. Eldred—Oceanside, N.Y.

1914 **Newspaper Audit**—newspaper circulation audit—Audit Bureau of Circulations—formed—Chicago, Ill.

1923 **Aviation** — airways illumination — attempted

1928 **Television—Telecast**—puppet show to be televised—WOR—Newark, N.J.

1933 **Science Advisory Board**—first meeting

1959 **State**—noncontiguous overseas state—Hawaii—admitted

AUGUST 22

1654 **Jews** — Jew — arrived — New Netherlands—Jacob Barsimson

1670 **Indians**—Indian preacher—of Christianity—Hiacoomes—ordained

1762 **Woman**—woman newspaper editor—Ann Franklin—*Newport Mercury*—Newport, R.I.

1771 **Dwarf**—exhibited—Boston, Mass.

1818 **Ship**—steamboat built in America to cross the Atlantic Ocean—"Savannah" launched

1822 **Printing Press**—printing press for printing "paper hangings"—(wall paper)—patented—Peter Force—Washington, D.C.

1851 **Yacht Race**—yacht race (international)—won by "America"

1865 **Soap**—soap in liquid form—patented—William Sheppard—New York City

1902 **President**—President to ride in an automobile — Theodore Roosevelt — Hartford, Conn.

1906 **Phonograph**—phonograph with an enclosed horn in the cabinet—manufactured—Victor Victrola—Camden, N.J.

1909 **Aviation—Races**—airplane race won by an American in Europe—G. H. Curtiss—Rheims, France

1928 **Television—Telecast**—presidential nomination notification ceremony to be televised—A. E. Smith—Albany, N.Y.

1940 **Aviation — Airplane** — naval patrol bomber — "Mars" — keel laid — Baltimore, Md.

AUGUST 23

1838 **College**—college for women—Mount Holyoke Seminary, South Hadley, Mass.—graduation

1853 **Bank** — clearing house — organized—New York City

1859 **Elevator**—elevator in a hotel—opened—Fifth Avenue Hotel—New York City

1865 **War Criminal Proceedings**—Henry Wirz trial

1892 **Street Car**—transfers (printed)—J. H. Stedman—patented

1904 **Automobile Tire Chain**—patented—H. D. Weed—Canastota, N.Y.

1912 **Commerce Department (U.S.)**—Foreign and Domestic Commerce Bureau —created

1916 **Submarine**—cargo submarine to cross the Atlantic Ocean—"Deutschland" returned to Germany—from Baltimore, Md.

1923 **Hospital**—cancer hospital (municipal)—New York City Cancer Institute—New York City—patient admitted

1935 **Bank Legislation**—bank guaranty legislation—insurance limited to $5000

1956 **Helicopter Flight** — transcontinental non-stop helicopter flight—San Diego, Calif., to Washington, D.C.

AUGUST 24

1675 **Catholic Holy Orders**—conferred—St. Augustine, Fla.

1676 **Court Martial Trial** — court martial trial—Newport, R.I.

1830 **Educational Association** — educational association (national) — constitution adopted

1853 **Pharmacy Society (national)**—American Pharmaceutical Association—annual meeting—Boston, Mass.

1853 **Village Improvement Society**—organized—Stockbridge, Mass.

1869 **Waffle Iron Patent** — Cornelius Swarthout—Troy, N.Y.

1903 **Horse**—horse to trot a mile in less than two minutes—Lou Dillon—Readville, Mass.

1912 **Postal Service**—parcel post service—authorized

1912 **Ship** — electrically propelled ship of the U.S. Navy—"Jupiter"—launched—Mare Island, Calif.

1932 **Aviation — Flights (transcontinental)** —transcontinental non-stop flight by a woman—A. E. Putnam—left—Los Angeles, Calif.

1932 **Golf Champion** — holes-in-one by a father and son—C. H. Calhoun, Sr. and Jr.—Washington, Ga.

1935 **Labor**—Labor Relations Act (national)—board appointed

1942 **Naval Officer**—woman naval inspector — Mrs. Jean Hales — appointed—Berkeley, Calif.

1950 **Diplomatic Service**—Negro delegate to the United Nations from the United States—E. S. Sampson—appointed

1951 **Medal**—Air Force Medal of Honor for action in the Korean War—L. J. Sebile—medal presented posthumously—Riverside, Calif.

1959 **Congressman (U.S.)**—congressman of Japanese ancestry elected to the House of Representatives—D. K. Inouye—sworn in

1959 **Senator (U.S.)** — senator of Asian ancestry—Hiram Fong—sworn in

AUGUST 25

1814 **President**—President to face enemy gunfire while in office—James Madison—Bladensburg, Md.

1828 **Labor Party (political)**—labor party (state) — Workingmen's Party — convention—Philadelphia, Pa.

1830 **Locomotive**—race between a locomotive and a horse-drawn vehicle—Relay, Md., to Baltimore, Md.

1840 **Seeding Machine (practical)** — patented — Joseph Gibbons — Adrian, Mich.

1843 **Ship**—frigate (American-built, steam-driven) to cross the Atlantic Ocean—arrived at Gibraltar

1886 **Polo**—international polo series—England vs. United States—Newport, R.I.

1902 **Newspaper** — Arabic daily newspaper —*Al-Hoda*—New York City

1916 **Park Service (national)** — National Park Service—authorized

1920 **Aviation—Flights**—New York-Alaska flight—arrived—Nome, Alaska

1924 **Automobile Bus**—bus operated by a railroad—highway operations began—Oregon and Washington

1925 **Television Tube** — miniature tube — patented—H. W. Weinhart, Elizabeth, N.J.

1940 **Wedding**—parachute wedding — New York City

1958 **President (U.S.)**—pension for Presidents—enacted

AUGUST 26

1748 **Lutheran Church**—Lutheran services in English—synod held—Philadelphia, Pa.

1776 **Pension**—pension act of the Continental Congress

1790 **Historical Society**—historical society (state)—Massachusetts Historical Society—organized—Boston, Mass.

1843 **Typewriter**—typewriter that successfully typed—patented—Charles Thurber—Norwich, Conn.

1857 **Teachers' Convention**—teachers' convention (national)—National Teachers Association—organized — Philadelphia, Pa.

1858 **Cable**—news dispatch by cable—received—New York *Sun*

1873 **Kindergarten** — public school kindergarten—authorized—St. Louis, Mo.

1884 **Typesetting Machine** — linotype machine — patented — O. Mergenthaler—Baltimore, Md.

1890 **Pan American Union** — Pan American Union—W. E. Curtis appointed director

1895 **Niagara Falls**—utilization of Niagara Falls waterpower (large scale)—power transmitted commercially

1920 **Olympic Games**—woman (American) to win an Olympic competition—Ethelda Bleibtrey

1920 **Woman Suffrage** — woman suffrage amendment approved by Congress—proclamation signed — Secretary of State Bainbridge Colby

1938 **Tape Recording** — radio broadcast from a tape recording—WQXR—New York City

1939 **Television—Telecast**—baseball games (major league) televised—Cincinnati Reds-Brooklyn Dodgers—New York City

1953 **Medal**—Medal of Honor awarded to a Nisei in the Korean War—H. H. Miyamura

1955 **Television—Telecast** — tennis tournament to be televised in color—Davis Cup matches—Forest Hills, N.Y.

AUGUST 27

1640 **College** — college — Henry Dunster —served Harvard University, Cambridge, Mass., as president

1650 **Expedition** — expedition — of Englishmen to cross Allegheny Mountains

1665 **Play (drama)**—play given by non-professional actors—*Ye Bare and Ye Cubb* —produced—Accawmack, Va.

1776 **Land Grant**—offered by Continental Congress to officers

1787 **Ship**—steamboat to carry a man—John Fitch—Delaware River

1856 **Manual Training** — industrial school for girls—incorporated as a state institution—Lancaster, Mass.

1858 **Cable**—news dispatch by cable—published—New York *Sun*

1859 **Oil**—oil well commercially productive —discovered—Titusville, Pa.

1867 **Railroad Crossing Gate Patent**—patent awarded—Boston, Mass.

1881 **Pure Food Law**—pure food and drug legislation (state) — effective — New York

1889 **Clarinet**—made exclusively of metal—patented—C. G. Conn—Elkhart, Ind.

1894 **Tax**—federal income tax—declared unconstitutional

1910 **Radio Broadcast**—radio broadcast sent from an airplane—J. A. Macready

1915 **Automobile Bus**—bus with cross seats —single-deck bus—New York City

1932 **Autogiro**—autogiro to loop the loop publicly—J. M. Miller—Cleveland, Ohio

1959 **Ship**—ship to fire a Polaris missile— "Observation Island"

AUGUST 28

1784 **Ship**—trading ship sent to China— "Empress of China"—arrived—Canton, China

1798 **Vineyard (successful)** — established— J. J. Dufour—Lexington, Ky.

1830 **Locomotive**—locomotive built in the United States to pull passengers— "Tom Thumb"—Baltimore, Md.

1838 **Music Instruction**—music instruction (public schools) — appointment of teacher authorized

1862 **Engraving and Printing Bureau (U.S.)**—operations began

1864 **Postal Service**—railroad post office for the general distribution of mail—service tested—Chicago, Ill., to Clinton, Iowa

1894 **Steel**—manganese steel for railroad tracks—manufactured — High Bridge, N.J.

1897 **Horse**—horse to pace better than 2:00—Star Pointer—Readville, Mass.

1911 **Gyro Compass** — gyro compass installed on an American naval vessel—"Delaware"—tested at sea

1919 **Actors' Union** — Associated Actors and Artists of America—incorporated

1922 **Golf Tournament**—international golf match—for Walker Cup—Southampton, N.Y.

1922 **Radio Broadcast**—advertising or commercial radio broadcast—WEAF—New York City

1938 **Degrees (academic and honorary)**—degree awarded a ventriloquist's dummy — Northwestern University — Evanston, Ill.

AUGUST 29

1758 **Indian Reservation**—Indian reservation (state) — established — Indian Mills, N.J.

1817 **Newspaper** — abolition newspaper — *Philanthropist*—published—Mt. Pleasant, Ohio

1828 **Brake Patent**—brake patent—Robert Turner—Ward, Mass.

1850 **Museum** — college museum — curator authorized—Charleston, S.C.

1866 **Railroad**—cog railroad—public demonstration—Mount Washington, N.H.

1885 **Prize Fight**—prize fight of importance under the Marquis of Queensberry rules—Cincinnati, Ohio

1889 **Tennis Match**—professional lawn tennis contest (international)—Newport Casino—Newport, R.I.

1892 **Baseball Player**—baseball player to catch a ball dropped from the Washington Monument — Billy ("Pop") Schriver—Washington, D.C.

1896 **Chop Suey** — concocted — New York City

1916 **Aviation**—Coast Guard aviation unit—authorized

1916 **Ship**—ambulance ship designed and built as a hospital—"Relief"—authorized

1920 **Aviation—Flights**—New York-Alaska flight—expedition left Nome, Alaska

1929 **Aviation — Passenger** — dirigible passenger transfer to an airplane—A. W. Gorton—Cleveland, Ohio

1934 **Bird Sanctuary** — Hawk Mountain Sanctuary—Drehersville, Pa.—options received

1938 **Building**—building devoted entirely to highway traffic — cornerstone laid — Saugatuck, Conn.

1950 **Tennis Match**—national tennis tournament of the United States Lawn Tennis Association in which a Negro woman competed—Forest Hills, N.Y.

1958 **Air Force Academy (U.S.)**—Air Force Academy—Colorado Springs, Colo.—received first Air Force cadets

AUGUST 30

1637 **Congregational Church** — Congregational Church council — Cambridge, Mass.

1842 **Narcotic**—narcotic tariff—enacted

1842 **Tariff**—tariff to prevent the importation of obscene literature and pictures—enacted

1875 **Music Instruction** — college music chair—established — Harvard University—Cambridge, Mass.

1890 **Meat Inspection Legislation (federal)**—enacted

1909 **Continuation School**—apprentice continuation school—established—Cincinnati, Ohio

1926 **Horse Race** — harness horse race (Hambletonian) for three-year-olds—Syracuse, N.Y.

1929 **Automobile** — automobile (new type gasoline-electric combination) delivered—E. H. R. Green—Schenectady, N.Y.

1929 **Submarine "Lung"** — tested — U.S. Navy

1931 **Aviation — Races** — airplane race (of importance) in which both men and women were contestants — Los Angeles, Calif., to Cleveland, Ohio

1961 **Judge** — Negro judge of a District Court (U.S.) — J. B. Parsons — confirmed

AUGUST 31

1809 **Catholic Magazine** — Catholic magazine in English—*Michigan Essay* — Detroit, Mich.

1826 **Ship**—warship to circumnavigate the globe—"Vincennes"—left—New York City

1842 **Navy**—Bureau of Medicine and Surgery—authorized

1842 **Nut and Bolt Machine** — Micah Rugg—patent

1852 **Postage Stamp** — stamped envelopes (U.S.)—authorized

1853 **Bank**—clearing house—plan presented—New York City

1881 **Tennis Match**—lawn tennis national championship matches—Newport, R.I.

1886 **Earthquake**—of importance—Charleston, S.C.

1910 **Aviation—Flights**—over-water flight—G. H. Curtiss — Cleveland-Sandusky, Ohio

1920 **Radio Broadcast** — election returns broadcast—Detroit, Mich.

1920 **Radio Broadcast**—news program—Detroit, Mich.

1935 **Skeet** — national skeet tournament — Indianapolis, Ind.

1955 **Automobile**—sun-powered automobile —demonstrated—Chicago, Ill.

1955 **Television Station** — microwave television station — KTRE-TV — Lufkin, Tex.

SEPTEMBER 1

1803 **Tract Society**—tract society—Massachusetts Society for Promoting Christian Knowledge—instituted—Boston, Mass.

1808 **Religious Publication** — religious review—*Herald of Gospel Liberty*—published—Portsmouth, N.H.

1819 **Plow** — plow with interchangeable parts—patented—J. J. Wood—Poplar Ridge, N.Y.

1836 **Colonist**—women to cross the continent—reached Fort Walla Walla, Wash.

1855 **Book Trade Magazine** — successful book trade magazine—*American Publishers' Circular and Literary Gazette*—New York City

1859 **Sleeping Car**—Pullman sleeping car—in service—Bloomington, Ill., to Chicago, Ill.

1862 **Tobacco** — tobacco tax for internal revenue—effective

1869 **Postal Service**—money order system agreement effective—Switzerland

1878 **Telephone Operator** — woman telephone operator—E. M. Nutt—Boston, Mass.

1880 **Tennis Match**—lawn tennis tournament of national scope—Staten Island, N.Y.

1887 **Accident Report**—industrial accident reports—law effective—Massachusetts

1890 **Single Tax**—single tax national conference—New York City

1894 **Health Laboratory**—health laboratory (state)—Providence, R.I.

1897 **Subway**—municipal subway — opened for traffic—Boston, Mass.

1898 **Forestry School**—forestry school dealing exclusively with problems of forestry—Biltmore Forest School—Biltmore, N.C.

1907 **Court** — night court — opened — New York City

1907 **Tunnel**—freight delivery tunnel system—completed—Chicago, Ill.

1910 **Woman**—woman horseback rider to make a solo transcontinental trip—N. J. Aspinwall—left—San Francisco, Calif.

1913 **Civic Design Chair**—C. M. Robinson served—Urbana, Ill.

1916 **Bird Legislation (international)**—migratory bird treaty—ratified

1916 **Child Labor Law**—child labor law (federal)—enacted

1916 **Road** — federal grant-in-aid — project approved

1917 **Child Labor Law**—child labor law (federal)—in force

1919 **Communist Labor Party of America** —convention—Chicago, Ill.

1920 **Aviation—Airplane**—airplane used by a newspaper—*Sun*—Baltimore, Md.

1920 **Postal Service**—postage meter—approved

1922 **Radio Broadcast** — news program (daily)—broadcast—New York City

1925 **Electric Lighting**—glass light bulb machine—patented—B. D. Chamberlin—Washington, D.C.

1931 **Anthropology Laboratory**—opened— Sante Fe, N.M.

1948 **Air Mail Service**—parcel post domestic air service—began

1948 **Supreme Court (U.S.)**—Negro clerk of the Supreme Court—W. T. Coleman—appointed

1949 **Bicycle Trip**—bicycle rider to cross the continent in less than three weeks — Eugene McPherson — left Santa Monica, Calif.

1954 **Television**—Telecast—prize fight in a "studio"—Philadelphia, Pa.

1955 **Ship**—roll-on roll-off carrier—in service—Hyannis and Nantucket, Mass.

SEPTEMBER 2

1775 **Ship**—warship regularly commissioned —"Hannah"—Marblehead, Mass.

1789 **Comptroller** — comptroller of the United States Treasury — office authorized

1789 **Treasury Department (U.S.)**—Treasury Department (U.S.)—organized

1858 **Cigar Band**—cigar band of special interest—C. W. Field—New York City

1884 **Electrical Show** — exhibition — Philadelphia, Pa.

1895 **College**—Catholic college for women —College of Notre Dame of Maryland—Baltimore, Md.—opened

1914 **Insurance**—war risk insurance bureau —established

1919 **Communist Party of America**—formed —Chicago, Ill.

1930 **Aviation** — Flights (transatlantic) — transatlantic non-stop flight from Europe to the United States—Coste and Bellonte arrived—Valley Stream, N.Y.

1936 **Aviation** — Flights (transatlantic) — transatlantic round-trip flight from the United States — Richard Merrill and Harry Richman—left—New York City

1937 **Game Preserve**—game preserve appropriation (federal)—enacted

1938 **Railroad Car** — car with fluorescent lighting—in service—New York Central

1952 **Surgical Operation** — heart operation in which the deep freezing technique was employed—F. J. Lewis

SEPTEMBER 3

1639 **Lawyer**—lawyer disbarred—Thomas Lechford—Massachusetts

1777 Flag—American flag flown in battle—Cooch's Bridge, Del.

1783 Treaty — treaty between the United States Government and a nation with which it had been at war—signed—Paris, France

1833 Newspaper—penny daily newspaper—New York *Sun* — published—successful

1872 Presidential Candidate — presidential candidate who was a Catholic—Charles O'Conor—nominated

1885 Naval War College—Naval War College—opened

1890 Single Tax—single tax national conference — platform adopted — New York City

1894 Golf Tournament — national championship stroke-play golf match — Newport, R.I.

1895 Football Game — professional football game—Latrobe, Pa.

1898 Subway—municipal subway — opened to North Station—Boston, Mass.

1900 Union Reform Party — convention — Baltimore, Md.

1919 Army Officer—General of the Armies of the United States—rank authorized

1934 Salvation Army—woman commander of the Salvation Army — Elizabeth Booth

1935 Automobile — automobile to exceed the speed of 300 miles an hour—Sir Malcolm Campbell — Bonneville Salt Flats, Utah

1935 Brokerage — woman stock exchange member (commodity exchange) — admitted—New York Cocoa Exchange—New York City

1936 Aviation — Flights (transatlantic) — transatlantic round-trip flight from the United States — Richard Merrill and Harry Richman—arrived—Wales

1940 Ship—navy vessel constructed as a minelayer—"Terror"—keel laid—Philadelphia, Pa.

1940 Television—Telecast—color television demonstration of high-definition electronically scanned images—New York City

1955 State Department (U.S.) — woman Acting Assistant Secretary of State—Florence Kirlin

1958 War (Quemoy) — American casualty of the Red Chinese bombardment—G. W. Johnston

SEPTEMBER 4

1645—Lutheran Church—Lutheran Church building—dedicated—Essington, Pa.

1777 Flag—American flag on the high seas —"Raleigh"—encounter with a British vessel

1813 Religious Publication—religious weekly newspaper—*Religious Remembrancer* —published—Philadelphia, Pa.

1820 Military School—military school—first class—enrolled—Norwich, Vt.

1833 Newsboy — Barney Flaherty — New York City

1856 Flag—American flag raised in Japan —flown

1877 Library Society—library association (national)—American Library Association—annual convention—New York City

1882 Electric Company—electric station (central) to supply light and power—Edison Electric Illuminating Company —New York City

1885 Restaurant—self-service restaurant—Exchange Buffet—opened—New York City

1888 Camera—roll film camera—patented—George Eastman—Rochester, N.Y.

1906 Election Law—primary election (statewide)—Wisconsin

1908 Automobile Tire — non-skid tire — patent applied for

1917 World War I—American Army soldiers killed in World War I—Dannes, France

1919 Army Officer—General of the Armies of the United States—J. J. Pershing confirmed

1921 Radio Broadcast—police broadcast—St. Louis, Mo.

1923 Aviation—Airship—dirigible (American-built rigid)—ZR1—tested—Lakehurst, N.J.

1933 Aviation—Flights—airplane to exceed the speed of 300 miles per hour—J. R. Wedell—Glenview, Ill.

1935 Automobile Truck—automobile truck completely streamlined — Cleveland, Ohio

1935 Labor—Labor Relations Act (national)—National Labor Relations Board—first meeting

1936 Aviation — Airplane — hydroplane of stainless steel—"Sea Bird"—tested—Bristol, Pa.

1937 Bicycle Racer—woman bicycle champion of the National Amateur Bicycle Association—Doris Kopsky—Buffalo, N.Y.

1948 Air Mail Service—parcel post international air service—inaugurated—to South America

1950 Helicopter—helicopter rescue of an American pilot behind enemy lines—Paul Van Boven

1951—Television—Telecast — telecast using coaxial cable—coast-to-coast transmission

1951 Television—Telecast—transcontinental telecast received on the east coast—from San Francisco, Calif.

SEPTEMBER 5

1721 Art Commission (public)—order given —Gustavus Hesselius—Maryland

1774 Continental Congress — Continental Congress—assembled — Philadelphia, Pa.

1774 President of the Continental Congress—Peyton Randolph—Virginia—elected

1776 Navy—naval uniforms (standardized)—adopted

1836 President of the Republic of Texas—Sam Houston—elected

1853 Village Improvement Society—Laurel Hill Association—Stockbridge, Mass.—incorporated

1854 Publishing Society—Seventy-Six Society—organized—Philadelphia, Pa.

1882 Holiday—Labor Day holiday parade—New York City

1883 Civil Service—Civil Service woman appointee—M. F. Hoyt—appointed

1885 Pump—gasoline pump—delivered—S. F. Bowser—Fort Wayne, Ind.

1901 Baseball League—baseball league association—National Association of Professional Baseball Leagues—organized—Chicago, Ill.

1923 Smoke Screen—demonstrated—Cape Hatteras, N.C.

1925 Golf Champion—golf champion to win the United States National Amateur Tournament two years in succession—R. T. Jones

1925 Photography—demonstration of rapid aerial photography — Fort Leavenworth, Kan.

1934 Aviation—floating seaplane ramp (municipally owned) — dedicated — New York City

1943 Aviation—airplane human pick-up—Wilmington, Ohio

1953 Atomic Reactor—atomic reactor (privately operated)—Raleigh, N.C.

1958 Tape Recording—video recording on magnetic tape in color—Charlotte, N.C.

SEPTEMBER 6

1810 Colonist—colonists to reach the Pacific coast—left New York City

1819 Lathe—patented—Thomas Blanchard—Middlebury, Conn.

1837 College—coeducational college—Oberlin Collegiate Institute—Oberlin, Ohio—equal status to women

1866 Political Convention—Negro delegate to a national political convention—Frederick Douglass—Philadelphia, Pa.

1882 Bicycle Trip—bicycle trip of 100 miles sponsored by a club—Worcester to Boston, Mass.—Boston Bicycle Club

1892 Automobile Tractor—gasoline tractor—sold—John Froelich—Froelich, Iowa

1909 Expedition—polar expedition of which a woman was a member—North Pole discovery announced

1919 Actors' Union—strike settled

1920 Radio Broadcast—prize fight broadcast—WWJ—Detroit, Mich.

1947 Ship—ship from which a long-range rocket was launched—"Midway"

1954 Electric Power Plant—atomic electric generating station (full scale)—ground breaking—Shippingport, Pa.

1958 Pipeline — pipeline (interstate) to transport ethylene—in operation—Orange, Tex.

SEPTEMBER 7

1724 Baptist Church—German Baptists—Coventry Congregation

1774 Continental Congress — Continental Congress to be opened with prayer—Philadelphia, Pa.

1776 Submarine—submarine built for use in war—"American Turtle"—attempt to sink "Eagle"

1797 Ship—ship to capture an enemy ship after the Revolution—"Constellation"—launched—Baltimore, Md.

1822 Treadmill — completed — New York City

1876 Piano Player—piano player—patent application — John McTammany — Cambridge, Mass.

1880 Trapshooting—clay pigeon target—patent—George Ligowsky—Cincinnati, Ohio

1888 Incubator for Infants — used — New York City

1892 Prize Fight—prize fight of importance under the Marquis of Queensberry rules—Sullivan-Corbett—New Orleans, La.

1896 Automobile Race—automobile race on a track—Cranston, R.I.

1899 Automobile Parade—Newport, R.I.

1903 Motorcycle Association — Federation of American Motorcyclists—organized—Manhattan Beach, N.Y.

1908 Esperanto Club—Esperanto club (national organization) — organized — Chautauqua Lake, N.Y.

1916 Shipping — United States Shipping Board—authorized

1923 Electric Generator — mercury boiler turbine—installed—Hartford, Conn.

1927 Boat Race—international lifeboat race—New York City

1936 Medical Congress — cancer institute (convention)—Madison, Wis.

1948 Road—synthetic rubber in an asphaltic concrete resurfacing mixture—Akron, Ohio

SEPTEMBER 8

1565 Catholic Parish—St. Augustine, Fla.

1565 Colonist—permanent white settlement—founded—St. Augustine, Fla.

1636 College—college—Harvard College—appropriation—Cambridge, Mass.

1729 Jewish Congregation—Jewish congregation—foundation stones laid—Shearith Israel—New York City

1866 Births—sextuplets — born — Bushnell family—Chicago, Ill.

1868 **Sports** — athletic club — organized — New York City

1879 **Ship**—steam whaler built as a whale boat — "Mary and Helen" — built — Bath, Me.—registered—New Bedford, Mass.

1920 **Air Mail Service**—air mail transcontinental service — (combination airplane-railroad)—New York to San Francisco, Calif.

1939 **Autogiro**—autogiro rotary wing aircraft fellowship—S. B. Sherwin—enrolled

1945 **Radio Telephone** — two-way radio equipped bus—in service—Washington, D.C.

1948 **Air Force Officer**—Judge Advocate General of the U.S. Air Force—R. C. Harmon—nominated

1953 **Automobile Bus**—transcontinental no-change bus service—instituted—New York City to San Francisco, Calif.

SEPTEMBER 9

1753 **Steam Engine**—steam engine—Josiah Hornblower—arrived

1776 **United States**—"United States"—authorized

1830 **Balloon Flight** — balloon flight by a native-born American—C. F. Durant —New York City

1833 **Drydock** — federal drydocks—Boston drydock—delivery accepted

1841 **Ship**—iron vessel built for the United States Navy—"Michigan"—authorized

1850 **State**—state admitted to the union on the Pacific coast—California

1885 **Economics Association** — American Economic Association — founded — Saratoga, N.Y.

1886 **Copyright Law** — international copyright agreement—convention at Berne, Switzerland

1893 **Births** — child born in the White House, Washington, D.C., the offspring of a President—Esther Cleveland—born

1895 **Bowling Rule Standardization** — convention—American Bowling Congress —New York City

1895 **Bowling Tournament** — bowling convention — of importance — American Bowling Congress—New York City

1898 **Log Rolling (Birling) National Championship**—Omaha, Neb.

1901 **Automobile Hill Climbing Contest** — Peekskill, N.Y.

1901 **Automobile Race** — automobile race (long distance)—New York City to Buffalo, N.Y.

1908 **Aviation — Passenger** — airplane passenger (official)—F. P. Lahm—Fort Myer, Va.

1908 **Aviation—Flights**—airplane endurance flight exceeding one hour—Fort Myer, Va.

1914 **Ship**—steamboat to pass through the Panama Canal — army transport — "Buford"

1929 **Konel**—announced—Pittsburgh, Pa.

1942 **World War II** — bombing on continental American soil—Mount Emily, Ore.

1959 **Diplomatic Service** — ambassador to Nepal—H. E. Stebbins—confirmed

SEPTEMBER 10

1785 **Treaty**—treaty entered into by the United States after the treaty of peace —with Prussia—signed at The Hague

1794 **College** — non-denominational college — Blount College — Knoxville, Tenn. —chartered

1813 **War (1812)**—defeat in history of a British squadron—O. H. Perry

1815 **Ship** — steamboat (double decked) — "Washington" — keel laid—Wheeling, W.Va.

1862 **Army Officer**—chaplain (Jewish) of the U.S. Army—Jacob Frankel appointed

1875 **Forestry Society** — national forestry association—American Forestry Association—organized—Chicago, Ill.

1884 **Historical Society**—historical society (general)—American Historical Association—founded—Saratoga, N.Y.

1889 **Freemasons** — Grotto—formal organization—Hamilton, N.Y.

1913 **Road** — coast-to-coast paved road — Lincoln Highway — proclamation of opening

1923 **Moving Picture**—moving picture of an eclipse of the sun taken from an airplane—Santa Catalina, Calif.

1942 **Aviation**—Women's Auxiliary Ferrying Squadron—N. H. Love—appointed

1951 **Woman**—American woman to swim the English Channel from both coasts —Florence Chadwick — England to France

SEPTEMBER 11

1723 **Physician**—doctor to receive an honorary medical degree—Daniel Turner —New Haven, Conn.

1789 **Comptroller** — Comptroller of the United States Treasury — Nicholas Eveleigh—served

1789 **Internal Revenue Commissioner** — Commissioner of the Revenue—Tench Coxe—served

1789 **Treasury Department (U.S.)**—Secretary of the Treasury—Alexander Hamilton—appointed

1789 **War Department (U.S.)** — War Department (U.S.) — Secretary—Henry Knox—appointed

1812 **Russian Settlement**—dedicated—Cazadero, Calif.

1841 **Tube** — collapsible tube—patented—John Rand

1850 **Railroad Car**—private railroad car—Jenny Lind—appearance at Castle Garden—New York City

1850 **Ticket Speculators**—Jenny Lind—appearance at Castle Garden—New York City

1862 **Brokerage**—exchange to specialize in mining securities — San Francisco, Calif.

1875 **Cartoon** — newspaper cartoon strip—*Daily Graphic*—New York City

1883 **Postal Service**—mail chute—patented—J. G. Cutler—Rochester, N.Y.

1910 **Street Car**—trackless trolley system—operated—Laurel Canyon, Calif.

1928 **Automobile Bus**—coast to coast through bus line—operated—Los Angeles, Calif., to New York City

1928 **Television**—**Telecast**—play to be televised—*The Queen's Messenger*—Schenectady, N.Y.

1933 **Federal Deposit Insurance Corporation**—directors met

1946 **Telephone**—mobile long distance car-to-car telephone conversation—Houston, Tex., to St. Louis, Mo.

1947 **Isotope**—radioactive isotopes exported—Oak Ridge, Tenn.—received at Canberra, Australia

1948 **Air Mail Service**—parcel post international air service — inaugurated — to Pacific area

1950 **Typesetting Machine**—typesetting machine to dispense with metal type—exhibited—Chicago, Ill.

1952 **Surgical Operation**—artificial aortic valve—C. A. Hufnagel—Washington, D.C.

1953 **Television Station**—television stations to share the same time and frequency—Salinas, Calif., and Monterey, Calif.

SEPTEMBER 12

1789 **War Department (U.S.)**—War Department (U.S.)—Secretary Henry Knox—served

1793 **Health Board**—health board (local)—quarantine imposed—Baltimore, Md.

1808 **Bible**—Bible translated into English in America—copyrighted

1866 **Play (drama)**—burlesque show—of importance—*The Black Crook*—New York City

1869 **Prohibition Party (national)**—organized—Chicago, Ill.

1873 **Typewriter**—typewriter that was practical—Sholes machine — completed — Ilion, N.Y.

1916 **Motorcycle Trip**—motorcycle transcontinental trip by a woman—arrived—San Diego, Calif.

1918 **Army Armored Tank**—used—St. Mihiel, France

1941 **World War II**—German ship captured in World War II—"Busko"—captured

1952 **Railroad Car** — "compartmentizer" freight cars—in service between Chicago, Ill., and San Francisco, Calif.

1956 **Coal**—commercial coal pipeline—completed—Eastlake, Ohio

SEPTEMBER 13

1788 **Election** — federal election in the United States

1789 **Loan**—loan to the United States

1791 **Academy**—University of Pennsylvania and College Academy and Charitable School of Philadelphia—united

1814 **National Anthem**—"Star Spangled Banner"—written—F. S. Key

1826 **Animals**—rhinoceros—exhibited—New York City

1842 **Prize Fight**—prize fight fatality—Hastings, N.Y.

1853 **Bank**—clearing house—plans adopted

1882 **Country Club**—country club to remain in existence eighty years—Country Club—Brookline, Mass.—organized

1898 **Photographic Film**—celluloid photographic film—patent—H. W. Goodwin—Newark, N.J.

1899 **Automobile Fatality**—H. H. Bliss killed—New York City

1925 **College**—Negro university (Catholic)—Xavier University—New Orleans, La.—college department opened

1928 **Railroad Car**—rail detector car—demonstrated—Poughkeepsie, N.Y.

1936 **Aviation** — **Flights (transatlantic)** — transatlantic round trip flight—return trip — Southport, England — Richard Merrill and Harry Richman

1948 **High School**—public high school to specialize in the performing field—New York City

1948 **Senator (U.S.)**—woman senator elected without having previously served an appointed term—M. C. Smith—Maine

1954 **National Security Council**—national security council meeting held outside Washington, D.C.

1956 **Taconite**—taconite — large-scale commercial project—Silver Bay, Minn.

SEPTEMBER 14

1716 **Lighthouse**—lighthouse — kindled — Little Brewster Island, Mass.

1778 **Diplomatic Service**—minister plenipotentiary—Benjamin Franklin—elected

1861 **Civil War**—naval engagement in the Civil War—Pensacola, Fla.—"Colorado" *vs.* "Judah"

1886 **Typewriter Ribbon**—typewriter ribbon patent — G. K. Anderson — Memphis, Tenn.

1892 **Bacteriology Laboratory**—bacteriology diagnostic laboratory—H. M. Biggs—served—New York City

1908 **Journalism Course**—journalism school—University of Missouri—Columbia, Mo.

1909 **Election Law**—preferential ballot system—charter adopted—Grand Junction, Colo.

1910 **Aviation—Airport** — airport municipal legislation—ratified—Modesto, Calif.

1915—**Sound Absorbing Material**—patent—C. G. Muench—St. Paul, Minn.

1922 **Aviation — Flights (transcontinental)** —transcontinental dirigible flight (non-rigid dirigible)—C2—left Newport News, Va.

1929 **Horse Race**—horse to win a $100,000 purse in one race—Whichone—Belmont, N.Y.

1936 **Art Course**—art course—fresco painting—Louisiana State University—University, La.

1940 **Conscription** — peacetime conscription bill—enacted

1956 **Surgical Operation**—lobotomy (prefrontal)—J. W. Watts and Walter Freeman—Washington, D.C.

SEPTEMBER 15

1777 **Catholic Funeral**—Catholic funeral attended by the U.S. Continental Congress—Tronson du Coudray—drowned

1812 **Political Convention**—political nominating caucus — Democratic-Republican Party—New York City

1817 **Iron**—iron mill to puddle and roll iron—in operation—Redstone Creek, Pa.

1830 **Negro**—national colored convention—Philadelphia, Pa.

1843 **Ship**—naval vessel of the United States to sail around the Cape of Good Hope to the west coast of the United States—anchored at Monterey Bay, Calif., on return voyage

1847 **Labor Law**—ten-hour-day law—effective—New Hampshire

1853 **Librarians' Convention**—New York City

1853 **Woman**—woman ordained a minister —A. B. Blackwell—South Butler, N.Y.

1857 **Typesetting Machine**—typesetting machine — patented — Timothy Alden — New York City

1858 **Postal Service**—overland mail service —Tipton, Mo., and San Francisco, Calif.

1863 **Habeas Corpus**—habeas corpus suspension order—proclamation suspending habeas corpus during military strife—Abraham Lincoln

1890 **Architect**—woman architect — elected —American Institute of Architects—L. B. Bethune

1896 **Hospital**—cancer home for incurables (free)—established—New York City

1901 **Architectural School**—landscape architecture course for women—Groton, Mass.

1913 **Goat Show**—of importance—Rochester, N.Y.

1929 **Aviation** — airplane "fly-it-yourself" system—started—Kansas City, Kan.

1930 **Mortuary** — cooperative — opened — Toledo, Ohio

1934 **Radio Broadcast** — musical comedy broadcast — *The Gibson Family* — New York City

1939 **College**—woman dean of a graduate school—F. Wunderlich—took office—New York City

1947 **Aviation — Airplane** — jet propelled fighter airplane (four-engine)—tested —Columbus, Ohio

1953 **Submarine**—submarine powered by a liquid metal-cooled atomic reactor—"Seawolf"—laid down

1955 **Cantor**—Jewish woman cantor—Betty Robbins — first service — Oceanside, N.Y.

1957 **Telephone**—air-to-ground public telephone service—Chicago-Detroit area

SEPTEMBER 16

1833 **Crime Prevention and Detection**—interstate crime pact—signed by New York and New Jersey

1891 **Woman**—white woman to become an Indian chief—H. M. Converse—Six Nations tribe

1908 **Esperanto Course**—Esperanto course carrying college credit—Clark University, Worcester, Mass.

1912 **Quarantine**—plant quarantine legislation (national) — white-pine blister rust quarantine effective

1918 **Aviation—Flights** — airplane altitude flight to exceed 28,000 feet—R. W. Schroeder—Fairfield, Ohio

1919 **War Veterans' Society**—American Legion—incorporated

1923 **Catholic Seminary**—for education of Negro priests—dedicated—Bay St. Louis, Miss.

1946 **College**—college principally for war veterans—opened—Plattsburg, N.Y.

1947 **Automobile**—automobile to exceed the speed of 400 miles an hour—Bonneville, Utah

SEPTEMBER 17

1607 **Slander Proceedings** — instituted — Jamestown, Va.

1777 **Catholic Funeral**—Catholic funeral attended by the U.S. Continental Congress—Philadelphia, Pa.

1778 **Treaty**—treaty entered into by the United States with Indian tribes—Delaware nations

1787 **Constitution of the United States**—Constitution (federal)—signed—Philadelphia, Pa.

1792 **Protestant Episcopal Bishop**—Protestant Episcopal bishop consecrated in the United States—T. J. Claggett consecrated

1844 **Printing Press**—printing press for polychromatic printing—patented—T. F. Adams

1861 School—Negro school for freedmen—established—Fortress Monroe, Va.

1872 Sprinkler—sprinkler system patent—P. W. Pratt—Abington, Mass.

1895 Ship — battleship of importance — "Maine"—commissioned

1901 Electric Lighting — mercury vapor lamp—patent — P. C. Hewitt — New York City

1908 Aviation — airplane fatality — Fort Myer, Va.

1911 Aviation — Flights (transcontinental)—transcontinental airplane flight—C. P. Rodgers—take-off Sheepshead Bay, N.Y.

1920 Football Club — football association (professional)—formed—Canton, Ohio

1938 Building—building built inside a factory—towed across Illinois River

1942 Dental Corps (U.S. Army)—Army Dental Corps Major General—R. H. Mills

1947 Defense Department (U.S.)—J. V. Forrestal—sworn in

1953 Siamese Twins—Siamese twins separated successfully by surgery—operation performed

SEPTEMBER 18

1634 Club Woman—Anne Hutchinson—arrived—Boston, Mass.

1679 Ship—Great Lakes commercial vessel —"Le Griffon"—sank

1769 Piano—piano—John Harris—described in newspaper—Boston, Mass.

1793 Capitol (of the United States)—cornerstone laid—Washington, D.C.

1883 Diplomatic Service—Korean embassy —received at Washington, D.C.

1895 Chiropractor—D. D. Palmer—adjustment treatment

1901 Commission Form of Government—operated—Galveston, Tex.

1915 Automobile Race Track—automobile race track (asphalt covered)—opened —Cranston, R.I.

1918 Aviation — Flights—airplane altitude flight to exceed 28,000 feet—R. W. Schroeder—Fairfield, Ohio

1932 Greek College and Orphanage—dedicated—Gastonia, N.C.

1937 Skywriting—skywriting at night—exhibited—Andy Stinis—New York City

1947 Air Force—Air Force Secretary—W. S. Symington—sworn in—Washington, D.C.

1947 Defense Department (U.S.)—Secretary of the Navy and Secretary for Air—sworn in

1948 Medical Society—woman president of a state medical society—L. S. Kent

SEPTEMBER 19

1772 Protestant Church—Protestant church — west of Pennsylvania — Schoenbrunn, Ohio

1787 Constitution of the United States—Constitution of the United States was first published—in a newspaper—*Pennsylvania Packet and Daily Advertiser*—Philadelphia, Pa.

1838 Brake Patent—railroad brake patent—Ephraim Morris—Bloomfield, N.J.

1854 Sleeping Car—sleeping car patent—H. B. Myer—Buffalo, N.Y.

1876 Carpet Sweeper—patent—M. R. Bissell—Grand Rapids, Mich.

1891 Tunnel — subaqueous railroad tunnel to a foreign country — Port Huron, Mich., to Sarnia, Ontario

1898 Forestry School—forestry school of collegiate character — established — Cornell University—Ithaca, N.Y.

1928 Aviation — airplane Diesel engine — tested—Detroit, Mich.

1928 Moving Picture — animated cartoon talking picture—*Steamboat Willie*—exhibited—New York City

1951 Valeteria—displayed—Cleveland, Ohio

SEPTEMBER 20

1565 War (colonial) — intercolonial war — Fort Caroline, Fla.

1848 Science Association—scientific society (national organization)—American Association for the Advancement of Science—organized—Philadelphia, Pa.

1850 Hospital — homeopathic hospital — Homeopathic Hospital of Pennsylvania — Philadelphia, Pa. — incorporated

1850 Land Grant—railroad land grant of importance—authorized

1853 Railroad Station—union passenger station—opened—Indianapolis, Ind.

1859 Electric Stove — electric range—patented—G. B. Simpson—Washington, D.C.

1860 Visiting Celebrities—Prince of Wales —arrived—Detroit, Mich.

1884 Equal Rights Party — formed — San Francisco, Calif.

1892 Glass—wire glass — patented — Frank Schuman—Philadelphia, Pa.

1915 Chiropody School—chiropody school as a regular division of a university —opened—Temple University—Philadelphia, Pa.

1916 Science Association — National Research Council—first meeting — New York City

1946 Television—Telecast—moving picture trailer to be televised—New York City

1951 Aviation—Flights — North Pole jet crossing—Fairbanks, Alaska

SEPTEMBER 21

1782 Bible—Bible printed in English—authorized by Congress

1784 Newspaper—daily newspaper—*Pennsylvania Packet and Daily Advertiser*—Philadelphia, Pa.

1872 **Naval Academy**—Negro midshipman in the United States Naval Academy —J. H. Conyers

1875 **Gas**—water gas production—patent— T. S. C. Lowe—Norristown, Pa.

1883 **Engineering College**—electrical engineering course—Cornell University— Ithaca, N.Y.

1895 **Automobile Company**—Duryea Motor Wagon Company — incorporated — Springfield, Mass.

1949 **Bicycle Trip**—bicycle rider to cross the continent in less than three weeks —Eugene McPherson—arrived—New York City

1954 **Submarine** — atomic-powered submarine—"Nautilus"—commissioned

1958 **Aviation—Flights**—airplane endurance flight exceeding 1,200 hours — Jim Heth and Bill Burkhart — landed— Dallas, Tex.

SEPTEMBER 22

1656 **Jury**—jury composed of women—Patuxent, Md.

1734 **Moravian**—George Boehnisch—arrived

1789 **Post Office**—Post Office Department of the United States—established

1789 **Postmaster** — postmaster general of the United States—office authorized

1851 **Telegraph**—telegraph in railroading— Goshen, N.Y.

1862 **Emancipation Proclamation (preliminary)**—Abraham Lincoln

1890 **Business School**—business high school —opened—Washington, D.C.

1926 **Book Course** — instruction — Rollins College—Winter Park, Fla.

1945 **Horse Race**—race track at which more than $5,000,000 was bet in one day— Belmont Park, N.Y.

1947 **Aviation—Airplane** — transatlantic robot pilotless airplane—take-off—Newfoundland

1950 **Aviation—Flights (transatlantic)**—jet transatlantic non-stop flight east to west—D. C. Schilling—to Limestone, Me.

SEPTEMBER 23

1642 **College**—college—commencement exercises—Harvard College—Cambridge, Mass.

1642 **Degrees (academic and honorary)**— Bachelor of Arts degree—conferred— Harvard College—Cambridge, Mass.

1745 **Knighthood**—knighthood conferred on a native-born American for military leadership—Sir William Pepperell

1806 **Expedition**—expedition across the continent to the Pacific coast—returned to St. Louis, Mo.

1845 **Baseball Rules**—baseball rule code— adopted

1845 **Baseball Team** — baseball team — Knickerbocker Club—organized—New York City

1879 **Deaf—Hearing Aid**—hearing aid of interest—patented—R. S. Rhodes— River Park, Ill.

1885 **Biology**—biology course (general) offered in a college—Bryn Mawr College—Bryn Mawr, Pa.

1897 **Holiday**—Frontier Day—celebration— Cheyenne, Wyo.

1898 **Hospital** — tuberculosis sanatorium (state)—completed—Rutland, Mass.

1911 **Air Mail Service**—air mail pilot—E. L. Ovington—sworn in

1922 **Aviation — Flights (transcontinental)** — transcontinental dirigible flight (non-rigid dirigible) — landed — Arcadia, Calif.

1926 **Prize Fight**—prize fight to attract 100,000 spectators — Dempsey-Tunney fight—Philadelphia, Pa.

1930 **Photography**—photographic flashlight lamps—patent

1932 **Baseball Manager**—baseball manager to win pennants in both leagues—J. V. McCarthy

1934 **Radio Broadcast** — radio broadcast heard in both the Arctic and the Antarctic regions—Schenectady, N.Y.

1951 **Television—Telecast**—transcontinental telecast received on the west coast— "Crusade for Freedom"

1952 **Television—Telecast** — pay television presentation of a sporting event— Philadelphia, Pa.

1954 **Court Martial**—court martial trial of an officer for collaborating with his captors—Fort Sheridan, Ill.

1954 **Television — Telecast** — medical symposium televised coast-to-coast on a closed circuit—New York City

SEPTEMBER 24

1657—**Autopsy**—autopsy and verdict of a coroner's jury—recorded—Maryland

1789 **Attorney General**—attorney general— of the United States—office created

1789 **Congress of the United States**—congressional act declared unconstitutional by the Supreme Court of the United States

1789 **Justice Department (U.S.)**—office of attorney general created

1789 **Supreme Court (U.S.)**—Chief Justice of the Supreme Court—John Jay— appointed

1789 **Supreme Court (U.S.)** — Supreme Court justice who was nominated but who did not serve—R. H. Harrison

1789 **Supreme Court (U.S.)** — Supreme Court of the United States—authorized

1858 **Hospital**—inebriates' asylum—United States Inebriate Asylum—cornerstone laid—Binghamton, N.Y.

1889 **Time Recorder**—dial time recorder— patented—Alexander Dey

1906 **Monument**—national monument—Devils Tower, Wyo.—established

1917 College—Negro university (Catholic)
—two year normal department—
opened—New Orleans, La.

1929 Aviation—Flights—all blind flight—Lt.
J. H. Doolittle—Mitchel Field, N.Y.

1932 Toyery—opened—New York City

1933 Radio Broadcast — drama broadcast
from a regular stage—WABC—New
York City

1934 Theatrical School—theater and dramatic criticism course—established —
Yale University—New Haven, Conn.

1938 Tennis Player—lawn tennis champion
to win four major titles—J. D. Budge
—Forest Hills, N.Y.

1958 Bridge—welded aluminum girder-type
highway bridge — completed—Urban-
dale, Iowa

1960 Ship—aircraft carrier (atomic powered)—"Enterprise"—launched

SEPTEMBER 25

1690 Newspaper — newspaper publisher —
Publick Occurrances — issued—Benjamin
Harris—Boston, Mass.

1753 Steam Engine—steam engine—delivered—North Arlington, N.J.

1789 Constitutional Amendment—constitutional amendments—submitted to the
states

1804 Presidential Election — presidential
election in which candidates had been
nominated for the vice presidency—
twelfth amendment to constitution

1877 Cream Separator—centrifugal cream
separator patent

1918 Cooperatives Convention—Springfield,
Ill.

1924 Paleontology Course—micropaleontology course—Columbia University—
New York City

1933 Poorhouse (state)—opened—Smyrna,
Del.

1940 Archival Administration — complete
course—School of Public Affairs—
Washington, D.C.

1956 Telephone — telephone conversation
over the transoceanic telephone cable

SEPTEMBER 26

1772 Medical Legislation—law to license
the practice of medicine—New Jersey

1789 Attorney General—attorney general of
the United States—E. J. Randolph—
appointed

1789 Attorney of the United States—Samuel Sherburne, Jr.—appointed

1789 Postmaster—postmaster general of the
United States—Samuel Osgood—appointed

1831 Anti-Masonic Party — convention—
Baltimore, Md.

1831 Play (drama) — play performed 1,000
times—*The Gladiator*—New York City—
opened

1871 Cement — patent — D. O. Saylor —
Allentown, Pa.

1872 Freemasons—Ancient Arabic Order
of Nobles of the Mystic Shrine—
temple instituted—New York City

1874 Rifle Tournament—rifle tournament
(international)—Creedmoor, N.Y.

1903 Boycott Law—enacted—Alabama

1914 Federal Trade Commission—Federal
Trade Commission—authorized

1931 Ship—aircraft carrier—"Ranger"—keel
laid—Newport News, Va.

1955 Bank—bank to operate a window in
a subway station for the convenience
of subway riders—New York City

1960 Presidential Candidate — presidential
candidate debate series on television
—first Nixon-Kennedy debate— Chicago, Ill.

SEPTEMBER 27

1792 Postmaster — woman postmaster appointed after the adoption of the Constitution—Sarah De Crow—Hertford,
N.C.

1879 Sports—amateur athletic competition
(inter-club)—Mott Haven, N.Y.

1892 Match — "book matches" — patent —
Joshua Pusey—Lima, Pa.

1915 College—Negro university (Catholic)
—Xavier University—New Orleans—
opened as a high school

1922 Radar—radar observations—Anacostia, D.C.

1930 Golf Champion—golf champion to
hold the four highest golf titles—R.
T. Jones, Jr., won United States Amateur—Philadelphia, Pa.

1934 Abrasive—boron carbide—announced

1937 Santa Claus School—opened—Albion,
N.Y.

1939 Aviation—License — airplane instructor's license—under C.A.A.—issued—
A. J. Banks—Atlanta, Ga.

1941 Ship—Liberty ship—"Patrick Henry"
—launched—Baltimore, Md.

1944 Medal—Legion of Merit medal awarded
to a Women's Army Corps member—
presented—W. B. Boyce

SEPTEMBER 28

1542 Discovery—discovery of land on the
United States Pacific Coast—J. R.
Cabrillo—landed—San Diego, Calif.

1800 Fireboat—fireboat — imported — New
York City

1849 Army Officer—chaplain (Catholic) of
the United States Army—S. H. Milley
—served—Monterey, Calif.

1924 Aviation — Flights (world) — world
flight—round-the-world flight completed—Seattle, Wash.

1940 Aviation—Airport—airport (federally
owned and operated)—cornerstone
laid—Washington, D.C.

1944 Television—Telecast—musical comedy (full length) written especially for television—*Boys From Boise*—presented —New York City

1945 Opera—Negro to sing a white role with a white cast in an opera company — R. T. Duncan — Washington, D.C.

1955 Television—Telecast—baseball world series game televised in color—New York City—New York Yankees-Brooklyn Dodgers

SEPTEMBER 29

1784 Freemasons—Negro mason—warrant to African Lodge

1789 Army—medical corps—Richard Allison—appointed surgeon

1789 Pension—pensions paid by the United States Government—authorized

1892 Football Game — football game at night—Mansfield, Pa.

1904 Monument—monument to the memory of the soldiers and sailors of the Spanish-American war—Monroeville, Ohio

1915 Radio Telephone — transcontinental radio telephone demonstration—New York City

1918 Protestant Episcopal Bishop—Negro suffragan—E. T. Demby—appointed

1930 Radio Instruction — radio-advertising course—in a college—instituted—New York City

1938 Archival Course — offered—Columbia University—New York City

1942 Ship—merchant ship of the U.S. commanded by a Negro captain—"Booker T. Washington"—launched—Wilmington, Del.

1951 Television—Telecast—football game televised in color on a network—Philadelphia, Pa.

1953 Business—department store to sell insurance—Carson Pirie Scott & Co.—Chicago, Ill.

SEPTEMBER 30

1630 Execution — execution in America — John Billington—Plymouth, Mass.

1641 Fair—annual fair — New Netherlands —New York City

1787 Ship—ship to carry the United States flag around the world—sailed—Boston, Mass.

1791 Export — export report — by federal government

1811 Export — exports from the United States to exceed the imports

1841 Pin—machine "for sticking pins into paper"—patented—Samuel Slocum — Poughkeepsie, N.Y.

1877 Swimming Championship (amateur open)—New York City

1882 Electric Power Plant — hydroelectric power plant—opened—Appleton, Wis.

1902 Rayon—rayon patent

1906 Balloon Race — balloon cup race — James Gordon Bennett Aeronautic Cup—Paris, France

1909 City Planning Instruction — Harvard University—Cambridge, Mass.

1912 Safety Congress—safety congress (national)—Cooperative Safety Congress —convention—Milwaukee, Wis.

1914 Flag—American flag flown in World War I over a band of fighting Americans—Toulouse, France

1935 Electric Power Plant—hydroelectric power plant to produce a million kilowatts—dedicated

1936 Aviation—Races — airplane passenger race around the world — started — Lakehurst, N.J.

1939 Television—Telecast — football game (collegiate) to be televised — New York City

1943 Merchant Marine Academy — Merchant Marine Academy (U.S.) — Kings Point, N.Y.—dedicated—F. D. Roosevelt

1947 Television—Telecast — baseball world series game televised — New York City—New York Yankees-Brooklyn Dodgers

1950 Medal—Medal of Honor awarded in the Korean War—presented

OCTOBER 1

1779 Medal—medal awarded by the Continental Congress to a foreigner — presentation made—F. L. T. de Fleury

1785 Directory (city) — published — Philadelphia, Pa.

1810 Fair — agricultural fair — Pittsfield, Mass.

1811 Ship — steamboat to sail down the Mississippi — arrived — New Orleans, La.

1823 Gymnasium—gymnasium to offer systematic instruction — Round Hill School—Northampton, Mass.—opened

1834 Locomotive—locomotive with six or eight driving wheels—patented—Ross Winans

1848 School—school for the mentally retarded—opened—Boston, Mass.

1861 Army Balloon Corps—organized

1875 Agricultural Experiment Station — state agricultural experiment station—appropriation—Connecticut

1875 Meat — beef exported — from New York City—to England

1880 Electric Lighting — electric incandescent lamp factory — Edison Lamp Works—Menlo Park, N.J.—opened

1883 Bible School — Missionary Training College—opened—New York City

1884 Theatrical School—theatrical school—exclusively for stage training—opened —New York City

1885 Newspaper—newspaper daily railroad delivery service—*Morning News*—Dallas, Tex.

1885 **Postal Service**—special delivery service—special delivery stamp issued

1887 **Insurance**—mutual liability insurance company—opened—Boston, Mass.

1888 **Arbitration**—interstate carrier arbitration law—enacted

1890 **Narcotic**—narcotic regulation (federal)—enacted

1892 **Sociology Professor**—A. W. Small—appointed professor—Chicago, Ill.

1896 **Postal Service**—rural free delivery—established

1904 **Library** — business library supported by taxes—Newark, N.J.

1908 **Nursing School**—university school of nursing—as part of a university—Minneapolis, Minn.

1909 **Research Institute**—institute for research in nervous diseases—Neurological Institute of New York—New York City—opened

1911 **Insurance** — workmen's compensation insurance law (state) — effective — Washington

1912 **Quarantine**—plant quarantine legislation (national)—effective

1913 **Monument**—monument to a bird—unveiled—Salt Lake City, Utah

1917 **Post Office**—open air post office—opened—St. Petersburg, Fla.

1918 **Hygiene Instruction** — hygiene and public health school—Johns Hopkins University—Baltimore, Md.—opened

1929 **Air Mail Service**—airplane mail pickup—demonstrated—Washington, D.C.

1934 **College**—college to dispense with the system of credits, hours, points, grades, etc. — in operation — Olivet, Mich.

1934 **Federal Credit Union Act**—charter No. 1—Texarkana, Tex.

1934 **Periodical**—sectarian magazine printed in rotogravure—*Catholic Missions*—issued—New York City

1937 **Trailer Church**—operated

1940 **Army Parachute Troops**—battalion organized—Fort Benning, Ga.

1942 **Aviation—Airplane**—jet propelled airplane—flown—Muroc, Calif.

1946 **Baseball Game**—baseball playoff series—St. Louis, Mo.

1947 **Air Mail Service**—helicopter air mail and express service—Los Angeles, Calif.

1949 **Television Tube**—rectangular television tube (practical)—deliveries made

1951 **Treaty**—treaty signed by a woman ambassador—Eugenie Anderson

1952 **Television—Telecast** — husband and wife to broadcast a religious program —Dr. and Mrs. Norman Vincent Peale —New York City

1952 **Television Station**—ultra high frequency commercial television station —KPTV—Portland, Ore.

1957 **Installment Sales Law** — effective— New York

OCTOBER 2

1721 **Animals** — camel imported — Boston, Mass.—advertised

1831 **Catholic Nuns**—Catholic nuns (colored community)—order approved

1866 **Cans**—can (tin) with a key opener—patented—J. Osterhoudt—New York City

1889 **Conference**—Pan American Conference—opened—Washington, D.C.

1903 **Turbine**—steam turbine generator of large capacity for commercial service —opened—Chicago, Ill.

1936 **Alcohol**—power alcohol plant—power alcohol sold—Atchison, Kan.

1937 **X-Ray**—X-ray moving pictures (successful) of the action of the human heart—exhibited—New York City

1943 **Aviation — Airplane** — rocket airplane (military)—tested as a glider

1955 **Methodist**—Negro Methodist minister of an all-white congregation—S. P. Montgomery—Old Mystic, Conn.

1956 **Clock**—clock to operate by atomic power—exhibited—New York City

OCTOBER 3

1632 **Tobacco**—tobacco tax (colonial)—authorized—Massachusetts

1789 **Holiday**—Thanksgiving Day — presidential proclamation issued

1805 **Pharmacopoeia**—pharmacopoeia (prepared by a medical association)—authorized—Boston, Mass.

1824 **Engineering College**—engineering college—Rensselaer Polytechnic Institute —Troy, N.Y.—founded

1824 **Treaty**—treaty with a South American country—signed—Bogotá, Colombia

1825 **Annual**—published—Philadelphia, Pa.

1852 **Deaf—Church Service**—church services for the deaf—New York City

1859 **Cricket Tournament** — international cricket tournament—Hoboken, N.J.

1863 **Holiday**—Thanksgiving Day national proclamation—Abraham Lincoln

1875 **Jewish College** — Jewish college to train men for the rabbinate—Hebrew Union College — established—Cincinnati, Ohio

1877 **Blind**—school for the blind—Perkins Asylum—changed name

1898 **Hospital** — tuberculosis sanatorium (state) — Massachusetts Hospital for Consumptives — Rutland, Mass. — opened

1899 **Vacuum Cleaner**—motor-driven vacuum cleaner — patented — J. S. Thurman—St. Louis, Mo.

1910 **Dental School**—dental assistants' and nurses' course—Ohio College of Dental Surgery—Cincinnati, Ohio

1919 **Federal Trade Commission**—Federal Trade Commission trade practice conference—Omaha, Neb.

1922 **Radio Facsimile Transmission**—photographs sent over a city telephone—transmitted — C. F. Jenkins—Washington, D.C.

1922 **Senator (U.S.)**—woman to occupy a seat in the Senate — R. L. Felton — appointed—Georgia

1924 **Citizenship and Public Affairs School** —opened—Syracuse, N.Y.

1942 **Medal** — Silver Star Army Medal awarded to a civilian—Vern Haugland

1943 **Television** — Telecast — missing persons telecast—New York City

1947 **Army** — Reserve Officers Training Corps course in mountain and winter warfare—Norwich University—Northfield, Vt.

1947 **Telescope**—telescope lens two hundred inches in diameter—completed

1949 **Radio Station**—radio station owned and operated by Negroes—WERD—Atlanta, Ga.

1951 **Television—Telecast**—prize fight televised coast-to-coast — Sands-Olson fight—Chicago, Ill.

1952 **Tape Recording**—video recording on magnetic tape—Los Angeles, Calif.

OCTOBER 4

1810 **Actor**—English actor of note—sailed to New York City—from Liverpool, England

1829 **Catholic Provincial Council** — convened—Baltimore, Md.

1830 **Printing Press**—power printing press capable of fine book work—patented—Isaac Adams—Boston, Mass.

1861 **Ship**—iron-clad turreted vessel in the U.S. Navy — "Monitor" — contract signed

1870 **Solicitor General of the United States** —B. H. Bristow—appointed

1878 **Chinese Embassy**—received — Washington, D.C.

1881 **Cream Separator** — continuous flow centrifugal cream separator—patented —C. G. P. de Laval

1881 **Piano Player**—piano player (completely automatic)—patented

1887 **Newspaper**—European edition of an American newspaper—*Herald*

1890 **Niagara Falls**—utilization of Niagara Falls waterpower (large scale)—ground broken

1895 **Golf Tournament**—open championship (official)—Newport, R.I.

1909 **Balloon Race**—dirigible balloon race—St. Louis, Mo.

1932 **Play (drama)**—anti-vivisection play—*Woven Dreams*—presented—Philadelphia, Pa.

1933 **Federal Surplus Relief Corporation**—incorporated—Delaware

1940 **Birds**—quetzal bird—imported—New York City

1954 **Supreme Court (U.S.)**—Negro page of the Supreme Court—C. V. Bush—served

1955 **Telephone** — telephone conversation (commercial) using electricity generated by the sun's rays—Americus, Ga.

1958 **Aviation—Flights (transatlantic)**—jet passenger commercial service—New York City-London

OCTOBER 5

1646 **Bounty**—granted—Virginia

1853 **College**—college to grant women absolutely equal rights—non-sectarian college of high rank—Antioch College —Yellow Springs, Ohio—opened

1853 **College** — woman college professor — R. M. Pennell—Antioch College—Yellow Springs, Ohio

1853 **Didactics Course**—didactics course in a college — Antioch College — Yellow Springs, Ohio—opened

1853 **Hygiene Instruction**—physiology and hygiene courses — offered — Antioch College—Yellow Springs, Ohio

1854 **Baby Show**—Springfield, Ohio

1869 **Bicycle Patent**—water velocipede patent—awarded—Columbus, Ohio

1871 **Unitarian Minister**—woman ordained to the Unitarian ministry—C. C. Burleigh—Brooklyn, Conn.

1881 **Immigration**—Chinese labor immigration act—ratifications proclaimed

1918 **Aviation** — war night-flying scout group—assigned to France

1919 **Radio Telephone**—two-way radio conversation between a submerged submarine and another vessel — New York City

1921 **Radio Broadcast**—baseball world series broadcast—New York City

1922 **Aviation — Passenger** — woman airplane passenger (transcontinental)—started—San Francisco, Calif.

1930 **Aviation—Flights (transcontinental)**—transcontinental airplane flight by a woman—Laura Ingalls—left Roosevelt Field, N.Y.

1931 **Aviation — Flights (transpacific)** — transpacific non-stop flight—landed at Wenatchee, Wash.—from Japan

1933 **Aviation**—airplane sleeping berths—introduced—Atlanta, Ga., to New York City

1936 **Television—Telecast**—telecast using coaxial cable — intercity telecast — Philadelphia, Pa., and New York City

1947 **Television—Telecast**—presidential address televised from the White House —H. S. Truman—Washington, D.C.

1953 **Baseball Team**—baseball team to win five World Series in succession—New York Yankees

OCTOBER 6

1683 **Mennonites** — Mennonites — arrived from Germany

1766 **Actor**—matinee idol—John Henry——American debut—Philadelphia, Pa.

1780 **Prison**—American imprisoned in the Tower of London—Henry Laurens

1783 **Clock**—self-winding clock—patent application—Benjamin Hanks—Litchfield, Conn.

1825 **Giant** — Patrick Magee — exhibited — New York City

1837 **Locomotive Steam Whistle**—used—Paterson, N.J.

1848 **Ship**—steamboat service (regular) to California via Cape Horn—"California"—sailed—New York City

1852 **Pharmacy Society (national)**—American Pharmaceutical Association—organized—Philadelphia, Pa.

1857 **Chess Champion**—P. C. Morphy—New York City

1857 **Chess Tournament**—of importance—American Chess Congress — New York City

1863 **Bathhouse**—Turkish bath—opened—Brooklyn, N.Y.

1868 **Nickel Plating**—patent—W. H. Remington—Boston, Mass.

1873 **Balloon**—balloon Atlantic crossing attempt—"Daily Graphic"—Brooklyn, N.Y.

1876 **Library Society**—library association (national)—American Library Association—organized—Philadelphia, Pa.

1884 **Naval War College**—naval war college—established—Newport, R.I.

1917 **Employment Service** — Employment Service (U.S.)—act approved

1955 **Army Officer**—male nurse—E. L. T. Lyon—sworn in

OCTOBER 7

1816 **Ship**—steamboat (double decked)—"Washington" — arrived — New Orleans, La.

1826 **Railroad**—railroad for freight transportation to celebrate its centenary—Granite Railway—completed—Quincy, Mass.

1856 **Folding Machine** — patent — Cyrus Chambers, Jr.—Kennet Square, Pa.

1863 **Charity Board (state)**—sworn in—Massachusetts

1868 **Veterinary School**—veterinary department of collegiate character—Ithaca, N.Y.

1922 **Radio Broadcast**—chain broadcast—New York City

1924 **Aviation—Flights (transcontinental)**—transcontinental airship voyage — "Shenandoah — started — Lakehurst, N.J.

1929 **Congress of the United States**—Prime Minister of England to address the Congress of the United States—Ramsay MacDonald—Washington, D.C.

1930 **Aviation—License**—glider pilot's license—awarded—L. A. Wiggins—Akron, Ohio

1931 **Photograph**—infra-red photograph—taken—Rochester, N.Y.

1939 **Electric Starting Gate (race track)**—full-sized gates used—San Francisco, Calif.

1942 **Dental Corps (U.S. Army)**—army dental corps major general—date of rank—R. H. Mills

1942 **Medal**—Distinguished Service Medal (merchant marine)—awarded—E. F. Cheney

1950 **War (Korean)**—American tank crew to cross the 38th parallel in Korea

1951 **Hotel**—hotel with all foam-rubber mattresses, pillows and furniture cushions—opened—Fort Worth, Tex.

1959 **Television**—Telecast—auction of federal property to be televised

1960 **Presidential Candidate**—presidential candidate debate series on television—second Nixon-Kennedy debate — Washington, D.C.

OCTOBER 8

1818 **Medical Instruction**—hygiene lectures offered—Cambridge, Mass.

1873 **Prison**—prison built for women and managed exclusively by women—Indianapolis, Ind.

1904 **Automobile Race** — Vanderbilt Cup Race—Hicksville, N.Y.

1909 **Aviation — Airplane** — airplane purchased by the United States Government—flight—College Park, Md.

1919 **Aviation—Races**—transcontinental air race—start—San Francisco, Calif.

1922 **Aviation—Passenger**—woman airplane passenger (transcontinental)—landed—Mineola, N.Y.

1929 **Aviation** — airplane moving picture show

1929 **Aviation** — automatic pilot— tested—Trow Sebree—Cleveland, Ohio

1936 **Visiting Celebrities**—pontiff—Eugenio Pacelli (later Pius XII)—arrived

1956 **Baseball Player**—baseball pitcher to pitch a perfect no-hit, no-run, no-walk World Series game—Don Larsen—New York City

OCTOBER 9

1780 **Astronomical Expedition** — sailed — Cambridge, Mass.

1792 **Money** — silver half dimes — coined —Philadelphia, Pa.

1855 **Calliope**—patented—J. C. Stoddard—Worcester, Mass.

1855 **Sewing Machine**—sewing machine motor patent — I. M. Singer — New York City

1865 **Oil**—oil pipeline of importance—completed—Titusville, Pa.

1876 **Telephone** — telephone conversation over out-of-door wires — Boston to Cambridge, Mass.

1877 **Humane Society**—humane association national organization—American Humane Association —organized—Cleveland, Ohio

1888 Monument — monument to George Washington (national)—Washington, D.C.—public admitted

1892 Hospital—tuberculosis hospital — National Jewish Hospital—Denver, Colo. —cornerstone laid

1894 Magic Lantern Show—magic lantern feature show — "Miss Jerry" — previewed—New York City

1915 Fingerprint Society—fingerprint society (international)—International Association for Criminal Identification—formed—Oakland, Calif.

1930 Aviation—Flights (transcontinental)—transcontinental flight by a woman—Laura Ingalls—left Roosevelt Field, N.Y.

1938 Baseball Team—baseball team to win three world series in succession—third series won

1946 Blanket—electronic blanket—manufactured—Petersburg, Va.

1947 Telephone—mobile telephone conversation—moving automobile to airplane —Wilmington, Del.

OCTOBER 10

1802 Jewish Congregation—Jewish congregation (Ashkenazic)—Rodeph Shalom—Philadelphia, Pa.—founded

1818 Ship—steamboat on the Great Lakes —"Walk-in-theWater"—trip

1843 Horse Race—futurity race—Nashville, Tenn.

1845 Naval Academy — naval academy (U.S.)—officially opened—Annapolis, Md.

1857 Chess Tournament—American Chess Association—formed—New York City

1863 Catholic Church — Catholic parish church for Negroes—purchased—Baltimore, Md.

1865 Billiard Ball—of composition material resembling ivory — patented — J. W. Hyatt

1886 Coat—tuxedo coat—introduced—Tuxedo Park, N.Y.

1896 Book Review—book review newspaper supplement — published — New York City

1918 Indian Church—Indian church organized by Indians — First American Church — incorporated — El Reno, Okla.

1920 Baseball Game—triple play unassisted in a world series— Bill Wambsganss—Cleveland, Ohio

1923 Aviation—Airship—dirigible (American-built rigid) — christened — Lakehurst, N.J.

1923 Baseball Game—world series baseball games to gross a million dollars — New York City

1933 Detergent—synthetic detergent—for home use—marketed

1934 Archivist of the United States—R. D. W. Connor—appointed

1934 Humanist Society—Humanist National Assembly—New York City

1937 Radio Broadcast—cooperative radio show—Hollywood, Calif.

OCTOBER 11

1753 Arbitration—colonial arbitration law—enacted—New Haven, Conn.

1802 Army School—Army school graduates—West Point, N.Y.

1811 Ferryboat—steam-propelled ferryboat —operated—Hoboken, N.J. to New York City

1853 Bank — clearing house — exchange opened—New York City

1881 Photographic Film—roll film for cameras — patented — D. H. Houston — Cambria, Wis.

1886 College—college for women to affiliate with a university—H. Sophie Newcomb Memorial College—New Orleans, La.

1887 Adding Machine—adding machine absolutely accurate at all times—patent —D. E. Felt—Chicago, Ill.

1910 President—President to fly—Theodore Roosevelt—St. Louis, Mo.

1919 Aviation—Races—transcontinental air race — completed — San Francisco, Calif.

1924 Aviation — Flights (transcontinental) —transcontinental airship voyage—"Shenandoah"—arrived—San Diego, Calif.

1932 Television—Telecast — political campaign telecast—New York City

1933 Poorhouse (state)—Smyrna, Del.—dedicated

1935 Crime Prevention and Detection—national conference on crime—Trenton, N.J.

1938 Glass Wool—patented—Newark, Ohio

1945 Army Officer—general to be consecrated a bishop—W. R. Arnold—consecrated—New York City

1948 Television — Telecast — stratovision world series telecast—Boston, Mass.

OCTOBER 12

1773 Hospital—insane hospital (state)—Williamsburg, Va.—opened

1792 Monument—monument to Christopher Columbus—dedicated—Baltimore, Md.

1794 African Church—received in full fellowship in Methodist Episcopal Church

1802 Army School—Army school graduate (Jewish)—Simon M. Levy—commissioned

1802 Army School—Army school graduates —commissioned

1845 Labor—labor congress (national)—First Industrial Congress—convened —New York City

1869 Horse Race—trotting futurity—New York City

1876 **Bridge**—cantilever bridge — construction started

1878 **Bridge** — railway all-steel bridge — bridge contract signed

1895 **Golf Tournament**—amateur golf tournament (official)—Newport, R.I.

1920 **Tunnel**—twin-tube subaqueous vehicular tunnel—Holland tunnel—Jersey City, N.J. and New York City—construction began

1924 **Aviation—Airship**—dirigible merchandise equipment—left Germany

1925 **Heresy Trial**—of a bishop—W. M. Brown—deposed—New Orleans, La.

1928 **Respirator (iron lung)**—used at hospital—Boston, Mass.

1932 **Diplomatic Service**—American legation in which a woman assumed charge—Stockholm, Sweden—F. E. Willis

1937 **Electric Generator**—hydrogen-cooled turbine generator—used—Millers Ford station, Ohio

1945 **Medal**—Medal of Honor awarded to a conscientious objector—D. T. Doss at Washington, D.C.

1949 **Diplomatic Service**—ambassador (woman)—Eugenie Anderson

OCTOBER 13

1775 **Navy**—naval fleet—authorized

1778 **Freemasons**—masonic grand lodge—organized—Williamsburg, Va.

1792 **Building**—building erected by the Government in Washington, D.C.—Executive Mansion—cornerstone laid

1843 **Jews**—Jewish fraternal society— B'nai B'rith founded

1853 **Zinc**—zinc commercial production—Pennsylvania and Lehigh Zinc Company Mill erected—Bethlehem, Pa.

1857 **Horse Race**—American-bred horse to win a major race abroad—Prioress—Newmarket, England

1860 **Photograph**—aerial photograph—Boston, Mass.

1894 **Golf Tournament**—amateur golf tournament (unofficial)—Yonkers, N.Y.

1915 **Chamber of Commerce**—junior chamber of commerce — organized — St. Louis, Mo.

1922 **League of Nations**—representative (unofficial)—Grace Abbott—appointed

1939 **Aviation—License**—airplane instructor's license—under CAA—issued to a woman—E. P. Kilgore—San Bernardino, Calif.

1940 **Deaf—Transmission**—visible and oral communication by the deaf over distance—accomplished—New York City

1951 **Football**—football with a rubber covering used in a major collegiate game—Atlanta, Ga.

1953 **Burglar Alarm**—burglar alarm operated by ultrasonic or radio waves—patented—Samuel Bagno—New York City

1955 **Medical Society**—woman president of a major medical society—E. S. Moss

1960 **Presidential Candidate** — presidential candidate debate series on television—third Nixon-Kennedy debate—New York City and Hollywood, Calif.

OCTOBER 14

1774 **Declaration of Rights**—enacted—Philadelphia, Pa.

1816 **Evangelical Church General Conference**—convened—Buffalo Valley, Pa.

1834 **Patent**—Negro to obtain a patent—Henry Blair—Glenross, Md.

1840 **Second Advent Believers** — general conference—Boston, Mass.

1879 **Ship**—steamboat to employ electric lights—"Jeannette"—attempt to use electric lights

1884 **Photographic Film** — transparent paper strip photographic film—patent—George Eastman—Rochester, N.Y.

1902 **Arbitration**—arbitration proceeding—court award made

1915 **Ship**—warship propelled by electricity—keel laid—"New Mexico"—New York City

1916 **Golf Tournament**—Professional Golfers Association tournament—Mount Vernon, N.Y.

1922 **Aviation—Flights**—airplane to exceed the speed of 200 miles an hour—L. J. Maitland

1928 **Wedding** — television wedding — Des Plaines, Ill.

1947 **Aviation—Flights**—airplane to exceed the speed of sound—Muroc, Calif.—C. E. Yeager

OCTOBER 15

1565 **Treaty**—treaty violation — occurred — Florida

1725 **Evangelical and Reformed Church**—Reformed Church in the United States — organized — Montgomery County, Pa.

1789 **President**—President to tour the country—George Washington—tour of New England states

1840 **Evangelical and Reformed Church**—Evangelical Synod of North America—organized—Mehlville, Mo.

1862 **Agriculture Bureau**—agriculture bureau scientific publication—dated—Washington, D.C.

1878 **Electric Company**—electric company—Edison Electric Light Company—New York City—incorporated

1881 **Fishing Magazine**—*American Angler*—Philadelphia, Pa.—published

1910 **Aviation — Flights (transatlantic)** — transatlantic dirigible flight—attempted—Walter Wellman

1917 **Army Camp**—army camp for training Negro officers—Fort Des Moines—Des Moines, Iowa—commissions granted

1918 **Judge**—woman judge of a juvenile court—Kathryn Sellers—appointed

1919 **Horse race** — three-hundred-mile endurance run—start—Burlington, Vt.

1924 **Aviation—Airship**—dirigible merchandise shipment — from Germany — landed—Lakehurst, N.J.

1927 **Radio License**—international broadcasting license—issued—New York City

1932 **Opera**—opera house municipally owned—opened—San Francisco, Calif.

1940 **Art Course** — industrial camouflage course—Kansas City, Mo.

1940 **Conscription** — peacetime conscription bill—C. A. Dykstra—confirmed as director

1946 **Glider**—powered soaring glider commercially licensed — San Fernando, Calif.

1948 **Naval Officer**—woman doctor in the regular U.S. Navy—F. L. Willoughby

1950 **Radio Paging Service** — instituted — New York City

OCTOBER 16

1629 **Agriculture**—crop limitation law—enacted—Virginia

1829 **Annunciator**—used—Tremont House, Boston, Mass.

1829 **Hotel**—hotel—Tremont House, Boston, Mass.—celebrated opening

1829 **Hotel**—hotel to install bathrooms—Tremont House—Boston, Mass.—opened

1844 **Psychiatric Association** — formed—Philadelphia, Pa.

1846 **Anesthesia**—painless surgery demonstration—Boston, Mass.

1848 **Medical School**—homeopathic college —Homeopathic Medical College of Pennsylvania — opened — Philadelphia, Pa.

1891 **Correspondence School**—International Correspondence Schools — Scranton, Pa.—student enrolled

1899 **Radio Broadcast**—yacht race broadcast—Sandy Hook, N.J.

1911 **Ship**—electrically propelled ship of the United States Navy—keel laid—Mare Island, Calif.

1916 **Medical Clinic**—birth control clinic—opened—New York City

1917 **Army**—gas regiment—battalion organized

1928 **Electric Lighting**—electric lamp bulb frosted on the inside—patented—Marvin Pipkin

1933 **Commodity Credit Corporation (U.S.)** —created

1936 **Vice President of the United States**— Vice President to leave the United States while the President was away— J. N. Garner—sailed—Seattle, Wash.

1948 **Cantor**—school for cantors—opened— New York City

1951 **Moving Picture**—moving picture of the inside of a living heart (of a dog) —shown—New York City

1956 **Ship**—gyro-stabilized American liner— "Mariposa" — christened — Portland, Ore.

OCTOBER 17

1777 **Holiday**—Thanksgiving Day celebration (nationwide, colonial)—surrender of Burgoyne

1834 **Gas**—gas meter (dry)—patented— James Bogardus—New York Ctiy

1839 **Building**—building with a high steeple —Trinity Church—New York City— begun

1855 **Jews**—Jewish Rabbinical Conference —Cleveland, Ohio

1888 **Bank**—bank for Negroes privately operated by Negroes—Capitol Savings Bank—Washington, D.C.—organized

1888 **Ship** — battleship of importance — "Maine"—keel laid—Brooklyn, N.Y.

1907 **Radio Broadcast**—transatlantic radio message of the regular westward service—received—New York City

1939 **Television—Telecast**—telecast (long distance) received in an airplane— Washington, D.C.—from New York City

1941 **World War II**—American destroyer torpedoed—"Kearny"—attacked

OCTOBER 18

1648 **Labor Union**—labor organization—authorized

1842 **Cable**—cable—laid—S. F. B. Morse

1852 **Play (drama)**—Chinese theatrical performance—San Francisco, Calif.

1870 **Sand Blasting**—patent—B. C. Tilghman—Philadelphia, Pa.

1873 **Football Rules** — formulated — New York City

1888 **Agricultural School**—vocational agricultural school—department of state university—St. Paul, Minn.

1891 **Bicycle Race**—international six-day bicycle race—New York City

1904 **Bibliography Society (national)** — Bibliographical Society of America— organized—St. Louis, Mo.

1904 **Newspaper**—Hungarian daily newspaper—published—New York City

1916 **Road**—federal grant-in-aid to states for roads—project approved

1929 **Medical Instruction**—History of Medicine Department — Johns Hopkins University—Baltimore, Md.

1930 **Jockey**—jockey to win seven races in one day—Joseph Sylvester—Ravenna, Ohio

OCTOBER 19

1790 **War**—battle fought by United States troops—Ohio

1839 **Iron**—iron blast furnace—using anthracite coal—Pottsville, Pa.

1874 **Wedding**—balloon wedding—Cincinnati, Ohio
1911 **Aviation**—Flights (transcontinental)—transcontinental airplane flight (eastbound)—R. G. Fowler—left Los Angeles, Calif.
1914 **Postal Service**—collection and delivery of mail in automobiles—owned by the U.S. Government
1918 **Army Insignia**—shoulder sleeve insignia—"shoulder patch"—authorized
1919 **Medal**—Distinguished Service Medal awarded to a woman—Evangeline Booth
1926 **Ordnance**—semi-automatic rifle—patented—J. C. Garand
1936 **Aviation**—Races—airplane passenger race around the world—completed—Lakehurst, N.J.
1936 **Fingerprinting**—high school to fingerprint its students—Watertown, S.D.
1937 **Soilless Culture of Plants**—commercial hydroponicum (large) — Montebello, Calif.—company incorporated
1941 **Electric Power Plant**—wind turbine—for alternating current power plant—in service—Grandpa's Knob, Vt.
1950 **Television Station**—illegal television station—Johnstown, Pa.
1953 **Aviation**—Flights (transcontinental)—transcontinental non-stop eastward scheduled service—Los Angeles, Calif., to New York City

OCTOBER 20

1817 **Theater**—showboat—floating theater—left Nashville, Tenn.
1846 **College**—college to grant women absolutely equal rights—Mount Union College, Alliance, Ohio—founded
1852 **Factory**—steam-heated factory—sold at auction—Burlington, Vt.
1860 **Visiting Celebrities**—Prince of Wales—left—Portland, Me.
1862 **Presidential Executive Order**—to be numbered—issued—Abraham Lincoln
1870 **Labor Union**—labor organization to admit workmen other than craft workmen—Noble Order of Knights of Labor
1883 **Manual Training** — manual training school entirely financed by public taxes—authorized—Baltimore, Md.
1888 **Baseball Team**—baseball teams to go on a world tour
1906 **Radio Tube**—three-element vacuum tube—announced—Lee De Forest
1910 **Baseball**—cork center baseball—used in world series—Chicago, Ill.
1916 **Bird Legislation (international)**—Migratory Bird Treaty—ratified—Great Britain
1920 **Aviation**—Flights—New York-Alaska flight—returned—Mitchel Field, N.Y.
1922 **Aviation**—Parachute—aviator to bail out of a disabled airplane—H. R. Harris—Dayton, Ohio

1925 **Compotype** — patented—Clifton Chisholm—Cleveland, Ohio
1929 **Hospital** —community hospital —organized—Elk City, Okla.
1960 **Post Office**—post office fully mechanized—opened—Providence, R.I.

OCTOBER 21

1639 **Medical Legislation**—medical law—enacted—Virginia
1849 **Tattoo**—tattooed man—J. F. O'Connell—appearance—New York City
1861 **Hospital**—military hospital on the modern pavilion plan—Poolesville, Md.
1871 **Sports** — amateur outdoor athletic games—New York City
1879 **Electric Lighting**—electric incandescent lamp—practical value—invented—T. A. Edison—Menlo Park, N.J.
1893 **Monument**—monument to a woman financed by women—M. B. Washington —Fredericksburg, Va. —cornerstone laid
1907 **Balloon Race**—balloon cup race—St. Louis, Mo.
1915 **Radio Telephone**—transatlantic radio telephone message—transmitted—Arlington, Va.—to Paris, France
1916 **Army**—Reserve Officers Training Corps Units—established
1917 **World War I**—American division in the trenches in World War I—Luneville, **France**
1921 **Radio** Broadcast—program theme song—"The Happiness Boys"
1925 **Photoelectric Cell**—photoelectric cell —publicly demonstrated—New York City
1929 **Aviation**—ambulance air service—organized—New York City
1931 **Autogiro** — autogiro manufactured with a closed cabin—flown—Philadelphia, Pa.
1947 **Aviation — Airplane** — bomber (allwing jet)—tested—Hawthorne, Calif.
1948 **Radio Facsimile Transmission**—facsimile high-speed transmission — Washington, D.C.
1960 **Presidential Candidate** — presidential candidate debate series on television —fourth Nixon-Kennedy debate—New York City

OCTOBER 22

1746 **College**—college charter granted by a governor or acting governor with only the assent of his council—Princeton, N.J.
1812 **War (1812)**—prisoners in the War of 1812—captured—St. Regis, N.Y.
1819 **Canal**—canal of importance—first boat between Rome and Utica, N.Y.
1836 **President of the Republic of Texas**—**Sam Houston**—sworn in—Columbia, **Texas**

1861 **Ship**—iron-clad turreted vessel in the U.S. Navy—"Monitor"—keel laid—Greenpoint, N.Y.

1883 **Horse Show**—horse show of national scope—opened—New York City

1883 **Opera**—opera at the Metropolitan Opera House—*Faust*

1885 **College**—state college for women—opened—Columbus, Miss.

1897 **Zionist Society**—Zionist national organization—United American Zionists—formed—New York City

1934 **Railroad**—streamlined Pullman train (six cars)—left Los Angeles, Calif.

1939 **Snow Cruiser (automobile)**—moved by its own power—Chicago, Ill.

1939 **Television—Telecast** — football game (professional) to be televised—New York City

OCTOBER 23

1810 **Horse Breeding Society**—Massachusetts Society for Encouraging the Breed of Fine Horses—annual trial—Boston, Mass.

1824 **Locomotive**—locomotive to pull a train on a track—built—John Stevens—Hoboken, N.J.

1850 **Woman Suffrage**—convention (national) of women advocating woman suffrage—Worcester, Mass.

1885 **College**—graduate school for women—Bryn Mawr College—Bryn Mawr, Pa.—college opened

1902 **Baseball League**—baseball league association — National Association of Professional Baseball Leagues—annual meeting—New York City

1910 **Aviation—Aviator**—woman aviator to make a public flight—B. S. Scott—Fort Wayne, Ind.

1915 **Horseshoe Pitchers' Association (national)** — championship tournament — Kellerton, Iowa

1917 **World War I**—American shot fired in World War I—sixth field artillery

1919 **Insurance**—fire and tornado insurance fund (state)—loss paid—Conway, S.D.

1919 **Ship**—concrete ship built for the United States Shipping Board—"Polias"—delivered—Brunswick, Ga.

1924 **Radio Broadcast**—network broadcast received on the Pacific Coast—Los Angeles, Portland, Seattle

1936 **Old Age Colony**—dedicated—Millville, N.J.

1947 **Nobel Prize**—husband and wife in the United States to receive a joint Nobel prize—C. F. Cori and G. T. Cori—St. Louis, Mo.—award announced

1956 **Tape Recording**—video recording on magnetic tape televised coast-to-coast Jonathan Winters show

OCTOBER 24

1812 **Historical Society**—historical society (national)—American Antiquarian Society—formed

1828 **Fair**—manufacturers' fair—New York City

1836 **Match**—match patent—A. D. Phillips—Springfield, Mass.

1849 **Disciples of Christ**—general convention—Cincinnati, Ohio

1861 **Telegram** — transcontinental telegram—San Francisco, Calif., to New York City

1861 **Telegraph**—telegraph line to the Pacific coast—in operation

1876 **Clock** — clock (one-day back-wind alarm clock) — patented — S. E. Thomas—New York City

1878 **Electric Company**—electric company—Edison Electric Light Company — organized—New York City

1893 **Niagara Falls**—utilization of Niagara Falls waterpower (large-scale)—contract for equipment executed

1901 **Niagara Falls**—person to go over Niagara Falls in a barrel—A. E. Taylor

1941 **Army Officer**—air surgeon of the War Department—D. N. W. Grant

1943 **Medal** — Distinguished Service Cross awarded to an animal—Chips—authorized

1945 **Television** — **Telecast** — department store sales demonstrations (large-scale)—Gimbel Brothers—Philadelphia, Pa.

1945 **Television** — **Telecast** — stratovision flight test—experimental license granted

1956 **Presbyterian Church** — woman ordained a minister—M. E. Towner—ordained—Syracuse, N.Y.

OCTOBER 25

1761 **Knighthood**—knighthood conferred in America—presented to Jeffery Amherst—Staten Island, N.Y.

1848 **Railroad**—railroad to run west, out of Chicago

1870 **Trademark** — registered — Averill Chemical Paint Co.—New York City

1881 **Air Brush Patent** — L. L. Curtis—Cape Elizabeth, Me.

1888 **Ferryboat** — double deck ferryboat — launched—Newburgh, N.Y.

1905 **Ferryboat**—municipally owned ferryboats—operated—New York City

1919 **Periodical** — photo-engraved magazine—*Literary Digest*—New York City

1924 **Aviation** — **Flights (transcontinental)** —transcontinental airship voyage—return voyage—"Shenandoah"

1929 **Cabinet of the U.S.**—cabinet member convicted of a crime—A. B. Fall—found guilty

1930 **Aviation** — **Flights (transcontinental)** —transcontinental regularly scheduled through air service—New York City to Los Angeles, Calif.

1940 **Army Officer**—brigadier general (Negro)—B. O. Davis—appointed
1945 **Flag**—President's flag—48 stars—authorized—H. S. Truman
1954 **Television—Telecast** — cabinet session to be televised—Washington, D.C.
1955 **Stove**—electronic range for domestic use—introduced—New York City
1960 **Clock**—electronic wrist watch — produced—New York City

OCTOBER 26

1785 **Animals** — mule — imported — Boston, Mass.
1825 **Canal** — canal of importance — Erie Canal opened
1858 **Washing Machine**—rotary motion washing machine — patent — H. E. Smith—Philadelphia, Pa.
1869 **Steeplechase** — Jerome Park, New York City
1909 **Aviation—Aviator**—Army aviator to solo—F. E. Humphreys—College Park, Md.
1933 **Industrial Recovery Act**—compliance board under the National Industrial Recovery Act—established
1956 **Ship**—gyro-stabilized American liner —"Mariposa"

OCTOBER 27

1780 **Astronomical Expedition** — observed eclipse—Boston, Mass.
1812 **Ship**—naval vessel of the United States to display the American flag around Cape Horn — left Delaware capes
1866 **Yacht Race**—yacht race across the Atlantic Ocean—agreement made
1869 **Agricultural Society**—agricultural society for dairymen—Vermont Dairymen's Association—organized—Montpelier, Vt.
1889 **Lithuanian Church**—organized—Plymouth, Pa.
1904 **Street Car**—aluminum street car—aluminum used in subway car construction
1904 **Subway**—subway (rapid transit)—Interborough Rapid Transit—New York City
1909 **Aviation—Passenger**—woman airplane passenger—College Park, Md.
1920 **Radio License**—radio station licensed —Pittsburgh, Pa.
1922 **Holiday**—Navy Day—celebrated
1948 **Economic Cooperation Administration**—industrial guaranty contract of investment of American capital in ERP (European Recovery Program) countries
1953 **Medal**—Medal of Honor awarded to a Nisei in the Korean War—presented —Washington, D.C.
1954 **Army Officer**—brigadier general (Negro) in the Air Force—B. O. Davis, Jr.

OCTOBER 28

1788 **Naval Officer**—naval chaplain (Continental navy)—Benjamin Parks—appointed
1799 **Aviation**—aeronautical patent—Moses McFarland
1863 **Water Conduit**—water supply tunnel for a city—Chicago, Ill.—contract
1867 **Jewish College**—Jewish college—Maimonides College—opened
1886 **Monument**—statue presented by a foreign country—Statue of Liberty—New York harbor
1904 **Fingerprinting**—police department to adopt the fingerprinting system—St. Louis, Mo.
1919 **Prohibition**—prohibition law (national) —Volstead Act enacted
1922 **Radio Broadcast**—football game (collegiate) coast-to-coast broadcast—New York City
1927 **Aviation—Airport**—air passenger international station — opened — Key West, Fla.
1929 **Births**—child born in an airplane—Miami, Fla.
1933 **Emergency Housing Corporation** (U.S.)— authorized
1934 **Indians**—Indian tribal constitution—under Indian Reorganization Act—signed
1935 **Indians**—Indian tribal constitution—signed—Washington, D.C.
1946 **Atomic Energy Commission**—Atomic Energy Commission—appointed
1958 **Brokerage**—woman director of a stock exchange—M. G. Roebling

OCTOBER 29

1766 **Fox Hunting Club**—preliminary meeting—Philadelphia, Pa.
1796 **Ship**—ship from the Atlantic coast to anchor in a California port—"Otter" —arrived—Monterey, Calif.
1814 **Ship**—steam-propelled frigate—"Demologos"—launched—New York City
1833 **Fraternity (Greek letter)**—fraternity house—Kappa Alpha Society—Williamstown, Mass.—chapter founded
1834 **College**—coeducational college—Oberlin Collegiate Institute—Oberlin, Ohio —graduation
1836 **Animals** — cattle (shorthorn) public auction sale—Chillicothe, Ohio
1904 **Automobile Trucking Service**—automobile inter-city trucking service—Colorado City, Colo.-Snyder, Tex.
1928 **Aviation—Passenger**—woman Zeppelin passenger (paying)— Clara Adams —sailed—Lakehurst, N.J.
1940 **Conscription**—peacetime conscription bill—drawing of numbers—Washington, D.C.
1945 **Medal**—Medal of Freedom awarded to a woman—Anna Rosenberg

1947 **Forest Fire**—forest fire drenched by man-made rain—Concord, N.H.

1959 **Television — Telecast —** stockholders' meetings televised coast-to-coast simultaneously

OCTOBER 30

1768 **Methodist Chapel —** dedicated — New York City

1794 **Ball Bearing**—commercial installation —Lancaster, Pa.

1799 **Naval Officer**—naval chaplain—William Balch—commissioned

1888 **Pen**—ball-point pen patent—J. J. Loud—Weymouth, Mass.

1894 **Time Recorder**—card time recorder—patented—D. M. Cooper—Rochester, N.Y.

1903 **Traffic Regulation Pamphlet**—printed traffic regulations — enacted — New York City

1912 **Vice Presidential Candidate —** vice presidential nominee to die before the meeting of the electoral college—J. S. Sherman—died

1917 **Naval Officer**—naval chaplain who was Jewish—David Goldberg

1941 **World War II**—American destroyer torpedoed and sunk while on convoy duty—"Reuben James"

1953 **Television—Telecast —** color telecast on a closed circuit local station—Philadelphia, Pa.

OCTOBER 31

1777 **Holiday**—Thanksgiving Day celebration (nationwide, colonial) — committee appointed to draft recommendation

1835 **Insurance**—mutual fire insurance company—Manufacturers' Mutual Fire Insurance Company of Rhode Island —incorporated

1838 **School**—model school—opened—Lafayette College—Easton, Pa.

1868 **Postal Service —** letter-carriers' uniforms approved

1883 **Temperance Society**—women's temperance society (national)—World Woman's Christian Temperance Union—organized

1892 **Street Car**—transfers (printed)—used —Rochester, N.Y.

1952 **Atomic Bomb**—atomic fusion (thermonuclear) bomb—detonated—Marshall Islands

1953 **Television—Telecast**—opera (major) televised in color—*Carmen*—New York City

1956 **Discovery**—American to land by air at the South Pole—G. J. Dufek

NOVEMBER 1

1776 **Lottery**—lottery held by the Continental Congress—lottery approved

1777 **Flag**—American flag saluted by a foreign nation—"Ranger"—sailed for France

1778 **Holiday**—Thanksgiving Day celebration (nationwide, colonial)—resolution accepted

1781 **Bank**—bank chartered by Congress—Bank of North America—organized—Philadelphia, Pa.

1781 **Medical Society —** medical society (state)—Massachusetts Medical Society—incorporated—Boston, Mass.

1784 **Citizenship —** citizenship (colonial) conferred by special grant—Maryland —session held

1848 **Medical School —** women's medical school — Boston Female Medical School—organized

1853 **Water Cures —** introduced — R. T. Trall—New York City

1864 **Postal Service**—money order system —established

1870 **Weather Bureau —** weather bureau (U.S.)—weather observations made—signal corps—War Department

1873 **Wire**—barbed wire — manufacturing began—De Kalb, Ill.

1879 **Bridge —** railway all-steel bridge — Glasgow, Mo.

1879 **Indian School —** Indian school of prominence—opened—Carlisle, Pa.

1895 **Automobile Club —** American Motor League—meeting—Chicago, Ill.

1901 **Ship**—schooner (seven masted, steel) —keel laid—Quincy, Mass.

1904 **Army War College —** first class — Washington, D.C.

1904 **Police**—police bureau of identification —Henry fingerprinting system added —Chicago, Ill.

1920 **Aviation**—hydroplane commercial line service (international) — Key West, Fla.

1932 **Pump**—computer pump—marketed—Fort Wayne, Ind.

1937 **Insurance**—group hospital-medical cooperative—Washington, D.C.

1939 **Impregnation —** impregnation (artificial)—rabbit exhibited — New York City

1940 **Air Raid Shelter**—air raid shelter—completed—Fleetwood, Pa.

1941 **Army Language School —** began courses—San Francisco, Calif.

1942 **Church of England**—American bishop to become bishop of a British Church of England—Spence Burton

1944 **Births**—quadruplets delivered by Caesarean operation—Philadelphia, Pa.

1950 **Basketball**—National Basketball Association Negro player—C. H. Cooper—played—Fort Wayne, Ind.

1951 **Atomic Bomb —** atomic explosion witnessed by troops—New Mexico

1951 **Coal**—coal pipeline unit (demonstration)—in operation—Cadiz, Ohio

1955 **Ship**—guided missile cruiser—"Boston"—converted—Philadelphia, Pa.

NOVEMBER 2

1776 Traitor—William Dement—deserted

1824 **Presidential Candidate** — presidential candidate to receive the greatest number of popular and electoral votes and yet fail of election

1824 **Presidential Popular Vote**—vote recorded

1833 **Animals**—cattle importation of purebred shorthorns—Ohio Company for Importing English Cattle—organized —Chillicothe, Ohio

1886 **Automobile Tractor** — endless chain tractor—patent—Charles Dinsmoor— —Warren, Pa.

1886 **Governor** — gubernatorial election in which two brothers were the opposing candidates— R. L. Taylor and A. A. Taylor—Tennessee

1904 **Fingerprinting** — federal penitentiary fingerprinting—Leavenworth, Kan.

1909 **Election Law**—preferential ballot system—election—Grand Junction, Colo.

1915 **Election Law**—proportional representation—Ashtabula, Ohio

1917 **World War I**—American Army soldiers killed in combat—France

1918 **World War I**—German spy to receive a death sentence from the American forces during World War I— death sentence confirmed

1929 **Theater**—newsreel theater—opened— —New York City

1931 **Rubber**—synthetic rubber produced on a commercial scale—Wilmington, Del.

1933 **Surgical Operation** — epileptic case treated by elevation of the skull cap— demonstrated—New York City

1936 **Theater**—state-owned theater—performance of *The Comedy of Errors*— Seattle, Wash.

1945 **Industrial and Labor Relations School** —registration began

1947 **Aviation** — **Airplane** — airplane with eight engines—tested—Long Beach, Calif.

1948 **Senator (U.S.)**—senator to win a seat which had been occupied by his father and mother—Russell Long—elected— Louisiana

1954 **Senator (U.S.)**—senator elected by a write-in-vote—J. S. Thurmond

1957 **Titanium** — titanium mill — opened — Toronto, Ohio

NOVEMBER 3

1803—**Evangelical Association Council** — meeting—Bucks County, Pa.

1863 **Yeast**—yeast preparation patent—J. T. Alden—Cincinnati, Ohio

1881 **Coast Guard** — inland U.S. Coast Guard station — opened — Louisville, Ky.

1889 **State**—states admitted to the Union simultaneously—North and South Dakota

1892 **Telephone**—automatic telephone system (successful)—opened—La Porte, Ind.

1899 **Moving Picture**—moving picture of a real pugilistic encounter taken at night —Coney Island, N.Y.

1900 **Automobile Show**—New York City

1911 **Continuation School** — continuation school established by state law— opened—Racine, Wis.

1930 **Tunnel**—vehicular tunnel to a foreign country—Detroit, Mich.

1945 **Judge** — Negro judge of a Customs Court (U.S.)—I. C. Mollison—inducted—U.S. Customs Court—New York City

1952 **Bread** — frozen bread — marketed — Port Chester, N.Y.

1953 **Navy**—podiatry section of the Navy —established—

1953 **Television** — **Telecast** — color coast-to-coast live telecast—New York City

1954 **Horse Race**—horse race in which the British Royal Silks participated— Laurel, Md.

1955 **Virus**—virus (human- or animal-infecting virus) to be crystallized—Berkeley, Calif.

NOVEMBER 4

1780 **Diplomatic Service**—consul to die in service — William Palfrey — elected consul

1846 **Leg (artificial)** patent—B. F. Palmer —Meredith, N.H.

1862 **Ordnance**—machine gun (rapid fire) —patent—R. J. Gatling—Indianapolis, Ind.

1873 **Dentistry**—patent for a gold crown— J. B. Beers—San Francisco, Calif.

1873 **Slicing Machine** — patent — Anthony Iske—Lancaster, Pa.

1879 **Cash Register**—patent—J. J. Ritty— Dayton, Ohio

1880 **Engineering Society**—mechanical engineering national society—American Society of Mechanical Engineers—annual meeting—New York City

1913 **Senator (U.S.)**—senators "elected by the people"—election

1914 **World War I**—American ship lost in World War I—"William P. Frye" cleared from Seattle, Wash.

1924 **Governor**—woman governor of a state —N. T. Ross—elected governor of Wyoming

1933 **Railroad** — gasoline-driven stainless steel, air-conditioned, pneumatic-tired, two-car train—delivered—Dallas, Tex.

1939 **Automobile**—air-conditioned automobile—exhibited—Chicago, Ill.

1943 **Medal**—combat infantry badge—authorized

1775 **Postal Service**—mail franking privilege—authorized

1791 **Academy**—meeting held — Philadelphia, Pa.

1805 **Expedition** — expedition across the continent to the Pacific coast—Lewis and Clark—reached Columbia River

1825 **Art Organization**—artists' society of importance—New York Drawing Association—organized—New York City

1837 **College**—college for women—Mount Holyoke Seminary, South Hadley, Mass.—opened

1864 **Army Vote**—election

1898 **Initiative and Referendum** — amendment submitted to state—South Dakota

1904 **Electric Attachment Plug (separable)** —patented—Harvey Hubbell—Bridgeport, Conn.

1910 **Insect Electrocutor Patent**—W. M. Frost—Spokane, Wash.

1926 **Ferryboat**—ferryboat built exclusively for motor vehicle transportation— in service — Weehawken, N.J. and New York City

1938 **Legislator (state)** — Negro woman state legislator — C. B. Fauset — elected—Philadelphia, Pa.

1941 **Aviation—Airplane** — naval patrol bomber—"Mars"—christened — Baltimore, Md.

1950 **Aviation—Aviator**—jet plane combat victor in the Korean War—R. J. Brown—over North Korea

1954 **Senator (U.S.)**—woman senator to succeed a woman senator—H. H. Abel

NOVEMBER 9

1748 **College**—college charter granted by a governor or acting governor with only the assent of his council—first commencement—College of New Jersey—Princeton, N.J.

1756 **Stage Coach Inter-City Service**—between New York City and Philadelphia—inaugurated

1790 **President**—President who had been a senator — James Monroe — served — Virginia

1820 **Library**—mercantile library — organized—New York City

1821 **Pharmacy College**—pharmacy college — Philadelphia College of Apothecaries—opened—Philadelphia, Pa.

1835 **Police**—state police—G. W. Davis authorized to raise twenty more Texas Rangers

1842 **Patent** — design patent — issued — George Bruce—New York City

1877 **Chemical Society** — chemical society (national)—American Chemical Society—incorporated

1911 **Electric Sign**—neon tube advertising sign—George Claude—patent application

1930 **Aviation—Flights**—New York-Panama non-stop flight—R. W. Ammel

1933 **Civil Works Administration (U.S.)**—established

1961 **Aviation—Flights**—airplane to exceed the speed of 4,000 miles an hour— flown — Edwards Air Force Base, Calif.—Robert White

NOVEMBER 10

1775 **Marines**—American marines—organized

1798 **Nullification Proceedings**—Kentucky Resolutions adopted—Lower House

1801 **Dueling Legislation (state)**—enacted —Knoxville, Tenn.

1814 **Conscription** — wartime conscription bill—passed

1817 **Trust**—trust—organized — Kanawha, W.Va.

1865 **War Criminal Proceedings** — Henry Wirz hanged

1868 **Knights of Pythias** — constitution adopted for Supreme Lodge—Wilmington, Del.

1891 **Temperance Society** — women's temperance society (national) — World Woman's Christian Temperance Union — convention — Boston, Mass.

1895 **Monument** — statue officially sanctioned by Rome—blessed—New Orleans, La.

1899 **Anesthesia** — spinal anesthesia report —Rudolph Matas treated case—New Orleans, La.

1914 **Bank**—bank established in a foreign country—Buenos Aires, Argentina

1919 **War Veterans' Society** — American Legion—national convention—Minneapolis, Minn.

1951 **Telephone** — dial telephone service coast-to-coast without the aid of operators—Englewood, N.J.

1959 **Submarine**—submarine with two nuclear reactors — "Triton" — commissioned

1959 **Submarine**—submerged circumnavigation of the earth—"Triton"—commissioned

NOVEMBER 11

1647 **School Law (compulsory)**—enacted— Massachusetts

1817 **Sword Swallower**—exhibition—Senaa Samma—New York City

1839 **Military School**—state military school —cadets mustered into service—Lexington, Va.

1851 **Telescope**—telescope patent — Alvan Clark—Cambridge, Mass.

1868 **Sports**—amateur indoor athletic games —New York City

1919 **Holiday**—Armistice Day—celebrated

1919 **Ship**—concrete ship built for the United States Shipping Board—"Atlantus" —delivered

1920 **Aviation — Aviator** — naval ace in World War I—awarded Distinguished Service Medal—D. S. Ingalls

1921 **Monument**—monument to the "unknown soldier" (national)—burial of "unknown soldier"—Arlington, Va.

1925 **Cosmic Ray**—discovery announced at Madison, Wis.

1926 **Dance Course**—with collegiate credit —University of Wisconsin—Madison, Wis.

1933 **Electrical Contract**—by city with federal government — signed — Tupelo, Miss.

1934 **Railroad**—streamlined all-steel diesel motor train—Lincoln, Neb., to Kansas City, Mo.

1935 **Balloon Flight**—balloon flight to exceed an altitude of 70,000 feet—O. A. Anderson and A. W. Stevens—Rapid City, S.D.

1935 **Photograph**—photograph showing the lateral curvature of the horizon—Rapid City, S.D.

NOVEMBER 12

1799 **Astronomy**—meteoric display — Florida

1843 **Jews**—Jewish fraternal society—B'nai B'rith — first lodge founded — New York City

1861 **Petroleum Exported to Europe**—shipped—Philadelphia, Pa.

1881 **Quarantine**—plant quarantine legislation (state)—rules and regulations issued—California

1885 **Library Society** — library society (local)—New York Library Club—general meeting—New York City

1903 **Humane Society**—humane association national organization—American Humane Association—incorporated

1911 **Aviation—Flights (transcontinental)**—transcontinental airplane flight—C. P. Rodgers—crashed—Compton, Calif.

1912 **Aviation—Flights**—airplane catapulted —Washington, D.C.

1915 **Nobel Prize**—Nobel prize in chemistry—T. W. Richards

1920 **"Baseball Dictator"**—K. M. Landis—elected

1921 **Conference**—conference of great powers—Conference on the Limitation of Armaments—Washington, D.C.

1926 **Aviation — Airplane Bombing** — airplane bombing in the United States—Williamson County, Ill.

1928 **Skeet** — college skeet tournament — Princeton, N.J.

1932 **President** — President to invite the President-elect for discussion—H. C. Hoover

1940 **Health Museum**—not connected with another museum—Cleveland Health Museum—opened—Cleveland, Ohio

1941 **Aviation—Aviator**—woman test pilot —Alma Heflin—Lock Haven, Pa.

1941 **Medical Clinic** — heredity clinic — opened—Ann Arbor, Mich.

1946 **Bank**—"autobank" complete service—Chicago, Ill.

1947 **Medal**—Agriculture Department distinguished service gold medal—awarded

1948 **Betatron**—mobile betatron—placed in service—White Oak, Md.

NOVEMBER 13

1749 **Academy** — Benjamin Franklin appointed president—Academy and College of Philadelphia

1798 **Nullification Proceedings**—Kentucky Resolutions—adopted—Upper House

1839 **Anti-Slavery Party** — Liberty Party convention—Warsaw, N.Y.

1865 **Money**—gold certificates—issued

1868 **Philological Society**—national philological Association — organized — New York City

1875 **Bowling Rule Standardization** — undertaken—New York City

1913 **Medical Society**—American College of Surgeons—annual convocation — Chicago, Ill.

1927 **Tunnel**—twin-tube subaqueous vehicular tunnel—Holland tunnel—opened —Jersey City, N.J. to New York City

1930 **Milking Platform (rotating)**—housed —Plainsboro, N.J.

1931 **Senator (U.S.)**—woman elected to the Senate—H. O. W. Caraway—appointed—Arkansas

1933 **Strike**—modern sit-down strike—Austin, Minn.

1938 **Catholic Beatification**—Catholic beatification of an American citizen—Mother Frances Xavier Cabrini

1945 **Radio Telephone** — two-way equipped bus—license granted to operate—Washington, D.C.

1946 **Snow** — artificial snow — produced — Mt. Greylock, Mass.

1955 **Television—Telecast**—live telecast from a noncontiguous foreign country—Havana, Cuba

NOVEMBER 14

1732 **Librarian**—librarian—Louis Timothee —hired—Philadelphia, Pa.

1784 **Protestant Episcopal Bishop**—Protestant Episcopal bishop—Samuel Seabury—consecrated

1825 **Ship**—iron vessel (sheet iron)—"Codorus"—tested

1832 **Street Car**—street car—used—New York City

1868 **Farmers' Institute**—farmers' institute sponsored by a college—Manhattan, Kan.

1878 **Humane Society**—humane association national organization—American Humane Association — constitution adopted

1889 **Tour of the World**—tour of the world made by a woman traveling alone—Nellie Bly—left New York City

1906 **President**—President to visit a foreign country — Theodore Roosevelt — at Panama

1910 **Aviation — Flights —** airplane flight from a ship—Eugene Ely

1921 **Opera**—opera broadcast in its entirety by a professional cast—*Samson et Dalila*—Chicago, Ill.

1931 **Animals**—cattle (Africander cattle)—shipment left Capetown, South Africa

1934 **Symphony —** symphony on a Negro folk theme—presented—Philadelphia, Pa.

1935 **Photograph**—portrait (life-size) of a human in a newspaper—Larry Quinn—San Francisco, Calif.

1937 **Church**—children's church—dedicated—Milton, Mass.

1941 **Business**—department store to hold a public art auction—Gimbel Brothers—New York City

1954 **Protestant Church**—Reformed Dutch Church Negro pastor—New York City

NOVEMBER 15

1681 **Shorthand Report**—St. Johns, Md.

1777 **Articles of Confederation**—adopted—Philadelphia, Pa.

1791 **College**—Catholic college — Georgetown College—opened — Washington, D.C.

1806 **Periodical**—college magazine—*Literary Cabinet*—published—New Haven, Conn.

1807 **Evangelical Conference**—assembled — Kleinfeltersville, Pa.

1849 **Poultry Show**—Boston, Mass.

1860 **Lighthouse** — iron pile lighthouse — light operated—new lighthouse—Minot's Ledge, Mass.

1864 **Mines School** — opened — Columbia University—New York City

1882 **Naval Officer**—naval attaché—F. E. Chadwick—sent to London

1884 **Newspaper Syndicate —** newspaper syndicate to supply articles—S. S. McClure—New York City

1896 **Niagara Falls**—utilization of Niagara Falls waterpower (large scale) — power transmitted to Buffalo, N.Y.

1898 **Foreign Service School** — School of Comparative Jurisprudence and Diplomacy — opened — George Washington University—Washington, D.C.

1899 **Newspaper**—newspaper published at sea (radio news service)—*Trans-Atlantic Times* issued

1914 **World War I**—American combatant casualty in World War I—France

1917 **Army Officer —** regimental Jewish chaplain—E. C. Voorsanger—commissioned

1919 **Congress (U.S.)—Senate**—Senate cloture resolution — invoked — Washington, D.C.

1928 **Railroad Car**—rail detector car in commercial service—in service—Montpelier, Ohio

1931 **Aviation—Parachute**—parachute jump from an autogiro—Frankie Hammond—Caldwell, N.J.

1935 **Social Security Act (U.S.)**—unemployment compensation law—approved—Washington, D.C.

1937 **Congress of the United States**—congressional session in air-conditioned Senate and House chambers—Washington, D.C.

1938 **Television — Telecast —** unscheduled event to be televised—Ward's Island, N.Y.

1940 **Conscription —** peacetime conscription bill—call for men

1948 **Locomotive**—gas turbine-electric locomotive—track-tested—Erie, Pa.

1949 **Aviation**—aviation trainer (jet)—flight evaluation test

1950 **Hockey**—Negro player in organized hockey—Arthur Dorrington—signed

1954 **Aviation — Flights (world) —** round-the-world flight over the North Pole on a regularly scheduled commercial air route — Copenhagen, Denmark — Los Angeles, Calif.

1960 **Submarine**—ballistic missile submarine—"George Washington"—on patrol duty

NOVEMBER 16

1676 **Prison**—prison — William Bunker—hired—Nantucket, Mass.

1776 **Flag**—American flag saluted by a foreigner—Johannes de Graeff—St. Eustatius, Dutch West Indies

1786 **Spinning, Carding and Roping Machines —** compensation granted to manufacturers—Bridgewater, Mass.

1798 **Nullification Proceedings**—Kentucky Resolutions—approved by governor

1810 **Actor**—English actor of note—G. F. Cooke—arrived—New York City

1841 **Life Preserver**—life preserver of cork—patented—N. E. Guerin

1875 **Dental Mallet**—dental mallet patented—W. G. A. Bonwill—Philadelphia, Pa.

1898 **Library Society**—state librarians' society—Washington, D.C.

1901 **Automobile**—automobile to exceed the speed of a mile a minute—A. C. Bostwick—Brooklyn, N.Y.

1914 **Bank**—federal reserve system — in operation

1920 **Postal Service**—postage meter—officially set—Stamford, Conn.

1925 **Atheism Society —** of importance — American Association for the Advancement of Atheism—incorporated—New York

1945 **Element**—element 95 — americium — announced

1945 **Element**—element 96 — curium — announced

1945 **Jewish College**—Jewish college of liberal arts and sciences under Jewish auspices—became Yeshiva University—New York City

1946 **Evangelical United Brethren Church** —formed—Johnstown, Pa.

1955 **Aquatic Mammals**—dugong—arrived —San Francisco, Calif.

1955 **Ship**—speed-boat to exceed 200 miles an hour—D. M. Campbell

NOVEMBER 17

1637 **Club Woman**—Anne Hutchinson— brought to trial—Cambridge, Mass.

1774 **Military Organization**—military organization (anti-British)—Light Horse of the City of Philadelphia—organized —Philadelphia, Pa.

1785 **Church of England**—Church of England organized in New England— James Freeman ordained

1797 **Clock**—clock patent—Eli Terry—East Windsor, Conn.

1800 **Congress of the United States**—Congress of the United States—first session—Washington, D.C.

1800 **Congress (U.S.)—House of Representatives**—House of Representatives— session in Washington, D.C.

1851 **Postage Stamp**—postage stamps depicting the American eagle—issued

1875 **Theosophical Society**—American Theosophical Society — founded — New York City

1880 **Immigration**—Chinese labor immigration act—treaty with China

1886 **Newspaper**—newspaper association— American Newspaper Publishers Association organized

1889 **Railroad**—daily railroad service to the Pacific coast—through service—Chicago, Ill. to Portland, Ore.

1909 **Fraternity (Greek letter)**—inter-fraternity council—meeting—New York City

1913 **Dental School** — dental hygienists' course—Fones Clinic — Bridgeport, Conn.

1917 **Ship**—naval vessels to sink an enemy submarine—"Fanning" and "Nicholson"

1933 **National Emergency Council (U.S.)**— authorized

1943 **Medal**—Soldier's Medal awarded to a Women's Army Corps member—presented—M. H. Maloney

1945 **Wedding**—wedding in the United States Occupation Forces in Korea

NOVEMBER 18

1787 **Unitarian Minister**—James Freeman —ordained—Boston, Mass.

1805 **Women's Club** — women's club — Female Charitable Society—Wiscasset, Me.

1820 **Discovery**—discovery of Antarctica— N. B. Palmer

1874 **Temperance Society**—women's temperance society (national)—National Woman's Christian Temperance Union—organized—Cleveland, Ohio

1883 **Time (standard)**—adopted

1890 **Ship** — battleship of importance — "Maine"—launched—New York City

1894 **Newspaper**—newspaper Sunday comic section—published—New York *World*

1899 **Hospital**—tuberculosis hospital operated by the government—patients received—Fort Stanton, N.M.

1913 **Aviation—Flights**—airplane loop the loop—Lincoln Beachey—San Diego, Calif.

1921 **Fencing**—international fencing championship competition — Washington, D.C.

1933 **Emergency Housing Corporation (U.S.)**—organized

1943 **Cabinet of the United States**—cabinet officer to address a joint session of Congress—Cordell Hull

1943 **Diplomatic Service**—ambassador to Canada—Ray Atherton—nominated

1948 **Vice President of the United States**— Vice President to marry in office— A. W. Barkley

1950 **X-Ray**—fluoro-record reflector camera —announced

NOVEMBER 19

1777 **Army**—brevet conferred upon an American — Walter Stewart — Continental Congress

1794 **Extradition**—extradition treaty with a foreign country—signed—Great Britain—London, England

1812 **Historical Society**—historical society (national)—American Antiquarian Society—first meeting—Boston, Mass.

1850 **Magic Lantern Slides (glass plate)**— patent—Frederick Langenheim—Philadelphia, Pa.

1872 **Adding Machine**—adding machine to print totals and sub-totals—patented— E. D. Barbour—Boston, Mass.

1893 **Newspaper**—newspaper colored supplement—issued—New York *World*

1895 **Pencil**—paper pencil—patented—F. E. Blaisdell—Philadelphia, Pa.

1916 **Aviation—Flights**—airplane to fly a distance exceeding 500 miles—Chicago, Ill., to Hornell, N.Y.—Ruth Law

1928 **Caterpillar Club**—father and son Caterpillar Club members — father jumped

1941 **Brokerage**—woman to sell securities on the floor of the New York Curb Exchange—Linda Darnell

1942 **Cemetery**—foreign service women interred in the Arlington National Cemetery—Arlington, Va.

1954 **Toll Collector (automatic)—Garden** State Parkway, N.J.

NOVEMBER 20

1789 **Constitutional Amendment (U.S.)**— constitutional amendments—first state to ratify—New Jersey

1866 **Bicycle**—bicycle with a rotary crank —patented—Pierre Lallemont

1866 **College**—Negro university to establish undergraduate, graduate and professional schools—Howard University—founded—Washington, D.C.

1866 **War Veterans' Society**—Grand Army of the Republic—national convention—Indianapolis, Ind.

1888 **Time Recorder**—employees' time recorder—patented—W. L. Bundy—Auburn, N.Y.

1909 **Medal**—National Institute of Arts and Letters gold medal—awarded—posthumously—Augustus Saint-Gaudens

1914 **Passport**—passport photographs—required

1919 **Aviation—Airport** — airport municipally owned—Tucson, Ariz.

1925 **Photograph**—photograph from an airplane at night—Rochester, N.Y.

1931 **Teletype Service** — teletype service (commercial) — American Telegraph and Telephone Company

1953 **Aviation—Flights**—airplane to exceed the speed of 1,300 miles an hour—Scott Crossfield

NOVEMBER 21

1766 **Theater**—theater building (permanent)—Southwark Theatre—Philadelphia, Pa.

1810 **Actor**—English actor of note—debut—G. F. Cooke—New York City

1824 **Jewish Congregation**—Jewish congregation (reform)—Charleston, S.C.

1871 **Cigar Lighter Patent**—M. F. Gale—New York City

1918 **Prohibition**—prohibition law (national)—enacted

1922 **Senator (U.S.)**—woman to occupy a seat in the Senate—R. L. Felton—served

1922 **Ship**—cruise ship to circumnavigate the world—"Laconia"—left New York City

1933 **Commercial Policy Executive Committee**—organized

1933 **Diplomatic Service** — ambassador to the Union of Soviet Socialist Republics—W. C. Bullitt—served

1936 **Degrees (academic and honorary)**—American awarded honorary degrees from three of England's leading universities—R. W. Bingham—Oxford University

1936 **Degrees (academic and honorary)**—husband and wife awarded honorary degrees—Mr. and Mrs. J. N. Garner—Waco, Tex.

1938 **Radio Station** — municipal school-owned ultra-high frequency radio station—WBOE—Cleveland, Ohio

1942 **Submarine**—submarine built on the Great Lakes—"Peto"—accepted

1946 **President**—President to travel underwater in a captured enemy submarine—H. S. Truman—Key West, Fla.

1951 **Atomic Energy Commission**—Atomic Energy Commission Patent Compensation Board—award—C. E. McClellan

1952 **Postage Stamp**—postage stamp in two colors produced by the rotary process at the Bureau of Engraving and Printing — International Red Cross issue

NOVEMBER 22

1809 **Pen**—steel pen patent—Peregrine Williamson—Baltimore, Md.

1842 **Volcano**—eruption—recorded — Lassen Peak, Calif.

1906 **Radio Distress Signal**—radio distress signal—SOS signal adopted

1910 **Golf Clubs**—steel shaft for a golf club—patented—A. F. Knight—Schenectady, N.Y.

1923 **World War I**—German spy to receive a death sentence from the American forces during World War I—pardon granted by President Coolidge

1929 **Congress (U.S.) — Senate** — Senate hearing in which women, other than members of Congress, were permitted on the floor—Washington, D.C.

1930 **Football Game**—football game played in the United States to be broadcast in England—New Haven, Conn.

1932 **Pump**—computer pump—patented

1935 **Air Mail Service**—Pacific air mail flight—"China Clipper" — left — San Francisco, Calif.

1943 **Marines**—woman marine major—R. C. Streeter—advanced to lieutenant-colonel

1955 **Air Mail Service**—helicopter air mail and express service to carry passengers—service Los Angeles—Long Beach, Calif.

1955 **Cabinet of the United States**—cabinet session held at a place other than the seat of the United States Government—Gettysburg, Pa.

NOVEMBER 23

1765 **Stamp Act Repudiation** — Frederick, Md.

1835 **Horseshoe Manufacturing Machine**—patented—Henry Burden—Troy, N.Y.

1848 **Medical Society**—women's medical society—organized—Boston, Mass.

1876 **Football Club**—intercollegiate football association — formed — Springfield, Mass.

1925 **Theater**—state-owned theater dedicated to its own drama—opened—Chapel Hill, N.C.

1935 **Musician** — woman conductor-composer—to write and conduct an opera—Ethel Leginska—*Gale*—sung—Chicago, Ill.

1942 **Coast Guard (U.S.)** — Coast Guard Women's Reserve — "SPARS" — authorized

1948 **Lens**—lens to provide zoom effects—patented—F. G. Back

NOVEMBER 24

1703 **Lutheran Church** — Lutheran pastor ordained in America—Justus Falckner

1827 **Horticultural Society** — horticultural society (permanent) — Pennsylvania Horticultural Society—organized

1871 **Rifle Association** — rifle association (national) — National Rifle Association—incorporated

1874 **Wire**—barbed wire—patented—J. F. Glidden—De Kalb, Ill.

1885 **Nurses' Society**—nurses' society (local) Philomena Society — organized — New York City

1896 **Election Law**—absentee voting law (state)—enacted—Vermont

1903 **Automobile Electric Self-Starter** — automobile electric self-starter patent —C. J. Coleman—New York City

1942 **Coast Guard (U.S.)**—Coast Guard Women's Reserve—D. C. Stratton—assumed command

1947 **Postmaster**—postmaster general appointed from the ranks—J. M. Donaldson

1954 **President**—presidential airplane (turbocompound powered)

NOVEMBER 25

1715 **Patent**—English patent granted to a resident of America—Thomas Masters

1834 **Opera**—opera singer (American) to sing in an Italian opera in Italian—Julia Wheatley—New York City

1837 **Silk** — silk power loom — patented — William Crompton—Taunton, Mass.

1850 **Museum** — college museum — F. S. Holmes elected curator

1874 **Greenback Party**—Independent Party —organized—Indianapolis, Ind.

1884 **Milk**—evaporated milk—patented—J. B. Meyenberg

1903 **Prize Fight**—pugilist to win three world championships—R. P. (Bob) Fitzsimmons—light heavyweight championship won—San Francisco, Calif.

1912 **Medical Society**—American College of Surgeons — incorporated — Springfield, Ill.

1920 **Radio Broadcast**—football game (collegiate) broadcast—College Station, Tex.

1925 **Newspaper**—composograph photograph in a newspaper—published—New York City

1960 **Atomic Reactor**—atomic reactor for research and development—in operation—Richland, Wash.

NOVEMBER 26

1716 **Animals**—lion — exhibited — Boston, Mass.

1722 **Art Commission (public)**—Gustavus Hesselius—"The Last Supper"—painting hung

1758 **Holiday**—Thanksgiving Day sermon —west of the Alleghenies—delivered—Charles Beatty—Pittsburgh, Pa.

1789 **Holiday**—Thanksgiving Day—holiday —designated by presidential proclamation

1825 **Fraternity (Greek letter)**—social fraternity—Kappa Alpha—established—Schenectady, N.Y.

1832 **Street Car**—street car—service begun —New York City

1867 **Railroad Car**—refrigerator car patent —J. B. Sutherland—Detroit, Mich.

1896 **Football Game**—indoor football game (large)—Chicago, Ill.

NOVEMBER 27

1676 **Fire**—fire of serious consequence—Boston, Mass.

1779 **College**—university legally designated as a university—University of Pennsylvania

1820 **Library**—mercantile library—Mercantile Library Association of the City of New York—constitution adopted

1839 **Statistical Society**—of importance—American Statistical Association—organized—Boston, Mass.

1901 **Army War College** — authorized — Washington, D.C.

1921 **Radio Church** — Radio Church of America—New York City

1940 **Ship**—merchant ship formally blessed at a launching ceremony—"Rio Hudson"—Chester, Pa.

1951 **Rocket**—rocket to intercept an airplane—White Sands Proving Grounds, N.M.

NOVEMBER 28

1895 **Automobile Race**—automobile race—Chicago to Waukegan, Ill.

1922 **Skywriting**—skywriting—demonstrated —Cyril Turner—New York City

1929 **Aviation—Flights**—South Pole flight —take-off—R. E. Byrd

1953 **Television — Telecast** — pay television presentation of a moving picture shown simultaneously in theaters—Palm Springs, Calif.

NOVEMBER 29

1775 **Diplomatic Service**—foreign service committee—formed

1775 **Ink**—invisible ink—Committee of Secret Correspondence—formed

1816 **Bank**—savings bank—Bank for Savings in the City of New York—conceived—New York City

1825 **Opera**—opera (Italian)—performed—New York City

1890 **Football Game**—Army-Navy football game—West Point, N.Y.

1895 **Catholic Apostolic Delegate**—Francesco Satolli—appointed cardinal

1929 **Aviation—Flights**—South Pole flight—R. E. Byrd—flew over pole

1932 **Electric Bridge Table** — patented — Laurens Hammond—Chicago, Ill.

1933 **Liquor Stores (state)**—authorized—Pennsylvania

1948 **Television** — **Telecast** — opera (complete) to be televised from the Metropolitan Opera House—New York City

1951 **Atomic Bomb**—atomic bomb underground explosion—Frenchman Flat, Nev.

1953 **Aviation—Flights (transcontinental)**—transcontinental regularly scheduled two-way non-stop service—Los Angeles, Calif., and New York City

NOVEMBER 30

1782 **Treaty**—treaty between the United States Government and a nation with which it had been at war—with Great Britain—preliminary articles signed

1803 **Territorial Expansion**—annexation of territory — Spain ceded Louisiana claims to France

1804 **Impeachment**—impeachment proceedings against a Justice of the Supreme Court of the United States—Samuel Chase

1866 **Tunnel**—subaqueous highway tunnel—work started—Chicago, Ill.

1875 **Oat-Crushing Machine** — patented — A. J. Ehrrichson—Akron, Ohio

1886 **Electric Power Plant** — alternating current power plant commercially successful—operated—Buffalo, N.Y.

1887 **Softball** — indoor baseball game—played—Chicago, Ill.

1899 **Aluminum**—aluminum used commercially in a transmission conductor—Hartford, Conn.

1924 **Radio Facsimile Transmission**—photograph sent by radio across the Atlantic as a public demonstration—received—New York City

1939 **President**—President to hold an airplane pilot's license — D. D. Eisenhower

1950 **Milk** — concentrated milk — sold — Wilmington, Del.

1954 **Meteorite**—meteorite known to have struck a woman—Sylacauga, Ala.

1958 **Ship** — guided missile destroyer — "Dewey"—launched—Bath, Me.

DECEMBER 1

1751 **Manual Training**—school to offer courses in manual training—opened—Talbot County, Md.

1841 **Normal School**—normal school instruction course given at a university—Wesleyan University—Middletown, Conn.

1841 **Ship**—steamboat engine built in America for a screw-propelled vessel—"Vandalia"—launched

1842 **Naval Officer** — naval officer condemned for mutiny—hanged

1843 **Insurance**—mutual life insurance company to be chartered—New England Life Insurance Company—Boston, Mass.—organized for business

1896 **Accountant**—C.P.A.'s conferred—New York

1904 **Pressing Machine (steam-operated)**—patent application—A. J. Hoffman

1909 **Bank** — Christmas savings club — payment made—Carlisle, Pa.

1913 **Automobile Service Station**—drive-in service station—opened—Pittsburgh, Pa.

1914 **Aviation—School**—naval air training school—opened—Pensacola, Fla.

1919 **Woman**—American-born woman to become a member of Parliament—Lady Astor—sworn in

1921 **Balloon**—balloon filled with helium gas—flight from Hampton Roads, Va., to Washington, D.C.

1921 **Postal Service**—philatelic agency—opened—Washington, D.C.

1924 **Corn Husking Championship Contest (national)**—Alleman, Iowa

1930 **Aviation—Flights (transcontinental)**—transcontinental airplane flight by a woman—Ruth Nichols—arrived—Burbank, Calif.

1932 **Medal** — platinum medal — made by U.S. mint—presented to President Hoover

1936 **Soilless Culture of Plants**—commercial hydroponicum (large)—patent

1938 **Legislator (state)** — Negro woman state legislator—assumed office—C. B. Fauset

1941 **Civil Air Patrol (U.S.)**—organized

1941 **Glider**—glider (all plywood-plastic)—tested—San Fernando, Calif.

1956 **Brokerage**—woman president of a major stock brokerage concern—J. P. Bay—New York City

1959 **Photograph**—photograph in color of the earth from outer space—missile launched—Cape Canaveral, Fla.

DECEMBER 2

1816 **Bank**—savings bank actually to receive money on deposit—Philadelphia Savings Fund Society—Philadelphia, Pa.—opened

1852 **Railroad**—railroad to run west of the Mississippi River—Pacific Railway of Missouri—test run

1908 **Federal Council of the Churches of Christ in America**—organized—Philadelphia, Pa.

1926 **Street Car**—aluminum street car—service—Cleveland, Ohio

1933 **Industrial Recovery Act**—conviction under a National Industrial Recovery Code—New York City

1933 Wedding—transatlantic telephone wedding—Detroit, Mich.

1934 Telescope—telescope lens two hundred inches in diameter—molten glass poured—Corning, N.Y.

1939 Woman — woman presidential campaign co-manager—R. H. M. Simms

1941 Aviation — Flights (world) — world flight by a commercial airplane—"Pacific Clipper"—left San Francisco, Calif.

1942 Atomic Energy—self-sustaining nuclear chain reaction demonstration—Chicago, Ill.

1952 Television—Telecast—birth (human) to be televised for the public—Denver, Colo.

1957 Electric Power Plant—atomic electric generating station (full scale)—operated—Shippingport, Pa.

1957 Ship—atomic-powered cruiser—"Long Beach"—keel laid—Quincy, Mass.

DECEMBER 3

1750 Opera—opera performed by a professional visiting troupe—*Beggar's Opera* —New York City

1825 Fraternity (Greek letter)—social fraternity—Kappa Alpha—Schenectady, N.Y.—initiation

1833 College—coeducational college—Oberlin Collegiate Institute—Oberlin, Ohio —opened

1834 Dental Society—dental society (local) —Society of Surgeon-Dentists formed —New York City

1835 Insurance—mutual fire insurance company—policy issued — Manufacturers' Mutual Fire Insurance Company

1875 Coaching Club—formed—New York City

1922 Moving Picture—Technicolor motion picture film—successful—*Toll of the Sea*—released

1948 Army Officer—woman army officer— M. A. Hallaren—sworn in

DECEMBER 4

1776 Ship—warship (American built) to enter European waters—"Reprisal"— sailed

1779 Law School—law school in a college— George Wythe appointed professor of law

1812 Mower (horsepower) — patented — Peter Gaillard—Lancaster, Pa.

1839 Political Convention — unit rule— adopted—Harrisburg, Pa.

1843 Paper—manila paper—patented—J. M. & L. Hollingsworth—South Braintree, Mass.

1867 Agricultural Society—agricultural society of national importance—National Grange of the Patrons of Husbandry —organized—Washington, D.C.

1875 Intercollegiate Athletic Association— organization meeting—Saratoga, N.Y.

1918 President—President to visit a European country—Woodrow Wilson—left Washington, D.C.

1918 Ship—concrete ship built for the United States Shipping Board—"Atlantus"—launched—Brunswick, Ga.

1922 Diplomatic Service—woman legation secretary—Lucille Atcherson—Columbus, Ohio—appointed

1933 Federal Alcohol Control Administration—authorized

1935 College—college classes to combat the influence of communism—instituted— St. Joseph's College—Philadelphia, Pa.

1942 Citizenship—citizenship granted to an alien on foreign soil—conferred—Panama Canal Zone

DECEMBER 5

1776 Fraternity (Greek letter)—scholastic fraternity—Phi Beta Kappa—founded —Williamsburg, Va.

1782 President—President born a citizen of the United States—Martin Van Buren —Kinderhook, N.Y.

1786 War—rebellion against the federal government—Daniel Shays—Worcester, Mass.

1831 Congress of the United States—Congress in which 1,000 bills were introduced

1843 Ship—iron vessel built for the United States Navy—"Michigan" launched— Pittsburgh, Pa.

1846 Cellulose Nitrate Patent — C. F. Schoenbein

1854 Chair—folding theater chair—patented —A. H. Allen—Boston, Mass.

1868 Bicycle School—velocipede riding— opened—New York City

1876 Wrench—pipe or screw wrench (practical)—patented—D. C. Stillson—Somerville, Mass.

1879 Telephone—automatic telephone system patent—Daniel Connolly—Philadelphia, Pa.

1905 Medal—Interstate Commerce Commission Medal of Honor—awarded—G. H. Poell—Grand Island, Neb.

1906 Young Women's Christian Association —national convention — New York City

1908 Football Uniform Numerals—used— University of Pittsburgh—Pittsburgh, Pa.

1927 King—king born in the United States —Rama IX of Thailand

1929 Nudist Organization — American League for Physical Culture—organized—New York City

1933 Constitutional Amendment (U.S.)— constitutional amendment submitted to the states for repeal—amendment ratified

1935 **Soilless Culture of Plants**—commercial hydroponicum (large)—established—Montebello, Calif.

1948 **Television**—Telecast—church service televised in sign language—Jamaica, N.Y.

1950 **Television**—Telecast — X-ray fluoroscopy television discussion—Baltimore, Md.

1951 **Garage**—completely automatic push-button controlled garage—Washington, D.C.—opened

1955 **Television**—Telecast—murder trial to be televised—Waco, Tex.

DECEMBER 6

1732 **Play (drama)**—play acted by professional players—*The Recruiting Officer*—New York City

1787 **Methodist College** — opened — Cokesbury College—Abingdon, Md.

1787 **State**—state to ratify the federal Constitution—Delaware

1790 **Congress of the United States**—Congress of the United States—first session in Philadelphia, Pa.

1825 **Conference**—conference of American Republics—appointment of delegates confirmed

1830 **Observatory** — observatory (national)—established—Washington, D.C.

1866 **Water Conduit**—water supply tunnel for a city—completed—Chicago, Ill.

1873 **Football Game**—international football game—New Haven, Conn.

1876 **Crematory**—crematory—incineration—Baron de Palm—Washington, Pa.

1884 **Monument** — monument to George Washington (national)—aluminum tip set—Washington, D.C.

1922 **Electric Transmission**—electric power line commercial carrier—operated—Utica, N.Y.

1923 **Radio Broadcast**—presidential message to be broadcast—Calvin Coolidge—Washington, D.C.

1929 **Congress (U.S.)**—Senate — senatorial controversy in which no candidates were seated after a recount

1935 **Air Mail Service**—Pacific air mail flight—"China Clipper"—return—San Francisco, Calif.

1946 **Medal**—soldier to receive seven decorations at once—L. M. Chilson

1949 **Television**—Telecast—medical intra-city color telecast—Johns Hopkins Hospital—Baltimore, Md.

DECEMBER 7

1787 **State**—state to ratify the federal Constitution—signed—Delaware

1841 **Newspaper Syndicate**—syndication of newspaper material—M. Y. Beach—New York City

1848 **Senator (U.S.)**—father and son senators at the same session—Henry Dodge and A. C. Dodge

1881 **Insurance**—bonding company (exclusive)—American Surety Company—New York City—incorporated

1887 **Hospital**—cancer hospital—opened for patients—New York City

1891 **Congress of the United States**—Congress to appropriate a billion dollars—session opened—Washington, D.C.

1891 **Tunnel**—subaqueous railroad tunnel to a foreign country—opened for passenger traffic—Port Huron, Mich.

1903 **Radio Distress Signal**—radio distress signal (CQD) from an American ship—"Kroonland"

1909 **Plastic**—thermosetting man-made plastic—patented — L. H. Baekeland — Yonkers, N.Y.

1916 **Bird Legislation (international)**—international treaty for the protection of wild birds—ratifications exchanged—United States and Great Britain

1917 **World War I**—United States declaration of war against Germany (World War I)—declaration against Austria-Hungary

1926 **Refrigerator**—gas refrigerator (household)—patented

1930 **Radio Broadcast**—submarine (submerged) broadcast—New London, Conn.

1932 **Ship**—gyro-stabilized vessel to cross the Atlantic Ocean—"Conte di Savoia"—arrived—New York City

1938 **Newspaper**—radio facsimile newspaper daily—St. Louis *Post-Dispatch*

1939 **Aviation**—Passenger—woman flown in a U.S. Army plane from one country to another—left Mitchel Field, N.Y.

1941 **Naval Officer**—admiral killed in action in World War II—I. C. Kidd—Pearl Harbor, Hawaii

1941 **Radar**—radar used to detect enemy airplanes—Pearl Harbor, Hawaii

1941 **World War II**—air hero—G. S. Welch

1941 **World War II**—Japanese attack in World War II

1941 **World War II**—Japanese submarine sunk by an American ship—"Ward"

1942 **Coast Guard (U.S.)**—Coast Guard Women's Reserve—"SPARS"—first recruit—D. E. L. Tuttle

1951 **Television**—Telecast—surgical operation televised on a coast-to-coast closed circuit in color—Los Angeles, Calif.

1953 **Automobile**—transparent-top automobile—"Sun Valley" manufactured—Detroit, Mich.

1954 **Heliport**—military heliport—dedicated

1959 **Ship** — guided missile destroyer — "Dewey"—commissioned— Bath, Me.

DECEMBER 8

1792 **Cremation**—Henry Laurens—died

1863 **Amnesty** — proclamation — Abraham Lincoln

1863 Farmers' Institute—farmers' institute sponsored by a state—Springfield, Mass.

1869 Naval Academy (U.S.)—Japanese midshipman in the United States Naval Academy—Z. Z. Matzmulla— admitted

1886 Labor Union—labor union of importance—adopted name American Federation of Labor

1890 Woman—woman labor delegate to a national convention—of the American Federation of Labor—Mary Burke— Detroit, Mich.

1909 Bird Banding Society—bird banding society—American Bird Banding Association—formed—New York City

1916 Bird Legislation (international)—Migratory Bird Treaty—proclaimed

1928 Physician—Capitol physician—G. W. Calver

1929 Radio Telephone—radio telephone ship-to-shore commercial service— New York City

1931 Cable—coaxial cable—patented

1939 Television — Telecast — telecast produced for a tri-city gathering— Schenectady, N.Y.

1941 Congressman (U.S.)—congresswoman to vote twice against the entry of the United States into war—Jeannette Rankin

1941 Ordnance—tank (heavy 60-ton)—delivered—Eddystone, Pa.

1946 Aviation—Airplane — rocket plane — tested—Muroc, Calif.

1946 Snow Melting Apparatus—snow-melting apparatus (practical) with pipe imbedded in the sidewalk—tested— New York City

1948 Television—Telecast—split-screen image —exhibited—New York City

1959 Moving Picture—moving picture with scent—*Behind the Great Wall*—presented —New York City

DECEMBER 9

1621 Sermon Printed (American)—Robert Cushman—Plymouth, Mass.

1814 Conscription — wartime conscription bill—approved by House of Representatives—but not enacted into law

1845 Suture—silver wire suture—J. M. Sims —experimented—Montgomery, Ala.

1869 Labor Union—labor organization to admit workmen other than craft workmen—Noble Order of the Knights of Labor—founded—Philadelphia, Pa.

1884 Roller Skate—ball-bearing skate patent—L. M. Richardson—Chicago, Ill.

1901 Bicycle Race—paired six-day bicycle race—New York City

1907 Seal—Christmas seals of the modern variety sold to raise funds to fight tuberculosis—Wilmington, Del.

1909 Aviation — Airplane — monoplane (American)—flown—Mineola, N.Y.

1930 Labor Department (U.S.) — native-born Secretary of Labor—W. N. Doak —sworn in

1934 Autogiro—autogiro (wingless direct control)—flown—Philadelphia, Pa.

1939 Aviation—Passenger—woman flown in a U.S. Army plane from one country to another—arrived—Santiago, Chile

1940 Radio Advertising—radio advertising contract for frequency modulation broadcasts—signed—New York City

1941 World War II—American bombing mission in the Orient—Vigan, Philippines

1945 Television — Telecast — stratovision flight test—Middle River, Md.

1960 Computer—electronic computer to employ Thin-Film memory—announced

DECEMBER 10

1672 Postal Service — postal route — announced

1690 Loan—state loan—authorized—Massachusetts

1792 Insurance—life insurance — Insurance Company of North America—organized—Philadelphia, Pa.

1815 Naval Officers' Training School— naval officers' training school—established—Boston, Mass.

1843 Ship—warship with propelling machinery below the waterline—"Princeton"—launched—Philadelphia, Pa.

1869 Woman Suffrage—state to grant suffrage to women—vote extended to women by territorial legislature—Wyoming

1879 Library Society—library association (national)—American Library Association—incorporated

1888 Baseball Team—baseball teams to go on a world tour—first game abroad— Auckland, New Zealand

1896 Basketball—basketball intercollegiate game—New Haven, Conn.

1899 Hospital—tuberculosis hospital—National Jewish Hospital—Denver, Colo. —opened

1931 Nobel Prize — Nobel Peace Prize awarded an American woman—Jane Addams

1941 Civil Air Patrol (U.S.)—national commander J. F. Curry—appointed

1950 Nobel Prize—Negro to win the Nobel Peace Prize—R. J. Bunche

1951 Helicopter — gas-turbine helicopter (turborotor)—tested—Windsor Locks, Conn.

DECEMBER 11

1719 Aurora Borealis—recorded

1839 Statistical Society—American Statistical Association—constitution adopted —Boston, Mass.

1844 Anesthesia—anesthetic in dentistry— Horace Wells—extraction

1866 **Yacht Race**—yacht race across the Atlantic Ocean

1872 **Governor**—Negro governor (acting) —P. B. S. Pinchback—Louisiana

1882 **Theater**—theater lighted by electricity —Bijou Theater—Boston, Mass.

1901 **Radio Broadcast**—transatlantic radio signal—Guglielmo Marconi—England to Newfoundland

1909 **Moving Picture**—colored moving pictures—exhibited—New York City

1919 **Monument**—monument to an insect— dedicated—Enterprise, Ala.

1931 **Animals**—cattle (Africander cattle)— arrived—New York City

1952 **Television — Telecast** — pay television presentation of an opera—*Carmen*—New York City

1954 **Ship**—aircraft carrier with an angle deck—"Forrestal"—launched — Newport News, Va.

DECEMBER 12

1796 **Nail Cutting and Heading Machine**— patented—G. Chandler—Maryland

1808 **Bible Society** — Bible society — Bible Society of Philadelphia—organized

1862 **Torpedo**—torpedo mine attack—Civil War — against war vessel — Yazoo River—"Cairo"

1870 **Congressman (U.S.)**—Negro congressman—J. H. Rainey—sworn in

1889 **Sanitary District**—Chicago, Ill.—special election

1893 **Photographic Patent**—aerial photography patent—C. B. Adams

1899 **Golf Tee**—patented—G. F. Grant— Boston, Mass.

1902 **Multigraph**—commercial manufacture —Cleveland, Ohio

1906 **Cabinet of the United States**—cabinet member who was Jewish—O. S. Straus—appointed

1937 **Television Mobile Unit**—mobile television unit—New York City

1941 **Aviation—Aviator**—American Ace in World War II—B. D. Wagner—attacked Japanese planes

1941 **World War II**—American general killed in World War II—H. A. Dargue

DECEMBER 13

1621 **Furs**—exported—Boston, Mass.

1766 **Fox Hunting Club**—Gloucester Fox Hunting Club—meeting

1774 **Revolutionary War**—incident in the Revolutionary War — New Castle, N.H.

1809 **Surgical Operation**—abdominal operation—performed—Danville, Ky.

1816 **Bank**—savings bank to become a corporation—Provident Institution for Savings—Boston, Mass.—chartered

1816 **Drydock Patent**—issued—John Adamson—Boston, Mass.

1853 **Hospital**—women's infirmary staffed by women physicians—New York Infirmary—incorporated

1855 **Ship**—turreted frigate in the U.S. Navy—"Roanoke"—launched

1864 **Naval Officer**—naval officer to become an admiral—D. G. Farragut advanced to vice admiral

1879 **Ship**—fish hatching steamer (federal) —"Fishhawk"—launched

1893 **Tuberculosis Laboratory**—tuberculosis diagnostic community laboratory—authorized—New York City

1918 **President**—President to visit a European country—Woodrow Wilson—arrived—Brest, France

1918 **World War I**—American Army division to cross the Rhine River—First Division

1920 **Astronomer**—astronomer to measure the size of a fixed star—A. A. Michelson—Mount Wilson, Calif.

1933 **Medal**—Air Mail Flyer's Medal of Honor—presented—M. B. Freeburg

1938 **Casein Fiber**—patented

DECEMBER 14

1793 **Road**—state road authorization—Kentucky

1798 **Nut and Bolt Machine**—nut and bolt machine—patented—David Wilkinson

1798 **Screw**—screw patent—David Wilkinson

1849 **Music**—chamber music organization— concert—Boston, Mass.

1889 **Political Science Society**—political and social science society (national)— American Academy of Political and Social Science—organized—Philadelphia, Pa.

1902 **Cable**—cable across the Pacific Ocean —paid out

1934 **Locomotive**—streamlined steam locomotive—introduced—Albany, N.Y.

1944 **Army Officer**—generals to wear the five-star insignia—grade approved

1944 **Naval Officer**—naval officers to wear the five-star insignia—grade approved

1945 **Naval Officer**—naval nurses' corps (woman member)—S. S. Dauser—received Distinguished Service Medal

1952 **Siamese Twins**—Siamese twins to survive a separation operation and live for one year—born

DECEMBER 15

1778 **Arbitration**—state arbitration law—enacted—Maryland

1791 **Constitutional Amendment (U.S.)**— constitutional amendments—declared in force

1792 **Insurance**—life insurance—first policy —Insurance Company of North America—Philadelphia, Pa.

1810 **Irish Magazine**—*The Shamrock*—published—New York City

1820 **Pharmacopoeia**—pharmacopoeia (general)—published—Boston, Mass.

1854 **Street Cleaning Machine** — used — Philadelphia, Pa.

1872 **Fraternity Magazine**—fraternity journal—*Beta Theta Pi*—published—Alexandria, Va.

1874 **Visiting Celebrities**—king (reigning) to visit the United States—David Kalakaua of Hawaii received by U. S. Grant

1886 **Brokerage**—stock exchange at which more than a million shares were traded in one day—New York City

1906 **Medal**—National Geographic Society gold medal—Hubbard Medal presented —R. E. Peary—Washington, D.C.

1925 **Road**—road with a depressed trough— opened to traffic—Texas

1931 **Congress (U.S.)**—House of Representatives—congressional committee headed by a woman—M. T. Norton— became chairman

1939 **Nylon**—nylon yarn manufacture (commercial)—begun—Seaford, Del.

1942 **Automobile — License Plates** — plastic license plate tabs—issued—Massachusetts

1943 **Marines**—marine officer of Chinese descent—W. C. Sze—commissioned

1944 **Naval Officer**—naval officers to wear the five-star insignia — appointments ratified

1798 **Impeachment**—impeachment proceedings against a United States Senator —William Blount—trial held

1821 **Debtors' Prison**—abolished—legislation enacted—Kentucky

1880 **Electric Company**—electric company —Edison Electric Illuminating Company—incorporated

1895 **Paper Twine Machinery**—patented— G. L. Brownell—Worcester, Mass.

1895 **Temperance Society** — Anti-Saloon League (national organization)—Anti-Saloon League of America—formed— Washington, D.C.

1903 **Aviation**—**Airplane**—airplane to receive national acclaim—Wright brothers—flight—Kitty Hawk, N.C.

1906 **Cabinet of the United States**—cabinet member who was Jewish—O. S. Straus—began service

1924 **Locomotive**—diesel-electric locomotive —in service—Central Railroad of New Jersey

1937 **Newspaper** — radio facsimile newspaper—KSTP—St. Paul, Minn.

1946 **Money**—coin bearing the portrait of a Negro—issued

1948 **Television**—**Telecast**—airplane telecast (network)—Washington, D.C.

1959 **Moving Picture**—moving picture presented simultaneously in major cities throughout the world—*On the Beach*

DECEMBER 16

1835 **Fire**—fire of great destructive force— New York City

1851 **Brass Spinning**—patent—H. W. Hayden—Waterbury, Conn.

1891 **Immigration** — immigration bureau superintendent — W. D. Owen — appointment confirmed

1897 **Submarine**—submarine fitted with an internal combustion engine—demonstration—Patapsco River

1903 **Theater**—theater to employ women ushers—Majestic Theater—New York City

1907 **Radio Broadcast**—singer to broadcast —E. H. Farrar

1908 **Credit Union Association**—founded— Manchester, N.H.

1912 **Postage Stamp**—postage stamps to picture an airplane—issued

1922 **Judge**—woman associate justice of a state supreme court—F. E. Allen— elected—Cleveland, Ohio

1941 **World War II**—air hero—G. S. Welch —awarded Distinguished Service Cross

DECEMBER 17

1679 **Trust**—manufacturers' price regulation agreement—coopers—New York City

1791 **Traffic Regulation**—one-way traffic regulation—New York City

DECEMBER 18

1777 **Holiday**—Thanksgiving Day celebration (nationwide, colonial)

1796 **Newspaper**—newspaper to appear on Sunday—*Monitor*—Baltimore, Md.

1839 **Photograph** — celestial photograph — J. W. Draper—New York City

1862 **Hospital** — orthopedic hospital — New York Society for the Relief of the Ruptured and Crippled—organized— New York City

1865 **Animals** — cattle importation law (U.S.)—enacted

1917 **Prohibition**—prohibition amendment to the Constitution—submitted to the states

1935 **Money**—bill to depict both the face and the reverse side of the Great Seal of the United States—issued

1936 **Animals**—giant panda—arrived—San Francisco, Calif.

1953 **Television**—**Telecast**—color telecast by a local station—WPTZ-TV—Philadelphia, Pa.

DECEMBER 19

1620 **Colonist**—English settlement in America (permanent)—left Blackwell, England

1683 **Architect**—landscape architect—John Reid—arrived

1795 **Road**—state road appropriation of a specific sum—enacted—Kentucky

1799 **Forestry Legislation**—federal forestry legislation—land purchased—Grover's Island, Ga.

1823 **Birth Registration**—birth registration law (state)—enacted—Georgia

1854 **Sewing Machine**—sewing machine to sew curving seams—patented—A. B. Wilson—Watertown, Conn.

1871 **Paper**—corrugated paper—patented—A. L. Jones—New York City

1877 **Cattle Club**—cattle club (Guernsey cattle)—American Guernsey Cattle Club—annual meeting

1891 **Catholic Priest**—Negro Catholic priest ordained in the United States—C. R. Uncles—Baltimore, Md.

1903 **Bridge**—suspension bridge of importance having steel towers—opened—New York City

1910 **Rayon** — rayon — commercially produced—American Viscose Company—Marcus Hook, Pa.

1910 **Supreme Court (U.S.)**—Associate Justice of the Supreme Court to become Chief Justice—E. D. White—took seat as chief justice

1920 **Curling Rink**—indoor curling rink—Country Club—Brookline, Mass.

1927 **Aviation**—air control municipal board —formed—San Diego, Calif.

1928 **Autogiro**—autogiro—flown — Philadelphia, Pa.

1933 **Electric Home and Farm Authority, Inc.**—authorized

1933 **Radio Facsimile Transmission**—facsimile broadcast in ultra high frequencies—Milwaukee, Wis.

1939 **Television—Telecast**—moving picture premiere festivities to be televised—New York City

1958 **Radio Broadcast**—outer space broadcast—tape recording broadcast from rocket—D. D. Eisenhower

DECEMBER 20

1669 **Rebellion**—rebellion of colonists against the English—Marcus Jacobson—condemned for insurrection

1780 **Conscientious Objectors** — released from prison—Albany, N.Y.

1790 **Cotton Mill**—cotton mill to spin cotton yarn successfully—started—Samuel Slater—Pawtucket, R.I.

1803 **Territorial Expansion**—annexation of territory—France ceded Louisiana territory

1820 **Tax**—bachelor tax—levied—Missouri

1837 **College** — city college — College of Charleston—became municipal university—Charleston, S.C.

1860 **Secession**—secession act — enacted—South Carolina

1864 **Postal Service**—railroad post office for the general distribution of mail—G. B. Armstrong—appointed general superintendent

1870 **Farmers' Institute**—farmers' institute held by a land grant agricultural college off its campus—Cedar Falls, Iowa

1870 **Impeachment**—impeachment and removal from office of a state governor —proceedings against W. W. Holden —North Carolina

1879 **Electric Lighting**—electric incandescent lamp — demonstration — Menlo Park, N.J.

1880 **Electric Company**—electric company —president chosen—Edison Electric Illuminating Company

1887 **Time Recorder**—autograph time recorder — patented — B. F. Merritt—Newton, Mass.

1892 **Automobile Tire**—pneumatic tire patent—Syracuse, N.Y.

1893 **Lynch Law (state)**—enacted—Georgia

1928 **Postal Service**—international dog sled mail—left Lewiston, Me.

1938 **Television**—electronic television system—patented—V. K. Zworykin—Wilkinsburg, Pa.

1944 **Medal**—Navy unit commendation decoration—established

1951 **Atomic Energy**—electric power from nuclear energy—100,000 watts—Idaho Falls, Idaho

DECEMBER 21

1620 **Physician**—doctor in New England—Samuel Fuller—arrived

1784 **State Department (U.S.)**—state department (U.S.) secretary—John Jay —served

1829 **Bridge**—stone arch railroad bridge—Carrollton viaduct—Baltimore, Md.—opened

1849 **Ice Skating Club**—ice skating club formed—Philadelphia, Pa.

1861 **Medal**—Medal of Honor awarded to a member of the Naval Service—authorized

1909 **High School**—junior high schools—authorized—Berkeley, Calif.

1913 **Crossword Puzzle**—published—New York *World*

1914 **Moving Picture**—six-reel feature-length comedy—*Tillie's Punctured Romance*—released

1929 **Insurance**—group hospital insurance plan—Dallas, Tex.

1933 **Blood Bank**—blood serum (human) (dried)—prepared

1937 **Moving Picture** — animated cartoon in color (Technicolor) of feature length with sound—exhibited

DECEMBER 22

1772 **Schoolhouse** — west of the Allegheny Mountains — started — Schoenbrunn, Ohio

1775 **Naval Officer**—commander-in-chief of the Continental Navy—Esek Hopkins —served

1775 **Navy**—naval fleet—Continental Navy organized

1807 **Embargo Act**—enacted

1831 **Street Car**—street car company—New York and Harlem Railway—franchise received

1877 **Bicycle Magazine**—*American Bicycling Journal*—published—Boston, Mass.

1885 **Railroad**—switchback railway—patent —L. A. Thompson — Coney Island, N.Y.

1886 **Accountants' Society** — accountants' society to become a national organization—American Association of Public Accountants — formed — New York City

1894 **Golf Club**—golf association (national) —United States Golf Association—formed—New York City

1910 **Postal Savings Stamps**—issued

1914 **Prohibition**—prohibition vote—showing dry majority in House of Representatives

1920 **Radio Broadcast**—prize fight broadcast from the ringside—New York City

1922 **Wedding**—double radio wedding—New York City

1936 **Automobile License (federal)**—common carrier license—granted—Rodger's Motor Lines—Scranton, Pa.

1943 **Arts and Letters Society** — Negro member of the National Institute of Arts and Letters—W. E. B. Du Bois —elected

1944 **Medal**—combat decoration—for Army personnel—authorized

1956 **Animals**—gorilla born in captivity—Colo—Columbus, Ohio

DECEMBER 23

1776 **Loan**—loan for war purposes—authorized

1780 **Diplomatic Service**—consul to die in service—left Wilmington, Del.

1852 **Theater**—Chinese theater—"Celestial John" opened—San Francisco, Calif.

1873 **Degrees (academic and honorary)**—Bachelor of Music degree—awarded—M. P. Lowrie

1907 **Railroad Car**—steel passenger railroad coach — all-steel car completed — Altoona, Pa.

1913 **Bank**—bank established in a foreign country—Federal Reserve Act approved

1913 **Bank**—federal reserve system—Federal Reserve Act—approved

1919 **Ship**—ambulance ship, designed and built as a hospital—"Relief" launched

1930 **Police**—police bureau of criminal alien investigation — organized—New York City

1943 **Television** — Telecast — opera (complete) to be televised—*Hansel and Gretel*

DECEMBER 24

1733 **Map** — war map — published—New *York Weekly Journal*

1784 **Methodist** — Methodist bishop—Francis Asbury—elected—Baltimore, Md.

1832 **Hospital**—Negro hospital and asylum —Georgia Infirmary—Savannah, Ga. —incorporated

1889 **Bicycle**—bicycle with a back pedal brake—patented

1906 **Radio Broadcast** — radio program broadcast—R. A. Fessenden—Bryant Rock, Mass.

1936 **Isotope**—radioactive isotope medicine —administered—Berkeley, Calif.

1948 **Building** — house completely sun-heated—occupied—Dover, Mass.

1948 **Television**—Telecast—Catholic Mass (midnight) to be televised — New York City

1951 **Television**—Telecast—opera written for television — *Amahl and the Night Visitors*—New York City

1953 **Television**—Telecast—color and black-and-white telecast to be sponsored—"Dragnet"

DECEMBER 25

1723 **Baptist Church**—German Baptists — first immersion—Philadelphia, Pa.

1780 **Universalist Church of America** — church dedicated—Gloucester, Mass.

1818 **Oratorio**—oratorio performance (complete)—*The Messiah*—Boston, Mass.

1894 **Football Game**—midwestern football team to play on the Pacific coast—San Francisco, Calif.

1917 **Play (drama)** — drama to win a Pulitzer prize—*Why Marry?*—opened—New York City

1930 **Bobsled Run**—Lake Placid, N.Y.—open to public

1931 **Opera**—opera broadcast in its entirety by the Metropolitan Opera Company —*Hansel and Gretel* — New York City

DECEMBER 26

1799 **Presidential Eulogy**—Henry Lee

1805 **Art Organization**—art organization—Pennsylvania Academy of Fine Arts established—Philadelphia, Pa.

1833 **Annunciator**—patented—Seth Fuller—Boston, Mass.

1854 **Paper**—wood pulp paper—exhibited John Beardsley—Buffalo, N.Y.

1862 **Ship**—hospital ship of the U.S. Navy —"Red Rover"—converted into a hospital ship

1865 **Coffee Percolator Patent** — J. H. Nason—Franklin, Mass.

1877 **Socialist Labor Party of North America**—national convention — Newark, N.J.

1878 **Electric Lighting**—electric light in a store—installed—Philadelphia, Pa.

1917 **Railroad**—government operation of railroads — proclamation made — Woodrow Wilson

1931 **Play (drama)**—musical play to win a Pulitzer prize—*Of Thee I Sing*—opened —New York City

DECEMBER 27

1845 **Anesthesia** — ether administered in childbirth—C. W. Long—Jefferson, Ga.

1892 **Psychological Society**—psychological society (national organization) — American Psychological Association— scientific meeting — Philadelphia, Pa.

1894 **War Veterans' Society**—Military Order of Foreign Wars—founded—New York City

1906 **Sociological Society**—sociological society (national) — annual meeting — American Sociological Society — Providence, R.I.

1934 **Youth Hostel** — opened — Northfield, Mass.

1938 **Skimobile**—in operation—North Conway, N.H.

1941 **Railroad**—railroad to be completely equipped with diesel-electric engines— diesel unit placed in service

1945 **Bank** — world bank — International Bank for Reconstruction and Development—organized

1951 **Automobile** — right-hand-drive automobile for the delivery of mail—in service—Cincinnati, Ohio

DECEMBER 28

1784 **Ship**—trading ship sent to China— "Empress of China" — left China bound for the United States

1832 **Vice President of the United States**— Vice President to resign—J. C. Calhoun

1869 **Chewing Gum**—chewing gum patent — W. F. Semple — Mount Vernon, Ohio

1869 **Holiday** — Labor Day holiday — inaugurated—Philadelphia, Pa.

1877 **Flour Mill**—flour rolling mill—John Stevens—patent application

1912 **Street Car**—municipally owned street car—operated—San Francisco, Calif.

1920 **Ship**—ambulance ship, designed and built as a hospital—"Relief" delivered to U.S. Navy

1935 **Works Progress Administration** — Works Progress Administration Federal Art Project Gallery—opened— New York City

1942 **Aviation**—Aviator—aviator to fly one hundred times across the Atlantic Ocean—R. O. D. Sullivan

DECEMBER 29

1782 **Almanac** — nautical almanac — published—Boston, Mass.

1837 **Thresher**—threshing machine to employ steam—patented—J. A. Pitts

1848 **Gas**—gas light in the White House, Washington, D.C.

1851 **Young Men's Christian Association**— organized—Boston, Mass.

1867 **Telegraph**—telegraph ticker used by a brokerage concern — installed — New York City

1891 **Radio Patent**—T. A. Edison—Menlo Park, N.J.

1908 **Automobile Brake**—four-wheel brake patented

1913 **Moving Picture**—serial moving picture — *Adventures of Kathlyn* — released

1914 **Organists' Society**—organists' society (national) — convention — New York City

1931 **Water**—heavy water—discovery announced

1936 **Automobile License (federal)**—contract carrier license—issued

1938 **Bridge**—pontoon bridge of reenforced concrete—Lake Washington Floating Bridge—work begun—Seattle, Wash.

1949 **Television Station**—ultra high frequency television station to operate on a regular daily basis—KC2XAK — Bridgeport, Conn.

1952 **Deaf—Hearing Aid** — transistorized hearing aid—offered for sale—Elmsford, N.Y.

1955 **Helicopter**—aerocycle—purchased by U.S. Army

DECEMBER 30

1731 **Music**—concert—Boston, Mass.

1799 **Musician** — Negro-song popularizer— J. C. G. Graupner—Boston, Mass.

1854 **Oil**—oil company—Pennsylvania Rock Oil Company incorporated

1869 **Labor Union**—labor organization to admit workmen other than craft workmen—first candidate elected—Philadelphia, Pa.

1873 **Weights and Measures Standardization**—national organization to improve systems of weights, measures, and moneys—American Metrological Society—formed—New York City

1887 **Physiological Society** — physiological society national organization—American Physiological Society—formed — New York City

1903 **Political Science Society**—political science association—American Political Science Association—founded — New Orleans, La.

1913 **Crepe**—"Crepe Georgette" trademark registered

1913 **Tungsten**—ductile tungsten—patented —W. D. Coolidge—Schenectady, N.Y.

1941 **Ship**—Liberty ship—"Patrick Henry" —delivered—Baltimore, Md.

1954 **Sports Trophy**—Negro to win the James E. Sullivan Memorial Trophy— M. G. Whitfield

1955 **Army Officer**—Army Medical Specialist Corps male officer—Sheldon Saffren—commissioned

1959 **Submarine** — ballistic missile submarine — "George Washington" — commissioned—Groton, Conn.

DECEMBER 31

1776 **Price Regulation Law**—price regulation law (colonial)—enacted—Rhode Island

1800 **Book** — book with color plates — *The City of Philadelphia*—published—Philadelphia, Pa.

1830 **Parade**—street parade held by a mystic society—Mobile, Ala.

1841 **Dental Legislation**—legislation (state) regarding dental surgery — enacted — Alabama

1877 **President**—President to celebrate his silver wedding anniversary at the White House—R. B. Hayes

1879 **Electric Lighting** — electric incandescent lamp — public demonstration — Menlo Park, N.J.

1923 **Radio Broadcast**—transatlantic broadcast of a voice—KDKA—Pittsburgh, Pa.

1934 **Aviation**—**Aviator**—woman aviator to pilot an air-mail transport — Helen Richey

1944 **Medal**—Distinguished Service Medal (Army) awarded to a woman—O. C. Hobby

1948 **Senator (U.S.)** — Senator to win a seat which had been occupied by his father and mother—Russell Long

1951 **Battery**—battery to convert radioactive energy into electrical energy—announced—P. E. Ohmart

1953 **Jockey**—jockey to ride 400 winners in one year—Willie Shoemaker

1955 **Corporation** — corporation to earn more than $1 billion in one year

Index to Personal Names

To obtain a complete account of the various items, the reader should consult the main body of the text. The **boldface** type shows the alphabetical heading under which each item may be found. If an item appears in the text under a general heading, the specific heading is noted below after the general heading. The individuals listed in this index are associated in some way with the events described; they are not necessarily the persons referred to in the headings.

Adams, Nathan—**Federal Home Loan Bank Board**

Adams, Samuel — **Holiday** — Thanksgiving Day celebration (nation-wide, colonial)

Adams, Samuel—**Medical Society**—medical society (state)

Adams, Thomas F.—**Printing Press**—printing press for polychromatic printing

Adamson, John—**Drydock Patent**

Addams, Jane—**Nobel Prize**—Nobel Peace Prize awarded an American woman

Adler, Cyrus—**Jewish College**—Jewish non-sectarian college

Adler, Felix—**Ethical Culture Society**

Adler, Max—**Planetarium**—planetarium open to the public

Adler, Peter Herman—**Television**—**Telecast** —opera (major) televised in color

Adt, John—**Wire**—wire cutting machine and automatic straightener

Affel, Herman A.—**Cable**—coaxial cable

Agassiz, Louis—**Science School**—natural science summer school

Aitken, Jane—**Bible**—Bible translated into English in America

Aitken, R.—**Trade Register**

Aitken, Robert—**Bible**—Bible printed in English

Aitken, Robert—**Military Drill Manual**— military drill manual devoted to field strategy

Aitken, Robert—**Money**—fifty-dollar gold pieces minted by the United States

Akeley, Carl Ethan—**Taxidermy Method (sculptural)**

Akin, Irwin—**Curling Championship (national)**

Akin, William B.—**Map**—automobile road map

Albanese, Licia—**Television**—**Telecast**—opera (complete) to be televised from the Metropolitan Opera House

Albee, Fred Houdlett—**Medical Clinic**—flying medical clinic

Albright, Jacob — **Evangelical Association Council**

Albright, Jacob—**Evangelical Church**

Albright, Jacob—**Evangelical Conference**

Albright, Tenley—**Ice Skating Champion**— American world figure skating champion

Albrizio, Conrad—**Art Course**—art course

Alcock, John—**Aviation**—**Flights (transatlantic)**—transatlantic non-stop flight from America

Alcott, William Andrus—**Physiological Society**—physiological society

Alda, Robert — **Television**—**Telecast**—color program (commercial)

Alden, J. T.—**Yeast**—yeast preparation patent

Alden, Timothy — **Typesetting Machine** — typesetting machine

Alden, William Livingston—**Canoe Association**

Ale, Fern—**Woman**—woman secretary of a state senate

Alexander, Ben — **Television** — **Telecast** — color and black-and-white telecast to be sponsored

Alexander, Harry Louis—**Medical Periodical**—allergy magazine

Alexander, Lucy Maclay—**Medal**—Agriculture Department distinguished service gold medal presented to a woman

Alexander, Moses—**Governor**—Jewish governor

Alexander, William — **Aviation** — **Flights** — New York-Bermuda flight

Alexanderson, Ernst Fredrik Werner—**Television**—**Telecast**—speaker to address an organization by television

Alexanderson, Ernst Fredrik Werner—**Theater**—television theater demonstration

Alger, Cyrus—**Ordnance**—gun (rifled)

Alison, Francis—**Insurance**—life insurance company

Allcock, Thomas—**Adhesive and Medicated Plaster**—adhesive and medicated plaster patent

Allen, Aaron H.—**Chair**—folding theater chair

Allen, Andrew—**Cricket Club**—cricket club

Allen, Arthur Augustus—**Birds**—ptarmigan (Eskimo chicken)

Allen, Chet — **Television** — **Telecast** — opera written for television

Allen, Florence Ellinwood—**Judge**—woman associate justice of a state supreme court

Allen, Florence Ellinwood—**Judge**—woman associate justice of the circuit court of appeals

Allen, Florence Ellinwood—**Judge**—woman judge to sentence a man to death

Allen, George—**Book**—book on vellum

Allen, George—**President**—presidential airplane (turbo-compound powered)

Allen, Herman—**Diplomatic Service**—ministers plenipotentiary to South and Central America

Allen, Horatio—**Locomotive**—locomotive for railroad use

Allen, Horatio — **Locomotive Headlights** — locomotive illumination

Allen, J.—**Music Book**—hymn book with music

Allen, James—**Aviation**—aeronautical division of the United States War Department

Allen, John — **Agricultural Book** — agricultural book

Allen, John—**Business Manual**

Allen, John—**Dental Code of Ethics**

Allen, John—**Farrier's Guide**

Allen, Lewis Falley—**Herd Book**

Allen, Macon B.—**Lawyer**—Negro lawyer formally admitted to the bar

Allen, Nathan—**Phrenology Magazine**

Allen, Richard—**African Church**

Allen, Richard—**Methodist Episcopal Church** —African Methodist Episcopal church

Allen, Richard—**Negro**—national colored convention

Allen, Stephen—**Treadmill**

Allen, Tom — **Prize Fight** — international fight, with bare knuckles

Allen, William—**Insurance**—life insurance company

Allen, Zachariah—Insurance—mutual fire insurance company

Allerton, Isaac—Orphanage—orphanage

Allgood, Howard Ray—Fingerprinting—community to fingerprint its citizens

Allison, Fran—Television—Telecast — color network telecast in compatible color

Allison, Fred—Element—element 87

Allison, Richard—Army—medical corps

Allman, David Bacharach—Television—Telecast—surgical operation televised on a closed circuit in color

Alston, Anna—Nurses' Society—society for superintendents of nursing schools

Altamirano, Frai Juan Cabezas de—Catholic Bishop—Catholic bishop

Altmeyer, Arthur Joseph—Social Security Act (U.S.)

Alvord, Henry Elijah—Animal Industry Bureau (U.S.)—dairy division

Ambler, Richard—Customhouse

Ameche, Don—Television—Telecast—color coast-to-coast telecast from the west coast

American, Sadie—Women's Club—Jewish women's organization (national)

Ames, David—Arsenal

Ames, David—Ordnance—muskets

Ames, John—Shovel—shovel (steel)

Ames, Nathan—Escalator—escalator patent

Amherst, Jeffery—Knighthood—knighthood conferred in America

Ammel, Roy W.—Aviation—Flights—New York-Panama non-stop flight

Ammen, Daniel—Fishes—goldfish industry

Amoros, Sandy (Edmundo Isasi Amoros)—Baseball Game—major league game in which the majority of the players were Negroes

Anagnos, Michael — Kindergarten — kindergarten for the blind

Anderson, Alexander—Engraving—wood engraving made with an engraving tool

Anderson, Broncho Billy. See Aronson, Max

Anderson, Carl David—Physics—positron

Anderson, Charles Alfred—Aviation—Flights (transcontinental)—transcontinental flight made by Negroes in their own plane

Anderson, Ellie Mae—Submarine—ballistic missile submarine

Anderson, Eugenie—Diplomatic Service—ambassador (woman)

Anderson, Eugenie—Treaty—treaty signed by a woman ambassador

Anderson, G. M. See Aronson, Max

Anderson, George K.—Typewriter Ribbon—typewriter ribbon patent

Anderson, Humphrey S.—Baseball Game—intercollegiate baseball game

Anderson, James—Newspaper — newspaper published at sea

Anderson, Louis Francis—College—dean of men

Anderson, Marian—Opera—Negro singer of the Metropolitan Opera

Anderson, Mary—Labor Department (U.S.) —Women's Bureau

Anderson, Max. See Aronson, Max

Anderson, Orvil A.—Balloon Flight—balloon flight to exceed an altitude of 70,000 feet

Anderson, Richard Clough — Conference — conference of American republics

Anderson, Richard Clough — Diplomatic Service — ministers plenipotentiary to South and Central America

Anderson, Richard Clough—Treaty—treaty with a South American country

Anderson, Robert — Civil War — act that marked the inauguration of the War of 1861-1865

Anderson, Violette Neatly—Lawyer—Negro woman lawyer to practice before the United States Supreme Court

Anderson, William Robert—Medal—presidential citation in peacetime

Anderson, William Robert — Submarine — submarine crossing of the North Pole under water

Anderson, Willie—Golf Tournament—professional open championship

Andrew, John Albion — Unitarian Church Convention (national)

Andrews, Ebenezer T.—Gazetteer—American gazetteer

Andrews, Jedidiah — Presbyterian Presbytery

Andrews, William—Book—Book of Common Prayer (in the Mohawk Indian language)

Angell, James Rowland—Radio Broadcast—dinner broadcast round-the-world

Angle, Edward Hartley—Dental Society—orthodontists' society

Anson, Adrian Constantine—Baseball Team —professional league baseball team to win three pennants in succession

Antheil, George — Symphony—symphonic work to call for an airplane propeller

Anther, Georg—Opera—opera composed by a woman performed at the Metropolitan Opera House

Anthony, Susan Brownell—Temperance Society—women's temperance society (state)

Anthony, Susan Brownell — Woman Suffrage—woman suffrage associations (national)

Anthony, William Arnold — Dynamo — dynamo for a direct-current outdoor lighting system

Appert, François—Canning Book

Appleton, Edward — Railroad Commission (state)

Appleton, Nathan — Cotton Mill — cotton mill in the world in which the whole process of cotton manufacturing from spinning to weaving was carried on by power

Appleton, William Henry — Book Trade Magazine—successful book trade magazine

Apponyi, Geraldine — Woman — woman of American descent to become a queen

Arcaro, Eddie—**Jockey**—jockey (American-born) to win 3,000 races

Arcaro, Eddie—**Jockey**—jockey to win the Kentucky Derby four times

Arcaro, Eddie—**Jockey**—jockey to win the triple crown twice

Arch, Alexander—**World War I**—American shot fired in World War I

Archer, Fred—**Horse Race**—American-bred horse to win the English Derby

Archer, John — **Physician** — doctor to receive a bachelor of medicine degree

Argall, Samuel — **Navy** — naval expedition (colonial)

Argall, Samuel — **War (colonial)** — colonial warfare between England and France for the possession of North America

Arlin, Harold W.—**Radio Broadcast**—presidential inauguration

Armstrong, George Buchanan—**Postal Service**—railroad post office for the general distribution of mail

Armstrong, Henry Jackson—**Prize Fight**—pugilist to hold three titles simultaneously

Armstrong, Samuel T.—**Cable (telegraph)**—submarine telegraph cable to be insulated with gutta percha

Arnett, Benjamin William — **Legislator (state)**—Negro legislator

Arnheim, William—**Aviation—School**—high school aviation course

Arnold, Charles — **Journalism Course** — journalism school

Arnold Frank Atkinson—**Radio Instruction**—radio-advertising course

Arnold, Henry Harley—**Army Officer**—generals to wear the five-star insignia

Arnold, Henry Harley—**Aviation**—Women's Auxiliary Ferrying Squadron

Arnold, Henry Harley — **Medal** — Distinguished Service Medal (Army) awarded to a woman

Arnold, Lewis Golding — **Prison**—military prison of the United States

Arnold, Ross Harper — **Pump** — computer pump

Arnold, William Richard—**Army Officer**—general to be consecrated a bishop

Arnson, Ludwig—**Radio Distress Signal**—radio distress signal (CQD) from an American ship

Aronson, Max—**Moving Picture**—moving picture with a plot

Aronson, Max — **Moving Picture Actor** — moving picture star

Arpin, Paul — **Newspaper** — French daily newspaper (successful)

Arthur, Chester Alan—**Diplomatic Service**—Korean embassy received

Arthur, Chester Alan — **Immigration** — Chinese labor immigration act

Arthur, Chester Alan—**Labor**—labor bureau (federal)

Arthur, Robert—**Dental School**—dental college

Arthur, Robert—**Dentistry**—gold used for the filling of dental cavities

Asbury, Francis — **Methodist** — Methodist bishop

Asbury, Francis — **Periodical** — sectarian magazine

Ashburner, Charles E.—**City Manager**

Ashford, Emmett Littleton—**Baseball Umpire**—Negro umpire in organized baseball

Ashmun, Jehudi—**College**—Negro university

Aspinwall, Nan Jane — **Woman** — woman horseback rider to make a solo transcontinental trip

Assing, Norman — **Play (drama)** — Chinese theatrical performance

Astaire, Fred — **Moving Picture** — moving picture presented simultaneously in major cities throughout the world

Astor, John Jacob—**Colonist**—colonists to reach the Pacific coast

Astor, Mary—**Moving Picture**—talking picture

Astor, Nancy Witcher Langhorne (Lady Astor)—**Woman**—American-born woman to become a member of Parliament

Atcherson, Lucille — **Diplomatic Service** — woman legation secretary

Athenagaros, Archbishop — **Greek College and Orphanage**

Atherton, Ray — **Diplomatic Service** — ambassador to Canada

Atkins, Captain—**Animals**—bear (white)

Atkins, Charles Grandison—**Fish Hatchery (federal)**

Atkinson, Eudora Clark—**Prison**—reformatory (state) conducted for women

Atkisson, Earl James—**Army**—gas regiment

Attwater, Henry Smith — **College** — college course without Greek or Latin

Atwater, Robert—**Glider**—seaplane glider

Atwater, Wilbur Olin — **Agricultural Experiment Station**—state agricultural experiment station

Atwood, Harry N.—**Aviation**—airplane to land on the White House lawn

Atwood, Luther—**Coal Oil Factory**

Atwood, Margaret — **Automobile Transcontinental Trip**—transcontinental automobile trip by a woman

Atwood, N. E.—**Fish Commission (state)**

Atwood, Wallace Walter — **Geography School**

Aubin, Paul Myers — **Glider** — glider commercial freight service

Audubon, John James—**Bird Banding**—bird banding

Auer, Florence — **Television—Telecast**—musical comedy telecast (one-hour)

Austin, Ann—**Quakers**—Quakers to arrive in America

Austin, C.—**Melodeon Patent**

Austin, William A. — **Motorcycle**—motorcycle (steam-driven)

Averill, D. R.—**Paint**—paint (ready-mixed)

Axson, A. Forster—**Health Board**—health board (state) to regulate quarantine

Axtater, Karl S. — **Aviation—Airship**—dirigible transfer of mail to a train

Axton, John Thomas—**Army Officer**—chaplain (chief) of the U.S. Army

Ayllón, Lucas Vásquez de—**Catholic Mass**—Catholic Mass

Aymer, Gilbert Henry — **Moving Picture** — colored moving pictures

Ayres, Thomas N.—**Insurance**—mutual life insurance company to operate

B

Babbitt, Benjamin Talbert—**Baking Powder Manufacturer**

Babbitt, Benjamin Talbert—**Band Wagon**

Babbitt, Benjamin Talbert—**Premium**—premiums given with merchandise

Babbitt, Benjamin Talbert — **Soap** — soap powder in packages

Babbitt, Isaac—**Britannia Ware**

Babcock, Clifford D.—**Radio Tube**—three-element vacuum tube

Babcock, Stephen Moulton—**Milk Tester**

Bache, Alexander Dallas—**Science Association**—National Academy of Sciences

Bache, Benjamin Franklin—**Cryptography Chart**

Bache, Franklin—**Medical Book**—dispensatory (American)

Bache, Richard—**Birds**—partridge propagation

Bacher, Robert Fox—**Atomic Energy Commission**—Atomic Energy Commission

Back, Frank Gerard—**Lens**—lens to provide zoom effects

Bacon, Richard—**Fuse**—safety fuse

Bacon, Theodore C.—**Billiard Match**—intercollegiate billiard match

Bacon, Thomas—**Manual Training**—school to offer courses in manual training

Badin, Stephen Theodore—**Catholic Priest**—Catholic priest ordained in the United States

Baekeland, Leo Hendrik—**Plastic**—thermosetting man-made plastic

Baer, Arthur ("Bugs") — **Television**—**Telecast**—demonstration of home reception of television

Baer, Max — **Television** — **Telecast** — prize fight to be televised

Bagley, Sarah G.—**Woman**—woman telegrapher

Bagley, Worth—**Spanish-American War**—naval officer killed in the Spanish-American war

Bagno, Samuel — **Burglar Alarm** — burglar alarm operated by ultrasonic or radio waves

Bailey, Charles Franklin—**Museum**—maritime museum

Bailey, Ezekiel—**Oilcloth Factory**

Bailey, Francis—**Directory (city)**

Bailey, Jim—**Runner**—runner to run a mile under four minutes

Bailey, Joshua—**Knitting Machine (power)**

Bailey, Theodorus—**Treason**—citizen of the United States to be tried for treason, convicted, and hanged

Bailey, Timothy—**Knitting Machine (power)**

Bainard, Lawrence—**Republican Party**—Republican Party meeting (national)

Bainbridge, Charles T.—**Paper**—crepe paper

Bainbridge, William—**Naval Officers' Training School**—naval officers' training school

Baine, John—**Bible**—Catholic Bible

Baird, John Logic—**Television**—**Telecast**—transoceanic television image

Baird, Robert Atkinson—**Air Mail Service**—jet propelled airplane to transport mail

Baird, Spencer Fullerton—**Fish and Fisheries Commissioner**

Baird, Spencer Fullerton—**Fish Protection**—fish protection office (federal)

Baker, Belle—**Radio Broadcast**—radio broadcast from a moving train of a regular program on a national network

Baker, Bernard Nadel—**Shipping**—United States Shipping Board

Baker, Elisha — **Dental Magazine** — dental journal

Baker, Ellis Benjamin — **Telephone** — coin telephone

Baker, Eugene Voy—**Football Game**—intercollegiate football championship

Baker, Newton Diehl — **Medal** — Distinguished Service Medal awarded to a woman

Baker, Newton Diehl—**Nursing School**—Army school of nursing

Baker, Richard Freligh—**Photograph**—photograph of genes

Baker, Sara Josephine—**Child Hygiene Bureau**

Balbo, Italo—**Aviation**—**Flights (transatlantic)**—transatlantic foreign squadron flight to the United States

Balch, Emily Greene—**Fellowship**—fellowship (graduate) awarded by a women's college

Balch, William—**Naval Officer**—naval chaplain

Balchen, Bernt — **Aviation** — **Airplane**—airplane equipped with radio to cross the Atlantic Ocean

Balchen, Bernt — **Aviation** — **Flights**—South Pole flight

Baldwin, Caroline Willard—**Degrees (academic and honorary)**—Doctor of Science degree earned by a woman

Baldwin, Cyrus W.—**Elevator**—elevator patent, for a vertical-geared hydraulic electric elevator

Baldwin, Helen—**Bicycle Race**—women's six-day bicycle race

Baldwin, James Fowle—**Engineering Society**—engineering society

Baldwin, John—**Abolition Society**

Baldwin, Loammi—**Drydock**—federal drydocks

Baldwin, Luke—**Rubber**—rubber company

Baldwin, Simeon Eben—**Aviation**—**Legislation**—aviation legislation (state)

Baldwin, Simeon Eben—**Lawyers' Association**—lawyers' association (national)

Baldwin, Thomas Scott—**Aviation**—**Airship**—dirigible balloon contracted for by the United States Government

Baldwin, Thomas Scott—**Balloon**—balloon circular flight

Balfour, George—**Naval Officer**—naval surgeon of the U.S. Navy

Ball, Neal—**Baseball Game**—triple play unassisted in a modern major league game

Ball, Sarah B.—**Library**—business library supported by taxes

Ballantyne, William—**Aviation**—aeronautical stowaway

Ballenger, Edgar Garrison — **Photograph**—cystoscopic photographs in color

Ballentine, John Jennings—**Ship**—ship from which a long-range rocket was launched

Balsley, H. Clyde — **Aviation** — **Aviator** — American aviator shot down in World War I

Bancroft, Aaron—**Historical Society**—historical society (national)

Bancroft, Aaron—**Unitarian Society**—national organization of the Unitarian Churches of the United States and Canada

Bancroft, George—**Gymnasium**—gymnasium to offer systematic instruction

Bancroft, Jane M.—**Fellowship**—resident fellowship for women awarded by a women's college

Bancroft, Priscilla—**Births**—sextuplets

Bandmann, Julius—**Dynamite**

Banks, Arthur J.—**Aviation—License**—airplane instructor's license

Banneker, Benjamin—**Clock**—clock to strike the hours

Bannister, Marion Glass—**Treasury Department (U.S.)**—woman assistant treasurer of the United States

Banvard, John—**Chromo**

Baptist, John—**Boat Club**—boat club

Barber, Red (Walter Ranier Barber)—**Television—Telecast**—baseball games televised in color

Barbour, Edmund D.—**Adding Machine**—adding machine to print totals and subtotals

Barbour, William—**Linen Thread Factory** (successful)

Barclay, Edwin—**Visiting Celebrities**—president of a Negro country

Barclay, Thomas—**Diplomatic Service**—consular officer detailed for duty in the Department of Foreign Affairs

Bard, John—**Medical Book**—dissection essay

Bard, Samuel—**Medical Book**—obstetrics book

Bard, William—**Bank**—trust company

Bardeen, John—**Transistor**—transistor

Barker, James Nelson—**Play (drama)**—play about an Indian

Barkley, Alben William—**Vice President of the United States** — Vice President to marry in office

Barnaby, Hattie Meyer—**Aviation—License**—glider license class "C"

Barnaby, Ralph Stanton—**Aviation—License**—glider license class "C"

Barnaby, Ralph Stanton—**Glider**—amphibious seaplane glider

Barnaby, Ralph Stanton—**Glider**—glider released from a dirigible

Barnard, Frederick Augustus Porter—**Weights and Measures Standardization**—national organization to improve systems of weights, measures, and moneys

Barnard, Henry—**Teachers' Institute**

Barnard, Tobias—**Degrees (academic and honorary)**—Bachelor of Arts degree

Barnes, Albert—**Lecture Series (endowed)**

Barnes, Alfred Smith—**Book Trade Magazine**—successful book trade magazine

Barnes, Charles E.—**Ordnance**—machine gun

Barnes, George—**Moving Picture**—moving picture with a plot

Barnes, Gladeon Marcus—**Ordnance**—tank (heavy 60-ton)

Barnes, Howard Turner—**Thermit**

Barnes, James—**Golf Tournament**—Professional Golfers Association tournament

Barnes, Martin—**Nut and Bolt Factory**

Barnes, Ross (Roscoe C. Barnes)—**Baseball Player**—baseball player to hit over .400

Barnes, W. M.—**Laundry**—rough dry laundry service

Barnes, William—**Insurance**—insurance department (state)

Barney, Everett Hosmer—**Skate** (all-metal)

Barnhart, Harry—**Music**—community chorus

Barnsdall, William—**Oil**—oil refinery (commercial)

Barnwell, Barbara Olive—**Medal**—Navy-Marine Corps medal for heroism awarded to a woman

Baron, Alexander—**Museum**—public museum

Baron, Francis Le—**Army**—medical corps

Barr, Alexander—**Spinning, Carding and Roping Machines**

Barr, Asa—**Music**—music convention

Barr, Robert—**Spinning, Carding and Roping Machines**

Barras, Charles M.—**Play (drama)**—burlesque show

Barrere, Francis Maria—**Passport**—passport

Barrett, George W.—**Capital Punishment**—capital punishment—federal law

Barrett, Nathaniel—**Diplomatic Service**—consuls of the United States appointed after the adoption of the Constitution

Barron, James—**Melons**

Barron, John H.—**Farm Bureau**

Barron, Samuel—**Ship**—ship constructed by the federal government

Barrow, Adele Lauriat—**Radio Church**

Barry, John—**Book**—book entered for copyright

Barry, John—**Naval Officer**—naval officer to become a commodore

Barry, John—**Ship**—frigate

Barry, John—**Ship**—revenue cutter and Navy cooperation

Barry, John—**Ship**—warship captured by a commissioned officer of the U.S. Navy

Barry, William Taylor—**Postmaster**—postmaster general of the United States to become a member of the cabinet

Barrymore, John—**Moving Picture**—talking picture

Barsimson, Jacob—**Jews**—Jew

Barsimson, Jacob—**Jews**—Jew to win all the rights and perform all the duties of citizenship

Becker, Samuel—**Evangelical Conference**

Becket, Welton — **Building**—circular office building

Beckley, John—**Congress (U.S.)—House of Representatives** — House of Representatives

Beckley, John — **Librarian** — Librarian of Congress

Beckwith, G. — **Ferryboat** — double-deck ferryboat

Beebe, Richard—**Ordnance**—muskets

Beecher, Henry Ward—**Premium**—premiums given by publishers

Beekman, James—**Greenhouse**

Beers, Alanson — **Colonial Government** — government on the Pacific coast

Beers, John B. — **Dentistry** — patent for a gold crown

Beissel, Johann Conrad — **Communistic Society**—communistic society

Beissel, Johann Conrad — **German Book** — German book printed in America

Belcher, Jonathan — **Freemasons** — mason (native born)

Belfer, Ben William — **Degrees (academic and honorary)**—master of arts degree in sacred music

Belknap, Jeremy — **Historical Society**—historical society (state)

Belknap, Morris B. — **File Manufacturing Machine**

Bell, Alexander Graham — **Deaf—School**—oral instruction for the deaf

Bell, Alexander Graham — **Phonograph** — phonograph that was practical

Bell, Alexander, Graham—**Telephone**—interstate telephone call

Bell, Alexander Graham — **Telephone**—telephone conversation over out-of-door wires

Bell, Alexander Graham — **Telephone**—telephone message

Bell, Alexander Graham — **Telephone**—telephone patent

Bell, Alexander Graham — **Telephone**—telephone used by a railroad company

Bell, Alexander Graham—**Telephone**—transcontinental telephone demonstration

Bell, Bernard L. — **World War II**—American bombardier over German occupied territory

Bell, Bobby — **Television—Telecast**—prize fight in a "studio"

Bell, Charles Heffelfinger — **Television — Telecast**—stockholders' meetings televised coast-to-coast simultaneously

Bell, Chichester—**Phonograph**—phonograph that was practical

Bell, John—**Constitutional Union Party**

Bell, Robert—**Architectural Book**—architectural book printed in America

Bell, Robert Mowry—**Esperanto Course**— Esperanto course carrying college credit

Bellew, Frank Henry Temple — **Cartoon** — "Uncle Sam" cartoon

Bellinger, Patrick Nelson Lynch—**Aviation** —gyroscope automatic stabilization

Bellingham, Samuel — **Degrees (academic and honorary)**—bachelor of arts degree

Bellini, Carlo — **Language Instruction** — Italian instruction in a college

Bellonte, Maurice — **Aviation — Flights (transatlantic)** — transatlantic non-stop flight from Europe to the United States

Bellows, Henry Adams—**Radio Commission (U.S.)**

Belmont, Raymond — **Polo** — international polo series

Belshe, Thomas — **President** — presidential airplane (turbo-compound powered)

Ben, Apache — **Indian Church** — Indian church organized by Indians

Benedict, William Pershing — **Aviation — Flights**—North Pole landing by an airplane at the geographic pole

Benedict, Zadoc—**Hat Factory**

Benesch, Alfred A.—**Traffic Light**—electric traffic signal lights

Benjamin, Asher — **Architectural Book** — architectural book distinctly American

Bennett, Miss—**Oratorio**—oratorio performance (complete)

Bennett, Elbert Gladstone—**Federal Deposit Insurance Corporation**

Bennett, Elizabeth Hog—**Surgical Operation** —Caesarean operation (successful)

Bennett, Floyd — **Aviation—Flights**—North Pole flight

Bennett, Hugh Hammond — **Medal** — Agriculture Department distinguished service gold medal

Bennett, James Gordon, Sr.—**News Correspondent**—Washington correspondent of importance

Bennett, James Gordon—**Coaching Club**

Bennett, James Gordon—**Polo**—polo

Bennett, James Gordon—**Ship** — steamboat to employ electric lights

Bennett, James Gordon—**Yacht Race**—yacht race across the Atlantic Ocean

Bennett, Jessee — **Surgical Operation**—Caesarean operation (successful)

Bennie, James Richardson — **Chiropody School**—chiropody school as a regular division of a university

Benson, Ezra Taft—**Cabinet of the United States**—cabinet conference telecast

Benson, William Shepherd — **Radio Telephone**—radio telephone ship-to-shore conversation

Bent, Florence — **Monument**—monument to the American flag

Bent, Josiah—**Cracker**—hard water crackers

Benton, James Gilchrist — **Ordnance** — sea coast gun carriage

Benz, Karl — **Automobile**—foreign automobile exhibited

Berenson, Senda — **Basketball** — basketball played at a women's college

Bergen, Edgar — **Degrees (academic and honorary)** — degree awarded a ventriloquist's dummy

Berger, Victor Louis—**Congressman (U.S.)** —Socialist congressman

Berger, Victor Louis — **Social Democratic Party of America**

Berger, Victor Louis—**Socialist Party**

Bishop, Nathaniel Holmes—**Canoe Association**

Bishop, Samuel — **Money** — copper cents minted by a state

Bispham, David — **Opera**—opera composed by a woman performed at the Metropolitan Opera House

Bissell, Daniel—**Medal**—Order of the Purple Heart

Bissell, Emily Perkins — **Seal** — Christmas seals of the modern variety sold to raise funds to fight tuberculosis

Bissell, George Henry—**Oil**—oil company

Bissell, Melville Reuben—**Carpet Sweeper**

Bittencourt, Amaro Soares—**Medal**—Legion of Merit Medal awarded to a foreign national

Black, Alexander—**Magic Lantern Show**—magic lantern feature show

Black, Frank Swett—**Forestry School**—forestry school of collegiate character

Black, J. W.—**Photograph**—aerial photograph

Black, James—**Prohibition Party** (national)

Black, Robert Glennwood—**Navy**—atomic submarine division

Black, William Henry — **Animals** — cattle (Africander cattle)

Blackfan, Joseph H.—**Civil Service**—Civil Service Commission

Blackford, Isaac—**Court**—court of claims

Blackton, James Stuart—**Moving Picture**—animated cartoon

Blackwell, Antoinette Brown — **Woman** — woman ordained a minister

Blackwell, Edward—**Fencing Book**

Blackwell, Elizabeth — **Hospital** — women's infirmary staffed by women physicians

Blackwell, Elizabeth — **Physician** — woman physician

Blackwell, Emily — **Hospital** — women's infirmary staffed by women physicians

Blackwell, H. M.—**Radio Broadcast**—advertising or commercial radio broadcast

Blackwell, Henry—**Fencing Book**

Blackwell, Robert—**African Church**

Blaine, James Gillespie — **Conference** — Pan American Conference

Blaine, James Gillespie — **Pan American Union**

Blair, Charles Francis—**Aviation**—**Flights**—North Pole flight in a single-engine airplane

Blair, Henry—**Patent**—Negro to obtain a patent

Blair, James — **College** — college charter granted by the Crown

Blair, James—**College**—college proposed

Blair, John — **Freemasons** — Masonic Grand Lodge

Blair, John—**Supreme Court (U.S.)**—Supreme Court of the United States

Blair, Joseph Cullen—**Civic Design Chair**

Blair, Montgomery—**Postal Service**—railroad post office

Blair, William Reid—**Animals**—okapi

Blaisdell, Frederick E.—**Pencil**—paper pencil

Blake, Eli Whitney—**Caster**

Blake, Eli Whitney—**Lock**—mortised lock

Blake, Eli Whitney—**Stone Crusher**

Blake, James—**Genealogy**—genealogy

Blake, John A.—**Caster**

Blake, John Harrison—**Engineering Society**—engineering society

Blake, Lemuel—**Rubber**—rubber company

Blake, Lyman Reed—**Shoe Manufacturing Machine**

Blake, Philos—**Caster**

Blake, Philos—**Lock**—mortised lock

Blalock, Alfred—**Television**—**Telecast**—surgical operation televised on a closed circuit

Blanchard, Jean Pierre — **Balloon Flight**—balloon flight in which a presidential order was carried

Blanchard, Thomas—**Lathe**

Blanchfield, Florence Aby—**Army Officer**—woman to be appointed a regular Army officer (colonel)

Bland, Edward—**Expedition**—expedition

Bland, Theodore—**Diplomatic Service**—Pan American delegates (American)

Bland, Theodoric—**Congressman (U.S.)**—congressman to die

Blass, Robert—**Opera**—opera composed by a woman performed at the Metropolitan Opera House

Blatch, Nora Stanton—**Engineering Society**—woman elected to the American Society of Civil Engineers

Blavatsky, Helena Petrovna—**Theosophical Society**

Blayton, Jesse Bee—**Radio Station**—radio station owned and operated by Negroes

Bleibtrey, Ethelda—**Olympic Games**—woman (American) to win an Olympic competition

Blickensderfer, George C. — **Typewriter** — portable typewriter

Bliss, Eleanor—**Sulfanilamide**—sulfanilamide as a treatment for infections of streptococcic origins

Bliss, Henry H.—**Automobile Fatality**

Bliss, Raymond Whitcomb—**Building**—solar-heated and radiation-cooled house

Blodget, Samuel—**Engraving**—historical print engraved in America

Blodget, Samuel—**Marble Building**

Blodgett, Joseph R.—**Indians**—Indian tribal constitution

Blok, Adrianen—**Ship**—decked ship

Blondel, John F.—**Doughnut Cutter**

Blondin, Émile (Jean Francois Gravelet)—**Niagara Falls**—person to cross Niagara Falls on a tightrope

Blong, Joseph Myles—**Baseball Game**—no-run nine-inning baseball game

Bloomer, Amelia Jenks—**Bloomers**

Bloomer, Melville H. — **Plow** — submarine cable plow

Bloomer, Reuben—**Marble Quarry**

Blount, William — **Impeachment** — impeachment proceedings against a United States Senator

Blow, Susan Elizabeth—**Kindergarten**—public school kindergarten

Blumenthal, Mark—**Hospital**—Jewish hospital

Blunt, Edward March—**Coast Survey Book**

Bly, Nellie—**Tour of the World**—tour of the world made by a woman traveling alone

Boardman, Alexander—**Boardwalk**

Bobbs, John Stough—**Surgical Operation**—gallstone operation

Bocock, Thomas Salem—**Congress of the Confederate States**

Bodfish, Morton—**Federal Home Loan Bank Board**

Boehm, John Philip—**Evangelical and Reformed Church**

Boehm, Martin—**Church of the United Brethren in Christ**

Boehnisch, George—**Moravian**

Boepple, John F.—**Button**—buttons of fresh water pearl

Boettner, John—**Caterpillar Club**—caterpillar club member

Bogardus, James—**Building**—building constructed wholly of cast iron

Bogardus, James—**Gas**—gas meter (dry)

Boger, Frederick—**Medical Periodical**—optometry magazine

Bohune, Lawrence—**Physician**—doctor in the colony of Virginia

Bolin, Jane Matilda—**Judge**—woman judge (Negro)

Bolívar, Simón—**Conference**—conference of American Republics

Bolles, Frank—**Cooperative**—college cooperative store

Bolles, Jenette Hubbard—**Medical Periodical**—osteopathy magazine

Bolles, Jenette Hubbard—**Physician**—osteopath (woman)

Bolling, William — **Deaf — School** — oral school for the deaf (still existing)

Bolster, Calvin—**Aviation—Passenger**—dirigible passenger transfer to an airplane

Bolter, James—**Insurance**—accident insurance policy

Bolton, Elmer K.—**Rubber**—synthetic rubber produced on a commercial scale

Bolton, Frances Payne—**Congressman (U.S.)**—mother and son simultaneously elected to Congress

Bolton, John—**Glass**—stained figure glass

Bolton, Oliver Payne—**Congressman (U.S.)**—mother and son simultaneously elected to Congress

Bolton, William Jay—**Glass**—stained figure glass

Bonaparte, Charles Joseph—**College**—Catholic college for women

Bond, Thomas—**Hospital**—hospital in America

Bond, William Cranch—**Photograph**—photograph of a star

Bonelli, Richard — **Opera**—opera broadcast over a national network from an American opera house

Bonelli, Richard — **Television — Telecast —** opera telecast

Bonner, James—**Town Named for George Washington**

Bonstelle, Jessie—**Theater**—municipal theater

Bonwill, William Gibson Arlington—**Dental Mallet**—dental mallet

Bonzano, John—**International Eucharistic Congress** in America

Booth, Elizabeth—**Salvation Army**—woman commander of the Salvation Army

Booth, Evangeline — **Medal** — Distinguished Service Medal awarded to a woman

Booth, James Curtis—**Chemical Laboratory**—chemical laboratory

Booth, Oliver—**Ice Yacht**

Booth, William—**Salvation Army**

Borcherdt, Victor—**Zoological Garden**—barless zoological garden of naturalistic rock construction

Bordelon, Guy — **Aviation — Aviator**—naval ace in Korea

Borden, Gail—**Cracker**—meat biscuit

Borden, Gail—**Medal**—medal awarded to an American food producer

Borden, Gail—**Milk**—condensed milk (commercial)

Borden, Joseph E.—**Baseball Game**—no-hit nine-inning baseball game

Borden, Simeon—**Geodetic Survey**

Boren, Horace C.—**Tour of the World**—passenger to fly around the world on commercial airlines in less than 100 hours

Borgfeldt, Nicholas H.—**Snow-Melting Apparatus**—snow-melting apparatus

Bosenberg, Henry F.—**Patent**—plant patent

Bostwick, A. C.—**Automobile**—automobile to exceed the speed of a mile a minute

Boswell, William—**Censorship**—state board of censorship on literature

Botetourt, Lord—**College**—college to confer medals as prizes

Bouchard, Emile—**Television**—television eyewitness allowed to testify in a federal court

Bouchet, Edward Alexander—**Degrees (academic and honorary)**—doctor of philosophy degree awarded to a Negro

Bouck, Zeh—**Aviation—Flights**—New York-Bermuda flight

Boudinot, Elias—**Bible Society**—Bible society (national organization)

Boudinot, Elias—**Lawyer**—lawyers admitted to the Supreme Court of the United States

Boudinot, Elias—**Newspaper**—Indian newspaper

Bouligny, Corporal—**World War I**—American combatant casualty in World War I

Bourne, Sylvanus—**Diplomatic Service**—consuls of the United States appointed after the adoption of the Constitution

Bouton, J. W.—**Book Trade Magazine**—book collectors' magazine

Boutwell, George Sewall—**Education**—compulsory school attendance law (state)

Boutwell, George Sewall—**Internal Revenue Commissioner**

Bouvier, John—**Law Dictionary (American)**

Bovay, Alvan Earle—**Republican Party**—Republican Party meeting (local)

Bowden, Don—**Runner**—runner (American) to run a mile in less than four minutes

Bowditch, E. B.—**Oil**—oil well commercially productive

Bowditch, Henry Ingersoll—**Health Board**—health board (state)

Bowditch, Nathaniel—**Astronomer**—astronomer to acquire fame after the Revolution

Bowditch, Nathaniel—**Bronze Statue**

Bowdoin, James—**Arts and Science Society**—arts and science society (national)

Bowen, Anthony—**Young Men's Christian Association**—Young Men's Christian Association (for Negro members)

Bowen, James Klein—**Moving Picture**—colored moving pictures

Bowers, Joseph Oliver—**Catholic Bishop**—Catholic bishop (Negro) consecrated in the United States

Bowers, Joseph Oliver—**Catholic Seminarians (Negro)** to be ordained to the priesthood by a Negro bishop

Bowie, James—**Bowie Knife**

Bowker, Richard Rogers—**Library Society**—library society (local)

Bowlus, William Hawley—**Glider**—powered soaring glider commercially licensed

Bowman, James E.—**Helicopter Flight**—transcontinental non-stop helicopter flight

Bowring, Eve—**Governor**—governor to appoint two United States senators in one year for interim terms

Bowser, Sylvanus F.—**Pump**—gasoline pump

Boxrud, Christ—**Ski Club**—ski club (local) that was active

Boyce, Westray Battle—**Medal**—Legion of Merit medal awarded to a Women's Army Corps member

Boyce, William—**Music**—patriotic American song

Boyd, Albert—**Aviation** — **Flights** — airplane to exceed the speed of 600 miles per hour

Boyd, Ernest—**Television**—**Telecast** — book review to be televised

Boyd, Glen R.—**Motorcycle Race**—motorcycle race (300 miles)

Boyd, James—**Fire Hose** of rubber-lined cotton web

Boyd, John—**Presbyterian Presbytery**

Boyden, Seth—**Iron**—iron castings (malleable)

Boyden, Seth—**Leather**—patent leather

Boyden, Uriah Atherton—**Turbine**—turbine successfully operated by water power

Boyle, Francis Edward—**Army Officer**—chaplain (Catholic) appointed by the President

Boyle, George L.—**Air Mail Service**—air mail experimental route

Boyle, James—**Bed**—box spring

Boyle, Robert—**Indian School**—Indian school (permanent)

Boylston, Thomas—**Vaccination for smallpox**

Boylston, Zabdiel—**Vaccination for smallpox**

Boynton, Charles Brandon—**College**—Negro university to establish undergraduate, graduate and professional schools

Boyton, Paul—**Shoot-the-Chutes**

Brackett, Anna Callender—**Normal School**—woman principal of a normal school

Braden, J. Noble—**Arbitration Association**—arbitration association

Bradford, Andrew — **Periodical** — magazine published in America

Bradford, Vincent L. — **Hospital** — homeopathic hospital

Bradford, William—**Book**—Book of Common Prayer (in the Mohawk Indian language)

Bradford, William—**Congregational Church**—Congregational Church

Bradford, William—**Duel**—duel

Bradford, William—**Earthquake**—earthquake description

Bradford, William—**Law Book**—law book

Bradford, William—**Paper Mill**

Bradford, William—**Play (drama)**—printed American play

Bradford, William—**Tax**—property tax law (colonial)

Bradley, Henry W.—**Oleomargarine**—oleomargarine patent

Bradley, Omar Nelson — **Army Officer** — woman army officer

Bradstreet, Anne Dudley—**Author**—woman author

Brady, Mathew B.—**Money**—coin bearing the portrait of a President

Brady, Mathew B. — **Photograph** — news photographs of distinction

Brady, Mathew B. — **Photograph** — photograph of a President (in office)

Bragg, Walter Lawrence—**Interstate Commerce Act**

Braham, Horace—**Television**—**Telecast**—play to be televised as a full-hour program

Braidwood, John — **Deaf** — **School** — oral school for the deaf (still existing)

Brainard, John—**Indian Reservation**—Indian reservation (state)

Brallier, John K.—**Football Game**—professional football game

Brand, Charles John—**Agriculture Department (U.S.)**—Office of Markets

Brandeis, Louis Dembitz—**Insurance**—savings bank life insurance

Brandeis, Louis Dembitz—**Supreme Court (U.S.)**—associate justice of the Supreme Court who was Jewish

Brantley, William Theophilus—**College**—city college

Brattain, Walter Houser—**Transistor**—transistor

Brattle, William—**Degrees (academic and honorary)**—Doctor of Sacred Theology degree

Brattle, William—**Logic Book**

Brown, Edgar — **Senator** (U.S.)—Senator elected by a write-in-vote

Brown, Edward Fisher—**Medical "Rogues' Gallery"**

Brown, Edwin Lee—**Humane Society**—humane association national organization

Brown, Elisha — **Cheese Factory** — cheese factory co-operative

Brown, Felix—**Nail Machine (Wire)**

Brown, Gerald—**Glass**—invisible glass installation

Brown, James — **Law Book**—law compilation of United States laws

Brown, Jesse Leroy — **Aviation**—**Aviator**—Negro flier of the U.S. Naval Reserve

Brown, Joe E. — **Moving Picture** — talking picture entirely in color

Brown, John D. — **Trademark Lawsuit** — trademark controversy involving a newspaper

Brown, Joseph Mansfield—**Boat Race**—intercollegiate boat race

Brown, M. O.—**Aviation**—**Flights (transcontinental)** — transcontinental commercial overnight transport service

Brown, Melvin L.—**Medal**—Medal of Honor awarded in the Korean War

Brown, Moses—**Bridge**—pontoon bridge

Brown, Moses—**Money**—deposit of gold bullion

Brown, O. B.—**Moving Picture Projector**—moving picture projector patent

Brown, Russell John—**Aviation**—**Aviator**—jet plane combat victor in the Korean War

Brown, Samuel Robbins—**Chinese Students**

Brown, Samuel Robbins — **College**—educational institution exclusively for women

Brown, Saul—**Jewish Congregation**—Jewish congregation

Brown, Solyman—**Dental Book**—orthodontia treatise

Brown, Solyman—**Dental Magazine**—dental journal

Brown, Solyman — **Dental Society** — dental society (local)

Brown, Thomas—**Postal Service**—mail box

Brown, Thornberry Bailey — **Civil War** — Union soldier killed by enemy action in the Civil War

Brown, W. R. — **Horse Race** — three-hundred-mile endurance run

Brown, Wesley Anthony—**Naval Academy**—Negro midshipman in the U.S. Naval Academy to graduate

Brown, William—**Medal**—Order of the Purple Heart

Brown, William — **Pharmacopoeia**—pharmacopoeia

Brown, William Henry—**Yacht Race**—yacht race (international)

Brown, William Hill — **Novel** — American novel published in America

Brown, William Montgomery—**Heresy Trial** of a bishop

Brown, William Wells—**Novel**—novel by a Negro

Browne, Joseph — **Medical Book** — medical book for army medical use

Browne, William W.—**Bank**—bank for Negroes operated by Negroes

Brownell, George Loomis — **Paper Twine Machinery**

Brownell, Herbert—**Cabinet of the United States**—cabinet conference telecast

Brownie, Leon—**Shooting Gallery (mechanized)**

Bruce, Archibald—**Mineralogy Magazine**

Bruce, David—**Stereotype**—stereotypers

Bruce, George—**Patent**—design patent

Bruce, George—**Stereotype**—stereotypers

Bruce, Nigel—**Moving Picture**—three-dimensional feature moving picture

Bruce, Philip Alexander—**Play (drama)**—play given by non-professional actors

Brucker, Wilber Marion—**Atomic Reactor**—military nuclear power plant

Brucker, Wilber Marion—**Flag**—Army flag (official)

Brundin, Ernest Walfrid—**Soilless Culture of Plants** — commercial hydroponicum (large)

Brunel, Isambard Kingdom — **Ship**—steamboat service (regular) across the Atlantic

Brunner, Edward—**College**—Negro university (Catholic)

Brunschweyler, John—**Wedding**—double radio wedding

Brush, Charles Francis—**Electric Lighting**—electric arc lights

Bryan, Otis Frank — **Aviation** — **Flights (transcontinental)**—transcontinental commercial overnight transport service

Bryan, William — **Cooperative** — consumers' cooperative society

Bryan, William Jennings—**Silverites**

Bryant, Alice Gertrude—**Medical Society**—women members of the American College of Surgeons

Bryant, Charles—**Petroleum Exported to Europe**

Bryant, Gridley — **Railroad** — railroad for freight transportation to celebrate its centenary

Bryant, Ralph Clement—**Forestry School**—forestry school of collegiate character

Bryant, William Cullen — **Poem** — by an American

Bryner, Vera—**Television**—**Telecast**—opera (major) televised in color

Buchanan, Franklin — **Naval Academy** — Naval Academy (U.S.)

Buchanan, James—**Cable (telegraph)**—cable across the Atlantic Ocean was completed

Buchanan, James—**President (U.S.)**—President who was a bachelor

Buck, Dudley Allen—**Cryotrons**—publicly reported

Buck, John Kill—**Treaty**—treaty entered into by the U.S. with Indian tribes

Buck, Solon Justus—**Archival Course**

Bucke—**Legislative Assembly**

Buckner, Simon Bolivar—**Election Law**—Australian ballot system

Budge, Don (John Donald Budge)—**Tennis Player**—lawn tennis champion to win four major titles

Bushnell, Edward W.—**Ice Skating Club**—ice skating club

Bushnell, H. L.—**Ship**—iron-clad warship for service at sea

Bushnell, James—**Births**—sextuplets

Bushnell, Jennie A.—**Births**—sextuplets

Bushnell, Laberto—**Births**—sextuplets

Bushnell, Lucy—**Births**—sextuplets

Bushnell, Norberto—**Births**—sextuplets

Bute, George H.—**Medical Society**—homeopathic medical society

Butler, Benjamin Franklin—**Anti-Monopoly Party**

Butler, Benjamin Franklin—**Crime Prevention and Detection**—interstate crime pact

Butler, Benjamin Franklin—**Treason**—citizen of the United States to be tried for treason, convicted, and hanged

Butler, Henry Varnum — **Naval Officer**—naval officer designated Commander, Aircraft Battle Force

Butler, John—**Stage Coach Inter-City Service**

Butler, John Washington—**Evolution Law (state)**

Butler, Nicholas Murray—**Nobel Prize**—Nobel Peace Prize awarded an American woman

Butler, Nicholas Murray—**Novel**—novel to win the Pulitzer prize in letters

Butler, William Orlando—**Political Convention**—national committee of a political organization

Butterfield, Daniel—**Taps (military signal)**

Butterick, Ebenezer—**Paper Patterns**

Buttolph, Nicholas—**Book**—miniature book

Button, Richard—**Olympic Games**—figure skating Olympic champion (American)

Buzennokami, Niimi—**Japanese Ambassador**

Byrd, Andrew D.—**Court Martial**—court martial trial at which enlisted men were allowed to sit as members of the court

Byrd, Richard Evelyn—**Aviation**—**Airplane**—airplane equipped with radio to cross the Atlantic Ocean

Byrd, Richard Evelyn—**Aviation**—**Flights**—North Pole flight

Byrd, Richard Evelyn—**Aviation**—**Flights**—South Pole flight

Byrd, Richard Evelyn—**Radio Broadcast**—radio broadcast heard in both the Arctic and the Antarctic regions

Byrn, M. L. —**Corkscrew Patent**

Byrne, Ethel—**Medical Clinic**—birth control clinic

C

Cabot, George — **Navy** — Secretary of the Navy

Cabot, Godfrey Lowell—**Traffic Regulation Course**—air traffic regulation course

Cabrillo, Juan Rodríguez—**Discovery**—discovery of land on the United States Pacific coast

Cabrini, Frances Xavier—**Catholic Beatification**—Catholic beatification of an American citizen

Cabrini, Frances Xavier—**Saint (Catholic)**

Cady, Hamilton Perkins—**Helium**—helium

Caille, Adolph—**Pinball Game**—pinball game machine (toy)

Caines, George—**Law Book**—law book (text)

Calahan, Edward A.—**Telegraph**—telegraph call boxes

Calder, William Musgrave—**Daylight Saving**

Calderón, Gabriel Díaz Vara—**Catholic Holy Orders**

Caldwell, Charles—**Medical Book**—pediatrics monograph

Caldwell, Eunice—**College**—college for women

Caldwell, Harry Howard—**Fingerprint Society**—fingerprint society (international)

Caldwell, Joseph—**Observatory**—observatory (astronomical) connected with an institution of learning

Caldwell, Orestes Hampton—**Radio Commission (U.S.)**

Calhoun, Charles H. Sr.—**Golf Champion**—holes-in-one by a father and son

Calhoun, Charles H. Jr.—**Golf Champion**—holes-in-one by a father and son

Calhoun, John Caldwell — **Vice President (U.S.)**—Vice President to resign

Callahan, Americus F.—**Envelope**—envelope with an outlook or window

Callsen, Peter—**Ship**—rotor ship

Calthorp, Samuel R.—**Railroad**—streamlined railroad train

Calver, George Wehnes—**Physician**—Capitol physician

Calverly, Edmund — **Court Martial Trial** — court martial trial

Camadine, Frank—**Theater**—television theater demonstration

Cameron, Simon—**Spoils System**

Camp, Walter—**Football Book**

Campanella, Roy—**Baseball Game**—major league game in which the majority of the players on one team were Negroes

Campanini, Italo—**Opera**—opera at the Metropolitan Opera House

Campanius, Johannes—**Book**—book intended for circulation in the English colonies

Campanius, Johannes—**Lutheran Church**—Lutheran church building

Campbell, Alexander—**Disciples of Christ**

Campbell, Alexander—**Milk**—milk delivery in glass bottles

Campbell, David—**Physiological Society**—physiological society

Campbell, Donald Malcolm—**Ship**—speedboat to exceed 200 miles an hour

Campbell, Douglas — **Aviation** — **Aviator**—American ace

Campbell, Douglas—**World War I**—air combat of an American organization in World War I

Campbell, George Washington—**Duel**—duel between congressmen

Campbell, John — **Newspaper** — newspaper (successful)

Campbell, Malcolm—**Automobile**—automobile to exceed the speed of 300 miles an hour

Campbell, Samuel—**Tennis Society**—tennis society (national)

Campbell, Thomas—**Disciples of Christ**

Camras, Marvin—**Wire Recorder**

Canby, Edward—**Scale**—computing scales

Canby, Henry Seidel—**Book Club**—Book-of-the-Month Club

Candee, Leverett—**Rubber** — rubber shoe manufacturer

Candlish, Alexander H.—**Research Institute**—institute for research in nervous diseases

Canfield, Dorothy—**Book Club**—Book-of-the-Month Club

Cannon, Martha Hughes—**Senate (state)**—woman state senator

Canter, William—**Chenille Manufacturing Machine**

Cantrell, J. F.—**Washing Machine**—washing machine for public use

Capron, Allen Kissam—**Spanish-American War**—army officer killed in battle in the Spanish-American war

Capron, Henri — **Music** — music publishers (exclusive)

Caraway, Hattie Ophelia Wyatt—**Senator (U.S.)**—woman elected to the Senate

Caraway, Hattie Ophelia Wyatt—**Senator (U.S.)**—woman senator to preside over the Senate

Cardozo, Benjamin Nathan—**Cabinet of the United States**—full cabinet sworn in at the same time and place

Carey, A. L.—**Insurance**—bonding law (state)

Carey, Alice—**Women's Club**—women's professional club

Carey, Mathew—**Book Fair**

Carey, Mathew—**Booksellers' Association**

Carey, Mathew—**Maternity Book**

Carkhuff, Stacy G.—**Automobile Tire**—non-skid tire

Carl, William Crane—**Organ School**

Carleton, Guy—**Salute** (complimentary)

Carlisle, David—**Herbal Book**

Carlson, Sigrid Sophia Margarete—**Wedding**—transatlantic telephone wedding

Carmody, John Michael—**Federal Works Agency**

Carmody, John Michael—**Labor**—Labor Relations Act (national)

Carnegie, Andrew—**Carnegie Hero Fund Commission**

Carnes, Burrell—**Diplomatic Service**—consuls of the United States appointed after the adoption of the Constitution

Carney, Joseph P.—**Factory**—factories operated by the United States Government

Carothers, Wallace Hume—**Nylon**—nylon

Carpenter, Arthur Schuyler—**Ship**—naval vessels to sink an enemy submarine

Carpenter, Charles Milton—**Diathermy Machine**

Carpenter, Malcolm Scott—**Astronauts**—astronauts

Carpenter, Samuel—**Paper Mill**

Carpentier, Georges — **Prize Fight** — prize fight to gross a million dollars

Carpentier, Georges — **Radio Broadcast** — prize fight (heavyweight championship) broadcast

Carr, Benjamin—**Opera**—opera by an American composer

Carr, Mary—**Moving Picture**—talking picture of more than 6,000 feet

Carrel, Alexis—**Artificial Heart**

Carrel, Alexis—**Nobel Prize**—Nobel Prize in medicine and physiology

Carrick, Samuel—**College** — non-denominational college

Carrington, James—**Coffee Mill Patent**

Carrington, Louis H. — **Aviation** — Flights (transpacific) — jet transpacific non-stop flight

Carrington, M. D.—**Ship**—schooner (five masted)

Carroll, Charles—**Bridge**—stone arch railroad bridge

Carroll, Daniel — **Senator (U.S.)**—Catholic senator

Carroll, Howard—**Bridge**—wrought iron lattice girder railroad bridge

Carroll, John—**Catholic Bishop** — Catholic bishop appointed to serve in the United States

Carroll, John—**Catholic Work**

Carroll, John Lee—**Strike**—strike in which federal troops were called in peacetime

Carroll, Robert W.—**Rocket**—space capsule recovered from an orbiting satellite

Carson, Jack — **Television** — **Telecast**—pay television

Carter, John—**Civil Government in America**

Carter, John Garnet—**Golf Course**—midget golf course

Carter, John Pym—**College**—Negro university

Carter, Mamie B.—**Physician**—osteopath (woman)

Carter, Robert — **Swedenborgian or New Church**—Swedenborgian or New Church Temple

Carter, Samuel Powhatan—**Army Officer**—general to become a rear admiral

Carter, Thomas Henry—**Bank**—postal savings bank

Cartwright, Alexander Joy—**Baseball Team**—baseball team

Carty, John Joseph—**Radio Broadcast**—coast-to-coast hook-up

Caruana, Frank—**Bowler**—bowler to roll two perfect games

Caruso, Enrico—**Opera**—opera broadcast in part

Carver, Carl F.—**Wedding**—wedding broadcast

Carver, George Albert—**Wedding**—wedding broadcast

Carver, George Washington—**Monument**—national monument dedicated to a Negro

Carver, Robin—**Baseball Book**

Carvill, William — **Cricket Tournament** — cricket game played by a college team

Cary, Samuel Fenton—**Greenback Party (or Independent Party)**

Case, Theodore W.—**Moving Picture**—talking pictures of presidential candidates

Cash, Ida—**Toyery**

Cashin, Thomas A.—**Street Car**—municipally owned street cars

Casiles, David—**Ship**—ship outfitted for hurricane research

Cass, Lewis—**Political Convention**—national committee of a political organization

Castor, Jesse—**Building and Loan Association**

Catchpole, Hubert Ralph—**Pituitary Hormone**—pituitary hormone (isolated)

Catchpole, Judith—**Jury**—jury composed of women

Caton, John Dean—**Game Preserve**—game preserve

Cattell, Alexander Gilmore—**Civil Service**—Civil Service Commission

Cattell, James McKeen—**Psychology Professor**

Caut, John—**Ship**—iron vessel

Cavert, Samuel McCrea—**Television—Telecast**—religious services to be televised

Cawston, Edwin—**Birds**—ostrich farm

Cayven, Georgia—**Glass Dress of spun glass**

Cehanovsky, George—**Television—Telecast**—opera telecast

Cella, Caesar — **Fingerprinting** — fingerprint conviction

Center, Robert—**Ship**—iron sloop yacht

Cervantes, Antonio de — **Catholic Mass** — Catholic Mass

Chabanel, Noel—**Catholic Canonization of North Americans**

Chace, M. G.—**Tennis Match**—lawn tennis champions who were brothers

Chadwick, Florence — **Woman** — American woman to swim the English Channel from both coasts

Chadwick, French Ensor—**Naval Officer**—naval attaché

Chaffee, Edwin M.—**Rubber**—rubber company

Chamberlain, Alexander Francis—**Degrees (academic and honorary)**—anthropology doctorate

Chamberlin, Benjamin D.—**Electric Lighting**—glass light bulb machine

Chambers, Benjamin — **Ordnance** — cannon (breech loading)

Chambers, Cyrus—**Folding Machine**

Chambers, John—**Boat Club**—boat club

Chambers, Washington Irving—**Aviation—Flights**—airplane catapulted

Chambers, William—**Boat Club**—boat club

Chandler, Charles deForest—**Aviation**—aeronautical division of the United States War Department

Chandler, Charles deForest—**Aviation—Airplane**—airplane outfitted with a machine gun

Chandler, George—**Nail Cutting and Heading Machine**

Chandler, Lloyd Horwitz—**Radio Telephone**—radio telephone ship-to-shore conversation

Chandler, William Eaton—**Naval Officer**—Judge Advocate of the Navy

Chaney, James Eugene—**Air Defense Command (U.S.)**

Chang—**Siamese Twins**—Siamese twins

Channing, William Francis—**Fire Alarm System (electric)**

Channing, William H.—**Woman Suffrage**—convention (national) of women advocating woman suffrage

Chanute, Octave—**Aviation—Expositions and Meets**—air conference (international)

Chanute, Octave—**Glider**—glider with cambered wings

Chapin, Charles Value—**Health Laboratory**—health laboratory (municipal)

Chapin, Charles Willard—**Disease (distinctly American)**

Chapin, Daniel M. —**Match**—friction matches

Chapin, Daryl M.—**Battery**—solar battery

Chapin, William—**Blind**—state school for the blind

Chaplin, Charles—**Moving Picture**—six-reel feature-length comedy

Chapman, Mathias Farrell—**Animals**—chinchilla farm

Chapman, Nathaniel—**Medical Book**—therapeutics and materia medica book

Chapman, R. A.—**Fish Commission (state)**

Chapman, Victor Emmanuel—**Aviation—Aviator**—American aviator killed while a pilot in the Lafayette Escadrille

Charlie, Kiowa—**Indian Church** — Indian church organized by Indians

Charlo, Martin—**Indians**—Indian tribal constitution

Chase, Charles M.—**Forest Service**—forest commission (state)

Chase, John Paul—**Capital Punishment**—capital punishment authorized by federal law

Chase, Salmon Portland — **Impeachment** — impeachment proceedings against a President of the United States

Chase, Salmon Portland—**Money**—coin to use "In God We Trust"

Chase, Samuel — **Impeachment** — impeachment proceedings against a Justice of the Supreme Court of the United States

Cheever, Ezekiel—**Grammar**—Latin grammar textbook

Cheney, Edwin Fox—**Medal**—Distinguished Service Medal (Merchant Marine)

Chenoweth, William B.—**Automobile Trucking Service**—automobile inter-city trucking service

Cheplin, Harry—**Milk**—acidophilus milk

Chesbrough, Ellis Sylvester—**Water Conduit**—water supply tunnel for a city

Chesebrough, Robert Augustus—**Petroleum Jelly**

Chestnut, Ike—**Television—Telecast**—prize fight in a "studio"

Clay, Henry — **Political Convention** — unit rule

Clay, Henry—**Political Platform (national)**

Clay, Henry—**President (U.S.)**—President to receive fewer popular and electoral votes than an opponent

Clay, Lucius Du Bignon—**Television**—Telecast—transcontinental telecast received on the west coast

Claypoole, David C.—**Constitution of the United States**—Constitution of the United States was first published in a newspaper

Claypoole, David C. — **Newspaper** — daily newspaper

Clayton, Henry Holm—**Balloon Race**—balloon cup race

Clayton, Powell—**Political Convention**—national nominating convention presided over by a Negro

Clemens, Samuel Langhorne—**Arts and Letters Society**—arts and letters society (national)

Clemens, Samuel Langhorne—**Typewritten Book Manuscript**

Clement, L. M.—**Radio Telephone**—radio telephone communication between the ground and an airplane

Clemons, Lucian M. — **Medal** — lifesaving medal

Clemson, Thomas Green—**Agriculture Bureau**—agriculture bureau

Clerc, Laurent—**Deaf—School**—school for the deaf

Cleveland, Clement—**Hospital**—cancer hospital

Cleveland, Esther—**Births**—child born in the White House, Washington, D.C., the offspring of a President

Cleveland, Frances Folsom—**Births** — child born in the White House, Washington, D.C., the offspring of a President

Cleveland, Grover—**Agriculture Department (U.S.)**—Secretary of the Department of Agriculture

Cleveland, Grover—**Births**—child born in the White House, Washington, D.C., the offspring of a President

Cleveland, Grover — **Interstate Commerce Act**

Cleveland, Grover—**President (U.S.)**—President elected for two non-consecutive terms

Cleveland, Grover—**President (U.S.)**—President to visit a foreign country while President

Cleveland, Grover—**Wedding**—White House wedding of a President

Clifford, Hadley — **Street Car** — interurban street car line

Cline, Genevieve Rose—**Judge**—woman associate justice on the federal bench

Clinton, De Witt — **Freemasons** — Knights Templar Grand Encampment

Clinton, De Witt—**Political Convention**—nominating convention (state)

Clinton, De Witt—**Political Convention**—political nominating caucus

Clinton, George — **Congressional Caucus**—congressional caucus (open, not secret)

Clinton, George—**Political Convention**—political nominating caucus attended by party leaders

Clinton, George—**Presidential Candidate**—presidential candidate nominated at a caucus

Clinton, George — **Presidential Election** — presidential election in which candidates had been nominated for the vice presidency

Clinton, George—**Salute** (complimentary)

Clinton, George — **Vice President of the United States** — Vice President to be nominated

Clinton, George — **Vice President of the United States**—Vice President to die in office

Clinton, George — **Vice President of the United States**—Vice President to serve under two Presidents

Clippinger, Arthur Raymond — **Evangelical United Brethren Church**

Clymer, George—**Art Organization**—art organization

Clymer, George — **Treasury Department (U.S.)**—Treasurer of the United States

Clymer, George E.—**Printing Press**—printing press invented in America

Coates, George Henry—**Clipper for Cutting Hair**

Coats, Moses—**Apple Parer**

Cobb, Jerrie—**Woman**—woman to undergo astronaut tests

Cobb, John—**Automobile**—automobile to exceed the speed of 400 miles an hour

Cobb, Ty (Tyrus Raymond Cobb)—**Baseball Player**—baseball player to score more than 4,000 hits

Cobb, Ty—**Hall of Fame**—hall of fame (baseball)

Cobb, William G.—**Automobile**—sun-powered automobile

Cobbett, William—**Fruit Culture Treatise**

Cochran, Jacqueline — **Aviation — Aviator** — woman to pilot an airplane faster than the speed of sound

Cochrane, Elizabeth—**Tour of the World**—tour of the world made by a woman traveling alone

Code, William Edward—**Codeball**

Cody, William Frederick—**Wild West Show**

Coe, Israel—**Brass Kettles**

Coe, Walter Hamilton—**Gold Leaf**

Coffin, Frank Trenholm—**Moving Picture**—moving picture from an airplane

Coffin, James Henry—**Manual Training**—manual training institute

Coffin, William—**Nautical School**—nautical school

Cogswell, John Green—**Gymnasium**—to offer systematic instruction

Cogswell, Mason Fitch — **Deaf — School** — school for the deaf

Cohen, Charles Joseph — **Normal School** — teachers' training school (Jewish)

Cohen, Mendes I. — **Egyptian Antiquities Collection**

Conroy, John M.—**Aviation—Flights (transcontinental)** — transcontinental round-trip solo flight between sunrise and sunset

Contini, Ludovico — **Opera** — opera at the Metropolitan Opera House

Converse, Frederick Shepherd — **Opera** — opera by an American composer performed at the Metropolitan Opera House of New York

Converse, Harriet Maxwell—**Woman**—white woman to become an Indian chief

Converse, James C.—**Railroad Commission (state)**

Conway, Phip—**Skeet**—national skeet tournament

Conwell, Christopher Columbus—**Newspaper** —penny daily newspaper

Conyers, James Henry—**Naval Academy**— Negro midshipman in the United States Naval Academy

Cook, Cordelia E. — **Medal** — Bronze Star presented to a woman

Cook, Frederick—**Cotton-Bale Metallic Tie**

Cook, S. M.—**High School**—county high school

Cooke, George Frederick — **Actor**—English actor of note

Cooke, Josiah Parsons—**Chemical Laboratory**—chemical laboratory in a collegiate institution

Cooke, William D.—**Deaf—Students' Magazine**—magazine for deaf students

Cooley, James P.—**Toothpick Manufacturing Machine Patent**

Cooley, Lyman Edgar—**Sanitary District**

Cooley, Thomas McIntyre—**Interstate Commerce Act**

Coolidge, Calvin—**Money**—coin bearing the portrait of a living President

Coolidge, Calvin — **Moving Picture**—talking pictures of presidential candidates

Coolidge, Calvin—**President (U.S.)**—President born on Independence Day

Coolidge, Calvin—**Radio Broadcast**—network broadcast received on the Pacific coast

Coolidge, Calvin—**Radio Broadcast**—political convention broadcast

Coolidge, Calvin—**Radio Broadcast**—political speech by a President on radio

Coolidge, Calvin—**Radio Broadcast**—President to broadcast from the White House

Coolidge, Calvin—**Radio Broadcast**—presidential inauguration

Coolidge, Calvin — **Radio Broadcast**—presidential message to be broadcast

Coolidge, Calvin—**Radio Facsimile Transmission**—photograph sent by radio across the continent

Coolidge, Mrs. Calvin — **Fair** — Woman's World Fair

Coolidge, William David—**Tungsten**—ductile tungsten

Cooney, Frank Buckley—**Ink**—ink paste

Coontz, Robert Edward—**Radio Facsimile Transmission**—transpacific and transcontinental facsimile transmission

Cooper, Charles Henry — **Basketball** — National Basketball Association Negro player

Cooper, Daniel M. — **Time Recorder**—card time-recorder

Cooper, Elias Samuel — **Medical School**— medical college on the Pacific coast

Cooper, George Marion—**Medical Clinic**— contraceptive clinic (state)

Cooper, Leroy Gordon, Jr.—**Astronauts**— astronauts

Cooper, Peter—**Building**—building in which wrought iron beams were used

Cooper, Peter—**College**—college to prohibit discrimination because of race, religion or color

Cooper, Peter—**Greenback Party**

Cooper, Peter — **Locomotive** — locomotive built in the United States to pull passengers

Cooper, Peter—**Locomotive**—race between a locomotive and a horse-drawn vehicle

Copeland, Charles W.—**Ship**—fish hatching steamer (federal)

Copley, John Singleton — **Artist**—American artist of importance

Copson, John — **Insurance** — fire insurance agent

Corbett, James John — **Moving Picture Actor**—actor to have an exclusive contract

Corbett, James John—**Prize Fight**—openair arena especially built for a prize fight

Corbett, James John — **Prize Fight**—prize fight of importance under the Marquis of Queensberry rules

Corbin, Austin—**Bank**—national bank

Corcoran, Larry—**Baseball Player**—baseball pitcher to pitch three no-hit games

Cori, Carl Ferdinand—**Nobel Prize**—husband and wife in the United States to receive a joint Nobel Prize

Cori, Gerty Theresa—**Nobel Prize**—husband and wife in the United States to receive a joint Nobel Prize

Cornelia, Miss—**Cripples**—private school for cripples

Cornelissen, Jan—**Insane Patient's Maintenance Act**

Cornelius, Robert—**Photograph**—photograph taken in the United States

Cornell, Ezra—**Cable**—submarine telegraph cable that was practical

Cornish, James—**Surgical Operation**—suture of the human heart (successful)

Cornish, John—**Wool**—worsted mill

Cornish, Samuel E. — **Newspaper** — Negro newspaper

Cornwallis, Charles—**Flag**—American flag flown in battle

Corrigan, Michael Augustine—**Catholic Student**

Corson, Juliet—**Cooking School**

Cortelyou, George Bruce—**Commerce and Labor Department (U.S.)**

Costa, Adele—**Deaf—Transmission**—visible and oral communication by the deaf over distance

Costabile, Alphonse—**Bicycle Traffic Court**

Cross, Robert — **Insurance** — life insurance company

Cross, Thaddeus M. B.—**Medical Book**—neurology textbook

Crossfield, Scott — **Aviation** — **Flights** — airplane to exceed the speed of 1,300 miles an hour

Crossman, William—**Britannia Ware**

Crothers, Rachel — **Television** — **Telecast** — play to be televised with its original Broadway cast

Crotty, Burke—**Television**—**Telecast**—President to appear on television

Crowell, Luther Childs—**Paper Bag Manufacturing Machine**—square-bottom paper bag machinery

Crowley, John G.—**Ship**—schooner (six masted)

Crowninshield, George—**Ship**—yacht

Crowninshield, Jacob—**Animals**—elephant

Cruger, John—**Chamber of Commerce**—chamber of commerce (state)

Crukshank, Joseph—**Botany Book**—botany book strictly American

Crukshank, Joseph—**Trade Register**

Crumrine, Clarence E.—**Aviation**—**Flights**—New York-Alaska flight

Cull, Dan B.—**Court**—conciliation tribunal for small claims

Culley, Langley B.—**Ship**—iron vessel built of American iron

Cullum, Elizabeth Hamilton—**Hospital**—cancer hospital

Culver, H. Paul—**Air Mail Service**—air mail experimental route

Cummings, Alma—**Dance Marathon**

Cummings, Irving—**Moving Picture**—talking picture taken outdoors (full length)

Cummings, Thomas Seir—**Art Organization**—artists' society of importance

Cummings, Walter Joseph—**Federal Deposit Insurance Corporation**

Cummings, William Arthur ("Candy")—**Baseball Player**—baseball pitcher

Cummins, Benjamin—**Saw** (circular)

Cummins, Clessie Lyle—**Diesel Engine**—diesel engine automobile trip

Cummins, Clessie Lyle—**Diesel Engine**—diesel engine speed record (official)

Cunningham, Alfred Austell—**Marines**—marine aviator

Cunningham, Charles E.—**Union Labor Party**

Cunningham, Harold A. —**Radio Telephone**—radio telephone ship-to-shore commercial service

Curry, Duncan F.—**Baseball Team**—baseball team

Curry, John Francis—**Civil Air Patrol (U.S.)**

Curtice, Cooper — **Zoological Laboratory (U.S.)**—zoological laboratory (U.S.) for the study of the parasites of livestock

Curtis, Augustus Darwin—**Electric Lighting**—electric indirect lighting demonstration

Curtis, Austen M.—**Radio Telephone**—transatlantic radio telephone message

Curtis, Charles—**Congress (U.S.)—Senate**—broadcast from the Senate chamber

Curtis, Charles—**Senator (U.S.)**—Indian senator

Curtis, Charles—**Vice President of the United States**—Indian Vice President

Curtis, Charles—**Woman**—woman secretary to a Vice President of the United States

Curtis, George—**Bank**—clearing house

Curtis, George William—**Civil Service**—Civil Service Commission

Curtis, George William—**Political Convention**—nominating convention presided over by a Negro

Curtis, John—**Chewing Gum**—chewing gum

Curtis, Leslie L.—**Air Brush Patent**

Curtis, William Eleroy—**Pan American Union**

Curtiss, Glenn Hammond—**Aviation**—aeronautical trophy

Curtiss, Glenn Hammond—**Aviation—Airplane**—airplane sold commercially

Curtiss, Glenn Hammond—**Aviation—Airplane**—hydroplane

Curtiss, Glenn Hammond—**Aviation—Airplane Bombing**—airplane bombing experiment

Curtiss, Glenn Hammond—**Aviation—Expositions and Meets**—aviation meet

Curtiss, Glenn Hammond—**Aviation—Flights**—hydroplane flight to and from a ship

Curtiss, Glenn Hammond—**Aviation—Flights**—over-water flight

Curtiss, Glenn Hammond—**Aviation—License**—pilot's license issued by the Aero Club of America

Curtiss, Glenn Hammond—**Aviation—Races**—airplane race won by an American in Europe

Curtiss, Glenn Hammond—**Aviation—Races**—airplane to race a train

Curtiss, Glenn Hammond—**Aviation—School**—airplane flying school

Curtiss, Glenn Hammond—**Motorcycle Hill-Climbing Contest**

Cushing, Jack—**Moving Picture**—moving picture of a staged prize fight

Cushing, Richard James—**Television—Telecast**—Catholic mass televised from a studio

Cushing, William—**Supreme Court of the United States**—Supreme Court of the United States

Cushman, Robert—**Furs**

Cushman, Robert—**Sermon Printed** (American)

Cutbush, Clara F.—**Fireworks Book**

Cutbush, Edward — **Naval Officer** — naval medical officer to write a book

Cutbush, James—**Fireworks Book**

Cutler, Abner—**Desk with roll top**

Cutler, James Goold—**Postal Service**—mail chute

Cutler, Manasseh—**Botanic Scientific Expedition**

D

Davis, Paulina W.—**Woman Suffrage**—convention (national) of women advocating woman suffrage

Davis, Phineas—**Locomotive**—locomotive bid

Davis, Phineas—**Locomotive**—locomotive to burn coal (practical, American made)

Davis, Raymond Cazallis — **Bibliography Course**

Davis, Samuel—**Presbyterian Presbytery**

Davis, Stephen Brooks—**Television**—Telecast—telecast of an object in motion

Davis, William Augustine—**Postal Service**—railroad post office

Davis, William Hammatt—**Industrial Recovery Act**—compliance board under the National Industrial Recovery Act

Davison, James J.—**Aviation**—Airplane—jet airplane to land on a ship

Dawes, Charles Gates—**Budget Bureau (United States)**

Dawes, Charles Gates—**Congress (U.S.)**—Senate—broadcast from the Senate chamber

Dawes, Charles Gates—**Radio Broadcast**—political convention broadcast

Dawes, Charles Gates—**Radio Broadcast**—presidential inauguration

Dawes, Robert G.—**College**—college principally for war veterans

Dawson, Benjamin Frederick—**Medical Periodical**—medical periodical devoted to diseases of women and children

Dawson, John—**Disciples of Christ**

Dawson, William Levi—**Congress (U.S.)**—House of Representatives—congressional standing committee headed by a Negro

Dawson, William Levi—**Symphony**—symphony on a Negro folk theme

Day, Benjamin Henry—**Newspaper**—penny daily newspaper

Day, Benjamin Henry — **Periodical** — illustrated weekly

Day, Edmund Ezra—**Industrial and Labor Relations School**

Day, Horace Harrel—**Adhesive and Medicated Plaster**—adhesive and medicated plaster patent

Day, Stephen (Steeven Daye)—**Book**—book (full size)

Day, Stephen—**Children's Book**

Day, Stephen—**Hebrew Type**

Day, Stephen—**Music Book**—hymn book

Day, Stephen—**Printing**—document printed in America

Day, Stephen—**Spelling Book**

Day, Stephen—**Thesis Directory**

Dayton, William Lewis—**Republican Party**—Republican Party national convention

Dean, William Frische—**Medal**—Medal of Honor awarded in the Korean War

Deane, Charles—**Book**—book (pamphlet) on vellum

Deane, Samuel — **Dictionary** — agricultural dictionary

Deane, Silas—**Ink**—invisible ink

Deane, Silas—**Navy**—naval fleet

Deane, Silas—**Treaty**—treaty entered into by the United States

Deane, Silas—**United States**—nation to recognize the independence of the United States

Deans, Leroy—**Medal**—Order of the Purple Heart awarded in the Korean War

Debel, Niels Henriksen — **Strike**—modern sit-down strike

De Blauw, John—**Air Mail Service**—helicopter air mail and express service

DeBlois, Thomas A. — **Navy**—naval militia (state)

De Bow, James Dunwoody Brownson — **Business Economics Course**

De Brebeuf, John—**Catholic Canonization of North Americans**

Debrett, J.—**Bibliography**—bibliography of Americana in English

Debs, Eugene Victor — **Social Democratic Party of America**

Debs, Eugene Victor—**Socialist Party**

Decatur, Stephen — **Navy** — prize money awarded by the United States Navy

Decker, John Wright—**Dairy School**

De Crow, Sarah—**Postmaster**—woman postmaster appointed after the adoption of the Constitution

Deere, John—**Steel**—cast steel for plows

De Felitta, Frank P.—**Television**—Telecast—opera written for television on commission for a commercial sponsor

Defoe, Daniel — **Newspaper** — newspaper serial story

De Forest, Lee—**Moving Picture**—sound on film moving picture

De Forest, Lee — **Moving Picture**—talking pictures of presidential candidates

De Forest, Lee—**Radio Broadcast**—singer to broadcast

De Forest, Lee—**Radio Microphone** (carbon)

De Forest, Lee—**Radio Society**

De Forest, Lee — **Radio Tube** — three-element vacuum tube

Defrees, John Dougherty — **Government Printing Office**—Government Printing Office

De Gersdorff, George Bruns—**Stadium**—cement stadium

De Grasse, John Vancerlle—**Physician**—Negro doctor to become a member of a medical association

Delafield, Edward—**Hospital**—eye hospital (permanent)

Delafield Edward—**Physician**—ophthalmologist of note

Delamotte, Charles—**Sunday School**—Sunday school

Delano, Frederic Adrian—**National Planning Board (U.S.)**

De Lanoy, William C.—**Insurance**—war risk insurance bureau

Delany, Martin Robinson—**Army Officer**—major (Negro)

Delcambre, Adrien—**Typesetting Machine**—typesetting machine patent

De Long, George Washington — **Nautical School**—nautical municipal school

De Long, George Washington — **Ship** — steamboat to employ electric lights

Del Puente, Giuseppe—**Opera**—opera at the Metropolitan Opera House

De Luce, Nathaniel—**Opera**—opera (Italian)

De May, Philip—**Automobile Transcontinental Trip**—transcontinental family automobile requiring only a month

Demby, Edward Thomas—**Protestant Episcopal Bishop**—Negro suffragan

Deming, William Champion—**Incubator for Infants**

Demont (Dement), William—**Traitor to the American cause**

Dempsey, Jack (William Harrison Dempsey)—**Prize Fight**—prize fight to attract 100,000 spectators

Dempsey, Jack—**Prize Fight**—prize fight to gross a million dollars

Dempsey, Jack—**Radio Broadcast**—prize fight broadcast

Dempsey, Jack—**Radio Broadcast**—prize fight (heavyweight championship) broadcast

Denby, Mrs. Edwin—**Aviation**—**Airship**—dirigible (American-built rigid)

Denman, James — **Public School** — public school for Chinese

Denman, William—**Shipping**—United States Shipping Board

Dennet, William—**Navy**—navy yard

Denney, Oswald Evans — **Hospital** — leper hospital

Denning, M. Leslie—**Telephone**—dial telephone service coast-to-coast without the aid of operators

Dennison, Aaron Lufkin — **Clock** — watch (eight day)

Dennison, Cora—**Wedding**—television wedding

Dennison, Warren Hathaway — **Church** — General Council of Congregational and Christian Churches

Denny, Jack—**Radio Broadcast**—radio broadcast from a moving train, of a regular program on a national network

De Paolis, Alessio—**Television**—**Telecast**—opera telecast

De Priest, Oscar Stanton — **Congressman (U.S.)** — Negro congressman from the North

Derbigny, Pierre—**Law Codification** (state)

Derby, George—**Balloon**—balloon destroyed by enemy gun fire

Derby, George — **Health Board** — health board (state)

Derham, James—**Physician**—Negro doctor

De Rosich—**Opera**—opera (Italian)

Desjardins, Alphonse—**Credit Union Association**

De Smedt, Joseph — **Road**—sheet asphalt pavement

Desmond, Connie — **Television**—**Telecast**—baseball games televised in color

De Soto, Fernando—**Flood**

Destinn, Emmy — **Opera** — opera broadcast in part

Deutsch, Bernard Seymour — **Aviation** — floating seaplane ramp (municipally owned)

Devan, William M.—**Coast Guard (U.S.)**—inland U.S. Coast Guard station

Devaney, Frances Teresa—**Naval Officer**—women sworn into the regular U.S. Navy

De Vilbiss, Allen — **Scale**—automatic computing pendulum-type scales

Devine, Edward T.—**College**—university extension summer meeting

De Vry, Herman Adolf—**Moving Picture Projector**—moving picture projector (portable)

Dewey, Charles Augustus—**College Alumni Association**—college alumni association

Dewey, George—**American Expeditionary Force**—American Expeditionary Force

Dewey, George—**Medal**—"campaign medal"

Dewey, George—**Naval Officer**—naval officer to become "Admiral of the Navy"

Dewey, Joseph—**Steel**—steel

Dewey, Martin — **Dental Magazine**—orthodontia magazine

Dewey, Melvil—**Library Chair**

Dewey, Melvil—**Library Society**—library association (national)

Dewey, Melvil—**Library Society**—state library society

Dewey, Melvil—**Library Training (systematic)**

Dewey, Thomas Edmund — **Labor** — labor anti-discrimination commission (state)

Dewey, Thomas Edmund—**Woman**—woman presidential campaign co-manager

De Witt, John H.—**Radar**—radar signal to the moon

De Wolf, Oscar Coleman—**Medical Instruction**—state medicine and public hygiene professorship

Dexter, Gregory—**Dictionary** — Indian-English dictionary

Dey, Alexander—**Time Recorder**—dial time recorder

Dey, John—**Time Recorder**—dial time recorder

Dey, Robert—**Time Recorder**—dial time recorder

Diamond, Harry — **Aviation** — **Flights**—all blind cross-country test

Dice, Lee Raymond—**Medical Clinic**—heredity clinic

Dickins, John—**Book Publisher** of denominational books

Dickinson, Charles—**Duel**—duel in which a future President of the United States participated

Dickinson, John—**Diplomatic Service** — foreign service committee

Dickinson, John — **Music**—patriotic American song

Dickinson, Jonathan—**College**—college charter granted by a governor or acting governor with only the assent of his council

Dickinson, Samuel—**School Superintendent**—school superintendent (city)

Dickinson, Thomas Herbert — **Theatrical School**—theatrical school sponsored by an institution of higher learning

Dickson, Sarah E.—**Woman**—woman Presbyterian elder

Dickson, William Kennedy Laurie — **Moving Picture**—moving picture "close-up"

Dielman, Henry—**Degrees (academic and honorary)**—doctor of music degree

Diesel, Rudolf—**Engine**—diesel engine built for commercial service

Dietz, Howard—**Radio Broadcast**—musical comedy broadcast

Dietz, Mildred Marie—**Bicycle Racer**—woman bicycle champion of the National Amateur Bicycle Association to win twice

Digges, Thomas Atwood — **Novel** — novel written in America

Dillon, John Forrest—**Radio Commission (U.S.)**

Dilworth, Thomas—**Textbook**

Dingee, Charles Hazard—**Pharmacy College** —pharmacy college

Dinsmoor, Charles — **Automobile Tractor**— endless chain tractor

Disney, Walt — **Moving Picture** — animated cartoon in color (Technicolor) of feature length with sound

Disney, Walt — **Moving Picture** — animated cartoon talking picture

Disney, Walt — **Moving Picture** — animated three-dimensional cartoon in Technicolor (modern)

Disturnell, J. — **Railroad Guide** — railroad guide

Dittenhoefer, Isaac—**Jews**—Jewish fraternal society

Dix, Dorothea Lynde — **Woman** — woman lobbyist

Dix, John Adams—**Political Machine**

Dixon, Brandt Van Blarcom—**College**—college for women to affiliate with a university

Dixon, Emmet—**Congress of the Confederate States**

Dixon, George — **Submarine**—submarine to sink a man-of-war

Dixon, Thomas—**Boat Club**—boat club

Dixwell, Epes Sargent—**Football Club**—football club

Doak, Samuel — **College** — college named after George Washington

Doak, William Nuckles — **Labor Department (U.S.)**—native-born Secretary of Labor

Dobson, J.—**Cranioscopy Book**

Dobson, Judah—**Embalming Book**

Dobson, Thomas—**Bible**—Hebrew Bible

Dobson, Thomas—**Encyclopedia**—encyclopedia

Dobson, Thomas — **Medical Book**—anatomy book

Dobson, Thomas—**Medical Book**—anatomy book (American)

Dobson, Thomas—**Medical Book**—dispensatory

Dobson, Thomas—**Music Book**—secular song book by a native American

Dock, Christopher—**Teaching Methods Book**

Dod, Daniel — **Ship** — steamboat built in America to cross the Atlantic Ocean

Dodd, Mrs. John Bruce—**Holiday**—Father's Day

Dodge, Augustus Caesar—**Senator (U.S.)**— father and son senators at the same session

Dodge, David Low—**Peace Society**

Dodge, Grace Hoadley—**Young Women's Christian Association**

Dodge, Henry—**Army**—cavalry unit

Dodge, Henry—**Senator (U.S.)**—father and son senators at the same session

Dodge, Homer Levi—**Army**—Reserve Officers Training Corps course in mountain and winter warfare

Dodge, Nehemiah—**Jewelers' Supply House**

Dodge, Philip Tell—**Voting Machine Commission (state)**

Dodrill, Forest Dewey—**Surgical Operation** —mitral valve exposure (prolonged) in a human patient

Doering, William von Eggers—**Quinine**— synthetic quinine

Doggett, John — **Railroad Guide** — railroad guide that printed the time schedule

Doheny, Edward Laurence—**Cabinet of the United States**—cabinet member convicted of a crime

Dolan, Thomas P.—**Manufacturers' Association**

Dollenberg, Fred Paul—**Glider**—glider commercial freight service

Dollier de Casson, François—**Oil**—oil spring

Dolph, William B.—**Radio Broadcast**—news program (cooperative)

Donahue, Peter M.—**Ship**—steamboat built on the Pacific coast for the government

Donald, John A.—**Shipping**—United States Shipping Board

Donald, Mrs. W. F.—**Holiday**—mother-in-law day

Donaldson, James—**Sugar**—sugar beets

Donaldson, Jesse Monroe — **Postmaster** — postmaster general appointed from the ranks

Donaldson, Washington Harrison—**Balloon** —balloon Atlantic crossing attempt

Donelson, Andrew Jackson—**American Party**

Donlon, Mary Honor—**Woman**—woman editor-in-chief of a law review

Donovan, Florence F.—**Arbitration**—state board of mediation and arbitration

Donovan, William Joseph—**Medal**—recipient of the four highest decorations awarded by the United States

Doolittle, Amos—**Music Magazine**—music magazine

Doolittle, James Harold—**Aviation—Flights** —all blind flight

Doolittle, James Harold—**Aviation—Flights (transcontinental)** — transcontinental one-stop flight

Doolittle, Sylvester—**Ship**—steamboat engine built in America for a screw-propelled vessel

Doran, A. J.—**Old Age Home for Pioneers**

Doremus, Sarah B.—**Missionary Society**— foreign missionary society organized by women

Doremus, Sarah Platt—**Hospital**—children's hospital

Dorr, Ebenezer—**Ship**—ship from the Atlantic coast to anchor in a California port

Dorrington, Arthur—**Hockey**—Negro player in organized hockey

Dorsey, Herbert Grove—**Fathometer**

Doss, Desmond T.—**Medal**—Medal of Honor awarded to a conscientious objector

Doster, Alexis—**Aviation**—airplane human pick-up

Dotey, Edward—**Duel**—duel

Doubleday, Abner—**Baseball Game**—baseball

Doughty, Thomas—**Periscope**

Douglas, Alexander—**Bustle**—patented

Douglas, Findlay S.—**Golf Champion**—golf champion (American born)

Douglas, Howard—**Aviation**—**Flights**—New York-Alaska flight

Douglas, James Henderson—**Air Force Academy (U.S.)**—Air Force Academy

Douglas, Paul—**Television — Telecast** —pay television presentation of a moving picture shown simultaneously in theaters

Douglas, Robert—**Forestry Society**—national forestry association

Douglas, William P.—**Coaching Club**

Douglass, David—**Theater**—theater building (permanent)

Douglass, Frederick—**Political Convention** —Negro delegate to a national political convention

Douglass, Frederick—**Presidential Candidate** —presidential candidate of Negro blood nominated

Douglass, Frederick—**Vice Presidential Candidate**—Negro vice presidential candidate

Dowd, Charles Ferdinand—**Time (standard)**

Dowd, Denis Patrick—**World War I**—American to sail to Europe to enlist in World War I

Downing, Andrew Jackson — **Botanist** — botanist

Downing, George—**Degrees (academic and honorary)**—Bachelor of Arts degree

Dows, Gustavus D.—**Soda Fountain**—ornamented soda fountain

Doyle, John Joseph—**Baseball Player**—baseball "pinch hitter"

Drake, E. F.—**Forestry Society**—state forestry association

Drake, Edwin Laurentine—**Oil**—oil well commercially productive

Drake, Samuel Gardner—**Book Store (antiquarian)**

Draper, Dorothy Catherine—**Photograph**—photograph taken in the United States

Draper, Eben Sumner—**Credit Union Law**

Draper, Henry—**Photograph**—photograph of a stellar spectrum showing the dark lines

Draper, John William—**Chemical Society**—chemical society (national)

Draper, John William—**Photograph**—celestial photograph

Draper, John William—**Photograph**—photograph taken in the United States

Draper, Richard — **Engraving** — historical print engraved in America

Drayton, William Henry—**Colonial Government**—independent government in any of the American colonies

Dreisbach, John—**Evangelical Church Building**

Dreisbach, Martin—**Evangelical Church General Conference**

Dressler, Marie—**Moving Picture**—six-reel feature-length comedy

Drew, Daniel—**Telegraph**—telegraph ticker used by a brokerage concern

Drinker, Philip—**Respirator** (iron lung)

Dripps, Isaac—**Locomotive Cowcatcher**

Dropsie, Moses Aaron—**Jewish College**—Jewish non-sectarian college

Dropsie, Moses Aaron—**Normal School**—teachers' training school (Jewish)

Drown, L. L.—**Nurses' Society**—society for superintendents of nursing schools

Dryden, Hugh Latimer — **Space Agency (U.S.)**

Duane, William—**Dictionary**—military dictionary

Duane, William—**Gymnastics Book**

Duane, William—**Library Catalog**—catalog of the Library of Congress

Duane, William—**Publishing Society**

Du Bois, Mrs. Cornelius—**Hospital**—children's hospital

Du Bois, William Edward Burghardt—**Arts and Letters Society**—Negro member of the National Institute of Arts and Letters

Duché, Jacob—**Continental Congress**—Continental Congress to be opened with prayer

Duckering, Florence West—**Medical Society** —women members of the American College of Surgeons

Dudley, Homer Walter—**Voice Mechanism** —voice mechanism capable of creating the complex sounds of speech

Dudley, William L.—**Golf Magazine**

Duenas, Tony—**Medal**—Silver Star Medal awarded to a civilian by the U.S. Navy in World War II

Dufek, George John—**Discovery**—American to land by air at the South Pole

Duffield, Howard—**Organ School**

Dufour, John James—**Vineyard** (successful)

Dufriche, Eugene—**Opera**—opera composed by a woman performed at the Metropolitan Opera House

Duggan, Pat — **Television — Telecast** — pay television presentation of a moving picture shown simultaneously in theaters

Duggar, Benjamin Minge—**Aureomycin**—aureomycin chlortetracycline

Duhring, Louis Adolphus—**Medical Book**—dermatology treatise

Dulany, Richard Hunter—**Horse Show**

Dulty, George—**Soda Fountain**—soda fountain patent

Dumas, Charles—**High Jump**

Dumont, Marjorie—**Wedding**—airplane wedding

Dunant, Jean Henri—**American Red Cross**

Dunbar, Charles Franklin—**Political Economy Course**—political economy chair

Dunbar, Edward Lucian—**Spring Manufacturer**

Dunbar, Robert—**Elevator**—grain elevator operated by steam

Duncan, Joseph Smith—**Addressograph**

Duncan, Robert Todd—**Opera**—Negro to sing a white role with a white cast in an opera company

Dunham, Alanson Millen—**Snowshoe**

Dunham, Isaac—**Lighthouse**—iron pile lighthouse

Dunham, Otis Emerson—**Animals**—reindeer

Dunklee, Ernest Walter—**Strike**—anti-sit-down strike legislation (state)

Dunlap, John—**Constitution of the United States**—Constitution of the United States was first published in a newspaper

Dunlap, John—**Newspaper**—daily newspaper

Dunlap, Maxine—**Aviation—License**—glider license awarded a woman

Dunlap, William—**Etcher**

Dunlap, William — **Opera** — opera by an American composer

Dunlap, William—**Playwright** (professional)

Dunlap, William—**Theater History**

Dunlop, John—**Declaration of Independence (American)**—Declaration of Independence was first printed

Dunn, James Clement—**Telephone**—mobile transatlantic telephone conversation between two telephone-equipped automobiles

Dunn, Nathan—**Book**—book for the blind

Dunn, Willie—**Golf Tournament**—open championship (official)

Dunster, Henry—**College**—college

Dunster, Henry — **Corporation** — corporate body

Dunster, Henry—**Missionary Society**—missionary society (colonial)

Dunton, Jacob—**Pill**—compressed pills or tablets

Du Pont, E. Paul, Jr.—**Aviation—Flights**—sky-train international round trip flight

Durand, Elias—**Soda Water**—soda water commercially bottled

Durand, Elie Magloire—**Bottler of Mineral Water**

Durant, Charles Ferson—**Balloon**—balloon flight by a native-born American

Durant, Mrs. Henry Fowle—**Young Women's Christian Association**

Durant, Howard M.—**Hotel**—hotel to install electric lights

Durell, William—**Engraving**—wood engraving made with an engraving tool

Durfee, William Franklin—**Copper Refinery Furnace**

Durfee, William Franklin—**Steel**—Bessemer steel converter

Durfee, William Franklin—**Steel Analysis Laboratory**

Durocher, Leo—**Television—Telecast**—baseball games (major league) televised

Duryea, Charles Edgar—**Automobile**—automobile regularly made for sale

Duryea, Charles Edgar—**Automobile Club**

Duryea, Charles Edgar—**Aviation—Expositions and Meets**—air conference (international)

Duryea, James Franklin—**Automobile Race**—automobile race

Dusenbury, William C.—**Credit Protective Group**

Duston, Hannah—**Woman**—heroine

du Vigneaud, Vincent—**Pituitary Hormone**—polypeptide hormone synthesized

Dwight, Edmund—**Normal School**—normal school (state)

Dwight, John—**Baking Soda**

Dwyer, Michael—**Horse**—horse whose total purses exceeded $100,000

Dwyer, Philip—**Horse**—horse whose total purses exceeded $100,000

Dyan, Hubert—**Censorship**—state board of censorship on literature

Dyar, Harrison Gray—**Telegraph**—telegraph

Dykstra, Clarence Addison—**Conscription**—peacetime conscription bill

Dykstra Clarence Addison—**Navy "E" Award**—Navy "E" certificates of meritorious service presented to an institution of higher learning

E

Eads, James Buchanan—**Bridge**—steel arch bridge

Eads, James Buchanan — **Medal** — Albert medal presented to a native-born American

Eads, James Buchanan — **Ship** — iron-clad naval vessels

Eagan, Edward F.—**Bobsled Competition**—four-man bob-team competition

Eagan, Michael—**Handball** national championship match for amateurs

Eagle, Frank—**Indian Church**—Indian church organized by Indians

Eales, Joseph—**Fuse**—safety fuse

Eames, A. G.—**Locker**—public locker plant

Eames, Wilberforce—**Bibliography Society** (national)

Earhart, Amelia. *See* Putnam, Amelia Earhart

Earl, Effie—**Baseball Team**—women's baseball team

Earle, Parker—**Railroad Car**—refrigerator car shipment of fresh fruit

Earle, Richard Blair — **Rubber** — synthetic rubber

Earle, Sarah H.—**Woman Suffrage**—convention (national) of women advocating woman suffrage

Eastman, George—**Camera**—roll film camera

Eastman, George — **Photographic Film** — transparent paper strip photographic film

Eastman, George Washington — **Business School**—business school

Eastman, Joseph Bartlett—**Transportation Coordination**—transportation coordination (federal)

Eisenhower, Dwight David—**Radio Broadcast**—outer space broadcast

Eisenhower, Dwight David—**State**—noncontiguous overseas state

Eisenhower, Dwight David—**State**—noncontiguous state

Eisenhower, Dwight David—**Television—Telecast**—cabinet session to be televised

Eisenhower, Dwight David—**Television—Telecast**—President to appear on television in color

Eisenhower, Dwight David — **Television — Telecast**—presidential news conference filmed for television and newsreels

Eisenhower, Mrs. Dwight David—**Ship**—atomic-powered merchant ship

Eisenhower, Mrs. Dwight David—**Submarine** —atomic-powered submarine

Ekins, Herbert Roslyn—**Aviation—Races**—airplane passenger race around the world

Ela, Jacob E.—**Insurance**—insurance board (state)

Eldred, Arthur Rose—**Boy Scouts of America**—Boy Scout to become an eagle scout

Elgar, John—**Ship**—iron vessel (sheet iron)

Eliot, Benjamin—**Grammar**—Latin grammar textbook

Eliot, Jared — **Agricultural Book** — agricultural book distinctly American

Eliot, John—**Bible**—Bible in an Indian language

Eliot, John—**Book**—book privately printed

Eliot, John—**Grammar**—Indian grammar

Eliot, John—**Indian Church**—Indian church

Eliot, John—**Indians**—Indian preacher

Eliot, John—**Missionary Society**—missionary society (colonial)

Eliot, John—**Primer**—primer in an American Indian dialect

Eliot, Samuel Atkins—**Music Instruction**—musical pedagogy school

Elizabeth II, Queen of Great Britain—**Canal** —Saint Lawrence Seaway

Elizabeth II — **Television—Telecast**—telecast received from England

Elizabeth, Consort of George VI, King of Great Britain—**Television—Telecast**—king and queen to be televised

Elizabeth, Consort of George VI—**Visiting Celebrities**—King and Queen of England

Elkes, Harry—**Bicycle Race**—motorcycle-paced bicycle race

Ellet, Charles—**Bridge**—railway suspension bridge

Ellet, Charles — **Bridge** — wire suspension bridge for general traffic

Ellicott, Andrew — **Astronomy** — meteoric display

Ellicott, Edward Beach—**Automobile License Board**

Elliot, Eugene S.—**Bridge Whist Organization**

Elliott, E. B.—**Civil Service**—Civil Service Commission

Ellis, Richard Gailard—**Ship**—Liberty ship

Ellis, Seth Hockett—**Union Reform Party**

Ellmaker, Amos—**Anti-Masonic Party**

Ellsworth, Annie — **Telegram**—telegram inaugurating commercial service

Ellsworth, Henry Leavitt—**Agricultural Seed Distribution** (national)

Ellsworth, Henry Leavitt—**Patent Commissioner**

Ellsworth, Oliver—**Congress (U.S.)—Senate** —Senate

Ellsworth, Oliver—**Supreme Court (U.S.) Decision**—Supreme Court decision between states

Ellyson, Theodore Gordon — **Aviation—Airplane**—naval airplane

Ellyson, Theodore Gordon — **Aviation — Flights**—airplane catapulted

Elman, Mischa—**Moving Picture**—talking picture

Elmen, Gustaf Waldemar—**Permalloy**

Elmer, Lucius Quintius Cincinnatus—**Crime Prevention and Detection** — interstate crime pact

Elmore, Francis Edward—**Mineral Segregation**

Elsberg, Louis — **Medical Clinic**—laryngology clinic

Elsberg, Louis—**Medical Instruction**—laryngology instruction

Elsberg, Louis—**Medical Periodical**—laryngology magazine

Elsberg, Louis—**Medical Society**—laryngology society (national)

Ely, Eugene — **Aviation — Flights** — airplane flight from a ship

Ely, Eugene — **Aviation — Races** — intercity airplane race

Ely, William H. J.—**Old Age Colony**

Emanuel, David — **Governor** — Jewish governor

Embree, Elihu—**Slavery**—anti-slavery magazine

Embury, Philip — **Methodist** — Methodist preacher

Embury, Philip—**Methodist Chapel**

Emerich, Charles Rulf — **Football Game** — Army-Navy football game

Emerich, James—**War (Korean)**—American tank crew to cross the 38th parallel in Korea

Emerson, Faye—**Television—Telecast**—color program (commercial)

Emerson, Gladys Anderson—**Vitamin**—vitamin E

Emerson, H. D.—**Automobile Club**

Emerson, Oliver Hudleston—**Vitamin**—vitamin E

Emerson, Ralph — **Television—Telecast**—phase-contrast cinemicrography film (American-made) telecast

Emma, Queen (Hawaii)—**Visiting Celebrities** —Queen to visit the United States

Emmes, Thomas—**Engraving**—engraving of any artistic merit

Emmett, Daniel Decatur—**Ministrel Show Troupe**

Emmett, Daniel Decatur—**Music**—war song of the Confederate States

End, George Kenneth—**Rattlesnake Meat**

Endicott, John—**Apples**

F

Farmer, John—**Genealogy**—genealogical collective work

Farmer, Moses Gerrish—**Electric Lighting** —electric light

Farmer, Moses Gerrish—**Fire Alarm System (electric)**

Farmer, Robert—**Expedition**—expedition

Farnham, Ivan Richard—**Pump**—computer pump

Farnsworth, Willis S.—**Locker**—locker (coin vender)

Farquhar, George—**Play (drama)**—play acted by professional players

Farr, John—**Quinine**—quinine

Farragut, David Glasgow—**Naval Officer**— naval officer to become an admiral

Farragut, David Glasgow—**Treason**—citizen of the United States to be tried for treason, convicted and hanged

Farrar, Eugenia H.—**Radio Broadcast**— singer to broadcast

Farrington, Wallace Rider—**Radio Facsimile Transmission**—transpacific and transcontinental facsimile transmission

Fascinato, John—**Television**—**Telecast**—color network telecast in compatible color

Fauset, Crystal Bird—**Legislator (state)**— Negro woman state legislator

Faust family—**Supreme Court (U.S.)**—members of a family admitted simultaneously to practice in the Supreme Court of the United States

Fauvel-Gouraud, François—**Photographic Pamphlet**

Fayssoux, Peter—**Museum**—public museum

Featherstonhaugh, George William—**Geological Survey**—geological survey appropriation (U.S.)

Fechner, Robert—**Civilian Conservation Corps (U.S.)**

Feezor, Betty—**Tape Recording**—video recording on magnetic tape in color

Fehrenbach, John—**Hospital**—tuberculosis hospital (municipal) for consumptive poor

Fell, Jesse—**Coal**—anthracite coal burned experimentally

Fellowes, Cornelius—**Horse Show**—horse show of national scope

Fellows, Alvin J.—**Tape Measure Patent**

Felt, Dorr Eugene—**Adding Machine**—adding machine absolutely accurate at all times

Felton, Rebecca Latimer—**Senator (U.S.)**— woman to occupy a seat in the Senate

Fendall, Josias—**Shorthand Report**

Fenger, Christian—**Hospital**—interracial hospital

Fenno, John—**Newspaper**—political newspaper

Fenwick, Joseph—**Diplomatic Service**—consuls of the United States appointed after the adoption of the Constitution

Ferebee, Thomas W.—**Atomic Bomb**—explosion over enemy territory

Ferentinos, Paisios—**Greek Orthodox Church**

Ferguson, Homer Lenoir—**Museum**—maritime museum

Ferguson, Mrs. Homer Lenoir—**Ship**—airconditioned naval ship

Ferguson, Samuel David—**Protestant Episcopal Bishop**—Protestant Episcopal bishop (Negro)

Fernald, Walter Elmore—**School**—school for the mentally retarded

Fernow, Bernhard Eduard—**Forest Service** —Forest Service (U.S.)

Fernow, Bernhard Eduard—**Forestry School** —forestry school of collegiate character

Ferris, George Washington Gale—**Ferris Wheel**

Fessenden, Reginald Aubrey—**Radio Broadcast**—radio program broadcast

Few, William—**Congress (U.S.)**—**Senate**— Senate

Few, William—**Hospital**—eye hospital (permanent)

Fickel, Jacob Earl—**Aviation**—**Aviator**— aviator to fire a gun from an airplane

Fiedler, Arthur—**Television**—**Telecast**—color network telecast in compatible color

Field, Ben—**Sleeping Car**—Pullman sleeping car

Field, Cyrus West—**Cable**—cable across the Atlantic Ocean was completed

Field, Cyrus West—**Cigar Band**—cigar band of special interest

Field, James Gaven—**People's Party**

Field, Pattie Hockaday—**Diplomatic Service** —woman vice consul

Field, Stephen Dudley—**Street Car**—electric street car successfully run with current generated by a stationary dynamo

Field, Stephen Johnson—**Telegram**—transcontinental telegram

Field, Stephen Johnson—**Telegraph**—telegraph line to the Pacific coast

Fields, Kate—**Women's Club**—women's professional club

Fieser, Louis Frederick—**Vitamin**—synthetic vitamin K

Fillmore, Millard—**American Party**

Finch, William Bolton—**Ship**—warship to circumnavigate the globe

Fink, Colin Garfield—**Chromium Plating process (commercial)**

Finletter, Thomas Knight—**Air Force**—Air Force Secretary

Finley, James—**Bridge**—suspension bridge

Finn, William Joseph—**Television**—**Telecast** —religious services to be televised

Finney, John Miller Turpin—**Medical Society**—American College of Surgeons

Firmstone, William—**Coke**

Firth, Abraham—**Humane Society**—humane association national organization

Fischer, Isaac—**Sandpaper Patent**

Fischer, Karl M.—**Television**—**Telecast**— commercial filmed by a camera operated by atomically generated electricity

Fischer, Louis R.—**Frog Jumping Jubilee**

Fisher, Alva J.—**Washing Machine**—complete, self-contained electric washing machine

Forrest, Nathan Bedford—**Ku Klux Klan**

Forrestal, James Vincent—**Defense Department (U.S.)**

Forrestal, Mrs. James Vincent—**Ship**—aircraft carrier with an angle deck

Forsyth, Ann J.—**Normal School**—woman principal of a normal school

Forsyth, William—**Fruit Culture Treatise**

Forsythe, Albert Ernest—**Aviation—Flights (transcontinental)**—transcontinental flight made by Negroes in their own plane

Fort, Franklin William—**Federal Home Loan Bank Board**

Fort, Franklin—**Home Owners Loan Corporation**

Foster, George G.—**Periodical**—comic weekly

Foster, George Gale—**Business**—installment finance company

Foster, John—**Disciples of Christ**

Foster, John—**Engraving**—engraving

Foster, John—**Map**—map made in the United States published in a book

Foster, John—**Poet**—American poet

Foster, John Gibbons—**Aviation—Flights**—North Pole jet crossing

Foster, M. G.—**Deaf—Hearing Aid**—electrical hearing aid

Foster, Robert Frederick—**Bridge Whist Organization**

Foster, Thomas Jefferson—**Correspondence School**

Foster, William—**Animals**—sheep (Merino sheep)

Foulois, Benjamin Delahauf—**Aviation—Flights**—inter-city airplane flight

Fourdrinier, Henry—**Paper-Making Machinery**—paper-making machine (Fourdrinier) imported

Fourdrinier, Sealy—**Paper-Making Machinery**—paper-making machine (Fourdrinier) imported

Fowler, George Ryerson—**First Aid Instruction**—first aid instruction

Fowler, Robert Grant—**Aviation—Flights (transcontinental)**—transcontinental airplane flight (eastbound)

Fowlkes, James—**Wedding**—television wedding

Fox, Annie G.—**Medal**—Order of the Purple Heart award to a nurse

Fox, Edward—**Insurance**—fire insurance joint-stock company

Fox, John D.—**Spiritualist**

Fox, Joseph—**Brass and Copper Seamless Tubes**

Fox, Philip—**Planetarium**—planetarium open to the public

Fraenkel-Conrat, Heinz Ludwig—**Virus**—virus separated into component parts

Francen, Victor—**Television—Telecast**—moving picture premiere performance to be televised (feature-length foreign film)

Frances, Mary—**College**—Negro university (Catholic)

Franchessin, Jacques Antoine de—**Army**—brevet

Francis I, king of France—**Kidnapping**—kidnapping

Francis, Edward—**Disease** (distinctly American)

Francis, James Bichens—**Sprinkler**—sprinkler

Francis, Joseph—**Lifeboat**—lifeboat (corrugated)

Francis, Tench—**Bank**—bank chartered by Congress

Frank, Glenn—**Medical Congress**—cancer institute (convention)

Frank, Morris S.—**Animals**—dogs trained to guide the blind

Frank, Walter H.—**Medal**—Medal of Honor awarded in World War II

Franke, Mrs. William Birrell—**Ship**—aircraft carrier (atomic powered)

Frankel, Jacob—**Army Officer**—chaplain (Jewish) of the United States Army

Frankenberg, J.—**Aviation**—airplane moving picture show

Franklin, Ann—**Woman**—woman newspaper editor

Franklin, Benjamin—**Academy**

Franklin, Benjamin—**Book**—translated classic published

Franklin, Benjamin—**Cartoon**—newspaper cartoon

Franklin, Benjamin—**Chair**—rocking chair

Franklin, Benjamin—**Chess Book**

Franklin, Benjamin—**Diplomatic Service**—foreign service committee

Franklin, Benjamin—**Diplomatic Service**—minister plenipotentiary

Franklin, Benjamin—**Electric Cooking Experiment**

Franklin, Benjamin—**Execution**—electrocution experiment

Franklin, Benjamin—**Hospital**—hospital in America

Franklin, Benjamin—**Insurance**—fire insurance company to receive a charter

Franklin, Benjamin—**Lens**—eyeglass bifocals

Franklin, Benjamin—**Library**—circulating library

Franklin, Benjamin—**Lightning Demonstration**

Franklin, Benjamin—**Lightning Rod**

Franklin, Benjamin—**Masonic Book**

Franklin, Benjamin—**Medal**—Copley medal awarded to an American

Franklin, Benjamin—**Money**—Continental coin

Franklin, Benjamin—**Newspaper**—German newspaper

Franklin, Benjamin—**Postage Stamp**—postage stamps issued by the Post Office Department

Franklin, Benjamin—**Postmaster**—postmaster general under the Continental Congress

Franklin, Benjamin—**Science Association**—scientific society of importance

Franklin, Benjamin—**Spelling Reform Advocate**

Franklin, Benjamin—**Stove**—stove

G

Gage, John H.—**Tool Factory**

Gage, Katherine Augusta—**Fellowship**—resident fellowship for women awarded by a women's college

Gage, Thomas—**Freemasons**—Negro mason

Gaillard, Peter—**Mower (horsepower)**

Gaine, Hugh—**Medical Book**—croup report (printed)

Gaines, Hugh—**Book Fair**

Gale, Joseph—**Colonial Government**—government on the Pacific coast

Gale, Moses F.—**Cigar Lighter Patent**

Galjour, Warren — **Television** — **Telecast**—opera (major) televised in color

Gallagher, Jack S.—**Helicopter**—helicopter passenger service

Gallagher, James—**Aviation**—**Flights (world)**—round-the-world non-stop airplane flight

Gallagher, Michael—**Television**—**Telecast**—birth (human) to be televised (closed circuit)

Gallagher, P. B. — **Radar**—radar signal bounced off the sun

Gallardo, Gregorio—**Bullfight**—bullfight

Gallatin, Abraham Alfonse Albert—**Congress (U.S.)**—**Senate**—contested election

Gallatin, Abraham Alfonse Albert—**Congress (U.S.)**—**Senate** session to which the public was admitted

Gallatin, Abraham Alfonse Albert—**Glass Factory**—glass factory west of the Allegheny Mountains

Gallaudet, Edward Miner—**Deaf**—**School**—institution in the world for the higher education of the deaf

Gallaudet, Thomas—**Deaf**—**Church Service**—church services for the deaf

Gallaudet, Thomas Hopkins—**Deaf**—**Church Service**—prayers in the sign language of the deaf

Gallaudet, Thomas Hopkins—**Deaf**—**School**—institution in the world for the higher education of the deaf

Gallaudet, Thomas Hopkins—**Deaf**—**School**—school for the deaf (permanent)

Gallaudet, Thomas Hopkins—**Teachers' Institute**

Gallery, Daniel V.—**Submarine**—submarine captured and boarded on the high seas

Gallitzin, Demetrius Augustine—**Catholic Priest**—Catholic priest to receive his full theological training in the United States

Gallo, Fortune—**Moving Picture**—moving picture of a complete grand opera

Galloway, Jesse James—**Paleontology Course**—micropaleontology course

Gallup, George B.—**Library Society**—state library society

Galphin, George—**Baptist Church**—Baptist Church (Negro)

Galston, Clarence G.—**Industrial Recovery Act**—conviction under a National Industrial Recovery Code

Gamble, John—**Theater**—television theater demonstration

Gammeter, Harry Christian—**Multigraph**

Gannal, Jean Nicolas—**Embalming Book**

Gannett, Ezra Stiles—**Unitarian Society**—national organization of the Unitarian churches of the United States and Canada

Gannon, Oscar B.—**Court Martial**—court martial trial at which enlisted men were allowed to sit as members of the court

Garand, John C.—**Ordnance**—semi-automatic rifle

Garber, Clarence Zent—**Medicine**—bone bank

Garcia, Manuel, Jr.—**Opera**—opera (Italian)

Garcia, Maria Felicita—**Opera**—opera (Italian)

Gardener, Helen Hamilton—**Civil Service**—woman Civil Service commissioner

Gardenier, Barent—**Duel**—duel between congressmen

Gardette, E. B.—**Melons**

Gardette, Emile B.—**Dental Society**—dental society of importance

Gardiner, Julia—**President (U.S.)**—President married while in office

Gardiner, Robert Hallowell—**Technical Institute**

Gardner, Ava—**Moving Picture**—moving picture presented simultaneously in major cities throughout the world

Gardner, Dozier—**Tennis Match**—intercollegiate court tennis match

Gardner, Ed. V.—**Air Mail Service**—air mail regular service

Gardner, Eleazer A.—**Street Car**—cable car

Gardner, Gideon—**Lifeboat**—lifeboat

Gardner, Helen Hunt. *See* Gardener, Helen Hamilton

Gardner, Henry Joseph—**Dairy Legislation (state)**

Gardner, James—**Golf Club**—golf club

Gardner, Lester Durand—**Radio Broadcast**—radio broadcast (two-way) from an airplane

Garfield, Eliza Ballou—**President (U.S.)**—President whose mother lived at the Executive Mansion

Garfield, James Abram—**Monument**—statue cast by the United States Government

Garfield, James Abram—**President (U.S.)**—President to use a telephone

Garfield, James Abram—**President (U.S.)**—President whose mother lived at the Executive Mansion

Garfield, James Abram—**Presidential Candidate**—presidential candidate to campaign and make speeches in a foreign language

Garlow, Melvin C. — **Aviation** — **Aviator**—aviator to fly a million miles in a jet airplane

Garner, John Nance—**Degrees (academic and honorary)**—husband and wife awarded honorary degrees

Garner, John Nance—**Vice President of the United States**—Vice President to leave the United States while the President was away

Garner, Mrs. John Nance—**Degrees (academic and honorary)**—husband and wife awarded honorary degrees

Gibson, Althea—**Tennis Match**—national tennis tournament of the United States Lawn Tennis Association in which a Negro woman competed

Giessenbier, Henry—**Chamber of Commerce**—junior chamber of commerce

Gifford, Walter Sherman—**Radio Telephone**—radio telephone ship-to-shore commercial service

Gifford, Walter Sherman — **Telephone** — round-the-world telephone conversation

Gifford, Walter Sherman—**Telephone**—transatlantic telephone service

Gilbert, B. H.—**Opera**—opera broadcast in its entirety

Gilbert, Edwin—**Sieve**—wire sieves

Gilbert, Richard Stuart—**Navy**—podiatry section of the Navy

Gilbert, Timothy—**Medical Society**—women's medical society

Gilchrist, John James—**Court**—court of claims

Gilchrist, William—**Disciples of Christ**

Gildersleeve, Virginia Crocheron—**Treaty**—treaty (federal) signed by a woman

Giles, Harriet E.—**Nursing School**—training school for Negro nurses

Gill, John—**Ordnance**—gun (revolving)

Gillespie, James Milligan—**Aviation—Airplane**—transatlantic robot pilotless airplane

Gillespie, Joe—**Horse Race**—horse race of a thousand miles

Gillespy, Edward—**Irish Magazine**

Gillette, Arthur Jay — **Hospital** — crippled children's hospital (state)

Gillette, King Camp—**Razor**—safety razor to be successfully marketed

Gilliam, Jim—**Baseball Game**—major league game in which the majority of the players on one team were Negroes

Gilliland, Alan Victor—**Poorhouse** (state)

Gillingham, J. E.—**Animals**—cattle tuberculosis test

Gillis, James Melville—**Astronomical Observations Book**

Gilmore, George William—**Lacrosse Association (intercollegiate)**

Gilpen, Thomas—**Paper-Making Machinery**—paper-making machine (cylinder)

Ginter, Philip—**Coal**—anthracite coal

Girstner, Margaret—**Wedding**—double radio wedding

Gissendanner, Charles — **War (Korean)** — American tank crew to cross the 38th parallel in Korea

Givens, Joseph E. — **Helicopter Flight**—transcontinental non-stop helicopter flight

Gleitsmann, William—**Hospital**—tuberculosis sanatorium (private)

Glenn, John Herschel, Jr.—**Astronauts**—American astronaut to orbit the earth

Glenn, John Herschel, Jr.—**Astronauts**—astronauts

Glennan, Thomas Keith—**Space Agency (U.S.)**

Glidden, Joseph Farwell—**Wire**—barbed wire

Glover, J. N.—**Brick**—terra cotta factory

Glover, Jesse — **Printing Press** — printing press

Glover, John—**Court Martial**—military court martial

Glover, Townend—**Entomologist** — federal entomologist

Goddard, George—**Photograph**—photograph from an airplane at night

Goddard, George W.—**Photography**—demonstration of rapid aerial photography

Goddard, Henry Herbert—**Intelligence Test**

Goddard, Luther—**Clock**—watchmaker

Goddard, Mary Katherine — **Postmaster** — woman postmaster (colonial)

Goddard, Robert Hutchins—**Rocket**—liquid fuel rocket flight

Goddard, Robert Hutchins—**Rocket**—liquid fuel rocket patent

Goddard, Thatcher — **Bicycle Society** — bicycle club

Godfrey, Alexander—**Brokerage**—stock order from a Zeppelin

Godfrey, Arthur—**Television—Telecast**—color program (commercial)

Godfrey, Thomas—**Quadrant**

Godwin, Mary—**Woman Suffrage**—woman suffrage book

Goff, Frederick Harris—**Community Trust**

Goffigan, Laban—**Lighthouse** — lighthouse built after American independence

Goldberg, David — **Naval Officer** — naval chaplain who was Jewish

Goldberger, Joseph—**Public Health**—pellagra experiment

Golden, John—**Television—Telecast**—play to be televised with its original Broadway cast

Goldmark, Peter Carl—**Television—Telecast**—color television demonstration of high-definition electronically scanned images

Goldsborough, Louis Malesherbes—**Observatory**—observatory (national)

Goldschmidt, Jenny Maria Lind. *See* Lind, Jenny

Goldstein, Isidore—**Eye**—identification system

Goler, George Washington—**Milk Station (municipal)**

Golitzyn, Dmitri Augustin—**Catholic Priest**—Catholic priest to receive his full theological training in the United States

Golubok, Leon—**Play (drama)**—Hebrew professional acting troupe

Goodale, Samuel D.—**Moving Picture**—peep show machine

Goodale, William—**Paper Bag Manufacturing Machine**—paper bag manufacturing machine

Goodall, Harvey L.—**Livestock Market Paper**

Goodall, Thomas—**Blanket**—blanket robe and carriage lap robe business

Goodall, Thomas—**Blanket**—horseblankets

Goodlin, Chalmers ("Slick") — **Aviation — Airplane**—rocket plane

Goodman, Louis—**Air Mail Service**—rocket air mail flight

Goodnow, Frank Johnson—**Political Science Society**—political science association

Goodrich, Annie Warburton — **Nursing School**—army school of nursing

Goodrich, Benjamin Franklin — **Rubber** — rubber company west of the Allegheny Mountains

Goodrich, J. Z.—**Republican Party**—Republican Party meeting (national)

Goodrich, John — **Money** — copper cents minted by a state

Goodrich, Joseph—**Building**—monolithic concrete building

Goodwin, George—**Law Book**—law book containing the federal laws of the United States

Goodwin, George — **Periodical** — children's magazine

Goodwin, George W.—**Ship**—steel sailing vessel

Goodwin, Hannibal Williston—**Photographic Film**—celluloid photographic film

Goodwin, Isabella—**Police**—woman detective

Goodwin, Nat C.—**Play (drama)**—drama to win a Pulitzer prize

Goodwin, William Nelson—**Photography**—camera exposure meter

Goodyear, Charles—**Rubber**—rubber patent of importance

Goodyear, Charles—**Rubber**—vulcanized rubber

Gordon, Hugh—**Aviation—Flights (world)**—round-the-world civil air service

Gordon, Louis—**Aviation—Passenger**—woman airplane passenger to cross the Atlantic Ocean

Gordon, Maurice Kirby — **War Veterans' Society**—American Legion

Gordon, Nathaniel — **Execution** — execution (federal) for slave trading

Gordon, Samuel George—**Fluorescent mineral exhibit**

Gore, Sammy—**Revolutionary War**—martyr in the Revolutionary war

Gorges, Ferdinando—**City (incorporated)**

Gorges, Ferdinando—**Water Power**—water power development grant

Gorham, Nathaniel—**Land Office**

Gorrie, John—**Refrigerator**—mechanical refrigerator patent

Gorringe, Henry Honeychurch—**Monument**—obelisk to be brought to the United States

Gorsuch, Robert Bennett—**Engineering Society**—civil engineering national society

Gorton, Adolphus W.—**Aviation—Passenger**—dirigible passenger transfer to an airplane

Gosnold, Bartholomew—**Colonial Government**—colonial council in America

Gosnold, Bartholomew — **Colonist** — English settlement in America (permanent)

Gosnold, Bartholomew—**Discovery**—discovery of New England by an Englishman

Gossling, Frederick W.—**Sugar**—sugar and glucose from cornstarch

Gottschalk, Louis Moreau—**Musician**—musician (native-born American) to achieve European fame

Gougelman, Pierre—**Eye**—artificial eyes

Goulaine de Laudonnière, René. *See* Laudonnière, René Goulaine de

Gould, Helen Miller—**Hall of Fame**—hall of fame (university)

Gould, Stephen Philip—**Casein Fiber**

Gounder, Howard Moyer—**Air Raid Shelter**—air raid shelter

Gounod, Charles François—**Opera**—opera at the Metropolitan Opera House

Goupil, René—**Catholic Canonization of North Americans**

Govern, S. K.—**Baseball Team**—baseball team (Negro professional)

Grace, Robert—**Stove**—stove

Grace, William Russell—**Monument** — obelisk to be brought to the United States

Graeff, Johannes de—**Flag**—American flag saluted by a foreigner

Graham, Charles M.—**Dentistry**—patent for artificial teeth

Graham, Evarts—**Surgical Operation**—lung removal

Graham, John — **Diplomatic Service** — Pan American delegates (American)

Graham, Sylvester—**Bread**—bread

Graham, William J.—**Insurance**—group insurance policy

Gram, Hans—**Music**—orchestral song

Gram, Hans Birch—**Homeopathy**—homeopathy

Gram, Hans Birch—**Medical Book**—homeopathic treatise

Grandon, F. J.—**Moving Picture**—serial moving picture

Granger, Austin—**Collar Factory**

Granger, Francis—**Whig Party**

Grant, Annie — **Baseball Team** — women's baseball team

Grant, David Norvell Walker—**Army Officer**—air surgeon of the War Department

Grant, George—**Animals**—cattle (Aberdeen-Angus)

Grant, George F.—**Golf Tee**

Grant, Kittie — **Baseball Team** — women's baseball team

Grant, Lawrence Harry—**Aviation—Flights (transatlantic)**—jet transatlantic non-stop flight west to east

Grant, Ray—**Television—Telecast** — variety talent show series with an all-Negro cast

Grant, Ulysses Simpson—**Army Officer**—general of the U.S. Army

Grant, Ulysses Simpson—**Civil Service**—Civil Service Commission

Grant, Ulysses Simpson—**Fish Protection**—fish protection office (federal)

Grant, Ulysses Simpson—**Indians**—Indian Affairs Commissioner (U.S.) who was an Indian

Grant, Ulysses Simpson—**Solicitor General of the United States**

Grant, Ulysses Simpson, III—**Swimming Pool in the White House**

Grant, William West—**Surgical Operation**—appendicitis operation (appendectomy)

Gras, Norman Scott Brien—**Business History Chair**

Gratz, Rebecca — **Sunday School** — Jewish Sunday school

Grauer, Ben—**Television**—**Telecast**—moving picture premiere festivities to be televised

Graupner, Johann Christian Gottlieb—**Musician**—Negro-song popularizer

Graupner, Johann Christian Gottlieb—**Orchestra**—orchestra

Gravelet, Jean François—**Niagara Falls**—person to cross Niagara Falls on a tightrope

Graveley, Samuel L.—**Naval Officer**—commander of a combat ship who was a Negro

Gray, Adeline—**Aviation**—**Parachute**—nylon parachute jump

Gray, Carl Raymond—**Railroad**—streamlined light-weight high-speed three-car passenger train

Gray, Clifford B.—**Bobsled Competition**—four-man bob-team competition

Gray, Elisha—**Telautograph**

Gray, Harold Edwin—**Aviation**—**Flights**—airplane flight (commercially scheduled) over a single route linking four continents

Gray, Hawthorne C.—**Balloon Flight**—balloon flight to exceed an altitude of 40,000 feet

Gray, John F.—**Medical Periodical**—homeopathic magazine

Gray, Leon—**Aviation**—**Flights (transcontinental)**—transcontinental round-trip airplane flight within one day

Gray, Robert—**Ship**—ship to carry the United States flag around the world

Gray, William—**Telephone**—coin telephone

Graydon, William—**Law Digest**

Greelet, Stephen—**Treadmill**

Greeley, Horace—**Book Review**—book review editor

Greeley, Horace—**Liberal Republican Party**

Green, B.—**Book Auction Catalog**—book auction printed catalog

Green, Bartholomew—**Book**—book of folio size

Green, Bartholomew—**Business Manual**

Green, Bartholomew—**Genealogy**—genealogy

Green, Bartholomew — **Grammar** — Latin grammar textbook

Green, Bartholomew—**Music Book**—hymn book with music

Green, Edward Howland Robinson—**Automobile**—automobile (new type gasoline-electric combination)

Green, George F.—**Drill**—dental drill (electric)

Green, George J.—**Benevolent and Protective Order of Elks**

Green, Horace—**Medical Book**—bronchitis treatise

Green, John—**Ship**—trading ship sent to China

Green, Norvin—**Electric Company**—electric company

Green, Philip Leonard—**Periodical**—Spanish magazine published by students

Green, Philip Leonard—**Students' Federation (international)**

Green, Robert M.—**Ice Cream Soda**

Green, Roy M.—**Federal Crop Insurance Corporation**

Green, S.—**History**—History of New England

Green, Samuel—**Bible**—Bible in an Indian language

Green, Samuel—**Children's Book**

Green, Samuel—**Newspaper**—newspaper

Green, T.—**Book**—miniature book

Green, Theodore Francis—**Army Exclusion Law**

Green, Timothy—**Fishing Treatise**

Green, Timothy—**Religious Publication**—religious journal

Green, William—**Aviation**—automatic pilot

Greene, Jacob Lyman—**President (U.S.)**—President to ride in an automobile

Greene, John S.—**Photostat**—photographic copying machine

Greenleaf, Halbert—**Lock**—time-lock

Greenough, Horatio—**Marble Statuary Group**

Greenough, John James—**Sewing Machine**—sewing machine patent

Greenwood, Chester—**Earmuff**

Greenwood, Edith—**Medal**—soldier's medal awarded to a woman

Greenwood, Isaac—**Arithmetic** — American arithmetic

Greenwood, John—**Dentistry** — porcelain teeth

Greenwood, John—**Drill**—dental drill

Greenwood, Miles—**Fire Department**—fire department to be paid a salary

Greer, James Richard—**Radio Facsimile**—radio facsimile long distance transmission of a medical subject

Gregory, Samuel—**Medical School**—women's medical school

Gregory, Samuel—**Medical Society**—women's medical society

Greig, Alexander M.—**Postage Stamp**—adhesive stamps

Grenville, William Wyndham, Baron Grenville—**Extradition**—extradition treaty with a foreign country

Gresham, James B.—**World War I**—American Army soldiers killed in combat

Grice, Charles C.—**Veterinary Hospital**

Gridley, Jeremy—**Freemasons**—military masonic lodge

Gridley, Richard—**Army**—Army Engineering Department

Gridley, Richard—**Army Officer**—chief engineer

Gries, John Matthew—**Federal Home Loan Bank Board**

Griffin, Lloyd Dean — **Aviation** — **Flights (transatlantic)**—jet transatlantic non-stop flight west to east

Griffith, Robert E.—**Archery Club**—archery club

Griffith, Samuel P.—**Archery Club**—archery club

Griffiths, Hall McAllister — **Presbyterian Church**—Presbyterian Church of America

Griffitts, Samuel Powel—**Pharmacy Professor**

Grilley, Henry—**Button**—pewter or block tin buttons

Grilley, Samuel—**Button**—pewter or block tin buttons

Grilley, Silas—**Button**—pewter or block tin buttons

Grissom, Virgil Ivan—**Astronauts**—astronauts

Griswold, Roger—**Congress (U.S.)—House of Representatives**—brawl

Gross, Samuel David—**Adhesive and Medicated Plaster**—adhesive and medicated plaster

Grosvenor, Gilbert—**Medal**—National Geographic Society gold medal

Grosvenor, Melville Bell—**Photograph**—photograph in natural colors taken in the air

Grote, Augustus Radcliffe — **Entomology Magazine**

Grotecloss, Harriet Elizabeth—**Fellowship**—fellowship awarded a woman

Grout, Jonathan—**Semaphore Telegraph System**

Grover, Edwin Osgood—**Book Course**

Groves, Ernest Rutherford — **Marriage Course**

Groves, John—**Aviation — Airport**—airport (federally owned and operated)

Grow, Malcolm Cummings—**Air Force Officer**—Air Force Surgeon General

Grushkin, Benjamin — **Chlorophyll** — chlorophyll

Gual, Pedro—**Treaty**—treaty with a South American country

Guerin, Napoleon E.—**Incubator (Eggs) Patent**

Guerin, Napoleon E.—**Life Preserver**—life preserver of cork

Guggenheim, H. Robert—**Automobile Race**—transcontinental automobile race

Guille, Charles—**Aviation—Parachute**—parachute jump from a balloon

Guilmant, Alexandre—**Organ School**

Gulick, Mrs. Luther Halsey—**Camp Fire Girls Organization**

Gummere, William Stryker—**Football Game**—intercollegiate football contest

Gumper, Jake D.—**Pump**—gasoline pump

Gunn, Frederick William—**Camp for Boys**

Gunnells, Leonard Blake—**Birth Registration**—birth registration uniform system for the numbering of birth certificates

Gunter, Thomas—**Carillon**—carillon

Guthrie, Samuel—**Chloroform**

Guthrie, Samuel—**Glucose**

Guyot, Arnold—**Lecture Series** (endowed)

Gwinn, Mary—**Fellowship**—resident fellowship for women awarded by a women's college

H

Haag, Mack—**Indian Church**—Indian church organized by Indians

Haas, Robert—**Book Club**—Book-of-the-Month Club

Haase, J. M. F.—**Moving Picture**—moving pictures of an eclipse of the sun taken from an airplane

Haasis, Dunbar Ferdinand—**Lacrosse Association** (intercollegiate)

Habersham, James—**Orphanage**—orphanage with a continuous existence

Hachard, Sister St. Stanislas—**Catholic Nuns**—nun who professed her vows

Hackelton, Thomas—**Lime**

Hackett, Charles—**Opera**—opera broadcast over a national network from an American opera house

Hackett, James Henry—**Actor**—American actor to appear abroad

Hadaway, William S.—**Electric Stove**—electric stove

Hadenwater, Harry—**Radio Station**—radio station operating a 100-kilowatt transmitter

Hadley, John—**Quadrant**

Hadley, William Aaron—**Blind**—correspondence school for the blind to offer instruction in the Braille system

Haefner, Ralph—**Primer**—typewriting primer

Haeterick, Robert—**Stove Patent**

Hagen, Hermann August—**Entomology Professor**

Hagner, Charles V.—**Drug Mill**

Hahnenmann, Christian Friedrich Samuel—**Medical Book**—homeopathic treatise

Hains, Dan—**Water Ski Association (national)**-

Hakanson, Walter C.—**Softball**

Hale, Benjamin—**Technical Institute**

Hale, George Ellery—**Telescope**—telescope lens two hundred inches in diameter

Hale, H. S.—**Bed**—folding bed manufacture

Hale, John Parker—**Senator (U.S.)**—senator elected on an anti-slavery ticket

Hale, Sarah Josepha—**Periodical**—magazine for women

Hale, Mrs. Stephen—**Flag**—American flag over a schoolhouse

Hall, Mr.—**Ice Cream**—ice cream

Hall, Charles — **Aviation — Aviator**—Negro Army aviator to down an Axis airplane

Hall, Charles Bingley—**Bankers' Association**—national bankers' association

Hall, Charles Corydon—**Rock Wool Factory**

Hall, Charles Martin—**Aluminum**—aluminum

Hall, Glenn—**Opera**—opera by an American composer performed at the Metropolitan Opera House of New York

Hall, Granville Stanley—**Psychological Society**—psychological society (national organization)

Hall, Granville Stanley—**Psychology Laboratory**

Hall, Granville Stanley—**Psychology Magazine**

Hall, Henry—**Book**—book set by linotype

Hall, Henry—**Cranberry Cultivation**

Hall, Henry—**Fishing Line Factory**

Hall, John Elihu—**Law Magazine**

Hall, Joseph—**Newspaper**—newspaper published west of the Alleghenies

Hall, Juanita—**Radio Station**—Negro network

Hall, Peleg—**Periodical**—sectarian magazine

Hall, Prince — **Masonry** — Negro Masonic Grand Lodge (not Free and Accepted Masons)

Hall, Samuel Read—**Educational Book**

Hall, Samuel Read—**Normal School**—normal school established exclusively for the preparation of teachers

Hall, Thomas S.—**Railroad Signal System**—railroad signal system (automatic electric block)

Hall, William Alden—**World War I**—shot fired by the American Navy in World War I

Hallam, Lewis—**Play (drama)**—native American play successfully acted on a regular stage

Hallam, Lewis—**Theater**—theater building (permanent)

Hallaren, Mary Agnes—**Army Officer**—woman army officer

Halleck, Fitz-Greene — **Monument**—monument to an American poet

Hallidie, Andrew Smith—**Street Car**—cable street car

Hallock, William—**Physics**—national physics association

Hallock, William Allen—**Tract Society**—tract society (national)

Halsey, Francis Whiting—**Book Review**—book review newspaper supplement

Halsey, Lewis Benjamin—**Milk**—milk pasteurized commercially

Halsted, William Stewart—**Suture**—silk suture

Halvey, Nina—**Play (drama)**—anti-vivisection play

Halvorson, Kittel—**Congressman (U.S.)**—congressman elected by the prohibitionists

Hambrick, George Okie—**Helicopter Flight**—helicopter transatlantic flight

Hamilton, Alexander—**Bank**—Bank of the United States

Hamilton, Alexander—**Cabinet of the United States**—cabinet

Hamilton, Alexander—**Congressional Caucus**—congressional caucus

Hamilton, Alexander—**Loan**—loan to the United States

Hamilton, Alexander—**Mint (U.S.)**—Mint of the United States

Hamilton, Alexander—**Newspaper**—political newspaper

Hamilton, Alexander—**Treasury Department**—Secretary of the Treasury

Hamilton, Alexander—**War Veterans' Society**—Society of the Cincinnati

Hamilton, Andrew—**Postal Service**—parliamentary act to establish a post office

Hamilton, Andrew—**Postmaster**—postmaster general (colonial)

Hamilton, Charles Keeney—**Aviation—Expositions and Meets**—aviation meet

Hamilton, Charles Keeney — **Aviation — Flights**—airplane round trip

Hamilton, Frank Hastings—**Surgical Operation**—skin grafting

Hamilton, James—**Insurance**—fire insurance company to receive a charter

Hamilton, John—**College**—college charter granted by a governor or acting governor with only the assent of his council

Hamilton, Samuel—**Postal Service**—Pony Express mail

Hamilton, Mrs. William—**Holiday**—Navy Day

Hammerstein, Oscar—**Cigar Rolling Machine**

Hammond, Elisha—**Library**—library building (university)

Hammond, Frankie—**Aviation—Parachute**—parachute jump from an autogiro

Hammond, Graeme M.—**Fencing**—fencing league (national)

Hammond, John—**Park**—park land

Hammond, John Hays—**Aviation**—airplane tank discharger

Hammond, Laurens—**Electric Bridge Table**

Hammond, Laurens—**Organ**—pipeless organ

Hammond, William Alexander — **Medical Book**—neurology textbook

Hampson, John—**Venetian Blinds**—Venetian blind patent

Hampton, John—**Presbyterian Presbytery**

Hance, William A.—**Bicycle**—bicycle with a back pedal brake

Hancher, Virgil Melvin—**Air Force Academy (U.S.)**—Air Force Academy

Hanchett, Henry Granger—**Organists' Society**—organists' society (national)

Hanchett, M. Waldo—**Dental Chair**

Hancock, George W.—**Softball**

Hancock, John—**Declaration of Independence (American)**—Declaration of Independence was signed

Hancock, John—**Medical Society**—medical society (state)

Hancock, John—**State**—state constitution

Hancock, Thomas — **Bibliography** — bibliography of theological and biblical literature

Hand, Thomas J.—**Cattle Club**—cattle club (Jersey cattle)

Handy, William Christopher—**Musician**—composer of jazz music

Hanes, Horace Albert—**Aviation—Flights**—airplane to exceed the speed of 800 miles an hour

Haney, David Jacob—**Aviation—Flights**—North Pole jet crossing

Hanger, Glossbrenner Wallace William—**Strike**—strike settlement

Hanks, Benjamin—**Chimes**

Harrison, Benjamin—**Diplomatic Service**—foreign service committee

Harrison, Benjamin—**Forest Reserve**—forest reserve (national)

Harrison, Benjamin—**State**—states admitted to the Union simultaneously

Harrison, Bertram—**Theater**—municipal theater

Harrison, Earl Grant—**Immigration**—alien registration

Harrison, John—**Sulphuric Acid**

Harrison, Joseph—**Naval Officer**—naval doctor

Harrison, Rex—**Television**—**Telecast**—moving picture premiere performance to be televised (major film)

Harrison, Richard—**Lawyer**—lawyers admitted to the Supreme Court of the United States

Harrison, Robert Hanson—**Supreme Court (U.S.)**—Supreme Court justice who was nominated but who did not serve

Harrison, Robert Hanson—**Supreme Court (U.S.)**—Supreme Court of the United States

Harrison, William Henry—**Political Convention**—unit rule

Harrison, William Henry—**President (U.S.)**—President to die in Washington, D.C.

Harrison, William Henry—**President (U.S.)**—President whose grandson became president

Harrison, William Henry—**Whig Party**

Harroun, Ray—**Automobile Race**—automobile race on a track (long distance)

Hart, Edwin Giles—**Citron**

Hart, Robert M.—**Television**—**Telecast**—transoceanic television image

Hartford, George Huntington—**Business**—chain store organization

Hartle, Russell Peter—**World War II**—American expeditionary force to land on the European continent

Hartley, David—**Treaty**—treaty between the U.S. Government and a nation with which it had been at war

Hartly, Thomas—**Lawyer**—lawyers admitted to the Supreme Court of the United States

Hartranft, John—**Strike**—strike in which federal troops were called in peacetime

Harts, Rutherford B.—**Photograph**—photograph showing air in motion

Hartsfield, William Berry—**Pinball Game**—pinball legislation enacted by a major city prohibiting the machines

Hartshorn, Orville Nelson—**College**—college to grant women absolutely equal rights with men

Hartshorne, Richard—**Crime Prevention and Detection**—crime prevention commission for interstate cooperation

Hartswick, F. Gregory—**Crossword Puzzle Book**

Harvard, John—**College**—college

Harvey, Bernard George—**Element**—element 99

Harvey, Bernard George—**Element**—element 101

Harvey, Charles T.—**Elevated Railroad**—elevated railroad

Harvey, George Brinton McClellan—**Esperanto Club**—Esperanto club (national organization)

Harvey, John—**Salt**—salt works

Harvey, John—**Treason**—treason trial (colonial)

Haskell, Ella Louise Knowles—**Attorney General**—assistant attorney general (state) who was a woman

Haskell, Emma—**Cripples**—public school for cripples

Haskell, James Richards—**Ordnance**—cannon (steel, breech loading, rifled)

Haskin, Dewitt Clinton—**Air (compressed)**

Haskins, Charles Waldo—**Accountancy Law** (state)

Haskins, Charles Waldo—**Accountants' Society**—accountants' society formed by a state group

Haskins, Roswell Willson—**School Superintendent**—school superintendent (city)

Haslett, Lewis Phectic—**Gas Mask**—gas mask

Hassall, Albert — **Zoological Laboratory (U.S.)**—zoological laboratory (U.S.) for the study of the parasites of livestock

Hassler, Ferdinand Rudolph—**Coast Survey Superintendent**

Hasson, Esther Voorhees — **Navy** — naval nurses' corps

Hastie, William Henry—**Governor**—Negro governor appointed by the President of the United States

Hastie, William Henry — **Judge** — Negro judge of a Circuit Court of Appeals

Hastings, Ernest—**Magic Lantern Show**—magic lantern feature show

Haswell, Charles Haynes—**Naval Officer**—naval officer to become an engineer

Hatch, Charles P.—**Oil**—oil tank cars

Hatch, Fred L.—**Silo**

Hatch, Julius—**Patent**—patent re-issue

Hatton, Anne Julia Kemble—**Opera**—opera of a serious nature

Haubner, Theodore D.—**Radio Distress Signal**—radio SOS from an American ship

Haubold, R. O.—**Fencing**—fencing league (national)

Haugh, Daniel (Howe)—**Military Organization**—military organization

Haughland, Vern — **Medal** — Silver Star Army Medal awarded to a civilian

Havemeyer, Theodore Augustus—**Cream Separator** — continuous flow centrifugal cream separator

Havemeyer, Theodore A.—**Golf Club**—golf association (national)

Hawes, Harriet Boyd—**College**—women's volunteer college unit to serve overseas

Hawes, Russell L. — **Envelope** — envelope folding machine

Hawkins, John F.—**Reaper**—reaper

Hawks, Frank Monroe—**Glider**—glider towed across the continent

Hawks, Frank Monroe—**Glider**—seaplane glider

Hawley, Gideon—School Superintendent—school superintendent (state)

Hawley, Ichabod—Temperance Society—temperance society (union)

Hawley, R. S.—Dog Race Track

Hay, John—American (as an adjective)

Hay, John—Arts and Letters Society—arts and letters society (national)

Hay, Merle D.—World War I—American Army soldiers killed in combat

Hayden, Hiram Washington—Brass Spinning

Hayden, Horace Henry—Dental School—dental college

Hayden, Horace Henry—Dental Society—dental society of importance

Hayden, Joel—Button—cloth-covered buttons

Hayes, Maximilian Sebastian—Farmer Labor Party

Hayes, Rutherford Birchard—Cabinet of the United States—Confederate to serve in the cabinet

Hayes, Rutherford Birchard—Chinese Embassy

Hayes, Rutherford Birchard—Easter Egg Roll

Hayes, Rutherford Birchard—Monument—monument to an American poet

Hayes, Rutherford Birchard — President (U.S.)—President to celebrate his silver wedding anniversary at the White House

Hayes, Rutherford Birchard—Strike—strike in which federal troops were called in peacetime

Hayes, Rutherford Birchard—Supreme Court (U.S.)—woman admitted to practice before the Supreme Court of the United States

Hayhurst, C. W.—Radio Telephone—military portable

Hayhurst, Elias Hicks—Baseball League—baseball league of importance

Hayhurst, Susan—Pharmacist—pharmacist (woman graduate)

Haynesworth, George E.—Civil War—act that marked the inauguration of the War of 1861-1865

Hays, Harold—Euthanasia Society

Hays, Isaac—Medical Book—medical encyclopedia

Hays, Will—Moving Picture—talking picture

Hayward, Ann—Wedding—parachute wedding

Hazard, Ebenezer—Insurance—life insurance

Hazard, Erskine—Bridge—iron wire suspension bridge

H'Doubler, Margaret Newell—Dance Course

Healy, James Augustine—Catholic Bishop—Catholic bishop (Negro)

Hearst, Phoebe Apperson—Parent-Teacher Association (national)

Hearst, Phoebe Apperson—Women's Club—women's club federation

Heath, Reverend—Methodist College

Heath, Frederick—Stadium—school stadium

Heath, George—Automobile Race—Vanderbilt cup race

Heatherton, Ray — Television — Telecast—operetta to be televised

Hebert, Paul Octave—Health Board—health board (state) to regulate quarantine

Heck, Barbara — Methodist — Methodist preacher

Heco, Joseph—Citizenship—Japanese granted citizenship

Heflin, Alma — Aviation—Aviator — woman test pilot

Hegenberger, Albert Francis—Aviation—Flights—all blind solo flight by the U.S. Army

Hegenberger, Albert Francis—Aviation—Flights (transpacific) — California-Hawaii flight

Heikes, Rolla O.—Trapshooting Tournament—trapshoot (Grand American) with clay targets

Heinemann, Edward H.—Aviation—Flights—airplane to exceed the speed of 1,300 miles an hour

Heinisch, Rochus—Cutlery Shears

Heinz, Henry John—Foodstuffs Producer

Helen, Sister—Hospital Record

Heminway, Merritt—Thread—silk thread on spools

Hemmestvedt, Torjus—Ski Club—ski club (local) that was active

Hendee, George M.—Motorcycle—motorcycle with built-in gas engine

Henderson, George—College—college extension courses

Henderson, James Arnold—Animal Breeding Society—artificial animal breeding cooperative

Henderson, John Brooks—Political Convention—national nominating convention presided over by a Negro

Henderson, Lawrence Joseph—Science Association—history of science society

Hendricks, Gerhard—Slavery—slavery protest

Hendrix, Eugene Russell—Federal Council of the Churches of Christ in America

Henenberg, Hattie L.—Court—state supreme court composed entirely of women

Henke, Milburn—World War II—American expeditionary force to land on the European continent

Henley, David — Court Martial — military court martial

Hennepin, Louis—Coal—coal

Hennock, Frieda B.—Federal Communications Commission—Federal Communications Commission woman member

Henriques, C. R.—Wedding—airplane wedding

Henry, Charles Lewis—Street Car—interurban street car line

Henry, Frederick F.—Medal—Medal of Honor awarded in the Korean War

Henry, John—Actor—matinee idol

Henry, John—Play (drama)—native American play successfully acted on a regular stage

Henry, Joseph—Electric Bell

Henry, Joseph—Electric Magnet

Henry, Joseph—**Radio Impulse Transmission (wireless)**

Henry, Joseph—**Telegraph**—telegraph (electro-magnetic)

Henry, Lou. *See* Hoover, Mrs. Herbert Clark

Henry, William—**Ship**—steamboat

Henry, William Elmer—**Library Society**—state librarians' society

Hensley, William Nicholas—**Radio Broadcast**—radio broadcast (two-way) from an airplane

Henson, Matthew Alexander—**Discovery**—discovery of the North Pole

Herbert, F. Hugh—**Moving Picture**—talking picture of more than 6,000 feet

Herbert, H. L.—**Polo Club**—polo association (national)

Herbert, Henry William—**Author**—sports writer

Herbert, Hilary Abner—**Submarine**—submarine contract of the U.S. Navy

Herbert, Xavier — **Hospital** — hospital in America

Herbertson, John—**Bridge**—cast iron bridge

Hererra, Enrique Olaya—**Diplomatic Service**—chief executive-elect of a foreign country

Hering, Constantine — **Medical School** — homeopathic school

Hering, Constantine — **Medical Society** — homeopathic medical society

Herman, Peter — **Radio Broadcast**—prize fight broadcast from the ringside

Hern, George C.—**Radio Broadcast**—submarine (submerged) broadcast

Herndon, Hugh—**Aviation—Flights (transpacific)**—transpacific non-stop flight

Herren, Thomas Wade—**War (Korean)**—Korean war hero buried in Arlington cemetery

Herreshoff, John Brown—**Ship** — torpedo boat

Herreshoff, Nathanael Greene—**Catamaran**

Herreshoff, Nathanael Greene—**Ship**—torpedo boat

Herring, Elbert—**Indians**—Indian Affairs Commissioner

Herrington, Carl D.—**Helicopter Flight**—transcontinental non-stop helicopter flight

Hersey, Henry Blanchard—**Balloon Race**—balloon cup race

Hershfield, Harry — **Television** — **Telecast**—demonstration of home reception of television

Herskovitz, Anatol—**Moving Picture**—moving picture of the inside of a living heart (of a dog)

Hertz, Alfred—**Opera**—opera composed by a woman performed at the Metropolitan Opera House

Herz, Wilhelm—**Motorcycle Race**—motorcycle to exceed 200 miles an hour

Hessel, John—**Radio Telephone**—military portable

Hesselius, Gustavus—**Art Commission (public)**

Heth, Jim—**Aviation—Flights**—airplane endurance flight exceeding 1,200 hours

Hetzel, Henry W.—**Moving Picture**—talking picture in Esperanto

Hewitt, James—**Opera**—opera of a serious nature

Hewitt, John Hill—**Music**—secular song hit

Hewitt, Peter Cooper—**Electric Lighting**—mercury vapor lamp

Heyl, Henry Renno—**Moving Picture**—animated photographic picture projection before a theater audience

Heyward, Thomas—**Museum**—public museum

Hiacoomes—**Indians**—Indian preacher

Hiawatha—**Indians**—Indian league of nations

Hibbard, Frederick Cleveland—**Monument**—statue to commemorate literary characters

Hickey, Thomas—**Army Execution**

Hicks, George—**Radio Broadcast**—submarine (submerged) broadcast

Hicks, Xen—**Judge**—woman associate justice of the Circuit Court of Appeals

Higgins, Lorenzo—**Cable (telegraph)**—submarine telegraph cable to be insulated with gutta percha

Higgins, Thomas Joseph—**College**—college classes to combat the influence of communism

Higley, John—**Money**—copper coins

Higley, Samuel—**Steel**—steel

Hildebrandt, Martin—**Tattoo**—tattoo shop

Hill, Alfred—**Animals**—pronghorn antelope

Hill, Charles—**Telephone**—telephone conversation over the transoceanic telephone cable

Hill, Clyde E.—**Birds**—snow goose

Hill, David—**Colonial Government**—government on the Pacific coast

Hill, Frank A.—**World War II**—American pilot to shoot down a German fighter plane

Hill, Ira A.—**Globe Factory**

Hill, J. D.—**Air Mail Service**—air mail long-distance night service

Hill, John—**Business Manual**

Hill, Ramsay—**Moving Picture**—three-dimensional feature moving picture

Hill, Samuel Eugene—**Bible**—Bibles in hotel rooms

Hill, Samuel Lapham—**Kindergarten**—free kindergarten

Hill, Walter — **War (Korean)** — American tank crew to cross the 38th parallel in Korea

Hillegas, Michael—**Music**—musical instrument dealer

Hillegas, Michael — **Treasury Department (U.S.)**—Treasurer of the United States

Hillquit, Morris—**Socialist Party**

Hilton, William—**Forest Fire**—forest fire lookout tower

Hine, Thomas Buck—**Smoke Screen**

Hines, Edward Norris—**Traffic Lines**

Hines, John Leonard — **Radio Facsimile Transmission**—transpacific and transcontinental facsimile transmission

Hines, Paul—**Baseball Game**—triple play unassisted

Hinman, L. R.—**Opera**—opera broadcast in its entirety

Hinton, Walter—**Aviation**—**Flights (transatlantic)**—transatlantic hydroplane flight

Hires, Charles Elmer—**Root Beer**

Hitchcock, Edward — **Geological Survey** — geological survey (state)

Hitchcock, Edward—**Hygiene Instruction**—hygiene and physical education professorship

Hitchcock, Elizabeth—**Christmas Carols Association (national)**

Hitchcock, Frank Harris—**Air Mail Service**—air mail pilot

Hitchcock, Lambert—**Chair Factory**

Hitchcock, Thomas—**Polo**—international polo series

Hittell, John Shentzen—**Volcano**

Hitz, John—**Zinc**—zinc

Hitz, William—**Cabinet of the United States**—cabinet member convicted of a crime

Hoagland, H. C.—**Moving Picture**—newsreel

Hoballah, Mahmoud—**Mosque**

Hoban, James—**Building**—building erected by the Government in Washington, D.C.

Hobbs, Lucy B.—**Dentist**—woman dentist to obtain a D.D.S. degree

Hobby, Oveta Culp—**Army Auxiliary Corps**—Women's Army Auxiliary Corps (WAAC)

Hobby, Oveta Culp—**Cabinet of the United States**—cabinet conference telecast

Hobby, Oveta Culp—**Cabinet of the United States**—Secretary of Health, Education and Welfare

Hobson, Frank M.—**Submarine "Lung"**

Hobson, Henry Wise—**Trailer Church**

Hobson, Joseph—**Tunnel**—subaqueous railroad tunnel to a foreign country

Hobson, Richard Pearson—**Prohibition**—prohibition vote

Hodder, James—**Arithmetic**—arithmetic

Hodge, Paul Rapsey—**Fire Engine**—steam fire engine

Hodges, Charles Edward—**Insurance**—mutual liability insurance company

Hodges, Edwin—**Wire**—brass wire

Hodges, Elizabeth — **Meteorite** — meteorite known to have struck a woman

Hodges, Leonard B.—**Forestry Society**—forestry association

Hodges, Paul Chesley—**Television**—**Telecast**—X-ray fluoroscopy television discussion

Hodgman, Amanda A.—**College**—college for women

Hodgson, Ralph—**Oiled Silk Patent**

Hoe, Richard March—**Printing Press**—rotary type printing press

Hoe, Robert—**Printing Press**—cylinder and flat bed combination printing press

Hoeney, Winfield — **Television** — **Telecast**—musical comedy telecast (one-hour)

Hoevenbergh, Henry Van—**Flicker**

Hoey, James Alexander Finnell—**Citizenship**—citizenship granted to an alien on foreign soil

Hoffman, Adon J.—**Pressing Machine (steam-operated)**

Hoffman, David—**Law School**—law school of collegiate rank

Hoffman, Edward L.—**Aviation**—**Parachute**—parachute

Hoffman, Harold Giles—**Crime Prevention and Detection**—crime prevention commission for interstate cooperation

Hoffman, Jacob Rosecrans—**Sawmill**—band sawmill

Hoffman, Paul Gray—**Economic Cooperation Administration**—Economic Cooperation Administration

Hoffman, William Joseph—**X-Ray**—X-ray moving pictures (successful) of the action of the human heart

Hoge, David—**Land Grant**—district land office

Holbrook, Amos—**Vaccination Legislation**—vaccination legislation (state)

Holbrook, Josiah—**Lyceum**

Holbrook, Josiah—**Manual Training**—industrial school

Holcomb, Amasa—**Photograph**—photograph taken in the United States

Holcomb, Amasa—**Telescope**—reflecting telescope

Holden, Paul Robert—**War (French Indo-China)**—American civilian pilot wounded in Indo-China

Holden, William — **Television** — **Telecast** — pay television presentation of a moving picture shown simultaneously in theaters

Holden, William Woods—**Impeachment**—impeachment and removal from office of a state governor

Holland, Andrew M.—**Moving Picture**—peep show

Holland, Clifford Milburn—**Tunnel**—twin-tube subaqueous vehicular tunnel

Holland, David—**Bicycle Race**—women's six-day bicycle race

Holland, John Philip—**Submarine**—submarine contract of the United States Navy

Holland, John Philip—**Submarine**—submarine that was practical and able to submerge

Hollerith, Herman—**Tabulating Machine**

Holley, Alexander Lyman—**Engineering Society**—mechanical engineering national society

Hollingshead, Richard Milton—**Moving Picture Theater**—drive-in moving picture theater

Hollingsworth, John Mark—**Paper**—manila paper

Hollingsworth, Lyman—**Paper**—manila paper

Hollis, Thomas—**Planetarium**—planetarium or orrery

Holly, Birdsall—**Heating System**—heating system from a central station

Holm, Hanya — **Copyright** — choreographic score copyrighted

Holman, Francis—**Stage Coach Inter-City Service**

Holman, Nat—**Basketball**—basketball collegiate team to win the National Invitation Tournament and the National Collegiate Athletic Association trophy

Holmes, Edwin Thomas—**Burglar Alarm**—burglar alarm

Holmes, Edwin Thomas—**Telephone**—telephone switchboard or exchange

Holmes, Edwin Thomas—**Telephone Operator**—woman telephone operator

Holmes, Francis Simmons—**Museum**—college museum

Holmes, Israel—**Brass Wire Drawing and Tube Making Machinery**

Holmes, Joseph Austin — **Mines Bureau (U.S.)**

Holmes, Oliver Wendell—**Stereoscope**

Holt, Mr.—**Puppet Show**

Holt, Benjamin — **Oratorio** — oratorio performance (complete)

Holt, Hamilton—**Book Course**

Holt, Hamilton—**College**—"Unit Cost Plan"

Holt, Hamilton—**Walk of Fame**

Holt, Harold G.—**Army Armored Car Unit**

Holt, J.—**Grammar**—English grammar by an American published in America

Holt, John—**Jewish Prayer Book**—published in the United States

Holt, John—**Medical Book**—surgery manual

Holt, Lewis B.—**Medal**—Agriculture Department distinguished service gold medal

Holt, Luther Emmett — **Medical Book**—pediatrics book of importance

Homer, Louise—**Opera**—opera by an American composer performed at the Metropolitan Opera House of New York

Hone, John—**Hospital**—eye hospital (permanent)

Hook, Albert H.—**Cigarette Manufacturing Machine**

Hooker, John Worthington—**Hygiene Instruction**—hygiene and physical education professorship

Hooper, Elihu Morgan — **Hospital** — leper hospital

Hoover, Herbert Clark—**Congress (U.S.)—Senate**—broadcast from the Senate chamber

Hoover, Herbert Clark—**Medal**—National Geographic Society special gold medal

Hoover, Herbert Clark—**Medal**—platinum medal

Hoover, Herbert Clark—**President (U.S.)**—President to invite the president-elect

Hoover, Herbert Clark—**Radio Conference**—national radio conference

Hoover, Herbert Clark—**Radio Facsimile Transmission**—photograph sent overland by radio to a distant point

Hoover, Herbert Clark—**Television—Telecast**—telecast of image and sound

Hoover, Herbert Clark—**Visiting Celebrities**—absolute monarch

Hoover, Herbert Henry—**Aviation—Flights**—airplane to exceed the speed of sound which was piloted by a civilian

Hoover, Mrs. Herbert Clark—**Geology**—woman graduate in geology

Hopkins, B. B.—**Bible Society**—Bible society

Hopkins, Esek—**Naval Officer**—commander-in-chief of the Continental Navy

Hopkins, Esek—**Navy**—naval fleet

Hopkins, Esek—**War (colonial)**—marine engagement in battle

Hopkins, Harry Lloyd—**Civil Works Administration (U.S.)**

Hopkins, Harry Lloyd—**Federal Emergency Relief Administration**

Hopkins, Harry Lloyd—**Federal Surplus Relief Corporation**

Hopkins, Harry Lloyd—**Works Progress Administration**—Works Progress Administration

Hopkins, John Burroughs—**Navy**—naval fleet

Hopkins, Joseph — **Money** — copper cents minted by a state

Hopkins, Mary Gross—**Village Improvement Society**

Hopkins, Samuel—**Patent**—patent granted by the United States government

Hopkinson, Francis—**Music**—secular song

Hopkinson, Francis—**Music Book**—secular song book by a native American

Hopkinson, Francis — **Musician** — composer (native-born American)

Horgan, Stephen Henry—**Engraving**—halftone engraving

Horlick, William—**Milk**—malted milk

Hornblower, Josiah—**Steam Engine**—steam engine

Horner, William Edmonds—**Medical Book**—pathology textbook

Hornsby, Joseph Allan—**Automobile Club**

Horrocks, Jeremiah—**Building and Loan Association**

Horton, Everett—**Fishing Rod of telescoping steel tubes**

Hosford, Mary—**College**—coeducational college

Hoskin, E. William—**Newspaper**—French daily newspaper (successful)

Hoskins, Timo—**Insurance**—insurance board (state)

Hosmer, Bradley C.—**Air Force Academy (U.S.)**—Air Force Academy

Hosmer, Mrs. Craig—**Ship**—atomic-powered cruiser

Houdry, Eugene—**Gasoline**—aviation gasoline

Hough, Franklin Benjamin—**Forestry Legislation**—federal forestry supervision

House, Henry Alonzo—**Automobile**—steam automobile

House, James A.—**Automobile**—steam automobile

House, Royal Earl—**Telegraph**—telegraph ticker to print letters of the alphabet

Houston, Abner — **Locomotive** — locomotive with a cab

Houston, David Franklin—**Road**—federal grant-in-aid

Houston, David Henderson—**Photographic Film**—roll film for cameras

Humphreys, Frederic E.—**Aviation—Aviator** —Army aviator to solo

Humphreys, James—**Chess Book**

Humphreys, Joshua—**Ship**—frigate

Humphreys, Joshua — **Shipping** — warship builder

Humphreys, Richard Franklin—**Atomic Reactor**—nuclear reactor built for private industrial research

Hunnewell, Hollis—**Tennis**—court tennis

Hunt, Pearson—**Railroad Charter**

Hunt, Richard Morris—**Building**—apartment house with a modern lay-out

Hunt, Robert—**Protestant Episcopal Church** —Protestant Episcopal church

Hunt, Walter—**Collar**—paper collar

Hunt, Walter—**Pin**—safety pin

Hunt, Walter—**Sewing Machine**—lock stitch sewing machine

Hunter, Dard—**Book**—book (of size) completed entirely by one man

Hunter, Dard—**Museum**—museum devoted exclusively to paper-making

Hunter, David—**Civil War**—Negro regiment in the Civil War

Hunter, James Bradbridge—**Hospital**—cancer hospital

Hunter, Robert—**Siamese Twins**—Siamese twins

Hunter, Robert — **Play (drama)** — printed American play

Hunter, Robert Mercer Taliaferro—**Congress of the Confederate States**

Hunter, William—**Medical Book**—croup report (printed)

Huntington, Anna Hyatt—**Museum**—maritime museum

Huntington, Archer Milton—**Museum**—maritime museum

Huntington, Mrs. Collis Potter—**Cancer Research Fund**

Hunton, William Alphaeus—**Young Men's Christian Association**—Young Men's Christian Association (for Negro members)

Hurd, Nathaniel—**Book Plate**

Hurd, Nathaniel—**Caricature**

Hurlbut, Stephen Augustus—**War Veterans' Society**—Grand Army of the Republic

Hurley, Edward Nash—**Federal Trade Commission**—Federal Trade Commission

Hurt, John—**Army Officer**—chaplain of the United States Army

Hurwitt, Elliott Samuel—**Moving Picture**— moving picture of the inside of a living heart (of a dog)

Husband, William Walter—**Border Patrol**— border patrol organization

Huss, Dwight B.—**Automobile Race**—transcontinental automobile race for a time record

Hüster, Mr.—**Tile**—brick roofing tile

Huston, John—**Moving Picture Actor**—moving picture actor and son to receive "Oscars"

Huston, Walter—**Moving Picture Actor**— moving picture actor and son to receive "Oscars"

Hutchins, Levi—**Clock**—alarm clock

Hutchins, Thomas — **Geographer of the United States**

Hutchinson, Anne—**Club Woman**

Hutchinson, Anne—**Congregational Church**— Congregational Church council

Hutchinson, Jock—**Golf Tournament**—Professional Golfers Association tournament

Hutchinson, Miller Reese—**Deaf—Hearing Aid**—electrical hearing aid

Hutchinson, Sam—**Iron**—exportation of iron

Hutchison, Joseph Chrisman—**Surgical Operation**—mastoid operation

Hutin, Francisquy—**Ballet**

Hyatt, George William—**Medicine**—tissue bank

Hyatt, Isaiah Smith—**Celluloid**

Hyatt, John Wesley—**Billiard Ball** of composition material resembling ivory

Hyatt, John Wesley—**Celluloid**

Hyde, D.—**Fountain Pen Patent**

Hyde, James M.—**Mineral Segregation**

Hyer, Lawrence—**Theater**—panorama show

I

Ickes, Harold Le Claire—**Emergency Housing Corporation (U.S.)**

Ickes, Harold Le Claire—**Federal Surplus Relief Corporation**

Ickes, Harold Le Claire—**Indians**—Indian tribal constitution

Ickes, Harold Le Claire—**Public Works Administration (U.S.)**

Ihm, Carl—**Medical Society**—homeopathic medical society

Ik, Min Yong—**Diplomatic Service**—Korean embassy

Imlay, Richard—**Railroad Car**—double-deck railroad coaches

Impellitteri, Vincent R.—**Telephone**—mobile transatlantic telephone conversation between two telephone-equipped automobiles

Ingalls, David Sinton—**Aviation—Aviator**— naval ace in World War I

Ingalls, Esther Abbie—**Skeet**—national skeet tournament

Ingalls, Laura—**Aviation—Flights (transcontinental)**—transcontinental non-stop east-west flight by a woman

Ingalls, Laura—**Aviation—Flights (transcontinental)**—transcontinental airplane flight by a woman

Ingersoll, Edward P.—**Automobile Magazine**

Ingersoll, Jared—**Political Convention**—political nominating caucus

Inouye, Daniel Ken—**Congressman (U.S.)**— Congressman of Japanese ancestry elected to the House of Representatives

Interranti, Giuseppe—**Moving Picture**—moving picture of a complete grand opera

Ireland, John—**Temperance Society**—Anti-Saloon League (national organization)

Irsay, Stephen d'—**Medical Instruction**—History of Medicine Department

Irvine, Callender—**Factory Standardization of Production**

Irving, Leslie Le Roy—**Aviation**—**Parachute** —parachute

Irving, Walter Edward—**Bridge**—bridge with open mesh steel flooring

Irwin, Bernard John Dowling—**Hospital**— army field hospital

Irwin, Bernard John Dowling—**Medal**— Medal of Honor action

Isabella, Queen of Spain—**Money**—coin bearing the portrait of a foreign monarch

Isabella, Queen of Spain—**Postage Stamp**— postage stamps to picture a woman

Isbell, Zachariah — **Civil Government in America**

Isham, Ralph N.—**Hospital**—interracial hospital

Iske, Anthony—**Slicing Machine**

Ives, Irving McNeil—**Industrial and Labor Relations School**

Ives, Norman S.—**Radio Broadcast**—submarine (submerged) broadcast

Izumeda, Rinban—**Buddhist Temple**

J

Jabara, James—**Aviation**—**Aviator**—American ace (jet)

Jackson, Andrew—**Cabinet of the United States**—cabinet appointee rejected by the Senate

Jackson, Andrew—**Cabinet of the United States**—cabinet member who was a Catholic

Jackson, Andrew—**Duel**—duel in which a future President of the United States participated

Jackson, Andrew—**Monument**—bronze equestrian statue

Jackson, Andrew—**Political Convention**— two-thirds rule

Jackson, Andrew — **Postmaster** — postmaster general of the United States to become a member of the President's cabinet

Jackson, Andrew—**President (U.S.)**—President born posthumously

Jackson, Andrew—**President (U.S.)**—President to receive fewer popular and electoral votes than an opponent

Jackson, Andrew—**President (U.S.)**—President to ride on a railroad train

Jackson, Andrew—**President (U.S.)**—President whose assassination was attempted

Jackson, Andrew—**Presidential Candidate**— presidential candidate nominated at a national convention

Jackson, Andrew—**Presidential Candidate**— presidential candidate to receive the greatest number of popular and electoral votes and yet fail of election

Jackson, Andrew—**Presidential Popular Vote**

Jackson, Andrew—**Presidential Protest**

Jackson, Andrew—**Spoils System**

Jackson, Benjamin—**Mustard**

Jackson, Charles Thomas—**Chemical Laboratory**—chemical laboratory

Jackson, Dale—**Aviation**—**Flights**—airplane endurance flight exceeding 400 hours

Jackson, Daniel—**Cotton Spinning Jenny**

Jackson, Frank—**Horseshoe Pitchers' Association (national)**

Jackson, Frank—**Horseshoe Pitching Contest (international)**

Jackson, Horatio Nelson—**Automobile Transcontinental Trip**—transcontinental automobile trip

Jackson, James A.—**Ambulance**—hospital ambulance service

Jackson, James—**Medical Instruction**—hygiene lectures

Jackson, James — **Pharmacopoeia** — pharmacopoeia prepared by a medical association

Jackson, John Barnard Sweet—**Medical Instruction**—pathology chair

Jackson, Jonathan—**Iron**—iron slitting mill

Jackson, Patrick Tracy—**Cotton Mill**—cotton mill in the world in which the whole process of cotton manufacturing from spinning to weaving was carried on by power

Jackson, Samuel—**Pharmacy College**—pharmacy college

Jackson, William — **Constitution of the United States**—Constitution (federal)

Jacobi, Abraham—**Medical Clinic**—children's clinic

Jacobi, Abraham—**Medical Instruction**—pediatrics professor

Jacobi, Abraham—**Medical Periodical**—medical periodical devoted to diseases of women and children

Jacobs, Israel—**Congressman (U.S.)**—Jewish congressman

Jacobson, Leon Orris—**Hospital**—hospital completely devoted to the study of the atom in the treatment of cancer

Jacobson, Marcus—**Rebellion**—rebellion of colonists against the English

Jadlowker, Herman—**Opera**—opera singer to sing two major roles on the same day

Jahns, Hermine—**Automobile Transcontinental Trip**—transcontinental automobile trip by a woman

James, Burton Wakeley—**Theater**—stateowned theater

James, Edmund Janes—**Political Science Society**—political and social science society (national)

James, Henry—**Arts and Letters Society**— arts and letters society (national)

James, Ralph Arthur—**Element**—element 95

James, Ralph Arthur—**Element**—element 96

James, Thomas Lemuel — **Freemasons** — Grotto

Janes, Thomas P.—**Agriculture Department (state)**—state department of agriculture

Janney, Eli Hamilton—**Railroad Coupler**

Jannings, Emil—**Moving Picture Actor**— moving picture actors to receive "Oscars"

Jannus, Antony (Tony)—**Aviation**—hydroplane commercial line service

Jaques, William Henry—**Nautical School**—nautical municipal school

Jarboro, Caterina — **Opera** — Negro prima donna of an opera company

Jardine, Robert Anderson—**Wedding**—American woman married to a former king of England

Jarvis, Anna—**Holiday**—Mother's Day

Jarvis, James—**Money**—Continental coin

Jastrow, Joseph—**Psychological Society**—psychological society (national organization)

Jastrow, Marcus—**Jewish College**—Jewish college

Jauch, Robert Joseph — **Pump** — computer pump

Jay, James—**Ink**—invisible ink

Jay, John—**Diplomatic Service**—foreign service committee

Jay, John—**Extradition**—extradition treaty with a foreign country

Jay, John—**State Department (U.S.)**—State Department (U.S.) Secretary

Jay, John—**Supreme Court (U.S.)**—Chief Justice of the Supreme Court

Jay, John—**Supreme Court (U.S.)**—Supreme Court of the United States

Jay, Peter Augustus — **Crime** — interstate crime pact

Jay, Pierre—**Credit Union Law**

Jay, William—**Coaching Club**

Jeffers, Harry Celestine—**Helicopter Flight**—helicopter transatlantic flight

Jeffers, Henry W.—**Milking Platform** (rotating)

Jeffers, William Martin—**Railroad**—streamlined light-weight high-speed three-car passenger train

Jefferson, Thomas—**Alfalfa**

Jefferson, Thomas—**Cabinet of the United States**—cabinet

Jefferson, Thomas—**Congressional Caucus**—congressional caucus (open, not secret)

Jefferson, Thomas—**Embargo Act**

Jefferson, Thomas—**Mint (U.S.)**—Mint of the United States

Jefferson, Thomas—**Parliamentary Rules of Order**

Jefferson, Thomas—**Patent**—patent granted by the United States government

Jefferson, Thomas—**Patent**—patent law (national)

Jefferson, Thomas—**Political Convention**—political nominating caucus attended by party leaders

Jefferson, Thomas—**President (U.S.)**—President elected by the House of Representatives

Jefferson, Thomas—**President (U.S.)**—President inaugurated in the city of Washington

Jefferson, Thomas—**President (U.S.)**—President to review the military forces

Jefferson, Thomas—**Presidential Candidate**—presidential candidate nominated at a caucus

Jefferson, Thomas—**Presidential Election**—presidential election in which candidates had been nominated for the vice presidency

Jefferson, Thomas—**State Department (U.S.)**—State Department (U.S.) Secretary

Jefferson, Thomas—**Territorial Expansion**—annexation of territory

Jefferson, Thomas—**Treaty**—treaty entered into by the United States after the treaty of peace with Great Britain

Jeffries, H. B.—**Wedding**—balloon wedding

Jeffries, Jim (James Jackson Jeffries)—**Moving Picture**—moving picture of a real pugilistic encounter taken at night

Jeffries, Jim—**Prize Fight**—Negro heavyweight champion of the world

Jellison, A. C.—**Bowling Tournament**—gold medal award to a perfect-score bowler

Jencks (Jenckes, Jenkes, Jenks), Joseph—**Brass and Iron Foundry**

Jencks, Joseph—**Fire Engine**—fire engine

Jencks, Joseph—**Money**—dies for coins in America

Jencks, Joseph—**Patent**—machine patent

Jenkins, Charles Francis—**Radio Facsimile Transmission**—photographs sent over a city telephone

Jenkins, Charles Francis—**Television—Telecast**—telecast of an object in motion

Jenkins, Charles Francis—**Television License**—television license

Jenney, William Le Baron—**Building**—building known as a skyscraper

Jenner, Edward—**Vaccination for smallpox**

Jernigin, J. D. ("Duke")—**Glider**—glider towed across the continent

Jerome, Chauncy—**Clock**—brass clock works

Jervis, John Bloomfield—**Locomotive**—locomotive with a four-wheeled front truck

Jessel, George—**Radio Broadcast** — cooperative radio show

Jessel, George—**Television—Telecast**—demonstration of home reception of television

Jester, Maurice D.—**Medal**—Navy Cross awarded to a Coast Guard officer in World War II

Jeter, Helen Rankin—**Degrees (academic and honorary)**—Doctor of Social Science degree

Jewell, Izetta—**Television—Telecast**—play to be televised

Jewell, Pliny—**Belting**

Jewett, Charles Coffin—**Librarians' Convention**

Jewett, John P.—**Medical Society**—women's medical society

Jogues, Isaac — **Catholic Canonization of North Americans**

John, Augustus—**Radio Facsimile Transmission**—drawing sent by radio across the Atlantic

Johnson, Andrew—**Impeachment**—impeachment proceedings against a President of the United States

Johnson, Andrew—**Labor Law**—eight-hour day for government laborers and mechanics

Johnson, Andrew—**President (U.S.)**—President to become a senator

Johnson, Byron Bancroft ("Ban")—**Baseball League**—American league

Johnson, Charles Eneu—**Printer's Ink**

Johnson, Clarence—**War (Korean)**—American tank crew to cross the 38th parallel in Korea

Johnson, Clarence L.—**Aviation—Airplane**—jet propelled fighter plane

Johnson, Eads—**Ferryboat**—ferryboat built exclusively for motor vehicle transportation

Johnson, Edward—**Gas**—gas ordinance (city)

Johnson, Edward — **Television — Telecast** —opera telecast

Johnson, George Arthur—**Water Purification**—water supply chemically treated with chlorine compounds

Johnson, George Washington—**Croquet League**

Johnson, Henry—**Medal**—Croix de Guerre awarded to a Negro

Johnson, Herbert Lester—**Peritonitis**—peritonitis preventive (successful)

Johnson, Hiram Warren—**Progressive Party**

Johnson, Hugh Samuel—**Industrial Recovery Act**—compliance board under the National Industrial Recovery Act

Johnson, Hugh Samuel—**Industrial Recovery Act**—industrial recovery act (national)

Johnson, Hugh Samuel—**Industrial Recovery Act**—postage stamps commemorating the National Recovery Act

Johnson, Jack—**Prize Fight**—Negro heavyweight champion of the world

Johnson, James B.—**Fish Hatchery**—fish hatchery

Johnson, James Weldon—**Poet**—Negro poet to be employed to teach creative writing

Johnson, Jerome—**Young Men's Christian Association**—Young Men's Christian Association (for Negro members)

Johnson, John—**Carpeting**—carpeting (velvet)

Johnson, Lewis Jerome—**Stadium**—cement stadium

Johnson, Louisa Catherine. *See* Adams, Mrs. John Quincy

Johnson, M. — **History** — History of New England

Johnson, Marmaduke—**Bible**—Bible in an Indian language

Johnson, Marmaduke—**Book**—book privately printed

Johnson, Marmaduke — **Grammar** — Indian grammar

Johnson, Marmaduke—**Primer**—primer in an American Indian dialect

Johnson, Mordecai Wyatt—**College**—Negro university to establish undergraduate, graduate and professional schools

Johnson, Morris—**Ship**—roll-on roll-off carrier

Johnson, Neils—**Helicopter**—helicopter passenger service

Johnson, Opha May—**Marines**—woman marine reserve

Johnson, Philip—**Building**—bronze and glass skyscraper

Johnson, Richard Mentor—**Vice President of the United States**—Vice President elected by the Senate

Johnson, Robert Wood—**Adhesive and Medicated Plaster**—adhesive and medicated plaster with a rubber base

Johnson, Roswell Hill—**Oil and Gas Production Course**

Johnson, Roy Lee—**Ship**—aircraft carrier with an angle deck

Johnson, Rudy F.—**Court Martial**—court martial trial in the United States at which enlisted men were allowed to sit as members of the court

Johnson, Samuel—**Grammar**—English grammar by an American published in America

Johnson, Thomas Loftin—**Coin Box**

Johnson, Walter—**Hall of Fame**—hall of fame (baseball)

Johnson, William H.—**City** (Lilliputian city)

Johnson, William Samuel—**Congress (U.S.)**—Senate—Senate

Johnson, William Samuel—**Diplomatic Service**—foreign service committee

Johnson, Woolsey—**Medical Society**—laryngological society (state)

Johnston, George W.—**War (Quemoy)**—American casualty of the Red Chinese bombardment

Johnston, Henrietta—**Artist**—woman painter

Johnston, Henrietta—**Pastellist**

Johnston, Joseph Eccleston—**Civil War**—serious engagement in the Civil War

Johnston, Thomas — **Engraving** — historical print engraved in America

Jokes, Joseph—**Whips**

Jon, Gee—**Execution**—lethal gas execution

Jonas, Karel—**Dictionary**—Bohemian-American dictionary

Joncaire, Chabert—**Niagara Falls**—utilization of Niagara Falls waterpower

Jones, Albert L.—**Paper**—corrugated paper

Jones, Alice — **Newspaper** — composograph photograph in a newspaper

Jones, Billy — **Radio Broadcast** — program theme song

Jones, Doris—**Streptomycin**

Jones, Emeline Roberts—**Dentist**—woman dentist

Jones, George William—**Farmers' Institute**—farmers' institute held by a land grant agricultural college off its campus

Jones, H. S.—**Basketball**—basketball team (college)

Jones, Henry—**Jews**—Jewish fraternal society

Jones, Hugh—**Grammar**—English grammar by an American

Jones, James I. — **Hospital** — eye hospital (permanent)

Jones, John—**Medical Book**—surgery manual

Jones, John Clifton—**Television—Telecast**—surgical operation televised on a coast-to-coast closed circuit in color

Jones, John Paul—**Flag**—American flag displayed on a man-of-war

Jones, John Paul—**Flag**—American flag saluted by a foreign nation

Jones, Orlando—**Cornstarch**—cornstarch patent

Jones, Pauline L.—**Library Society**—state librarians' society

Jones, Richard Watson—**College**—state college for women

Jones, Robert Tyre (Bobby)—**Golf Champion**—golf champion to hold the four highest golf titles

Jones, Robert Tyre—**Golf Champion**—golf champion to win the United States National Amateur Tournament two years in succession

Jones, Ruel B.—**Lunch Wagon**

Jones, William—**Insurance**—fire insurance joint-stock company

Jones, William H.—**Ice Skating Club**—ice skating club

Jordan, Cicely—**Breach of Promise Suit**

Josepho, Anatol M.—**Photography**—film developing machine

Joshee, Anandibai—**Physician**—Hindu woman to receive a doctor of medicine degree

Joubert de la Muraille, Jacques Hector Nicholas—**Catholic Nuns**—Catholic nuns (colored community)

Judson, Whitcomb L.—**Fastening**—hookless fastening

Juett, Howard W.—**Automobile License (federal)**—contract carrier license

Julius, George—**Totalisator**

Jump, William Ashby—**Medal**—Agriculture Department distinguished service gold medal

June, Harold Irving—**Aviation—Flights**—South Pole flight

Junkin, George — **Normal School** — normal school instruction offered by a college

Junkin, George—**School**—model school

Junkin, Sam F.—**World War II**—American pilot to shoot down a German fighter plane

Jurgensen, Walter Herman—**Legislature**—unicameral legislature (state)

Justine, George—**Television—Telecast**—prize fight in a "studio"

K

Kaercher, Grace—**Woman**—woman clerk of a state supreme court

Kahnweiler, David—**Life Preserver**—life preserver of cork

Kalakaua, David—**Visiting Celebrities**—king (reigning) to visit the United States

Kalisch, Isidor—**Jews**—Jewish Rabbinical Conference

Kalmus, Herbert Thomas—**Moving Picture**—Technicolor motion picture film

Kan, Edward Bing—**Citizenship**—Chinese granted citizenship

Kane, Delancey Astor—**Coaching**

Kane, Elisha Kent—**Expedition**—Arctic expedition

Kanouse, Edna Beecham—**Births**—quintuplets

Kanouse, Edward Cole—**Births**—quintuplets

Kantrowitz, Adrian—**Moving Picture**—moving picture of the inside of a living heart (of a dog)

Karpeles, Leopold—**Medal**—Medal of Honor awarded to a Jewish soldier

Kaufman, George Simon—**Play (drama)**—musical play to win a Pulitzer prize

Kaufman, Irving Robert—**Television**—television eyewitness allowed to testify in a federal court

Kaufman, Irving Robert—**Treason**—execution for treason in peacetime

Kean, Thomas—**Opera**—opera performed by a professional visiting troupe

Kean, Thomas — **Play (drama)** — Shakespearean play

Kean, Thomas—**Theatrical Advance Publicity Man**

Keayne, Robert — **Military Organization** — military organization

Keel, Elmo Woodrow—**War Veterans' Society**—World War II veterans' society officially recognized by Congress

Keeler, Leonarde—**Lie Detector**

Keeler, Sarah Warren—**Deaf—School**—lip reading instruction for the deaf

Keene, Edmund—**Actor**—actor to receive curtain applause

Keene, Foxhall—**Automobile**—automobile to exceed the speed of a mile a minute

Keene, Foxhall P.—**Polo**—international polo series

Keep, Nathan Cooley—**Dental School**—dental school permanently established by a university

Keim, Elwood — **Aviation** — **Flights** — "airplane train"

Keim, Elwood — **Aviation—Flights** — skytrain international round-trip flight

Keim, Jacob—**Boardwalk**

Keimer, S.—**Insurance Book**—insurance proposal

Keimer, S.—**Shorthand Book**

Keimer, Samuel — **Newspaper** — newspaper serial story

Keith, A. E.—**Telephone**—automatic telephone system (successful)

Keith, Benjamin Franklin—**Vaudeville**

Keller, Frances—**Arbitration Association**—arbitration association

Keller, Franklin J. — **High School** — public high school to specialize in the performing field

Keller, Kaufman Thuma—**Air Force Academy (U.S.)**—Air Force Academy

Kelley, John F.—**Aviation Magazine**—aviation magazine devoted primarily to airplanes

Kelley, Oliver Hudson—**Agricultural Society**—agricultural society of national importance

Kellogg, Albert — **Forest Service** — forest Commission (state)

Kellogg, Frank Billings—**Woman**—woman passport division chief

Kellogg, Mary Fletcher—**College**—coeducational college

Kelly, Grace—**Moving Picture Actor**—moving picture actress depicted on a postage stamp

Kelly, John Patrick—**Army Officer**—flight surgeon

Kelly, Oakley G.—**Aviation—Flights (transcontinental)** — transcontinental non-stop flight

Kelly, William—**Immigration**—Chinese labor immigration

Kelpius, Magister—**Ancient Mystical Order Rosae Crucis**

Kelsey, Benjamin — **Aviation—Flights**—all-blind flight

Kemmler, William—**Execution**—electrocution of a human being

Kemper, W. H.—**Court**—small debtors' court established by state law

Kempon, G. S.—**Radio Broadcast**—transatlantic radio signal

Kendall, Amos—**Telegraph**—telegraph company

Kendall, George—**Colonial Government**—colonial council in America

Kendall, George—**Rebellion (colonial)**

Kendrick, Captain—**Ship**—ship to carry the United States flag around the world

Kenison, Nehemiah—**Chiropodist**

Kennedy, Bernard Reilly — **Codification Board (United States)**

Kennedy, Gerald S.—**Television—Telecast**—stockholders' meetings televised coast-to-coast simultaneously

Kennedy, Henry Peres—**Chair**—recumbent chair patent

Kennedy, John Fitzgerald—**Cabinet of the United States**—cabinet member who was a brother of a President

Kennedy, John Fitzgerald—**Medal**—National Aeronautics and Space Administration Distinguished Service Medal

Kennedy, John Fitzgerald—**Presidential Candidate**—presidential candidate debate series on television

Kennedy, John Fitzgerald — **Television — Telecast**—presidential news conference to be televised live

Kennedy, John Fitzgerald—**Water**—sea water conversion plant (practical)

Kennedy, Robert Francis—**Cabinet of the United States**—cabinet member who was a brother of a President

Kennedy, W. Ashton—**Chiropody School**—chiropody school as a regular division of a university

Kensett, Thomas—**Canning**—canning

Kent, Billy—**Television—Telecast**—musical comedy telecast (one-hour)

Kent, Leslie Swigart—**Medical Society**—woman president of a state medical society

Kenyon, Helen—**Church**—woman moderator of the General Council of Congregational and Christian Churches

Kenyon, William Orlin—**Sponge**—oxidized cellulose (sponge)

Kephart, Calvin Ira—**Radio Broadcast**—debate over the radio

Kepley, Ada H.—**Lawyer**—woman lawyer graduated from a law school

Kepner, William E.—**Aviation—Airship**—dirigible made completely of metal

Kern, Mrs. Lou J.—**Physician**—osteopath (woman)

Kernodle, George Riley—**Theatrical School**—theater and dramatic criticism course

Kerns, James N.—**Baseball League**—baseball league of importance

Kerr, George—**Tennis Match**—professional lawn tennis contest (international)

Kerr, Gordon Campbell—**Television—Telecast**—birth (human) to be televised for the public

Kerr, R.—**Button**—buttons of fresh water pearl

Kerr, William T.—**Monument**—monument to the American flag

Kerst, Donald William—**Betatron**

Kesselering, Boyd—**Air Mail Service**—helicopter air mail and express service

Kessler, Frido W.—**Air Mail Service**—rocket air mail flight

Ketler, Weir Carlyle—**Radio Broadcast**—speaker to address an organization by radio

Kettering, Charles Franklin — **Automobile Electric Self-Starter**—automobile electric self-starter applied commercially

Key, David McKendree—**Cabinet of the United States**—Confederate to serve in the cabinet

Key, Francis Scott—**National Anthem**

Keys, Geoffrey—**Medal**—Bronze Star presented to a woman

Keys, John—**Civil War**—regiment to respond to President Abraham Lincoln's proclamation

Keys, Leota—**Quadruplets to Complete a College Course**

Keys, Mary—**Quadruplets to Complete a College Course**

Keys, Mona—**Quadruplets to Complete a College Course**

Keys, Roberta—**Quadruplets to Complete a College Course**

Kidd, Isaac Campbell—**Naval Officer**—admiral killed in action in World War II

Kidd, William—**Workmen's Compensation**—workmen's compensation agreement

Kidder, Alfred Vincent—**Anthropology Laboratory**

Kieft, Wilhelm—**Curfew Bell**

Kier, Samuel M.—**Oil**—oil refinery

Kiernan, John James—**News Agency**—financial news agency

Kiernan, Leo — **Aviation — Races** — airplane passenger race around the world

Kies, Mary—**Woman**—woman granted a patent

Kikuchi, Takeo—**Lawyer**—Japanese lawyer

Kilby, Thomas Erby—**Money**—coin bearing the portrait of a living person

Kilgallen, Dorothy — **Aviation—Races** — airplane passenger race around the world

Kilgore, E. W.—**Wedding**—airplane wedding

Kilgore, Evelyn Pinckert—**Aviation—License** —airplane instructor's license

Killebrew, Emmet Stephen—**Electric Power Plant**—hydroelectric power plant (county-owned)

Kilpatrick, Judson—**Civil War**—bloodshed north of the Mason-Dixon line

Kilton, John—**Physiological Society**—physiological society

Kimball, Ernest—**Cafeteria**

Kimball, Justin Ford—**Insurance**—group hospital insurance plan

Kimball, Sumner Increase—**Life Saving Service**—life saving service

Kind, Johann Friedrich—**Opera**—grand opera sung in English

Kinder, Arthur—**Hair Cloth**

King, Charles Brady—**Automobile**—automobile with left-hand steering

King, Charles Brady—**Automobile Club**

King, Charles Brady—**Hammer (pneumatic)**

King, Chow—**Hospital**—Chinese hospital

King, Clarence—**Geological Survey**—geological survey director (U.S.)

King, Ernest Joseph—**Naval Officer**—naval officers to wear the five-star insignia

King, Samuel Archer—**Photograph**—aerial photograph

King, William—**Cork Manufacturer**

King, William Rufus de Vane—**Vice President of the United States**—Vice President sworn in on foreign soil

Kingsford, Thomas — **Cornstarch** — starch made commercially from Indian corn

Kinney, Dita H. — **Army Nurse Corps (female)**

Kinney, James—**Aviation—Flights**—all blind cross-country test

Kip, Charles Hayden—**Cooperative**—college cooperative store

Kirby, Ephraim—**Law Reports**

Kirby, Fred Morgan—**Civil Rights Chair**

Kirby, Rollin—**Cartoon**—cartoon awarded a Pulitzer prize

Kirk, Edward Cameron—**Dental Book**—book for dental hygienists (text)

Kirkbride, Raymond Watson — **College** — "Junior Year Abroad"

Kirkbridge, Thomas Story—**Psychiatric Association**

Kirkham, Charles — **Aviation — Airplane** — fighter airplane

Kirkham, Charles — **Aviation — Airplane**—molded plywood airplane

Kirkham, Thomas—**Horse Race**—futurity race

Kirkpatrick, Ross C.—**Aviation—Flights**—New York-Alaska flight

Kirkwood, James Pugh—**Water Purification** —water purification by filtration

Kirlin, Florence—**State Department (U.S.)** —woman Acting Assistant Secretary of State

Kisters, Gerry — **Medal** — Medal of Honor awarded to a soldier who already had received a Distinguished Service Cross

Kitchen, Stuart Fordyce—**Vaccine**—yellow fever vaccine for human immunization

Klemm, Johann Gottlob—**Organ**—organ built in the United States

Klenle, Gustave A.—**Wedding**—television wedding

Kliegl, Anton Tiberius—**Electric Lighting**—klieglight lighting unit

Kliegl, John Hugh—**Electric Lighting**—klieglight lighting unit

Kline, A. C.—**Postage Stamp Catalog**

Knapp, James Henry—**Hat**—derby hat

Knapp, Joseph Gillett—**Forest Service**—forestry inquiry commission (state)

Kneeland, Samuel—**Fishing Treatise**

Kneeland, Samuel—**Religious Publication**—religious journal

Knight, Arthur F.—**Golf Clubs (or golf sticks)**—steel shaft for a golf club

Knight, Frederick Irving—**Medical Periodical**—laryngology magazine

Knight, James—**Cripples**—private school for cripples

Knight, James—**Hospital**—orthopedic hospital

Knight, Jonathan—**Medical Society**—medical society (national)

Knowles, Asa Smallidge—**College**—college principally for war veterans

Knox, Clarence Moore—**Aviation—Legislation**—aviation legislation (state)

Knox, Henry—**Cabinet of the United States** —cabinet

Knox, Henry—**Patent**—patent law (national)

Knox, Henry—**War Department (U.S.)**—War Department (U.S.)

Knox, Henry—**War Veterans' Society**—Society of the Cincinnati

Knox, William—**Bowler**—bowler to make a perfect score of 300 in an American Bowling Congress tournament

Knox, William—**Diplomatic Service**—consuls of the United States appointed after the adoption of the Constitution

Knudsen, William Signius—**Army Officer**—general appointed from civilian rank

Knyphausen, Wilhelm, Baron von—**Flag**—American flag flown in battle

Koelsch, John Kelvin—**Medal**—Medal of Honor awarded to a helicopter pilot

Koenig, Alfred J.—**Radio Facsimile Transmission**—transpacific and transcontinental facsimile transmission

Koenig, George Augustus—**Diamond**—diamonds in a meteorite

Koester, Heinrich Bernhard — **Lutheran Church**—Lutheran services in English

Koester, Mrs. M.—**Bowling Tournament**—bowling tournament for women

Kolb, Lawrence—**Narcotic**—narcotic sanatorium (federal) for drug addicts

Kolb, Robert—**Army**—helicopter battalion

Koller, Helen—**Wedding**—double radio wedding

König, Paul—**Submarine**—cargo submarine to cross the Atlantic Ocean

Koons, Franklin M.—**World War II**—American to land on French soil

Koos-ta-ta, Paul — **Indians** — Indian tribal constitution

Kopsky, Doris—**Bicycle Racer**—woman bicycle champion of the National Amateur Bicycle Association

Korda, Alexander — **Television** — **Telecast**—moving picture premiere performance to be televised (major film)

Korizek, Frank — **Newspaper** — Czech language newspaper

Korn, Arthur—**Radio Facsimile Transmission**—photograph sent by radio across the Atlantic from Europe

Krafft, Michael—**Parade**—street parade held by a mystic society

Krafft, Michael August—**Distilling Book**

Kramer, John Franklin—**Prohibition**—prohibition bureau (federal)

Kramer, Stanley—**Moving Picture**—moving picture presented simultaneously in major cities throughout the world

Krantz, John Christian — **Anesthesia** — trifluoroethyl vinyl ether

Krauskopf, Joseph—**Jewish College**—Jewish college to train men for the rabbinate

Krebs, George—**Aviation** — **Airplane** — jet propulsion four-engine bomber

Kreusi, John—**Phonograph**—phonograph

Krigbaum, William Lutz—**Army Camp**—army camp for "limited service"

Krueger, Otto E.—**Orchestra**—radio orchestra

Kuchins, Harry — **Glider** — glider flight indoors

Kuhn, Adam—**Botany Professor**

Kump, Herman Guy—**Industrial Recovery Act**—state to place all its employees under the blanket code of the National Recovery Act Code

Kunzi, Abraham—**Quinine**—quinine

Kuskof, Ivan Alexandrovich—**Russian Settlement**

Kyrides, Lucas Petrou—**Rubber**—synthetic rubber

L

Labadie, Jean de—**Labadist Community**

Lablache, Louise — **Opera** — opera at the Metropolitan Opera House

La Farge, John—**Arts and Letters Society**—arts and letters society (national)

Lafayette, Marquis de — **Citizenship** — citizenship (colonial) conferred by special grant

Lafayette, Marquis de—**Land Grant**—special land grant to a foreigner

La Follette, Philip—**Insurance**—unemployment insurance act

La Follette, Robert Marion—**Moving Picture**—talking pictures of presidential candidates

Lagan, M. D.—**Hospital**—leper hospital

Lahm, Frank Purdy—**Aviation—Airplane**—airplane purchased by the United States Government

Lahm, Frank Purdy—**Aviation—Aviator**—Army aviator to solo

Lahm, Frank Purdy—**Aviation—Passenger**—airplane passenger (official)

Lahm, Frank Purdy—**Balloon Race**—balloon cup race

Laird, John—**Ship**—iron vessel

Lake, Simon—**Submarine**—submarine fitted with an internal combustion engine

Lake, Simon—**Telephone**—telephone message from a submarine under water

Lalande, John — **Catholic Canonization of North Americans**

Lalemant, Gabriel—**Catholic Canonization of North Americans**

Lallemont, Pierre—**Bicycle**—bicycle with a rotary crank

Lamar, Gazaway Bugg—**Ship**—iron vessel

Lamar, Mirabeau Buonaparte—**President of the Republic of Texas**

Lamb, John—**Employment Service**—municipal employment office

Lambert, Albert Bond — **Army Balloon School**

Lambrecht, John Osgo—**Ship**—aircraft carrier to sail around Cape Horn

La Mountain, John—**Ship**—balloon carrier

Lamson, Eleanor Annie—**Astronomer**—woman astronomer employed in the United States Naval Observatory

Land, Edwin Herbert—**Camera**—camera to take, develop and print pictures on photographic paper

Land, Frank Sherman—**Freemasons**—Order of De Molay

Landis, Cullen — **Moving Picture** — talking picture of more than 6,000 feet

Landis, James McCauley—**Securities and Exchange Commission (U.S.)**

Landis, Kenesaw Mountain—**Baseball Dictator**

Landis, Merkel—**Bank**—Christmas savings club

Landreth, David—**Seed Business**

Lane, Benjamin J.—**Gas Mask**—gas mask with a self-contained breathing apparatus

Lane, Dick—**Television Station**—commercial television station west of the Mississippi River

Lane, Ephraim—**Tungsten**—tungsten and tellurium

Lane, Ralph — **Letter** — letters written in English

Lane, William Coolidge—**Bibliography Society** (national)

Lanergan, Andrew—**Rocket**—rocket patent

Langdon, John—**Congress (U.S.)—Senate**—president pro tempore of the United States Senate

Langdon, John—**Congress (U.S.)—Senate—**Senate

Langdon, John—**Navy**—naval fleet

Langdon, John—**Vice Presidential Candidate**—vice presidential nominee to decline nomination

Langdon, Kay Louise—**Naval Officer**—women sworn into the regular U.S. Navy

Langenheim, Frederick — **Magic Lantern Slides** (glass plate)

Langenheim, Frederick—**Photograph**—photograph to gain world fame

Langenheim, William—**Photograph**—photograph to gain world fame

Langford, Nathaniel Pitt—**Park**—park (national)

Langhorne, Nancy Witcher. *See* Astor, Nancy Witcher Langhorne

Langley, Samuel Pierpont—**Aviation—Airplane**—airplane (heavier-than-air) to make any long sustained flight

Langley, Samuel Pierpont—**Aviation—Expositions and Meets**—air conference (international)

Langloiserie, Louis—**Language Instruction**—French instruction

Laning, Richard Boyer—**Submarine**—submarine powered by a liquid metal-cooled atomic reactor

Lansdowne, Zachary—**Aviation—Airship**—dirigible (American-built rigid)

Lansdowne, Zachary — **Aviation — Flights (transcontinental)** — transcontinental airship voyage

Lanston, Tolbert—**Typesetting Machine**—monotype

Lapham, Increase Allen—**Forest Service**—forestry inquiry commission (state)

La Porte, Arthur Earl—**Aviation—Flights (transatlantic)**—Atlantic Ocean scheduled air service

Larkin, Thomas Oliver—**Diplomatic Service**—consul to California

Larsen, Don — **Baseball Player** — baseball pitcher to pitch a perfect no-hit, no-run, no-walk World Series game

Larsen, Paul J.—**Civil Defense Director**

Larsh, Almon E.—**Element**—element 103

La Salle, Robert Cavelier, Sieur de—**Ship**—Great Lakes commercial vessel

Lasswell, Harold Dwight — **Propaganda Course** (college)

Latham, Woodville—**Moving Picture**—moving picture on film shown on a screen

Lathrop, Julia Clifford—**Children's Bureau (U.S.)**

Lathrop, Mary Florence—**Lawyer**—woman lawyer to become a member of the American Bar Association

Lathrop, Rose Hawthorne—**Hospital**—cancer home for incurables (free)

Latimer, Robert M.—**Element**—element 103

La Tour, Sieur le Blond de—**Levees**

Latrobe, Benjamin Henry—**Bridge**—wooden railroad bridge of a purely truss type

Latta, Alexander Bonner—**Fire Engine**—fire engine that was practical

Lauber, Harold—**Curling Championship (national)**

Lauber, Louis—**Curling Championship (national)**

Laudonnière, René Goulaine de—**War (colonial)**—intercolonial war

Laughlin, James—**Tennis Match**—intercollegiate court tennis match

Laurens, Henry—**Colonial Government**—independent government in any of the American colonies

Laurens, Henry—**Cremation**

Laurens, Henry—**Prison**—American imprisoned in the Tower of London

Laurie, James—**Engineering Society**—civil engineering national society

Laval, Carl Gustaf Patrik de—**Cream Separator**—continuous flow centrifugal cream separator

La Violette, William—**Aviation—Flights**—all-blind cross-country test

Law, Frederick Rodman—**Moving Picture Actor**—stunt actor

Law, James—**Veterinary School**—veterinary department of collegiate character

Law, Ruth—**Aviation—Flights**—airplane to fly a distance exceeding 500 miles

Lawler, Richard Harold—**Surgical Operation**—kidney transplanting

Lawless, Henry—**Colonist**—civilian settlement west of the Allegheny Mountains

Lawrence, Cornelius Van Wyck—**Election**—mayor elected by popular vote in a city

Lawrence, Ernest Orlando—**Physics**—cyclotron

Lawrence, Florence—**Moving Picture Actor**—moving picture star (female)

Lawrence, Gertrude—**Television—Telecast**—play to be televised with its original Broadway cast

Lawrence, John Hunsdale—**Isotope**—radioactive isotope medicine

Lawrence, Joseph—**Bank**—trust company

Lawrence, Richard — **President** — President whose assassination was attempted

Lawrence, W. G.—**Golf Tournament**—national championship stroke-play golf match

Lawson, Alfred William—**Aviation—Magazine**—aviation magazine devoted primarily to airplanes

Lawton, Chester S.—**Plow**—submarine cable plow

Laydon, John—**Wedding**—wedding in Virginia

Lea, Robert Wentworth—**Industrial Recovery Act**—compliance board under the National Industrial Recovery Act

Leahy, William Daniel—**Naval Officer**—naval officers to wear the five-star insignia

Leason, George—**Calico**

Leavitt, Samuel—**Press Clipping Bureau**

Lechford, Thomas — **Lawyer** — lawyer disbarred

Levy, Asser—**Jews**—Jew to win all the rights and perform all the duties of American citizenship

Levy, Bert ("Yank")—**Army School**—army training school

Levy, Louis—**Air Mail Service**—autogiro mail delivery direct to a post office

Levy, Simon Magruder—**Army School**—Army school graduate (Jewish)

Levy, Simon Magruder—**Army School**—army school graduates

Levy, Uriah Phillips—**Naval Officer**—captain in the U.S. Navy who was Jewish

Lewi, Maurice J.—**Chiropody School**—chiropody school of note

Lewin, Richman—**Television Station**—microwave television station

Lewis, Andrew—**Treaty**—treaty entered into by the United States with Indian tribes

Lewis, Colby—**Television**—college credit course in television

Lewis, Floyd John—**Surgical Operation**—heart operation in which the deep freezing technique was employed

Lewis, Fulton—**Radio Broadcast**—news program (cooperative)

Lewis, George Hill—**Radio License**—radio license

Lewis, Jacobs—**Milestones**

Lewis, Josephine Miles—**Fine Arts Department**—fine arts department in a college

Lewis, Kate (Mrs. William Lewis)—**Wedding**—wedding abroad of a soldier in the American Expeditionary Force

Lewis, Kate—**Births**—World War baby

Lewis, Meriwether—**Expedition**—expedition across the continent to the Pacific coast

Lewis, O.—**Horse Race**—horse race (Kentucky Derby)

Lewis, Sinclair—**Nobel Prize**—Nobel Prize in literature

Lewis, Thomas—**Treaty**—treaty entered into by the United States with Indian tribes

Lewis, Winford Lee—**Lewisite**

Ley, Willy—**Air Mail Service**—rocket air mail flight

Lideen, Clifford L.—**Degrees (academic and honorary)**—degree conferred by radio

Lieber, Francis—**Encyclopedia**—American encyclopedia

Liele, George—**Baptist Church**—Baptist church (Negro)

Ligowsky, George—**Trapshooting**—clay pigeon target

Lilienthal, David Eli—**Atomic Energy Commission**—Atomic Energy Commission

Lilienthal, David Eli—**Electric Home and Farm Authority, Inc.**

Lilly, Chris—**Prize Fight**—prize fight fatality

Lincoln, Abraham—**Agricultural Land Grant**

Lincoln, Abraham—**Amnesty**

Lincoln, Abraham—**Army**—law (federal) authorizing military service for Negroes

Lincoln, Abraham—**Civil War**—call for Union troops in the Civil War

Lincoln, Abraham—**Emancipation Proclamation (preliminary)**

Lincoln, Abraham—**Freedmen's Bureau (U.S.)**

Lincoln, Abraham—**Habeas Corpus**—habeas corpus suspension order

Lincoln, Abraham—**Holiday**—Thanksgiving Day national proclamation

Lincoln, Abraham—**Money**—coin bearing the portrait of a President

Lincoln, Abraham—**Monument**—monument by a woman ordered by the U.S. Government

Lincoln, Abraham—**Naval Officer**—Judge Advocate of the Navy

Lincoln, Abraham—**Postage Stamp**—memorial stamp

Lincoln, Abraham—**Postage Stamp**—mourning stamp

Lincoln, Abraham—**President (U.S.)**—President born beyond the boundaries of the original thirteen states

Lincoln, Abraham—**President (U.S.)**—President to be assassinated

Lincoln, Abraham—**President (U.S.)**—President to rest in state in the United States Capitol rotunda

Lincoln, Abraham—**President (U.S.)**—President who had received a patent

Lincoln, Abraham—**Presidential Executive Order to be numbered**

Lincoln, Abraham—**Telegram**—telegram dispatched from an aerial station

Lincoln, Abraham—**Telegram**—transcontinental telegram

Lincoln, Abraham—**Telegraph**—telegraph line to the Pacific coast

Lincoln, Mrs. Abraham—**Pension**—pension to the widow of a President

Lincoln, Charles—**Dog Show**

Lincoln, Enoch—**Governor**—brothers to serve simultaneously as governors of their respective states

Lincoln, Levi—**Governor**—brothers to serve simultaneously as governors of their respective states

Lincoln, Levi—**Park**—park land

Lincoln, William E.—**Moving Picture Machine**—machine to show animated pictures

Lind, Jenny—**Railroad Car**—private railroad car

Lindbergh, Anne Morrow—**Medal**—National Geographic Society gold medal

Lindbergh, Charles Augustus—**Air Force Academy (U.S.)**—Air Force Academy

Lindbergh, Charles Augustus—**Artificial Heart**

Lindbergh, Charles Augustus—**Aviation-Flights (transatlantic)**—transatlantic solo flight

Lindbergh, Charles Augustus—**Medal**—Distinguished Flying Cross

Lindbergh, Charles Augustus—**Postage Stamp**—postage stamp on which was inscribed the name of a living American

Linderman, Henry—**Assay Office Building (federal)**

Lindley, Jacob—**College**—university founded by a federal land grant

Lineback, John—**Cottonseed Hulling Machine**

Lovelace, Francis—**Rebellion**—rebellion of colonists against the English

Lovell, Joseph—**Army**—medical corps

Lovell, Joseph—**Army Officer**—surgeon general of the U.S. Army

Lovering, William Croad—**Insurance**—mutual liability insurance company

Low, Albert William—**Television—Telecast**—Catholic mass televised from a studio

Low, Mrs. Edward Gilchrist—**Architectural School**—landscape architecture course

Low, Frederick—**Election Law**—fraudulent election law (state)

Low, Josiah O.—**Squash Club**—squash tennis organization (national)

Low, Juliette Gordon—**Girl Scouts**

Lowe, Bobby (Robert Lincoln Lowe)—**Baseball Player**—baseball player to hit four home runs in one game

Lowe, Edmund—**Moving Picture**—talking picture taken outdoors (full length)

Lowe, Thaddeus Sobieski Coulincourt—**Army Balloon Corps**

Lowe, Thaddeus Sobieski Coulincourt—**Gas**—water gas plant

Lowe, Thaddeus Sobieski Coulincourt—**Gas**—water gas production

Lowe, Thaddeus Sobieski Coulincourt—**Telegram**—telegram dispatched from an aerial station

Lowell, Francis Cabot—**Cotton Mill**—cotton mill in the world in which the whole process of cotton manufacturing from spinning to weaving was carried on by power

Lowell, Percival—**Astronomy**—planet

Lowrie, Mattie Pease—**Degrees (academic and honorary)**—Bachelor of Music degree

Lowry, Edward George—**Federal Alcohol Control Administration**

Lowry, Erwin Foster—**Konel**

Loy, Myrna—**Moving Picture**—talking picture

Lubcke, Harry R.—**Television—Telecast**—television images received in an airplane

Lucas, Fielding — **Medical Book** — ophthalmology book

Lucas, Robert—**Political Convention**—two-thirds rule

Luce, Stephen Bleecker—**Naval War College**—naval war college

Luckett, Hubert—**Photograph**—photograph of a beam of 1 billion-volt X-rays

Ludlow, Noah Miller—**Theater**—showboat

Ludlow, Roger—**Constitution**—Constitution

Luhring, Marie—**Woman**—woman automotive engineer

Luke, Frank—**Aviation—Aviator**—pilot to receive the Congressional Medal of Honor

Lukens, Charles—**Boiler Plates**

Lumbrozo, Jacob—**Physician**—Jewish doctor

Lunt, George Ashton—**Balloon**—balloon Atlantic crossing attempt

Lunt, H. R.—**Trapshooting**—trapshooting intercollegiate association

Lussier, Jean—**Niagara Falls**—person to go over Niagara Falls in a rubber ball

Lutter, Grover Cleveland—**Bicycle Traffic Court**

Lutz, Frank Eugene—**Museum**—outdoor museum (or nature trail)

Lutz, Isaac C.—**Monument**—monument to George Washington

Lykins, Johnston — **Periodical**—Indian-language monthly

Lyle, Alexander Gordon—**Dental Corps (U.S. Navy)**—admiral in the dental corps (U.S. Navy)

Lyle, Benjamin—**Hospital**—tuberculosis hospital (municipal) for consumptive poor

Lyle, Ethel Hedgeman—**Sorority**—Negro sorority

Lyman, Edward Hutchinson Robbins—**Theater**—municipal theater

Lyman, William—**Iron**—iron blast furnace

Lynch, Joe—**Radio Broadcast**—prize fight broadcast from the ringside

Lynch, John Roy—**Political Convention**—national nominating convention presided over by a Negro

Lynk, Vandahurst—**Medical Periodical**—Negro medical journal

Lyon, Edward L. T.—**Army Officer**—male nurse

Lyon, Frank Farrington—**Soilless Culture of Plants**—commercial hydroponicum (large)

Lyon, James—**Music Book**—music book by a native American

Lyon, Mary—**College**—college for women

Lyon, Matthew—**Congress (U.S.)—House of Representatives**—brawl

Lyon, Matthew—**Congressman (U.S.)**—congressman elected who served time in prison

M

Maas, J. C. W.—**Postal Service**—postage canceling machine patent

Mabie, Hamilton Wright—**Social Science Society (national)**

McAdoo, William Gibbs—**Railroad**—government operation of railroads

McAfee, Henry H.—**Forestry Society**—national forestry association

McAfee, Mildred Helen—**Naval Officer**—woman naval officer commissioned in the U.S. Naval Reserve

McAlister, Hill—**Enclave**—municipal enclave of economic ground rent

MacAllan, Jack—**Farriers' Course in a College**

McAllister, James W.—**Entomology Magazine**

McAllister, Ralph C.—**College Alumni Association**—college alumni association secretary (full-time paid position)

McAlpin, Harry—**News Correspondent**—Negro news correspondent accredited to the White House

McAnnally, David R.—**Journalism Course**—history of journalism course

MacArthur, Arthur — **Governor** — governor removed from office by a state supreme court

MacArthur, Douglas—**Army Officer**—generals to wear the five-star insignia

MacArthur, Douglas — **Medal** — Silver Star Army Medal awarded to a civilian

Macatee, Charles—**Aviation—Flights (transcontinental)** — jet passenger commercial transcontinental service

McBride, John—**Employment Service**—state employment service

McCabe, Lorenzo Dow—**President (U.S.)** —President to celebrate his silver wedding anniversary at the White House

McCaffery, Dominick F.—**Prize Fight**—prize fight of importance under the Marquis of Queensberry rules

McCarl, John Raymond—**Comptroller General of the United States**

McCarthy, George Lewis—**Check Photographing Device**

McCarthy, Joseph Vincent—**Baseball Manager**—baseball manager to win pennants in both leagues

McCarthy, William—**Air Mail Service**—air mail pilot

McClellan, Cyril Elwin—**Atomic Energy Commission**—Atomic Energy Commission Patent Compensation Board—award

McClellan, General George Brinton—**Army Ambulance Corps**

McClellan, General George Brinton—**Telegraph**—Army field telegraph used in warfare

McClellan, George Brinton — **Automobile Race**—transcontinental automobile race

McClintock, Miller — **Traffic Regulation Course**—graduate course in traffic engineering and administration

McCloskey, John—**Catholic Priest**—Catholic priest to be elevated to the cardinalate

McClure, Donald—**World War I**—American Army division to cross the Rhine River

McClure, Samuel Sidney—**Newspaper Syndicate**—newspaper syndicate to supply articles

McComb, John — **Lighthouse** — lighthouse built after American independence

McConnell, Joseph Christopher—**Aviation—Aviator**—American ace (triple jet) in Korea

McConnell, Matthew—**Brokerage**—stock exchange

McCoole, Mike—**Prize Fight**—international fight, with bare knuckles

McCormick, Charles H.—**Pharmacy College** —pharmacy college

McCormick, Cyrus Hall — **Reaper** — reaper that was practical

McCormick, Patricia—**Bull Fight**—woman bull fighter (professional)

McCormick, Robert Rutherford—**Newspaper** —illustrated tabloid

McCoy, George Walter—**Disease (distinctly American)**

McCoy, Michael Norman Wright—**Aviation —Flights (transatlantic)**—jet transatlantic non-stop flight west to east

McCoy, Tom—**Prize Fight**—prize fight fatality

McCracken, Henry Mitchell—**Hall of Fame** —hall of fame (university)

McCracken, Naomi M.—**Air Force Academy** —Air Force Academy woman officer

MacCracken, William Patterson—**Aviation— License**—pilot's license issued by the U.S. Department of Commerce

McCreary, Conn — **Television** — **Telecast** — sports event televised in color

McCulloch, Hugh—**Bank Legislation**—national banking system

McCulloch, Hugh—**Comptroller**—Comptroller of the Currency

McCullough, W. T.—**Garage** (public)

McCunn, Adia—**Wedding**—wedding broadcast

McCunn, Bertha Annie—**Wedding**—wedding broadcast

McCurdy, James A. D.—**Aviation**—airplane rescue at sea

McDaniel, Carl B.—**Aviation—Flights**—all-blind distance flight by the United States Army

McDaniel, Hattie—**Moving Picture Actor**— Negro to win an "Oscar"

McDermott, John J.—**Golf Champion**—golf champion (American born professional) to win the United States Open Tournament

McDermott, John J.—**Marathon Race (annual)**

MacDonald, Allan—**Ship**—concrete seagoing ship

Macdonald, Charles Blair—**Golf Course**— eighteen-hole golf course

Macdonald, Charles Blair—**Golf Tournament** —amateur golf tournament (official)

Macdonald, Charles Blair—**Golf Tournament** —amateur golf tournament (unofficial)

Macdonald, Charles Blair—**Golf Tournament** —national championship stroke-play golf match

MacDonald, Eleanor — **Submarine-Escape Training Tank**—women to take the submarine-escape test

McDonald, Harold Paul—**Photograph**—cystoscopic photographs in color

McDonald, J. B.—**Automobile**—electric storage battery automobile

McDonald, Marshall—**Aquarium**—aquarium (inland salt water)

McDonald, Marshall—**Fish and Fisheries Commissioner**

MacDonald, Ramsay — **Congress of the United States**—Prime Minister of England to address the Congress of the United States

MacDonald, Wilson—**Monument**—monument to an American poet

McDougall, Alexander—**War Veterans' Society**—Society of the Cincinnati

MacDowell, Edward—**Arts and Letters Society**—arts and letters society (national)

McDowell, Ephraim—**Surgical Operation**—abdominal operation

McDowell, Irvin—**Civil War**—serious engagement in the Civil War

McDowell, John Huber—**Theatrical School**—theater and dramatic criticism course

McDowell, Mary Lou—**Naval Officer**—woman to preside as law officer

McEachern, Archie—**Bicycle Race**—paired six-day bicycle race

McElroy, Mary—**Kidnapping**—death penalty for kidnapping

McEntire, George W. — **Aviation** — **Flights (transcontinental)** — transcontinental dirigible flight (non-rigid dirigible)

Macfadden, Bernarr — **Restaurant** — penny restaurant

McFarland, David Ford—**Helium**—helium

McFarland, Irene—**Caterpillar Club**—woman caterpillar club member

McFarland, Moses—**Aviation**—aeronautical patent

McFatrick, James D.—**Optometry Instruction**—optometry school

McGaffey, Ives W.—**Vacuum Cleaner**—suction-type vacuum cleaner

McGay, James—**Game Protection Society**

M'Geary, James—**Camp Meeting**

McGee, Anita Newcomb — **Army Nurse Corps (female)**

McGee, John—**Camp Meeting**

McGee, Walter H. — **Kidnapping** — death penalty for kidnapping

McGee, William—**Camp Meeting**

McGinnis, Knefler—**Aviation**—**Flights (transpacific)**—Honolulu squadron flight

McGivney, Michael Joseph—**Knights of Columbus**

McGovern, Vincent Howard — **Helicopter Flight**—helicopter transatlantic flight

McGowan, John—**Civil War**—act that marked the inauguration of the War of 1861-1865

MacGrath, Harold—**Moving Picture**—serial moving picture

McGrath, Paul—**Television**—**Telecast**—play to be televised with its original Broadway cast

McGraw, John Joseph—**Baseball Game**—world series baseball games to gross a million dollars

McIntyre, James Francis—**Catholic Priest**—Catholic cardinal whose see was west of the Rockies

Mackall, R. Covington — **Dental School** — dental college

Mackay, Clarence Hungerford — **Cable** — cable across the Pacific Ocean between Honolulu, Midway, Guam and Manila

Mackay, James—**Ship**—racing shell

McKean, Thomas — **Declaration of Independence (American)**—Declaration of Independence was first ordered "to be fairly engrossed on parchment"

McKean, Thomas—**President (U.S.)**—President elected

McKechnie, William — **Television — Telecast**—baseball games (major league) telecast

McKenzie, John—**Free Port**

Mackie, John—**Medal** — Medal of Honor awarded to a marine

McKim, Isaac—**Ship**—clipper ship

McKinley, Ashley C.—**Aviation**—**Flights**—South Pole flight

McKinley, William — **President (U.S.)** — President who had used a telephone for campaigning

McKinley, William—**Voting Machine**—voting machines for use in federal elections

McLaughlin, Frank — **Automobile Service Station**—drive-in service station

McLaurin, John Lowndes—**Senator (U.S.)**—senators censured

Maclay, William—**Congress (U.S.)**—**Senate**—Senate

McLean, Edith Eleanor—**Incubator for Infants**

McLean, James—**Insurance**—insurance rate standardization

McLean, James Sylvanus — **Piano** — piano patent

McLean, John—**Eye**—eye bank

McLean, John—**History Instruction**—ancient and modern history chair

McLoughlin, John — **Game Manufacturing Company**

Maclure, William—**Geological Society (national)**

Maclure, William—**Geology Book**—geology book

McMahan, John Wood—**Degrees (academic and honorary)**—Doctor of Philosophy in Accounting degree

McMath, Robert Reynolds—**Moving Picture**—moving picture of the sun

McMillan, Edwin Mattison—**Element**—element 93

McMillan, Edwin Mattison—**Element**—element 94

McNair, Alexander—**State**—state admitted to the Union west of the Mississippi River

McNair, Lesley James—**Medal**—Expert Infantryman's Badge

McNamee, Graham—**Radio Broadcast**—chain broadcast

McNamee, Graham — **Radio Broadcast**—political convention broadcast

McNamee, Graham—**Television**—**Telecast**—high-definition telecast

McNary, Charles Linza—**Television**—**Telecast**—political convention to be televised

McNeill, George E.—**Labor**—labor bureau (state)

McNish, George—**Presbyterian Presbytery**

McNutt, Paul Vories — **Federal Security Agency**

McNutt, Paul Vories—**Governor**—governor granted almost dictatorial power

McPherson, Eugene—**Bicycle Trip**—bicycle rider to cross the continent in less than three weeks

McPherson, John—**Directory** (city)

McQuiston, James—**Electric Power Plant**—municipally owned electric power plant

McRae, V. H.—**Phonograph Trade Magazine**

Marshall, George Catlett—**Army Officer**—generals to wear the five-star insignia

Marshall, George Catlett — **Medal** — Distinguished Service Medal (Army) awarded to a woman

Marshall, Humphry—**Botany Book**—botany book strictly American

Marshall, James Wilson—**Gold**—gold discovered in California

Marshall, John—**Commerce Case**

Marshall, John—**Supreme Court (U.S.) Decision**—Supreme Court decision establishing the power of the United States

Marshall, John Sayre—**Dental Corps (U.S. Army)**—Dental Corps of the U.S. Army

Marshall, Lois I. Kimsey—**Vice President of the United States**—Vice President's widow to receive a pension

Marshall, Roy Kenneth — **Planetarium** — planetarium owned by a university

Marshall, Thomas Riley—**Vice President of the United States**—vice president's widow to receive a pension

Marston, Sarah H.—**Missionary Society**—foreign missionary society organized by women

Martell, Charles Bowling—**Ship**—guided missile cruiser

Martell, Belle—**Woman**—woman prize fight referee (licensed)

Martin, Charles—**Photograph**—photographs taken under the sea in natural colors

Martin, David H.—**United Christian Party**

Martin, Edwin—**Play (drama)**—play given by non-professional actors

Martin, Glenn Luther—**Aviation—Flights**—over-water round trip flight

Martin, Henry—**Brick Machine**

Martin, Henry Newell—**Physiological Society**—physiological society (national organization)

Martin, John—**Actor**—actor of American birth

Martin, John—**Colonial Government**—colonial council in America

Martin, Joseph—**Ship**—clipper ship

Martin, Keith—**Art Course**—industrial camouflage course

Martin, Riccardo — **Opera** — opera by an American composer performed at the Metropolitan Opera House of New York

Martin, Truman J.—**Insurance**—automobile insurance policy

Martin, William—**Bicycle Race**—international six-day bicycle race

Martinelli, Giovanni — **Moving Picture** — talking picture

Mary, John—**Grammar**—French grammar

Mason, Eben—**Veterinary School**—veterinary college of importance

Mason, Edith—**Opera**—opera broadcast over a national network from an American opera house

Mason, Ellen H. B.—**Missionary Society**—foreign missionary society organized by women

Mason, George Thompson—**War (Mexican)**—Mexican war shots

Mason, John—**Street Car**—street car company

Mason, Leonard—**Wrestling**—intercollegiate wrestling association

Mason, Lowell—**Music Instruction**—music instruction (public school)

Mason, Lowell—**Music Instruction**—musical pedagogy school

Maspero, Pierre—**Free Lunch**—free lunch

Massasoit—**Treaty**—colonial treaty with the Indians

Massey, John—**Fox Hunting Club**

Masters, Thomas—**Patent**—English patent granted to a resident of America

Matas, Rudolph—**Anesthesia**—spinal anesthesia report

Matchett, Charles Horatio—**Socialist Labor Party of North America**

Matheny, William A.—**Aviation—Flights**—all blind distance flight by the United States Army

Mather, Cotton—**Bibliography**—bibliography of theological and biblical literature

Mather, Cotton—**Paleontology Report**

Mather, Increase—**Degrees (academic and honorary)**—doctor of sacred theology degree

Mather, Ralph — **Swedenborgian or New Church**—Swedenborgian or New Church Temple

Mather, Samuel — **Corporation** — corporate body

Mathews, George — **Telephone** — telephone conversation (commercial) using electricity generated by the sun's rays

Mathews, Henry Mason—**Strike**—strike in which federal troops were called in peacetime

Mathews, James—**Farmers' Institute**—farmers' institute held by a land grant agricultural college off its campus

Mathewson, Christy—**Hall of Fame**—hall of fame (baseball)

Matlack, Charles F.—**Medical Society**—homeopathic medical society

Matthews, Annabel—**Woman**—woman tax appeals board member

Matthews, Clarence—**Football Game**—football game between Negro colleges

Matthews, Edmund O.—**Torpedo**—torpedo manufacturing station

Matthews, John — **Soda Water Machine Manufacturer**

Matthews, Thomas—**Bridge Whist Rule Book**

Matzmulla, Zun Zow—**Naval Academy**—Japanese midshipman in the United States Naval Academy

Mauchly, John W. — **Computer**—electronic computer

Maugham, Russell Lowell — **Aviation — Flights (transcontinental)**—transcontinental flight within 24 hours

Maury, James—**Diplomatic Service**—consuls of the United States appointed after the adoption of the Constitution

Miller, George—**Evangelical Conference**

Miller, George J.—**Automobile Race**—automobile race from New York to Paris

Miller, Gerrit Smith—**Football Club**—football club

Miller, Mrs. Hugh—**Television**—**Telecast**—play to be televised

Miller, James Arthur—**Tape Recording**—radio broadcast from a tape recording

Miller, James Francis—**Bankers' Association**—bankers' association formed by a state group

Miller, James M.—**Catholic Magazine**—Catholic magazine in English

Miller, John—**State**—states admitted to the Union simultaneously

Miller, John MacDonald—**Air Mail Service**—autogiro mail delivery regular service

Miller, John MacDonald—**Autogiro**—autogiro to loop the loop publicly

Miller, John MacDonald—**Autogiro**—autogiro to tow a glider

Miller, John MacDonald—**Autogiro**—transcontinental autogiro flight

Miller, Lewis—**Chautauqua Organization**

Miller, Lewis—**College**—college summer school

Miller, Mary P.—**Aviation**—**Airship**—woman airship passenger

Miller, Max—**Air Mail Service**—air mail regular service

Miller, Robert F.—**Radio Contest**

Miller, T. G.—**Telephone**—round-the-world telephone conversation

Milley, Samuel H.—**Army Officer**—chaplain (Catholic) of the United States Army

Millholland, James—**Bridge**—tubular plate girder bridge

Millikan, Robert Andrews—**Cosmic Ray**

Milliken, John F.—**Boat Race**—international lifeboat race

Milling, Thomas de Witt—**Aviation**—**Airplane**—airplane outfitted with a machine gun

Mills, Anson—**Cartridge Belt Patent**

Mills, Clark—**Monument**—bronze equestrian statue

Mills, Hiram Francis—**Water Purification**—municipal filtration system

Mills, Robert—**Atlas**

Mills, Robert—**Building**—building of fireproof construction

Mills, Robert H.—**Dental Corps (U.S. Army)**—Army Dental Corps Major General

Milnor, George Sparks—**Grain Stabilization Corporation**

Milton, Jefferson Davis—**Border Patrol**—border patrolman

Mindell, Fania—**Medical Clinic**—birth control clinic

Miner, Roy Waldo—**Coral Reef Barrier**

Mingus, Nathan—**Freemasons**—Negro masonic lodge

Minot, Charles—**Telegraph**—telegraph in railroading

Minot, George Dexter—**Engineering Society**—engineering society

Minuit, Peter—**Swedes**

Miske, Billy—**Radio Broadcast**—prize fight broadcast

Miskey, John A.—**Squash Racquets Champion**—squash racquets champion

Mitchel, John Purroy—**Telephone**—transcontinental telephone demonstration

Mitchel, Ormsby MacKnight—**Astronomy Magazine**

Mitchell, Charles Lewis—**Legislator (state)**—Negro representatives to sit in any state legislature

Mitchell, Harold E.—**Rocket**—space capsule recovered in mid-air from an orbiting satellite

Mitchell, Margaret—**Television**—**Telecast**—moving picture premiere festivities to be televised

Mitchell, Maria—**Arts and Science Society**—woman elected to the American Academy of Arts and Sciences

Mitchell, Matthew—**Election**—election in defiance of the Royal Courts

Mitchell, Noel—**Aviation**—hydroplane commercial line service

Mitchell, Rose—**Baseball Team**—women's baseball team

Mitchell, Samuel Augustus—**Entomology Book (comprehensive)**

Mitchell, Samuel Weir—**Physiological Society**—physiological society (national organization)

Mitchell, Virne Beatrice (Jackie)—**Baseball Player**—woman baseball pitcher

Mitchell, Wesley Clair—**National Planning Board (U.S.)**

Mitchill, Samuel Latham—**Agriculture Professor**

Mitchill, Samuel Latham—**Medical Periodical**—medical magazine

Mitchill, Samuel Latham—**Pharmacopoeia**—pharmacopoeia prepared by a hospital staff

Miyamura, Hiroshi Hershey—**Medal**—Medal of Honor awarded to a Nisei in the Korean War

Moedy, Henry—**Book Auction**

Moffat, John L.—**Mint (U.S.)**—private mint authorized by the United States Government

Moffett, James Andrew—**Emergency Housing Corporation (U.S.)**

Mokarzel, Naoum Anthony—**Newspaper**—Arabic daily newspaper

Moley, Raymond—**Community Trust**

Molis, William—**Button**—buttons of fresh water pearl

Moller, John C.—**Music**—music publishers (exclusive)

Mollison, Amy Johnson—**Aviation**—**Aviator**—woman aviator to fly across the Atlantic Ocean east to west

Mollison, Irving Charles—**Judge**—Negro judge of a customs court (U.S.)

Mollison, James Allan—**Aviation**—**Flights (transatlantic)**—transatlantic solo westward flight

Morris, Joshua H.—**Insurance**—title guaranty insurance company

Morris, Kate Eugenia—**Degrees (academic and honorary)**—Doctor of Philosophy degree awarded to a woman by a women's college

Morris, Nelson—**Animals**—cattle exportation to Great Britain

Morris, Robert—**Congress (U.S.)—Senate**—Senate

Morris, Robert—**Flag**—American flag

Morris, Robert—**Mint (U.S.)**—Mint of the United States

Morris, T. A.—**Railroad Station**—union passenger station

Morris, William—**Photograph**—photograph of a beam of 1 billion-volt X-rays

Morris, William E.—**Cotton**—cotton acreage reduction payment

Morrison, Effie—**Old Age Colony**

Morrison, Herbert—**Radio Broadcast**—recorded coast-to-coast broadcast

Morrison, Hugh Alexander—**Almanac**—almanac bibliography

Morrison, Sarah Parke—**College**—state university to grant equal privileges to women

Morrison, William — **Automobile** — electric storage battery automobile

Morrison, William Newton—**Dentistry**—gold crown tooth

Morrison, William Ralls—**Interstate Commerce Act**

Morschauser, Joseph—**Newspaper**—composograph photograph in a newspaper

Morse, Jedidiah—**Gazetteer**—American gazetteer

Morse, Jedidiah—**Geography**

Morse, Samuel Finley Breese—**Art Organization**—artists' society of importance

Morse, Samuel Finley Breese—**Cable**—cable

Morse, Samuel Finley Breese—**Cable**—submarine telegraph cable that was practical

Morse, Samuel Finley Breese—**Photograph**—photograph taken in the United States

Morse, Samuel Finley Breese—**Telegram**—telegram inaugurating commercial service

Morse, Samuel Finley Breese—**Telegraph**—telegraph station

Mortimore, Alice—**Public School**—public school classes for epileptic children

Morton, George—**Skimobile**

Morton, George Arthur—**Electron Tube**

Morton, Julius Sterling — **Holiday**—Arbor Day

Morton, Ladislaus — **Microscope** — electron microscope

Morton, Levi Parsons—**Accountancy Law (state)**

Morton, Nathaniel—**History**—history of New England

Morton, Samuel George—**Cranioscopy Book**—published

Morton, Sarah Wentworth Apthorp—**Novel**—American novel published in America

Morton, Thomas—**Cod Liver Oil**

Morton, Thomas—**Deportation**

Morton, Thomas George—**Anti-Vivisection Society**

Morton, William James—**X-Ray**—X-ray of the entire body of a living person

Moscona, Nicola—**Television—Telecast**—opera (complete) to be televised from the Metropolitan Opera House

Mosher, Jesse Montgomery—**Hospital**—psychiatric ward

Mosher, William Eugene—**Citizenship and Public Affairs School**

Moskovics, Fred Evans—**Automobile Race Track** — automobile speedway (board track)

Moss, Emma Sadler—**Medical Society**—woman president of a major medical society

Moss, Isaac M.—**Bridge Whist Rule Book**

Mott, John—**Money**—trade tokens

Mott, Lucretia—**Woman Suffrage**—convention of women advocating woman suffrage

Mott, Lucretia—**Woman Suffrage**—woman suffrage associations (national)

Mott, William—**Money**—trade tokens

Moulton, Frances Estelle—**Bank**—national bank woman president

Mouton, Carolyn Anne—**Siamese Twins**—Siamese twins separated successfully by surgery

Mouton, Catherine Anne—**Siamese Twins**—Siamese twins separated successfully by surgery

Mudd, Stuart—**Blood Bank**—blood serum (human) (dried)

Mudge, Genevra Delphine — **Automobile Driver (woman)**

Muehlenberg, Henry Melchior—**Lutheran Church**—Lutheran services in English

Muench, Carl Gebhard—**Sound-Absorbing Material**

Muhlenberg, Frederick Augustus Conrad—**Congress (U.S.)—House of Representatives**—House of Representatives

Muhlenberg, Frederick Augustus Conrad—**Congress (U.S.)—House of Representatives**—Speaker of the House

Muhlenberg, William Augustus—**Vacation Fund**

Mühlmann, Adolph — **Opera** — opera composed by a woman performed at the Metropolitan Opera House

Mullanphy, Bryan—**Travelers Aid**

Mulliken, Samuel—**Patent**—patentee to obtain more than one patent

Mulzac, Hugh—**Ship**—merchant ship of the U.S. commanded by a Negro captain

Mumford, Stephen—**Baptist Church**—Seventh Day Baptist Church

Mumford, William Bruce—**Treason**—citizen of the United States to be tried for treason, convicted and hanged

Mundt, Karl Earl—**Television—Telecast**—split-screen image

Munemori, Nawa—**Medal**—Medal of Honor awarded to a Nisei

Munemori, Sadao S. — **Medal** — Medal of Honor awarded to a Nisei

Munk, Max Michael—**Wind Tunnel**—wind tunnel of variable air density

Munroe, C. K.—**Bicycle Society**—bicycle society (national organization)

Munsey, Frank Andrew—**Periodical**—all-fiction pulp magazine

Munters, Georg—**Refrigerator**—gas refrigerator (household)

Muraille, Jacques Hector Nicholas Joubert de la. *See* Joubert de la Muraille, Jacques Hector Nicholas

Muratore, Lucien—**Opera**—opera broadcast in its entirety by a professional cast

Murdock, Jacob M.—**Automobile Transcontinental Trip**—transcontinental family automobile trip requiring only a month

Murphy, Charles Minthorn—**Bicycle Racer**—bicycle racer

Murphy, Charles W.—**Employment Service**—state employment service

Murphy, Edgar Jackson—**Element**—element 87

Murphy. Isaac—**Horse Race**—horse race (American Derby)

Murray, George Evelyn Pemberton—**Telephone**—transatlantic telephone service

Murray, Hannah L.—**Kindergarten**—nursery school

Murray, James—**Workmen's Compensation**—workmen's compensation lawsuit

Murray, Marie—**Moving Picture**—moving picture with a plot

Murray, Walter—**Opera** — opera performed by a professional visiting troupe

Murray, Walter — **Play (drama)** — benefit performance

Murray, Walter — **Play (drama)** — Shakespearean play

Murray, Walter—**Theatrical Advance Publicity Man**

Musial, Stan (Stanley Frank Musial)—**Baseball Player**—baseball player to win the Most Valuable Player Award three times

Musick, Edwin Charles—**Aviation—Airplane**—transport airplane designed especially for transoceanic service

Musick, Edwin Charles—**Air Mail Service**—Pacific air mail flight

Musser, John Herr—**Medical Instruction**—medical research chair

Mustin, Henry Croskey—**Aviation—School**—naval air training school

Muths, Johann Cristoph Friedrich Guts—**Gymnastics Book**

Muybridge, Eadweard—**Photograph**—photograph showing action (not moving pictures)

Myer, Albert James—**Army**—signal corps

Myer, Albert James—**Weather Bureau (U.S.)**

Myer, Henry B.—**Sleeping Car**—sleeping car patent

Myerhofer, "Swede" — **Aviation—Airport**—airport municipally owned

Myers, Edward—**World War II**—American ship sunk by a U-boat

Myers, Henry—**Strike**—union strike benefit

Myers, Jacob H.—**Voting Machine**—voting machines were authorized

Myers, John — **Aviation—Airplane**—rocket airplane (military)

N

Nagel, Charles—**Chamber of Commerce**—Chamber of Commerce of the United States of America

Nagel, Conrad—**Theater**—municipally owned and operated summer theater-in-the-round

Naismith, James—**Basketball**—basketball

Naismith, James—**Basketball Rules**—basketball rule book

Nancrède, Paul Joseph Guérard de—**Catholic Magazine**—Catholic magazine

Nanney, J. P.—**Electrical Contract**

Nash, Gary—**Tennis Match**—intercollegiate court tennis match

Nash, James H.—**Congress of the Confederate states**

Nash, Simon Augustine—**Court**—domestic relations court

Nasmyth, James—**Pile Driver**—steam pile driver patent

Nason, J.—**Railroad Crossing Gate Patent**

Nason, James H.—**Coffee Percolator Patent**

Nason, Joseph—**Heating System**—heating system (steam)

Nast, Thomas—**Cartoon**—Democratic cartoon

Nast, Thomas—**Cartoon**—Republican cartoon

Naugle, Harry Merrill—**Building**—building of pressed structural steel

Neal, Roy — **Television — Telecast** — color coast-to-coast telecast from the West Coast

Neale, Thomas—**Postal Service**—parliamentary act to establish a post office

Neel, Carr Baker—**Tennis Match**—lawn tennis champions who were brothers

Neel, Samuel R.—**Tennis Match**—lawn tennis champions who were brothers

Neeley, Richard Cox—**Aviation—Flights**—North Pole jet crossing

Neff, Mary—**Woman**—heroine

Neff, Pat Morris — **Court** — state supreme court composed entirely of women

Neiligan, Raymond J.—**Telephone**—dial telephone service coast-to-coast without the aid of operators

Nelson, C. Alexander—**Library Society**—library society (local)

Nelson, Christian K.—**Eskimo Pie**

Nelson, Erik Henning—**Aviation—Flights**—New York-Alaska flight

Nelson, Erik Henning—**Aviation—Flights (world)**—world flight

Nelson, Frankie—**Bicycle Race**—women's six-day bicycle race

Nelson, Murray—**Sanitary District**

Nelson, Ray—**Television—Telecast**—musical comedy (full-length) written especially for television

Nerinck, Charles—**Convent**—Catholic convent to admit colored women as sisters

Nesbitt, John Maxwell—**Insurance**—life insurance

Neuberger, Maurine Brown — **Legislator (state)**—husband and wife simultaneously elected to both chambers of a state legislature

Neuberger, Richard Lewis — **Legislator (state)**—husband and wife simultaneously elected to both chambers of a state legislature

Neumann, Gustav Adolf—**Newspaper**—German daily newspaper

Newbold, Charles—**Plow**—plow patent

Newcombe, Don — **Baseball Game**—major league game in which the majority of the players on one team were Negroes

Newcombe, Henry—**Expedition**—expedition

Newell, William Allan—**Medical Legislation** — law (state) requiring serological blood tests of pregnant women

Newhouse, Sewell — **Traps** — steel animal traps

Newlands, Francis Griffith—**Silverites**

Newman, Philip James—**Wedding**—wedding in the United States Occupation Forces in Korea

Newman, Samuel—**Bible Concordance**

Newman, William—**Shoe Measuring Stick**

Newport, Christopher—**Colonial Government** —colonial council in America

Newport, Christopher — **Colonist** — English settlement in America (permanent)

Newton, Hubert Anson — **Weights and Measures Standardization** — national organization to improve systems of weights, measures, and moneys

Newton, John Thomas — **Ship** — frigate (American-built steam-driven) to cross the Atlantic Ocean

Newton, Maurice — **Air Mail Service** — air mail regular service

Newton, Mortimer W.—**Insurance**—health insurance law (state)

Ney, Karl Winfield—**Surgical Operation**—epileptic case treated by elevation of the skull cap

Neyhart, Amos Earl—**Automobile Driving Course**

Neyhart, Amos Earl—**Traffic Regulation Course**—teacher training course in "training traffic safety"

Ng, Yee Y.—**Hospital**—Chinese hospital

Nicholas, Samuel—**War (Colonial)**—marine engagement in battle

Nichols, Anna R. G.—**Patent Examiner**—woman patent examiner

Nichols, William—**Animals**—lion

Nicholson, Charles Ambrose—**Aviation—Flights**—airplane catapulted from a dirigible

Nicholson, Francis—**Capitol**

Nicholson, Francis—**Treason**—American colonist hanged for treason

Nicholson, L. A.—**Stadium**—school stadium

Nicholson, R. F.—**Ship**—battleship built on the Pacific coast

Nicholson, Samuel T.—**Union Reform Party**

Nicholson, William—**Conchology Report**

Nicholson, William—**File Factory**—file factory (machine cutting) to attain success

Nicola, Lewis—**Engineering Book**

Nicoll, Allardyce—**Theatrical School**—theater and dramatic criticism course

Nilsson, Christine—**Opera**—opera at the Metropolitan Opera House

Nimitz, Chester William—**Naval Officer**—naval officers to wear the five-star insignia

Nininger, Alexander Ramsey ("Sandy")—**Medal**—Medal of Honor awarded in World War II

Nitschmann, David—**Moravian Bishop**

Nixdorff, Charles Edward—**Euthanasia Society**

Nixon, John—**Declaration of Independence (American)**—Declaration of Independence was first read publicly

Nixon, Richard Milhous—**Flag**—Army flag (official)

Nixon, Richard Milhous—**Postage Stamp**—postage stamp to bear the likeness of a Vice President of the United States issued by a foreign country

Nixon, Richard Milhous—**Presidential Candidate**—presidential candidate debate series on television

Nixon, Richard Milhous—**Vice President of the United States**—Vice President to preside at a National Security Council meeting

Nixon, Richard Milhous—**Vice President of the United States**—Vice President to preside over a cabinet meeting

Noah, Manuel Mordecai—**Diplomatic Service**—Jewish diplomatic representative

Noah, Mordecai M.—**Trademark Lawsuit**—trademark controversy involving a newspaper

Noble, Silas—**Toothpick Manufacturing Machine Patent**

Nobles, Charles Edward—**Television-Telecast**—stratovision flight test

Noeggerath, Emil Jacob—**Medical Periodical** —medical periodical devoted to diseases of women and children

Nolan, Mae Ella—**Congressman (U.S.)**—congresswoman elected to serve in the place of her husband

Norcross, Leonard—**Diving Suit**—(practical) for submarine diving

Norcross, Otis—**Charity Board** (state)

Norman, J.—**Architectural Book**—architectural book printed in America

Normand, Mabel—**Moving Picture**—six-reel feature-length comedy

Norris, George William—**Farm Loan Board (federal)**

Norris, George William—**Legislature**—unicameral legislature (state)

North, Elisha—**Hospital**—eye infirmary

North, Elisha—**Medical Book**—typhus fever treatise

North, Simeon—**Factory Standardization of Production**

North, Simeon—**Pistol**—government contract for pistols

North, Stephen—**Pharmacy College**—pharmacy college

Norton, Charles Eliot—**Archaeological Society**—archaeological society (national)

Norton, John—**Latin Book**

Norton, Lewis Mills — **Cheese**—pineapple cheese

Norton, Mary Teresa—**Congress (U.S.)— House of Representatives**—congressional committee (woman chairman)

Norton, Mary Teresa — **Woman** — woman state committee chairman

Norton, Oliver Willcox—**Taps**

Norton, Thomas—**Nail Machine (Wire)**

Norton, William—**Glass Bead**

Norwood, William A.—**Skee Ball Alley**

Nova, Lou — **Television** — **Telecast** — prize fight to be televised

Novara, Franco—**Opera**—opera at the Metropolitan Opera House

Novella, Alba—**Moving Picture**—moving picture of a complete grand opera

Noville, George O.—**Aviation—Airplane**—airplane equipped with radio to cross the Atlantic Ocean

Novy, Frederick George—**Medical Instruction**—bacteriology courses in a college

Noyes, Enoch—**Comb Factory**

Nusbaum, Jesse Logan—**Anthropology Laboratory**

Nuthead, Dinah—**Woman**—woman printer

Nutt, Clifford Cameron—**Aviation—Flights**—New York-Alaska flight

Nutt, Emma M.—**Telephone Operator**—woman telephone operator

Nutting, Mary Adelaide—**Nurse**—nurse appointed to a university professorship

O

Oakley, Jessie—**Soap**—cakes of soap of uniform weight and individually wrapped

Oakman, Wheeler—**Moving Picture**—talking picture of more than 6,000 feet

Oaks, Orion O.—**Liquid Heat**

O'Bannon, Presley Neville—**Flag**—American flag flown over a fortress of the Old World

Oboler, Arch—**Moving Picture**—three-dimensional feature moving picture

O'Brien, Edmond—**Moving Picture**—three-dimensional feature moving picture produced and released by a major company

O'Brien, Jay—**Bobsled Competition**—four-man bob-team competition

O'Brien, Jeremiah—**Revolutionary War**—naval battle of the Revolution

O'Brien, John—**Revolutionary War**—naval battle of the Revolution

O'Brien, Parry—**Shot-Put**—shot-put toss over 60 feet

O'Brien, Thomas Charles—**National Union for Social Justice**

O'Brien, Thomas Charles—**Union Party**

O'Brine, Forest—**Aviation—Flights**—airplane endurance flight exceeding 400 hours

O'Callahan, Joseph Timothy—**Naval Officer**—chaplain to win a Congressional Medal of Honor

O'Connell, James F.—**Tattoo**—tattooed man

O'Connor, B. F.—**Fencing**—fencing league (national)

O'Connor, James Francis Thaddeus—**Federal Deposit Insurance Corporation**

O'Connor, W. Scott — **Fencing** — fencing league (national)

O'Conor, Charles—**Presidential Candidate**—presidential candidate who was a Catholic

Odlum, Mrs. Floyd Bostwick. *See* Cochran, Jacqueline

O'Donnell, Bertha — **Deaf—Transmission**—visible and oral communication by the deaf over distance

Oelrichs, Mrs. Hermann—**Automobile Parade**

Ofeldt, F. W.—**Motor Boat**—motor boat pleasure craft

Ogden, Aaron—**Commerce Case**

Ogle, Henry—**Reaper**—reaper that actually worked

Ogle, Samuel—**Horse** — horse (thoroughbred)

Oglethorpe, James Edward — **Moravian Church**

O'Hare, Edward Henry—**Aviation—Aviator**—naval ace in World War II

O'Hern, Michael W.—**Kidnapping**—death penalty for kidnapping

Ohi, K. Elizabeth—**Lawyer**—Japanese woman lawyer

Ohmart, Philip Edwin—**Battery**—battery to convert radioactive energy into electrical energy

Oland, Warner—**Moving Picture**—talking picture

Olcott, Henry Steele—**Theosophical Society**

Old, Archie J.—**Aviation—Flights (world)**—jet round-the-world non-stop flight

Olds, Robin—**Aviation—Flights (transcontinental)**—transcontinental round-trip airplane flight within one day

Oliver, Anna—**Theological School**—theological school to admit women

Oliver, Henry Kemble—**Labor**—labor bureau (state)

Oliver, Robert Shaw—**Tennis**—lawn tennis

Oliver, Robert Shaw—**Tennis Society**—tennis society (national)

Oliver, Robert T.—**Dental Corps (U.S. Army)**—Dental Corps of the U.S. Army

Olson, Carl ("Bobo")—**Television—Telecast**—prize fight televised coast-to-coast

Olson, John—**Fuller's Earth**

O'Meara, Jack—**Aviation—Flights**—"airplane train"

O'Meara, Jack—**Aviation—Flights**—sky-train international round-trip flight

O'Meara, Jack—**Radio Telephone**—two-way conversation between a glider and the land

Omlie, Phoebe Fairgrave—**Aviation**—**License**—pilot's license granted to a woman by the U.S. Dept. of Commerce

Omlie, Phoebe Fairgrave—**Aviation**—**Races**—airplane race (of importance) in which both men and women were contestants

O'Neall, Belton—**Workmen's Compensation**—workmen's compensation lawsuit

Opper, Frederick Burr—**Periodical**—comic books

Oram, James—**Business Publication**

Orbach, Harold—**Television**—**Telecast**—Jewish temple services (complete) to be televised

O'Reilly, Samuel F.—**Tattoo**—electric tattoo machine

O'Rielly, Henry—**Telegraph**—telegraph convention (national)

Ormandy, Eugene—**Television**—**Telecast**—symphonic concerts to be televised

Ormsby, Waterman L.—**Patent**—design patent

Orr, Hugh—**Spinning, Carding, and Roping Machines**

Orr, Robert—**Arsenal**

Orr, Robert—**Ordnance**—muskets

Orr, William—**Paper**—wood-pulp and rag paper

Orton, Edward—**Ceramics School**

Osborn, Charles — **Newspaper** — abolition newspaper

Osborn, Frank P.—**Telephone**—dial telephone service coast-to-coast without the aid of operators

Osborn, James Butler—**Submarine**—ballistic missile submarine

Osborn, James Butler—**Submarine**—submerged submarine to fire a Polaris missile

Osborne, Harold M.—**Olympic Games**—American decathlon champion

Osborne, Ralph—**Medal**—Medal of Honor awarded to a Nisei in the Korean War

Osborne, Richard—**Bridge**—iron truss bridge

Osgood, George—**Yacht Race**—yacht race across the Atlantic Ocean

Osgood, Samuel—**Cabinet of the United States**—cabinet

Osgood, Samuel — **Postmaster**—postmaster general of the United States

Osler, William — **Medical Clinic**—medical clinic (general)

Ossoli, Marchioness. *See* Fuller, Margaret

Osterhaus, Hugo — **Aviation** — **Expositions and Meets**—aeronautic international exposition

Osterheld, G.—**Hat Blocking and Shaping Machine**

Osterhoudt, J.—**Cans**—can (tin) with a key opener

Ostermeier, Johannes—**Photography**—photographic flashlight lamps

O'Sullivan, Humphrey—**Rubber**—rubber heel

Otis, Bass—**Lithograph**

Otis, Elisha Graves—**Elevator**—elevator with completely enclosed car

Otis, Elisha Graves—**Elevator**—elevator with safety devices

Otis, William S.—**Steam Shovel**

Ott, Elsie S.—**Medal**—Air Medal (U.S.) awarded to a woman

Ott, Fred—**Copyright**—motion picture film copyrighted

Ott, Fred—**Moving Picture**—moving picture "close-up"

Otterbein, Philip William—**Church of the United Brethren in Christ**

Otto, Dr.—**Cottonseed Oil**

Otto, John Conrad—**Medical Book**—hemophilia treatise

Outcault, Richard Felton — **Newspaper** — newspaper Sunday comic section

Outerbridge, Mary Ewing—**Tennis**—lawn tennis

Ovington, Earl Lewis—**Air Mail Service**—air mail pilot

Owen, Marie—**Police**—policewoman to be appointed

Owen, Robert—**Communistic Society**—communistic non-religious settlement

Owen, Robert—**Printing Instruction**—printing instruction

Owen, Ruth Bryan—**Diplomatic Service**—woman diplomat to represent the United States in the capacity of a minister

Owen, William D.—**Immigration**—immigration bureau superintendent

Owens, Jesse—**Olympic Games**—American athlete to win four prizes at the Olympic games

Owens, Michael Joseph—**Glass Blowing Machine**

P

Pace, Frank—**War (Korean)**—Korean war hero buried in Arlington Cemetery

Pacelli, Eugenio. *See* Pius XII, Pope

Pacheco, Mr. — **Advertisement** — advertisement to occupy a half-page

Pacheco, Mr.—**Automaton**—automaton

Packard, Sophia Booker—**Nursing School**—training school for Negro nurses

Page, Albert B.—**Diathermy Machine**

Page, Charles Grafton—**Locomotive**—electric locomotive

Page, George—**Plow**—plow for pulverizing the soil

Page, James—**Ice Skating Club**—ice skating club

Page, John Wallace—**Wire**—woven wire fence industry

Page, Joseph—**Planetarium**—planetarium or orrery

Paget, Percy Wright—**Radio Broadcast**—transatlantic radio signal

Paine, Cassius M.—**Bridge Whist Organization**

Paine, John Knowles—**Music Instruction**—college music chair

Paine, John Knowles—**Oratorio**—oratorio by an American

Paine, John Knowles — **Symphony**—symphonic work by an American composer

Painter, William—**Bottle Cap**

Palfrey, William—**Diplomatic Service**—consul to die in service

Palisan, Johann—**Astronomy**—planet (asteroid) named for an American President

Palm, Joseph Henry Louis de, Baron—**Crematory**—crematory

Palmer, Mr. — **Baptist Church** — Baptist church (Negro)

Palmer, Benjamin F.—**Leg (artificial) patent**

Palmer, Daniel David—**Chiropractic School**

Palmer, Daniel David—**Chiropractor**

Palmer, John F.—**Bicycle Tire**—bicycle tire (cord)

Palmer, John McAuley—**Labor Law**—women's equal employment legislation

Palmer, Nathaniel Brown—**Discovery**—discovery of Antarctica

Palmer, Potter—**Hotel**—fireproof hotel

Palmer, Volney B.—**Advertising Agency**

Palmerton, John—**Boat Club**—boat club

Palmerton, Thomas—**Boat Club**—boat club

Pandit, Shrimati Vijaya Lakshmi—**Diplomatic Service**—woman ambassador from a foreign country

Pangborn, Clyde—**Aviation**—**Flights (transpacific**—transpacific non-stop flight

Paraf, Alfred—**Oleomargarine**—oleomargarine manufacturer (successful)

Pardee, Charles Laban—**Heresy Trial**

Park, James Alan—**Insurance Treatise**

Park, Jesse K.—**Envelope**—envelope machine patent

Park, Roswell—**Cancer Laboratory**

Park, Thomas—**Library**—library building (university)

Park, William Hallock—**Antitoxin Laboratory**

Park, William Hallock—**Vaccine**—tuberculosis vaccine

Parker, Dr.—**Madstone**

Parker, Angie — **Baseball Team**—women's baseball team

Parker, Benjamin Clarke Cutler—**Church**—floating church

Parker, Bruce—**Water Ski Tournament (national)**

Parker, Charles Wallace—**Carrousel**—carrousel with the jumping horse mechanism

Parker, Charles Wallace—**Shooting Gallery (mechanized)**

Parker, Ely Samuel—**Indians**—Indian Affairs Commissioner (U.S.) who was an Indian

Parker, James—**Crime Prevention and Detection**—interstate crime pact

Parker, James—**Music Book**—music book printed from type

Parker, Joel—**Labor Party (political)**—labor party (national)

Parker, John—**Revolutionary War**—armed conflict in the Revolutionary War

Parker, Joseph—**Blotting Paper**

Parker, Samuel—**Leather**—leather-splitting machine

Parker, Willard — **Health Board**—health board (municipal) armed with sufficient powers

Parker, Willard — **Medical Clinic**—college medical clinic

Parker, William T.—**Carrousel**—carrousel with the jumping horse mechanism

Parks, Benjamin—**Naval Officer**—naval chaplain (Continental Navy)

Parks, Charles Henry—**Naval Officer**—naval chaplain who was Catholic

Parks, William—**Cook Book**—cook book

Parks, William—**Fencing Book**

Parks, William — **Newspaper** — newspaper published south of the Potomac River

Parmelee, DuBois D.—**Adding Machine**—adding machine to employ depressible keys

Parmelee, Henry S.—**Sprinkler**—sprinkler head

Parmelee, Philip—**Aviation**—airplane merchandise shipment

Parmelee, Philip O. — **Aviation**—**Airplane Bombing**—airplane bombing experiment with explosives

Parmly, Eleazar—**Dental Magazine**—dental journal

Parmly, Eleazar—**Dental Society**—dental society (local)

Parmly, Eleazar—**Dental Society**—dental society of importance

Parnell, Garvey—**Senator (U.S.)**—woman elected to the Senate

Parnell, Thomas—**Music**—secular song

Parr, George—**Cricket Tournament**—international cricket tournament

Parrish, Donald E.—**Moving Picture**—talking picture in Esperanto

Parrish, Samuel L.—**Golf Club**—golf association (national)

Parrott, William Pearce—**Engineering Society**—engineering society of importance

Parry, Will H.—**Federal Trade Commission**—Federal Trade Commission

Parsons, Harry de Berkeley—**Voting Machine Commission (state)**

Parsons, James Benton—**Judge**—Negro judge of a District Court (U.S.)

Parsons, John E.—**Hospital**—cancer hospital

Parsons, Le Roy Edward—**Television**—community television antenna system

Partridge, Alden — **Engineering College** — civil engineering course

Partridge, Alden—**Military School**—military school

Pastorius, Francis Daniel—**Slavery**—slavery protest

Pastorius, Francis Daniel — **Theological Treatise**

Patch, Rex—**Radio Broadcast**—speaker to address an organization by radio

Paton, Richard Townley—**Eye**—eye bank

Patrick, J. T.—**Enclave**—municipal enclave of economic ground rent

Patrick, Mason Mathews—**American Expeditionary Force**—American Expeditionary Force Air Service chief

Patt, Arthur P.—**Insurance**—health insurance law (state)

Patten, Richard—**Observatory**—observatory (national)

Patterson, John Clarke—**Archival Administration**

Patterson, Joseph Medill—**Newspaper**—illustrated tabloid

Patterson, William — **Gas** — gas ordinance (city)

Pattison, Edward—**Tinware Manufacturers**—tinware manufacturers

Pattison, William—**Tinware Manufacturers**—tinware manufacturers

Paul, Almarin B.—**Silver Mill**

Paul, Oglesby—**Trapshooting**—trapshooting intercollegiate association

Paul, William M.—**Navy**—naval militia (state)

Paulding, James Kirke—**History**—comic history of the United States

Paulhan, Louis—**Aviation**—**Aviator**—aviator (American) to establish an altitude record

Paulhan, Louis—**Aviation**—**Expositions and Meets**—aviation meet

Paulsen, Carl Christian von—**World War II**—German ship captured in World War II

Paxton, Donald—**Building**—commercial building heated by the sun

Paxton, John—**Moving Picture**—moving picture presented simultaneously in major cities throughout the world

Payne, William Harold—**Pedagogy Chair**—pedagogy chair (permanent)

Payson, Henry—**Gas**—gas ordinance (city)

Peabody, Amelia — **Building** — house completely sunheated

Peabody, Elizabeth Palmer—**Kindergarten**—American kindergarten

Peake, Mary S.—**School**—Negro school for freedmen

Peale, Franklin—**Archery Club**—archery club

Peale, Norman Vincent—**Television**—**Telecast**—husband and wife to broadcast a religious program

Peale, Rembrandt—**Gas**—gas company

Peale, Rembrandt—**Museum**—museum especially constructed as a museum and art gallery

Peale, Ruth—**Television**—**Telecast**—husband and wife to broadcast a religious program

Peale, Titian Ramsey—**Archery Club**—archery club

Pearce, Richard Mills—**Medical Instruction**—medical research chair

Pearson, Gerald Leondus—**Battery**—solar battery

Pearson, Humphrey—**Moving Picture**—talking picture entirely in color

Pearson, John—**Cloth**—cloth mill

Pearson, Leonard—**Animals**—cattle tuberculosis test

Pearson, Theodore—**Cracker Bakery**

Peary, Josephine—**Expedition**—polar expedition of which a woman was a member

Peary, Robert Edwin—**Discovery**—discovery of the North Pole

Peary, Robert Edwin — **Medal** — National Geographic Society gold medal

Pease, Daniel Chapin—**Photograph**—photograph of genes

Pease, Francis Gladheim—**Astronomer**—astronomer to measure the size of a fixed star

Pease, Titus—**Whips**

Peawa, William — **Indian Church** — Indian church organized by Indians

Peay, Austin—**Evolution Law (state)**

Peck, Frederick M.—**Rifle Association**—rifle association (national)

Peck, Gregory—**Moving Picture**—moving picture presented simultaneously in major cities throughout the world

Peek, George Nelson—**Bank**—Export-Import Bank

Peek, George Nelson—**Commercial Policy Executive Committee**

Peer, Lyle Hudson Bennett—**High Jumping Standards using electric eye detectors**

Peirce, Isaac—**Chemical Magazine**

Peirce, William—**Almanac**—almanac

Pelham, Peter—**Engraver**

Pelham, Peter—**Music**—concert

Pelham, Richard—**Minstrel Show Troupe**

Pellicier, Anthony Domenic Ambrose—**Catholic Bishop**—native bishops of the south

Pemberton, Bennett—**Road**—state road authorization

Pendergast, William Wirt — **Agricultural School**—vocational agricultural school

Penington, Henry—**Publishing Society**

Penman, Edward—**Golf Club**—golf club

Penn, William—**Law Book**

Penn, William—**Mennonites**—Mennonites

Pennant, Elias—**Expedition**—expedition

Pennell, Rebecca Mann—**College**—woman college professor

Pennell, Rebecca Mann—**Didactics Course**—didactics course in a college

Pennell, Rebecca Mann—**Hygiene Instruction**—physiology and hygiene courses

Penniman, Anson W.—**Blind**—state school for the blind

Pennock, Cyril—**Military School**—military school

Pennypacker, Samuel Whitaker—**Sterilization Legislation**

Pepperell, William — **Knighthood** — knighthood conferred on a native-born American for military leadership

Percy, Samuel R.—**Milk**—dried milk patent

Perham, Josiah—**Railroad Excursion**—railroad excursion rates

Perkings, Jay—**Health Laboratory**—health laboratory (state)

Perkins, Anthony—**Moving Picture**—moving picture presented simultaneously in major cities throughout the world

Picket, John W.—**Educational Magazine**—educational magazine

Picket, John W.—**Educational Magazine**—educational magazine to achieve success

Pierce, Bradford K.—**Manual Training**—industrial school for girls

Pierce, Clinton Albert—**World War II**—American general wounded in action in World War II

Pierce, Cyrus—**Normal School**—normal school (state)

Pierce, Franklin—**Court**—court of claims

Pierce, Franklin—**Fair**—industrial exposition

Pierce, George Foster—**College**—women's college chartered

Pierce, Hugh Franklin—**Air Mail Service**—rocket air mail flight

Pierce, R.—**Schoolbook**

Pierce, Roger—**Telephone**—mobile telephone conversation overseas

Pierson, Mr.—**Envelope Manufacturer**

Pierson, Henry L.—**Railroad Passenger**—railroad honeymoon trip

Pierson, Josiah Gilbert—**Rivet**

Pierson, Warren Lee—**Bank**—Export-Import Bank

Pietersen, Evert—**School**—evening school

Pike, Nicholas—**Algebra Book**—algebra book by a native American

Pike, Nicholas—**Birds**—sparrows

Pike, Sumner Tucker—**Atomic Energy Commission**—Atomic Energy Commission

Pilling, Samuel—**Building and Loan Association**

Pillsbury, Moody Adams—**Animals**—cattle (Guernsey cattle)

Pin, Chen Lan—**Chinese Embassy**

Pinchback, Pinckney Benton Stewart—**Governor**—Negro governor (acting)

Pinchot, Gifford—**Liquor Stores** (state)

Pinchot, Gifford—**Radio Facsimile Transmission**—photograph sent overland by radio to a distant point

Pinckney, Charles Cotesworth—**Museum**—public museum

Pinckney, Thomas—**Diplomatic Service**—ambassador to England

Pincus, Gregory—**Impregnation**—impregnation (artificial)

Pinkerton, Allan—**Army Secret Service Bureau**

Pintard, John Marsden—**Diplomatic Service**—consuls of the United States appointed after the adoption of the Constitution

Pinto, Isaac—**Jewish Prayer Book** published in the United States

Pipe, Captain—**Treaty**—treaty entered into by the United States with Indian tribes

Pipestem, George—**Indian Church**—Indian church organized by Indians

Pipkin, Marvin—**Electric Lighting**—electric lamp bulb frosted on the inside

Piquet, La Motte—**Flag**—American flag saluted by a foreign nation

Pitcairn, Harold Frederick—**Autogiro**—autogiro

Pitcairn, John—**Revolutionary War**—armed conflict in the Revolutionary war

Pitkin, Henry—**Clock**—watch made by machinery

Pitkin, James—**Clock**—watch made by machinery

Pitkin, Timothy—**History**—political history

Pitts, Hiram Abial — **Thresher** — threshing machine to employ steam

Pitts, John A.—**Thresher**—threshing machine to employ steam

Pius VI, Pope—**Catholic Bishop**—Catholic bishop appointed to serve in the United States

Pius XI, Pope—**Radio Facsimile Transmission**—photograph sent by radio across the Atlantic from Europe

Pius XII, Pope—**Visiting Celebrities**—pontiff

Place, Martha M.—**Execution**—execution of a woman

Plant, Joseph Theophilus Kirk—**Knights of Pythias**

Platen, Baltzar Carl von—**Refrigerator**—gas refrigerator (household)

Platt, Sarah M.—**Normal School**—woman principal of a normal school

Plaza Lasso, Galo—**President of a South American Country Born in the United States**

Plimpton, James Leonard—**Skating Rink**—roller skating rink (public)

Poe, Edgar Allan—**Detective Story**

Poell, George H.—**Medal**—Interstate Commerce Commission Medal of Honor

Polacco, Giorgio—**Opera**—opera broadcast in its entirety by a professional cast

Polacco, Giorgio—**Opera**—opera broadcast over a national network from an American opera house

Polk, James Knox—**Photograph**—photograph of a President (in office)

Polk, James Knox—**President (U.S.)**—President who was a "dark horse"

Pollak, Simon—**Blind**—school for the blind to adopt the Braille system

Pollard, Alfred William—**Microfilm**—book series microfilmed

Pollard, Edward—**Glass**—invisible glass installation

Pollard, Othello—**Animals**—leopard

Pollard, Thomas—**Hotel**—hotel to install bathrooms

Pomeroy, Dorothy—**Church**—children's church

Pomeroy, Vivian Towse — **Church** — children's church

Pond, H. Chester—**Clock**—watch movement to be electrically wound

Pool, Mr.—**Equestrian Exhibition**

Poole, Ernest—**Novel**—novel to win the Pulitzer prize in letters

Poole, William Frederick—**Periodical Index**

Pooley, Greville—**Breach of Promise Suit**

Poore, Benjamin Perley—**Congressional Directory**

Poore, Benjamin Perley—**Index of Government Publications**

Pope, Albert Augustus—**Bicycle Factory**

Ransom, Brayton Howard—**Zoological Laboratory (U.S.)** — zoological laboratory (U.S.) for the study of the parasites of livestock

Raphall, Morris Jacob—**Congress (U.S.)— House of Representatives**—Jewish rabbi to open the House of Representatives with prayer

Rapp, George—**Communistic Society**—communistic non-religious settlement

Ratcliffe, John — **Colonist** — English settlement in American (permanent)

Ratcliffe, John—**Colonial Government**—colonial council in America

Rathbone, Justus Henry—**Knights of Pythias**

Ratliffe, John—**Book Binder**

Ravdin, Isador Schwaner—**Television—Telecast**—surgical operation televised on a local program

Ravenscroft, Edward A.—**Bottle**—screw cap bottle with a pour lip

Rawle, Francis—**Insurance Book**—insurance proposal

Rawlins, Horace—**Golf Tournament**—open championship (official)

Rawson, Albert Leighton—**Freemasons**—Ancient Arabic Order of Nobles of the Mystic Shrine

Rawson, Edward — **Ordnance** — gunpowder mill

Ray, Charlotte E.—**Lawyer**—Negro woman lawyer

Ray, James Garrett—**Air Mail Service**—autogiro mail delivery direct to a post office

Ray, James Garrett—**Autogiro**—autogiro to land on the White House lawn

Ray, James Garrett—**Autogiro**—autogiro to land packages on a moving ship

Ray, Nat—**Horse Race**—harness horse race (Hambletonian) for three-year olds

Raymond, Eleanor—**Building**—house completely sunheated

Raymond, Julius—**Hospital**—Jewish hospital

Raymond, William—**Lifeboat**—lifeboat

Rea, Henry B.—**Horse Race**—harness horse race (Hambletonian) for three-year olds

Reach, Alfred James—**Baseball Player**—professional baseball player

Read, Albert Cushing—**Aviation—Flights (transatlantic)** — transatlantic hydroplane flight

Read, Daniel — **Music Magazine** — music magazine

Reading, Oliver Scott—**Camera**—aerial camera (nine-lens) for large-scale mapping

Ream, Vinnie (Mrs. Richard Leveridge Hoxie) — **Monument** — monument by a woman ordered by the U.S. Government

Ream, Vinnie (Mrs. Richard Leveridge Hoxie)—**Monument**—statue cast by the U.S. Government

Rechten, Philip—**Whaling**—whale-killing machine (electric)

Reckenzaun, Anthony—**Motor Boat**—storage battery motor boat

Reckenzaun, Frederick—**Motor Boat**—storage battery motor boat

Reddington, George—**Alligator Farm**

Redfield, William Charles—**Science Association**—scientific society (national organization)

Redfield, William Cox — **Commerce and Labor Department (U.S.)**

Redfield, William Cox—**Commerce Department (U.S.)**—Commerce Department (U.S.)

Redgrave, Gilbert Richard—**Microfilm**—book series microfilmed

Redpath, James—**Novel**—novel by a Negro

Reece, Ernest James—**Library Chair**

Reed, William Bradford—**History Instruction**—American history chair

Reeder, Alner—**Railroad Charter**

Reese, J. E.—**Wedding**—airplane wedding

Reese, James—**Slate**

Reese, Warren Snyder—**Lens**—plastic lens

Reese, William—**Slate**

Reeve, Tapping—**Law School**—law school

Regal, Betty — **Play (drama)** — burlesque show

Reichers, Lou—**Aviation—Flights**—airplane flight with an auto slung beneath the fuselage

Reid, John—**Architect**—landscape architect

Reid, John—**Radio Telephone**—military portable

Reilly, H. Christine—**Streptomycin**

Reinagle, Alexander—**Music Book**—secular song book

Reinecke, Mabel Gilmore—**Woman**—woman internal revenue collector

Reiner, Fritz — **Television** — **Telecast** — pay television presentation of an opera

Reinhardt, Aurelia Henry—**Unitarian Society**—woman moderator of the Unitarian Church

Remington, William H.—**Nickel Plating**

Remsen, Ira—**Saccharin**

Renick, Felix—**Animals**—cattle importation of purebred shorthorns

Renick, Felix—**Animals**—cattle (shorthorn) public auction sale

Reno, John—**Railroad Train Robbery**—railroad train robbery of a train in motion

Reno, Simeon—**Railroad Train Robbery**—railroad train robbery of a train in motion

Renoe, A. J.—**Fingerprint Society**—fingerprint society (international)

Renwick, James—**Brick**—terra cotta

Ressegue, H.—**Animals**—fur-bearing animals

Rettger, Leo Frederick—**Milk**—acidophilus milk

Reuss-Belce, Luisa—**Opera**—opera composed by a woman performed at the Metropolitan Opera House

Revel, Bernard—**Jewish College**—Jewish college of liberal arts and sciences under Jewish auspices

Revels, Hiram Rhodes—**Senator (U.S.)**—Negro senator

Reyburn, Robert—**Medical Society**—Negro medical society

Reyes, J. Antonio—**Students' Federation** (international)

Reymert, James De Noon—**Newspaper**—Norwegian-American newspaper

Reynolds, Arthur Rowley—**Automobile License Board**

Reynolds, Samuel Williams — **Governor**—governor to appoint two United States senators in one year for interim terms

Reynolds, Virginia Elizabeth—**Wedding**—wedding in the United States Occupation Forces in Korea

Reynolds, Winchester Englebert—**Public Buildings Administration**

Rhinelander, Leonard Kip—**Newspaper**—composograph photograph in a newspaper

Rhoads, Eugene Saylor—**Aviation**—**Flights (transatlantic)** — transatlantic hydroplane flight

Rhodes, Cecil—**Rhodes Scholar**—Rhodes scholars

Rhodes, Richard S.—**Deaf**—**Hearing Aid**—hearing aid of interest

Rhodes, Thomas E.—**Radio Broadcast**—debate over the radio

Ribaut, Jean—**Ship**—ship built to cross the Atlantic Ocean

Rice, Allen Thorndike—**Election Law**—Australian ballot system

Rice, David—**College**—university west of the Allegheny Mountains

Rice, Edwin Wilbur—**Industrial Research Laboratory**

Rice, Emery—**World War I**—shot fired by the American Navy in World War I against a known German submarine

Rich, Comly—**Building and Loan Association**

Richard, Gabriel—**Congressman (U.S.)**—Roman Catholic priest to serve in Congress

Richards, George—**Masonic Magazine**

Richards, George Warren—**Evangelical and Reformed Church**

Richards, Linda—**Hospital Record**

Richards, Theodore William—**Nobel Prize**—Nobel Prize in chemistry

Richardson, Ebenezer—**Revolutionary War**—martyr in the Revolutionary war

Richardson, Holden Chester—**Aviation**—**Flights**—airplane catapulted

Richardson, Jack—**Aviation**—**Flights (transcontinental)**—transcontinental round-trip airplane flight within one day

Richardson, Levant M.—**Roller Skate**—ball-bearing skate patent

Richardson, William—**Postal Service**—Pony Express Mail

Richey, Helen—**Aviation**—**Aviator**—woman aviator to pilot an air-mail transport

Richman, Harry—**Aviation**—**Flights (transatlantic)**—transatlantic round-trip flight from the United States

Richmond, Bill—**Prize Fight**—American to win distinction in the prize ring

Richmond, James N.—**Glass**—plate glass

Richmond, Lee—**Business**—installment finance company

Richter, John Paul—**Aviation**—refueling attempt in mid-air

Rickenbacker, Edward Vernon—**Aviation**—airplane sleeping berths

Rickenbacker, Edward Vernon—**Aviation**—**Aviator**—American ace of aces

Ricketts, John Bill—**Circus**—circus

Ricketts, Palmer Chamberlaine—**Voting Machine Commission (state)**

Rickover, Hyman George — **Submarine** — atomic powered submarine

Riddell, R. R.—**Freemasons**—Grotto

Riddle, George—**Play (drama)**—Greek play

Rider, Fremont—**Microcard**—book on microcards

Rider, John—**Pistol**—revolver

Rider, William—**Gutta Percha**

Ridley, Frederick Thomas—**Lens**—plastic lens

Riedel, Karl—**Opera**—opera broadcast in its entirety by the Metropolitan Opera Company

Riefler, Winfield William—**Central Statistical Board (U.S.)**

Rienhoff, William Francis—**Surgical Operation**—lung removal carried out according to pre-operative plans

Riesz, Robert Richard—**Voice Mechanism**—voice mechanism capable of creating the complex sounds of speech

Riggs, John M.—**Anesthesia**—anesthetic in dentistry

Rihbany, Abraham Mitrie—**Arabic Magazine**

Riker, A. L.—**Automobile Race**—automobile race on a track

Rintoul, Norman—**Aviation**—airplane human pick-up

Riotte, C. C.—**Boat Race**—motor boat race under organized rules

Rittenhouse, David — **Building** — building erected in the United States for public use

Rittenhouse, David — **Mint (U.S.)**—mint (U.S.) director

Rittenhouse, William—**Mennonites**—Mennonite church meeting-house

Rittenhouse, William—**Paper Mill**

Rittenhouse, William—**Watermark**

Ritty, James J. (Jake)—**Cash Register**

Ritty, John—**Cash Register**

Roach, Elizabeth—**College**—women's college (chartered)

Roane, Archibald — **Dueling Legislation (state)**

Robb, Al—**Electric Power Plant**—municipally owned electric power plant

Robb, Lotus—**Play (drama)**—drama to win a Pulitzer prize

Robbins, Betty (Mrs. Sheldon Robbins)—**Cantor**—Jewish woman cantor

Roberdeau, Daniel—**Holiday**—Thanksgiving Day celebration (nationwide, colonial)

Robert, Nicholas Louis—**Paper-Making Machinery**—paper-making machine (Fourdrinier) imported

Robert, René—**Ship**—Great Lakes commercial vessel

Rommel, George McCullough—**Book**—book on cornstalk paper

Ronaldson, James—**Dollar Marks**

Ronaldson, James—**Type Specimen Book**

Ronan, George—**Army School**—army school graduate killed

Roosevelt, Anna Eleanor—**Post Office**—airplane post office

Roosevelt, Ellen—**Tennis Match**—women's national championship lawn tennis matches

Roosevelt, Franklin Delano — **Archivist of the United States**

Roosevelt, Franklin Delano—**Aviation—Airport**—airport (federally owned and operated)

Roosevelt, Franklin Delano—**Cabinet of the United States**—full cabinet sworn in at the same time and place

Roosevelt, Franklin Delano—**Cabinet of the United States**—woman cabinet member

Roosevelt, Franklin Delano — **Diplomatic Service**—ambassador to the Union of Soviet Socialist Republics

Roosevelt, Franklin Delano—**Electric Power Plant**—hydroelectric power plant to produce a million kilowatts

Roosevelt, Franklin Delano—**Federal Alchohol Control Administration**

Roosevelt, Franklin Delano—**Federal Works Agency**

Roosevelt, Franklin Delano—**Home Owners Loan Corporation**

Roosevelt, Franklin Delano—**Industrial Recovery Act**—industrial recovery act (national)

Roosevelt, Franklin Delano—**Industry**—Industrial Advisory Board (federal)

Roosevelt, Franklin Delano—**Judge**—woman associate justice of the Circuit Court of Appeals

Roosevelt, Franklin Delano—**Labor Department (U.S.)**—woman Secretary of Labor

Roosevelt, Franklin Delano—**Merchant Marine Academy**—Merchant Marine Academy (U.S.)

Roosevelt, Franklin Delano—**Olympic Games**—winter Olympic games competition

Roosevelt, Franklin Delano—**President (U.S.)**—President elected for a fourth term

Roosevelt, Franklin Delano—**President (U.S.)**—President inaugurated on January 20

Roosevelt, Franklin Delano—**President (U.S.)**—President to become a godfather to a member of the English royal family

Roosevelt, Franklin Delano—**President (U.S.)**—President to broadcast from a foreign country

Roosevelt, Franklin Delano—**President (U.S.)**—President to broadcast in a foreign language

Roosevelt, Franklin Delano—**President (U.S.)**—President to fly in an airplane while in office

Roosevelt, Franklin Delano—**President (U.S.)**—President to go through the Panama Canal

Roosevelt, Franklin Delano — **President (U.S.)**—President to invite the President-elect

Roosevelt, Franklin Delano—**President (U.S.)**—President to visit a foreign country in wartime

Roosevelt, Franklin Delano—**President (U.S.)**—President to visit Hawaii while President

Roosevelt, Franklin Delano—**President (U.S.)**—President to visit South America while President

Roosevelt, Franklin Delano—**President (U.S.)**—President whose mother saw her son inaugurated President of the United States for a second term

Roosevelt, Franklin Delano—**Presidential Candidate**—presidential candidate to fly to a political convention

Roosevelt, Franklin Delano—**Presidential Candidate**—presidential candidate to make a speech of acceptance at a nominating convention

Roosevelt, Franklin Delano—**Public Works Administration**

Roosevelt, Franklin Delano—**Securities and Exchange Commission (U.S.)**

Roosevelt, Franklin Delano—**Television—Telecast**—President to appear on television

Roosevelt, Franklin Delano—**Veto (presidential)**—veto message read by a President

Roosevelt, Grace—**Tennis Match**—women's national championship lawn tennis matches

Roosevelt, Hilborne Lewis—**Organ**—electric organ

Roosevelt, Isaac—**Dental Dispensary**—dental dispensary

Roosevelt, Nicholas J.—**Ship**—steamboat to sail down the Mississippi

Roosevelt, Sarah Delano—**President (U.S.)**—President whose mother saw her son inaugurated President of the United States for a second term

Roosevelt, Theodore—**Cabinet of the United States**—cabinet member who was Jewish

Roosevelt, Theodore — **Cable**—cable across the Pacific Ocean between Honolulu, Midway, Guam and Manila

Roosevelt, Theodore — **Children's Welfare Congress (international)**

Roosevelt, Theodore—**Election Law**—corrupt election practices law (state)

Roosevelt, Theodore—**Forest Service**—Forest Service (U.S.)

Roosevelt, Theodore—**Medal**—National Geographic Society gold medal

Roosevelt, Theodore — **Monument**—national monument

Roosevelt, Theodore—**Nobel Prize**—Nobel Prize

Roosevelt, Theodore—**Political Convention**—national nominating convention presided over by a Negro

Roosevelt, Theodore—**President (U.S.)**—President to fly

Roosevelt, Theodore—**President (U.S.)**—President to ride in an automobile

Roosevelt, Theodore—**President (U.S.)**—President to visit a foreign country while President

Roosevelt, Theodore—**Progressive Party**

Rutledge, John—**Supreme Court (U.S.)**—Chief Justice whose nomination was not confirmed

Rutledge, John—**Supreme Court (U.S.)**—Supreme Court of the United States

Rutledge, William J.—**War Veterans' Society**—Grand Army of the Republic

Ryan, Harriet—**Hospital**—tuberculosis home for the care of consumptives

Ryan, Harry—**Football Game**—professional football game

Rynder, Isaiah—**Horse Race**—trotting futurity

Ryskind, Morrie—**Play (drama)**—musical play to win a Pulitzer prize

S

Sabin, Florence Rena—**College**—woman professor at a first class medical school

Sabin, Florence Rena—**Science Association**—woman elected to the National Academy of Sciences

Sadove, Max Samuel—**Anesthesia**—trifluoroethyl vinyl ether

Saffren, Sheldon—**Army Officer**—army medical specialist corps male officer

St. Clair, Arthur—**Congress of the United States**—congressional investigation

St. Clair, Arthur—**Territorial Expansion**—acquisition of land by the federal government

Saint-Gaudens, Augustus—**Arts and Letters Society**—arts and letters society (national)

Saint-Gaudens, Augustus—**Medal**—National Institute of Arts and Letters gold medal

St. Goddard, Emile—**Dog Sled Race**—dog sled race on an Olympic demonstration program

St. John, William Pope—**Silverites**

St. Leger, Francis—**Television—Telecast**—opera telecast

Salmon, Daniel Elmer—**Animal Industry Bureau (U.S.)**—Bureau of Animal Industry

Salter, Susanna Medora—**Woman**—woman mayor

Saltonstall, Dudley—**Navy**—naval fleet

Saltonstall, Henry—**Degrees (academic and honorary)**—Bachelor of Arts degree

Samma, Senaa—**Sword Swallower**

Sampson, Edith Spurlock—**Diplomatic Service**—Negro delegate to the United Nations from the United States

Samson, Job—**Tunnel**—tunnel

Samuelson, Frank — **Rowing**—transatlantic trip by row boat

Sanders, Homer — **Bowling Tournament** — gold medal award to a perfect-score bowler

Sanders, Jared Young — **Price Regulation Law**—price regulation law (state)

Sanders, Millard F.—**Horse**—horse to trot a mile in less than two minutes

Sanders, Nathaniel—**Road**—state road authorization

Sanderson, Ivan T.—**Television—Telecast**—color program (commercial) to be presented daily

Sandford, Nathan — **Trademark Lawsuit**—trademark controversy involving a newspaper

Sands, Charles E.—**Golf Tournament**—amateur golf tournament (official)

Sands, Dave — **Television—Telecast**—prize fight televised coast-to-coast

Sandys, George — **Book** — profane poetry translation prepared in the colonies to be published

Sanford, Elias Benjamin—**Federal Council of the Churches of Christ in America**

Sanford, Harold — **Television — Telecast** — operetta to be televised

Sanger, Margaret—**Medical Clinic**—birth control clinic

Sarasohn, Kasriel Hersch—**Newspaper**—Yiddish daily newspaper

Sarazen, Gene—**Golf Champion**—golf champion to win the United States Open and the Professional

Sargeant, John—**Conference**—conference of American republics

Sargent, Edith — **Public School** — public school classes for epileptic children

Sargent, Franklin Haven—**Theatrical School**—theatrical school

Sargent, James—**Lock**—time-lock

Sargent, Nan C.—**Golf Tournament**—women's tournament golf championship

Sarnoff, David—**Radio Facsimile Transmission**—facsimile high-speed transmission

Sarnoff, David—**Television**—high-definition telecast

Satolli, Francesco—**Catholic Apostolic Delegate**

Sauer, Christoph—**Bible**—Bible printed in German

Sauer, Christoph—**German Book**—German book printed in German type in America

Sauer, Christoph — **Type Foundry** — type foundry to be permanently established in America

Saund, Dalip Singh—**Congressman (U.S.)**—congressman of Asian ancestry

Saunders, Clarence — **Business**—Keedoozle store

Saunders, William—**Agricultural Society**—agricultural society of national importance

Saunders, William—**Oranges**—seedless navel oranges

Savage, Abraham — **Freemasons** — military masonic lodge

Savage, Arthur—**Animals**—lion

Sawyer, Wilbur Augustus—**Vaccine**—yellow fever vaccine for human immunization

Saxe, Alfred — **Normal School** — normal school instruction given at a university

Saxon, B. F.—**Wedding**—double radio wedding

Saxton, Joseph — **Photograph** — photograph taken in the United States

Say, Thomas—Conchology Report

Say, Thomas—**Entomology Book (comprehensive)**

Saylor, David Oliver—**Cement**—cement

Sayre, Lewis Albert—**Medical Instruction**—orthopedics chair

Scalchi, Sofia—**Opera**—opera at the Metropolitan Opera House

Scanlin, Jack—**Radio Station**—naval radio station

Scannell, Clinton G.—**Punchboards**

Scarborough, George P.—**Court**—court of claims

Schade, Arnold—**Air Mail Service**—missile mail (official)

Schaefer, Vincent Joseph—**Snow**—artificial snow

Schatz, Albert—**Streptomycin**

Schayes, Dolph — **Basketball** — basketball player (professional) to score more than 15,000 points

Schelling, Felix Emmanuel—**Novel Course**—lecture course on the English novel

Schenck, Carl Alvin—**Forestry School**—forestry school dealing exclusively with problems of forestry

Scherman, Harry—**Book Club**—Book-of-the-Month Club

Scherzer, William — **Bridge** — rolling lift bridge

Schick, Jacob—**Razor**—electric dry shaver

Schilling, David Carl—**Aviation—Flights (transatlantic)** — jet transatlantic flight west to east

Schilling, David Carl—**Aviation—Flights (transatlantic)**—jet transatlantic non-stop flight east to west

Schimmoler, Laurette—**Aviation—Airport**—airport manager (woman)

Schippers, Thomas—**Television—Telecast**—opera written for television

Schirra, Walter Marty, Jr.—**Astronauts**—astronauts

Schley, Winfield Scott—**Ship**—navy vessel equipped to lay mines

Schneider, Walter Arthur—**Colorscope**

Schneider, Willhelm — **Carrousel**—carrousel patent

Schoenbein, Christian Frederick—**Cellulose Nitrate Patent**

Schoenleber, Gretchen B.—**Brokerage**—woman stock exchange member (commodity exchange)

Scholfield, Arthur—**Broadcloth**

Scholfield, Arthur—**Wool**—wool carding machine

Scholfield, John—**Broadcloth**

Scholfield, John—**Wool**—wool carding machine

Scholz, Roy Philip—**Suture**—fiberglas sutures

Schoonmaker, Augustus—**Interstate Commerce Act**

Schrack, Christian—**Varnish (manufacturer)**

Schratz, Paul Richard—**Submarine**—leaping submarine

Schriver, Billy ("Pop")—**Baseball Player**—baseball player to catch a ball dropped from the Washington Monument

Schroeder, Rudolph William—**Aviation—Flights**—airplane altitude flight to exceed 28,000 feet

Schulte, Paul — **Catholic Mass** — Catholic Mass in an airship over the ocean

Schultz, Augustus—**Leather**—chrome tanning process

Schultz, George—**Schwenkfelder**

Schultz, Jackson Smith—**Health Board**—health board (municipal) armed with sufficient powers

Schuman, Frank—**Glass**—wire glass

Schuyler, Eugene—**Degrees (academic and honorary)**—doctor of philosophy degree

Schuyler, John—**Steam Engine**—steam engine

Schwab, Charles M.—**Corporation**—corporation incorporated with a capitalization of $1 billion

Schwab, Harvey A.—**Monument**—monument to the American flag

Schwartz, Arthur—**Radio Broadcast**—musical comedy broadcast

Schwartz, Russell Plato—**Electrobasograph**

Schwarzwalder, John—**Television Station**—noncommercial educational television station

Schwerdt, Carlton Everett—**Virus**—virus (human or animal-infecting virus) to be crystallized

Scopes, John Thomas — **Evolution law (state)**

Scot, Robert — **Money** — half cent of the United States

Scott, Albert S.—**Insurance**—insurance board (state)

Scott, Bert W.—**Automobile Race**—transcontinental automobile race

Scott, Blanche Stuart—**Aviation—Aviator**—woman aviator to make a public flight

Scott, George Herbert—**Aviation—Airship**—airship (lighter-than-air)

Scott, John Walter—**Postage Stamp**—public exhibition of postage stamps

Scott, John Welwood—**Religious Publication**—religious weekly newspaper

Scott, Norman—**Skating Tournament**—figure skating international championship tournament

Scott, Walter—**Lunch Wagon**

Scott, Winfield—**Political Convention**—unit rule

Scott-Browne, D. L.—**Typewriting School**

Scull, John—**Newspaper**—newspaper published west of the Alleghenies

Seaborg, Glenn Theodore—**Element**—element 94

Seaborg, Glenn Theodore—**Element**—element 95

Seaborg, Glenn Theodore—**Element**—element 96

Seaborg, Glenn Theodore—**Element**—element 97

Seaborg, Glenn Theodore—**Element**—element 98

Seaborg, Glenn Theodore—**Element**—element 101

Seabury, George J.—**Adhesive and Medicated Plaster**—adhesive and medicated plaster with a rubber base

Seabury, Samuel — **Protestant Episcopal Bishop**—Protestant Episcopal bishop

Seaby, Diana — **Television**—Telecast—demonstration of home reception of television

Seagers, Paul William—**School**—school to have all classroom lights controlled by electric eyes

Seaman, Valentine—**Nursing School**—instruction for nurses

Seaman, Valentine—**Pharmacopoeia**—pharmacopoeia prepared by a hospital staff

Searle, William—**Ship**—revenue cutter

Sears, Eleanora R.—**Squash Racquets Champion**—woman to win the U.S.A. Women's Squash Racquets Singles championship

Sears, Richard D.—**Tennis Match**—lawn tennis national championship matches

Seaver, Lucas—**Almanac**—patent medicine almanac

Sebile, Elizabeth J. — **Medal** — Air Force Medal of Honor for action in the Korean War

Sebile, Louis J.—**Medal**—Air Force Medal of Honor for action in the Korean War

Sebree, Trow—**Aviation**—automatic pilot

Seccombe, Joseph—**Fishing Treatise**

Secker, William—**Book**—miniature book

Sedgwick, Theodore—**Fair**—industrial exposition

Sedgwick, Theodore—**Village Improvement Society**

Sedgwick, Thomas—**Slavery**—slave emancipated

Seely, Henry W.—**Electric Flatiron**

Seereiter, John—**Billiard Match**—billiard match to attain international prominence

Segar, Elzie Crisler—**Monument**—monument to a comic character

Segrave, Henry O'Neil de Hane—**Automobile**—automobile to exceed the speed of 200 miles an hour

Seid, B. S.—**Hospital**—Chinese hospital

Seiffert, Anton—**Moravian Bishop**

Selden, George Baldwin—**Automobile Patent**

Selfridge, Thomas Etholen—**Aviation**—airplane fatality

Selfridge, Thomas Oliver—**Torpedo**—torpedo mine

Sellers, Coleman—**Moving Picture**—photographic attempt to show motion

Sellers, John—**Sieve**—sieve

Sellers, Kathryn—**Judge**—woman judge of a juvenile court

Seltzer, Leo A.—**Skating**—roller derby

Selznick, David Oliver — **Television**—Telecast—moving picture premiere festivities to be televised

Semmes, Raphael—**Ship**—Confederate cruiser to raid Union commerce

Semple, Robert — **Newspaper** — newspaper published on the Pacific coast

Semple, William Finley—**Chewing Gum**—chewing gum patent

Sennett, Mack — **Moving Pictures**—six-reel feature-length comedy

Sergeant, John—**Political Platform (national)**

Serra, Junipero—**California Mission**

Servoss, Thomas Lowery—**Shipping**—coastal shipping service

Sevier, Electa—**Ship**—gyro-stabilized American liner

Sevier, John—**Civil Government in America**

Sewall, Arthur—**Silverites**

Sewall, Mary Wright—**Women's Club**—women's club federation

Sewall, Samuel—**Bridge**—pile bridge

Sewall, Stephen—**Astronomical Expedition**

Seymour, Henry—**Crime Prevention and Detection**—interstate crime pact

Seymour, Joseph H.—**Book**—book printed on American paper with American-made plates and bound in America

Seymour, Richard—**Holiday**—Thanksgiving Day service

Shade, James—**Aviation**—Airship—airship to land on a roof

Shadid, Michael Abraham—**Hospital**—community hospital

Shadrick, Kenneth—**War (Korean)**—soldier killed in the Korean War

Shaler, Nathaniel Southgate—**Science School**—natural science summer school

Shallenberger, Oliver B.—**Electric Meter**

Shallus, Jacob—**Constitution of the United States**—printed copies of the Constitution

Shank, Robert F.—**Air Mail Service**—air mail regular service

Shanks, David Carey—**Medal**—Distinguished Service Medal awarded to a woman

Sharkey, Tom—**Moving Picture**—moving picture of a real pugilistic encounter taken at night

Sharkey, William L.—**Vice President of the United States**—Vice President sworn in on foreign soil

Sharp, George—**Disciples of Christ**

Sharp, J.—**Oratorio**—oratorio performance (complete)

Sharp, John—**Equestrian Exhibition**

Sharp, William—**Pharmacy College**—pharmacy college

Sharpless, Samuel J.—**Cattle Club**—cattle club (Jersey cattle)

Shattuck, George Cheyne—**Medical Instruction**—pathology chair

Shaw, Lewis Agassiz—**Respirator** (iron lung)

Shaw, Samuel—**Diplomatic Service**—consul under the Department of State

Shays, Daniel—**War**—rebellion against the federal government

Shea, John M.—**Fingerprinting**—police department to adopt the fingerprinting system

Shecut, W. H.—**Adhesive and Medicated Plaster**—adhesive and medicated plaster patent

Sheehan, Joseph Eastman—**Medical Instruction**—plastic surgery professor

Sheen, Fulton John—**Television—Telecast**—religious services to be televised

Sheffield, George St. John—**Billiard Match**—intercollegiate billiard match

Sheldon, Charles Monroe—**Book**—best seller other than a text or purely theological work

Sheldon, Edward Austin—**Normal School**—normal school (state) at which students actually conducted classes

Sheldon, Harold Horton—**Colorscope**

Sheldon, John P.—**Typewriter**—typewriter

Sheldon, W. E.—**Teachers' Convention**—teachers' convention (national)

Shepard, Alan Bartlett, Jr.—**Astronauts**—astronauts

Shepard, Alan Bartlett, Jr.—**Astronauts**—space flight by an American astronaut

Shepard, Alan Bartlett, Jr.—**Medal**—National Aeronautics and Space Administration distinguished service medal

Shepard, Charles H.—**Bathhouse**—Turkish bath

Shepard, Mr.—**Congregational Church**—Congregational Church council

Shepard, Mrs. Finley Johnson—**Hall of Fame**—hall of fame (university)

Shepherd, Lemuel Cornick—**Medal**—Navy-Marine Corps medal for heroism awarded to a woman

Sheppard, Jeanie Ramsey—**Woman**—woman state liquor board member

Sheppard, William—**Soap**—soap in liquid form

Sherburne, Samuel—**Attorney of the United States**

Sheridan, Bernard—**Embossing Press**

Sherman, James Schoolcraft—**Vice Presidential Candidate**—vice presidential nominee to die before the meeting of the electoral college

Sherman, John—**Territorial Expansion**—island territory

Sherman, John Ames—**Envelope**—envelope folding and gumming machine

Sherwin, Samuel B.—**Autogiro**—autogiro rotary wing aircraft fellowship

Shibe, Benjamin F.—**Baseball**—cork center baseball

Shield, Lansing Peter—**Business**—"Food-O-Mat"

Shields, James—**Senator (U.S.)**—senator to serve three states

Shilders, J.—**Labadist Community**

Shipley, Ruth Bielaski—**Woman**—woman passport division chief

Shippee, Amasa—**Flag**—American flag over a schoolhouse

Shippee, Lois—**Flag**—American flag over a schoolhouse

Shippee, Rhoda—**Flag**—American flag over a schoolhouse

Shippen, William—**Medical Instruction**—anatomy lectures (scientific)

Shippen, William—**Medical School**—medical college

Shireman, Eugene Curtis—**Fish Hatchery**—goldfish hatchery

Shive, John Northrup—**Transistor**—photo-transistor

Shockley, William—**Transistor**—junction transistor

Shoemaker, Thomas Buckman—**Citizenship**—citizenship granted to an alien on foreign soil

Shoemaker, Willie—**Jockey**—jockey to ride 400 winners in one year

Shoemaker, Willie—**Jockey**—jockey to win the national riding championship four times

Sholes, Christopher Latham—**Typewriter**—typewriter that was practical

Shook, Frederic W.—**Aviation—Flights (transpacific)**—jet transpacific non-stop flight

Short, Shirley—**Air Mail Service**—air mail long-distance night service

Shotwell, Luman W.—**Indians**—Indian tribal constitution

Shotwell, William—**Hair Cloth**

Shoukletovich, Doushan Jefta—**Serbian Orthodox Cathedral**

Shreeve, Herbert E.—**Radio Telephone**—transatlantic radio telephone message

Shreve, Henry Miller—**Ship**—steamboat (double decked)

Shryrock, George A.—**Paper**—straw paper

Shu, Loo Kum—**Telephone**—telephone switchboard or exchange for Chinese subscribers

Shuckburgh, Richard—**"Yankee Doodle"**

Shuler, Marjorie—**Aviation—Passenger**—woman to fly entirely around the world by commercial heavier-than-air plane

Shulze, John Andrew—**Tax**—inheritance tax (state)

Shunk, Francis Rawn—**Child Labor Law**—child labor law restricting the age of the worker

Shuster, George—**Automobile Race**—automobile race from New York to Paris

Shute, Nevil—**Moving Picture**—moving picture presented simultaneously in major cities throughout the world

Sibert, William Luther—**World War I**—American troops to land in France

Siddall, Joseph S.—**Insurance**—title guaranty insurance company

Sidney, Sylvia—**Theater**—municipally owned and operated summer theater-in-the-round

Sievert, Frances—**Telephone**—telephone switchboard with Braille markings

Sik, Hong Yong—**Diplomatic Service**—Korean embassy

Sikkeland, Torbjørn—**Element**—element 103

Sikorsky, Igor Ivan—**Helicopter**—helicopter (direct-lift-aircraft)

Sikorsky, Igor Ivan—**Helicopter Flight**—helicopter flight from water

Sikorsky, Igor Ivan—**Helicopter Flight**—helicopter flight of one-hour duration

Silliman, Benjamin—**Chemistry Professor**—professorship of applied chemistry

Silliman, Benjamin—**Science Magazine**—science magazine

Silver, George — **Moving Picture** — moving picture of a real pugilistic encounter taken at night

Simmons, Amelia—**Cook Book**—cook book of American authorship

Simmons, John—**College**—technical college for women

Simms, Ruth Hanna McCormick—**Woman**—woman presidential campaign co-manager

Simon, Carleton—**Eye**—identification system

Simon, Irving B.—**Periodical**—Spanish magazine published by students

Simon, Rene—**Aviation**—airplane rescue at sea effected by another airplane

Simon, William—**Pharmacy College**—pharmacy college to make analytical chemistry a required course

Simons, Charles Caspar—**Judge**—woman associate justice of the Circuit Court of Appeals

Simons, David Goodman—**Balloon Flight**—balloon flight to exceed an altitude of 100,000 feet

Simpson, Albert Benjamin—**Bible School**

Simpson, Garry—**Television**—**Telecast**—opera written for television on commission for a commercial sponsor

Simpson, George B.—**Electric Stove**—electric range

Simpson, Michael Hodge—**Bunting**

Simpson, Michael Hodge—**Library**—library newspaper room

Simpson, Wallis Warfield—**Wedding**—American woman married to a former king of England

Simpson, William—**Root Beer**

Sims, James Marion—**Hospital**—women's hospital

Sims, James Marion — **Impregnation** — impregnation (human) by means of artificial insemination

Sims, James Marion—**Suture**—silver wire suture

Sims, Julia Isabelle—**Jury**—woman grand jury foreman

Simson, Sampson—**Hospital**—Jewish hospital

Sinclair, Richard L. — **Garage** — completely automatic push-button controlled garage

Singer, Isaac Merritt—**Sewing Machine**—sewing machine equipped with a rocking treadle or double treadle

Singer, Isaac Merritt—**Sewing Machine**—sewing machine manufacturer

Singer, Isaac Merritt—**Sewing Machine**—sewing machine motor—patent

Sinnett, Walter—**Television** — **Telecast**—X-ray fluoroscopy television discussion

Sinnock, John Ray—**Medal**—woman to have her likeness on a medal issued by the United States Mint

Skeldon, Joseph — **Ship** — schooner (five masted)

Skene (Skeen) John—**Freemasons**—mason

Skinner, Frederick Henry—**Museum**—maritime museum

Skinner, Halcyon — **Carpet Loom** — carpet power loom to weave Axminster carpets

Skinner, John Stuart—**Agricultural** Journal—agricultural journal to attain prominence

Skinner, John Stuart—**Sports Magazine**

Skinner, Richard Cort—**Dental Book**—book on dentistry

Skipwith, Fulwar—**Diplomatic Service**—consuls of the United States appointed after the adoption of the Constitution

Slack, Leslie—**Ship**—ship to fire a Polaris missile

Slade, Daniel Denison—**Veterinary School**—veterinary college

Slade, Frederick J.—**Steel**—open hearth furnace

Slate, Thomas Benton—**Ice**—dry ice

Slater, Bill—**Television**—**Telecast**—baseball World Series game televised

Slater, Ellis — **President** — presidential airplane (turbo-compound powered)

Slater, Samuel—**Cotton Mill**—cotton mill to spin cotton yarn successfully

Slaughter, Alanson—**Creamery**

Slaughter, Louis N.—**Single Tax**—single tax political ticket

Slayter, Games—**Glass Wool**

Slayton, Donald Kent—**Astronauts**—astronauts

Slifer, Eli—**Civil War**—regiment to respond to President Abraham Lincoln's proclamation

Sloat, Jacob—**Cotton Twine Factory**

Slocum, Joshua—**Ship**—ship to circumnavigate the world with but one in the crew

Slocum, Samuel—**Pin**—machine for sticking pins into paper

Slocum, Samuel—**Pin**—pins manufactured with a solid head

Slowe, Lucy—**Sorority**—Negro sorority

Small, Albion Woodbury—**Sociology Professor**

Small, Elisha—**Naval Officer**—naval officer condemned for mutiny

Smalley, Daniel S. — **Dictionary** — phonetic dictionary

Smith, Alex—**Golf Tournament**—professional open championship

Smith, Alfred Emanuel—**Arbitration**—state arbitration law (modern)

Smith, Alfred Emanuel—**Television**—**Telecast**—presidential nomination notification ceremony to be televised

Smith, Arthur—**Automobile Fatality**

Smith, C. James—**Automobile Race**—transcontinental automobile race

Smith, Campbell—**Army Officer**—judge advocate of the U.S. Army

Smith, Charles—**Atheism Society**

Smith, Charles—**Paper-Making Machinery**—paper-making machine (Fourdrinier)

Smith, Charles Louis—**Police**—policewoman on the aerial force

Smith, Charles Shaler—**Bridge**—cantilever bridge

Smith, Charles Shaler — **Bridge** — hanging railroad bridge

Snelling, Lillia—**Opera**—opera by an American composer performed at the Metropolitan Opera House of New York

Snider, Christopher—**Revolutionary War**—martyr in the Revolutionary war

Snider, Jacob—**Book**—book for the blind

Snider, Peter—**Boat Club**—boat club

Snorro — **Births** — child born of European parents on American soil

Snowdon, John—**Bridge**—cast iron bridge

Snowden, Thomas — **Trademark Lawsuit** — trademark controversy involving a newspaper

Sola, Abraham de—**Congress (U.S.)**—House of Representatives—foreign clergyman to open the House of Representatives with prayer

Solberg, Thorvald—**Copyrights Registrar of the United States**

Soley, John Codman—**Navy**—naval militia (state)

Solis-Cohen, Jacob—**Medical Periodical**—laryngology magazine

Solomon, Hannah Greenebaum—**Women's Club**—Jewish women's organization (national)

Sonnenberg, Albert—**Whaling**—whale-killing machine (electric)

Sordelet, James Robert—**Navy**—naval man to reenlist while under the North Pole

Sothell, Seth—**Indigo**

Soto, Hernando de—**Discovery**—discovery of the Mississippi River by a European

Souder, Frank A.—**Pier**—ocean pier of steel

Sousa, John Philip—**Sousaphone**

Southworth, Effie A.—**Fellowship**—resident fellowship for women awarded by a women's college

Southworth, Evelyn — **Congress (U.S.)** — Senate—Senate session in which women, other than members of Congress, were permitted on the floor

Spaatz, Carl—**Air Force Academy (U.S.)**—Air Force Academy

Spafford, George—**Paper-Making Machinery**—paper-making machine (Fourdrinier)

Spafford, George—**Paper-Making Machinery**—paper-making machine (Fourdrinier) imported

Spalding, Eliza Hart—**Colonist**—women to cross the continent

Spalding, Lyman—**Pharmacopoeia**—pharmacopoeia (general)

Spangenberg, August Gottlieb — **Moravian Church**

Sparkes, Leonora — **Opera** — opera by an American composer performed at the Metropolitan Opera House of New York

Sparks, Frank—**Railroad Train Robbery**—railroad train robbery of a train in motion

Sparks, Jared—**History Instruction**—ancient and modern history chair

Speakman, Townsend—**Soda Water**—soda water

Spears, C. B.—**Trapshooting**—trapshooting intercollegiate association

Spencer, Dolly—**Police**—woman chief of police

Spencer, Philip—**Naval Officer**—naval officer condemned for mutiny

Spencer, Sara Andrews—**Political Convention**—presidential convention (national) addressed by a woman

Sperry, Charles Stillman — **Ship** — warship fleet to circumnavigate the globe

Sperry, Elmer Ambrose—**Railroad Car**—rail detector car

Sperry, Lawrence B.—**Aviation**—gyroscope automatic stabilization

Sperry, Thomas Alexander—**Trading Stamp**

Spiedel, Robert C.—**Heliport**—military heliport

Spiegler, Caesar — **Aviation**— **Airship**— dirigible

Spofford, F. A. — **Bicycle Patent** — water velocipede patent

Spooner, Eliakim—**Seeding Machine Patent**

Spotswood, Alexander—**Theater**—theater

Sprague, J. Russel—**Woman**—woman presidential campaign co-manager

Sprague, William Peter—**Carpet Factory**—carpet mill

Spurrier, John—**Alfalfa**

Spurzheim, Johann Gaspar—**Phrenologist**

Spurzheim, Johann Gaspar — **Phrenology Book**

Squires, Tilloah—**Librarians' Union**

Stack, Robert—**Moving Picture**—three-dimensional feature moving picture

Stackpole, William—**Billiard Match**—intercollegiate billiard match

Stafford, Ward—**Church**—Mariners' church

Stagg, Amos Alonzo—**College "Lettermen's Club"**

Stagg, Amos Alonzo—**Football Dummy**

Stagg, Amos Alonzo—**Physical Culture Department**

Stagg, Charles—**Theater**—theater

Stagg, Mary—**Theater**—theater

Staley, Augustus Eugene—**Soybean Processing Plant**

Stalker, Milliken—**Veterinary School**—veterinary school (state)

Standish, Miles—**Military Leader**

Stanek, Fred—**Corn Husking Championship Contest (national)**

Stanford, John—**Deaf**—**School**—instruction for the deaf

Stanford, Leland—**Railroad**—railroad to run west, out of Chicago

Stange, Stanislaus—**Phonograph Record**—phonograph record of a stage performance by the original cast

Stanley, Robert Morris—**Aviation**—**Airplane**—jet propelled airplane

Stanley, Wendell Meredith—**Virus**—virus obtained in crystalline form

Stanley, William—**Electric Power Plant**—alternating current power plant

Stansbury, Abraham—**Law Book**—law book (text)

Stansbury, Arthur—**Law Book**—law book (text)

Still, Andrew Taylor — **Physician** — osteopathic physician

Stillman, Alfred—**Squash Club**—squash tennis organization (national)

Stillman, Alfred — **Squash Tournament** — squash tennis tournament

Stillman, George F.—**Automobile Tire**—pneumatic tire patent

Stillson, Daniel C.—**Wrench**—pipe or screw wrench (practical)

Stimson, Henry Lewis — **Army Auxiliary Corps**—Women's Army Auxiliary Corps (WAAC)

Stimson, Henry Lewis—**Conscription**—peacetime conscription bill

Stimson, Henry Lewis — **Medal** — Distinguished Service Medal (Army) awarded to a woman

Stimson, Henry Lewis — **President** — presidential airplane

Stimson, Julia Catherine—**Army Officer**—woman with rank corresponding to major

Stinis, Andy — **Skywriting** — skywriting at night

Stinson, Emma B.—**Aviation**—**School**—airplane flying school operated by a woman

Stockton, Robert Field—**Ship**—warship with propelling machinery below the waterline

Stockton, Samuel Witham—**Agricultural Society**—agricultural society

Stoddard, Joshua C.—**Calliope**

Stoddard, Lawrence B.—**Golf Tournament**—amateur golf tournament (unofficial)

Stoddard, Sampson Vryling—**Tract Society**—tract society (national)

Stoddert, Benjamin—**Navy**—Secretary of the Navy

Stokowski, Leopold—**Symphony**—symphony on a Negro folk theme

Stone, A. P.—**Republican Party**—Republican Party meeting (national)

Stone, Charles Pomeroy—**Hospital**—military hospital on the modern pavilion plan

Stone, Edward Mandell—**World War I**—American combatant to die in World War I

Stone, Ellen R.—**Tuberculosis School**—outdoor school for tubercular children

Stone, Elmer Fowler—**Aviation**—**Flights** (transatlantic) — transatlantic hydroplane flight

Stone, John—**Pile Driver**—pile driver

Stone, John—**Radio Society**

Stone, John Osgood—**Health Board**—health board (municipal) armed with sufficient powers

Stone, Marvin Chester—**Straws** (artificial) for drinking

Stone, Mary (Shih Mai-yu)—**Physician**—Chinese woman to receive a doctor of medicine degree

Stone, Roy—**Road**—federal road agency

Stoneman, George—**Telegraph**—Army field telegraph used in warfare

Stoney, Thomas B. — **Aviation** — **Flights** (transatlantic)—jet passenger commercial service

Stoughton, Israel—**Bridge**—bridge

Stover, Daniel C.—**Bicycle**—bicycle with a back pedal brake

Stow, Marietta Lizzie Bell—**Equal Rights Party**

Strang, Kate Depew—**Medical Clinic**—cancer prevention clinic for children

Strang, Robert Hallock Wright—**Dental Book**—book for dental hygienists (text)

Strang, W. H.—**Horse Race**—harness race driver to win the Hambletonian four times

Stratton, Dorothy Constance—**Coast Guard** (U.S.)—Coast Guard Women's Reserve

Stratton, Samuel Wesley—**Standards Bureau** (U.S.)

Stratton, William Grant—**Automobile Legislation**—automobile seat belt safety legislation

Straus, Isidor—**Business History Chair**

Straus, Nathan—**Hospital**—tuberculosis preventorium for children

Straus, Oscar Solomon—**Cabinet of the United States**—cabinet member who was Jewish

Straus, Oscar Solomon—**Diplomatic Service**—Jewish ambassador

Strauss, Harold A. — **Aviation** — **Flights** (transcontinental) — transcontinental dirigible flight (non-rigid dirigible)

Strauss, Joseph Baermann—**Bridge**—bridge with piers sunk in the open sea

Strauss, Lewis Lichtenstein—**Atomic Energy Commission**—Atomic Energy Commission

Strawbridge, Robert Early—**Foxhound Master (American)**

Street, Kenneth—**Element**—element 98

Streeter, Alson Jennes—**Union Labor Party**

Streeter, Ruth Cheney—**Marines**—woman marine major

Streett, St. Clair—**Aviation**—**Flights**—New York-Alaska flight

Strelitzer, Hugh — **Public School** — public school opera studio

Strickland, William—**Railroad Technical Report**

Stringham, James — **Medical Instruction** — medical jurisprudence course

Strong, Alexander—**Aviation**—airplane sleeping berths

Strong, Caleb—**Congress (U.S.)**—**Senate**—Senate

Strong, Caleb—**Election Law**—registration law (state)

Strowger, Almon B.—**Telephone**—automatic telephone system (successful)

Strube, Gustav—**Orchestra**—municipal orchestra supported by taxes

Stuart, James Ewell Brown—**Civil War**—bloodshed north of the Mason-Dixon line

Stubblefield, Nathan B.—**Radio Broadcast**—radio broadcast demonstration

Stubblefield, Nathan B.—**Radio Telephone**—radio telephone marine demonstration

Stultz, Wilmer — **Aviation** — **Passenger** — woman airplane passenger to cross the Atlantic Ocean

Sturgis, Norman R.—**Trailer Church**

Stuyvesant, Peter—**Fire Department**—fire department established by municipal action

Stuyvesant, Peter—**Jews**—Jew

Stuyvesant, Peter—**Orphanage**—orphanage

Stuyvesant, Rutherford — **Building** — apartment house with a modern lay-out

Suderman, Henry Leonard—**Christmas Tree**

Sullivan, Albert Leo — **Ship** — naval vessel with a plural name

Sullivan, Ed — **Television** — **Telecast** — color program (commercial)

Sullivan, Francis Henry—**Ship**—naval vessel with a plural name

Sullivan, George Thomas—**Ship**—naval vessel with a plural name

Sullivan, Henry F.—**Swimmer**—American to swim the English Channel

Sullivan, John—**Revolutionary War**—incident in the Revolutionary war

Sullivan, John Laurence—**Defense Department (U.S.)**

Sullivan, John Lawrence—**Prize Fight**—prize fight of importance under the Marquis of Queensberry rules

Sullivan, Joseph Eugene—**Ship**—naval vessel with a plural name

Sullivan, Madison Abel—**Ship**—naval vessel with a plural name

Sullivan, Philip—**Capital Punishment**—capital punishment authorized by federal law

Sullivan, Robert Oliver Daniel—**Aviation**—**Aviator**—aviator to fly one hundred times across the Atlantic Ocean

Sullivan, Robert Oliver Daniel—**Aviation**—**Flights (transatlantic)**—transatlantic regular commercial airplane service

Sully, Thomas—**Archery Club**—archery club

Sulzberger, David—**Normal School**—teachers' training school (Jewish)

Summerfield, Arthur Ellsworth—**Air Mail Service**—missile mail (official)

Summerford, Gene — **Telephone** — telephone conversation (commercial) using electricity generated by the sun's rays

Summers, Rachael—**Woman**—women to become federal government employees

Sumner, Miss—**Oratorio**—oratorio performance (complete)

Sundback, Gideon—**Fastening**—hookless fastening for universal use

Sutherland, J. B.—**Railroad Car**—refrigerator car patent

Sutter, John Augustus—**Gold**—gold discovered in California

Sutter, John Augustus—**Russian Settlement**

Swaine, Charles—**Expedition**—arctic expedition to seek the northwest passage, for the £20,000 reward

Swaine, John—**Law Book**—law book containing the federal laws of the United States of more than one session of Congress

Swallow, Silas Comfort—**United Christian Party**

Swan, Abraham—**Architectural Book**—architectural book printed in America

Swan, Caleb—**Army Officer**—paymaster

Swan, William G.—**Glider**—rocket glider flight

Swarthout, Cornelius—**Waffle Iron Patent**

Swarts, Gardner Taber—**Health Laboratory**—health laboratory (municipal)

Swarts, Gardner Taber—**Health Laboratory**—health laboratory (state)

Swayze, John Cameron—**Television**—**Telecast**—split-screen image

Sweeney, Michael Francis — **Automobile** — armored commercial car completely protected

Sweet, John Edson—**Caliper** (screw)

Swift, Gustavus Franklin — **Railroad** — railroad shipments of dressed beef (year-round long-distance)

Swift, Joseph Gardner—**Army School**—army school graduates

Swift, William Henry — **Lighthouse** — iron pile lighthouse

Swinburn, John—**Boat Club**—boat club

Swinnerton, James—**Periodical**—comic books

Swinton, George R.—**Old Age Colony**

Swords, J.—**Railroad Treatise**

Swords, T.—**Railroad Treatise**

Sykes, Eugene Octave—**Federal Communications Commission**

Sykes, Eugene Octave—**Radio Commission (U.S.)**

Syle, Henry Winter—**Deaf**—**Church Service**—ordained deaf clergyman

Sylvester, Joseph—**Jockey**—jockey to win seven races in one day

Symington, William Stuart—**Air Force**—Air Force Secretary

Symington, William Stuart—**Defense Department (U.S.)**

Symmes (Syms), Benjamin — **Educational Endowment**

Symmes, John Cleves—**Land Pre-emption Act (federal)**

Sze, Wilbur Carl—**Marines**—marine officer of Chinese descent

T

Taft, Mrs. Josiah—**Woman**—woman whose vote was recorded

Taft, William Howard—**Bank**—postal savings bank

Taft, William Howard—**Cable**—cable across the Pacific Ocean between Honolulu, Midway, Guam and Manila

Taft, William Howard—**Chamber of Commerce** — Chamber of Commerce of the United States of America

Taft, William Howard—**Naval Officer**—admiral who was Jewish

Taft, William Howard—**President (U.S.)**—President buried in the National Cemetery at Arlington, Va.

Taft, William Howard—**President (U.S.)**—President to become Chief Justice of the United States

Taft, William Howard—**President (U.S.)**—President to pitch a ball to open the baseball season

Taggart, William H.—**Dentistry**—gold inlay

Tainter, Charles Sumner — **Phonograph** — phonograph that was practical

Taitt, Francis—**Ship**—merchant ship formally blessed at a launching ceremony

Talbot, Ethelbert—**Heresy Trial**

Talley, Lynn Porter — **Commodity Credit Corporation (U.S.)**

Talley, Marion — **Moving Picture** — talking picture

Tallmadge, Benjamin—**Secret Service**—secret service (colonial)

Tallmadge, Henry O.—**Golf Club**—golf association (national)

Tally, Thomas Lincoln—**Moving Picture Theater**—moving picture theater

Talmadge, Norma—**Radio Broadcast**—cooperative radio show

Talon, Jean—**Oil**—oil spring

Taney, Roger Brooke—**Cabinet of the United States**—cabinet appointee rejected by the Senate

Taney, Roger Brooke—**Cabinet of the United States**—cabinet member who was a Catholic

Taney, Roger Brooke — **Supreme Court (U.S.)** — Chief Justice of the Supreme Court who was Catholic

Taney, Roger Brooke — **Supreme Court (U.S.) Decision**—Supreme Court decision in a state boundary suit

Tanner, Zera Luther—**Ship**—fish hatching steamer (federal)

Tapp, Jesse Washington—**Federal Crop Insurance Corporation**

Tappan, D.—**Tract Society**—tract society

Tappan, Lewis—**Business**—commercial rating agency

Tappan, Lewis—**Unitarian Society**—national organization of the Unitarian Churches of the United States and Canada

Tatham, Charles—**Fencing**—fencing league (national)

Taub, Sam—**Television—Telecast**—prize fight to be televised

Taussig, Helen Brooke—**Medical Society**—woman member of the Association of American Physicians

Taylor, Albert Hoyt—**Radar**—radar detection of airplanes

Taylor, Albert Hoyt—**Radar**—radar observations

Taylor, Albert Hoyt—**Radio Facsimile Transmission** — photographs sent over a city telephone

Taylor, Alfred Alexander—**Governor**—gubernatorial election in which two brothers were the opposing candidates

Taylor, Anna Edson—**Niagara Falls**—person to go over Niagara Falls in a barrel

Taylor, Carl Rutherford—**Ice Cream Cone**—ice cream cone-rolling machine

Taylor, Estelle—**Moving Picture**—talking picture

Taylor, Frederick W.—**Tennis Match**—lawn tennis national championship matches

Taylor, Howard Augustus—**Tennis Match**—intercollegiate lawn tennis match

Taylor, John—**Iron**—rolling mill

Taylor, Maxwell Davenport—**Flag**—Army flag (official)

Taylor, Napoleon Edward—**World War II**—American expeditionary force to land in Africa

Taylor, Nathaniel—**Presbyterian Presbytery**

Taylor, Robert Love—**Governor**—gubernatorial election in which two brothers were the opposing candidates

Taylor, Ruth Carol—**Aviation**—air stewardess (Negro)

Taylor, Theophilus Mills — **Presbyterian Church**—moderator of the United Presbyterian Church

Taylor, Zachary—**Interior Department (U.S.)**—Interior Department Secretary

Taylor, Zachary—**War (Mexican)**—Mexican war shots

Teagle, Walter Clark—**Industry**—Industrial Advisory Board (U.S.)

Tekakwitha, Kateri—**Catholic Beatification**—Catholic beatification of an American Indian

Telkes, Maria—**Building**—house completely sunheated

Tellefsen, Carl—**Ski Club**—ski club association

Tellegen, Lou—**Moving Picture**—foreign feature film exhibited

Temple, Mary B.—**Women's Club**—women's club federation

Ten Broeck, Richard—**Horse Race**—American-bred horse to win a major race abroad

Tennent, John Van Brugh—**Medical Instruction**—midwifery professor

Tenney, William H.—**College**—college principally for war veterans

Terry, Eli—**Clock**—clock patent

Terry, Silas Burnham—**Spring Manufacturer**

Teschemacher, H. F.—**Telegraph**—telegraph line to the Pacific coast

Thach, John Smith—**Navy**—task force to fight undersea craft

Thacher, James—**Medical Book**—hydrophobia book

Thacher, Thomas—**Medical Book**—medical pamphlet

Thatcher, Linden A.—**Postal Service**—coin-operated mailbox

Thayer, Abbott Henderson—**Camouflage**

Thayer, Frederick Winthrop — **Baseball Catcher's Mask**

Thelander, Hulda—**Naval officer**—woman physician in the Medical Corps Reserve of the U.S. Navy

Thiess, Ruth Hammond — **Opera** — opera broadcast in its entirety

Thiry, John Henry—**Bank**—savings group

Thomas, Mr.—**Library**—book-wagon

Thomas, Allan M.—**Incubator for Infants**

Tiffin, Edward—**College**—university founded by a federal land grant

Tilghman, Benjamin Chew—**Sand Blasting**

Tillman, Benjamin Ryan—**Senator (U.S.)**—senators censured

Tillstrom, Burr—**Television—Telecast**—color network telecast in compatible color

Tilton, James—**Army**—medical corps

Tilton, James—**Army Officer**—surgeon general of the U.S. Army

Timby, Theodore Ruggles—**Ordnance**—revolving gun turret

Timms, Ross L.—**Valeteria**

Timothee, Louis—**Librarian**—librarian

Tinker, Clarence Leonard—**World War II**—American general missing in action in World War II

Tipton, William D.—**Aviation—Airplane**—airplane used by a newspaper

Tkach, M. — **Newspaper** — Ukrainian daily newspaper

Todd, Libanus McLouth—**Check Protectors**

Todd, Thomas — **Wedding** — White House wedding

Todd, William Cleaves—**Library**—library newspaper room

Tokatyan, Armand—**Television—Telecast**—opera telecast

Tolton, Augustus — **Catholic Priest** — Negro Catholic priest

Tombaugh, Clyde William—**Astronomy**—planet

Tomlinson, Homer — **Wedding** — parachute wedding

Tomlinson, William—**Colonist**—civilian settlement west of the Allegheny Mountains

Tompkins, Charles H.—**Civil War**—skirmish in the Civil War

Tompson, Benjamin—**Poet**—American poet

Toney, Fred—**Baseball Game**—double no-hit nine-inning baseball game

Toniski, William J.—**Television—Telecast**—play to be televised

Topliff, Samuel—**News Agency**—news agency

Torkillus, Reorus—**Lutheran Church**—Lutheran pastor

Torrey, John—**Assay Office Building** (federal)

Toscanini, Arturo—**Television—Telecast**—symphonic concerts to be televised

Totter, Audrey—**Moving Picture**—three-dimensional feature moving picture produced and released by a major company

Towers, John Henry—**Aviation—Airplane**—naval airplane

Town, Ithiel — **Building** — building in all-Gothic architecture

Towner, Margaret Ellen — **Presbyterian Church**—woman ordained a minister

Townsend, E. Price—**Bridge Whist Tournament**—duplicate whist tournament

Toy, John D.—**Atlas**

Toy, John D.—**Medical Book**—ophthalmology book

Tracy, Susan Edith—**Occupational Therapy Treatment**

Trainer, Merrill—**Theater**—television theater demonstration

Trall, Russell Thacher—**Water Cures**

Tranchepain, Marie—**Convent**—convent

Travell, Janet Graeme—**Physician**—woman appointed "personal physician to the President"

Treadwell, Daniel—**Printing Press**—power or steam printing press

Tresse, Thomas—**Paper Mill**

Trik, Carl A.—**Bridge**—concrete arch highway bridge

Tripler, Charles Eastman—**Air (liquid)**

Tripler, Charles Stuart—**Hospital**—military hospital on the modern pavilion plan

Tronson du Coudray, Philippe Charles Jean Baptiste—**Catholic Funeral**—Catholic funeral attended by the U.S. Continental Congress

Troost, Gerardt—**Pharmacy College**—pharmacy college

Troxel, Dorothy A. — **Dictionary** — Mongolian-English, English-Mongolian dictionary

Troy, Laura—**Wedding**—airplane wedding

Troy, Willie—**Television—Telecast** — prize fight televised in color

Troyanovsky, Alexander Antonovich—**Diplomatic Service**—ambassador to the Union of Soviet Socialist Republics

Trudeau, Edward Livingston—**Health Society**

Trudeau, Edward Livingston—**Hospital**—tuberculosis sanatorium (modern)

Trudeau, Edward Livingston—**Tuberculosis Laboratory**—tuberculosis research laboratory

Trueblood, Thomas Clarkson—**Public Speaking Department**

Truman, Harry S.—**Air Force Officer**—Judge Advocate General of the U.S. Air Force

Truman, Harry S. — **Diplomatic Service** — woman ambassador from a foreign country

Truman, Harry S.—**Flag**—President's flag

Truman, Harry S.—**Governor**—Negro governor appointed by the President of the United States

Truman, Harry S.—**Medal**—Medal of Freedom

Truman, Harry S.—**Medal**—Medal of Honor awarded in the Korean War

Truman, Harry S.—**Medal**—Reserve Officers Association medal

Truman, Harry S.—**Money**—coin bearing the portrait of a Negro

Truman, Harry S.—**Postmaster**—postmaster general appointed from the ranks

Truman, Harry S.—**President (U.S.)**—President to travel underwater in a captured enemy submarine

Truman, Harry S. — **Submarine** — atomic-powered submarine

Truman, Harry S.—**Television—Telecast**—presidential address televised from the White House

Truman, Harry S.—**Television—Telecast**—transcontinental telecast received on the east coast

Trumbull, Earl—**Bridge**—cast iron girder bridge

Truscott, Lucian — **Medal** — Distinguished Service Cross awarded to an animal

Truxton, Thomas—**Ship**—ship to capture an enemy ship after the Revolution

Tucker, John—**Supreme Court (U.S.)**—Supreme Court of the United States

Tucker, Richard—**Television—Telecast**—pay television presentation of an opera

Tucker, Stephen D.—**Printing Press**—rotary printing press

Tucker, Tommy—Radio Broadcast—cooperative radio show

Tucker, William Ellis—**Porcelain (hard)**

Tudor, Frederick—**Ice**—export of ice

Tudor, William—**Army Officer**—judge advocate

Tufts, John—**Music Book**—vocal instruction book

Tulley, John—**Map**—road map for public use

Tunney, Gene—**Prize Fight**—prize fight to attract 100,000 spectators

Tunnicliffe, George—**Hotel**—hotel to install electric lights

Turner, Charles W. — **Medal** — Medal of Honor awarded in the Korean War

Turner, Christopher—**Ship**—yacht

Turner, Cyril—**Skywriting**—skywriting

Turner, Daniel—**Physician** — doctor to receive an honorary medical degree

Turner, George A.—**Education**—war orphans education law

Turner, Henry C.—**Labor**—labor anti-discrimination commission (state)

Turner, Henry McNeal—**Army Officer**—chaplain (Negro) of the United States Army

Turner, James Edward—**Hospital**—inebriates' asylum

Turner, Lana — **Television — Telecast** — pay television

Turner, Robert—**Brake**—brake patent

Turner, Robert—**Paper Mill**

Turner, William G.—**Education**—war orphans education law

Turpin, Mary—**Catholic Nuns**—nun who was born in the United States

Tuthill, Richard Stanley—**Court**—juvenile court

Tuttle, Dorothy Edith Lorne—**Coast Guard (U.S.)**—Coast Guard Women's Reserve

T'Vault, William G.—**Newspaper**—newspaper published on the Pacific coast

Twain, Mark. *See* Clemens, Samuel Langhorne

Twining, Nathan Crook—**Aviation—Flights**—airplane catapulted

Twining, Nathan Farragut—**Air Force Officer**—Air Force chairman of the Joint Chiefs of Staff

Twombly, John Fogg—**Esperanto Club**

Twomey, Jeremiah F.—**Medical Legislation**—law (state) requiring serological blood tests of pregnant women

Tyler, John—**Political Convention**—unit rule

Tyler, John—**President (U.S.)**—President married while in office

Tyler, John—**President (U.S.)**—President to serve as an official of the Confederate States

Tyler, John — **Presidential Commission** — President requested by Congress to justify the creation of a presidential commission

Tyler, John—**Veto (presidential)**—legislation passed over a President's veto

Tyler, John—**Vice President of the United States**—Vice President to become President automatically

Tyler, Joseph—**Ship**—revenue cutter

Tyler, Royall—**Novel**—American novel republished in England

Tyler, Royall—**Play (drama)**—native American play successfully acted on a regular stage

Tyndale, Sarah—**Woman Suffrage**—convention (national) of women advocating woman suffrage

Tyng, James Alexander—**Baseball Catcher's Mask**

Tytus, John Butler—**Steel**—continuous sheet steel mill

U

Uelses, John—**Pole Vaulter**—pole vault jump indoors over 16 feet

Ullery, John Calvin — **Births** — quadruplets delivered by Caesarean operation

Uncles, Charles Randolph—**Catholic Priest**—Negro Catholic priest ordained in the United States

Underhill, Isaac—**Marble Quarry**

Underwood, Oscar Wilder — **Conference** — conference of great powers

Unterberg, Mrs. Israel—**Young Women's Hebrew Association**

Updike, Daniel Berkeley—**Printing Instruction**—printing lecture course in a college

Upson, Ralph Hazlett—**Aviation—Airship**—airship to land on a roof

Upton, Robert—**Theatrical Advance Publicity Man**

Upton, Roger—**Glue Factory (animal products)**

Urban, Charles—**Moving Picture**—colored moving pictures

Urey, Harold Clayton—**Water**—heavy water

Usher, Hezekiah—**Bookseller**

Usher, Hezekiah—**Children's Book**

Usher, Hezekiah—**Law Book**—compilation of colonial laws

Usher, John—**Copyright Law**—copyright law

Usher, John — **History** — History of New England

V

Vail, Alfred—**Telegram**—telegram inaugurating commercial service

Vail, Alfred—**Telegraph**—telegraphic communication system in which dots and dashes represented letters

Vail, Edwin—**Television**—**Telecast**—musical comedy telecast (one-hour)

Vaili, Mario—**Moving Picture**—moving picture of a complete grand opera

Vallentine, Edward—**Silk**—silk dyers

Van Bokkelen, Libertius—**Military School**—church military school

Van Boven, Paul—**Helicopter**—helicopter rescue of an American pilot behind enemy lines

Van Buren, Adelina—**Motorcycle Trip**—motorcycle transcontinental trip by women

Van Buren, Augusta—**Motorcycle Trip**—motorcycle transcontinental trip by women

Van Buren, Martin—**Free Soil Party**

Van Buren, Martin—**Political Convention**—two-thirds rule

Van Buren, Martin—**Political Machine**

Van Buren, Martin — **President (U.S.)** — President born a citizen of the United States

Van Buren, Martin—**Presidential Candidate**—presidential candidate nominated at a national convention

Van Buren, Martin—**Treaty**—treaty with a Far Eastern country

Vance, Claire K.—**Air Mail Service**—air mail transcontinental through regular service

Van Dam, Anthony—**Chamber of Commerce**—chamber of commerce (state)

Van Deman, Mrs. Ralph Henry—**Aviation-Passenger**—woman airplane passenger

Vandenberg, Hoyt Sanford — **Flag** — Air Force flag

Vandenberg, Hoyt Sanford — **Medal** — Air Force Medal of Honor for action in the Korean War

Vanderbilt, George Washington — **Forest Management**

Vanderbilt, William Henry—**Monument**—obelisk to be brought to the United States

Vandergrift, Alexander Archer—**World War II**—American offensive in the Pacific area

Vander Meer, Johnny—**Baseball Player**—major league baseball player to pitch two successive no-hit no-run games

Van de Waeter, Jan Hendricksen—**Swedes**

Van Dusen, John—**Insurance**—plate glass insurance

Van Etten, Edwin Jan—**Radio Broadcast**—religious service broadcast

Van Gieson, Ira—**Medical Instruction**—Psychiatric Institute

Van Hulsteyn, J. C.—**Orchestra**—municipal orchestra supported by taxes

Van Kannel, Theophilus—**Door**—door (revolving)

Vanni-Marcoux — **Opera** — opera broadcast over a national network from an American opera house

Van Reypen, William Knickerbocker—**Ship**—ambulance ship

Van Sant, Samuel Rinnah—**Optometry Legislation**

Van Syckel, Samuel—**Oil**—oil pipeline of importance

Van Twiller, Wouter—**Building**—brick building

Van Vechten, Carl—**Book**—book bound with a pre-printed offset cloth

Vare, William Scott—**Congress (U.S.)**—**Senate**—senatorial controversy in which no candidates were seated after a recount

Vaughan, Henry G.—**Foxhound Association**

Vaughan, Victor Clarence—**Medical Instruction**—bacteriology courses in a college

Vaughn, Jim—**Baseball Game**—double no-hit nine-inning baseball game

Veatch, John A.—**Borax**

Venima, Pieter—**Algebra Book**—algebra book

Vening-Meinesz, Felix Andries—**Astronomer**—woman astronomer employed in the United States Naval observatory

Vernon, Ambrose White—**Biography Course**—biography department

Vernon, Fortesque—**Astronomical Expedition**

Verplanck, Gulian Crommelin—**Election**—mayor elected by popular vote in a city

Verrazano, Giovanni da—**Kidnapping**—kidnapping

Vianesi, Augusto—**Opera**—opera at the Metropolitan Opera House

Vicente, Manuel de Populo—**Opera**—opera (Italian)

Victoria, Queen of Great Britain—**Cable (telegraph)**—cable across the Atlantic Ocean was completed

Viets, Simeon—**Cigar Factory**

Vilhelm, Prince of Sweden—**Lecturer**—lecturer of royal blood to speak for personal profit

Villiers, Coulon de—**War (colonial)**—French and Indian war battle

Vinay, Ramon—**Television**—**Telecast**—opera (complete) to be televised from the Metropolitan Opera House

Vincent, Ambrose—**Book Auction Catalog**—book auction catalog

Vincent, George Edgar—**Radio Broadcast**—dinner broadcast round-the-world

Vincent, John Heyl—**Chautauqua Organization**

Viner, D. D. ("Jimmy")—**Air Mail Service**—helicopter air mail delivery

Vinson, Frederick Moore—**Air Force**—Air Force Secretary

Vinson, Frederick Moore—**Defense Department (U.S.)**

Vivian, Charles A. S.—**Benevolent and Protective Order of Elks**

Vlasto, Solon John — **Newspaper** — Greek newspaper

Von Braun, Wernher—**Rocket**—rocket to reach outer space

Von Hagen, Victor Wolfgang—**Birds**—quetzal bird

Voorsanger, Elkan Cohen—**Army Officer**—regimental Jewish chaplain

Vorstman, P.—**Labadist Community**

Vosburg, R. J.—**Radio Distress Signal**—radio SOS from an American ship

Votey, Edwin S.—**Piano Player**—pneumatic piano player

Vredenburgh, Dorothy McElroy—**Woman**—woman secretary of a national political party

Vreeland, Jeanette—**Radio Broadcast**—radio concert from an airplane

W

Wade, John—**Ship**—iron vessel

Wade, Leigh—**Aviation—Flights (world)**—world flight

Wadleigh, George Henry—**Nautical School**—nautical municipal school

Wadsworth, Henry—**Television—Telecast**—play to be televised as a full-hour program

Wadsworth, Jeremiah—**Wool**—worsted mill operated by water power

Wadsworth, W. Austin—**Foxhound Association**

Waesche, Russell Randolph—**Coast Guard (U.S.)**—Vice Admiral in the Coast Guard

Wagner, Boyd D. — **Aviation — Aviator** — American ace in World War II

Wagner, Clinton—**Medical Society**—laryngological society (state)

Wagner, Herman L. — **Typewriter** — typewriter to produce a line of writing visible as it was being typed

Wagner, Honus—**Hall of Fame**—hall of fame (baseball)

Wagner, John—**Beer**—lager beer

Wagner, Robert Ferdinand—**Labor**—Labor Board (national)

Wagoner, Clyde Decker—**Radio Broadcast**—round the world broadcast

Wait, William E.—**Labor**—labor congress (national)

Waite, Charles C.—**Baseball Glove**

Wakefield, William H. T.—**United Labor Party**

Waksman, Selman Abraham—**Microbiology Laboratory**

Waksman, Selman Abraham—**Streptomycin**

Walcott, Joe — **Television — Telecast** — pay television presentation of a sporting event

Waldauer, Abe D.—**Enclave**—municipal enclave of economic ground rent

Walden, Henry W.—**Aviation—Airplane**—monoplane (American)

Waldrake, Sarah—**Woman**—women to become federal government employees

Waldseemüller, Martin H.—**"America"**

Waldseemüller, Martin H.—**Map**—globular map published showing the western hemisphere

Wales, Thomas Crane—**"Artics"**

Walker, Aldace Freeman—**Interstate Commerce Act**

Walker, Charles Duy—**Fraternity Magazine**—fraternity journal

Walker, D. A.—**Civil Service**—Civil Service Commission

Walker, Edwin Garrison—**Legislator (state)**—Negro representatives to sit in any legislature

Walker, Francis Amasa—**Economics Association**

Walker, Frank Comerford—**National Emergency Council (U.S.)**

Walker, George Herbert—**Golf Tournament**—international golf match

Walker, John—**Dictionary**—rhyming dictionary

Walker, John—**Senator (U.S.)**—senator appointed by a governor

Walker, John (John Pearson)—**Fingerprinting**—international exchange of fingerprints

Walker, Joseph—**Shoe Peg**

Walker, Maggie Lena—**Bank**—bank president (Negro woman)

Walker, Mary Edwards—**Army Officer**—woman assistant army surgeon

Walker, May—**Librarians' Union**

Walker, Moses Fleetwood—**Baseball Player**—Negro baseball player

Walker, Samuel Hamilton—**Temperance Society**—Anti-Saloon League

Walker, Thomas—**Colonist**—civilian settlement west of the Allegheny Mountains

Walker, William—**Land Office**

Walker, William H.—**Rayon**—rayon patent

Wallace, Henry—**Postal Service**—Pony Express mail

Wallace, Henry Agard—**Agricultural Adjustment Administration**

Wallace, Henry Agard—**Cabinet of the United States**—father and son to occupy the same cabinet posts

Wallace, Henry Agard—**Federal Surplus Relief Corporation**

Wallace, Mrs. Henry Agard—**Ship**—Liberty ship

Wallace, Henry Cantwell—**Cabinet of the United States**—father and son to occupy the same cabinet posts

Wallace, John Hankins—**Horse Register**—trotting register

Wallace, Lewis—**War Criminal Proceedings**

Wallace, Robert — **Spoons** — nickel silver spoons

Waller, Frank—**Bicycle Race**—motorcycle-paced bicycle race

Waller, William—**Stage Coach Inter-City Service**

Wallington, James—**Radio Broadcast**—submarine (submerged) broadcast

Wallington, James—**Television—Telecast**—color coast-to-coast telecast from the west coast

Walmesley, Charles — **Catholic Bishop** — Catholic bishop appointed to serve in the United States

Walsh, F. W.—**Temperance Society**—Anti-Saloon League (national organization)

Walsh, Mary—**Wedding**—balloon wedding

Walsh, Raoul—**Moving Picture**—talking picture taken outdoors (full length)

Walsh, Robert—**Periodical**—quarterly magazine

Walter, Eugene—**Radio Broadcast**—drama (full-length melodrama) broadcast

Walter, John—**Evangelical Association Council**

Walter, Thomas—**Music Book**—music book printed with bars

Walters, Bernice Rosenthal—**Naval Officer**—woman medical officer assigned to a naval vessel

Walthour, Robert—**Bicycle Race**—paired six-day bicycle race

Walvisch, Jonas—**Television**—television eye-witness allowed to testify in a federal court

Walworth, James Jones—**Heating System**—heating system (steam)

Wambsganss, Bill (William Wambsganss)—**Baseball Game**—triple play unassisted in a World Series

Wanamaker, John—**Electric Lighting**—electric light in a store

Wanamaker, Rodman—**Aviation**—**Airplane**—hydroplane with a multi-engine

Wang, Theodora Chan—**Women's Club**—Chinese women's club incorporated

Warbasse, James Peter—**Cooperatives Convention**

Ward, Aaron Montgomery—**Business**—mail order house

Ward, Artemas—**Army Officer**—Major General

Ward, August—**Cattle Club**—cattle club (Guernsey cattle)

Ward, Charles S.—**World War II**—American expeditionary force to land in Africa

Ward, Donald Gordon—**Radio Facsimile Transmission**—photograph sent by radio across the Atlantic as a public demonstration

Ward, Henry Dana—**Second Advent Believers General Conference**

Ward, Holcombe—**Tennis Match**—lawn tennis matches for the Davis Cup

Ward, Hortense—**Court**—state supreme court composed entirely of women

Ward, Lester Frank—**Sociological Society**—sociological society (national)

Ward, Richard Jay—**Radio Church**

Ward, Robert De Courcy—**Climatology Professor**

Warder, John Aston—**Forestry Society**—national forestry association

Ware, Bruce Richardson—**World War I**—shot fired by the American Navy in World War I against a known German submarine

Ware, W. H.—**Dental Corps (U.S. Army)**—dentist officially employed in the U.S. Army

Ware, William Robert—**Architectural School**—architectural school

Waring, George E.—**Cattle Club**—cattle club (Jersey cattle)

Waring, George Edwin—**Sewage**—separate system of sewage disposal

Waring, Hank—**Aviation**—**Airplane**—turbine propeller light-airplane

Warmerdam, Cornelius—**Pole Vaulter**—pole vaulter to clear the bar at 15 feet

Warner, Amos Griswold—**Corporation Course**—industrial corporation course

Warner, Charles Joseph—**Legislature**—unicameral legislature (state)

Warner, Ira DeVer—**Corset**

Warner, Lucien Calvin—**Corset**

Warner, Maurice—**Orchestra**—radio orchestra

Warren, Edward—**Balloon**—balloon flight

Warren, Fred Marshall—**Medal**—Reserve Officers Association medal

Warren, James—**Army Officer**—Paymaster General

Warren, John Collins—**Anesthesia**—painless surgery demonstration

Warren, John Collins — **Pharmacopoeia** — pharmacopoeia prepared by a medical association

Warren, Josiah—**Anarchist**

Warren, Leonard — **Television** — **Telecast** — opera (complete) to be televised from the Metropolitan Opera House

Warren, Lillie Eginton—**Deaf**—**School**—lip reading school for adults

Warren, Mercy Otis — **History** — American history of importance written by a woman

Washburn, Cadwallader Colden—**Congressman (U.S.)**—congressmen (brothers) to serve simultaneously

Washburn, Harry—**Television**—**Telecast**—murder trial to be televised

Washburn, Ichabod—**Wire**—piano wire

Washburn, Ichabod—**Wire Gauge**

Washburn, Israel—**Congressman (U.S.)**—congressmen (brothers) to serve simultaneously

Washburne, Elihu Benjamin—**Congressman (U.S.)**—congressmen (brothers) to serve simultaneously

Washington, Booker Taliaferro—**Money**—coin bearing the portrait of a Negro

Washington, Booker Taliaferro — **Postage Stamp**—Negro depicted upon a U.S. postage stamp

Washington, George—**Animals**—mule

Washington, George—**Army Officer**—General (Continental Army)

Washington, George—**Army Uniform**

Washington, George — **Attorney General** — Attorney General

Washington, George — **Balloon** — balloon flight in which a presidential order was carried

Washington, George—**Cabinet of the United States**—cabinet

Washington, George—**Capitol of the United States**

Washington, George — **Congress of the United States**—joint meeting of the Senate and the House of Representatives

Washington, George—**Constitution of the United States**—Constitution (federal)

Washington, George — **Copyright Law** — copyright law of the United States

Washington, George — **Degrees (academic and honorary)**—honorary degree granted George Washington

Wignell, Thomas—**Play (drama)**—native American play successfully acted on a regular stage

Wilbour, Charlotte Beebee—**Women's Club** —women's professional club

Wilbur, Curtis Dwight—**Television—Telecast**—telecast of an object in motion

Wilbur, James H.—**Indian School**—Indian school (boarding) on a reservation

Wilcox, John W.—**Electrotype**—electrotype manufacturing

Wilcox, L. S.—**Tung**

Wilde, Francis E. J.—**Electric Sign**—electric sign flasher

Wildey, Thomas—**Odd Fellows Lodge**

Wildman, Ernest Atkins—**Conscientious Objectors' Camp**

Wiley, David—**Agricultural Journal**—agricultural journal

Wiley, Herbert Victor—**Glider**—glider released from a dirigible

Wilhelmina, Queen of the Netherlands—**Congress of the United States**—reigning queen to address a joint session of Congress

Wilkes, Charles—**Expedition**—scientific expedition fitted out by the United States Government

Wilkins, James Ernest—**Cabinet of the United States**—Negro sub-cabinet member

Wilkinson, David—**Nut and Bolt Machine**

Wilkinson, David—**Screw**—screw patent

Wilkinson, Eugene Parks—**Navy**—atomic submarine division

Wilkinson, Eugene Parks—**Submarine**—atomic-powered submarine

Wilkinson, Hannah—**Thread**—cotton thread

Wilkinson, Jeremiah—**Nails**—nails

Willard, Charles Foster—**Aviation—Expositions and Meets**—aviation meet

Willard, Emma Hart—**College**—school for the higher education of women

Willard, Frances Elizabeth—**College**—woman college president

Willard, Frances Elizabeth—**Monument**—statue of a woman in National Statuary Hall

Willard, Samuel—**Book**—book of folio size

Willard, Simon—**Clock**—banjo clock patent

Willerup, Christian B.—**Methodist Episcopal Church**—Scandinavian Methodist Episcopal Church

Willets, Edward—**Animals**—monkey trained to perform

Willets, Gilson — **Moving Picture** — serial moving picture

Williams, Charles—**Railroad**—railroad to run west of the Mississippi River

Williams, Charles — **Telephone** — telephone for domestic use

Williams, Daniel Hale—**Hospital**—interracial hospital

Williams, Daniel Hale—**Surgical Operation** —suture of the human heart (successful)

Williams, Elkanah—**Medical Instruction**—ophthalmology professor

Williams, Ella C.—**Fellowship**—resident fellowship for women awarded by a women's college

Williams, Harvey—**Radio Contest**

Williams, Henry J.—**Publishing Society**

Williams, Horatio Burt—**Stethoscope**—electrical stethoscope (portable)

Williams, Isaac—**Neutrality Regulation**

Williams, J. A.—**Welsh Magazine**

Williams, Jesse—**Cheese Factory**—cheese factory of consequence

Williams, Jesse Lynch—**Play (drama)**—drama to win a Pulitzer prize

Williams, John—**Medal**—Medal of Honor awarded to a member of the Naval Service

Williams, John Foster—**Ship**—revenue cutter

Williams, Jonathan—**Army**—engineer corps

Williams, Jonathan—**Army School**—army school

Williams, Joseph Ricketson—**Agricultural School**—agricultural college (state) to open

Williams, Kathlyn—**Moving Picture**—serial moving picture

Williams, Lola M.—**Woman**—woman secretary to a Vice President of the United States

Williams, Nellie—**Baseball Team**—women's baseball team

Williams, Richard F.—**Hospital**—Negro hospital and asylum

Williams, Robley Cook—**Virus**—virus separated into component parts

Williams, Roger—**Baptist Church**—Baptist Church

Williams, Roger—**Dictionary**—Indian-English dictionary

Williams, Samuel—**Astronomical Expedition**

Williams, Samuel Wells—**Chinese Language and Literature Lectureship**

Williams, Sydney Augustus—**Insurance**—mutual liability insurance company

Williams, Thomas Robinson—**Felt**—manufacturing mechanical process

Williams, Thomas W.—**Ship**—steam whaler

Williams, Walter—**Journalism Course**—journalism school

Williamson, James De Long—**Community Trust**

Williamson, John Ernest—**Photograph**—photographs taken under the sea

Williamson, John Finley—**Television—Telecast**—religious services to be televised

Williamson, Peregrine—**Pen**—steel pen patent

Williamson, Walter—**Medical School**—homeopathic college

Willich, Anthony Florian Madinger—**Agricutural Encyclopedia**

Willing, Thomas—**Bank**—bank chartered by Congress

Willingham, Harris Emanuel—**Federal Alcohol Control Administration**

Winthrop, John — **Colonial Government** — colonial government union

Winthrop, John—**Copper Mine**

Winthrop, John—**Degrees (academic and honorary)**—doctor of laws honorary degree

Winthrop, John—**Election**—accredited colonial election

Winthrop, John—**Expedition**—scientific expedition

Winthrop, John—**Fork**

Winthrop, John—**Iron**—iron works (successful)

Wirt, William—**Anti-Masonic Party**

Wirt, William—**Platoon School**

Wirz, August Herman—**Tube**—machine designed to produce collapsible tubes

Wirz, Henry—**War Criminal Proceedings**

Wisden, J.—**Cricket Tournament**—international cricket tournament

Wise, Isaac Mayer—**Jewish College**—Jewish college to train men for the rabbinate

Wise, John — **Aviation** — **Airship** — airship bombing

Wise, John—**Aviation**—**Airship**—dirigible

Wise, John—**Balloon**—balloon flight carrying mail

Wistar, Caspar—**Medical Book**—anatomy book (American)

Wistar, Isaac Jones—**Research Institute**—anatomy research institute

Wister, William—**Cricket Club**—cricket club to own its own clubhouse

Withers, Clark—**Radio Telephone**—two-way radio conversation between a submerged submarine and another vessel

Witherspoon, Herbert—**Opera**—opera by an American composer performed at the Metropolitan Opera House of New York

Witsell, Edward Fuller — **Army Officer** — woman army officer

Wittenmyer, Annie T.—**Temperance Society**—women's temperance society (national)

Wittich, Jean Wetterau—**Woman**—woman state budget commissioner

Witzke, Lothar—**World War I**—German spy to receive a death sentence from the American forces during World War I

Wolber, Joseph Gustave—**Crime Prevention and Detection**—crime prevention commission for interstate cooperation

Wolcott, Alexander S.—**Photographic Patent**

Wold, Peter Irving—**Television**—**Telecast**—speaker to address an organization by television

Wolf, Ludwig Martin Nicolaus—**Sewing Machine**—sewing machine lamp holder

Wolfe, Richard—**Church**—church without theology, creed or dogma

Wolff, Julius—**Canning**—sardine cannery

Wolfson, Arthur M.—**Degrees (academic and honorary)**—master of arts degree in sacred music

Woll, Frederic Albert—**Optometry Instruction**—optics and optometry courses

Wollstonecraft, Mary—**Woman Suffrage**—woman suffrage book

Wolman, Leo — **Labor** — Labor Advisory Board (U.S.)

Wood, Abraham—**Expedition**—expedition

Wood, Charles Raymond—**Helicopter**—ram-jet helicopter

Wood, Edward Stickney—**Medical Instruction**—medical chemistry course (systematic)

Wood, Fernando—**Telegram**—transcontinental telegram

Wood, Fernando—**Telegraph**—telegraph line to the Pacific coast

Wood, George Bacon—**Medical Book**—dispensatory (American)

Wood, Harold L. — **Discovery** — northwest passage

Wood, Henry Alexander Wise—**Labor-Saving Device**

Wood, Henry Alexander Wise—**Stereotype**—automatic plate-casting and finishing machine for stereotype printing

Wood, John—**Printing Press**—rotogravure press

Wood, John Jethro—**Plow**—plow with interchangeable parts

Wood, Sally Sayward—**Women's Club**—women's club

Wood, Stuart—**Political Science Society**—political and social science society (national)

Wood, Walton J.—**Public Defenders' Office**

Wood, William M.—**Navy**—naval militia (state)

Wood, William Maxwell—**Naval Officer**—Surgeon General of the Navy

Woodbridge, Benjamin—**Degrees (academic and honorary)**—Bachelor of Arts degree

Woodbridge, Timothy—**Physician**—doctor to receive an honorary medical degree

Woodbridge, William—**Educational Association**—educational association (local)

Woodhouse, James—**Chemical Laboratory Manual**

Woodhouse, James — **Chemical Society** — chemical society

Woodhull, Victoria Claflin—**Brokerage**—woman brokerage office owner

Woodhull, Victoria Claflin — **Presidential Candidate**—woman presidential candidate

Woods, Kate Tanett—**Women's Club**—women's club federation

Woods, Leslie G.—**World War I**—American Army soldiers killed in combat

Woods, Persis C. — **College** — college for women

Woods, William—**Steel**—cast steel for plows

Woodward, Artemas—**Brushes**

Woodward, George B.—**Bicycle Society**—bicycle club

Woodward, John Blackburne—**Rifle Association**—rifle association (national)

Woodward, Robert Burns—**Chlorophyll**—chlorophyll "a"

Woodward, Robert Burns — **Quinine** — synthetic quinine

Woodward, Samuel B.—**Psychiatric Association**

Woodworth, John Maynard—**Public Health**—Public Health Service (U.S.)

Woolfolk, Marie—**Sorority**—Negro sorority

Woolley, John Granville—**United Christian Party**

Woolley, Leonidas G.—**Locomotive Headlight**—electric locomotive headlight

Woolworth, Frank Winfield — **Business** — five-cent store

Woorn, Joseph — **Wedding** — double radio wedding

Worden, John Lorimer — **Ship** — iron-clad turreted vessel in the U.S. Navy

Workman, Sonny — **Horse Race** — horse to win a $100,000 purse in one race

Worthington, Henry Rossiter — **Pump**—independent single direct-acting steam power pump

Worthington, John — **Health Board**—health board (local)

Worthylake, George — **Lighthouse** — lighthouse

Wortman, Jacob L. — **Typewriter Ribbon**—typewriter "copy" ribbon

Wouves, P. R.—**Cryptography Chart**

Wrabetz, Voyta—**Insurance**—unemployment insurance act

Wren, Edward—**Medal**—Distinguished Service Cross awarded to an animal

Wrenn, Robert D. — **Tennis Match** — lawn tennis champions who were brothers

Wright, Arthur Williams—**Degrees (academic and honorary)**—doctor of philosophy degree

Wright, Carroll Davidson — **Labor**—labor bureau (federal)

Wright, Carroll Davidson — **Vending Machine**—vending machine (coin operated) to dispense postage stamps

Wright, Elizur — **Insurance**—non-forfeiture insurance law (state)

Wright, George — **Baseball Team**—baseball team to receive a regular salary

Wright, George Green — **Vaccine** — anthrax vaccine for humans

Wright, Harry — **Baseball Team** — baseball team to receive a regular salary

Wright, James Hood—**Electric Lighting**—electric light from a power plant in a residence

Wright, John D.—**Hospital**—inebriates' asylum

Wright, Orville—**Aviation**—airplane fatality

Wright, Orville — **Aviation — Airplane**—airplane to receive national acclaim

Wright, Orville — **Aviation — Flights** — airplane endurance flight exceeding one hour

Wright, Orville—**Aviation — Flights**—intercity airplane flight

Wright, Orville — **Aviation—License**—Civil Aeronautics Administration honorary license

Wright, Silas—**Political Machine**

Wright, Wilbur — **Aviation — Airplane**—airplane purchased by the United States Government

Wright, Wilbur — **Aviation — Airplane**—airplane to receive national acclaim

Wright, William Hammond—**Moving Picture**—moving picture of the planets

Wunderlich, Frieda — **College**—woman dean of a graduate school

Wyatt, Ben Harrison — **Moving Picture** — moving picture of an eclipse of the sun taken from an airplane

Wyatt, Francis — **Prohibition** — prohibition enforcement officers

Wyatt, Francis—**Temperance Law (colonial)**

Wyatt, James—**Wax Works Museum**

Wyckoff, Henry I.—**Hospital**—eye hospital (permanent)

Wye, Thomas E.—**Factory**—factories operhospital operated by the government

Wyman, George A. — **Motorcycle Trip** — motorcycle transcontinental trip

Wyman, Morrill—**Medical Book**—hay fever book

Wyman, Walter — **Hospital** — tuberculosis hospital operated by the Government

Wynn, Ed — **Television**—**Telecast** — high-definition telecast

Wynne, Arthur—**Crossword Puzzle**

Wynne, Shirley Wilmotte — **Television** — **Telecast**—demonstration of home reception of television

Wythe, George—**Law School**—law school in a college

Y

Yalden, James—**Accountants' Society**—accountants' society to become a national organization

Yale, Linus—**Lock**—lock ("clock")

Yancey, Lewis Alonzo—**Aviation**—**Flights**—New York-Bermuda flight

Yancey, Wallace D. — **Aviation** — **Flights (transpacific)**—jet transpacific non-stop flight

Yates, Esther—**Water Ski Tournament (national)**

Yeager, Charles E.—**Aviation**—**Flights**—airplane to exceed the speed of sound

Yeardley, George—**Legislative Assembly**

Yeaton, Hopley—**Naval Officer**—naval officer commissioned

Yolton, John Maloney—**Aviation**—**Airship**—airship with an enclosed cabin

Yost, Doris—**Surgical Operation**—lung removal carried out according to pre-operative plans

Youmans, Edward Livingston — **Science Magazine**—science magazine (popular)

Young, Achsah—**Witchcraft Execution**

Young, Brigham — **Business** — department store

Young, Clarence Marshall—**Aviation**—**License**—glider pilot's license (honorary)

Young, Edna Earle—**Naval Officer**—women sworn into the regular U.S. Navy

Young, James Hadden—**Typesetting Machine**—typesetting machine patent

Young, John Richardson—**Medical Book**—gastroenterology treatise

Young, Leo C.—**Radar**—radar detection of airplanes

Young, Leo C.—**Radar**—radar observations

Young, Mahonri—**Monument**—monument to a bird

Young, Perry H.—**Aviation—Aviator**—Negro airplane pilot on a scheduled passenger line

Young, Samuel Baldwin Marks—**Army War College**

Young, William G.—**Ice Cream Freezer**

Yulee, David Levy—**Senator (U.S.)**—Jewish senator

Yung, Wing—**Chinese Embassy**

Yung, Wing—**Chinese Students**

Z

Zacharie, Issachar—**Medical Book**—chiropody book

Zachos, John Celinergos—**Stenotype**

Zachow, Otto—**Automobile Brake**

Zaharias, Babe Didrikson—**Golf Champion**—woman golfer (American born) to win the British Women's Amateur Golf Tournament

Zahn, Albert Francis—**Aviation—Expositions and Meets**—air conference (international)

Zakrzewska, Marie Elizabeth—**Hospital**—women's infirmary staffed by women physicians

Zamenhof, Lazaro Ludovico—**Esperanto**

Zane, Ebenezer—**Land Grant**—special land grant

Zeisberger, David—**Protestant Church**—Protestant church

Zeisberger, David—**Schoolhouse**

Zenger, John Peter—**Map**—war map

Zenger, John Peter—**Newspaper**—political newspaper

Zenger, Peter—**Algebra Book**—algebra book

Zentzytzki, Stanislaus—**Bobsled Run**

Zerega, Antoine—**Macaroni Factory**

Zettlein, George—**Baseball Game**—no-run nine-inning baseball game

Zieber, George B.—**Sewing Machine**—sewing machine manufacturer

Zimmerman, Andrew—**Oil**—oil well (flowing)

Zimmermann, Cyrus Johnston—**Air Mail Service**—air mail service to a steamer at sea

Zinzendorf, Benigna von—**School**—school for Protestant girls

Zoller, Frederick—**Business**—installment finance company

Zukor, Adolph—**Moving Picture**—foreign feature film exhibited

Zumwalt, Elmo Russell, Jr.—**Ship**—guided missile destroyer

Zwicky, Fritz—**Submarine**—submarine jet propulsion device patent

Zworykin, Vladimir Kosma—**Electron Tube**

Zworykin, Vladimir Kosma—**Microscope**—electron microscope

Zworykin, Vladimir Kosma—**Road**—electronic highway system

Zworykin, Vladimir Kosma—**Television**—electronic television system

Geographical Index

To obtain a complete account of the various items, the reader should consult the main body of the text. The **boldface** type shows the alphabetical heading under which each item may be found. If an item appears in the text under a general heading, the specific heading is noted below after the general heading.

ALABAMA

Boycott Law—enacted—Sept. 26, 1903

Dental Legislation—legislation (state) regarding dental surgery—enacted—Dec. 31, 1841

Ship—tugboat (diesel electric)—1929

Television Station—state-wide and state-supported educational television network —opened—Aug. 9, 1956

Trust—anti-trust law (state)—approved— Feb. 23, 1883

Woman—woman secretary of a national political party—D. M. Vredenburgh—appointed

Auburn

Element—element 87—francium—announced —Feb. 8, 1930

Birmingham

Photograph—cystoscopic photographs in color—publicly exhibited—March 11, 1940

Enterprise

Monument—monument to an insect—dedicated—Dec. 11, 1919

Fairhope

Enclave—established—Jan. 5, 1895

Fort Rucker

Helicopter—Flight—helicopter refueling flight (successful)—Aug. 14, 1956

Mobile

Catholic Bishop—native bishops of the South—ordained—Aug. 15, 1850

Money—confederate currency—authorized— March 9, 1861

Parade—parade with float tableaux—Feb. 24, 1868

Parade—street parade held by a mystic society—Dec. 31, 1830

Montgomery

Aviation—Flights—night flight—W. R. Brookins—April 18, 1910

Building—"White House of the Confederacy"—used—Feb. 18, 1861

Congress of the Confederate States—provisional session—Feb. 4, 1861

Constitution of the Confederate States of America—adopted—March 11, 1861

Flag—Confederate States flag—adopted— March 4, 1861

President of the Confederate States—Jefferson Davis—took office—Feb. 18, 1861

Suture—silver wire suture—used—J. M. Sims—1849

Prattville

Birth Registration Law—birth registration uniform system for the numbering of birth certificates—lowest number assigned

Sylacauga

Meteorite—meteorite known to have struck a woman—Nov. 30, 1954

ALASKA

State—noncontiguous state—admitted—Jan. 3, 1959

Fairbanks

Aviation—Flights—North Pole jet crossing —Sept. 20, 1951

Metlakahtla

President (U.S.)—President to visit Alaska and Canada while President—W. G. Harding—July 8, 1923

ARIZONA

Apache Pass

Medal—Medal of Honor action—B. J. D. Irwin—Feb. 13, 1861

Ashfork

Dam—steel dam—built—1898

Canon Diablo

Diamond—diamonds in a meteorite—found —June 1891

ARIZONA—*Continued*

Flagstaff

Astronomy—planet—found beyond Neptune Feb. 18, 1930

Phoenix

Aviation—Aviator—pilot to receive the Congressional Medal of Honor—posthumous award—May 29, 1919

Prescott

Old Age Home for Pioneers—approved— March 10, 1909

Rodeo—July 4, 1888

Tucson

Aviation — Airport — airport municipally owned—Nov. 20, 1919

Building—solar-heated and radiation-cooled house—built—R. W. Bliss—Jan. 15, 1955

ARKANSAS

Park—park (national)—Hot Springs National Park—March 4, 1921

Protestant Episcopal Bishop—Negro suffragan—Rev. E. T. Demby—appointed—Sept. 29, 1918

Senator (U.S.)—woman elected to the Senate—H. O. W. Caraway—Jan. 12, 1932

Benton

Fuller's Earth—discovered—1891

Fayetteville

Army—Reserve Officers Training Corps Units—authorized—Oct. 21, 1916

Hot Springs

Hospital—hospital for the military and naval forces—opened—Jan. 17, 1887

Murfreesboro

Diamond—diamond in actual rock — discovered—1906

Wilmar

Turbine—gas turbine to pump natural gas— installed—May 13, 1949

CALIFORNIA

Alfalfa—introduced—1854

Congressman (U.S.)—congressman of Asian ancestry—D. S. Saund—elected—Nov. 6, 1956

Congressman (U.S.)—congresswoman elected to serve in the place of her husband— Jan. 23, 1923

Dock—state-owned docks—authorized—April 24, 1863

Election Law—fraudulent election law (state)—enacted—March 26, 1866

Forest Service—forest commission (state)— permanent—authorized—March 3, 1885

Homestead Act—homestead act (desert)— enacted—March 3, 1875

Oyster Cocktail—originated—1866

Park—park (national) containing an active volcano—established—Aug. 9, 1916

Park—state park—Yosemite Valley park— 1865

Price Regulation Law—resale price maintenance law (state)—"Fair Trade Act"— approved—May 8, 1931

Quarantine — plant quarantine legislation (state)—enacted—March 4, 1881

State—state admitted to the Union on the Pacific coast—Sept. 9, 1850

Volcano—eruption—recorded—1694

Woman—woman District Attorney of the United States—A. A. Adams—served— July 25, 1918

Alameda

Telephone—dial telephone service coast-to-coast without the aid of operators—to Englewood, N.J.—Nov. 10, 1951

Angels Camp, Calaveras County

Frog Jumping Jubilee—May 19-20, 1928

Arcadia

Aviation—Flights (transcontinental)—transcontinental dirigible flight (non-rigid dirigible)—from Newport News, Va.—Sept. 23, 1922

Berkeley

Aviation—Airship—airship disaster—May 23, 1908

Bevatron—in operation—Feb. 15, 1954

Element—element 93—neptunium—discovery announced—June 8, 1940

Element — element 94 — plutonium — discovered—1940

Element—element 96—curium—discovered— 1944

Element—element 97—berkelium—identified —Dec. 1949

Element—element 98—californium identified and produced—Jan. 1950

Element—element 99—einsteinium—identified —Dec. 1952

Element—element 101—mendelevium—discovered—Feb. 1955

Element—element 103—produced—Feb. 14, 1961

High School—junior high schools—authorized—Dec. 21, 1909

CALIFORNIA—*Continued*

Hollywood

See under Los Angeles

Honey Lake

Moving Picture—moving picture of an eclipse of the sun taken from an airplane—April 28, 1930

Inglewood

Electric Starting Gate—race track—installed—May 8, 1939
Horse—horse to win a million dollars in races—Citation—July 14, 1951
Jockey—jockey to win 4,000 races—Johnny Longden—May 15, 1952

La Habra

Citron—commercially grown in large quantity—1925

La Jolla

Oceanography Institution—established—1912

Long Beach

Air Mail Service—helicopter air mail and express service to carry passengers—to Los Angeles—Nov. 22, 1955
Aviation—Airplane—airplane with eight engines—tested—Nov. 2, 1947
Aviation—Flights (transcontinental)—transcontinental airplane flight—completed—C. P. Rodgers—Dec. 10, 1911

Los Angeles

Air Mail Service—helicopter air mail and express service—service inaugurated—Oct. 1, 1947
Air Mail Service—helicopter air mail and express service to carry passengers—to Long Beach, Calif.—Nov. 22, 1955
Animals—chinchilla farm—established—Feb. 22, 1923
Automobile Bus—bus night coach—to San Francisco—July 1929
Automobile Bus—coast to coast through bus line—to New York City—Sept. 11, 1928
Automobile Race Track—automobile speedway (board track)—opened—April 7, 1910
Automobile Transcontinental Trip—gas turbine automobile to make a transcontinental trip—arrived from New York City—March 30, 1956
Automobile Transcontinental Trip—transcontinental family automobile trip requiring only a month—left for New York City—April 24, 1908
Aviation—Aviator—aviator (American) to establish an altitude record—Louis Paulhan—Jan. 12, 1910
Aviation—Expositions and Meets—aviation meet—Jan. 10, 1910

Aviation—Flights (transcontinental)—transcontinental airplane flight (east-bound)—R. G. Fowler—Oct. 19, 1911
Aviation—Flights (transcontinental)—transcontinental commercial overnight transport service—from Newark, N.J.—Aug. 2, 1934
Aviation—Flights (transcontinental)—transcontinental flight made by Negroes in their own plane—arrived—July 19, 1933
Aviation—Flights (transcontinental)—transcontinental non-stop eastward scheduled service—to New York City—Oct. 19, 1953
Aviation—Flights (transcontinental)—transcontinental non-stop flight by a woman—A. E. Putnam—Aug. 24, 1932
Aviation—Flights (transcontinental)—transcontinental regularly scheduled through air service—Oct. 25, 1930
Aviation—Flights (transcontinental)—transcontinental regularly scheduled two-way non-stop service—Nov. 29, 1953
Aviation—Flights (transcontinental)—transcontinental round-trip solo flight between sunrise and sunset—May 21, 1955
Aviation—Flights (world)—round-the-world flight over the North Pole on a regularly scheduled commercial air route—Nov. 15, 1954
Aviation—Parachute—aviator to bail out of an airplane flying at supersonic speed—G. F. Smith—Feb. 26, 1955
Aviation—Parachute—parachute jump from an airplane by a woman—Georgia Broadwick—June 21, 1913
Aviation—Races—airplane race (of importance) in which both men and women were contestants—commenced—Aug. 30, 1931
Buddhist Temple—established—July 15, 1904
Building—circular office building—dedicated—April 6, 1956
Catholic Priest—Catholic cardinal whose see was west of the Rockies—J. F. McIntyre—elevated—Jan. 12, 1953
Fog Disposal Unit—accepted by test—March 29, 1949
Football—football with a rubber covering—manufactured—March 1936
High Jump—over seven feet—Charles Dumas—June 29, 1956
Humanist Society—established—Jan. 13, 1929
Moving Picture—animated cartoon in color (Technicolor) of feature length with sound—exhibited—Dec. 21, 1937
Moving Picture—animated cartoon talking picture—produced—1928
Moving Picture—animated three-dimensional cartoon in Technicolor (modern)—premiere—May 28, 1953
Moving Picture Actor—moving picture actor and son to receive "Oscars"—John and Walter Huston—March 24, 1949
Moving Picture Actor—moving picture actors to receive "Oscars"—May 16, 1929
Moving Picture Actor—Negro to win an "Oscar"—Feb. 29, 1940
Moving Picture Theater—moving picture theater—opened—April 2, 1902

Photograph — photograph of genes — announced—Jan. 7, 1949

Presidential Candidate—Presidential candidate debate series on television—third debate, Kennedy in New York City and Nixon in Hollywood—Oct. 13, 1960

Public Defender's Office—created—June 13, 1913

Public School—public school opera studio—opened—Oct. 1937

Radio Broadcast—cooperative radio show—Oct. 10, 1937

Radio Broadcast—network broadcast received on the Pacific Coast—Oct. 23, 1924

Radio Telephone—radio telephone service (commercial)—July 16, 1920

Railroad—streamlined Pullman train (six cars)—to New York City—Oct. 22, 1934

Railroad Car—air-conditioned cars—installed —to Chicago—1914

Runner—runner to run a mile under four minutes—Jim Bailey—May 5, 1956

Ship — gyro-stabilized American liner — "Mariposa"—sailed—Oct. 26, 1956

Shot-Put—shot-put toss over 60 feet—Parry O'Brien—May 8, 1954

Sleeping Car—transcontinental through Pullman sleeping car service—to New York City—inaugurated—March 30, 1946

Sports Trophy—Negro to win the James E. Sullivan Memorial Trophy—M. G. Whitfield—1954

Street Car—trackless trolley system—operated—Sept. 11, 1910

Surgical Operation—lung tumor operation in which the patient was under hypnosis—Jan. 1955

Tape Recording—video recording on magnetic tape—Oct. 3, 1952

Television—Telecast—atomic explosion telecast—Feb. 1, 1951

Television—Telecast—stockholders' meetings televised coast-to-coast simultaneously—Oct. 29, 1959

Television—Telecast—surgical operation televised on a coast-to-coast closed circuit in color—Dec. 7, 1951

Television—Telecast — telecast images received in an airplane—May 21, 1932

Television Station—commercial television station west of the Mississippi River—Jan. 22, 1947

Theater—theater provided with scientific air distribution—1921

Mare Island

Ship—electrically propelled ship of the U.S. Navy—launched—Aug. 24, 1912

Submarine—streamlined submarine of the U.S. Navy—"Nautilus"—launched—March 15, 1930

Submarine—submarine expressly designed and built to fire guided missiles—"Grayback"—launched—July 2, 1957

Merced

Aviation—Flights (world)—jet round-the-world non-stop flight—Jan. 1957

Modesto

Aviation—Airport—airport municipal legislation—ratified—Sept. 14, 1910

Montebello

Soilless Culture of Plants—commercial hydroponicum (large)—established—Dec. 5, 1935

Monterey

Army Officer—chaplain (Catholic) of the U.S. Army—S. H. Milley—served—Sept. 28, 1849

Newspaper—newspaper published on the Pacific coast—*Californian*—Aug. 15, 1846

Ship—naval vessel of the United States to sail around the Cape of Good Hope to the west coast of the United States—arrived —Sept. 15, 1843

Ship—ship from the Atlantic coast to anchor in a California port—"Otter"—Oct. 29, 1796

Television Station—television stations to share the same time and frequency—KMBY-TV and KSBW-TV (Salinas)—Sept. 11, 1953

Mount Hamilton

Moving Picture—moving picture of the planets—Oct. 1926

Seismograph—exhibited—June 1, 1888

Mount Ophir

Mint (U.S.)—private mint authorized by the United States Government—built—1850

Money—fifty-dollar gold pieces—minted—Feb. 20, 1851

Mount Wilson

Astronomer—astronomer to measure the size of a fixed star—F. G. Pease—Dec. 13, 1920

Muroc

Aviation—Airplane—bomber with the flying wing design—landed—June 25, 1946

Aviation—Airplane—gas turbine propeller-driven airplane—tested—Feb. 11, 1945

Aviation—Airplane—jet propelled airplane—flown—Oct. 1, 1942

Aviation—Airplane—jet propulsion four-engine bomber—flown—March 6, 1947

Aviation—Flights—airplane to exceed the speed of 600 miles per hour—Albert Boyd —June 19, 1947

Aviation—Flights—airplane to exceed the speed of sound—C. E. Yeager—Oct. 14, 1947

Aviation—Flights—airplane to exceed the speed of 1,300 miles an hour—Scott Crossfield—Nov. 20, 1953

CALIFORNIA—*Continued*

Newport Bay

Aviation — Flights — over-water round-trip flight—to Catalina Island—May 10, 1912

Oakland

Aviation—Airport—airport hotel—opened— July 15, 1929
Aviation—Aviator—woman aviator to fly solo across the Pacific Ocean—A. E. Putnam—arrived—Jan. 12, 1935
Aviation—Flights (transpacific)—California-Hawaii flight—June 28, 1927
Balloon—balloon circular flight—Aug. 3, 1904
Bird Refuge—authorized by a state—Feb. 14, 1872
Fingerprint Society—fingerprint society (international)—formed—Oct. 9, 1915
Forest Service—aircraft owned by the Forest Service—in service—Aug. 17, 1938
Laundry—commercial power laundry—1851
Unitarian Society—woman moderator of the Unitarian Church—A. H. Reinhardt—1940

Otay

Glider—glider flight—J. J. Montgomery— March 17, 1884

Palm Springs

Television—Telecast—pay television presentation of a moving picture shown simultaneously in theaters—Nov. 28, 1953

Palmdale

Aviation—Flights—airplane to exceed the speed of 800 miles an hour—H. A. Hanes —Aug. 20, 1955

Palo Alto

Geology—woman graduate in geology—Lou Henry—1898
Photograph—photograph showing action (not moving pictures)—Eadweard Muybridge— 1872

Palomar Mountain

Telescope—telescope lens two hundred inches in diameter—installed—1947

Pasadena

Cosmic Ray—discovered—R. A. Millikan— 1925
Moving Picture—newsreel in color—taken— Jan. 1, 1948
Physics—positron—recognized—C. D. Anderson—1934
Submarine—submarine jet propulsion device patent—Fritz Zwicky—Feb. 15, 1949

Television—Telecast—color coast-to-coast telecast from the West Coast—Tournament of Roses—Jan. 1, 1954
Tournament of Roses—Jan. 1, 1890
Virus—virus (human- or animal-infecting virus) to be crystallized—poliomyelitis virus—announced—Nov. 3, 1955

Petaluma

Locker—locker (coin vender)—patented— W. S. Farnsworth—March 7, 1911

Playa Del Rey

See under Los Angeles

Redwood City

Ship—concrete seagoing ship—"Faith"— launched—March 14, 1918
Tape Recorder—magnetic tape recorder (commercial) of sound and picture— demonstrated—April 14, 1956

Riverside

Aviation—Flights (transcontinental)—transcontinental round-trip airplane flight within one day—to Andrews Field, Md.— June 13, 1946
Forest Service—forest service aerial patrol— established—June 1, 1919
Medal—Air Force Medal of Honor for action in the Korean War—presented posthumously—Aug. 24, 1951
Oranges (seedless navel)—grown—1873

Rogers Dry Lake

Aviation—Aviator—woman to pilot an airplane faster than the speed of sound— Jacqueline Cochran—May 18, 1953

Sacramento

Camel Race—April 7, 1864
Library Catalog—union catalog of books in a state library—undertaken—1909
Postal Service—Pony Express mail—to St. Joseph, Mo.—April 3, 1860

Salinas

Television Station—television stations to share the same time and frequency— KSBW-TV and KMBY-TV (Monterey) —Sept. 11, 1953

San Bernardino

Aviation—License—airplane instructor's license—under C.A.A.—issued to a woman —E. P. Kilgore—Oct. 13, 1939

San Diego

Autogiro—transcontinental autogiro flight— J. M. Miller—landed—May 28, 1931

Aviation—air control municipal board—Dec. 19, 1927

Aviation—jet drone target missile—manufactured

Aviation—Airplane—hydroplane — that was successful—flown—Jan. 26, 1911

Aviation—Airplane—jet propelled landing on an aircraft carrier—Nov. 6, 1945

Aviation—Airplane—twin-engine pressurized airplane—flown—March 16, 1947

Aviation—Flights—airplane loop the loop—Lincoln Beachey—Nov. 18, 1913

Aviation—Flights—hydroplane flight to and from a ship—Feb. 17, 1911

Aviation—Flights (transcontinental)—transcontinental airship voyage—"Shenandoah" —from Lakehurst, N.J.—arrived—Oct. 11, 1924

Aviation—Flights (transcontinental)—transcontinental flight in 24 hours flying time—to Jacksonville—take off—Feb. 21, 1921

California Mission—dedicated—July 16, 1769

Discovery—discovery of land on the United States Pacific coast—J. R. Cabrillo—Sept. 28, 1542

Glider—glider towed across the continent—piloted by F. M. Hawks—take off—March 30, 1930

Helicopter Flight—transcontinental non-stop helicopter flight—left—Aug. 23, 1956

Lighthouse—lighted beacon on the Pacific coast—1855

Motorcycle Trip—motorcycle transcontinental trip by a woman—from New York City—arrived—Sept. 12, 1916

Photograph—photograph from an airplane—Jan. 10, 1911

Street Car—double-deck street car—operated —July 4, 1892

San Fernando

Glider—glider (all plywood-plastic)—tested Dec. 1, 1941

Glider—powered soaring glider commercially licensed—licensed—Oct. 15, 1946

Gold—gold discovered in California—1842

San Francisco

Air Mail Service—air mail transcontinental flight—to New York City—left—Feb. 22, 1921

Air Mail Service—air mail transcontinental service—from New York City—Sept. 8, 1920

Air Mail Service—air mail transcontinental through regular service—from New York City—July 1, 1924

Air Mail Service—Pacific air mail flight—left—Nov. 22, 1935

American Expeditionary Force—sailed—May 25, 1898

Animals — giant panda — arrived — Dec. 18, 1936

Aquatic Mammals—dugong—arrived—Nov. 16, 1955

Army Language School—began courses—Nov. 1, 1941

Automobile Bus—bus night coach—to Los Angeles—July 1929

Automobile Transcontinental Trip—transcontinental automobile trip—by a nonprofessional driver—started—May 23, 1903

Automobile Transcontinental Trip—transcontinental automobile trip by a woman—arrived—Aug. 6, 1909

Aviation—air stewardess—May 15, 1930

Aviation—Airplane—transport airplane designed especially for trans-oceanic service —flight—to Hawaii—April 16, 1935

Aviation—Airplane Bombing—airplane bombing experiment with explosives—Jan. 7, 1911

Aviation—Flights (transcontinental)—transcontinental flight within 24 hours—landed —June 23, 1924

Aviation—Flights (transpacific) — Honolulu squadron flight—Jan. 10, 1934

Aviation—Flights (world)—world flight by a commercial airplane—left—Dec. 2, 1941

Aviation—Passenger—woman airplane passenger (transcontinental)—left—Oct. 5, 1922

Aviation—Races—transcontinental air race—Oct. 8, 1919

Bed—"concealed bed"—manufactured—1909

Bicycle Race Track of Wood—opened—July 1, 1893

Bicycle Trip—bicycle trip around the world —Thomas Stevens—started—April 22, 1884

Billiard Match—billiard three-ball match on a six-by-twelve carom table—April 30, 1855

Book—Book of Common Prayer—used—June 24, 1579

Bridge—bridge with piers sunk in the open sea—commenced—Jan. 5, 1933

Brokerage—exchange to specialize in mining securities—Sept. 11, 1862

Cable—cable across the Pacific ocean—completed—Jan. 1, 1903

Chinese Embassy—landed—July 25, 1878

Dentistry—patent for a gold crown—J. B. Beer—Nov. 4, 1873

Dock—state-owned docks—Board of State Harbor Commissioners meeting—Nov. 4, 1863

Dynamite—manufactured—1866

Electric Company—electric company organized to produce and sell electricity—June 30, 1879

Equal Rights Party—formed—Sept. 20, 1884

Flea Laboratory—opened—Jan. 1, 1939

Football Game—midwestern football team to play on the Pacific coast—Univ. of Chicago—game—Dec. 25, 1894

Forest Service—forest commission (state)—(permanent)—meeting—April 1, 1885

Hospital—Chinese hospital—opened—April 18, 1925

Immigration—Chinese immigrants—arrived —1848

Japanese Ambassador—arrived—March 9, 1860

Labor Union Label—adopted—Cigar Makers' International Union—1874

CALIFORNIA—San Francisco—Continued

Money—fifty-dollar gold pieces minted by the United States—coined—June 15, 1915

Motorcycle Trip—motorcycle transcontinental trip—to New York City—left—May 16, 1903

Naval Officer—woman physician in the Medical Corps Reserve of the U.S. Navy—Hulda Thelander — commissioned — April 19, 1944

Newspaper—Chinese daily newspaper—published—Feb. 16, 1900

Opera—opera house municipally owned—opened—Oct. 15, 1932

Photograph—portrait (life-size) of a human in a newspaper—Larry Quinn—Nov. 14, 1935

Play (drama)—Chinese theatrical performance—Oct. 18, 1852

Postal Service—overland mail service—to Tipton, Mo.—Sept. 15, 1858

President (United States)—President and President's wife to die during the term for which he had been elected—W. G. Harding—Aug. 2, 1923

Prize Fight—pugilist to win three world championships — Bob Fitzsimmons — won third—Nov. 25, 1903

Public School—public school for Chinese—opened—Sept. 1859

Radio Broadcast—all-Chinese commercial radio program—April 22, 1940

Radio Facsimile Transmission—photograph sent by radio across the continent (commercial)—to New York City—April 18, 1925

Railroad Car—"compartmentizer" freight cars—in service—Sept. 12, 1952

Railroad Excursion — railroad excursion (transcontinental) of an organization—from Boston—arrived—May 31, 1870

Rat Extermination (city-wide) to avert bubonic plague—accomplished—1907-1908

Road—coast-to-coast paved road—opened—Sept. 10, 1913

Ship—aircraft carrier to sail around Cape Horn—arrived—Aug. 7, 1952

Ship—naval ship with a plural name—"The Sullivans"—launched—April 4, 1943

Ship—steamboat built on the Pacific coast for the government—"Saginaw"—1860

Ship—steamboat service (regular) to California via Cape Horn—established—Feb. 18, 1849

Ship — steamboat service round-the-world (regular passenger service)—sailed—Feb. 1924

Ship—steamboat to employ electric lights successfully—"Columbia"—lights in operation—May 2, 1880

Stadium—municipal stadium—completed—1907

Street Car—cable street car—in service—Aug. 1, 1873

Street Car—municipally owned street cars—operated—Dec. 28, 1912

Telegram — transcontinental telegram — to New York City—Oct. 24, 1861

Telegraph—telegraph line to the Pacific coast—from New York City—in operation—Oct. 24, 1861

Telephone—telephone switchboard or exchange for Chinese subscribers—established—1894

Telephone—transcontinental telephone demonstration—from New York City—Jan. 25, 1915

Television — Telecast — phase-contrast cinemicrography film (American-made) telecast —The Birth of a Plant—Feb. 28, 1954

Television—Telecast—stockholders' meetings televised coast-to-coast simultaneously—Oct. 29, 1959

Television—Telecast—telecast using coaxial cable—coast-to-coast transmission to New York City—Sept. 4, 1951

Television—Telecast—transcontinental telecast received on the east coast—Sept. 4, 1951

Theater—Chinese theater—"Celestial John" —opened—Dec. 23, 1852

Tong (Chinese secret society)—organized—1870

Treaty—treaty (federal) signed by a woman —Charter of the United Nations—V. C. Gildersleeve—June 26, 1945

United Nations Conference on International Organization—April 25, 1945

Woman—woman horseback rider to make a solo transcontinental trip—to New York City—left—Sept. 1, 1910

San Leandro

Automobile Tractor—steam tractor—manufactured—1886

Santa Barbara

Avocado—planted—1833

Santa Catalina Island

Aviation—Flights — over-water round-trip flight—from Newport Bay—May 10, 1912

Moving Picture—moving pictures of an eclipse of the sun taken from an airplane—Sept. 10, 1923

Radio Telephone—radio telephone service (commercial)—to Los Angeles—inaugurated—July 16, 1920

Santa Clara

Medical School—medical college on the Pacific coast—opened—1858

Santa Cruz

Loganberry—introduced—J. H. Logan—1881

Santa Monica

Automobile—automobile-airplane combination—manufactured—Feb. 20, 1937

Bicycle Trip—bicycle rider to cross the continent in less than three weeks—Eugene McPherson—left—Sept. 1, 1949

President (United States)—presidential airplane—built—1944

Santa Susana Mountains

Atomic Reactor—sodium reactor (experimental)—operated—April 25, 1957

South Pasadena

Birds—ostrich farm—established—1886

Stanford

Radar—radar signal bounced off the sun—April 7, 1959

Stockton

Runner—runner (American) to run a mile in less than four minutes—Don Bowden—June 1, 1957

Summerland

Oil—offshore oil wells successfully drilled in the ocean—1896

Tulare County

Disease (distinctly American)—tularemia—recognized—1910

Tuscan Springs

Borax—discovered—Jan. 8, 1856

Van Nuys

Aviation—Airplane—plastic bonded airplane—built—July 1940

Woman—woman prize fight referee (licensed)—Belle Martell—April 30, 1940

Venice

Automobile Transcontinental Trip—transcontinental automobile group tour—concluded—Aug. 13, 1911

Washington

Canning—salmon cannery—erected—1864

COLORADO

Child Delinquency Law (state)—passed—April 28, 1909

Expedition—exploration of the Grand Canyon of the Colorado—J. W. Powell—May 24, 1869

Canon City

Bridge—hanging railroad bridge—built—1879

Castlewood

Dam—rock-filled dam—opened—Nov. 1890

Colorado City

Automobile Trucking Service—automobile inter-city trucking service—to Snyder, Texas—Oct. 29, 1904

Colorado Springs

Air Force Academy (U.S.)—Air Force Academy—cadets received—Aug. 29, 1958

Denver

Air Force Academy (U.S.)—Air Force Academy—temporary headquarters—July 11, 1955

Air Force Academy (U.S.)—Air Force Academy woman officer—N. M. McCracken—April 26, 1957

Animals — pronghorn antelope — bred and reared in captivity—1903

Birds—snow goose—bred and hatched in captivity—1934

Church—church without theology, creed or dogma—organized—1912

Hospital—tuberculosis hospital—non-sectarian—opened—Dec. 10, 1899

National Security Council—national security council meeting held outside Washington, D.C.—Sept. 13, 1954

Opera—opera broadcast in its entirety—Martha—May 19, 1921

Television—Telecast—birth (human) to be televised for the public—G. C. Kerr—Dec. 2, 1952

War Veterans' Society—Veterans of Foreign Wars of the United States—organized—Aug. 18, 1913

Zoological Garden—barless zoological garden of naturalistic rock construction—completed—1918

Gilman

Zinc—underground mill for the separation of zinc and lead—completed—1929

Grand Junction

Election Law—preferential ballot system—first election—Nov. 2, 1909

Telluride

Electric Transmission—alternating current power transmission—installation—1890

CONNECTICUT

Arbitration—colonial arbitration law—enacted—1753

Automobile Legislation—state motor car legislation—May 21, 1901

Automobile License Plates—permanent license plates—March 1, 1937

CONNECTICUT—*Continued*

Aviation — Legislation — aviation legislation (state)—June 8, 1911

Boiler Legislation—approved—July 9, 1864

Branding Legislation—enacted—Feb. 5, 1644

Constitution—constitution—"fundamental orders"—passed—Jan. 14, 1639

Copyright Law—copyright law (state)—passed—Jan. 8, 1783

Dental Legislation—legislation (state) regarding dental hygienists—approved—May 19, 1915

Extradition — extradition—established—New England Confederation—1643

Pound (enclosure for animals)—authorized—May 1650

Supreme Court (U.S.) Decision—Supreme Court decision between states—Connecticut vs. New York—commenced—Aug 5, 1799

Ansonia

Bicycle—bicycle with a rotary crank—demonstrated—1866

Copper Refinery Furnace—to use gaseous fuel—1878

Avon

Sewing Machine—sewing machine lamp holder—patented—L. M. N. Wolf—May 13, 1873

Berlin

Tinware Manufacturers—Pattison brothers—1740

Bloomfield

Helicopter—helicopter fully operated by remote control—built—1953

Helicopter—helicopter with a fully servo-controlled intermeshing rotor—built—1947

Helicopter—twin gas-turbine helicopter (turborotor)—flown—March 26, 1954

Bridgeport

Air Mail Service—helicopter air mail delivery—July 5, 1946

Automobile — steam automobile — H. A. House—1866

Aviation—Flights—airplane flight—Gustave Whitehead—Aug. 14, 1901

Dental School—dental hygienists' course—commenced—Nov. 17, 1913

Electric Attachment Plug (separable)—patented—Harvey Hubbell—Nov. 8, 1904

Electric Light Socket with pull chain—patented—Harvey Hubbell—Aug. 11, 1896

Helicopter — helicopter commercially designed—initial flight—Feb. 16, 1946

Ordnance—bazooka rocket gun—produced—June 14, 1942

Phonograph Record — long-playing microgroove records—manufactured—1948

Television Station—ultra high frequency television station to operate on a regular daily basis—KC2XAK—Dec. 29, 1949

Trading Stamp—originated—T. A. Sperry—1891

Bristol

Clock—brass clock works—invented—1837

Fishing Rod of telescoping steel tubes—patented—Everett Horton—March 8, 1887

Spring Manufacturer—E. L. Dunbar—1845

Brooklyn

Unitarian Minister—woman ordained to the Unitarian ministry—C. C. Burleigh—parish—Oct. 5, 1871

Centerbrook

Comb—ivory comb—manufactured—1789

Danbury

Hat Factory—established—Zadoc Benedict—1780

Danielson

Dentist—woman dentist—E. R. Jones—began practice—May 1855

Derby

Animals—sheep (merino sheep)—imported—1802

Manual Training—industrial school—Josiah Holbrook—1819

Pin—machine for manufacturing pins—patented—J. I. Howe—June 22, 1832

East Windsor

Clock—clock patent—Eli Terry—Nov. 17, 1797

Farmington

Cattle Club—cattle club (Guernsey cattle)—formed—March 1, 1876

Georgetown

Sieve—wire sieves—manufactured—1834

Granby

Copper Mine—company chartered—1709

Money—copper coins—1737

Greenwich

Squash Racquets Champion—woman to win the U.S.A. Women's Squash Racquets Singles championship—E. R. Sears—Jan. 19, 1928

Groton

Engine—diesel engine in a submarine—submarines commissioned—Feb. 14, 1912

Submarine — atomic-powered submarine — "Nautilus"—launched—Jan. 21, 1954

Submarine—atomic-powered turbine electric-drive submarine—"Tullibee" — launched—April 27, 1960

Submarine — ballistic missile submarine — "George Washington"—launched—June 9, 1959

Submarine—submarine powered by a liquid metal-cooled atomic reactor—"Seawolf"—launched—July 21, 1955

Submarine—submarine with two nuclear reactors—"Triton"—launched—Aug. 19, 1958

Television—submarine with closed-circuit television—"Tullibee"—launched—April 27, 1960

Gurleyville

Silk—silk dyers—1838

Hamden

Rubber—rubber shoe manufacturer—Leverett Candee—1842

Hartford

Aluminum—aluminum used commercially in a transmission conductor—Nov. 30, 1899

Anesthesia—anesthetic in dentistry—used—Horace Wells—Dec. 11, 1844

Automobile Tire—pneumatic tire—manufactured—1895

Aviation—Parachute—nylon parachute jump —June 6, 1942

Belting—manufactured—1826

Bible—Bible translation by a woman—J. E. Smith—published—1876

Bicycle Factory—established—1877

Brick Machine—installed—1857

Clock—watch made by machinery—1838

Cook Book—cook book of American authorship—published—1796

Cryptography Book—published—1805

Deaf—Church Service—prayers in the sign language of the deaf—1817

Deaf—School—school for the deaf—Connecticut Asylum—opened—April 15, 1817

Electric Alternator—successfully operated in parallel—installed—1896

Electric Generator—mercury boiler turbine—placed in service—Sept. 7, 1923

Electric Power Plant—hydroelectric power plant to use a storage battery—1896

Electric Transmission—three-phase alternating high frequency current transmission—operated—March 1893

Genealogy—genealogy—of American family —published—1771

Gyroscope—gyroscopes—commercially manufactured—June 1857

Insurance—accident insurance company—chartered—June 17, 1863

Insurance—accident insurance policy—issued —1864

Insurance—accident insurance policy (printed)—issued—April 1, 1864

Insurance—aircraft liability and property damage insurance—1919

Insurance—automobile insurance policy—Feb. 1, 1898

Insurance—boiler insurance company—chartered—June 1866

Law Book—law book containing the federal laws of the United States—published—1791

Periodical—children's magazine — Children's Magazine—published—Jan. 1789

President (U.S.)—President to ride in an automobile—Theodore Roosevelt—Aug. 22, 1902

Silver Plating Factory—successful—Rogers Brothers—1847

Teachers' Institute—Oct. 1839

Telephone—coin telephone—patented—William Gray—Aug. 13, 1889

Tennis Match—intercollegiate lawn tennis match—June 7, 1883

Torpedo—underwater torpedo operated by electric current—invented—Samuel Colt—1841

Turbine — steam turbine — installed — April 1901

Wool—worsted mill operated by water power —organized—April 15, 1788

Huntington

Tungsten—tungsten and tellurium—found—1819

Ivoryton

Comb-Cutting Machine—patented—April 12, 1799

Kensington

Monument—monument to commemorate the Civil War—dedicated—July 25, 1863

Killingworth

Gem-Cutting Machine—lapidary—invented—Abel Buell—1766

Type Foundry—type foundry—Abel Buell—April 1, 1769

Lakeville

Cutlery Factory—cutlery factory for the manufacture of pocket cutlery—1845

Litchfield

Anthology (American)—published—1793

Clock—self-winding clock—1783

Law Reports—published—1789

Law School—law school—opened—Judge Tapping Reeve—1784

Temperance Society—temperance organization (local)—formed—1789

Mansfield

Silk—silk mill—erected—1810

Thread—silk thread—manufactured—1819

Marion

Nut and Bolt Factory—established—1840

CONNECTICUT—*Continued*

Meriden

Piano Player—piano player (completely automatic)—manufactured—Feb. 1897

Middlebury

Lathe—profile lathe patent—Thomas Blanchard—Sept. 6, 1819

Middletown

Agricultural Experiment Station—state agricultural experiment station—approved—July 20, 1875

Educational Association—educational association (local)—organized—May 1799

Elastic Webbing—produced—Russell Manufacturing Co.—1841

Factory Standardization of Production—interchangeable parts contract with U.S. government—April 16, 1813

Normal School—normal school instruction course given at a university—Dec. 1, 1841

Milford

Camp for Boys—established—Aug. 1861

Mystic

Ship—iron-clad warship for service at sea—"Galena"—launched—Feb. 14, 1862

Naugatuck

Trade Association—American Brass Association—organized—Feb. 1853

New Haven

Baseball Batting and Fielding Cage—built—1885

Basketball—basketball intercollegiate five-man team game—March 20, 1897

Basketball—basketball intercollegiate game—Dec. 10, 1896

Bicycle—bicycle with a rotary crank—demonstrated—1866

Blotting Paper—manufactured—1856

Building—building in all-Gothic architecture—Trinity Episcopal Church—designed—1814

Caster—for furniture—patented—June 30, 1838

Chemistry Professor—professorship of applied chemistry—granted—Yale University—1846

Chinese Language and Literature Lectureship—Yale University—1877

Chinese Students—college graduate—Yung Wing—Yale University—1854

Confectionery Machine—lollipop machine—used—1908

Degrees (academic and honorary)—Doctor of Philosophy degree — awarded — Yale University—1861

Degrees (academic and honorary)—Doctor of Philosophy degree awarded to a Negro—Yale University—1876

Extradition—extradition—New England Confederation—1643

Fine Arts Department—fine arts department in a college—School of Fine Arts—established—1864

Football Dummy—improvised by A. A. Stagg—1889

Football Game—football game played in the United States to be broadcast in England—Nov. 22, 1930

Football Game—intercollegiate football championship—1876

Football Game—international football game—Yale—Dec. 6, 1873

Geography—printed—1784

Geological Society (national)—founded—1819

Glider—amphibious seaplane glider—manufactured—1943

History—political history—Timothy Pitkin—published—1828

Knights of Columbus—founded—Jan. 16, 1882

Map—map of the United States—engraved—Abel Buell—1783

Milk—acidophilus milk—devised—1920

Money—Continental coin — manufactured — 1787

Music Magazine—*American Musical Magazine.*—published—May 1786

Newspaper—college daily—*Yale News*—published—Jan. 28, 1878

Novel Course—course on the contemporary novel—W. L. Phelps—1895

Paleontology Chair—in a college—established—1866

Periodical—college magazine—*Literary Cabinet*—published—Nov. 15, 1806

Physician—doctor to receive an honorary medical degree—Daniel Turner—Sept. 11, 1723

Physiological Laboratory—established—1874

Pituitary Hormone—pituitary hormone isolated—announced—July 23, 1937

Planetarium—planetarium or orrery built in America—Thomas Clap—1743

Rowing—college to feature rowing—1844

Skating Tournament—figure skating international championship tournament—March 20, 1914

Sprinkler—sprinkler head—patented—H. S. Parmelee—Aug. 11, 1874

Stone Crusher—patented—E. W. Blake—June 15, 1858

Tape Measure Patent—patented—A. J. Fellows—July 14, 1868

Telephone—pay station telephone service—June 1, 1880

Telephone—telephone switchboard or exchange (commercial)—installed—Jan. 28, 1878

Telephone Directory—issued—Feb. 21, 1878

Theatrical School—theater and dramatic criticism course—to award a Ph.D.—established—Sept. 24, 1934

Tornado—June 10, 1682

Trapshooting—trapshooting intercollegiate association—meet held—May 7, 1898

New London

Hospital—eye infirmary—established—Elisha North—1817

Mine Barrage—David Bushnell—Aug. 1777

Navy—atomic submarine division—formed—March 31, 1958

Radio Broadcast—submarine (submerged) broadcast—Dec. 7, 1930

Ship—steam whaler—"Pioneer"—converted by T. W. Williams—1865

Submarine-Escape Training Tank—in operation—Aug. 15, 1930

Submarine-Escape Training Tank—women to take the submarine-escape test—certified—July 12, 1943

New Milford

Electric Lighting—street light of an automatic system—installed—March 2, 1949

North Canaan

Insurance—hail insurance—on growing tobacco crops—1880

North Windham

Paper-Making Machinery—paper-making machine (Fourdrinier) imported—installed—Jan. 1828

Norwich

Typewriter—typewriter that successfully typed—patented—Charles Thurber—Aug. 26, 1843

Old Mystic

Methodist—Negro Methodist minister of an all-white congregation—S. P. Montgomery—Oct. 2, 1955

Putnam

Thread—non-twisted sewing thread—manufactured—1946

Riverton

Chair Factory—Lambert Hitchcock—established 1818

Rocky River

Electric Power Plant—hydroelectric power plant to use water pumped into a reservoir—Connecticut Light and Power Co.—1927

Salem

Music Instruction—music school authorized to confer degrees—established—Oramel Whittlesey—1835

Salisbury

Library—youth's library—established—Jan. 1803

Saugatuck

Building—building devoted entirely to highway traffic—completed—July 1, 1939

Saybrook

Submarine—submarine for use in war—"American Turtle"—built—David Bushnell—1776

Seymour

Auger (screw auger)—manufactured—Walter French—1810

Simsbury

Fuse—Cordeau-Bickford detonating fuse—introduced—1913

Fuse—safety fuse—manufactured—1836

Fuse — textile-wrapped detonating fuse — manufactured—1936

Steel—steel—manufactured—Samuel Higley—May 1728

South Killingly

Woman—woman granted a patent—Mary Kies—May 5, 1809

South Norwalk

Hat—derby hat—manufactured—1850

South Windham

Paper-Making Machinery — paper-making machine (Fourdinier) — manufactured — 1829

Stamford

Crane—crane—manufactured—1883

Postal Service—coin-operated mailbox—patented—L. A. Thatcher—July 28, 1942

Postal Service—postage meter—officially set—Nov. 16, 1920

Railroad Signal System—railroad signal system (automatic electric block)—patented—T. S. Hall—June 7, 1870

Razor—electric dry shaver—manufactured—March 18, 1931

Shoe Measuring Stick—introduced—1657

Telegraph—telegraph code converter—announced—Oct. 1854

Typewriter—portable typewriter—patented—G. C. Blickensderfer—April 12, 1892

CONNECTICUT—*Continued*

Stanfield

Cider Mill—patented—Isaac Quintard—April 5, 1806

Stonington

Discovery—discovery of Antarctica—July 25, 1820—expedition sailed

Stratford

Aviation—Aviator—woman aviator to fly across the Atlantic Ocean east to west—A. J. Mollison—crashed—July 23, 1933

Aviation—Flights (transatlantic)—transatlantic solo westward flight—J. A. Mollison—July 23, 1933

Helicopter—helicopter (direct-lift-aircraft)—constructed—Oct. 1939

Helicopter Flight—helicopter flight (cross country)—May 13, 1942

Helicopter Flight—helicopter flight from water—April 17, 1941

Helicopter Flight—helicopter flight of one-hour duration—April 15, 1941

Suffield

See West Suffield

Tariffville

Aluminum—aluminum used commercially in a transmission conductor—Hartford Electric Light Co.—Nov. 30, 1899

Thomaston

Clock—clock (one-day back-wind alarm clock)—in metal case—1876

Torrington (Wolcottville)

Brass Kettles—made—Coe Brass Co.—1834
Brass Rod—drawn—Coe Brass Co.—1873
Brass Spinning—process used—1851
Milk—condensed milk (commercial)—condensery established—1856
Needles (machine made)—manufactured—1866
Wire—wire-cutting machine and automatic straightener—invented—1866

Trumbull

Fluorspar—commercial mining—1837

Wallingford

Coffee Mill Patent—James Carrington—April 3, 1829
Spoons—nickel silver spoons—manufactured—Robert Wallace—1835

Waterbury

Brass—rolled—Abel Porter & Co.—1802
Brass Spinning—patented—H. W. Hayden—Dec. 16, 1851
Brass Wire Drawing and Tube Making Machinery—imported—1831
Button—gilt buttons to be commercially manufactured—Abel Porter & Co.—1802
Button—pewter or block tin buttons—manufactured—1790
Fastening—hooks and eyes—successfully manufactured—1836

Watertown

Sewing Machine—sewing machine to sew curving seams—patented—A. B. Wilson—Dec. 19, 1854
Thread—silk thread on spools—Merritt Heminway—1849

West Haven

Photoelectric Cell—photoelectric cell installed commercially—June 19, 1931

West Suffield

Cigar Factory—of importance—established—Simeon Viets—1810

West Torrington

Wire — brass wire — manufactured — Edwin Hodges—1840

Westville

Lock — mortised lock — introduced — Blake Bros.—1835

Wethersfield

Election—election in defiance of the Royal Courts—April 11, 1640

Windsor

Umbrella—used—1740

Windsor Locks

Helicopter—gas-turbine helicopter (turbo-rotor)—tested—Dec. 10, 1951
Helicopter—helicopter fully operated by remote control—flown—July 1953
Helicopter—helicopter with a fully servo-controlled intermeshing rotor—flown—Jan. 1947

Wolcottville

See Torrington and West Torrington

DELAWARE

Electric Home and Farm Authority—incorporated—Jan. 17, 1934

Fertilizer Law (state)—enacted—March 16, 1871

Poorhouse (state)—replaced by state home —closed—Dec. 1933

Rebellion—rebellion of colonists against the English—Marcus Jacobson—condemned— Dec. 20, 1669

Single Tax—single tax political ticket— formed—Sept. 1896

State—state to ratify the federal Constitution—Dec. 7, 1787

Brandywine

Paper-Making Machinery — paper-making machine (cylinder) — manufactured — Thomas Gilpen—Aug. 1817

Cooch's Bridge

Flag—American flag flown in battle—Sept. 3, 1777

Fort Christina

Lutheran Church—Lutheran pastor—Reorus Torkillus—arrived—April 17, 1640

Newark

College—"Junior Year Abroad"—instituted —University of Delaware—July 7, 1923

Seaford

Nylon—nylon yarn manufacture (commercial)—commenced—Dec. 15, 1939

Wilmington

Lucite (polymethyl methacrylate) production (commercial)—May 21, 1936

Milk—concentrated milk—sold—Nov. 30, 1950

Nylon—nylon—patented—W. H. Carothers —Feb. 16, 1937

Radio Telephone—radio telephone communication (one way)—from Montauk Point, N.Y.—April 4, 1915

Rubber—synthetic rubber produced on a commercial scale—Nov. 2, 1931

Seal—Christmas seals of the modern variety, sold to raise funds to fight tuberculosis— designed—E. P. Bissell—sold—Dec. 9, 1907

Ship—iron steamship built for transatlantic service—"Bangor"—launched—May 1844

Ship—merchant ship of the U.S. commanded by a Negro captain—"Booker T. Washington"—launched—Sept. 29, 1942

Sulfanilamide — sulfanilamide — produced— Dec. 1930

Swedes—landed—1638

Telephone—mobile telephone conversation with commercial equipment—automobile to an airplane—Oct. 9, 1947

DISTRICT OF COLUMBIA

Anacostia

See under Washington

Georgetown

See under Washington

Washington

Agricultural Journal—agricultural journal— issued—July 4, 1810

Agricultural Society—agricultural society of national importance—organized—Dec. 4, 1867

Agricultural Soil Conference—June 13, 1917

Agriculture Bureau—agriculture bureau scientific publication—issued—Oct. 15, 1862

Air Force—Air Force Secretary—W. S. Symington—sworn in—Sept. 18, 1947

Air Force Officer—Air Force chairman of the Joint Chiefs of Staff—N. F. Twining— sworn in—Aug. 15, 1957

Air Force Officer—Brigadier General (Negro) in the Air Force—B. O. Davis, Jr. —appointed—Oct. 27, 1954

Air Mail Service—air mail experimental route—to New York City and Philadelphia —May 15, 1918

Air Mail Service—airplane mail pick-up —demonstrated—Oct. 1, 1929

Almanac—almanac bibliography—published —1907

American Red Cross—organized—Clara Barton—May 21, 1881

Archival Administration—course offered— Sept. 25, 1940

Army Auxiliary Corps—woman to become a member of the Women's Army Corps— sworn in—July 8, 1948

Army Officer—Chaplain (Catholic) appointed by the President—June 13, 1862

Army Officer—Chaplain (Negro) of the U.S. Army—H. M. Turner—commissioned— 1863

Army War College—cornerstone laid—Feb. 21, 1903

Astronomical Observations Book—published —1838

Autogiro—autogiro to land on the White House lawn—J. G. Ray—April 22, 1931

Aviation—airplane high-speed tank to test airplanes—completed—May 1931

Aviation—airplane to land on the White House lawn—H. N. Atwood—July 14, 1911

Aviation—Airport—airport (federally owned and operated)—Washington National Airport—opened—June 16, 1941

Aviation—Aviator—woman aviator to pilot an air-mail transport—Helen Richey—to Detroit, Mich.—Dec. 31, 1934

Aviation—Flights—airplane catapulted—successfully—Nov. 12, 1912

Aviation—License—glider license class "C" —first woman—H. M. Barnaby—Aug. 12, 1931

DISTRICT OF COLUMBIA—Washington
—*Continued*

Bank—bank for Negroes privately operated by Negroes—organized—Oct. 17, 1888

Bank — Export-Import bank — organized — Feb. 8, 1934

Bank—Freedmen's bank—Freedman's Savings and Trust Co.—chartered—March 3, 1865

Baseball Player—baseball player to catch a ball dropped from the Washington Monument—Aug. 29, 1892

Baseball Umpire—baseball umpire (major league) to wear eyeglasses—E. A. Rommel—April 18, 1956

Bird Legislation (international)—Migratory Bird Treaty—signed—Aug. 16, 1916

Births—child born in the White House, Washington, D.C.—Jan. 17, 1806

Births—child born in the White House, Washington, D.C., the offspring of a President—Sept. 9, 1893

Boy Scouts of America—Boy Scouts of America—incorporated—Feb. 8, 1910

Building—atom bomb-resistant federal building—dedicated—May 23, 1955

Building—building erected by the government in Washington, D.C.—Executive Mansion—cornerstone laid—Oct. 13, 1792

Building—building with prefabricated walls of mosaic concrete—completed—Feb. 1935

Business School—business high school—opened—Sept. 22, 1890

Cabinet of the U.S.—cabinet conference telecast—June 3, 1953

Cabinet of the U.S.—cabinet member convicted of a crime—A. B. Fall—Oct. 25, 1929

Cabinet of the U.S.—full cabinet sworn in at the same time and place—March 4, 1933

Cabinet of the U.S.—Negro sub-cabinet member—J. E. Wilkins—sworn in—March 18, 1954

Cabinet of the U.S.—Secretary of Health, Education and Welfare—O. C. Hobby—sworn in—April 11, 1953

Capitol (of the United States)—cornerstone laid—Sept. 18, 1793

Casein Fiber—patented—Dec. 13, 1938

Catholic Apostolic Delegate—permanent—arrived—Jan. 24, 1893

Cemetery—congressional cemetery—1804

Cemetery—national cemeteries—authorized—July 17, 1862

Chamber of Commerce—Chamber of Commerce of the United States of America headquarters dedicated—May 20, 1925

Children's Welfare Congress (international) —March 10-17, 1908

Chinaware—dishes (complete set) made in America for the Executive Mansion—delivered—July 31, 1918

Chinese Embassy—Oct. 4, 1878

Civil Service—woman Civil Service commissioner—H. H. Gardener—sworn in—April 13, 1920

College—Catholic college—Georgetown College—opened—Nov. 15, 1791

College—Negro university to establish undergraduate, graduate, and professional schools—Howard University—founded—Nov. 20, 1866

Conference—conference of great powers—Nov. 12, 1921

Conference — Pan American Conference — opened—Oct. 2, 1889

Congress of the U.S.—congressional session in air-conditioned Senate and House chambers—Nov. 15, 1937

Congress (U.S.)—House of Representatives —House of Representatives—first session in Washington—Nov. 17, 1800

Congress (U.S.)—House of Representatives —Negro preacher to deliver a sermon in the House of Representatives—Feb. 12, 1865

Congress (U.S.)—Senate—broadcast from the Senate chamber—March 4, 1929

Congress (U.S.)—Senate—loud-speaker—installed—May 15, 1933

Conscription—peacetime conscription bill—numbers drawn—Oct. 16, 1940

Court—commerce court (U.S.)—established —June 18, 1910

Deaf—School—institution in the world for the higher education of the deaf—National Deaf Mute College—incorporated—Feb. 16, 1857

Degrees (academic and honorary)—Doctor of Music degree—conferred—Georgetown University—July 24, 1849

Diplomatic Service—chief executive-elect of a foreign country—to serve in Washington —April 20, 1930

Diplomatic Service—woman career diplomat advanced to the rank of ambassador—F. E. Willis—Aug. 10, 1953

Easter Egg Roll—April 2, 1877

Electric Lighting—glass light bulb machine —patented—Sept. 1, 1925

Electric Stove—electric range—patented—G. B. Simpson—Sept. 20, 1859

Esperanto Club—Esperanto Congress in the U.S.—Aug. 14, 1910

Federal Communications Commission—Federal Communications Commission woman member—Frieda B. Hennock—sworn in —July 6, 1948

Fencing—international fencing championship —competition—Nov. 18, 1921

Flag—American flag made of American bunting to fly over the Capitol, Washington, D.C.—hoisted—Feb. 24, 1866

Flag—Army flag (official)—established—June 12, 1956

Foreign Service School—School of Comparative Jurisprudence and Diplomacy—opened —Nov. 15, 1898

Garage—completely automatic push-button controlled garage—opened—Dec. 5, 1951

Garage—hydraulic lift parking device—installed—Oct. 1954

Gas—gas light in the White House—Dec. 29, 1848

Girl Scouts—incorporated—June 10, 1915

Government Printing Office — Government Printing Office—plant opened—1861

Hall of Fame—hall of fame (national)—established—July 2, 1864

Health Society—annual meeting—May 18, 1905

Helicopter Flight—transcontinental non-stop helicopter flight—from San Diego, Calif.—arrived—Aug. 24, 1956

Holiday—Labor Day holiday (federal)—authorized—June 28, 1894

Humane Society—humane association national organization—American Humane Association—incorporated—Nov. 12, 1903

Index of Government Publications—published—1885

Indians—Indian tribal constitution—signed—Oct. 28, 1935

Industrial Recovery Act—postage stamps commemorating the National Recovery Act —sold—Aug. 15, 1933

Insurance—group hospital-medical cooperative—opened—Nov. 1, 1937

Judge—woman judge of a juvenile court—Kathryn Sellers—appointed—Oct. 15, 1918

Knights of Pythias—founded—Feb. 19, 1864

Lawyer—Negro woman lawyer—C. E. Ray —admitted to bar—April 23, 1872

Legislative Conference (interstate)—assembled—Feb. 3, 1933

Lewisite—developed—W. L. Lewis—Feb. 1918

Library—Library of Congress—established—April 24, 1800

Library Catalog—catalog of the Library of Congress—printed—1802

Library Society—state librarians' society—formed—Nov. 16, 1898

Locomotive—electric locomotive—trial trip—April 29, 1851

Locomotive—streamlined electric engine—in service—Jan. 28, 1935

Marines—woman marine reserve—enrolled—Aug. 12, 1918

Medal—Distinguished Service Medal (Army) awarded to a woman—O. C. Hobby—Dec. 31, 1944

Medal—Distinguished Service Medal (Merchant Marine)—presented—Oct. 8, 1942

Medal—Medal of Freedom awarded to a woman—Anna Rosenberg—Oct. 29, 1945

Medal—Medal of Honor awarded to a Marine in the Korean War—H. A. Commiskey—Aug. 1, 1951

Medal—Medal of Honor awarded to a Nisei in the Korean War—presented—Oct. 27, 1953

Medal—National Aeronautics and Space Administration Distinguished Service Medal —presented—A. B. Shepard—May 8, 1961

Medal—National Geographic Society gold medal—Hubbard medal—presented—R. E. Peary—Dec. 15, 1906

Medal—National Geographic Society special gold medal—presented—A. E. Putnam—June 21, 1932

Medal—Navy-Marine Corps medal for heroism awarded to a woman—awarded—B. O. Barnwell—Aug. 7, 1953

Medal—Reserve Officers Association medal presented—H. S. Truman—Jan. 15, 1953

Medal—soldier to receive seven decorations at one time—L. M. Chilson—Dec. 6, 1946

Medical Congress—Mental Hygiene International Congress—opened—May 4, 1930

Medical Society—American College of Surgeons—organized—May 5, 1913

Medical Society—Negro medical society—organized—April 24, 1884

Microfilm—microfilm reading device—patented—B. A. Fiske—March 28, 1922

Monument—bronze equestrian statue—unveiled—January 8, 1853

Monument—monument by a woman ordered by the U.S. Government—July 28, 1866

Monument—monument to George Washington (national)—capstone set—Dec. 6, 1884

Monument—statue cast by the U.S. Government—accepted—April 25, 1881

Monument—statue of a woman in National Statuary Hall—dedicated—Feb. 17, 1905

Mosque—Islamic Center—cornerstone laid—Jan. 11, 1949

Moving Picture—talking pictures of presidential candidates—taken—Aug. 11, 1924

Naval Officer—chaplain to win a Congressional Medal of Honor—J. T. O'Callahan —presentation—Jan. 23, 1946

News Correspondent—White House reporter —W. W. Price—employed—April 24, 1897

Newspaper—newspaper with perfumed advertising page—issued—March 25, 1937

Nursing School—Army School of Nursing —authorized—May 25, 1918

Observatory — observatory (national) — established—Dec. 6, 1830

Pan American Union—established—April 14, 1890

Parent-Teacher Association (national)—organized—Feb. 17, 1897

Parliamentary Rules of Order—printed—1801

Periodical—magazine of the United States Government—issued—March 14, 1936

Photograph—photograph bounced off the moon—received—Jan. 28, 1960

Photograph—photograph showing air in motion—1918

Physician—Capitol physician—G. W. Calver —Dec. 8, 1928

Plow—plow for pulverizing the soil—patented —George Page—Aug. 7, 1847

Political Convention—political nominating caucus attended by party leaders—Feb. 25, 1804

Political Platform (national)—adopted—May 11, 1832

Post Office—airplane post office—dedicated —May 15, 1938

Postage Stamp—postage stamp in two colors produced by the rotary process at the Bureau of Engraving and Printing—1952

Postage Stamp—postage stamp on which was inscribed the name of a living American—issued—June 18, 1927

DISTRICT OF COLUMBIA—Washington
—*Continued*

Postage Stamp—postage stamps in coils—issued—Feb. 18, 1908

Postal Directory—printed—1855

Postal Service—collection and delivery of mail in automobiles—Oct. 19, 1914

Postal Service—dead letter office—organized —1825

Postal Service—Highway Post Office Service—route to Harrisonburg, Va.—established—Feb. 10, 1941

President (U.S.)—President buried in Washington, D.C.—Woodrow Wilson—Feb. 5, 1924

President (U.S.)—President inaugurated in the city of Washington—Thomas Jefferson —March 4, 1801

President (U.S.)—President inaugurated on January 20—F. D. Roosevelt—1937

President (U.S.)—President inaugurated on March 5—James Monroe—1821

President (U.S.)—President to be assassinated—Abraham Lincoln—died—April 15, 1865

President (U.S.)—President to broadcast in a foreign language—F. D. Roosevelt— Nov. 7, 1942

President (U.S.)—President to celebrate his silver wedding anniversary at the White House—R. B. Hayes—Dec. 31, 1877

President (U.S.)—President to die in Washington, D.C.—W. H. Harrison—April 4, 1841

President (U.S.)—President to fly in a helicopter—D. D. Eisenhower—July 12, 1957

President (U.S.)—President to fly in a twin-engined airplane—D. D. Eisenhower— June 3, 1955

President (U.S.)—President to reside in Washington, D.C.—John Adams—June 3, 1800

President (U.S.)—President to rest in state in the United States Capitol rotunda— Abraham Lincoln—April 15, 1865

President (U.S.)—President to review the military forces—at his residence—Thomas Jefferson—July 4, 1801

President (U.S.)—President to visit a European country while President—Woodrow Wilson—left—Dec. 4, 1918

President (U.S.)—President whose assassination was attempted—Andrew Jackson— Jan. 30, 1835

President (U.S.) — presidential airplane (turbo-compound powered)—christened— Nov. 24, 1954

Presidential Candidate—presidential candidate debate series on television—second debate—Nixon-Kennedy—Oct. 7, 1960

Presidential Candidate—presidential candidate nominated at a caucus—Thomas Jefferson—Feb. 25, 1804

Printing Press—printing press for printing "paper hangings"—patented—Peter Force —Aug. 22, 1822

Radar—radar detection of airplanes—June 24, 1930

Radar—radar observations—Sept. 27, 1922

Radio Broadcast—debate over the radio— WJH—May 23, 1922

Radio Broadcast—news program (cooperative)—Nov. 1937—Fulton Lewis, Jr.

Radio Broadcast—President to broadcast from the White House—Calvin Coolidge —Feb. 22, 1924

Radio Broadcast—presidential inauguration —Calvin Coolidge—March 4, 1925

Radio Broadcast—presidential message to be broadcast—Calvin Coolidge—Dec. 6, 1923

Radio Conference—National Radio Conference—Feb. 27, 1922

Radio Facsimile Transmission — facsimile high-speed transmission—demonstrated— Oct. 21, 1948

Radio Facsimile Transmission — facsimile transmitted to a moving train—June 4, 1946

Radio Facsimile Transmission—photograph sent by radio across the continent—March 4, 1925

Radio Facsimile Transmission—photograph sent overland by radio to a distant point— March 3, 1923

Radio Facsimile Transmission—photographs sent over a city telephone—transmitted— Oct. 3, 1922

Radio Station—sea-going radio broadcasting station—"Courier" — dedicated — March 4, 1952

Railroad—air-conditioned train—installed— May 24, 1931

Railroad—railroad to run trains to Washington, D.C.—trial trip—July 1, 1835

Sewing Machine—sewing machine patent— J. J. Greenough—Feb. 21, 1842

Sorority — Negro sorority — Alpha Kappa Alpha—founded—Jan. 15, 1908

Supreme Court (U.S.)—Negro page of the Supreme Court—C. V. Bush—served— Sept. 27, 1954

Surgical Operation—artificial aortic valve— C. A. Hufnagel—fitted—Sept. 11, 1952

Surgical Operation—lobotomy (prefrontal) —Drs. J. W. Watts and Walter Freeman —Sept. 14, 1956

Swimming Pool in the White House—formally accepted—June 2, 1933

Telegram—news dispatch telegram—to Baltimore, Md.—May 25, 1844

Telegram—telegram inaugurating commercial service—May 24, 1844

Telegraph — telegraph appropriation (federal)—March 3, 1843

Telegraph—telegraph station—opened—1844

Telephone—commercial telephone service on railroad trains for passengers—in operation —Aug. 15, 1947

Telephone—underground cable long distance telephone conversation—to Boston, Mass. —Feb. 26, 1914

Television—Telecast—airplane telecast (network)—Dec. 17, 1948

Television—Telecast—cabinet session to be televised—Oct. 25, 1954

Television—Telecast—medical intracity color telecast—from Johns Hopkins Hospital, Baltimore, Md.—Dec. 6, 1949

Television — Telecast — presidential address televised from the White House—H. S. Truman—Oct. 5, 1947

Television—Telecast—presidential news conference filmed for television and newsreels —Jan. 19, 1955

Television—Telecast—presidential news conference to be televised live—J. F. Kennedy—Jan. 25, 1961

Television—Telecast—prize fight (heavyweight championship bout) to be televised —received—Louis-Conn fight—June 19, 1946

Television — Telecast — telecast (long distance) received in an airplane—Oct. 17, 1939

Television—Telecast—telecast of an object in motion—June 13, 1925

Television—weather map telecast—received —Aug. 18, 1926

Television License—television license—issued—Feb. 25, 1928

Temperance Society—Anti-Saloon League (national organization)—formed—Dec. 17-18, 1895

Time (standard)—adopted—Nov. 18, 1883

Typesetting Machine—monotype—patented —Tolbert Lanston—June 7, 1887

Veto (presidential)—veto message read by a President—May 22, 1935

Vice President of the U.S.—Vice President to die in office—George Clinton—April 20, 1812

Vice President of the U.S.—Vice President to preside at a National Security Council meeting—R. M. Nixon—July 14, 1953

Vice Presidential Candidate—vice presidential nominee to decline nomination—John Langdon—May 12, 1812

Visiting Celebrities—king (reigning) to visit the United States—David Kalakaua of Hawaii—Dec. 15, 1874

Visiting Celebrities—president of a Negro country to visit the United States—President Edwin Barclay of Liberia—May 1943

War Criminal Proceedings—Henry Wirz—tried—Aug. 23-Nov. 4, 1865

Wedding—White House wedding—March 29, 1812

Wedding—White House wedding of a President — Grover Cleveland — June 2, 1886

Woman Suffrage—woman suffrage association (international)—organized—Feb. 1902

Young Men's Christian Association—Young Men's Christian Association for Negro members—organized—1853

Zinc—zinc—produced—John Hitz—1835-1836

Zoological Laboratory (U.S.)—zoological laboratory (U.S.) for the study of parasites of man—started—Aug. 16, 1902

Zoological Laboratory (U.S.)—Zoological Laboratory (U.S.) for the study of the parasites of livestock—opened—Aug. 1, 1886

FLORIDA

Artist—artist—to arrive in America—Jacques Le Moyne de Morgues—June 22, 1564

Artist—English artist—John White—drew—1585-1590

Astronomy — meteoric display — "shooting stars"—recorded—Nov. 12, 1799

Bird Reservation (national)—Pelican Island —authorized—March 14, 1903

Catholic Bishop—Catholic bishop—Frai Juan Cabezas de Altamirono—visited—1607

Photograph—photographs taken under the sea in natural colors—July 16, 1926

Senator (U.S.)—Jewish senator—D. L. Yulee —served—July 1, 1845

Treaty—treaty violation—Pedro Menéndez de Avilés—Oct. 15, 1565

Anastasia Island

Alligator Farm—established—1892

Apalachicola

Refrigerator—mechanical refrigerator patent —John Gorrie—May 6, 1851

Arcadia

Rattlesnake Meat—in cans—March 1931

Belle Glade

Kenaf Fiber—planting of commercial importance—July 1951

Cape Canaveral (Cape Kennedy)

Astronauts—American astronaut to orbit the earth—take-off—Feb. 20, 1962—J. H. Glenn, Jr.

Astronauts—space flight by an American astronaut—A. B. Shepard—May 5, 1961

Photograph—photograph in color of the earth from outer space—Dec. 1, 1959

Rocket—American satellite to reach the moon—Ranger IV—launched—April 23, 1962

Rocket—intermediate range ballistic missile —Jupiter—fired—May 31, 1957

Rocket—rocket cone recovery—Aug. 8, 1957

Rocket—satellite placed in orbit—Explorer I —Jan. 31, 1958

Rocket—satellite placed in solar orbit—Pioneer V—launched—March 11, 1960

Rocket—satellite to transmit photographs of the earth—Aug. 7, 1959

Ship—ship to transport fresh orange juice in stainless steel tanks—Feb. 16, 1957

Submarine—submerged submarine to fire a Polaris missile—"George Washington"—July 20, 1960

Television—Telecast—transoceanic television program—satellite launched—July 10, 1962

Daytona Beach

Automobile—automobile to exceed the speed of 200 miles an hour—H. O. Segrave—March 29, 1927

Diesel Engine—diesel engine speed record (official)—C. L. Cummins—March 20, 1930

Fort Caroline

Births—white child of French Protestant parentage—born—1565

War (colonial)—intercolonial war—commenced—Sept. 20, 1565

Fort Jefferson

Prison—military prison of the United States on an island—construction started—1846

Hialeah

Camera—photo-finish camera (electric eye) installed at a race track—Jan. 16, 1936

Jacksonville

Air Mail Service—missile mail (official)—landed—June 8, 1959

Aviation—Flights (transcontinental)—transcontinental airplane flight (eastbound)—R. G. Fowler—landed—Feb. 8, 1912

Aviation—Flights (transcontinental)—transcontinental flight in 24 hours flying time —from San Diego—landed—Feb. 24, 1921

Key Largo

Park — underseas park (federal) — Key Largo Coral Reef Preserve—established —March 15, 1960

Key West

Aviation—airplane rescue at sea—J. A. D. McCurdy—Jan. 30, 1911

Aviation—hydroplane commercial line service (international)—established—Nov. 1, 1920

Aviation—Airport—air passenger international station—opened—Oct. 28, 1927

Aviation—Flights—sky-train international round-trip flight—started—May 14, 1935

President—President to travel underwater in a captured enemy submarine—H. S. Truman—Nov. 21, 1946

Telephone—telephone cable service (deep sea)—established—April 11, 1921

Marineland

Aquarium—aquarium for monsters of the deep—opened—June 23, 1938

Aquatic Mammals—porpoise—born in captivity—Feb. 14, 1940

Miami

Air Mail Service—air mail service between North and South America—May 14, 1929

Births—child born in an airplane—Oct. 28, 1929

Federal Savings and Loan Association—created—Aug. 8, 1933

Greyhound Racing Association—formed—March 3, 1926

President (U.S.)—president to fly in an airplane while in office—F. D. Roosevelt—Jan. 14, 1943

Ship—woman to sail solo across the Atlantic Ocean—Ann Davidson—arrived—Aug. 12, 1953

Television—Telecast—live telecast from a non-contiguous foreign country—received Nov. 13, 1955

Totalisator—used—Jan. 14, 1932

Miami Beach

Medal—Legion of Merit Medal awarded to a foreign national—presentation—Nov. 7, 1942

Pelican Island

Bird Reservation (national)—established—March 14, 1903

Pensacola

Aviation—Airship—airship of the U.S. Navy —flown—April 1917

Aviation—School—naval air training school —opened—Dec. 1, 1914

Civil War—naval engagement in the Civil War—Sept. 14, 1861

Port Canaveral

See under Cape Canaveral

St. Augustine

Billiards—introduced—1565

Catholic Bishop—Catholic bishop—to exercise episcopal functions—1607

Catholic Holy Orders—conferred—Aug. 24, 1675

Catholic Parish—founded—Sept. 8, 1565

Catholic Priest—native Catholic priest—born —1620

Catholic Settlement—1565

Colonist — permanent white settlement — Sept. 8, 1565

Map—map of a city—engraved—1588

St. Petersburg

Aviation—hydroplane commercial line service—Jan. 1, 1914

Post Office—open air post office—opened—Oct. 1, 1917

San Mateo

War (colonial)—intercolonial war—commenced—Sept. 20, 1565

Tampa

Aviation—hydroplane commercial line service—Jan. 1, 1914

Medal—Medal of Honor awarded in World War II—presented posthumously—Feb. 10, 1942

Winter Park

Book Course—Rollins College—1926

College—"Unit Cost Plan"—Rollins College—Sept. 1933

Degrees (academic and honorary)—honorary degree awarded a Negro woman—M. M. Bethune—Feb. 21, 1949

Walk of Fame—Rollins College—1929

Woman—woman coxswain of a men's collegiate varsity team—Sally Stearns—May 27, 1936

GEORGIA

Agriculture Department (state)—state department of agriculture—created—Feb. 28, 1874

Birth Registration—birth registration law (state)—enacted—Dec. 19, 1823

Censorship—state board of censorship on literature—act approved—Feb. 19, 1953

Governor—Jewish governor—David Emanuel—March 3, 1801

Lynch Law (state)—enacted—Dec. 20, 1893

Moravian Bishop—David Nitschmann—arrived—1736

Railroad Legislation—railroad legislation (state)—enacted—March 5, 1856

Senator (U.S.)—woman to occupy a seat in the Senate—R. L. Felton—appointed—Oct. 3, 1922

Ship—steamboat patent—issued—Feb. 1, 1788

State—state to abolish both entail and primogeniture—Feb. 5, 1777

Americus

Telephone—telephone conversation (commercial) using electricity generated by the sun's rays—Oct. 4, 1955

Athens

College—state university chartered—Jan. 27, 1785

Atlanta

Aviation—airplane sleeping berths—nonconvertible—service to New York City—Oct. 5, 1933

Aviation—License—airplane instructor's license—A. J. Banks—Sept. 27, 1939

Football—football with a rubber covering used in a major collegiate game

Football Game—football game between Negro colleges—Jan. 1, 1897

Nursing School—training school for Negro nurses — Spelman Seminary — founded — 1881

Photographic Patent—aerial photography patent—awarded—C. B. Adams—Dec. 12, 1893

Pinball Game—pinball legislation enacted by a major city prohibiting the machines—effective—July 1, 1939

Prison—penitentiary building (national)—completed—Jan. 1902

Prison—prisoners (federal) employed in industry—July 11, 1919

Radio Station—radio station owned and operated by Negroes—WERD—Oct. 3, 1949

Augusta

Aviation—airplane in actual military operation—Army Aviation School—1913

Brunswick

Ship—concrete ship built for the United States Shipping Board — "Atlantus" — launched—Dec. 4, 1918

Cartersville

Automobile License (federal)—contract carrier license—awarded—H. W. Juett—Dec. 29, 1936

Crisp County

Electric Power Plant—hydroelectric power plant (county-owned)—placed in operation—Aug. 1, 1930

Fort Benning

Army Parachute Troops—battalion formed—Oct. 1, 1940

Grover's Island

Forestry Legislation—federal forestry legislation—reservation of public timber land—purchase—Dec. 19, 1799

Jefferson

Anesthesia — anesthetic (general) — C. W. Long—Dec. 1841

Anesthesia—ether administered in childbirth—Dec. 27, 1845

La Fayette

Carpeting—carpeting of tufted plastic—offered for sale—Jan. 4, 1953

Macon

Baptism—March 1540

College—women's college (chartered)—1836

Women's Club—women's secret society—organized—May 15, 1851

Mulberry Grove

Cotton Gin—patented—Eli Whitney—March 14, 1794

GEORGIA—*Continued*

New Echota

Newspaper — Indian newspaper — *Cherokee Phoenix*—Feb. 21, 1828

Rome

Bauxite—discovered—1887

Savannah

Agricultural Experiment Station—agricultural experiment farm—1735
Animals—cattle exportation—1755
Girl Scouts—founded—March 12, 1912
Hospital—Negro hospital and asylum—chartered—Dec. 24, 1832
Meat—beef export—1755
Moravian Church—built—1735
Orphanage—orphanage with a continuous existence—1740
Ship—iron vessel—"John Randolph"—1834
Ship—steamboat built in America to cross the Atlantic Ocean—sailed—May 22, 1819
Silk—silk exportation—1735
Sunday School—established—John Wesley—1736

Soperton

Newspaper—newspaper printed on pine-pulp paper—*Soperton News* — published — March 31, 1933

Washington

Golf Champion—holes-in-one by a father and son—C. H. Calhoun, Sr. and Jr.—Aug. 24, 1932

HAWAII

Congressman (U.S.)—Congressman of Japanese ancestry elected to the House of Representatives—D. K. Inouye—July 28, 1959
Senator (U.S.)—Senator of Asian ancestry—H. L. Fong—elected—July 29, 1959
State—noncontiguous overseas state—admitted—Aug. 21, 1959

Hilo

President (U.S.)—President to visit Hawaii while President—F. D. Roosevelt—landed—July 25, 1934

IDAHO

Governor—Jewish governor—elected for full term—Moses Alexander—Jan. 4, 1915

Arco

Electric Power Plant—electric power generated from atomic energy to illuminate an entire town—July 17, 1955

Boise

Air Raid Shelter—air raid community shelter —completed—July 1, 1961

Idaho Falls

Atomic Energy—electric power from nuclear energy—100,000 watts power—Dec. 20, 1951

Kellogg

Newspaper—mimeographed daily newspaper —July 25, 1923

ILLINOIS

Automobile Legislation—automobile seat belt safety legislation—enacted—June 27, 1955
Judge—Negro judge of a District Court (U.S.)—J. B. Parsons—appointment confirmed—Aug. 30, 1961
Labor Law—labor law prohibiting the employment of women—effective—July 1, 1879
Labor Law—women's equal employment legislation—enacted—March 22, 1872
Land Grant—railroad land grant of importance
Plumbing—state plumbing legislation—enacted—May 30, 1881
Railroad—state aid to railroads—enacted—March 2, 1833
Woman—woman internal revenue collector —M. G. Reinecke—served—June 1, 1923
Woman Suffrage—woman suffrage amendment approved by Congress—ratified—June 10, 1919

Aurora

Railroad Car—car with an observation dome

Belleville

Aviation—Airship—dirigible transfer of mail to a train—June 15, 1928

Bloomington

Corn—shipment of hybrid seed corn—April 13, 1916
Sleeping Car—Pullman sleeping car—service to Chicago—Sept. 1, 1859

Brookfield

Horse—forest horse—foaled—May 18, 1956

Chicago

Adding Machine—adding machine absolutely accurate at all times—patented—Oct. 11, 1887
Addressograph — commercial production — July 26, 1893

ILLINOIS—Chicago—*Continued*

Electric Lighting—electric indirect lighting demonstration—Oct. 1908

Electric Power Plant—rotary converter power plant—operated—May 16, 1896

Elevated Railroad—electric elevated railroad —June 2, 1883

Envelope—envelope with an outlook or window—patented—A. F. Callahan—June 10, 1902

Fair—Woman's World Fair—April 18-25, 1925

Farmer Labor Party—organized—June 12, 1920

Fastening—hookless fastening—patented— W. L. Judson—March 31, 1896

Ferris Wheel—exhibited—1893

Football Game—indoor football game (large) —Nov. 26, 1896

Forestry Society—national forestry association—America Forestry Assn.—organized —Sept. 10, 1875

Gasoline—cracking process used to obtain gasoline from crude petroleum—patented —W. M. Burton—Jan. 7, 1913

Greenback Labor Party—national convention—June 9-10, 1880

Horse Race—horse race (American Derby) —June 28, 1884

Horse Race—horse race of a thousand miles —from Chadron, Neb.—completed—June 27, 1893

Hospital—hospital completely devoted to the study of the atom in the treatment of cancer—Argonne Cancer Research Hospital— opened—March 13, 1953

Hospital—interracial hospital—Provident Hospital—opened—May 4, 1891

Hotel—fireproof hotel—Palmer House— opened—Nov. 1873

Insurance—group insurance contract of importance—Montgomery Ward & Co.—July 1, 1912

International Eucharistic Congress—June 20-24, 1926

Insurance—insurance policy to be illustrated —April 8, 1947

Jockey—jockey (American-born) to win 3,000 races—Eddie Arcaro—June 24, 1952

Kapok—commercially introduced—May 1, 1893

Lawyer—Japanese woman lawyer—K. E. Ohi—admitted to practice—June 10, 1937

Lawyer—Negro woman lawyer to practice before the United States Supreme Court— V. N. Anderson—Jan. 29, 1926

Lawyer—woman lawyer graduated from a law school—A. H. Kepley—Union College of Law—June 30, 1870

Lens—bifocal contact lens—N. K. Wesley— 1958

Lie Detector—invented—Leonarde Keeler

Livestock-Market Paper—*Drover's Journal*— published—Jan. 11, 1873

Madstone—sale recorded—1804

Medical Instruction—public hygiene professor—Thomas Bevan—appointed—1868

Medical Instruction—state medicine and public hygiene professorship—established— 1882

Medical Legislation—premature baby health law—enacted—March 5, 1935

Medical Society—American College of Surgeons—annual convocation—Nov. 13, 1913

Models' Training School—1928

Moving Picture—foreign feature film exhibited—commercial—Aug. 12, 1912

Moving Picture—serial moving picture—issued

Moving Picture Projector—moving picture projector (portable)—invented—H. A. De Vry—1913

Musician—woman conductor-composer— major opera house—*Gale*—Nov. 23, 1935

News Correspondent—woman news reporter at a political convention—M. A. R. Livermore—May 12-18, 1860

Newspaper—newspaper rotogravure sections —published—*Tribune*—March 29, 1914

Newspaper Audit—newspaper circulation audit—Audit Bureau of Circulations— formed—Aug. 21, 1914

Nobel Prize—Nobel prize in physics awarded to an American—A. A. Michelson —1907

Nurses' Society—society for superintendents of nursing schools—formed—June 15-17, 1893

Opera—opera broadcast in its entirety by a professional cast—*Samson et Dalila*—Nov. 14, 1921

Opera—opera broadcast over a national network from an American opera house— *Faust*—Jan. 21, 1927

Optometry Instruction—optometry school— founded—1872

Organ—pipeless organ—patented—Laurens Hammond—April 24, 1934

Physical Culture Department—established— A. A. Stagg—appointed—1892

Pinball Game—pinball game machine—manufactured—1930

Planetarium—planetarium open to the public —Adler Planetarium—opened—May 10, 1930

Police—police bureau of identification—established—Jan. 1, 1884

Political Convention—national nominating convention presided over by a Negro—J. R. Lynch—June 3, 1884

Postal Service—railroad post office for the general distribution of mail—to Clinton, Iowa—Aug. 28, 1864

Presidential Candidate—presidential candidate debate series on television—first debate—Sept. 26, 1960

Presidential Candidate—presidential candidate of Negro blood nominated—Frederick Douglass—June 23, 1888

Presidential Candidate—presidential candidate to fly to a political convention—from Albany, N.Y.—F. D. Roosevelt—July 2, 1932

Presidential Candidate—presidential candidate to make a speech of acceptance at a nominating convention—F. D. Roosevelt— July 2, 1932

Printing Press—web-fed four-color rotary printing press—operated—*Inter-Ocean*—1892

Progressive Party—national convention—Aug. 6, 1912

Prohibition Party (national)—organized—Sept. 12, 1869

Propaganda Course (college)—University of Chicago—1927

Punchboards—patented—Jan. 17, 1905

Radio Broadcast—coast-to-coast hook-up—J. J. Carty—Feb. 8, 1924

Radio Receiver—radio receiver with an auxiliary silicon unit to convert the rays of the sun into electrical power—April 16, 1956

Railroad—daily railroad service to the Pacific Coast—to Portland, Ore.—through service without change—Nov. 17, 1889

Railroad—electrically lighted train—"Pennsylvania Limited"—service to New York—June 1887

Railroad—railroad shipments of dressed beef (year-round long-distance)—G. F. Swift—1877

Railroad—railroad to run west, out of Chicago—C.N.W.—Oct. 25, 1848

Railroad Car—air-conditioned cars—service to Los Angeles—A.T.&S.F.—1914

Railroad Car—"compartmentizer" freight cars—in service to San Francisco, Calif.—Sept. 12, 1952

Railroad Car—dining car—operated—1868

Railroad Car—dining car (all-electric)—in service between Chicago and St. Louis, Mo.—March 9, 1949

Railroad Car—observation cars (super dome)—built—1952

Railroad Car—passenger car (ACF-Talgo for use in the U.S.)—in service to Peoria, Ill.—Feb. 11, 1956

Railroad Car—Pullman train completely equipped with roller bearings—to St. Paul, Minn.—May 21, 1927

Railroad Car—refrigerator car shipment of fresh fruit—Parker Earle—1872

Railroad Track—railroad rails of Bessemer steel—made—May 24, 1865

Roller Skate—ball-bearing skate patent—L. M. Richardson—Dec. 9, 1884

Rotary Club—organized—Feb. 23, 1905

Sanitary District—authorized—Nov. 5, 1889

Sewage—underground comprehensive sewer system (city)—grid pattern—1856

Sidewalk (traveling)—sidewalk (traveling)—1893

Skating—roller derby—opened—Aug. 13, 1935

Sleeping Car—Pullman sleeping car—service to Bloomington—Sept. 1, 1859

Sleeping Car—Pullman sleeping car that was comfortable—built—1865

Snow Cruiser (automobile)—operated—Oct. 22, 1939

Social Democracy of America Party—national convention—June 7, 1898

Sociology Professor—A. W. Small—appointed—Oct. 1, 1892

Softball—indoor baseball game—played—Nov. 30, 1887

Stethoscope—electrical stethoscope (portable)—exhibited—June 10, 1924

Surgical Operation—kidney transplanting—June 17, 1950

Surgical Operation—suture of the human heart (successful)—D. H. Williams—July 9, 1893

Tape Recorder—magnetic tape recorder (commercial) of sound and picture—demonstrated—April 14, 1956

Taxidermy Method (sculptural)—devised—C. E. Akeley—1902

Telephone—air-to-ground public telephone service—Chicago-Detroit area—Sept. 15, 1957

Telephone—telephone switchboard or exchange (multiple)—Jan. 1879

Teletypesetter — teletypesetter — manufactured—1932

Television—Telecast—pay television—Phonovision—demonstrated—Jan. 1, 1951

Television—Telecast—prize fight televised coast-to-coast—Sands-Olson—Oct. 3, 1951

Television — Telecast — stockholders' annual meeting televised on a closed circuit—April 16, 1957

Television—Telecast — stockholders' meetings televised coast-to-coast simultaneously—Oct. 29, 1959

Television—Telecast—surgical operation televised coast-to-coast—June 10, 1952

Television—Telecast—variety talent show series with an all-Negro cast—April 1, 1949

Television Station—all-color station to televise live local programs—WNBQ-TV—April 15, 1956

Tunnel—freight delivery tunnel system—Aug. 15, 1906

Tunnel—subaqueous highway tunnel—commenced—Nov. 30, 1866

Turbine—steam turbine generator of large capacity for commercial service—Oct. 2, 1903

Typesetting Machine—typesetting machine to dispense with metal type—exhibited—Sept. 11, 1950

Vacuum Cleaner — suction-type vacuum cleaner—patented—June 8, 1869

Washing Machine—complete self-contained electric washing machine—1907

Water Conduit—water supply tunnel for a city—completed—Dec. 6, 1866

Wire Recorder—patented—Marvin Camras—June 13, 1944

Women's Club—Jewish women's organization (national)—National Council of Jewish Women—formed—Jan. 1894

Decatur

Soybean Processing Plant—commercially successful—1922

War Veterans' Society—Grand Army of the Republic—established—April 6, 1866

ILLINOIS—*Continued*

De Kalb

Wire—barbed wire—patented—J. F. Glidden —Nov. 24, 1874

Des Plaines

Building—building for telephone directory compilation and printing — dedicated — April 30, 1953
Wedding—television wedding—Oct. 14, 1928

East Peoria

See also Peoria

Bank—bank payments to depositors of a closed insured bank—July 3, 1934
Building—building built inside a factory— Sept. 17, 1938

Evanston

College—woman college president—Feb. 1871
Degrees (academic and honorary)—degree awarded a ventriloquist's dummy—Aug. 28, 1938

Fort Chicago

See also Chicago

Army School—Army school graduate killed —in military action—George Ronan—Aug. 15, 1812

Fort Sheridan

Court Martial—court martial trial of an officer for collaborating with his captors— Sept. 23, 1954

Freeport

Bicycle—bicycle with a back pedal brake— patented—Dec. 24, 1889

Glencoe

Bottle—screw cap bottle with a pour lip— patented—E. A. Ravenscroft—May 5, 1936
Golf Champion—golf champion to win the United States Open and the Professional —Gene Sarazen

Glenview

Aviation—Flights—airplane to exceed the speed of 300 miles per hour—J. R. Wedell —Sept. 4, 1933

Highland Park

Telautograph—patented—Elisha Gray—Feb. 7, 1893

Kankakee

School—circular school building—opened— Feb. 6, 1956

Lake Forest

Golf Champion—golf champion (American born)—H. M. Harriman—won U.S. Amateur Golf Championship—July 8, 1899

La Salle

Coal—coal—discovered—Louis Hennepin— 1673

Lemont

Element—element 102—nobelium—announced —Argonne National Laboratory—July 9, 1957

McHenry County

Silo (of record)—constructed—F. L. Hatch —1873

Miller's Station

Glider—glider with cambered wings—invented—Octave Chanute—1895

Morrison

Lock—time-lock—installed in bank—May 1874

North Chicago

Bottle—screw cap bottle with a pour lip— manufactured—1936

Ottawa

Coal—coal—discovered — Louis Hennepin— 1673
Game Preserve—game preserve—established —c.1860

Peoria

See also East Peoria

Automobile—armored car—manufactured— 1898
Automobile Tractor—diesel-powered tractor —commercial manufacture—1931
Railroad Car—passenger car (ACF-Talgo for use in the U.S.)—in service to Chicago, Ill.—Feb. 11, 1956

Pullman

Locomotive—electric freight locomotive— built—1888
Sleeping Car—Pullman sleeping car made entirely of steel—manufactured—1907

Quincy

Catholic Priest—Negro Catholic priest—ordained to work in U.S.—April 24, 1886

River Park

Deaf—Hearing Aid—hearing aid of interest —patented—R. S. Rhodes—Sept. 23, 1879

Rock Island

Bridge—railway bridge across the Mississippi River—completed—to Davenport, Iowa—April 21, 1856

Canal Locks—on concrete—Hennepin canal—to Chicago, Ill.—section opened—April 17, 1895

United Christian Party—first convention—May 2, 1900

Scott Field

Balloon—balloon flight to exceed an altitude of 40,000 feet—ascended—H. C. Gray—May 4, 1927

Spring Grove

Horse—Haflinger horse—imported—Aug. 18, 1958

Springfield

Aviation—airplane fatality (woman)—Julie Clark—killed—June 17, 1912

Cooperatives Convention—Sept. 25, 1918

Medical Society—American College of Surgeons—incorporated—Nov. 25, 1912

President (United States)—President who had received a patent—Abraham Lincoln—May 22, 1849

War Veterans' Society—Grand Army of the Republic—first state convention—July 12, 1866

Urbana

Betatron—betatron—operated—July 15, 1940

Civic Design Chair—established—University of Illinois—1912

Degrees (academic and honorary)—doctor of philosophy in accounting degree—June 12, 1939

Vandalia

Road—federal highway—from Cumberland, Md.—authorized—March 29, 1806

Waukegan

Automobile Race—automobile race—from Chicago—Nov. 28, 1895

Wheaton

Golf Champion—golf champion (American born professional) to win the United States Open Tournament—June 26, 1911

Golf Course—eighteen-hole golf course—opened—1893

Williamson County

Aviation — Airplane Bombing — airplane bombing in the United States—Nov. 12, 1926

Wilmette

Baha'i House of Worship—opened—May 1, 1931

Winnetka

Blind—correspondence school for the blind to offer instruction in the Braille system—Aug. 1921

INDIANA

Governor—governor granted almost dictatorial power—P. V. McNutt—Feb. 1933

Sterilization Legislation—act passed—March 9, 1907

Tax—chain stores tax (state)—effective—July 1, 1929

Alexandria

Rock Wool Factory—Crystal Chemical Works—opened—June 1, 1897

Street Car—interurban street car line—to Anderson—June 1, 1898

Anderson

Headlight—automatic headlight control—"Autronic-Eye"—offered to public—Jan. 25, 1952

Street Car—interurban street car line—to Alexandria—June 1, 1898

Bloomington

College—state university to grant equal privileges to women—first woman graduated—1869

Medal—Medal of Honor awarded to a soldier who already had received a Distinguished Service Cross—in World War II—June 21, 1943

Vocational Guidance Chair—Indiana University—June 1914

Bluffton

Platoon School—established—1899

Columbus

Automobile Tractor—diesel engine tractor—assembled—May 1930

Diesel Engine—diesel engine automobile trip—to New York City—left—Jan. 3, 1930

Crawfordsville

Archery Club—archery association (national)—formed—Jan. 23, 1879

Elkhart

Clarinet—made of metal—patented—Aug. 27, 1889

Railroad Apprentice School—railroad apprentice school—established—1872

Sarrusophone—manufactured—1921

Saxophone—manufactured—1888

Sousaphone—modern—manufactured—1908

Evansville

Refrigerator—gas refrigerator (household)—marketed—1926

Vitamin—synthetic vitamin—D—commercially manufactured—1927

INDIANA—*Continued*

Fort Wayne

Aviation—Aviator—woman aviator to make a public flight—B. S. Scott—Oct. 23, 1910
Baseball Game—baseball game at night—June 2, 1883
Basketball—National Basketball Association Negro player—C. H. Cooper—played—Nov. 1, 1950
Pump—computer pump—sold—Nov. 1, 1932
Pump—gasoline pump—installed—Sept. 5, 1885
Sawmill—band sawmill—operated—1867

Franklin

Money—scrip money to be self-liquidating—issued—March 8, 1933

Gary

Railroad—railroad freight yard fully automatic—in operation—Jan. 25, 1952

Greencastle

Sorority—sorority—Kappa Alpha Theta—Jan. 27, 1870

Indianapolis

Automobile Race—automobile race on a track (long distance)—May 30, 1911
Greenback Party—organized—Nov. 25, 1874
Naval Officer—Negro commissioned officer in the regular U.S. Navy—John Lee—March 15, 1947
Ordnance—machine gun (rapid fire)—patented—Nov. 4, 1862
Prison—prison built for women and managed exclusively by women—Oct. 8, 1873
Radio Receiver—transistor radio receiver—manufactured—1954
Railroad Station—union passenger station—opened—Sept. 20, 1853
Socialist Party—formed—March 25, 1900
Surgical Operation—gallstone operation—Dr. J. S. Bobbs—June 15, 1867
War Veterans' Society—Grand Army of the Republic—national convention—Nov. 20, 1866
Woman—woman secretary of a state senate—Fern Ale—Jan. 6, 1927

Jasper

Garbage Collection—city to discontinue garbage collection—Aug. 1, 1950

Lafayette

Balloon—balloon flight carrying mail—John Wise—started—Aug. 17, 1859

La Porte

Telephone—automatic telephone system (successful)—installed—1892

Martinsville

Fish Hatchery—goldfish hatchery—successfully operated—1899

Michigan City

Gas—gas storage tank (waterless)—placed in service—Feb. 10, 1925

New Harmony

Communistic Society—communistic non-religious settlement—1825
Printing Instruction—printing instruction—Robert Owen—1826

Richmond

Automobile—miniature automobile manufactured in the U.S.—Crosley—offered for sale—April 28, 1939

South Bend

Automobile—automobile-airplane combination—delivery received—Aug. 15, 1937

Vincennes

Book—book printed in the Indiana Territory—1804

Wabash

Electric Lighting—street lighting (electric) by a municipality—March 31, 1880

IOWA

Cigarette Tax—cigarette tax (state)—April 11, 1921

Alleman

Corn Husking Championship Contest (national)—Dec. 1, 1924

Ames

Cornstone—Maizolith—made—1922
Veterinary School—veterinary school (state)—established—May 23, 1879

Cedar Falls

Farmers' Institute—farmers' institute held by a land grant agricultural college off its campus—by Iowa State College—Dec. 20, 1870

Cedar Rapids

Photograph—photograph bounced off a satellite—beamed—Aug. 18, 1960
Radio Sextant—announced—July 14, 1954

Davenport

Bank—national bank—opened—under law of 1863—June 29, 1863

Bridge—railway bridge across the Mississippi River—to Rock Island, Ill.—completed—April 21, 1856

Camera—moving picture camera (portable)
—manufactured—1923

Carrousel—carrousel patent—July 25, 1871

Chiropractic School—opened—1900

Chiropractor—D. D. Palmer—adjustment
treatment—Sept. 18, 1895

Surgical Operation—appendicitis operation
(appendectomy)—Jan. 4, 1885

Des Moines

Army Auxiliary Corps—Women's Army
Auxiliary Corps (WAAC) training course
—July 20, 1942

Army Camp—army camp for training Negro
officers—June 15, 1917

Automobile—electric storage battery automobile—built—1891

Radio Facsimile Transmission—radio facsimile broadcasting on the regular broadcasting band—Feb. 4, 1938

Dubuque

Ship—warship built on inland waters—
"Ericsson"—launched—May 12, 1894

Fairfield

Electric Power Plant—municipally owned
electric power plant—purchased—1882

Froelich

Automobile Tractor—gasoline tractor—manufactured—1892

Iowa City

Degrees (academic and honorary)—degree
conferred by radio—June 9, 1925

Education—chair in education—permanently
established—1873

Kellerton

Horseshoe Pitchers' Association (national)—
championship tournament—Oct. 23, 1915

Marion

Bridge—concrete cantilever bridge—erected
—1905

Mount Pleasant

Lawyer—woman lawyer—admitted to practice—A. A. Mansfield—June 1869

Photograph—photograph of a total solar
eclipse—E. C. Pickering—Aug. 7, 1869

Muscatine

Button—buttons of fresh water pearl—1890

Onawa

Eskimo Pie—patented—C. K. Nelson—Jan.
24, 1922

Oskaloosa

Fingerprinting—community to fingerprint its
citizens—May 21, 1934

Sioux City

Addressograph—invented—J. S. Duncan—
1892

Bank—joint stock land bank—chartered—
April 24, 1917

Urbandale

Bridge—welded aluminum girder-type highway bridge—completed—Sept. 24, 1958

KANSAS

Impeachment — impeachment proceedings
against a state governor—acquittal—1862

Trust — anti-trust law (state)—general—
enacted—March 9, 1889

Trust—blue-sky laws—enacted—March 10,
1911

Abilene

Carrousel—portable carrousel—manufactured
—1896

Shooting Gallery (mechanized)—invented—
C. W. Parker—1890

Argonia

Woman—woman mayor—S. M. Salter—April
4, 1887

Atchison

Alcohol—power alcohol plant—established
—Oct. 2, 1936

Bronson

Horseshoe Pitching Contest (International)
—1909

Dexter

Helium—helium—discovered as a constituent
of natural gas—1905

Chapman

High School—county high school—Dickinson County Community High School—
opened—Sept. 1889

Dodge City

Bullfight—bullfight—July 4, 1884

Motorcycle Race—motorcycle race (300
miles)—July 4, 1914

Fort Riley

Army Officer—brigadier general (Negro)—
appointed—Oct. 25, 1940

KANSAS—*Continued*

Garden City

Aviation—air-rail passenger transcontinental service—plane service from Cleveland—June 14, 1929

Kansas City

Aviation—airplane "fly-it-yourself" system—Fairfax Airport—Sept. 15, 1929
Horseshoe Pitchers' Association (National)—formed—May 16, 1914

Leavenworth

Carrousel—carrousel with the jumping horse mechanism—manufactured—1896
Fingerprinting—federal penitentiary fingerprinting—United States Penitentiary—Nov. 2, 1904
Photography—demonstration of rapid aerial photography—Sept. 5, 1925
Prison—penitentiary building (national)—completed—Feb. 1, 1906

Manhattan

Farmers' Institute—farmers' institute sponsored by a college—held—Nov. 14, 1868

Topeka

Court—small debtors' court established by state law—1913

Victoria

Animals—cattle (Aberdeen-Angus) importation—1873

Wichita

Aviation—Airplane—turbine propeller light-airplane—flown—Nov. 5, 1952
Railroad Car—freight car (Adapto car)—in service to St. Louis, Mo.—July 24, 1956

KENTUCKY

Debtors' Prison—abolished by legislation—Dec. 17, 1821
Election Law—Australian ballot system—adopted for Louisville—Feb. 24, 1888
Nullification Proceedings—approved—Nov. 16, 1798
Road—state road appropriation of a specific sum—Dec. 19, 1795
Road—state road authorization—Dec. 14, 1793

Ashland

Steel—continuous sheet steel mill—built—1922

Barbourville

Colonist—civilian settlement west of the Allegheny Mountains—April 23, 1750

Churchill Downs

See Louisville

Danville

College—university west of the Allegheny Mountains—chartered—1783
Surgical Operation—abdominal operation—ovariotomy—Dr. E. McDowell—Dec. 13, 1809

Fort Knox

Woman—woman to have her name placed on the cornerstone of a United States government building—N. T. Ross—April 1936

Harrison's Mills

Duel—duel in which a future President of the United States participated—May 30, 1806

Harrodsburg

Bridge — cantilever bridge — construction started—Oct. 12, 1876

Hodgenville

President (United States)—President born beyond the boundaries of the original thirteen states—Abraham Lincoln—Feb. 12, 1809

Lexington

Narcotic—narcotic sanatorium (federal) for drug addicts—opened—May 29, 1935

Logan County

Camp Meeting—1803

Loretto

Convent—Catholic convent to admit colored women as sisters—May 1824

Louisa

Dam—needle-type dam—constructed—1900

Louisville

Brick—terra cotta factory—to be successful —1867

Coast Guard (U.S.)—inland U.S. Coast Guard station—opened—Nov. 3, 1881

Coin Box—for street cars—invented—T. L. Johnson—1870

Gas Mask—gas mask—resembling modern type—patented—L. P. Haslett—June 12, 1849

Horse Race—filly to win the Kentucky Derby—May 8, 1915

Horse Race—horse race (Kentucky Derby) —May 17, 1875

Jockey—jockey to win the Kentucky Derby four times—Eddie Arcaro

Medal—Air Medal (U.S.) awarded to a woman—presentation—March 26, 1943

Presidential Candidate—presidential candidate who was a Catholic—Charles O'Conor —nominated—Sept. 3, 1872

Telegraph—telegraph ticker which successfully printed type—patented—D. E. Hughes —May 20, 1856

Telephone—multiple common battery switchboard—in service—1897

Ludlow

Railroad—municipal railroad—from Cincinnati—service—July 23, 1877

Somerset

Railroad—municipal railroad—from Cincinnati—service—July 23, 1877

LOUISIANA

Governor—Catholic governor—E. D. White —1835

Governor—Negro governor (acting)—P. B. S. Pinchback—Dec. 11, 1872

Health Board—health board (state) to regulate quarantine

Law Codification (state)—promulgated— June 13, 1825

Price Regulation Law (state)—approved— July 2, 1908

Prize Fight—state legislation concerning prize fighting—May 12, 1890

Senator (U.S.)—Senator to win a seat which had been occupied by his father and mother—Russell Long—elected—Nov. 2, 1948

Sugar—sugar cane—imported—1751

Sulphur Mine (offshore)—Louisiana coast— March 14, 1960

Calcasieu Parish

Sulphur Deposit—discovered—1869

Carville

Hospital—leper hospital—founded—1894

Protestant Church—Protestant Church for Lepers—dedicated—June 14, 1915

Lake Charles

Pipeline—pipeline (interstate) to transport ethylene—in operation—to Orange, Texas —Sept. 6, 1958

New Orleans

Anesthesia — spinal anesthesia report — Rudolph Matas—1900

Business Economics Course—Tulane University—1849

Catholic Nuns—nun who professed her vows in the United States—March 15, 1729

Catholic Nuns—nun who was born in the United States—novitiate—July 2, 1749

College—college for women to affiliate with a university—established—Oct. 11, 1886

College — Negro university (Catholic) — Xavier University—college department opened—Sept. 13, 1925

Convent—convent—opened—Aug. 6, 1727

Cotton-Bale Metallic Tie—patented—March 2, 1858

Craps—introduced—1813

Free Lunch—free lunch—Pierre Maspero— 1838

Greek Orthodox Church—founded—1867

Heresy Trial of a bishop—Oct. 12, 1925

Holiday—Mardi Gras of New Orleans, La.— 1827

Levees—on Mississippi River—built—1724

Methodist—Methodist missionary—Ebenezer Brown—1819

Money—Confederate coinage—1861

Monument—statue officially sanctioned by Rome—blessed—Nov. 10, 1895

Political Science Society—political science association—founded—Dec. 30, 1903

Prize Fight—prize fight of importance under the Marquis of Queensberry rules—Sept. 7, 1892

Road—mosaic pavement—completed—Feb. 4, 1930

Ship—Confederate cruiser to raid Union commerce—fitted out—1861

Ship—steamboat (double decked)—"Washington"—arrived—Oct. 7, 1816

Ship—steamboat to sail down the Mississippi —"New Orleans"—arrived—Oct. 1, 1811

Shipping—coastal shipping service—T. L. Servoss—1831

Siamese Twins—Siamese twins separated successfully by surgery—Sept. 17, 1953

Street Car—street car tracks which were tieless, soundless and shockless—1930

Sugar—sugar refinery—practical—1791

Treason—citizen of the United States to be tried for treason, convicted, and hanged— W. B. Mumford—hanged—June 7, 1862

Venetian Blinds—venetian blind patent— John Hampson—Aug. 21, 1841

Water—heavy water—discovery announced —Dec. 29, 1931

University

Art Course—art course—true fresco painting course—Louisiana State University—Sept. 14, 1936

MAINE

Births—child born of European parents on American soil—Snorro—1007

Congressman (U.S.)—congressmen (brothers) to serve simultaneously

Governor—brothers to serve simultaneously as governors of their respective states— Levi Lincoln (Massachusetts) and Enoch Lincoln

Senator (U.S.)—woman senator elected without having previously served an appointed term—M. C. Smith—Sept. 13, 1948

Ship—ship built by the English in the American colonies—launched—1607

Andover

Television—Telecast—transoceanic television program—July 10, 1962

Augusta

Fur Trading Post—established—1628

Bangor

Chewing Gum—manufactured—1848

Bar Harbor

Radio Facsimile Transmission—photograph sent by radio across the Atlantic from Europe—received—June 11, 1922

Bath

Ship—guided missile destroyer—"Dewey"

Ship—schooner (four masted)—"William J. White"—launched—June 1880

Ship—steam whaler built as a whale boat— "The Mary and Helen"—built—1879

Ship—steel sailing vessel—"Dirigo"— launched—Feb. 3, 1894

Ship—turbine-propelled ship of the U.S. Navy—"Chester"

Bristol

Pirate—on the Atlantic seaboard—Dixie Bull—looted—1632

Brunswick

Negro—Negro college graduate—J. B. Russwurm—graduated—1826

Bucksport

Fish Hatchery (federal)—established—1872

Calais

Colonist—colonial white settlement (north of Florida)—founded—1604

Telephone—international telephone conversation—to St. Stephen—July 1, 1881

Camden

Ship—schooner (six masted)—launched— July 1, 1900

Cape Elizabeth

Air Brush Patent—L. L. Curtis—Oct. 25, 1881

Cape Porpoise

Discovery—discovery of New England by an Englishman—Bartholomew Gosnold— landed

Dixfield

Diving Suit (practical) for submarine diving —patented—Leonard Norcross—June 14, 1834

Eastern Egg Rock

Birds—bird for which a definite crossing of the Atlantic has been recorded—banded— July 3, 1913

Eastport

Canning—sardine cannery—1876

Farmington

Earmuff—patented—Chester Greenwood— March 13, 1877

Gardiner

Technical Institute—Gardiner Lyceum— founded—1822

Greenville

Forest Fire—forest fire lookout tower—service began—June 10, 1905

Lake Sebago

Camp Fire Girls organization—announced— March 17, 1912

Lewiston

Postal Service—international dog sled mail —left—Dec. 20, 1928

Limerick

Bank—national bank woman president— elected—Jan. 11, 1938

Limestone

Aviation—Flights (transatlantic)—jet transatlantic non-stop flight east to west—D. C. Schilling—Sept. 22, 1950

Aviation—Flights (transatlantic)—jet transatlantic non-stop flight west to east—April 7, 1953

Machias

Revolutionary War—naval battle of the Revolution—"Unity" and "Margaretta"— June 12, 1775

Mount Desert

Park—park (national) east of the Mississippi—established—July 8, 1916

War (colonial)—colonial warfare between England and France for the possession of North America—took place—1613

Newfield

Methodist—Negro minister with two white congregations—J. R. Washington—June 3, 1958

Norway

Snowshoe—commercial production—A. M. Dunham, Jr.—1862

Orono

Army—Reserve Officers Training Corps Units—authorized—Oct. 21, 1916

Pemaquid

Road—road pavement—laid—1625

Phippsburg

Holiday—Thanksgiving Day service—Aug. 9, 1607

Portland

Brokerage—stock order from a Zeppelin—received—Aug. 8, 1930

Catholic Bishop—Catholic bishop (Negro)—consecrated—1875

Oratorio—oratorio by an American—performed—June 3, 1873

Railroad—international railroad—to Montreal—service—July 18, 1853

Sanford

Blanket—blanket robe and carriage lap robe business—successfully undertaken—1867

South Berwick

Blanket—blanket factory—Burleigh Blanket Mills—1854

Water Power—water power development grant—established—1620

Thomaston

Doughnut Cutter—patented—J. F. Blondel—July 9, 1872

Togus

Soldiers' Homes (national)—Eastern Home—authorized—March 21, 1866

West Newfield

Methodist—Negro minister with two white congregations—J. R. Washington—June 3, 1958

Winthrop

Oilcloth Factory—successful—established—1845

Thresher—threshing machines to employ steam—patented—Dec. 29, 1837

Wiscasset

Women's Club—women's club—Female Charitable Society—organized—Nov. 18, 1805

York

Bridge—pile bridge—constructed—1761

City (incorporated)—March 1, 1642

MARYLAND

Arbitration—state arbitration law—Dec. 15, 1778

Autopsy—autopsy and verdict of a coroner's jury—Sept. 24, 1657

Citizenship—citizenship (colonial) conferred by special grant—session—Nov. 1, 1784

Nail Cutting and Heading Machine—patented—George Chandler—Dec. 12, 1796

Physician—Jewish doctor—Jacob Lumbrozo—arrived—Jan. 24, 1656

Religious Liberty Act (colonial)—Tolerance Act—enacted—April 1649

Senator (U.S.)—Catholic senator—Daniel Carroll—March 4, 1789

Woman Suffrage—woman suffrage advocate—Margaret Brent—demanded vote—June 24, 1647

Abingdon

Methodist College—Cokesbury College—building opened—Dec. 6, 1787

Alberton (Elysville)

Bridge—wooden railroad bridge of a purely truss type—1838

Annapolis

Army—Reserve Officers Training Corps Units—authorized—Oct. 21, 1916

Catholic Work—1784

Marines—marine aviator—assigned—July 9, 1912

Naval Academy—Japanese midshipman in the U.S. Naval Academy—admitted—Dec. 8, 1869

Naval Academy—Naval Academy (U.S.)—opened—Oct. 10, 1845

Naval Academy—Negro midshipman in the U.S. Naval Academy—J. H. Conyers—attended—Sept. 21, 1872

Naval Academy—Negro midshipman in the U.S. Naval Academy to graduate—W. A. Brown—June 3, 1949

Woman—woman printer—Dinah Nuthead—petitioned—May 5, 1696

MARYLAND—*Continued*

Baltimore

Agricultural Journal—agricultural journal to attain prominence—April 2, 1819

Anti-Masonic Party—presidential candidates nominated—Sept. 26, 1831

Atlas—issued by a state—1825

Aviation—Airplane—airplane used by a newspaper—Sept. 1, 1920

Aviation—Airplane—naval patrol bomber—christened—Nov. 8, 1941

Balloon—balloon flight—June 23, 1784

Bottle Cap—with crown cork—patented—Feb. 2, 1892

Bridge—stone arch railroad bridge—Dec. 21, 1829

Cathedral—cathedral — building dedicated — May 31, 1821

Catholic Church—Catholic parish church for Negroes—dedicated—Feb. 21, 1864

Catholic Diocese—established—April 6, 1789

Catholic Nuns—Catholic nuns (cloistered community)—founded—April 24, 1922

Catholic Nuns—Catholic nuns (colored community)—Oct. 2, 1831

Catholic Priest—Catholic priest ordained in the U.S.—May 25, 1793

Catholic Priest—Catholic priest to receive his full theological training in the U.S.—ordained—March 18, 1795

Catholic Priest—Negro Catholic priest ordained in the U.S.—Dec. 19, 1891

Catholic Provincial Council—convened—Oct. 4, 1829

Citizenship—Japanese granted citizenship—June 30, 1858

Civil War—bloodshed in the Civil War—April 19, 1861

College—Catholic college for women—College of Notre Dame of Maryland—opened—Sept. 2, 1895

College—woman professor at a first-class medical school—1901

Constitutional Union Party — organized — May 9, 1860

Country Day School—opened—Sept. 1897

Democratic National Convention—May 1832

Dental School—dental college—Baltimore College of Dental Surgery—degrees conferred—March 9, 1841

Egyptian Antiquities Collection—imported—1835

Gas—gas company—incorporated—Feb. 5, 1817

Gas—gas ordinance (city)—approved—June 19, 1816

Health Board—health board (local)—appointed—1792

Humane Society—humane association national organization—American Humane Association—constitution adopted—Nov. 14, 1878

Hygiene Instruction—hygiene and public health school—established—1916

Ice Cream—ice cream wholesale dealer—Jacob Fussel—1851

Ice Cream Freezer—patented—W. G. Young—May 30, 1848

Labor Law—eight-hour day—uniform action—Aug. 20, 1866

Law Magazine—*American Law Journal*—published—1808

Locomotive—locomotive bid—solicited—Jan. 4, 1831

Locomotive—locomotive built in the United States to pull passengers—"Tom Thumb"—test—Aug. 28, 1830

Locomotive—race between a locomotive and a horse-drawn vehicle—to Relay—Aug. 25, 1830

Manual Training—manual training school entirely financed by public taxes—established—1884

Medical Book—aviation medicine book—*Aviation Medicine*—published—1926

Medical Book—ophthalmology book—published—1823

Medical Clinic—medical clinic (general)—of importance—Johns Hopkins—opened—Oct. 1889

Medical Instruction—History of Medicine Department—Johns Hopkins University—Oct. 18, 1929

Medical Instruction—ophthalmology course (regular)—Ophthalmic Clinic—established—1823

Medical Instruction—pathology chair—modern pathology chair—W. H. Welch—Johns Hopkins University—1883

Methodist—Methodist Bishop—Francis Asbury—appointed—1784

Monument—monument to Christopher Columbus—dedicated—Oct. 12, 1792

Monument—monument to George Washington (city or state)—cornerstone laid—July 4, 1815

Museum—museum especially constructed as a museum and art gallery—Aug. 15, 1814

Newspaper—newspaper to appear on Sunday—*Monitor*—Dec. 18, 1796

Odd Fellows Lodge—established—April 26, 1819

Orchestra—municipal orchestra supported by taxes—first concert—Feb. 11, 1916

Patent—label patent—issued—Aug. 1, 1874

Pen—steel pen patent—Peregrine Williamson—Nov. 22, 1809

Pharmacy College—pharmacy college to make analytical chemistry a required course—Maryland College of Pharmacy—March 20, 1872

Pharmacy Professor—pharmacy professorship—David Stewart—April 24, 1844

Political Convention—national committee of a political organization—formed—May 22, 1848

Political Convention — two-thirds rule—adopted—May 21, 1832

Polo—polo game played outdoors at night—July 2, 1931

Postmaster—woman postmaster (colonial)—M. K. Goddard—1775

MARYLAND—*Continued*

Cambridge

Automobile Trucking Service—automobile trucking service—by railroad—to Salisbury and Tyaskin, Md.—Jan. 8, 1923

Cardiff

Slate—for roofing material—1734

Catonsville

Military School—church military school—founded—1845

College Park

Army Officer—flight surgeon—J. P. Kelly—reported for duty—June 30, 1911
Aviation—Airplane—airplane outfitted with a machine gun—flown—May 7, 1912
Aviation—Aviator—Army aviator to solo—F. E. Humphreys—Oct. 26, 1909
Aviation—Flights—all blind cross-country test—to Newark, N.J.—March 21, 1933
Aviation—Passenger—woman airplane passenger—Oct. 27, 1909
Helicopter Flight—helicopter flight—of importance—June 16, 1922

Cumberland

Bottle—milk bottles—manufactured—L. P. Whiteman—1879
Road—federal highway—Cumberland road—to Vandalia, Ill.—appropriation—March 29, 1806

Elkridge Landing

Clock—clock to strike the hours—constructed—Benjamin Banneker—1754

Ellicott's Mills

President (United States)—President to ride on a railroad train—Andrew Jackson—June 6, 1833
Railroad Car—double-deck railroad coaches—to Baltimore, Md.

Elysville

See Alberton

Fort George G. Meade

Army Armored Car Unit—organized—1928

Frederick

Carpet Factory—carpet mill to make ingrain carpets—established—1810
Stamp Act Repudiation—Nov. 23, 1765
Supreme Court of the United States—Chief Justice of the Supreme Court who was Catholic—R. B. Taney—appointed—March 28, 1836

Glenross

Patent—Negro to obtain a patent—Henry Blair—Oct. 14, 1834

Hagerstown

Library—book-wagon—service—April 1905

Hyattsville

Single Tax—city to adopt the single tax for local revenue purposes—July 1892

Laurel

Horse Race—horse race in which the British Royal Silks participated—Nov. 3, 1954
Radio Broadcast—radio broadcast from a moving train, of a regular program on a national network—pick up—March 27, 1932

Middle River

Television—Telecast—stratovision flight test—Dec. 9, 1945

Mount Savage

Brick—fire brick to withstand high heat—manufactured—1841
Railroad Track—railroad rails of iron—rolled—1844

Patuxent

Jury—jury composed of women—ordered—Sept. 22, 1656

Poolesville

Hospital—military hospital on the modern pavilion plan—Oct. 21, 1861

Prince Georges County

Art Commission (public)—contract placed—Sept. 5, 1721

Relay

Conscientious Objectors' Camp—opened—May 15, 1941
Locomotive—race between a locomotive and a horse-drawn vehicle—from Baltimore—Aug. 25, 1830

St. Johns

Shorthand Report—Nov. 15, 1681

Salisbury

Automobile Trucking Service—automobile trucking service—by railroad—to Cambridge and Tyaskin, Md.—Jan. 8, 1923

Silver Spring

Radio Station—all-local network—May 15, 1950

Somerset

Ordnance—semi-automatic rifle—patented—J. C. Garand—Oct. 19, 1926

Sykesville

Railroad—railroad to carry troops—B.&O.—June 30, 1831

Talbot County

Manual Training—school to offer courses in manual training—opened—Dec. 1, 1751

Tyaskin

Automobile Trucking Service—automobile trucking service—by railroad—to Cambridge and Salisbury, Md.—Jan. 8, 1923

Upper Marlborough (Marlboro)

Orchestra—orchestra used in conjunction with an opera—1752

White Oak

Betatron—mobile betatron—operated—Nov. 12, 1948

MASSACHUSETTS

Accident Report—industrial accident reports —required—Sept. 1, 1887

Animals—cows—imported—March 1624

Apples—imported—John Winthrop—1629

Army Insignia—special insignia—authorized —July 5, 1775

Automobile License Plates—plastic license plate tabs—issued—Dec. 15, 1942

Aviation—aeronautical patent—Moses McFarland—Oct. 28, 1799

Charity Board (state)—established—April 29, 1863

Child Labor Law—child labor law regulating hours of employment—March 3, 1842

Child Labor Law—child labor law to include educational provision—effective—April 1, 1837

Copyright Law—copyright law—May 15, 1672

Credit Union Law—approved—May 21, 1909

Dairy Legislation (state)—May 30, 1856

Education—compulsory education law—June 14, 1642

Education—compulsory school attendance law (state)—May 18, 1852

Education—state board of education—established—April 30, 1837

Election—accredited colonial election—May 18, 1631

Election Law—registration law (state)—March 7, 1801

Epidemic — smallpox epidemic — of importance—1616

Expedition—scientific expedition—outfitted—1761

Extradition — extradition — New England Confederation—1643

Fish Commission (state)—authorized—May 16, 1856

Forestry Legislation—colonial forestry legislation—March 29, 1626

Fork—imported—1630

Furs — exported — Robert Cushman — Dec. 1621

Game Law—game law (state)—1817

Gas Commission (state)—legislation approved—June 11, 1885

Geological Survey—geological survey (state) —1830-1833

Governor—brothers to serve simultaneously as governors of their respective states—Levi Lincoln and Enoch Lincoln (Maine)

Health Board—health board (state)—approved—June 21, 1869

Horse—horses—imported—April 17, 1629

Horse Race—horse race prohibition legislation—June 4, 1674

Hurricane—recorded—Aug. 15, 1635

Insurance—automobile compulsory insurance act (state)—effective—Jan. 1, 1927

Insurance—government insurance—1636

Insurance—insurance regulation (state)—legislation—Feb. 13, 1799

Insurance—marine insurance law (state)—approved—Feb. 16, 1818

Insurance — non-forfeiture insurance law (state)—approved—April 10, 1861

Insurance—savings bank life insurance—approved—June 26, 1907

Labor — labor bureau (state) — approved — June 23, 1869

Labor Law—factory inspection law—April 30, 1879

Labor Law—minimum wage law—June 4, 1912

Lawyer—lawyer disbarred—Thomas Lechford—Sept. 3, 1639

Legislature—legislature with two chambers —March 1644

Life Saving Stations for Distressed Mariners —established—1787

Literacy qualification for voting—amendment—May 1, 1857

Loan—state loan—authorized—Dec. 10, 1690

Medical Legislation—law to regulate the practice of medicine (colonial)—enacted—May 3, 1649

Military Leader—of Puritans—Miles Standish—1621

Milk Inspectors—authorized—April 6, 1859

Missionary Society—missionary society organized in the U.S.—1762

Money—paper money—issued—1690

Nautical School—nautical state school—established—June 11, 1891

Patent—machine patent — granted — Joseph Jencks—March 6, 1646

Patent—patent granted by the colonies—Samuel Winslow—1641

MASSACHUSETTS—*Continued*

Physician—doctor in New England—Samuel Fuller—arrived—Dec. 21, 1620

Physician—Negro doctor to become a member of a medical association—J. V. De Grasse—1854

Post Office—post office (colonial)—established—Nov. 5, 1639

Probation—probation legislation for juvenile delinquents—enacted—June 23, 1869

Quakers—Quakers to arrive in America—July 1656

Quarantine—quarantine legislation (colonial) —March 1647

Railroad Commission (state)—established—July 1, 1869

School Law (compulsory)—enacted—Nov. 11, 1647

State—state constitution—adopted—May 16, 1775

Tax—property tax law (colonial)—enacted—May 14, 1634

Tobacco—tobacco tax (colonial)—authorized—Oct. 3, 1632

Vaccination Legislation—vaccination legislation (state)—enacted—March 6, 1810

Witchcraft Execution—Achsah Young—May 27, 1647

Abington

Shoe Manufacturing Machine—patented—L. R. Blake—July 6, 1858

Sprinkler—sprinkler system patent—P. W. Pratt—Sept. 17, 1872

Amherst

Hygiene Instruction—hygiene and physical education professorship—established—1860

Arlington

Loop the Loop Centrifugal Railway—patented—Edwin Prescott—Aug. 16, 1898

Auburn

Brake Patent—brake patent—Robert Turner —Aug. 29, 1828

Rocket—liquid fuel rocket flight—March 16, 1926

Belchertown

Semaphore Telegraph System—invented—Jonathan Grout—1799

Beverly

Cotton—cotton goods to be trademarked —June 6, 1788

Cotton Mill—established—Beverly Cotton Manufactory—1788

Billerica

Leather—leather-splitting machine—patented —Samuel Parker—July 9, 1808

Boston

Actor—actor to receive curtain applause—Edmund Keene—1821

Adding Machine—adding machine to print totals and subtotals—patented—Nov. 19, 1872

Advertisement—advertisement—*News-Letter* —May 1-8, 1704

Agricultural Book—agricultural book—*The Husbandman's Guide*—published—1710

Agricultural Book—agricultural book distinctly American—published—1760

Almanac — nautical almanac — published — Dec. 29, 1782

"America"—publicly sung—July 4, 1832

American Language—book on Americanisms—published—1816

Anesthesia—painless surgery demonstration —Oct. 16, 1846

Animals—bear (white)—exhibited—Jan. 18, 1733

Animals—camel imported—advertised—Oct. 2, 1721

Animals—cattle (Guernsey cattle)—imported —1831

Animals—leopard—exhibited—Feb. 2, 1802

Animals—lion—exhibited—Nov. 26, 1716

Animals—mule—imported—Oct. 26, 1785

Annunciator—patented—Dec. 26, 1833

Archaeological Society—archaeological society (national)—founded—May 10, 1879

Architectural School—architectural school—of collegiate rank—Massachusetts Institute of Technology—established—Feb. 20, 1865

Arithmetic—American arithmetic—by a native American —published—1729

Arithmetic—arithmetic—printed—1719

Artist—American artist of importance—J. S. Copley

Arts and Science Society—arts and science society (national)—chartered—May 4, 1780

Automobile School—automobile school—established—1903

Aviation—airplane commutation tickets—to Newark, N.J.—May 1, 1929

Aviation—Flights—airplane night scheduled passenger flight—left—April 1, 1927

Bank—savings bank to become a corporation—chartered—Dec. 13, 1816

Baseball Book—published—1834

Baseball Glove—worn—C. C. Waite—1875

Baseball Player—baseball player to hit four home runs in one game—Bobby Lowe—May 30, 1894

Bathhouse—bathhouses owned and operated by a municipality—built—1865

Bibliography—bibliography of theological and biblical literature—printed—1726

Bicycle Magazine—*American Bicycling Journal*—Dec. 22, 1877

Bicycle Society—bicycle club—formed—Feb. 11, 1878

Bicycle Trip—bicycle trip of 100 miles sponsored by a club—from Worcester, Mass. —Sept. 6, 1882

MASSACHUSETTS—Boston—Continued

Grammar—Latin grammar textbook—Ezekiel Cheever—published—1709

Greenhouse—erected—Andrew Faneuil—1737

Heating System—heating system (steam)—installed—1844

High School—high school—English Classical School—opened—May 1820

High School—high school for girls—established—1826

High School—vocational high school for girls—opened—July 1904

Historical Society—historical society (state)—Massachusetts Historical Society—organized—Aug. 26, 1790

History—American history of importance written by a woman—published—M. O. Warren—1805

Horse Breeding Society—Massachusetts Society for Encouraging the Breed of Fine Horses—formed—1810

Hospital—tuberculosis home for the care of consumptives—Channing Home—opened—May 1857

Hotel — hotel — Tremont House—opened—Oct. 16, 1829

Hotel—hotel to install bathrooms—Tremont House—opened—Oct. 16, 1829

Hotel—hotel to install radio reception—Hotel Statler—May 10, 1927

Hygiene Instruction—School Department of Hygiene—established—1907

Ice—export of ice—to Martinique—Aug. 1805

Insurance—health insurance company—organized—April 21, 1847

Insurance—mutual liability insurance company—organized—April 21, 1887

Insurance—mutual life insurance company to be chartered—April 1, 1835

Kindergarten — American kindergarten — 1868

Labor Union—labor organization—shoemakers—Oct. 18, 1648

Lawyer—Japanese lawyer—graduated—June 5, 1877

Legislator (state)—Negro representatives to sit in any state legislature—1866

Lighthouse—lighthouse—in operation—Sept. 14, 1716

Logic Book—published—1735

Map—map made in the United States published in a book—1677

Map—road map for public use—published—1698

Marathon Race (annual)—April 19, 1897

Masonry—Negro Masonic Grand Lodge (not Free and Accepted Masons)—organized—June 24, 1791

Medical Book—bacteriology textbook—published—1880

Medical Book—medical pamphlet—treatise on smallpox—published—Jan. 21, 1677

Medical Instruction — medical chemistry course (systematic) — Harvard Medical School—1871

Medical School—coeducational medical school—Boston University School of Medicine—1874

Medical School—women's medical school—Boston Female Medical School—organized—Nov. 1, 1848

Medical Society—medical society—founded

Medical Society—medical society (state)—of importance—incorporated—Nov. 1, 1781

Medical Society—women's medical society—organized—Nov. 23, 1848

Medicine Ball—invented—1895

Military Organization—military organization—Ancient and Honorable Artillery Company—chartered—March 13, 1638

Milk Inspector—appointed—Aug. 10, 1859

Missionary Society—foreign missionary society organized by women—organized—Nov. 1860

Money—deposit of gold bullion—made—Feb. 12, 1795

Motorcycle Endurance Run—motorcycle endurance run—to New York City—July 4, 1902

Music—chamber music organization—concert—Dec. 14, 1849

Music—concert—Dec. 30, 1731

Music—music convention—Aug. 16, 1838

Music—music festival—Feb. 16, 1815

Music—music printed in a magazine—published—April 1774

Music—orchestral song—published—March 1791

Music—patriotic American song—published—July 1768

Music—secular song hit—published—1827

Music—war song—"Chester"—published—William Billings—1778

Music Book—hymn book with music—published—1798

Music Book—music book printed with bars—published—1721

Music Book—music composition book—published—1770

Music Book—vocal instruction book—published—1721

Music Instruction—music instruction (public school)—Hawes School—Nov. 1837

Music Instruction—musical pedagogy school—Boston Academy of Music—founded—Jan. 8, 1833

Musician—Negro-song popularizer—J. C. G. Graupner—Dec. 30, 1799

Musician—orchestra leader to conduct without using a baton—G. J. Webb—1843

Naval Officers' Training School—naval officers' training school—established—Dec. 10, 1815

Navy—naval militia (state)—Massachusetts Naval Battalion—organized—March 18, 1890

News Agency—established—1811

Newspaper—newspaper printed on woodpulp paper—Boston Morning Journal—Jan. 15, 1863

Newspaper — newspaper publisher—Benjamin Harris—Sept. 25, 1690

Newspaper—newspaper rotogravure sections—published—Sun-Herald—March 29, 1914

Newspaper—newspaper (successful)—News-Letter—April 17, 1704

MASSACHUSETTS—Boston—*Continued*

Telephone—telephone switchboard or exchange—May 17, 1877

Telephone—underground cable long distance telephone conversation—to Washington, D.C.—Feb. 26, 1914

Telephone Operator—woman telephone operator—E. M. Nutt—Sept. 1, 1878

Television—Telecast—Catholic mass televised from a studio—WBZ-TV—June 10, 1953

Television—Telecast—color network telecast in compatible color—June 7, 1953

Television—Telecast—stockholders' meetings televised coast-to-coast simultaneously—Oct. 29, 1959

Television — Telecast — stratovision World Series telecast—Oct. 11, 1948

Tennis — court tennis — introduced — Hollis Hunnewell—1876

Theater — television theater — licensed — opened—July 13, 1938

Theater—theater destroyed by fire—Federal Street Theater—Feb. 2, 1798

Theater—theater lighted by electricity—Bijou Theater—Dec. 11, 1882

Theological School—theological school to admit women—Boston University School of Theology—formed—March 30, 1871

Theological School—theological school to present regular courses by scholars representing different denominations—Boston Theological Seminary—opened—Sept. 1867

Tract Society—tract society—formed—Sept. 1, 1803

Unitarian Minister — Unitarian minister — James Freeman—ordained—Nov. 18, 1787

Unitarian Prayer Book—*A Liturgy*—published —1785

Unitarian Society—national organization of the Unitarian Churches of the United States and Canada—American Unitarian Association—organized—May 25, 1825

Vaudeville—originated—1883

Vending Machine—vending machine (coin operated) to dispense postage stamps—manufactured—1892

Veterinary School—veterinary college—Boston Veterinary Institute—incorporated—April 28, 1855

Voting Machine—electric vote recorder—patented—T. A. Edison—June 1, 1869

Water—municipal water supply system—built—1652

Water Conduit—drinking water conduit—built—1848

Wool—worsted mill—established—John Cornish—1695

Young Men's Christian Association—Young Men's Christian Association—organized—Dec. 29, 1851

Young Women's Christian Association—organized—1866

Bradford

Missionary Society—foreign missionary society—organized—June 29, 1810

Brant Rock

Radio Broadcast—radio program broadcast —Dec. 24, 1906

Bridgewater

Spinning, Carding and Roping Machines—manufactured—1786

Brockton

Refrigerator—household refrigerating machine patent—A. T. Marshall—Aug. 8, 1899

Brookline

Country Club—country club to remain in existence eighty years—organized—Sept. 13, 1882

Curling Rink—indoor curling rink—opened —Dec. 19, 1920

Tennis Match—lawn tennis matches for the Davis Cup—Aug. 8-10, 1900

Buckland

Bridge—bridge of flowers—to Shelburne, Mass.—1929

Byfield

Wool—wool carding machine—installed—1793

Cambridge

Almanac—by William Peirce—1639

Astronomer—astronomer of note in the American colonies—observations made—April 19, 1739

Astronomical Expedition—left—Oct. 9, 1780

Aviation—School — aeronautical engineering course—complete college course—1913

Baseball Catcher's Mask—manufactured—1876

Bible—Bible in an Indian language—translation—1661

Bible Concordance—published—1683

Book—book (full size)—published—July 1640

Book—book (pamphlet) on vellum—published—1854

Book—book privately printed—1665

Bookseller—of importance—Hezekiah Usher —1639

Bronze Statue—full length statue—1847

Business History Chair—established—1923

Camera—non-electronic device for observing in total darkness—announced—Feb. 15, 1956

Chemical Laboratory—chemical laboratory in a collegiate institution—1858

Children's Book—published—1641

Chlorophyll—chlorophyll "a"—synthesized—R. B. Woodward—June 27, 1960

City Planning Instruction—offered—1909

Climatology Professor—appointed—1910

College—college—established—Sept. 8, 1636

College—college entrance requirement, other than Greek, Latin, and arithmetic—1807

College Student—college student to work his way through college—Zechariah Brigden—1657

Congregational Church — Congregational Church council—met—Aug. 30, 1637

Cooperative—college cooperative store—Feb. 28, 1882

Corporation—corporate body—Harvard chartered—May 30, 1650

Court Martial—military court martial—commenced—Jan. 20, 1778

Cryotrons—publicly reported—D. A. Buck—Feb. 6, 1957

Degrees (academic and honorary)—Bachelor of Arts degree—conferred—Harvard College—Sept. 23, 1642

Degrees (academic and honorary)—Doctor of Laws honorary degree—Harvard—July 21, 1773

Degrees (academic and honorary)—Doctor of Sacred Theology degree—Harvard—Increase Mather—1692

Degrees (academic and honorary)—honorary degree granted George Washington—Harvard—April 3, 1776

Divinity Professor—E. Wigglesworth—appointed—Jan. 24, 1722

Entomology Professor—H. A. Hagen—1870

Fire Prevention Legislation—enacted—March 17, 1631

Football Game—rugby contest (international)—with McGill University—May 14, 1874

Football Goal Post—football goal post—used —May 14, 1874

Gas Mask—gas mask with a self-contained breathing apparatus—patented—B. J. Lane —July 2, 1850

Grammar—Indian grammar—John Eliot—published—1666

Gymnastics Instruction—gymnastics instruction at a college—1826

Hebrew Type—used—1640

History—History of New England—published—1669

History Instruction—ancient and modern history chair—1838

Impregnation — impregnation (artificial) — Nov. 1939

King—king born in the United States—Rama IX of Thailand—Dec. 5, 1927

Language Instruction—French instruction—1733

Law Book—compilation of colonial laws—published—1648

Law School—law school of collegiate rank—Harvard College School of Law—opened —1817

Medical Instruction—bacteriology lectures—H. C. Ernst—1885

Medical Instruction—dermatology chair—Dr. J. C. White—1871

Medical Instruction—hygiene lectures—Dr. J. Jackson—1818

Medical Instruction—pathology chair—J. B. S. Jackson—1847

Museum—museum devoted exclusively to paper-making—opened—June 5, 1939

Music Book—hymn book—published—1640

Music Instruction—college music chair—established—Aug. 30, 1875

Naval Officer—Negro commissioned officer in the Naval Reserve—B. W. Robinson—commissioned—June 18, 1942

Newspaper — newspaper — Samuel Green — 1689

Nobel Prize—Nobel prize in chemistry—T. W. Richards—1914

Orchestra — college orchestra — founded — March 6, 1808

Photograph—photograph of a star (other than the sun)—July 17, 1850

Photograph — photograph (taken in the United States) on which a meteor was found—Aug. 10, 1889

Piano Player—piano player—patented—John McTammany, Jr.—June 14, 1881

Planetarium — planetarium or orrery — imported—1732

Play (drama) — Greek play — produced—Oedipus Tyrannus—May 1881

Play (drama)—play of note written by an American and acted in America—Gustavus Vasa—presented—1690

Political Economy Course—political economy chair—C. F. Dunbar—1871

Primer—primer in an American Indian dialect—Indian Primer—published—1669

Printing—document printed in America—"Oath of a Free Man"—March 1639

Printing Instruction—printing lecture course in a college—Feb. 1911

Printing Press—printing press—operated—March 1639

Quinine—synthetic quinine—produced—April 10, 1944

Spelling Book—printed—Stephen Day—1643

Stadium—cement stadium—completed—1904

Telephone—telephone conversation over out-of-door wires—Oct. 9, 1876

Telescope—telescope patent—Alvan Clark—Nov. 11, 1851

Theological School—theological school (non-sectarian)—organized—1816

Thesis Directory—published—Stephen Day —1642

Traffic Regulation Course—graduate course in traffic engineering and administration—Aug. 16, 1937

Vitamin—synthetic vitamin K—made—Dr. L. F. Fieser—Aug. 1, 1939

Windmill—erected—1632

Cambridgeport

Lens—achromatic lenses—made—1844

Camp Devens

Horse Race—three-hundred-mile endurance run—from Burlington, Vt.—Oct. 15, 1919

MASSACHUSETTS—*Continued*

Cape Ann

See Gloucester

Cape Cod

Radio Broadcast—transatlantic broadcast (not experimental)—to England—Jan. 19, 1903

Cheshire

Cheese Factory—cheese factory cooperative —1801

Glass—plate glass—manufactured—c. 1853

Chicopee

Match — friction matches — manufactured — 1834

Clinton

Gingham Factory—opened—E. B. Bigelow —1846

Paper Bag Manufacturing Machine—paper bag manufacturing machine—patented— William Goodale—July 12, 1859

Colrain

Flag—American flag over a schoolhouse— May 1812

Concord

Army School—army training school—to teach security troops—formed—June 13, 1942

Pencil Factory—established—William Monroe—June 1812

Pile Driver—pile driver—patented—March 10, 1791

Dartmouth

Discovery—discovery of New England by an Englishman—Bartholomew Gosnold— landed—May 15, 1602

Dedham

Canal—canal for creating water power—ordered constructed—March 25, 1639

Dennis

Cranberry Cultivation—attempted—1820

Dorchester

"Artics"—patented—T. C. Wales—Feb. 2, 1858

Bridge—bridge—erected—to Milton—1634

Chocolate Mill—erected—1765

Music—singing contest—1790

Public School—public school supported by direct taxation—authorized—May 20, 1639

School Committee—elected—1645

Dover

Building—house completely sunheated—occupied—Dec. 24, 1948

East Watertown

Rubber—synthetic rubber—manufactured— L. P. Kyrides and R. B. Earle—1913

Easthampton

Button—cloth-covered buttons—Mrs. Samuel Williston—1826

Fairhaven

Immigration—Japanese to enter the United States—Nakahama Manjiro—1841

Ship—ship to circumnavigate the world with but one in the crew—trip completed— July 3, 1898

Fitchburg

Factory—windowless factory—erected—1930

Florence

Kindergarten—free kindergarten—opened— Jan. 3, 1876

Franklin

Coffee Percolator Patent—Dec. 26, 1865

Gloucester

Aviation—airplane tank discharger—patented—J. J. Hammond—April 28, 1936

Carillon (modern)—installed—July 2, 1922

Ship—schooner built in America—launched —1714

Universalist Church of America (Independent Christian Church, Universalist)— church dedicated—Dec. 25, 1780

Granville

Toothpick Manufacturing Machine Patent— Feb. 20, 1872

Great Barrington

Electric Power Plant—alternating current power plant—commercially operated— March 20, 1886

Greenfield

Architectural Book distinctly American— printed—1797

Cutlery Factory—of importance—c.1833

File Manufacturing Machine—invented—M. B. Belknap—1812

Manual Training—manual training institute —opened—1829

Groton

Architectural School—landscape architecture course for women—certificates awarded—June 10, 1903

Hamilton

Golf Tournament—professional open championship—June 14, 1901

Haverhill

Woman—heroine—publicly rewarded—Hannah Duston—1697

Holyoke

Telephone—toll line commercial telephone service—instituted—April 2, 1879

Volley Ball—developed—W. G. Morgan—1895

Hopkinton

Marathon Race (annual)—to Boston—April 19, 1897

Ship—roll-on roll-off carrier—in service—to Nantucket—Sept. 1, 1955

Shoe Peg—invented—Joseph Walker—1818

Ipswich

Botanic Scientific Expedition—started—July 19, 1784

Lancaster

Genealogy—genealogical collective work—published—1829

Manual Training—industrial school for girls—incorporated—Aug. 27, 1856

Lawrence

Mohair — commercially manufactured — Arlington Mills—1872

Water Purification—municipal filtration system—completed—Sept. 1893

Leicester

Geology Book—geology textbook—published—1818

Leominster

Baby Carriage Factory—F. W. & F. A. Whitney—1858

Lexington

Normal School—normal school (state)—opened—July 3, 1839

Revolutionary War—armed conflict in the Revolutionary War—April 19, 1775

Telephone—common battery (non-multiple) switchboard—operated—Jan. 9, 1894

Little Brewster Island

Lighthouse—lighthouse—built—1716

Lowell

Belts of Leather—for transmitting power—1828

Carpet Loom—carpet power loom—used—Lowell Manufacturing Co.

Carpet Loom—carpet power loom to weave ingrain carpets—1841

Cash Carrier System—installed—Feb. 1879

Ordnance—machine gun—patented—C. E. Barnes—July 8, 1856

Rubber—rubber heel—manufactured—patent—Jan. 24, 1899

Soda Fountain—ornamented soda fountain—manufactured—1858

Sprinkler—sprinkler—installation—1852

Turbine—turbine successfully operated by water power—1844

Woman—woman telegrapher—S. G. Bagley—Feb. 21, 1846

Lynn

Baseball Catcher's Mask—used—April 12, 1877

Blackout—blackout lighting demonstration—May 14, 1941

Brass and Iron Foundry—Joseph Jencks—1645

Bridge—pontoon bridge—1804

Fire Engine—constructed—Joseph Jencks—1654

Iron—exportation of iron—1650

Labor Union—women's labor organization (national)—convention—July 28, 1869

Money—dies for coins in America—made—Joseph Jencks—1652

Welding by the electric process—patented—Elihu Thomson—Aug. 10, 1886

Malden

Clock—clock to operate by atomic power—Atomicron manufactured

Moving Picture Projector—moving picture projector patent—O.B. Brown—Aug. 10, 1869

Marblehead

Ship—warship regularly commissioned—"Hannah"—Sept. 2, 1775

Mare Mount

Deportation—Thomas Morton—June 9, 1628

Martha's Vineyard

Indians—Indian preacher—of Christianity—ordained—Aug. 22, 1670

Medfield

Brushes — manufactured — Artemas Woodward—1808

Medford

Fishery (commercial)—established—1629

MASSACHUSETTS—*Continued*

Meeting House Pond

World War I—shots to land on American soil—July 21, 1918

Melrose

Patent Examiner—woman patent examiner—A. R. G. Nichols—served—July 1, 1873

Millbury

Lyceum—organized—Oct. 1826

Millville

Factory—factories operated by the United States Government—project commenced—June 4, 1934

Milton

Bridge—bridge erected—to Dorchester—1634
Church—children's church—dedicated—Nov. 14, 1937
Cracker—hard water crackers—manufactured—1801
Iron—iron slitting mill—established—1710

Minot's Ledge

Lighthouse—iron pile lighthouse—completed—Jan. 1, 1850

Mount Greylock

Snow—artificial snow—produced—Nov. 13, 1946

Nantucket

Lifeboat—lifeboat—built—1807
Nautical School—nautical school—established—May 29, 1827
Prison—prison—constructed—1676
Ship—roll-on roll-off carrier—in service—to Hyannis, Mass.—Sept. 1, 1955
Whale—sperm whale—captured—1711
Whaling — whaling expedition — started — c.1715

Natick

Indian Church—Indian church—in New England—established—1600

New Bedford

Coast Guard (U.S.)—Coast Guard officers' training school—established—July 31, 1876
Helicopter—helicopter to deliver material across a picket line—March 9, 1947

Newburyport

Algebra Book—algebra book by a native American—published—1788

Astronomer—astronomer to acquire fame after the Revolution—Nathaniel Bowditch—1802
Coast Survey Book—published—March 1796
Cracker Bakery—Theodore Pearson—1792
Library—library newspaper room—dedicated—April 28, 1882
Ship — revenue cutter — "Massachusetts"—keel laid—1791
Wool—wool carding machine—built—1793

Newport

Pushball—invented—M. G. Crane—1894

Newton

Time Recorder—autograph time recorder—B. F. Merritt—Dec. 20, 1887

Newtowne

See Cambridge

North Beverly

Animals—reindeer—born—May 31, 1929

Northampton

Basketball—basketball played at a women's college—Smith College—1892
College—women's volunteer college unit to serve overseas—Smith College Relief Unit—1917
Deaf—School—oral school for the deaf (still existing)—Clarke School for the Deaf—founded—1867
Degrees (academic and honorary)—Doctor of Philosophy degree awarded to a woman by a women's college—K. E. Morris—June 21, 1882
Gymnasium—gymnasium to offer systematic instruction—Round Hill School—opened—Oct. 1, 1823
Pencil — indelible pencil — patented — E. P. Clark—July 10, 1866
Sugar—sugar beets—factory—D. L. Child—erected—1838
Theater — municipal theater — Academy of Music—Feb. 9, 1893

Northfield

Biblical Students Summer Conference—organized—July 7, 1886
Youth Hostel—opened—Dec. 27, 1934

Orleans

World War I—shots to land on American soil—fired at tugs near Nauset Bluffs—July 21, 1918

Paxton

Radio License—frequency modulation (FM) construction permit—WIXOJ—Aug. 18, 1937

Pecoit

Ordnance—gunpowder mill—operated—1639

Penikese Island

Science School—natural science summer school—opened—1873

Pittsfield

Animals—sheep (Merino sheep) exhibition—1807
Baseball Game — intercollegiate baseball game—Amherst vs. Williams—July 1, 1859
Broadcloth—produced—1793
Fair—agricultural fair—Oct. 1, 1810
Lightning (artificial)—demonstrated—June 10, 1932
Lightning Observatory — erected — General Electric Company—1935

Plymouth

Chimes—chimes and bells manufactured—Benjamin Hanks
Congregational Church — Congregational Church—founded—1620
Congressman (U.S.)—congressman who had been a President of the U.S.—served—March 4, 1831
Duel—duel—recorded—June 18, 1621
Earthquake—earthquake description—June 1, 1638
Execution—execution in America—John Billington—hanged—Sept. 30, 1630
Furs—exported—Robert Cushman—Dec. 13, 1621
Governor—native-born governor of New England—Josiah Winslow—elected—1673
Leather—leather tanning—first tanner—Experience Miller—1623
Medical Book—hydrophobia book—*Observations on Hydrophobia*—published—1812
Pension—pension act—1636
Physician—doctor in New England—Samuel Fuller—arrived—Dec. 21, 1620
Sermon Printed (American)—delivered—Dec. 9, 1621
Treaty—colonial treaty with the Indians—April 1, 1621

Quincy

Granite—quarried—1820
Radar—off-shore radar warning station—built—1955
Railroad — railroad — for freight transportation to celebrate its centenary—Granite Railway Co.—road completed—Oct. 7, 1826
Railroad Accident—railroad accident—July 25, 1832
School—school to operate on the one-class-to-a-room basis—established—1846
Ship—air-conditioned ship—"Mariposa"—keel laid—May 17, 1930

Ship — atomic-powered cruiser — "Long Beach"—launched—July 14, 1959
Ship—schooner (seven masted, steel)—"Thomas W. Lawson"—launched—July 10, 1902
Ship—warship named for a Negro—"Harmon"—launched—July 25, 1943
Typesetting Machine—photo-engraving high-speed process for making half-tones—in operation—Feb. 26, 1954

Readville

Horse—horse to pace better than 2:00—Star Pointer—Aug. 28, 1897
Horse—horse to trot a mile in less than two minutes—Lou Dillon—Aug. 24, 1903

Rowley

Bridge—toll bridge—erected—1654
Cloth—cloth mill—John Pearson—1638
Wool—fulling mill—established—1643

Roxbury

Christmas Cards — manufactured — Louis Prang—1874
Clock—watch (eight day)—manufactured—A. L. Dennison—1850
Kindergarten—kindergarten for the blind—opened—May 2, 1887
Railroad — streamlined railroad train — patented—S. R. Calthorp—Aug. 8, 1865
Rubber—rubber company—Roxbury India Rubber Co.—formed—1832
School—endowed school—Free Schoole in Roxburie—established—1645

Rutland

Hospital—tuberculosis sanatorium (state)—completed—Sept. 23, 1898

Salem

Autopsy—autopsy—Sept. 1639
Brick Kiln—established—1629
Electric Lighting—electric light—household illumination—M. G. Farmer—July 1859
Fire Alarm System (electric)—patented—M. G. Farmer—May 19, 1857
Potter—John Pride—1641
Ship — yacht — "Jefferson" — constructed — 1801
Telephone—news dispatch by telephone—to Boston *Globe*—Feb. 12, 1877
Telephone—telephone patent—A. G. Bell—March 7, 1876

Saugus

Escalator—escalator patent—Nathan Ames—Aug. 9, 1859
Iron—iron works (successful)—constructed—1643

MASSACHUSETTS—*Continued*

Saxonville

Bunting—manufactured—1838

Scituate

Quakers—Quakers' annual meeting—1660

Sheffield

Slavery—slave emancipated—1780

Shelburne

Bridge—bridge of flowers—to Buckland, Mass.—1929

Sherborn

Prison—reformatory (state) conducted for women—opened—Nov. 7, 1877

Shrewsbury

Clock—watchmaker—1809

Somerville

Brass and Copper Seamless Tubes—manufactured—1851

Telephone—telephone for domestic use—installed—April 1877

Wrench—pipe or screw wrench (practical)—D. C. Stillson—Dec. 5, 1876

South Braintree

Paper — manila paper — patented — Dec. 4, 1843

South Hadley

Canal—canal—1793

College—college for women—Mount Holyoke Seminary—opened—Nov. 8, 1837

Gymnastics Instruction—gymnastics instruction at a college for women—1862

Southborough

Cream Separator—centrifugal cream separator—installed—1879

Southwick

Telescope — reflecting telescope — manufactured—Amasa Holcomb—1826

Springfield

Arsenal—established—April 2, 1794

Automobile—automobile regularly made for sale—C. E. Duryea—April 19, 1892

Automobile Catalog—Duryea Motor Wagon Company—1895

Automobile Company—Duryea Motor Wagon Co.—incorporated—Sept. 21, 1895

Basketball — basketball — game invented—James Naismith—1892

Basketball Rules—basketball rule book—*Rules for Basketball*—published—1892

Basketball Rules—basketball rules—published—Jan. 15, 1892

Envelope—envelope with an outlook or window—manufactured—July 1902

Farmers' Institute—farmers' institute sponsored by a state—opened—Dec. 8, 1863

Football Club—intercollegiate football association—formed—Nov. 23, 1876

Kindergarten Manual—*The Paradise of Childhood*—published—1869

Match—match patent—phosphorous friction matches—A. D. Phillips—Oct. 24, 1836

Meat Packer—William Pynchon—1636

Motorcycle—motorcycle (twin-cycle)—manufactured—1905

Motorcycle—motorcycle with built-in gas engine—manufactured—1901

Ordnance—metal cartridge—patented—D. B. Wesson—Aug. 8, 1854

Ordnance — muskets — made — Springfield Armory—1795

Skate (all-metal)—marketed—E. H. Barney—1864

Telephone—toll line commercial telephone service—instituted—April 2, 1879

Wrench—wrench patent—Solyman Merrick Aug. 17, 1835

Sterling

Paper Patterns — manufactured — Ebenezer Butterick—1863

Stockbridge

Village Improvement Society—with a continued existence—formed—Aug. 24, 1853

Taunton

Britannia Ware—manufactured—1824

Silk—silk power loom—patented—William Crompton—Nov. 25, 1837

Uxbridge

Woman—woman whose vote was recorded—1756

Waltham

Coal Oil Factory—to manufacture coal oil from coal tar—1853

Cotton Mill—cotton mill in the world in which the whole process of cotton manufacturing from spinning to weaving was carried on by power—incorporated—Feb. 23, 1813

Ward

See **Auburn**

Watertown

See Cambridge

Waverly

Baseball Catcher's Mask—patented—F. W. Thayer—Feb. 12, 1878

Wellesley

Spectrophotometer—patented—A. C. Hardy Jan. 8, 1935

West Boylston

Carpet Loom—carpet power loom—patented —E. B. Bigelow—April 20, 1837

West Bridgewater

Shovel—shovel (steel)—manufactured—John Ames—1774

West Lynn

Vectolite—manufactured—Feb. 27, 1935

West Newbury

Comb Factory—1759

Westborough

Prison—reformatory for boys (state)—authorized—April 9, 1847

Westfield

Whips—manufactured commercially—1801

Westford

Television—Telecast — transcontinental telecast by means of an orbiting satellite—received—April 24, 1962

Westover Air Force Base

Helicopter Flight—helicopter transatlantic flight—left for Germany—July 15, 1952

Weymouth

Pen—ball-point pen patent—J. J. Loud—Oct. 30, 1888

Whitman

Insurance—savings bank life insurance—bank to establish department—June 18, 1908

Williamstown

College Alumni Association—college alumni association—formed—Williams College—Sept. 1821

Fraternity (Greek letter)—fraternity house —occupied—1839

Winthrop

Motorcycle—motorcycle (steam-driven)—invented—W. A. Austin—1868

Woods Hole

Ship—ship outfitted for hurricane research—"Crawford"—July 3, 1956

Worcester

Abrasive—manufactured—1934

Bible—Bible in folio size to be illustrated—published—1791

Bible—Greek testament—printed—1800

Bicycle Trip—bicycle trip of 100 miles sponsored by a club—to Boston—Sept. 6, 1882

Billiard Match — intercollegiate billiard match—July 25, 1860

Boat Race—intercollegiate regatta—July 26, 1859

Book—book printed on American paper with American-made plates and bound in America—*Elegiac Sonnets and Other Poems* —1795

Calliope—patented—Oct. 9, 1855

Clipper for Cutting Hair—manufactured— G. H. Coates—1876

Degrees (academic and honorary)—anthropology doctorate—Clark University—March 9, 1892

Dictionary — agricultural dictionary — *The New England Farmer*—published—1790

Dictionary—dictionary published in the United States—published—1788

Dictionary—pocket dictionary—*Royal Standard English Dictionary*—published—1788

Envelope—envelope folding and gumming machine—patented—J. A. Sherman—Feb. 8, 1898

Envelope—envelope folding machine—practical—patented—R. L. Hawes—Jan. 21, 1853

Esperanto Course—Esperanto course carrying college credit—Clark University—Sept. 16, 1908

Geography School — Clark University — opened—1921

Historical Society—historical society (national)—American Antiquarian Society—incorporated—Oct. 24, 1812

Lawyer—Negro lawyer formally admitted to the bar—M. B. Allen—passed examination—May 3, 1845

Paper Twine Machinery—patented—G. L. Brownell—Dec. 17, 1895

Park—park land—purchased by a city—March 17, 1854

Printing History — Isaiah Thomas — published—1810

Psychological Society — psychological society (national organization) — American Psychological Association — organized — July 8, 1892

Rocket—liquid fuel rocket patent—R. H. Goddard—July 14, 1914

Sewage—sewage disposal by chemical precipitation—1890

MASSACHUSETTS—Worcester—*Cont.*

Silk—silk loom—of importance—Gem Silk Loom—built—1887

Spring Winding Machine—built—1892

War—rebellion against the federal government—Daniel Shays—1786

Wire—piano wire—produced—1850

Wire Gauge—developed—1849

Woman Suffrage—convention (national) of women advocating woman suffrage—Oct. 23-24, 1850

MICHIGAN

Capital Punishment—death penalty was first abolished—March 1, 1847

Cooperative—cooperative state law—effective —March 20, 1865

Fireworks Legislation—fireworks legislation (state)—enacted—March 29, 1929

Woman Suffrage—woman suffrage amendment approved by Congress—ratified— June 10, 1919

Adrian

Degrees (academic and honorary)—Bachelor of Music degree—awarded M. P. Lowrie— Dec. 23, 1873

Seeding Machine (practical) — patented — Joseph Gibbons—Aug. 25, 1840

Wire—woven wire fence industry—factory— J. W. Page—1883

Ann Arbor

Bibliography Course—University of Michigan—1878

College—college entrance "certified school plan"—introduced—Sept. 1871

College—honors course—University of Michigan—Sept. 1882

College—state university supported by a direct property tax—approved—March 15, 1867

College Alumni Association—college alumni association secretary (full time paid position)—established—June 30, 1897

Forestry School—forestry course in a university—established—1881

History Instruction—history seminar—University of Michigan—1869

Medical Clinic—heredity clinic—opened— Nov. 12, 1941

Medical Instruction—bacteriology courses in a college—Jan. 1889

Microfilm—book series microfilmed—microfilmed—1935

Microfilm—microfilm machine to project enlarged images on ceilings—1945

Microfilm—microfilms of U.S. Government publications or documents—April 1952

Pedagogy Chair—pedagogy chair (permanent)—established—1879

Physician—Chinese woman to receive a doctor of medicine degree—Mary Stone—June 22, 1896

Public Speaking Department—established— 1892

Battle Creek

Microfilm—microfilm machine to project enlarged images on ceilings—installed— March 21, 1946

Bay City

Crane—wrecking crane—built—1883

Benton Harbor

House of David—established— May 1, 1903

Dearborn

Automobile—plastic automobile—manufactured—Aug. 1941

Detroit

Automobile—automobile with left hand steering—manufactured—1907

Automobile—free piston automobile—announced—April 15, 1956

Automobile—gas turbine automobile operated on city streets—April 19, 1955

Automobile—production of more than one million passenger cars of one make in one year—Chevrolet—1949

Automobile—sedan type automobile

Automobile—transparent-top automobile— "Sun Valley"—manufactured—Dec. 7, 1953

Automobile Bus—gas turbine bus—announced—June 10, 1954

Automobile Electric Self-Starter—automobile electric self-starter applied commercially—May 1911

Aviation—airplane diesel engine—1928

Aviation—Airship—dirigible made completely of metal—tested—Aug. 19, 1929

Aviation—Aviator—woman aviator to pilot an air-mail transport—from Washington, D.C.—landed—Dec. 31, 1934

Billiard Match—billiard match to attain international prominence—April 12, 1859

Catholic Magazine—Catholic magazine in English—issued Aug. 31, 1809

Corporation—corporation to earn more than $1 billion in one year—General Motors— 1955

Electric Transmission—substation with a rotary converter completely unattended— April 1914

Hammer (pneumatic)—patented—C. B. King —Jan. 30, 1894

Medical Book—hydrotherapy book—published—1892

Newspaper—newspaper association—American Newspaper Publishers Association— organized—1886

Newspaper—newspaper printed on a train —*Weekly Herald*—Feb. 3, 1862

Orchestra—radio orchestra—May 28, 1922

Piano Player—pneumatic piano player—patented—E. S. Votey—May 22, 1900

Pinball Game—pinball game machine (toy) —manufactured—1910

Police—policewoman to be—appointed—1893

Public School—public school classes for epileptic children—organized—Jan. 1935

Radio Broadcast—election returns broadcast—Aug. 31, 1920

Radio Broadcast—news program—Aug. 31, 1920

Radio Broadcast—prize fight broadcast—Sept. 6, 1920

Radio Station—commercial radio station—daily service—WWJ—Aug. 20, 1920

Railroad Car—refrigerator car patent—awarded—J. B. Sutherland—Nov. 26, 1867

Sponge—oxidized cellulose (sponge) for medical and surgical use—marketed—June 5, 1946

Surgical Operation—mitral valve exposure (prolonged) in a human patient and corrective surgery—July 3, 1952

Telephone—air-to-ground public telephone service—Chicago-Detroit area—Sept. 15, 1957

Trailer Church—St. Paul's Wayside Cathedral—in operation—Oct. 1, 1937

Tunnel—vehicular tunnel to a foreign country—opened—Nov. 3, 1930

Visiting Celebrities—Prince of Wales—Albert Edward—arrived—Sept. 20, 1860

Wedding—transatlantic telephone wedding—Dec. 2, 1933

Woman—woman labor delegate to a national convention—of the AFL—Mary Burke Dec. 8, 1890

East Lansing

Farriers' Course in a College—Michigan State College—1930

Flint

Automobile — plastic laminated fiberglas body sports car—manufactured—June 30, 1953

Grand Rapids

Baseball Game—baseball game at night by a regular league team—July 8, 1909

Carpet Sweeper—practical—M. R. Bissell—1876

Electric Power Plant—hydroelectric power plant (commercial) — organized — March 22, 1880

Game Warden (salaried game and fish warden)—W. A. Smith—1887

Water—community to fluoridate its municipal water—Jan. 25, 1945

Grosse Ile

Aviation—Airship—dirigible made completely of metal—tested—Aug. 19, 1929

Holland

Chloromycetin—chloromycetin laboratory—March 13, 1952

Ishpeming

Ski Club—ski club association—meeting—Jan. 16, 1891

Kalamazoo

Drill—dental drill (electric)—patented—G. F. Green—Jan. 26, 1875

Lansing

Agricultural School — agricultural college (state) to open—Agricultural College of Michigan—May 13, 1857

Mendon

Locomotive Headlight—electric locomotive headlight—patented—May 3, 1881

Mount Clemens

Aviation—Flights—airplane to exceed the speed of 200 miles an hour—L. J. Maitland—Oct. 14, 1922

Aviation—Flights (transatlantic)—jet transatlantic flight west to east—to Odiham, England—July 20, 1948

Mount Vernon

Typewriter—typewriter — patented — W. A. Burt—July 23, 1829

Olivet

College—college to dispense with the system of credits, hours, points, grades, etc.—Olivet College—Oct. 1, 1934

Pontiac

Aviation—Airport—airport to receive an AI-A rating—Feb. 11, 1930

Curling Club—organized—1831-32

Moving Picture—moving picture of the sun—June 19, 1934

Port Huron

Newspaper—newspaper printed on a train—*Weekly Herald*—Feb. 3, 1862

Tunnel—subaqueous railroad tunnel to a foreign country—opened—Sept. 19, 1891

Royal Oak

National Union for Social Justice—formed—Nov. 1934

Wayne County

Road—concrete rural road—laid—1909

Traffic Lines—painted—1911

Wyandotte

Steel—Bessemer steel converter—erected—1864

Steel Analysis Laboratory — established — W. F. Durfee—1862

MINNESOTA

Election Law—primary election law—enacted—April 20, 1899

Optometry Legislation — state — enacted — April 13, 1901

Austin

Strike—modern sit-down strike—G. A. Hormel & Co.—Nov. 13, 1933

Crosby

Balloon—balloon flight to exceed an altitude of 100,000 feet—D. G. Simons—Aug. 19, 1957

Duluth

Bridge—aerial ferry—opened—April 9, 1905

Canal—Saint Lawrence Seaway—opened—April 25, 1959

Ship—whaleback steamer to cross the Atlantic—sailed—June 11, 1891

Faribault

Cathedral—Episcopal cathedral—Cathedral of Our Merciful Saviour—completed—1869

Minneapolis

Automobile—armored commercial car completely protected — construction commenced—March 1919

Book Index—monthly cumulative index of books—published—Feb. 1898

Electric Toaster—electric toaster—household-type—marketed—June 1926

Ink—ink paste—patented—F. B. Cooney—Jan. 1, 1924

Library—children's department in a library —Minneapolis Public Library

Medical Society—immunology society—organized—June 19, 1913

Nursing School—university school of nursing—authorized—Oct. 1, 1908

Railroad Car—chapel car—"Evangel"—services

Railroad Car—Pullman train completely equipped with roller bearings—May 21, 1927

Surgical Operation—heart operation in which the deep freezing technique was employed—Sept. 2, 1952

Television—Telecast—stockholders' meetings televised coast-to-coast simultaneously—Oct. 29, 1959

War Veterans' Society—American Legion—first national convention—Nov. 10, 1919

Woman—woman state budget commissioner —J. W. Wittich—served—March 16, 1931

Minnesota Point

Bridge—aerial ferry—opened—April 9, 1905

New Ulm

Religious Hillside Shrine—"The Way of the Cross"—built—1884

Northfield

Biography Course—biography department—Carleton College—1919

Ortonville

Woman—woman clerk of a state supreme court—G. F. Kaercher—elected—Nov. 7, 1922

Red Wing

Ski Club—ski club (local) that was active —Aurora Ski Club—organized—Jan. 19, 1886

St. Paul

Agricultural School—vocational agricultural school—opened—Oct. 18, 1888

Army—Reserve Officers Training Corps Units—authorized—Oct. 21, 1916

Automobile—armored commercial car completely protected—in service—Feb. 1, 1920

Computer—electronic computer to employ Thin-Film Memory—announced—Dec. 9, 1960

Forestry Society—state forestry association —organized—Jan. 12, 1876

Hospital—crippled children's hospital (state) —authorized—April 23, 1897

Newspaper — radio facsimile newspaper — KSTP—Dec. 17, 1937

Railroad Car—chapel car—"Evangel"—services

Railroad Car — Pullman train completely equipped with roller bearings—May 21, 1927

Sound-Absorbing Material—rigid insulating board—patented—Sept. 14, 1915

Silver Bay

Taconite—taconite — large-scale commercial project

MISSISSIPPI

Senator (U.S.)—Negro senator—H. R. Revels—elected—Jan. 20, 1870

State—state to repudiate a debt—1842

Bay St. Louis

Catholic Bishop—Catholic bishop (Negro) consecrated in the U.S.—J. O. Bowers—Apr. 22, 1953

Catholic Seminarians (Negro) to be ordained to the priesthood by a Negro bishop—June 29, 1953

Catholic Seminary—for Negro priests—Sept. 16, 1923

Clarksdale

Cotton—cotton crop commercially produced entirely by machinery—1944

Columbus

College—state college for women—established—March 12, 1884

Holiday—Decoration day—celebrated—May 30, 1868

Jackson

Public Health—pellagra experiment—of note —Joseph Goldberger—test—Feb. 4, 1915

Meridian

Jewish Congregation—Jewish congregation to call a woman to exercise a rabbi's function—Jan. 26, 1951

Moss Point

Bank—national bank branch legally operated —chartered—March 14, 1907

Natchez

Ship—battleship to visit an inland city— "Mississippi"—May 20, 1909

Rodney

College—Negro land grant college—established—1871

Tupelo

Electrical Contract—with federal government—signed—Nov. 11, 1933

Washington

College—women's college chartered—Elizabeth Female Academy—Feb. 17, 1819

MISSOURI

Dentistry—gold crown tooth—process described—May 1869

Senator (U.S.)—senator to serve three states —James Shields

State—state admitted to the Union west of the Mississippi River—Aug. 10, 1821

Tax—bachelor tax—effective—Jan. 1, 1821

Arcadia

Railroad Excursion—railroad excursion (mystery)—from St. Louis—May 21, 1932

Columbia

Journalism Course—history of journalism course—University of Missouri—1879

Journalism Course—journalism school—University of Missouri—opened—Sept. 14, 1908

Crystal City

Sash—wrought iron window sash installation —Pittsburgh Plate Glass Co.—1929

De Soto

Newspaper—newspaper published by soldiers in the field—*United States American Volunteer*—May 21, 1861

Glasgow

Bridge—railway all-steel bridge—in service —Nov. 1, 1879

Hannibal

Monument—statue to commemorate literary characters—erected—May 27, 1926

Postal Service—railroad post office—mail car built—1862

Jefferson Barracks

Army—cavalry unit—Regiment of Dragoons —organized—August 1833

Aviation—Parachute—parachute jump from an airplane—March 1, 1912

Kansas City

Art Course—industrial camouflage course— Kansas City Art Institute—Oct. 15, 1940

Freemasons—Order of De Molay—founded —1919

Kidnapping—death penalty for kidnapping —imposed—July 27, 1933

Newspaper—newspaper rotogravure sections —published—*Star*—March 29, 1914

Railroad—streamlined all-steel diesel motor train—Nov. 11, 1934

Railroad Car—train with fluorescent lights —from St. Louis, Mo.—April 30, 1939

War Veterans' Society—World War II veterans' society officially recognized by Congress—amalgamation of 11 groups—Dec. 12, 1944

Kirksville

Medical Periodical—osteopathy magazine— *Journal of Osteopathy*—published—May 1894

Medical School — osteopathy school — chartered—May 10, 1892

Physician—osteopath (woman)—J. H. Bolles —graduated—March 1, 1894

Louisiana

Patent—fruit tree patent—J. E. Markham— Feb. 16, 1932

Macon

Physician—osteopathic physician—A. T. Still—treatment—June 22, 1874

Newton County

Monument—national monument dedicated to a Negro—G. W. Carver—authorized— July 14, 1943

Philadelphia

College—Masonic college—Masonic College of Missouri—opened—May 12, 1844

MISSOURI—*Continued*

St. Joseph

Postal Service—Pony Express mail—service to Sacramento, Calif.—April 3, 1860

St. Louis

See also Jefferson Barracks, Mo.

Adding Machine—adding machine successfully marketed—patented—W. S. Burroughs—Aug. 21, 1888

Animals—cow flown in an airplane—milk parachuted—Feb. 18, 1930

Army Balloon School—established—April 6, 1917

Aviation—Flights—airplane endurance flight exceeding 400 hours — landed — July 30, 1929

Balloon Race—dirigible balloon race—Oct. 4-9, 1909

Baseball Game—baseball playoff series—Oct. 1, 1946

Baseball Game—no-run nine-inning baseball game—May 11, 1875

Baseball Player—baseball player to win the Most Valuable Player Award three times—Stan Musial

Bibliography Society (national) — Bibliographical Society of America—organized Oct. 18, 1904

Blind—school for the blind to adopt the Braille system—1859

Bohemian American Church—opened—April 20, 1855

Bowling Tournament—bowling tournament for women—March 17, 1917

Bridge—steel arch bridge—opened—July 4, 1874

Chamber of Commerce—Junior Chamber of Commerce—organized—Oct. 13, 1915

Christmas Carols Association (national)—organized—Jan. 20, 1947

Dental Magazine—orthodontia magazine—*International Journal of Orthodontia*—published—Jan. 1915

Dental Society — orthodontists' society — American Society of Orthodontists — founded—June 1900

Electron Tube — announced — meeting of American Association for the Advancement of Science—Jan. 2, 1936

Engine—diesel engine built for commercial service—Sept. 1898

Expedition—expedition across the continent to the Pacific coast—Lewis and Clark expedition started—May 14, 1804

Fingerprinting—international exchange of fingerprints—July 6, 1905

Fingerprinting—police department to adopt the fingerprinting system—Oct. 28, 1904

Glider—glider flight indoors—in "dead air"—Harry Kuchins—March 2, 1930

Helicopter—helicopter with a twin-engine—XHJD-1—tested—March 1946

Helicopter — ram-jet helicopter — tested — May 5, 1947

Ice Cream Cone—ice cream cone—introduced—1904

Incinerator—successful—1897

Insurance—baby sitters' insurance policy—Jan. 26, 1950

Insurance—insurance service offered by a newspaper—*Star*—April 14, 1919

Jai-Alai—pelota game—introduced—1904

Kindergarten—public school kindergarten—authorized—Aug. 26, 1873

Law School—law school (university) to admit women—first woman graduate—June 15, 1871

Medical Periodical—allergy magazine—*Journal of Allergy*—published—Nov. 1929

Milk—evaporated milk—J. B. Meyenberg—patented—Nov. 25, 1884

Newspaper—newspaper rotogravure sections—published—*Post-Dispatch*—March 29, 1914

Newspaper—radio facsimile newspaper (daily)—*Post-Dispatch*—Dec. 7, 1938

Nobel Prize—husband and wife in the United States to receive a joint Nobel Prize award announced—Oct. 23, 1947

Normal School—woman principal of a normal school—A. C. Brackett—Jan. 5, 1863

Olympic Games—Olympic celebration—May 14, 1904

President (U.S.)—President to fly—Theodore Roosevelt—Oct. 11, 1910

Prize Fight—international fight, with bare knuckles—June 15, 1869

Radio Broadcast—police broadcast—WIL—Sept. 4, 1921

Radio Broadcast — weather broadcasts — WEW—April 26, 1921

Railroad—railroad to run west of the Mississippi River—Pacific Railway of Missouri—incorporated—March 12, 1849

Railroad Car—dining car (all-electric)—in service to Chicago, Ill.—March 9, 1949

Railroad Car—freight car (Adapto Car)—in service to Wichita, Kan.—July 24, 1956

Railroad Car—train with fluorescent lights—to Kansas City—April 30, 1939

Railroad Excursion — railroad excursion (mystery)—to Arcadia, Mo.—May 21, 1932

Sash—wrought iron window sash installation—constructed—1929

Sewing Machine—sewing machine to stitch buttonholes — patented — Charles Miller—March 7, 1854

Ship — iron-clad naval vessels — accepted — Jan. 15, 1862

Silverites — first national convention — July 22, 1896

Street Car—light-weight one-man street car—built

Surgical Operation — lung removal — performed—April 5, 1933

Suture—fiberglas sutures—used—mastoid operation—July 19, 1939

Telephone — mobile telephone commercial service—inaugurated—June 17, 1946

Telephone — mobile telephone conversation overseas—July 16, 1946

Telephone—mobile telephone news dispatch—May 15, 1946

Travelers Aid—instituted—1851

Vacuum Cleaner — motor-driven vacuum cleaner—patented—J. S. Thurman—Oct. 3, 1899

Vice President of the United States—Vice President to marry in office—A. W. Barkley

Springfield

Cemetery—federal cemetery in the U.S. to contain graves of both Union and Confederate soldiers—March 3, 1911

City (Lilliputian city)—built—June 6, 1925

Tipton

Postal Service—overland mail service—Butterfield stage lines—to San Francisco—Sept. 15, 1858

Washington

Pipe—corncob pipe commercial manufacture —Henry Tibbe—1869

Westport Landing

Road—overland wagon road across the Rocky Mountains—to Vancouver, Wash.—1842

MONTANA

Attorney General—assistant attorney general (state) who was a woman—E. L. K. Haskell—1892

Congressman (U.S.) — Congresswoman elected—Jeannette Rankin—March 4, 1917

Congressman (U.S.) — Congresswoman to vote twice against the entry of the U.S. into war—Jeannette Rankin

Pension — old age pension laws (state) — March 5, 1923

Butte

Mineral Segregation—by flotation—commercial operation—J. M. Hyde—1911

Superior

Bible—Bibles in hotel rooms—Oct. 1908

NEBRASKA

Forest Service—federal planting of trees—1891

Governor—governor to appoint two United States Senators in one year for interim terms—Robert Crosby—1954

Holiday—Arbor Day—celebration—April 10, 1872

Legislature—unicameral legislature (state) —adopted—Nov. 6, 1934

Beatrice

Homestead—taken—Jan. 1, 1863

Chadron

Horse Race—horse race of a thousand miles —to Chicago—started—June 13, 1893

Grand Island

Medal—Interstate Commerce Commission Medal of Honor—awarded—G. H. Poell—Dec. 5, 1905

Lincoln

Corporation Course—industrial corporation course—University of Nebraska—1888

Railroad—streamlined all-steel diesel motor train—to Kansas City, Mo.—Nov. 11, 1934

North Platte

Wild West Show—prepared and exhibited—July 4, 1883

Omaha

Federal Trade Commission—Federal Trade Commission trade practice conference—Oct. 3, 1919

Log Rolling (Birling) National Championship—Sept. 9, 1898

Railroad—streamlined light-weight high-speed three-car passenger train—operated —March 2, 1934

Vending Machine—vending machine law—enacted—May 10, 1898

NEVADA

Narcotic—narcotic regulation (state)—adopted—March 10, 1933

Pension—old age pension laws (state)—March 5, 1923

Boulder City

Electric Power Plant—hydroelectric power plant to produce a million kilowatts—June 1943

Carson City

Execution—lethal gas execution—Gee Jon—Feb. 8, 1924

Prize Fight—open-air arena especially built for a prize fight

Elko

Air Mail Service—air mail contractor (domestic)—plane operation to Pasco, Wash. —April 6, 1926

Frenchman Flat

Atomic Bomb—atomic bomb underground explosion—detonated—Nov. 29, 1951

Ordnance — atomic cannon — electronically fired—May 25, 1953

Henderson

Titanium—titanium plant fully self-contained and fully integrated—opened—June 1, 1951

NEVADA—*Continued*

Lake Mead

Ship—speed-boat to exceed 200 miles an hour —"Bluebird"—Nov. 16, 1955

Las Vegas

Locomotive—gas turbine propane-fueled locomotive—in service—June 8, 1953

News Nob

Television—Telecast—atomic explosion telecast on a network—April 22, 1952

Reno

Prize Fight—Negro heavyweight champion of the world—Jack Johnson—July 4, 1910

Virginia City

Silver Mill—to treat silver ore successfully —opened—Aug. 11, 1860

Yucca Flat

Rocket—rocket with an atomic warhead— fired—July 19, 1957

NEW HAMPSHIRE

Attorney of the United States — Samuel Sherburne, Jr.—appointed—Sept. 26, 1789
Indians — Indian scalping—by white men— Feb. 20, 1725
Insurance—insurance board (state)—established—July 1, 1851
Labor Law—ten-hour-day law—enacted— July 9, 1847
Library Law enacted by a state—July 7, 1849
Naval Officer—naval officer commissioned— Hopley Yeaton—March 21, 1791
Senator (U.S.)—senator elected on an anti-slavery ticket—J. P. Hale—June 9, 1846
Washing Machine—washing machine patent —Nathaniel Briggs—March 28, 1797

Berlin

Ski Club—ski club (local)—Nansen Ski Club—formed—Jan. 15, 1882

Concord

Clock—alarm clock—made—Levi Hutchins —1787
Forest Fire—forest fire drenched by man-made rain—Oct. 29, 1947
Melodeon Patent—C. Austin—June 19, 1849

Derry

Potato—potato cultivation—1719

Dover

Strike—strike of women operatives—1828

Dublin

Library—free public library—1822

Goodrich Falls

Skimobile—invented—George Morton—1937

Grafton

Mica—mica—obtained—Ruggles mine—1803

Lake Winnepesaukee

Animals—cattle (Guernsey cattle)—imported —1831
Boat Race—intercollegiate boat race—Aug. 3, 1852

Manchester

Credit Union Association—founded—Dec. 16, 1908

Meredith

Leg (artificial) patent—B. F. Palmer—Nov. 4, 1846

Mount Washington

Railroad—cog railroad—demonstrated—Aug. 29, 1866

Nashua

Tool Factory—machinists' tools—1838

New Castle

Revolutionary War—incident in the Revolutionary War—Dec. 13, 1774

Newington

Forest—community forest—1710

North Conway

Skimobile—in operation—Dec. 27, 1938

Orford

Engine—internal combustion engine—Samuel Morey—patented—April 1, 1826

Peterborough

Library—free public library (town supported)—April 9, 1833

Portsmouth

Flag—American flag displayed on a man-of-war—July 4, 1777
Navy—navy yard—purchased—June 12, 1800

Religious Publication — religious review — *Herald of Gospel Liberty*—published—Sept. 1, 1808

Submarine—leaping submarine—"Pickerel" —commissioned—April 4, 1949

Troy

Blanket — horseblankets — manufactured — Thomas Goodall—1852

Walpole

Herbal Book—*The American Herbal*—published—1801

Novel—American novel republished in England—originally published—1797

Washington Center

Seventh Day Adventist Church—1844

NEW JERSEY

Animal Breeding Society—artificial animal breeding cooperative society—organized— May 16, 1938

Crime Prevention and Detection—crime prevention commission for interstate cooperation—March 12, 1935

Holding Company authorization (state)— enacted—April 4, 1888

Labor Law—labor discrimination law (state)—enacted—May 15, 1894

Labor Union — labor union legalization (state)—enacted—Feb. 14, 1883

Medical Legislation—law to license the practice of medicine—enacted—Sept. 26, 1772

Moving Picture—moving picture with a plot *The Great Train Robbery*—filmed—1903

Piano—piano patent—J. S. McLean—May 27, 1796

Railroad Charter—granted—Feb. 6, 1815

Reaper—reaper—patent—May 17, 1803

Road—law regarding state aid for roads— enacted—April 14, 1891

Toll Collector (automatic)—Garden State Parkway—Nov. 19, 1954

Woman Suffrage—colony to grant suffrage to women—constitution adopted—July 2, 1776

Arlington

Nylon—nylon bristle filament production for toothbrushes—Feb. 24, 1938

Athenia

Animals—sheep (karakul fur sheep)—quarantined—1908

Atlantic City

Automobile Transcontinental Trip—transcontinental automobile group tour—commenced—June 26, 1911

Aviation—Flights—airplane to exceed a mile in altitude—W. R. Brookins—July 9, 1910

Aviation—Flights (transatlantic)—transatlantic dirigible flight—attempted—Oct. 15, 1910

Aviation—Flights (transcontinental)—transcontinental flight made by Negroes in their own plane—left—July 17, 1933

Boardwalk—completed—June 26, 1870

Glider—rocket glider flight—successful— June 4, 1931

Health Society—National Tuberculosis Association—organized—June 6, 1904

Medical Society—woman member of the Association of American Physicians—H. B. Taussig—elected—May 3, 1950

Pier—ocean pier—built—Howard's pier— 1881

Pier—ocean pier of steel—opened—June 18, 1898

Television—Telecast—birth (human) to be televised (closed circuit)—June 14, 1951

Television—Telecast—surgical operation televised on a closed circuit in color—June 6, 1949

Atlantic Highlands

Radio Beacons—installed—fog signals—tests —1916

Bayonne

Radio Broadcast—radio police system (two-way three-way)—construction permit application—Oct. 7, 1932

Belmar

Radar—radar signal to the moon—Jan. 10, 1946

Beverly

Birds — partridge propagation — encouraged 1790

Bloomfield

Brake Patent — railroad brake patent — Ephraim Morris—Sept. 19, 1838

Electric Lighting—electric sterilamp—introduced—March 1938

Bordentown

Locomotive Cowcatcher—used— to Hightstown—1833

Bound Brook

Railroad Signal System—railroad signal system of interlocking signal apparatus operated by compressed air—installed—1883

Burlington

See also West Burlington

Educational Trust Fund—created—1682

Freemasons—mason—to arrive in America— John Skene—1682

NEW JERSEY—Burlington—*Continued*

Plow—plow patent—Charles Newbold—June 26, 1797
Pottery—pottery—Daniel Coxe—1680
Windmill—windmill driven by rotor power—tested—July 1933

Caldwell

Aviation—Parachute—parachute jump from an autogiro—Nov. 15, 1931

Caldwell Township

Mica—synthetic mica—May 17, 1956

Camden

Air Mail Service—autogiro mail delivery regular service—from Philadelphia—July 6, 1939
Ferryboat—ferryboat built exclusively for motor vehicle transportation—1926
Microscope—electron microscope — invented —V. K. Zworykin—1940
Moving Picture Theater—drive-in moving picture theater—opened—June 6, 1933
Pen—steel pens commercially produced—Richard Esterbrook—1858
Phonograph—phonograph with an automatic record-changer—introduced—March 1927
Phonograph—phonograph with an enclosed horn in the cabinet—Aug. 22, 1906
Phonograph Record—phonograph record of a stage performance by the original cast—1904
Radio Broadcast—ship launching broadcast—April 7, 1925
Television Mobile Unit—mobile television unit—manufactured—1937

Camp Kilmer

Helicopter—aerocycle—tested

Carlstadt

Business—"Food-O-Mat"—May 24, 1945

Coytesville

Television—Telecast—standard broadcast station to transmit a television image—WRNY—Aug. 13, 1928

Deepwater

Rubber—synthetic rubber (neoprene)—produced commercially—1931

East Orange

Adhesive and Medicated Plaster—adhesive and medicated plaster with a rubber base —1874

Edgewater

Ferryboat—ferryboat built exclusively for motor vehicle transportation—in service—Nov. 8, 1926

Elizabeth

Flicker — patented — Henry Van Hoevenbergh—May 16, 1882
Television Tube—miniature tube—patented—H. W. Weinhart—Aug. 25, 1925

Elizabethport

Cutlery Shears—manufactured—1825
Sewing Machine—electric sewing machine—manufactured—1889

Englewood

Telephone—dial telephone service coast-to-coast without the aid of operators—Nov. 10, 1951

Fort Lee

Cable—submarine telegraph cable that was practical—Ezra Cornell—1845

Fort Monmouth

Radio Telephone — military portable — "Walkie-Talkie"—constructed—1933

Greenville

Revolver Shooting Tournament (intertional)—June 16, 1900

Hadley Field

Aviation—Flights—airplane night scheduled passenger flight—to Boston—April 1, 1927

High Bridge

Steel — manganese steel — manufactured — 1892
Steel—manganese steel for railroad tracks—manufactured—Aug. 28, 1894

Hightstown

Aviation—Parachute—parachute tower for training parachute jumpers—built—April 1935
Locomotive Cowcatcher—used—to Bordentown—1833

Hoboken

Air (compressed)—for tunnel construction—1879
Cricket Tournament—international cricket tournament—Oct. 3, 1859
Engineering Society—mechanical engineering national society—organization meeting—April 7, 1880
Fastening—hookless fastening for universal use—invented—1906
Ferryboat—double-deck ferryboat with the propeller-type steel hull—to New York City—1891

Ferryboat — steam-propelled ferryboat — to New York City—Oct. 11, 1811

Ferryboat—steel-hull ferryboat—operated to New York City—1881

Locomotive—locomotive to pull a train—built—John Stevens—Oct. 23, 1824

Mechanical Engineering Laboratory for research work—established—1874

Radio Station—sea-going radio broadcasting station—"Courier"—commissioned — Feb. 15, 1952

Ship—steamboat to make an ocean voyage—"Phoenix"—built

Ship—steamboat with a twin-screw propeller —built—1803

Holmdel

Rocket—communications satellite—message received from Goldstone, Calif.

Indian Mills

Indian Reservation — Indian reservation (state)—established—Aug. 29, 1758

Jersey City

Adhesive and Medicated Plaster—adhesive and medicated plaster patent—March 26, 1845

Cornstarch—starch made commercially from Indian corn—Thomas Kingsford—1842

Drydock — drydock — constructed — Robert Fulton—1805

Handball national championship match for amateurs—Jan. 7, 1897

Prize Fight—prize fight to gross a million dollars—Dempsey-Carpentier—July 2, 1921

Radio Broadcast—prize fight (heavyweight championship) broadcast—July 2, 1921

Sidewalk (Traveling)—sidewalk (traveling) in a railroad station—May 24, 1954

Tunnel—tunnel under the Hudson River—to New York City—opened—Feb. 25, 1908

Tunnel—twin-tube subaqueous vehicular tunnel—Holland tunnel—opened—Nov. 13, 1927

Water Purification—water supply chemically treated with chlorine compounds—1908

Kearny

Linoleum—linoleum machine (fully automatic)—installed—1911

Lakehurst

Aviation — Airship — dirigible (American-built rigid)—tested—Sept. 4, 1923

Aviation — Airship — dirigible merchandise shipment—arrived—Oct. 15, 1924

Aviation—Flights (transatlantic)—Atlantic Ocean regular commercial airship service —"Hindenburg"—arrived—May 9, 1936

Aviation—Flights (transcontinental)—transcontinental airship voyage—commenced—Oct. 7, 1924

Aviation—Passenger—woman Zeppelin passenger (paying)—Oct. 29, 1928

Aviation—Races—airplane passenger race around the world—start—Sept. 30, 1936

Glider—glider released from a dirigible—Jan. 31, 1930

Lakewood

Hospital — tuberculosis preventorium for children—established—1909

Lebanon

Cash Carrier System—patented—David Brown—July 13, 1875

Lynn

Money—dies for coins in America—Joseph Jencks—1652

Mahwah

Cream Separator—continuous flow centrifugal cream separator—installed—1881

Menlo Park

Electric Lighting — electric incandescent lamp—invented—T. A. Edison—Oct. 21, 1879

Electric Lighting — electric incandescent lamp factory — Edison Lamp Works — opened—Oct. 1, 1880

Mimeograph—patented—T. A. Edison—Aug. 8, 1876

Phonograph—phonograph—patented—T. A. Edison—Feb. 19, 1878

Photograph—photograph taken by incandescent electric light—Dec. 1879

Radio Patent of importance—T. A. Edison—Dec. 29, 1891

Millville

Old Age Colony—dedicated—Oct. 23, 1936

Moorestown

Horse—horse (Percheron horse) importation)—1839

Morristown

Telegraph—telegraphic communication system in which dots and dashes represented letters—invented—Alfred Vail—Sept. 1837

Murray Hill

Transistor—junction transistor — invention announced—July 5, 1951

Transistor—phototransistor—invention announced—March 30, 1950

Transistor — transistor — demonstrated — June 30, 1948

Navesink

Radio Station—naval radio station—established—1903

New Brunswick

Football Game—intercollegiate football contest—Nov. 6, 1869

Microbiology Laboratory—dedicated—June 7, 1954

Patent—plant patent—H. F. Bosenberg—Aug. 18, 1931

Radio Facsimile Transmission—photograph sent by radio across the Atlantic—transmitted to England—July 6, 1924

Telephone—interstate telephone call—to New York City—May 17, 1877

Newark

Aviation—airplane commutation tickets—to Boston—May 1, 1929

Aviation—Flights—all blind cross-country test—from College Park, Md.—March 21, 1933

Aviation—Flights (transcontinental)—transcontinental commercial overnight transport service—inaugurated—Aug. 1, 1934

Aviation—Flights (transcontinental)—transcontinental non-stop flight by a woman—completed—Aug. 25, 1932

Carpeting — carpeting (velvet) — manufactured—1855

Fertilizer (artificial) — developed — J. J. Mapes—1847

Fire Extinguisher using vaporized chemical —manufactured—1905

Iron—iron castings (malleable)—produced—July 4, 1826

Jury—woman grand jury foreman—served—April 6, 1937

Jury School—jury school—opened—Jan. 16, 1937

Leather—patent leather—tanned—Seth Boyden—1819

Library—business library supported by taxes —opened—Oct. 1, 1904

Motor Boat—storage battery motor boat—"Magnet"—built—1888

Photographic Film—celluloid photographic film—patented—H. W. Goodwin—Sept. 13, 1898

Photography—camera exposure meter—patented—Feb. 21, 1932

Radio Broadcast—baseball world series broadcast—WJZ—Oct. 5-13, 1921

Radio Broadcast—chain broadcast—Oct. 7, 1922

Road—sheet asphalt pavement—laid—July 29, 1870

Socialist Labor Party of North America—national convention—Dec. 26, 1877

Telegraph—duplex telegraph (practical)—patented—Aug. 9, 1892

Television—Telecast—puppet show to be televised—WOR—Aug. 21, 1928

North Arlington

Steam Engine—steam engine—delivered—Sept. 25, 1753

Oceanport

Television—Telecast—sports event televised in color—July 14, 1951

Passaic

Insurance—group insurance policy—Pantasote Leather Company insured—June 1, 1911

Paterson

Linen Thread Factory (successful)—established—1865

Locomotive Steam Whistle—used—Oct. 6, 1837

Pistol—pistol—with revolving barrel—patented—Samuel Colt—Feb. 25, 1836

Silk—silk loom of importance—ordered—April 23, 1887

Strike—strike in which the militia was called —July 21, 1828

Paulsboro

Gasoline — aviation gasoline — produced — June 6, 1936

Perth Amboy

Election Law—Negro to vote under authority of the Fifteenth Amendment—voted—March 31, 1870

Pitman

Naval Officer—woman doctor in the regular (U.S.) Navy — appointed — F. L. Willoughby—Oct. 15, 1948

Plainfield

Printing Press—web-fed four-color rotary printing press—manufactured—1890

Plainsboro

Milking Platform (rotating) — installed — Nov. 13, 1930

Princeton

College—college charter granted by a governor or acting governor with only the assent of his council—issued—Oct. 22, 1746

College—university to adopt the preceptorial system—1905

College Literary Society—college literary society—1765

Lacrosse Association (intercollegiate)—Intercollegiate Lacrosse Association—organized—March 11, 1882

Radio Impulse Transmission (wireless)—Joseph Henry—Dec. 1840

Road—electronic highway system—demonstrated—June 1953

Skeet—college skeet tournament—Nov. 12, 1928

Virus—virus obtained in crystalline form—reported—June 28, 1935

Rahway

Hair Cloth—manufactured—1813

Streptomycin—commercially manufactured—Sept. 1944

Ridgewood

Cable (telegraph)—coaxial cable—patented—Dec. 8, 1931

Plow—submarine cable plow—patented—Jan. 12, 1937

Sandy Hook

Radio Broadcast—yacht race broadcast—Oct. 16, 1899

Summit

Liquid Heat—system operated—Jan. 7, 1942

Trenton

Army Officer—chaplain killed in action—John Rosbrugh—Jan. 2, 1777

Building—building in which wrought iron beams were used—rolled—1854

Chinaware—chinaware for restaurant use—made—1862

Crime Prevention and Detection—national conference on crime—Oct. 11-12, 1935

Freemasons—Negro Masonic lodge—Alpha Lodge of New Jersey—warrant granted—Jan. 19, 1871

Pottery—pottery to make sanitary ware—founded—1853

Steel—open hearth furnace—built—1868

Water Ski Association (national)—American Water Ski Association—formed—April 1939

Woman—woman state committee chairman—M. T. Norton—elected—May 22, 1934

Tuckerton

Brokerage—stock order from a Zeppelin—message picked up—Aug. 8, 1930

Vineland

Intelligence Test—introduced—Aug. 1908

Weehawken

Ferryboat—ferryboat built exclusively for motor vehicle transportation—in service—Nov. 8, 1926

West Burlington

See under Burlington

West Orange

Moving Picture—moving picture "close-up"—Feb. 2, 1893

Moving Picture—moving picture of a staged prize fight—July 1894

Moving Picture "Studio"—erected—1892

Woodbridge

Brick—fire brick—manufactured—1825

Iron—iron patent—S. Broadmeadow—Jan. 6, 1844

NEW MEXICO

Atomic Bomb—atomic explosion witnessed by troops—Nov. 1, 1951

Alamogordo

Atomic Bomb—atomic bomb explosion—July 16, 1945

Aviation—jet drone target missile—flown—April 23, 1954

Rocket Sled—rocket-driven sled on rails—tested—March 19, 1954

Albuquerque

Building—commercial building heated by the sun—Aug. 1, 1957

Woman—woman to undergo astronaut tests—Jerrie Cobb—Feb. 15, 1960

Fort Stanton

Hospital—tuberculosis hospital operated by the government—opened—April 27, 1899

Sante Fe

Anthropology Laboratory—opened—Sept. 1, 1931

White Sands Proving Grounds

Photograph—ultraviolet pictures of the sun—March 13, 1959

Rocket — ballistic missile — fired—May 22, 1947

Rocket—rocket to attain a 100-mile altitude—July 30, 1946

Rocket—rocket to exceed a 150-mile altitude—Viking XI—May 24, 1954

Rocket—rocket to intercept a low-flying airplane—May 1958

Rocket—rocket to intercept an airplane—Nov. 27, 1951

Rocket—rocket to reach outer space—Feb. 24, 1949

NEW YORK

Accountancy Law (state)—April 17, 1896

Advertising Law — advertising legislation (state)—April 30, 1898

Advertising Law—outdoor advertising legislation (state)—March 28, 1865

Agricultural Appropriation—for state extension training—May 12, 1894

NEW YORK—*Continued*

Agricultural "Board" (state)—organized—Jan. 20, 1820

Arbitration—state arbitration law (modern)—April 19, 1920

Arbitration—State Board of Mediation and Arbitration—organized—June 1, 1886

Automobile License Plates—automobile license plates—required by law—April 25, 1901

Bank Legislation—bank legislation (state)—enacted—April 2, 1829

Bathhouse — legislation concerning public baths—passed—April 18, 1895

Census—state to exceed 5,000,000 in population—1880

Census—states to exceed 1,000,000 in population—1820

Crematory — crematory (state) — authorized—May 21, 1888

Dog License—dog license law (state)—enacted—March 8, 1894

Election—federal election in the U.S.—authorized—Sept. 13, 1788

Election Law—corrupt election practices law (state)—enacted—April 4, 1890

Entomologist — state entomologist — Asa Fitch—appointed—May 4, 1854

Farm Bureau—state assistance—appropriation enacted—May 24, 1913

Fire Escapes—for tenements—required by law—April 17, 1860

Forest Reserve—forest reserve (state)—designated—May 15, 1885

Game Law—hunting license fee (state)—law enacted—April 30, 1864

Installment Sales Law—enacted—April 17, 1957

Insurance — credit insurance — attempted — 1887

Insurance—insurance department (state)—authorized—April 15, 1859

Labor—labor anti-discrimination commission (state)—appointed—July 1, 1945

Labor Union—labor union to nominate its own political candidates—Mechanics Union—1784

Labor Union—labor union to nominate its own political candidates and win an election — Ebenezer Ford — elected — Nov. 7, 1829

Library Loan—made by a state library to a community—Feb. 8, 1892

Medical Legislation—blood grouping test laws (state)—enacted—March 22, 1935

Medical Legislation—law (state) requiring marriage license applicants to undergo medical tests—enacted—April 12, 1938

Medical Legislation—law (state) requiring serological blood tests of pregnant women—enacted—March 18, 1938

Missionary—Negro missionary—John Marrant—ordained—May 15, 1785

Oleomargarine — oleomargarine legislation (state)—enacted—June 5, 1877

Pharmacy Legislation (state) — enacted — May 3, 1904

Pure Food Law—pure food and drug legislation (state)—enacted—May 28, 1881

Railroad—railroad merger—of importance—May 17, 1853

School Superintendent—school superintendent (state)—Gideon Hawley—served—Jan. 14, 1813

Supreme Court (U.S.) Decision—Supreme Court decision between states—action commenced—Aug. 5, 1799

Territorial Expansion—acquisition of land by the federal government—New York ceded land—1781

Trademark Lawsuit—trademark controversy involving a newspaper—decision—Jan. 31, 1825

Traitor to the American cause—William Demont—Nov. 2, 1776

Treason—American colonist hanged for treason—Jacob Leisler—May 16, 1691

Truancy Legislation (state)—enacted—April 12, 1853

Voting Machine—voting machines were authorized—March 15, 1892

Voting Machine Commission (state)—authorized—May 17, 1897

Wire—legislation (state) requiring wires to be placed underground—enacted—June 14, 1884

Woman—woman state liquor board member—J. R. Sheppard—appointed—April 12, 1933

Albany

Aviation—Races—airplane to race a train—G. H. Curtiss—May 29, 1910

Baseball Team — baseball team to tour — played—July 1860

Canal—canal of importance — to Buffalo, N.Y.—opened—Oct. 26, 1825

Celluloid—patented—June 15, 1869

College Academic Costume Standardization—May 16, 1895

Cracker—cracker (sweet)—manufactured—1865

Electric Magnet—invented—Joseph Henry—June 1828

Hospital—psychiatric ward—associated with a general hospital—opened—1901

Library Society—state library society—formed—July 11, 1890

Locomotive — locomotive to attain the proved speed of 112.5 miles an hour

Locomotive—streamlined steam locomotive—introduced—Dec. 14, 1934

Medical Book—medical jurisprudence treatise (authoritative)—published—1823

Paleontology Report—based on Albany discovery—prepared—1713

Paper — perforated wrapping paper — patented—Seth Wheeler—July 25, 1871

Political Machine—well organized—Albany Regency—1820

Potato Chips—manufacturing plant—1925

Presidential Candidate—presidential candidate to fly to a political convention—to Chicago—July 2, 1932

Presidential Candidate—presidential candidate to make a speech of acceptance at a nominating convention—F. D. Roosevelt —Chicago—July 2, 1932

Telegraph—telegraph (electro-magnetic)— exhibited—Joseph Henry—1831

Television—Telecast — presidential nomination notification ceremony to be televised —A. E. Smith—Aug. 22, 1928

Whig Party—convention—Feb. 3, 1836

"Yankee Doodle"—written—Richard Shuckburgh—1755

Albion

Santa Claus School—opened—C. W. Howard—Sept. 27, 1937

Ardsley-on-Hudson

Golf Club—intercollegiate golf association—tournament—May 13-14, 1897

Ashville

Fire Department—fire department composed entirely of women—Feb. 1943

Attica

Bank—national bank failure—April 14, 1865

Auburn

Execution—electrocution of a human being —William Kemmler—Aug. 6, 1890

Prison—organization of a prison—into "community" groups—1914

Time Recorder—employees' time recorder—patented—W. L. Bundy—Nov. 20, 1888

Auriesville

Catholic Beatification—Catholic beatification of an American Indian—May 9, 1939

Batavia

Almanac—patent medicine almanac — published—1843

Beacon

Railroad Car—rail detector car—tested—June 13, 1928

Theater—therapeutic theater — "psycho-dramatic shock treatment"—1937

Bedloe Island

See Liberty Island

Belmont Park

See Elmont

Bentonsville

Saw (circular)—manufactured—c. 1814

Binghamton

Aviation—aviation trainer—used in a school —1929

Aviation—aviation trainer (jet)—completed —1949

Farm Bureau—established—March 20, 1911

Hospital — inebriates' asylum — organized— May 15, 1854

Oleomargarine — oleomargarine patent — H. W. Bradley—Jan. 3, 1871

Bloomville

Milk—milk pasteurized commercially—1895

Blue Mountain Lake

Elevator—elevator with an electric light—installed—July 12, 1882

Hotel—hotel to install electric lights—1881

Bronx

See New York City

Brooklyn

See New York City

Buchanan

Atomic Reactor—thorium-uranium reactor (privately owned)—construction began—Jan. 28, 1958

Buffalo

Almanac—patent medicine almanac—issued —1843

Architect—woman architect—L. B. Bethune —opened office—1881

Automobile Race—automobile race (long distance)—completed—Sept. 14, 1901

Aviation—Airplane — rocket plane — built — 1946

Bicycle Racer—woman bicycle champion of the National Amateur Bicycle Association —Doris Kopsky—Sept. 4, 1937

Bowler—bowler to roll two perfect games—Frank Caruana—March 5, 1924

Bowler—woman bowler to obtain a perfect score—Emma Fahning—March 4, 1930

Canal—canal of importance—to Albany—opened—Oct. 26, 1825

Cancer Laboratory—established—University of Buffalo—May 1898

Cellophane—manufactured—Du Pont Cellophane Co.—1924

Court—domestic relations court—established —1909

Desk—with roll top—invented—c. 1850

Drydock—timber drydock—erected—1840

Electric Power Plant—alternating current power plant commercially successful—built —Nov. 1886

Elevator—grain elevator operated by steam —built—1842

NEW YORK—Buffalo—*Continued*

Free Soil Party—organized—Aug. 9, 1848

Herd Book—*American Herd Book*—published —1846

Library Society—woman to become president of the American Library Association —T. H. W. Elmendorf—served—May 24, 1911

Medical Society—laryngological society (national)—American Laryngological Association—founded—June 3, 1878

Microscope—microscope for examining structure of materials—built—American Optical Company—1951

Motorcycle—motorcycle (practical)—E. R. Thomas Motor Co.—1900

Paper—wood-pulp paper—basswood — John Beardsley—exhibited—Dec. 26, 1854

School Superintendent—school superintendent (city)—R. W. Haskins—appointed— 1836

Ship—steamboat on the Great Lakes— launched—April 4, 1818

Sleeping Car—sleeping car patent—H. B. Myer—Sept. 19, 1854

Surgical Operation — skin grafting — suggested—F. H. Hamilton—1847

Television—Telecast—stockholders' meetings televised coast-to-coast simultaneously— Oct. 29, 1959

Television—Telecast—telecast transmitted to Canada—Jan. 20, 1953

Canastota

Automobile Tire Chain—patented—H. D. Weed—Aug. 23, 1904

Cato

School—school completely irradiated with germicidal lamps—installed—Jan. 3, 1945

Chautauqua

See also Fair Point

Esperanto Club—Esperanto club (national organization)—formed—Sept. 7, 1908

Home Study Course—serious nature—Aug. 10, 1878

Cohoes

Knitting Machine (power)—operated—1832

Coney Island

See New York City

Cooperstown

Baseball Game—baseball—played—1839

Hall of Fame—hall of fame (baseball)— dedicated—June 12, 1939

Corning

Glass—photosensitive glass — manufactured —Nov. 1937

Telescope — telescope lens two hundred inches in diameter—molded—Dec. 2, 1934

Creedmoor

Rifle Association—rifle association (national) —shooting meet—April 25, 1873

Rifle Association—rifle tournament (international)—Sept. 26, 1874

Crown Point

Freemasons — military Masonic lodge — formed—April 13, 1759

Cuba

Oil—oil spring—recorded—1627

Dexter Park

See New York City

Eastchester Township

Radio Broadcast—radio police system (two-way three-way)—placed in operation—July 10, 1933

Elizabethport

Cracker—meat biscuit—patented—Gail Borden, Jr.—July 30, 1850

Elmira

College—educational institution exclusively for women—opened—1855

Ordnance — automatic aircraft cannon — manufactured for U.S. Army — May 16, 1941

Elmont

Horse—horse to win the triple crown—Sir Barton—Belmont Park—1919

Horse Race—horse to win a $100,000 purse in one race—Whichone—Belmont Park— Sept. 14, 1929

Horse Race—race track at which more than $5,000,000 was bet in one day—Belmont Park—Sept. 22, 1945

Elmsford

Cocktail—introduced—1776

Deaf—Hearing Aid—transistorized hearing aid—offered for sale—Dec. 29, 1952

Fair Point

See also Chautauqua

Chautauqua Organization—organized—Aug. 4, 1874

Farmingdale

Bicycle Racer—to attain the speed of a mile a minute—C. M. Murphy—June 30, 1899

Fayetteville

Cement—natural cement rock—discovered—1818

Fishkill

War Veterans' Society—Society of the Cincinnati—instituted—May 10, 1783

Floyd Bennett Field

See New York City

Forest Hills

See New York City

Fort Washington

See New York City

Frankfort

Bridge—cast iron girder bridge—built—1840

Fredonia

Gas—natural gas corporation—organized—1865
Gas—natural gas used as an illuminant—1824

Garden City

Air Mail Service—air mail pilot—E. L. Ovington—to Mineola, L.I.—Sept. 23, 1911
Aviation—Airplane—airplane (commercial) stabilized—built—1931
Aviation—Airplane—fighter airplane—Kirkham Fighter—tested—Aug. 19, 1918
Aviation—Airplane—molded plywood airplane—"Whistling Bill"—built—1918

Geneva

College—college course without Greek or Latin—established—1824
Physician — woman physician — Elizabeth Blackwell—graduated—Jan. 23, 1849

Goshen

Telegraph—telegraph in railroading—used—Sept. 22, 1851

Governors Island

Army Officer—male nurse—E. L. Lyon—sworn in—Oct. 6, 1955
Court Martial—court martial trial in the United States at which enlisted men were allowed to sit as members of the court—Feb. 3, 1949

Greenpoint

See New York City

Greenwood Lake

Air Mail Service—rocket air mail flight—Feb. 23, 1936

Hamilton

Freemasons—Grotto—formal organization—Sept. 10, 1889
Freemasons—Grotto—Veiled Prophets—instituted—June 13, 1890

Hammondsport

Aviation—gyroscope automatic stabilization—demonstrated—Aug. 1913
Aviation—Airplane—airplane sold commercially—June 16, 1909
Aviation — Airplane — hydroplane with a multi-engine—christened—June 22, 1914
Aviation—Airplane—naval airplane — tested—1911
Aviation — Airplane Bombing — airplane bombing experiment—G. H. Curtiss—June 30, 1910
Aviation—School—airplane flying school—opened—Sept. 1910
School—school to have all classroom lights controlled by electric eyes—lights in operation—Jan. 4, 1936

Harlem

See New York City

Hartsdale

Television—Telecast—transoceanic television image—received—Feb. 8, 1928

Hastings

Prize Fight—prize fight fatality—Sept. 13, 1842

Hastings-on-Hudson

Photograph—photograph of a stellar spectrum showing the dark lines—1872

Hempstead Plains

Horse Race—horse race—on regular basis—1665

Hicksville

Automobile Race—Vanderbilt cup race—Oct. 8, 1904

Hornell

Aviation—Flights—airplane to fly a distance exceeding 500 miles—from Chicago, Ill.—Ruth Law—Nov. 19, 1916

NEW YORK—*Continued*

Hydeville

Spiritualist—J. D. Fox—1848

Ilion

Computer—solid-state electronic computer—built—1958

Pistol — revolver — self-cocking — manufactured—1856

Typewriter—typewriter that was practical—patented—C. L. Sholes—June 23, 1868

Ithaca

Aviation—air stewardess (Negro)—R. C. Taylor—to New York City—Feb. 11, 1958

Birds — ptarmigan (Eskimo chicken) — hatched—July 24, 1934

Caliper (screw)—constructed—J. E. Sweet—1874

Degrees (academic and honorary)—Doctor of Science degree earned by a woman—C. W. Baldwin—Cornell University—June 20, 1895

Dynamo—dynamo for a direct-current outdoor lighting system—built—1875

Engineering College—electrical engineering course—established—Sept. 21, 1883

Fellowship—fellowship awarded a woman—granted—H. E. Grotecloss—June 19, 1884

Forestry School—forestry school of collegiate character—established—Sept. 19, 1898

Hotel Administration College Course—offered—1922

Ice Cream Sundae—originated—1897

Industrial and Labor Relations School—opened—Nov. 2, 1945

Teletypesetter—teletypesetter installed in a school—July 5, 1933

Veterinary School—veterinary department of collegiate character—opened—Oct. 7, 1868

Woman—woman editor-in-chief of a law review—M. H. Donlon—Nov. 1919

Jamaica

See New York City

Johnstown

Axe—manufacturing plant—erected—1800

Gloves—commercial manufacture—1809

Leather—leather tanning by the "oil tan" method—originated—Talmadge Edwards—1810

Karner

Locomotive—streamlined steam locomotive—introduced—Dec. 14, 1934

Kinderhook

President (U.S.)—President born a citizen of the United States—Martin Van Buren—Dec. 5, 1782

Kings Point

Merchant Marine Academy—Merchant Marine Academy (U.S.)—dedicated—F. D. Roosevelt—Sept. 30, 1943

Merchant Marine Academy—Merchant Marine Cadet Corps (U.S.)—established—March 15, 1938

La Guardia Field

See New York City

Lackawanna

Catholic Church—Catholic Church raised to the dignity of a Basilica—dedicated—May 25, 1926

Lake George

Canoe Association—American Canoe Association—formed—Aug. 3, 1880

Lake Placid

Auction Bridge Championship (duplicate)—July 9, 1914

Bobsled Competition—four-man bob-team competition—Feb. 14-15, 1932

Bobsled Competition — two-man bob-team competition—Feb. 9-10, 1932

Dog Sled Race—dog sled race on an Olympic demonstration program—Feb. 6-7, 1932

Olympic Games—Winter Olympic Games competition—opened—Feb. 4, 1932

Ski Meet (international)—of importance—Feb. 10-13, 1932

Lansingburgh

Oiled Silk Patent—Ralph Hodgson—Feb. 1, 1793

Lewiston

Railroad—inclined railway— erected—1764

Liberty Island

Monument—statue presented by a foreign country—Statue of Liberty—unveiled—Oct. 28, 1886

Moving Picture Actor—stunt actor—F. R. Law—parachute jump—Feb. 2, 1912

Lockport

Heating System—heating system from a central station—installed—Birdsall Holly—1877

Voting Machine—voting machines were authorized for use—machines used—April 12, 1892

Locust Grove

Bank—trailer bank—opened—May 26, 1956

McGraw

Corset—health corset—manufactured—July 1874

Manchester

Church of Jesus Christ of Latter Day Saints —organized—April 6, 1830

Mineola

Aviation—Passenger—woman airplane passenger (transcontinental)—Lillian Gatlin—landed—Oct. 8, 1922

Monroe

Cheese—Liederkranz brand cheese—produced—1892

Montauk Point

Moving Picture—moving picture of an eclipse of the sun taken from a dirigible —Jan. 24, 1925

Radio Telephone — radio telephone communication (one way)—to Wilmington, Del.—April 4, 1915

Mount Lebanon

See New Lebanon

Mount Vernon

Golf Tournament—Professional Golfers Association tournament—Siwanoy Golf Club —Oct. 14, 1916

New Lebanon

Shaker Society—organized community— established—1788

New Paltz

Adding Machine—adding machine to employ depressible keys—patented—D. D. Parmelee—Feb. 5, 1850

New Russia

Organ—color organ — patented—Bainbridge Bishop—Jan. 16, 1877

New York City

Abrasive—boron carbide—announced—Sept. 27, 1934

Accountant—C.P.A.—licensed—Dec. 1, 1896

Accountants' Society—accountants' society—organized—July 28, 1882

Accountants' Society—accountants' society formed by a state group—organized—March 30, 1897

Accountants' Society—accountants' society to become a national organization — formed—Dec. 22, 1886

Actor—English actor of note—arrived—Nov. 16, 1810

Actors' Union—chartered—Jan. 4, 1896

Advertisement—advertisement to occupy a half-page—July 18, 1743

Advertisement—automobile advertisement—July 30, 1898

Advertisement—magician's advertisement—March 18, 1734

Advertising Magazine—published—1865

Advertising Organization—to combat business abuses—organized—December 1911

Agriculture Professor—appointed—July 9, 1792

Air (compressed)—for tunnel construction—used 1879

Air (liquid)—practical production—1895

Air Defense Command (U.S.)—created—Feb. 26, 1940

Air Mail Service—air mail experimental route—May 15, 1918

Air Mail Service—air mail long-distance night service—established—July 1, 1925

Air Mail Service—air mail regular service—established—Aug. 12, 1918

Air Mail Service—air mail service from ship to shore—inaugurated—Aug. 13, 1928

Air Mail Service—air mail service to a steamer at sea—Aug. 14, 1919

Air Mail Service—air mail transcontinental flight—Feb. 22, 1921

Air Mail Service—air mail transcontinental service—(combination airplane-railroad)—to San Francisco—Sept. 8, 1920

Air Mail Service—air mail transcontinental through regular service—to San Francisco —July 1, 1924

Air Rights Lease—Feb. 1910

Algebra Book—algebra book—published—1730

Animals—cattle (Africander cattle)—arrived —Dec. 11, 1931

Animals—elephant—arrived—April 13, 1796

Animals—monkey trained to perform—exhibited—Feb. 25, 1751

Animals—okapi—imported—August 4, 1937

Animals—rhinoceros—exhibited—Sept. 13, 1826

Animals—sheep (Karakul fur sheep)—imported—1908

Anti-Slavery Party—national convention—May 12, 1841

Antitoxin Laboratory — established — Sept. 1894

Aquatic Mammals—platypus (duck-billed)—exhibited—July 15, 1922

Arabic Magazine—*Star of America*—published —1892

Arbitration—arbitration tribunal—established —May 3, 1768

Arbitration Association—arbitration association—Arbitration Society of America, Inc. —formed—May 15, 1922

Architect—landscape architect—John Reid —arrived—Dec. 19, 1683

Archival Course — Columbia University — Sept. 29, 1938

Army Execution—Thomas Hickey—June 27, 1776

Art Organization—artists' society of importance—organized—Nov. 8, 1825

NEW YORK—New York City—*Continued*

Baseball Player—baseball "pinch hitter"—used—June 7, 1892

Baseball Player—baseball pitcher—to curve a ball—Arthur Cummings—1866

Baseball Player—baseball pitcher to pitch a perfect no-hit, no-run, no-walk World Series game—Don Larsen—Oct. 8, 1956

Baseball Player — major league baseball player to pitch two successive no-hit no-run games—June 11, 1938—June 15, 1938

Baseball Player—Negro major league baseball player — Jackie Robinson — played — April 11, 1947

Baseball Rules—baseball rules—standardization—National Baseball Assn.—May 1858

Baseball Team — Knickerbocker Club—organized—Sept. 23, 1845

Baseball Team—baseball team (Negro professional)—organized—1885

Baseball Team — baseball team to tour — Brooklyn team—left for Albany—June 30, 1860

Baseball Team—baseball team to win five World Series in succession—New York Yankees—Oct. 5, 1953

Baseball Team—baseball team to win three World Series in succession—New York Yankees—1936, 1937, 1938

Basketball—basketball collegiate team to win the National Invitation Tournament and the National Collegiate Athletic Association trophy—March 28, 1950

Bathhouse—public bath and washhouse—opened—Jan. 1, 1852

Bathhouse — public baths with showers — opened—Aug. 17, 1891

Bathhouse—Turkish bath opened—Oct. 6, 1863

Battery — solar battery — announced—April 25, 1954

Bed—box spring—imported—1857

Benevolent Protective Order of Elks—organized—Feb. 16, 1868

Bible—Bible for the blind in embossed form —issued—1835

Bible School—Missionary Training College —opened—Oct. 1, 1883

Bible Society—Bible society (national organization) — American Bible Society — formed—May 8, 1816

Bicycle — bicycle velocipedes — imported — 1819

Bicycle Patent—W. K. Clarkson, Jr.—June 26, 1819

Bicycle Race—intercollegiate bicycle race—May 27, 1896

Bicycle Race—international six-day bicycle race—Oct. 18, 1891

Bicycle Race—motorcycle-paced bicycle race—July 29, 1899

Bicycle Race—paired six-day bicycle race—Dec. 9-14, 1901

Bicycle Race—women's six-day bicycle race—Jan. 6-11, 1896

Bicycle School—opened—Dec. 5, 1868

Bicycle Tire — bicycle tire (pneumatic) — manufactured—April 1891

Bicycle Trip—bicycle rider to cross the continent in less than three weeks—Eugene McPherson—arrived—Sept. 21, 1949

Billiard Ball of composition material resembling ivory—patented—Oct. 10, 1865

Billiard Book—*Billiards Without A Master*—published—1850

Bird Banding Society—formed—Dec. 8, 1909

Birds—quetzal bird—imported—Oct. 4, 1940

Birds—sparrows—imported—1850

Boat Club—boat club—Knickerbocker Boat Club—organized—1811

Boat Club—boat club association of amateur clubs—1834

Boat Race—international lifeboat race—Sept. 7, 1927

Boat Race—motor boat race under organized rules—June 23-24, 1904

Book—book bound with a pre-printed offset cloth—*Portraits and Prayers*—published—Nov. 7, 1934

Book—Book of Common Prayer (in the Mohawk Indian language)—published—1715

Book—book on cornstalk paper—printed—June 1928

Book—book set by linotype—published—1887

Book—stereotyped book—stereotyped—June 1813

Book Auction—authorized—April 18, 1662

Book Catalog—*The Uniform Trade List Annual*—published—1873

Book Club — Book-of-the-Month Club — formed—April 1926

Book Fair—June 1, 1802

Book Index—*American Book Circular*—published—1843

Book Publisher of denominational books—organized—May 1789

Book Review—book review editor—Margaret Fuller—appointed—Dec. 1844

Book Review—book review newspaper supplement—published—Oct. 10, 1896

Book Trade Magazine—book collectors' magazine — *The Philobiblion* — published — 1861

Book Trade Magazine—book trade magazine—issued—Jan. 1, 1834

Book Trade Magazine—successful book trade magazine—weekly—issued—Sept. 1, 1855

Booksellers' Association—American Company of Booksellers—organized—June 7, 1801

Booksellers' Catalog—published—Leon & Brother—1885

Bottle—milk bottles—used—1879

Bowling Magazine—*Gut Holz*—issued—Aug. 9, 1893

Bowling Rule Standardization — National Bowling Assn.—Nov. 13, 1875

Bowling Tournament—bowling convention—of importance—Sept. 9, 1895

Bowling Tournament—bowling match—Jan. 1, 1840

NEW YORK—New York City—*Continued*

Church—universal chapel embracing eight faiths—Universalist Church of the Divine Paternity—dedicated—April 8, 1956

Cigar Band—cigar band of special interest—C. W. Field—Sept. 2, 1858

Cigar Lighter Patent—Nov. 21, 1871

Cigar Rolling Machine—practical—patented—Feb. 27, 1883

Cigarette Manufacturing Machine—invented—1872

Clock—clock to operate by atomic power—Atomicron—exhibited—Oct. 2, 1956

Clock—electronic wrist watch—produced—Oct. 25, 1960

Coaching—tallyho trip—May 1, 1876

Coaching Club—formed—Dec. 3, 1875

Cobra—King cobra snakes—born in captivity—July 4, 1955

Collar—paper collar—patented July 25, 1854

College—college to prohibit discrimination because of race, religion or color—Cooper Union—April 29, 1851

College—woman dean of a graduate school—Frieda Wunderlich—elected—Jan. 4, 1939

Colonist—colonists to reach the Pacific coast—left New York City—Sept. 6, 1810

Colorscope—public demonstration—June 5, 1930

Congress (U.S.)—Congress of the United States—March 4, 1789

Congress (U.S.)—congressional act—June 1, 1789

Congress (U.S.)—joint meeting of the Senate and the House of Representatives—April 6, 1789

Congress (U.S.)—House of Representatives—committee of the House of Representatives—appointed—April 2, 1789

Congress (U.S.)—House of Representatives—contested election—April 18, 1789

Congress (U.S.)—House of Representatives—House of Representatives—meeting—March 4, 1789

Congress (U.S.)—House of Representatives—House of Representatives—quorum assembled—April 1, 1789

Congress (U.S.)—Senate—Senate—meeting—March 4, 1789

Congress (U.S.)—Senate—Senate—quorum assembled—April 6, 1789

Congressman (U.S.)—congressman to die—Theodoric Bland—June 1, 1790

Conscientious Objectors—arrived August 6, 1774

Cooking School—New York Cooking School—Nov. 1876

Cooperative—consumers' cooperative society—organized—1830

Copyright—choreographic score copyrighted—Hanya Holm—Feb. 25, 1952

Coral Reef Barrier—exhibition completed—July 1934

Cork—for steam pipe covering—manufactured—1894

Cork Manufacturer—1850

Corkboard Patent—John T. Smith—July 14, 1891

Corkscrew Patent—M. L. Byrn—March 27, 1860

Corporation—commercial corporation—New York Fishing Co.—Jan. 8, 1675

Court—night court—opened—Sept. 1, 1907

Cranberry Treatise—published—1856

Credit Protective Group—formed—1842

Credit Report Book—published—1844

Crepe—imported—1912

Cricket Tournament—cricket match—May 1, 1751

Crime—interstate crime pact—signed—Sept. 16, 1833

Cripples—private school for cripples—opened—May 1, 1863

Crossword Puzzle—published—Dec. 21, 1913

Crossword Puzzle Book—published—April 18, 1924

Curfew Bell—introduced—Wilhelm Kieft—1638

Dacron—dacron men's suits—introduced—May 8, 1951

Dance Marathon—March 30, 1923

Deaf—Association—national social organization for the hard of hearing—formed—Feb. 27, 1919

Deaf—Church Service—church services for the deaf—Thomas Gallaudet—Oct. 3, 1852

Deaf—School—instruction for the deaf—John Stanford—1807

Deaf—School—lip reading instruction for the deaf—S. W. Keeler—1882

Deaf—School—lip reading school for girls—established—L. E. Warren—1890

Deaf—Transmission—visible and oral communication by the deaf over distance—by television—Oct. 13, 1940

Degrees (academic and honorary)—Bachelor of Sacred Music degree—conferred—June 10, 1953

Degrees (academic and honorary)—Doctor of Military Science degree—J. J. Pershing—April 11, 1930

Degrees (academic and honorary)—law degree of LL.M. (Master of Laws)—conferred by Columbia University—June 29, 1864

Degrees (academic and honorary)—Master of Arts degree in Sacred Music—conferred—June 6, 1956

Degrees (academic and honorary)—Master of Hebrew Literature degree awarded a woman—H. H. Levinthal—May 28, 1939

Dental Book—book on dentistry—strictly American—R. C. Skinner—published—1801

Dental Book—dental textbook—*A System of Dental Surgery*—published—1829

Dental Book—orthodontia treatise—Solyman Brown—published—1841

Dental Dispensary—dental dispensary—City Dispensary for the Medical Relief of the Poor—opened—Feb. 1, 1791

Dental Magazine—dental journal—*American Journal of Dental Science*—published—1839

NEW YORK—New York City—*Continued*

Fencing—fencing league (national)—Amateur Fencers League of America—organized—May 6, 1891

Fencing—intercollegiate fencing championship competition—May 5, 1894

Ferryboat—double-deck ferryboat with the propeller-type steel hull—built—1891

Ferryboat—municipally owned ferryboats—operated—Oct. 25, 1905

Ferryboat—steam-propelled ferryboat — to Hoboken, N.J.—operated—Oct. 11, 1811

Ferryboat—steel-hull ferryboat—operated to Hoboken, N.J.—1881

Fingerprinting—fingerprint conviction—May 19, 1911

Fire—fire of great destructive force—Dec. 16, 1835

Fire Department—fire department established by municipal action—1659

Fire Department—fire department to be paid—1697

Fire Engine—steam fire engine—tested—March 27, 1841

Fire Patrol—fire patrol to receive a salary—organized—1835

Fireboat—used—1800

Fish Hatchery—fish hatchery—to breed salmon—1864

Fish Protection—fish legislation—May 28, 1734

Fishing Line Factory—established—Henry Hall—1859

Flag—flag displayed from the right hand of the Statue of Liberty—June 13, 1927

Flashlight—manufactured—1898

Flea Circus—opened—Jan. 1835

Flowers — tetraploid flower — publicly exhibited—Jan. 29, 1940

Fly Casting Tournament—indoor fly casting tournament—March 15-20, 1897

Football Book—football book—*American Football*—published—1891

Football Game—indoor football game—1891

Football Goal Post—football goal posts of collapsible folding metal—installed—June 1936

Football Rules—formulated—Oct. 18, 1873

Fountain Pen—practical—L. E. Waterman—1884

Foxhound Association—Masters of Fox Hounds Assn.—formed—Feb. 14, 1907

Fraternity (Greek letter)—inter-fraternity council—assembled—Nov. 17, 1909

Free Lunch—free lunches to aid convalescents—N.Y. Diet Kitchen Assn.—opened—April 24, 1873

Free Port—opened—Stapleton, Staten Island, N.Y.—Feb. 1, 1937

Freemasons—Ancient Arabic Order of Nobles of the Mystic Shrine—established—June 16, 1871

Freemasons—Knights Templar Grand Encampment—Jan. 22, 1814

Game Manufacturing Company—organized by J. McLoughlin—1828

Game Protection Society—formed—May 20, 1844

Gardener's Manual—Thomas Bridgeman—published—1835

Gas—gas meter (dry)—patented—James Bogardus—Oct. 17, 1834

Gas Engine—patented—S. Perry—May 25, 1844

Giant—exhibited—Oct. 6, 1825

Glass—invisible glass installation—Sept. 1935

Glider—glider towed across the continent—landed—April 6, 1930

Golf Book—J. P. Lee—published—May 25, 1895

Golf Club—golf association (national)—United States Golf Assn.—formed—Dec. 22, 1894

Golf Clubs (or golf sticks)—golf clubs (or golf sticks)—described—1729

Golf Magazine—*Golfing*—published—1894

Grammar—English grammar by an American published in America—Samuel Johnson—1765

Greenhouse — erected — James Beekman — 1764

Gutta Percha—imported—1840

Hall of Fame—Hall of Fame (university)—dedicated—May 30, 1901

Hat—soft felt hats for women—introduced—J. N. Genin—1851

Health Board—health board (municipal) armed with sufficient powers—authorized—Feb. 26, 1866

Health Instruction in connection with the schools—undertaken—Oct. 1902

Health Ordinance prohibiting spitting—on the sidewalks—passed—May 12, 1896

Hebrew Book—published—1860

Helicopter—helicopter licensed for commercial use—March 8, 1946

Helicopter—helicopter passenger service—July 9, 1953

High School—public high school to specialize in the performing field—Sept. 13, 1948

History—comic history of the United States—published—1812

Holiday—Labor Day holiday parade—Sept. 5, 1882

Homeopathy—introduced—H. B. Gram—1825

Horse Race—trotting course—established—Jamaica—1825

Horse Race—trotting futurity—Oct. 12, 1869

Horse Register—horse pacing register—*American Race-Turf Register*—published 1833

Horse Register—trotting register—*American Trotting Register*—published—1871

Horse Show—horse show of national scope—Oct. 22-26, 1883

Horticultural Society—horticultural society—New York Horticultural Society—founded—1818

Hospital—babies' hospital designed exclusively for infants—chartered—June 23, 1887

Hospital—cancer home for incurables (free)—established—Sept. 15, 1896

NEW YORK—New York City—*Continued*

Library — mercantile library — organized— Nov. 9, 1820

Library Chair—established—Columbia University—April 4, 1938

Library Society — library society (local) — New York Library Club — formed—June 18, 1885

Library Training (systematic) — courses — Columbia University—Jan. 5, 1887

Libretto — libretto — *The Disappointment* — published—1767

Life Preserver—life preserver of cork—patented—N. E. Guerin—Nov. 16, 1841

Life Preserver—life preserver of cork approved by the Board of Supervising Inspectors—patented—David Kahnweiler — July 10, 1877

Lifeboat—lifeboat (corrugated)—patented— Joseph Francis—March 26, 1845

Linoleum—linoleum—manufactured—1873

Liquor Reform Movement—1623

Locomotive — diesel-electric locomotive—in service—Dec. 17, 1924

Loop the Loop Centrifugal Railway—installed—Coney Island—1900

Macaroni Factory — established — Antoine Zerega—1848

Magic Lantern Show—magic lantern feature show—Oct. 9, 1894

Map—road map—published—1789

Map—war map—published—Dec. 24, 1733

Marines—Marine corps—organized—1740

Meat—beef exported—to England—Oct. 1, 1875

Mechanics Textbook—*The Elements of Analytical Mechanics*—published—1853

Medical Book—bronchitis treatise—Horace Green—published—1846

Medical Book — chiropody book — Issachar Zacharie—published—1860

Medical Book — croup report (printed) — Richard Bayley—published—1781

Medical Book—dissection essay—1750

Medical Book — hay fever book — Morrill Wyman—published—1872

Medical Book — hemophilia treatise—published—1803

Medical Book—homeopathic treatise—C. F. S. Hahnemann—published—1825

Medical Book—medical book for army medical use—published—1790

Medical Book—neurasthenia book—G. M. Beard—published—1880

Medical Book—neurology textbook—W. A. Hammond—published—1871

Medical Book—obstetrics book—Samuel Bard—published—1807

Medical Book—pediatrics book of importance—L. E. Holt—published—1894

Medical Book—surgery manual—John Jones —published—1775

Medical Clinic—birth control clinic—opened —Oct. 16, 1916

Medical Clinic—cancer prevention clinic for children—opened—Jan. 3, 1947

Medical Clinic—children's clinic—established —1862

Medical Clinic—college medical clinic— established—1840

Medical Clinic — laryngology clinic — established—March 1863

Medical Clinic—ophthalmology clinic—Fifth Avenue Hospital—Sept. 1932

Medical Congress—Fever Therapy International Conference—March 29, 1937

Medical Instruction—clinical instruction and bedside demonstration—A. H. Stevens— 1818

Medical Instruction—laryngology instruction —University of the City of New York— Louis Elsberg—1861

Medical Instruction—medical jurisprudence course—James Stringham—1813

Medical Instruction—midwifery professor— J. V. B. Tennent—1767

Medical Instruction—orthopedics chair—established—Bellevue Hospital Medical College—1861

Medical Instruction—pediatrics professor— Abraham Jacobi—1870

Medical Instruction—plastic surgery professor—J. E. Sheehan—1926

Medical Instruction—Psychiatric Institute— authorized—May 12, 1896

Medical Legislation—chiropody law governing the study of chiropody—passed—1895

Medical Legislation—law to regulate the practice of medicine (actually enforced)— June 10, 1760

Medical Periodical—homeopathic magazine —*American Journal of Homeopathia*—published—1835

Medical Periodical—laryngology magazine— *Archives of Laryngology*—published—1880

Medical Periodical—medical magazine—*Medical Repository*—published—Aug. 8, 1797

Medical Periodical—medical periodical devoted to diseases of women and children— *American Journal of Obstetrics*—published —May 1868

Medical Periodical—optometry magazine— *The Optician*—published—Jan. 1891

Medical "Rogues' Gallery" — started — Jan. 1930

Medical School — naval medical school — opened—Aug. 1, 1893

Medical Society — laryngological society (state)—organized—October 1873

Medicine — bone bank — established — April 1946

Methodist—Methodist preacher—Philip Embury—arrived—Aug. 11, 1760

Methodist Chapel—dedicated—Oct. 30, 1768

Microfilm—magazine on microfilm offered to subscribers—*Newsweek*—June 1, 1949

Microfilm—newspaper to microfilm its current issues—New York *Herald Tribune*— Jan. 1, 1936

Microfilm—newspaper to microfilm its past issues—New York *Times*—Nov. 1935

Milk—condensed milk (commercial)—patent granted—Gail Borden—Aug. 19, 1856

Milk—dried milk patent—S. R. Percy—April 9, 1872

NEW YORK—New York City—*Continued*

Newspaper — Greek newspaper — *Atlantis* — published—March 3, 1894

Newspaper — Hungarian daily newspaper — *Amerikai Magyar Népszava*—published— Oct. 18, 1904

Newspaper — illustrated daily newspaper — *Daily Graphic*—published—March 4, 1873

Newspaper — illustrated tabloid — *Illustrated Daily News*—published—June 26, 1919

Newspaper—Italian newspaper—*Il Progresso Italo-Americano*—published—Sept. 1880

Newspaper — Negro newspaper — *Freedom's Journal*—published—March 16, 1827

Newspaper—newspaper colored supplement— *World*—published—Nov. 19, 1893

Newspaper—newspaper rotogravure sections —published—*Times*—March 29, 1914

Newspaper—newspaper Sunday comic section —published—*World*—1893

Newspaper—penny daily newspaper—successful —*Sun*—Sept. 3, 1833

Newspaper — political newspaper — *Gazette of the United States*—published—April 11, 1789

Newspaper—Spanish newspaper—*El Redactor* —published—July 1, 1827

Newspaper — transoceanic newspaper — *Daily Mail*—Jan. 5, 1944

Newspaper—Ukranian daily newspaper—*Ukranian Daily News*—published—Jan. 31, 1920

Newspaper—Yiddish daily newspaper—*Yiddishes-Tageblatt*—published—1885

Newspaper Index—newspaper index separately published—1866

Newspaper Syndicate—newspaper syndicate to supply articles—S. S. McClure—Nov. 8, 1884

Newspaper Syndicate—syndication of newspaper material—M. Y. Beach—Dec. 7, 1841

Novel—novel to win the Pulitzer prize in letters—*His Family*—award announced— June 3, 1918

Nudist Organization—American League for Physical Culture—founded—Dec. 5, 1929

Nurse—district nurse—employed—1877

Nurse—nurse appointed to a university professorship—M. A. Nutting—1910

Nurses' Magazine—*The Nightingale*—published—March 6, 1886

Nurses' Society—nurses' society (local)— Philomena Society—organized—Nov. 24, 1885

Nursing School—instruction for nurses— systematic—New York Hospital—1798

Nylon—nylon stretch yarn—introduced— 1952

Oleomargarine—oleomargarine manufacturer (successful)—A. Paraf—1871

Opera—grand opera sung in English—*Der Freischutz*—March 2, 1825

Opera—Negro prima donna of an opera company—Caterina Jarboro—July 22, 1933

Opera—Negro singer of the Metropolitan Opera—Marian Anderson—Jan. 7, 1955

Opera—Negro to sing a white role with a white cast in an opera company—R. T. Duncan—Sept. 28, 1945

Opera—opera at the Metropolitan Opera House—*Faust*—Oct. 22, 1883

Opera — opera broadcast in its entirety by the Metropolitan Opera Company—*Hansel and Gretel*—Dec. 25, 1931

Opera—opera broadcast in part—from Metropolitan Opera House—Jan. 13, 1910

Opera—opera by an American composer— *The Archers*—performed—April 18, 1796

Opera—opera by an American composer performed at the Metropolitan Opera House of New York—*The Pipe of Desire*— March 18, 1910

Opera—opera composed by a woman performed at the Metropolitan Opera House— *Der Wald*—E. M. Smyth—March 11, 1903

Opera—opera (Italian)—*Il Barbiere di Siviglia*—Nov. 29, 1825

Opera—opera of a serious nature—*Tammany* —March 3, 1794

Opera—opera performed by a professional visiting troupe—*The Beggar's Opera*—Dec. 3, 1750

Opera—opera singer (American) to sing in an Italian opera in Italian—Julia Wheatley—Nov. 25, 1834

Opera—opera singer to sing two major roles on the same day—Herman Jadlowker—Metropolitan Opera House—March 22, 1911

Optometry Instruction—optics and optometry courses—Columbia University—1910

Orchestra—orchestra (American) to make a European tour — Symphony Society of New York—sailed—April 22, 1920

Orchestra—orchestra in a theater—1750

Organ — electric organ — installed — Chickering Hall—1876

Organ—organ built in the U.S.—installed— Trinity Church—May 1740

Organ—pipeless organ—exhibited—April 15, 1935

Organ School—Guilmant Organ School— established—1899

Orphanage—orphanage — established — June 1654

Paint—paint (ready-mixed)—patented—July 16, 1867

Paleontology Course — micropaleontology course—Columbia University—Sept. 25, 1924

Paper—corrugated paper—patented—Dec. 19, 1871

Paper—crepe paper—manufactured—1890

Paper — toilet paper — manufactured—J. C. Gayetty—1857

Patent—design patent—George Bruce—Nov. 9, 1842

Pawnbroking Ordinance—enacted—July 13, 1812

Peace Society—New York Peace Society— organized—Aug. 16, 1815

Periodical—all-fiction pulp magazine—*Argosy* —published—1896

Periodical—comic books—published—1904

Periodical—electrical journal — *Electro-Magnetic and Mechanics Intelligencer*—published —Jan. 18, 1840

Periodical—illustrated weekly—*Brother Jonathan*—published—Jan. 1, 1842

Periodical—magazine containing a fashion plate—*The Port Folio*—June 1809

Periodical—magazine to contain a phonograph record—*Pageant*—Nov. 1955

Periodical—photo-engraved magazine—*Literary Digest*—published—Oct. 25, 1919

Periodical—sectarian magazine printed in rotogravure—*Catholic Missions*—published—Oct. 1, 1934

Periodical—Spanish magazine published by students—*El Estudiante Comercial*—published—1917

Periodical Index—W. F. Poole—published—1848

Permalloy—developed—G. W. Elmen—June 7, 1913

Petroleum Jelly—manufactured—1870

Pharmacopoeia—pharmacopoeia prepared by a hospital staff—published—1816

Philological Society—national philological society—American Philological Association—organized—Nov. 13, 1868

Phonograph Trade Magazine—*The Phonogram*—published—Jan. 1891

Photoelectric Cell—photoelectric cell—publicly demonstrated—Oct. 21, 1925

Photograph—celestial photograph—of the moon—Dec. 18, 1839

Photograph—news photographs of distinction—Mathew B. Brady—studio opened—1844

Photograph—photograph of a President (in office)—J. K. Polk—Feb. 14, 1849

Photograph—photograph taken in the United States—Aug. 19, 1839

Photographic Patent—photographic patent—A. S. Wolcott—May 8, 1840

Photography—film developing machine—fully automatic—patented—A. M. Josepho—Jan. 17, 1928

Physician—ophthalmologist of note—Edward Delafield—1864

Physics—national physics association—American Physical Society—formed—May 20, 1899

Physiological Society—physiological society (national organization)—American Physiological Society—organized—Dec. 30, 1887

Pin—safety pin—patented—Walter Hunt—April 10, 1849

Pituitary Hormone—polypeptide hormone synthesized—1953

Play (drama)—aquatic play—*The Pirate's Signal*—July 4, 1840

Play (drama)—benefit performance—Jan. 7, 1751

Play (drama)—burlesque show—of importance—*The Black Crook*—Sept. 12, 1866

Play (drama)—drama to win a Pulitzer prize—opened—Dec. 25, 1917

Play (drama)—Hebrew professional acting troupe—performed—Aug. 12, 1882

Play (drama)—musical play to win a Pulitzer prize—*Of Thee I Sing*—opened—Dec. 26, 1931

Play (drama)—native American play successfully acted on a regular stage—*The Contrast*—April 16, 1787

Play (drama)—play acted by professional players—*The Recruiting Officer*—Dec. 6, 1732

Play (drama)—play performed 1,000 times—*The Gladiator*—opened—Sept. 26, 1831

Play (drama)—printed American play—*Androboros*—printed—1714

Play (drama)—Shakespearean play—*King Richard III*—March 5, 1750

Play (drama)—theatrical presentation sponsored by the federal government—*The Family Upstart*—Jan. 20, 1934

Pole Vaulter—pole vault jump indoors over 16 feet—John Uelses—Feb. 2, 1962

Police—police Bureau of Criminal Alien Investigation—Dec. 23, 1930

Police—police uniforms—authorized—July 8, 1693

Police—traffic police squad—"Broadway Squad"—organized—1860

Police—woman detective—Isabella Goodwin—appointed—March 1, 1912

Political Convention—political nominating caucus—Sept. 15-16, 1812

Political Economy Course—college chair of political economy—Columbia College—1818

Polo—intercollegiate indoor polo championship—Princeton vs. Yale—March 18, 1922

Polo—polo—introduced—J. G. Bennett—1876

Polo Club—polo association (national)—United States Polo Association—formed—June 6, 1890

Polo Club—polo club—organized—1876

Post Office—Post Office Department of the United States—established—Sept. 22, 1789

Postage Stamp—adhesive stamps—City Despatch Post—Feb. 15, 1842

Postage Stamp—imperforated ungummed sheet of postage stamps—issued—Feb. 10, 1934

Postage Stamp—sheet of postage stamps to contain more than one variety—sold—May 9, 1936

Postage Stamp—stamped envelopes (U.S.)—manufactured

Postal Service—coin-operated mailbox—installed—May 17, 1939

Postal Service—letter to encircle the world by commercial airmail—dispatched—April 19, 1937

Postal Service—ocean mail contracts—authorized—March 3, 1845

Postal Service—postal route—to Boston—Jan. 22, 1673

Postal Service—"V" mail film—to London—June 22, 1942

President of a South American Country Born in the United States—Galo Plaza Lasso—born—Feb. 17, 1906

President (U.S.)—President elected—George Washington—inaugurated—April 30, 1789

President (U.S.)—President married while in office—John Tyler—June 25, 1844

NEW YORK—New York City—*Continued*

President (U.S.)—President to receive the unanimous vote of the presidential electors —George Washington

Presidential Candidate—Presidential candidate debate series on television—third debate, Nixon in New York City and Kennedy in Hollywood, Calif.—Oct. 13, 1960— fourth debate—Oct. 21, 1960

Presidential Candidate—woman presidential candidate—V. C. Woodhull—nominated— May 10, 1872

Presidential Inaugural Ball—May 7, 1789

"Presidential Mansion"—occupied by George Washington—April 23, 1789

Press Clipping Bureau—opened—April 15, 1884

Primer—typewriting primer—*Ted and Polly* —published—Nov. 1933

Printing Press—cylinder and flat bed combination printing press—patented—April 17, 1844

Printing Press—cylinder printing press— manufactured—1831

Printing Press—printing press invented in America that was practical and successful —Washington Press—1827

Printing Press—printing press operated by electricity—Thomas Davenport—1839

Printing Press—quadruple newspaper press —constructed—1887

Printing Press—rotary printing press—with continuous roll feed—produced—1871

Printing Press—rotary type printing press— manufactured—R. M. Hoe—1846

Printing Press—sextuple printing press— constructed—R. Hoe & Co.—1891

Prison—prison matrons—appointed—American Female Guardian Society—1845

Prison—reformatory for juvenile delinquents under legislative control—New York House of Refuge—opened—Jan. 1, 1825

Prize Fight—prize fight at which admission tickets sold at $100—Louis-Conn fight— June 19, 1946

Prize Fight—pugilist to hold three titles simultaneously—H. J. Armstrong—Aug. 17, 1938

Protestant Church—Reformed Dutch Church Negro pastor—J. J. Thomas

Protestant Episcopal Bishop—Protestant Episcopal bishop consecrated in the U.S.— T. J. Claggett—Sept. 17, 1792

Protestant Episcopal Bishop—Protestant Episcopal bishop (Negro)—S. D. Ferguson—consecrated—June 24, 1885

Pump—independent single direct-acting steam power pump—patented—H. R. Worthington—July 24, 1844

Puppet Show—Feb. 12, 1738

Quinine—quinine sulphate—manufactured— 1823

Radio Advertising—radio advertising contract for frequency modulation broadcasts —Dec. 9, 1940

Radio Broadcast—advertising or commercial radio broadcast—WEAF—Aug. 28, 1922

Radio Broadcast—chain broadcast—Polo Grounds—from Newark, N.J.—Oct. 7, 1922

Radio Broadcast—drama broadcast from a regular stage—WABC—Sept. 24, 1933

Radio Broadcast—football game (collegiate) coast-to-coast broadcast—Oct. 28, 1922

Radio Broadcast—foreign language course broadcast—WJZ—March 21, 1924

Radio Broadcast—network sponsored broadcast—Feb. 12, 1924

Radio Broadcast—news program (daily)— Sept. 1, 1922

Radio Broadcast—political speech by a President on radio—Calvin Coolidge— Feb. 12, 1924

Radio Broadcast—prize fight broadcast from the ringside—Dec. 22, 1920

Radio Broadcast—radio broadcast sent from an airplane—J. A. Macready—Sheepshead Bay, N.Y.—Aug. 27, 1910

Radio Broadcast—radio broadcast (two-way) from an airplane—Aug. 14, 1924

Radio Broadcast—radio concert from an airplane—April 14, 1922

Radio Broadcast—radio program simultaneously transmitted—over AM and FM stations and telecast—March 20, 1948

Radio Broadcast—recorded coast-to-coast broadcast—Hindenburg explosion—May 6, 1937

Radio Broadcast—ship-at-sea broadcast from an ocean liner—"Europa"—March 25, 1930

Radio Broadcast—singer to broadcast—E. H. Farrar—Dec. 16, 1907

Radio Broadcast—transatlantic radio message of the regular westward service— Oct. 17, 1907

Radio Church—established—Nov. 27, 1921

Radio Distress Signal—radio SOS from an American ship—"Arapahoe"—Aug. 11, 1909

Radio Facsimile Transmission—check sent by radio across the Atlantic Ocean— against Bankers Trust Co.—April 20, 1926

Radio Facsimile Transmission—drawing sent by radio across the Atlantic—transmitted—May 2, 1926

Radio Facsimile Transmission—photograph sent by radio across the Atlantic—July 6, 1924

Radio Facsimile Transmission—photograph sent by radio across the Atlantic as a public demonstration—Nov. 30, 1924

Radio Facsimile Transmission—photograph sent by radio across the Atlantic inaugurating commercial service—April 30, 1926

Radio Facsimile Transmission—photograph sent by radio across the continent (commercial)—from San Francisco, Calif.— April 18, 1925

Radio Facsimile Transmission—radio facsimile long distance transmission of a medical subject—May 28, 1925

Radio Facsimile Transmission—transpacific and transcontinental facsimile transmission—May 6, 1925

NEW YORK—New York City—*Continued*

Ship—radar installation aboard a commercial carrier—"African Star"—April 27, 1946

Ship—rotor ship—arrived—May 9, 1926

Ship—ship permitted to enter port without stopping for quarantine procedure — "Cameronia"—arrived—Feb. 1, 1937

Ship—ship to transport fresh orange juice in stainless steel tanks—"Tropicana"—arrived—Feb. 19, 1957

Ship—steam-propelled frigate—"Demologos"—launched—Oct. 29, 1814

Ship — steamboat built in America to cross the Atlantic Ocean — "Savannah"—launched—Aug. 22, 1818

Ship—steamboat service (regular) across the Atlantic—arrived—April 23, 1838

Ship—steamboat to make an ocean voyage —to Philadelphia—June 10, 1809

Ship — steamboat to make regular trips — "Clermont"—trial trip—Aug. 7, 1807

Ship — steamship passenger line between United States ports and Europe to fly the American flag—sailed—June 1, 1847

Ship—trading ship sent to China — "Empress of China"—left—Feb. 22, 1784

Ship — tugboat (steam) — "Rufus King"—built—1825

Ship — warship propelled by electricity — "New Mexico"—launched—April 23, 1917

Ship—warship to circumnavigate the globe —"Vincennes"—left—Aug. 31, 1826

Shipping — coastal shipping service—established—T. L. Servoss—to New Orleans—1831

Shoe Pegging Machine — operated—C. D. Bigelow—1852

Shoot-the-Chutes—built—Paul Boyton—1894

Single Tax—single tax national conference —assembled—Sept. 1, 1890

Skating Rink—ice skating rink (indoor)—built—1879

Skee Ball Alley—built—1914

Skywriting—skywriting—Nov. 28, 1922

Skywriting—skywriting at night—Sept. 18, 1937

Sleeping Car—transcontinental through Pullman sleeping car service—to Los Angeles—March 30, 1946

Snow-Melting Apparatus—snow-melting apparatus—patented—N. H. Borgfeldt—April 6, 1869

Snow-Melting Apparatus—snow-melting apparatus (practical) with pipe imbedded in the sidewalk—tested—Dec. 8, 1946

Soap—soap in liquid form — patented —William Sheppard—Aug. 22, 1865

Soap Manufacturer—to render fats in his plant—William Colgate—1806

Social Register—*Society List and Club Register*—published—1886

Social Science Society (national) — American Social Science Association—founded —1865

Soda Water Machine Manufacturer—John Matthews—1834

Soup Company—Franco-American Food Co. —organized—Nov. 1886

Sports—amateur athletic competition (interclub)—Sept. 27, 1879

Sports—amateur indoor athletic games—Nov. 11, 1868

Sports—amateur outdoor athletic games—Oct. 21, 1871

Sports—athletic club—New York Athletic Club—organized—Sept. 8, 1868

Sports—cross country championships—Nov. 6, 1883

Sports—sports trainer (professional)—Bob Rogers—May 1, 1883

Sports Book—of importance—*The Sportsman's Companion*—published—1783

Squash Club—squash tennis organization (national)—formed—March 20, 1911

Squash Tournament—April 8-10, 1911

Stage Coach Inter-City Service—to Philadelphia—Nov. 9, 1756

State Department (U.S.)—State Department (U.S.)—established—July 27, 1789

State Department (U.S.)—State Department (U.S.) Secretary — Thomas Jefferson — March 22, 1790

Steam Distribution Plant—formed—July 26, 1880

Steam Engine—steam engine—imported—Sept. 9, 1753

Steeplechase—Jerome Park—Oct. 26, 1869

Stenotype—patented—J. C. Zachos—April 11, 1876

Stereotype—automatic plate-casting and finishing machine for stereotype printing—invented—H. A. W. Wood—1900

Stereotype—curved stereotype plate—cast—Charles Craske—1854

Stereotype—stereotypers—successful—D. & G. Bruce—1813

Stock Quotation Board—automatic electric stock quotation board—installed—May 21, 1929

Stock Quotation Board—stock quotation boards—manufactured—1889

Stove—electronic range for domestic use—introduced—Oct. 25, 1955

Street Car—electric street car successfully run with current generated by a stationary dynamo—invented—S. D. Field—1874

Street Car—street car—Nov. 14, 1832

Street Car—street car company—incorporated—April 25, 1831

Strike—strike—bakers—1741

Students' Federation (international)—Pan American Student League—founded—1920

Submarine—submarine contract of the U.S. Navy—J. P. Holland Torpedo Boat Co.—March 13, 1895

Submarine—submarine that was practical and able to submerge—submerged—March 17, 1898

Subway—pneumatic subway—invented—A. E. Beach—in operation—Feb. 26, 1870

Subway—subway (rapid transit)—opened—Oct. 27, 1904

Subway—train to run automatically without conductors or motormen—Jan. 4, 1962

Sugar—sugar and glucose from cornstarch—manufactured

Sulfanilamide—sulfanilamide as a treatment for infections of streptococcic origins—used—1935

Supreme Court (U.S.)—Chief Justice of the Supreme Court—John Jay—appointed—Sept. 24, 1789

Supreme Court (U.S.)—Supreme Court justice who was nominated but who did not serve—R. H. Harrison—Sept. 24, 1789

Supreme Court (U.S.)—Supreme Court of the U.S.—first session—Feb. 1, 1790

Surgical Operation—epileptic case treated by elevation of the skull cap—demonstrated—Nov. 2, 1933

Surgical Operation—mastoid operation—performed—June 15, 1859

Swedish Magazine—*Skandinavia*—published—Jan. 15, 1847

Swimming Championship (amateur open)—Sept. 30, 1877

Sword Swallower — Senaa Samma — performed—Nov. 11, 1817

Symphony—symphonic work to call for an airplane propeller—*Ballet Mécanique*—performance—April 10, 1927

Tabulating Machine — patented — Herman Hollerith—Jan. 8, 1889

Talking Book—for the blind—issued—July 1934

Tape Recording—radio broadcast from a tape recording—WQXR—Aug. 26, 1938

Tape Recording—video recording on magnetic tape televised coast-to-coast—Oct. 23, 1956

Tariff—tariff legislation—July 4, 1789

Tattoo—electric tattoo machine—used—1875

Tattoo—tattoo shop—opened—1846

Tattoo — tattooed man — exhibited—J. F. O'Connell—Oct. 21, 1849

Teachers' Death Benefit—1869

Teachers' Pension Fund—authorized—April 14, 1894

Teachers' Sick Benefit Funds—established—1887

Telegram — singing telegram — introduced—Feb. 10, 1933

Telegraph—telegraph — constructed—H. G. Dyar—1827

Telegraph—telegraph call boxes—installed—June 22, 1872

Telegraph—telegraph convention (national)—July 17, 1850

Telegraph—telegraph line to the Pacific coast—in operation—Oct. 24, 1861

Telegraph—telegraph ticker to operate at high speed—installed—Nov. 1929

Telegraph—telegraph ticker to print letters of the alphabet—R. E. House—patented—April 18, 1846

Telegraph — telegraph ticker used by a brokerage concern—installed—Dec. 29, 1867

Telephone—commercial telephone service on railroad trains for passengers—Aug. 15, 1947

Telephone—interstate telephone call—from New Brunswick, N.J.—May 17, 1877

Telephone—mobile transatlantic telephone conversation between two telephone-equipped automobiles—from Milan—June 26, 1947

Telephone—round-the-world telephone conversation—April 25, 1935

Telephone—telephone conversation over the transoceanic telephone cable—to London, England—Sept. 25, 1956

Telephone — telephone switchboard with Braille markings—installed—April 1, 1928

Telephone—transatlantic telephone service—commercial—Jan. 7, 1927

Telephone—transcontinental telephone demonstration—Jan. 25, 1915

Television—municipal television film unit—established—Feb. 15, 1949

Television—television eyewitness allowed to testify in a federal court—Jan. 29, 1951

Television—Mobile Unit—mobile television unit—delivered—Dec. 12, 1937

Television—Mobile Unit—mobile television units (color)—WNBT—Jan. 1, 1954

Television—Telecast—art auction televised on a coast-to-coast circuit—April 27, 1960

Television—Telecast—audience participation telecast—Aug. 7, 1941

Television—Telecast—baseball game (collegiate) telecast—May 17, 1939

Television—Telecast—baseball games (major league) televised—Aug. 26, 1939

Television—Telecast—basball games televised in color—Aug. 11, 1951

Television—Telecast—baseball World Series game televised—Sept. 30, 1947

Television—Telecast—baseball World Series game televised in color—Sept. 28, 1955

Television—Telecast—basketball game to be televised—Feb. 28, 1940

Television—Telecast—book review to be televised—May 3, 1938

Television—Telecast—Catholic Mass (midnight) to be televised—Dec. 24, 1948

Television—Telecast—church service televised in sign language—Dec. 5, 1948

Television—Telecast—circus telecast—April 25, 1940

Television—Telecast—color and black-and-white telecast to be sponsored—Dec. 24, 1953

Television — Telecast — color coast-to-coast live telecast—to Burbank, Calif.—Nov. 3, 1953

Television—Telecast—color commercial televised on a local show—commissioned—March 9, 1954

Television—Telecast—color program (commercial)—June 25, 1951

Television—Telecast—color television demonstration of high definition electronically scanned images—Sept. 3, 1940

Television—Telecast—color television demonstration (public)—June 27, 1929

Television—Telecast—demonstration of home reception of television—Aug. 20, 1930

Television—Telecast—fashion show telecast—May 17, 1939

NEW YORK—New York City—*Continued*

Television—Telecast—football game (collegiate) to be telecast—Sept. 30, 1939

Television—Telecast—football game (professional) to be televised—Oct. 22, 1939

Television—Telecast—high definition telecast —June 29, 1936

Television—Telecast—hockey game to be televised—Feb. 25, 1940

Television—Telecast—husband and wife to broadcast a religious program—Dr. and Mrs. N. V. Peale—Oct. 1, 1952

Television—Telecast—Jewish temple services (complete) to be televised—Nov. 4, 1951

Television—Telecast—king and queen to be televised—June 10, 1939

Television — Telecast — medical symposium televised coast to coast on a closed circuit —Sept. 23, 1954

Television—Telecast—missing persons telecast—Oct. 3, 1943

Television—Telecast—moving picture premiere festivities to be televised—Dec. 19, 1939

Television—Telecast—moving picture premiere performance to be televised—April 10, 1944

Television—Telecast—moving picture premiere performance to be televised (feature-length foreign film)—Jan. 1, 1948

Television—Telecast—moving picture premiere performance to be televised (major film)—Nov. 6, 1955

Television—Telecast—moving picture trailer to be televised—Sept. 20, 1946

Television—Telecast—musical comedy (full length) written especially for television— Sept. 28, 1944

Television—Telecast—musical comedy telecast (one-hour)—July 25, 1939

Television—Telecast—newsreel telecast presented daily—Feb. 16, 1948

Television—Telecast—opera (complete) to be televised from the Metropolitan Opera House—Nov. 29, 1948

Television—Telecast—opera (major) televised in color—*Carmen*—Oct. 31, 1953

Television—Telecast—opera telecast—March 10, 1940

Television—Telecast—opera written for television—*Amahl and the Night Visitors*—Dec. 24, 1951

Television—Telecast—opera written for television on commission for a commercial sponsor—*The Parrot*—March 24, 1953

Television—Telecast—operetta to be televised—June 20, 1939

Television—Telecast—outdoor scenes to be televised—July 12, 1928

Television—Telecast—pay television presentation of an opera—closed circuit—Dec. 11, 1952

Television—Telecast—play to be televised as a full-hour program—June 29, 1939

Television—Telecast—play to be televised with its original Broadway cast—June 7, 1938

Television — Telecast — political campaign telecast—Oct. 11, 1932

Television—Telecast—President to appear on television—F. D. Roosevelt—April 30, 1939

Television—Telecast—prize fight (heavyweight championship bout) to be televised —Joe Louis-Billy Conn—June 19, 1946

Television—Telecast—prize fight televised in color—March 19, 1954

Television—Telecast—prize fight to be televised—Lou Nova-Max Baer—June 1, 1939

Television—Telecast—religious services to be televised—March 24, 1940

Television—Telecast—sales meeting televised—Jan. 9, 1940

Television — Telecast — simulcast presented regularly by a sponsor—Feb. 21, 1940

Television—Telecast — split-screen image — exhibited—Dec. 8, 1948

Television — Telecast — standard broadcast station to transmit a television image— received—Aug. 13, 1928

Television—Telecast — stockholders' annual meeting televised on a closed circuit—April 16, 1957

Television—Telecast—stockholders' meetings televised coast-to-coast simultaneously— Oct. 29, 1959

Television—Telecast—symphonic concerts to be televised—March 20, 1948

Television — Telecast — telecast (long distance) received in an airplane—Oct. 17, 1939

Television—Telecast—telecast of image and sound—transmitted over any considerable distance—from Washington, D.C.—April 7, 1927

Television—Telecast—telecast (public) over telephone wires—May 20, 1939

Television—Telecast—telecast received from England—June 18, 1959

Television—Telecast—telecast using coaxial cable—June 10, 1936

Television—Telecast—tennis tournament to be televised in color—Davis Cup matches —Aug. 26, 1955

Television—Telecast—track meet (intercollegiate) to be televised—March 2, 1940

Television—Telecast—transcontinental telecast received on the west coast—Sept. 23, 1951

Television—Telecast — two-way demonstration of television in a theatre—April 9, 1930

Television—Telecast — under-water telecast from a submarine—April 10, 1947

Television—Telecast—unscheduled event to be televised—Nov. 15, 1938

Television—Telecast—weather map telecast to a transatlantic steamer—June 20, 1930

Television License—commercial television license—granted—July 1, 1941

Television License—construction permit—for commercial station—June 17, 1941

Television Receiver—coin-operated television receiver—exhibited—Nov. 7, 1946

Television Receiver—television receiver to permit two audiences to see and hear two different programs at the same time—demonstrated—**Jan. 7, 1954**

Tennis — lawn tennis — introduced — M. E. Outerbridge—March 1874

Tennis Match—intercollegiate court tennis match—May 4, 1954

Tennis Match—lawn tennis tournament of national scope—Staten Island Club—Sept. 1, 1880

Tennis Match—national tennis tournament of the United States Lawn Tennis Association in which a Negro woman competed —Aug. 1950

Tennis Player—lawn tennis champion to win four major titles—J. D. Budge—Sept. 24, 1938

Tennis Player—Negro tennis player to participate in a U.S. indoor Lawn Tennis Association championship tournament— Reginald Weir—March 11, 1948

Tennis Society—tennis society (national)— United States Lawn Tennis Association —formed—May 21, 1881

Terramycin—announced—Jan. 27, 1950

Theater—newsreel theater—Nov. 2, 1929

Theater—panorama show—1790

Theater—television theater demonstration of a sports event on a full-size screen—April 14, 1948

Theater—theater lighted by gas—Chatham Garden—May 8, 1825

Theater—theater to employ women ushers —Majestic Theater—Dec. 16, 1903

Theater History—of importance—published —William Dunlap—*History of the American Theatre*—1832

Theatrical Advance Publicity Man—Robert Upton—1750

Theatrical School—devoted exclusively to training for the professional stage—founded—Oct. 1, 1884

Theological School — theological school — founded—1784

Theosophical Society—American Theosophical Society—founded—Nov. 17, 1875

Ticket Speculators—operated—Sept. 1850

Tightrope—woman tightrope performer— performance—June 1, 1819

Tinware Manufacturers—successful tinware manufacturers — factory opened — Woodhaven—1860

Tour of the World—passenger to fly around the world on commercial air lines in less than 100 hours—H. C. Boren—landed— June 25, 1953

Tour of the World—tour of the world made by a woman traveling alone—Nelly Bly— left—Nov. 14, 1889

Toyery—opened—Sept. 24, 1932

Tract Society—tract society (national)— American Tract Society—organized—May 11, 1825

Trademark (U.S.)—registered—Oct. 25, 1870

Traffic Regulation—one-way traffic regulation—Dec. 17, 1791

Traffic Regulation—traffic law—enacted— June 27, 1652

Traffic Regulation Pamphlet—printed traffic regulations—issued—Oct. 30, 1903

Traitor to the American cause—William Demont—Nov. 2, 1776

Trapshooting—trapshooting intercollegiate association—formed—March 25, 1898

Trapshooting Tournament—trapshoot (Grand American) with clay targets—June 12, 1900

Trapshooting Tournament—trapshoot (Grand American) with live birds—March 1893

Travelers Aid Society—Travelers Aid Society (national)—founded—1904

Treadmill—used—New York City Prison— Sept. 7, 1822

Treason—American colonist hanged for treason—Jacob Leisler—May 16, 1691

Trust — manufacturers' price regulation agreement—coopers—Dec. 17, 1679

Tuberculosis Circular—issued—July 1889

Tuberculosis Laboratory—tuberculosis diagnostic community laboratory—authorized —Dec. 13, 1893

Tunnel—tunnel under the Hudson River— opened officially—Feb. 25, 1908

Tunnel—twin-tube subaqueous vehicular tunnel—Holland Tunnel—opened—Nov. 13, 1927

Typesetting Machine—linotype machine used commercially—installed—July 1, 1886

Typesetting Machine—photographic type-composing machine—book set by the Photon process—*The Wonderful World of Insects*—1953

Typesetting Machine—typesetting machine —practical — patented — Timothy Alden— Sept. 15, 1857

Typewriter—typewriter to produce a line of writing visible as it was being typed— patented—May 16, 1893

Typewriting School—opened—1878

Unitarian Church Convention (national)— assembled—April 5, 1865

Vacation Fund—established—1847

Vaccine—poliomyelitis vaccine—produced— Feb. 1933

Vaccine—tuberculosis vaccine—effective—developed—1928

Veterinary Hospital—opened—C. C. Grice— 1830

Veterinary School—veterinary college of importance—incorporated—April 6, 1857

Vice Presidential Candidate—Negro vice presidential candidate—nominated—May 10, 1872

Visiting Celebrities—absolute monarch— King Prajadhipok—arrived—April 1931

Visiting Celebrities—queen to visit the U.S. —Queen Emma—arrived—Aug. 8, 1866

Vivisection—to show process of life—J. C. Dalton—1855

Voice Mechanism—voice mechanism capable of creating the complex sounds of speech —exhibited—June 5, 1938

War Veterans' Society—Military Order of Foreign Wars—founded—Dec. 27, 1894

Water Cures—introduced—Nov. 1, 1853

Water Ski Tournament (national)—June 22, 1939

Wax Works Museum—opened—June 1749

Wedding—double radio wedding—Dec. 22, 1922

NEW YORK—New York City—*Continued*

Wedding—parachute wedding—August 25, 1940

Weights and Measures Standardization—national organization to improve systems of weights, measures, and moneys—American Metrological Society—formed—Dec. 30, 1873

Welsh Magazine—*Cymro Americaidd*—published—1832

Woman—woman automotive engineer—received M.E. degree—June 5, 1922

Woman—woman horseback rider to make a solo transcontinental trip—N. J. Aspinwall—arrived—July 8, 1911

Woman—woman sculptor honored by membership in the National Academy of Design—1919

Woman Suffrage—woman suffrage association (national)—American Equal Rights Association—constitution adopted—May 10, 1866

Women's Club—Chinese women's club incorporated—June 10, 1936

Women's Club—women's club federation—organized—March 20, 1890

Women's Club—women's professional club—founded—March 21, 1868

Works Progress Administration—Works Progress Administration Federal Art Project Gallery—officially opened—Dec. 28, 1935

World War I—American troop contingent to arrive in France—left—May 8, 1917

World War I—American troops to land in England—sailed—May 28, 1917

World War II—American ship sunk by a U-boat—sailed—May 6, 1941

X-ray—fluoro-record reflector camera—announced—Nov. 18, 1950

X-Ray—X-ray machine—exhibited—Jan. 18, 1896

X-Ray—X-ray moving pictures (successful) of the action of the human heart—exhibited—Oct. 2, 1937

X-Ray—X-ray of the entire body of a living person—taken—April 1897

Yacht Club—New York Yacht Club—organized—July 30, 1844

Yacht Race—regatta—of importance—July 16, 1845

Yiddish Professorship—established—Columbia University—Feb. 11, 1952

Young Men's Hebrew Association—founded—March 22, 1874

Young Women's Hebrew Association—organized—Feb. 6, 1902

Zionist Society—Zionist national organization—United American Zionists—formed—Oct. 22, 1897

Newburgh

Botanist—botanist—landscape gardener—A. J. Downing—1841

Ferryboat—double-deck ferryboat—launched—Oct. 25, 1888

Ferryboat—double-deck ferryboat with the propeller-type steel hull—built—1891

Ferryboat—steel-hull ferryboat—"Lackawanna"—built—1881

Medal—Order of the Purple Heart—established—Aug. 7, 1782

Soap—cakes of soap of uniform weight and individually wrapped—manufactured—Jessie Oakley—c. 1830

Newport

Lock—lock ("clock")—double locks—patented—Linus Yale—May 6, 1851

Newton Creek

Oil—oil (kerosene)—patent—Abraham Gesner—March 27, 1855

Niagara County

Fruit Spraying—with Paris green—1878

Niagara Falls

Bridge—railway suspension bridge—completed—1854

Niagara Falls—person to cross Niagara Falls on a tightrope—J. F. Gravelet—June 30, 1859

Niagara Falls—person to go over Niagara Falls in a barrel—A. E. Taylor—Oct. 24, 1901

Niagara Falls—person to go over Niagara Falls in a rubber ball—Jean Lussier—July 4, 1928

Niagara Falls—utilization of Niagara Falls waterpower—1757

Niagara Falls—utilization of Niagara Falls waterpower (large scale)—June 13, 1889

Photograph—photograph to gain world fame—taken—July 1845

Visiting Celebrities—King and Queen of England—arrived—June 7, 1939

Nieuw Amsterdam

See New York City

North Elba

Bobsled Run—of international specifications—opened—Dec. 25, 1930

Oceanside

Boy Scouts of America—Boy Scout to become an eagle scout—A. R. Eldred—Aug. 21, 1912

Cantor—Jewish woman cantor—Betty Robbins—first service—Sept. 15, 1955

Olean

Gas—natural gas for manufacturing—used—1870

Oneida Community

Traps—steel animal traps—commercially manufactured—Sewell Newhouse—1855

Oneida County

Animals—fur-bearing animals—raised commercially—1866

Ossining

Execution—execution (federal) for the killing of a Federal Bureau of Investigation agent—Gerhard Puff—Aug. 12, 1954

Execution—execution of a woman—M. M. Place—March 20, 1899

Fingerprinting—state prison to take fingerprints—Sing Sing Prison—March 3, 1903

Treason—execution for treason in peacetime —June 19, 1953

Oswego

Normal School—normal school (state) at which students actually conducted classes —established—May 1, 1861

Ship—steamboat engine built in America for a screw-propelled vessel—ship enrolled April 14, 1842

Oyster Bay

Cable—cable across the Pacific Ocean between Honolulu, Midway, Guam, and Manila—official message sent—July 4, 1903

Pearl River

Aureomycin—aureomycin chlorotetracycline —released—1948

Peekskill

Automobile Hill Climbing Contest—Sept. 9, 1901

"First Aid" Instruction—given—1885

Pelham Manor

Glass—stained figure glass—manufactured— 1844

Plattsburg

College—college principally for war veterans —opened—Sept. 16, 1946

Physiologist—of note—William Beaumont— report published—1833

Poplar Ridge

Plow—plow with interchangeable parts— patented—J. J. Wood—Sept. 1, 1819

Port Chester

Bread—frozen bread—marketed—Nov. 3, 1952

Port Washington

Aviation—Flights (transatlantic) — Atlantic ocean scheduled air service—left—May 20, 1939

Aviation—Flights (transatlantic) — transatlantic regular commercial airplane service —left—June 28, 1939

Aviation—Passenger—woman to fly entirely around the world by commercial heavier-than-air plane—last lap—June 17, 1939

Glider—seaplane glider—flight—March 15, 1930

Poughkeepsie

Ice Yacht—built—Oliver Booth—1790

Ice Yacht Club—organized—1861

Insurance—group insurance policy for college students—Feb. 1, 1936

Philological Society—national philological society—American Philological Association—convention—July 27, 1869

Pin—machine "for sticking pins into paper" —patented—Samuel Slocum—Sept. 30, 1841

Pin—pins manufactured with a solid head— Samuel Slocum—1838

Railroad Car—rail detector car—demonstrated—Sept. 13, 1928

Water Purification—water purification by filtration—1870

Riverdale

See New York City

Rochester

Automobile Patent—G. B. Selden—May 8, 1879

Business — installment finance company — meeting—April 7, 1904

Business School—business school—opened— 1842

Camera — roll film camera — announced — George Eastman—June 1888

Check Photographing Device—patented— Feb. 25, 1930

Check Protectors—manufactured—1870

Communion Cup—individual communion cups—introduced—May 1894

Electrobasograph—invented—R. P. Schwartz 1933

Goat Show—(of milch goats)—Sept. 15-27, 1913

Lock—time-lock—manufactured—Sargent & Greenleaf—1874

Milk Station (municipal)—established—1897

Music—community chorus — established — 1912

Newspaper—newspaper association—convention—Feb. 16, 1887

Photograph — infra-red photograph — taken —Oct. 7, 1931

Photograph—photograph from an airplane at night—taken—Nov. 20, 1925

Photographic Film — moving picture film (commercial) — manufactured—March 26, 1885

Photographic Film—transparent paper strip photographic film — patented — George Eastman—Oct. 14, 1884

NEW YORK—Rochester—*Continued*

Photostat — photographic copying machine —commercially manufactured—1910

Postal Service—mail chute—patented—J. G. Cutler—Sept. 11, 1883

Presidential Candidate—presidential candidate of Negro blood nominated — Frederick Douglass—June 23, 1888

Railroad Car—glass-lined tank car—built—1910

Social-Democratic Party of America—convention—Jan. 27, 1900

Street Car—transfers (printed)—used—Oct. 31, 1892

Temperance Society—women's temperance society (state)—founded—April 20, 1852

Time Recorder—card time recorder—patented—D. M. Cooper—Oct. 30, 1894

Vending Machine—vending machine—automatically operated—produced—1897

X-Ray—X-ray photograph of the entire body taken in a one-second exposure—A. W. Fuchs—July 1, 1934

X-Ray—X-ray photograph showing the complete arterial circulation—completed—July 16, 1936

Rome

Cheese Factory—cheese factory of consequence—established—1851

Roosevelt Field

See Garden City

Rye

Television—Telecast—tennis tournament to be televised—Aug. 9, 1939

Sackets Harbor

Chloroform — distilled — Samuel Guthrie — 1831

Glucose—from potato starch—refined—Samuel Guthrie—1831

Saint Regis

War (1812)—prisoners in the War of 1812—captured—Oct. 22-23, 1812

Saranac Lake

Hospital—tuberculosis sanatorium (modern)—opened—Feb. 1, 1885

Tuberculosis Laboratory—tuberculosis research laboratory—established—1894

Saratoga Springs

Bankers' Association—national bankers' association—convention—July 20, 1875

Economics Association—American Economic Association—founded—Sept. 9, 1885

Historical Society—historical society (general)—American Historical Association—founded—Sept. 10, 1884

Intercollegiate Athletic Association—organized—June 1876

Lawyers' Association—lawyers' association (national)—American Bar Association—organized—Aug. 21, 1878

Temperance Society — temperance society (union) — Union Temperate Society — organized—April 13, 1808

Time (standard)—suggested—C. F. Dowd—1870

Track Meet (intercollegiate)—July 20-21, 1876

Schenectady

Air Brake—patented—George Westinghouse, Jr.—April 13, 1869

Air Mail Service—jet propelled airplane to transport mail—June 22, 1946

Automaton—automaton to operate by long-distance control — announced — May 23, 1956

Automobile—automobile (new type gasoline-electric combination) — delivered — Aug. 30, 1929

Automobile License Plates—plastic license plate tabs—manufactured—1942

Bridge—wrought iron lattice girder railroad bridge—1859

Diamond—pilot plant for the actual production of man-made diamonds—production announced—Feb. 15, 1955

Diathermy Machine — practical — manufactured—Dec. 1928

Electric Lighting—sodium vapor lamps—installed—June 13, 1933

Electric Power Plant—mobile electric power plant—delivered—Jan. 10, 1944

Fraternity Catalog—published—1830

Fraternity (Greek letter)—social fraternity—Kappa Alpha—established—Nov. 26, 1825

Golf Clubs (or golf sticks)—steel shaft for a golf club—patented—A. F. Knight—Nov. 22, 1910

High Jumping Standards—using electric eye detectors—used—May 31, 1941

Industrial Research Laboratory—opened—Sept. 1900

Light Beam Communication—from a dirigible—May 19, 1932

Locomotive — duplex compound locomotive (Mallet)—built—1904

Locomotive — rack-rail diesel-electric locomotive—built—1939

Locomotive Headlight—talking headlight—installed—Nov. 6, 1934

Microscope—microscope for examing structure of materials—installed—Sept. 1951

Photograph—photograph of a beam of 1 billion-volt X-rays—made—Oct. 1946

Photography—photographic flashlight lamps —manufactured—1930

Radio Broadcast—dinner broadcast round the world—April 20, 1927

Radio Broadcast—drama (full-length melodrama) broadcast—Aug. 3, 1922

Radio Broadcast—radio broadcast heard in both the Arctic and the Antarctic regions —Sept. 23, 1934

Radio Broadcast—round the world broadcast W2XAD—June 30, 1930

Radio Station—radio station operating a 50-kilowatt transmitter—2XAG—in operation —July 29, 1925

Radio Station—radio station operating a 100-kilowatt transmitter—2XAG—Aug. 4, 1927

Radio Telephone—two-way radio conversation between a brakeman in a caboose of a moving freight train and an engineer in the cab of a locomotive—demonstrated—June 15, 1927

Radio Tube—radio tube—of metal—announced—April 1, 1935

Ship—radar installation aboard a commercial carrier—General Electric Co.—April 27, 1946

Stroboradiograph—announced—Aug. 14, 1956

Television—Telecast—moving picture premiere performance to be televised—April 10, 1944

Television—Telecast—opera (complete) to be televised—presented—Dec. 23, 1943

Television—Telecast—play to be televised—Queen's Messenger—Sept. 11, 1928

Television—Telecast — presidential nomination notification ceremony to be televised —Aug. 22, 1928

Television—Telecast — programs regularly televised—WGY—May 11, 1928

Television—Telecast—speaker to address an organization by television—April 1, 1930

Television—Telecast—telecast produced for a tri-city gathering—Dec. 8, 1939

Television — Telecast — television network demonstration (long distance)—Feb. 1, 1940

Theater—television theater demonstration—May 22, 1930

Theatrical School—theatrical school sponsored by an institution of higher learning —courses—July 2, 1935

Tungsten — ductile tungsten — produced — W. D. Coolidge—1908

Seneca Falls

Bloomers—introduced—July 19, 1848

Woman Suffrage—convention of women advocating woman suffrage—July 19-20, 1848

Sheepshead Bay

See New York City

Sloatsburg

Cotton Twine Factory—Jacob Sloat—1839

South Butler

Woman—woman ordained a minister—A. B. Blackwell—Sept. 15, 1853

Southampton

Golf Tournament—international golf match —Aug. 28-29, 1922

Whaling—whaling (systematic)—March 7, 1644

Spuyten Duyvil

See New York City

Staten Island

See New York City

Syracuse

Automobile Tire—pneumatic tire patent—Dec. 20, 1892

Basketball—basketball player (professional) to score more than 15,000 points—Dolph Schayes

Billiard Match — of importance — May 13, 1854

Citizenship and Public Affairs School—Oct. 3, 1924

Dental Chair—patented—M. W. Hanchett—Aug. 15, 1848

Fine Arts Department — fine arts department in a college to grant degrees—established—June 24, 1873

Horse Race—harness horse race (Hambletonian) for three-year-olds—Aug. 30, 1926

Presbyterian Church—woman ordained a minister—M. E. Towner—Oct. 24, 1956

Road—plank road—completed—July 18, 1846

Time Recorder—dial time recorder — company formed—1893

Typewriter — electric portable typewriter — placed on sale—Feb. 4, 1957

Ticonderoga

Graphite—commercially produced—1840

Troy

Boy Scouts of America—Boy scout uniformed troop—1911

Collar—detached—made—H. L. Montague —1825

Collar Factory—1833

Collar Manufacturer—of detachable collars —Ebenezer Brown—1829

Engineering College—engineering college—Rensselaer School—founded—Nov. 5, 1824

Fraternity (Greek letter)—professional fraternity—Theta Xi—founded—April 29, 1864

Horseshoe Manufacturing Machine—patented —Henry Burden—Nov. 23, 1835

Laundry—established—Independence Starks —1835

Paper—wood-pulp and rag paper — for printing—manufactured—1854

Waffle Iron Patent—Cornelius Swarthout—Aug. 24, 1869

NEW YORK—*Continued*

Tuxedo Park

Building—building of pressed structural steel—June 1907

Coat — tuxedo coat — introduced—Oct. 10, 1886

Museum—outdoor museum (or nature trail) —established—1925

Utica

Business—five-cent store—opened—Feb. 22, 1879

Electric Transmission—electric power line commercial carrier—operated—Dec. 6, 1922

Fly Casting Tournament—June 18, 1861

Political Convention—nominating convention (state)—1824

Teachers' Convention—teachers' convention (state)—Jan. 1831

Valley Stream

Autogiro—autogiro to tow a glider—May 23, 1933

Aviation—Flights (transatlantic) — transatlantic non-stop flight from Europe to the United States—arrived—Sept. 2, 1930

Waddington

Thermit—used to break ice jams—Feb. 24, 1925

Wallkill

Creamery—established—1861

Warsaw

Anti-Slavery Party—first convention—Nov. 13, 1839

Watertown

Breakfast Food—shredded wheat biscuits—patented—Aug. 1, 1893

Watervliet

Conscientious Objectors—settled—1776

Shaker Society—Shaker "Family"—formed —1776

West Milton

Electric Power Plant—electric power generated from atomic energy to be sold commercially—July 18, 1955

Television—Telecast—commercial filmed by a camera operated by atomically generated electricity—televised—July 24, 1955

West Point

Army School—Army school—Military Academy of the United States—established—March 16, 1802

Army School—Army school graduate (Jewish)—S. M. Levy—Oct. 11, 1802

Army School—Army school graduate (Negro)—H. O. Flipper—June 1877

Army School — Army school graduates—Oct. 11, 1802

Blockade—across Hudson River—April 30, 1778

Football Game—Army-Navy football game —Nov. 29, 1890

Television—Telecast—President to appear on television in color—D. D. Eisenhower —June 7, 1955

Westbury

Golf Tournament—women's tournament golf championship—Nov. 1895

Whitestone

See New York City

Woodhaven

See New York City

Yonkers

Carpet Loom—carpet power loom to weave Axminster carpets — invented — Halcyon Skinner—1876

Golf Tournament—amateur golf tournament (unofficial)—Oct. 13, 1894

Hat Blocking and Shaping Machine—patented—April 3, 1866

Horse Race—harness race driver to win the Hambletonian four times—B. F. White—Aug. 11, 1943

Plastic—thermosetting man-made plastic — developed—L. H. Baekeland—1906

NORTH CAROLINA

Civil Government in America — Watauga Commonwealth—May 1772

Impeachment — impeachment and removal from office of a state governor—W. W. Holden—March 22, 1871

Nurse—nurses' registration law (state) — March 3, 1903

President (United States)—President born posthumously—Andrew Jackson—March 15, 1767

Asheville

Forest Management — professional scale — 1891

Hospital—tuberculosis sanatorium (private) —opened—1875

Biltmore

Forestry School—forestry school dealing exclusively with problems of forestry—Biltmore Forest School — opened — Sept. 1, 1898

Blakely

Railroad—interstate railroad—opened—1833

Cabarrus County

Gold—gold nugget—found—1799

Cape Hatteras

Radio Distress Signal—radio SOS from an American ship—received—Aug. 11, 1909
Smoke Screen—demonstrated—Sept. 5, 1923

Chapel Hill

Grammar Instruction in a College—University of North Carolina—1795
Marriage Course in a college—1924
Observatory — observatory (astronomical) connected with an institution of learning —University of North Carolina—1830
Planetarium—planetarium owned by a university—opened—May 10, 1949
Theater—state-owned theater dedicated to its own drama — Playmakers Theatre — opened—Nov. 23, 1925

Charlotte

Computer—mobile computer center—assignment undertaken—March 27, 1961
Declaration of Independence—declaration of independence by a colony—Mecklenburg declaration—adopted—May 20, 1775
Jewish Congregation—Jewish mobile synagogue—in operation—April 4, 1955
Tape Recording—video recording on magnetic tape in color—Sept. 5, 1958
Teletypesetter—teletypesetter circuit operated by a news agency—April 23, 1951

Davidson

X-Ray — X-ray photograph — made — Dr. H. L. Smith—Jan. 12, 1896

Fort Bragg

Army—helicopter battalion—activated—April 1, 1954
Court Martial—court martial trial in the United States at which enlisted men were allowed to sit as members of the court—Feb. 3, 1949
Medal — Expert Infantryman's Badge — awarded—W. L. Bull—March 29, 1944

Gastonia

Factory — air-conditioned factory — Gray Manufacturing Co.—1905
Greek College and Orphanage—dedicated—Sept. 18, 1932

Halifax

Declaration of Independence (American)— declaration of independence by a colony— authorized—April 12, 1776

Hertford

Postmaster—woman postmaster appointed after the adoption of the Constitution— Sarah De Crow—Sept. 27, 1792

Kitty Hawk

Aviation—Airplane—airplane to receive national acclaim—Wright brothers—flight— Dec. 17, 1903

Lexington

Silver Mine—Silver Hill Mine—discovered— 1838

Morehead City

Aviation—Coast Guard air station—opened —March 24, 1920

Newberne (New Bern)

Ordnance — gun (revolving) — made — John Gill—1829

Raleigh

Atomic Reactor—atomic reactor (privately operated)—Sept. 5, 1953
Blind—school for the Negro blind—opened —Jan. 4, 1869
Deaf—Students' Magazine—magazine for deaf students—*Deaf Mute Casket*—published —1851
Medical Clinic—contraceptive clinic (state) —opened—March 15, 1937
Nuclear Engineering College Course—students enrolled—June 12, 1950

Roanoke Island

Births—child born of English parents in America—Virginia Dare—Aug. 18, 1587

Salem

Cottonseed Hulling Machine — patented — John Lineback—March 31, 1814

Spray

Acetylene—manufactured—T. L. Willson— May 4, 1892
Carbide Factory—established—1894

Washington

Town Named for George Washington—1775

NORTH DAKOTA

Insurance—bonding law (state)—enacted— March 1, 1913
Insurance—fire and tornado insurance fund (state)—July 1, 1919
Insurance—hail insurance law (state)—enacted—March 18, 1911

NORTH DAKOTA—*Continued*

Legislator (state)—woman speaker of a state house of representatives—Jan. 3, 1933

State—states admitted to the Union simultaneously—North and South Dakota—Nov. 3, 1889

Portal

Visiting Celebrities — absolute monarch — King Prajadhipok of Siam—arrived in U.S.—April 19, 1931

OHIO

Employment Service — state employment service—authorized—April 28, 1890

High School Legislation—authorizing night classes—March 16, 1829

Judge—woman associate justice of a state supreme court—F. E. Allen—elected—Dec. 16, 1922

Labor Law—labor law regulating the working hours of women—March 29, 1852

Land Grant—land subsidy for internal improvements—April 30, 1802

Legislator (state)—Negro legislator (state)—Jan. 6, 1885

Telephone—telephone company answering service—March 1951

Territorial Expansion—acquisition of land by the federal government—Northwest Territory—established—July 13, 1787

War—battle fought by United States troops—after formation of Union—Oct. 19, 1790

Akron

Automobile Police Patrol Wagon—operated—1899

Automobile Tire—balloon tire production—introduced—April 5, 1923

Automobile Tire — clincher tire — manufactured—1899

Automobile Tire—cord tire—manufactured—1910

Automobile Tire—non-skid tire—patented—April 14, 1914

Automobile Tire—synthetic rubber tire—marketed—June 5, 1940

Automobile Tire—tubeless automobile tires—announced—May 11, 1947

Aviation—Airship—airship of the U.S. Navy that was successful—May 30, 1917

Aviation—Airship—airship to land on a roof—took off—May 23, 1919

Aviation—Airship—airship with an enclosed cabin—flight—June 3, 1925

Aviation—Airship—dirigible for private commercial operation—built 1930

Aviation—License—glider pilot's license—awarded—Oct. 7, 1930

Belt Conveyor System—belt conveyor more than four miles long

Bicycle Tire—bicycle tire (cord)—manufactured—B. F. Goodrich Co.—1892

Oat Crushing Machine—patented—Nov. 30, 1875

Road—synthetic rubber in asphaltic concrete resurfacing mixture—Sept. 7, 1948

Rubber—rubber company west of the Allegheny mountains—established—1870

Alliance

Basketball — basketball team (college) — formed—1892

College — college summer school — Mount Union College—1870

College—college to grant women absolutely equal rights — Mount Union College — founded—Oct. 20, 1846

Ashtabula

Election Law — proportional representation election—Nov. 2, 1915

Athens

College—university founded by a federal land grant—Ohio University—opened—June 1, 1808

Barberton

Match—"book matches"—made—1896

Bellefontaine

Road—concrete road—1892

Cadiz

Coal—coal pipeline unit (demonstration)—in operation—Nov. 1, 1951

Coal—commercial coal pipeline—in operation—June 4, 1957

Canton

Football Club—football association (professional)—formed—Sept. 17, 1920

President (United States)—president who had used a telephone for campaigning--William McKinley—1896

Chillicothe

Animals—cattle importation of purebred shorthorns—1834

Animals—cattle (shorthorn) public auction sale—Oct. 29, 1836

Book—book (of size) completed entirely by one man—Dard Hunter—1923

Cincinnati

Ambulance—hospital ambulance service

Anarchist — Josiah Warren — "time store"—opened—1827

Astronomy Magazine—*Sidereal Messenger*—published—July 1846

Automobile — right-hand-drive automobile for the delivery of mail—in service—Dec. 27, 1951

Baseball Game—baseball game at night by major league teams — played — May 24, 1935

Baseball Player — major league baseball player to pitch two successive no-hit no-run games—first game—June 11, 1938

Baseball Team—baseball team to receive a regular salary—1869

Battery—battery to convert radioactive energy into electrical energy—announced —P. E. Ohmart—Dec. 31, 1951

Caterpillar Club—woman Caterpillar Club member—Irene McFarland—June 28, 1925

Continuation School — apprentice continuation school—established—Aug. 30, 1909

Dental School—dental assistants' and nurses' course—Oct. 3, 1910

Dentist—woman dentist to obtain a D.D.S. degree—graduated—Feb. 21, 1866

Detergent—synthetic detergent—for home use—marketed—Oct. 10, 1933

Dictionary—phonetic dictionary — published —1855

Fire Department—fire department to be paid a salary—April 1, 1853

Fire Engine—fire engine that was practical —tested—Jan. 1, 1853

Hospital—tuberculosis hospital (municipal) for consumptive poor — opened — July 8, 1897

Jewish College—Jewish college to train men for the rabbinate—Hebrew Union College —established—Oct. 3, 1875

Liberal Republican Party—convention—May 1, 1872

Manufacturers' Association — national organization—formed—Jan. 22, 1895

Medical Instruction—ophthalmology professor—Elkanah Williams—1865

Moving Picture—peep show machine—patented—S. D. Goodale—Feb. 5, 1861

Music—saengerfest—1849

People's Party—organized—May 19, 1891

Political Convention — presidential convention (national) addressed by a woman— S. A. Spencer—June 15, 1876

Prize Fight—prize fight of importance under the Marquis of Queensberry rules — Aug. 29, 1885

Radio License—radio license—G. H. Lewis —1911

Railroad—municipal railroad—service commenced—July 23, 1877

Railroad Car—chapel car—"Evangel"—dedicated—May 23, 1891

Shortening—shortening made by the hydrogenation process—Aug. 15, 1911

Soap—soap to float—manufactured—1878

Trapshooting—clay pigeon target—patented —George Ligowsky—Sept. 7, 1880

Union Labor Party—formed—Feb. 22, 1887

Union Reform Party—platform adopted— March 1, 1899

United Labor Party—organized—May 16, 1888

Wedding—balloon wedding—Oct. 19, 1874

Woman—woman Presbyterian elder — permission granted—May 31, 1930

Yeast—compressed fresh yeast—introduced —Charles Fleischmann—1868

Yeast—yeast preparation patent—J. T. Alden—Nov. 3, 1863

Cleveland

Advertisement—automobile advertisement— Winton Motor Car Co.—July 30, 1898

Autogiro—autogiro to loop the loop publicly Aug. 27, 1932

Automobile Mail Wagon—constructed—1899

Automobile Truck—automobile truck completely streamlined—Sept. 4, 1935

Aviation—air-rail passenger transcontinental service—June 14, 1929

Aviation—automatic pilot—tested—Oct. 8, 1929

Aviation—Airship—airship to land on a roof —Hotel Statler—May 23, 1919

Aviation—Flights—over-water flight—G. H. Curtiss—Aug. 31, 1910

Aviation — Passenger — dirigible passenger transfer to an airplane—August 29, 1929

Aviation—Races—airplane race (of importance) in which both men and women were contestants—from Los Angeles, Calif. —Aug. 30, 1931

Baseball Game—triple play unassisted in a world series—Oct. 10, 1920

Baseball Game—triple play unassisted in a modern major league game—Neal Ball— July 19, 1909

Community Trust—Cleveland Foundation— established—Jan. 2, 1914

Compotype—patented—Oct. 20, 1925

Court—conciliation tribunal for small claims —established—March 15, 1913

Cripples—kindergarten for crippled children —opened—1900

Electric Lighting—electric arc lights—for public street lighting—April 29, 1879

Evangelical and Reformed Church—organized—June 26, 1934

Fireworks Legislation—fireworks legislation enacted by a large city—July 18, 1908

Health Museum—Cleveland Health Museum —opened—Nov. 12, 1940

Humane Society—humane association national organization—American Humane Association—organized—Oct. 9, 1877

Ice Cream Cone—ice cream cone-rolling machine—patented—C. R. Taylor—Jan. 29, 1924

Jews—Jewish Rabbinical Conference—Oct. 17, 1855

Judge—woman judge to sentence a man to death—F. E. Allen—May 14, 1921

Multigraph—patented—H. C. Gammeter— March 10, 1903

National Union for Social Justice—national convention—Aug. 14, 1936

Newspaper—newspaper rotogravure sections published—*Plain Dealer*—March 29, 1914

Ordnance—submachine gun—invented—J. T. Thompson—1915

Paint—paint prepared from standard formulas—1880

OHIO—Cleveland—*Continued*

Radio Broadcast—political convention broadcast—June 10, 1924

Radio Station — municipal school-owned ultra-high frequency radio station — WBOE—licensed—Nov. 21, 1938

Road—brick pavement on a rural road—completed—1895

Seal—seals for raising funds—organization formed—April 20, 1861

Siamese Twins—Siamese twins to survive a separation operation and live for one year —born Dec. 14, 1952

Street Car—aluminum street car—in service —Dec. 2, 1926

Surgical Operation—heart operation for the relief of angina pectoris—Dr. C. S. Beck—Feb. 13, 1935

Surgical Operation—heart operation in which the elective cardiac arrest technique was employed—May 1956

Temperance Society—women's temperance society (national)—organized—Nov. 18, 1874

Traffic Light—electric traffic signal lights—installed—Aug. 5, 1914

Union Party—convention—August 15, 1936

Valeteria—displayed—Sept. 19, 1951

Clyde

Spanish-American War—soldier killed in the Spanish-American war—monument erected

Columbus

Animals—gorilla born in captivity—Colo—Dec. 22, 1956

Aviation—airplane merchandise shipment—Nov. 7, 1910

Aviation—Airplane—jet propelled fighter airplane (four-engine)—tested—Sept. 15, 1947

Bicycle Patent—water velocipede patent—Oct. 5, 1869

Blind—state school for the blind—opened July 4, 1837

Ceramics School—Ohio State University—1894

Labor Party (political)—labor party (national)—formed—Feb. 22, 1872

Prohibition Party (national)—first national convention—Feb. 22, 1872

Dayton

Aviation—airplane merchandise shipment—to Columbus—Nov. 7, 1910

Aviation—physiological research laboratory of the U.S. Army Air Corps—completed —Jan. 1, 1937

Aviation—Airplane—airplane purchased by the U.S. Government — tested — July 30, 1909

Aviation—Airplane — fighter airplane carrying a cannon—tested—April 6, 1938

Aviation—Flights—all blind solo flight by the U.S. Army—May 7, 1932

Aviation—Parachute—aviator to bail out of a diasabled airplane—H. R. Harris—Oct. 20, 1922

Aviation — Parachute — parachute — "free type"—used—April 28, 1919

Cash Register—patented—J. J. Ritty—Nov. 4, 1879

Electric Generator—hydrogen-cooled turbine generator—in service—Oct. 12, 1937

Gasoline—ethyl gasoline—marketed—Feb. 2, 1923

Helicopter Flight—helicopter flight (cross-country)—from Stratford, Conn.—landed —May 17, 1942

Scale—computing scales—company incorporated—March 20, 1891

Soldiers' Homes (national)—in operation—1867

Eastlake

Coal—commercial coal pipeline—in operation—June 4, 1957

Fairfield

Aviation—Flights—airplane altitude flight to exceed 28,000 feet—R. W. Schroeder—Sept. 18, 1918

Gambier

Camera—tintype camera—patented—H. L. Smith—Feb. 19, 1856

Jacobsburg

Corn—shipment of hybrid seed corn—April 13, 1916

Kent

Forestry School — forestry correspondence course in tree surgery—1914

Forestry School—forestry school to give scientific training in the care and preservation of trees — incorporated—Feb. 9, 1909

Kings Mills

Ordnance—cartridge-loading machinery—installed—G. M. Peters—1885

Ordnance—shot tower—erected—1895

Kirtland

Mormon Temple — dedicated — March 27, 1836

Mansfield

Stove—electronic range for domestic use—manufactured—1955

Marblehead

Medal — lifesaving medal — awarded by Treasury Dept.—to L. M. Clemons—June 19. 1876

Marion

President (United States)—President and President's wife to die during the term for which he had been elected—Mrs. W. G. Harding died—Nov. 21, 1924

Milford

Police—woman chief of police—Dolly Spencer—1914

Monroeville

Monument—monument to the memory of the soldiers and sailors of the Spanish-American war—unveiled—Sept. 29, 1904

Montpelier

Railroad Car—rail detector car in commercial service—Nov. 15, 1928

Mount Pleasant

Newspaper—abolition newspaper—*Philanthropist*—published—Aug. 29, 1817

Mount Vernon

Chewing Gum—chewing gum patent—W. F. Semple—Dec. 28, 1869

Nela Park

Electric Lighting—electric lamp bulb frosted on the inside—patented—Marvin Pipkin—Oct. 16, 1928

Newark

Glass Wool—patented—Oct. 11, 1938

North Bend

Railroad Train Robbery—railroad train robbery of a disabled train—May 5, 1865

Oberlin

College — coeducational college — opened — Dec. 3, 1833
Temperance Society—Anti-Saloon League—founded—May 24, 1893

Oxford

Fraternity (Greek letter)—fraternity west of the Alleghenies—founded—Aug. 8, 1839

Port Bucyrus

Aviation—Airport—airport manager (woman)—appointed—May 28, 1932

Ravenna

Jockey—jockey to win seven races in one day—Joseph Sylvester—Oct. 18, 1930

Riverside

See Cincinnati

Sandusky

Aviation—Flights—over-water flight—G. H. Curtiss—Aug. 31, 1910

Schoenbrunn

Protestant Church—west of Pennsylvania—communion service—June 9, 1772
Schoolhouse—west of the Allegheny mountains—completed—July 29, 1773

Solon

Skeet—national skeet tournament—Aug. 31, 1935

Springfield

Baby Show—Oct. 5, 1854

Steubenville

Land Grant—district land office—opened—July 2, 1800

Toledo

Aviation—propeller blade of hollow steel—manufactured—June 1942
Baseball Player—Negro baseball player—M. F. Walker—1884
Bowler—bowler to make a perfect score of 300 in an American Bowling Congress tournament—William Knox—March 10, 1913
Building—all-glass windowless structure—completed—Jan. 15, 1936
Employment Service—state employment service—office opened—June 4, 1890
Glass Blowing Machine—patented—M. J. Owens—Feb. 26, 1895
Glass Dress of spun glass—manufactured—1893
Greenback Labor Party—organized—Feb. 22, 1878
Lutheran Church—American Lutheran Church—organized—Aug. 11, 1930
Mortuary—cooperative—Sept. 15, 1930
Paint Spraying Device—employed—1909
Scale—automatic computing pendulum-type scales—patented—Allen De Vilbiss—May 22, 1900
Ship — schooner (five masted) — "David Dows"—launched—April 21, 1881
Television Receiver—television receivers to project large images—built—1955
Television Tube—rectangular television tube (practical)—announced—July 10, 1949

Toronto

Titanium—titanium mill—opened—Nov. 2, 1957

OHIO—*Continued*

Van Wert

Library—county library—successfully conducted—organized—1898

Wilmington

Aviation—airplane human pick-up—Sept. 5, 1943

Xenia

Ordnance — cartridge-loading machinery — patented—G. M. Peters—July 7, 1885

Yellow Springs

College—college to grant women absolutely equal rights with men — non-sectarian — Antioch College—opened—Oct. 5, 1853
College—woman college professor — accorded same privileges as men professors—appointed—Sept. 1852
College Literary Society—college literary society (coeducational)—founded—1853
Didactics Course—didactics course in a college—Antioch College—1853
Hygiene Instruction—physiology and hygiene courses—Antioch College—Oct. 5, 1853

Zanesville

Bridge—"Y" bridge—authorized — Jan. 21, 1812
Sawmill—sawmill engine — portable —constructed—1858

OKLAHOMA

El Reno

Indian Church—Indian church organized by Indians—incorporated—Oct. 10, 1918

Elk City

Hospital—community hospital—dedicated—Aug. 13, 1931

Oklahoma City

Esperanto Magazine—published—Oct. 1906
Medical Clinic—cancer clinic (traveling)—established—Feb. 14, 1946
Parking Meter (automatic)—installed—July 16, 1935
Turbine—gas turbine used by an electrical utility company—in service—July 29, 1949

Tonkawa

Medical Clinic—cancer clinic (traveling)—opened—1946

OREGON

Gasoline Tax—gasoline tax (state)—Feb. 25, 1919

Holiday—Labor Day law (state)—state holiday—enacted—Feb. 21, 1887
Labor Law—minimum wage law—commission authorized—Feb. 17, 1913
Legislator (state)—husband and wife simultaneously elected to both chambers of a state legislature—Nov. 7, 1950
Money—paper money issued by the American Indians—c.1840

Albany

Molybdenum—molybdenum centrifugal casting—Nov. 4, 1958

Astoria

Television—community television antenna system—Dec. 1949

Champoeg

Colonial Government—government on the Pacific coast—authorized—May 2, 1843

Medford

Medical Society—woman president of a state medical society—L. S. Kent—elected—Sept. 18, 1948

Mount Emily

World War II—bombing on continental American soil—Sept. 9, 1942

Oregon City

Newspaper—newspaper published on the Pacific coast—*Oregon Spectator*—Feb. 5, 1846

Portland

Automobile Bus—bus operated by a railroad—service—Aug. 25, 1924
Automobile Race—transcontinental automobile race (for a time record)—from New York City—arrived—June 21, 1905
Aviation—airplane take-off from a hotel roof—Silas Christoferson—June 11, 1912
Electric Power Plant—alternating current hydroelectric power plant to operate over a long distance—current from Willamette Falls, Ore.—June 2, 1889
Radio Broadcast—network broadcast received on the Pacific coast—Oct. 23, 1924
Railroad—daily railroad service to the Pacific coast—through service without a change—Nov. 17, 1889
Servite Church—Marian Congress—Aug. 12, 1934
Ship—steamboat to employ electric lights successfully—to San Francisco—May 2, 1880
Television Station—ultra high frequency commercial television station—KPTV—regular commercial service—Oct. 1, 1952

St. Johns

Plywood—Douglas fir plywood—commercial production—1905

Salem

College—university on the Pacific coast—Willamette University—organized—Feb. 1, 1842

Willamette Falls

Electric Power Plant—alternating current hydroelectric power plant to operate over a long distance—supplied current to Portland, Ore.—June 2, 1889

PENNSYLVANIA

Bible—Bible translated into English in America—copyrighted—Sept. 12, 1808

Census—states to exceed 1,000,000 in population—1820

Child Labor Law—child labor law restricting the age of the worker—approved—March 28, 1848

Congressman (U.S.)—Catholic congressman—Thomas Fitz-Simons—March 4, 1789

Congressman (U.S.)—Jewish congressman—Israel Jacobs—March 4, 1791

Election—printed ballot—authorized—Feb. 15, 1799

Governor—governor of a territory and a state—J. W. Geary

Holiday—Flag Day—as a legal holiday—authorized—May 7, 1937

Liquor Stores (state)—opened—Jan. 2, 1934

Moravian—George Boehnich—arrived—Sept. 22, 1734

Moving Picture Censorship—moving picture censorship board (state)—June 19, 1911

Music Instruction—State Supervisor of Music—P. E. Beck—appointed—July 1, 1915

Patent—English patent granted to a resident of America—issued—Nov. 25, 1715

Railroad—state-owned railroad—opened—April 2, 1834

Railroad—railroad to install gasoline-mechanical cars—Feb. 1923

Slavery—law (state) abolishing slavery—enacted—March 1, 1780

Sterilization Legislation—vetoed—1905

Stove Patent—Robert Haeterick—June 11, 1793

Tax—inheritance tax (state) —enacted — April 7, 1826

Allentown

Cement—cement—patented—D. O. Saylor—Sept. 26, 1871

Medical School—homeopathic school — founded—April 10, 1835

Transistor—transistors produced commercially for a specific product—Oct. 1951

Altoona

Railroad Car—steel passenger railroad coach—built—1902

Railroad Track—railroad rails of steel—manufactured—1864

Telephone—telephone used by a railroad company—tested—May 21, 1877

Ardmore

Automobile—automobile with a circulating lubrication system—1904

Automobile—shaft-driven automobile—constructed—Autocar Co.—1901

Beaver Falls

Corkboard (impregnated)—manufactured—1900

Bedford

Automobile School—truck-driving training school—class graduated—July 31, 1954

Berwick

Railroad Car—Freight car (Adapto Car)—built—1956

Railroad Car—passenger car (ACF-Talgo)—built—1949

Railroad Car—passenger car (ACF-Talgo for use in the United States)—completed—April 22, 1955

Bethlehem

See also South Bethlehem

Cottonseed Oil—produced—1768

Moravian Easter Service—1742

Orchestra—symphony orchestra—1744

Steel—vacuum-cast steel—poured—July 2, 1957

Trombone—used in liturgical services—Nov. 15, 1754

Water—water pumping plant—May 27, 1755

Zinc—zinc commercial production — mill erected—Oct. 13, 1853

Zinc—zinc patent—Samuel Wetherill—Jan. 6, 1857

Zinc—zinc sheet mill—in production—1865

Braddock

Steel—steel mill to install an electrical machine—1882

Bristol

Aviation—Airplane—hydroplane of stainless steel—flown—Sept. 4, 1936

Ship—torpedo boat of importance—"Cushing"—keel laid—1888

PENNSYLVANIA—*Continued*

Brownsville

Bridge—cast iron bridge—Dunlap's Creek—1835

Brush Run

Disciples of Christ—church established—May 4, 1811

Bryn Mawr

Biology—biology course (general) offered in a college—Sept. 23, 1885

College—"dean of the faculty"—Jan. 1884

College—graduate school for women—Oct. 23, 1885

College Self-Government Organization—chartered—Feb. 23, 1892

Fellowship—fellowship (graduate) awarded by a women's college—June 6, 1889

Fellowship—resident fellowship for women awarded by a women's college—1884

History Instruction—history course (integrated) in a women's college—1885

Bucks County

Evangelical Association Council—Nov. 3, 1803

Carbon County

Coal—anthracite coal — accidentally discovered—Philip Ginter—1791

Carbondale

Locomotive—locomotive for railroad use—"Stourbridge Lion"—first run to Honesdale—Aug. 9, 1829

Carlisle

Bank—Christmas savings club—in operation—Dec. 1, 1909

Declaration of Independence (American)—Declaration of Independence—July 12, 1774

Indian School—Indian school of prominence—opened—Nov. 1, 1879

Chambersburg

Paper—straw paper—manufactured—1829

Sleeping Car—sleeping car—to Harrisburg, Pa.—1836

Chester

Iron—rolling mill—established—1746

Ship—iron sloop yacht—"Vindex"—built—1871

Ship—merchant ship formally blessed at a launching ceremony—Nov. 27, 1940

Ship—seatrain—built—1928

Ship—steamboat to employ electric lights successfully—"Columbia"—built

Chester County

Stove—stove — "Pennsylvania fireplace" — manufactured—1742

Coatesville

Boiler Plates—manufactured—1816

Connellsville

Iron—iron mill to puddle and roll iron—operated—Sept. 15, 1817

Creighton

Glass—plate glass produced on a large scale—1883

Crum Creek

Railroad—railroad for freight transportation—to Ridley Creek—1809

Delaware County

Insane Patient's Maintenance Act—1676

Delta

Slate—used for roofing material—obtained—1734

Downington

Apple Parer—invented—Moses Coats—Feb. 14, 1803

Drehersville

Bird Sanctuary—established—Aug. 29, 1934

Dusboro

Iron—iron casting—Joseph Mallinson—1739

East Pittsburgh

Elevator—dual elevator—placed in service—1931

Easton

Civil Rights Chair—established

Normal School—normal school instruction—Lafayette College—cornerstone laid—July 4, 1838

Philology Chair — comparative philology chair—Lafayette College—1856

School—model school—opened—Oct. 31, 1838

Eddystone

Ordnance—tank (heavy 60-ton)—built—1941

Emporium

Television Station—illegal television station—closed—Oct. 19, 1950

Ensfield

Sugar—sugar beets—grown—c.1830

Ephrata

Communistic Society—communistic society 1733

Erie

Locomotive—gas turbine-electric locomotive —track-tested—Nov. 15, 1948

Essington

Lutheran Church—Lutheran Church building —dedicated—Sept. 4, 1645

Fairmount

Bridge—wire suspension bridge for general traffic—opened—Jan. 2, 1842

Fleetwood

Air Raid Shelter—air raid shelter—completed—Nov. 1, 1940

Fort Necessity

War (colonial)—French and Indian war battle—July 3, 1754

Frankford

Building and Loan Association—organized —Jan. 3, 1831

Franklin

Aviation—Airship—woman airship passenger—M. P. Miller—Aug. 11, 1906

Germantown

See Philadelphia

Gettysburg

Cabinet of the United States—Cabinet session held at a place other than the seat of the United States Government—Nov. 22, 1955
President (U.S.)—President to fly in a twin-engined airplane—from Washington, D.C. —D. D. Eisenhower—June 3, 1955

Great Bend

Patent—patent re-issue—Julius Hatch—Jan. 9, 1838

Grove City

Radio Broadcast—speaker to address an organization by radio—W. C. Ketler—April 20, 1920

Hanover

Civil War—bloodshed north of the Mason-Dixon line—June 30, 1863

Harrisburg

Law Digest—published—1803
Political Convention—unit rule—adopted—Dec. 4, 1839
Sleeping Car—sleeping car—to Chambersburg—1836

Haverford

Cricket Tournament—cricket game played by a college team—1836

Honesdale

Locomotive—locomotive for railroad use—to Carbondale—Aug. 9, 1829

Johnstown

Evangelical United Brethren Church—formed—Nov. 16, 1946
Tunnel—railroad tunnel—built—1831

Kennet Square

Folding Machine—patented—Cyrus Chambers—Oct. 7, 1856

Kleinfeltersville

Evangelical Conference—Nov. 15, 1807

Kobuta

Plastic—expandable polystyrene production (commercial)—1954

Lancaster

Ball Bearing commercial installation—Oct. 30, 1794
Brick—brick insulating—Armstrong Cork Co.—June 1913
Church of the United Brethren in Christ—May 18, 1766
Clock—electric watch—introduced—Jan. 3, 1957
Linoleum—embossed inlaid linoleum—introduced—1925
Mower (horsepower) — patented — Peter Gaillard—Dec. 4, 1812
Road—macadam road—Lancaster turnpike —to Philadelphia—completed—Dec. 1795
Ship—steamboat—built — William Henry — 1763
Slicing Machine—patented—Anthony Iske —Nov. 4, 1873

Latrobe

Football Game—professional football game —Sept. 3, 1895

Lebanon County

Evangelical Church—first annual conference —1807

PENNSYLVANIA—*Continued*

Leechburg

Gas—natural gas for manufacturing—in iron and puddle mill furnaces—1873

Tin Factory—to manufacture black plate, tin and terne plate—1874

Lewiston

Railroad Signal System—railroad signal system of continuous cab signals—July 11, 1923

Library

Coal—coal pipeline loops (experimental)—built—May 23, 1950

Mansfield

Football Game—football game at night—Sept. 29, 1892

Marcus Hook

Rayon—rayon—production—Dec. 19, 1910

Mauch Chunk

Coal—anthracite coal used in smelting iron ore—1837

Tunnel—mining tunnel (large)—commenced—1824

Meadville

Fastening — hookless fastening — manufactured—1893

Monongahela City

Carborundum—invented—E. G. Acheson—1891

Montgomery County

Bird Banding—bird banding—1803

Tile—brick roofing tile—manufactured—1735

New Berlin

Evangelical Church Building—dedicated—March 2, 1817

New Geneva

Glass Factory—glass factory west of the Allegheny mountains—established—1794

Newton Wells

Gas—pipeline (long distance)—for natural gas — to Titusville — completed — Aug. 1, 1872

Norristown

Gas—water gas production—patented—T. S. C. Lowe—Sept. 21, 1875

Oakmont

Golf Champion—golf champion to win the United States Open and the Professional—Gene Sarazen — Professional Golfers' Tournament—Aug. 18, 1922

Oil Creek

Oil—oil pipeline of importance—completed—Oct. 9, 1865

Oil—oil pipeline within the oil regions—to Plumer, Pa.—1862

Oil—oil refinery (commercial) — erected — June 1860

Orwigsburg

Tunnel—tunnel—opened to traffic—1821

Philadelphia

Abolition Society—formed—April 14, 1775

Academy — founded — Benjamin Franklin — 1749

Accordion Patent—issued—Anthony Faas—Jan. 13, 1854

Actor—matinee idol—John Henry—American debut—1766

Adhesive and Medicated Plaster—adhesive and medicated plaster—used in the treatment of fractures—reported—1830

Advertisement—automobile advertisement—in a national magazine—March 31, 1900

Advertising Agency—V. B. Palmer—opened—1841

African Church—founded—Richard Allen—1793

Agricultural Encyclopedia—published—1804

Agricultural Society—agricultural society—Philadelphia Society for the Promotion of Agriculture—formed—March 1, 1785

Air Mail Service—air mail experimental route—May 15, 1918

Air Mail Service—autogiro mail delivery direct to a post office—May 25, 1935

Air Mail Service—autogiro mail delivery regular service—July 6, 1939

American Party—national convention—June 5, 1855

Ancient Mystical Order Rosae Crucis—lodge, temple, and laboratories erected—1694

Annual—*Le Souvenir*—published—1825

Anti-Masonic Party—national convention—Sept. 1830

Anti-Vivisection Society—organized Feb. 23, 1883

Arcade—completed—Sept. 1827

Archery Club—archery club—founded—1825

Architectural Book — architectural book printed in America—1775

Army Officer—Army Medical Specialist Corps male officer—Sheldon Saffren—commissioned—Dec. 30, 1955

Army Officer — chaplain (Jewish) of the U.S. Army—appointed—Sept. 10, 1862

PENNSYLVANIA—Philadelphia—*Cont.*

Medical Book—mental diseases book—published—1812

Medical Book—pathology textbook — *Treatise on Pathological Anatomy*—published—1829

Medical Book — pediatrics book — *Maternal Physician*—published—1810

Medical Book — pediatrics monograph —published—1796

Medical Book—therapeutics and materia medica book—*Discourses on the Elements of Therapeutics*—published—1817

Medical Book—typhus fever treatise—*History of the Typhus Petechialis*—published—1809

Medical Instruction — anatomy lectures (scientific)—Dr. William Shippen—1762

Medical Instruction—medical research chair—University of Pennsylvania—1910

Medical School — homeopathic college — Homeopathic Medical College of Pennsylvania—incorporated—April 8, 1848

Medical School — medical college — established—May 3, 1765

Medical School—naval medical school (unofficial)—authorized—May 19, 1823

Medical School — women's medical school (still in existence as an independent institution) — Women's Medical College—organized—1850

Medical Society—homeopathic medical society—Hahnemann Society—organized — April 10, 1833

Medical Society—medical society (national)—American Medical Association—organized—May 5, 1847

Medical Society—woman physician admitted to the American Institute of Homeopathy —M. B. Jackson—1871

Medical Society — woman physician elected a member of the American Medical Association—S. H. Stevenson—1876

Medical Society—women members of the American College of Surgeons—A. C. Bryant and F. W. Duckering—admitted—June 22, 1914

Melons—grown—1818

Mennonites — Mennonite church meeting-house—built—1708

Mennonites—Mennonites — arrived — Oct. 6, 1683

Methodist Conference—July 16, 1773

Methodist Episcopal Church—African Methodist Episcopal Church — established — April 9, 1816

Microscope — electron microscope—demonstrated—April 20, 1940

Milestones—erected—May 15, 1764

Military Drill Manual—military drill manual —published—1779

Military Drill Manual—military drill manual devoted to field strategy—printed—Robert Aitken—1775

Military Organization — military organization (anti-British) — organized—Nov. 17, 1774

Mint (U.S.)—Mint of the United States—cornerstone laid—July 31, 1792

Mint (U.S.)—mint (U.S.) director—David Rittenhouse—appointed—April 14, 1792

Money—coin (United States) to use "E Pluribus Unum" — authorized — April 2, 1792

Money—silver coins — authorized — April 2, 1792

Money—silver dollar—authorized—1792

Money—silver half dimes—coined—Oct. 9, 1792

Moving Picture — animated photographic picture projection before a theater audience—Feb. 5, 1870

Moving Picture—photographic attempt to show motion—patented—Feb. 5, 1861

Museum—commercial museum — Philadelphia Commercial Museum — organized— June 15, 1894

Music—long distance telephone concert—March 31, 1877

Music—music publishers (exclusive)—Moller & Capron—established—1790

Music—musical instrument dealer—Michael Hillegas—1759

Music Book — music book by a native American—*Urania*—published—1761

Music Book—secular song book—*Selection of the Most Favorite Scots Tunes*—published— Aug. 1787

Music Book—secular song book by a native American—published—1788

Musician—composer (native-born American)—Francis Hopkinson—song—1759

Mustard—manufactured—Benjamin Jackson —1768

Naval Officer—naval doctor—Joseph Harrison—appointed—1775

Naval Officer—naval medical officer to write a book — Edward Cutbush—published— 1808

Negro—national colored convention—Sept. 15, 1830

News Correspondent—woman news correspondent accredited to the White House —E. E. Briggs—Jan. 1866

Newspaper—Arabic daily newspaper—*Al-Hoda*—founded—Feb. 22, 1898

Newspaper—daily newspaper — *Pennsylvania Packet and Daily Advertiser*—published— Sept. 21, 1784

Newspaper — democratic newspaper — *Democratic Press*—published—March 27, 1807

Newspaper—French daily newspaper—*Courrier Français*—established—April 15, 1794

Newspaper—French newspaper—*Courier de l'Amérique*—July 27, 1784

Newspaper — German newspaper — *Philadelphische Zeitung*—published—May 6, 1732

Newspaper—newspaper editorial apology —published—April 20, 1721

Newspaper—newspaper rotogravure sections —published—*Public Ledger*—March 29, 1914

Newspaper — newspaper serial story — *Pennsylvania Gazette*—appeared—1729

Newspaper — penny daily newspaper — *The Cent*—published—1830

Normal School—teachers' training school (Jewish)—trustees elected—Feb. 17, 1895

Novel Course—lecture course on the English novel—University of Pennsylvania—1889

Nursing School—school for nurses to award a diploma—chartered—March 22, 1861

Oil—oil tank cars—introduced—1864

Opera—opera by an American composer (important) — *Leonora*—performed—June 4, 1845

Opera—opera (comic) — *The Disappointment* —scheduled—April 20, 1767

Organ—organs imported—1700

Organists' Society—organists' society (national)—branch chapter formed—June 10, 1902

Paper Mill—built—1690

Patent—patent granted jointly to a father and son—Aug. 2, 1791

Patent—patentee to obtain more than one patent—Samuel Mulliken—March 11, 1791

Pencil—paper pencil—patented—F. E. Blaisdell—Nov. 19, 1895

Pencil—pencil with an attached eraser—patented—March 30, 1858

Periodical — comic weekly — *John Donkey* — published—Jan. 1, 1848

Periodical—magazine containing a fashion plate—*The Port Folio*—June 1809

Periodical — magazine for the blind — *Student's Magazine*—published—Jan. 1837

Periodical — magazine published for mental patients—*Illuminator*—April 1, 1843

Periodical—magazine published in America —*American Magazine* — published—Feb. 13, 1741

Periodical — quarterly magazine — *American Review of History*—published—Jan. 1811

Periodical — sectarian magazine — *Arminian Magazine*—published—Jan. 1789

Petroleum Exported to Europe—boat chartered—Nov. 12, 1861

Pharmacist—pharmacist (woman) — Elizabeth Marshall—1804

Pharmacist—pharmacist (woman graduate) —Susan Hayhurst—graduated—March 16, 1883

Pharmacopoeia — pharmacopoeia — William Brown—published—1778

Pharmacy College—pharmacy college—Philadelphia College of Apothecaries—organized—Feb. 23, 1821

Pharmacy Magazine—pharmacy magazine— *Journal of the Philadelphia College of Pharmacy*—published—Dec. 1825

Pharmacy Professor—pharmacy professor— S. P. Griffitts—1789

Pharmacy Society (national) — American Pharmaceutical Association — organized — —Oct. 6, 1852

Phrenology Magazine—*American Phrenological Journal*—published—Oct. 1838

Physician—doctor to receive a bachelor of medicine degree—John Archer—graduated —June 21, 1768

Physician—Hindu woman to receive a doctor of medicine degree—Anandibai Joshee —graduated—March 11, 1886

Physician—Negro doctor—James Derham

Pill—compressed pills or tablets—commercially manufactured—1863

Play (drama)—anti-vivisection play—*Woven Dreams*—produced—Oct. 4, 1932

Play (drama)—play about an Indian— *The Indian Princess*—produced—April 6, 1808

Political Convention—Negro delegate to a national political convention—Frederick Douglass—Sept. 6, 1866

Political Science Society—political and social science society (national)—American Academy of Political and Social Science— organized—Dec. 14, 1889

Porcelain (hard)—manufactured successfully—W. E. Tucker—1825

Postage Stamp—public exhibition of postage stamps—May 10, 1876

Postage Stamp—stamped envelopes issued to commemorate an event—printed—May 10, 1876

Postage Stamp Catalog—*Stamp Collector's Manual*—published—1862

Postal Service—street letter box—patented —Albert Potts—March 9, 1858

Presbyterian Church—Presbyterian Church of America—formed—June 11, 1936

Presbyterian General Assembly—meeting— May 22, 1789

Presbyterian Presbytery—assembled—1705

Printer's Ink—manufactured—C. E. Johnson —1804

Printing Magazine (professional) — *Typographic Advertiser*—published—April 1855

Printing Press—high-speed newspaper printing and folding machine—installed—1876

Printing Press—printing press for polychromatic printing—patented—T. F. Adams— Sept. 17, 1844

Printing Press—printing press invented in America—G. E. Clymer—1816

Printing Press—rotogravure press — imported—1904

Prison—prison to have individual cells— system introduced—1790

Prison Reform Society—formed—May 8, 1787

Prize Fight—prize fight to attract 100,000 spectators—Dempsey-Tunney fight—Sept. 23, 1926

Protestant Episcopal Catechism—Episcopal catechism—published—1785

Psychiatric Association—formed—Oct. 16, 1844

Psychological Society—psychological society (national organization)—American Psychological Association—scientific meeting —Dec. 27, 1892

Psychology Professor—J. M. Cattell—1888

Publishing Society—Seventy-Six Society— organized—Sept. 5, 1854

Quinine—quinine—manufactured—1822

Radio Broadcast—radio broadcast demonstration—voice heard—May 30, 1902

Radio Broadcast—stereophonic sound program broadcast by separately owned stations—Nov. 5, 1955

Radio Contest—held—Feb. 23, 1910

PENNSYLVANIA—Philadelphia—*Cont.*

Radio Facsimile Transmission—photograph sent overland by radio to a distant point—from Anacostia, D.C.—March 3, 1923

Radio License—experimental radio license—issued by Dept. of Commerce—Aug. 13, 1912

Railroad—gasoline-driven, stainless steel, air-conditioned, pneumatic-tire, two-car train—built—1933

Railroad—railroad to install gasoline-mechanical cars—Feb. 1923

Railroad—streamlined all-steel diesel motor train—built—1934

Railroad Signal System—railroad signal system (manual block)—installed—1863

Railroad Technical Report—published—1826

Railroad Track—railroad track (practical) —July 31, 1809

Religious Publication—religious weekly news paper—*Religious Remembrancer*—published— Sept. 4, 1813

Republican Party—Republican Party national convention—June 17, 1856

Research Institute—anatomy research institute—Wistar Institute of Anatomy and Biology—established—July 20, 1891

Restaurant—restaurant with an automatic arrangement for vending food—opened— June 1902

Road—macadam road—work commenced— Feb. 1793

Root Beer—manufactured—1866

Rubber—rubber patent—J. F. Hummel— April 29, 1813

Sand Blasting—patented—B. C. Tilghman —Oct. 18, 1870

School—school for Protestant girls—established—1742

Schwenkfelder—George Schultz—arrived— 1731

Science Association—scientific society of importance—American Philosophical Society —organized—1743

Science Association—scientific society (national organization)—American Association for the Advancement of Science—organized—Sept. 20, 1848

Seed Business—established—David Landreth —Jan. 7, 1784

Ship—frigate—"United States"—launched— May 10, 1797

Ship—guided missile cruiser—"Boston"— converted—Nov. 1, 1955

Ship—navy vessel constructed as a mine layer—"Terror"—launched—June 6, 1941

Ship—steamboat to make an ocean voyage —to Philadelphia—June 1809

Ship—warship captured by a commissioned officer of the U.S. Navy—conveyed to Philadelphia—battle—April 1776

Ship—warship with propelling machinery below the waterline — "Princeton" — launched—Dec. 10, 1843

Shorthand Book—published—1728

Shorthand Magazine—*American Phonographic Journal*—published—July 1848

Sieve—sieve—produced—John Sellers—1768

Slavery—slavery protest—of importance— Feb. 18, 1688

Sociology Treatise—*Treatise on Sociology*— published—1854

Soda Water—soda water—prepared

Soda Water—soda water commercially bottled—Elias Durand—1835

Stage Coach Inter-City Service—to New York City—inaugurated—Nov. 9, 1756

Steam Engine—steam engine that was practical—manufactured—Oliver Evans—1795

Steam-Operated Amphibious Vehicle—invented—Oliver Evans—1805

Steam Shovel—patented—W. S. Otis—Feb. 24, 1839

Stereotype—stereotype printing—Benjamin Mecom—1745

Stomach Washing—P. S. Physick—1800

Street Car—cable car—patented—March 23, 1858

Street Car—street car—constructed—1832

Street Cleaning Machine—used—Dec. 15, 1854

Street Cleaning Service—instituted—Benjamin Franklin—1757

Strike—union strike benefit—authorized— May 31, 1786

Sulphuric Acid—produced—John Harrison —1793

Sunday School—Jewish Sunday school—society organized—March 4, 1838

Symphony—symphony on a Negro folk theme—W. L. Dawson—presented—Nov. 14, 1934

Teachers' Convention—teachers' convention (national)—Aug. 26, 1857

Teaching Methods Book—*Schul-ordnung*— published—1770

Telephone—automatic telephone system patent—Dec. 5, 1879

Television—Telecast—color telecast by a local station—WPTZ-TV—Dec. 18, 1953

Television—Telecast—color telecast on a closed circuit local station—WPTZ-TV— Oct. 30, 1953

Television — Telecast — department store sales demonstrations (large-scale)—Gimbel Bros.—Oct. 24, 1945

Television—Telecast—football game televised in color on a network—Sept. 29, 1951

Television—Telecast—moving picture premiere performance to be televised—WPTZ —April 10, 1944

Television—Telecast—pay television presentation of a sporting event—Walcott-Marciano fight—Sept. 23, 1952

Television—Telecast—political convention to be televised—June 24, 1940

Television—Telecast—prize fight in a "studio"—televised—Sept. 1, 1954

Television—Telecast—surgical operation televised on a local program—March 16, 1952

Television—Telecast—symphonic concerts to be televised—March 20, 1948

Television—Telecast—telecast using coaxial cable—inter-city telecast to New York City —Oct. 5, 1936

Tennis Match—women's national championship lawn tennis matches—1887

Textbook printed in America—*A New Guide to the English Tongue*—reprinted—1747

Textile Machinery Patent—James Davenport—Feb. 14, 1794

Theater—municipally owned and operated summer theater-in-the-round — opened — June 30, 1951

Theater—theater building (permanent) — Southwark Theatre—opened—Nov. 21, 1766

Theological Treatise—of importance—published—1690

Tile—wall and floor tiles—manufactured—1845

Trade Register—*Aitken's General American Register*—published—1773

Tube—machine designed to produce collapsible tubes—built—1873

Tuberculosis Society—tuberculosis society—Pennsylvania Society for the Prevention of Tuberculosis—founded—April 10, 1892

Turnstile (electric)—used—May 10, 1876

Type Foundry—type foundry to be permanently established in America—Christopher Sauer—erected—1771

Type Specimen Book—published—Binny & Ronaldson—1812

Typewriter Ribbon—typewriter "copy" ribbon—patented—Jan. 24, 1888

Vaccine—yellow fever vaccine for human immunization—announced—April 28, 1932

Varnish Manufacturer—Christian Schrack—1815

Venetian Blinds—venetian blinds—installed—1761

Wallpaper — wallpaper — manufactured — Plunkett Fleeson—1739

War Veterans' Society—Society of the Cincinnati—general meeting—May 7, 1784

Washing Machine—rotary motion washing machine—patented—H. E. Smith—Oct. 26, 1858

Watermark—in paper—William Rittenhouse—1690

White Lead Manufacturer—Samuel Wetherill—1789

Woman—women to become federal government employees—1795

Woman Suffrage—woman suffrage book—*A Vindication of the Rights of Women*—published—1792

Wrestling—intercollegiate wrestling association—formed—April 7, 1905

Zoological Garden—opened to public—July 1, 1874

Phoenixville

Gas—water gas plant—built—1874

Pithole

Oil—oil pipeline of importance—completed Oct. 9, 1865

Pittsburgh

Automobile Robbery—armored commercial car hold-up—March 11, 1927

Automobile Service Station—drive-in service station—opened—Dec. 1, 1913

Automobile Truck—built—1898

Aviation—automatic pilot — tested — from Cleveland, Ohio—Oct. 8, 1929

Bowling Tournament—gold medal award to a perfect-score bowler—roll-off—March 11, 1909

Bridge—wire cable suspension aqueduct bridge—completed—May 1845

Building—aluminum-faced building — Alcoa Building—completed—Aug. 1, 1953

Commercial High School—commercial high school—established—1868

Electric Meter—commercial production — Aug. 1888

File Factory (hand cutting)—established—1829

Fire—fire in a mine—recorded—1765

Football Uniform Numerals—used—Dec. 5, 1908

Glass Crystal Chandelier—1810

Glass Factory—flint glass factory—successful—1807

Holiday—Saturday half holiday—introduced—June 1871

Holiday—Thanksgiving Day sermon—West of the Alleghenies—Nov. 26, 1758

Ice Loading Machinery — operated — May 1917

Immigration—Chinese labor immigration—William Kelly—1854

Iron—angle iron—rolled—Samuel Leonard—1819

Konel—discovery announced—Sept. 9, 1929

Labor Union—labor union of importance—organized—1881

Map—automobile road map—published—1914

Monument—monument to the American flag—dedicated—June 14, 1927

Moving Picture Theater—theater in the world devoted exclusively to the exhibition of motion pictures — "Nickelodeon" — opened—June 1905

News Correspondent—Negro news correspondent—J. A. Rogers—assigned to Ethiopia—Oct. 1935

Newspaper—newspaper published west of the Alleghenies—*Pittsburgh Gazette*—July 29, 1786

Oil—oil refinery—S. M. Kier—1855

Oil and Gas Production Course—in a college—1912

Patent—print patent—H. J. Heinz Co.—March 7, 1893

Petroleum Refining Course—collegiate grade—1922-23

Presbyterian Church—Moderator of the United Presbyterian Church—elected—T. M. Taylor—May 28, 1958

Printing Press—printing press to use a continuous web or roll of paper—Bullock Press—manufactured—1865

Radio Broadcast—baseball game broadcast with a play-by-play description—Aug. 5, 1921

Radio Broadcast—religious service broadcast—Jan. 2, 1921

PENNSYLVANIA—Pittsburgh—*Cont.*

Radio Broadcast—transatlantic broadcast of a voice—KDKA—Dec. 31, 1923

Radio License—radio station licensed—Oct. 27, 1920

Radio Station—radio station with 500,000-watt power—June 12, 1936

Railroad—railroad to install track water tanks—1870

Railroad Car—mail car (steel)—built

Republican Party—Republican Party meeting (national)—Feb. 22, 1856

Ship—iron vessel built for the the U.S. Navy —"Michigan"—sections built—1842

Ship—steamboat to sail down the Mississippi—"New Orleans"—sailed—Sept. 1811

Steel—cast steel for plows—1846

Street Car—street cars with clear-vision windows—in operation—1929

Television—Telecast—stratovision flight public demonstration—June 23, 1948

Television Station—city to have two educational television channels

Wedding—wedding broadcast—Nov. 7, 1922

Pleasant Hills

Building—house with a built-in nuclear bomb shelter—exhibited—May 24, 1959

Plumer

Oil—oil pipeline within oil regions—from Oil Creek, Pa.—1862

Plymouth

Lithuanian Church—St. Casimir's Lithuanian Church—organized—Oct. 27, 1889

Port Royal

Organ—organs imported—Episcopal Church —1700

Pottstown

Bridge—iron truss bridge—trusses constructed—March 1845

Pottsville

Iron—iron blast furnace—used anthracite successfully—blown—Oct. 19, 1839

Reading

Civil War—regiment to respond to President Lincoln's proclamation—Ringgold Light Artillery

Fountain Pen Patent—D. Hyde—May 20, 1830

Ridley Creek

Railroad—railroad for freight transportation —to Crum Creek—1809

Rochester

Electric Meter—patented—O. B. Shallenberger—Aug. 14, 1888

Glass—cut glass — manufactured from pressed blanks—1902

Radio Facsimile Transmission—radio facsimile patent—C. D. Ehret—March 28, 1905

Rouseville

Oil—oil well fire—April 17, 1861

Rush

Vending Machine—vending machine to sell from bulk—invented—T. S. Wheatcraft—1897

Saxonburg

Wire—wire rope factory—erected—J. A. Roebling—1841

Scranton

Automobile License (federal)—common carrier license—license issued to Rodger's Motor Lines—Dec. 22, 1936

Correspondence School—student enrolled—1891

Railroad—railroad operated by an electric third rail system—operated—May 25, 1903

Sewickley

Radio Broadcast—tennis match broadcast—Aug. 4, 1921

Sharpsburg

Foodstuffs Producer—to achieve great commercial success—H. J. Heinz—opened factory—1869

Shippingport

Electric Power Plant—atomic electric generating station (full scale)—power generated—Dec. 2, 1957

Shuman's Station

Bridge—timber trestle pier of lattice construction—started—June 1840

South Bethlehem

Armor Plate Contract (U.S. Navy)—awarded—June 1, 1887

State College

Agricultural School—agricultural college (state) to be chartered—opened—Feb. 16, 1859

Automobile Driving Course—State College High School—Feb. 1934

Traffic Regulation Course—teacher training course in "Training Traffic Safety"—Pennsylvania State College—1936

Sunbury

Electric Company—three-wire central station incandescent electric lighting plant—operated—July 4, 1883

Railroad Signal System—railroad signal system of continuous cab signals—installation—July 11, 1923

Tidioute

Gas—natural gas for manufacturing—1870

Titusville

Gas—pipeline (long distance)—to Newton Wells—completed—Aug. 1, 1872

Oil—oil well commercially productive—discovered—Aug. 27, 1859

Oil—oil well drilled by torpedoes—Jan. 21, 1865

Troy

Cheese—pineapple cheese—made—1808

Union County

Evangelical Church General Conference—Oct. 14-17, 1816

Uniontown

War (colonial)—bloodshed in the French and Indian war—May 28, 1754

Villa Nova

Animals—cattle tuberculosis test—March 3, 1892

Warren

Automobile Tractor—endless chain tractor—patented—Nov. 2, 1886

Washington

Crematory—crematory—erected—1876

Disciples of Christ—organized—Aug. 17, 1809

Waynesburg

Baseball League—juvenile baseball league—formed—1908

Westmoreland County

Bridge—suspension bridge—James Finley—1796

Wildwood

Coal Mine—designed for 100 per cent mechanical operation—opened—Oct. 1930

Wilkes-Barre

Coal—anthracite coal burned experimentally—Feb. 11, 1808

Wilkinsburg

Television—electronic television system—patented—V. K. Zworykin—Dec. 20, 1938

York

Locomotive—locomotive to burn coal (practical, American-made) — built — Phineas Davis—tested—Feb. 19, 1831

Ship—iron vessel (sheet iron)—"Codorus"—built

RHODE ISLAND

Army Exclusion Law — enacted — May 5, 1908

Insurance—health insurance law (state)—effective—May 10, 1942

Nut and Bolt Machine—nut and bolt machine—patented—Dec. 14, 1798

Oyster Propagation—state—June 1779

Screw—screw patent — granted — Dec. 14, 1798

Bellefonte

Screw—screw factory—established—1810

Bristol

Ship—torpedo boat—"Lightning"—built—J. B. Herreshoff—1876

Conanicut Island

Movable Church—consecrated—June 3, 1899

Cranston

Automobile Race — automobile race on a track—Sept. 7, 1896

Automobile Race Track—automobile race track (asphalt covered) — opened — Sept. 18, 1915

Cumberland

Nails — cold cut — manufactured—Jeremiah Wilkinson—1777

Goat Island

Torpedo—torpedo manufacturing station — established—1869

Greenwich

Building—building known as a Quonset hut—built—Sept. 1941

Newport

Automobile Parade—Sept. 7, 1899

Baptist Church — Seventh Day Baptist Church—organized—1671

Bicycle Society—bicycle society (national organization)—formed—May 31, 1880

RHODE ISLAND—Newport—*Continued*

Candle Factory—established—1748

Cattle Club—cattle club (Jersey cattle)—formed—July 1868

Court Martial—court martial trial—Aug. 24, 1676

Felt manufacturing mechanical process—invented—T. R. Williams—1820

Gas—gas lights (street)—installed—1806

Golf Course—golf course (nine holes)—completed—1890

Golf Tournament—amateur golf tournament (official)—Oct. 12, 1895

Golf Tournament — national championship stroke-play golf match—Sept. 3-4, 1894

Golf Tournament—open championship (official)—Oct. 4, 1895

Naval War College—naval war college—opened—Sept. 1885

Polo—international polo series—England vs. America—Aug. 25, 1886

Post Office—post office building (U.S.)—built—1829

Skating Rink—roller skating rink (public)—opened—1866

Slavery—non-importation of slaves act—enacted—June 13, 1774

Tennis Match—lawn tennis champions who were brothers—won—Aug. 18, 1896

Tennis Match—lawn tennis national championship matches—Aug. 31, 1881

Tennis Match — professional lawn tennis contest (international)—Aug. 29, 1889

Woman — woman newspaper editor — Ann Franklin— Newport *Mercury*—Aug. 22, 1762

Pawtucket

Cotton Mill — cotton mill to spin cotton yarn successfully—1790

Strike—strike in which women participated —1824

Thread — cotton thread — made — Hannah Wilkinson—1793

Providence

Baptist Church — Baptist Church — established—1639

Baseball Game—triple play unassisted—May 8, 1878

Catamaran—patented—N. G. Herreshoff — April 10, 1877

Cotton Spinning Jenny—operated—1786

File Factory—file factory (machine cutting) to attain success—Nicholson File Co. — organized—1864

Gold Leaf—in roll form—patented—W. H. Coe—April 5, 1892

Hat—straw hats—produced—June 1798

Health Laboratory—health laboratory (municipal)—established—Jan. 1, 1888

Health Laboratory — health laboratory (state)—established—Sept. 1, 1894

Insurance—mutual fire insurance company —incorporated—Oct. 31, 1835

Jewelers' Supply House — established — Nehemiah Dodge—1794

Lime—manufactured—Jan. 27, 1662

Lunch Wagon—introduced—1872

Mineralogy Instruction—Rhode Island College—1786

Moving Picture Machine—machine to show animated pictures — patented — April 23, 1867

Price Regulation Law—price regulation law (colonial)—effective—Jan. 8, 1777

Screw — screw machine — to manufacture pointed screws—patented—Cullen Whipple—June 3, 1856

Sociological Society — sociological society (national)—first annual meeting—Dec. 27, 1906

Street Car—gas-powered street car—operated —1873

Tuberculosis School — outdoor school for tubercular children—opened—Jan. 27, 1908

Quonset Point

Navy—air squadron of jets (U.S. Navy)—July 23, 1947

Warwick

Election Law—fraudulent election law (colonial)—enacted—May 22, 1649

Post Office—post office fully mechanized—opened—Oct. 20, 1960

Slavery — law regulating slavery—prohibitory law—enacted—May 18, 1652

SOUTH CAROLINA

Civil War—Negro regiment in the Civil War—organized—July 1862

Indigo—planted—c.1690

Naval Academy—Negro midshipman in the U.S. Naval Academy—J. H. Conyers—appointed—1872

Secession—secession act—Dec. 20, 1860

Senator (U.S.)—Senator elected by a write-in vote—J. S. Thurmond—elected—Nov. 2, 1954

Slavery—insurrection of Negro slaves—1739

Workmen's Compensation—workmen's compensation lawsuit—trial—July 1838

Chapin

Road—cotton fabric used on a road — to Prosperity, S.C.—1926

Charleston

Army — Reserve Officers Training Corps Units—authorized—Oct. 21, 1916

Building—building of fireproof construction —1822

College—city college—opened—April 1, 1838

Colonial Government—independent government in any of the American colonies—formed—March 1776

Cotton exported—to England—1764

Golf Club—golf club—formed—1786

Ice—commercial transportation of ice—from New York City—1799

Insurance—fire insurance company — organized—1735

Jewish Congregation—Jewish congregation (Reform)—organized—Nov. 21, 1824

Library—library—established—1698

Museum — college museum — curator appointed—Nov. 25, 1850

Museum—public museum—Charleston Museum—organized—Jan. 12, 1773

Music Society—music society of importance (local)—organized—1737

Opera—opera performed in America—Feb. 18, 1735

Railroad Passenger — railroad honeymoon trip—to Hamburg, S.C.—Jan. 15, 1831

Ship — rivetless cargo vessel — launched — Feb. 1930

Submarine—submarine to sink a man-of-war—Feb. 17, 1864

Weather Observations—weather systematically recorded—John Lining—Jan. 1738

Clemson

Textile School—textile school in a college —established—1899

Columbia

Library—library building (university)—University of South Carolina — completed — May 6, 1840

Medical School—medical summer school — opened—1853

Dillon

Paprika Mill—incorporated—March 25, 1941

Fort Sumter

Civil War—attack in the Civil War—April 12, 1861

Hamburg

Railroad Passenger — railroad honeymoon trip—from Charleston—Jan. 15, 1831

James Island

Cotton Mill—established—Frances Ramage —1789

Middleton Barony

Tea Shrub—planted—F. A. Michaux—1802

Morris Island

Civil War—act that marked the inauguration of the War of 1861-1865—Jan. 9, 1861

Port Royal

Ship—ship built to cross the Atlantic Ocean —1562

Prosperity

Road—cotton fabric used on a road — to Chapin, S.C.—1926

Silver Bluff

Baptist Church—Baptist Church (Negro)— established—1773

Sumter

City Manager Plan—adopted—June 1912

SOUTH DAKOTA

Initiative and Referendum — legislation passed—Jan. 27, 1897

State—states admitted to the union simultaneously—North and South Dakota — Nov. 3, 1899

Rapid City

Balloon Flight—balloon flight to exceed an altitude of 70,000 feet—O. A. Anderson and A. W. Stevens—Nov. 11, 1935

Photograph—photograph showing the lateral curvature of the horizon—balloon take-off—Nov. 11, 1935

Watertown

Fingerprinting—high school to fingerprint its students — Watertown Senior High School—Oct. 19, 1936

White Lake

Photograph—photograph showing the lateral curvature of the horizon—balloon landed—Nov. 11, 1935

TENNESSEE

Army—law (state) conferring military privileges and duties on the Negro—enacted— June 28, 1861

Civil Government in America — Watauga Commonwealth—May 1772

Dueling Legislation (state)—enacted—Nov. 10, 1801

Evolution law (state)—enacted—March 23, 1925

Governor—gubernatorial election in which two brothers were the opposing candidates—R. L. Taylor and A. A. Taylor— Nov. 2, 1886

President (U.S.)—President to become a senator—Andrew Johnson—1875

Prohibition—prohibition state—legislation enacted—Jan. 26, 1838

State—state re-admitted to the Union—July 24, 1866

Chattanooga

Baseball Player—woman baseball pitcher— engaged by organized male team—April 1, 1931

Golf Course—midget golf course—1929

TENNESSEE—*Continued*

Clinton

Element—element 95—americium—formed

Collierville

Enclave — municipal enclave of economic ground rent—authorized—April 21, 1933

Jackson

Medical Periodical—Negro medical journal —*Medical and Surgical Observer*—published —1892

Jonesboro

Slavery—anti-slavery magazine—*The Emancipator*—published—April 30, 1820

Kingsport

Sponge—oxidized cellulose (sponge)—manufactured—1936

Knoxville

College — non-denominational college — Blount College—chartered—Sept. 10, 1794

Memphis

Business—Keedoozle store — opened — May 15, 1937
Sewage—separate system of sewage disposal—started—Jan. 21, 1880
Typewriter Ribbon—typewriter ribbon patent—G. K. Anderson—Sept. 14, 1886

Nashville

Animals—dogs trained to guide the blind—taught—1928
Fraternity (Greek letter)—scholastic fraternity chapter established at a Negro university—Phi Beta Kappa—Fisk University—April 4, 1953
Horse Race—futurity race—Oct. 10, 1843
Poet—Negro poet to be employed to teach creative writing — J. W. Johnson — Jan. 1932
Radio License—frequency modulation transmitter to receive a commercial license—W47NV—operated—March 1, 1941
Theater—showboat—floating theater—commenced tour—Oct. 20, 1817

Oak Ridge

Isotope — radioactive isotopes exported — produced—1947
Museum—museum devoted exclusively to atomic energy—opened—March 19, 1949

Pulaski

Ku Klux Klan—organized—1865

Rogersville

Periodical—trade journal—*Rail-road Advocate* —published—July 4, 1831

Shiloh

Hospital—Army Field Hospital—established —April 1862

Washington College

College—college named after George Washington—Washington College—July 8, 1795

TEXAS

Bowie Knife—invented—1835
Cotton-Boll Weevil—introduced—1892
Court—state supreme court composed entirely of women—appointed—Jan. 8, 1925
Police—state police—Texas Rangers—organized—1835

Amarillo

Holiday — mother-in-law day — celebrated— March 5, 1934

Belton

Road—road with a depressed trough—opened to traffic—Dec. 5, 1925

College Station

Army—Reserve Officers Training Corps Units—authorized—Oct. 21, 1916
Radio Broadcast—football game (collegiate) broadcast—Nov. 25, 1920

Columbia

President of the Republic of Texas—Sam Houston—oath of office—Oct. 22, 1836

Crystal City

Monument—monument to a comic character —"Popeye" statue—unveiled—March 26, 1937

Dallas

Aviation—Flights—airplane endurance flight exceeding 1,200 hours—Jim Heth and Bill Burkhart—began—Aug. 2, 1958
Insurance—group hospital insurance plan—Baylor University Hospital—Dec. 21, 1929
Newspaper—newspaper daily railroad delivery service—*Morning News*—Oct. 1, 1885
Newspaper—newspaper printed on pine-pulp paper in color—*News*—March 31, 1937

Photograph—photograph bounced off a satellite—received—Aug. 18, 1960
Radio Station—municipal radio station—1920
Sidewalk (traveling)—two-way moving walk—in service—Jan. 30, 1958

Floydada

Federal Crop Insurance Corporation—first indemnity payment—April 14, 1939

Fort Bliss

Army—ballistic missile operational unit—completed training—Nov. 1954

Fort Sam Houston

World War I—German spy to receive a death sentence from the American forces during World War I—sentenced—Aug. 16, 1918

Fort Worth

Aviation—Flights (world)—round-the-world non-stop airplane flight — completed — March 2, 1949
Helium—helium plant of the United States—completed—April 1921
Helium — helium plants (experimental) — erected—1917
Hotel—hotel to establish a heliport—May 20, 1953
Hotel—hotel with all foam rubber mattresses, pillows and furniture cushions—Oct. 7, 1951
Railroad—gasoline-driven, stainless steel, air-conditioned, pneumatic-tired, two-car train —in service—to Texarkana—1933
Street Car—light-weight one-man street car —placed in operation—Nov. 1916
Washing Machine—washing machine for public use — "washateria" — introduced — April 18, 1934

Freeport

Magnesium—commercially produced from sea water—extracted—Jan. 21, 1941
Water—sea water conversion plant (practical)—opened—May 8, 1961

Galveston

Commission Form of Government—inaugurated—Sept. 18, 1901
Newspaper—newspaper delivery train—to Houston—1883

Holliday

Animals—sheep (Karakul fur sheep)—imported—1908

Houston

Boiler—carbon monoxide boiler—in operation—Nov. 1953
Newspaper—newspaper delivery train—from Galveston—1883

Postal Service—mail box (drive-up)—installed—July 1927
Telephone—mobile long distance car-to-car telephone conversation—to St. Louis—Sept. 11, 1946
Television Station—noncommercial educational television station—KUHT—May 12, 1953
Wedding—airplane wedding—May 31, 1919

Indianola

Animals—camels imported for commercial purposes—May 14, 1856

Kingsville

Animals — cattle (Africander cattle) — imported—March 14, 1932

Lampasas

Bankers' Association—bankers' association formed by a state group—July 23, 1885

Lufkin

Television Station—microwave television station—KTRE-TV—Aug. 31, 1955

Nueces County

Cotton—cotton acreage reduction payment—received—July 28, 1933

Orange

Pipeline—pipeline (interstate) to transport ethylene—in operation—Sept. 6, 1958

Panhandle

Federal Crop Insurance Corporation—first application made—M. L. Purvines—May 18, 1938

Petrolia

Helium—helium plants (experimental) — erected—1917

Randolph Air Force Base

Space Cabin—used—1956

San Angelo

School — air-conditioned public elementary school—Oct. 1955

San Antonio

Aviation—School — airplane flying school operated by a woman—1914
Building—air-conditioned office building—opened—Jan. 1, 1928

TEXAS—*Continued*

Snyder

Automobile Trucking Service—automobile inter-city trucking service—to Colorado City, Colo.—Oct. 29, 1904

Temple

Road—road with a depressed trough—opened—Dec. 15, 1925

Texarkana

Federal Credit Union Act—charter No. 1—granted—1934

Railroad—gasoline-driven, stainless steel, air-conditioned, pneuamatic-tired, two-car train—in service—to Fort Worth—1933

Waco*ff*

Degrees (academic and honorary)—husband and wife awarded honorary degrees—Vice President and Mrs. J. N. Garner—Nov. 21, 1936

Quadruplets to Complete a College Course—Keys sisters—graduated—May 31, 1937

Television—Telecast—murder trial to be televised—Dec. 5, 1955

Weatherford

Cotton Picker (mechanical)—built—J. D. Rust—1928

UTAH

Game Preserve—game preserve appropriation (federal)—state aid project approved—July 23, 1938

Moving Picture—talking picture taken outdoors (full length)—*In Old Arizona*

Senate (state)—woman state senator—M. H. Cannon—served—Jan. 11, 1897

Bonneville Salt Flats

Automobile—automobile to exceed the speed of 300 miles an hour—Sir Malcolm Campbell—Sept. 3, 1935

Automobile—automobile to exceed the speed of 400 miles an hour—John Cobb—Sept. 16, 1947

Fort Bridger

Cartridge Belt patent—Anson Mills—Aug. 20, 1867

Salt Lake City

Business—department store—Zion's Cooperative Mercantile Institution—1868

Monument—monument to a bird—sea gull monument—unveiled—Oct. 1, 1913

Wendover

Motorcycle Race—motorcycle to exceed 200 miles an hour—Wilhelm Herz—Aug. 4, 1956

VERMONT

Congressman (U.S.)—congressman elected who served time in prison—Matthew Lyon

Election Law—absentee voting law (state)—enacted—Nov. 24, 1896

Emancipation Act (state)—enacted—July 2, 1777

Money—copper cents minted by a state—authorized—June 1785

Patent—patent granted by the United States government—to Samuel Hopkins—July 31, 1790

Seeding Machine Patent—Eliakim Spooner—Jan. 25, 1799

State—state admitted to the Union—after the ratification of the Constitution—March 4, 1791

Strike—anti-sit-down strike legislation (state)—enacted—April 9, 1937

Bradford

Globe Factory—to manufacture terrestrial and celestial globes—1813

Burlington

Factory—steam-heated factory—Burlington Woolen Company—1846

Horse Race—three-hundred-mile endurance run—to Camp Devens, Mass.—held—Oct. 15, 1919

Concord

Normal School—normal school established exclusively for the preparation of teachers—Concord Academy—opened—March 11, 1823

Dorset

Marble Quarry—operated—Isaac Underhill—1785

Grandpa's Knob

Electric Power Plant—wind turbine—to generate energy for an alternating current power system—operated—Oct. 19, 1941

Middlebury

College—school for the higher education of women—Emma Willard—1814

Horse—horse farm operated by the United States government—established—1907

Montpelier

Agricultural Society—agricultural society for dairymen—organized—Oct. 27, 1869

Northfield

Army — Reserve Officers Training Corps course in mountain and winter warfare—Norwich University—announced—Oct. 3, 1947

Traffic Regulation Course—air traffic regulation course—endowed—1934

Norwich

Engineering College — civil engineering course—Norwich University—1819

Military School—military school—American Literary, Scientific and Military Academy —founded—Aug. 6, 1819

Plymouth

President (U.S.)—President born on Independence Day—Calvin Coolidge—July 4, 1872

Proctor

Nurse—nurse employed by an industrial organization—Ada Stewart—1896

Randolph

Horse—horse (Morgan horse) — foaled — 1789

Rutland

Epidemic—poliomyelitis epidemic—June 17, 1894

St. Johnsbury

Scale — platform scale — built — Thaddeus Fairbanks—1830

Scale—railway track scale — patented — Jan. 13, 1857

Springfield

Sandpaper Patent—Isaac Fischer—June 14, 1834

Wallingford

Epidemic—poliomyelitis epidemic—June 17, 1894

Windsor

Suffrage—state to provide universal manhood suffrage—constitution enacted—July 28, 1777

Woodstock

Ski Tow (rope)—in operation—Jan. 28, 1934

VIRGINIA

Agriculture—crop limitation law—enacted—Oct. 16, 1629

Agriculture—crop surplus destruction — ordered—Jan. 6, 1639

Artist — English artist — John White — arrived—1585

Beer—brewed—Roanoke Colony—1587

Blue Law—blue law—enacted—1619

Blue Law—blue law regulating gambling — 1624

Census—states to exceed 1,000,000 in population—1820

Game Law — game law (colonial)—enacted —March 24, 1629

Horse—horse (thoroughbred)—Bulle Rock —imported—1730

Labor Law—convict labor law—enacted—March 2, 1642

Lottery—lottery—of importance — June 26, 1614

Medal—Indian medals—authorized—1661

Medical Legislation—medical law — enacted —Oct. 21, 1639

Physician—doctor in the colony of Virginia —Lawrence Bohune—arrived—1610

Potato—potato—introduced—Dec. 1621

Presbyterian Church—Presbyterian Church —established—1611

Prohibition — prohibition enforcement officers—authorized—June 21, 1622

Rice—imported—1647

Road—highway legislation (colonial)—enacted—Sept. 4, 1632

Salt—salt works—established—1630

Senator (U.S.) — senator appointed by a governor—John Walker—March 31, 1790

Silk—silk culture—started—1623

Surveyor—Thomas Hariot—arrived—1585

Tax — inheritance tax (colonial) — levied—1687

Temperance Law (colonial) — signed — March 5, 1623

Treason—treason trial (colonial)—May 7, 1634

War (colonial)—Indian war of importance fought by English colonists—May 27, 1607

Wedding—wedding in Virginia—1609

Accomac (Accawmack)

Play (drama)—play given by nonprofessional actors—performance—Aug. 27, 1665

Alexandria

Aviation—Flights—inter-city airplane flight —from Fort Myer—July 30, 1909

Fraternity Magazine—fraternity journal—*Beta Theta Pi*—published—Dec. 15, 1872

Radio Station—all-local network—May 15, 1950

Railroad Coupler — railroad coupler — patented—E. H. Janney—April 29, 1873

Road—toll road — to Snicker's Gap — Oct. 1785

School — Negro school (state) — Snowden School—authorized—July 11, 1870

Arlington

Cemetery—foreign service women interred in the Arlington National Cemetery — Nov. 19, 1942

Monument — monument to the "Unknown Soldier" (national)—Nov. 11, 1921

VIRGINIA—Arlington—*Continued*

President (U.S.)—President buried in the National Cemetery at Arlington, Va.— W. H. Taft—March 11, 1930

Radio Station—all-local network—May 15, 1950

Radio Telephone—transatlantic radio telephone message—to Paris—Oct. 21, 1915

Radio Telephone — transcontinental radio telephone demonstration—Sept. 29, 1915

Television—Telecast—weather map telecast —to Washington, D.C.—Aug. 18, 1926

War (Korean)—Korean war hero buried in Arlington Cemetery—H. G. Thomas, Jr.— Aug. 14, 1950

Bath

See Berkeley Springs, W.Va.

Bull Run

Civil War—serious engagement in the Civil War—July 21, 1861

Cape Henry

Aviation—Airplane—jet airplane to land on a ship—July 21, 1946

Lighthouse—lighthouse built after American independence—finished—1792

Protestant Episcopal Church — Protestant Episcopal Church—established—1607

Charles City

Breach of Promise Suit—June 14, 1623

Chesapeake Bay

Photograph—photographs taken under the sea—J. E. Williamson—1913

Craney Island

Lightship—July 14, 1820

Edom

Surgical Operation—Caesarean operation (successful)—Dr. Jessee Bennett—Jan. 14, 1794

Fairfax

Civil War—Confederate officer killed in the Civil War—J. Q. Marr—June 1, 1861

Civil War—skirmish in the Civil War—June 1, 1861

Falling Creek

Iron—iron works—erected—1619

Lead—mined and smelted—1620

Falls Church

Radio Station—all-local network—May 15, 1950

Fort Belvoir

Atomic Reactor—military nuclear power plant—dedicated—April 29, 1957

Fort Eustis

Heliport—military heliport—dedicated—Dec. 7, 1954

Fort Henry

Expedition—expedition—of Englishmen—to cross Allegheny Mountains—started—Aug. 27, 1650

Fort (Fortress) Monroe

Chaplains' School—Army school for chaplains—Feb. 9, 1918

Fire Extinguisher Patent—Alanson Crane— Feb. 10, 1863

School—Negro school for freedmen—established—Sept. 17, 1861

Ship — balloon carrier — observed military positions—Aug. 3, 1861

Fort Myer

Aviation—airplane fatality—T. E. Selfridge —Sept. 17, 1908

Aviation—Airship—dirigible balloon contracted for by the U.S. government—demonstrated—Aug. 1908

Aviation—Flights—airplane endurance flight exceeding one hour—Sept. 9, 1908

Aviation—Flights—inter-city airplane flight —to Alexandria—July 30, 1909

Aviation—Passenger — airplane passenger (official) Sept. 9, 1908

Fredericksburg

Monument—monument to a woman financed by women—dedicated—May 10, 1894

Gosport

Ship—ship constructed by the federal government—1794

Hampton

Educational Endowment—Benjamin Syms— 1634

Hampton Roads

Aviation—battleship sunk by an airplane— July 21, 1921

Aviation—Flights—airplane flight from a ship—Eugene Ely—take-off—Nov. 14, 1910

Balloon—balloon filled with helium gas— Dec. 1, 1921

Civil War—conflict between iron-clad vessels in the Civil War—"Merrimac" and "Monitor"—March 9, 1862

Expedition—scientific expedition fitted out by the United States Government—sailed —Aug. 18, 1838

Ordnance—revolving gun turret—"Monitor" —engagement—March 9, 1862
Radio Telephone—radio telephone ship-to-shore conversation—May 6, 1916
Ship—warship fleet to circumnavigate the globe—returned—Feb. 22, 1909

Harrisonburg

Postal Service—Highway Post Office Service—route to Washington, D.C. established —Feb. 10, 1941

Harrison's Landing

Taps (military signal)—played—July 1862

James City

Bounty—authorized—Oct. 5, 1646
Road—highway legislation (colonial)—passed —Sept. 4, 1632

Jamestown

Animals—sheep—imported—1609
Bottle—bottle—blown—1608
Colonial Government—colonial council in America—May 13, 1607
Colonist—English settlement in America (permanent)—May 13, 1607
Glass Bead—manufactured—1608
Glass Factory—glass factory—established— Oct. 1608
Indians—Indian massacre of white people— March 22, 1622
Legislative Assembly—July 30, 1619
Maize—Indian corn—planting—1609
Rebellion (colonial)—George Kendall—1607
Slander Proceedings—John Robinson—Sept. 17, 1607
Slavery—slaves—introduced—Aug. 1619
Tobacco—tobacco—cultivated—1612

Langley Field

Aviation—Flights—all blind distance flight by the U.S. Army—April 6, 1940
Radio Telephone—radio telephone communication between the ground and an airplane—July 2, 1917
Wind Tunnel—full-scale wind tunnel for testing airplanes—in operation—May 27, 1931
Wind Tunnel—high-speed jet wind tunnel— completed—June 29, 1929
Wind Tunnel—propeller research tunnel— completed—1927
Wind Tunnel—wind tunnel of variable air density—completed—April 1923

Lexington

Journalism Course—journalism course — Washington University (now Washington and Lee University)—1869
Military School—state military school—Virginia Military Institute — established — March 29, 1839

Luray

Civilian Conservation Corps (U.S.)—camp opened—April 17, 1933

Mechanicsville

Telegraph—Army field telegraph used in warfare—May 24, 1862

Mill Point

Sewing Machine—chain-stitch single-thread sewing machine (practical)—patented—J. E. A. Gibbs—June 2, 1857

Newport News

Aviation—Flights (transcontinental)—transcontinental dirigible flight (non-rigid dirigible)—started—Sept. 14, 1922
Museum—maritime museum—established— June 2, 1930
Ship—air-conditioned naval ship—"Newport News"—launched—March 6, 1947
Ship—aircraft carrier—launched—Feb. 25, 1933
Ship—aircraft carrier (atomic powered)— "Enterprise"—launched—Sept. 24, 1960
Ship—aircraft carrier with an angle deck— "Forrestal"—launched—Dec. 11, 1954
Ship—ship equipped with a masthead sea anchorage for a dirigible—dirigible landing—Aug. 15, 1925

Norfolk

Aviation—Flights—airplane flight from a ship—Eugene Ely—landed—Nov. 14, 1910
Chaplains' School—naval chaplains' school— Feb. 23, 1942
Drydock—federal drydocks—Norfolk Dry Dock—completed—March 15, 1834
Hospital—marine hospital (U.S.)—Norfolk Naval Hospital deeded to U.S.—April 20, 1801
Radio Compass—used on airplane—flight to battleship—July 7, 1920
Ship—frigate (American-built steam-driven) to cross the Atlantic Ocean—sailed—Aug. 5, 1843
Ship—turreted frigate in the U.S. Navy— "Roanoke"—launched—Dec. 13, 1855

Petersburg

Blanket—electronic blanket—manufactured— Oct. 9, 1946
Cottonseed Oil Mill—Francis Follet—1829
Railroad—interstate railroad—opened—1833

Portsmouth

Drydock—national ship in a federal drydock—"Delaware"—June 17, 1833
Hospital—naval hospital—completed—1833

VIRGINIA—*Continued*

Richmond

Bank—bank for Negroes operated by Negroes—opened—April 3, 1889

Bank—bank president (Negro woman)—M. L. Walker—July 28, 1903

Cans—beer in cans—placed on sale—Jan. 24, 1935

Congress of the Confederate States—under permanent constitution—meeting—Feb. 18, 1861

Roanoke

Locomotive—locomotive (super-giant)—operated—Jan. 27, 1948

Snicker's Gap

Road—toll road—to Alexandria—1785

Staunton

City Manager—elected—April 2, 1908

Upperville

Horse Show—Upperville Colt and Horse Show—1853

Wallops Island

Rocket—satellite placed in orbit by an all-solid propellant rocket—launched—Feb. 16, 1961

Walnut Grove

Reaper—reaper that was practical—C. H. McCormick—1831

Wheeling

See Wheeling, W.Va.

Williamsburg

Capitol—erected—1698

College—college charter granted by the Crown—Feb. 8, 1693

College—college proposed—William and Mary—1617

College—college to confer medals as prizes —1770

College—college to have a full faculty—William and Mary

College—college to receive a coat-of-arms from the College of Heralds—May 14, 1694

College—elective system of study—introduced—1779

Cook Book—*Compleat Housewife*—published —1742

Fencing Book—*Compleat System of Fencing* —published—1734

Fraternity (Greek letter)—scholastic fraternity—Phi Beta Kappa—founded—Dec. 5, 1776

Freemasons—Masonic Grand Lodge—organized—Oct. 13, 1778

Grammar—English grammar by an American—Hugh Jones

History Instruction—school of modern history—1803

Honor System—of conducting examinations —introduced—1779

Hospital—insane hospital (state)—opened—Oct. 12, 1773

Indian School—Indian school (permanent) —established—1720

Language Instruction — modern language school—in a college—1779

Newspaper—newspaper published south of the Potomac River—*Virginia Gazette*—published—Aug. 5, 1736

Political Economy Course—political economy course—1784

Theater—theater—built—1718

Yorktown

Customhouse—1706

WASHINGTON

Insurance—workmen's compensation insurance law (state)—passed—March 14, 1911

Bremerton

Ferryboat—streamlined ferryboat—commercial service to Seattle—July 4, 1935

Cape Disappointment

Colonist—colonists to reach the Pacific coast —from New York City—landed—April 12, 1811

Hanford

Element—element 95—americium—formed

Houghton

Ferryboat — streamlined ferryboat — completed—1935

Pasco

Air Mail Service—air mail contractor (domestic)—plane to Elko, Nev.—April 6, 1926

Renton

Aviation—Airplane—jet transport commercial airplane built in the United States—tested—July 15, 1954

Richland

Atomic Reactor—atomic reactor for research and development—Nov. 25, 1960

Atomic Reactor—atomic reactor to produce plutonium—operated—Sept. 1944

Seattle

Air Mail Service—international air mail—to Victoria, B.C.—March 3, 1919

Automobile Bus—bus operated by a railroad —service commenced—Aug. 25, 1924

Automobile Race—transcontinental automobile race—completed—June 22, 1909

Aviation—Flights (world)—world flight—ended—Sept. 28, 1924

Blackout—blackout outdoor light control—instituted—May 11, 1942

Bridge—bridge with open mesh steel flooring—opened—April 7, 1933

Bridge—pontoon bridge of reenforced concrete—dedicated—July 2, 1940

Church—General Council of Congregational and Christian Churches—formed—1931

Employment Service—municipal employment office—opened—April 1, 1894

Ferryboat—streamlined ferryboat—commercial service—to Bremerton—July 4, 1935

Police—policewoman on the aerial force—appointed—July 13, 1934

Pressing Machine (steam-operated)—patented—A. J. Hoffman—July 13, 1909

Radio Broadcast—network broadcast received on the Pacific coast—Oct. 23, 1924

Ship—battleship built on the Pacific coast—"Nebraska"—keel laid—July 4, 1902

Soilless Culture of Plants—commercial hydroponicum built on the roof—erected—1936

Theater — state-owned theater — opened — Nov. 2, 1936

Vice President of the United States—Vice President to leave the United States while the President was away—J. N. Garner—sailed for Japan—Oct. 16, 1936

World War I—American ship lost in World War I—sailed—Nov. 4, 1914

Spokane

Automobile Bus—bus operated by a railroad —service commenced—Aug. 25, 1924

Holiday—Father's Day—June 19, 1910

Insect Electrocutor Patent—W. M. Frost—Nov. 8, 1910

Tacoma

Stadium—school stadium—dedicated — June 10, 1910

Tenino

Money—wooden money—issued—Feb. 1932

Vancouver

Army Field Range—introduced—May 1908

Road—overland wagon road across the Rocky Mountains—from Westport Landing, Mo.—1842

Ship—steamboat on the Pacific coast—tested —May 16, 1836

Walla Walla

College—college comprehensive senior examination program—adopted—May 26, 1913

College—dean of men—B. H. Brown—appointed—1901

Colonist—women to cross the continent—arrived—Sept. 1, 1836

Wenatchee

Aviation—Flights (transpacific)—transpacific non-stop flight—landed—Oct. 5, 1931

Yakima County

Indian School—Indian school (boarding) on a reservation—Yakima Agency Boarding School—opened—1860

WEST VIRGINIA

Industrial Recovery Act—state to place all its employees under the blanket code of the National Recovery Act Code—July 27, 1933

Tax—sales tax (state)—effective—July 1, 1921

Charles Town

Postal Service—rural free delivery—Oct. 1, 1896

Beverley Springs

Spa—opened to the public—1756

Charleston

Road—brick pavement—1870

Salt—salt well—west of Alleghenies—1808

Fetterman

Civil War—Union soldier killed by enemy action in the Civil War—T. B. Brown—May 22, 1861

Halltown

Postal Service—rural free delivery—Oct. 1, 1896

Institute

Coal—coal hydrogenation chemicals pilot plant (large)—opened—May 8, 1952

Kanawha

Trust—trust—organized—Nov. 10, 1817

Mullens

Locomotive — locomotive (super-giant) — placed in service—Jan. 27, 1948

WEST VIRGINIA—*Continued*

Parkersburg

Vitrolite—manufactured—1907

Uvilla

Postal Service—rural free delivery—Oct. 1, 1896

Wheeling

Gas—municipal gas plant—acquired—1871

Nails—steel-cut nails—manufactured—1883

Ship—steamboat (double decked)—"Washington"—launched—June 4, 1816

Soda Fountain — soda fountain patent — granted—April 24, 1833

WISCONSIN

Congressman (U.S.)—Socialist congressman —V. L. Berger

Election Law—primary election (state-wide) —Sept. 4, 1906

Forest Service—forestry inquiry commission (state)—authorized—March 23, 1867

Governor—governor removed from office by a state supreme court—W. A. Barstow— 1856

Insurance—unemployment insurance act— Jan. 28, 1932

Insurance—workmen's compensation insurance law (state)—effective—May 3, 1911

Woman Suffrage—woman suffrage amendment approved by Congress—ratified— June 10, 1919

Appleton

Electric Power Plant—hydroelectric power plant—opened—Sept. 30, 1882

Cambridge

Methodist Episcopal Church—Scandinavian Methodist Episcopal church—organized— April 1851

Camp McCoy

Army Camp—army camp for "limited service"—1942

Chippewa Falls

Ski Jump (steel)—built—Nov. 1908

Clintonville

Automobile Brake—(four wheels)—patented —Dec. 29, 1908

La Crosse

Microcard—book on microcards—*The Scholar and the Future of the Research Library*— 1947

Lake Geneva

Automobile—armored car—used—1898

Automobile—field hospital automobile with X-ray equipment—used—May 1915

Bicycle Corps (military)—organized—1894

Radio Car (military)—designed—R. P. Davidson—1911

Madison

Animal Husbandry—animal husbandry professor—J. A. Craig—1890

Brick—light-weight brick—developed—1927

Dairy School—of collegiate rank—University of Wisconsin—opened—Jan. 3, 1890

Dance Course—with collegiate credit—University of Wisconsin—approved—Nov. 11, 1926

Game Management Chair—University of Wisconsin—established—Aug. 1933

Medical Congress—cancer institute (convention)—Sept. 7, 1936

Milk Tester—of value—invented—S. M. Babcock—1890

Navy "E" Award—Navy "E" certificates of meritorious service presented to an institution of higher learning—awarded—June 1, 1942

Manitowoc

Submarine—submarine built on the Great Lakes—launched—April 30, 1942

Menasha

Servite Church—Servite church in America —established—Aug. 1870

Milton

Building—monolithic concrete building — built—1845

Milwaukee

Baseball Game—major league game in which the majority of the players on one team were Negroes—July 17, 1954

Bridge Whist Organization — American Whist League—formed—April 14, 1891

Bridge Whist Tournament—duplicate whist tournament—April 15, 1891

Electrobasograph—exhibited—June 12, 1933

Engine — outboard motor — commercially successful—developed — Ole Evinrude — 1909

Engine — outboard twin-cylinder motor (light)—developed—1921

Newspaper—newspaper advertisement printed on aluminum foil—*Sentinel*—March 18, 1958

Newspaper—newspaper to insert an aluminum foil sheet—*Sentinel*—April 2, 1957

Occupational Therapy Course—Milwaukee-Downer College—1913

Radio Facsimile Transmission — facsimile broadcast in ultra high frequencies — W9XAF—Dec. 19, 1933

Safety Congress—safety congress (national)—convened—Sept. 30, 1912

Soldiers' Homes (national) — Northwestern Home—1867

Telephone — automatic telephone system (successful)—exchange equipped with rotating dial—installed—1896

Television—college credit course in television—Marquette University—1951

Woman—woman Presbyterian elder—S. E. Dickson—elected—June 2, 1930

Muskego

Newspaper—Norwegian-American newspaper—*Nordlyset*—July 29, 1847

Neenah

Flour Mill—flour rolling mill — patented — March 23, 1880

Portage

Lie Detector — Keeler Polygraph—tested—Feb. 2, 1935

Racine

Bicycle Traffic Court—held—June 18, 1936

Confectionery Machine—for making "suckers"—manufactured—1908

Continuation School — continuation school established by state law—opened—Nov. 3, 1911

Dictionary—Bohemian-American dictionary—published—1876

Milk — malted milk — invented — William Horlick—1882

Newspaper — Czech language newspaper — *Slovan Amerikansky* — published — Jan. 1, 1860

Ripon

Republican Party—Republican Party meeting (local)—name "Republican" suggested—March 20, 1854

Watertown

Births—quintuplets—Feb. 13, 1875

Waukesha

Advertisement — three-dimensional newspaper advertisement—*Daily Freeman*—June 12, 1953

WYOMING

Governor—woman governor of a state—N. T. Ross—Jan. 5, 1925

Woman Suffrage—state to grant suffrage to women—July 10, 1890

Cheyenne

Aviation—air stewardess—flight from San Francisco—May 15, 1930

Holiday — Frontier Day—celebrated—Sept. 23, 1897

Devils Tower National Monument

Monument — national monument — established—Sept. 24, 1906

Laramie

Recreational Ranching Course—in a college—B.S. degree awarded—June 6, 1938

Yellowstone National Park

Park—park (national)—authorized—March 1, 1872

R
031
K
KANE, JOSEPH NATHAN
Famous first facts

DATE DUE			
MAY 20			
			ALESCO